Heads Up, Entertainment Hounds!

(We've got your passions covered)

VideoHound's® Golden Movie Retriever™ 1997

The biggest is better than ever in this new edition, and it still has *plenty* of attitude. *VideoHound 1997*, with lots of new movies and outrageous film categories, tons of astounding trivia and an inviting new page design, continues to run circles around other video guides in fun and entertainment value. Fully expanded and updated with 1,000 new reviews, the *Hound* provides information and opinions on 22,000-plus videos—more than any other guide on the market.

Paperback • 1,600 pages • **ISBN 0-7876-0780-0** • Sept 1996 • **$19.95**

CyberHound's Web Guide
8,000 Sites with Bite

As any cybersurfer knows, all Internet sites were not created equal. Fortunately, *CyberHound* unknots the 'Net for you by selecting and reviewing 8,000 of the most interesting and informative sites. Covers a wide variety of subject areas, from entertainment to politics to personal home pages, plus some that are particularly controversial or bizarre.

Paperback • 1,450 pages • 1996
• **ISBN 0-7876-1017-8 • $34.95**

musicHound rock

The Essential Album Guide

edited by Gary Graff

foreword by Marshall Crenshaw

DETROIT • NEW YORK • TORONTO • LONDON

musicHound **rock**
The
Essential
Album
Guide

Most Visible Ink Press™ books are available at special quantity discounts when purchased in bulk by corporations, organizations, or groups. Customized printings, special imprints, messages, and excerpts can be produced to meet your needs. For more information, contact Special Markets Manager, Gale Research, 835 Penobscot Bldg., Detroit, MI 48226. Or call 1-800-776-6265.

Library of Congress Cataloging-in-Publication Data

Graff, Gary
MusicHound rock: the essential album guide / by Gary Graff.
P. cm.
Includes indexes.
ISBN 0-7876-1037-2 (alk. paper)
1. Rock music—Discography. I. Title.
ML156.4R6G73 1996
781.66'0266—dc20

96-31449
CIP
MN

ISBN 0-7876-1037-2
Printed in the United States of America

10 9 8 7 6 5 4 3 2 1

musicHound **credits**

THE AUTHOR

Gary Graff turned his attention to journalism after an unsatisfying encounter with ninth grade biology convinced him that it might be wise to steer a career path away from medicine. Over the years, Graff has written award-winning music articles and criticism for *Guitar World, Rolling Stone, Creem, People, Reuters, Replay, Request, Hit Parader, Hits, Billboard, Country Song Roundup, ICE, BMI Music World,* Mr. Showbiz, Compuserve WOW!, the Microsoft Network and for myriad newspapers, including the *San Francisco Chronicle*, the *Dallas Morning News*, the *Boston Globe*, the *Detroit Free Press*, the *Pittsburgh Post-Gazette*, the *Atlanta Journal-Constitution*, the *San Diego Union Tribune*, the *Oakland Press* (Mich.) and the *Detroit Journal* and *Sunday Journal*. Graff is also a co-founder and board member of the Motor City Music Awards Foundation, and he reports on rock news for Detroit's WRIF-FM. A graduate of the University of Missouri-Columbia, Graff lives with his wife, daughter and twin stepsons in suburban Detroit, where he can sometimes be found coaching kids sports teams and flailing at racquetballs, golf balls, softballs, floor hockey pucks and bass guitars.

MANAGING EDITOR

Hilary Weber

ASST. MANAGING EDITOR

Christopher P. Scanlon

ASSOCIATE EDITORS

Peggy Castine has been a writer and editor for more than 20 years. She's worked for the *New York Times*, the *Detroit Sunday Journal* and the *Detroit Free Press*. She will cheer loudly when the Packers win the Super Bowl.

Bob Cronin bats right, throws right and has held various reporting and high-ranking editing positions at the *Detroit Journal*, the *Detroit Free Press*, the *Sedalia Democrat* (Mo.) and the *Greenville News* (S.C.). He also worked spotlights and dropped a lot of band gear at rock concerts in St. Louis.

Jim Schaefer is a reporter at the *Toledo Blade* who has also worked as a writer and copy editor for the *Detroit Journal* and *Sunday Journal*, and the *Detroit Free Press*. He's a Buckeye but was granted special dispensation to cross the line into Michigan.

MUSICHOUND STAFF

Michelle Banks, Jim Craddock, Dean Dauphinais, David Kunath, Beth Fhaner, Bryan Lassner, Leslie Norback, Brad Morgan, Rebecca Nelson, Carol Schwartz, Devra Sladics, Christine Tomassini

PRODUCTION

Mary Beth Trimper, Dorothy Maki, Evi Seoud, and Shanna Heilveil

TYPESETTING

Marco Di Vita, The Graphix Group

ART DIRECTION

Tracey Rowens

MARKETING & PROMOTIONAL WRITING

Susan Stefani, Lauri Taylor, and Jenny Sweetland

TECHNOLOGY

Jeffrey Muhr

RESEARCH

Jennifer Lund, Gary J. Oudersluys, and Maureen Richards, *Research Specialists;* Julia C. Daniel, Tamara C. Nott, and Michelle P. Pica, *Research Associates*

DATA ENTRY

Kenneth Benson

CONTRIBUTORS

Grant Alden is the managing editor of *huH* magazine and co-editor of the alternative country bimonthly *No Depression.*

Gil Asakawa is the Content Editor for America Online's Digital City Denver, co-author of *The Toy Book* and has written for *Rolling Stone, Pulse, Creem, No Depression, New Country* and other publications.

Tracey Birkhenhauer is a reporter at the *Lansing State Journal* (Mich.).

Peter Blackstock is co-editor of *No Depression*, a senior editor at Northwest music biweekly *The Rocket* and a columnist for the *Seattle Post-Intelligencer.*

Mike Brown is a DJ, a rave organizer and a system administrator for Hyperreal, an Internet web site that provides a home for alternative culture and expression.

Carl Cafarelli is a frequent contributor to *Goldmine* and the *Syracuse New Times.*

JD Cantarella works in the media department of American Recordings.

Roger Catlin is the rock critic at the *Hartford Courant* (Conn.).

Thor Christensen is the pop music writer at the *Dallas Morning News.*

Martin Connors created VideoHound, loves Celtic music, enjoys his pints, and with the publication of MusicHound, feels his life's work is completed, leaving more time for daytime television. He's looking forward to Bruce reuniting with the E Street Band, is glad Iggy is still alive, and hopes one day to learn how to play his banjo.

Jim Craddock is the current editor of *VideoHound's Golden Movie Retriever,* and just wants to ride his machine without getting hassled by the man.

Jim Cummer manages Madhatter Music Co., a record store in Bowling Green, Ohio.

Dean Dauphinais is an associate editor for Visible Ink Press and could survive just fine on a steady diet of Marvin Gaye, Frank Sinatra, Lyle Lovett, and (pre-symbol) Prince. He is the co-author of *Astounding Averages!* and *Car Crazy.*

Tim Davis is a consultant with Jacobs Media, a suburban Detroit firm that created the modern rock format The Edge as well as Classic Rock.

Eric Deggans is the pop music critic for the *St. Petersburg Times* (Fla.). His work has also appeared on Rolling Stone Online and in *Hit, Modern Drummer, P.C. Novice* and *Rockrgrl* magazines.

Joshua Freedom du Lac is the pop music critic for the *Sacramento Bee* and frequently appears on the Sacramento PBS affiliate.

Daniel Durchholz is the editor of *Replay* magazine and a contributing editor of *Request* magazine.

Brian Escamilla is the editor of *Contemporary Musicians*, a biographical reference series, and a musician.

Shane Faubert played in a band called Cheepskates during '80s and is presently a solo artist in Montvale, N.J.

Marc Fenton is the publicist for Razor & Tie Records in New York.

Kim Forster is editor of *WTCA World Business Directory* and the *Companies International* CD-ROM.

Christina Fuoco is a music journalist for the *Observer & Eccentric Newspapers* in suburban Detroit.

Larry Gabriel is a Detroit-based writer, poet and musician who has been covering music and issues for more than 20 years. His work has appeared in the *Detroit Sunday Journal*, the *Detroit Metro Times* and the *Detroit Free Press.*

David Galens is the editor of *Contemporary Authors* on CD and a regular contributor to the *Contemporary Theatre, Film, and Television and Contemporary Authors* print series. He is also a member of the Detroit-based band The Civilians.

Anna Glen is the former managing editor of *URB Magazine* in Los Angeles. Currently, she is freelancing and working on her first novel.

Simon Glickman is the lead singer and lyricist for the L.A. band Spanish Kitchen. He has written for *Contemporary Musicians, Uncommon Heroes, Entertainment Today, Rockrgrl,* and other publications, and served as co-editor of *Native North American Biography.*

Gary Pig Gold is a musician and songwriter who has published the music fanzine *The Pig Paper* since 1975.

David Goldberg is director of new business ventures for JAM Productions in Chicago.

Mike Greenfield plays guitar, writes songs and works in advertising and public relations in Youngstown, Ohio.

Jill Hamilton is a Los Angeles-based freelance writer whose stories have appeared in the the *Ann Arbor News* (Mich.), *Rolling Stone* and other publications.

William Hanson is a movie critic for the *Detroit Sunday Journal* and has written for the *Ann Arbor News* and *Detroit Free Press.*

Steve Holtje is freelance writer and editor in New York whose work has appeared in *Creem, New Power Generation,* the *New Review* and other publications.

Peter J. Howard is the editor and publisher of *ICE: The CD News Authority.*

Michael Isabella is a radio account manager in Detroit whose love of music was nurtured in his native Cleveland.

Mike Joiner is an advertising copywriter and music collector in New York.

Keith Klingensmith is an avid power pop fan and a member of the Detroit area group the Phenomenal Cats.

Steve Knopper is a Chicago-based freelance writer who has contributed to *Rolling Stone, Newsday, Request, Billboard,* the *Chicago Tribune,* the *Chicago Reader* and the *Rocky Mountain News.*

Greg Kot is the rock critic for the *Chicago Tribune* and has contributed to *Rolling Stone, Request, Replay* and other music publications.

Bryan Lassner is a student at the University of Michigan, and in his spare time, enjoys playing and composing on the piano and keyboard.

Liz Lynch is an Evanston, Ill., writer and novelist who has written for the *Chicago Sun-Times,* the *Miami Herald,* the *Fort Lauderdale Sun-Sentinel* and *Replay* magazine.

Brian Mansfield is the Nashville editor of *New Country* magazine and has written for *Request, CCM, The Tennessean, Spin* and *Country America.*

Patrick McCarty has written about rock 'n' roll for the past 20 years for publications including the *Richmond Times-Dispatch* (Va.), the *Richmond News Leader* and *Style Weekly.* He's a classically trained musician, producer and songwriter, but we don't hold that against him.

Adam McGovern is a cultural critic as well as curator for the 10 on 8 Public Art Windows in Manhattan and communications director at Alliance for Art Education/N.J.

David Menconi is the music critic at the *Raleigh News & Observer* (N.C.) and has written for *Spin, Billboard* and *Request.*

Matthew Merta has written for *Home and Studio Recording* and the *Detroit Metro Times.* He is also a music promoter, booking agent and member of the band The Masons (of Detroit).

Judy Miller is a publicist who runs Motormouth Media in Los Angeles.

Brad Morgan is a senior editor with Visible Ink Press who will listen to anything once (twice, if he likes it). He is editor of *The Vampire Book,* among others, and currently kills time surfing the Internet.

J. Christopher Newberg is a member of the Detroit rock band the Vudu Hippies.

John Nieman works for Ticketmaster's Detroit office and contributes to Clublands, a weekly listing on Ticketmaster's World Wide Web site.

Allan Orski, in addition to freelance writing, is an associate editor at the *New Review* in New York City. He is also an actor and a vegan. Allan has been pounding out reviews from his warehouse loft in Brooklyn for exactly one year.

Jordan Oakes lives in St. Louis, where he publishes a fanzine and produces a CD sampler series, both called *Yellow Pills.* He also contributes to the *Riverfront Times.*

David Okamoto is the music editor for the *Dallas Morning News* and a contributing editor to ICE. His work has also appeared in *Jazziz, Rolling Stone* and *CD Review.*

Tamara Palmer is the associate editor of *URB Magazine* in Los Angeles. Her work has appeared in *Rolling Stone, Wired, Option,* MTV Online, *Raygun* and the *LA Weekly.*

Alan Paul is a senior editor of *Guitar World* magazine and the executive editor of Guitar World Online. His has also appeared in the *New Yorker* and *Mojo.*

James E. Person, Jr. is a senior editor at Gale Research and a musician who has written songs for small gatherings.

Mark J. Petracca is the publisher and editor of *New Power Generation* and the former editor in chief of *Creem.* He currently fronts a band called the WrightBrothers.

Doug Pippin is an advertising copywriter in New York and a drummer who ran the band music practice facility Jamland.

Gary Plochinski is a advertisting copywriter at the BBDO advertising agency in Detroit and was a founding member of the Polish Muslims.

Doug Pullen is the music and media writer for the *Flint Journal* (Mich.) and Booth Newspapers.

Jack Rabid is founder and publisher of the underground magazine *The Big Takeover.* He's also played drums for Springhouse, Even Worse, and The Leaving Trains.

Bob Remstein is a keyboardist and composer who was music editor for *Los Angeles View* before he began writing for publications in cyberspace, where he now resides.

Chris Richards is the main buyer for the Repeat the Beat record store chain in Michigan and a member of the band the Phenomenal Cats.

Leland Rucker has been writing about popular music since 1975. He is co-author of *The Toy Book* (Knopf, 1992), a study of baby boomer toys, and managing editor of *Blues Access,* a quarterly journal of blues music published in Boulder, Colo.

Christopher Scanlon is co-editor of *MusicHound Rock* as well as *Magill's Cinema Annual* and is editor of *The Video Source Book.*

Christopher Scapelliti is the editor of *On-the-Town* magazine, a monthly arts journal in West Michigan.

Joel Selvin has covered pop music for the *San Francisco Chronicle* since 1970 and is the author of six books on the subject. He co-produced Dick Dale's *Tribal Thunder* album.

Brandon Trenz is a contributing editor to Gale Research's *Contemporary Authors* series, as well as a freelance writer and film reviewer.

Aidin Vaziri is a freelance journalist in California whose work has been published in the *San Francisco Chronicle, Guitar Player* and *Vibe.*

Polly Vedder is an associate editor for Gale Research with a passion for musics that most of her acquaintances have never heard of — notably Scottish folk, contemporary Christian and off-the-beaten-track pop and rock.

Dan Weber is a copywriter at the J. Walter Thompson advertising agency in Detroit.

Hilary Weber is editor of *VideoHound's Movie LaughLines* and *VideoHound's Idiot's Delight.* She is also a contributing reviewer for *Magill's Cinema Annual* and *VideoHound's Golden Movie Retriver.*

Sarah Weber is a freelance writer who frequently contributes to Gale Research and Visible Ink Press publications.

Todd Wicks is a Detroit area freelance writer whose work has appeared for fanzines the *Jam Rag* and the *Renegade,* the *Detroit Jewish News* and the *Observer & Eccentric* newspapers in suburban Detroit.

David Yonke writes about popular music for *The Toledo Blade.*

Joshua Zarov works for Ticketmaster's Chicago office and writes for Clublands, a weekly listing on Ticketmaster's World Wide Web site.

There was no formal agenda to the meeting that spawned MusicHound on one of the coldest days of the Detroit winter in January 1996. It was more of a casual get-together between myself and Visible Ink Press' Martin Connors and Terri Schell; if nothing else, it was a chance for three Bruce Springsteen fans — in the afterglow of two superlative Detroit concerts during his recent solo acoustic tour — to reflect on those and other Springsteen shows we'd seen over the years. I don't think any of the three of us had any idea we'd wind up creating the critter you hold in your hands right now, the product of an offhand remark towards the end of the conversation.

Marty and Terri have been particularly generous in their support of the MusicHound concept and in giving me a crash course in the idiosyncracies of the book publishing business. As fellow music fans (and sports devotees), they've guarded the idea as much as if it was their own, eager to present a record guide markedly different and more utilitarian than anything else on the market. Their enthusiasm makes me look forward to the growth of MusicHound in the future.

Hilary Weber, MusicHound's managing editor, was the book's indispensable taskmaster, keeping the creative dishes full and yanking on the leash when she had to. She had the unenviable task of working to keep all aspects of the Hound in control and on target (if not always on schedule — not her fault), and she accomplished that with grace and admirable patience. Also working on the Hound's behalf at Visible Ink, putting in considerable time and effort, were Christopher Scanlon, MusicHound's co-editor and much needed support system, Bryan Lassner, an unflagging contributor and researcher, and Dean Dauphinais and Jim Craddock, who aided in creating the concept of MusicHound. Non-editorial kudos go to Jeffrey Muhr, whose technical knowledge and support were unparalleled, and Tracey Rowens, who literally gave MusicHound its exceptional look and feel. Thanks also go to Larry Baker, Don Boyden, and Mike LeBlanc, who gave valuable input on our artist list, and our MusicHound advisory board, including Steve Bergman of Schoolkids Records, Ann Delisi from CIDR-FM, Martin Bandyke at WDET, Kim Heron, and Tony Gadson from Harmony House, Berkley (Mich.).

On my side of the fence were the more than five dozen MusicHound contributors, many of whom have busy day jobs at newspapers and magazines but nonetheless set aside large chunks of their free time to perform the rigorous (but not unpleasurable) research it took to put these entries together. Many are musicians as well, and some are music enthusiasts gifted with good ears and the ability to express their opinions clearly. I've made new friends during this project, and I'm honored that all of these folks participated.

Bob Cronin, Jim Schaefer and Peggy Castine were a formidable copy editing team who brought their exceptional skills into play for MusicHound's great benefit. Bob in particular invested an incredible amount of time and emotional energy into the project, treating it as seriously as the myriad daily newspaper front pages he's put out — and then, glutton for punishment that he is, said he couldn't wait for the next one!

Chris Richards, main buyer for Repeat the Beat chain, was our one-man Minister of Information, handling myriad inquiries and double-checking lots of facts. He also helped bring some exceptional writers to MusicHound. He more than earned his five bones. Many others in the music industry offered salient advice and served as sounding boards for this project. Thanks go to: Brian Caillovette of Sprockets; Fred, Paul and Bill Jacobs, Tim Davis, Shirley Wilson, Joyce Koja and Jennifer Sabo at Jacobs Media; Drew Lane, Mike Clarke, Trudi Daniels, Rob Schaeffer, Doug Podell, Tom Bender, and Ralph Cipolla at WRIF-FM; Mike and Sandra Watts, Doug Banker, Walter and Susan Barnowski, Kathy Banker, Al Wilson and the rest of the Motor City Music Awards Foundation board; Dick Kernan and Nancy Schoenhiede of the Specs Howard School; Todd Schenkenberger and Michael Taub at RCA Records; Marc Fenton at Razor & Tie; Steve Karas at A&M Records; Kevin Kennedy at Geffen Records; Bill Schulte at PGD; Phil Ober at Belkin Productions; Rick Franks, John Itsell, Gary Meyer, Melissa Matuzak, Jennifer Bedikian and Carrie Rosol at Cellar Door Productions; Amir Daiza, Perry Lavoisne, Maureen McCurdy and Dianna Frank at Ritual Productions; Mark Campana and Jason Wright at Nederlander Productions; Bill Blackwell, Punch Andrews, Mike Boila, Frank Copeland, Kim Blackwell and Kathleen Kapelczak at Punch Enterprises; Jeff Elwood, Bob Fox, Rick Kay, Michael Tinik, Mike Novak and Marguerite Rose at Brass Ring Productions; Dave Clark and Lee Berry at Prism Productions; Dave and Anya Siglin at the Ark; Dave Zainea at the Majestic; and special thanks to Marshall Crenshaw, a personal favorite, for the dynamite foreword.

Thanks also go to the scores of record label publicists who provided CDs and other information to the contributors. Too many to mention without inadvertently offending someone, they — and their postal accounts — know who they are. On the personal front, I enjoyed the backup — professional and emotional — of many good friends: Stephen Scapelliti, my personal Minster of Law; Kent Woodman, my Minister of Karma; and Dan Durchholz, Jim and Elizabeth Lynch, and Jeff Brown, who dispensed support and good vibes. Thanks also to Vince Mogos, the always on-call Minister of Technology.

Other colleagues rallied around the project — and cut me valuable slack — including: Erik Flanigan at Mr. Showbiz; Brad Tolinski, Tom Beaujour, Harold Steinblatt, Alan Paul and Chris Gill at *Guitar World*; Sal Cirrincione at MJI; Joel Selvin at the *San Francisco Chronicle*; Tim Sheridan and Ginger Pullen at Compuserve WOW!; John Shelton Ivany and Becky Luening at *Country Song Roundup*; John Abell at Reuters; Mike Crowell and George Varga at the *San Diego Union-Tribune*; Marylynn Hewitt at the *Oakland Press*; Allan Walton and Scott Mervis at the *Pittsburgh Post-Gazette*; Tom Sabulis at the *Atlanta Journal-Constitution*; and Doug Carroll of Phoenix Newspapers.

Assorted family, friends and neighbors became part of MusicHound simply through their sincere support and regular inquiries. Thanks go to: the Galantys; Amy, Evan and Jonah Scapelliti; the Mandells; the Brysks; the Schoutens; the Woodmans; the Huszczos; Christopher Scapelliti; the Ehrlicmans; the Browns; Phil Jacobs and his family; the Logans; the Jenkins; the Keslers; the Wiles; the Isabellas; the Ceriers; the Emorys; the Arroyos; the Wershbales; the McBrooms; the Plochinskis; Howard Glanz and his family; Deborah Brown; Rob Musial; Jeff Supowit; Steve Waronoff; Brad Wasserman; Jeff Corey; Charlie Hunt; Bob Wagner; Bob and Nita Seger; Alto Reed; Chris Campbell; Craig Frost; Ted Nugent; Toby Mamis; Alice Cooper; the Tuesday night floor hockey gang; and the Yakima, Ottawa and Choctaw gangs. Propers also to the memory of the late Richard Wells, one of the finest teachers anyone could ever have. My brothers and sisters in the Metropolitan Council of Newspaper Unions — particularly Newspaper Guild Local 22 and the staff of the Detroit Sunday Journal and Detroit Journal online — provided less tangible but equally important support for MusicHound. Ours has been a just, if difficult, struggle, and it's been a privilege standing next to you all.

My greatest thanks and love go to my family, without whose indulgence MusicHound could not have been realized. Betty Schuman made sure the house stayed afloat. My grandmother, Bertha Galanty, passed away while MusicHound was being put together, but the memory of her love and support helped push me through some of the book's most difficult times. My brother Harvey and his wife Vicki offered the benefit of their publishing experiences. My stepsons Ben and Josh Rocher had the good sense to get out of town during much of the summer, while my daughter Hannah did an admirable job of checking her exasperation at my unavailability while paging through the Kiss concert program in my office (quite a sight, that). My wife, Judy Brysk, was a tremendous font of love and inspiration as the book wound itself through the spring and summer. And finally, to my parents Milton and Ruthe Graff — to whom this book is dedicated — all my love and my sincere thanks for letting me keep the stereo up loud.

Gary Graff

I'm a professional rock musician, and in order to keep the big bucks flowing in my direction, I'm on a constant search for fresh inspiration, and for new and different sounds. Here are some places and situations that I've been in where I've had my musical horizons broadened. If you're interested in music like I am then maybe you'd like to try some of these yourself:

The Elko, NV, Public Library. Back in the second half of 1977, I was traveling around the western U.S. playing in a C&W lounge band. I found myself stuck in Elko, NV., for two weeks and ran out of things to do in my spare time in about a day and a half. So, one afternoon I wandered into the public library and was pleasantly surprised to discover that they had a modest-sized but excellent selection of record albums. It was here that I first heard Wynonie Harris, Cecil Gant, and other 1940s rock 'n' rollers; The Boswell Sisters; "I'm Nuts About Screwy Music" by Jimmie Lunceford; and, best of all, "Prelude to a Kiss" by Duke Ellington. All this and slot machines in the laundromats too, in Elko, NV.

Being in a Band. If you were to ransack the luggage of a rock 'n' roll band on the road, you'd find that everyone was carrying along a slew of CDs and tapes to listen to. Of course everyone has lots of Johnny Paycheck records, but look again: one guy's got AC/DC, Lyn Collins, and Charles Mingus, another person's got The Shangri-Las and Asha Bhosle, somebody else has Skinny Puppy and Astrid Gilberto, etc., etc. I've learned a lot about music, literature, and films from people that I've gone on tours with.

Hanging Around with Cub Koda. I once spent a weekend visiting this Stratocaster stylist and *Goldmine* magazine columnist and I'm still shaking my head in disbelief over the great 45s that we listened to: "Cherokee Dance" by Bob "Froggy" Landers, "The Hunch" by Hasil Adkins, "Love Me" by The Phantom, and "The Dream" by Eugene Fox. To paraphrase Salvador Dali, you don't need drugs to enjoy records like these; these records ARE drugs. Name a record made by an American psychopath within the last seventy-five years and I'll bet that Cub has got a copy.

Another way to possibly broaden your musical horizons is to check out a book like this one. The people who wrote this book spend their professional lives listening to rock music, so you won't have to. Within these pages they're offering you information and opinion about which records are essential and which ones aren't.

Suppose that there's an era of rock music that you missed the first time around (maybe because you weren't born yet, or whatever) and now, for some reason, you're curious about it. Again, take me for example. In 1969 I was fifteen years old and one of the biggest rock music fans on two legs. Then 1970-71 rolled around and I felt like the ground had been pulled out from under me! The Beatles were broken up, Jimi Hendrix was dead, southern soul music was kind of over (for the moment). And not only that (I figured this out later), the technology of record making had changed almost overnight from tube equipment to transistors (now it's changing back), and from 4-track and 8-track tape machines (which required people to work together in groups) to 16 and 24 tracks (which enabled all the instruments to be isolated from one another), and suddenly records were starting to sound sort of cold and alienating. FM rock radio was changing as well; The Dumb-Ass Brigade (the folks that still want to hear the same ten records over and over again, year in and year out) was moving in and demanding sweeping changes, like no more blues, R&B, or jazz. So I drifted away from FM rock radio during the '70s—and got more into music than I'd ever been before. But now a lot of time has passed and I'd really like to know: which Blue Oyster Cult album is the best? Which Lynyrd Skynyrd album? (I might buy one, but I'm not going to buy them all, for God's sake.) So a book like this one would come in handy for me; I only hope that a copy of *MusicHound Rock* is heading toward my mailbox right now.

Someone once said that "writing about music is like dancing about architecture," but what the hell is that supposed to mean, anyhow? I know that if it weren't for writers like Nick Tosches, Dan Forte, and many others, I might have missed out on some of my all-time favorite records. But enough of my yakkin'... If you want to see dancing about architecture done with a vengeance, then look no further than the pages of *MusicHound Rock*.

Marshall Crenshaw

Record shops and book stores share a unique kind of shopping sensibility. The folks you see milling in the aisles and eyeing the product are *interested*. They're passionate. Fanatical in some cases. They're not figuring out whether a tie goes with the shirts they own or if a pair of shoes matches enough of the rest of the wardrobe—not that those are easy choices, either. These folks are making decisions about whether a piece of artistry fits with their *lives*. These are high stakes we're talking about. It's about how they'll be investing their time—and feeding their psyche. So it's not surprising that a kind of joyous intensity is palpable in these places. Oh, there's the odd customer who rushes in, makes a decisive purchase and gets out quickly. But there are many more who linger, browsing the shelves and racks for some new highlight or a previously unheard-of gem. It's both relaxing and tense; the purchase matters, but there's something soothing about working your way through the myriad choices.

Where the record and book shops differ is in environment. Book stores are a little like libraries; there's a hushed quality, and the shopping experience is more individual. In a record store, on the other hand, music blasts in the background, and the energy level is entirely different—active, visceral, partisan. Communication differs as well; if book store patrons acknowledge each other with the quiet nod, record shoppers are more prone to discuss their tastes and selections. You'll be flipping through an act's section, checking out a particular album, and the person next to you offers a comment. Someone across the aisle chimes in with an observation, and you're in the midst of a conversation—or a debate, depending on the opinions present. The goal of these discussions is uniform, however. What should I buy? What's good? What's not? Basic stuff—but big decisions, nonetheless.

That's where MusicHound comes in.

What you hold in your hands is *MusicHound Rock*, the first of a series of album guides that will examine various forms of music with an eye towards helping the buyer—novice and fanatic alike—make that crucial purchase decision. Imagine the MusicHound as those other people striking up a conversation with you—except in this case it's a canine with limitless time to prowl the aisles and sniff out everything that's there. Like any good dog, its hearing is keen; it will wag its tail when it finds something good. But its teeth are sharp, too, and the Hound isn't afraid to take a big chunk out of something that doesn't make the grade.

MusicHound, of course, is kind of a wonder-dog amalgamation of music experts and devotees from around the country. We've assembled writers and critics from a variety of magazines, newspapers and on-line publications. We've brought in folks from the radio world. All of them listen to music on a daily basis; they have expertise and perspective (they're well-trained, to belabor the doggie metaphor). They hear it all, and if they say it's good, you know it stands out from amongst the dozens of albums that land on their desks and in their CD players every day.

We've also invited plain old music fans, whose exuberance doesn't interfere with their critical ears, to lend their opinions as well. What they've created in MusicHound is a pup who *likes* music and proceeds under the premise that all music is worth hearing unless, through listening, it proves itself otherwise.

Without slighting any of our worthy running buddies in the album guide field, we think we've taken a unique and refreshing approach to dealing with the glut of rock 'n' roll out there.

The Hound, by the way, has made its own decision about what's rock and what isn't. It's no easy task; the scent spills over into some areas of the hip-hop, jazz, country and other speciality sections. The criteria is purposely general and vague—you know it when you hear it—but there's a sensibility that unites these entries under the Rock mantle; and yes, some of the choices may (and should) surprise you. Neil Diamond, for instance, is in the book; his work hails from the same roots (Hank Williams, Woody Guthrie) as any number of rockers and displays a rock 'n' roll orientation. Barry Manilow, however, comes from more of a Tin Pan Alley background, more pop than rock and is therefore passed over by the Hound.

So what's the best way to let MusicHound romp through the record store with you? First sit back and page through the book. You'll find two different kinds of entries: detailed assessments for acts with lengthy histories and/or large bodies of work; and shorter assessments reserved for fledgling acts with only a few releases or for older artists who just don't have much left in print anymore. Each entry tells you a little something about the act, more a perspective on its music than a full-blown biography (this is a guide, after all, not an encyclopedia). Still, the entries provide invaluable information and perhaps even a new way of thinking about that particular band or artist.

MusicHound then gets down to the main task of helping you make that decision about what to buy, what to avoid and so on. You'll find those recommendations herein, with opinions that are neither mushy nor tentative. Trust the Hound reviewers; if they say get it, then do so. If they say skip it, avoid it like the plague. In making their recommendations, the MusicHound considered not just what an act's best work is but also what the most representative work might be. For instance, Bruce Springsteen's "The Ghost of Tom Joad" might be a magnificent artistic and thematic piece. But is it the first thing a Springsteen buyer should get? How should you make your way through the Beatles' catalog when most folks would deem each of the Fab Four's 13 titles essential listening? You may simply sit back and reap the benefits brought to you by the brave Hounds who had to paw through the ample litter of albums by giants such as Elvis Presley or Ray Charles or James Brown or Johnny Cash.

Now, you ask, what's with those bones? It's not hard to figure out, rating on a scale from 0-5—five bones ⟡⟡⟡⟡⟡ is nirvana (not Nirvana), a WOOF! is dog food. Keep in mind that the bone ratings don't pertain just to the act's own catalog but also to it's worth in the whole music realm. Therefore a lesser act's **What to Buy** choice might rate no more than three bones ⟡⟡⟡; some even rate two and a half bones ⟡⟡▿, a not-so-subtle sign of the act's placement in the rock spectrum. **What to Buy Next** means what it says; these works are worthwhile once you've listened to the **What to Buy** selections and decided whether or not you like the act. **What to Avoid** is pretty clear, too, though in cases where the trusted Hound reviewer thinks the subject hasn't released a bad album, it refers to an act's *least* essential work. You'll also find ratings for the rest of the act's catalog—in most cases we list only what remains in print rather than sending you on a wild goose chase (the Hound *hates* those)—and for solo projects by individual members of bands. The **Worth Searching For** designation sends you hunting for out-of-print treasures, bootlegs, imports and other hard-to-find items that the Hounds sniffed out. Each of the major entries ends with categories maked by Fast Forward and Rewind symbols. The former gives a sense of who the act has influenced or what other acts you might like if you like this one. Rewind is just the opposite, a quick look back at influences that shaped the act's sound or style. As with any opinions, all of what you're about to read is subjective and personal. MusicHound has a bit of junkyard dog in it, too; it likes to start fights.

We hope it does, too. Ultimately, we think the Hound will point you in the right direction, and if you buy the five bone and four bone choices, you'll have an album collection to howl about. But if you've got a bone to pick, the Hound wants to hear about it. If you think we're wagging our tails in the wrong direction or lifting our leg at something that doesn't deserve it, let us know. If you think an act has been capriciously excluded—or charitably included—tell us.

After all, there will be more MusicHounds coming your way in the future—and we want those jazz, blues, country and other music fans to get the benefit of the rock hounds' experience. And MusicHound will revisit the rock world in the not-too-distant future. So strap a leash on this puppy and take it out for your next trip through the record store. The Hound travels well, and we bet it will be a pretty productive stroll.

Though Bruce Springsteen has told the story differently, God did not declare, "Let there be rock 'n' roll," and there it was. Rock evolved from a hybrid of assorted folk musics, rural blues, R&B, jazz and the twangy sounds of country and pre-country hillbilly music. It's the ultimate mongrel music.

The following performers cannot be considered rock 'n' rollers, but they did exert significant influence on its development. Any rock fan would do well to pick up the recommended purchases to get a sense of the disparate places rock 'n' roll hail hailed from.

Laurel Aitken

Born 1928 in Cuba

A precursor of reggae, ska and dancehall, Aitken is known for works both serious ("Judgment Day," "Landlords and Tenants"), light ("Bartender," "Bugaboo") and downright rude ("Pussy Price"). Aitken—who moved to Jamaica during the early 50s—made the first Jamaican record released in Britain ("Little Sheila"), and he eventually moved to London during the 60s to become a touchstone for ska and punk artists of the late 70s.

what to buy: *The Blue Beat Years* (Moon, 1996).

Chet Atkins

Born June 20, 1924 in Luttrell, Tenn.

A Nashville guitar trend-setter, Atkins is an acknowledged influence on rockers both obvious (George Harrison, Dire Straits' Mark Knopfler, Leo Kottke) and unexpected (Neil Diamond, George Benson). As a player, Atkins developed a dry, plucky finger-picking style drawn from influences such as Merle Travis and Django Reinhardt. As a producer (mostly at RCA Records), he dressed up performances in sweet, lush arrangements that came to define the pop-oriented Nashville sound of the 60s and early 70s—which in itself bucked country tradition in the same way that Willie Nelson and Waylon Jennings did with their "outlaw" movement. Atkins remains a force today, recording his own albums and occasionally collaborating with admirers such as Knopfler.

what to buy: *The RCA Years: 1947-1981* (RCA, 1992).

Lavern Baker

Born Nov. 11, 1929 in Chicago, Ill.

Baker, the niece of blues great Memphis Minnie, made her mark during the 50s with hits such as "Tweedlee Dee," "I Cried a Tear" and "Jim Dandy"—the latter revived by Black Oak Arkansas in 1975. With a big voice honed in gospel choirs, Baker disappeared from the charts during the early 60s, and by the end of the decade she was living and running a nightclub in the Phillippines, where she moved after being treated there for a case of pneumonia she developed in 1969. Baker began a comeback at the Atlantic Records' 40th anniversary concert in 1988, and in recent years she's been honored by the Rhythm & Blues Foundation and the Rock and Roll Hall of Fame, and her albums and live performances have shown she's still a force to be reckoned with.

what to buy: *Soul on Fire: The Best of Lavern Baker* (Rhino, 1991).

Jesse Belvin

Born Dec. 15, 1933 in Texarkana, Ark. Died Feb. 6, 1960 in Los Angeles, Calif.

More than his own music, Belvin is remembered as the father figure of Los Angeles' doo-wop scene during the 50s—a writer, producer, arranger, de facto manager and occasional member. His biggest hit was a writer of the Penguins' 1955 smash "Earth Angel," while his own hits stayed on the R&B charts. Sadly, his greatest success—"Guess Who" in 1959—hit the R&B Top 10 just nine months before he died in an auto accident.

what to buy: *Goodnight, My Love* (Flair/Virgin, 1991).

Tony Bennett

Born Anthony Dominick Benedetto, August 13, 1926, Queens, N.Y.

Bennett is a definitive vocal stylist whose appeal crosses generations. A 50s and early 60s crooner whom Frank Sinatra has called his personal favorite, Bennett owns a litany of pop hits ("Because of You," "Stranger in Paradise," "I Left My Heart in San Francisco") in addition to estimable credentials as a jazz singer. Though rock 'n' roll ran roughshod over his career (he didn't record between 1978-85), Bennett has lately become something of a beloved uncle for the modern rock generation. He's appeared on "The Simpsons," on "Late Night with David Letterman" and on the MTV Music Video Awards, dressed like Public Enemy's Flavor Flav and mugging with some of the Red Hot Chili Peppers. For his "MTV Unplugged" episode, Bennett was joined by k.d. lang, Elvis Costello and Dinosaur Jr.'s J Mascis. He's not quite ready for Lollapalooza, but Bennett is unquestionably cool.

what to buy: *MTV Unplugged* (Columbia, 1994).

Bobby "Blue" Bland

Born Jan. 27, 1930 in Rosemark, Tenn.

Breaks occur in strange ways; in Bland's case, it was being hired as B.B. King's chauffeur, which gave him entree to record company executives. One from Duke Records heard Bland sing, and in 1955 he was on the charts with "It's My Life, Baby." Dynamic and resonant, Bland helped define classic soul singing, influencing not only R&B performers but also any number of rockers who drew their inspiration from the soul side of the fence.

what to buy: *I Pity the Fool/The Duke Recordings, Vol. 1* (MCA, 1992).

Earl Bostic

Born April 25, 1913 in Tulsa, Okla. Died Oct. 28, 1965 in New York, N.Y.

Rock and soul saxophone players—from King Curtis to Jr. Walker to Maceo Parker to Clarence Clemons—all owe a debt to Bostic, whose honking alto sax provided the foundation for their approaches. Bostic worked with Lionel Hampton and Cab Calloway, among others. He put his own band together in 1951 and scored R&B chart hits such as "Flamingo" and "Sleep."

what to buy: *16 Sweet Tunes of the Fantastic 50s* (Hollywood/Rounder, date N/A).

Charles Brown

Born 1922 in Texas City, Texas

Sam Cooke, Bruce Springsteen, Bonnie Raitt, B.B. King and Fats Domino have recorded his songs. Ray Charles cites him as a vocal influence. Clearly, Brown's importance goes well beyond his own hits, which included a handful of R&B chart successes during the late 40s and early 50s ("Trouble Blues," "Black Night," "Seven Long Days" and "Merry Christmas Baby"). As a singer, Brown was neither a belter nor a shouter; rather, he helped pioneer the smooth, jazzy style known as "ballad blues," an approach that's touched several generations of slow songs. You'll still find Brown out on the road, often with chief patron Raitt.

what to buy: *Driftin' Blues: The Best of Charles Brown* (EMI, 1992).

Roy Brown

Born Sept. 10, 1925 in New Orleans, La. Died May 25, 1981 in Los Angeles, Calif.

A blues belter of the first order, Brown was a seminal influence on the Sun Records crowd—and Elvis Presley in particular. Brown's 1947 hit "Good Rocking Tonight" was one of the early songs Presley cut at Sun and one of the staples of his live show. The Robert Plant-led Honeydrippers, meanwhile, revived Brown's "Rockin' at Midnight" in 1984. Brown also boasted hits such as "Long About Midnight," "Hard Luck Blues" and "Boogie at Midnight," and his energetic stage shows laid the foundation for rock 'n' roll showmen such as James Brown and Little Richard.

what to buy: *Good Rocking Tonight: The Best of Roy Brown* (King/Rhino, 1994).

Ruth Brown

Born Jan. 30, 1928 in Portsmouth, Va.

From church choirs to big bands to Broadway, Brown has been a vital presence in R&B, blues, pop and jazz since the late 40s. Nicknamed "Miss Rhythm," she was one of Atlantic Records' first major stars—in fact, the label was known as "The House That Ruth Built" during its early days. During the mid-80s, Brown added theater to her repertoire, and in 1989 she won a Tony Award for her performance in the musical "Black and Blue." She still hits the road, performing with proteges such as Bonnie Raitt.

what to buy: *Miss Rhythm (Greatest Hits and More)* (Rhino, 1989).

Cab Calloway

Born Cabell Calloway, Dec. 25, 1097 in Rochester, N.Y. Died Nov. 18, 1994.

Embraced by both jazz and R&B fans, Calloway distinguished himself with stylish, energetic performances and a crowd-pleasing exuberance, best displayed in his signature hit "Minnie the Moocher" and its "hi de hi de hi de hi" call-and-response refrain. Calloway's showmanship probably made a greater mark on the rock world than his music, though his songwriting adheres to universal conventions that are as familiar to pop fans in the 90s as they were to Calloway's crowd during the 30s and 40s.

what to buy: *Are You Hep to the Jive?* (Columbia/Legacy, 1994).

The Carter Family

Formed 1926 in Maces Spring, Va. Disbanded 1943.

A vocal group that broke ground with its full-scale chorale arrangements of folk songs, the Carter Family was a progenitor of what we now call country music and also influenced the way pop groups approached music-making. Led by A.P. Carter and his wife, Sara Dougherty, the Carters during the 20s created definitive versions of such standards as "Will the Circle Be Unbroken," "Wabash Cannonball," "Wildwood Flower" and "Keep on the Sunny Side." It also gave the world two more generations of singing stars, including the Carter Sisters—a troupe that included Johnny Cash's wife June—and Carlene Carter.

what to buy: *Anchored in Love: Their Complete Victor Recordings 1927-28* (Rounder).

Charlie Christian

Born 1919 in Dallas, Texas. Died march 2, 1942 in New York, N.Y.

Though primarily a jazz artist who worked with Benny Goodman, Dizzy Gillespie and others, Christian's ascent coincided with the emergence of the electric guitar. With his lucid, melodic playing—including a picking technique that's copied to this day—Christian established the guitar's place as a solo instrument after years of being relegated to the rhythm section.

what to buy: *The Genius of the Electric Guitar* (Columbia, 1987).

Nat "King" Cole

Born Nathaniel Adams Cole, March 17, 1919, Montgomery, Ala. Died February 15, 1965 in Los Angeles, Calif.

Perhaps better remembered for his warmly voiced baritone vocals on such ballads as "Mona Lisa," "Ramblin' Rose" and "When I Fall in Love," pianist Cole was initially an instrumental performer. His playing influenced such legendary jazz pianists as Art Tatum, Oscar Peterson and Erroll Garner, while Cole's original trio—with Wesley Prince on bass and Oscar Moore on guitar—offered a hot-house melding of jazz and R&B. Cole's influence on the pop world was mostly as a singer, however; his smooth ballads and peppy uptempo stylings established a number of vocal conventions that can be heard from Morrissey to Montell Jordan. His daughter Natalie's "duet" with him on "Unforgettable" was the big Grammy winner of 1992.

what to buy: *The Greatest Hits* (Capitol, 1994).

Son House

Born Eddie House, March 21, 1902 in Riverton, Miss. Died Oct. 19, 1988 in Detroit, Mich.

House's 1965 release declared him the "Father of the Folk Blues," and that about sums it up. An acknowledged influence on Robert Johnson, Muddy Waters and the rest of the Delta blues community, House was a Baptist minister who taught himself to play guitar and began working house parties around rural Mississippi. His own mentor was Charley Patton, who produced House's first recordings for Paramount Records in 1930.

what to buy: *Delta Blues: The Original Library of Congress Sessions from Field Recordings 1941-1942* (Biograph, 1991).

The Ink Spots

Formed 1928 in Indianapolis, Ind.

Arguably the first doo-wop group, the Ink Spots began recording during the mid-30s and had a million-seller, "If I Didn't Care," by 1939. The group's other hits—"Maybe," "We Three," "To Each His Own" and "I Don't Want to Set the World on Fire"—flaunted smooth harmonies and a lushness created by the voices rather than instruments. With lineups too numerous to count over the years, new versions of the Ink Spots still pop up periodically, though their association to the original is usually tenuous.

what to buy: *Greatest Hits: The Original Recordings 1939-1946* (MCA, 1989).

Blind Lemon Jefferson

Born July 1897 in Couchman, Texas. Died December 1930 in Chicago, Ill.

Jefferson's country blues of the 20s was a seminal influence on other rock 'n' roll forebears such as John Lee Hooker, Lightin' Hopkins, T-Bone Walker, B.B. King and Big Joe Williams. The term boogie woogie is an outgrowth of booger rooger, which he coined in his hit "Booger Rooger Blues."

what to buy: *King of the Country Blues* (Yazoo, 1990).

Robert Johnson

Born May 8, 1911 in Hazelhurst, Miss. Died August 16, 1938 in Greenwood, Miss.

Although he recorded just 29 songs, Johnson's influence on blues and rock 'n' roll is immense. A street singer who became a leading figure of the sacred Delta blues scene, Johnson composed an inordinate share of songs—"Dust My Broom," "Sweet Home Chicago," "Ramblin' on My Mind," "Love in Vain" and "Terraplane Blues"—that are rock and blues staples, covered by the likes of the Rolling Stones, Cream and the Allman Brothers Band, among others. His legion of vociferous proteges includes Eric Clapton, Jimmy Page, Keith Richards and, if they're smart, any other guitarist who has the good taste to listen to his *King of the Delta Blues Singers*.

what to buy: *The Complete Recordings* (Columbia, 1990).

Louis Jordan

Born July 8, 1908 in Brinkley, Ark. Died Feb. 4, 1975 in Los Angeles, Calif.

Beginning as a jazz saxophonist, Jordan developed a bluesy, spirited and good-humored style that was a direct precursor to R&B and rock 'n' roll. Chuck Berry, Ray Charles and Little Richard sang Jordan's praises early in their careers; producer Milt Gabler acknowledged that the records he produced for Bill Haley and His Comets were lifted from earlier works he did with Jordan. Joe Jackson saluted Jordan's influence with his 1981 album *Jumpin' Jive*, while the hit Broadway musical *Five Guys Named Moe* mined the Jordan songbook for a latter day revival.

what to buy: *No Moe! Louis Jordan's Greatest Hits* (Verve, 1992).

Leadbelly

Born Hudie Ledbetter, circa 1885 in Mooringsport, La. Died Dec. 6, 1949 in New York, N.Y.

There's much debate about whether the songs that made Leadbelly famous—"Goodnight Irene," "The Midnight Special," "Rock Island Line"—were original or simply adaptations of old folk and slave songs he picked up during his travels. No matter; Leadbelly—with help from folklorists John and Alan Lomax—provided a vital link in American musical traditions, offering a gutbucket brand of rural blues and introducing the 12-string guitar as accompaniment.

what to buy: *King of the 12-String Guitar* (Legacy, 1991).

Junior Parker

Born Herman Parker, March 3, 1927 in West Memphis, Ark. Died November 18, 1971 in Blue Island, Ill.

Blues harmonica player and vocalist Parker began his career in 1948 at a Sonny Boy Williamson show, raising his hand when Williamson asked for a harmonica player. Parker joined Williamson's band and went on to play with Howlin' Wolf, Johnny Ace and B.B. King. He's also the author of the Elvis Presley hit "Mystery Train" and had lengthy career of his own with hits such as "Driving Wheel," "Annie Get Your Yo-Yo" and "Barefoot Rock."

what to buy: *Junior's Blues: The Duke Recordings, Vol. 1* (Duke/MCA, 1992).

Charley Patton

Born April 1981 in Bolton, Miss. Died April 28, 1934 in Indianola, Miss.

An innovative songwriter and guitar player—including his signature bottleneck slide style—Patton was a gutsy rock 'n' roll grandparent who influenced such rock forebears as Howlin' Wolf and Son House. Among those dubbed "King of the Delta Blues," Patton played complex, original music that eschewed standard blues progressions and incorporated early polyrhythmic techniques and aspects of African and South American musics.

what to buy: *King of the Delta Blues: The Music of Charley Patton* (Yazoo, 1991).

Les Paul

Born Lester Polfus, January 9, 1915 in Waukesha, Wisc.

A player and innovator, Paul is responsible for many of the "toys" that have been part of the rock guitar world for decades. Paul created the solid body electric guitar (Gibson's Les Paul model is still one of the most popular), electronic echo, overdubbing studio multi-tracking techniques and a variety of pickups for guitars. His recorded output—mostly with his wife, singer Mary Ford—can seem a bit lightweight compared to his other credentials, but Paul has showed his playing mettle on albums such as *Chester and Lester* and *Guitar Monsters* with Chet Atkins on Al DiMeola's *Splendido Hotel.*

what to buy: *Les Paul: The Legend and the Legacy* (Capitol, 1991).

Doc Pomus

Born Jerome Solon Felder, June 27, 1925 in Brooklyn, N.Y. Died March 14, 1991 in New York, N.Y.

Though a singer in his own rite, Pomus is best known as a songwriter whose catalog—on his own and with partner Mort Shuman—includes "Viva Las Vegas," "Save the Last Dance For Me" and "There Must Be a Better World Somewhere." His death was one of the inspirations for the Lou Reed album, "Magic + Loss."

what to buy: N/A

Ma Rainey

Born Gertrude Melissa Nix Pridgett, April 16, 1886 in Columbus, Ga. Died Dec. 22, 1939 in Columbus.

Rainey carved out a place for blues in the vaudeville tradition, serving as a direct mentor for Bessie Smith and, in turn, an influence on Dinah Washington, Sippie Wallace and others. Her "See See Rider Blues" evolved into the rock staple "C.C. Rider."

what to buy: *Ma Rainey* (Milestone, 1974/1992).

Jimmy Reed

Born Sept. 6, 1925 in Dunleith, Miss. Died Aug. 29, 1976 in Oakland, Calif.

Elvis Presley, the Rolling Stones and Aretha Franklin are only some of the artists who have covered Reed staples such as "Big Boss Man," "Honest I Do" and "Baby, What You Want Me to Do." A blues harpist and singer, Reed began scoring hits during the mid-50s, though he was among the veterans pushed aside by the British Invasion during the 60s.

what to buy: *The Classic Recordings* (Tomato, 1994).

Jimmie Rodgers

Born September 8, 1897 in Meridian, Miss. Died May 26, 1933 in New York, N.Y.

If the Carter Family represents the "clean" side of modern country music, Rodgers is its "dirty" counterpart. Adding rural blues to the mix—which Rodgers picked up as a railroad brakeman during the early 20s—he crafted a grittier kind of music that affected not only Nashville but also the Memphis musicians who would make their mark at Sun Records. With the short film "The Singing Brakeman" in 1929, Rodgers can also be considered one of music's video pioneers as well.

what to buy: *The Best of Jimmie Rodgers* (Rhino, 1990).

Pete Seeger /the Weavers

Born May 3, 1919 in New York, N.Y.

Having outlived Woody Guthrie, Leadbelly and many of his other contemporaries, Seeger remains the embodiment of the pure folk spirit that moved first Bob Dylan and then a legion of other singer-songwriters. Seeger's parents were on the faculty of the Julliard School of Music, and he was already something of a scholar when he began making music as a teenager. His outspoken social and political views made the Harvard-educated Seeger a no-brainer for the House Un-American Activities Committee's blacklist during the 50s, but Seeger never broke stride and was fully redeemed by 1965, when the Byrds turned his "Turn! Turn! Turn!" into a No. 1 hit. Seeger first recorded that song with the Weavers—Ronnie Gilbert, Fred Hellerman and Lee Hays—which was America's chief folk revival troupe between 1949-58 and an equally important touchstone for the folk-rock music.

what to buy: *We Shall Overcome: The Complete Carnegie Hall Concert* (Columbia, 1989); *The Best of the Weavers* (MCA, 1987).

Frank Sinatra

Born Francis Albert Sinatra, Dec. 12, 1915 in Hoboken, N.J.

Ol' Blue Eyes—or, if you prefer, The Chairman—has been no great friend to rock 'n' roll. He was one of its most outspoken critics during the early days—particularly when it knocked him and his Rat Pack contemporaries off the pop charts. That said, he's covered more than a few rock hits over the years, and his recent series of "Duets" albums has featured a litany of rockers that includes U2 singer Bono and the Pretenders' Chrissie Hynde. And there's no denying Sinatra's influence; he's one of—if not *the*—finest pop stylists of our time, blending influences from Bing Crosby to Billie Holiday and honing his loose, improvisatory style with big band leaders Harry James and Tommy Dorsey. Sinatra also set standards for pop iconolatry (he was the Michael Jackson of *his* day) and tough-guy cool; any rocker that dons a leather jacket owes something, at least indirectly, to Sinatra. He still performs, but don't expect to see him turn up on "MTV Unplugged."

what to buy: (with Tommy Dorsey): *All-Time Greatest Hits, Vol. 1* (RCA, 1988); *The Capitol Years* (Capitol, 1990); *Sinatra: Soundtrack to the CBS Mini-Series* (Reprise, 1992).

Bessie Smith

Born April 15, 1894 in Chattanooga, Tenn. Died September 26, 1937 in Clarksdale, Miss.

Smith's gravestone—which was co-financed by Janis Joplin—declares her "The Greatest Blues Singer in the World," and you'll be hard-pressed to argue the point. Mentored by Ma Rainey and schooled in vaudeville, Smith stepped out on her own following World War I and created a body of work that made her the top black entertainer of the early 20th century and a touchstone for any blues-inclined singer to come along since. During the early 30s Smith was singing pop standards, but they never overshadowed her dazzling blues repertoire. Columbia Records has released four box sets of Smith's work in recent years, and their consistently high quality is a testament to her talents.

what to buy: *The Collection* (Columbia, 1989).

Huey "Piano" Smith

Born Jan. 26, 1934 in New Orleans, La.

Acknowledging his limited talent as a singer, pianist Smith formed a group called the Clowns, and the ensemble created some early R&B classics during the 50s that helped establish New Orleans as a rock 'n' roll hotbed, opening the door for Fats Domino and Frankie Ford, among others. In fact, it's the Clowns who backed Ford on his 1969 smash "Sea Cruise." Smith—who retired from music to become a Jehovah's Witness during the early 70s—is best known for "Rockin' Pneumonia and the Boogie Woogie Flu," a song as important to New Orleans' rock legacy as "Blueberry Hill" or "Iko Iko."

what to buy: *Rock & Roll Revival* (Ace U.K., 1991).

The Soul Stirrers

Formed early 30s in Texas.

Best known as the onetime home of Sam Cooke, this gospel group's real leader was Robert H. Harris. Harris' innovative vocal arrangements provided a bridge for gospel to evolve into soul ensemble singing. Besides Cooke, the Soul Stirrers also included, at various times, Johnnie Taylor, James Medlock and Julius Cheeks.

what to buy: *The Original Soul Stirrers featuring Sam Cooke* (Speciality).

T-bone Walker

Born Aaron Thibeaux Walker, May 28, 1910 in Linden, Texas. Died March 16, 1976 in Los Angeles, Calif.

Like Charlie Christian in jazz, Walker pioneered a role for the electric guitar in his milieu—the blues. By plugging in, Walker gave rootsy Delta blues a sharp, urban feel; in doing so, he also laid the groundwork for R&B and rock 'n' roll. Every early electric blues hero (B.B. King, Buddy Guy, Albert Collins, Albert King, Freddie King) took a lead from Walker, while Chuck Berry's style can be traced directly back to Walker's recordings.

His biggest hit, "Call it Stormy Monday" (aka simple "Stormy Monday") is a blues and rock staple.

what to buy: *The Complete Imperial Recordings, 1950-1954* (EMI, 1991).

Dinah Washington

Born Ruth Lee Jones, August 29, 1924 in Tuscaloosa, Ala. Died Dec. 14, 1963 in Detroit, Mich.

Washington's hallmark was versatility; she could handle jazz, blues, gospel and pop with equal facility, and when she let them blend into each other, she crafted a wholly distinctive style. She sang first in church but during the mid-40s worked with Lionel Hampton before going solo and earning the mantle "Queen of the Harlem Blues." She was also one of the R&B singers most heard by fledgling rock singers thanks to pop crossover hits such as "A Rockin' Good Way," "What a Diff'rence a Day Makes" and, with Brook Benton, "Baby (You've Got What it Takes").

what to buy: *First Issue: The Dinah Washington Story* (Mercury, 1993).

Jimmy Yancey

Born Feb. 20, 1898 in Chicago, Ill. Died Sept. 17, 1951 in Chicago.

A lifelong Chicago resident—who took a 15-year hiatus to be a groundskeeper for the White Sox—pianist Yancey is considered the father of boogie woogie, a style that was popular in Chicago but really took hold in the South, particularly New Orleans.

what to buy: *In the Beginning.*

Gary Graff with Steve Holtje,
Patrick McCarty and Leland Rucker

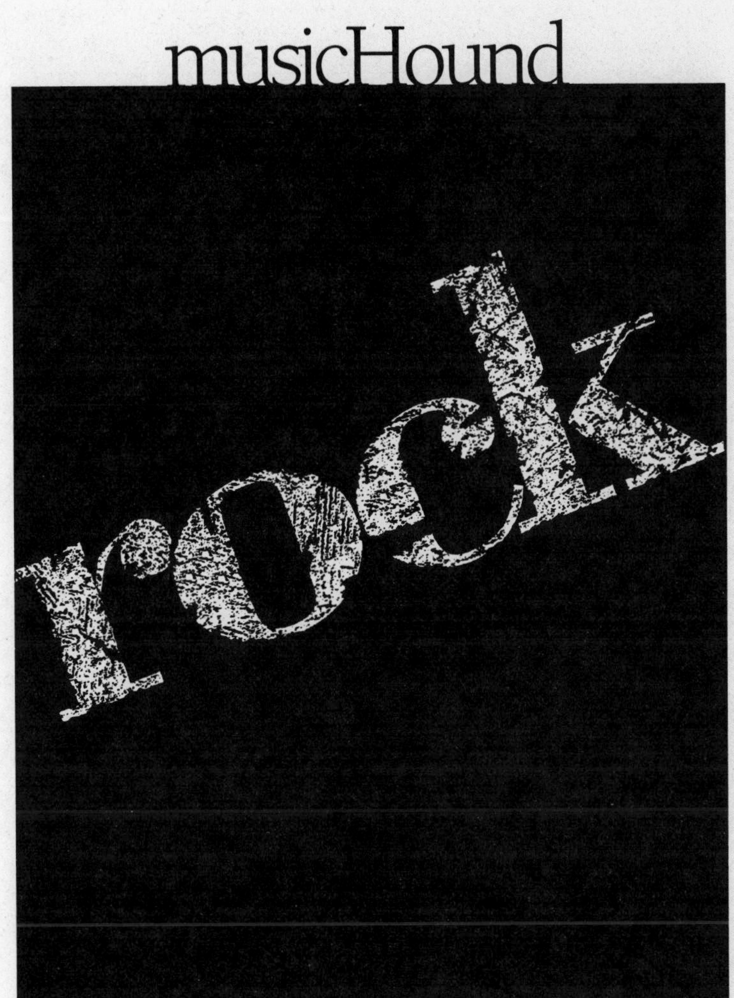
musicHound
rock

A House

Formed 1985 in Dublin, Ireland

Dave Couse, vocals, guitar; Fergal Bunbury, guitar; Martin Nealy, bass; Dermot Wylie, drums

Although not quite as popular as their Irish brethren, U2, A House also can write catchy, tuneful pop with a Celtic flavor. Their four-man lineup cuts to the chase in creating standard guitar rock with interesting lyrics that often touch upon a variety of meaningful or at least potentially controversial issues. Their first single was titled, "Kick Me Again, Jesus" while another song, "That's Not the Truth," attacks journalists. Some songs paint a violent picture—"I Want to Kill Something," "Violent Love"—yet the band isn't afraid to show some emotion as on "My Little Lighthouse." Their strong first album, *On Our Big Fat Merry-Go-Round,* (Sire, 1988) proved that Ireland has more to offer than just that other band. This album is especially impressive for a debut as it contains a song which rose to number 9 on Billboard's Modern Rock chart. *I Want Too Much* (Sire, 1990) is no sophomore slump as it offers more catchy guitar hooks and witty lyrics that translate to meaningful pop tunes. Their third offering, *I Am the Greatest,* (Radioactive, 1992) is more diverse than the previous two with some melodious tracks and other more noisy cuts. The arrogant-sounding title is actually a song about the price of fame. The literary nature of the Irish is readily apparent in this band.

Christopher Scanlon

ABBA

Formed 1971 in Sweden

Benny Andersson, keyboards, vocals; Bjorn Ulvaeus, guitar, vocals; Agnetha "Anna" Faltskog, vocals; Anni-Frid "Frida" Lyngstad, vocals

Like the Volvo of the band's homeland—the only Swedish export bigger than this group during the 70s—ABBA's well-oiled pop machine was very nearly a perfectly manufactured product. Heavily layered vocals and synthesizers delivering conversely simple lyrics and melodies made the band's music enormously successful around the world. ABBA was bigger abroad than in the U.S. and charted 14 Top 20 hits there. Anna, Benny, Bjorn and Anni-Frid were individual stars in Sweden before they joined forces (and first initials) to form ABBA, which first drew worldwide attention with "Waterloo," the winner of the 1974 Eurovision Song Contest. After the group's 1982 breakup (said to be necessitated by the members' wealth, which drew death and kidnapping threats), ABBA nostalgia only grew. A decade later, greatest hits compilations topped the charts worldwide, while the music was covered by all manner of artists and frequently popped up in film soundtrack. It may be slick and sugary, but the very optimism of their voices and tunefulness of their songs makes ABBA's music very hard to dislike.

what to buy: Because it was a singles band, ABBA's *Gold* (Polydor, 1992, prod. Benny Andersson and Bjorn Ulvaeus) is a glittering array of highlights and party sure-things, with 19 tracks ranging from "Dancing Queen" and "Knowing Me, Knowing You" to "S.O.S" and "Waterloo." So sweet you may feel your teeth start to decay.

what to buy next: For those who need more, get *Thank You for the Music,* (A&M, 1995, prod. Benny Andersson and Bjorn Ulvaeus) a four-disc boxed set with one full disc of unreleased tracks, B-sides and foreign language versions. *More ABBA Gold* (Polydor, 1996, prod. Benny Andersson and Bjorn Ulvaeus) ♪♪♪ features a lot of wonderful and overlooked ABBA ditties, including a few hits such as "I Do, I Do, I Do, I Do, I Do." For those who wonder what an original ABBA album sounds like, *Arrival* (Polydor, 1977, prod. Benny Andersson and Bjorn Ulvaeus) ♪♪♪, timed to concur with ABBA's first international tour, finds the band at its peak, with the hits "Dancing Queen" and "Knowing Me, Knowing You."

what to avoid: *Ring Ring* (Atlantic, 1973/Polydor, 1995, prod. Benny Andersson and Bjorn Ulvaeus) ♪♪ begins the story a little too early. The band hasn't quite found itself yet.

the rest: *Waterloo* (Atlantic, 1974/Polydor, 1995) ♪♪♪ *ABBA* (Atlantic, 1975/Polydor, 1995) ♪♪♪ *The Album* (Atlantic, 1977/Polydor, 1995) ♪♪♪ *Voulez-Vous* (Atlantic, 1979/Polydor, 1995) ♪♪♪ *Super Trouper* (Atlantic, 1980/Polydor, 1995) ♪♪ *The Visitors* (Atlantic, 1981/Polydor, 1995) ♪♪

worth searching for: *Selections from Thank You for the Music* (Polydor, 1995) ♪♪♪♪ a promotional sampler from the box set that features "Abba Undeleted," a specially crafted 23-minute "Stars on Abba" medley of hits.

solo outings:

Frida Lyngstad: Something's Goin' On (Atlantic, 1982) ♪♪♪

▶▶ Ace of Base, the Real McCoy, Bjorn Again, Erasure

◀◀ Blue Swede, 1910 Fruitgum Co., the Archies, the Fifth Dimension

Roger Catlin

ABC

Formed 1980 in Sheffield, England

Martin Fry, vocals; Mark White, guitar, keyboards; Mark Lickley, bass (1980); David Robinson, drums (1980); Stephen Singleton, saxophone (1980-84); David Palmer, drums (1980-83); Eden, vocals (1983-90); David Yarritu, keyboards (1983-90)

Amid the fashion conscious music scene of post-punk England, ABC matched luxuriant pop writing with its wardrobe, crafting one bona fide classic of the period before shifting gears awkwardly to rock, then back to campy pop, then over to dance. The band's career has been in limbo since its stylish frontman and mainstay, Martin Fry, was diagnosed with Hodgkin's disease in 1987.

what to buy: *The Lexicon of Love* (Mercury, 1982, prod. ABC) ♪♪♪♪ holds up in an era of very flimsy fashion music as a self-assured, tuneful, classy stab into heartfelt emotion tied up with a lot of strings—literal and metaphoric.

what to buy next: *Absolutely* (Mercury, 1990, prod. Various) ♪♪♪♪ is a greatest hits album that seems a little premature but captures the high points nicely.

what to avoid: *Beauty Stab* (Mercury, 1983, prod. ABC) ♪♪, the follow-up to *Lexicon of Love* that suffered for the decision to turn ABC into a heavier guitar band.

the rest: *How to Be a Zillionaire* (Mercury, 1985) ♪♪♪ *Abracadabra* (Mercury, 1991) ♪♪

worth searching for: *Alphabet City* (Mercury, 1987, prod. Martin Fry and Mark White) ♪♪♪♪ is a return to form, now out of print, that featured "When Smokey Sings," an infectious tribute to Smokey Robinson.

▶▶ George Michael, Pulp, Love Jones

◀◀ Roxy Music, David Bowie, Motown

Roger Catlin

Paula Abdul

Born June 19, 1962 in Los Angeles, Calif.

Chosen as a choreographer for the Los Angeles Lakers basketball team cheerleaders at age 17, Abdul found herself rubbing shoulders with the town's most famous citizens—eventually attracting interest from the Jacksons, who hired her to choreograph a video. From there, she guided Janet Jackson's dance-heavy breakthrough videos, becoming a star herself when the clips exploded on MTV. After doing similar work for the Pointer Sisters, ZZ Top and "The Tracey Ullman Show," among others, Abdul signed a recording deal herself—releasing a critically drubbed but commercially successful debut album, filed with disposable dance/pop. Most potshots regarding that and subsequent albums centered on Abdul's singing—a thin, nasal wail that needed lots of processing to sound listenable. Still, her stylized videos saturated MTV, pushing her into the pop stratosphere. A second record also did well, but trouble loomed when a backup singer on Abdul's first record claimed to have sung lead vocals on all the tunes. Given Abdul's lack of vocal talent, it was a serious charge, but a Los Angeles court eventually decided in Abdul's favor. But by the time the suit was resolved, younger, hip hop-influenced dance divas were ruling the charts, and Abdul's 1995 album came and went without much notice.

what to buy: Her debut, *Forever Your Girl,* (Virgin, 1988, prod. Various) perfectly distills the tenor of the MTV-fed pop market of the time. It's basically a record featuring a boatload of producers and even more studio musicians, crafting a raft of tracks designed to provide a sonic artifact to go along with an incredibly videogenic star. The songs seem like an afterthought, momentarily enjoyable but ultimately forgettable.

what to avoid: *Shut Up and Dance (The Dance Mixes)* (Virgin, 1990, prod. Various) WOOF!, which just provided another excuse for MTV put an Abdul video in heavy rotation.

the rest: *Spellbound* (Virgin, 1991) *Head Over Heels* (Virgin, 1995)

worth searching for: The collection of videos from her debut disc, also called "Straight Up" (Virgin, 1990), if only to see the real reason why she got a record deal—videogenic dance moves and well-packaged video showcases.

▶▶ Mariah Carey, Gillette

◀◀ Janet Jackson, Madonna, Donna Summer

Eric Deggans

AC/DC

Formed 1973 in Sydney, Australia

Angus Young, guitar; Malcolm Young, guitar; Dave Evans, vocals (1973-74); Ronald Belford "Bon" Scott, vocals (1974-80, died Feb. 19, 1980); Brian Johnson, vocals (1980-present); Peter Clark, drums (1973-74); Phillip Rudd, drums (1974-82, 1995-present); Simon Wright, drums (1982-89); Chris Slade, drums (1989-95); Rob Bailey, bass (1973-74); Mark Evans, bass (1974-77); Cliff Williams, bass (1977-present)

One of the most popular and influential hard rock bands in the world, AC/DC has enjoyed success for more than two decades without straying from the brand of straightforward, electrified boogie it began with during the mid-70s. Founding members and brothers Angus and Malcolm Young were influenced at an early age by their uncle George, a member of the Easybeats (known for the hit "Friday on My Mind"). With George's musicianship and music industry savvy to guide them, the Young brothers soon assembled a group that was filling the Australian bar circuit. Many of AC/DC's fans came to witness Angus' hyperkinetic onstage antics: clad in his signature schoolboy uniform and clutching a Gibson SG (the only guitar he ever plays), little Angus would thrash, bob, crawl and duck-walk his way through the band's sets, pausing occasionally to moon the audience. After two Australian albums, the band scored overseas and quickly became a worldwide sensation, seemingly immune to even the greatest adversity in 1980, at the peak of their success, singer Scott died, choking on his own vomit in the back seat of a friend's car. The band pressed on, adding ex-Geordie vocalist Johnson to the lineup; the first album with Johnson, *Back in Black,* was its best-seller yet. AC/DC has since churned out a succession of popular albums that remain true to its raunchy, guitar-fueled formula, for which it's been rewarded with a steadily increasing army of fans and a string of successful world tours.

what to buy: For many fans, there are two AC/DCs: the Bon Scott band and the Brian Johnson band. For fans of Scott's bluesy style, *Let There Be Rock* (Atlantic, 1977, prod. Harry Vanda and George Young) and *Powerage* (Atlantic, 1978, prod. Harry Vanda and George Young) reign supreme, showcasing both Scott's solid lyrics and Angus' crunching guitar. However, even fans who prefer Scott can't deny the power of *Back in Black,* (Atlantic, 1980, prod. Robert John "Mutt" Lang) by far the best of the albums that feature Johnson's whiskey-soaked growl.

what to buy next: The live *If You Want Blood...You've Got It* (Atlantic, 1978, prod. Harry Vanda and George Young) finds the Scott-fronted band in fine form, while Johnson's sophomore effort, *For Those about to Rock, We Salute You* (Atlantic, 1981, prod. Robert John "Mutt" Lang) is one of AC/DC's most solid recordings.

what to avoid: *Flick of the Switch* (Atlantic, 1983, prod. AC/DC) is one of the group's more lackluster albums.

the rest: *High Voltage* (Atlantic, 1976) *Dirty Deeds Done Dirt Cheap* (Atlantic, 1976) *Highway to Hell* (Atlantic, 1979) *'74 Jailbreak* (Atlantic EP, 1984) *Fly on the Wall* (Atlantic, 1984) *Who Made Who* ("Maximum Overdrive" film soundtrack) (Atlantic, 1986) *Blow Up Your Video* (Atlantic, 1988) *The Razor's Edge* (Atlantic, 1990) *Live* (Atlantic, 1992) *Ballbreaker* (EastWest, 1995)

worth searching for: The two-disc collector's edition of *Live* (Atlantic, 1992, prod. Bruce Fairbairn) provides several essential performances missing from the single-disc edition.

Soundgarden, Guns N' Roses, The Cult, Joan Jett, Rhino Bucket

Led Zeppelin, Yardbirds, Cream, the Who

Brandon Trenz

The Accelerators

Formed 1983 in Raleigh, N.C. Disbanded 1992.

Gerald Duncan, vocals, guitar; Chris Moran, guitar (1983-87); Brad Rice, guitar, vocals (1988-91); Doug Welchel, drums (1983-90); Jon Wurster, drums (1990-91); Skip Anderson, bass (1983-87); Mike Johns, bass, vocals (1988-91)

From the Georgia Satellites to Webb Wilder, most 80s roots rock bands got by more on good intentions than actual songcraft. The Accelerators' underrated Duncan is slyer than most, a songwriter equipped with enough smarts and droll humor to pull off songs as emotionally outlandish as "Two Girls in Love" (which is about exactly what the title implies). That never helped Duncan or the Accelerators find an audience, however. But they left behind some fine records, especially the swan song, *Dream Train* (Profile, 1991, prod. Dick Hodgin) with a dozen sharp songs—including the best-ever theft of the "Bang a Gong (Get It On)" riff on the shoulda-been-a-hit-single "Boy & Girl." The Accelerators' uneven debut album, *Leave My Heart*, (Dolphin, 1983, prod. Don Dixon) wears its period power pop uneasily, but it has an ace version of the aforementioned "Two Girls in Love." The middle album, *The Accelerators*, (Profile, 1988, prod. Dick Hodgin, Don Dixon and Rod Abernathy) is better, although it has one too many throwaway covers. After the Accelerators broke up, drummer Wurster joined Superchunk, and guitarist Rice resurfaced in the hardcore honkytonk band the Backsliders.

David Menconi

Ace

See: Paul Carrack

Ace of Base

Formed 1990 in Göteborg, Sweden

Jenny Cecilia Berggren, vocals; Malin Sofia Datarina "Linn" Berggren, vocals; Jonas Petter "Joker" Berggren, keyboards; Ulf Gunnar "Buddha" Ekberg, keyboards

It's appropriate that you can file Ace of Base's albums right after ABBA's in your collection. Like the Swedish Europop pioneer that preceded it, Ace of Base consists of two men and two women playing insidiously catchy pop songs that are guilty pleasures, pure and simple. The group's debut, *The Sign* (Arista, 1993, prod. Joker/Buddha) offers a trio of massive international hits—"All That She Wants," "Don't Turn Around" and the title track—all of which sound remarkably alike, a curious mix of toy reggae, Eurodisco and new wave synth-pop bouncing along at 95 or so beats per minute. (The European version of *The Sign* is available in a slightly different configuration under the title *Happy Nation*.) Despite, or perhaps because of, its adherence to the group's hit formula, *The Bridge* (Arista, 1995, prod. Joker/Buddha) failed to ignite much excitement stateside. (A European version is available in another slightly different configuration.) The 1995 remix album, *Aced! The Unreleased Mixes*, is available as an import.

Daniel Durchholz

Adam and the Ants

See: Adam Ant

Bryan Adams

Born Bryan Guy Adams, Nov. 5, 1959, in Kingston, Ontario

Adams started out like everybody's kid brother—nice enough, harmless, but kind of an annoyance. Dressed in blue jeans, T-shirts and leather jackets, he was a radio-friendly alternative to the era's true heartland-rock hitmaker, Bruce Springsteen. Yet there's something to be said for Adams' hooky, unpretentious singles; they stuck in your ears to the extent that you can probably still sing along to "Cuts Like a Knife" and "Summer of '69," which now are more than a decade old. Adams will never be accused of being a great artist, but give him this: he knows the craft. In recent years, two major shifts have occurred with Adams: Once a rocker, his hits now are frequently ballads, and movie themes at that—and he has thrown off the jeans-and-T-shirt look for expensive suits, greasy hair and an unshaven face, looking disturbingly like Kurt Cobain had the late Nirvana leader sold out to the idea of playing the dissolute pop star. As the saying goes, know thyself.

what to buy: From his third album on, Adams has enjoyed enviable success on the singles chart. *So Far So Good* (A&M, 1993, prod. Various) does a pretty good job of summarizing his career to that point. And since Adams is a hitmaker, not an album-oriented artist, this is the only essential purchase.

what to buy next: The album on which Adams found his mission as a man with a dependable hook, simple lyric and memorable chorus was *Cuts Like a Knife,* (A&M, 1983, prod. Bryan Adams and Bob Clearmountain) which features the singles "This Time," "Straight from the Heart" and the memorable title cut. *Reckless* (A&M, 1984, prod. Bryan Adams and Bob Clearmountain) is Adams' best album overall, mostly thanks to a plethora of hits such as "Heaven," "Summer of '69" and "Run to You." After a disappointing half-decade, Adams came roaring back with *Waking Up the Neighbours,* (A&M, 1991, prod. Robert John "Mutt" Lange and Bryan Adams) a worldwide smash that produced still more hits, including the monstrous "(Everything I Do) I Do It for You" from the film "Robin Hood, Prince of Thieves."

what to avoid: The overblown, hamhanded *Into the Fire* (A&M, 1987, prod. Bryan Adams and Bob Clearmountain) offered ample proof that Adams should be making singles, not statements.

the rest: *You Want It, You Got It* (A&M, 1981, prod. Bryan Adams and Bob Clearmountain) *Live! Live! Live!* (A&M, 1986, prod. Bryan Adams) *18 til I Die* (A&M, 1996, prod. Robert John "Mutt" Lange and Bryan Adams)

worth searching for: His debut, *Bryan Adams,* (A&M, 1980, prod. Bryan Adams and Jim Vallance) can only be found these days in the Great White North.

▶▶ Steve Perry, Michael McDermott, Bon Jovi, Skid Row

◀◀ Joe Cocker, Bruce Springsteen, John Cougar (Mellencamp), the Beatles, the Guess Who, Fleetwood Mac

By Daniel Durchholz

Terry Adams

See: NRBQ

Barry Adamson

See: Magazine; Nick Cave and the Bad Seeds

The Adverts

Formed 1976 in London, England. Disbanded 1979.

Tim "T.V." Smith, vocals; Howard Pickup (born Howard Boak), guitar; Gaye Advert (born Gaye Black), bass; Laurie Driver (born Laurie Muscat), drums (1976-78); John Towe, drums (1978); Rod Latter, drums (1978-79); Tim Cross, keyboards (1979)

Whenever someone wants to know about the intellectual edge even the crudest English punk of '76-78 had, the Adverts are the best place to start. The group's songs were skillfully catchy, despite the raw edges and sometimes tattered sound. More importantly, in T.V. Smith it had perhaps the keenest social critic in a time that was overflowing with them. And for such a short-lived band, with only two proper LPs to its credit, the Adverts produced some of the most fondly remembered, enduring classics of the genre in the incredible "Gary Gilmour's Eyes" "No Time to Be 21" and "One Chord Wonders"—the first two of which were even Top 40 hits in the U.K., despite their contentious subject matter. Fortunately, all three are found on the reissued versions of the band's fabulous (also) U.K. Top 40 debut LP that truly captures those times, *Crossing the Red Sea With the Adverts* (Bright Records U.K., 1978, prod. John Leckie). These songs, and the equally thought-provoking societal analysis/distaste found in the killer "Bombsight Boy," "New Church" and "The Great British Mistake," have held up over nearly two decades. One other single from the LP, "Safety in Numbers," even has the foresight and temerity to criticize the punk scene itself, prophetic when one considers how punk eventually lost its way. The follow-up, *Cast of Thousands* (RCA U.K., 1979, prod. Tom Newman) couldn't match the immediacy in production; in fact, Newman needlessly mutes the LP in his way too polite mix. Nevertheless, such faults in no way obscure Smith's first-rate songwriting and typically strong lyrical prowess. The generous use of synthesizers add a new wrinkle, proving the Adverts were also an ambitious group, not afraid to adapt and grow while still retaining their direct drive. Years after the group's demise, two live documents—*The Peel Sessions* (Strange Fruit U.K. EP, 1987) and *Live at the Roxy* (Receiver U.K., 1990)—paid tribute to the Adverts' spark and energy.

T.V. Smith has had a long and respectable solo career under a variety of monikers. As T.V. Smith's Explorers: *Last Words of the Great Explorer.* (Epic, 1981) As T.V. Smith: *Channel Five* (Expulsion U.K., 1983) *March of the Giants* (Cooking Vinyl U.K., 1992) *Immortal Rich.* (Thirsty Ear, 1996) As T.V. Smith's Cheap: *RIP...Everything Must Go.* (Griffin, 1994)

Jack Rabid

Aerosmith

Formed 1970 in Sunapee, N.H.

Steven Tyler, vocals, keyboards; Joe Perry, guitar (1970-79; 1985-present); Brad Whitford, guitar (1970-81; 1985-present); Jimmy Crespo,

guitar (1979-84); Rick Dufay, guitar (1982-84); Tom Hamilton, bass; Joey Kramer, drums

When Aerosmith released its first album in 1973, there was little to distinguish the band from a hundred other hard rock outfits that could cover old Yardbirds tunes (which Aerosmith did with "Train Kept a Rollin'.") Within three years, however, the Boston quintet had infused a bit more soul and swing into its crunch and evolved from just another blues 'n' boogie band into arguably America's most important hard rockers. But by the 80s, the group had all but flushed its career down the toilet; some of its members had turned into junkies (Tyler and Perry weren't nicknamed "The Toxic Twins" for nothing), ego problems threatened to tear the group apart and the music went limp. Yet in the late 80s, Aerosmith—buoyed by a Run-D.M.C. remake of its hit "Walk This Way"—detoxed, reunited and launched one of the most impressive comebacks in rock history.

what to buy: *Rocks* (Columbia, 1976, prod. Jack Douglas and Aerosmith) didn't spawn any big hits, but raunchy rave-ups like "Last Child" and "Rats in the Cellar" make it the mother of all American hard rock albums. *Toys in the Attic* (Columbia, 1975, prod. Jack Douglas) is almost as nasty, thanks to unapologetically raunchy rave-ups such as "Walk This Way," "Sweet Emotion" and "Big Ten Inch."

what to buy next: *Pump* (Geffen, 1989, prod. Bruce Fairbairn) gave Aerosmith another shot at packing arenas, and rightfully so: "Janie's Got a Gun" and "What It Takes" are as good as anything the band has done.

what to avoid: Recorded after Perry and Whitford first quit, *Rock in a Hard Place* (Columbia, 1984, prod. Jack Douglas and Steven Tyler) was more like schlock in soft space.

the rest: *Aerosmith* (Columbia, 1973) *Get Your Wings* (Columbia, 1974) *Draw the Line* (Columbia, 1977) *Live Bootleg* (Columbia, 1978) *A Night in the Ruts* (Columbia, 1979) *Aerosmith's Greatest Hits* (Columbia, 1980) *Classics Live* (Columbia, 1984) *Done With Mirrors* (Geffen, 1985) *Classics Live II* (Columbia, 1987) *Permanent Vacation* (Geffen, 1987) *Gems* (Columbia, 1988) *Pandora's Box* (Columbia, 1991) *Get a Grip* (Geffen, 1993) *Big Ones* (Geffen, 1984)

worth searching for: *Train Kept a Rollin'* (Pluto, 1991), a powerful bootleg of a British concert that featured Jimmy Page on versions of "Train Kept a Rollin' " and "Walk this Way."

solo outings:

Joe Perry Project: Let the Music Do the Talking (Columbia, 1980) *I've Got the Rock 'n' Rolls Again* (Columbia, 1981) *Once a Rocker, Always a Rocker* (Columbia, 1984)

Whitford-St. Holmes: Whitford-St. Holmes (Columbia, 1981)

Die Kreuzen, Tesla, Ratt, Guns N' Roses

Rolling Stones, Led Zeppelin, Yardbirds

Thor Christensen

The Afghan Whigs

Formed 1986 in Cincinnati, Ohio

Greg Dulli, vocals, guitar; Rick McCollum, guitars; John Curley, bass; Steve Earle, drums (1986-95); Paul Buchignani, drums (1995-present)

Often labeled the bastard son of Sub Pop, the Afghan Whigs didn't exactly fit the pre-grunge profile of its Seattle-based label's artistic repertoire. The Whigs almost always relied on an organic formula of passionate rock and soul, a far cry from the Marshall-stacked guitar pummelings of soon-to-be-famous labelmates Nirvana and Soundgarden. It has been long rumored that scratchy-throated vocalist Dulli met guitarist McCollum in an Ohio jail cell, and the pair later became acquainted with bassist Curley and drummer Earle, thus rounding out what would be the Whigs permanent line-up until 1995. Despite early detractors, the Whigs recorded heroic garage music that often played homage to the amorous sounds of soul. As a frontman, Dulli—who sang on the soundtrack for the Beatles film "Backbeat"—developed a tortured persona that won him a legion of female fans who swooned over his lyrical honesty (see *Gentlemen*) and Midwestern, demented-boy-next door charm. Most notably, the Whigs should be listened to for its sense of cinematic adventure; hearing to their best is like listening to the soundtrack of your secret desires.

what to buy: *Congregation* (Sub Pop, 1992, prod. Ross Ian Stein and Greg Dulli) begins what is essentially the Whigs' foray into climactic orchestration, with each song contributing to a larger thematic picture and exhibiting a fearless musical passion and skill that no earlier releases matched. *Gentlemen,* (Sub Pop/Elektra, 1993, prod. Greg Dulli) the Whigs major label debut, again highlights the group's own special brand of guitar-driven angst, this time with cleaner production. *Gentlemen* glides the listener through a shocking landscape of fear ("What Jail Is Like"), abuse ("Fountain and

Fairfax") and rejection ("Now you Know"), dressing up the group's guitar attack with touches of mellotron and piano.

what to buy next: Punky, grungey and lots of fun, *Up In It* (Sub Pop, 1990, prod. Jack Endino) exposes the garage glory of the early Whigs. Songs such as "White Trash Party" and "Retarded" are anthemic rockers, though they bear little resemblance to the Whigs' later, more sophisticated, work. *Black Love* (Sub Pop/Elektra, 1996, prod. Greg Dulli) is infinitely more sinister and less accessible than previous works. Still, the Whigs propensity for storytelling remains intact and songs such as "Honkey's Ladder," and "My Enemy" are notable. *The Uptown Avondale* (Sub Pop EP, 1992, prod. Afghan Whigs) is a pleasing four-song diversion that finds the Whigs covering soul classics by the Supremes ("Come See About Me"), Freda Payne ("Band of Gold") and Al Green ("Beware").

what to avoid: The *What Jail Is Like* EP (Sub Pop/Elektra, 1994, prod. Greg Dulli) is merely a bone-throw to Whigs fans after *Gentlemen* began attracting attention, a hodgepodge of live tracks, covers and previously released material.

worth searching for: *Big Top Halloween* (Ultrasuede, 1988, prod. Afghan Whigs) is the Whigs' first release, chock-full of fuzzy guitars and garagey glory but burdened by raw, amateurish production.

▶▶ Howlin' Maggie, Jonny Polonsky, D Generation, Super 8

◀◀ The Beatles, the Replacements, Hüsker Dü, Motown

Judy Miller

Agent Orange

Formed 1979 in Fullerton, Calif.

Mike Palm, vocals, guitars; Steve Soto, bass, vocals; James Levesque, bass, vocals; Brent Liles, bass; Scott Miller, drums (1979-85); Derek O'Brian, drums (1985-present)

One of the first bands to pair punk sensibilities with 60's surf music, Agent Orange often sounds as close to "Wipeout" as it does to "Anarchy in the UK"—but at the same time it's more melodic and easily accessible than either. A little too rough for the surf dudes on the beach, Agent Orange was adopted by landlubbing skate punks, who found its twangy guitars and unusually harmonious punk vocals a perfect soundtrack for their brand of surfing.

what to buy: *This Is the Voice* (Restless, 1986, prod. Daniel Van Patten) remains Agent Orange's best and most accessible release, a bit mellower than its predecessors with touches of everything from 80s pop to 60s psychedelic guitar solos.

what to buy next: *Living In Darkness* (Rhino, 1981, prod. Robbie Fields, Jay Lansford and Daniel Van Patten) is a solid album on its own, but the CD version adds the songs from the 1982 EP *Bitchen' Summer* Don't miss the terrific take of Dick Dale's "Misirlou."

the rest: *When You Least Expect It* (Restless EP, 1984) *Real Live Sound* (Restless, 1991)

▶▶ The Adolescents, Christian Death, Game Theory

◀◀ Fear, Minor Threat, Jefferson Airplane, the Ventures, the Sex Pistols

Bryan Lassner

a-ha

Formed 1982 in Oslo, Norway

Morton Harket, vocals; Magne "Mags" Furuholmen, keyboards; Pal Waaktaar, guitar

a-ha is living proof that the world is a really big market. Emerging rapidly with a cutting edge video for the single "Take On Me," a technological marvel that depicted a romantic adventure starring lead singer Harket as a comic book hero who comes to life. The combination of live action and animation garnered heavy MTV airplay and success in the U.S. during the summer of 1985. Although a-ha made a valiant effort to sustain that level of success, its commercial status in North America diminished as quickly as it came—though a-ha remained popular around the world. Subsequent albums continued to demonstrate a-ha's pop hooks blended with Hacket's poetic vocals over a layer of synthesizer-heavy electropop. Other highlights included the theme song for the 1987 James Bond Film "The Living Daylights" and record-breaking crowds at the 1991 "Rock In Rio" festival.

what to buy: *Hunting High and Low* (Warner Bros., 1985, prod. Alan Tarney) features "Take On Me" as well as other strong material such as the title track and "The Sun Always Shines On T.V.," which demonstrates Harket's magnificent vocal range. *Scoundrel Days* (Warner Bros., 1986, prod. Alan Tarney and a-ha) continues in the same vein, putting a slightly softer and more soothing varnish on the group's characteristically engaging melodies.

what to buy next: *Headlines and Deadlines: The Hits of a-ha*(Warner Bros. 1991, prod. Various) ♪♪♪ is a best-of package that culls all the singles released worldwide, along with some remixes, for a complete taste of a-ha.

what to avoid: On *Memorial Beach,* (Warner Bros., 1993 prod. David Z and a-ha) ♪ a-ha tries to be U2 and it does not work.

the rest: *Stay On These Roads* (Warner Bros., 1988 prod. Alan Tarney) ♪♪ *East of the Sun, West of the Moon* (Warner Bros., 1991 prod. Chris Neil and Ian Stanley) ♪♪

worth searching for: The 45rpm single for "Take On Me" (Warner Bros., 1985, prod. Alan Tarney) ♪♪♪♪ complete with the comic book and storyboards from the song's celebrated video.

▶▶ Ace of Base

◀◀ Simple Minds, Duran Duran, Roxy Music, David Bowie

John Nieman

Air Supply

Formed 1976 in Melbourne, Australia. Disbanded 1988. Re-formed 1991.

Graham Russell, vocals, guitar; Russell Hitchcock, vocals

Air Supply warbled highly produced, sugary love ballads to massive radio play at the end of the 70s; by the early 80s, a syrupy string of hits made them middle-of-the-road radio staples. The millions of Air Supply records sold are into double digits, proving there may, in fact, be no limit to the public's appetite for schmaltz.

what to buy: *Greatest Hits.* (Arista, 1983, prod. Robie Porter) ♪ Certainly not album-oriented musicians, Air Supply is best taken in one quick gulp. "Lost in Love," "Every Woman in the World," "Making Love Out of Nothing at All" are here for your romantic nights in front of the Duraflame log.

what to buy next: *Lost in Love* (Arista, 1980, prod. Porter) ♪ is the album that sent upper-middle class 7th-grade girls lip-synching down the hallways.

what to avoid: *The Christmas Album.* (Arista) WOOF! Wasn't giving ballads a bad name enough?

the rest: *Love and Other Bruises* (Columbia, 1977) ♪ *Now and Forever* (Arista, 1982) ♪ *The Earth Is* (Giant, 1991) ♪ *The Vanishing Race* (Giant, 1993) ♪ *News from Nowhere* (Giant, 1995) ♪ *Greatest Hits Live...Now And...* (Giant, 1996) ♪

worth searching for: Ha!

▶▶ Christopher Cross, Mariah Carey

◀◀ The Captain and Tennille

Allan Orski

The Alarm

Formed 1978 in Rhyl, Wales. Disbanded 1992.

Mike Peters, vocals; Eddie McDonald, bass; Dave Sharp, guitar; Nigel Twist, drums

With idealistic overtones and stadium-style rockers, the Alarm initially sought to bring punk's spirit to its acoustic strumming. Inspired by U2 and the Clash, the lofty political messages were vague and unrealized compared with those bands'. Subsequently, the Alarm rocked with climatic urgency that pinnacled every three minutes with feverish sturm and drang. The band eventually plugged in, turning out mainstream rock, but never shook the U2 comparisons.

what to buy: *Standards* (I.R.S., 1990, prod. Various) ♪♪♪♪ The Alarm was most effective on its singles, and this has them all. "The Stand" and "Sixty-Eight Guns" are early blazers; the partly successful commercial bid of the highly produced "Rain in the Summertime" and the blues-edged "Sold Me Down The River" are also represented, along with three new tracks recorded for the disc.

what to buy next: *Strength* (I.R.S., 1985, prod. Mike Howlett) ♪♪♪♪ is one of the band's most consistent albums, featuring the title track and "Spirit of '76." *Change* (IRS, 1989, prod. Tony Visconti) ♪♪♪ is a harbinger of change indeed, revealing a tougher sound with more electric guitar bite than anything the Alarm had recorded previously.

what to avoid: *Raw* (IRS, 1991, prod. ??) ♪♪ Oh, the dreary business of fulfilling contractual obligations. And why cover Neil Young's "Rockin' in the Free World"—to point arrows at the band's own lack of depth?

the rest: *The Alarm* (I.R.S., 1983) ♪♪♪ *Declaration* (I.R.S., 1984) ♪♪♪ *Eye of the Hurricane* (I.R.S., 1987) ♪♪♪ *Electric Folklore: Live* (I.R.S., 1988) ♪♪ *Newid* (I.R.S., 1989) ♪♪

worth searching for: *Second Generation: Rare Songs of the Alarm,* (MPO, 1995) ♪♪♪♪ a collection of re-recorded Alarm rarities and B-sides that Peters recorded and distributed through the band's fan club after the Alarm broke up.

solo outings:

Dave Sharp: Downtown America (Dinosaur Entertainment, 1996)

Hothouse Flowers, Midnight Oil

U2, the Clash, the Sex Pistols

Allan Orski

Arthur Alexander

Born May 10, 1940 in Florence, Ala. Died June 9, 1993 in Nashville, Tenn.

Alexander wrote songs that helped define early 60s popular music, yet he never achieved a wide or sustaining notoriety beyond the music industry. With a smooth and plaintive vocal style, Alexander wedded country with soul to create music that was unique, outstanding and enduring. His first hit, 1962's "You Better Move On," was recorded in Muscle Shoals, Ala., and helped to establish that locale as a hotbed of soul and R&B talent. Alexander's music was also an early influence on John Lennon and Paul McCartney, who covered his biggest hit, "Anna (Go To Him)," on the Beatles' 1963 debut album; two years later, the Rolling Stones used Alexander's "You Better Move On" on *December's Children.* Bob Dylan ("Sally Sue Brown"), Elvis Presley ("Burning Love") and Otis Redding ("Johnny Heartbreak") were among the other pop luminaries who recorded Alexander's works. But his own career languished, due mainly to substance abuse and a record industry that insisted on pegging him as a country artist. Disillusioned, he retired from recording and moved to Cleveland, Ohio, where he drove a bus for a social services agency. Marshall Crenshaw kept Alexander's music alive by covering "Soldier of Love (Lay Down Your Arms)" on his 1982 debut album, and in 1991, Alexander was coaxed into performing at a songwriters workshop at The Bottom Line in New York. That sparked him to record a new album and resume his career though, tragically, he suffered a fatal heart attack on the eve of a concert tour to celebrate his return. Alexander was never really a household name, but he'll always be remembered as one of the great early influences on rock & roll.

what to buy: *The Ultimate Arthur Alexander* (Razor & Tie, 1993, prod. Various) is an outstanding compilation that houses Alexander's original versions of the songs that were covered and by so many influential artists of the 60s. These are mostly mid-tempo ballads featuring great melodies and lyrics that are hauntingly personal and direct, with a recurring theme of relationships gone wrong.

what to buy next: *Lonely Just Like Me* (Elektra Nonesuch, 1993, prod. Ben Vaughn and Thomas Cain) was recorded shortly before Alexander's death and offers some great new originals in the style of his best work, along with some updated versions of his older songs. This was an unexpected treasure for fans who had assumed Alexander would never record again. *Adios Amigo: A Tribute to Arthur Alexander* (Razor & Tie, 1994, prod. Various) is a memorable tribute from a wide range of artists paying their respects in song. Elvis Costello's burning version of "Sally Sue Brown" is worth the price of admission alone.

what to avoid: While there are some great moments, *Rainbow Road: Arthur Alexander: The Warner Brothers Recordings* (Warner Bros., 1994, prod. Tommy Cogbill) is inconsistent and for major fans and completists only.

the rest: *Soldier of Love* (Ace, 1987)

worth searching for: *A Shot of Rhythm and Soul,* (Ace, 1982) a well-annotated vinyl only collection that contains all the big hits and some great songs such as "Sally Sue Brown," which are not represented on *The Ultimate Arthur Alexander*

The Beatles, Marshall Crenshaw, Elvis Costello, the Rolling Stones, Otis Redding, Ike & Tina Turner, Humble Pie, Ry Cooder, the Bee Gees, Rod Stewart

Eddy Arnold, Hank Williams, Elmore James, Jimmy Reed, B.B. King, Junior Parker, the Drifters, the Clovers, Billy Ward and the Dominos

Michael Isabella

Alice in Chains

Formed 1987 in Seattle, Wash.

Jerry Cantrell, guitar; Layne Staley, vocals; Sean Kinney, drums; Mike Starr, bass (1987-92); Mike Inez, bass (1992-present)

Drugs, sad to say, are what makes Alice in Chains stand out from its more conventional contemporaries in grunge and metal bands. Staley airs his private battle with addiction publicly in the band's gloomy songs and layers his vocals so they sound like the moaning you might hear in a haunted house; and when they're wrapped around "Junkhead," "Hate to Feel" and "Sickman," they sound positively frightening. Otherwise, Alice In Chains, which began as a hard rock band opening shows for Anthrax, Metallica and Slayer, is simply Pearl Jam with shorter hair. As the commercial market shifted from speed metal to grunge, Alice in Chains shifted, too, lodging "Would?" on the lucrative "Singles" soundtrack and eventually following Nirvana to the top of the alternative-rock sweepstakes—even taking its own turn on "MTV Unplugged" in 1996.

what to buy: *Dirt*, (Columbia, 1992, prod. Bryan Carlstrom) despite its mopey metallic sound, builds the hits "Rooster," "Junkhead" and "Would?" around transfixing dark melodies.

what to buy next: *Jar of Flies* (Columbia EP, 1993, prod. Alice in Chains) is most notable for its doo-wop vocals from Hell—which sound, oddly enough, like the vocals on a couple of Hootie and the Blowfish hits.

what to avoid: The debut, *Facelift*, (Columbia, 1990, prod. Dave Jerden) gave the band a crucial commercial buzz, but it sure sounds bland in retrospect.

the rest: *Sap* (Columbia EP, 1991) *Alice In Chains* (Columbia, 1995) *MTV Unplugged* (Columbia, 1996)

worth searching for: *We Die Young* (Columbia EP, 1990) was a promotional EP that predicted the grunge curve long before Alice in Chains joined it.

Stone Temple Pilots, Bush, Korn, Hootie and the Blowfish

Nirvana, Pearl Jam, Led Zeppelin, Black Sabbath, Metallica

Tracey Birkenhauer and Steve Knopper

Gregg Allman

See: Allman Brothers Band

Allman Brothers Band

Formed 1969 in Jacksonville, Fla. Disbanded 1982. Reformed 1989.

Duane Allman, guitar (died Oct. 29, 1971); Gregg Allman, keyboards, vocals, Dickey Betts, guitar, vocals; Berry Oakley, bass (d. Nov. 11, 1972); Butch Trucks (drums); Jaimoe Johanson (drums); Chuck Leavell, keyboards (1972-76); Lamar Williams, bass (1972-76, d. Jan. 25, 1983); Bonnie Bramlett, vocals, (1979-80); Dan Toler, guitar (1979-82); David Goldflies, bass (1979-82); David "Frankie" Toler, drums (1981-82); Johnny Neel, keyboards (1989-90); Warren Haynes, guitar (1989-present); Allen Woody, bass (1989-present); Marc Quinones, percussion (1991-present)

The Allman Brothers Band was formed in 1969 by Duane Allman, a young session guitarist who had recorded with Wilson Pickett, Aretha Franklin, King Curtis and other r&b greats. Returned to Jacksonville, Fla., to strike out on his own, Allman enlisted a collection of players with a wide range of experiences: bassist Oakley and guitarist Betts led the psychedelic band the Second Coming; drummer J. Johnny "Jaimoe" Johnson was an r&b veteran who had toured with Otis Redding and Percy Sledge; drummer Butch Trucks played with the Jacksonville folk-rock band The 31st of February; and organist/vocalist Gregg Allman had recorded two albums with his brother Duane in the Los Angeles-based blues-rock band, Hourglass.

Together, this eclectic bunch created an utterly distinctive, highly improvisational style which rocks hard while reflecting a profound understanding of virtually every indigenous American musical form—blues, country, R&B, jazz and rock. Driven by Trucks' and Jaimoe's relentlessly propulsive, inventive twin drumming, Gregg Allman's bluesy organ comping and Oakley's free-range bass lines, Betts and Duane Allman crafted a remarkable twin lead guitar approach. Taking cues from jazz horn players, particularly Miles Davis and John Coltrane, and the twin fiddles of Western Swing music, they rewrote the rule book on how rock guitarists can play together, paving the way for every two-guitar band that has followed. But Hall Of Fame careers are not built on instrumental virtuosity alone, and the root of the Allman Brothers' success has been a strong, varied songbook.

The band has overcome a variety of obstacles, most notably the deaths of Duane and Oakley and two breakups. They've returned to nearly peak form during the 90s, a development few could have predicted.

what to buy: *At Fillmore East* (Capricorn, 1971, prod. Tom Dowd) captured the band's instrumental glory and improvisatory magic remarkably well. Arguably rock's greatest record, the double album holds only seven very long songs—including the epic "Whipping Post"—and nary a wasted note. *Eat a Peach* (Capricorn, 1972, prod. Tom Dowd) includes more tunes from the Fillmore shows, including the 33-minute "Mountain Jam" (which back in the days of vinyl consumed two sides!) as well as great new tunes like "Melissa" and "Blue Sky." *Brothers and Sisters*, (Capricorn, 1975, prod. Johnny Sandlin and the Allman Brothers Band) the Allmans' first post-Duane album, includes the band's biggest hits—"Ramblin' Man," "Jessica" and "Southbound." If you want to see what Allmans are up to now, *An Evening With, First Set* (Epic, 1992, prod. Tom Dowd) provides a pretty good glimpse.

what to buy next: *Beginnings* (Capricorn, 1973, prod. Joel Dorn and Tom Dowd) combines the band's first two albums in full. Once you're hooked, you won't want to be without *Dreams* (Polydor, 1989, prod. Various), a four-volume anthology that does everything a boxed set should. *Where it All Begins* (Epic, 1994, prod. Tom Dowd), while somewhat inconsistent, contains the best material the new Brothers have produced.

what to avoid: The Allmans' worst albums, on Arista during the early 80s, are blessedly out of print, with the best moments preserved on the retrospective *Hell and High Water* (Arista, 1994, prod. Various)

the rest: *The Allman Brothers Band* (Capricorn, 1969) *Idlewild South* (Polygram, 1970) *Win, Lose or Draw* (Capricorn, 1975) *The Road Goes on Forever* (Capricorn, 1976) *Wipe the Windows, Check the Oil, Dollar Gas* (Capricorn, 1976) *Enlightened Rogues* (Capricorn, 1979) *Best of the Allman Brothers Band* (Polydor, 1981) *Live at Ludlow Garage* (Polydor, 1970/1990) *Seven Turns* (Epic, 1990) *Shades of Two Worlds* (Epic, 1991) *Decade of Hits (1969-79)* (Polydor, 1991) *The Fillmore Concerts* (Polygram Chronicles, 1992) *An Evening With, Second Set* (Epic, 1995)

worth searching for: *The Allman Brothers Band at the R&R Cafe* (Epic, 1992) was a promo-only acoustic performance (shared with the Indigo Girls) which is well worth the effort to find. Excellent live bootlegs abound, but *New York City Blues*, recorded in 1970, is exceptional.

solo outings:

Gregg Allman: *Laid Back* (Capricorn, 1973) *The Gregg Allman Tour* (Polygram, 1974) *Playin' Up a Storm* (Capricorn, 1977/Razor & Tie, 1996) *I'm No Angel* (Epic, 1987) *Just before the Bullets Fly* (Epic, 1988) *One More Try* (Polydor, 1996)

Govt Mule (Haynes and Woody): *Govt Mule* (Relativity, 1995)

Dickey Betts: *Highway Call* (Capricorn, 1974) *Pattern Disruptive* (Epic, 1988)

The Eagles, Lynyrd Skynyrd, Little Feat, .38 Special, Black Oak Arkansas, The Black Crowes

Albert King, Cream, Miles Davis, Bob Willis and the Texas Playboys

Alan Paul

Marc Almond Band

Formed 1970 in London, England. Disbanded 1973. Re-formed 1975. Disbanded 1979.

Jon Marc, vocals, guitar; Johnny Almond, reeds and vibes; Dannie Richmond, drums (1970-73); Ken Craddock, keyboards, guitar (1972); Tommy Eyre, keyboards; Colin Gibson, bass (1972); Roger Sutton, bass, cello (1970-73); Geoff Condon, brass, reeds (1972); Alun Davies, guitar (1973); Bobby Torres, percussion (1973)

Marc and Almond enjoyed their first fame as sidemen to John Mayall on the acclaimed 1969 *Turning Point* album. Banding together, they pursued a non-commercial, highly acoustic folk-rock-jazz fusion. Their light, improvisational sound was among the earliest fusion approaches and a precursor to the New Age sound which would rise during the late 70s. Marc Almond almost always wrote and recorded suites rather than songs; the band's most celebrated pieces, "The City" and "One Way Sunday," are included on the *The Best of Marc Almond* (Rhino, 1980, prod. Various) An attempt to revive the group, *To the Heart*, (ABC, 1976, prod. Roy Halee) included a bunch of jazz stars and resulted in some pretty melodies but ultimately unengaging music.

Lawrence Gabriel

Herb Alpert /Herb Alpert & the Tijuana Brass

While 60s teenagers were turning on to the British invasion, their mothers were grooving out to the smooth, Ameriachi jazz rhythms of Alpert and the Tijuana Brass. A first-class trumpeter, Alpert was managing the rock 'n' roll duo Jan & Dean when he took a demo of his instrumental "Twinkle Star," added bullfight noises and created his first No. 1 record, "The Lonely Bull," in 1962. The song exemplified the style that he was to popularize for the next 15 years: saucy, Latinate arrangements of standards and contemporary pop songs, performed in a mood that was by turns unleashed and wild or laid-back and sexy. With his the Tijuana Brass, Alpert produced a string of hit instrumentals throughout the 60s that neatly crossed the line between ethnic novelty music and contemporary pop. His label, A&M records—formed with producer Jerry Moss in 1962—became home to many similar acts (usually produced by Alpert), like Sergio Mendes and the Baja Marimba Band (and later became a rock powerhouse with the Police, Bryan Adams and Styx). Alpert ditched the Brass during the 70s, sold the record company (to form the new Almo Sounds label) and continues his long successful run to this day.

what to buy: While you can't go wrong buying either *The Lonely Bull* or *Whipped Cream (& Other Delights)*, you're better off with *Classics, Vol. 1,* (A&M, 1987, prod. Herb Alpert) a hip and lively compilation of Alpert & Co. classics from the 60s through the 70s. With up-tempo hits ("Casino Royale," "A Taste of Honey"), sexed-up jazz ("Love Potion No. 9," "The Lonely Bull") and sly ballads (witness Alpert's charmingly shy vocal debut on "This Guy's in Love with You)," this is the trumpet-pop album to own.

what to buy next: After years of languishing at the bottom of (or off) the charts, the Brass-less Alpert scored with the jazz-funk fusion of *Rise,* (PGD/A&M, 1979, prod. Herb Alpert) his biggest seller and simply one of his finest, most sophisticated albums.

what to avoid: *North on South St.* (A&M, 1991, prod. Chris Boyd) milks a late-80s jazz lite formula that constrains his trademark Latin bravado.

the rest: Herb Alpert & The Tijuana Brass: *The Lonely Bull* (A&M, 1962) *Whipped Cream (& Other Delights)* (A&M, 1965) *Greatest Hits* (A&M, 1970) *Greatest Hits #2* (A&M, 1973) *Four Sider* (A&M, 1973) Herb Alpert: *Herb Alpert Classics, Vol. 20* (A&M, 1987) *Keep Your Eye on Me* (PGD/A&M, 1987) *Midnight Sun* (PGD/A&M, 1992) *Second Wind* (Almo Sounds, 1996)

worth searching for: Alpert teamed up with South African trumpet master Hugh Masekela for *Herb Alpert/Hugh Masekela,* (Horizon, 1977) a remarkable meeting of pop music's two premiere trumpet plays that smoothly melds Masekela's charismatic Afro-pop and Alpert's well-mannered Latin stylings.

▶▶ Sergio Mendes, Baja Marimba Band, Hugh Masekela, Chuck Mangione, Dirty Dozen Brass Band, Chicago

◀◀ Tito Puente, Louis Prima

Christopher Scapelliti

The Alpha Band

Formed 1976 during Bob Dylan's Rolling Thunder Revue tour. Disbanded 1979.

T Bone Burnett (born John Henry Burnett), vocals, guitar, piano; Steven Soles, vocals, guitar, piano; David Mansfield, violin, mandolin, guitar, dobro, viola, steel guitar, cello, piano

As Bob Dylan's freewheeling Rolling Thunder Revue wound down, three of its supporting members banded together to form the Alpha Band, a trio that ultimately may have been too smart for its own good. Operating on a vaguely country-rock groove—though not nearly as laid-back as is usual for the genre—the group output is eclectic, eccentric and a wonderful reminder that not everything recorded in America during the late 70s was meant to deliver a peaceful easy feelin'. Burnett's contributions stand out, though his occasional proselytizing will likely turn some listeners off. And Mansfield's excursions on all things stringed are always entertaining. The group recorded a trio of albums—*The Alpha Band,* (Arista, 1976, prod. Larry Hirsch) *Spark in the Dark* (Arista, 1977, Arista, prod. Larry Hirsch) and *The Statue Makers of Hollywood* (Arista, 1978, prod. Larry Hirsch and the Alpha Band) —all of which stiffed and are out of print today. All of them are worth searching the used-album bins, though.

see also: *T Bone Burnett*

Daniel Durchholz

Alphaville

Formed 1981 in Berlin, Germany

This atrocious mid-80s synthesizer art group fronted by singer Marian Gold is of no consequence save its appalling attempts to craft egocentric dance music. At one time the band boasted 31 musicians (in addition to the core members), lending new meaning to the word bombast. All four Atlantic releases have been deleted. If you must have one—and believe us, you mustn't—look for *The Breathtaking Blue,* (Atlantic, 1989, prod. Klaus Shulze) a slightly more stylized effort than the other three.

Allan Orski

Alt

See: Split Enz

Altered Images

Formed 1979 in Glasgow, Scotland. Disbanded 1984.

Clare Grogan, vocals; Tony McDaid, guitar; Jim McKinnon, guitar (1979-83); Stephen Lironi, keyboards (1984); Johnny McElhone, bass; Tich Anderson, drums (1979-83); Gerry McElhone, drums (1984)

Rising out of the working-class burg of Glasgow at the height of New Wave, Altered Images embodied that genre's most (and least) successful characteristics: punky dance music, charmingly novice musicianship and, most importantly, youthful exuberance. With her cutesy, boop-de-boop voice, Grogan sounded a tad too much like Shirley Temple to be awakening young men's libidos; she could be both coquettishly alluring and childishly annoying. Neither Grogan nor any of the other band members showed especially strong musical talent, but for two years Altered Images spun out a steady string of plucky tunes in the most saccharine style of New Wave. The best of its lot is *Bite,* (Epic, 1983, prod. Tony Visconti and Mike Chapman) ♪♪♪ a plush disco collection that predated that genre's revival by nearly a decade. Grogan's voice is at its least cloying, and most of the songs ("Change of Heart," "Thinking About You," "Another Lost Look," and the UK hit "Don't Talk to Me About Love") still shimmer and pop. *Pinky Blue* (Epic, 1982, prod. Martin Rushent) ♪♪ is also worth grabbing. The bulk of the songs ("I Could Be Happy," "See Those Eyes") leap about, screaming "hit single," and Rushent's kicky production is appropriate to the band's quirky style. Altered Images ended after *Bite* fizzled, with Grogan pursuing a film career and Johnny McElhone forming the more earnest group Texas.

the rest: *Happy Birthday* (Epic, 1981) ♪ *Collected Images* (Epic, 1984) ♪♪ *Best of* (Pinnacle, 1994) ♪♪

see also: *Texas*

Christopher Scapelliti

Alvin & the Chipmunks

See: The Chipmunks

Dave Alvin

Born Nov. 11, 1955 in Los Angeles, Calif.

As a member of the Blasters, guitarist Alvin coined the term "American Music," and he has spent the rest of his career defining the term, crafting a distinctive brand of music now most commonly known as roots—drawing on such solidly domestic forms as country, vintage R&B, rockabilly and blues. After a split with his brother Phil ended the Blasters' too-brief run, Alvin joined X for one album, then began a solo career which has been defined by songs with a gift for narrative and a fine poetic sense that cuts through Alvin' brusk delivery. And he plays a mean lead guitar. Of late, Alvin has gained a reputations as producer of West Coast roots music, and he also put together the excellent Merle Haggard tribute, *Tulare Dust*, in 1994.

what to buy: *Blue Blvd.* (HighTone, 1991, prod. Chris Silagyi, Dave Alvin and Bruce Bromberg) ♪♪♪♪ reads like a book of short stories and rocks like nobody's business. "Haley's Comet," co-written with Tom Russell, recounts the dubious end of rock 'n' roll legend Bill Haley, while "Andersonville" is the most vivid song about the Civil War since "The Night They Drove Old Dixie Down." *King of California* (HighTone, 1994, prod. Greg Leisz) ♪♪♪♪ is an acoustic-based album on which Alvin finally grew into his voice, allowing the quieter arrangements to show off its distinctiveness rather than its limitations. You could carp about Alvin taking still another run at "Fourth of July," but songs such as "Barn Burning," which rolls like a freight train, and the lush title track, Alvin's best ballad ever, more than make up for the repetition.

what to buy next: *Romeo's Escape* (Epic, 1987, prod. Steve Berlin and Mark Linnett) ♪♪♪ contains some of Alvin's finest songs, including several reprised from the Blasters' albums. And while some of the arrangements, notably "Border Radio," cast the songs in new light, Alvin's limited vocal abilities hold him back. *Museum of Heart* (HighTone, 1993, prod. Chris Silagyi, Bruce Bromberg and Dave Alvin) ♪♪♪ is a wrenching album of heartbreak, sifting through the shards of a shattered relationship. The best of the lot, "Don't Talk About Her" and "A Woman's Got a Right," could be seen as the laments of a man smart enough to see both sides of the story.

the rest: (with the Guilty Men): *Interstate City* (HighTone, 1996, prod. Dave Alvin and the Guilty Men) ♪♪♪

worth searching for: *The Pleasure Barons Live in Las Vegas* (Hightone, 1993 prod. Mark Linnett and Country Dick Montana) ♪♪♪ is of more interest to serious fans of any one of the principals—Alvin, Mojo Nixon, Country Dick Montana—than to the general populace. Alvin's cover versions of "Closing Time" and "Gangster of Love" stand out, but the late, lamented Country Dick's Tom Jones medley has to be heard to be believed.

▶▶ Big Sandy & His Fly Right Boys, the Reverend Horton Heat, Jason & the Scorchers

◀◀ Big Joe Turner, Sonny Burgess, Hank Williams

see also: *The Blasters*

Daniel Durchholz

Phil Alvin

See: The Blasters

Eric Ambel

See: The Del Lords

Ambitious Lovers

Formed 1984 in New York, N.Y. Disbanded.

Arto Lindsay, vocals, guitar; Peter Scherer, keyboards, synthesizer bass, drum programming, sampling

DNA visionary Lindsay and musical renaissance man Scherer combined their disparate talents to produce a polyglot sound whose elements found no parallel in the music scene of the time. The gnarled, compact songs bursting with jack-in-the-box energy that typified DNA rested alongside coiled funk and languid Brazilian music—Lindsay was raised in Brazil and sang the later material in Portuguese. After albums named for three of the Seven Deadly Sins, the duo (always joined on album by an array of guests) split due to a desire to pursue differing musical interests and the economic burden of paying hired guns rather than working with a cooperative band.

what to buy: *Greed* (Virgin, 1988 prod. Peter Scherer) contains the best funk track this group ever released, "Love Overlap," plus the most impressive roster of guests—including Vernon Reid, Bill Frisell, John Zorn, John Lurie and Nana Vasconcelos.

what to buy next: *Envy* (EG, 1984, prod. Peter Scherer, M.E. Miller and Arto Lindsay) was shocking in its juxtapositions, with some of Lindsay's most twisted guitar fragments followed by romantic, poignant ballads. *Lust* (Elektra, 1991, prod. Peter Scherer) avoided the overtly avant-garde snippets in favor of a smoother sound, though Lindsay's guitar squiggles remain prominent. A cover of Jorge Ben's soccer tribute "Umbabarauma" was a local club hit.

worth searching for: Those who think Scherer was a moderating influence on Lindsay should check import bins for *Pretty Ugly,* (Made to Measure (Belgium), 1990, prod. Peter Scherer and Arto Lindsay) largely comprised of instrumental ballet and theater music that's as raw and uncompromised as DNA. Not an Ambitious Lovers project, it's jointly credited to Lindsay and Scherer.

solo outings:

Arto Lindsay Trio: Aggregates 1-26 (Knitting Factory Works, 1995)

Peter Scherer: Very Neon Pet (Metro Blue/Capitol, 1995)

David Byrne, Cameo

Caetano Veloso, Gilberto Gil, James Brown, Derek Bailey

see also: *DNA, Golden Palominos*

Steve Holtje

Ambrosia

Formed 1971 in Los Angeles, Calif. Disbanded 1983. Reunited 1996.

David Pack, guitar; Joe Puerta, bass; Christopher North, keyboards (1971-77); Burleigh Drummond, drums (1977-83); David Lewis, keyboards (1980-82); Royce Jones, percussion, vocals (1980-82)

Until 1975, Britain had the art-rock music scene pretty much to itself. Enter Ambrosia, four accomplished vocalists and multi-instrumentalists who performed a rock-fusion debut of Leonard Bernstein's "Mass" with the L.A. Philharmonic in 1973, well before they began recording as a group. Ambrosia's early albums showed a successful synthesis of rock and classical training, often with intentionally humorous results (as on the comically baroque track "Dance with Me George," from the group's 1976 album *Somewhere I've Never Traveled*). North's keyboard contributions on the first two albums did much to broaden Ambrosia's sound and made the group sound more like an ensemble than a typical four-piece rock band. Following his departure in 1977, the group's music became more slick and mainstream, with mellow hits such as "How Much I Feel," "You're the Only Woman" and "The Biggest Part of Me." Of Ambrosia's work, its earliest tongue-in-cheek recordings are the most enduring. But wherever you look in the band's catalog there is excellent musicianship and spot-on composition. The bad news is that as of this writing, only the middling fourth album, *One Eighty,* (Warner Bros., 1980, prod. Freddie Piro and Ambrosia) remains in print; despite the hits "Biggest Part of Me" and "You're the Only Woman," the album's eccentric nature suggests the group wasn't quite ready to leave behind its tongue-in-cheek art rock farces or to fully embrace its new status as an adult contemporary light-rock band. The good news is that in November 1996, Warner Bros. is slated to release a retrospective of tracks from Ambrosia's five albums, including three new songs from the newly reunited group.

Christopher Scapelliti

America

Formed 1969 in London, England

Dewey Bunnell, vocals, guitar, drums; Gerry Beckley, guitar, vocals; Dan Peek, guitar, vocals (1969-77)

America was folk-rock's Fabian—tuneful and easy on the ears, not terribly subversive and, therefore, more commercial. The trio, which formed on a U.S. armed forces base, enjoyed a string of hit singles during the 70s, beginning by aping Neil Young on "A Horse With No Name" and hitting a few other high points—including some sides produced by Beatles collaborator George Martin—along with the drivel of "Muskrat Love." After Peek left, however, the bottom seemed to drop out. With the exception of the 1982 hit "You Can Do Magic," Bunnell and Beckley simply soldier along on the oldies circuit, pairing up with fellow travelers such as the Beach Boys and Three Dog Night.

what to buy: *History: America's Greatest Hits* (Warner Bros., 1975, prod. Various) has everything you'd want—and need—from the group's peak period.

what to buy next: *Encore! More Greatest Hits* (Rhino, 1990, prod. Various) provides a nice addendum for those who want more of the story.

what to avoid: *Alibi* (Capitol, 1980, prod.) **WOOF!** the worst of the myriad sub-par albums America, as a duo, has recorded during 80s and 90s.

the rest: *America* (Warner Bros., 1972) *Homecoming* (Warner Bros., 1972) *Hat Trick* (Warner Bros., 1973) *Holiday* (Warner Bros., 1974) *Hearts* (Warner Bros., 1975) *Hideaway* (Warner Bros., 1976) *Harbor* (Warner Bros., 1976) *Silent Letter* (Capitol, 1979) *View From the Ground* (Capitol, 1982) *Your Move* (Capitol, 1983) *Perspective* (Capitol, 1984) *Hourglass* (American Gramophone, 1994)

Firefall, McGuinn, Clark & Hillman

James Taylor, the Eagles, Jackson Browne, Crosby, Stills, Nash and Young, Poco the Kingston Trio

Gary Graff

What Album Changed Your Life?

"There was a blues record that came out by Junior Wells called Hoodoo Man Blues (Delmark, 1965)...It was just a really spare blues quartet, with Junior Wells, Buddy Guy on guitar, Sam Lee on drums and I forgot who on bass. That's all there was to it. I liked that simplicity."

Bob Weir, (Grateful Dead, Ratdog)

American Music Club /Mark Eitzel

Formed 1983 in San Francisco, Calif.

Mark Eitzel, acoustic guitar, keyboards, vocals; Bruce Kaphan, pedal steel, keyboards, guitars, vocals; Mark "Vudi" Pankler, guitars, vocals; Danny Pearson, bass, guitars, mandolin, vocals; Tim Mallon, bass, drums (1985-88); Mike Simms, drums (1989-1992) Tim Mooney, drums (1993-95)

AMC is a brooding, thought-provoking quintet which created dazzling emotional landscapes drawn by the evocative singing and obtuse songwriting of frontman Eitzel. This former punk rocker from Columbus, Ohio, found the perfect marriage with guitarist Vudi and multi-instrumentalist Kaphan for his tortured musings on life and love. Drawing its musical form from folk, country and rock with a pinch of psychedelic texture, AMC has never fit comfortably into any cliched radio programmer's format. Sadly, Eitzel's departure in 1995 for a solo career marks the end of an era, if not the band.

what to buy: *Everclear* (Alias, 1991, prod. Bruce Kaphan) is a tour de force that perfectly captures the dynamics of Eitzel's songs with the band's playing, from the raucously punky "Crabwalk" to the poignant ballad "Ex-Girlfriend" to "What the Pillar of Salt Held Up," a stripped-down voice-and-guitar piece that's one of Eitzel's best ballads. *San Francisco* (Reprise, 1994, prod. Joe Chiccarelli and AMC) is the band's last album before Eitzel split. A return to form reuniting the band with *Everclear* engineer Joe Chiccarelli, it features more moody, dark acoustic tunes ("Fearless," "Cape Canaveral"), twisted mid-tempo songs with cool titles ("How Many Six Packs Does It Take to Screw in a Light") and plenty of spirited rockers ("It's Your Birthday" "Wish the World Away" and "Hello Amsterdam"). On his solo debut, *60 Watt Silver Lin-*

ing, (Warner/Reprise, 1996, prod. Mark Eitzel) Eitzel explores the aching ruminations of Chet Baker with spare, melancholy arrangements that highlight the prominent trumpet solos.

what to buy next: *Engine* (Frontier, 1987, prod. Tom Mallon) is on a par with *Everclear* and includes concert favorites "Big Night" and "Nightwatchman."

the rest: *Engine* (Frontier, 1987) *California* (Frontier, 1988) *Mercury* (Reprise, 1993)

worth searching for: *California/United Kingdom,* (Demon, 1989) a British import combo, or the vinyl only *The Restless Stranger* (Grifter, 1985) which, according to some, may get a CD release in the near future).

▶▶ Red House Painters, Swell, Idaho

◀◀ Nick Drake, Tim Buckley, Love, Big Starr

Mark J. Petracca

aMiniature

Formed 1988 in San Diego, Calif.

John Lee, vocals, guitar; Kevin Wells, guitar (1993); Tony Rotter guitar (1994); Devon Goldberg, guitar (1992-94); Mark Monteith, guitar (1995-present); Colin Watson, bass; Christian Hoffman, drums (1992-94); Mark Trombino, drums (1995); Johnny Schier, drums (1995-present)

aMiniature—the a is silent; it's there to differentiate the group from a jazz ensemble named Miniature—is Korean-American Lee's baby; he writes all the music and is the only original member still in the group, which undergoes a dizzying number of personnel changes every year with bassist Watson the only other constant. The dark energy and tempered hope of Lee's densely layered songs are built with two or three hooks going at once; the bass parts alone would make some songs memorable. Equally adept at building a memorable sound and solid structures, Lee fluctuates a song's intensity by thickening or paring down the arrangement, intertwining simple but distinctive guitar riffs that provide an irresistible momentum. Lee's vocals are like another instrument equal to the guitar, nearly shouted yet at the same time melodic in a blunt, minimal way. *Murk Time Cruiser* (Restless, 1995, prod. John Lee & Mark Trombino) surpasses the group's other efforts due to perfectly proportioned and paced material from start to finish; the hooks are all knockout punches, and the sound is distinctive and instantly classic.

the rest: *Plexiwatt* (Scheming Intelligentsia, 1991) *Depth Five Rate Six* (Restless, 1994)

Steve Holtje

Tori Amos

Born Myra Ellen Amos, Aug. 22, 1963 in Newton, N.C.

A singer, pianist and songwriter, Amos is Barbra Streisand by way of Wendy O. Williams—her confessional piano-fired ballads can be sweet and delicate, but what Amos really wants to do is raise hell. The daughter of a Methodist preacher, the classically-trained Amos writes weird, compelling tunes about sex, religion and all points in between. Her idiosyncratic style borders on the annoying at times, but at its best, Amos' piano-rock is every bit as good Elton John's mid-70s work, and she's particularly adept at individualizing other artists' songs (she's recorded versions of Nirvana's "Smells Like Teen Spirit" and the Rolling Stones' "Angie"). *Little Earthquakes* (Atlantic, 1991, prod. Davitt Sigerson, Eric Rosse, Ian Stanley and Tori Amos) remains her benchmark, a 12-song act of high drama. "Me and a Gun," "Crucify" and "Silent All These Years" are the aural equivalent of reading someone's diary a week after a suicide.

the rest: *Y Kant Tori Read* (1988, Atlantic) *Crucify* (Atlantic EP, 1992) *Under the Pink* (Atlantic, 1994) *Boys For Peie* (Atlantic, 1996 *Hey Jupiter* (Atlantic, 1996)

Thor Christensen

Amps

See: The Breeders

Trey Anastasio

See: Phish

Al Anderson

See: NRBQ

Eric Anderson

Born Feb. 14, 1943 in Pittsburgh, Penn.

Anderson hit the folk circuit during the 60s, becoming one of the first "new " Dylans, a label that is somewhat short-sighted. Anderson is similar to Dylan only in his phrasing; but where

Dylan is elusive and biting, Anderson is open and thoughtful. His vision is nowhere near as far reaching, however, as he prefers to stick to more romantic themes. His career was thrown off track in the 70s after the master tapes for his follow up to his masterful *Blue River* album were inexplicably lost. After meandering for a decade or so, Anderson appears to be back on track, recently releasing some of the most focused work of his career.

what to buy: *Blue River* (Columbia, 1972) is undoubtedly his greatest work and stands alongside anything that the singer-movement produced during the 70s. Once located, the tapes for *Stages: The Lost Album* (Columbia, 1991, prod Amy Herot) proved as complete and substantial as the rumors indicated. Certainly "Baby, I'm Lonesome" is one of the more moving love songs he's recorded. Also included are some strong new recordings with guests Garth Hudson, Rick Danko, Shawn Colvin and the Hooters' Eric Bazilian.

what to buy next: *Ghosts Upon the Road* (Gold Castle, 1988, prod. Steve Addabbo and Eric Anderson) marks a full-force comeback. It's a mature, vast record with vivid, literate songs including the 10-minute title track. *The Best of Eric Anderson* (Vanguard, 1970, prod. Various) is a solid intro to his coffee house folk beginnings, containing his signature "Thirsty Boots."

what to avoid: *More Hits From Tin Can Alley* (Vanguard, 1968, prod. Al Gorgoni) is not without its moments, but the Beatlesque production will be a bit florid for the purists and is certainly incongruous with anything else in his catalogue.

the rest: *'Bout Changes and Things* (Vanguard, 1966) *Today is the HIghway* (Vanguard, 1965, prod. Maynard Solomon)

worth searching for: *Anderson, Danko, Fjeld* (Rykodisc, 1993), a wonderfully intimate and understated album recorded with The Band's Rick Danko and Jonas Fjeld.

▶▶ James Taylor, Jackson Browne, Bruce Springsteen, John Mellencamp, Tom Petty, James McMurtry

◀◀ Bob Dylan, Woody Guthrie, Hank Williams

Allan Orski

Ian Anderson

See: Jethro Tull

Jon Anderson

See: Yes

Laurie Anderson

Born June 5, 1947, in Chicago, Ill.

Anderson has challenged the conventions of musical performance with thematic stage shows that employ dramatic lighting, theatrical pacing and a variety of media (including film, video and written text) to get her ideas across. Her impressive list of collaborators includes beat author William S. Burroughs, photographer Robert Mapplethorpe and progressive classical composer Philip Glass. Her themes encompass—but are not limited to—women's rights, the place of art in society, issues of censorship and myriad variations on the mysteries of human relations; her landmark stage show "United States" sought to delve into nothing less than the collective American consciousness. Impressive credentials, but with all this conceptual stuff going on, Anderson's music could easily get lost in the shuffle. Because she is commonly referred to as a "performance artist"—a label that inspires as much audience dread as the word "mime"—Anderson's music is often written off as merely one element in the patchworks that are her multi-media presentations. While much of her work does benefit from both seeing *and* hearing, her recordings still have much to offer.

what to buy: Anderson's early recordings strongly rely on her trademark spoken/sung vocal delivery, a technique best described as monologues with musical accompaniment. Of these, *Mr. Heartbreak* (Warner Bros., 1984, prod. Bill Laswell) fares the best. This is due, in large part, to her collaborators—which include Burroughs, guitarist Adrian Belew and former Material bassist Laswell. The well-chosen musicians on *Mr. Heartbreak* flesh out Anderson's typically cold electronic soundscapes, adding a welcome warmth to the palette. Peter Gabriel also turns up for two duets, "Gravity's Angel" and "Excellent Birds," a song that appears on his *So* album—with a slightly different arrangement—as the song "This Is the Picture." On *Strange Angels,* (Warner Bros., 1989, prod. Laurie Anderson) Anderson's vocals are more musical and she pursues more conventional song structures—particularly on the title and "Beautiful Red Dress."

what to buy next: If *Mr. Heartbreak* is to your liking, the next logical step is the live album *Home of the Brave* (Warner Bros., 1986, prod. Laurie Anderson) which features many of the same players from *Mr. Heartbreak* The concert setting allows the musicians a chance to stretch out a bit, and the results—

particularly Belew's guitar playing and singing—are decidedly looser and more groove-oriented than any of Anderson's studio fare. For more of the musical stylings of *Strange Angels*, *Bright Red* (Warner Bros., 1994, prod. Laurie Anderson and Brian Eno) ♪♪♪ is a good choice.

what to avoid: While impressive in its scope and Herculean length, *United States Live* (Warner Bros., 1984, prod. Laurie Anderson and Roma Baran) ♪♪ is definitely one of those "you had to be there" experiences. The version of "O Superman" is quite good, but the four-plus hours of music here really need the complement of Anderson's arresting visual style to get the maximum bang.

the rest: *Big Science* (Warner Bros., 1982) ♪♪♪ *The Ugly One with Jewels* (Warner Bros., 1995) ♪♪♪

worth searching for: While there is no authorized audio version of *Stories from the Nerve Bible*(the piece initially appeared in print and was followed by a Voyager CD-ROM), Anderson did a performance tour of the work, which as cropped up on various bootlegs.

▶▶ Adrian Belew, Mae Moore

◀◀ William S. Burroughs, experimental theater, Talking Heads, Brian Eno

David Galens

Anderson, Wakeman, Bruford and Howe

See: Yes

Angel

Formed 1975 in Washington, D.C. Disbanded 1981.

Frank DiMino, vocals; Gregg Giuffria, keyboards; Punky Meadows, guitar; Mickey Jones, bass (1975-77); Barry Brandt, drums; Felix Robinson, bass (1975-1981)

Angel was something of a mess, with its glammy, all-white attire and albums full of bloated pomp-rock that was intended to sound majestic but instead came off as Grade B Genesis or Yes. The group, which was discovered by Kiss' Gene Simmons, released seven albums in its seven years together, none of which made substantial impact on the masses. *An Anthology* (Mercury, 1992, prod. Various) ♪♪♪ preserves the best of the albums—which, unfortunately, isn't saying much—and also includes the group's title them for the film "Foxes." Giuffria went on to minor success with his own band and later joined the group House of Lords.

Gary Graff

Animal Logic

See: Stewart Copeland

The Animals /Eric Burdon and the Animals /Eric Burdon /Alan Price

Formed 1962 in Newcastle upon Tyne, England. Disbanded 1969. Reformed 1976 and 1983.

Eric Burdon, vocals; Alan Price, keyboards (1962-65); Bryan "Chas" Chandler, bass (1962-66, died July 17, 1996); John Steel, drums (1962-66); Hilton Valentine, guitar (1962-66); Dave Rowberry, keyboards (1965-66); Barry Jenkins, drums (1966-); John Weider, guitar (1966-); Danny McCullough, bass (1966-68); Tom Parker, organ (1966-67); Vic Briggs, guitar (1967-68); Zoot Money, keyboards (1968-69); Andrew Somers, guitar (1968-69)

During the early 60s British Invasion, the Animals prided themselves on being one of the stalwarts of the blues, even after the Rolling Stones went pop. Yet the band will be remembered as one of the first to marry a folk song to a rock beat for its breakthrough hit, "House of the Rising Sun." Frontman Burdon was one of the great vocalists of the era, with gritty, soulful delivery and his James Brown-style collapse routine on stage. The original Animals split up in 1966, but an altered band—billed with Burdon's name out front—was at the front line of West Coast psychedelia, having been to the Monterey Pop Festival (and writing a hit single about it) and later singing convincingly of such American concerns as Vietnam and San Francisco nights. As they left, the individual Animals made their marks elsewhere in rock: Chandler was Jimi Hendrix' first manager; Price scored the soundtrack to "O Lucky Man!"; Somers became Andy Summers and joined the Police; and Burdon went on to a solo career, with War as his first backing band. The Animals' reunions have never stuck, but the group's performances showed it could still call up the ferocious attack of its 60s peak at will.

what to buy: There's never been a fully satisfying Animals collection—at least not on these shores. But *The Best of the Animals* (MGM, 1966/Abkco, 1987, prod. Mickie Most) ♪♪♪♪♪ covers the extraordinary early singles, the Abkco set in digitally remastered sound.

what to buy next: *The Best of Eric Burdon and the Animals, Vol. 2* (MGM, 1967, prod. Various) captures the later, psychedelicized version of the band. *Animalization* (MGM, 1966, prod. Mickie Most) is the most fully realized early album.

what to avoid: Of Burdon's many mediocre solo albums, *Black Man's Burdon* (MGM, 1971/Avenue, 1993, prod. Jerry Goldstein) —his second with War—was incredibly indulgent and self-consciously arty.

the rest: *The Animals* (MGM, 1964) *The Animals on Tour* (MGM, 1965) *Animal Tracks* (MGM, 1965) *Animalism* (MGM, 1966) *Every One of Us* (MGM, 1968/One Way, 1994) *Love Is* (MGM, 1969/One Way, 1994) *The Greatest Hits of Eric Burdon and the Animals* (MGM, 1969) *Before We Were So Rudely Interrupted* (United Artists, 1977) *Ark* (I.R.S., 1983) *Rip It to Shreds: Greatest Hits Live* (I.R.S., 1984) *Winds of Change* (One Way, 1995)

worth searching for: That illusive, 1962-69 Animals collection exists in the form of the strong Australian import *The Most of the Animals,* (Raven, 1989, prod. Various) which tracks the hits from "House of the Rising Sun" through the group's resurrections of Johnny Cash's "Ring of Fire" and Traffic's "Coloured Rain."

solo outings:

Eric Burdon: Eric Burdon Declares War (Polydor, 1970/Avenue, 1993) *Guilty* (MGM, 1971) *Sun Secrets* (Capitol, 1975) *Love is All Around* (Avenue, 1976/1993) *That's Live* (Inakustik, 1985) *Wicked Man* (GNP/Crescendo, 1988) *Eric Burdon Sings The Animals Greatest Hits* (Rhino, 1998/1994) *Unreleased Burdon* (Blue Wave, 1993) *Sun Secrets/Stop* (Avenue, 1993) *The Best of Eric Burdon and War* (Avenue, 1995) *Eric is Here* (One Way, 1995)

Alan Price: The Price to Play (Decca, 1966) *A Price on His Head* (Decca, 1967) *The Price is Right* (Parrot, 1968) *Fame and Price* (Columbia, 1971) *O Lucky Man!* (Warner Bros., 1973/1995) *Between Yesterday and Today* (Warner Bros., 1974)

▶▶ Bruce Springsteen, John Mellencamp, Blue Oyster Cult

◀◀ John Lee Hooker, Alex Korner.

see also: *War*

Roger Catlin

Paul Anka

Born July 30, 1941, in Ottawa, Canada

One of the few 50s teen idols with a long career in music, Anka has proven resilient and resourceful. He broke through in 1957 with the No. 1 hit "Diana," a song he wrote about a babysitter, and became a heartthrob almost immediately. He had a few more hits during this era, including "Lonely Boy" and "Puppy Love," before he tried acting in such movies as "The Longest Day," for which he wrote the theme song. Anka has had some hits since then, including the controversial "(You're) Having My Baby," which some took as sexist, others as anti-abortionist (others as just really, really bad). Today he is mostly known for his songwriting and business dealings; he'll forever be an asterisk in the Frank Sinatra story for taking a French song and rearranging it into the lounge-lizard standard "My Way."

what to buy: Most of Anka's albums are either collections of hits or live recordings, and most of them are out of print. The most exhaustive of his several anthologies is the *30th Anniversary Collection,* (Rhino, 1989, prod. Various) which spans his career evolution from a sweet-voiced teen star to a suave crooner who can write. All the hits and near hits, from "Diana" to "My Way," are included on this thoughtfully assembled package.

what to avoid: Anka's chart resurgence during the early 70s was good for his bank account, bad for our ears. Most of that swill was released during his years with United Artists, and were collected on the anthology *The Best of the United Artists Years* (EMI, 1996, prod. Various)

the rest: *21 Golden Hits* (RCA, 1963) *Classic Hits* (Curb, 1992) *Paul Anka Sings His Big Ten, Vol. 1* and *Vol. 2* (Curb, 1992)

▶▶ Neil Diamond, Barry Manilow, Julio Iglesias

◀◀ Frank Sinatra, Nat King Cole

Doug Pullen

Phil Anselmo

See: Pantera

Adam Ant /Adam and the Ants

Born Stuart Leslie Goddard, Nov. 3, 1954, in London, England

One of the more colorful figures on the British New Wave scene, Ant has made dashing forays into post-punk, mainstream pop and even adult alternative. Under the auspices of former Sex Pistols manager Malcolm McClaren, Adam and the Ants were a gimmicky cartoon outfit dressed in pirate clothes and war paint, hawking itself in self-promoting songs such as "Antmusic" and "Antrap." Replete with tribal double drumming and yodels, the Ants made the British charts but were never taken seriously in the U.S. In a bid for more commercial acceptance, Ant went solo and took passing shots at sex symboldom with sophomoric odes to the flesh. He also built a modest acting career.

what to buy: The Ants' *Kings of the Wild Frontier* (Epic, 1980, prod. Chris Hughes) is driven by pounding rhythms and Ant's fantasy world of pirates and Indians rifling through Marco Pirroni's 50s influenced guitar. Cheap thrills abound on "Jolly Roger," "Los Rancheros" and the signature tune, "Antmusic." *Friend or Foe* (Epic, 1982, prod. Chris Hughes) is Ant's first and best solo effort, with a more restrained pop feel that helps "A Place in the Country" and "Goody Two Shoes." *Wonderful* (Capitol, 1995, prod. David Tickle) is a solid return to his recording career. Marked by a more adult approach and a focused pop sound, Ant still focuses on his libido and all its needs, but isn't quite as crass as his previous work.

what to buy next: The Ants' *Prince Charming* (Epic, 1981, prod. Chris Hughes) follows the same path as *Kings*, with some of the group's finest moments in the title track and "Stand and Deliver." *Antics in the Forbidden Zone* (Epic, 1990, prod. Various) compiles all the hits for a decent if occasionally tedious sampler.

what to avoid: *Vive Le Rock* (Epic, 1985, prod. Tony Visconte) is a faceless trash-heap release that finds Ant in black leather, vainly trying to rock—without memorable tunes, a decent backing band or even a good gimmick to push it over.

the rest: *Dirk Wears White Sox* (Epic, 1979) *Strip* (Epic, 1983) *Manners & Physique* (Epic, 1988) *Peel Sessions* (Dutch East India, 1991) *B-side Babes* (Epic/Legacy, 1994)

worth searching for: The import *Antmusic: The Very Best of Adam Ant* (Arcade, 1993, prod. Various) is a generous and wide-ranging compilation that comes with a live disc recorded at a 1992 radio concert.

Sigue Sigue Sputnik, Elastica, the Bogmen

New York Dolls, Kiss

Allan Orski

Antenna /Velo-Deluxe/Mysteries of Life

Antenna—John Strohm, guitar, vocals; Jacob Smith, guitar, vocals; Freda Love, drums; Patrick Spurgeon, drums; Vess Ruhtenberg, guitar (1992); Ed Ackerson, guitar (1993). Velo-Deluxe—John Strohm, guitar, vocals, piano, loops; Lenny Childers, bass, baritone guitar, vocals; Mitch Harris, drums. Mysteries of Life—Jake Smith, lead vocals, guitar; Freda Love, drums, vocals; Geraldine Haas, cello; Tina Barbieri, bass, vocals

After the demise of the Blake Babies, Juliana Hatfield moved on to a successful, tumultuous solo career. Strohm and Love formed Antenna with Jacob Smith (Love's husband), with Strohm strongly in the spotlight. Love, who had been frequently spelled by Patrick Spurgeon, and Smith then took time off for further college studies and to have a child, while Strohm formed Velo-Deluxe to pursue the perfect indie guitar sound. Love and Smith reappeared in Mysteries of Life.

what to buy: *Sway* (Mammoth, 1991, prod. Paul Mahern) is as anthemic as any Blake Babies album while covering a broader stylistic range.

what to buy next: Velo-Deluxe's *Superelastic* (Mammoth, 1994, prod. John Strohm and Anjali Dutt) has lots of guests besides the core trio, including Smith on two tracks (he wrote "Alibi"), a horn section, and a pedal steel guitarist. The sound is generally darker, denser, and practically psychedelic at times thanks to Strohm's guitar textures. Mysteries of Life's debut, *Keep a Secret* (RCA, 1996, prod. Paul Mahern and Mysteries of Life) is janglier than Blake Babies or Antenna, with a sunnier disposition. The prominent cello is a nice touch, well-integrated into the sound. "Alibi" resurfaces.

the rest: Antenna: *Sleep* (Mammoth, 1992) *Hideout* (Mammoth, 1993) *(For Now)* (Mammoth EP, 1993)

R.E.M., Keith Richards, Buffalo Tom, Velvet Underground, Feelies

see also: *Blake Babies, Juliana Hatfield*

Steve Holtje

Anthrax

Formed 1981 in New York, N.Y.

Scott Ian, guitar; Dan Spitz, guitar; Dan Lilker, bass (1981-84); Charles Benante, drums; Neil Turbin, vocals (1981-84); Joey Bel-

laDonna, vocals (1984-92); Frank Bello, bass (1984-present); John Bush, vocals (1992-present)

Along with Slayer, Metallica and Megadeth, Anthrax was once at the forefront of thrash metal—a much-accelerated version of the Ted Nugent, Alice Cooper, Kiss, Black Sabbath and Led Zeppelin music that had come before. The band was more interesting in theory than in practice, and its early albums were average despite the funky bass creeping in to make the Satanic grooves swing. Public Enemy, the influential hardcore rap band, sampled an Anthrax song on its 1988 hit "Bring Tha Noise." which brought respect and the merger of the two bands for a powerful new version of that song, followed by a national tour. Anthrax gradually tightened its sound under the leadership of Ian, but as it started to gain commercial clout, personnel problems flared and Anthrax changed lead singers in 1992. By then the marketplace had changed, and despite a couple of strong Anthrax albums, only Metallica continued to earn commercial success in the thrash metal market.

what to buy: *Among the Living* (Island, 1987, prod. Eddie Kramer and Anthrax) is the band's funniest and most diverse album, with songs based on Stephen King's novels, rhythms that lurch from fast to slow, the headbanging classic "Caught In a Mosh" and language borrowed from hip-hop culture.

what to buy next: The first albums, *Fistful of Metal* (Megaforce, 1984, prod. Carl Cannedy) and *Spreading the Disease*, (Island, 1985, prod. Anthrax and Carl Cannedy) are solid, if one-dimensional, thrash records, perfect for headbanging. The *Attack of the Killer B's (EP)* (Island, 1991, prod. Anthrax, Mark Dodson and Charles Benante) is full of interesting scraps, including "N.F.B. (dallabnikcufeciN)," which ends with the satirical sound of a pop-metal band crying through a power ballad and Ian sniffing, "Joey, pass me a tissue."

what to avoid: *State of Euphoria* (Island, 1988, prod. Anthrax and Mark Dodson) is strong evidence that a band can go only so far with thrash-metal, no matter what weird things it tries to add to it, before the whole business goes stale.

the rest: *Persistence of Time* (Island, 1990) *Sound of White Noise* (Elektra, 1993) *Live: The Island Years* (Island, 1994) *I'm the Man* (Island EP, 1987) *Armed and Dangerous* (Megaforce, 1989) *Stomp 442* (Elektra, 1995)

solo outings:

Joey Belladonna: *Belladonna* (Mausoleum, 1995)

Scott Ian (with Stormtroopers of Death): *Speak English or Die* (Megaforce, 1985/1995)

Type O Negative, Gravity Kills, Pantera, GWAR, Slayer, Megadeth, Red Hot Chili Peppers

Black Sabbath, Public Enemy, Alice Cooper, Sex Pistols, Ramones, P-Funk, KISS, Ted Nugent, Motorhead, Metallica, Fishbone

Steve Knopper

Anti-Nowhere League

Formed early 80s in Tunbridge Wells, England. Disbanded 1988.

Mike "Animal" Kramer, vocals; Magoo, guitar, Winston, bass, P.J., drums

In the aftermath of the initial punk explosion, various mutant bands sprung up like deformed ironweeds. Amidst England's debris stood the Anti-Nowhere League, a bile-spitting, goofy hate machine. Fueled with raucous energy and noxious diatribes, the band brought its Sex Pistols influence into the distilled but free-floating hate inherent in 80s punk. The group would mellow its attitude and polish its music further into the decade, but what remains in print is the ramshackle first album, *We Are...the League* (Dojo, 1984/1996) obnoxious, misogynistic, and funny, it's like vandalism with a backbeat. Play it loud. Offend the neighbors.

Allan Orski

Arc Angels

Formed 1992 in Austin, Texas

Charlie Sexton, vocals, guitar; Doyle Bramhall II, guitar, vocals; Tommy Shannon, bass; Chris "Whipper" Layton, drums

Arc Angels came together following Stevie Ray Vaughan's tragic death for one album, *Arc Angels.* (DGC, 1992, prod. Little Steven) Shannon and Layton were the rhythm section for Vaughan's band Double Trouble, Bramhall was a longtime Vaughan collaborator (and son of another well-known Austin musician) and Sexton was a teen rock prodigy burned out on the hype and looking for a situation in which he could grow. The album reflects the band's Texas blues-rock background and is obviously meant as a tribute and final farewell to Stevie Ray; in fact, you can almost hear his voice on the track that laments his death, "See What Tomorrow Brings." The Fabulous Thunderbirds (Jimmie Vaughan's former band) are also a touchstone, particularly on "Shape I'm In." A musical therapy session in the tradition of Vaughan's "Life Without You" and "Life By the Drop," this honors its subject by not bringing down the mood. In 1996, a recovering Bramhall voiced hopes of getting the group back together again.

see also: *Stevie Ray Vaughan, Charlie Sexton*

Jim Craddock

Arcadia

See: Duran Duran

Arcana

See: Bill Laswell

Tasmin Archer

Born (date N/A) in England

With her silky voice and acoustic/synth-pop soul, British vocalist/songwriter Archer evokes the intimate spirit common to Joan Armatrading and Seal. Far from merely imitating their efforts, Archer manages to make distinctive if only mildly derivative music on themes that are both confessional and inspirational. *Great Expectations* (Capitol, 1993, prod. Steve Fitzmaurice, John Hughes, Peter Kaye, Julian Mendelsohn and Paul "Wix" Wickens) is a promising but (despite its optimistic title) certainly not ground-breaking debut that places her in the pantheon of other British soul artists. The compelling opener, "Sleeping Satellite" (a hit in much of Europe), roots into the brain with a melody that grows organically from Archer's rich voice. It's a hard act to follow, as the rest of the album proves, although the sparely arranged "In Your Care" and the soul-bearing "Ripped Inside" are nicely done. Archer fares a little better with *Shipbuilding,* (Capitol EP, 1994, prod. Julian Mendelsohn) on which she hones her interpretative skills with capable covers of Elvis Costello songs ("Shipbuilding," "Deep Dark Truthful Mirror," "All Grown Up," "New Amsterdam") in addition to three live cuts and an acoustic version of "Sleeping Satellite."

Christopher Scapelliti

Archers of Loaf

Formed 1991 in Chapel Hill, N.C.

Eric Bachmann, guitar, vocals; Eric Johnson, guitar; Mark Price, drums; Matt Gentling, bass

Along with the Grifters and Pavement, Archers of Loaf are frequently cited as one of indie rock's Great Hopes. Like those bands, the Archers go heavy on the open-tuned guitar drones and obtuse lyrics, and they're not above using the rock underground itself as subject matter. But principle songwriter Bachmann has a flair for bubblegum hooks at odds with his own artier leanings. Even at its skronkiest, the Archers are hook machines. The full-length debut *Icky Mettle* (Alias, 1993, prod. Caleb Southern) is the Archers at their catchiest and most accessible. The single "Web in Front" (with the immortal chorus, "All I ever wanted was to be your spine") carved the group's niche with college radio. *Vee Vee* (Alias, 1995, prod. Archers of Loaf and Bob Weston) is almost as strong as *Icky Mettle* but not quite as inviting and perhaps a shade too tribal for those whose indie-rock credentials aren't in order. *Barry Black* (Alias, 1995, prod. Caleb Southern) is a Bachmann solo side project in which he lets his Tom Waits influence range far and wide.

the rest: *Archers of Loaf vs. The Greatest of All Time* (Alias, 1994) *The Speed of Cattle* (Alias, 1996)

David Menconi

The Archies

Formed 1968 in Riverdale, N.Y.

Members Ron "Archie" Dante (born Carmine Granito), vocals; Andy Kim (born Andrew Joachim), vocals; Ellie Greenwich, vocals; Toni Wine, vocals; Tony Passalacqua, vocals

The Archies, who with the bubblegum classic "Sugar Sugar" were responsible for the top-selling American single of 1969, were often referred to within the music industry as "Kirshner's Revenge"—Kirshner being music mogul Don Kirshner, the self-proclaimed Man With The Golden Ears who until recently had been the musical director behind the Monkees' phenomenally successful television series. Frequent creative clashes with Michael Nesmith in particular brought a rude end to Kirshner's Monkee business by early '67, but within a year he'd confidently bounced back with his own label and a new band of TV popsters upon whom to work his charms. Only this time, he made sure there would be no chance of "artistic differences" soiling his master plan. His new band would never, ever be able to question his decisions, musical or otherwise, for the Archies were merely comic book characters and soon-to-be-stars of their own Saturday morning cartoon series. When it came time to create hit records for this inanimate band, Kirshner, as he had with the Monkees, assembled a crack team of songwriters (Jeff Barry, Andy Kim) and session players (Dave Appell, Hugh McCracken) who, with Dante's lead vocals, quickly scored a Number 1 with the Barry-Kim composition "Sugar Sugar" (originally planned as a vehicle for Monkee Davy Jones). Other frothy Barry-produced (and Kirshner-published) hits followed ("Bang-Shang-a-Lang", "Jingle Jangle") before The Archies inevitably gave way to such real-life radio confections as the Osmonds and Bobby Sherman. All even the most discerning student of cartoon rock need own is *The Archies,* (Sony, 1992, prod. Various) which includes every hit and then some ("Waldo P. Emerson Jones"). Dante went on to create many successful records for Cher, Barry Manilow and Pat Benatar as well as being the voice behind McDonald's "You Deserve A Break Today" jingle. Kim enjoyed a string of hits such as "Rock Me Gently" and a fine cover of Phil Spector's "Baby I Love You". And as for The Man With The Golden Ears, he arranged his greatest-ever marriage between television and rock in the mid-Seventies as creator and host of the "Don Kirshner's Rock Concert" series, and in some quarters now has the dubious honor of being called the Father of MTV.

Gary Pig Gold

Jann Arden

Born Jann Arden Richards, March 27, 1962, in Calgary, Alberta, Canada

Arden writes and performs convincing, heart-felt tales of heartbreak, though critics have been quicker to notice than listeners. Her debut album, *Time For Mercy* (A&M, 1993, prod. Ed Cherney) earned her two Juno Awards (the Canadian version of the Grammys) for Most Promising Solo Performer and Best Video for "I Would Die For You." A collection of beautifully structured, full-throated pop songs, her second album —*Living Under June* (1994, A&M, prod. Ed Cherney) —made her a minor force in the burgeoning AAA radio format. Her songwriting, as in the delicate but spiteful ode to an ex-lover, "Insensitive" ("I'm out of vogue/I'm out of touch/I fell too fast/I feel too much/I hope that you might have some advice to give/on how to be insensitive"), shows a gem that's been shining from the beginning.

Christina Fuoco

Argent

Formed 1969 in London, England. Disbanded 1976.

Rod Argent, keyboards, vocals; Russ Ballard, guitar, vocals (1969-74); Jim Rodford, bass, vocals; Bob Henrit, drums; John Grimaldi, guitar, strings (1974-76); John Verity, guitar, bass, vocals (1974-76)

Arising from the ashes of the Zombies, Argent took the former's ethereal, minor-key approach a step further by adopting a more "progressive" approach, balancing Argent's tasteful keyboards with Ballard's guitar. All of its first album (*Argent*) and most of its second (*Ring of Hands*) are wondrous, harmony-laden delights, with songs such as "Like Honey," the original "Liar," "Bring You Joy," "Celebration," and "Pleasure" particular standouts; unfortunately, you can only get them these days via the import route. By the time of its third album, Argent began sacrificing their vocal and songwriting strengths in favor of a slide down the Emerson, Lake and Palmer chute of wretched keyboard excess, though that path did yield the defining hit "Hold Your Head Up." Regrettably, the only domestically-available Argent CD, *The Argent Collection* (Epic, 1978) gives short shrift to those first two albums in favor of this later output, which from the fourth album on is virtually unlistenable.

see also: *The Zombies*

Mike Greenfield

Joan Armatrading

Born Dec. 9, 1950 in Basseterre, St. Kitts, West Indies

Armatrading's loyal cult following has kept her touring and recording for more than 25 years. Her revealing, emotionally charged lyrics and excellent though underrated guitar playing reveal a solid, consistent talent. Raised in England, Armatrading's first public notice came in 1970, when she appeared in "Hair" and began a folk collaboration with songwriter Pam Nestor. After one duo album, Armatrading went solo with a sound that blended jazz, Caribbean and rock influences into a folk format; she was also among the first to bring synthesizers into an essentially acoustic setting. Her later work featuring electric guitars is less satisfying, but her steady songwriting skills have maintained the integrity of the music. The coordination and interplay between her vocals and her guitar playing lends distinction to much of her work.

what to buy: *Joan Armatrading* (A&M, 1976, prod. Glyn Johns) is full of pining lyrics and sparse arrangements that color and enhance her pleasing, husky voice. The anthemic gospel ending to "Love and Affection" just tops off one of the most joyous and revealing ever looks at the effects of love. Some of her electric stuff does hit, and *The Key* (A&M, 1983 prod. Steve Lillywhite and Val Garay) is one of Armatrading's least introspective forays. There's a taste of the old Joan on "Drop the Pilot," "(I Love It When You) Call Me Names" and the title song, but she also casts an eye on the social ravages of drugs and violence. *Greatest Hits* (A&M, 1996, prod. Various) is exactly what it says.

what to buy next: Much of what fans like most about Armatrading is on *Back To the Night* (A&M, 1975, prod. Pete Gage) a spare, folkish work with great songs such as 'Dry Land," "Cool Blue Stole My Heart" and "Body to Dust."

what to avoid: Armatrading's ability to produce a hook or memorable line largely evaded her songs on *Hearts and Flowers*, (A&M, 1990 prod. Joan Armatrading) although the title tune is a keeper.

the rest: *Whatever's For Us* (A&M, 1972) *Show Some Emotion* (A&M, 1977) *To the Limit* (A&M, 1978) *Me, Myself and I* (A&M, 1980) *Walk Under Ladders* (A&M, 1981) *Track Record* (A&M, 1983) *Sleight of Hand* (A&M, 1986) *Classics, Vol. 21* (A&M, 1986) *The Shouting Stage* (A&M, 1988) *Square the Circle* (A&M, 1992) *What's Inside* (A&M, 1995)

worth searching for: The hard-to-find *Secret Secrets* (A&M, 1985, prod. Mike Howlett) contains some of Armatrading's most densely produced music, including horns, but the change does her good. There's a pervasive joy here so that even a bluesy lyric such as "Friends Not Lovers" gets delivered with a bouncy, infectious beat.

▶▶ Tracy Chapman, Dionne Farris

◀◀ Odetta, Joni Mitchell

Lawrence Gabriel

Louis Armstrong

Born Aug. 4, 1901 in New Orleans, La. Died July 6, 1971 in New York, N.Y.

Armstrong stands out as one of the giants of 20th century music. A trumpeter, vocalist and entertainer par excellence, Armstrong put the stamp on all jazz singing and improvisation that would come after him; his stylings also made their mark in the pop and rock communities, where his hit "What a Wonderful World"—which took on a new life after its inclusion in the film "Good Morning Vietnam"—has become a popular cover choice. Born and raised in New Orleans as the jazz age was taking off, Armstrong was the first improviser to tie together various riffs and accents into extended solos that still hung together as a unified musical statement. This was obvious during his early days with the King Oliver and Clarence Williams groups, but his recordings with his own bands—Hot Five and Hot Seven—are some of the most important works of any music. These were just studio bands, but their musical treatments took New Orleans jazz out of the collective improvisation mode into that of the featured solo improviser. Pieces such as "Potato Head Blues," "Hotter Than That" and "Cornet Chop Suey" set standards for improvisation and composition. "Heebie Jeebies" put him on the map as a vocalist and popularized scat singing; Armstrong's gruff voice could wring emotion out of jazz, blues, ballad or pop song. Armstrong put it all together with an unequaled technical mastery that so overshadowed his contemporaries that he was held as a model for all to follow.

what to buy: Armstrong's early recordings are historic, and many of them are included on the four-CD set *Portrait of the Artist As a Young Man, 1923-1934* (Columbia/Legacy, 1994, comp. Nedra Olds-Neal) This is an essential Armstrong collection with recordings from his Oliver and Williams days in addition to seminal collaborations with Bessie Smith ("St. Louis Blues"), Lonnie Johnson, Jimmie Rogers (yes, the country-western guy) and others. The Hot Five/Seven stuff is here, along with some of his early big band work. *The Complete Studio Recordings of Louis Armstrong and the All Stars* (Mosaic, 1993, comp. Michael Cuscuna) completes the picture with a six-CD set of Armstrong recordings spanning 1950-58. This is a great collection showing the band in top form with the likes of Earl Hines, Jack Teagarden, Trummy Young, Barney Bigard, Lucky Thompson and Gene Krupa on board. Many of the standards ("Muskrat Ramble," "Struttin' With Some Barbecue," "Body and Soul," "Lazy River") are here, captured fresh without the burden of an audience to entertain. "Baby, You're Slip Is Showing" provides a taste of how Armstrong could still capture the old feeling. Both sets include excellent booklet essays and photos.

what to buy next: *Hot Fives and Hot Sevens -Vol. 2* (CBS, 1926/Columbia, 1988, prod. Various) shows Armstrong's first flush of maturity and defining of the art of jazz.

what to avoid: *What A Wonderful World* (Decca, 1970, prod. Bob Thiele) **WOOF!** contains little of what made Armstrong great, pandering to the rock generation with electric bass and guitar on covers that include "Give Peace a Chance" and "Everybody's Talking."

the rest: *Louis Armstrong and Earl Hines* (CBS, 1927/Columbia

Jazz Masterpieces, 1989) *The Essential Louis Armstrong* (Vanguard, 1987) *Stardust* (CBS, 1988) *Laughin' Louie* (RCA, 1989) *The Sullivan Years* (TVT, 1990) *Mack the Knife* (Pablo, 1990) *Rhythm Saved the World* (Decca, 1991) *In Concert With Europe 1* (RTE, 1992) *Blueberry Hill* (Milan, 1992) *The California Concerts* (MCA, 1992) *Sings the Blues* (BMG, 1993) *Young Louis Armstrong—(1930-1933)* (BMG, 1993) *Louis Armstrong and His Friends (Pasadena Civic Auditorium, 1951)* (GNP, 1993) *Happy Birthday Louis* (Omega, 1994) *Swing that Music* (Drive, 1994) *Pocketful of Dreams, Vol. III* (Decca, 1995) *Satchmo At Symphony Hall* (MCA, 1996) *Disney Songs the Satchmo Way* (Disneyland, 1968/Walt Disney Records, 1996)

worth searching for: *Ella Fitzgerald and Louis Armstrong* (Verve, 1957, prod. Norman Granz) offers a double treat with two of the world's greatest classic jazz singers swinging together. A great cast of Oscar Peterson, Herb Ellis, Ray Brown and Buddy Rich back them up.

▶▶ Bix Beiderbecke, Dizzy Gillespie, Wynton Marsalis, Victoria Williams, Buster Poindexter, Chicago, Blood, Sweat & Tears

◀◀ Joe "King" Oliver, Buddy Bolden, Kid Rena

Lawrence Gabriel

Arrested Development /Speech/Dionne Farris

Formed 1988 in Atlanta, Ga. Disbanded 1994.

Speech (born Todd Thomas) vocals; Headliner (born Tim Barnwell),DJ; Rasa Don (born Donald Jones), vocals, drums; Aerle Taree, vocals,dancer, stylist (1988-94); Montsho Eshe, dancer, choreographer; Baba Oje,spiritual adviser; Dionne Farris, vocals (1992-94); Ajile, vocals, dancer(1994-present); Kwesi, DJ, vocals (1994-present); Nadirah, vocals(1994-present)

Billed as the positive rap band to counter the negative gangstas and braggarts, Arrested Development borrowed liberally from Sly and the Family Stone and built on De La Soul to make one of 1992's best albums. Led by Speech, an upbeat young rapper with dreadlocks, the band eschewed violence, hatred and misogyny and played up African-American self-esteem and even Christianity. Drawing a connecting line through the history of 20th Century black music, AD built its songs out of blues samples and 70s funk riffs; Spike Lee was so impressed with the band's sense of history that he gave AD the leadoff track ("Revolution") to his jazz- and R&B-dominated "Malcolm X" soundtrack. Unfortunately, the band had little staying power, splintering after its tedious sophomore album. Farris, a part-time singer with the band, surprisingly outshone Speech when her solo album was better received and a bigger hit than his.

what to buy: The hit single "Tennessee," packed with sunny chants and Farris' strong singing, was just one of the many highlights on AD's terrific debut, *3 Months, 5 Months & 2 Days in the Life of....* (Chrysalis/EMI, 1992, prod. Speech) "Mr. Wendal," "People Everyday" and "Fishin' 4 Religion" showed AD to be a group of rare conscience and melodic sensibility.

what to buy next: Farris' solo debut, *Wild Seed—Wildflower,* (Columbia, 1995, prod. Dionne Farris, Randy Jackson and Michael Simanga) a mature, acoustic-oriented record marked by that year's funkiest hit, "I Know."

what to avoid: *Unplugged* (Chrysalis, 1993, prod. Alvin Speights and Speech) doles out inferior alternate versions of the debut's fresh songs.

the rest: *Zingalamaduni* (Chrysalis, 1994, prod. Speech)

worth searching for: Spike Lee's "Malcolm X" soundtrack (Reprise/Warner Bros., 1992, prod. Spike Lee and Quincy Jones) brilliantly lines up AD's "Revolution" (also released on an extended EP) alongside blues, jazz and R&B luminaries.Solo Outings: Speech—*Speech* (Chrysalis, 1996, prod. Speech)

▶▶ Fugees, Digable Planets, Basehead, Spearhead

◀◀ Public Enemy, De La Soul, Sly & the Family Stone, Gangstarr, Jungle Brothers, Dream Warriors

Tracey Birkenhauer and Steve Knopper

The Art of Noise

Formed 1983 in London, England. Disbanded 1990.

Anne Dudley, keyboards, string arrangements; J.J. Jeczalik, Fairlight, keyboards; Gary Langan, engineer (1983-86)

Hailed by hip-hop and techno musicians for its pioneering use of samplers as song construction tools rather than random noise boxes, The Art of Noise were formed in 1983 as a side project of studio wizards Jeczalik, Langan and Dudley, who had been brought together by Horn for the production of Yes' *90125* album and Frankie Goes to Hollywood's *Welcome to the Pleasuredome* sessions. The group's first experiments, captured on *Into Battle* and *Who's Afraid*, were catchy, arty instrumentals assembled almost entirely from pre-recorded sound snippets via Horn's newly-purchased Fairlight sampling keyboard—one of the first such devices ever made. After scoring dance club and chart success with "Beat Box" and its drastically remixed counterpart, "Close (to the Edit)," the Art of Noise split from the ZTT camp in 1985 over creative differences. Its subsequent releases through China Records, although generally well-received, included dodgy novelty collaborations (a dance track featuring manufactured media personality Max Headroom, a cover of Prince's "Kiss" featuring Tom Jones and the Grammy award-winning "Peter Gunn" remake with twang legend Duane Eddy), syrupy orchestral arrangements and an uninteresting trough of remixes, compilations, and repeated reissues of the same material. An amicable parting in 1990 allowed Dudley and Jeczalik to pursue solo projects; Dudley continued her orchestral work for film soundtracks, while Jeczalik collaborating with Ten Years After's Alvin Lee before entering the techno scene in 1995-96 with The Art of Silence.

what to buy: An electronic music classic, the concept album *Who's Afraid Of? (The Art of Noise!)* (ZTT/Island, 1984, prod. Trevor Horn, Paul Morley and Art of Noise) has itself been sampled by scores of musicians in tribute. *In Visible Silence* (China/Chrysalis/Off Beat, 1986, prod. Art of Noise) is more accessible and equally competent, although it is markedly different from—in fact, almost a parody of—the band's ZTT-era sound. Although bombastic at times, *In No Sense? Nonsense!* (China/Chrysalis, 1987, prod. Anne Dudley and J.J. Jeczalik) is an engaging, stereophonic tour de force, seamlessly gliding from string interludes to boys choirs to dance tracks and beyond; worlds away from "Beat Box," it is the cream of the post-ZTT Art of Noise.

what to buy next: Dismissed as "pretentious" by some critics, *Below The Waste* (China/Polydor, 1989, prod. Anne Dudley and J.J. Jeczalik) is the least experimental of the band's output but makes a good followup to *In No Sense? Nonsense!* The African-influenced tracks—"Dan Dare", "Chain Gang" and "Yebo!"—are well worth the price.

what to avoid: All the post-ZTT cash-in compilations—*The Best of the Art of Noise,* (China/Polydor, 1988) *The Ambient Collection* (China/Polydor, 1990) and *The FON Mixes* (China, 1991)

the rest: *Into Battle with the Art of Noise* (ZTT/Island, 1983) *Re-Works of Art of Noise* (China/Chrysalis, 1986) *The Best of the Art of Noise* (China, 1992)

worth searching for: The import-only compilation *Daft,* (ZTT/Warner, 1986) which contains all of *Who's Afraid...* plus remixes of "Moments In Love" and a long version of "Snapshot."

solo outings:

Anne Dudley (with Jaz Coleman): *Songs from the Victorious City* (China/Polydor/TVT, 1991) *Alice In Wonderland: Symphonic Variations* (Sound Stage, 1994) *Ancient and Modern* (The Echo Label, 1995)

J.J. Jeczalik: *The Art of Sampling* (AMG, 1994) (with Art of Silence) *artofsilence.co.uk* (Permanent, 1996)

▶▶ Future Sound of London, The Orb, 808 State, William Orbit, Yello, Shinjuku Thief, Global Communication, Severed Heads

◀◀ Kraftwerk, Tangerine Dream, Mike Oldfield, John Cage, environmental noise recordings

Mike Brown

Ash

Formed early 90s in Northern Ireland

Tim Wheeler, guitar, vocals; Mark Hamilton, bass, Rick McMurray, drums

Barely old enough to shave, England's teenage trio pops out engaging hard-pop that skirts along the edges of punk. Wheeler has a ready skill for penning immediately melodic tunes and the band plays with a varied, if not radio-friendly, post-punk fervor. They can whip it up with the big boys and sound somewhat fresher than the average alterna-rock slacker. *Trailer* (Reprise, 1995, prod. Various) is a clean-hitting debut of sharp distortion and pop melodics that hang in the air, though Ash really sounds best when it plays falt-out. *1977* (Reprise, 1996, prod. Owen Morris and Ash) has a lighter punch but the same sing-along economic pop-fests. "Girl From Mars" and "Kung Fu" highlight this catchy batch.

Allan Orski

Daniel Ash

See: Love and Rockets

Asia

Formed 1981 in Los Angeles, Calif.

Carl Palmer, drums; Geoff Downes, keyboards; John Wetton, bass, vocals (1981-83, 1985-92); Steve Howe, guitar (1981-85, 1992); Greg Lake, bass, vocals (1983-85); Mandy Meyer, guitar (1985-86); Pat Thrall, guitar (1990-92); John Payne, bass, vocals (1992) Al Pitrelli, guitar (1992)

Formed from alumni of 70s art-rock bands such as Emerson Lake and Palmer, Yes and King Crimson, Asia became the last true supergroup of that era, cranking out albums that vacillated between arty instrumental pretension and intermittent stabs at pop success. Though its debut record launched two huge hits, each subsequent album seemed less and less focused, probably because of the revolving door of members that saw both Wetton and Howe leave and rejoin the group twice each. By the mid-90s, the band was intermittently active and propped up by various studio musicians and road hacks—a brand name good for nostalgia tours and anthology records only.

what to buy: With two hit singles and a few listenable instrumental excursions, *Asia* (Geffen, 1982, prod. Mike Stone) is the best example of the group's formula, a precarious balance between arty rock ambition and bombastic pop appeal. Sure, it's crass and pretentious, but "Heat of the Moment" and "Only Time Will Tell" are the most appealing tunes this band has ever produced

what to buy next: To save endless plodding through pointless collections of instrumental noodling and directionless art-pop compositions, the compilation-of-sorts *Then and Now* (Geffen, 1990, prod. Various) collects Asia's six most successful tunes with four new ones. Of course, this means you'll have to wade through the new stuff, co-written by the likes of teen idol David Cassidy and Sex Pistol Steve Jones and about as brainless as art rock gets.

what to avoid: *Aqua* (JRS, 1992, prod. Geoff Downes) **WOOF!** is the worst of a bad lot, a pointless excursion that misses Wetton's vocals and suffers for ex-Alice Cooper guitarist Al Pitrelli's hamhanded noodling.

the rest: *Alpha* (Geffen, 1983) *Astra* (Geffen, 1985) *Live In Moscow* (Rhino, 1990) *Aria* (JRS, 1994)

worth searching for: Without exception, Asia bandmembers did their best work elsewhere. Check out the catalogs of Yes (Howe, Downes), U.K. (Wetton), Emerson, Lake and Palmer (Palmer) and the Buggles (Downes) to hear these musicians in their primes.

Zebra, Marillion, Saga, Dream Theater

Yes, King Crimson, Emerson Lake and Palmer, Kansas, Styx

see also: *Yes, King Crimson, the Buggles, Roxy Music, Uriah Heep, Emerson, Lake and Palmer*

Eric Deggans

Asleep at the Wheel

Formed 1970 in Paw Paw, Va.

Ray Benson, guitar, vocals; Lucky Oceans, pedal steel; Leroy Preston, drums; dozens of others over the years

Texas-based Asleep at the Wheel has carved out one of the most unique niches in contemporary country music with its twist on Texas swing, blues, boogie, rock and pop. Largely the brainchild of its towering frontman and sole founding member, Benson, the group has managed to weather myriad personnel changes and still stay true to its vision of bringing countrified swing to just about anyone who'll listen. Its various lineups have included fiddle, accordion, pedal steel, saxophone and mandolin, with each new face bringing something fresh to the mix. Recognition has come slowly to this eclectic, elastic band (now based in Austin, Texas), but it has come; its last album, a Bob Wills tribute, won a couple of Grammy Awards.

what to buy: For pure Wheel fun, check out the *Still Swingin'*, box set (Liberty, 1994, prod. Various) which features a wide range of material from previously unreleased obscurities to remakes of AATW staples by high-profile guests such as Garth Brooks and Dolly Parton. A total of 51 tracks is featured on this exhaustive collection, including such Wheel hits as "Take Me Back to Tulsa," "Route 66," "The Letter That Johnny Walker Read."

what to buy next: *Asleep at the Wheel Tribute to the Music of Bob Wills* and the Texas Playboys (Liberty, 1993, prod. Ray Benson and Allen Reynolds) is the most ambitious album this little ol' swing band from Texas ever attempted. Wills is the band's sturdiest musical root, so, with the help of surviving Playboys Johnny Gimble and Eldon Shamblin, the Wheels and guests (Lyle Lovett, Chet Atkins, Vince Gill, George Strait and Garth Brooks) eloquently recreated such Wills signatures as "Red Wing" and "Corine, Corina." The album won a pair of Grammys and spawned a line dance version, *Asleep at the*

Wheel Tribute to the Music of Bob Wills and the Texas Playboys (Dance Versions), (Liberty, 1994, prod. Benson, Reynolds) with a few club remixes on it.

what to avoid: Creatively moribund, much of AATW's 90s output has consisted of hits collections and live albums. The worst is the live collection of hits, *Greatest Hits (Live & Kickin')* (Arista, 1992, prod. Ray Benson) which doesn't do the band's live show—or its legacy—any justice.

the rest: *Asleep at the Wheel* (MCA, 1985) *10* (Epic, 1987) *Western Standard Time* (Epic, 1988) *Keepin' Me Up Nights* (Arista, 1990) *The Swingin' Best Of* (Epic, 1992) *The Wheel Keeps On Rollin'* (Capitol, 1995)

worth searching for: The Wheel's earliest, edgier efforts are long out of print. One vinyl album worth tracking down is *Collision Course*, (Capitol, 1978, prod. Ray Benson) which captured the band in all its stylistic diversity. And what a great band it was at the time, with two fiddlers, velvet-voiced singer Chris O'Connell and pedal steel guitarist extraordinaire Lucky Oceans.

▶▶ Lyle Lovett and His Large Band, Marty Stuart, Mark O'Conner, Alison Krauss

◀◀ Bob Wills, Phil Harris, Count Basie, Merle Haggard

Doug Pullen

The Associates (aka Associates)

Formed 1976 in Dundee, Scotland

Billy Mackenzie, vocals, all instruments; Alan Rankine, all instruments except drums (1976-82)

The early-80s music of the Associates would sound just fine at any rave today. At the earliest part of the group's career, lyricist Mackenzie and composer Rankine produced some impressive dance music, distinguished by Rankine's tuneful arrangements and Mackenzie's theatrical voice, which was only somewhat less high and shrill than that of the Cure's Robert Smith. As the Associates, they wrote gloomy, nihilistic music about rejection and doomed relationships. Uncharacteristic of many bands from this period, the group shied away from synthesizers, concentrating arrangements on solid dance rhythms driven by percussion and bass. The music could be harsh and stark ("Tell Me Easter's on Friday," "It's Better This Way," but the duo also was capable of producing well-textured dance pop devoid of the usual techno-synth excesses, as it did on the excellent single "Party Fears Two." But by the group's first American release, 1982's *Sulk*, Rankine had succumbed to the lure of synthesizers, and Mackenzie had subverted his intellectual perspective on relationships to shallow, self-conscious posturing. The duo split on the eve of its first major British tour in 1982. Rankine moved to Brussels, where he has worked extensively with ex-Josef K member Paul Haig on a number of solo recordings. Mackenzie continued recording and performing solo under the name Associates and later The Associates, teaming up with guitarist Steve Reid and producers Martin Rushent and Julian Mendelsohn. While Mackenzie's musical output has at times been surprisingly strong (as on the 1985 flop *Take Me to the Girl*), his better instincts have been undone repeatedly by his Eurodisco fascination. *Popera: The Singles Collection* (Sire/Warner Bros. 1990, prod. Various) compiles the essential material from the Associates' unsteady career (including "Party Fears Two"), although the omission of "It's Better This Way" is unforgivable. Now out of print, you'll have to dig around to find this one.

Christopher Scapelliti

The Association

Formed 1965 in Los Angeles, Calif. Disbanded mid-70s. Reformed 1981.

Russ Giguere, guitar (1965-68, 1981-present); Brian Cole (d. Aug. 2, 1972 of heroin overdose), bass; Terry Kirkman, woodwinds; Gary Alexander, guitar (1965-68); Jim Yester, guitar, sax); Ted Bluechel, drums; Terry Ramos, guitar (1968-present); Richard Thompson, guitar (1970-73)

The Association is remembered today as wimp-rock specialists, but the group made its early reputation as progressive folk-rockers with a counterculture message, albeit a rumored one: "Along Comes Mary," the group's peppy first hit in 1966, was supposedly about marijuana, and some radio stations refused to play it. The group made a more overt statement with the funereal anti-Vietnam War ode "Requiem for the Masses" in 1967. But its biggest hits were memorable for their keen melodies and airy, chorale-like harmonies, though the songs that have lasted are indeed sappy puffs of pop—"Cherish," "Windy," "Never My Love." The Association can be found these days on the oldies circuit.

what to buy: *Greatest Hits* (Warner Brothers/Seven Arts, 1968, prod. Various) has all the chart-climbers plus the lofty-minded but ponderous "Requiem for the Masses" and the generational anthem "Enter the Young."

what to buy next: If you want to dig a little deeper than the hits, *The Association Live* (Warner Brothers/Seven Arts, 1970. prod. The Association) ♪♪ is an interesting document of its folk-rock times, the fuzzed-out guitars contrasting with the sweet singing. History buffs can enjoy rocking versions of "Along Comes Mary" and "Windy" (the Association played the first day of the festival, but the collection is more notable for other artists) on the Rhino Records' *Monterey International Pop Festival* boxed set (Rhino, 1992, prod. Stephen K. Peeples and Geoff Gans, exec. prod. Lou Adler) ♪♪♪½.

what to avoid: The group in one form or another continues to release albums. Don't bother with *Association 1995: A Little Bit More* (On Track, 1995, prod. Stan Vincent and John Allen) **WOOF!**, a vile album of mostly Vegas-style oldies covers that only serves to stain the original group's accomplishments with a greasy veneer of cheap nostalgia.

the rest: *And Then...Along Comes the Association* (Valiant, 1966) ♪ *Renaissance* (Valiant, 1966) ♪ *Insight Out* (Warner Bros./Seven Arts, '67) ♪ *Birthday* (Warner Bros./Seven Arts, 1968) ♪ *The Association* (Warner Bros./Seven Arts, 1969) ♪ *Stop Your Motor* (Warner Bros./Seven Arts, 1971) ♪ *Waterbeds in Trinidad!* (Columbia, 1972) ♪.

▶▶ The Carpenters, Bread, Up with People

◀◀ The Weavers, Kingston Trio, Peter, Paul & Mary, Simon & Garfunkel, The Mamas & The Papas, The Byrds

Gil Asakawa

Rick Astley

Born Feb. 6, 1966, in Newton-le-Willows, England

Discovered by the production team of Stock, Aitken and Waterman, Rick Astley sent many teenage girls' hearts aflutter with his soulful voice and patented dance songs, but it never got deeper than that. His debut *Whenever You Need Somebody* (RCA, 1987, prod. Phil Harding, Ian Curnow and Daize Washbourn) ♪♪♪ made him a certified teeny-bop star with the hits "Never Gonna Give You Up," "Together Forever," "It Would Take A Strong, Strong Man" and the oft-covered "When I Fall In Love." Astley's fans got older and his crack production team got weaker—all of which dampened his sophomore effort, *Hold Me In Your Arms* (RCA, 1988, prod. Matt Aitken, Rick Astley, Ian Curnow, Phil Harding, and Daize Washbourn) ♪♪ "She Wants to Dance With Me" inundated the airwaves, but the album's success ended there. For his third album, *Free*, (RCA, 1991, prod. Henrik Nilson and Gary Sevenson) ♪♪½ Astley dumped SAW and the majority of his fans with his newfound adult contemporary direction.

Christina Fuoco

Astronauts

Formed 1961 in Boulder, Colo. Disbanded 1966.

Rich Fifield, guitar; Jim Gallagher, drums; Bob Demmon, guitar; Dennis Lindsey, guitar (died 1992); Jon "Stormy" Patterson, bass

A surf band? From Boulder, Colorado? The lack of water didn't deter the Astronauts, who during the early 60s was a legitimate rival to the Beach Boys. Fifield's echoey, staccato plucking - part of the band's three-guitar attack - drew heavily from the king, Dick Dale. The young, primly dressed band quickly strung together a big Colorado following before RCA decided to make the musicians stars. The 'nauts briefly tasted national fame, when its 1963 version of Lee Hazelwood's "Baja" hit No. 64. *Surfin' With the Astronauts* (RCA Victor, 1963, prod. Al Schmitt) ♪♪♪½ and *Competition Coupe* (RCA Victor, 1964, prod. Schmitt) ♪♪♪ are both worth picking up, and "Baja" and "Hot-Doggin' " still show up frequently on surf and guitar compilations. Fifield still plays in Boulder classic-rock cover bands.

Steve Knopper

Aswad

Formed 1975 in Ladbroke Grove, England

Brinsley Forde, vocal, guitar; Courtney Hemmings, vocal, keyboard (1975-78); Donald Benjamin, vocal, guitar, (1975-83); Ras George Levi, bass (1975-80); Angus "Drummie" Zeb, vocal, drums; Tony Gad Robinson, vocal, keyboards, bass (1979-present)

Aswad ranks among the best and most long-lived of British reggae bands. The band first hit the scene with a militant brand of reggae, though later it proved itself adept at rock, too. It was the first U.K. reggae group to sign with a major recording company, Island, in 1976. Although a hit among reggae enthusiasts, Aswad aspired to larger audiences. During the 80s, the group began adding pop influences to the music. The results were uneven, though crossover stardom never came and reggae purists charged that the group had lost its roots; a trio since 1986, Aswad's recent return to more rootsy music has gained some critical attention, but the outside influences remain. As Forde says: "We're driving a reggae vehicle, but we're carrying a lot of passengers."

what to buy: The group has been through a lot of changes, but

What Album Changed Your Life?

"An Otis Redding album, Live in Europe (Atco, 1966) was the name of it. It was him at his peak. I had seen him at the Fillmore, and I knew he was big and playing powerful music. On this live record, he really connected that night. What it did was reinforce my feelings for live music and being able to capture that one, special, miraculous moment. He never sounded that good again. It was a great record."

Mickey Hart (Grateful Dead, Mystery Box)

Aswad (Island, 1976, prod. Tony Platt and Aswad) captures the uncompromising stance of mid-70s reggae—guys with guitars who had something to say. "I A Rebel Soul," "Can't Stand the Pressure" and "Back To Africa" are all classics, and the band showed some dubability on "Ethiopian Rhapsody" and "Red Up." *Crucial Tracks - The Best of Aswad* (Mango, 1989, prod. Various) culls the best from the 80s work and pulls out some pearls. "Gimme the Dub," a U.K.-only single included here, is a dance club slammer.

what to buy next: *Rise and Shine Again* (Mesa, 1995, prod. Various) is full of uplifting messages and upbeat dance grooves. "Shine," "Warriors" and "Pickin' Up" move the militant attitude into a self-improvement mode.

what to avoid: *Distant Thunder* (Mango, 1988, prod. Aswad) aimed at an elusive crossover audience it never reached.

the rest: *Hulet* (Mango, 1979) *A New Chapter of Dub* (Mango, 1982) *Live and Direct* (Mango, 1983) *Rebel Souls* (Mango, 1984) *Going To the Top* (Simba, 1986) *To the Top* (Mango, 1989) *Too Wicked* (Mango, 1990) *Showcase* (Mango, 1990) *Rise and Shine* (Mesa, 1994)

worth searching for: *Dub: The Next Frontier* (Mesa, 1995, prod. Aswad) takes the music on a P-Funk-like space voyage. Vocal additions to the mix are a delight.

▶▶ Patra, Big Mountain

◀◀ Toots and the Maytals, Freddie McGregor

Lawrence Gabriel

Atlanta Rhythm Section /ARS

Formed 1971 in Doraville, Ga. Disbanded 1981. Re-formed as ARS in 1989.

Barry Bailey, guitar; Rodney Justo, vocals (1971-72); Paul Goddard, bass; Robert Nix, drums (1971-77); J.R. Cobb, guitar; Dean Daughtry, keyboards; Ronnie Hammond, vocals (1972-present); Roy Yeager, drums (1978-81); Steve Stone, guitar (1989-93; Sean Burke, drums, (1989-93); Justin Senker, bass (1989-93)

Fomer studio cats with a flair for slippery Southern boogie, the Atlanta Rhythm Section made a name for itself in the late 70s with buttered-up, fluid guitar lines and a smooth, restrained musical tone. Although Hammond is an unremarkable frontman and the band never really forged a strong identity, it did garner several hit singles as well as gold and platinum albums. *A Rock and Roll Alternative* (Polydor, 1976, prod. Buddy Buie) is its most fully realized blend of harder jams and ballads and contains its biggest hit, the smoky "So Into You." The million-selling follow-up *Champagne Jam* (Polydor, 1978, prod. Buddy Buie) has the "So Into You" rewrite "Imaginary Lover" as well as the near-reckless "I'm Not Gonna Let it Bother Me Tonight." *The Best of Atlanta Rhythm Section* (Polydor, 1991, prod. Buddy Buie) tracks the band's less distinguished early material through its peak years and shortly thereafter in an ample hour-plus sampler.

the rest: *Quinella* (Columbia, 1981)

Allan Orski

The Au Pairs

Formed 1978 in Birmingham, England

Leslie Woods, vocals, guitar; Jane Munro, bass, vocals; Paul Foad, guitar, vocals; Pete Hammond, drums

This band featured the female vocals and feminist perspective of Woods, with her dissections of male-female relations and women's place in society, role-playing her way through situations rather than delivering screeds. Accused of being humorless, her lyrics were often quite funny in the blackest, most sardonic way, delivered in a grating voice that demands attention. Rhythmically similar to the herky-jerky avant-funk of Gang of Four, the Au Pairs' music was generally sparer, and the politics less radical and strident, though just as left-leaning. After placing singles in the indie charts, getting censored by the BBC and touring as the opener for Gang of Four and later UB40, the band released *Playing with a Different Sex* (Human U.K., 1981/RPM U.K., 1992, prod. Au Pairs and Ken Thomas) offers thoughtful yet danceable punk fun—fleshed out to a full 72 minutes on the CD reissue. Unfortunately neither that nor the group's second album, *Sense and Sensuality,* (Kamera U.K., 1982/RPM U.K., 1993) were ever released in the U.S. They're worth searching for.

Steve Holtje

Brian Auger

Born July 18, 1939 in London, England

During the mid-60s, Auger teamed up with vocalist Julie Driscoll in England and created music that introduced elements of progressive rock, blues and R&B with jazz. When he formed Oblivion Express in 1970, Auger—along with artists such as Herbie Hancock, Chick Corea, and Stanley Clarke—helped usher in and popularize the jazz-rock fusion era of the early 70s. After making three albums between 1971-72, Auger reshuffled his Oblivion Express line-up (which over the years included super drummer Steve Ferrone, future Santana singer Alex Ligertwood and future Average White Band drummer Robbie McIntosh), took over lead vocals, and headed back into the studio intending only to record his version of Marvin Gaye's "Inner City Blues." But the studio chemistry was so strong that Auger wrote more songs and wound up with the band's finest album, *Closer To It,* in 1973. The propulsive first track "Whenever You're Ready" is actually the first studio take and it clearly offers a more supple and mainstream sound, while the second, "Happiness is Just Around the Bend," found its way onto some progressive American rock stations and helped put the band on the map. Essentially the same line-up returned for *Straight Ahead,* (RCA, 1975/1995, prod. Brian Auger) an equally impressive release that included a terrific version of Wes Montgomery's "Bumpin' on Sunset". The band also recorded material at Los Angeles' Whiskey A Go Go in 1974, which were later released in two volumes. Auger's Oblivion Express days are captured on *The Best of Brian Auger's Oblivion Express* (Chronicles, 1996, prod. Various) a smart two-disc set that should whet appetites for the (hopefully) inevitable re-release of some of the group's other individual albums. After Oblivion Express splintered, Auger continued to tour and record as a solo act; these days he occasionally teams up with formal Animals singer Eric Burdon and tours with a band that includes his son and daughter.

Michael Isabella

The Auteurs

Formed 1992 in London, England

Luke Haines, vocals, piano, guitar; Alice Readman, bass; Glenn Collins, drums (1992-94); Barney Crockford, drums (1994-present); James Banbury, cello, organ (1993-present)

After a stint as guitarist with the 80s band The Servants, Haines formed The Auteurs with girlfriend Readman and Collins. Named after the art cinema of the 50s, The Auteurs were quickly touted as intelligent English pop by the music press. Now considered one of the leaders of Brithop, The Auteurs remain true to their essence by blending offbeat, sometimes cynical lyrics with aching pop melodies. Its stunning first release *New Wave* (Hut, 1993, prod. Phil Vinall and Luke Haines) introduces the band's strong songwriting skills. *Now I'm A Cowboy* (Hut, 1994, prod. Phil Vinall and Luke Haines) offers a scornful set of social commentary. µ *Ziq vs. The Auteurs* (Hut, 1994, prod. Michael Paradinas) is an album of Auteurs songs covered and reconstructed by electronic musician Michael Paradinas, aka Mu-Ziq. *After Murder Park* (Hut, 1996, prod. Steve Albini) is their latest album. The combination of Albini's sonic production and Luke Haines' sarcasm creates tense, unforgettable songs. From the atmospheric "Dead Sea Navigators" to the Beatles-influenced "Unsolved Child Murder," Haines sings his private obsessions with a sneer in his voice and a melody in his heart.

Anna Glen

Average White Band

Formed 1972 in Scotland. Disbanded 1981. Reformed 1989.

Alan Gorrie, bass, vocals; Onnie McIntyre, guitar, vocals; Roger Ball, keyboards, saxes; Malcom Duncan, tenor saxophone (1972-80); Robbie McIntosh, drums (1972-74, died Sept. 23, 1974 in Los Angeles, Calif.); Hamish Stuart, guitar, vocals (1972-80); Steve Ferrone, drums (1974-80); Alex Ligertwood, vocals (1989-present)

Heralded as a bunch of Scottish guys who played funk like they were born in one of America's Chocolate Cities (with a name supposedly bestowed by Bonnie Bramlett of Delaney and Bonnie), the Average White Band came together with members from several Scottish soul tribute groups. Though a 1973 debut failed to catch fire, AWB soon struck gold with Atlantic Records in 1974, concocting a mix of James Brown-style funk and old-school R&B that captivated the then-emerging disco movement. Unfortunately, success took its toll, as drummer McIntosh died at a Hollywood party, snorting a fatal mix of heroin and morphine (Gorrie reportedly inhaled the same mixture but was kept awake by Cher and survived). Friend and Bloodstone member Ferrone replaced McIntosh, helping the band sharpen its focus on authentic funk sounds. But as disco waned, AWB's material became curiously focused on that dying genre—until fans of its original funk flavor stopped buying records. Disbanded in 1980, AWB was revived by Gorrie, Ball and McIntyre in 1989, with former Santana vocalist Ligertwood as lead singer, though the relative failure of its comeback album doomed the band to the nostalgia circuit.

what to buy: Fans of 70s funk must own the group's first two Atlantic albums, *Average White Band* (Atlantic, 1974, prod. Arif Mardin) and *Cut the Cake.* (Atlantic, 1975, prod. Arif Mardin) Both helped set the tone for 70s funk, ranging from horn-fueled workouts such as the instrumental hit "Pick Up the Pieces" to silky slow jams like "Schoolboy Crush," "If I Ever Lose This Heaven" and "Person to Person." Unlike many Europeans trying to do funk, AWB sounded as authentic as every other act on R&B radio—a feat as impressive as it was surprising.

what to buy next: Greatest hits packages, when done well, are the best way to get the good stuff from an artist's career without the clinkers. And few collections do this job better than *Pickin' Up the Pieces: The Best of the Average White Band, 1974-1980.* (Rhino, 1992, prod. Various) Here, fans can check out the group's biggest successes and album cuts on one 18-track excursion.

what to avoid: The band's reunion effort, *Aftershock* (Track Record, 1989, prod. John Robie) WOOF! reached new depths of disappointment. Featuring just three original members and a formulaic sound, the album reminds everybody why the group broke up in the first place.

the rest: *Show Your Hand* (MCA, 1973) *Put It Where You Want It* (MCA, 1975) *Soul Searching* (Atlantic, 1976) *Person to Person* (Atlantic, 1977) *Benny and Us* (Atlantic, 1977) *Warmer Communications* (Atlantic, 1978) *Feel No Fret* (RCA, 1979) *Average White Band, Vol. 8* (Atlantic, 1980) *Shine* (Arista, 1980) *Cupids In Fashion* (RCA, 1982) *Best of the Average White Band* (RCA, 1984)

worth searching for: Members of AWB have lent their talents as session musicians to works by several artists, including Chaka Khan, Paul McCartney, Eric Clapton, Duran Duran and Tom Petty—often making better contributions there than on their own records. Particularly worthwhile is *Benny and Us* (Atlantic, 1977) with R&B great Ben E. King.

Prince, K.C. & the Sunshine Band, Little Steven & the Disciples of Soul

James Brown, Tower of Power, Brian Auger, Ben E. King.

Eric Deggans

Aztec Camera

Formed 1980, Glasgow, Scotland

Roddy Frame, guitar and vocals; Alan Welsh, bass (1980); Dave Mulholland, drums (1980-81); Campbell Owens, bass (1980-86); Craig Gannon, guitar (1981-83); David Ruffy, drums (1982-86); Malcolm Ross, guitar (1983-86)

Emerging from Scotland's fledgling New Wave movement, Aztec Camera demonstrated a level of compositional excellence and performance virtuosity lacking in much of this period's pop music. Built around Roddy Frame's ample songwriting and guitar-playing talents, the band—its members still in their teens—showed an ability to turn out sophisticated, jazzy, acoustic-oriented guitar pop without falling on its face. Frame's fragile, enchanting voice engaged in clever word play that made him sound like the optimistic kid brother of Elvis Costello (who, notably, gave the band a plug in 1983 when he dubbed Frame the most promising songwriter of the day). Although well-received in Britain, the group had less success in the U.S., where Frame's ambitious mix of genres made the group difficult to pigeonhole. By 1987, with his ever-increasing musical interests spread to house and rap music, Frame jettisoned the band, making Aztec Camera essentially a recurring front for his solo efforts.

what to buy: Aztec Camera's debut effort, *High Land, Hard Rain,* (Sire, 1983, prod. John Brand and Bernie Clark) bubbles over with jangly pop and jazz-guitar riffing. "Oblivious" and "Pillar to Post" are particularly lovely and memorable, evoking the naivete of early New Wave while rising above the preciousness typical of the genre.

what to avoid: Recorded in the U.S. with studio musicians and a half-dozen different producers, *Love* (Sire, 1987, prod. Various) 🦴 is a misguided trip down Philly-soul lane, its heavy production obscuring Frame's earnest, boyish voice. On the other hand, U.K. record buyers made this Frame's biggest commercial hit to date.

the rest: *Knife* (Sire, 1984) 🦴🦴 *Stray* (Sire, 1990) 🦴🦴🦴🦴 *Dreamland* (Sire, 1993) 🦴🦴🦴 *Frestonia* (Reprise, 1995) 🦴🦴🦴

worth searching for: Two promotional-only compilations—Japan's *The Best of Aztec Camera* (WEA, 1993) 🦴🦴🦴🦴, prod. Various→ and its U.S. counterpart, *Retrospect.* (Sire/Reprise, 1993, prod. Various) 🦴🦴🦴▽ Both deliver worthy overviews of the group's catalog and include Frame's humorously deadpan take on Van Halen's "Jump."

▶▶ 10,000 Maniacs, Nick Heyward, The Style Council, The Housemartins

◀◀ The Byrds, Elvis Costello, Dire Straits

Christopher Scapelliti

Babe the Blue Ox

Formed 1989 in Brooklyn, N.Y.

Rose Thomson, vocals, bass; Tim Thomas, vocals, guitar; Hanna Fox, vocals, drums

This bass-heavy alternative power trio with a high skronk factor and a wry sense of humor incorporates a broad range of disparate sounds into a seamless, distinctive style. The members trade off vocals in the same casual yet energetic way they blast through their loose-limbed grooves, with Thomson's high vocals recalling Juliana Hatfield. Thomas and Fox had to deal with carpal tunnel syndrome, a result not of musical endeavors but of heavy typing at their full-time day jobs (Fox had to quit drumming for four months). *Color Me Babe* (Homestead, 1994, prod. Bruce Hathaway and Babe the Blue Ox) 🦴🦴🦴🦴 shows the band's highest development of its indie sound. *[BOX]* (Homestead, 1993, prod. Bruce Hathaway, Garris Shipon and Babe the Blue Ox) 🦴🦴🦴▽ was the band's first non-single release and has a winningly raw sound.

the rest: *Je m'Appelle Babe* (Homestead EP, 1993) 🦴🦴🦴▽ *People* (RCA, 1996) 🦴🦴🦴

Steve Holtje

Babes in Toyland

Formed 1987 in Minneapolis, Minn.

Katherine "Kat" Bjelland, vocals, guitar; Lori Barbero, drums; Michelle Leon, bass (1987-92); Maureen Herman, bass (1992-present)

Babes in Toyland make a racket. First among the riot grrrl groups (Bjelland wore baby doll dresses *before* Courtney Love, thank you), the trio rages against the machine and everything else, including mates, parents, rivals, Barbie dolls. It's primal scream therapy with electric guitars, and an emphasis on the primal—often it sounds like Chrissie Hynde singing in front of the (old) Sex Pistols. Bjelland came to Minneapolis from San Francisco, where she was in the band Sugar Baby Doll with Courtney Love of Hole and Jennifer Finch of L7. Babes earned its indie credibility quickly, winning a powerful patron in Sonic Youth—and, in 1993, a spot on the Lollapalooza tour.

what to buy: On its major label debut, *Fontanelle* (Reprise, 1992, prod. Lee Ranaldo and Kate Bjelland) 🦴🦴🦴▽, the group tones down the rage just a bit and makes the most of strong songs and production help from Sonic Youth's Ranaldo.

what to buy next: *Spanking Machine* (Twin/Tone, 1990, prod. Jack Endino) 🦴🦴🦴 is an assured debut, all spite and bile in anticipation of the big grunge breakthrough the following year. *Painkillers* (Reprise EP, 1993) 🦴🦴🦴, released to coincide with the Lollapalooza tour, features five standard songs and a sneaky sixth track that's actually a 35-minute live set.

what to avoid: *To Mother* (Twin/Tone EP, 1991, prod. John Loder) 🦴🦴▽ has the sound and feel of an exercise in treading water.

the rest: *Nemesisters* (Reprise, 1995) 🦴🦴▽

worth searching for: *Live at the Academy,* (Reprise, 1992) 🦴🦴🦴 another live collection—this one promotion only—only with the *Fontanelle* single "Won't Tell."

▶▶ Hole, 7 Year Bitch, Veruca Salt

◀◀ The Stooges, the Pretenders, Sonic Youth, the Pixies

Gary Graff

Bachman-Turner Overdrive

Formed 1972 in Winnipeg, Manitoba, Canada. Disbanded 1980. Periodic reunions.

Randy Bachman, guitar, vocals (1972-77); Tim Bachman, guitar, vocals (1972-73); Robbie Bachman, drums, vocals; C.F. (Fred) Turner, bass, vocals; Blair Thornton, guitar, vocals (1974-80); Jim Clench, bass, vocals (1977-80)

The prairie city of Winnipeg spawned two of the most successful rock bands of the 70s: the Guess Who and Bachman-Turner Overdrive. Guitar legend Randy Bachman had a large hand in both. By 1970, Guess Who co-founders Bachman and singer Chad Allan had quit the band they started in 1962. They reunited, and in 1971 formed Brave Belt with Bachman's brother Robbie on drums. After two records, another Bachman brother, Tim, and Turner replaced Allan, and the new band became Bachman-Turner Overdrive. (Legend has it that the band drew inspiration for its name after it visited a truck stop in Windsor, Ontario, and noticed a copy of Overdrive magazine, a trucking industry trade journal.) As he had done in the Guess Who, Bachman was able to craft great rock songs on simple guitar riffs; by 1977 that skill had netted the band sales of 7 million records in the U.S. BTO disbanded in 1980 but has regrouped for tours in various configurations ever since. Randy Bachman also records as a solo artist—often with countrymate Neil Young as a guest—and also occasionally tours with various versions of the Guess Who.

what to buy: *Bachman-Turner Overdrive II* (Mercury, 1973, prod. Randy Bachman) ♪♪♪♪ Every teenager in North America was aware of this record after its release, and the five opening guitar notes on "Takin' Care of Business" can still make heads bob today. It also contains the hits "Welcome Home," a jazzy homage to the rock life, and the Doobie Brothers-influenced "Let It Ride." The band followed with another strong record, *Not Fragile,* (Mercury, 1974, prod. Randy Bachman) ♪♪♪♪ which features the still-popular hits "You Ain't Seen Nothing Yet" and "Roll On Down the Highway."

what to buy next: *Bachman-Turner Overdrive: The Anthology* (Mercury, 1993, prod. Randy Bachman, BTO and Jim Vallance) ♪♪♪♪ is a whopping two-disc set with a nicely chosen chunk of material from the group's heyday and afterwards.

what to avoid: *All Time Greatest Hits - Live* (Curb, 1990) ♪ is not exactly the band's all-time greatest performance.

the rest: *Bachman-Turner Overdrive* (Mercury, 1973) ♪♪ *Four Wheel Drive* (Mercury, 1975) ♪♪♪ *BTO's Greatest* (Mercury, 1981) ♪♪♪ *You Ain't Seen Nothing Yet* (Polygram, 1993) ♪♪ *Best Of - Live* (Curb, 1994) ♪♪♪

worth searching for: Bachman's *Plugged In—The Garage Tapes,* (Ranbach EP, 1993) ♪♪♪ a Canadian import of a relaxed sounding Bachman solo performance in Seattle, featuring "You Ain't Seen Nothin' Yet," "Takin' Care of Business" and three Guess Who favorites.

solo outings:

Randy Bachman: *Any Road* (Guitar Recordings, 1994) ♪♪♪

▶▶ The Smithereens, Soundgarden, Stone Temple Pilots

◀◀ Box Tops, Free, the Who

William Hanson

Bad Brains

Formed 1979 in Washington, D.C.

H.R. (born Paul D. Hudson, a.k.a. Joseph I), vocals (1979-83, 1986-87, 1988-89, 1994-95); Dr. Know (born Gary Wayne Miller), guitar (1979-95); Darryl Aaron Jenifer, bass (1979-95); Earl Hudson, drums (1979-83, 1986-87, 1989, 1994-95); Israel Joseph-I (born Dexter Pinto), vocals (1992-94); Mackie Jayson, drums (1983-86, 1988-89, 1992-93)

Bad Brains are the most influential band in hardcore, often overlooked due to an all-black lineup that's out of synch with punk stereotype. But the Brains' pioneering mix of punk with reggae also makes it an unusual giant of world music and a founder of the barrier-breaking aesthetic now spreading through all forms of art. The group's explosive sound has the creative tension of cultures actually facing each other for the first time—call it Hard World. The Brains' sensibility stems from an upbringing in the ghettos around the capital of the free world; it embodies the past shame and future promise of American multiculturalism—bassist Jenifer even traces his lineage from a slave-owning signer of the Constitution. Reversing rock's usual trend, Bad Brains were not amateurs who gradually built up their sound but fusion-jazz types who learned the value of simplicity from the late-70s punk revolution. When they discovered the beliefs and music of Rastafarianism, the Brains set their cultural blender on high and threw away the knob. The creative energies involved are a volatile brew, and since 1983 the band has literally made albums between breakups, with vocalist H.R. and his brother Earl departing regularly to pursue more straightforward reggae recordings. Narrowly marketed to the punk audience, portrayed more as historical figures than contemporary players and eclipsed by violent incidents involving an unbalanced H.R., the Brains have been in limbo since its last album in 1995. Its fullest success may be ahead of the group, but its accomplishments are left behind for all to hear.

what to buy: The debut, *Bad Brains* (ROIR, 1982/1996, rec. by Jay Dublee) ♪♪♪♪♪ is not only the authoritative hardcore album, but the standard by which all non-conformist music can be measured. With oddly melodic power chords and vocal wails, polyphonic noise guitar, unpredictable acrobatics of rhythm and tempo, and precociously expert reggae, the Brains transcended a genre even as they defined it. On *I Against I*, (SST, 1986, prod. Ron St. Germain) the band grounds metal-leaning rock with the syncopation of funk, takes pop to blistering extremes and keeps its playing tight while ambitiously stretching out their song-structure. H.R. turns in his best lyrics and inflects his singing with a rich soul texture (after a drug bust, the vocals for "Sacred Love" were resourcefully recorded by phone from prison). The stunning *Quickness* (Caroline, 1989, prod. Ron St. Germain) shifts genres within individual songs. The prodigal H.R. returned to create the lyrics and vocal melodies in one night; some remnants of his a cappella demos contrast the otherwise fat production sound with a fabulous rawness. His sometimes overly macho lyrics, and a few repeated musical ideas from *I Against I*, are the only things which qualify the album's success.

what to buy next: *God of Love* (Maverick, 1995, prod. Ric Ocasek) slows the pace of experimentation a bit and may seem to lack the other albums' visionary sweep. But it marks the band's most decisive same-song synthesis of hard rock and reggae yet, and features the must-have, ambient reggae odyssey "How I Love Thee" and the metal-gospel, country-western prayer call (believe it!) of "Thank JAH." *Live* (SST, 1988, prod. Phil Burnett) is a sterling example of the Brains on stage.

what to avoid: Even a bad album for the Brains would be a good one for many others. But *Rock for Light* (PVC, 1983/Caroline, 1991, prod. Ric Ocasek) is packed with inferior versions of songs from the (then-rare) first album.

the rest: *Bad Brains* (Alternative Tentacles EP, 1982) *I and I Survive/Destroy Babylon* (Important EP, 1982) *Attitude: The ROIR Session* (ROIR/Important, 1989) *The Youth Are Getting Restless: Live in Amsterdam* (Caroline, 1990) *Spirit Electricity* (SST EP, 1991) *Rise* (Epic, 1993)

worth searching for: The soundtrack for *Pump Up the Volume*, (MCA, 1990, prod. Various) which features a cover of the MC5's "Kick Out the Jams" with Henry Rollins on vocals.

Living Colour, Beastie Boys, Consolidated, Bad Religion, Cornershop, Goldfinger, Sting, Babe the Blue Ox

Bob Marley, Parliament/Funkadelic, The Sex Pistols, The Clash, The Damned, The Ramones, Mahavishnu Orchestra, Return to Forever

Adam McGovern

Bad Company

Formed 1973 in London, England. Disbanded 1983. Reformed 1986.

Mick Ralphs, guitar; Simon Kirke, drums; Paul Rodgers, vocals, guitar, keyboards (1973-82); Boz Burrell, bass (1973-82); Brian Howe, vocals (1986-92); Rick Wills, bass (1992-present); Robert Hart, vocals (1992-present); Dave "Bucket" Colwell, guitar (1992-present)

Like Led Zeppelin (with whom they shared a record label and manager), Bad Company was the culmination of the British blues-rock scene, a "supergroup" formed with a conscious eye towards the sales charts and an ear for radio-ready songwriting. The group was formed by two members of Free, throaty vocalist Paul Rodgers and drummer Simon Kirke, after that more quirky hard rock group broke up. They lured Mick Ralphs from Mott the Hoople, who was disgruntled with his group's turn towards glam-rock with their hit version of David Bowie's "All the Young Dudes." Bassist Boz Burrell of King Crimson rounded out the lineup. Bad Company's first album was a machismo-dripping blueprint for post-blooz FM rock. Subsequent records continued the hits and made the group one of the 70s biggest concert attractions, but the mega-touring took its toll. The original group called it quits after the 1982 album *Rough Diamonds*. Rodgers has gone his own way since, but Simon and Ralphs reconvened Bad Company in 1986. The group is still trotting out the macho moves and pounding away with hard-rock riffs, and the albums have been nothing if not predictable.

what to buy: The biggest hit on *Bad Company* (Swan Song, 1974, prod. Bad Company) was the lusty "Can't Get Enough," but several others—the slow-grinding "Rock Steady," the pretty Mott the Hoople remake "Ready for Love," the brooding "Bad Company" and the gleeful "Movin' On"—remain part of the foundation of the classic rock canon. It never got any better.

what to buy next: *Straight Shooter* (Swan Song, 1975, prod. Bad Company) and *Run with the Pack* (Swan Song, 1976, prod. Bad Company) both have strong songs to recommend them—if nothing else, Bad Company knew how to build an entire song instead of just jamming on a riff. *Straight Shooter's* "Feel Like Makin' Love" rose to #10 on the Billboard charts, making it the group's biggest hit after "Can't Get Enough," which hit #5.

what to avoid: *What You Hear is What You Get: The Best of Bad Company Live* (Atlantic, 1993, prod. Simon Kirke) **WOOF!** is a shrill live set featuring shrill vocalist Brian Howe that's so cliched it's almost a parody of arena rock. Except Spinal Tap did that better.

the rest: *Burnin' Sky* (Swan Song, 1977) *Desolation Angels* (Swan Song, 1979) *Rough Diamonds* (Swan Song, 1982) *10 from 6* (Atlantic 1985) *Fame and Fortune* (Atlantic, 1986) *Dangerous Age* (Atlantic, 1988) *Holy Water* (Atco, 1990) *Here Comes Trouble* (Atco, 1992) *Company of Strangers* (EastWest, 1995, prod. Bad Company) WOOF!

worth searching for: *Can't Get Enough of That Stuff,* (Oh Boy) a bootleg from a 1974 concert in Boston that finds Bad Company at its tough, rocking best.

solo outings:

Paul Rodgers: Cut Loose (Atlantic, 1983) *Muddy Waters Blues* (Victory, 1993) *The Hendrix Set" Victory, 1993) (with The Firm)*The Firm *(Atlantic, 1985)* Mean Business *(with The Law)* The Law" (Atlantic, 1991)

Bon Jovi, Def Leppard, Black Crowes

Alexis Korner, Yardbirds, Fleetwood Mac, Free, Led Zeppelin

Gil Asakawa

Bad Manners

Formed 1978 in London, England

Buster Bloodvessel (born Doug Trendle), vocals; Louis Cook, guitar; Davis Farren, bass; Martin Stewart, keyboards, Brian Tuitti, drums; Gus Herman, trumpet; Chris Kane, saxophone; Andrew Marson, saxophone

The two-ton girth of cue-ball Bloodvessel and his goofy onstage antics helped make Bad Manners one of the leading post-Specials ska bands of the 80s. Sporting a hyper novelty sound that resulted in a string of U.K. hits, Bad Manners continued the ska revival of the 70s throughout most of the 80s and remained a touring band into the 90s, despite recent years of commercial indifference that's left most of its albums out of print on these shores. *Return of the Ugly* (Blue Beat-Relativity, 1989/Lagoon Reggae, 1995) even has a skank version of the "Bonanza" theme, while *Forging Ahead* (Portrait, 1982/Magnet, 1995) is a killer that contains the band's goofy take on the classic (retitled) "My Girl Lollipop."

the rest: *Fatty Fatty* (Lagoon Reggae, 1993) *Fat Sound* (Triple X Records, 1993)

Allan Orski

Bad Religion

Formed 1980 in Los Angeles, Calif.

Greg Graffin, lead vocals; Brett Gurewitz, guitar, vocals (1980-94); Greg Hetson, guitar, vocals (1984-present); Brian Baker, guitar (1994-present); Jay Bentley, bass; Jay Ziskrout, drums (1980-81); Peter Finestone, drums (1981-91); Bobby Schayer, drums (1992-present)

From its first album, *How Could Hell Be Any Worse?* in 1982, through 1993's *Recipe for Hate*, Bad Religion issued its records on its own label, Epitaph, which became a huge indie success story, also putting out albums by the Offspring, Rancid, Down By Law, L7, Dag Nasty and others. Along with Fugazi, Bad Religion stood as the epitome of indie-ness, so its signing by Atlantic Records in 1993 came as a shock. The most intellectual punk band since Gang of Four, Bad Religion features a lead singer (Graffin) who interrupted the band's career to get a graduate degree in sociology and who subsequently structured the band's tours around his teaching schedule. Graffin offers penetrating analyses of socio-political issues, frequently sending listeners to their dictionaries with polysyllabic words never used before or since in popular music, The group is hardly a bunch of eggheads, however, producing some of the most intense, hard-rocking punk ever made. 1988's *Suffer* had just one song longer than 2:02), but then came a gradual progression to increased stylistic versatility, with harmony vocals and more varied tempos added to the fury—which neatly folded into the group's decision to go with a major label.

what to buy: *Generator* (Epitaph, 1992, prod. Bad Religion) is one of the most majestic punk albums ever, with "Atomic Garden" dissecting the infantilism of doomsday diplomacy and "Fertile Crescent" putting the Persian Gulf War in historical perspective. Schayer proves himself one of the greatest punk drummers throughout.

what to buy next: *80-85* (Epitaph, 1991, prod. Jim Mankey and Bad Religion) collects the debut album *How Could Hell Be Any Worse?* plus EPs and compilation tracks of the first phases of the group's career. *Recipe for Hate* (Epitaph, 1993, prod. Bad Religion) shows how Bad Religion has changed in 10 years, though with 14 hard-fast songs in 37:42, it's still securely punk. But the band manages to add intricacy with simple ingredients such as trademark harmony vocals; the guitar riffs are solid, and the lyrics are simpler, more direct and as dead-on analytical as always.

what to avoid: *All Ages* (Epitaph, 1995, prod. Bad Religion) is compiled from the five in-print Epitaph albums and baited with a mere two live tracks. At just 50 minutes, it's not a good value despite a well-chosen program.

the rest: *Suffer* (Epitaph, 1988) *No Control*(Epitaph, 1989) *Against the Grain* (Epitaph, 1990) *Stranger Than Fiction* (Atlantic, 1994) *The Gray Race* (Atlantic, 1995)

worth searching for: *Into the Unknown*, (Epitaph, 1983) the second album Bad Religion has disowned, is long out of print. Occasionally there's talk of reissuing it in a remixed form, presumably with the prog-rock keyboards buried or erased, since there's nothing else about this album that the group could be ashamed of.

▶▶ Offspring, Pennywise, NOFX

◀◀ The Clash, Crass, the Buzzcocks, Bad Brains

Steve Holtje

Badfinger /Joey Molland

Formed 1968 in London, England. Disbanded 1975. Reformed 1978.

Pete Ham, vocals, guitar, piano (1968-75, died April 23, 1975); Tom Evans, vocals, guitar, bass (1968-83, died Nov. 23, 1983); Mike Gibbins, drums (1968-75); Ron Griffiths, bass (1968); Joey Molland, vocals, guitar, keyboards (1968-74, 1978-81); Bob Jackson, keyboards (1974-75); Joe Tanzin, guitar (1978); Kenny Harck, drums (1978); Tony Kaye, keyboards (1981); Glenn Sherba, guitar (1981); Richard Bryans, drums (1981)

Originally called the Iveys, Badfinger signed with the Beatles' Apple Records in 1968 after Paul McCartney discovered its demo. With a power pop sound derivative of its famous mentors, the group produced some wonderful songs during the early 70s, including "Come And Get It," "No Matter What," "Day After Day" and "Baby Blue," but suffered a tragic and short-lived existence. The Badfinger song "Without You" was covered by Harry Nilsson on his "Nilsson Schmilsson" album and hit No. 1 on the charts in 1972. The group backed ex-Beatles on tours and albums, and it performed at George Harrison's landmark benefit concert for Bangladesh in 1971. Clouds appeared on the horizon in 1974 when Molland, upset over bungled management at Warner Bros., quit the band. The deluge came soon after, when bandleader and chief songwriter Ham hanged himself in his London home in 1975, forcing the band to disband. Molland and Evans revived the band in 1978, but business problems continued, and Evans took his own life in 1983, also by hanging. Molland and Gibbins now live in the U.S. and tour periodically under the Badfinger moniker.

what to buy: *No Dice*, (Apple, 1970, prod. Geoff Emerick and Mal Evans) Badfinger's glorious second album, contains beautifully layered pop songs and established Ham as a versatile rock vocalist and imaginative songwriter. It spawned the classic hit "No Matter What" and the original version of "Without You." The band's third album, *Straight Up*, (Apple, 1971, prod. Todd Rundgren, George Harrison and Geoff Emerick) assured it a spot in pop history, with guest artists Leon Russell on piano and Harrison on slide guitar, as well as the unforgettable "Baby Blue" and "Day After Day."

what to buy next: *Come and Get It: The Best of Badfinger* (Capitol, 1995, prod. Various) is a comprehensive collection with all the big hits.

what to avoid: *Magic Christian Music* (Apple, 1970, prod. Paul McCartney) The band's debut album was a soundtrack for the Peter Sellers-Ringo Starr film "The Magic Christian." The songs aren't horrible so much as inconsistent, though it produced the group's first hit, the McCartney-penned "Come and Get It."

the rest: *The Best of Badfinger, Volume 2* (Rhino, 1989)

worth searching for: *Day After Day* (Rykodisc, 1990, prod. Mark Healey and Joey Molland) is a decent recording of a 1974 concert.

solo outings:

Joey Molland: The Pilgrim (Rykodisc, 1992)

▶▶ Teenage Fanclub, Suede, Del Amitri, Oasis

◀◀ The Beatles, Manfred Mann, Herman's Hermits

William Hanson

Badlands

Formed 1988 in Los Angeles, Calif. Disbanded 1991.

Jake E. Lee, guitars; Ray Gillen, vocals; Greg Chaisson, bass; Eric Singer, drums (1989-91); Jeff Martin, drums (1991-92)

A throwback to bombastic arena supergroups of the 70s, Badlands—along with bands such as Cinderella and Mr. Big—attempted to lead a blues-rock resurgence during the late 80s and early 90s, a movement that quickly fizzled out. Former Ozzy Osbourne guitarist Lee recruited former Black Sabbath fill-in vocalist Gillen for a rootsy, blues-based group that would contrast against the frilly pop of then-big sellers such as Whitesnake and Bon Jovi. With Singer and Chaisson, *Badlands* (Atlantic, 1989, prod. Paul O'Neill and Badlands) featured plenty of acoustic balladry and electric crotch rock that was supposedly Free-influenced but had Led Zeppelin stamped all over it. Former Racer X singer Jeff Martin replaced Singer on drums for *Voodoo Highway,* (Atlantic, 1991, prod. Jake E. Lee) which featured an unsuccessful and ill-advised cover of James Taylor's "Fire and Rain." Soon after, Badlands died a quiet death. Singer replaced the late Eric Carr in Kiss but was on the sidelines of the 1996 makeup-and-all reunion tour. Singer and Chaisson are now in smaller metal bands, while Lee is working on his own.

Todd Wicks

Joan Baez

Born Jan. 9, 1941, in Staten Island, N.Y.

Baez symbolized the 60s socially conscious folkie: warm voiced, young and relentlessly humanitarian in her political concerns. More of a voice for the downtrodden than a singular creative force, Baez has nonetheless became Earth mother to the newly crowned queens of heartfelt acoustics. Throughout her career she has been celebrated and chastised for her association with Bob Dylan, which has resulted in some of her song writing credits being questioned. If there is any punishment to be dealt, it should come from her atrocious, life-sucking rendition of The Band's "The Night They Drove Old Dixie Down." Although her recording career has been spotty of late, Baez has stayed politically active and steadfast in her humanitarian ideas—which is more than Bobby Seale can say. At last report, Baez is planning to cool the social consciousness in order to concentrate more on the music.

what to buy: *Diamonds and Rust* (A&M, 1975, prod. David Kershenbaum and Joan C. Baez) signaled Baez' commercially minded break from her traditional beginnings, and she hit the height of her powers both as a songwriter and as an interpreter of top-shelf writers such as Jackson Browne, John Prine and Dylan. *The First 10 Years* (Vanguard, 1993, prod. Various) chronicles her early Vanguard days, from her reverent traditional folk beginnings to her (then) contemporary topical material.

what to buy next: *Farewell, Angelina* (Vanguard, 1965) finds Baez branching out into contemporary folk, covering Donovan and Dylan—notably in the former's sublime title track. *Rare, Live and Classic* (Vanguard, 1993, prod. Various) provides a three-disc mix of rarities—including unreleased material with Dylan —along with her better-known work to provide a welcome addition to her canon of albums.

what to avoid: The title track of *Where Are You Now My Son* (A&M, 1973, prod. Joan Baez and Norbert Putnam) takes up half the disc, chronicling her '72 Christmas trip to Hanoi. It threatens to never end.

the rest: *Joan Baez in Concert* (Parts 1 and 2) (Vanguard, 1963) *5* (Vanguard, 1964) *Noel* (Vanguard, 1966) *Joan* (Vanguard, 1967) *Any Day Now* (Vanguard, 1968) *Baptism* (Vanguard, 1968/1995) *David's Album* (Vanguard, 1968/1995) *One Day At a Time* (Vanguard, 1970/1996) *Carry It On* (Vanguard, 1971/1996) *Hits, Greatest & Others* (Vanguard, 1973) *Best of Joan C. Baez* (A&M, 1977/1987) *Very Early Joan Baez* (Vanguard, 1983) *Recently* (Gold Castle, 1988) *The Joan Baez Country Music Album* (Vanguard, 1993) *Play Me Backwards* (Virgin, 1993) *From Every Stage* (A&M, 1993) *Ring Them Bells* (Guardian/Angel, 1995) *Greatest Hits* (A&M, 1996)

worth searching for: *Live in Europe 83: Children of the Eighties,* (Ariola, 1983) a live import recorded while she was without a major U.S. label.

Indigo Girls, Dar Williams, Mary Chapin Carpenter, Tracy Chapman

Bob Dylan, Woody Guthrie, Odetta

Allan Orski

Chris Bailey

See: The Saints

Philip Bailey

See: Earth, Wind & Fire

Bailter Space

Formed 1987 in New Zealand

John Halvorsen, guitar, bass, vocals; Alister Parker, guitar, bass, vocals; Hamish Kilgour, drums, samples (1987-89); Brent McLachlan, drums (1990-present)

Growing out of the seminal guitar-noise band the Gordons, and eventually replicating the Gordons lineup, Bailter Space has soldiered on, gradually building up an alternative following in the U.S. The Gordons did clangorous, non-chordal guitar sound-sculptures before Sonic Youth saw the inside of a studio, and the comparison is obvious. But Bailter Space is more consistently excellent and less annoyingly self-conscious, though a Bailter Space track such as *Vortura*'s "Voices" suggests the influence eventually went both ways. The music is dark and guitar-oriented, often with bass-heavy, minor-key riffs and hauntingly minimal melodies. Oblique song titles and buried vocals emphasize the tone of angst and confusion.

what to buy: *Wammo* (Matador, 1995, prod. Rod Hui, Bailter Spae) ♪♪♪♪ has the group's most radio-friendly song, "Splat," and its most abrasively forbidding, "Voltage," thus offering a good cross-section of the band's styles and virtues. *Vortura* (Matador, 1994, prod. Bailter Space and Paul Berry) ♪♪♪♪ is just as good in its subtle sonic variations.

what to buy next: *Thermos* (Flying Nun, 1990/Matador, 1991, prod. Bailter Space and Nick Roughan) ♪♪♪½ witnesses the early development of the above albums' virtues.

the rest: *Nelsh/Tanker* (Matador, 1995) ♪♪♪ *Aim* (Matador EP, 1992) ♪♪♪ *Robot World* (Matador, 1993) ♪♪♪

▶▶ Sonic Youth, Band of Susans, Come, Nirvana

◀◀ Velvet Underground, Stooges, Television

Steve Holtje

Dan Baird

See: Georgia Satellites

The Balancing Act

Formed 1984 in Los Angeles. Disbanded 1989.

Willie Aron, guitars, keyboards, percussion, vocals; Robert Blackmon, drums; Jeff Davis, guitars, vocals; Steve Wagner, bass, guitars, vocals

The Balancing Act achieved cult status during the 80s with its brainy brand of folk-pop, which boasted distinctive vocal harmonies, offbeat and often humorous lyrics, avant-garde sonic forays and eclectic instrumentation. As enjoyable as the band's original material often was, it showed even greater invention in its choice and arrangement of cover tunes. The group's debut EP was produced by once and future Plimsoul Peter Case, and they later hired Gang of Four's Andy Gill to work behind the boards on an album. While tireless touring with such acts as They Might Be Giants and 10,000 Maniacs endeared the band to underground rock fans around the country—especially on college campuses—The Balancing Act broke up before alternative music stood a chance on mainstream radio. The essential purchase is *Three Squares and a Roof/New Campfire Songs,* (I.R.S., 1988, prod. Vic Abascal and The Balancing Act/Peter Case) ♪♪♪ which pairs the first full-length album with the debut EP and is a worthy introduction to the group's not inconsiderable charms.

the rest: *Curtains* (I.R.S., 1988) ♪♪½

Simon Glickman

Marty Balin

See: Jefferson Airplane

Hank Ballard

Born Nov. 18, 1936, in Detroit, Mich.

Radio may have banned his biggest 50s hits and Chubby Checker cashed the big paycheck for "The Twist," but Ballard towered on the R&B landscape of the day. His 1954 record, "Work With Me Annie," proved too hot for the timid times, but the song inspired many sanitized rewrites and answer records. Censorship didn't slow down Ballard, who followed the record that blared out of jukeboxes across the country with "Annie Had a Baby" and the even more incendiary "Sexy Ways." While Ballard and the Midnighters served as a fixture on the R&B charts through the 50s, the group didn't hit home on the pop Top 10 until 1960 with "Finger Popping Time" and "Let's Go, Let's Go, Let's Go." Ballard joined doo-woppers the Royals in time to cut the group's first R&B chart entry, "Get It," in 1953 and set the stage for the historic recordings they made together. The group finally disbanded in '65, and Ballard went on to tour and record with James Brown before reviving the Midnighters during the 80s and recreating his classic 50s stage show. By bucking the sexual mores of the times, he may have been denied his just due on the charts, but Ballard's records serve to demonstrate an important point—rock 'n' roll never got any better than this, only different.

what to buy: *Sexy Ways: The Best Of Hank Ballard and the Midnighters* (Rhino, 1993, prod. Various) ♪♪♪♪♪ is the only Midnighters collection necessary. The 20 tracks cover all the highlights of his original King sessions.

what to buy next: An English import, *Live At the Palais,* (Charly, 1987, prod. John White) ♪♪♪½ captures Ballard's current stage show, merrily mixing his classic rhythm and blues with more contemporary soul.

the rest: *Their Greatest Jukebox Hits* (King, 1956) *Spotlight On Hank Ballard* (King, 1960) *Hank Ballard and the Midnighters* (King, 1961) *What You Get When the Gettin' Gets Good* (Charly U.K., 1986) *Singin' and Swingin' the Twist* (King, 1990) *Naked in the Rain* (After Hours, 1993) *Let 'em Roll* (Charly, 1993) *Sings 24 Hit Tunes* (King, NA) *Spotlight On* (King, NA) *And His Midnighters* (King, NA) *The One and Only* (King, NA)

worth searching for: The Midnighters' 1954 10-inch album *Their Greatest Jukebox Hits* is one of the prime collector's items of 50s R&B, invariably bringing more than $1,000 for a copy in reasonable condition.

James Brown, Swamp Dogg, John Fogerty

Gene Autry, Jimmy Rushing, Five Royales

Joel Selvin

Bananarama /Shakespear's Sister

Formed 1981 in London, England

Bananarama: Sarah Dallin, vocals; Karen Woodward, vocals; Siobhan Fahey, vocals (1981-87); Jacqui Sullivan, vocals (1988-91). Shakespear's Sister: Siobhan Fahey, vocals; Marcella Detroit (born Marcella Levy), vocals, guitar

The advent of MTV surely lent an upper hand to acts with charm and visual appeal, and the ladies of Bananarama had that in abundance. They also had songs with plenty of hooks and danceable accessibility—sweet cotton candy for the ears. Bananarama enjoyed a handful of hits before splintering, with Fahey starting the artsier Shakespear's Sister with former Bob Seger/Eric Clapton backup singer Detroit; self-conscious where Bananarama was light and airy, the duo had far less commercial action before splitting up itself.

what to buy: Bananarama's *Greatest Hits Collection* (London, 1988, prod. Various) isn't quite comprehensive, but it has the major hits and offers a painless listen.

what to buy next: Shakespear's *Hormonally Yours* (London, 1991, prod. Alan Moulder, Chris Thomas and Shakespear's Sister) features a more grown-up kind of pop that produced the polished "Stay" and "I Don't Care." *True Confessions,* (London, 1986/Razor & Tie, 1995 prod. Stock/Aitken/Waterman) Bananarama's last real success in the marketplace, contains its hit rendition of Shocking Blue's "Venus."

what to avoid: *Pop Life* (London, 1991, prod. Youth) can be very cruel indeed when you're out of fashion.

the rest: *Ultraviolet* (Curb, 1996)

worth searching for: Bananarama's U.S. debut, *Deep Sea Skiving,* (London, 1983) is really a collection of its early singles: "He Was Really Sayin' Somethin'" (with Fun Boy Three), "Shy Boy" and "Na Na Hey Hey (Kiss Him Goodbye)," all gushing group vocal confections.

solo outings:

Marcella Detroit: Jewel (London, 1994)

Go-Go's, Wilson Phillips, Milli Vanilli

Mamas and the Papas, the Chiffons, the Shangri-La's

Allan Orski

The Band

Formed 1967 in Woodstock, N.Y.

Robbie Robertson, vocals, guitar (1967-1976); Levon Helm, vocals, drums (1967-present); Rick Danko, vocals, bass, guitar (1967-present); Richard Manuel, vocals, piano (1967–1986); Garth Hudson, keyboards, saxophone (1967-present); Jim Weider, guitar (1983-present); Randy Ciarlante, vocals, percussion (1983-present); Richard Bell, vocals, piano (1986-present)

By the time they became known as simply The Band, the four cocky, young Canadians with the drummer from Arkansas had played together for almost seven years. As part of Ronnie Hawkins' back-up group and later on their own as the Hawks, they had became the baddest of the bad-ass bands that roamed the lounge-lizard circuit from Ontario and Quebec in Canada through the Rust Belt and the American South in the early sixties, garnering a well-deserved reputation as the party band.

But they worked as hard as they played, and by the time Bob Dylan tapped them as his electric backing band for a world tour in the summer of 1965, the Hawks had become a quite sophisticated quintet, with several unique secret weapons: three equally distinct lead singers, including Manuel's seductive soul pipes; Hudson's multi-instrumental mastery; Robertson's pinpoint guitar and increasingly incisive song lyrics; and the well-lubricated rhythm section of Helms and Danko.

After working with Dylan on what became known as *The Basement Tapes,* they released *Music From Big Pink* in 1967 and began a chain of distinctly American short stories told in a musical language that seemed able to bridge the growing generation gap. (Is there anybody under 50 who doesn't know what it feels like to pull into Nazareth a' feelin' about half past dead?) The Band subsequently emerged as a live unit, and the high expectations were never met again. The group toured sporadically and sputtered and coughed through a series of less and less interesting albums; the best of their later work mostly would be reworkings of its early bedrock material.

They ended it all in 1976 by throwing and filming and recording a huge farewell party dubbed "The Last Waltz" which, as it turns out, hid the serious acrimony that had developed among the members, especially between Helm and Robertson. It would be the last time the five of them would appear on stage together. Listening to any of their post-Band efforts, the sad irony is inescapable: Robertson has become a songwriter without musicians, and the others became musicians without a voice.

what to buy: Fortunately, all their music is readily available. You still can't beat *Music From Big Pink* (Capitol, 1968, prod. John Simon) and *The Band,* (Capitol, 1969, prod. Simon) two of rock's most original, imaginative, enduring and enigmatic albums and bookends for the group's short-lived collective muse. *Moondog Matinee* (Capitol, 1973, prod. The Band) is a rousing return to their roadhouse days, a set of old favorites that perfectly evokes their youthful charisma by utilizing their mature sophistication. *Rock of Ages,* (Capitol, 1972, prod. The Band) is a superb live recording filtered through Allen Toussaint's soulful horn charts.

what to buy next: *Stage Fright,* (Capitol, 1970, prod. The Band) their third album, includes several classics, including "The Shape I'm In," "W.S. Wolcott Medicine Show" and the autobiographical title track. *Across the Great Divide,* (Capitol, 1995, prod. Various) is a three-disc retrospective with more than a third devoted to rarities and early recordings.

what to avoid: *Islands,* (Capitol, 1977, prod. The Band) an uneven plate of leftovers that, as the title suggests, demonstrates the huge divisions that had isolated the group members.

the rest: *Northern Lights - Southern Cross* (Capitol, 1975) *Cahoots* (Capitol, 1971) *The Best of the Band* (Capitol, 1976) *The Last Waltz* (Capitol, 1978) *To Kingdom Come* (Capitol, 1991) *Jericho* (Pyramid/Rhino, 1993) *The Band Live at Watkins Glen* (Capitol, 1995) *High on the Hog* (Pyramid/Rhino, 1996)

worth searching for: Any of the myriad bootlegs from *The Concert at Royal Albert Hall* from the concert Dylan and the Band played in England in 1965 capture them at their most musically adventurous at a time—when hostile audiences were booing them.

solo outings:

Robbie Robertson: *Robbie Robertson,* (Geffen, 1987) *Storyville* (Geffen, 1991) *Music for The Native Americans* (Capitol, 1995)

Rick Danko: *Rick Danko* (Arista, 1977) *Rick Danko, Eric Anderson/Jonas Fjeld* (Rydodisc, 1991)

Levon Helm: *Levon Helm and the RCO All-Stars* (ABC, 1977) *American Son* (MCA, 1980) *Levon Helm* (Capitol, 1982)

▶▶ Graham Parker, the Rumour, Eric Clapton, McGuinness-Flint, Long Ryders, Uncle Tupelo, Wilco, Son Volt, subdudes

◀◀ Clarence "Frogman" Henry, Bobby "Blue" Bland, the Impressions, Chuck Berry, the Miracles, Marvin Gaye, Booker T and the MGs

Leland Rucker

Band of Susans

Formed 1986 in New York, N.Y.

Robert Poss, guitar, vocals; Susan Stenger, bass, vocals; Ron Spitzer, drums; Susan Lyall, guitar, vocals (1986-87); Susan Tallman, guitar, vocals (1986-87); Alva Rogers, vocals (1986-87); Page Hamilton, guitar, vocals (1988-89); Karen Haglof, guitar, (1988-89); Mark Lonergan, guitar, (1989-95); Anne Husic, guitar, (1989-95)

This downtown Manhattan band goes the Sonic Youth-Live Skull distortion-feedback-drone crowd one better. Not only does Band of Susans have three guitarists, but it also has monolithic songs based on intertwining or alternating riff patterns rather than standard rock song progressions. Leaders Stenger (who has an alternate career as a flutist) and Poss (who worked with Rhys Chatham) have strong backgrounds in the avant garde. Still, no BOS stuff is beyond open-minded rock listeners, though the heavy, dense sound is hardly easy listening. Poss's fascination with guitar sound produces the aural equivalent of an Ad Reinhardt painting in which different shades of black are subtly contrasted. Stenger stepped increasingly to the fore—vocally, instrumentally and compositionally—during the band's latter days, but has since moved to England. There, she and Poss have collaborated with former Wire idea-man Bruce Gilbert, among others.

what to buy: *The Powerful Veil* (Restless, 1993, prod. Robert Poss) ♪♪♪♪ has the most memorable riffs and patterns in the group's catalog, including "Mood Swing," "The Red and the Black" (*not* the Blue Oyster Cult song), the implacably spooky "Following My Heart" and the anthemic, oddly uplifting "Blind." This is the most perfect, consistent and original expression of the sound at the core of the BOS sonic juggernaut.

what to buy next: *The Word and the Flesh* (Restless, 1991, prod. Robert Poss) ♪♪♪♪ has a greater sense of space, spreading out rather than compacting the guitar assault. The minimal melodies are more memorable than before, especially on "Now Is Now." *Here Comes Success* (Restless, 1995, prod. Robert Poss) ♪♪♪ stretches out the structures, injects different rhythms—"Hell Bent's" proto-funk riff, the Bo Diddley beat of "Stone Like a Heart"—tries out a few new ideas ("Elizabeth Stride (1843-1888)," a descriptive, menacing tribute to a Jack the Ripper victim) and indulges in a short study of feedback ("As Luck Would Have It"). If it's the final BOS album, it's a worthy valedictory.

what to avoid: Poss' second solo album, *Inverse Guitar* (Trace Elements, 1988) ♪ is less grounded in rock than BOS, more for lovers of feedback, distortion and sampling.

the rest: *Love Agenda* (Blast First, 1989) ♪♪♪ *The Peel Sessions* (Strange Fruit, 1992) ♪♪♪ *Now* (Restless EP, 1992) ♪♪♪

worth searching for: All four songs on the *Blessing and Curse* EP (Trace Elements, 1987, prod. Robert Poss) ♪♪♪ are included on *Hope Against Hope,* (Blast First, 1988, prod. Robert Poss) ♪♪ offering the early manifestations of the group's dark sound (the actual B&C versions of two are here; the other two are on Love Agenda). The import compilation *Wired for Sound* (Blast First, 1995, prod. Robert Poss) ♪♪♪♪ may be the easiest way to hear material from the out-of-U.S.-print first two releases.

solo outings:

Robert Poss: Sometimes (Trace Elements, 1986) ♪♪

▶▶ aMiniature

◀◀ Rolling Stones, Wire, Rhys Chatham, Psychedelic Furs, Joy Division, Live Skull

see also: *Helmet*

Steve Holtje

Bangles

Formed in 1981 in Los Angeles, Calif.

Susanna Hoffs, guitar; Vicki Peterson, lead guitar; Debbi Peterson, drums; Michael Steele, bass (1984-88); and Annette Zilinskas, bass (1981-82)

If the Go-Go's were new-wave's giddy girl group, the Bangles were their leather-jacketed, street-smart cousins. Originally known as the Bangs, the all-female band charged onto the indie scene as a Beatlesque pop group with psychedelic overtones. Signing by Columbia Records in 1984, they added former Runaways member Steele and scored a radio hit in 1986 with "Manic Monday," written specially for them by The Artist Then Known As Prince Who Cleverly Credited Himself As Christopher. With guitarist-singer Susanna Hoffs emerging as the star in a band that shared everything from lead vocals and songwriting duties to interviews (on their first national tour as Cyndi Lauper's opening act, the group would only talk to the press if all four were present), the Bangles imploded from the internal friction and split up in 1988.

what to buy: *All Over the Place,* (Columbia, 1984, prod. David Kahne) ♪♪♪♪ their major-label debut, blends "Revolver"-era guitars with luscious Mamas & Papas harmonies on such jangly gems as "James," "Hero Takes a Fall" and a charming cover of Katrina and the Waves' "Going Down to Liverpool." Their swan song, *Everything* (Columbia, 1988, prod. Davitt Sigerson), ♪♪♪ gets dismissed as the source of their sappiest single, "Eternal Flame," but it also houses their darkest, hardest-rocking material ("Watching the Sky," "Glitter Years").

what to buy next: *Greatest Hits* (Columbia 1990, prod. Various) ♪♪♪ gathers such favorites as "If She Knew What She Wants," "In Your Room" and "Walk Like an Egyptian" and adds such non-album tracks as "Hazy Shade of Winter" (from the "Less Than Zero" soundtrack) and a lovely cover of the Grass Roots' "Where Were You When I Needed You" (the B-side of "Hero Takes a Fall").

what to avoid: *When You're a Boy* (Columbia, 1991, prod. David Kahne) **WOOF!**, Hoffs' 1991 solo album, plays to her sexpot image ("My Side of the Bed") and penchant for oddball covers

(David Bowie's "Boys Keep Swinging") but also buries her charm under glossy, keyboard-driven production. A sellout that didn't sell.

the rest: *The Bangles* (Faulty Products EP, 1983) *Different Light* (Columbia, 1986)

worth searching out: *Rainy Day* (Rough Trade, 1983, prod. Various), a compilation of psychedelic folk covers by L.A.'s "Paisley Underground" scene (including members of the Three O'Clock and Rain Parade) that features Hoffs singing a gorgeous version of Bob Dylan's "I'll Keep It With Mine."

solo outings:

Vicki Peterson (with Susan Cowsill and Peter Holsapple): *Continental Drifters* (Monkey Hill, 1994)

Debbie Peterson (with Kindred Spirit): *Kindred Spirit* (Gai Saber, 1995)

▶▶ Gin Blossoms, L7, Hole, Veruca Salt

◀◀ The Beatles, the Mamas and the Papas, Big Star, The Go-Go's

David Okamoto

Tony Banks

See: Genesis

Barefoot Servants

See: Jon Butcher Axis

Barenaked Ladies

Formed 1990 in Toronto, Ontario, Canada

Stephen Page, vocals, guitar; Ed Robertson, guitar, vocals; Jim Creeggan, bass; Tyler Stewart, drums; Andrew Creeggan, keyboards (1990–94)

Perhaps the most talented group of musicians to come out of Toronto since Rush, Barenaked Ladies (BNL for short) has, with just three albums, attracted a rabidly loyal group of fans and amassed a slew of Canadian music awards. Founding members Page and Robertson, who had grown up together in suburban Toronto, began playing together as a musical comedy duo, opening for minor acts in Toronto clubs. With the additions of the Creeggan brothers and drummer Stewart, the band began writing music that blended pop, rock, jazz, rap and just about every other musical style in various configurations. Based upon the success of their five-song independent cassette and a cover of Bruce Cockburn's "Lovers in a Dangerous Time" (featured on a tribute album), BNL won funding from Toronto radio station CFNY's "Discovery-to-Disc" program to record its debut album, *Gordon* The ensuing tour established a record for most sellouts in Canadian music history, chiefly due to the group's highly energetic and entertaining performances—typified by Page and Robertson's humorous banter and the band's penchant for launching seamlessly into a host of ad-libbed songs, as well as the audiences' habit of hurling macaroni and cheese at the stage during the song "If I Had $1,000,000," which prominently mentions Kraft Dinner mix. Unfortunately, the silliness of some of the band's first singles—"Be My Yoko Ono" and "$1,000,000"—hung it with a novelty act tag, unfair since even a casual listen to their albums reveals the group's copious, if quirky, songwriting talents. In 1994, keyboardist Andrew Creeggan left to continue his academic studies; though the band took a new keyboardist on tour, BNL has remained a foursome.

what to buy: It is best to begin at the beginning, with *Gordon* (Sire/Reprise, 1992, prod. Michael-Philip Wojewoda). Though a bit lighter in spots than its later recordings, BNL's debut captures the group's wide-ranging mix of earnest ("What a Good Boy", "Enid", "Blame It on Me"), musically-referential ("Brian Wilson", "New Kid on the Block", "Box Set") and humorous ("This Is Me in Grade 9", "King of Bedside Manner").

what to buy next: *Born on a Pirate Ship* (Sire, 1996, prod. Michael-Philip Wojewoda) is more serious than BNL's previous recordings, featuring ambitious writing, experimentation with nontraditional instruments and some of Page's most impressive singing.

the rest: *Maybe You Should Drive* (Sire, 1994) *Shoe Box* (Sire EP, 1996)

worth searching for: The soundtrack to the film "Coneheads" (Warner Bros., 1993) features the band doing a cool—and surprisingly faithful—rendition of Public Enemy's "Fight the Power."

◀◀ Beach Boys, B-52s, Bruce Cockburn, Beatles

Brandon Trenz

Barnes and Barnes

Formed 1970 in Los Angeles, Calif.

Bill Mumy and Robert Haimer

Friends since grammar school, Mumy (Will Robinson of "Lost in Space" fame) and Haimer decided to channel their shared fondness of science fiction, DC comics and warped humor into music. They took on the identities of Art and Artie Barnes, brothers from the planet Lumania. Novelty songs such as "Boogie Woogie Amputee", "Swallow My Love" and "Party in My Pants" made them a big favorite on Dr. Demento's syndicated radio show, and the video for their 1979 hit, "Fishheads" still gets play on MTV and VH1. Although Rhino has currently deleted all Barnes and Barnes titles from its catalog, a CD and video retrospective are planned for the near future.

Gary Plochinski

Barnstorm

See: Joe Walsh

The Barracudas

Formed 1979 in London, England

Jeremy Gluck, vocals; Robin Wills, guitar, vocals; David Buckley, bass, vocals (1979-82); Nicky Turner, drums, vocals (1979-82); Jim Dickson, bass, vocals (1982-84); Graeme Potter, drums (1982); Chris Wilson, guitar, vocals (1983-84); Terry Smith, drums (1983-84); Jay Posner, drums, vocals (1989-present); Steve Robinson, bass, vocals (1989-present)

The Barracudas scored exactly one British hit—the Kenny Laguna-produced "Summer Fun" in 1980—before bidding farewell to the charts and getting on with the business of being an underappreciated cult act. The group never made any impression at all in the U.S., where its debut album remains the only domestic Barracudas product available. But what a debut it was—*Drop Out with the Barracudas,* (Voxx, 1981/1984, prod. Various) was a non-stop barrage of punk-pop energy, surf 'n' sun hooks and an overriding death wish that would be frightening if it weren't so damn catchy. Those hooked by the debut can look for: *Mean Time,* (Closer, 1983, prod. Peter Gage) the French import of the group's second album; *Endeavour to Persevere,* (Closer, 1984, prod. John David) another French import, or the British title *Wait for Everything,* (Shake, 1991, prod. not listed) which, while not in *Drop Out's* league, marks a welcome return.

see also: *Flamin' Groovies, Lords of the New Church*

Carl Cafarelli

Paul Barrere

See: Little Feat

Syd Barrett

Born Jan. 6, 1946 in Cambridge, England

Listening to Barrett is like watching a condemned house fall to pieces. His flaming disintegration led to the former Pink Floyd leader's dismissal after the group's first album. Propped up by his bandmates, he managed two fleeting albums before completely submerging into the LSD netherworld. The first, *The Madcap Laughs* (Harvest, 1970, prod. David Gilmour and Roger Waters) is a harrowing set of rough sonic quality, full of false starts and half-finished compositions that harshly illuminate the demise of a bright talent. *Barrett* (Harvest, 1970, prod. David Gilmour and Richard Wright) is a deceptively more cohesive effort, displaying the psychedelic musings that ear marked Floyd's debut. The fuller sound is credited to the producers, who sweetened it after Barrett recorded his parts. *Crazy Diamond—The Complete Syd Barrett* (Capitol, 1994, prod. Various) collects practically every snippet Barrett recorded onto three CDs, mostly in the form of alternate takes, along with a detailed booklet.

the rest: *Opel* (Capitol, 1988) *Octopus: The Best of Syd Barrett* (Cleopatra, 1992)

see also: *Pink Floyd*

Allan Orski

Dave Bartholomew

Born Dec 24, 1940, in Edgard, La.

One of the true unsung heroes of rock 'n' roll, bandleader Bartholomew laid one of the music's cornerstones with the records he made with Fats Domino starting in 1949. But as the New Orleans-based artist and repertoire director for Imperial Records, the trumpeter and songwriter conducted a series of rich, vibrant recordings with dozens of lesser known artists throughout the 50s that never traveled far beyond jukeboxes in the deep South. While the Domino million-sellers were Bartholomew's only taste of nationwide success as a producer, he made equally satisfying records, steeped in the traditional sounds of New Orleans, with the same studio musicians backing himself, Smiley Lewis, Tommy Ridgely, The Spiders and Earl King, as well as visiting R&B dignitaries such as Big Joe Turner, Roy Brown, T-Bone Walker and Charles Brown. His solo records have been covered by a scattered but select few such as the Fabulous Thunderbirds—who did a marvelous job with "The Monkey"—Elvis Costello and Buster Poindexter. He went into semi-retirement during the early 60s, though he continued to play music around New Orleans and occasionally joined Fats Domino's band on tour. But his work as one of the prime designers of the New Orleans rhythm and blues sound echoes throughout the rock world to this day.

what to buy: A double-disc set, *The Spirit Of New Orleans: The Genius of Dave Bartholomew,* (EMI, 1992, prod. Dave Bartholomew) ♪♪♪♪♪ blends his solo recordings with his productions of other artists, a detailed panoramic look at his landmark work.

what to buy next: Bartholomew's work hovers over the four-disc boxed set, *Crescent City Soul: The Sound Of New Orleans 1947-1974,* (EMI, 1996, prod. Various) ♪♪♪½ like one of those floats on Macy's Thanksgiving Day parade. The set samples not only his work with artists such as Fats Domino, Smiley Lewis and many lesser-knowns, but key Bartholomew productions such as "Lawdy Miss Clawdy" by Lloyd Price. Unfortunately, the set duplicates many of the selections from *The Spirit Of New Orleans* and ranges far beyond only Bartholomew's work.

worth searching for: His early solo recordings for the DeLuxe and King labels were collected on a British CD, *In the Alley.* (Charly, 1991, prod. Various) ♪♪♪

▶▶ Allen Toussaint, Paul McCartney, Dirty Dozen Brass Band

◀◀ Louis Armstrong, Fats Pinchon, Louis Jordan

Joel Selvin

Basehead

Formed 1990 in Washington, D.C.

Michael Ivey, vocals, guitar, bass, keyboards, drum programs; Brian Hendrix, drums; Paul "DJ Unique" Howard, turntables (1990-92); Bill Conway, bass (1992-present); Marco Delmar, guitar (1990-93); Bob DeWald, bass (1990-93); Bruce "Cool Aid" Gardner, drums (1990-93); Clarence "Citizen Cope" Greenwood, turntables (1992-present); Keith Lofton, guitar, 1992-present

Basehead, the brainchild of the multi-talented Ivey, impressed critics and a small cult of fans during the early 1990s with its moody, psychedelic blend of hip-hop and rock. Ivey's cynical and self-deprecating manner and somnambulistic vocals worked in striking contrast to his frequently trenchant lyrics, and Basehead's sleepy grooves, redolent of pot smoke and dorm-room angst, have an insinuating power. Basehead's debut, *Play With Toys,* (Imago, 1992, prod. Michael Ivey) ♪♪♪ is a compelling mix of phat grooves, lean Hendrix and Zep-inspired guitar lines, edgy sarcasm and hilarious sketches.

the rest: *Not in Kansas Anymore* (Imago, 1993) ♪♪½ *Faith* (Imago, 1996) ♪♪♪ Ivey solo—*B.Y.O.B.* (13/Rykodisc, 1994) ♪♪½

Simon Glickman

A Dozen Great Girl Group Albums

Growin' Up Too Fast: The Girl Group Anthology
Various Artists (Mercury/Chronicles)

The Best of the Girl Groups, Vol. 1 and 2
Various Aritsts (Rhino)

Atlantic Sisters of Soul
Various Artists (Rhino/Atlantic & Atco Remasters)

Anthology
The Supremes (Motown)

Best of the Ronettes
(Abcko)

Best of the Crystals
(Abcko)

Anthology (1959-1967)
The Shirelles (Rhino)

Milestones
Martha & the Vandellas (Motown)

Deliver: The Singles (1961-1971)
The Marvelettes (Motown)

Greatest Hits Collection
Bananarama (London)

Very Necessary
Salt-N-Pepa (London)

CrazySexyCool
TLC (LaFace)

Bash and Pop

See: The Replacements

Basia

Born Basia Trzetrzelewska, Sept. 30, 1956 in Jaworzno, Poland

If there is such a thing as a truly international sound, it should be found somewhere in the music of Basia. Born in Poland, where she performed with the female trio Alibabki, Basia toured the Soviet Union and later lived in Chicago, where she soaked up American R&B and blues, and in London, where she joined the band Matt Bianco, whose album *Whose Side Are You On?* (now out of print) was a hit in England and Europe. She went solo in 1985, continuing to collaborate with Matt Bianco keyboardist Danny White. On her own albums, Basia surveys an intriguing mix of pop-jazz and especially Latin styles such as samba, and bossa nova.

what to buy: Recorded during a 1994 stint at New York City's Neil Simon Theater, *Basia on Broadway* (Epic, 1995, prod. Danny White and Basia) 𝄢𝄢𝄢𝄢 is a de facto greatest hits package, featuring Basia's best-known numbers ("Copernicus," "Cruising for Bruising," "Baby You're Mine," "New Day for You," "Time and Tide") and several new songs. In concert, Basia's classy sound comes through loud and clear. Spyro Gyra saxophonist Jay Beckenstein sits in on "Yearning."

what to buy next: *London Warsaw New York* (Epic, 1989, prod. Basia and Danny White) 𝄢𝄢𝄢𝄢 is the album on which Basia's sound truly came of age, kicking off with the slick pop-jazz of "Cruising for Bruising," a bittersweet lover's kiss-off. "Best Friends" apes ebullient Gloria Estefan-style pop, but the soaring self-actualization "Brave New Hope," the Aretha Franklin cover "Until You Come Back to Me" and the rhythmic hands-across-the-water "Copernicus" make this a fine effort. *The Sweetest Illusion* (Epic, 1994, prod. Danny White and Basia) 𝄢𝄢𝄢½ is nearly that album's equal, thanks to the optimistic "Third Time Lucky," the grooving "Drunk on Love" and the elegant "Yearning."

the rest: *Time and Tide* (Epic, 1987, prod. Basia and Danny White) 𝄢𝄢𝄢 *Brave New Hope* (Epic EP, 1991, prod. Basia and Danny White) 𝄢𝄢𝄢

worth searching for: The great, lost Matt Bianco album *Whose Side Are You On?* (Atlantic, 1984, prod.Mark Reilly)

▶▶ Swing Out Sister, Lisa Stansfield

◀◀ Astrud Gilberto, Gloria Estefan, Sade

Daniel Durchholz

Fontella Bass

Born July 3, 1949 in St. Louis, Mo.

Born into a gospel singing family, Bass turned her back on that music to play piano in a series of blues bands during the early 60s. She stumbled into singing after filling in one night for a drunk Little Milton and later became a featured vocalist in the Oliver Sain Revue. Bass brought a brassy gospel voice to her blues and R&B singing; her biggest hit came in 1965, when "Rescue Me" hit the top of the R&B charts and garnered a Grammy nomination. Her marriage to avant garde trumpeter Lester Bowie led to life in Paris from 1968-71 and a largely unrecognized body of jazz work—although the powerful "Theme De Yoyo" on the Art Ensemble of Chicago's *Les Stances A Sophie* album shows her in top form. After divorcing Bowie, Bass was off the scene during most of the 70s and 80s raising her family, and when she returned, she slipped back into gospel. Her 60s work is compiled on *Rescued - The Best of Fontella Bass,* (MCA, 1992, prod. Various) 𝄢𝄢𝄢𝄢½ a good accounting of gospel-influenced 60s soul with "Don't Mess With a Good Thing" and "Joy of Love." Her recent gospel work still touches the jazz world. *No Ways Tired* (Nonesuch, 1995, prod. Wayne Horvitz) 𝄢𝄢𝄢𝄢 features jazzmen Bowie, David Sanborn and Hamiett Blueitt. She also injects some soul into a couple of songs on the World Saxophone Quartet's 1994 release *Breath of Life. Everlasting Arms* (Silver Spring, 1991, prod. Fontella Bass and Leroy Jodie Pierson) 𝄢𝄢𝄢𝄢 is an unusually naked performance of Bass singing traditional gospel songs accompanied only by herself on piano.

Lawrence Gabriel

Stiv Bators

See: Dead Boys

Bauhaus

Formed 1979 in Northampton, England. Disbanded 1983.

Peter Murphy, vocals; Daniel Ash, guitar and vocals; David J(ay) (born David Haskins), bass; Kevin Haskins, drums

Bauhaus led and begat what would come to be called gothic rock, a genre that's been slammed as gloom or death rock but actually has intellect, theatrics and an ethereal, brooding emotion. Bauhaus was not without a sense of humor; when detractors accused it being too Bowie-esque, it responded by covering T-Rex's "Telegram Sam." Due to Murphy's bout with pneumonia during the recording of the final album, *Burning From the Inside,* J and Ash took over vocal responsibilities, which stoked Ash's desire for creative control, which prompted the break-up of the band and the pursuit of new careers by all parties.

what to buy: *Mask* (Beggars Banquet, 1981/1995, prod. Bauhaus) is Bauhaus' finest, showing a variety of styles and extremes in both musicianship and verse. *In The Flat Field* (4AD, 1980, prod. Bauhaus) burrowed into the human mind to uncover the density and raw force that was to become a signature of Bauhaus.

what to buy next: *Burning From The Inside* (Beggars Banquet/A&M, 1983/1989, prod. Bauhaus) is more the work of a collective than a band, with Ash and J singing on various tracks and a new, acoustic bent to some of the material. A definite stepping stone towards Love and Rockets.

what to avoid: *The Sky's Gone Out* (Beggars Banquet/A&M, 1982, prod. Bauhaus) lacks the pensive and tongue-in-cheek lyrics that define so much of Bauhaus' best work.

the rest: *Press The Eject and Give Me The Tape* (Beggars Banquet, 1982) *Kick in the Eye (Searching for Satori)* (Beggars Banquet 1982) *Ziggy Stardust* (Beggars Banquet EP, 1982) *Lagartija Nick* (Beggars Banquet EP, 1982) *4AD* (4AD EP, 1983) *The Singles 1981-1983* (Beggars Banquet, 1983) *1979-1983* (Beggars Banquet, 1985) *1979-1983, Vol. 1 and Vol. 2* (Beggars Banquet, 1986) *Swing the Heartache: The BBC Sessions* (BBC/Beggars Banquet, 1989) *Rest in Peace: The Final Concert* (Nemo/Beggars Banquet, 1992)

worth searching for: *Bela Lugosi's Dead,* (Small Wonder, 1979) a 12" single that also includes "Boys" and "Dark Entries." It was produced on six colors of vinyl - black, clear, red, green, blue and glow-in-the-dark (our favorite).

Christian Death, Alien Sex Fiend, Sisters of Mercy

David Bowie, Pere Ubu, John Cale

see also: *Love and Rockets, Peter Murphy, Dali's Car*

JD Cantarella

Bay City Rollers

Formed 1970 in Edinburgh, Scotland. Disbanded 1982. Reformed 1993.

Leslie McKeown, vocals (1970-78); Stuart Wood, guitar; Ian Mitchell, bass (1976-78); Eric Faulkner, guitar; Derek Longmuir, drums (1970-78); Alan Longmuir, bass (1970-76, 1993-present); Nobby Clarke, vocals (1971-73); John Devine (1971-73); Pat McGlynn, bass (1977-78); Duncan Faure, vocals (1978); Kass, drums, vocals (1993-present)

From the Longmuir Brothers to Saxon, the name Bay City Rollers was chosen by pointing at random to a spot in Michigan on the map of the United States. Aimed at Britain's massive teenybopper market and surrounded by hype, the Bay City Rollers had some success in the U.K. market. The band's first U.S. hit, "Saturday Night," was pure bubblegum. *Greatest Hits* (Arista, 1977, prod. Various) should suffice for the curious.

the rest: *Bay City Rollers* (Arista, 1974) *Rock N' Roll Love Letter* (Arista, 1975) *Dedication* (Arista, 1976) *It's A Game* (Arista, 1977) *Strangers In The Wind* (Arista, 1978) *Elevator* (Arista, 1979) *Ricochet* (Epic, 1981)

Anna Glen

Be Bop Deluxe

Formed 1972 in Wakefield, England. Disbanded 1979.

Bill Nelson, guitar, vocals, keyboards; Ian Parkin, guitar (1972-74); Rob Bryan, bass (1972-74); Nicholas Catterton-Drew, drums (1972-74); Richard Brown, keyboards (1972-74); Milton Reame-James, keyboards (1974); Paul Jeffreys, bass (1974); Simon Fox, drums (1974-79); Andrew Clark, keyboards (1975-79); Charles Tumahai, bass, vocals (1974-79)

When he chose to play it, Be Bop Deluxe founder Nelson produced some stunning music with an electric guitar. Unfortunately, Nelson's tendency toward overwrought production, quirky arrangements and lyrical visions of the future obscured some of the fiercest guitar licks in mid-70s rock. After releasing *Axe Victim* (1974) and *Futurama* (1975) in the members' native England, Be Bop Deluxe issued its first U.S. release, *Sunburst Finish* (1976), which produced a minor hit with "Ships in the Night." But the band never quite connected with the average suburban Jimmy Page fan, even though Be Bop Deluxe toured the United States widely during 1976, opening for bands as diverse as Patti Smith, Golden Earring and Electric Light Orchestra. *Modern Music* was released that same year and stands as the band's best effort and one of the lost treasures of mid-70s rock. The final studio album, *Drastic Plastic,* was released in 1978. Nelson has produced and recorded prolifically over the years and while many of his albums are now keyboard based, you can sometimes hear a glimpse of his guitar mastery.

what to buy: With the vast majority of the Be Bop Deluxe catalog tragically out of print, fans have to be content with some concert recordings. *Be Bop Deluxe Radioland - BBC Radio One Live in Concert* (Griffin, 1995) comes from excellent shows recorded during 1976 and 1978, featuring a generous sampling of songs from the seminal *Modern Music* album.

what to buy next: *Live! in the Air Age* (Harvest/One Way, 1977) is another fine live concert performance, though at this point we're really crying for some of the studio material to be made available.

what to avoid: *Axe Victim* (Harvest, 1974) is available via import CD. Save your money.

worth searching for: Too much, unfortunately. But *Sunburst Finish* (Harvest, 1976) is available on an import and essential for fans of melodic guitar rock, though the even better *Modern Music* (Harvest, 1976) remains inexplicably in the vaults. *Raiding the Divine Archive: The Best of Be Bop Deluxe* (Harvest/Capitol, 1990) isn't preferable, but it was out on CD once and may show up in used bins. There's also a good Nelson solo album, *On a Blue Wing,* (Portrait, 1986) that has yet to be issued on CD.

solo outings:

Bill Nelson: Red Noise (Cocteau, 1979) *Vistamix* (Epic, 1982) *The Love that Whirls (Diary of a Thinking Heart)* (Cocteau, 1989) *Blue Moons & Laughing Guitars* (Virgin, 1992) *Practically Wired* (All Saints, 1995) *After the Satellite Sings* (Caroline, 1996)

▶▶ A Flock of Seagulls, the Fixx, Joe Satriani

◀◀ Jimi Hendrix, Jeff Beck, David Bowie, Roxy Music

Michael Isabella

The Beach Boys

Formed 1961 in Hawthorne, Calif.

Brian Wilson, piano, guitar, bass, vocals; Carl Wilson, guitar, vocals; Dennis Wilson, drums, vocals (died December 28, 1983); Mike Love, vocals; Alan Jardine, guitar, vocals (1961-62, 1963-present); David Marks, guitar (1962-63); Bruce Johnston (1965-72, 1978-present), keyboards, vocals; Blondie Chaplin, guitar, vocals (1971-74); Ricky Fataar, drums, vocals (1972-74)

The Beach Boys were America's first major and longest-running 'n' roll band/soap opera. Led by reclusive, unstable prodigy Brian Wilson, group peaked early and has sustained a substantial career that, at least as a live act, continues long after its members became Beach Men. Rising from the sun-and-cars culture of post-war Southern California and careening off Chuck Berry's small-combo rock 'n' roll, pristine Four Freshman harmonies and the surf craze of the early 60s, the Beach Boys' early hits—"Surfin' U.S.A.," "Be True to Your School," "Fun, Fun, Fun," "Help Me, Rhonda," "I Get Around," "California Girls"—remain colorful aural descriptions of teen-age life circa 1962-63, before the J.F.K. assassination and Vietnam. Brian Wilson was an auteur, a sensitive, intelligent kid whose fun-and-sun themes were a kind of smokescreen for a darker side (in the person of Murry Wilson, a violent, abusive musician wannabe who was particularly jealous of his oldest son's gifts), exposed in prescient songs like "In My Room." Though deaf in one ear, Wilson's writing, arranging and production skills grew with each album and hit single. Inspired by the equally groundbreaking work of the Beatles and Phil Spector, Wilson found himself locked in musical competition with them. He responded with "The Beach Boys Today" and "Summer Days and Summer Nights" in 1965 and "Pet Sounds," the group's masterpiece which, in 1966, also became its first commercial failure. The pressures of producing a sequel, the never-officially-released "Smile," left Wilson in a state of severe emotional duress (accentuated by drug use) from which he seems still to be recuperating. With Brian in well-publicized seclusion—he's only been an occasional member since 1966—the group tried to carry on as a recording unit while waiting for Brian to return, with less than convincing results, increasing friction among the members and distressingly fallow albums. They haven't had a hit in years, but Brian Wilson's best recordings with the Beach Boys rank among the 60s finest music.

what to buy: *Pet Sounds,* (Capitol, 1966, prod. Brian Wilson) recorded in monaural, still sounds fresh and young and irresistibly romantic. (It's slated to be the subject of an expansive boxed set, *The Pet Sounds Sessions,* (Capitol, 1996, prod. Brian Wilson) with outtakes, noodling, studio chatter and even a stereo version of the album for comparison, although it's still better in mono.) Capitol has released all the original albums as two-fer bargains, and most of them really are, especially *Smiley Smile/Wild Honey* (Capitol, 1967, prod. Brian Wilson) which includes the scrambled remnants of *Smile* and the ragged soul of *Wild Honey*, considered by many fans to be the band's best recorded moments. *Surf's Up* (Caribou/Epic, 1971, prod. the Beach Boys) is the group's most interesting album and a fascinating puzzle, with contributions from all the Beach Boys as well as two of Brian's all-time best tunes,

"Until I Die" and "Surf's Up," written with Van Dyke Parks and originally slated for *Smile*.

what to buy next: *Good Vibrations*, (Capitol, 1993, prod. Brian Wilson) a cluttered, eccentric boxed set that's a blast, with a fascinating collage of hits, remixes, studio talk, interviews and other arcane material, beginning with a young Brian pounding out "Surfin' U.S.A." and including a "version" of *Smile* that offers a taste of that great lost album. Some aficionados prefer *The Beach Boys Today/Summer Days and Summer Nights*, (Capitol, 1965, prod. Brian Wilson) the two albums leading up to *Pet Sounds*, to their more-hyped successor; either way, don't pass up "I'm Bugged at My Old Man." *Beach Boys Love You* (Caribou/Epic, 1977, prod. Brian Wilson) is a low-key, congenial partial return-to-earth from Brian isolated in the general dreck of the other albums that surround it.

what to avoid: Take your pick of those surroundings: the woefully mistitled *15 Big Ones* (Caribou/Epic, 1976, prod. Beach Boys) *M.I.U.* (Caribou/Epic, 1978, prod. Beach Boys) or *L.A. (Light Album)*, (Caribou/Epic, 1979, prod. Beach Boys) which finds the group hard in the grip of Love's meditation obsession.

the rest: *Surfin' Safari/Surfin' U.S.A.* (Capitol, 1962/1963) *Surfer Girl/Shut Down Vol. 2* (Capitol, 1963) *Little Deuce Coupe/All Summer Long* (Capitol, 1963/1964) *Beach Boys Concert/Beach Boys '69—Live in London* (Capitol, 1964/1969) *Party/Stack-O-Tracks* (Capitol, 1965/1968) *Friends/ 20/20* (Capitol, 1968/1969, 1990) *Sunflower* (Caribou/Epic, 1970) *Holland* (Caribou/Epic, 1973) *Carl and the Passions—So Tough* (Caribou/Epic, 1972) *Beach Boys in Concert* (Caribou/Epic, 1973) *Endless Summer* (Capitol, 1974) *Spirit of America* (Capitol, 1975) *Ten Years of Harmony* (Caribou/Epic, 1979) *Keepin' the Summer Alive* (Caribou/Epic, 1980) *Sunshine Dream* (Capitol, 1982) *Rarities* (Capitol, 1983) *Made in the U.S.A.* (Capitol, 1986) *Still Cruisin'* (Capitol, 1989) *20 Good Vibrations* (Capitol, 1995)

worth searching for: *The Best of the Beach Boys*, (Capitol, 1995, prod. Various) a two-disc British compilation that's better than the myriad too-skimpy hits collections and offers plenty for someone who doesn't want to for out for the *Good Vibrations* box.

solo outings:

Dennis Wilson: *Pacific Ocean Blue* (Caribou, 1977)

Mike Love: *Looking Back With Love* (Boardwalk, 1981)

The Beatles, the Byrds, Jan and Dean, the Eagles, Porno For Pyros

Four Freshmen, Chuck Berry, the Lettermen, the Everly Brothers, Phil Spector

see also: *Brian Wilson*

Leland Rucker

Beastie Boys

Formed 1981 in New York, N.Y.

Adam Yauch, a.k.a. MCA, vocals, bass; Michael Diamond, a.k.a. Mike D., vocals, drums; Adam Horovitz, a.k.a. King Ad-Rock, vocals, guitar (1982-present); John Berry, guitar (1981-82); Kate Schellenbach, drums (1981-82)

Formed as a punk outfit, the Beasties turned to rap after meeting Def Jam Records co-owner Rick Rubin during the mid-80s. All sons of affluent New Yorkers, the core trio developed a uniquely in-your-face style that mixed suburban references such as Led Zeppelin and Budweiser with hip-hop vernacular and attitude. Accordingly, the group's first album drew a sharp line between hip-hop fans attracted by the trio's outlaw style and outspoken critics who felt these three white guys' exaggerated style was an insult to the rap genre. Thanks to a couple of MTV-fed hits, the Beasties' debut became one of the best-selling rap albums, but the Beasties proved with their next record—an in-depth exploration of 70s influences—that they weren't just dilettantes, weaving their obnoxious image into a funky sound pastiche. By the third record, the band had picked up its instruments again, adding punk sounds and trippy instrumentals into their arsenal and showing that, despite attempts to write them off as an untalented publicity stunt, the Beastie Boys were a group deserving of serious props.

what to buy: *Licensed to Ill* (Def Jam, 1986, prod. Rick Rubin) caught pop audiences flatfooted with the Beastie's baldfaced rhymes about drugs, drinking and crimes, along with dope beats and an engaging lyrical style. Forget about the frat rock anthem "(You Gotta) Fight For Your Right (to Party)"; instead, check out high-octane jams such as "She's Crafty" (fueled by a spot-on Led Zeppelin sample) and the hip-hop outlaw tale "Paul Revere" (backward drum machine parts make the groove here). The inspired followup, *Paul's Boutique*, (Capitol, 1989, prod. the Beastie Boys and the Dust Brothers) is even better, mixing a 70s vibe with a flood of pop culture references and a psychedelic-style wash of sonics. DJs and rappers of today are still trying to catch up with the densely layered beats and broad stylistic sweep captured on this record.

what to buy next: With instruments in hand, the Beasties hopscotch from raps to 70s jazz/soul shadings to full-out punk abandon on *Ill Communication,* (Grand Royal/Capitol, 1994, prod. the Beastie Boys and Mario Caldato Jr.) cranking out groundbreaking jams such as the rocked-out "Sabotage" and the funkified "Root Down."

what to avoid: The EP featuring the early hardcore punk singles, *Some Old Bullshit,* (Capitol, 1994, prod. The Beastie Boys, Scott Jarvis and Dug Pomeroy) WOOF! is aptly named, with tunes that barely hint at the ambitions that lay ahead.

the rest: *Check Your Head* (Capitol, 1992) *Root Down* (Grand Royal/Capitol EP, 1995)

worth searching for: For some perspective on how different the Beasties' sound was for fans of mid-80s rap, the three-CD collection *Def Jam Music Group: 10th Year Anniversary* (Def Jam, 1995, prod. Various) spreads the most interesting tracks from *Licensed To Ill* over a volume that includes cuts from the company's decade-long history and performers such as LL Cool J, Slick Rick, Onyx and Montell Jordan.

⏩ G. Love and Special Sauce, Disposable Heroes of Hiphoprisy, Consolidated

⏪ Led Zeppelin, Run-D.M.C., Public Enemy

Eric Deggans

The Beat Farmers

Formed 1983 in San Diego, Calif.

Jerry Raney, vocals, guitar; Rolle Dexter, bass; Country Dick Montana (born Dan McClain), drums, vocals (died Nov. 8, 1995); Buddy Blue, guitar, vocals (1983-86); Joey Harris, vocals, guitar (1986-95)

The mid-80s were an optimistic period in underground American music, a time when it was possible to stay blissfully ignorant of the mainstream and find comforting sustenance from such bands as X or the Long Ryders. The Beat Farmers, a crack country-rock crew from the West Coast, were as good as any of them—the last word in beer-soaked good times. Unfortunately, its live appeal never came through as well on records. And as time wore on, their onstage alcoholic excesses (which could make even the Replacements look sober in comparison) ceased being funny and took on an aura of human sacrifice. Years of self-abuse finally caught up with drummer/ringleader Country Dick Montana in 1995, when he died onstage in Canada of heart failure at age 40, leaving behind a partially finished solo album that his bandmates and friends helped complete for posthumous release.

what to buy: For pure unpretentious charm, it's tough to top the Beat Farmers' debut, *Tales of the New West.* (Rhino, 1985, prod. Steve Berlin and Mark Linett) Along with ace originals, the album includes covers of everybody from the Velvet Underground to John Stewart. Every note rings perfectly true—even Montana's goofy frog-voiced star turns on "California Kid" and "Happy Boy."

what to buy next: Although one hesitates to encourage the Beat Farmers' boozy mythology, *Loud and Plowed and . . . LIVE!!* (Curb, 1990, prod. Denny Bruce) does make for a representative sampler. Recorded before a well-oiled New Year's Eve home town crowd, it captures the band in prime form on a career-spanning selection of material.

what to avoid: By any standard, *Best of the Beat Farmers* (Curb, 1995, prod. Various) is appallingly shoddy—10 tracks, none from their best album, and just 35 minutes long. Awful. If you want a compilation, stick with the live album.

the rest: *Glad 'n' Greasy* (Demon EP, 1986/Rhino, 1991) *Van Go* (Curb/MCA, 1986) *The Pursuit of Happiness* (Curb/MCA, 1987) *Poor & Famous* (Curb/MCA, 1989)

solo outings:

Joey Harris: *Joey Harris and the Speedsters* (MCA, 1983)

The Jacks (Buddy Blue): *Jacks Are Wild* (Rounder, 1988) *Guttersnipes 'n' Zealots* (Rhino, 1991)

Country Dick Montana: *The Devil Lied to Me* (Bar None, 1996)

worth searching for: *Live in Las Vegas,* (Hightone, 1993, prod. Mark Linett and Country Dick Montana) a relaxed and friendly outing by the Pleasure Barons, an ad hoc outfit that features Montana and Harris with Mojo Nixon, Dave Alvin, John Doe and others.

⏩ Go to Blazes, Old 97s, Backsliders, Uncle Tupelo

⏪ Flying Burrito Brothers, Neil Young, Rolling Stones

David Menconi

Beat Happening

Formed 1984 in Olympia, Wash.

Calvin Johnson, vocals, guitar, drums; Heather Lewis, vocals, guitar, drums; Bret Lunsford, vocals, guitar, drums

Besides heavily influencing Nirvana and spawning the independent K Records label, Beat Happening is most notable for being perhaps the only band whose members regularly swap all vocal and instrumental duties. Deep-voiced Johnson (kind of a modern rock Barry White) used to walk around Olympia in "Hello Kitty" accessories and was the de facto leader of the Calvinists, a mini-movement of adults who aspired to be childlike. He took the same approach with Beat Happening's music: using simple tom-tom drumbeats and rudimentary guitar, all very low-fi, with the musicians droning or awkwardly croon over the music. The results range from hypnotic to simply boring. Johnson's K Records was also a groundbreaking label, pre-dating the more celebrated Sub Pop and releasing early music by Nirvana, Screaming Trees and Beck. Beat Happening was last heard from (on record) in 1992, but the group has not formally disbanded.

what to buy: *Dreamy* (K/Sub Pop, 1991, prod. Steve Fisk) ♪♪♪ is a short and sweet example of the band's whimsical charm. Songs such as "Hot Chocolate Boy" and "Redhead Walking" could be radio hits in an alternate—not just alternative—universe.

what to buy next: The anthology *1983-85* (K, 1990, prod. Various) ♪♪♪ collects the best of the rest, the sound of the beginning of grunge.

what to avoid: *You Turn Me On* (K/Sub Pop, 1992) ♪♪ comes off like an old joke repeated once too often.

the rest: *Beat Happening* (K, 1985) ♪♪ *Jamboree* (K/Rough Trade, 1988) ♪♪ *Black Candy* (K, 1989) ♪♪♪

worth searching for: *Beat Happening/Screaming Trees*, (K-Homestead EP, 1988) ♪♪♪ a lumbering but fun four-song joint project by two of Olympia's chief exports.

▶▶ Beck, Nirvana, the Spinanes

◀◀ The Doors, the Stooges

Todd Wicks

The Beat /Paul Collins

Formed 1979 in Los Angeles, Calif.

Paul Collins, lead vocals, guitar; Steven Huff, bass, vocals; Larry Whitman, guitar, vocals, (1979-82); Jimmy Ripp, guitar (1983); Michael Ruiz, drums (1979-82); Jay Dee Daugherty, drums (1983)

Power popster Collins formed the Beat after the Nerves, for whom he drummed, broke up in 1978. Collins' new group struck it big in San Francisco, with Bill Graham agreeing to manage the band after it opened for Eddie Money at Graham's Kabuki Theater. Collins and Money co-wrote "Let Me Into Your Life," which made it onto the debut album, as did "Rock 'n' Roll Girl," which has since been covered by the Muffs. The second album was credited to Paul Collins' Beat to differentiate it from the group known on this side of the Atlantic as the English Beat. Columbia dropped the group soon after issuing its sophomore effort. After personnel changes, the group's final U.S. release came out, but no offers were forthcoming. A number of Collins' solo albums released in Europe may eventually be released in the the United States by Wagon Wheel.

what to buy: *The Beat* (Columbia, 1979/Wagon Wheel, 1994, prod. Bruce Botnick) ♪♪♪♪ sounds a bit thin but has plenty of energy. The reissue adds "There She Goes" from the "Caddyshack" soundtrack.

what to buy next: *The Kids Are the Same* (Columbia, 1982, prod. Bruce Botnick) ♪♪♪ improves on the sound, but slips a bit in the songwriting.

the rest: *To Beat or Not to Beat* (Passport EP, 1983) ♪♪♪

solo outings:

Paul Collins Band: From Town to Town (Wagon Wheel, 1993) ♪♪♪♪

▶▶ The Rubinoos, the Romantics, the Plimsouls, Material Issue

◀◀ The Beatles, the Hollie, the Byrds, the Shoes, Dwight Twilley

Steve Holtje

The Beatles

Formed 1960 in Liverpool, England. Disbanded 1970.

John Lennon, guitar, vocals (1960-70); Stuart Sutcliffe, bass (1960-61); Paul McCartney (b. James Paul McCartney), bass, guitar, keyboards, vocals (1960-70); George Harrison, guitar, vocals (1960-70); Pete Best, drums (1960-62); Ringo Starr (b. Richard Starkey), drums, vocals (1962-1970)

At a time when rock music and its creators could be described as one-dimensional, the Beatles were intelligent, innovative, and perceptive interpreters of their generation. In the 40-year history of rock, no one has matched the group's far-reaching impact and enduring influence. From infectious three-minute pop songs to sophisticated studio production and trend-setting fashions and album art, the Beatles revolutionized popular music by forever liberating rock and roll from its once-narrow definitions.

Lennon met fellow Liverpool teens McCartney and Harrison in 1957 while seeking members for his skiffle group, the Quarrymen. Sharing a fondness for black R&B, the trio weathered personnel changes and initially lackluster critical response to forge a uniquely aggressive sound based on driving guitars, a solid backbeat, and high vocal harmonies. With Starr on drums, the newly dubbed "Fab Four" took Britain by storm with its debut LP and soon after became the first rock group to gain international fame as Beatlemania swept Europe, Asia, and America.

As composers, Lennon and McCartney blew away rock's artless image, giving the genre credibility with sophisticated chord structures, innovative lyrics, and intricate three-part harmonies. By 1966, fed up with the pressures of touring, the Beatles committed to studio work, ushering in a revolutionary era in audio recording. With producer George Martin, the group advanced the concept of "recording studio as laboratory," furthering the art of audio production with multitrack recording and tape-loop effects. As founders of Apple Records in 1968, the Beatles were the first group to create their own label, with acts that included Liverpool's Badfinger and U.S. folk singer James Taylor.

Solo projects, clashing egos, and family life began dividing the group in 1968, and by early 1970 the end was official. Solo careers followed, Lennon's and McCartney's being the most consistently noteworthy. All hopes of a Beatles reunion ended with Lennon's 1980 assassination in NYC, although a "reunion" was effected via the studio when the three remaining members added their voices instruments to two Lennon demos to create new songs for *The Beatles Anthology* documentary.

what to buy: As milestones go, there is little to compare with *Sgt. Peppers Lonely Hearts Club Band* (Parlophone, 1967, prod. George Martin). Rock and roll's first concept album, *Sgt. Pepper* simmers with confidently adventurous songwriting and production while it marks a major progression in the group's development. A fascinating listen even by today's standards. *Abbey Road* (Apple, 1969)—dubbed "Sgt. Pepper Mark II" by Martin—can hardly be beat for sheer songwriting excellence and audio sophistication. Amidst internal animosity and feuds, the Beatles shone one last time as a group, showing mastery of their craft most notably on Lennon's "Come Together," McCartney's "Oh! Darling," and Harrison's "Here Comes the Sun" and "Something." *Revolver,* (Parlophone, 1966, prod. Martin) while musically uneven, shows an emerging sophistication in the group's songwriting ("Eleanor Rigby," "I'm Only Sleeping") and recording techniques ("Tomorrow Never Knows") without the self-consciousness that marred later efforts. For a look at the group's early years, *A Hard Day's Night* (Parlophone, 1964, prod. Martin) shows the band at the peak of its Beatlemania-era productivity and talents. More than 30 years on, it holds its own as a solid and satisfying rock artifact.

what to buy next: While self-indulgent and at moments unlistenable, the double CD *The Beatles* (a.k.a. *The White Album*) (Apple, 1968, prod. Martin) is a necessary taproot to the freeform nihilism echoed ever since in the punk and alternative music genres. Among the thirty songs, a few fascinating standouts—"While My Guitar Gently Weeps," "Happiness Is a Warm Gun," and "Helter Skelter"—make this worth owning. *Past Masters Volume II* (Parlophone, 1988, prod. Martin)—a compilation of non-LP singles from 1966-1970—provides crucial creative links between this period's albums while demonstrating the group's giddy mastery of the 45 rpm pop song format (most notably "Lady Madonna" and "Revolution").

what to avoid: *Let It Be* (Apple, 1970, prod. Phil Spector) is a grim reminder that there is nothing so depressing as the sound of breaking up. A salvage effort by Spector renders the LP's few worthy tunes unlistenable with lush strings and choirs.

the rest: *Please Please Me* (Parlophone, 1963) *With the Beatles* (Parlophone, 1963) *Beatles for Sale* (Parlophone, 1964) *Help!* (Parlophone, 1965) *Rubber Soul* (Parlophone, 1965) *Magical Mystery Tour* (Parlophone, 1968) *Yellow Submarine Soundtrack* (Apple, 1969) *The Beatles 1962-1966* (Apple, 1973) *The Beatles 1967-1970* (Apple, 1973) *The Beatles : In the Beginning: Early Tapes (Circa 1960)* (Polygram, 1984) *Past Masters: Volume One* (Apple, 1988) *Live at the BBC* (Apple, 1994) *Anthology I* (Apple, 1995) *Anthology II* (Apple, 1996)

worth searching for: The bootleg *Posters, Incense, and Strobe Candles* (Vigotone, 1993) offers a 1969 radio broadcast of "Get Back," the album that many overdubs later would become *Let It Be.* A fascinating relic from rock's psychedelic era.

solo outings:

See: George Harrison, John Lennon, Paul McCartney/Wings, Ringo Starr

▶▶ Badfinger, Big Star, Utopia, the Jam, Squeeze, XTC, the dBs, Crowded House, Oasis

◀◀ Lonnie Donegan, Elvis Presley, Buddy Holly, Carl Perkins, Chuck Berry, Little Richard, the Coasters, the Everly Brothers, Roy Orbison, Arthur Alexander

Christopher Scapelliti

Beatnigs

Formed 1986 in San Francisco, Calif.

Michael Franti, vocals, bass; Rono Tse, percussion; Henry Flood, percussion; Andre, keyboards and samples; Kevin, percussion

Franti used to dream about becoming an NBA star; these days, the 6-foot-6 news junkie probably dreams about keeping a band together for more than one album. Like the Disposable Heroes of Hiphoprisy and the original Spearhead lineup that would follow, the Beatnigs lasted just one recording: *The Beatnigs* (Alternative Tentacles, 1988, prod. Not Listed) which stands as the most interesting and innovative album any of the three Franti-led groups has made. Although not endlessly listenable, the experimental album is full of surprising sonic twists and turns, blending vocal and found-sound samples, occasional electronic keyboard flurries, wandering bass lines, distorted choruses, industrial percussion (buzzsaws, chains whipped against tire rims, clanging metal pipes) and an odd rhythmic foundation. On top of the pulsating, pre-Consolidated soundscape, Franti goes into Gil Scott-Heron/quasi-rap mode, compassionately but pointedly attacking greed ("When You Wake Up In the Morning"), the nuclear arms race ("Rooticus Sporaticus"), the hypocrisy of hunger in America ("Burritos") and, most notably, "Television," where "Sesame Street is more real than "Hill Street." Despite that strong political bent, Franti thankfully manages to generally avoid the sort of pedantry that too often marks his later groups.

see also: *Disposable Heroes of Hiphoprisy/Spearhead*

Joshua Freedom du Lac

The Beau Brummels

Formed 1964 in San Francisco. Disbanded 1968. Reformed 1974.

Sal Valentino (born Sal Spampinato), vocals; Ron Elliott, guitar, vocals; Declan Mulligan, guitar, bass, vocals (1964-65, 1974-75); Ron Meagher, bass (1964-67); John Petersen, drums (1964-66, 1974-75)

The first San Francisco roc, group, well before the Summer of Love gang, the Beau Brummels were also one of the very first self-contained groups from America to respond to the British onslaught (with "Laugh, Laugh" in the fall of 1964)—though paradoxically it initial image and sound tricked many into thinking the Brummels were British, too. The Brummels were among the few to successfully make the transition (artistically, at least) from Top 40 popsters to respected "serious" rock musicians. The group boasted one of rock's most distinctive vocalists in Valentino and one of its finest guitarists and songwriters in Elliot. And finally, you can listen to Beau Brummels music from any era—the group pops up frequently, with varying line-ups—and come away satisfied that it was among the best at what it was doing.

what to buy: For a sampling of prime Brummels Mark I, *The Best of The Beau Brummels, 1964-1968* (Rhino, 1987, prod. Sly Stone) will do nicely. The Top 40 hits "Laugh Laugh" and "Just a Little" are here, along with "Don't Talk to Strangers," a song that defines folk-rock perhaps even better than the Byrds' "Turn, Turn, Turn."

what to buy next: *Autumn Of Their Years* (Big Beat, 1994, prod. Sly Stone) collects unreleased songs and alternate takes from the group's early period on the Autumn label.*San Francisco Sessions* (Sundazed, 1996, prod. Sly Stone) has even more of the same.

the rest: The Beau Brummels first two LPS, *Introducing the Beau Brummels* (Autumn, 1965/Sundazed, 1994, prod. Sly Stone) and *You Tell Me Why/Don't Talk to Strangers* (Autumn, 1965/Sundazed, 1994, prod. Sly Stone) are worth having for LP tracks not collected elsewhere.

worth searching for: During the late 60s, a pared-down Beau Brummels released two highly-regarded albums that sold zilch but enhanced the band's cachet among the lucky few who knew of them. *Triangle* (Warner Bros., 1967, prod. Lenny Waronker) has a mystic slant to much of it, while *Bradley's Barn* (Warner Bros., 1968, prod. Lenny Waronker) was recorded at that very locale in Nashville and is more country-oriented. Both have recently been reissued on CD in Great Britain.

▶▶ Toad the Wet Sprocket, Del Amitri

◀◀ The Beatles, the Searchers

Mike Greenfield

Beck

Born Beck Hansen, July 8, 1970 in Los Angeles, Calif.

Best known for the rock/folk/hip-hop marriage on his brilliant single, "Loser," the ultra-prolific Beck changes musical genres almost as often as he does record labels. The son of hip, punk-rock parents, he first gained recognition as an eccentric folkie songwriter/performer in Los Angeles. Finding his niche mixing creaky acoustic guitar with oddball, stream-of-consciousness lyrics, Beck recorded several hard-to-find singles and independently-released albums until the intentionally goofy "Loser"—with Beck rapping badly over a hip-hop beat—set off a bidding war between labels. *Mellow Gold* (DGC, 1994, prod. Various) offers a style-hopping cornucopia of sounds that establishes him as more than a one-hit wonder. His deal with DGC allowed him to continue recording for small labels, and he did so with the pure folk of *One Foot in the Grave* (K Records, 1994, prod. Beck) and the noisy, avant rock of *Steropathetic Soul Manure.* (Flipside, 1994, prod. Beck) The masses of "Loser" fans who saw him doing scissor kicks and the splits during his manic Lollapalooza sets in 1995 were cool to those releases, however, and Beck's next DGC outing, *Odelay,* (DGC, 1996, prod. Dust Brothers) is closer to the melodic eclecticism of its predecessor.

Todd Wicks

Jeff Beck

Born June 24, 1944 in Surrey, England

Beck might be the least-known of the three guitar heroes who populated the Yardbirds, but as sonic innovator he eclipses Jimmy Page and Eric Clapton—and most others—with his explosive, avant-noise style. Beck's post-Yardbirds career has been an erratic one filled with tempestuous behavior, long gaps between albums and with lead vocalists who never quite mesh with his playing (though Rod Stewart came pretty close). As a result, many of Beck's best albums are all-instrumental, though he's also veered off into soundtracks ("Twins," "Frankie's House") and salutes to his influences (*Crazy Legs*).

what to buy: *Truth,* (Epic, 1968, prod. Mickie Most) is the first Jeff Beck Group album and boasts a young Rod Stewart vocals. It's been been dubbed the first true heavy metal album, and while that's misleading, this blues-rock workout certainly reset the limits on just how guttural and raunchy a guitar could sound. The jazz and funk-oriented *Blow By Blow* (Epic, 1975, prod. George Martin) is Beck's all-instrumental masterpiece and features the crowd favorite "Freeway Jam."

what to buy next: *Rough and Ready* (Epic, 1971, prod. Jeff Beck), featuring singer Bobby Tench, chronicles Beck's first foray into soulful jazz-metal, while *There and Back* (Epic, 1980, prod. Jeff Beck and Ken Scott) is a collection of Beck's potent instrumentals, with backing from the sympathetic rhythm section of drummer Simon Phillips and keyboardist Tony Hymas.

what to avoid: *Jeff Beck with the Jan Hammer Group Live* (Epic, 1977, prod. Jan Hammer) provides several strong arguments for banning synthesizer solos.

the rest: *Beck-Ola* (Epic, 1969) *Jeff Beck Group* (Epic, 1972) *Beck, Bogert and Appice* (Epic, 1973) *Wired* (Epic, 1976) *Flash* (Epic, 1985) *Jeff Beck's Guitar Shop* (1989) *Beckology* (Epic, 1991) *Frankie's House* (soundtrack) (Epic, 1992) *Crazy Legs* (Epic, 1993) *Best of Beck* (Epic, 1995)

worth searching for: *Rock 'n' Roll Spirit Vol. II: Jeff Beck Session Works* (Epic, 1994, prod. Various), a Japanese import that studies his contributions to various works by Malcolm McLaren, Donovan, Stanley Clarke and others.

▶▶ Eddie Van Halen, Joe Satriani, Stevie Ray Vaughan, Vernon Reid

◀◀ Cliff Gallup, James Burton, Les Paul, Buddy Guy

Thor Christensen

Walter Becker

See: Steely Dan

George Bedard and the Kingpins

Formed in Ann Arbor, Mich.

George Bedard, guitar, lead vocals; Randy Tessier, bass, vocals; Richard Dishman, drums and vocals

Great music transcends boundaries of age, genre and preconception for a simpler, universal appeal. Listeners who subscribe to this school of thought will see Bedard and the Kingpins as a great band; those who think the opposite will more than likely dismiss them as just another retro band. That's their loss, because the Kingpins boast excellent songs, searing chops and a nearly religious conviction in the redemptive power of rock 'n' roll. Long a sideman in lesser outfits such as Tracy Lee and the Leonards, Bedard is a veritable lexicon of hot guitar licks and early rock cool; his style seamlessly incorporates the influences of such rock guitar pioneers as James Burton, Dick Dale and Scotty Moore, while his vocals evoke Buddy Holly with light shades of Elvis Presley. Like the Stray Cats, the Kingpins use the aesthetic of late 50s/early 60s rock as a starting point, not as an end unto itself. Tessier and Dishman are far more aggressive than many early rock rhythm sections, and their propulsive force drives Bedard's fiery fretwork, creating a sound that is simultaneously nostalgic and fresh. Like the Cats, the Kingpins are not striking a pose; they believe in this music, and the trio's enthusiasm is an infectious, tangible element in their recordings and live shows.

A longtime favorite on the Ann Arbor club circuit, the Kingpins managed the rare feat of capturing their live energy on a studio disk with their debut recording *Upside*. (Schoolkids Records, 1994, prod. George Bedard) ♪♪♪♪ The album features seven original tracks, including the should-be classics "You Put the Hurt on Me" and "I'm My Own Dog." Alongside the originals are a tasty handful of early rock chestnuts that are often the high point of the band's live shows—most notably an incendiary version of the surf classic "Pipeline." That these standards sit comfortably next to Bedard's own songs is a testament to the band's talent and accomplished knowledge of rock history.

David Galens

The Bee Gees

Formed 1958 in Brisbane, Australia

Barry Gibb, vocals, guitar; Robin Gibb, vocals (1958-69, 1970-present); Maurice Gibb, vocals, bass, keyboards, guitar, percussion

Before John Travolta strode down the sidewalk eating pizza to the disco sway of "Stayin' Alive," the Bee Gees were regarded as a pop vocal group of estimable talent that could take a good song and make it sound great. The trio had a few of those early on—"New York Mining Disaster 1941," "To Love Somebody," "Run to Me"—but it wasn't until the group recorded a few songs for the "Saturday Night Fever" soundtrack that they became a phenomenon, making hits not just for itself but also for singer Yvonne Elliman and their late younger brother Andy Gibb. The brothers Gibb are, first and foremost, pop craftsman with an intuitive knack for harmonies and decent melodic sensibilities. Were it not for the film—and the subsequent co-starring role in the disastrous "Sgt. Peper's Lonely Hearts Club Band"—the Bee Gees likely would have remained modest also-rans in the pop pantheon, neither celebrated nor scorned. Now they have a lot of money, but also an artistic albatross that they haven't been able to shake since 1977.

what to buy: *Main Course* (RSO, 1975/Polydor, 1994, prod. Arif Mardin) ♪♪♪♪ is a transitional album, pop with R&B touches that would turn into a full-fledged disco movement for "Saturday Night Fever." On *Main Course*, however, it's a welcome switch from the bland pop path the Bee Gees were on before, yielding tuneful hits such as "Jive Talkin' " and "Nights on Broadway." *Bee Gees Gold* (Polydor, 1976, prod. Various) ♪♪♪½ is a solid gathering of pre-"Fever" favorites.

what to buy next: Worth considering—but carefully—is the box set *Tales From the Brothers Gibb*. (Polydor, 1990, prod. Various) ♪♪♪ It covers everything you'd want, but its four discs have plenty that you don't too.

what to avoid: *Spirits Having Flown*, (RSO, 1979/Polydor, 1994, prod. the Bee Gees, Karl Richardson and Albhy Galuten) ♪ the slick, calculated and vapid follow-up to the "Fever" success.

the rest: *Bee Gees 1st* (Atco, 1967/Rebound, 1994) ♪♪½ *Odessa* (Atco, 1969/Polydor, 1988) ♪½ *Best of the Bee Gees, Vol. 1* (Atco/Polydor, 1969); *To Whom it May Concern* (Atco, 1972/Polydor, 1992) ♪♪ *Best of the Bee Gees, Vol. 2* (Atco/Polydor, 1973); *Mr. Natural* (RSO, 1974/Polydor, 1992) ♪♪ *Children of the World* (RSO, 1976/Polydor, 1994) ♪♪♪ *Here at Last...Live* (RSO, 1977/Polydor, 1990) ♪♪♪ *Size Isn't Everything* (Polydor, 1993) ♪♪

worth searching for: The *veddy* late 60s *Cucumber Castle*, (Atco, 1970, prod. Robert Stigwood and the Bee Gees) ♪♪½ recorded by Barry and Maurice during Robin's brief hiatus from the band, has hysterical Medieval cover art that company will get a kick out of.

⏩ Yvonne Elliman, Andy Gibb, Air Supply, Bread, Mr. Mister

⏪ The Four Freshmen, the Kingston Trio, the Beatles, the Beach Boys

Gary Graff

Adrian Belew /The Bears

Born Robert Steven Belew, Dec. 23, 1949 in Covington, Ky.

Adrian Belew, guitar, vocals; Rob Fetters, guitar, vocals; Bob Nyswonger, bass; Chris Arduser, drums

A journeyman guitar virtuoso, Belew has always been at his

best supporting other players—beginning with his first step into the big leagues, a spot in Frank Zappa's mid-70s band. Launched into that gig when the rock orchestrator saw him performing in a Cincinnati club band, Belew became a sideman extraordinaire, lending his amazing arsenal of sounds to David Bowie, Talking Heads and the Tom Tom Club before helping to reinvent King Crimson for the 80s. As a solo artist, his material has usually emphasized instrumental craft and creative abstraction over accessible melodies, hampering any commercial success. Getting together with pals from an old Cincinnati band called the Raisins, Belew developed a commercial venue for arty rock/pop tunes—kind of a New Wave Beatles—dubbed The Bears in 1986. But the concept didn't catch on, so after two appealing yet underpromoted records, Belew returned to his own erratic recording projects, most recently using guitar synthesizers to perform original orchestral works and reuniting with King Crimson in 1994.

what to buy: His first solo album, *Lone Rhino,* (Island, 1983, prod. Adrian Belew) is an engaging showcase for Belew's astounding guitar abilities, showing off arty rock and funk tunes written and produced by the guitarist himself. From the haunting title track—complete with guitar-produced Rhinoceros bellows—to the rocking "Big Electric Cat," Belew served notice that he was an artist to be watched. Unfortunately, it took another 10 years before the guitarist would live up to that promise with *Inner Revolution,* (Atlantic, 1992, prod. Adrian Belew) a Beatles pastiche record that allows him to stretch his instrumental capabilities (he plays every instrument and produces) and compositional skills.

what to buy next: The two Bears albums, *The Bears* (Primitive Man/I.R.S., 1987, prod Adrian Belew) and *Rise and Shine,* (Primitive Man/I.R.S., 1988, prod. Adrian Belew) are the next-best examples of Belew in pop mode, whipping out intelligent, accessible tunes with a Beatle-esque flair), spiced with some burning chops. His backing musicians are no slouches either, offering spot-on support throughout these guitar-fueled rock tunes—material that failed only because it was probably 10 years ahead of its time.

what to avoid: Belew's biggest mistakes come when he allows his own virtuosity and musical smarts to get ahead of good songwriting. As a solo artist, those missteps were most glaring on *Young Lions* (Atlantic, 1990, prod. Adrian Belew) WOOF! and *Twang Bar King* (Island, 1983, prod. Adrian Belew) WOOF! On both records, he lets his own complex ideas and innovative playing get away from him—surrounding mediocre compositions with top-notch playing and production.

the rest: *Desire Caught By The Tail (Island, 1986)* Mr. Music Head *(Atlantic, 1989)* Desire of the Rhino King *(Island, 1991)* Here *(Plan 9/Caroline, 1994)* The Guitar as Orchestra *(Adrian Belew Presents, 1995)* Op Zop Too Wah *(Passenger, 1996) not available for rating*

worth searching for: Belew's guitar trickery lights up the classic record but hard to find live album *The Name of This Band is the Talking Heads,* (Sire, 1992) particularly on the funky World Music cut "I Zimbra."

▶▶ John Frusciante, Beck

◀◀ Frank Zappa, King Crimson, the Beatles

see also: *King Crimson*

Eric Deggans

Bell Biv Devoe

See: New Edition

Chris Bell

See: Big Star

Joey Belladonna

See: Anthrax

Belly

Formed 1991 in Providence, R.I.

Tanya Donelly, vocals, guitar; Thomas Gorman, guitar, organ, piano; Fred Abong, bass (1991-93); Leslie Langston, bass (1992); Gail Greenwood, bass (1993-present); Chris Gorman, drums

After years of seeing only a few of her standout songs appear on each Throwing Muses album (and then on Breeders releases), Donelly put her own group together with the Gorman brothers, borrowing Muses bassist Abong (earlier Muses bassist Langston filled in for a while but has not recorded with the group). With vocals nearly as distinctively quirky as the Muses' Kristin Hersh, but with a brighter sound, Donelly parlayed play on suddenly influential college radio into broader success with her first album, *Star,* (Sire/Reprise, 1993, prod. Various) which contains "Feed the Tree" and "Gepetto," with lots of fine, elliptical lyrics set to billowy alternative rock. *King* (Sire/Reprise, 1995, prod. Glyn Johns) continues the familiar sound; if nothing is as immediately catchy as the debut's highlights, the production is more varied.

the rest: *Slow Dust* (Sire/Reprise EP, 1992) ♪ *Geppeto* (Sire/Reprise, EP 1992) ♪♪♪ *Feed the Tree* (Sire/Reprise, EP 1992) ♪♪½ *Moon* (Sire/Reprise EP, 1993) ♪♪♪ *Now They'll Sleep* (Sire/Reprise, EP 1995) ♪♪ *Judas My Heart* (Sire/Reprise EP, 1995) ♪♪♪

Steve Holtje

Ben Folds Five

Formed 1994 in Chapel Hill, N.C.

Ben Folds, piano, vocals; Robert Sledge, bass, vocals; Darren Jessee, drums, vocals

Irony abounds in the world of Ben Folds Five. The group is actually a trio, not a quintet, and the its lead instrument is a piano, not a guitar—which is no small feat, considering it hails from Chapel Hill, N.C., considered in many circles to be jangle-pop's ground zero. And while frontman Folds characterizes his music as "punk rock for sissies," songs such as "Underground"—which takes the piss out of the oh-so-hip alternative rock scene—and the hilarious "Julianne" actually contain plenty of attitude. Musically, the songs range from vintage Todd Rundgren to early Squeeze and Joe Jackson, with hints of Brian Wilson and Queen thrown in. Sledge's fuzz-toned bass drives the songs forward, and the group's crack harmonies lend even the more raucous moments a sheen of professionalism. *Ben Folds Five* (Passenger/Caroline, 1995, prod. Caleb Southern) ♪♪♪♪ is a winner all the way.

Daniel Durchholz

Pat Benatar

Born Pat Andrzejewski, Jan. 10, 1953 in Brooklyn, N.Y.

A classically-trained singer in her teens, Benatar was headed for the Julliard School of Music as the daughter of an opera singer until her rock 'n' roll attitude got in the way. Instead, she married Army recruit Dennis Benatar and followed him to Virginia, only to move back to her native New York a few years later. Eventually divorcing Dennis (but keeping his surname), Benatar caught the eye of Catch a Rising Star owner Rick Newman, who became her manager. Though a few record labels turned down her tough-girl rocker material, Chrysalis Records signed the diminutive vocalist in 1978. Debuting as a sexpot singer more likely to sing uptempo rock tunes about beating up men than loving them, Benatar exploded onto the charts with energetic tunes powered by her impressive vocals. Her reign as the queen of hard-headed rock 'n'roll continued through most of the 80s, even as she and producer Neil Giraldo (who eventually became her second husband) added more keyboards and pop elements to her arena rock sound. By the early 90s, as the grunge revolution made such pop-rockers passe, Benatar released a blues record that drove off the few fans who were left, putting the brakes on a career that had already been slowed by time off to raise children.

what to buy: Benatar's first two albums—*In the Heat of the Night* (Chrysalis, 1979, prod. Mike Chapman and Peter Coleman) ♪♪♪♪ and *Crimes of Passion* (Chrysalis, 1980, prod. Keith Olsen) ♪♪♪♪—are her most consistent. Arena rock classics like "Heartbreaker," "Hit Me With Your Best Shot" and John Cougar's "I Need a Lover" cemented her reputation as a toughie with pipes of solid brass—an antidote to the coy and antiseptic female pop stars of the time.

what to buy next: Since Benatar's records grew increasingly more inconsistent through during 80s, her first hits collection, *Best Shots* (Chrysalis, 1989, prod. Various) ♪♪♪♪ remains the best way to sample everything. Featuring many significant hits from her career, including a live version of "Hell Is For Children" and the "Legend of Billie Jean" soundtrack hit "Invincible," its a cheap and easy way to skim the cream of Benatar's mid-to-late 80s work without wading through every album.

what to avoid: It's pretty obvious that Benatar's ill-fated blues record *True Love* (Chrysalis, 1991, prod. Neil Geraldo) WOOF! was the biggest nail in her career coffin. Filled with awkward, clueless versions of B.B. King and Albert King tunes, this is that most horrible of rock star indulgences—a blues album by players who never bothered learning how to play them.

the rest: *Precious Time* (Chrysalis, 1981) ♪♪♪½ *Get Nervous* (Chrysalis, 1982) ♪♪½ *Live From Earth* (Chrysalis, 1983) ♪♪½ *Tropico* (Chrysalis, 1984) ♪♪ *Seven the Hard Way* (Chrysalis, 1985) ♪♪½ *Wide Awake in Dreamland* (Chrysalis, 1988) ♪♪ *Gravity's Rainbow* (Chrysalis, 1993) ♪♪ *Very Best Of: All Fired Up* (Chrysalis, 1994) ♪♪♪½

worth searching for: Benatar was a regular guest of such 80s-era television music series as "In Concert" and "Don Kirshner's Rock Concert." Catching her on reruns of either is a guaranteed hoot, if only to see her macho posturing and drummer Myron Grombacher's New Wave Keith Moon impersonation.

▶▶ Scandal, 4 Non Blondes, Melissa Etheridge

◀◀ Janis Joplin, Grace Slick, Patti Smith

Eric Deggans

Brook Benton

Born Benjamin Franklin Peay, Sept. 19, 1931 in Camden, S.C. Died April 9, 1988 in New York, N.Y.

With his satin-smooth baritone and easygoing delivery, Benton became one of the few black crooners of the 50s to successfully cross over into the pop-rock realm. Benton cut his teeth first on the gospel circuit and later with writer/producer Clyde Otis, singing and co-writing of demos for hundreds of other musicians (including Nat King Cole and Clyde McPhatter). By the late 50s, Benton was signed by Otis to Mercury, where he put his deep, rich voice to work on lushly orchestrated R&B songs. The arrangements were the perfect showcase for Benton's intimate vocal style, and he scored an impressive 21 gold records in five years. In a move typical of record labels of this period, Mercury teamed Benton with a popular female singer—his label mate Dinah Washington—whose easygoing voice meshed delightfully with Benton's. Together they scored a number of hits on the R&B charts ("Baby (You've Got What It Takes),") "A Rockin' Good Way") until Washington's untimely death in 1963. Benton's encore was the 1970 hit "A Rainy Night in Georgia," an emotionally powerful deep-blues ballad that is the finest recording of his career. Although he never charted again, he remained a popular tour attraction into the early 80s.

what to buy: *Anthology* (Rhino, 1986, prod. Various) [3 bones] is a fine 24-track retrospective of Benton's long and varied career, but it loses points for excluding Benton's mid-60s stint at RCA, where he made a number of excellent recordings of pop standards. But it does serve up the early hits ("It's Just A Matter Of Time," "Kiddio," "Fools Rush In"), the duets with Washington ("Baby (You've Got What It Takes)," "A Rockin' Good Way") and his later classic recordings for Atlantic's Cotillion label, including the hit "Rainy Night in Georgia."

what to buy next: *This Is Brook Benton* (BMG/RCA, 1989, prod. Various) [3 bones] fills the gaps in Rhino's *Anthology* This 20-track compilation of his 1965-66 recordings for RCA features Benton backed by a full orchestra on a wide number of pop standards of the day, including "Call Me Irresponsible," "A Nightingale Sang In Berkeley Square" and Nat King Cole's signature tune "Unforgettable." A pleasant reminder that Benton could croon as well as he could swing.

what to avoid: It is, in all likelihood, impossible to put out a bad album of Benton hits. So while *Greatest Hits* (WEA/Atlantic/Curb, 1991, prod. Various) [2 bones] isn't necessarily poor, it is a lackluster sampling of Benton's catalog. Any of the other compilations listed here would make a stronger choice.

the rest: *Best of Brook Benton* (Polygram, 1987) [4 bones] *All His Best* (Charly Budget, 1992) [3 bones] *Greatest Songs* (WEA/Atlantic/Curb,1995) [3 bones]

worth searching for: *40 Greatest Hits* (Mercury, 1989, prod. Clyde Otis) [4 bones] is the best retrospective of Benton's Mercury years ever assembled. Although the album is out of print, sharp shoppers can usually locate unpurchased or used copies.

▶▶ Etta James, Ray Charles, Clyde McPhatter, Joe South

◀◀ Arthur Prysock, Frank Sinatra, Nat King Cole

Christopher Scapelliti

Chuck Berry

Born Charles Edward Anderson Berry, Oct. 18, 1926, in St. Louis, Mo.

Next to Elvis Presley, Berry is rock 'n' roll's most influential performer; yet in terms of innovation, he stands second to no one. Berry's ringing guitar gave the nascent genre its most identifiable sound, and his wide-ranging, poetic lyrics gave it a vision. A black man with a taste for country music as well as the blues, Berry's souped-up anthems to teendom were irresistible because of his well-enunciated, theoretically raceless vocals, acceptable for airplay on radio stations that refused to broadcast R&B. But how the mighty have fallen; beyond the staggering accomplishments mentioned, Berry's contributions to rock 'n' roll include sexual deviancy—he was jailed for transporting a teenage prostitute across state lines during the early 60s and fined for videotaping the bathroom activities at his Wentzville, Mo., restaurant in the early 90s—and tax evasion, for which he was sent to prison during the late 70s. Embittered, perhaps justifiably so, at the treatment he has received in exchange for his music, Berry for years has toured in a mercenary fashion, insisting on payment in cash, not rehearsing the pickup bands that back him and phoning in his performances. He was the father of rock 'n' roll, but somehow he's turned into its deadbeat dad.

what to buy: Featuring 71 cuts over a span of three discs, *The Chess Box* (Chess/MCA, 1988, prod. Leonard and Phil Chess) [5 bones] is an essential purchase for any serious fan of rock 'n' roll. It covers all his essential hits—too numerous to mention here—and delves into other areas, such as his blues playing, and includes some of the instrumental jams that the Chess brothers would record surreptitiously in the studio and use to flesh out Berry's albums. The set may be long for the novice listener, but Berry's accomplishments are so staggering that it seems superfluous to note that this book would not have been necessary had he not existed. Those on a tighter budget are directed to *The Great Twenty-Eight* (Chess, 1982, prod. Leonard and Phil Chess) which gets right down to business of Berry's best, with no frills and some essential material missing. Still, it's solid from start to finish.

what to buy next: Berry wasn't really an album-oriented artist, so which of his individual albums you might care to own largely depends on the hits contained therein. *St. Louis to Liverpool* (Chess, 1964, prod. Leonard and Phil Chess) is probably his best single album, featuring "Promised Land," "Little Marie," "No Particular Place to Go" and "You Never Can Tell," plus a couple of good covers and a slow blues tune. For someone who owns the box set, it's worth checking out the rarities series—*Rock 'n' Roll Rarities* (Chess, 1986, prod. Leonard and Phil Chess), *More Rock 'n' Roll Rarities* (Chess, 1986, prod. Leonard and Phil Chess) and *Missing Berries: Rarities, Vol. 3* (Chess/MCA, 1990, prod. Leonard and Phil Chess) After that, the early albums *After School Session* (Chess, 1957, prod. Leonard and Phil Chess), *One Dozen Berrys* (Chess, 1958, prod. Leonard and Phil Chess) and *Chuck Berry is on Top* (Chess, 1959, prod. Leonard Chess) are all worthwhile.

what to avoid: Berry left Chess during the mid-60s to record for Mercury, and most of the undistinguished work he turned in there is justifiably out of print. Still available, though, are *Golden Hits* (Mercury, 1967, prod. Chuck Berry) **WOOF!** which features needless re-recordings of his seminal hits, and *Live at the Fillmore Auditorium* (Mercury, 1967, prod. Abe Kesh) an unimpressive concert recording. Also avoid *Chuck Berry On Stage* (Chess, 1963, prod. Leonard and Phil Chess) **WOOF!** which is not what its title advertises but rather studio recordings with a dubbed-in audience. *The London Chuck Berry Sessions* (Chess, 1972, prod. Esmond Edwards) yielded one of Berry's biggest hits, the novelty song "My Ding-a-Ling," but the album is a marginal effort nonetheless. Finally, Berry's work has been repackaged many times on many labels. Unless you know enough to know what you're looking at, unless it's on the Chess label, don't buy it.

the rest: *Rockin' at the Hops* (Chess, 1960) *New Juke Box Hits* (Chess, 1961) *Twist* (aka *More Chuck Berry*) (Chess, 1962) *Chuck Berry's Greatest Hits* (Chess, 1963) *Two Great Guitars* (with Bo Diddley) (Checker, 1964) *Chuck Berry in London* (Chess, 1965) *Fresh Berry's* (Chess, 1966) *Chuck Berry's Golden Decade* (Chess, 1967) *Back Home* (Chess, 1970) *Chuck Berry's Golden Decade, Vol. 2* (Chess, 1973) *Chuck Berry's Golden Decade, Vol. 3* (Chess, 1974) *San Francisco Dues* (Chess, 1971) *Bio* (Chess, 1973) *Chuck Berry* (Chess, 1975) Rockit *(Atco, 1979)* Hail! Hail! Rock 'n' Roll *(MCA, 1987)*

worth searching for: *Chuck Berry is On Top* (Chess, 1959) and *Rockin' at the Hops,* (Chess, 1960) two of Berry's best albums that are available, in original mono, via French imports.

The Beatles, the Rolling Stones, the Beach Boys, Bob Dylan and everyone else who has ever played rock 'n' roll.

Muddy Waters, Louis Jordan, T-Bone Walker, Hank Williams

Daniel Durchholz

Cindy Lee Berryhill

Born in Los Angeles, Calif.

Originally running with the post-punk folk crowd that included Kirk Kelly and Roger Manning, San Diego-based Berryhill was one of the first new acts signed to reissue kingpin Rhino Records. Her first two albums were suitably driven by attitude ("Damn, I Wish I Was a Man," "Baby, Should I Have the Baby?") but overloaded with yippie-skippy, Beat-poetry earmarks. However, *Garage Orchestra* (Cargo, 1994, prod. Cindy Lee Berryhill and Michael Harris) marked a groundbreaking shift toward a bigger sound and an outlook that was more playful than ponderous, following Alejandro Escovedo's chamber-rock lead by enhancing her swooping soprano with a swirling mix of cellos, tympanis, violins, vibraphones and offbeat percussion. Such engaging numbers as "I Wonder Why," "Song For Brian" (a love letter to Brian Wilson) and "UFO Suite" dabble in avant-garde dissonance but mostly demonstrate the tasteful, textural range that strings can bring to pop music.

the rest: *Cindy Lee Berryhill* (Rhino, 1987) *Naked Movie Star* (Rhino, 1989) *Straight Outta Maryville* (Cargo, 1996)

David Okamoto

Better than Ezra

Formed 1988 in New Orleans, La.

What Album Changed Your Life?

"The first Bob Wills album (Bob Wills and His Texas Playboys (MCA, 1958)). Someone in the Cody band found it in a cutout bin, a cheapie. It had 'Fat Boy Rag' on it, and 'New San Antonio Rose,' great stuff. We'd never heard anything like that. We didn't know from Western swing. We started going wild, going 'Hee-yah!' and yelling 'flea bite!' after solos."

Bill Kirchen,Commander Cody's Lost Planet Airmen

Kevin Griffin, vocals, guitars; Cary Bonnecaze, drums, vocals (1988-96); Travis Aaron McNabb, drums (1996-present); Tom Drummond, bass

Tragedy has followed Better Than Ezra since its early days as a Dinosaur Jr.-influenced combo. Drummer Bonnecaze was shot the back as a teen, though he fully recovered. And its original lead singer, Joel Rundell, died accidentally. The remaining trio forayed into modern rock, picking up early support from college radio stations. *Deluxe* (Elektra, 1995, prod. Dan Rothchild) elevated the band to the pop mainstream thanks to the infectious wuh-huh choruses of "Good." A sophomore effort, *Friction Baby,* was slated for release in late summer, 1996.

Christina Fuoco

Dickey Betts

See: Allman Brothers Band

Bewitched

See: Sonic Youth

The B-52's /Fred Schneider

Formed 1976 in Athens, Ga.

Fred Schneider, vocals; Cindy Wilson, vocals (1976-90, 1994-present); Kate Pierson vocals, keyboards; Keith Strickland, drums, guitar; Ricky Wilson, guitar (died Oct. 12, 1985)

The B-52's, the second most popular band to come out of Athens, Ga., had its roots in parties, so the best of the band's sounds—particularly the oddball hits "Rock Lobster," "Private Idaho" and "Planet Claire"—go after an off-beat, whacky kind of fun. It's also one of the first rock bands to be affected directly by AIDS; guitarist Wilson died of the disease in 1985. The rest of the group, including his sister Cindy, decided to go on without replacing him (drummer Strickland learned the guitar) and wound up with the biggest album of the group's career, 1989's *Cosmic Thing*, and the smash hits "Love Shack" and "Roam." The B-52's haven't reached that pinnacle since, but it can still be counted on to get a crowd to "dance this mess around."

what to buy: *The B-52's* (Warner Bros., 1979, prod. Chris Blackwell and Robert Ash) is the indispensable New Wave party record. Its stripped-down, surf-twang retro makes it sound ever-modern, and its party chants still rule the floor.

what to buy next: *Cosmic Thing,* (Reprise, 1989, prod. Don Was and Nile Rogers) the sprightly comeback with "Love Shack," "Roam" and "Deadbeat Club." *Whammy!,* (Warner Bros. 1983, prod. Steven Stanley) a solid but overlooked mid-period album the revealed a mastery of computer noises.

what to avoid: *Good Stuff* (Reprise, 1992, prod. Don Was and Nile Rogers) found the band down to just three B-52's, and the lackluster songs made its title was misleading at best.

the rest: *Wild Planet* (Warner Bros., 1980) *Bouncing Off the Satellites* (Warner Bros., 1986) *Party Mix/Mesopotamia* (Warner Bros., 1991)

worth searching for: The British import *Dance This Mess Around,* (Island, 1990, prod. Various) a superlative collection from the pre-*Cosmic Thing* albums that should keep the party out of bounds for its duration.

solo outings:

Fred Schneider: Fred Schneider and the Shake Society (Reprise, 1991) *..Just Fred* (Reprise, 1996)

▶▶ Deee-Lite, Cibo Matto, Technotronic

◀◀ Yoko Ono, Dick Dale, Shangri-La's, Ricky Ricardo

Roger Catlin

Jello Biafra

See: Dead Kennedys

Big Audio Dynamite /B.A.D. II, Big Audio

Formed 1984 in London, England

Mick Jones, vocals, guitars; Don Letts, keyboards (1984-90); Leo Williams, bass (1984-90); Greg Roberts, drums (1984-90); Dan Donovan, keyboards (1984-90); Gary Tonadge, bass (1991-present)

Unceremoniously booted from the Clash, Jones—who was responsible for some of that band's more adventurous music—put together this multimedia, multi-genre ensemble that's become one of the longest-running parties of the post Clash bunch. Jones blended his rock instincts with his growing interests in hip-hop, rave and dance fads of the day. And while Big Audio Dynamite has changed personnel almost as often as it changed band names, it has been a dependable source for a good single every couple of years, even as Jones slowly returned to the ragged guitar sound of his roots.

what to buy: *Planet B.A.D.: Greatest Hits* (Columbia, 1995, prod. Various) ℛℛℛℛ goes above and beyond such collections by including not only the crucial cuts from every Columbia album, but also leasing one from the label he defected to, "I Was a Punk," to bring the chronicle full circle.

what to buy next: *This is Big Audio Dynamite* (Columbia, 1985, prod. Mick Jones) ℛℛℛℛ seemed a little bareboned at the time; its atmosphere is as stark as the Spaghetti Western milieu it reflected in its tracks—not so far from Jones' work in Clash, but a definite jump to something new, a mix of rock and dance that sounded natural and still sounds fresh many years later.

what to avoid: *F-Punk*, (Radioactive, 1995, prod. Mick Jones and Andre Shapps) ℛℛ a rote return to the more guitar-oriented music of Jones' Clash past.

the rest: *No. 10 Upping Street* (Columbia, 1986) ℛℛℛ *Tighten Up, Volume '88* (Columbia, 1988) ℛℛℛ *Megatop Phoenix* (Columbia 1989) ℛℛℛ *B.A.D. II* (Columbia, 1991) ℛℛℛ

worth searching for: *Looking for a Song 2 CD Set*, (Columbia, 1994) ℛℛℛℛ a promotion-only set with three versions of the band's last single for Columbia, paired with a succinct greatest hits collection.

▶▶ Soup Dragons, Jesus Jones, EMF

◀◀ The Clash, the Who, Chicago house music, Detroit techno

Roger Catlin

The Big Bopper

Born Jiles Perry "J.P." Richardson, Oct. 24, 1930 in Sabine Pass, Texas. Died Feb. 3, 1959 near Clear Lake, Iowa

Was he for real or a joke? We never got the answer to that question, because the Big Bopper died in the same plane crash that took the lives of Buddy Holly and Ritchie Valens, less than a year after J.P. Richardson from KTRM radio in Beaumont, Texas, came to international prominence with his hit, "Chantilly Lace." The truth is, Richardson—who began writing songs during a stint in the army —was an entertainer. His other songs were novelties—"The Purple People Eater Meets the Witch-Doctor," "The Big Bopper's Wedding," "Little Red Riding Hood." His stage show played on his radio persona, a big man with a big voice and that famous come-hither call of "Helloooo baby!" *Hellooo Baby! The Best of Big Bopper* (Rhino, 1989) ℛℛℛ has 'em all—and probably more than you ever wanted. The original but skimpier *Chantilly Lace* (Mercury, 1958/1994) ℛℛ is also available.

Gary Graff

Big Brother and the Holding Company

See: Janis Joplin

Big Chief

Formed 1989 in Ann Arbor, Mich.

Barry Henssler, vocals; Mark Dancey, guitar; Matt O'Brien, bass; Phil Durr, guitar; Mike Danner, drums

Paying tribute to its geographical roots, Big Chief took the hard edge of Ann Arbor legends the Stooges and the MC5 and combined it with the Motor City funk sounds of George Clinton's Parliament-Funkadelic projects. The result was an aggressive, powerful mix as much hardcore funk as funky hardcore. Big Chief tempered its big sounds with liberal doses of humor (the members also worked on the popular underground humor/culture mag Motorbooty). The album *Platinum Jive*, for example, was a mock greatest hits collection with booklet pictures of the members' purported solo outings—such as Henssler's *The Sexual Intellectual*. But due to low record sales, Big Chief was dropped by Capitol Records in 1995, and it remains unclear what the band's next move will be.

what to buy: *Mack Avenue Skullgame* (Sub Pop, 1993, prod. Big Chief and Al Sutton) is the funky "original soundtrack" to the non-existent movie of the same name. Judging by the music, the movie would have been a gritty, violent 70s flick with plenty of females, flares and 'fros.

what to buy next: *Face* (Sub Pop, 1992, prod. Al Sutton and Big Chief) came out on a Seattle label in the prime days of grunge, but Big Chief rises above the fray with more of an in-your-face, heavy metal/soul melange.

what to avoid: Big Chief choked on its major label debut. The lightheartedness of the concept of *Platinum Jive* (Capitol, 1994, prod. Phil Nicolo and Big Chief) didn't translate to the generally heavy-handed music.

the rest: *Drive It Off* (Get Hip, 1991)

worth searching for: Big Chief was a big supporter of vinyl and put out several limited edition singles, most of them on colored vinyl. The most coveted of these is the band's first, the "Brake Torque" b/w "Superstupid" (Big Kiss, 1989, prod. Big Chief) 7-inch on mauve and green vinyl.

◀◀ Parliament-Funkadelic, James Brown, MC5, Stooges

Jill Hamilton

Big Head Todd and the Monsters

Formed 1987, Boulder, Colo.

Todd Park Mohr, guitar, vocals; Brian Nevin, drums; Rob Squires, bass

Dominated by "Big Head" Todd Park Mohr, a fan of old blues, soul and funk records, the Monsters developed a jazzy rock style. In concert, Mohr's guitar solos go off on never-ending tangents, sounding like Stevie Ray Vaughan or Dire Straits' Mark Knopfler, and Nevin and Squires fall in behind him, improvising like the Grateful Dead when necessary. On record, they're much tighter: Mohr writes strong songs with good detail and sings them with a booming, friendly voice, while the versatile rhythm section knows when to be dominant and when to back off.

what to buy: *Sister Sweetly* (Giant, 1993, prod. David Z) is a straightforward, finely polished rock album with the catchy, bluesy singles such as "Broken Hearted Savior" and "Bittersweet."

what to buy next: The self-produced albums *Another Mayberry* (Big Records, 1989/Giant, 1994) and *Midnight Radio* (Big Records, 1990/Giant, 1994) attracted loyal followings in Colorado and Chicago.

what to avoid: *Sister Sweetly* (Giant EP, 1993), with bland live versions of Monsters' songs and Sly Stone's "Everyday People."

the rest: *Strategem* (Giant, 1994)

▶▶ Dave Matthews Band, Rusted Root, Widespread Panic

◀◀ Buddy Guy, Albert Collins, Sly and the Family Stone, Stevie Ray Vaughan, Blues Traveler

Steve Knopper

Big Star /Chris Bell

Formed 1971, Memphis, Tenn. Disbanded 1975.

Chris Bell, guitar, vocals (1971-73, died Dec. 27, 1978); Alex Chilton, guitar, vocals; Andy Hummell, bass (1971-74); Jody Stephens, drums and vocals

Big Star helped define the subgenre known as power pop. Mining the exuberant melodicism and vocal harmonies of The Beatles but adding a liberal amount of crunchy guitar, glam-era sexuality, and the R&B grit of their native Memphis, the group cranked out two albums of essential, dynamic pop before taking a detour into melancholy on their third record. The band was fronted by singer-guitarist Chilton, who'd scored hits as a youth with The Box Tops ("The Letter"); his tremulous vocals pack an emotional wallop. Singer-guitarist Bell contributed some lovely vocals and songwriting to Big Star's debut but left after its release. Big Star fell apart in the mid-70s after languishing in cultdom; Chilton embarked on a mercurial solo career and also produced a number of other artists. Big Star's reputation continued to grow, however, and after myriad young bands saluted the Memphis popsters as a seminal influence, Chilton and Stephens agreed in 1992 to perform as Big Star with the help of two members of acolytes The Posies. The concert was recorded and appeared on CD in 1993.

what to buy: Pop fans will find the bargain of a lifetime with the combination of *#1 Record/Radio City.* (Stax, 1992, prod. John Fry) The first two albums sport such Big Star perennials as "Back of a Car," "September Girls," "Thirteen," "The Ballad of El Goodo" and "Mod Lang."

what to buy next: *Third/Sister Lovers* (Rykodisc, 1992, prod. Jim Dickinson) is not a combination but Big Star's long-delayed third album bearing both of its titles. Generally downbeat, it features some of Chilton's most emotionally wrenching work, notably "Holocaust." Bell's *I Am the Cosmos* (Rykodisc, 1992, prod. Chris Bell) is worth having for its incandescent title track alone, but it features several other lovely songs.

the rest: *Big Star Live* (Rykodisc, 1992) *Columbia: Live at Missouri University* (Zoo, 1993)

worth searching for: *Big Star's Biggest* (Line, 1988, prod. Various) is a German import compilation that has all the right selections.

Posies, Raspberries, Elvis Costello, Replacements, Marshall Crenshaw, dB's, R.E.M., Tommy Keene, Matthew Sweet, Teenage Fanclub, Game Theory, Loud Family, Jellyfish, Aimee Mann, Letters to Cleo

The Beatles, Rolling Stones, Byrds, Hollies, Kinks, Moby Grape, Otis Redding, Booker T. and the MGs, Badfinger, Beach Boys, Move

see also: *Alex Chilton*

Simon Glickman

Bikini Kill

Formed 1990 in Olympia, Wash.

Kathleen Hanna, vocals; Kathi Wilcox, bass; Tobi Vail, drums; Billy Karren, guitar

The house band for the riot grrrrl movement of the early 90s, Bikini Kill served notice on its first EP that not only can women rock, they can rock with a vengeance. Hanna's outrageous Johnny Rotten vocal stylings, combined with her band's Iggy Pop-meets-X-Ray Spex rock assault, leave no doubt that women in punk rock have arrived. *Bikini Kill* (Kill Rock Stars, 1992, prod. Bikini Kill) combines the first two EPs for an instant punk classic, a melody infused treatise that's instantly memorable and features the fist-flinging manifesto "Double Dare Ya" and the incestuous "Suck My Left One." *Pussy Whipped* (Kill Rock Stars, 1992, prod. Stuart Hallerman) keeps the rage intact but adds a bit of studio polish. *Reject All American* (Kill Rock Stars, 1996, prod. John Goodmanson) features greater songwriting contributions from all the band members, though Hanna's remain the standouts.

Jim Cummer

Birthday Party

Formed in 1980 in Melbourne, Australia. Disbanded in 1983.

Nick Cave, vocals; Mick Harvey, guitar, drums, keyboard; Rowland S. Howard, guitar; Tracey Pew, bass (1980-81); Phil Calvert, drums (1980-82); Barry Adamson, bass (1982-83)

The Birthday Party was born out of Cave and Harvey's Boys Next Door, which was formed by the two while at a Melbourne boarding school in the late 70s. That band released a single and an EP before moving to London and changing their name to Birthday Party. Under this deceivingly tame name, Birthday Party created some of the darkest, most violent and raucous music of the time. Cave's poetic yet disturbing lyrics often dealt with love, death and religion, themes that would continue throughout his career. Their reputation and live shows matched their abbrasive, perverse sound and garnered a cult following of British punks. Their first album, *Prayers on Fire*, received critical and popular acclaim. The band's legendary excesses led to personnel changes (bassist Pew was imprisoned for drug and alcohol charges) and they moved to Berlin after recording their second album, *Junkyard*. In Berlin, they experimented with post-punk acts like Lydia Lunch and Einsturzende Neubauten and recorded an EP, *The Bad Seed*. However, continued drug and personal problems led to the band's demise while recording their final album, *Mutiny!* All of the band members went on to other projects with Nick Cave and the Bad Seeds faring the best.

what to buy: Although purists might disagree, *Hits*, (4AD, 1992, prod. N/A) a sort of best-of compilation from a band that had no actual hits, provides an excellent representation of their blistering punk/blues/noise assualt.

what to buy next: *Prayers on Fire*, (4AD, 1981, prod. N/A) the BP's debut, features Caves's spooky, howling vocals supported by Pew's throbbing bass and Richardson's fire and brimstone guitar fury; it burst onto the post-punk scene with a reckless abandon not seen since the Stooges.

the rest: *Junkyard* (4AD, 1982) *Drunk on the Pope's Blood EP* (4AD, 1982) *Mutiny! EP* (4AD, 1983) *It's Still Living* (Missing Link, 1985) *A Collection* (Missing Link, 1985)

The Birthday Party: The Peel Sessions (Strange Fruit, 1987) *Hee Haw* (4AD, 1980/1989)

worth searching for: Of their many EPs, *The Bad Seed* (4AD, 1983) is the best, showcasing the band at its peak shortly before its demise.

The Sex Pistols

The Stooges, The Doors

see also: *Nick Cave and the Bad Seeds*

Christopher Scanlon

Elvin Bishop

Born Oct. 21, 1942 in Tulsa, Okla.

To many, Bishop is "Fooled Around and Fell in Love," the 1976 smash that put his name in the Top 40—for a second. The real story is that Bishop is one of the most gifted and tasteful guitarists to come out of the 60s blues-rock movement. Paul Butterfield, a college buddy from the University of Chicago, invited Bishop to join his Paul Butterfield Blues Band—which also included another hotshot guitarist, Michael Bloomfield. Bishop wisely accepted a back seat and soaked up some of Bloomfield's magic; when Bloomfield left, Bishop's playing on 1967's *The Resurrection of Pigboy Crabshaw* was transcendent, and he opted to go solo afterwards. "Fooled Around..." was something of an aberration; Bishop's path has stayed fairly honest to the blues, and he remains an exemplary stylist and a quiet senior statesman of the scene.

what to buy: *Tulsa Shuffle: The Best of Elvin Bishop* (Epic/Legacy, 1994, prod. Various) compiles tracks from Bishop's first four solo albums, including the monster instrumental "Hogbottom" and soul-styled raver "Be With Me." *Sure Feels Good: The Best of Elvin Bishop* (Polydor, 1979/1992, prod. Various) gets you "Fooled Around..." and the cream from his 1974-79 albums.

what to buy next: Bishop is still alive and well—as evidenced on *Don't Let the Bossman Get You Down,* (Alligator, 1991/1993, prod. ??) the best of the yeoman-like blues albums he's released during the 90s.

what to avoid: *Let it Flow* (PolyGram Special Products, date N/A) WOOF! a skimpy best-of that's an insulting redundancy.

the rest: *Crabshaw Rising: The Best of Elvin Bishop* (Epic, 1972/1996) *Back to Back* (K-Tel, 1992) *Big Fun* (Alligator, 1993) *Ace in the Hole* (Alligator, 1994)

worth searching for: Of his many guest appearances, check out Bishop's playing on James Cotton's *Three Harp Boogie* (Tomato, 1994), which includes a rootsy acoustic set recorded in 1963.

Canned Heat, Jimmie Vaughan, Stevie Ray Vaughan

B.B. King, Albert King, Freddie King, Albert Collins, Elmore James, Lightnin' Hopkins

see also: *Paul Butterfield Blues Band*

Gary Graff

Bjork /Sugarcubes

Formed 1987 in Reykjavik, Iceland. Disbanded 1992.

Bjork Gudmundsdottir, vocals, keyboards; Einar Orn, vocals, trumpet; Bragi Olafsson, bass; Thor Eldon, guitar; Margaret (Magga) Ornolfsdottir, keyboards; Sigtryggur (Siggi) Baldursson, drums

The Sugarcubes promoted the primal anarchy embraced by U.S. groups like the Pixies; that they hailed from Iceland only made the music that much more exotic to American ears. Punctuated by a meandering, atonal trumpet and stellar Neanderthal drumming, the 'cubes produced a feisty mix of dance-oriented rhythms and glowering Teutonic moodiness (imagine Hitler Youth on Ecstasy.) Making it all accessible was lead singer Bjork, an imp of a young woman whose intoxicating vocal range extends from cooing child to growling animal and everything in between. A promising debut album gave way to bland self-imitation, although the group's third and, to date, final album showed evidence that it had learned how to harness its erratic talent. The Sugarcubes' breakup in 1992 seems to have done well by Bjork, whose solo career has shown moments of buoyant and inspired strokes of genius. The group reformed without Bjork in 1995 but nothing has been heard from it yet.

what to buy: *Stick Around for Joy* (Elektra, 1992, prod. Paul Fox) is the band's most accessible and, true to its name, happiest sounding album, packed end to end with lively and tuneful dance pop. Producer Fox lightens up the group's sound, revealing inspired rhythmic grooves ("Hit," "Lucky Night," and "Walkabout") while providing a perfect showcase for Bjork's amazing wail of a voice. Bjork's appropriately titled solo premiere,*Debut* (Elektra, 1993, prod. Bjork and Nellee Hooper) , is a sonically beautiful work that finds the young singer stretching artfully into jazz-funk stylings ("Big Time Sensuality") and haunting torch songs ("Venus As a Boy"). Bjork scored a minor hit here with the whimsical "Human Behavior."

what to buy next: The Sugarcubes' debut,*Life's Too Good,* (Elektra, 1988, prod. R. Shulman and Derek Birkett) , is a satisfying bite of everything that made the group so exciting: punchy rhythms, inspired singing, and a compelling sense of the surreal. "Motorcrash" and "Blue Eyed Pop" are fun and funky, while "Birthday" is simply the most gorgeous piece of debauchery ever wrought in the name of rock music.

what to avoid: The Sugarcubes' unenthusiastic sophomore effort,*Here Today, Tomorrow, Next Week!,* (Elektra, 1989, prod. Derek Birkett) has none of its predecessor's charm and far too much of Einar Orn's affected, "Velcome to Shprockets"-style utterances—though two of the songs, "Regina" and "Planet," are gems.

the rest: Sugarcubes: *It's-It* (Elektra, 1992) Bjork: *Post* (Elektra, 1995, prod. Various)

worth searching for: *Illur Arfur!* (One Little Indian, 1989) offers the same tracks as the group's second album but sung in Icelandic. A fascinating listen. Issued abroad under the group's native name, Sykurmolarnir.

Dee-Lite, Pizzicato 5, Shelleyan Orphan

Cocteau Twins, Dead Can Dance, Joy Division, Siouxsie and the Banshees

Christopher Scapelliti

Frank Black

Born Charles Michael Kitteridge Thompson IV, 1965 in Los Angeles, Calif.

Black Francis, the former frontman for the Pixies, went solo in 1993, inverting his pseudonym along the way to become Frank Black. In this latest guise, Black emphasizes the innovative melodicism that was always lurking in the dark background of the Pixies' music. While his lyrics continue to draw from such murky references as spies, outer space, UFOs and (as always) Los Angeles, he's more focused musically, playing up his finely tuned pop sensibilities on his first two solo efforts. As if to contradict all expectations, Black returned to the post-punk fray with his 1995 release, *The Cult of Ray.* One can't even begin to guess where he'll go next.

what to buy: Black put all of his pop music references into one basket on his eponymous debut, *Frank Black.* (4AD/Elektra, 1993, prod. Eric Drew Feldman and Frank Black) A few songs ("Los Angeles" and "Ten Percenter") harken back to the full-throttle rage of the Pixies, but most of the tunes show a surprising range of 1960s influences, including Bowie, Lennon and Brian Wilson.

what to buy next: Clocking in at over an hour, *Teenager of the Year* (4AD/Elektra, 1994, prod. Eric Drew Feldman, Frank Black and Al Clay) is an ambitious and frequently restrained followup. Black keeps his erratic tendencies in check and delivers back-to-back beauties with "(I Want to Live on An) Abstract Plain," "Calistan," "Speedy Marie" and "Headache."

the rest: *The Cult of Ray* (American Recordings, 1995) *The Black Sessions/Live in Paris* (Anoise Annoys, 1995)

worth searching for: Black is joined by members of Teenage Fanclub for *The John Peel Sessions,* (Strange Fruit, 1995, prod. Ted de Bono) a terrific four-song EP featuring punked-out versions of Del Shannon's "Sister Isabel" and the Otis Blackwell chestnut "Handyman."

Dinosaur Jr., the Feelies, the Flaming Lips, Nirvana, Sonic Youth, Throwing Muses, Belly, Weezer, the Lemonheads, the Sugarcubes, Husker Du, the Pixies, Jonny Polonsky

Dick Dale & His Del-Tones, the Ventures, Brian Wilson, the Beatles, the Velvet Underground, David Bowie, Iggy Pop, the Ramones, Jonathan Richman, Iggy Pop

see also: *The Pixies*

Christopher Scapelliti

The Black Crowes

Formed 1988 in Atlanta, Ga.

Chris Robinson, vocals; Rich Robinson, guitar; Jeff Cease guitar (1988-91); Johnny Colt, bass; Steve Gorman, drums; Marc Ford, guitar (1991-present), Eddie Harsch, keyboards (1991-present)

The Black Crowes made a stunningly confident, complete debut with 1990's *Shake Your Money Maker.* The fact that the group didn't seem to have an original musical idea was irrelevant in the face of seeing a young band with such good taste in who to rip off (the underrated Faces and Humble Pie, along with the Rolling Stones) and enough moxie to credibly take Otis Redding's "Hard to Handle" to the top of the charts during an era dominated by soulless corporate rock. Since then, the Crowes have gone their own way, veering into hard rock briefly before delving whole-hog into trippy, flowing jams. Ironically, as the group has become more original, it hasn't always remained as memorable; the songwriting has grown spotty, with not enough tunes that resonate as much as *Moneymaker* gems such as "Twice as Hard," "Seeing Things" and "She Talks to Angels." The Crowes seem to be in it for the long haul, however, and there is every reason to believe that the band has plenty of good music left in it.

what to buy: *Shake Your Money Maker* (Def American, 1990, prod. George Drakoulias) won't win any points for originality, but who needs 'em, when you've got this much swagger, energy and soul? *Three Snakes and One Charm* (American, 1996, prod. Jack Joseph Puig and the Black Crowes) finds the band getting ever-more psychedelic, stretching out into straight funk, loping country and searing Southern rock. An ambitious success.

what to buy next: *Amorica* (American, 1994, prod. Jack Joseph Puig and the Black Crowes) sounds great, with malleable song structures and a smooth, flowing sound that includes mandolin and pedal steel. But there are few songs here that stick in the cranium. An in-your-face, bone-dry production makes *The Southern Harmony and Musical Companion* (Def American, 1992, prod. George Drakoulias and the Black Crowes) a bit harder to listen to all the way through, but it has plenty of high points.

worth searching for: *Grits 'n Gravy*, (American, 1994, prod. George Drakoulias, Jack Joseph Puig and the Black Crowes) a 13-song promotional sampler from the Crowes' first three albums.

▶▶ Blues Traveler, Widespread Panic, Primal Scream, the Quireboys

◀◀ The Allman Brothers Band, the Faces, Humble Pie, Led Zeppelin, Little Feat, the Rolling Stones, Rod Stewart, War, Aerosmith

Alan Paul

Black Flag

Formed 1977 in Hermosa Beach, Calif. Disbanded 1986.

Greg Ginn, guitar; Charles (Chuck) Dukowski, bass (1977-84); Kira Roessler, bass (1983-86); C'el, bass (1986); Dez Cadena, guitar (1981-83); Robo, drums (1978-83); Keith Morris, vocals (1977-78); Chavo Pederast, vocals (1978-81); Henry Rollins (born Henry Garfield), vocals (1981-86); Brian Migdol, drums (1977-78); Bill Stevenson, drums (1981, 1983-85); Emil, drums (1982); Chuck Biscuits, drums (1982); Anthony Martinez, drums (1985-86)

The original purveyors of the DIY work ethic, Black Flag was formed in 1977 by Ginn, who founded the SST label as a vehicle to release his band's material. The group's loud, testosterone-laced attack made Black Flag the country's premier hardcore punk band during the early 80s. The band went through a series of vocalists, including Keith Morris, who went on to form the Circle Jerks, before Washington, D.C., punker Rollins jumped on board—literally, by leaping on stage during a show. His would be the career that took off after Black Flag called it quits.

what to buy: After wandering into jazz and other styles, Black Flag returned to its abrasive punk roots for *In My Head* (SST, 1985, prod. Dave Tarling, Greg Ginn and Bill Stevenson) The lyrics' unyielding attitude is expressed with the rage of an animal ready to pounce on its prey. This is Black Flag at its finest.

what to buy next: The live album *Who's Got the 10 1/2?* (SST, 1986, prod. Greg Ginn) captures the concert spirit of Black Flag, including Rollins' vein-popping intensity and angst-ridden lyrics and Ginn's crafty guitar work.

what to avoid: *Family Man* (SST, 1984, prod. Spot) is an oddity, half group instrumentals and half Rollins reading poetry—before he became a proficient spoken word performer.

the rest: *Damaged I* (SST, 1981) *Everything Went Black* (SST, 1983) *The First Four Years* (SST, 1984) *Live '84* (SST 1984) *My War* (SST, 1984) *Slip It In* (SST, 1984) *Loose Nut* (SST, 1985) *Wasted ... Again* (SST, 1987)

worth searching for: Rollins' journals from his days in Black Flag, published as "Get in the Van" (2.13.61, 1994)

solo outings:

Greg Ginn: My War (SST, 1984) *In My Head* (SST, 1985) *Let's Get Real, Real Gone for a Change* (SST, 1986) *Gone II, But Never Too Gone!* (SST, date N/A) *Who's Got the 10 1/2?* (SST, date N/A) *Getting Even* (Cruz, 1993) *Dick* (Cruz, 1993) *Let it Burn (Because I Don't Live)* (Cruz, 1994) *Belly to the Ground* (Cruz, 1994) *Red Dog* (New Alliance, 1994) *All The Dirt That's Fit to Print* (SST, 1994) *Just Do It* (SST EP, 1995) *House* (SST, 1995)

▶▶ Circle Jerks, Green Day, the Offspring, NOFX, Pennywise, Wayne Kramer

◀◀ The Ramones, the Sex Pistol, MC5, the Stooges

see also: *Henry Rollins, Circle Jerks*

Christina Fuoco

Black 47

Formed 1989 in New York City, N.Y.

Larry Kirwan, guitar, keyboards, percussion, lead vocals; Chris Byrne,

uilleann pipes, tin whistle, bodhran, vocals; Fred Parcells, trombone, tin whistle, vocals; Geoffrey Blythe, saxaphone, clarinet;Thomas Hamlin, drums, percussion; Andrew Goodsight, bass (1995-present); Kevin Jenkins bass, (1993-1995), David Conrad, bass, 1985-1993)

Black 47 is an Irish-American band combining the attitude of the Big Apple with the pride of Ireland. Essentially an extremely rowdy bar band in the best sense, Black 47 is so named for the peak year of the Irish famine in the 19th century. Larry Kirwan, erstwhile playwright hailing from the Emerald Island, and Chris Byrne, a New York City cop with a passion for Irish traditional, rap, and punk music, shared several pints at the hole-in-the-wall Paddy Reilly's while complaining about the dismal state of modern music. At some point that evening, Black 47 was born, and soon thereafter, Paddy Reilly's became the band's home. Kirwin and company's reputation for original music and a confrontational attitude soon attracted a loyal following in the city. Kirwin's songs, crowded with lyrics and ecstatic horn arrangments, tended toward the rousing anthem as the band wailed like a Memphis soul band trapped in the body of an Irish folk singer. The band's first recording was a self-produced independent release that was basically sold by hand as the band toured Irish hotspots around the country, always landing back at Paddy's. After catching the band one evening, Ric Ocasek volunteered to polish that first album, and *Fire of Freedom* was completed in a mere three weeks. The CD caught the attention of the New York media, and soon the band found itself a rising star, while still fulfilling its dates at Paddy's. Jerry Harrison arrived for production duty on the second album, and appearances on the "Tonight Show" and other national media soon led to more widespread recognition. Still a regular at Paddy's, Black 47 recently released their third major label album.

what to buy: The first release is the essential Black 47 album. *Fire of Freedom* (SBK Records, 1992, prod. Ric Ocasek and Larry Kirwin) ♪♪♪ is Celtic to its core, while still strongly suggesting the band's American roots. Songs range from the swing of "Funky Ceili" to the rabble rousing pint raising of "James Connelly." While the production seems a bit crowded and thin, the band's exhuberant personality is well captured. The independent label version of this album, eponomously titled, contains a slightly different song list. An EP version of the SBK album also is available, with a selection of songs from both versions of the first release.

what to buy next: *Green Suede Shoes* (SBK Records, 1996, prod. Larry Kirwin) ♪♪♪ returns to the band's pub roots, supplying a sweaty, passionate sound supporting the usual free the Irish or we'll really bang on the bodhran anthems ("Bobby Sands MP").

the rest: *Home of the Brave* (SBK Records, 1994) ♪♪

▶▶ Goats Don't Shave

◀◀ The Pogues, Enemy Orchard, Them, Bruce Springsteen, Booker T and the Mgs

Martin Connors

Black Grape

See: Happy Mondays

Black Oak Arkansas

Formed in Black Oak, Ark., 1969. Disbanded 1980.

Jim (Dandy) Mangrum, vocals; Harvey Jett, guitar (1969-74); James Henderson, guitar (1974-80); Stanley Knight, guitar, fiddle and saxophone (1969-1976); Jack Holder, guitar (1976-80); Rickie Reynolds, guitar (1969-76); Greg Reding, guitar (1976-80); Pat Daugherty, bass (1969-76); Andy Tanas, bass (1976-80); Wayne Evans, drums (1969-75); Thomas Aldrich, drums (1975-76); Joel Williams, drums (1976-80); Ruby Starr, vocals (1973-80)

Before Lynyrd Skynyrd or .38 Special began making their cases on the radio, Black Oak Arkansas offered the purest distillation of 100-proof boogie ever produced south of the Mason-Dixon line. Lead singer Mangrum was a David Lee Roth-Ted Nugent wildman, whose rough, good ol' boy holler paved every three-guitar monster riff with tar and gravel. The group's rough-and-ready attitude resulted in some good-and-greasy party music, although the occasional dip into the murky pools of Southern mysticism suggests the group was probably hoping for greater credibility. The band's music gained considerable breadth when Mangrum brought in Starr, a gutsy vocalist whose saucy come-ons made a good foil for his sexed-up persona. With Starr in tow, the group solidified its name with a hit remake of LaVern Baker's "Jim Dandy." Extensive touring (50 weeks per year) took its toll on the members, resulting in numerous personnel changes through the late 70s. BOA called it quits in 1980 after Mangrum suffered a heart attack; after recovering, he continued with solo work but never re-established his presence after BOA. *Hot & Nasty: The Best of Black Oak Arkansas* (WEA/Atlantic/Rhino, 1992, prod. Various) ♪♪♪♪ picks the plums from BOA's erratic catalog, from the hits ("Hot & Nasty," "Jim Dandy," "Strong Enough to be Gentle") to a fascinating selection of bizarre covers such as the Byrds' "(So You Want to be a)

Rock & Roll Star" and the Beatles' "Taxman." *Jim Dandy* (WEA/Atlantic/Rhino, 1996, prod. Various) pares things down to 10 essential tracks, while *High on the Hog,* (WEA/Atlantic/Rhino, 1973, prod. Ed Barton, Ron Albert and Howie Albert) the album that put BOA on the map, remains in print to demonstrate the high-livin', hard-drinkin', good-lovin' hellraising at the heart of BOA.

Christopher Scapelliti

Black Sabbath

Formed 1967 in Birmingham, England

Ozzy Osbourne, vocals (1967-79); Ronnie James Dio, vocals (1979-82, 1991-92); Tony Iommi, guitar; Bill Ward, drums (1967-81, 1982-85); Terry "Geezer" Butler, bass (1967-85, 1991-95); Vinnie Appice, drums (1981-82, 1991-93); Dave Donato, vocals (1982-83); Ian Gillan, vocals (1983-84); Glenn Hughes, vocals (1985-87); Geoff Nichols, keyboards, (1985-89, 1990); Dave Spitz, bass (1985-87, 1989); Eric Singer, drums (1985-87); Tony Martin, vocals (1987-91, 1993-present); Bev Bevan, drums (1987); Bob Daisley, bass (1987); Cozy Powell, drums (1989-91); Lawrence Cottle, bass (1989); Neil Murray, bass (1990); Bob Rondinelli, drums (1993-present)

Ominous, menacing and deafeningly loud, Black Sabbath was in many ways the prototypical heavy metal band. While much of the band's infamy centered on Osbourne's pseudo-Satanic howlings (he insisted the band's lyrics were anti-Lucifer), it was Iommi's narcotic guitar work the made up the backbone of the Sabbath sound: if not for his dark, fuzz-toned riffs and solos, speed, thrash and death metal would never exist, and grunge would still be a synonym for grime. Sabbath created some truly devastating metal with Osbourne, but the singer left in the late 70s to launch a succesful solo career. The band stayed afloat for awhile by recruiting ex-Rainbow singer Dio, but after he quit Sabbath became self-parody with a revolving door lineup. At least four vocalists (including ex-Deep Purple wailer Ian Gillan) tried to replace the Great Oz, and a battalion of drummers and bassists came and went. The only constant has been Iommi, who seems more than willing to slog away under the Sabbath mantle as long as the headbangers will take it.

what to buy: Metal doesn't get more frightening than *Paranoid,* (Warner Bros., 1971, prod. Roger Bain) which features the title track and "Iron Man." *Master of Reality* (Warner Bros., 1971, prod. Roger Bain) was another brilliant skull-crusher, featuring the timeless "Children of the Grave" and "Sweet Leaf." The 16-song best-of, *We Sold Our Soul For Rock And Roll* (Warner Bros., 1976, prod. Various) is a thorough introductory to early Sabbath.

what to buy next: *Black Sabbath* (Warner Bros., 1970, prod. Roger Bain) the band's opening salvo, includes the wicked psycho-blooze instrumental "The Wizard." On *Sabbath Bloody Sabbath* (Warner Bros., 1973, prod. Black Sabbath) the band successfully mixed its stun-gun guitars with synthesizers. If Dio's faux operatic wailing doesn't turn you off, *Heaven and Hell* (Warner Bros., 1980, prod. Martin Birch) made it seem as if there was indeed life after Ozzy. Briefly.

what to avoid: *Seventh Star* (Warner Bros., 1986, prod. Jeff Glixman) WOOF! and *Headless Cross* (I.R.S., 1989, prod. Tony Iommi and Cozy Powell) WOOF! were Black Sabbath albums in name only as Iommi and his faceless cohorts sank lower then Hades itself.

the rest: *Black Sabbath, Vol. 4* (Warner Bros., 1972) *Sabotage* (Warner Bros., 1975) *Technical Ecstasy* (Warner Bros., 1976) *Never Say Die!* (Warner Bros., 1978) *The Mob Rules* (Warner Bros., 1981) *Live Evil* (Warner Bros. 1982) *The Eternal Idol* (Warner Bros. 1987) *T Y R* (I.R.S.,1990) *Dehumanizer* (Reprise, 1992) *Cross Purposes* (I.R.S., 1994)

worth searching for: *Between Heaven and Hell* (Castle, 1995, prod. Various), a British collection—compiled by Osbourne and Butler—that culls the cream of the Osbourne-Dio years.

▶▶ Soundgarden, Nirvana, Metallica, Megadeth, Anthrax

◀◀ Cream, Muddy Waters, Bela Lugosi

Thor Christensen

Black Uhuru

Formed 1979 in Jamaica

Duckie Simpson, vocals; Michael Rose, lead vocals (1979-86); Puma Jones, vocals (1979-87); Don Carlos, lead vocals (1987-present); Junior Reid, vocals (1986-87); Garth Dennis, vocals (1987-present); Sly Dunbar, drums (1979-86); Robbie Shakespeare, bass (1979-86)

With incisive vocal harmonies, a legendary rhythm section and excellent songwriting, Black Uhuru—reggae's first Grammy winner—was one of the biggest post-Bob Marley acts of the 80s. The only constant through several incarnations of the vocal trio has been harmony singer Simpson. Black Uhuru peaked with lead singer and songwriter Rose and harmonist

Jones; Dunbar and Shakespeare—known best as producers and session players—were equal members of the group during the Rose years, and their skills helped Black Uhuru become a dub pioneer. Still, the essential vocal drive of the group is often lost in that highly instrumental reggae offshoot.

what to buy: *Red* (Mango, 1981, prod. Sly Dunbar and Robbie Shakespeare) 🦴🦴🦴🦴🦴 is the group's slam-dunk best. All the songs are written or co-written by Rose, and the high harmony singing on "Youth of Eglington" shows what made the group great. There's more of the same on the superbly produced *Chill Out,* (Island, 1982, Island, prod. Sly Dunbar and Robbie Shakespeare) 🦴🦴🦴🦴 with a slicker sound and a higher profile for the rhythm section.

what to buy next: *The Dub Factor* (Mango, 1983, prod. Sly Dunbar and Robbie Shakespeare) 🦴🦴🦴🦴 re-works past material with tricky dub effects, but it keeps you dancing.

what to avoid: The title gives you a hint; *Brutal* (Ras, 1986, prod. Various) 🦴½ was the only outing by short-lived lead singer Reid. The dub version of this was better.

the rest: *Sensimilla* (Mango, 1980) 🦴🦴🦴🦴 *Tear It Up—Live* (Mango, 1982) 🦴🦴🦴🦴 *Brutal Dub* (Ras, 1986) 🦴🦴🦴 *Guess Who's Coming To Dinner* (Heartbeat, 1987) 🦴🦴🦴🦴 *Black Uhuru* (Mango, 1989) 🦴🦴🦴🦴 *Now* (Mesa, 1990) 🦴🦴🦴 *Now Dub* (Rhino, 1990) 🦴🦴🦴 *Black Sounds of Freedom* (Shanachie, 1990) 🦴🦴🦴½ *Iron Storm Dub* (Mesa, 1992) 🦴🦴🦴 *Mystical Truth Dub* (Mesa, 1993) 🦴🦴🦴½ *Liberation—The Island Anthology* (Mango, 1993) 🦴🦴🦴🦴½

worth searching for: *Iron Storm* (Mesa, 1991, prod. Black Uhuru) 🦴🦴🦴 and *Mystical Truth* (Mesa, 1992, prod. Black Uhuru) 🦴🦴🦴🦴 show these guys can still put out quality, though no longer groundbreaking, reggae.

solo outings:

Sly & Robbie: Rhythm Killers (Island, 1987) 🦴🦴🦴🦴

⏩ Fugees, UB40

⏪ Burning Spear, The Wailers

Lawrence Gabriel

The Blackgirls /Dish

Formed 1986 in Raleigh, N.C. Disbanded 1990.

Dana Kletter, piano, vocals; Eugenia Lee, guitar, vocals; Hollis Brown, violin, backup vocals

Truly, the blackgirls was years ahead of is time. Where the trio's gothic, women-on-the-verge-of-nervous-breakdowns chamber pop once seemed uncomfortably weird and atonal, nowadays it sounds perfect for radio segues between Tori Amos and Beck. Most blackgirls songs proceed at a jittery pace driven by Kletter's piano, with Brown's Celtic-influenced fiddle providing atmosphere. Kletter's rich, piercing voice is the group's best instrument, (she sang backup on Hole's *Live Through This*) although Lee's nervous jabbering is more striking (in both bad and good ways). *Procedure* (Mammoth, 1989, prod. Joe Boyd) 🦴🦴🦴🦴 is the definitive blackgirls album, a series of wild mood swings. Lee sounds almost unhinged ("I am a loser" and "I am waiting for you to realize that I'm alive" are just two of her declarations), while Kletter comes across as calm in the face of rising panic. Dish, Kletter's new band, adds rocked-up guitar and drums to the basic blackgirls sound on the brilliant *Boneyard Beach.* (Interscope, 1995, prod. John Agnello) 🦴🦴🦴🦴

the rest: *Speechless* (Black Park/Tom Tom EP, 1987) 🦴🦴🦴 *Happy* (Mammoth, 1991) 🦴🦴🦴½

David Menconi

Ruben Blades

Born July 16. 1948, in Panama City, Panama

A Harvard-trained lawyer and movie star, the singing Blades emerged with the mid-70s Fania label that popularized much of the New York salsa scene. After a stint with trombonist Willie Colon, Blades eschewed the jazz influence in salsa for a more pop-oriented sound incorporating synthesizers and working with the band Son/Seis Del Solar. Blades' music is hugely popular among Latin Americans due to his lyrics, which peer in on some the sadder realities of life in those areas; he's closer to the Nuevo Cancion (New Song) movement of Latino leftists than to the exuberant party salsa of New York. For non-Spanish speakers Blades always provides translations of his songs with the albums. Major movie roles in "Crossover Dreams," "The Milagro Beanfield Wars" and others has given him a public profile well beyond music. And his social concerns have taken him into politics; Blades came in second in 1994 elections for Panama's presidency, which is better than Joe Walsh ever did in his periodic campaigns to run the U.S..

what to buy: Blades took a piercing look at hard lives on *Buscando America (Searching For America)*. (Elektra, 1984, prod.

Ruben Blades) ✪✪✪✪ "Decisions" spotlights a pregnant teenage girl and a philandering husband. "Disappearances" depicts loved ones searching for disappeared family members, and the title song despairs that the promise of America has been kidnapped by dictators. Throughout, Blades avoids preachiness by letting his characters tell their own stories. The Colon-Blades collaboration *Siembra* (Fania, 1978, prod. Willie Colon) ✪✪✪✪ is a more traditional salsa scorcher, with the Fania Crew providing grooves and Colon's trombone adding a jazzy touch. This disc is legendary among salsa fans.

what to buy next: *Nothing But the Truth* (Elektra, 1988, prod. Various) ✪✪✪ is Blades' first all-English outing, with songs written by Sting, Lou Reed and Elvis Costello. Not one for the salsa fans, but it merits listening.

what to avoid: *Agua De Luna (Moon Water)* (Elektra, 1987, prod. Ruben Blades) ✪✪ features less-than-memorable arrangements and conceptual lyrics that seldom feel lived in by the songs' characters.

the rest: *Crossover Dreams* soundtrack (Elektra, 1986) ✪✪✪ *Antecedente* (Elektra, 1988) ✪✪✪ *Escenas* (Elektra, 1985) ✪✪ *Amor Y Control* (Sony Discos, 1992) ✪✪✪✪

worth searching for: *Ruben Blades and Son de Solar . . . Live* (Elektra, 1990, prod. Ruben Blades) ✪✪✪✪ features a smoking dance set still driven by the salsa ethos of his earlier work.

▶▶ Victor Manuel, Jon Secada, Robbie Robertson

◀◀ Celia Cruz, Fania All Stars

Lawrence Gabriel

Blake Babies

Formed 1986 in Boston, Mass. Disbanded 1991.

Juliana Hatfield, vocals, bass, guitar, piano (1986-90); John Strohm, guitar, vocals; Freda (Boner) Love, drums; Andrew Mayer, bass (1986); Seth White, bass (1987); Evan Dando, bass, (1988); Mike Leahy, guitar (1990-91)

Ironically, Juliana Hatfield was studying voice at Berklee College of Music when she united with Indiana natives Boner and Strohm (who's had two stints as a Lemonhead, first on drums and later on guitar, as well as time with Evan Dando in the Hatin' Spores, a Black Sabbath cover band) to form Blake Babies, whose sound was largely defined by Hatfield's erratic, seemingly untrained singing (even more apparently strained on stage than on record). She frequently swerved out of tune but conveyed utter sincerity and a newly emerging female toughness epitomized by the bitter, spit-out lyrics of Sunburn's "I'm Not Your Mother" and "Sanctify's" line "kick a boy and teach him how to cry." Hatfield's departure in 1990 effectively ended the group; she went on to a more celebrated solo career, while Boner and Strohm went on to other bands—Antenna, Velo-Deluxe and Mysteries of Life.

what to buy: The album that broke the group through to a sizable audience, *Sunburn*(Mammoth, 1990, prod. Gary Smith) ✪✪✪✪✪ is chock-full of great songs, including "Out There," "Star," "Look Away" and "Train." Strohm's guitar sound—mixing electric sinew and acoustic jangle—is at its apex here.

what to buy next: On CD, *Earwig* (Mammoth, 1989, prod. Gary Smith) ✪✪✪✪ incorporates the album of that name plus the *Slow Learners* EP recorded the previous year. *Earwig* has the same merits as *Sunburn* but is slightly less consistent. A rowdy cover of the Stooges' "Loose" fits Hatfield's persona well. *Rosy Jack World*, (Mammoth, 1991, prod. Gary Smith, Paul Mahern and Blake Babies) ✪✪✪ a five-song EP, was a worthy swan song highlighted by Hatfield's "Nirvana" (a tribute to Cobain and company before most of the world had heard of Nirvana) and a brilliant cover of the Grass Roots' "Temptation Eyes."

the rest: *Nicely, Nicely*(Chew-bud, 1987/Mammoth, 1984) ✪✪ *Innocence and Experience* (Mammoth, 1993) ✪✪✪

▶▶ Jill Sobule, Lemonheads

◀◀ R.E.M., Keith Richards, Buffalo Tom, Velvet Underground, Feelies

see also: *Juliana Hatfield, Antenna/Velo-Deluxe/Mysteries of Life*

Steve Holtje

The Blasters

Formed 1979 in Los Angeles, Calif. Disbanded 1986.

Phil Alvin, vocals, guitar; Dave Alvin, guitar; John Bazz, bass; Bill Bateman, drums; Gene Taylor, piano

The Blasters may have been at the forefront of the late 70s/early 80s rockabilly revival, but that's not the whole story. It's instructive to remember that Blasters were contemporaries with X and Dwight Yoakam, and equally conversant with both. The group combined the energy of the burgeoning L.A. punk scene with a solid base in rock 'n' roll history and a taste for R&B and country. Theirs was not a simple revivalism, but a genuine expression of a shared musical sensibility that drew on, but didn't ape, Jerry Lee Lewis, Big Joe Turner and many others. Unfortunately only two of the group's albums are in print today. *The Blasters* (Slash/Warner Bros., 1981, prod. the Blasters) is the group's major label debut, and also its best single effort, thanks to such memorable songs as "Marie Marie," "So Long Baby Goodbye" and the genre-defining "American Music." A definitive overview, *The Blasters Collection* (Slash/Warner Bros., 1990, prod. the Blasters and Jeff Eyrich) is the place to start. True believers will want to search out the bands other out-of-print albums on vinyl: *Over There: Live at the Venue, London,* (Slash/Warner Bros., 1982, prod. the Blasters) a jumping live recording; *Non Fiction,* (Slash/Warner Bros., 1983, prod. the Blasters) an over-reaching stab at socially conscious topics; and *Hard Line,* (Slash/Warner Bros., 1985, prod. Jeff Eyrich) a slight return to form. The group's independently released debut, *American Music* (Rollin' Rock, 1980, prod. The Blasters) is a highly sought-after collectors item.

solo outings:

Phil Alvin: Un "Sung Stories" (Slash, 1986) *County Fair 2000* (HighTone, 1994)

see also: *Dave Alvin*

Daniel Durchholz

Blind Melon

Formed 1990 in Los Angeles, Calif.

Shannon Hoon, vocals (died October 21, 1995); Rogers Stevens, guitar; Christopher Thorn, guitar; Brad Smith, bass; Glen Graham, drums

Blind Melon's mix of hippie style and moderately hard rock didn't seem to have much of a future until the video for its sprightly single "No Rain," with its indelible image of a bespectacled little girl in a bee costume, took MTV by storm and made the group's debut album, *Blind Melon,* (Capitol, 1992, prod. Rick Parasher) a hit. The first release also includes some heavy jams and the piercing vocals of Hoon, a friend of Guns N' Roses frontman Axl Rose (to whom he was often compared as both singer and prima donna). Hoon and company pursued a more eclectic range of material on their sophomore effort, *Soup,* (Capitol, 1995, prod. Andy Wallace and Blind Melon) the album tanked commercially, however. Sadly, Hoon was found dead of a drug overdose on Blind Melon's tour bus in 1995.

Simon Glickman

Blondie /Deborah Harry, Jimmy Destri

Formed 1975 in New York, N.Y. Disbanded 1983.

Deborah Harry, vocals; Chris Stein, guitar, vocals; Clem Burke, drums; Jimmy Destri, keyboards; Gary Valentine, bass (1975-76), bass; Frank Infante, bass, guitar (1975-83); Nigel Harrison, bass (1978-83)

Blondie's emergence paralleled the rise of punk rock and new wave, but even though the group drew on the energy and attitude of these scenes, it had a more eclectic sensibility, charm galore and pronounced pop songwriting chops. Drawing on British Invasion melodicism, the teenage devotional tunes of Brian Wilson and Phil Spector, horror-movie kitsch and punk's defiant posturing, Blondie crafted a commercially appealing hybrid that rarely lost its subversive edge. After releasing a spiky debut on an indie label, the band signed with Chrysalis Records; its second album for the major, *Parallel Lines,* achieved widespread success on the strength of the disco-pop crossover smash "Heart of Glass." More hits followed—"Dreaming," "Sunday Girl," the Eurodisco "Call Me," the proto-rap gem "Rapture" and the calypso cover "The Tide is High"—and Blondie rode the new wave to megastardom until Chris Stein was struck by a debilitating illness, forcing a breakup. Harry nursed her husband-bandmate back to health and pursued careers as a solo musician and film actor. Blondie's powerful influence on a new generation of bands, notably such Brit-pop outfits as Elastica and Sleeper, has been chronicled via a handful of compilations in the 90s.

what to buy: *Parallel Lines* (Chrysalis, 1978, prod. Mike Chapman) encompasses everything that made the band great: winsome pop, exhilarating guitar rock, danceable grooves, some arty touches and Harry's tough, droll, infinitely appealing persona. "Lines" includes the dance floor standard "Heart of Glass," the rocking "Hangin' on the Telephone" and the luminous pop ditty "Picture This" among its outstanding tracks.

what to buy next: For a collection of the band's hits—which in Blondie's case means some of their finest work—pick up *The Best of Blondie,* (Chrysalis, 1981, prod. Various) which tracks the group's hits through its peak years, including "Call Me" from the "American Gigolo" soundtrack. The more interested should check out the double-CD *The Platinum Collection* (EMI, 1994,. prod. Various) *Eat to the Beat* (Chrysalis, 1979, prod. Mike Chapman) has fewer highlights but is a solid effort and features the engaging pop songs "Dreaming" and "Atomic." *Plastic Letters* (Chrysalis, 1977, prod. Richard Gottehrer) is hit-and-miss and marred occasionally by intrusive synthesizers, but contains several intimations of greatness, notably "(I'm Always Touched by Your) Presence, Dear," "Fan Mail" and "I Didn't Have the Nerve to Say No."

what to avoid: *The Hunter* (Chrysalis, 1982, prod. Mike Chapman) chronicles the band's rapid dissolution amid commercial and other pressures—a sign that not only Blondie but the whole new wave was moribund. Redeemed solely by "Island of Lost Souls," which is available on a few compilations. Steer clear also of Harry's solo efforts *KooKoo* (Chrysalis, 1981, prod. Mike Chapman) and *Def, Dumb, and Blonde* (Sire, 1989, prod. by Mike Chapman), both of which are rife with gimmickry and lack all of Blondie's finesse.

the rest: *Blondie* (Chrysalis, 1976) *Autoamerican* (Chrysalis, 1980) *Once More Into the Bleach* (Chrysalis, 1988) *Blonde and Beyond* (Chrysalis 1993) *The Remix Project* (Chrysalis, 1995)

worth searching for: *The Complete Picture: The Very Best of Deborah Harry and Blondie* (Chrysalis, 1991, prod. Various), a British compilation that, while not as complete as *The Platinum Collection*, is still the best single-CD collection.

solo outings:

Deborah Harry: *Rockbird* (Chrysalis, 1986) *Debravation* (Sire/Reprise, 1993)

Jimmy Destri: *Heart on a Wall* (Chrysalis, 1982)

Checquered Past (Burke and Harrison): *Checquered Past* (EMI, 1984)

Bangles, Elastica, Sleeper, Echobelly, Letters to Cleo

Phil Spector, Brian Wilson, Beatles, Motown, James Brown, Toots and the Maytals, David Bowie, T. Rex, Television, Ramones, Iggy Pop, Grandmaster Flash and the Furious Five, Marilyn Monroe

Simon Glickman

Blood, Sweat and Tears

Formed 1967 in New York, N.Y.

Al Kooper, keyboards, vocals (1967-68); Steve Katz, guitar, vocals (1967-72); Fred Lipsius, saxophone, piano (1967-72); Jim Fielder, bass (1967-73); Bobby Colomby, drums (1967-76); Dick Halligan, keyboards, trombone, flute (1967-72); Randy Brecker, trumpet, flugelhorn (1967-68); Jerry Weiss, trumpet, flugelhorn (1967-68); David Clayton-Thomas, vocals (1968-72, 1974-present); Chuck Winfield, trumpet, flugelhorn (1968-72); Lew Soloff, trumpet, flugelhorn (1968-73); Jerry Hyman, trombone (1968-70); Dave Bargero, trumpet, trombone, tuba (1970-76); Bobby Dole, vocals (1972); Lou Marini, Jr., reeds (1972-73); Georg Wadenius, guitar (1972-75); Jerry Fisher, vocals (1972-74); Tom Malone, trumpet, flugelhorn, trombone, saxophone (1972-73); Ron McClure, bass (1973-75); Jerry LaCroix, vocals, reeds, harmonica (1973-74); Joe Giorgianni, trumpet, flugelhorn (1974-75); and many others over the years

Horns were not strangers to pop music in 1967, but horn sections weren't commonplace in rock 'n' roll bands; there was something Vegas-y and adult about the concept. But Blood, Sweat & Tears sought to change that by bringing its particular big band idea into play as a way to effectively merge styles—in this case rock, jazz and blues. Formed by Blues Project refugees Kooper and Katz, BS&T did succeed in making one landmark album—*Child is Father to the Man*— and in assembling a volatile bunch of artistic personalities that wouldn't be able to stay together much longer than one album. Kooper was one of the first out, bristling over group demands that he step aside from or at least share the vocal spot. This became a trend; over the years BS&T would shift personnel with almost every album, becoming something of a musical lab for hot young players. That is, in fact, how frontman Clayton-Thomas—the voice behind hits such as "Spinning Wheel," "You've Made Me So Very Happy" and "Hi-De-Ho"—runs the band these days. Ironically, BS&T has in fact become what it set out not to be—a family oriented show band playing big, brassy hits in casinos, nightclub and parks.

what to buy: *Child is Father to the Man* (Columbia, 1968, prod. John Simon) is indeed a landmark synthesis of styles and musical sensibilities, winding jazzy horn charts, lush string sections and a soulful rock 'n' roll rhythm section into the same song. It still sounds fresh today though, to be honest, Kooper's thin vocals do keep the album just a wee bit earthbound. *The Best of Blood, Sweat & Tears: What Goes Up!* (Columbia/Legacy, 1995, prod. Various) is a strong two-CD that tracks the group's recordings up to 1976, when drummer Colomby was the final original member to leave the band.

what to buy next: The bands that recorded *Live & Improvised* (Columbia/Legacy, 1991, prod. Bobby Colomby) in 1975 may not resemble the first two or three BS&T lineups at all, but they're still hot ensembles (including Clayton-Thomas and guitarists Mike Stern and Steve Kahn) that wail away on long, jammy versions of some of BS&T's best-known songs.

what to avoid: Things get a little bit out there on *Blood, Sweat*

& *Tears 3*, (Columbia, 1970, prod. Bobby Colomby and Roy Halee) especially on the ill-advised "Symphony for the Devil/Sympathy for the Devil" suite. Mick Jagger at least got a good laugh out of it.

the rest: *Blood, Sweat & Tears* (Columbia, 1969/1988) *BS&T 4* (Columbia, 1971/Legacy, 1996) *Greatest Hits* (Columbia, 1972) *Found Treasures* (Columbia Special Products, 1972) *Live* (Avenue, 1980/1994) *Nuclear Blues* (Avenue, 1980/1995)

worth searching for: The out-of-print *Mirror Image*, (Columbia, 1974) which features an interesting version of the band fronted by full-throated singer Jerry LaCroix, a musician who brings more of a player's sensibility to the group.

Chicago, Michael Bolton, the Brecker Brothers, Stevie Wonder

The Blues Project, the Electric Flag, Duke Ellington, Count Basie, the Beatles, Ike Turner's Kings of Rhythm

see also: *Al Kooper, the Blues Project*

Gary Graff

Luka Bloom

Born Barry Moore, May 23, 1955, in Newbridge, County Kildare, Ireland

Brother of Irish minstrel Christy Moore, Barry Moore began his career in the pubs of Dublin before moving to Washington, D.C. in 1987. There he became Luka Bloom and a favorite on the Eastern Seaboard club circuit, perfecting an intense, explosive rythmic guitar attack and a mix of introspective and socially aware folk-rock. His style owes as much to the romanticism and mysticism of his Irish roots as it does to traditional folk balladeers like Woody Guthrie and modern folksters such as Joan Armatrading and Joni Mitchell. A charismatic, riveting live performer, Bloom's recordings have increasingly emphasized somber melodies and reflective lyrics that only suggest the power he brings on stage. "Life is not a sterile business," he says, explaining his love of performing. "Life is blood and guts and shit and heartbreak, and it's fucked up, and it's a mess. I think you can articulate that better sweating in a club with a wooden instrument in your hand."

what to buy: Although Bloom's debut album is stirring, his second, *The Acoustic Motorbike* (Reprise, 1992, prod. Paul Barrett) is more immediately engaging. Recorded in Ireland with musical assists by brother Christy and the Hothouse Flowers, the album peaks with the passionate Celtic rap of L.L. Cool J's "I Need Love," and the strumming charm of the title song.

what to buy next: Bloom came to national note with *Riverside* (Reprise, 1990, prod. Jeffrey Wood) for good reason: it's a striking first album, notable for its earnestness, melodies, and Irish soul. "You Couldn't Have Come At a Better Time" and "Delirious" immediately grab the listener, while the remainder of the album stands up to repeated listening. Contributors include Irish American fiddle whiz Eileen Ivers and Liam 'O Maonlai on bodhran.

the rest: Turf (Reprise, 1994)

Tracey Chapman, Hothouse Flowers, Sinead O'Connor

Boomtown Rats, The Cowboy Junkies, Joan Armatrading, Susan Vega, Michelle Shocked, Joni Mitchell

Martin Connors

Michael Bloomfield

Born July 28, 1944 in Chicago, Ill. Died Feb. 15, 1981 in San Francisco, Calif.

Look no further than Bloomfield to understand the beginning of the electric blues rock craze that began during the 60s. Expressive and passionate, Bloomfield combined a sincere understanding of blues guitar technique with a signature style. With a solid rock punch, Bloomfield maintained a singular grace and fluidity. He backed Bob Dylan on *Highway 61 Revisited* and was a frequent contributor to James Cotton's recordings. His earliest and perhaps most potent work was as lead guitarist for the Paul Butterfield Blues Band. The debut *The Paul Butterfield Blues Band* and the follow-up *East-West* are landmark recordings. Powerhouse blues, Eastern modal accents and tinges of psychdelia melded for the imaginative and compelling albums. Commercial success followed when he joined Al Kooper for the *Super Session* album, around the same time he formed Electric Flag with ex-Butterfield Blues Band drummer Buddy Miles. Their ambitious debut *A Long Time Comin'* further broadened Bloomfield's musical scope, with a mix of soul, funk, rock and blues. His work after Electric Flag was sporadic and commercially unsuccessful.

what to buy: *Don't Say That I Ain't Your Man!* (Legacy, 1994, comp. Bob Irwin) is a compilation of most of Bloomfield's finest moments.

what to buy next: Though he flaked out and left the session early, *Super Session* (Columbia, 1968, prod. Al Kooper) 🦴🦴🦴🦴 has some of Bloomfield's most relaxed and inspired solos.

what to avoid: *Triumverate,* (Columbia, 1973) 🦴🦴 a slipshod jam session with John Hammond, Jr., and Dr. John.

the rest: *A Long Time Comin'* (Columbia, 1968) 🦴🦴🦴🦴 *Between the Hard Place and the Ground* (Takoma, 1979) 🦴🦴🦴 *Living in the Fast Lane* (ERA, 1992) 🦴🦴🦴 *Old Glory: The Best Of Electric Flag* (Legacy, 1995) 🦴🦴🦴🦴 *The Original Lost Elektra Sessions* (Rhino, 1995) 🦴🦴🦴🦴

worth searching for: *The Trip* (Edsel, 1967) An instrumental soundtrack composed and performed by Electric Flag, it's a wild and untethered collision of styles that works well, particularly given this drug exploitation film's subject matter.

▶▶ Peter Green, Shuggie Otis

◀◀ Robert Johnson, Muddy Waters

see also: *Paul Butterfield Blues Band, Al Kooper*

Patrick McCarty

Blotto

Formed 1979 in Albany, New York. Disbanded 1986.

Blanche Blotto, vocals, keyboards (1979–80); Bowtie Blotto, vocals, guitar; Broadway Blotto, vocals, guitar; Cheese Blotto, vocals, bass; Lee Harvey Blotto, vocals, drums; Sergeant Blotto, vocals, percussion; Chevrolet Blotto, vocals, keyboards (1980–81)

Blotto was the flat-out funniest rock 'n' roll band of all time, with a hilarious live act and sufficient musical prowess to back up the laughs with rockin' pop panache—evidenced by the surf 'n' swim put-on "I Wanna Be a Lifeguard" and the spy thriller knockoff "Goodbye, Mr. Bond." *Collected Works* (One Way, 1994, prod. Various) 🦴🦴🦴🦴 gives you the whole story, reprising in their entirety the group's two EPs and one album, along with a 45 B-side ("The B-Side"), a live track, a non-album cover of Lou Christie's "Lightning Strikes" and a karaoke version of "I Wanna Be a Lifeguard." Often silly, frequently downright goofy, Blotto steamrolls through its material with a wink and a smirk, but also with unerring style and elan.

Carl Cafarelli

Kurtis Blow

Born Kurt Walker, Aug. 9, 1959 in New York, N.Y.

Blow is certainly not one of the most talented or distinctive rappers the music world has ever seen. But he still owns an important place in pop music history as one of rap's most accomplished and influential pathbreakers. He was the first rapper to land a major label deal (with Mercury Records in 1979), the first rapper to earn a gold record for a 12-inch single ("The Breaks" in 1980) and the first bona fide rap superstar. Blow was also one of the genre's most directly influential lyricists; among those his simple but resonant style touched were L.L. Cool J, Kool Moe Dee and Run-D.M.C., whose Joseph Simmons (Run) originally called himself Son of Kurtis Blow. But Blow's time in the spotlight didn't last long; he was gradually surpassed, commercially and stylistically, by his hip-hop disciples, and he saw his recording career come to a halt in 1988 after his eighth album—the stale-sounding *Back By Popular Demand*—flopped. Blow now works as a DJ on a Los Angeles radio station and promotes occasional old-school rap concerts. As with most early rappers, Blow was a singles-oriented artist whose studio albums (all of which are out of print) typically were uneven collections loaded with forgettable filler. So the only Blow album you'll ever need to hear is *The Best of Kurtis Blow,* (Mercury, 1994, prod. Various) 🦴🦴🦴🦴 a 14-track collection with the essential hits ("The Breaks," "Hard Times," "Basketball") as well as "Street Rock," which features a cameo by Bob Dylan.

Joshua Freedom du Lac

The Blue Aeroplanes

Formed 1981 in Bristol, England

Gerard Langley, vocals; Ian Kearey, guitar, banjimer, harmonium; Nick Jacobs, guitar, vocals; Dave Chapman, guitar, bass, harmonica, mandolin, vocals; Angelo Bruschini, guitar, accordion, vocals; John Langley, drums, keyboards, vocals; Wojtek Dmochowski, dancer; John Stapleton, records, tapes

A musical consortium with few fixed members, the Blue Aeroplanes are among the least definable and most tenacious pop groups to come along. With vocalist Langley as the only constant, the Aeroplanes have somehow managed to sound consistent over some 10 albums and more than a dozen changes in personnel. While guitars are the dominating instrument, the group generously blends in hurdy-gurdy, melodeon, bagpipes and other old-world instrumentation, creating a rustic rock-pop that is both fresh and nostalgic. There is little to compare to it. Langley, the main songwriter, alternately snaps out his lyrics in a scouse snarl or sings them in a voice pleasantly chaffed with whisky and wind. His themes tend toward love on the brink, but he can just as easily create a somber and romantic mood of reverie, using fractured phrases a drunk might have the luck to spout as the last bar closes. Heady and moving stuff.

what to buy: *Spitting Out Miracles* (Fire, 1987, prod. Gerard Langley and Charlie Llewellin) is a friendly place to check out the Aeroplanes' stuff. Langley's singing-talking vocals work to great effect across many styles here, including laidback folk ("Cowardice and Caprice"), cajun-rock ("Spitting Out Miracles") and lovely waltz-time reveries ("Ceiling Roses"). It's an amazingly well-paced record, given its alphabet-soup eclecticism, with fast and happy rockers like "Winter Sun" and "Bury Your Love Like Treasure" punctuating the calmer moments.

what to buy next: Following a three-year period during which it released no new material, the band returned in full force on *Swagger,* (Chrysalis, 1990, prod. Gil Norton) a 12-song extravaganza driven by pure pop power. Layers of guitars create a lovely chiming wash for Langley's introspections on relationships. The usual cavalcade of Aeroplane friends gets bit of star power from R.E.M.'s Michael Stipe and ex-Belle Stars saxophonist Clair Hirst.

what to avoid: Not bad so much as unnecessary, *World View Blue* (Ensign, 1990) is a lackluster collection of live tracks, leftovers and covers, including "Sweet Jane" and a live version of Dylan's "I Wanna Be Your Lover."

the rest: *Tolerance* (Fire, 1986) *Friendloverplane* (Fire, 1988) *Beatsongs* (Ensign-Chrysalis, 1991) *Friendloverplane 2 (Up In A Down World)* (Ensign-Chrysalis, 1992) *Life Model* (Beggars Banquet, 1994) *Rough Music* (Beggars Banquet, 1995)

worth searching for: Long out of print, the Aeroplanes' first album, *Bop Art,* (Regeneration, 1984, prod. Blue Aeroplanes) has been re-released as a mail-order CD via its Blue Aeroplanes Information service in Bristol England. Filled with the trademark sounds that would define the group's later work, *Bop Art* is a highly accessible record that's every bit as good as *Spitting Out Miracles.*

▶▶ Nick Cave and the Bad Seeds

◀◀ Velvet Underground, Leonard Cohen, Paul Winter Consort, Fairport Convention

Christopher Scapelliti

What Album Changed Your Life?

"Definitely Sly & the Family Stone's There's a Riot Goin' On (Epic, 1971). I learned every part from every instrument on that record. My older brother had a paper route when I was a kid, and he joined the Columbia Record Club. After he spent that penny on nine or 10 records, he didn't keep up with it, so they would just send him records...I was like eight years old, and he got There's a Riot Goin' On. He thought it was O.K., but I loved that song 'Family Affair.' I remember asking him about some words in that song, where it says 'blood is thicker than mud,' what did it mean? He said...'If you've got a glass of mud and a glass of blood, then blood is thicker.' It was a ridiculous explanation, but I loved that song, so he gave me the album."

Harold Chichester (Howlin' Maggie, Afghan Whigs, Royal Crescent Mob)

Blue Cheer

Formed 1967 in Boston, Mass. Disbanded 1971. Re-formed 1985.

Dickie Petersen, bass, vocals; Bruce "Leigh" Stephens, guitar (1967-68); Paul Whaley, drums (1968-69, 1985-89); Randy Holden, guitar (1968-69); Norman Mayell, drums (1969-71); Bruce Stephens, guitar, vocals (1969-70); Ralph Burns Kellogg, keyboards (1969-); Gary Yoder, guitar (1970-71); Tony Rainier, guitar (1985-present)

Blue Cheer epitomized acid rock, the forerunner to heavy metal. The power trio, which took its name from a potent form of LSD, played hard, loud and fast. Its remake of Eddie

Cochran's "Summertime Blues" in 1968 is considered one of the first heavy metal songs ever recorded. The group moved to San Francisco shortly thereafter, but after six average-selling albums, it broke up in 1971. Blue Cheer has regrouped on occasion, and its latest incarnation has produced three new albums, though only one was released in the U.S. Most of Blue Cheer's albums are long out of print, but *The Good Times Are So Hard to Find: The History of Blue Cheer* (Mercury, 1988, prod. Various) pulls together largely overlooked originals and choice covers—and, of course, "Summertime Blues"—on one budget-priced CD.

the rest: *Vincebus Eruptum* (Mercury, 1968) *Outsideinside* (Mercury, 1968)

Doug Pullen

The Blue Nile

Formed 1982 in Glasgow, Scotland

The Blue Nile—Paul Buchanan (vocals, guitar), Robert Bell (bass) and Paul Joseph (keyboards)—started out playing nearly entirely sampled and synthesized music. Buchanan's whispery vocals, over the layered textures of synthesized strings and horns, programmed drums and turned-down electric guitars, evoke that moment when the late of the night changes to the early morning. Not a prolific group, the trio let five years lapse between its first two albums, and seven years went by between its second and third. The middle album, *Hats* (Linn/Virgin, 1989, prod. the Blue Nile) is the one to buy. It relies heavily on synthesized instruments and Buchanan's restrained singing, but the melodies are well-defined and accessible, with major chord arrangements at least providing a bit—and only a bit—more oomph to the proceedings.

the rest: *A Walk Across the Rooftops* (Linn/Virgin, 1983, prod. the Blue Nile) *Peace At Last* (Warner Bros., 1996, prod. the Blue Nile)

Joshua Zarov

Blue Oyster Cult

Formed 1970 in Stony Brook, N.Y.

Eric Bloom, vocals, "stun" guitar, keyboards, bass; Donald (Buck Dharma) Roeser, guitar, keyboards, vocals, bass; Allen Lanier, guitar, keyboards (1970-84, 1987-present); Tommy Zvonchek, keyboards (1984-86); Joe Bouchard, bass, vocals (1970-86); Jon Rogers, bass, vocals (1992-present); Albert Bouchard, drums, synthesizer, vocals (1970-81, 1986-88); Rick Downey, drums (1981-84); Tommy Price, drums (1984-85); Jimmy Wilcox, drums (1985-86); Ron Riddle, drums (1989-92); Chuck Burgi, drums, vocals (1992-present)

This was the 70s heavy metal band that critics could respect. In fact, seminal rock critic Richard Meltzer co-wrote songs with the band, as did British fantasy author Michael Moorcock and Patti Smith, during her relationship with guitarist Allen Lanier. Initially featuring a three-guitar attack and black-humored satire, BOC—which grew out of the Long Island college-town band Soft White Underbelly—explored the supernatural, pondered mortality and mocked the gullible in an odd combination of progressive rock, hippie concerns, camp and down-and-dirty club rock. Incessant touring and its sinister, sardonic live presentation cemented BOC's reputation, and increased musical sophistication paid off on the fourth album, *Agents of Fortune*, which went platinum partly on the strength of Dharma's surprise hit "Don't Fear the Reaper." The band has existed fitfully in recent years, and its only new recording has been the curiousity *Cult Classic*, a studio re-recording of the band's hits made partly for use in the Stephen King TV movie "The Stand;" vocal-less "TV mix" tracks of "Don't Fear the Reaper" and "Godzilla" will delight the karaoke-inclined.

what to buy: *Agents of Fortune* (Columbia, 1976, prod. Murray Krugman, Sandy Pearlman and David Lucas) is perhaps the most sophisticated metal album ever. "Don't Fear the Reaper" and "E.T.I." are the favorites, but every cut is good. This is also where Patti Smith's presence is strongest. *Spectres* (Columbia, 1976, prod. Murray Krugman, Sandy Pearlman, David Lucas and Blue Oyster Cult) is just as good but funnier, with "Godzilla" and "Golden Age of Leather" a riotous one-two punch and "R.U. Ready 2 Rock" an anthem. *Workshop of the Telescopes* (Legacy, 1996, prod. Various) is an exemplary two-CD compilation that supplements the obvious choice songs with rare items and cherry-picks the post-*Spectres* albums for their only worthwhile cuts.

what to buy next: The first three albums—*Blue Oyster Cult*, (Columbia, 1973, prod. Murray Krugman and Sandy Pearlman) *Tyranny & Mutation* (Columbia, 1974, prod. Murray Krugman and Sandy Pearlman) and *Secret Treaties* (Columbia, 1974, prod. Murray Krugman amd Sandy Pearlman)—can be bought together in a slipcase for $25, a bargain for the group's hardest-rocking work.

what to avoid: *Career of Evil: The Metal Years* (Columbia, 1990, prod. Various) fails as a compilation, selecting only from the albums you'll want anyway while ignoring the later releases from which you'll want only one or two songs each. *Club Ninja* (Columbia, 1986, prod. Sandy Pearlman) WOOF! is uninspired, by-the-numbers rock by a lineup that includes neither Albert Bouchard nor Allen Lanier and depends heavily on mediocre outside songwriting.

the rest: *On Your Feet or On Your Knees* (Columbia, 1975) *Some Enchanted Evening* (Columbia, 1978) *Mirrors* (Columbia, 1979) *Cultosaurus Erectus* (Columbia, 1980) *Fire of Unknown Origin* (Columbia, 1981) *Extraterrestrial Live* (Columbia, 1982) *Revolution By Night* (Columbia, 1983) *Imaginos* (Columbia, 1988) *Cult Classic* (Herald, 1994)

solo outings:

Buck Dharma: Flat Out (Portrait/Sony, 1982)

▶▶ Judas Priest, Metallica, Minutemen/fIREHOSE, Def Leppard

◀◀ Led Zeppelin, Steppenwolf

Steve Holtje

Blue Rodeo

Formed 1984 in Toronto, Canada

Greg Keelor, vocals, guitar; Jim Cuddy, vocals, guitar; Bazil Donovan, bass; Kim Deschamps, pedal and lap steel (1991-present); Bob Wiseman, keyboards (1984-92); James Gray, keyboards (1992-present); Mark French, drums (1984-91); Glenn Milchem, drums (1991-present)

One of Canada's most successful bands, Blue Rodeo continues to develop its sound over the course of each new song. A contemporary of fellow country-oriented Canadian acts such as k.d. lang and the Cowboy Junkies, Blue Rodeo has established a large and loyal following across Canada and in border cities in the U.S. The group's gritty, guitar-based debut album, *Outskirts* (Atlantic, 1987, prod. Terry Brown) is a good place to start, with Beatle/Byrds-style harmonies and songs—"Try" and "Heart Like Mine"—that still sound fresh. With *Casino*, (Atlantic, 1991, prod. Pete Anderson) the band's sound takes on more country touches, while *Five Days in July* (Discovery, 1993, prod. Blue Rodeo) marks the addition of Deschamps and a more acoustic approach.

the rest: *Diamond Mine* (Atlantic, 1989) *Lost Together* (Discovery, 1992) *Nowhere to Here* (Discovery, 1995)

Matt Merta

The Bluebells

Formed 1982 in Glasgow, Scotland. Disbanded 1984.

Kenneth McCluskey, vocals, harmonica; Robert Hodgens, guitar, vocals; Russell Irvin, guitar (1982-83); Craig Gannon, guitar (1983-84); Lawrence Donegan, bass (1982-83); Neil Baldwin, bass (1983-84); David McCluskey, drums, vocals, guitar

While much of the music world was revelling in New Wave electronica, a small movement was quietly at work in Scotland to move pop away from synthesizers and back to its guitar-driven roots. Like its Glaswegian compatriots Aztec Camera, the Bluebells crafted rustic, jangly music awash with tempting hooks and utterly wonderful melodies. Formed by songwriter and ex-fanzine publisher Hodgens, the Bluebells made marvelous music and earned an impressive amount of support from the industry in a short time. (Among the group's producers and fans were Colin Fairley and Elvis Costello.) Although the Bluebells managed to place two singles ("I'm Falling" and "Young at Heart") in the U.K. Top 10 during 1984, the group disbanded soon afterward, leaving everyone to wonder what might have been. *Bluebells* (Sire, 1983, prod. Various) is the masterful five-song EP that put the group on the map. Standouts among the pack are the lovely Scottish folk-rocker "Cath," the up-tempo "Everybody's Somebody's Fool" and the anthemic "Sugar Bridge." *Sisters* (London, 1984, prod. Various) is the group's first full-length album. In addition to including three tracks from *Bluebells*, the album features seven new tracks, among the best of which is "I'm Falling (Down Again)." The songs interweave seamlessly in an appealing wash of chiming guitars, fiddles and mandolin, spilling over with memorable hooks and infectious choruses. *Second* (London, 1992, prod. Various) gathers previously unreleased recordings for a convincingly cohesive "second" album.

Christopher Scapelliti

The Blues Brothers

Formed 1977 in New York City, N.Y.

Jake Blues (aka John Belushi), vocals; Elwood Blues (aka Dan Aykroyd), harmonica, vocals

During "Saturday Night Live's" heyday, pals and blues enthusiasts Belushi and Aykroyd came up with a revue-style act to perform on the show. Backed by authentic soul veterans (including Booker T. & the MGs alums Steve Cropper and Donald "Duck" Dunn), the two adopted dark-suited, sunglassed personas and performed enthusiastic (if not always accomplished) renditions of R&B classics. The Blues Brothers became a popular recurring segment of SNL and even toured behind its million-selling albums; in 1980, director John Landis turned the concept into a hit film. Belushi's death from a drug overdose in 1982 cemented the Blues Brothers as cult legends. Aykroyd used his Elwood persona to promote his House of Blues nightclub chain and plans to re-launch the Blues Brothers on film and record with actors James Belushi (John's brother) and John Goodman.

what to buy: *The Definitive Collection* (Atlantic, 1992, prod. Various) contains all the favorites, including their popular versions of Sam and Dave's "Soul Man," the Spencer Davis Group's "Gimme Some Lovin' " and the quirkier numbers sung by Aykroyd.

the rest: *Briefcase Full of Blues* (Atlantic, 1978) *Made in America* (Atlantic, 1980) *The Blues Brothers* soundtrack (Atlantic, 1980) *The Best of the Blues Brothers* (Atlantic, 1980)

Blues Traveler, Treat Her Right

Ray Charles, James Brown, Sonny Boy Williamson, The Blues Project, Stax

Todd Wicks

Blues Project

Formed 1965 in New York. Disbanded 1972.

Danny Kalb, guitar; Roy Blumenfeld, drums; Andy Kulberg, bass, flute (1965-67); Steve Katz, guitar, harmonica (1965-67); Tommy Flanders, vocals (1965-66, 1972); Al Kooper, keyboards, vocals (1965-67); Don Kretmar, bass, saxophone (1971-72); David Cohen, piano (1972); Bill Lussenden, guitar (1972)

"The Jewish Beatles," as this 60s New York-based band was once dubbed, was more important and influential than its lack of success might first indicate. The Project was a transitional phase for many of its members: Kooper and Katz went on to found Blood, Sweat & Tears; Kooper became successful as a producer; Kulberg and Blumenfeld headed for Seatrain. The members, individualists all, came up with a potent, sophisticated, East Coast blast of blues, folk and rock with slightly jazzy overtones that found adherents from all genres and helped cross-pollinate them into rock. Flanders left early on; the rest toiled together little more than two years after they first got together. Still, after Paul Butterfield and along with English bands like Cream, the group was instrumental in educating the rock audience to blues—at the same time they were learning it themselves.

what to buy: *The Best of the Blues Project* (Rhino, 1989, prod. Various) is a 16-track overview that includes all the essentials—"No Time Like the Right Time,""Wake Me, Shake Me," "Flute Thing" in its studio and live incarnations.

what to buy next: *Projections,* (Verve-Forecast, 1967, prod. Tom Wilson) their only real studio album, is still the best indication of the breadth of their eclectic talent, from the lilting jazz melody of "Flute Thing" (sampled on "Flute Loop" from the Beastie Boys' *Ill Communications* album) to their intense, 10-minute-plus kidnaping of Muddy Waters' "Two Trains Running."

what to avoid: *Lazarus,* (Capitol, 1971, prod. Shel Talmy) an uninspired attempt by Kalb, Blumenfeld and Flanders to bring back the magic.

the rest: *Live at Town Hall* (Verve-Forecast, 1967); *Planned Obsolescence* (Verve-Forecast, 1968) *Reunion in Central Park,* (MCA, 1973) *Best of the Blues Project* (Verve-Forecast, 1969)

worth searching for: *Live at the Cafe Au Go Go,* (Verve-Forecast, 1966) featuring Flanders, is a gritty document of their early, blues/folk synthesis. Who else would have chosen "Catch the Wind" and "Violets of Dawn" alongside "Spoonful" and "Who Do You Love?"

Blood, Sweat & Tears, Seatrain

Muddy Waters, Willie Dixon, Chuck Berry, Bob Dylan, the Rolling Stones

Leland Rucker

Blues Traveler

Formed 1985 in Princeton, N.J.

John Popper, vocals, harmonica, guitar; Chan Kinchla, guitar; Bobby Sheehan, bass; Brendan Hill, drums, percussion

In a lesson learned from the Grateful Dead, Blues Traveler found that it was possible to sustain a musical career without the benefit of hit singles or huge album sales. Instead, they built an often fanatical following by touring relentlessly and stressing musicianship over songsmithery. Of the so-called "jam" bands that emerged in the early to mid-90s, Blues Traveler is the one to watch, in large part due to frontman Popper, whose harmonica playing is distinctive and astonishingly dexterous. Vocally, Popper makes up with moxie what he lacks in range, though his lyrics are often ponderous. Bassist Sheehan and drummer Hill provide a solid groove, while guitarist Kinchla's lightning-fast runs complement Popper's harp nicely. The group eventually did hit the airwaves in 1995 with "Run-Around" from *Four,* but popular success altered their style not a whit.

what to buy: *Four* (A&M, 1994, prod. Steve Thompson & Michael Barbiero) contains what's easily the band's most memorable song, "Run-Around" which comes off like a bastard son of the Grateful Dead's "Uncle John's Band" and Bruce Springsteen's "Rosalita." The album also includes the punchy "Stand" and the self-effacing "Hook." *Blues Traveler* (A&M, 1990, prod. Justin Niebank) includes Blues Traveler's other signature song, "But Anyway," plus a number of songs—including "Gina," "100 Years," and "Sweet Talking Hippie"—which are still live staples.

what to buy next: *Live From the Fall,* (A&M, 1996, prod. Dave Swanson, Rich Vink and Blues Traveler) a two-disc concert recording that captures Blues Traveler in its element, stretching out their arrangements—several beyond the 15-minute mark—and showing off their often impressive chops. The set does act as a serviceable retrospective, even if, as with most live albums, you probably had to be there. Fans will cherish this; detractors will find it pointless.

the rest: *Travelers & Thieves* (A&M, 1991) *Save His Soul* (A&M, 1993)

▶▶ Spin Doctors, Joan Osborne, Screaming Cheetah Wheelies, The Why Store

◀◀ The Grateful Dead, David Peel, The Blues Brothers, Allman Brothers Band

Daniel Durchholz

Bluestime

See: J. Geils Band

Colin Blunstone

Born June 24, 1945, in Hatfield, England

Blunstone first found fame in 1965 as the husky-voiced lead singer of the British Invasion group the Zombies. With Rod Argent's electric piano riff flowing underneath, Blunstone's romantic tenor phrased his plaintive questions on "She's Not There." His solo debut *One Year* (Epic, 1971) combined the flattering elements of a wistful tone, romantic focus and sympathetic arrangements. The best of that era may be heard on *Some Years: It's The Time Of Colin Blunstone,* (Epic/Legacy, 1995, prod. Various) which features his early solo hit "She Loves the Way They Love Her." Blunstone was a frequent choice of producer Alan Parsons for his Alan Parsons Project recordings; he can be heard on any of the Project's compilations.

see also: *The Zombies, Alan Parsons Project*

Patrick McCarty

Blur

Formed 1988 in London, England

Damon Albarn, vocals, piano, organ, synthesizers; Graham Coxon, electric and acoustic guitars, banjo, backing vocals; Alex James, bass guitar; Dave Rowntree, drums

Blur started its career as a Stone Roses/Charlatans/Happy Mondays clone at the height of Britain's Manchester frenzy. But hailing from London, the shtick didn't last too long. By its third album, Blur had emerged from the shadow of that scene with its own singular identity. On *Parklife*, the pivotal disc in the group's career, Blur completely changed its sound and attitude; mixing up musical styles and focusing on the British middle-class ideal, the group quickly gained acclaim for its lyrical depth and musical precision. Blur's looming celebrity even inspired a Rolling Stones/Beatles caliber rivalry with chart-mates Oasis, whose songwriter Noel Gallagher went as so far to wish the AIDS virus on Albarn and James. Blur, of course, came out unscathed in the end and remains one of England's most important bands.

what to buy: It took Blur two albums before it finally found its niche in the British pop sweepstakes with *Parklife.* (Food/SBK, 1994, prod. Stephen Street) Blending tight punk rhythms with lush melodies and lyrics that heralded the virtues of life in Britain, the group finally hit its stride with remarkable songs such as "Girls & Boys," "End of the Century" and "London Loves." Its follow-up, *The Great Escape* (Food/Virgin, 1995, prod. Stephen Street) held the stylistic ground of the previous disc, but ushered in more refined songwriting on exquisite tracks like "Country House" and "The Universal."

what to buy next: Even though the group was merely trying to cash-in on Britain's exploding Manchester scene with its baggy rhythms and indifferent melodies, Blur's debut, *Leisure,* (Food/SBK, 1991, prod. Stephen Street) includes charming pop songs ("She's So High," "Bang") that initially made people take notice of the band.

what to avoid: Although it features some pivotal songs from the Blur catalog ("Chemical World," "Oily Water"), the spiritless *Modern Life Is Rubbish* (Food/SBK, 1993, prod. Stephen Street) ♪ tracks the group's difficult transitional period between its shoegazing and mod phase.

worth searching for: *Blur-ti-go* (Food/SBK, 1992) is a raucous live EP that signals the group's move away from its dream-pop origins. It also includes two dance mixes of "Bang."

▶▶ Elastica, These Animal Men, Shed Seven

◀◀ Buzzcocks, The Jam, The Who, XTC, The Kinks

Aidin Vaziri

Bodeans

Formed 1985 in Waukesha, Wisc.

Kurt Neuman, guitar, vocals; Sam Llanas, guitar, vocals; Bob Griffin, bass; Guy Hoffman, drums (1985-89); Michael Ramos, keyboards (1989-95); Rafael "Danny" Gayol, drums (1991-93)

Hailing from the American heartland, BoDeans offered a fresh, straightforward and slightly twangy brand of rock that was missing from the pop scene at the time. The combination of songcraft and beautiful harmonies led to instant critical acclaim for the debut album, *Love&Hope&Sex&Dreams*, but not an instant audience. Rather, BoDeans have slogged it out for a decade—trying various top-shelf producers, lineups and stylistic tweakings—before the mass audience embraced "Closer to Free," a 1993 song that became a hit two years later as the theme for the Fox TV show "Party of Five." Meanwhile, BoDeans could console themselves with a role as a necessary touchstone for mid-90s explosion of American roots rock in the form of bands such as The Jayhawks, Uncle Tupelo, Wilco, Son Volt and the Bottle Rockets.

what to buy: *Love&Hope&Sex&Dreams* (Slash/Warner Bros., 1986, prod. T-Bone Burnett) ♪♪♪♪ starts off with a 1-2-3 punch of "She's a Runaway," "Fadeaway" and 'Still The Night"—earthy, guitar-driven rockers whose feel was decidedly—and distinctively—American Midwestern. BoDeans' second album, *Outside Looking In* (Slash/Reprise, 1987, prod. Jerry Harrison), ♪♪♪♪ was even better, a lively sophomore effort with strong, vivid songs about hard-working characters and their high hopes for life ("Dreams") and romance ("Say About Love"). *Joe Dirt Car* (Slash/Reprise, 1995, prod. Various) ♪♪♪♪ is a double disc live retrospective that features most of the band's key tracks in performances that often best their studio counterparts.

what to buy next: *Go Slow Down* (Slash/Reprise 1993, prod. T-Bone Burnett) ♪♪♪ takes a slightly more acoustic path. It has "Closer to Be Free," but the album's real highlight is the harmony laden "Idaho."

the rest: *Home* (Slash/Reprise, 1989) ♪♪♪ *Black and White* (Slash/Reprise, 1991) ♪♪♪

worth searching for: *Live @ Tower 10/11/93* (Slash/Reprise, 1994, prod. Mark McGraw), a promotional-only live recording that was a nice stop-gap until *Joe Dirt Car* came along and that still holds up as a strong representation of BoDeans in concert.

▶▶ Big Head Todd & The Monsters, Freddy Jones Band, The Jayhawks, Uncle Tupelo, Wilco, Son Volt and the Bottle Rockets

◀◀ The Band, The Byrds, Everly Brothers, Buffalo Springfield

John Nieman

Body Count

Formed 1991 in Los Angeles, Calif.

Rapper and free speech poster boy Ice-T (real name Tracy Marrow) had what seemed like a brilliant idea; on his last good rap album, *O.G.(Original Gangster),* (Sire, 1991, prod. Ice-T) ♪♪♪ he introduced a heavy metal band on one raw but potentially cool song. Then he unveiled the band during the first Lollapalooza tour and quickly won over amphitheater crowds across the country. Body Count's debut, *Body Count* (Sire/Warner Bros., 1992, prod. Ice-T/Ernie C.) ♪♪♪♪ is a terrific metal album because it's the sound of raw, untrained enthusiasm instead of slick speed-metal or bland pop-metal. Its music wasn't what sold records, however; shortly after its release, police groups began protesting the uncompromising attack on inner-city police brutality, "Cop Killer," saying it encouraged violence against officers. Ice-T protested their protests, but he couldn't stop the massive wave of backlash, and a cornered Warner Bros. eventually re-released the album without the song and then dropped Ice-T. Body Count resurfaced with *Born Dead,* (Virgin, 1994, prod. Ice-T/Ernie-C) ♪♪ a flimsy album of bad metal and boring social commentary despite a slightly interesting version of "Hey Joe."

the rest: *Violent Demise* (Virgin, 1996) not available for rating.

Steve Knopper

Tommy Bolin

Born Thomas Richard Bolin, Aug. 1, 1951 in Sioux City, Iowa. Died December 4, 1976 of a drug overdose in Miami, Fla.

Bolin was a self-taught guitar hero whose crying, slashing signature slide sound didn't fit any of the stylistic molds of his day (or even the present day, for that matter). Never a huge hitmaker while alive, his body of work has become the object of a cult of fret-heads who worship his still-unique sound, which throughout his career managed to bounce between bluesy hard-rock riffing and intense jazz fusion a la John McLaughlin and Larry Coryell. A teenaged rebel who quit high school when ordered to cut his hair, he migrated to Colorado in 1968 and formed a heavy blues-rock band called Zephyr and established a reputation as a flashy dresser and even flashier guitarist in and around the Boulder scene. The group never caught on commercially despite several albums for ABC/Probe (Candy Givens' vocals were too often unfavorably compared to Janis Joplin), and Bolin moved on to form an early jazz-rock fusion group called Energy, which never recorded for a label.

His natural ability and instinctively progressive musicality caught the attention of sometime-Boulder resident Joe Walsh, who recommended Bolin as Domenic Troiano's replacement in Walsh's old group, the James Gang. Bolin gave the James Gang a second commercial life during 1973 and 1974 with the albums *Bang* and *Miami;* at the same time he played on jazz drummer Billy Cobham's ground breaking 1973 album *Spectrum.* Though Bolin was frustrated as a backup player, he accepted another replacement job in 1975, when Ritchie Blackmore left Deep Purple. He wrote the majority of the songs on Deep Purple's 1975 album *Come Taste the Band* at the same time he was recording his solo debut, *Teaser,* a remarkably commercial funk-rock collection that showcased his sensual vocals, slinky, soul-based songwriting and that ever-present, instantly identifiable guitar style.

He juggled his two careers until Deep Purple broke up (for the first time), allowing Bolin to pursue his own music. Bolin released *Private Eye* in 1976, but he died of a drug overdose in a Miami hotel room after the first concert of what should have been a breakout tour, opening for Jeff Beck. His music is still commemorated by hardcore collectors all over the world, some of whom helped Geffen Records compile a boxed set in 1989 that included music from all phases of his short but exciting career. Bolin was a prolific guest artist as well—his fretwork appears on various albums from the mid-70s by artists such as Dr. John and a forgotten rock group, Moxy.

what to buy: *Teaser* (Nemperor, 1975, prod. Bolin and Lee Kiefer) and *Private Eyes* (Columbia, 1976, prod. Bolin and Dennis McKay) display Bolin's songwriting skill and instrumental chops at their peak.

what to buy next: Billy Cobham's *Spectrum* (Atlantic, 1973, prod. William E. Cobham, Jr.) shows Bolin's dexterity at music more complex than hard rock. *The Ultimate...* boxed set (Geffen, 1989, prod. Various) is a scattershot but ultimately fascinating overview of Bolin's music that includes wistful demos, rare tracks from Energy and long out-of-print material by Zephyr. *Tommy Bolin: From the Archives Volume 1* (Rhino, 1995, prod. Mike Drumm and Bob Ferbrache) gathers together more demos and alternate takes, odds and ends that don't work together as an album, but it's welcome manna for Bolin's cult devotees.

the rest: With Zephyr: *Zephyr* (ABC/Probe 1970) *Going Back To Colorado* (Warner Bros., 1971) With The James Gang: *Bang* (Atco, 1973) *Miami* (Atco, 1974) With Deep Purple: *Come Taste the Band* (Warner Bros., 1975)

worth searching for: *Live,* a single-CD bootleg, has varying sound quality but includes two tracks recorded during a May 1976 concert at a tiny Denver nightclub, Ebbet's Field that's still talked-about in Colorado music circles as well as amongst Bolin fans. Narada Michael Walden was on drums for the performance, and complete tapes of the show are also floating around.

Eddie Van Halen, Stevie Ray Vaughan, Randy Rhodes, Motley Crue

Elvis Presley, Jimmy Hendrix, Eric Clapton, Jeff Beck, David Bowie

Gil Asakawa

The Bolshoi

Formed in 1984 in London, England. Disbanded 1988.

Trevor Tanner, vocals, guitar; Nick Chown, bass; Jan Kalicki, drums; Paul Clark, keyboards

While not technically a one-hit wonder (it had two: "Away" and "Please") the Bolshoi pounced on the British music scene with an interesting cover of Jimi Hendrix's "Crosstown Traffic." It wasn't until after another EP, *Giants,* that the band finally got around to a full-length recording, *Friends* (I.R.S./Beggars Banquet, 1986, prod. Mick Glossip and Andy Warwick) and made a commercial impact. Sounding like a cross between vintage Cure and *Love*-era Cult, the brooding dance hit "Away" received airplay on college radio and MTV. The album, meanwhile, is a strong example of dark, danceable New Wave from the mid-80s.. But its successor, *Lindy's Party* (I.R.S./Beggars Banquet, 1987, prod. the Bolshoi) was an odd mix of even darker rock (listen to "Barrowlands") with a smattering of comical, novelty songs ("TV Man") that confused its fans.

Tim Davis

Michael Bolton

Born Michael Bolotin, Feb. 26, 1953, in New Haven, Conn.

A screamer on the New England hard rock circuit for years, Bolton split for Los Angeles to concentrate on songwriting and was churning out emotional hits for others before someone noticed he had a pretty stirring voice himself on those demo tapes. With long hair flowing and a strong chin, he became a middle-of-the-road matinee idol, a Fabio for former Barry Manilow fans. His over-the-top style (and penchant for re-making classic soul songs) earned him sneers from critics and swoons from his fans. He got kudos from Ray Charles and Otis Redding's widow for his soul re-makes, but the Isley Brothers successfully sued over the similarities between Bolton's 1991 hit "Love is a Wonderful Thing" and one of their 1966 songs. Bolton still resides and records in Connecticut, where he spends a lot of time on charitable activity.

what to buy: The essence of Bolton is almost too strong to take an album at a time, but *The Greatest Hits, 1985-1995* (Columbia, 1995, prod. Various) covers the highlights, though the five new cuts don't compare to the proven hits.

what to buy next: *Soul Provider* (Columbia, 1989, prod. Peter Bunetta) finds Bolton at the height of his powers, before the arrogance and bombast became a problem. This includes his cover of "Georgia on My Mind" and his own "How Am I Supposed to Live Without You?"

what to avoid: *Timeless: The Classics* (Columbia, 1992 prod. David Foster) Accused of ripping off the past, Bolton decides to rub his critics' faces in an entire album of inferior cover tunes. He even misspells Levi Stubbs' name in the credits. Ouch.

the rest: *The Hunger* (Columbia, 1987) *Time, Love and Tenderness* (Columbia, 1991) *The One Thing* (Columbia, 1993)

worth searching for: If you're a fan and want a taste of Bolton with more hair and less ego, try *Michael Bolton*, (Columbia, 1983) his first, and worst-selling, album on the label.

Mariah Carey, Celine Dion

Percy Sledge, Otis Redding, Patti LaBelle, Al Jolson

Roger Catlin

Bon Jovi

Formed 1983 in Sayreville, N.J.

Jon Bon Jovi (born John Francis Bongiovi), vocals, guitar; Richie Sambora, guitar, vocals; David Bryan (born David Rashbaum), keyboards, vocals; Alec John Such, bass guitar (1983-94); Tico Torres, drums

Formed in the rough-and-tumble heyday of New Jersey's bar band scene—in the same dives that gave us Bruce Springsteen and Southside Johnny & the Asbury Dukes—Bon Jovi won its record deal with PolyGram on the strength of a song called "Runaway," which turned into a regional hit after its inclusion on a radio station sampler of local music. Though the band enjoyed some initial success with its first two albums, the group really took off after Jon Bon Jovi—who picked up his pop smarts while sweeping floors at his cousin't New York recording studio, the legendary Power Station—enlisted gun-for-hire Desmond Child's help as a co-writer to help craft a hitmaking formula. Breaking big in 1986 on the strength of a videogenic good looks and hit singles that perfectly captured the pop/metal market that ruled MTV then, Bon Jovi reached heights it would rarely scale again. By the late 80s, both Bon Jovi and Sambora were itching to try solo projects, though the group survived and came back back together in the early 90s, creatively weaker but still a commercial force to be reckoned with around the world.

what to buy: Bon Jovi's triumphant, multi-million selling *Slippery When Wet* (Mercury, 1986, prod. Bruce Fairbairn) totally focuses the band's appeal into concise, innovative pop/metal nuggets that don't lose palooka joyousness of a good Jersey Shore bar band. Hit singles such as "Wanted: Dead or Alive," "You Give Love a Bad Name" and "Livin' on a Prayer" defined the spirit of mid-80s commercial metal.

what to buy next: The hits collection *Cross Road: 14 Classic Grooves* (Mercury, 1994, prod. Various) offers all of the best singles in one volume, skipping the pointless filler weighing down many of the original albums.

what to avoid: *7800 Fahrenheit* (Mercury, 1985, prod. Lance

Quinn) **WOOF!** is simply lousys. Forgettable and formulaic, it gave little hint to the success that would shortly follow.

the rest: *Bon Jovi* (Mercury, 1984) *New Jersey* (Mercury, 1988) *Keep the Faith* (Jambco/Mercury, 1992) *These Days* (Jambco/Mercury, 1995)

worth searching for: *Most Requested*, (Jambco/Mercury, prod. Various) a promotional sampler that rivals the publicly released hits set *Cross Road*.

solo outings:

Jon Bon Jovi: Young Guns II: Blaze of Glory (Mercury, 1990)

Richie Sambora: Stranger in This Town (Jambco/Mercury, 1991)

David Bryan: Netherworld (Moonstone, 1992)

▶▶ Ratt, Poison, Alice Cooper, Aerosmith, Winger, Warrant

◀◀ Aerosmith, Cheap Trick, Kiss, Bruce Springsteen, the Asbury Jukes, Aerosmith, Alice Cooper

Eric Deggans

Gary U.S. Bonds

Born Gary Anderson, June 6, 1939 in Jacksonville, Fla.

Regardless of what Bruce Springsteen may think, it just may be that Bonds is little more than a cipher, a singer with a gritty and soulful but ultimately unexceptional voice, who happened to be in the right place at the right time—twice. His first 15 minutes of fame came thanks to producer Frank Guida, who multitracked Anderson's voice and added a party ambience to songs such as "New Orleans," "Quarter to Three" and "School Is Out." Bonds' albums are out of print, but the hits are collected on *The Best of Gary U.S. Bonds* (Rhino, 1990, prod. Various) Bonds hit the oldies circuit until the early 80s, when Springsteen—who frequently performed "Quarter to Three" in concert—got Bonds a record deal and co-produced a pair of albums for him. *Dedication* (EMI America, 1981/Razor & Tie, prod. Bruce Springsteen and Miami Steve Van Zant) features the hit "This Little Girl," which Springsteen wrote, and "Jole Blon," on which he shares vocals with Bonds. The follow-up, *On the Line*, (EMI America, 1982/Razor & Tie, 1988, prod. Bruce Springsteen and Miami Steve Van Zant) was written almost entirely by Springsteen, and Bonds causes a few sparks with the minor hit "Out of Work" and "Rendezvous." The best of these albums are collected on *The Best of Gary U.S. Bonds*, (EMI, 1996, prod. Bruce Springsteen and Miami Steve Van Zant) which is padded with live versions of "New Orleans" and "Quarter to Three."

Daniel Durchholz

The Bongos /Richard Barone

Formed 1981 in Hoboken, N.J. Disbanded 1986.

Richard Barone, vocals, guitar; Rob Norris, bass; Frank Giannini, drums; James Mastro (1981-1986)

Part of the unusual New York-area power-pop scene (which included the dBs, the Individuals and the Necessaries), the early Bongos combined the unbridled energy of punk with boyish vocals, a 60s-pop sensibility and jittery rhythms. The group's later work was lusher and more ambitious. On his own, songwriter Richard Barone went on to record some beautiful chamber pop and the occasional Bongos-ish rocker.

what to buy: The Bongos' *Drums Along the Hudson* (PVC, 1982, prod. Ken Thomas, Mark Abel and the Bongos) is the band's definitive statement, collecting the group's first singles and EPs and adding some brilliant newer songs. The sound is part *Rubber Soul*, part *Electric Warrior*, part Velvet Underground and part urban art-noise—and it's as pop as anything by the Knack. *Numbers With Wings* (RCA EP, 1983, prod. Richard Gottehrer and John Jansen) boasts a wet, ornate sound that's a contrast to the debut's punky rawness. The highlight of the five-song EP is "Barbarella," which matches a "Sunshine Superman"-ish melody with tribal rhythms that don't beat down the hook.

what to buy next: *Beat Hotel* (RCA, 1985, prod. John Jansen) is the Bongos' vision fully realized, a catchy musical fantasy of a rock record that suffers only from a lack of depth and surprise. Barone's solo *Primal Dream* (MCA, 1990, prod. Richard Gotterher and Don Dixon) contains the brisk, yearning "Where the Truth Lies" and the desperate, naked power-pop of "I Only Took What I Needed."

the rest: Richard Barone—*Cool Blue Halo* (Passport, 1987) *Clouds Over Eden* (Line, 1992, prod. Hugh Jones)

worth searching for: Barone's *From Heaven To Cello*, (Line, 1994) an import live album that showcases Barone's gift for intimate, uninhibited performance, though acoustic guitars and cellos make it seem a serious affair compared to the glam-tinged rock of the Bongos.

▶▶ Michael Penn

◀◀ Marc Bolan, the Beatles, Donovan, the Velvet Underground

Jordan Oakes

Karla Bonoff /Bryndle

Born Dec. 27, 1951 in Los Angeles, Calif.

A singer/songwriter who came to prominence when Linda Ronstadt chose three of her songs to perform on her *Hasten Down the Wind* album, Bonoff has had a solo career marked by consistently good material but precious little public acclaim. As a performer, Bonoff—who first hit the stage with the singer-songwriter collective Bryndle (which also included Kenny Edwards, Andrew Gold, Wendy Waldman)—displays considerable charm and intellect, if not overpowering expressiveness. In other words, it's clear why her chief success has been as a songwriter. Still, her albums have their moments, and looking back on them now—particularly the first three—they recall a time during the late-70s when and an El Lay singer/songwriter was something to be. Songs from that first trio of albums were covered by Nicolette Larson, Bonnie Raitt, Maria Muldaur, Kim Carnes and Judy Collins, among others. In recent years, Bonoff has turned her eye toward Nashville; Wynonna scored a country smash with "Tell Me Why" and Bonoff has written for and performed on albums by Reba McEntire, Kathy Mattea and Wynonna, among others. That makes perfect sense, given that Bonoff's brand of West Coast pop is what passes for Nashville country these days. What goes around comes around.

what to buy: *Karla Bonoff* (Columbia, 1977, prod. Kenny Edwards) ♪♪♪♪ reprises versions of the Ronstadt-covered "Someone to Lay Down Beside Me," "Lose Again" and "If He's Ever Near." But the surprise here is that, in taking those three, Ronstadt didn't exhaust Bonoff's supply of good songs; the album also features the lovely waltz "Home," the lightly rocking "I Can't Hold On" and "Isn't It Always Love," and the yearning "Falling Star."

what to buy next: *New World* (Gold Castle, 1988/MusicMasters, 1995, prod. Mark Goldenberg) ♪♪♪½ predated the adult-contemporary format by enough to keep it from getting the attention it deserves. Goldenberg's too-rich production aside, the album contains Bonoff's best batch of songs since her debut, including "All My Life"—which Ronstadt and Aaron Neville turned into a Grammy-winning hit. Bryndle, which re-formed in 1993, finally put out an album with *Bryndle* (MusicMasters, 1995, prod. Josh Leo and Bryndle) ♪♪♪½ Written in almost total collaboration, the album sounds like it could be the result of an old-fashioned guitar pull. All four members trade lead vocals and contribute honeyed harmonies.

what to avoid: *Restless Nights,* (Columbia, 1979, prod. Kenny Edwards) ♪♪½ is pleasant but is carried mostly by its two covers—the Searchers "When You Walk in the Room" and the traditional "The Water is Wide"—than by Bonoff's originals.

the rest: *Wild Heart of the Young,* (Columbia, 1982) ♪♪♪

worth searching for: The soundtrack for the TV series "Thirtysomething" (Geffen, 1991, prod. Various) ♪♪½ on which Bonoff performs "The Water is Wide."

▶▶ Kathy Mattea, Wynonna, Trisha Yearwood

◀◀ Stone Poneys, Laura Nyro, Wendy Waldman

Daniel Durchholz

Bonzo Dog Band

Formed 1965 in London, England. Disbanded 1971.

Vivian Stanshall, vocals, trumpet, ukelele; Neil Innes, vocals, guitar, keyboards; Roger Ruskin Spear, kazoos, Jew's harp (1965-70); Rodney Slater, saxophone (1965-70); Vernon Dudley Bohay-Nowell, guitar (1965-68); "Legs" Larry Smith, drums (1965-70); Sam Spoons, percussion (1965-70); Dennis Cowan, bass (1968-71); Bubs White, guitar (1971); Andy Roberts, guitar, fiddle (1971); Dave Richards, bass (1971); Dick Parry, flute (1971); Hughie Flint, drums (1971).

The only other band to appear in a movie by the Beatles (they were in the nightclub scene in "Magical Mystery Tour"), the Bonzo Dog Band—originally the Bonzo Dog Doo Dah Band—mined a rare humor in rock in a series of albums generally ignored beyond the English borders. The group, born out of art college, was about the size of an orchestra before it was honed to creative forces Stanshall and Innes and a band that included Ruskin Spear and Smith. Originally formed to recreate big band, jazz, vaudeville and 50s rock touches, the group eventually used conventional rock sounds in pursuit of its always amusing songs. Some were just one gag (an intro to "I Left My Heart in San Francisco," a cacophony of "A Sound of Music"), but there was also some extraordinary pop ("Ready Mades"). The band's humor had a direct influence on Monty Python, especially since Innes was called on for music (and eventually came up with the brilliant Beatle knockoffs for The Rutles).

Stanshall's voice became best known as the narrator on Mike Oldfield's "Tubular Bells."

what to buy: *Urban Spaceman,* (Liberty, 1968, prod. Apollo C. Vermouth (aka Paul McCartney)) the U.S. version, more or less, of the album known as *The Doughnut in Granny's Greenhouse* is the group's funniest, most assured album, with a Top 5 U.K. single in the title track.

what to buy next: *Best of the Bonzo Dog Band* (Rhino, 1990, prod. Various) is a decent enough compilation, with a couple of examples of solo work.

what to avoid: *Let's Make Up and Be Friendly* (Liberty, 1972) is a half-hearted attempt at a reunion, with just Stanshall and Innes returning from the original lineup.

the rest: *Tadpoles* (Liberty, 1969) *Gorilla* (Liberty, 1967) *Keynsham* (Liberty, 1970)

worth searching for: The more broad-reaching double-length collection, *Bestiality of Bonzo Dog Doo Dah Band* (Liberty, 1990, prod. Various) which offers even more Bonzo gonzo.

▶▶ Monty Python, the Rutles, Weird Al Yankovic

◀◀ Spike Jones, the Beatles

Roger Catlin

Betty Boo

Born Alison Moira Clarkson, 1970 in Kensington, London, England

British soul/rap singer Boo is one part hooky hip-hop artist and one part kooky novelty tune writer. Mostly, her music is about dancing, and Boo whips up plenty of exuberant booty-shaking rhythms. Originally performing under the name of cartoon character Betty Boop (legalities forced her to drop the "p"), Boo established herself with inventive hooks and comic-style videos that showed off exotic Scottish-Malaysian beauty. Her career began to flounder when, while lip-synching on live British TV, she dropped her microphone, revealing a canned vocal track. No great crime, but the public was still shaking its head over the Milli Vanilli scandal. Boo disappeared after her poorly received sophomore release, but news of a renewed career surfaced when she was signed to Madonna's Maverick label in early 1996. There's no word yet on her next release, but *Boomania* (Rhythm King, 1990, prod. Various) still simmers with layers of guitar licks, keyboard riffs and bass lines, the whole of which conspire to blow the roof off your sugar shack—from the Top 10 raps "Doin' the Do" and "Where Are You Baby?" to the an ace instrumental ("Boo's Boogie") and a straightforward dance number ("24 Hours"), on which she sounds uncannily like Paula Abdul. *Grrr! It's Betty Boo* (Sire, 1992, prod. Betty Boo) continues in the vein of *Boomania* but offers mellower tunes such as "Close the Door" and "Let Me Take You There." Boo shows especially good form on "I'm on My Way"; instead of sampling the brass on the Beatles' "Lady Madonna," she brings in the original sax players (including Ronnie Scott) to reprise their parts. That's class.

Christopher Scapelliti

The Boo Radleys

Formed 1988 in Liverpool, England

Martin Carr, guitar; Sice, vocals, guitar; Tim Brown, bass; Steve Hewitt, drums (1988-90); Rob Ceika, drums (1990-present)

Debuting from the land of the Beatles with *Ichabod and I* (Action U.K., 1990), boasting a low-fi yet frantic sound. It evolved into a more straightforward pop approach, which in turn led to the brilliant and varied *Giant Steps.* (Columbia, 1993, prod. Martin Carr, Tim Brown and Andy Wilkinson) The song "Lazarus" is the Boo Radleys at its lush and visionary best.

the rest: *Everything's Alright Forever* (Creation, 1992) *Wake Up!* (Creation, 1995)

Anna Glen

James Booker

Born Dec. 17, 1939 in New Orleans, La. Died Nov. 8, 1983 in New Orleans.

Booker stood in for Huey "Piano" Smith on tour and Fats Domino in the studio, and the Clash covered his theme song, "Junco Partner," on *Sandinista!* There are many authorities who gladly testify to his amazing abilities, from Dr. John to Harry Connick, Jr. In a city noted for great piano players, Booker was the greatest—if judged on sheer technique, not on hits or personal stability. Born into a musical family, Booker had an amazing musical memory and excelled at classical piano (giving recitals at age six) but was seduced by boogie woogie. By the age of 11 he was playing regularly on a local radio station, and at 14 he cut his first single, "Doing the Hambone/Thinkin' About My Baby," for Imperial Records, produced by Rock & Roll

Hall of Famer Dave Bartholomew—who gave Booker session work based on his ability copy anybody's style instantly.

But though he had a hit with his 1960 record "Gonzo," made singles for a variety of labels during the 50s and 60s (often under aliases) and was a sideman on records by everyone from Joe Tex, Bobby Bland and Lloyd Price to Maria Muldaur, the Doobie Brothers and Ringo Starr, Booker didn't record an album of his own until 1976, partly because he spent the middle of the 60s in prison. He went through periods of drug abuse, though New Orleans guitarist Earl King backs up Booker's contention that he wasn't an addict but that his metabolism allowed him to quit with no ill effects.After his prison stint, Booker did a little session work and then more or less retired, but reappeared in 1975 for a European package tour which garnered him recording offers. He played regularly in New Orleans thereafter, until his death.

what to buy: Every Booker album is great and precious, and full of awe-inspiring keyboard feats, but *New Orleans Piano Wizard: Live!* (Rounder, 1981, prod. Bernard Henrion) wins top recommendation for the crucial repertoire it includes: "Come Rain or Come Shine," "Please Send Me Someone to Love" and especially his diametrically opposed favorites "On the Sunny Side of the Street" and the heartfelt "Black Night." His vocals have a narrow stylistic range but are utterly appropriate. *Spiders on the Keys* (Rounder, 1993, prod. Scott Billington and John Parsons) draws on hours and hours of recordings at the Maple Leaf Bar to present a fascinating picture of Booker as strictly a pianist. His left hand is so strong that he makes even the Beatles' "Eleanor Rigby" totally fonky.

what to buy next: *Junco Partner* (Hannibal, 1976, prod. Joe Boyd and John Wood) was Booker's first album and one of only two studio albums. It's crucial not only for "Black Minute Waltz" (showing his classical side) and a great "Junco Partner" but also for George Winston's liner notes, analyzing the pianistic and compositional particulars of each performance. The other studio effort is *Classified*, (Rounder, 1982, prod. Scott Billington and John Parsons) the only album available in the U.S. on which Booker recorded with a band (including saxophonist Alvin "Red" Tyler, long Booker's bandleader); the album's highlight is his tune "Classified," which Dr. John covered. For the feeling of an all-stops-out club date, *Resurrection of the Bayou Maharajah* (Rounder, 1993, prod. Scott Billington and John Parsons) can't be beat. The rowdy, rollicking set (at 76+ minutes the most generous in his catalog) of Maple Leaf Bar performances has lots of vocal tunes (everything from "St. James Infirmary" to "Bony Maronie") and a total lack of inhibition or playing it safe.

worth searching for: Any of Booker's original vinyl singles, which carry collector's values—and fetch collector's prices, for sure.

Little Richard, Dr. John, Allen Toussaint, Henry Butler, George Winston

Huey "Piano" Smith, Tuts Washington, Professor Longhair, Jelly Roll Morton, Frederic Chopin, Louis Moreau Gottschalk, Meade Lux Lewis

Steve Holtje

Booker T. and the MG's

Formed 1961 in Memphis, Tenn.

Booker T. Jones, organ; Steve Cropper, guitar; Al Jackson Jr., drums (died Oct. 1, 1975); Lewis Steinberg, bass (1961-63); Donald "Duck" Dunn (1963-present); Willie Hall, drums (1975-77); James Gadson, drums (1994); Steve Potts, drums (1994)

This racially-integrated quartet mapped out the instrumental blueprint of 60s Southern soul not only on deceptively simple ensemble instrumental sides, but as the house band at Stax/Volt recording studios. These four musicians appear to interact on an practically instinctual level, stitching together tight, intricate musical lines with evident ease. The band's 1962 Top 10 hit "Green Onions" put the small regional soul label on the nationwide map, setting the stage for a soul music uprising that echoes ever more resonant through the years. At the core of this signature sound was the collaborative backbone of Booker T. and the MG's, whose members often ended up as part-writers of the many classics they created in the studio with giants like Otis Redding ("Dock Of the Bay") or Albert King ("Born Under a Bad Sign").

On their own, the band members sculpted a trademark sound—a churning, throbbing tidy knot of sound topped by Jones' mellifluous organ and tacked together by Al Jackson Jr.'s left foot—a style they became comfortable and conversant enough with to stretch out considerably on later albums. In the wake of Stax's dissolution in the early 70s, the band also disintegrated. Jones moved to the West Coast and produced hit Willie Nelson albums. Cropper and Dunn joined the Blues Brothers. Al Jackson Jr., who carried on the tradition playing on Al Green recordings, was murdered in his home in 1975. The other three members began performing together again in 1990 and have appeared notably as the house band at the Bob Dylan tribute at Madison Square Garden in 1992 and at the 1995 Rock and Roll Hall of Fame concert in Cleveland, as well as backing Neil Young on a 1994 summer tour. But none of the MG's many latter-era accomplishments match the towering contributions of the Memphis recordings.

what to buy: The band's fourth album, *Hip Hug-Her,* (Stax, 1967/Rhino, 1992 prod. Jim Stewart) ♫♫♫♫♫ brims with confidence and seamless instrumentals—from succulent originals like the haunting title track, the rousing "Double Or Nothing" or the cool "Slim Jenkins' Joint" to radically transformed covers like "Groovin' " and "Sunny."

what to buy next: The jazzy *Melting Pot* (Stax, 1983, prod. Booker T. and the MG's) ♫♫♫♫ and the tour-de-force instrumental rendering of the Beatles *Abbey Road* titled *McLemore Avenue,* (Stax, 1971, prod. Booker T. and the MG's) ♫♫♫♫ named after the street where the Stax studios were located in Memphis, capture the mature, confident band stretching their sound into new, rich realms.

what to avoid: The reincarnation's major label outing, *The Way It Should Be,* (Columbia, 1994, prod. Booker T. Jones) ♫♪ suffers from over-directing by the Columbia A&R department and a palpable lack of spirit.

the rest: *Green Onions* (Atlantic, 1962) ♫♫♫♪ *Soul Dressing* (Atlantic, 1965) ♫♫♫♪ *And Now* (Atlantic, 1966) ♫♫♫ In The Christmas Spirit (Atlantic 1966) ♫♫♫ *The Mar-Keys and Booker T. and the MG's: Back To Back* (Atlantic 1967) ♫♫♫ *Doin' Our Thing* (Atlantic, 1968) ♫♫♫ *Soul Limbo* (Stax, 1968/1991) ♫♫♫ *Booker T Set* (Stax, 1969/1987) ♫♫♫ *The Best of Booker T & the MG's* (Atlantic, 1984) ♫♫♫ *The Best of Booker T. and the MG's* (Stax, 1986) ♫♫♫♪

worth searching for: While the two volumes of the 1967 European tour by the Stax/Volt entourage, *The Stax/Volt Revue: Volume One—Live In London* (Atlantic, 1967, prod. Jim Stewart) ♫♫♫♫ and *The Stax/Volt Revue: Volume 2—Live In Paris* (Atlantic 1967, Prod. Jim Stewart) ♫♫♫♪ captures Booker T. and the MGs serving as the protean house band for the Memphis soul caravan, *The Complete Stax/Volt Singles 1959-1968* (Atlantic 1991, prod. Various) ♫♫♫♫ is really nothing more than a nine-disc tribute to the greatest soul accompanists of all-time.

▶▶ Creedence Clearwater Revival, Elvis Costello and the Attractions

◀◀ The Mar-Keys, Cannonball Adderley

see also: *The Blues Brothers*

Joel Selvin

The Boomtown Rats /Bob Geldof

Formed 1975 in Dun Laoghaire, Ireland. Disbanded 1986

Bob Geldof (born Oct. 5, 1954 in Dublin, Ireland) vocals; Johnny Fingers, keyboards; Pete Briquette, bass; Simon Crowe, drums; Gerry Cott, guitar (1975-81); Garry Roberts, guitar

Geldof made his name more for his humanitarian efforts—organizing the Live Aid concerts and the all-star "Do They Know it's Christmas" single—than for his nasal delivery and outspoken lyrics. With a Nobel Peace Prize nomination in the late 80s, Geldof seemed light years from "I Don't Like Mondays," the Rats biggest U.S. hit. A spare, piano based single concerning a murder spree, the song and the album, *The Fine Art of Surfacing* (Columbia, 1980, prod. Phil Wainman) ♫♫♫ was the band's high water mark both commercially (especially in the U.S.) and artistically. Although the Rats career began on the punk/new wave crest, it was, in fact, a more indebted to Van Morrison and Bruce Springsteen. The group released six other uneven albums (all out of print) before disbanding in 1986. Geldof's three solo albums—*Deep in the Heart of Nowhere,* (Atlantic, 1986) ♫♫♫ *Vegetarians of Love,* (Atlantic, 1990) ♫♫♪ *The Happy Club* (Polydor, 1993) ♫♫♪—are even more straightforward, but they're also out of print. Import hunters are well-served by the British compilation *Loudmouth: The Best of the Boomtown Rats & Bob Geldof.* (Vertigo, 1994, prod. Various) ♫♫♫♪

Allan Orski

Pat Boone

Born Charles Eugene Boone, June 1, 1934 in Jacksonville, Fla.

Though he's now known best for his gospel albums and support for Republican politicians, Boone was once nearly crowned the king of rock 'n' roll—with more pop hits during the late 50s and early 60s than any artist, save Elvis Presley. Raised in rural Tennessee, Boone parlayed an appearance on the "Ted Mack Amateur Hour" television show into a year-long stint on Arthur Godfrey's amateur show and a recording contract. Boone enjoyed a few pop hits with songs such as "Two Hearts, Two Kisses" in 1955, but it wasn't until he began recording sanitized, de-ethnicized versions of R&B and rock hits—including

Little Richard's "Tutti Frutti" and "Long Tall Sally"—that Boone's place in history was assured. With his crewcut and white buckskin shoes, Boone was the perfect bridge between early rock 'n' roll "race records" the white pop mainstream, covering tunes by Fats Domino, Ivory Joe Hunter and others. Beatlemania eventually made his efforts irrelevant, but not before Boone had moved on to his own television show and movie soundtrack work. In all, Boone enjoyed 38 chart topping hits. In 1996, however, he began preparing an album of heavy metal covers while also working the infomercial circuit, proving himself an opportunist of the highest caliber. Most of what's available are retrospectives, holiday collections and Christian recordings. Many—though not all—of the hits are on *Pat Boone's Greatest Hits* (MCA, 1993, prod. Various) ♪♪♪ There's also a video anthology of his chart successes, *40 Years of Hits,* (Rhino, 1995) ♪♪♪ or you can dig for the hard-to-find *Jivin' Pat* (Bear Family, 1986) ♪♪♪♪ a sardonic collection of all his rock covers.

Eric Deggans

Boston

Formed 1975 in Boston, Mass.

Members (1975-early 80s): Tom Scholz, guitars, keyboards; Brad Delp, vocals, guitar; Barry Goudreau, guitar; Fran Sheehan, bass; John "Sib" Hashian, drums

While critics and fans have poked fun at Boston leader Scholz's legendary finicky behavior—some called the eight-year delay between the group's second and third records "the other Boston Marathon"—there's no doubt it gets results. A graduate of Massachusetts Institute of Technology who worked by day as an engineer for Polaroid, Scholz spent years cobbling together a series of demos on his basement 12-track recorder that eventually snagged a deal with Epic Records. With a few additional parts added here and there, those demos became the group's multi-platinum debut album, recently certified as one of the best-selling rock records of all time. Based on the twin towers of Delp's high, powerful vocals and Scholz's wall of guitars and harmonized lead passages, Boston's signature sound struck a chord with fans. All its records have featured this formula, and nearly all have sold in multi-platinum numbers. The only problem, it seems, was Scholz's perfectionism, which has made it hard to keep a regular group of musicians together (not that they contribute significantly to the albums, anyway). Sony Music, Epic's parent company, sued Scholz for breach of contract; Scholz won the suit and continues to put out albums—for another label, mind you—whenever he's satisfied he has something good enough to release. Meanwhile, he concentrates on social action projects and on developing musical equipment; his Rockman personal amplifier is one of the best-selling rock toys of all time.

what to buy: The Scholz formula sounds freshest on the debut, *Boston* (Epic, 1976, prod. by John Boylan and Tom Scholz) ♪♪♪ Bouncy, slick tracks such as "More Than a Feeling" and "Peace of Mind" defined new parameters for rock radio during the 70s, with soaring vocals, searing guitars and trite lyrics.

what to buy next: *Don't Look Back* (Epic, 1978, prod. Tom Scholz) ♪♪♪ is a rote continuation of the predictable path laid out on the debut, with songs that don't quite hold up to the standard of its predecessor.

what to avoid: *Walk On,* (MCA, 1994, prod. Tom Scholz) ♪ the first Boston album devoid of Delp's bionic yelping, sounds like absolutely irrelevant 90s post-punk.

the rest: *Third Stage* (MCA, 1986) ♪♪♪

worth searching for: *We Found it in the Trashcan, Honest!,* (Ruthless Rhymes, 1977) ♪♪♪ a bootleg of some of Scholz' demos, with slightly different lyrics and a rawer sound than the Teflon perfection of the *Boston* album.

▶▶ Foreigner, Survivor, Night Ranger

◀◀ Led Zeppelin, the Beatles, Yes

Eric Deggans

The Bottle Rockets

Formed 1993 in Festus, Mo.

Like Ronnie Van Zandt and Lynyrd Skynyrd before them, guitarist/vocalist Brian Henneman and the Bottle Rockets are not the unreconstructed hawbucks they seems at first glance. Henneman's songs, are populated with hot-to-trot trailer mamas and Confederate-flag-waving idiots, conveying a deeply conflicted sense of small town values, offering alternate celebrations and condemnations of redneck culture.

After an apprenticeship with Uncle Tupelo, Henneman signed up guitarist Tom Parr, drummer Mark Ortmann, and bassist Tom Ray (the former two from Henneman's previous outfit, Chicken Truck), for *The Bottle Rockets*(East Side Digital, 1993, prod. John Keane) ♪♪♪♪ which offers plenty of lusty low humor ("Gas Girl," "Every Kinda Everything") and high drama ("Kerosene" in which a family dies in a senseless trailer fire, and "Wave That

Flag" which chastises four wheelin' faux rebels). *The Brooklyn Side* (East Side Digital, 1994/Tag Atlantic, 1995 prod. Eric "Roscoe" Ambel) continues in the same vein, imparting social justice ("Welfare Music") folk wisdom ("1000 Dollar Car"), and genuine desperation ("Sunday Sports") but adding a radio ready pop sheen to songs such as "I'll Be Comin' Around" and "Gravity Fails." These guys may yet take their brand of country grunge to the charts.

Daniel Durchholz

Jean-Paul Bourelly

Born Nov. 23, 1960 in Chicago, Ill.

Jazz fans know this guitarist for his work on Miles Davis, McCoy Tyner/Elvin Jones, Muhal Richard Abrams and Cassandra Wilson albums (he co-produced Wilson's *Dance to the Drums Again*), while R&B/hip-hop fans have heard him on records by Jody Watley, DJ Jazzy Jeff & Fresh Prince, Bel Biv Devoe and Charles & Eddie. Unbelievably, he's only been able to put out albums on German and Japanese labels (Enemy at least has a New York office). He has combined the influences of a number of greats to invent his own distinctive, uniquely rich guitar sound. Mixing jazz/blues/rock playing and his gruffly soulful vocals with funk and hip-hop rhythms, often with his group Blue Wave (sometimes Bluwave) Bandits, he builds dense, complex music he calls "New Breed Funk Jazz." Bassists Melvin Gibbs (Rollins Band), Darryl Jones (Rolling Stones) and Me'shell NdegoCello all passed through his groups prior to their more famous gigs, and "Kundalini" Mark Batson of the hip-hop group Get Set VOP plays Sly Stonesque keyboards and sometimes raps for Bourelly's Blue Wave Bandits.

what to buy: *Saints & Sinners* (DIW, 1993, prod. Jean-Paul Bourelly and Kazunori Sugiyama) distills the core of his stylistic fusion on "Got to Be Able to Know" and "Rumble in the Jungle," while "Muddy Waters (Blues for Muddy)" is a slow, simmering update of the blues. Many tracks, especially "Skin I'm In," show his matter-of-fact socio-political/racial consciousness without being preachy.

what to buy next: *Trippin'* (Enemy, 1991, prod. Jean-Paul Bourelly) features some of Bourelly's best guitar playing, focusing on his integration of lead and rhythm, and some of his tighter material. The lush, intensely lovely instrumental rave-up "Love Crime" is especially memorable.

what to avoid: *Tribute to Jimi* (DIW, 1994)

the rest: *Blackadelic-Blu* (DIW, 1994) isn't awful, but it enforces a stylistic when Bourelly is better given free rein.

worth searching for: Bourelly's debut as a leader, *Jungle Cowboy,* (JMT, 1987, prod. Stefan Winter and Jean-Paul Bourelly) is his best album and definitely the easiest way in for the uninitiated, so it's unfortunate that JMT's U.S. distributor, Verve, doesn't make it available. It predates Bourelly's incorporation of hip-hop beats, with late jazz sax great Julius Hemphill guested. As of this writing, Bourelly's *Fade to Cacophony,* (DIW, 1995) with seven live tracks and two previously unreleased studio tracks, is available only as an import.

▶▶ Milo Z

◀◀ Muddy Waters, Jimi Hendrix, Wes Montgomery, Jimmy Page, John McLaughlin, Sly & the Family Stone, Frank Zappa, Miles Davis

see also: *Defunkt*

Steve Holtje

Bow Wow Wow

Formed 1979 in London, England. Disbanded 1983.

Annabella Lwin, vocals; Matthew Ashman, guitar; Leigh Gorman, bass; David Barbarossa, drums

The pet project of Sex Pistols manager Malcolm McLaren, Bow Wow Wow was comprised of singer Lwin (a 14-year-old Burmese immigrant that McLaren found waiting on tables) and the Ants from Adam and the Ants. The band's incorporation of Burundi "Afrobeat" drumming into its pissed-off punk tunes, coupled with McLaren's publicity-hound instincts, won instant attention. When McLaren vacated the producer's chair to be replaced by Kenny Laguna and, later, Mike Chapman of Blondie fame, the novelty of Bow Wow Wow began to wear thin. The band dissolved in 1983.

what to buy: Bow Wow Wow was best at its inception, when the group was still, um, safely under McLaren's wing. Its debut, *Your Cassette Pet,* (EMI, 1980, prod. Malcolm McLaren) provides the most consistently palatable collection of Afrobeat pop. To further churn the publicity mill, McLaren released the album—with its pro-taping single "C-30, C-60, C-90, Go!"—during the midst of the British recording industry's accusations that home recording was killing sales. Most of *Your Cassette Pet* was later released on *12 Original Recordings,* (Capitol, 1982, prod. Malcom McLaren) along will a few b-sides.

Ways to Know Your Doo Wop

The Doo Wop Box
(Rhino)

Greatest Hits 1939-1946
the Ink Spots (MCA)

Best of a Capella
(Relics)

Doo Wop Delights
(Relics)

Best of Marcels
(Rhino)

Wimoweh: The Best of the Tokens
(RCA)

Very Best of the Drifters
(Rhino)

The Doo Bop She Bop: Best of the Flamingos
(Rhino)

The Best of the Belmonts
(Relics)

The Very Best of the Drifters
(Rhino)

Magic Touch: An Anthology
the Platters (Mercury)

50 Coastin' Classics
the Coasters (Rhino)

Blue Velvet: The Ultimate Collection
the Moonglows (Chess)

For Collectors Only
Frankie Lymon & the Teenagers (Collectables)

The Best of the Del Vikings: The Mercury Years
(Mercury/Chronicles)

The Best of The Penguins: The Mercury Years
(Mercury/Chronicles)

what to buy next: The unmarketably-titled *See Jungle! See Jungle! Go Join Your Gang, Yeah! City All Over! Go Ape Crazy!* (RCA, 1981, prod. Malcolm McLaren) ♪♪♪ comes the closest to the successful formula originated on *Your Cassette Pet*.

what to avoid: Though its title song, a thumping cover of the Strangeloves' beach-pop hit, has become a retro favorite—and a fixture at sporting events—*I Want Candy* (RCA, 1982, prod. Various) ♪♪ is a tired re-release of *Last of the Mohicans* (RCA EP, 1982) ♪♪ with a handful of sub-par b-sides tacked on.

the rest: *When the Going Gets Tough (the Tough Get Going)* (RCA, 1983) ♪♪ *Best of Bow Wow Wow* (Receiver, 1989) ♪♪♪

solo outings:

Annabella Lwin: *Fever* (RCA, 1986) ♪

▶▶ Oingo Boingo, Siouxsie and the Banshees, Belly

◀◀ Adam and the Ants, Sex Pistols, Bo Diddley

Brandon Trenz

David Bowie

Born David Robert Jones, Jan. 8, 1947 in London, England

Bowie was an indispensable voice of the 70s, pursuing a rare compositional and emotional balance as he adopted a variety of guises and experimented with different styles of music. He rarely faltered; songs such as "Space Oddity," "Moonage Daydream" and "Young Americans" remain as moving today as they were when they were originally released, matching even John Lennon and Paul McCartney in their intensity and inventive popcraft. He also presented some of the most elaborately staged concerts of the era. During the the 80s, however, Bowie adopted a more straightforward pop approach with less satisfying results—though his work with a cauterwaling side band called Tin Machine explored a more avant noise tip. Unfortunately, most of Bowie's recent releases are embarrassingly bad, the work of someone who's clearly lost the plot.

what to buy: *The Rise and Fall of Ziggy Stardust and the Spiders from Mars* (RCA, 1972, prod. David Bowie and Ken Scott) ♪♪♪♪♪ is Bowie's crowning achievement, his finest fusion of concept and songs ("Moonage Daydream," "Suffragette City," "Starman"). Driven by exquisite melodies, stellar playing and the songwriter's singular vision, it is one of the finest albums of the 70s. Its follow-up, *Aladdin Sane*, (RCA, 1973, prod. David Bowie and Ken Scott) ♪♪♪♪♪ pushes the boundaries of pop music by prominently incorporating jazzy pianos in the rock 'n' roll mix. Written during Bowie's *Ziggy Stardust* tour, the album focuses on the singer's peculiar view of life in America, as captured in songs such as "Drive-In Saturday" and "Panic In Detroit." To get a better taste of Bowie's experimental side, *Station To Station* (RCA, 1976, prod. David Bowie and Harry

Maslin) ℓℓℓℓℓ is a vital beginning, marking Bowie's first real attempts at deconstructionism—which, in turn, led to the Bowie/Brian Eno collaborative trilogy of *Low, Heroes,* and *Lodger,* though it also included ace pop tunes like "Golden Years" and "Wild is the Wind." Bowie also released several greatest hits packages throughout his career, which serve as excellent primers to the dynamic span of his work. *The Singles 1969-1993* (Rykodisc, 1993, comp. Jeff Rougvie) ℓℓℓℓℓ is the best, a double-album set that touches on every crucial move forward.

what to buy next: On *Young Americans,* (RCA, 1975, prod. Tony Visconti) ℓℓℓℓ Bowie delves into soul grooves, with dazzling results. It includes such sensuous groovers as the title track and "Fame." *Hunky Dory* (RCA, 1971, prod. Ken Scott) ℓℓℓℓ was a similarly moving affair, with meditative melodies and lush string arrangements for "Changes," "Oh, You Pretty Things" and "Life On Mars?" As for the Bowie/Eno collaborations, *Heroes* (RCA, 1977, prod. David Bowie and Tony Visconti) ℓℓℓℓ is the highlight, incorporating some of Bowie's finest melodies into the atmospheric soundscapes. The title track is stellar, as are "Beauty and the Beast" and "Joe The Lion." Bowie's debut, *Space Oddity,* (originally released as *Man of Words, Man of Music*) (RCA, 1969, prod. Tony Visconti and Gus Dudgeon) ℓℓℓℓ still stands as a masterpiece. Psychedelic, innocent and suggestive, it captures just the right balance of wide-eyed wondering and young man coming of age, particularly on such stirring songs as "Letter To Hermione" and "An Occasional Dream."

what to avoid: Most of Bowie's later recordings are criminally bland, the biggest culprit of the lot being the insipid *Never Let Me Down* (EMI, 1987, prod. David Bowie and David Richards) WOOF!, with its listless single "Day In Day Out." The vulgar "Glass Spider" tour that promoted it wasn't much better.

the rest: *The Man Who Sold the World* (RCA, 1970) ℓℓℓℓ *Pin Ups* (RCA, 1973) ℓℓℓ *Diamond Dogs* (RCA, 1974) ℓℓℓℓ *David Live* (RCA, 1974) ℓℓℓ *Low* (RCA, 1977) ℓℓℓℓ *Stage* (RCA, 1977) ℓℓℓ *Lodger* (RCA, 1979) ℓℓℓ *Scary Monsters* (RCA, 1980, prod. David Bowie/Tony Visconti) ℓℓℓ½ *Ziggy Stardust: The Motion Picture* (RCA, 1983) ℓℓℓ *Let's Dance* (EMI, 1983) ℓℓ *Tonight* (EMI, 1984) ℓ *Sound + Vision* (Rykodisc, 1989/1994) ℓℓℓ½ *Black Tie White Noise* (Savage, 1993) WOOF! *Santa Monica '72* (Griffin, 1995) ℓℓℓ½ *The Buddha of Suburbia* (Virgin, 1993/1995) WOOF! *Outside* (Virgin, 1995) WOOF! (with Tin Machine): *Tin Machine* (EMI, 1989) WOOF! *Tin Machine II* (Victory, 1991) WOOF! *Tin Machine Live: Oy Vey, Baby* (Victory, 1992) WOOF!

worth searching for: The deluxe edition of *Ziggy Stardust...* (Rykodisc, 1990, prod. David Bowie and Ken Scott) ℓℓℓℓℓ gives this wondrous album a royal treatment with superior sound quality, bonus tracks and a lavish booklet to enhance an already marvelous listening experience.

▶▶ Duran Duran, Suede, The Smiths, Smashing Pumpkins, Nirvana

◀◀ Pink Floyd, the Yardbirds, the Who, the Kinks, the Easybeats

Aidin Vaziri

The Box Tops

See: Alex Chilton

Boy George

See: Culture Club

Terry Bozzio

See: Missing Persons

Brad

See: Pearl Jam

Billy Bragg

Born Dec. 20, 1957 in Essex, England

The sight of this brash Brit busking with an electric guitar and speakers mounted on his backpack was an irresistible image in 1983. His fiery mixture of the Clash's energy and Woody Guthrie's political fervor was an equally irresistible image. Since he often performs solo, Bragg could be dismissed as just another angry folk singer, but underneath the sometimes laborious left-wing rhetoric is a startling command of pop music that made his better albums a fascinating tug-of-war between message and melody. His best known song, "A New England," was turned into a British radio hit by Kirsty MacColl and was recently ransacked by American punk-pop act Too Much Joy.

what to buy: *Back to Basics* (Elektra, 1987, prod. Kenny Jones) ℓℓℓℓ compiles his first three British releases ("Life's a Riot

With Spy Vs. Spy," "Brewing Up" and "Between the Wars") and offers the most cohesive look at Bragg's earlier, gruff appeal. "Talking With the Taxman About Poetry" (Elektra, 1986, prod. Kenny Jones and John Porter) reflects a marked jump in maturity as a songwriter ("Levi Stubbs' Tears," "Greetings to the New Brunette") and the start of a warmer, more-fleshed out sound that reaches fruition on *Don't Try This at Home*, (Elektra, 1991, prod. Grant Showbiz). The latter includes his prettiest, most reflective material and backing from members of R.E.M. on "You Woke Up My Neighborhood."

what to buy next: *Workers Playtime* (Elektra, 1988, prod. Joe Boyd) is Bragg's first attempt to integrate a band sound with help from noted British folk producer Boyd. Such infectious tunes as "Life With the Lions," "She's Got a New Spell" and "Waiting for the Great Leap Forwards" foreshadow what he will achieve on "Don't Try This At Home"

what to avoid: *The Internationale* (Elektra, 1990, prod. Wiggy and Grant Showbiz) , a turgid EP which finds Bragg on his socialist soapbox offering heavy-handed adaptations of protest anthems dating back to the Industrial Revolution of the 19th century.

the rest: *Help Save the Youth of America* EP (Elektra, 1988) *William Bloke* (Electra, 1996) not available for rating

worth searching for: *Let Them Eat Bingo* (Elektra, 1990), the debut album by Beats International, finds guest vocalist Bragg mustering up a convincing falsetto on the Philly soul-flavored "Won't Talk About It."

Hammell On Trial, John Wesley Harding

The Clash, Woody Guthrie, Elvis Costello

David Okamoto

Laura Branigan

Born July 3, 1957 in Brewster, N.Y.

Branigan blurted out overly dramatic, studio-pumped pop hits during the early to mid-80s with enough studio sheen to guarantee at least a few singles before fading away. Whether her healthy set of pipes could have been used to better effect is a moot question now that her decade-plus career has yet to produce anything even remotely organic.

what to buy: *The Best of Branigan* (Atlantic, 1995, prod. Various) offers the radio dramas all in a row, including her first hit, "Gloria," the quicky follow-up "Solitaire" and "Self Control."

what to buy next: *Branigan*, (Atlantic, 1982, prod. Jack White) her debut album, contains "Gloria" (*not* the Them stomper), which showcases her flair for bluster and willingness to be submerged in glossy production.

what to avoid: *Branigan 2*. (Atlantic, 1983, prod. Jack White) Covering The Who's "Squeeze Box" could be deemed imaginative. Right. And maybe Joni Mitchell should try "Me So Horny."

the rest: *Self Control* (Atlantic, 1984) *Touch* (Atlantic, 1987, prod. various) *Over My Heart* (Atlantic, 1994)

Alanis Morrisette, Joan Osborne

Tina Turner, Donna Summer, Hall and Oates, Irene Cara

Allan Orski

Brave Combo

Formed 1979 in Denton, Texas

Carl Finch, vocals, accordion and guitar; Bubba Hernandez, bass and vocals; and Jeffrey Barnes, saxophone, clarinet and percussion

A self-described "nuclear polka" band, Brave Combo is often shortchanged as a novelty act since its frenetic live shows zigzag from stampede-inducing romps through "Who Stole the Kishka" and "The Happy Wanderer" all the way to a surf version of "Oh, What a Beautiful Morning" and a swinging take on Wayne Newton's "Danke Schoen." But over the years, the Combo—a revolving six-piece band built around the nucleus of Finch, Hernandez and Barnes—has evolved into a versatile outfit capable of being both faithful and funky as they parade through polkas, rancheras, sambas, cumbias and anything else you can dance to. Once a band to simply get wrecked to, Brave Combo is now a group to be reckoned with.

what to buy: *No, No, No, Cha Cha Cha* (Rounder, 1993, prod. Brave Combo) focuses on the group's Latin influences and boasts a seamless medley of the Rolling Stones' "Satisfaction" and Ringo Starr's "No No Song, " a festive salsa version of Cher's "The Way of Love" and a boss bossa-nova rendition of "Fly Me to the Moon." *Polkas for a Gloomy World* (Rounder, 1995, prod. Brave Combo) is their Grammy-nominated return to straight-ahead polka, mixing infectious originals like "Flying Saucer" with traditional Mexican, Russian and German polkas. *It's Christmas, Man!* (Rounder, 1992, prod. Brave Combo) is an irreverent antidote to all those Mannheim Steamroller holiday albums thanks to the delightful title track, a ska version of "The Christmas Song" and an inspired reading of "Must Be Santa," once recorded by Lorne Greene.

what to buy next: *Girl*, a surprisingly listenable collaboration with Tiny Tim (Rounder, 1996, prod. Brave Combo and Bucks Burnett) demonstrates the depth of Brave Combo's musical vocabulary and its astounding ability to make anyone sound good. Check out the hepcat-jazz version of "Stairway to Heaven" and the "Wooly Bully"-like reworking of "Bye Bye Blackbird."

what to avoid: *Musical Varieties*, (Rounder, 1988, prod. Brave Combo) a compilation of pre-Rounder tracks from the early '80s. Although hardly horrid, they lean toward predictable gimmickry ("People Are Strange" and "Sixteen Tons" as polkas), sideswiping genres the band would eventually tackle head-on.

the rest: *Polkatharsis* (Rounder, 1987) *Humansville* (Rounder, 1989) *A Night on Earth* (Rounder, 1990)

Worth Searching Out: *The Hokey Pokey* (denTone, 1994, prod. Brave Combo), a self-released EP of wacky concert favorites like "The Hava Nagila Twist," "The Jeopardy Schottische" and a Devo-like demolition of the title track.

The New Orleans Klezmer All Stars

You name it

David Okamoto

Bread

Formed 1969 in Los Angeles, Calif. Disbanded 1973. Reunited 1976.

David Gates, vocals, guitar, bass, keyboards, violin; James Griffin, vocals, guitar, keyboards; Robb Royer, guitar, bass, keyboards, flute (1969-71); Larry Knechtel, keyboards, bass, guitar, harmonica (1972-77); Jim Gordon, drums (1969); Mike Botts, drums (1970-77)

Bread was put together by three veteran session musicians and songwriters (whose credits include Lesley Gore, the Monkees, Bobby Darin and Connie Stevens) to take advantage of music trends they saw coming. Their foresight was accurate, as the group scored 11 Top 40 hits. But the hit singles, all penned by Gates, caused critics to reject them with the label "soft rock," and the group is thought of mostly for ballads perceived as saccharine, insincere odes written solely to achieve commercial success. Though there's some truth to the accusation, since a few of Gates's biggest hits are almost unbearably sappy, other Gates tunes, and some Griffin efforts, are pop masterpieces. Bread started its hit parade on its second album, when the single "Make it With You" hit No. 1 on the strength of Gates' casual declaration of love; intended as a change of pace on a relatively intense album that belies the perceived image of the quartet, it ended up defining Bread's sound. The string continued with "Baby I'm-a Want You," "Everything I Own" and "It Don't Matter to Me," though before long tension arose between Gates and Griffin, who wanted to pursue more rock-oriented directions. (It also must have hurt that none of the 10 singles Griffin had a hand in writing made the Top 40.) In 1973, the group broke up after an incredibly productive run. A 1976 reunion suffered from the same tensions and produced one hit. Gates, not surprisingly, had the most successful post-Bread solo career (his big hit was the title song for the film "The Goodbye Girl" in 1978), though it hardly matched Bread's accomplishments. Griffin began concentrating on country work during the 80s, and spent time in an all-star band called Black Tie that featured alumni of Poco, the Eagles and the Beach Boys.

what to buy: *On the Waters* (Elektra, 1970, prod. David Gates, James Griffin and Robb Royer) has many of Gates's best ballads ("Been Too Long on the Road," "Make It With You," "In the Afterglow," "The Other Side of Life") and the peaks of the Griffin/Royer collaboration ("Why Do You Keep Me Waiting," "Look What You've Done," "I Am That I Am," "Coming Apart," "Call On Me"). It's a superb mix of mellow tracks and more intense numbers, with nobody pigeonholed into a role yet and no cloying songs. *Guitar Man* (Elektra, 1972, prod. David Gates) stands out thanks to the title track, "Make It By Yourself," "Fancy Dancer," "Let Me Go" and Knechtel's "Picture in Your Mind."

what to buy next: The two-CD *Retrospective* (Elektra/Rhino, 1996, prod. Bread, David McLees and Bill Inglot) is a model set, with all the Bread hits plus samples of the solo work by Gates and Griffin (including the demo of "For All We Know").

what to avoid: The reunion album *Lost Without Your Love* (Elektra, 1977, prod. David Gates) was tepid and uninspired.

the rest: *Bread* (Elektra, 1969) *Manna* (Elektra, 1971) *Baby I'm-a Want You* (Elektra, 1972) Gates' *First* (Elektra, 1973) *Never Let Her Go* (Elektra, 1975) *Love is Always Seventeen* (Discovery, 1994, prod. Gates)

worth searching for: Gates' *Goodbye Girl* (Elektra, 1979, prod. David Gates) skims tracks from his first two solo albums (like this one, long out of print) and adds the hit title track and a few new songs of similar vintage. Griffin's *Breakin' Up is Easy* (Polydor, 1973, prod. James Griffin and Robb Royer) suffers from dated production but has some good material, and Griffin sings well. Two tracks here with Gates and Knechtel were left over from an aborted Bread album.

solo outings:

David Gates: First (Elektra, 1973) *Never Let Her Go* (Elektra, 1975) *Love is Always Seventeen* (Discovery, 1994)

▶▶ America, Air Supply, Chris von Sneidern, Matthew Sweet

◀◀ Chet Atkins, the Association, Beatles

Steve Holtje

Breeders /Amps

The Breeders (1990-present): Kim Deal, vocals, guitar; Tanya Donnelly, vocals, guitar (1990-93); Josephine Wiggs, bass; Shannon Doughton (born Britt Walford, alias Mike Hunt), drums 1990-93; Kelley Deal, guitar, vocals (1992-present); James Macpherson, drums 1993-present. The Amps (1995-present): Kim Deal, vocals, guitar; Nathan Farley, vocals, guitars, bass; Luis Lerma, bass; James Macpherson, drums

Once a side project for Kim Deal to escape from Black Francis' dominance in the Pixies—and for Donnelly, who moved on to Belly, to find a respite for similar circumstances in Throwing Muses—the Breeders quickly transcended that group's commercial success with the transfixing rock 'n' roll single "Cannonball," which earned the band a spot on the 1994 Lollapalooza tour. Shortly after that, however, Deal's guitarist sister Kelley encountered drug problems and dropped out of the band, forcing Deal to start over yet again with the Amps, which is a bit more spacey but still rocked. But with Kelley's subsequent treatment—she also formed a side band, the Kelley Deal 6000—the siblings have openly discussed the possibility of more Breeders work.

what to buy: The Breeders' *Last Splash* (4AD/Elektra, 1993, prod. Kim Deal and Mark Freegard) finds Deal wriggling away from Black Francis and proving her love of twisted pop melodies was a key driving force behind the Pixies; the dripping strawberry heart on the album cover somehow perfectly captures the juicy hooks in "Cannonball," "Drivin' on 9," "I Just Wanna Get Along" and "No Aloha."

what to avoid: The Amps' *Pacer* (4AD/Elektra, 1995, prod. Various) sound like a transitional album before the talented Deal figures out a more creatively lucrative directions.

the rest: Breeders: *Pod* (4AD/Elektra, 1990) Kelly Deal 6000: *Go to the Sugar Alter* (Nice, 1996)

worth searching for: The Breeders' four-song EP, *Safari* (4AD/Elektra, 1992) is the sound of a new band getting its act together. "Don't Call Home" is the spookiest thing Deal ever wrote, and its explosive cover of the Who's "So Sad About Us" makes a case for that song's forgotten greatness.

▶▶ Juliana Hatfield, Belly

◀◀ Ramones, the Beach Boys, the Jesus and Mary Chain, the Who, Husker Du, Throwing Muses, Raincoats, the Replacements

Steve Knopper

Edie Brickell & New Bohemians

Formed 1985 in Dallas, Texas. Disbanded 1991.

Edie Brickell (born March 10, 1966), vocals, guitar; Kenny Withrow, guitar, vocals; Brad Houser, bass; Wes Burt-Martin, guitar, vocals; Matt Chamberlain, drums; John Bush, percussion

Meet the new boho, same as the old boho. Like the eternal hipoisie from whom they take their name, Edie Brickell and New Bohemians were merely unconventional as opposed to revolutionary, and merely clever as opposed to smart. Brickell's shy-girl personality comes through in her vocals, which are low-key and charmingly unassuming, and in her lyrics, which read like pages of a schoolgirl's journal. And while the group displayed undeniable instrumental chops in its laid-back mix of rock, folk and jazz, it was a pretty faceless bunch, which led to discord when Brickell—who, after all, first sat in with the band on a dare—became its unmistakable star and, ultimately a solo artist. *Shooting Rubberbands at the Stars* (Geffen, 1988, prod. Pat Moran) contains the hit "What I Am." a loping bit of anti-intellectualism driven by Withrow's neo-Garcia guitar noodlings, and "Little Miss S.," a tribute to bohemian shooting star Edie Sedgewick. *Ghost of a Dog* (Geffen, 1990, prod. Tony Berg) produced no hits, but it's a less-studied outing, with the nursery-rhyme rocker "Black & Blue" and accordionist Jo-el Sonnier sitting in on "Carmelito." After New Bohemians split, and Brickell married Paul Simon, and for good and ill—mostly the latter—her writing has picked up his habits of detailing the intricacies of quotidian ups and downs. Her solo debut, *Picture Perfect Morning,* (Geffen, 1994, prod. Paul Simon and Roy Halee) features a funkier sound and a host of guest stars, including Dr. John, Barry White, Art and Cyrille Neville, the Dixie

Cups and Simon himself. Unfortunately, the material is generally too weak to support the cast.

Daniel Durchholz

Eddie Brigati

See: The Young Rascals

David Bromberg

Born September 19, 1945 in Philadelphia, Pa.

Known as the consummate "musician's musician," multi-instrumentalist Bromberg is a virtual jukebox of American roots music. Equally at home in folk, blues, rock, jazz, country, bluegrass, Texas swing and Irish traditional, a Bromberg album is like a musical stew. Drawn to the Greenwich Village folk scene of the mid-'60s, Bromberg—who was studying to be a musicologist—dropped out of Columbia University to work full time as a performer. His proficiency as a guitarist combined with his eclectic range of styles led to a substantial career as a session musician, appearing on close to 80 albums for the likes of Bob Dylan, Jerry Jeff Walker, Ringo Starr, Phoebe Snow and others. Following a stunning last-minute performance at the 1970 Isle of Wight Festival, Bromberg was offered his own recording contract with Columbia. In 1976 he moved to the Fantasy label and formed the David Bromberg Band which featured, on any given tune, a bluesy assault of electric guitars or a blend of fiddles, mandolin, clarinet, trombone, and acoustic guitar. An electrifying performer, it's no accident that many of Bromberg's albums include live performances, both solo and with his tight-knit band. Currently semi-retired (his last album was in 1989, and he rarely performs), Bromberg lives in Chicago where he buys, sells and builds violins.

what to buy: His debut, *David Bromberg* (Columbia, 1971, prod. David Bromberg), showcases all of his influences with a mostly acoustic album of blues, folk, rock and a tune co-written with George Harrison ("The Holdup"). "The Holdup" surfaces again on *Wanted Dead or Alive* (Columbia, 1974, prod. David Bromberg), along with a Bob Dylan tune ("Wallflower"), a Blind Willie McTell classic ("Statesboro Blues") and Bromberg's own blend of acoustic folk/blues ("The New Lee Highway Blues"). *How Late'll Ya Play Til?* (Fantasy, 1976, prod. David Bromberg and Steve Burgh) is available as a two-disc set or individually. One disc is a studio recording, the other live, and both show Bromberg and his band in top form.

what to buy next: *Out of The Blues: The Best of David Bromberg* (Columbia, 1977, prod. David Bromberg) provides a good introduction, but unfortunately it relies too much on novelty tunes such as "Sharon" and "The Holdup," and not enough on the rootsier side of Bromberg's music. It's still worth for a great rendition of "Mr. Bojangles."

what to avoid: *Bandit in a Bathing Suit* (Fantasy, 1978, prod. David Bromberg and Hugh McDonald). Perhaps it was an attempt to sound more commercial, but the unemotional pop songs included on this album don't even approach the capabilities of this band.

the rest: *Demon in Disguise* (Columbia, 1972) *Midnight on the Water* (Columbia, 1975) *Reckless Abandon* (Fantasy, 1977) *My Own House* (Fantasy, 1978) *You Should See the Rest of the Band* (Fantasy, 1980) *Long Way From Here* (Fantasy, 1986) *Sideman Serenade* (Rounder, 1989)

worth searching for: Fiddler Vassar Clements' *Hillbilly Jazz* (Flying Fish, 1974), which features Bromberg on a nice western swing recording.

▶▶ David Grisman, Chris Whitley

◀◀ The Beatles, Rev. Gary Davis, Bob Dylan, Jerry Jeff Walker

Brian Escamilla

Bronski Beat /Jimmy Somerville/Communards

Born June 22, 1961, in Glasgow, Scotland

Bronski Beat (1982-86)—Sommerville, vocals (1982-85); Steve Bronski, keyboards, percussion; Larry Steinbachek, keyboards, percussion; John Jon Foster, vocals (1985-86) Communards (1985-87)—Sommerville, vocals; Richard Coles, keyboards

Although Boy George, Morrissey, the Pet Shop Boys and Frankie Goes to Hollywood each struck musical blows on behalf of gay rights in England during the 80s, none made as extreme an impact as the voice of Somerville, original lead singer of Bronski Beat, co-leader of the Communards and, finally, successful solo artist. When the singles "Smalltown Boy" and "Why?" pounded dance floors in 1984, nothing had existed to compare with his piercing, yet not quite unpleasant, falsetto voice—except perhaps an operatic countertenor. By 1985, he had left Bronski Beat to form the Communards; he had (along with Billy Bragg and Paul Weller, among others) become an active part of the socialist Red Wedge movement that was sweeping Britain at the time, and though politics didn't play a direct role in the group's music, he was clearly developing his art. In 1990, he put out his first solo album, and it expressed an even wider musical scope. His hitmaking days may be over at this point, but his sonic and stylistic influence cannot be overstated. His voice and genre may not be for all tastes, but without him, dance-club music would be very different.

what to buy: *The Singles Collection 1984-90* (FFRR/London, 1990, prod. Various) 🦴🦴🦴🦴 offers nearly everything you could possibly want, including wistful Bronski Beat hits such as "Why?" and "Smalltown Boy," plenty of Communards cuts (especially the furious dance remake of "Never Can Say Goodbye"), and five from his first solo disc, *Read My Lips*.

what to buy next: Although most of the best cuts from *Read My Lips* (London, 1990, prod. Jimmy Somerville, Pascal Gabriel and Stephen Hague) 🦴🦴🦴 are contained on *The Singles Collection*, this album features quite a stylistic range and makes for an impressive listening experience on its own.

what to avoid: More than 10 years after Bronski Beat first astonished the dance-pop scene with its hyper-trebliness, Sommerville's *Dare to Love* (London, 1995, prod. Various) 🦴🦴 sounds awfully dated. He's a pro, and his voice is as cutting as ever, but the new songs just don't measure up.

the rest: Bronski Beat: *The Age of Consent* (MCA, 1984) 🦴🦴🦴 *Truthdare Doubledare* (MCA, 1986) 🦴🦴 Communards: *Communards* (MCA, 1986) 🦴🦴 *Red* (MCA, 1987) 🦴🦴🦴

▶▶ Cece Peniston, Cathy Dennis

◀◀ Donna Summer, Giorgio Moroder, Thelma Houston, Alison Moyet, Q-Feel

Bob Remstein

Jonatha Brooke and the Story

Formed 1990 in Boston, Mass.

Jonatha Brooke, vocals, guitar, piano; Jennifer Kimball (1990-94), harmony vocals

The Story's self-consciously arty yet still compelling debut *Grace in Gravity* (Green Linnet/Elektra, 1991, prod. Ben Wittman) 🦴🦴🦴 caught the attention of veteran jazz producer Tommy LiPuma, who helped to hook the duo up with Elektra. What he must have noticed was the sweet but edgy pairing of Brooke's Sarah McLachlan-like lead vocals and Kimball's tight harmonies, as well as the Jane Siberry-like humor of "Dog Dreams" and the Joni Mitchell-influenced poetry of "Damn Everything But the Circus." With *The Angel in the House*, (Green Linnet/Elektra, 1993, prod. Alain Mallet and Ben Wittman) 🦴🦴🦴🦴 the duo really hit its mark, scoring an adult-alternative hit with the poignant and striking "So Much Mine." Besides other gorgeous cuts such as "The Gilded Cage," the album features the Brazilian-influenced "At the Still Point," and the hilarious, salsa-fied "Fatso," in which the duo sing out of tune for a stretch to illustrate the weakening effects of a starvation diet. Elektra, not happy with the group's sales, dropped the Story, which led to Kimball leaving to sing backup for fellow Boston folkie Patti Larkin. Brooke returned in 1995 with a longer group name and a jazzier new album, *Plumb*. (Blue Thumb/GRP, 1995, prod. Alain Mallet) 🦴🦴🦴 Now married to Mallet, she allowed him to add an over-the-top bebop piano solo to "Inconsolable" as well as a lovely string arrangement for "Paris." Without Kimball to provide her half of those alluring two-part vocal textures, the album suffers a bit, but clearly Brooke is able to make artful, highly desirable music on her own, thank you very much.

Bob Remstein

Gary Brooker

See: Procol Harum

Arthur Brown

Born June 24, 1942, in Whitby, England

One of the first truly theatrical rockers, Brown was using fire in his act before either Jimi Hendrix or Kiss did. His first band, the Crazy World of Arthur Brown, was also his most successful, scoring a Top 10 hit with the novel "Fire" and its ominous intro: "I am the God of burning fire!!" That band included drummer Carl Palmer, later of Emerson, Lake and Palmer. Brown never did much after that. He put together an electronic band, Kingdom Come, during the early 70s and all but disappeared until the 80s, when the Englishman once favored by the Who's Pete Townshend relocated to Austin, Texas, and hooked up with former Mothers of Invention drummer Jimmy Carl Black. Their *Brown, Black and Blue* (BlueWave) 🦴🦴 marked a return to Brown's bluesier roots. It's the only album of his work in print today.

▶▶ Alice Cooper, David Bowie, Sensational Alex Harvey Band

◀◀ London's West End theaters.

Doug Pullen

Bobby Brown

See: New Edition

James Brown

Born May 3, 1933, in Barnwell, S.C.

In terms of soul music, nobody can top the contributions or the pervasive influence of Brown. He is a living link between the R&B swing bands of Louis Jordan and today's rap minimalists. The great soul singers of the middle and late 60s—and more than a few rockers—took lessons from his early records and that animalistic scream he called a voice. Brown literally invented funk, still the dominant influence on black music—especially disco and rap. Like no one, save Ray Charles, Brown faced off the spiritual passion and cadences of black gospel preachers with the supercharged sexual beat and rhythms of R&B. "Please, Please, Please," "Try Me" and "Think" introduced Brown's considerable skills to a generation of budding soul stars that would explode in the mid-60s. His stage show, from the corny-yet-effective cape routines to the rigorously rehearsed, ultra-professional, dapper Famous Flames revue, set a sweaty standard. Nobody worked harder than the self-dubbed Hardest Working Man in Show Business (a.k.a. Mr. Dynamite, the Godfather of Soul). Beginning in 1965, he began treating the recording studio with the same precision and exuberance of an Apollo midnight performance, and his incredibly high standards for band membership paid off with "Papa's Got a Brand New Bag (1965) and "It's a Man's, Man's, Man's World" (1966), music as revolutionary and innovative as any from the better-known and higher-praised Beatles, Rolling Stones or Bob Dylan. As the 60s wore on, Brown's lyrics became more strident and often focused on the civil rights movement. As the lyrics eschewed sex and romance to stress black individualism ("Say It Loud, I'm Black and I'm Proud"), the music turned in on itself in ever more primal ways. Brown's band became an incubator of soul, home to innovative, talented musicians—Maceo Parker, Bobby Byrd, Fred Wesley and Bootsy Collins—as stubborn, professional, moody and self-determined as their boss. Solos and verse-chorus patterns were dumped in favor of extended, repetitive grooves pushed to fever pitch by Brown's call-and-response vocal chants ("Take me to the bridge!" "Give the drummer some!"). Before long, every instrument was playing some sort of percussion role—an approach that evolved into the dance music that became known as funk, then disco and then the even more fragmented hip-hop styles. Brown has achieved enormous wealth and success, but he's also been dogged by drug addictions and personal problems that landed him in prison during the late 80s. But there's no denying Brown's importance, the proof of which is found in 40 years of solid, ground-breaking grooves.

what to buy: Brown's recorded output is as fragmented as the funk he created. Fortunately, he was more a singles artist, and whether you're at all interested in his importance or just want to shake your booty, nothing can possibly top *Star Time* (Polydor, 1991, prod. Various) This is a comprehensive, chronological and funkifying solid four discs of his very best and most important works, with many of the singles expanded back to their original lengths and liner notes that detail his accomplishments. If you're a bit more cautious, you shouldn't be without *Solid Gold 30 Golden Hits,* (Polydor, 1986, prod. Various) which boasts about half of those incredibly visionary, exhausting and shake-your-booty singles. *Live at the Apollo* (King, 1963/Polydor, 1990, prod. James Brown) captures the midnight show on Aug. 24, 1962, that put Brown on the national map, an electrifying documentation of pure show-time from the best live act of its time.

what to buy next: When Sid Nathan of King Records wouldn't release an instrumental called "(Do The) Mash Potatoes," Brown put it out on another label under a pseudonym (Nat Kendrick & the Swans). Not surprisingly, it was a hit. His limitless proficiency on instrumental tracks matches (or at least augments) the creativity of the vocal hits, and many of his bands' finest performances are featured on *Soul Pride: The Instrumentals 1960-1969* (Polydor, 1993, prod. James Brown) The insights are tremendous; Brown, for instance, stands out as an intuitive organ player whose fluid style is perfectly suited to the music. *Roots of a Revolution* (Polydor, 1983, prod. Tim Rogers) is a producer's choice of recordings from 1956-64, showing how Brown and his Famous Flames went from imitative to innovative in the years leading up to "Papa's Got a Brand New Bag." His blues side gets a rare spotlight on *Messing with the Blues,* (Polydor, 1990, prod. James Brown) which illuminates his individualistic approach toward cover material and proves him as impressive a stylist as Ray Charles.

what to avoid: *Black Caesar* and *Slaughter's Big Rip-Off* (both Polydor, 1973, prod. James Brown) are two blaxploitation film soundtracks that prove Brown was mortal after all.

the rest: Brown's albums number at least into the 80s, ranging from the imaginative to the perfunctory, and from the superficial to the redundant. Never pass up any of his releases on vinyl, however, and all of the following weigh in at three bones or better: *Please Please Please* (King, 1959/PolyGram Chronicles, 1996); *Think* (King, 1960/PolyGram Chronicles, 1996); *Papa's Got a Brand New Bag* (King/PolyGram Special Products, 1965); *Sex Machine* (King, 1970/PolyGram Chronicles, 1996); *Hell* (Polydor, 1975); *20 All-Time Greatest Hits* (Polydor, 1991); *Love Power Peace: Live at the Olympia, Paris, 1971* (Polydor, 1992); *Funk Power 1970: A Brand New Thang* (Polydor Chronicles, 1996)

worth searching for: If you're interested in Brown's early recordings, the out of print collection *The Federal Years—Parts One and Two* (Solid Smoke, 1984) offers nascent versions of Brown's early vision and the growing pangs of the Famous Flames. Also look for his collaboration with hip-hop pioneer Afrika Bambaataa, *Unity,* (Tommy Boy, 1984, prod. Tom Silverman and Afrika Bambaataa) just in case you were wondering about Brown's connection to rap.

Michael Jackson, Otis Redding, Sly and the Family Stone, Jimi Hendrix, Mick Jagger, Parliament-Funkadelic, George Clinton, Bootsy Collins, Peter Wolf (J. Geils Band), Isaac Hayes, Chic, Afrika Bambaataa, Prince, Eric B. and Rakim, Hammer, Rod Stewart

Hank Ballard & the Midnighters, Ray Charles, Louis Jordan, Bo Diddley, Wynonie Harris, Roy Brown, the Dominos, Five Royales.

Leland Rucker

Jackson Browne

Born Oct. 9, 1948 in Heidelberg, West Germany

Jackson Browne was the right artist for his times—during a decade in which rock fans were growing up and dealing with real-life problems for the first time, Browne's thoughtful personal reflection seemed, well, thoughtful. When he titled his second LP *For Everyman,* a generation of fans took it for granted that they were the "everyman" Browne was writing about. At his best, he's a powerful songwriter because he writes personal truths and sings realistically about love from a post-collegiate point of view (Joni Mitchell was the female equivalent emotionally, though musically she was much more complex and experimental). His early songs such as "Ready or Not" and "Take It Easy" may have been sexist drivel, but guys were like that then. And over the course of his albums, you could watch Browne grow up; his best work—songs such as "Fountain of Sorrow" or "For a Dancer" —weren't macho manifestos, but thoughtful (there's that word again) ruminations of lost love that went well beyond the simple romanticism of Top 40 radio.

But on *Late For the Sky*—the same album that yielded "For a Dancer"—Browne planted the seeds of his ultimate downfall as an artist. His socio-political conscience, revealed on the anti-nuke song "Before the Deluge," powerful and moving as an album closer, was the beginning of Browne's immersion in issues of the day. By the 1980s, Browne's somewhat one-dimensional sound sounded strident because of his insistence in using his position as a pop star to issue political harangues, albeit important ones, about Central America, the environment and modern America in general. Most of his recent output makes him sound as tedious and preachy as Bruce Cockburn, even though he's tried to reach back to earlier styles and musical values.

what to buy: *Late for the Sky* (Asylum, 1974, prod. Jackson Browne and Al Schmitt) is a bit mopey, but it hangs together as Browne's strongest and most melodious album, with a couple of rockers thrown in to perk up the listeners. The best song, the fondly reflective "Fountain of Sorrow," is typical of Browne's ability to make personal experience seem universal.

what to buy next: *The Pretender* (Asylum, 1976, prod. Jon Landau) gets a little ponderous on songs such as "Sleep's Dark and Silent Gate" and the title track, Browne's first rant at middle America, but it also was emotionally powerful, with songs of regret ("Your Bright Baby Blues," "Here Come Those Tears Again") and hope for the future ("The Only Child," "Daddy's Tune") following his first wife's 1976 suicide. It also solidified his commercial cachet and was his first platinum LP.

what to avoid: *Running on Empty* (Asylum, 1977, prod. Browne) was hailed at the time as a brilliant concept album about life on the road, but it hasn't held its luster. It now sounds like an indulgent pastiche thrown together with second-rate, emotionally uncompelling material, and a couple of curio-like cover songs ("Rev. Gary Davis," "Cocaine" and the Zodiacs' "Stay," with a cameo vocal by guitarist David Lindley)

the rest: *Jackson Browne* (Asylum, 1972) *For Everyman* (Asylum, 1973) *Hold Out* (Asylum, 1980) *Lawyers in Love* (Asylum, 1983) *Lives in the Balance* (Asylum, 1986) *World in Motion* (Elektra, 1989) *I'm Alive* (Elektra, 1993) *Looking East* (Elektra, 1996)

worth searching for: The promotional CD for Browne's 1993 single *I'm Alive" (Elektra, prod. Jackson Browne and Scott*

Thurston) *was accompanied by a well-chosen 12-song retrospective that was digitally remastered to sound better than Browne's regular CDS.*

▶▶ David Wilcox, Garth Brooks, Natalie Merchant, Alanis Morissette

◀◀ Leonard Cohen, Eric Andersen, Phil Ochs

Gil Asakawa

Brownsville Station /Cub Koda

Formed 1969 in Ann Arbor, Mich. Disbanded 1979.

Cub Koda (born Michael Koda), guitar, vocals; Michael Lutz, guitar, bass, vocals; T.J. Cronley, drums (1969-72); Tony Driggins, bass (1969-73); Henry (H-Bomb) Weck, drums (1972-1979); Bruce Nazarian, guitar, bass, vocals (1975-79)

Following the lead of fellow Ann Arborites Iggy Pop and the Stooges, Brownsville Station was a punk-rock pioneer, serving up raw-edged guitar tunes that featured the quirky snarl of lead singer Koda. The band hit its commercial apex with the 1974 smash "Smokin' In the Boys' Room," the snot-nosed anthem for a generation of teens and pre-teens that reached No. 3 on the charts. The Koda-penned song, also a hit for Motley Crue in 1985, provides the title for the excellent compilation album *Smokin' in the Boys' Room: The Best of Brownsville Station* (Rhino, 1993, prod. Various) The smartly packaged disc includes the wonderful "Let Your Yeah Be Yeah," the wacky "Martian Boogie" and "I'm the Leader of the Gang," a punk-rock prototype from the band's 1974 LP *School Punks.* On his own, Koda has released the well-received *Welcome to My Job—The Cub Koda Collection 1963-1993* (Blue Wave, 1993) and *Abba Dabba Dabba—A Bananza of Hits* (Schoolkids, 1994)

William Hanson

Jack Bruce

Born May 14, 1943, in Glasgow, Scotland

Awarded a scholarship for cello and composition, Bruce dropped out of the Royal Scottish Academy of Music to play jazz bass, then moved to London and hooked up with some of the key players of the 60s British blues boom—Alexis Korner, John Mayall and Graham Bond. He also was with Manfred Mann before teaming up with Eric Clapton and Ginger Baker to form the influential blues-rock power trio Cream in 1966. It was Bruce's clear tenor voice, pop sensibilities and improvisational jazz spirit that set a solid foundation for Clapton's aggressive guitar explorations. After the supergroup split up in 1968, Bruce went on to create a powerful mix of blues, pop, rock and jazz. He's also worked with such premier guitarists as John McLaughlin, Larry Coryell, Gary Moore and Robin Trower. But he's never come close to the synthesis of power, art and public acclaim he enjoyed with Clapton and Cream.

what to buy: *A Question of Time* (Epic, 1989, prod. Joe Blaney and Jack Bruce) features subtly compelling melodies, superb vocals, a balance of scorching rock and soothing acoustic guitars, and a challenging mix of styles. In other words, it is a microcosm of Bruce's diverse post-Cream solo career.

what to buy next: The two-disc set *Willpower* (Polydor, 1989, prod. Various) is a solid retrospective whose 17 songs cover Bruce's broad spectrum of styles. Eric Clapton guests on two songs. *Cities of the Heart* (CMP, 1994, prod. Jack Bruce) was recorded live in Cologne, Germany, in 1993, and features some tasty Cream morsels including, "Spoonful," "Sunshine of Your Love" and "Politician."

what to avoid: *How's Tricks,* (Polydor, 1977, prod. Bill Halverson) an uninspired set of 10 lackluster tunes performed by a thankfully short-lived version of the Jack Bruce Band.

the rest: *Songs for a Tailor* (Polydor, 1969) *Things We Like* (Polydor, 1970) *Harmony Row* (Polydor, 1971) *Out of the Storm* (Polydor, 1974) *Somethinels* (CMP, 1993)

▶▶ Ozzy Osbourne, Robert Plant, Geddy Lee, Stanley Clarke, Rob Wasserman, Jaco Pastorius, Jack Casady

◀◀ Willie Dixon, John Mayall, Charlie Parker, Dizzy Gillespie

see also: *Cream*

David Yonke

Lindsey Buckingham

Born October 3, 1947 in Palo Alto, Calif.

Although it's hard to separate Buckingham from his years with Fleetwood Mac, it's the only way to fully appreciate his impact on that band as well as his achievements as a solo artist. By the time that he and girlfriend Stevie Nicks joined Fleetwood Mac in 1974, the two had already spent time together in the acid rock band Fritz and recorded a mostly folk-rock collection under the billing Buckingham/Nicks. It was this album that brought them to the attention of Mick Fleetwood; Nicks gave

Fleetwood Mac it's first sex symbol, but it was Buckingham's brilliant musicianship, luscious arrangements and studio craft that influenced the sound of the band and led Fleetwood Mac to the top of the charts. Inspired by the punk rock movement and given the role as musical director for the band, Buckingham began to push the group's music into more adventurous directions, which met with some resistance from the rest of the group after the *Tusk* album failed to reach the same commercial heights as its record-setting predecessor, *Rumours* Buckingham released his first two albums while still part of Fleetwood Mac, but in 1987 the longing to spend more time in the studio crafting his own sound got the best of him and Buckingham formally left the band.

what to buy: *Out of the Cradle* (Reprise, 1992, prod. Linsdey Buckingham and Richard Dashut) ♪♪♪♪♪ is Buckingham's finest moment, full of sophisticated arrangements, lush harmonies and vocal treatments, classic finger-picked guitar work and smart pop craftsmanship.

what to buy next: *Law And Order,* (Asylum, 1981, prod. Lindsey Buckingham and Richard Dashut) ♪♪♪♪ his first solo outing, is fun, quirky and quick. The singles "Trouble" and "Bawana" and his re-make of "A Satisfied Mind" insure a winner on their own.

the rest: *Buckingham/Nicks* (Polydor, 1973) ♪♪♪ *Go Insane* (Elektra, 1984) ♪♪♪

worth searching for: The soundtrack to "National Lampoon's Vacation" (Warner Bros., 1983) ♪♪♪ includes the Buckingham songs "Dancing Across the U.S.A." and "Holiday Road," which could have fit perfectly on *Law and Order* or Fleetwood Mac's *Tusk.*

▶▶ John Stewart, Matthew Sweet, Marshall Crenshaw

◀◀ Brian Wilson, Kingston Trio, the Sex Pistols, The Clash

Mike Joiner

The Buckinghams

Formed mid-1965 in Chicago, Ill. Disbanded 1970. Re-formed 1980.

Denny Tufano, vocals; Carl Giannarese, lead guitar; Nick Fortune (born Nicholas Fortuna), bass; Dennis Miccolis, keyboards (1965-67); Marty Grebb (1967-69), organ; Jon-Jon Poulos, drums; John Turner, keyboards (1969-70)

Although the group changed its name from the Pulsations to the Buckinghams to glom onto the British Invasion, this quintet from northwest Chicago sounded more like the West Coast acts emerging at the time, most notably Paul Revere & the Raiders and Gary Puckett & the Union Gap. Tufano's pleasantly engaging voice and the group's punchy combination of guitar, organ and brass made for some stirring white-boy soul stylings, but much of the group's success was owed to outside forces: songwriter Jim Holvay, whose talent for crafting hooky melodies resulted in a string of highly durable hit singles for the group; and ex-Mother of Invention James William Guercio, who acted as something of a sixth member, producing, arranging, conducting and even composing for the band. While its 18 songs are something of an overindulgence, *Mercy Mercy Mercy (A Collection)* (Legacy, 1991, prod. Various) ♪♪♪ features all of the Buckinghams' bona fide hits—"Kind of a Drag," "Don't You Care," "Hey Baby (They're Playing Our Song)" and "Susan." A pleasant reminder of a fun and wistful period in rock's history.

Christopher Scapelliti

Jeff Buckley

Born 1968; place of birth N/A

Buckley is the son of legendary experimental folk artist Tim Buckley, and, as Julian Lennon will tell you, having a famous father can be both a blessing and a curse. As the inheritor of such a legacy, Buckley must endure comparisons to his late father and the expectations of fans eager for the progeny to take up where the sire left off. Like his father, Buckley does possess an ethereal voice capable of dramatic sweeps of range; his singing uncannily evokes Tim's. However, Buckley the junior clearly has a musical agenda quite apart from his father's. In fact, Jeff claims very little musical influence from his father, who died before his son was old enough to remember him. While his material tangentially recalls Tim's florid romanticism, Jeff's musical direction—especially with a band—leans more toward 70s album-rock than folk ballads. *Grace* (Columbia, 1994, prod. Andy Wallace and Jeff Buckley) ♪♪♪♪ is Buckley's second recording, and his first with a full band following the more intimate solo coffee house recording *Live at Sin-E.* (Big Cat/Columbia 1993) ♪♪♪ The material ranges from progressive rock ("So Real") to mediative ballads (a stunning voice and guitar arrangement of Leonard Cohen's "Hallelujah"), to dreamy psychedelia ("Mojo Pin"), yet the album impresses as a cohesive work. The unifying principle is Buckley's versatile singing; his voice can sinuously twine itself around a beautiful melody, hover with growling menace and swoop to startling falsetto heights, often within the same song. The most pop-friendly material here ("Last Goodbye," "Grace") boasts smart hooks, inventive arrangements and restrained, yet aggressive playing. Buckley's writing on *Grace* shows a distinct knack for interesting melodies and haunting lyricism, and the album stands as an impressive early achievement.

David Galens

Tim Buckley

Born Feb. 14, 1947 in Washington, D.C. Died June 29, 1975 in Santa Monica, Calif.

One of numerous folk singer/songwriters to surface in Dylan's mid-60's wake, Buckley soon parted company with his peers to chart a path very much his own. Though his earliest records seem innocently romantic today (he was just 19 when his first album appeared), his turn towards a more free-form, jazz-influenced sound pushed his introspective and always impassioned vocals right off the map. For it was Buckley's voice, above all, that distinguished him—a stunning, four-octave wonder that ranged from angelic tenderness to blistering passion. Recording for Frank Zappa's Straight label from 1970-73, his folk/jazz experimentation—and angst-ridden, sexually direct material (eg. "Get On Top Of Me Woman")—was critically admired but found little commercial acceptance. By 1975, Buckley was dead of a heroin overdose. Ironically, his underappreciated legacy is being rediscovered today through the popularity of his son Jeff Buckley (who sounds uncannily like his father).

what to buy: Oddly, for a singer of Buckley's improvisatory talents, no live recordings appeared during his lifetime. Two recent releases have remedied that - and are a perfect place for the uninitiated to start. *Dream Letter: Live In London, 1968* (Manifesto, 1990, prod. Bill Inglot and Lee Hammond) is a two-CD set recorded by the BBC, generously capturing the passion of Buckley's early performances, with jazz-textured guitar, bass and vibraphone backing. *Honeyman* (Manifesto Records, 1995) is from a 1973 New York radio show—and an altogether edgier, more incendiary affair from a man who had now left his 60s innocence far behind.

what to buy next: Adventurous listeners should proceed directly to *Starsailor* (Rhino, 1970, prod. Tim Buckley), Buckley's most uncompromising work—by a long shot. Consciously experimental, its raw passion still outweighs its avant-garde pretensions. The more accessible, languidly melancholy *Blue Afternoon* (Straight, 1969) is the best of the '60's discs. *Greetings From LA* (Straight, 1972, prod. Jerry Goldstein) is gloriously decadent late-era Buckley, in full carnal heat.

what to avoid: Near the end, the inspiration was sadly lacking; *Look At The Fool* (Planet 3 Records, 1974, prod. Joe Falsia) provides the evidence.

the rest: *Tim Buckley* (Elektra, 1966) *Goodbye And Hello* (Elektra, 1967) *Happy/Sad* (Elektra, 1969) *Lorca* (Elektra, 1970) *Sefronia* (Planet 3 Records) *The Peel Sessions* (Dutch East India, 1991) *Live At The Troubadour, 1969* (Rhino, 1994)

worth searching for: Buckley's soundtrack for the 1969 Hall Bartlett film "Changes" (1969).

This Mortal Coil, Bono, Patti Smith, Jeff Buckley

Bob Dylan, Leadbelly, Miles Davis, John Coltrane

Doug Pippin

Buffalo Springfield

Formed 1966 in Los Angeles, Calif. Disbanded 1968

Stephen Stills, guitar, vocals; Neil Young, guitar, vocals; Richie Furay, guitar, vocals; Dewey Martin, drums, vocals; Bruce Palmer, bass, vocals (1966), Jim Fielder, bass, vocals (1967), Ken Koblun, bass (1967); Jim Messina, bass, vocals (1968)

A transitional group almost more important for what its members did after they left this seemingly jinxed band, especially Stills (Crosby, Stills and Nash), Furay (Poco) and Young. Short-time bassist Fielder went on to Blood, Sweat and Tears, and Messina, after a stint with Poco, hooked up with Kenny Loggins. Still, its traumatic, short career doesn't take away from the charm of Buffalo Springfield's music. "There's something happening here/What it is ain't exactly clear," from the band's first hit single, "For What It's Worth," became a catch-phrase for the growing counterculture and introduced Stills as a songwriter. Young's contributions, from "I Am a Child" to "Broken Arrow" and "Mr. Soul," are nascent blueprints of his formidable talent. There are kernels of CSN, Poco, the Eagles and every other West Coast rock group in the Springfield's mostly pleasant soft folk and country-flavored rock.

what to buy: *Buffalo Springfield Again* (Atco, 1967, prod. York/Pala) is the group's strongest effort song-wise, with great contributions from Young ("Mr. Soul," "Broken Arrow," "Expecting to Fly") and Stills ("Rock and Roll Woman," "Bluebird"). *Retrospective* (Atco, 1969, prod. Various) released soon after the group broke up, will have to do until the overdue boxed set comes out.

what to buy next: *Buffalo Springfield,* (Atco, 1966, prod. Charles Greene and Brian Stone) ♪♪♪♪ is a surprising debut, with "For What It's Worth," "Go and Say Goodbye," "Sit Down I Think I Love You," "Nowadays Clancy Can't Even Sing" and "Burned."

the rest: *Last Time Around* (Atco, 1968) ♪♪♪

worth searching for: Bootlegs of *Stampede*, the group's aborted final album ♪♪♪ which boasts a few keepers such as "Neighbor Don't Worry" and "Down to the Wire."

▶▶ Crosby, Stills and Nash, Poco, Flying Burrito Brothers, Linda Ronstadt, Eagles, Loggins and Messina, Warren Zevon, Uncle Tupelo

◀◀ Everly Brothers, Beatles, Byrds

see also: *Crosby, Stills and Nash, Neil Young, Poco, Loggins and Messina*

Leland Rucker

Buffalo Tom

Formed 1986 in Boston, Mass.

Bill Janovitz, vocals, guitar; Chris Colbourn, bass; Tom Maginnis, drums

Dinosaur Jr. frontman J Mascis co-produced Buffalo Tom's first two albums; that and sonic similarities at first led critics to tag the trio Dinosaur Jr. Jr. Minimal melodies carried by Janovitz's everyman vocals generally rise out of an inexorable wash of sound rather than a messy din, though the debut's "Reason Why" gets kind of rowdy; contrarily, there are periodic acoustic forays later on. These ordinary Joes have cultivated an unpretentious, song-driven, jangle-crunch guitar band destined by its unprepossessing attitude to be perpetually underrated.

what to buy: On the group's third album, *Let Me Come Over,* (Beggars Banquet, 1992, prod. Paul Kolderie, Sean Slade and Buffalo Tom) ♪♪♪♪♪ the distinctive musical personality first heard on *Birdbrain* blossoms fully, typified by a jangly acoustic/electric blend ("Taillights Fade" has a Neil Young-ish guitar solo, "Mountains of Your Head" is as catchy as the Lemonheads and "Larry" is positively anthemic), with variety coming from the changing proportions. The emphasis on songs increases with the higher profile of the vocals.

what to buy next: *Birdbrain* (Beggars Banquet, 1990, prod. Buffalo Tom and J Mascis with Sean Slade) ♪♪♪♪ mixed in more acoustic guitar and upped the hummability quotient several notches over the debut while maintaining its power. Of note are two bonus tracks—a quieter "Reason Why" and a totally acoustic cover of Psychedelic Furs' "Heaven" (with cello). *[big red letter day]* (Beggars Banquet, 1993, prod. the Robb Brothers and Buffalo Tom) ♪♪♪♪ picks up where *Let Me Come Over* left off, if somewhat less distinctively.

what to avoid: *Buffalo Tom,* (SST, 1989/Beggars Banquet, 1992) ♪♪ the debut, isn't bad, but they still sound too much like an aspiring Dinosaur Jr. at this point.

the rest: *Sleepy Eyed* (EastWest, 1995) ♪♪♪

▶▶ Grant Lee Buffalo

◀◀ Dinosaur Jr., Mission of Burma, Husker Du

Steve Holtje

Jimmy Buffett

Born Dec. 25, 1946 in Pascagoula, Miss.

Buffett's tropical tunes and seafaring tales offer a temporary escape for every office-bound baby boomer with a mortgage, a two-car garage and a surly boss. Few can resist the singer-songwriter's balmy fantasyland filled with palm trees, sandy beaches, cold beer, fast boats, cheeseburgers, margaritas and romance. Sure, there are sharks to reckon with and volcanoes to flee and broken hearts to mend. But—Buffett's message dictates—they can be dealt with. Buffett majored in journalism at Auburn University and the University of Southern Mississippi, working briefly at Billboard magazine before launching his career as a folk and country singer and songwriter. A failed marriage and a move from Nashville to Key West, Fla., triggered a new appreciation for the healing powers of the tropical sun. Buffett started writing earnest, positive songs with humor and wit, and his audiences grew slowly but steadily. He scored his first hit in 1974 with the wonderfully wistful ballad "Come Monday," but it was the booze-in-the-blender philosophical shrug of "Margaritaville" that put the wind in Buffett's sails. With little radio play and a glaring shortage of hit singles—but with a loyal and large group of Parrothead fans—Buffett has become one of the wealthiest beach bums in history.

what to buy: *Songs You Know By Heart: Jimmy Buffett's Greatest Hit(s)* (MCA, 1985, prod. Jimmy Buffett) ♪♪♪♪♪ is an essential first step for anyone curious about the Parrothead phenomenon. The album includes the hit(s) ("Margaritaville," "Cheeseburger in Paradise") and concert favorites ("Fins," "Volcano," "Pencil Thin Mustache"). Buffett's breakthrough album,

Changes in Latitudes, Changes in Attitudes (MCA, 1977, prod. Norbert Putman) is a perfect sampler of feel-good folk-rockers (the title track, "Margaritaville") and pensive ballads ("Biloxi," "Wonder Why We Ever Go Home"). Another good overview is *Feeding Frenzy,* (MCA, 1990, prod. Michael Utley and Elliot Scheiner) a live recording featuring 72 minutes' worth of classic concert craziness.

what to buy next: If Buffett has cast his spell on you, you won't mind indulging in the four-disc boxed set *Boats Beaches Bars & Ballads,* (Margaritaville/MCA, 1992, prod. Various) an extensive retrospective dividing the 72 songs by the categories listed in the title. *Living and Dying in 3/4 Time* (MCA, 1974, prod. Don Gant) captures the lyrical charm of early Buffett ("Come Monday," "The Wino and I Know"), while *Banana Wind* (MCA, 1996, prod. Russ Kunkel) shows some justifiable crankiness ("Jamaica Mistaica," "Cultural Infidel") along with the steel-drum calypso instrumental title track, a first for Buffett.

what to avoid: *Last Mango in Paris* (MCA, 1985, prod. Jimmy Bowen) WOOF! and *Off To See the Lizard* (MCA, 1989, prod. Elliot Scheiner) wander around in a sea of overly slick production losing sight of Buffett's laid-back charm.

the rest: *A White Sport Coat and a Pink Crustacean* (MCA, 1973) *A-1-A* (MCA, 1974) *Havana Daydreamin'* (MCA, 1976) *Son of a Son of a Sailor* (MCA, 1978) *You Had To Be There* (MCA,1978) *Volcano* (MCA, 1979) *Coconut Telegraph* (MCA, 1981) *Somewhere Over China* (MCA, 1981) *One Particular Harbor* (MCA, 1983) *Riddles in the Sand* (MCA, 1985) *Floridays* (MCA, 1986) *Hot Water* (MCA, 1988) *Before the Beach* (Margaritaville/MCA, 1993) *Fruitcakes* (Margaritaville/MCA, 1994) *Barometer Soup* (Margaritaville/MCA, 1995)

worth searching for: *All the Great Hits,* (Prism Leisure, 1994, prod. Various) a British hits collection that's a bit more generous than *Songs You Know By Heart*

▶▶ The Iguanas, subdudes, Blues Traveler

◀◀ Gamble Rogers, Irma Thomas, Benny Spellman, Jerry Jeff Walker

David Yonke

The Buggles

Formed 1979 in London, England. Disbanded 1981.

Trevor Horn, vocals, keyboards; Geoffrey Downes, vocals, keyboards

The Buggles earned a footnote in rock history by having the dubious honor of being the first video played on MTV—the aptly titled "Video Killed the Radio Star." It's a catchy enough tune, although much of the credit goes to its then high tech production—an ominous prelude to the hollow electronic pop that was to ensue throughout the first half of the 80s. Similarly, the rest of *The Age of Plastic,* (Island, 1979, prod. The Buggles) has about the same texture of its title. Horn and Downes shockingly agreed to join prog-rock stalwarts Yes in 1980, an experiment that ended a year later. Downes went on to the band Asia, while Horn has become an in-demand producer who's helped guide Seal to stardom.

Allan Orski

Nicholas James Bullen & Bill Laswell

See: Bill Laswell

Bulletboys

Formed in Los Angeles, CA

Marq Torien, vocals; Tommy Pittam, guitar (1994-present); Lonnie Vencent, bass; Rob Karras, drums (1994-present); Mick Sweda, guitar (1988-94); Jimmy D Anda, drums (1988-94)

Bulletboys, like most of its late-Eighties metal peers, shone brightest with its debut album. With Torien's David Lee Roth-like vocals, Ted Templeman producing and a contract with Warner Bros. all pointed to a neo-Van Halen image, but *Bulletboys* (Warner Bros., 1988) actually delivers the raunchy goods. The hits, "Smooth Up In Ya" and a cover of the O'Jays' "For the Love of Money," were harder and grittier than those by hair-metal counterparts, and remain mindlessly entertaining.

the rest: *Freakshow* (Warner Bros., 1991) *Za-Za* (Warner Bros., 1993) *Acid Monkey* (Perris, 1995)

Todd Wicks

Eric Burdon and the Animals

See: The Animals

Sonny Burgess

Born Albert Burgess, May 28, 1931, Newport, Ark.

With his flaming red suit, red shoes, red guitar and dyed red hair,

Burgess probably looked like the devil incarnate to audiences in Arkansas and Tennessee circa 1956. And he pretty much sounded like him on the records he made for Sun between 1956-58. *We Wanna Boogie, Red Headed Woman* and *Ain't Got a Thing* featured shouted, nearly unintelligible vocals, slapback bass, thundering drums, pounding piano, machine-gun bursts of guitar and a blurting, out-of-context trumpet. Burgess' records were wild even by Sun standards—perhaps too wild, for his intense mix of rockabilly boogie and white-boy rhythm & blues never made him more than a regional hit. The best of his Sun sides can be found on *Hittin' that Jug! The Best of Sonny Burgess*, (AVI, 1995, prod. Sam Phillips and Jack Clement) ♪♪♪♪ more than a hour's worth of glorious chaos, in two-and-a-half minute bursts; many of those same tracks are also available on the compilation *We Wanna Boogie* (Rounder, 1990, prod. Sam Phillips and Jack Clement) ♪♪♪♪ After Sun, Burgess retreated to playing in Conway Twitty's band and eventually took a day job until he was coaxed out of rock 'n' roll retirement in 1986 to play with the Sun Rhythm Section. His comeback effort, *Tennessee Border*, (HighTone, 1992, prod. Dave Alvin) ♪♪♪ is a roadhouse gem that proves Burgess has still got it, even at age 60. *Sonny Burgess* (Rounder, 1996, prod. Garry Tallent) ♪♪♪½ is even better, with spirited performances by Burgess on songs by Bruce Springsteen, Steve Forbert, Radney Foster, Dave Alvin and Chris Gaffney, among others. As a special treat, the Jordanaires and Scotty Moore sit in on "Bigger Than Elvis."

Daniel Durchholz

Solomon Burke

Born 1936 in Philadelphia, Pa.

Upon this rock they built the church. Burke, one of the crucial transitional figures in classic 60s Southern soul, has seldom been recognized or celebrated for the key role he played in shaping the music's firmament. His 60s hits on Atlantic Records were largely products of a fruitful creative association with songwriter-producer Bert Berns, who launched his own estimable career with Burke's 1961 version of his "Cry To Me." Berns wrapped Burke's gospel fervor—the former "Wonder Boy Preacher"—in crisp, churchy sounds inflected with Afro-Cuban accents, driving Burke to the edge of heartbreak in the songs. Together they mapped out a unique sound that bridged the gap between the mannered 50s studio-conceived R&B of Leiber and Stoller and the rich, earthy Southern soul of Stax/Volt and Muscle Shoals. Burke's figure loomed large in the South during his heyday, when he was known as "King Of Soul" on the chitlin' circuit. During the four years he worked with Berns, Burke put out extraordinary record after extraordinary record, some of the definitive R&B recordings of their time. He also later made other fine records, including his biggest hit, "Got To Get You Off My Mind," but nothing equaled the drama and raw passion, the almost gothic soul, of his records with the brilliant producer. Burke virtually disappeared from the scene, tending to his large family, businesses and his church in Los Angeles. But in recent years, Burke has returned with several worthy albums for small independent labels that have helped him back into the spotlight and resuscitated a nearly forgotten but glorious career.

what to buy: The current double-disc retrospective of his Atlantic years, *Home In Your Heart*, (Rhino, 1992, prod. Various) ♪♪♪♪ covers the full expanse, though its deleted predecessor, a single-disc, 20-song collection, *The Best Of Solomon Burke* (Atlantic, 1989, prod. Various) ♪♪♪♪♪ might be more precisely to the point.

what to buy next: The whole sweaty, breathless majesty of his live performances gives Burke's music persuasive new dimensions, evidenced satisfactorily on *Live At the House Of Blues*. (Black Top, 1994) ♪♪♪

what to avoid: After leaving Atlantic, Burke made a modestly successful cover of "Proud Mary" for Bell records, but his subsequent work on MGM Records clearly shows a compromised artist lost in a sea of changing musical fashions.

the rest: *Soul Alive!* (Rounder, 1985) ♪♪♪ *A Change Is Gonna Come* (Rounder, 1986) ♪♪♪ *Home Land* (Bizarre/Straight 1991) ♪♪ *Soul Of the Blues* (Black Top, 1993) ♪♪♪

worth searching for: His first album, *Rock 'N Soul*, (Atlantic, 1961) ♪♪♪♪♪ a pricey collector's item these days, is one of the unrecognized landmarks of the golden age of soul.

▶▶ Otis Redding, Joe Tex, Bruce Springsteen

◀◀ Robert Blair and the Fantastic Violinaires, the Rev. Julius Cheeks

Joel Selvin

T-Bone Burnett

Born John Henry Burnett, Jan. 14, 1948 in St. Louis, Mo.

Spiritual yet sharp-tongued, witty but sometimes preachy and oblique, T-Bone Burnett has all the qualities of a down-to-earth Episcopalian preacher. Burnett first came to public attention through Bob Dylan's Rolling Thunder Revue in the 70s and has created a distinctive body of work coming from a folk-country base. Though he's managed only a cult audience as a performer, Burnett has found considerable success as a producer, working with such acts as Bruce Cockburn, Los Lobos, Elvis Costello, Counting Crows and Marshall Crenshaw.

what to buy: Always adept at exposing moral charlatans, Burnett turns his gaze inward on *The Criminal Under My Own Hat*, (Columbia, 1992, prod. T-Bone Burnett) ♪♪♪♪ in the process creating an album that utilizes his most creative musical and lyrical tendencies.

what to buy next: Burnett's first solo album, *Truth Decay*, (Takoma, 1980, prod. Reggie Fisher) ♪♪♪ goes for a post-Sun era rockabilly sound with a four-piece band and features some of Burnett's simplest and most pointed songs like "Madison Avenue," "Talk Talk Talk" and "Boomerang." *Trap Door*, (Warner Bros., 1984, prod. Reggie Fisher and T-Bone Burnett) ♪♪♪½ the six-song EP which followed, is even better—especially a sarcastic, spoken rendition of "Diamonds Are a Girl's Best Friend."

what to avoid: *The Talking Animals*. (Columbia, 1988, prod. T-Bone Burnett) ♪♪½ Burnett's sometimes criticized for preachiness, but he's even worse when he gets obtuse, as he did on this currently out-of-print album.

the rest: *Behind the Trap Door* (Demon, 1984) ♪♪♪ *Proof Through the Night* (Demon, 1983) ♪♪♪ *T-Bone Burnett* (Dot, 1986) ♪♪♪

worth searching for: *Spark in the Dark* (Arista, 1977), the best of Burnett's three albums with the Alpha Band, his post-Rolling Thunder trio with Steve Soles and David Mansfield.

▶▶ Sam Phillips, Los Lobos, Counting Crows

◀◀ Bob Dylan, Elvis Costello

Brian Mansfield

Johnny Burnette

Born Mar. 24, 1934, in Memphis, Tenn. Died Aug. 1, 1964, in Clear Lake, Calif.

Burnette went to the same high school in Memphis as Elvis Presley. He and his brother Dorsey Burnette were troubled boys, sent to Catholic schools for discipline, not religion. But these two hard-scrabble sometime prizefighters—with guitarist Paul Burlison—led the Rock and Roll Trio, one of Memphis' first rockabilly outfits that emerged from working at local hillbilly roadhouses. Although the trio cut one of the great rock 'n' roll albums of the 50s, the Burnettes had very little to show for it. None of the singles for Coral Records even nicked the charts, and the band spent the better part of '56, a crucial year, touring with the Ted Mack Amateur Hour traveling show after winning three consecutive weeks on the televised talent contest. When the band broke up shortly thereafter—during an onstage fist fight between the two brothers—the two Burnettes moved their families to Los Angeles, where they showed up on Ricky Nelson's door one day offering to write songs for the burgeoning teen idol. Burnette compositions such as "Waitin' In School," "It's Late" and "Believe What You Say" became landmarks in the Nelson repertoire. But Johnny Burnette was destined to become best known for sappy teen pop that he recorded—but did not write—under the supervision of producer Snuff Garrett, particularly the two Top 10 hits "You're Sixteen" and "Dreamin'." When he died in a boating accident in '64, his career was in decline. But Burnette was one of rock 'n' roll's great originals—a burly, feisty hard-luck loser who never got credit for his most genuine accomplishments. His years at Liberty Records have been scrupulously covered with *You're Sixteen: The Best Of Johnny Burnette*, (EMI, 1992, prod. Various) ♪♪½ 25 songs and a 13-minute interview, although his best known material is not necessarily his best. Germany's Bear Family compiled all the 1956-57 sessions by the Johnny Burnette Trio on one CD, *Rockabilly Boogie*, (Bear Family, 1989, prod. Bob Thiele and Paul Cohen) ♪♪♪♪½ that leaves little doubt how masterful Burnette's early recordings were.

Joel Selvin

What Album Changed Your Life?

"The first time I heard (Prince's) Purple Rain (Warner Bros., 1984), it just blew me away. It was one of those breaking down a few barriers type of records. There were elements of rock, of funk, of dance--of everything, really. I really dug it for its bravery and open-mindedness. It was its own thing."

Phil Collen (Def Leppard)

Bush

Formed 1994 in London, England

Gavin Rossdale, vocals, guitar; Nigel Pulsford, guitar; Dave Parsons, bass; Robin Goodridge, drums

Probably the most well-known grunge band to come out of England, Bush exploded onto the American music scene in 1994 with *Sixteen Stone.* (Trauma, 1994, prod. Clive Langer and Alan Winstanley) Dismissed by some critics as a Nirvana rip-off and not taken seriously by the music press in its homeland, Bush's album was a multi-million sales smash, driven by energetic, angst-filled hits such as "Everything Zen," "Come Down" and "Little Things."

Anna Glen

Kate Bush

Born July 30, 1958, in Surrey, England

Depending on your temperament for eclectic art rock, Bush is either going to come across like an angel or like that weird drama teacher from your high school; she is an individualist who wears her creativity without shame. Despite obvious eccentricities, however, she is a unique and frequently compelling artist. Discovered by Pink Floyd guitarist David Gilmour, Bush's material has drawn heavily from Elizabethan stage dramas and Medieval fantasy, as well as British art rock and traditional Celtic music. Where her male contemporaries often sully the art rock banner with flatulent instrumental excess, however, she is more concerned with narrative flow, character motivation and the emotional depth of romantic relationships. Her work achieves this with a keen talent for musical hybridization and an understanding of theatrical pacing and tension. In many of her songs, Bush assumes multiple roles, playing out mini-dramas against ambitious sonic backdrops. Essential in Bush's delivery is her multifarious voice, an instrument which can, by turns, evoke childlike wonder, irresistible seduction, heartrending sadness and chilling malevolence. To her many fans, it is this unique voice that defines the Bush experience; for others, it is her flair for the dramatic (an accomplished scenarist, Bush designed and staged a landmark tour in 1979—her only one to date—and wrote, directed and starred in the 1993 film "The Line, The Cross, The Curve," a companion piece to her 1993 album *The Red Shoes* Bush's rise to mainstream success guaranteed a host of imitators swimming in her wake (most notably Tori Amos), but their work pales in comparison to the originality and style of Bush's best music.

what to buy: *Hounds of Love* (EMI America, 1985, prod. Kate Bush) rode to the number one spot on the British album charts in 1985, and the singles "Running up That Hill" and "Cloudbusting" propelled Bush to her greatest U.S. success since "Wuthering Heights" in 1978. The hoopla was justified; with *Hounds*, Bush finally struck the perfect balance, leavening the melodrama with canny Celtic touches and sensual polyrhythms, and tempering her penchant for fantasy with more corporeal concerns—from the lulling warmth of "Mother Stands for Comfort" to the eerie beauty of "And Dream of Sheep" to the propulsive fury of "Jig of Life."

what to buy next: While sonically similar to *Hounds of Love*, *The Sensual World* (Columbia, 1989, prod. Kate Bush) finds Bush dealing with much more mature subject matter. Still preoccupied with romance, the relationships depicted in *The Sensual World* are decidedly more earthbound than those in Bush's past recordings. But she still infuses songs such as "The Fog" and the title track with enough mystery and foreboding to recall her chimerical work. And in "Love and Anger," she delivers a dynamic anthem for the complications and compensations of modern romance. Also of interest is the greatest hits package *The Whole Story,* (EMI, 1986, prod. Various) which provides an excellent overview of Bush's first five albums. While each song is a standout, the album as a whole lacks the thematic unity that Bush's individual albums boast.

what to avoid: *Lionheart* (EMI America, 1978, prod. Andrew Powell) is a hastily put-together album that attempted to quickly cash-in on Bush's success with the single "Wuthering Heights" (off of her debut album *The Kick Inside* and later covered by Pat Benatar) and a clear example of her indulgence to excess. While the album does boast the outstanding cut "Wow," to reach it you must first brave the 101 sentimentality of "Symphony in Blue" and "In Search of Peter Pan."

the rest: *The Kick Inside* (EMI America, 1978) *Kate Bush on Stage* (EMI America, 1979) *Never for Ever* (EMI America, 1980) *The Dreaming* (EMI America, 1982) *This Woman's Work* (Columbia, 1990) *The Red Shoes* (Columbia, 1993)

worth searching for: *Aspects of the Sensual World,* (Columbia EP, 1990) a collection of unreleased material that coincided with the release of *The Sensual World* In addition to two versions of the title song, the EP contains the previously unavailable cuts "Be Kind to My Mistakes" (from the 1987 Nicolas Roeg film "Castaways"), "I'm Still Waiting," and "Ken."

Sinead O'Connor, Tori Amos, Dolores O'Riordian (the Cranberries), Siouxsie Sioux (Siouxsie and the Banshees)

Pink Floyd, the Moody Blues, Fairport Convention, Sandy Denny, Genesis, Peter Gabriel, Celtic folk music

David Galens

Jon Butcher Axis /Jon Butcher/Barefoot Servants

Formed 1980 in Boston, Mass. Disbanded 1985.

Jon Butcher, guitar, vocals; Derek Blevins, drums; Chris Martin, bass (1980-84); Jimmy Johnson, bass (1984-85)

Because he was a black guitarist leading a trio with the word Axis in its name, Butcher was pushed as a New Hendrix. He's actually more of a cross between Jeff Beck, Eric Johnson and Pat Metheny, with a better feel for textured ambient pop than high-voltage riffing. As a consequence, almost every Butcher album has a handful of decent tracks, but they're all unfocused and not fully realized. If ever a proper best-of compilation emerges, it would probably top anything else in his catalog.

what to buy: Between them, *Jon Butcher Axis* (Polydor, 1983, prod. Pat Moran) and the followup, *Stare at the Sun,* (Polydor, 1984, prod. Pat Moran) add up to one really good record. They haven't aged particularly well, but the synth-pop atmospherics of "Life Takes a Life" and "Walk on the Moon" show promise and would have been a direction worthy of further pursuit.

what to avoid: Butcher's solo effort *Pictures from the Front,* (Capitol, 1989, prod. Glen Ballard, Jon Butcher and Spencer Proffer) a desperate-sounding grab bag. Also forgettable is the eponymous debut of Butcher's most recent band, *Barefoot Servants,* (Columbia, 1994, prod. Michael Frondelli) a misguided super session with assorted studio hacks.

the rest: Jon Butcher Axis: *Along the Axis* (Capitol, 1985) Jon Butcher: *Wishes* (Capitol, 1987)

Living Colour

Jeff Beck, Pat Metheny, Jimi Hendrix Experience, Robin Trower, Mahogany Rush

David Menconi

Jerry Butler

See: Curtis Mayfield

The Paul Butterfield Blues Band

Formed 1963 in Chicago, Ill. Disbanded 1972.

Paul Butterfield, vocals, harp (died May 4, 1987 in North Hollywood, Calif.); Michael Bloomfield, guitar (1963-66, died Feb. 16, 1981 in San Francisco, Calif.); Elvin Bishop, guitar (1963-67); Mark Naftalin, keyboards; Jerome Arnold, bass; Sam Lay, drums (1963-65); Billy Davenport, drums (1965-72); Buzz Feiten, guitar (1968-72)

British Invasion bands such as the Rolling Stones are deservedly credited for awakening America to its own electric blues traditions. But it was a band from Chicago—schooled in South Side clubs by such masters as Muddy Waters and Little Walter—that made the blues rock like never before. Its debut album made the blues come powerfully alive for a new generation of young, white rock fans; featuring Butterfield's astonishing blues harp and bruising vocals—and sizzling, faster-than-light guitarist Bloomfield—the band had a profound and lasting impact on blues and rock musicians alike. But the original lineup would not last long; Bloomfield became an immediate star and soon departed. By 1968, Butterfield was leading a new band, with a horn section that featured a young David Sanborn. By the early 70s, the band had broken up, but not before leaving their mark on virtually every electric blues band since.

what to buy: The first two cuts alone on *The Paul Butterfield Blues Band* (Elektra, 1965, prod. Paul Rothchild) attest to how influential this record became—versions of "Born In Chicago" and "Shake Your Moneymaker" that have become standards for the thousands of bar-circuit blues bands that followed in Butterfield's wake. This is the album that unleashed Bloomfield's guitar legend and Butterfield's vastly imitated blues harp style. It's no wonder that Bob Dylan chose the band's powerhouse rhythm section of Sam Lay and Jerome Arnold to back him in his electric debut at Newport in 1965.

what to buy next: *East-West* (Elektra, 1966, prod. Paul Rothchild and Mark Abramson) showed the influence of 60s rock on the band, with extended soloing, Eastern touches in Bloomfield's playing and even a bit of psychedelia. After the departure of most of the original group, Butterfield reconfigured the band, adding horns and toning down the guitars on *The Resurrection of Pigboy Crabshaw.* (Elektra, 1968, prod. John Court)

what to avoid: Some of the original band's earliest demo sessions, previously unreleased, are available on *The Lost Elektra Sessions,* (Rhino, 1995, prod. Various) which is of interest mostly to collectors and hard-core fans.

the rest: *Strawberry Jam* (Winner, 1995)

worth searching for: A long out-of-print Elektra Records compilation from 1966, *What's Shakin'*, which contains five excellent outtakes from the band's debut album, including versions of "Spoonful" and "One More Mile."

solo outings:

Paul Butterfield's Better Days: *Better Days* (Bearsville, 1973/Rhino, 1991) *It All Comes Back* (Bearsville, 1973/Rhino 1991)

Paul Butterfield: *The Legendary Paul Butterfield Rides Again* (Amherst, 1986)

The Electric Flag, Blood, Sweat and Tears, Chicago, Aerosmith, Bad Company, the Fabulous Thunderbirds, the Black Crowes

Muddy Waters, Sonny Boy Williamson, Little Walter, Buddy Guy, Junior Wells

see also: *Michael Bloomfield, Elvin Bishop*

Doug Pippin

Butthole Surfers

Formed 1981 in San Antonio, Texas

Gibby Haynes, vocals; Paul Leary, guitar; King Coffee (King Koffy), drums (1983-present); Theresa Nervosa, drums (1983-1989); Jeff Pinkus, bass (1986-present)

This Texas group—whose name can only be broadcast on brave radio stations—staked its reputation by flouting a lack of polite taste and an embrace of anything remotely vulgar. Its music can wildly change; imagine rockabilly, 70's art rock and post-punk, trashy lyrics about drug abuse and the decline of suburban America, and some unclassifiable avant-garde noise—at once. Then you might be able to sum up the extent of the Surfers' wide music repertoire. The Surfers consider themselves shock-punk band that doesn't play punk. Featuring stiff, repetitive percussion, jagged, colliding and twangy guitars, and often nasal, abrasive singing (but with a certain melody and infectious quality nonetheless), the group often grates on conventional pop/rock tastes. Its an acquired taste, in other words. But these musicians are never killjoys; they make music to amuse themselves, and at its best, they give us enough berth to get a sense of the joke, too.

what to buy: *Locust Abortion Technician* (Touch & Go, 1987, prod. Butthole Surfers) is the Surfers' most direct and concentrated album; all of the songs make a point without dragging on or becoming dull experiments in sound manipulation (as many Surfers' records do). The lyrics often contain a fascinating, albeit grotesque, appeal, while others are truly disturbing. Musical influences still swing from one side of the pendulum to the other, but always come back to a fixed center. *The Hole Truth and Nothing Butt* (Trance Syndicate, 1995, prod. Butthole Surfers) compiles many of the Surfers' best singles along with some live performances and B-sides. Despite that, it's more cohesive than most of the other albums, with a few more catchy tracks than the average Surfers album. *Hairway to Steven* (Touch & Go, 1988, prod. Butthole Surfers) features a messed up, distorted 70s feel and includes some of Leary's best guitar work.

what to buy next: *Independent Worm Saloon*, (Capitol, 1993, prod. John Paul Jones) is one of the Surfers' hardest-rocking albums, and the band finally gets around to playing a few songs that actually sound like punk music. *Electriclarryland-MDBR* (Capitol, 1996, prod. Paul Leary and Steve Thompson) grows the fan base with even more accessible songs and a bona fide modern rock radio hit, "Peppers."

what to avoid: On *Pioughd* (Rough Trade, 1991, prod. Butthole Surfers) (pronounced P.O.'d), it sounds like the band is just going through the motions of making an album, despite the college radio hit version of "Hurdy Gurdy Man."

the rest: PCPPEP Live *(Alternative Tentacles, 1984)* Rembrandt Pussyhorse/Cream Corn from the Socket of DavisMDBR *(Touch & Go, 1986/85)* Psychic... Powerless...Another Man's Sac *(Touch & Go, 1985)* Double Live *(Latino Buggerveil, 1989)*

worth searching for: The out-of-print debut, *Butthole Surfers,* (Alternative Tentacles, 1983, prod. Butthole Surfers) is one of the band's finest, rawest recordings.

solo outings:

Paul Leary: *History of Dogs* (Rough Trade, 1990)

Gibby Haynes and Jeff Pinkus: *Jack Officers* (Rough Trade, 1990, prod. Leary)

⏩ Ween, NoMeansNo, Killdozer, Reverend Horton Heat, Cherubs, Alice Donut

⏪ 10cc, Hawkwind, Fall, Flipper

Bryan Lassner

Buzzcocks

Formed 1976 in Manchester, England. Disbanded 1981. Reformed 1993.

Steve Diggle, lead guitar, vocals; John Maher, drums (1976-81); Pete Shelley, guitar, vocals; Howard Devoto, vocals (1976-77); Garth Smith, bass (1976-77); Steve Garvey, bass (1977-81); Tony Barber, bass (1993-present); Phil Barker, drums (1993-present)

Created after they saw the Sex Pistols perform in February 1976, the Buzzcocks became the harmonic side of punk minimalism, blending buzz-saw guitars with sweet vocals like the Kinks at warp speed. The first of a succession of punk groups from Manchester, the Buzzcocks became one of the most successful singles bands in one of the great ages of English singles, right up there alongside the Jam, Clash and Pistols. Shelley's brash love songs and deadpan delivery were kick-started by Diggle's erratic, brawny guitar and a rhythm section in permanent overdrive. Like many first-era punk bands, the Buzzcocks put a premium on attire and on the art and design of their singles and albums. After undistinguished solo work, the band reformed in the early 90s and continue to tour.

what to buy: Since the Buzzcocks were a singles band first and foremost, their first American album, *Singles Going Steady,* (I.R.S., 1979, prod. Martin Rushent) is the most appropriate choice, collecting eight singles—A sides and B sides. It's one of punk's best documents. *Product,* (Restless Retro, 1989, prod. Martin Rushent) offers three discs of most of their classic material dressed up in artsy, somewhat confusing packaging.

what to buy next: *A Different Kind of Tension,* (I.R.S., 1980, prod. Martin Rushent) a lofty attempt to get away from their pop origins. *Another Music in Another Kitchen,* (I.R.S., 1980, prod. Martin Rushent) their first album without original member Devoto, catches Shelley at his best.

the rest: *Love Bites* (I.R.S., 1978) *Lest We Forget* (ROIR, 1980) *The Peel Sessions Album* (Strange Fruit/Dutch East India, 1991) *Live at the Roxy Club: April '77 (Trojan, 1989)* Operator's Manual: The Buzzcock's Best *(I.R.S., 1991)* Entertaining Friends *(I.R.S., 1992)* Trade Test Transmission *(Caroline, 1993)* French *(I.R.S., 1995)* All Set *(I.R.S., 1996)*

worth searching for: *Spiral Scratch* (New Hormones EP, 1977, prod. Martin Rushent) many consider this raw power EP with original member Devoto to be the group's best moment.

solo outings:

Pete Shelley: *Homosapien* (Genetic/Arista, 1982) *XL1* Genetic/Arista)

Steve Diggle and John Maher (with Flag of Convenience): *Life on the Telephone* (PVC/Sire EP, 1982)

⏩ Magazine, Husker Du

⏪ Sex Pistols, Ramones, Stooges, Television

Leland Rucker

The Byrds

Formed 1964, in Los Angeles, Calif. Disbanded 1973.

Roger McGuinn (born James Joseph McGuinn III), guitars, vocals; Chris Hillman, bass, vocals (1964-68); Gene Clark (born Harold Eugene Clark), vocals (1964-66, died May 24, 1991); David Crosby (born David Van Cortland), guitar, vocals (1964-67); Michael Clarke, drums, vocals (1964-67); Kevin Kelley, drums (1967-68); Gram Parsons (born Ingram Cecil Connor III), guitar, vocals (1967-68); Gene Parsons, drums, vocals (1968-72); Skip Battin, bass, vocals (1968-73); John York, bass (1968); Clarence White, guitar, vocals (1968-73); John Guerin, drums (1972-73)

In terms of guitar sound, the Byrds—along with Neil Young and, perhaps, the Allman Brothers Band—was the most important American rock 'n' roll entity of the 1960s. Inspired by the Beatles' film "A Hard Day's Night"—particularly the Rickenbacker 12-string George Harrison occasionally shouldered—McGuinn and company jump-started a hazy, Bob Dylan tune called "Mr. Tambourine Man," initiating a challenge that would ring back and forth across the Atlantic. Someone else might have stumbled onto playing folk songs on an electric guitar, but it was McGuinn and his cohorts who defined an entirely new direction for rock. And while any number of other Byrds made significant contributions to the Byrds sound, it was McGuinn—whose eclectic tastes ranged from Pete Seeger to bluegrass and whose proficiency on the Rickenbacker 12-string was far beyond most pop practitioners of the time—who established the flight pattern. The Byrds became a jumping-off place for Clark, Hillman, Crosby and Clarke, but McGuinn and whoever was with him added jazz, Moog synthesizers and psychedelia before stripping it all away back to country music with *Sweetheart of the Rodeo*. It's not hard to hear echoes of their music almost everywhere today. (Note: In 1996, Columbia reissued the first four Byrds albums with appropriate bonus tracks added to each title.)

what to buy: *Mr. Tambourine Man* (Columbia, 1965, prod. Terry Melcher) provided mystery, harmonies, intrigue and electrified Dylan songs in one of rock's all-time great debuts. *Sweetheart of the Rodeo* (Columbia, 1968, prod. Gary Usher) was flawed but remains a landmark that steered rock back towards country. *The Byrds* (Columbia, 1990, prod. Various) is a boxed set actually worth its price, with four discs that cover the band's output—including the long-awaited and well-worth-it original version of the *Sweetheart of the Rodeo* album.

what to buy next: *Younger Than Yesterday* (Columbia, 1967, prod. Gary Usher) features "So You Want to Be a Rock 'n' Roll Star," a hit that still rings true today along with the rest of this quiet album. *The Notorious Byrd Brothers* (Columbia, 1968, prod. Gary Usher) is the prequel to *Sweetheart of the Rodeo* and is an interesting transitional effort. *20 Essential Tracks From the Boxed Set: 1965-1990* (Columbia, 1992, prod. Various) is a formidable collection of hits, but only if you don't splurge for the whole box. *The Byrds (Untitled)* (Columbia, 1970, prod. Terry Melcher and Jim Dickson) includes McGuinn's ethereal equine meditation, "Chestnut Mare," and a stunning live recording of Dylan's "Positively 4th Street."

what to avoid: *The Byrds,* (Asylum, 1973, prod. David Crosby) like the pictures of the individual members on the front cover, this was stitched together, with no group identity remaining.

the rest: *Turn! Turn! Turn!* (Columbia, 1966) *Fifth Dimension* (Columbia, 1966) *Byrds Greatest Hits* (Columbia, 1967) *Dr. Byrds and Mr. Hyde* (Columbia, 1969) *Preflyte* (Together, 1969/Columbia, 1973) *The Ballad of Easy Rider* (Columbia, 1970) *Byrdmaniax* (Columbia, 1971) *Farther Along* (Columbia, 1971) *The Best of the Byrds (Greatest Hits Vol. 2)* (Columbia, 1972) *The Byrds Play Dylan* (Columbia, 1980) *The Original Singles 1965-1967* (Columbia, 1981) *The Very Best of the Byrds* (Pair, 1986)

worth searching for: *Never Before,* (Re-flyte, 1988/Murray Hill, 1989, prod. Various) a pre-boxed set collection of rarities whose best moment is an alternate version of "Eight Miles High." The CD adds seven tracks to the original album's 10.

solo outings:

Roger McGuinn: *Roger McGuinn* (Columbia, 1973) *Peace on You* (Columbia, 1974) *Roger McGuinn and Band* (Columbia, 1975) *Cardiff Rose* (Columbia, 1976) *Thunderbyrd* (Columbia, 1977) *Back From Rio* (Arista, 1991) *Born to Rock and Roll* (Columbia Legacy, 1991)

McGuinn, Clark and Hillman: *McGuinn, Clark and Hillman* (Capitol, 1979)

McGuinn and Hillman: *City* (Capitol, 1980)

Gene Clark: *Two Sides to Every Story* (Polydor, 1977) *Echoes* (Legacy, 1991) *Looking for a Connection* (Dos, 1994)

Bob Dylan, Flying Burrito Brothers, Desert Rose Band, Beatles, R.E.M., Buffalo Springfield, Crosby, Stills & Nash, Poco, Eagles, Blue Oyster Cult, Searchers, Gin Blossoms, Tom Petty & the Heartbreakers, Elvis Costello & the Attractions, Soul Asylum, Uncle Tupelo, Wilco, Son Volt, Jayhawks

New Christy Minstrels, Beatles, Bob Dylan, John Coltrane, Ravi Shankar, Merle Haggard

see also: *Gram Parsons, Flying Burrito Brothers*

Leland Rucker

David Byrne

Born May 14, 1952, in Dumbarton, Scotland

As the main man of the Talking Heads, brainy Byrne's solo work hasn't been nearly as successful, although a lot of the music from the performer Time magazine called "Rock's Renaissance Man" has been easily as good. A voracious student of all cultures, Byrne was sometimes criticized for often adapting it for his own purposes—though rarely did he get complaints from the Brazilians from whom he took rhythms and Cubans whose music he reintroduced—via his Luaka Bop label—in the U.S. following a more than 20-year ban. More recently, his four-piece rock approach has come closer to the Heads than anything he's done previously.

what to buy: *My Life in the Bush of Ghosts,* (Sire, 1981, prod. David Byrne and Brian Eno) a collaboration with Eno while Byrne was still in the Talking Heads, began the groundbreaking work incorporating found rhythms, odd radio transmissions and a dance beat a decade before such practices became commonplace in pop.

what to buy next: Byrne's pop-oriented albums are surprisingly consistent and strong, but *Rei Momo* (Luaka Bop/Sire, 1989, prod. Steve Lillywhite and David Byrne) is a fully realized work, incorporating his cracked lyrics with a full-blown Latin band that he took on a splendid tour.

what to avoid: Byrne's artsy works for the avant-garde theater can be deadly listening, none moreso than the score for Robert Wilson's *The Forest* (Luaka Bop/Sire, 1991)

the rest: *The Complete Score from the Broadway Production of The Catherine Wheel* (Sire, 1981) *Music for The Knee Plays* (ECM, 1985) *Uh-Oh* (Luaka Bop/Sire) *David Byrne* (Luaka Bop/Sire)

worth searching for: *Hanging Upside Down* (Sire, 1992, prod. Nick Launay) is an import CD single that includes Byrne's first stab at an old Talking Heads song, "(Nothing But) Flowers," while on his *Uh-Oh* tour.

▶▶ Primitive Radio Gods, Beck, Hayden

◀◀ Terry Allen, Robert Wilson, Desi Arnaz

see also: *Talking Heads, Brian Eno*

Roger Catlin

C & C Music Factory

Formed 1990 in New York, N.Y. Disbanded 1995.

Although packaged in videos as a group featuring singer Zelma Davis and rapper Freedom Williams, C&C Music Factory actually was the brainchild of remix producers Robert Clivilles and David Cole—an ace team that had re-worked hits for artists such as Natalie Cole, Luther Vandross and Grace Jones. Determined to make a hit or two for themselves, they called together an army of studio musicians, singers and rappers to strike an inspired balance between the worlds of rap, crossover R&B, dance and pop with their debut, *Gonna Make You Sweat* (Columbia, 1990, prod. Robert Clivilles and David Cole) Buoyed by hits such as the title track and the freewheeling groove thang "Things That Make You Go, Hmmm..." the pair rocketed to the top of the charts—bolstered by slashing synthesizer hits, percolating drum programs and soulful vocals. As the album's success played out, controversy arose when it was revealed that Davis, the woman featured in the videos (Clivilles and Cole were not) didn't sing the powerhouse soul vocal licks that proved the selling point for the "...Sweat" single. The vocals had instead been handled by veteran Martha Wash of the Weather Girls. As the group's obviously calculated origins began to wear on fans, frictions arose among the performers. It took four years to assemble a follow-up record—without Williams, who'd already gone solo—and by then, no one cared. Cole died in 1995 of an AIDS-related illness.

the rest: *Anything Goes* (Columbia, 1994)

solo outings:

***Clivilles and Cole:** Greatest Remixes, Vol. 1* (Columbia, 1992)

***Freedom Williams:** Freedom* (Columbia, 1993)

Eric Deggans

Chris Cacavas and Junkyard Love

See: Green on Red

J.J. Cale

Born Jean Jacques Cale, Dec. 5, 1938 in Oklahoma City, Okla.

Cale is a lo-fi roots rocker and songwriter who, besides having more success with other artists covering his songs, can whip up some brilliant guitar playing when so desired. He's also one of the first artists to utilize drum machines and other new technology without losing the organic sensibilities of his songs about honky tonk livin' and wonder. A limited vocalist but an overachiever as a tunesmith, Cale can lull you into an ambient splendor. His best known covers include: Eric Clapton's interpretations of "Cocaine" and "After Midnight;" Lynyrd Skynyrd and, recently, The Mavericks' takes on "Call Me the Breeze;" Bryan Ferry and Captain Beefheart's renditions of "Same Old Blues;" The Band's crackling "Crazy Mama;" and Randy Crawford's jazzed-up version of "Cajun Moon." His 1982 song "A Thing Going On" from his *Grasshopper* album was recently featured in the hit movie "Phenomenon."

what to buy: *Naturally...J.J. Cale* (Mercury, 1972, prod. Audie Ashworth) is a cornucopia of roots rockin' tunes that features the hit song "Crazy Mama" (one of the first songs to utilize a drum machine) and stellar backing from Tim Drummond and Carl Radle on bass, and David Briggs on piano and organ. *Special Edition* (Mercury, 1984, prod. Audie Ashworth and J.J.

Cale) is a 14-track best-of collection from Cale's Mercury albums, boasting the well-covered hits plus less-known but equally compelling songs such as "Money Talks," "Don't Cry Sister" and "Carry On." *Closer to You* (Virgin, 1994, prod. J.J. Cale) is Cale's first album for Virgin and his 11th overall, another display of top-notch guitar playing and songwriting.

what to buy next: *Number 10* (Silvertone, 1992, prod. J.J. Cale) may be a just a notch below *Naturally* in the song department but more than makes up for it with Cale's guitar heroics throughout.

what to avoid: There's nothing terribly wrong with *Five,* (Mercury, 1979, prod. Audie Ashworth and J.J. Cale) but there's a sense of interchangeability about the albums Cale recorded around this time.

the rest: *Really, J.J. Cale* (Mercury, 1972) *Okie* (Mercury, 1974) *Troubadour* (Mercury, 1976) *Shades* (Mercury, 1980) *Grasshopper* (Mercury, 1982) *Eight* (Mercury, 1983) *Travel-Log* (Silvertone, 1990) *Guitar Man* (Virgin, 1996)

worth searching for: *Naturally,* (Shelter, 1972) Cale's debut and one of the first releases on Shelter Records, co-owned by fellow Oklahoman Leon Russell.

Dire Straits, Eric Clapton, Wilco, Uncle Tupelo, John Campbell

Chet Atkins, Grand Ole Opry

Mark J. Petracca

John Cale

Born March 9, 1942, in Garnant, South Wales

Few figures in rock history have had the wide-reaching influence and broad background of musician/composer/producer Cale. A classically trained pianist and violist, the Welsh-born Cale has been a vital player in American music's avant garde, first as a student and cohort of jazz artist/minimalist LaMonte Young and later as a founding member of the seminal pre-punk group the Velvet Underground. As producer for artists such as Iggy Pop, Patti Smith and Jonathan Richman, Cale defined the raw, sonic excesses that would shape punk music. Throughout the 70s, his associations with the likes of Brian Eno and Roxy Music guitarist Phil Manzanera put him at the center of rock music's most bizarre and experimental period. His own solo work has been eccentric and unpredictable, marked by flashes of brilliance and artistic malaise. Cale's post-Velvet albums saw him venturing into British folk of the haunted, Nick Drake variety, but by the early 70s (his most productive period) he seemed to have found his niche, writing morbidly fascinating rock songs about murder and debauchery that consolidated his tastes for rock, folk, classical and electronic music. His post-punk work is erratic and uninspired, although recent collaborations with former musical partners Lou Reed and Eno, as well as his own return to his classical roots, have resulted in some fine recordings.

what to buy: If there is a central work in Cale's opus, it is *Fear,* (Island, 1974, prod. John Cale) an album of savage excesses and pastoral reflections. Joined by Eno and Manzanera, Cale builds an intensely claustrophobic atmosphere that evokes both fright and nervous laughter. The songs are terrific and cover a wide range of styles, from demented rockers such as "Fear Is a Man's Best Friend" and "Gun" to lovely ballads like "Buffalo Ballet" and "Ship of Fools." An engagingly weird and disturbing recording. Cale lowered the tension slightly on his next album, *Slow Dazzle,* (Island, 1975, prod. John Cale) which plays out like an honest effort at recording a rock album, with fine arrangements and broader themes on many of the songs. Among the treats are "Mr. Wilson" (a clever tribute to Brian Wilson), the raunchy barrel-house rocker "Dirty-Ass Rock 'n' Roll," a dirge-like cover of Elvis Presley's "Heartbreak Hotel" and "The Jeweler," a recitation that recalls Cale's work with the Velvet Underground.

what to buy next: Recorded shortly after *Slow Dazzle, Helen of Troy* (Island, 1975, prod. John Cale) melds its predecessor's pop sensibilities with the brooding pain of *Fear.* The result is an intensely personal album of gripping themes and compelling arrangements, kicking off with the anthem-like "My Maria" (complete with operatic chorus) and rolling with engaging morbidity through the gentle string-infused ballad "I Keep a Close Watch" and a gripping cover of Jonathan Richman's "Pablo Picasso." For a look at Cale's lighter work, check out *Paris 1919.* (Reprise, 1973, prod. Chris Thomas) Recorded in California with members of Little Feat, the album is an enigmatic and breathtaking work, beautifully orchestrated and featuring lovely songs throughout—most notably "Hanky Panky Nohow," "The Endless Plain of Fortune" and "Andalucia."

what to avoid: Like several of the albums from Cale's post-punk period, *Caribbean Sunset* (ZE-Island, 1984, prod. John Cale) is too erratic and unfocused to hold much interest. Aside from the strong title track, the rest of the album plods along without much aim or enthusiasm.

the rest: *Vintage Violence* (Columbia, 1969) *Church of Anthrax* (Columbia, 1971) *The Academy in Peril* (Edsel, 1972) *Honi Soitx* (A&M, 1981) *Music for a New Society* (ZE-Passport, 1982) *Artificial Intelligence* (Beggars Banquet-PVC, 1985) *Words for the Dying* (Opal/Warner Bros., 1989) *Even Cowgirls Get the Blues* (ROIR, 1991) *Fragments of a Rainy Season* (Hannibal/Carthage, 1992) *Seducing Down the Door: A Collection 1970-1990* (Rhino, 1994) *Walking on Locusts* (Hannibal/Rykodisc, 1996) (with Kevin Ayers, Eno and Nico): *June 1, 1974* (Island, 1974) (with Lou Reed): *Songs for Drella* (Sire-Warner Bros., 1990)

worth searching for: After years of assisting with each other's albums, Cale and Eno finally collaborated on the brilliant but out of print *Wrong Way Up*, (Opal-Warner Bros., 1990, prod. Brian Eno) resulting in one of the best albums either artist has ever made.

▶▶ Nick Drake, King Crimson, Robert Fripp, Pink Floyd, Roxy Music, Brian Eno, Patti Smith, Tom Waits, Television, Tom Verlaine, Robert Wyatt

◀◀ John Cage, LaMonte Young, The Beach Boys, the Beatles, the Velvet Underground

see also: *The Velvet Underground*

Christopher Scapelliti

Randy California

See: Spirit

The Call

Formed 1980 in Los Angeles, Calif.

Michael Been, vocals, guitar; Scott Musick, drums, vocals; Tom Ferrier, guitar, vocals; Greg Freeman, bass; Jim Goodwin, keyboards

The Call carved its mark with an apocalyptic post-punk steely aggressiveness, propelled in large part by Been. A limited but passionate singer, he attracted the likes of the Band's Garth Hudson, who lent his hand to a number of songs. Standing apart from the early 80s New Wave scene, the Call have much more in common, ideaologically, with 70s punk in its uncompromising drive and railings against the status quo.

what to buy: *The Walls Came Down: Best of the Mercury Years* (Mercury, 1991, prod. Various) is Been's own compilation from from the Call's first three albums, providing an excellent intro to the band's work—especially the scathing title track and the floor-shaking indictments of "Turn a Blind Eye."

what to buy next: *Reconciled* (Elektra, 1986, prod. Michael Been and the Call) features guest shots from Robbie Robertson, Peter Gabriel and Simple Minds' Jim Kerr, which can't help but tip the scales in the right direction.

what to avoid: *The Call* (Mercury, 1982, prod. Hugh Padgham) is tentative, with the band just finding its style and sound—though completists shouldn't be too disappointed.

the rest: *Modern Romans* (Mercury, 1983) *Scene Beyond Dreams* (Mercury, 1984) *Red Moon* (MCA, 1990) *Into the Woods* (Elektra, 1987)

worth searching for: *Let the Day Begin* (MCA, 1989) didn't get much recognition, but it's full of hard-hitters in addition to the title track.

▶▶ The Alarm, nine inch nails

◀◀ The Clash, Joy Division

Allan Orski

Camel

Formed 1971 in London, England

One of the more ethereal of Britain's progressive rock bands of the 70s, Camel created ambitious, conceptual pieces that never quite found an audience in the U.S. Lacking a strong visionary, such as Pink Floyd's Roger Waters or Genesis' Peter Gabriel, the group simply never got much attention. But its keyboard washes, layered guitars and breezy vocals made for some of the most pleasant, entrancing music of the prog rock era and prefaced the New Age movement. Bardens went on to acclaim as the keyboardist on Van Morrison's "Wavelength" album, while Collins' feverish, high-pitched tenor sax solo was a highlight of the Rolling Stones' hit "Miss You."

what to buy: Most of Camel's records are out of print now, including its best album, the Brian Eno collaboration *Rain Dances*. Fortunately, there are a few anthologies out there, including the two-CD collection *Echoes: The Retrospective*, (Deram/Chronicles, 1993, prod. Various) a far-ranging collection that manages to string together some of its best mid-70s work with hard-to-find songs from its 80s and early 90s.

the rest: Breathless *(Deram/One Way, 1978)* I Can See

Your House from Here *(Deram/One Way, 1979)* A Compact Compilation *(Rhino, 1985)* Collection *(Griffin Music, date N/A)* Pressure Points *(Deram, date N/A)*

Cocteau Twins, Dead Can Dance, Enya

Pink Floyd (with Syd Barrett); Genesis (with Peter Gabriel); King Crimson, Procol Harum

Doug Pullen

Ali Campbell

See: UB40

Glen Campbell

Born April 22, 1936 in Billstown, Ark.

Although best remembered as a somewhat ingratiating, over-the-top cornball cowboy (his hugely successful CBS series "The Glen Campbell Goodtime Hour" can still strike terror into the faint-of-heart), Campbell's long and successful career as an entertainer is testament to the obvious drive and abundant talent behind the rhinestones. First leaving home as a teen to tour behind his uncle Dick Campbell, Campbell landed in Los Angeles in 1960 at the perfect time to make use of his growing prowess on the guitar. Over the next five years, he was one of the city's most sought-after studio musicians, performing behind everyone from Spector to Sinatra; he was even a bona fide Beach Boy for a while. Signed to Capitol Records in 1962, he first hit the Top 50 in 1965 with a version of Donovan's "Universal Soldier," and two years later his signature tune, John Hartford's "Gentle On My Mind," hit No. 39. But it wasn't until he began recording the brilliant songs of Jimmy Webb that Campbell became a regular visitor to the Top 10; "By The Time I Get To Phoenix," "Wichita Lineman" and "Galveston" remain classics of the country-pop genre). After several years spent entertaining on both the small and big screens (his motion picture debut was alongside John Wayne in "True Grit"), Campbell returned to the top of the charts in 1975 ("Rhinestone Cowboy") and 1977 ("Southern Nights") before hitting the scandal sheets with Tanya Tucker and letting years of pharmaceutical dabbling get the better of him. The 90s, however, found Campbell both physically and spiritually cleansed and refreshed, and he remains a popular performer—and red-hot guitarist—to this day. The recent *Essential Glen Campbell* series (Liberty/Capitol Nashville, 1995, prod. Various) gathers, in three volumes, all the hits in gorgeous sound as well as just enough rarities, instrumentals and live recordings to demonstrate both the depth and scope of this decidedly all-round entertainer.

Gary Pig Gold

Camper Van Beethoven /Cracker

Camper Van Beethoven (1984-91): David Lowery, vocals, guitar; Chris Molla, vocals, guitar, drums (1984-86); Victor Krummenacher, bass, vocals; Jonathan Segel, violin, keyboards, mandolin (1984-89); Greg Lisher, guitar; Chris Pederson, drums (1986-90); Morgan Fichter, violin (1989). Cracker (1992-present): David Lowery, vocals, guitar; Johnny Hickman, guitar, vocals; Davey Faragher, vocals, bass; Michael Urbano, drums (1992-93); Charlie Quintana, drums (1993-95); Johnny Hott, drums (1996-present)

With Lowery's nerdy voice and sarcastic sense of humor, plus an enthusiasm for Middle Eastern rhythms and unusual rock instruments, Camper Van Beethoven staked its spot as the "funny band" to R.E.M.'s "serious band" in the independent underground. The band's early albums were the sounds of surfing ska fans trying to crack each other up, and sometimes they did it in a hilariously lazy way. "Take the Skinheads Bowling," a dumb joke that lampooned racist punk concert-goers, became Camper's college-radio hit. Gradually, the members began incorporating more complex songwriting and relying more on the violins and mandolins that were novelties on early albums. The band got very good, but also very serious; eventually tension about the group's direction led to a breakup. Members went in all directions. The first post-Camper band was the Monks of Doom, featuring Lisher, Krummenacher, Pedersen and sort-of Camper member David Immerglick; that band rocked but had trouble writing good, tight songs. Lowery's band, Cracker, didn't have that problem. Drawing from punk persona non grata Tom Petty, Lowery cut out the fat and put together Cracker's three albums of snappy, bluesy pop songs, some of which became MTV-driven hits.

what to buy: *Telephone Free Landslide Victory* (Independent Project/Rough Trade, 1985/I.R.S., 1993) is a refreshing blast of humor given the angst-ridden drunkenness that characterized so much 80s post-punk, and it has both "Where the Hell Is Bill" and "Take the Skinheads Bowling." The swan song, *Key Lime Pie,* (Virgin, 1989, prod. Dennis Herring) features a brilliant, stomping cover of Strawberry Alarm Clock's "Pictures of Matchstick Men" and a new Lowery political edge in "Jack Ruby," "When I Win the Lottery" and "(I Was Born In a) Laundromat." Cracker's debut, *Cracker* (Virgin, 1992, prod. Don Smith) contains several songs that sound great on the radio, including the propulsive "Teen Angst (What the World Needs Now)" and the new birthday classic "Happy Birthday to Me."

what to buy next: Cracker's *Kerosene Hat (Virgin, 1993, prod. Don Smith) adds "Low," "Get Off This" and "Movie Star," which finally gave the underappreciated Lowery a presence on MTV and in national music magazines. Camper's* Our Beloved Revolutionary Sweetheart, *(Virgin, 1988, prod. Dennis Herring) the band's major-label debut, continued to mix all sorts of psychedelic, Indian and traditional rock sounds that sometimes went together and sometimes didn't.*

what to avoid: *Vampire Can Mating Oven* EP (Pitch-A-Tent/Rough Trade, 1987, /I.R.S., 1993) clears the closet before Camper moved to a major label, sounding sometimes like that last box of found junk you toss together and know you might never open in the new place.

the rest: Camper Van Beethoven: *Camper Van Beethoven II & III* (Pitch-A-Tent/Rough Trade, 1986/I.R.S., 1993) *Camper Van Beethoven* (Pitch-A-Tent/Rough Trade, 1986/I.R.S., 1993) Cracker—*The Golden Age* (Virgin, 1996)

worth searching for: *Camper Van Chadbourne,* (Fundamental, 1987) a collaboration with equally twisted guitarist Eugene Chadborne. *Camper Vantiquities,* (I.R.S., 1993) a rarities collection put out when I.R.S. re-released all the group's old Rough Trade albums, is worth a few extra bucks for a version of the Animals' "I'm Not Like Everybody Else."

solo outings:

Jonathan Segel: Storytelling (Pitch-A-Tent/Rough Trade, 1989) Monks of Doom: *Breakfast on the Beach of Deception* soundtrack (Pitch-A-Tent/Rough Trade, 1988) *The Cosmodemonic Telegraph Company* (Pitch-A-Tent/Rough Trade, 1989)

▶▶ Dead Milkmen, Presidents of the United States of America, Sublime, Mighty Mighty Bosstones

◀◀ Tom Petty, Grateful Dead, Indian raja music, Bob Marley, the Specials, R.E.M., Jan & Dean

Steve Knopper

Candlebox

Formed 1991 in Seattle, Wash.

Kevin Martin, vocals, guitar; Peter Klett, guitar; Scott Mercado, drums; Bardi Martin, bass

Candlebox may have started in Seattle, but it wasn't part of the city's exploding angst-fuzz-and-flannel grunge scene. The quartet plays straightforward, muscular arena rock with a wisp of the blues. Named after a Midnight Oil lyric, Candlebox was the first rock band Madonna signed to her Maverick label after the quartet built a grass-roots following among hard-rock fans with its dynamic live shows. What helps Candlebox stand out from the hordes of guitar-driven rock quartets is the music's compelling ebb and flow, paced by Klett's strategically sharp guitar attacks and Kevin (no relation to Bardi) Martin's emotionally intense, tempered vocal screams. The debut, *Candlebox* (Maverick, 1993, prod. Kelly Gray, Jon Plum and Candlebox) is a solid mix of guitar energy and power ballads, highlighted by pensive lyrics ("Mother's Dream," "Far Behind") and well-crafted melodies ("You," "Rain"). Except for the steady rise of "Understanding," there's less restraint or melodic wit on *Lucy,* (Maverick, 1995, prod. Kelly Gray, Jon Plum and Candlebox) as Candlebox cranks out high-voltage guitars and screeching vocals, hitting peak form on the patient thumper, "Bothered."

David Yonke

Canned Heat

Formed 1966 in Los Angeles, Calif.

Bob "Bear" Hite, vocals, harmonica (1966-81, died April 45, 1981); Al "Blind Owl" Wilson, guitar, vocals, harmonica (1966-70, died Sept. 3, 1970); Henry "The Sunflower" Vestine, guitar (1966-69, 1970); Frank Cook, drums (1966-68); Larry Taylor (born Samuel Taylor), bass (1966-70, 1994-present); Adolpho "Fito" de la Parra, drums (1968-present); Harvey Mandel, guitar (1969-70); Antonio de la Barreda, bass (1970-72); Richard Hite, bass (1972-91); James Thornbury, guitar, hamonica, vocals (1984-present); Junior Watson, guitar, vocals (1994-present); Ron Shumake, bass, vocals (1994-present)

The boogie, ever since John Lee Hooker created it during the late '40s in Detroit, has been a timeless thing. So it is that this bunch of players from Southern California plugged in their jug band and started playing the rolling, loose-limbed blues they loved so much on their John Lee Hooker records. If Canned Heat were a new band today, it would be part of the H.O.R.D.E. festival. As it is, the group continues—though without its original frontmen, Bob Hite and Al Wilson but with an increasing number of original and prime-time members each year, as if they're coming back to the mothership for a bit of boogie nourishment.

what to buy: *Uncanned! The Best of Canned Heat* (Liberty/EMI,

1994, prod. Various) is an expansive two-disc, 41-song set that has the hits ("On the Road Again," "Going Up the Country," "Fannie Mae") and a disarming number of highly listenable jams. How quickly we forget.

what to avoid: *The King Biscuit Flower Hour Presents Canned Heat,* (KBFH, 1996) a radio concert taken from a flat and forgettable 1979 show.

the rest: *The Best of Canned Heat* (EMI America, 1987) *Internal Combustion* (River Road, 1994) *Gamblin' Woman* (Mausoleum, 1996)

worth searching for: One of the group's most consistent albums, *Future Blues,* (Liberty, 1970/See For Miles, 1993, prod. Skip Taylor and Canned Heat) which is available as an import.

The Grateful Dead, Fabulous Thunderbirds, Blues Traveler

John Lee Hooker, Howlin' Wolf, Sonny Boy Williamson

Gary Graff

Captain Beefheart & His Magic Band

Formed 1964 in Lancaster, Calif.

Captain Beefheart (born Don Van Vliet), vocals, harmonica, tenor and soprano sax, bass clarinet. Notable Magic Band alumni include: Zoot Horn Rollo (born Bill Harkleroad), guitar, (1969-73); Winged Eel Fingerling (born Eliot Ingber), guitar (1968-73); Antennae Jimmy Semens (born Jeff Cotton), guitar (1966-70); Alex St. Claire, guitar (1966-70); Ry Cooder, guitar, (1966); Gary Lucas, guitar, (1978-80); Jeff Morris Tepper, guitar, (1978-82); Rockette Morton (born Mark Boston), bass, (1969-72); Orejon (born Roy Estrada), bass, (1972); Eric Drew Feldman, keyboards, (1978-82); Bruce Lambourne Fowler, trombone, (1978-82); Drumbo (born John French), drums (1966-82); Ed Marimba (born Art Tripp), drums, (1972); Robert Arthur Williams, drums (1978-82)

The profoundly playful godfathers of all things alternative in rock, Captain Beefheart & His Magic Band stripped songs down to their bare bones and let them run free. Though clearly rooted in the most primitive blues, Beefheart's music is full of angles and cross rhythms, stuttering, snaky guitar lines and free jazz dissonance—a fitting backdrop for the holy terror of the Captain's Howlin' Wolf-on-acid vocals and hilarious, dadaist lyrics. While his early recordings were marred by record company-induced compromise, in 1969 he was given carte blanche by longtime friend Frank Zappa's Bizarre label. The result was the enormously influential "Trout Mask Replica," a still-crucial art-rock reference point. Despite some mid-70's stumbles, Beefheart returned with a new Magic Band in 1978 to make music as challenging as ever—though its point was somewhat blunted by the advent of punk. The Captain, who last recorded in 1983, has moved to the northern California coast, where he paints full-time.

what to buy: Fractured, ferocious and full of Delta Blues meets Sun Ra surprises—along with Beefheart's wondrously surreal and goofy lyrics —*Trout Mask Replica* (Reprise, 1969, prod. Frank Zappa) remains the indisputable benchmark for what lurks under, over and beyond rock. Almost 30 years later, the music still sounds as if it was made tomorrow.

what to buy next: Beefheart followed up *Trout Mask Replica* with the self-produced and only marginally less turbulent *Lick My Decals Off Baby* (Bizarre, 1970, prod. Don Van Vliet) His next two albums, *The Spotlight Kid/Clear Spot,* (Reprise, 1972, prod. Ted Templeman) now available on one CD, found the Captain and his band rocking a little harder and in a more recognizable rock song format—which is why these records are the more accessible favorites of many fans. Of Beefheart's recordings with the reincarnated Magic Band, *Doc At The Radar Station* (Blue Plate, 1980, prod. Don Van Vliet) marked the most powerful return of his "fast and bulbous" sound.

what to avoid: *Bluejeans & Moonbeams* (Blue Plate, 1974, prod. Don Van Vliet) was Beefheart's overt and truly dubious attempt to make a "pop" record.

the rest: *Safe As Milk* (One Way Records, 1967) *Mirror Man* (One Way Records, 1973) *Unconditionally Guaranteed* (Blue Plate, 1974) *Shiny Beast (Bat Chain Puller)* (Bizarre, 1978) *Ice Cream For Crow* (Blue Plate, 1982) *The Legendary A&M Sessions* (A&M, 1984)

worth searching for: A seminal early Beefheart recording, *Strictly Personal* (Blue Thumb, 1968) is available as a British import on Liberty Records. Outtakes from those sessions can be heard on a French import, *I May Be Hungry, But I Sure Ain't Weird* (Sequel, 1993)

solo outings:

The Captain often popped up on Zappa records, including *Hot Rats* and *The Lost Episodes.* But on Zappa's live album *Bongo*

Fury, (Rykodisc, 1975, prod. Frank Zappa) ♪♪♪ Beefheart takes over as lead vocalist and chief provocateur.

▶▶ Sonic Youth, The Residents, Nick Cave, Tom Waits, Eugene Chadbourne, PJ Harvey

◀◀ Howlin' Wolf, Bo Diddley, Ornette Coleman, Eric Dolphy, Sun Ra, Karlheinz Stockhausen

see also: *Frank Zappa*

Doug Pippin

The Captain and Tennille

Formed 1974 in Los Angeles, Calif.

A partnership often better known for its industry savvy and knack for making the most of career opportunities, the Captain and Tennille—a.k.a. Daryl Dragon and Catheryn Antoinette "Toni" Tennille—made their name by scoring a series of pop hits during the mid- and late-'70s. The duo pushed an inoffensive brand of pop-rock built on catchy melodies and Tennille's expert if generic vocal abilities. Both students of classical piano for nearly a decade each, Dragon and Tennille met when the singer developed a musical, "Mother Earth," for which her husband-to-be played keyboards. When the show closed days after opening, Dragon took Tennille along as a backing vocalist on his new gig, as keyboardist for the Beach Boys. By 1974, the two had recorded a single together, "The Way I Want to Touch You." But it was a year later that their recording of Neil Sedaka's "Love Will Keep Us Together" exploded onto the pop charts. By the year's end, both songs would be Top 10 hits. The next year, a version of Smokey Robinson's "Shop Around" became another big hit, allowing the duo to land an ABC television series that lasted two years. The couple also had great success with a remake of America's "Muskrat Love," but its 15 minutes ran out after the 1979 smash "Do That to Me One More Time." Tennille released occasional albums of big band tunes while Dragon helmed the pair's Nevada studio, producing albums and writing film soundtracks. Never an album-oriented act, it's no surprise that all that's left is *Captain and Tennille's Greatest Hits*, (A&M, 1977, prod. Darryl Dragon) ♪♪♪ which came out too early to include "Do That to Me. . ." Aw, shucks.

Eric Deggans

Caravan

Formed 1968 in England

Pye Hastings, guitar,vocals; David Sinclair, keyboards; Richard Sinclair, bass, vocals; Richard Coughlan, drums

This was the freshest-sounding, least self-absorbed of the progressive rock bands from England during the late 60s. Using English folks and renaissance music styles along with superior musicianship, Caravan was adept at performing tight song structures and creating exciting vamps in suite-like arrangements. *Canterbury Tales: The Best of Caravan* (Deram/Chronicles, 1994) ♪♪♪♪ is a fine two-disc sampling of Caravan's first seven albums. It's also worth searching for the deleted *For Girls Who Grow Plump in the Night* (London, 1973), the band's smartest, most powerful album.

Patrick McCarty

Mariah Carey

Born March 27, 1970 on Long Island, N.Y.

A product of a black Venezuelan father and Irish-American mother, Carey seemed born to be a pop star—wielding a soulfully astonishing seven-octave voice while offering a supermodel look that barely hints at her ethnic origins. Working as a backup singer for various R&B sessions around Manhattan in her late teens—while supporting herself as the self-described "world's worst waitress"—the singer honed her songwriting talents with keyboardist Ben Margulies. On one such gig, backing R&B one hit wonder Brenda K. Starr at a party, Carey got her big break; Starr presented a demo tape of hers to Columbia Records chief Tommy Mottola, who was so taken with the material while driving home, he headed back to the party to meet Carey. Before long, with Mottola guiding her career—eventually named Sony Music president, he married Carey in 1993—the singer released a single, "Visions of Love," that shot to No. 1 on the pop charts in 1990. Carey would eventually earn five consecutive No. 1 pop singles over two albums, along with two Grammy Awards. From that point, Carey—most often compared to fellow hitmaking diva Whitney Houston—could do no wrong, offering an appealing pop sound leavened with touches of soul. An EP version of her *MTV Unplugged* performance soared to the top of the charts in 1992, along with her third record a year later. Though her first-ever concert tour in 1993 met with mixed reviews, a chart-topping duet with Boyz II Men in 1995 proved she still retained her golden touch.

what to buy: For anyone looking at Carey's catalog, this answer depends on what the collector wants. Fans of her treacly pop sound—a generically accessible approach that nearly suffocates her amazing vocal abilities—will want *Mariah Carey* (Columbia, 1990, prod. Mariah Carey, Walter Afanasieff, Rhett Lawrence, Narada Michael Walden, Ben Margulies and Ric Wake) ♪♪♪♪ Featuring the hits "Vision of Love" and "Love Takes Time," it's the most vibrant of her studio discs.

what to buy next: For those who yearn to hear Carey break free of her commercial prison, the closest she comes is *MTV Unplugged.* (Columbia EP, 1992, prod. Mariah Carey and Walter Afanasieff) ♪♪♪♪ Though the 26-plus people performing on this disc seem to belie the unplugged ethic, Carey's vibrant live delivery is nearly worth the heresy. As schmaltzy as it might seem, her take on the Jackson 5's MDBR*"I'll Be There" really does impress—at least on the first hundred listens.*

what to avoid: For fans of truly expressive soul music, everything in Carey's catalog goes down like a sawdust sandwich. But *Merry Christmas,* (Columbia, 1994, prod. Walter Afanasieff) ♪♪♪ mixing standards such as "Silent Night" with originals like "All I Want For Christmas Is You," is enough to make anyone reach for a few stiff shots of egg nog.

the rest: *Emotions* (Columbia, 1991) ♪♪♪ *Music Box* (Columbia, 1993) ♪♪♪ *Daydream* (Columbia, 1995) ♪♪♪

worth searching for: A videotape of the 1995 Grammy awards telecast, if only to see the consternation on Carey's face as she is consistently edged out (and eventually shut out, despite four nominations) by Alanis Morissette and Annie Lennox.

⏩ Toni Braxton, Celine Dion

⏪ Whitney Houston, Minnie Ripperton, Irene Cara

Eric Deggans

Belinda Carlisle

See: The Go-Go's

Eric Carmen

See: The Raspberries

Mary Chapin Carpenter

Born Feb. 21, 1958, Princeton, N.J.

Though signed to Columbia Records' Nashville division, Carpenter is no more country than Nick Lowe —another power-pop specialist whose lyrics seem perfectly suited for short, fast rock 'n' roll songs. Though her voice has a hint of a Southern twang and her lyrics occasionally focus on honky-tonks and highways, Carpenter studies the Beatles and Joni Mitchell much more than Merle Haggard or Johnny Cash. Either way, she has managed to build a substantial crossover audience of mainstream country fans and neo-folkies clinging to albums by Carpenter's friends, Shawn Colvin and Rosanne Cash. Her best songs, including "I Feel Lucky" and a polished version of Lucinda Williams' "Passionate Kisses," have hit the top of the country charts and she consistently racks up Grammys and Country Music Awards.

what to buy: *Come On Come On* (Columbia, 1992, prod. John Jennings and Mary Chapin Carpenter) ♪♪♪♪ produced seven country hits (which also received substantial pop airplay), including "Passionate Kisses" and "I Feel Lucky," which drops the names of Lyle Lovett and Dwight Yoakam.

what to buy next: *Shootin' Straight in the Dark* (Columbia, 1990, prod. John Jennings and Mary Chapin Carpenter) ♪♪♪ began Carpenter's commercial breakthrough with the romping "Down at the Twist and Shout." *Stones in the Road* (Columbia, 1994, prod. John Jennings and Mary Chapin Carpenter) ♪♪♪♪ had generally quieter and more introspective—but still engaging—songs.

the rest: *Hometown Girl* (Columbia, 1988) ♪♪♪ *State of the Heart* (Columbia, 1989) ♪♪♪

worth searching for: *On Location: Conversation and Music By Mary Chapin Carpenter,* a one-hour radio special on CD from 1992 that features Carpenter performing and talking about the songs from her first four albums.

⏩ Shawn Colvin, Trisha Yearwood, Patty Loveless, Suzy Bogguss, Dar Williams

⏪ Carlene Carter, the Beatles, Joni Mitchell, Bob Dylan, Rosanne Cash

Tracey Birkenhauer and Steve Knopper

The Carpenters

Formed 1969 in Downey, Calif.

Richard Carpenter, vocals, keyboards; Karen Carpenter, vocals, drums (died Feb. 4, 1983 in Los Angeles, Calif.)

The best Carpenters songs weren't the sappy, perky mega-hits the duo specialized in during the mid-70s—such as "Top of the World," "Can't Smile Without You," "Sing" or "Touch Me When We're Dancing." Rather, they were the sad numbers on which Karen's pure voice conveyed restrained yet heart-wrenching agony or wistful nostalgia. Only Richard's slick arrangements could get such downbeat lyrics on the radio. In fact, the juxtaposition of Karen's melancholy sound with Richard's lush settings lends many tracks an oddly menacing irony in view of Karen's 1983 death from cardiac arrest connected to anorexia. The Carpenters' rise from child prodigies to superstardom and the duo's subsequent fall has been well-chronicled, in the 1988 TV movie "The Karen Carpenter Story" and in a biography by Ray Coleman. Although much was made of Karen being a drummer (a genuine oddity back then), most of the best drum parts on the first half-decade's albums are by studio great Hal Blaine; in fact they redefined the art and sound of studio drumming. But Karen nonetheless assumed iconic significance as a feminist symbol.

what to buy: *Carpenters* (A&M, 1971, prod. Jack Daugherty) is by far the group's pinnacle, with "Rainy Days and Mondays," "Let Me Be the One," "For All We Know," "Superstar," "One Love" and "Sometimes." The production may sound dated, but it still has a fresh innocence only slightly tainted by Richard's whiny anti-groupie screed "Druscilla Penny." *Yesterday Once More* (A&M, 1985, prod. Various) is a two-CD compilation that, though it includes some of the more cloying hits, largely avoids the out-and-out dross.

what to buy next: *Close to You,* (A&M, 1970, prod. Jack Daugherty) with "We've Only Just Begun" and "I'll Never Fall in Love Again," and *A Song for You,* (A&M, 1972, prod. Jack Daugherty) with "Hurting Each Other" and the great "Goodbye to Love," with its brilliant outro of fuzz guitar solo over massed oohs-n-aahs, have the same dewy freshness as *Carpenters*, though with less consistent material. A large proportion of the Carpenters' pop prowess was based on Richard's ear for great songs by other writers, as documented on *Interpretations* (A&M, 1995, prod. ??). It's interesting to hear Karen's pure voice on music identified more with other performers ("This Masquerade," "When I Fall in Love," "Tryin' to Get the Feeling Again").

what to avoid: *Now and Then: The Singles 1969-1973* (A&M, 1973, prod. Various) is from the group's most listenable period, but it overlaps the songs in a no-gap flow and has been superseded by *Yesterday Once More. Once from the Top: The Ultimate Retrospective* (A&M, 1991, prod. Various) is a four-CD set with more merit for the die-hard fans (most people will find it overkill), but Richard overdubbed parts in a decades-late, obsessive attempt to improve some songs.

What Album Changed Your Life?

"It seems weird, but I only discovered Pet Sounds (Capitol, 1966) and Surf's Up (Reprise, 1971) four or five years ago. I'd heard early Beach Boys when I was young, very young--the surfing stuff. I'd heard Holland as well. But when I missed those two albums, and when I heard them, I was in tears. I could not believe what I was hearing, things like the track 'Surf's Up' and 'God Only Knows,' just one after another. I wouldn't have thought that at this stage of my life I could be affected so much by music--and music that had been made 20 or more years before I'd heard it."

Howard Jones

the rest: *Ticket to Ride* (A&M, 1969) *Passage* (A&M, 1977) *Made in America* (A&M, 1981) *Lovelines* (A&M, 1989) *Horizon* (A&M, 1975) *A Kind of Hush* (A&M, 1976) *Voice of the Heart* (A&M, 1983)

worth searching for: *If I Were a Carpenter,* (A&M, 1994, exec. prod. Matt Wallace and David Konjoyan) an all-star tribute album helps 90s ears appreciate the Carpenters' material. The stellar lineup—including Sonic Youth ("Superstar"), the Cranberries ("Close to You"), and Matthew Sweet (a sweet, pedal steel-drenched "Let Me Be the One")—makes this rank way above the average tribute album.

▶▶ Air Supply, Sheryl Crow

◀◀ Beatles, Burt Bacharach, Mantovani, the Association

Steve Holtje

Detroit Rock City

Face
Big Chief (Sub Pop, 1992)

Robert Bradley's Blackwater Surprise
Robert Bradley's Blackwater Surprise (RCA, 1996)

Marshall Crenshaw
Marshall Crenshaw (Warner Bros., 1982)

The Queen of Soul
Aretha Franklin (Rhino, 1992)

Grand Funk
Grand Funk Railroad (Capitol, 1970)

John Lee Hooker on Vee-Jay 1955-1958
John Lee Hooker (Vee-Jay, 1993)

Alive
Kiss (Casablanca/Mercury, 1975)

Kick Out the Jams
MC5 (Elektra, 1969)

Rock Action
The Scott Morgan Band (Revenge, 1985)

Free For All
Ted Nugent (Epic, 1976)

Rev it Up: The Best of Mitch Ryder and the Detroit Wheels
Mitch Ryder and the Detroit Wheels (Rhino, 1989)

Live Bullet
Bob Seger (Capitol, 1976)

Wax Ecstatic
Sponge (Columbia, 1996)

Fun House
The Stooges (Elektra, 1970)

Detroit Underground, Vol 1
Various Artists (Razor Cut, date N/A)

Celtic Rock Classics

The Alarm
The Alarm (I.R.S. EP, 1983)

High Land, Hard Rain
Aztec Camera (Sire 1983)

The Long Black Veil
The Chieftains (RCA Victor, 1995)

The Crossing
Big Country (Mercury, 1983)

Change Everything
Del Amitri (A&M, 1992)

Too-Rye-Ay
Dexys Midnight Runners (Mercury, 1982)

Troubadour: The Definitive Collection 1964-1976
Donovan (Epic, 1992)

Watermark
Enya (Geffen, 1988)

Home
Hothouse Flowers (London, 1990)

His Band and the Street Choir
Van Morrison (Warner Bros., 1970)

I Do Not Want What I Haven't Got
Sinead O'Connor (Ensign/Chrysalis, 1990)

Rum, Sodomy & the Lash
The Pogues (MCA, 1985)

Every Picture Tells a Story
Rod Stewart (Mercury, 1971)

The Joshua Tree
U2 (Island, 1987)

Room to Roam
The Waterboys (Ensign/Chrysalis, 1990)

What Album Changed Your Life?

"An X record, probably Wild Gift. It's as simple as 'I got it.' It hit me in the spine. Once you get that high, it's like being a junkie; you need it again and again. You expect that of music. Once I heard that, I couldn't really go back and...listen to anything stupid ever again."

Kristen Hersh (Throwing Muses)

Paul Carrack /Ace

Born April 1951 in Sheffield, Yorkshire, England

Gifted with a spine-tingling, blue-eyed soul voice and an unassuming, workmanlike approach to music, Carrack has assembled an impressive musical resume—despite his knack for making the least of any commercial success. He first came to national attention via the pub rock group Ace, bringing his emotive, soulful vocals to bear on its monster 1974 hit, "How Long." When the band failed to match that success in subsequent work, Carrack briefly joined Frankie Miller's band before signing up for two albums with Roxy Music. Though he next released his first solo album, it wasn't long before Carrack was back in a band—this time with Squeeze, contributing to its landmark album *East Side Story* and singing lead vocals on its biggest hit, the R&B-influenced ballad "Tempted." Carrack's subsequent work included stints with Eric Clapton and a permanent spot with Genesis guitarist Mike Rutherford's Mike and the Mechanics, as well as an intermittently successful solo career and guest spots on albums by the Pretenders, Roger Waters, Elton John and the Smiths.

what to buy: His impressive *One Good Reason* (Chrysalis, 1987, prod. Christopher Neal) is the Carrack album every fan hoped for—good songs, impressive performances and lots of gritty, blue-eyed soul shouting from the man himself. The cry-in-your-beer single "Don't Shed a Tear" is worth the price of admission alone.

what to buy next: The only thing better than a good Carrack album is a collection of all the cool work he's done with other people. *Collection: Twenty-One Good Reasons* (Chrysalis, 1994, prod. Various) features his solo best plus the hits he sang with with Ace, Squeeze, Mike and the Mechanics and a couple songs from his brief stint in Carlene Carter's band.

what to avoid: Nothing stinks worse than a halfhearted greatest hits package, and *The Carrack Collection* (Chrysalis, 1988, prod. Various) WOOF! reeks. This skimpy assemblage feels like a dress rehearsal for the more complete 1994 collection.

the rest: *Nightbird* (Vertigo, 1980) *Suburban Voodoo* (Epic, 1982) *When You Walk In The Room* (Chrysalis, 1987) *Ace Mechanic* (Demon, 1987) *Groove Approved* (Chrysalis, 1989) (with Ace): *Best of Ace: How Long* (See For Miles, 1988/1994)

worth searching for: The original Ace albums—the best being *Five-A-Side*— (Anchor, 1974) for a taste not only of Carrack's early days but also of the roots from which he and a good chunk of what became known as New Wave sprang from.

Michael Bolton, Little River Band

Jackie Wilson, Otis Redding, Ray Charles

see also: *Squeeze, Mike and the Mechanics (Genesis)*

Eric Deggans

Joe "King" Carrasco

Born Joseph Teutsch, 1954 in Dumas, Texas

With various incarnations of his band the Crowns (or Las Coronas), Carrasco has steadfastly sustained a career playing a rockified version of Tex-Mex, the rhythmic music he heard growing up. Like Doug Sahm a generation before him, Carrasco soaked up the Spanish influence of his native Texas, applied it to rock 'n' roll and revived it with the accordion metamorphosing into cheeseball Farfisa organ bleats during the punk heyday, and later replacing the organ once again with the more traditional (and cooler) accordion. Early in his career, the irrepresible Carrasco was famous for crazy antics like leaping from the stage (this was a long time before stage-diving was adopted by thrashers) or running through a club or concert hall with an incredibly long guitar chord so he could play from a balcony, a bathroom or outside the lobby. In recent years, Carrasco's also added more reggae influence to his music, a reflection of the time he spends hanging out in the Caribbean and in Central America. But no matter how he filters his energy, Carrasco's trademark enthusiasm and yelping vocals still remain undiluted.

what to buy: *Tales from the Crypt* (ROIR Cassette, 1984, prod. Joe Gracey) is the long-awaited release of the demo tapes that got Carrasco his original notoriety and, ultimately, his record deal. It was recorded in bits and pieces during the late 70s (whenever Carrasco could only afford time in a basement studio in Austin) and passed around to New York rock critics in 1979, when the Crowns made their first attack on the Manhattan clubs. It's a distillation of Carrasco's lifelong immersion in both Tex-Mex and roots rock 'n' roll, featuring covers such as "Sweet Little Rock 'n' Roller" alongside wild-eyed orignals like "Caca de Vaca." Writer John Morthland hit it on the head in the liner notes, when he called this cassette release "garage-band heaven."

what to buy next: *Joe 'King' Carrasco and the Crowns,* (Hannibal, 1981, prod. Billy Altman) the first official U.S. release by the band, is cleaner than the cassette demos. And almost as fun.

what to avoid: *Party Weekend* (MCA, 1983), a passable but flat album—particularly compared to Carrasco's other efforts.

the rest: *Party Safari* (Hannibal, 1981) *Synapse Gap* (MCA, 1982) *Joe "King" Carrasco and El Molino* (ROIR, 1984) *Border Town* (New Rose/Big Beat, 1985) *Bandito Rock* (Rounder, 1987) *Royal, Loyal & Live* (Royal Texicali Records, 1990) *Dia de las Muertos* (Royal Texicali Records, 1994) *Anthology* (One Way, 1995)

worth searching for: The British import version of *Joe "King" Carrasco and the Crowns* (Stiff, 1980, prod. Billy Altman) pressed on lavender vinyl so repugnant it's desireable.

▶▶ Doug Sahm, Flaco Jimenez, Texas Tornados

◀◀ Sir Douglas Quintet, ? and the Mysterians, Sam the Sham & the Pharoahs, Flaco Jimenez

Gil Asakawa

Jim Carroll

Born 1950 in New York, N.Y.

After squandering a promising future in basketball, surviving addiction and incarceration, and enjoying literary fame from age 16, poet and novelist Carroll still had time for a career in rock 'n' roll from 1979-85. A fine writer who now thinks his poetic rhythm had to recover from rock song-structure, his three albums' significance is more stylistic and historical than literary. A makeshift but powerful kind of punk plainsong made the Jim Carroll Band one of the first (and still only) acts to widen the form's audience but not sell it out. Carroll has influenced the do-it-yourself grunge generation who paid him homage on the soundtrack to the 1995 film version of his memoir, "The Basketball Diaries," though they have yet to match his ambition. Other than a remake, with Pearl Jam, of his song "Catholic Boy," and some spoken-word tracks on that album, Carroll has concentrated since 1985 on his truest love, the word, publishing books and releasing an album of readings, *Praying Mantis*, in 1991. He remains an inspiration to the sadder and wiser alike. that rare rebel icon less fascinating for his tragedy than his survival.

what to buy: Carroll's best albums are the first and last. *Catholic Boy* (Atco, 1980, prod. Earl McGrath and Bob Clearmountain) features his one hit, "People Who Died," a cathartic bon voyage to lost young friends which has only gained resonance in the age of AIDS and juvenile gunplay. After a slight decline, *I Write Your Name* (Atlantic, 1984, prod. Earl McGrath) regained the spontaneity and coiled energy of the first album and headed off in other directions, most of them fruitful. "Voices" is excessively Devo-derivative, and his rendition of "Sweet Jane" joins a whole sub-genre of unnecessary Velvet Underground covers. But the title track is an improbable masterwork of gutsy New Wave, and the ghostly choral vocal arrangement blowing through "Hold Back the Dream" marks a complete breakaway from Carroll's punky precedent. As good an album song-for-song as *Catholic Boy* is for overall atmosphere.

what to buy next: While only one of the songs demoed for *Catholic Boy* made it to that album, *Dry Dreams* Atco, 1982, prod. Earl McGrath) found Carroll doing his exploring in public, with mixed results. The second half in particular suffers for his standardized, yelpy vocals, drawn-out Jersey Shore-style arrangements and often diluted production.

what to avoid: *A World Without Gravity: The Best of The Jim Carroll Band* Rhino, 1993, prod. Larry Lieberman and David McLees) misses many of the highs and keeps many of the lows, including two inconsequential unreleased studio tracks. You're better off hunting down the original albums.

the rest: *Praying Mantis* (Giant, 1991) *The Basketball Diaries: Original Motion Picture Soundtrack* (Island, 1995)

Pearl Jam, Soundgarden, Alice in Chains

Sex Pistols, Leonard Cohen, Jim Morrison, Graham Parker, Bruce Springsteen, Lou Reed

Adam McGovern

The Cars

Formed 1976 in Boston, Mass. Disbanded 1988.

Ric Ocasek (born Richard Otcasek), vocals, guitar; Ben Orr (born Benjamin Orzechowski); bass, vocals; Elliot Easton (born Elliot Steinberg) guitar; Greg Hawkes, keyboards; David Robinson, drums

Combining smart, artful and accessible pop songs with a clickety New Wave sound, the Cars quickly became one of America's top bands during the late 70s and early 80s. With its debut album, the band single-handedly crafted some of the genre's best sounding and best-selling songs. Peppered with lite keyboards, drum machines and airy background vocals, the Cars' sound had an almost aloof, detached feel that made the songs instantly recognizable. After a short venture into an even more synthesized sound with 1980's *Panorama*, the Cars quickly bounced back to their pop sensibilities and became more popular than ever with its 1984 release *Heartbeat City*. By 1988, however, the band was ready to call it quits; machines had all but replaced Robinson and Easton, and personal conflicts and made the recording of its final album, *Door To Door*, a difficult process. Of the individual members, Ocasek has had the greatest success, producing albums for Weezer, Bad Brains and other modern rock groups.

what to buy: *The Cars* (Elektra, 1978, prod. Roy Thomas Baker) remains the group's finest album. Kicking off with "Let the Good Times Roll," "My Best Friend's Girl" and "Just What I Needed," the album sounds more like a greatest hits collection than a debut. Before long, its teflon production became state-of-the-art for sonic wannabes. *The Cars Anthology: Just What I Needed* (Elektra Traditions/Rhino, 1995, prod. Various) is a splendid collection of all the right tracks and even non-album gems such as "Breakaway."

what to buy next: *Heartbeat City* (Elektra 1984, prod. Robert John "Mutt" Lange and the Cars) rivals *The Cars* for freshness and churned out four hits, each with its own trend-setting video.

what to avoid: *Panorama* (Elektra, 1980, prod. Roy Thomas Baker) isn't different enough to sound experimental, though that seems to be the intent. Mostly it sounds like a collection of half-finished ideas.

the rest: *Candy O* (Elektra, 1979) *Shake It Up* (Elektra, 1981) *Greatest Hits* (Elektra, 1985) *Door to Door* (Elektra, 1987)

solo outings:

Ric Ocasek: *Beatitude* (Geffen, 1983) *This Side of Paradise* (Geffen, 1986) *Fireball Zone* (Geffen, 1991) *Quick Change World* (Reprise, 1993)

Ben Orr: *The Lace* (Elektra, 1986)

Greg Hawkes: *Niagra Falls* (Passport, 1983)

Elliot Easton: *Change No Change* (Elektra, 1985)

Weezer, Matthew Sweet, Lloyd Cole, Bad Religion, Afghan Whigs

Blondie, Talking Heads, Modern Lovers, Kraftwerk, the Velvet Underground

Mike Joiner

Clarence Carter

Born Jan. 14, 1936, in Montgomery, Ala.

Carter sure did a lot of cheatin' and homewreckin', according to his songs. That's bad for the monogamous, good for us, as his leacherous ways produced a bona fide classic, "Slip Away." A backdoor proposition with Carter woefully copping to the tawdriness of it all as he slides his foot in the door, the song is a close second to "Dark End of the Street" as the greatest stolen-love soul song ever. The rest of his body of work follows the tracks that "Slip Away" laid down, with no less lascivious results. He still releases albums sporadically, and his trademark "heh-heh-heh" growl can still make the dudes pull their girlfriends a little closer.

what to buy: *Snatching it Back: The Best of Clarence Carter* (Rhino, 1992, comp. Rick Hall) is a solid 21-track compilation that contains "Slip Away" and "Patches" as well as other important tracks, such as his absurdly profound reworking of "Dark End of the Street."

what to buy next: *Dr. C.C.* (Ichiban, 1987, prod. Clarence Carter) is highlighted by the gloriously lewd "Strokin'."

what to avoid: *The Dr.'s Greatest Prescriptions* (Ichiban, 1990) isn't a bad compilation, but the Rhino package renders it obsolete.

the rest: *Have You Met Clarence Carter* (Ichiban, 1992) *Between a Rock and a Hard Place* (Ichiban, 1990) *Touch of Blues* (Ichiban, 1988) *Hooked on Love* (Ichiban, 1988) *Messin' With My Mind* (Ichiban, 1988) *Legendary* (MCA Special Products, 1995)

worth searching for: *Sixty Minutes with Clarence Carter,* (Fame, 1973, prod. Rick Hall) Carter's out-of-print final session with the Muscle Shoals gang, which brought some new and more modern sonic elements into his mix.

Rick James, Aerosmith, Keith Sweat, R. Kelly

Lightnin' Hopkins, Otis Redding, Solomon Burke

Allan Orski

Peter Case /The Plimsouls

Peter Case (born April 5, 1954, in Buffalo, N.Y.), vocals, guitar; Eddie Munoz, guitar, vocals; Dave Pahoa, bass; Lou Ramirez, drums (1978-84); Clem Burke, drums (1995-present)

Starting out as the bassist for San Francisco punk-pop band the Nerves during the mid-70s and later fronting influential Los Angeles underground group the Plimsouls, Case gradually evolved into an acoustic troubadour, though he never really abandoned his rockin' roots (indeed, a reunited Plimsouls surfaced in 1995, seeking a new record deal). The Plimsouls were one of the great early-80s little trains that couldn't: Its two major-label albums floundered amidst the arena-rock climate of the era. During the mid-80s, Case married Victoria Williams (they divorced at the end of the decade), became a born-again Christian and went out on his own musically, establishing himself as one of the most powerful solo acoustic acts on the club circuit. He released three albums for Geffen, never quite making a commercial impact; in the mid-90s, he signed with folk-oriented independent label Vanguard.

what to buy: *Blue Guitar* (Geffen, 1989, prod. J. Steven Soles, Larry Hirsch and Peter Case) is a folk-rock classic, an impassioned 10-song portrait of down-and-out losers and star-crossed lovers seeking redemption. *Peter Case* (Geffen, 1986, prod. T Bone Burnett and Mitchell Froom) is slightly less focused but loaded with first-rate songwriting. The Plimsouls *Everywhere at Once* (Geffen, 1983, prod. Jeff Eyrich) includes the group's two best-known songs, "A Million Miles Away" and "Oldest Story in the World" (both of which were also featured in the movie "Valley Girl").

what to buy next: *Torn Again* (Vanguard, 1995, prod. Larry Hirsch and J. Steven Soles) was a fine return to form for Case, featuring some of the best songs he'd written in years. *Sings Like Hell* (Vanguard, 1994, prod. Marvin Etzioni) was recorded live in a living-room studio and features mostly traditional tunes performed solo acoustic; it's hit-and-miss, but worth seeking out for the inclusion of the longtime concert favorite "Lakes of Ponchartrain."

what to avoid: *Six-Pack of Love* (Geffen, 1992, prod. Mitchell Froom and Peter Case) seems in retrospect like an attempt to save the major-label deal with a more commercially viable effort, but the beefed-up arrangements didn't cotton to a set of songs that was sub par by Case's standards.

the rest: The Plimsouls: *Zero Hour* (Beat EP, 1980) *The Plimsouls* (Planet, 1981) *The Plimsouls ... Plus* (Rhino, 1992)

The Replacements, Alejandro Escovedo

Woody Guthrie, Blind Lemon Jefferson

Peter Blackstock

Johnny Cash

Born Feb. 26, 1932, in Kingsland, Ark.

A larger-than-life figure who looms over the history of rock 'n' roll and country music as well, Cash scarcely needs an introduction to anyone whose ears have been open during the past 40 years. Yet for someone who is as recognizable as Mount Rushmore, Cash has always been surprisingly mercurial; He was the most country-leaning of the Sun rockabilly crowd, yet his pill-popping, hell-raising lifestyle would likely make any of today's alternarockers blanch. Once he crossed over to country, he threw over Nashville early, moving instead to California, where he remained, for better and worse, his own man. Amid the politically conservative world of country music, Cash has always been a firebrand, championing minority rights—especially for Native Americans—and condemning the Vietnam War. And he traded songs with the rock world, notably with Bob Dylan and, in later years, with Bruce Springsteen and U2. Yet for all that, he is a passionately evangelical Christian whose best friends are the Rev. Billy Graham on the one hand and fellow hellraiser Waylon Jennings on the other. Not for nothing did

Kris Kristofferson celebrate him as "a walking contradiction." A member of the Rock and Roll Hall of Fame, the Country Music Hall of Fame and Nashville's Songwriter's Hall of Fame—the only one who has been so honored—Cash casts as long a shadow as anyone over almost the whole of American popular music.

what to buy: Cash's Sun material has been worked to death on a variety of reissues, but rock fans should be satisfied with *The Sun Years,* (Rhino, 1990, prod. Jack Clement) which shows off Cash's trademark boom-chicka-boom rhythm on classics such as "Folsom Prison Blues," "Hey Porter," "Get Rhythm" and "I Walk the Line." The fruits of Cash' labors at his second home are amply covered on *Columbia Records, 1958-1986,* (Columbia, 1987, prod. Various) a three-disc set that belongs in every serious rock and country collection. For the budget-minded, a better place to start is *The Essential Johnny Cash, 1955-1983* (Columbia/Legacy, 1992, prod. Various) a single-disc collection that will suffice but will likely whet your appetite for the larger set. Cash's roots are in folk music as much as in country, and *American Recordings* (American, 1994, prod. Rick Rubin) —comprised of raw solo performances—returns him to the form he had not explored extensively since the early part of his Columbia era.

what to buy next: *At Folsom Prison and San Quentin* (Columbia, 1975, prod. Bob Johnston) compiles two of Cash's legendary concert albums onto one CD, constitutings some of the bravest recordings ever made. Before the very definition of a captive audience. *Classic Cash* (Mercury, 1988, prod. Johnny Cash) is one of those rare occasions when an album featuring re-recordings not merely averts disaster, but actually offers a few new insights into well-worn favorites such as "Get Rhythm" and "Sunday Morning Coming Down." Another exception to the rule, *Water From the Wells of Home* (Mercury, 1988, prod. Jack Clement) transcends the usual empty hype that attends most duet albums—this one with performances by Emmylou Harris, Tom T. Hall, Hank Williams Jr., the Everly Brothers and Paul McCartney, among others.

what to avoid: Some of Cash's work is downright bizarre and finds him stretching, yes, but in ways that simply don't work. Steer clear of: *Mean as Hell!,* (Columbia, 1966, prod. Don Law and Frank Jones) **WOOF!** *Everybody Loves a Nut,* (Columbia, 1966, prod. Don Law and Frank Jones) **WOOF!** *The Holy Land,* (Columbia, 1968, prod. Bob Johnston) *Any Old Wind That Blows,* (Columbia, 1973, prod. not listed) *Sunday Morning Coming Down,* (Columbia, 1973, prod. Bob Johnston) *Ragged Old Flag,* (Columbia, 1974, prod. not listed) and *The Junky and the Juicehead Minus Me* (Columbia, 1974, prod. not listed).

the rest: *Hymns by Johnny Cash* (Columbia, 1959) *Ride This Train* (Columbia, 1960) *Hymns From the Heart* (Columbia, 1962) *Blood, Sweat, and Tears* (Columbia, 1963) *Ring of Fire: The Best of Johnny Cash* (Columbia, 1963) *I Walk the Line* (Columbia, 1964) *Bitter Tears: Ballads of the American Indian* (Columbia, 1964) *Johnny Cash Sings the Ballads of the True West* (Columbia, 1965); *Greatest Hits, Vol. 1* (Columbia, 1967) *Hello, I'm Johnny Cash* (Columbia, 1970) *The World of Johnny Cash* (Columbia, 1970) *Man in Black* (Columbia, 1971) *His Greatest Hits, Vol. 2* (Columbia, 1971) *Johnny Cash Sings Precious Memories* (Columbia, 1972) *Johnny Cash and His Woman* (with June Carter Cash) (Columbia, 1973) *Five Feet High and Rising* (Columbia, 1974) *John R. Cash* (Columbia, 1975) *Look at Them Beans* (Columbia, 1976) *Strawberry Cake* (Columbia, 1976) *One Piece at a Time* (Columbia, 1976) *The Last Gunfighter Ballad* (Columbia, 1976) *The Rambler* (Columbia, 1977) *Gone Girl* (Columbia, 1978) *Greatest Hits, Vol. 3* (Columbia, 1978) *I Would Like to See You Again* (Columbia, 1978) *Silver* (Columbia, 1979) *Rockabilly Blues* (Columbia, 1980) *The Baron* (Columbia, 1981) *The Survivors* (with Jerry Lee Lewis and Carl Perkins) (Columbia, 1982) *The Adventures of Johnny Cash* (Columbia, 1982) *Biggest Hits* (Columbia, 1982) *Rainbow,* (Columbia, 1985) *Highwayman* (with Waylon Jennings, Kris Kristofferson and Willie Nelson) (Columbia, 1985) *Believe in Him* (Word, 1986) *Heroes* (with Waylon Jennings) (Columbia, 1986) *Johnny Cash is Coming to Town* (Mercury, 1987) *Patriot* (Columbia, 1990) *Boom Chicka Boom* (Mercury, 1990) *Highwayman 2* (with Waylon Jennings, Kris Kristofferson and Willie Nelson) (Columbia, 1990) *The Mystery of Life* (Mercury, 1991) *The Gospel Collection* (Columbia/Legacy, 1992) *Wanted Man* (Mercury, 1994) *The Road Goes On Forever* (with Waylon Jennings, Kris Kristofferson and Willie Nelson) (Liberty, 1995)

worth searching for: Many of Cash's Columbia albums are out of print, but nearly all of them, save those mentioned above, are worth a listen if you can find them in the used-album bins. Of special interest to rock fans may be *Orange Blossom Special* (Columbia, 1965) on which Cash covers three Dylan tunes, and *Johnny 99* (Columbia, 1983, prod. Brian Ahearn) on which he tries two by Bruce Springsteen.

⏩ Bob Dylan, Waylon Jennings, Kris Kristofferson, Marty Stuart, Hank Williams Jr., Bruce Springsteen, Rosanne Cash, Carlene Carter, Nick Lowe

⏪ The Louvin Brothers, the Carter Family, Jimmie Rodgers

Daniel Durchholz

Rosanne Cash

Born May 24, 1956 in Memphis, Tenn.

Cash survived her Nashville Royalty pedigree (her dad is Johnny Cash) to carve out an identity in the 80s as an innovative and remarkably successful country artist. On a string of records starting in 1979, Cash and producer/husband Rodney Crowell progressively expanded the boundaries of what a female performer could accomplish in Nashville. Her emphatic fusion of hard-hitting rock and classic country, maverick for that time, still scored big on the hidebound Nashville radio charts. But Cash's critically acclaimed balancing act crashed in 1990. With her marriage to Crowell dissolving and her affinity for the country establishment plummeting, Cash released the somber, commercially disastrous *Interiors* and packed it in for life in a Greenwich Village brownstone. She has concentrated since on raising her three daughters, writing fiction (her first collection, "Bodies of Water," appeared in 1996) and recording spare, ironic songs with a lyric confessionalism that's about as far from conventional Nashville tunesmithing as you can get. It's also awfully good.

what to buy: *King's Record Shop* (Columbia, 1988, prod. Rodney Crowell) 🦴🦴🦴🦴🦴 is unquestionably the summation of Cash's Nashville work. It arcs smoothly from wistful pop ("If You Change Your Mind") to playful nostalgia ("Tennessee Flat Top Box") to edgy social balladry ("Rosie Strike Back," a call to arms for battered wives). Cash authoritatively demonstrates that she could take everything Nashville threw at her and throw it right back. Her first major effort, 1979's *Right or Wrong* (Columbia, 1979, prod. Rodney Crowell) 🦴🦴🦴🦴 still sounds surprisingly fresh, with the title tune's ironic exploration of adultery and the first of Cash's sassy take-that-guys anthems, "Man Smart, Woman Smarter." Cash's current incarnation is best represented by *Ten Song Demo* (Capitol, 1996, prod. John Leventhal and Roseanne Cash) 🦴🦴🦴🦴, a stripped-down collection redolent of her frank, biting wit. After listening to "Take This Body," just try looking at a cosmetic-surgery ad without wincing.

what to buy next: *Seven Year Ache* (Columbia, 1981, prod. Rodney Crowell) 🦴🦴🦴🦴 features some of the trenchant songwriting (the title track and "Blue Moon With Heartache") that would blossom more fully for Cash once she began leaving the country-heartbreak constraints behind. She also has gender-bending fun with "My Baby Thinks He's a Train" and "What Kinda Girl?"

what to avoid: *Interiors*. (Columbia, 1990, prod. Rosanne Cash) 🦴 As the analysts say, Cash had some issues to work through, and by God, she did—with a frankness that teeters into the maudlin. Significant in that it marks Cash's definitive break with Nashville power pop, but not a pretty sight. Or sound.

the rest: *Somewhere in the Stars* (Columbia, 1982) 🦴🦴🦴 *Rhythm and Romance* (Columbia, 1985) 🦴🦴🦴 *The Wheel* (Columbia, 1993) 🦴🦴🦴🦴

worth searching for: *Live at the Bottom Line* (RSM) is a clean-sounding bootleg of a hot 1988 performance in New York.

⏩ Mary Chapin Carpenter, Shawn Colvin

⏪ Roy Orbison, the Everly Brothers, Emmylou Harris, Joni Mitchell. Oh yeah, and The Man in Black—what was his name again?

Elizabeth Lynch

Cast

See: The La's

Catherine Wheel

Formed 1990 in Yarmouth, England

Rob Dickinson, vocals, guitar; Brian Futter, guitar; Dave Hawes, bass; Neil Sims drums

Hailing from a small seaside town in England, Catherine Wheel were able to develop a unique sound by being so removed from London. Attempts to classify their three astonishingly strong albums have met roadblocks at every turn, thanks to the mix of styles and approaches. *Ferment* (Mercury, 1992, prod. Tim Friese-Greene) 🦴🦴🦴🦴½ certainly hinted at the then-current U.K. "shoegaze" or "dreampop" sound, but there was more of a House of Love guitar feel (and other more shimmering, subconscious, pastoral influences) than the hazy, blurred My Bloody Valentine style. Furthermore, the vocals and words of singer Rob Dickinson—ironically, a first cousin of ex-Iron Maiden leader Bruce Dickinson—are both out front and discernible. Thus, two memorable singles, "I Want to Touch You" and the hypnotic, repetitive epic "Black Metallic" helped establish the quartet in America in a time where British acts were mostly unwelcome.

Its follow-up, *Chrome* (Mercury, 1993, prod. Gil Norton) ♪♪♪♪ toughens up the sound and even adds minor metal touches the elder Dickinson might favor, without diluting the group's overall immediacy or strengths. Such mighty, steely bombs as "I Confess" and "Broken Head" are offset by the straight-ahead drive of "Strange Fruit" and "Chrome," while the more ponderous side two dabbles in bits of Pink Floyd and later (more ambient) Talk Talk, babbling mood setters they carry off as convincingly. Finally, *Happy Days*, (Mercury, 1995, prod. Gil Norton and Rob Dickinson) ♪♪♪♪ proves no letup. Not so much a departure from *Chrome* as an even harder version, several tracks—"Little Muscle," "Kill My Soul," "Receive," and the scary single "Way Down"—push the envelope on the group's odd ability to make harsh hard rock and post-punk seem so compatible in one blasting number after another. Yet it still show a more tender side on the melancholic "Heal" and a sparkling anti-heroin single "Judy Staring at the Sun" that pairs Dickinson in a duet with Belly's Tanya Donelly.

the rest: *Like Cats & Dogs* (Mercury, 1996) not available for rating.

Jack Rabid

Felix Cavaliere

See: The Young Rascals

Nick Cave and the Bad Seeds

Formed 1984 in London, England

Nick Cave (born Nicholas Edward Cave), vocals, piano, organ; Mick Harvey, drums, keyboard, guitar; Blixa Bargeld, guitar, vocals; Barry Adamson, guitar, piano (1984-86); Hugo Race, guitar (1984-86); Tracy Pew, bass (1984-86); Thomas Wydler, drums (1986-present); Kid Congo Powers, guitar (1986-1990); Martyn P. Casey, bass (1992-present); Conway Savage, piano (1992-present)

Cave and Harvey met in their Melbourne, Australia, high school and formed their first band, The Boys Next Door, during the late 70s. In 1980, that band dissolved into the Birthday Party and moved to London, where it released three albums over the next three years and influenced the burgeoning British New Wave scene. In 1983, the group moved to West Berlin, where the musicians' notorious indulgences in alcohol and drugs lead them to break up. Cave, Harvey and Adamson persevered, added Bargeld of Einstuerzende Neubauten and Hugo Race to form The Bad Seeds. The group has released nine albums of Cave's morose and poetic lyrics—many of them ruminating on love and death—and took a turn on the Lollapalooza main stage in 1994. The lineup has changed considerably since 1984, but Cave—who's also dabbled in writing, acting and filmmaking—Harvey and Bargeld remain the unflappable core.

what to buy: *Kicking Against the Pricks* (Homestead, 1986, prod. Nick Cave and the Bad Seeds) ♪♪♪♪♪ is an all-covers album featuring Cave's dark, theatrical renditions of songs ranging from blues standards ("Muddy Water") to gospel to rock classics ("Hey Joe"). Vocally and musically, Cave and the Bad Seeds have never sounded better. *Your Funeral ... My Trial* (Mute/Homestead, 1986, prod. Nick Cave and the Bad Seeds) ♪♪♪♪ is an eight-song double EP of original material that is the clearest and most straightforward of Cave's albums and showcases his greatest talent: chilling storytelling.

what to buy next: The Bad Seeds' debut, *From Here to Eternity*, (Mute, 1984, prod. Nick Cave and the Bad Seeds) ♪♪♪♪ establishes a strong foundation of themes (i.e. love, murder, religion and a fascination with Americana, including Elvis Presley) that every subsequent album would build upon. Cave's desperate vocals are highlighted as the Bad Seeds merely provide background music. *Tender Prey* (Mute/Enigma, 1988, prod. Not listed) ♪♪♪♪ is another excellent album featuring a richer sound due to unusually bottom-heavy production. The opening track, "Mercy Seat" may be Cave's best song ever. *Let Love In* (Mute/Elektra, 1994, prod. Tony Cohen and the Bad Seeds) ♪♪♪ is something of a rebound album after three unremarkable predecessors.

what to avoid: *Live Seeds*, (Mute/Elektra, 1993, prod. Nick Cave and the Bad Seeds) ♪♪ an unremarkable concert souvenir.

the rest: *The Firstborn Is Dead* (Mute/Homestead, 1985) ♪♪♪ *The Good Son* (Mute/Elektra, 1990) ♪♪♪ *Henry's Dream* (Mute/Elektra, 1992) ♪♪♪ *Murder Ballads* (Mute/Elektra, 1996) ♪♪♪

worth searching for: *Tupelo* (Homestead EP, 1985) ♪♪♪ features the opening number from *The Firstborn is Dead* and adds some non-album tracks, including a remake of the Birthday Party favorite "The Six Strings That Drew Blood."

solo outings:

***Nick Cave, Mick Harvey and Blixa Bargeld:** Ghosts...of the Civil Dead* (Mute, 1989) ♪♪♪

Barry Adamson: Mass Side Story (Mute/Restless, 1989) 𝄞𝄞𝄞 "Delusion" soundtrack (Mute, 1991) 𝄞𝄞 *Oedipus Schmoedipus* (Mute, 1996) 𝄞𝄞𝄞

▶▶ Tori Amos

◀◀ The Clash, the Doors, Leonard Cohen, Nick Drake

see also: *The Birthday Party, Einstuerzende Neubauten*

Christopher Scanlon

Exene Cervenka

See: X

Peter Cetera

See: Chicago

Chad & Jeremy

Formed 1963 in London, England

Chad Stuart, vocals, guitar, piano; Jeremy Clyde, vocals, guitar

Chad & Jeremy were second only to fellow London folk-rockers Peter & Gordon in the quest to be the most popular Everly Brothers knock-offs of the original British Invasion. Although probably more talented and certainly more qualified to reinterpret the Odetta songbook Merseybeat-style than P&G, the duo had an undeniable disadvantage in the quest for *new* material (Peter's sister was dating Paul McCartney at the time). So immediately following their first appearance on the American charts with "Yesterday's Gone" in 1964, Stuart and Clyde relocated to the U.S. where they quickly became fixtures on the small screen ("Hullabaloo," "Shindig," even "The Dick Van Dyke Show"). Their biggest hit, "A Summer Song", came soon afterwards, before Jeremy returned to England to take a role in a London musical. That left Chad to form a duet with his wife until his partner returned in '67. What followed were their two heavy-handed but well-meaning stabs at the post-*Sgt. Pepper's* sweepstakes, *Of Cabbages And Kings* (1967) and *The Ark* (1968), after which Jeremy again returned to the world of musical-comedy. Chad briefly served as musical director on the Smothers Brothers' first TV series and, like Jeremy, began dabbling in the theater. The two still reunite occasionally on stage and on record, and they can still sing the Everlys better than Peter & Gordon ever could.

what to buy: 20-track *Best Of Chad & Jeremy* (One Way, 1994, prod. Various) 𝄞𝄞𝄞𝄞 features not only their greatest hits but also the delightful "My How The Time Goes By" that, as The Redcoats, they used to serenade Rob and Laura Petrie.

what to buy next: Fans of the dreaded Concept Album must have *Of Cabbages And Kings,* (Columbia, 1967, prod. Chad Stuart and Jeremy Clyde) 𝄞𝄞𝄞𝄞 if only for the 17-minute-plus "Progress Suite," which mixes nuclear explosions with the first-ever appearance on record by The Firesign Theatre. Bones are also awarded for the ultra-cheesy, sub-*Satanic Majesties Request* cover shot, which brings all new meanings to the question "Why do you think they call it dope?"

what to avoid: *Chad Stuart And Jeremy Clyde* (Rocshire, 1983, prod. by Chad Stuart) 𝄞𝄞 is yet another misguided reunion album which proves, as so many such projects do, that you cannot re-heat a soufle.

worth searching for: *Before And After* (Columbia, 1965) 𝄞𝄞𝄞 and *Distant Shores* (Columbia, 1966) 𝄞𝄞𝄞 are both well-intentioned and well-sung, if a tad on the pedestrian side—like Simon & Garfunkel Lite.

▶▶ Boyce & Hart, Wham!, The Proclaimers

◀◀ Peter, Paul & Mary, The Everly Brothers, Flanders & Swann

Gary Pig Gold

Chairmen of the Board

Formed 1969 in Detroit, Mich. Disbanded 1976.

"General" Norman Johnson, vocals; Danny Woods, vocals; Harrison Kennedy, vocals (1969-72); Eddie Curtis, vocals (1969-72)

Time didn't favor the Chairmen of the Board. One of the last great Motown vocal groups of the 60s, the quartet found its smooth brand of dance-floor soul falling out of favor almost as soon as it scored its first hit, 1969's "Give Me Just a Little More Time." Originally named the Gentlemen, the Chairmen became the biggest group on the Invictus label, a company formed by the legendary Holland/Dozier/Holland songwriting team after they left Motown Records. Johnson, the Chairmen's founder, handled most of the lead vocal duties, and his impassioned hiccup of a voice became the group's most distinctive sound. As more-popular Motown acts such as Marvin Gaye and Stevie Wonder progressed into urban and ecological themes, the Chairmen's traditional vocal sound became passe. Johnson and Woods hung on as a duo, fueled by their popularity in England, where they made a lasting impression on white soul fans such as Dexy's Midnight Runners' Kevin Rowland and the Jam's Paul Weller. It was Weller who gave Johnson a career boast in 1986 when he scored a U.K. hit with a remix of his song "Loverboy." The group's greatest hits package *Soul Agenda* (HDH, 1992, prod. Various) ♪♪♪♪ is the requisite retrospective, but the songs (including "Give Me Just a Little More Time," "Everything's Tuesday" and the group's biggest hit, "Pay to the Piper," sung by Woods) are soul-coaxing reminders that the Chairmen of the Board could have been leaders of the pack.

Christopher Scapelliti

The Chambers Brothers

Formed early 1960s in Mississippi

George Chambers, bass; Willie Chambers, guitar; Lester Chambers, harmonica; Joe Chambers,guitar; Brian Keenan, drums

With their roots in gospel, The Chambers Brothers would seem unlikely funk-psychedelic crossover pioneers, providing a reference point for other crossover groups beginning to hit their stride at the same time, includinge Parliament/Funkadelic and Sly and the Family Stone. The acoustic gospel band made its first amplified appearance at the 1965 Newport Folk Festival to great acclaim. White drummer Brian Keenan had joined and the band hit the rock club circuit, where a typical set would include any number of lengthy jams that would have made another young southern brother act, the Allman's, proud. In 1968, The Brothers had a hit single with "The Time Has Come Today," an edited version of the powerful 12-minute pyschedelic epic on their Columbia debut, the first of six releases to chart. The band pulled from equal parts Otis Redding, Wilson Pickett, and Haight Ashbury, always with a nod back to their beginning at the Mount Calvary Baptist Church near Carthage in Lee County, Mississippi. A terrific sampling of the band is available on *The Chambers Brothers' Greatest Hits,* (Columbia, 1971, prod. David Rubinson, The Chambers Brothers, and Tim O'Brien) ♪♪♪♪ with the complete version of "Time Has Come Today" plus the blistering "I Can't Turn You Loose" and the more traditional gospel crooning of "People Get Ready."

the rest: *People Get Ready* (Vault, 1965) ♪♪♪ *Chambers Brothers Now* (Vault, 1966) ♪♪♪ *Time Has Come* (Columbia, 1967) ♪♪♪♪ *Shout!* (Vault, 1968) ♪♪♪ *Love, Peace and Happiness* ♪♪♪ (Columbia, 1969)

Feelin' the Blues ♪♪♪ (Vault, 1970) *Chambers Brothers Live at Fillmore East* ♪♪♪♪ (Columbia, 1970) *Unbonded* (Avco, 1974) ♪♪♪ *Right Move* (Avco, 1975) ♪♪♪

▶▶ George Clinton, Sly and the Family Stone, Run DMC, War

◀◀ Wilson Pickett, Otis Redding, James Brown, The Animals

Martin Connors

The Chameleons

Formed 1980 in Manchester, England. Disbanded 1986.

Mark Burgess, vocals, bass; Dave Fielding, guitars, keyboards; Reg Smithies, guitar; John Lever, drums

This is one of those bands with the distinction of having more records released after it broke up than before. The group has three official studio albums, but almost a dozen after-the-fact releases are available. During the band's heyday in the mid- to late-80s, the British music press frequently called the Chameleons "sonic architects," which is an apt description. The four-piece band created sounds and atmospheres that were unparalleled, while Burgess' lyrics and vocals were remarkably expressive. As a whole, the band easily ranks as one of the best—if also one of the most under-appreciated—of the decade. The downfall tragically centers around Burgess' excessive drinking; his binges, along with wild mood swings and abusive behavior toward his bandmates, finally created a rift so great that a lifetime friendship with guitarist Smithies ended along with the band shortly after the release of 1986's *Strange Times.* While drawing on the bleak industrial landscapes that surrounded them, the Chameleons did not become weighed down by the environment, but attempted to overcome it; despite the dark sound, Burgess kept his lyrics generally bright and hopeful.

what to buy: *Script Of The Bridge* (Statik/MCA, 1983, prod. the Chameleons and Colin Richardson) ♪♪♪♪♪ is a brilliant album. From classic songs like "Second Skin" to the inspired "As High As You Can Go" this takes the brooding sounds of Joy Division and the Smiths to the next level.

what to buy next: *Strange Times,* (Geffen, 1986, prod. David Allen) ♪♪♪♪♪ the band's first proper release in the U.S., was a college radio sensation with the epic "Swamp Thing," an inspired cover of David Bowie's "John, I'm Only Dancing" and an alternate version of the beautiful "Tears." The band's debut, *What Does Anything Mean? Basically* (Statik/MCA, 1981, prod. the Chameleons and Colin Richardson) ♪♪♪♪ isn't quite as phenomenal as the other two but is still a strong set.

what to avoid: Generally approach posthumously released live albums and radio show released with caution. They tend to be imports only and vary in quality. Smithies' label Imaginary is usually the most reputable source for these recordings.

the rest: *The Peel Sessions* (Strange Fruit, 1990) ♪♪♪ *Here Today...Gone Tomorrow (Live)* (Imaginary, 1992) ♪♪♪♪ *Live In Toronto* (Imaginary, 1992) ♪♪♪♪ *Dali's Picture/Live In Berlin* (Imaginary, 1993) ♪♪♪

worth searching for: *The Fan And The Bellows*, (Hybrid/Caroline, 1986) ♪♪♪♪ billed as "a collection of classic early recordings," it gathers out-of-print early singles and demos (later versions appear on *What Does Anything Mean? Basically*) into one volume. With a more raw, less produced sound, these songs paint a picture closer to what the band is like live.

solo outings:

The Reegs (Reg Smithies): *Return Of The Seamonkeys* (Imaginary, 1988) ♪♪♪

▶▶ Bush, the Smiths, the Afghan Whigs, James, Green Day

◀◀ Joy Division, Peter Gabriel/Genesis, King Crimson

Tim Davis

James Chance /James White

Born James Siegfried, April 20, 1953 in Milwaukee, Wisc.

Bullshit artist or inspired genre mutator? Supreme ironist or self-deluding "White Negro?" Probably all four, this pompadoured, multiply-monickered saxophonist/keyboardist/vocalist comes off as utterly self-indulgent and personal, yet possibly the most intense vocalist on the New York punk scene, epitomized by the tortured screams on his frequently recorded anthem "Contort Yourself." He started out sitting in on the jazz loft scene and was in an early version of Lydia Lunch's Teenage Jesus & the Jerks, and her use of slide guitar was a major influence of the sound he pursued with his band, the Contortions. Harshly dissonant, jerky organ chords (whether by White or, at first, Adele Bertai), White's squealing alto sax, clanging guitar riffs and slippery, atonal slide guitar combined in frenzied abandon held together by rock-solid bass and drums. White's obvious self-loathing and obsession with James Brown's "King Heroin" (which appears on all four of his live albums) suggest reasons for the constant turnover of his groups (one guitarist who passed through his band dubbed him a "major league asshole"). His stylistic range on sax and organ were severely limited, and after awhile he slipped into an overly ironic parody of himself—though he *was* great at what he did. In 1995, he resumed regular performance in New York. (His first three albums—*Buy the Contortions, Off White* and *Sax Maniac*—have been reissued, with bonus tracks, by the Henry Rollins-Rick Rubin label Infinite Zero.)

what to buy: The Contortions' *Buy the Contortions* (Ze, 1979, prod. James White) ♪♪♪♪♪ is the single greatest studio product of No Wave, a groundbreaking shotgun wedding of New York post-punk with sped-up funk and disco rhythms topped off with abrasive, unsettling N.Y.C. sullenness. White never again matched the overwhelming intensity and jagged nastiness of his debut, though he would come close on some live albums. James Chance & the Contortions' *Soul Exorcism* (ROIR, 1991, prod. James White) ♪♪♪♪ has fairly good sound (the best of the domestically available live albums) and a must-hear cover of Michael Jackson's "Don't Stop Till You Get Enough."

what to buy next: Instead of the hard rhythms of *Buy*, James White & the Blacks' *Off White* (Ze, 1979, prod. James White) ♪♪♪ mostly uses a simple, campy disco beat, accenting the increasingly sleazy White persona heard on "Stained Sheets" and other tracks. Pat Place's slippery slide guitar riffs are conceptually more subversive given this musical context. James White & the Blacks' *Sax Maniac* (Animal/Chrysalis, 1982, prod. James White) is a compromise between *Buy* and *Off White*, and was White's only flirtation with a major label.

what to avoid: *Live in New York* (ROIR, 1981, prod. James Chance and John Hanti) ♪♪ has the worst sound of any of the live albums and can safely be bought last. But on two tracks it does document a particularly interesting 1980 band with guitarist Bern Nix (Ornette Coleman's Prime Time) and trombonist/vocalist Joseph Bowie (Defunkt), as well as an otherwise unavailable song, "Sophisticated Cancer."

the rest: James Chance & the Contortions: *Lost Chance* (ROIR, 1995) ♪♪♪

worth searching for: The Contortions' four tracks on *No New York* (Antilles, 1978, prod. Brian Eno) ♪♪♪♪ show the early group at its confrontational, raggedy best.

▶▶ Defunkt, Raybeats, Bush Tetras, Living Colour, Tar Babies, Minutemen

◀◀ James Brown, Albert Ayler, Teenage Jesus & the Jerks

Steve Holtje

Chaos Face

See: Bill Laswell

Harry Chapin

Born December 7, 1942 in New York City. Died July 16, 1981.

During the pre-Live Aid era when it wasn't cool to care, Chapin invested much of his time and energy into raising awareness of world hunger. More than half of his annual concerts were benefits for the cause, and in 1978, prodded by Chapin's relentless badgering on Capitol Hill, President Jimmy Carter appointed him to the Presidential Commission on World Hunger. His humanitarian passions mixed with his irreverent sense of humor to transform his underrated live shows into intimate, captivating experiences that were rarely duplicated on his uneven studio albums. Chapin scored Top 40 hits with "Taxi," "Cat's in the Cradle" and "W.O.L.D.," despite a penchant for lengthy narratives that unfolded more like musical short stories than songs. Such tenacious but taxing melodramas as "Sniper," "What Made America Famous" and "The Mayor of Candor Lied" became his trademarks, but they also branded him a heavy-handed overachiever. Indeed, Chapin was at his most affecting when he scaled back his dramatic ambitions and simply tapped into the everyday doubts and dreams that fuel such heartfelt ballads as "Any Old Kind of Day," "If My Mary Were Here," "I Wonder What Happened to Him," "Last Stand" and his stirring ode to 60s idealism, "Remember When the Music."

what to buy: Musically diverse and politically aware, *Dance Band on the Titanic* (Elektra, 1977, prod. Stephen Chapin) is the closest Chapin ever got to making a solid studio album. The rollicking title track raises a convincing ruckus; "One Light in a Dark Valley" and the achingly vulnerable "I Wonder What Happened to Him" rank among his most touching performances. And the 14-minute "There Only Was One Choice"—an autobiographical art-rock collage—eerily foreshadows the car crash that killed him. *Legends of the Lost and Found* (Elektra, 1979, prod. Stephen Chapin) is an enjoyable live album that mixes new material—including the hilarious "Get On With It" and the rousing "Old Folkie," dedicated to Pete Seeger—with both stripped-back ("Mail Order Annie," "Tangled Up Puppet") and fleshed-out ("Corey's Coming," "Flowers Are Red") renditions of favorites that eclipse their studio versions.

what to buy next: *Greatest Stories Live* (Elektra, 1976, prod. Stephen Chapin and Fred Kewley) infuses such favorites as "Taxi," "Cat's in the Cradle," "30,000 Pounds of Bananas" and "Better Place to Be" with Chapin's manic stage energy. The CD reissue mercifully removes two of the strained studio cuts that filled out the original double-LP set, although it retains the unlistenable "Shortest Story."

what to avoid: Commemorating his posthumous awarding of the Congressional Gold Medal, the two-CD *Gold Medal Collection* (Elektra, 1988, prod. Various) slaps together singles, album tracks, live performances and interview/speech snippets with no regard for context or content. Chapin's legacy deserves better preservation.

the rest: *Heads and Tales* (Elektra, 1972) *Sniper and Other Love Songs* (Elektra, 1972) *Short Stories* (Elektra, 1973) *Verities and Balderdash* (Elektra, 1974) *Portrait Gallery* (Elektra, 1975) *On the Road to Kingdom Come* (Elektra, 1976) *Living Room Suite* (Elektra, 1978) *Sequel* (Boardwalk, 1980) *Anthology of Harry Chapin* (Elektra, 1985) *Remember When the Music* (DCC, 1987; reissue of "Sequel" with two bonus tracks) *The Last Protest Singer* (DCC, 1988)

worth searching for: Pat Benatar, the Hooters, Judy Collins, Richie Havens and others perform Chapin's tunes on *Harry Chapin Tribute* (Relativity, 1990, prod. Stephen Chapin), recorded live at Carnegie Hall. But the most inspired match is Bruce Springsteen's touching rendition of "Remember When the Music," complete with a monologue about Chapin's commitment to keeping "a good clear eye on the dirty ways of the world" that stands as his finest epitaph.

Mary Chapin Carpenter, James McMurtry, John Mellencamp, Sheryl Crow

Phil Ochs, Pete Seeger

David Okamoto

Tracy Chapman

Born 1964 in Cleveland, Ohio

On the heels of Suzanne Vega's breakthrough with "Luka," Boston coffeehouse singer Tracy Chapman snared the attention of Elektra Records in 1988 and scored an unlikely Top 10 hit with "Fast Car," a gently rendered treatise on soured dreams driven by a captivating depth rarely heard on radio. The momentum of that shortlived pre-Alanis Morissette women's movement, coupled with Chapman's skilis at examining such emotionally charged topics as domestic violence and racial injustice without preaching, made her an instant star: the alternative band Thelonious Monster covered her "For My Lover,"

Neil Diamond recorded "Baby Can I Hold You" and she joined a high-profile Amnesty International tour with Sting, Peter Gabriel and Bruce Springsteen. Despite her lyrical strengths and good intentions, Chapman still hasn't made another album as riveting as her self-titled 1988 debut. But then, few artists have.

what to buy: *Tracy Chapman* (Elektra, 1988, prod. David Kershenbaum) ♪♪♪♪ is an impressive calling card, detailing the frustrations of inner-city life while championing inner strength. There's a quiet, compelling sense of dignity bubbling under the fear and futility of "Fast Car," "Behind the Wall" and "Across the Lines."

what to buy next: *New Beginnings* (Elektra, 1996, prod. Don Gehman) ♪♪♪ finds Chapman on the artistic rebound thanks to Gehman's mostly acoustic production and the singer's ability to rally attention for her causes without railing.

what to avoid: *Matters of the Heart*, (Elektra, 1992, prod. Chapman and Jimmy Iovine) ♪♪ settles for easy targets like yuppie materialism and grumpy sketches instead of her usually thoughtful portraits.

the rest: *Crossroads* (Elektra, 1989) ♪♪♪

worth searching for: On *Rubaiyat*, a double-CD commemorating Elektra Records' legacy, Chapman performs an upbeat, "Fever"-like cover of "House of the Rising Sun" with help from E-Street Band pianist Roy Bittan.

▶▶ Jewel, Ani DiFranco, Poe, Patty Griffin, Dionne Farris

◀◀ Joan Armatrading, Joan Baez, Joni Mitchell

David Okamoto

Craig Chaquico

See: Jefferson Starship

The Charlatans UK

Formed 1988 in Manchester, England

Tim Burgess, vocals; Martin Blunt, bass; Mark Collins, guitar; Jon Baker, guitar (1988-91); Rob Collins, keyboards; Jon Brookes, drums

The Charlatans UK, much like their American namesake, get their kicks from psychedelic jams. They provided the Farfisa-fueled grooves that served as the soundtrack to England's momentary Summer of Love revival at the outset of the 90s. Along with the Happy Mondays and the Stone Roses, the group heralded Britain's much-celebrated Manchester scene, driven by all-night Ecstasy parties, swirl-happy British dance currents and a wah-wah fervor. The Charlatans' early albums became the definitive sound of the British indie scene. But as the times changed, so did the Charlatans. The bang of Manchester's heyday soon became a distant memory. The bleary-eyed quintet of foppish hairdos and beestung lips moved on to the imminent Altamont revival. On its fourth album—quaintly self-titled—the group spent most of its time excavating the rough sonic bits from the Stone's "Exile on Main Street," with a dash of the Faces and a sprinkle of the Who thrown in for good measure—making it a considerably darker episode than the adolescent rock thrills of earlier singles like "The Only One I Know" and "Weirdo." The last album consisted of languid, acoustic-tinged melodies and a moody, power-chord thrust that drove numbers like "Crashin' In" and "No Fiction" to imposing proportions. It was the sound of lads turning into men.

what to buy: The Charlatans' debut, *Some Friendly* (Beggar's Banquet/RCA, 1990, prod. The Charlatans) ♪♪♪♪♪ was packed with youthful energy and unforgettable melodies. It also merged house rhythms, psychedelic keyboards and jangly guitars, creating the perfect soundtrack for England's Summer Of Love revival in 1990. Songs like "The Only One I Know" and "Then" are considered modern British pop classics. The group moved further into dance music territory with *Between 10th and 11th* (Beggar's Banquet/RCA, 1992, prod. Flood), ♪♪♪♪ which remains the group's most polished record to date, as well as its most infectious. Songs like "Weirdo" and "Tremolo Song" showcased a jazzier edge to the Charlatans sound.

what to buy next: The Charlatans' fourth album, *The Charlatans* (Beggar's Banquet/Atlantic, 1995, prod. The Charlatans, Dave Charles and Steve Hillage), ♪♪♪ was considered a return to form for the group after a few minor disasters. Its straight-ahead rock sound on songs like "Crashin' In" and "Here Comes a Soul Saver" courted comparisons to rock greats such as the Who and the Small Faces. However, it lacked the vibrant dance grooves of previous outings.

what to avoid: The Charlatans momentarily lost direction on *Up To Our Hips* (Beggar's Banquet/Atlantic, 1994, prod. Steve Hillage) ♪. Recorded mostly while keyboardist Collins was serving time in prison for an armed-robbery offense, it features the group's most lethargic grooves and half-hearted attempts at songwriting. "Patrol" blatantly borrows its chorus from De La Soul's "Eye Patch," released only a year earlier.

worth searching for: *Isolation 21.2.91* (Live Live Good, 1992) was recorded live at the Chicago Metro during the Charlatans' first tour of the States and features energetic re-interpretations of songs from the debut album as well as rare tracks like "Indian Rope" and "10th and 11th."

The Bluetones, Northern Uproar, Milltown Brothers.

Deep Purple, Stevie Wonder, the Who, Rolling Stones.

Aidin Vaziri

Ray Charles

Born Ray Charles Robinson, Sept. 23, 1930, in Albany, Ga.

Not for nothing was Charles known as "the Genius." In his extraordinary recording career, he's done more than almost any other artist to obliterate the lines that once existed between genres such as R&B, gospel, country, pop, jazz and rock. Beginning as an imitator of the smooth styles of Nat "King" Cole and Charles Brown, Charles eventually forged his own style, combining gospel music and harmonies with decidedly earthier lyrics reflecting love, lust, heartbreak and hard times. Charles rightly commented in his autobiography that his work had little to do with rock 'n' roll; it contained too much despair to compete on the charts with the up tempo ravings of Little Richard, Jerry Lee Lewis, and Elvis Presley. Yet Charles' work was intensely rhythmic and had a profound impact on rock, if only as an influence. A bigger leap still was when Charles recorded two albums of soulful country & western music. A man of Herculean determination, few opponents have faced him down. Not all of his decisions have been right ones, but he stands behind them all. And why not? His voice is one of the most recognizable in all of music, thanks to such timeless hits as "I Got a Woman," "What'd I Say," "The Night Time Is the Right Time," "Hit the Road Jack," "Georgia On My Mind," "Unchain My Heart," "You Don't Know Me," "Busted" and countless others, to say nothing of his famous Diet Pepsi commercials. There is no one else like him.

what to buy: Because Charles' classic material is divided into two principal periods—the years he spent recording for Atlantic, and those spent on ABC—no comprehensive greatest hits package exists since *A 25th Anniversary in Show Business* went out of print. So the likely place to start is with the purchase of both *Anthology* (Rhino, 1988, prod. Various) and *The Best of Ray Charles: The Atlantic Years.* (Rhino, 1994, prod. Jerry Wexler, Zenas Sears, Neshui Ertegun and Ahmet Ertegun) The 20-track *Anthology* contains some of the ABC material, including "Georgia On My Mind," "Let's Go Get Stoned," "Eleanor Rigby," "Hit the Road Jack" and "Unchain My Heart." *The Atlantic Years* which also contains 20 tracks, features "I Got a Woman," "What'd I Say," "The Night Time Is the Right Time" and "Drown in My Own Tears." For those wanting to delve a little deeper in to the Atlantic material, you can't go wrong with *The Birth of Soul: The Complete Atlantic Rhythm & Blues Recordings, 1952-1959,* (Rhino, 1991, prod. Various) a three-CD chronicle tracking Charles' development from his years as a Cole imitator to his breakout as a talent of almost unparalleled intuition and ability.

what to buy next: Charles expanded his R&B material with influences from various genres, but when he took on country & western, as it was then called, he proved that no barrier in music cannot be breached. *Modern Sounds in Country and Western Music* (ABC, 1962, prod. Sid Feller and Joe Adams) and *Modern Sounds in Country and Western Music, Vol. 2* (ABC, 1963, prod. Sid Feller and Joe Adams)—since compiled on single CD (Rhino, 1988)—are staggering achievements for their innovation and sheer audacity. An explosive live performers, two of Charles best in-concert albums are *Ray Charles at Newport* (Atlantic, 1958, prod. Neshui Ertegun) and *Ray Charles in Person* (Atlantic, 1960, prod. Zenas Sears) (now available as the 2CD set *Live* (Atlantic, 1987, prod. Neshui Ertegun and Zenas Sears)). The experiments Charles was carrying out in the studio are extended to the stage, and his feverish versions of "The Right Time," "What'd I Say" and "Drown in My Own Tears," among others, shout, plead, testify, and rock.

Five Essential 50s Collections

Billboard Top Hits 1955-59
(individual volumes) (Rhino)

Space Age Pop, Vol. 1-3
(RCA)

Chess Rhythm 'n' Roll
(Chess)

The Sun Story
(Rhino)

The Doo Wop Box
(Rhino)

what to avoid: Some of Charles' albums are ill-conceived or poorly executed, but none are truly wretched. Beware of numerous, cheap repackagings of his hits; if it's not on Atlantic, ABC, Rhino or DCC, proceed with caution.

the rest: *Hallelujah, I Love Her So* (Atlantic, 1957) *The Great Ray Charles* (Atlantic, 1957) *Ray Charles* (Atlantic, 1957) *Yes Indeed!!* (Atlantic, 1958) *What'd I Say* (Atlantic, 1959) *The Genius of Ray Charles* (Atlantic, 1960) *The Genius Hits the Road* (ABC, 1960) *The Genius Sings the Blues* (Atlantic, 1961) *The Genius After Hours* (Atlantic, 1961) *Dedicated to You* (ABC, 1961) *Genius + Soul = Jazz* (Impulse, 1961) *The Ray Charles Story, Vol. 1* (Atlantic, 1962) *The Ray Charles Story, Vol. 2* (Atlantic, 1962) *Greatest Hits* (ABC, 1962) *Ingredients in a Recipe for Soul* (ABC, 1963) *The Ray Charles Story, Vol. 3* (Atlantic, 1963) *The Ray Charles Story, Vol. 4* (Atlantic, 1964) *Sweet and Sour Tears* (ABC, 1964) *Have a Smile With Me* (ABC, 1964) *Live in Concert* (ABC, 1965) *Country & Western Meets Rhythm and Blues* (aka *Together Again*) (ABC, 1965) *Crying Time* (ABC, 1966) *Ray's Moods* (ABC, 1966) *Ray Charles Invites You to Listen* (ABC, 1967) *A Portrait of Ray* (ABC, 1968) *I'm All Yours, Baby* (ABC, 1969) *Doing His Thing* (ABC, 1969) *My Kind of Jazz* (Tangerine, 1970) *Love Country Style* (ABC, 1970) *Volcanic Action of My Soul* (ABC, 1971) *A 25th Anniversary in Show Business Salute to Ray Charles* (ABC, 1971) *Through the Eyes of Love* (ABC, 1972) *Jazz Number II* (Tangerine, 1972) *Come Live With Me* (Crossover, 1974) *Renaissance* (Crossover, 1975) *My Kind of Jazz, Part 3* (Crossover, 1975) *Porgy and Bess* (with Cleo Laine) (RCA, 1976) *True to Life* (Atlantic, 1977) *Love and Peace* (Atlantic, 1978) *Ain't It So* (Atlantic, 1979) *Brother Ray Is At It Again!* (Atlantic, 1980) *A Life in Music, 1956-59* (Atlantic, 1982) *Wish You Were Here Tonight* (Columbia, 1983) *Do I Ever Cross Your Mind?* (Columbia, 1984) *Friendship* (Columbia, 1984) *The Spirit of Christmas* (Columbia, 1985) *From the Pages of My Mind* (Columbia, 1986) *His Greatest Hits, Vol. 1 (1960-71)* (DCC, 1987) *His Greatest Hits, Vol. 2 (1960-72)* (DCC, 1987) *Just Between Us* (Columbia, 1988) *Greatest Country & Western Hits (1962-1965)* (DCC, 1988) *Soul Brothers/Soul Meeting* (Rhino, 1989) *Seven Spanish Angels and Other Hits* (Columbia, 1989) *Would You Believe?* (Warner Bros., 1990) *My World* (Warner Bros., 1993) *Classics* (Rhino, 1995) *Strong Love Affair* (Qwest, 1996)

worth searching for: Even though he owns the masters himself, nearly all of Charles' ABC work is out of print, which is disappointing since it features some of his finest small combo work, and many of his greatest hits. *A Message From the People,* (ABC, 1972) is a protest album of sorts (including "Abraham, Martin and John," "There'll Be No Peace Without All Men As One" and brilliant readings of "Look What They Done to My Song, Ma" and "America the Beautiful") from a man whose politics before this album—and since—have seldom been on display.

Van Morrison, Joe Cocker, Billy Joel

Nat "King" Cole, Charles Brown, Count Basie, the Grand Ole Opry, Louis Jordan, Claude Jeter

Daniel Durchholz

Charm Farm

Formed 1991 in Grosse Pointe Woods, Mich.

Dennis White, vocals, guitar, keyboards, drums; Steve Zuccaro, guitars; Dean "Dino" Zoyes, bass; Eric Meyer (born Eric Hogemeyer), drums; Tom Onyx (born Tom Munnell), keyboards (1991-93); Ken Roberts, keyboards, (1994-present); Taj Bell, backing vocals (1994-present)

Formed by ex-Inner City music directors White and Onyx, Charm Farm won over hometown fans in Detroit through its blend of techno-pop and guitar-driven modern rock. The mixture, found on its major-label debut *Pervert,* (Mercury, 1996 prod. Dennis White) produces hypnotic ear candy. The sensual slow groove of the title track, the guitar-heavy "Sick" and the disco-pop song "Superstar"—which pokes fun at the New York's Studio 54 scene of the 70s of Andy Warhol's club scene—are the highlights.

Christina Fuoco

Cheap Trick

Formed 1974 in Rockford, Ill.

Rick Nielsen, guitar and vocals; Robin Zander, vocals and guitar; Tom Petersson, bass, vocals (1974-80, 1986-present); Pete Comita, bass (1980-81); Jon Brant, bass (1981-86); Bun E. Carlos, drums

The new wave movement gets credit for puncturing the stuffy, humorless corporate-rock mentality that ruled the airwaves during the late-70s, but Cheap Trick fired the first salvo. While many bands had lead singers you couldn't tell apart from the roadies, Cheap Trick—pretty boys Zander and Petersson flanked by the nerdy Nielsen, who looked like a demonic paper boy, and Carlos, who could pass for a chain-smoking CPA—offered a goofy respite that made its merger of Beatlesque pop and heavy metal thunder even more endearing. Japanese audiences caught on first, prompting the group to put out *Live at Budokan* overseas in 1978. Epic released the album stateside a year later, and its platinum success has made it the band's signature work. Since then, Cheap Trick has floundered from producer to producer (Todd Rundgren, George Martin, Roy Thomas Baker, Ted Templeman) in search of the magical combination that will recapture the success of their early albums. Save for the occasional killer tune ("She's Tight," "If You Want My Love," "Let Go"), they still haven't found what they're looking for.

what to buy: Aerosmith producer Jack Douglas brought a crunchy credibility to *Cheap Trick,* (Epic, 1977) which introduced the group as a metal act. But *In Color* (Epic, 1977, prod. Tom Werman) brings out the band's pop instincts via "Southern Girls," "So Good to See You" and "I Want You to Want Me." That album just beats out *Heaven Tonight,* (Epic, 1978, prod. Werman) whose overbearing rockers ("Stiff Competition," "Auf Wiedersehen") are overshadowed by such power-pop anthems as "Surrender" and a blistering cover of the Move's "California Man."

what to buy next: A one-two punch of *Live at Budokan* (Epic, 1978, prod. Cheap Trick) —a live album with audience screams that make the Beatles' "Live at the Hollywood Bowl" sound like a Marcel Marceau performance—and *Budokan II* (Epic, 1993, prod. Cheap Trick) were released 15 years apart but recorded mostly during the same tour. Designed to be played back-to-back (*Budokan II* begins with Track 11), the two documents capture Cheap Trick in its roaring prime.

what to avoid: Despite the dream pairing with Beatles producer George Martin, *All Shook Up* (Epic, 1980) falls flat as the band chokes under the pressure of meeting its spiritual mentor.

the rest: *Dream Police* (Epic, 1979) *One on One* (Epic, 1982) *Found All the Parts* (Epic EP, 1980) *Next Position Please* (Epic, 1983) *Standing on the Edge* (Epic, 1985) The Doctor4 (Epic, 1986) *Lap of Luxury* (Epic, 1988) *Busted* (Epic, 1990) *The Greatest Hits* (Epic, 1991) *Woke Up With a Monster* (Warner Bros., 1994) *Sex, America, Cheap Trick* (four-CD box set) (Epic Legacy, 1996)

solo outings:

Robin Zander: *Robin Zander* (Interscope, 1993)

worth searching for: *Working Class Hero: A Tribute to John Lennon* (Hollywood, 1995) boasts the Cheap Trick's ferocious cover of "Cold Turkey."

Enuff Z'Nuff, Material Issue, Johnny Bravo

The Move, the Beatles, the Who

David Okamoto

Chubby Checker

Born Oct. 3, 1941 in Andrews, S.C.

Checker is a fair to middling singer who happened to get extremely lucky when his version of Hank Ballard's "The Twist" hit the No. 1 (in both 1960 and in 1962) and spawned an unparrelled dance craze whose presence can still be felt in films such as "Pulp Fiction" and at any wedding or Bar Mitzvah reception. Unfortunately, Checker had little to say after "The Twist." Not that it mattered, as it's been a consistent meal ticket, and he even turned it into a hit *again* in 1988, this time as a duet with rappers the Fat Boys. *Chubby Checker's Dance Party* (K-tel, date N/A, prod. Various) is the most extensive compilation, with the innocent insistence of "The Twist" and its follow-up "Let's Twist Again."

the rest: *All Time Greats* (Special Music, date N/A) *Mr. Twister* (Charly, 1992)

Allan Orski

Cher

See: Sonny and Cher

Neneh Cherry

Born Neneh Mariann Karlsson, March 10, 1964 in Stockholm, Sweden

"You never seen a girl like this before/Because she's so sassy and completely secure" rapper Guru comments in the lead track of Neneh Cherry's sophomore album—perhaps as accurate and concise a summation of the singer/rapper's appeal as is possible. The daughter of Swedish artist Moki Cherry and West African percussionist Amadu Jah, Cherry is also the stepdaughter of avant-garde jazz trumpeter Don Cherry, and all of their work seems to have made an impact on her innovative, rhythmic and jazz-inflected hip-hop/pop. Cherry performed with the ska band the Nails and with the punk act the Slits before recording several albums as a percussionist with the irreverent jazz-fusion outfit Rip, Rig + Panic, which in turn evolved into Float Up CP (both of the latter two bands' albums are out of print. Going solo, Cherry threw down *Raw Like Sushi,* (Virgin, 1989, exec. prod. Cameron "Booga Bear" McVey) which leads off with the irrepressible and street-smart "Buffalo Stance," a hit single that blazed several hip-hop trials by incorporating jazz riffs, a sung chorus and a strong, self-assured female perspective. The rest of the album doesn't quite rise to that standard, but it has many fine moments. *Homebrew* (Virgin, 1992, prod. Cameron "Booga Bear" McVey, Johnny Dollar and Neneh Cherry) doesn't contain as obvious a single, though "Trout"—with its thundering John Bonham drum sample, a riff from Steppenwolf's "The Pusher" and a duet with R.E.M.'s Michael Stipe—comes close. The album is as uneven as *Sushi,* but it's a harder and ultimately more mature album. Unfortunately, since *Homebrew,* Cherry has been strangely silent.

Daniel Durchholz

Vic Chesnutt

Born Nov. 12, 1964 in Jacksonville, Fla.

With his raw, acoustic music and heart-tugging songs, Athens, Ga.-based Chesnutt has become a cult figure. Half court jester and half tragic hero, the wheelchair-bound Chesnutt (he was paralyzed in a 1983 drunk driving accident) is a brilliant and eccentric singer/songwriter who combines beautiful melodies and lyrics that lay truths uncomfortably bare. His eloquent songs tell stories about fellow eccentrics and document his drunken screw-ups and hopes for transcendence. In 1996, Chesnutt's songs were covered by various admirers, including Madonna and the Smashing Pumpkins on the benefit album *Sweet Relief II: Gravity of The Situation, The Songs of Vic Chesnutt* (Columbia, 1996, prod. Various)

what to buy: The stripped-down yet rich sound of *West of Rome* (Texas Hotel, 1992, prod. Michael Stipe) is Chesnutt at his best—sad, funny and poignant.

what to buy next: In 1988, Chesnutt was content getting drunk and playing his profound little songs at Athens' 40 Watt Club. R.E.M.'s Michael Stipe dragged him into a studio, and a day later they emerged with Chesnutt's stark, raw debut *Little* (Texas Hotel, 1990, prod. Michael Stipe) *Drunk* (Texas Hotel, 1994, prod. Vic Chesnutt) was the result of a few drunken weekend recording sessions. Like many drunken experiences, it's a mix of highlights (the haunting "Supernatural") and the embarrassing (the repetitive title track).

what to avoid: Chesnutt's collaboration with the group Widespread Panic on *Nine High a Pallet* (Capricorn, 1995, prod. Scott Stuckey) ends up sounding like Vic lite.

the rest: *Is The Actor Happy?* (Texas Hotel, 1995)

worth searching for: Chesnutt does a poker-faced version of "The Night The Lights Went Out in Georgia" on the campy K-Tel style compilation *Super Fantastic Mega Smash Hits!* (Pravda/Backyard Records, 1995, prod. Various).

Victoria Williams, Joe Henry, Gillian Welch

Bob Dylan, Leonard Cohen

Jill Hamilton

Chic

Founded 1977 in New York City, N.Y. Disbanded 1984. Reformed 1992.

Nile Rodgers, guitar; Bernard Edwards, bass; Tony Thompson, drums; Alfa Anderson, vocals; Norma Jean Wright (1977), vocals; Luci Martin, vocals (1978-79); Luther Vandross, cameo vocals (1978-79)

From their first mega-hit single "Dance, Dance, Dance" in 1977 until the end of the disco Chic dominated the airwaves and the dance floors. Chic created some of the best bass-lines and grooves in the history of the industry; not just a 70s throwaway/one-hit-wonder, Chic has been sampled by everyone from Queen to the Sugarhill Gang. Combined with Rodgers' ear for a good riff, and a healthy injection of Vandross' vocals, Chic can still hold its own to any modern pop band.

what to buy: *Dance, Dance, Dance: The Best Of Chic* (Atlantic, 1991, prod. Nile Rodgers, Bernard Edwards, Kenny Lehman) has all the major hits from one of the best pop groups ever. Take some great guitar work, a good groove, crisp production, with a little funk and you've got a hypnotic rhythm laid under some of the best dance songs around. *Best of Chic, Vol. 2* (Rhino, 1992, prod. Nile Rodgers, Bernard Edwards, Kenny Lehman, Bob Edwards) follows up on the first *Best Of* with a series of deeper album cuts. They weren't all big hits, but these tracks are no less worthy of praise, they remain beat-heavy enough for any dance floor, yet are still musically innovative and sufficiently varied to be enjoyed in any setting.

what to buy next: *Everybody Dance* (Rhino, 1995, prod. Nile Rodgers, Bernard Edwards, Kenny Lehman) is a budget priced compilation of most of the hit songs plus a few seemingly random tracks to fill out the album; a good starting point to hear some of Chic's best hits without spending a lot of money. *C'est Chic* (Atlantic, 1978, prod. Nile Rodgers, Bernard

Edwards) 𝄞𝄞𝄞 catches Chic at the height of the era. With both Anderson and Wright still on vocal duties, and Luther Vandross' sublime backing help, Chic spawned their best LP and two hugely popular songs: "Dance, Dance, Dance (Yowsah, Yowsah, Yowsah)" and "Le Freak." Taking cues from the retro movement Chic reformed after eight years to record *Chic-Ism*. (Warner, 1992, prod. Nile Rodgers, Bernard Edwards) 𝄞𝄞𝄞 Years of producing acts like David Bowie and Madonna have left Rodgers' with a keen sense of what goes into a good pop song. While there's nothing revolutionary on here all the tracks are well crafted. If this had been released in the 70s it would have been a big hit, but as it is the album provides a pleasant nostalgic feeling. If you want to hear some new disco songs, this is a good place to get them.

what to avoid: *Chic* (Atlantic, 1977, prod. Bernard Edwards, Nile Rodgers, Kenny Lehman, Bob Edwards) 𝄞𝄞 is not exactly bad, but then again beyond "Dance, Dance, Dance" it's not exactly good. With "Dance...." on so many other, better, albums there should be no reason to take a second look at this one.

the rest: *Risque* (Atlantic, 1979, prod. Bernard Edwards, Nile Rodgers) 𝄞𝄞𝄞 and *Real People* (Atlantic, 1980, prod. Bernard Edwards, Nile Rodgers) 𝄞𝄞𝄞

worth searching for: A few albums were released on vinyl but never made the conversion over to CD. These LP are all currently out of print but if you happen to see one in the bargain bin, pick it up. *Chic Chic* (Atlantic, 1981, prod. Bernard Edwards, Nile Rodgers) 𝄞𝄞𝄞 *Take It Off* (Atlantic, 1981, prod. Bernard Edwards, Nile Rodgers) 𝄞𝄞 *Tongue In Chic* (Atlantic, 1982, prod. Bernard Edwards, Nile Rodgers) 𝄞𝄞𝄞 *Believer* (Atlantic, 1984, prod. Bernard Edwards, Nile Rodgers) 𝄞𝄞𝄞

▶▶ Mick Jagger, Madonna, David Bowie, Queen, Sugarhill Gang, Peter Gabriel, Bryan Ferry, Duran Duran, Al Jarreau, Philip Bailey, Sister Sledge, Diana Ross, Robert Palmer, Blondie

◀◀ Parliament/Funkadelic, James Brown, Sylvester

Bryan Lassner

Chicago /Peter Cetera

Formed 1967 in Chicago, Ill.

Terry Kath, guitar, vocals (1967-78, died Jan. 28, 1978); Peter Cetera, bass, vocals (1967-84); Robert Lamm, piano, vocals; Walter Parazaider, reeds; Danny Seraphine, drums (1967-89); James Pankow, trombone; Lee Loughnane, trumpet; Lauder De Oliveira, percussion (1974-80); Donnie Dacus, guitar, vocals (1978-79); Chris Pinnick, guitar (1979-81); Bill Champlin, vocals, guitar, keyboards (1981-present); Jason Scheff, bass, vocals (1984-present; DaWayne Bailey, guitar (1988-present); Tris Imboden, drums (1990-present); Keith Howland, guitar (1995-present)

Rock bands with horn sections were not commonplace when Chicago came along, though Blood, Sweat & Tears and the Electric Flag had already begun using them. Christened first the Big Thing and then Chicago Transit Authority, Chicago played a more down-the-middle brand of brass-fueled rock than its predecessors, using the horns for additional rhythmic pump as well as for solos and melodic accents. Its lyrics were counterculture friendly, but the tunes were as palatable to an adult audience as it was to the kids, giving Chicago a wide commercial berth and a string of hit singles throughout the 70s—as well as remarkably good album sales considering its first three albums (all with numbered titles) were double-record sets and the fourth was a four-record live set. But Kath died after accidentally shooting himself in the head in 1978, and the group was never quite the same. Chicago's commercial success has come in fits and starts, but much of its music during the past decade and a half has been adult-contemporary pabulum, a far cry from the bolder sonic adventures of its earlier releases.

what to buy: *Chicago IX: Chicago's Greatest Hits* (Columbia, 1975/Chicago Records, 1995, prod. James William Guercio) 𝄞𝄞𝄞𝄞 is the essential singles collection, a testament to the commercial force Chicago was during the late 60s and early 70s. *Chicago II* (Columbia, 1970/Chicago Records, 1995, prod. James William Guercio) 𝄞𝄞𝄞𝄞 provides the best exhibition of the group's early ambitions, via Kath's epic guitar solo in "25 or 6 to 4" and the pop suite "Ballet For a Girl in Buchannon."

what to buy next: *Chicago V* (Columbia, 1972/Chicago Records, 1995, prod. James William Guercio) 𝄞𝄞𝄞 is a more modest affair but still has plenty of melodic clout with "Saturday in the Park" and the charmingly dated "Dialogue, Parts I and II." The boxed set *Group Portrait* (Columbia/Legacy, 1991, prod. Various) 𝄞𝄞𝄞 is comprehensive but gets a little weak on the later discs.

what to avoid: Lots, really, but *Night & Day (Big Band)* (Giant, 1995, prod. Bruce Fairbairn) WOOF! is a wretched and ill-conceived collection of swing era covers, with little of the grace or subtlety that marked the original recordings.

the rest: *Chicago Transit Authority* (Columbia, 1969/Chicago

Records, 1995) *Chicago III* (Columbia, 1971/Chicago Records, 1995) *Chicago at Carnegie Hall* (Columbia, 1971/Chicago Records, 1995) *Chicago VI* (Columbia, 1973/Chicago Records, 1995) *Chicago VII* (Columbia, 1974) *Chicago VIII* (Columbia, 1975) *Chicago X* (Columbia, 1976/Chicago Records, 1995) *Chicago XI* (Columbia, 1977/Chicago Records, 1995) *Hot Streets* (Columbia, 1978/Chicago Records, 1995) *Chicago 13* (Columbia, 1979/Chicago Records, 1995) WOOF! *Chicago XIV* (Columbia, 1980/Chicago Records, 1995) *Greatest Hits, Vol. II* (Columbia, 1981/Chicago Records, 1995) *Chicago 16* (Full Moon/Warner Bros., 1982) *If You Leave Me Now* (Columbia, 1983) *Chicago 17* (Full Moon/Warner Bros., 1984) *Chicago 18* (Full Moon/Warner Bros., 1986) *Chicago 19* (Full Moon/Warner Bros., 1988) *Greatest Hits 1982-1989* (Full Moon/Warner Bros., 1989) *Twenty 1* (Full Moon/Warner Bros., 1991) WOOF!

worth searching for: The slightly bizarre *Chicago/Blood, Sweat & Tears Live Toronto '69/Live Frankfurt 80* (K-Tel, 1986) is, if nothing else, a brief look at Chicago in its fledgling state.

solo outings:

Peter Cetera: Peter Cetera (Full Moon/Warner Bros., 1981) *Solitude/Solitaire* (Warner Bros., 1986) *One More Story* (Warner Bros., 1988) *World Falling Down* (Warner Bros., 1992) (River North, 1995)

▶▶ Grass Roots, American Breed, Uptown Horns, UB40

◀◀ Maynard Ferguson, Herb Alpert & the Tijuana Brass, Blood, Sweat & Tears, Electric Flag

Gary Graff

Toni Childs

Born 1958, in California

Singer-songwriter Childs grew up in small towns all over the U.S.; her parents, missionaries for the Assemblies of God, moved the family on a regular basis, preaching their beliefs to as many as possible—and not letting much popular culture into the household. It's no wonder she became a bit rebellious. After spending three months in prison on a drug charge, Childs first moved to London, then to Los Angeles where she met David Ricketts of David + David. *Union* (A&M, 1988, prod. David Tickle and David Ricketts) chronicles their broken love affair, with songs that examine the different aspects of love and relationships. Impressive enough, but Childs' seamless fusion of blues, folk, pop and world music on this one record is an amazing achievement. After a slight let-down on the follow-up, *House of Hope,* (A&M, 1991, prod. David Ricketts, Toni Childs and Gavin MacKillop) Childs offered *The Woman's Boat,* (DGC, 1994, prod. David Bottrill and Toni Childs) a concept album that takes the listener through a spiritual journey of life, from a woman's point of view, all done in Childs' unique style of rock and world music. The album features guest appearances by Peter Gabriel, Karl Wallinger (World Party), Robert Fripp and Nusrat Fatah Ali Khan.

Joshua Zarov

The Chills

Formed 1981 in Dunedin, New Zealand. Disbanded 1992.

Martin Phillips, guitar, vocals; Justin Harwood, bass; Andrew Todd, keyboards; Caroline Easther, drums (1987-90); Jimmy Stephenson, drums (1990-92)

Like its Dunedin compatriots—the Verlaines and the Clean—the Chills made pretty, hook-laden pop awash with chiming guitars and interwoven harmonies. In character with its frigid name, the group embraced topics of death and broken hearts, setting them in rain and frost on New Zealand's remote Otago Peninsula and dressing them up with cool, pastel production. But while the themes tended toward hurt and loss, Phillips kept his lyrics a good 12 steps away from cloying sentiment and pathos, writing straightforward lyrics devoid of pretension. Although *Submarine Bells* (the Chills' first American released) garnered praise from critics and play on college radio, it failed to solidify an American audience. The group's next effort, *Soft Bomb,* bombed softly, and in 1993 Phillips iced the Chills.

what to buy: *Kaleidoscope World* (Homestead, 1986, prod. Various) is a worthy and valued collection of singles the group cut for Flying Nun, New Zealand's influential independent record label; it also includes songs from the group's *Lost* EP (Homestead, 1988) including "Pink Frost," a chilling song about death and one of the band's best pieces of music. On *Submarine Bells,* (Slash/Warner Bros., 1990, prod. Gary Smith) the Chills for once establish a full and cohesive sound over the expanse of an entire album, with individual gems such as "Heavenly Pop Hit," the title track and the punky change-of-pace tracks "The Oncoming Day" and "Familiarity Breeds Contempt."

what to buy next: *Brave Words* (Homestead, 1987, prod. Mayo Thompson) is the group's first real album, 13 insidious little pop songs that work their way slowly through your skin, as if by osmosis.

what to avoid: With its unfortunately prescient title, *Soft Bomb* (Warner Bros., 1992, prod. Gavin MacKillop) found the Chills abandoning its diamond-edged pop for something lighter and quieter. But certainly nothing among these 17 tracks suggests that the Chills should have called it a day.

▶▶ Sundays, the Posies, the Cranberries

◀◀ Split Enz, Cocteau Twins, the Easybeats

Christopher Scapelliti

Alex Chilton /The Box Tops

Born Dec. 28, 1950, in Memphis, Tenn.

With the possible exception of Rod Stewart, no artist has betrayed his talent so completely as Chilton. After the quiet demise of the commercially ignored but creatively astounding Big Star, Chilton set out on a course of perverse artistic self-destruction, with a flagrant disregard for record making. The bittersweet pop gems he previously penned mutated into trashy toss-offs, and on tour he reverted to sets filled with standards and oldies. As legions began to discover the brilliance of Big Star, they were often greeted with insolent indifference and sporadic, off-the-cuff record releases. One needs only to hear seconds of the Box Tops material to catch the full sweep of this demise; a gruff-voiced, teenage Chilton belting out blue-eyed soul took to the charts a number of times in the band's brief career. Bristling under the heavy production of Dan Penn and Chips Moman, Chilton soon departed for more autonomous—but not always furtile—pastures.

what to buy: *The Ultimate Box Tops* (Warner Special Products, 1987, prod. Dan Penn, Tommy Cogbilland Chips Moman) shines with over-the-top emotion from Chilton and such top-notch material as "The Letter," "Cry Like a Baby," and "Soul Deep." *19 Years: A Collection* (Rhino, 1991, prod. Various) presents a tellingly scattershot picture of Chilton's slipshod solo career. Some late-period Big Star material (which was essentially a solo project by then) is included, and occasionally his exuberance pops up like sparks from a burning building.

what to buy next: *High Priest/Black List.* (Razor & Tie, 1994, prod. Alex Chilton) A two-fer reissue of his comeback (of sorts) in 1987 and the 1990 follow-up finds Chilton rocking in good humor all over the map from his Memphis soul beginnings to garage thumpers. Unexpected takes of "Volare" and Charlie Rich's "Lonely Weekends" are pleasant surprises.

what to avoid: *Like Flies on Sherbet,* (Aura, 1979, prod. Jim Dickinson) a drunken spree that tramples potentially good material, best showcases Chilton's disintegration.

the rest: *Bach's Bottom* (Razor & Tie, 1981) *Feudalist Tarts/No Sex* (Razor & Tie, 1994) *Cliches* (Ardent, 1994) *A Man Called Destruction* (Ardent, 1995) *1971* (Ardent, 1996)

worth searching for: *Alex Chilton's Lost Decade,* a sprawling 1985 French fan club release that features obscurities and tracks Chilton produced for other singers.

▶▶ The Replacements, R.E.M., the dB's, the Posies

◀◀ Otis Redding, the Beatles

see also: *Big Star*

Allan Orski

China Crisis

Formed 1979 in Liverpool, England

Garry Daly, vocals, keyboards; Eddie Lundon, guitar, vocals; Gary "Gazza" Johnson, bass, programming; Kevin Wilkinson, drums, percussion

Quiet philosophers with a yen for lightly funky dance-pop, China Crisis found it difficult to compete commercially with its early 80s Brit-pop brethren. As a result, its earlier semi-hits (1983's "Working With Fire and Steel," from the album of the same name) tended towards annoying over-the-top New Romanticism. But with *Flaunt the Imperfection,* (Warner Bros., 1985, prod. Walter Becker) they achieved a subtler, more muted sound, aided immeasurably by the then-former Steely Dan member Becker. With the follow-up, *What Price Paradise,* (A&M, 1986, prod. Clive Langer and Alan Winstanley) the group opted for a more straightforward approach which removed most of what little personality it once had to offer. Those listeners beguiled by *Imperfection* may want to search for the U.K.-only *The China Crisis Collection,* (Virgin, 1990, prod. Various) otherwise, one can rest easy knowing that China Crisis, despite the name, was a small but pleasantly plaintive chapter in the hustle and bustle of 80s British pop.

Bob Remstein

The Chipmunks /Alvin & The Chipmunks

Created 1958 in Hollywood, Calif. by David Seville (born Ross Bagdasarian, 1919 in Fresno, Calif. Died 1972 in Beverly Hills, Calif.)

Oddly enough, this is where many adults got their initiation to contemporary music. The Chipmunks are an anonymous vocal trio whose Munchkin-like voices (the result of recording at half speed and playing back at full speed) graced a slew of hit records from 1958 to the present. The group is the handiwork of Bagdasarian, a composer, author, actor and cousin of playwright William Saroyan who, under the pseudonym David Seville, wrote a number of novelty records during the early 50s, including Rosemary Clooney's 1951 hit "Come On-A My House." By and large a children's sing-along act, the Chipmunks—individually named Alvin, Simon and Theodore—jumped on the Beatlemania bandwagon in 1964 with *The Chipmunks Sing the Beatles Hits* More recently, Bagdasarian's son revived the group for a million-selling series of albums covering punk and country-western classics. The hits just keep on coming.

what to buy: *Sing-Alongs* (Chipmunk Records, 1993, prod. Various) ♫♫♫♫ is a tempting collection of classic children's songs. *Here's Looking at Me* (Sony Wonder, 1994, prod. Various) ♫♫♫ is a 35-year retrospective that includes 80's rock ("Uptown Girl," "Girls Just Wanna Have Fun"), country-western ("On the Road Again"), and the song that started it all, Bagdasarian's 1958 hit "Witch Doctor."

what to buy next: What holiday season would be complete with *A Very Merry Chipmunk*," (Sony Wonder, 1994, prod. Ross Bagdasarian, Janice Karman and Steve Lindsey) ♫♫♫ on which the trio's cute performances even cover the adult-contemporary blather of Celine Dion, Patty Loveless and Kenny G. The versatile rodents' country side is showcased best on *Urban Chipmunk*, (Epic, 1981, prod. Ross Bagdasarian) ♫♫♫ which makes good fun of the early-80s cowboy craze with redneck tunes like "The Gambler" and "On the Road Again."

what to avoid: And break all the kids hearts? Forget it!

the rest: *Christmas with the Chipmunks* (EMI America, 1962) ♫♫ *Christmas with the Chipmunks, Vol. 2* (EMI America, 1963) ♫♫ *A Chipmunk Christmas* (Sony Kids, 1981) ♫♫♫ *Chipmunks in Low Places* (Sony Kids, 1992) ♫♫♫

influences: Geddy Lee (Rush)

influenced by: "The Wizard of Oz" and all of your favorite singers, from every generation.

Christopher "il Rodento" Scapelliti

The Chocolate Watch Band

Formed 1965 in Los Altos, Calif.. Disbanded 1968.

Dave Aguilar, vocals (1965-66); Chris Flinders, vocals (1967); Danny Phay, vocals (1968); Mark Loomis, lead guitar (1965-66, 1968); Tim Abbot, lead guitar (1967); Phil Scoma, lead guitar (1968); Sean Tolby, guitar; Bill Flores, bass; Gary Andrijasevich, drums (1965-66, 1968); Mark Whittaker, drums (1967)

The quintessential 60s psychedelic group, the Chocolate Watch Band was not that genre's best-known band (that would be the Standells), but its legacy has survived longer and stronger than most. Sounding like a punkier version of the Rolling Stones, the Watch Band combined English-style R&B with quasi-mysticism, rendering it in a blaze of fuzz guitar, sitar and hallucinogenic lyrics. While most of the group's releases were cover versions, its excellent ensemble musicianship and distinctively upstart sound earned it a spot in the 1966 cult film "Riot on Sunset Strip" and a contract with Tower Records that same year. The group was already breaking up by the time it released its full-length debut, *No Way Out*, (Sundazed Records, 1967, prod. Ed Cobb) ♫♫♫♫ perhaps the finest major-label example of garage-punk. Opening with the now-classic "Let's Talk About Girls," this trippy little time capsule album dips deeply into the underbelly of the American dream on such tracks as "Dark Side of the Mushroom" and "Are You Gonna Be There (At the Love-In)." Producer/manager Cobb reassembled Flores, Tolby, Andrisevich, Loomis (later replaced by Scoma) and the group's original vocalist, Danny Phay, for *The Inner Mystique*. (Sundazed Records, 1968, prod. Cobb) ♫♫ While not as focused as its predecessor, it still satisfies with a raucous collection of cover tunes (the Kinks' "I'm Not Like Everybody Else," Dylan's "It's All Over Now, Baby Blue," and the Standell's "Medication") and hip-to-the-bone acid-trip noodling, most successfully on the neat little gem, "In the Past." Cobb had one more shot at milking money from the group's name with *One Step Beyond* (Sundazed Records, 1969, prod. Cobb) ♫♫ which, in spite of some bottom-of-the-barrel tunes, is rescued by Aguilar's punchy "Don't Need Your Lovin'," killer bonus tracks ("Sitting There Standing"), and comprehensive liner notes that put a tidy close to the Watch Band trilogy.

Christopher Scapelliti

Lou Christie

Born Lugee Alfredo Giovanni Sacco, Feb. 19, 1943 in Glen Willard, Pa.

In the spirit of the great falsettos Del Shannon and Frankie Valli, 60s heartthrob Christie wailed his way to stardom with a

string of distinctive hit songs. From his early start as Roulette Records' first breakthrough artist in 1962, Christie cut a figure as a tough-but-sensitive crooner, infusing his repertoire of "boy meets girl" tunes with just a blush of sexual urgency via his distinctive falsetto. By the late 60s, he was part of the stable at bubblegum label Buddah Records, where he enjoyed one last hit ("I'm Gonna Make You Mine") before becoming a fixture in traveling revues. His best songs ("The Gypsy Cried," "Two Faces Have I," "Rhapsody in the Rain" and his ambitious million-seller "Lightnin' Strikes") are dutifully collected in *Enlightenment: The Best of Lou Christie* (Rhino, 1991, prod. Various) 🦴🦴🦴

Christopher Scapelliti

The Church

Formed 1980 in Sydney, Australia

Steven Kilbey, bass, vocals, keyboards; Marty Willson-Piper, guitar, vocals; Peter Koppes, guitar, vocals (1980-92); Richard Ploog, percussion, drums, vocals (1981-90); Jay Dee Daugherty, drums (1990-92)

Almost as catchy as the Beatles and almost as lush and dense as the Cocteau Twins, the Church dragged a bunch of guitars from Australia and have churned out more than more than a dozen albums. Founders Koppes and Willson-Piper sometimes focus on sprightly pop and other times make music so gloomy and dark it would embarrass the Sisters of Mercy. The Church has been popular in its homeland since it began recording, but U.S. audiences didn't catch on until 1988, when "Under the Milky Way" courted some radio attention. That was hardly a permanent breakthrough; despite sporadic subsequent radio play, the Church remains a cult-level band at best on these shores.

what to buy: *Starfish,* (Arista, 1988, prod. Waddy Wachtel and Danny Kortchmar) 🦴🦴🦴🦴 the Church's international breakthrough, is a soothing, ethereal album with the cleanly produced, radio-friendly hits"Under the Milky Way" and "Destination."

what to buy next: *Heyday* (Warner Bros., 1986/Arista, 1988, prod. Peter Walsh) 🦴🦴🦴 is one of the group's most straightforward and hard-hitting albums. *Priest=Aura* (Arista, 1992, prod. Gavin MacKillop) 🦴🦴🦴 is appealingly woozy and ambient.

what to avoid: *Remote Luxury* (Warner Bros., 1984/Arista, 1988, prod. Ken Perry) 🦴🦴 compiles two inconsequential Australian EPs.

the rest: *Of Skins and Heart* (Parlophone, 1981/Arista, 1988, prod. Chris Gilbey and Bob Clearmountain) 🦴🦴 *The Blurred Crusade* (Carrere, 1982/Arista, 1988) 🦴 *Seance* (Carrere,1983/Arista, 1988) 🦴🦴 *Gold Afternoon Fix* (Arista, 1990) 🦴🦴🦴 *Sometime Anywhere* (Arista, 1994) 🦴🦴

worth searching for: *Almost Yesterday 1981-1990,* (Raven, 1991, prod. Various) 🦴🦴🦴🦴 an Australian best-of collection, contains all the key tracks through *Gold Afternoon Fix.*

solo outings:

Steve Kilbey: *Unearthed* (Enigma, 1987) 🦴🦴 *Earthed* (Rykodisc, 1988) 🦴🦴 *The Slow Crack* (Rough Trade, 1989) 🦴🦴🦴 *Transaction* (Red Eye-Polydor EP, 1989) 🦴🦴 *Remindlessness* (Red Eye-Polydor, 1990) 🦴🦴🦴

Jack Frost (Kiley and Grant McLennan): *Jack Frost* (Arista, 1991) 🦴🦴🦴 *Snow Job* (Beggars Banquet, 1996) 🦴🦴🦴

Peter Koppes: *Manchild & Myth* (Rykodisc, 1988) 🦴 *From the Well* (TVT, 1989) 🦴🦴

Marty Willson:Piper: *In Reflection* (Chase, 1987) 🦴 *Art Attack* (Rykodisc, 1988) 🦴🦴 *Rhyme* (Rykodisc, 1989) 🦴🦴 *Spirit Level* (Rykodisc, 1992) 🦴🦴

⏩ Stone Roses, Galaxie 500, Luna, Lush, Ride, Slowdive

⏪ The Byrds, the Beatles, David Bowie, Cocteau Twins, the Fall, Leonard Cohen

see also: *Grant McLennan*

Tracey Birkenhauer and Steve Knopper

Ciccone Youth

See: Sonic Youth

Cinderella

Formed 1983 in Philadelphia, Pa.

Tom Keifer, guitar, keyboards, vocals; Eric Brittingham, bass; Jeff LeBar, guitar; Tony Destra, drums (1983-86); Jody Cortez, 1986); Fred Coury, (1986-90)

Cinderella was a big-haired heavy metal band that immediately clicked thanks to Keifer's banshee wail and a searing guitar attack that must have seemed particularly heavy to the pop-metal Bon Jovi/Def Leppard crowd that lapped it up. Ultimately, Cinderella proved its mettle with its third album, *Heartbreak Station,* (Mercury, 1990, prod. John Jansen and Tom Keifer)

𝅘𝅥𝅘𝅥𝅘𝅥𝅘𝅥 an impressively varied set that mixed rootsy touches—plus strings, horns and gospel choruses—with the pro-forma crunch of previous albums. It's exactly what you need from this band's sporadic output, though it's worth hunting for the Japanese import *Live Train to Heartbreak Station*, (Mercury EP, 1991) 𝅘𝅥𝅘𝅥𝅘𝅥 an exuberant, if brief, look at the band in concert.

the rest: *Night Songs* (Mercury, 1986) 𝅘𝅥𝅘𝅥 *Long Cold Winter* (Mercury, 1988) 𝅘𝅥𝅘𝅥𝅘𝅥 *Still Climbing* (Mercury, 1994) 𝅘𝅥𝅘𝅥

Gary Graff

John Cipollina

See: Quicksilver Messenger Service

Circle Jerks

Formed 1980 in Hollywood, Calif.

Keith Morris, vocals; Greg Heston, guitar; Zander Schloss, bass, baritone guitar; Keith Clark, drums, background vocals

Formed by ex-Black Flag headman Morris and former Redd Kross guitarist Heston, the Circle Jerks have become one of the oldest and most respected hardcore bands from the first wave of American punk. The band's brutal style has helped to define the melodic music that became known as California surf punk. The group takes the standard "screw the establishment" punk message and puts on its own special twist, infusing the lyrics with a wise guy persona of bad jokes—often in bad taste. The music is fast, hard-hitting and unpolished, but the band's best offers quick, melodic riffling of guitars, incorporating a variety of stylings while still maintaining a consistent—and heavy—feel.

what to buy: *Golden Shower of Hits* (Rhino, 1983, prod. Gary Hirstius, David Anderle and the Circle Jerks) 𝅘𝅥𝅘𝅥𝅘𝅥𝅘𝅥 contains a huge selection of the Jerks best material—a whirlwind of vulgar thrash rock, with a little social commentary thrown in to balance things out.

what to buy next: *Group Sex/Wild in the Streets* (Frontier, 1986, prod. Cavy Markoff) 𝅘𝅥𝅘𝅥𝅘𝅥𝅘𝅥 combines and remixes the group's first two albums for a 30-track feast—though the *Group Sex* material is clearly weaker. *VI* (Relativity, 1987, prod. Circle Jerks) 𝅘𝅥𝅘𝅥𝅘𝅥𝅘𝅥 takes the band back to its punk roots, raging full-on for the Jerks' finest post-*Golden Shower* release.

what to avoid: *W"nderful* (Relativity, 1985, prod. Circles Jerks) 𝅘𝅥 is anything but. The band sounds timid and unassuming, and the guitarists play unimaginative, standard punk chord progressions.

the rest: *Group Sex* (Frontier, 1980) 𝅘𝅥𝅘𝅥𝅘𝅥 *Wild in the Streets* (Frontier, 1982) 𝅘𝅥𝅘𝅥𝅘𝅥𝅘𝅥 *Oddities, Abnormalities, and Curiosities* (Mercury, 1985) 𝅘𝅥𝅘𝅥𝅘𝅥 *Gig* (Relativity, 1992) 𝅘𝅥𝅘𝅥𝅘𝅥

▶▶ Bad Religion, Dead Kennedys, Husker Du, Agent Orange

◀◀ XTC, Jefferson Airplane, Kinks, Cramps, Rolling Stones, Dictators, Sex Pistols

Bryan Lassner

Eric Clapton

Born March 30, 1945 in Surrey, England

Clapton's reputation as a great guitarist and a towering figure has overtaken reality to such a large extent that it is nearly impossible to consider his music objectively—which may help explain how Clapton has remained so revered over the past 20 years as he has released one middling album after another, with occasional forays into outright wretchedness. Clapton's work with Cream and Blind Faith is truly brilliant and groundbreaking, and his sole studio album with Derek and the Dominos, *Layla and Other Assorted Love Songs*, is a certifiable masterpiece. And his first few solo albums range from very good to pretty good, as he seemed to be settling into a laid-back singer-songwriter groove, something which he did well, even if it displeased old fans waiting to hear fiery, innovative guitar soloing. In retrospect, these early and mid-70s albums, most of which were largely dismissed at the time, sound like high points. Since then, he has made some truly despicable albums. In 1989, Clapton seemed content with the comfortable plateau he had reached, actually titling an album *Journeyman*. His next release, *Unplugged*, catapulted him to international stardom greater than any he had previously known. Clapton *can* still play, and he continues to sparkle sporadically—largely on guest appearances such as Chuck Berry's "Hail, Hail Rock and Roll" and Jimmie Vaughan's *Tribute to Stevie Ray Vaughan*—but he seems to have long since stalled creatively. 1996 saw PolyGram release newly re-mastered versions of much of Clapton's solo work.

what to buy: On Derek and the Dominos' *Layla and Other Assorted Love Songs*, (Polydor, 1970, prod. Tom Dowd) 𝅘𝅥𝅘𝅥𝅘𝅥𝅘𝅥𝅘𝅥 Clapton was spurred to perhaps the greatest playing of his career by the presence of Duane Allman. The results speak for themselves. *461 Ocean Boulevard* (Polydor, 1974, prod. Tom Dowd) 𝅘𝅥𝅘𝅥𝅘𝅥𝅘𝅥 and *Slowhand* (Polydor, 1977, prod. Glyn Johns)

are the best of Clapton's mellow-period albums. *Crossroads* (Polydor, 1988, prod. Various) is close to a model boxed set, though the heavily padded fourth CD illustrates Clapton's decline.

what to buy next: *Eric Clapton* (Polydor, 1970, prod. Delaney Bramlett) is loose and filled with great playing, though it in many ways sounds more like a Delaney Bramlett album than a Clapton recording. *The Rainbow Concert,* (Polydor, 1973/1995, prod. Glyn Johns/Jon Astley and Andy Macpherson) which marked Clapton's reappearance after several years of drug-induced hiatus, sounds much better today than it did in 1973.

what to avoid: *Behind the Sun* (Duck/Warner Bros., 1985) and *August,* (Duck/Warner Bros., 1986) both produced by Phil Collins, are vile albums: soulless, pandering, overdone and inexcusable. *From the Cradle* (Warner Bros., 1994, prod. Eric Clapton and Russ Titelman) was hailed as Clapton's return to his blues roots, and it includes lots of great guitar playing. Unfortunately, his all-English backing band wouldn't know a groove if it fell into one, and Clapton's singing is over-emotive, patronizing blues belting at its worst.

the rest: *There's One in Every Crowd* (Polydor, 1974) *E.C. Was Here* (Polydor, 1975) *No Reason to Cry* (Polydor, 1976) *Backless* (Polydor, 1978) *Just One Night* (Polydor, 1980) *Another Ticket* (Polydor, 1981) *Timepieces (The Best of Eric Clapton)* (Polydor, 1982) *Timepieces Vol. II: Live in the Seventies* (Polydor, 1983) *Money and Cigarettes* (Duck/Warner Bros., 1983) *Journeyman* (Reprise, 1989) *24 Nights* (Reprise, 1991) , *Rush* soundtrack (Reprise, 1992) *Unplugged* (Reprise, 1992) *Crossroads 2 (Live in the Seventies)* (Polydor, 1996)

worth searching for: *The Unsurpassed Eric Clapton: The Delany* (sic) *Mix of His First Solo Album,* (Yellow Dog, 1992) a bootleg title featuring a somewhat looser and more freewheeling version of the *Eric Clapton* album.

▶▶ Stevie Ray Vaughan, the Allman Brothers Band

◀◀ Albert King, Freddie King, Muddy Waters, Jimi Hendrix, the Band, J.J. Cale

see also: *Cream, Blind Faith, the Yardbirds, John Mayall*

Alan Paul

Dave Clark Five

Formed 1961 in Tottenham, England. Disbanded 1970.

Dave Clark, vocals, drums, percussion; Mike Smith, vocals, piano, organ; Lenny Davidson, guitars, vocals; Dennis Payton, saxophone, harmonica, acoustic guitar, vocals; Rick Huxley, bass, acoustic guitar, vocals

While the Dave Clark Five has been roundly dismissed as a pale imitation of the Beatles, you have to give drummer Clark credit for being a talented songwriter and a savvy businessman. In addition to writing much of the group's hit material, Clark (a former movie stuntman with more than 40 film credits) managed and produced the band himself. He was smart enough to set his sights on the U.S. after the Beatles' 1964 concert tour, making the DCF the first British group to break into the American charts after the Beatles. With 17 Top 40 hits between 1964-967 (including "Do You Love Me," "Bits and Pieces," "Glad All Over" and "Catch Us If You Can"), the band was considered the only true contender to the Beatles' throne. And while its music was never as sophisticated as the Fab Four's, DCF had a good sense of melody and a well-tuned ear for harmony that was supported by Smith's raucous vocals and Clark's solid, heavy backbeat. The group had a rather successful foray into film ("Catch Us If You Can," an imitation of the Beatles' "A Hard Day's Night") and television (the British TV sensation "Hold On, It's the Dave Clark 5" and more appearances on the "Ed Sullivan Show" than any other rock act). With perhaps fitting timing, the group disbanded in 1970, the same year the Beatles broke up. Clark has continued to be a successful producer in TV and music, while his legacy as a marketer of prefab pop remains in evidence in such groups as Menudo, New Kids on the Block and Milli Vanilli—to name but a few. *The History of the Dave Clark Five* (Hollywood, 1993, prod. Dave Clark) offers a whopping 50 tracks, including all the hits, plus a 32-page booklet featuring rare photos, interviews and a history of the band. Enough bits and pieces to make you glad all over.

Christopher Scapelliti

Gene Clark

See: The Byrds

Petula Clark

Born Nov. 15, 1932 in Epsom, Surrey, England

Riding in on the last wave of the 60s British Invasion, film actress-singer Clark confided a sense of homespun reassurance during one of rock's most turbulent periods (1964-72). A precursor to the Carpenters and Olivia Newton-John, Clark was blessed with a clear, precision voice and wholesome good looks that gave her instant access to the adult pop market. With producer-arranger-composer Tony Hatch, she spun out a string of chirpy hits—"Downtown," "My Love," "This Is My Song," all No. 1 hits in the States—whose melding of strings and brass with basic pop rhythm sections recalled the sprightly music of a 60s Broadway musical. (Not surprisingly, it was in a hit Broadway musical, "Blood Brothers," that Clark revived her career during the mid-90s.)

what to buy: *The Pye Years Vol. 1/Don't Sleep in the Subway* (RPM, 1996, prods. Various) ♪♪♪♪ is an excellent reissue the combines two of Clark's albums (*The International Hits* and *These Are My Songs*) with extra singles. In addition to numerous standards of the day, the CD contains two of Clark's biggest hits, "Don't Sleep in the Subway" and "This Is My Song." The hits continue with *The Pye Years Vol. 2/Wind of Change*, (RPM, 1996, prod. Various) ♪♪♪♪ featuring Clark's final Pye album, *Pet '71*, all relevant singles from this period and several alternate takes made for a never-issued American version of the LP. All of the RPM reissues feature extensive liner notes, original LP art, rare singles sleeves and lavish photo spreads. A first-class job all the way.

what to buy next: If the above mentioned albums whet your appetite, then jump for *Greatest Hits*, (GNP/Crescendo, 1986, prod. Various) ♪♪♪♪ a first-rate retrospective of her early years featuring all the essential Clark classics ("Don't Sleep in the Subway," "Downtown," "A Sign of the Times," "My Love").

what to avoid: Given the plethora of Clark reissues, don't bother wasting your money on *Treasures Vol. 1* (WEA/Scotti Bros., 1992, prod. Various) ♪ The record skimps on essential cuts and, despite the suggestive title, there is no Vol. 2 to round out the collection. Stick with the recommended picks.

the rest: *I Know a Place* (Sequel, 1965) ♪♪♪ *My Love* (Sequel, 1966) ♪♪♪ *Other Man's Grass Is Always Greener* (See for Miles Records, 1968) ♪♪ *Portrait of Petula* (Sequel, 1969) ♪♪ *Live at the Royal Albert Hall* (GNP/Crescendo, 1972) ♪♪ *The Polygon Years Vol. 1* (RPM, 1996) ♪♪ *The Polygon Years Vol. 2* (RPM, 1996) ♪♪ *The Nixa Years Vol. 1/Another Door Opens* (RPM, 1996) ♪♪♪ *The Nixa Years Vol. 2/Gonna Find Me a Bluebird* (RPM, 1996) ♪♪♪

worth searching for: The three-CD package *I Love to Sing* (Sequel, 1995, prod. Various) ♪♪♪ is a comprehensive retrospective that includes the hits, the misses and the rare. For diehards only.

▶▶ The Carpenters, Olivia-Newton John, Anne Murray, Linda Ronstadt

◀◀ Lulu

Cristopher Scapelliti

Gilby Clarke

See: Guns N' Roses

The Clash

Formed 1976 in London, England. Disbanded 1985.

Joe Strummer (born John Graham Mellor), vocals, guitar; Mick Jones, guitar (1976-84); Paul Simonon, bass; Tory Crimes (born Terry Chimes), drums (1976-77, 1982-85); Nicky "Topper" Headon, drums (1976-82); Pete Howard, drums (1984-85); Vince White and Nick Sheppard, guitars (1984-85)

Along with the Ramones and Sex Pistols, the Clash were one of the three touchstones of punk rock. From the start, the group played a similar sort of buzzsaw, power-chord driven distorted rock. But it also had a genuine political sense—with Joe Strummer railing against commercial culture, American imperialism and the abuses of capitalism—as well as open, non-doctrinaire musical minds that shot everything from reggae to rap and disco to rockabilly into the band's sound. These same traits which helped separate the Clash from the pack eventually turned around and bit it on the ass; its open-minded ambition led to overblown, maddeningly inconsistent efforts like the three-album set *Sandanista!* its political awareness made some songs just so much sloganeering and eventually even led Strummer to fire founding guitarist Jones for some sort of political incorrectness. The Clash only lasted one album after that split, however, and, unlike the Pistols, has so far resisted big money reunion pitches from Lollapalooza and other concert promoters.

what to buy: *London Calling* (Epic, 1979, prod. Guy Stevens) ♪♪♪♪♪ is the band's masterpiece, balancing high energy punk efficiency with forays into roots rock, blues and reggae. Less intense than its debut, but also more accessible, this is simply a great collection of songs. *The Clash* (CBS U.K., 1977/Epic, 1979, prod. M. Foote, L. Perry, The Clash and B. Price) ♪♪♪♪ is pure punk heaven—overdriven fury, tuneful reggae, snarled vocals, great guitar riffs. *The Story of the Clash, Volume One* (Epic, 1988, prod. Various) ♪♪♪♪♪ is a first-rate, double-length compilation.

what to buy next: The band's U.S. debut, *Give 'Em Enough Rope* (Epic, 1978, prod. Sandy Pearlman) borders on the over-produced, but the results work surprisingly well: it's arena punk! *Combat Rock* (Epic, 1982, prod. Glyn Johns) was both the band's commercial breakthrough—including "Should I Stay or Should I Go?" and "Rock the Casbah"—and its last worthwhile creative grasp.

what to avoid: Cut after Strummer and Simonon fired Jones, *Cut the Crap* (Epic, 1985, prod. Jose Unidos) is a hollow echo of a once-great band.

the rest: *Sandanista!* (Epic, 1980) *Super Black Market Clash* (Epic, 1980/1994) *Return to Brixton* (Epic EP, 1990) *The Clash on Broadway* (Epic/Legacy, 1991)

worth searching for: The vinyl only promotional sampler *Sandanista Now!* (Epic, 1980, prod. the Clash) is the magnificent 12-song single album *Sandanista* could have been.

solo outings:

Topper Headon: Waking Up (Mercury, 1986)

Havana 3 A.M. (Paul Simonon): Havana 3 A.M. (I.R.S., 1991)

Joe Strummer: Walker (Virgin, 1987) *Earthquake Weather* (Epic, 1987) *Gangsterville* (Epic, 1989) *Island Hopping* (Epic, 1989)

▶▶ Rancid, Nada Surf, Green Day, the Pogues

◀◀ the Sex Pistols, the Ramones, Bo Diddley, Eddie Cochran, Junior Marvin, David Bowie, the Who

see also: *Big Audio Dynamite*

Alan Paul

Classics IV

Formed 1965 in Jacksonville, Fla. Disbanded early 70s.

Dennis Yost, vocals; James R. Cobb, guitar; Wally Eaton, guitar; Joe Wilson, bass; Kim Venable, drums

The smooth rock sound of Classics IV predated the adult contemporary category by several years. The group established its mellow pop style with U.S. hits such as "Spooky," "Stormy" and "Traces," its last million-seller. Most of the band's songs were co-written by Cobb and producer Buddy Buie, whose own group, the Atlanta Rhythm Section, revived "Spooky" in 1979. Both *Greatest Hits* (Capitol Special Products, 1992, prod. Buddy Buie) and *Very Best of the Classics IV* (EMI America, 1988, prod. Buddy Buie) are solid compilations that comprise both the group's big hits and lower chart entries ("Soul Train," "Every Day with You, Girl" and "Change of Heart"). Oddly, neither album offers "What Am I Crying For?" the group's final Top 40 entry and a fine example of this group's distinctive, easygoing sound.

Christopher Scapelliti

Josh Clayton-Felt

See: School of Fish

Johnny Clegg & Savuka /Juluka

Born June 7, 1953, in Rochdale, England

Johnny Clegg & Savuka (1986-95)—Clegg, vocals, guitar, mouth bow; Steve Mavuso, keyboards; Keith Hutchinson, keyboards, saxophone, flute; Derek De Beer, drums, percussion; Solly Letwaba, bass; Dudu Zulu, percussion. Juluka (1979-85, 1996)—Clegg; De Beer; Sipho Mchunu, vocals, guitar, concertina; Gary Van Zyl, bass, percussion (1981-85); Scorpion Madondo, flute, saxophone (1982-85); Cyril Mnculwana, keyboards (1983-85); Glenda Millar, keyboards (1982-85)

Born in England but raised in Zimbabwe and South Africa, Clegg learned Zulu dancing at an early age and, depending on which version of the story you believe, he either met Sipho Mchunu when Mchunu heard about this white boy who could dance like a Zulu, or when Clegg, already a lecturer in anthropology, was sought out by Mchunu because of Clegg's reputation as a hotshot guitarist. The first story maintains that the two met as teenagers around 1970 and worked together for nine years before hooking up with producer/impresario Hilton Rosenthal. The second one likely would indicate that they had only worked together for a little while before they started making records in 1979. Either way, the idea of a white man and a black man co-leading a South African band was a political statement in itself, and in some ways became more important than their novel melding of South African mbaqanga or "township" music, Western pop/rock and Zulu chants. By 1981, the duo put together a backup band, and before long Juluka's colorful and energetic performances made it a hot concert draw—and also brought them into direct conflict with the racist practices of South Africa's apartheid government. By 1982, it was wowing audiences in Britain, and soon after, Juluka was signed to an American major label. Commercial success never came, and after the group broke up, Clegg returned in as sole leader of a new ensemble, Savuka. Blander and more formulaic than Juluka, Clegg and Savuka became a serious concert draw across the world, but its albums never really rose above the level of stylish professionalism, and the group was dropped by Capitol after 1993's *Heat, Dust, and Dreams* Meanwhile, Clegg and Mchunu have reunited for some concerts and are reportedly planning a new Juluka album.

what to buy: More energetic and a bit more focused than Clegg and Savuka's earlier work, *Cruel, Crazy, Beautiful World* (Capitol, 1989, prod. Hilton Rosenthal and Bobby Summerfield) in some ways parallels the rising tide of optimism that was about to overtake South Africa when the album was released.

what to buy next: Highlighted by Juluka's South African breakthrough hit, "Impi," *African Litany* (Rhythm Safari, 1982/1991, prod. Hilton Rosenthal) offers a view of the earlier band just as it was about to make the jump from national to international status.

what to avoid: Tame and somewhat disappointing coming after the breakup of Juluka, Savuka's debut, *Third World Child* (Capitol, 1987, prod. Hilton Rosenthal) is fairly pleasant but unremarkable stuff.

the rest: Juluka—*Ubuhle Bemvelo* (Rhythm Safari, 1982/1991) *Scatterlings* (Warner Bros., 1983) *Stand Your Ground* (Warner Bros., 1984) Johnny Clegg & Savuka—*Shadow Man* (Capitol, 1988) *Heat, Dust, and Dreams* (Capitol, 1993)

worth searching for: *The Best of Juluka* (Rhythm Safari, 1991, prod. Hilton Rosenthal) provides a nice initiation to Clegg's international pop style, though the final track—"Scatterlings of Juluka (Mega-Mix)—can be skipped.

▶▶ Paul Simon (circa "Graceland"), Dave Matthews Band, Rusted Root

◀◀ Mahlathini & the Mahotella Queens, Ladysmith Black Mambazo, The Police, Men At Work, Aswad

Bob Remstein

Clarence Clemons

See: Bruce Springsteen

Jimmy Cliff

Born James Chambers, April 1, 1948 in St. Catherine, Jamaica

Along with Bob Marley, singer-songwriter Cliff is most responsible for popularizing reggae worldwide. He was one of Island Records' first artists and, in 1965, moved to England, where he achieved moderate success. In 1969, *Wonderful World, Beautiful People* hit the UK Top 10 even got recognition in the U.S. Ironically, it was his appearance as the lead character in the 1972 film "The Harder They Come" that really put him over the top; the soundtrack featured his music which yielded hits on the title tune and the searingly beautiful "Many Rivers To Cross" and "Sitting In Limbo." Cliff has a clear and flexible voice which is at home singing R&B as well as reggae, and his music has some overt West African influences. While his songwriting has always been strong and his work has been covered by Desmond Dekker, Bruce Springsteen, Linda Rondstadt, Keith Richards, Joe Cocker, UB40 and others, Cliff's acclaim never again peaked as high as it did just after the film.

what to buy: Cliff has written many wonderful songs, but the music on the soundtrack to *The Harder They Come* (Island, 1972, prod. Various) ripples with the film's urgency. The title cut is a wail of rebellion that speaks for the downtrodden anywhere. But it's in searching ballads such as "Many Rivers To Cross" that fit Cliff's voice and songwriting talents best in years to come. On *Give Thankx* (Warner Bros., 1978, prod. Bob Johnston and Jimmy Cliff), Cliff captures all the key themes in reggae—rebellion ("Stand Up and Fight Back"); repatriation ("Bongo Man," "Meeting In Africa"); and love ("She Is A Woman," "Universal Love") both sexual and spiritual.

what to buy next: *In Concert - The Best of Jimmy Cliff* (Reprise, 1976, prod. Andrew Loog Oldham and Jimmy Cliff) covers most of the film's key material plus early hits such as "Wild World" and "Wonderful World, Beautiful People."

what to avoid: Cliff's themes tend not to stray far afield, and they don't ring as true as usual on *Images*, (Cliff Sounds and Films, 1989, prod. Various) although his voice generally raises the album to a listenable level.

the rest: *Wonderful World, Beautiful People* (A&M, 1970) *Harder* (Mango, 1972) *Give the People What They Want* (MCA, 1981) *The Power and the Glory* (Columbia, 1983) *Hanging Fire* (Columbia, 1988) *Cliff Hanger* (Columbia, 1989) *Breakout* (JBS, 1992) *Live 1993* (Lagoon Reggae, 1993)

worth searching for: *I Am the Living* (MCA, 1980, prod. Jimmy Cliff and Oneness) is on a more spiritual tip, with good tunes such as "Gone Clear" "Morning Train" and "Love Again."

Maxi Priest, Third World, UB40, English Beat, Big Mountain

Toots and the Maytals, Desmond Dekker

Lawrence Gabriel

Patsy Cline

Born Sept. 8, 1932, in Winchester, Va. Died March 5, 1963.

One of the premier voices in country music, Cline wielded an influence that transcended style and genre and was felt in the folk, rock and the singer-songwriter communities. During her brief, six-year recording career—cut short by a fatal plane crash—Cline displayed a daring talent and acumen for lush pop, honky tonk and rock 'n' roll as well as straight country. A warm and self-reliant vocal tone marks the bulk of Cline's material, and her strength helped break down barriers for women, particularly in country music. Almost all of her recordings contain excellent performances, so rating them is a relative exercise. Cline's catalogue is fairly extensive—almost 50 titles still in print—and mostly comprises greatest hits collections, so only the cream of the crop is dealt with below.

what to buy: *The Patsy Cline Story* (MCA, 1988, prod. Owen Bradley) ♪♪♪♪♪ is a sterling 25-track collection of her biggest hits ("Crazy," "Walkin' After Midnight," "She's Got You") from her final period at Decca. It's an excellent introduction to Cline's sprightly colored palette. *The Patsy Cline Collection* (Country Music Foundation/MCA, 1991, prod. Various) ♪♪♪♪♪ is a 104-track bonanza that covers her complete Decca recordings, 51 songs from her 4 Star Music period and plenty of rare material. The remastered box set also contains a detailed booklet with rare photos.

what to buy next: *Walkin' Dreams: Her First Recordings, Vol. 1,* (Rhino, 1989, prod. Owen Bradley) ♪♪♪♪♪ *Hungry for Love: Her First Recordings, Vol. 2,* (Rhino, 1989, prod. Owen Bradley) ♪♪♪♪½ and *Rockin' Side: Her First Recordings, Vol. 3.* (Rhino, 1989, prod. Owen Bradley) ♪♪♪♪½ These three discs represent Cline's output from 1955-59—hits and otherwise— when she tackled a wide array of styles.

what to avoid: *The Best of Patsy Cline* (Curb, 1991, prod. N/A) ♪♪ is a skimpy, unrevealing 12-track disc that only hints at the scope of Cline's talent.

the rest: *A Portrait of Patsy Cline* (MCA, 1988) ♪♪♪♪ *The Last Sessions* (MCA, 1988) ♪♪♪♪½ *12 Greatest Hits* (MCA, 1988) ♪♪♪♪ *Live at the Opry* (MCA, 1988) ♪♪♪♪½ *Live, Vol. 2* (MCA, 1988) ♪♪♪ *The Patsy Cline Collection* (MCA, 1991) ♪♪♪♪♪ *Greatest Hits* (MCA Masterdisc, 1993) ♪♪♪♪ *Patsy Cline: The Birth of a Star* (Razor & Tie, 1996) ♪♪♪½

Linda Ronstadt, Lucinda Williams, Mary Chapin Carpenter, Loretta Lynn, Dolly Parton, k.d. lang, Cowboy Junkies

Hank Williams, Bob Wills, Cole Porter

Allan Orski

George Clinton /Parliament-Funkadelic

Born July 22, 1940 in Kannapolis, N.C.

MusicHound, meet the Atomic Dog. It's not like there weren't other funk bands around, but P-Funk distilled it to its purest elements and gave it metaphysical properties. For all the funk bands in the world, no other group has mastered the intricacy of layered rhythms, grooves and vocals into a sophisticated whole the way Clinton and his P-Funk mob has done. And no other group has influenced black pop music as strongly over the last 20 years. After migrating to Detroit from New Jersey and flunking out at Motown during the mid-60s, George Clinton and his Parliament pals (at that time a vocal group formed during the mid-50s in Plainfield, N.J.) decided to loosen up their music and take on a wild street image—in the process they revolutionized popular music and added multiple new agendas to black music. Clinton's rock-tinged raw music and irreverent black consciousness was like a breath of fresh air to the slick and suited veneer of most R&B acts.

While P-Funk's antics spawned a growing underground buzz and occasional pop airplay, it wasn't until 1975's *The Clones of Dr. Funkenstein* that its heavy bass, chanted lyrics, wriggling guitars and phat horn lines went over the top. From 1975-80, the P-Funk mob churned out hit after hit with the added spinoff groups, Bootsy's Rubber Band and the Brides of Funkenstein. In 1976, the group—a collective that rivals James Brown's assorted bands, with celebrated tenures by bassist Bootsy Collins, keyboardists Bernie Worrell and Walter "Junie" Morrison, guitarist Eddie Hazel, saxophonist Maceo Parker and percussionist Larry Fratangelo—released five albums under four names for three different labels. Common belief is that Clinton used the name Parliament for his more R&B, dance club-oriented records and Funkadelic for his rock side. That may be, but the Funkadelic appeared when Clinton temporarily lost legal rights to the Parliament name. And when he lost legal

What Album Changed Your Life?

"I don't know why, but one of the most killer albums I ever heard was Muddy Waters' Hard Again (Blue Sky, 1977) album. It's one of the most incredible blues albums I ever heard--maybe one of the best of all times. Not too many people talk about it, and I don't know why. They did it all live in the studio, with James Cotton, Pine Top Perkins, Johnny Winter playing guitar. It was an incredible band and they just kicked ass."

Kenny Wayne Shepherd

rights to both names in the 1980s started recording under his own name. Regardless of the title, it's basically the same band; even after the group splintered in 1981, Clinton's records have featured many of the same musicians. Legal hassles dogged Clinton and other funkateers through much of the 80s, and the hits disappeared after 1982's "Atomic Dog"—though Clinton produced hit records for Thomas Dolby, the Red Hot Chili Peppers and others. It was "Atomic Dog" that brought Clinton back in the 80s as rapper after rapper sampled the track. Other P-Funk grooves followed and the funk presence brought Clinton back as an elder statesman. Not content to be just nostalgia, 1993's *Hey, Man...Smell My Finger* showed he could still throw down, while "If Anybody Gets Funk Up (It's Gonna Be You)" from *T.A.P.O.A.F.O.M.* signaled a full-scale return to form.

what to buy: Almost anything from the 70s is a good choice, but Parliament's *Mothership Connection* (Casablanca, 1975, prod. George Clinton) lays out the P-Funk philosophy in a capsule with relentless grooves and happy horns. "Give Up the Funk (Tear the Roof Off the Sucker)" is the big hit, but the title tune is like losing yourself in a bumping cartoon. Funkadelic gets on the good foot, too, with *One Nation Under a Groove* (Warner Bros., 1987/Priority, 1993, prod. George Clinton) If you didn't like this record, you weren't dancing when you heard it.

what to buy next: For the early years, *Funkadelic's Greatest Hits* (Westbound, 1975, prod. George Clinton) covers things pretty well with "Can You Get To That," "I'll Bet You" and "I Got a Thing..." The only essential early hit missing is the Parliament's "I Wanna Testify." The 10-minute title track of Funkadelic's *Maggot Brain* (Westbound, 1971, prod. Clinton) proves that Jimi Hendrix wasn't the only black freaky rock guitarist.

what to avoid: Things looked bad for Funkadelic with *The Electric Spanking of War Babies,* (Warner Bros., 1980, prod. George Clinton) which produced no jams and Sly Stone's pathetic bleating on "Funk Gets Stronger."

the rest: Parliament—*Up for the Down Stroke* (Casablanca, 1974) *Chocolate City* (Casablanca, 1975) *Clones of Dr. Funkenstein* (Casablanca, 1976) *Funkentelechy Vs. the Placebo Syndrome* (Polygram, 1977) *P-Funk Earth Tour* (Warner Bros., 1977) *Motor Booty Affair* (Casablanca, 1978) *Gloryhallastupid* (Casablanca, 1979) *Tear the Roof Off 1974-1980* (Casablanca/Chronicles, 1993) *The Best of Parlet featuring Parliament* (Casablanca/Chronicles, 1994) *The Best of Parliament: Give Up the Funk* (Casablanca/Chronicles, 1995) Funkadelic—*Funkadelic* (Westbound, 1971) *Free Your Mind and Your Ass Will Follow* (Westbound, 1970) *America Eats Its Young* (Westbound, 1972) *Cosmic Slop* (Westbound, 1973) *Standing on the Verge of Gettin' It On* (Westbound, 1974) *Let's Take It to the Stage* (Westbound, 1975) *Hardcore Jollies* (Warner Bros., 1976) *Uncle Jam Wants You* (Warner Bros., 1979) *Music for Your Mother* (Westbound, 1992) George Clinton—*Computer Games* (Capitol, 1982) *U Shouldn't-Nuf Bit Fish* (Capitol, 1983) *Some of My Best Jokes Are Friends* (Capitol, 1985) *R&B Skeletons from the Closet* (Capitol, 1986) *The Best of George Clinton* (Capitol, 1986) *The Cinderella Theory* (Paisley Park, 1989) *P. Funk All-Stars Live* (Westbound, 1990) *Hey, Man . . . Smell My Finger* (Paisley Park, 1993) *George Clinton Family Series Vol. 1-5* (AEM, 1992/1994) *George Clinton's Sample Some of Disc, Sample Some of D.A.T. Series Vol. 1-6* (AEM, 1992/1994) *Live Greatest Hits, 1972-1993* (AEM, 1993) *T.A.P.O.A.F.O.M. (The Awesome Power of a Fully Operational Mothership)* (Sony 550, 1996)

worth searching for: *Music For Your Mother,* (Ace/WEstbound,

1992, prod. Various) an import collection of Funkadelic singles, an interesting but valid perspective on what's definitely an album-oriented band.

Dr. Dre, Prince, Groove Collective, Eric B & Rakim, Digital Underground, Red Hot Chili Peppers

James Brown, Screamin' Jay Hawkins, Ike Turner, Sun Ra

see also: *Bootsy Collins, Maceo Parker*

Lawrence Gabriel

Clivilles & Cole

See: C&C Music Factory

Club Nouveau

Formed 1986 in Sacramento, Calif. Disbanded 1990.

Jay King, vocals; Valerie Watson, vocals; Alex Hill, keyboards

If you blinked, you missed this band, which started in the mid-80s as a spinoff from the Timex Social Club, a group that had its own out-of-nowhere hit with "Rumors" in 1986. One of the first producer-driven non-bands of the mid-80s R&B-pop era, Club Nouveau featured three Timex members—King, Watson and Hill, joined by the production team of Thomas McElroy and Denzil Foster. *Life, Love and Pain* (Warner Bros., 1986, prod. Jay King, Thomas McElroy and Denzil Foster) was an unqualified success, fueled by a monster hit cover of Bill Withers' "Lean on Me." Unfortunately, McElroy and Foster left soon after to mastermind R&B divas En Vogue's success, taking their New Jack pop smarts with them. Although Club Nouveau released records in 1988 and 1989 (now out of print), it turns out the party had left this nightspot a long time ago.

Eric Deggans

The Coasters

Formed 1955 in Los Angeles, Calif. Disbanded 1976

Carl Gardner, tenor vocals; Billy Guy, baritone vocals (1955-65); Bobby Nunn, bass vocals (1955, died Nov. 5, 1986); Leon Hughes, tenor vocals (1955); Will "Dub" Jones, bass vocals (1956-1965); Cornell/Cornelius Gunter, tenor vocals (1956-60, died Feb. 26, 1990); Earl "Speedo" Carroll, tenor vocals, (1961-76); Ronnie Bright, tenor vocals (1965-76); Jimmy Norman, baritone (1965-76)

At the end of the white-bread 50s, America's mainstream chose the comical Coasters as their most beloved black entertainers. Under the watchful eye of writer-producers Jerry Leiber and Mike Stoller, the Coasters issued a number of playful singles, which kept the group at the top of the charts well into the early 60s. Although the contribution of Leiber and Stoller can't be overstated, the group's sound was just as earmarked by Nunn's low bottoms and Gardner's wolf-in-sheep's-clothing tenor. *50 Coastin' Classics: Anthology,* (Rhino, 1992, prod. Various) by far the best Coasters compilation on the market, is nearly overwhelming; going back to the pre-Coasters group, the Robins, the album has a wealth of obscurities and ample liner notes, with comments by Leiber and Stoller. *The Very Best of the Coasters* (Rhino, 1993, prod. various) offers a compact version of the above that focuses on such chart-toppers as "Yakety-Yak," "Charlie Brown" and "Poison Ivy," as well as "What About Us," a track that argues that the band had more to offer than just yuks.

Allan Orski

Eddie Cochran

Born Oct. 3, 1938, in Oklahoma City, Okla. Died on April 17, 1960, in Bristol, England

Cochran is probably the most overrated member of the early rock 'n' roll pantheon. He is remembered more for his suave, Elvis-like style than the enduring quality of his songs, although a handful —"Summertime Blues," "20 Flight Rock," "Somethin' Else," "Teenage Heaven," "C'mon Everybody" —are certified classics. His influence was felt more in England, where he died in the same car crash that crippled Gene Vincent. Such British rock stars as Rod Stewart, the Rolling Stones, the Who and even the Sex Pistols have kept his songs in the book. By the time British reissue labels finished sorting through his work, the entire body looked rather less than impressive; Ricky Nelson records held up better. There are certain recordings that stand up against any from his time, but just don't dig too deep.

what to buy: The 20-song collection *Eddie Cochran: The Legendary Masters Series* (EMI, 1990, prod. Various) focuses on his signature driving rock sound and includes a bare minimum of the schlocky ballads.

what to buy next: *The Early Years* (Ace, 1988, prod. Various) is a slapdash collection of his experiments in country music mixed with some rock. The coupling of *Singin' to My Baby* and *Never to Be Forgotten* (EMI, 1993, prod. Various) sticks a dreadful teen pop album with a posthumous collection of worthy, lesser known rockers.

the rest: *Greatest Hits* (Curb, 1990)

worth searching for: Airchecks from 1960 British television programs collected for one side of a major label album, *Eddie Cochran: On the Air* (EMI, 1987, prod. Not Listed) gets across some of Cochran's personality that often got stifled on recordings. Who let this one out? Take a bow.

▶▶ Ricky Nelson, Paul McCartney, Brian Setzer

◀◀ Elvis Presley

Joel Selvin

Bruce Cockburn

Born May 27, 1945 in Ottawa, Ont., Canada

Bruce Cockburn has had a fascinating musical development, starting as a folk singer in the early 70s but eventually incorporating rock and world music elements to create a more complex style. His maturation came on 1979's *Dancing in the Dragon's Jaws,* when he was being influenced by reggae, jazz and African pop while also discovering world politics (the album also featured his only American Top 40 hit, "Wondering Where the Lions Are"). He fully realized that sound with 1984's *Stealing Fire* and would eventually turn his music inward again to American folk and blues. Cockburn is limited as a vocalist, but his spiritual convictions shine through his music, making him an incredibly emotional singer at times.

what to buy: *Stealing Fire,* (Columbia, 1984, prod. Jon Goldsmith and Kerry Crawford) which came out of Cockburn's visits to Central American refugee camps, is one of the most moving works of politically motivated rock ever created. Instead of launching into polemics, Cockburn personalizes the songs, singing about love during wartime in "Lovers in a Dangerous Time" and dreaming visions of vengeance in the shattering "If I Had a Rocket Launcher." Incorporating worldbeat rhythms into his own folk experience, Cockburn makes powerfully emotional melodies, even turning the line "Who put the bullet hole in Peggy's kitchen wall?" into an unforgettable hook.

what to buy next: Working with a band that included Booker T. Jones and Nashville fiddle virtuoso Mark O'Connor, Cockburn did for inner spiritual turmoil what he had done for Latin American politics in *Nothing but a Burning Light,* (Columbia, 1991, prod. T-Bone Burnett) weaving original songs and old gospel blues into a phosphorescent statement of faith.

what to avoid: Though the albums aren't bad, Cockburn's two earliest releases—*Bruce Cockburn* (True North, 1970, prod. Eugene Martynec) and *High Winds, White Sky* (Columbia, 1971) — are folk singer/songwriter albums that exhibit little of the eclecticism that would make some of Cockburn's later work so involving.

the rest: *Sunwheel Dance* (Columbia, 1972) *Night Vision* (Columbia, 1973) *Salt, Sun & Time* (True North, 1974) *Joy Will Find a Way* (True North, 1975) *In the Falling Dark* (True North, 1977) *Circles in the Stream* (True North, 1977) *Further Adventures Of* (True North, 1978) *Dancing in the Dragon's Jaws* (Columbia, 1979) *Humans* (Columbia, 1980) *Inner City Front* (Columbia, 1981) *The Trouble With Normal* (Columbia, 1983) *World of Wonders* (Columbia, 1986) *Big Circumstance* (Columbia, 1989) *Bruce Cockburn Live* (True North, 1990) *Christmas* (Columbia, 1993) *Dart to the Heart* (Columbia, 1994)

worth searching for: *Mummy Dust,* (True North, 1981) also released as *ResumFigure 1,* and *Waiting for a Miracle,* (True North, 1987) two best-ofs from Cockburn's Canadian label that collect the singer's most popular works from different periods in his career.

▶▶ Mark Heard, Billy Bragg, Tragically Hip

◀◀ Gordon Lightfoot, Bob Dylan, The Weavers

Brian Mansfield

Joe Cocker

Born John Robert Cocker, May 20, 1944 in Sheffield, England

With his gruff voice and passion-fueled delivery, Cocker is one of rock's great stylists—which can be as much a curse as a blessing. Because he seldom writes his own material, Cocker is usually at the mercy of the material and the producers who help him choose it and then craft his sound at that particular time. With sympathetic cohorts—Denny Cordell and Leon Russell at the start of his career, for instance—Cocker's brilliance, schooled in the classic blues and R&B of Ray Charles and Big Joe Turner, shines through; it takes *cajones* and rare talent to not only cover but to also re-invent prior hits such as the Beatles' "With a Little Help From My Friends" and Traffic's "Feelin' Alright." But Cocker has also laid his estimable pipes on some real schmaltz, even though sometimes it's brought him tremendous success ("Up Where We Belong" from the film *An Officer and a Gentleman*). In his fifties now, Cocker still has the voice—and his distinctive spastic air guitar performing style—that he began with in 1969. But each new venture is a crap-shoot, and we can only hope that he again finds the right combination of songs and collaborators to fulfill his potential.

what to buy: With a signature tune, "Delta Lady," as well as another hot Beatles cover ("She Came in Through the Bathroom Window"), *Joe Cocker!* (A&M, 1969, prod. Denny Cordell and Leon Russell) built on Cocker's triumphant Woodstock appearance and marked the arrival of a tremendous new talent. Though the band Russell assembled for the live *Mad Dogs and Englishmen* (A&M, 1970, prod. Denny Cordell and Leon Russell) at times seems loose and intrusive, Cocker really shows his mettle by never letting it overwhelm him. *Classics Volume 4* (A&M, 1987, prod. Various) offers the best of his early period.

what to buy next: *The Best of Joe Cocker* (Capitol, 1993, prod. Various) captures the best of his spotty later work, though every collection should have his rendition of "Unchain My Heart" and "You Can Leave Your Hat On." At four CDs, *The Long Voyage Home: The Silver Anniversary Collection* (A&M, 1995, prod. various) is flabby in spots, but there are more than enough electrifying moments to compensate.

what to avoid: Tepid originals and vapid cover choices dog Cocker's last two albums, *Night Calls* (Capitol, 1992, prod. Various) and *Have a Little Faith* (Sony 550, 1994, prod. Chris Lord-Alge and Roger Davies) WOOF!

the rest: *With a Little Help From My Friends* (A&M, 1969) *Joe Cocker* (A&M, 1972) *I Can Stand a Little Rain* (A&M, 1974) *Jamaica Say You Will* (A&M, 1975) *Sting Ray* (A&M, 1976) *Live in L.A.* (A&M, 1976) *Greatest Hits* (A&M, 1977) *Luxury You Can Afford* (A&M, 1978) *Sheffield Steel* (Island, 1982) *Civilized Man* (Capitol, 1984) *Cocker* (Capitol, 1986) *Unchain My Heart* (Capitol, 1987) *One Night of Sin* (Capitol, 1989) *Joe Cocker Live* (Capitol, 1990)

worth searching for: *Woodstock Twenty Fifth Anniversary Collection* (Atlantic, 1994) which features portions of the performance that launched Cocker's career in the U.S.

Kim Wilson (Fabulous Thunderbirds), Roger Daltrey (the Who), Robert Palmer, Bryan Adams

Ray Charles, Big Joe Turner, James Brown, the Beatles, B.B. King

Gary Graff

The Coconuts

See: Kid Creole and the Coconuts

Cocteau Twins

Formed 1980 in Grangemouth, Scotland

Elizabeth Fraser, vocals; Robin Gutherie, guitars; Will Heggie, bass (1980-83); Simon Raymonde, bass (1984-present)

For the better part of a decade, the Cocteau Twins represented not only 4AD Records as the label's anchor act, but also the British commercial avant-garde. Laying the groundwork for virtually every female-fronted band that used atmospheric guitars and moody synthesizers was tough work—so tough, in fact, that virtually no Cocteau Twins song has proper lyrics. Fraser sings from a stream of consciousness in most cases, and her verbal repertoire consists almost exclusively of made-up sounds she finds pleasing to her ears. While there are moments when proper English comes into play, they tend to be infrequent. Along with contemporary Kate Bush, Fraser also laid the groundwork for a more classical approach to modern music—not symphonic a la Yes or the Moody Blues, but in a more daring attempt to convey emotions and ideas. In the beginning, the Cocteaus were a stripped-down unit creating dark and sinister music using a keyboard, drum machine, some guitar effects and Fraser's voice. When bassist Heggie left to start his own band, Lowlife, it was obvious he had been holding the group back; once Raymonde joined the band, Fraser and Gutherie both cut loose. The songs began to shimmer, which had a positive effect—during the mid-80s, the group began to sell hundreds of thousands of records in the U.S. As imports. Ironically, the Twins' deal with Capitol Records marked the beginning of the end qualitatively. Perhaps the Twins have succumbed to the pressures of a major label. Or perhaps the group ran out of new ideas. But the next three releases were syrupy-pop records, and with the number of female chanteuses on the rise, the originals need to stay a step ahead. And the Cocteau Twins just aren't doing it.

what to buy: *Treasure* (Capitol, 1984, prod. Ivo Watts Russell) set the sonic standard for the shoegazer movement of the late 80s. But the bulk of the band's best material appeared on the two EPs it released in Britain each year through the 80s; they've been compiled for the U.S. on *The CD Single Box Set* (4AD/Capitol, 1991, prod. Various)

what to buy next: *Garlands* (Capitol, 1980, prod. Ivo Watts Russell and the Cocteau Twins) sounds like the soundtrack to a nightmare; Fraser's vocals are raspy and harsh, and the music is scary and cold. *The Pink Opaque,* (4AD/Relativity, 1986) technically the band's first U.S. release, collects tracks from each previous album as well as several EPs. To date it stands as the Cocteau's only official compilation.

what to avoid: *The Moon and the Melodies* (4AD/Relativity, 1986) was not recorded under the name the Cocteau Twins, but rather as Harold Budd, Elizabeth Fraser, Robin Gutherie and Simon Raymonde. Whether it was an attempt to blossom as artists or just to make a buck hooking up with New Age pianist and Brian Eno pal Budd, the project is uninspired and features Fraser's singing on only three songs.

the rest: *Head over Heels* (Capitol/4AD, 1983) *Victoria-land* (Capitol/4AD, 1987) *Blue Bell Knoll* (Capitol/4AD, 1988) *Heaven or Las Vegas* (Capitol/4AD, 1990) *Four Calendar Cafe* (Capitol, 1993) *Milk and Kisses* (Capitol, 1996)

worth searching for: *Cocteau Twins Collector Disc* (4AD/Capitol, 1994, prod. Various) is a promotional-only release recapping the band's history in conjunction with *The CD Single Box Set.*

▶▶ Curve, Tori Amos, Dead Can Dance, This Mortal Coil, the Cranes

◀◀ Kate Bush, Simple Minds, Joy Division, Siouxsie and the Banshees

see also: *This Mortal Coil*

Tim Davis

Phil Cody

Born Oct. 18, 1968, in Cleveland, Ohio

Calling Cody a folk singer is a tempting but too limiting a term; he's more a ragtag patchwork of folk, punk and rock 'n' roll, all balled up under his wool cap. *The Sons of Intemperance Offering* (Interscope Records, 1996, prod. Thom Wilson) is a hiccuping, no-frills debut recorded live in the studio. The whizzing-by details of the opening jig "House of Lust" nearly trip over themselves under Cody's rushed delivery. With a vivid eye for detail, Cody writes pungent story-songs that are the mark of many a folk singer, minus the sanctimony. Any further doubters are referred to his acoustic cover of The Clash's "Straight to Hell," which retains its martial atmosphere while also giving license to Cody's freewheeling bursts of singing.

Allan Orski

Leonard Cohen

Born Sept. 21, 1934, in Montreal, Canada

Cohen was a published poet and novelist in his native Canada well before Judy Collins first recorded his songs in 1966. He was 34 years old when his debut album appeared in 1968, and though he was often grouped with such songwriters as Joni Mitchell, he seemed wiser, like a far worldlier uncle. His most popular early songs—"Suzanne" and "Bird on the Wire"—stamped him as the ultimate long-suffering romantic and erotic victim of countless beautiful women. But as his lyrics grew darker and more obsessive through the 70s, his fans dwindled; he was simply too depressing, many complained. Yet Cohen continues to be rediscovered by younger listeners who are drawn to his poetic artistry as much as his romanticized gloom. And, in fact, his work over the past decade is some of his strongest. Two tributes albums— 1991's *I'm Your Fan* and 1995's *Tower of Song* (with Cohen tunes done by REM, Nick Cave and the Pixies, among others)—revealed his influences on a new generation of songwriters.

what to buy: The best place to start is with two albums that span nearly 30 years of Cohen's output. His debut, *Songs of Leonard Cohen* (Columbia, 1968, prod. John Simon) immediately established his credentials as an utterly original lyricist, while producer Simon's arrangements gave a romantic shimmer (which Cohen, at the time, detested) to the music's deep melancholia. On *The Future,* (Columbia, 1992, prod. Various) Cohen casts an unsparing eye on the state of the world and the hopeless politicians, priests and lovers who inhabit it. Musically, it's his most adventurous album ever—and it shows his wit is definitely improving in middle age. *Best of Leonard Cohen* (Columbia, 1975, prod. Various) is a fine introduction to his work, though it only covers his first five albums (put Cohen high on the list of artists deserving of a box set).

what to buy next: *Songs From a Room* (Columbia, 1969, prod. Bob Johnston) is perhaps Cohen's most haunting record, with very spare, sympathetic production ("Bird on the Wire" debuted here). Cohen released little in the U.S. during the 80s, but re-emerged with the stunning *I'm Your Man,* (Columbia, 1988, prod. Leonard Cohen) featuring an entirely new palette of sounds in his musical backing—and an uncharacteristically bold sense of humor.

what to avoid: One of the oddest collaborations in pop music annals, *Death of a Ladies' Man* (Columbia, 1977, prod. Phil Spector) paired Cohen with producer Spector. Truly bizarre.

the rest: *Songs of Love and Hate* (Columbia, 1971/1995) *New Skin For the Old Ceremony* (Columbia, 1975/1995) *Recent Songs* (Columbia, 1979/1990) *Various Positions* (Columbia, 1985/1995) *Cohen Live* (Columbia, 1994)

worth searching for: On the all-star tribute *Weird Nightmare: Meditations on Mingus,* (Columbia, 1992) Cohen teams with performance artist Diamanda Galas for a compellingly oddball version of "Eclipse."

Nick Cave, the Sisters of Mercy, Morrissey

Hank Williams, Leadbelly, Jacques Brel, Bob Dylan

see also: *Jennifer Warnes*

Doug Pippin

Cola Boy

See: St. Etienne

Jude Cole

Born in East Moline, Ill.

A former member of the British power-pop band the Records, Cole has all the makings of a successful singer-songwriter—a good voice, good musical ideas and a strong perspective—but he just can't seem to get attention. Cole left the Records after one release and showed some promise with *Jude Cole.* (Reprise, 1987, prod. Russ Titleman) But he really scored with *A View from 3rd Street.* (Reprise, 1990, prod. David Tyson and Michael Ostin) Although the sweet "Baby It's Tonight" and the heartfelt "Time For Letting Go" were Top 40 hits, the album could have spawned three more "House Full of Reasons."

the rest: *Start The Car* (Reprise, 1992) *I Don't Know Why I Act This Way* (Island, 1995)

Christina Fuoco

Lloyd Cole

Born Jan. 31, 1961 in Buxton, England

Scottish singer-songwriter Cole garnered considerable attention in the mid-1980s with his band The Commotions. His mordant wit and flair for sparkling, folk-flavored pop melodies earned favorable comparisons to Elvis Costello, though Cole's sensibility was generally more languorous than vitriolic, and his croaky voice and penchant for literary allusions at times suggest Lou Reed. Cole and the Commotions released their heralded debut, *Rattlesnakes*, in 1984; but despite faring well in the U.K., the band failed to crack U.S. radio. It recorded two more albums before Cole embarked on a solo career, edging away from the poppier material he'd limned with the band and flirting with a variety of styles, notably soul and fussily arranged chamber pop. 1995's *Love Story* marked a tentative return to his earlier form, though with a new maturity.

what to buy: *Rattlesnakes* (Capitol, 1984, prod. Paul Hardiman) is a seamless debut album, filled with bristling pop creations such as "Perfect Skin," "Are You Ready to Be Heartbroken" and the title track. It rewards compulsive listening.

what to buy next: *1984-1989* (Capitol, 1989, prod. Various) gathers some superb tracks from Rattlesnakes and some of Cole's best work during the rest of the decade. *Love Story* (Rykodisc, 1995, prod. Lloyd Cole & Friends) is a welcome and consistently strong return to pop form. *Easy Pieces* (Capitol, 1985, prod. Clive Langer and Alan Winstanley) falls far short of the standard set by *Rattlesnakes* but has several excellent tracks, including "Rich," "Brand New Friend" and the bouncy "Lost Weekend." Ditto for *Mainstream,* (Capitol, 1987, prod. Ian Stanley) which boasts "Jennifer She Said," the powerful title song and the wistful "29."

the rest: *Don't Get Weird on Me Babe* (Capitol, 1991) *Lloyd Cole* (Capitol, 1990) *Bad Vibes* (Rykodisc, 1993)

worth searching for: The CD-5 for the track "Like Lovers Do" (Rykodisc, 1995, prod. Lloyd Cole & Friends) from the *Love Story* album. It features three solid non-album tracks.

Pete Droge, Toad the Wet Sprocket

Beatles, Bob Dylan, Hank Williams, Jimmy Webb, Leonard Cohen, Al Green, Nick Drake, Neil Young, Lou Reed, Big Star, Elvis Costello

Simon Glickman

Paula Cole

Born 1969 in Rockport, Mass.

Trained in jazz vocal technique at the Berklee College of Music in Boston, Cole moved to New York, where she was spotted by Imago Records chief Terry Ellis. But before her debut CD, *Harbinger* (Imago, 1994/Warner Bros, 1995, prod. Kevin Killen) hit the marketplace, Peter Gabriel heard the disc and asked Cole to join his 1993 "Secret World Tour" to portray "a Jungian vision of womanhood," as she says. A year later, her entrancing brand of art/pop was released, ranging from the atmospheric lament "I Am So Ordinary" to more syncopated, funk-tinged tunes such as "Chiaroscuro" and "Hitler's Brothers." Hampered by Imago's 1995 bankruptcy, Cole toured with Sarah McLachlan and Melissa Etheridge before negotiating a new record deal with Warner Bros., which thankfully re-released *Harbinger* so the album could get its due.

Eric Deggans

Jaz Coleman

See: Killing Joke

Collective Soul

Formed 1990/1993 in Stockbridge, Ga.

Ed Roland, vocals, guitar; Dean Roland, guitar; Will Turpin, bass; Shane Evans, drums; Ross Childress, guitar

For Collective Soul, the big break came after it had broken up, prompting Ed Roland to get back together with his younger brother, Dean, and resurrect the band. A college radio station in Atlanta acquired a demo tape Roland put together in hopes of landing a songwriting contract, and the song "Shine," with its vocal warmth and chugging, stutter-step guitars, became an instant sensation. That twist of fate led to a major-label contract and demands for a tour, spurring the rebirth of Collective Soul. The group, named after a phrase from Ayn Rand's "Atlas Shrugged," rocks with restraint, alternating fluid rhythms with timely bursts of guitar power. Roland structures the songs on solid melodies and delivers his deftly phrased lyrics with vocal charm. "Shine" provided an impressive kickoff to *Hints Allegations and Things Left Unsaid,* (Atlantic, 1993, prod. Ed Roland, Matt Serletec and Joe Randolph) and the band shows more of the same rhythmic verve and pop melodicism on "Breathe" and "Goodnight, Good Guys"—though those come between failed sonic explorations such as the orchestral "Pretty Donna" and the Beatlesque "All." Much better is *Collective Soul,* (Atlantic, 1995, prod. Ed Roland and Matt Serletec) which is actually Collective Soul's first album written and performed as a band. More focused, it features the band's melodic surge-rock ("Gel," "December") along with crunching rockers ("Untitled," "Where the River Flows") and dreamy power ballads ("The World I Know," "She Gathers Rain").

David Yonke

Bootsy Collins

Born William Collins, Oct. 26, 1951, in Cincinnati, Ohio

First known as a session musician in Cincinnati, Collins came to the national spotlight when James Brown recruited him for his backing band in 1969. After fueling Brown's band for two years, the bassist left to join George Clinton's Parliament-Funkadelic menagerie. Within a few years, the colorful bassist—taken to wearing glitzy, sequined clothes with stars all over and playing a bass shaped like a huge star—became one of P-Funk's most popular ingredients, leading to a solo deal with his Bootsy's Rubber Band in 1976. Featuring fellow P-Funkers such as Bernie Worrell and past Brown sidemen Fred Wesley and Maceo Parker, the Rubber Band presented a boatload of cartoon-like space-based tunes grounded in seriously psychedelic funk grooves. After six solo records filled with the same science-fiction funk, Bootsy turned to session work with artists such as Malcolm McLaren and Dee-Lite. But the funk returned again during the late 80s, with Collins presenting a series of records even trippier than before, courtesy of his collaborations with avant-garde producer Bill Laswell.

what to buy: Collins' solo debut *Stretching Out in Bootsy's Rubber Band* (Warner Bros, 1976, prod. George Clinton and Bootsy Collins) is one of the bassist's most consistent records, showcasing both his nimble, effects-filled bass work and out-of-this-world sense of humor. You have to fast-forward 12 years to get to his next-best effort, the aptly titled *What's Bootsy Doin'?* (Columbia, 1988, prod. Bootsy Collins and Bill Laswell) Recorded after a six-year layoff, it features some of the bassist's tightest, most powerful funk grooves, including the expansive workout "Party on Plastic."

what to buy next: As a convenient way to get the real funk without time-consuming detours, Collins' greatest-hits record *Back in the Day: The Best of Bootsy* (Warner Bros., 1994, prod. Various) offers plenty of bang for the buck, collecting near-legendary singles such as "Bootzilla," "The Pinocchio Theory" and "Hollywood Squares" in the same package.

what to avoid: As an artist, consistent focus has never been one of Collins' strong points. Still, the all-over-the-place *Ultra Wave* (Warner Bros., 1980/1996, prod. Bootsy Collins and George Clinton) sets new lows for lack of direction and less-than-distinctive material. Collins' live album, *Keepin' Dah Funk Alive 4 1995* (Rykodisc, 1995, prod. At'c Inoue) WOOF! presents a mediocre band trying its best to re-create the bassist's legendary grooves.

the rest: *Ahh ... the Name is Bootsy Baby* (Warner Bros.,

1977/1996) ♪♪♪♪ *Bootsy? Player of the Year* (Warner Bros., 1978) ♪♪♪♪ *This Boot is Made for Fonk-N* (Warner Bros., 1979) ♪♪♪ *The One Giveth, The Count Taketh Away* (Warner Bros., 1982) ♪♪♪ *Jungles Bass* (4th and Broadway, 1990) ♪♪♪ *Blasters of the Universe* (Rykodisc, 1994) ♪♪ *Zillatron, Lord of the Harvest* (Rykodisc, 1994) ♪♪♪

worth searching for: *Funk Power 1970: A Brand New Day* (Polydor/Chronicles, 1996) ♪♪♪♪ chronicles Collins' term as a JB, showing the roots of the "space bass" style that would drive P-Funk and the Rubber Band in later years.

▶▶ T.M. Stevens, Rick James, Flea (Red Hot Chili Peppers)

◀◀ James Brown, George Clinton, Larry Graham

Eric Deggans

Edwyn Collins

Born Aug. 23, 1959 in Glasgow, Scotland

From 1979-85, Collins was a member of the seminal Scottish pop-punk band Orange Juice, whose singles "Rip It Up," "Felicity" and "Louise Louise" were sunny pop at its best. After the group broke up, Collins released two solo albums in the U.K.—*Hope and Despair* (Demon, 1989) ♪♪♪♪ and *Hellbent on Compromise* (Demon, 1990) ♪♪♪ His most fully realized album to date, *Gorgeous George* (Bar/None, 1995, prod. Edwyn Collins) ♪♪♪♪ is Collins at his best—cynical, honest, ironic and funny. From the memorable hit "A Girl Like You" to the social commentary of "The Campaign For Real Rock" and "Low Expectations," the album mixes 60s soul with Euro-pop and balladry.

Anna Glen

Judy Collins

Born May 1, 1939, in Seattle, Wash.

With her delicate tone, interpretive skills and ear for good to great material, Collins' contributions cover folk, folk-rock, pop, show tunes and country-tinged rock. She debuted on piano with the Denver Symphony Orchestra at age 13 and during the mid-60s, she began recording folk albums, selecting songs by aspiring songwriters such as Leonard Cohen ("Suzanne") and Joni Mitchell ("Both Sides Now"); she recorded Roger McGuinn's "Bells of Rhymney" before he re-arranged it for his band, the Byrds. By the late 60s, Collins had effortlessly segued from folk to pop, and although her songs usually remained in gentle settings, her own political songwriting was pointed and uncompromising. Stephen Stills dedicated his "Suite: Judy Blue Eyes" to her. In 1970, she recorded the traditional "Amazing Grace" in St. Paul's Chapel at Columbia University, her pristine soprano without instrumental embellishment creating one of the most masterful renditions of that song ever. It was a Top 20 hit in this country and one of the longest-charting singles in U.K. history. Having already recorded cabaret and show tunes, including work by Jacques Brel, Collins landed a hit in 1975 with Stephen Sondheim's "Send in the Clowns" on *Judith*, her last gold album. But even though commercial success has eluded her during the past two decades, Collins has always exhibited a sense of grace, refinement and timeliness that transcends generational and stylistic boundaries.

what to buy: *Who Knows Where the Time Goes* (Elektra, 1968, prod. David Anderle) ♪♪♪♪♪ is a culmination of pop, folk and country styles, in step with the musical movement of the times. With Buddy Emmons on pedal steel, James Burton on electric guitar and dobro, Chris Etheridge on bass, Van Dyke Parks on piano and Michael Stahl on organ, Collins was cast in a warm, glowing light. Along with the title track, memorable songs include "My Father," "Poor Immigrant," "Story of Isaac" and "Pretty Polly."

what to buy next: *Wildflowers*, (Elektra, 1967, prod. Mark Abramson) ♪♪♪♪ an elegant recording that includes her hit version of "Both Sides Now" as well as "Michael from the Mountains," "Sisters of Mercy" and "La Chanson Des Vieux Amants." Joshua Rifkin's deft orchestration is harmonious and complements Collins' vocals and material. *In My Life* (Elektra, 1966, prod. Mark Abramson) ♪♪♪♪ features songs by Bob Dylan, Leonard Cohen, Bertolt Brecht and Kurt Weill. This is also Collins' first recording to include her own work. *Whales & Nightingales* (Elektra, 1970, prod. Mark Abramson) ♪♪♪♪ includes her rendition of "Amazing Grace," which sets the tone for an introspective recording on which nearly every selection is tenderly wrought.

what to avoid: *Hard Times For Lovers* (Elektra, 1979) WOOF! is slick, pretentious, woefully outdated and imminently forgettable. *Shameless* (Mesa/Bluemoon 1995) ♪ is an ambitious but flawed effort, blunted by keyboard layers, a drum machine and a full boys choir.

the rest: *Recollections* (Elektra, 1969) ♪♪ *5th Album* (Elektra, 1965) ♪♪♪♪ *Living* (Elektra, 1971) ♪♪♪♪ *Colors of the Day: The Best of Judy Collins* (Elektra, 1972) ♪♪♪ True Stories and Other Dreams *(Elektra, 1973)* ♪♪ Judith *(Elektra, 1975)* ♪♪♪♪ Times of Our Lives *(Elektra, 1982)* ♪♪ Home Again *(Elektra, 1984)* ♪♪♪ Come Rejoice! A Judy Collins Christmas *(Mesa/Bluemoon, 1986)*

Fires of Eden *(Columbia, 1990)* Wind Underneath My Wings *(Laserlight, 1992)* Judy Sings Dylan: Just Like A Woman *(Geffen, 1993)* Baby's Morningtime *(Lightyear, 1993)* Baby's Bedtime *(Lightyear, 1993)* Live at Newport *(Vanguard, 1994)*

worth searching for: On *Innervoices* (RCA, 1989), Collins joins clarinetist Richard Stoltzman for a lovely and haunting set of songs.

Linda Ronstadt, Cowboy Junkies, Emmylou Harris

Woody Guthrie, Pete Seeger, Bob Dylan

Patrick McCarty

Phil Collins

Born Jan. 31, 1951 in London, England

The only thing more surprising than Collins' seamless shift from drummer to lead vocalist after Genesis frontman Peter Gabriel's 1974 departure, was the balding percussionist's transformation into a solo artist more successful than the band. Crafting a stark sound filled with powerhouse drums—Collins was among the first to develop the wide open, reverb-drenched drum sounds that dominated 80s-era records—scratchy guitars, moody keyboards and his own reedy, yet muscular, wail, Collins exploded onto the rock charts with a debut effort that veered from R&B/funk to atmospheric art-rock. Injecting his work with increasing amounts of pop songcraft, Collins was rewarded with a succession of 13 straight Top 10 hits and records that rode a fine line between commercial appeal and creative vision. Eventually, his distinctive sound seeped into Genesis' work, giving the group's albums at least a flavor of his solo efforts. In 1996, his place among the biggest names in rock assured, Collins announced he was leaving the band he'd performed with for more than two decades in order to concentrate on his solo career.

what to buy: As a near-perfect marriage of Collins' emerging songwriting and production chops, *Face Value* (Atlantic, 1981, prod. Phil Collins and Hugh Padgham) details the disintegration of Collins' first marriage through innovative tunes that range from the atmospheric bombast of "In the Air Tonight" to the greasy, horn-drenched funk of "I Missed Again/Behind the Lines." Nearly as impressive is Collins' third solo outing, *No Jacket Required*, (Atlantic, 1985, prod. Phil Collins and Hugh Padgham) which presents the singer's aggressively commercial formula in full bloom—as evidenced by hits such as the danceable "Sussudio" and the heartbreak ballad "One More Night."

what to buy next: As the next step in Collins' seemingly unshakeable domination of 80s-era pop radio, *...But Seriously* (Atlantic, 1989. prod. Phil Collins and Hugh Padgham) featured his take on somber subjects, ruefully addressing homelessness in the smash hit "Another Day in Paradise."

what to avoid: Generally, Collins' attempts to step outside the traditional album format have brought terrible results. Several of his efforts—the collection of 12-inch dance remixes *12ers*, (Atlantic, 1988, prod. Phil Collins and Hugh Padgham) WOOF! the soundtrack to the film *Buster* (Atlantic, 1988, prod. Various) WOOF! and a live record *Serious Hits...Live!* (Atlantic, 1990, prod. Phil Collins and Robert Colby) WOOF!—are serious wastes of recording tape.

the rest: *Hello, I Must Be Going* (Atlantic, 1982) *Both Sides* (Atlantic, 1993)

worth searching for: To get an idea of just how good a drummer Collins is, check out his work with the 70s-era British jazz-fusion band Brand X, conveniently collected on the compilation *Xtrax* (Passport, 1986, prod. Brand X)

Seal, Howard Jones, Mike + the Mechanics

Peter Gabriel, Earth Wind and Fire, Motown

see also: *Genesis*

Eric Deggans

Paul Collins Band

See: The Beat

Christine Collister

See: Clive Gregson & Christine Collister

Shawn Colvin

Born Shanna Colvin, Jan. 10, 1958 in Vermillion, S.D.

Colvin picked up her first guitar when she was 10, and after high school she chose to pursue music full-time. During 70s, she moved to Texas to join a swing band, the Dixie Diesels, then spent a few years in San Francisco before settling in New York. There she played in the Buddy Miller Band, a pop group, before deciding to start working on her own. Influenced by the likes of Joni Mitchell, and later, Suzanne Vega—a patron of sorts who used Colvin for backup vocals on the hit "Luka" and as an opening act on tour—Colvin's poetic lyrics, flawless finger-picking and alternately guitar tunings gave her songs a distinctive character, while her voice, breathy and gentle, is capable of swelling with strength and emotion when necessary. An independently released live album in 1988 attracted attention from the record industry, as did thorough gigging on the East Coast club circuit. Though she tends to take her time between albums, Colvin remains a writer and performer of rare and special abilities.

what to buy: Colvin's debut, *Steady On,* (Columbia 1989, prod. Shawn Colvin, John Leventhal and Steve Addabbo) ♪♪♪♪ offers an excellent balance of Colvin's crystal clear vocals, poetic lyrics and folk influences, along with the accompaniment and contributions of a full band—plus guests David Sandborn, Bruce Hornsby and Vega. Nearly every song's gem, though the album closes on a yawn with the string-laden "The Dead of Night"—which was, unfortunately, a sign of things to come.

what to avoid: *Cover Girl* (Columbia 1994, prod. Shawn Colvin, Stewart Smith and David Kahne) ♪ seemed promising on paper, with Colvin covering songs by others, including personal favorites from Bob Dylan, The Police, Talking Heads and Tom Waits. But she doesn't deliver. The same over-production that burdened "The Dead of Night" hamper Colvin's renditions on this album. Take "Every Little Thing (He) Does Is Magic," in which lush strings divert the ears from her beautiful guitar picking. In concert she has done these songs with just her acoustic guitar, and that's been fine. Sometimes more isn't better.

the rest: *Fat City* (Columbia, 1992) ♪♪ *A Few Small Repairs* (Columbia, 1996) not available for rating

worth searching for: *Live '88* (Plump Records, 1988/1995. prod. Carol Young) ♪♪♪♪ is Colvin's live independent album, which has been reissued on CD. Many of the songs wound up on *Steady On*, and while we miss some of the arrangements from that album, Colvin still carries the songs with the purity of her guitar and vocals.

▶▶ Jewel, Amanda Marshall, Natalie Merchant

◀◀ Tom Waits, Joni Mitchell, Suzanne Vega

Joshua Zarov

Combustible Edison

Formed 1992 in Providence, R.I.

Liz Cox (a/k/a "Miss Lily Banquette"), vocals; Michael Cudahy (a/k/a "The Millionaire"), guitar; Peter Dixon, keyboards; Aaron Oppenheimer, vibes, drums; Nicholas Cudahy, bass

Combustible Edison, along with a handful of other eccentric bands, helped spearhead the retro lounge craze of the mid-90s. Finding its sound and inspiration in the work of "Hi-Fi" pioneers of the 1960s such as Esquivel, Martin Denny, and Les Baxter, as well as atmospheric film composers like Nino Rota and Ennio Morricone, the group fused faux-Polynesian exotica, bachelor pad jazz and creepy, twangy movie music into a bizarre stew that, remarkably, has a consistent vibe of its own without devolving too frequently into kitsch. Guitarist Cudahy offers some pointed, melodically intriguing work; the singing of Cox, unfortunately, is for the most part too mannered to transcend the genre. *I, Swinger* (Sub Pop, 1994, prod. Carl Plaster) ♪♪♪ is a generally engaging effort, featuring the truly unsettling theme from the low-budget horror classic "Carnival of Souls" and the Weill/Brecht number "Surabaya Johnny." *Schizophonic* (Sub Pop, 1996, prod. Carl Plaster and Combustible Edison) ♪♪♪ shows the formula already running out of steam, but still serves its function at a party with a well-stocked bar.

Simon Glickman

Come

Formed 1990 in Boston, Mass.

Thalia Zedek, guitar, vocals; Chris Brokaw, guitar, vocals; Sean O'Brien, bass (1990-95); Arthur Johnson, drums (1990-95)

Lesbian and recovering junkie Zedek, formerly of Live Skull, Uzi, Via and Dangerous Birds, joined with Brokaw (ex-Codiene drummer) and Athens, Ga. musicians O'Brien (Kilkenny Cats) and Johnson (Bar-B-Q Killers); after one Sub Pop 7" ("Cars") the buzz was awesome, but despite rumors of intense major label interest, Zedek's experience with Matador owner Gerard Cosley when he was at Homestead and she was in Live Skull made the decision easy. The band's darkly menacing sound was not constructed from grunge influences but is emotionally akin, with Zedek apparently drawing from her own tortured past life, snarling and spitting the resulting lyrics over gnarled guitar Sonic Youth could envy. After O'Brien and Johnson quit in the summer of '95, Zedek and Brokaw soldiered on with a variety of Chicago rhythm sections.

what to buy: *Eleven:Eleven* (Matador, 1992, prod. Come, Tim O'Heir and Carl Plaster) ♪♪♪♪ delivers Come's sonic bludgeoning in its purest, most compelling form. A cover of the Rolling Stones' "I Got the Blues" pays tribute to one of the band's strongest conceptual sources.

what to buy next: *Don't Ask Don't Tell* (Matador, 1994, prod. Carl Plaster, Mike McMackin, Bryce Goggin and Come) is slightly more aggressive and less drone-oriented than the debut. *Near Life Experience* (Matador, 1996, prod. Not listed) gains stylistic and textural flexibility from the rotating rhythm sections (borrowed from indie stalwarts including Jesus Lizard, Gastr del Sol, and Rachel's). For the first time, Brokaw lead vocals supplement Zedek's exquisitely ravaged singing.

the rest: *The Come EP* (Matador, 1994)

worth searching for: The non-album track "Cimmaron" can be found on the women's causes benefit compilation *Ain't Nothing But a Girl Thing* (London, 1995).

Steve Wynn

Rolling Stones, Neil Young, Live Skull, Swans, Velvet Underground

Steve Holtje

Commander Cody and His Lost Planet Airmen

Formed 1967 in Ann Arbor, Mich.

Commander Cody (George Frayne), piano, vocals; John Tichy, guitar; West Virginia Creeper, steel guitar (1967-70); Billy C. Farlow, harmonica, vocals (1968-76); Bill Kirchen, guitar (1968-76); Bruce Barlow, bass (1968-76); Lance Dickerson, drums (1968-76); Andy Stein, fiddle, saxophone (1968-76); Bobby Black, steel guitar (1970-76); plus others over the years

A band before its time, Commander Cody and the Lost Planet Airmen can be seen as a precursor to the Austin music scene of the 80s. In fact, Austin kingpins Asleep At the Wheel first moved to San Francisco under the influence of the Cody outfit and worked clubs there as a kind of satellite of the pioneering rockabilly/western swing revivalists. The band's first four classic albums laid the groundwork for a whole wing of retro-revisionists in country-rock, as far as possible from the slick Los Angeles hybrid practiced by the Byrds, Poco and others. Cody's crew practiced a loose-jointed, rollicking brand of barroom boogie that sounded like it had been steeped in beer fumes in front of rowdy crowds as ready to fight as dance. Despite scoring a Top 10 hit ("Hot Rod Lincoln") off its debut album, Cody's band was never accorded appropriate acclaim, and the original players splintered in disarray in 1976—though the Commander continues to record and tour with an always changing squadron of Airmen.

what to buy: The first three albums have been cannibalized for an inconsistent collection, *Too Much Fun: The Best Of Commander Cody and his Lost Planet Airmen* (MCA, 1990, prod. Various)

what to buy next: The fourth album, a jaunty concert recording originally titled *Live From Deep In the Heart Of Texas,* has been reissued as *Sleazy Roadside Stories,* (Relix, 1995, prod. S. Jarvis) hard evidence of the original lineup's swinging blend of country and rock 'n' roll.

what to avoid: Without the balance of the Lost Airmen personalities, Cody's solo albums have suffered from contrivance and the unmitigated dominance of his personality, none more so than *Let's Rock* (Blind Pig, 1987), despite the presence of Airmen Kirchen and Barlow.

the rest: *We Got a Live One Here* (Warner Bros., 1976) *Lost In Space* (Relix, 1993) *Relix's Best Of Commander Cody* (Relix, 1995)

worth searching for: The first two, long-deleted albums, *Lost In the Ozone* (Paramount, 1971) and *Hot Licks, Cold Steel and Trucker's Favorites,* (Paramount, 1972) qualify as certified classics in the field. During that period, the band cut a spectacular Christmas song, "Daddy's Drinking Up Our Christmas," which has been rescued from obscurity by *Hillbilly Holiday.* (Rhino, 1988, prod. Various)

solo outings:

Commander Cody: *Ace's High* (Relix, 1990)

Bill Kirchen: *Tombstone Every Mile* (Black Top, 1994) *Have Love Will Travel* (Black Top, 1996)

Asleep At the Wheel, Nick Lowe

Bob Wills, Moon Mullican, Dave Dudley

Joel Selvin

The Commodores /Lionel Richie

Formed 1968 in Tuskegee, Ala.

Lionel Richie Jr., (born 1950 in Tuskegee, Ala.), vocals, piano, saxophone (1968-82); Walter "Clyde" Orange, drums, vocals; Milan Williams, keyboards, trombone, guitar (1968-89); Ronald LaPread,

bass, trumpet (1968-86); William King, Jr., brass, vocals; Thomas McClary, guitar (1968-83); James Dean "J.D." Nicholas, vocals, keyboards (1984-present)

You can mark the evolution of the Commodores' sound by the height of frontman Richie's afro. He piled it high in the early days, when the Commodores were a high-stepping funk outfit following the rock 'n' R&B path paved by Sly & the Family Stone and James Brown, testifying with crotch-thrusters such as "Machine Gun" and "Slippery When Wet" that tested the limits of the family crowds at concerts by the Jackson 5, who the Commodores opened for between 1971-73. Towards the end of the 70s, however, Richie took over and the group took a softer, more conservative trail, specializing in soft—but undeniably melodic—ballads such as "Sail On," "Still" and "Three Times a Lady." In true Motown fashion, it was only a matter of time until Richie spun off into a solo career, which he did with remarkable success during the 80s. The Commodores live on, though the group has never again been the chart denizen it was during the late 70s.

what to buy: *The Commodores Anthology* (Motown, 1995, prod. Various) has it all; the early funk hits, the latter day love songs, the handful of post-Richie triumphs ("Nightshift," "Reach High"). A solid overview of one of the 70s top acts.

what to buy next: *Caught in the Act* (Motown, 1975, prod. James Anthony Carmichael and the Commodores) is vintage, fiery Commodores, before the mush took over. Richie became an obnoxiously ubiquitous presence during the 80s, but his second solo album, *Can't Slow Down* (Motown, 1983, prod. Lionel Richie and James Anthony Carmichael) is a well-crafted, melodic affair loaded with hits such as "All Night Long (All Night)," "Hello" and "Stuck on You."

what to avoid: *Commodore Hits Vol. 1* and *Vol. 2* (both Sound Barrier, 1992, prod. the Commodores) **WOOF!** find the remaining Commodores trio clearly out of ideas, so they re-recorded the group's 70s and early 80s hits. Pathetic.

the rest: *Hot on the Tracks* (Motown, 1976) *Commodores* (Motown, 1977) *All the Great Hits* (Motown, 1982) *All the Great Love Songs* (Motown, 1984) *Nightshift* (Motown, 1985) *Greatest Hits* (Motown, 1991) *Commodores Christmas* (Sound Barrier, 1992) *No Tricks* (Sound Barrier, 1993)

worth searching for: The out-of-print *Midnight Magic* (Motown, 1979, prod. James Anthony Carmichael and the Commodores) is a worth-hearing transitional album that finds the Commodores beginning the shift into highly commercial ballad mode.

solo outings:

Lionel Richie: Lionel Richie (Motown, 1982) *Dancing on the Ceiling* (Motown, 1986) *Back to Front* (Motown, 1992) *Louder Than Words* (Mercury, 1996, prod. Various)

▶▶ Prince, Steve Arrington, Frankie Beverly & Maze

◀◀ Sly & the Family Stone, James Brown, the Temptations, Blood, Sweat & Tears

Gary Graff

Communards

See: Bronski Beat

Concrete Blonde

Formed 1981 in Los Angeles, Calif. Disbanded 1994

Johnette Napolitano, vocals, bass; Jim Mankey, guitar; Harry Rushakoff, drums (1981-89, 1992); Paul Thompson, drums (1989-92, 1993-94); Alan Bloch, bass (1989-90)

Concrete Blonde was built on Napolitano's spooky, quavering voice, which sounds like Chrissie Hynde if she were a practicing witch—a sound that connected seamlessly with Halfnelson/Sparks progressive-rock guitarist Jim Mankey's dramatic plucking. Though the band had one Top 20 hit—the yearning "Joey"—it never fully overcame its complex financial problems. As a result, the trio put out several almost-great albums, sometimes with two or three incredible, distinctively gloomy pop songs, but never fulfilled its potential. The group split up in 1994, with Napolitano forming a new band called Pretty & Twisted.

what to buy: Though overproduced and too polished, *Bloodletting* (I.R.S., 1990, prod. Concrete Blonde with Chris Tsangarides) showcases Napolitano's invitingly dark songwriting. "Tomorrow, Wendy" is a chilling hymn about a woman dying from AIDS, and the stomp of "Days and Days" complements the more measured hit "Joey."

what to buy next: *Walking in London,* (I.R.S., 1992, prod. Concrete Blonde with Chris Tsangarides) which features a downright weird version of James Brown's "It's a Man's Man's Man's World," could have been a successful album but for lack of support from the band's unfocused label.

what to avoid: *Mexican Moon* (Capitol, 1993, prod. Concrete Blonde with Sean Freehill) has some nice ideas, including a snippet of actual conversation by infamous cult killer Jim Jones, it's clearly the band's last gasp.

the rest: *Free* (I.R.S., 1989) *Still in Hollywood* (Capitol, 1994)

worth searching for: Unfortunately, the band never put its soaring version of Leonard Cohen's "Everybody Knows," on a record, though the "Pump Up the Volume" movie and soundtrack (MCA, 1990, prod. Various) used it to great effect.

solo outings:

Johnette Napolitano (with Holly Vincent): ***Vowel Movement*** (Atlantic, 1995) (with Pretty & Twisted): *Pretty & Twisted* (Warner Bros., 1995)

⏩ 4 Non Blondes, Alanis Morissette

⏪ Patti Smith, Pretenders, James Brown, Leonard Cohen

Steve Knopper

Arthur Conley

Born April 1, 1946, in Atlanta, Ga.

Otherwise a relatively minor star, Conley did assure his place in the Southern soul pantheon with "Sweet Soul Music;" a true 60s horn-pumping, soul anthem, it's a literal roll call of homage to the decade's best soul men, name checking Sam Cooke (who is actually responsible for the song's melody) and Otis Redding, who co-wrote the song. Conley's career seemed to lose focus after Redding's death, despite a few minor singles such as "Funky Street" and a cover of the Beatles' "Ob-la di, Ob-la da." Conley eventually moved to Europe. *Sweet Soul Music: The Best of Arthur Conley* (Ichiban, 1995, prod. David Nathan and Harry Young) is an excellent overview, containing many worthwhile lesser-known songs and a detailed history of the artist.

Allan Orski

The Connells

Formed 1984 in Raleigh, North Carolina

Mike Connell guitar, vocals; Doug MacMillan vocals, guitar; George Huntley guitar, vocals; David Connell bass; Peele Wimberley drums; Steve Potak keyboards, organ (1991-present).

Started by two brothers, the Connells quickly struck a responsive chord with the college crowd thanks to its irresistible melodies and jangly guitars. With a solid foundation of songwriting, the Connells had excellent timing as a rush of indie and major label signings swept through the region fueled by R.E.M.'s growing reputation, though the group would never enjoy the same success as many swept along in the same wake. The Connells' rootsy brand of power pop rode the wave of the college charts as "alternative" music went through its changes. With a strong cult audience and a continuous touring schedule, the group enjoyed some regional success and even had some modest commercial success with the 1993 album *Ring* and the singles "Slackjawed" and "74-75." If nothing else, the Connells are survivors, continuing to make viable music both on record and on stage.

what to buy: The Connells' sophomore outing *Boylan Heights* (TVT, 1987 prod. Mitch Easter) is a lively record with catchy songs and exciting harmonies, making for one of the most distinctive college rock albums of the 80s. Highlights include "Scotty's Lament," "Over There" and "Pawns." The follow-up, *Fun & Games,* (TVT, 1989 prod. Gary Smith) continues down the same path, with greater group contributions—in particular more vocals by Huntley.

what to buy next: *One Simple Word* (TVT, 1990, prod. Hugh Jones) has a more commercial feel and really shows off the skilled guitar work of Mike Connell.

what to avoid: Compared to later releases, *Darker Days,* (Black Park, 1986/TVT, 1987, prod. Dave Adams, Steve Gronback, Ron Dash and Don Dixon) the group's debut, sounds like the skeletal outline for what would become a more compelling sound.

the rest: *Ring* (TVT, 1993, prod. Lou Giordano and The Connells) *Weird Food And Devastation* (TVT, 1996, prod. Tim Harper)

worth searching for: The 12-inch single for "Hats Off," (Black Park, 1986, prod. Steve Gronback, Ron Dash, Don Dixon and Joe Harvard) which features re-mixes of the title track, "Darker Days" and an early version of "If It Crumbles."

⏩ Gin Blossoms, Freddy Jones Band, Wilco, Son Volt, Jayhawks

⏪ R.E.M., dBs, Wire Train

John Nieman

Gary Lee Conner

See: Screaming Trees

Van Conner

See: Screaming Trees

Continental Drifters

Formed 1990 in Los Angeles, Calif.

Peter Holsapple, guitar, keyboards, vocals; Susan Cowsill, vocals, guitar, mandolin; Vicki Peterson, vocals, guitar; Mark Walton, bass; Robert Mache, guitar; Rob Ladd, drums; Carlo Nuccio, drums (1990-95); Gary Eaton, vocals, guitar (1990-94); Ray Ganucheau, guitar (1990-94)

On the strength of a 1992 single and a 1994 indie album, the Drifters were named one of Rolling Stones' "Best Unsigned Bands" of 1994. That's a lot of hype to live to, but the band members can handle the pressure: between them they've lived through several lifetimes of hype as members of other bands. Holsapple was a founder of the celebrated early 80s power pop band the dBs; Cowsill was the ingenue in the 60s pop band with her mom and brothers, the Cowsills; Peterson was the underrated lead guitarist in the Bangles; and Nuccio used to play in a New Orleans bar band called the Continental Drifters that eventually evolved into the subdudes. Despite its power-pop pedigree, these Drifters play a rambling survey of American music that recalls nothing short of The Band and includes folk, rock, pop, country and soul in its stylistically mixed bag. The group is in the midst of a major-label feeding frenzy and is dogged by constant rumors that Holsapple—who has done stints as keyboardist for R.E.M. and Doobie... er, Hootie and the Blowfish during 1996—has become a permanent Blowfish and that the Drifters have broken up. Not true: there's too much promise for this band to give up yet.

what to buy: *Continental Drifters* (Monkey Hill/Ichiban, 1994, prod. Continental Drifters) ♪♪♪♪ is the group's only full release to date, and it's a must-own for any fan of roots-rock. It features catchy originals like "Mixed Messages" but also covers Michael Nesmith's almost-forgotten chestnut "Some of Shelly's Blues" and even the Box Tops' "Soul Deep."

worth searching for: The original lineup worked the LA club scene and created a buzz at the start of the 90s, and released one single, *The Mississippi* b/w *Johnny Oops* (Singles Only Label, 1992), a label based in New York.

solo outings:

Peter Holsapple and Chris Stamey: *Mavericks* (Rhino New Artists, 1991, prod. Holsapple and Stamey) ♪♪♪

▶▶ Son Volt, Wilco, Jayhawks, subdudes

◀◀ The Byrds, the Band, Gram Parsons, Nitty Gritty Dirt Band

see also: *dBs, The Bangles*

Gil Asakawa

Ry Cooder

Born Ryland Peter Cooder, March 15, 1947 in Los Angeles, Calif.

Eschewing trends and sticking stubbornly to the roots, guitarist Ry Cooder was exploring indigenous North American and world music long before it became fashionable. But Cooder's no scholarly purist. From his first recordings with Taj Mahal and Rising Songs during the 60's, his guitar work—particularly his slide playing—has been as earthy and intuitive as the deepest blues and has led to countless "hired gun" studio gigs with the Rolling Stones, Eric Clapton and Little Feat, among others). On his solo outings, Cooder invariably uncovers and reinterprets lost gems of country and urban blues, r&b, gospel and Tex Mex, often blending in textures and mixing styles from a global melting pot of rootsy sources. He is one of the few musicians who could bring Eddie Vedder and Pakistani singer Nusrat Fateh Ali Khan together—as he did for the "Dead Man Walking" soundtrack—and make the synthesis work. Cooder has also composed numerous film scores, and in 1992 he joined longtime cohorts Jim Keltner, John Hiatt and Nick Lowe in the band Little Village. He remains one of America's truest musical treasures.

what to buy: Of his many fine solo records, *Paradise & Lunch* (Reprise, 1974, prod. Lenny Waronker and Russ Titelman) ♪♪♪♪♪ is Cooder's warmest and most enduring—a peerless collection of remakes ("Fool For A Cigarette," "It's All Over Now," "If Walls Could Talk") performed by an extraordinary group of musicians from widely divergent backgrounds - a Cooder trademark. With its rougher-edged mix of vintage blues, barroom laments, Tex-Mex accordion and Hawaiian slack-key guitar, *Chicken Skin Music* (Reprise, 1976, prod. Ry Cooder) ♪♪♪♪ is also highly recommended.

what to buy next: *Music By Ry Cooder* (Warner Archives, 1995, prod. Various) ♪♪♪♪ is a superb two-CD sampler of Cooder's atmospheric soundtrack work from films such as "Paris, Texas," "The Long Riders" and "Southern Comfort." Some of Cooder's greasiest guitar playing can be heard on *Live & Let Live,* (Rounder, 1993, prod. Ry Cooder) a record he produced for bluesmen Bobby King & Terry Evans. *Talking Timbuktu* (Hannibal, 1994, prod. Ry Cooder) is Cooder's masterful collaboration with Malian guitarist Ali Farka Toure - backed by a band combining African musicians and blues-rooted local talent such as Gatemouth Brown and Jim Keltner.

what to avoid: Compared to his usual high standards, *The Slide Area* (Reprise, 1982, prod. Ry Cooder) falls flat.

the rest: *Ry Cooder* (Reprise, 1970) *Into The Purple Valley* (Reprise, 1972) *Boomer's Story* (Reprise, 1972); *Jazz* (Reprise, 1978) *Bop Till You Drop* (Reprise, 1978) *Borderline* (Reprise,1980) *Get Rhythm* (Reprise, 1987) *Pecos Bill* (with Robin Williams) (Windham Hill, 1988, prod. Mark Sottnick and Ry Cooder) *A Meeting By The River* with V.M. Bhatt (Water Lily Acoustics, 1993)

worth searching for: The one live album in Cooder's catalog, *Show Time* (Reprise, 1976) is also his only album not available on CD. The vinyl or cassette is well worth a search.

▶▶ John Hiatt, Los Lobos, Jim Dickinson, Daniel Lanois, Robbie Robertson

◀◀ Blind Willie Johnson, The Golden Gate Quartet, Gabby Pahinui, Sleepy John Estes, Joseph Spence, Little Walter

see also: *Little Village*

Doug Pippin

Sam Cooke

Born Jan. 22, 1935 in Chicago, Ill. Died Dec. 11. 1964 in Los Angeles, Calif.

Producer Jerry Wexler always thought Cooke has the greatest voice of his generation. Considering Wexler made all those great records with Ray Charles and Aretha Franklin, among others, that's quite a recommendation. Cooke's life story is practically a parable for the story of soul music itself—from the innocence of shouting gospel to a sordid death outside a hooker's seedy hotel room. He became one of the first major black artists to establish his creative self-determination with a major label. He laid the cornerstones of the music called soul.

As the lead vocalist (and sex symbol) of a top sanctified gospel group, the Soul Stirrers, Cooke had to hold his first pop sessions in secret, releasing the results under a pseudonym to relative indifference. But his next single, "You Send Me," went No. 1 in 1957, and Cooke never looked back. He not only expertly explored a vast broad cross-section of music on his own recordings—blues, supper club pop, epic ballads, Top 40 jive—but he wrote and produced brilliantly for other artists. His extraordinary impact cannot be over estimated; the pure sound in his throbbing, sensual voice intoxicated so many other vocalists—as well as listeners—that his style continues to echo throughout the pop scene long after his death. But his many and momentous accomplishments still live, well preserved in a number of different collections of his work.

what to buy: *The Man And His Music* (RCA Victor, 1986, prod. Various) documents his commercial successes, from the early Soul Stirrers records to the towering final ballad, "A Change Is Gonna Come," over the chronological course of 28 selections. But no picture of Sam Cooke can be complete without *One Night Stand: Live At the Harlem Square Club 1963,* (RCA Victor, 1985, prod. Hugo & Luigi) which provide sweaty, smoky persuasive evidence of his mesmerizing powers over an audience from the scene of the crime.

what to buy next: His expressions covered so many different areas, there are at least three immediately rewarding areas to investigate. *Night Beat,* (Abkco, 1995, prod. Al Schmidt) his 1963 small combo late-night blues album, was one of soul's lost masterpieces until its digital release. *Sam Cooke With the Soul Stirrers* (Specialty, 1991, prod. Various) is surely some of the most sublime gospel vocals ever put to record. And *Sam Cooke's SAR Story* (Abkco, 1994, prod. Various) is a two-disc box that commemorates his skills as a writer and producer on one disc of rare gospel and another disc of obscure pop songs that originally appeared on his own record label.

what to avoid: The man could sing pages from the phone book and make it sound wonderful, although *Hits Of the '50s* (RCA Victor 1961 prod. Hugo and Luigi) is as close to a pointless exercise of his talents as anything Cooke ever did.

the rest: *The Best Of Sam Cooke* (RCA Victor, 1963) *At the Copa* (Abkco, 1987) *The Rhythm and the Blues* (RCA Victor, 1995)

worth searching for: A number of rewarding selections that did not find their way onto CD remain resting on the original vinyl version of his album *Shake,* (RCA Victor, 1965) a collector's item that draws large bounties in record stores these days.

▶▶ Otis Redding, Marvin Gaye, Rod Stewart, Steve Perry

R.H. Harris, Kylo Turner, Charles Brown

Joel Selvin

Alice Cooper

Born Vincent Furnier, Feb. 4, 1948 in Detroit, Mich.

Cooper wasn't the world's first shock rocker; Screamin' Jay Hawkins and Arthur Brown and his Crazy World were direct forebears. But Cooper was the first to take it to theatrical extremes with the snakes, hacked-up baby dolls, guillotines and gallows that populate his stage shows. With Cooper, the show was the thing—particularly during his early 70s heyday—and that usually obscured some good rock 'n' roll he and his band were cranking out at the time. Though raised in Phoenix, Cooper brought his band to Detroit during the late 60s, and the group schooled itself on the burgeoning Motor City rock of the MC5 and Stooges. Guitarist Michael Bruce, Cooper's main foil in the early days, churned out Stones-ish guitar hooks and taught rock melodies, over which the singer laid out his macabre tales of "Dead Babies" and "Sick Things." But with "I'm Eighteen," Cooper created a "Smells Like Teen Spirit" for the post-hippie generation, and his well-orchestrated shock spectacle took things from there, generating controversy over issues that seem comparatively tame today. Over the years, Cooper's music has been as good as his collaborators; guitarists Dick Wagner and Steve Hunter filled in after Cooper dropped his original band, and gun-for-hire Desmond Child helped craft some 80s hits. But while he continues to record, Cooper will always be the guy with the girl's name, who wore mascara, played with snakes and alternately entertained and freaked out audiences of a quarter century ago.

what to buy: Absent a good box set—which has been rumored to be coming for several years now—*Alice Cooper's Greatest Hits* (Warner Bros., 1974, prod. Various) is the essential singles collection and proof that there's more to Cooper than a cheap-thrills horror show. Of the individual albums, *Love it to Death* (Warner Bros., 1971, prod. Bob Ezrin) still holds its own as an early angst rock touchstone, with "I'm Eighteen" and "Black JuJu" among the standout tracks.

what to buy next: *Killer,* (Warner Bros., 1971, prod. Bob Ezrin) *School's Out* (Warner Bros., 1972, prod. Bob Ezrin) and *Billion Dollar Babies* (Warner Bros., 1973, prod. Bob Ezrin) are all entertaining efforts with songs to serve both radio listeners and concert attendees. *Classicks* (Epic, 1995, prod. Various) highlights Cooper's brief 80s resurgence ("Poison," "Hey Stoopid"), though nothing holds up to the six older songs that are represented via live renditions.

What Album Changed Your Life?

"Neil Young's Tonight's the Night (Reprise, 1975). It was just like, I couldn't believe it. It was so intense, yet still had some kind of whacked sense of humor to it. It was an amazingly scary album but you could still laugh at it because everyone sounded so fucked up. It was funny and frightening at the same time."

Brian Henneman (The Bottle Rockets, Uncle Tupelo)

what to avoid: Either of Cooper's mid-80s "comeback" albums—*Constrictor* (MCA, 1986, prod. Beau Hill and Michael Wagener) or *Raise Your Fist and Yell* (MCA, 1987, prod. Michael Wagener) WOOF!—that mistakenly tried to maneuver him into the heavy metal camp.

the rest: *Pretties For You* (Straight, 1969/Enigma Retro, 1989) *Easy Action* (Straight, 1970/Enigma Retro, 1989) *Muscle of Love* (Warner Bros., 1974) *Welcome to My Nightmare* (Warner Bros., 1975) *Alice Cooper Goes to Hell* (Warner Bros., 1976) *Lace and Whiskey* (Warner Bros., 1977) *The Alice Cooper Show* (Warner Bros., 1977) *From the Inside* (Warner Bros., 1978) *Flush the Fashion*(Warner Bros., 1980) *Special Forces* (Warner Bros., 1981) *Zipper Catches Skin* (Warner Bros., 1982) WOOF! *DaDa* (Warner Bros., 1983) WOOF! *Prince of Darkness* (MCA, 1989) *Trash* (Epic, 1989) *Hey Stoopid* (Epic, 1991) *Lie at the Whiskey A-Go-Go 1969* (Rhino EP, 1992) *The Last Temptation* (Epic/Sony, 1994)

worth searching for: *The Beast of Alice Cooper,* (Warner Bros., 1989, prod. Various) an import collection that's slightly more thorough than *Greatest Hits* But, please, bring on that box set already!

Ozzy Osbourne, Kiss, Motley Crue, Gwar, Guns N' Roses

Little Richard, the Crazy World of Arthur Brown, the Stooges, the MC5, Boris Karloff, Bela Lugosi

Gary Graff

Julian Cope /Teardrop Explodes

Born October 21, 1957, in Deri, Mid Glamorgan, Wales. Teardrop Explodes formed 1979, in Liverpool, England. Disbanded 1983.

Julian Cope (, vocals, bass, synthesizers; David Balfe, organ, piano, marimba; Gary Dwyer, drums; Michael Finkler, guitar (1979-1981); Troy Tate, guitar (1981-1982)

If high aspirations and good intentions were everything, Cope would be one of the world's greatest popular musical figures. An iconoclast with a spaced-out head and a heart of gold, the one-time frontman for Liverpudlian psychedelic pop/rockers The Teardrop Explodes has neither an interesting enough singing voice nor the musical smarts to bring his wild-eyed concepts to complete fruition. And yet, for music fans seeking edgy guitar pop placed in the service of global concerns, Cope offers occasional bursts of genius within an oeuvre that is never simply ordinary. Along with Echo and the Bunnymen and to some extent the Psychedelic Furs, The Teardrop Explodes helped usher in the spacier side of post-punk. Unlike the other groups, though, its music was bright and straightforward; only its lyrics were fuzzy and complex. The band quickly built a large following in Britain, and Cope, true artiste that he is, became uneasy and broke up the group. He soon surfaced with two very strange and decidedly uncommercial albums, *World Shut Your Mouth* (which does not include the hit song of the same name) and *Fried.* Apparently having changed his mind about being a smug, self-indulgent auteur, Cope rebounded with his two most accessible efforts, 1987's *Saint Julian* (which *does* include the driving, sassy "World Shut Your Mouth") and the more laidback, 60s-ish *My Nation Underground*, which is probably the best Cope album for non-Cope fans. Since then, he's entered a period of utter conceptual weirdness, beginning with two "official" bootlegs, *Skellington* and *Droolian,* both of which are better left to die-hard collectors. Next up was his massive trilogy dedicated to the planet's environmental and spiritual problems, followed most recently by the more upbeat *20 Mothers* On it, at least the bouncy "Try, Try, Try" presented new evidence that Saint Julian still has a few infectious numbers left in him.

what to buy: After a period of drug-induced haziness, *Saint Julian* (Island, 1987, prod. Ed Stasium and Warne Livesey) 𝄞𝄞𝄞𝄞 marked Cope's return to form. "World Shut Your Mouth," one of his best singles, is the best-known track, but "Trampolene" heads a list of several other memorable cuts.

what to buy next: *Floored Genius: The Best of Julian Cope and the Teardrop Explodes, 1979-91* (Island, 1992, prod. Various) 𝄞𝄞𝄞½ provides a good overview, although it stops short of his three most recent albums. Also, the concepts which have been so important to his recent work are lost in a compilation format. Of the three releases since, *Jehovahkill* (Island, 1992, prod. Julian Cope and Donald Ross Skinner) 𝄞𝄞𝄞½ is the best—more listenable than the extravagant *Peggy Suicide,* yet more ambitious and varied than *Autogeddon,* the entire three-phase magnum opus features strong material and savvy production. Of The Teardrop Explodes' two original releases, the debut, *Kilimanjaro* (Mercury, 1980, prod. Bill Drummond and David Balfe, Clive Langer and Alan Winstanley) 𝄞𝄞𝄞½ was the more consistent. Once somewhat groundbreaking, this album now seems moderate in its power pop approach, especially in light of Cope's 90s work.

what to avoid: Wildly self-indulgent and uncompromising in its weirdness, the double-LP *Peggy Suicide* (Island, 1991, prod. Julian Cope and Donald Ross Skinner) 𝄞𝄞 generally goes too far off the deep end, although the guitars snarl ferociously and there are a few strong tunes (the Caribbean-influenced "Beautiful Love," for instance).

the rest: The Teardrop Explodes: *Wilder* (Mercury, 1981) 𝄞𝄞𝄞 Julian Cope: *World Shut Your Mouth* (Mercury, 1984) 𝄞𝄞𝄞 *Fried* (Mercury, 1985) 𝄞𝄞½ *My Nation Underground* (Island, 1988) 𝄞𝄞𝄞½ *Autogeddon* (American, 1994) 𝄞𝄞𝄞 *20 Mothers* (American, 1995) 𝄞𝄞½

Icicle Works, Inspiral Carpets, Psychedelic Furs, the Outfield

The Jam, Syd Barrett, the Kinks, the Doors

Bob Remstein

Stewart Copeland /Klark Kent/Animal Logic

Born on July 16, 1952 in Alexandria, Egypt

Interviewed for a technical magazine, Copeland once said his compositional technique consisted of playing rhythms into a computer and assigning pitches later—an approach that makes a strange kind of sense, considering the drummer's bent toward creating herky-jerky, eccentric sounds. Born the son of a CIA official, Copeland moved in the mid 70s to England, where he joined progressive rockers Curved Air. Once that band dissolved in 1986, he assembled the Police with a former schoolteacher on bass (Sting) and an ex-Animals member on guitar (Andy Summers). Continually frustrated by Sting's exercise of control, Copeland turned to solo projects early on to satisfy his songwriting muse. Working as Klark Kent, he released a punky, off-kilter album in 1982 before composing the score for Francis Ford Coppola's film "Rumble Fish." In 1985, the same year Sting announced a sabbatical from the group that would turn into a full-fledged departure, Copeland offered another solo record—this time under his own name—documenting his collaborations with various African musicians. Soundtracks for the films "Wall Street" and "Talk Radio" expanded his film credentials just before the drummer formed another rock band, Animal Logic, with bassist Stanley Clarke and vocalist-songwriter Deborah Holland. But the group collapsed after two albums, unable to reconcile Copeland's and Clarke's unique instrumental approaches into songs radio-friendly enough to make a difference. Instead, Copeland found success composing "King Lear" for the San Francisco Ballet and writing two operas—"Holy Blood and Crescent Moon" and "Horse Opera."

what to buy: Certainly Copeland's most listenable post-Police work came with Animal Logic, the only thing approaching a pop project he's tackled since his first band's demise. Animal Logic's second record, *Animal Logic II*, (I.R.S., 1991, prod. Animal Logic, Tony Berg and Frankie Blue) ♪♪♪½ finds the band getting over the initial shock of playing together and digging into the compositions more, adding subtle textures to moody laments like "Through a Window" and "Rose-Colored Glasses."

what to buy next: As the perfect extension of his white-guy reggae grooving with the Police, Copeland's *The Rhythmatist* (A&M, 1985, prod. Stuart Copeland and Jeff Seitz) ♪♪♪ neatly presages future pop stars' preoccupation with Third World flavors. Be warned, though, that this is heady and adventurous stuff, channeling mind-blowing African influences through Copeland's own twisted vision of rhythm and melody.

what to avoid: Copeland's early punk work as Klark Kent was particularly stinky—immortalized on the collection *Kollected Works*, (I.R.S. 1995, prod. Stewart Copeland) WOOF! as tuneless and non-sensical as the Police were melodic and well-crafted.

the rest: *Klark Kent* (I.R.S., 1980) ♪½ *Rumble Fish* (A&M, 1983) ♪♪½ *The Equalizer and Other Cliff Hangers* (I.R.S., 1988) ♪♪½ *Animal Logic* (I.R.S., 1989) ♪♪♪

worth searching for: The Police's "Synchronicity Concert" video (A&M, 1983), for a look at the drummer in his most effective element—behind a drum kit driving one of the greatest rock bands ever.

▶▶ Manu Katche, Jars of Clay

◀◀ Edgar Varese, Frank Zappa

Eric Deggans

Corrosion of Conformity

Formed 1982 in Raleigh, N.C.

Woody Weatherman, guitar; Reed Mullin, drums, vocals; Mike Dean, bass, vocals (1982-90, 1994-present); Phil Swisher, bass (1990-94); Eric Eycke, vocals (1982-86); Simon Bob, vocals (1986-90); Karl Agell, vocals (1990-94); Pepper Keenan, vocals, guitar (1990-present)

Corrosion of Conformity merit respect simply by not sitting still, by not finding one particular metal groove comfort zone and staying there ad nauseum. When it started, C.O.C. played a blazing blend of punk and metal—one of the first to do so. But when others followed, C.O.C. slowed the tempos and mined a more dark and ominous vein; pre-grunge, if you will. But when everyone and their flannel shirt followed that route, C.O.C. switched again, broadening its sonic palette just in time for its major label debut, *Deliverance*. Without question one of the most ambitious and inventive hard rock bands in the land, C.O.C. has influenced many of those who have leaped beyond it in the sales column. Its day will come, too.

what to buy: *Deliverance* (Columbia, 1994, prod. John Custer) ♪♪♪♪ steps away from grunge mode and finds C.O.C. adding more subtle sounds to its attack, such as the weepy pedal steel of "Shelter," though the thundering "Heaven's Not Overflowing" and "Pearls Before Swine" prove C.O.C. hasn't gone soft on us.

what to buy next: *Deliverance's* predecessor, *Blind* (Relativity, 1991/Columbia, 1995, prod. John Custer and C.O.C.) ♪♪♪½ thrashes a bit more, though "Dance of the Dead" and "Vote With a Bullet" won over traditional metal audiences and even the harder edge of the metal crowd.

what to avoid: With 21 songs, *Eye For an Eye* (Caroline, 1983/1995, prod. C.O.C.) ♪♪ is an impressively prolific debut, but it's also a lot of songs played pretty much the same way.

the rest: *Animosity* (Metal Blade, 1985) ♪♪♪ *Technocracy*

(Metal Blade, 1987) *Wise Blood* (Columbia, 1996) not available for rating

worth searching for: *Nola,* (Elektra, 1995) from a surprisingly cohesive side project called Down formed by Keenan, Pantera singer Phil Anselmo and members of Crowbar and Eye Hate God.

Pantera, Soundgarden, Alice in Chains

MC5, Black Sabbath, ZZ Top, Lynyrd Skynyrd, Black Flag, Samhain

Gary Graff

Elvis Costello

Born Declan Patrick McManus, Aug. 25, 1954 in London, England

Costello and his band, The Attractions (keyboardist Steve Nieve, bassist Bruce Thomas and drummer Pete Thomas), were among the chief proponents of the British new wave. Emerging during the height of the punk era, Costello combined that form's anger with an astonishing sense of songcraft that combined beautiful melody with a smart and biting lyricism; it's no accident that Paul McCartney invited Costello to collaborate with him during the late '80s and into the '90s. Costello's two decades of recording, with and without the Attractions, has generated an impressive output of pop music as any of his contemporaries. His first three albums—*My Aim Is True*, *This Year's Model* and *Armed Forces*, all produced by fellow new waver and erstwhile pub-rocker Nick Lowe—form one of the most impressive pop trilogies ever. Since then, Costello has remained an intriguing, important and changing artist, unafraid to cover country songs (*Almost Blue*) or to record with a string quartet (*The Juliet Letters*). We may not always like it, but we always check it out. (Note: Costello's Columbia catalog was reissued by Rykodisc during 1993-94, with appropriate bonus tracks for each album.)

what to buy: *This Year's Model* (Columbia, 1978, prod. Nick Lowe) —Costello's second album and first with the Attractions—is Costello's first great album, showcasing spectacular hooks, a delightfully venomous tone and ace songs such as "Pump it Up," "Radio Radio" and "The Beat.' '*Armed Forces* (Columbia, 1979, prod. Nick Lowe) brilliantly continues along the same vein, with instant classics such as "Oliver's Army," "Accidents Will Happen" and the Lowe-penned "What's So (Funny 'bout Peace Love and Understanding)." *Imperial Bedroom* (Columbia, 1982, prod. Geoff Emerick) is as impassioned and varied an album as you'll find in his ouevre, a collection of lushly produced pop songs, aching ballads and film noir-influenced narratives. *King Of America* (Columbia, 1986, prod. J. Henry (T- Bone Burnett) and Declan Patrick Aloysius MacManus) is an exceptional album, marked by Costello's decision to record with T-Bone Burnett and use three members of the other Elvis (Presley)'s T.C.B. band. The ventures into rockabilly territory, along with biting commentaries on American culture, are worth the price of admission.

what to buy next: *My Aim is True* (Columbia, 1977, prod. Nick Lowe) is a phenomenal debut album notable for the Costello classics "(The Angels Wanna Wear My) Red Shoes," "Alison" and "Watching The Detectives." As is typical for the best Costello albums it sounds as good today as it did when it was originally released. *Get Happy!* (Columbia, 1980, prod. Nick Lowe) is a purely fun Costello outing, remarkably consistent over its whopping 21 songs—including excellent covers (Sam and Dave's "I Can't Stand Up For Falling Down," the Merseybeats' "I Stand Accused") and fine Costello originals such as "High Fidelity" and "Riot Act." *Blood and Chocolate* (Columbia, 1986, prod. Nick Lowe and Colin Fairley) marks something of the end of an era; it was Costello's final album for Columbia, and his last with the Attractions for eight years. But with Lowe back in the producer's chair, it contained all the elements that had won Costello notoriety in the first place.

what to avoid: *Goodbye Cruel World* (Columbia, 1984, prod. Clive Langer and Alan Winstanley) is the one Costello album that should never have been made, listless and uninspired and one he even acknowledges is his worst album with The Attractions.

the rest: *Taking Liberties* (Columbia, 1980) *Almost Blue* (Columbia, 1981) *Trust* (Columbia, 1981) *Punch The Clock* (Columbia, 1983) *The Best of Elvis Costello and the Attractions* (Columbia, 1985) *Out of Our Idiot* (Demon U.K., 1987) *Girls, Girls, Girls* (Columbia, 1989) *Spike* (Warner Bros., 1989) *Mighty Like A Rose* (Warner Bros, 1991) *The Juliet Letters* (Warner Bros., 1993) *2 1/2 Years* (Rykodisc, 1993) *Brutal Youth* (Warner Bros., 1994) *The Very Best of...Elvis Costello and the Attractions 1977-86* (Rykodisc, 1994) *Kojak Variety* (Warner Bros., 1995) *All This Useless Beauty* (Warner Bros., 1996)

worth searching for: The bootleg *Our Aim Is True* (Slipped Disc) contains the demos Costello did with his first band, Flip City. Highlights include his rendition of "Knockin' On Heaven's Door" and early versions of "Radio, Radio" ("Radio Soul") and "Living In Paradise."

▶▶ The Clash, The Jam, Richard Thompson, Joe Jackson, Nick Lowe, Rockpile, Dave Edmunds, Graham Parker, Madness, The Specials, The English Beat, Squeeze, The Pogues, Kirsty MacColl, Any Trouble, Ian Dury, Wreckless Eric, Billy Bragg, Paul McCartney, T-Bone Burnett, John Hiatt, Crowded House, Peter Case, John Wesley Harding, Roger McGuinn, Aimee Mann

◀◀ Hank Williams, The Beatles, The Rolling Stones, The Byrds, Stax, Motown Booker T & the MGs, George Jones, Johnny Cash, Bob Dylan, The Band, Randy Newman, Gram Parsons, Brinsley Schwarz, Van Morrison, Bruce Springsteen

Marc Fenton

Count Five

Formed 1965 in San Jose, Calif.

Ken Ellner, vocals; John Michalski, guitar; Sean Byrne, guitar; Roy Chaney, bass; Craig Atkinson, drums

If you've got to be a one-hit wonder, you couldn't do better than Count Five's "Psychotic Reaction" in 1966. Like some twisted Yardbirds cover band sprinting on high octane, the harp, thump and wail of this single still packs a wallop. This single is available on numerous compilations. You may be better off with the various artists collection *Nuggets: Classics from the Psychedelic 60s* (Rhino, 1986, comp. Bill Inglot) ♪♪♪♪ rather than the import *Psychotic Reaction: The Complete Psychotic Reaction* (Performance, 1994) which gives you the hit plus 17 other songs—which may be about 17 more than you want from this band.

Patrick McCarty

Counting Crows

Formed 1991 in San Francisco, Calif.

Adam Duritz, vocals, piano, harmonica; David Bryson, guitar, vocals; Dan Vickrey, guitar; Charlie Gillingham, keyboards, vocals; Matt Malley, bass, guitar, vocals; Steve Bowman, drums (1991-94); Ben Mize, drums (1994-present)

Counting Crows first made news subbing for Van Morrison and performing his "Caravan" at a Rock and Roll Hall of Fame induction ceremony, but the band established itself as a pop powerhouse with their guest-filled debut album, *August and Everything After (DGC, 1993, prod. T-Bone Burnett)* The Crows' rootsy, melodic rock draws heavily—almost to derivative levels—on the work of Morrison and Bob Dylan, as well as other classic rock icons. The single "Mr. Jones" (with its ironic line "I wanna be Bob Dylan") was a smash hit, though the band is taking its time finishing a follow-up.

Simon Glickman

Country Joe and the Fish

Formed 1966 in Berkeley, Calif. Disbanded 1970. Re-formed 1977.

Country Joe McDonald, vocals, guitar; Barry Melton, guitar; David Cohen, keyboards, guitar (1965-69); Bruce Barthol, bass (1965-68); John Francis Gunning, drums (1965-66); Paul Armstrong, washboard (1965-1966); Chicken Hirsh, drums (1965-69); Mark Ryan, bass (1968-69).

Largely forgotten as one of the giants of psychedelic rock, Country Joe and the Fish towered over their contemporaries and left behind one masterpiece album, their first—*Electric Music for the Mind And Body*—one of the definitive albums of American acid rock. Like the psychedelic scene itself, the album mixed the trippy and bizarre with the jocular and whimsical, and crafted folk-pop with adventuresome experimentation, electric blues with political satire. Both McDonald and Melton, who grew up next door to Woody Guthrie in Brooklyn, brought decided folk backgrounds with them to the free-wheeling band they founded. The Berkeley-based group qualified as one of the original five Fillmore headliners, although these days the Fish are not regarded in the same breath as the Grateful Dead and Jefferson Airplane. The original, high-spirited group of hippies began to dissolve after its third album; by the time the group made its famous appearance at the 1969 Woodstock Festival, only McDonald and Melton remained. The group disappeared altogether the following year, although McDonald continued a fruitful and active musical career. Melton was recently appointed a public defender attorney in Mendocino County, Calif.

what to buy: Even the official greatest hits collection includes seven of the 11 tracks from the band's 1967 debut, *Electric Music for the Mind and Body,* (Vanguard, 1967, prod. Sam Charters) ♪♪♪♪♪ one of the first albums to carry the sound of the San Francisco ballrooms across the country.

what to buy next: The band's second album was recorded so quickly after the debut that the group made do with less potent pieces from its existing repertoire. At least it saved the Vietnam era's No. 1 anthem, "I-Feel-Like-I'm-Fixin'-to-Die Rag," for this album. Coupled with McDonald's elegant elegy to his romance with the girl singer from Big Brother and the Holding Company, "Janis," the two side-openers lifted *I-Feel-Like-I'm-Fixin'-To-Die Rag* (Vanguard, 1967, prod. Charters) above the ordinary.

what to avoid: By the time the original group started to fall apart, the band had recorded three albums, and nothing on the subsequent two albums, *Here We Are Again* (Vanguard, 1968) and *C.J. Fish*, (Vanguard, 1970, prod. Tom Wilson) added anything to the band's repertoire.

the rest: *Together* (Vanguard, 1968) *The Life and Times of Country Joe and the Fish* (Vanguard, 1971) *The Collected Country Joe and the Fish* (Vanguard, 1987)

worth searching for: Two authentic Country Joe and the Fish psychedelic artifacts have been brought into the digital domain. *Collectors Items: The First Three EPs* (One Way, 1994, prod. Not Listed) captures the early Berkeley records that launched the band in the Bay Area, while *Live! At the Fillmore West* (Vanguard, 1996, prod. Bill Belmont) may want for superb sonics but contains the rare sound of a genuine ballroom jam—a free-for-all celebrating the original group's final performance with such guests as Steve Miller, Jerry Garcia, Jorma Kaukonen, Jack Casady and Mickey Hart joining the fray.

solo outings:

Country Joe McDonald: *The Best of Country Joe* (Vanguard, 1990) *Thinking of Woody Guthrie* (Vanguard, 1970) *Paradise with an Ocean View* (Fantasy, 1975) *Country Joe Classics* (Fantasy, 1989) *Tonight I'm Singing Just for You* (Vanguard, 1970/One Way, 1995) *Into the Fray* (Rag Baby, 1981) *Peace on Earth: The Vietnam Experience* (Rag Baby 1985/One Way 1995) *Superstitious Blues* (Rykodisc, 1991) *Carry On* (Line, 1994)

▶▶ B-52's, Boomtown Rats, Tom Robinson Band

◀◀ Woody Guthrie, Reverend Gary Davis, Big Brother and the Holding Company

Joel Selvin

Dave Cousins

See: The Strawbs

Cowboy Junkies

Formed 1979 in Toronto, Ontario, Canada

Margo Timmins, vocals; Michael Timmins, guitar; Peter Timmins, drums; Alan Anton, drums

Teetering between hypnotic and narcoleptic, ambient and ambivalent, the Cowboy Junkies snared attention in the late-80s by reducing such hallowed country and rock staples as Neil Young's "Powderfinger," the Velvet Underground's "Sweet Jane," Patsy Cline's "Walking After Midnight" and Hank Williams' "I'm So Lonesome I Could Cry" to moody shadows of their former selves. After two failed rock bands, guitarist Michael Timmins drafted siblings Margo and Peter to join him and drummer Alan Anton in the Cowboy Junkies, which debuted on Canada's Latent Records in 1986 with *Whites Off Earth Now*, consisting mostly of covers of blues classics and Bruce Springsteen's "State Trooper." The group's major-label debut, 1988's *The Trinity Session*, was recorded direct to DAT in an abandoned church for $250 and spotlighted Margo Timmins' trance-like murmuring against a gloomy backdrop of fiddles, mandolins and pedal steel guitars. When it explores the thin line between regret and anguish, pain and suffering, the Cowboy Junkies offer an ethereal catharis. But when the group starts fumbling around in its self-created darkness, it sometimes forget the difference between chilling and merely cold.

what to buy: Listeners who prefer Bruce Springsteen's *Ghost of Tom Joad* to *Born to Run* no doubt worship *The Trinity Session*, (RCA, 1988, prod. Peter Moore) which established the Junkies as minimalist visionaries. But *Black Eyed Man* (RCA, 1992, prod. Michael Timmins) remains the group's masterpiece, swinging rather than lurching and tweaking its atmospheric sound by adding two missing ingredients—melody and hope. Highlights include "If You Were the Woman and I Was the Man," a duet with John Prine, and "A Horse in the Country," a stirring lament about marital restlessness.

what to buy next: Switching to a new label and new producer, the Junkies experiment with strings and a more traditional rock approach on *Lay It Down* (Geffen, 1996, prod. Michael Timmins and John Keane) "A Common Disaster" rocks without sacrificing the group's trademarks, "Angel Mine" is sweetly melodic and "Speaking Confidentially" borders on funk. At last, a Junkies album you can listen to while operating heavy machinery.

what to avoid: *200 More Miles: Live Performances 1985-1994* (RCA, 1995, prod. Michael Timmins) is a tepid two-CD collection released solely to fulfill the band's contract with RCA.

the rest: *Whites Off Earth Now* (RCA, 1990) *The Caution Horses* (RCA, 1990) *Pale Sun, Crescent Moon* (RCA, 1993)

worth searching for: A haunting treatment of another sacred country-rock cow, the Rolling Stones' "Dead Flowers," turns up on the 12-inch promotional single for *'Cause Cheap Is How I Feel* (RCA, 1990)

⏩ Lisa Germano, Dead Can Dance

⏪ Hank Williams, Velvet Underground, Patsy Cline

David Okamoto

The Cowsills

Formed 1965, in Newport, R.I.

Barbara Cowsill, vocals (died Jan. 31, 1985); Bill Cowsill, guitar, vocals; Bob Cowsill, guitar, vocals; Dick Cowsill, vocals; Paul Cowsill, keyboards, vocals; Barry Cowsill, bass, vocals; John Cowsill, drums; Susan Cowsill, vocals

They proudly called themselves America's First Family of Song, and though some Jacksons might take issue, there's no denying that for two brief years during the late 60's, these all-singing, all-playing Rhode Islanders made musical history (they were MGM Records' top-selling act in 1968) along with some undeniably sunshine-sweet music. Formed by father William "Bud" during the mid-60s, the Cowsill clan was a fixture on the (all-ages) New York club scene before releasing its first record in late 1967. Within a year, the group produced two innovative, harmony-drenched Top 10 hits of distinction, "Indian Lake" and the classic "The Rain, The Park and Other Things." Sporting the same genetic blend that has always been the trademark of the best musical households—from the Beach Boys to the Bee Gees and beyond—the clan had in Bill and Bob two writers and arrangers of sufficient merit to make even its albums' filler tracks surprisingly solid (for example, the near-Brian Wilsonesque complexities of "Poor Baby"). Unfortunately, after one last hit in 1969 (the theme from the musical "Hair"), the Cowsills' fresh-scrubbed, milk-boosting image began to work against them, unfairly tossing the group into the unhip heap long before its time—but not before they'd been Xeroxed and made into a weekly television series (yes, those Partridges were but a poor Hollywood imitation Cowsill Family). *The Best Of The Cowsills* (Polydor, 1988/Rebound, 1994, prod. Various) ♪♪♪♪ is just what it says: the songwriting and choice of cover material is strong throughout, the playing is joyful and spirited, the singing is truly breath-taking—and li'l Susie sure could beat a mean tambourine, couldn't she? For a step beyond that, *The Cowsills In Concert* (Razor & Tie, 1993, prod. Bill and Bob Cowsill) ♪♪♪ captures all the action circa '69 of a shriek-drenched public appearance by this First Family. Following their mother's death, various Cowsills continued performing and recording, both together and separately. Susan worked not only with husbands Dwight Twilley and Peter Holsapple, but in the Psycho Sisters and Continental Drifters with ex-Bangle Vicki Peterson. Bill, meanwhile, has spent the past decade in Canada with his band The Blue Shadows, which are rightly hailed as one of the architects of the new-country scene.

Gary Pig Gold

Cracker

See: Camper Van Beethoven

The Cramps

Formed 1975 in New York, N.Y.

Lux Interior (born Erick Lee Purkhiser), vocals; Poison Ivy Rorschach (born Christine Marlana Wallace), guitar; Brian Gregory, guitar (1976-80); Pam Gregory, drums (1975); Miriam Linna, drums (1975-77); Nick Knox (born Nicholas Stephanoff), drums (1977-90); Kid Congo Powers (born Brian Tristan), guitar (1980-82); Candy Del Mar, bass (1990-present)

In the explosion of punk, this neo-rockabilly band seemed to emerge from some sort of primeval ooze, its members as scary as the swampy music they played. First under the control of the mysterious Brian Gregory (who left one day and was never seen again), the band sails along in the 90s under the unerring leadership of junk culture lovers Lux Interior and Poison Ivy Rorschach (who has moved from second guitar to lead guitar, writer, producer and cover model). Few other couples have been further steeped in the arcane world of trash culture, and their music is all the better for it, virtually creating the tasty subgenre of psychobilly.

what to buy: *Bad Music for Bad People* (I.R.S., 1984, prod. the Cramps and Alex Chilton) ♪♪♪♪ is an early compilation from the Cramps' first few recordings, not a bad place to start exploring the swampy, murky early stuff. After years of legal wrangling and a virtual disappearance from U.S. releases, *Stay Sick!* (Restless, 1990, prod. the Cramps) ♪♪♪♪ brings the band's power and edge back stronger than ever on funny, uncompromising rockers.

what to buy next: *Songs the Lord Taught Us,* (I.R.S., 1980/1989, prod. Alex Chilton) ♪♪♪ an album as important for its historical significance—it's the Cramps full-length debut—

as well as for its throbbing version of "Tear It Up" and "T.V. Set."

what to avoid: *Psychedelic Jungle,* (I.R.S., 1981/1989, prod. the Cramps) while not a horrible album, seems to find the band a bit dazed, minus Gregory and with the addition of Kid Congo Powers from Gun Club. It's made a bit more worthwhile when paired with the *Gravest Hits* EP (I.R.S., 1979, prod. Alex Chilton) on the 1989 CD reissue.

the rest: *Smell of Female* (Enigma EP, 1983) *A Date with Elvis* (Big Beat, 1986); *Look Mom, No Head!* (Restless, 1991) *Flame Job* (Medicine, 1994)

worth searching for: *Rockin' 'n' Reelin' in Auckland New Zealand,* (Vengenance, 1987) an authorized bootleg from one night on the *A Date with Elvis* tour, with two otherwise unavailable Presley covers—"Do the Clam" and "Heartbreak Hotel."

▶▶ Reverend Horton Heat, Jason and the Scorchers

◀◀ Hasil Adkins, Ed Wood, Ed Gein

Roger Catlin

The Cranberries

Formed 1990 in Limerick, Ireland

Dolores O'Riordan, vocals, guitar; Noel Hogan, guitar; Mike Hogan, bass; Feargal Lawler, drums

When former church choir member O'Riordan joined with the brothers Hogan and Lawler, the band's name was The Cranberry Saw Us (say the last name fast). They gave her a tape of guitar chords, and O'Riordan came up with "Linger," one of the hits from the group's debut *Everybody Else Is Doing It, So Why Can't We.* (Island, 1993, prod. Stephen Street) That album introduced the band's lush folk-pop style to the world, and the world bought it—making the Cranberries one of the most popular newcomers of the decade. It remains the essential purchase, though the group's two succeeding albums are also worthwhile. *No Need To Argue* (Island, 1994, prod. Stephen Street) is a continuation of the group's gentle, Celtic-influenced music, though the hit "Zombie" hits hard, both sonically and politically. *To The Faithful Departed* (Island, 1996, prod. Bruce Fairbairn) goes even further in that direction, with a rawer sound that reflects hard rock producer's Fairbairn's touch.

Anna Glen

Cranes

Formed 1986 in Portsmouth, England

Alison Shaw, vocals, bass; Jim Shaw, drums, piano, guitar; Mark Francome, guitar (1989-present); Matt Cope, guitar (1989-present)

The Shaw siblings bought an eight-track recorder during the late 80s and made private cassettes before their 1989 vinyl release *Self Non Self* was played by taste-making BBC deejay John Peel, who did a session with the Shaws. They made the cover of Melody Maker and Dedicated Records signed them, after which Francombe and Cope were drafted into the group. Alison Shaw's breathy, shy vocals are easily overwhelmed, so much of the instrumentation is subdued, with lots of acoustic guitar strumming, harpsichord-style keyboards and string arrangements, with screaming shards of electric guitar usually entering only between verses.

what to buy: *Wings of Joy* (Dedicated/Arista, 1991, prod. Cranes) is delicate, at times almost frightened, but includes some impressive guitar maelstroms. Considering that the songs on the sturdier *Forever* (Dedicated/Arista, 1993, prod. Cranes) have titles such as "Cloudless," "Jewel" and "Far Away," the textures (and the matching stasis-evoking chord progressions) seem appropriate. If Shaw's hyper-girlish singing makes it nearly impossible to understand what everything's about, this is so masterfully constructed that it's highly evocative even if you don't really know what of.

What to Buy Next *Loved* (Dedicated/Arista, 1994, prod. Cranes) is confident and more instrumentally competent, though in a way, that drains some of the uniqueness that gives this band its charm.

the rest: *Self Non Self* (Biteback!, U.K., 1989/Dedicated-Arista, 1992)

▶▶ Mazzy Star

◀◀ Cocteau Twins, Joy Division, Foetus, Lydia Lunch

Steve Holtje

Crash Test Dummies

Formed late 80s in Winnipeg, Manitoba, Canada

Brad Roberts, vocals, guitar, piano; Benjamin Darvill, mandolin, harmonica; Ellen Reid, piano, keyboards, accordion, vocals; Dan Roberts, bass; Michel Dorge, drums

This folk-influenced pop outfit took Canada by storm in 1991 with its debut album, *The Ghosts That Haunt Me,* (Arista, 1991, prod. Steve Berlin) which featured the Canadian smash hit "Superman's Song." Although the band hails from Winnipeg, which spawned the Guess Who and BTO, it owes more stylistically to XTC, Leonard Cohen and Talking Heads; songwriter-leader-singer Brad Roberts possesses a lush baritone with remarkable range and sounds a bit like Bauhaus vocalist Peter Murphy. With the release of the second album, *God Shuffled His Feet,* (Arista, 1993, prod. Jerry Harrison and Crash Test Dummies) the group scored a pair of international hits—"MMM MMM MMM MMM" and "Afternoons & Coffee Spoons"—that boosted its stature beyond its homeland.

the rest: *A Worm's Life* (Arista, 1996) not available for rating.

William Hanson

Robert Cray

Born August 1, 1953 in Columbus, Ga.

From the minute Cray arrived on the national scene, with 1983's *Bad Influence,* he was marked as the blues' best hope for mass appeal. He was, after all, a handsome man with a soulful, pleasing voice, a stinging, true blues guitar attack and an ear for nifty pop hooks. Indeed, Cray became the blues' first modern pop star three years later with *Strong Persuader*, his major label debut. Since then, his music has become ever more R&B-based and, unfortunately, largely less interesting. While his guitar playing and singing have only improved over the years, he has sadly lost some of the sense of fun and buoyancy which made his early music so special. But the strength of his most recent effort, *Some Rainy Morning,* provides hopeful indications that Cray may have turned the corner on creative stagnation. His success on early albums—and on 1996's *Tribute to Stevie Ray Vaughan*—suggests that one way he may enliven his work in the future is to occasionally turn to the past for material.

what to buy: *Bad Influence* (Hightone, 1983, prod. Bruce Bromberg and Dennis Walker) is illuminated by that special spark which separates great music from good. Some of the performances may be a tad sloppy, but the album swings with a robust energy while spotlighting Cray's songwriting, his sense of humor ("So Many Women, So Little Time") and his ability to seamlessly incorporate soul, rock and pop touches into his blues. *Strong Persuader* (Hightone/Mercury, 1986, prod. Bruce Bromberg) contains most of the same traits as well as better production values and a more pristine sound. Cray proved his true blue mettle with *Showdown!,* (Alligator, 1985, prod. Bruce Iglauer and Dick Shurman) his sparkling collaboration with Albert Collins and Johnny Copeland.

what to buy next: On *Some Rainy Morning,* (Mercury, 1995, prod. Robert Cray) Cray rebounds nicely after several mediocre albums, ditching the horn section and producing a taut, fiery album.

what to avoid: Cray followed *Strong Persuader*'s success by trying to force out pop songs on *Don't Be Afraid of the Dark,* (Hightone/Mercury, 1988) a bad move for a guy who is basically a natural pop tunesmith anyhow.

the rest: *Who's Been Talkin'* (Tomato, 1980/ Atlantic, 1986) *False Accusations* (Hightone, 1985) *Midnight Stroll* (Mercury, 1990) *I Was Warned* (Mercury, 1992) *Shame + A Sin* (Mercury, 1993)

worth searching for: *Black Heart White Hand,* (Buccaneer, 1991) a solid bootleg from a 1987 show in Philadelphia which offers a good indication of Cray's live skills as well as an encore version of "The Crawl" with the Fabulous Thunderbirds.

▶▶ Joe Louis Walker, Kenny Wayne Shepherd

◀◀ Hubert Sumlin, Eric Clapton, B.B. King, Albert Collins, Magic Sam, O.V. Wright, Johnny "Guitar" Watson, Howlin' Wolf

Alan Paul

Crazy Horse

Formed 1969 in Calif.

Ralph Molina, drums; Billy Talbott, bass; Frank "Pancho" Sampedro, guitar (1975-present); Danny Whitten, vocals, guitar (1969-1972)

Called the "greatest garage band of all-time," Crazy Horse is best know as the powerful backing band on many of Neil Young's most memorable albums. Talbott, Molina, and Whitten first came together in 1962 as Danny and the Memories and were briefly known as The Rockets before hooking up with Young on the seminal album *Everybody Knows This Is Nowhere.* Powerful three-chord guitar work, feedback, and just plain noise (in the best sense of the word) are the band's sonic trademarks. While the band has released several solo outings (none since 1981's *Left for Dead,*) it's best work has definitely been backing Young, with whom the band has recorded 14 albums, including two live sets. Original member Whitten died of a drug overdose in 1972, a death that was eulogized on vinyl in Young's "The Needle and the Damage Done" off 1975's *Tonight's the Night.*

what to buy: *Crazy Horse* (Reprise, 1971, prod. Bruce Botnick) is the band's first outing without Young as a frontman. The presence of Jack Nitzsche and Nils Logren make this the only consistently strong Crazy Horse solo album—later efforts were unfocused and rambling, especially when compared to the band's very strong performances behind Young.

what to avoid: *At Crooked Lake* (Epic, 1973) is unfocused, rambling and is plagued by unusually sloppy guitar work.

the rest: *Loose* (Reprise, 1971) *Crazy Moon* (RCA, 1978) *Left for Dead* (Curb, 1981)

▶▶ Black Crowes, Jayhawks

◀◀ Rolling Stones, Yardbirds, Buffalo Springfield

see also: *Neil Young*

Brad Morgan

Cream

Formed 1966 in London, England. Disbanded 1968.

Eric Clapton, guitar, vocals; Jack Bruce, bass, harmonica, vocals; Ginger Baker, drums, vocals

During its relatively short lifespan, Cream revolutionized rock 'n' roll. For the first time, three established rock stars left three separate groups and joined forces—Clapton from the Yardbirds and John Mayall's Bluesbreakers, Baker from the Graham Bond Organization and Bruce from Graham Bond and the Manfred Mann band. They opted for the demanding trio format instead of the standard four- or five-piece band. In the span of just two years and four albums (more were released afterward), Cream blazed a trail for power trios, supergroups and wide-ranging, adventuresome music making. The group created crisp pop songs that were perfect for radio as well as fierce, rambling jams that combined the brute force of rock with the technical demands of jazz improvisation and a touch of the blues' emotional depth. The trio's excessive volume and exceptional talent set new standards for rock, and its music remains a major influence even 30 years later. Superstar egos, as well as Clapton's ravenous demands for new challenges, prompted Cream to split up in November 1968. (A box set anthology is expected in late 1996 or early 1997.)

what to buy: Cream's dual identities—disciplined singles band and full-tilt concert jammers— merge magnificently on *Wheels of Fire* (Polydor, 1968, prod. Felix Pappalardi) The first disc is a solid studio session ("White Room," "Born Under a Bad Sign," "Sitting on Top of the World") but it's the four-song second disc that captures the trio at maximum power, swooping and diving like jet fighters in an aerial display. Clapton's explosive lead halfway through "Crossroads," lightning fast with startling tone, is one of the greatest rock-guitar solos ever recorded.

what to buy next: Although trapped in 60s psychedelia, *Disraeli Gears* (Polydor, 1967, prod. Felix Pappalardi) displays Cream's pop sensibility ("Strange Brew," "Tales of Braves Ulysses") without any loss of its blues-rock power ("Sunshine of Your Love," "Outside Woman Blues"). The band's debut, *Fresh Cream*, (Polydor, 1966, prod. Robert Stigwood) offers melodic, blues-based rock with what would prove to be uncharacterisitc restraint. *Strange Brew: The Very Best of Cream* (Polydor, 1983, prod. Felix Pappalardi and Robert Stigwood) is a fine compilation focusing on the singles.

what to avoid: The spirit was gone when Cream bade farewell in concert at Royal Albert Hall on November, 26, 1968, and it shows in the four self-indulgent live tunes on *Goodbye* (Polydor, 1969, prod. Felix Pappalardi)

the rest: *Live* (Polydor, 1970) *Live, Volume 2* (Polydor, 1972); *The Very Best of Cream* (Polydor, 1995)

worth searching for: *Secret History*, a two-disc bootleg of studio outtakes and BBC radio performances that's an illuminating complement to Cream's legitimate releases.

▶▶ The Jimi Hendrix Experience, Mountain, ZZ Top, Van Halen

◀◀ Robert Johnson, Muddy Waters, Willie Dixon, Alexis Korner, Charlie Parker

David Yonke

Creedence Clearwater Revival

Formed 1959 in El Cerrito, Calif. Disbanded 1972

John Fogerty, guitar, vocals; Tom Fogerty, guitar (1959-71); Stu Cook, bass; Doug Clifford, drums

Widely dismissed as a Top 40 band at the time, the work of Creedence Clearwater has endured to become recognized as classic American rock. At the height of the group's career, Creedence outsold the Beatles and auteur rocker John Fogerty crafted a dozen or more records that would be known as rock standards. When the band first began, it was an after-school enterprise conducted in one of their parents' garages called the

Blue Velvets. But when John's older brother joined, the band turned more professional; Tommy Fogerty and the Blue Velvets notched a modest 1961 hit on local radio, before returning to the realm of high school dances and frat parties as the Golliwogs.

But when John Fogerty cut an eight and a half-minute version of the Dale Hawkins oldie, "Suzie Q," and the tape landed on the legendary San Francisco underground radio station KMPX, the newly named Creedence Clearwater Revival vaulted from playing tiny unknown clubs to the marquee of the Fillmore Auditorium almost overnight. An edited version became the group's first nationwide hit, but in 1969, "Proud Mary" exploded Creedence into the top ranks of rock bands of the day.

Nine consecutive Top 10 hits later, the band began to disintegrate when Tom Fogerty left the group and the other three members agreed to equally share songwriting responsibilities. One album after that, the band was finished and mastermind John Fogerty entered the studio by himself to record an album of country and western staples. But Creedence left behind a luminous body of work that has only grown more lustrous over the years—one of the great American rock and roll originals.

what to buy: Author Stephen Kings thinks *Cosmo's Factory* (Fantasy, 1970, prod. John Fogerty) ♪♪♪♪♪ is the best rock album ever. He may be right. The group's sixth album finds the band at the peak of its powers on an album crowded with five hit singles, reworkings of first-generation rock gems and an epic eleven-minute workout on "I Heard It Through the Grapevine."

what to buy next: Although *Chronicle* (Fantasy, 1976, prod. John Fogerty) ♪♪♪♪ offers a fairly comprehensive overview on the band's hits, the prime Credence albums—*Born On the Bayou*, (Fantasy, 1969, prod. John Fogerty) ♪♪♪♪ *Green River*, (Fantasy, 1969, prod. John Fogerty) ♪♪♪♪ *Willy and the Poor Boys* (Fantasy, 1969, prod. John Fogerty) ♪♪♪♪—provide a deeper, richer look at the band with album tracks every bit as persuasive as the hit singles.

what to avoid: The last album, *Mardi Gras* (Fantasy, 1971, prod. John Fogerty) WOOF!, featured only the three Blue Velvets and may have been one of the worst albums ever released by a major band.

the rest: *Creedence Clearwater Revival* (Fantasy, 1968) ♪♪♪ *Live In Europe* (Fantasy, 1987) WOOF! *The Concert* (Fantasy, 1980) ♪ *Chronicle, Volume Two* (Fantasy, 1986)

worth searching for: The bootleg *Fantasy Session '70* (Main Street) ♪♪♪♪ features nearly 70 minutes of CCR jamming with hero Booker T. Jones on a combination of Fogerty originals and soul covers.

▶▶ The Hollies, Bob Seger, Bruce Springsteen

◀◀ Booker T. and the MGs, Elvis Presley, Little Richard

see also: *John Fogerty*

Joel Selvin

Marshall Crenshaw

Born Nov. 11, 1953 in Detroit, Mich.

Since he wears glasses, writes and sings mostly his own material, and plays guitar, Crenshaw was likened to Buddy Holly when his debut album was released in 1982. And while artists have every reason to resent being called "the next" anybody, in this case the reference did legitimately point to Crenshaw's musical roots; for further proof, check out the hard-to-find promotional single for "Cynical Girl," which features a live and very evocative performance Holly's "Rave On." And let's not forget that he portrayed Holly in the Ritchie Valens bio-flick, "La Bamba." But Crenshaw's roots include all great pop music that preceded him, including the Beatles; he played John Lennon in one production of Beatlemania. The *Marshall Crenshaw* album instantly established him as a comer, but it was also Crenshaw's commercial peak; never an MTV favorite, he explored various nuances of sophisticated pop music-making to (mostly) critical raves and little more than cult-level notoriety. Crenshaw has soldiered on nonetheless, continuing to record as well as writing a book about the evolution of rock music in film ("Hollywood Rock")

what to buy: *Marshall Crenshaw* (Warner Bros., 1982, prod. Richard Gottherer and Marshall Crenshaw) ♪♪♪♪♪ is filled with catchy, up-tempo pop songs that sound as vibrant today as they did in 1982. An essential album for any rock collection.

what to buy next: For some reason, *Field Day* (Warner Bros., 1983, prod. Steve Lillywhite) ♪♪♪♪ was attacked by many of the same people who championed Crenshaw's first album—a bunch of hooey, since the album, while not as polished as the debut, is another collection of excellent songs. After a bit of stylistic drifting in the interim, *Life's Too Short* (Paradox/MCA, 1991, prod. Ed Stasium) ♪♪♪♪ (MCA) marks a return to form that should please long-time fans and newcomers alike. Ditto *Miracle of Science*, (Razor & Tie, 1996, prod. Marshall Crenshaw) ♪♪♪♪ which boasts many of Crenshaw's most celebrated attributes and enjoys a tighter focus as his first self-produced album.

what to avoid: *Good Evening* (Warner Bros., 1989, prod. David Kershenbaum and Paul McKenna) is the weakest of the lot, with the best songs coming from other writers.

the rest: *Downtown* (Warner Bros., 1985) *Mary Jean & 9 Others* (Warner Bros., 1987) *Live...My Truck is My Home* (Razor & Tie, 1994)

worth searching for: Prior to the release of *Life's Too Short*, MCA released the excellent—but promotional only—career retrospective *Marshall Crenshaw: A Collection.* (Paradox/MCA, 1991, prod. Various)

▶▶ Matthew Sweet, BoDeans, Hootie & the Blowfish, Toad the Wet Sprocket

◀◀ The Beatles, Buddy Holly, the Everly Brothers, Arthur Alexander, Motown

Michael Isabella

Peter Criss

See: Kiss

Jim Croce

Born Jan. 19, 1943 in Philadelphia, Penn. Died Sept. 20, 1973 in Natchitoches, La.

By the end of the 60s, folk music had evolved from themes of social relevance to issues of personal introspection at the hands of artists such as Joni Mitchell and Gordon Lightfoot. Enter Jim Croce, a singer-songwriter from the East who captured everyman themes in his easygoing folk-pop music. Croce's warm, reassuring voice gave his songs a universal appeal, and he enjoyed tremendous success during the early 70s with humorous uptempo hits ("Bad, Bad Leroy Brown," "Workin' at the Car Wash Blues") and heartfelt ballads ("Operator (That's Not the Way It Feels)," "Time in a Bottle"). His career was cut painfully short in 1973 when a plane carrying Croce and his lead guitarist Maury Muehleisen crashed. His death was a major loss to music, a fact that is proven by the enduring quality and timeless appeal of his songs.

what to buy: *Photographs & Memories: His Greatest Hits* (WEA/Atlantic, 1974, prod. Terry Cashman and Tommy West) is a must-have compilation that gives ample evidence of Croce's humorous side ("Bad, Bad Leroy Brown," "You Don't Mess Around with Jim," "Workin' at the Car Wash Blues") and his soft, romantic side ("Operator," "Time in a Bottle," "New York's Not My Home"). All the cuts are remastered, and the sound is terrific. *24 Carat Gold in a Bottle* (Digital Compact Classics, 1994, prod. Terry Cashman and Tommy West) is a 24K gold disc that ups the ante with 24 tracks of hits and lesser-known songs.

what to buy next: *50th Anniversary Collection* (WEA/Atlantic, 1992, prod. Terry Cashman and Tommy West) is a comprehensive two-CD set covering Croce's career, from 1969-73. In addition to the hits, the collection features many lesser-known LP tracks, including "Rapid Roy (The Stock Car Boy)" and a cover of the Red Ingles novelty hit "Cigarettes, Whiskey and Wild, Wild Women." All tracks have been digitally remastered from the original master tapes, and the set includes vital liner notes from Croce's wife, Ingrid.

what to avoid: *Down the Highway* (WEA/Atlantic, 1975, prod. Terry Cashman and Tommy West) is a slick compilation that offers too few hits and too many lesser-known songs that offer little insight to Croce's mastery.

the rest: *I Got a Name* (Capitol, 1973) *Time in a Bottle: Greatest Love Songs* (Atlantic, 1976)

worth searching for: Recorded during Croce's last tour in the summer of 1973, *Live: the Final Tour* (Saja, 1973, prod. Terry Cashman and Tommy West) is an intimate look at the singer-songwriter's ability to hold an audience and turn a tale. While it's light on the hits, many of the other tunes (including "New York's Not My Home" and "Hard Time Losin' Man") receive nice turns.

▶▶ Don McLean, Cat Stevens, Jackson Browne, Jesse Winchester, Dan Fogelberg, Lyle Lovett

◀◀ Paul Simon, Gordon Lightfoot, Joni Mitchell, James Taylor

Christopher Scapelliti

David Crosby

See: Crosby, Stills and Nash

Crosby, Stills and Nash /Crosby, Stills, Nash and Young/David Crosby/Crosby & Nash/Graham Nash/Stephen Stills

Formed 1968 in Los Angeles, Calif.

David Crosby (born August 14, 1941 in Los Angeles, Calif.), guitar, vo-

cals; Stephen Stills (born January 3, 1945 in Dallas, Texas), guitar, bass, keyboards, vocals; Graham Nash (born February 2, 1942 in Blackpool, England) guitar, keyboards, vocals; Neil Young (born November 12, 1945 in Toronto, Canada), guitar, vocals

One of the most celebrated and enduring of the late '60s supergroups, Crosby, Stills and Nash—with and without Neil Young—continued and built on musical foundations initiated with their previous bands. Crosby was in the Byrds, Stills and Young formed Buffalo Springfield and Nash was a signature voice in the Hollies. The decision to use their last names, in fact, stemmed from the desire not to be thought of as just another band but as a group of individuals who worked together when it felt right. Formed as a trio to record their first album, the blend of CSN's voices combined with the songwriting skills of each—as well as Stills' musical proficiency—became a cornerstone of the Southern California folk-rock movement. With the addition of Young and his darker, more contemplative songs, CSNY became a powerful voice of the times, infusing desperate love songs and political theory with the same emotional harmonies. Though dogged by periodic personality conflicts and assorted substance abuse addictions (which necessitated Crosby's liver transplant in 1994), the original trio seems inextricably drawn together, though their last work with Young was in 1988.

what to buy: *Crosby, Stills & Nash* (Atlantic, 1969, prod. CSN) is an impressive blend of voice and guitar, beginning with Stills' complex and timeless "Suite: Judy Blue Eyes" and continuing through Nash's bouncy "Marrakesh Express," Crosby's paean to Robert Kennedy, "Long Time Gone," and the apocalyptic fairy tale, "Wooden Ships." The first album with Young, *Deja Vu* (Atlantic, 1970, prod. CSNY) solidified the quartet's status as *the* superstar American band of the Woodstock generation. With a hippie anthem by Crosby ("Almost Cut My Hair"), Stills' guitar heroics ("Carry On"), Nash's sing-along tunes ("Our House," "Teach Your Children") and Young's introspective "Helpless," they still found room for another songwriter's work (Joni Mitchell's "Woodstock"). *So Far,* (Atlantic, 1974, CSNY and Bill Halverson) a greatest hits package after only two albums, contains the high points of the first two releases as well as the scathing single that came out in the wake of the Kent State shootings, "Ohio/Find the Cost of Freedom"

what to buy next: The four-CD box set *CSN* (Atlantic, 1991, prod. Graham Nash and Gerry Tolman) is filled with strong material from all of the musicians' incarnations—solo and apart—but may be for serious fans only. The first two discs are essential; it's the final one, comprised of latter day solo and CSN recordings, that's hard to listen to all the way through. The live *4 Way Street* (Atlantic, 1971, prod. CSNY) became more attractive after it was expanded with four more songs on the 1992 CD reissue in 1992, but it may put off casual listeners who prefer the polish of the group's studio work. Crosby, Stills and Nash's solo albums have seldom been as satisfying as the group efforts, but a few worthwhile, notably: Crosby's *If I Could Only Remember My Name* (Atlantic, 1971, prod. David Crosby) Stills' *Stephen Stills* (Atlantic, 1972, prod. Stephen Stills and Bill Halverson) and *Manassas* (Atlantic, 1972, prod. Chris Hillman, Dallas Taylor and Stephen Stills) and the short-lived Stills-Young Band's *Long May You Run* (Reprise, 1976, prod. Stephen Stills)

what to avoid: *Live It Up,* (Atlantic, 1990, prod. CSN, Joe Vitale and Stanley Johnston) a phone-in effort where the voices sound as synthetic as the layered keyboards backing them up. The exception: Stills' "Haven't We Lost Enough?"

the rest: CSNY: *American Dream* (Atlantic, 1988) CSN: *CSN* (Atlantic, 1977) *Replay* (Atlantic, 1980) *Daylight Again* (Atlantic, 1982) *Allies* (Atlantic, 1983) *After the Storm* (Atlantic, 1994)

worth searching for: The promotional CD single for *Chippin' Away,* (Atlantic, 1989, prod. CSN, Stanley Johnston and Craig Doerge) a song the trio—with guest James Taylor—recorded as a reaction to the fall of the Berlin Wall. It was rush-released to radio but never made it on a CSN album.

solo outings:

David Crosby: *Oh Yes I Can* (A&M, 1989) *Thousand Roads* (Atlantic, 1993) *It's All Coming Back To Me Now* (Atlantic, 1995)

Crosby & Nash: *Graham Nash/David Crosby* (Atlantic, 1972) *Crosby-Nash Live* (Atlantic, 1975) *Wind on the Water* (MCA, 1973) *Whistling Down the Wire* (ABC, 1976) *Best of Crosby & Nash* (Atlantic, 1978)

Graham Nash: *Songs for Beginners* (Atlantic, 1972) *Wild Tales* (Atlantic, 1974) *Earth and Sky* (Capitol, 1980) *Innocent Eyes* (Atlantic, 1986)

Stephen Stills: *Stephen Stills 2* (Atlantic, 1971) *Down the Road* (Atlantic, 1973) *Stills* (Columbia, 1975) *Illegal Stills* (Columbia, 1976) *The Best of Stephen Stills* (Atlantic, 1977) *Thoroughfare GapMDBR* (Columbia, 1978)

Live (Atlantic, 1979) *Right by You* (Atlantic, 1984) *Stills Alone* (Vision, 1991)

America, the Eagles, Poco, Michael Hedges

The Beatles, Bob Dylan, the Everly Brothers, Fred Neil

see also: *Neil Young*

Brian Escamilla

Christopher Cross

Born Christopher Geppert, 1951 in San Antonio, Texas

Once considered a promising pop/rock artist, Cross eventually became the quintessential two-hit wonder, capturing five Grammy awards and millions of record sales with *Christopher Cross,* (Warner Bros., 1980, prod. by Michael Omartian) an effort buoyed by the hits "Ride Like The Wind" and "Sailing," along with guest appearances by Nicolette Larson and Michael McDonald. Signed to Warner Bros. after an apprenticeship in a popular Austin, Texas, cover band, Cross proved his pop smarts again with the 1981 hit "Arthur's Theme (The Best That You Can Do)," from the film "Arthur." But the new wave revolution made Cross' easygoing pop sound quite irrelevant, with subsequent efforts such as *Back of My Mind* (Warner Bros., 1988, prod. Michael Omartian) or his latest, *Window,* (Rhythm Safari, 1995) falling on deaf ears. A German compilation *Ride Like the Wind* (Warner Bros., 1992, prod. Various) puts all the hits in one place.

Eric Deggans

Sheryl Crow

Born Feb. 2, 1962 in Kennett, Mo.

In the early 90s, when the term "girls with guitars" implied either glowering punkettes or retiring folkies, Crow emerged as something else entirely. A former backup singer for Michael Jackson, Don Henley, Rod Stewart and others, Crow joined a loose-knit group of musicians that jammed on Tuesday nights, eventually resulting in the songs on her debut, *Tuesday Night Music Club.* (A&M, 1993, prod. Bill Bottrell) By and large, the songs are emotionally raw, literate, and stylistically various. Standouts include: "All I Wanna Do"—essentially Wyn Cooper's poem "Fun" set to a Stealer's Wheel groove—which won a Grammy as 1994's Record of the Year; "What I Can Do For You," which capitalized on the country's growing awareness of sexual harassment; and "Leaving Las Vegas," which captures in three lines—"Such a muddy line between/The things you want/And the things you have to do"—the morality play Joe Eszterhas claims he was staging in *Showgirls.*

Daniel Durchholz

Crowded House

Formed 1985 in Melbourne, Australia. Disbanded 1996.

Neil Finn, vocals, guitar, keyboards; Paul Hester: drums, vocals, keyboards (1985-94); Nick Seymour, bass, vocals; Tim Finn: piano, guitar, vocals (1991-93); Mark Hart (1993-96)

Crowded House sprang from the ashes of Split Enz, which Neil Finn joined as second fiddle to his brother Tim but eventually became chief songwriter. The new band took its name from the cramped Hollywood bungalow where it rehearsed its 1985 debut. Those quarters may have been a creative asset because Crowded House went on to produce some of the most melodically stunning pop this side of John Lennon and Paul McCartney. Airplay and attention built slowly for the first release, but eventually the singles "Don't Dream Its Over" and "Something So Strong" won an audience. Crowded House would never be so commercially successful again, though its music continued to evolve and become more sophisticated. The group finally fizzled in 1996, though it was probably over a couple of years before. Still, lovers of well constructed and intensely melodic post-Beatles pop should find every Crowded House album a treasure.

what to buy: On *Woodface,* (Capitol, 1991, prod. Mitchell Froom and Neil Finn) Tim Finn joins brother Neil for a blend of uptempo, quirky numbers ("Chocolate Cake," "Italian Plastic") with gorgeous ballads such as "Four Seasons in One Day", "Fall At Your Feet" and "Weather With You." This is not only Crowded House's finest, but also one of the very best of the post-Beatles anglo-pop releases.

what to buy next: *Crowded House* (Capitol, 1985, prod. Mitchell Froom) is a fine debut and has the big hits ("Something So Strong," "Don't Dream Its Over"). *Together Alone* (Capitol, 1993, prod. Youth) is very nearly on par with *Woodface* and features the outstanding Finn ballads "In My Command," "Fingers of Love," "Private Universe" and "Distant Sun." *Recurring Dream: The Very Best of Crowded House* (Capitol, 1996, prod. Various) is a generous (19 songs) collection that lives up to its title.

what to avoid: *Temple of Low Men* (Capitol, 1988, prod. Mitchell Froom) is a solid work, but it may be a bit dark and stylistically obscure for the casual fan.

worth searching for: The CD single for "I Feel Possessed," (Capitol, 1989) which includes three Byrds classics recorded in concert with Roger McGuinn.

▶▶ The Rembrants, Oasis

◀◀ The Beatles, the Everly Brothers, the Byrds, Procol Harum, Split Enz

see also: *Split Enz*

Michael Isabella

Julee Cruise

Born Dec. 1, 1956 in Creston, Iowa

Cruise was a French-horn protege as a child growing up in Iowa who apprenticed with the Chicago Symphony Orchestra. But she was drawn to acting and musical theater, performing off-Broadway and in radio and TV commercials before film director David Lynch discovered her and used her wispy vocals on the "Blue Velvet" soundtrack. Lynch called upon her again when making the unconventional television series "Twin Peaks," and he found more avenues for her ethereal vocals, teaming with composer Angelo Badalamenti to write an entire album for her, *Floating*, (Warner Bros., 1989, prod. David Lynch and Angelo Badalamenti) released at the height of the "Twin Peaks" hype in 1989. The album perfectly captured the eerie, haunting nature of the freaky "Twin Peaks," especially on the sadly narcotic "Falling," which was featured on the show. The coolly detached, retro lounge lizard jazz quality of the record presaged today's cocktail scene. They strung her up, literally, for "Industrial Symphony #1," staged later that year at the Brooklyn Academy of Music, and Cruise subbed for Cindy Wilson during the B-52s 1992 tour. The Lynch-Badalamenti partnership reunited for a second Cruise album, *The Voice of Love*, (Warner Bros, 1993, prod. David Lynch and Angelo Badalamenti) which unfortunately didn't measure up to *Floating's* standard.

▶▶ Tori Amos

◀◀ Cocteau Twins

Doug Pullen

Cry of Love

Formed 1990 in Raleigh, N.C.

Audley Freed, guitar; Jason Patterson, drums; Robert Kearns, bass; Kelly Holland, vocals (1990-94)

Made up of longtime veterans of numerous Tarheel bands, Cry of Love plays accomplished bluesy rock tailor-made for traditional album-rock. Released into the teeth of alternative rock's early-90s onslaught, its debut album, *Brother* (Columbia, 1993, prod. John Custer) sounds strangely out of time—decidedly unfashionable mainstream guitar rock of a piece with Bad Company or Humble Pie. Incessant touring earned Cry of Love some rock radio success with "Bad Thing" and "Peace Pipe," but proved too much for vocalist Holland, who quit in late 1994. At the time of this writing, the rest of the band is still together and actively recruiting a replacement. While waiting you might want to scare up a copy of *August 25, 1993*, (Columbia, 1993, prod. Mitch Maketansky) a promo-only four-track EP featuring live versions of three *Brother* tracks plus a nifty cover of Willie Dixon's "I Ain't Superstitious."

David Menconi

Crystal Waters

Born 1964 in Philadelphia, Pa.

Waters' "la da dee, la da dah" chorus in the song "Gypsy Woman (She's Homeless)," was intensely catchy, a natural summer dance hit, and it made this unknown Washington, D.C., singer-songwriter a star. Waters has at least as much dance hall savvy as Paula Abdul, and she's a better lyric writer, but she still hasn't been able to click for more than a hit or two per album. "100% Pure Love," another catchy song from her 1994 follow-up, hit No. 11 on the pop singles charts—but it was "I Believe I Love You," buried between mostly overproduced dance music on her second album, that truly showcased her talent. The song is a Stax-Motown-style soul classic, with perfect sound effects, a funky groove and a Janet Jackson-style delivery. Waters' debut, *Surprise*, (Mercury, 1991, prod. Basement Boys) went gold on the strength of "Gypsy Woman," a story-song told from the perspective of a Washington, D.C., homeless woman. *Storyteller* (Mercury, 1994, prod. Basement Boys) is full of much stronger songwriting, especially the wonderful "I Believe I Love You," but its electro-dance-funk production wears thin too fast.

Steve Knopper

The Cult /The Holy Barbarians

Formed 1983, Brixton (London), England. Disbanded 1995

Ian Astbury (born Ian Lindsay), vocals, tambourine; Billy Duffy, guitar; Jamie Stewart, bass (1983-89); Les Warner, drums (1983-87);

Six Essential 60s Collections

The British Invasion: The History of British Rock Vol. 1-9
(Rhino, 1992)

16 No. 1 Hits From the Early 60s/Late 60s
(Motown, 1995)

Nuggets, Vol 1
(Rhino, 1986)

Highs of the 60s
(Warner Special Products, 1986)

Frat Rock, Vol. 1
(Rhino, 1991)

Woodstock: Twenty Fifth Anniversary Collection
(Atlantic, 1994)

Matt Sorum, drums (1989-90); Craig Adams, bass (1991-95); Scot Garrett, drums (1991-95)

Out of the ashes of Astbury's Southern Death Cult and Duffy's Nosebleed came the Cult, a hard rocking quartet that at times flirted with great commercial success but never quite achieved it. Combining Astbury's love of Native American imagery (fire, Phoenixes, etc.) with Duffy's penchant for blockbuster riffs, the Cult's early albums were subversive before alternative rock became a marketing category. Ironically, its later efforts were more forthright at a time when mainstream ears finally opened to what The Cult was doing early on. Its popularity peaked in 1989 with heavy MTV and rock radio play for the anthem "Fire Woman" and a well-timed tour opening for the about-to-be-huge Metallica. But Astbury and Duffy publicly feuded, and there were several lineup changes and far too many fallouts and reunions between its principals for The Cult to remain healthy for long. The band formally disintegrated in 1995, with Astbury moving on to the Holy Barbarians.

what to buy: *Sonic Temple* (Sire, 1989, prod. Bob Rock) ♪♪♪♪ is an excellent introduction to the band's irresistible brand of mystic, stomping hard rock, containing not only "Fire Woman" but also "Sweet Soul Sister" and "Edie (Ciao Baby)."

what to buy next: On *Electric,* (Sire, 1987, prod. Rick Rubin) ♪♪♪♪ producer Rubin helps The Cult pare away the dense psychedelia that marked its albums to that point and comes up with perhaps the best AC/DC album that band never made.

what to avoid: *Ceremony* (Sire, 1991, prod. Richie Zito) ♪♪ is occasionally stirring but too often a yawn.

the rest: *Dreamtime* (Beggars Banquet, 1984) ♪♪♪ *Love* (Sire, 1985) ♪♪♪ *The Cult* (Sire, 1994) ♪♪♪

worth searching for: *Pure Cult* (Beggars Banquet, 1992, prod. Various) ♪♪♪♪ is an import collection that compiles the singles and best material up through the early 90s. The first copies came with a limited-edition live CD

solo outings:

The Holy Barbarians (Astbury): *Cream* (Reprise, 1996) ♪♪♪♪

▶▶ Bush, Candlebox, Alice in Chains, Guns N' Roses

◀◀ Led Zeppelin, AC/DC, the Doors, Sex Pistols, Killing Joke

Todd Wicks

Culture Club /Boy George

Formed 1981 in London, England. Disbanded 1987.

Boy George (born George O'Dowd), vocals; Roy Hay, guitar, keyboards; Mikey Craig, bass; Jon Moss, drums

Culture Club frontman Boy George brought pure ear candy with a healthy dose of androgyny to the top of the U.S. charts. Part of a long line of adrogynous rock singers, Boy George took it to the extreme, primping himself with makeup, braided hair and tunics. The fad wore off after the group's first two albums—which launched a string of hit singles and earned the group a Grammy for Best New Artist in 1983. Personal dissensions and drug addictions eventually brought the group to an end. After a dry spell, Boy George's career was temporarily revived when his hit cover of Dave Berry's 1964 British hit "The Crying Game" was featured in the 1992 movie of the same name.

what to buy: Pop music doesn't get much better than *Colour By Numbers* (Virgin, 1983, prod. Steve Levine) ♪♪♪♪ and its danceable singles "Karma Chameleon," "Church of the Poison Mind" and "Miss Me Blind."

what to buy next: Culture Club's debut album *Kissing to Be Clever* (Virgin, 1982, prod. Steve Levine) ♪♪♪♪ disarmed the masses with George's appearance and the plucky hits "Do You Really Want to Hurt Me?" "Time (Clock of the Heart)" and "I'll Tumble 4 Ya."

what to avoid: *From Luxury to Heartache* (Virgin, 1986, Virgin, prod. Arif Mardin and Lew Hahn) You can smell the end of the band coming on this one.

the rest: *Waking Up With the House on Fire* (Virgin, 1984) *This Time: The First Four Years* (Virgin, 1987) *At Worst ... The Best of Boy George and Culture Club* (SBK, 1993)

solo outings:

Boy George: Sold (Virgin, 1987) *High Hat* (Virgin, 1989) *The Martyr Mantras* (Virgin, 1991); *Cheapness and Beauty* (Virgin, 1995)

Right Said Fred, Pulp, Rupaul, Madonna

Queen, David Bowie, Bow Wow Wow, the Village People

Christina Fuoco

Burton Cummings

See: The Guess Who

The Cure

Formed 1976 in Crawley, England

Robert Smith, vocals, guitar; Michael Dempsey, bass (1976-80); Laurence "Lol" Tolhurst, drums, keyboards (1976-91); Porl Thompson, guitar (1984-94); Simon Gallup, bass (1980-present); Mathieu Hartley, keyboards (198); Boris Williams, drums (1984-); Roger O'Donnell, keyboards (1988-91); Perry Bamonte, guitar, keyboards (1991-present)

While nowhere near as heady or neo-apocalyptic as early 80s bands such as Bauhaus, Sisters Of Mercy or Joy Division, the Cure has managed to get rich, which makes the band different. Having established a fan base early on with the winsome British hit "Boys Don't Cry," not to mention bandleader Smith's connection to another British favorite, Siouxsie And The Banshees, with whom he had toured, the Cure took the small independent label Fiction Records and catapulted it into a multimillion-dollar enterprise almost overnight. With a unique brand of gloomy, overly romanticized music dealing with love, loss and sex in almost every song, the Cure managed to capture the heart of every angst-filled British teenager possible. Once the band members determined the British Isles were too small to confine them, they set their eyes on the U.S., where they quickly gained cult status and eventually superstardom despite little radio airplay during the earliest days of the assault. Despite a chaotic—at best—personnel situation, Smith maintained the integrity of the band's musical style across a dozen albums with at least as many different members. While not necessarily redundant or derivative, virtually every LP has a consistent style and quality that does not disappoint. Smith's lyrics sometimes border on the droll, making Morrissey seem chipper and positive in comparison, but he's never really veered into the self-pitying school of songwriting. Despite the gloom and angst that dominates the work, Smith frequently sneaked in a playful and more upbeat song that invariably was a hit ("Love Cats," Why Can't I Be You," "Let's Go To Bed," "Friday I'm In Love"). Although nowhere on par with U2 or R.E.M. at this point, the Cure is still putting up an admirable fight to prove its relevance in a world where Pearl Jam and Nirvana rule. Despite lackluster sales and airplay from more recent efforts, the band still packs 'em in for concerts—although Smith regularly opines that each tour may be the Cure's last, which surely puts a few folks in the seats.

what to buy: *Staring At The Sea* (Elektra, 1986, prod. Various) is a singles package collecting U.K. hits up the mid-80s, a good way to introduce the band to U.S. audiences. The CD has a few bonus tracks, while the cassette version adds a full dozen extra B-sides.

what to buy next: Smith's doom and gloom is nowhere more apparent than in the frighteningly somber *Faith*, (Elektra, 1981, prod. Mike Hedges and The Cure) a great Halloween soundtrack or mood music for a seance. It doesn't get loud or fast, but rather provides a deluge of gray sound; *Kiss Me, Kiss Me, Kiss Me* (Elektra, 1987, prod. Allen Smith) is a little lighter, with a higher bop quotient in "Hot, Hot, Hot" and "Just Like Heaven."

what to avoid: *Paris*, (Elektra, 1993, prod. Robert Smith and Bryan New) taken from a Paris live show in 1992, with only average sound quality and a middling selection of tracks.

the rest: *Boys Don't Cry* (Elektra, 1980) *Seventeen Seconds* (Elektra, 1980) *Pornography* (Fiction/A&M, 1982) *Japanese Whispers* (Fiction/Sire, 1993) *Head On The Door* (Elektra, 1985) *Disintegration* (Elektra, 1989) *Mixed Up* (Elektra, 1990) *Wish* (Elektra, 1992) *Thirteen* (Elektra, 1996)

solo outings:

Presence (Tolhurst): *Inside* (Smash, 1993)

The Glove (Smith): *The Glove* (Rough Trade, 1990)

The Essence, Siouxsie And The Banshees, Jesus & Mary Chain

Genesis, Joy Division, the Sex Pistols

Tim Davis

Curve

Formed 1990 in London, England. Disbanded 1993.

Toni Halliday, vocals; Dean Garcia, bass, guitars, keyboards, programming

Halliday and Garcia were introduced by Dave Stewart of the Eurythmics and played together in a band called State of Play, which released one album and a couple of singles during the late 80s before dissolving. Reuniting a few years later to form Curve, Halliday and Garcia again experienced only marginal success. While not overtly bad, Curve's recipe of fuzzy guitar, moody vocals and danceable electronic drums was hardly original; the group was simply one of the myriad British "shoe-gazing," pop bands that saturated the record racks during the early 90s. *Doppleganger* (Charisma, 1992, prod. Curve and Flood) hit No. 1 in the U.K. and produced a semi-hit single, "Split into Fractions;" *Pubic Fruit* (Charisma, 1992) collects tracks from some early EPs. Curve's second album, *Cuckoo* (Charisma, 1993, prod. Curve) is similar to *Doppleganger* and made little impact, prompting the duo to split several months after its release.

Christopher Scanlon

Cypress Hill

Formed 1988 in Los Angeles, Calif.

B-Real (born Louis Freese), vocals; Sen Dog (born Senen Reyes), vocals; DJ Muggs (born Lawrence Muggerud), turntables and samples

Championing a style known as Spanish "lingo," Cypress Hill emerged in the just-emerging gangsta rap explosion, vacillating between derivative street tales and material celebrating how much fun it is to get high—all combining potent, bass-heavy instrumental tracks with B-Real's nasal lyrical delivery. The group's 1992 debut was a hit in the rap community, setting the stage for their sophomore record, which took the hip edge of the rock mainstream by storm. High-profile contributions to the soundtracks for films such as "Judgment Night" and "Last Action Hero" only increased the trio's exposure, along with coveted spots on the Woodstock '94 concert and on Lollapalooza '95 bills. While some criticize the band's use of violent imagery and its advocacy of the legalization of marijuana, it ultimately uses taut, textured jams to hold its place in the pop culture mainstream.

what to buy: The platinum-plus *Black Sunday* (Ruffhouse/Columbia, 1993, prod. DJ Muggs and T-Ray) refines the mix of lazy, bass-heavy (and jeep-ready) sonics and B-Real's almost Beastie Boys-style delivery. Buoyed by engaging hit singles such as "Insane in the Brain" and "I Ain't Goin' Out Like That."

what to buy next: The impact of the debut title, *Cypress Hill* (Ruffhouse/Columbia, 1991, prod. DJ Muggs) cannot be understated. As the first album to kick the red-eyed, stoned funk that powers the trio's unique sound, this disc opened the ears of rap—and a few savvy rock—fans everywhere. Muggs' music provided the hazy, drugged-out feel, while B-Real's gangsta fantasies ("How I Could Just Kill a Man") brought some much-needed spice to the party.

what to avoid: Cypress Hill's flat contribution to the "Last Action Hero" soundtrack, "Cock The Hammer." (Columbia, 1993, prod. DJ Muggs) WOOF! One listen and it's obvious why the group didn't want this for one of its own projects.

the rest: *Temple of Boom* (Ruffhouse/Columbia, 1995)

worth searching for: The trio's duet with grunge rockers Pearl Jam on the soundtrack for the film "Judgment Night" soundtrack. (Immortal/Epic Soundtrax, 1993, prod. Pearl Jam and Cypress Hill) Combining B-Real's incendiary vocals with a mean groove by the P-Jammers, this track nearly jumps off the disc.

House of Pain, Funkdoobiest

N.W.A., Kid Frost, Mellow Man Ace

Eric Deggans

The Cyrkle

Formed 1961 in Easton, Pennsylvania. Disbanded 1968.

Don Dannemann, vocals, guitar; Tom Dawes, bass; Marty Fried, drums

Despite some impressive music-biz connections (Brian Epstein, Paul Simon) and a more-than-sufficient modicum of ability, this New York-based trio spent barely a year in the spotlight before plunging back into obscurity faster than one could say "Where are they now?" It all began on the coffee house/frat circuit during the early 60s where, as The Rhondells, the group honed its close-knit vocal and instrumental style before hitting the Eastern club circuit seriously in 1963. Like so many others, the

British Invasion taught it to electrify their act, and by 1965 it had become an accomplished, if not necessarily original unit. The group caught Beatle manager Epstein's ear (and eye) the following year and, having been re-christened the Cyrkle by none other than John Lennon, was signed to Columbia Records and given a Simon & Garfunkel reject, "Red Rubber Ball", to record. Although Paul Simon to this day claims it's the worst song he's ever written, it quickly hit the #2 spot on the charts. By the time the Cyrkle was warming up for the Fab Four on its final American tour, it had placed another song into the Top 20 (the splendid "Turn Down Day"). It was the last hit. They continued touring throughout 1967, did a bit of soundtrack work in '68, and had disbanded by the turn of the decade, leaving behind a small but pretty worthy recorded legacy represented by the solid overview *Red Rubber Ball: A Collection.* (Columbia, 1991, prod. Various) ♪♪♪♪

Gary Pig Gold

dada

Formed 1990 in Los Angeles, Calif.

Joie Calio, vocals, bass; Michael Gurley, vocals, guitars; Phil Leavitt, drums

A powerhouse trio of virtuoso musicians, dada prides itself on smartly written lyrics that overflow with hooks. The sprightly tune "Dizz Knee Land" off its debut album, *Puzzle,* (I.R.S., 1992, prod. Ken Scott) ♪♪♪ pushed the pop-rock band into the public eye. Although deserving of the same acclaim, its next two releases *American Highway Flower* (I.R.S., 1994, prod. Jason Corsaro) ♪♪♪ and *El Subliminoso* (I.R.S., 1996, prod. dada) ♪♪♪ failed to make the same impact, which is a shame; the latter, which explores western funk in "Bob The Drummer," acoustic lushness in "Star You Are" and raw pop in "I Get High" should have been a mainstream smash.

Christina Fuoco

Dick Dale

Born Richard Anthony Monsour, May 4, 1937 in Boston, Mass.

Until 1994, when Quentin Tarantino's smash film "Pulp Fiction" stuck the 1962 surf instrumental "Misirlou" in the opening credits, Dale was a tremendously overlooked rock 'n' roll trailblazer. The surfer-guitarist's early hits, including "Let's Go Trippin' " and "Misirlou," not only invented the entire genre of surf music, but also influenced such younger legends as Jimi Hendrix and Brian Wilson. Dale's style, which he said was an approximation of the sound a wave makes when it's next to your ear, has a natural rumble and sometimes sounds like a person screaming. As "King of the Surf Guitar" in the early 60s, Dale was one of the few rock celebrities to gain fame between Buddy Holly's death and the birth of the Beatles—Life magazine ran a huge spread of Dale at home, surrounded by his pet lions. Eventually, the Beach Boys and the rest of the''60s thing eclipsed Dale, who survived a major spread of cancer in his intestines, and he faded into obscurity. He continued to tour with the Del-tones and in 1986 released a "comeback" record which went nowhere. He also recorded with Stevie Ray Vaughan. But Dale's second comeback, *Tribal Thunder*, got people listening again and recast him as a forebear of heavy-metal guitar. Then came "Pulp Fiction" and the smiling, pony-tailed Dale, last seen touring in nightclubs around the country, had a meal ticket once again.

what to buy: *King of the Surf Guitar: The Best of Dick Dale and His Del-Tones* (Rhino, 1989, prod. Various) ♪♪♪♪♪ has all the early hits, including "Let's Go Trippin'," "Riders in the Sky," "Mr. Eliminator" and, of course, "Misirlou." They all have a snap that sounds fresh today and must have seemed positively out of this world in 1961. Dale's comeback, *Tribal Thunder* (Hightone, 1993, prod. Scott Mathews and Joel Selvin) ♪♪♪♪ shows he has been paying attention to his proteges all these years, and without sacrificing his style, he pays homage to heavy metal and the British Invasion.

the rest: *Unknown Territory* (Hightone, 1994) ♪♪♪ *Calling Up Spirits* (Beggars Banquet, 1996) ♪♪♪

worth searching for: Dale's early albums are difficult to find, but snap 'em up—particularly if you come across *Surfer's Choice* (Deltone, 1962) ♪♪♪ or *King of the Surf Guitar* (Capitol, 1963) ♪♪♪

▶▶ Beach Boys, Chantays, Ventures, Jimi Hendrix, Van Halen, Metallica, Man ... Or Astroman?

◀◀ Link Wray, Duane Eddy, Chuck Berry, Chet Atkins, Merle Travis

Steve Knopper

Dali's Car

See: Peter Murphy

Roger Daltrey

See: The Who

Damn Yankees /Night Ranger/Shaw-Blades

Night Ranger (formed 1981 in San Francisco, Calif.)—Jack Blades, bass, vocals (1981-89); Kelly Keagy, drums, vocals; Brad Gillis, guitar, vocals; Alan Fitzgerald, keyboards (1981-88); Jeff Watson, guitar. Damn Yankees (formed 1989 in New York, N.Y.)—Jack Blades, bass, vocals; Ted Nugent, guitar, vocals; Tommy Shaw, guitar, vocals; Michael Cartellone, drums

Night Ranger was the transitional rock-radio band between Foreigner, Journey and the other early-80s hard-rock balladeers and the hair-pop-glam-metal bands that replaced them. Led by charismatic bassist Blades—who's best with a ballad—the band had hits with "Sister Christian" and "(You Can Still) Rock in America." Blades later hooked up with Styx' Shaw and Motor City Madman Nugent and formed the reasonably popular late-80s hard-rock band Damn Yankees. The band took a break—mostly to let Nugent run off his mouth about hunting rights and how stupid Kurt Cobain was to commit suicide—and during that time, Shaw and Blades collaborated for one bland album.

what to buy: Night Ranger's *Greatest Hits* (MCA, 1989, prod. Various) ♪♪ is a solid collection of radio-friendly pop-metal, mostly ballads, with bonus tracks "Eddie's Comin' Out Tonight" and "Rumours in the Air." It also saves you the trouble of tracking down the band's bland studio albums. Damn Yankees' two albums, *Damn Yankees* (Warner Bros., 1990, prod. Ron Nevison) ♪♪♪ and *Don't Tread* (Warner Bros., 1992, prod. Ron Nevison) ♪♪ have a touch of attitude thanks to the Nuge's calculated insanity and still-innovative metal guitar licks.

what to avoid: Night Ranger's *Feeding off the Mojo* (Drive Entertainment, 1995, prod. David Prater) ♪ and *Live in Japan* (MCA, 1990, prod. Night Ranger) ♪ are excessive no matter how great your Night Ranger jones.

the rest: Night Ranger: *Dawn Patrol* (Boardwalk/MCA, 1982) ♪♪ *Midnight Madness* (MCA, 1983) ♪♪ *7 Wishes* (Camel/MCA, 1985) ♪♪ *Man in Motion* (Camel/MCA, 1988) ♪♪ Shaw/Blades: *Hallucination* (Warner Bros., 1995) ♪♪

▶▶ Hootie and the Blowfish, Bon Jovi, Warrant, Motley Crue, Poison

◀◀ Kiss, Ted Nugent, Journey, Foreigner, Styx, REO Speedwagon

see also: *Styx, Ted Nugent*

Tracey Birkenhauer and Steve Knopper

The Damned

Formed 1976 in London, England. Disbanded 1989.

Dave Vanian (born David Letts), vocals; Brian James (born Brian Robertson), guitar (1977-79); Captain Sensible (born Ray Burns), bass, guitar (1976-84); Rat Scabies (born Chris Miller), drums (1976-77, 1979-89); Lu (Robert Edmunds), guitar (1977-79); Jon Moss, drums (1977-78); Alistair Ward, bass (1979-80); Paul Grey, bass (1980-82); Roman Jugg, keyboards, guitar (1981-89); Bryan Merrick, bass (1984-85)

Never mind the Sex Pistols; here's the Damned. By one month, the Damned were the first punk band to put out an album, and the first to tour the U.S. The Damned was certainly a colorful bunch—Vanian in his vampire get-up, Sensible in his tutu, Scabies diving into the audience for punch-ups. The music, though, was prototypical—hard and fast, with a fourth chord allowed only after arduous decision making. What the Damned didn't do is flame out quickly; despite significant personnel changes the group soldiered on and, in fact, put out some of its bigest hits (and best material) during the mid-70s, with "Smash it Up" and "Love Song." The Damned outlived the Pistols, the Clash and its other punk peers, finally breaking up in 1989 but leaving behind a fairly inspiring collection of music.

what to buy: *Damned, Damned, Damned* (Stiff U.K., 1977/Frontier, 1993, prod. Nick Lowe) ♪♪♪♪♪ is the Damned's blazing debut and the only studio recording by the original quartet. Like the early Stooges and MC5 albums, it retains its power and freshness two decades after the fact. After several personnel changes, *Machine Gun Etiquette* (Chiswick/Roadrunner, 1979) ♪♪♪♪♪ came as a surprise. As loud and proud as *Damned, Damned, Damned*, there's just a touch more sophistication and, dare we say, songcraft on tracks such as "Smash it Up," "Love Song" and "I Just Can't be Happy Today."

what to buy next: *The Light at the End of the Tunnel* (MCA, 1987, prod. Various) ♪♪♪♪ is a well-selected retrospective that also includes B-sides and other rarities. *The Final Damnation* (Restless, 1989) ♪♪♪♪ is a worthy representation of the Damned's adrenalin-rush live show—though by the time it was recorded in 1988, the group had even slowed the tempos a bit to reveal lean, tightly written virtues of its songs.

what to avoid: Vanian's Dracula fixation takes over on *Phantasmagoria*, (MCA, 1985/Off Beat, 1994, prod. Jon Kelly) ♪♪ the aural equivalent of a late-night horror flick that comes off as intolerably silly.

the rest: *The Best of the Damned* (Roadrunner, 1980/1993)

Live at the Lyceum (REstless, 1981/1990) *Strawberries* (Bronze, 1982/Cleopatra, 1993) *Damned But Not Forgotten* (Dojo, 1985/One Way, 1994) *Anything* (MCA, 1986) *The Peel Sessions* (Dutch East India, 1991) *Sessions of the Damned* (Dutch East India, 1993) *Tales From the Damned* (Cleopatra, 1993) *Collection* (Griffin, 1995)

worth searching for: The British issue of *The Black Album*, (I.R.S., 1980) which pairs one of the group's most musically sophisticated albums with a concert recording.

▶▶ The Germs, the Offspring, NOFX

◀◀ The Stooges, the Ramones, the Sensational Alex Harvey Band

Gary Graff

Charlie Daniels Band

Formed 1970 in Nashville, Tenn.

Charlie Daniels (born 1937 in Wilmington, N.C.), vocals, fiddle, guitar; Joel "Taz" DiGregorio, keyboards, vocals; Jack Gavin, drums; Bruce Ray Brown, guitar, vocals; Chris Wormer, guitar, saxophone, vocals; Charlie Haywood, bass (plus numerous others over the years)

A North Carolina native who became a popular session fiddler in Nashville, Daniels is best known for his 1979 hit "The Devil Went Down to Georgia," which country music fans and detractors alike cite to support their cases. Daniels, along with Lynyrd Skynyrd, was one of the early Southern rockers, building his Charlie Daniels Band in the Allman Brothers Band's image but keeping a little more twang in his guitars and a bit more weep in his fiddle. Hard touring in the 70s led to radio play for "Uneasy Rider" and "The Legend of Wooly Swamp," as well as a moving Vietnam vets' tribute "Still in Saigon." Unfortunately, his stay-out-of-my-backyard myopia and lunkheaded jingoism (his anti-drug diatribes would embarrass even Nancy Reagan) has helped undercut his earlier accomplishments. Daniels has been off the charts for well more than a decade and makes his living touring the country's most yee-hawlering country bars.

what to buy: *A Decade of Hits* (Epic, 1983, prod. Various) features many of the intermittent gems Daniels fiddled onto the radio. The consistent *Million Mile Reflections* (Epic, 1979, prod. John Boylan) has "The Devil Went Down to Georgia."

what to buy next: *Full Moon* (Epic, 1980, prod. John Boylan) is Daniels' most successful album, featuring "In America" and"The Legend of Wooly Swamp."

what to avoid: *Super Hits* (Epic, 1994, prod. Various) is a skimpy best-of. For all his flaws, Daniels deserves better.

the rest: *Te John, Grease and Wolfman* (Kama Sutra,1970) *Honey in the Rock*, aka *Uneasy Rider* (Buddah-Kama Sutra, 1973/Epic, 1977) *Fire on the Mountain*, aka *Simple Man* (Buddah-Kama Sutra, 1974/Epic, 1989) *Way Down Yonder* aka *Whiskey* (Buddah-Kama Sutra, 1974/Epic, 1977) *Night Rider* (Buddah-Kama Sutra, 1975) *Saddle Tramp* (Epic, 1976) *High Lonesome* (Epic, 1977) *Midnight Wind* (Epic, 1977); *Volunteer Jam III and IV* (Epic, 1978) *Volunteer Jam VI* (Epic, 1980) *Windows* (Epic, 1982) *Me and the Boys* (Epic, 1985) *Powder Keg* (Epic, 1987) *Homesick Heroes* (Epic, 1988) *Christmas Time Down South* (Epic, 1990) *Renegade* (Epic, 1991) *America, I Believe in You* (Liberty, 1993) *The Door* (Sparrow, 1994) *Same Ol'Me* (Capitol, 1995, prod. Barry Beckett)

worth searching for: *Volunteer Jam*, (Capricorn, 1976) which chronicles the first of Daniels' long-running all-star festivals, an idea that sounded tapped out on subsequent editions.

solo outings:

Charlie Daniels: Charlie Daniels (Capitol, 1971)

▶▶ Marshall Tucker Band, Lynyrd Skynyrd, Alabama, Oak Ridge Boys, Little Texas, Brooks & Dunn

◀◀ Allman Brothers Band, Waylon Jennings, Hank Williams Jr., Merle Haggard

Steve Knopper and Gary Graff

Danzig /Samhain

Formed 1986 in Los Angeles, Calif.

Glenn Danzig, vocals; John Christ, guitar; Eerie Von, bass; Chuck Bisquits, drums (1986-93); Joey Castillo, drums (1994-present)

From the burnt offerings of the Misfits came the short-lived full-metal bore of Samhain, which evolved into the more varied but no less threatening Danzig. Oh, how the PMRC must get its morals all cinched up over the evil obscenities bellowing from the muscle-bound, tattooed Danzig. The openly throttled demonic aura of the band, tempered with a forked tongue-in-cheek bravado, captured the hearts (if not the souls) of critics—and Beavis and Butt-Head, thanks to heavy MTV rotation for a live version of the song "Mother." Fire is cool, heh-heh.

what to buy: The richly textured *4* (American, 1994, prod. Glenn

Danzig and Rick Rubin) is the band's most ambitious album. *Danzig* (Def American, 1988, prod. Glenn Danzig) has enough five-pointed imagery to Aleister Crowley cringe as well as the original take on "Mother."

what to buy next: *Danzig III: How the Gods Kill* (Def American, 1992, prod. Glenn Danzig) pushes the mainstream envelope with tighter songs and more polished production.

what to avoid: *Black Aria*, (Plan 9/ Caroline, 1993, prod. Glenn Danzig) an operatic experimentation whose artiness would have Beavis shrieking in real horror.

the rest: Samhain: *November-Coming-Fire* (Plan 9/Caroline, 1986) *Final Descent* (Plan 9/Caroline, 1990) Danzig: *Danzig II: Lucifuge* (Def American, 1990) *Thrall: Demonsweatlive* (Def American, 1993)

worth searching for: The first Samhain release, *Initium*, (Plan 9/Caroline, 1984/1986, prod. Glenn Danzig) a punkier effort than either the latter-day Misfits or Danzig would offer.

▶▶ Metallica, Slayer

◀◀ Black Sabbath, Led Zeppelin, AC/DC

see also: *Misfits*

Allan Orski

Terence Trent D'Arby

Born March 15, 1962 in New York, N.Y.

Known for bringing the original grit of soul and funk back to popular music during the mid-80s, D'Arby—an American and former journalist who moved to Britain during the mid-80s—scored quickly with his first album, *Introducing the Hardline According to Terence Trent D'Arby*, but then encountered difficulties. Fans and reviewers were put off by his overwhelming arrogance and, later, by his misguided musical experiments. Still—following the spirit of headstrong R&B greats Prince and Marvin Gaye—D'Arby continues to do things his own way despite a continual lack of commercial triumphs.

what to buy: *Introducing the Hardline According to Terence Trent D'Arby* (Columbia, 1987, prod. Martyn Ware and Terence Trent D'Arby) is a remarkable document of D'Arby's expansive range and sonic breadth. Highlights include the urgent "If You Let Me Stay," the cool "Wishing Well" and the mournful "Let's Go Forward."

what to buy next: Despite the critical and commercial disregard, D'Arby continued to put out solid, interesting material after his more popular debut. *Neither Fish Nor Flesh* (Columbia, 1989, prod. Terence Trent D'Arby) contains several moving and innovative tracks, including "This Side of Love" and "To Know Someone Deeply Is to Know Someone Softly." Likewise, *Symphony or Damn* (Columbia, 1993, prod. Terence Trent D'Arby) features many fiery soul cuts, including the immaculate "Do You Love Me Like You Say?" and "Wet Your Lips."

what to avoid: While still bolstered by D'Arby's vast creative vision, *Vibrator* (Work, 1995, prod. Terence Trent D'Arby) suffers from a distinct lack of focus. Songs like "Supermodel Sandwich" and "Surrender" simply don't pack the same appeal as past works.

worth searching for: The Bruce Springsteen bootleg *New York City Night* (Crystal Cat, 1993) features D'Arby—who was rudely booed by the crowd at this 1993 benefit concert—joining the Boss for some inspired duets.

▶▶ Lenny Kravitz, Seal, Living Colour

◀◀ Stevie Wonder, Marvin Gaye, Prince, Rolling Stones

Aidin Vaziri

Bobby Darin

Born Walden Robert Cassotto on May 14, 1936 in Bronx, N.Y. Died Dec. 20, 1973 in Los Angeles, Calif.

Although he never reached his lofty goal of being "bigger than Sinatra," Darin influenced a generation of American pop singers—Dion, Fabian and Frankie Avalon, to name a few. He's remembered primarily as a teen idol of the 50s, but Darin was also an accomplished musician and a fine writer who penned more than 75 songs, including his first hit, "Splish Splash," which reached No. 3 in 1958. Several more gold singles followed: "Queen of the Hop," his own "Dream Lover," and "Mack the Knife," which sold more than two million copies in 1959. The hits continued during the early 60s with "Beyond the Sea," "Bill Bailey," "Things" and "Artificial Flowers," on which he never sounded better. Darin had a folk-rock hit in 1966 with Tim Hardin's "If I Were A Carpenter;" He also had stints as an actor and worked for Robert Kennedy's presidential campaign in 1968. Darin died much too early, in 1973, from complications during surgery to repair a faulty heart valve. In 1990 he was inducted into the Rock and Roll Hall of Fame.

what to buy: *As Long As I'm Singing: The Bobby Darin Collection* (Rhino, 1995, prod. Various) is a four-disc boxed set well worth the money for serious fans. It features an all-star cast of musicians and some great liner notes. *That's All* (Atco, 1959, prod. Ahmet Ertegun, Nesuhi Ertegun and Jerry Wexler) is Darin's first album and features the classics "Beyond the Sea" and "Mack the Knife."

what to buy next: *Two Of A Kind: Bobby Darin with Johnny Mercer,* (Atco, 1961, prod. Ahmet Ertegun) an arresting collaboration, and *The Bobby Darin Story,* (Atco, 1961, prod. Various) a concise but rewarding disc loaded with big hits.

what to avoid: *Best of Bobby Darin* (Curb, 1990, prod. Various) is a skimpy discount offering. There are plenty of better choices.

the rest: *This Is Darin* (Atlantic, 1960) *25th Day of December* (Atco, 1961) *Darin, 1936-1973* (Motown, 1974) *Capitol Collector's Series* (Capitol, 1989) *The Ultimate Bobby Darin* (Warner Special Products, 1986) *Splish Splash: The Best of Bobby Darin, vol. 1* (Atco, 1991) *Mack the Knife: The Best of Bobby Darin, vol. 2* (Atco, 1991) *Spotlight On Bobby Darin* (Capitol, 1995)

worth searching for: *Darin At the Copa* (Atco, 1960, prod. Ahmet Ertegun and Nesuhi Ertegun) is a fine live recording that includes Darin signature songs "Mack the Knife" and "Bill Bailey."

Harry Connick Jr., Burton Cummings, Brian Setzer, Billy Joel

Frank Sinatra, Ella Fitzgerald, Bing Crosby

William Hanson

David David /David Baerwald

Boomtown (A&M, 1986, prod. Davitt Sigerson), the lone album released by David Baerwald and David Ricketts, presents a desolate picture of life during the Reagan years. Beneath the smooth production and winning melodies lie horror stories, replete with drug dealers and spouse beaters. The sharp display of moral bankruptcy won the duo a Top 40 hit with "Welcome to the Boomtown," after which they soon disbanded. Baerwald has since continued to reveal unsettling slices of the American underbelly in a commercially fruitless solo career. Largely ignored by the buying public (one bitter pill is enough, thank you), both of his out-of-print albums, *Bedtime Stories* (A&M, 1990, prod. Larry Klein) and *Triage* (A&M, 1992, prod. Bill Bottrell, David Baerwald and Dan Schwartz) are compelling enough to root around for.

Allan Orski

Ray Davies

See: The Kinks

Miles Davis

Born May 26, 1926, in Alton Ill. Died. Sept. 28, 1991, in Santa Monica, Calif.

By the late 60s, jazz trumpeter Davis had accomplished enough to fill the careers of three or four lesser greats, but his restless genius and thirst for continuing relevance led him beyond acoustic jazz into electric territory barely explored by his peers. Just adding electric guitar and electric piano was enough to incite cries of "sell-out," and Davis went further with electric bass, synthesizer, even a wah-wah attachment for his trumpet. But while he incorporated rock and funk rhythms into his music, he never watered down his style; actually, it became denser and more complex, even more forbidding. If Davis' bold action caused a schism in the jazz world that still inspires impassioned debate today, it also sparked an entire new style—fusion—whose major players were groomed in Davis' bands: Herbie Hancock, Joe Zawinul and Wayne Shorter of Weather Report, Billy Cobham, Jack deJohnette, John McLaughlin and Chick Corea. Fusion also revived jazz's commercial fortunes, while Davis and producer Teo Macero pioneered what for jazz was a new and equally controversial method of recording, laying down hours and hours of improvisation (in the studio or in concert) and then constructing tracks by splicing different segments together—an anethma to purists. It remains only to be pointed out that years before any of this happened, the one-time boxer had already perfected an attitude the haughtiest rock star could envy—playing with his back to the audience, disdaining to announce tunes or speak at all, dressing to kill, driving extremely expensive cars extremely fast, dating models and movie stars (eventually marrying Cicely Tyson), and generally taking no guff from anyone, especially record company executives. There were also drugs, but that was a problem he conquered repeatedly; more serious were recurring hip problems. By the mid-70s, Davis was using so high a dosage of pain killers to perform that he didn't notice bleeding sores on his feet. His music of the time gave that peculiar mixture of pain and numbness exquisite expression; soon after the concerts that gave us the epic *Agharta* and *Pangaea* albums, his health forced a six-year retirement. He returned in 1981, and if he was no longer on the edge, neither was he standing still; his last studio album incorporated elements of hip-hop and rap.

what to buy: Though not the first fusion album, *In a Silent Way*

(Columbia, 1969, prod. Teo Macero) is the first of great lasting value. The playing—Davis' and Wayne Shorter's plangent tones, the shimmering electric keyboards of Joe Zawinul and Chick Corea, the steady but subtly varied pulses of drummer Tony Williams, John McLaughlin's guitar filigree and the rock-solid bass lines of Dave Holland—weaves a meditative spell not of new-agey emptiness but rather of ecstatically infinite interest and tonal beauty. *Bitches Brew* (Columbia, 1969, prod. Teo Macero) supplements all the previous album's players except Williams with more future fusion all-stars—including multiple drummers who add layers of rhythmic complexity on one of the greatest albums made in any genre. The live albums *Agharta* (Sony, 1976, prod. Teo Macero) and *Pangaea* (Sony, 1975, prod. Teo Macero) were recorded on the same day, at, respectively, afternoon and evening concerts in Japan that showcased electric guitarists Pete Cosey and Reggie Lucas and reeds player Sonny Fortune.

what to buy next: *A Tribute to Jack Johnson* (Columbia, 1970, prod. Teo Macero) has a side of funky aggression (featuring MacLaughlin's great riffing) and a side of meditative tranquility, with references to Davis' earlier work. *Get Up With It,* (Columbia, 1974, prod. Teo Macero) dedicated to the recently deceased Duke Ellington, features the fantastically atmospheric, side-long tribute "He Loved Him Madly." *On the Corner* (Columbia, 1972, prod. Teo Macero) is Davis' most rhythmic album and, in a way, his most avant-garde, structurally and sonically influenced by the sound sculptures of classical avant-gardist Karlheinz Stockhausen without ever sounding directly like the German's work.

what to avoid: *The Man With the Horn* (Columbia, 1980, prod. Teo Macero) was Davis' comeback from retirement, and his chops were rusty.

the rest: *At Fillmore* (Columbia, 1970) *Black Beauty: At The Fillmore West* (CBS/Sony, 1970) *Live Evil* (Columbia, 1970) *Big Fun* (Columbia, 1974) *In Concert* (Columbia, 1973) *Dark Magus* (CBS/Sony, 1977) *We Want Miles* (Columbia, 1981) *Star People* (Columbia, 1982) *Decoy* (Columbia, 1984) *You're Under Arrest* (Columbia, 1985) *Tutu* (Warner Bros., 1986) *The Columbia Years 1955-1985* (Columbia, 1988) *Amandla* (Warner Bros., 1989) *Doo-Bop* (Warner Bros., 1992) *Live Around the World* (Warner Bros., 1996) (Note: Davis albums not covered here do not fall within the stylistic scope of this book.)

worth searching for: One of the few Davis rarities (Columbia/Sony know a cash factory when they see it, but this slipped through the cracks) is *Time After Time,* (Columbia EP, 1984, prod. Miles Davis and Robert Irving III) which features a longer, earlier, superior version of the Cyndi Lauper hit, which Davis twists into a beautiful ballad.

▶▶ Weather Report, Mahavishnu Orchestra, Herbie Hancock, Bill Laswell/Material, Jon Hassell, Grassy Knoll, Ice Burn, Vernon Reid/Living Colour

◀◀ Freddie Webster, Charlie Parker, Cannonball Adderley Quintet, James Brown, Sly & the Family Stone, Ornette Coleman, Karlheinz Stockhausen

Steve Holtje

Morris Day

See: The Time

Taylor Dayne

Born Leslie Wunderman, March 7, 1963 in Baldwin, N.Y.

Wielding a powerful voice molded in the spirit of the R&B and soul records she idolized as a child, Dayne offered the perfect package for crossover success from the dance world to the pop charts. A performer since age six, she kicked around in rock and pop bands after graduating from high school, eventually changing her name on the advice of friend Dee Snider of Twisted Sister. Paying her dues singing in Russian-American nightclubs throughout Brighton Beach, Dayne joined forces with producer Ric Wake to create a percolating dance version of a ballad called "Tell It to My Heart." That single became Dayne's first Top 10 hit, paving the way for an album that fused her powerhouse blue-eyed soul vocal licks to full-throttle 80s-style disco grooves. The result was a string of seven Top 10 singles through the end of the 80s. But the fickle marketplace that dampened many a dance diva's career during the early 90s crippled Dayne's, too—a problem that wasn't helped by her participation in the soundtrack for the ill-fated film, "The Shadow."

what to buy: Like that of all great dance divas, the appeal of Dayne's work lies mostly in her singles—making her career ripe for a good greatest-hits record. And there is one—*Taylor Dayne: Greatest Hits* (Arista, 1995, prod. Various) which sandwiches classic Dayne cuts such as "Tell It to My Heart" and the frenetic "Don't Rush Me" with her remake of Barry White's "Can't Get Enough of Your Love."

what to buy next: For those who can stand the singer's formula—teen-friendly lyrics about love, love and more love set to a mindless, mechanical dance-pop groove—there's her debut album, *Tell It to My Heart* (Arista, 1987, prod. Ric Wake) ♪♪♪ It best sums up this approach, offering four of her biggest hits and the least amount of filler in her catalog.

what to avoid: *Soul Dancing,* (Arista, 1993, prod. Various) WOOF! for which she hired every hitmaker in sight to save her career from the ash heap of pop music that had already claimed such quick hits as Tiffany, Debbie Gibson and Shanice Wilson. Alas, all they could do was prolong the inevitable with a bunch of pop tunes no one cared to hear.

the rest: *Can't Fight Fate* (Arista, 1989) ♪♪♪

▶▶ Celine Dion, Mariah Carey

◀◀ Madonna, Janet Jackson, Donna Summer

Eric Deggans

The dB's /Peter Holsapple/Will Rigby

Formed 1978 in New York, N.Y. Disbanded 1987.

Chris Stamey, vocals, guitar, organ (1978-83); Peter Holsapple, vocals, guitar, organ, drums; Gene Holder, bass, guitar (1978-87); Rick Wagner, bass (1984); Jeff Beninato, bass (1984-87); Will Rigby, drums, vocals

After working together in various North Carolina bands, Holsapple, Stamey and Rigby reunited after they each had separately moved to New York. Their referential rock, constructed from allusions to British Invasion bands, roots rock and various 60s styles, made the dB's critical favorites, but the group remained obscure; the first two albums originally were issued only in England. The band experienced some bad luck when the video of the sophomore release's catchy "Amplifier" was rejected by MTV for its depiction of a hanging suicide. Stamey then left for an equally off-the-radar-screen solo career, and Holsapple soldiered on, again encountering bad luck when, after releasing the group's third album on Bearsville, label boss Albert Grossman died and operations were halted. The band more or less broke up after 10 years, though there have been fitful reunions. Holsapple has rented his instrumental abilities out to everyone from R.E.M. to Hootie & the Blowfish, and in his free time leads the mini-supergroup Continental Drifters with wife Susan Cowsill. Rigby has played with Matthew Sweet, while Holder joined the Individuals and became a producer.

what to buy: *Repercussion* (Albion, U.K., 1982/I.R.S., 1989, prod. Scott Litt) ♪♪♪♪ contains the original, notorious "Amplifier" and features sturdy production. *Like This* (Bearsville, 1984/Rhino, 1988, prod. Chris Butler and the dB's) ♪♪♪♪ is much more American-sounding with Stamey gone, proving Holsapple's songwriting is strong enough to stand alone. What to Buy Next: *Stands for deciBels* (Albion, U.K., 1981/I.R.S., 1989, prod. Alan Betrock & band) ♪♪♪♪ is a great debut full of singalong melodies. *Ride the Wild TomTom* (Rhino, 1993) ♪♪♪ gathers 26 early recordings and demos, most of which didn't made it onto the albums.

what to avoid: *Paris Avenue* (Monkey Hill, 1994) ♪♪ has a somewhat hollow sound and Holsapple's voice is ragged, though there are some good songs such as "Girlfriend."

the rest: *The Sound of Music* (I.R.S., 1987)

solo outings:

Peter Holsapple and Chris Stamey: *Mavericks* (Rhino, 1991) ♪♪♪♪

Will Rigby: *Sidekick Phenomenon* (Egon, 1985) ♪♪

Chris Stamey: *Wonderful Life* (ESD, 1982/1992) ♪♪♪♪ *Christmas Time* (ESD EP, 1986) ♪♪♪ *It's Alright* (A&M, 1987) ♪♪♪♪ *Fireworks* (Rhino, 1991) ♪♪♪♪ (with Kirk Ross) *The Robust Beauty of Improper Linear Models in Decision Making* (ESD, 1995) ♪♪♪

▶▶ R.E.M., Continental Drifters, Individuals, Wygals, Schramms

◀◀ Big Star/Alex Chilton, the Beatles, the Nazz, Elvis Costello, Grass Roots

see also: *Continental Drifters, Chris Stamey*

Steve Holtje

Chris DeBurgh

Born Oct. 15, 1948, in Argentina

A storyteller of depth and detail, DeBurgh brings an Old World sensibility to much of his work, a solidly crafted oeuvre that blends folk, pop and rock styles. He's long had followings abroad, and with his hit "Lady in Red," from the 1986 album *Into the Light,* he finally achieved recognition in the U.S.—briefly. Ballads set in the worlds of legend or in the future are his hallmark; he's written about everything from the death of a mysterious maiden whose grave sprouts flowers in a frozen land to the last broadcast from Planet Earth. An incurable romantic who nevertheless recognizes and wrestles intelligently and sensitively with the darker sides of life, de Burgh has a strong interest in spirituality and the personal and religious aspects of war. Born to British parents and now living in Ireland, he might appeal to those who enjoy the Moody Blues or Gordon Lightfoot, but like those artists he creates a body of work very much his own rather than chasing trends. On *The Getaway,* (A&M, 1982, prod. Rupert Hine) DeBurgh grabs the ears with the rousing rock folktale "Don't Pay the Ferryman," a strong opening to an album that shows off his range of power and sensitivity. *Crusader* (A&M, 1979, prod. Andrew Powell) is anchored by an emotional and thoughtful three-part epic on the Third Crusade that focuses largely on spiritual and personal concerns.

the rest: *Into the Light* (A&M, 1986) *Flying Colors* (A&M, 1988) *High On Emotion: Live From Dublin* (Avalanche, date N/A)

Polly Vedder

De La Soul

Formed 1985 in Amityville, N.Y.

Psdŋous (born Kevin Mercer); Trugoy the Dove (born David Jolicoeur); P.A. Pasemaster Mase (born Vincent Mason)

De La Soul single-handedly paved a new direction for hip-hop, away from a dead-end urban street of violence, misogyny and tired rhymes. With producer Prince Paul, the trio of suburban high school friends crafted a new, no-holds-barred bed for their thoughtful, funny, laid-back rhymes. Everything was game—French instruction records, Hall and Oates beats and even a Turtles song (which caused the 60s band to sue). De La Soul's debut, *3 Feet High and Rising,* with its flowers and primary colors, psychedelic swirl of sound and promotion of "the D.A.I.S.Y. Age (Da Inner Sound Y'all)," had people talking about their hippie-hop. And while the album produced a couple of hits in "Me Myself and I" and "Buddy," the band felt it had to retreat and act tougher on subsequent releases to maintain street credibility. A spotty live act, De La Soul was loosely associated, on and off, with other articulate and committed East Coast acts, including A Tribe Called Quest, the Jungle Boys and Queen Latifah. By 1996, it was recording without the eccentric turns of Prince Paul and was rapping over funk provided by a live band.

what to buy: *3 Feet High and Rising* (Tommy Boy, 1989, prod. Prince Paul and De La Soul) is a hip-hop classic that is still as fresh and fun to listen to as when it came out.

what to buy next: Most De La Soul albums hold their listenability over the years, and the multi-faceted messages are worth rehearing. But *Stakes Is High,* (Tommy Boy, 1996, prod. De La Soul) its first without Prince Paul, is strikingly direct. The rhymes are still surprising, but the group has matured, with fewer jokey asides.

what to avoid: De La Soul's guest spots on other albums by A Tribe Called Quest and Queen Latifah are usually disappointing.

the rest: *De La Soul is Dead* (Tommy Boy, 1991) *Buhloone Mindstate* (Tommy Boy, 1993)

worth searching for: The seven-track CD single for "Ego Trippin" (Part Two), (Tommy Boy, 1993, prod. Prince Paul and De La Soul) a single from *Buhloone Mindstate,* is, at more than 30 minutes, longer than some albums used to be.

▶▶ Jungle Brothers, A Tribe Called Quest

◀◀ KRS-One, Ritz Brothers, Stetsasonic

Roger Catlin

Deacon Blue

Formed 1986, Glasgow, Scotland

Ricky Ross, lead vocals; James Prime, keyboards; Graeme Kelling, guitars; Lorraine McIntosh, vocals; Ewen Vernal, bass; Douglas (Dougie) Vipond, drums & percussion

Although this sextet is named after a well-known Steely Dan hit, the group is in no way influenced by the sophisticated jazz/rock or the wry lyrics of Becker and Fagen. Instead they go for a typically Northern heart-on-sleeve approach, which works as long as they don't try to show how soulful they are. With its hint of gravel, Ross' voice is a dead ringer for Grant McLennan's (formerly of the Go-Betweens), but unlike McLennan, he doesn't indicate much emotional connection to the melodies he sings. Lyrically, Ross attempts to be both poetic and socially conscious, but too often winds up writing lines like "Let freedom unfurl" (from 1993's "All Over the World"). After a flurry of rave reviews in London following a show there in late 1986, the group scored a hit in the U.K. with the leaden "Dignity" from its debut album, *Raintown,* and soon its albums were debuting on the British charts at #1. Yet even with the more commercially viable material on its fourth album, *Whatever You Say, Say Nothing,* the group has never managed to make a name for itself in the U.S.

what to buy: On *Fellow Hoodlums,* (Columbia, 1991, prod. Jon

Kelly) Deacon Blue achieved whatever artistic heights it's ever likely to hit. "The Wildness" comes close to reaching Van Morrison-like charm, and "Your Swaying Arms" is another strong, yet romantic track. Finally, Ross and McIntosh created a distinctive vocal sound here, moving away from the Prefab Sprout/Go-Betweens approach that made their earlier work seem derivative.

what to buy next: If you like the looseness of "Hoodlums," you may want to check out the band's debut, *Raintown.* (Columbia, 1988, prod. Jon Kelly) For something more exciting and more pop/dance oriented (although it has slightly slimy, near-INXS overtones), try *Whatever You Say, Say Nothing* (Chaos/Columbia, 1993, prod. by Steve Osborne and Paul Oakenfold) the percolating opening track "Your Town" is the band's best single, and both "Only Tender Love" and "Last Night I Dreamed of Henry Thomas" are compelling.

what to avoid: *When the World Knows Your Name* (Columbia, 1989, prod. Warne Livesey, David Kane and Deacon Blue) may have been the band's big-time breakthrough in England, but the album sounds stiff and dated, with only the perky "Real Gone Kid" to recommend it.

worth searching for: *Our Town: The Greatest Hits* (Columbia, 1994, prod. Various) a generous (19 tracks) British import that nicely surveys the group's four albums.

▶▶ Goodbye Mr. Mackenzie, Oasis

◀◀ Simple Minds, The Go-Betweens, Prefab Sprout, Jackson Browne

Bob Remstein

Dead Boys /Stiv Bators/Lords of the New Church

Formed 1976 in Cleveland, Ohio. Disbanded 1979. Re-formed 1987.

Dead Boys: Stiv Bators, (born Stivin Bator; died June 4, 1990, in Paris, France) vocals; Cheetah Chrome (born Gene Connor), guitar; Jimmy Zero, guitar; Jeff Magnus, bass; Johnny Blitz, drums. Lords of the New Church (1981-85): Bator; Brian James, guitar; Dave Tregunna, bass; Nick Turner, drums

Shot like a big gob in punk's infancy, the Dead Boys' *Young Loud and Snotty* (Sire, 1977, prod. Genya Ravan) is actually more vulgar than the Sex Pistols. The gnashing artlessness of the band's attack and Bators' guttural roar remains pungent, like urine on a radiator. After disbanding in 1979, Bators dropped the s, recorded a solo album—the import-only *Disconnected* (Bomp/Line, 1980) —and then formed Lords of the New Church, a less entertaining (but just as obnoxious) punk-meets-sludge metal hybrid that can still be heard on *Killer Lords* (I.R.S., 1985, prod. Various) and *Lords of the New Church.* (I.R.S., 1982) Bators died in the midst of a Dead Boys reformation, following complications after being hit by a car in 1990.

Allan Orski

Dead Can Dance

Formed 1983 in London, England

Brendan Perry and Lisa Gerrard, voices and instruments; Peter Ulrich, percussion

Easily one of the most influential and recognizable bands of the modern gothic scene, Dead Can Dance (DCD) has built a significant career by using French depressive poetry (Charles Baudelaire) and Eastern European field chants, along with baroque instrumentation and religious symbolism. Listeners who coddled artists such as Enya and Enigma might find DCD a bit challenging, but if those artists leave you flat or longing for something along the same lines with a little more substance, DCD would likely fill the bill. As one of the earliest members of the elite 4AD record label, the band served to bolster the company's image of releasing arty, if pretentious, material. DCD's following is small but fervent, and it wasn't until 1994 that the group's catalog was available domestically in the U.S.

what to buy: The Baudelaire-inspired *Spleen And Ideal* (4AD, 1985, prod. Dead Can Dance and John Rivers) is the keystone to the band's style—brooding music in a minor key with beautifully atmospheric male and female vocals. While more stylized as almost pop-Gregorian music, *Dead Can Dance* (4AD, 1984, prod. Dead Can Dance and John Rivers) is less lush and more synthesizer-driven than later efforts, but it's still a brilliant piece of work. The CD includes the band's first EP *In The Garden Of Arcane Delights* as a bonus—the only way to get these songs domestically.

what to buy next: The band's progression form the early goth/baroque influences into a fully cohesive two-piece of Perry and Gerrard is realized on *Aion.* (4AD, 1990, prod. Dead Can Dance) This album shows the full pursuit of organic instrumentation and strong medieval ties, along with field chants, may pole dances, flutes and stunning vocal arrangements.

what to avoid: *The Serpent's Egg* (4AD, 1988, prod. Dead Can Dance and John Rivers) 🦴🦴 finds the band at a turning point that muddles the album's cohesiveness.

the rest: *Within The Realm Of A Dying Sun* (4AD, 1987) 🦴🦴🦴▽ *Into The Labyrinth* (4AD, 1993) 🦴🦴🦴 *A Passage In Time* (Rykodisc, 1994) 🦴🦴🦴 *Toward The Within* (4AD, 1994) 🦴🦴🦴🦴 *Spiritchaser* (4AD, 1996) 🦴🦴🦴🦴

worth searching for: *Dead Can Dance* (4AD, 1994) a self-titled promotional only 13-track sampler recapping the band's history up to 1994, to introduce the previously import-only material to radio programmers upon the release of *Into The Labyrinth*

solo outings:

Lisa Gerrard: *The Mirror Pool* (4AD, 1995) 🦴🦴🦴▽

Peter Ulrich: *Ta!aquaha's Leaving* (12" single)(Corner Stone, 1990) 🦴🦴🦴🦴▽

▶▶ Enigma, Enya, Deep Forest, Cocteau Twins, This Mortal Coil (features DCD), SPK, Cindytalk, Le Mystere De Voix Bulgare

◀◀ Gregorian chants, Bauhaus, medieval minstrels, chamber orchestras, Sisters Of Mercy, Johan Sebastian Bach

Tim Davis

Dead Kennedys

Formed 1978 in San Francisco, Calif. Disbanded 1991

Jello Biafra, vocals (born Eric Boucher); East Bay Ray, guitar; Klaus Fluoride, bass; J.H. Pelligro, drums

Biafra, a rabble-rouser from hippie-happy Boulder, Colo., connected early with punk rock's angry young men and political possibilities. Armed with a sarcastic sense of humor and a belief that all politicians were stupid (especially Republicans), he moved to San Francisco to form a band and possibly run for office. He did both. His Dead Kennedys, purposely provocative with their name, album covers and titles like "In God We Trust Inc.," were more influential for what they did than how they sounded. Biafra's nasal whines didn't so much sing as lecture, and his lyrics didn't so much rhyme as proselytize, but his points were usually effective and necessary. Sonically, the hardcore punk is so dense and intense on some Kennedys' albums you can barely listen to them today. But when Biafra makes his mark—on the minute-long "Nazi Punks Fuck Off" or the essay "Chickenshit Conformist"—he's tough to ignore. He ran unsuccessfully for San Francisco's mayor. Later, his influential and fiercely independent underground label, Alternative Tentacles, was charged with distributing pornography for reproducing H.R. Giger's "Landscape #XX" (nicknamed "penis landscape") in an album cover. The charges were eventually dropped, but the Kennedys broke up shortly thereafter. Biafra then struck out on the lecture circuit, relentlessly trashing the Persian Gulf War and, of course, conservative political and social agendas. Pathetically, after befriending Ice-T and speaking to the first Lollapalooza crowds, some San Francisco punks broke his leg and beat him up at a concert just after Nirvana-punk hit the mainstream.

what to buy: The best expression of Biafra's bizarre yodel and the Kennedy's faster-than-anything rhythm section came on the debut, *Fresh Fruit For Rotting Vegetables* (I.R.S., 1980/Alternative Tentacles, 1993, prod. Norm) 🦴🦴🦴, which contains such sarcastic titles as "Kill the Poor" and "California Uber Alles."

what to buy next: You only need one or two of the Kennedys' albums, equally hilarious, powerful and unlistenable. The *In God We Trust Inc.* EP (Alternative Tentacles, 1981, prod. Thom Wilson and Dead Kennedys) 🦴🦴🦴 and *Plastic Surgery Disasters* (Alternative Tentacles, 1982, prod. Thom Wilson and Dead Kennedys) 🦴🦴▽ are the best.

what to avoid: Too much Jello Biafra spoken word; though his rambling speeches deservedly make mincemeat of George Bush and the Persian Gulf War, and occasionally come up with a pretty good band name suggestion, one of these mouthfests ought to be plenty—draw the line at *High Priest of Harmful Matter* and *Tales From the Trial* (Alternative Tentacles, 1989) 🦴▽

the rest: *Frankenchrist* (Alternative Tentacles, 1985) 🦴🦴▽ *Bedtime for Democracy* (Alternative Tentacles, 1986) 🦴🦴▽

worth searching for: *Virus 100* (Alternative Tentacles, 1992, prod. Greg Werckman with John Yates and Jason Traeger) 🦴🦴🦴 is a top-notch tribute album, with NoMeansNo doing an a cappella version of "Forward to Death" and the Disposable Heroes of Hiphoprisy rapping on "California Uber Alles."

solo outings:

Jello Biafra: *No More Cocoons* (Alternative Tentacles, 1987) 🦴🦴 *I Blow Minds for a Living* (Alternative Tentacles, 1991) 🦴🦴 (with D.O.A.): *Last Scream of the Missing Neighbors* (Alternative Tentacles EP, 1989) (🦴🦴 (with NoMeansNo): *The Sky Is Falling and I Want My Mommy* (Alternative Tentacles, 1991) 🦴🦴🦴 (with Mojo Nixon): *Prairie Home Invasion* (Alternative Tentacles, 1994) 🦴🦴

⏩ Rage Against the Machine, Ice-T, Disposable Heroes of Hiphoprisy, Bikini Kill, Black Flag

⏪ MC5, Iggy Pop, Sex Pistols, Avengers, Dickies, Germs, X

Steve Knopper

The Dead Milkmen

Formed 1983 in Philadelphia, Penn. Disbanded 1995

Dean Clean, drums, vocals; Joe Jack Talcum, vocals. guitar; Dave Blood, bass, vocals; Rodney Anonymous, vocals

Punk rock cleared the way for forceful social leaders who screamed angst and bled fingers. It also gave smart-ass teenagers with warped senses of humor an equal chance for stardom. The Dead Milkmen, whose wit runs from cheap butt jokes to incisive parodies of mindless punk-rock kids, almost became stars. Instead, like so many other bands that rely on the one-liner instead of the right note, they grew up, became unfunny, broke up and petered out. Before that, though, the group managed to do some wonderful things. Its college radio hit "Bitchin' Camaro" lampooned underground apathetic slacker culture even before it officially arrived; the song was so stupid it was hilarious. After that came a career of great titles—"Methodist Coloring Book" (chorus: "But if you color outside the lines/Then God will send you to Hell"), "(Theme From) Blood Orgy of the Atomic Fern," "Let's Get the Baby High." In the end, the Milkmen weren't as musically creative as contemporaries such as They Might Be Giants, Camper Van Beethoven or even Too Much Joy, so their demise was inevitable. Fun concerts, though.

what to buy: *Big Lizard In My Back Yard* (Fever/Restless, 1985, prod. the Dead Milkmen and John Wicks) ♪♪♪ establishes the sound—sloppy experiments with rambling rap, reggae and loungey jazz, along with a hint of hardcore, plus "Bitchin' Camaro" and lots of good offensive jokes such as "Takin' Retards to the Zoo." *Eat Your Paisley!* (Fever-Restless, 1986, prod. John Wicks, Dead Milkmen and Dave Reckner) ♪♪♪ and *Bucky Fellini* (Fever-Enigma, 1987, prod. Brian "Mud Lounge" Beattie) ♪♪♪ are more of the same, with slightly more interesting humor ("The Thing That Only Eats Hippies").

what to buy next: *Beelzebubba* (Fever-Enigma, 1988, prod. Brian "Orchid Breath" Beattie and Mike Stewart) ♪♪♪ contains the band's second "hit," "Punk Rock Girl," later ripped accurately on "Beavis and Butt-head," and a hilarious "Ringo Buys a Rifle," with the lines "Hey Paul! You asshole!" *Metaphysical Graffiti* (Enigma, 1990, prod. Brian "Bongwizard" Beattie) ♪♪♪, whose cover is a spoof of the similarly named Led Zeppelin album, takes on Yes, Sha Na Na, brownnosers, political correctness and Methodists.

what to avoid: The Milkmen probably should have quit after, oh, *Bucky Fellini*—and the creative well was really dry for *Not Richard, But Dick* (Hollywood, 1993, prod. Dead Milkmen and Jon Lupfer). ♪

the rest: *Instant Club Hit (You'll Dance to Anything)* (Fever-Enigma EP, 1987) ♪♪ *Chaos Rules: Live at the Trocadero* (Restless, 1994) ♪♪ *Stoney's Extra Stout (Pig)* (Restless, 1995) ♪

⏩ Presidents of the United States of America, King Missile, Too Much Joy, Beastie Boys

⏪ Minutemen, They Might Be Giants, Dead Kennedys, Run-D.M.C.

Steve Knopper

Deadline

See: Bill Laswell

Kim Deal

See: The Pixies

Paul Dean

See: Loverboy

Death Metal

Thrash plus hardcore plus growling unintelligible vocals combined with a healthy dose of Satanic imagery sums up the typical death metal band. Its roots can be traced back to the 70s when Black Sabbath introduced a new kind of rock music—heavy metal with a gloomy surface and references to the occult and the dark side of the spiritual world. It was a great posture, but it was almost another decade before death metal took it's next embryonic step. In 1979 black metal was born from the lips and guitar strings of its first practitioner, Venom. Venom moved the genre forward by creating faster songs with high-pitched screaming for vocals and lyrics that dealt more openly with Satan and mythology. After Venom's demise, dark metal went underground—more specifically, to Scandinavia, where Norwegian bands such as Bathory and Hellhamer sang about death and dismemberment in the long, dark Norse nights. The latest revival began during the late 80s, after speed and thrash metal took on more mainstream forms in the hands of bands such as Metallica and Megadeth. Concurrently, Florida became a hotbed for up and coming death bands, including groups such as Morbid Angel, Death and Deicide. Already accustomed to the gothic stylings of Danzing and the speed metal of Slayer and Motörhead, death metal didn't *sound* appreciably different to the metal crowd, and it was certainly more subversive than going to see Metallica in a giant stadium with Guns 'N Roses, but as bands started to grow beyond local phenomenons they quickly became targets for censorship by Christian and parental advocacy groups. Cannibal Corpse in particular came to national awareness when their albums were banned in many areas. As U.S. death metal started to wear thin, attention was soon placed on foreign groups; Brazil's Sepultura gained a U.S. following after touring with Pantera, and the prolific Scandinavian death metal scene became the focus of many collectors. For the most part, however, death metal remains a cult-level phenomenon; most metal fans dismiss the music as too rudimentary and repetitive, while the mainstream audience simply has no appetite for songs about cannibalism and ritual slaughter. Death metal is now being written off by its own insiders as uninspiring and unemotional, but the music seems to be taking a turn for the better as the more melodic and innovative black metal and its varieties come back into vogue.

what to buy: *Black Metal* (Combat, 1982) is Venom's genre-defining record, although like many pioneering efforts it sounds different from more contemporary releases. Cannibal Corpse's *Butchered At Birth* (Metal Blade, 1991) is death metal's most infamous album; banned in many parts of the U.S. and Europe, it drew attention and followers to the genre and set the template for a host of imitators. It's a brutal record; titles such as "Meat Hook Sodomy" and "Covered With Sores" pretty much sum it up. Morbid Angel's *Covenant* (Giant, 1994, prod. Morbid Angel, Flemming, Rasmussen) is that band's finest release—not very innovative, but definitely a ferocious rocker. Bathory's *Under the Sign of a Black Mark* (New Renaissance, 1986) is one of the first releases from the new wave of black metal; raw evil oozes from these songs, and the album is already a classic in the genre. *Nordic Metal - A Tribute to Euronymous* (Necroplois, 1996, prods.?) is a comprehensive sampling of the new school of Norse black/death metal; it contains a variety of progressive acts that invoke the Viking spirit through battle hymns and tales of the cold north. Artists featured include Marduk, Emperor, and Mortiis.

what to buy next: My Dying Bride's *Turn Loose the Swans* (Futurist, 1994, prod.?) and Emperor's *In the Nightside Eclipse* (Century Black, 1994, prod.?) are two far-reaching and innovative albums. Both have set new trends in motion. *Turn Loose the Swans* liberal use of violins adds a sad, funereal ambience to the music, while *In the Nightside Eclipse* creates a hauntingly evil, yet paradoxically beautiful and rich musical landscape via keyboards. Both approaches have been heavily copied, but few match up to the originals. Hellhammer's *Apocalyptic Raids 1990 AD* (Noise, 1990), another defining album for the genre, is somewhat slow and simple, but the music hits hard. Sepultura's *Beneath the Remains* (Roadrunner, 1989) brings a consciousness to death metal, albeit a morbid one; it manages to speak out against political conditions in Brazil while maintaining death metal's distinctive musical signature. Cradle of Filth's *Vempire or Dark Faerytales in Phallustein* (Cacophonous, 1996) is surprisingly interesting black metal from England (which has a reputation for not having much of a death/black metal scene). But this album's songs range from speed 'n' grind to gothic orchestral pieces, generously overlayed with a female choir that gives a full and haunting atmosphere to the album.

worth searching for: If you aren't above having a few laughs with your death metal, check out Lawnmower Deth's *Ooh Crikey It's...Kids in America* (Combat, 1991) for some hilarious thrash/death metal parody. Or even better yet, try anything from Gwar; the music is at times barely listenable but the liner notes and comics included with the CDS are hysterical. But Gwar's real forte is for live shows, in which the group stages epic battles between space aliens, pimps, demons and O.J. Simpson for the right to copulate and destroy the earth.

Bryan Lassner

Deee-Lite

Formed 1988 in New York, N.Y.

Lady Keir, vocals; Dmitry, programming, various instruments; DJ Towa Tei (1988-92), turntables; DJ On-e (1992-present), turntables

A New York underground club sensation for years before releasing its first album, *World Clique* (Elektra, 1990, prod. Dee-Lite) to rave reviews, Deee-Lite brought together house, hip-hop, funk and disco with a 70's fashion sense. Not only is the music danceable, but the songs are virulently catchy. "Power of Love" and the guitar-inspired funk of the hit "Groove is in the Heart" are instantly appealing, and "Smile On" proves the trio can just as deftly handle songs that are slower and more melodic. The follow-up, *Infinity Within* (Elektra, 1992, prod. Dee-Lite) is not nearly as successful; a heavy political message and cold, studio precision weighs down many of the tracks, and the spontaneity and upbeat grooves of *World Clique* is nowhere to be found. *Dewdrops in the Garden* (Elektra, 1994, prod. Super DJ Dmitry) brings in newcomer DJ On-e and returns Deee-Lite to its dance floor roots.

solo outings:

DJ Towa Tei: Future Listening (Elektra, 1995)

Bryan Lassner

Deep Purple

Formed 1968, Hertford, England

Ritchie Blackmore, guitar (1968-75, 1984-94); Jon Lord, keyboards (1968-present); Ian Paice, drums (1968-present); Rod Evans, vocals (1968-69); Nick Simper, bass (1968-69); Ian Gillan, vocals (1969-73, 1984-89, 1993-present); Roger Glover, bass (1969-73, 1984-present); David Coverdale, vocals (1973-76); Glenn Hughes, bass, vocals (1973-76); Tommy Bolin, guitar (1975-76); Joe Lynn Turner, vocals (1989-93); Steve Morse, guitar (1994-present)

Scoring first with the lava-lamp special "Hush," Deep Purple quickly evolved into one of rock's heaviest bands, churning out dense, crushing slabs of metallic fury (the loudest band in the world, according to the Guinness Book of World Records) with great drama and an endless array of solos from Blackmore, whose mercurial temper harnessed him to the second strata of guitar heroedom. Purple's heyday came during the early 70s—when "Smoke on the Water" entered the pantheon of hard rock classics—but frequent personnel changes always seemed to hamper the group's forward progress. Purple disbanded in 1976 but enjoyed a much ballyhooed reunion of its "Smoke on the Water" lineup six years later. Since then, however, the group has lumbered along with middling material and still-shifting lineups, though it remains more popular in Japan and Europe than in North America.

what to buy: *Machine Head* (Warner Bros., 1972, prod. Deep Purple) is Purple's definitive moment, a powerful and seamless document of a band at its peak with all-time power tracks such as "Smoke on the Water," "Space Truckin' " and "Highway Star." Those tracks are highlights of *Made in Japan,* (Warner Bros., 1972, prod. Deep Purple) a molten live album that also features Gillan's piercing, tortured screams on "Child in Time." Considering the circumstances—Gillan and Glover's departure—*Burn* (Warner Bros., 1974, prod. Deep Purple) is a remarkable feat, bringing Coverdale and Hughes into the group without losing stride.

what to buy next: *Fireball* (Warner Brothers, 1971, prod. Deep Purple) is the "Machine Head" sound in evolution; Purple still plays with an appealingly raw abandon. *Come Taste the Band,* (Warner Bros., 1975, prod. Martin Birch and Deep Purple) Bolin's only studio album with the band, brings an interesting R&B flavor to the Purple attack. *When We Rock, We Rock and When We Roll, We Roll* (Warner Bros., 1978, prod. Deep Purple) is incomplete as a retrospective but is still the most palatable way to get "Hush" and Purple's rendition of Neil Diamond's "Kentucky Woman" into the collection.

what to avoid: *Concerto for Group and Orchestra* (Warner Bros., 1970, prod. Deep Purple) WOOF! is a misbegotten exercise in highbrow pretension. Emerson, Lake & Palmer they weren't.

worth searching for: *Purple Chronicle* (Purple/Warner Bros., 1994, prod. Various) is a lovingly compiled three-volume Japanese box set that collects all the key tracks plus alternate versions and rare songs ("Painted Horse," "Cry Free"). A definitive Purple chronicle—even if the accompanying booklet is in Japanese.

What Album Changed Your Life?

"Ornette Coleman, Change of the Century (Atlantic, 1959). To this very day, my favorite song would have to be 'Lonely Woman,' along with a track called 'Ramblin' that was just incredible. I've never, since the day I heard it, had that album out of my mind; it has a permanent residence in my head. Hearing that free jazz improvisation, it really changed my way of thinking about music."

Lou Reed

the rest: *Shades of Deep Purple* (Tetragrammaton, 1968) *Book of Taliesyn* (Tetragrammaton, 1968) *Deep Purple* (Tetragrammaton, 1969) *Deep Purple In Rock* (Warner Bros., 1970) *Purple Passages* (Warner Bros., 1972) *Who Do We Think We Are!* (Warner Bros., 1973) *Stormbringer* (Warner Bros., 1974) *24 Carat Purple* (Warner Bros., 1975) *Made in Europe* (Warner Bros., 1976) *Deepest Purple* (Warner Bros., 1980) *In Concert* (Portrait, 1982) *Perfect Strangers* (Mercury, 1984) *The House of Blue Light* (Mercury, 1987) *Nobody's Perfect* (Mercury, 1988) *Slaves and Masters* (RCA, 1990) *Purple Rainbows* (EMI, 1991) *Knocking On Your Back Door: The Best of Deep Purple in the '80s* (Mercury, 1992) *The Deep Purple Family Album* (Connoisseur, 1993) *The Battle Rages On* (Giant, 1993) *Come Hell or High Water* (RCA, 1994) *King Biscuit Flower Hour Presents Deep Purple* (KBFH Records, 1995) *Purpendicular* (CMC International, 1996) *Live at the California Jam* (Mausoleum Classix, 1996)

solo outings:

Ian Gillan: *Jesus Christ Superstar* (MCA, 1972) *Ian Gillan Band: Child in Time* (Oyster, 1976) *Clear Air Turbulence* (EMI, 1977) *Scarabus* (Island, 1978) *Live at Budokan* (Virgin, 1979) *Glory Road* (Virgin, 1980) *Future Shock* (Virgin, 1981) *Double Trouble* (Virgin, 1981) *Magic* (Virgin, 1982) *Naked Thunder* (EastWest, 1990) *Tool Box* (EastWest, 1991)

Roger Glover: *Roger Glover* (Oyster, NA) *The Butterfly Ball and the Grasshopper's Feast* (Oyster, 1974) *Elements* (Oyster, 1978) *The Mask* (PolyGram, 1984)

Ian Gillan and Roger Glover: *Accidentally on Purpose* (Virgin, 1988)

Metallica, Iron Maiden, Rainbow, Dio, Guns 'N Roses, Dokken, UFO, Whitesnake

Johnny Kidd & the Pirates, The Yardbirds, Screaming Lord Sutch & the Savages, The Animals, Mahler

see also: *Rainbow, Tommy Bolin, Whitesnake, Black Sabbath*

Gary Graff

Def Leppard

Formed 1977 in Sheffield, England

Joe Elliot, vocals; Steve Clark, guitar, vocals (1977-91, died Jan. 8, 1991); Rick Allen, drums; Rick Savage, bass; Pete Willis, guitar, vocals (1977-81); Phil Cohen, guitar, vocals (1981-present), Vivian Campbell, guitar (1992-present)

In addition to being the most successful pop-metal act of the 80s, Def Leppard has also weathered more setbacks than Job—drummer Allen losing his arm in a New Year's Eve 1985 auto accident, founding guitarist Clark's fatal substance abuse addictions. Instead of the usual guitar flash and mudraking rhythm section of most metal bands, Leppard's main assets have been studio craft and songwriting skills, first evidenced on *High 'n' Dry's* "Bringin' on the Heartbreak." Much of the credit goes to producer Robert John "Mutt" Lange, an instrumental force in developing the band's trademark crystalline, bubble gum crunch, which helped bring the girls into the metal party—thereby doubling the group's audience. The group's meticulous work habits often result in long spells between albums, which sometimes works to its disadvantage, but Def Leppard soldiers on, increasing its radio-friendly studio layering with each subsequent release.

what to buy: The compilation *Vault 1980-1995* (Mercury, 1995, prod. Various) delivers a potent hook fest, eschewing the faceless tracks which subtract from even the band's better albums. *Hysteria* (Mercury, 1987, prod. Robert John "Mutt" Lange) hits the high water mark as studio prowess and songcraft blend into a tuneful froth with "Pour Some Sugar On Me" and "Armageddon It."

what to buy next: *Pyromania* (Mercury, 1983, prod. Robert John "Mutt" Lange) marked the real break from other heavy metal acts, with its clean production tempered with just enough crunch to make "Photograph" a powerfully efficient and, for metal, technically complex single.

what to avoid: The first two releases, *On Through the Night* (Mercury, 1980, prod. Tom Allom) and *High 'n' Dry* (Mercury, 1981 prod. Robert John "Mutt" Lange) contain neither the melodies nor the polished riffs to hold anybody's attention, except perhaps air guitarists lurking below the "Wayne's World" level.

the rest: *Adrenalize* (Mercury, 1992) *Retro Active* (Mercury, 1993) *Slang* (Mercury, 1996)

worth searching for: Import versions of *Vault* are considerably different and have more to offer than the U.S. release. Our favorite is the Japanese edition, with its nine-track bonus live CD and excellent booklet.

Bon Jovi, Poison, Ratt, Candlebox, Shania Twain

⏪ Kiss, Boston, Sweet, Slade, AC/DC, the Beatles

Allan Orski

Desmond Dekker

Born Desmond Dacres July 16, 1941, in Kingston, Jamaica

One of reggae's seminal forces, Dekker started out with famed producer Leslie Kong in a group called the Aces. It was the release of the startling "The Israelites" that brought Dekker to international fame; a pioneering, herky-jerky Biblical song that sold more than a million copies and went to No. 1 in Britain, it still stands as one of the finest reggae songs ever. Moreover, it has saved him from bankruptcy with its recent reissue. *Rockin' Steady: The Best of Desmond Dekker* (Rhino, 1992, prod. Leslie Kong) ♪♪♪♪ contains his first single, "Honour Your Mother and Father" and his first hit, "007 (Shanty Town)," as well as his work with his backing band the All-Stars and "The Isrealites." *Shanty Town Original* (Drive Archive, 1994) ♪♪♪ contains "You Can Get it if You Really Want It," written for him by Jimmy Cliff—who later had more success with it on the soundtrack for "The Harder They Come."

Allan Orski

Del Fuegos

Formed 1980 in Oberlin, Ohio. Disbanded 1989.

Dan Zanes, guitar, vocals; Tom Lloyd, bass, vocals; Warren Zanes, guitar; Brent "(Woody)" Giessmann, drums

Mere children when they began appearing in Boston clubs at the turn of the 80s (Warren Zanes was recruited the day he graduated from high school), these musicians formed a white garage band that thought it was an R&B outfit. The young quartet made its reputation by covering Elvis Presley and Sam and Dave songs; Zanes snarled rather than sang, and his original lyrics were matched by wrenching guitars and a crazy rhythm section. Simplicity was the key to the group's success, epitomized by the raucous, twitching "Nervous and Shakey," "Longest Day" and "Don't Run Wild." Known for its anything-goes lifestyle, the band came quickly, burned brightly and flamed out.

what to buy: Until a good best-of comes along, it's a toss-up between the first two albums. Both *Boston, Massachusetts* (Warner Bros., 1985, prod. Mitchell Froom) ♪♪♪♪ and *The Longest Day* (Warner Bros., 1984, prod. Mitchell Froom) ♪♪♪♪♪ offer the above-mentioned songs and best capture the group's charismatic, explosive strength. Dan Zanes' solo album *Cool Down Time* (Private, 1995, prod. Mitchell Froom) ♪♪♪♪♪ is a stripped-down, wryly humorous concept album that sounds like a soul band in love with Jamaican dub.

what to buy next: *Stand Up,,* (Warner Bros., 1987, prod. Mitchell Froom) ♪♪♪ though the production values often will draw chuckles (check the background voices that wind down "A Town Called Love"). Songs such as "Wear It Like a Cape" and the harrowing, prescient "He's Had a Lot to Drink Today" are among Zanes's best efforts.

what to avoid: *Smoking in the Fields* (RCA, 1989, prod. ??) ♪, recorded after Warren Zanes and Giessmann left the group. Even Dan Zanes considers this one forgettable.

⏩ The Jayhawks, Afghan Whigs

⏪ Bo Diddley, Chuck Berry, Stax, Tom Petty and the Heartbreakers

Leland Rucker

The Del Lords /Eric Ambel/Scott Kempner

Formed 1982 in New York, N.Y. Disbanded 1991.

Eric Ambel, guitar, vocals; Scott Kempner, guitar, vocals; Manny Caiati, bass, vocals; Frank Funaro, drums, vocals

Not quite anarchic enough to be considered punk, and slightly too urban to be lumped in with the countrified roots movement, the Del Lords slipped between the cracks during the absurdly fickle 80s. That's too bad, because former Dictator Kempner's songs of love and determination set against a backdrop of hard times were far more relevant than anything that made it onto MTV back then. The group came to an end after Ambel left, but our loss is also our gain, since he and Kempner have both started ambitious solo careers.

what to buy: The group's debut, *Frontier Days* (Enigma/EMI America, 1984, prod. Lou Whitney and the Del Lords) ♪♪♪♪ contains its best material, including "Get Tough," "Burning in the Flame of Love" and a smoking cover of Alfred Reed's "How Can a Poor Man Stand Such Times and Live." Ambel's aptly titled *Loud & Lonesome* (East Side Digital, 1995, prod. Eric Ambel) ♪♪♪♪ cranks the volume a few notches and partners Ambel with ace songwriters Kevin Salem, Terry Anderson, Dan Baird and Dan Zanes. Ambel's whinny is further left of center than Neil Young's, but his guitar work will blister your wallpaper.

what to buy next: Hiring Pat Benatar's husband Neil Geraldo to produce two of its albums—including *Based on a True Story,* (Enigma, 1988, prod. Neil Geraldo) brought a metallic sheen to the Del Lords' sound. Likely a stab at gaining radio play, it ultimately failed, albeit without significant damage to the band's down-the-middle sound. The wistful "Cheyenne" and the hard-rocking "Judas Kiss" are especially fine. Kempner's sole solo effort (so far), *Tenement Angels* (Razor & Tie, 1992, prod. Lou Whitney, Manny Caiati and Scott Kempner) hearkens back to the classic sound of the Del Lords' debut album, thanks in large part to producer Whitney and his band, the Skeletons, which performs bar-band magic on Kempner's three-chord rockers.

what to avoid: The live mini-album *Howlin' at the Halloween Moon* (Restless, 1989) is a disappointment, offering a relatively bland selection of originals and covers.

the rest: *Johnny Comes Marching Home* (Enigma/EMI America, 1986) *Lovers Who Wander* (Enigma, 1990)

solo outings:

Eric Ambel: Roscoe's Gang (Enigma, 1988)

see also: *The Dictators*

Daniel Durchholz

Delaney & Bonnie

Formed 1967 in Los Angeles, Calif.

Delaney Bramlett (born July 1, 1939 in Pontotoc County, Miss.) and Bonnie Bramlett (born Nov. 8, 1944 in Acton, Ill.)

This duo was married, but divorced after a recording career that lasted from the late 60s to early 70s. Something of an offshoot of such traveling bands as Leon Russell and Joe Cocker's Mad Dogs and Englishmen, they relied on the same stable of musicians—including Russell, Carl Radle (bass), Rita Coolidge (vocals), Jim Gordon (drums) and Bobby Keys (saxophone)— to create their powerhouse and grit-stained rocking blues with a Southern-fried edge. *Delaney & Bonnie & Friends on Tour with Eric Clapton* (Atco, 1970. prod. Jimmy Miller and Delaney Bramlett) is a joyous live romp tinged with soul-satisfying gospel. Clapton is loose and plays at his searing best, while Delaney's forceful vocal delivery and Bonnie's lead and harmony vocals sway between over-the-top dynamics and reflective balladry. *The Best Of Delaney & Bonnie* (Rhino, 1990, prod. Various) is a terrific compilation of memorable songs and high-stepping performances.

Patrick McCarty

Victor Delorenzo

See: Violent Femmes

Iris Dement

Born 1961, Paragould, Ark.

A songwriter with a distinctive voice that seems to embody the entire tradition of American folk music and an unerring ability to tell moving and believable stories, DeMent is an anomaly in the music business. She was raised the youngest of eight children born in Arkansas and raised in California in a strict Pentecostal family, and she had never thought of being a musician until she was in her late 20s. She now finds herself filtering singer-songwriters such as Joni Mitchell through her childhood love for the likes of Kitty Wells, and delivers her story-songs with her charmingly unpolished, real voice cracking past notes without ever sounding like affectations. She's got fans in high places, including John Prine, who wrote the liner notes for her debut, Merle Haggard, who collaborated on a song for her third album, Emmylou Harris and Nanci Griffith. DeMent's songs on her debut, *Infamous Angel* (Philo, 1992, prod. Jim Rooney) —including "Let the Mystery Be" and "Our Town" (later used over the credits for the final episode of the TV show "Northern Exposure") already sound like Smoky Mountain traditionals. Warner Bros. signed her and re-released that album and its followup, *My Life,* (Warner Bros., 1994, prod. Jim Rooney) a thoughtful though implacably sad and deeply moving collection of autobiographical songs and fictional sketches. Her third album, *The Way I Should* (Warner Bros., 1996, prod. Randy Scruggs) lacks the inspired starkness of her earlier work, but loosens up DeMent's style in appealing ways, with free-wheeling honky-tonk riffs and trenchant social commentary.

Gil Asakawa and Elizabeth Lynch

Sandy Denny

See: Fairport Convention

Depeche Mode

Formed 1980 in Basildon, England

Martin Gore, keyboards, vocals; David Gahan, vocals and guitar; Andy Fletcher, percussion; Vince Clark, keyboards (1980-81); Alan Wilder, drums, keyboards, vocals (1982-95)

Depeche Mode can make a convincing case as the biggest New

Wave band of the 80s; the sheer influence and weight the band enjoyed within the music industry was on par with any of the more mainstream superstar acts of the era. This once-obscure artsy-synth band brought electronic music to the mainstream through catchy hooks, obtuse lyrics, instantly danceable rythms and world-weary lyrics that, while simple in retrospect, were groundbreaking for the time. Born of England's New Romantic movement, Depeche was the cornerstone of Mute Records, one of a number of independent British labels that would control the music scene there for years. Depeche has gone through many many phases since its inception—from the esoteric electro-pop of its first few releases to the more industrial, rock-with-a-conscience leanings during the latter part of the decade. But during the 90s, when guitars reclaimed dominance over the modern rock scene, Depeche's style seemed stale and predictable. But the group proved up to the challenge with *Songs Of Faith And Devotion*, which is marked by the prominent use of guitar and walls of feedback noise. Still, Depeche is trying to assess its spot in the new world musical order. Compounding this mission even further is the departure of Wilder, plus singer Gahan's suicide attempt and subsequent drug bust in 1996.

what to buy: *Catching Up With Depeche Mode* (Mute/Sire, 1985, prod. Various) is a safe singles collection designed to introduce the group to the U.S. audience.

what to buy next: For a taste of early 80s electro-pop heaven, don't miss *Speak and Spell,* (Mute/Sire, 1981, prod. Daniel Miller) which is the band's first full release and features Vince Clark, who would soon leave the band to form Yaz and then Erasure. Fluffy from start to finish despite attempts at Cabaret Voltaire-style found sounds and apocalyptic subtlies, this is pure ear candy. The band's midpoint is found on *People Are People,* (Mute/Sire, 1984, prod. Depeche Mode and Daniel Miller) featuring the breakthrough U.S. single of the same name. This release finds the band farming in more industrial territory but still maintaining its pop sensibilities. If you're looking for that record to listen to when you think your life is as bad as it can get, *Black Celebration* (Mute/Sire, 1986, prod. Depeche Mode and Daniel Miller) may just what you're looking for. Somber and brooding from start to finish, this record shows a bleak side of the band that had only been hinted at before.

what to avoid: *Violator* (Mute/Sire, 1990, prod. Daniel Miller) is nothing but pure pop. It lacks the distinct stylization of the band's earlier releases that, while light, were not formulaic. That said, it was also the band's biggest commercial success in the U.S.

the rest: *A Broken Frame* (Mute/Sire, 1982) *Construction Time Again* (Mute/Sire, 1983) *Some Great Reward* (Sire Mute, 1984) *Music For The Masses* (Mute/Sire 1994) *101 Live* (Mute/Sire, 1989) *Box Set Of Singles 1-3* (Mute/Sire, 1991) *Songs Of Faith And Devotion* (Sire/Mute, 1993) *Songs Of Faith And Devotion: Live* (Mute/Sire, 1994)

worth searching for: A limited edition pairing *Songs of Faith and Devotion* and its live follow-up in one CD package, done for 1994 tour for a spring 1994 tour of Australia.

solo outings:

Martin Gore: *Counterfeit* (Mute/Sire EP, 1989)

Recoil (Andy Fletcher): *Hydrology 1 + 2* (Mute/Enigma, 1989)

Soft Cell, Erasure, Yaz, Recoil, the Orb, Orbital

Kraftwerk, Throbbing Gristle, Silicon Teens, Cabaret Voltaire

Tim Davis

Rick Derringer /The McCoys

Born Aug. 5, 1947 in Union City, Ind.

(1960-70) Rick Zehringer (later Derringer), guitar, vocals and keyboards; Randy Hobbs, bass; Robert Peterson, keyboards; Randy Zehringer, drums

Typical of 60s garage-rock groups, the McCoys made simple, straightforward pop-rock in the vein of "Louie Louie" and "La Bamba." While still in high school, the quartet was pegged by the Strangeloves production team of Feldman-Goldstein-Gottehrer to record for Bang Records; the group's first single, "Hang on Sloopy," was a No. 1 smash built around a monotonous three-chord riff and a nonsense sing-along chorus. Unfortunately, the group's producers confined the McCoys' output to vapid clones of this prototype; the group's most original material, the folk-driven "Sorrow," ended up being a hit for the English group the Merseys. The group broke with Bang Records during the 60s, finding its voice as a psychedelic progressive-rock group. Most of the band members joined up with guitarist Johnny Winter during the early 70s. Zehringer, now known as Rick Derringer, left Johnny to join brother Edgar Winter's group as guitarist before embarking on a solo career in 1974. Derringer also continued to produce and play sessions, working with a wide range of acts including Steely Dan, Cyndi Lauper and Weird Al Yankovic.

what to buy: Derringer's *All American Boy* (Blue Sky, 1973, prod. Rick Derringer and Bill Szymczyk) ♪♪♪♪♪ is a classic power-rock album that shows inspired genius over 12 tracks, beginning with the hit "Rock and Roll Hootchie Koo" and continuing through pop dramas ("The Airport Giveth," "Teenage Queen"), dark ballads ("Jump, Jump, Jump" and "Hold," cowritten with Patti Smith) and gloriously hooky rock ("Slide on Over, Slinky," "Teenage Love Affair"). He even manages to sneak in two of the most infectious Latin rhythm instrumentals ever committed to tape—"Joy Ride" and "Time Warp."

what to buy next: *The Best of the McCoys* (Legacy Rock Artifacts, 1995, prod. Feldman-Goldstein-Gottehrer) ♪♪♪ is a comprehensive collection of the group's Bang Records catalog, with 22 tracks that include all the group's significant A- and B-sides (including "Hang on Sloopy" and "Sorrow," of course) as well as two previously unreleased cuts ("Gaitor Tails and Monkey Ribs" and "Bald Headed Lena"). *The Psychedelic Years* (One Way, 1994, prod. the McCoys) ♪♪♪ shows the band in all its post-Bang Records glory, a nearly complete compendium of its work from 1968-70 with masterpieces such as "Faces," "Resurrection," "Daybreak" and "Love Don't Stop." Derringer's mid-90s R&B excursions—*Back to the Blues* (Blues Bureau International, 1994, prod. Rick Derringer) ♪♪♪ and *Electra Blues* (Blues Bureau International, 1994, prod. Rick Derringer) ♪♪♪—mark a mighty and meaty return to form with interpretations of "Blue Suede Blues," "Blue Velvet" and "Meantown Blues."

worth searching for: Derringer's self-named band of the mid-70s was a solid rock outfit given to invigorating performances. Either *Derringer* (Blue Sky, 1976) ♪♪♪½ and *Live* (Blue Sky, 1977) ♪♪♪♪ are well worth the hunt.

▶▶ Cyndi Lauper, Slash (Guns 'N Roses), Bryan Adams, Billy Squier

◀◀ Chuck Berry, Jerry Lee Lewis, Carl Perkins, the Kingsmen Johnny Winter, Edgar Winter

see also: *Johnny Winter, Edgar Winter*

Christopher Scapelliti

Jackie DeShannon

Born Aug. 21, 1944, in Hazel, Ky.

A talented, pioneering singer and early women songwriters in the rock era, DeShannon never achieved the fame of some of her contemporaries, though she's had two Top 10 hits in 1965's "What the World Needs Now is Love" (the Burt Bacharach-Hal David theme from the movie "Bob and Carol and Ted and Alice") and her own "Put a Little Love in Your Heart" in 1969. She began writing at an early age, and her songs have been recorded artists such as Kim Carnes ("Bette Davis Eyes"), Brenda Lee ("Dum-Dum"), the Byrds ("Don't Doubt Yourself Babe"), Marianne Faithful ("Come Stay With Me"), the Searchers ("When You Walk Into the Room"), the Carpenters ("Boat to Sail"), and Annie Lennox and Al Green ("Put a Little Love in Your Heart"). Though often uncredited, she has produced her own material, worked with Jimmy Page, Van Morrison and Ry Cooder, wrote themes for films ("Splendor in the Grass" and "C'mon, Let's Live a Little") and was an opening act on the Beatles first American tour. Two compilations remain available; each is worthwhile, and between them they tell the DeShannon story: *What the World Needs Now Is—Jackie DeShannon: The Definitive Collection* (EMI, 1994, comp. Bruce Harris) ♪♪♪♪½ only covers her Liberty/Imperial years (1958-69); and *The Best of Jackie DeShannon* (Rhino, 1991, prod. Various) ♪♪♪♪ is more expansive and includes her version of "Bette Davis Eyes."

Leland Rucker

Mink Deville

See: Willy Deville

Willy Deville /Mink Deville

Born Aug. 27, 1953 in New York, N.Y.

Numerous label changes coupled with industry blackball due to previous drug problems have left Deville's catalogue woefully depleted despite its solid foundations. Mink Deville began in the midst of the late 70s punk scene, an inauspicious spot for a street-inflected R&B group with a Latino flair. The fusion of those styles, matched with Deville's romantic songwriting and the grit-grease of his impassioned vocals, brought a credible grandeur to the well-mined soul trove. Although it costs a bit more, the import-only *Spanish Stroll 1977-1987* (Raven, 1993, prod. Various) ♪♪♪♪ is worth tracking down as it recaps the singer's early years onto a generous 21-song disc. The slinky title track, the easy roll of " 'A' Train Lady" and all his majestic early ballads demand attention. Of Deville's solo work, which remains rooted in R&B roots, only his last two releases are in print—which is unfortunate as they do not demonstrate the full depth of his work. *Backstreets of Desire* (Forward, 1992, prod. Various) is a fairly rigorous comeback but lacks the leanness of his best work. *Loup Garou* (EastWest, 1995/Discovery, 1996, prod. John Phillip Shenale and Willy DeVille) finds the singer returning to New Orleans (where he's recorded and lived), and although "When You're Away From Me" shines, a number of the ballads seem overwrought and rehashed.

Allan Orski

The Devlins

Formed 1989 in Dublin, Ireland

Colin Devlin, vocals, guitar, keyboards; Peter Devlin, bass, guitar, mandolin, vocals; Sean Devitt, drums, percussion, vocals; Niall Macken, keyboards

The Devlin's fresh, dreamy folk-rock made its debut, *Drift*, Capitol, 1993, prod. Malcolm Burn and Robert Bell) a critical favorite. But the Irish group, centered around the Devlin brothers, hasn't been able to turn its acclaim into significant record sales, at least not in the U.S. *Drift* was sent adrift after its completion in 1992, delayed until April of the next year while Capitol's front-office played musical chairs. Good reviews and persistent touring with the likes of Sheryl Crow and Sarah McLachlan built a small U.S. following—the band's a bit bigger in Ireland—but it hasn't been heard from much since. The group's recorded output also includes the *Live Bait, Dead Bait* EP, released in the U.K. prior to "Drift," and an edgy, synth-heavy track ("Crossing the River") on the "Batman Forever" soundtrack.

Doug Pullen

Devo

Formed 1972 in Akron, Ohio

Mark Mothersbaugh, vocals, guitar, keyboards; Gerald V. Casale, vocals, bass, keyboards; Bob Mothersbaugh, guitar, vocals; Bob Casale, keyboards, guitar; Alan Myers, drums (1972-88); David Kendrick, drums (1988-present

Possibly the most unlikely success story in pop, Devo's music, wardrobe, stage show, interviews and mini-movies all preached a vague philosophy of "de-evolution," the dehumanization of mankind by technology, industry and apathy—an idea Devo alternately praised and derided. Formed on the campus of Kent State University (shortly after the shooting of four students by the National Guard), Devo gained underground popularity during the mid-70s due to its bizarre stage shows, in which the musicians would dress in identical yellow jumpsuits, plastic masks and fake hair, sometimes accompanied by the helmeted "General Boy" (actually Mark and Bob's father). Playing an early form of synth-pop, the group won a contract with Warner Bros. in 1978, bowing before a quizzical public with *Q: Are We Not Men? A: We Are Devo* and its kinetic cover of the Rolling Stones' "(I Can't Get No) Satisfaction." Devo was a curiosity until it won over the masses with its 1980 single, "Whip It," but the spotlight faded fast. Though its never officially disbanded—Devo performed at the 1996 Sundance Film Festival—the musicians have since 1990 concentrated on film, TV and multi-media projects, including the animated children's series "Rugrats."

what to buy: Nowhere is Devo more Devo than on its first album, *Q: Are We Not Men? A: We Are Devo.* (Warner Bros., 1978, prod. Brian Eno) Containing songs both curious ("Mongoloid," "Space Junk," "(I Can't Get No) Satisfaction") and perverse ("Uncontrollable Urge," "Sloppy (I Saw My Baby Gettin')"), it is a much better rebellion against the stagnant music of the 70s than many of the most celebrated punk albums.

what to buy next: *Oh, No! It's Devo* (Warner Bros.,1983, prod. Roy Thomas Baker) displays the band's ability to create catchy tunes without watering down its trademark philosophy.

what to avoid: *Total Devo,* (Virgin, 1988, prod. Devo) while featuring some strong songs, is burdened by poor production that renders the songs flat and lifeless. (Fortunately, many of them appear in better form on the live recording *Now It Can Be Told.*)

the rest: *Duty Now for the Future* (Warner Bros., 1979) *Freedom of Choice* (Warner Bros., 1980) *Live* (Warner Bros. EP, 1981) *New Traditionalists* (Warner Bros., 1981) *Shout* (Warner Bros., 1984) *Now It Can Be Told* (Enigma, 1989) *Smooth Noodle Maps* (Enigma, 1990) *Hardcore Devo, Volume 1, 1974-1977* (Rykodisc, 1990); *Devo's Greatest Hits* (Warner Bros., 1990) *Devo's Greatest Misses* (Warner Bros., 1990) *Hardcore Devo, Volume 2, 1974-1977* (Rykodisc, 1991); *Devo Live: The Mongoloid Years* (Rykodisc, 1992)

worth searching for: The satiric *Devo E-Z Listening Disk* (Rykodisc, 1987, prod. Devo) features the band performing elevator music versions of its songs, muzaking its own work before Muzak can get it.

▶▶ They Might Be Giants, The Residents, Tony Basil, Nirvana, Foo Fighters

◀◀ Kratfwerk, Can, Brian Eno, Robert Fripp, the Rolling Stones

Brandon Trenz

Dexy's Midnight Runners /Kevin Rowland & Dexy's Midnight Runners

Formed 1979 in Birmingham, England

Kevin Rowland, vocals; Billy Adams, banjo and guitar; Giorgio Kilkenny, bass; Micky Billingham, accordion, piano and organ; Seb Shelton, drums; Big Jimmy Patterson, trombone; Paul Speare, flute, tin whistle and saxophone; Brian Maurice, saxophone

When New Wave raised its ugly commercial voice in 1980, punk singer Rowland answered back with Dexy's Midnight Runners, a high-octane mix of traditional Irish music, soul and rock. Although Rowland's vision was inevitably short-sighted (he burned bridges with his first label and abused journalists and band members), he managed to find success producing honest, hard-working soul music at a time when it was anything but the fashion. For the group's 1982 hit album *Too-Rye-Ay* and its hit "Come On Eileen," Rowland re-configured Dexy's as dungaree-clad Celtic rock group, featuring two-piece fiddle section, vocal trio, and the occasional horn backup. Sadly, Dexy's catalog is out of print in the U.S.; all that remains here is the spirit but sloppy *BBC Radio One Live in Concert,* (Griffin, 1995) 🦴🦴🦴 taken from a 1982 concert. Of the imports, *Searching for the Young Soul Rebels* (EMI U.K., 1980) 🦴🦴🦴🦴 is a foot-stomping rave-up of earnest soul tributes, while *Too-Rye-Ay,* (Mercury U.K. 1982) 🦴🦴🦴 isn't as focused but has some great moments shifting between rustic folk-rock ("The Celtic Soul Brothers") to blazing soul (a cover of Van Morrison's "Jackie Wilson Said") and rollicking pop (the international hit "Come On Eileen"). *Geno* (Old Gold UK, 1983, prod. Various) 🦴🦴🦴 is a worthwhile compilation of early singles. After a poor 1988 solo showing, Rowland has remained out of sight and ear shot. There's no word yet on his next move.

Christopher Scapelliti

Dennis Deyoung

See: Styx

Buck Dharma

See: Blue Oyster Cult

Dharma Bums

Formed 1988 in Portland, Oregon

Jeremy Wilson, vocals; Eric Lovre, guitar; Jim Talstra, bass; John Moen, drums

With a name taken from the classic Jack Kerouac novel and band members that have the ability to range from drawling hillbillies, to post-punkers, to REM wannabe's, it is shockingly surprising how often Dharma's music tends to blend together into a drone of mediocre modern rock, or worse yet, poorly executed country. Some of the songs do have instant appeal and are catchy, (which may help explain the amount of college-radio air-play they receive) but after a few listenings most quickly break down into simple chords and uninspired lyrics. *Bliss* (Frontier, 1990, prod. Dharma Bums) 🦴🦴🦴 is their strongest and most varied album; a few tracks like "Pumpkinhead" manage to hold their own, and while there's certainly nothing innovative going on, they mix things up enough to maintain a good flow. Thankfully, the country influences are fairly subdued (though a few tracks will have you pining for the big city). *Welcome* (1991, Frontier, prod. Ed Brooks) 🦴🦴🦴 may hold a few people interested for the plain fact that they rock a heck of lot more this time out. Sure the songs follow an identical format, but the increased tempo should at least keep you awake. *Haywire: Out Through the Indoor* (Frontier, 1989, prod. Dharma Bums) 🦴🦴½ exudes more of a country vibe, but is fundamentally the same; a few decent songs to keep the record from sinking, but too many no-shows. The Dharma Bums never really sound bad, they can play their instruments reasonably well, but it would be nice to know if they can write a song.

Bryan Lassner

Neil Diamond

Born Jan. 24, 1941 in Brooklyn, N.Y.

Diamond has been so entrenched in pop's middle-of-the-road mainstream for so long that it's easy to forget he was—for a time—a decent rock songwriter and something of a maverick whose material was more personalized than most of what came out of the Brill Building song factory where Diamond began his career. A former premed student (he attended New York University on a fencing scholarship), Diamond can lay claim to one of pop's great three-chord wonders (1966's

"Cherry, Cherry") as well as to a string of songs covered by a wide swatch of performers, including the Monkees ("I'm a Believer"), Deep Purple ("Kentucky Woman"), UB40 ("Red Red Wine"), Chris Isaak ("Solitary Man") and Urge Overkill ("Girl, You'll Be a Woman Soon"). These days he's more defined by the schmaltzier portion of his ouvre ("You Don't Bring Me Flowers," "Heartlight"), but his 30 years of recording—and worldwide record sales of nearly 100 million—merit respect.

what to buy: *Classics—The Early Years* (Columbia, 1983, prod. Various) ♪♪♪♪♪ contains all of his wonderful late 60s hits, laying a claim for Diamond up as one of the finest pop craftsmen of the era.

what to buy next: *His Twelve Greatest Hits* (MCA, 1974, prod. Tom Catalano) ♪♪♪ captures the next evolution of Diamond's career, a commercial peak even though the singalong slickness of "Sweet Caroline" and "Song Sung Blue" is a dramatic comedown from the *Classics* selection. *Beautiful Noise* (Columbia, 1976, prod. Robbie Robertson) ♪♪♪ is a concept album about the Brill Building/Tin Pan Alley scene, an ambitious and listenable venture that stands apart from the lackluster albums that preceded and followed it.

what to avoid: *Heartlight* (Columbia, 1982, prod. Burt Bacharach, Carole Bayer Sager and Neil Diamond) WOOF! is emblematic of how slight and lightweight the bulk of Diamond's albums have been.

the rest: *Velvet Gloves and Spit* (Uni, 1968) ♪♪ *Brother Love's Traveling Salvation Show* (Uni, 1969) ♪♪♪ *Touching You, Touching Me* (Uni, 1969) ♪♪ *Neil Diamond Gold* (Uni, 1970) ♪♪♪ *Tap Root Manuscript* (Uni, 1970) ♪♪♪ *Stones* (MCA, 1971) ♪♪♪ *Moods* (MCA, 1972) ♪♪ *Hot August Night* (MCA, 1972) ♪♪♪ *Rainbow* (MCA, 1973) ♪♪ *Jonathan Livingston Seagull* (Columbia, 1973) WOOF! *Serenade* (Columbia, 1974) ♪♪ *And the Singer Sings His Songs* (MCA, 1976) ♪♪ *Love at the Greek* (Columbia, 1977) ♪♪♪ *I'm Glad You're Here With Me Tonight* (Columbia, 1977) ♪ *You Don't Bring Me Flowers* (Columbia, 1978) ♪ *September Morn* (Columbia, 1979) WOOF! *The Jazz Singer* (Capitol, 1980) ♪♪♪ *On the Way to the Sky* (Columbia, 1981) ♪ *12 Greatest Hits, Volume 2* (Columbia, 1982) ♪♪ *Primitive* (Columbia, 1984) WOOF! *Love Songs* (MCA, 1985) ♪♪♪ *Headed for the Future* (Columbia, 1986) ♪ *Hot August Night II* (Columbia, 1987) ♪♪ *The Best Years of Our Lives* (Columbia, 1988) WOOF! *Lovescape* (Columbia, 1991) WOOF! *The Greatest Hits 1966-1992* (Columbia, 1992) ♪♪♪ *Glory Road—1968 to 1972* (MCA, 1992) ♪♪♪ *The Christmas Album* (Columbia, 1992) ♪♪ *Up on the Roof: Songs from the Brill Building* (Columbia, 1993) ♪♪ *Live in America* (Columbia, 1994) ♪♪♪ *The Christmas Album, Volume II* (Columbia, 1994) ♪♪ *Tennessee Moon* (Columbia, 1986) ♪♪♪

worth searching for: Diamond's earliest albums—*The Feel of Neil Diamond* (Bang, 1966) ♪♪♪ and *Just for You* (Bang, 1967) ♪♪♪—have collector's value as well as their share of those early hits.

▶▶ Barry Manilow, Mary's Danish, Michael Bolton

◀◀ Bob Dylan, Hank Williams, George and Ira Gershwin, Elvis Presley, Barbra Streisand

Gary Graff

Bruce Dickinson

See: Iron Maiden

The Dictators

Formed 1974 in the Bronx, N.Y. Disbanded 1980.

Handsome Dick Manitoba (born Richard Blum), vocals; Andy Shernoff, vocals, bass, keyboards; Ross "The Boss" Funichello, guitar; TopTen (born Scott Kempner), guitar; Mark "The Animal" Mendoza, bass (1975-77); Stu Boy King, drums (1974-75); Richie Teeter, drums, vocals (1975-80)

It's been argued (most strongly by critic/booster Richard Meltzer) that this was the first punk group. If it's admitted that Television was too arty and musically adept, and that the New York Dolls were really glam, then the argument stands up. Of course, many would say there was too much heavy metal in the Dictators' music—especially Ross the Boss's frenetic "quantity is quality" solos—for the group to be considered punk. But, punk was as much attitude as anything else, and the 'tators had attitude out the wazoo. Manitoba, who certainly doesn't sound like a singer, started as the band's roadie, but with his parodistic wrestling image made a perfect "secret weapon" comic-macho frontman (just how macho was up for measurement when he heckled transvestite Wayne County at CBGB one night; County whacked his head with the microphone stand, sending Manitoba to the hospital).

The group was put together by fanzine (Teenage Wasteland Gazette) editor Shernoff, Kempner and Funichello and quickly became a mainstay of the early CBGB scene. Shernoff's songs (he wrote all the originals, very occasionally in collaboration) were irreverently referential to the history and iconography of rock, as on the debut album's "(I Live For) Cars and Girls" (as well as its covers of Sonny & Cher's "I Got You Babe" and "California Sun"). *Go Girl Crazy!,* like all the group's studio efforts, was produced by the same team (Murray Krugman and Sandy Pearlman) that made Blue Oyster Cult stars; the Dictators had to settle for commercially unsuccessful critic's faves. Since breaking up in 1980, the Dictators have sporadically and temporarily reunited, using any handy excuse (the 10th anniversary of punk, the 20th anniversary of CBGB or for no reason at all.

what to buy: The perfect blend of 60s pop takeoffs and aggressive punk humor on *Go Girl Crazy!* (Epic, 1975, prod. Murray Krugman and Sandy Pearlman) shows the group at its crudest and funniest, often skirting the limits of taste but so goofy ("Master Race Rock") that it undermined any attempt to mold the jokes into ideology.

what to buy next: *Fuck 'Em If They Can't Take a Joke* (ROIR, 1981, prod. Not listed) comes from an early ('81) reunion show. The early tunes are less punk and more metal at this juncture, and highlights include "Loyola," covers of Mott the Hooples' "Moon Upstairs" and Velvet Underground's "What Goes On," and a funny lounge-style opening verse to open "Search and Destroy."

worth searching for: The long out-of-print *Manifest Destiny,* (Asylum, 1977, prod. Murray Krugman and Pearlman) features slightly better songwriting than the debut but not quite as hilarious. Ditto *Bloodbrothers,* (Asylum, 1978, prod. Murray Krugman and Sand Pearlman) which boasts another great cover (the Flamin' Groovies' "Slow Death") and the anthem of purpose "Faster & Louder." Both long-out-of-print Asylum albums have never been digitalized.

solo outings:

Wild Kingdom (Manitoba, Shernoff, Funichello): *. . And You?* (MCA, 1990, prod. Andy Shernoff)

The Ramones, the Surf Punks, Circle Jerks, Twisted Sister, Motley Crue

The Stooges, Flamin' Groovies, Kinks, Who, Seeds, Mott the Hoople, Blue Oyster Cult

see also: *The Del-Lords, Twisted Sister*

Steve Holtje

Bo Diddley

Born Elias Bates, Dec. 30, 1928, in McComb, Miss.

Unarguably one of the most-influential musicians in rock 'n' roll, Diddley's distinctive "chunka, chunka" rhythm guitar riff is the stuff of which rock's bedrock was made. Born near the Mississippi Delta, Diddley was raised by sharecroppers and earned his nickname in school. The family that adopted him—and changed his last name to McDaniel—moved to Chicago, where Diddley began making his guitars and playing them on the street and in small clubs. He signed with Checker Records during the mid-50s and released a string of albums and singles through the mid-60s that would influence countless rockers, from Elvis Presley and Buddy Holly to the Rolling Stones and Jimi Hendrix. Diddley's recorded output since then has been erratic, and most of what he has released has been either uninspired, ill-advised or both—though the star-studded 1996 *A Man Amongst Men,* his first for a major label in 25 years, showed there's life in the old man yet. Diddley, a member of the Rock and Roll Hall of Fame, has stayed active on the concert trail, his rectangular guitars and Coke-bottle glasses as familiar to generations of admirers as that gritty voice and gut-bucket guitar sound.

what to buy: *Bo Diddley/Go Bo Diddley* (Chess, 1958 and 1959/1987) capture the primal "Bo Diddley Beat" in all its fever. Some of Diddley's greatest songs appeared on these records, including "Bo Diddley," "I'm a Man," "Who Do You Love" and "Crackin' Up."

what to buy next: If you're willing to shell out a few more bucks, check out *The Chess Box,* (Chess, 1990, comp. Andy McKaie) an exhaustive warehouse of Diddley's early and influential work for the famous Chicago label. All his most popular and important work is here, as well as worthwhile obscurities and previously unreleased material.

what to avoid: Just about anything Diddley did for the small, well-meaning Triple X Records label—most of them well-intentioned but poorly executed attempts to make Diddley relevant. Among them: *Breakin' Through the B.S.* (Triple X, 1989, prod. Scott Free); *The Mighty Bo Diddley* Bokay Productions, 1985) and *This Should Not Be* (Triple X, 1993, prod. Scott Free)

the rest: *Bo Diddley* (Chess, 1958) *Bo Diddley is a Gunslinger* (Chess, 1960) *In the Spotlight* (Chess, 1960) (with Chuck Berry): *Two Great Guitars*(Chess, 1964) *Superblues* (with Muddy Waters and Little Walter) (Chess, 1967) (with Muddy Waters and Howlin' Wolf): *The Super Super Blues Records*(Chess, 1968) *The London Bo Diddley Sessions* (Chess, 1973) *His Greatest Sides, Vol. 1* (Chess,

1986, cassette only) ♪♪♪ *Rare and Well Done* (Chess, 1991) ♪♪♪ *A Man Amongst Men* (Code Blue/Atlantic, 1996) ♪♪

worth searching for: Completists just have to track down one of Diddley's most opportunistic albums, *Surfin' with Bo Diddley*, (Chess, 1963) ♪ a record that proved that Bo knows trends, but doesn't always know when to avoid them.

▶▶ The Rolling Stones, Eric Burdon, Jimi Hendrix, Buddy Holly, Elvis Presley, Bow Wow Wow, U2

◀◀ Louis Jordan, Muddy Waters, John Lee Hooker

Doug Pullen

Difford and Tilbrook

See: Squeeze

Ani DiFranco

Born 1970 in Buffalo, N.Y.

In an industry ruled by pigeonholes and demographics, Ani DiFranco has built a rabid cult following of old folkies and young punks, men and women, gays and straights by recording fiercely personal music on her own label, Righteous Babe, at a staggering rate of two albums per year. In between tackling abortion, sexuality, stereotypes and decaying relationships in striking, stream-of-consciousness detail, DiFranco has also emerged as an underground heroine with such savage salvos at the corporate music industry as "Egos Like Hairdos," "The Next Big Thing" and "The Million You Never Made," which baits the major record companies sniffing at her backstage door ("I don't prefer obscurity/but I'm an idealistic girl"). DiFranco's visibility has been boosted by three mighty forces: the World Wide Web, where you can find more than five home pages dedicated to her; the "angry woman" movement spearheaded by Alanis Morissette; and torrents of 1995 accolades from the mainstream press, which is always eager to rally around a young rebel with a cause. But artistic integrity is more than just a stance to DiFranco, who walks it like she balks at it.

what to buy: DiFranco has been fleshing out her aggressive solo acoustic sound with other instruments since her third album. But *Out of Range* (Righteous Babe, 1994, prod. Ani DiFranco and Ed Stone) ♪♪♪♪ marks a pivotal move toward a band feel without overwhelming the bite of her voice, especially on the electric version of the title track. *Not a Pretty Girl* (Righteous Babe, 1995, prod. Ani DiFranco) ♪♪♪♪ is a hard-nosed hybrid of jagged confessionals, poetic imagery and punkish diatribes ranging from social inadequacy ("This Bouquet") to capital punishment ("Crime for Crime"). *Dilate* (Righteous Babe, 1996, prod. DiFranco) ♪♪♪♪ is both her noisiest and most unsettling album, challenging her voice with multi-textured arrangements and quashing any fears about her new-found fame tempering her attitude in the unquotable chorus of "Untouchable Face."

what to buy next: From the days when she was more folk than punk, the solo acoustic *Ani DiFranco* (Righteous Babe, 1990, prod. Ani DiFranco and Dale Anderson) ♪♪♪♪ displays the influence of everyone from Rickie Lee Jones to Phoebe Snow and exudes a faint sense of innocence bubbling under the already-calloused skin. The harrowing highlight is "Lost Woman Song," which captures the narrator's contempt for protesters blocking her way into an abortion clinic, her revulsion of the lover who insists on waiting with her and her respect for the nurse who helps her get through it.

what to avoid: *Like I Said* (Righteous Babe, 1993, prod. Ani DiFranco and Ed Stone) ♪♪♪, a compilation of re-recorded versions of songs from her first two albums. Faster, but not necessarily better, than the originals.

the rest: *Not So Soft* (Righteous Babe, 1991) ♪♪♪ *Imperfectly* (Righteous Babe, 1992) ♪♪♪ *Puddle Dive* (Righteous Babe, 1993) ♪♪♪

▶▶ Dar Williams, Alanis Morissette

◀◀ Joni Mitchell, Rickie Lee Jones, Tracy Chapman, Fugazi

David Okamoto

Dim Stars

See: Richard Hell & the Voidoids

Dinosaur Jr. /J Mascis

Formed 1984 in Amherst, Mass.

J Mascis (born Joseph D. Mascis), guitar, vocals; Lou Barlow, bass (1984-88); Donna Biddell, bass (1989); Van Connor, bass (1991); Mike Johnson, bass (1992-present); Murph, drums (1984-94)

Dinosaur Jr. (the Jr. was appended after a similarly named bunch of veteran San Francisco musicians objected) is directly or indirectly one of the most influential bands of the late 80s, inspiring sounds in both the U.S. and Great Britain. The enigmatic, untalkative Mascis—often deemed the ultimate slacker as much for his lazy vocals as for his diffidence—is a powerful guitarist whose Neil Young (circa *Zuma*)-inspired feedback fests and high-volume distortion assaults resulted in some of the most intense underground rock of the mid-80s. Long before grunge was an acknowledged genre, the term was frequently used to describe the thick, messy, guitar-heavy sound of this trio, which through it all still managed to maintain a modicum of pop catchiness. During the 90s Mascis began using more acoustic guitar, an approach culminating in his 1996 solo album. Mascis has also demonstrated some acumen as a drummer, playing on Dinosaur Jr. albums as well as with Deep Wound (with Barlow), Gobblehoof (with Deep Wound's Charles Nakajima), Upside Down Cross and others. Original bassist Barlow, frustrated by Mascis' unrelenting control, eventually bolted to form Sebadoh. A succession of bassists followed before Johnson nailed down the role.

what to buy: *Bug* (SST, 1988, prod. Not Listed) features the college radio hit "Freak Scene" and the thickest guitar sound of Mascis's career—"No Bones" is a firestorm of distortion and Young-esque reverb splashes—as well as primal hooks on nearly every chorus and quite a few verses, too. Only the shapeless closer "Don't" keeps this from 5 bone perfection. Mascis' solo album, *Martin and Me* (Reprise, 1996, prod. Not Listed) is a live solo acoustic set (with guitarist Kurt Fedora joining on the last two tracks), a logical progression which works superbly thanks to the sturdiness of Mascis's originals as well as an inspired assortment of covers that includes Greg Sage's "On the Run," Carly Simon's "Anticipation," Lynyrd Skynrd's "Every Mother's Son" and the especially apt Smiths' selection "The Boy with the Thorn in His Side."

what to buy next: *Green Mind* (Sire/Warner Bros., 1991, prod. J Mascis), the first post-Barlow album after a three-year gap, is practically a Mascis solo album, with Murph drumming on only three songs and guests Don Fleming and Jay Spiegel (both from Velvet Monkeys, which Mascis played with on *Rake*) filling in some textures. The electric/acoustic mix is a startling but effective change.

what to avoid: The two best tracks from *You're Living All Over Me* (SST, 1987, prod. Not Listed)—"Little Fury Things" and "In a Jar"—are also on *Fossils*, the two Barlow tracks are utter crap and some of the other Mascis songs sound suspiciously like second-rate heavy metal riffing (especially the end of "SludgeFest").

the rest: *Dinosaur* (Homestead, 1985) *Fossils* (SST, 1991) Wagon *(Blanco y Negro/Warner Bros. EP, 1991)* Where You Been *(Sire/Warner Bros., 1993);* Without a Sound *(Sire/Reprise, 1994)*

worth searching for: The three-song European EP "I Don't Think So" (Warner Bros., 1994) features long, furious live versions of "What Else Is New" and "Sludge."

My Bloody Valentine, Buffalo Tom, Afghan Whigs, Sebadoh/Folk Implosion

Neil Young, Velvet Underground, Black Flag, Cure, R.E.M.

see also: *Mike Johnson, Sebadoh*

Steve Holtje

Dio

Formed 1983, location N/A.

Dio is a band but mostly a man—singer Ronnie James Dio, who was discovered when Deep Purple guitarist Ritchie Blackmore snared Dio from the band Elf to front Blackmore's solo project, Rainbow. With his gutsy, melodramatic delivery, Dio fit the role perfectly and stayed with the irascible Blackmore until 1978, when he replaced Ozzy Osbourne in Black Sabbath. By 1982, Dio was done with that and had moved on to his solo career, sounding more like the big, Mahler-esque epic rock of Rainbow than the leaner high-seed model he pursued with Sabbath. Dio has gone through its share of members—even a hiatus when Dio returned to Sabbath from 1991-93—and was for a while the home of future Whitesnake and Def Leppard guitarist Vivian Campbell. The latest version of the band includes former Sabbath drummer Vinny Appice and ex-Dokken bassist Jeff Pilson.

what to buy: Dio's albums are largely interchangeable, so stick with the first, *Holy Diver,* (Warner Bros., 1983) which benefits from the sound of a charged-up Dio and his band lighting out on a new adventure.

what to avoid: The live *Intermission* (Warner Bros., 1986) a disappointment in that there are far better recordings of Dio in concert with Rainbow and Sabbath.

the rest: *Last in Line* (Warner Bros., 1984) *Sacred Heart* (Warner Bros., 1985) *Dream Evil* (Reprise/Warner Bros., 1987) *Lock Up the Wolves* (Reprise, 1990) *Strange Highways* (Reprise, 1994)

worth searching for: *Hear 'n Aid,* (Mercury, 1986, prod. Various) the hard rock all-star project for famine relief—"We Are the World" in leather—that features "Stars," the communal song that Dio co-wrote and produced.

James Hetfield (Metallica), Dave Meniketti (Y&T), Geoff Tate (Queensryche), Chris Cornell (Soundgarden), Eddie Vedder (Pearl Jam)

Led Zeppelin, Deep Purple, Rainbow, Arthur Brown, King Crimson

Gary Graff

Dion

Born Dion DiMucci, July 18, 1939 in the Bronx, N.Y.

Training on street corners, DiMucci and his band the Belmonts won national acclaim with the hit "I Wonder Why" in 1959; the group was also the fourth-billed act for the tour on which Buddy Holly died. But unlike the innumerable doo-wop stars of the era that came and went in a flash, Dion showed staying power by forging a solo career. Effectively beginning in 1960 with the No. 1 hit "Runaround Sue," he continued into various styles of rock 'n' roll and R&B. Maintaining a streetwise soulfulness, he has remained a figure in the fickle music industry for more than 30 years.

what to buy: *Runaround Sue,* (Laurie, 1961/The Right Stuff, 1993, reissue prod. Eli Okun) his early 60s solo break, is highlighted by the title track, "The Wanderer," "The Majestic" and "Little Star." Classic stuff.

what to buy next: *Bronx Blues: The Columbia Recordings* (Columbia/Legacy, 1991, comp. Greg Geller) From 1962-65, Dion branched out to sing blues, gospel and country, and the best songs of that period are found here in sterling sound quality and accompanied by informative liner notes.

what to avoid: *When You Wish Upon a Star* (Collectables, 1983/1960) for its absolutely crappy sound.

the rest: *Dion* (Columbia, 1968/The Right Stuff, 1994) *The Return of the Wanderer* (Lifesong, 1978/DCC, 1990) *Lovers Who Wander* (Laurie, 1962/The Right Stuff, 1993) *Velvet and Steel* (Columbia, 1986/1991) *Yo, Frankie* (Arista, 1989) *Reunion: Live at the Madison Square Garden 1972* (Rhino, 1993)

worth searching for: *The Fabulous Dion* (Ace, date N/A) is a solid import greatest hits collection with "Runaround Sue" and "The Wanderer."

Lou Reed, Billy Joel, Paul Simon

The Orioles, the Cadillacs, the Del-Vikings

Allan Orski

Celine Dion

Born March 30, 1968, in Charlemagne, Quebec, Canada

Although American audiences only became aware of Dion's five-octave vocal power in 1991 (she sang mostly in French until that point), she had been winning accolades as a singer since her teenage years in her native Canada. The child of working-class parents in a small town east of Montreal, Dion was introduced to current manager/husband Rene Angelil via a demo tape sent by her brother Michel. According to legend, Angelil was so taken by her ability that he mortgaged his home to pay for her first record date. Through the 80s she built a strong following in Canada, but it wasn't until she sang the theme for Disney's hit animated film "Beauty and the Beast" in 1991 that Dion won o'er the masses. She's only become more popular with each successive album, with only minor interferences—critical derision, disagreements with Phil Spector during the making of her *Falling Into You* album—sullying her rise. Her next English-language record, released in 1992, pushed her success further, but it was her 1993 album that truly made her a stateside star—featuring the schmaltzy duet "When I Fall In Love" from the film "Sleepless in Seattle" and the hit single, "Power of Love." While fans fell for her VH-1-style pop sound, critics disparaged her overtly commercialized focus, penchant for cover tunes and a soulless vocal dexterity that brought little passion to her work. Poised for a big splash with a 1996 English-language record, Dion's reputation was sullied slightly by a conflict with legendary producer Phil Spector, who dropped out of work on the album after tusseling with her management over the record's focus. Still, the album remained among the country's ten best-selling records more than 18 weeks after its release.

what to buy: As a true pop diva, Dion's best work is the one that has the most hit singles, *Celine Dion* (Epic, 1992, prod. Ric Wake, Humberto Gatica, Walter Afanasieff and Guy Roche) Produced by many of the same people who made Mariah Carey a household name, this record did the same for Dion—powered by singles such as "Beauty and the Beast" and "Love Can Move Mountains."

what to buy next: The next-biggest collection of hits, of course. For Dion, that would be *The Colour of My Love,* (550 Music/Epic, 1993, prod. Various) featuring the smash hit

"Power of Love" along with her maudlin duet with singer Clive Griffin, "When I Fall In Love," from the film "Sleepless in Seattle."

what to avoid: Dion's weakness is the same shared by many producer-created, hit-driven divas; in the search for ever-broader appeal, true emotion and passion and creativity can get lost. Nowhere is that more apparent than on *Falling Into You* (Epic, 1996, prod. Various) WOOF!, a soulless collection of pop pap aimed at baby boomers' wallets with more movie treacle such as "Because You Loved Me" from the film "Up Close and Personal."

the rest: *D'eux* (Sony Music Canada, 1995) ♪♪♪ *Celine Dion A L'Olympia* (Sony Music Canada, 1994) ♪♪½ *Dion Chante Plamondon* (Sony Music Canada, 1991) ♪♪♪ *Unison* (Epic, 1990) ♪♪♪½ *Incognito* (Sony Music Canada, 1988) ♪♪♪

worth searching for: Legendary producer Spector claims to have masters from his sessions with Dion for *Falling Into You*—some recorded with a 60-piece orchestra. After his falling out with the singer, he threatened to mix them himself and release them on his own label.

▶▶ Donna Lewis

◀◀ Mariah Carey, Barbra Streisand, Carly Simon

Eric Deggans

Dire Straits

Formed 1977 in London, England

Mark Knopfler, guitar, vocals; John Illsley, bass, vocals; David Knopfler, guitar (1977-80); Pick Withers, drums (1977-82); Hal Lindes, guitar (1980-85); Alan Clark, keyboards (1981-present); Terry Williams, drums (1982-86); Guy Fletcher, keyboards, vocals (1983-present)

During the late 70's most new bands out of England fit into the punk/new wave category. Against the grain, Dire Straits released a self-titled LP, introducing the world to the double-fingered guitar picking of Mark Knopfler, a former school teacher whose skillful work showed country/blues influences, with a rock and roll sensibility. Knopfler, with his brother David, a social worker, and friend and sociology student Illsley began rehearsing Mark's compositions during late 1977 with drummer Withers, a session man from Dave Edmund's studios. The group's brand of rock—loaded with extended pieces considered passe at the time—took the U.K. and U.S. by storm with its first single "Sultans of Swing" charting extremely well in both countries. It wasn't until 1985, however, that Dire Straits would become a supergroup thanks to its *Brothers in Arms* album—20 million copies sold worldwide—and the massive hit single, "Money For Nothing." Since then, however, the group's output has been spare, with Mark Knopfler seemingly more interested in his solo career and soundtrack work than in the band.

what to buy: *Making Movies* (Warner Bros., 1980, prod. Jimmy Iovine and Mark Knopfler) ♪♪♪♪♪ is one of rock's great records. The songwriting and expert musicianship, combined with Knopfler's gruff vocals, display an impressive range from the thematic "Tunnel of Love" and "Romeo and Juliet" to the irreverent "Skateaway" and the aptly named "Solid Rock." The band's debut, *Dire Straits* (Warner Bros., 1978, prod. Muff Winwood) ♪♪♪♪ hinted at what the band could do with solid tracks such as "Sultans of Swing" and "Water of Love," and Knopfler's guitar work instantly put him in a league with rock's masters. *Brothers in Arms* (Warner Bros., 1985, prod. Mark Knopfler and Neil Dorfsman) ♪♪♪♪ was the watershed point for the band, a shimmering, full-digital production—one of rock's first—that made Knopfler's evocative guitar parts seem like lyrics themselves. The songs were as strong as the sound, though, offering searing commentary in the anti-rock star anthem "Money for Nothing" (with guest vocalist Sting) and on power and politics in "The Man's Too Strong."

what to buy next: *Love over Gold* (Warner Bros., 1982, prod. Jerry Wexler and Barry Beckett) ♪♪♪½ contains some solid tracks—including the epic "Telegraph Road" and "Private Investigations"—even if it isn't quite in the same league as the above picks. *Money for Nothing* (Warner Bros., 1988, prod. Various) ♪♪♪½ is a retrospective with loads of good numbers, although it lacks the cohesion of their finer studio records.

what to avoid: The band's most recent studio release, *On Every Street* (Warner Bros., 1991) ♪ was six years in the making, and perhaps that was the problem for a prolific songwriter and producer like Knopfler. To follow up *Brothers in Arms* was a daunting task, and Knopfler choked.

the rest: *Communique* (Warner Bros., 1980) ♪♪♪ *Alchemy* (Warner Bros., 1984) ♪♪½ *On the Night* (Warner Bros., 1993) ♪♪ *Live at the BBC* (Warner Bros., 1995) ♪♪♪

worth searching for: *Twisting by the Pool* (Warner Bros., 1983, prod. Mark Knopfler) ♪♪♪ is a four-song EP that hints at the more pop-infused direction that was coming with *Brothers in Arms*

solo outings:

Mark Knopfler: *Screenplaying* (Warner Bros., 1993, prod. Mark Knopfler) *Golden Heart* (Warner Bros., 1996) (with The Notting Hillbillies) *Missing...Presumed Having a Good Time* (Warner Bros., 1990) (with Chet Atkins) *Neck and Neck* (Columbia, 1990)

David Knopfler: *The Giver* (Mesa/Bluemoon, 1994) *Small Mercies* (Mesa/Bluemoon, 1995)

▶▶ Aztec Camera, John Hiatt, Mary Chapin Carpenter, The Mavericks

◀◀ Chet Atkins, Ry Cooder, Bob Dylan, Van Morrison

David Goldberg

Dirty Dozen Brass Band

Formed 1975 in New Orleans, La.

Gregory Davis, trumpet (1975-present); Efrem Jones, trumpet (1978-present); Kevin Harris, tenor sax (1975-present); Roger Lewis, baritone and soprano sax (1975-present); Charles Joseph, trombone (1975-90); Kirk Joseph, sousaphone (1975-92); Jenell Marshall, snare drum (1975-95); Benny Jones, bass drum (1975-84); Lionell Batiste, bass drum (1985-95); Raymond Webster, drums (1991- ??); Keith Anderson, sousaphone and trombone, (1993); Revert Andrews, trombone (1996); Julius McKee, sousaphone & basses (1996); Richard Knox, keyboards (1996); Terence Higgins, drums (1996)

Of the masses of musical traditions that flow through New Orleans, one of the deepest is the brass marching band. The Dirty Dozen Brass Band spurred a new generation of players and audiences that give life to this immediate predecessor and midwife of jazz. But rather than rest as a historical repertory band, members of the Dirty Dozen have put their own imprint on the music by composing titles with more modern approaches and covering bebop, R&B and pop titles. But as much fun and as great as they can be live, the recordings seldom elicit the same emotional response. Still, with solicitous use of such guests as Danny Barker, Eddie Bo, Dr. John, Elvis Costello, David Bartholomew and others, the Dirty Dozen has managed to keep the records varied and entertaining although laying in the same groove much of the time. The band made a sharp turn in 1996, dropping the Brass Band label and changing instrumentation for a more conventional sound with trap drums and keyboards in addition to a guest guitarist on several pieces.

what to buy: The Dozen came up with an excellent vehicle for its skills with *Jelly,* (Columbia, 1993, prod. Scott Billington) a tribute to the incomparable Jelly Roll Morton. Interspersed with octogenarian Danny Barker's reminiscences of the self-proclaimed creator of jazz, the songs maintain the loose group feel of Morton's ensembles and the Spanish tinge so important to the New Orleans sound. Lewis' soprano saxophone work on "The Pearls" is a highlight. The band burst onto the recording scene with *My Feet Can't Fail Me Now,* (Concord Jazz, 1984, prod. Quint Davis) featuring a novel lineup and sound. This record set the tone that the band has seldom gone beyond, and tells you exactly what Dirty Dozen music is all about.

what to buy next: The band's biggest change of pace came on *ears to the wall* (Mammoth, 1996, prod. the Dirty Dozen) which tosses out the traditional beats for a modern funky sound close to that of Maceo Parker. All the tunes here are originals, and the remake of "My Feet Can't Fail Me Now" from the first album shows the group slicker but still willing to have fun.

what to avoid: Though it holds up on its own, *Voodoo* (Columbia, 1989, prod. Scott Billington) finds the band reworking territory they've pretty much covered before, despite appearances by Dizzy Gillespie and Branford Marsalis.

the rest: *Live: Mardi Gras at Montreux* (Rounder, 1986) *The New Orleans Album* (Columbia, 1990)

▶▶ Rebirth Brass Band

◀◀ Olympia Brass Band

Larry Gabriel

Dish

See: The Blackgirls

Disposable Heroes of Hiphoprisy /Spearhead

Formed 1990 in Oakland, Calif. Disbanded 1990. Spearhead formed 1993 in Oakland Calif.

Disposable Heroes: Michael Franti, vocals; Rono Tse, DJ, percussion. Spearhead: Michael Franti, vocals; Mary Harris, vocals; Le Le Jamison, keyboards; Keith McArthur, bass; David James, guitar; James Gray, drums; Sub Commander Ras I Zulu, vocals

Singer-rapper Franti first gained attention for his confrontational but articulate political rapping, which owed a massive

What Album Changed Your Life?

"Meet the Beatles, but it wasn't the album; it was seeing them on TV, on the Ed Sullivan show. It was like a combination of religion and music and I don't know what else. The clock stopped for me; everything stopped. It was like in '2001' when the apes went up to the monolith and touched it --just a quantum leap forward. All of a sudden I understood what my fate was, what I had to do."

Gene Simmons (Kiss)

debt to Gil Scott-Heron and The Last Poets. The Disposable Heroes of Hiphoprisy, which sought to replace the boasting and misogyny of mainstream rap with substantive argument, essayed such topics as U.S. foreign policy, homophobia and the corrosive effects of television. Franti's tract-like rhymes were placed in a sonic collage influenced by punk and free jazz more than R&B. The result, though admirable in its intent, was too mired in political correctness and in-your-face indie cred to be very enjoyable. Franti dissolved the outfit after one release and returned in 1994 with something entirely different—and better. Spearhead allowed him to mingle the political and the personal in a powerful new way, and instead of samples and *musique concrete*, his new musical context was a band that played warm, emotionally powerful soul and funk. On *Home*, (Capitol, 1994, prod. Joe Nicolo) ♪♪♪♪ he stretches out lyrically and displays a surprisingly effective singing voice. The band's other main vocalist, Mary Harris, meanwhile provided powerhouse accompaniment and a wry, sly counterpoint to Franti's sincere persona. Spearhead, unable to capture the gangsta-loving rap audience, was marketed to an alternative rock audience with some success, thanks in part to its insinuating single and video "Hole in the Bucket."

the rest: Disposable Heroes of Hiphoprisy: *Hiphoprisy is the Greatest Luxury* (4th & Broadway, 1992) ♪♪♪ Spearhead: *Hole in the Bucket* (Capitol EP, 1995) ♪♪♪

Simon Glickman

Divination

See: Bill Laswell

Divinyls

Formed 1980 in Sydney, Australia

Christina Amphlett, vocals; Mark McEntee, guitar; Bjarre Ohlin, guitar, keyboards (1980-91); Rick Grossman, bass (1980-91); Richard Harvey, drums (1980-91)

The widespread audience that discovered Divinyls through its 1991 hit "I Touch Myself" likely knew little about the Australian band's long past or four previous albums. Songwriters and onstage foils Amphlett and McEntee quickly became the most visible members of the group—she as a female Angus Young in a sexy schoolgirl getup, he as the stoic blond guitarist. Their music—a sometimes sweet, sometimes sleazy brand of Stone-sish rock—was much hyped during the 80s Australian mini-invasion spearheaded by INXS and Men at Work. Unfortunately, Divinyls had its one hit, placed a song on 1994 "Melrose Place" soundtrack and hasn't been heard from since.

what to buy: *Divinyls* (Virgin, 1990, prod. Divinyls and David Tickle) ♪♪♪♪ not only has the novelty value "I Touch Myself" but also a consistent batch of lean rockers and cool ballads.

what to buy next: *Essential Divinyls* (Chrysalis, 1991, prod. Various) ♪♪♪ doesn't have the same level of as easy melodicism as *Divinyls* but still gleans the cream from the group's releases prior to that breakthrough.

what to avoid: *What a Life!* (Chrysalis, 1985, prod. Mark Opitz, Mike Chapman and Gary Langan) ♪ is a distressingly anonymous album that sounds more like the work of the production team than the band.

the rest: *Monkey Grip* (WEA, 1982) ♪♪♪ *Desperate* (Chrysalis, 1983) ♪♪ *Temperamental* (Chrysalis, 1988) ♪♪♪

worth searching for: *Divinyls Live*, an official but unmarked 1991 release that features concert renditions of "I Touch Myself," "Tempermental" and "Guillotine."

▶▶ Hole, Magnapop

AC/DC, the Rolling Stones, Pat Benatar

Todd Wicks

Dixie Dregs /The Dregs

Formed 1973 in Florida. Disbanded 1982. Re-formed 1992.

Steve Morse, guitar (1973-82, 1992-94); Andy West, bass (1973-82); Rod Morgenstein, drums (1973-82, 1992-present); Steve Davidowski, keyboards (1973-77); T Lavitz, keyboards (1978-82, 1992-present); Allen Sloan, electric violin (1973-80, 1992); Mark Parrish, keyboards (1977-82); Mark O'Conner, violin, guitar (1980-82); David LaRue, bass (1992-present); Jerry Goodman, violin (1992-present)

With a wild inventive streak, brilliant musicians, serious/serio-comic arrangements and flawless execution, the Dixie Dregs showered listeners with an explosion of notes on its dynamic 1977 debut *Free Fall.* Frontman and lead guitarist Morse assembled the heart of the band while studying at University of Miami's School of Music. What separates the Dregs (which dropped Dixie in 1981) from a host of other fusion bands is its sense of humor; complex, cosmic jazz-inflected boogie performed at warp-speed envelopes popular music melodies and careens into percussive, highly textured jazz, rock and country romps. It's heady music, steered with a firm hand by Morse. There is plenty of subtlety to be detected, too—though that detection must be made at a frenetic pace. Simply put, Morse is a guitar guru whose mantra does not include the word restraint, though, thankfully, it does include melody. A proof of the Dregs artistry is found in its live recordings; with fast tempo, rhythm, melody and key changes, the group member's potent musicianship rings clear without a lot of processing or chicanery. An odd career excursion took Morse into the fold of the middle-weight rock group Kansas for two ignored albums during the mid 80s, and now he's gone on to take the guitar chair in Deep Purple.

what to buy: *Divided We Stand: Best of the Dixie Dregs* (Arista, 1989, prod. Steve Morse) ♪♪♪♪ offers a solid sampling of the Dregs formative work on Capricorn during the late 70s and early 80s. Included are such well structured and executed songs as "Cruise Control," "Take It Off the Top' and "Twiggs Approved." But at 44 minutes, it's a little sparse. With today's technology, it could be nearly double in length. The Dregs deserve it.

what to buy next: *What If* (Polydor, 1978) ♪♪♪½ With its funky, shifting tempos on "Ice Cakes," a country, funk grin on "Gina Lola Breakdown" and the sweeping "Night Meets Light," the Dregs flex an impressive amount of creative muscle. Morse's solo album, *Structural Damage,* (High Street, 1995, prod. Steve Morse and Dave LaRue) ♪♪♪♪ finds him working in a trio format, soaring on his guitar with the encumberance of keyboards.

the rest: *Night of the Living Dregs* (Polydor, 1979) ♪♪♪½ *Bring 'Em Back Alive* (Capricorn, 1992) ♪♪♪ *Full Circle* (Capricorn, 1994) ♪♪♪½

solo outings:

Steve Morse: The Introduction (Elektra Musician, 1984) ♪♪½ *High Tension Wires* (MCA, 1989) ♪♪ *Southern Steel* (MCA 1991) ♪♪ *Coast to Coast* (MCA, 1992) ♪♪♪½ *Stress Fest* (High Street, 1996) ♪♪♪½

Col. Bruce Hampton & the Aquarium Rescue Unit, Michael Hedges

The Flock, Frank Zappa, Mahavishnu Orchestra, Weather Report

see also: *Deep Purple, Kansas*

Patrick McCarty

Don Dixon

Born in Dec. 13, 1950 in Lancaster, S.C.

Dixon's name appears in fine print on some of the finest pop albums of the 80s, from his engineering stint with Mitch Easter on R.E.M.'s *Reckoning* to production credits on the Smithereens' *Especially for You*, Marshall Crenshaw's *Mary Jean and 9 Others*, Guadalcanal Diary's *Flip Flop* and wife Marti Jones' *Used Guitars.* But the former lead singer for the North Carolina rock band Arrogance has made his best music on the other side of the mixing board, where his affection for British Invasion pop, Memphis soul and new-wave quirkiness has resulted in a small but smartly crafted catalog of solo albums that proudly rank with the best work of fellow pop purists Crenshaw and Nick Lowe. Recently, Dixon became the first pop act signed to country-bluegrass label Sugar Hill Records, and he has been winning rave reviews for his role in a musical called "King Mackerel and the Blues Are Running," which also stars Bland Simpson of the Red Clay Ramblers and "Pump Boys and Dinettes" composer Jim Wann.

what to buy: *Most of the Girls Like to Dance But Only Some of the Boys Like To* (Enigma, 1985, prod. Don Dixon) ♪♪♪½ is mostly demos and live tracks but the ragged charms of "Praying Mantis," "You're a Big Girl Now," "Southside Girl" and the marvelous title track make this sound more like the product of a playground than a studio. *EEE* (Enigma, 1989, prod. Don Dixon) is the most consistent example of his offbeat production style and musical range, including the Elvis Costello-like "Oh Cheap Chatter" and soulful covers of James Carr's "Dark End of the Street," Brenton Wood's "Gimme Little Sign" and John Hiatt's "Love Gets Strange."

what to buy next: A fine retrospective, *If I'm a Ham, Well, You're a Sausage* (Restless, 1992, prod. Don Dixon) gathers 15 of his best songs and adds the previously unreleased "Teenage Suicide (Don't Do It)," which he penned and performed for the dark teen comedy "Heathers."

what to avoid: *The Chi-Town Budget Show* (Enigma, 1989, prod. Don Dixon) is a live radio broadcast replete with muffed lyrics and frenetic pacing that makes it more of a souvenir than a statement.

the rest: *Romeo at Julliard* (Enigma, 1987) *Romantic Depressive* (Sugar Hill, 1995)

worth searching for: The jangling chemistry between Dixon and wife Marti Jones is captured on her *Live at Spirit Square* (Sugar Hill, 1996, prod. Don Dixon), a 1990 show featuring Dixon on bass and prominent backing vocals. He also wrote or co-wrote 10 of the 18 songs.

▶▶ Marti Jones, Hootie & the Blowfish

◀◀ Percy Sledge, the Searchers, Nick Lowe

David Okamoto

DJ Quik

Born David Blake in 1971 in Compton, CA

DJ Quik (born David Blake) has been labeled a gangsta rapper, but his lyrics are more about sex-trippin' than set-trippin'. Like a rapping version of Steve (Wild Man) Gallon or Rudy Ray Moore, Quick tells raunchy, explicit tales of sexual conquests past and future, setting them to self-produced music that blends taut, hard-hitting beats with the sweaty, sanctified wah-wah swagger of Stax/Volt and the sweet dance-funk grooves of Parliament. Quik's debut, *Quik Is the Name* (Profile, 1991, prod. DJ Quik) stands as his finest moment, partly because he hadn't yet become completely obsessed with raunch, but mostly because of his deft and confident production touch. It's telling that he shrugs off expected criticism—"Now, in my lyrics, I kick the shit that the critics debate to/But I can create the shit that the brothers relate to."—because his subsequent releases became even more explicit, threatening to turn Quik into a caricature of himself.

the rest: *2nd II None* (Profile, 1991) *Way 2 Fonky* (Profile, 1992) *Safe & Sound* (Profile, 1995)

Joshua Freedom du Lac

Dj Towa Tei

See: Deee-Lite

DMZ

Formed 1976 in Boston, Mass. Disbanded 1978.

Jeff "Mono Mann" Conolly, vocals, keyboards; J.J. Rassler, guitar; Peter Greenberg, guitar (1976); Mike Lewis, bass (1976); Mike Lewis (no relation), drums (1976); Adam Schwartz, vocals (1976); David Robinson, drums (1976); Rick Coraccio, bass (1976-78); Paul Murphy, drums (1976-78); Preston Wayne, guitar (1978)

DMZ was one of the first bands to make an overt connection with the original punk rock of the 60s—the brash, sloppy party music slurred through by the likes of the Standells, the Seeds, the Raiders, the Sonics and the 13th Floor Elevators. Fronted by maniacal raver Conolly, DMZ reveled in trash aesthetic but eschewed any trace of condescension or camp. How could it be otherwise, given Conolly's stated goal "of trying to fuse the Chocolate Watch Band with the Stooges?" Conolly could wail like a man possessed (or like Roky Erickson of the 13th Floor Elevators—same thing, really) while showing off the depth of his cool record collection with dips into the Pretty Things, Troggs, Flamin' Groovies and Wailers songbooks, and with rampaging original tunes of an identical garage-punk mindset. *When I Get Off* (Voxx, 1993) is the essential DMZ set, collecting 18 primal sides—some previously unreleased—but all crackling with vibrant, grungedelic shake 'n' sweat. If you're in search-mode, you might want to track down *DMZ*,, (Sire, 1978, prod. Flo and Eddie) the group's sole official album, but it doesn't even come close to matching the intensity of *When I Get Off.*

see also: *The Lyres*

Carl Cafarelli

DNA

Formed 1977 in New York, N.Y. Disbanded 1982.

Arto Lindsay, guitar, vocals; Ikue Ile Mori, drums; Robin Crutchfield, keyboards (1977-78); Tim Wright, bass, guitar (1978-82)

Rejecting rock norms, DNA stood in the forefront of the late 70s downtown Manhattan movement dubbed No Wave, which went past punk and new wave into more radical recastings of musical structure while still using rock instrumentation. This trio was the first context of Lindsay's astonishingly non-chordal, self-taught guitar style. Basically linear, albeit knotty, it leaves lots of space for the other musicians, whose parts intertwine rather than being stacked within a hierarchy. Such an approach implies conciseness and equality, which on a piece such as "Calling to Phone" can strip the music down to a collection of discrete rhythmic outbursts. The way Lindsay sings often matches this guitar style as he compacts lyrics and blurts them out in a rush, like bursts of electronic information coming across in bunched form rather than smoothly. It's as close as rock has come to the ultra-expressive miniatures of serialist composer Anton Webern and is unrelated to the equally short but more conventionally structured mini-song thrashings of hardcore punk. The extreme spareness of DNA's material, in which no sound is casual or superfluous, heightens the impact of every single moment and action. After DNA broke up, Lindsay played with the Lounge Lizards and James Chance before forming a new group, Ambitious Lovers, and working under his own name. Wright played with David Byrne and Brian Eno. Mori played violin, viola, and cello with Mars and recorded a solo album.

what to buy: The four-band compilation *No New York* (Antilles, 1978, prod. Brian Eno) ♪♪♪♪ shows the early DNA lineup with keyboardist Crutchfield, playing closer to normal rock structures than on later efforts but still far from the mainstream. *Live at CBGB* (Avant, 1993, prod. DNA) ♪♪♪♪, documenting the group's 1982 farewell concert, offers concert versions of all six pieces on *A Taste of DNA* as well as another nine tracks, all showing the final evolution of the group's sound.

worth searching for: The single "Little Ants/You and You" (Medical Records/Lust\Unlust Music, 1978, prod. Robert Quine) ♪♪♪, the group's debut, shows it at its most aggressive and unschooled. *A Taste of DNA* (American Clave, 1980, prod. DNA) ♪♪♪♪♪, with six songs in less than 10 minutes, severely deconstructs rock gestures and then compacts them into a new musical language. It's the pinnacle of DNA's aesthetic, and to this day there's never been anything quite like it.

solo outings:

Ikue Ile Mori: Painted Desert (DIW, 1995, prod. John Zorn) ♪♪♪

▶▶ Lounge Lizards, John Zorn, Marc Ribot, Bill Frisell

◀◀ Derek Bailey, Television, Pere Ubu

see also: *Arto Lindsay*

Steve Holtje

Dr. Buzzard's Original Savannah Band

See: Kid Creole and the Coconuts

Dr. Dre

Born Andre Young, c. 1965 in Compton, Calif.

Dr. Dre is to rap what Phil Spector was to 60s pop. While Spector's Wall of Sound production style changed the face of pop during the early 60s, upping the creative stakes and spawning a wave of imitators, Dre's pioneering G-Funk production touch has similarly altered the course of rap. Every album the former N.W.A. member has produced—including his own sonically brilliant *The Chronic* (Death Row/Interscope, 1992, prod. Dr. Dre) ♪♪♪♪♪—has gone gold or platinum, and countless other producers (including his half-brother, Warren G) have rushed to copy his trademark blend of concise Parliament-Funkadelic beats, thick bass lines, descending synthesizer runs, seductive samples and melodic choruses, making it the dominant style in rap. No wonder several pop and rock stars (including Madonna) have expressed interest in collaborating with Dre, who began his career as part of the DJ collective the World Class Wreckin' Cru. Of course, his production touch on *The Chronic* masks the fact that he's only an average lyricist at best, and that his thematic concerns about gangsta lifestyle—so groundbreaking when his former group, the seminal gangsta rap outfit N.W.A., debuted during the late 80s—are now standard. But the appeal of the album, and his follow-up of sorts for protege Snoop Doggy Dogg, is not what Dre's saying, but in how he's saying it. By providing a soothing, easy-listening musical foundation for his tense words, he manages to make the killing fields of Compton, Calif., sound sexy and alluring—no small feat, and a significant departure from N.W.A.'s gangsta classic, *Straight Outta Compton,* (Ruthless/Priority, 1988, prod. Dr. Dre and DJ Yella) ♪♪♪♪♪ which sounded as dangerous as any punk record.

Joshua Freedom du Lac

Dr. John

Born Malcolm John "Mac" Rebennack Jr., Nov. 21, 1940, in New Orleans, La.

With his spooky, voodoo-drenched debut as The Night Tripper in 1967 and his guided tour of New Orleans roots music on *Dr. John's Gumbo* in 1972, Dr. John paved the way for America's discovery of the Crescent City's rich musical heritage. It was Dr. John who led listeners to legendary New Orleans artists such as Professor Longhair and Huey (Piano) Smith. And his 1973 hits "Right Place, Wrong Time" and "Such A Night" helped bring national attention to regional stars such as The Meters and Allen Toussaint. Born and raised in New Orleans, Rebennack already was performing and recording in his teens, mainly as a guitarist. But it was his funky piano and distinctive, gravelly drawl that made him a star with the release of the *In The Right Place* album in 1973. Financial and drug problems plagued him well into the 80s, but the growing popularity of New Orleans music helped him regain his stride. Today, he reigns as the acknowledged master of the New Orleans sound; no one has done more to popularize it.

what to buy: *Mos' Scocious* (Rhino, 1993, prod. Various) ⚶⚶⚶⚶⚶ is the definitive Dr. John anthology—a two-CD set that begins with rare early sides cut with local bands such as Ronnie & The Delinquents, then marches on through more than 30 years of the doctor's finest. A virtual encyclopedia of the New Orleans sound. *The Very Best Of Dr. John* (Rhino, 1995, prod. Various) ⚶⚶⚶⚶ is a single CD collection that skims the cream of *Mos' Scocious Dr. John's Gumbo* (Atlantic, 1972, prod. Jerry Wexler and Harold Battiste) ⚶⚶⚶⚶ is Dr. John's landmark tribute to the Crescent City's R&B roots—while, a year later, *In The Right Place* (Atco, 1973, prod. Allen Toussaint) ⚶⚶⚶⚶ gave him a hit. (Both *Gumbo* and *In The Right Place* are combined on a Mobile Fidelity Sound Lab 24K disc.)

what to buy next: *Goin' Back To New Orleans* (Warner Bros., 1992, prod. Stewart Levine) ⚶⚶⚶⚶ is another fine reflection of his early influences, with lots of stellar guest artists. *In A Sentimental Mood* (Warner Bros., 1989, prod. Tommy LiPuma) ⚶⚶⚶⚶ is Rebennack's career-reviving take on standards such as "Makin' Whoopee" (a Grammy-winning duet with Rickie Lee Jones) and "Accentuate The Positive." And have your mojo ready should you fall under the hoodoo spell of The Night Tripper on *Gris Gris* (Atco, 1968). ⚶⚶⚶

what to avoid: *At His Best,* (Special Music Co., 1989) ⚶⚶⚶ a set that's been rendered redundant by the several more complete best-ofs.

the rest: *The Ultimate Dr. John* (Warner Bros., 1987) ⚶⚶⚶ *At His Best* (Special Music Co., 1989) ⚶⚶⚶ *The Brightest Smile In Town* (Clean Cuts, 1989) ⚶⚶⚶ *Afterglow* (Blue Thumb, 1995) ⚶⚶⚶

worth searching for: An import CD of formative, loose-limbed 60s sessions, *Cut Me While I'm Hot* (Magnum America, date N/A).

▶▶ The Neville Brothers, Marcia Ball, The Radiators

◀◀ Professor Longhair, James Booker, Tuts Washington, Joe Liggins, Huey (Piano) Smith

Doug Pippin

John Doe

See: X

Dogmatics

Formed 1981 in Boston, Mass. Disbanded 1986.

Pete O'Halloran, guitar, vocals; Paul O'Halloran, bass, vocals; Jerry Lehane, guitar, vocals; Tommy Long, drums

Mainly a local attraction in Boston's mid-80s modern rock scene, the Dogmatics was a decidedly less polished bunch of slopmeisters than most of its peers. The band slapped together rudimentary, beer-spittin' rock 'n' roll with a ruckus-making disregard for anything other than a garage band's clanging. Therein lies the charm: The Dogmatics apparently had no artistic ambitions. Paul O'Halloran was killed in a motorcycle wreck in 1986, which effectively ended the band. *The Dogmatics: 1981-86* (Vagrant Records, 1995, prod. Johnny Angel) ⚶⚶⚶ is a career-spanning, 20-track sampler covers the band's lewd three-chord bursts and proto-punk rockabilly and presents the band in its proper (dirty basement window) light.

Allan Orski

Dokken

Formed 1979 in Hollywood, Calif. Disbanded 1988. Re-formed 1992.

Don Dokken, vocals; George Lynch, guitar; Juan Croucier, bass (1979-83); Jeff Pilson, bass; (1983–present); Mick Brown, drums

Though undeniably a product of the big-hair glam rock scene that exploded in Los Angeles during the early 80s, Dokken displayed a little more talent and musicianship than many of its peers—due mostly to Don Dokken's strong, versatile vocals and Lynch's flashy, melodic guitar work. After several years of relative success, including a slot alongside Metallica, Scorpions and Van Halen in 1988's "Monsters of Rock" tour, friction between Dokken and Lynch peaked, causing the band to split up. Lynch and Brown formed a new band, Lynch Mob, while Dokken recorded a solo album. In 1992 the band reformed, but its once-rabid fans barely noticed.

what to buy: *Tooth and Nail,* (Elektra, 1984, prod. Tom Werman) the first album with Pilson (original bassist Croucier left to join Ratt), is probably as good as Dokken is capable of. With radio hits such as "Into the Fire" and "Alone Again (Without You)," Lynch emerged as a standout in the crowded field of speedy Hollywood guitarists.

what to buy next: Though not as consistently satisfying as *Tooth and Nail, Under Lock and Key* (Elektra, 1985, prod. Neil Kernon and Michael Wagner) features some of the band's best songs, "In My Dreams" and "It's Not Love."

what to avoid: *Back for the Attack* (Electra, 1987, prod. Neil Kernon) appears to be where the band ran out of ideas. It's disjointed, derivative, and dull, dull, dull.

the rest: *Back on the Streets* (Carrere, 1979) *Breaking the Chains* (Elektra, 1983) *Beast from the East* (Elektra, 1988) *Dysfunctional* (Columbia, 1995, prod. Don Dokken)

solo outings:

George Lynch: Sacred Groove (Elektra, 1993)

Lynch Mob (Lynch & Brown): Wicked Sensation (Elektra, 1990) *Lynch Mob* (Elektra, 1992)

Don Dokken: Up from the Ashes (Geffen, 1990)

◄◄ AC/DC, Van Halen, Black Sabbath, Ozzy Osbourne, Judas Priest

Brandon Trenz

Don Dokken

See: Dokken

Thomas Dolby

Born Thomas Morgan Robertson, Oct. 14, 1958 in Cairo, Egypt, 1958

Raised the son of a respected British archaeologist, Dolby made his reputation as songwriter/producer/backing musician for New Wave siren Lena Lovich, mainstream rockers Foreigner, singer/songwriter Joan Armatrading and even rappers Whodini. Stepping out on his own during the early 80s, Dolby became known as a wirehead extraordinaire, creating witty, extravagant synth-pop singles filled with electronic keyboards, percussion and his own frantic vocals. His solo efforts benefited from forays into film soundtracks and outside production work, with later efforts integrating more organic sounds and complex sonic textures. By the 90s, Dolby had also branched into computer programs, presenting the soundtrack to a video game as his most recent solo release.

what to buy: Dolby's breakthrough debut, *The Golden Age of Wireless* (Capitol, 1982, prod. Thomas Dolby and Tim Friese-Green), cements his image as a synth-pop mad scientist, fueled by the success of the whimsical single, "She Blinded Me With Science" Harnessing an impressive array of keyboards to service an inventive and hook-laden collection of songs, the album serves as a perfect introduction to Dolby's twisted sonic world.

what to buy next: His third full-length release, *Aliens Ate My Buick* (EMI Manhattan, 1988, prod. Thomas Dolby and Bill Bottrell) brings all of Dolby's disparate artistic sides together—the wittily acerbic rock/pop of "Airhead," the complex atmospherics of "Budapest By Blimp" and members of George Clinton's P-Funk All Stars on "May the Cube Be With You."

what to avoid: Generally, Dolby's soundtrack work has been the weak link in his efforts, with the 1986 soundtracks for the movies "Gothic" and "Howard the Duck" filled with pointless atmospherics and pointless pop tunes, respectively.

the rest: *The Flat Earth* (EMI, 1984) *Astronauts and Heretics* (Giant, 1992) *The Gate to the Mind's Eye* (Giant, 1994) *The Best of Thomas Dolby: Retrospectacle* (Capitol, 1995)

worth searching for: "Live Wireless," an extended video tour document from the early 80s, provides a fascinating look at Dolby's creative process, while "The Gate," (Miramar Productions, 1994) is a full-length video album available on video and laserdisc with breathtaking visuals to accompany the "Mind's Eye" sonics.

►► Trent Reznor, Beck, Self

◄◄ Frank Zappa, George Clinton, Gary Wright

Eric Deggans

Dolenz and Jones

See: The Monkees

Domino

Born Shawn Ivy

Long Beach, Calif., artist Shawn (Domino) Ivy is neither a good singer nor a good rapper, so he goes halfway, delivering his vocals—mostly about getting paid and getting laid—in the singsong drawl that's also favored by the likes of Bone Thugs-N-Harmony, Da Brat, Ahmad, Warren G and, most notably, Snoop Doggy Dogg. But Domino's vocals lack the danger, tension and (misleading) playfulness that make Snoop Doggy Dogg's lyrics compelling. As such, the focus turns to his backing music, an oft-languid Parliament-Ohio Players-Zapp hybrid that blends horn blasts, mesmerizing piano and organ vamps, tweaked rhythm guitar riffs, synth squiggles, electro-funk fuzz and loose-and-airy beats like a low-rent Dr. Dre production. *Domino* (OutBurst, 1993, prod. DJ Battlecat) is notable mostly for its two ear-candy singles, "Sweet Potato Pie," which essentially updates the Stones' "Brown Sugar" recipe, and "Getto Jam," a summer groove that contains some surprising jazz-like scats. The rest of the material pales, though the use of a Hi Records-type Hammond loop does makes the painfully materialistic "Money Is Everything" sonically worthy. On *Physical Funk,* (OutBurst, 1996, prod. Domino) Domino sounds as if he's resting on all two of his past hits: "Hennessy" should be retitled "Getto Jam (Part II)," and "So Fly" should be "(More) Sweet Potato Pie." In the opening "Microphone Musician," Domino even seems to point out that his best songs might already be behind him, saying: "Now look into my past and see the work I've done/I'm up in Billboard, six weeks at No. 1."

Joshua Freedom du Lac

Fats Domino

Born Antione Domino on Feb. 26, 1928, in New Orleans, La.

Not only is Domino responsible for an astounding 63 charted singles and more than 65 million in record sales, but he did it with nothing more than pure musical charm. A short-statured man of ample girth, Domino possessed none of the titillating antics or wild personality traits of contemporaries such as Little Richard and Chuck Berry. Instead, he smiled and let the rolling triplets of his piano and his warm New Orleans drawl steer his never-ending string of self-penned hits. Nearly everything the man recorded has a rollicking charm and gentleness, and they retain their impact and innocence to this day. He cut his first hit, "The Fat Man," in 1949, predating both Bill Haley and Elvis Presley by several years and therefore making it arguably the first rock 'n' roll song. From that point on, Domino's influence and importance as a musical force cannot be overstated.

what to buy: The four-disc box set *They Call Me the Fat Man* (EMI, 1991, prod. Dave Bartholomew) chronicles his stay at the Imperial label and renders almost every other release redundant with hit such as "Blueberry Hill," "Ain't That a Shame" "Walkin' to New Orleans," "I'm Walkin' " and "Whole Lotta Lovin'." *My Blue Heaven* (EMI, 1990, prod. Dave Bartholomew) is a fine introductory single-disc sampler to the warm Creole sound of the Fat Man.

what to buy next: *Antione "Fats" Domino* (Tomato, 1992, prod. Kevin Eggers and Robert G. Vernon) is a vivacious live document, recorded when Domino was 61 and still in full possession of all his friendly energy. Plus, it offers a good version of "Red Sails in the Sunset."

what to avoid: *Christmas Is a Special Day* (The Right Stuff/EMI, 1993) Yes it is. So buy the box set and leave the caroling to cardigan-clad setsters such as Perry Como.

the rest: *The Best of Fats* (Pair, 1990) *All-Time Greatest Hits* (Curb, 1991) *Best of Fats Domino Live Vol. 1* (Curb, 1992) *Best of Fats Domino Live Vol. 2* (Curb, 1992) *Fats Domino: The Fat Man: 25 Classics* (EMI, 1996) *That's Fats! A Tribute to Fats Domino* (EMI, 1996)

worth searching for: *Out of New Orleans,* (Bear Family, 1993) an eight-disc import that presents the complete Imperial recordings, along with unedited alternate takes and a 72-page book containing extensive liner notes and a complete sessionography.

Van Morrison, Paul Simon, Billy Joel, Bruce Hornsby, the Neville Brothers, Allen Toussaint

Big Joe Turner, Louis Jordan, Professor Longhair

Allan Orski

Lonnie Donegan

Born Anthony James Donegan, 1931, Glasgow, Scotland

Scottish guitarist Donegan plundered the catalogs of American folk singers (such as Leadbelly and Woody Guthrie) and in turn inspired a generation of British rock heroes (like Cliff Richard and John Lennon). A regular performer on Britain's jazz circuit—he supposedly took his stage name from blues guitarist Lonnie Johnson—Donegan was England's undisputed leader of skiffle, a down-and-dirty brand of uptempo folk played on acoustic guitars, washboards, and tea-chest bass. His version of "Rock Island Line" became an instant U.K. hit in 1955, and skiffle groups appeared practically overnight throughout the country thanks to the music's simplicity and the high availability of common instruments. The craze lasted through 1959, when Donegan was knocked out of the charts by the very rock 'n' roll acts he helped to inspire. Following a lengthy absence due to a heart attack, he returned in 1978 with "Putting on the Style," an all-star skiffle record featuring Ringo Starr, Brian May, Elton John and other musicians inspired by his music. For a solid introduction to Donegan, check out *Collection,* (Castle Communications, 1989) ♪♪♪♪ a single-disc sampler of essential Donegan tracks. If that whets your appetite—in a big way only—move on up to the import *More than Pie in the Sky,* (Bear Family, 1993) ♪♪♪♪ a massive eight-CD box set stuffed to the gills with 209 tracks. Given the strengths of these two packages, the three-CD set *Putting on the Styles* (Sequel) ♪♪ seems unnecessary, with too many novelty tunes and no "Rock Island Line."

Christopher Scapelliti

Donovan

Born Donovan Leitch, Feb. 10, 1946, in Glasgow, Scotland

An early British folky turned pop star, Donovan incorporated rock and psychedelic elements during the mid- and late-60s. From such tender ditties as "Catch the Wind" in 1965 to the grinding buzz of 1968's "Hurdy Gurdy Man" (with guitarist Jeff Beck), Donovan was all over the stylistic map. His credibility suffered from an early and much-hyped comparison to Bob Dylan, but producer Mickie Most molded Donovan from a reformed folkie to a pop singer with clever lyrics and wit—which started the "e-lect-ri-cal banana" craze of "Mellow Yellow." From pop star, Donovan changed colors again and turned himself into a into an early New Ager. And all of these transitions took place in a span of only four or five years. From 1965-69, he released 14 albums, making him something of a one-man British Invasion with hits such as "Universal Soldier," "Colours," "Wear Your Love Like Heaven," "Season of the Witch," "Atlantis" and "Barabajagal." But after that his career declined rapidly, as if so much work so soon had sapped Donovan of his creative strength. Later 70s and occasional 80s work was imminently forgettable, and in 1996 plotted a comeback with modern rock and rap producer Rick Rubin and a new album *Sutras.*

what to buy: *Troubadour: The Definitive Collection 1964-1976* (Legacy, 1992, prod. Various) ♪♪♪♪♪ is the one stop to hear his best. This comprehensive collection—handpicked by Donovan—includes 44 songs and all of his hits.

what to avoid: *The Classics Live* (Great Northern Arts Ltd., 1991) WOOF! is an unfortunate concert recording, best left unheard.

the rest: *Barabajagal* (Epic, 1969/1987) ♪♪♪ *Catch The Wind* (Hickery, 1965/Sandstone, 1992) ♪♪♪ *Hurdy Gurdy Man* (Epic, 1968/1986) ♪♪♪ *Sunshine Superman* (Epic, 1966/1990) ♪♪♪ *Sutras* (American, 1996) ♪♪

worth searching for: *Mellow Yellow,* (Epic, 1967) ♪♪♪♪ one of his more consistent 60s albums that has yet to see the laser light of CD re-issue. Its title track is a defining piece of the 60s pop counterculture.

▶▶ David Crosby, XTC/Dukes of Stratosphear, the Housemartins

◀◀ Bob Dylan, the Beatles

Patrick McCarty

The Doobie Brothers

Formed 1970 in San Jose, Calif. Disbanded 1982. Reformed in 1987.

Tom Johnston, guitar, vocals (1970-77, 1987-present); Patrick Simmons, guitar vocals (1970-82, 1987-present); John Hartman, drums (1970-78, 1987-present); Dave Shogren, bass (1970-71); Tiran Porter, bass, vocals (1971-81, 1987-present); Michael Hossack, drums (1971-73, 1987-present); Keith Knudsen, drums (1973-83); Jeff "Skunk" Baxter, guitar (1974-78); Michael McDonald, keyboards, vocals (1975-82, 1995-present); John McFee, guitar (1979-82); Chet McCracken, drums, (1979-82); Cornelius Bumpus, sax, keyboards (1979-82); Willie Weeks, bass (1982); Bobby LaKind, percussion, (1987-present)

The Doobie Brothers thought themselves bad-boys at the start of their career, flaunting their friendship with the San Jose biker scene and naming themselves—nudge, nudge, wink, wink—after a slang name for a marijuana joint. Like the Allman Brothers, they had a multiple-guitar front flanked by a double-drum foundation. But by the end of the group's first run at the charts, the Doobies were chasing after mainstream acceptance with pop pap, and their musical base was the electric keyboard. The balance switched with the mid-career addition of Michael McDonald, the sultry-voiced singer and keyboardist who joined the group after several years of singing with Steely Dan. McDonald's first album, "Takin' It to the Streets," steered the Doobies away from their double-guitar country-boogie into an urbane, faux-sophisticated R&B style. Early fans cried sellout;

new fans thought early FM hits such as "China Grove" and "Long Train Runnin' " were gauche and trashy. Truth be told, neither version of the group made music for the ages, though their hits—especially those written by Pat Simmons, whose love for folk music led to the prettiest picking and melodies throughout the Doobies' career—are fun to hear again. Once in a while, anyway. Like many 70s groups that broke up in the early 80s, the Doobies (more or less the original version), reunited in 1987 for a couple more albums and money-making tours.

what to buy: *Toulouse Street* (Warner Bros., 1972, prod. Ted Templeman) the strongest of the pre-McDonald group. Though it didn't include the biggest hits, it did have a nice balance of hard rock a la "Rockin' Down the Highway" and folksiness in the better-known version of the Byrds' "Jesus Is Just Alright." *Takin' It To the Streets* (Warner Bros., 1976, prod. Ted Templeman) is the first and best of the latter-day Doobies, with McDonald bringing his voice to hits like "It Keeps You Running" and the title track, with Johnston still around to add a little rock 'n' roll grit.

what to buy next: You can't lose with hits compilations for a band whose strength was singles—*Best of the Doobies* (Warner Bros., 1976, prod. Ted Templeman) and *The Best of the Doobies Volume II* (Warner Bros., 1981, Ted Templeman)

what to avoid: Tired, retread ideas are all you'll hear on the reunion albums *Cycles* (Capitol, '89, prod. Rodney Mills) WOOF! and *Brotherhood.* (Capitol, 1991, prod. Rodney Mills) WOOF!

the rest: *Doobie Brothers* (Warner Bros., 1971) *The Captain and Me* (Warner Bros., 1973) *What Were Once Vices Are Now Habits* (Warner Bros., 1974) *Stampede* (Warner Bros., 1975) *Livin' on the Faultline* (Warner Bros., 1977) *Minute By Minute* (Warner Bros., 1978) *One Step Closer* (Warner Bros., 1980) *The Doobie Brothers Farewell Tour* (Warner Bros., 1983) *Rockin' Down the Highway: The Wildlife Concert* (Legacy, 1996)

worth searching for: *Listen to the Music* (Warner Bros., 1993, prod. Ted Templeman) is a British best-of that's fatter and more complete than either of its domestic counterparts.

solo outings:

Tom Johnston: *Everything You've Heard Is True* (Warner Bros., 1979) *Still Feels Good* (Warner Bros., 1981)

Patrick Simmons: *Arcade* (Elektra, 1983)

Michael McDonald: *If That's What It Takes* (Warner Bros., 1982) *No Lookin' Back* (Warner Bros., 1985) *Take It To Heart* (Reprise, 1990) *Blink of An Eye* (Reprise, 1993)

▶▶ Georgia Satellites, Black Crowes, Screaming Cheetah Wheelies

◀◀ Allman Brothers Band, Moby Grape, Hot Tuna

Gil Asakawa

The Doors

Formed 1965 in Los Angeles, Calif. Disbanded 1973.

Jim Morrison, vocals (died July 3, 1971), Robby Krieger, guitar; John Densmore, drums; Ray Manzarek, keyboards

Who but the Doors could have comfortably covered both Weill/Brecht ("Alabama Song") and Howlin' Wolf ("Back Door Man") on the same album? That they did it on their debut, in between their own masterpieces like "Break on Through" and "Light My Fire" only makes it all the more impressive. The Doors were true originals—nobody before or after has ever sounded quite like them. The band's music tended toward the dark even while most of their peers were preaching all-we-need-is-love utopianism, prefiguring the grisly, violent end of the peace-and-love era. They also brought the seamy underside of Southern California to light at a time when the nation was California dreamin'. The focus rightly tends to go to Morrison, the hyper-charismatic and super-pretty frontman who was also a commanding, dramatic singer and fine rock poet—which should not be confused with a real poet, by the way. The minimalist, atmospheric music created by Krieger, Manzarek and Densmore created the perfect frame for Morrison's lyrics. The band's love for the blues became increasingly clear over the course of their amazingly prolific career—six studio albums in five years. In a strange way, the band's sloppy original take captured the spirit of the blues better than any of their peers' slavish, overly reverential imitations. It's pointless to speculate what the future may have held for the Doors, but the fact that the band's last album before Morrison's death, *L.A. Woman*, was one of its best certainly indicates that there was plenty of good music left.

what to buy: As a starting point, you couldn't do better than to begin at the beginning. All of the Doors' most notable traits are apparent on *The Doors* (Elektra, 1967, prod. Paul Rothchild) —acid-on-the-beach philosophy ("Break on Through"), palatable avant gardism ("The Crystal Ship"), a unique take on the blues ("Back Door Man"), paisley pop masterpieces ("Light

My Fire") and extended mind trips ("The End"). *Morrison Hotel* (Elektra, 1970, prod. Paul Rothchild) kicks off with "Roadhouse Blues" and never really looks back, as the Doors sound more and more like a hard-hitting rock band. Its swan song, *L.A. Woman* (Elektra, 1971, prod. Bruce Botnick) is also a masterpiece, all the more poignant for the fact that Morrison sounds distinctly tired throughout—in a good way. It's looser, bluesier and more bare-bones than anything that preceded it.

what to buy next: *Strange Days* (Elektra, 1967, prod. Paul Rothchild) lacks some of the debut's swagger, but it's still quite fine. The heavily orchestrated *The Soft Parade* (Elektra, 1969, prod. Paul Rothchild) is uneven, but tends toward the great and includes some of the band's most ambitious, original material.

what to avoid: *American Prayer* (Elektra, 1978/1995, prod. The Doors), featuring Morrison reading poetry to the Doors' musical accompaniment is for cult members only.

the rest: *Waiting for the Sun* (Elektra, 1968) *Thirteen* (Elektra, 1970) *Best of the Doors* (Elektra, 1980) *Classics* (Elektra, 1985) *In Concert* (Elektra, 1991)

worth searching for: The out-of-print compilation *Weird Scenes Inside the Gold Mine* (Elektra, 1972, prod. Various) is a perfect overview, though the regular albums are still the way to go.

solo outings:

Robbie Krieger: RKO Live (One Way, 1995)

Ray Manzarek (with Michael McClure): Love Lion (Shanachie, 1993)

▶▶ Jane's Addiction, Patti Smith, the Cult, INXS, Marilyn Manson, Lords of the New Church

◀◀ Willie Dixon, Howlin' Wolf, Jimmy Reed, Bertolt Brecht

Alan Paul

Lee Dorsey

Born Dec. 24, 1926, in New Orleans, La. Died Dec. 1, 1986 in New Orleans

Dorsey's Allen Toussaint-produced sessions sound almost like collaborations between the two—Toussaint fitting his own high, light, almost faint vocals against Dorsey's on monuments such as "Workin' In a Coal Mine" and "Yes We Can." But it is easy to understand the producer's attraction to Dorsey's rough-hewn, chunky vocal style, sharpened considerably on a series of vernacular rhythm and blues hits in the early 60s, notably "Ya Ya." When the hits ran dry for Dorsey, who continued to occasionally make fine records with Toussaint long past his chart life, he simply relied for a livelihood on his prosperous New Orleans auto body shop, where Dorsey banged out dents for all the city's taxi cabs. But he remained a popular figure, cutting a duet with Southside Johnny and Ashbury Jukes and opening a 1980 U.S. tour for The Clash, not to mention his virtually annual appearances at the New Orleans Jazz and Heritage Festival.

what to buy: His 1970 masterpiece *Yes We Can* — also a high-water mark for producer-arranger-writer Toussaint—has been released on CD in expanded form, *Yes We Can ... And Then Some* (Polydor, 1993, prod. Allen Toussaint) The album should be owned, though it wasn't necessarily improved by adding outtakes and miscellaneous singles never before released on a collection. The frequently covered "Freedom For the Stallion" is a welcome, fitting inclusion, however.

what to buy next: *Golden Classics* (Collectable, date N/A, prod. Various) has mid-60s Toussaint-produced tracks ("Workin' In a Coal Mine," "Holy Cow") along with samples of his worthy earlier work from the "Ya Ya" era, when he recorded for Bobby Robinson's Fury label.

worth searching for: The final Dorsey-Toussaint collaboration, *Night People*, (ABC, 1978, prod. Allen Toussaint) is one of the great lost R&B albums of the disco era—not that Toussaint's supple funk has anything to do with disco.

▶▶ Pointer Sisters, Robert Palmer, Devo

◀◀ Professor Longhair, Ray Charles

Joel Selvin

Nick Drake

Born June 19, 1948 in Rangoon, Burma. Died November 25, 1974 in Tanworth-in-Arden, England

Of all the names to come out of the English folk movement of the late '60s, only Drake had to wait some 20 years after his death to be recognized for his achievements and impact. During his brief life, Drake released three touching, heartfelt albums that met critical adulation and public dismissal. This lack of commercial acceptance sent the already melancholy Drake into an even deeper state of depression. Through his pain, or perhaps because of it, Drake was able to write songs that were at times personal, often mystical, sometimes tragic and always enchanting. Behind the English lilt of his hush-be-quiet voice was Drake's radiant and hypnotic guitar playing, a lyrical triad of alternate tunings, complex chord progressions, and intricate finger picking. But, his chronic shyness and aversion to performing live did little to get his name in front of those who could have appreciated him while he was alive. A few months after beginning to record his fourth album, Drake overdosed on Tryptizol, an anti-depressant medication. The coroner declared it a suicide, though friends and family disagree. Today, interest in Drake far surpasses that of when he was alive, with his CDs reaching a new audience as well as talk about tribute albums and a feature film about his life.

what to buy: *Bryter Layter* (Island/Hannibal, 1970, prod. Joe Boyd). ♪♪♪♪♪ Even with the lush background of Robert Kirby's string arrangements, the delicate power of Drake's acoustic guitar rings through. The jazzy "One of These Things First" and "At the Chime of the City Clock" share space with haunting instrumentals and emotionally intense love songs such as "Northern Sky." Drake reportedly recorded the songs on *Pink Moon* (Island/Hannibal, 1972, prod. Nick Drake) ♪♪♪♪♪ in two days, just with his voice and a guitar, then without a word dropped the tape off at the Island Records reception desk and disappeared. After several days someone opened the package and realized they had the new Nick Drake album. After a few listens, this scenario makes perfect sense; he said all he needed to with one voice, six strings and 11 songs.

what to buy next: Drake's first album, *Five Leaves Left* (Island/Hannibal, 1969, prod. Joe Boyd), ♪♪♪♪ was recorded when he was just 20 years old. But he belies his youth with skillful playing, and the production blends his guitar, voice and string arrangements magnificently. "Cello Song" is as close to perfection as it gets. *Time of No Reply* (Hannibal, 1986, prod. Joe Boyd and Frank Kornelussen) ♪♪♪♪ consists of unreleased songs recorded during the *Five Leaves Left* sessions, as well as home recordings and four songs recorded in 1974 which were to be included on Drake's fourth album. All are solo acoustic performances except an alternate version of "The Thoughts of Mary Jane," which features Richard Thompson on electric guitar. Once you're hooked, splurge for *Fruit Tree* (Hannibal, 1986, prod. Joe Boyd), ♪♪♪♪ a four-CD box set that contains all three original releases and *Time of No Reply* along with a 16-page booklet.

the rest: *Way to Blue: An Introduction to Nick Drake* (Hannibal, 1994) ♪♪♪♪

worth searching for: *Tanworth-in-Arden 1967/68* ♪♪♪♪, an Italian bootleg that features 18 tracks, mostly cover songs, from a homemade tape. *The Complete Home Recordings* (Boyds Music), ♪♪♪♪ a German bootleg, features 24 tracks.

▶▶ Jeff Buckley, the Cure, Mark Eitzel, J Mascis, R.E.M., the Smiths, Paul Weller

◀◀ The Beatles, Tim Buckley, Bob Dylan, Tim Hardin, John Renbourn, Joni Mitchell

Brian Escamilla

Dramarama

Formed 1982 in Wayne, N.J. Disbanded 1994.

John Easdale, vocals, acoustic guitar; Chris Carter, bass; Mark "Mr. E. Boy" Englert, guitar, e-bow, mandolin; Peter Wood, guitar; Theothorous Athanasious Ellenis, keyboards (1982-87); Jesse Farbam, drums (1982-90); Tim Edmondson, drums (1990); Brian Macleod, drums (1990); Clem Burke, drums (1993-94)

Full of pop culture references and the sounds of 60s and 70s mainstream rock, this group's trademark mixture of Beatles melodicism, Rolling Stones energy and New York Dolls glam-punk never quite earned it the attention it deserved, though Los Angeles DJ Rodney Bingenheimer's enthusiasm and support made the first album's "Anything, Anything (I'll Give You)" a local hit. But the group's first two albums had to be made for French labels, and when it did get signed in America, it was by a label (Chameleon) that led an intermittent existence. Drummer Farbam (who was always credited as simply Jesse) quit just before the *Vinyl* sessions to join an Eastern religious sect and was replaced by Wire Train's Macleod for the recording and by Edmondson on tour; ex-Blondie skinsman Burke joined for the group's swan song. Chameleon went under for the last time in 1993, and the group dissolved the following year.

what to buy: The six-song *Live at the China Club* (Chameleon EP, 1990, prod. Val Garay) ♪♪♪♪♪ is the perfect introduction to the band, with frenetic, barely controlled energy harnessed to the band's most memorable tunes ("Last Cigarette" is the highlight) plus a cover of the New York Dolls' "Private World." *Vinyl* (Chameleon, 1991, prod. Don Smith, Chris Carter and John Easdale) ♪♪♪♪ is most consistent full-length album, a fuller embodiment of the band's belief in the rock verities.

what to buy next: Besides "Anything, Anything," the best tunes on the low-budget debut *Cinema Verite* (New Rose, France, 1985/Chameleon, 1991, prod. Chris Carter and John Easdale) ♪♪♪♪ are "Scenario," "Some Crazy Dame" and "All I Want."

what to avoid: *Looking Through ...*, (Eggbert, 1994, prod. Chris Carter and John Easdale) ♪♪ which is actually credited to The Bent Backed Tulips (it's a Beatles reference) collects 1988 outtakes from *Stuck in Wonderamaland*, some of which came out in France on a shorter 1992 album of the same name. The grab-bag aspects make it uneven, but there are some good tunes, with more acoustic-based songs than usual.

the rest: *Box Office Bomb* (Questionmark, France, 1987/Chameleon,1991) ♪♪♪ *Stuck in Wonderamaland* (Chameleon, 1989) ♪♪♪½ *Hi-Fi Sci-Fi* (Chameleon, 1993) ♪♪½

▶▶ Gin Blossoms, Tragically Hip, Velvet Crush

◀◀ Rolling Stones, New York Dolls, Neil Young, Mott the Hoople, Blondie, dB's

Steve Holtje

Dread Zeppelin

Formed 1989 in Los Angeles, Calif.

Fresh Cheese & Cheese, drums (1989-91); Butt Boy (aka Gary B.I.B.B.), "porn bass," lead vocals (as B.I.B.B. in 1992), guitar; Jah Paul Jo, guitar (1989-95); Carl Jah, guitar (1989-94); Tortelvis, vocals, tacos (1989-91, 1993-present); Ed Zeppelin, congas, reggae love vibes (1989-91, 1993-94); Spice, drums (1992-94); Rasta Li-Mon, keyboards (1992—present); Fernandez (Ed Zeppelin's "twin brother"), congas (1994—present); Derf Nasna-Haj, bass (1995—present); SilverShower Raven, drums (1995-present)

WARNING! If you're religious in your love for the music of Led Zeppelin, then you may want to avert your eyes from this entry. This is the story of Dread Zeppelin, a band of fellas who thought it would be a good idea to re-record some of Led Zeppelin's material ... as reggae songs ... with an overweight, jumpsuit-era Elvis impersonator singing. Guess what? It was a good idea. The Wagnerian pomposity of Led Zeppelin was ripe for satire, and Dread Zeppelin's irreverent wit (its 1995 album is titled *No Quarter Pounder* was just the ticket. With the corpulent talents of vocalist Tortelvis out front, this merry band of genre-confused lads offer some of the most creative and hilarious rock parody this side of Spinal Tap. Not content with the mere gimmick of their delivery, Dread Zeppelin also took the pains to create an entire faux history for the band, replete with seamy pasts, illegitimate offspring, and overripe indulgences (band lore also states that the band played their first live gig on Elvis's birthday, January 8th, which, using the transatlantic time difference to fudge the numbers, is also Led Zeppelin founder Jimmy Page's birthday). Tortelvis briefly left the building in 1991—to return two years later—and the general Dread Zeppelin sound stayed consistent. Or, if you will, the song remained the same (ouch!).

what to buy: Of its available catalog, Dread Zeppelin's major label debut—the prophetically titled *Un-Led-Ed* (I.R.S., 1990, prod. Rasta Li-Mon and Jah Paul Jo) ♪♪♪♪ is easily its most inspired and enjoyable recording. The wacko hybrid of Zeppelin stompers and reggae rhythms is deliciously effective and, at times, induces an epiphanous delirium—you listen to this stuff enough and you may start to believe that nature intended "Heartbreaker" to segue into Elvis Presley's "Heartbreak Hotel." Irie!

what to buy next: *5,000,000* (IRS, 1991, prod. Jah Paul Jo and Rasta Li-Mon) ♪♪♪ is more of the same from the calypso-crazed hammer of the gods. This release finds the band still mining (and having its rasta way with) the classic Led Zeppelin catalog—including a typically goofball mauling of "Stairway to Heaven" —along with some non-Zeppelin tunes such as the Yardbirds' "Train Kept a Rollin'." By the end of this album, however, the joke is beginning to repeat itself.

what to avoid: *It's Not Unusual* (I.R.S., 1992, prod. Jah Paul Jo and Rasta Li-Mon) WOOF! is a misguided attempt to apply the band's schtick to disco hits of the 1970s, with Butt Boy (transformed to Gary B.I.B.B.) vainly attempting to fill the considerable girth of Tortelvis's jumpsuit.

the rest: *Hot and Spicy Beanburger* (Birdcage, 1993) ♪♪♪ *The First No-Elvis* (Birdcage, 1994) ♪♪♪ *No Quarter Pounder* (Birdcage, 1995) ♪♪♪ *The Fun Sessions* (Cash Cow, 1995) ♪♪½

worth searching for: *Live on Blueberry Cheesecake*, (Cash Cow, 1996) a live set that offers a neat snapshot of the spectacle that is a Dread Zeppelin concert—though Tortelvis really must be *seen* to truly be believed.

solo outings:

There is a much rumored solo album by Tortelvis, but it is apparently only available from an overweight, sideburned guy in sunglasses who works as a fry cook at some burger joint.

▶▶ Are you kidding? Nobody sounds like these guys.

◀◀ Vegas-era Elvis Presley, Led Zeppelin, Bob Marley, Weird Al Yankovic, Spinal Tap

Dave Galens

Dream Academy

Formed 1983 in London, England

Gilbert Gabriel, keyboards; Nick Laird-Clowes, vocals, guitar; Kate St. John, vocals, oboe, saxophone

Adhering to a 60s pyschedelic-pop aesthetic (Pink Floyd's David Gilmour was a patron), the nostalgic "Life in a Northern Town," with its dreamlike chanting "Hey-ah ma-ma-ma" chorus, got this trio a lucky break in 1985. The employment of a timpani and cellos almost cover up Laird-Clowes' bland singing, which typifies the group's sophisticated but pointless and backward-looking meanderings. All of its subsequent recordings followed suit, with justifiably lesser results. As all of their material is out of print, the easiest place to find "Life in a Northern Town" (the name supposedly suggested by Paul Simon to save fans the embarrassment of walking up to the record counter and just chanting) is on *Living in Oblivion: The 80s Greatest Hits, Vol. 3.* (EMI, 1994) 🦴🦴🦴

Allan Orski

The Dream Syndicate /Steve Wynn/Opal/Guild of Temporal Adventurers/Kendra Smith

Formed 1981 in Los Angeles, Calif. Disbanded 1989.

Steve Wynn, guitar, vocals; Karl Precoda, guitar (1981-84); Paul Cutler, guitar (1985-89); Kendra Smith, bass, vocals (1981-83); Dave Provost, bass (1983-84); Mark Walton, bass (1985-89) Dennis Duck, drums

The name came from Faust-member Tony Conrad's album *Outside the Dream Syndicate,* which ironically was a reference (apparently unknown to Wynn) to a 60s band that featured Conrad, minimalist composer LaMonte Young and John Cale, who went on to join the Velvet Underground—a group that Wynn's Dream Syndicate continually was compared to, though he brazenly denied any influence. Lumped in with the so-called Paisley Underground of the early 80s West Coast, despite a less psychedelic sound, the band basically did what Wynn felt like doing (which led Smith and then Precoda to quit), with Wynn's muse eventually taking him into more of a country-rock sound. It might have worked if the quality of his writing hadn't faded. After Dream Syndicate broke up, Wynn went on to an intermittent solo career, sometimes guesting in the mid-90s with Walton's Continental Drifters. Smith went on, for a time, to the somnolent Opal.

what to buy: The original quartet's debut, *The Days of Wine and Roses,* (Slash/Ruby, 1982, prod. Chris Desjardins) 🦴🦴🦴🦴 remains the group's finest moment, thanks to Wynn's haunting songs ("Tell Me When It's Over," "When You Smile") and the perfect VU-style reproduction.

what to buy next: In the absence of most of the catalog, *Tell Me When It's Over: The Best of Dream Syndicate* (Rhino, 1992, prod. Various) 🦴🦴🦴🦴 will have to do. *The Day Before Wine and Roses* (Atavistic, 1995) 🦴🦴🦴🦴 is an incidiery 1982 radio gig; all three of the live tracks on the *Tell Me When It's Over* EP (Rough Trade, 1983) 🦴🦴🦴 were from this concert and are on the CD. Smith's *Five Ways of Disappearing* (4AD, 1995, prod. Kendra Smith and A. Phillip Uberman) 🦴🦴🦴🦴 radiates the expected VU-like drones, but with a stronger love of melody and instrumental variety than in her Dream Syndicate and Opal incarnations. The frequent use of pump organ embodies the brooding twilight tone of the album, and her pure, gorgeous voice lends a cool grace to all tracks.

what to avoid: The overrated *Out of the Grey,* (Big Time, 1986/1987, prod. Paul Cutler) 🦴🦴 delivers tepid, amorphous country rock of no distinction.

the rest: *Medicine Show/This is Not the New Dream Syndicate Album...Live!* (A&M, 1984/1985) 🦴🦴🦴🦴: The Lost Tapes 1983-1988 *(Atavistic, 1996)* 🦴🦴🦴 Ghost Stories *(Enigma, 1988)* 🦴🦴 Live at Raji's *(Restless, 1989)* 🦴🦴🦴 *Opal:* Happy Nightmare Baby *(SST, 1987)* 🦴🦴

worth searching for: The raw four-song *Dream Syndicate,* EP (Down There, 1982, prod. Not Listed) 🦴🦴🦴🦴 the band's first release, has a jagged conceptual integrity that equals the album's. *Rainy Day* (Llama/Enigma, 1983, prod. David Roback) 🦴🦴🦴🦴 was a pre-trend tribute album on which Smith, Precoda, and Duck joined members of Bangles, Rain Parade and 3 O'-Clock to record covers of songs by artists who inspired the Paisley Underground scene—from the Byrds and Jimi Hendrix to the Beach Boys and the Who. Opal's out-of-print compilation *Early Recordings* (Rough Trade, 1989, prod. Various) 🦴🦴🦴 includes the two non-album tracks from the *Northern Line* EP (One Big Guitar, 1985) and all four songs from the precursor group's *Fell From the Sun* EP (Serpent-Enigma, 1984). Smith's *Kendra Smith Presents the Guild of Temporal Adventurers* (Fiasco, 1992, prod. Kendra Smith) 🦴🦴🦴🦴 is a low-key but subtly brilliant amalgam that at one turn anticipates the neo-lounge sound and at another recalls early Eno.

solo outings:

Steve Wynn: *Flourescent* (Mute, 1994) 🦴🦴🦴 *Melting in the Dark* (Zero Hour, 1996) 🦴🦴🦴🦴

▶▶ R.E.M., American Music Club, Red House Painters, the Continental Drifters

◀◀ The Velvet Underground, Neil Young, the Rolling Stones, Brian Eno

see also: *The Continental Drifters*

Steve Holtje

The Drifters

Formed 1953 in New York, N.Y.

Key Lead Vocalists: Clyde McPhatter (1953-54, died June 13, 1972); David Baughan (1954-55); Johnny Moore (1955-57, 1964-65); Bobby Hendricks (1957-58); Ben E. King (1959-60); Rudy Lewis (1961-64, died 1964)

The Drifters are to doo wop what Elvis Presley is to rock 'n' roll; it could have existed without them, but a big ol' chunk would be missing. The Drifters were actually two different groups of two different eras—the classic doo wop of the McPhatter-Moore group of 1953-58 and the more pop-oriented lineups led by Ben E. King, Rudy Lewis and Johnny Moore 1959-1964. Both incarnations were giants of their time; few groups, after all, could have survived the departure of a talent such as McPhatter, who sang lead on hits such as Money Honey," "Honey Love" and "White Christmas." But the harmony lineup of the group proved they could go on, backing Moore on "Adorable," Ruby Baby" and You Promise To Be Mine." Manager George Treadwell disbanded the group in 1958 and signed the Five Crowns to perform as the Drifters. First King led the group on "There Goes My Baby," "This Magic Moment" and "Save the last Dance for Me." Then Lewis took the lead for "Sweets for My Sweet," "Under the Boardwalk" and "On Broadway." Finally, Moore returned to the group in time for "Up On the Roof." Since about 1967, the Drifters have been more a name than a group, with makeshift lineups packaged to play the supper club and hotel circuit. At times there were two so-called Drifters groups playing at the same time, a sad way to carry on a truly legendary legacy.

what to buy: The Drifters that most will remember come through on *1959-1965 All-Time Greatest Hits and More,* (Atlantic, 1988, prod. Bob Porter and Kim Cook) a compilation whose sonic re-engineering puts a new sheen on the group's immaculate harmonies. The other side of the coin gets its due on *Let the Boogie Woogie Roll,* (Atlantic, 1988, prod. Various) covering the harmony heavy doo wop of the 50s.

what to buy next: There are lots of crummy collections of the same rehashed songs available, but the three-disc set *Rockin' and Driftin': The Drifters Box* (Atlantic & Atco Remasters, 1996, prod. Various) is excellent, rightly emphasizing the McPhatter years (and his solo work) and featuring a booklet full of great photos.

what to avoid: *Up On the Roof, Under the Boardwalk and On Broadway* (Rhino, 1993, prod. Various) trades on the title tunes, but after those three there's not a lot to recommend.

the rest: *16 Greatest Hits* (Deluxe) *Greatest Hits* (Hollywood/Rounder) *Live at Harvard University* (Rose, 1993) *Save the Last Dance For Me* (Avid, 1995)

worth searching for: *The Very Best of the Drifters* (Rhino, 1993, prod. Mike Stoller) compiles the hits and only the hits for those who just want to dance and not delve into the intricacies of doo wop,

▶▶ The Temptations, the Four Tops, the Parliaments, Boyz II Men

◀◀ The Ink Spots, the Orioles, the Ravens

see also: *Clyde McPhatter, Ben E. King*

Lawrence Gabriel

Drivin' N' Cryin' /Kevn Kinney/Kathleen Turner Overdrive/Toenut

Formed 1985, Atlanta, Ga.

Kevn Kinney, guitar, vocals; Tim Nielsen, bass, mandolin; Jeff Sullivan, drums; Buren Fowler, guitar (1989-94); Joey Huffman, keyboards (1994-present).

Formed in the midst of the fertile Atlanta/Athens scene of the mid-80s, Drivin' N' Cryin' broke the region's jangle-pop prototype with an unlikely blend of country-folk that emphasized acoustic instrumentation and hard-rock that bordered on heavy metal. DNC started out on independent label 688 Records but quickly jumped to the major-label ranks in 1988 for a deal with Island that lasted until the mid-90s, when the group moved to Geffen. An opening slot for pals R.E.M. on a 1989 arena tour helped expose the band to wider audiences; its records have sold reasonably well, though it continues to be primarily a club-level draw. Frontman Kinney also has released a couple of solo albums that veer specifically toward his more acoustic inclinations, while bassist Nielsen and drummer Sullivan are work in the outside groups Kathleen Turner Overdrive and Toenut, respectively.

what to buy: *Mystery Road* (Island, 1989, prod. Scott MacPherson, Kinney and Nielsen) is the band's best overall collection of songs and the one that suffers least from its often-jarring juxtaposition of soft and hard styles. It includes the concert-favorite anthem "Straight to Hell." *Wrapped in Sky* (Geffen, 1995, prod. John Porter) marks a welcome return to form after a noticeable slide during its latter years with Island. Ironically, both of Kinney's solo releases—*MacDougal Blues* (Island, 1990, prod. Peter Buck) and *Down Out Law*—(Mammoth, 1994, prod. Kevin Kinney) are head-and-shoulders above anything he's ever done with his band. *MacDougal Blues,* which features acoustic accompaniment by all of his bandmates, plus Buck, John Keane and other Georgia scene standbys, has the wonderfully comfortable feel of a late-night hootenanny, while *Down Out Law* is a deeply affecting and personal work recorded almost entirely solo acoustic.

what to buy next: *Scarred But Smarter* (688 Records, 1986/Island, 1989, prod. George Pappas) is a fine first record, rawer and gutsier than their subsequent efforts, if a little less refined. *Whisper Tames the Lion* (Island, 1988, prod. Anton Fier) offers a clear representation of what the band is all about by sequencing the hellfire screamer "Powerhouse" directly after the sprightly, countryish ditty"Catch The Wind."

what to avoid: *Smoke* (Island, 1993, prod. Geoff Workman and Drivin' N' Cryin') is a glaring low point, with hardly a single memorable song and an unhealthy turn toward a harder-edged sound that ultimately sold the band short of its more significant melodic talents.

the rest: *Fly Me Courageous* (Island, 1990) *Live on Fire* (Island EP, 1991)

solo outings:

Kevin Kinney (with Frank French): *Everything Looks Better in the Dark* (Twilight, 1987)

Tim Nielsen (with Kathleen Turner Overdrive): *Kathleen Turner Overdrive* (Booger's Banquet, 1994)

Jeff Sullivan (with Toenut): *Information* (Mute, 1994)

▶▶ Indigo Girls, Black Crowes

◀◀ Hank Williams, Bob Dylan, Ramones, John Denver

Peter Blackstock

Pete Droge

Born. March 11, 1969, Eugene, Ore.

With a lyrical gift that says "folkie," and a band that answers "rock 'n' roll," Droge can have it both ways. But he mostly plays it down the middle, creating solid, acoustic-based rockers that are literate, soulful and earnest to a fault. Considering he began his career in Seattle and later moved to Portland, it's surprising that he chose not to hide his lyrics in a sea of sonic sludge or adorn them with coy love-rock. But Droge has the air of an iconoclast about him, and, backed by his simple guitar-bass-drums-keyboard arrangements, his laconic delivery makes him sound like Tom Petty backed by the Band. On *Necktie Second,* (American, 1994, prod. Brendan O'Brien) Droge indulges in a fair amount of self-pity, but at least some of the time, as on the rocking opening cut, "If You Don't Love Me (I'll Kill Myself)," he plays if for yuks. Elsewhere, he engages in a bit of Dylanesque wordplay ("Sunspot Stopwatch") and proves himself a capable storyteller ("Fourth of July"). The album is suffused with regret and longing, yet there is just enough humor to keep things moving. On *Find a Door,* (American, 1996, prod. Brendan O'Brien) Droge's backing outfit has solidified into a band he calls the Sinners, but the sound is no less than heavenly, particularly on the rocking single "Wolfgang," which coasts along on a George Harrison-style slide guitar. The horn-augmented "Mr. Jade" rants at a clueless yuppie, and is perhaps Droge's own "Ballad of a Thin Man." And on "Dear Diane," Droge regresses to the wise-ass moroseness of his debut, instructing "Dear Diane/Today was worse/Call the Reverend and a hearse." This kid's gonna go places.

Daniel Durchholz

The Dukes of Stratosphear

See: XTC

Slim Dunlap

See: The Replacements

Duran Duran

Formed 1979 in Birmingham, England

Simon Le Bon, vocals; Nick Rhodes, keyboards; John Taylor, bass, vocals; Andy Taylor, guitar, vocals (1979-85); Roger Taylor, drums (1979-85); Warren Cuccurullo, guitar, (1987-present); Steve Ferrone, drums (1986-88); Sterling Campbell, drums (1990-present)

For a band that spent the better part of its career frolicking on tropical beaches, marrying supermodels and creating videos that put Randal Kleiser to shame, Duran Duran devoted an incomprehensible amount of passion to its music. At the turn of the 80s, the group blended funk rhythms with glam posturing, punk attitude with New Romantic daring, and invented a sound and style that set new standards for pop music. The group's ability to turn out simple songs—coupled with the band members' good looks and video acumen that made it an early MTV favorite—relegated it to teen idoldom early on, but Duran overcame that stigma and has enjoyed one of the longest-running careers in recent rock history.

what to buy: *Rio* (Capitol, 1982, prod. Colin Thurston) ♪♪♪♪♪ blended tropical themes, savvy synthesizer work and catchy melodies to become one of the defining records of the early 80s. Songs like "Hungry Like The Wolf" and "Save A Prayer" showcased the dynamic powers at work behind this band and proved there was much more to Duran than pretty faces and fancy videos. However, Duran was primarily a singles band, and *Decade* (Capitol, 1991) ♪♪♪♪♪ collects some of its most stellar recordings, including "Is There Something I Should Know," "A View To A Kill" and "Skin Trade."

what to buy next: The debut, *Duran Duran* (Capitol, 1981, prod. Colin Thurston) ♪♪♪♪, made it clear that this was a band that was serious about its music. Songs like "Girls On Film" and "Planet Earth" are still staples on modern rock radio. Even though it was a commercial bomb, *Big Thing* (Capitol, 1988, prod. Duran Duran, Jonathan Elias and Daniel Abraham) ♪♪♪ represented a new level of maturity for Duran. Balanced by lush ballads ("Land," "Palomino") and introspective rockers ("I Don't Want Your Love," "All She Wants Is"), it marked one a creative peak.

what to avoid: *Thank You* (Capitol, 1995, prod. Duran Duran) WOOF!, the group's covers album, was its most unnecessary exercise in self-mutilation. Hearing the former teen idols take on songs as bewildering as Public Enemy's "911 Is A Joke," The Doors' "Crystal Ship" and Elvis Costello's "Watching The Detectives," proved nothing more than laughable.

the rest: *Seven and the Ragged Tiger* (Capitol, 1983) ♪♪ *Arena* (Capitol, 1984) ♪ *Notorious* (Capitol, 1986) ♪ *Liberty* (Capitol, 1990) ♪♪ *Duran Duran* (Capitol, 1993) ♪♪♪.

worth searching for: *Carnival* (Capitol, 1982), ♪♪♪♪ a vinyl EP of extended remixes of four songs from Duran Duran's first two albums, captures the excitement the group brought to dance clubs during the early 80s.

solo outings:

Arcadia (Le Bon, Rhodes): *So Red The Rose* (Capitol, 1985) ♪♪♪

The Power Station (Andy Taylor, John Taylor): *The Power Station* (Capitol, 1985) ♪

Andy Taylor: *Thunder* (MCA, 1986) WOOF!

▶▶ Blur, Hole, Stone Temple Pilots, Live

◀◀ David Bowie, Roxy Music, Chic, Sex Pistols

Aidin Vaziri

Seven Essential 70s Collections

The Disco Years, Vol. 1-2 (Rhino)

Reservoir Dogs Soundtrack (MCA)

Classic Rock of the 70s (Warner Bros.)

Dazed and Confused Soundtrack (Giant)

New Wave Hits, Vol. 1-4 (Rhino)

Smooth Grooves, Vol. 1-7 (The Right Stuff)

Funky Stuff: The Best of Funk Essentials (Mercury/Chronicles)

Bob Dylan

Born Robert Allen Zimmerman, May 24, 1941 in Duluth, Minn.

Decades from now, when all the dust has settled and the rock music revolution is viewed with historical hindsight, Dylan will stand out as one of the three most important people to ever pick up a guitar. George Harrison feels even more strongly; he's been quoted as saying that 500 years from now, Dylan will be the most remembered and revered name from this era, eclipsing even the Beatles. Unlike the Fab Four and Elvis Presley,

Dylan's profound influence on the music world—and society in general—was never matched by his sales. Nonetheless, his key material truly serves as the soundtrack for a generation, and is deeply ingrained in our daily lives. Phrases like "The Times They Are A-Changin' " have worked their way into everyday journalistic vernacular; his song "Like A Rolling Stone" even helped give a moniker to our biggest music magazine.

Dylan's most important contribution was giving the voice of social consciousness to contemporary music lyrics, starting with folk music and then evolving into rock. When girl groups and teenage idols were topping the charts in 1962 and '63, Dylan woke up a sleeping public with songs about racial injustice and the ravages of war. All of this has earned Dylan a continuing level of respect that is on a par with greats like Duke Ellington, Leonard Bernstein and Miles Davis. His influence may be best illustrated by the fact that one scholarly study concluded that he was the one person, from all walks of life, most responsible for stopping the Vietnam war.

what to buy: To this day, Dylan's legacy is still very much that of a folk artist, and his key work in that genre is *The Freewheelin' Bob Dylan* (Columbia, 1963, prod. John Hammond) This album single-handedly launched the mid-60s protest movement with such venerable songs as "Blowin' In The Wind" and "A Hard Rain's A-Gonna Fall." Once Dylan started rocking full-time, he made *Highway 61 Revisited* (Columbia, 1965, prod. Bob Johnston and Tom Wilson), which many pundits feel is one of the greatest albums ever released, perhaps even tying the Beatles' *Sgt. Pepper's Lonely Hearts Club Band* for the all-time crown. It is hard to overpraise an album that opens with "Like A Rolling Stone" and closes with "Desolation Row," and doesn't have an ounce of fat in between. Directly following that was *Blonde On Blonde* (Columbia, 1966, prod. by Bob Johnston), another highly regarded album that always winds up in the top 10 of any greatest albums of all-time poll. Probably Dylan's most popular record among his legions of hard-core fans, the album is a folk-rock masterpiece featuring "Rainy Day Women #12 & 35," "I Want You" and "Just Like A Woman." Although Dylan's creative output peaked with that record, nine years later he shocked everyone with the brilliance of *Blood On The Tracks* (Columbia, 1975, prod. Bob Dylan) As his marriage started to crumble, Dylan wrote and sang songs like "Tangled Up In Blue" and "Idiot Wind" from the soul, causing critics everywhere to pull out and dust off the "masterpiece" moniker once again.

what to buy next: *Bringing It All Back Home* (Columbia, 1965, prod. by Tom Wilson) is many fans' favorite Dylan album and literally kick-started the folk-rock movement with "Mr. Tambourine Man" and "It's Alright, Ma (I'm Only Bleeding)." Before that, however, *The Times They Are A-Changin'* (Columbia, 1964, prod. by Tom Wilson) set the music world on fire with its title song and "With God On Our Side," and *Another Side Of Bob Dylan* (Columbia, 1964, prod. by Tom Wilson) showed his softer—though no less ingenious—side with "It Ain't Me Babe" and "Chimes Of Freedom." The double-disc *Basement Tapes* (Columbia, 1975, prod. Bob Dylan and The Band) was recorded in 1967 with The Band and has achieved legendary status with off-the-wall, yet compelling, songs like "Please, Mrs. Henry" and "Nothing Was Delivered" (plus the brilliant "Tears Of Rage"). If it's an overview of Dylan's career that you need, however, nothing beats the *Biograph* box set (Columbia, 1985, prod. Various), featuring three CDs full of his most compelling material, spanning all of his most important phases.

what to avoid: Without Dylan's consent, his former record label released the unfortunately titled *Dylan* album (Columbia, 1973, prod, by Bob Johnston) WOOF! only after he had jumped ship to David Geffen's Asylum label. It was a dirty trick that now stands alone as a black eye in Dylan's canon. The album is so insignificant that, to this day, Columbia still hasn't reissued it on CD in America.

the rest: *Bob Dylan* (Columbia, 1962) *Bob Dylan's Greatest Hits* (Columbia, 1967) *John Wesley Harding* (Columbia, 1968) *Nashville Skyline* (Columbia, 1969) *Self Portrait* (Columbia, 1970) *New Morning* (Columbia, 1970) *Greatest Hits Vol. II* (Columbia, 1971) *Pat Garrett & Billy The Kid* soundtrack (Columbia, 1973) *Planet Waves* (Asylum, 1974) *Before The Flood* (Asylum, 1974) *Desire* (Columbia, 1976) *Hard Rain* (Columbia, 1976) *Street Legal* (Columbia, 1978) *Bob Dylan At Budokan* (Columbia, 1979) *Slow Train Coming* (Columbia, 1979) *Saved* (Columbia, 1980) *Shot Of Love* (Columbia, 1981) *Infidels* (Columbia, 1983) *Real Live* (Columbia, 1985) *Empire Burlesque* (Columbia, 1985) *Knocked Out Loaded* (Columbia, 1986) *Down In The Groove* (Columbia, 1988) *Dylan & The Dead* (Columbia, 1989) *Oh Mercy* (Columbia, 1989) *Under The Red Sky* (Columbia, 1990) *The Bootleg Series Vols. 1-3 1961-1991* (Columbia, 1991) *Good As I Been To You* (Columbia, 1992) *World Gone Wrong* (Columbia, 1993) *Greatest Hits Vol. 3* (Columbia, 1994) *MTV Unplugged* (Columbia, 1995)

worth searching for: DCC Compact Classics' gold-disc version of *Highway 61 Revisited*, remastered in the early 90s with sparkling sound is well worth its $25-$30 price tag. Also, *The Concert For Bangla Desh* (Apple/Capitol, 1971), with its five-song, highly-charged Dylan acoustic set that features his greatest-ever live reading of "Just Like A Woman."

▶▶ The Byrds, Sonny & Cher, Joan Baez, Tom Petty & the Heartbreakers, Bruce Springsteen, John Mellencamp, Garth Brooks, Joe Henry, Bob Seger, Joan Osborne

◀◀ Woody Guthrie, Hank Williams, Leadbelly, Little Richard, Elvis Presley, the Weavers, Joan Baez

Pete Howard

The Eagles

Formed 1971, Los Angeles, Calif.

Don Felder, guitar and vocals (1974-present); Glenn Frey, vocals, guitar and keyboards (1971-present); Don Henley, vocals and drums (1971-present); Bernie Leadon, guitar, banjo, mandolin and vocals (1971-76); Randy Meisner, bass and vocals (1971-77); Timothy B. Schmit, bass and vocals (1977-present); Joe Walsh, guitar and vocals (1976-present)

Bred in Los Angeles' fertile country-rock community, the Eagles came together first as the backing band for Linda Ronstadt's *Silk Purse* album in 1970; individually, the musicians had already played with the Flying Burrito Brothers, Poco, Rick Nelson's Stone Canyon Band and Bob Seger. But it was the Eagles sound—smooth harmonies and polished, twangy arrangements—that defined Southern California rock during the 70s. By the time they rolled out the seminal *Hotel California* album, Henley and Frey had become astute social commentators—despite a bit of cynicism that lent a nasty edge to some of their songs. Always too serious, the Eagles succumbed to the pressures of success and called it quits in 1981. But after 13 years of solo recordings they reunited for an MTV concert that yielded the top-selling *Hell Freezes Over* album and a phenomenally successful world tour (with $100+ tickets). It still appears unlikely they'll record another full album of new music again, however.

what to buy: A little inconsistent during their early years, the Eagles are best served by *Their Greatest Hits, 1971-75* (Asylum, 1975, prod. Glyn Johns and Bill Szymczyk), an awesome collection of singles—from "Take it Easy" to "One of These Nights"—that established the Eagles as one of rock's top groups of the time. *Hotel California* (Asylum, 1976, prod. Szymczyk) made the most of that momentum. Bolstered by the addition of Walsh's stinging guitar solos and a collection of poignant, pointed songs, it's as much a cultural barometer as a great rock 'n' roll album.

what to buy next: *The Long Run* (Asylum, 1979, prod. Szymczyk) is another sharp, skillful work marked by the title track and Schmit's aching love song *"I Can't Tell You Why." One of These Nights* (Asylum, 1975, prod. Szymczyk) is the apex of the Eagles' twang time with some truly gorgeous moments in "Lyin' Eyes" and "Take it to the Limit."

what to avoid: *Desperado* (Asylum, 1973, prod. Johns) is a misbegotten concept album whose best songs can be found on *Their Greatest Hits.*

the rest: *Eagles* (Asylum, 1972) *On the Border* (Asylum, 1974) *Live* (Asylum, 1980) *Greatest Hits, Vol. 2* (Asylum, 1982) *Hell Freezes Over* (Geffen, 1994).

worth searching for: *Peaceful Easy Feeling* (Cuttlefish bootleg) is one of many recordings of a landmark 1974 show at New York's Bottom Line, at which Rondstadt and Jackson Browne joined the Eagles for a rendition of "Take it Easy."

solo outings:

Don Felder: *Airborne* (Elektra, 1983)

Glenn Frey: *No Fun Aloud* (Asylum, 1982) *The Allnighter* (MCA, 1984) *Soul Searchin'* (MCA, 1988) *Strange Weather* (MCA, 1992) *Live* (MCA, 1993) *Best of* (MCA, 1995)

Don Henley: See separate entry

Randy Meisner: *One More Song* (Epic, 1980) *Randy Meisner* (Epic, 1982)

Timothy Schmit: *Playin' it Cool* (Asylum, 1984) *Timothy B* (MCA, 1987) *Tell the Truth* (MCA, 1990)

Joe Walsh: See separate entry

▶▶ Travis Tritt, Garth Brooks, Mavericks, Gin Blossoms, Uncle Tupelo, Jayhawks, Vince Gill

◀◀ Byrds, Gram Parsons, Beatles, Everly Brothers, Hank Williams

Gary Graff

Steve Earle

Born Jan. 17, 1955 in Fort Monroe, Va.

The son of an air traffic controller, Steve Earle infiltrated Nashville in 1986 with a twangy, hardcore-hillbilly sound filtered through the heartland rock 'n' roll of John Mellencamp and *Nebraska*-era Bruce Springsteen. Although signed to mainstream MCA Records, Earle quickly established himself as a rebel without a pause by worshiping Townes Van Zandt, opening shows for the Replacements and eventually battling cocaine and heroin addictions. Despite a string of powerful albums—capped by 1990's underrated *The Hard Way*—radio resisted the big, bad good ol' boy and the back-to-back releases of a live album and a greatest-hits collection confirmed that even MCA had lost patience with him. But Earle has confronted and apparently conquered his demons: Now clean and sober, he released a 1996 comeback album called *I Feel Alright* that confirms the title with a hearty, hard-rocking relish. Simultaneously, such Nashville stalwarts as Travis Tritt, the Highwaymen, Gretchen Peters and Emmylou Harris are covering his songs, giving him a rare second chance for commercial redemption.

what to buy: *Guitar Town* (MCA, 1986, prod. Emory Gordy, Jr., and Tony Brown) is an auspicious debut of small-town frustration ("Someday") and romantic yearning ("Fearless Heart"). *The Hard Way* (MCA, 1990, prod. Earle and Joe Hardy) slipped out when even his staunchest fans had forgotten about him, but "Promise You Anything," "The Other Kind" and "Billy Austin" are as trenchant as any songs he's recorded. *I Feel Alright* (Warner Bros., 1996, prod. Richard Dodd, Ray Kennedy and Richard Bennett) finds him defiantly addressing his past in "Cocaine Can't Kill My Pain" and "The Unrepentant." But the brightest signs are the brash but breezy twang-pop confections "Hard-Core Troubador," "More Than I Can Do" and "You're Still Standin' There" (a duet with Lucinda Williams).

what to buy next: *Copperhead Road* (MCA, 1988, Earle and Tony Brown) finds him ditching his country roots and heading into darker territory with such venomous rockers as "Snake Oil," "Johnny Come Lately" and a barnstorming remake of his own "Devil's Right Hand."

what to avoid: *Early Tracks* (Columbia, 1987, prod. Roy Dea and Pat Carter) is a hurriedly compiled collection of tepid unreleased material designed to cash-in on his "Guitar Town" accolades.

the rest: *Exit O* (MCA, 1987) *BBC Live* (Windsong, 1988) *Shut Up and Die Like an Aviator* (MCA, 1991) *Essential Steve Earle* (MCA, 1993) *Train a Comin'* (Winter Harvest, 1995)

Worth Searching For: A self-titled three-song EP (MCA, 1986) with a remixed "Someday" and a live version of Bruce Springsteen's "State Trooper."

Travis Tritt, Todd Snider, Dale Watson

Townes Van Zandt, Waylon Jennings, Bruce Springsteen, Bob Dylan

David Okamoto

Earth Wind & Fire /Philip Bailey/Maurice White

Formed 1969 in Chicago, Ill. Disbanded 1984. Re-formed 1987.

Maurice White, drums, vocals, kalimba; Philip Bailey, vocals, percussion (1972-present); Verdine White, bass; Donald Whitehead, keyboards (1969-72); Wade Felmons, vocals, keyboards (1969-72); Michael Beal, guitar, harmonica (1969-72); Yackov Ben Israel, percussion (1969-72); Chet Washington, tenor sax (1969-72); Alex Thomas, trombone (1969-72); Sherry Scott, vocals (1969-72); Larry Dunn, keyboards (1972-83); Ralph Johnson, percussion (1972-83); Roland Bautista, guitar (1972, 1981-84); Ronnie Laws, sax, flute (1972); Jessica Cleaves, vocals (1972); Andrew Woolfolk, soprano sax, flute (1973-present); Al McKay, guitar (1973-81); Sheldon Reynolds, guitar (1987-present); Johnny Graham, guitar (1973-83); Freddie White, drums (1974-75)

One of the most successful bands of the 70s, EWF is a smooth funk band that plays songs, not just grooves. Anchored by blues/soul drummer Maurice White—a former Chess Records session drummer and a member of Ramsey Lewis' trio—and his brother Verdine on bass, the band soared on Philip Bailey's angelic falsetto and a series of well-written and sumptuously crafted singles that made the most of the group's formidable instrumental skills. Embellishing the catchy tunes and propulsive rhythms is a nebulous but colorful Afrocentrism and cosmology, which enliven not only the album covers but also the concerts—vast communal affairs of astonishing precision yet compelling impact. The group adjusted easily to disco, but further developments in R&B left it behind as it was unwilling to jettison elements that had worked so well for so long. Bailey already had a florishing solo career by the time the group broke up in 1984, but the 1987 album sounded more like vintage EWF than subsequent efforts. The group continues to tour, with either Maurice White or Bailey (whose falsetto, though still impressive, isn't what it used to be) acting as frontman and Verdine usually on bass, and remains an impressive concert experience.

what to buy: The big hit on *Spirit* (Columbia, 1976, prod. Maurice White and Charles Stepney) was "Getaway," but it's the album's seamlessness that stands out—as well as Bailey's greatest vocal performance, "Imagination." *All 'n' All* (Columbia, 1977, prod. Maurice White) has "Serpentine Fire" (one of the most original funk tracks EWF made), a strong Brazilian flavor (Paulinho da Costa, Eddie Del Barrio and Deodato contribute) and "Fantasy."

what to buy next: *Head to the Sky* (Columbia, 1973, prod. Joe Wissert) is great except for the long closing instrumental, with "Keep Your Head to the Sky" and "Evil" pointing toward the group's future sound. *Open Our Eyes* (Columbia, 1974, prod. Earth Wind & Fire) doesn't have many hits, but is a wonderfully coherent yet also varied album. *That's the Way of the World* (Columbia, 1975, prod. Sig Shore) boasts the seminal hits "Reasons" and "Shining Star," while *I Am* (ARC/Columbia, 1979, prod. Maurice White) moved smoothly into the disco era with "Boogie Wonderland," "In the Stone" and the slow groove "After the Love Is Gone."

what to avoid: *Last Days and Time* (Columbia, 1972, prod. Joe Wissert) misfires with covers of "Where Have All the Flowers Gone" and "Make It With You" and has even less memorable originals. *Faces* (ARC/Columbia, 1980) is rather faceless; bland and overlong are a bad combination. *Heritage* (ARC/Columbia, 1990, prod. Various) uses a wide variety of producers in a desperate effort to seem contemporary and relevent. Two guest spots by M.C. Hammer are particularly pathetic.

the rest: *Earth, Wind & Fire* (Warner Bros, 1970) *The Need of Love* (Warner Bros, 1972) *Gratitude* (Columbia, 1975) *The Best of Earth, Wind & Fire Vol. 1* (ARC/Columbia, 1978) *Raise* (ARC/Columbia, 1981) *Powerlight* (ARC/Columbia, 1983) *Electric Universe* (ARC/Columbia, 1983) *Touch the World* (ARC/Columbia, 1987) *The Best of Earth, Wind & Fire Vol. 2* (ARC/Columbia, 1988) *Millenium* (Warner Bros., 1993) *The Eternal Dance* (Columbia Legacy, 1992)

worth searching for: *Star Box*, (Sony, 1993) a 16-song Japanese hits collection that does far better than any of its U.S. single disc counterparts.

solo outings:

Maurice White: *Maurice White* (Columbia, 1985) ***Philip Bailey:*** *Continuation* (Columbia, 1983) *Chinese Wall* (Columbia, 1984) *Inside Out* (Columbia, 1986) *Philip Bailey* (Zoo, 1994) (Note: Bailey also releases regular gospel recordings that aren't listed here.)

Brothers Johnson, Brand New Heavies, Incognito, Kim Pensyl

James Brown, Sly & the Family Stone, Ohio Players

Steve Holtje

Elliot Easton

See: The Cars

The Easybeats

Founded 1963 in Australia. Disbanded 1969.

Stevie Wright, vocals; George Young, guitar, vocals; Harry Vanda, guitar, vocals; Dick Diamonde, bass; Gordon (Snowy) Fleet, drums (1963-66); Tony Cahill, drums (1966-69)

While the Beatles were taking the world by storm, the Easybeats were having a heyday in Australia. Formed by friends who met in a youth hostel, the group became the most successful Australian group of the 60s, scoring a string of seven Top 10 Down Under singles that fused the Merseybeat pop of the Beatles with the amphetamine drive of the Who and the Kinks. The group came to London in 1966, where, under the guiding hand of producer Shel Talmy, it cracked the international pop market with the herky-jerky rave-up "Friday on My Mind" in 1967. The songwriting/production team of Young and Vanda came up with fine, adventurous music that was right in step with the ambitious musical trends of the period. But while the group earned raves from contemporaries such as Paul McCartney and Lou Reed, listeners' ears were tuned elsewhere. Oddly, the group's best support came from cover versions of its songs performed by the Lemon Pipers, the Buckinghams, the Music Explosion and Los Bravos. Vanda and Young continued working together after the breakup, masterminding the new wave group Flash and the Pan and assisting Young's brothers Angus and Malcolm in starting Australia's most successful group, AC/DC. The Easybeats' influence remained in evidence throughout the 80s in groups such as the Three O'Clock, the Plimsouls, Divinyls and INXS, all of which have covered its songs. *Absolute Anthology* (EMI, 1980, prod. Various) is a two-CD set that offers everything you could ever want (and more); those with less prodigious appetites will prefer the more compact *The Best of the Easybeats,* (Rhino, 1985, prod. Various) which includes all of the group's essential cuts.

Christopher Scapelliti

Echo & the Bunnymen /Electrafixion

Formed 1978 in Liverpool, England. Disbanded 1991.

Ian McCulloch, vocals, (1978-89); Pete De Freitas, drums (1978-89, died June 15, 1989); Will Sergeant, guitar; Les Pattinson, bass; Noel Burke, vocals (1989-91); Damon Reece, drums

Musicians can't grow up in Liverpool without feeling some influence from you-know-who, so it's no surprise that there's more than a little tunefulness in the music of Echo & the Bunnymen. But there's a dark melancholia, too; lest we forget, this was the punk era, and group leaders McCulloch and Sergeant also shared a fondness for the Doors' moody tone poems. McCulloch set Echo in motion after getting the boot from an early incarnation of Teardrop Explodes, and the group's original lineup included a drum machine named Echo until De Freitas joined in. With the textured, ambient wash of hits such as "The Killing Moon," "Silver" and "Bring on the Dancing Horses," Echo joined Depeche Mode and the Cure in defining a particularly strong wave of British rock during the early 80s. McCulloch left for a solo career in 1989, and the group unravelled shortly thereafter. But in 1994, McCulloch and Sergeant were back together again in a new, every Echo-ish band Electrafixion.

what to buy: *Ocean Rain* (Sire, 1984, prod. David Lord and Echo & the Bunnymen) is the pinnacle of the group's gorgeously moody approach. Sergeant blends his guitar with a full string section to create enduring gems such as "Seven Seas," "Silver" and "The Killing Moon." *Songs to Learn & Sing* (Sire, 1985, prod. Various) has those and eight others in a stunning best-of that more than validates the title.

what to buy next: Few debut albums have the potent flavor of a major new talent arriving as does *Crocodiles.* (Sire, 1980, prod. David Balfe and Bill Drummond) McCulloch voices his angst before it became a cliche, while Sergeant's guitar playing has an appealing roughness to it. Electrafixion's *Burned* (Sire, 1995, prod. Ian McCulloch and Will Sergeant) is, despite the duo's denial, a de facto Bunnymen album, with many of the same melodic virtues though it tends to rock a little harder.

what to avoid: *Reverberation,* (Sire, 1990) the album after McCulloch left the group, has its good points but the group ultimately sounds like a diluted version of its former self.

the rest: *Heaven Up Here* (Sire, 1981/1988) *Echo & the Bunnymen* (Sire, 1987) *BBC Live* (Windsong, 1993)

worth searching for: McCulloch's solo catalog is out of print, but his first effort, *Candleland* (Sire, 1989, prod. Ray Shulman) is a fine, Echo-ish album with a somewhat more personal touch to the lyrics.

Suede, Oasis, Happy Mondays, Stone Roses

The Beatles, the Doors

Gary Graff

Echobelly

Formed 1993 in London, England

Sonya Aurora Madan, vocals; Glenn Johansson, guitar, vocals; Debbie Smith, guitar, Alex Keyser, bass and keyboards; Andy Henderson, drums

Based in England and showcasing the ethnic diversity that is a key to that country's ongoing musical vitality, Echobelly craft melodic, driving new-waveish pop-with-an-attitude that also manages to be tender and introspective. Thanks in large part to the commanding vocals of Anglo-Indian frontwoman Madan, the group has earned an enthusiastic cult following the U.S. and more solid success in the U.K. and Japan. Influenced strongly by the archly self-conscious singing of the Smiths' Morrissey, Madan can convey yearning and *ennui* in the same breath. The group's debut EP *Bellyache* (Rhythm King, 1993) made them the darlings of the notoriously fickle British press, and it gathered more converts with their 1994 debut album. But its sophomore effort, *On,* (550 Music/Epic, 1995, prod. Sean Slader and Paul Koldierie) demonstrated a greater maturity of vision, showcasing gigantic hooks and Madan's infectious, clarion vocals and incisive lyrics.

the rest: *Everybody's Got One* (Rhythm King, 1994)

Simon Glickman

Eddie & the Hot Rods

Formed 1975 in Southend, Essex, England. Disbanded 1981

Barrie Masters, vocals; Dave Higgs, guitar, vocals, piano; Graeme Douglas, guitar (1977-80); Paul Gray, bass, vocals (1975-80); Tony Cranney, bass (1980-81); Steve Nicholl, drums, vocals; Lew Lewis, harmonica (1975-76)

One of the main links between pub rock and punk, Eddie & the Hot Rods were formed by ex-amateur boxer Masters and quickly found success playing the London pub circuit, showcasing a mix of rock and soul covers and originals. There was no Eddie in the group, though manager/producer Ed Hollis was practically a member; onstage a life-size dummy named Eddie was regularly beaten up as part of the group's high-energy show. Island signed them and by 1976 the group scored British hits with a cover of "Wooly Bully," and Higgs's "Teenage Depression." The Island album of the same name was issued in England that year, though it wouldn't come out in the U.S. until 1977. Ex-Kursaal Flyer Douglas came on board in '76 and became an instant factor, co-writing most of the best songs on the group's second album. But by the late 70s the group was splintering, and in 1981 Masters split up what remained of the group and joined the Inmates. There have been intermittent partial Hot Rods reunions, the fruits of which have not made it across the Atlantic.

what to buy: *Life on the Line* (Island, 1977, prod. Ed Hollis) ♫♫♫♫♫ is an absolutely crucial document of its time and still stands up musically and lyrically. Hollis and Douglas form an ace songwriting team, and songs such as "Do Anything You Wanna Do," "Quit This Town," "Ignore Them (Still Life)," the title track and "[And] Don't Believe Your Eyes" are enduring standouts.

what to buy next: *BBC Radio One Live in Concert* (Windsong, 1994, prod. Jeff Griffin) ♫♫♫ contains 1977-78 appearances recorded for British radio. The boisterous energy invigorates some of the Higgs tunes (though they blur together). It's particularly good to have his "I Might Be Lying," a fine non-album single, in two versions here.

What to Avoid The Hot Rods' final album, *Fish 'n' Chips* (EMI, 1980, prod. Al Kooper) **WOOF!** was made without Douglas and Gray. Nobody has ever had a good word to say about this pallid, misguided effort.

the rest: *Teenage Depression* (Island, 1977) ♫♫ *Thriller* (Island, 1979, prod. Peter Kerr) ♫♫♪

Worth Searching For: *One Story Town* (Waterfront EP, 1985) ♫♫♫♪, a six-song British import documenting a spirited reunion gig led by Masters and Nicol.

▶▶ Rockpile, Buzzcocks, Graham Parker and the Rumour

◀◀ Bob Seger, Rolling Stones, the Who, Dr. Feelgood

Steve Holtje

Eddie Floyd

Born June 25, 1935, in Montgomery, Ala.

Calling Floyd a second-rate talent amongst his Stax peers is a bit like chiding the sluggishness of a Carrera next to a Ferrari. He simply had the historical misfortune of being a very good singer-songwriter on a label with artists who made the earth move. That's not to say his signature song, "Knock on Wood" doesn't jar the Richter scale; it does, and the countless cover versions that have abounded over the years are further testaments to its power. But Floyd simply didn't reach those dazzling results with the same frequency of Otis Redding or Sam & Dave. Not too shabby at all.

what to buy: *Rare Stamps* (Stax/Fantasy, 1993, prod. Steve Cropper) ♫♫♫♫♪ compiles two 60s albums—*I Never Found a Girl* and *Rare Stamps*—into a stunning 25-track disc. Backed by the peerless Booker T. and The MG's, Floyd kicks out his best material, including "Knock on Wood," a lively version of Sam Cooke's "Bring it on Home to Me" and the pre-metal lament "Big Bird." The reissue also contains two hot duets with Mavis Staples.

what to buy next: *Knock on Wood* (Stax, 1967/Rhino, 1991 reissue, prod. Yves Beauvais) ♫♫♫♫ is Floyd's strongest studio album, highlighted by the title track, "634-5789" and the sublime "I've Just Been Feeling Bad." *Chronicle: Greatest Hits* (Stax, 1991, prod. Various) ♫♫♫♫ collects some of the *Rare Stamps* material along with "My Girl" and the Memphis funk of "Soul Street."

what to avoid: *Baby Lay Your Head Down,* (Stax, 1973) ♫♫ since deleted, contains the weakest material of his career.

the rest: *California Girl/Down to Earth* (Stax, 1996) ♫♫♫♫

worth searching for: *You've Got to Have Eddie* (Stax, 1969), *Soul Street* (Stax, 1974) and *Experience* (Malaco, 1977)—all deleted (*Soul Street* is available on cassette) albums whose highlights are available on the aforementioned collections but are still worth hearing, anyway.

▶▶ Commodores, Rick James, Bruce Springsteen, Toots and the Maytals, Eric Clapton

◀◀ Sam Cooke, Lou Rawls, Otis Redding

Allan Orski

Duane Eddy

Born on April 26, 1938, in Corning, N.Y.

"The Twangiest Guitar of Them All" was a red Gretsch 6120 wielded by Eddy. Not well remembered today, Eddy ruled the guitar scene of the late 50s with his tremolo-heavy instrumentals. His shadow fell especially long in England, where a generation of young guitar players—from Hank Marvin of the Shadows to George Harrison—came under his spell. His records essentially came down to duets between Eddy, who scrupulously and carefully stated the melodic themes drenched in ringing, "twangy" tones, and saxophonist Steve Douglas, who replied in squawking, screeching blasts that came to define the sound of rock 'n' roll saxophone. Douglas went on to record all the solos on the famous Phil Spector records and, with King Curtis, supplied one of the two fountainheads of the instrument's rock vocabulary. The man behind the hits, producer Lee Hazlewood, parlayed his Eddy success into a career as one of Hollywood's masterful pop visionaries on records with Nancy Sinatra—work as fully realized and imaginative in scope as contemporary productions by such well-recognized *auteurs* as Spector and Brian Wilson. Eddy drifted into an uncomfortable obscurity, settling in Lake Tahoe, touring as guitarist for Italianate pop vocalist Al Martino and shunning the spotlight. Sporadic efforts to revive his career have been made—a 1976 single with then-hot Willie Nelson and Waylon Jennings providing lead vocals, a short-lived 1983 reformation of his vintage studio band with the addition of Ry Cooder on second guitar, a re-make of "Peter Gunn" in 1986 by the British dance band the Art of Noise, a 1987 album featuring help from Paul McCartney, John Fogerty, George Harrison, Steve Cropper and others. But as Eddy's contributions drift further beyond the horizon, he seems to be all the more neglected despite his work in the very foundations of rock guitar.

what to buy: The double-disc retrospective, *Twang Thing: The Duane Eddy Anthology,* (Rhino, 1993, prod. Various) ♪♪♪♪♪ covers the full breadth of his career—from the earliest hits and album sides to 80s recordings with McCartney, Harrison and Cooder.

what to buy next: Still want more? *Twangin' from Phoenix to Los Angeles* (Bear Family, 1994, prod. Various) ♪♪♪½ is a five-disc box from Europe that collects virtually the complete Jamie Records sessions and more.

what to avoid: Beware the abbreviated, cut-price collections that don't even scrape beneath the top of the surface of Eddy's remarkable body of work.

worth searching for: His debut album, *Have Twangy Guitar Will Travel,* (Jamie, 1958, prod. Lee Hazlewood) ♪♪♪♪♪ is one of the keystone landmarks of modern rock guitar. Also, his 80s comeback effort, *Duane Eddy,* (EMI, 1987, prod. Various) ♪♪♪♪ is not one to pass up in a cut-out bin.

▶▶ George Harrison, John Entwistle, John Fogerty, George Thorogood

◀◀ Chet Atkins, Les Paul, Jerry Byrd

Joel Selvin

The Edge

See: U2

Dave Edmunds /Rockpile

Born April 15, 1943 in Cardiff, Wales

Edmunds is the quintessential musician's musician—a producer, performer, lead guitarist, sideman, frontman. He's done them all, and all of them well—even if he's still a cult item to the masses. You'd never believe it from his early efforts in the band Love Sculpture, but his surprise first (and biggest) hit single, 1971's "I Hear You Knocking" contained the core of every track he recorded afterwards, a modern sound based in the rhythms of rockabilly that he made into his own. Edmund's name will always be associated with Rockpile—the super-players group that included Nick Lowe on bass, Terry Williams on drums and Billy Bremner on guitar. The band kick-started the sound of the 50s, equal parts Chuck Berry and the Everly Brothers, but adding a 70s pub rock sensibility. Rockpile only released one disappointing album under its own name, but due to contractual difficulties and solo career conflicts, the band enjoyed a fruitful period between 1977-80, recording on a total of six Edmunds and Lowe solo albums that still sound as fresh as the day they were recorded. Since, Rockpile, Edmunds' solo albums seemed to lose direction; *Information*, for instance, embraces synthesizers and computers in a clear bid for hit singles. His myriad production credits include the Stray Cats' first two (British) albums, the Everly Brothers' comeback effort *EB '84* and Lowe's *Party of One*.

what to buy: Edmunds Swan Song albums are uniformly excellent. *Get It* (Swan Song, 1977, prod. Dave Edmunds) ♪♪♪♪♪, is the first actual Rockpile collaboration and includes "I Knew the Bride," "Get Out of Denver" and "JuJu Man." *Tracks on Wax 4* (Swan Song, 1978, prod. Dave Edmunds) ♪♪♪♪♪ is Rockpile's hardest rocking collection, while *Repeat When Necessary*

(Swan Song, 1979, prod. Dave Edmunds) is amazingly sharp considering the band also recorded Lowe's *Labour of Lust* at the same time.

what to buy next: *The Dave Edmunds Anthology (1968-90)* (Rhino, 1993, prod. Various), a 41-track overview that includes too much Love Sculpture among its many gems. *D-E7* (Columbia, 1982, prod. Dave Edmunds), which includes the Bruce Springsteen-composed "From Small Things, Big Things Come." *The Best of Dave Edmunds* (Swan Song, 1981, prod. Dave Edmunds), which features all tracks from his classic period.

what to avoid: Anything by Love Sculpture, Edmunds' first real band, most of which approaches headache-inducing guitar music.

the rest: *Rockpile* (MAM, 1972) *Subtle as a Flying Mallet* (RCA, 1975) *Twangin'* (Swan Song, 1981) *Information* (Columbia, 1983) *Riff Raff* (Columbia, 1984) *I Hear You Rockin'* (Columbia, 1988 (with Rockpile) *Seconds of Pleasure* (Columbia, 1980) *Closer to the Flame* (Capitol, 1990) *Plugged In* (Pyramid, 1994)

worth searching for: Rockpile bootlegs—in particular *I Hear You Rocking* (GLR, 1991) and *Provoked Beyond Endurance* (Oh Boy)—that capture the Rockpile experience better than *Seconds of Pleasure Rocking* features guest appearances by Robert Plant and the Rolling Stones' Keith Richards.

▶▶ Stray Cats, Blasters, Bottle Rockets

◀◀ Les Paul and Mary Ford, Chet Atkins, Elvis Presley, Gene Vincent, Ricky Nelson, Smiley Lewis, Jerry Lee Lewis, Chuck Berry, Everly Brothers

Leland Rucker

801

See: Phil Manzanera

Mark Eitzel

See: American Music Club

Elastica

Formed 1992 in London, England

Justine Frischmann, guitar, vocals; Donna Matthews, guitar, vocals; Annie Holland, bass (1994-95); Abby Travis, bass (1995-1996); Sheila Chipperfield, bass (1996-present); Justin Welch, drums; Dave Bush, keyboards (1996-present)

Elastica's cool and crafty new wave revivalism made it a modern rock sensation in the mid-90s. Founded by Frischmann, a former member of U.K. glam aspirants Suede (and live-in mate of Blur's Damon Albarn), the quartet parlayed its catchy, nervous pop—distinguished by Frischmann's sultry and occasionally apathetic vocals—into international success. After releasing a string of singles that endeared it to U.K. pop fans and the mercurial music press, Elastica released its debut album, *Elastica,* (Geffen, 1995, prod. Marc Waterman and Elastica) a generally solid effort, though its coldness at times diminishes its impact. Nonetheless, the group knows how to write pop hooks—or steal them; the groups Wire and the Stranglers, which Frischmann freely acknowledged as influences, scored a share of the royalties thanks to the sonic similarity of Elastica hits such as "Connection" and "Stutter" to their music.

Simon Glickman

Electric Hellfire Club

See: My Life with the Thrill Kill Kult

Electric Light Orchestra /Jeff Lynne/ ELO II

Formed 1971 in Birmingham, England. Disbanded 1990. Re-formed as ELO II in 1991.

Jeff Lynne, guitar, vocals, synthesizers (1971-90); Bev Bevan, drums; Rick Price, bass (1971-72); Roy Wood, guitar, vocals (1971-72); Richard Tandy, guitar, keyboards (1972-90); Michael D'Albuquerque, bass (1972-74); Mike Edwards, cello (1972-74); Colin Walker, cello (1972-73); Wilf Gibson, violin (1972-73); Hugh McDowell, cello (1973-77); Mik Kaminsky, violin (1973-77, 1991-present); Kelly Groucutt, bass, vocals (1974, 1991-present); Melvyn Gale, bass, vocals (1974-77); Eric Troyer, keyboards, vocals (1991-present); Phil Bates, guitar, vocals (1991-present)

Formed out of the ashes of successful 60s British rockers the Move, ELO began as a idea by Wood to carry the orchestral ideas of *Sgt. Pepper*-era Beatles further. But Wood was gone before the group bagged its first big single, a heavily orchestrated version of Chuck Berry's "Roll Over Beethoven." With Wood gone, Lynne began to emerge as the group's sole producer and creative leader, refining the band's blend of classical string sounds and Beatle-esque rock/pop tunes. As one of the only rock bands experimenting with strings that actually tried to tour, ELO met with horrible results in early concerts, eventually resorting to taped backing tracks as 70s-era sound technology lagged behind the group's vision. After hitting a creative stride during the 70s—17 Top 40 hits between 1975-81—ELO became the victim of changing tastes, watching its slick, seamless pop sound sell fewer and fewer records, until the notoriously stage-shy Lynne abandoned the band in favor of a growing career as a producer. A short, misguided attempt to continue without him as ELO II produced two stiff albums and some lame live performances.

what to buy: The band's formula first jelled into a sleek hit-making machine with *Face The Music*, (Jet, 1975, prod. Jeff Lynne) an album on which Lynne's producing chops first match his songwriting prowess—fueled by songs such as the radio staple "Evil Woman" and dreamy ballad "Strange Magic." The precision of that record was quickly surpassed by *A New World Record*, (Jet, 1976, prod. Jeff Lynne) which ranges from the operatic rock of "Rockaria" to the mournful "Telephone Line" and a remake of an early Move hit, "Do Ya."

what to buy next: To avoid the moribund filler that often hampers even the best ELO records, seek out its second greatest hits compilation, *ELO's Greatest Hits*, (Jet, 1979, prod. Jeff Lynne) which collects classics such as "Telephone Line," "Rockaria" and "Evil Woman" on a single album. For more, the two-CD *Strange Magic: The Best of Electric Light Orchestra* (Legacy/Epic, 1995, prod. Jeff Lynne) cobbles together every interesting cut the band ever released, excluding only the ELO II efforts.

what to avoid: Basically, any ELO album released after 1980. All of them—*Time* (Jet, 1981, prod. Jeff Lynne) WOOF!, *Secret Messages* (Jet, 1983, prod. Jeff Lynne) WOOF! and *Balance of Power* (Epic, 1986, prod. Jeff Lynne) WOOF!—represent the drawn-out decline and death of Lynne's slicked-up ultra-pop vision, made impossibly obsolete by newer, more vibrant rock flavors. The only thing worse is Lynne's former bandmates' baldfaced attempt to cash in on the group's 20-year legacy with *Part 2* (Scotti Bros., 1991, prod. Jeff Glixman) WOOF! featuring a new lineup without the one guy who made it all happen. Predictably, it falls flat in the worst way.

the rest: *No Answer* (Jet, 1972) *ELO II* (Jet, 1973) *On the Third Day* (Jet, 1973) *Eldorado* (Jet, 1974) *Ole' ELO* (Jet, 1976) *Out of the Blue* (Jet, 1977) *Discovery* (Jet, 1979) *Afterglow* (Epic, 1990) *ELO Classics* (Sony, 1990)

worth searching for: Lynne's excruciatingly overproduced contributions to the soundtrack for Olivia Newton-John's film "Xanadu," (MCA, 1980) if only to laugh at the outdated fashions on the album cover and in the grooves.

solo outings:

Jeff Lynne: Armchair Theater (Reprise, 1989)

Traveling Wilburys, Enya, Eurythmics

The Beatles, the Move, Roy Orbison

see also: *The Move, the Traveling Wilburys*

Eric Deggans

Electronic

Formed 1989 in Manchester, England

Johnny Marr, guitar, keyboard, programming; Bernard Sumner, vocals, keyboard, programming

Electronic was formed in 1989 as an interim project by two members of Britain's most innovative bands of the 80s—guitarist Marr from the Smiths and vocalist Sumner of New Order. But the experiment quickly turned into a legitimate gig for the pair after topping the U.K. charts and hitting the American Top 40 with their debut single, "Getting Away With It." *Electronic* (Warner Bros., 1990, prod. Bernard Sumner and Johnny Marr) mixes contemporary acid house rhythms with Marr's innovative guitar playing and Sumner's effervescent vocals, perfectly capturing the sound of the moment on singles like "Get The Message" and "Feel Every Beat." But six years later, on the duo's follow-up disc, *Raise The Pressure*, (Warner Bros., 1996, prod. Electronic) the formula just didn't click. Working with former Kraftwerk member Karl Bartos and sounding hooked on Prozac, the British pop veterans turned out a lackluster set of dance floor anthems.

see also: *The Smiths, New Order, Joy Division*

Aidin Varizi

Eleventh Dream Day

Formed 1983 in Chicago, Ill.

Janet Beveridge Bean, drums and vocals; Rick Rizzo, guitar and vocals; Shu Shubat, bass (1983-85); Douglas McCombs, bass (1985-present); Baird Figi, guitar (1985-91); Matthew "Wink" O'Bannon, guitar (1991-94)

Long before alternative rock became a marketing catch phrase and the Chicago underground scene became nationally renowned, Eleventh Dream Day was at the leading edge of both. The guitar front line of primary songwriter Rizzo and Figi fused the twisted, spiraling interplay of Television to the barbed-wire stomp of Crazy Horse and became the focal point of a scorching live act that attained legendary status in Chicago. On record, the quartet prefigured grunge —- Nirvana once opened for them in Chicago —- and then, as grunge became popular, outgrew it. The band, now reduced to its core of husband-and-wife Rizzo and Janet Bean, plus Doug McCombs, continues to make accomplished music, though it records less frequently and never tours. Side projects have brought further acclaim —- McCombs with the avant-garde instrumental group Tortoise and Bean with the roots-country band Freakwater.

what to buy: *Prairie School Freakout* (Amoeba, 1988 prod. Eleventh Dream Day and Matthew "Wink" O'Bannon) ♫♫♫♫ was recorded in one beer-soaked session with a buzzing amplifier, and it comes the closest to capturing the guitar-fired frenzy of the quartet in its concert prime. The darkly beautiful *Ursa Major* (Atavistic, 1994, prod. John McEntire) ♫♫♫♫ is a major departure from the band's country- and Neil Young-tinged earlier output, with producer McEntire and the band exploring more atmospheric terrain.

what to buy next: *Beet* (Atlantic, 1989, prod. Gary Waleik) ♫♫♫♪ finds the band reining in the guitars slightly to emphasize Rizzo's turbulent song narratives.

the rest: *Eleventh Dream Day* (Amoeba EP, 1987) ♫♫♫ *Lived to Tell* (Atlantic, 1991) ♫♫♫ *El Moodio* (Atlantic, 1993) ♫♫♫♪

worth searching for: The hard-to find *Wayne* (Amoeba EP, 1989, prod. Eleventh Dream Day) contains the 10-minute guitar burner "Tenth Leaving Train," a cover of Neil Young's "Southern Pacific" and a ripping punk-Young homage, "Go."

▶▶ Grunge

◀◀ Neil Young, Television

Greg Kot

Danny Elfman

See: Oingo Boingo

Joe Ely

Born Feb. 9, 1947, in Amarillo, Texas

Too rock for country, too country for rock, Texan Ely has managed to exist somewhere in the middle, touring with both Merle Haggard and the Clash. He's never turned all of his critical acclaim into record sales, but he's managed to make a living. Ely blew out of the hot, windy south plains of Lubbock—Buddy Holly's home town—during the late 70s. A prolific writer who had wandered the wilds of the Southwest as a teenager, Ely had the gritty voice and raucous mix of honky-tonk country, blues-rock and Tex-Mex to turn those experiences into vivid songs. The earlier, New Wave honky-tonk sound gave way to a harder edge by the time he moved from MCA to Hightone. Ely returned to MCA in 1990, releasing a second live album before he returned to the more contemplative side first heard on *Down on the Drag.* Ely surrounds himself with resourceful musicians (band members have included guitarists David Grissom and Charlie Sexton, accordionist Ponty Bone and steel guitarist Lloyd Maines).

what to buy: *Love and Danger* (MCA, 1992, prod. Joe Ely and Tony Brown) ♫♫♫♪ was a return to form for Ely after he'd ventured away from his honky tonk roots to a rootsy blues-rock sound during his stretch with Hightone. Ely's at his best when he's writing compelling narratives or interpreting songs by wonderful but overlooked Texas writers—Robert Earl Keen, in this case.

what to buy next: The smoky, sweaty bars, hot summer nights and desperate characters are all there on *Honky Tonk Masquerade,* (MCA, 1978, prod. Chip Young) ♫♫♫ the product of Ely's restless spirit and his tenure as the king of West Texas honky tonks. Ely classics "West Texas Waltz" and "Fingernails" ("I keep my fingernails long so they click when I play the piano," goes the song's opening line) are among the album's most colorful inclusions.

what to avoid: The raucous rockabilly of *Must Notta Gotta Lotta* (MCA/Southcoast, 1981, prod. Joe Ely and Michael Brovsky) ♫♫ *is fun but not as memorable as his best work.*

the rest: *Joe Ely* (MCA, 1977) ♫♫♫ *Down on the Drag* (MCA, 1979) ♫♫♪ *Live Shots* (MCA/Southcoast, 1980) ♫♫♪ *Lord of the Highway* (Hightone, 1987) ♫♫♫ *Dig All Night* (Hightone, 1988) ♫♫ *Live at Liberty Lunch* (MCA, 1990) ♫♫♪ *Letter to Laredo* (MCA, 1995) ♫♫♫

worth searching for: All but one of Ely's albums are available on CD. The exception: 1984's experimental *Hi-Res,* which marked Ely's one and only plunge into the world of computers and synthesizers. It's pretty clunky, but there are some superb songs under the layers of electronics, including "Cool Rockin'

Loretta," which appears on his *Live at Liberty Lunch*, and "Letter to Laredo," recast as the title song of his Mexican-flavored 1995 album.

▶▶ Buddy Holly, Hank Williams

◀◀ Sun Volt, Uncle Tupelo, Alejandro Escovedo

see also: *The Flatlanders*

Doug Pullen

Emerson, Lake & Palmer /Emerson, Lake & Powell, 3

Formed 1970 in London, England. Disbanded 1979. Re-formed 1986.

Keith Emerson, keyboards; Greg Lake, bass, guitar, vocals; Carl Palmer, drums, percussion (1972-79, 1987, 1992-present); Cozy Powell, drums (1986)

Few bands can match ELP's ability to elicit an equal amount of thrills and yawns with its version of progressive rock. Emerson, who was in the Nice, and Lake, who left King Crimson, auditioned drummers and chose the powerhouse style of Palmer, who had played with the Crazy World of Arthur Brown and Atomic Rooster. The trio of veterans had all the musical skills, dynamic range and practiced showmanship to ignite a crowd; what they lacked was a modicum of restraint, which often led to marathon pomp-rock displays of shallow flash, especially in their pseudo-rock interpretations of classical music. The trio was at its best on majestic ballads ("Lucky Man") or when turning with controlled aggression to vaguely ominous rockers framed with classical structure ("The Endless Enigma"). Palmer's industrial-strength drums provided the foundation as Emerson opened the floodgates on his synthesizers and Lake floated through the mix with his velvety vocals and deft bass lines. ELP's stage shows were legendary for their theatrics, including Palmer and his drums twirling in mid-air and Emerson throwing knives at his fire-breathing keyboards. Eventually ELP's musical strengths lost out to circus-like concerts and misguided classical ambitions. The rise of punk rock was largely a revolt against the bloated, scripted, stilted rock the punkers saw in ELP and Pink Floyd. The trio disbanded in 1978, and in 1986, Emerson and Lake briefly tried to resurrect ELP with veteran drummer Cozy Powell. The three originals met for a soundtrack project in 1991 and decided to give ELP another shot.

what to buy: *Trilogy* (Atlantic, 1972, prod. Greg Lake) 3½ bones is bold without getting boorish, featuring one of ELP's finest ballads ("From the Beginning"), a convincing fusion of rock and classical ("The Endless Enigma"), plus one of Emerson's zippiest synthesizer discourses on Aaron Copland's "Hoedown." *Emerson, Lake and Palmer* (Atlantic, 1971, prod. Greg Lake) 3 bones offers the signature song "Lucky Man" and the dynamic tension of "Knife Edge." *The Best of ELP* (Atlantic, 1980, prod. Greg Lake) 3 bones offers a concise review of ELP's first incarnation.

what to buy next: *The Return of the Manticore* (Victory, 1993/Rhino, 1995, prod. Various) 4 bones is a four-disc boxed set that differs from the usual retrospective because it not only covers ELP's 1970-78 heyday but adds some worthwhile new material from the band's second incarnation, including the hefty "Black Moon" and fresh covers of "Fire" from Palmer's days with the Crazy World of Arthur Brown, "21st Century Schizoid Man," which Lake wrote with King Crimson, and "Touch and Go," from Emerson's old band the Nice.

what to avoid: *Pictures at an Exhibition* (Atlantic, 1971, prod. Greg Lake) 1 bone is a contrived concept album recorded live that puts a stale rock spin on Russian composer Mussorgsky's great classical work. It has neither the majesty of the original nor the earthy power of rock and roll.

the rest: *Tarkus* (Atlantic, 1971/Rhino, 1996) 2 bones *Brain Salad Surgery* (Atlantic, 1973/Rhino, 1996) 2½ bones *Welcome Back My Friends to the Show that Never Ends* (Atlantic, 1974/Rhino, 1996) 2 bones *Works Volume I* (Atlantic, 1977/Rhino, 1996) 2 bones *Works Volume II* (Atlantic, 1977/Rhino, 1996) 2 bones *Love Beach* (Atlantic, 1979/Rhino, 1996) 1½ bones *Works Live* (Atlantic, 1979/Rhino, 1996) 1½ bones *Black Moon* (Victory, 1992) 2½ bones *Live at the Royal Albert Hall* (Victory, 1994/Rhino, 1996) 2 bones *The Best of Emerson, Lake and Palmer* (Rhino, 1996) 3 bones

worth searching for: The deluxe edition of *Brain Salad Surgery*, (Victory, 1992/Rhino, 1996) 3 bones which re-creates the original album's slick, fold-out graphics in the CD format.

solo outings:

Greg Lake: King Biscuit Flower Hour Presents Greg Lake (KBR, 1995) 1½ bones

▶▶ Yes, Asia, David Bowie, U2, Kansas, Mission UK, Depeche Mode

◀◀ Charlie Parker, Prokofiev, King Crimson, the Nice, Jerry Lee Lewis.

see also: *King Crimson, Asia*

David Yonke

An Emotional Fish

Gerald Whelan, vocals; Enda Wyatt; David Frew; Martin Murphy

A moody Irish quartet given to brooding and rueful examinations, An Emotional Fish drew on such influences as U2, Lou Reed and a generally 60s pop aesthetic. *Sloper* (Pure, 1996, prod. Emotional Fish) has a garage-like rustic countryside feel (it was recorded on a friend's 8-track in a garage in Dublin) that gels with Whelan's nasal delivery. With guitar jangle and moody melodicism in tow, the band has ingredients for chart-busting but lacks a clear identity of its own

Allan Orski

English Beat /General Public

English Beat (1978-83)—Andy Cox, guitar; Everett Morton, drums; David Steele, bass; Dave Wakeling, guitar, vocals; Ranking Roger (born Roger Charlery, vocals, percussion (1979-83); Saxa, saxophone (1979-82). General Public (1984-87, 1994-present)—Wakeling; Ranking Roger; Micky Billingham, keyboards, vocals (1984-87); Horace Panter, bass (1984-87); Kevin White, guitar (1984-85); Stoker, drums (1984-85); Gianni Minardi, guitar (1986-87); Mario Minardi, drums (1986-87); Michael Railton, keyboards, programming, vocals (1994-present); Wayne Lothian, bass (1994-present); Dan Chase, drums (1994-present); Norman Jones, percussion, vocals (1994-present)

One good thing to come out of the racial strife that engulfed England during the late 70s and early 80s was the two-tone movement, a cluster of racially mixed bands dedicated to uniting British youth through song and dance. Followers of the music, which was a hybrid of punk rock and Jamaican ska, sported black-and-white clothing and short hair, as did the musicians. Among the best and most important of these bands was the English Beat, known simply as the Beat everywhere but in America due to trademark concerns. The Beat, which formed in 1978, released its first single in 1979, Smokey Robinson's "Tears of a Clown," on the 2-tone record label owned by another key band in the movement, the Specials. The single went to No. 6 on the British charts and featured the frenetic saxophone work of veteran Jamaican musician Saxa, who had played with the Beatles and the ska stars Desmond Dekker and Prince Buster. Saxa later joined the band full time, as did Ranking Roger, a young Birmingham percussionist whose specialty was toasting (melodic chanting). The Beat generated a string of U.K. hits, including "Hands Off . . . She's Mine," "Mirror in the Bathroom," "Best Friend" and the politically charged "Stand Down Margaret," which pleaded for "peace, love and unity" as well as the departure of the British Prime Minister. The Beat enjoyed a loyal following in the U.S., too, scoring its biggest hits with 1982's "I Confess" and "Save It for Later." The band broke up in 1983, resulting in two new outfits. Cox and Steele formed Fine Young Cannibals, while Wakeling and Ranking Roger became General Public. Wakeling and Roger split up in 1988 after a falling out but have since reformed General Public, enjoying a hit remake of the Staple Singers' "I'll Take You There" in 1994, when it was featured in the film "Threesome."

what to buy: *I Just Can't Stop It* (Sire, 1980, prod. Bob Sargeant) is the English Beat's debut album and one of the best records of the 80s. Mixing Chuck Berry-like guitar sounds, Beach Boyish harmonies, sizzling sax lines and Caribbean rhythms, this spellbinding record sounds as good today as it did 16 years ago. *Special Beat Service* (I.R.S., 1982, prod. Bob Sargeant) is the English Beat's third record and features the band's best-known singles in the U.S., "Save It for Later" and "I Confess," as well as the verbal acrobatics of Ranking Roger and guest Pato Banton in the delightful "Pato and Roger Ago Talk."

what to buy next: Wakeling and Roger's first effort as General Public, . . *All the Rage*, (I.R.S., 1984, producers General Public, Gavin MacKillop and Colin Fairley) has harder edges than anything the Beat did. The two excellent singles from the record, "Tenderness" and "Never You Done That," have a distinctly Motown feel.

what to avoid: The English Beat compilation *What Is Beat?* (I.R.S., 1983, producers Bob Sargeant, the English Beat, Mike Hedges and David Peters) provides some answers to that question, but earlier records offer a clearer picture.

the rest: The English Beat—*Wha'ppen* (I.R.S., 1981) General Public—*Hand to Mouth* (I.R.S., 1986) *Rub It Better* (Epic, 1995) The International Beat—*The Hitting Line* (Triple X, 1986)

worth searching for: *The Beat Goes On* (I.R.S., 1991) features some of the English Beat's biggest hits as well songs by Fine Young Cannibals, Wakeling, Ranking Roger and the International Beat.

solo outings:

Ranking Roger: Radical Departure (I.R.S., 1988)

Dave Wakeling: No Warning (I.R.S., 1991)

▶▶ Barenaked Ladies, Dave Matthews Band, Rancid

◀◀ Prince Buster, Desmond Dekker, Smokey Robinson, Sly and the Family Stone

see also: *Fine Young Cannibals*

William Hanson

Enigma

Formed 1990 in Ibiza, Spain

Curly M.C. (Michael Cretu), programming, guitars, keyboards, percussion; F. Gregorian (Frank Peterson), songwriting (1990); Sandra Lauer, vocals; David Fairstein, songwriting; Angel (Andy Hard), vocals (1993); Jens Glad, guitar (1993)

Cretu, a classically trained pianist and respected European producer and engineer, created Enigma in order to experiment combining diverse types of musical styles and influences. It was intended to be an anonymous project to force listeners to instinctively react only to the music, not the people behind it. With the single "Sadeness" already a hit, Enigma's debut album *MCMXC a.D.* (Charisma, 1990, prod. Michael Cretu) combines French spoken-word, hip-hop and keyboards, all layered on top of one another while Gregorian chants and flute loops help bring life giving a rich, warm organic feel to what could otherwise be synthetic sounding music. The album plays like an extended song as tracks merge together. *The Cross of Changes* (Charisma, 1993, prod. Michael Cretu) —billed to Enigma 2 due to new players and a different direction—uses various indigenous sounds—most notably the Indian lapp chant—in place of the Gregorian chants. It doesn't have quite the same richness or flow as *MCMXC a.D.*, and engrossing tracks such as "Return to Innocence" are the exception. (Note: Each album was also released in "Limited Edition" packages with remixes.)

Bryan Lassner

Brian Eno

Born Brian Peter George St. John le Baptiste Eno, May 15, 1948, in Suffolk, England

Eno began his professional music life with the rock group Roxy Music but has gone on to become an innovator of enormous influence in pop, progressive electronic and new age music circles. Eno became enamored of synthesizers during the late 60s and entered Roxy as a technical aide, though his role grew. He left the band in 1973 to produce his own quirky rock, which became more and more experimental with ambient sounds and minimalist techniques. Rather than songs, Eno produced sound landscapes meant to be experienced as much as heard, to serve as part of the background texture of a room. Eno is also a visual artist and has created ambient music to be played at his art installations. Even though his own muse leads along more esoteric line, Eno has also produced highly popular recordings for the likes of Talking Heads, U2, David Bowie and Devo, and he's engaged in critically acclaimed collaborations with Robert Fripp, David Byrne and John Cale, among others.

what to buy: Before he took a sharp turn to ambience Eno did some incisive experimental rock work. His ear for melody and musical hooks show through on *Another Green World,* (Island, 1975, prod. Brian Eno and Rhett Davies) with its thick mixes and otherworldly atmosphere. The hook on "Sky Saw" seems capable of ripping the heavens apart. and "I'll Come Running" shows how he can turn out a banal pop lyric, then twist it into a comment on the whole genre. The David Byrne collaboration *My Life In the Bush of Ghosts* (Sire, 1981, prod. Brian Eno and David Byrne) mixes Byrne's world music fascination with Eno's bag of ambient tricks. It contains dense, African-like rhythms mixed in a danceable format with the authors' cache of found sounds, prepared instruments and synthesized riffs.

what to buy next: Airy and spare, *Music For Airports* (PVC, 1978, prod. Brian Eno) shows the side of Eno that eventually influenced new age sounds—incidental music that is not meant to be listened to closely, yet sets an overall calming mood.

the rest: *Taking Tiger Mountain (By Strategy)* (Caroline, 1974) *Discreet Music* (Caroline, 1987) *Before and After Science* (Island, 1978) *Music for Films* (Antilles, 1978) *On Land* (Caroline, 1982) *Desert Island Selection* (Editions EG, 1989) *Wrong Way* (Warner Bros., 1990) *Nerve Net* (Opal, 1992) *Brian Eno* (Virgin, 1994) (with Keith Levene): *Spinner* (Gyroscope, 1995) (with U2, et al): *Passengers: Original Soundtracks 1* (Island, 1995, prod. Brian Eno)

worth searching for: His first record out of the gate, *Here Come the Warm Jets* (Island, 1973, prod. Brian Eno) is a pastiche of quirky rock tunes with cunning lyrics. "Baby's On Fire," "Cindy Tells Me" and "On Some Faraway Beach" show a pop sensibility but always with a twist that pokes a stick in the eye of tradition.

▶▶ Talking Heads, David Arkenstone, Michael Brook, U2

◄◄ Soft Machine, King Crimson, John Cage

see also: *Roxy Music, Robert Fripp, Passengers*

Lawrence Gabriel

John Entwistle

Born Oct. 9, 1944, in London, England

Within the flash 'n' trash world of the Who, Entwistle perhaps played his role as the stolid, quiet bassist a bit too well, for he is still the one member of the legendary band who could probably ride a crowded elevator without being noticed. However, being noticed is precisely the reason behind, and purpose of, Entwistle's ultimately frustrating quarter-century-plus solo career. For a man of such large talent and stature, it must be difficult to consider he can still be found, between Who reunions, touring America in an Econo-van, playing 200-seat sports bars. Like Ringo Starr, he threatens to remain simply a footnote to, and bit player in, a larger-than-life showbiz entity, with all that entails—and implies. John Entwistle deserves better; he did as much as James Jamerson and, yes, Beatle Paul to redefine the way rock 'n' roll bass was played, and his sick 'n' funny songs were easily the highlights of many a Who record. He possesses a remarkable singing voice as well—one minute rumbling from the depths of hell ("Boris The Spider"), the next minute soaring magnificently into the nosebleed heights of the harmonies ("A Quick One While He's Away"). Still, his career outside of the Who has failed to carve his much-deserved niche in the grand scheme of rock things, despite an abundance of fine songs, fine performances and hilarious cover art.

what to buy: *Tales From The Ox: The Best Of John Entwistle* (Rhino, 1996, prod. John Entwistle, John Alcock and Cy Langston) 🦴🦴🦴🦴 deftly spans a decade of Ox-rock, from 1971-81, though it leans heavily, as it should, towards selections from his first two albums.

what to buy next: *Smash Your Head Against The Wall* (Decca, 1971/Rhino, 1996, prod. John Entwistle) 🦴🦴🦴🦴 and *Whistle Rymes,* (Decca, 1972/Rhino, 1996, prod. John Entwistle and John Alcock) 🦴🦴🦴🦴 the first two solo releases, are wry, hard-hitting collections of bottom-heavy rock with the odd - in more ways than one - ballad thrown in, just to throw you off. Peter Frampton actually plays his guitar tastefully throughout the latter.

what to avoid: *Too Late The Hero* (Atco, 1981/Rhino, 1996, prod. John Entwistle and Cy Langston) **WOOF!** is a misguided, over-blown collaboration with the severely unwitty Joe Walsh. The sound of two old rockers creaking on the front porch.

the rest: *John Entwistle's Rigor Mortis Sets In* (Track, 1973/Rhino, 1996) 🦴🦴🦴 *Mad Dog* (Track, 1975/Rhino, 1996) 🦴🦴🦴 *The Rock* (Griffin, 1996) 🦴🦴

worth searching for: Who albums.

►► Jack Bruce, Geddy Lee, Bruce Foxton

◄◄ Duane Eddy, Bob Bogle, Boris Karloff

see also: *The Who*

Gary Pig Gold

Enuff Z'nuff

Formed mid-80s in Chicago, Ill.

Donnie Vie (guitar, vocals); Derek Frigo (guitar); Chip Z'Nuff (bass, guitar, vocals); Vikki Foxx (drums)

What initially gave Enuff Z'Nuff a commercial identity came back to haunt the band later, when heavy metal—so big (like its singers' hair) during the mid-80s—corroded in the 90s. Enuff Z'Nuff was never a metal band anyway; it was a Beatles-influenced power-pop combo that often watered down its potent songs with generic, grating guitar solos. By contrast, fellow Illinois rockers Cheap Trick also had thundering, metal-influenced riffs but wove them into the fabric of the band's sound. In the case of Enuff Z'Nuff, the riffing was often painfully extraneous—the band could have fired its guitarist and been a better band. Still, the sparkling songs shone through the rusty metal, and there are enough of them to make the band one of the bright lights of recent power-pop.

what to buy: *1985* (Big Deal, 1994) 🦴🦴🦴🦴 gathers some of the group's first recordings in a cohesive package of pure pop, catching the group before it grasped the metal mantle. Down to a two-piece —founders Donnie Vie and Chip Z'Nuff—*Tweaked* (Mayhem, 1995, prod. Enuff Z'Nuff) 🦴🦴🦴🦴 shows what the group can do without the riffing that filled its major label releases. The songs are melodic confessions that evoke the dreaminess of classic ELO ("My Dear Dream") and the horrors of substance abuse (the appropriately bluesy "My Heroin").

what to buy next: *Enuff Z'Nuff,* (Atco, 1989, prod. Enuff Z'Nuff and Ron Fajerstein) 🦴🦴🦴 which contains the melodically euphoric "New Thing," the group's best song and one of the best pop songs in recent memory. *Strength* (Atco, 1991, prod. Enuff Z'Nuff and Paul Lani) 🦴🦴🦴 has nothing as stunning as "New

What Album Changed Your Life?

"The first Led Zeppelin album was such raw, relentless sexuality. It was just staggering--as close to knocking me off my feet as music can come. The first time I heard 'Good Times, Bad Times' I thought someone had unleashed an animal in the speaker. Something was going on there that hit everything primal, sonic, intellecutal, visceral."

Paul Stanley (Kiss)

Thing" but is a more consistent record, beautifully haunted by the ghost of John Lennon.

the rest: *Animals With Human Intelligence* (Arista, 1992) *Peach Fuzz* (Big Deal, 1986-1990)

⏩ Jellyfish

⏪ The Beatles, Mott the Hoople, Badfinger, Off Broadway, Cheap Trick

Jordan Oakes

Enya

Born Eithne Ni Bhraonain, May 17, 1961 in Gweedore, County Donegal, Ireland.

Enya began her music career in her family's Irish folk band Clannad, but after two years she left to pursue a solo career that began with television music for the BBC. It wasn't until she started working with producer Nicky Ryan and lyricist Roma Ryan that Enya achieved critical and commercial success. Her ethereal, New Agey sound incorporated elements of traditional Celtic musics, which in 1988 resulted in the worldwide smash "Orinoco Flow." Enya tends to take her time between albums, but she always seems to find an audience anxiously awaiting them. "Orinoco Flow's" home, *Watermark* (Reprise, 1988, prod. Nicky Ryan) showcases Enya's beautiful, trance-inducing voice, weaving warm, flowing aural landscapes that elicit pictures of a lush, clover-covered Irish countryside. *Shepherd Moons* (Reprise, 1991, prod. Nicky Ryan) continues along the same gently-flowing river of dreamy soundscapes, with some tracks sung in Gaelic.

the rest: *Enya* (Atlantic, 1987 *The Memory of Trees* (Reprise, 1995)

Christopher Scanlon

Epic Soundtracks

Born Paul Godley, in London, England.

His friends often are punks and hardcore noise people, but Soundtracks emulates good old-fashioned soul and pop singing. An ex-member of a buffet of underground bands—he drummed in the Swell Maps, played in Red Crayola, Crime and the City Solution and the Jacobites—Soundtracks began performing during the 70s and went solo in 1992. He says his influences are hardcore punk bands and legendary rock 'n' rollers, from Big Star to Dion, but you can hear Carole King, Billy Joel and Queen creeping up in his lush, sometimes syrupy piano pop. Not surprisingly, he has generated a handful of terrific songs. *Change My Life* (Bar/None, 1996, prod. Henry Olsen) is his best thanks to the terrific lead-off rocker, "You Can Be My Baby," and a terrific cover of Big Star's "Nighttime"—though the album too frequently devolves into Al Stewart-style bland pop-folk.

the rest: *Rise Above* (Bar/None, 1992) *Sleeping Star* (Bar/None, 1994)

Steve Knopper

Erasure

Formed 1985 in London, England

Vince Clarke, synthesizer; Andy Bell, vocals

After splitting from Yaz, Clarke paired up with the flamboyantly gay Bell to form another synthesizer duo—this one characterized by bouncy synth-pop and Bell's distinctive flair for melodrama. Riding one approach—more or less—since its inception, the group has successfully wooed the jilted club kids with lovelorn pop confections and catchy dance piffle.

what to buy: *Pop!: The First 20 Hits* (Mute/Sire/Reprise, 1992, prod. Various) offers a Nutrasweet collection of the band's singles, including "Chains of Love," "Victim of Love" and "Oh L'Amour." Its U.S. breakthrough, *The Innocents* (Mute/Sire/Reprise, 1988, prod. Stephen Hague) is the pseudo-soul dance peak of the band, containing "A Little Respect" and "Ship of Fools" in addition to "Chains of Love."

what to buy next: *Wonderland,* (Mute/Sire, 1986, prod. Flood) the band's debut, comes off like Yaz Part 2, more as an extension of Clarke's electronic inventions than a mere rehashing of his former work.

what to avoid: On *Circus,* (Mute/Sire, 1987, prod Flood) Clarke's synth work is frothy as ever but Bell's woe-is-me delivery is too self-indulgent for even the heaviest dose of ecstasy.

the rest: *The Two Ring Circus* (Mute/Sire, 1987) *Wild!* (Mute/Sire/Reprise, 1989) *Crackers International* (Mute/Sire/Reprise EP, 1989) *Chorus* (Mute/Sire/Reprise, 1991) *Abba-esque* (Elektra EP, 1992) *I Say, I Say, I Say* (Mute/Elektra, 1994) *Erasure* (Mute/Elektra, 1995)

▶▶ New Order, Simply Red, Electronic

◀◀ Yaz/Yazoo, Depeche Mode, Abba

Allan Orski

Roky Erickson

Born July 15, 1947, in Dallas, Texas

A blindingly disturbed singer who makes Daniel Johnston seem like a pillar of stability, Erickson's songwriting prowess is not so much the gurgling of an idiot savant as it is the few salvaged remains from a mind wiped out by acid and mental institutions. From the wellsprings of his formative band, the truly psychedelic 13th Floor Elevators, came a piddly pot charge that he inexplicably pleaded insanity to and was thus institutionalized. Upon release, Erickson's erratic solo career began with horrifying rock 'n' roll; the demonic dementia that inhabits much of his material is heightened by his belief that he and Satan are in cahoots. Amidst the true-life tribulations that make up his daily existence, he has penned an arresting number of staggering rockers and disarmingly sweet acoustic ballads that have influenced a couple generations of rockers—evidence the contributions of groups as diverse as ZZ Top and R.E.M. to *Where the Pyramid Meets the Eye: A Tribute to Roky Erickson* (Sire, 1990, prod. Various) Numerous unauthorized releases have been in circulation since the early 80s, making his catalogue as difficult to define as his songs are, sometimes, to comprehend.

what to buy: *You're Gonna Miss Me: The Best of Roky Erickson* (Restless, 1991, prod. Various) makes the publicity-seeking Satanism of most metal bands seem like a childproof lighter compared to this searing document of rock 'n' roll dementia. Underneath B-movie titles such as "Two Headed Dog" and "I Walked With a Zombie" is shuddering conviction matched with crack delivery. It's a bracing representation of his 80s output.

what to buy next: *All That May Do My Rhyme* (Trance Syndicate, 1995, prod. Various) is a surprisingly cohesive, acoustically based effort compiled of new material and some decade-old recordings. His childlike tenor gives the melodic tunes a ringing note of sincere frailty that most folk singers would trade their tea bags for.

what to avoid: Although documentation is impossible, any release not listed in this entry should be approached with caution, as much of his material has been recorded with varying degrees of mental health.

the rest: *Holiday Inn Tapes* (Fan Club, 1987) *Beauty and the Beast* (Sympathy For The Record Industry, 1993) *The Evil One* (Restless, 1993) (with the 13th Floor Elevators) *The Magic of Pyramids* (Collectables) Worth Searching For: *Gremlins Have Pictures,* (Pink Dust, 1986) and import of live recordings that reveal his fragile emotional state more than anything else.

▶▶ R.E.M., Daniel Johnston, Katy McCarty

◀◀ 13th Floor Elevators, Black Sabbath

Allan Orski

Alejandro Escovedo

Born Jan. 10, 1951, San Antonio, Texas

At first, nattily dressed Escovedo's concerts sound like any country-tinged singer-songwriter—the songs are a bit downbeat, a bit rocking. By the time he reaches his droning version of Iggy Pop's "I Wanna Be Your Dog," though, he gives himself away. Despite three moody, pristinely written solo albums, Escovedo hangs tightly to his roots as a Texas punk rocker. Escovedo, whose niece, Sheila E., was a Prince percussionist and solo artist, played in the Nuns, Rank and File and the True Believers (with his brother, Javier) throughout the 80s. He has never, unfortunately, tasted any significant commercial success.

what to buy: *Gravity,* (Watermelon, 1992, prod. Turner Stephen Bruton) a hushed, moody album written after Escovedo's wife committed suicide, contains the explosive rocker "One More Time" and the chanting tear-jerker "Bury Me." Escovedo co-founded the terrific New York City country-punk band Rank and File, with Dils members Tony and Chip Kinman in 1981, and stuck around for the band's terrific debut, *Sundown* (Slash/Warner Bros., 1982, prod. David Kahne)

what to buy next: Escovedo's second solo album, *Thirteen Years* (Watermelon, 1993, prod. Bruton) is overly repetitive and harder to listen to than *Gravity*, but "Ballad of the Sun and the Moon" is one of many well-written highlights.

worth searching for: Both catchy, rocking self-titled True Believers' albums (the first was out-of-print, the second never released) came out as the *Hard Road* reissue (Rykodisc, 1994, prods. Jim Dickinson/Jeff Glixman)

the rest: *With These Hands* (Rykodisc, 1996, prod. Bruton)

Blasters, Jimmie Dale Gilmore, Buddy Holly, Richie Valens, Iggy Pop, X

Uncle Tupelo, Jason and the Scorchers, Wilco, Bottle Rockets

Gloria Estefan /Miami Sound Machine

Born Gloria Fajardo, Sept. 1, 1957 in Havana, Cuba

Simply put, Estefan has terrific pipes that were co-opted—willingly—away from Miami's Cuban dance scene into the blander but phenomenally successful realm of middle-of-the-road pop. The Cuban native, who fled that country's revolution with her family and moved to the U.S. when she was two, started out fronting the Miami Sound Machine, a former wedding band led by husband Emilio Estefan, Jr., whose South of the Equator polyrythms provided an interesting mainstream pop alternative during the mid-80s. It didn't last long; as Estefan's voice grew from chirpy to assured, the Miami Sound Machine moniker gradually disappeared from the album covers in order to showcase the singer. During 1990, Estefan's tour bus was hit by a tractor-trailer, fracturing one of her vertebrae; but a year later, she was back in action, singing "Coming Out of the Dark," a song inspired by the accident, to No. 1. Give Estefan this much; she's no producer's tool, writing many of her own lyrics and checking off on the creative decisions. If only one of those decisions would be a return to the those irresistible club grooves...

what to buy: *Eyes of Innocence* (Epic, 1984/1989, prod. Emilio and the Jerks) had only the minor hit "Dr. Beat," but the Miami Sound Machine's debut is an intoxicating blend of Caribean rhythms. You won't find anything from that album on *Greatest Hits* (Epic, 1992, prod. Emilio Estefan) but you do get her best, a largely upbeat collection that includes "Conga," "Rhythm is Gonna Get You" and "Get On Your Feet."

what to avoid: *Hold Me, Thrill Me, Kiss Me* (Epic, 1994, prod. Various) There are lots of songs Estefan can probably sing very well. Why'd they pick these?

the rest: *Primitive Love* (Epic, 1985) *Let it Loose* (Epic, 1987) *Cuts Both Ways* (Epic, 1989) *Into the Light* (Epic, 1981) *Mi Tierra* (Epic, 1993) *Christmas Through Your Eyes* (Epic, 1993) *Abriendo Puertas* *Destiny* (Epic, 1996)

worth searching for: Estefan's guest vocal on the song "Africa" from Arturo Sandoval's *Dayon* (GRP, 1994, prod. Arturo Sandoval and Richard Eddy)

Debbie Gibson

Carmen Miranda, Tito Puente, Herb Alpert & the Tijuana Brass, Aretha Franklin, Donna Summer

Gary Graff

Melissa Etheridge

Born May 29, 1961 in Leavenworth, Kan.

Raised on heartland rock, Etheridge delivers the sort of music that sounds perfect from the vantage point of a bar stool after a couple of cold ones on a hot summer night. But like a few too many brews, Etheridge's songs can leave a bad taste in your mouth and make you wonder what all the fuss was about the night before. Her best attribute is her powerful, gritty voice that's part Janis Joplin, part Rod (the Mod) Stewart. But her writing often bogs down in arena-rock cliches, and her specialty—odes to lost love rendered carefully in gender-neutral terms—is ultimately too limiting. Still, when Etheridge calms down and realizes she doesn't always have to play to the back rows, she can be an insightful and affecting artist.

what to buy: The title of *Yes I Am* (Island, 1993, prod. Hugh Padgham and Melissa Etheridge) is a coy reference to her coming out as a lesbian, which she addresses in various asides throughout the album. "I'm the Only One" is in the too-familiar vein of Etheridge's songs of unrequited lust; so is "Come to My Window," but at least that has a rich melody and memorable chorus that makes it Etheridge's best composition. What makes the album her most listenable, though, is Padgham's measured production, which reins in Etheridge's tendencies to *rawk* out aimlessly. Her debut, *Melissa Etheridge,* (Island, 1988, prod. Craig Krampf, Kevin McCormick, Melissa Etheridge and Niko Bolas) alternates between earnest ballads and acoustic-based rockers, but it's the trio of pissed-off anthems—"Similar Features," "Like the Way I Do" and "Bring Me Some Water"—that made some rock radio inroads.

what to buy next: The material on *Your Little Secret* (Island, 1995, prod. Hugh Padgham and Melissa Etheridge) is nearly the equal of that on *Yes I Am*, especially "Nowhere to Go" and "I Want to Come Over." But the album has the feeling of a sequel, making it a less-than-essential purchase.

what to avoid: *Never Enough* (Island, 1992, prod. Kevin McCormick and Melissa Etheridge) earned Etheridge a Grammy for the song "Ain't It Heavy," but on this album she gives in to all of her worst tendencies—overreaching, overemoting and writing nary a memorable tune. And the neo-*Born in the U.S.A.* shot on the cover (Springsteen is a hero and buddy) is just too much.

the rest: *Brave and Crazy* (Island, 1989)

worth searching for: Either—or both—of the promotion-only *Melissa Etheridge Live,* CDs (Island, 1988, prod. Kevin McCormick and Melissa Etheridge) and (Island, 1989, prod. Kevin McCormick and Melissa Etheridge) which give a sense of her gutsy and robust concert performances.

▶▶ Sass Jordan, Sheryl Crow, Joan Osborne, Alanna Myles

◀◀ Bruce Springsteen, John Mellencamp, Janis Joplin, Suzi Quatro

Daniel Durchholz

Marvin Etzioni

See: Lone Justice

Eugenius

See: The Vaselines

Eurythmics

Formed 1980 in London, England. Disbanded 1990.

Dave Stewart, guitar, keyboards; Annie Lennox, vocals, flute, keyboards

Emerging from the ashes of British folk/psychedelic/New Wave rock band The Tourists, Lennox and Stewart became the oddest of couples—breaking up as lovers before forming Eurythmics together. Melding New Wave synth-pop sounds with Lennox's 60s soul vocal influences, the pair scored big once Stewart took full control of their sound as producer, recording their breakthrough record on an eight-track machine with arrangements emphasizing his partner's amazing vocals. Tired of the baby doll blonde image she'd fostered in The Tourists, Lennox appeared in men's suits and dressed as Elvis in the group's early years. As synth-pop began to take a back seat on the charts, Stewart leavened the group's sound with garage rock and earthier soul touches, only to try a return to techno form just before the duo went on indefinite hiatus in 1990.

what to buy: The pair's breakthrough album *Sweet Dreams (Are Made of This)* (RCA, 1983, prod. Dave Stewart) provides a neat summation of the group's appeal. Stewart's eerily emotionless, synthesizer-bred arrangements stand in stark contrast to Lennox's expressive vocals—making the hit title track, along with the driving dance cut "Love Is a Stranger," sizzle with the friction. With full band backing, *Be Yourself Tonight* (RCA, 1985, prod. Dave Stewart) enjoys an energetic, live group flavor with the charging "Would I Lie to You?", the midtempo hit "It's Alright (Baby's Coming Back)" and Lennox's muscular duet with Aretha Franklin, "Sisters Are Doin' It For Themselves."

what to buy next: For an overview of the duo's biggest commercial triumphs, it's hard to beat *Greatest Hits* (RCA, 1991, prod. Various), a collection of the group's top. The best 90s-era representation of the Eurythmics' sound is on Lennox' first solo album, *Diva* (Arista, 1992, prod. Stephen Lipson), a record that blends the updated synth-pop of "Legend in My Living Room" with the pop-rock of "Walking on Broken Glass"—a potent reminder why we liked the group so much in the first place.

what to avoid: As a film soundtrack that even the director denounced publicly, *1984* (RCA, 1984, prod. Dave Stewart) **WOOF!** upsets Eurythmics' delicate stylistic balance, drowning Lennox's evocative vocals in an oppressive flood of downbeat techno-pop.

the rest: *In The Garden* (RCA UK, 1981) *Touch* (RCA, 1983) *Revenge* (RCA, 1986) *Savage* (RCA, 1987) *We Too Are One* (Arista, 1989) *Live 1983-1989* (Arista, 1993)

worth searching for: *Rough & Tough at the Roxy* (RCA, 1986), a promotional EP sporting four live cuts recorded with Eurythmics best-ever touring band.

solo outings:

Annie Lennox: *Medusa* (Arista, 1995)

Dave Stewart: *Lily Was Here* soundtrack (Anxious, 1989) *Dave Stewart and the Spiritual Cowboys* (Arista, 1990) *Honest* (Arista, 1991) *Greetings From the Gutter* (EastWest, 1995)

▶▶ Garbage, Roxette

◀◀ Lene Lovich, Aretha Franklin, Kraftwerk, Can

Eric Deggans

Everclear

Formed 1991 in Portland, Ore.

Art Alexakis, vocals, guitar; Craig Montoya, bass; Scott Cuthbert (1991-94), drums, vocals; Greg Eklund (1994-present), drums

The center of this group, Alexakis, was 34 when it finally broke through in 1996 after MTV picked up the video to the casually apocalyptic "Santa Monica." He'd grown up in the housing projects of Culver City, Calif., in a broken family; his older brother was involved in dealing heroin and ODed. Art soon was doing and dealing a multiplicity of drugs himself, and after a girlfriend ODed, he tried to commit suicide. At age 22, he survived his own overdose and then went cold turkey on everything. He traveled the West Coast, leading a band (Colorfinger) and an indie label (Shindig), both of which failed. In 1991 he followed his wife-to-be to Portland and soon formed Everclear with Montoya (formerly of Soul Hammer) and Cuthbert.

Alexakis' material draws heavily on his background without necessarily being autobiographical. The Everclear sound (especially Alexakis's vocals) and sensibility owe a debt to Nirvana but stop just short of derivativeness—it's a power trio that learned some lessons and uses them towards distinctive ends. One of its most effective tactics is to contrast the verses and choruses not with the now-cliched quiet/loud dichotomy, but instead with spareness shifting into density. Tight, tuneful songwriting and ferociously powerful guitar riffs and drumming complete the picture—all of which is best illustrated on the breakthrough *Sparkle and Fade* (Capitol, 1995, prod. Art Alexakis)

the rest: *World of Noise* (Tim/Kerr, 1993) *Nervous & Weird* (Tim/Kerr EP, 1993)

Steve Holtje

Everly Brothers

Don Everly, born Feb. 1, 1937 in Brownie, Ky.; Phil Everly, born Jan. 19, 1939 in Brownie, Ky.

The blood harmonies of the Everly Brothers may be the main tributary feeding all rock vocal styles; The Beatles, among many others, styled their harmony sound after the Everlys. Having begun their singing careers as children on their parents' radio program, the two brothers qualified as veterans by the time their first records hit the charts eight years later, their deeply entwined high mountain harmonies practically instinctual.

After a couple of little known sides recorded for Columbia Records, the Everlys first made their mark with a series of hit records on the Cadence Records label beginning with "Bye Bye Love" in 1957—most written specifically for the brothers by the husband-wife songwriting team of Boudleaux and Felice Bryant (often with guitarist Chet Atkins playing on the sessions). After moving to Warner Bros. Records in 1960, the duo continued to make hit records, notably "Cathy's Clown," although the Everlys slowly disappeared from the charts, victims of changing popular tastes.

But Don and Phil Everly never stopped making heart-stoppingly beautiful records. When matched with the right piece of material and sympathetic production, the brothers cut records that matched the finest work of their early years, right up the modest 1984 comeback with Paul McCartney's "On the Wings Of a Nightingale" (produced by Dave Edmunds) and beyond. The act split bitterly in 1973, breaking up literally in front of a Knott's Berry Farm audience with Don splintering a guitar across his brother's back and walking offstage. After discovering that nobody wanted to hear one Everly brother sing alone, they reunited for a sentimental 1983 Royal Albert Hall concert, recorded and filmed for posterity, and apparently found an uneasy truce that allowed them to continue to perform and record together.

what to buy: *Cadence Classics: Their 20 Greatest Hits* (Rhino, 1985, prod. Archie Bleyer) contains the basic fundamentals of the Everlys repertoire, from the acoustic guitar accented rockabilly of "Wake Up Little Susie" and "Claudette" to almost ethereal ballads like "Let It Be Me."

what to buy next: *Walk Right Back: The Everly Brothers On Warner Bros 1960 To 1969* (Warner Archives, 1993, prod. Various) is a 50-song survey that begins where the Cadence era left off and takes the Everlys through the flowering of Los Angeles country-rock that their early work did so much to inspire. The four-disc boxed set, *Heartaches and Harmonies* (Rhino, 1994, prod. Various) , offers a detailed retrospective that smoothly covers nearly forty years of Everlys recordings.

what to avoid: In the mid-sixties, the brothers re-recorded a set of their Cadence hits for Warners, released as *The Very Best of the Everly Brothers* (Warner Brothers, 1964, prod. Various) that pales vastly in comparison to the original versions.

the rest: *The Fabulous Style of the Everly Brothers* (Cadence, 1960/Rhino, 1988) *Songs Our Daddy Taught Us* (Cadence, 1958/Rhino, 1988) *Roots* (Warner Bros., 1968) *Reunion Concert* (Mercury, 1984) *EB 84* (Mercury, 1984; Razor & Tie, 1994) "The Mercury Years" (Mercury, 1993)

worth searching for: In assembling the label's Everlys reissues of the Cadence material, the Rhino Records researchers unearthed a set of unreleased demo tapes, *All They Had To Do Was Dream* (Rhino, 1985, prod. Archie Bleyer) , that showcase the pure vocal sound of the brothers—in perhaps some of rock's first "unplugged" sessions—that glisten with the maturity and depth of artists far beyond their years.

▶▶ Simon and Garfunkel, The Beatles

◀◀ Stanley Brothers, Louvin Brothers

Joel Selvin

Everything But the Girl

Formed in 1983 in London, England

Tracey Thorn, vocals; Ben Watt, guitar and vocals

Naming themselves after a London boutique claiming to sell everything but the girl behind the counter, former Marine Girls singer Tracey Thorn and Ben Watt joined Sade and Matt Bianco as the most visible proponents of London's early-80s jazz-pop movement. Although their engaging sound—a sensitive, savvy blend of Stan Getz-inspired Brazilian jazz and acoustic guitar-driven pop—won over U.K. audiences, Americans enamored by the chanteuse-like Sade weren't as quick to embrace Everything But the Girl's dour outlook and moody, often mopey image. So it was black-clad teens with Bauhaus T-shirts and Smiths albums who first recognized the alternately soothing and aching beauty of Thorn's cool but emotive alto. However, after 10 years of vainly cramming everything from orchestras to dance rhythms onto their subtle sound, EBTG scaled the Billboard charts with the groove-enhanced remix of "Missing," a late-blooming single from 1994's *Amplified Heart* album that made them one of pop's oldest overnight success stories. Sometimes there is justice in the world.

what to buy: *Amplified Heart* (Atlantic, 1994, prod. Ben Watt and Tracey Thorn) deftly blends every style that the duo has experimented with into a cool, cohesive whole—it's beautiful music in every sense of the phrase. The beat-heavy followup, *Walking Wounded* (Atlantic, 1996, prod. Ben Watt and Spring Heel Jack) , builds upon the house remixes of "Missing" and Thorn's collaborations with trip-hop group Massive Attack for a seductive, sonically captivating work. *Love Not Money* (Sire, 1985, prod. Robin Millar) forsakes the heavy jazz leanings of their debut album for jangling pop with a social conscience that includes a lovely cover of the Pretenders' "Kid."

what to buy next: Thorn's interpretive skills are spotlighted on *Acoustic* (Atlantic, 1992, prod. Tracey Thorn and Ben Watt) , which includes covers of Elvis Costello's "Alison," Cyndi Lauper's "Time After Time" and Bruce Springsteen's "Tougher Than the Rest."

what to avoid: *Language of Life* (Atlantic, 1990, prod. Tracey Thorn, Ben Watt and Tommy Lipuma) teams them with LiPuma, the late Stan Getz and several American jazz session players—but the result is all surface and little substance.

the rest: *Everything But the Girl* (Sire, 1984) *Baby, the Stars Shine Bright* (Sire, 1986) *Idlewild* (Sire, 1988) *Worldwide* (Atlantic, 1991)

worth searching for: Thorn's pre-EBTG solo album, *A Distant Shore* (Cherry Red, 1982) , offers a gorgeous reading of the Velvet Underground's "Femme Fatale" that shames all other covers.

solo outings:

Ben Watt: ***North Marine Drive*** (Cherry Red, 1983)

▶▶ Eddi Reader, Tanita Tikaram

◀◀ Astrud Gilberto, Stan Getz, Massive Attack

David Okamoto

Extreme

Formed 1987 in Boston, Mass.

Nuno Bettencourt, guitar; Gary Cherone, vocals; Pat Badger, bass; Paul Geary, drums.

Distinguished from the hard-rock pack by arty ambitions, choirboy harmonies and the ferociously inventive fretwork of guitarist Bettencourt, Extreme enjoyed both chart success and critical plaudits during the early 90s. The quartet came together when singer Cherone met Portuguese-born Bettencourt while the two were in separate bands; their immediate chemistry led to a large early catalog of material, some of which appeared on Extreme's eponymous 1989 A&M debut. But it was the sophomore effort, *Pornograffitti*, that caught the ears of reviewers and discriminating rock fans; with its hard-hitting yet thoughtful rock—a mix of prog-rock virtuosity, feel-good funk-rock and power-pop sweetness—the album demonstrated the group's potential. Ironically, it was the yearning acoustic ballad "More Than Words" that brought Extreme mass success. Subsequent records saw the band moving into even more stylistically adventuresome territory, and becoming increasingly preachy in lyrical content. But the advent of "alternative" rock soon dampened its appeal, though its well-crafted albums retained an enthusiastic core following.

what to buy: *Extreme II: Pornograffitti* (A&M, 1990, prod. Michael Wagener) is chock full of radio-friendly hooks and shows Bettencourt in full feather. "Get the Funk Out" is a party anthem that would make the Red Hot Chili Peppers proud.

what to buy next: *III Sides to Every Story* (A&M, 1992, prod. Nuno Bettencourt) errs on the side of self-indulgence but shows an admirable eagerness to experiment, when cranking out more power ballads would've been easy.

what to avoid: *Waiting for the Punchline* (A&M, 1995, prod. Nuno Bettencourt) misses the songwriting and thematic unity of its predecessors.

the rest: *Extreme* (A&M, 1989)

worth searching for: The Japanese import *Extragraffitti*, (A&M, 1990) which gathers some interesting and hard-to-find B-sides.

Dream Theater, Spacehog, Deftones, Jars of Clay

Queen, The Beatles, Van Halen, ELO, Red Hot Chili Peppers

Simon Glickman

Fabian

Born Fabiano Forte Bonaparte, Feb. 6, 1943, in Philadelphia, Pa.

Although Fabian was not a powerful, skillful vocalist, his records have been unjustly maligned. Crafted by sturdy studio professionals and frequently written by the respected team of Mort Shuman and Doc Pomus, his Chancellor Records singles, fodder for 50s teenyboppers, hold up remarkably well more than 30 years after their release. Discovered as a teenager by a pair of music business entrepreneurs, Fabian came to epitomize the cultivated teen idol whose pinup-boy looks were more important to his success than talent. After several years of Top 40 hits, "American Bandstand" appearances and grueling national tours on package shows, he eased into a motion picture career in which he appeared as the youthful foil to such older stars as John Wayne, Jimmy Stewart and Bing Crosby. During the 80s, much to his own amazement, he experienced a singular comeback as part of "The Golden Boys of Bandstand" with Frankie Avalon and Bobby Rydell, an act that would headline Atlantic City and Las Vegas casinos. No lesser a contemporary than Dion transformed Fabian's "Turn Me Loose" into a minor gem for the 1995 Doc Pomus tribute album. Unfortunately, the only thorough examination of Fabian's work is a British import, *This Is Fabian!*, (Ace, 1991, prod. Various) that collects virtually his entire singles output. The domestic *Greatest Hits* (Curb, 1992, prod. Various) is, at a mere 10 songs, skimpy even for a figure as peripheral to the history of rock 'n' roll as Fabian ultimately was.

Joel Selvin

The Fabulous Thunderbirds

Formed 1974 in Austin, Texas

Kim Wilson, vocals, harmonica; Jimmie Vaughan, guitar, vocals (1974-90); Michael "Duke" Robillard, guitar (1990-93); Doug "The Kid" Bangham (1990-93); Kid Ramos, guitar (1994-Present); Keith Ferguson, bass (1974-86); Preston Hubbard, bass (1986-93); Harvey Brooks, bass (1994-95); Willie J. Campbell, bass (1996-present); Mike Buck, drums (1974-80); Fran Christina, drums (1980-95); Jimmy Bott, drums (1995-present); Gene Taylor, keyboards (1994-present)

Bringing hard rock muscle to Chicago blues, the Fabulous Thunderbirds were the hottest band on Texas' spicy rock 'n' blues bar circuit during the 70s, when disco was king and nobody in Texas thought they had a snowball's chance in, well, Texas to make it big. But word spread, the band got a deal with the independent label Takoma Records (home to John Fahey and Leo Kottke), then signed with the major label Chrysalis a year later. Its 1986 hit "Tuff Enuff" brought the group mainstream success and helped spur a surge of interest in the blues, but all the years of hard work that founders Wilson and Vaughan (Stevie Ray Vaughan's older brother) had put into it began to unravel. The group started repeating itself, Vaughan left to pursue a solo career and personnel changes persisted. Wilson, an expert harmonica player, put the band on hold to cut a couple of overlooked solo albums, then put together a new version the band, which signed to Private Music and released the Danny Kortchmar-produced *Roll of the Dice* in 1995. More personnel changes followed, with longtime drummer Christina departing, but the new lineup plans to remain active as a touring and recording unit.

what to buy: *The Essential Fabulous Thunderbirds Collection* Chrysalis, 1991, prod. Denny Bruce and Nick Lowe) ♪♪♪ is prime stuff from the band's early days, when it still played smokey bars and didn't even think about writing a hit song. The collection is drawn from its first four albums, including their debut on Takoma, all of which are now out of print.

what to buy next: *Tuff Enuff* Columbia, 1986, prod. Dave Edmunds) ♪♪♪ is slick, but not so much so that it hides the T-Birds' usual virtues. The title track and a re-make of Sam and Dave's "Wrap it Up" sound terrific on the radio, too.

what to avoid: *Powerful Stuff,* Epic, 1989, prod. Tony Manning) ♪♪ Vaughan's last with the band, is quite the opposite of its title.

the rest: *Hot Number* Epic/Associated, 1987) ♪♪ *Walk That Walk, Talk That Talk* Epic, 1991) ♪♪ *Hot Stuff: The Greatest Hits* Epic, 1992) ♪♪ *Roll the Dice* Private Music, 1995) ♪♪♪

solo outings:

Kim Wilson: Tigerman Antone's, 1993) ♪♪ *That's Life* (Antone's, 1994) ♪♪

▶▶ Stevie Ray Vaughan and Double Trouble, the Red Devils

◀◀ Muddy Waters, Bo Diddley, Slim Harpo, Freddie King

Doug Pullen

The Faces /The Small Faces

Formed 1965 in London, England. Disbanded 1976. Small Faces reformed 1976-79.

Steve Marriott, guitar, vocals (1965-69, 1976-79, died April 20, 1991); Jimmy Winston, keyboards (1965); Ian McLagan, keyboards (1965-79); Ronnie Lane, bass, (1965-73); Kenney Jones, drums (1965-79); Rod Stewart, vocals (1969-74); Ron Wood, guitar (1969-75); Tetsu Yamauchi, bass (1973-76); Rick Wills, bass (1976-79); Joe Brown, guitar (1976-78); Jimmy McCulloch, guitar (1978-79, died Sept. 27, 1979)

The Small Faces became popular in England as much for their natty Mod outfits and short stature as for their raw, R&B-based rockers. The group recorded its first hit single ("Whatcha Gonna Do About It?") just weeks after forming, though it never made much of a dent in the U.S. When Marriott left in 1969 to form Humble Pie, he was replaced by the taller duo of Rod Stewart and Ronnie Wood, and the new band shortened its name to the Faces. The group had fun onstage and off, crafting a loose, boozy, occasionally sloppy kind of rock that was marked by Stewart's scratchy voice, Wood's sinewy guitar riffs and McLaglan's rock-boogie piano. Stewart eventually launched a dual career as a solo artist, but when his solo projects began eclipsing the band's popularity it put a strain on the Faces that ultimately pulled the group apart. Wood went on to join the Rolling Stones, Jones hooked up with the Who and Lane began suffering from multiple sclerosis and became an activist fighting against the disease. The Small Faces were considering yet another reunion when Marriott died in a 1991 house fire.

what to buy: *A Nod Is As Good As A Wink ... to a Blind Horse* (Warner Bros., 1971, prod. Glyn Johns and the Faces) ♪♪♪♪ offers all of the Faces' best sides, from Wood's slashing slide guitar on "That's All You Need" to Lane's sensitive ballad "Debris" to Stewart's macho boasts on "Stay With Me."

what to buy next: *Long Player* (Warner Bros., 1971, prod. the Faces) ♪♪♪♪ captures the party-hearty sound of the Faces, highlighted by boisterous live versions of Paul McCartney's "Maybe I'm Amazed" and Big Bill Broonzy's "I Feel So Good."

what to avoid: Growing tensions in the band stifle *Ooh-La-La,* (Warner Bros., 1973, prod. Glyn Johns) ♪♪ whose 10 tracks sound flat despite the opening track's title, "Silicone Grown."

the rest: Small Faces: *There Are But Four Small Faces* (Immediate, 1967/Sony Music Special Products, 1991) ♪♪♪ *Ogden's Nut Gone Flake* (Immediate, 1968/Sony Music Special Products, 1991) ♪♪♪ *All or Nothing* (Sony Music Special Products, 1992) ♪♪♪ Faces: *First Step* (Warner Bros., 1970) ♪♪♪ *Coast to Coast: Overtures and Beginnings* (Warner Bros., 1974) ♪♪ *Snakes and Ladders: The Best of the Faces* (Warner Bros., 1978) ♪♪♪

worth searching for: *Singles A's and B's,* (See For Miles, 1990, prod. Various) ♪♪♪♪ a solid and relatively comprehensive import collection of the Small Faces' hits, which will have to do until a decent domestic compilation comes out.

solo outings:

Ronnie Lane: Anymore for Anymore (GM, 1974) ♪♪ *Ronnie*

Lane's Slim Chance (A&M, 1975) *Mahoney's Last Stand* (Atlantic, 1976) (with Pete Townshend) *Rough Mix* (MCA, 1977)

Ian McLaglan: *Troublemaker* (Mercury, 1979) *Bump in the Night* (Mercury, 1981)

The Black Crowes, the London Quireboys

Muddy Waters, Sam Cooke, Otis Redding, Elvis Presley, Jerry Lee Lewis, Lonnie Donnegan

see also: *Rod Stewart, Humble Pie, Ron Wood*

David Yonke

Donald Fagen

See: Steely Dan

John Fahey

Born Feb. 28, 1939, in Takoma Park, Md.

A folk/blues guitarist, producer, scholar and founder of the Takoma label, Fahey's first interest was in traditional country music. He traveled extensively through the South, searching for obscure country and blues recordings. As much a historian of early blues guitarists as he is a proficient practitioner of the art, he wrote a definitive biography of blues musician Charley Patton. From blues, country, folk and spirituals, Fahey turned his attention to Brazilian music during the 80s. His open-tuned acoustic guitar work was the progenitor for such guitarists as Leo Kottke (who first recorded on the Takoma label) and William Ackerman.

what to buy: *The Essential John Fahey* (Vanguard, 1974/1993, prod. John Fahey, Barry Hansen and Sam Charters) is a 13-track overview of Fahey's career that hits most of his high points. Combining such disparate elements as hymns, blues and trippy accents, Fahey's methodical approach transcends to an elegant vision. On two tracks, supporting musicians include members of Spirit, which adds to the diverse styles.

what to buy next: *The John Fahey Christmas Album* (Burnside, 1991, prod. Terry Robb and Don MacLeod) collects 24 tracks of Christmas hymns and secular music are finely polished to a warm sheen. *Transfiguration Of Blind Joe Death* (Takoma, 1967) Refined with an effortless melding of blues and spirituals, this is Fahey's most ambitious work.

what to avoid: *Old Girlfriends & Other Horrible Memories,* (Varrick, 1993) though accomplished, is an odd bit of stream of consciousness without the meat of his voluminous and better work.

the rest: God, Time and Casualty (Shanachie, 1990) Christmas Guitar (Vanguard, 1974) *The Yellow Princes* (Vanguard, 1968) *Fare Forward Voyagers* (Takoma, 1974) *I Remember Blind Joe Death* (Rounder, 1987)

worth searching for: The soundtrack to *Country.* (Windham Hill, 1984) With the most memorable results, Fahey participates on this highly atmospheric and moody soundtrack.

Leo Kottke, William Ackerman, Richard Thompson, Jorma Kaukonen

Lightin' Hopkins, Robert Johnson, Leadbelly, Julian Bream

Patrick McCarty

Fairground Attraction /Eddi Reader

Formed 1988 in London, England. Disbanded 1989.

Eddi Reader, vocals; Mark E. Nevin, guitar; Simon Edwards; Will Hasley.

This short-lived British skiffle-swing quartet lasted for one album, but *First of a Million Kisses* (RCA, 1988, prod. Kevin Moloney and Fairground Attraction) happens to be one of the most gorgeous, unabashedly romantic works to ever drift across the Atlantic. Blending the finger-snapping cool of early Rickie Lee Jones with the hushed, elegant folk-pop of Everything But the Girl, Fairground Attraction relied on acoustic instrumentation ranging from mandolins and guitarrons to vibraphones and clarinets. The giddy "Perfect" was a minor MTV hit, but the band's main virtues were songwriter Nevin's gift for imagery ("A Smile In a Whisper" "Moon on the Rain") and Reader's sensual, soaring voice. Since the band broke up, Nevin has collaborated with Kirsty MacColl, while Reader has launched a solo career that's spawned the moody, import-only *Mirmama* (RCA, 1992, prod. the Patron Saints of Imperfection and others) and *Eddi Reader,* (Reprise, 1994, prod. Greg Penny) the latter a soothing, soulful pop triumph whose strongest songs were contributed by Nevin and the prolific Boo Hewerdine.

David Okamoto

Fairport

See: Fairport Convention

Fairport Convention/Fairport/Sandy Denny/Fotheringay

Formed 1967 in London, England. Disbanded 1976. Re-formed 1985.

Richard Thompson, guitar, vocals (1967-71); Simon Nicol, guitar, banjo, bass, vocals (1967-71); Judy Dyble, piano, vocals (1967-68); Ashley "Tyger" Hutchings, bass, guitar, vocals (1967-69); Martin Lamble, drums (1967-69); Iain Matthews (born Ian MacDonald), vocals, percussion, guitar (1967-68); Sandy Denny, vocals, guitar, keyboards (1968-69, 1974-76); Dave Swarbrick, violin, mandolin, vocals (1969-present); Dave Mattacks, drums, keyboards, vocals (1969-74, 1985-present); Dave Pegg, guitar, viola, vocals (1969-present); Roger Hill, guitar, mandolin (1971-72); Tom Farnell, drums (1972); David Rea, guitar (1972); Trevor Lucas, guitar (1972-76); Jerry Donahue, guitar, vocals (1972-76); Paul Warren, drums (1974); Bruce Rowland, drums (1974-76); Martin Allcock, bass, guitar, bouzouki (1985-present); Ric Sanders, violin (1985-present)

Bringing Celtic folk traditions to the forefront, Fairport Convention used made its mark with the evanescent vocals of Sandy Denny and Richard Thompson's brave, soulful songwriting and guitar work. Though Denny and Thompson departed after a handful of releases, the group soldiered on through the next decade with a huge, rotating cast of players. Initially called Tim Turner's Narration, the group was named for the "convention" of musicians at founder Hutchings's house in Muswell Hill, a London suburb. It was Denny's entrance —replacing Dyble— that helped change the group from American folk acolytes to English folk-rock pioneers. The collective became simply Fairport in 1976, split in 1979—overwhelmed briefly by the lack of commercial success that has always been its lot—but reformed in 1985 and has released records periodically ever since. Because of Denny's unique style, the group chose never to install another female lead singer, but let the musicians take over vocal chores themselves. The group reunited briefly with Denny during the 70s. Members of Fairport have also been part of Jethro Tull, Soft Machine, Richard and Linda Thompson's band, and several have done extensive session work. Thompson continues to win fans for his solo work, and Fairport stages an annual picnic/anniversary concert that brings many of its old members back into the fold for one night.

what to buy: Recorded with Fairport's best lineup—including Thompson, Denny and fiddler Swarbrick — *Liege and Leaf* (A&M, 1969, prod. Joe Boyd) is a fully realized fusion of folk and rock sensibilities best heard on songs such as "Tam Lin" and "Crazy Man Michael." *Unhalfbricking* (Hannibal, 1969, prod. Joe Boyd, Simon Nicol and Fairport Convention) is a stunning mix of Thompson and Denny originals, traditional songs and several renditions of Bob Dylan tunes—notably a French version of "If You Gotta Go." Denny's debut, *What We Did on Our Holidays* (Hannibal, 1969, prod. Joe Boyd) is a standout that mixes great songs both old ("She Moves Through the Fair") and new ("Fotheringay," "Meet on the Ledge").

what to buy next: *House Full,* (Hannibal, 1986, prod. Joe Boyd and Frank Kornelussen) revises a 1977 live album that showcases another of Fairport's formidable units. *Five Seasons* (Rough Trade, 1990, prod. Fairport Convention) and *Jewel in the Crown* (Green Linnet, 1995, prod. Fairport Convention) are latter day Fairport releases—the latter with a pronounced political edge—that show the group hasn't lost much.

what to avoid: *In Real Time: Live '87* (Island, 1989, prod. Dave Mattacks) is a pleasant enough reunion album, but hardly shows the fire and invention of the group's best work.

the rest: *Fairport Convention* (Polydor, 1968) *Full House* (Hannibal, 1970) *Angel Delight* (A&M, 1971) *Babbacombe Lee* (A&M, 1971) *Rosie* (A&M, 1973) *Nine* (A&M, 1973) *A Fairport Live Convention* (Island, 1974) *Rising for the Moon* (Island, 1975) *Fairport Chronicles* (A&M, 1976) *Gottle O' Geer* (island, 1976) *Bonny Bunch of Roses* (Vertigo, 1977) *Live at L.A. Troubadour* (Island, 1977) *Tipplers Tales* (Vertigo, 1978) *Farewell, Farewell* (Simon's, 1979) *Moat on the Ledge* (Stony Plain, 1982) *Glady's Leap* (Varrick, 1985) *Expletive Delighted!* (Varrick, 1986); *Heyday* (Hannibal, 1987) *In Real Time: Live '87* (Island, 1987) *Red & Gold* (Rough Trade, 1989)

worth searching for: *25th Anniversary Concert,* (Woodworm, 1993, prod. Dave Pegg) the import document of the jovial 1992 celebration that brought back a good chunk of the band's past—including Thompson and Swarbrick—as well as admirers such as Robert Plant.

solo outings:

Fotheringay (Denny, Jerry Donahue): *Fotheringay* (Hannibal, 1970)

Sandy Denny: *All Our Own Work* (Pickwick, 1968) *Sandy Denny* (Saga, 1970) *North Star Grassman and the Ravens* (Hannibal, 1971) *The Bunch* (A&M, 1972) *Sandy*

(A&M, 1972) ♪♪♪ *Like an Old Fashioned Waltz* (Hannibal, 1973) ♪♪♪ *Rendezvous* (Hannibal, 1977) ♪♪♪ *Sandy Denny & The Strawbs* (Hannibal, 1985) ♪♪♪ *Who Knows Where the Time Goes* (Hannibal, 1986) ♪♪♪♪ *The Best of Sandy Denny* (Hannibal, 1989) ♪♪♪♪ *Original Sandy Denny* (Trojan, 1991) ♪♪♪

▶▶ Andy and The Marksman, Bradford F.C. and The Pyramid, Captain Rugeley's Blues, Doctor K's Blues Band and Ethnic Shuffle Orchestra, King Crimson, Led Zeppelin, Pioneers, Soft Machine, Steeleye Span, Jethro Tull, Whippersnapper, Nick Drake, Dire Straits

◀◀ Bob Dylan, Donovan, Joni Mitchell, the Byrds, Pentangle, the Chieftains

Sarah Weber and Simon Glickman

Faith No More /Mr. Bungle

Formed 1982 in Los Angeles, Calif.

Faith No More—Mike Bordin, drums; Roddy Bottum, keyboards; Billy Gould, bass; Chuck Mosely, vocals (1983-88); Jim Martin, guitar (1984-94); Mike Patton, vocals (1989—present); Dean Menta, guitar (1994-present). Mr. Bungle—Mike Patton, vocals; Trey Spruance, guitar; Trevor Dunn, bass; Clinton McKinnon, tenor sax, clarinets; I Quit, percussion; Theo, reeds

Faith No More rose out of the early 80s post-punk scene in Los Angeles. The initial lineup, with original singer/shouter Chuck Mosely, yielded two albums that were notable only for their funk-tinged hard rock grooves. Mosely was sent packing in 1988 (he subsequently went on to a brief stint fronting seminal punkers Bad Brains) and the band, sans singer, began work on the album *The Real Thing*. Vocalist Patton was brought aboard in 1989 with the daunting task of quickly composing the lyrics for the near-finished album; he did so with considerable flourish, and the recording yielded the smash single "Epic." Patton's wild antics, broad vocal abilities and conceptual facility took the band to a new level that successfully combined such disparate elements as funk, metal, rap, jazz, art rock and theater of the absurd. Using his newfound clout, Patton secured a deal for his side project, Mr. Bungle, a band whose no-rules approach was highly influenced by the scatter-jazz aesthetics of saxophonist John Zorn (who produced its debut). The line between Faith No More and Mr. Bungle blurred somewhat in 1994 when Faith's guitarist Jim Martin was fired and Mr. Bungle guitarist Spruance filled in on the group's latest album. By the early 90s, both bands—while still exhibiting the considerable might of the musicians—had primarily become arenas for the prolific imagination of Patton.

what to buy: Faith No More's *Angel Dust* (Slash/Reprise, 1992, prod. Matt Wallace and Faith No More) ♪♪♪♪ took the concepts that were hinted at on *The Real Thing* and exploded them to gargantuan proportions. This album finds the band at the height of their powers, playing material that is caustically aggressive, psychically violent and compulsively listenable. Songs such as "Midlife Crisis," "Caffeine," "Smaller and Smaller" and "Everything's Ruined" are both harrowing and irresistible. Martin's guitar is loud and chunky, Bordin and Gould's rhythm section is solid and insistent, and keyboardist Bottum supplies eclectic subtleties. Best of all is Patton, who displays frightening growth in his lyrical vision and vocal delivery; his *The Real Thing* persona of a schizophrenic imp is wiped away and replaced with that of a ghoulish cynic lurking in the shadows of a dark subculture. *Mr. Bungle* (Warner Bros., 1991, prod. John Zorn and Mr. Bungle) ♪♪♪♪ takes the darker fringe elements of Faith No More's sound and brings them to the fore; the result is something very close to stream of consciousness music, with ideas and musical genres zooming in and out at a relentless pace. Much like producer Zorn's work (particularly with his band Naked City), the music careens deliriously from fast to slow, jackhammer loud to lullaby soft. To say that the material is restless is a gross understatement; the myriad styles crowding the songs conjure images of a psychotic calliope while the lyrics examine society's slimy underbelly with darkly comic effects. Granted this is not music for the faint of heart, but it is musically challenging, rewarding, and, like fear, never boring.

what to buy next: *King for a Day ... Fool for a Lifetime* (Slash/Reprise, 1995, prod. Andy Wallace and Faith No More) ♪♪♪ and *Disco Volante*, (Warner Bros., 1995, prod. Mr. Bungle) ♪♪♪ the follow-up albums from Faith No More and Mr. Bungle, respectively, both deliver pleasures similar to their predecessors. Unfortunately, these albums bear the cross of following brilliant outings, and the results are neither as fresh nor as diverse. Both, however, come highly recommended to anyone who enjoyed *Angel Dust* and *Mr. Bungle*.

what to avoid: Faith No More's *Introduce Yourself* (Slash/Reprise, 1987, prod. Steve Berlin, Matt Wallace and Faith No More) ♪♪ is a frustrating album that just evades being listenable. The musicianship is solid and inventive, although the band is clearly still searching for its own turf. The problem lies with Mosely's vocals, which veer from whiny to wailing without much musicality in between.

the rest: Faith No More: *We Care a Lot* (Mordam, 1985) *The Real Thing* (Slash/Reprise, 1989)

worth searching for: In 1993, Faith No More recorded a cover version of the Commodores hit "Easy" for a limited EP release; it also appeared on later import copies of the *Angel Dust* album. Like the version of the theme from "Midnight Cowboy" that closes *Angel Dust*, this is a fairly straightforward rendering of the song that still manages a good dose of ironic humor.

White Zombie, Tool, Therapy?, Primus

Black Sabbath, Public Enemy, Parliament, Frank Zappa, Black Flag; John Zorn/Naked City, Frank Zappa, Roky Erikson, William S. Burroughs, Tom Waits

Dave Galens

Marianne Faithfull

Born Dec. 29, 1946 in London, England

The daughter of a British college lecturer and an Austrian baroness, Faithfull was a beautiful young model with no real singing aspirations until she fell in love with Mick Jagger. He wrote her first hit, 1964's "As Tears Go By" with fellow Rolling Stone Keith Richards. She helped write their "Sister Morphine," but went uncredited until a few years ago. Faithfull's various descents into drug addiction hell are now legendary, including a nearly fatal bout with heroin at the time she broke up with Richards. But she's always managed to land on her feet, and her ragged, haggard, Dietrich-like voice powerfully reflects her painful experiences. The infamous lady in the rug—Faithfull was found clad in nothing but a floor covering during a drug bust at Richards' home—became a singer in her own right during the late 70s but succumbed to chemical temptations several times during the 80s. She emerged clean, clear-headed and candid in her 1994 autobiography, which was accompanied by a greatest hits album. Faithfull followed it a year later with her most ambitious and conceptual album, *A Secret Life*, on which she collaborated with director David Lynch's musical collaborator, Angelo Badalamenti ("Twin Peaks," "Blue Velvet").

what to buy: *Faithfull: A Collection of Her Best* (Island, 1994) is a surprisingly cohesive 11-song collection that draws from the various and varied aspects of Faithfull's 32-year recording career. Selections range from that first innocent blush of "As Tears Go By" to the bitterly vulgar "Why'd Ya Do It" (from *Broken English*), the moody "Trouble in Mind" theme song, torch numbers from the Hal Willner-produced "Strange Weather" and a sample from the then-upcoming album *A Secret Life*.

what to buy next: *Broken English* (Island, 1979, prod. Mark Miller Mundy) couldn't possibly have the dramatic impact today that it did when it was released 17 years ago. There was no way then to be prepared for the stark deterioration of Faithfull's formerly breathy voice, a withered but powerful emotive tool ravaged by drugs and a beautiful life turned hard. Producer Mundy and guitarist Barry Reynolds showcased that voice without obstructing it. *Blazing Away* (Island, 1990) is a powerful live album that showcases Faithfull at her dramatic best, backed by people such as Dr. John, former Tom Waits and Elvis Costello guitarist Mark Ribot and the Band's Garth Hudson. Powerful stuff.

what to avoid: Faithfull's collaboration with "Twin Peaks" and "Blue Velvet" composer Angelo Badalamenti, *A Secret Life*, (Island, 1995) is an interesting idea that doesn't work. Both make haunting music on their own, but this is just a little too dull.

the rest: *Marianne Faithfull's Greatest Hits* (Abkco, 1969) *Dangerous Acquaintances* (Island, 1981) *A Child's Adventure* (Island, 1983) *Strange Weather* (Island, 1987)

worth searching for: High-quality sound (at a high price) is the lure of Mobile Fidelity's Ultradisc combination of *Broken English* and *Strange Weather* (1995). Real collectors might have a tough time hunting down three rarities—the import-only *Faithless*, (Sony, 1978) which broke an 11-year recording gap, and her long out-of-print 60s albums *Come My Way* (Decca, 1965) and *Faithfull Forever* (London, 1966)

Bjork, Rickie Lee Jones

Joan Baez, Buddy Holly, Everly Brothers, Charlie Parker

Doug Pullen

The Fall

Formed 1976 in Manchester, England

Mark E. Smith, vocals, guitar, keyboards, tapes; Una Baines, keyboards (1976-78), keyboards; Yvonne Pawlett, electric piano (1978-79); Marcia Schofield, keyboards, vocals (1987-90); David Bush, keyboards (1991-present); Martin Bramah, guitar, vocals (1976-78, 1989-90); Craig Scanlan, guitar (1979-present); Brix Smith, guitar, key-

board, vocals (1983-89, 1994); Tony Friel, bass (1976-78); Marc Riley, keyboards, guitar, bass (1978-83); Steve Hanley, bass, guitar (1979-present); Simon Rogers, bass, keyboards, guitar (1984-87); Karl Burns, drums, bass (1976-79, 1981-86, 1993-present); Mark Leigh, drums (1979-80); Paul Hanley, drums, keyboards (1980-84); John Simon Wolstencroft, drums (1986-present); Kenny Brady (a.k.a Nigel Kennedy), violin (1990)

Mark E. Smith was working on the docks when punk hit. Reacting against some of the mundane examples of the genre, he formed his own group, simultaneously informed by his love of German experimentalists such as Can and of American rockabilly. He's reputedly tone deaf, and has said his sing-songy spoken vocal style is inspired by reggae toasters—in other words, he's a rapper, with an extra "uh" added to the ends of words being his trademark. It's a gloriously confrontational style that conveys his cranky spirit even when American listeners haven't the slightest idea what he's talking about—and when the odd one-liner cracks you up, so much the better. Debuting with one of the finest albums to come out of punk, the Fall has lasted longer than all but a few bands, and has been more productive (more than 30 albums if compilations are counted) and consistent than any of them. The group's name came from the existential Albert Camus album of the same title, and Smith makes no effort to hide his high opinion of himself and low opinion of most music fans. There's a socio-political edge to many of his lyrics, refracted so eccentrically as to avoid preachiness. Thus, after an initial progression into more forbiddingly dissonant and ragged sound, it was a shock when the group developed a cleaner style that was occasionally even catchy. An appreciation for guitar hooks and something approximating a steady rhythm remain, and there's even a bit of synthesizer, all making Smith's rants a little more accessible. The Fall is an acquired taste, to be sure, (especially for Americans), but one worth the effort.

what to buy: *The Infotainment Scan* (Matador/Atlantic, 1993, prod. Rex Sargeant, Mark E. Smith and Simon Rogers) contains some recent Fall standards. "Paranoia Man in Cheap Sh*t Room" is a classic semi-intelligible Smith rant. "Glam-Racket No. 3" wittily rips the contemporary British music trend, and the cover of Sister Sledge's disco anthem "Lost in Music" shows a sense of humor.

what to buy next: *Twenty-Seven Points* (Permanent/BMG, 1995, prod. Not Listed) is the group's seventh live album, a two-CD compilation covering the years 1992-95 on which the Fall revamps a few earlier songs and captures the loose spirit that makes this band great.

worth searching for: Either the stunning debut *Live at the Witch Trials* (Step Forward, U.K., 1978/I.R.S., U.S., 1979, prod. Bob Sargeant) or the somewhat overlapping compilation *Early Fall 77-79* (Faulty Products/I.R.S., 1981, prod. Not Listed) should be in the collection of anyone who cares about punk even slightly. A new sound, a new attitude—it was the beginning of a great run but never quite equalled thereafter in impact or purity of vision.

what to avoid: *The Frenz Experiment* (Beggars Banquet/RCA, 1988, prod. Simon Rogers) matches rants that are incoherent with music so bare there's nothing to hold onto. Most of the songs on *Middle Class Revolt* (Matador, 1994, prod. Rex Sargeant) leave no impression.

the rest: *Grotesque (After the Gramme)* (Rough Trade, 1980) *A Part of America Therein, 1981* (Cottage/Rough Trade, 1982) *Perverted by Language* (Rough Trade, 1983) *Palace of Swords Reversed* (Cog-Sinister/Rough Trade, 1987) *The Wonderful and Frightening World of The Fall* (Beggars Banquet/WEA, 1984) *This Nation's Saving Grace* (Beggars Banquet/PVC, 1985) *The Fall* (PVC EP,1986) *The Domesday Payoff* (Big Time/RCA, 1987) *I Am Kurious Oranj* (Beggars Banquet/RCA, 1988) *Seminal Live* (Beggars Banquet/RCA, 1989) *A Sides* (Beggars Banquet/RCA, 1990) *B Sides* (Beggars Banquet/RCA, 1990) *Extricate* (Cog-Sinister/Fontana, 1990) *Shift-Work* (Cog-Sinister/Fontana, 1991) *Code: Selfish* (Cog-Sinister/Fontana, 1992) *Kimble* (Peel Sessions) (BBC Ent./Dutch East India, 1993) *Cerebral Caustic* (Permanent/Caroline, 1995) *BBC Radio 1 Live in Concert* (Windsong U.K., 1993/Griffin, 1995)

▶▶ Joy Division, Public Image Ltd., Sugarcubes, Sonic Youth, Swans, Pavement, Trumans Water

◀◀ Sex Pistols, Can, Faust, Velvet Underground, Gene Vincent, Kinks

Steve Holtje

Mark Farner

See: Grand Funk Railroad

Fastbacks

Formed early 80s in Seattle, Wash.

Kim Warnick bass, vocals; Lulu Gargiulo guitar; Kurt Bloch guitar, drums

Pre-dating its more famous Seattle brethren isn't what this group should be known for; out-rocking them is. Dripping energy and always sounding like they're having the time of their lives, Fastbacks are powered by songwriter and Young Fresh Fellow Bloch's punkish pop gems, which Sub Pop secretary Warnick tackles with vigor. Gargiulo adds occasional guitar and vocal support, while the list of former Fastbacks drummers—which includes a pre-Guns N' Roses Duff McKagen—rivals Spinal Taps'. The place to start is the Sub Pop collection *The Question Is No,* (Sub Pop, 1992, prod. Various) which gathers some of the group's best songs and loose ends from 1980-92 and is guaranteed to get you out of your seat. "Lose" is a pop punk classic, and "Everything That I Don't Need" just plain rocks. *Fastbacks...and his Orchestra* (Pop Llama, 1987, prod. Various) adds nine more songs to the original *...And His Orchestra* LP and features such Fastback classics as "Seven Days" and the super catchy "In America." *New Mansions in Sound* (Sub Pop, 1996) shows the group is still in good form, sliding slightly more towards a power pop direction.

Keith Klingensmith

The Feelies

Formed 1976 in Haledon, New Jersey. Disbanded 1991.

Bill Million (born William Clayton), guitar, vocals; Glenn Mercer, guitar, vocals; John J., bass (1976-77); Dave Weckerman, drums, percussion (1976-77, 1986-91); Keith Clayton (born Keith DeNunzio), bass (1977-86); Vinny D (born Vincent DeNunzio), drums (1977-78); Anton Fier, drums (1978-86); Stanley Demeski, drums (1986-91); Brenda Sauter, bass, violin (1986-91)

Using the sound of the Velvet Underground's rapidly strummed, trancy guitars on "What Goes On" as a blueprint, the Feelies became the stuff of cult legend in the New Jersey-New York area with the members' numerous side projects (the Trypes, Yung Wu, Speed the Plough), rare live performances and even less frequent recordings. The debut album, *Crazy Rhythms*, remains a landmark of jittery American post-punk guitar rock, even if the shy monotone vocals were all but an afterthought. But it was six years before the Feelies would record again, returning in 1986 with a new lineup and more pastoral sound on *The Good Earth*, co-produced by kindred spirit Peter Buck of R.E.M. During this period, the Feelies appeared in Jonathan Demme's movie "Something Wild" as a cover band at a high school reunion, performing deadpan covers of the Monkees' "I'm a Believer" and David Bowie's "Fame." Subsequent albums failed to capitalize on this glimmer of mainstream attention, and the group disbanded after the 1991 release, "Time for a Witness," with Mercer and Weckerman forming Wake OoLoo, Sauter re-emerging as the lead vocalist of Wild Carnation and Demeski joining Luna.

what to buy: The debut, *Crazy Rhythms* (A&M, 1980, prod. Bill Million and Glenn Mercer) opens with a song called "The Boy With Perpetual Nervousness," and the band did indeed project a nerdy, caffienated energy that echoed punk but also looked back to embrace the Velvets, the Stones, Neil Young and the Beatles (whose "Everybody's Got Something to Hide" is covered). The guitars of Million and Mercer trace twisted, giddy spirals around the—you guessed it—crazy rhythms of future Golden Palominos founder Fier.

what to buy next: *The Good Earth* (Coyote-Twin/Tone, 1986, prod. Bill Million, Glenn Mercer and Peter Buck) evokes early R.E.M. Buck's production eases the band into an electro-folk groove, and with the steady Demeski replacing the more free-form Fier on drums, the pulse gets downright trancy at times. The group's pinnacle is "Slipping (Into Something)," which surges from chamber pop into a transcendent, Eastern-tinged guitar workout.

the rest: *No One Knows* (Coyote-Twin/Tone EP, 1986) *Only Life* (Coyote-A&M, 1988) *Time for a Witness* (Coyote-A&M, 1991)

worth searching for: *Four Free Feelies Songs* (A&M, 1989, prod. Various) a promotional disc that includes covers of the Patti Smith Group's "Dancing Barefoot" and live renditions of the Beatles' "Everybody's Got Something to Hide" and Jonathan Richman's "Egyptian Reggae."

▶▶ Wild Carnation, Luna, Wake OoLoo, Yo La Tengo

◀◀ Velvet Underground, Wire, Neil Young, Rolling Stones, Monkees, Brian Eno, Patti Smith Group, The Beatles, R.E.M.

Greg Kot

Don Felder

See: The Eagles

Jay Ferguson

See: Spirit

Steve Ferguson

See: NRBQ

Melissa Ferrick

Among the flurry of women in rock stories that dominated music media in the past couple of years, one name that was, in most cases, overlooked was Ferrick's. Too bad, because Ferrick's powerful, dramatic voice and talent for writing memorable melodies and incisive lyrics are worthy of attention. A violin prodigy who later attended the Berklee School of Music on a trumpet scholarship, Ferrick played guitar during her college years, garnering attention from mope-rock maven Morrissey, for whom she opened a show in Boston. Morrissey took her along for the rest of his tour, including a stop at Madison Square Garden, which landed Ferrick a recording contract of her own. *Massive Blur* (Atlantic, 1993, prod. Gavin MacKillop) shows Ferrick's considerable range, rocking it up on "Happy Song" and tugging at heartstrings with "Hello Daddy," about an unloving, alcoholic father. The album stiffed, as did her sophomore effort, *Willing to Wait,* (Atlantic, 1995) a quieter acoustic affair that is markedly different from her debut. "Willing to Wait" and "I Am Done" are the standouts. Ferrick was released from her Atlantic contract in July 1996, but let's hope we haven't heard the last of this smart, talented artist.

Daniel Durchholz

Bryan Ferry

Born Sept. 26, 1945 in Washington, England

Ferry's slick, doomed romantic persona doesn't jibe with his upbringing as a British coal miner's son. His artsy ways were cultivated at the University of Newcastle, where he studied art and played in his first bands. Ferry formed the influential British avant-pop band Roxy Music in 1970, and guided it through several personnel changes (producer Brian Eno was a member) and musical incarnations. Ferry started making solo records early into Roxy's run, at first to do something decidedly different from the group's edgy, sometimes tongue-in-cheek rock. But the lines began to blur late in Roxy's life, and by the early 80s there wasn't much difference between what he was doing under the group's name or his own.

what to buy: *Boys and Girls* (Warner Bros., 1985, prod. Rhett Davies and Bryan Ferry) took the lush, layered sound Ferry had begun perfecting on Roxy's *Flesh + Blood* and *Avalon* albums and tweaked it a notch, piling gently plucky guitars on shifting rhythms and washes of keyboards, topped by Ferry's pained tenor. There are no big hits on this, but there's not a weak link in the bunch. *Bete Noire* (Reprise, 1988, prod. Patrick Leonard and Bryan Ferry) updated the sleek, silky sound of its predecessor with a slightly darker, more detached edge. The title cut, which closes the album, has a tasty gypsy violin part that just bores into your brain.

what to avoid: There's hardly a weak link in Ferry's post-Roxy solo work, but the one exception, *Taxi* (Reprise, 1993, prod. Various) is a real let-down. Ferry had reached an impasse on a project (which eventually evolved into the recent *Mamouna* album), so he resorted to his old trick of interpreting other people's songs. But what worked on occasion doesn't work over the course of an entire album.

the rest: *These Foolish Things* (Atlantic, 1973) *Another Time, Another Place* (Atlantic, 1974) *Let's Stick Together* (Atlantic, 1976) *In Your Mind* (Atlantic, 1977) *The Bride Stripped Bare* (Atlantic, 1978) *Mamouna* (Virgin, 1994)

worth searching for: The Japanese "single" for his cover of "Girl of My Best Friend" from *Taxi* is actually a 13-song disc (Virgin, 1993, prod. Various) that mixes *Taxi* tracks and B-sides with live recordings form a 1988 show in Glasgow, Scotland.

▶▶ ABC, A-ha, Duran Duran, Edwyn Collins

◀◀ Frank Sinatra, Tony Bennett, David Bowie

Doug Pullen

Fifth Dimension

Formed 1966 as the Versatiles in Los Angeles, Calif.

(all vocalists) Marilyn McCoo (1966-75); Florence LaRue Gordon; Billy Davis Jr. (1967-75); Ronald Townson; Lamonte McLemore. (Additional members: Danny Beard, Marjorie Barnes, Michael Bell, Phyllis Battle, Greg Walker)

The slick California soul of the Fifth Dimension took the world by storm with 1967's prophetically titled "Up, Up and Away," which swept its way through the 1968 Grammys with five awards. With that seal of approval for its smiley pop, the group went on to score hits with "Stoned Soul Picnic," "Aquarius/Let the Sunshine In," "Wedding Bell Blues" and others. In 1975, McCoo and Davis—who had married in 1969—left the group for solo careers. The band replaced them and had a hit with "Love Hangover" in 1976, but it never returned to its former luster. McCoo and Davis had their best success as a team, scoring a No. 1 hit with "You Don't Have To Be A Star" in 1977. While it was at its peak, the Fifth Dimension offered plenty of memorable hits; they're all collected on *Anthology 1967-1973* (Rhino, 1986, prod. Various)

the rest: *Greatest Hits on Earth* (Bell, 1972/Arista, 1987) *In the House* (Click, 1995)

Lawrence Gabriel

54.40

Formed 1980, in Vancouver, Canada

Neil Osborne, vocals, guitar; Brad Merritt, bass guitar; Phil Comparelli, trumpet, guitar; Ian Franey, drums (1980-83); Daryl Neudorf, drums (1983-84); Matt Johnson, drums (1984-present)

Born out of the Vancouver underground scene during the era of the Sex Pistols and the Clash, 54.40 has been one of Canada's most influential bands since the early 1980s. Early years saw the band honing a gritty and sometimes confrontational guitar-driven sound that drew heavily from R.E.M. and other guitar pop bands. Major label success in the 1980s led to a slicker, synthesizer-backed sound that turned off some early fans but gained success on college radio in the United States. The 1990s has seen the band reinvent itself more than once, first opting for a rawer, more bluesy sound, and then returning to its roots for its most recent releases. Frontman and lyricist Osborne is well-known throughout Canada for leading the battle to maintain Canadian content standards on Canadian radio and television stations.

what to buy: *54.40,* (Warner/Reprise, 1986, prod. 54.40 and Dave Ogilvie) also known as "The Green Album," is the band's major label debut and most representative of its earlier sound. Features the song "I Go Blind," later covered by phenom band Hootie and the Blowfish and featured on the television show "Friends." *Smilin' Buddha Cabaret* (Sony Canada, 1994, prod. Don Smith) is called the band's "K-Tel album" by drummer Johnson because no two songs are alike. Written largely while on a European tour, the album is a return to the band's early Vancouver roots and is considered to be its best work.

what to buy next: *Show Me* (Warner Brothers, 1987, prod. Dave Jerden) is the band's first album made entirely after signing with Warner Brothers. Far slicker than their independent releases and featuring synthesizers and heavily processed guitar and drum sounds, the album's highlight is the anthemic "One Gun."

what to avoid: *Fight for Love* (Reprise, 1989, prod. Neil Osborne and Dave Ogilvie) failed to capitalize on the success of *Show Me* and alienated some fans with its acoustic focus and long guitar solos.

the rest: *Things Are Still Coming Ashore* (MO=DA=MU, 1981) *Selection* (MO=DA=MU, 1982) *Set the Fire* (MO=DA=MU, 1984) *Sweeter Things—A Compilation* (Warner Music Canada, 1991) *Trusted by Millions* (Sony Canada, 1996)

worth searching for: *Dear, Dear* (Sony Canada, 1992, prod. Don Smith) was released in Canada only, where it yielded a slew of radio hits featuring a more stripped down sound. The hits included "She La," "Nice to Luv You," "Music Man," and "You Don't Get Away (That Easy)."

▶▶ Hunters & Collectors, The Tragically Hip

◀◀ R.E.M.

Brad Morgan

What Album Changed Your Life?

"I think probably Bitches Brew by Miles Davis. That was, I suppose, the beginning of rock 'n' roll and jazz mixed up, which thrilled me. It still does, actually."

Sting

Fight

See: Judas Priest

Fine Young Cannibals

Formed 1984 in London, England

Andy Cox, guitar; David Steele, bass, keyboards; Roland Gift, vocals

Following the break-up of the English Beat, Cox and Steele lit out on their own and teamed up with singer/actor Gift. Their debut, *Fine Young Cannibals* (I.R.S., 1985, prod. Robin Millar, Pela and Fine Young Cannibals) is a stylish demonstration of the group's style of dance-pop fused with Motown-style R&B. Gift's richly emotional vocals shine on "Johnny Come Home" and "Don't Ask Me To Choose." But FYC's second album, *The Raw & The Cooked* (I.R.S., 1989, prod. Fine Young Cannibals) provided the breakthrough thanks to the massive hits "She Drives Me Crazy" and "Good Thing." Since then, however, the group has been dormant save *The Raw & The Remix* (I.R.S., 1990, prod. Various) an unnecessary assemblage of remixes from the album.

see also: *English Beat*

Anna Glen

Tim Finn

See: Split Enz

Finn Brothers

See: Split Enz

Firefall

Formed 1974 in Boulder, Colo.

Rick Roberts, guitar, vocals (1974-83); Jock Bartley, guitar, vocals (1974-present); Larry Burnett, guitar, vocals (1974-83); Mark Andes, bass (1974-80); Michael Clarke, drums (1974-83); David Muse, sax, flute, (1977-83); Steven Weinmeister, vocals, guitars (1983-present); Sandy Ficca, drums (1983-present); Bil Hopkins, bass, vocals (1983-present); Stephen Thomas Manshel, vocals, guitars (1983-present); Dan Clawson, saxophone, flute, harmonica, keyboards (1983-present)

Firefall is perhaps the nadir of the folk- and country-rock evolution sparked by the Byrds. The formula was perfect; bring together veteran country-rockers from the Byrds (Clarke), Flying Burrito Brothers (Roberts, who took over the Burritos after Gram Parsons went solo), Gram Parson's Fallen Angels Band (Bartley, who had been jamming with Tommy Bolin before joining Parsons in mid-tour) and even the psychedelic band Spirit (Andes), and give them a flawlessly glossy commercial surface for the hits to skate on. The formula was too good: skate is exactly what they did, with Top 40 hits from the harmless "You Are the Woman" and the amazingly misogynistic "Cinderella" to the wimpy "Just Remember I Love You" and the weird "Strange Way." The music was catchy but insincere, and it doesn't come close to matching the quality of any of these guys' original bands. At best, they helped perpetuate a breezy, beautiful Boulder, Colo. ethos by capturing something of the town's freewheeling spirit. Andes left the band to join Heart full-time in 1980; Roberts was last heard writing children's music; Bartley still leads a harder-rocking version of Firefall in the Boulder area.

what to buy: *The Best of Firefall* (Atlantic, 1981, prod. Various) gathers together the hits, which dabbled on into the early 1980s (*Always*, from 1983, was the last), and is mostly listenable.

what to buy next: *Firefall* (Atlantic, 1976, prod. Jim Mason) is the best of the rest, although it's nearly fatally flawed by some really dumb songs such as "Cinderella," "No Way Out" and "Sad Ol' Love Song" (all written by the machismo-stricken Burnett).

what to avoid: *Messenger* (Redstone, 1994, prod. Jim Mason and Jock Bartley) WOOF! is a completely lame collection under Bartley's leadership. Though it has all the right stylistic elements, the songs are empty-headed — including one wretched, unsubtle ode against child abuse.

the rest: *Luna Sea* (Atlantic, 1977) *Elan* (Atlantic, 1978) *Undertow* (Atlantic, 1980) *Clouds Across the Sun* (Atlantic, 1981) *Break of Dawn* (Atlantic, 1983)

solo outings:

Rick Roberts: Windmills (A&M, 1972) *She Is a Song* (A&M, 1973)

▶▶ Brooks & Dunn, Shenandoah

◀◀ The Byrds, Flying Burrito Brothers, Poco

see also: *The Byrds, Flying Burrito Brothers, Gram Parsons, Heart, Spirit*

Gil Asakawa

fIREHOSE /Minutemen/Minuteflag/Mike Watt

Minutemen (1979-85) — D. Boon (born Dennes Dale Boon), guitar, vocals (died Dec. 23, 1985); Mike Watt, bass, vocals; George Hurley, drums; fIREHOSE (1986-94) — Watt; Hurley; Ed fROMOHIO (born Ed Crawford), guitar, vocals

Perhaps the greatest band to come out of the California hardcore punk scene, the Minutemen charged out of San Pedro as a quartet called the Reactionaries (with Martin Tamburovich on vocals and saxophone). The new name was chosen not only as a wry comment on hard-core song lengths, which the group certainly honored early on, but also as a slap at a California-based ultra-conservative group. There was always a strong socio-political edge in Boon's lyrics—sometimes couched sardonically, sometimes explicatively, sometimes in a broader context. But what made the Minutemen stand out was the music, which was never formulaic and managed to incorporate funk and jazz so deeply that all the pieces emerged in organic wholes of startling clarity and directness. Minutemen music can stand on its own as abstract art, though it's much more than that. After Boon was killed in a car crash, Crawford, a Minutemen fan from Ohio, persuaded the surviving members to continue with him. Crawford had his merits but was no match for Boon, and Watt's fIREHOSE material tends to sit comfortably at a respectable plateau rather than scale the heights. The band broke up in 1994, and Watt re-surfaced in 1995 with an alternative all-star project called *Ball-hog or Tugboat?* He toured with a band that included Pearl Jam's Eddie Vedder and Dave Grohl from Nirvana and Foo Fighters, and the following year Watt joined Perry Farrell's band Porno for Pyros.

what to buy: The Minutemen album *Post-Mersh Vol. I* (SST, 1987, prod. Spot) combines the EPs *Punchline* (SST, 1981, prod. Spot) and *What Makes Makes a Man Start Fires?,* (SST, 1982, prod. Spot) which both distill the hardcore ethic to its sharpest essence with short, tight, unusual structures and poetic but no-bull lyrics.

what to buy next: fIREHOSE's *if'n* (SST, 1987, prod. Mike Watt and Ethan James) is the group's most varied and inspired album by a wide margin, including everything from Watt's dead-on parody of R.E.M. to Crawford's acoustic finger-picking folk tribute "In Memory of Elizabeth Cotton." The *Sometimes* EP (SST, 1988, prod. Watt and Ethan James) has two outtakes from the same sessions that should've been added to the 40-minute album.

what to avoid: *MinuteFlag* (SST EP, 1986, prod. Greg Ginn) is a collaboration between Minutemen and Black Flag that gels only on the one track Henry Rollins and D. Boon sing on (the other three are instrumentals). fIREHOSE's *Mr. Machinery Operator* (Columbia, 1993, prod. J Mascis) subjects some (if not enough) decent material to sludgy production.

the rest: Minutemen: *Post-Mersh Vol. II* (SST, 1987) *Post-Mersh Vol. III* (SST, 1989) *The Politics of Time* (New Alliance, 1984) *Ballot Result* (SST, 1986) fIREHOSE: *Ragin' Full-on* (SST, 1986) *fROMOHIO* (SST, 1989) *Flyin' the Flannel* (Columbia, 1991) *Live Totem Pole* (Columbia EP, 1992) Mike Watt: *Ball-hog or Tugboat?* (Columbia, 1995)

worth searching for: Get the double LP of Minutemen's *Double Nickels on the Dime,* (SST, 1985, prod. Ethan James) since the single CD didn't have room for everything, and you don't want to miss the menacing "Little Man with a Gun in His Hand." In terms of stylistic coherence, this is the greatest punk album ever made.

▶▶ Victim's Family, Tar Babies, Jane's Addiction, UYA, Universal Congress of...

◀◀ Wire, the Clash, Effigies, Dils, Blue Oyster Cult, Bob Dylan, Richard Hell & the Voidoids, Ornette Coleman

Steve Holtje

Fish

See: Marillion

Fishbone

Formed 1980 in Los Angeles, Calif.

John (Norwood) Fisher, bass vocals; Phillip Dwight (Fish) Fisher, drums; Kendall Rey Jones (1994-present), guitar, vocals; Angelo Christopher Moore, vocals, saxophone; Christopher Gordon Dowd, trombone, keyboards; Walter Adam Kibby, trumpet, John Bigham, guitar, keyboards (1990-present)

Without benefit of mainstream radio play, Fishbone has built its fan base on the strength of blistering live performances. Were the band able to bring some focus to its hyper blend of punk, ska, hardcore and funk long enough to sufficiently focus, Fishbone might achieve the transcendence it's been threatening for quite some time. Instead, the music is most often a supercharged hodgepodge of styles and social messages, which creates an air of rootlessness covered up by fiery chops.

what to buy: *The Reality of My Surroundings* (Columbia, 1991, prod. Fishbone and David Kahne) is arguably the band's best and is certainly its most ambitious effort, one that won over modern rock fans with the tunes "Everyday Sunshine" and "Sunless Saturday." *Truth and Soul* (Columbia, 1988, prod. David Kahne) is another mixed bag, featuring a steroid take on Curtis Mayfield's "Freddie's Dead" and scorchers such as "Bonin' in the Boneyard" mixed in with some forgettable riff-o-ramas.

what to buy next: *In Your Face* (Columbia, 1986, prod. David Kahne) is a slicked-up bid for commercial play, but it *is* Fishbone at its most accessible as the band keeps (more or less) a ska-inflected backbeat to "A Selection" and "Cholly."

what to avoid: *Give a Monkey a Brain and He'll Swear He's the Center of the Universe* (Columbia, 1993, prod Terry Date and Fishbone) is as obtuse as the title, overreaching, schizophrenic and frustrating.

the rest: *Fishbone* (Columbia EP, 1985) *It's a Wonderful Life (Gonna Have a Good Time)* (Columbia EP, 1987) *Bonin' in the Boneyard* (Columbia EP, 1990) *Chim Chim's Badass Revenge* (Rowdy, 1996)

worth searching for: *Singles,* (Sony, 1993, prod. Various) a Japanese collection of some of Fishbone's best tracks, highlighted by a handful of fiery live performances.

▶▶ Living Colour, Weapon of Choice

◀◀ Curtis Mayfield, Rush, James Brown, Sly Stone

Allan Orski

Matthew Fisher

See: Procol Harum

The Fixx

Formed 1980 in London, England

Cy Curnin, vocals; Jaime West-Oram, guitars; Adam Woods, drums; Rupert Greenall, keyboards; Charlie Barrett, bass (1980-83); Dan K. Brown, bass (1983-1991)

Initiated by a college friendship between Curnin and Woods, the remaining members joined in answer to a newspaper advertisement. After a short stint under a different name, the quintet recorded a demo of its first single, "Lost Planes" and snagged a record deal. For a brief moment during the early 80s, the group's calculated brand of synth-pop found an audience, back in the days when Flock of Seagulls seemed like the wave of the future. But as that cold brand of keyboard-dominated rock began to fall off the charts, so did the Fixx. A belated attempt to change sounds by casting off longtime producer Rupert Hine (now closely involved with Rush) didn't help, and by the early 90s, the Fixx had faded into pop music oblivion.

what to buy: It isn't often that a band's most commercial record is its best, but in the Fixx's case, the million-selling *Reach the Beach* (MCA, 1983, prod. Rupert Hine) turned out to be the band's most consistent, engaging work—led by the singles "One Thing Leads to Another" and "Saved By Zero." Here, the formula of cascading guitars, spacey keyboards and urgent vocals reached its peak. Best of all, the band's greatest-hits album *One Thing Leads to Another: Greatest Hits* (MCA, 1989, prod. Rupert Hine and Hugh Padgham) highlights its best work without the album filler—also including tunes such as "Secret Separation," "Stand or Fall" and "Red Skies."

what to buy next: Some dismiss it as a collection of synth-pop curiosities, but the moody, keyboard-drenched tunes on *Phantoms* (MCA, 1984, prod. Rupert Hine) strike a creative, complex chord—including 80s hits such as "Are We Ourselves?" and "Sunshine In the Shade."

what to avoid: The band always had trouble reproducing its lush, complex recorded sound in concert, so it's no surprise that the band's live album *React* (MCA, 1987, prod. Hugh Padgham) WOOF! falls flat.

the rest: *Shuttered Room* (MCA, 1982) *Walkabout* (MCA, 1986) *Calm Animals* (MCA, 1988) *Ink* (Impact, 1991) *The King Biscuit Flower Hour Presents The Fixx* (KBFH, 1996)

worth searching for: For a taste of a Fixx concert that wasn't quite so bad, check out *Live in the U.S.A.* (MCA, 1991) a live video that, while heavy on material from *Phantoms,* is a sympathetic rendering of the group's concert skills.

▶▶ Erasure, Howard Jones

◀◀ Gary Numan, Ultravox, David Bowie

Eric Deggans

Flag of Convenience

See: Buzzcocks

The Flamin' Groovies

Formed 1966 in San Francisco, Calif. Disbanded 1992.

George Alexander, bass, vocals; Cyril Jordan, guitar, vocals; Roy Loney, vocals, guitar (1966-71); Tim Lynch, guitar, vocals (1966-71); Danny Mihm, drums (1966-73, 1982); James Farrell, guitar (1971-76); Chris Wilson, vocals, guitar (1971-81); Terry Rae, drums (1973-75); David Wright, drums (1975-80); Mike Wilhelm, guitar (1976-82); Mark Dunwoody, keyboards, vocals (1980-82); Paul Zahl,drums (1983-921); Jack Johnson, guitar, vocals (1984-92); Ron Ronco, vocals (1989)

It could be argued that no rock 'n' roll act was ever so good and simultaneously so commercially ignored as San Francisco's legendary Flamin' Groovies. Throughout its long history and many personnel changes, the group (which added the apostrophe to

Flamin' during the mid-70s) was consistently out of step with the times. While its contemporaries were properly freaking out and endlessly jamming in a tedious soundtrack to an emerging counterculture, the Groovies drew on its unfashionable rock'n' roll roots, alternately purveying good-time jug band music a la the Lovin' Spoonful and rockin' the mother-lovin' house down with a ferocity to rival the Stones and Stooges. By the time reduced-frills rock started making a comeback in the 70s, a new incarnation of theGroovies was dressed up in Mod clothing and playing polished power-pop as if it were 1965 and the band was some mythic combination of the Beatles, Byrds, Beach Boys and Rolling Stones heading into the studio for a session with Phil Spector. And by the time "jangly pop" becamea buzz phrase, the Flamin' Groovies were so far underground that no amount of excavating could bring it to the surface, let alone to the pop stardom that should have been its divine right. As it is, the Groovies produced some unforgettable work, including three oft-covered classics—"Slow Death," "Teenage Head" and the incomparable, booming "Shake Some Action," which sounded like the eleventh-hour announcement of pop-rock Armageddon. Groovies fansare generally divided into two camps: those who favor the manic-rockin' original Groovies fronted by Loney, and those who prefer the pop perfection of the Sire years (1976-79) with Wilson. In each incarnation, Jordan and Alexander kept the flame burning brightly. While the world at large remains criminally unaware of the group's virtues, an ever-faithfulbloc of fans retains its affection for all things red-hot and groovy.

what to buy: *Groovies' Greatest Grooves* (Sire, 1989, prod. Various) does a fine job of anthologizing the Sire years, including the Loney-sung "Teenage Head" and scattered non-LP singles (including "Slow Death"). *Teenage Head* (Kama Sutra/One Way, 1971, prod. Richard Robinson) is the Loney-era Groovies' crowning achievement, a triumphant Stonesy swagger that Keith Richards is said to have preferred to *Sticky Fingers*.

what to buy next: *Rock Juice* (National, 1992, prod. Cyril Jordan and Karl Derfler) offers a swell swan song for the Groovies, with a batch of fine Cyril Jordan originals (bolstered by the prerequisite covers) serving notice that the Flamin' Groovies weregonna go out in style. *California Born and Bred* (Norton, 1995, prod. Various) is a rock 'em-sock 'em set of 23 revved-up teenage blasts from the vaults, chronicling the original Groovies via a collection of hard-to-find and previously-unreleased Loney-eragoodies.

what to avoid: *A Collection of Rare Demos & Live Recordings* (Marilyn, 1993, prod. Not listed) is licensed by Chris Wilson, but it's muddy sounding bootleg material just the same.

the rest: *Sneakers* (Snazz, 1968) *Supersnazz* (Epic, 1969) *Flamingo* (Kama Sutra, 1970) *Now* (Sire, 1978) *Jumpin' in the Night* (Sire, 1979) *Bucketful of Brains* (Voxx, 1983) *Rockin' at the Roundhouse* (Mystery, 1993)

worth searching for: *Shake Some Action,* (Sire, 1976, prod. Dave Edmunds) now available on import recordings, is the quintessential Flamin' Groovies pop record, and a vital part of any respectable power-pop fan's permanent record library.

solo outings:

Roy Loney and the Phantom Movers: *Out After Dark*(Solid Smoke, 1979) *Phantom Tracks* (Solid Smoke, 1980) *Contents Under Pressure* (War Bride, 1981) *Having a Rock 'n' Roll Party* (WarBride, 1982) *Fast & Loose* (Double Dare, 1983) *TheScientific Bombs Away!!!* (Norton, 1989) *Action Shots!* (Marilyn, 1993)

Chris Wilson: *Random Creatures* (Marilyn, 1993) (with the Sneetches): *Pop!* (Marilyn, 1993) *Back on the Barbary Coast* (Marilyn, 1993)

▶▶ The Hoodoo Gurus, R.E.M., Tommy Keene, the LongRyders, the Sneetches, the Plimsouls

◀◀ The Rolling Stones, the Lovin' Spoonful, the Beatles, the Byrds, Phil Spector, the Beach Boys, Eddie Cochran

see also: *The Barracudas*

Carl Cafarelli

Flaming Lips

Formed 1984 in Oklahoma City, Okla.

Wayne Coyne, vocals, guitar; Mark Coyne, vocals (1984-86); Michael Ivins, bass; Richard English, drums (1984-89); John "Dingus" Donahue, guitar (1989-90); Nathan Roberts, drums (1989-90); Ronald Jones, guitar (1990-present); Steven Drozd, drums (1990-present)

Isolation such as that imposed on bands who choose to live and record in Oklahoma City can be an incubator for originality, genius or just plain weirdness. In the case of the Flaming Lips, it's a little of all three. The group genially shares the crackpot wing of rock's psychedelic fringe with founding father Syd Barrett and elder statesmen such as Julian Cope, Robyn Hitchcock and the Meat Puppets. With its blend of acid-rock and bubblegum, spaced-out jams that run for 20 minutes or more (check "Hell's Angel's Cracker Factory" from *Telepathic Surgery*) and relatively concise folk ballads, the Lips' albums can be bewildering to neophytes. But spend a little time with the best records and the group becomes rock's version of a Fellini movie, in which the most mundane details —- a trip to the grocery store, a postal carrier making his rounds, a cloud pattern —- are made wondrous, strange, awesome. With the addition of guitar-effects maestro Jones and the Bonham-like Drozd on drums in 1990, the group's sometimes fragmented ideas coalesced into consistently evocative songs, and its live shows attained a power few rock bands have approached in recent years.

what to buy: *Transmissions from the Satellite Heart* (Warner Bros., 1993, prod. Flaming Lips and Keith Cleversly) is one of the decade's finest rock records. It includes the band's fluke hit, "She Don't Use Jelly," hardly the disc's best, or even catchiest, song. Amid a dazzling funhouse of 3-D sound ideally suited for headphone listening but also rocking enough to blast at a beach party, Coyne's oblique lyrical imagery and wobbly voice resonate almost in spite of themselves. The Lips' strangely optimistic songs suggest that to survive the world, sometimes you have to imagine a more fantastic one.

what to buy next: *In a Priest Driven Ambulance* (Restless, 1990, prod. Flaming Lips and Dave Fridmann) is the band's first great leap forward in songwriting. The sleeve (misleadingly) lists the running times for all 10 tracks as 3:26, but the disc is among the group's most successful stabs at writing more concise (albeit enticingly odd) pop songs and concludes with the Lips' unoffical anthem, a relatively straight reading of the standard "What a Wonderful World."

what to avoid: *Telepathic Surgery* (Restless, 1989, prod. Flaming Lips) isn't a total disaster, but for a group that thrives on wild stylistic and sonic experimentation, this is surprisingly tame, one-dimensional rock.

the rest: *The Flaming Lips* (Restless, 1985) *Hear It Is* (Restless, 1986) *Oh My Gawd!!! ... the Flaming Lips* (Restless, 1987) *Unconsciously Screamin'* (Atavistic EP, 1990) *Hit to Death in the Future Head* (Warner Bros., 1991) *Clouds Taste Metallic* (Warner Bros., 1995)

worth searching for: *Providing Needles For Your Balloons* (Warner Bros. EP, 1994) spans a generous 44 minutes with eight tracks, largely self-recorded at radio stations and in-store performances, including the essential talking blues, "Put the Waterbug in the Policeman's Ear," about grocery shopping on acid.

Pavement, Presidents of the United States of America

Syd Barrett, Plastic Ono Band, Echo and the Bunnymen, Hawkwind

Greg Kot

The Flatlanders

Formed 1970 in Lubbock, Texas

Jimmy Dale Gilmore, vocals, guitar; Joe Ely, vocals, harmonica, dobro, guitar; Butch Hancock, vocals, guitar; Tommy Hancock, fiddle; Syl Rice, string bass; Tony Pearson, mandolin; Steve Wesson, musical saw.

Spawned in roughly the same era as the Byrds and the Flying Burrito Brothers, the Flatlanders represented that period's clash of values between the traditional and the radical, the search to build on the legacies of Jimmie Rodgers and Hank Williams while seeking a higher consciousness and rejecting the values of a bygone era. Perhaps the fatal error was to attempt this in Nashville, which didn't want to hear about such nonsense, rather than L.A., which likely would have taken to the band's lonesome West Texas warblings like it took to the Eagles and the Nitty Gritty Dirt Band. *More a Legend Than a Band* (Rounder, 1990, prod. Royce Clark), a reissue of the Flatlanders' original 1971 album, only saw the light of day on 8-track and is one of the great lost albums and contains the seeds of a generation of West Texas talent that since has gone on to fame if not fortune. Gilmore's tremulous voice hovers above the proceedings on most of the tracks, including two of his finest songs, "Dallas" and "Tonight I'm Gonna Go Downtown." Wesson's musical may as well be a sitar amid these country & Eastern musings. Hancock contributes a handful of tunes, including the mournful "She Had Everything," while Ely settles mostly for being the session's hotshot guitarist. Prompted by the growing reputation of these three as solo artists, Charley reissued the album in 1980, and Rounder a decade later in a slightly different configuration.

see also: *Joe Ely, Butch Hancock, Jimmie Dale Gilmore*

Daniel Durchholz

Mick Fleetwood

See: Fleetwood Mac

Fleetwood Mac

Formed 1967 in London, England

Mick Fleetwood, drums; John McVie, bass; Peter Green, guitar, vocals (1967-69); Jeremy Spencer, guitar, vocals, piano (1967-70); Danny Kirwan, guitar, vocals (1968-72); Christine McVie, piano, vocals (1970-present); Bob Welch, guitar, vocals (1971-74); Dave Walker, guitar, vocals, harmonica (1972-73); Bob Weston, guitar, banjo, harmonica (1972-73); Lindsay Buckingham, guitar, vocals (1975-87); Stevie Nicks, vocals (1975-90); Billy Burnette, guitar, vocal (1987-present); Rick Vito, guitar (1987-91); Bekka Bramlett, vocals (1993-present); Dave Mason, guitar, vocals (1994-present)

From 1975 to 1982, a band that started out playing pure blues had 12 consecutive Top 20 singles, and overall has totaled 18 Top 40 hits despite personnel turmoil and turnover that make Spinal Tap seem stable. Fleetwood Mac went from being the Green-founded blues group—which was very popular in the British blues scene—to a bland, West Coast pop outfit under the lead of guitarist Welch. The crucial evolution came when Welch was replaced in 1975 by two fellow Californians, Buckingham and Nicks, who had recently recorded the fine album *Buckingham Nicks* (which inexplicably remains un-reissued). Buckingham was capable of incindiery guitar work and in concert proved himself worthy of Green's legacy on older material. But he would ultimately contribute much more with his disarmingly accessible pop stylings that made Fleetwood Mac one of pop's hottest groups during the 70s. *Fleetwood Mac* in 1975 launched three hit singles and broke the band in America. The follow-up, *Rumours*—inspired by the break-ups in the various intra-band couples (Buckingham and Nicks, the McVies)—remains the second-highest-selling album ever, behind Michael Jackson's *Thriller.* Ultimately, the magic of this incarnation slowly fizzled when subsequent albums didn't equal *Rumours'* once-in-a-lifetime standard, and when Buckingham and Nicks became more interested in their solo careers. Both eventually quit the group—though the lineup reunited to perform the hit "Don't Stop" during one of President Bill Clinton's 1993 inaugural galas—replaced by journeyman rocker Mason and Bramlett, the daughter of the rock duo Delaney & Bonnie. The new lineup (which includes Christine McVie for recording only) has recorded one album, which didn't sell quite like *Rumours* either.

what to buy: *Rumours,* (Warner Bros., 1977, prod. Fleetwood Mac, Richard Dashut, Ken Caillat and Cris Morris) with 11 great songs and no duds, is as good as mainstream pop gets. *Fleetwood Mac,* (Reprise, 1975, prod. Fleetwood Mac and Keith Olsen) with "Landslide," "Rhiannon," "Over My Head" and "I'm So Afraid," nearly matches that standard. *Tusk* (Warner Bros., 1979, prod. Fleetwood Mac, Richard Dashut, and Ken Caillat) is more an eccentric masterpiece than a pop masterpiece, with Buckingham running wild and reinventing lo-fi on his pieces while Nicks ("Sara") and Christine McVie ("Think About Me") keep the group in the mainstream.

what to buy next: Fleetwood Mac's blues period can be comfortably sampled on *English Rose,* (Blue Horizon, 1969, prod. Mike Vernon) known in the U.K. in somewhat different form as *Mr. Wonderful* If Green and Spencer weren't always convincing blues singers, they were gifted guitarists. The double album *Fleetwood Mac in Chicago 1969,* (Blue Horizon/Sire, 1975, prod. Mike Vernon, Marshall Chess) with guests Otis Spann, Willie Dixon, Shakey Horton, Honeyboy Edwards, Buddy Guy, and other bluesmen, is also a good context in which to hear the Brits' six-string blues expertise with more competent singers to the fore. *Future Games,* (Reprise, 1971, prod. Fleetwood Mac) with both Welch and Kirwan, has an appealingly spacy sound, plus Christine's pretty "Show Me a Smile."

what to avoid: *Kiln House* (Reprise, 1970, prod. Fleetwood Mac) is a rudderless album drifting aimlessly in search of a tunesmith. *Penguin* (Reprise, 1973, prod. Fleetwood Mac and Martin Birch) is the sort of nondescript album on which the only moments that stand out are howlingly obvious lapses in taste and judgment. *Tango in the Night* (Warner Bros., 1987, prod. Lindsay Buckingham and Richard Dashut) is so enervated it's downright annoying once the first three tracks, which at least are familiar, are done.

the rest: *Fleetwood Mac* (Blue Horizon, 1968) *Then Play On* (Reprise, 1969) *Bare Trees* (Reprise, 1972) *Mystery to Me* (Reprise, 1973) *Heroes Are Hard to Find* (Reprise, 1974) *Live* (Warner Bros., 1980) *Mirage* (Warner Bros., 1982) *Behind the Mask* (Warner Bros., 1990) *25 Years—The Chain* (Warner Bros., 1992) *Time* (Warner Bros., 1995) *Peter Green's Fleetwood Mac Live at the BBC* (Castle, 1995)

worth searching for: *The Chain Sampler,* (Warner Bros., 1992, prod. Various) an 18-song promotional sampler from the box set that's a fine retrospective unto itself.

solo outings:

Mick Fleetwood: *The Visitor* (RCA, 1981) *Mick Fleetwood's Zoo: Shakin' the Cage* (Warner Bros., 1992)

Christine McVie: *The Legendary Christine Perfect Album* (Blue

Horizon, 1969/Sire, 1976) *Christine McVie* (Warner Bros., 1984)

Matthew Sweet, Tori Amos

Elmore James, Etta James, John Mayall, the Beach Boys

see also: *Lindsay Buckingham, Stevie Nicks, Bob Welch*

Steve Holtje

The Fleshtones

Formed 1976 in Queens, N.Y.

Peter Zaremba, vocals, harmonica, organ; Keith Streng, guitar; Danny Gilbert, guitar (1976); Jimmy Bosco, drums (1976); Jan Marek Pakulski, bass (1976-87); Lenny Calderone, drums (1976-79); Bill Milhizer, drums (1979-present); Brian Spaeth, horns (1978-79); Gordon Spaeth, alto sax, organ, harmonica (1978-90); Kenny Fox, bass (1990-present)

The Fleshtones rose from New York's punk/New Wave movement during the late 70s and have since been touring almost non-stop preaching the gospel of fun 60s garage rock. The band's experience hasn't translated into commercial success, but the band members have learned how to put on quite a show; a typical Fleshtones performance includes go-go dance moves, silly Farfisa organ jams and a relentless party atmosphere. Its campy, hedonistic music never quite made it with the early 80s MTV crowd, and it's now an absolute anomaly in an era dominated by angst-ridden bands. Despite various hopeful signs—such as singer Peter Zaremba's stint hosting MTV's 80s new wave show "The Cutting Edge"—the Fleshtones seem destined to remain an under-appreciated bar band.

what to buy: The Fleshtones have a reputation for being a band that can't recreate the fire in the studio. An exception is *Powerstance,* (Ichiban, 1991, prod. Dave Faulkner) which sounds like it was recorded in the middle of sweaty concert ecstasy.

what to buy next: *Laboratory of Sound* (Ichiban, 1995, prod. Steve Albini) also rises above typical Fleshtones fare with the band's most mature songwriting efforts to date.

what to avoid: *Blast Off* (RIOR/Danceteria, 1982, prod. Various) is a collection of early material, much of it taken from low-quality audio cassettes. For fans only.

the rest: *Up Front* (I.R.S., 1980) *Roman Gods* (I.R.S., 1981) *Hexbreaker* (I.R.S., 1983) *Speed Connection 1: Live In Paris* (I.R.S., 1985) *Speed Connection II: The Final Chapter* (I.R.S., 1985) *Time Bomb-Big Band Theory* (compilation of side projects) (Skyclad, 1988) *Living Legends* (I.R.S., 1989) *Angry Years '84-86* (Impossible Records, 1993)

worth searching for: The out-of-print *Fleshtones Vs. Reality* (Emergo, 1987, prod. James Ball and The Fleshtones) is arguably the band's finest recorded moment.

solo outings:

Keith Streng (with Full Time Men): *Your Face My Fist* (Coyote/Twin/Tone, 1988)

Peter Zaremba (with Love Delegation): *Spread The Word* (Celluloid/Moving Target, 1986) *Delegation Time* (Accord, 1988)

Green Day, The Mighty Mighty Bosstones, the Dead Milkmen

Zombies, The Monks, Dick Dale, The Dictators

Jill Hamilton

Flo & Eddie

See: The Turtles

A Flock of Seagulls

Formed 1980 in Liverpool, England

Mike Score, vocals, keyboards; Ali (Alistair) Score, drums; Paul Reynolds, guitar (1980-84); Frank Maudsley, bass; Gary Steadin, guitar (1984-87); Chris Chryssaphis, keyboards (1984-87)

With sculpted hair and lite synthesizer pluckiness, A Flock of Seagulls typified the lightweight side of the new wave craze of the early 80s. England's punk scene dissolved into congenial pop, and parents all breathed a sigh of relief when the kids started singing "I Ran" instead of "White Riot." The former was a big smash, as was the group's self titled debut (Jive, 1982, prod. Mike Howlett). Although you can actually hear the guitar lines, keyboards and contrived sci-fi imagery ("Telecommunications," "Space Age Love Song") are at the heart of the group's songs. The band scored minor hits with "Wishing" and "Nightmares" (melodic, but not too scary) from *Listen* (Jive, 1983, prod. Mike Howlett) before disbanding in 1987 (it's since gotten back together, with little impact.) *The Best of A Flock of Seagulls* (Jive, 1991, prod. Various) pulls the group's most listenable tunes into a spacey, dance-pop package.

the rest: *The Story of a Young Heart* (Jive, 1984) *Dream Come True* (Jive, 1986)

Allan Orski

Flop

Formed 1989 in Seattle, Wash.

Rusty Willoughby, guitar, vocals; Bill Campbell, guitar; Paul Schurr, bass; Nate Johnson, drums

Flop's spiky power-pop emerged in the shadow of Seattle's grunge-rock scene; while Nirvana meshed similar influences with a noisier attack and angst-ridden worldview and other Seattleites looked to 70s arena rock for inspiration, the Flopsters paired a sly, sarcastic outlook with a punk-pop that owes much to English bands from The Kinks to the Buzzcocks. The quartet came together with refugees from bands such as The Fastbacks and Pure Joy; after releasing some indie singles the band released its debut album, *Flop & the Fall of the Mopsqueezer,* (Frontier, 1992, prod. Karl Bloch) still the best showcase of Flop's perverse but irresistible pop-punk. The debut earned them a substantial cult following—and the presence of Seattle rock superstars at their shows—but the group has failed to gain a larger audience since. Nonetheless, Flop's infectious attack and cheeky absurdism deserve a listen.

the rest: *Whenever You're Ready* (Frontier/550/Epic, 1993) *World of Today* (Frontier, 1995)

Simon Glickman

The Fluid

Formed 1985, Denver, Colo. Disbanded 1994.

John Robinson, vocals; James Clower, guitar and vocals; Richard Kulwicki, vocals and guitar; Matt Bischoff, vocals and bass; Garrett Shavlik, drums

Plagued with poor producers and bad business advisors, the Fluid narrowly missed being the right grungey punk band at the right time. They recorded several terrific early singles for Sub Pop Records—the Seattle label that launched Nirvana and Soundgarden—but never gained enough momentum to gain success outside of Denver or Seattle. Their live shows were spectacular, with Robinson wearing lacy undergarments and commanding center stage like Iggy Pop, while the rest of the band skated through its loud-guitar punk music with charisma and confidence. They recorded one album for Hollywood Records, which went nowhere, and they broke up shortly after that.

what to buy: *Glue/Roadmouth* (Sub Pop, 1990, prod. Butch Vig (*Glue*), Jack Endino and the Fluid (*Roadmouth*)) collects two raw, wonderful albums of sloppy guitar muscle and great melodies that, when it peaks—on "Girl Bomb"and the Troggs' "Our Love Will Still Be There"—collides the Monkees against Slayer.

what to buy next: *Purplemetalflakemusic* (Hollywood, 1993, prod. Mike Bosley and the Fluid) is uneven, but has "Mister Blameshifter," "On My Fee" and "My Kind," which are almost at the level of the Fluid's early rivals/friends Nirvana.

what to avoid: The debut, *Punch n Judy* (Rayon Records, 1986) is boring, derivative and, fortunately, hard to find in stores.

the rest: *Clear Black Paper* (Sub Pop, 1988)

worth searching for: *The Grunge Years,* (Sub Pop, 1991, prod. Various) a compilation that stacks the Fluid's "Tomorrow" with early songs by Babes in Toyland, Afghan Whigs, Screaming Trees, L7, Love Battery and, of course, Nirvana.

solo outings:

Garrett Shavlik (with Spell): Mississippi (Island, 1994)

▶▶ Nirvana, L7, Baldo Rex

◀◀ Iggy Pop, MC5, Troggs, David Bowie, Sex Pistols

Steve Knopper

Flying Burrito Brothers

Formed 1968 in Los Angeles, Calif.

Gram Parsons, vocals, guitar (1968-1970), Chris Hillman, vocals, guitar, bass (1968-72); Chris Etheridge, bass (1968-75); "Sneaky" Pete Kleinow, steel guitar (1968-71, 1974-present); Michael Clarke, drums, harmonica (1969-72); Bernie Leadon, guitar, banjo, dobro, vocals (1969-71); Rick Roberts, guitar, vocals (1970-73); Al Perkins, pedal steel (1971-72); Byron Berline, fiddle (1971-73); Roger Bush, bass (1971-73); Kenny Wertz, guitar (1971-73); Al Munde, banjo, guitar (1972-73); Don Beck, pedal steel (1972-73); Erik Dalton, drums (1972-73); John Beland, guitar (1981—present); Joe Scott Hill, bass, vocals (1974-present); Floyd "Gib" Gilbeau, fiddle, guitar, vocals (1974-present); Gene Parsons, drums, (1974-present); Skip Battin, bass, (1976-present); Ed Ponder, drums; Jim Goodall (1985-88)

Formed by ex-Byrds Chris Hillman and Gram Parsons, the Flying Burrito Brothers are generally considered a transition period for Gram Parsons between the Byrds and his solo work. But the group, arguably first to play what's now considered country-rock, still performs despite the absence of the two founders. During the early 80s, a version of the group relocated to Nashville and released a series of moderately successful country singles as the Flying Burrito Brothers and simply the Burrito Brothers (the biggest of which, "She Belongs to Everyone but Me," reached #16 in 1981). A group including Sneaky Pete, Skip Battin, Greg Harris and Jim Goodall also recorded as the Flying Brothers.

what to buy: *The Gilded Palace of Sin* (A&M, 1969, prod. The Flying Burrito Brothers, Larry Marks and Henry Lewy) was a grand experiment that fused notions of country music, California hippie rock and Southern soul. Parsons and Hillman were writing some of their best songs—among them "Sin City" (later cut by Dwight Yoakam) and "Hot Burrito #1" (covered by Elvis Costello)—and also covered Muscle Shoals classics "Do Right Woman" and "Dark End of the Street." For a thorough overview, *Farther Along: The Best of the Flying Burrito Brothers* (A&M, 1988, prod. Various) contains 21 cuts, including nine from "The Gilded Palace of Sin" and some rare outtakes.

what to buy next: Not quite the groundbreaker that *The Gilded Palace of Sin* was, *Burrito Deluxe* (A&M/Edsel, 1970, prod. Jim Dickson and Henry Lewy) nevertheless offered some fine moments in the same vein. It also contains the Burritos' version of "Wild Horses," which Mick Jagger and Keith Richards allegedly wrote for Parsons (according to the same legend, he re-arranged "Honky Tonk Woman" as "Country Honk" for the Rolling Stones).

what to avoid: The quality of the band's recordings took a sharp drop after Parsons left, so all but the most die-hard fans could live without anything recorded after the group left A&M. Be especially wary of *Eye of a Hurricane*, (One Way, 1994) a European-only release that finds the band a shell of its former self.

the rest: *The Flying Burrito Bros.* (A&M/Mobile Fidelity Sound Lab Recordings, 1971) *Airborne* (Columbia, 1976) *Flying Again* (Columbia, 1975) *Close Up the Honky Tonks* (A&M, 1974) *Last of the Red Hot Burritos* (A&M/Rebound, 1972) *Sleepless Nights* (A&M, 1976) *From Another Time* (Shiloh, 1976) *Back to the Sweethearts of the Rodeo* (Appaloosa, 1987) *Cabin Fever* (Relix, 1989) *Close Encounters to the West Coast* (Relix) *Hollywood Nights 1979-'82* (Sundown/Magnum) *Live From Europe* (Relix, 1986) *Sin City* (Relix) *Relix Records Best of the Flying Burrito Brothers* (Relix)

worth searching for: *Dim Lights, Thick Smoke and Loud, Loud Music* (Edsel, 1993)

solo outings:

Chris Hillman: Morning Sky (Sugar Hill, 1982) *Desert Rose* (Sugar Hill, 1984) (with the Desert Rose Band): *The Desert Rose Band* (Curb, 1987) *Running* (Curb, 1988) *Pages of Life* (Curb, 1990) *A Dozen Roses: The Best of* (Curb, 1991) *True Love* (Curb, 1991)

The Eagles, Gram Parsons, Desert Rose Band, Jayhawks, Uncle Tupelo, Wilco, Son Volt

The Byrds, Hank Williams, Memphis/Muscle Shoals soul

see also: *The Byrds, Gram Parsons*

Brian Mansfield

Dan Fogelberg

Born Aug. 13, 1951, in Peoria, Ill.

Fogelberg was raised in the Midwest, rose to prominence on the West Coast amidst Southern California's burgeoning folk-rock singer-songwriter scene of the early 70s, and ended up in Boulder, Colo.—a fitting final destination for "a quiet man of music," to borrow one of his better-known lyrics. He dropped out of art school at the University of Illinois in 1971 and moved to Los Angeles to try his hand at a music career; he earned a deal with Columbia (eventually settling on the CBS subsidiary Full Moon/Epic). On his early records, he was backed by the likes of Joe Walsh, Russ Kunkel, Graham Nash and Al Perkins; as his career progressed, his music veered away from the West Coast's country-pop stylings and more toward an unlikely mix of sentimental ballads and atmospheric prog-rock. The ballads are what eventually made him famous, likely on the strength of Fogelberg's distinctive high-tenor voice. He became a staple of adult-contemporary radio stations during the late 70s and early 80s with hits such as "Longer" and "Leader of the Band." Since the mid-80s, Fogelberg has shown an increasing and generally healthy willingness to experiment with other styles—sometimes with refreshing results such as 1985's bluegrass-oriented *High Country Snows*, other times less successfully (1993's world-music influenced *River of Souls*).

what to buy: Even after a quarter-century and more than a dozen albums, Fogelberg's debut, *Home Free*, (Columbia, 1972, prod. Norbert Putnam) still stands as his best work—simply because it's so unaffected by the more commercial considerations of his subsequent efforts. Songs such as "To the Morning" and "Hickory Grove" capture the innocence of his Illinois youth at an early enough stage in his career that he could still feel it pulling on him. Ironically, he seemed about as far removed from those roots as possible when he released *The Innocent Age*, (Full Moon/Epic, 1981, prod. Dan Fogelberg) 𝄞𝄞𝄞½ the most ambitious project of his career. The two-record song-cycle, released at the peak of his mainstream popularity, could easily have been a pompous and pretentious disaster (and, at times, it hints at that). But it succeeds, as its title suggests, because of its earnest attempt to recapture lost innocence—the same spirit that made *Home Free* such a treasure, only this time through the distorted reflection of a decade-long rearview mirror. If you care less about albums as entities unto themselves and more about just getting the hits, try *Greetings from the West*, (Full Moon/Epic, 1991, prod. Dan Fogelberg) 𝄞𝄞𝄞½ a live album recorded at the Fox Theater in St. Louis that includes most of his best-known songs (Sony Music Video also released a video of the concert).

what to buy next: A couple of Fogelberg's earlier albums — *Souvenirs* (Full Moon/Epic, 1974, prod. Joe Walsh) 𝄞𝄞𝄞 and *Nether Lands* (Full Moon/Epic, 1977, prod. Dan Fogelberg and Norbert Putnam) 𝄞𝄞𝄞—have their moments of fine songcraft that predate his gradual slide into schlockdom. And *High Country Snows* (Full Moon/Epic, 1985, prod. Dan Fogelberg and Marty Lewis) 𝄞𝄞𝄞 was a welcome venture into bluegrass, with guest appearances by the likes of Doc Watson, David Grisman, Chris Hillman and Herb Pedersen. For a straightforward, non-live collection of chart successes, *Greatest Hits* (Full Moon/Epic, 1982, prod. Various) 𝄞𝄞𝄞 is a serviceable document, despite its revealingly yuppified cover photo.

what to avoid: *Windows and Walls* (Full Moon/Epic, 1984, prod. Dan Fogelberg) 𝄞 represents the depths of Fogelberg's shallowness; hardly a song here is even worth hearing. *Love Songs* (Full Moon/Epic, 1995, prod. Various) 𝄞½ isn't so much bad as it is unnecessary, an apparent attempt by the label to rehash Fogelberg's hits one more time after he'd moved on to a different record company.

the rest: *Captured Angel* (Full Moon/Epic, 1975) 𝄞𝄞½ *Phoenix* (Full Moon/Epic, 1979) 𝄞𝄞 *Exiles* (Full Moon/Epic, 1987) 𝄞½ *The Wild Places* (Full Moon/Epic, 1990) 𝄞𝄞½ *River of Souls* (Full Moon/Epic, 1993) 𝄞𝄞 (with Tim Weisberg): *Twin Sons of Different Mothers* (Full Moon/Epic, 1978) 𝄞𝄞 *No Resemblance Whatsoever* (Giant, 1995) 𝄞𝄞

▶▶ Dan Hill, David Wilcox, James McMurtry

◀◀ Bruce Cockburn, James Taylor, Jackson Browne, the Cascades

Peter Blackstock

John Fogerty

Born May 28, 1945 in Berkeley, Calif.

Since Creedence Clearwater Revival's 1972 breakup, Fogerty has led a frustrating solo career, plagued by crippling writer's block and labyrinthine lawsuits. His 1985 No. 1 comeback album, *Centerfield*, was nothing less than a personal triumph over haunting demons. But his first solo outing was a recreation of classic country and western standards, with Fogerty playing all the instruments himself under the pseudonym Blue Ridge Rangers. His first authentic solo album returned to the Creedence sound, but with only modest success. A second "proper" solo album was delayed for nine years, until *Centerfield* came, seemingly out of nowhere, with the hit, "Old Man Down the Road." That was a success Fogerty's subsequent solo album did not duplicate. He remains a fussy, intense craftsman with an unparalleled flair for treating classic themes in a timeless way—someone who could clearly turn out another landmark tomorrow.

what to buy: *Centerfield* (Warner Bros., 1985, prod. John Fogerty) 𝄞𝄞𝄞𝄞 is a jaunty celebration of Americana, shaded lightly by some dark undertones.

what to buy next: Although he didn't write a single song on the set, Fogerty's *Blue Ridge Rangers* (Fantasy, 1972, prod. John Fogerty) 𝄞𝄞𝄞½ gives country numbers from the songbooks of Merle Haggard, George Jones and others a glistening pop radio sound.

what to avoid: His *Centerfield* follow-up, *Eye of the Zombie* (Warner Bros., 1986, prod. John Fogerty) 𝄞𝄞 despite a couple of high spots, didn't really do his talents justice.

the rest: *John Fogerty* (Asylum 1975) 𝄞𝄞½

worth searching for: A couple of his Warner Brothers singles contain highly worthy non-LP B-sides, especially his rollicking take on the zydeco hit, "My Toot Toot" on the flip of "Change In the Weather" (Warner Bros., 1985, prod. John Fogerty).

▶▶ Dave Edmunds, Southern Culture On the Skids

◀◀ Creedence Clearwater, Dave Edmunds

Joel Selvin

Foghat

Formed 1971 in London, England

"Lonesome" Dave Peverett, vocals, guitar (1971-84, 1993-present); Rod Price, guitar (1971-80, 1993-present); Tony Stevens, bass (1971-73, 1993-present); Roger Earl, drums (1971-84, 1993-present); Nick Jameson, bass, keyboards (1973-75); Craig MacGregor, bass (1975-84); Erik Cartwright, guitar (1980-84)

Formed by Savoy Brown refugees Peverett, Stevens and Earl, Foghat dished up a basic, straightforward brand of blues-oriented boogie, both in its own crunchy originals and in revved-up covers oldies such as "Maybelline," "Sweet Home Chicago" and its first big it, Willie Dixon's "I just Want to Make Love to You." Foghat was blessed with good producers (Dave Edmunds, Dan Hartman), and Earl's slide guitar work helped raise Foghat's music above the pedestrian. The group's zenith—artistic and commercial—with the 1975 album, *Fool for the City,* which contained the hit "Slow Ride." But this kind of stuff gets old fast, and by the late 70s Foghat had become an also-ran. It broke up during the early 80s, but the original foursome regrouped in 1993 to mine the classic rock oldies circuit.

what to buy: *The Best of Foghat* (Bearsville/Rhino, 1989, prod. Various) and *The Best of Foghat, Volume 2" (Bearsville/Rhino, 1992, prod. Various)* are fine samplers of Foghat's output. The former has all the hits, while the latter dishes up worthwhile album tracks such as "Step Outside."

what to buy next: *Fool For the City* (Bearsville, 1975, prod. Nick Jameson) is Foghat's best album and houses hits in the funk-rocker "Slow Ride" and the driving title track. Its successor, *Night Shift,* (Bearsville, 1976, prod. Dan Hartman) doesn't have hits but is a consistent serving of meat and potatoes hard rock.

what to avoid: *Zig-Zag Walk* (Bearsville, 1983, prod. Nick Jameson) WOOF! proved beyond a doubt that Foghat had overstayed its welcome on the scene.

the rest: *Foghat* (Bearsville, 1972) *Foghat* (aka *Rock and Roll*) (Bearsville, 1973) *Energized* (Bearsville, 1974) *Rock and Roll Outlaws* (Bearsville, 1974) *Live* (Bearsville, 1977) *Stone Blue* Bearsville, 1978) *Boogie Motel* (Bearsville, 1979) *Tight Shoes* (Bearsville, 1980) *Girls to Chat and Boys to Bounce* (Bearsville, 1981) *In the Mood for Something Rude* (Bearsville, 1982)

Georgia Satellites, Brother Cane, Badlands, Black Crowes, Lenny Kravitz, Pearl Jam

Savoy Brown, Fleetwood Mac, Rolling Stones, John Mayall's Bluesbreakers, Chuck Berry, Howlin' Wolf, Willie Dixon, John Lee Hooker

see also: *Savoy Brown*

Gary Graff

Wayne Fontana & the Mindbenders

Formed 1963 in Manchester, England

Wayne Fontana (born Glynn Geoffrey Ellis), vocals: Eric Stewart, guitar; Bob Lang, bass; Ric Rothwell, drums

For solid, straightforward, meat 'n' potatoes British Beat, one need look no further than the Mindbenders: for what these guys may have lacked in the songwriting department, the group more than made up for with loads of good, old-fashioned panache and exuberance. It was at a 1963 audition in Manchester's Oasis club that Ellis' band the Jets was discovered by Philips Records and brought to London to record—but not before Glynn was renamed Wayne Fontana by a rep from, you guessed it, Philips' Fontana division. The group first entered the U.K. charts in 1964 with a cover of Major Lance's "Um, Um, Um, Um, Um, Um," and within a year had a worldwide hit with the infectious "Game Of Love." Soon afterward Fontana left to pursue a solo career (his only minor hit being "Pamela, Pamela") while the Mindbenders, as a three-piece, soon scored another transatlantic smash with "A Groovy Kind Of Love," a song so durable it withstood a 1988 cover by Phil Collins. After appearing with Lulu in the film "To Sir With Love," the Mindbenders recruited songwriter-extrodinaire ("For Your Love," "Bus Stop") Graham Gouldman in 1967, who remained with the group for two years until he and Eric Stewart left to form the incredible Hotlegs ("Neanderthal Man") and then 10cc. To this day, however, Wayne Fontana can still be found touring the European cabaret circuit with pickup groups of Mindbenders. *The Best Of Wayne Fontana and the Mindbenders* (Fontana, 1994, prod. Various) features all the hits, all the shoulda-beens ("It's Just A Little Bit Too Late" and the wistful "Ashes To Ashes") and even the song Sidney Poitier valiantly tried to frug to in "To Sir With Love." It's also worth searching for the group's debut, *Wayne Fontana and the Mindbenders* (Fontana, 1965) which, like the first Beatles and Stones albums, provides a perfect, rock-hard snapshot of a group of kids with brand new guitars and electricity to burn.

Gary Pig Gold

For Against

Formed 1984 in Lincoln, Neb.

Jeffrey Runnings, bass, guitar, vocals; Harry Dingman, guitar (1984-89); Steven "Mave" Hinrichs, guitar (1990-present); Jeff Gaskins, bass (1989-91); Greg Hill drums (1984-89); Steve Schultz drums (1989-91); Paul Engelhard drums (1991-present)

For Against has long suffered in relative obscurity despite releasing four fine, very different albums—records well appreciated by those who've heard them, but sadly, too few have. Part of the problem is geography; it's hard to get noticed when you hail from Nebraska. The rest has been bad luck, lack of resources, poor timing and the crime of making independent-minded atmospheric, aggressive pop when the U.S. market wants punk and grunge. After an early self-released single "Autocrat" drew the attention of Independent Projects Records, For Against released two albums, 1987's *Echelons* and 1988's *December* with its original lineup before the personnel changes began. The results since have been even more impressive, with some of the most inwardly affecting music made so far in the 90s, as the group presses on through its second decade undeterred so far by their lack of commercial success. In particular, few write more soul-searching lyrics without a trace of self-indulgence than the melancholic-voiced Runnings, who's been known to reduce some of the fans the band has managed to garner to actual tears with his more recent work.

what to buy: *Mason's California Lunchroom* (Rainbow Quartz Records, 1994, prod. For Against with Tom Ware) ♪♪♪♪♪ may be the arrival at the place Runnings's always envisioned in his head. This is one of those rare LPs that combines an attack-oriented, post-punk rhythm section on half the songs (such gassed burners as the standout, "Tagalong," plus "Seesick," "Crossed," "Coursing" and "Reinventing the Wheel") with some surprisingly beautiful guitar playing. Hinrichs spits out a variety of tones, alternately biting, shimmering, ringing, distorting and flanging, a one-man tour de force. And on the slower stuff, such as "Blow," "Vacuum," and especially the moving, vulnerable "Hindsight," the overall mood is gentle, poignantly fragile, evocative and spellbinding.

what to buy next: *Aperture* (Rainbow Quartz Records, 1992, prod. For Against and Randy Watson) ♪♪♪♪ is more patchwork but still convincing. "Today Today" is as startling as "Hindsight" in its harrowing melancholy, and there are plenty more insidious melodies and sonorous bangers such as "Mindframed" and the single "Don't Do Me any Favors." For those who want a more dense and complicated thrill ride, *December* (Independent Projects Records, 1988, prod. For Against and Randy Watson) ♪♪♪♪ is a claustrophobic but enveloping guitar record with occasional, curious neo-reggae rhythms undercutting the solid punch of post-punk pop in "Stranded in Greenland," "Clandestine High Holy" and "The Last Laugh," astride the moody title track, and the introspective "The Effect."

what to avoid: A 10-inch vinyl only mini-LP of the groups's pre-first album days called "In the Marshes" (Independent Projects Records, 1990, prod. For Against) ♪♪♪ is the least of their works, though if one has already procured and dug all four albums, this more early-4AD side of the group as a studio project of sorts—complete with drum machine—is occasionally fascinating, particularly the relentless, hypnotic "Purgatory Salesman" and "Amnesia."

the rest: *Echelons* (Independent Projects Record, 1987) ♪♪♪♪ *Shelflife* (Independent Projects/World Domination, 1996) ♪♪♪♪

▶▶ Springhouse, Half String, Scenic

◀◀ Comsat Angels, Lowlife, Joy Division

Jack Rabid

For Squirrels

Formed: 1993 in Gainesville, Fla.

John Francis Vigliatura, IV, vocals (d. Sept. 8, 1995); Travis Michael Tooke, guitar; William Richard White, bass (d. Sept. 8, 1995); Thomas Jacob Griego, Jr., drums

Few things are sadder in music than a promising career that is cut short before it is allowed to really begin. That is the sorrowful legacy of For Squirrels, a promising Gainesville, Florida, band that was about to release its major label debut when its tour van blew a tire, causing vocalist Jack Vigliatura, who was driving, to lose control of the vehicle. It flipped over, killing Vigliatura, bassist Bill White and tour manager Tim Bender. The group's first two releases, *Bay Path Road* (self-released, 1994, prod. For Squirrels) ♪♪ and *Plymouth EP* (Y&T, 1994, prod. For Squirrels) ♪♪ which are fairly derivative of R.E.M. jangle-rock, but *Example* (550/Epic, 1995, prod. Nick Launay) ♪♪♪ proved that they were on the verge of transcending their influences (including other obvious reference points such as Live's dramatic tension and release, and Soul Asylum's punky garage pop) and truly coming into their own. "8.02 PM" and "Long Live the King," for example thrash about impressively "Superstar" is a triumphant anthem, and "Under Smithville" and "Mighty K.C."

are ringing, melodic, power pop. Following the accident, guitarist Tooke and drummer Griego vowed to carry on, but in what form and with whom in place of Vigliatura and White, remains to be seen.

Daniel Durchholz

Steve Forbert

Born 1955 in Meridian, Miss.

Already saddled with the "New Dylan" tag because of his raspy voice and guitar-harmonica accompaniment, Forbert debuted in 1978 with *Alive on Arrival*, a charming concept album celebrating his country-boy-moves-to-the-Big-Apple dreams. His proclamations of peach-fuzzed optimism were so earnest and life-affirming that the scores of critics who adopted him as their folk-rock Peter Pan didn't want him to ever grow up. Forbert managed to score one hit single, 1980's "Romeo's Tune," and send a not-so-subtle declaration of maturity via the snide title of his 1980 album, *Little Stevie Orbit*, before a six-year feud with Columbia Records kept him out of the record stores. Forbert re-emerged on Geffen Records—older, wiser and, no surprise, much more cynical. But like John Hiatt's recent work, such albums as *Mission of the Crossroad Palms* and *The American In Me* are short on dreams but still full of hope, the work of a battle-scarred veteran who is learning to adapt his idealistic beliefs to the daunting pressures of adulthood.

what to buy: *Alive on Arrival* (Nemperor, 1978, prod. Steve Burgh) remains a joyful testament to youthful idealism, thanks to such timeless songs as "Goin' Down to Laurel," "Steve Forbert's Midsummer Night's Toast" and "What Kinda Guy?" *Little Stevie Orbit* (Nemperor, 1980, prod. Pete Solley) ushers in the harder-rocking, more-mature Forbert with "Get Well Soon," "If You Gotta Ask, You'll Never Know" and the gorgeous "Song For Katrina." *Steve Forbert* (Nemperor, 1982, prod. Steve Burgh) is an unjustly forgotten album that features the rousing "Ya Ya (Next to Me)" and his funniest song, "He's Gotta Live Up to His Shoes." *The American in Me* (Geffen, 1992, prod. Pete Anderson) is the grown-up bookend to *Alive on Arrival*, using the reflection and self-doubt of "You Cannot Win 'Em All" and "Responsibility" as tools for resilience, not resignation.

what to buy next: Forbert's 1982 tour with his road band, the Flying Squirrels (anchored by future Shawn Colvin/Rosanne Cash producer John Leventhal), produced his most memorable rock 'n' roll-driven shows. *King Biscuit Flower Hour Presents* (KBFH/BMG, 1996) captures a fiery set at Long Island's My Father's Place, mixing his best-known material with convincing romps through Chuck Berry's "Too Much Monkey Business," the Searchers' "When You Walk in the Room" and a lovely reading of the Troggs' "Love Is All Around."

what to avoid: *Jackrabbit Slim* (Nemperor, 1979, prod. John Simon) spawned his hit, "Romeo's Tune," but compared to the rest of his catalog, the horn-driven, string-drenched production now sounds more syrupy than soulful.

the rest: *Streets of This Town* (Geffen, 1988) *What Kinda Guy: The Best of Steve Forbert* (Epic/Legacy, 1993) *Mission of the Crossroad Palms* (Giant, 1995)

worth searching for: *Arriving Live* (Nemperor, 1978) a promotional EP with live versions of "You Cannot Win If You Do Not Play," "Steve Forbert's Midsummer Night's Toast" and the unreleased "Steve Forbert's Moon River."

▶▶ Michael McDermott, Joe Henry, Will T. Massey

◀◀ Jimmie Rodgers, Bob Dylan, Chuck Berry

David Okamoto

Lita Ford

Born Rosanna Ford, Sept. 23, 1959 in London, England

Without the inherent pop sense of her Runaways mate Joan Jett, Ford has languished as something of a token metal pin-up, as much a precursor to the riot grrrl groups as Jett but not quite as durable. She does enjoy the distinctions of being the first woman to appear on the cover of Hit Parader and the first woman inducted into Circus magazine's Hall of Fame in 20 years—as well as a member of the house band for comedian Howie Mandel's "Howie" on CBS. That can probably carry you through a lot of world's great hard rock dive clubs.

what to buy: *Lita* (RCA, 1988, prod. Mike Chapman) has everything Ford has to offer—including her hits "Kiss Me Deadly" and "Close My Eyes" (with Ozzy Osbourne), as well as a songwriting collaboration with Motorhead's Lemmy Kilmister on "Can't Catch Me."

what to buy next: *Greatest Hits* (RCA, 1993, prod. Various) and *The Best of Lita Ford* (RCA, 1992, prod. Various) each do an adequate job of winnowing the best of Ford's output.

what to avoid: Ford's first couple of solo albums—*Out for Blood* (Mercury, 1983/1990, prod. Neil Merryweather) and

Dancin' on the Edge (Mercury, 1983/1990, prod. Lance Quinn) WOOF!— make the Runaways sound like the Beatles.

the rest: *Stiletto* (RCA, 1990) *Dangerous Curves* (RCA, 1991) *Black* (ZYX, 1995)

L7, 7 Year Bitch, Hole

Jimi Hendrix, Suzi Quatro, Black Sabbath, Motorhead, Slade

Gary Graff

Julia Fordham

Born Aug. 10, 1962, Portsmouth, Hampshire, England

Is Fordham a jazz, pop or folk singer? In truth, she's all three, which makes her one of those artists with considerable talent who fall between the cracks of regimented radio formats. Possessed of a rich contralto voice that at time is reminiscent of jazz diva Nina Simone, Fordham rose through the ranks, singing backup for Mari Wilson and Kim Wilde. She's been a songwriter since her teens, and her experience is plainly in evidence on her four albums; for though her songs tend focus mostly on lost love, the situations never repeat themselves, and Fordham injects surprising insights and pathos into each of them. Still, it's understandable that some listeners find her a bit of a cold fish, mostly due to the studied, every-hair-in-place production of her first three albums. *Porcelain* (Virgin, 1989, prod. Grant Mitchell and Hugh Padgham) is the exception, an adult-contemporary and VH-1 favorite thanks to the exquisite title track, the gentle Latin rhythms of "Genius" and the lyrically compelling "Girlfriend." *Falling Forward* (Virgin, 1994, prod. Larry Klein and Julia Fordham) benefits from slightly less restrained performances that show off the extraordinary range and expressiveness of Fordham's voice.

the rest: *Julia Fordham* (Virgin, 1988) *Swept* (Virgin, 1991)

Daniel Durchholz

Foreigner

Formed 1976 in New York, N.Y.

Mick Jones, guitar, vocals; Lou Gramm (born Louis Grammatico), vocals (1976-90, 1992-present); Ian McDonald, flute, keyboards, reeds, guitar and vocals (1976-80); Al Greenwood, keyboards, synthesizers (1976-80); Ed Gagliardi, bass (1976-79); Dennis Elliot, drums (1976-92); Rick Wills, bass (1979-92); Johnny Edwards, vocals (1990-92); Mark Schulman, drums (1994-present); Jeff Jacobs, keyboards (1994-present); Bruce Turgon, bass (1994-present)

One of the most successful purveyors of Album Oriented Rock sounds during the 70s and 80s, Foreigner started as a project organized by ex-Spooky Tooth and Leslie West guitarist Jones. Stumbling on ex-King Crimson keyboardist Ian McDonald, Jones handpicked the other members for his group—including a little-known singer named Lou Grammatico, then fronting a New York cover band. Foreigners 1977 debut sold more than 4 million copies on the strength of Jones' power pop arrangements and Gramm's incendiary pop-metal vocals. The hits kept coming through the 80s—from the keyboard-drenched "Cold As Ice" to the rocker "Dirty" to the majestic ballad "I Want to Know What Love Is." Jones streamlined the band as time went on—including a two-year split with Gramm, who tried his hand at a solo career. Foreigner continues to release albums, but its greatest success these days is on the summer oldies circuit.

what to buy: A band like Foreigner is all about hits, so it makes sense that its best album would be *The Very Best...And Beyond.* (Atlantic, 1992, prod. Various) From 70s rock hits like "Hot Blooded" and "Head Games" to the band's mellower 80s smashes such as "Waiting For a Girl Like You' and "I Want To Know What Love Is," this offers the most complete chronicle of the group's prolonged classic rock dominance—though a few flaccid new tunes don't make much of a case for its future.

what to buy next: For a taste of the band's status as sorta-metal, sorta classic rockers, try the sophomore album, *Double Vision.* (Atlantic, 1978, prod. Mick Jones, Ian McDonald and Keith Olsen) Fortified with hits such as "Blue Morning, Blue Day" and the title track, it's a prototypical 70s arena rock album. If the group's crafted, pop-oriented material is more your style, then *4* (Atlantic, 1981, prod. Mick Jones and John "Mutt" Lange) dishes up slick hits such as "Waiting For a Girl Like You" and the anthemic "Jukebox Hero."

what to avoid: The worn-out performances filling its only live record, *Classic Hits Live* (Atlantic, 1993, prod. Bud Prager) WOOF! serve as ample evidence that Foreigner is but a hair's breadth away from opening for the Beach Boys or Chicago on the VH1 nostalgia circuit.

the rest: *Foreigner* (Atlantic, 1977) *Head Games* (Atlantic, 1979) *Records* (Atlantic, 1982) *Agent Provocateur* (Atlantic, 1984) *Inside Information* (Atlantic, 1987) *Unusual Heat* (Atlantic, 1991) *Mr. Moonlight* (Rhythm Safari, 1994)

Eight Essential 80s Collections

VH-1: The Big 80s
(Rhino)

Get Into the Greed: 80s Hits
(Risky Business)

Sedated in the 80s, Vol. 1-4
(Capitol)

New Wave Hits, Vol. 5-15
(Rhino)

Living in Oblivion, Vol. 1-5
(EMI)

Def Jam Box
(Def Jam)

Youth Gone Wild, Vol. 1-3
(Rhino)

Valley Girl Soundtrack
(Rhino)

solo outings:

***Lou Gramm:** Ready or Not* (Atlantic, 1987) *Foreigner in a Strange Land* (Collectables, 1988) *Long Hard Look* (Atlantic, 1989)

***Mick Jones:** Mick Jones* (Atlantic, 1989)

worth searching for: *Foreigner Profiled!* (Atlantic, 1991) is a promotion-only interview disc that's amusing in hindsight for its declarations that short-time singer Edwards was the future of Foreigner.

⏩ Cutting Crew, Survivor, Loverboy

⏪ The Shadows, Elton John, Spooky Tooth, Mountain, Jefferson Airplane

Eric Deggans

Robert Forster

See: The Go-Betweens

Foster and Lloyd

Formed 1987 in Nashville, Tenn. Disbanded in 1992.

Radney Foster (born July 20, 1959 in Del Rio, Texas), vocals, guitar; Bill Lloyd (born Dec. 6, 1955, in Bowling Green, Ky.) vocals, guitar

Foster and Lloyd's run was short-lived but of high quality. They specialized in country-tinged romantic angst cut with a healthy dose of wry detachment. Listening to the three albums they made together summons up wistful memories of one of those heady five-minute timeouts in Nashville (in this case, post-Barbara Mandrell, pre-Garth Brooks) when it seemed as if off-center artists might possibly find a niche. Lyle Lovett, Dwight Yoakam and Steve Earle were shaking things up, and Rosanne Cash hadn't yet fled to New York. Out of this interesting atmosphere came Foster and Lloyd and the O'Kanes—sharp-eyed songwriting teams who turned to performing with the blessing, and creative license, of major recording labels.

Foster, a lawyer's son, and Lloyd, an army brat and communications major, didn't fit the traditional country-act mold, coveting greater pop and rock influences than Nashville tolerated at the time. They were, however, writers of hit songs for the likes of the Sweethearts of the Rodeo and Holly Dunn, which gave them strong potential as a recording act. *Foster and Lloyd* (RCA, 1987, prod. Radney Foster and Bill Lloyd) is a charmer—deft songwriting, tight arrangements, enough rockabilly backbeat to keep things hopping and enough engaging harmony to keep things down-home. The pleading "Don't Go Out with Him," for instance, almost sounds like something the Ronettes could have sung.

The duo's other releases—*Faster and Llouder* (RCA, 1989, prod. Radney Foster, Bill Lloyd and Rick Will) and *Version of the Truth* (RCA, 1990, prod. Radney Foster, Bill Lloyd and Rick Will) —weren't quite as good but were still compelling. After the duo split, Foster followed a more traditional country path, while Lloyd kept a foot (or more) in pop with *Set to Pop*, (ESD, 1994, prod. Bill Lloyd) which features guest appearances by Marshall Crenshaw, Al Kooper and Big Star's Jody Stephens.

Elizabeth Lynch

Fotheringay

See: Fairport Convention

The Foundations

Formed 1967 in London, England. Disbanded 1970.

Clem Curtis, vocals (1967-68); Colin Young, vocals (1969-70); Allan Warner, guitar, vocals; Peter Macbeth, bass; Tim Harris, drums; Tony Gomez, organ; Pat Burke, tenor sax; Mike Elliott, tenor sax; Eric Allandale, trombone

Predating such racially integrated British groups as the Specials and the English Beat, the Foundations combined three white Londoners, two Jamaicans, a Trinidadian, a Dominican and a Ceylonese for a brief but successful foray into R&B-pop. Britain had been importing soul acts for years, but the Foundations marked one of the first home-grown outfits. The group was signed to Pye Records by Tony Macauley, who basically ordered it to sing and play his songs. With Curtis on vocals, the Foundations enjoyed a string of U.K. hits beginning with the Motown-influenced "Baby, Now That I've Found You," a No. 1 record in England. Young sang the group's U.S. smash, "Build Me Up, Buttercup," a feisty soul-pop record that demonstrated an excellent balance of organ, brass and call-and-response vocals. *The Very Best of the Foundations* (Taragon, prod. Various) is a worthy compilation of the group's upbeat and uptempo tunes that should appeal to fans of such later British acts as the English Beat, Fine Young Cannibals and General Public.

Christopher Scapelliti

Four Seasons /Frankie Valli

Formed as the Four Lovers, 1956 in Newark, N.J. Disbanded 1974. Reformed 1980.

Frankie Valli, vocals; Tommy Devito, guitar (1956-70); Nick Devito, guitar (1956-60); Hank Majewski, bass, (1956-60); Bob Gaudio, keyboards (1960-74); Nick Massi, bass (1960-65); others

Spanning 40 years and more than 100 million record sales, the Four Seasons are the longest surviving and most successful doo-wop ever. The main focus has always been Valli and his soaring three-octave tenor, which shifts with frightening ease. Hopping constantly over the years from frontman to solo performer, Valli has nearly always struck commercial gold, whether it be with the street-corner harmonies of "Sherry" or the unbearable disco dreck of "Grease." The Four Seasons has reformed countless times, (usually for the worse) but by 1976 it was still capable of something as engaging as "December 1963 (Oh What a Night)" which hit No. 1 and has re-charted with an inhuman regularity ever since—most recently as part of the soundtrack for "Forrest Gump."

what to buy: Since the band's catalogue is a virtually endless stream of repackaged collections of their greatest hits, only the most noteworthy are listed. Pinning down what to buy is maddening as every album has a gem like "Big Girls Don't Cry" and something exacerable like "Grease." *25th Anniversary,* (Rhino, 1987, prod. Various) a three-disc set, is by far the most comprehensive document of the band's output (including Valli's solo excursions) and contains virtually everything you do and don't want to hear. *Anthology* (Rhino, 1988, prod. Bill Inglot) is a more streamlined 26 track single disc that doesn't wallow too long in the disco years.

what to buy next: *Greatest Hits Vol. 1* (Rhino, 1991, prod. Bob Crewe) compacts most of the early hits like "Walk Like a Man" and "Sherry." *Greatest Hits Vol. 2* (Rhino, 1991, prod. Various) focuses more on the later material. If you must own "Swearin' to God" and "Who Loves You," this is probably the most painless of the later era compilations on the market.

what to avoid: *Dance Album* (Curb, 1993, prod. Not Listed) We could dance to the originals just fine, thank you.

the rest: *Christmas Album* (Rhino, 1967) *Working My Way Back to You and More* (Rhino, 1966) *Rarities Vol. 1* (Rhino, 1990) *Rarities Vol. 2* (Rhino, 1990)

The Beach Boys, the Beatles, Billy Joel

The Drifters, the Platters, the Penguins

Allan Orski

The Four Tops

Formed 1954 in Detroit, Mich.

Levi Stubbs; Abdul "Duke" Fakir; Lawrence Payton; Renaldo "Obie" Benson

One of Motown's two mightiest male vocal groups, the Four Tops held its power by remaining intact, while Temptations, by contrast, came and went. The gruff authority of Stubbs' voice has been a wondrous thing, celebrated in songs by other artists years later. As a group, few in Motown exemplified the real powerhouse of the label—the songwriting of Holland-Dozier-Holland and the power of the in-house band—as the Tops did. Amid a flurry of mid-60s hits, the highlight may have been "Reach Out I'll Be There," which kicked off with its heralding flutes and military drumbeats; few songs of support and solidarity have been so grippingly recorded. The group relied on its strong vocals and less on dancing, ala the Temps, with whom the Tops staged a friendly rivalry at various song "showdowns." But the Tops didn't enjoy a second run of psychedelic hits as did their Motown rivals; in fact, when Holland-Dozier-Holland left the label, so did Stubbs and company. The Tops came back quickly with a couple of quick hits in "Keeper of the Castle" and "Ain't No Woman (Like the One I've Got)" in 1972 but had little else on the pop charts afterwards. The 1990 Rock and Roll Hall of Fame inductees continue to tour—often with the Temptations—showing remarkable durability for a group consigned to the oldies circuit.

what to buy: The double-length *Anthology* (Motown, 1989, prod. Various) spans the Top's hits on Motown and other labels, showcasing the group's awesome run of hits.

what to buy next: For a more intense rush of the group's heyday, the silver-covered *Greatest Hits* (Motown, 1967/1987, prod. Holland-Dozier-Holland) is relentless. *Until You Love Someone: More of the Best* (Rhino, 1993) is worthwhile for those who want to delve deeper than the hits.

what to avoid: The group's latest, *Four Tops Christmas* (Motown, 1995, prod. Four Tops) is a lame holiday effort in which each of the members produces his own selection and nothing but a visit from Aretha Franklin helps them.

the rest: *Four Tops* (Motown, 1965) *Second Album* (Motown, 1966) *On Top* (Motown, 1966) *Live* (Motown, 1967/1991) *Four Tops Reach Out* (Motown, 1967/1983) *Yesterday's Dreams* (Motown, 1968 *Four Tops Now* (Motown, 1969) *Soul Spin* (Motown, 1969) *Still Waters Run Deep* (Motown, 1970/1982) *Changing Times* (Motown, 1970) *The Magnificent Seven* (with The Supremes) (Motown, 1970) *The Return of the Magnificent Seven* (with the Supremes) (Motown, 1971) *Dynamite* (with the Supremes) (Motown, 1972) *Nature Planned It* (Motown, 1972) *Greatest Hits (1972-76)* (MCA, 1982/1987) *Back Where I Belong* (Motown, 1983) *Great Songs* (Motown, 1983/89) *Magic* (Motown, 1985) *Ain't No Woman...* (MCA, 1987/1994) *Indestructible* (Arista, 1988) *When She Was My Girl* (Mercury, 1992) *Motown Legends* (Esx Entertainment, 1994)

worth searching for: The soundtrack for the film version of *Little Shop of Horrors,* (Geffen, 1986, prod. Bob Gaudio) which features Stubbs as the wickedly soulful voice of the man-eating plant.

▶▶ The Temptations, Darius Rucker (Hootie and the Blowfish), Boyz II Men

◀◀ The Orioles, the Drifters, the Moonglows

Roger Catlin

Samantha Fox

Born April 15, 1966, in London, England

Discovered by photographers for the Daily Sun newspaper at the tender age of 16, Fox posed topless for the British publication's notorious Page Two pinup portrait enough times to become the most popular model ever featured there. From that point, it was a short hop to a career as a producer-developed dance diva. Her debut single in 1986, "Touch Me," traded on the same trend that made sexy dance sirens such as Madonna and Taylor Dayne worldwide hits—solid grooves, sexually charged lyrics and barely-there melodies. Although that record did well, it wasn't until her album *Samantha Fox* (Jive, 1987, prod. Various) that the former model hit big, welding her sultry image to a perfectly suitable song, "Naughty Girls (Need Love Too)." Continuing her production-by-committee approach to assembling albums (15 different producers), Fox offered two more albums of new music. But since all that really mattered were the singles, a fan's best bet is her *Greatest Hits* (Jive, 1992, prod. Various) When the bottom fell out of dance pop in the early 90s, Fox's singing career went with it, though she gamely tried her hand at acting. There's always newspapers to be sold...

Eric Deggans

Peter Frampton

Born April 22, 1950 in Beckenham, England

It would have taken a certain prescience to peg Frampton as pop music's biggest superstar of the pre-*Thriller* era. Before 1976, when *Frampton Comes Alive* made him a mass market phenomenon, Frampton enjoyed a reputation as an estimable guitarist, singer and songwriter, logging moderately successful tenures with The Herd and Humble Pie. After leaving the latter in 1971, Frampton embarked on a solo career that was only modestly successful—but building—until the live album heard 'round the world. Some bad decisions followed that breakthrough, however, including the fallow follow-up ballad "I'm in You" and an ill-advised starring role in the wretched *Sgt. Pepper's Lonely Hearts Club Band* movie. Those undermined whatever cache Frampton had built for himself, and through the 80s and 90s he's mostly been the answer to a "What ever happened to...?" question. None of his periodic comebacks—including a spot in David Bowie's band during 1987 and a *Frampton Comes Alive II* release in 1995—have taken flight, and a reunion with Humble Pie mate Steve Marriott tragically crashed when Marriott died in 1991 house fire.

what to buy: *Shine On: A Collection* (A&M, 1992, various prod.) offers a solid overview of Frampton's career, making a case for the strong—if not overwhelming—solo albums that preceded *Frampton Comes Alive*. It also includes two songs he recorded with Marriott during early 1991.

what to buy next: Go ahead; everybody else owns *Frampton Comes Alive* (A&M, 1976, prod. Frampton) and you should, too. Its energetic performances are still infectious, even if the "spontaneous" crowd outbursts do get tired.

what to avoid: Just about anything after *Frampton Comes Alive*.

the rest: *Wind of Change* (A&M, 1972) *Frampton's Camel* (A&M, 1973) *Something's Happening* (A&M, 1974) *Frampton* (A&M, 1975) *I'm In You* (A&M, 1977) *Where I Should Be* (A&M, 1979) *Breaking All the Rules* (A&M, 1981) *The Art of Control* (A&M, 1982) *Premonition* (Atlantic, 1986) *When All the Pieces Fit* (Atlantic, 1989) *Peter Frampton* (Relativity, 1994) *Frampton Comes Alive II* (Relativity, 1995)

worth searching for: If you must own it, the British edition of *Comes Alive II* includes four extra tracks not found on the U.S. volume.

Bryan Adams, Tom Cochrane

The Shadows, the Beatles, The Searchers

Gary Graff

Frankie Goes to Hollywood

Formed 1982 in Liverpool, England. Disbanded 1988.

William "Holly" Johnson, vocals; Mark O'Toole, bass; Paul Rutherford, vocals, dancing; Brian Nash, guitar; Peter Gill, drums

Frankie Goes to Hollywood changed the landscape of British pop music when it released the double-length debut, *Welcome to the Pleasuredome* in 1984. Mixing bombastic attitude, overtly hedonistic themes and unorthodox covers (Bruce Springsteen's "Born to Run?!") with irresistible originals, the record was nothing short of a revelation at a time when England was overflowing with tame synthesizer bands. Frankiemania lived, including a series of T-shirts and badges bearing legends such as "Frankie Say War! Arm Yourself." What started out with a bang, however, ultimately ended in a bust. Due to its massive exposure with the first LP and growing dissension within the group, FGTH's second and final disc, *Liverpool*, died quietly shortly after its release in 1986. While various members of the group tried to carry on with solo careers, none ever came close to repeating the success of FGTH's debut.

what to buy: *Welcome to the Pleasure Dome* (ZTT/Island, 1984, prod. Trevor Horn) was very much a product of producer and ZTT head Horn's studio adventures. A majority of the songs on the double-album surfaced in the British charts following the album's release, and for good reason. Singles such as "Relax," "Two Tribes" and "The Power of Love" were immaculate slices of pop, mixing a gritty disco bite with charming melodies and smart sonic finesse.

what to avoid: *Liverpool* (ZTT/Island, 1986, prod. Stephen Lipson and Trevor Horn) captured the band at an obvious creative void. Containing only eight tracks and offering a pair of insignificant singles ("Watching the Wildlife" and "Rage Hard"), it served as a pathetic finale to the group's fleeting career.

solo outings:

Holly Johnson: Blast (Uni, 1989) *Hollelujah* (MCA EP, 1990) *Dreams That Money Can't Buy* (MCA, 1991)

Paul Rutherford: Oh World (ZTT/Island, 1989) WOOF!

worth searching for: *Bang!...The Greatest Hits of Frankie Goes to Hollywood*, (ZTT, 1993, prod. Various) a European collection that presents an agreeably tight winnowing of the group's flash 'n' bang success.

Sigue Sigue Sputnik, Pet Shop Boys, Seal

Village People, Duran Duran, Sex Pistols, Burt Bacharach

Aidin Vaziri

Aretha Franklin

Born March 25, 1942 in Memphis, Tenn.

For the daughter of the famous Detroit preacher C.L. Franklin, gospel was second nature. Having achieved young stardom in the gospel world, her first venture to the secular world was an uneasy one at Columbia Records. But Atlantic's Jerry Wexler pursued her after her contract ran out. Together they made an astounding string of classics during the late 1960s that not only defined soul music but also crowned Aretha "Queen of Soul" for life. Besides being a joy to hear, Franklin's work was also culturally significant, helping to define black self-awareness at a time when a little bit of R-E-S-P-E-C-T was much needed. Franklin's success seems tied to her various recording companies; none could match Atlantic, but she enjoyed odd bouts of success once more on Arista during the early 80s. Her love for gospel remains strong, and she continues to be an ambassador for soul music from her home in the Detroit area.

what to buy: *I Never Loved a Man (the Way I Loved You)* (Atlantic, 1967, prod. Jerry Wexler) is a startling achievment. There's no way her Atlantic debut could have been more electrifying. With the Muscle Shoals backing and Jerry Wexler producing, the album includes her searing "Respect" as well as the enduring "Do Right Woman, Do Right Man" and "Dr. Feelgood."

what to buy next: If your billfold is thick enough, the opulently packaged box set *The Queen of Soul* (Rhino/Atlantic, 1992, prod. Various) has it all—the hits, the surprises, the achievements of her career. In an economic pinch, *30 Greatest Hits* (Atlantic, 1985, prod. Various) distills the hit period. *Lady Soul* (Atlantic, 1968, prod. Jerry Wexler) is also from her greatest period. *Amazing Grace* (Atlantic, 1972, prod. Jerry Wexler, Arif Mardin and Aretha Franklin) is her triumphant return to gospel. *Aretha's Greatest Hits (1980-1994)* (Arista, 1994, prod. Various) shows she's still able to sing with soul even when the material is uneven.

what to avoid: On *La Diva* (Atlantic, 1979) Lady Soul gets stuck in the disco period.

the rest: *Aretha* (Columbia, 1961) *The Electrifying Aretha Franklin* (Columbia, 1962) *Laughing on the Outside* (Columbia, 1963) *The Tender, the Moving, the Swinging Aretha Franklin* (Columbia, 1963 *Unforgettable: A Tribute to Dinah Washington* (Columbia 1964) *Running Out of Fools* (Columbia, 1964) *Yeah! Aretha Franklin in Person* (Columbia, 1965) *Soul Sister* (Columbia, 1966) *Greatest Hits* (Columbia, 1967) *Take It Like You Give It* (Columbia, 1967) *Take a Look* (Columbia, 1967) *Aretha Arrives* (Atlantic, 1967) *Aretha Now* (Atlantic, 1968) *Aretha in Paris* (Atlantic, 1968) *Greatest Hits, Vol. 2* (Columbia, 1968) *Soul '69* (Atlantic, 1969) *Aretha's Gold* (Atlantic, 1969) *This Girl's in Love with You* (Atlantic, 1970) *Spirit in the Dark* (Atlantic, 1970) *Live at the Fillmore West* (Atlantic, 1971) *Greatest Hits* (Atlantic, 1971) *Young, Gifted and Black* (Atlantic, 1972) *Hey Now Hey (The Other Side of the Sky)* (Atlantic, 1973) *The First Twelve Sides* (Columbia, 1973) *The Best of Aretha Franklin* (Atlantic, 1973) *Let Me in Your Life* (Atlantic, 1974) *With Everything I Feel in Me* (Atlantic, 1974) *You* (Atlantic, 1975) *Sparkle* (Atlantic, 1976) *Ten Years of Gold* (Atlantic, 1976) *Sweet Passion* (Atlantic, 1977) *Almighty FireMDBR* (Atlantic, 1978) *Love All the Hurt Away* (Arista, 1981) *Jump to It* (Arista, 1982) *Sweet Bitter Love* (Columbia, 1982) *Get It Right* (Arista, 1983) *Aretha's Jazz* (Columbia, 1984) *Who's Zoomin' Who* (Arista, 1985) *Aretha Sings the Blues* (Columbia, 1985), *Aretha* (Arista, 1986) *After Hours* (Columbia, 1987) *One Lord, One Faith, One Baptism* (Arista, 1987) *Through the Storm* (Arista, 1989) *What You See Is What You Sweat* (Arista, 1991) *Jazz to Soul* (Columbia Legacy, 1992)

worth searching for: *The Gospel Sound of Aretha Franklin* (Checker, 1956) captures Aretha tearin' it up in church at age 14.

▶▶ Whitney Houston, Anita Baker, Chaka Khan

◀◀ Celia Ward, Ruth Brown, the Rev. C.L. Franklin, Sam Cooke

Roger Catilin

Freakwater

Formed 1983 in Louisville, Ky.

Catherine Irwin, vocals, guitar; Janet Bean, vocals, guitar; David Gay, bass (1989-present)

Friends from childhood, Irwin and Bean began blending their voices to old Carter Family and Loretta Lynn songs in Bean's parents' basement and continued to collaborate when Bean moved to Chicago to join her future husband, Rick Rizzo, in the acclaimed rock band Eleventh Dream Day, for whom she played drums and sang backing vocals. Freakwater anticipated the rise of the insurgent-country movement—a reaction to Nashville-bred commercialism led by the underground rock community during the 90s. *Freakwater* (Amoeba, 1989, prod. James Bond and Bobbie Drinkwater) includes a countryfied remake of Bean's bad seed portrait, "Albert C. Sampson," that was initially recorded as a blazing rocker by Eleventh Dream Day. With *Dancing Under Water* (Amoeba, 1991, prod. Brad Wood) and *Feels Like the Third Time,* (Thrill Jockey, 1993, prod. Brad Wood and Freakwater) the duo's splendid high-and-lonesome harmonies and string band instrumentation are split between a batch of well-chosen covers and a handful of Irwin originals, most notably "Drunk Friend" from the latter. On *Old Paint,* (Thrill Jockey, 1995, prod. Brad Wood and Freakwater) ♪♪♪♪ Irwin's songs dominate and with good reason; their spiritual resolve in the face of tragic circumstances is timeless.

Greg Kot

Freddie & the Dreamers

Formed 1960 in Manchester, England. Disbanded 1968. Re-formed 1976.

Freddie Garrity, vocals; Derek Quinn, guitar, harmonica; Roy Crewsdon, guitar, piano; Pete Birrell, bass; Bernie Dwyer, drums

Garrity and his band seemed content to be the clowns princes of the British Invasion, leap-frogging into the hearts of the least musically discriminating during the mid-60s with a string of cotton-candy hits and dozens of film and television appearances. Today, such an outfit would undoubtedly tour alongside Weird Al Yankovic—between guest spots on The Kids Network, that is—but back in their glory days, the Dreamers racked up impressive sales both overseas and in the U.S. It all began when, tiring of life as a milkman, Freddie used his resemblance to Buddy Holly to front various bands in the north of England before forming what eventually became the Dreamers. A successful audition for the BBC in 1962 lead to a contract for the band with Columbia Records. Beatles manager Brian Epstein stepped in the help the group score its first U.S. hit, "I'm Telling You Now," and a savvy record company executive decided to fashion the Garrity's gyrations into a dance craze, and a ditty entitled "Do The Freddie" was quickly recorded (with nary a Dreamer in sight). The success was short-lived, however, and by 1968 the band was no more. Garrity continues to leap through Merseybeat reunions and similar nostalgia-fests, seemingly as energetically as he did in his long-lost youth. The suspiciously titled *Best of Freddie & The Dreamers* (EMI, 1992, prod. Various) ♪♪♪ is an adequate, if slightly padded, sampling of the band's work. Freddie's act was as much visual as it was musical, so the various "Hullabaloo" and "Shindig" video compilations might help the curious to understand, and perhaps even appreciate, the Dreamers' own particular brand of acrobatic pop.

Gary Pig Gold

Free

Formed 1968 in London, England. Disbanded 1971. Re-formed 1972. Disbanded 1973.

Paul Rodgers, vocals; Paul Kossoff, guitar (1968-72, died March 19, 1976 in New York, N.Y.); Andy Fraser, bass, (1968-71); Simon Kirke, drums; Tetsu Yamauchi, bass (1972-73); John "Rabbit" Bundrick, keyboards (1972-73)

Along with Cream, Free's tough, spartan brand of hard rock provided a prototype for 70s arena rock—a model its own members would follow in groups such as Bad Company and Backstreet Crawler. Formed in the blues-drenched London pubs—and named by British music icon Alexis Korner—the quartet's assets were the envy of its colleagues: Rogers was one of the scene's richest, most passionate singers; Kirke was as solid a drummer as you'd find; Kossoff was an estimable guitar player; and Fraser crafted inventive, lyrical bass parts. It all coalesces on Free's enduring hit, "All Right Now," in which Rodgers wails over a taught groove provided by Kossoff and Kirke, while Fraser's bass swoops in on the choruses to drive the song into another dimension. Free split up briefly in 1971, and when it got back together the following year, Kossoff and Fraser had moved on to Backstreet Crawler and the Sharks, respectively. Rogers and Kirke kept Free alive until 1973, when they became part of the burgeoning Bad Company.

what to buy: The two-disc *Molten Gold: The Anthology* (A&M/Chronicles, 1993, prod. Various) ♪♪♪♪ is a well-chosen overview of Free favorites, its only mistake being the inclusion of a live rendition of "Fire and Water" rather than the more economical studio version.

what to buy next: *Fire and Water* (A&M, 1970, prod. Free) ♪♪♪♪ is as good an album as Free produced, featuring the title track and the seminal "All Right Now."

what to avoid: *Heartbreaker* (Island, 1973, prod. Free and Andy Johns) ♪♪ has an ace in "Wishing Well" but mostly makes you wonder why the group got back together to make this diminished work.

the rest: *Best of Free* (A&M, 1975) ♪♪♪♪

worth searching for: *Message to Love: The Isle of Wight Festival 1970* (Essential/Castle, 1995, prod. Jon Astley and Andy Macpherson) ♪♪♪♪ opens with Free performing a hot rendition of "All Right Now."

▶▶ Bad Company, Backstreet Crawler, Foreigner, Kiss

◀◀ John Mayall's Bluesbreakers, the Yardbirds, the Rolling Stones, Sonny Boy Williamson, John Lee Hooker

see also: *Bad Company*

Gary Graff

Ace Frehley

See: Kiss

Frente

Formed 1989 in Melbourne, Australia

Angie Hart, vocals; Simon Austin, guitars, piano, vocals; Alastair Barden, drums; Tim O'Connor, bass (1989-95); Bill McDonald, bass, guitar (1995-present)

With Hart's sweet, angelic vocals and Austin's shimmering guitar tones, Frente is a breath of fresh air in the primarily stagnant alternative rock scene. Frente's debut *Marvin: The Album* (Mammoth/Atlantic, 1994, prod. Michael Koppelman and Frente) spawned two hits: "Labour of Love" and an acoustic cover of New Order's "Bizarre Love Triangle." Its sophomore long-player *Shape* (Mammoth/Atlantic, 1996, prod. Bill McDonald and Cameron McVey, a.k.a. Booga Bear) expands the band's acoustic-based songs to include elements of trip-hop and power pop.

Christina Fuoco

Glenn Frey

See: The Eagles

Robert Fripp /League of Crafty Guitarists/Fripp & Eno/Sylvian & Fripp/Fripp & Summers

Born May 16, 1946, in Dorset, England

Primarily known and revered as the leader of King Crimson, Fripp is a tireless musician/producer/collaborator whose love of playing and challenging new situations (not to mention the demand for his distinctive guitar styles) has led to a bulging solo catalog and a vast array of collaborations. He's teamed with musical conceptualist Brian Eno of Roxy Music, former Japan frontman David Sylvian and guitarist Andy Summers of the Police. He started a New Wave-ish dance rock quartet, The League of Gentlemen, with ex-XTC keyboardist Barry Andrews, Gang of Four bassist-to-be Sara Lee and drummer Jonny Toobad, and also formed the League of Crafty Guitarists, an outgrowth of his Guitar Craft school. Fripp has also remixed his catalogs, including all of King Crimson's output, for CDs, finally starting his own label, Discipline. Even as King Crimson continues to release albums on a major label (currently Virgin). Discipline has enabled Fripp to issue more from his various projects.

what to buy: *The Essential Fripp and Eno* (Caroline, 1994) collects both side-long tracks from 1973's *(No Pussyfooting)*, half of 1975's *Evening Star* and four linked tracks from an unissued third album. The '73 album is the most essential; towering edifices of sound are constructed by putting Fripp's soaring guitar lines through Eno's processing. Fripp's first solo album, *Exposure,* (EG, 1979, prod. Robert Fripp) features Peter Gabriel (the best version of his "Here Comes the Flood"), Eno, Phil Collins, Peter Hammill and Terre Roche, among others. Running the gamut from nearly mainstream to just plain weird, it's a brooding album of great intensity. *The League of Gentlemen* (EG, 1981, prod. Robert Fripp) anticipates future dance trends on a conceptual level while at the same time creating Frippertronic-sounding pieces in real time.

what to buy next: The first part of of Fripp's *God Save the Queen/Under Heavy Manners* (EG, 1979, prod. Robert Fripp) is solo Frippertronics loops; the second half is Discotronics, Fripp's repetitively structured dance music, featuring a hilariously alienated recitative by the Talking Heads' David Byrne. Sylvian and Fripp's *The First Day* (Virgin, 1993, prod. David Sylvian and David Botrill) mixes Frippertronics with ambient and new age production on a beautiful, tuneful and emotional triumph.

what to avoid: The League of Gentlemen bootleg *The Bunch of Women,* (Editions EF, 1981) supposedly capturing the group's 22nd gig. Fripp despises bootlegs, and if anything gets enough attention, he'll issue something comparable with better sound.

the rest: Robert Fripp: *Let the Power Fall* (EG, 1981) Soundscapes: *Live in Argentina* (Discipline, 1994) *Radiophonics* (Discipline, 1996) *Blessing of Tears* (Discipline, 1996) Fripp & Brian Eno: *Evening Star* (Island, 1975) Sunday All Over the World: *Kneeling at the Shrine* (EG, 1991) Fripp & Andy Summers: *I Advance Masked* (A&M, 1982) *Bewitched* (A&M, 1984) League of Gentlemen: *THRANG THRANG GOZINBULX* (Discipline, 1996) League of Crafty Guitarists: *Live!* (EG/Caroline, 1986) *Show of Hands* (EG/Caroline, 1991) *Intergalactic Boogie Express* (Discipline, 1995) Toyah and Fripp: *The Lady or the Tiger* (EG, 1986) Robert Fripp String Quartet: *The Bridge Between* (Discipline, 1994)

worth searching for: Sylvian and Fripp's limited-edition *Damage* (Live) (Virgin, 1994) mixes five tracks from *The First Day* with three from Sylvian's *Gone to Earth* and four others (including Rain Tree Crow's "Every Colour You Are"). The live setting lends new urgency, and Fripp hardly repeats himself.

Iceburn, His Name Is Alive, the Orb, Living Colour

Jimi Hendrix, Beatles, John McLaughlin, Phillip Glass

see also: *King Crimson*

Steve Holtje

Fripp & Eno

See: Robert Fripp

Fripp & Summers

See: Robert Fripp

John Frusciante

See: Red Hot Chili Peppers

Fugazi

Formed 1987 in Arlington, Va.

Ian MacKaye, vocals and guitar; Guy Picciotto, vocals and guitar; Joe Lally, bass; Brendan Canty, drums

MacKaye, former leader of Washington hardcore legends Minor Threat—not to mention the lesser-known Teen Idols, Egg Hunt and Embrace—set out with Fugazi to create the ultimate independent punk-rock band. Fugazi has never once compromised—its songs are harsh and raw, its melodies are sometimes catchy but often dense, and it has never considered signing with a major record label. MacKaye, to the delight of his loyal fans, has refused to let concert tickets rise above $5. This has resulted in less money for the band-owned record label, Dischord, but at least nobody has ever accused Fugazi of selling out.

what to buy: *13 Songs*, (Dischord, 1989, prod. Various) combines the debut album *Fugazi* (Dischord, 1988, prod. Ted Nicely and Fugazi) and the followup EP *Margin Walker*. (Dischord, 1989, prod. John Loder) It opens with Fugazi's best songs, the catchy "Waiting Room" and "Bulldog Front," which sound like hardcore-and-uncheesey extensions of Queen.

what to buy next: *Repeater*, (Dischord, 1990, prod. Ted Niceley) which includes the "3 Songs" 7-inch single, is the sound of a great band aiming all its weapons in the same direction—the bass and drums create a glorious cacophony, and MacKaye's forceful, slightly whiny vocals slip nicely on top.

the rest: *Steady Diet of Nothing* (Dischord, 1991) *In On the Kill Taker* (Dischord, 1993) *Red Medicine* (Dischord, 1995)

worth searching for: The Picciotto-led band Rites of Spring lacks punch and noodles a bit too much, but its only album, *Rites of Spring*, (Dischord, 1985, prod. Ian MacKaye and Michael Hampton) is a decent complement to a Fugazi-Minor Threat collection.

Offspring, Nirvana, Soundgarden, Guns N' Roses, Pearl Jam, Nada Surf

Queen, Motorhead, Dead Kennedys, Minutemen, Descendents, Sex Pistols

see also: *Minor Threat*

Steve Knopper

The Fugees

Formed 1989 in South Orange, N.J.

Wyclef "Clef" Jean, vocals, guitar, keyboards, bass; Lauryn "L" Hill, vocals; Prakazrel "Praz" Michael, vocals, keyboards

The group name is short for refugees, a reminder of the Haitian heritage of cousins Clef and Praz. The Fugees' brand of hip-hop is musical and fully conscious, but the Fugees are no sucker M.C.s: in the struggle to keep it real, its music places the group squarely between the hardcore jeep beats of gangsta rap and the flaccid alterna-rap of Arrested Development and De La Soul. *Blunted on Reality* (Ruffhouse/Columbia, 1993, prod. LeJam Productions, Inc.) failed to gain much attention on release, until a remix of "Nappy Heads" took off. "Vocab" is the track that showed them the way to the future, though, as it combined raggamuffin vocals with a percussive acoustic guitar figure. *The Score* (Ruffhouse/Columbia, 1996 prod. the Fugees) shows remarkable growth, moving hip-hop forward even as it looks back to pays tribute to influences such as Bob Marley and Roberta Flack. The covers of Marley's "No Woman, No Cry" and Flack's "Killing Me Softly" are less than revelatory, but the original tracks "Fu-Gee-La," "Ready or Not" and "Family Business" prove the Fugees are worthy successors to those heroes. The group earns extra points for according L as much mic time as Clef and Praz, a rare act of gender equality in the rap game.

Daniel Durchholz

The Fugs

Formed 1965 in New York, N.Y. Disbanded 1969. Re-formed 1984 and 1994.

Tuli Kuferberg, vocals, percussion (1965-69); Ed Sanders, guitar, vocals (1965-69, 1984-present); Ken Weaver, drums, vocals (1965-66); John Anderson, bass (1965-67); Vinnie Leary, guitar (1965-67); Pete Stampfel, guitar, fiddle (1965-66); Steve Weber, guitar (1965-66); Lee Crabtree, keyboards (1966-67); Pete Kearney, guitar (1966-67); Charles Larkey, bass (1967-68); Dan Kootch, guitar (1967); Ken Pine, guitar (1967-68); Bill Wolf, bass (1968); Bob Mason, drums (1968); Richard Lee, organ (1968); Howard Johnson, tuba, saxophone (1968); Julius Watkins, french horn (1968)

The Fugs were possibly the first punk band of the rock era. Hardly able to play instruments, the Fugs traded on a raw folk-rock sound that backed neo-beat poets Sanders and Kuferberg, who wrote most of the band's material. The songs went beyond drugs, sex and anti-war paeans to deliberate filth ("Coca-Cola Douche") that was calculated to shock. Still, there was a method to its madness, grounded in the 50s beat scene. Poet Allen Ginsberg contributed to the Fugs' lyrics, and one of the few songs that received radio play, "How Sweet I Roamed From Field To Field," was an adaptation of a work by romantic poet William Blake. Of what remains available, *The Fugs First Album*" (ESP, 1965/Fantasy, 1994 prod. Harry Smith) ♫♫♫♫ has plenty of antisocial sentiments via "Slum Goddess," "I Couldn't Get High" and more. *The Fugs Second Album* (Fantasy, 1994, prod. Harry Smith) ♫♫♫♫ is pretty much the same though a little less self-concerned with "Kill For Peace" and "Morning, Morning," their most popular ballad.

Lawrence Gabriel

The Bobby Fuller Four

Formed 1963 in El Paso, Texas

Bobby Fuller, guitar, vocals (died July 18, 1966); Randy Fuller, bass, vocals; Jim Reese, guitar; Dalton Powell, drums (1963-64); DeWayne Querico, drums (1964-66)

The Bobby Fuller story reads like a treatment for a major motion picture. Fade in: Young man growing up in a Texas town falls in love with rock 'n' roll, particularly that of fellow Texan Buddy Holly. In time, the young man—a musical prodigy—forms his own band and starts attracting attention. He and his band tour, make records and television appearances, and even have a smash hit across the country. But with fame come the pleasures and perils of fame, and a young man is unlikely to resist the charms of the many women now enamored of this new pop star. The young man runs into trouble with one such woman, a woman linked to a reputed mobster. One morning, the young man is found dead in his parked car, his body bruised, beaten and covered with gasoline. Though the young man obviously was murdered, the police officially list the death as accidental and privately call it a suicide. With justice not served, the questions linger for decades, never to be answered. The music, meanwhile, lives on as well, never to be forgotten. Fade out. The tabloid aspects of Fuller's demise may yet draw Hollywood's interest (and, lest this be written off as another crackpot conspiracy theory, let there be no mistake about our position: Paul ain't dead, Elvis ain't alive, but Bobby Fuller was murdered), it is Fuller's music that continues to entertain and fascinate fans 30 years after his death. The unforgettable "I Fought The Law," itself a cover of a song by the Crickets, was the Bobby Fuller Four's only Top 40 entry, though there were scattered regional hits—notably the sublime "Let Her Dance." The cream of this excellent body of work is collected on *The Best of the Bobby Fuller Four,* (Rhino, 1990, prod. Bob Keane and Bill Inglot) ♫♫♫♫ an essential set of American mid-60s rock 'n' roll surviving and thriving in the wake of the British Invasion. (At this writing, Fuller's original label, Del-Fi, has announced plans for a Fuller boxed set and a new series of reissues. We'll recommend 'em all here, sight unseen.)

Carl Cafarelli

Fun Boy Three

Formed 1981 in Coventry, England. Disbanded 1983.

Lynval Golding, vocals; Terry Hall, vocals; Neville Staples, guitar, vocals

Formed by three ex-members of The Specials, Fun Boy Three retained the ska sound but showed more of an African-based influence. *Waiting* (Chrysalis, 1983, prod. David Byrne) ♫♫♫♫ is their strongest album, marked by the slowed-down version of the Go-Go's "Our Lips Are Sealed."—which Hall co-wrote. The group disbanded in 1983, and Hall went on to form the Colour Field.

the rest: *The Fun Boy Three* (Chrysalis, 1982) ♫♫♫ *The Best of the Fun Boy Three* (Chrysalis, 1984) ♫♫♫♫ Terry Hall: *The Collection* (Chrysalis, 1993) ♫♫♪

Anna Glen

Richie Furay

See: Poco

Future Sound of London

Formed 1988 in Manchester, England

Gary Cobain, keyboards; Brian Dougan, keyboards

Cobain and Dougan have recorded under numerous aliases in their explorations of electronic music (Stakker Humanoid, Semi Real, Yage, Metropolis, Art Science Technology, Mental Cube, Candese, Intelligent Communication, Smart Systems, Far Out Son of Lung, Amorphous Androgynous and other "secret projects"). Each has had varying degrees of underground success, but it is their primary project, Future Sound of London, that has attracted the most worldwide attention. In 1988, their early anthem "Humanoid" (as Stakker Humanoid) hit just as the acid house movement exploded in the U.K. From there, FSOL was born, and alongside it the single "Papua New Guinea," considered by many of rave's historians to be one of the defining songs of the phenomenon. That was enough to place FSOL at the forefront of techno, and its position hasn't wavered.

what to buy: *Accelerator* (Virgin U.K., 1992/Cleopatra, 1996, prod. Gary Cobain and Brian Dougan) is worth any price based solely on the singular, orgasmic beauty of "Papua New Guinea," with its heavenly vocals (borrowed from Dead Can Dance) and sinful bass line (borrowed from Meat Beat Manifesto). Oh yeah, it's also got great songs like "Moscow," "Central Industrial" and "It's Not My Problem," but you'll be too stuck on "Papua New Guinea" to care. As Amorphous Androgynous, Cobain and Dougan recorded *Tales of Ephidrena* (Virgin U.K., 1993, prod. Gary Cobain and Brian Dougan), an album of ambient techno that gracefully covered the spectrum between beatless soothers and dance floor movers.

what to buy next: *Lifeforms* (Astralwerks, 1994, prod. Gary Cobain and Brian Dougan), the follow-up to *Accelerator*, features the ethereal vocal talents of the Cocteau Twins' Liz Fraser, manipulated in ways you'd never thought they could go.

what to avoid: The duo's lackluster house full-length release as *Humanoid* (Jumpin' and Pumpin' U.K., 1989, prod. Gary Cobain and Brian Dougan) WOOF! Fortunately, it's extremely hard to find.

the rest: As Various Artists: *Earthbeat* (Jumpin' and Pumpin' U.K., 1992) As FSOL: *Art Futura* (Astralwerks, 1996) not available for rating

worth searching for: *ISDN* (Astralwerks, 1995, prod. Gary Cobain and Brian Dougan), a limited edition release of their live ISDN transmission events.

Small Fish With Spine

Brian Eno, Tangerine Dream, Master Musicians of Jajouka

Tamara Palmer

G. Love and Special Sauce

Formed 1993 in Boston, Mass.

G. Love (born Garrett Dutton, Oct. 3, 1972) vocals, guitar, harmonica; Jeffrey Clemens drums, backing vocals; Jimmy Prescott, stand-up bass

Straight out of a coffee house, G. Love and Special Sauce sold fans on its fusion of rag-mop, blues, rap and swing with the release of its self-titled debut (Okeh, 1994, prod. Stiff Johnson and G. Love and Special Sauce) G. Love, in his fire-engine red silk suits and Elvis-like stage presence, sings of shooting hoops, hanging out on the street and enjoying a refreshing drink. The group did something that's traditonally avoided blues artists—bringing to radio hook-laden odes such as the back porch rap of "Cold Beverage" and "The Things That I Used To Do." The group's sophomore effort, *Coast to Coast Motel* (Okeh, 1995, prod. Jim Dickinson and G. Love and Special Sauce) serves up healthy portions of funk ("Sweet Sugar Mama"), New Orleans R&B groove ("Kiss and Tell" and "Bye Bye Baby") and stripped-down acoustic sounds ("Coming Home").

Christina Fuoco

Peter Gabriel

Born Feb. 13, 1950 in London, England

Made a star as the first lead singer for British art-rockers Genesis, Gabriel gained attention as much for his outlandish stage outfits (including a way-early mohawk haircut and a flower suit) as his forward-thinking songwriting ideas. Feeling stifled by the group's growing commercial success, Gabriel struck out on his own in 1975, eschewing the theatrics to focus on a style that melded his art-rock and folk roots with a strong social conscience and desire to push creative boundaries. Building critical and commercial success with each release, Gabriel (who named his first four solo records *Peter Gabriel* like issues in a magazine) refined his style into an amazingly creative blend of rock, soul and worldbeat styles—mixing Eurocentric rock touches with tribal music conventions and commercial rock tunes with messages on Apartheid, Native American issues and his own divorce. Eventually, he channeled his own success into a world music label, Real World, along with an annual world music festival, called WOMAD.

what to buy: Though his first two solo releases set the stage, it wasn't until his third *Peter Gabriel* album (Geffen, 1980, prod. Steve Lillywhite) that the singer fully stepped away from his art-rock roots to craft pop music unlike anything made before. Forbidding drummers Phil Collins and Jerry Marotta to use cymbals, Gabriel combined unorthodox percussion parts, brittle guitar textures and outlandish synthesizer sounds to create edgy, arty classics such as the hit "Games Without Frontiers" and the majestic tribute to slain anti-Apartheid activist Steven Biko, "Biko."

what to buy next: Gabriel's commercial breakthrough, *So* (Geffen, 1986, prod. Daniel Lanois and Peter Gabriel) melds the singer's arresting creative vision with actual hit songs, from the soulful celebration "Sledgehammer" to the percolating, ironic take on rock star ego, "Big Time." Add the mesmerizing, worldbeat flavored ballad "In Your Eyes," a tender duet with Kate Bush, "Don't Give Up" and the powerful, passionate groove "Red Rain" and you have the makings of an instant classic. As a showcase for Gabriel's growing sonic palette, the fourth *Peter Gabriel* (aka *Security*) (Geffen, 1982, prod. Peter Gabriel and David Lord) bounds from an epic Native American tale ("San Jacinto") to the buoyant "Kiss of Life" and the kinetic single, "Shock the Monkey."

what to avoid: The singer's two stabs at film scoring, *Music From the Film Birdy* (Geffen, 1984, prod. Peter Gabriel) and *Passion: Music for the Last Temptation of Christ* (Geffen, 1989, prod. Peter Gabriel) do little more than cobble together reworked versions of songs from whatever album preceded them. You'd be better off buying the records that inspired them.

the rest: *Peter Gabriel* (Atco, 1977) *Peter Gabriel* (Atlantic, 1978) *Plays Live* (Geffen, 1983) *Shaking the Tree: Sixteen Golden Greats* (Geffen, 1990) *Revisited* (Atlantic, 1992) *Us* (Geffen, 1992) *Secret World Live* (Geffen, 1994)

worth searching for: The import *SW Live EP* (RealWorld/Virgin, 1994, prod. Peter Gabriel and Peter Walsh) adds two songs, "San Jacinto" and "Mercy Street," not found on *Secret World Live*.

George Michael, Paula Cole, Daniel Lanois, Youssou N'-Dour

Sam Cooke, Otis Redding, King Crimson, David Bowie, Brian Eno

Eric Deggans

Galaxie 500

Formed 1986 in Boston, Mass. Disbanded 1990.

Dean Wareham, vocals, guitar; Naoimi Yang, bass; Damon Krukowski, drums

These three are Harvard grads, yet they played unsophisticated, lo-fi slacker dirges like they didn't have the energy to sit up, much less graduate. In its more inspired and tuneful moments, Galaxie 500 approached (from a distance) the slower drudge of the Velvet Underground. The mopey charm of "Tugboat Captain," from their debut album *Today* (Aurora, 1987/Rough Trade, 1991, prod. Kramer) will shrug its way into your heart, but the less melodic groans leave you feeling like you've been drinking too much cough syrup. After Galaxie split up, Wareham went on to found Luna.

the rest: *On Fire* (Rough Trade/Giant-Rockville, 1989) *This is Our Music* (Rough Trade/Giant-Rockville, 1990)

see also: *Luna*

Allan Orski

Rory Gallagher

Born March 2, 1949, in Ballyshannon, Ireland. Died June 14, 1995 in London, England.

A blues-rock guitarist and singer, Gallagher had a lengthy career beginning with his trio Taste, was something of an Irish response to the success of England's Cream, in 1969. After disbanding, Gallagher became a solo artist and fronted bands under his own name for the rest of his career. One of the most aggressive guitarists in this genre, his style wasn't diluted by changing musical tastes and attitudes. Given some of the experimentation he had done with Taste, it's a pity that Gallagher didn't spread his creative wings further; while his recordings were accomplished, there is a strong similarity to them. He penned most of the blues songs, which tended to be lengthy with increasingly dynamic improvisations. Unlike contemporaries such as Eric Clapton, Jeff Beck, Jimmy Page and Jimi Hendrix, Gallagher experimented little and always stayed close to his blues roots. If nothing else, with Gallagher you always knew what to expect.

what to buy: *The Best of Taste Featuring Rory Gallagher* (Polydor, 1994) 𝄞𝄞𝄞𝄞 is a solid sampling of his earlier, raw-boned blues guitar and vocal attack. These recordings were long out of print; they are a welcome return and the linchpin to Gallagher's career.

what to buy next: *Tattoo,* (Polydor/Griffin, 1973) 𝄞𝄞𝄞𝄞 Gallagher's fifth solo album, contains a number of strong songs, including "Cat Cradle," "Living Like a Trucker" and "They Don't Make It Like That Anymore."

what to avoid: *Blueprint,* (Polydor/Griffin, 1973) 𝄞𝄞 one of those moribund, same-sounding collections.

the rest: *Irish Tour '74* (Polydor/I.R.S., 1974) 𝄞𝄞𝄞 *Against the Grain* (Chrysalis/Griffin, 1975) 𝄞𝄞𝄞 *Calling Card* (Chrysalis/I.R.S., 1976) 𝄞𝄞𝄞 *Top Priority* (Chrysalis/I.R.S., 1979) 𝄞𝄞𝄞 *Defender* (I.R.S., 1987) 𝄞𝄞𝄞 *Fresh Evidence* (I.R.S., 1991) 𝄞𝄞𝄞 *Live in Europe/Stage Struck* (I.R.S., 1991) 𝄞𝄞𝄞

⏩ Gary Moore, George Thorogood & The Destroyers

⏪ Albert King, Freddie King, Muddy Waters, Bo Didley

Patrick McCarty

Gallon Drunk

Formed 1990 in London, England

James Johnston, vocals, guitar, organ; Mike Delanian, bass; Max Decharne, drums; Joe Byfield, maracas; Terry Edward, horns (1993-present)

Since its beginning, Gallon Drunk's musical style has stayed the same: dark, boozy, rock 'n' roll soundtracks for a lounge generation. Its debut album *Tonite . . . the Singles Bar* (Rykodisc, 1992, prod. Gallon Drunk) 𝄞𝄞𝄞 remains the best introduction to its primal sound—by a hair, that is. *You, the Night . . . & the Music* (Rykodisc, 1992, prod. Gallon Drunk and Tony Harris) 𝄞𝄞𝄞 adds traces of Memphis soul and rockabilly, while *From the Heart of Town* (Sire, 1993, prod. Phil Wright) 𝄞𝄞𝄞 is highlighted by the larger-than-life sound of "Jake on the Make."

Anna Glen

Game Theory /Loud Family

Formed 1982 in northern California

Does Scott Miller use power pop as a tool for conveying his emotions, or are his emotional lyrics an excuse for great power-pop? Whatever the case, he's one of the few in the genre who has a sound all his own; whatever influences he has are sublimated within his originality. Miller's melodies are the musical equivalent of intricate math problems, and his vocals—often compared to Chris Stamey's and Alex Chilton's—launch into emotional falsettos at the drop of a hat (or, considering Miller's allusiveness, the drop of a reference). Repeat plays are essential to understanding his songs.

what to buy: Game Theory's *Real Nighttime* (Enigma, 1984, prod. Mitch Easter) 𝄞𝄞𝄞𝄞 is full of Big Starrish melodies and lyrics reflecting rejection, dejection and young adult confusion. *Lolita Nation* (Enigma, 1987, prod. Mitch Easter) 𝄞𝄞𝄞𝄞 is a self-indulgent but gorgeous double-length album. The Loud Family's *Plants & Birds & Rocks & Things* (Alias, 1993, prod. Mitch Easter) 𝄞𝄞𝄞𝄞 is a richly textured pop masterpiece; it contains some of Miller's best songs, and the arrangements are chilling. *Distortion of Glory* (Alias, 1993, prod. Michael Quercio and Scott Miller) 𝄞𝄞𝄞𝄞 combines Game Theory's first album (though many songs were clinically re-recorded) with two subsequent (and excellent) EPs and bonus tracks.

what to buy next: *Tinkers To Evers To Chance* (Enigma, 1990, prod. Various) 𝄞𝄞𝄞𝄞 is a Game Theory compilation with fairly well-chosen tracks—including a couple of new recordings of pre-Game Theory songs—but you'd do better with one of the regular albums. Game Theory's *Big Shot Chronicles,* (Rational/Enigma, 1985, prod. Mitch Easter) 𝄞𝄞𝄞𝄞 to use vinyl talk, has a great Side 1 and a disappointing Side 2. *Two Steps From the Middle Ages* (Rational/Enigma, 1988, prod. Mitch Easter) 𝄞𝄞𝄞 has some of Miller's best songs but also some that don't quite connect. The Loud Family's *Tape of Only Linda* (Alias, 1994, prod. Mitch Easter) 𝄞𝄞𝄞𝄞 is denser than *Plants & Birds...*" but almost as good; ultimately, the other members' contributions only blur his vision.

worth searching for: A vinyl import called *Dead Center* (Lolita, 1994) 𝄞𝄞𝄞𝄞 combines the EP tracks with an otherwise-unavailable Game Theorized cover of the Box Tops' "The Letter."

⏩ Ultra Vivid Scene, the Posies

⏪ Big Star, the dB's, Roxy Music

Jordan Oakes

Gang of Four /Shriekback

Formed 1977 in Leeds, England. Disbanded 1984. Reformed 1990.

Gang of Four—Jon King, vocals, melodica; Andy Gill, guitar and vocals; Dave Allen, bass (1977-81); Hugo Burnham, drums, (1977-82); Busta "Cherry" Jones, bass, (1981-82); Sara Lee, bass, vocals (1982-84). Shriekback (Formed 1981 in London, England. Disbanded 1989. Reformed 1992)—Dave Allen, bass (1981-86, 1992-94); Carl Marsh, guitar, vocals (1981-85); Barry Andrews, vocals, keyboards; Martyn Barker, drums; Mike Cozzi, guitar (1985-89, 1992-present); Doug Wimbush, bass (1986-89)

Gang of Four number among the most important post-punk bands to emerge from England, departing from the thrashing nihilism of punk and pursuing a stark sound influenced by funk and avant-garde music, along with lyrics from an analytical, leftist point of view. Formed by art students King, Gill and Burnham, the trio came into focus with the arrival of experienced pro Allen. Gill's minimalist guitar work rebelled against rock's traditional chordal barrage, scattering dissonant shards over the uptight grooves of Burnham and Allen while King punctuated his chanted critiques with ghostly bursts of melodica. The space opened up by Gill's crafty restraint ratcheted up the tension level of the music immeasurably. The group's 1979 debut album, *Entertainment!*, has since earned classic status among alternative music fans.

Allen departed after Gang of Four's second album, citing the liberal drift of King's thinking, and formed the dance-oriented Shriekback. With Talking Heads veteran Jones, the Gang continued touring until bassist-singer Lee was brought in to add an appealing pop presence to the more melodic *Songs of the Free*" and its mini-hit, "I Love a Man in Uniform." The group took an ill-fated turn toward processed alterna-soul with 1984's *Hard*, however, and after the firing of Burnham (who became an A&R executive) and the release of a live album recorded in Los Angeles, the Gang disbanded. Gill pursued a career in film scoring and record producing. During the intervening years, the group's contribution to modern rock and to the stripped-down grooves of rap was recognized, and a Gill-King reunion in 1991 yielded a Gang of Four reunion.

Shriekback, meanwhile, enjoyed its own bit of radio success, particularly with the nightmarish anthem "Nemesis." Mixing funk and soul grooves with post-punk songcraft and industrial soundscapes, the group enjoyed moderate success throughout the decade—as well as a brief breakup and subsequent reunion. Allen also founded the modern rock label World Domination, which released Shriekback's 1992 effort *Sacred City*

what to buy: Gang of Four's *Entertainment!* (Warner Bros., 1979, prod. Andy Gill, Jon King, Rob Warr and Rick Walton) is a spellbinding collection of politicized, funky post-punk. Because the lyrics are fragmented and opaque, they largely avoid the truisms that befall preachier songwriters. Shriekback's *Oil & Gold* (Island, 1985, prod. Barry Andrews) catches the band at its noisy but pop-savvy peak and features the unstoppable "Nemesis."

what to buy next: Gang of Four's *Solid Gold* (Warner Bros., 1981, prod. Jimmy Douglass and Gang of Four) continues in the debut's uncompromising vein, while *Songs of the Free* (Warner Bros, 1982, prod. Mike Howlett, Andy Gill and Jon King) moves in a somewhat more melodic direction and shows greater stylistic breadth. Those wanting to dabble first should obtain *A Brief History of the Twentieth Century*, (Warner Bros., 1990, prod. Various) a compilation that gathers the band's finest moments. Shriekback's *Dancing Years* (Island, 1990, prod. Barry Andrews) is a diverse anthology, featuring remixes, unreleased material and live tracks.

what to avoid: Gang of Four's initial reunion effort *Mall* (Polydor, 1991, prod. Andy Gill) lacked the chemistry of the early releases, leaning on programmed and sampled drums and sound collages.

the rest: Gang of Four: *Gang of Four* (Warner Bros EP, 1980) *Hard* (Warner Bros., 1984) *At the Palace* (Mercury, 1984) *Shrinkwrapped* (Castle, 1995) Shriekback—*Care* (Warner Bros., 1983) *Jam Science* (Arista, 1984) *Big Night Music* (Island, 1986) *Go Bang!* (Island, 1988) *Sacred City* (World Domination, 1992)

worth searching for: *The Peel Sessions* (Strange Fruit, 1990) which contains interesting alternate versions of some of the key early songs.

▶▶ Red Hot Chili Peppers, Rage Against the Machine, Disposable Heroes of Hiphoprisy, Nine Inch Nails, Ministry

◀◀ James Brown, Funkadelic, Jimi Hendrix, Marxism-Leninism, Sex Pistols, Mekons, Pere Ubu

Simon Glickman

Gang Starr

Formed 1988 in Brooklyn, N.Y.

Guru (born Keith Elam), vocals; DJ Premier (born Chris Martin) production

Although the hip-hop one-two punch of Guru and DJ Premier use the moniker Gang Starr, the two aren't gangstas; Guru's consciousness-raising lyrics recall Grandmaster Flash and KRS-One more so than Spice 1, while the gritty, jazzbo-cool backing music supplied by Premier is miles closer to "Doo Bop"-era Miles Davis than "F—- Tha Police"-era N.W.A. Influenced by jazz more than any other hip-hop group, Gang Starr also understands better than the rest the correlation between jazz and rap—two black art forms with similar cadences that thrive on spontaneous innovation. The group's songs typically feature jazzy basslines, horn riffs and obscure jazz samples laid out over loose hip-hop beats; many could probably work as instrumental tracks. Yet Guru's conversational, laconic vocals weave perfectly through Premier's raw, soulful and simple constructions, with neither music nor lyrics fighting for attention. Outside of the Gang Starr format, Brooklyn native and onetime computer science major Premier has become one of the most sought-after producers in East Coast rap, working with the likes of KRS-One, Nas, Jeru the Damaja and Group Home, while Guru—the son of Boston's first black judge—has coordinated two jazz-meets-rap projects under the name Jazzmatazz.

what to buy: The minimalist *Daily Operation,* (Chrysalis, 1992, prod. DJ Premier and Guru) 𝅘𝅥𝅘𝅥𝅘𝅥𝅘𝅥 which samples artists from Charles Mingus to Donald Byrd, is Gang Starr's best, most consistent album. The thoughtful "Soliloquy of Chaos" which warns against the cycle of violence, and the tender, respectful "Ex Girl to the Next Girl" serves almost as antidotes to the killing and misogyny of gangsta-rap. *Guru's Jazzmatazz: Vol. I* (Chrysalis, 1993, prod. Guru) 𝅘𝅥𝅘𝅥𝅘𝅥𝅘𝅥 falls on the other side of the jazz-hop fence, as it features new contributions from jazz legends (Roy Ayers, Byrd, Lonnie Liston Smith) and comers (Ronny Jordan, N'Dea Davenport, Carleen Anderson) rather than samples and swings more than any Gang Starr album.

what to buy next: The upbeat *No More Mr. Nice Guy* (Wild Pitch/EMI, 1989, prod. DJ Premier and Guru) 𝅘𝅥𝅘𝅥𝅘𝅥½ features the tone-setting history lesson, "Jazz Thing," which is based on a poem by the longtime jazz publicist Elliot Horne, and the hip-hop classic, "Manifest," which makes excellent use of a Dizzy Gillespie sample. On *Hard to Earn,* (Chrysalis/ERG, 1994, DJ Premier and Guru) 𝅘𝅥𝅘𝅥𝅘𝅥 Premier strips away much of the jazz influence to reveal his old-school hip-hop roots, but Guru's cautionary tone of "Tonz 'O' Gunz" is decidedly 90s.

what to avoid: *Jazzmatazz Vol. II: The New Reality* (Chrysalis/EMI, 1995, prod. Guru) 𝅘𝅥𝅘𝅥 shares many of its predecessor's virtues but doesn't make nearly the same impact.

the rest: *Step In the Arena* (Chrysalis, 1990) 𝅘𝅥𝅘𝅥𝅘𝅥

worth searching for: *Guru Presents Ill Kid Records* (Payday, 1995, prod. Various) 𝅘𝅥𝅘𝅥𝅘𝅥 features lyrics from several Gang Starr associates, including the excellent Jeru the Damaja and Bahamadia.

▶▶ Buckshot LeFonque, the Roots, Ronny Jordan, Bahamadia, Digable Planets, Us3, Dream Warriors, A Tribe Called Quest, Jeru the Damaja

◀◀ Miles Davis, Donald Byrd, Roy Ayers, Lonnie Liston Smith, Jungle Brothers, Eric B and Rakim, Poor Righteous Teachers

Joshua Freedom du Lac

Jerry Garcia

See: Grateful Dead

Art Garfunkel

Born Arthur Garfunkel, Nov. 5, 1941 in New York, N.Y.

The masterful harmony singer with Paul Simon in Simon and Garfunkel through the 60s, Garfunkel's solo albums concentrate on his main asset—his choir boy voice. That worked up to a point. Without Simon as an artistic foil and songwriter, Garfunkel's work reached an artistic dead-end during the 80s.

what to buy: *Garfunkel,* (Columbia, 1990, prod. Various) 𝅘𝅥𝅘𝅥𝅘𝅥½ a best-of that covers the bases and includes all his Top 40 hits save 1974's "I Shall Sing."

what to buy next: *Angel Clare* (Columbia, 1973, prod. Roy Halee and Art Garfunkel) 𝅘𝅥𝅘𝅥𝅘𝅥 is his most powerful solo recording, with nice versions of Van Morrison's "I Shall Sing" and Randy Newman's "Old Man." *Watermark* (Columbia, 1977, prod. Phil Ramone) 𝅘𝅥𝅘𝅥𝅘𝅥 is a worthy collaboration with writer Jimmy Webb.

what to avoid: *Lefty* (Columbia, 1988, prod. Various) 𝅘𝅥 if for no other reason than his treacly version of "When a Man Loves a Woman."

the rest: *Breakaway* (Columbia, 1975) 𝅘𝅥𝅘𝅥 *Fate for Breakfast* (Columbia, 1979) 𝅘𝅥𝅘𝅥 *Scissors Cut* (Columbia, 1981) 𝅘𝅥½ *Up 'Til Now* (Sony, 1993) 𝅘𝅥𝅘𝅥

▶▶ Stephen Bishop, Babyface, Jackson Browne, Bobby Kimball

◀◀ Sam Cooke, Judy Garland, the Beach Boys

Leland Rucker

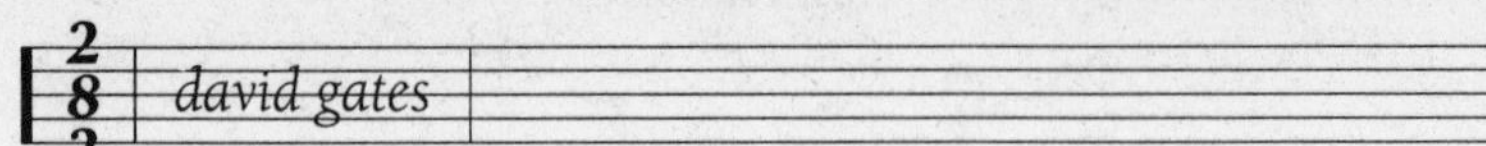

David Gates

See: Bread

Danny Gatton

Born 1945 in Washington, D.C.. Died October 20, 1994.

One of the most talented instrumentalists ever to pick up a guitar, Gatton combined lightning-fast chops with an encyclopedic knowledge of jazz, blues, country, rockabilly and swing. Anything that could be done on the guitar, Gatton could do it better, faster and cooler. Something of a child prodigy, Gatton played in several bands during the late 50s, 60s and 70s, including the Offbeats, Redneck Jazz Explosion and The American Music Company. But his fame never extended far beyond his home territory of Washington, D.C., even though in 1989 he was deemed "The World's Greatest Unknown Guitarist" in Guitar World magazine ("... but what famous guitarist could outplay him?" the mag pointed out)—an accolade which led to a two-record deal with Elektra, his first major label contract, at the age of 44. Though the resulting albums, *88 Elmira St.* and *Cruisin' Deuces,* earned Gatton critical praise and a somewhat larger audience, both financial success and fame continued to elude him. He committed suicide at his home in October, 1994.

what to buy: First-timers should begin with *88 Elmira St.* (Elektra, 1990, prod. Danny Gatton) a well-produced collection that features Gatton's best band (Bill Holloman, horns and keyboards; John Previti, bass; Shannon Ford, drums). Gatton's mile-wide range is well represented here, from the Eddie-Cochran-on-speed licks of "Elmira St. Boogie" to the gorgeous cover of the Beach Boys' "In My Room." If you don't like this, you don't like guitar, period.

what to buy next: Gatton's second record for Elektra, *Cruisin' Deuces,* (Elektra, 1994, prod. Danny Gatton and Billy Windsor) continues where *Elmira St.* left off, using Gatton's masterful guitar playing to weave a tapestry of various musical styles. *Unfinished Business* (NRG, 1987, prod. Danny Gatton) displays more of Gatton's jazz influences and features his takes on the classics "Cherokee," "Melancholy Serenade," "Sleepwalk" and "Georgia on My Mind."

what to avoid: The American Music. Co.'s *American Music* (Aladdin, 1975) has moments, but it's the work of a fledgling player who's a few steps away from the mature talent Gatton would become.

the rest: With Danny and the Fat Boys: *Vintage Masters, 1976-78* (Hippo, 1989) *Redneck Jazz* (NRG, 1978) (with Tom Principato): *Blazing Telecasters* (POW, 1990) (with others): *New York Stories* (Blue Note, 1992) (with Joey DeFrancesco): *Relentless* (Big Mo, 1994) *Redneck Jazz Explosion* (NRG, 1996)

worth searching for: Guitarists would be wise to look for Gatton's two "Hot Licks" instructional video tapes, "Licks & Tricks" and "Strictly Rhythm Guitar."

Vince Gill, Brian Setzer, Junior Brown

Les Paul, Carl Perkins, Chet Atkins, Roy Clark, Roy Buchanan, Dave Brubeck, Thelonius Monk, Charlie Christian, Albert Lee, Duane Eddy, Gene Vincent

Brandon Trenz

Marvin Gaye

Born Marvin Pentz Gay, Jr., April 21, 1939 in Washington, D.C. Died Sept. 1, 1984 in Los Angeles, Calif.

A moody, mercurial soul, who always seemed to be searching for some elusive happiness but reveled in—and sometimes seemed to invent—his own personal miseries, Gaye was Motown's most ambivalent pop star. His real desire, so he said, was to be a crooner along the lines of Frank Sinatra and Nat King Cole. But his fame—and, indeed, his best music—came from his early pop hits and his socially conscious spiritual journeys, culminating in the 1971 masterpiece *What's Going On* Gaye came to Motown via the Marquees (a group that enjoyed the patronage of Bo Diddley) and the Moonglows; it was during one of the latter's performances in Detroit that Berry Gordy, Jr., heard Gaye and signed him to his burgeoning label. Starting as a session drummer and marrying Gordy's sister Anna (their breakup would be the focus of his harrowing 1978 album *Here, My Dear*), Gaye began his string of hits in 1962 with "Stubborn Kind of Fellow," a run that would last into the mid-70s. Gaye also established himself as a generous duet partner, scoring hits with Mary Wells, Kim Weston, Tammi Terell and Diana Ross. Gaye's biggest solo hit, "I Heard it Through the Grapevine" in 1968, signaled a shift into deeper material—and darker subject matter; he fought hard to get Motown to release *What's Going On*, an epic song cycle on which Gaye took total control and weaved his observations about inner city youth, the ecology and race relations. He followed that with *Let's Get it On*, an immersion in eroticism that remained a focus through his last big hit, 1982's "Sexual Healing." Addled by drugs and depression, Gaye was in the midst of a career comeback when his father shot him after an argument. His has been one of the most lamented of the Motown passings, commemorated every year in Detroit with a special ceremony or concert.

what to buy: You have to ask? *What's Going On* (Motown, 1971, prod. Marvin Gaye) is not just a great Gaye album but is one of the great pop albums of all time. (Splurge and get the deluxe edition.) *The Master 1961-1984* (Motown, 1995, prod. Various) is one of those rare box sets that sustains its quality over the course of four discs. *Superhits* (Motown, 1970/1991, prod. Various) isn't the most comprehensive of Gaye's collections, but it was *the* Gaye album to own at the time and is still worth having for its cheesy superhero caricature on the cover.

what to buy next: *Let's Get it On* (Motown, 1973, prod. Marvin Gaye) offers the visceral desire of a man in serious heat. *Midnight Love* (Columbia, 1992, prod. Marvin Gaye) is much the same, though it's a little softer and just a touch more subtle. *Marvin Gaye & His Girls* (Motown, 1969/1990, prod. Various) is a nice collection of his duets with Wells, Weston and Terrell, missing only Diana Ross to make it a complete overview.

what to avoid: *Dream of a Lifetime* (Columbia, 1985) a posthumous release of material Gaye was working on at the time of his death, as bald a violation of his artistry as the releases that came out after Jimi Hendrix' death.

the rest: *Together With Mary Wells* (Motown, 1964/1991) *A Tribute to the Great Nat King Cole* (Motown, 1965/1989) *The Soulful Moods of Marvin Gaye* (Motown, 1966/1994) *Heard it Through the Grapevine* (Motown, 1968/1989) "Trouble Man" soundtrack (Motown, 1972/1989) *Live* (Motown, 1974) *I Want You* (Motown, 1976) *Greatest Hits* (Motown, 1976/1989) *Live at the London Palladium* (Motown, 1977) *Here, My Dear* (Motown, 1978/1994) *In Our Lifetime: The Final Motown Sessions* (Motown, 1981/1994) *Every Great Motown Hit* (Motown, 1983) *Romantically Yours* (Columbia, 1985/1989) *Great Songs & Performances that Inspired Motown 25* (Motown, 1983) *A Musical Testament* (Motown, 1988) *The Marvin Gaye Collection* (Motown, 1990) *The Last Concert Tour* (Giant, 1991) *Adults* (Hollywood/Rounder, 1992) *See and You Shall Find: More of the Best* (Rhino, 1993) *The Norman Whitfield Sessions* (Motown, 1994) *Motown Legends* (ESX, 1994) *Classics Collection* (Motown, 1994) *When I'm Alone I Cry* (Motown, 1994) *Anthology* (Motown, 1995) *Vulnerable* (Motown, 1996)

What Album Changed Your Life?

"Blue--it just hit me. I was a Joni Mitchell fan from day one. I was on boats and out there, and that was the background music to what I was doing in my life at the time. If I carry 10 CDs in my case, Blue and Court and Spark are two of them. It was the biggest thing since the first Gordon Lightfoot album I heard."

Jimmy Buffett

worth searching for: In 1986, Motown put both *What's Going On* and *Let's Get it On* on a single CD. The fidelity isn't quite up to the standards of later CD releases, but it's still a wonderful trip to slap it on and hear two of Gaye's finest albums flow back-to-back.

▶▶ Stevie Wonder, Frankie Beverly, Rick James, Terence Trent D'Arby, Barry White, Al B. Sure!, Keith Sweat, El DeBarge

◀◀ Nat King Cole, Frank Sinatra, Billie Holiday, Ray Charles, Clyde McPhatter, Little Willie John, Rudy West, the Orioles, the Capris

Gary Graff

Gear Daddies

See: Martin Zellar

J. Geils Band /Bluestime

Formed 1967 in Boston, Mass. Disbanded 1985.

J. (Jerome) Geils, guitar; Peter Wolf (born Peter Blankfield), vocals (1967-83); Seth Justman, keyboards, vocals (1968-85); Magic Dick (Salwitz), harmonica; Danny Klein, bass; Stephen Jo Bladd, drums

Part barroom blues ensemble, part soul revue, part arena rabble rousers, the J. Geils Band was a quintessentially American rock 'n' roll band, drawing from sources that stretched from Mississippi Delta blues to Motown to the Rolling Stones. During its 18 years together, the Geils gang was always painfully inconsistent, and for a minute—with 1981's multi-million selling *Freeze-Frame*— it was the hottest band in the land. The inconsistency was always frustrating for fans, because Geils had a loaded arsenal of talent—the motor-mouthed histrionics of former disc jockey Wolf, the sharp melodic sense of Justman, the truly enchanting harp skills of Magic Dick. When it clicked, few could beat Geils, and its concerts were usually 'til-we-all-drop marathons. The bottom fell out when the group was at the top, when Wolf left in 1983. The Geils chemistry was never the same without him, and a break-up was inevitable. Wolf has had a middling solo career, while Geils and Magic Dick went on to form the rootsier group Bluestime. There's periodic talk of a Geils reunion, but it has yet to transpire.

what to buy: The two-CD *Houseparty: The J. Geils Band Anthology* (Atlantic & Atco Remasters/Rhino, 1993, prod. Various) nails it, housing all the truly great Geils moments (though we'd rather have the full-length version of the 70s hit "Give it to Me"); it's essential either on its own or as a guide for future purchases. *Monkey Island* (Atlantic, 1977, prod. J. Geils Band) and *Love Stinks* (EMI, 1980, prod. Seth Justman) are the best of the studio sets, both of them marked by adventures sonic forays that don't abandon the group's melodic roots.

what to buy next: *Freeze-Frame* (EMI, 1981, prod. Seth Justman) was Geils' smash and remains entertaining, if not as consistently fresh as *Love Stinks*. No Geils collection is complete without a live recording; *Blow Your Face Out* (Atlantic, 1976/Rhino, 1993, prod. Allen Blazek, Bill Szymczk and the J. Geils Band) is the choice there, a rowdy representation of the group's onstage charisma, including Wolf's stream-of-consciousness raps.

what to avoid: *Hotline* (Atlantic, 1975/1990, prod. Bill Szymczk and Allen Blazek) is typical of the ineffectual studio work Geils was capable of during the early and mid-70s.

the rest: *The J. Geils Band* (Atlantic, 1970) *The Morning After* (Atlantic, 1971) *Full House* (Atlantic, 1972) *Bloodshot* (Atlantic, 1973) *Ladies Invited* (Atlantic, 1973) *Nightmares...and Other Tales From the Vinyl Jungle* (Atlantic, 1974) *Sanctuary* (EMI, 1978) *The Best of the J. Geils Band* (Atlantic, 1979) *You're Getting Even While I'm Getting Odd* (EMI, 1984) *Flashback: The Best of the J. Geils Band* (EMI, 1985)

worth searching for: Available only as an import, the live *Showtime!* (EMI, 1982/BGO, 1995, prod. Seth Justman) isn't quite as definitive as *Blow Your Face Out*, but it catches an exuberant Geils stand at the end of its triumphant *Freeze-Frame* tour.

solo outings:

Bluestime (J. Geils and Magic Dick): Bluestime (Rounder, 1994) *Little Care of Blues* (Rounder, 1996)

⏩ Aerosmith, Bruce Springsteen and the E Street Band, Michael Stanley Band, the Iron City Houserockers, Blues Traveler

⏪ James Brown, Jackie Wilson, the Yardbirds, John Mayall, the Rolling Stones, John Lee Hooker, Motown, Stax, Bill Haley & the Comets

see also: *Peter Wolf*

Gary Graff

Bob Geldof

See: The Boomtown Rats

Gene

Formed 1993 in London, England

Martin Rossiter, vocals; Steve Mason guitar; Kevin Miles bass; Matt James drums

While some quarters have attempted to write off this British quartet as mere Smiths copyists, there have been as many championing them as one of the few acts to convey sweeping emotion with intelligence, wit, charm (like the Smiths before them) and guts. The latter of these contrasting views is in fact more the case. The debut album *Olympian* (A&M, 1995, prod. Phil Vinall) actually encompasses many great influences in pop history, from mod to punk, soul, rockabilly and glam, all with effortless dexterity. Best of all, Rossiter turns out to be a singular human-relationship lyricist, with as much humor and eye for detail as empathy. Behind him, Mason is a wonderkind, mixing delicate and pounding riffs, with brilliantly understated runs and a knack for moodsetting, while the rhythm section handles hush as well as harsh with equal effectiveness. Their versatility thus encompasses the bounce of the opening "Haunted By You" through the more epic feel of "London, Can You Wait" and the title track. Also worth picking up is an import-only collection of British B-sides and live/demo/BBC session versions of "Olympian" material called *To See The Lights* (Costermonger Records U.K., 1996) ♪♪♪♪ that even betters the proper LP for consistent highs.

Jack Rabid

Generation X

See: Billy Idol

Genesis

Formed 1966 in Godalming, England

Tony Banks, keyboards; Mike Rutherford, guitar, bass, vocals; Peter Gabriel, vocals (1966-75); Anthony Phillips, guitar (1966-70); Chris Stewart, drums (1966-68); John Silver, drums (1968-69); John Mayhew, drums (1969-70); Phil Collins, drums, vocal (1970-96); Steve Hackett, guitar (1970-77)

Formed at England's private Charterhouse secondary school, Genesis is the most enduring group of the art rock movement, having not only survived but becoming more popular with each significant personnel change. The group's early touchstone was Jonathan King's hit "Everyone's Gone to the Moon," and its earliest recordings ape that song's pastoral psychedelia. But a later influence, King Crimson's *In the Court of the Crimson King*, was more profound; Genesis began crafting longer, more intricate pieces, combining together individual "bits" and ideas into suite-like compositions that featured Banks layered keyboards and the ambient guitars of Hackett and Rutherford. This reached a peak on the 23-minute opus "Supper's Ready" and the 1974 concept album *The Lamb Lies Down on Broadway*, after which original singer Gabriel—whose elaborate costumes and theatrical sense resulted in captivating concerts—left for a celebrated solo career. With Collins in front, Genesis never abandoned its longer compositions but made room for more pop fare and became a consistent resident of the Top 40 with hits such as "Follow You, Follow Me," "Invisible Touch" and "Land of Confusion." As Collins' solo career reached phenomenon peaks (Rutherford had a more modest success with his side band, Mike & the Mechanics, while Banks concentrated on film soundtracks) Genesis albums came further and further apart. His departure in 1996 could well be the band's death blow, though Rutherford and Banks have vowed to continue on—and Genesis has shown nothing if not a track record for resilience, particularly in the face of adversity. (Note: During 1994-95, Atlantic re-released most of Genesis' catalog in a Definitive Edition Remaster series. The titles are clearly marked, and all others should be avoided.)

what to buy: Genesis' sound truly gels on *Foxtrot* (Atlantic, 1972, prod. David Hitchcock) ♪♪♪♪ Gabriel's array of voicings give depth to the characters in "Get 'em Out by Friday" and the massive "Supper's Ready," while "Watcher of the Skies" is one of the majestic classics of art rock. Because its narrative is fairly oblique, *The Lamb Lies Down on Broadway* (Atlantic, 1974, prod. John Burns and Genesis) ♪♪♪♪ works as a flowing, almost formless concept piece, a musical journey rather than a dogmatic treatise. *A Trick of the Tail* (Atco, 1976, prod. David Hentschel and Genesis) ♪♪♪♪ quickly establishes that the group could survive Gabriel's departure, and the comparative brevity of songs such as "Squonk" and the title track is actually a welcome change of pace after the sprawl of *The Lamb. Abacab* (Atlantic, 1981, prod. Genesis) ♪♪♪♪ is the sonic pinnacle of the Collins years, a smart pop album that flows from the taut title track to the muscular swell of "Dodo/Lurker" to straightforward hit fare such as the horn-laden "No Reply at All" and the spare "Man on the Corner."

what to buy next: The politically pointed *Selling England by the Pound* (Atlantic, 1973, prod. John Burns and Genesis) ♪♪♪♪ refines many of *Foxtrot's* virtues but without the same sense of drama. *Wind & Wuthering* (Atco, 1977, prod. David Hentschel and Genesis) is, in hindsight, the final work of Genesis as a full-scale "progressive" rock band. *Seconds Out* (Atco, 1977, prod. David Hentschel and Genesis) ♪♪♪♪ is the best of Genesis' several live albums.

what to avoid: A transitional album following Hackett's departure, *...And Then There Were Three...* (Atlantic, 1978, prod. David Hentschel and Genesis) ♪♪ put Genesis on the radio with "Follow You, Follow Me" but lacked the meaty songcraft and ambitious arrangements of its predecessors—and of its successors.

the rest: *From Genesis to Revelation/In the Beginning* (PolyGram, 1968) ♪ *Trespass* (Charisma/MCA, 1970) ♪♪♪ *Nursery Cryme* (Atlantic, 1971) ♪♪♪ *Duke* (Atlantic, 1980) ♪♪♪♪ *Three Sides Live* (Atlantic, 1982) ♪♪♪♪ *Genesis* (Atlantic, 1983) ♪♪♪♪ *Invisible Touch* (Atlantic, 1986) ♪♪♪ *We Can't Dance* (Atlantic, 1991) ♪♪♪♪ *Live/The Way We Walk, Vol. 1: The Shorts* (Atlantic, 1992) ♪♪♪ *Live/The Way We Walk, Vol. 2: The Longs* (Atlantic, 1993) ♪♪♪

worth searching for: The import collection *Turn it On Again: Best of '81-'83* (Vertigo, 1991, prod. Genesis and Hugh Padgham) ♪♪♪♪ takes a nice snapshot of this three-year period, fleshing it out with some non-album singles ("Paperlate") and live tracks, including the entertaining "Turn it On Again" medley.

solo outings:

Tony Banks: A Curious Feeling (Charisma, 1979) ♪♪ *The Fugitive* (Charisma, 1983) ♪♪♪ *The Wicked Lady* (Atlantic, 1983) ♪♪ *Quicksilver* (Atlantic, 1986) ♪♪♪ *Bankstatement* (Atlantic, 1989) ♪♪

Steve Hackett: Voyage of the Acolyte (Chrysalis, 1976/Blue Plate, 1991) ♪♪♪ *Please Don't Touch* (Chrysalis, 1978/Caroline, 1991) ♪♪♪ *Spectral Mornings* (Charisma U.K., 1979/Blue Plate, 1991) ♪♪♪ *Defector* (Chrysalis, 1980/Blue Plate, 1991) ♪♪ *Cured* (Epic, 1981/Caroline, 1991) ♪♪♪ *Highly Strung* (Caroline, 1985/1991) ♪♪♪ (with GTR): *GTR* (Arista, 1986) ♪ *Time Lapse* (Blue Plate, 1992), ♪♪ *Guitar Noir* (Viceroy, 1993) ♪♪ *Gallery of Dreams* (Eurock, 1993) ♪♪ *Momentum* (Herald/Caroline, 1994) ♪♪ *Till We Have Faces* (Herald/Caroline, 1994) ♪♪♪ *Bay of Kings* (Caroline, 1994) ♪♪ *Blues With a Feeling* (Caroline, 1995) ♪

Mike Rutherford (with Mike & the Mechanics): Mike + the Mechanics (Atlantic, 1985) ♪♪♪♪ *The Living Years* (Atlantic, 1988) ♪♪ *Word of Mouth* (Atlantic, 1991) ♪♪ *Beggar on a Beach of Gold* (Atlantic, 1995) ♪♪

▶▶ Marillion, Styx, Kansas, Saga

◀◀ Jonathan King, King Crimson, Procol Harum, The Beatles

see also: *Phil Collins, Peter Gabriel, Mike Rutherford/Mike & the Mechanics*

Gary Graff

Lowell George

See: Little Feat

Georgia Satellites /Dan Baird

Formed 1983 in Atlanta, Ga. Disbanded 1991. Re-formed 1993.

Dan Baird, vocals, guitar (1979-91); Rick Richards, guitar; Mauro Megellan, drums (1979-91); Rick Price, bass; Joey Huffman, keyboards (1993-present); Billy Pitts, drums, (1993-present)

Unfairly written off as one-hit wonders ("Keep Your Hands to Yourself") the Georgia Satellites did have more to say than its ode to unrequited amore implied. After releasing three competent albums, the best of which stand as classic examples of white trash rock 'n' roll, the band fell commercially flat and disbanded in 1991 (but partially regrouped in 1993). *Let it Rock: The Best of The Georgia Satellites* (Elektra, 1993, prod. Various) ♪♪♪ is all that remains, and it's a decent sampler of their backwoods roots rock; still, it's worth searching for the group's excellent third album, *In the Land of Salvation and Sin.*(Elektra, 1989, prod. Joe Hardy and the Georgia Satellites) ♪♪♪♪ Singer Baird is having better luck solo, scoring a minor hit with the dumb "I Love You Period" from *Love Songs for the Hearing Impaired.* (Def American, 1992, prod. Brendan O'Brien) ♪♪♪ He struck again with the equally raucous *Buffalo Nickel* (American, 1996, prod. Brendan O'Brien) ♪♪♪

Allan Orski

Lisa Germano

Born 1958, in Mishawaka, Ind.

The daughter of classical musicians, Germano and her five siblings were all expected to learn an instrument—so the shy brunette studied the violin from age 7 to 18. Though she started playing classical music, her efforts eventually turned to country sounds, culminating in a gig at the Little Nashville Opry in Indiana. In these circles, she eventually befriended John Cougar Mellencamp drummer Kenny Aronoff, who in turn brought her to Mellencamp's attention when the Indiana rocker needed violin sounds for 1987's *The Lonesome Jubilee* album. Germano spent the next few years touring and recording with Mellencamp, squeezing in work with acts such as Simple Minds, Bob Seger and Billy Joel before releasing her first solo record in 1991. By now a multi-instrumentalist who could play piano, mandolin, guitar, accordion and harmonica as well, Germano recorded the entire record on her own—a feat she would repeat on subsequent releases. Crafting an intense, introspective style, Germano's own music offers an oddball mix of traditional instruments used in non-traditional ways. Signed to Capitol Records for her second solo record, the singer/songwriter grew frustrated with the label and eventually moved to 4AD Records, which re-released her second album before offering her third solo disc several months later.

what to buy: Though she clashed repeatedly with her label while making it, *Happiness* (Columbia, 1993, prod. Lisa Germano and Malcolm Burn) ♪♪♪♪ remains the best combination of Germano's quirky vision and an oddball, accessible appeal. Veering from a stark cover of Nancy Sinatra's "These Boots Are Made For Walkin' " to the percolating sound collage "Sycophant," Germano makes dissonance and dark thoughts an appealing prospect.

what to buy next: As the sonic tale of a young woman's coming of age, *Geek The Girl* (4AD, 1994, prod. Lisa Germano and Malcolm Burn) stands as a rich, darkly textured sonic journey. Blending a sample of a terrifying 911 call into the herky-jerky tune "A Psychopath"—inspired by her own longtime problems with a stalker—and enlisting a pennywhistle to kick off the dark brooding of "My Secret Reason," Germano makes disparate sounds serve a single purpose. At once earthy folk and dreamy performance art-style atmospherics, this record stands out as an intense, complex work.

what to avoid: Despite its delicate, darkly disturbing beauty, *On the Way Down From the Moon Palace* (Major Bill, 1991, prod. by Lisa Germano) is by far the slightest of her solo efforts.

the rest: *Excerpts From a Love Circus* (4AD, 1996)

worth searching for: Germano's many contributions to other's records, including Mellencamp's *The Lonesome Jubilee* and *Big Daddy* albums, the Indigo Girls' *Swamp Ophelia* and Bob Seger's *The Fire Inside*.

Michelle Malone, Mae Moore

Indigo Girls, Aimee Mann, Patti Smith

Eric Deggans

The Germs

Formed 1977 in Los Angeles, Calif. Disbanded 1980.

Darby Crash (born Paul Beahm), vocals (died Dec. 6, 1980); Pat Smear, guitar; Lorna Doom, bass; Donna Rhia, drums (1977); Don Bolles, drums (1977-79); Nicky Beat, drums (1979-80)

The Germs were America's punk rockers. Let the Sex Pistols put safety pins in their clothes; the Germs—particularly frontman Darby Crash—staged food fights and wore leopard fur jock straps. The Germs' story is almost prototypical punk legend: kindred spirits get together, can't really play or sing but do so anyway. A cult scene sprouts up around the group, which records one album and flames out, with one member (in this case Crash) winding up dead from a drug overdose. The music the Germs left behind is also prototypical—brutal, driving punk songs that blaze for a couple of minutes (or less) before a martial count launches the next one. It's captured in all its noisy and low-fi glory on *Germs (MIA): The Complete Anthology*, (Slash, 1993, prod. Various) a 30-track wonder that contains the group's legendary 1979 album *(GI)* and an assortment of other tracks including the "Forming/Sex Boy" single and a so-sloppy-it's-fun rendition of Chuck Berry's "Round and Round" that features X's D.J. Bonebrake on drums. *(MIA)* renders the rarities collection *Media Blitz* (Cleopatra, 1993) redundant. *Germicide—Live at the Whisky 1977* (ROIR, 1982) is tough to listen to, since the band hasn't quite gelled yet; but it does have a guest shot by one Dottie Dagger, better known later as Belinda Carlisle of the Go-Go's. The Germs didn't quite get its due while it was together, but the group is finally getting some recognition thanks to Smear's involvment in Nirvana and Foo Fighters and the tribute album *The Germs (Tribute) A Small Circle of Friends*, (Grass, 1996, prod. Various) which features performances by L7, Matthew Sweet, the Meat Puppets, the Posies, Thurston Moore and Kim Gordon, J Mascis and other modern rockers who have felt the Germs touch.

Gary Graff

Lisa Gerrard

See: Dead Can Dance

Gerry & the Pacemakers

Formed 1959 in Liverpool, England. Disbanded 1966.

Gerry Marsden, vocals; Les Maguire, piano; Les Chadwick, bass; Freddie Marsden, drums

Like their fellow Liverpudlians, the Beatles, Gerry & the Pacemakers found roots in Britain's late-50s skiffle craze. The group cut its teeth in the same Hamburg clubs where the Beatles played, and it was the first group signed by Brian Epstein after he secured the Beatles. But that's where the two groups parted ways. The music of Gerry and the Pacemakers was softer; Marsden's gentle vocals were sunny and reassuring, and only rarely did he cut loose into raunchier styles. Ironically, the group had its first hit with a number recorded but rejected by the Beatles—the 1963 U.K. hit "How Do You Do It?" The band made music history as the first rock group to have its first three records reach No. 1: "How Do You Do It?" and "I Like It," both written by Mitch Murray, and the unlikely Rodgers & Hammerstein ballad "You'll Never Walk Alone." Marsden went solo in 1967 and enjoyed success in stage work ("Charlie Girl") and children's TV. He has occasionally reformed the group for revival shows. *Gerry Cross the Mersey: All the Hits of Gerry and the Pacemakers* (Razor & Tie, 1995, prod. George Martin and

Ron Richards) is a worthy compilation filled with the sun-behind-the-clouds hopefulness that permeates the band's catalog. The 16 tracks include the group's U.K. and American hits ("How Do You Do It?," "You'll Never Walk Alone," "Don't Let The Sun Catch You Cryin'") plus some excellent B-sides, including the wistful and lovely "Ferry Cross the Mersey."

Christopher Scapelliti

Johnny Gill

See: New Edition

Ian Gillan

See: Deep Purple

Jimmy Dale Gilmore

Born May 6, 1945 in Amarillo, Texas

Blessed with a voice of extraordinary range and expressiveness—think Roy Orbison if he'd wanted to be Jimmie Rodgers instead of Mario Lanza—and a lyrical vision that is equal parts West Texas lonesome and the sound of one hand clapping, Gilmore is a unique presence in contemporary music. Silent for nearly two decades after his abortive debut with the supergroup-in-retrospect Flatlanders, Gilmore's solo career began in fairly conventional country territory and moved further left-of-center with each release. Gilmore's interpretive skills have led him to become the definitive interpreter of songs by fellow Texas visionary (and former Flatlander) Butch Hancock, while Gilmore's own songs have been covered by Natalie Merchant and David Byrne.

what to buy: *After Awhile* (Elektra Nonesuch American Explorer Series, 1991, prod. Stephen Bruton) is a stunning showcase for Gilmore's original artistry, notably the elliptical, Zen-like "Tonight I Think I'm Gonna Go Downtown" and "Treat Me Like a Saturday Night." But the album's otherworldly feel is nicely undercut by the gentle humor of Gilmore's own "Go to Sleep Alone" and the not-so-gentle humor of Hancock's "My Mind's Got a Mind of Its Own." To complete the package, the blazing "Midnight Blues" proves Gilmore can play with intensity. Just try keeping your jaw from dropping repeatedly while listening to this one. *Spinning Around the Sun* (Elektra, 1993, prod. Emory Gordy, Jr.) relies more heavily on covers than its predecessor, and it would rate as a superior work if it only contained Gilmore's near-definitive take on Hank Williams' "I'm So Lonesome I Could Cry," but that's only the tip of the iceberg. There's also a loping cover of the Elvis B-side "I Was the One" and Hancock's devastating lover's put-down "Just a Wave." If anything proves Gilmore's artistic mettle, its his cover of ex-wife Jo Carol Pierce's "Reunion," which imagines a couple sundered on earth to be reunited in the hereafter.

what to buy next: *Braver Newer World* (Elektra, 1996, prod. T-Bone Burnett) If "Magical Mystery Tour" had been recorded in Austin, Texas, it might sound something like this. Producer Burnett removes Gilmore almost entirely from a country context, surrounding him instead with saxophones, echo-laden drums and stinging, sitar-like guitar leads, making explicit Gilmore's country & Eastern leanings. It's a radical experiment, but it works.

the rest: *Fair & Square* (HighTone, 1988, prod. Joe Ely) *Jimmy Dale Gilmore* (HighTone, 1989, prod. Bruce Bromberg and Lloyd Maines)

worth searching for: The *Mudhoney/Jimmie Dale Gilmore* EP, (Sub Pop, 1994, prod. Various) a peculiar artifact on which Gilmore and the Seattle grunge pioneers cover each others' songs and team up for Townes Van Zandt's "Buckskin Stallion Blues."

Jim Lauderdale, Kevin Welch, Iris DeMent, Gillian Welch

Hank Williams, Roy Orbison, Buddy Holly, Jimmie Rodgers, Willie Nelson

see also: *The Flatlanders*

(By Daniel Durchholz)

David Gilmour

See: Pink Floyd

Gin Blossoms

Formed 1987 in Tempe, Ariz.

Robin Wilson, vocals (1988-present); Douglas Hopkins, guitar (1987-91, died 1993); Scott Johnson, guitar, vocals (1991-present); Jesse Valenzuela, guitar, vocals; Bill Leen, bass, vocals; Phillip Rhodes, drums, vocals (1988-present)

Friends Hopkins and Leen had played together in Tempe bands for years when, on a Christmas night, they debuted the Gin Blossoms with Valenzuela on lead vocals. Within months, Wilson had joined and gradually took over on lead vocals, his plaintive high voice becoming the group's sonic trademark. But Hopkins's drinking, chronicled perhaps too much on the first album's songs, had increasingly made him unreliable, and he was replaced between the first EP—*Up and Crumbling* (A&M, 1991, prod. Gin Blossoms) ♪♪♪—the end of recording for the first album. The writer of "Hey Jealousy" and "Found Out About You," the group's first two hits, Hopkins played on *New Miserable Experience* (A&M, 1992, prod. John Hampton and the Gin Blossoms) ♪♪♪½ and received all due songwriting credits, but there are no playing credits listed—just a band member list with his replacement, Johnson. It took over a year for the band's singles to become hits, but A&M stuck with it and ultimately the material, whose jangley guitars and tight harmonies certainly would have been radio-friendly in the 70s, benefited from changing formats and spearheaded the return of a sound once again considered commercial—the friendly side of the modern rock/alternative coin. Hopkins, despite the success of his songs, committed suicide shortly before Christmas 1993. Though his quirky outlook is missed on *Congratulations I'm Sorry,* (A&M, 1996, prod. John Hampton and the Gin Blossoms) ♪♪♪ the sophomore album is generally more consistent, and the gorgeous chorus of "As Long As It Matters" and the up-tempo guitar riff of "Whitewash" prove the remaining band members can write catchy material, too.

Steve Holtje

Ginger

Formed 1992, in Vancouver, British Columbia, Canada

Tom Hooper, vocals, bass, guitars; Chris Hooper, drums; Vincent Jones, keyboards

This trio took the lush sound of its former band, the Grapes of Wrath, a step further, retaining the The jangley guitars and moody vocals but giving wider berth to Jones' keyboard. *Ginger* (Nettwerk EP, 1994, prod. John Leckie) ♪♪♪♪ is a fine representation of that sound, with biting lyrics that are perhaps a reflection of the tumultuous relationship between the three and their former Grapes of Wrath bandmate, Kevin Kane ("I've given up something/I thought it was real/Now I don't care if I spend it with you/I'm tired of your problems/The earth revolves around you.") The anger seems to have subsided on Ginger's full-length debut *Far Out,* (Nettwerk, 1995, prod. Jim Rondinelli) ♪♪♪½ which has a personality similar to the earthy, acoustic-minded infancy of the Grapes—as well as a short CD-ROM presentation about the recording of the album.

Christina Fuoco

Girls Against Boys

Formed 1990 in Washington, D.C.

Scott McCloud, vocals, guitar; Eli Janney, bass, organ, vibraphone; Brendan Canty, drums (1990-92); Johnny Temple bass, keyboards, samples (1992-present); Alexis Fleisig, drums (1992-present)

Girls Against Boys (GvsB) all have hardcore backgrounds—McCloud, Temple and Fleisig were in Soulside, Canty is Fugazi's drummer—and while GvsB incorporate hardcore elements, their slower, darker, and groovier bass-lines set them far apart from their more traditional roots. Although they never intended to maintain a full-time band, GvsB have recently been taking metal to new extremes. Dubbed "ultra-rock" by the band—electronic music combined with a heavy but melodic rhythm section—is a hard, yet surprisingly sensual sound. Their secret lies in duel bass players, and being able to maintain the delicate balance of using tape loops and synthesizers, while keeping enough power and human element to still rock a live show. With their musical balance perfected and the band's recent move to a major label it would seem GvsB are poised to storm the modern rock world.

what to buy: *House of GvsB* (Touch and Go, 1996, Ted Nicely) ♪♪♪♪ polishes their "ultra-rock" to a smooth, sexy finish, but *House* takes GvsB beyond their normal boundaries to effortlessly incorporate elements of techno, jazz, and art-rock into their impressive range of musical styles.

what to buy next: *Cruise Yourself* (Touch and Go, 1994, prod. Ted Nicely) ♪♪♪½ is all about dark lyrics and industrial strength rhythm; the beat is hard and slow, but if it were any faster and it would be causing nose bleeds. *Venus Luxure No. 1 Baby* (Touch and Go, 1994, prod. Ted Nicely) ♪♪♪ the beats are kept bold and the humor dark, but a lack of variety forces the record to loose too much steam.

the rest: *Nineties vs. Eighties* (Adult Swim, 1991, prod. McCloud, Janney) ♪♪½

◀◀ Fugazi, Ministry, Einstrüzende Neubauten, Skinny Puppy, Soulside

Bryan Lassner

Glass Eye

See: Kathy McCarty

Gary Glitter

Born Paul Francis Gadd, May 8, 1940 in Banbury, England

An important figure in the era of glam rock—though not nearly as influential as David Bowie or T. Rex—Glitter was the third incarnation of aspiring pop star Paul Gadd. After years of toiling in a ballad-heavy teen pop-star mode, Gadd reinvented himself as Glitter and charted 11 consecutive Top 10 singles in the U.K. His trademarks were cheesy handclap effects, sleazy guitar riffs and massive, singalong choruses—basically rock 'n' roll sports cheers. Glitter's legacy is mostly wrapped up in one song—"Rock and Roll Part II"—whose rousing "Hey!" chorus is played at virtually every sporting event. Appearing onstage in tacky, sparkling outfits which often showcased his growing girth, Glitter nevertheless seemed in on the joke and could be a hilarious, rousing stage performer. While critics and other musicians sniggered, he inspired a manic following which inevitably departed as his fame fleeted. He declared bankruptcy in 1980 but soon came out of retirement to begin touring again to cash in on "Rock and Roll's" burgeoning popularity.

what to buy: *Greatest Hits* (Rhino, 1991, prod. Michael Leander) ♪♪♪♪ not only showcases his chart-topping run of great singles but is as infectious a singalong record as any you'll encounter.

the rest: *Gary Glitter Gangshow: The Gang, the Band, the Leader* ♪♪♪ (Castle Communications, 1989)

▶▶ Kiss, Joan Jett, Def Leppard, Oasis

◀◀ David Bowie, T. Rex

Todd Wicks

The Glove

See: The Cure

Roger Glover

See: Deep Purple

The Go-Betweens /Robert Forster

Formed 1977 in Brisbane, Australia. Disbanded 1990.

Grant McLennan, vocals, bass, guitar (1978-90); Robert Forster, vocals, guitar (1978-90); Lindy Morrison, drums (1980-90); Robert Vickers, bass (1983-88); Amanda Brown, violin, oboe, vocals (1986-90); John Willsteed, bass (1988-90)

The story of the Go-Betweens is one that should inspire all young musicians. Starting out as a slightly Dylan-influenced duo, Forster and McLennan flew off to the U.K. in 1982 to take their shot at creating a lasting musical career for themselves. But rather than getting caught up in the syrupy synth-pop scene that held sway in Britain at the time, they blazed their own trail to develop a coarse, bittersweet post-punk sound during the early 80s through tentative ornamentalism in the mid-80s until they finally produced a mini-classic, *16 Lovers Lane*, for their swan song. Early on, it was Forster, with his frank, occasionally out-of-tune vocals, who dominated; McLennan took over later, as he began to find his compositional and stylistic voice. The band broke up in 1990, and while Forster and McLennan have released several solo albums, McLennan has received greater acclaim—particularly for 1995's impressive *Horsebreaker Star*

what to buy: *16 Lovers Lane* (Beggars Banquet/Capitol, 1988, prod. Mark Wallis) ♪♪♪♪ is a gem from start to finish. McLennan's driving, straightforward and jangly pop tunes ("Streets of Your Town," "Is There Anything I Could Do?") are balanced beautifully by Forster's pensive, more puzzling material ("Clouds," "Love Is a Sign"), and producer Wallis helps the band create gorgeously hazy arrangements, using airy backup vocals, warm violin lines and incisive oboe parts to support a mesmerizing group of songs.

what to buy next: *The Go-Betweens/1978-1990* (Beggars Banquet/Capitol, 1990, prod. Various) ♪♪♪♪ surveys the band's career, though with a bit too much space allotted to early singles and less-than-stunning B-sides. *Liberty Belle and the Black Diamond Express* (Beggars Banquet, 1986, prod. Richard Preston) ♪♪♪♪ marks the band's transition from loose experimentalism to a more structured approach; McLennan's "In the Core of a Flame" is especially strong, and Forster's "Head Full of Steam" ranks among his best.

what to avoid: Poorly recorded and somewhat amateurish in execution, the band's debut, *Send Me a Lullaby*, (Beggars Banquet, 1981) ♪♪ will be of interest only to completists.

the rest: *Before Hollywood* (Beggars Banquet, 1983) ♪♪♪ *Spring Hill Fair* (Beggars Banquet, 1984) ♪♪♪ *Tallulah* (Beggars Banquet, 1987) ♪♪♪♪

worth searching for: *Metals and Shells* (PVC, 1985, prod. Various) ♪♪♪ a pithy but out-of-print compilation drawn from the group's first four albums.

solo outings:

Robert Forster: Danger in the Past (Beggars Banquet/RCA,

1991) ♪♪♪ *I Had a New York Girlfriend* (Beggars Banquet, 1994, prod. Robert Forster) ♪♪♪♪

▶▶ Deacon Blue, Downy Mildew, Poi Dog Pondering

◀◀ Echo and the Bunnymen, the Cure, Bob Dylan

see also: *Grant McLennan*

Bob Remstein

The Go-Go's

Formed 1978 in Hollywood, Calif. Disbanded 1984. Reunited in 1990 and 1994.

Belinda Carlisle, vocals; Charlotte Caffey, guitar; Jane Wiedlin, guitar (1978-84, 1990-94); Margot Olaverra, bass (1978-80); Elissa Bello, drums (1978-79); Gina Schock, drums (1979-present); Kathy Valentine, bass (1980-present)

Not the first all-female rock band, but certainly the most popular, the Go-Go's began in the late 70s Los Angeles punk scene and honed its act in clubs and on tour in England. Its debut album went to No. 1 and produced two enduring anthems, "We Got the Beat" and "Our Lips Are Sealed," providing inspiration for untold numbers of future female rockers. The group's subsequent two albums were considered relative failures but managed to produce some solid singles as well. Each member has dabbled in music since the 1984 breakup, including a serious solo career for lead singer Carlisle. The group reunited for a tour in 1990 and again in 1994, when they recorded a few new songs to accompany a compilation.

what to buy: The group's buoyant, giddy fun is captured perfectly on the delicious first album, *Beauty and the Beat,* (I.R.S., 1981, prod. Richard Gottehrer and Rob Freeman) ♪♪♪♪♪ and not just in the hit singles; check out "This Town," "Lust to Love," "Skidmarks on My Heart," "Tonight" and "Fading Fast."

what to buy next: *Greatest* (I.R.S., 1990, prod. Various) ♪♪♪♪ covers the high points, with lots from the first album and essentials from the next two (which are out of print), including "Turn to You," "Head Over Heels" and "Vacation."

what to avoid: *Return to the Valley of the Go-Go's* (I.R.S., 1994, prod. Various) ♪♪♪ is recommended for firm fans only. It goes beyond the greatest hits to present revealing early punk incarnations of the group and decent but unexceptional reunion recordings.

worth searching for: An acoustic solo performance of "We Got the Beat" climaxes guitarist Wiedlin's best-of compilation *The Very Best of Jane Wiedlin: From Cool Places to Worlds on Fire* (EMI, 1993, prod. Various) ♪♪♪♪

solo outings:

Belinda Carlisle: *Belinda Carlisle* (I.R.S., 1986) ♪♪♪ *Heaven on Earth* (MCA, 1987) ♪♪♪♪ *Runaway Horses* (MCA, 1989) ♪♪♪ *Her Greatest Hits* (MCA, 1992) ♪♪♪♪ *Real* (Virgin, 1993) ♪♪

Jane Wiedlin (with froSTed): *Cold* (DGC, 1996) ♪♪♪♪

▶▶ The Bangles, Bikini Kill, Tiger Trap

◀◀ The Chordettes, the Shangri-La's, the Germs

Roger Catlin

Go West

Formed 1980 in Twickenham, England. Disbanded 1993.

Peter Cox, lead vocals, keyboards, guitar, programming; Richard Drummie, guitar, keyboards, backing vocals, programming

Friends since discovering an early, shared interest in the rock band Free, Cox and Drummie made their partnership official in 1980, scored a publishing deal in 1982 and released their first record two years later. Blending Cox's powerhouse vocals with a blend of highly-produced, synthesizer-heavy dance-pop, the duo made a minor U.S. splash with its well-crafted debut. Fearing its teen-idol good looks and seamless pop sound would get them tagged as the next Wham!, the duo turned in a sophomore record that was more arty and adventurous—and watched as its minor U.S. following evaporated in its wake. Its career got a second boost with 1990's "King of Wishful Thinking," mostly due to its prominence in the hit film "Pretty Woman." The duo's last release surrounded that single with similarly crafted, horn-drenched soul/pop—kind of like Phil Collins with earthier singing—but its relatively modest success didn't keep Cox from ditching Drummie to go it alone for a 1996 release.

what to buy: For those who enjoy the duo's agonizingly crafted sound—and it's definitely an acquired taste—the debut *Go West* (Chrysalis, 1984, prod. Gary Stevenson) ♪♪♪♪ offers an impressive sample of its strengths, namely, interesting grooves, spot-on playing and Cox's amazingly soulful and skillful belting. Hearing his impassioned performance on the ballad "Goodbye Girl"—perhaps the best blue-eyed soul workout in recent memory—is worth owning the album alone.

what to buy next: The retrospective *Aces and Kings: The Best of Go West* (ERG, 1993, prod. Gary Stevenson) ♪♪♪♪ gathers the group's many sterling film soundtrack contributions—including hip-shaking songs from "Rocky IV," "White Men Can't Jump" and "Pretty Woman"—in one package.

what to avoid: Though Go West was consistent in its mediocrity, its second album, *Dancing on the Couch* (Chrysalis, 1987, prod. Gary Stevenson) suffers for its artsy and insincere efforts to get away from the group's commercial sound.

the rest: *Bangs and Crashes* (Chrysalis, 1985) *Indian Summer* (EMI, 1992)

worth searching for: Cox's unmistakable backing vocals make the hip-hop-tinged "Come the Revolution" the coolest cut on former Tears for Fears bassist Curt Smith's solo album *Soul on Board.* (Mercury, 1993)

▶▶ Seal, the Rembrandts

◀◀ Smokey Robinson, Earth Wind and Fire, Gary Numan

Eric Deggans

God Street Wine

Formed 1990 in New York, N.Y.

Lo Faber, vocals, guitar; Aaron Maxwell, vocals, guitar; Dan Pifer, bass, vocals; Jon Bevo, keyboards, vocals; Tomo, drums, vocals

One of the many 90s bands chasing the jam-happy ideals (and the audience) of the Grateful Dead, God Street Wine plays a loose-limbed kind of rock but goes a step or two further than some of its peers by embracing a variety of styles—though it also falls victim to concentrating too much on tones and not enough on tunes. But GSW is certainly on a learning curve, as evidenced by *Red* (Mercury, 1996) The songs are getting mildly tighter and more focused ("RU4 Real" borders on power pop), while its stylistic reach is broader than ever, moving from blues shuffles to percolating reggae. Always better live (so far), *Who's Driving* (Ripe & Ready, 1993) captures GSW at its indulgent best, though its earnest spirit compensates for some of the more interminable jams.

the rest: *Bag* (Ripe & Ready, 1992) *$1.99 Romances* (Geffen, 1994)

Gary Graff

The Golden Palominos

Formed 1981 in New York, N.Y.

"These records are totally self-indulgent projects for me. I don't make my living off of them and I never have. They're just ways to explore different processes and ways for me to learn about different elements of music, ways to learn about different elements of process," says Palominos ringleader, percussionist Anton Fier, whose drumming and producing gigs would keep two ordinary men busy. Furthermore, he leads a "group" of himself and whomever he feels like working with; the other near-constants are fellow eclectics Bill Laswell on bass and Nicky Skopelitis on guitar. Not surprisingly, the Palominos sound changes from album to album, from the downtown New York City avant-gardisms of the group's 1983 debut, through four albums that were more song-oriented yet still stylistically varied, and then dreamy ambient-influenced work.

what to buy: *A History (1982-1985)* (Metrotone/Restless, 1992, prod. Various) contains all but one track ("Clean Plate," worth seeking out) of the debut album, *The Golden Palominos,* (Celluloid, 1981, prod. Anton Fier and Bill Laswell) and the entire sophomore effort *Visions of Excess,* (Celluloid, 1985, prod. Anton Fier) both masterpieces in entirely different ways. The former features the avant-garde shenanigans of guitarist/vocalist Arto Lindsay and John Zorn, who toots not only alto sax and clarinet but also game calls. Bassist Jamaaladeen Tacuma (Ornette Coleman's Prime Time) and guitarist Fred Frith show up on a few tracks too. It's structured improvisation in which any sound may happen. *Visions of Excess* tackles mainstream rock from the periphery and makes more explicit the rotating-cast concept, with vocalists alone including Michael Stipe (R.E.M.), John Lydon (Sex Pistols/Public Image Ltd.), Jack Bruce (Cream), Syd Straw and Lindsay. The largely collaborative songwriting is strong enough that every tune is memorable.

what to buy next: On the spacey *This Is How It Feels,* (Restless, 1993, prod. Anton Fier) Laswell's dub-like bass lines, Fier's super-steady rhythms, Bernie Worrell's swirling Hammond organ licks and the breathy vocals of Lori Carson (who recorded a 1990 singer-songwriter album, *Shelter*, for Geffen) and Lydia Kavanagh (of She Never Blinks) combine to flirt with a sort of real-time ambient/trip-hop feel. The Lyrics are based on Graham Greene's 1951 novel "The End of the Affair," except for a striking cover of Jackson Browne's "These Days."

what to avoid: *A Dead Horse* (Celluloid, 1989, prod. Anton Fier) is as tired and uninspired as its title suggests.

the rest: *Blast of Silence* (Celluloid, 1986) *Drunk With Passion* (Charisma, 1991) *A History (1986-1989)* (Metrotone/Restless, 1992) *Prison of the Rhythm—The Remixes* (Restless, 1993) *Pure* (Restless, 1994) Prison of the Rhythm-The Remixes (Restless, 1993) *No Thought, No Breath, No Eyes, No Heart* (Restless, 1995)

worth searching for: The "Omaha" 12" (Celluloid, 1985) is notable for a non-album B-side cover of Ennio Morricone's movie theme "For a Few Dollars More" produced by Material/OAO. The flip side of "The Animal Speaks" 12" (Celluloid, 1985) includes a version with vocals by Bruce instead of Lydon.

Hector Zazou, Jeff Buckley, Matthew Sweet

Steely Dan, DNA, Bill Laswell, David Sylvian, Cocteau Twins

Steve Holtje

Golden Smog

Formed 1992 in Minneapolis, Minn.

Jeff Tweedy (a.k.a. Scot Summit), vocals, guitar; Dan Murphy (David Spear), vocals, guitar; Gary Louris (Michael Macklyn), vocals, guitar; Marc Perlman (Jarret Decatur), vocals, bass; Kraig Johnson, vocals, guitar; Noah Levy (Leonardson Saratoga), drums (1993-present); Chris Mars, drums (1992)

Golden Smog is a supergroup of punk-inspired rockers—most of whom have major record label contracts—obsessed with twangy, genuine country music. It began as an experiment, a way to slip away from the spotlight and pressure the members felt with their better-known bands. At first, the band was Jayhawks Louris and Perlman messing around with their Minneapolis friends, including Soul Asylum's Murphy and Dave Pirner; its rapidly rotating lineup grew to encompass ex-Replacement Mars, Wilco/Uncle Tupelo's Tweedy, Run Westy Run's Johnson and, later, the Honeydogs' Levy. After *On Golden Smog*, (Crackpot, 1992/Rykodisc, 1996, prod. James Bunchberry Lane) a goofy EP of country-rock covers, the band played a few shows for laughs. The ramshackle side project later became legitimate business: the more consistent and almost offhandedly casual *Down by the Old Mainstream* (Rykodisc, 1996, prod. James Bunchberry Lane) solidified the side project's hip cache.

Steve Knopper

Goo Goo Dolls

Formed in 1986 in Buffalo, N.Y.

Johnny Rzeznik, guitar and vocals; Robby Takac, bass; George Tutuska, drums (1986-95); Mike Malinin, drums (1995-present)

Diehard Replacements fans (are there any other kind?) write this trio off as Paul Westerberg wanna-be's, but they're not listening closely. Pulling themselves out of the speed-metal/thrash heap with 1990's *Hold Me Up*, the Goos have emerged as a brash but bracing power-pop outfit that is far more tuneful and optimistic than the 'Mats ever wanted to be. Beneath the crunching guitars, frat-pack stage antics and lunkheaded garage-band charm lies guitarist Rzeznik's simple but heartfelt proclamations of romantic and youthful desire. When you call yourselves the Goo Goo Dolls and frequently encore with Tommy Tutone's "867-5309," you can't expect people to take you seriously. But then, that's why unexpected lines like "I don't even know what to say so I'm thinking out loud" resonate long after the last power chord has faded away.

what to buy: *Superstar Car Wash* (Warner Bros., 1993, prod. Gavin MacKillop) sustains the guitar-driven assault tactics of earlier albums but tightens the arrangements, brightens the choruses and dares to invite even more Replacements comparisons by co-writing one tune ("We Are the Normal") with Paul Westerberg. The band teams with noted producer Lou Giordano for its platinum breakthrough, *A Boy Named Goo* (Warner Bros., 1995), which contains the hit "Name" and a ragged cover of the obscure "Slave Girl" by the Australian band Lime Spiders.

what to buy next: The fascinating sound of a young band in transition is captured on *Hold Me Up* (Warner Bros., 1990, prod. Armand John Petri) which combines tough-rocking originals like "Just the Way You Are" and "There You Are" with covers of the Plimsouls' "A Million Miles Away" and Prince's "I Could Never Take the Place of Your Man" (with guest vocals by Buffalo lounge lizard Lance Diamond).

what to avoid: Recorded before Rzeznik matured as the band's visionary, the thrashy *Goo Goo Dolls* (Celluloid/Metal Blade, 1987, prod. Goo Goo Dolls) has little in common with the Dolls you know now, save for a penchant for cool covers (in this case, Blue Oyster Cult's "Don't Fear the Reaper" and Cream's "Sunshine of Your Love").

the rest: *Jed* (Metal Blade, 1989)

worth searching for: The soundtrack of "Ace Ventura: When Nature Calls" (MCA, 1995, prod. Various) boasts the Goos' killer version of INXS' "Don't Change."

Triplefast Action, Goldfinger

The Replacements, Cheap Trick

David Okamoto

Steve Goodman

Born July 25, 1948 in Chicago, Ill. Died September 20, 1984 in Seattle, Wash.

Goodman was a folk singer from Chicago and good friend of John Prine who emerged in the early 70s with a great gift for blues guitar playing and, like Prine, compassionate and humorous songwriting. His compositions have been recorded often—by Jimmy Buffett, Prine, David Allen Coe and the Clancy Brothers, among others. His classic, "The City of New Orleans" has been done by Arlo Guthrie, John Denver and Willie Nelson. After a bout with major labels, Goodman settled into a groove with his own Red Pajamas imprint until he died in 1984 of leukemia at age 36.

what to buy: *No Big Surprise* (Red Pajamas, 1994, prod. Various) ♪♪♪♪♪ is a worthy anthology, with a disc each of Goodman in the studio and onstage. *Somebody Else's Troubles,* (Buddah, 1972, prod. Arif Mardin) ♪♪♪♪½ an early collection that includes "The Dutchman," "The Loving of the Game" and the powerful "The Ballad of Penny Evans." *Santa Ana Winds* (Red Pajamas, 1980, prod. Steve Goodman) ♪♪♪♪ is his best collection produced the way it ought to be.

what to buy next: *Affordable Art* (Red Pajamas, 1983, prod. Steve Goodman and Dan Einstein) ♪♪♪½ includes "Talk Backwards," "Watching Joey Glow" and "A Dying Cub Fan's Last Request," one of the most poignant of all baseball songs.

what to avoid: Like many good songwriters, Goodman had problems with major labels who had no easily marketable niches for him. *High and Outside* (Asylum, 1979, prod. Steve Goodman) ♪ is a prophetic title; though the songs aren't bad, this stab at slick arrangements (the soul wanna-be "Just Lucky I Guess," for instance) strangles them in a death grip.

the rest: *Words We Can Dance To* (Asylum, 1976) ♪♪♪ *Say It In Private* (Asylum, 1977) ♪♪♪ *Hot Spot* (Asylum, 1980) ♪♪♪ *The Essential Steve Goodman* (Buddah, 1976) ♪♪♪ *The Best of the Asylum Years Vol. 1* (Red Pajamas, 1988) ♪♪♪ *The Best of the Asylum Years Vol. 2* (Red Pajamas, 1989) ♪♪♪ *The Original Steve Goodman* (Buddah, 1989) ♪♪♪ *Steve Goodman* (Buddah, 1972) ♪♪ *Jessie's Jig and Other Favorites* (Asylum, 1975) ♪♪♪½ *Artistic Hair* (Red Pajamas, 1983) ♪♪♪ *Unfinished Business* (Red Pajamas, 1987) ♪♪♪

worth searching for: *Tribute to Steve Goodman* (Red Pajamas, 1985, prod. Al Bunetta) ♪♪♪♪½ is a loving salute with lots of special guests, with Prine, Arlo Guthrie, John Hartford, Bonnie Raitt and David Bromberg among those performing some of Goodman's best tunes.

James McMurtry, Michael Penn, Steve Forbert

Bob Gibson, Josh White, Woody Guthrie, Bob Wills, Hank Williams, Big Bill Broonzy, Jethro Burns, Bob Dylan

Leland Rucker

Lesley Gore

Born May 2, 1946, in New York, N.Y.

The unlikely pairing of teenager Gore and producer Quincy Jones resulted in a flurry of Top 10 hits in 1963—"It's My Party," "Judy's Turn to Cry," "She's a Fool" and "You Don't Own Me" were memorable bright spots in her shooting-star career. The latter single found Gore using a surprisingly independent tone for that era. Gore had a few other hits, but after "California Nights" in 1967 the party was over. Compilations range from affordable to over-the-top. *It's My Party: The Mercury Years* (Mercury, 1996) ♪♪♪♪ and *The Lesley Gore Anthology* (Rhino, 1986) ♪♪♪½ are your best best. *The Golden Hits of Lesley Gore* (Mercury, 1987) ♪♪♪ is comparatively skimpy. And for fanatics, there's a five-disc box set import available on the Bear Family label for $124.99, Judy won't be the only one crying.

Patrick McCarty

Martin Gore

See: Depeche Mode

John Gorka

Born July 27, 1958, in Edison, N.J.

With dark good looks, subtle humor and a rich, sensitive baritone, Gorka has become one of the best-known names in the American folk scene of the 80s and 90s. A native of New Jersey who works out of steel country in Pennsylvania, his most touching songs often personalize those displaced by changing times. He first gained attention by winning the New Folk Award at the Kerrville Folk Festival in 1984 and has since released a number of albums that showcase his voice as well as his songs.

It's the quietly emotional nature of his music that has won him fans outside the usual folk circles.

what to buy: *Jack's Crows* (High Street, 1991, prod. Dawn Atkinson and Will Akerman) is perhaps the most intimate of Gorka's albums, highlighted by "Houses in the Fields," a heart-wrenching take on the development of America's farmland that extended Gorka's popularity well beyond the New England folk circuit.

what to buy next: *Out of the Valley* (High Street, 1994, prod. John Jennings) is Gorka's first album with a full band, a host of Nashville musicians who help provide a different slant to his songs.

the rest: *I Know* (Red House, 1987) *Land of the Bottom Line* (Windham Hill, 1990) *Temporary Road* (High Street, 1992) *Between Five and Seven* (High Street, 1996)

worth searching for: *Motor Folkin',* (High Street, 1994) a promotional CD containing a live version of "Furniture" recorded at a Seattle radio station.

Bill Morrissey, Peter Keane

Stan Rogers

Brian Mansfield

Govt Mule

See: Allman Brothers Band

Lou Gramm

See: Foreigner

Grand Funk Railroad

Formed March 1969 in Flint, Mich. Disbanded 1976. Re-formed 1980. Disbanded 1983. Re-formed 1996.

Mark Farner, guitar, vocals, keyboards, harmonica; Don Brewer, drums, vocals; Mel Schacher, bass (1969-76; 1996-present); Craig Frost, keyboards (1972-76); Dennis Bellinger, bass (1981-83)

Grand Funk Railroad was one of the loudest, rawest and most successful rock bands to ever rumble out of Michigan. Formed in the blue collar town of Flint—home to General Motors and the United Auto Workers—Grand Funk was rooted in the aggressive guitar rock of then-dominant power trios such as Cream and the Jimi Hendrix Experience, as well as nearby Motown. Mark, Don and Mel—as fans often referred to them—were one of the first groups to be known as a "people's band," meaning critics hated it. The group made a reported $5 million in 1971 alone, the same year it broke the Beatles' gross ticket sales mark at New York's Shea Stadium—a show that sold out faster than the Fab Four's 1965 appearance there. GFR's first 11 albums went either platinum or gold, with more than 20 million sold by the time the band broke up after the Frank Zappa-produced *Good Singin' Good Playin'* in 1976. A brief early 80s reunion, with former band tech Bellinger taking a reluctant Schacher's place, fell flat, but the original trio reunited in 1996 with plans to record again—including new songs for a planned 1997 box set—while Capitol Records is remastering and re-releasing nine of the group's classic titles.

what to buy: Because only a handful of the group's titles are available domestically on CD, there aren't many to choose from. The compilation *Grand Funk Railroad* (Capitol Collectors Series, 1991, prod. Various) is an effective time capsule of its 70s heyday, collecting singles from 1969's quasi-psychedelic "Time Machine" to 1974's sweet "Bad Time" and chronicling the band's transition from underground heroes ("Inside Looking Out," "Heartbreaker") to Top 40 sell-outs ("Some Kind of Wonderful," "The Loco-Motion").

what to buy next: Capitol, the band's label home from 1969-75, is re-mastering and re-issuing 11 Grand Funk titles as part of a budget CD line, but it's been a slow process. *Closer to Home* (Capitol, 1970, prod. Terry Knight) is the best of what's out, a solid studio effort notable for its inspirational centerpiece, "Closer to Home/"I'm Your Captain."

what to avoid: Either of the band's reunion albums—*Grand Funk Lives* (Full Moon/Warner Bros., 1981, prod. Grand Funk and Andrew Cavaliere) and *What's Funk* (Full Moon/Warner Bros., 1983, prod. Various) —which, like the last couple of albums before the 1976 breakup, found the group searching for direction. Its rendition of "Queen Bee," however, did get some notice, thanks to its appearance on the "Heavy Metal" soundtrack.

the rest: *E Pluribus Funk* (Capitol, 1971/1995) *We're An American Band* (Capitol, 1973/1996) *Caught in the Act* (Capitol, 1975/1995) *More of the Best* (Rhino, 1991)

worth searching for: *Grand Funk Railroad,* (Capitol, 1970) also known as "The Red Album" because of its bright red cover, is the group's best studio effort and will be part of the reissue series. Those who can't wait might want to hunt down a Canadian edition on the Collector's Pipeline label, though the art reproduction is horrid. Many of Grand Funk's original albums are also available via Japanese import, but beware the inferior sound quality.

solo outings:

Mark Farner: Mark Farner (Atlantic, 1977) *No Frills* (Atlantic, 1978) *Just Another Injustice* (Frontline, 1988)

Kiss, Bon Jovi, Foreigner, Boston, Soul Asylum

Motown, Cream, Hendrix

Doug Pullen

Grandmaster Flash and the Furious Five

Formed 1977 in New York, N.Y. Disbanded 1983. Reunited 1987.

Grandmaster Flash (born Joseph Sadler); Melle Mel (born Melvin Glover); Kidd Creole (born Nathaniel Glover); Scorpio a.k.a. Mr. Ness (born Eddie Morris); Rahiem (born Guy Todd Williams); Cowboy (born Keith Wiggins, died Sept. 8, 1989)

Grand Wizard Theodore may have invented the art of scratching, but it was Grandmaster Flash who brought punch phrasing—a precursor to sampling—to the masses. Of course, as the first DJ to break out of the New York underground, Flash also introduced the music-buying world to back-spinning (manually rewinding record, then repeating the break or groove) and phasing (record-speed manipulation), as well as scratching. After earning legendary status for his innovative mixing and scratching techniques in the underground—where he had performed since the mid-70s with various rappers, including Kurtis Blow—Flash and his rap accompanists, the Furious Five, took the plunge into the realm of recorded music with 1979's long-lost "Superrappin'," followed by 1980's better-known single, "Freedom." But it was 1981's groundbreaking "The Adventures of Grandmaster Flash on the Wheels of Steel" that finally introduced the world to the previously unheard (on record) mixing and scratching techniques that were popular at hip-hop parties. The layered collage included breaks and bits of Chic's "Good Times," Queen's "Another One Bites the Dust," Blondie's "Rapture" (with Deborah Harry chanting "Flash is bad" over and over) and a children's recording for a piece that remains endlessly rewarding and fascinating. But Flash, who studied electronics in school and essentially built the first hip-hop-era mixing board out of spare parts and glue, wasn't the only star of his records; the Furious Five, led by Melle Mel and Cowboy, also earned an important place in the rap pantheon, introducing groundbreaking vocal routines and harmonizing on 1982's "Flash to the Beat." The Furious Five also occasionally moved away from the typical rap party themes: The edgy, apocalyptic 1982 single, "The Message," for instance, focused on social decay and despair in the inner cities and was the first successful political rap song, while 1983's "White Lines (Don't Don't Do It)," which would become a modern-rock and dance club standard, addressed the destructive nature of cocaine and examined racial and socioeconomic injustice. After recording "White Lines," however, Grandmaster Flash and the Furious Five splintered into two groups, with Flash, Rahiem and Kidd Creole going one way and Melle Mel, Scorpio and Cowboy another. Melle Mel also collaborated with Chaka Khan on the 1984 hit "I Feel For You." Although Mel's post-Flash trio retained the Furious Five name, with Mel adding "Grandmaster" to his own moniker, Flash's group (which included the forgettable likes of Larry Love, Lavon, Mr. Broadway and Shame) also billed itself as the Furious Five—until Flash lost a lawsuit against Sugarhill Records. After recording several poor-selling and poor-quality albums each, the two sides reunited for a 1987 charity concert and recorded a new album. Ironically, though, by that time, the sampling and production technology that Flash had anticipated with his pioneering mixing techniques had passed the group by. Aside from a few greatest hits collections, all albums by Grandmaster Flash and the Furious Five and Grandmaster Melle Mel and the Furious Five are out of print. That, however, is not a bad thing, since Flash and Co. come from the singles-oriented rap era. The best bets are *Message From the Beat Street: The Best of Grandmaster Flash, Melle Mel and the Furious Five* (Rhino, 1994, prod. Various) and *The Adventures of Grandmaster Flash, Melle Mel and the Furious Five: More of the Best.* (Sugarhill/Rhino, 1996, prod. Various) The first set includes most of the group's key songs, including "The Message," "White Lines (Don't Don't Do It)" and the amusing "Showdown," which features the studio-created Sugarhill Gang. The second set is worth buying simply for the otherwise impossible-to-find "The Adventures of Grandmaster Flash on the Wheels of Steel."

Joshua Freedom du Lac

Eddy Grant

Born March 5, 1948 in Plaisance, Guyana, West Indies

Grant emerged in 1968 as a dreadlocked one-man-band and corporation, playing all the instruments and releasing his albums on his own Ice label. More pop star than reggae purist, he hit it big in 1983 with "Electric Avenue," a funky single that earned him a shot at the title track for the film "Romancing the Stone"—which, as fate would have it, was rejected. Grant's Ice catalog is available via import, but there's nothing currently in print in the U.S. Check the racks for *Killer on the Rampage* (Epic, 1982) and *Going for Broke* (Epic, 1984) for the above mentioned tracks.

Allan Orski

Grant Lee Buffalo

Formed 1991 in Los Angeles, Calif.

Grant Lee Phillips, guitar, vocals; Paul Kimble, bass, keyboards; Joey Peters, drums

Grant Lee Buffalo emerged from the L.A. club scene in 1993 with the release of its first album, *Fuzzy.* The band's style, though rootsy, boasts modern influences such as David Bowie and R.E.M. As a songwriter, Phillips isn't afraid to tackle social and political views, but he presents them with the flavor of an intimate disucssion rather than a stirring oratory. With just three albums, the trio has grown considerably: *Mighty Joe Moon* (Slash/Reprise, 1994, prod. Paul Kimble) reflects the energy of songs Grant Lee Buffalo conceived while on the road; while *Copperopolis* (Slash/Reprise, 1996, prod. Paul Kimble) is a more layered and multi-dimensional sonic experience, the result of more relaxed, off-tour time spent constructing and arranging the songs. The debut, *Fuzzy*, (Slash, 1993, prod. Paul Kimble) is no slouch, establishing Grant Lee Buffalo as a rip-roaring and outspoken rock band ("America Snoring") and Phillips as a formidable new songwriting voice in the narrative "Dixie Drug Store."

Kim Forster and Gary Graff

The Grapes of Wrath

Formed 1983 in Kelowna, British Columbia, Canada. Disbanded 1992.

Tom Hooper, vocals, bass, marimba; Chris Hooper, drums; Kevin Kane, vocals, piano, guitar; Vincent Jones, keyboards (1989-92)

The Hooper brothers, along with childhood friend Kane, spent time playing—separately and together—with a series of art, punk and hardcore bands before forming the Grapes of Wrath. The musicians raised money to record its four-song demo through yard sales and flea, and what was supposed to be an independent EP went national (in Canada) when it was swept up by Terry McBride for his then-fledgling label Nettwerk records. But it was seven years later when the group recorded its definitive work, *These Days.* (Capitol, 1991, prod. John Leckie) This stellar effort showcases The Grapes' finest traits—picturesque storytelling, gorgeous harmonies and lush arrangements, especially in the songs "You May Be Right," "I Am Here" and "Travelin.'" Sadly, the band broke up the following year. The Hoopers and Jones have carried on as Ginger, while Kane works as a producer and solo musician.

the rest: *The Grapes of Wrath* (Nettwerk EP, 1984) *September Bowl of Green* (Nettwerk, 1985/Capitol, 1986) *Treehouse* (Capitol, 1987) *Now and Again* (Capitol, 1989) *Seems Like Fate 1984-1992* (Nettwerk/EMI, 1994)

see also: *Ginger*

Christina Fuoco

The Grass Roots

Formed 1966 in Los Angeles, Calif.

Warren Entner, guitar, vocals, keyboards; Creed Bratton, guitar, banjo, sitar (1966-69); Ricky Coonce, drums (1966-72); Rob Grill, bass, vocals (1966-75); Dennis Provisor, organ (1969-72); others over the years

This band was the brainchild of songwriters and producers P.F. Sloan and Steve Barri. Needing a band to front their material, the members were assembled after the 1966 hit "Where Were You When I Needed You." The band's style shifted from a folk-rock beginning to a nearly power-pop/soul sound by its end. From socially aware tunes to dewy-eyed ballads and romantic pop, the Grass Roots hit with "Let's Live for Today," "Midnight Confessions," "I'd Wait a Million Years" and "Sooner or Later." The best collection so far of the band's mid-60s to early 70s work is *Anthology: (1966-1975)* (Rhino, 1991, prod. P.F. Sloan)

the rest: *Where Were You When I Needed You* (Dunhill, 1966/Varese Vintage, 1994) *Greatest Hits, Vol. 1* (MCA, 1988) *Greatest Hits, Vol. 2* (MCA, 1988)

Patrick McCarty

Grateful Dead

Formed 1965 in San Francisco, Calif.

Jerry Garcia, guitar, vocals (died Aug. 9, 1995); Bob Weir, guitar, vocals; Phil Lesh, bass, vocals; Bill Kreutzmann, drums; Mickey Hart,

What Album Changed Your Life?

"Do you know that record, Leftism by Left Field? I thought a lot of that club and techno music you could only listen to in a club, but that record seems to sustain for 35 minutes' running time, and it seems to get better every time I hear it."

Adam Clayton, U2

drums (1967-69, 1974-present); Ron (Pig Pen) McKernan, vocals, keyboards (1965-1972, died March 8, 1973); Tom Constanten, keyboards (1968-70); Keith Godchaux, keyboards (1972-1979, died July 23, 1980); Donna Godhcaux, vocals (1972-1979); Brent Mydland, keyboards, vocals (1979-1990, died July 26, 1990); Vince Welnick, keyboards, vocals (1990-present)

Separating the sociological phenomenon from the musical force has always been difficult with the Grateful Dead. In a single performance, few groups could span an equivalent breadth of 20th century music, as the Dead merrily careened from the delta blues of Robert Johnson through the pure sonics of Karlheinz Stockhausen, from the giddy Gypsy jazz of Django Reinhardt to the cheery rock and roll of Chuck Berry. The musicians' commitment to the art of ensemble improvisation produced some extraordinary bursts of imagination, but the delicate chemistry of the Grateful Dead never translated well to the recorded medium. That they came to represent a quickly bygone era of San Francisco 60s utopianism never less than bewildered the band members, who unceremoniously followed their own path in blissful indifference to the commercial conventions of the music business until the death of the group's central figure, guitarist Garcia, finally spelled an end to their adventures in 1995.

what to buy: A live recording using the finest modern technology to wring fine-point detail out of relatively ancient source tape, *Two From the Vault* (Grateful Dead Records, 1992, prod. Dan Healy) is Grateful Dead 101—a two-disc set that covers the band's basic 1968 repertoire and abundantly displays the band's occasionally extravagant gifts. Of course, *Workingman's Dead* (Warner Bros., 1970, prod. Grateful Dead) remains the crucial studio work, inspired by the clapboard honesty of "Music From Big Pink" by The Band.

what to buy next: The follow-up to *Workingman's*, *American Beauty* (Warner Bros. 1970, prod. Grateful Dead) also managed to convey the band's fluid lyricism with somewhat darker undertones. *The History Of the Grateful Dead, Vol. 1 (Bear's Choice)* (Warner Bros., 1973, prod. Owsley Stanley) is a selection of live recordings taken from an epic series of shows at the Fillmore East in 1970, fully released on a three-disc set from the band's mail order label, *Dick's Picks Vol. 4* (Grateful Dead Records, 1996, prod. Owsley Stanley and Dick Latvala)

what to avoid: The live record from the band's 1974 Winterland stand also filmed for a concert movie, *Steal Your Face* (Grateful Dead, 1976, prod. Grateful Dead) has long been a source of embarrassment to the band because of the badly botched sound quality, but the hackneyed attempts at commercial relevance in which the band indulged in the late 70s—*Terrapin Station* (Arista, 1977, prod. Keith Olsen) *Shakedown Street* (Arista, 1978, prod. Lowell George and Dan Healy) *Go To Heaven* (Arista, 1980, prod. Gary Lyons) WOOF!—have even less to do with what the band is really about.

the rest: *Grateful Dead* (Warner Bros., 1967) *Anthem Of the Sun* (Warner Bros., 1968) *Aoxomoxoa* (Warner Bros., 1969) *Live Dead* (Warner Bros., 1970) *Grateful Dead* (aka Skull & Roses) (Warner Bros., 1971) *Europe '72* (Warner Bros., 1972) *Wake Of the Flood* (Grateful Dead, 1973) *From the Mars Hotel* (Grateful Dead, 1974) *Blues For Allah* (Grateful Dead, 1975) *Reckoning* (Arista, 1981) *Dead Set* (Arista 1981) *In the Dark* (Arista, 1987) *Dylan and the Dead* (Columbia, 1989) *Built To Last* (Arista, 1989) WOOF! *Without a Net* (Arista, 1990) *One From the Vault* (Grateful Dead, 1991) *Dick's Picks Volume One* (Grateful Dead, 1993) *Infrared Roses* (Grateful Dead, 1994) *Dick's Picks Volume Two* (Grateful Dead, 1995) *Dick's Picks Volume Three* (Grateful Dead, 1995) *Hundred Year Hall* (Grateful Dead, 1995) *Grayfolded* (Plunderphonics, 1995) *Dick's Picks Volume Five* (Grateful Dead, 1996) *Best of the Grateful Dead* (Arista, 1996) not available for rating

worth searching for: In 1965, the Dead and author Ken Kesey and his band of Merry Pranksters dropped acid and entered a recording studio for several hours of noodling and assorted craziness, editing the mass of tapes down to a strange album, *The Acid Test* (A Sound City Production, 1965) virtually impossible to find but a priceless relic of the mishigass out of which the Dead was born.

solo outings:

Jerry Garcia: *Garcia* (Warner Bros. 1970) *Compliments Of Garcia* (Grateful Dead, 1974) *Reflections* (Grateful Dead, 1976) *Cats Under the Stars* (Arista, 1976) *Run For the Roses* (Arista, 1982) *Jerry Garcia Band* (Arista 1991) (with Howard Wales): *Hooteroll* (Douglas, 1970) (with Merl Saunders and Tom Fogerty): *Fire Up* (Fantasy, 1973) *Live At Keystone Berkeley* (Fantasy, 1973) (with Old and In the Way) *Old and In the Way* (Grateful Dead, 1975) (with David Grisman): *Jerry Garcia/David Grisman* (Acoustic Disc, 1991) *Not For Kids Only* (Acoustic Disc, 1993) (with Old and In The Way) *That High Lonesome Sound* (Acoustic Disc, 1996)

Bob Weir: *Ace* (Warner Bros., 1970) *Heaven Help the Fool* (Arista, 1978) *Bobby and the Midnites* (Arista 1981)

Kingfish: *Kingfish* (Grateful Dead, 1976) *Live 'N' Kickin'* (United Artists, 1977) *King Biscuit Flower Hour Presents Kingfish* (KBR Records, 1995)

Mickey Hart: *Rolling Thunder* (Warner Bros., 1972) *Dafos* (Reference Recordings, 1983) *Rhythm Devils Play River Music: The Apocalypse Now Sessions* (Passport, 1980) *Music To Be Born By* (Rykodisc, 1989) *At the Edge* (Rykodisc, 1990) *Planet Drum* (Rykodisc, 1991) *Mickey Hart's Mystery Box* (Rykodisc, 1996)

▶▶ Allman Brothers, Los Lobos, Spin Doctors, Phish, Blues Traveler

◀◀ Cannon's Jug Stompers, Le Hot Club de France, Jimmy Reed, Rolling Stones, Bob Dylan

Joel Selvin

Great White

Formed 1981 in Los Angeles, Calif.

Jack Russell, vocals; Mark Kendall, guitars; Michael Lardie, keyboards; Audie Desbrow, drums; Teddy Cook, bass

One of the many faceless hair bands that emerged from Los Angeles during the late 80s, Great White combined titillation with a straightforward blues-influenced hard rock. After an EP produced by then-hot Don Dokken went nowhere, the band wound up at Capitol Records, where it slowly built a following, culminating in the platinum sales of its *Once Bitten, Twice Shy* (out of print) and *Hooked* albums. *Hooked* (Capitol, 1991, prod. Alan Niven and Michael Lardie) caught the band at its most cocky and confident, bolstered by the mounting buzz created by the two albums that preceded it and seasoned by extensive touring and the groupiedom that goes with it.

the rest: *Once Bitten* (Capitol, 1987) *Best of Great White* (Capitol, 1993) *Sail Away* (Zoo, 1994) WOOF! *Stage* (Zoo, 1995) *Let it Rock* (Imago, 1996)

Doug Pullen

Al Green

Born April 13, 1946 in Forrest City, Ark.

When soul music began to shift gears as the 60s became the 70s, a new voice emerged with a sweetness and hoist not quite heard since Sam Cooke's death in 1964. Green brought a freshness and tradition to soul music that had otherwise attempted to get harder or funkier or jump into the pools of psychedelia. With superb, subtle production by Willie Mitchell and a crack Memphis band, Green made enduring classics celebrating love's exuberance and pain throughout the 70s, even as he made his way back to gospel in the latter part of the decade. His unbridled joy and soulful instincts made his sacred material worth a listen, and when he returned more solidly to the secular world with new work during the 90s, it was as if he hadn't gone away. In a way he hadn't; as a singer who grew up in the church, he frequently included praise to Jesus even during his most sexy soul workouts, and he sang of romance in the middle of his gospel work. Even after becoming a minister of his own church, Green continues to administer the gospel of soul, with most of his best-loved albums back in print.

what to buy: *Greatest Hits*, (Hi, 1975/The Right Stuff-Capitol, 1995, prod. Willie Mitchell and Al Green) a superb collection of the hit singles was made even better in its latest incarnation by adding later recordings "L-O-V-E," and "Belle" to what was already one of the great romantic soul albums of all times.

what to buy next: For a one-album slice of how wonderful Green can be, you can do no better than *Call Me* (Hi, 1973/The Right Stuff-Capitol, 1994, prod. Willie Mitchell and Al Green) In addition to the hits "You Ought to Be with Me," "Here I Am (Come and Take Me)" and the title song, this record explores Green's love for country in versions of Hank Williams' "I'm So Lonesome I Could Cry" and Willie Nelson's "Funny How

Time Slips Away," which Green would re-record 20 years later with Lyle Lovett. There's also a powerful gospel workout, "Jesus is Waiting." *One in a Million* (Word/Epic, 1991) ᏗᏗᏗᏗ compiles the best of his gospel recordings.

what to avoid: *White Christmas* (Word/Epic, 1983/1991 prod. Moses C. Dillard Jr.) ᏗᏗ Deep in his gospel period, Green failed to infuse sufficient cheer into these seasonal standards.

the rest: *Al Green Gets Next to You* (Hi, 1970) ᏗᏗᏗᏗ *Let's Stay Together* (Hi, 1971) ᏗᏗᏗᏗ *I'm Still in Love With You* (Hi, 1972/The Right Stuff-Capitol, 1993) ᏗᏗᏗᏗᏊ *Livin' for You* (Hi, 1973) ᏗᏗᏗᏗ *Al Green Explores Your Mind* (Hi, 1974/The Right Stuff-Capitol, 1994) ᏗᏗᏗᏗ *Al Green is Love* (Hi, 1975/The Right Stuff-Capitol, 1994) ᏗᏗᏗᏊ *Full of Fire* (Hi, 1976/The Right Stuff-Capitol, 1994) ᏗᏗᏗ *The Belle Album* (Hi, 1977/The Right Stuff-Capitol, 1995) ᏗᏗᏗᏗ *Tokyo...Live* (Cream, 1978/The Right Stuff-Capitol, 1994) ᏗᏗᏗᏗᏊ *Precious Lord* (Myrrh, 1982) ᏗᏗᏊ *I'll Rise Again* (Myrrh, 1983, Word/Epic, 1991) ᏗᏗᏗ *Soul Survivor* (A&M Records, 1987) ᏗᏗᏗ *Your Heart is In Good Hands* (MCA, 1995) ᏗᏗᏗᏗ

worth searching for: *Love Ritual: Rare and Previously Unreleased 1968-76* (MCA, 1989, prod. Colin Escott) ᏗᏗᏗᏗ Leftover tracks from sessions originally produced by Green and Mitchell, dating from his first single (a surprising cover of the Beatles' "I Want to Hold Your Hand") to an alternate mix of "Love Ritual" from the *Al Green is Love* sessions and an astounding 15 minute track, "Beware."

▶▶ Luther Vandross, Prince, Otis Clay, Terence Trent D'Arby

◀◀ Sam Cooke, Otis Redding, Clyde McPhatter

Roger Catlin

Green Day

Formed 1989 in Berkeley, Calif.

Billie Joe Armstrong, guitar, vocals; Mike Dirnt (born Mike Pritchard), bass, vocals; Al Sobrante, drums (1989-90); John Kiftmeyer, drums (1990); Tre Cool (born Frank Edwin Wright III), drums (1990-present)

With a cheeky mixture of punk energy and power-pop smarts, Green Day blasted out of Berkeley's fertile punk scene and scored a multi-platinum smash in 1994 with its major label debut, *Dookie.* In its wake—and in the wake of similar success by Orange County-based kindred spirits The Offspring—numerous self-styled punk outfits gained mainstream attention. Of course, the debate raged about whether Green Day was "real punk"—a claim the band members never made. In fact, Green Day frontman Armstrong described the group as sounding like what would happen "if The Ramones and The Partridge Family got into a bus accident." Still, the trio had underground credibility, thanks to two early releases on the independent Lookout label, and its irreverent spirit was in full view during the band's mud fight with the crowd at Woodstock '94. *Dookie's* follow-up, *Insomniac*, didn't hit with the same magnitude, but it didn't damage Green Day's reputation for catchy and occasionally ferocious tunes.

what to buy: *Dookie* (Reprise., 1994, prod. Rob Cavallo) ᏗᏗᏗᏊ is packed with the trio's hummable, adrenalized pop and features the hits "Longview," "Basket Case" and "When I Come Around."

what to buy next: *Insomniac* (Reprise, 1995, prod. Rob Cavallo and Green Day) ᏗᏗᏗ is darker and less ingratiating but shows the band attempting to grow stylistically.

the rest: *Kerplunk* (Lookout, 1992) ᏗᏗᏗ *39/Smoothed Out Sappy Hour* (Lookout, 1991) ᏗᏗᏊ

worth searching for: The Japanese release *Live Tracks* (Reprise EP, 1995, prod. Rob Cavallo and Green Day) ᏗᏗᏗᏊ which offers a six-song sample of Green Day's fiery concert skills.

◀◀ Ramones, Dickies, Buzzcocks, Clash, Only Ones, Undertones, Redd Kross, Cheap Trick

Simon Glickman

Green Jelly

Formed 1981 as Green Jello in Kenmore, N.Y.

Developed more as a practical joke than a band, Green Jello was named after a flavor the whole band hated, a reflection of the work they expected to produce. The group prided itself on being the world's worst band during a mid-80s appearance on "The Gong Show," but it wasn't until they began making their own onstage props that it began to join the realm of such shtick rockers as Gwar and the Impotent Sea Snakes. Building an entire album around a heavy metal version of the "Three Little Pigs" story, the group crafted a clever Claymation video for the song that went into heavy rotation on MTV and made them modern rock's most unlikely stars. Forced by legal concerns to change the name to Green Jelly, the group produced a highly entertaining debut album, *Cereal Killer Soundtrack,* (Zoo, 1993, prod. Sylvia Massy and C.J. Buscaglia) ᏗᏗᏗ which was fortified by a cover of the Sex Pistols' "Anarchy in the U.K." Though the group released a much more forgettable album in 1994, only time will tell if it will live down to Rolling Stone magazine's 1993 designation of the group as "this year's musical lowpoint."

Eric Deggan

Green on Red

Formed 1980 in Tucson, Arizona. Disbanded 1992.

Dan Stuart, lead vocals, guitar (1980-92); Chuck Prophet IV, guitar, vocals (1985-92); Chris Cacavas, piano, organ, harmonica, vocals (1980-88); Jack Waterson, bass, vocals (1980-88); Van Christian, drums (1980-81); Alex MacNicol, drums (1981-86); Keith Mitchell, percussion (1987-88)

Starting out as an Arizona punk group called The Serfers, the band had already become Green On Red by the time it hit Los Angeles in 1981. Within a few years, it was lumped in with the area's burgeoning psychedelic rock scene—the so-called Paisley Underground that also included Dream Syndicate, the Three O'Clock, the Rain Parade and the Long Ryders. And yet, by 1985, it had—with the help of guitarist Prophet IV—eliminated most of its psychedelic trappings in favor of a hard-hitting country-rock sound that recalled Neil Young, Bob Dylan and even the Velvet Underground. Finally, whiny-voiced and somewhat contrived lead singer Stuart had a strong foil to play off of, although Cacavas' organ and piano work remained the band's most colorful ingredient. A pair of releases for major label Mercury Records followed, and though they include some strong moments, those albums proved to most that the band was out of its league. Stuart and Prophet apparently thought so too, firing the rest of the band but continuing to make records without garnering much attention along the way. They eventually called it quits in 1992. Since then, Prophet has released a few solo records, Stuart just one. Cacavas and MacNicol each put out records on their own during the late 80s. Although Green on Red never quite achieved modern rock iconhood, it did prefigure the mid-90s movement back to country-rock.

what to buy: In retrospect, *Gas Food Lodging* (Enigma, 1985, prod. Paul Cutler) 𝄞𝄞𝄞½ seems to have been the album where Green On Red found its rough-and-ready country-rock sound: On it, "Hair of the Dog" cranks along in riproaring fashion, while "That's What Dreams" is surprisingly touching in a proto-New Sincerity style. *Here Come the Snakes* (Restless, 1989, prod. Jim Dickenson and Joe Hardy) 𝄞𝄞𝄞½ represents Stuart and Prophet's best effort after they fired the rest of the band.

what to buy next: *The Best of Green On Red* (Off Beat, 1994, prod. Various) 𝄞𝄞𝄞 provides a decent overview, although it's weighted heavily towards material from 1989 on and includes no tracks from either of the Mercury releases. The band's major label debut, the mini-LP *No Free Lunch* (Mercury, 1985, prod. Dan Stuart) 𝄞𝄞𝄞 has enough twangy character that it borders on the ridiculous at times, including a version of Willie Nelson's "Funny How Time Slips Away" that borders on parody but which somehow works.

what to avoid: *The Killer Inside Me* (Mercury, 1987, prod. Jim Dickenson) 𝄞𝄞 suffers equally from forgettable songwriting and heavyhanded production. The gloriously soulful gospel backup singers only served to emphasize how ludicrous Stuart's lead vocals could sometimes be.

the rest: *Green On Red* (Green On Red EP, 1981) 𝄞½ *Green On Red* (Down There/Enigma, 1982) 𝄞𝄞 *Gravity Talks* (Slash, 1983) 𝄞𝄞½ *Live at the Town and Country Club* (China/Polydor, 1989) 𝄞𝄞𝄞 *This Time Around* (Off Beat, 1989) 𝄞𝄞½ *Scapegoats* (Off Beat, 1991) 𝄞𝄞𝄞

worth searching for: Danny and Dusty's *The Lost Weekend* (A&M, 1985, prod. Paul Cutler) 𝄞𝄞𝄞𝄞 is the great urban twang-rock album that Green On Red never quite made on its own. Featuring the alternating lead vocals of Stuart and Dream Syndicate's Steve Wynn, plus instrumental contributions by members of both of their bands and The Long Ryders, the disc is loose and fun, but it's got some anger and heart too.

solo outings:

Dan Stuart: Can O' Worms (Monkey Hill, 1995)

Chuck Prophet IV: Brother Aldo (Fire, 1990) *Feast of Hearts* (1995)

Chris Cacavas and Junkyard Love: Chris Cacavas and Junkyard Love (Heyday, 1989)

Jack Waterson: Whose Dog? (Heyday, 1988)

▶▶ Uncle Tupelo, Son Volt, Blue Mountain

◀◀ Neil Young, Violent Femmes, The Faces

Bob Remstein

Green River

See: Pearl Jam

Greg Kihn

Born 1952 in Baltimore, Md.

Slightly more subtle in his sonic thievery (and less effective) than Steve Miller, Kihn has similarly made his mark with recycled riffs and a 60s pop aesthetic. Those virtues culminated in a handful of singles, the best of which is 1981's "The Breakup Song (They Don't Write 'Em). Comparisons to Bruce Springsteen, Tom Petty and Buddy Holly have abounded over the years, but those are inflated, as Kihn's straightforward vision is clearly limited and certainly tamer—and is hampered by an annoying tendency towards wussy pop. After the MTV hit "Jeopardy" in 1983, Kihn all but dropped off the charts. All of his albums from the 70s and 80s on the Beserkley are deleted, but Kihn is best heard as a singles artist anyway. So *Kihnsoilidation: The Best of Greg Kihn* (Rhino, 1989, prod. Various) 🦴🦴🦴🦴 is the best place for an introduction, as it contains all his chart hits, plus "Testify" (it almost rocks) and his earnest turn on Springsteen's "For You." *Unkihntrollable Live* (Rhino, 1989) 🦴🦴🦴 is a spirited concert set, while the spartan acoustic folks of *Mutiny* (Clean Cuts, 1994, prod. Various) 🦴🦴🦴🦴 marks a drastic departure from wimpdom, and suggests the presence of a viable artist who's been submerged for too long.

Allan Orski

Clive Gregson & Christine Collister

Formed 1985 in Manchester, England; Clive Gregson born January 4, 1955, in Manchester, England;Christine Collister born on the Isle of Man, UK

Between 1980 and 1984, Clive Gregson led an offbeat pub-rock band called Any Trouble. Clever and attractive, but neither groundbreaking nor commercial, the band eventually broke up without leaving Gregson in any position to carve out a hitmaking solo career. Sizing up his options, he happened to hear Christine Collister performing in a small bar and was immediately taken with her smoky alto voice and impassioned delivery. He agreed to produce some tracks for her, and the pair began performing in clubs. Soon, both were on tour as members of Richard Thompson's backup band, and with that extra experience behind them, they launched what would be a seven-year period of smart, poignant folk/rock. Because they were romantically linked during that time, the story of their musical career parallels that of their affair, shifting from tentative (*Mischief,* highlighted by the lovely, but cutting "I Specialise") to self-assured and powerful (1989's classic *A Change in the Weather*) to sniping and bitter (1992's *The Last Word*). Like Thompson, Gregson is a terrific guitarist, and he's not a bad singer, but his real skill lies in his ability to pen canny and insightful country/rock and pop/rock tunes. He has gone on to record several rather impressive solo albums, but he'll probably never again have as potent an instrument to write for as Collister's voice. She recently put out a live album that, sadly, shows what can happen when someone with great pipes loses their direction. The sound is there, but the feeling and intent are not.

what to buy: Varied and peppy, but often melancholy and/or dramatically moving, *A Change in the Weather* (Rhino, 1989, prod. Clive Gregson) 🦴🦴🦴🦴🦴 features two absolutely heartstopping vocal performances by Collister, plus a host of other strong numbers, particularly "This Is the Deal," a touching tale of domestic abuse. Either "A Blessing in Disguise" or "How Weak I Am" would be worth the price of admission for any disc; together, they beautifully demonstrate the magic of Gregson's songwriting and Collister's singing.

what to buy next: Darker than *Weather, The Last Word* (RNA/Rhino, 1992, prod. Clive Gregson) 🦴🦴🦴🦴 was the album Gregson and Collister made after their relationship had come to an end. You may want to sit down for this one.

what to avoid: An album of cover tunes by Jackson Browne, Bruce Springsteen, Aztec Camera, Merle Haggard, and others, *Love Is a Strange Hotel* (RNA, 1990, prod. Clive Gregson & Christine Collister) 🦴🦴🦴 should have been brilliant. But both Gregson's arrangements and Collister's vocals are too tame, too reverent, and other than Browne's "For a Dancer," the album floats along without making much of an impression.

the rest: *Home and Away* (Cooking Vinyl, 1987, prod. Clive Gregson) 🦴🦴🦴 *Mischief* (Rhino, 1988, prod. Clive Gregson) 🦴🦴🦴🦴

solo outings:

Clive Gregson: *Strange Persuasions* (Demon/Compass, 1985/1995, prod. Clive Gregson); *Welcome to the Workhouse* (Special Delivery, 1990, prod. Clive Gregson); *Carousel of Noise* (Compass, 1994, prod. Clive Gregson); *People & Places* (Compass, 1995, prod. Clive Gregson); *I Love This Town* (Compass, 1996, prod. Garry West)

Christine Collister: *Live* (Green Linnet, 1995)

⏩ John Wesley Harding, Eleanor McEvoy, Matt Keating

⏪ Richard & Linda Thompson, Hank Williams, Sandy Denny, Nick Drake

Bob Remstein

Nanci Griffith

Born July 16, 1954 in Seguin, Texas

Griffith has spent a career bridging the uneasy gap between country and folk, earning critical praise, devoted fans and minimal mass market success. Emerging from the Austin folk scene during the mid-70s, she recorded two albums for tiny labels and crisscrossed the country performing at festivals. By the time she cut her first Nashville album in 1984, she had a reputation as a writer of tight, insightful songs. Griffith released her first work for MCA in 1987, but big-label backing did not translate into chart success for her idiosyncratic style (in the U.S., anyway; Griffith has consistently topped charts in Ireland and Britain). Her songs, meanwhile, became Top 10 country hits for other singers (Kathy Mattea, Suzy Bogguss). A move to MCA's pop division in 1989 pointed Griffith toward a mass audience emphasis that better suited both her distinctive voice and the burgeoning adult-contemporary format. Griffith held this course while changing labels to Elektra and remains in demand as a collaborator for everyone from the Chieftains to R.E.M. Still, she's best known as a musical storyteller whose slice-of-life vignettes like "Trouble in the Fields," "Love at the Five and Dime" and "It's a Hard Life," which only gain impact with repeated handlings by other singers.

what to buy: Merely mentioning *Last of the True Believers* (Rounder/Philo, 1986, prod. Jim Rooney and Nanci Griffith) reduces many Griffith fans to mindless mush. It is a beauty, with a supporting cast of musicians' musicians (Bela Fleck, Roy Huskey Jr., Maura O'Connell, Lyle Lovett) and a fistful of classic Griffith songs ("Love at the Five and Dime," "More than a Whisper," "Lookin' for the Time"). Another fine introduction to the Griffith songbook is the live *One Fair Summer Evening*, (MCA, 1988, prod. Nanci Griffith and Tony Brown) with moving versions of much of her best material and an understated reading of Julie Gold's "From a Distance" that eclipses Bette Midler's mawkish rendition.

what to buy next: *Other Voices, Other Rooms* (Elektra, 1993, prod. Jim Rooney) a Griffith record devoid of Griffith material, is a study of her interpretative abilities, featuring 17 songs by everyone from Woody Guthrie to John Prine to (yep) Janis Ian. On *Late Night Grande Hotel*, (MCA, 1992, prod. Peter Van-Hooke and Rod Argent) the most successful to date of Griffith's VH1-style albums, Phil Everly duets on the nervous, driving "It's Just Another Morning Here," and Griffith continues her tradition of incisive political commentary with "One Blade Shy of a Sharp Edge."

what to avoid: The problem with *Lone Star State of Mind* (MCA, 1987, prod. Tony Brown and Nanci Griffith) isn't material; nor is it collaborators (Fleck, Huskey et al). It's the production, which attempts to jam Griffith's music into a pair of pink sequined cowboy boots. Lots of twangin' that's annoyin'.

the rest: *Poet in my Window* (Philo/Rounder, 1982) *Once in a Very Blue Moon* (Philo/Rounder 1984) *Little Love Affairs* (MCA, 1988) *Storms* (MCA, 1989) The MCA Years: A Retrospective *(MCA, 1993)* Flyer *(Elektra, 1995)*

worth searching for: *There's a Light Beyond These Woods* (MCA U.K., 1982, prod. Mike Williams and Nanci Griffith) is a British re-release of Griffith's first album, recorded live in an Austin studio and originally released in 1978.

▶▶ Lucinda Williams, Iris DeMent, Gillian Welch

◀◀ Carolyn Hester, Bill Staines, the Weavers, Judy Collins, Tom Paxton

Elizabeth Lynch

The Grifters

Formed 1989 in Memphis, Tenn.

David Shouse, guitar and vocals; Scott Taylor, guitar and vocals; Tripp Lamkins, bass; Stan, drums

Beginning as a three-piece outfit called Bud in 1989, the Grifters released an independent cassette and two EPs before putting out its first full-length album, *So Happy Together* (Sonic Noise, 1992, prod. Various) On its next release, *One Sock Missing* (Shangri-La Records, 1993, prod. Doug Easley) the Grifters established a lo-fi identity, letting its music wander far from the typical blues and rock patsh. Voices and guitars blend and crash over bluesy rhythms covered by a thick layer of feedback and distortion. The Grifters next album, *Crappin' You Negative* (Shangri-La, 1994, prod. Doug Easley) had many of the same attributes and drew the attention of Seattle's uber-indie, Sub Pop. The result is the cleaner, more pop-oriented *Ain't My Lookout* (Sub Pop, 1996, prod. Doug Easley) although songs such as "Return to Cinder" and "Boho/Alt" show that the band is determined to maintain a sarcastic tone in their lyrics and at least a slightly subversive edge to its music.

Kim Forster

Grin

See: Nils Lofgren

Dave Grohl

See: Nirvana

Groove Collective

Formed 1990 in New York, N.Y.

Gordon "Nappy G" Clay, timbales, bongos, percussion, vocals; Jonathan Maron, bass; Fabio Morgera, trumpet, flugelhorn; Jay Rodriquez, reeds; Josh Roseman, trombone; Itaal Shur, piano, keyboards; Genji Siraisi, drums; Chris Theberge, congas, percussion; Bill Ware, vibraphones, percussion; Richard Worth, flute, alto flute, piccolo, bonsuri, kalimba.

Groove Collective is a hybrid of two factions of New York City jazz groups—Giant Step and the Club Bird All-Stars—which often found themselves billed together at the Metropolis Cafe. After a few months, they merged as Groove Collective, combining the old-school flavor of John Coltrane and Thelonious Monk with contemporary hip-hop styles for something closer to traditional than acid jazz. *Groove Collective* (Reprise, 1993, prod. Gary Katz) ♪♪♪♪ was recorded live at the Metropolis and captures the band's fluid, energetic mix of jazz, rap and head-bobbing grooves. *We the People* (Giant Step, 1996, prod. N/A) ♪♪♪½ hits more of a straightforward dance groove, making it just a touch less intriguing.

Christopher Scanlon

Joe Grushecky /Iron City Houserockers

Born May 6, 1948 in Pittsburgh, Pa.

Like Michael Stanley and early Bob Seger, Grushecky exudes a kind of everyman quality, even when he's on an arena stage. With the Iron City Houserockers, the band he formed in Pittsburgh in 1976, Grushecky played tough, workmanlike barroom rock, steeped in R&B and early rock 'n' roll roots (Chuck Berry meets Sam and Dave). On his own, Grushecky—who has worked as a special education teacher during down times in his music career—is a somewhat more reflective troubadour; he still rocks, mind you, but songs cut a bit deeper, with more observations about the vaugaries of life and the *American Babylon* he sings about on his latest album.

what to buy: The aptly titled *Pumping Iron & Sweating Steel: The Best of the Iron City Houserockers* (Rhino, 1992, prod. Various) ♪♪♪♪ is filled with high-energy performances that convey an it's-the-weekend exuberance. Every city might have a band (or three) like this, but the Houserockers blow with a steel mill toughness that separates it from that pack.

what to buy next: Grushecky's *End of the Century* (Razor & Tie, 1992, prod. Joe Grushecky and Rick Witkowski) ♪♪♪½ is a thoughtful work whose best songs ("No Man's Land," "Talking to the King," the title track) make sharp observations about the human spirit.

what to avoid: Sad to say, *American Babylon* (Razor & Tie, 1995, prod. Bruce Springsteen, Joe Grushecky and Rick Witkowski) ♪♪ too often sounds like a Springsteen wanna-be—a critcism Grushecky's heard before.

the rest: *Rock & Real* (Rounder, 1987) ♪♪♪ *Swimming With the Sharks* (Rounder, 1988) ♪♪♪

worth searching for: The Houserocker's second album, *Have a Good But...Get Out Alive!*, (MCA, 1980) ♪♪♪½ another tough-spirited album that's the most consisted of the group's individual titles.

▶▶ Hootie & the Blowfish

◀◀ Stax-Volt, Bruce Springsteen, Mitch Ryder & the Detroit Wheels, the Rockets

Gary Graff

The Guess Who

Formed 1962 in Winnipeg, Manitoba, Canada. Disbanded 1975. Reformed 1979.

Chad Allan (born Allan Kobel), vocals, guitar (1962-66); Bob Ashley, piano (1962-65); Randy Bachman, guitar, vocals (1962-70); Garry Peterson, drums; Jim Kale, bass (1962-72, 1979-present); Burton Cummings, vocals, keyboards, flute (1965-75); Bruce Dekker, vocals (1966); Greg Leskiw, guitar, vocals (1970-72); Kurt Winter, guitar, vocals (1970-74); Don McDougall, guitar, vocals (1972-74); Bill Wallace, bass, vocals (1972-75); Dominic Troiano, guitar, vocals (1974-75)

In 1968, convinced that the Guess Who was destined for stardom, record producer Jack Richardson mortgaged his house to finance a New York recording session for the band. The fruits of that trip were realized the next year when the group enjoyed a string of gold hits south of the border with "These Eyes," "Laughing" and "Undun," and Richardson hasn't worried about house payments since. Guitarist and co-founder Bachman and lead singer-keyboardist Cummings (who replaced co-founder Chad Allan) formed one of the most successful songwriting duos of the era and put Canada on the pop music map for good. In 1970 the band scored a #1 hit with the politically charged "American Woman," and a #5 hit with "No Time." But both men were immensely talented musicians and were often at odds over band matters. Bachman quit the Guess Who in 1970, later forming Bachman-Turner Overdrive. Cummings replaced Bachman with two guitarists, Winter and Leskiw, and answered Bachman's departure with a string of hits that included "Share the Land," "Hand Me Down World" and "Clap For the Wolfman." Kale, who owns Guess Who name, re-formed band in 1979 with McDougall; there have been several different configurations since then.

what to buy: *The Best Of the Guess Who* (RCA, 1971, prod. Jack Richardson) ♪♪♪♪♪ is a compact collection of some of the best AM radio rock hits of all time. The guitar-hook rich *Share The Land* (RCA, 1970, prod. Jack Richardson) ♪♪♪♪ is significant because it was the band's first album without Bachman. New guitarists Kurt Winter and Greg Leskiw deliver big-time on such gems as "Hand Me Down World," "Bus Rider" and the title track.

what to buy next: *Track Record* (RCA, 1988, prod. Jack Richardson) ♪♪♪♪ is a two-disc set with all the hits and some interesting liner notes from Cummings and Richardson. It will leave ardent fans craving a full-scale boxed set, though. *Canned Wheat* (RCA, 1969, prod. Jack Richardson) ♪♪♪ and *Wheatfield Soul* (RCA, 1969, prod. Jack Richardson) ♪♪♪ are two strong early outings.

what to avoid: *Lonely One* (Intersound, 1995) WOOF! features original members Kale and Peterson, who had little to do with shaping the Guess Who sound.

the rest: *All This For a Song* (Valley Vue, 1979) ♪ *The Greatest Of the Guess Who* (RCA, 1988) ♪♪♪♪ *American Woman, These Eyes & Other Hits* (RCA, 1990) ♪♪ *At Their Best* (RCA, 1993) ♪♪♪

worth searching for: Canadian CD imports of the original albums—*So Long, Bannatyne* (RCA, 1971) ♪♪♪♪ *Rockin'* (RCA, 1972) ♪♪♪♪ *#10* (RCA, 1973) ♪♪♪♪ and *Road Food* (RCA, 1974) ♪♪♪

solo outings:

Burton Cummings:*The Burton Cummings Collection* (Rhino, 1994) ♪♪♪

▶▶ Queen, Pearl Jam, Blues Traveler, Del Amitri

◀◀ Big Joe Turner, Buddy Holly, Gerry and the Pacemakers, the Beatles

William Hanson

Guided by Voices

Formed 1983 in Dayton, Ohio

Robert Pollard, vocals and guitar (1983-1996); Jim Pollard, guitar and bass; Tobin Sprout, guitar, vocals, bass, drums, piano; Mitch Mitchell, guitar; Kevin Fennell, drums; Don Thrasher, drums; Dan Toohey, bass (1983-94); Greg Demos, bass (1994, 1996-present); Jim Greer, bass (1994-95)

Less a band than a hobby for a loose aggregation of drinking buddies, Guided By Voices is the obsession of prolific songwriter Robert Pollard. While teaching elementary school in Dayton, Pollard wrote and recorded with his accomplices on four-track tape a private history of rock 'n' roll, which mashed together three decades of influences culled from his massive record collection. It wasn't until they were in their mid-to-late 30s and had released a half-dozen albums over 10 years that the members of GBV attracted notice with their first nationally distributed release, *Vampire on Titus*. Even as the critical acclaim started to roll in and a deal with Matador Records was clinched, GBV continued to make engaging if eccentric low-fi records characterized by insidious melodies, ripping guitars, terse arrangements (many under 2 minutes in length), tape hiss and Pollard's elliptical, fairy-tale lyrics, sung in a fake British accent. During the mid-90s, GBV stood as perhaps the most celebrated cult band in North America.

what to buy: The two-albums-on-one-CD *Vampire on Titus/Propeller* (Scat, 1993, prod. Guided By Voices) ♪♪♪♪ is the breakthrough, with Pollard's prog-rock and British Invasion flourishes —- evoking early Genesis, the Syd Barrett-led Pink Floyd and the mid-60s Who —- delivered with punkish brevity and a thrilling sense of spontaneity. Rather than detracting from the allure, the dim, tinny sound gives the discs an otherworldly cohesiveness. *Bee Thousand* (Scat/Matador, 1994, prod. Guided By Voices) ♪♪♪♪ answered the critical hype with what is arguably the band's most consistent batch of pop songs, including the indie-rock classic "I Am a Scientist." *Under the Bushes Under the Stars* (Matador, 1996, prod. Kim Deal and Steve Albini) ♪♪♪♪ moves subtly toward a richer sound and longer, more fully realized songs, with help from the group's first pair of outside producers.

what to buy next: *Alien Lanes* (Matador, 1995, prod. Guided By Voices) ♪♪♪ is a more hit-and-miss affair, with several brilliant tunes: "My Valuable Hunting Knife," "Striped White Jets," "Closer You Are" and "Motor Away." *Box* (Scat/Matador, 1995, prod. Guided By Voices) ♪♪♪ is a five-CD collection that gathers the band's early, highly uneven albums and some unreleased songs.

worth searching for: *Crying Your Knife Away,* (Lo-Fi, 1994, prod. Guided By Voices) a reckless, beer-soaked live document, with Pollard's humorous banter an added bonus.

solo outings:

Robert Pollard: Not in My Airforce (Matador, 1996) not available for rating

Presidents of the United States of America

Pink Floyd, The Who, Genesis, Sex Pistols, The Jam, The Damned

Greg Kot

Guild of Temporal Adventurers

See: The Dream Syndicate

Guns N' Roses

Formed 1985 in Los Angeles, Calif.

W. Axl Rose (born William Bailey), vocals; Slash (born Saul Hudson), guitar; Izzy Stradlin (born Jeff Isabelle), guitar, vocals (1985-92); Gilby Clarke, guitar, vocals (1992-94); Duff "Rose" McKagan (born Michael McKagan), bass, vocals; Dizzy Reed, keyboards (1991–present); Steven Adler, drums, (1985-89); Matt Sorum, drums, (1989–present)

The rise of Guns N' Roses during the late 80s signalled the demise of the big hair glam-metal bands—the Warrants, the Cinderellas, the Bon Jovis—that had dominated the hard rock scene for the previous few years. Formed by Rose and Stradlin, who had grown up together in Indiana, and joined by Slash and McKagan, Guns sought to distance itself from the pop-metal scene, eschewing slick ballads in favor of songs about the seamy, destructive underbelly of cities like Hollywood. Its first full-length album, *Appetite For Destruction*, offered a ferocious tireless litany of indulgence, corruption and abuse—and sold several million copies. Guns was in a position to take over the world, to, in effect, be the Led Zeppelin for a new generation. Instead it fumbled the opportunity with inner-band feuds, overindulgence (the two separate *Use Your Illusion* albums) and concerts that started late and always risked the temperamental Rose walking off at any given time. As the lineup shifted, the cohesion that was so vital to the group disappeared, and by the early 90s Guns began an extended hiatus that showed no signs of ending soon.

what to buy: Truly a landmark album, *Appetite For Destruction* (Geffen, 1987, prod. Mike Clink) offers the Gunners at their best, before ego and eccentricity caused them to come unglued. Many of the band's seminal tunes ("Welcome to the Jungle," "Sweet Child o' Mine," "Paradise City") can be found in a package that is solid from start to finish.

what to buy next: Though often self-indulgent, much of the material on the expansive *Use Your Illusion I* and *Use Your Illusion II* (Geffen, 1991, prod. Mike Clink and Guns N' Roses) is of high enough quality to compensate. Slicker and more tempered than *Appetite*, the *Illusion* set is also darker and more mature. Start with the first volume if you can only buy one at a time, but be sure to get both.

what to avoid: McKagan's guest-saturated solo album *Believe in Me* (Geffen, 1994, prod. Jim Mitchell and Duff McKagan) is a dull, pedestrian affair that misses the collaboration of his bandmates.

the rest: *G'n'R Lies* (Geffen, 1988) *The Spaghetti Incident?* (Geffen, 1993)

worth searching for: To date, the most recent recording by Guns N' Roses is a cool cover of the Rolling Stones' "Sympathy for the Devil," included on the soundtrack to the film *Interview with the Vampire* (Geffen, 1994).

solo outings:

Slash's Snakepit (Slash, Sorum, Clarke): It's Five O'clock Somewhere (Geffen, 1995)

Gilby Clarke: Pawn Shop Guitars. (Virgin, 1995) Izzy Stradlin: *Izzy Stradlin & the JuJu Hounds* (Geffen, 1992) Neurotic Outsiders (McKagan, Sorum): *Neurotic Outsiders* (Maverick, 1996)

AC/DC, Aerosmith, Rolling Stones, Nazareth, Frank Zappa, David Bowie, Brian Eno

Brandon Trenz

Arlo Guthrie

Born July 10, 1947 in Coney Island, N.Y.

Think being called the next Bob Dylan is tough? How about the next Woody Guthrie? To his credit, Arlo Guthrie never traded on his father's legend; humble and grateful for the man, the younger Guthrie stayed close to his father's peers (particularly Pete Seeger) and developed his own relaxed style of folk-rock. The 18-minute "Alice's Restaurant Massacree" was a fine introduction, a winding, humorous narrative that encapsulated the generational struggles and draft paranoia that were so prevalent during the mid-60s. Guthrie scored a couple of other hits with the Woodstock nation—"Coming Into Los Angeles," Steve Goodman's "The City of New Orleans"—before settling into a niche. When Warner Bros. dropped him from its roster, Guthrie formed his own label, Rising Son, bought up his old recordings and continues to make music and do charitable works bsed out of upstate New York.

what to buy: *Alice's Restaurant* (Reprise, 1967/88, prod. Fred Hellerman) isn't the kind of thing you listen to every day, but it's always an entertaining listen when you get the hankering. *The Best of Arlo Guthrie* (Warner Bros., 1977/1989, prod. Various) has the other important hits. On *Woody's 20 Grow Big Songs,* (Rising Son, 1992) Arlo and the extended Guthrie clan pay homage to his father with a conceptually inspired children's album that works for adults, too.

what to buy next: *Amigo* (Warner Bros., 1976/Rising Son, 1990) is Guthrie's hardest rocking and most focused collection, with a killer cover of the Rolling Stones' "Connection." *Mystic Journey* (Rising Son, 1996, prod. Arlo and Abe Guthrie) is a richly crafted and introspective record that shows he's hardly played out.

what to avoid: *Alice's Restaurant: The Massacree Revisited* (Rising Son, 1995) updates the sonics of the original but can't quite capture its same moment-in-time quality. *Power of Love* (Warner Bros., 1981/Rising Son, 1990) isn't bad so much as it is anonymous, without the warm character of his better albums.

the rest: *Arlo* (Reprise, 1968/Rising Son, 1991) *Running Down the Road* (Reprise, 1969/Rising Son, 1991) *Washington County* (Reprise, 1970/Rising Son, 1991) *Hobo's Lullabye* (Reprise, 1972/Rising Son, 1990) *Last of the Brooklyn Cowboys* (Reprise, 1973/Risng Son, 1991) *Arlo Guthrie* (Reprise, 1974/Rising Son, 1991) *One Night* (Reprise, 1978/Rising Son, 1991) *Outlasting the Blues* (Reprise, 1979/Rising Son, 1991) *Power of Love* (Reprise, 1981/Rising Son, 1990) (with Pete Seeger) *Precious Friend* (Warner Bros., 1982/1988) *Someday* (Reprise, 1986/Rising Son, 1990) *Baby's Storytime* (Lightyear, 1990/1993) *All Over the World* (Rising Son, 1991/1993) *Son of the Wind* (Rising Son, 1992) (with Pete Seeger) *More Together Again in Concert* (Rising Son, 1994)

worth searching for: Arlo duets with Nanci Griffith on Townes Van Zandt's "Tecumseh Valley" for her album *Other Songs, Other Rooms* (Elektra, 1993, prod. Jim Rooney)

▶▶ Tom Petty, John Mellencamp, Jackson Browne, the Eagles

◀◀ Woody Guthrie, Pete Seeger, Leadbelly, Bob Dylan

Gary Graff

Gwar

Formed 1985 in Richmond, Va.

Odorus Urungus (David Brockie), vocals; Balsac the Jaws of Death (Michael Derks), guitar; Flattus Maximus (Peter Lee), guitar; Beefcake the Mighty (Michael Bishop), bass; Jizmak the Gusha (Brad Roberts), drums; Slymenstra Hymen (Danyelle Stampe), whips; Sexicutioner (Charles Varga), chains; Sampler Sound-EFX (David Musel), electronic devices; Techno-Destructo (Hunter Jackson), vocals; Sleazy P. Martini (Don Drakulich), manager

With shows that resemble performance art more than heavy metal concerts, this group of creatively twisted Richmond college students declared itself the most disgusting band of all time and set out to prove it—or, more accurately, they declared themselves aliens from Venus, led by singer Odorus Urungus, clothed themselves in futuristic caveman outfits with giant phalluses and bizarre weapons, and put on some outrageously terrific shows. Gwar changes themes with every tour, but generally the musicians lop off the heads of costumed nemeses on stage (sometimes the Pope, sometimes the President) and send quarts of fake blood spurting into the audience. The first thing you notice at a GWAR show is everything, from the speakers to the overhead lights, is covered in plastic; later, when the fluids start gushing from the stage, you understand why. Many critics rip the band's music, but occasionally, as on the hilarious "Slaughterama" and "Beavis and Butt-head" favorite "Jack the World," they're as tight and destructive, not to mention imaginative, as any good metal band.

what to buy: The definitive GWAR album is *Scumdogs of the Universe,* (Metal Blade, 1990, prod. Ron Goudie) which contains "Maggots," "Vlap the Impaler," "Sexecutioner" and the anti-hippie game-show parody "Slaughterama."

what to buy next: *This Toilet Earth* (Metal Blade, 1994, prod. Scott Wolfe) has a few good songs—including "Jack the

World," a rip against the band's laughable Grammy video nomination—but it is incredibly sick and enthusiastically makes fun of rape and pedophilia.

what to avoid: *Hell-o* (Shimmy Disc, 1988, prod. Kramer) WOOF! Gwar's debut, is absolutely unlistenable.

the rest: *America Must Be Destroyed* (Metal Blade, 1992) *The Road Behind* (Metal Blade, 1993)

The Tubes, Motorhead, Alice Cooper, Kiss, the Dead Kennedys

My Life With the Thrill Kill Kult, Marilyn Manson, nine inch nails, "Beavis and Butt-head."

Steve Knopper

Steve Hackett

See: Genesis

Sammy Hagar

Born Oct. 13, 1947, in Monterey, Calif.

Before joining the Van Halen party in 1985, Hagar was a member of Montrose, which he left to begin cultivating a middling solo career, opening for acts such as Boston, Kiss and Foghat during the late 70s. "The Red Rocker" (nicknamed for his penchant for wearing all things red—spandex, headbands, socks has decent metal-lite vocal chops (like Journey with chest hair), but his right-wing politics and altogether lack of panache and subtlety make for some tedious expressions of "hard" rock. He and Van Halen split unexpectedly in 1996, making Hagar a free agent again. Montrose reunion, anyone?

what to buy: *Standing Hampton* (Geffen, 1982, prod. Keith Olsen) is easily the most consistent album of Hagar's career; "I'll Fall in Love Again" is his best song and as good as anything he and Van Halen ever did together, and the under-appreciated "Heavy Metal" rocks harder than Eddie Van Halen's recent smiley-faced fingerflash.

what to buy next: *Unboxed* (Geffen, 1994, prod. Various) is a fair summation of his Geffen years with "I'll Fall in Love Again," "Heavy Metal" and the rigid "There's Only One Way to Rock." Strangely, it omits the pop hit "Your Love is Driving Me Crazy" from "Three Lock Box."

what to avoid: *I Never Said Goodbye* (originally titled *Sammy Hagar*) (Geffen, 1987/1992, prod. Sammy Hagar and Eddie Van Halen) finds Hagar was obviously fulfilling contractual obligations here with slack, uninspired pop and overwrought power ballads.

the rest: *Three Lock Box* (Geffen, 1983) *VOA* (Geffen, 1984) *The Best of Sammy Hagar* (Capitol, 1992) *Red Hot* (CEMA Special Products, 1994)

worth searching for: *The Anthology (1973-84)*, (Connoisseur Collection, 1994, prod. Various) an import retrospective that's a notch better than its domestic counterparts thanks to the inclusion of some Montrose tracks.

Van Halen, Journey, Loverboy

Montrose, Foghat, Kiss

Allan Orski

Nina Hagen

Born March 11, 1955, in East Berlin, Germany

Hagen's eccentric wailing may not be the stuff you'd normally associate with the Eastern bloc, but her German-sung version of The Tubes' "White Punks on Dope" will dispel any illusions of alternate citizenship. Musically, her daredevil experiments embraced themes of religion and space saucers, and she recorded with the dispirate likes of Paul Schaffer, Chris Spedding and Giorgio Moroder. *14 Friendly Abductions: The Best of Nina Hagen* (Legacy, 1996, prod. Various) is a career-spanning disc capturing the caterwauling Hagen in all her hyper-intensity. The diversity of her takes on the club scene ("New York, New York") and other cover version deconstructions ("My Way," "Spirit in the Sky") careen over the line of sacrilege with glee.

the rest: *Nunsexmonkrock* (Legacy, 1991/1982)

Allan Orski

Haircut 100 /Nick Heyward

Formed late 1970s in England. Disbanded 1984.

Nick Heyward (born May 20, 1961 in Beckenham, England), guitar, vocals; Graham Jones, guitar; Les Nemes, bass; Memphis Blair Cunningham, drums; Phil Smith, saxophone; Mark Fox, percussion

Perhaps the cleanest-cut group of the New Wave era, Haircut 100 made a pretty-boy fusion of light funk with jazz and pop. Heyward had a touchingly youthful voice with an ear-catching marbles-in-the-mouth inflection. Although not as gutsy as either the Style Council or the English Beat, Haircut 100 would in all likelihood appeal to fans of those groups. The band was briefly hot in Britain during 1982 with the hit song "Love Plus One." When Heyward left to pursue a solo career in 1983, the group carried on without him, but broke up after its second album, *Paint on Paint.* The still in print *Pelican West* (Arista, 1982, prod. Bob Sargeant) is a slick little mixture of pop, jazz and Latin rhythms. "Lemon Firebrigade," "Love Plus One" and "Favourite Shirts (Boy Meets Girl)" in particular are snappy numbers with enough hooks to pull in the most jaded listener.

On his own, Heyward began with an album that sounded amazingly like—a Haircut 100 record. Although *North of a Miracle,* (Arista, 1983, prod. Geoff Emerick and Nick Heyward) did little to remove Heyward from the light funk-jazz-pop fusion of his former group, it did establish him as a talented and sophisticated songwriter on the order of Aztec Camera's Roddy Frame. After years of silence, Heyward re-surfaced with the back-to-basics *From Monday to Sunday,* (Epic, 1993, prod. Nick Heyward) which features chiming Merseybeat guitars and flourishes of brass and string, ear candy that any popster would be proud to call his own.

Christopher Scapelliti

Bill Haley

Born July 6, 1925, in Highland Park, Mich. Died Feb. 9, 1981, in Harlingen, Texas.

Rock 'n' roll's first monarch only reigned briefly. But from 1955, when his "Rock Around the Clock" became the first No. 1 rock 'n' roll hit, until the ascendancy of Elvis Presley the following year, Haley was the undisputed king. Virtually forgotten today, Haley was an unlikely figure—30 years old at the time, cherubic features, a spit curl on his forehead, invariably dressed in a tuxedo. But blaze the trail he did. As a country singer with a fondness for cutting R&B songs, Haley first dabbled in cultural miscegenation with a 1951 recording of the Jackie Brenston R&B hit, "Rocket 88," as Bill Haley and the Saddlemen. The first record by the renamed Bill Haley and the Comets, "Crazy Man Crazy," on the independent Essex Records label, became the first rock 'n' roll record to make the nationwide Top 20. After signing to Decca Records in 1954, he recorded the epochal "Rock Around the Clock," which failed on its initial release but scorched up the charts after a film, "The Blackboard Jungle," used the song as a theme the following year. Haley's records tended toward the cutesy ("Skinny Minnie") and novelty ("Mambo Rock"), but Decca producer Milt Gabler, a savvy veteran, sagaciously styled Haley's sound after another one of his charges, the rollicking Louis Jordan, and came up with some stunning, underrated pieces; Haley's "Rip It Up," for instance, may actually out-rock the Little Richard original. Ultimately, however, his career amounted to little more than "Rock Around the Clock," and he spent many years living in Mexican exile before settling in Texas, where a bitter, deranged Haley would show strangers his driver's license to prove who he was.

what to buy: *From the Original Master Tapes* (MCA, 1985, prod. Various) provides adequate detail for most libraries.

what to buy next: The evolution of Haley as a country singer to the first rock 'n' roll star is examined in fine-point detail on *Rock the Joint! The Original Essex Recordings 1951-1954,* (Schoolkids, 1994, prod. Various) an historic 24-song collection that hews closely to Haley's developing rock 'n' roll style.

what to avoid: An unilluminating late 60s interview with Haley, interspersed with snatches of music, *The Haley Tapes,* (Jerden, 1995) WOOF! does not make an interesting or rewarding CD.

the rest: *Bill Haley's Greatest Hits!* (MCA, 1991)

worth searching for: The German reissue specialists Bear Family did produce a five-disc boxed set, *The Decca Years And More,* (Bear Family, 1994, prod. Various) though that may be overkill in this case.

▶▶ Pat Boone, Carl Perkins, Bruce Springsteen, the Ramones

◀◀ Big Joe Turner, Bob Wills, Louis Jordan

Joel Selvin

Daryl Hall

See: Hall and Oates

Daryl Hall & John Oates

Formed 1972 in Philadelphia, Pa.

Daryl Hall (born Oct. 11, 1949, in Pottstown, Pa.), vocals, guitar, keyboards; John Oates (born April 7, 1949 in New York, N.Y.), vocals, guitar

The most commercially successful duo in rock history, Hall & Oates has had 29 Top 40 hits, six of them No. 1, and have come to epitomize the term "blue-eyed soul" (in other words, they're white guys who sound black, or at least soulful). They did this not by playing it safe, but by sometimes innovating and thus creating trends in popular music. The two singers met at Temple University after growing up in Philadelphia suburbs, and Oates joined Hall's failed group Gulliver in 1969 just before it fell apart. They then went separate ways but reunited and signed with Atlantic Records. Atlantic never quite knew what to do with them, and they bounced from near-folk to soul to rock. Their sole Atlantic hit, "She's Gone," charted only after they'd switched to RCA, riding the coattails of the hit from their first RCA album, "Sara Smile." For several years after that, though they charted, their experimental tack dampened their commercial success; in fact, RCA long refused to issue Hall's first solo album, an adventurous effort produced by Robert Fripp. Hall & Oates recovered from their commercial slump not by going along with the record company, but rather by producing their 1980 album *Voices* themselves. Inventing a perky pop style particularly distinctive for its bouncy, percolating electric keyboard parts, but with plenty of room for Hall's virtuosic vocal fillips and melismas, it yielded four Top 40 hits, including the No. 1 "Kiss on My List." That launched a four-year string during which Hall & Oates' dominated radio playlists, pop charts and even MTV. But by the late 80s, the duo was, if not over, at least spent. These days they work together intermittently, and their music—together and apart—no longer causes the stir it once did.

what to buy: *Rock 'n' Soul, Part 1* (RCA, 1983, prod. Various) couldn't possibly contain all the hits—that would take two CDs, and aren't these guys due for a box set?—but it does go the extra mile by including the Atlantic track "She's Gone" and a fairly crucial selection of RCA material. Hall's *Sacred Songs* (RCA, 1980, prod. Robert Fripp) in a way proved RCA right: it isn't at all commercial or even pop. But its chilly contrast to his usually passionate vocal style makes it great, and it's not an off-putting listen.

what to buy next: *Voices* (RCA, 1980, prod. Hall & Oates) and *Private Eyes* (RCA, 1981, prod. Hall & Oates) have far more good tunes than could go on any compilation, and the production style has held up well over the years.

what to avoid: The debut *Whole Oats* (Atlantic, 1972, prod. Arif Mardin) **WOOF!** is lame singer-songwriter mellowness having nothing to do with the duo's later strengths.

the rest: *Abandoned Luncheonette* (Atlantic, 1973) *War Babies* (Atlantic, 1974) *Daryl Hall & John Oates* (RCA, 1975) *Bigger Than Both of Us* (RCA, 1976) *Beauty on a Back Street* (RCA, 1977) *Livetime* (RCA, 1978) *Along the Red Ledge* (RCA, 1978) *X-Static* (RCA, 1979) *H2O* (RCA, 1982) *Bigbamboom* (RCA, 1984) *Live at the Apollo* (RCA, 1985) *Ooh Yeah!* (Arista, 1988) *Change of Season* (Arista, 1990)

worth searching for: With 18 tracks, the import best-of *Looking Back* (RCA/Arista, 1991, prod. Various) is even better than *Rock 'n' Soul, Part 1*

solo outings:

Daryl Hall: Three Hearts in the Happy Ending Machine (RCA, 1986) *Soul Alone* (Epic, 1993)

▶▶ Charles & Eddie, Boyz II Men

◀◀ The O'Jays, Gamble & Huff, Sam and Dave

Steve Holtje

John S. Hall & Kramer

See: King Missle

Hamilton's Pool

See: Iain Matthews

Col. Bruce Hampton /Aquarium Rescue Unit/Fiji Mariners

Born Bruce Hampton in Atlanta, Ga.

It's hard to believe that Hampton ever heard a musical style he didn't like. His work is a boiling pot of eccentric takes on familiar genres—a unique melding of rock, R&B, country, soul, swing, bluegrass, psychedelic and jazz influences stirred for a seamless shower of musical exuberance. In a lesser artist the result could be rampant pandemonium; in Hampton's skewed vision, it is a magical, vibrant listening experience. A cult figure on the Southern music scene, he fronted the Hampton Grease Band, which released *Music to Eat* in 1969 (re-released in 1996). His involvement with such projects as New Ice Age and Late Bronze Age during the 70s and early 80s paved the way for what would prove to be some of his best work yet. *Col. Bruce Hampton & The Aquarium Rescue Unit* (Capricorn, 1992, prod. Johnny Sandlin) recorded live at the Georgia Theatre in Athens, begins as Hampton and his band open with a percussive, rambling vamp while introductions are made. The show has definitely begun, and along the way, Hampton conjures up sonic memories of everything from the early Allman Brothers, Weather Report and Les McCann to latter day Dregs.

Mirrors of Embarrassment (Capricorn, 1993) ♪♪♪♪ is solid, but lacks the live, whirling dervish effect of the debut. The side project *Fiji Mariners Featuring Col. Bruce Hampton* (Capricorn, 1996, prod. Bruce Hampton and Dr. Dan Matrazzo) ♪♪♪ is his hardest rocking effort, with lots of vamps and trippy accents, but some of the song structures and lyrics sound as though they are the germination of an idea, not the fruition. A lot of vamps with trippy accents makes for a good listen.

▶▶ Blues Traveler, Screaming Cheetah Wheelies, Dave Matthews Band

◀◀ Captain Beefheart, Root Boy Slim, Frank Zappa

Patrick McCarty

The Hang Ups

Formed 1988 in Minneapolis, Minn.

Brian Tighe, guitar, vocals, sax; Jeffrey Kearns, bass; Stephen Ittner, drums, vocals; John Crozier, guitar, harmonica (1992-present)

The core of this band met at Minneapolis College of Art and Design, and Tighe's senior project was the Hang Ups' first real demo tape. The inclusion of Muskellunge guitarist Crozier added density and complexity. The group's sound is classic American jangle-pop augmented with inventiveness and imagination, insuring that this won't sound like just another Minneapolis raw power band; the Hang Ups' twilight moodiness suggests more the influence of the English shoe-gazer scene. *He's After Me* (Clean/ Twin/Tone, 1993, prod. Ed Ackerson) ♪♪♪♪ is catchy in a casual way, the songs hanging in the air like vapour until suddenly condensing into fluid choruses. The *Comin' Through*, EP (Clean/ Twin/Tone, 1993, prod. Various) ♪♪♪ released prior to the album, includes a cover of "Eight Miles High" from a Husker Du tribute and three non-album songs.

Steve Holtje

Happy Mondays

Formed 1985 in Manchester, England

Shaun Ryder, lead vocals; Paul Ryder, bass; Paul Davis, keyboards; Gary Whelan, drums; Mark Day, guitar; Mark "Bez" Berisford, percussion and dancer

Riding on the euphoric wave of good vibes that swept Britain at the outset of the 90s, the Happy Mondays provided a perfectly suited soundtrack for loose-limbed kids who embraced Ecstasy culture and 18-inch flares. But there was much more to the group than its frivolous music suggested. Mainly, it exhibited an unyielding knack for turning out songs of substantial caliber. Then there was the lure of rock 'n' roll recklessness that surrounded it, often portraying the members as the rough and tumble equivalent of the Rolling Stones to contemporaries The Stone Roses' fey Beatles. Success came at the group with blinding intensity, and the working-class Manchester natives of which the band consisted espoused its evils with not one second thought. Soon enough, the strain of overnight success started to unravel the Happy Mondays at the core. "We all hated each other," singer Ryder said after the group's split. "I just started speaking to me brother again." Ryder and Berisford, however, have kept the spirit alive in their new group, Black Grape.

what to buy: While Happy Mondays had its fair share of decent album tracks, the group's strength was primarily in its remarkable string of singles. *Double Easy: The U.S. Singles* (Elektra, 1993, prod. Various) ♪♪♪♪♪ is the perfect showcase for the Manchester group's chaotic chemistry, collecting impeccable groove-oriented guitar numbers like "Hallelujah," "Kinky Afro" and "Loose Fit" on one exhaustive package. *Pills 'N' Thrills and Bellyaches* (Elektra, 1990, prod. Paul Oakenfeld and Steve Osborne) ♪♪♪♪ caught the group at the height of its creative apex, mixing funk rhythms, soulful backing vocals and classic melodies. "Bob's Yer Uncle" and "Step On" fulfilled the Happy Mondays' sonic objective.

what to buy next: For those who were tuned into Happy Mondays for rave appeal, there is no better document of the band's dance leanings than *Hallelujah*, (Elektra, 1989, prod. Martin Hannett) ♪♪♪♪ a seven-song disc comprised of remixes by club gurus Andrew Weatherall, Steve Lillywhite and Paul Oakenfeld ("Hallelujah," "Rave On" and "W.F.L.") and trance-inducing B-sides ("Clap Your Hands," "Holy Ghost").

what to avoid: By the time Happy Mondays got around to making its final album, *Yes, Please*, (Elektra, 1992, prod. Chris Frantz and Tina Weymouth) ♪♪ the members of the group had fallen victim to drug abuse and general disinterest in music. While a few noteworthy songs ("Sunshine and Love," "Cut 'em Loose Bruce") did rise out of the wreckage, the record was a mostly staid affair.

the rest: *Squirrel and G-Man Twenty-Four Party People Plastic Face Carnt Smile* (White Out) (Factory, 1987) ♪ *Bummed* (Elektra, 1988) ♪♪ *Live* (Elektra, 1991) WOOF!

worth searching for: *The Peel Sessions*, (Strange Fruit/Dutch

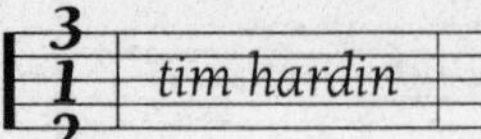

East India Trading, 1991, prod. Dale Griffin) recorded in 1986, captures the ramshackle glory of Happy Mondays right before the group fell into the habit of making production-heavy records.

solo outings:

Black Grape (Ryder and Berisford): *It's Great When You're Straight* (Radioactive, 1995)

Northside, The Farm, Northern Uproar

Beatles, Curtis Mayfield, Bee Gees, Donovan

Aidin Vaziri

Tim Hardin

Born Dec. 23, 1941 in Eugene, Ore. Died Dec. 29, 1980 in Los Angeles, Calif.

Hardin was a dark-hued and often mournful singer-songwriter whose place in the late 60s folksinger movement was ensured not so much by his own commercial success but by later versions of his songs covered by other artists. Hardin's originals were marked by spare performances—nearly outlines, really—and brief running times (most clock in at under two minutes). But the undeniable strength inherent in his sketchy yet potent style earned the singer substantial critical acclaim but relatively little else. By the early 70s, Hardin's career had been effectively wiped out from a nasty drug addiction which eventually killed him at age 39. *Hang on to a Dream: The Verve Recordings* (Polydor, 1994, prod. Erik Jacobsen) is a far-reaching and comprehensive document, collecting every Verve recording plus 17 unreleased tracks of pure melancholy. His most notable tracks, "Reason to Believe," "Misty Roses," "If I Were a Carpenter," and "Black Sheep Boy" are all included.

the rest: *Reason to Believe (Best of)* (Polydor, 1987) *Tim Hardin Live in Concert* (Polygram Special Products, 1968/1995)

Allan Orski

John Wesley Harding

Born 1965 in Hastings, England

Although he started his stateside career as a pop songsmith with Brian Wilson dreams and Elvis Costello pretensions, John Wesley Harding has reverted to his politically charged folk roots since parting ways with Sire Records in 1992. This isn't a shock to most fans; the brash singer-songwriter—who took his name from the classic Bob Dylan album—has always laced his shows with biting commentaries in the form of rambling monologues as well as such tersely but cleverly worded numbers as "Scared of Guns," "Hitler's Tears," "The Triumph of Trash" and "July 13th 1985" (about how Live Aid was really more about bloated egos than starving children). Over the years, the Costello comparisons have passed and Wes' upbeat, often frantic stage show has developed into a more thoughtful, though equally pointed platform that even caught the attention of Bruce Springsteen: The Boss, who rarely hires opening acts, invited Harding to join him on two 1995 West Coast dates during his solo acoustic tour.

what to buy: *Here Comes the Groom* (Sire, 1989, prod. Andy Paley) bubbles with the youthful fervor and manic wordplay of Costello's "My Aim Is True" (no surprise since the backing band includes Pete Thomas and Bruce Thomas of the Attractions) and the heel-clicking splendor of the Lovin' Spoonful. *John Wesley Harding's New Deal,* (Forward/Rhino, 1996, prod. Harding and Chris von Sneidern) his self-proclaimed antidote to Newt Gingrich's Contract With America, is clearly more Phil Ochs than Phil Spector. It's also his most relaxed record, with fiddles, mandolins, cellos, acoustic guitars and Hammond organs backing his delicate delivery on "Kiss Me, Miss Liberty," "Other's People Failure" and "The King Is Dead Boring."

what to buy next: Harding's straight-faced acoustic cover of Madonna's "Like a Prayer" is one of three non-LP oddities on *God Made Me Do It: The Christmas EP* (Sire, 1989, prod. John Wesley Harding). *Pett Levels: The Summer EP* (Sire, 1992, prod. Andy Paley, Steve Berlin and Scott Matthews) boasts five previously unreleased tracks highlighted by the glorious "Summer Single," his final flirtation with wall-of-sound pop, and the hardnosed live favorite "One Shot."

what to avoid: *It Happened One Night* (Rhino, 1991, prod. Wes Stace) a live solo acoustic album originally released in England in 1988, is driven more by adrenalin than vision.

the rest: *The Name Above the Title* (Sire, 1991) *Why We Fight* (Sire, 1992)

worth searching for: *Dynablob* (Mod Lang, 1996, prod. John Wesley Harding), a collection of studio outtakes and radio performances sold via his fan club and Mod Lang Records (P.O. Box 10111, Berkeley, CA 94709). It includes the original country version of "The Devil in Me" and his much-requested "Talking Return of the Great Folk Scare Blues."

◀◀ Phil Ochs, Bob Dylan, Elvis Costello

David Okamoto

Ben Harper

Born Oct. 28, 1969 in Pamona, Calif.

Harper made a critical splash with his debut album, *Welcome to the Cruel World,* (Virgin, 1994, prod. Ben Harper and J.P. Plunier) partly because it's still unusual these days for a young black man to sing reflective, bluesy acoustic folk-rock. Given the political bent of some of Harper's lyrics, it would be easy to tag him as a male version of Tracy Chapman, but his voice is less distinctive. Of course, Harper puts his own spin on things, keeping the instrumental arrangements simple but cleverly nuanced, and often adding choir-like backing vocals. Highlights range from the funny, reggae-ish "Mama's Got a Girlfriend Now" to the surprisingly upbeat "How Many Miles Must We March?" to the dreamy "I'll Rise." His followup, *Fight For Your Mind,* (Virgin, 1995, Ben Harper and J.P. Plunier) gets more electric on a few numbers, but mostly it sticks to the same Bob Marley- and Neil Young-influenced folk-rock. Occasionally, he gets too ambitious for his own good, adding a string quartet to the already dark "Power of the Gospel" and winding up with something tedious instead of stirring. Still, "Ground on Down" is powerful, damning stuff, and there's certainly going to be more where that came from.

Bob Remstein

Emmylou Harris

Born April 2, 1947, in Birmingham, Ala.

Her musical trademark is a pure, aching soprano, but Harris' defining musical characteristic is curiosity. It's led her to traditional country, new songwriters and maverick producers. Practically every hotshot on the country scene today, from Garth Brooks on down, claims Harris as an inspiration, but few can match her creative daring.

Harris began as a 60s-style folkie, working clubs around Washington, D.C. Through ex-Byrd Chris Hillman, she met Gram Parsons. Their duets on Parsons' *Grievous Angel* are pioneering moments in country-rock and brought a well-deserved spotlight to Harris' voice. Parsons' death in 1973 left Harris fiercely committed to continuing his vision in her solo work. With her 1975 major-label debut, *Pieces of the Sky*, she unveiled the sound that would become an influential trademark—classic country touches like galloping rhythm guitar and heartfelt vocals, cut with a driving rock backbeat. Early on, Harris demonstrated both her interest in country's past (i.e., the Louvin Brothers) and her commitment to new or unconventional material (i.e., the Beatles' "Here, There and Everywhere" or "Easy From Now On," by the young Carlene Carter).

Harris' Hot Band, which toured with her through the 80s, was an incubator of top talent; alumni include Ricky Skaggs, Vince Gill and Rodney Crowell, as well as producers Emory Gordy Jr. and Tony Brown. Opting for a bare-bones traditional sound during the 90s, Harris formed the Nash Ramblers and released the acclaimed *At the Ryman* in 1992. Her fan base is solid enough to offset country radio's indifference, and her most recent work reflects both a stronger rock flavor and a continued willingness to stretch the boundaries.

Nine Essential 90s Collections

MTV Buzz Bin, Vol. 1
(Rhino)

MTV Party to Go, Vol. 1-9
(Tommy Boy)

Big Ones of Alternative Rock
(Box Tunes)

X Games, Vol. 1
(Tommy Boy)

No Alternative
(Arista)

The Crow Soundtrack
(Atlantic)

Clerks Soundtrack
(Columbia)

Dead Presidents Soundtrack
(Capitol)

Natural Born Killers Soundtrack
(Interscope)

what to buy: For a warp-speed trip through Harris' early career, start with *Profile: The Best of Emmylou Harris,* (Warner Bros., 1978, prod. Various) which offers the cream of her early studio work. High points include covers of Dolly Parton's "To Daddy" and the Louvins' "If I Could Only Win Your Love." Fast forward to the daring *Wrecking Ball* (Asylum, 1995, prod. Daniel Lanois) to hear a Harris now completely confident in her musical impulses. Within rock producer Lanois' otherwordly arrangements, she pushes her voice to a raw, urgent edge and continues to dig up great material by underappreciated writers such as Lucinda Williams and Gillian Welch.

Two live albums provide excellent introductions to important phases of Harris' music: *Last Date,* (Warner Bros., 1982, prod. Brian Ahern) an exuberant country-rock manifesto, summarizes why Harris' Hot Band work had such impact; while *At the Ryman* (Reprise, 1992, prod. Allen Reynolds and Richard Bennett) offers Harris as acoustic purist, achieving an unplugged sound that is firmly traditional and astoundingly flexible, encompassing everything from Steve Earle to Stephen Foster.

what to buy next: Any would-be country traditionalist should own *Roses in the Snow,*(Warner Bros., 1980, prod. Brian Ahern) Harris' valentine to old-timey music (with assists from the likes of Parton, Skaggs, Linda Ronstadt and Johnny Cash). The ambitious concept album *The Ballad of Sally Rose* (Warner Bros., 1985, prod. Harris and Paul Kennerley) doesn't meld into a convincing dramatic whole, but features wonderful songwriting by Harris and Kennerley—"Woman Walk the Line" in particular has become a country standard. Two very different albums with spirituality as a theme are *Angel Band,* (Warner Bros., 1987, prod. Emmylou Harris and Emory Gordy, Jr.) a spare collection of country gospel hymns, and the introspective *Cowgirl's Prayer,* (Asylum, 1993, prod. Allen Reynolds and Richard Bennett) which features an eerie, ethereal version of Leonard Cohen's "Ballad of a Runaway Horse."

what to avoid: *Cimarron* (Warner, 1981, prod. Brian Ahern) is mostly listless Nashville-by-the-book—and Harris is infinitely better when she chucks the rulebook.

the rest: *Pieces of the Sky* (Reprise, 1975) Elite Hotel *(Reprise, 1976)* Luxury Liner *(Warner Bros., 1977)* Quarter Moon in a Ten Cent Town *(Warner Bros., 1978)* Blue Kentucky Girl *(Warner Bros., 1979)* Light of the Stable *(Warner Bros., 1980)* Evangeline *(Warner Bros., 1981)* White Shoes *(Warner Bros., 1983)* Profile II: The Best of Emmylou Harris *(Warner Bros., 1984)* Thirteen *(Warner Bros., 1986)* Bluebird *(Reprise, 1989)* Brand New Dance *(Reprise, 1990)* Duets *(Reprise, 1990)* Songs of the West *(Warner, 1994)*

worth searching for: *Gliding Bird,*(Jubilee, 1969) Harris' very first album, reportedly turns up from time to time in the record collections of Harris junkies. See if they'll let you tape it.

⏩ Alison Krauss, the Mavericks, the Cowboy Junkies

⏪ The Carter Family, Buck Owens, the Louvin Brothers, Hazel and Alice, Tom Rush, Gram Parsons

see also: *Gram Parsons*

Elizabeth Lynch

M.J. Harris & Bill Laswell

See: Bill Laswell

George Harrison

Born Feb. 25, 1943 in Liverpool, England

The Quiet Beatle was actually the first of the fabs to go solo, with one album of *Electronic Sounds* and an obscure soundtrack, *Wonderwall Music*, whose title was later borrowed for an Oasis hit. Creatively stymied by his former group, which only allowed one or two contributions per album, Harrison seemed the happiest to see the group break up—though he did bring Ringo Starr and Paul McCartney together again for his 1981 tribute to John Lennon, "All Those Years Ago." His pent-up creativity fairly burst upon release though, with the epic and audacious triple-album set *All Things Will Pass* It made way for his planning of rock's first huge benefit spectacle, The Concert for Bangladesh. But Harrison's output sputtered surprisingly quickly during the 70s and early 80s; his albums tend to have a couple of worthy tunes, but each is successively worse than its predecessor. Unlike Ringo Starr, Harrison never suffered the indignity of an album turned down for release, but it might have been close around the time of *Extra Texture* or *Gone Troppo* His five-year hiatus from music, when he became a movie producer, helped clear Harrison's head and helped make the 1987 comeback *Cloud Nine* a success—and the last album by a former Beatle to hit the Top 10. Perhaps superstitious, he has yet to follow it up, although a 1991 tour with Eric Clapton, which lasted only for a few dates in Japan, was captured for a worthy live album. Harrison was also responsible for starting the chain of events that led to the formation of the Traveling Wilburys—

him, Bob Dylan, Roy Orbison, Tom Petty and Jeff Lynne—in 1988.

what to buy: *All Things Must Pass* (Apple, 1970, prod. Phil Spector) remains one of the greatest Beatles solo recordings. With Spector creating his trademark wall of sound, the album spills over with ambitious, tuneful songs that were topped off by the extra album of jamming (something that doesn't work quite as well on the double-CD. Among the key tracks are "If Not for You," co-written with Dylan, and "My Sweet Lord," for which Harrison was found guilty of having "unknowingly" plagiarized the Shirelles' "He's so Fine."

what to buy next: *Cloud Nine* (Warner Bros., 1987, prod. Jeff Lynne) is a remarkable comeback album that spoke to several generations and had a few radio hits to boot in "Got My Mind Set on You" and "When We Was Fab." *Live in Japan* (Warner Bros., 1992, prod. George Harrison and Eric Clapton) is a remarkable live set, featuring Harrison backed by Clapton and his band and playing a repertoire that blends the best of his Beatles writing with his solo material.

what to avoid: *"Electronic Sounds"* (Apple, 1969) may interest students of early synthesizer experiments, but nobody else.

the rest: *Wonderwall Music* (Apple, 1968) *Concert for Bangladesh* (Apple, 1972) *Living in the Material World* (Apple, 1973) *Dark Horse* (Apple, 1974) *Extra Texture (Read All About It)*, (Apple, 1975) *33 1/3* (Dark Horse, 1976) *The Best of George Harrison* (Capitol, 1976) *George Harrison* (Dark Horse, 1979) *Somewhere in England* (Dark Horse, 1981) *Gone Troppo* (Dark Horse, 1982) *The Best of Dark Horse 1976-1989* (Capitol, 1989)

worth searching for: *Fourth Night Live* (Platypus, 1992) is a bootleg from the '91 Japanese tour, this one featuring Clapton's set—which was excluded from the legitimate album—and a reproduction of the tour program.

▶▶ Jeff Lynne, Paul Simon, Grant McLennan, Crowded House

◀◀ Chet Atkins, The Beatles, Carl Perkins, Ravi Shankar

Roger Catlin

Jerry Harrison

See: Talking Heads

Grant Hart

See: Hüsker Dü

Mickey Hart

See: Grateful Dead

PJ Harvey

Born Polly Jean Harvey, Oct. 9, 1969 in Yeovil, England

One of the most intriguing post-punk artists to emerge in years, Harvey makes blues-based rock that's raw, angry and challenging. But unlike her angst-merchant peers, she has the voice and the hooks to make her rage matter. Her band—also called PJ Harvey—included bassist Stephen Vaughan and drummer Rob Ellis until 1993, when both were replaced by studio musicians when Harvey veered into a more ambient, sonically experimental sound. That happened on *To Bring You My Love*, (Indigo, 1995, prod. Flood, PJ Harvey and John Parish) which was voted the best album of 1995 in the Village Voice Pazz & Jop Critics' Poll, and for good reason: even including a few duds, this strange collection of blues-punk is one of the most harrowing rock records ever made. Her debut, *Dry*, (Indigo, 1992, prod. Robert Ellis, PJ Harvey and Head) was recorded on a shoestring budget and didn't sell squat, but songs such as "Sheela-Na-Gig" and "Oh My Lover" come on with the force of a Mack truck. *Rid of Me*, (Indigo, 1993, prod. Steve Albini) is more abrasive than its predecessor, but "50 Ft. Queenie" and Harvey's deconstruction of Bob Dylan's "Highway 61 Revisited" rank with her best performances. *4-Track Demos* (Indigo, 1993) is an insightful collection of demos from *Rid of Me*, plus several previously unheard tracks.

the rest: (with John Parish): *Dance Hall at Louse Point* (Atlantic, 1996) not available for rating

Thor Christensen

Hater

See: Soundgarden

Juliana Hatfield

Born July 27, 1967 in Wiscasset, Maine

With her pixie voice, buzzed-out guitar, and brash, sometimes brutal, honesty, Hatfield presents a compelling clash of contradictions. She sounds like a fragile waif, plays guitar like a headbanger and writes songs with plenty of pop appeal and lyrical weight. The daughter of a Boston Globe reporter, Hatfield earned a degree in composition and writing at the prestigious Berklee College of Music. That's where she hooked up with two fellow students in 1987 to form the alternative rock trio the Blake Babies, in which she played bass and sang. Hatfield went solo in 1990 and has steadily gained confidence as a singer, songwriter and guitarist. She sent some shockwaves through the media—and asserted her independent spirit—when she told an interviewer in 1992 that she was a virgin at age 25. An update on her sexual status was unavailable at presstime.

what to buy: *Only Everything* (Atlantic/Mammoth, 1995, prod. Sean Slade, Paul Q. Kolderie and Juliana Hatfield) churns with metallic pop power as waves of guitars crash behind Hatfield's airy vocals. Her heart is broken on "My Darling" and "Universal Heart-Beat," but she bounces back, bruised but wiser ("What a trip/I'm better for it.") She also quiets down for a few relatively mellow ballads ("You Blues," "Live on Tomorrow").

what to buy next: *Become What You Are* (Atlantic/Mammoth, 1993, prod. Scott Litt) is more cryptic and less forceful than *Only Everything*, but Hatfield still puts her righteous indignation to good work in protesting women's vulnerability ("A Dame with a Rod") and superficiality ("Supermodel").

the rest: *Hey Babe* (Mammoth, 1992)

worth searching for: A limited edition of *Only Everything* featured fake fur on the cover's buffalo image.

▶▶ Alanis Morissette, Magnapop

◀◀ R.E.M., X, the Replacements, Patti Smith, 'til Tuesday

David Yonke

Havana 3 A.M.

See: The Clash

Richie Havens

Born January 21, 1941 in Brooklyn, N.Y.

Though he first established himself as a folk singer on the New York coffee house circuit, Havens' rich, craggy voice and prowess as an interpreter of others' material gained him national recognition during the late 60s. His first couple of albums stiffed, but subsequent releases for MGM/Verve—notably *Mixed Bag*—encapsulated the humanistic, progressive mood of the time. Almost distinctive as his clarion vocals was Havens' powerful guitar playing, which involved hooking his thumb over the open-tuned strings and strumming furiously. His moment of greatest visibility came with his extended improvisation on the old spiritual "Motherless Child" at the Woodstock festival in 1969. He scored several hit singles during the next few years, recording memorable renditions of songs by Bob Dylan and the Beatles, as well as his own material. After a decade-long hiatus from recording, he began turning out albums again in 1987 and has appeared frequently with other 60s pop veterans at nostalgic reunion concerts. Aside from his musical endeavors, Havens has long worked as an environmental activist and done commercial voice-over work (he's best known in this regard as the singer of the Amtrak train jingle), as well as some film acting.

what to buy: *Resume: The Best of Richie Havens* (Rhino, 1993, comp. Johanan Vigoda) is a generous anthology that draws from his best original songs and covers.

what to buy next: *Mixed Bag* (Verve, 1967, prod. Johanan Vigoda) is an early peak, boasting the anti-war classic "Handsome Johnny" and his versions of Dylan's "Just Like a Woman" and the Beatles' "Eleanor Rigby."

what to avoid: *Mixed Bag II* (Verve, 1974, prod. Johanan Vigoda) is, like so many sequels, inferior to the original.

the rest: *A Richie Havens Record* (Douglas, 1965) *Electric Havens* (Douglas, 1966) *Something Else Again* (Verve, 1968) *Stonehenge* (Stormy Forest, 1970) *State of Mind* (Verve, 1971) *Alarm Clock* (Verve, 1971) *Great Blind Degree* (Verve, 1971) *Richie Havens on Stage* (Verve, 1972) *Portfolio* (Verve, 1973) *Richie Havens* (Polydor, 1975) *The End of the Beginning* (A&M, 1976) *Mirage* (A&M, 1977) *Connections* (Elektra, 1980) *Richard P. Havens 1983* (Verve, 1969/1983) *Common Ground* (EMI, 1984) *Simple Things* (RBI, 1987) *Now* (Solar/Epic, 1991) *Cuts to the Chase* (Forward, 1994)

worth searching for: *Richie Havens Sings the Beatles and Bob Dylan* (Rykodisc, 1986, prod. Douglas Yeager and Richie Havens) is an album full of covers from Havens' favorite songwriters.

▶▶ Tracy Chapman, Ben Harper, Hootie and the Blowfish

◀◀ Bob Dylan, the Beatles, Sam Cooke, Leadbelly, Robert Johnson, Muddy Waters

Simon Glickman

Greg Hawkes

See: The Cars

Dale Hawkins

Born on Aug. 22, 1938, in Goldmine, La.

The guitar licks that anchored "Suzie Q," Hawkins' piece of rock 'n' roll immortality, were played by James Burton, who left Louisiana for Hollywood—where he backed Ricky Nelson for the next 10 years and ultimately joined Elvis Presley's band. But Hawkins, a first cousin of another wild Louisiana rocker, Ronnie Hawkins, replaced Burton with Roy Buchanan. Before his recording career at Chicago's Chess label ended, he would also have Elvis' original guitarist, Scotty Moore, backing him up, not to mention the great blues sidemen that peopled most of the Chess sessions in Chicago. "Suzie Q" resonated through rock annals; from the Rolling Stones' version to the first hit single by Creedence Clearwater. Hawkins gave up performing in favor of producing early in the 60s, but he was one of many unsung greats of early rock 'n' roll. An 18-song collection, *Oh! Suzie Q: The Best of Dale Hawkins,* (MCA Chess, 1995, prod. Various) ♪♪♪♪ has the cream of his two-year association (1956-58) with Chess, Burton, Buchanan and Moore featured on guitar.

Joel Selvin

Ronnie Hawkins

Born Jan. 10, 1935, in Fayetteville, Ark.

There was once one brief shining moment, circa 1960, when Rompin' Ronnie Hawkins was poised to take over the world. All the crucial elements were in place: he and drummer Levon Helm were slowly assembling one of the greatest bands of all time (someday to become legendary in its own right as The Band); the head of Hawkins' label Roulette was spreading the word that his boy "moved better than Elvis, looked better than Elvis and *sang* better than Elvis" (and you know, he wasn't that far off the mark); and most important of all, the stagnating state of rock simply begged for a talent like Hawkins' to grab it and shake it back to life. Unfortunately, Hawkins chose instead to remain in his adopted home of Toronto, Canada, where he spent the 60s buying up nightclubs and making money as opposed to making history. Oh sure, he made great music and even had a few hits ("Mary Lou," "Forty Days"), but unless you happened to be spending your Saturday nights on Toronto's Yonge Street strip, you would never know that the kind of rumble the Beatles were busy producing in Liverpool and that the Stones were starting outside London was already well under way wherever Ronnie & the Hawks were performing. Sadly, as one by one his musicians left to seek their deserved fortunes outside of Toronto (guitarists Robbie Robertson and Roy Buchanan among them), Hawkins stubbornly remained in Canada, only occasionally committing to tape his special brand of razor-backed rock. Still, when Toronto recently threw him a 60th birthday bash, Carl Perkins and even Jerry Lee Lewis felt they owed it to the Hawk to make an appearance, and that night the rafters shook as much as they had back in '60. Still not convinced Hawkins is one of the greatest talents ever to sing rock 'n' roll? Well, name one other singer Jerry Lee would fly 1,000 miles to play piano for. *The Best Of Ronnie Hawkins and The Hawks* (Rhino, 1990, prod. Various) ♪♪♪♪♪ contains a decade's worth of top-standard rock 'n' roll culminating with his 1970 comeback hit "Down In The Alley," produced in Muscle Shoals with Duane Allman. Robertson's guitar solo on "Who Do You Love" sounds no less awe-inspiring now as it must have back in '63. *Ronnie Hawkins: The Roulette Years* (Sequel, 1994, prod. Various) ♪♪♪♪♪ fleshes out the years 1959-63 and is of particular interest in that it demonstrates just how fully The Band's unique approach to music was in evidence long before Mr. Dylan hijacked them.

Gary Pig Gold

Screamin' Jay Hawkins

Born Jalacy Hawkins, July 18, 1929 in Cleveland, Ohio

Primarily known as one of early rock's great showmen, Hawkins found fame promoting himself as a rock 'n' roll lunatic—appropriate for both Wolfman Jack and Dr. Demento. A former Golden Gloves boxing champion, he embarked on a musical career working small clubs with an energetic R&B revue show that often found him carried onstage in a flaming coffin, using flash powder or waving spears with skulls on them at the audience. His work was attacked by the usual authorities; early singles, particularly the classic "I Put a Spell On You" (reportedly cut by a dead-drunk Hawkins), featured so much of his wild moaning and vocal thrashing that they were banned from some radio stations and therefore, sold little. He continues to record for various independent labels, still singing about such subjects as sex and cannibalism. A surprising cameo in Jim Jarmusch's 1989 cult "Mystery Train"—as well as a song for "The X-Files" album project *Songs in the Key of X* (Warner Bros., 1996) were enthusiastically received and led to a minor resurgence of interest in his career. *Portrait of a Man* (Demon Records, 1995, prod. Various) ♪♪♪ compiles his crucial tracks, with all the great histrionics of near-misses and should've-beens such as "The Whammy" and "Little Demon."

Todd Wicks

Sophie B. Hawkins

Born c. 1967

An accomplished musician who studied ethnic percussion and jazz, Hawkins prefers to call herself a songwriter. The New Yorker, who began her career as a percussionist for Bryan Ferry, covers the range of her talents—including a tendency towards exhibitionism (check the CD booklets)—on her debut *Tongues and Tails* (1992, Columbia, prod. Rick Chertoff and Ralph Schuckett) ꝜꝜꝜ and *Whaler* (1994, Columbia, prod. Stephen Lipson) ꝜꝜꝜ Her debut solo album spawned the dance-floor hit "Damn, I Wish I Was Your Lover," while "Tongues and Tails" showed her quieter side with "As I Lay Me Down" and "The Ballad of Sleeping Beauty." Dig farther than that and her abilities to seamlessly weave in and out of jazz, folk and dance, all driven by a kind of tribal percussion sensibility.

Christina Fuoco

Ted Hawkins

Born 1936 in Biloxi, Miss. Died Jan. 1, 1995, in Los Angeles, Calif.

Singer-songwriter Hawkins was one of the rawest and most unschooled musicians to ever record, yet he was able to convey deep emotions through his rudimentary vocal and guitar skills. Unknown for most of his life—though he recorded as early as 1971—Hawkins attracted attention as a street singer in the Venice Beach area near Los Angeles during the early 80s. His style is that of a country bluesman with a little city soul thrown in. Some of Hawkins' best work is on *Happy Hour* (Rounder, 1986/1993, Rounder, prod. Bruce Bromberg and Dennis Walker) ꝜꝜꝜꝜ where his vocals and guitar render such original tunes as "Bad Dog," Revenge of Scorpio," and the title song. The tune "Happy Hour" should be a country-western standard with its barroom-worthy heartbreak lyrics. Hawkins also kicks it out pretty good on *Songs From Venice Beach,* (Evidence, 1995, prod. H. Thorp Minister III) ꝜꝜꝜꝜ a spare solo outing where he puts the country soul touch on such Motown classics as "Too Busy Thinking" and "Just My Imagination," and shows the Sam Cooke side of his heart on other songs.

the rest: *Watch Your Step* (Rounder, 1982/1993) ꝜꝜꝜꝜ *The Next Hundred Years* (DGC, 1994) ꝜꝜꝜ

Lawrence Gabriel

Isaac Hayes

Born Aug. 6, 1938 in Covington, Tenn.

Along with partner David Porter, Hayes was one of the preeminent and most successful songwriters at Stax records, churning out hits for Sam and Dave, Johnnie Taylor, Carla Thomas and Mable John. But Hayes truly made his mark with his own recordings; his sweaty, epic productions featured extended sides of influential soul orchestration and ushered R&B into the concept album era, while his work on the Oscar- and Grammy-winning "Shaft" soundtrack paved the way for similar blaxploitation artists such as Curtis Mayfield and Marvin Gaye. Through his albums and performances, the shirtless, bald-headed, sunglass-wearing basso profundo transformed himself into the sexually charged Black Moses; his groundbreaking half-sung, half-spoken pillow-talk monologues became standard practice for 70s soul. Quickly, though, Hayes seemed to run out of creative gas, as the quality of his recordings began to decrease at an astonishing rate. Hayes also ran out of luck: In 1976, he declared bankruptcy. By the 80s, he had become seemingly more interested in Hollywood than Memphis, his acting credits ("Escape from New York," "I'm Gonna Git You Sucka," "Robin Hood: Men in Tights," "It Could Happen to You") accumulating more rapidly than his album sales. Hayes, who now works as a DJ at a New York radio station, also became active in the Church of Scientology. In 1995, he attempted a comeback with two albums, one of which included his first songwriting collaboration with Porter since the pair split during the late 60s.

what to buy: The seminal Hayes concept album, *Hot Buttered Soul* (Enterprise, 1969/Stax, 1987, prod. Al Bell, Marvell Thomas and Allen Jones) ꝜꝜꝜꝜꝜ contains just four songs, including the sprawling, nearly 19-minute interpretation of Jimmy Webb's "By the Time I Get to Phoenix," a loping, 12-minute cover of Burt Bacharach's "Walk on By" and the essential high-hat groove, "Hyperbolicsyllabicsesquedalymistic." For a slightly more traditional album, the "Shaft" soundtrack (Enterprise, 1971, prod. Isaac Hayes) ꝜꝜꝜꝜ features several shorter cuts, including the classic title track and a series of instrumentals. Yet it also features a lengthy workout, the nearly 20-minute vocal ramble, "Do Your Thing." While the soundtrack does not address social concerns, a la Curtis Mayfield's "Superfly," it still grooves hard. Both *Hot Buttered Soul* and "Shaft" feature a crack rhythm section, the Bar-Kays.

what to buy next: *The Isaac Hayes Movement* (Enterprise/Stax, 1970, prod. Isaac Hayes) ꝜꝜꝜꝜ features more orchestral, string-heavy soul, including a tremendous reading of Jerry Butler's "I Stand Accused" and the 12-minute cover of the Beatles' "Something." *Double Feature* (Enterprise, 1974/Stax, 1993, prod. Isaac Hayes) features the underheard soundtracks from "Truck Turner" and "Tough Guys."

what to avoid: Hayes' work is best digested whole; taking songs out of context can lessen their impact, particularly when they've been trimmed for commercial-radio purposes. As such, *Best of Isaac Hayes, Vol. 1*, (Stax, 1986, prod. Various) *Best of Isaac Hayes, Vol. 2* (Stax, 1986, prod. Various) and *Greatest Hit Singles* (Stax, 1991, prod. various) should be avoided, as seminal songs are edited down and sequenced haphazardly, making for a poor introduction to Hayes' work.

the rest: *Presenting Isaac Hayes* (Enterprise/Stax, 1967) *To Be* Continued *(Enterprise/Stax, 1970)* Black Moses *(Enterprise, 1971)* Live at the Sahara Tahoe *(Enterprise/Stax, 1973)* Joy *(Enterprise, 1973)* Hotbed *(Stax, 1978)* Don't Let Go *(PolyGram Special Products, 1979)* Enterprise: His Greatest Hits *(Stax, 1980)* Love Attack *(Columbia, 1988)* Branded *(Pointblank, 1995)* Wonderful *(Stax, 1995)* Movement: Raw and Refined *(Pointblank, 1995)* Soul Essentials: The Best of The Polydor Years *(Polydor/Chronicles, 1996)*

worth searching for: *Branded/Raw & Refined Sampler*, (Pointblank, 1995) a one-disc distillation of Hayes' two 1995 albums which, in effect, create the single disc set it should have been.

▶▶ Gamble and Huff, Barry White, Teddy Pendergrass, DJ Quik, Cypress Hill, Marvin Gaye, Al Green, Lenny Kravitz, Terence Trent D'Arby

◀◀ Henry Mancini, Nat King Cole, Burt Bacharach, Brook Benton, Rufus Thomas, Wilson Pickett, Percy Sledge, Motown

Joshua Freedom du Lac

Gibby Haynes & Jeff Pinkus

See: Butthole Surfers

Justin Hayward

See: Moody Blues

Topper Headon

See: The Clash

Jeff Healey Band

Formed 1985 in Toronto, Canada

Jeff Healey (born March 25, 1966), vocals, guitar; Joe Rockman, bass; Tom Stephen, drums

America's first glimpse of Healey's talent was in the Patrick Swayze movie "Road House," where the blind guitarist demonstrated his five-fingered (he uses his thumb for effects as well) lap-top guitar work. The widespread exposure has been a mixed blessing, as his unusual technique has received more attention than his legitimately exciting playing. His path to guitar wizardry is further hampered by his penchant for playing generally unchallenging album-rock songs which don't make the most of his talents; Healey often opens up more when he's jamming with others.

what to buy: *See the Light* (Arista, 1988, prod. Greg Ladanyi, Jimmy Iovine and Thom Panunzio) is a strong debut, with the sweet balladry of "Angel Eyes" and bar band rave-ups such as "Confidence Man."

what to buy next: *Hell to Pay* (Arista, 1990, prod. Ed Stasium) tightens up the sound with better straightforward rockers, although mawkish cameos by George Harrison (on "While My Guitar Gently Weeps") and others knock it back a bit.

what to avoid: *Cover to Cover* (Arista, 1995, prod. Thom Panunzio and the Jeff Healey Band) is an unremarkable, pedestrian album of cover versions.

the rest: *Feel This* (Arista, 1992)

worth searching for: The deleted "Road House" soundtrack (Arista 1987, prod. Various) finds Healey cutting loose with some of his best playing on cvoers of the Doors' "Roadhouse Blues," "Hootchie Cootchie Man" and Bob Dylan's "When the Night Comes Falling From the Sky." But beware the two Swayze songs lurking amidst other contributions from Bob Seger, Otis Redding and Little Feat.

◀◀ Eric Clapton, Willie Dixon, John Lee Hooker, Jeff Beck, Stevie Ray Vaughan

Allan Orski

Heart

Formed 1970 in Seattle, Wash.

Ann Wilson, vocals, guitar, flute; Nancy Wilson, guitar, mandolin, vocals; Howard Leese, guitar, keyboards; Roger Fisher, guitar (1970-

80); Michael Derosier, drums (1970-82); Steve Fossen, bass (1970-82); Mark Andes, bass (1982-93); Denny Carmassi, drums (1982-93)

Considering Heart's status as one of the rare female-fronted rock groups during the 70s, it's ironic that the band's history didn't begin until Ann Wilson decided to move to Vancouver, Canada, to live with her then-boyfriend, Fisher. Before long, they had sent for Ann's kid sister Nancy and formed Heart with some friends from Seattle. The group's debut album, combining the Wilsons' singer-songwriter material with harder-edged rock, sold slowly at first, eventually scoring three hit singles to sell more than three million copies. Through the 70s and early 80s, the band recorded several classic rock anthems, only to find its audience waning in the wake of heavy metal's new popularity during the 80s. Drafting a new rhythm section, the group turned to metalized power ballads and videos featuring Nancy's impressive good looks for a mid-80s career resurgence that lasted until grunge turned 90s radio upside down. With yet another rhythm section—bassist Fernando Saunders and drummer Denny Fongheiser—Leese and the Wilson sisters have developed a stripped-down, unplugged presentation for their most recent albums and shows.

what to buy: From the complex, synthesizer-drenched classic rock mysticism of "Magic Man" to the straight-up rock of "Crazy on You" and the dreamy title track, *Dreamboat Annie* (Capitol, 1976, prod. Mike Flicker) [rating: 4.5 bones] expertly melds a singer-songwriter's imagination with a rocker's muscle—adding three classic cuts to the 70s rock lexicon in the process.

what to buy next: Although less focused than the debut, *Little Queen* (Portrait, 1977, prod. Mike Flicker) [rating: 4 bones] brings more of what made Heart a groundbreaking arena rock band, with legendary workouts such as "Barracuda" and the title track powering the airwaves for years to come. Similarly, the first live record, *Heart Greatest Hits/Live* (Epic, 1980, prod. Various) [rating: 4 bones] brings together all the classic tracks from the group's first five albums along with a shot of moderately interesting live tracks that let you avoid the sometimes-embarrassing filler on past records.

what to avoid: Stung by reaction among the rock crowd to its mid-80s ballads, Heart tried to present a harder edge on *Brigade*, (Capitol, 1990, prod. Ritchie Zito) **WOOF!** a record that only wound up demonstrating how badly the group's songwriting skills had deteriorated. And since *Rock The House Live!* (Capitol, 1991, prod. Heart and Richard Erwin) **WOOF!** compounds the mistake by featuring six cuts from *Brigade*, its pathetic results are predictable.

the rest: *Magazine* (Mushroom, 1978) [rating: 2.5 bones] *Dog and Butterfly* (Portrait, 1978) [rating: 3 bones] *Bebe Le Strange* (Epic, 1980) [rating: 3 bones] *Private Audition* (Epic, 1982) [rating: 2 bones] *Passionworks* (Epic, 1983) [rating: 2.5 bones] *Heart* (Capitol, 1985) [rating: 3 bones] *Bad Animals* (Capitol, 1987) [rating: 2.5 bones] *Desire Walks On* (Capitol, 1993) [rating: 2 bones] *Road Back Home* (Capitol, 1995) [rating: 3.5 bones]

worth searching for: Heart is one of the first bands to issue a multimedia CD-ROM of its history, called "Heart: 20 Years of Rock N' Roll." It's a great way for novices to familiarize themselves with the group's exhaustive history.

[influenced:] Veruca Salt, Alannah Myles, 4 Non Blondes

[influences:] Led Zeppelin, Joni Mitchell, Janis Joplin

Eric Deggans

Heaven 17

Formed 1979 in Sheffield, England. Disbanded 1988.

Martyn Ware, synthesizers; Ian Craig Marsh, synthesizers; Glenn Gregory, vocals

A spinoff from the Human League, Heaven 17 was a synthesizer-driven techno-trio with a bit more to it than the average slick-boy outfit plucking single notes from racks of keyboards. It sought a more interesting, albeit less accessible and commercially rewarding, route of innovative electro-funk. And in Gregory it had a singer who could actually express himself, which is more than most of his electronic geek peers can warble in their one-note defense. Of course, this kind of thing can't go on forever, and the band called it quits in 1988, after failing to make sufficient forays into radio gaga. *The Best of Heaven 17: Higher and Higher* (Virgin, 1993, prod. Various) [rating: 3.5 bones] is almost all that remains of seven studio albums and proves the band's sophistication level was higher than it was given credit for. *Teddy Bear, Duke and Psycho* (Caroline/Virgin, 1988) [rating: 3.5 bones] is a solid last effort, full of highly crafted atmospheric soundscapes and out-and-out funk.

Allan Orski

Michael Hedges

Born Dec. 31, 1953 in Enid, Okla.

Hedges' radical approach to the acoustic guitar effectively transforms it into a different instrument, creating sounds no one else has attempted with six strings. He changes the tunings, hammers and pulls the chords, taps the frets, tosses off lightning leads and chooses unusual chord progressions. Hedges studied classical guitar, earned a degree in composition from the Peabody Conservatory and then attended Stanford University's electronic music department. At first, Hedge's meditative instrumentals were tagged New Age, but he soon became too bold and quirky for that, or any, label. His own descriptions, although told in jest, are the most accurate, including "violent acoustic," "heavy mental" and "wacka-wacka." Hedges' virtuoso technique led Guitar Player magazine to elect him to the "Gallery of the Greats," but he uses the instrument as a tool for artistic expression, not just to thrill guitar fans. Lately, Hedges has been adding more of his sonorous vocals, keyboards and percussion to his performances.

what to buy: *Live on the Double Planet,* (Windham Hill, 1987, prod. Michael Hedges) ♪♪♪♪ is a safe introduction to Hedges' unorthodox guitar style and compositional talents. His covers of rock classics ("All Along the Watchtower," "Come Together") show his ability to reinvent the obvious. The instrumental majesty of *Aerial Boundaries* (Windham Hill, 1984, prod. William Ackerman, Michael Hedges and Steven Miller) marks Hedges' emergence as a guitar rebel but is relatively tame and much more accessible than his later efforts.

what to buy next: *Taproot* (Windham Hill, 1990, prod. Michael Hedges) ♪♪♪♪ is a concept album in which Hedges' instrumental prowess explores "classic mythic archetypes" with themes centering on planting, growth, and harvesting. The concept is obscure but Hedges' guitar brilliance is not.

what to avoid: *Breakfast in the Field* (Windham Hill, 1981, prod. William Ackerman) ♪ his recording debut, *is* tepid New Age fare.

the rest: *Watching My Life Go By* (Windham Hill, 1985) ♪♪♪ *The Road To Return* (Windham Hill, 1994) ♪♪♪

worth searching for: The David Crosby solo album *Oh Yes I Can,* (Atlantic, 1989, prod. Various) ♪♪♪♪ on which Hedges' playing is a highlight.

▶▶ Chris Whitley, Ben Harper, Craig Chaquico

◀◀ Leo Kottke, Martin Carthy, John Martyn, Edgar Varese

David Yonke

Helium

Formed 1992 in Boston, Mass.

Mary Timony, guitar, vocals; Brian Dunton, bass (1992-95); Ash Bowie, bass (1995-present); Shawn King Devlin, drums

Timony, of the infamous D.C. band Autoclave, was asked to come in on a new project headed by Jason Hatfield (Julianna's brother) and backed by former Dumptruck rhythm section, Dunton and Devlin. Soon after, Hatfield was arrested for carjacking, so Timony took over as leader, renamed the band, and Helium was born. Wallowing in distortion-heavy punk, melancholy lyrics and Timony's paradoxically waifish yet powerful voice, the band produces a moderately unique, if not unusual, sound. *Pirate Prude* (Matador EP, 1994, prod. Adam Laus) ♪♪♪ offers a rich musical experience. Dissonant, moody guitar and sad, apocalyptic vocals tell the tragic tale of lost innocence and femininity. *Dirt of Luck* (Matador, 1995, prod. Adam Laus) ♪♪♪♪ deals with many of the same themes as *Pirate Prude,* but this time out Helium introduces a sound—with lush, interweaving hooks and notably improved musical prowess.

Bryan Lassner

Richard Hell & the Voidoids

Formed 1976 in New York, N.Y. Disbanded 1982.

Richard Hell (born Richard Meyers, Oct. 2, 1949 in Lexington, Ky.), vocals, bass; Robert Quine, guitar (1976-82); Ivan Julian, guitar (1976-79); Naux, guitar, (1980-82); Mike Paumgardhen, guitar (1983); Jeff Freeman, guitar (1983); Jody Harris, guitar (1985); Jerry Antonius, bass, keyboards (1978-79); John (or Jahn) Xavier (aka Xcessive), bass (1979); Ted Horowitz, bass (1985); Marc Bell, drums (1976-78); Frank Mauro, drums (1978-79); James Morrison, drums (1979); Fred Maher, drums (1980-82); Chuck Wood, drums (1983); Anton Fier, drums (1985)

Poet/writer Hell formed his own group after being a founding member of both the Neon Boys (in 1971), a band which by 1973 had turned into Television (the first punk band), and the Heartbreakers. The Neon Boys are heard on a posthumous 1980 EP on Shake Records, now out of print; Hell appears on Television's "Little Johnny Jewel" single and the bootleg album *Double Exposure*, consisting of demos produced by Brian Eno and live recordings. Famously, it was Hell's fashion sense—ripped clothes, slogans scrawled on T-shirts, safety pins—which influenced Malcolm McLaren's construction of the Sex Pistols' look. Even more influentially, Hell blurted out nihilistic, decadent lyrics ("Love Comes in Spurts") in a tuneless voice, epitomizing the attitude and sound of punk, with the band's rhythms matching his lurching cadences. A major collaborator in the Voidoids sound was guitarist Quine, who combined the choppy chording of Lou Reed in the Velvet Underground with the dissonant polytonality jagged lines of Miles Davis's 70s guitarists.

Myriad personnel changes found Hell the only constant (drummer Bell became Marky Ramone), though Quine figures in all the important lineups—which is to say all the lineups before the group basically split up in 1982. (Dare we say that fitful appearances of later Voidoids lineups were financially motivated? Hell's bad habits, which he has chronicled freely, required some cash flow.) After eventually retiring (more or less) from playing, Hell concentrated on writing and also got a few acting gigs, including a cameo in "Desperately Seeking Susan" as Madonna's boyfriend. A one-shot band, Dim Stars, was built around him by admirers from the next generation of downtown New York rockers—Sonic Youth's Thurston Moore and Steve Shelley and producer/Gumball leader Don Fleming.

what to buy: *Blank Generation* (Sire, 1977, prod. Richard Gottehrer and Richard Hell) ♪♪♪♪ is a seminal punk album showcasing Quine's guitar imagination. Though Hell has insisted that the title track speaks of the open possibilities of an unlabeled generation, it has inevitably been interpreted more cynically, which with the benefit of hindsight doesn't seem like a mistake. The CD varies from the original LP by adding two bonus tracks but also substituting an inferior version of "Down at the Rock and Roll Club" when, at less than 41 minutes, there's room for both.

what to buy next: *Destiny Street* (Red Star, 1982/Razor & Tie, 1994, prod. Alan Betrock) ♪♪♪½ is less reckless than *Blank Generation*, though "polished" would be an overstatement. Mostly it's more reflective, especially on "Time" and the funky title track, and the songwriting seems more thorough and less reliant on shock effects.

the rest: *R.I.P.* (ROIR, 1986) ♪♪♪ *Funhunt* (ROIR, 1990) ♪♪♪

worth searching for: If you ever find the Voidoids' debut 7" (Ork, 1976), be prepared to shell out a lot. Besides early versions of "Blank Generation" and "Another World," it includes the non-album "You Gotta Lose."

solo outings:

Richard Hell: *Go Now* (Tim Kerr, 1995) ♪♪½

Dim Stars (Hell, Quine): *Dim Stars* (Caroline, 1992) ♪♪

▶▶ Sex Pistols, DNA/Arto Lindsay, Contortions, Minutemen, Sonic Youth, Matthew Sweet

◀◀ Velvet Underground/Lou Reed, Stooges, Captain Beefheart, Arthur Rimbaud, Charles Baudelaire

Steve Holtje

Hellecasters

Formed 1994 in Los Angeles, Calif.

John Jorgenson, guitar; Will Ray, guitar; Jerry Donahue, guitar

While most three-guitar bands are prone to wayward, rambling jams, the Hellecasters are an exception. Comprised of three top country music session players (whose credits also include Bob Seger, Bob Dylan, George Harrison and Elton John), the Hellecasters—the name is a comical reference to the Fender Telecaster guitar—explore varying styles of music, including reggae and Middle Eastern, while still tenaciously clinging to their country-tinged roots and surf-rock influences. The results are the envy of anyone who has ever picked up a guitar. Each of the individual Hellecasters seems to be in friendly competition with his bandmates, drawing out some of the best country-influenced guitar playing set to tape. *The Return of the Hellecasters* (Rio, 1994, prod. Dan Fredman) ♪♪♪♪ sounds like the Ventures on speed, with each guitarist showing absolute mastery of his instrument while never interfering with the other two. The band's rendition of "Orange Blossom Special" is sure to make anyone's mouth drop in amazement. *Escape From Hollywood* (Rio, 1994, prod. Hellecasters) ♪♪♪½ contains more of the same, though it occasionally sounds repetitive.

Matt Merta

Helmet

Formed 1989 in New York, N.Y.

Page Hamilton, vocals, guitar; Peter Mengede, guitar (1989-94); Rob Echeverria, guitar (1994-present); Henry Bogdan, bass; John Stamier, drums

Helmet burst onto the rock scene quite literally—with a barrage of volume, riffs, rage and power. Led by ex-Band of Susans guitarist Hamilton, Helmet cranked out some of the heaviest, thickest power chord rock around. Dubbed the next Nirvana, Helmet was the subject of an intense major label bidding war and was saddled with astronomical expectations which it never lived up to in the commercial sense. What separated the group from the grunge scene was its short-haired, straight-edge appearance (a la Fugazi), and the fact that its members were university-educated musicians whose formal training made Helmet a tighter, more efficient unit—which in turn, only enhanced the power of its start-stop monster riffs and locomotive rhythms. *Meantime* (Interscope, 1992, prod. Steve Albini) is really all the Helmet one needs. Punctuated by short but beyond-powerful blasts of guitar fury, this album gets in and gets out quickly, leveling everything in its path with its molten, bare-bones attack.

the rest: *Born Annoying* (Amphetamine Reptile EP, 1989) *Strap It On* (Amphetamine Reptile, 1990) *Betty* (Interscope, 1994) *Aftertaste* (Interscope, 1996) not available for rating

Christopher Scanlon

Jimi Hendrix

Born James Marshall Hendrix, Nov. 27, 1943, in Seattle, Wash. Died Sept. 18, 1970, in London, England

The Experience, 1966: Jimi Hendrix, guitar, vocals; Noel Redding, bass, vocals; Mitch Mitchell, drums. Band of Gypsies: Jimi Hendrix, guitar and vocals; Billy Cox, bass; Buddy Miles, drums and vocals

Rock 'n' roll would not be what it is today without Hendrix's influence. He defined the electric guitar as the quintessential rock instrument in ways that no player before him did. As Charlie Parker's name is synonymous with the jazz saxophone, so is Hendrix's name with the rock electric guitar. While many guitarists deserve credit for various innovations during rock's infancy, it was Hendrix who assimilated the instrument's known vocabulary, exploded its preconceptions and, through his genius for color and sound, created for it a new sonic forum. Hendrix's singular style evolved from a heady brew of musical and cultural sources; his playing was influenced by both the blues and jazz, and his early professional outings—most notably as a member of the Isley Brothers' band—bore these influences out in a competent but unremarkable fashion. Increasingly, however, Hendrix was drawn to the evolving rock scene of the mid-60s; influenced by the flowering psychedelic scene and the social conscience of musicians such as Bob Dylan, he developed a philosophy of personal freedom and unfettered expression, a mission of universal emancipation through music. Armed with this world view and his technical skills, Hendrix approached the guitar as an extension of his own personality and beliefs, making it an instrument of emotional expression without boundaries. While he was undeniably a virtuoso on the instrument, it was not just his guitar playing that made Hendrix a rock legend. Perhaps just as important was his commitment to song structure and ideology; his songs served a purpose beyond being a forum for guitar histrionics. He did not see his guitar as an end unto itself but as just one part of a unified musical vision. In addition, he believed that his music should speak to people, challenge presentiments and provoke change; he was committed to the hippie ideal of making the world a better place through music. Also important to the Hendrix legend was the mythic gypsy persona he chose for himself and his bands (the Experience and Band of Gypsies), one that had great influence on fashion in the 60s and 70s. This canny incarnation—that of a colorful, fantastic character—helped him to straddle the color line and reach a vast white audience without compromising his musical roots. His ability to make a wide variety of musical styles widely accessible (notably his later forays into jazz) also made him an ideal musical ambassador and teacher. Hendrix's career as a solo artist lasted only three years; that he exercised such a tremendous influence on modern music—both sonically and visually—in that short period is just further evidence of his brilliance.

what to buy: *Electric Ladyland* (Reprise, 1968/MCA, 1993, prod. Jimi Hendrix) is Hendrix' masterpiece with the Experience (bassist Noel Redding and drummer Mitch Mitchell), the album that provided a breathtaking glimpse into the guitarist's future potential and ambitions. Just as the Beatles' *Sgt. Pepper's Lonely Hearts Club Band* raised the bar on what could be called pop, so did *Electric Ladyland* change the perception of what a rock record could be; sonically, the album is light-years ahead of any of its contemporaries, with Hendrix making copious use of then-new multi-track recording technology.

what to buy next: *Axis: Bold As Love* (Reprise, 1968/MCA, 1993, prod. Chas Chandler) preceded *Electric Ladyland* by less than a year, and it is an excellent illustration of the rate at which Hendrix and the Experience matured, sonically and thematically, between the two releases. This is not to say that *Axis* is any less of an album than its follow-up—many songs rival those found on *Electric Ladyland.* For those fond of Hendrix's gentle side, the album offers a bounty of beauty in the delicate chording and melodies of "Little Wing," "Castles Made of Sand" and the title song. There are also plentiful examples of the master's molten way with blues-rock, particularly "If 6 Was 9" and the warped "Up from the Skies."

what to avoid: *Voodoo Soup,* (MCA, 1994, prod. Alan Douglas) which claims to be the unfinished masterpiece that Hendrix was working on before his untimely death. Unfinished is what the material sounds like, despite the best efforts of studio swamis to conjure the spirit of Jimi in completing these tracks.

the rest: *Are You Experienced?* (Reprise, 1967/MCA, 1993) *Band of Gypsies* (Capitol, 1970/1994) *Blues* (MCA, 1994) *Live at Winterland* (Rykodisc, 1987) *Radio One* (Rykodisc, 1988) *Woodstock* (MCA, 1994) *The Ultimate Experience* (MCA, 1993)

worth searching for: If your mission is to search out Hendrix's out-of-print classics, you've got your work cut out for you. A morass of legal wranglings over ownership and MCA's purchase of his Reprise catalog have left many of his recordings in limbo. Of special note is the album he recorded with the Band of Gypsys lineup (bassist Billy Cox and singer-drummer Buddy Miles), *Cry of Love* The album is a nice primer on Hendrix's blues roots and the steps he was taking after the demise of the Experience.

Stevie Ray Vaughn, Robin Trower, Van Halen, Ernie Isley, Lenny Kravitz, Prince, Miles Davis, Carlos Santana, Eric Clapton, Sly Stone

Buddy Guy, Freddie King, The Beatles, Chuck Berry, Bob Dylan, The Yardbirds, Howlin' Wolf, Robert Johnson

David Galens

Nona Hendryx

Born on Aug. 18, 1945, in Trenton, N.J.

Hendryx spent 15 years with two groups—Patti Labelle & the Bluebells and Labelle, eventually becoming the latter's songwriter. After the very successful Labelle broke up in 1976, Hendryx switched from R&B to rock; with disco then peaking, neither labels nor radio could sell a black woman singing aggressive rock. But Hendryx's talents and refusal to be pigeonholed found a sympathetic milieu in the downtown Manhattan scene. Her backing vocals became an integral part of Talking Heads' sound (she's on the albums *Remain in Light*, *The Name of This Band Is Talking Heads* and *Speaking in Tongues*) and was a strong visual presence at T-Heads concerts. But the collaboration that would most influence Hendryx's career was with Material. She sang on its 1981 club hit "Bustin' Out" and its album *One Down*, and the Material production team (Bill Laswell, Michael Beinhorn) then resurrected her solo career with *Nona* and *The Art of Defense*, bringing her back on the R&B charts with "Keep It Confidential," "Transformation," "I Sweat," tough it's the rock and reggae tracks that hold up best. Since then, Hendryx has recorded sporadically, continuing as a studio vocalist while further expanding the stylistic range of her music and collaborations.

what to buy: *Female Trouble* (EMI America, 1987, prod. Various) combines excellent material, a freshly percolating sound and exciting guests (Peter Gabriel, Bernie Worrell, George Clinton, Mavis Staples and members of the Time). Every track is strong, particularly "I Know What You Need (Pygmy's Confession)," the hit "Why Should I Cry?," the title track and "Baby Go-Go," penned by Prince under the pseudonym J. Coco.

what to buy next: *Nona* (RCA, 1983, prod. Material and Nona Hendryx) may have benefitted from a long gap between albums. The high quality of the songwriting suggests Hendryx had a large stockpile of songs and could choose the best, while the Material production gives coherence to a broad stylistic range.

what to avoid: Hendryx's forceful vocals are stranded amid dry backing on *The Art of Defense*, (RCA, 1984, prod. Material and Nona Hendryx) with drum tracks that are downright boring.

the rest: *The Heat* (RCA, 1985) *Skindiver* (Private, 1989) *You Have to Cry Sometime* (with Billy Vera) (Shanachie, 1992)

worth searching for: The long out-of-print solo debut *Nona Hendryx* (Epic, 1977, prod. Michael Sherman) sounds a bit dated but it's made compelling by Hendryx's edgy vocals and strong personality.

Lisa Lisa & Cult Jam, Tasmin Archer, Neneh Cherry

Eurythmics, Mavis Staples

Steve Holtje

Don Henley

Born July 22, 1947 in Gilmer, Texas

Henley has had the greatest solo success of all the Eagles, both commercially and artistically. Not only has he scored substantial hits—"The Boys of Summer," "The End of the Innocence"—but he's also advanced a thoughtful, populist viewpoint that, unlike the cynical disdain of late-period Eagles, is filled with hope and a desire to affect change. Henley's solo career was slowed by a contractual battle with his label (he switched from Geffen to Warner Bros. in 1996) and by the Eagles' 1994 reunion, but "The Garden of Allah"—a new track on his 1995 best-of set, shows that his virtues remained intact.

what to buy: *Building the Perfect Beast*(Geffen, 1984, prod. Henley, Danny Kortchmar, Greg Ladanyi) mixes the high-tech sheen of its rockers ("The Boys of Summer," "All She

Wants to Do is Dance") with aching, gentle ballads. Painstakingly crafted, "Beast" propelled Henley from the shadow of the Eagles.

what to buy next: Any of the rest of his output will do. *I Can't Stand Still* (Asylum, 1982, prod. Henley, Kortchmar, Ladanyi) ♪♪♪ is an estimable solo debut. *The End of the Innocence* (Geffen, 1989, Henley, Kortchmar) ♪♪♪½ suffered a bit for following *Building the Perfect Beast* but was still solid; the title track and "The Heart of the Matter" are perhaps his finest ballads. *Actual Miles: Henley's Greatest Hits* (Geffen, 1995 prod. Various) ♪♪♪½ is a creditable, if incomplete, sampler, with new songs that are worth having.

worth searching for: *An Eagle Out East* (KTS, 1993) is a strong bootleg from a 1990 performance in Tokyo, a mini-greatest hits set that also includes Eagles favorites such as "Hotel California," "Life in the Fast Lane" and "Desperado."

▶▶ Tom Petty, Bryan Adams, Sheryl Crow, Mojo Nixon

◀◀ Henry David Thoreau, Leonard Cohen, Bob Dylan, Gram Parsons, the Byrds

see also: *Eagles, Bruce Hornsby, Joe Walsh, Sheryl Crow*

Gary Graff

Herman's Hermits

Formed 1963 in Manchester, England. Disbanded 1971.

Peter Noone, vocals, piano, guitar; Karl Green, guitar, harmonica; Keith Hopwood, guitar; Derek Leckenby (died June 4, 1994), guitar; Barry Whitwam, drums)

Twenty years later it would be the home of modern rock favorites such as Stone Roses and Happy Mondays, but in 1963, Manchester gave the world Herman's Hermits—smiling, happy people playing pop songs that practically commanded listeners to bop. Fronted by Noone and produced by Britain's reigning hitmaker Mickie Most, the Hermits reeled out a string of hits during the mid-60s that included "I'm Into Something Good," "Mrs. Brown You've Got a Lovely Daughter" and the Dr. Demento favorite "I'm Henry the Eight, I Am." The Hermits lived something of a charmed life; besides Most, the group had futrure Led Zeppelin members Jimmy Page and John Paul Jones play on its records; and the Kinks' Ray Davies penned one of its Top 5 hits, "Dandy." *Their Greatest Hits* (ABCKO, date N/A, prod. Mickie Most) ♪♪♪½ does the trick with 16 songs from the era—much better than the skimpy 10 tracks on *Greatest Hits*, (Hollywood/Rounder, date N/A) ♪♪½ which is the only other title currently available. Noone has had the most high-profile post-Hermits career, recording some solo albums (his big hit was David Bowie's "Oh! You Pretty Thing"), appearing in a Broadway production of "The Pirates of Penzance" and hosting the "My Generation" program on VH-1.

Gary Graff

Nick Heyward

See: Haircut 100

Richard X. Heyman

Born Aug. 16, 19— in Plainfield, N.J.

Fans of the Smithereens, World Party or Matthew Sweet ought to love Heyman, whose one-man-band pop records are as wonderful as they are undeservedly obscure. Heyman's prior stint as a drummer in Link Wray's touring band serves him well on *Living Room!!* (N.R. World Records Unlimited, 1988/Cypress, 1990, prod. Richard X. Heyman) ♪♪♪♪ Where the rhythms often seem like an afterthought on most homemade albums (and Heyman made this one in, yes, his living room), on these 14 songs they're just as solid as the to-die-for hooks. He even keeps time with a typewriter on one track, "Local Paper." The followup *Hey Man!* (Sire, 1991, prod. R.X. Heyman and Andy Paley) ♪♪♪½ is almost as strong, continuing Heyman's odd fondness for exclamatory titles and military metaphors ("Back to You," "Private Army," "Civil War Buff").

David Menconi

John Hiatt

Born 1952 in Indianapolis, Ind.

Few of rock's angstful young men have matured with the grace and dignity of John Hiatt. While other middle-aged rockers fret about their mortality and receding hairlines, this resilient singer-songwriter takes pride in his domestic bliss: "Bring the Family" and "Slow Turning" are filled with delightfully skewered observations of adulthood and passionate paeans to shaping up ("These days the only bar I ever see/has got lettuce and tomatoes") and settling down. A respected songwriter who has penned hits for everyone from Three Dog Night ("Sure As I'm Sittin' Here") to Rosanne Cash ("The Way We Make a Broken Heart") and Bonnie Raitt ("Thing Called Love"), Hiatt jumped on the new-wave bandwagon in the early 80s with such strained, strident efforts as "Slug Line" and "All of a Sudden."

His teaming with former mentor Ry Cooder, Jim Keltner and Nick Lowe in 1987 for "Bring the Family" stirred up some volatile creative chemistry (the four would later form the group Little Village) and reunited him with his country/blues roots.

what to buy: *Bring the Family* (A&M, 1987, prod. John Chelew) and *Slow Turning* (A&M, 1988, prod. Glyn Johns) trace Hiatt's development as a family man and a much-improved singer. Johns' crisp production lends the latter a tough-rocking edge on "Drive South," "Trudy and Dave," "Tennessee Plates" and the title track. On *Perfectly Good Guitar* (A&M, 1993, prod. Matt Wallace) Hiatt gets a hall pass from his parental duties and paints the town with Wallace, who beefs up Hiatt's country-tinged melodies with a barrage of fuzzy, feedback-drenched guitars that echo the reckless abandon of Neil Young's "Ragged Glory." *Walk On* (Capitol, 1995, prod. Don Smith) strikes a keen balance between his primitive and paternal sides with the barnstorming country-rock of "Good As She Could Be," the elegant "You Must Go" and the shimmering pop of "Shredding the Document."

what to buy next: *Riding With the King* (Geffen, 1983, prod. Ron Nagel, Scott Matthews and Nick Lowe) is the most listenable remnant from his "new wave" period, with backing from Nick Lowe and his Paul Carrack-led Cowboy Outfit on half the disc.

what to avoid: On *Slug Line* (MCA, 1979, prod. Denny Bruce) promising songs are drowned in cliche-ridden production that leaves him sounding more nerdy than nervy. At best, Elvis Costello Lite.

the rest: *Hanging Around the Observatory* (Epic, 1974) *Overcoats* (Epic, 1975) *Two Bit Monsters* (Geffen, 1980) *Warming Up to the Ice Age* (Geffen, 1985) *Y'All Caught?: The Ones That Got Away 1979-1985* (Geffen, 1989) *Stolen Moments* (A&M, 1990) *Hiatt Comes Alive at Budokan* (A&M, 1994).

worth searching for: *Love Gets Strange: The Songs of John Hiatt* (Rhino, 1993, prod. Various), a various-artists collection of diverse treatments by the Neville Brothers ("Washable Ink"), Rosanne Cash ("Pink Bedroom"), Jeff Healey ("Angel Eyes") and Marshall Crenshaw ("Someplace Where Love Can't Find Me").

▶▶ Joe Henry, Syd Straw, Bob Seger

◀◀ Ry Cooder, Stax/Volt soul, Elvis Costello, Bob Seger, Bob Dylan

David Okamoto

Dan Hicks

Born on Dec. 9, 1941, in Little Rock, Ark.

Hicks polished the old-timey style of the Charlatans, the little-known but influential San Francisco band on which he served as drummer, into a campy, acoustic-flavored cabaret act, Dan Hicks and His Hot Licks. The group would presage such full-blown period pieces as Bette Midler, the Pointer Sisters and the Manhattan Transfer by several years. Hicks' sarcastic persona and well-developed sense of irony gave him a determined deadpan attitude and helped obscure the fact that his songwriting was really first-rate. With his jazzy mien and caustic air, Hicks made a modest splash with his Blue Thumb albums of the early 70s, which had the zippy nonchalance of an R. Crumb cartoon come to life. He continues an active performing career, although his recordings have been few and far in between since the heyday of the Hot Licks.

what to buy: *Where's the Money* (MCA, 1971, prod. Tommy LiPuma) probably best reflects the zany intransigence of Hicks and company.

what to buy next: *Striking It Rich* (MCA, 1972, prod. Tommy LiPuma) captures the live ambiance of the band's appearances.

the rest: *Last Train to Hicksville* (MCA, 1973) *Shootin' Straight* (On the Spot, 1994)

worth searching for: His debut album, *Dan Hicks and His Hot Licks,* (Epic, 1969, prod. B. Johnston) is his best, with such signature songs as "How Can I Miss You When You Won't Go Away," "Canned Music" and "I Scare Myself" (later covered by Thomas Dolby).

▶▶ The Pointer Sisters, Thomas Dolby

◀◀ Le Hot Club de France, Andrews Sisters, the Charlatans

Joel Selvin

Chris Hillman

See: Flying Burrito Brothers

Peter Himmelman

Born Nov. 23, 1959 in Minneapolis, Minn.

A former Elvis Costello disciple in a Minneapolis power-pop band called Sussman Lawrence, Peter Himmelman changed his life and his sound after his father's death. He became an Orthodox Jew, married Bob Dylan's daughter, Maria, and started writing thoughtful examinations of emotional and spiritual strife and the resilience of the human spirit that have established him as one of rock's most passionate songwriters. He's also an intriguing paradox: Despite the brooding tone of his songs, his acclaimed live shows are part-performance art and part-"Let's Make a Deal" as he invites audience members onstage, makes up songs on the spot, hands out Play-Doh and exudes a hilarious brink-of-disaster spontaneity so sadly lacking in the modern-day concert experience. His solo acoustic shows give him more freedom, but on a good night, his longtime band—featuring Jeff Victor, Andy Kamman, Al Wolovitch and Kristin Mooney—provides tight, tenacious backing that rivals Tom Petty's Heartbreakers.

what to buy: The intimate *From Strength to Strength* (Epic, 1991, prod. Peter Himmelman) ♪♪♪♪ includes his near-hit, "Woman With the Strength of 10,000 Men" and such concert staples as "Only Innocent" and "Mission of My Soul." *Flown This Acid World* (Epic, 1992, prod. Don Smith and Peter Himmelman) ♪♪♪♪ is the hard-rocking follow-up, boasting blistering renditions of "Beneath the Damage and the Dust" and "Untitled," a harrowing story song about the night he rode in a taxi driven by a neo-Nazi. *This Father's Day,* (Island, 1986, prod. Peter Himmelman) ♪♪♪♪ reissued in 1995 by Razor and Tie, is his first post-Sussman Lawrence album and traces his evolution from sneering punk to soulful singer-songwriter. The title track is a heartfelt, guts-spilling demo written on Father's Day 1983 that captures him breaking down toward the end of the song.

what to buy next: *Skin* (Sony 550, 1994, prod. Peter Himmelman and Jeff Victor) ♪♪♪♪ is a daring concept album that follows the death and rebirth of a hedonistic egomaniac named Ted. More important, it rocks.

what to avoid: The keyboard-laden *Synesthesia* (Island, 1989, prod. Peter Himmelman) ♪♪ tries too hard for rock credibility and sounds distant, strained and overproduced—everything his other albums are not.

the rest: (with Sussman Lawrence) *Hail to the Modern Hero* (Regency 1980) ♪♪ *Pop City* (Orange, 1984) ♪♪♪ (solo) *Gematria* (Island, 1987) ♪♪♪♪ *Stage Diving* (Plump, 1996) ♪♪♪♪

worth searching for: *The Musings of Someone*, a 1991 promotional interview disc showcasing Himmelman's offbeat sense of humor interspersed with acoustic performances and the bane of his existence, a two-minute ditty about an independent dachshund called "Dixie the Tiny Dog" that still gets requested more than "Free Bird" at a Lynyrd Skynyrd concert.

◀◀ Bob Dylan, Elvis Costello

David Okamoto

Hindu Love Gods

Warren Zevon, vocals; Peter Buck, guitar; Mile Mills, bass; Bill Berry, drums

Originally one of the many aliases used for R.E.M. side projects, Hindu Love Gods was co-opted by Warren Zevon during his sessions for his *Sentimental Hygiene* album. Zevon was backed on that effort by R.E.M.'s instrumentalists, and the songs they used to warm up in the studio—Prince's "Raspberry Beret," the Georgia Satellite's "Battleship Chains" and blues covers such as "Mannish Boy" and "Crosscut Saw"—eventually wound up on *Hindu Love Gods,* (Giant, 1990, prod. Andrew Slater and Niko Bolas) ♪♪♪ somewhat to the dismay of the R.E.M. camp. The album is an enjoyable romp, however, and conveys the enthusiasm of musicians playing for each other and having fun.

Daniel Durchholz

His Name is Alive /Liquorice

Formed 1989 in Livonia, Mich.

Karen Oliver, vocals, cello; Angie Carozzo, vocals (1990); Warren Defever, guitar, bass, samples; Trey Many, drums (1993-present)

The eerie, foreboding sparseness of this band evokes existential angst as originally as anything out there, bringing post-punk principles to bear on progressive rock ideas, mixing acoustic and electric instruments in alternately cool and powerful sounds. Think of His Name is Alive as a sort of New Age college radio version of King Crimson. Similarities include rousing, guitar-powered rock alternating with quiet, sometimes drum-less chamber music; clearly articulated but deliberately obscure lyrics; and seemingly pointless filler to wade through on the way to the good parts. Dissimilar and frustrating is the brevity of many of those good parts on the first two albums. Defever played in his older brother's totally different band, Elvis Hitler, from which he borrowed the first album's guest drummer. He has put together a number of permutations of HNIA and produced guitarist Melissa Elliott's much louder

What Album Changed Your Life?

"There was an old blues compilation called Memphis Blues Again. It's a combination of all these Delta-tradition blues arists, mostly duets of guitar and harmonica or country blues solo artist. There was one song, 'Jelly Feelin' Woman,' about a prostitute. I was, like, 14 at the time, just getting into rock 'n' roll, so I had to find out about the blues. I was a kid looking under rocks for things."

Chris Barron (Spin Doctors)

HNIA offshoot, the Dirt Eaters; tracks Defever did with them were used on *Mouth By Mouth*, lending it more variety than other HNIA efforts. Current HNIA drummer Many was drafted into the indie super group Liquorice, with Jenny Toomey (Tsunami) and Dan Littleton (Hated).

what to buy: On *Mouth by Mouth*, (4AD, 1993, prod. His Name is Alive) ♪♪♪♪ some tunes are marginally more traditional than earlier efforts thanks to more prominent use of bass and drums, but surreal lyrics and juxtapositions place the results on a different plane from rock. On, for example, "Drink, Dress, and Ink" and "Can't Go Wrong Without You," the placid pulse and nearly New Age mellowness are countered by barbed bursts of electric guitar fuzz and disjunctive structure, resulting in compelling eeriness. A cover of Big Star's "Blue Moon" stands out.

what to buy next: *Stars on ESP* (4AD, 1996, prod. Warren Defever) ♪♪♪♪ isn't as singular a work of art, but is more accessible. Several of the songs draw heavily on recognizable styles—the Beach Boys ("Good Vibrations" is reworked as the basis of "Universal Frequencies"), surf guitar, Big Star desolation—and a high percentage of the material is fully developed into nearly normal song forms.

what to avoid: *Livonia* (4AD, 1990) ♪♪ is so fragmentary that it requires putting more into listening than anyone but fanatics should be willing to do.

the rest: *Home Is in Your Head* (4AD, 1991) ♪♪♪ *Universal Frequencies* (4AD EP, 1996) ♪♪♪

worth searching for: *King of Sweet*, (Perdition Plastics, 1993) ♪♪♪ available in a limited pressing of 2,000, collects outtakes of an obviously unfinished nature but will appeal to fans.

solo outings:

Liquorice (Trey Many): Listening Cap (4AD, 1995) ♪♪♪

◀◀ King Crimson, Led Zeppelin, Karlheinz Stockhausen, Brian Eno, Phillip Glass, Cocteau Twins, This Mortal Coil, Colin Newman, Guided By Voices, Brian Wilson, Big Star, King Tubby

Steve Holtje

Robyn Hitchcock (and the Egyptians)

Born 1953 in West London, England. The Egyptians formed 1985 in Cambridge, England

Robyn Hitchcock vocals, guitar; Andy Metcalfe bass, vocals; Morris Windsor drums, vocals; Roger Jackson keyboards (1985-86)

Robyn Hitchcock more or less retired from music after the Soft Boys dissolved. He painted, wrote songs for Captain Sensible and licked his wounds. Eventually the pull of songwriting and performing was too strong, and he began to return regularly to the studio as a solo act and with The Egyptians—who, for their part, were the Soft Boys minus lead guitarist Kimberly Rew. Regardless of the setting, Hitchcock writes songs which make inescapable the connection between West Coast psychedelia and folk music. They're sweet, idiosyncratic, sometimes dada, frequently surrealistic and often tainted with the odor of love (past, present or future). Always a critic's favorite (and rarely any kind of commercial success), Hitchcock has bounced from label to label. Throughout, his body of work (with one notable exception) has been first-rate. In live performance, he connects his songs with a stream-of-unconsciousness patter that is almost as fascinating as the songs are beautiful.

what to buy: Where to begin? *I Often Dream of Trains* (Midnight Music, 1984/Rhino 1995, prod. Robyn Hitchcock) ♪♪♪♪ is an exquisite album, relaxed and focused and studded with kind, wry, sad songs like "Sometimes I Wish I Was a Pretty Girl," the music hall-ish "Uncorrected Personality Traits" and the stunning title track. It is a simple, winsome record, and quite fetching. The Egyptians' college radio hit, "Balloon Man," from *Globe of Frogs* (A&M, 1988, prod. by The Egyptians) marked the group's ascension to a major label in the States. It is as quirky, eccentric and ebullient a record as the band would make. That *Perspex Island* (A&M, 1991, prod. Paul Fox) didn't produce a break-through hit—what with the likes of "So You Think You're In Love" and "She Doesn't Exist"—is a testimonial only to the unfairness of things.

what to buy next: The first Egyptians opus, *Fegmania!* (Midnight Music, 1985/Rhino 1995, prod. Pat Collier) includes the haunting (pun intended) "My Wife and My Dead Wife" and "The Man With the Lightbulb Head." *Element Of Light* (Relativity/Glass Fish, 1986/Rhino, 1995, prod. Robyn Hitchcock and Andy Metcalfe) features the most linear storytelling of the Hitchcock canon, including "Raymond Chandler Evening" and "Ted, Woody and Junior." Not to mention the laughably misunderstood "Tell Me About Your Drugs."

what to avoid: No question here. Mostly recently titled *Gravy Deco* (Rhino, 1995, prod. Matthew Seligman and Steve Hillage) the sessions for *Groovy Decay* (Albion, 1982) were so wretched Hitchcock reissued an alternate version titled *Groovy Decay* (Midnight Music, 1985)—and retired from music for three years, again. All right, so "Grooving On A Inner Plane" and "America" are worth hearing, but this is an assortment of bad ideas in which Hitchcock was a disinterested participant. Not a pretty picture, that.

the rest: *Black Snake Diamond Role* (Armageddon, 1981/Rhino, 1995) *Gotta Let This Hen Out!* (Midnight Music, 1985/Rhino, 1995) *Eye* (Twin/Tone, 1989/Rhino, 1995) *Queen Elvis* (A&M, 1989) *Respect* (A&M, 1993) *Invisible Hitchcock* (Rhino, 1995) *You And Oblivion* (Rhino, 1995)

worth searching for: Rhino produced a promotional sampler titled, well, *Catalog Sampler* in 1995 on the occasion of its reissue of Hitchcock and/or The Egyptians back catalogue in 1995, and it's a smashing greatest hits summation. A&M produced the promo-only seven-song *Live Death* in an edition of 1,000 or something equally ridiculous; it includes some Hitchcock standards as well as Richard Thompson's "Withered And Died" and the Lennon/McCartney "A Day In The Life."

▶ Crowded House, Blur, Everclear, Pete Droge

◀ John Lennon, Syd Barrett, Bob Dylan

Grant Alden

Roger Hodgson

See: Supertramp

Hole

Formed 1990 in Los Angeles, Calif.

Courtney Love, vocals, guitar; Eric Erlandson, guitar; Jill Emery, bass (1990-91); Caroline Rue, drums (1990-91); Patty Scheme, drums (1992-present); Kristen Pfaff, bass (1992-94, died June 16, 1994); Melissa Auf Der Maur, bass (1994-present)

With assertions such as "I want to be the girl with the most cake" and "I fake it so real I am beyond fake," Love exhibits two definite personal traits: an extraordinary degree of self-knowledge, and absolutely no shame. The most successful rock 'n' roll social climber in recent memory, Love, to her credit, was at least able to deliver the goods when it counted most. But it wasn't always that way. When she formed Hole after brief stints in an early incarnation of Faith No More and Sugar Baby Doll (with Kat Bjelland, later of Babes in Toyland, and L7's Jennifer Finch), the angry punk stance was there, but the songs and the performance were not. *Pretty on the Inside* (Caroline, 1991, prod. Don Fleming and Kim Gordon) is pretty tough to take. Love's vocals consist of uncontrolled screeching, and guitarist Eric Erlandson demonstrates a similar lack of control. "Good Sister/Bad Sister" and "Slut Kiss Girl" transcend the band's shortcomings, but the arty between-song experiments do not. After Love's marriage to Nirvana frontman Kurt Cobain made her the princess of grunge, her music took an unexpected turn for the better. *Live Through This* (DGC, 1994, prod. Paul Q. Kolderie and Sean Slade) benefits from her husband's undeniable influence in terms of song structure and dynamics. Love's voice, though still limited, is nuanced here, and her scream is used judiciously. Interestingly, her writing also took a quantum leap, and songs such as "Softer. Softest," "Plump," "Asking for It" and "Miss World" deal with a variety of feminist issues in a gut-wrenchingly personal fashion. Cobain's suicide a week before the album's release added resonance to every line, making the album a 90s punk classic. Avoid the EP *Ask For It* (Caroline, 1995, prod. Mike Robinson) WOOF! a brief, non-essential, and occasionally excruciating collection of leftovers, covers and live shots.

Daniel Durchholz

Jools Holland

See: Squeeze

The Hollies

Formed 1962 in Manchester, England. Disbanded 1981. Reunited 1983.

Graham Nash, vocals, guitar (1962-68, 1983); Allan Clarke, vocals, harmonica (1962-71, 1973-81, 1983); Anthony Hicks, guitar; Donald Rathbone, drums (1962-63); Eric Haydock, bass (1962-66); Robert Elliott, drums (1963-81, 1983); Bernard Calvert, bass (1966-81); Terry Sylvester, vocals, guitar (1968-81); Mikal Rikfors, vocals (1971-73)

Though the group is often dismissed as a lightweight singles band, the Hollies' devotees know better. The group's remarkable career spans many different phases, but the key through it all are those glorious three-part harmonies that instantly distinguish a Hollies song. No one else has ever or will ever sound quite like this band. In addition, the Hollies are seldom credited for the tightness of its instrumental attack; fueled by vastly underrated guitarist Hicks and propulsive drummer Elliot—universally acclaimed by his peers as a top stick man of the British beat era— this music has always had a thoroughly professional sheen to it, leavened by a great deal of infectious energy. Though the band's very early period, when it was covering well-worn American R&B songs, has little to recommend, once the Hollies started generating original material and getting top songs from other writers, the group never looked back. The pure pop songs are a delight; the experimentation with more open forms in the psychedelic era was usually interesting, and the band adapted to most future trends well—excepting perhaps disco.

what to buy: *The Hollies 30th Anniversary Anthology* (EMI, 1993, prod. Various) 🦴🦴🦴🦴 gathers material from all phases of the group's career and is the only official collection of pre-1967 output. It's hard to dislike a compilation with such a rich array of great tracks; on the other hand, the compilers chose to remix the pre-67 material into stereo—and despite their good intentions, it's a major mistake. The early tracks lose all sense of power and cohesiveness when they're broken apart into separate elements. Also, the emphasis is almost entirely on hit singles, while strong album tracks are ignored. *The Hollies Anthology* (Epic, 1990, prod. Various) 🦴🦴🦴🦴🦴 is a nicely-done package that covers the 1967-75 era, with better mixes and an acoustic take of "Magic Woman Touch."

what to buy next: Virtually all original Hollies albums have been re-released on CD in Great Britain in their original form, and while they're technically imports, many are distributed via a label (Beat Goes On) that's widely distrubted to North American retailers. Of special note is the second album *In The Hollies Style* (Beat Goes On, 1964) 🦴🦴🦴🦴 The *Sgt. Pepper's* influenced *Butterfly* (Beat Goes On, 1967) 🦴🦴🦴 is also a worthwhile purchase.

what to avoid: *All Time Greatest Hits,* (Curb, 1990) 🦴🦴🦴 which has the biggies but without the depth or the packaging of the 5-bone collections.

the rest: *Greatest Hits* (Columbia, 1987) 🦴🦴🦴🦴 *A Distant Light* (Epic, 1971/Columbia, 1991) 🦴🦴🦴 *The Hollies* (Epic, 1974/Columbia, 1974) 🦴🦴🦴 *The Best of* (Capitol, date N/A) 🦴🦴🦴🦴 *Looking Back* (CEMA Special Products, 1995) 🦴🦴🦴

worth searching for: For proof that The Hollies could cut it live just as surely as in the studio, an LP called *Hollies Live*, originally released in Canada in 1976, is the one to look for.

⏩ Crosby, Stills and Nash, The Posies, Material Issue, Barenaked Ladies

⏪ Buddy Holly, the Everly Brothers

see also: *Crosby, Stills and Nash*

Mike Greenfield

Holly and the Italians

See: Holly Vincent

Buddy Holly

Born Charles Hardin Holley, Sept. 7, 1936, in Lubbock, Texas. Died Feb. 3, 1959, near Clear Lake, Iowa

In the mere 22 months that Holly spent on the pop charts, he etched his name indelibly into the music's history with easy charm and tuneful mastery of rock's basics. Guileless but not naive, Holly captured the essential angst of young love with wit and an underlying aggressive edge that gave his simple songs a durability none of his contemporaries could match. As a young country singer, Holly fell under the sway of Presley when Elvis made one of his early concert stops in Holly's native Lubbock, Texas. A home movie caught the suddenly transformed Holly and his pals backstage at this crucial turning point in his life. His initial 1956 recording sessions with Nashville stalwart Owen Bradley survived the steely hand of the producer, unsympathetic to the emerging new music. Isolated numbers such as "Rock with Ollie Vee" display the exuberant joy Holly could bring to rock and roll. Under the less restraining influence of Norman Petty in his Clovis, N.M., studios, Holly found the free rein he needed to write his page in rock 'n' roll history. The re-recorded version of "That'll Be the Day," literally remade in its second incarnation, launched the chart career of the Crickets, as Holly and his associates were called by the record label. With "Peggy Sue" three months later, producer Petty used the same group of musicians to establish Holly as a solo artist. The Holly single was rising on the charts as the Crickets' single was slipping down. Although a plane crash ended his career at a time when Holly appeared to be turning a rewarding artistic corner—experimenting with saxophonist King Curtis and cutting ballads with New York session musicians—he had already left behind a legacy that would prove to be one of rock's most enduring treasures.

what to buy: Although at least three different boxed sets were released in the 70s covering, to different degrees, the complete works of Holly, the existing two-disc set, *The Buddy Holly Collection* (MCA, 1993, prod. Various) 𝅘𝅥𝅘𝅥𝅘𝅥𝅘𝅥𝅘𝅥 distills the essence into an admirable 50-song collection.

what to buy next: Holly's first two post-Nashville albums, *The Chirping Crickets* (MCA, 1958, prod. Norman Petty) 𝅘𝅥𝅘𝅥𝅘𝅥𝅘𝅥 and *Buddy Holly,* (MCA, 1958, prod. Norman Petty) 𝅘𝅥𝅘𝅥𝅘𝅥𝅘𝅥 have been made available as compact discs and are well worth picking up.

what to avoid: Although practically no Holly recording is entirely without merit, his early Nashville sessions—originally issued by the Decca label under the title "That'll Be the Day" to cash in on the success of the Clovis version of the song—have been reissued over the years as *The Great Buddy Holly,* (MCA, 1988, prod. Owen Bradley) 𝅘𝅥 although he was not yet that great on these often uncomfortable productions.

the rest: *Buddy Holly—From the Original Master Tapes* (MCA, 1985) 𝅘𝅥𝅘𝅥𝅘𝅥𝅘𝅥 *Oh Boy* (MCA, 1987) WOOF!

worth searching for: During a brief 1995 dalliance with audiophile vinyl pressings, MCA put out an absolutely gorgeous edition of *Buddy Holly* on its so-called "heavy vinyl" series—a breathtaking audio experience, like listening to the playbacks in the studio control room.

⏩ Bobby Vee, Waylon Jennings, the Beatles, the Rolling Stones

⏪ Hank Williams, Hank Ballard, Elvis Presley

Joel Selvin

Peter Holsapple and Chris Stamey

See: Continental Drifters

The Holy Barbarians

See: The Cult

The Hoodoo Gurus

Formed 1981 in Sydney, Australia

Dave Faulkner, vocals, guitar; Brad Shepherd. guitar, vocals; Clyde Bramley, bass (1981-88); James Baker, drums (1981-85); Mark Kingsmill, drums (1985-present); Rich Grossman, bass (1988-current)

A contemporary of INXS and Midnight Oil, the Hoodoo Gurus emerged from Australia's notoriously difficult club scene with a passel of wonderfully crafted songs, jangly guitars, an entertaining (and sometimes humorous) pop sensibility, splendid vocal harmonies, hooks that could grab any living creature out of the sea and an energetic performance style. The group has never quite cracked the U.S. mainstream—though the college radio audience has been receptive—and it's our loss more than anything else.

what to buy: The band's second album, *Mars Needs Guitars* (Elektra, 1985, prod. Charles Fisher) 𝅘𝅥𝅘𝅥𝅘𝅥𝅘𝅥 is a must-have thanks to irresistible pop/rock confections such as "Bittersweet," "Poison Pen," "Show Me Some Emotion" and "The Other Side Of Paradise." But it goes further, with humorous stories in "Hayride To Hell," "Like Wow-Wipeout" and the celestial solution offered in the title track. With help from the Bangles and other friends, *Blow Your Cool* (Elektra, 1987, prod. Mark Opitz and Hoodoo Gurus) 𝅘𝅥𝅘𝅥𝅘𝅥𝅘𝅥 turns the guitars up a notch with even more pop hooks. "What's My Scene" is the standout track.

what to buy next: The debut *Stoneage Romeos* (Big Time/A&M, 1983, prod. Alan Thorne) 𝅘𝅥𝅘𝅥𝅘𝅥½ is the zaniest of the Hoodoo Gurus' output, with off-beat classics such as "I Was A Kamikaze Pilot," "Zanzibar" and "I Want You Back." *Magnum Cum Louder* (RCA, 1989, prod. Hoodoo Gurus) 𝅘𝅥𝅘𝅥𝅘𝅥½ launches out of the box with "Come Any Time" and continues to roar with "Another World," "Shadow Me," and "All The Way," as well as the baseball ode "Where's That Hit?"—not bad for a band from Down Under. *Electric Soup* (RCA, 1992, prod. Various) 𝅘𝅥𝅘𝅥𝅘𝅥𝅘𝅥 is a shortcut to a Hoodoo Gurus experience, a singles collection that comprises most of the band's top tunes.

the rest: *Kinky* (RCA, 1991) 𝅘𝅥𝅘𝅥𝅘𝅥½ *Gloria Biscuit B-Sides and Rarities* (RCA, 1993) 𝅘𝅥𝅘𝅥𝅘𝅥 *Crank* (Zoo, 1994) 𝅘𝅥𝅘𝅥𝅘𝅥 *In Blue Cave* (Mushroom/Zoo, 1996) 𝅘𝅥𝅘𝅥𝅘𝅥½

worth searching for: Good quality recordings from the Hoodoo

Gurus' performances during the 1987-88 tour with the Bangles—extremely difficult to find since the band's lack of commercial success in the U.S. scares bootleg dealers away from them.

▶▶ The Smithereens, Jellyfish

◀◀ The Cramps, the Kinks, the Turtles, Skyhooks

John Nieman

Peter Hook

See: New Order

John Lee Hooker

Born—depending on your source—a) Aug. 22, 1920 in Clarksdale, Miss., b) Aug. 22, 1917 in Clarksdale, Miss., or c) before God.

Hooker is a giant of the blues and one of its most distinctive voices; he's also the father of the boogie, which makes him one of rock 'n' roll's great antecedents. Hooker's deep, primitive rhythms and his dark, growly, hypnotic vocals have inspired innumerable performers over his 50-plus year career. A semi-transient street musician from the age of 15, Hooker moved to Detroit in 1943. His recording career began in 1948 with "Boogie Chillen," a blues classic that topped the R&B charts in 1949. He was a raw, undisciplined musician who seldom played a song the same way twice, yet he managed to record prolifically through the 50s on a number of labels. His output—under such names as Johnny Lee, John Lee Booker, John Lee Chance, Birmingham Sam, Delta John, Texas Slim, Boogie Man and John Williams—is second only to Lightnin' Hopkins. His songs "Dimple" and "Boom Boom" made waves on the 60s British blues scene, and he went acoustic during the blues revival and played the hippest clubs in the U.S. and Europe. During the 70s, Hooker went electric and did records with Canned Heat, Elvin Bishop, Van Morrison and other rockers. The aging Hooker faded into semi-retirement during the 80s, but 1989's *The Healer,* featuring Bonnie Raitt, Carlos Santana, Robert Cray and George Thorogood, won a Grammy and put Hooker back at center stage. He's managed to remain there with two more solid albums since then. Although Hooker tends to recycle tunes, such classics as "Crawlin' King Snake," "I'm In the Mood," "One Bourbon, One Scotch, One Beer," "Little Wheel," "Boogie With the Hook" and "I'm Bad Like Jesse James" all bear re-telling. In 1996, B.B. King is the only living bluesman with the same stature as Hooker, and there are but a handful of others, period. His spots in the Rhythm and Blues Foundation's Hall of Fame and in The Rock and Roll Hall of Fame—among other honors—are well deserved.

what to buy: *The Ultimate Collection, 1948-1990* (Rhino, 1991, comp. James Austin) 🦴🦴🦴🦴🦴 lives up to its title, with 31 Hooker's best-known cuts and a bevy of guests such as Jimmy Reed, Willie Dixon and Raitt. The septuagenarian Hooker seems to boogie effortlessly on *Chill Out,* (Point Blank, 1995, prod. Roy Rogers) 🦴🦴🦴🦴🦴 and with Santana adds a Latin edge to his mantra-like boogie on "Chill Out (Things Gonna Change)."

what to buy next: Hooker is clearly having fun on *The Healer,* (Chameleon, 1989, prod. Roy Rogers) 🦴🦴🦴🦴½ the record that sprang him back into the limelight with friends like Raitt and Cray helping out.

what to avoid: Hooker may have presaged the funk, but the slick 70s edge on *Free Beer and Chicken* (ABC, 1974, prod. Ed Michel) 🦴🦴 just didn't fit, regardless of the rock and roll heavies in tow.

the rest: *Endless Boogie* (MCA, 1971) 🦴🦴🦴½ *Never Get Out of These Blues Alive* (Pickwick, 1978) 🦴🦴🦴½ *Real Folk Blues* (MCA, 1987) 🦴🦴🦴🦴½ *Simply the Truth* (One Way, 1988) 🦴🦴🦴 *Mr. Lucky* (Charisma, 1991) 🦴🦴🦴🦴½ *I Feel Good* (Jewel, 1995) 🦴🦴🦴½ *Boom Boom* (Capitol, 1995) 🦴🦴🦴🦴 *Alone,* (Blues Alliance, 1996) 🦴🦴🦴🦴

worth searching for: *Hooker 'N' Heat* (Liberty, 1971/EMI, 1991 prod. Skip Taylor and Robert Hite Jr.) 🦴🦴🦴🦴 was the equivalent of *The Healer* 20 years earlier. Though it's a rougher-edged affair, Hooker's collaboration with Canned Heat made the rock crowd take notice.

▶▶ James Brown, George Clinton, Bonnie Raitt, John Mayall, Savoy Brown, Canned Heat, Robert Cray, George Thorogood

◀◀ Robert Johnson, Charley Patton

Lawrence Gabriel

The Hooters

Formed 1978 in Philadelphia, Pa.

Rob Hyman, vocals, keyboards; Eric Bazilian, vocals, guitar; John Lilley, guitar; Rob Miller, bass (1978-87); David Uosikkinen, drums; Fran Smith Jr., bass, vocals (1987-present)

Presumably named after the nickname for the melodica—the musical instrument used on the hit "And We Danced"—the Hooters spent nearly a decade building a following in Philadelphia (it was reportedly considered a rite of passage for young area bands to open for them). With a wholesome image and radio-ready sound, the band sold 100,000 copies of a self-released album (1983's *Amore*), which caught the attenion of major labels and eventually netted the group a deal with Columbia. Though its debut *Nervous Night*, scored some hits and made the band a momentary Next Big Thing, it didn't quite hold onto the commercial cache. Meanwhile, Hyman and Bazilian built a legacy away from the band, writing more enduring hits for artists such as Cyndi Lauper ("Time After Time") and Joan Osborne ("One of Us").

what to buy: The group's debut, *Nervous Night,* (Columbia, 1985, prod. Rick Chertoff) was a breakthrough which launched the hits "And We Danced," "Day By Day" and "Where Do the Children Go."

what to buy next: *Zig Zag,* (Columbia, 1989, prod. Rick Chertoff) is a more mature, complex effort that was unjustly ignored by the masses.

what to avoid: None of the performances on *Greatest Hits II: The Hooters Live* (Sony International, 1994) are as interesting as their studio counterparts.

the rest: *Amore* (Antenna, 1983) *Out of Body* (MCA, 1993) (*Greatest Hits I* (Sony International, 1994)

worth searching for: The Japanese hits collection*Star Box*, (Sony, 1993, prod. Various) a generous (18 tracks) set that samples all of the Hooters' albums.

▶▶ The Levellers, Hot House Flowers

◀◀ Bruce Springsteen, The Band

Todd Wicks

Hootie & the Blowfish

Formed 1986 in Columbia, S.C.

Darius Rucker, vocals, guitar; Mark Bryan, guitar, keyboards, vocals; Dean Felber, bass, vocals; Brantley Smith, drums (1986-89); Jim "Soni" Sonefeld, drums, vocals (1989-present)

Hootie & the Blowfish's blend of bouncy folk-rock and hummable melodies seemed to leap out of nowhere to win America's hearts—and wallets—during 1995 as its major-label debut, *Cracked Rear View,* racked up sales of 14 million and counting. In reality, the group had been polishing its sound for years, graduating from a cover band at frat parties to a huge folk-rock favorite throughout the Carolinas and Mid-Atlantic states. Hootie is a group in the truest sense of the word, with all the pieces coming together to create a sound greater than the sum of its individual parts. Rucker's soulful baritone vocals are elevated by his colleagues' soaring background harmonies. Bryan's tactful, mild-thing guitars are gracefully supported by Felber's understated bass lines and Sonefeld's steady rhythmic kick. With roots spread across the spectrum—from Nanci Griffith and John Hiatt to R.E.M. and the Allman Brothers, Hootie & the Blowfish has forged a distinctive Southern folk rock sound that strikes a chord with the masses. After three independent releases, *Cracked Rear View* (Atlantic 1994, prod. Don Gehman) makes people feel good with the upbeat rhythms and stirring melodies of "Hold My Hand," "Hannah Jane" and "Only Wanna Be With You," while two ballads—"I'm Goin' Home" and "Not Even the Trees"—touch the heart as Rucker grieves his mother's death. The group's sophomore effort, *Fairweather Johnson,* (Atlantic, 1996, prod. Don Gehman) is lyrically darker than its debut but is brightened by the same brisk musical mix. Rucker tends to get sloppily emotional as he wails about lost love and emptiness ("When I'm Lonely," "Let It Breathe") but the jaunty "Old Man & Me" echoes the catchy southern spunk of the Allman Brothers, while "Tucker's Town" exemplifies Hootie at its best with its melodic hook, sweet harmonies, and balanced musicianship.

the rest: *Hootie & the Blowfish* (1990) *Time* (1992) *Kootchypop* (1993)

David Yonke

Jamie Hoover

See: The Spongetones

Mary Hopkin

Born 1950 in Pontardawe, Wales

Paul McCartney was seeking talent for the fledgling Apple Records label in 1968 when he struck gold with waif folksinger Hopkin. Blessed with a sweet country lass voice and a face of apple-pie purity, Hopkin (under McCartney's guidance) spun out a short but hit-studded career of precious Olde Worlde ballads and lilting folk-pop. *Post Card* (Capitol, 1969, prod. Paul McCartney) is a pretty album of twee but romantic confection that includes her hit "Those Were The Days," a terrific cover of Donovan's "Lord of the Reedy River" and a few odd novelty numbers ("Puppy Song," "Inchworm")—music the whole family can enjoy. Hopkin shed her woman-child image for *Earth Song/Ocean Song,* (Capitol, 1971, prod. Tony Visconti) a fine collection of lovely folk-rock tunes that are capably rendered. Hopkins subsequently married Visconti and retired from music, returning to active duty as a backup singer on David Bowie's *Low* and as a member of the short-lived trio Oasis (with Julian Lloyd Weber, brother of Andrew) in 1984.

Christopher Scapelliti

Lightnin' Hopkins

Born Sam Hopkins, March 15, 1912, Centerville, Texas. Died Jan. 30, 1982 in Houston, Texas

Hopkins stands with Blind Lemon Jefferson and T-Bone Walker as a giant of Texas blues and is the most prolifically recorded bluesman of all time. Largely a regional artist, Hopkin's laid-back style brought him recognition in Texas and the Southwest, particularly after "Katie May" was a hit in 1946. Although he recorded regularly, Hopkins mainly lived from playing parties, picnics and club dates throughout the region until being "re-discovered" by historian Sam Charters during the blues revival in 1959. From then until his death, Hopkins toured nationally and internationally as a solo artist and with many of the group tours promoting traditional blues. Hopkins used country techniques on acoustic and electric guitar as he sang songs about current and personal events ("Hurricane Betsy," "Dirty House Blues") much in the manner of traditional African griots. Most of his many recordings for small labels are out of print or in bargain bins, but much of it has been assembled into some well-researched collections. A seven-disc set, *The Complete Prestige/Bluesville Recordings* (Prestige, 1991, prod. Various) rounds up some of his best material and includes liner notes written by Charters. *The Complete Alladin Recordings* (Capitol, 1991) features Hopkins in a solo acoustic setting where he can ramble and improvise in his unique way.

Lawrence Gabriel

Bruce Hornsby

Born Nov. 23, 1954 in Richmond, Va.

Hornsby's deep, wide musical roots and professionalism have made him a studio favorite, guesting on more than 50 albums by artists ranging from Willie Nelson and Bob Dylan to Liquid Jesus and Squeeze. He co-wrote the Huey Lewis and the News hit "Jacob's Ladder" and assisted Don Henley with "The End of the Innocence," a track that defines Hornsby's writing style and piano playing. Hornsby's three albums with his band, the Range, featured laid-back, slickly crafted tunes that smoothly blended rock, blues, jazz and folk. For 18 months starting in September, 1990, Hornsby performed more than 100 concerts with the Grateful Dead, filling in after the death of Brent Mydland. Hornsby broke up the Range in 1993, finding inspiration for his solo albums with a stellar supporting cast that included Bonnie Raitt, Branford Marsalis, Jerry Garcia, Phil Collins and Pat Metheny.

what to buy: *Hot House* (RCA, 1995, prod. Bruce Hornsby) is an infectiously upbeat collection of dreamy melodies set against precise jazz-rock twists and turns reminiscent of Steely Dan. Hornsby's laid-back vocals and breezy keyboards also shine on *Harbor Lights,* (RCA, 1993, prod. Bruce Hornsby) offering the steamy rhythmic bop of "Talk of the Town," about an interracial couple, to sprawling, picturesque ballads such as the title track and "Fields of Gray."

what to buy next: Hornsby's debut, *The Way It Is,* (RCA, 1986, prod. Bruce Hornsby, Elliot Scheiner and Huey Lewis) established his talents early with a Grammy Award and three Top 10 singles in the title track, "Mandolin Rain" and "Every Little Kiss."

what to avoid: Polished production renders *Scenes from the Southside* (RCA, 1988, prod. Bruce Hornsby and Neil Dorfsman) slick and nondescript, lacking grit and personality.

the rest: *A Night on the Town* (RCA, 1990)

worth searching for: *Bruce Hornsby and the Range Live: The Way It Is Tour 1986-87,* (RCA, 1987) a promotion-only concert recording from the first tour that features a strong performance as well as Hornsby's dazzling piano solo that leads into "The Way it Is."

▶▶ Bonnie Raitt, Ben Folds Five

◀◀ Bob Dylan, the Grateful Dead, Steely Dan, Keith Jarrett

David Yonke

Hot Tuna

Formed 1969 in San Francisco, Calif.

Jorma Kaukonen, guitar, vocals; Jack Casady, bass; Will Scarlet, harmonica (1970-71); Papa John Creach, violin (1971-72); Sammy Piazza, drums (1971-74); Bob Steeler, drums (1974-77); Michael Falzarano, guitar, mandolin, harmonica, vocals (1990-present)

Formed in hotel rooms across the country after Jefferson Airplane concerts, when guitarist Kaukonen and bassist Casady couldn't stop playing, Hot Tuna slowly emerged into the public, first as an acoustic duo and then as an electric quartet appearing often as a support act for the mothership. Essentially a vehicle for Kaukonen's remarkable skills as a country blues guitarist, Tuna specialized in lengthy improvisations, in which Casady's fluid, inventive bass figures would wrap around Kaukonen's delta blues lines almost endlessly. The band, on one occasion at least, performed for eight hours straight. Friends since childhood, Kaukonen and Casady split in the late 70s and reformed about 10 years later. The original unplugged band, Tuna remains the sole surviving unit of the San Francisco psychedelic scene's heyday.

what to buy: Either *First Pull Up—Then Pull Down* (RCA, 1971, prod. Jorma Kaukonen) or *Burgers* (RCA, 1972, prod. Jorma Kaukonen) will provide the quintessential Tuna experience, mixing the Rev. Gary Davis/Mississippi John Hurt fingerpicking nobody does any better than Kaukonen with Casady's imaginative bass playing.

what to buy next: The duo's quiet acoustic debut, *Hot Tuna,* (RCA, 1970, prod. Al Scmitt) captured the lads, fresh out of the hotel rooms, in a small Berkeley nightclub playing relatively straight-ahead elaborations on traditional country blues, unplugged before its time.

what to avoid: The sound quality on *Classic Hot Tuna Acoustic,* (Relix, 1996, prod. Michael Falzarano) taken from a radio broadcast, leaves much to be desired, although the companion piece, *Classic Hot Tuna Electric,* (Relix, 1996, prod. Michael Falzarano) fared better since it was taken from multi-track recordings made during the 1971 final week at the Fillmore West.

the rest: *The Phosphorescent Rat* (RCA, 1973) *America's Choice* (RCA, 1975) *Yellow Fever* (RCA, 1975) *Hoppkorv* (RCA, 1976) *Double Dose* (RCA, 1977) *Pair a Dice Found* (Epic, 1991) *Live at Sweetwater* (Relix, 1992) *Live at Sweetwater Two* (Relix, 1993)

solo outings:

Jorma Kaukonen: Quah (Relix, 1974) *Magic* (Relix, 1985) *Too Hot to Handle* (Relix, 1986) *Land of Heroes* (American Heritage, 1995)

▶▶ Keb' Mo', Jeff Buckley, Chris Whitley, Jeff Healey

◀◀ Rev. Gary Davis, Mississippi John Hurt, Scott LeFaro

Joel Selvin

Hothouse Flowers

Formed in 1986 in Ireland

Liam 'O Maonlai, lead vocals, piano, hammond organ, wurlitzer, low whistle, bodhran, didjeridoo; Fiachna O'Braonain, electric and acoustic guitars, bouzouki, vocals; Peter O'Toole, bass guitar, bouzouki, backing vocals; Leo Barnes, saxaphone, hammond organ, wurlizter, backing vocals; Jerry Fehily, drums, percussion

More Memphis Stax than Dublin U2, Hothouse Flowers blends Celtic mysticism with R&B and gospel. The result is clearly Irish in its quest for the transcendental, though the band displays its spirituality more boldly than most. When the group gained critical acclaim for its debut, *People,* and a host of predictions that it would be the Emerald Isle's next big export, many of the reviews cited the Hothouse's apparent distain for U2's more mainstream heroic vision. Maybe it was the horns and the gritty sound, but though the influences might differ, both bands are obviously in search of something bigger than rock stardom. With Hothouse Flowers, the embrace of American soul and Irish traditional as the road to God is more consistent, and for that matter, much more Irish. Liam 'O Maonlai's impassioned vocals and the musicanship of guitarists Fiachna O'Braonain and Peter O'Toole frequently reach glorified heights, though occasionally 'O Maonlai has a tendency to over testify. The band is also reluctant to record, with three albums to its credit since 1988, though members appear on a host of recordings by others (well, they have the time).

what to buy: *People* (London, 1988, prod. Clive Langer and Alan Winstanley) is a beautiful merging of original vision and mainstream influences and became the best-selling debut in Irish pop history. Standout cuts include "The Older We Get," which speaks to wisdom hard earned.

what to buy next: With an effective reworking of Johnny Nash's chestnut "I Can See Clearly Now" and the gorgeous "Christchurch Bells," *Home* (London, 1990, prod. Paul Barrett, Pat McCarthy, Daniel Lanois, Clive Langer, Alan Winstanley, and Norman Verso) is a strong follow-up to the debut. Fiddler Steve Wickham, late of the Waterboys, guests on the live "Dance to the Storm."

the rest: *Songs From the Rain* (London, 1993)

▶▶ 54.40

◀◀ U2, The Waterboys

see also: Alt

Martin Connors

The House of Love

Formed 1986 in London, England. Disbanded 1993.

Guy Chadwick, vocals, guitar; Chris Groothuizen, bass guitar; Pete Evans, drums; Terry Bickers, guitar (1986-1990); Simon Walker, guitar (1990-1992); Andrea Heukamp, backing vocals (1986-1988, 1993)

Although never achieving widespread acclaim, Chadwick was one of the great songwriters of the late 80s and early 90s. With the House of Love (HOL), he helped usher in a new awareness of guitar rock in England and was partially responsible for launching the big Velvet Underground revival in his homeland. Even though HOL gained moderate alternative radio play with its remarkable single "I Don't Know Why I Love You," Chadwick struggled with the group's lack of all-out success and ended up dissolving the band in 1993 after years of internal conflict and self-doubt.

what to buy: The House of Love's American major label debut, *The House of Love (Butterfly)*, (Fontana/PolyGram, 1990, prod. Stephen Hague, Tim Palmer and Paul Staveley O'Duffy) 🦴🦴🦴🦴 captured the group's vision perfectly. It included such immaculate guitar rocks songs as "I Don't Know Why I Love You," "Beatles and the Stones" and "Shake and Crawl." Its studio follow-up, *Babe Rainbow*, (Fontana/Mercury, 1992, prod. Wayne Livesey) 🦴🦴🦴🦴 held the most promise of a commercial breakthrough for the group with such exquisite tracks as "You Don't Understand" and "Feel." But its moody thunder did not fit in well with pop radio's prevailing grunge fetish.

what to buy next: The House of Love's early albums were raw, but the songwriting was consistently excellent, particularly on *The House of Love (Faces)*, (Creation/Relativity, 1988, prod. the House of Love) 🦴🦴🦴½ which included an early version of "Shine On" and the monumental "Christine" single.

what to avoid: As a reaction to the House of Love's inability to break through to American ears, the group recorded an uncharacteristically dreary disc on the verge of its break-up. *Audience with the Mind* (Fontana/Mercury, 1993, prod. the House of Love) 🦴🦴 is a tough listen, but does contain occasional sparks ("Hollow," "You've Got To Feel").

the rest: *The House of Love (Group)* (Creation, 1987) 🦴🦴🦴 *A Spy in the House of Love* (Fontana/Mercury, 1990) 🦴🦴🦴

worth searching for: *The House of Love Live* (Fontana/PolyGram, 1990, prod. Timothy Powell) 🦴🦴🦴 was a promotional-only disc, recorded for radio off a live broadcast on WXRT-FM in Chicago. It includes blistering renditions of "Christine" and "Never."

⏩ Ride, Chapterhouse, the Stone Roses

⏪ Velvet Underground, the Smiths, the Beatles, the Church, Echo & the Bunnymen

Aidin Vaziri

House of Pain

Formed 1990 in Los Angeles, Calif.

Everlast (born Eric Schrody), vocals; Danny Boy (born Daniel O'Connor), vocals; D.J. Lethal (born Lear DiMant), D.J.

Unlike many white acts performing rap, House of Pain is no mere novelty. The trio's old-school rhymes, combined with a dense soundscape littered with heavy jeep beats and shrill effects (thanks in part to producer DJ Muggs from Cypress Hill) makes for a heady brew. And if you're buying, make theirs a Guinness Stout. The L.A. rappers wear their Irish heritage proudly, singing a snippet of "Danny Boy" here, or claiming "I never eat pig, but I can fuck up a potato" there. On the group's debut, *House of Pain*, (Tommy Boy, 1992, prod. DJ Muggs and DJ Lethal) 🦴🦴🦴 Everlast (a former member of Ice-T's Rhyme Syndicate) and Danny Boy prove they can flow, and DJ Lethal mostly lives up to his name. Irrepressible romps such as "Jump Around" and "Top o' the Morning to Ya" simply won't be denied. But despite those high points, the album also flaunts many of the hip-hop culture's worst tendencies—especially lyrics laced with homophobia, misogyny, racism and pointless posturing. Too bad. Nothing on *Same As It Ever Was*, (Tommy Boy, 1994, prod. The Baka Boys, DJ Muggs and DJ Lethal) 🦴🦴½ is as catchy as "Jump Around." To compensate, the group tries to come on even harder, but without the songs to back it up, who cares?

By Daniel Durchholz

The Housemartins /The Beautiful South/Beats International

The Housemartins (1984-88)—Paul Heaton, vocals, guitar; Stan Cullimore, bass; Ted Key, guitar (1984-85); Hugh Whitaker, drums (1984-86); Norman Cook, guitar (1985-88); Dave Hemingway, drums (1986-88). The Beautiful South (1988-present)—Heaton, vocals; Hemingway, vocals; David Rotheray, guitar; Sean Welch, bass; Briana Corrigan, vocals; David Stead, drums; Jacqueline Abbott, vocals; Damon Butcher, keyboards. Beats International—Cook, bass; Lindy Layton, vocals; Lester Noel, vocals; Andy Boucher, keyboards; MC Wildski, vocals

Named for the swallow known in this country as the purple martin, the Housemartins were a group of angry young fellows from Hull, England, proud of their Northern working-class roots and eager to chip at the excesses of booming Thatcherite England to the south. Singer-songwriter Heaton, whose voice lies somewhere between Morrissey and George Michael, crafted sweet-sounding songs with sarcastic and often bitter lyrics. His clever, socially conscious material met with mixed reviews in the English press, but the band enjoyed a fair amount of commercial success in Britain, scoring hits such as "Caravan of Love" and "Happy Hour;" the video of the latter was seen frequently on MTV in America. In 1988 the band split up. Heaton and drummer Hemingway formed the Beautiful South (the name is a sarcastic jab at London) while guitarist Cook created Beats International (not to be confused with the English Beat or the International Beat; see separate entries). Heaton has maintained his sharp pencil lyrically, but now points it more at the politics of love and relationships. Musically, the Beautiful South's songs combine strong melodies with lush orchestrations that recall late 60s American pop in the style of Jimmy Webb or Harry Nilsson. The band recorded a version of the 1969 Nilsson hit "Everybody's Talkin' " in an obvious tip of the cap to that period. The formula has worked well, and has earned the band a slew of hits in Britain. Cook's efforts with Beats International are decidedly more modern; the former DJ has experimented with samples, overdubbing and multiple vocalists to shape the band's techno-dance sound, which earned a British chart-topper with 1990's "Dub Be (cq) Good to Me." Neither group has made much impact in the U.S.; the silver lining is that because there's so little product available, it's all of a high quality, without anything to be avoided.

what to buy: *Carry On Up the Charts: The Best of the Beautiful South* (Mercury, 1995, prod. Various) is a sterling collection of perfect pop tunes, establishing Heaton and Rotheray among the premier league of British tunesmiths. (Note: The limited-edition Go! Discs import of "Charts" that offers a second disc of material, including a stripped-down and effective reworking of the Bee Gees' "I Started A Joke.") Beats International's *Let Them Eat Bingo* (Elektra, 1990, prod. Norman Cook) is a rhythmic rave of a record with samples galore and guests Billy Bragg and the Damned's Captain Sensible.

what to buy next: The Beautiful South's *0898* (Elektra, 1992, prod. Jon Kelly) features the British hits "Old Red Eyes Is Back," "We Are Each Other" and "Bell Bottomed Tear." The Housemartins' debut, *London 0 Hull 4*, (Elektra, 1986, prod. John Williams) features edgy, guitar-driven pop with the spry but tart anti-yuppie anthem "Happy Hour," and the Kinks-like "Anxious."

the rest: The Housemartins—*The People Who Grinned Themselves to Death* (Elektra, 1987) The Beautiful South—*Welcome to the Beautiful South* (Elektra, 1989) *Choke* (Elektra, 1990) Beats International—*Excursion On the Version* (Polygram, 1991)

worth searching for: The generous Housemartins' retrospective *Now That's What I Call Quite Good!* (Go! Discs, 1988, prod. Various) is only stocked as an import.

Green Day, Supergrass, Oasis, Blur

The Kinks, the Clash, the Specials, the English Beat

William Hanson

Whitney Houston

Born August 9, 1963 in Newark, N.J.

The daughter of soul and gospel singer Cissy Houston and cousin to pop vocalist Dionne Warwick, Whitney Houston's talent may be genetic. But you don't have to call cousin Didi's Psychic Friends Network to know that, in strong contrast to Houston's voice—one of the most powerful, yet supple, instruments in all of pop music—her albums have been less than spectacular thanks to vapid material and cheesy 80s synth-pop production that has not aged as gracefully as Houston herself. Like Michael Jackson, Houston is more interesting as a phenomenon than as an artist; her albums have sold in the tens of millions worldwide, and, along with Jackson, Houston helped break the racial barriers that once kept black artists off of MTV. Unlike the gloved one, however, Houston's success has spilled over onto the silver screen, and she has starred in two highly successful films, "The Bodyguard" and "Waiting to Exhale." She also has enjoyed massive non-album hits with "One Moment in Time," the theme to the 1988 Summer Olympics, and her Super Bowl rendition of "The Star Spangled Banner," which rode a wave of Desert Storm patriotism all the way to the bank.

what to buy: *Whitney Houston* (Arista, 1985, prod. L.A. Reid) rocketed the young singer to superstardom almost instantly, and not without reason. Houston demonstrates her astonishing talent as a balladeer on "Saving All My Love For You" and "You Give Good Love." "The Greatest Love of All" may be a little over the top in its vapid self-help message, Houston delivers it sincerely. And while it's but a bit of fluff, "How Will I Know" is Houston's most infectious single ever. After its release, copies of *The Bodyguard* soundtrack (Arista, 1992, prod. Various) were issued upon entrance to a shopping mall, or so it seemed at the time. Still, much of the attention was deserved; The album contains Houston's best vocal performance ever, a triumphant take on Dolly Parton's "I Will Always Love You" that you probably still haven't dislodged from your memory banks, even if you want to. The album also contains five other Houston performances, as well as contributions by Kenny G and Aaron Neville, Lisa Stansfield and Joe Cocker, among others.

what to buy next: The soundtrack to Houston's second film, *Waiting to Exhale* (Arista, 1995, prod. Babyface) is a tour de force for producer/songwriter 'Face, but it contains only three Houston tracks—one of them the too-slight "Exhale (Shoop Shoop)" and one of them a duet with CeCe Winans.

what to avoid: *I'm Your Baby Tonight* (Arista, 1990, prod. Various) is a mess, thanks to its crazy quilt of producers and the fact that, for a star of Houston's magnitude, the material is extraordinarily weak. The sole standout is the bombastic "He's All the Man I Need"—which refers to God, in case you were wondering.

the rest: *Whitney* (Arista, 1987, prod. Various)

Toni Braxton, Mariah Carey, Brandy

Aretha Franklin, Cissy Houston, Dionne Warwick, Chaka Khan, Diana Ross

Daniel Durchholz

Steve Howe

See: Yes

Howlin' Wolf

Born Chester Arthur Burnett, June 10, 1910 in West Point, Miss. Died Jan. 10, 1976 in Hines, Ill.

With all due respect to Willie Dixon and Muddy Waters, there was something *fearsome* about Howlin' Wolf and the particular kind of blues he created at Chess Records during the 50s. Maybe it's the name, a formidable handle even by gangsta rap standards. Maybe it was his size, a hulking 6-foot-3, 300-some pounds. Or maybe it was his performances, which were down, dirty and tough—"Spoonful," "Smokestack Lightnin'," "Little Red Rooster," "I Ain't Superstitious," "Killing Floor," "Back Door Man." You'll recognize those titles from lots of rock albums during the 60s and the 70s, and it's true—Wolf was perhaps *the* most seminal blues influence on rock 'n' roll, a performer whose ferocity spoke directly to the hearts of the proteges who were trying to create an even bigger noise. (They repaid the debt in 1971 by backing him up on *The London Howlin' Wolf Sessions*) The young Burnett was raised on a cotton plantation and learned to play guitar when he was a child. He soaked up influences from around the Mississipi Delta, particularly his half-sister's husband, Sonny Boy Williamson. His journeys north took him first to Memphis, where he recorded for Sun Records. Sun then leased those tapes to Chess, and Howlin' Wolf became part of that city's immense blues heritage. Simply put, there's practically nowhere in rock 'n' roll where Wolf's influence isn't felt; even artists who don't convey an overt blues influence reflect some of his performance standards.

what to buy: *The Chess Box* (Chess, 1991, prod. Various) fills three discs with Wolf's best. It's pricey. And long. But you won't be wasting a penny, or a minute.

what to buy next: The twofer *Howlin' Wolf/Moanin' in the Moonlight* (Chess, 1987) pairs two of his best albums for another captivating listening experience. *Cadillac Daddy* (Memphis Recordings, 1952/Rounder, 1989) offers a selection of Wolf's pre-Chess days. The *Real Folk Blues* (Chess, 1966/1988) and *More Real Folk Blues* (Chess, 1967/1988) albums are akin to audio texts on the form. *The London Howlin' Wolf Sessions* (Chess, 1971/1994) is flawed—Eric Clapton, Steve Winwood and the rest seem a bit awed and timid to be recording with their hero—but Wolf still manages a winning performance.

what to avoid: *Live and Cookin'* (Chess, 1972/1992) catches Wolf late in the game, when failing health was beginning to take a toll on his skills.

the rest: *The Back Door Wolf* (Chess, 1973/1995) *Change My Way* (Chess, 1975/1992) *Live in Cambridge* (NRR, 1992) *Wolf is at Your Door* (NRR, 1992) *Howlin' Wolf Rides Again* (Virgin, 1993) *Ain't Gonna Be Your Dog, Vol. 2* (Chess, 1994) *Chicago Blue* (Rhino, 1995) *Blues Master* (Chess, 1996) *Highway 49* (1996)

worth searching for: *The Howlin' Wolf Album* (Chess, 1969) The music is great, but the cover—with its simple legend "This is Howlin' Wolf's new album. He doesn't like it. He didn't like his electric guitar at first either."—speaks volumes about the man.

Eric Clapton, Cream, John Mayall, the Yardbirds, Jeff Beck, Led Zeppelin, the Doors, the rest of this book...

Sonny Boy Williamson, Robert Johnson, Charley Patton, Willie Dixon

Gary Graff

Howling Maggie (Harold Chichester)

See: Royal Crescent Mob

Human League

Formed 1977, Sheffield, England

Phil Oakey, vocals, synthesizer; Martyn Ware, synthesizer (1977-80); Ian Craig Marsh, synthesizer (1977-80); Ian Burden, bass, synthesizer (1980-present); Suzanne Sulley, vocals (1980-present); Joanne Catherall, vocals (1980-present); Jo Callis, synthesizer (1981-present)

The Human League reigned supreme over British New Wave pop groups of the early 80s with its slick, synth-driven radio hits. Although it began as a rather dour Kraftwerk-influenced group, its pop machine was in full gear by the time of its first U.S. release in 1982. By bringing various soul-inflected tunes to its programmed pop aesthetic, the band showed considerable more staying power and commercial viability than many of its foppish counterparts. However, the hollow emotional core inhabiting virtually all of 80s synth pop eventually took over. Most of its studio albums—1982's *Dare* being the most consistent—are out of print. *Greatest Hits* (A&M, 1988, prod. Various) 𝄞𝄞𝄞 is a fair reminder of a band that started out with great singles, only to descend into ill-conceived political stabs and empty funk. Some of the better tracks—"Fascination," "Mirror Man" and the group's first smash, "Don't You Want Me"—are included.

the rest: *Octopus* (EastWest America, 1995) 𝄞𝄞

Allan Orski

Humble Pie

Formed 1969 in Essex, England. Disbanded 1975. Re-formed 1980-81.

Steve Marriott, vocals, guitar, keyboards (died April 20, 1991); Peter Frampton, vocals, guitar (1969-1971); Greg Ridley, bass, vocals; Jerry Shirley, drums; David "Clem" Clempson, guitar, vocals; Bobby Tench, vocals, guitar (198-81); Anthony Jones, bass (1980-81)

When British pop stars Marriott and Frampton—from the Small Faces and the Herd, respectively—hooked up during the late 70s, few could have guessed that they were creating a prototypical, boogie 'n' blues-based hard rock outfit. The first few albums hinted at that direction, but it was the ferocious, molten jams of *Performance—Rockin' the Fillmore* that really staked Humble Pie's claim. Things got a bit too heavy for Frampton, who split for his own momentarily successful solo career, while Marriott guided Humble Pie into the realm of non-stop touring and workmanlike albums—though "30 Days in the Hole" endures. By the mid-70s, Humble Pie was pretty well spent (its role having been taken over by the likes of Foghat and REO Speedwagon), and the turn-of-the-decade attempt to revive it was inconsequential. Sadly, Marriott and Frampton had begun working together again when the former died in a house fire in 1991.

what to buy: *Performance—Rockin' the Fillmore* (A&M, 1971/1988, prod. Humble Pie) 𝄞𝄞𝄞𝄞 is Humble Pie's shining, triumphant moment, rocking up a fury with extended versions of "I Don't Need No Doctor," "I'm Ready" and nearly a half-hour of "I Walk on Gilded Splinters." You'll never believe that Frampton played like this. *Hot 'n' Nasty: The Anthology* (A&M/Chronicles, 1994, prod. Various) 𝄞𝄞𝄞𝄞 shows that Humble Pie was more than a boogie band, generously sampling from each of the group's albums for a consistently compelling overview.

what to buy next: *Rock On* (A&M, 1971/Rebound, 1994, prod. Glyn Johns and Humble Pie) 𝄞𝄞𝄞 and *Smokin'*, (A&M, 1972, prod. The Pie) 𝄞𝄞𝄞 which bookended *Performance*, are as consistent as Humble Pie ever got on its studio albums. The latter has "30 Days in the Hole."

what to avoid: The first comeback album, *On to Victory*, (Atco, 1980/1991, prod. Johnny Wright and Humble Pie) 𝄞 was a defeat. Lord knows why the group tried another one.

the rest: *Town and Country* (A&M, 1969/Griffin, 1994) 𝄞𝄞𝄞 *Humble Pie* (A&M, 1970/Griffin, 1994) 𝄞𝄞 *Go For the Throat* (Atco, 1981/1991) 𝄞 *The Best of Humble Pie* (A&M, 1982) 𝄞𝄞𝄞 *Classics Vol. 14* (A&M, 1987) 𝄞𝄞𝄞 *Early Years* (Griffin, 1994) 𝄞𝄞𝄞½ *Rock On* (Rebound, 1994) 𝄞𝄞𝄞

worth searching for: Humble Pie's first album, *As Safe as Yesterday*, (Columbia, 1969/Line, 1987, prod. Humble Pie) 𝄞𝄞𝄞½ currently available as an import, is an intriguing and sometimes trippy record that serves Frampton's more melodic sensibilities particularly well.

solo outings:

Steve Marriott: *30 Seconds to Midnite* (Griffin, 1989/1994) 𝄞𝄞½

Foghat, REO Speedwagon, Ted Nugent, the Black Crowes, Cry of Love

John Lee Hooker, Willie Dixon, the Beatles, Spooky Tooth

see also: *Peter Frampton, Small Faces*

Gary Graff

Ian Hunter

Born June 3, 1946 in Shrewsbury, England

When he left Mott the Hoople in 1974—after being hospitalized for exhaustion—Hunter moved to New York and continued along a similar musical path, basically a mix of rowdy, pub-style rockers and dramatic ballads, often dressed with literate and wry lyrics. In the years just before punk, Hunter's collaborations with former Bowie/Mott sidekick Mick Ronson were ill-timed for mass attention but unquestionably made an impact on what came later (the Clash's Mick Jones returned the favor by producing Hunter's *Short Back and Sides* in 1981). Since the early 80s, Hunter has surfaced infrequently, though he has popped up on albums by Def Leppard and on the late Ronson's final effort *Heaven and Hull* A good chunk of his recorded output is out of print, which truly is our loss.

what to buy: On his solo debut, *Ian Hunter,* (Columbia, 1975/Legacy, 1990, prod. Ian Hunter and Mick Ronson) [4 bones] Hunter sounds like a man with something to prove and comes out gangbusters with "Once Bitten, Twice Shy," "Who Do You Love" and the expansive tone poem "Boy." On *Short Back and Sides,* (Chrysalis, 1981/Griffin, 1995, prod. Mick Jones) [3½ bones] producer Jones' influence is clearly heard on the funk of "Noises," the reggae touches on "Gun Control" and the bop of "Lisa Likes to Rock 'n' Roll."

what to buy next: *You're Never Alone With a Schizophrenic* (Chrysalis, 1979/Razor & Tie, 1994, prod. Ian Hunter and Mick Ronson) [3½ bones] is a smart, snappy set of rockers ("Just Another Night," "Cleveland Rocks"), though it also includes "Ships"—a song so sappy that Barry Manilow covered it.

what to avoid: *Ian Hunter's Dirty Laundry* (Cleveland International, 1995) [2 bones] came after a decade and sounds as rusty as you'd imagine.

worth searching for: *Welcome to the Club,* (Chrysalis, 1980/1994, prod. Mick Ronson and Ian Hunter) [4 bones] sadly available only via import (though some tracks are on *Shades*), is spirited live album that features solo material, Mott favorites and even Ronson's "Slaughter on Tenth Avenue."

Graham Parker, Elvis Costello, Great White, Smashing Pumpkins, Def Leppard

Bob Dylan, David Bowie, Little Richard

Gary Graff

Hunters & Collectors

Formed 1980 in Melbourne, Australia.

Mark Seymour, vocals, guitar; Jack Howard, trumpet; Michael Waters, trombone, keyboards; Jeremy Smith, French horn, keyboards; John Archer, bass; Doug Falconer, drums; Greg Perano, percussion (1980-84); Martin Lubran, guitar (1980-84)

Starting out as an experimental blend of rugged Australian post-punk rock, tribal percussion jams and blaring horns, Hunters & Collectors quickly became a popular live act Down Under. But although 1982's fairly alluring single, "Talking to a Stranger," aired on MTV for a brief time, the band didn't really hit its mark until 1986's *Human Frailty* employed tighter song structures that merged the guitars, horns and rhythm more evenly behind Seymour's wailing, over-the-top vocals. An even better effort, *Fate,* followed, and around the same time the horn section made a significant contribution to Midnight Oil's best album, *Diesel and Dust.* But the creative spark seemingly departed soon after, and although the group remains a sizable draw in Australia, it never really did crack the U.S. market, nor has it released anything here for several years. Seymour's vocals can be too much at times; his feverish approach often sounds as though someone should be hunting for, and collecting, some oxygen for the poor guy. But at its best, the band combines stirring fervor with graceful elements. Plus, there's always that wild horn section and, most important of all, Archer's wiry, slamming bass parts grooving with Falconer's tom-heavy, tribal drums. It's a combo that's hard to beat.

what to buy: With its 60s-style blend of surf-influenced guitars and TV detective-show horn figures, *Fate* (IRS, 1988, prod. Greg Howard and Hunters & Collectors) [4 bones] is solid and energetic throughout. The almost Stonesy "Faraway Man" and the rather dark and oddly powerful "Wishing Well" are the standout tracks, but there are few weak cuts here, period.

what to buy next: Although it's less consistent than *Fate*, *Human Frailty* (IRS, 1986, prod. Gavin MacKillop and Hunters & Collectors) [3½ bones] opens up with three of the band's best, most crackling numbers—"Say Goodbye," "Is There Anybody in There?" and the elegant "Throw Your Arms Around Me." For those who want an overview, *Collected Works* (IRS, 1990, prod.

Various) offers five tracks each from *Fate* and *Human Frailty* along with hit and miss selections from other albums.

what to avoid: Despite backing vocals from Crowded House's Neil Finn, *Ghost Nation* (Atlantic, 1990) is a surprisingly lackluster effort, a strange and disappointing development following the band's two best albums.

the rest: *Demon Flower* (Shake the Record, 1994)

worth searching for: Those seeking something rawer and more industrial/percussion-driven may want to check out *Hunters & Collectors* (Oz/A&M, 1983) or its Australian counterpart, a double album with almost entirely different material).

▶▶ Hoodoo Gurus, Nick Cave

◀◀ Gang of Four, Midnight Oil, Bad Manners, Lords of the New Church, the Kinks

Bob Remstein

Hüsker Dü

Formed 1979 in St. Paul, Minn. Disbanded 1988.

Bob Mould, vocals, guitar; Grant Hart, vocals, drums; Greg Norton, bass, vocals

Hüsker Dü was simply one of the great rock bands of the 80s, truly communal in terms of band dynamics (at least in the beginning), blazingly intense and wildly prolific. Under a hail of scathing guitars and a battering rhythm section, the trio combined brute force with carefully constructed and often sweetly melodic songs. Although most punk bands spew their anger outward, Hüsker Dü's themes were painfully personal, displaying an often-unflinching self-awareness. While most critics would have you believe Hüsker Dü and the Replacements invented alternative rock (they didn't), the Hüskers' influence can't be overstated in both musical and commercial terms. One of the first alterna-bands to sign on to a major record label (Warner Bros.) without compromise, Hüsker Dü seemed poised for major recognition. But personal problems, power struggles and eventual label disagreements (Warner Bros. wanted to nix Hart in favor of programmed drums!) led to its ultimate dissolution. Mould has enjoyed success on his own and with the band Sugar Hart also went solo before forming Nova Mob; his post-Hüsker work has been less celebrated than Mould's but no less visceral.

what to buy: *Edson Arcade*, (SST, 1984, prod. Spot and Hüsker Dü) a double concept album, was to be the zenith of the band's collaborative powers. The result is an arresting roller coaster slash of epic proportions. Every subsequent release were designed to alternate between Mould and Hart's songs, but the scales tipped gradually towards Mould. *New Day Rising* (SST, 1984, prod. Spot and Hüsker Dü) focuses the band's sound with a set of songs of ferocious momentum. Inherently tuneful and blaring, "I Apologize," "Terms of Psychic Warfare" and "59 Times the Pain" all explode on impact. *Flip Your Wig* (SST, 1985, prod. Bob Mould and Grant Hart) is even more concise, played with screamingly tight precision, as if it had been recorded while the group went over a cliff. The airtight pop melodics of "Makes No Sense at All," "Green Eyes" and "Hate Paper Doll" only add to the supercharged atmosphere.

what to buy next: *Candy Apple Grey* (Warner Bros. 1986, prod. Bob Mould and Grant Hart) Moving to the majors with typical feral grace results in, if anything, a more emotionally intense map of bitterness and pounding rockers. Two fine acoustic songs mix quite well with the bristling vitriol. *Warehouse: Songs and Stories,* (Warner Bros., 1987) another double release, was compared to Derek and the Dominoes' *Layla* but it's more like the Beatles' *White Album.* The struggles within the band reached the breaking point with Mould and Hart (Norton's able writing abilities were silenced a long time ago) operating like separate entities. The tension is palpable, the implosion inevitable and the band goes down like titans clashing—a pretty exciting sound, actually.

what to avoid: *Land Speed Record* (SST, 1981, prod.Hüsker Dü) is by no means worthless, but the cheap recording of their live shows only hints at the band's power. Check out *The Living End* for a better idea.

the rest: *Everything Falls Apart and More* (Reflex, 1982/Rhino, 1995) *Metal Circus* (SST, 1983) *The Living End* (Warner Bros., 1994)

worth searching for: Grant Hart: *2541* (SST EP, 1988) was a first solo stab, with a touching acoustic title track.

solo outings:

Grant Hart: *Intolerance* (SST, 1989)

Nova Mob (Hart): *The Last Days of Pompeii* (Rough Trade, 1991) *Nova Mob* (Restless, 1994)

▶▶ Soul Asylum, Nirvana, the Pixies

◀◀ Black Flag

see also: *Bob Mould/Sugar*

Allan Orski

Janis Ian

Born Janis Eddy Fink, May 7, 1951 in New York, N.Y.

Ian was the Tiffany and Debbie Gibson of her time, with a crucial difference; her music was good, and serious. Ian was just 15 when she courted controversy with "Society's Child," her searing observation about interracial romance that was banned by some radio stations but finally won respect when Leonard Bernstein invited her to perform it on a 1967 TV special he hosted about rock. But the rest of Ian's career has been somewhat fitful, marked as much by commercial slumps and prolonged absences as by hits. She did return the charts in 1975 with her hit "At Seventeen," but not long after that she began a 12-year break from recording. When she returned, Ian came out, and though her subsequent albums have not launched hits, they have been among the most moving and resonant of her career.

what to buy: On *Between the Lines,* (Columbia, 1975) "At Seventeen" is only one of an album full of luminous, well-crafted songs. *Breaking Silence* (Morgan Creek, 1993, prod. Janis Ian and Jeff Balding) is a bold return to recording on which Ian, never one to scrimp on her emotions, is even more frank and pointed.

what to buy next: *Society's Child: The Verve Recordings,* (Polydor/Chronicles, 1995, prod. Various) because you have to have "Society's Child," although this two-disc set would have been better as a more judiciously selected single.

what to avoid: *Present Company* (Capitol, 1971/One Way, 1994) is a transitional effort between Ian's earnest teenage recordings and her more deeply rooted work of the mid-70s, an awkward phase in anybody's life, much less a recording artist.

the rest: *Revenge* (Beacon, 1995)

worth searching for: *Between the Lines'* predecessor, *Stars,* (Columbia, 1974) marked a new maturity in Ian's music. It also includes "Jesse," which was a hit for Roberta Flack.

▶▶ Suzanne Vega, Tracy Chapman, Shawn Colvin

◀◀ Joan Baez, Rev. Gary Davis, Ronnie Gilbert

Gary Graff

Jimmy Ibbotson

See: Nitty Gritty Dirt Band

Icehouse

Formed 1980 in Sydney, Australia

Iva Davies, vocals, guitars, keyboards, oboe, English horn; Robert Kretschmer, guitars (1982-present); Anthony Smith, keyboards (1981-82); Keith Welsh, bass (1981-82); Andy Qunta, keyboards (1982-87); Simon Lloyd, saxophone, trumpet, keyboards (1984-present); Guy Pratt, bass (1982-86); Stephen Morgan, bass (1987-89); John Lloyd, drums, percussion (1981-84); Paul Wheeler, drums (1987-present)

For a while in the mid-80s it seemed that Davies, the lead singer and head songwriter of Icehouse, was a poor man's version of Bryan Ferry. He had the soaring tenor voice, and like many other New Romantic groups of that era, Icehouse was influenced equally by the seductive, layered pop/rock of later Roxy Music and the sassier, glam-inflected rock 'n' roll of David Bowie. But Davies has never exhibited much personality, either on stage or on disc, and his albums have rarely featured more than two noteworthy songs apiece. Starting out as Flowers, Davies and his original cohorts received little attention until the band's debut was re-released under the name Icehouse. New Wavey and pointedly electronic, the album mixed elements of Ultravox and The Cars to good effect. On the follow-up, *Primitive Man,* the Ferry sound kicked in, with "Hey Little Girl" (a hit in Europe) and "Street Cafe." It wasn't until 1986, though, that the band found its mark with *No Promises,* a dazzling bit of mid-80s pop—moody, rangy and a terrific showcase for Davies' vocals. In 1987, the group scored two Top 10 U.S. hits, "Crazy" and "Electric Blue," one overwrought and the other (co-written with John Oates of Hall and Oates) forgettable. Legal problems with Chrysalis Records ensued, and the group never again regained its commercial momentum. After a break of a few years, the band apparently has returned to active duty and recently released (in Australia and Germany, at least) an album of covers entitled *The Berlin Tapes,* featuring songs made famous by Bowie, Lou Reed and Frank Sinatra. Be afraid. Be very afraid.

what to buy: Until a decent singles package is released domestically (and don't hold your breath), *Measure For Measure* (Chrysalis, 1986, prod. David Lord and Rhett Davies) is probably your best bet, and really only because it features the band's best single, the gloriously extravagant "No Promises." Brian Eno lends his sonic talents on a few cuts, but most of the songs just don't hold up.

what to buy next: *Icehouse* (Chrysalis, 1981, prod. Cameron Allan and Iva Davies) offers the band in its early, pre-Roxy Music-influenced version. With its coldly electronic approach, the album sounds like an Icehouse record (for once), and though Davies' vocals have that Midge Ure-like sheen, songs such as "I Can't Help Myself" and the title track are dark and rather interesting.

what to avoid: Wracked by fake Bowie-isms and short on compelling songs, *Sidewalk* (Chrysalis, 1984, prod. Iva Davies) WOOF! is better left in the gutter. And don't get suckered into picking up *Great Southern Land* (Chrysalis, 1989, prod. Various) although it was marketed as a greatest-hits package, the album leaves out "No Promises," includes cheesily re-recorded versions of first-album tunes and omits everything from *Man Of Colours,* the band's biggest-seller in the United States. Go figure.

the rest: *Primitive Man* (Chrysalis, 1982) *Man Of Colours* (Chrysalis, 1987)

worth searching for: The five-song *Fresco* EP (Chrysalis, 1983, prod. Iva Davies and Keith Forsey) is a less painful way of experiencing Icehouse, as only one real dud is included along with the two best (and most Roxy Music-influenced) songs from *Primitive Man,* "Hey Little Girl" and "Street Cafe."

▶▶ Cutting Crew, Talk Talk, Tears For Fears

◀◀ Roxy Music, David Bowie, The Cars, Alan Parsons Project, Ultravox

Bob Remstein

Idaho

Formed 1992 in Los Angeles, Calif.

John Berry, guitar, drums (1992-93); Jeff Martin, bass, vocals, four-string guitar, drums, keyboards; Mark Lewis, drums, trumpet (1995-present); Dan Seta, guitars (1995-present); Terrence Borden, bass, acoustic guitar (1995-present)

Founding members Berry and Martin knew each other for years on the L.A. punk scene before they started recording together around 1987. The duo often played all the instruments on its songs but occasionally used various temporary drummers. Berry, the son of TV actor Ken Berry ("Mayberry R.F.D.," "F Troop"), was an off-and-on heroin junkie who had served time in jail; after his problems forced him out of the band, Martin went on without him, eventually making some of the musicians he used full-time band members. Always he produces a shimmering sound with guitar effects and occasional outbursts set to slow but inexorable rhythms, topped off with his angst-laden vocals. This is an original and unique band, though its dark-hued songs can be hard on weaker psyches. *Year After Year* (Caroline, 1993, prod. Idaho and Martin Brumbach) is an intense, gorgeously moody album from the original duo. Martin's low vocal range, which he uses a lot, sounds at its darkest like Joy Division's Ian Curtis (his bass playing also recalls Joy Division's fat, round sound), while his upper range is a dead ringer for American Music Club's Mark Eitzel. The music, in fact, suggests a snarling, less-mellow AMC. *This Way Out* (Caroline, 1994, prod. Jeff Martin, Brumbach) opens up the sound a bit while continuing to explore angst and dolor. Martin's voice fits well with his tingling, shuddering guitar riffs and almost poppy melodies, like the Lemonheads on quaaludes.

the rest: *The Palms* (Caroline EP, 1993) *Three Sheets to the Wind* (Caroline, 1996)

Steve Holtje

What Album Changed Your Life?

"Probably (Stevie Wonder's) Innervisions, back when I was 8. It was just so amazingly musical, just perfections and so beautiful. It's a very spiritual record."

Lenny Kravitz

Billy Idol /Generation X

Formed 1976 in London, England. Disbanded 1981.

Billy Idol (born William Michael Albert Broad, Nov. 30, 1955 in Stanmore, Middlesex, England), vocals; Tony James, bass, vocals; Bob Andrews, guitar, vocals; John Towe, drums (1976-77); Mark Laff, drums (1977-81)

The first punk to enthusiastically court the mainstream pop audience, Idol first used his decent band Generation X, then catchy songs, spikey hair and a good sneer, to sell lots of records. During the mid-70s, avid trend follower Idol shifted allegiances from the Beatles to the Sex Pistols, hung out constantly at Malcolm McLaren's famous Sex shop and formed Generation X. Though many purists turned up their noses at the band of unashamed punks-for-profit, the group put out some excellent singles, including "Your Generation" and "Ready, Steady, Go," not to mention indirectly inspiring the name of a Douglas Coupland book and a marketing term for an actual generation. Idol's solo career began with a dance retread of the band's popular "Dancing With Myself," which became a huge hit—one of many in his lucrative 80s career. Punks, revolted by Idol's dominant presence on MTV, turned their backs on him, but the masses embraced him wholeheartedly. By the 90s, however, Idol was desperately searching for an audience and unsuccessfully tried to ride the cyberpunk movement's coattails, putting out a computer news release and an abysmal album called *Cyberpunk*.

what to buy: Generation X's *Perfect Hits 1975-1981* (Chrysalis, 1991, prod. Various) collects the band's best early singles, including "Ready, Steady, Go," "One Hundred Punks" and the original "Dancing With Myself."

what to buy next: Many punk fans still consider Idol verboten for shifting gears into bland pop hits in order to be a big star. Still, *Rebel Yell* (Chrysalis, 1983, prod. Michael Frondelli) —bolstered by the slash 'n' burn guitar attack of Steve Stevens—is a formidable commercial accomplishment, featuring a year's worth of smash hits in the title track, "Eyes Without a Face" and "Flesh For Fantasy."

what to avoid: Idol's *Cyberpunk* (Chrysalis, 1993, prod. Robin Hancock) unashamedly tries to cash in on a trend, but he forgot to bring the songs.

the rest: Idol: *Don't Stop* (Chrysalis EP, 1981) *Billy Idol* (Chrysalis, 1982) *Whiplash Smile* (Chrysalis, 1986) *Charmed Life* (Chrysalis, 1990) *Vital Idol* (Chrysalis, 1987) Generation X: *The Best of Generation X* (Chrysalis, 1985) *Valley of the Dolls* (Chrysalis, 1979)

worth searching for: *Idol Songs*, (Chrysalis, 1988, prod. Various) a British collection of Idol's hits, a better compilation than the *Vital Idol* remix collection. Also, *Generation X*, (Chrysalis, 1978) is among the best albums of the punk era, with a cover of John Lennon's "Gimme Some Truth" and the classic Generation X singles "Wild Youth" and "Your Generation."

▶▶ The Offspring, Sigue Sigue Sputnik, Sisters of Mercy, Green Day

◀◀ The Sex Pistols, Siouxsie and the Banshees, the Beatles, the Buzzcocks, the Clash

Tracey Birkenhauer and Steve Knopper

The Impressions

See: Curtis Mayfield

Indigo Girls

Formed 1984 in Decatur, Ga.

Amy Ray, guitar and vocals; Emily Saliers, guitar and vocals

Ray and Saliers easily won over sensitive folkies and alternative rockers alike with their 1989 major-label debut by baring their souls where others merely beat on their chests. Fusing Biblical imagery, feminist integrity and poetic pretensions, the Atlanta duo risked coming across as angstful overachievers, but their unflagging earnestness and soaring harmonies made an indelible impression. Since then, they have struggled to harness the power of their voices and their convictions: For every shimmering pop triumph like "Hammer and a Nail" or "Power of Two" there's a heavy-handed "The Girl With the Weight of the World in Her Hands" or "You and Me of 10,000 Wars." For every tasteful cover of Bob ylan's "All Along the Watchtower" or Elton John's "Mona Lisas and Mad Hatters," there's an overwrought take on Dire Straits' "Romeo and Juliet" and Buffy Sainte-Marie's "Bury My Heart at Wounded Knee." But 1994's hard-rocking "Swamp Ophelia" hit the emotional and artistic mark, proving that with each album, Saliers and Ray are indeed getting closer to fine.

what to buy: *Indigo Girls* (Epic, 1989, prod. Scott Litt) boasts help from R.E.M. and Hothouse Flowers, who lend an edge to "Closer to Fine," "Kid Fears" and "Tried to Be True." *Swamp Ophelia* (Epic, 1994, prod. Peter Collins) expands the duo's sound with horns, mandolins, African drums, accordions and other textures that for once are conducive, not cosmetic.

what to buy next: The range of styles covered in their live shows is documented on the sprawling two-CD *1200 Curfews* (Epic, 1995, prod. Indigo Girls and Russell Carter) but the intensity is stronger on the eight-song *Back on the Bus Y'all*, (Epic, 1991, prod. Timothy R. Powell) which also features the Ellen James Society.

what to avoid: *Strange Fire*, (Epic, 1989, prod. John Keane) a reissue of the Indigo's 1987 indie debut, is burdened by an underdeveloped vision and tentative vocals. Their idea of a statement at the time was covering the Youngbloods' "Get Together."

the rest: *Nomads Indians Saints* (Epic, 1990) ♪♪♪ *Rites of Passage* (Epic, 1992) ♪♪♪

worth searching for: *Jesus Christ Superstar: A Resurrection* (Daemon/Long Play, 1994, prod. Michael Lorant) ♪♪♪ is a rocking but uneven update of the Andrew Lloyd Webber-Tim Rice musical featuring Ray as Jesus Christ and Saliers as Mary Magdalene. Their duets on "Everything's Alright" and "What's the Buzz" top Saliers' shaky "I Don't Know How to Love Him."

⏩ The Story, Disappear Fear

⏪ Bob Dylan, R.E.M., Simon and Garfunkel

David Okamoto

Infectious Grooves

See: Suicidal Tendancies

Inspiral Carpets

Formed 1986 in Manchester, England

Stephen Holt, vocals (1986-88); Tom Hingley, vocals (1988-present); Clint Boon, keyboards, vocals; Graham Lambert, guitar; David Swift, bass (1986-88); Martyn Walsh, bass (1988-present); Craig Gill, drums

When the Manchester scene was at its dizzying height back during the late 80s, the Inspiral Carpets were a curious oddity, for they lacked the Stone Roses' charisma, the Happy Mondays' radical concepts and the Charlatans' instant catchiness. By fusing bare boned neo-psychedelic rock 'n' roll with themes of urban decay, prostitution and being downright miserable, the quintet's organ-fueled sound served as a reality check to the whole trippy scene. Despite contributing a few classic singles to the Britpop sweepstakes, the Inspiral Carpets eventually fell out of favor and into obscurity.

what to buy: The Inspiral Carpets' debut album, the colossally downtrodden *Life,* (Mute/Elektra, 1990, prod. Inspiral Carpets and Nick Garside) ♪♪♪♪ shows rare depth and maturity for such a young band. Layered with cascading feedback, whopping drums, haunting Doors-shaded organs and looping monotone vocals, the album features such splendid songs as "This Is How It Feels" and "She Comes In The Fall."

what to buy next: Despite their short tenure in the British pop charts, the Inspiral Carpets left behind a remarkable collection, *The Singles* (Mute, 1995, prod. Various) which compiles all of the group's finest material, including underrated tunes like "Move," "Bitches Brew" and "Biggest Mountain."

what to avoid: The group lost steam by its fourth album, the directionless *Devil Hopping.* (Mute/Elektra, 1994, prod. Pascal Gabriel) ♪

the rest: *The Beast Inside* (Mute/Elektra, 1991) ♪♪♪ *Revenge of the Goldfish* (Mute/Elektra, 1992) ♪♪

worth searching for: The import only *Plane Crash,* EP (Playtime, 1988, prod. Dave Fielding) ♪♪♪ the group's recording debut, features a crisp cover of "96 Tears" along with four originals.

⏩ Oasis, Supergrass

⏪ The Fall, The Doors, Joy Division

Aidin Vaziri

INXS

Formed 1977 in Sydney, Australia

Michael Hutchence, vocals (1977-96); Tim Farriss, guitar; Andrew Farriss, keyboards, guitar; Jon Farriss; drums; Gary Gary Beers, bass; Kirk Pengilly, guitar, saxophone

A durable group that kept its original lineup—including three brothers—together longer than most, INXS was able to keep an equinamity about it even after singer Hutchence became a sex symbol during the mid-80s (he once turned down a Rolling Stone cover because it wouldn't include his bandmates). After several long years toughening its act in front of surfers in Sydney pubs, the band first received widespread attention in the mid-80s as an opening act for (then) more successful countrymen Men at Work. One of alternative music's most commercial bands, INXS' ascension during the peaked when the 1985 single "What You Need" became an international smash and set up the multi-million selling triumph of the 1987 album *Kick* The group's popularity slowly waned after that, though the Hutchence-Andrew Farriss songwriting partnership continued to flourish with strong singles such as "Suicide Blonde," "Beautiful Girl" and the industrial-tinged "The Gift." By the mid-Nineties, Hutchence was regularly making gossip columns as the concubine of Bob Geldof's wife Paula Yates. The band, meanwhile, signed to another label (Capitol) with hopes of releasing an album in late 1996 or early 1997.

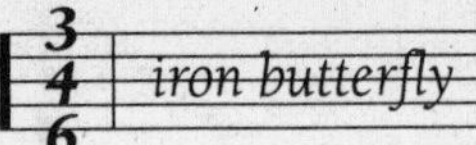

what to buy: *Kick,* (Atlantic, 1987, prod. Chris Thomas) which spawned four huge singles, is as radio-ready as an album can be, one of those wonderful 80s packages (a la Def Leppard's *Hysteria* or U2's *The Joshua Tree*) where each track could have been a legitimate single.

what to buy next: *Full Moon, Dirty Hearts* (Atlantic,1993, prod. Mark Opitz & INXS) is an unjustly overlooked entry in the band's catalog, offering caustic rockers ("Days of Rust") and the usual quality dance fare ("The Gift").

what to avoid: *Live Baby Live,* (Atlantic, 1991, prod. Mark Opitz) a head-scratching affair that reduces a usually rousing live act to stiff and bored, with terrible production to boot.

the rest: *INXS* (Deluxe, 1980/Atco, 1984) *Underneath the Colours* (Deluxe, 1981/Atco, 1984) *Shabooh Shoobah* (Atco, 1983) *Dekadance* (Atco EP, 1983) *The Swing* (Atco, 1985) *Listen Like Thieves* (Atlantic, 1986) *X* (Atlantic, 1990) *Welcome to Wherever You Are* (Atlantic, 1992) *Greatest Hits* (Atlantic, 1992)

worth searching for: *The Lost Boys* soundtrack (Atlantic, 1988, prod. Various) was a predecessor to today's chock-full-of-modern-rock movie soundtracks and features two fine INXS performances with Australian screamer Jimmy Barnes.

Jesus Jones, Charm Farm

Roxy Music, the Rolling Stones

Todd Wicks

Iron Butterfly

Formed 1966 in San Diego, Calif. Disbanded 1971. Re-formed 1974-75 and 1993-present.

Doug Ingle, keyboards, vocals; Ron Bushy, drums, vocals; Darryl DeLoach, vocals (1967); Jerry Penrod, bass (1967); Danny Weis, guitar (1967); Erik Braunn, guitar, vocals (1968-69, 1974-75); Lee Dorman, bass, guitar, piano (1968, 1993); Mike Pinera, guitar, vocals (1970-71, 1993); Larry "Rhino" Reinhardt (1970-71); Phil Kramer, bass (1974); Howard Reitzes, keyboards, guitar (1974-75); Derek Hilland, keyboards, vocals (1993-present); Eric Barnett, guitar (1996-present); Lee Dorman, bass, vocals (1993-present)

If not for the legendary excess of its 17-minute heavy-metal anthem, the now-comical "In-a-Gadda-Da-Vida," few would remember Iron Butterfly. But with its brash guitars, thudding drums and stilted vocals, the band helped define the heavy-metal era that followed. Its heyday was brief, but between 1967-69, Iron Butterfly toured with the Doors and the Jefferson Airplane and briefly was Atlantic Records' best-selling band, hitting the seven million mark in album sales. The group has gone through several ill-advised revivals, unable to face the fact that its appeal was limited to the jam-rock scene of the psychedelic 60s.

what to buy: Iron Butterfly's 17 minutes of fame has been perfectly preserved, in triplicate, via a reissue of *In-a-Gadda-Da-Vida* (Atco, 1968/Rhino, 1995, prod. Jim Hilton) The original six tunes have been remastered with two bonus takes of "Vida," including a 19-minute live jam and a 2:52 version (no drum solo?!) edited for radio.

what to buy next: Grudgingly, *Light and Heavy: The Best of Iron Butterfly* (Rhino, 1993, prod. Various) is a cost-effective way to sample the rest of the group's output—if you really want to.

what to avoid: The rest of Iron Butterfly's sludge-rock adventures (all WOOFS!): *Heavy* (Atco, 1968/Rhino, 1993); *Ball* (Atco, 1969/1991); *Metamorphosis* (Atco, 1970/Rhino, 1993); *Live* (Rhino, 1989); and *Scorching Beauty.* (MCA, 1993)

worth searching for: If you're gonna own it, go for the deluxe version of *In-a-Gadda-Da-Vida* (Rhino, 1995) with cool, hippie-like graphics and a new set of liner notes.

Black Sabbath, Judas Priest, Alice Cooper, Kiss

The Troggs, Blue Cheer, the Animals, the Yardbirds

David Yonke

Iron City Houserockers

See: Joe Grushecky

Iron Maiden /Bruce Dickinson

Formed 1976 in London, England

Paul Di'anno, vocals (1976-81); Bruce Dickinson, vocals (1982-92); Steve Harris, bass; Dave Murray, guitar; Clive Burr, drums (1980-82); Adrian Smith, guitar (1980-88); Janick Gers, guitar (1990-present); Blaze Bayley, vocals (1993-present); Nicko McBrain, drums (1983-present)

In an unapologetic nod to 70s metal, Maiden's guitar-enforced, wailing hard rock has scored numerous gold and platinum albums and a loyal headbanger base without the benefit of radio play or much MTV rotation. Anchored by Harris' somewhat obtrusive thumping, the band's literate approach of mythological themes and movie inspiration really took hold when Dickinson joined; one of the more dramatic poseurs in heavy metal, he nonetheless fronted the band throughout the most successful run of its career (1982-90), and his departure leaves the band's future uncertain. Castle Records has recently rehauled most of Maiden's catalogue, generously including a bonus disc of B-sides and live recordings with each release.

what to buy: With the hellish title track of *The Number of the Beast,* (Harvest, 1982/Castle, 1995, prod. Martin Birch, Iron Maiden and Doug Hall) the band hits a melodic peak, beginning its seven-album winning streak. A scorching brew of memorable tunes and catchy metalloid axe burners. On *Iron Maiden,* (Harvest, 1980/Castle, 1995, prod. Will Malone) original frontman Di'anno and Co. pull out all the stops in a frenzied guitar attack that laid the groundwork for all subsequent releases.

what to buy next: Di'anno's swan song, *Killers,* (Harvest, 1981/Castle 1995, prod. Martin Birch) is a flat-out screech fest, with only slightly less fiery results than the debut—plus a cool cover illustration of the band's rotting corpse mascot, Eddie. *Piece of Mind* (Harvest, 1983/Castle, 1995, prod. Martin Birch) is a solid mid-period release that introduces drummer McBrain and boasts excellent guitar work on "Where Eagles Dare" and "Flight of Icarus." The Castle bonus disc includes a crunching take on Jethro Tull's "Cross-Eyed Mary."

what to avoid: *Somewhere in Time* (Harvest, 1986/Castle, 1995, prod. Martin Birch) Who the hell let the keyboards in?

the rest: *Maiden Japan* (Harvest EP, 1981) *Powerslave* (Harvest, 1984/Castle, 1995) *Live After Death* (Harvest, 1985/Castle, 1995) *Seventh Son of a Seventh Son* (Harvest, 1988/Castle, 1995) *No Prayer for the Dying* (Epic, 1990/Castle, 1995) *Fear of the Dark* (Epic, 1992/Castle, 1995) *A Real Live One* (Capitol, 1993/Castle, 1995) *A Real Dead One* (Capitol, 1993/Castle, 1995) *The X-factor* (CMC International, 1995)

solo outings:

Bruce Dickinson: *Tattooed Millionaire* (Columbia, 1990) *Balls to Picasso* (Mercury, 1994) *Skunkworks* (Castle, 1996)

▶▶ Metallica, Megadeth, Slayer

◀◀ Led Zeppelin, Black Sabbath, Deep Purple

Allan Orski

Chris Isaak

Born June 6, 1956 in Stockton, Calif.

Someone has to keep alive the spirit of 1950s rock, and these days singer/songwriter Chris Isaak has the job pretty much to himself. Backed by guitarist James Calvin Wilsey, bassist Rowland Salley and drummer Kenney Dale Johnson, the Bay-area guitarist churns out stripped-to-the-roots rockers and sullen blues numbers that embody the pathos of Roy Orbison with the brooding of Elvis Presley. Isaak enjoyed commercial success after director David Lynch featured the sultry "Wicked Game" (from *Heart Shaped World*) in his 1990 film, *Wild at Heart.* The songwriter has also earned some recognition as an actor with roles in *Married to the Mob, Wild at Heart, The Silence of the Lambs,* and *Little Buddha.*

what to buy: True to its title, *San Francisco Days* (Reprise, 1993, prod. Erik Jacobsen) is a sunny divergence from the melancholy of Isaak's early albums. The sonic landscape opens up to offer some of his most vital and distinctive songs, including the title track and "Round 'N' Round." On the flip side, "Move Along," "5:15" and the vaguely psychotic "Can't Do a Thing (to Stop Me)" demonstrate Isaak's growing command over the deep-blues style that's at his roots.

what to buy next: *Forever Blue* (Reprise, 1995, prod. Erik Jacobsen) expands upon the broader soundscape of *San Francisco Days.* While the album tends toward quieter acoustic numbers, the rockers—"Baby Did a Bad Bad Thing," "Go Walking Down There," and "I Believe"—give compelling reason to get up and dance.

what to avoid: *Silvertone* (Warner Bros., 1985, prod. Erik Jacobsen) is an unpromising debut that isn't bad as much as it is one-dimensional. Isaak hit his stride later on, but the songs here lope along without much direction or, for that matter, variation.

the rest: *Chris Isaak* (Warner Bros., 1987) *Heart Shaped World* (Reprise, 1989)

worth searching for: *Wicked Game,* (Reprise, 1991) a solid import-only compilation of songs from Isaak's first three albums, put together to cash-in on the title track's success.

▶▶ Marshall Crenshaw, Dwight Yoakam

◀◀ Elvis Presley, Roy Orbison, Eddie Cochran, Neil Diamond

Christopher Scapelliti

Isley Brothers

Formed 1957 in Cincinnati, Ohio

Ronald Isley, vocals (1957-present); Rudolph Isley, vocals (1957-86, 1990-present); O'Kelly Isley, vocals (1957-1986, died March 31, 1986); Ernie Isley, guitar, drums (1969-84, 1996); Marvin Isley, bass (1969-84); Chris Jasper, keyboards (1969-84)

The Isley Brothers started out as a gospel group but didn't enjoy much success until—following the death of brother Vernon, who was killed in a 1955 bicycle accident—they brought gospel to the soul sound during the early 60s and then added hard rock in the 70s. The 1959 single "Shout," featuring their church organist, put the Isleys on the charts (and remains one of the most popular party anthems of all time). Sporadic success during the 60s, including a stint at Motown, left them bouncing from label to label until the band hit its stride in 1969 after reviving their own T-Neck label and releasing "It's Your Thing." The Isleys enjoyed considerable success throughout the 70s, particularly after younger brothers Ernie and Marvin and cousin Chris Jasper joined and add a harder rock edge to the sound. An acrimonious split with the younger trio yielded the moderately successful Isley-Jasper-Isley, while the older brothers soldiered on as a regular presence on the R&B charts. The group successfully sued pop star Michael Bolton for plagiarizing their song "Love is a Wonderful Thing" for his hit of the same name. Since O'Kelly's death in 1986, the group has featured Ronald with moderate success.

what to buy: Black rock music took a step forward with *3 + 3*, (T-Neck, 1973, prod. Isley Brothers) which featured Ernie Isley's screaming electric guitar on "That Lady" and acoustic, soulful treatments of folk-rock tunes such as "Don't Let Me Be Lonely Tonight" and "Summer Breeze." The Isleys crossed the line into funk with *The Heat Is On* (T-Neck, 1975, prod. Isley Brothers) and its hit "Fight the Power," though they also turned down the lights and crooned the sensual "For the Love of You."

what to buy next: *The Isley Brothers Story, Vol. 1: Rockin' Soul* (Rhino, 1991, comp. Bill Inglot) gathers the harmonies of the Isley's 60s output on tunes such as "This Ol' Heart of Mine" and "Shout."

what to avoid: *In the Beginning . . .* (T-Neck, 1972, prod. Isley Brothers) is a compilation that tries to capitalize on Jimi Hendrix's short stint with the band during 1964-65. Neither Hendrix nor the Isleys had really broken into their signature styles at this point.

the rest: *Harvest For the World* (T-Neck, 1976) *Winner Takes All* (Epic, 1979) *Go All the Way* (Columbia, 1980) *Between the Sheets* (Epic, 1983) *Smooth Sailin'* (Warner Bros., 1987) *Spend the Night* (Warner Bros., 1989) *The Isley Brothers Story, Vol. 2: The T-Neck Years* (Rhino, 1991) *Greatest Hits and Rare Classics* (Motown, 1991) *Tracks of Life* (Warner Bros., 1992) *The Isley Brothers Live* (Elektra, 1993) *Mission To Please* (Island, 1996) *Beautiful Ballads* (Legacy, 1994) *Funky Family* (Legacy, 1995) *Mission to Please* (Island, 1996)

worth searching for: Get an idea of where the Beatles learned their harmony style on *Twist and Shout,* (Sundazed, 1993, comp. Bob Irwin) which also features "Rubber Leg Twist," "Spanish Twist" and "Twistin' With Linda."

solo outings:

Isley:Jasper-Isley: *Caravan of Love* (Epic Associated, 1985)

Ernie Isley: *High Wire* (Elektra, 1990

▶▶ Funkadelic, Bone Maxwell, Boyz II Men

◀◀ The Drifters, Sam Cooke, James Brown, Jimi Hendrix, Sly & the Family Stone

Lawrence Gabriel

Ernie Isley

See: Isley Brothers

Isley-Jasper-Isley

See: Isley Brothers

David J

See: Love and Rockets

Jack Frost

See: The Church

Jackson 5 /The Jacksons

Formed 1964, Gary, Indiana

Jackie Jackson, vocals; Tito Jackson, guitar, vocals; Marlon Jackson, vocals; Jermaine Jackson, vocals, bass (1964-76, 1984-present); Michael Jackson, vocals (1964-85); Randy Jackson, vocals (1975-pre-

sent); Janet Jackson, Maureen Jackson and LaToya Jackson, vocals (mid-70s)

Although the recent years of infighting and controversy have eclipsed this family group's musical output, the Jacksons remain among the most successful vocal soul-pop groups ever. Schooled (some claim brow-beaten) by father Joe Jackson, the five oldest Jackson boys became a tight, slick performing unit when they were just adolescents and teenagers, with Michael demonstrating a stylistic maturity unfathomable for his age. Signed to Motown in 1969, the group became a sensation right away—four No. 1 hits in a row that injected fresh energy into the label, which was suffering from the graying of some of its most popular acts. The Jackson 5 became a Saturday morning cartoon and lunch box caricatures, though the formula was tapped out by the mid-70s. A move to Epic—after much legal wrangling and Jermaine's departure to stay with Motown and his father-in-law, Berry Gordy, Jr.—gave the newly christened Jackson's a chance to modernize, which it did as Michael and Randy in particular exercised more control over the writing and production. But at the beginning of the 80s, Michael's *Off the Wall* gave him a solo career even more successful than that of the group's, irreparably altering the chemistry of the clan and the band. The 1984 "Victory" tour was an arm-twisting last gasp in the wake of Michael's *Thriller* triumph, and the rest of the Jacksons faded into the background as Michael and Janet took off for the pop stratosphere.

what to buy: *The Ultimate Collection* (Motown, 1995, prod. Various) ♪♪♪♪♪ offers a crackling overview of Motown's last great singles group; the sheer exuberance of "ABC," "The Love You Save" and "I Want You Back" are hard to argue with, as is Michael's early solo stuff like "Rockin' Robin." The 82-song box set *Soulsation! The 25th Anniversary Collection* (Motown Records, 1995, prod. Various) ♪♪♪♪½ goes even deeper; it even has one of *Jackie's* solo cuts!

what to buy next: *Destiny* (Epic, 1978, prod. the Jacksons) ♪♪♪♪ marks the brothers' first attempt at the production/songwriting helm, and they come up triumphant with ace hits such as "Blame it on the Boogie" and "Shake Your Body (Down to the Ground)." *Triumph* (Epic, 1980, prod. the Jacksons) ♪♪♪♪ may be even more consistent, with a new element of tense foreboding that would crop up to even better effect on Michael's *Thriller*.

what to avoid: *The Jacksons: An American Dream*, (Motown, 1992) ♪♪½ an uneven live celebration of the group that adds nothing significant to the Jackson catalogue.

the rest: *Diana Ross Presents the Jackson 5* (Motown, 1969/1989) ♪♪♪ *ABC* (Motown, 1970/1989) ♪♪♪♪ *Third Album* (Motown, 1970/1989) ♪♪♪♪ *Christmas Album* (Motown, 1970/1986) ♪♪ *MaybeTomorrow* (Motown, 1971/1989) ♪♪♪ *Greatest Hits* (Motown Records, 1971) ♪♪♪½ *Skywriter* (Motown, 1973/1990) ♪♪ *Anthology* (Motown Records, 1976) ♪♪♪½ *The Jacksons* (Epic, 1976) ♪♪♪ *Goin' Places* (Epic, 1977) ♪♪♪ *Victory* (Epic, 1984) ♪♪½ *2300 Jackson Street* (Epic, 1989) ♪♪½ *Great Songs and Performances...* (Motown, 1991) ♪♪♪ *Pre-History: The Lost Steeltown Recordings* (Brunswick, 1996) ♪♪½

worth searching for: Led by the disco favorite title track—which approaches the vivaciousness of "ABC"—the now-deleted *Dancing Machine* (Motown, 1974) ♪♪♪♪ marks a strong finish of the Jacksons' Motown era.

solo outings:

Jermaine Jackson:Greatest Hits & Rare Classics (Motown Records, 1991) ♪♪½ LaToya Jackson—*You're Gonna Get Rocked* (Private I, 1988) ♪

▶▶ Boys II Men, New Edition, Jodeci

◀◀ The Temptations, Smokey Robinson, Frankie Lymon, James Brown, Jackie Wilson

see also: *Michael Jackson, Janet Jackson*

Allan Orski and Gary Graff

Janet Jackson

Born Janet Damita Jackson, May 16, 1966 in Gary, Ind.

Growing up the youngest daughter in the mega-successful Jackson clan, Janet Jackson stepped into the shadow of a monumental dynasty when she began performing with her brothers during the mid-70s. Indeed, it seemed at first that Janet's future lay in television, as she found minor success with roles in the sitcoms "Good Times" and "Diff'rent Strokes." But family patriarch Joe Jackson had other ideas, encouraging Janet to deliver her mostly-forgettable self-titled solo debut. A subsequent album produced by Time guitarist Jesse Johnson also stiffed, signaling what seemed the end of a vapid recording career. But then A&M executives got the idea to pair her with former Time members James "Jimmy Jam" Harris III and Terry Lewis, resulting in the singer first blockbuster success, *Control*. Backed by her producers' cutting edge dance grooves and a series of hyperkinetic videos choreographed by Paula Abdul, Janet became a major star in her own right. Taking the tone of her breakthrough record to heart, she jettisoned her father as manager and plowed into *Rhythm Nation 1814*, a further distillation of the percolating, Teflon dance formula that also tackled social issues. This record's success shot her into the pop culture stratosphere occupied by stars like Madonna and her brother, Michael—allowing the singer to negotiate a new, $60 million deal with Virgin Records. *janet.*, the first product of that deal, also did massive business, emphasizing the singer's smoldering sexuality while trafficking in the dance pop grooves of the day.

what to buy: No record in her limited catalog matches the impact of *Control*, (A&M, 1986, prod. Janet Jackson, James Harris III, Terry Lewis and Monte Moir) an album that virtually re-defined the world of dance-oriented R&B single-handedly. Fresh from work with R&B stalwarts The SOS Band, Harris and Lewis were ready to re-write the rules for contemporary soul; they just needed a good-looking, videogenic singer to help them do it. From the mechanized funk of the title track to the percolating, sultry grooves of "Nasty" and the sassy hit single "What Have You Done For Me Lately," the trio welds artsy, funky percussion grooves to slashing keyboard sounds and Jackson's breathy, insubstantial voice. The world of hi-tech funk would never be the same.

what to buy next: Jackson's sophomore record, *Rhythm Nation 1814* (A&M, 1989, prod. Janet Jackson, James Harris III, Terry Lewis and Jellybean Johnson) pushed the team's patented dance formula even further, nicking bits of an old Sly Stone tune for the title track's avalanche of percussive sounds. Forget about the clumsy lyrical references to ill-defined social problems such as homelessness and racism; what matters here are the grooves—from the direct, near-industrial flavor of the hit single "Miss You Much" to the rock-tinged "Black Cat" and frothy pop of "Escapade," every tune here will either make you want to hit the dance floor or the bedroom. And after all, isn't that what good dance jams are all about?

what to avoid: Jackson's second pre-Harris/Lewis solo record—*Dream Street* (A&M, 1984, prod. Jesse Johnson) WOOF!—reeks of formulaic pandering. Bereft of memorable cuts, it came before the days when a good MTV video could make anyone a star, so Jackson's talents as a videogenic dance diva couldn't even save the day.

the rest: *janet.* (Virgin, 1993) *Design of a Decade: 1986-1996* (A&M, 1996)

worth searching for: Jackson's potency as a performer can't really be judged until you see her in action—the complex choreography with a lone chair in the "Pleasure Principle" video; her army of military-style dance recruits in the "Rhythm Nation" clip; her sensuously curvy body moves in the film for "That's the Way Love Goes." That's why she's gathered video clips from every album onto separate anthologies—there are actually two for "Control"—and it's also why any fan worth their weight in 12-inch remix records will buy them.

Paula Abdul, Karyn White, Jody Watley

Michael Jackson, Prince, Madonna, Diana Ross

Eric Deggans

Jermaine Jackson

See: Jackson 5

Joe Jackson

Born Aug. 11, 1954 in Portsmouth, England

Touted with Elvis Costello and Graham Parker as the late 70s heirs to the angry young man throne, Jackson has proven far more eclectic and experimental (though not necessarily more talented) than his contemporaries, making his career a bumpy ride with minimal commercial success but tremendous artistic highs. He evolved from the successful power pop of his early albums and began his forays into jazz, big band swing, bossanova, reggae and ambient instrumental music. Jackson has never had trouble expressing his disdain for pop music marketing—nor his resentment over his own lack of commercial success—and though at times this has given his music a bile quotient that seems merely snide instead of passionate. Above all, Jackson has rarely been boring, which in this case is a compliment of the highest order.

what to buy: *Look Sharp* (A&M, 1979, prod. David Kershenbaum) presents hyper and bitter pop with a good beat. Jackson rails with intelligence and inspiration against numerous targets, scoring direct hits with the ugly-guy opus "Is She Really Going Out With Him?" and the vituperative white reggae of "Sunday Papers." *I'm the Man* (A&M, 1979, prod. David Kershenbaum) continues in the same vein, with a bit less focus but with outstanding songs—the propulsive title track, the biting "On Your Radio" and the pop perfection of "It's Different for Girls"—that more than compensate. *Night and Day* (A&M, 1982, prod. David Kershenbaum and Joe Jackson) is a gorgeous, minimalist excursion into jazz-tinged salsa and bossanova stylings, with the hits "Steppin' Out" and "Breaking

Us in Two." *Blaze of Glory* (A&M, 1989, prod. Joe Jackson and Ed Roynesdal) ♪♪♪♪ is a sharp autobiographical memoir whose individual songs hold their own outside that conceptual framework.

what to buy next: *Jumpin' Jive* (A&M, 1981, prod. Joe Jackson) ♪♪♪ is the first of Jackson's radical departures from the pop idiom, this time with a swingin' big band that hearkens back forty or fifty years. Atypically, Jackson seems to be having a great deal of fun.

what to avoid: *Night Music* (Virgin, 1994, prod. Joe Jackson and Ed Roynesdal) ♪ is pretentious and smug synthesizer music for the wine and cheese crowd. This is Jackson at his self-important worst.

the rest: *Beat Crazy* (A&M, 1980) ♪♪♪ *Body and Soul* ♪♪♪ *Big World* (A&M, 1986) ♪♪ *Will Power* (A&M, 1987) ♪ *Live...1980-1986* (A&M, 1988) ♪♪♪ *Laughter and Lust* (Virgin, 1991) ♪♪♪, *Greatest Hits* (A&M, 1996, prod. Various) ♪♪♪

worth searching for: The CD-5 for "Stranger Than Fiction" (Virgin, 1991, prod. Joe Jackson and Ed Roynesdal) ♪♪♪ includes a remake of "Different for Girls" that recasts the song as a duet' between Jackson and singer Joy Askew.

▶▶ Ben Folds Five

◀◀ Cole Porter, Louis Jordan, Bob Dylan

Allan Orski and Gary Graff

Michael Jackson

Born Michael Joseph Jackson, Aug. 29, 1958 in Gary Ind.

While others have worked years to win worldwide fame in the music business, for Jackson it seemed like a birthright. A founding member of the Jackson 5, he was bringing his powerful contralto vocals to bear as lead singer for the group at age four. By age 10 he was touring the country, opening for respected Motown acts such as Gladys Knight and the Pips and The Temptations. A year later, he was an international sensation as the Jackson 5 took over the charts with "I Want You Back," "ABC," "I'll be There" and more. Groomed by Motown mogul Berry Gordy, Jackson was encouraged to go solo in 1972, reportedly as an answer to Donny Osmond's rising popularity. His first solo record, like all of his early and mid-70s solo efforts, veered between schmaltzy ballads aimed at the pop audience and bits of lightweight fluff aimed at the teenyboppers. Though Jackson found some success during these times, his work always seemed guided by older, more domineering hands and overshadowed both by his brother Jermaine's ascent as a teen idol and by the continuing work of The Jacksons (as they were re-christened in 1976). It wasn't until 1979's *Off the Wall*—co-produced by Quincy Jones, who Michael had met while filming "The Wiz"—that the singer's own creative instincts began to emerge. Fusing an unerring pop sensibility with up-to-date R&B grooves and solid songs, that record set the stage for Michael's greatest triumph, 1982's *Thriller.* At more than 40 million copies sold, *Thriller* still stands as the most successful album ever; a phenomenon fed by Jackson's creative use of videos—from the dance showcase of the "Billie Jean" clip to the "West Side Story"-style moves of "Beat It" and the horror movie special effects extravaganza, "Thriller." But Jackson's tremendous success was dogged by speculation about his private life; his acquisition of most of the Beatles' song catalog spoke to his business acumen, but reports of severe plastic surgery, his alleged use of hyperbaric oxygen tents and his reclusive nature portrayed him as eccentric at best, disturbed at worst. His releases since *Thriller* have sold in the multi-millions, but they've been (wrongly) declared failures because they didn't match their predecessor's world-record sales. The shine really came off Jackson's star in 1993, when a 13-year-old boy accused the star of molesting him. The matter was settled out of court, but Jackson lost big: Pepsi-Cola canceled a decade-long endorsement deal; police raided his Los Angles home; and he admitted to having the skin-lightening disease vitiligo and to an addiction to painkillers. Interest in Jackson faded to the point where his two-CD set *HIStory: Past, Present and Future, Book 1*—which was attacked for anti-semitic lyrics in one song—fizzled in the amount of time it took to announce both his wedding and subsequent divorce from Elvis Presley's daughter, Lisa Marie.

what to buy: In this case, it's a no-brainer. The most artistically satisfying record of Jackson's career also happens to be his most successful, *Thriller.*" (Epic, 1982, prod. by Michael Jackson and Quincy Jones) ♪♪♪♪♪ From the sinewy funk of "Billie Jean" to the rock-tinged "Beat It" (with a guitar solo by Eddie Van Halen) and the epic title track, Jackson and Jones created a perfect fusion of commercial R&B and pop sensibilities—with the good luck to release it at a time when such naked ambition wasn't yet considered uncool.

what to buy next: As the record that first showed Jackson's promise as a solo artist, *Off The Wall* (Epic, 1979, prod. by Michael Jackson and Quincy Jones) ♪♪♪♪ lets the singer stretch beyond his teenybopper image. "Rock With You" is a slick, sensual piece of R&B-tinged pop, while "Wanna Be Starting Something" seems tailor-made for the kind of adult-oriented dance clubs that would never go near a Jackson 5 single. Best of all, by welding impressive, inventive production with solid songs, the pair showed hints of what a mature Jackson might be capable of.

what to avoid: In a bald-faced attempt to cash in on Jackson's explosive *Thriller* success, Motown assembled a bunch of lackluster unreleased tracks from 1975 on the album *One Day in Your Life*. (Motown, 1981, prod. Various) **WOOF!**

the rest: *Got to Be There* (Motown, 1972) *Ben* (Motown, 1972) *Music and Me* (Motown, 1973) *The Best of Michael Jackson* (Motown, 1975) *Anthology* (Motown, 1976) *Bad* (Epic, 1987) *Dangerous* (Epic, 1991) *HIStory: Past, Present and Future, Book I* (Epic, 1995)

worth searching for: *Remind: The Remix*, (FGP) a pleasingly bizarre bootleg disc featuring specially mixed medleys of Jackson's songs—some of which sound better in this context than they do on their original albums.

▶▶ Janet Jackson, Tevin Campbell, Mariah Carey

◀◀ Jackie Wilson, Diana Ross, Gene Kelly, James Brown

see also: *The Jackson 5*

Eric Deggans

The Jacksons

See: Jackson 5

Mick Jagger

Born July 26, 1943, Dartford, England

In the midst of his 80s estrangement from Keith Richards, the Rolling Stones frontman fought to stay current by launching a solo career. As the Stones floundered, Jagger enlisted a load of heavy hitters (Jeff Beck, Pete Townshend, Nile Rogers, Herbie Hancock) to reach more sophisticated heights. *She's the Boss* (Atlantic, 1985, prod. Mick Jagger, Bill Laswell and Nile Rogers) is all punchy sheen and studio gloss, replete with Jagger slinking away from his womanizing image with some sensitive, bloodless blather. *Primitive Cool* (Atlantic, 1987, prod. Keith Diamond and David A. Stewart) is more varied and less calculated, but clunkers such as "Let's Work" and "Shoot Off Your Mouth" are flailing, misbegotten attempts to top the charts. *Wandering Spirit* (Atlantic, 1993, prod. Rick Rubin and Mick Jagger) is by far his best effort. Sporting a much leaner sound, the bass nuances in Jagger's voice flourish throughout the rockers, country ballads and even the traditional "Handsome Molly." Finally committing to the music rather than keeping ahead of the young pups, Jagger captures his defiance of time passing in a resoundingly more honest album.

see also: *The Rolling Stones*

Allan Orski

The Jam /Paul Weller

Formed 1972 in Woking, Surrey, England. Disbanded 1982.

Paul Weller (born John William Weller), guitar, vocals; Bruce Foxton, bass, vocals; Rick Buckler, drums

Next to the Clash, the Jam was the most enduring group to emerge from England's punk scene. Unlike many of its contemporaries, the group wasn't merely a platform for the social ideals of the dispossessed: the songs were what mattered, ultimately, and Weller (the Jam's main songwriter) wrote terrific numbers drawn from such unlikely and disparate influences as the Small Faces and Curtis Mayfield. Not since the Beatles had a British rock group defined its times so well, and the Jam enjoyed huge success in its homeland. From the group's first release in 1977, its albums showed ever-increasing versatility and promise; thus it was a surprise when Weller broke up the Jam in 1982, at the peak of its popularity. Buckler went on to form Time (UK) with guitarist Danny Kustow (formerly of the Tom Robinson Band) and released a number of singles in the 1980s. Foxton's abortive solo career produced *Touch Sensitive* (out of print) for Arista Records in 1984, and in 1986 he founded the now-defunct band 100 Men. Weller continued to stretch his muse by forming soul-funk-jazz group the Style Council and in 1992 began a successful solo career in the U.K.

what to buy: *Compact Snap!* (Polydor, 1983, prod. Various) is an excellent sampler that gleans the gems from the band's many LPs, EPs and singles. Among the highlights are a spirited demo version of "That's Entertainment" as well as "The Bitterest Pill" and "Beat Surrender," both songs from out-of-print EPs. Inspired by the Beatles' "Revolver" album, *Sound Affects* (Polydor, 1980, prod. the Jam and Vic Coppersmith-Heaven) shows the Jam in a lively, adventurous mood. Known for writing songs with biting social commentary, Weller eases up here to deliver poppy, love-struck tunes such as "Start!," "Boy About Town" and "But I'm Different Now."

what to buy next: The few great songs missing from *Compact Snap!* can be found on *Extras* (Polydor, 1992, prod. Various), ♪♪♪♪ a compilation of EPs, obscure B-sides, and unreleased material. The inclusion of tracks from the group's 1982 *Beat Surrender* EP (notably "Shopping" and Curtis Mayfield's "Move on Up") make this a vital addition for fans. The Jam's final studio effort, *The Gift* (Polydor, 1982, prod. Peter Wilson and the Jam) ♪♪♪♪, is a worthy swan song that finds the group merging R&B funk ("Town Called Malice" and "Precious") with terrific soul rockers ("Happy Together").

what to avoid: A live retrospective recorded at various stages of the band's career, *Dig the New Breed!* (Polydor, 1982, prod. Vic Coppersmith-Heaven and Peter Wilson) ♪ is a neat idea that doesn't work. Never a strong singer while with the Jam, Weller seems to bark out his vocals, and while the songs are performed powerfully, they're better served by their studio counterparts. *Live Jam* (Polydor, 1993, prod. Vic Coppersmith-Heaven and Peter Wilson) ♪ is a set of entirely different material, suitable only for diehard fans.

the rest: *In the City* (Polydor, 1977) ♪♪ *This is the Modern World* (Polydor, 1977) ♪♪ *All Mod Cons* (Polydor, 1978) ♪♪♪ *Setting Sons* (Polydor, 1979) ♪♪♪ *Strange Fruit: The Peel Sessions* (Polydor, 1990) ♪♪♪ *Greatest Hits* (Polydor, 1992) ♪♪♪♪

worth searching for: *A-Bomb in Oxford Street* (Blue Moon Records, 1995) ♪♪♪ is a much-sought-after bootleg of the Jam's scorching 1977 concert at London's infamous punk haven, the 100 Club. Recorded by Polydor UK for distribution to a handful of British radio stations, the album shows the band in top form, blasting its way through 19 songs from *In the City* and *This is the Modern World* Sound quality is high overall. As an added bonus, the CD tacks on eight studio demos from the same period.

solo outings:

Paul Weller: *Paul Weller* (Go! Discs/London, 1992) ♪♪♪♪ *Wild Wood* (Go! Discs/London, 1992) ♪♪♪ *Stanley Road* (Go! Discs/London, 1995) ♪♪

▶▶ The Clash, Elvis Costello, Billy Bragg, Sugar, Oasis

◀◀ The Beatles, The Who, The Kinks, Small Faces, Curtis Mayfield, Motown, Booker T & the MGs, Traffic, Steve Winwood, Free

see also: *Style Council*

Christopher Scapelliti

James

Formed 1983, in Manchester, England

Tim Booth, vocals; Larry Gott, guitars; Jim Glennie, bass; Gavan Whelan, drums (1983-88); Saul Davies, violins, guitars, cowbells (1988-present); Andy Diagram, trumpet (1988-92); David Bayton Power, drums (1988-present); Mark Hunter, keyboards, accordion, (1988-present)

One of the purveyors of the Manchester music scene, James successfully marries new wave, pop, rock and folk. Although the group tends to go overboard with what seems like incessant jamming, James is an innovative band that improves with each release. Most of James' albums provide a handful of memorable songs, but Booth's schizophrenic vocals jump from one end of the scale to the other without warning, which gets old by the time the record ends.

what to buy: *James* (Fontana, 1990, prod. Tim Booth, Larry Gott, Jim Glennie, Nick Garside, Gil Norton and Flood) ♪♪♪♪ shows the band at its best. For this record, James added a trumpeter and violinist to fill out its folk-influenced arrangements. It also added a dramatic soundtrack to Booth's socially and politically conscious lyrics, resulting in the band's most consistently satisfying album, with a hit to boot in "Sit Down." Meanwhile, Booth's solo album, a collaboration with composer Angelo Badalamenti called *Booth and the Bad Angel,* (Mercury, 1996, prod. Angelo Badalementi) ♪♪♪♪ is the singer's most impressive work to date. The album, which features guest appearances by former London Suede guitarist Bernard Butler and Brian Eno, is filled with accessible pop gems.

what to buy next: On *Seven,* (Fontana, 1992, prod. Youth, Steve Chase and James) ♪♪♪ James puts aside its alterna-dance influences and concentrates more on the musical idiosyncrasies of its music. Cascading vocals over lush horns and guitars make "Born of Frustration" one of the best songs the group has ever recorded.

what to avoid: A few too many cooks and not enough first-tier songs make *Strip-Mine* (Sire, 1988, prod. Hugh Jones, Steve Power and Steve Lovell) ♪♪ a bit of a stumble on the way to better things.

the rest: *Stutter* (Sire, 1986) ♪♪♪ *Laid* (Mercury, 1993) ♪♪♪ *Wah Wah* (Mercury, 1994) ♪♪♪

worth searching for: The import live album *One Man Clapping* (Rough Trade, 1989) ♪♪♪ captures the soul-freeing spirit of James' live show and includes previously unreleased material.

▶▶ The Levellers, Altan

◀◀ Neil Young, Patti Smith, Nick Cave

Christina Fuoco

Elmore James

Born Elmore Brooks, January 27, 1918 in Richland, Miss. Died May 24, 1963.

In James' raunchy voice and buzzing electric slide-guitar riffs, you can hear the Chicago blues dissolving into early rock 'n' roll. Best known for "Dust My Broom," which he borrowed from Robert Johnson and souped up, "Shake Your Money Maker" and "Madison Blues," James' licks became as much part of blues and rock standard practice as Bo Diddley's beat and Chuck Berry's school stories. James, who like Muddy Waters was born in Mississippi and moved to Chicago to make his name, built his entire career on the electric boogie riff that pulses through his best hits. He also had the Broomdusters, the smokingest band this side of Waters' legendary combo during the early 50s. James influenced generations of bluesmen and rockers, from B.B. King and Jimmy Reed to the Rolling Stones, Jimi Hendrix, George Thorogood, Stevie Ray Vaughan and every band that picked up guitars and cranked up the amp volume.

what to buy: James recorded so many sessions with so many different record labels—he put out countless versions of "Dust My Broom," for example—that until 1992 it was tough to compile a definitive collection. *The Sky Is Crying: The History of Elmore James* (Rhino, 1993, comp. Robert Palmer and James Austin) solved that problem, collecting the best versions of "Dust My Broom," "The Sky Is Crying," "Shake Your Moneymaker" and the explosive "Rollin' and Tumblin'." Song completists will probably want *The Complete Elmore James Story,* (Capricorn/Warner Bros., 1992, prod. Various) which has many more songs but starts to drown you with slide after a while.

what to buy next: *The Complete Fire and Enjoy Sessions,* parts 1-4 (Collectables, 1989, prod. Bobby Robinson) are overwhelming but establish James as a crucial guitar pioneer whose wailing slide was as powerful as Howlin' Wolf, the Rolling Stones or anybody who has dabbled in the blues. *Street Talkin',* (Muse, 1973/1988, prod. Willie Dixon) also features bluesman Eddie Taylor.

what to avoid: Some of the early compilations—including *Anthology of the Blues: Legend of Elmore James,* (Kent, 1976, prod. Various) *Anthology of the Blues: Resurrection of Elmore James,* (Kent, 1976, prod. Various) *Red Hot Blues,* (Quicksilver, 1982, prod. Various) *The Classic Early Recordings, 1951-1956* (Atomic Beat, 1994, prod. Various)—are solid, but have been trumped by the superior Rhino and Capricorn collections.

the rest: *Blues Masters, Vol. 1* (Blues Horizon, 1966) *Tough* (Blues Horizon, 1970) *The Sky Is Crying* (Sphere Sound, 1971) *I Need You* (Sphere Sound, 1971)

worth searching for: "Whose Muddy Shoes" (Chess/MCA, 1969/1991, prod. Phile and Leonard Chess) contains songs by James and the obscure-but-great Chicago bluesman John Brim.

▶▶ The Rolling Stones, B.B. King, Jimi Hendrix, Stevie Ray Vaughan, George Thorogood, Allman Brothers, Johnny Winter

◀◀ Robert Johnson, Sonny Boy Williamson, Muddy Waters, Robert Nighthawk

Steve Knopper

Etta James

Born Jamesetta Hawkins, Jan. 25, 1938, in Los Angeles, Calif.

Is it heresy to suggest that it is Etta James—not schmaltzy Aretha—who rules as queen of soul these days? Not only does she come from the lineage, from her days as a 50s R&B teen queen through her time as a 60s soul shouter, but James has matured into one of the grand dames of R&B. She always sang with a great, intense passion, but the years only seem to have added depth of character and subtle, rich color and emotion. (And she did claim the title on her 1965 album *Queen of Soul*) Her first record, "Roll With Me Henry," was a simple answer to a popular Hank Ballard record that landed James on the road in 1954, where she has stayed since. She made one of the great gospel soul records, *Something's Got a Hold On Me* in 1961, and by 1967 could be found putting the fiery lead vocals on one of the landmarks of Southern soul, *Tell Mama.* By 1994, she could assay material some thought indelibly linked with Billie Holiday for *Mystery Lady*, an album that was at once a tribute to her earliest source of inspiration and a personal liberation. Through relentless determination and stubborn artistic strength, James has steered her own course through the rapid waters of the music's ever-changing path, relying always on instincts and bald-faced honesty.

what to buy: A double-disc retrospective of her 1960-74 tenure at Chicago's Chess Records, *The Essential Etta James,* (MCA/Chess, 1993) ♪♪♪♪ collects the backbone of her illustrious career.

what to buy next: *Mystery Lady* (Private, 1994, prod. J. Snyder) ♪♪♪♪♪ is a leap from her vernacular soul and blues outing into a realm of pure personal expression. With jazz pianist Cedar Walton at the bandstand, the resulting work defies easy categorization and gives James a platform to just be herself in a stunning triumph that finally earned her a Grammy Award.

what to avoid: Even her most paltry recent effort, *Stickin' To My Guns* (Island, 1990) ♪♪—a largely unsuccessful attempt to incorporate rap and hip-hop into a more traditional R&B context—is more of an aberration than an artistic misstep.

the rest: *The Right Time* (Elektra, 1992) ♪♪♪♪ *R&B Dynamite* (Flair, 1986) ♪♪♪♪ *The Second Time Around* (Chess, 1961) ♪♪♪♪ *Rocks the House* (Chess, 1964) ♪♪♪♪ *Tell Mama* (Chess, 1968) ♪♪♪♪ *Come a Little Closer* (Chess, 1974) ♪♪ *Deep In the Night* (Bullseye Blues, 1978) ♪♪♪ *Blues In the Night* (with Eddie (Cleanhead) Vinson) (Fantasy, 1986) ♪♪ *The Late Show* (with Eddie (Cleanhead) Vinson) (Fantasy, 1987) ♪♪ *Seven Year Itch* (Island, 1989) ♪♪♪ *How Strong Is a Woman: The Island Sessions* (Polydor, 1993) ♪♪♪ *These Foolish Things: The Classic Balladry of Etta James* (MCA, 1995) ♪♪♪ *Live In San Francisco* (On the Spot, 1994) ♪♪♪ *Time After Time* (Private, 1994) ♪♪

worth searching for: *Etta James Rocks the House,* (Cadet, 1963) ♪♪♪♪ an early album that more than lives up to its title.

▶▶ Tina Turner, Janis Joplin

◀◀ Billie Holiday, Hank Ballard

Joel Selvin

The James Gang

See: Joe Walsh

Rick James

Born James Johnson, Jr., Feb. 1, 1948 in Buffalo, N.Y.

After a decade of trying to make it—including a period in Toronto, Canada with roommate Neil Young in the Mynah Birds, which recorded unreleased material for Motown in 1968—James cracked through in 1977 when he formed the Stone City Band (featuring the Mary Jane Girls) and signed with Motown. With his "funk 'n' roll" sound patterned after Funkadelic, James traded in a raunchy rock that delighted in easy pre-AIDS era sex and drug use. By 1981, he was at the top of the charts with such naughty novelties as "Super Freak" and "Give It To Me Baby." He also produced 1983's *Cold Blooded,* a hit LP for his sexy Mary Jane Girls. James managed to keep his hand in things during the 80s, producing Eddie Murphy's hit "Party All the Time" in 1985. His influence was clear when M.C. Hammer grabbed James' "Super Freak" bass riff for his own smash, "U Can't Touch This." James, however, has been on ice since 1991, when drug addictions led to him being jailed on assault charges. He was due to be released in 1996.

what to buy: The super freaky, *Street Songs* (Motown, 1981, prod. Rick James) ♪♪♪♪♪ revels in the hedonism of the times with a self-satisfied smirk. In addition to the big hits, "Ghetto Life" and "Below the Funk" are top-flight songs that convey realistic ghetto scenes. James' debut, *Come Get It* (Motown, 1978, prod. Rick James) ♪♪♪♪ brought tracks such as "You and I" and "Mary Jane" that competed with Parliament-Funkadelic for the R&B limelight.

what to buy next: *The Flag* (Motown, 1986, prod. Rick James) ♪♪♪♪ doesn't have the fine-honed street sense of his earlier work, but the hard-driving funk grooves are intact.

what to avoid: *Throwin' Down* (Motown, 1982, prod. Rick James) ♪♪♪ seems lyrically uninspired next to "Street Songs" though the grooves are strong—if a bit redundant.

the rest: *Cold Blooded* (Motown, 1983) ♪♪♪ *Reflections* (Motown, 1984) ♪♪♪♪ *Bustin' Out! The Very Best of Rick James* (Motown, 1994) ♪♪♪♪ *Motown Legends: Give It To Me Baby—Cold Blooded* (ESX, 1994) ♪♪♪

worth searching for: *Bustin' Out of L7* (Motown, 1979, prod. Rick James) ♪♪♪♪ showed James on the way to *Street Songs* and had its own hits in "Bustin' Out" and "High On Your Love Suite."

solo outings:

Mary Jane Girls: *Only Four You* (Motown, 1985) ♪♪♪♪

▶▶ Prince, 2 Live Crew, Jodeci

◀◀ Parliament-Funkadelic, James Brown, Sly & the Family Stone

Lawrence Gabriel

Tommy James & the Shondells

Formed 1960 in Niles, Mich. Disbanded 1970.

Tommy James, vocals, guitar, keyboards; Eddie Gray, guitar, vocals; Ronnie Rosman, keyboards, vocals; Mike Vale, bass, vocals; Pete Lucia, drums, percussion, vocals

Of the groups dominating the bubblegum music genre during the late 60s, Tommy James and the Shondells was certainly the most sophisticated. Despite such featherweight entries as "Mirage" and "I Think We're Alone Now," the group turned out two of the most inventive pop music gems of the era: the tremolo-heavy "Crimson and Clover;" and a wispy, Philly soul-inflected bit of nonsense called "Crystal Blue Persuasion." The group began life in the garage-rock vein, with James' rough-edged vocals seared across the early R&B-flavored hits "Hanky Panky" (cut in 1963 but reissued as a No. 1 hit in 1966) and "Mony, Mony" (1967). Although both those singles made a significant stir in the U.S. and the U.K., the group abandoned R&B, first in favor of lightweight bubblegum hits such as "I Think We're Alone Now" and later to jump on the psychedelic bandwagon. Of this latter period, both "Crimson and Clover" and "Crystal Blue Persuasion" went into the top registers of the charts and displayed what was at the time an impressive use of sound effects and layered instruments and vocals. For all the group's teenybopper appeal, its music remains a delight to hear and has been covered heavily by a number of artists, including Billy Idol ("Mony, Mony"), Joan Jett ("Crimson and Clover"), Tiffany ("I Think We're Alone Now") and John Wesley Harding ("Crystal Blue Persuasion").

what to buy: *The Very Best of Tommy James and the Shondells* (Rhino, 1993, prod. Various) ♪♪♪♪ is a handy 10-track compilation of the group's best songs, including "Hanky Panky," "I Think We're Alone Now," "Mony, Mony," "Crimson And Clover" and "Crystal Blue Persuasion." True fans will have to have the 27-track *Anthology*, (Rhino, 1990, prod. Various) ♪♪♪♪ featuring all the hits and plenty more.

what to buy next: *Crimson & Clover/Cellophane Symphony* (Roulette/Rhino, 1969, prod. Tommy James) is a double-package reissue of the group's two 1969 albums that, like all Rhino releases, features completely remastered tracks. Among the gems are "Crimson & Clover" (the longer album version), "Crystal Blue Persuasion" and "Sweet Cherry Wine." A treasure chest of psychedelic bubblegum.

what to avoid: *Night in Big City* (Aura, 1995, prod. N/A) ♪ is an unambitious and completely unnecessary comeback album. In addition to the mediocre material, the band drums up reprised versions of "I Think We're Alone Now" and "Tighter, Tighter." If you hold your memories sacred, stick to the old hits.

the rest: *The Very Best of Tommy James and the Shondells* (Pair, 1990) ♪♪♪ *Hanky Panky/Mony Mony* (Sequel, 1994) ♪♪♪

worth searching for: What happened to Tommy James after 1970? Find out with *Discography: Deals & Demos '74-'92: The Complete Post-Roulette Compilation*, (Aura Records, 1993, prods. Various) ♪♪♪ a two-disc set that features James' complete solo recordings, including "Glory Glory," "Tighter, Tighter," and his 1981 Top 20 hit "Three Times in Love."

solo outings:

Tommy James: Tommy James Solo Years, 1970-1981 (Rhino, 1991, comp. Bill Inglot and Gary Peterson) ♪♪

⏩ The Grass Roots, the Monkees, the Troggs, Paul Revere & the Raiders, Strawberry Alarm Clock, 1910 Fruitgum Company, Tommy Roe, the Five Americans, XTC/the Dukes of Stratosphear

⏪ Elvis Presley, The Beatles, Motown, Jefferson Airplane

Christopher Scapelliti

Jan & Dean

Formed 1958 in Los Angeles, Calif.

Jan Berry, vocals, piano; Dean O. Torrence, vocals, guitar

The incredible California Saga of Jan & Dean began inconspicuously enough—under the showers at Emerson Junior High in Los Angeles, where Berry began leading his fellow footballers in after-game doo-wop sessions. By 1958, these sing-alongs had moved into Berry's garage where, with friends Torrence and Arnie Ginsburg (accompanied by drummer Sandy Nelson and future Beach Boy Bruce Johnston), songs were composed and painstakingly recorded. One of these, a ditty about a local stripper named "Jennie Lee," actually hit the Top 10 in 1958, and over the next several years Jan & Dean placed five songs on the charts before signing with Liberty Records in '61. The story would probably have ended there if Berry had not befriended Brian Wilson and composed with him the anthemic "Surf City" (Brian's first, and J&D's only, No. 1 hit). Shrewdly continuing to record Beach Boy outtakes and soundalikes, Jan & Dean enjoyed a string of hits throughout the mid-60s, each cleverly arranged and produced (by Berry) so as to withstand even the challenge of the British Invaders. But just as music began to change—and the duo seemed ready to pursue non-musical careers (Berry was in pre-med and Torrence was a graphic artist)—Berry, like the hero of his song "Dead Man's Curve," drove his Corvette under a parked truck at 65 m.p.h. and sustained head injuries so severe that they affect him to this day. It wasn't until more than a decade later, in the wake of a popular TV movie about the duo, that Jan & Dean began performing and even recording together again, their sense of self-humor amazingly intact and their timeless musical odes to sun, fun and surf still a powerful elixir.

what to buy: *Golden Hits* (One Way, 1995, prod. Various) ♪♪♪♪♪ squeezes the duo's three greatest hits collections onto two CDs, providing a comprehensive overview of the band's salad days.

what to buy next: *Teen Suite 1958-1962* (Varese Vintage, 1995, prod. Various) ♪♪♪♪ documents the pre-surf material so thoroughly it even includes a seven-minute session tape from one of their very first garage get-togethers. Until Phil Spector decides to unlock his vaults, this is the closest one can come to eavesdropping on the birth of West Coast rock. Side 4 of *Legendary Masters* (United Aritsts, 1971/One Way, 1996, prod. Various) ♪♪♪♪♪ includes a hilarious Zappa-meets-surf collage of vintage concert recordings.

the rest: *Surf City/Folk 'n' Roll* (One Way, 1996) ♪♪♪♪ *Drag City/Jan & Dean's Pop Symphony No. 1* (One Way, 1996) ♪♪♪♪ *Our Golden Summer Days*(Varese Vintage, 1996) ♪♪♪ *Our Golden Summer Nights* (Varese Vintage, 1996) ♪♪♪

worth searching for: *Jan & Dean Meet Batman* (Liberty, 1966, prod. Jan Berry) ♪♪♪♪ is the kind of musical tribute to the Caped Crusader that The Artist Formerly Known As Prince only *wishes* he could make.

▶▶ Flo & Eddie, Hall & Oates

◀◀ Dion & the Belmonts, Frankie Valli & the Four Seasons, the Lettermen, the Four Freshmen, Laurel & Hardy

Gary Pig Gold

Jane's Addiction

Formed 1986 in Los Angeles, Calif. Disbanded 1991.

Perry Farrell (born Perry Bernstein), vocals; Eric Avery, bass; Dave Navarro, guitars; Stephen Perkins, drums

Even though Jane's Addiction only had two proper albums, the Los Angeles art-rock band made its mark by blending heavy metal, glam and punk sensibilities with rhythmic funk strains—all under Lollapalooza co-founder Farrell's unique, high-pitched (some might say grating) warble. It was an enormously influential approach, and the band made people pay attention with its provocative album art—including a cover of *Ritual de lo Habitual*, whose images of full frontal nudity prompted some retailers to refuse to stock it, so a second cover was created that offers the text of the first amendment. *Jane's Addiction*, (Triple X, 1987, prod. Jane's Addiction) ♪♪ recorded live at the Roxy in Hollywood, introduced Farrell as a flamboyant lead singer, and resident eccentric who fancied wearing neon dreadlocks and dark eye makeup. That album drags, but *Nothing's Shocking* (Warner Bros., 1988 prod. Dave Jerden, Perry Farrell) ♪♪♪ is a better effort. The prize of the album, the rolling acoustic song "Jane Says," departs from the band's usual whomp with its acoustic guitar and chiming marimba. Heavier even than the debut, *Nothing's Shocking* has all the art-rock trimmings and Zeppelinesque guitar licks courtesy of Navarro. With *Ritual De Lo Habitual*, (Warner Bros., 1990, prod. Dave Jerden and Perry Farrell) ♪♪♪ Jane's Addiction met the mainstream halfway with more accessible melodies and rollicking tunes such as "Stop!" and "Been Caught Stealing." As on all the band's albums, Farrell's voice wears on the listener after a few songs, but *Ritual's* stronger songs make it a bit more tolerable. The band split at the end of summer 1991, after inaugurating the Lollapalooza series. Farrell formed Porno for Pyros, which also includes Perkins. Navarro and Avery joined drummer Michael Murphy in the band Deconstruction, whose lone album, *Reconstruction* (American, 1994 prod. Ron Champagne) ♪, is a grating experiment in sound, working with feedback and other dissonance. Navarro eventually wound up in the Red Hot Chili Peppers.

see also: *Porno for Pyros, Red Hot Chili Peppers*

Christina Fuoco

Japan /Rain Tree Crow/David Sylvian/Mick Karn/Polytown

Formed 1974 in London, England. Disbanded 1982. Re-formed as Rain Tree Crow, 1991. Disbanded 1992.

David Sylvian, vocals, guitar, keyboards; Steve Jansen, drums, percussion; Richard Barbieri, keyboards; Mick Karn, bass, saxophone

During four short years as a recording entity, Japan managed one of the most startling transformations in modern rock. Its 1979 debut came as part of the New Romantic movement, which was influenced by artists such as David Bowie and Roxy Music. Being a New Romantic basically boiled down to loud

Six Reasons Why You Need to Go to Memphis

The Complete Stax-Volt Singles 1959-1968
(Atlantic)

Hi Times: The Hi Records R&B Years
(Hi/The Right Stuff)

The Sun Records Story
(Rhino)

From Elvis in Memphis
Elvis Presley (RCA)

The Best of B.B. King, Volume 1
(Flair/Virgin)

The Rendezvous Barbeque (well, they do play records there....)

clothes and hair colors, melodramatic vocals and copious (and unoriginal) use of the synthesizer. By 1979, however, Japan had already moved beyond such superficial accoutrements and was concentrating on more sophisticated forms. Sparked by Sylvian's interest in Eastern song structure, the band experimented with micro-scales and polyrhythms. Utilizing sophisticated (for the time) synthesizer technology, Sylvian and Barbieri developed a shimmering, detuned keyboard sound. This, coupled with Sylvian's dramatic baritone, Karn's distinctive fretless bass and the unconventional drumming of Jansen (who is Sylvian's brother) gave Japan its sonic signature. As the band's music matured, so too did Sylvian's lyrics, which came to deal in dystopian imagery and fractal snapshots of modern culture. In 1982, however, just as the band reached its fertile peak, it disbanded. Its members pursued solo projects and occasionally worked together in various configurations. In 1991, they formed Rain Tree Crow, which stayed together just long enough to record one album.

what to buy: Released a year before the group disbanded, Japan's *Tin Drum* (Caroline, 1991, prod. Japan) bore the full fruit of its evolution from pop band to progressive art rock outfit. The material here is distinctive and ambiguously haunting, with Karn's melodic bass counterpointing Sylvian's vocals. Many of the songs, such as "Ghosts," achieve a dark, penetrating beauty, while more kinetic numbers such as "The Art of Parties" and "Still Life in Mobile Homes" examine the decadence of the late twentieth century culture.

what to buy next: *Gentlemen Take Polaroids* (Caroline, 1980, prod. John Punter) offers pleasures similar to those found on *Tin Drum* The material is slightly more upbeat, with Jansen delivering a number of propulsive performances—notably on the title cut and "Methods of Dance." There are also foreshadows of *Tin Drum's* more contemplative moments in material such as "My New Career" and "Taking Islands in Africa."

what to avoid: *Adolescent Sex* (Hansa, 1978/Caroline, 1994, prod. Ray Singer) is interesting only as a historical artifact. On its debut album, Japan is little more than a haircut band along the lines of Duran Duran or (gulp!) Flock of Seagulls. And this record is indistinguishable from the piles of synthpop belched up in the late 1970s.

the rest: Japan: *Obscure Alternatives* (Hansa, 1978/Caroline, 1991) *Quiet Life* (Hansa, 1979/Caroline, 1991) *Oil on Canvas* (Virgin, 1983/Caroline, 1991) Rain Tree Crow: *Rain Tree Crow* (Virgin, 1991)

worth searching for: There are a number of Japan recordings—as well as the individual members' solo albums—that are only available as imports. The best of these is the retrospective, *Exorcising Ghosts* (Virgin, 1984) Also of note is the live *Souvenir from Japan* (Hansa, 1989)

solo outings:

Mick Karn: Titles (Caroline, 1982) *Dreams of Reason Produce Monsters* (Caroline, 1987) (with Dali's Car) *The Judgment Is the Mirror* (Beggars Banquet, 1984) (with Polytown) *Polytown* (CMP, 1994) in 1994.

Depeche Mode, Bill Nelson, Midge Ure and Ultravox

Roxy Music, David Bowie, Can, Brian Eno, Bebop Deluxe, Lou Reed and the Velvet Underground

see also: *David Sylvian*

Dave Galens

Jason and the Scorchers

Formed 1981 in Nashville, Tenn. Disbanded 1990. Re-formed 1995.

Jason Ringenberg, vocals, harmonica and guitar; Warner Hodges, guitar and vocals; Jeff Johnson, bass; Perry Baggs, drums and vocals; Andy York, guitar (1989); Ken Fox, bass (1989)

The members of Jason and the Scorchers, along with the

Mekons and other punkish 80s bands, decided they understood Hank Williams Sr. better than the Eagles did. So they recreated country-rock in their own image. The Scorchers' name was not an exaggeration: led by Ringenberg's frenzied energy and herky-jerky stage movements, the band cranked up the guitars and turned Williams' music back into the honky-tonking classics they are. Ringenberg, as legend goes, grew up on his family's hog farm in Sheffield, Ill., then moved to Nashville to become a star. He hooked up with a few hillbillies who shared his love for Bob Dylan and the Ramones, and they set about crashing punk and country into each other. After opening for Dylan on his 1990 tour, the Scorchers were fed up with each other and the lack of commercial attention, so they broke up. They reformed, still-blazing, with a 1995 reunion album.

what to buy: *Essential Jason and the Scorchers, Vol. 1: Are You Ready for the Country* (EMI, 1992, prod. Jeff Daniel and Adam Block) ♪♪♪♪ collects two early albums, *Fervor* and *Lost & Found*, along with a bunch of rarities and live tracks. The reunion album, *A-Blazing Grace* (Mammoth, 1995, prod. Jason and the Scorchers) ♪♪♪½, is built around an incredible version of John Denver's formerly corny "Take Me Home, Country Roads" and George Jones' "Why Baby Why."

what to buy next: The debut EP, *Reckless Country Soul* (Praxis, 1992/Mammoth, 1996, prod. Jack Emerson, Jason and the Scorchers and Jim Dickinson) ♪♪♪, gets repetitive, but its barnstorming country-punk breathes life into Williams' "I'm So Lonesome (I Could Cry)," plus the consummate Scorchers classic, "Help! There's a Fire."

what to avoid: *Thunder and Fire* (A&M, 1989) ♪♪ is the sound of all the thunder and fire slipping away, just before the band broke up.

the rest: *Still Standing* (EMI, 1986) ♪♪½

worth searching for: *Lost & Found (EMI, 1985, prod. Terry Manning)* ♪♪♪ *and Fervor* (EMI EP, 1983, prod. Jim Dickinson, Jack Emerson, Chuck Ainlay and Terry Manning) ♪♪♪ are good but hard to find. Besides, *Essential* is a better deal.

solo outings:

Jason Ringenberg: One Foot in the Honky Tonk (Liberty, 1992) ♪♪

▶▶ Social Distortion, Uncle Tupelo, Golden Smog, Bottle Rockets

◀◀ Hank Williams Sr., Johnny Cash, Ramones, Mekons, Gram Parsons

Steve Knopper

The Jayhawks

Formed 1985 in Minneapolis, Minn.

Gary Louris, guitar, vocals; Mark Olson, guitar, vocals (1985-1995); Marc Perlman, bass; Thad Spencer, drums (1985-1990); Ken Callahan, drums (1990-present); Karen Grotberg, keyboards; Tim O'Regan

Hailed as the second coming of the Flying Burrito Brothers, the Jayhawks actually had the goods to hold up to the comparison. Not that the notion was completely off the mark: Mark Olson played Gram Parsons to Gary Louris' Chris Hillman, and the band played a musically sparse, emotionally packed music that tapped into the spirit of country music without ever reflecting Nashville's infatuation with the mainstream. Olson, who married singer-songwriter Victoria Williams, left the band in November 1995; the remaining line-up (Louris, Perlman, Grotberg and O'Regan) planned to change the band's name and continue recording.

what to buy: On *Tomorrow the Green Grass* (American, 1995, prod. George Drakoulias) ♪♪♪♪ the Jayhawks effectively start shaking off the Flying Burrito Brother comparisons, replacing it with—of all things—70s power-pop. With songs like "Blue" and a cover of Grand Funk's "Bad Time," the Jayhawks produce their best hooks without forsaking their country soul.

what to buy next: *Hollywood Town Hall* (American, 1993, prod. George Drakoulias) ♪♪♪♪ established the Jayhawks as the premiere country-rock (for lack of a better term) band of its time. The album made best-of lists in the "Village Voice," "Entertainment Weekly" and just about everywhere else.

the rest: *The Jayhawks* (Bunkhouse, 1986) ♪♪♪ *Blue Earth* (Twin/Tone, 1989) ♪♪♪½

worth searching for: The import CD-5 for "Waiting For the Sun" (American, 1993) ♪♪♪½ features four live songs, including a cover of Tim Hardin's "Reason to Believe."

▶▶ Golden Smog, Wilco, Son Volt, Victoria Williams, Joe Henry

◀◀ Gram Parsons, Neil Young

Brian Mansfield

Jefferson Airplane

Formed 1965 in San Francisco, Calif. Disbanded 1972.

Marty Balin, vocals (1965-70); Grace Slick, keyboards, vocals; Paul Kantner, guitar, vocals; Jorma Kaukonen, guitar, vocals; Jack Casady, bass; Skip Spence, drums (1965-66); Spencer Dryden, drums (1966-70); Joey Covington, drums (1970-71); Papa John Creach, violin (1971-72); John Barbata, drums (1971-72)

Although the band's reputation has diminished over the years (see: Jefferson Starship), the Jefferson Airplane ushered in the Summer Of Love with two hits that neatly encapsulated the feeling of the time, "Somebody To Love" and "White Rabbit." An iracsible, contentious group of strong-willed personalities, the Airplane led the San Francisco sound out of the provinces and around the world. Combining the pop sensibilities of founder and vocalist Marty Balin with the folky flavor of Paul Kantner, the peerless delta blues-based guitaristics of Jorma Kaukonen and the free-wheeling bass of Jack Casady, the band forged a unique signature style best revealed in live performance. Grace Slick may have been the most obvious component of the group, having provided lead vocals to the band's two best-known songs, but the strength of the Airplane was the ensemble collaboration, a tentative creative partnership responsible for some stunning high points in the band's estimable body of work.

what to buy: The pre-Grace Slick debut, *Jefferson Airplane Takes Off* (RCA Victor, 1966, prod. Matthew Katz and Tommy Oliver) 🦴🦴🦴🦴 has been freshly dusted off for the digital era, complete with one track censored off the initial issue for the inclusion of the word "trips." It's an album few noticed outside the San Francisco Bay Area that nevertheless retains some of the special flavor of the original band. *Surrealistic Pillow* (RCA Victor, 1967, prod. Rick Jarrard) 🦴🦴🦴🦴🦴 has been released in a gold disc edition that crystallizes one of the era's great albums in spectacular sonics. *Bless Its Pointed Little Head* (RCA Victor, 1969, prod. Al Schmitt) 🦴🦴🦴🦴 documents the powerful sweep of the band's epic live performances, including sterling samples of the band's often sprawling improvisations.

what to buy next: The three-disc boxed set, *Jefferson Airplane Loves You* (RCA Victor, 1992, prod. Various) 🦴🦴, contains some spectacular previously unreleased 1967 live recordings, a few rewarding out takes and early efforts and seemingly hours and hours of less interesting material from the band's latter stages. *Early Flight* (RCA Victor, 1974, prod. Jefferson Airplane) 🦴🦴🦴 contains a selection of rather more intriguing out takes and singles not released on other albums.

what to avoid: *Thirty Seconds Over Winterland* (RCA Victor, 1973) **WOOF!** captures the group in its final moments on one of the worst live albums ever released by a major act.

the rest: *After Bathing At Baxter's* (RCA Victor, 1967) 🦴🦴 *Crown Of Creation* (RCA Victor, 198) 🦴🦴🦴 *Volunteers*(RCA Victor, 1969) 🦴🦴🦴 *The Worst Of the Jefferson Airplane* (RCA Victor, 1970) 🦴🦴🦴 *Bark*(Grunt, 1971) 🦴 *Long John Silver* (Grunt, 1972) **WOOF!***2400 Fulton Street* (RCA, 1987) 🦴🦴½ *White Rabbit and Other Hits* (RCA Victor 1990) 🦴

worth searching for: The oddball David Crosby solo album, *If I Could Only Remember My Name,* (Atlantic, 1971, prod. David Crosby) 🦴🦴 is an eccentric collaboration between the Airplane, Grateful Dead and Santana, with cameos by Neil Young, Graham Nash and Joni Mitchell.

solo outings:

Paul Kantner: *Blows Against the Empire,* (RCA Victor, 1970) 🦴🦴

Paul Kantner and Grace Slick: *Sunfighter* (Grunt, 1971) **WOOF!***Baron Von Tollbooth and the Chrome Nun* (with David Freiberg) (Grunt, 1973) **WOOF!**

Grace Slick: *Manhole* (Grunt, 1974) 🦴*Dreams* (RCA, 1980) 🦴 *Welcome to the Wrecking Ball* (RCA, 1981) **WOOF!***Software* (RCA, 1984) 🦴½

Marty Balin: *Bodacious DF* (RCA, 1973) 🦴🦴 *Rock Justice* (EMI, 1980) 🦴🦴 *Balin* (EMI, 1981) 🦴🦴½ *Lucky* (EMI, 1983) 🦴 *Balince: A Collection* (Rhino, 1990) 🦴🦴½ *Better Generation* (GWE, 1991) 🦴🦴

KBC Band (Kantner, Balin, Casady): *KBC Band* (Arista, 1986) 🦴

▶▶ Jefferson Starship (ugh)

◀◀ The Weavers, Otis Redding, Eric Dolphy, Bob Dylan

see also: *Hot Tuna, Jefferson Starship*

Joel Selvin

Jefferson Starship

Formed 1974 in San Francisco, Calif.

Paul Kantner, guitar, vocals (1974-84, 1992-present); Grace Slick, vocals, keyboards (1974-78, 1982-88); Marty Balin, vocals (1975-78, 1994-present), David Freiberg, bass, vocals (1974-84); Craig Chaquico, guitar; John Barbata, drums (1974-78); Papa John Creach (1974-75, 1992-94); Pete Sears, bass, keyboards (1974-86); Aynsley Dunbar, drums (1978-83); Mickey Thomas, vocals (1978-1990); Donny Baldwin, drums (1983-89); Brett Bloomfield, bass (1990-91); Mark Morgan, keyboards (1990-91); Jack Casady, bass (1992-present); Tim

Gorman, keyboards (1992-present); Prairie Prince, drums (1992-present); Darby Gould, vocals (1992-present)

Nobody could have guessed that a wild, untamed band of resolute crazies like the Jefferson Airplane would have degenerated into an MTV coiffure band , churning out useless pre-fab radio fodder like "Find Your Way Back," "Jane" or "We Built This City." Outside of vocalist Marty Balin's three-album stint with this hapless hulk, which included his fairly sublime "Miracles," the Starship left little worth remembering, although the long run on the radio left the once glowing reputation of the mothership tarnished by association.

what to buy: If you must, *Gold* (RCA Victor, 1979, prod. Various) ♪♪ covers the early part of the Starship era, before the band succumbed to Hollywood session players and hot-rod producers like Ron Nevison or Narada Michael Walden. That latter period is duly chronicled on *Greatest Hits (Ten Years And Change 1979-1991)* (RCA Victor, 1991, prod. Various) ♪, for what it's worth.

what to avoid: Everything?

worth searching for: Grace Slick's penchant for acerbic wisecracks is well documented on a 1982 radio promotion RCA Victor album.

solo outings:

Paul Kantner: Planet Earth Rock and Roll Orchestra (RCA Victor, 1983) ♪♪♪

Mickey Thomas: As Long as You Love Me (MCA, 1971) ♪ *Alive Alone* (Elektra, 1981) ♪

Craig Chaquico: Acosutic Highway (Higher Octave, 1993) ♪♪ Acoustic Planet (Higher Octave, 1994) ♪♪ *A Thousand Pictures* (Higher Octave, 1996) ♪

▶▶ Jefferson Starship: The Next Generation

◀◀ Jefferson Airplane

Joel Selvin

Garland Jeffreys

Born mid-1940s in Brooklyn, N.Y.

Though critically acclaimed, singer-songwriter Jeffreys never seemed to catch on with the masses with the exception of the single "Wild In the Streets" in 1977. By and large, Jeffreys' low key rock and thematic tour of the life's downside didn't work in the disco and funk-crazed 70s. He first appeared on the New York music scene during the mid-60s, where he palled around with Lou Reed and Eric Burdon. He later assembled the band Grinder's Switch ,which recorded an eponymous LP in 1969. Jeffreys went solo in 1970 and recorded several albums through the early 80s, picking up a reggae influence along the way. Most of his albums are obscure or out of print, though the few songs that got notice are on *Matador and More* (A&M, 1992, prod. David Spinozza) ♪♪♪♪ The single "Matador," with its gospel reggae feel, was a hit across Europe. His best album, *Escape Artist* (Epic, 1981, prod. Garland Jeffreys and Bob Clearmountain) ♪♪♪♪ rides on several tales of twisted love and includes one of Jeffreys' rare cover efforts with "96 Tears."

Lawrence Gabriel

Jellyfish

Formed 1989, San Francisco, Calif. Disbanded 1994.

Andy Sturmer: vocals, drums, guitars, keyboards; Roger Manning, vocals, keyboards; Jason Falkner, guitar, bass (1989-91); Chris Manning, bass (1989-91); Tim Smith: bass (1991-94); Jon Brion, guitar (1991-94)

Put some Badfinger, Supertramp, Queen, Cheap Trick, and, of course, some Beatles into a blender and you get a tasty little pop treat called Jellyfish. This band burst onto the scene with a trippy 70s logo, retro clothing and a hit video for its first single, "The King is Half Undressed." But make no mistake—Jellyfish is more than cute visuals and a nod and a wink to some rock icons. The first release, *Bellybutton* (Charisma, 1990, prod. Albhy Galuten and Jack Joseph Puig) ♪♪♪♪♪ is loaded with strong songs that make reference to the past but also sound wholly fresh and original. Not so on *Spilt Milk,* (Charisma, 1993, prod. Jack Joseph Puig) ♪♪♪ which comes across slightly forced, bombastic and brittle, with far more obvious references to forebears, particularly Supertramp and Queen. Sadly, Jellyfish dissolved after touring in support of its sophomore release: Manning formed the band Imperial Drag; Brion and Falkners released an album as the Grays; and Sturmer is planning a solo career.

Michael Isabella

The Jesus and Mary Chain

Formed 1984 in East Kilbride, Scotland

William Reid, guitar, vocals; Jim Reid, guitar, vocals; Douglas Hart, bass (1984-89); Ben Lurie, bass, guitar (1994-present); Murray Dalglish, drums (1984); Bobby Gillespie, drums (1984-85); John

Moore, drums (1985-89); Richard Thomas, drums (1989-95); Steve Monti, drums (1995-present)

Years before grunge, the Jesus and Mary Chain got maximum mileage out of fuzzy, distorted guitars. They certainly weren't the first to explore guitar feedback and white noise: rock ensembles from the Jimi Hendrix Experience to Sonic Youth had perfected that. But the beauty behind the J&M Chain is its ability to balance the racket and morose lyrics against some of the prettiest melodies this side of the Beach Boys. The band—led by the Reid Brothers —nailed its approach from the get-go, though it didn't evolve much after that. But armed with such beautiful noise, they really didn't need to.

what to buy: The Chain found the perfect link on its very first album, *Psychocandy*, (Reprise, 1985, prod. The Jesus & Mary Chain) a masterful amalgam of pop, punk and sheer white noise, including the hypnotic hit "Just Like Honey."

what to buy next: *Darklands* (Warner Bros., 1987, prod. William Reid and Bill Price) was less of a downer than the band's debut LP, but almost as memorable thanks to gems like "April Skies." *Stoned and Dethroned*, (American, 1994, prod. Jim and William Reid) is their folkies effort to date and includes "Sometimes Always," their semi-hit duet with Hope Sandoval of Mazzy Star.

what to avoid: *Automatic* (Warner Bros., 1989, prod. Jim and William Reid) has some good songs but is marred by its stiff arrangements, which find the Reid brothers accompanied mostly by dry, electronic drum patterns.

the rest: *Barbed Wire Kisses* (Warner Bros., 1988) *Honey's Dead* (Def American, 1992) *Hate Rock 'N' Roll* (American, 1995)

worth searching for: The group switched labels with *10 Smash Hits/1985-1992*, (Def American, 1992, prod. Various) an enjoyable promotion-only retrospective

▶▶ My Bloody Valentine, Ride, Teenage Fanclub

◀◀ Velvet Underground, Jimi Hendrix, Beach Boys, Phil Spector

Thor Christensen

Jesus Jones

Formed 1988, London, England

Mike Edwards, vocals, guitars; Jerry De Borg, guitars; Barry D (born Iain Baker), keyboards; Al Jaworski, bass; Gen (born Simon Matthews), drums

Like fellow Brits EMF, Jesus Jones exposed strongly melodic, hook-filled electronic dance music to a commercial audience. Its second release, *Doubt* (SBK, 1991, prod. Mike Edwards), is its the most successful—commercial and artistically—with the spritely hits "Right Here, Right Now," a celebration of the end of the Cold War that was briefly Bill Clinton's 1992 campaign theme before he switched to Fleetwood Mac's "Don't Stop"). "International Bright Young Thing," and "Real, Real, Real" kept the group on the charts, but its third album bombed and Jesus Jones has kept a low profile since—though a new album is said to be in the works.

the rest: *Liquidizer* (SBK, 1989) *Perverse* (SBK, 1993)

Christina Fuoco

The Jesus Lizard

Formed 1989 in Chicago, Ill.

Duane Denison, guitar; Mac McNeilly, drums; David Wm. Sims, bass; David Yow, vocals

The Jesus Lizard blends the talents of three of the most accomplished instrumentalists in indie rock with the maniacal vocal spew of Yow, the clown prince of 90s concert showmen. The group is a legendary live act, but its merger of animal fury and angular intellect translates less persuasively on record, primarily because of Yow's unconventional non-singing style and his frequently dour, if not disgusting, subject matter. But for those with a taste for uncompromising hard rock, the quartet's albums for Touch & Go, all recorded with Chicago noise-guitar architect Steve Albini, are about as nasty as it gets.

what to buy: *Liar* (Touch & Go, 1992, rec. by Steve Albini) is where the band's songwriting catches up with the hide-and-shriek riffing of Sims and Denison. *Shot* (Capitol, 1996, prod. G.G. Garth Richardson), captures the group's extraordinarily refined yet powerful interplay with unsurpassed clarity.

what to buy next: *Down* (Touch & Go, 1994, rec. by Steve Albini) shows the band's instrumentalists flexing their chops without resorting to bombast, and introduces subtle keyboards.

what to avoid: *Pure* (Touch & Go EP, 1989, rec. by Steve Albini) was recorded before the addition of McNeilly, and the group misses his unerring sense of swing.

the rest: *Head* (Touch & Go, 1990) *Goat* (Touch & Go, 1991) *Lash* (Touch & Go EP, 1993) *Show* (Collison Arts)

worth searching for: The group's limited edition 1993 split single with Nirvana on the Touch & Go label. The Jesus Lizard track, the catchy-in-spite-of-itself "Puss," is from *Liar*, while the Nirvana cut, "Oh, The Guilt," is a previously unreleased heavy metal screed recorded in a Seattle laundry room with producer Barrett Jones.

◀◀ Birthday Party, Led Zeppelin, the Yow-Sims band Scratch Acid

Greg Kot

Jethro Tull /Ian Anderson

Formed 1967 in Blackpool, England

Ian Anderson (born August 10, 1947, Edinburgh, Scotland), vocals, flute, guitar, keyboards; Martin Barre, guitar (1968-present); Clive Bunker, drums (1967-71); Glen Cornick, bass (1967-71); Barriemore Barlow, drums (1971-76); John Evan, keyboards (1969-79); Jeffrey Hammond, bass (1971-76); David Palmer, keyboards (1977-80); John Glascock, bass, (1976-78, died 1979); Eddie Jobson, keyboards, violin (1980-81); Dave Pegg, bass (1979-91); Mark Craney, drums (1980-81); Peter-John Vettese, keyboards (1982-87, 1988-91); Jerry Conway, drums (1981-84); Doane Perry, drums (1987-91); Martin Allcock, keyboards (1988-91); Matt Pegg, bass (1991-present); Dave Mattacks, drums (1991-present)

Jethro Tull began as a psychedelic-blues quartet in the late 1960s and gained some attention thanks to singer-flautist Anderson's stage antics. Anderson's breathy histrionics on the flute owed much to jazz legend Rahsaan Roland Kirk, and on the band's debut he and original guitarist Abrahams mined a heavily jazz and blues-inflected brand of rock. After Abrahams moved on to greater obscurity with Blodwyn Pig, Anderson began taking the band in a new direction, aided by the heavier guitar stylings of Barre. Soon Tull was melding riff-rock, English folk and the new "progressive" style that hit pay dirt during the early 70s.

Their first three albums sold increasingly well, but their fourth, *Aqualung,* made them superstars. They followed this with back-to-back album-length songs, but moved toward AOR during the mid-70s, achieving radio hits with "Bungle in the Jungle" and "Too Old To Rock 'n Roll, Too Young to Die." The late 70s saw them pursuing the Elizabethan strain they'd hinted at earlier, after which time they tried on such diverse styles as space-age prog, mellow folk-rock and retooled metal. In 1988 Tull won a Grammy—to the astonishment of nearly everyone, and the dismay of Metallica and AC/DC fans— for Best Hard Rock/Heavy Metal Performance. The group remain a major international concert draw, thanks to a well-honed combination of instrumental flash and theatricality—and a willingness to play the old hits without complaint. The "Stonehenge" debacle in the rock film parody "This Is Spinal Tap" is a direct spoof of Tull's most grandiose moments.

Anderson's solo excursions, *Walk Into Light* and *Divinities*, have permitted him to explore his less bombastic side as a songwriter and his more pretentious side as a composer, respectively.

what to buy: *Aqualung* (Chrysalis, 1971, prod. Terry Ellis and Ian Anderson) remains Tull's crowning achievement, filled with passionate rock and quirky, melodic folk.

what to buy next: *Stand Up* (Chrysalis, 1968, prod. Terry Ellis and Ian Anderson) is less pompous—and less ambitious; it does, however, contain several potent rockers and the group's trademark rendition of Bach's "Bouree." *Living in the Past* (Chrysalis, 1972, prod. Various) is a generous sampler of the band's early work and contains some bona fide gems. The album-length song *Thick as a Brick* (Chrysalis, 1972, prod. Terry Ellis and Ian Anderson) isn't for everyone, but remains one of the more inventive pop creations of the period. *Benefit* (Chrysalis, 1970, prod. Ian Anderson) is a leaner, more rock-oriented collection that boasts the hit "Teacher."

what to avoid: *The Broadsword and the Beast* (Chrysalis, 1982, prod. Paul Samwell-Smith) WOOF! shows the band sliding into self-parody; while most of their subsequent work has been mediocre, the campy medievalism and paunchy riffage on display here are woeful.

the rest: *This Was* (Chrysalis, 1968) *A Passion Play* (Chrysalis, 1973) *WarChild* (Chrysalis, 1974) *Minstrel in the Gallery* (Chrysalis, 1975) *Too Old to Rock 'N' Roll, Too Young to Die* (Chrysalis, 1976) *M.U.: The Best of Jethro Tull* (Chrysalis, 1976) *Repeat: The Best of Jethro Tull, Volume 2* (Chrysalis, 1977) *Songs from the Wood* (Chrysalis, 1977) *Heavy Horses* (Chrysalis, 1978) *Bursting Out* (Chrysalis, 1978) *Stormwatch* (Chrysalis, 1979) *A* (Chrysalis, 1980) *Under Wraps* (Chrysalis, 1984) *Original Masters* (Chrysalis, 1985) *Classic Case* (RCA, 1985) *Crest of a Knave* (Chrysalis, 1987) *20 Years of Jethro*

Tull (Chrysalis, 1988) *Rock Island* (Chrysalis, 1989) *Catfish Rising* (Chrysalis, 1991) *A Little Light Music* (Chrysalis, 1992) *25th Anniversary Box Set* (Chrysalis, 1993) *Best of Jethro Tull: The Anniversary Collection* (Chrysalis, 1993) *Roots to Branches* (EMI, 1995)

solo outings:

Ian Anderson: Walk Into Light (Chrysalis, 1983) *Divinities; 12 Dances With God* (EMI, 1995)

worth searching for: "Another Christmas Song" (Chrysalis, 1989, prod. Ian Anderson), a promotional EP that features two versions of the single as well as homey, dressing room recordings of favorites such as "Mother Goose" and "Locomotive Breath."

Bloodwyn Pig, Heart, Spinal Tap

Beatles, Fairport Convention, Bach, Rahsaan Roland Kirk, Sonny Boy Williamson, The Move

Simon Glickman

Joan Jett

Born September 22, 1960 in Philadelphia, Pa.

Ever since her teenage apprenticeship in the all-girl rock band the Runaways, Joan Jett has provided a model for women in rock 'n' roll. Front and center, clad in leather and backed by the all-male Blackhearts, she thrashes away at her electric guitar, sweat and mascara streaming down her face like a river of redemption. Although she writes much of her material, Jett's strongest statements have been her cover songs: with the exception of Lesley Gore's feminist anthem "You Don't Own Me," Jett has doggedly tackled tunes associated strictly with male performers. Even the riot-grrrl acts that she inspired wouldn't have the nerve to cover the Rolling Stones' "Star Star," Jonathan Richman's "Roadrunner," Iggy Pop's "I Wanna Be Your Dog" and ZZ Top's "Tush," let alone pull them off. Although her last chart hit came in 1988 with the Bon Jovi-like "I Hate Myself For Loving You," Jett has survived passing trends. Her resilience was rewarded on 1994's *Pure and Simple*, which featured collaborations with members of Bikini Kill, Babes in Toyland and L7, bands that are now barreling through the doors that Jett kicked open.

what to buy: Opening with the bouncy, Ramones-like blitzkrieg of the title track, *Bad Reputation* (Blackheart, 1980, prod. Kenny Laguna and Ritchie Cordell) found Jett shrugging off her "jailbait-rock" past and asserting her independence via such punk-pop anthems as "You Don't Know What You've Got" and torrid versions of Gary Glitter's "Do You Wanna Touch Me," "Shout" and "Wooly Bully." *I Love Rock 'n' Roll* (Blackheart, 1981, prod. Kenny Laguna and Ritchie Cordell) contains the chart-topping title track and "Crimson and Clover, but "Victim of Circumstance"—a fiery kiss-off to her critics—is the linchpin. Despite a crunching cover of Sly Stone's "Everyday People," *Album* (Blackheart, 1983, prod. Kenny Laguna and Ritchie Cordell) paled commercially to its predecessor. But rock 'n' roll has produced few commentaries on coattail-riding leeches as pointed as "Fake Friends" and few covers as brave as her take on the Stones' "Star Star."

what to buy next: A 22-track collection of B-sides, bonus tracks and other rarities, *Flashback* (Blackheart, 1994, prod. Kenny Laguna, Ritchie Cordell and others) rescues such Jett staples as her version of Bruce Springsteen's "Light of Day," the 1910 Fruitgum Co.'s "Indian Giver," David Bowie's "Rebel Rebel" and a 1979 pre-Blackhearts recording of "I Love Rock 'n' Roll" featuring Steve Jones and Paul Cook of the Sex Pistols.

what to avoid: The lukewarm *Notorious* (Epic, 1991, prod. Kenny Laguna and Phil Ramone) pairs her with songwriting ringers Desmond Child and Diane Warren. Only "Backlash," a collaboration with Paul Westerberg, raises any semblence of a ruckus.

the rest: *Glorious Results of a Misspent Youth* (Blackheart, 1984) *Good Music* (Epic, 1986) *Up Your Alley* (Epic, 1988) *The Hit List* (Epic, 1990) *Pure and Simple* (Warner Bros., 1994) *Evil Stig* (with members of the Gits) (Warner Bros., 1995)

worth searching for: *The Best of the Runaways* (Mercury, 1987, prod. Earle Manke, Kent J. Smyth and Kim Fowley) is the strongest showcase of Jett's teen era, with original versions of "Cherry Bomb," "Wait for Me" and "I Love Playin' With Fire" that would resurface on later solo albums.

L7, Babes in Toyland, Bikini Kill

David Bowie, Rolling Stones, 60s bubblegum, Gary Glitter

see also: *The Runaways*

David Okamoto

Jewel

Born Jewel Kilcher, May 23, 1974 in Homer, Alaska

Produced by Neil Young collaborator Ben Keith and recorded

partly live and acoustic at a San Diego coffeehouse, Jewel's *Pieces of You* (Atlantic, 1994, prod. Ben Keith) introduced a sunny, sensitive folkie with a surfer-chick attitude and a poet's soul. But she immediately started bucking against the singer-songwriter pigeonhole: compared to the introspective sound of the album, Jewel's live shows were funny, funky and loose, liberally dosed with cheerful monologues, yodeling exercises and such sexually charged, unreleased rockers as "Race Car Driver" and the punk-pop "God's Gift to Women" (which can be found on a 1994 Atlantic promo-only EP titled *Save the Linoleum*—it's worth whatever you have to pay for it). Relentless touring as opening act for everyone from Peter Murphy to Bob Dylan, a role as Dorothy in a TBS-produced update of "The Wizard of Oz" and the hypnotic rhythms of her twice-released single, "Who Will Save Your Soul," helped goose her debut to gold status in 1996.

David Okamoto

Jo Jo Gunne

See: Spirit

Jodeci

Formed 1988 in Charlotte, N.C.

Cedric "K-Ci" Hailey, vocals; Joel "JoJo" Hailey, vocals; Donald "DeVante Swing" DeGrate, vocals, instruments; Dalvin "Mr. Dalvin" DeGrate, vocals

Frequently posited as ominous Rolling Stones figures next to Boyz II Men's clean cut Beatles, Jodeci plays out soul music's archetypal conflict between the sacred and the secular. All four members honed their vocal chops in church before coming together as Jodeci—to the severe disapproval of their deeply religious parents (who reportedly refuse to listen to any non-gospel music, even that of their own children). Their parents would probably approve even less if they actually heard Jodeci's highly explicit new-jack seduction ballads. Of Jodeci's three albums, the debut *Forever My Lady* (Uptown/MCA, 1991, prod. DeVante Swing and Al B. Sure!) is the most palatable because it finds room for some actual tender moments, such as the title track and "Stay." That album's success certainly didn't make Jodeci anymore generous toward the fairer sex, given the carnally demanding tone of the follow-up *Diary of a Mad Band.* (Uptown/MCA, 1993, prod. DeVante Swing and Mr. Dalvin) But that was just a warmup for *The Show, the After Party, the Hotel,* (Uptown/MCA, 1995, Prod. DeVante and Mr. Dalvin) an ill-tempered concept album about groupies. Jodeci also appears on the live various artists collection *Uptown MTV Unplugged,* (Uptown/MCA, 1993, prod. Andre Harrell) which includes tracks from Mary J. Blige, Heavy D & the Boyz, Christopher Williams and Father MC. Still, Jodeci's development should be fascinating to watch; DeVante has turned into a noted producer (for Al Green, among others), while Hailey is a frontman of volcanic charisma—who nevertheless seems, to borrow an Al Green metaphor, just a pot of boiling grits away from winding up back in the church choir.

David Menconi

Billy Joel

Born May 9, 1949 in the Bronx, N.Y.

Joel has described himself as "a melody freak," and it's that love of a hummable tune that has made him one of pop music's most enduring, and endearing, stars. From his early days playing in Long Island rock bands to his stretch as a story-telling piano man to a logical merger of both roles, Joel has consistently penned memorable melodies. He studied classical piano before rocking through the 60s with the Hassles and Attila, then worked briefly as a solo pianist in California, when he scored his first hit in 1973 with the ballad "Piano Man." Joel enjoyed moderate success with the next several albums but when he teamed up with noted producer Phil Ramone, the result was his 1977 pop-rock masterpiece *The Stranger,* Joel's breakthrough album highlighted by two exquisite odes to the fairer sex—"She's Always a Woman" and "Just the Way You Are." Joel's artistic growth continued as he stretched his lyrical sights to include topical issues ranging from unemployment to the plight of Vietnam veterans. Behind the scenes, Joel has filed several multi-million-dollar lawsuits against his former management over songwriting revenue and other income he was cheated out of, and he's has been through two failed marriages, including one to model Christie Brinkley. But whenever he has been knocked down, personally or professionally, the feisty former amateur boxer always manages to bounce back; his latest album, 1993's *River of Dreams,* was the first of his career to debut at No. 1 on the Billboard chart.

what to buy: With such a long record of chart success, the two-disc *Greatest Hits Volume I & II* (Columbia, 1985, prod. Phil Ramone) covers the highlights from 1973-85 in fine fashion, with 25 of Joel's most memorable songs. *River of Dreams* (Columbia, 1993, prod. Dan Kortchmar) matches soul-baring lyrics to masterful melodies ranging from minor-key blues of "Shades of Grey" to the exotic rhythms of the title track to Beatlesque rock and metaphorical angst of "Great Wall of China." There's more to *The Stranger* (Columbia, 1977, prod. Phil Ramone) than its four hit singles (the suite "Scenes From an Italian Restaurant," for one), making it a Joel classic.

what to buy next: *The Nylon Curtain* (Columbia, 1982, prod. Phil Ramone) is one of Joel's most ambitious and satisfying efforts, combining lyrical depth with radio-friendly tunes such as "Allentown" and "Goodnight Saigon." The rhythmic snare of "We Didn't Start the Fire" and the confessional bravado of "Shameless," covered later by Garth Brooks, highlight *Storm Front* (Columbia, 1989, prod. Billy Joel and Mick Jones) *An Innocent Man* (Columbia, 1983, prod. Phil Ramone) captures Joel reveling in the start of his relationship with Brinkley, singing feel-good anthems such as "Tell Her About It" and "Uptown Girl."

what to avoid: Joel sounds pretty green on his first album, *Cold Spring Harbor,* (Columbia, 1972, prod. Artie Ripp) **WOOF!** which also suffers from recording problems (his voice was mistakenly sped up). *Kohuept (In Concert)* (Columbia, 1987, prod. Jim Boyer and Brian Ruggles) was recorded live during a tour of the Soviet Union but was released against Joel's objections. They should have listened to him.

the rest: *Piano Man* (Columbia, 1973) *Streetlife Serenade* (Columbia, 1974) *Turnstiles* (Columbia, 1976) *52nd Street* (Columbia, 1978) *Glass Houses* (Columbia, 1980) *Songs in the Attic* (Columbia, 1981) *The Bridge* (Columbia, 1986)

worth searching for: *Live at the Bottom Line,* (Mistral, 1993) one of many bootlegs of Joel's live radio show on June 10, 1976—a show that was nearly as crucial to his career as Bruce Springsteen's radio broadcast from the same venue was a year earlier.

▶▶ Amy Grant, Garth Brooks, Barry Manilow, Richard Marx

◀◀ The Beatles, the Rolling Stones, Ray Charles, Bob Dylan, the Four Seasons, Dion & the Belmonts, George & Ira Gershwin, Elton John

David Yonke

David Johansen

Born January 9, 1950 in Staten Island, N.Y.

Known to most listeners as martini-swigging, hip-swiveling loungemeister Buster Poindexter, David Johansen began his career as the flamboyant, Mick Jagger-influenced frontman for the New York Dolls. Late guitarist Johnny Thunders is frequently heralded as the heroin-addicted hero of the short-lived glam-rock band, but Johansen was clearly its hungry heart: Never shy about his commercial aspirations, his subsequent solo career spawned one bona fide rock 'n' roll classic—his staggering 1978 self-titled debut—before he began flirting with disco and reggae on *In Style* and album-rock credibility on *Here Comes the Night.* He toured as Pat Benatar's opening act and became an early fixture on MTV with a cheesy "performance" video of his popular Animals medley before reinventing himself as Poindexter, the pompadour-wearing pride of Bogalusa, La. who accomplished with "Hot Hot Hot" what Johansen could never do: a Top 40 hit hit hit. The last laugh may be his, but the loss is ours.

what to buy: *David Johansen* (Sony/Razor and Tie, 1978, prod. Richard Robinson and David Johansen) combines frantic Dolls leftovers like "Girls" and "Funky But Chic" with surprisingly soulful ballads and a five-minute tour de force called "Frenchette." The Razor and Tie reissue adds the B-side "The Rope" as a bonus track. Recorded at New York's Bottom Line, *The David Johansen Group Live* (Epic/Legacy, 1978, prod. Johansen) was originally released as a radio promo but its legendary status among fans prompted Epic to reissue it on CD in 1993 with nine bonus tracks. Scorching covers of the Foundations' "Build Me Up Buttercup," Wilson Pickett's "I Found a Love" and Bonnie Tyler's "It's a Heartache" combine with a fistful of Dolls favorites to make this one of the fiercest live documents since Warren Zevon's "Stand in the Fire."

what to buy next: If you must sample Johansen's Poindexter repertoire, stick with the self-titled 1987 debut *Buster Poindexter* (RCA, 1987, prod. Hank Medress), which mines such cool R&B obscurities as the Jive Bombers' "Bad Boy," Freddie Scott's "Are You Lonely For Me Baby" and Wynonie Harris' "Good Morning Judge."

what to avoid: *Sweet Revenge* (Passport, 1984, prod. Joe Delia and Johansen), **WOOF!** a last-ditch stab at synth-pop that went directly to cutout bins.

the rest: As David Johansen: *In Style* (Sony/Razor and Tie, 1979) *Here Comes the Night* (Sony/Razor and Tie, 1981) *Live It Up* (Sony/Razor and Tie, 1982) *From Pumps to Pompadours: The David Johansen Story* (Rhino, 1995) As Buster Poindexter: *Buster Goes Berserk* (RCA, 1989) **WOOF!** *Buster's Happy Hour* (Forward/Rhino, 1994)

worth searching for: The 45 rpm release of *Funky But Chic,*

1978, Blue Sky, prod. Richard Robinson and David Johansen which adds female backing vocals to give the song a sassy Stones-like feel.

The modern lounge movement

The Four Tops, the Rolling Stones, Louis Prima

David Okamoto

Elton John

Born Reginald Kenneth Dwight, March 25, 1947, Pinner (London), England

After establishing himself as a gifted singer-songwriter and pianist during the early 70s, John attained superstar status by the middle of that decade with a non-stop string of hits and top-selling albums. With his mature pop songcraft, campy glam sensibility and funky virtuosity on the keyboard, John also served as an influence that can be heard all over the musical map, from hard rock uber-rockers Guns N' Roses to underground pop groups like Ben Folds Five. During the 80s, he more or less left the rock elements of his early work to reposition himself as a staple of the Adult Contemporary world, mostly through impeccably commercial though often syrupy ballads. By the mid-90s he was composing hits for family films (Disney's "The Lion King") and winning Grammys and Oscars for it. In 1994 he was inducted into the Rock and Roll Hall of Fame.

John began studying piano when he was four, and by 12 had won a scholarship to the Royal Academy of Music. During his teens, he joined a variety of R&B-influenced groups before auditioning for the record label Liberty, where he was paired via mail with lyricist Bernie Taupin. The two only met after collaborating on 20 songs, but their partnership—despite an interruption during the mid-1970s—would span several decades. John's early work showed the influence of master tunesmiths such as George and Ira Gershwin and The Beatles, but it also echoed the sound of Leon Russell and other soul and pop artists. By 1973's *Goodbye Yellow Brick Road* he exhibited greater ambition, both thematically and musically, and metamorphosed from self-effacing piano man to protean stadium rocker, sporting outrageous costumes and glitzy spectacles—both on his face and on stage. His role as the Pinball Wizard in Ken Russell's 1975 film of The Who's rock opera *Tommy* was the apotheosis of this phase. Over the years, John has transformed himself, cleaning up his substance addictions and coming to terms with his homesexuality. He's no longer the phenomenon he was during the 70s, but he's still one of the world's biggest pop stars. (Note: Most of the albums from the first six years of John's career have been reissued on Island/Rocket, many with bonus tracks.)

what to buy: The true marvel of *Goodbye Yellow Brick Road* (Uni, 1973, prod. Gus Dudgeon) is that despite a plethora of hits (the title track, "Saturday Night's Alright for Fighting," "Candle in the Wind"), it still function as an ambitious and coherent double-length album. *Greatest Hits Vol. 1* (Uni, 1974, prod. Gus Dudgeon) is an essential collection of his early hits.

what to buy next: *Tumbleweed Connection* (Uni, 1971; prod. Gus Dudgeon) is a superb early collection in which John explores blues-rock, soul and exquisite pop balladry. *Madman Across the Water* (Uni, 1971, prod. Gus Dudgeon) and *Honky Chateau* (Uni, 1972, prod. Gus Dudgeon) are also ambitious, powerful sets, while *Greatest Hits Vol. II* (MCA, 1977) affirms why John ruled the radio during the 70s. *11-17-70* (MCA, 1971; prod. Gus Dudgeon) is a scrappy live album that demonstrates his estimable piano chops and a boasts superlative renditions of "Take Me to the Pilot" and "Burn Down the Mission."

what to avoid: *The Complete Thom Bell Sessions* (MCA EP, 1989, prod. Thom Bell), the six songs from a wisely aborted experiment in R&B-pop with Philadelphia International producer Bell.

the rest: *Empty Sky* (DJM, 1969/MCA, 1975) *Elton John* (Uni, 1970) *Friends* (Paramount, 1971) *Don't Shoot Me I'm Only the Piano Player* (Uni, 1973) *Caribou*, (Uni, 1974) *Captain Fantastic and the Brown Dirt Cowboy* (Uni, 1975) *Rock of the Westies* (Uni, 1975) *Blue Moves* (Rocket/MCA, 1976) *Here & There* (MCA, 1976) (MCA, 1976/Island-Rocket, 1996) *A Single Man* (MCA, 1978) *Victim of Love* (MCA, 1979) *21 at 33* (MCA, 1980) *The Fox* (Geffen, 1981) *Jump Up!* (Geffen, 1982) *Too Low for Zero* (Geffen, 1983) *Breaking Hearts* (Geffen, 1984) *Ice on Fire* (Geffen, 1985) *Leather Jackets* (Geffen, 1986) *Greatest Hits, Vol. 3* (Geffen, 1986) *Live in Australia* (MCA, 1987) *Reg Strikes Back* (MCA, 1988) *Sleeping with the Past* (MCA, 1989) *To Be Continued...* (MCA, 1990) *The One* (MCA, 1992) *Greatest Hits 1975-86* (MCA, 1992) *Rare Masters* (Polydor, 1982) *Duets* (MCA, 1993) *Made in England* (Rocket/Island, 1995) *The Lion King* (Disney, 1995) *Love Songs* (Rocket, 1996)

worth searching for: *Reg Dwight's Piano Goes Pop* (RPM, 1994) is an oddball import title of pop and R&B covers John recorded for a budget label in England before starting his own career.

▶▶ Phil Collins, Guns N' Roses, George Michael, Jellyfish, Suddenly Tammy!, Ben Folds Five

◀◀ Fats Waller, Duke Ellington, Beatles, Motown, Stax, Rolling Stones, Lee Dorsey, Leon Russell

Simon Glickman

Little Willie John

Born William J. Woods, Nov. 15, 1937, in Cullendale, Ark. Died in May 26, 1968, in Walla Walla, Wash.

Little Willie John stood tall in the R&B world of the 50s. His intensity brought his vocal performances to the edge of hysteria. John was a constant presence on the R&B charts for six years beginning with his 1955 King Records debut, "All Around the World." John suffused his signature song, "Fever," with vivid eroticism. He sounded desolate beyond description moaning, "I Need Your Love So Bad." Whatever he sang, John put the full weight of his feelings behind it. Offstage he was a wild, untamed character who came to a sorry end, dying of a heart attack in Washington State Prison, where he was serving a 20-year sentence for manslaughter after being convicted of stabbing a man to death in a nightclub argument. Though he's not well-known these days, Little Willie John inspired and influenced a generation of black musicians whose names became household words. The owner of Harlem's famed Apollo Theater, who ought to know, believes John was the best male vocalist he ever heard. After years of his catalog being impossible to find, John finally received the long overdue treatment he deserves with *Fever: The Best Of Little Willie John* (Rhino, 1993, prod. H. Glover) ♪♪♪♪♪, a 20-song collection that details his glory years at King Records. Two of his original albums have also been reissued on CD—*Mister Little Willie John* (King, 1958, prod. H. Glover) ♪♪♪ and *Sure Things.* (King, 1961, prod. H. Glover) ♪♪♪

Joel Selvin

Eric Johnson

Born Aug. 17, 1954, in Austin, Texas

Like the Beatles, Jimi Hendrix's name is one of the most overused references in rock music. Many guitarists have been touted as "Hendrixian;" in reality, very few players have the talent and vision to merit comparison to Hendrix. Johnson, just like his Austin contemporary Stevie Ray Vaughn, is one of those players. What earns Johnson this distinction is not that he sounds or plays like Hendrix (although he can), but that he approaches the guitar with the same reverence, the same attention to detail and song structure. His playing crosses many styles, from country to blues to jazz to fiery rock, yet it always fits perfectly within his material. Like the great Danny Gatton, he seamlessly incorporates myriad references without descending to ostentation. In fact, Johnson's skills with melody and tone create guitar solos that are often more attractive for their melodic beauty and perfect context than for their breathtaking technical mastery. A notorious perfectionist, Johnson is known to work and re-work his albums until they meet his high standards. This time-consuming approach has yielded a remarkably small catalog for an artist who has been recording since the mid-70s. It has also delivered some of the most stunning guitar playing of the last two decades.

what to buy: *Ah Via Musicom* (Capitol, 1990, prod. Eric Johnson) ♪♪♪♪♪—which Johnson recorded three times before releasing—is the best-realized example of Johnson's musical vision, a recording that unites his virtuostic ability with tightly arranged compositions such as "Cliffs of Dover" and "Steve's Boogie." Smoothly shifting between a broad palette of guitar colors, Johnson creates a dynamic panorama of sound that conveys deep emotion and a unifying theme of music as a life force.

what to buy next: *Tones* (Capitol, 1986, prod. Eric Johnson) ♪♪♪♪ is the album that told the world what Austin had known for years: that Johnson is one masterful guitarist. Though less ambitious in scope than *Ah Via Musicom, Tones* displays Johnson's facility with Chet Atkins-like country picking, James Brown funk and shimmering psychedelic rock.

what to avoid: Nearly six years in the making, Johnson's third album, *Venus Isle,* (Capitol, 1996, prod. Eric Johnson) ♪♪ is an unruly mess—dense, overarranged and clearly hindered by his perfectionism.

worth searching for: Johnson's initial album, *Seven Worlds,* is not available through a label, but the album has been bootlegged fairly extensively. Those interested in his early years may want to seek it out.

▶▶ Vinnie Moore, Joe Satriani, Steve Vai, Ian Moore, Eric Gale, Steve Morse, Stevie Ray Vaughn, Shawn Lane

◀◀ Jimi Hendrix, Johnny Winter, Billy Gibbons (ZZ Top), Yardbirds, Cream, Eric Clapton, Freddie King, Elmore James, Jeff Beck, Nokie Edwards, Merle Travis, Danny Gatton, Chet Atkins, the Beatles, the Rolling Stones, Dixie Dregs

David Galens

Holly Johnson

See: Frankie Goes to Hollywood

Jesse Johnson

See: The Time

Johnnie Johnson

Born July 8, 1924 in Fairmont, W.Va.

Turnabout, as they say, is fair play, and it is sweet irony to note that the career of rock 'n' roll piano legend Johnson is flourishing these days, and that he is receiving the recognition he so richly deserves, while his former employer, Chuck Berry, can't get arrested (figuratively speaking, that is). For if Berry is the father of rock 'n' roll—or, more accurately, its deadbeat dad—then Johnson should be accorded credit as its stepfather at the very least. Berry may have been the crucible in which the blues and country gave birth to a new form which was further shaped by his wit and poetic sense, but it was Johnson who led his band and who contributed, uncredited, the music for some of the songs that are the very cornerstone of rock. Gracious to a fault, Johnson is willing to let bygones be bygones and let his music speak for itself. During the summer of 1996, former Grateful Dead guitarist Bob Weir tapped Johnson to be part of his band, Ratdog, on the summer's Furthur Festival.

what to buy: *Johnnie B. Bad* (Elektra Nonesuch American Explorer Series, 1991, prod. Terry Adams and Keith Richards) ♪♪♪♪ is Johnson's best album overall, thanks in part to an all-star cast that includes Keith Richards, Eric Clapton and members of NRBQ. "Tanqueray" and "Stepped in What!?" are Johnson's first vocal performances ever, and while far from spectacular, they capture perfectly his gentle, humorous, and self-effacing personality.

what to buy next: *Johnnie Be Back* (Musicmasters, 1995, prod. Jimmy Vivino) ♪♪♪ is another all-star affair, with Phoebe Snow, Buddy Guy, Al Kooper, John Sebastian and Max Weinberg all lending a hand. There's still plenty of room for Johnson to shine, though. *Rockin' Eighty-Eights* (Modern Blues, 1991, prod. Daniel Jacoubovitch) ♪♪♪ teams Johnson with two other St. Louis piano greats, Clayton Love, who played with Ike Turner during the 50s, and Jimmy Vaughn, who played with Albert King, Little Milton Campbell and Ike Turner, among others. The album is an interesting compendium of midwestern postwar blues styles. Of special note is Johnson's smoking take on "Frances," an instrumental track named for his wife.

What Album Changed Your Life?

"(Bob Dylan's) <u>Highway 61 Revisited</u> It's the greatest record ever made, that's why. I thought everybody knew that, that it's just common knowledge."

John Mellencamp

the rest: *Blue Hand Johnnie* (Pulsar, 1988, prod. Oliver Sain, Sam Valenti) ♪♪♪ *That'll Work* (with the Kentucky Headhunters) (Elektra Nonesuch American Explorer Series, 1993, prod. The Kentucky Headhunters) ♪♪♪

▶▶ Ian Stewart (Rolling Stones), Ian McLagan (Faces), Elton John

◀◀ Earl "Fatha" Hines, Count Basie, Bud Powell

Daniel Durchholz

Mike Johnson

Born Aug. 27, 1965

Johnson's slurred vocal style will elicit comparisons to his Dinosaur Jr. bandmate J Mascis, but his voice is lower and beefier, similar to Mark Eitzel's of American Music Club and exploring the same resigned emotional territory. Before Dinosaur Jr., Johnson was in the legendary Eugene, Ore., punk band Snakepit with Billy Karin (Bikini Kill), Al Larsen (Some Velvet Sidewalk), Joe Preston (Earth, Melvins) and Robert Christie (Oswald Five-O). Johnson has also worked as co-producer of both solo albums by Screaming Trees singer Mark Lanegan. *Where Am I?* (Up/Sub Pop, 1994, prod. Mike Johnson) ♪♪♪ teams Johnson with Screaming Trees drummer Barrett Martin (on bass, cello and piano as well as percussion) for a rootsy, sometimes almost unplugged collection that covers Townes Van Zandt, Lee Hazelwood and Gene Clark—although the song "Atrophy" is a blazing rocker. Johnson and Martin (who adds vibes to his instrumental duties)—with Mascis on drums—expand their sonic range even further on *Year of Mondays,* (TAG/Atlantic, 1996, prod. John Agnello and Mike Johnson) ♪♪♪ with sharper sound.

see also: *Dinosaur Jr.*

Steve Holtje

Daniel Johnston

Born 1961 in Sacramento, Calif.

Like Roky Erickson and Beach Boy Brian Wilson, Johnston is a hugely talented rock 'n' roller (and Austin, Texas, cult legend) whose troubled mind takes him farther beyond the cutting edge than most of us would like to go. He sings like a little kid—all wide-eyed, high-pitched and awestruck—then contradicts the innocence with either weird and biting sarcasm or a determined, fragile intensity. His songs are usually skeleton arrangements, based on a standard blues-rock riff or a bouncy electronic keyboard, and he makes fun of television cartoons ("Casper"), the Beatles (a clunky-but-great piano version of "I Saw Her Standing There"), Elvis Presley (a version of "Heartbreak Hotel") and Bruce Springsteen ("Funeral Home," a morbid rewrite of "Cadillac Ranch"). Johnston began his career recording lo-fi tapes on a home boombox and distributing them to friends. His work has been wildly uneven, but his moments of brilliance—when we're lucky, they encompass an entire album—vindicate his 16-year recording career. He also shares with Mick Jagger and Alex Chilton the ability to shout "yeah!" in that undefinable purely rocking way.

what to buy: *Yip/Jump Music* (Homestead, 1989, prod. Daniel Johnston) is a 1983 recording that contains "Speeding Motorcycle," which, like the best punk rock, creates the ultimate driving song and simultaneously undermines it. Though *Hi, How Are You,* (Homestead, 1988, prod. Daniel Johnston) another 1983 session, can be unsettling with its nervous spoken introductions, weird noises and sloppy carnival keyboards, it's incredibly powerful when it hits on "Hey Joe" and the truly desperate "Desperate Man Blues."

what to buy next: *Fun* (Atlantic, 1994, prod. Paul Leary) is Johnston's major-label debut, and it's weird to comprehend—the singer's simplistic pen-and-ink drawings are on the label next to Atlantic's logo and bar code. The best song is the throbbing rocker "Love Wheel." Recorded with the Austin band Texas Instruments, *Continued Story* (Homestead, 1992, prod. Joe Johnson) is particularly paranoid—nobody will ever record the Beatles' "I Saw Her Standing There" like this.

what to avoid: More than anything else, Johnston's music needs a good editor. His early tapes —*Live at SXSW* (Stress, 1990, prod. Daniel Johnston) and both *The Lost Recordings Vol. 1* and *The Lost Recordings Vol. 2* (Stress, 1983, prod. Daniel Johnston) —are just Johnston noodling around, not saying much of anything.

the rest: *Songs of Pain* (Stress, 1980) *More Songs of Pain* (Stress, 1981) *The What of Whom* (Stress, 1982) *Don't Be Scared* (Stress, 1982) *Retired Boxer* (Stress, 1984) *Respect* (Stress, 1985) *Jad Fair and Daniel Johnston* (50 Skadillion Watts, 1989) *1990* (Shimmydisc, 1990) *Artistic Vice* (Shimmydisc, 1991)

worth searching for: Though Yo La Tengo, Sonic Youth, Pearl Jam (on pirate radio), the Dead Milkmen and many other good bands have taken a crack at Johnston's ouevre, the only truly successful tribute came from ex-Glass Eye leader Kathy McCarty, whose *Dead Dog's Eyeball* (Bar/None, 1994, prod. Brian Beattie and Kathy. McCarty) draws out his songs' wonderful weirdness and raunchy rock.

Kathy McCarty, Yo La Tengo, Nirvana, Sonic Youth, Pearl Jam, Dead Milkmen

Beatles, Roky Erickson and 13th Floor Elevators, Beach Boys, Bob Dylan, Neil Young, Jerry Lee Lewis

Steve Knopper

Tom Johnston

See: The Doobie Brothers

Grace Jones

Born May 19, 1952, in Spanishtown, Jamaica

Haughty fashion model turned haughty chanteuse, Jones started as a disco diva, then moved into rock without abandoning her dance roots. She has enjoyed success on the R&B charts, though she has never managed to cross over to the pop Top 40 despite some visually stunning videos on MTV. Her tough, ultravixen image (she slapped around a British TV host in 1980 during a live program!) was vastly magnified by the arty cover photos and videos of Jean-Paul Goude, whom she married for a while. Jones has also done some film acting, most notably in "Conan the Destroyer" (Arnold Schwarzenegger reportedly complained she hit too hard in fight scenes), the James Bond flick "A View to a Kill" and the Eddie Murphy vehicle "Boomerang." Jones' music career started as more image than substance. Purveying a persona that appealed to the gay disco audience, she got over despite a distinct lack of singing ability, and in spite of producer Tom Moulton's by-the-numbers disco productions on her first three albums. *Fame's* mellow-disco version of "Autumn Leaves," partly in the original French (and with the tackiest rhythm track imaginable, like a setting on a cheap organ bought at the Wurlitzer shop in the local mall), demonstrates just how bad Jones' vocals could be. She has endured through a couple of hiatuses and a cocaine problem, though her musical output has slowed singificantly. Her only output during the 90s has been a cover of the Sheep on Drugs song *Sex Drive.*

what to buy: *Inside Story* (Manhattan, 1986, prod. Nile Rodgers and Grace Jones) is Jones' most consistent, coherent album as well as her most personal. Her lyrics draw on her experiences and work in an unpretentious, often wistful way, with complementary musical arrangements that are often stripped down for the more casual numbers.

what to buy next: *Island Life* (Island, 1986, prod. Various) is far from an adequate survey of the first two phases of her career, missing many crucial tracks but still offering a taste of Jones' particular *elan.*

what to avoid: *Muse* (Island, 1979, prod. Tom Moulton) features a lyrically overwrought, musically faceless sidelong concept/morality play medley—"Sinning/Suffer/Repentance (Forgive Me)/Saved"—with a pseudo-gospel section is unintentionally hilarious. Some tracks strain Jones way past whatever tiny degree of legitimate vocal technique she possessed.

the rest: *Portfolio* (Island, 1977) *Fame* (Island, 1978) *Warm Leatherette* (Island, 1980) *Nightclubbing* (Island, 1981) *Living My Life* (Island, 1982) *Slave to the Rhythm* (Manhattan/Island, 1985) *Bulletproof Heart* (Capitol, 1989) *Sex Drive* (Island, 1993)

▶▶ David Bowie, Black Box, Wally Badarou, Joan Armatrading, Fine Young Cannibals, Robert Palmer

◀◀ Gloria Gaynor, Andrea True, Pretenders, the Normal

Steve Holtje

Howard Jones

Born John Howard Jones, Feb. 23, 1955 in Southampton, England

Combine classical piano training with an interest in technology and a bunch of utopian, hippie ideals, and you get Howard Jones. He emerged in 1984 as a one-man band, singing about love and loving each other while creating multiple layers of synthesizer bop while a dancer named Jed gyrated around. Rolling Stone magazine called Jones "a synthesized Gilbert O'-Sullivan," but he's a bit better than that; his melodies are sturdy, and his arrangements, while relentlessly cheerful ("Things," he reminds us, "can only get better"), were certainly novel at the time. Jones had a run of hits during the mid-80s, culminating with the 1986 Top 5 hit "No One is to Blame"—on which he shared vocals with Phil Collins. But as the hits dried up, Jones' output became more sporadic, though most recently he's made a comeback with acoustic music.

what to buy: *Human's Lib* (Elektra, 1984, prod. Rupert Hine) is a pop confection that's gotten kind of charming with age. The tunes are still of a high quality—even the positively perky "New Song"—and it's nice to remember a time when synthesizers provided a light touch and not just the gloomy ambience of industrial or the bland wash of certain techno acts.

what to buy next: *The Best of Howard Jones* (Elektra, 1993, prod. Various) culls the highlights of Jones' career, a broader swatch than *Human's Lib*, though it's not quite as cohesive. *Acoustic Live in America* (Plump, 1995, prod. Howard Jones) is a shrewd move, stripping his songs down to just his voice, a piano and a percussionist to reveal that he's a not a bad tunesmith at all.

what to avoid: On *In the Running,* (Elektra, 1992, prod. Ross Cullum and Howard Jones) Jones goes for the big, lush pop hit, and his contrivance betrays him.

the rest: *Dream Into Action* (Elektra, 1985) *One to One* (Elektra, 1986) *Cross That Line* (Elektra, 1989)

worth searching for: *What is Love?,* (EastWest U.K., 1992, prod. Various) an import best-of that collects the better material from Jones' weaker later albums.

▶▶ Donnie Iris

◀◀ Kraftwerk, Joy Division, Depeche Mode

Gary Graff

John Paul Jones

See: Led Zeppelin

Marti Jones

Born N/A

After making an EP as part of the group Color Me Gone, Jones came out of Ohio and teamed up with North Carolina fixture Don Dixon, producer of R.E.M. and the Smithereens, among others (Dixon and Jones eventually married). The duo delighted critics with savvy cover choices from unlikely sources and discovering unknown talent; for instance, they recorded John Hiatt songs several years before the rest of the music world. They also began composing together, eventually no longer depending on outside writers. But Jones' lack of commercial success stalled her momentum, and her only new record since 1990 was actually recorded back then.

what to buy: *Used Guitars* (A&M, 1988, prod. Don Dixon) ♪♪♪♪ is the apex of Dixon and Jones's great covers choices, with standouts from John Hiatt ("The Real One," "If I Can Love Somebody"), Janis Ian, Jackie DeShannon and Graham Parker ("You Can't Take Love for Granted"). Dixon and Jones add some original tunes ("Tourist Town," "Twisted Vines"), and Marshall Crenshaw and Sonny Landreth kick in amazing guitar leads. *Any Kind of Lie* (RCA, 1990, prod. Don Dixon) ♪♪♪♪ is a bit too slick for its own good but finds Dixon and Jones carrying an album with almost no covers. Their title track is so catchy it should be illegal.

what to buy next: *Match Game* (A&M, 1986, prod. Don Dixon) ♪♪♪ shines on Elvis Costello's "Just a Memory" and Crenshaw's "Whenever You're on My Mind." *Live at Spirit Square,* (Sugar Hill, 1996, prod. Dixon) ♪♪♪♪ recorded in 1990, offers production that will never be dated, thanks to the concert/quintet setting. Plus, its whopping 17 tunes act as a fine career summary.

worth searching for: *Unsophisticated Time* (A&M, 1985, prod. Don Dixon) ♪♪♪ has cheesy production values, but the two Peter Holsapple tunes ("Lonely Is as Lonely Does," "Neverland") are worth the trouble of tracking down this out-of-print album.

▶▶ Bonnie Raitt, John Doe

◀◀ Judy Collins, Dusty Springfield, Jackie DeShannon, Petula Clark

Steve Holtje

Mick Jones

See: Foreigner

Rickie Lee Jones

Born Nov. 18, 1954 in Chicago, Ill.

A child of restless and volatile parents, Jones moved across the country with them until she got expelled from high school in Washington state, beginning a journey through the West Coast underclass that would fuel much of her finest work. Eventually spinning a job as a waitress into occasional stage appearances and a career as a singer-songwriter, Jones began hanging out in creative circles that included Tom Waits and Little Feat's Lowell George and scored a record deal of her own in the late 70s. Her first album, fueled by a jazzy R&B and a beat poetry vibe, made her an instant critic's darling and won an audience with the hit "Chuck E's in Love." Subsequent albums ranged from a refinement of the street stories presented on her debut to records filled with jazzy covers of old pop standards. Always, Jones managed to bring a creative, unconventional approach to the material, even when substance abuse problems, a marriage and the birth of her daughter threatened to distract her.

what to buy: Certainly, her debut, *Rickie Lee Jones,* (Warner Bros., 1979, prod. Lenny Waronker and Russ Titleman) ♪♪♪♪♪ provides the perfect distillation of Jones' unique approach, fusing her vivid portraits of street characters with supple vocals that can be innocent and knowing, soulful and awkward, breathless and powerful, all in the same moment.

what to buy next: The only record that comes close to matching the debut is Jones' sophomore album, *Pirates,* (Warner Bros., 1981, prod. by Russ Titleman and Lenny Waronker) ♪♪♪♪ a complex, open record that grows stronger with repeated listening. Filled with her off-kilter meditations on death and progression, the record offers an amazing peek at a songwriter who isn't afraid to bare her soul on wax.

what to avoid: For any other singer-songwriter, *The Magazine* (Warner Bros., 1984, prod. Rickie Lee Jones and James Newton Howard) WOOF! might have been a triumph. But with creative expectations of her so high, this mishmash of self-consciously pretentious material goes over like a lead zeppelin, as the saying goes. Not much better is *Traffic From Paradise,* (Geffen, 1993, prod. Rickie Lee Jones) WOOF! a collection of seemingly half-finished tunes that makes you wonder whether Jones has now resorted to releasing her demo tapes.

the rest: *Girl at Her Volcano* (Warner Bros., 1983) ♪♪♪♪ *Flying Cowboys* (Geffen, 1989) ♪♪♪♪ *Pop, Pop* (Geffen, 1991) ♪♪♪ *Naked Songs: Live and Acoustic* (Reprise, 1995) ♪♪♪♪

worth searching for: Jones turns in an inspired duet with soulful New Orleans pianist-singer Dr. John on the playful groove "Makin' Whoopee" from his *In a Sentimental Mood* (Warner Bros., 1989, prod. Tommy LiPuma) ♪♪♪♪

▶▶ Sheryl Crow, k.d. lang, Suzanne Vega

◀◀ Laura Nyro, Joni Mitchell, Tom Waits

Eric Deggans

Steve Jones

See: The Sex Pistols

Tom Jones

Born June 7, 1940, in Pontypridd, Wales

The bumping, the grinding, the bellowing: rarely has a singer been so equally admired and reviled as the hip-swinging Jones. Leering and pandering, he left the 60s pop charts ("What's New Pussycat," "It's not Unusual," "Delilah") for the cheese of Vegas. Making like Elvis without the fat, Jones led with his crotch in gleeful acts of self-parody. The Welshman made a blindsiding resurgence during the 80s, pairing himself with hip alternative acts such as Art of Noise, covering of Prince's "Kiss" and EMF's "Unbelievable," and guesting on "The Simpsons." His totally over-the-top emoting and complete immersion in his own hype have always been his most endearing qualities, and the ones that've kept him amazingly afloat all these years. Well into his 50s, the grandfather is still fog-horning for his supper in fishnet tank-tops and leather pants, oblivious to the rigors of aging.

what to buy: *The Complete Tom Jones* (Deram, 1993, prod. Various) offers the best cross-section of his work with the standards "It's Not Unusual," "Delilah" and "Green, Green Grass of Home," as well as his team-up with Art of Noise (!) for Prince's "Kiss."

what to buy next: *Things That Matter Most to Me* (Mercury, 1988/1993, prod. Various) is the best compilation of his country hits such as "Darlin'" and "Green, Green, Grass of Home," which argues that Jones can take his shtick pretty much anywhere for engaging results. *Move Closer* (Jive, 1989, prod. Various) is one of his more consistent studio efforts and the original home of "Kiss;" his take on the Stones' "Satisfaction," makes Mick Jagger seem downright demure.

what to avoid: *Greatest Songs* (Curb, 1995) Says who?

the rest: *Tom Jones Country* (Mercury, 1982/1993) *Love is On the Radio* (Mercury, 1984/1993) *Tender Loving Care* (Mercury, 1993/1985) *The Lead and How to Swing It* (Interscope, 1994)

worth searching for: *The Long Black Veil,* (RCA Victor, 1995, prod. Various) a Chieftains all-star outing which Jones joins for a delightful barrelling-through version of "Tennessee Waltz."

Michael Bolton, Buster Poindexter, Wham!

Elvis Presley

Allan Orski

Janis Joplin /Big Brother and the Holding Company

Born Jan. 19, 1943 in Port Arthur, Texas. Died October 4, 1970 in Hollywood, Calif.

Big Brother Members: Sam Andrew, vocals, guitar; James Gurley, guitars; Peter Albin, bass; David Getz, drums

When Janis Joplin left the nurturing fold of Big Brother and the Holding Company, she turned into a commodity. Her early recordings with the San Francisco ballroom band capture a raw Joplin, enmeshed in the passionate throes of an unequally untamed band. Ambition was her true weapon of self-destruction, not the drugs and ill-fated romances. But she left behind a frustrating glimpse of something powerful enough to ignite her enduring legend. Joplin exploded all over the crowd at the historic 1967 Monterey Pop Festival; in a single show she established her reputation. At that very moment, she also sowed the seeds of eventual departure from her helpless communal colleagues in Big Brother. The very week their *Cheap Thrills* album hit No. 1, Joplin announced her intention to go solo to her unsurprised bandmates.

As a solo artist, she was a disaster. Joplin made her debut performance after a mere two days rehearsal, headlining an authentic soul show to an indifferent audience at an annual Memphis black fundraiser. Her first band, the Kozmik Blues Band, never jelled, and although its successor, the Full Tilt Boogie Band, represented a substantial improvement, she didn't have time to build up a substantial enough body of work to support her looming posthumous stature. She was dead at age 28 before even finishing that final, second solo album.

what to buy: Even more than a quarter-century later, *Cheap Thrills* (Columbia, 1968, prod. John Simon) stills sounds nervy, rich and radical. The album rips along, high-voltage electricity charging every number, until it reaches its climax, "Ball and Chain," which Joplin turns into one of the high points of personal expression in rock history.

what to buy next: Although the band's debut album, *Big Brother and the Holding Company* (Mainstream, 1967, prod. B. Shad) was a shoddy and hasty affair made in a few days, the record captured nevertheless the warm, sloppy atmosphere of the band and some precious Joplin vocals.

what to avoid: *I Got Dem Ol' Kozmic Blues Again Mama!* (Columbia, 1970, prod. Gabriel Meckler) is a sprawling, awful mess of a pseudo-soul album that sounded forced and shrill at the time, and does not hold up over the years.

the rest: *Pearl* (Columbia, 1971) 🦴🦴🦴 *Joplin In Concert* (Columbia, 1972) 🦴🦴½ *Farewell Song* (Columbia, 1982) 🦴🦴🦴 *Janis Joplin* (Columbia, 1993) 🦴🦴🦴 *18 Essential Songs* (Columbia, 1995) 🦴🦴🦴🦴

worth searching for: Big Brother drummer David Getz released a particularly raw early live performance of this unruly and exciting young band on an album, *Cheaper Thrills* (Made To Last, 1982, prod. David Getz) 🦴🦴🦴½ that has been released on CD in England.

▶▶ Melissa Etheridge, Mariah Carey

◀◀ Memphis Minnie, John Coltrane, Lightnin' Hopkins

Joel Selvin

Journey

Formed 1973 in San Francisco, Calif. Disbanded 1987.

Neal Schon, guitar; Gregg Rolie, vocals, keyboards (1973-81); George Tickner, guitar (1973-75); Ross Valory, bass (1973-85); Aynsley Dunbar, drums (1973-79); Steve Perry, vocals (1978-87); Steve Smith, drums (1979-85); Jonathan Cain, keyboards (1981-87)

Carefully developing a trademark sound that made Journey one of the most popular rock groups of the early 80s, the band evolved from an instrumental ensemble with fusion leanings that rose from the ashes of the original Santana into a polished power pop hit machine that reflected some of the worst stylistic tendencies of the genre the band helped create. Journey might have invented the power ballad—a dubious contribution to the literature of pop—but the group's sweeping, pervasive influences on the rock scene of the early 80s may actually have perversely hastened the rise of more visceral, economical brands of rock influenced by the new wave movement.

Journey represented the absolute peak of stadium rock. In fact, the band's slow, inexorable rise paralleled the growth the arena rock business itself experienced during the 70s. Journey's gargantuan success was an inevitability with its steady refinements and the band's utter and complete devotion to shaping its craft to meet the curve of public appeal. The albums reflect that process, zeroing in on popular success with greater accuracy on each subsequent release up to the 1981 supernova, *Escape*, after which the typical diminishing returns led to the acrimonious dissolution of the group, followed by inescapable reunion talk a decade years later.

what to buy: While *Greatest Hits* (Columbia, 1988, prod. Various) 🦴🦴🦴 will probably spend eternity on the catalog charts, while *Escape* (Columbia, 1981, prod. Mike Stone and Kevin Elson) 🦴🦴🦴 probably shows the group to its best advantage.

what to buy next: The three-CD boxed set, *Time3* shown as mathematical symbol for to the third power (Columbia, 1993, prod. Various) 🦴🦴½ examines the group's career in fine-point detail, including many illuminating previously unreleased recordings.

what to avoid: As is so often the case, by the time the group recorded its final album, *Raised On Radio*, (Columbia, 1986, prod. Steve Perry) 🦴 ego conflicts and intra-band ambitions made the project more of a Steve Perry solo album than a group effort—although there are those who might argue that would be an improvement.

the rest: *Journey* (Columbia, 1975) 🦴🦴 *Into the Future* (Columbia, 1976) 🦴 *Next* (Columbia, 1977) 🦴 *Infinity* (Columbia, 1978) 🦴🦴 *Evolution* (Columbia, 1979) 🦴🦴 *Departure* (Columbia, 1980) 🦴🦴 *Captured* (Columbia, 1981) 🦴 *Frontiers* (Columbia, 1983) 🦴½

worth searching for: The Japanese-only soundtrack album *Dream After Dream* (Sony, 1980, prod. Kevin Elson and Geoff Workman) 🦴🦴🦴 captures *Escape*-era Journey in an atmospheric, Floydian mode.

solo outings:

Steve Perry: *Street Talk* (Columbia, 1984) 🦴🦴 *For Love Of Strange Medicine* (Columbia, 1994) **WOOF!**

Neal Schon: (with Sammy Hagar) *Through the Fire* (Geffen, 1984) 🦴 (with Jan Hammer): *Untold Passion* (Columbia, 1981) 🦴🦴 and *Made To Stay* (Columbia, 1982); (solo) *Beyond the Thunder* (Higher Octave, 1995) 🦴🦴🦴

▶▶ Michael Bolton, Survivor, Whitesnake, Bad English

◀◀ Santana, Queen, Boston

Joel Selvin

Joy Division

Formed 1977 in Manchester, England. Disbanded 1980.

Ian Curtis, vocals (died May 18, 1980); Bernard Albrecht (born Bernard Dicken, ala Bernard Sumner), guitar, vocals; Peter Hook, bass; Stephen Morris, drums

Sparked into existence by punk, Joy Division was an enormously influential group that connected the original punk revolution and the 80s sounds that came after, including industrial and various post-punk dance forms. Hook and Sumner, after attending the Sex Pistols' first concert in Manchester on June 4, 1976, and were inspired to start bands. Forming first as Warsaw, the quartet changed its name to the term given to the Nazi's involuntary concentration camp brothels. Barely able to play their instruments but immensely compelling nonetheless due to epileptic singer Curtis's dark, morbid lyrics, the group hooked up with local label Factory, and producer Martin Hannett. Hannett's contribution to the group's recorded sound cannot be understated; he took a musical concept that could have sounded merely sloppy and incompetent and made it unique with echo, a sense of vast space and a fattening and highlighting of elements such as Hook's bone-simple bass lines. Just as the second album was coming out, the always-disconsolate Curtis, devastated by the breakup of his marriage, hung himself at the age of 22. The rest of the band regrouped as New Order and, building on the dance elements inherent in Joy Division, once again created a new musical sound.

what to buy: *Unknown Pleasures* (Factory, 1979, prod. Martin Hannett) features "She's Lost Control" and is devastating in its nihilistic vision and raw, jagged sound. *Closer* (Factory, 1980, prod. Martin Hannett) is just as dark but with even better songs and arrangements.

what to buy next: *Substance* (QWest, 1988, prod. Joy Division and Martin Hannett) is a career overview that mostly avoids overlapping the albums, concentrating on singles (including the great "Love Will Tear Us Apart," a response to the Captain & Tennille hit "Love Will Keep Us Together") and rarities. *Still* (Factory, 1981, prod. Martin Hannett) collects live recordings and rarities, including a striking cover of the Velvet Underground's "Sister Ray."

what to avoid: Given the small number of Joy Division releases, *Permanent: Joy Division 1995* (QWest, 1995, prod. Various) is an unnecessary compilation feebly baited with a 1995 remix of "Love Will Tear Us Apart" tricked up for dance-club play but musically inferior.

the rest: *Peel Sessions* (Strange Fruit, 1990)

worth searching for: *Amsterdam*, a bootleg from an adrenalized live show that's done up to look like a Factory promo item.

The Cure, New Order, Bauhaus, Red Lorry Yellow Lorry, Sisters of Mercy/The Mission U.K., Teardrop Explodes/Julian Cope, nine inch nails, Nirvana, American Music Club/Mark Eitzel, Moby

Velvet Underground, Sex Pistols, Kraftwerk, David Bowie

see also: *New Order, Electronic*

Steve Holtje

Judas Priest

Formed 1969 in Birmingham, England

Alan Atkins, vocals (1969-72); Rob Halford, vocals (1971-92); K. K. Downing, guitar; Glenn Tipton, guitar; Ian Hill, bass; John Ellis, drums (1969-71); Alan Moore, drums (1971, 1974-77); Chris Campbell, drums (1971-72); John Hinch, drums (1973); Simon Phillips, drums (1977); Les Binks, drums (1978); Dave Holland, drums (1979-90); Scott Travis, drums (1990-92); Ripper Owens, vocals (1996-present)

One of heavy rock's pioneers of hard rock, Judas Priest was metal when metal wasn't cool—in fact, one could argue that the band, along with fellow Brits Deep Purple, Black Sabbath and Motörhead—*are* the ones that made it cool. Just about every heavy metal band since 1980 has borrowed from Priest's formula of crunching guitars and dark, Gothic lyrics, as well as its studded-leather wardrobe. Guitarist Downing and bassist Hill formed the band in 1969, but didn't begin recording until after vocalist Halford began his long tenure in 1971. It took several years for Judas Priest to find (some might say create) its niche, it didn't really take off in the U.S. until the early 80s. The group really earned its stripes of credibility due to inane controversies: it was accused by a Christian organization of recording subliminal messages backwards on its albums; it was targeted by the Washington D.C. wives' Parents Music Resource Center (PMRC) for its violent and sexually explicit lyrics; and in 1986, supposedly backward lyrics from the album *Stained Class* were said to have induced two boys to attempt suicide (one died). In 1992, singer Halford left to form Fight; the remaining members of Judas Priest vowed to continue, though they have yet to record with new vocalist Owens.

what to buy: By the time Priest recorded *Screaming for Vengeance*, (Columbia, 1982, prod. Tom Allom) the band had perfected its sound. The album opens with the thunderous instrumental "The Hellion" and rumbles through hits such as "Electric Eye" and "You've Got Another Thing Coming". Play it loud.

what to buy next: Priest's double-length live package, *Priest ... Live!* (Columbia, 1986, prod. Tom Allom) may be one of the best live heavy metal albums out there. Tipton and Downing ably duplicate their two-guitar attack, and Halford's piercing wail is unfailing.

what to avoid: *Painkiller* (Columbia, 1990, prod. Chris Tsangarides and Judas Priest) **WOOF!** is a dull, strident album that may have been the reason for Halford's departure two years later.

the rest: *Rocka Rolla* (RCA, 1974) *Sad Wings of Destiny* (RCA, 1976) *Sin After Sin* (Columbia, 1977) *Stained Class* (Columbia, 1978) *Best of Judas Priest* (RCA, 1978) *Hell Bent for Leather* (Columbia, 1978) *Unleashed in the East* (Columbia, 1979) *British Steel* (Columbia, 1980) *Point of Entry* (Columbia, 1981) *Defenders of the Faith* (Columbia, 1984) *Hero, Hero* (RCA, 1985) *Turbo* (Columbia, 1986) *Ram It Down* (Columbia, 1988) *Metalworks '73-'93* (Columbia, 1993)

worth searching for: Not only is the band's 1984 picture disc a neat collectors item, but it contains an excellent selection of its greatest hits (if you dare to actually put it on your turntable).

solo outings:

Fight (Halford & Travis): War of Words (Epic, 1993) *Mutations* (Epic EP, 1994) *A Small Deadly Space* (Epic, 1995)

Metallica, Slayer, Anthrax, Accept, Venom, Iron Maiden, Scorpions, Pantera, White Zombie, Tool

Led Zeppelin, Cream, the Who, Black Sabbath

Brandon Trenz

Juluka

See: Johnny Clegg & Savuka

Junk Monkeys

Formed 1986 in Dearborn, Mich.

David Bierman, vocals, guitar; Dave Boutette, guitar; Kevin Perri, bass; Dan Allen, drums, vocals (1986-91); Glynn Scanlan, drums, vocals (1992-present)

Building a Detroit-area following by developing the Minneapolis sound exemplified by the Replacements and Soul Asylum, this quartet's best album, *Bliss,* (Metal Blade Modern, 1993, prod. Michael Nehra, Al Sutton and David Bierman) is one of the best guitar-pop releases in a decade rife with great ones. The group augments its chunky rhythm-guitar riffing, hoarsely melodic vocals and a smidgen of syncopation with subtle touches of acoustic piano and organ courtesy of Todd McKinney. The simple but effective songs feature sing-along-inducing choruses while the witty or poignant verses often turn cliches sideways. The group is considerably less active than it used to be, but can still be found playing the odd Detroit club gig.

the rest: *Soul Cakes* (Metal Blade, 1989) *Five Star Fling* (Metal Blade, 1991)

Steve Holtje

Brenda Kahn

Born May 3, 1967 in Hartford, Conn.

Rising out of the Alphabet City "anti-folk" scene in late-80s Manhattan, singer-songwriter Kahn took lessons from folk scene veteran Dave Van Ronk but was equally influenced by punk—especially its DIY ethic and emotional directness. She chose the solo acoustic path because, while growing up in New Jersey, local bands resisted the idea of a female guitarist. She's persevered through horrible record label experiences and continues to put her vividly etched depictions of relationships and occasionally piquant political statements before the public, working solo or with a trio. Given the recent public acceptance of "angry women" a la Alanis Morrissette, the underexposed Kahn could, with luck, find a major audience.

what to buy: With minimal bass-and-drums backing, *Goldfish Don't Talk Back* (Community 3, 1990, prod. Albert Garzon) showcases fantastic songwriting (the elegiac "Winchester Chimes"), powerful politics (the viciously sarcastic "Eggs on Drugs") and in-your-face romantic plaints. *Epiphany in Brooklyn* (Chaos/Columbia, 1992, prod. David Kahne) is slightly less consistent, but some of Kahne's inspired touches allow Kahn to break out of the acoustic troubadour mold on quiet pieces full of atmosphere and foreboding ("Sleepwalking").

what to buy next: Columbia declined to issue *Destination Anywhere,* (Through Being Cool/Shanachie, 1996, prod. Tim Patalan) Kahn's rock album, but "Yellow Sun's" catchy enough to be a hit.

the rest: *Hey, Romeo/...and Door Locks* (Through Being Cool single, 1995, prod. Tim Patalan) *Life in the Drug War Trenches* (Crackpot EP, 1992)

worth searching for: "60 Second Critic" (Chaos/Columbia, 1992, prod. Brenda Kahn/Dave Pirner) a duet with Soul Asylum's Dave Pirner, was a promo-only cassette single bitterly commenting on the choices in the '92 Presidential election campaign.

Bessie Smith, Phil Ochs, Dave Van Ronk, Lou Reed, Elvis Costello, Clash, X-Ray Spex, Pretenders, Michelle Shocked, Roger Manning

Steve Holtje

Kajagoogoo

Formed 1982 in England. Disbanded 1986. Re-formed 1992.

Limahl, vocals (1982-84); Nick Beggs, bass; various others over the years

According to some, the word Kajagoogoo has now taken on a broader meaning than simply being the name of a foppish British quintet of the early 80s who were known as much for its teased-out, bushed-up hairdos as for its thoroughly disposable synth-pop music. Kajagoogoo now refers to anything trendy, false, ephemeral or faddish, particularly something associated with the New Romantic era in music/fashion/videos. Yes, for one brief, shining moment in early 1983, Kajagoogoo were on top of the pop charts—in the U.K., at least—with "Too Shy," a bubbly concoction of funky dance-lite, the sort of thing that by comparison lent importance to, say, "The Reflex" by Duran Duran. Not surprisingly, double-D's keyboard player Nick Rhodes co-produced Kajagoogoo's debut, *White Feathers,* (EMI, 1982, prod. Nick Rhodes, Colin Thurston, Tim Palmer and Kajagoogoo) WOOF! a fairly irredeemable dollop of slithery synth-pop goop. The Kajagoogoo album that followed, as well as a final release under the shorter, hipper (?) monicker Kaja, were completely irredeemable. By then, though, Limahl (an all-too-clever anagram of his real last name, Hamill) had left to put out a solo album, which featured his giddy, almost Germanic-pop hit theme song to the film, "The NeverEnding Story." Both hits, along with a few remixes and a host of unlistenable crap, are included on *Too Shy—The Singles.* (EMI, 1993, prod. Various) Smart retro 80s freaks will pick up those songs on either Rhino's *New Wave Hits* series or EMI's *Living In Oblivion* series. At least there, the songs are tempered by being placed in context with other better material from the same era.

Bob Remstein

Kansas

Formed 1972 in Topeka, Kan.

Kerry Livgren, guitar, keyboards (1972-1983, 1991); Steve Walsh, vocals, keyboards (1972-81, 1986-present); Robby Steinhardt, violin, vocals (1972-83); Richard Williams, guitar (1972-present); Phil Ehart, drums (1972-present); Dave Hope, bass (1972-83); John Elefante, vocals, keyboards (1981-83); Steve Morse, guitar (1985-88); Billy Greer, bass (1985—present); David Ragsdale, violin (1990-present)

Fusing the neo-classical sensibilities of progressive rock with an earthy Midwestern rock grind, Kansas enjoyed a brief period of mass popularity during the late 70s with hits such as "Carry On Wayward Son" and "Dust in the Wind." Though often held up as an example of faceless 70s album-rock, there's no faulting the players' chops, nor the creative ambitions that yielded a number of textured, multi-part suites. Ultimately, Walsh's initial departure in 1981 knocked the group off stride, and it's never regained its balance; these days it can be found reliving past glories with 70s kin such as Styx and the Alan Parson Project.

what to buy: Led by the hit "Carry on Wayward Son," *Leftoverture* (Kirshner, 1976, prod. Jeff Glixman) was Kansas' breakthrough album and a thorough representation of its assorted musical sensibilities, from the power ballad "The Wall" to the punchy rock of "What's on My Mind" to the long-winded pomp of "Magnum Opus." Less well-known—but just as good—is *Masque* (Kirshner, 1975, prod. Jeff Glixman), whose lengthier numbers ("Icarus," "The Pinnacle") have a more organic majesty.

what to buy next: The *Kansas* box set (Epic Associated/Legacy, 1995) captures the crucial tracks and winnows what's interesting from later releases. Those interested in Kansas at its most bombastic are well-served by *Song For America* (Kirshner, 1975, prod. Jeff Glixman and Wally Gold), whose title cut is still one of prog-rock's sonic gems.

what to avoid: John Elefante was a thin replacement for Walsh, and *Drastic Measures* (CBS Associated, 1983, prod. Kansas) WOOF! was a bottoming-out that led Kansas to split up for three years.

the rest: *Kansas* (Kirshner, 1974) *Point of Know Return* (Kirshner, 1977) *Two For the Show* (Kirshner, 1978) *Monolith* (Kirshner, 1979) *Audio-Visions* (Kirshner, 1980) *Vinyl Confessions* (Kirshner, 1982) *Power* (MCA, 1986) *In the Spirit of Things* (MCA, 1988) *Freaks of Nature* (Intersound, 1995)

worth searching for: The Japanese *Star Box* (Kirshner/Sony, 1993) is a more compact retrospective that offers a thorough selection of hits and a reasonable assortment of album tracks.

solo outings:

Kerry Livgren: Seeds of Change (Kirshner, 1980)

Steve Walsh: Schemer-Dreamer (Kirshner, 1979)

▶▶ The Livgren-Hope Christian rock band AD; Shooting Star; scads of '90s groups (Dave Matthews Band, Smashing Pumpkins) that added violins and cellos to their arrangements.

◀◀ Moody Blues, Procol Harum, King Crimson, Humble Pie, B.B. King, Elmore James, Ramsey Lewis, Dave Brubeck

Gary Graff

Paul Kantner

See: Jefferson Airplane

Mick Karn

See: Japan

Kathleen Turner Overdrive

See: Drivin' N' Cryin'

Katrina and the Waves

Formed 1981 in London, England

Katrina Leskanich, guitar, vocals; Kimberley Rew, guitar; Vince De la Cruz, bass; Alex Cooper, drums

A British-American pop-rock group, Katrina and the Waves formed in 1981 when Air Force brat Leskanich started playing with former Soft Boys member Rew. Four years and some independent recordings later, Capitol released the group's first album in the United States, producing a quick summer hit in "Walking on Sunshine." With Rew's undeniable songwriting skills, the group boasts a body of catchy power pop, though it's never repeated the same commercial impact.

what to buy: *Katrina and the Waves* (Capitol, 1985, prod. Pat Collier and Katrina and the Waves) contains "Walking on Sunshine" and another Top 40 hit, "Do You Want Crying," on an album loaded with cheery, unpretentious pop.

what to buy next: On *Break of Hearts,* (Capitol, 1986, prod. Katrina and the Waves, Pat Collier and Scott Litt) the band introduced Stax-influenced R&B grooves to mixed results. It worked more often than not, but just wasn't as effective as the previous album's ebullient pop.

what to avoid: By 1989, Katrina and the Waves had replaced the whimsical playfulness that had made the first records so joyous with the power-rock formula of *Breaking Hearts* (SBK, 1989, prod. Katrina and the Waves)

the rest: *Anthology* (One Way, 1995)

worth searching for: The group's first American album actually contained re-recordings of songs the band already had released in Canada or England. Those recordings included *Shock Horror* (Scoop, 1983, prod. Richard Bishop, Nick Cook, Pat Collier) (as the Waves): *Walking on Sunshine* (Attic, 1983) and *Katrina and the Waves 2* (Attic, 1984, prod. Pat Collier and Katrina and the Waves)

▶▶ Ace of Base, the Bangles

◀◀ The Soft Boys, Dusty Springfield

see also: *The Soft Boys*

Brian Mansfield

Jorma Kaukonen

See: Hot Tuna

John Kay

See: Steppenwolf

KBC Band

See: Jefferson Airplane

KC and the Sunshine Band

Formed 1973 in Hialeah, Fla.

Harry Wayne Casey, vocals, keyboards; Richard Finch, bass, percussion; Robert Johnson, drums; Jerome Smith, guitar; Fermin Goytisolo, percussion; Mike Lewis, tenor saxophone; Vinnie Tanno, trumpet; Ken Faulk, trumpet; Whit Sidener, baritone sax; Fire (Margret Reynolds, Beverly Champion & Jeannette Williams), background vocals

KC and the Sunshine Band was one of the most influential dance groups of the 70s, setting the precedent for what commercial disco should sound like, KC dominated the mid-70s with a rapid-fire succession of hit singles; songs such as "That's The Way (I Like It)," "Get Down Tonight" "Rock Your Baby" were the "Macarenas" of the 70s. The group brought a tropical, Carribean party flavor to its dance grooves and fueled its popularity with loud, tacky stage costumes, a soft-sell message of racial harmony and bright, cheerful lyrics. KC and Co. are still on the road, often touring with disco mates such as the Village People for crowds that still haven't tired of shake, shake, shaking their bootys.

what to buy: *Best of KC & The Sunshine Band* (Rhino, 1990, prod. Richard Finch,Bobby Martinez, Harry Wayne Casey and Amaury Lopez) has all of KC's hits that you can recall, plus a few you've probably forgotten. It doesn't just cover his 70s material (although all of the era-defining hits are included) but spans the scope of KC's work into the 80s with post-disco singles such "Give It Up."

what to buy next: *KC & The Sunshine Band...And More* (Rhino, 1995, prod. Harry Wayne Casey, Richard Finch and Steve Alaimo) combines the group's 1975 album with two tracks from KC's out of print *Space Cadet* (TK Records, 1981, prod. Harry Wayne Casey, Richard Finch) and two new cover songs. You get a true disco classic plus a sampling of KC's later material on one CD. *Part 3...And More* (Rhino, 1995, prod. Harry Wayne Casey and Richard Finch) takes the same format with covers and three tracks from the out-of-print *Do It Good* (TK Records, 1978, prod. Harry Wayne Casey and Richard Finch).

what to avoid: *Rhino Special Editions: The Best of KC & The Sunshine Band* (Rhino, 1990) is a skimpier hits collection. If you're gonna get down, don't be shy about it.

the rest: *Get Down Live* (Intersound, 1995) *Oh Yeah!* (ZYX, 1993)

▶▶ Fine Young Cannibals, Chic, Anita Ward, Gwen Guthrie, Sylvester, Miami Sound Machine

◀◀ Gwen McCrae, Betty Wright, George Clinton/Parliament-Funkadelic, Tito Puente

Bryan Lassner

Tommy Keene

Keene has such a classic pop voice—high but not squeaky, with enough character to skirt wimpiness but ooze sincere yearning—that even if he didn't write such killer jangle riffs, it would still be a joy to hear his records. The fact that his melodies are memorable and hummable and that he's an excellent finger-style electric guitarist with a distinctive arpeggiated sound just makes his obscurity that much harder to fathom. The title track of his well-received *Places That Are Gone* EP got Keene noticed; it was The Village Voice's 1984 Pazz & Jop winner in the EP category. Keene was signed by Geffen and released two fine albums and an EP, but got nowhere commercially and was dropped. He spent three years recording and shopping demos until some were picked up by Matador and released on a 1992 EP. Alias then put together a collection, including many of the unused demos, and in 1996 Matador put out a whole album's worth of new material, presenting hope that in the more pop-friendly alternative market (and the more alternative-friendly pop market) Keene would finally win the kudos due him.

what to buy: *Sleeping on a Rollercoaster* (Matador EP, 1992, prod. Tommy Keene and Steve Carr) has only five songs, but "Love Is a Dangerous Thing" might be the best he's ever done.

what to buy next: *The Real Underground* (Alias, 1993, prod. Tommy Keene and Ted Niceley) contains all six songs of the *Places That Are Gone* EP (Dolphin, 1984, prod. Tommy Keene and Ted Niceley) and some unreleased material.

what to avoid: Don't be tempted by the *Back Again (Try...)* (Dolphin EP, 1984, prod. Not Listed) just because it has two covers (Brian Ferry's "All I Want Is You" and the Rolling Stones' "When the Whip Comes Down") left off *The Real Underground*. Neither is a good song to begin with, they sound worse in these low-fi bar recordings.

the rest: *Strange Alliance* (Avenue) *Run Now* EP (Geffen, 1986) *Ten Years After* (Matador, 1996)

worth searching for: The out-of-print Geffen material can be found cheaply in used record stores and is must-own stuff for fans of jangly pop. *Based on Happy Times* (Geffen, 1980, prod. Geoff Emerick) included a new version of "Places That Are Gone" and a hard-rocking cover of Lou Reed's "Kill Your Sons" that shows off Keene's fine guitar style. *Songs from the Film* (Geffen, 1989, prod. Joe Hardy, John Hampton and Tommy Keene) has slightly tougher production and includes guest Peter Buck (R.E.M.) on two tracks, one an obscure Beach Boys tune.

▶▶ Gin Blossoms, Matthew Sweet, Young Fresh Fellows, Teenage Fanclub, Superchunk, Velvet Crush

◀◀ The Beatles, the Byrds, the Who, Big Star, the Shoes, Let's Active

Steve Holtje

Paul Kelly

Born Jan. 13, 1955, in Adelaide, Australia

Singer-songwriter Kelly pens incisive and mature tales to critical acclaim and weak record sales. Drawing comparisons to Graham Parker and Elvis Costello, Kelly's writing style is, in fact, more minimalist and mournful in its distillation of life's pivotal moments. He's had trouble getting noticed in the U.S., resulting in his being dropped from A&M in 1989. Kelly has recently been threatening to gain a wider audience, but his well-thought-out snapshots require too much concentration for the casual radio drone to appreciate.

what to buy: *Gossip,* (A&M, 1987, prod. Alan Thorn and Paul Kelly) the stunning U.S. debut that's loaded with dead-on portraits of the damage caused by an alcoholic father. On the lighter side, Kelly shows his gift for ballads ("Randwick Bells") and charming pop ("Don't Ever Harm the Messenger" and "Leaps and Bounds"). *Deeper Water,* (Vanguard, 1995, prod. Various) is a splendid return to form that shows Kelly has lost none of his insights during all the label-jumping; his gift for vivid detail seems bottomless in its inspiration.

what to buy next: *Comedy* (Doctor Dream, 1992, prod. Alan Thorne and Paul Kelly) runs the stylistic gamut from social commentary to pop gems and cover versions, making this sprawling record one of his strongest. *So Much Water So Close To Home,* (White Records, 1989, prod. Scott Litt and Paul Kelly) named after a short story by Raymond Carver, continues his poignant slices of songcraft—notably "Sweet Guy," a tale of domestic abuse from the woman's point of view, and "No You," an acoustically driven rocker.

what to avoid: *Wanted Man* (Vanguard, 1994) Not a complete washout, but not up to the level of his earlier work.

the rest: *Paul Kelly Live From the Continental and the Esplanade* (Vanguard, 1996)

worth searching for: The first-rate but out-of-print titles *Stand on the Positive Side* (Warner Bros., 1977) *Talk* (Mushroom, 1981) *Manila* (Mushroom, 1982) and *Post* (White Label, 1985)

⏩ Elvis Costello, Graham Parker, John Mellencamp

⏪ Bob Dylan, Raymond Carver

Allan Orski

Sean Kelly

See: The Samples

Scott Kempner

See: The Del Lords

Eddie Kendricks

See: The Temptations

Klark Kent Animal Logic

See: Stewart Copeland

Nik Kershaw

Born Nicholas David Kershaw, 1958, in Bristol, Somerset, England

The son of a classical musician and an opera singer, Kershaw must have raised some eyebrows when he taught himself guitar as a teen and began playing in a Deep Purple cover band. Before long, he'd moved on to jazz fusion and, later, pop. Following the breakup of a fusion band he'd recorded with, Kershaw signed to MCA Records in England and crafted a wonderful solo debut, showing off his penchant for inventive pop songwriting and production while enlisting such high-powered pals as Level 42 bassist Mark King. Though his first record failed to generate much interest, a 1984 follow-up, featuring a remixed version of the single "Wouldn't It Be Good," hit on both sides of the Atlantic, establishing Kershaw as a pop star. But subsequent albums didn't fare as well, prompting the singer-producer to craft tunes and albums for other artists, most notably Chesney Hawkes and his massive hit, "The One and Only."

what to buy: *Human Racing* (MCA, 1984, prod. Peter Collins) combines Kershaw's soaring vocal talents with ace production and inventive arrangements. Of particular interest is his the simmering "Bogart," a tribute to Humphrey, and the percussion-packed "Drum Talk."

what to buy next: Gathering together all of the notable work from his too-short career as a solo artist, *Anthology* (One Way, 1995, prod. Peter Collins) serves as a great sampling of a quality pop songwriter who never found a steady audience.

what to avoid: As the album where his muse begins to flag, *Radio Musicola* (MCA, 1986, prod. Peter Collins) WOOF! has the unenviable distinction of being the first bit of evidence that Kershaw may have made the right move when he stepped out of the spotlight.

the rest: *The Works* (MCA, 1989)

worth searching for: Listen to Petula Clark's *Treasures, Vol. 1* (Scotti Bros., 1992, prod. Various) and catch Kershaw singing backing vocals.

▶▶ Chesney Hawkes

◀◀ Elton John, Gary Numan

Eric Deggans

Chaka Khan

See: Rufus

Kid Creole and the Coconuts /Dr. Buzzard's Original Savannah Band

Formed 1974 in New York, N.Y.

Kid Creole (1980-present): Thomas August "Kid Creole" Darnell Browder, vocals; Andy "Coati Mundi" Hernandez, vibes, percussion (1980-87); Peter Schott, keyboards; Cheryl Poirier, vocals. Dr. Buzzard's (1974-80, 1984): Stoney Browder Jr., guitar, piano (1974-79, 1984); Thomas August Darnell Browder, bass (1974-79); Mickey Sevilla, drums (1974-79, 1984); Sugar Coated Andy Hernandez, vibes, marimba, accordion (1974-79); Corey Daye, vocals (1974-79, 1984); Don Armando Bonilla, percussion (1974-76); Mark Josephsberg, vibes (1984); Michael Almo, horns (1984); Roland Prince, guitars (1984); Michael Boone, bass (1984); Mark Radice, bass (1984)

Dr. Buzzard's Original Savannah Band brought 30s big band sounds to the disco era with a witty edge, scoring a hit with "Cherchez La Femme" on 1976's *Dr. Buzzard's Original Savannah Band* and enjoyed moderate success for a few years. The group broke up in 1980, although it resurfaced in 1984, minus Darnell and Hernandez, for the badly conceived *Calling All Beatniks* Kid Creole, on the other hand, based its sound in disco, with Latin and Caribbean rhythms added. That unique mixture was enhanced by Darnell's often tongue-in-cheek lyrics and his Caribbean Cab Calloway image, as well as the party hearty stage show featuring the beautiful Coconuts as backup singers and break dancing by Coati Mundi. With a sound that defies categorization, Kid Creole's is more of a cult following, although the music itself presaged salsa's popularity in U.S. pop circles. The band enjoyed some greater exposure when it backed Barry Manilow on a cut from his 1987 release *Swing Street*, and it's been featured in the films "Against All Odds," "Car 54 Where Are You" and "The Forbidden Dance." Darnell has also distinguished himself as a producer.

what to buy: *In Praise of Older Women and Other Crimes* (Sire, 1985, prod. August Darnell) finds the band in funky and fun form with "Endicott," a cry of independence from a henpecked husband and the group's best-known tune stateside. The cry becomes the coo of doo wop on "Particul'y Interested," and soulful on "Name It." The band even takes a break from its usual party mode for musically successful stabs at social concerns on "Caroline Was A Dropout" and "Dowopsalsaboprock (We're Fighting Back)." In an earlier, Caribbean party mode, *Wise Guy* (Sire, 1982, prod. August Darnell) landed Top 10 hits in the U.K. with "Annie, I'm Not Your Daddy" and "I'm a Wonderful Thing, Baby."

what to buy next: Both of these bands feature strong musicianship and production, and *Dr. Buzzard's Original Savannah Band* (RCA, 1976, prod. Sandy Linzer) is a well-played, disco-style delight.

what to avoid: *Calling All Beatniks* (Passport, 1984, prod. Sandy Linzer) WOOF! features bad 50s-style rock by Dr. Buzzard minus Darnell and Hernandez. It proves the fire in this group really came from Darnell.

the rest: *Dr. Buzzard's Original Savannah Band Meets King Penett* (RCA, 1978) Kid Creole: *Fresh Fruit In Foreign Places* (Sire, 1981) *Doppelganger* (Sire, 1983) *I, Too, Have Seen the Woods* (Sire, 1987) *You Should Have Told Me You Were . . .* (Columbia, 1991) *Kid Creole Redux* (Sire, 1992) *To Travel Sideways* (Atoll, 1994)

worth searching for: *Off the Coast of Me* (Antilles, 1980, prod. August Darnell) is the transitional album from Dr. Buzzard to the Coconuts. The Kid steps out front with his humor, but he hasn't dropped the big band feel yet.

solo outings:

The Coconuts: Don't Steal My Coconuts (EMI, 1983)

▶▶ Gloria Estefan, Buster Poindexter

◀◀ Machito and His Afro-Cubans, Cab Calloway

Lawrence Gabriel

Steve Kilbey

See: The Church

Killing Joke

Formed 1979 in London, England

Jaz Coleman, vocals, keyboards; Geordie (Walker), guitar, synthesizers; Youth (born Martin Glover), bass, vocals (1979-82, 1994-present); Guy Pratt, bass (1982); Paul Raven, bass (1983-88, 1990); Andy Rourke, bass (1988); Taff, bass (1988); Paul Ferguson, drums (1979-88); Martin Atkins, drums (1988, 1990)

Sounding like correspondents reporting on the Apocalypse, Killing Joke made, to quote its debut single "War Dance," "music to march to." From the first notes of its eponymous 1980 debut album—an inexorably pulsing synthesizer tone that practically bored holes in listeners' skulls—this band announced that there was no more business as usual, that the old forms and methods had to be revised for harder times. Rather than using synthesizers as a soothing wash, Killing Joke uses the instrument as a rhythmic tool, combining those sounds with coldly abrasive guitar chords, simple, brutal drum beats, analytical yet passionate lyrics and Coleman's rough, urgent vocals. Coming out of punk but aiming to make dance music, this influential band's secret talent is striking a balance between complexity and simplicity. Even when tarted up for the dance crowd, the menacing sound of this industrial originator is classic.

what to buy: *Killing Joke* (EG, 1980, prod. Killing Joke) is one of the purest visions in rock history, a staggering and revolutionary stripping away of all rock ornamentation, revealing the frightening skeleton underneath and then making it slam-dance.

what to buy next: The comeback *Extremities, Dirt, and Various Repressed Emotions* (Noise/BMG, 1990, prod. Various) takes the heavy guitar inherent in the group's sound and places it in an anthemic rock context devoid of indulgence and flash.

what to avoid: *Outside the Gate* (EG, 1988, prod. Jaz Coleman and Geordie Walker) was ostensibly planned as a Coleman solo album and features just the singer, Geordie and session drummer Jimmy Copley. It's full of bizarre, incohesive arrangements constructed with numerology.

the rest: *What's This For...!* (EG, 1981) *Revelations* (EG, 1982) *Birds of a Feather* EP (EG, 1982) *Fire Dances* (EG, 1983) *Night Time* (EG, 1985) *Brighter Than a Thousand Suns* (EG, 1987) *An Incomplete Collection 1980-85* (EG, 1990) *Laugh? I Nearly Bought One!* (EG, 1992) *Wilful Days* (Caroline Blue Plate, 1995) *Pandemonium* (Big Life/Zoo, 1994) *Democracy* (Big Life/Zoo, 1996)

worth searching for: The out-of-print *Ha* EP (EG, 1982, prod. Killing Joke and Konrad Plank) provides a taste of live Killing Joke, including "War Dance."

solo outings:

Jaz Coleman (with Anne Dudley): Songs from the Victorious City (China/TVT, 1991)

▶▶ nine inch nails, Ministry, Filter

◀◀ Joy Division, Can, Kraftwerk

Steve Holtje

Albert King

Born April 25, 1923, in Indianola, Miss. Died December 21, 1992 in Memphis, Tenn.

Never as well-known as his like-named contemporary, B.B. King, Albert King was nonetheless almost as big of an influence. In fact, more rock guitarists—notably Jimi Hendrix, Cream-era Eric Clapton and Stevie Ray Vaughan—have copped directly from Albert than from any other bluesman. Standing an imposing six-foot-five, 250-pounds, the former bulldozer driver played with brute force, bending the strings on his upside-down Gibson Flying V with a ferocity that could be downright frightening. King made his first recordings during the early 50s and cut some fantastic sides for Bobbin and King Records from 1959-63. But he really hit his stride when he signed with Stax Records in 1966 and began working with Booker T and the MG's and the Memphis Horns. For all his toughness, King's music swung, a fact well-documented on the excellent live albums where he recaptures the Stax albums' drive backed by a hornless quartet.

what to buy: King's Stax debut, *Born Under a Bad Sign* (Atlantic, 1967, prod. Al Jackson) is an undisputed classic. The two-CD compilation *The Ultimate Collection* (Rhino, 1992, prod. Various) offers a fine career overview. Any of the three live albums recorded at San Francisco's Fillmore West Auditorium in 1968 capture the full power of King in concert—*Live Wire/Blues Power,* (Stax, 1968, prod. Al Jackson) *Wednesday Night in San Francisco* (Stax, 1990, prod. Al Jackson) and *Thursday Night in San Francisco* (Stax, 1990, prod. Al Jackson).

what to buy next: *Let's Have a Natural Ball* (Modern Blues, 1989, prod. Various) collects King's late-50s/early-60s sides, where he was backed by a hard-charging horn section. *I'll Play the Blues For You* (Stax, 1972, prod. Allen Jones and Henry Bush) includes the killer title track as well as "Little Brother," perhaps King's most tender moment.

what to avoid: *Red House* (Castle Records, 1991, prod. Joe Walsh and Alan Douglas) is a misguided, probably well-intentioned attempt by producers Walsh and Douglas to help the great bluesman modernize his sound. Ugh.

the rest: *Jammed Together: Albert King, Steve Cropper, Pops Staples* (Stax, 1969) *Years Gone By* (Stax, 1969) *Lovejoy* (Stax, 1970) *I Wanna Get Funky* (Stax, 1973) *The Pinch* (Stax, 1977) *New Orleans Heat* (Tomato, 1979) *Montreaux Festival* (Stax, 1979) *Blues for Elvis* (Stax, 1981) *Crosscut Saw: Albert King in San Francisco* (Stax, 1983/1992) *I'm in a Phone Booth Baby* (Stax, 1984) *The Lost Session* (Stax, 1986) *Blues at Sunrise* (Stax, 1988)

worth searching for: Discreetly circulating tapes of King's 1992 performance at the Detroit Blues Festival, a fiery exhibition that shows he still had the fire just a few months before his death.

Otis Rush, Eric Clapton, Jimi Hendrix, Stevie Ray Vaughan, Buddy Guy, Billy Gibbons

B.B. King, Jimmy Reed, T-Bone Walker

Alan Paul

B.B. King

Born Sept. 16, 1925, near Itta Bena, Miss.

No other blues artist has ever entered mainstream American culture quite like King. He is the only one to step inside from the commercial cold that has long been the bluesman's fate, to receive presidential citations and honorary degrees and star in commercials for the likes of McDonald's and Northwest Airlines. He has become so omnipresent that it's easy to forget why he's so revered: because he fundamentally changed the way the electric guitar is played. The roots of any blues-based electric guitarist can be traced back to King, whether they know it or not. King took single-string electric lead guitar playing, pioneered by Charlie Christian and T-Bone Walker, and coated it with Mississippi grit. The result was a highly personalized style marked by stinging finger vibrato, incredible economy and uncannily vocal-like phrasing, which had tremendous impact on every electric blues guitarist to follow—including Buddy Guy, Albert King, Freddie King and Otis Rush. These players, in turn, inspired countless rock guitarists, notably Jimi Hendrix, Eric Clapton and Stevie Ray Vaughan. Though his 70s and 80s records are often burdened by over-production, King has not recorded an embarrassing album—and he's released more than 50.

What Album Changed Your Life?

"I love (the Who's) Quadrophenia. I just love the whole feel of it--the expression, the spirituality, even of Tommy as well."

John Power (The La's, Cast)

what to buy: The emergence of King's groundbreaking style can be heard on *The Best Of B.B. King, Volume One* (Flair/Virgin, 1991, comp. Malcolm Jones), an essential collection of fifties' recordings which includes his original versions of standard-bearers such as "Three O'Clock Blues," "You Upset Me Baby" and "Five Long Years." King's lyrical guitar playing is part and parcel of his rare ability to communicate intimately with an audience, a powerful rapport which is perfectly captured on *Live at the Regal* (MCA, 1971, prod. Johnny Pate), a document of a 1964 performance which is considered by many to be not only his finest recording, but the greatest album in all modern blues. This treasure-trove of sophisticated-yet-down home music includes such staples as "It's My Own Fault," "Every Day I Have The Blues" and "Sweet Little Angel." *Completely Well* (MCA, 1969, prod. Bill Szymczyk) contains King's only Top 20 hit, "The Thrill is Gone," and is solid through and through.

what to buy next: Sooner or later, you'll probably want the four-CD boxed set *King of the Blues* (MCA, 1992, comp. Andy McKaie), which provides an excellent summary of King's career. *Live at San Quentin* (MCA, 1990, prod. Trade Martin and Sidney Seidenberg) and *Blues Summit* (MCA, 1993, prod. Danny Diante), which features a host of guest stars, are King's best recent efforts, both showing that he's still got plenty of both sting in his vibrato and ideas in his head.

what to avoid: *B.B. King in London* (MCA, 1971, prod. Ed Michel and Joe Zagarino) is the usual pointless exercise of hooking the blues guy up with well meaning rockers who love him- but can't play his stuff half as well as his own band.

the rest: *Blues is King* (MCA, 1967) *Lucille* (MCA, 1968) *The Electric B.B. King—His Best* (MCA, 1968) *Live & Well* (MCA, 1969) *Incredible Soul of B.B. King* (MCA, 1970) *Indianola Mississippi Seeds* (MCA, 1970) *Live in Cook County Jail* (MCA, 1970) *Back in the Alley: The Classic Blues of B.B. King* (MCA, 1973) *The Best of B.B. King* (MCA, 1973) *To Know You is To Love You* (MCA, 1973) *Friends* (MCA, 1974) *B.B. King and Bobby Bland: Together for the First Time Live* (MCA, 1974) *Lucille Talks Back* (MCA, 1975) *B.B. King & Bobby Bland: Together Again...Live* (MCA, 1976) *King Size* (MCA, 1977) *Midnight Believer* (MCA, 1978) *Take it Home* (MCA, 1979) *Live at Ole Miss* (MCA, 1980) *Great Moments with B.B. King* (MCA, 1981) *There Must be a Better World Somewhere* (MCA, 1981) *Love Me Tender* (MCA, 1982) *Blues 'N' Jazz* (MCA, 1983) *Six Silver Strings* (MCA, 1985) *Do the Boogie: Early 50's Classics* (Flair/Virgin, 1988) *King of the Blues 1989* (MCA, 1989) *There is Always One More Time* (MCA, 1991) *The Fabulous B.B. King* (Flair/Virgin, 1991) *Singin' The Blues* (Flair/Virgin, 1991) *Live at the Apollo* (GRP, 1991) *Sweet Little Angel* (Flair/Virgin, 1992)

worth searching for: A single CD that combines the seminal *Live at the Regal* with the nearly as good *Live in Cook County Jail* (MCA, 1984) but was taken off the market in favor of the individual CDs. The united volume is nothing less than blues bliss.

▶▶ Buddy Guy, Eric Clapton, David Gilmour, Albert King, Otis Rush, Stevie Ray Vaughan, Kenny Wayne Shepherd

◀◀ Blind Lemon Jefferson, T-Bone Walker, Django Reinhardt, Lonnie Johnson, Clarence "Gatemouth" Brown

Alan Paul

Ben E. King

Born Sept. 23, 1938, in Henderson, N.C.

With its reverberating, four-note bass line, "Stand By Me" is a Hall of Fame song before King even starts singing; when he wraps his smooth tenor around the lyrics, it becomes a hymn for the ages. It's one of the most covered songs on the planet, and it enjoys regular boosts in popularity thanks to TV commercials and movies—most notably Rob Reiner's 1986 film of the same name. It's hardly all King has to offer, though. As one of the many fine lead singers in The Drifters' revolving door of frontmen, he sang lead on "There Goes My Baby," "Save The Last Dance For Me" and "I Count The Tears," and his solo career boasts "Spanish Harlem" and a handful of other pop-R&B gems. *The Ben E. King Anthology* (Rhino, 1993, prod. Various) covers all the aforementioned—plus non-album singles—across a remastered, double-length and nicely annotated package. It's what you need; the rest of the available titles are mostly second-rate compilations.

the rest: *The Ultimate Collection* (Atlantic, 1987) *The Best of Ben E. King* (Curb, 1993) *The Best of Ben E. King and the Drifters* (Dominion, 1993)

Allan Orski

Carole King

Born Carole Klein, Feb. 9, 1942, in Brooklyn, N.Y.

From the early 60s to the mid-70s, King was the champion of making musical memories. Like some favorite scent long gone but easily remembered, King and her then-husband Gerry Goffin covered a wide territory, placing a permanent stake wherever they went. Given pop music's far-flung scope and ever-changing tastes, King's accomplishments are extraordinary. From deft romantic ballads as realistic as they were heartfelt came such hits as "Take Good Care of My Baby," "Up on the Roof," "Crying in the Rain" and "Will You Love Me Tomorrow?" The British music invasion and a generation's mood swing didn't slow the tide. "Don't Bring Me Down," "I'm into Something Good," "I Wasn't Born to Follow" and "Pleasant Valley Sunday" circumnavigated a field of what were career-ending land mines for other songwriters. And to think that was only a hint of what was to come when she stepped out on her own...

what to buy: Her third release, *Tapestry,* (Ode, 1971, prod. Lou Adler) is a benchmark recording for King and for pop music. With her earnest yet vulnerable vocals, a fluid backup band and Adler's sure production, *Tapestry* combined a bit of classic King material ("(You Make Me Feel Like)A Natural Woman," "Will You Love Me Tomorrow?") with new, self-assured songs such as "I Feel the Earth Move," "So Far Away," "It's Too Late" and "Home Again." The album was on the charts, deservedly, for more than five years. *A Natural Woman: The Ode Collection 1968-1976* (Legacy, 1994, prod. Lou Adler) is a two-disc set that surrounds *Tapestry* with her better solo work and a previously unreleased live duet with James Taylor on "You've Got a Friend."

what to buy next: *City Streets*(Capitol, 1989) is an unjustifiably overlooked effort, with King unhesitatingly delivering her most powerful and passionate vocals ever. Eric Clapton guests, and the title track is a killer

what to avoid: *Fantasy* (Ode, 1973/Legacy, 1991) and *Rhymes and Reason* (Ode, 1972/Legacy 1991) go nowhere in the slow lane.

the rest: *Carole King: Writer* (Ode, 1970/Legacy, 1991) *Music* (Ode, 1971/Legacy, 1991) *Wrap Around Joy* (Ode, 1974/Legacy, 1991) *Really Rosie* (Ode, 1975/Columbia, 1986) *Thoroughbred* (Ode/Legacy, 1976) *Her Greatest Hits (1972-1978)* (Ode/Columbia, 1978) *In Concert* (King's X/Rhythm Safari, 1994)

worth searching for: King's first band, the City, stepped out front and center with her reflective debut *Now That Everything's Been Said.* (Ode, 1968) Overlooked but not forgotten, it was as careful as it was an appropriate first recording for King.

Carly Simon, Tori Amos, Bonnie Hayes

Doc Pomus, Mort Shuman

Patrick McCarty

Freddie King

Born Sept. 30, 1934, in Gilmer, Tex. Died Dec. 28, 1976 in Dallas, Texas

Not having the towering presence on ghetto jukeboxes of his namesake B.B. King or the sweeping influence of his Chicago blues elders Muddy Waters and Howlin' Wolf, Freddie King nevertheless eventually emerged as one of the great electric bluesmen. His melodic, driving shuffles struck a resonant chord with a younger generation of white blues-rock guitarists, who passed around his rare, out-of-print albums like sacred scriptures. His 1961 instrumental hit, "Hideaway," gave King a nationwide reputation, though none of his subsequent singles appeared on even the R&B charts after that year. But the blues boom of the late 60s rescued him from obscurity and he made a pair of modest albums under the aegis of saxophonist King Curtis and a series of more successful albums produced by Leon Russell. His stinging attack on loping instrumentals laid one of the cornerstones of moder blues guitar vocabulary. Although his reputation rests with his guitar, King also sang with an underrated, powerful style. His lasting influence has insured Freddie King's recognition as one of the great postwar blues masters.

what to buy: The best available overview of his long career, *Hideaway: The Best Of Freddie King,* (Rhino, 1993, prod. Various) includes three cuts from his later recording but concentrates on the fruitful abundance of his King years (1961-66).

what to buy next: A recently discovered tape, *Live At the Electric Ballroom 1974,* (Black Top, 1995, exec. prod. Hammond Scott) mixes a rare pair of acoustic numbers recorded on a radio show with a blasting, ripping concert appearance.

what to avoid: The two albums King recorded with the customarily savvy King Curtis, *Freddie King Is a Blues Master* (Cotillion, 1969) and *My Feeling For the Blues,* (Cotillion, 1970) both suffer from thin accompaniment, too little guitar and reedy vocals.

the rest: *King Of the Blues* (EMI, 1995) *17 Hits* (Federal, 1987) *1934-1976* (with Eric Clapton) (Polydor 1993)

worth searching for: All his original King Records albums remain highly prized collector's items, and his especially enduring debut, *Freddy King Sings,* (King, 1961/Modern Blues Recordings, 1989) is one of the great modern blues albums.

Eric Clapton, Jimi Hendrix, Stevie Ray Vaughan

Otis Rush, Eddie Taylor, Robert Jr. Lockwood

Joel Selvin

King Crimson

Formed 1969 in London, England

Robert Fripp, guitar, mellotron; Ian McDonald, keyboards, woodwinds (1969); Greg Lake, bass, vocals (1969); Michael Giles, drums; Peter Sinfield, lyricist (1969-72); Mel Collins, woodwinds (1971-72); Boz Burrell, bass, vocals (1971-72); Ian Wallace, drums (1971-72); David Cross, violin, viola, mellotron (1972-74); John Wetton, bass, vocals (1972-74); Bill Bruford, drums (1972-74, 1981-84, 1994-present); Jamie Muir, percussion, (1972-73); Richard Palmer-James, lyricist (1972-74); Adrian Belew, vocals, guitar, lyricist (1981-84, 1994-present); Tony Levin, Chapman Stick, bass, vocals (1981-84, 1994-present); Trey Gunn, guitar, bass (1994-present); Pat Mastelotto, drums (1994-present)

The band that almost gave art rock a good name, King Crimson grew out of a trio that couldn't sell more than 600 copies of its only album in its own country. Brothers Michael and Peter Giles teamed with young guitarist Fripp in Giles Giles & Fripp, whose 1968 album *The Cheerful Insanity of Giles Giles & Fripp* is a legendary flop. Musically more than a historical footnote but less than a revolution, the band's whimsical social commentary sounds too much of its time to be taken seriously. When Peter Giles chose to work as a computer operator (though he would continue playing sporadically), Lake joined up with Michael Giles, Fripp and new members McDonald and Sinfield. The new group's debut far surpassed its predecessor's. After one concert; audience member Jimi Hendrix asked Fripp to shake his left hand because it was the one closer to his heart. *In the Court of the Crimson King* showed that progressive rock could be as heavy as Led Zeppelin yet as intricate and full of dynamic contrasts as classical music (the howling, bludgeoning "21st Century Schizoid Man" was the first of many Crimson classics in unusual time signatures), and sometimes as tuneful as the Beatles. King Crimson has pursued an ideology of musical adventure ever since, through myriad line-up changes (Fripp's favorite is the original) and musical personalities. The group works and breaks at Fripp's whim—a formidable calling due to his many other musical projects. Currently, King Crimson is a six-piece "double trio" that performs in various configurations. There certainly are less-than-ideal aspects to the Crimson legacy; for instance, Fripp, by his preference for vocalists who also carry a heavy instrumental load, has consistently burdened the band with unsubtle singers and has seemed content to let the lyrics pursue the writers' fancies no matter how ephemeral or ridiculous. But the instrumental legacy is generally irreproachable, involving a willingness to explore new territory and take risks that most comparably successful bands shun.

what to buy: *In the Court of the Crimson King* (Atlantic, 1969/EG, 1989, prod. King Crimson) was influential and stands up well. *Red* (Atlantic, 1974/EG, 1989, prod. King Crimson) is the definitive statement by the most powerful Crimson lineup (Fripp, Wetton and Bruford). *Discipline* (Warner Bros./EG, 1981, prod. King Crimson and Rhett Davies) reinvents the group's principles in lither form. With these albums, the listener has the best of the three most important configurations.

what to buy next: *The Great Deceiver,* (Caroline, 1992) a live, four-CD cross-section of the most versatile and wonderfully bombastic band (the 1973-74 lineup) ever to command silence with passages for violin and mellotron and then blow minds with relentless crescendos. The best summary is *The Essential King Crimson: Frame by Frame,* (Caroline, 1991, prod. Various) which includes not only a chronological review over three CDs (including previously unreleased or revamped material) but also a fourth CD of live material, most newly issued. Fripp provides detailed liner notes.

what to avoid: *The Abbreviated King Crimson* (EG/Caroline, 1991, prod. Various) *The Compact King Crimson* (EG/Caroline, 1987, prod. Various) and *The Concise King Crimson,* (Blue Plate/Caroline, 1993, prod. Various) all made superfluous by the vastly better *Frame By Frame.*

the rest: *The Cheerful Insanity of Giles Giles & Fripp* (Deram/London, 1968/1992) *In the Wake of Poseidon* (Atlantic, 1970/EG, 1989) *Lizard* (Atlantic, 1971/EG, 1989) *Islands* (Atlantic, 1972/EG, 1989) *Lark's Tongues in Aspic* (Atlantic, 1973/EG, 1989) *Starless and Bible Black* (Atlantic, 1974/EG, 1989) *Beat* (Warner Bros./EG, 1982) *Three of a Perfect Pair* (Warner Bros./EG, 1984) *B'-Boom* (Discipline, 1995) *VROOM* (Discipline EP, 1994) *Thrak* (Virgin, 1995) *Thrak Attack* (Discipline, 1996)

worth searching for: The five live 1972 performances on the rare *Earthbound* (EG, 1972, prod. Robert Fripp) are sometimes overindulgent, and the sound can be clotted, but it documents a somewhat overlooked lineup of Fripp, Collins, Burrell and Wallace. Only one track of the live *USA* (Atlantic, 1975) made it onto *Frame By Frame,* not nearly enough for a powerful lineup's live swan song.

▶▶ Emerson Lake & Palmer, Foreigner, Bad Company, U.K., Helmet, Porcupine, No Man, Iceburn, Living Colour, His Name Is Alive

◀◀ Jimi Hendrix, Beatles, John McLaughlin

see also: *Robert Fripp, Emerson, Lake and Palmer, Bad Company, Adrian Belew, Yes*

Steve Holtje

King Curtis

Born Curtis Owsley, Feb. 7, 1934 in Ft. Worth, Texas. Died Aug. 14, 1971, in New York, N.Y.

Although he only rarely achieved fame on his own, King Curtis probably was the most influential rock/R&B saxophone player of his time. He began playing in Texas during the 40s, hooked up with Lionel Hampton in 1952 and later became one of New York's most desired session players. As leader of Atlantic Records' house R&B band, Curtis played some of the most famous sax breaks in pop music, among them the Coasters' "Yakety Yak" and Aretha Franklin's "Respect." Curtis also played for Nat King Cole, Buddy Holly, Sam Cooke and John Lennon and briefly roomed with Duane Allman. But Curtis, who came from the tradition of hard-blowing Texas blues saxophonists, also had his own hits. Three of his instrumental records reached the Top 40: *Soul Twist* in 1962 and *Memphis Soul Stew* and *Ode to Billie Joe* in 1967. Curtis was stabbed to death outside his New York City apartment in 1971, at age 37.

what to buy: *Instant Soul: The Legendary King Curtis* (Razor & Tie, 1994, prod. Not listed) is an excellent compilation that covers 1956-70 but concentrates on the recordings he made with the Muscle Shoals Rhythm Section. The 23 tracks include all three of his Top 40 hits.

what to buy next: During the session captured on *King Curtis & Champion Jack Dupree: Blues at Montreux,* (Atlantic, 1973, prod. King Curtis and Joel Dorn) Curtis is at his loosest, with a band that includes Cornell Dupree on guitar and Jerry Jemmott on bass.

what to avoid: *Soul on Soul,* (Pickwick, 1972, prod. Not listed) a cheapie posthumous compilation from Curtis' Capitol period, issued as part of Pickwick's "Harlem Hitparade" series. *The Best of King Curtis* (Collectables, 1989) doesn't nearly cover the claim of its title.

the rest: *The New Scene of King Curtis* (New Jazz-Prestige, 1960/Original Jazz Classics, 1992) *King Soul* (Prestige, 1960) *Soul Meeting* (Prestige, 1960) *Trouble in Mind* (Prestige, 1961/Original Blues Classic, 1992) *Old Gold* (Tru-Sound, 1962) *It's Party Time With King Curtis* (Tru-Sound, 1962) *Country Soul* (Capitol, 1965) *Soul Serenade* (Capitol, 1966) *That Loving Feeling* (Atco, 1966) *Live at Small's Paradise* (Atco, 1967) *King Curtis Plays the Great Memphis Hits* (Atco, 1967) *King Size Soul* (Atco, 1967) *Sweet Soul* (Atco, 1968) *Best of King Curtis* (Atco, 1968) *Sax in Motion* (RCA Camden, 1968) *Instant Groove* (Atco, 1969) *Everybody's Talkin'* (Atco, 1972) *Jazz Groove* (Prestige, 1973) *Soul Twist* (Collectables, 1988) *Soul Serenade* (JCI, 1991) *Home Cookin'* (Zillion, 1992) *Night Train* (Prestige, 1995) *The Capitol Years* (Blue Note, 1996)

worth searching for: *Live at the Fillmore West* (Atco, 1971, prod. King Curtis and Arif Mardin) captures a hot set when Curtis opened a Bay Area stand for Franklin, who was recording her own live album of the same name. The box set *Blow Man, Blow!* (Bear Family) compiles Curtis' recordings for Capitol from 1962-65 and includes 16 previously unreleased tracks.

▶▶ Clarence Clemons, Leroi Moore (Dave Matthews Band)

◀◀ Illinois Jacquet, Earl Bostic, Arnett Cobb

Brian Mansfield

King Missile

Formed 1986 in New York, N.Y. Disbanded 1994.

John S. Hall, vocals; Dogbowl, guitar (1987-88); Dave Rick, guitar (1990-94); Chris Xefos, bass, keyboards (1990-94); Roger Murdock, drums (1990-94)

There are often references to rock lyrics being the new poetry, but rarely in the past have poets fronted bands. The viewpoint of poet Hall (the middle initial differentiates him from the mellow-rock guitarist of the 70s), with his skewed yet peculiarly logical method of taking everyday situations or metaphors to extreme conclusions, fits well in front of a band, however, and for a while he was the most visible point in a trend reversing that situation. Starting out as a duo named King Missile (Dog Fly Religion) with Dogbowl on the local Shimmy-Disc label of producer Kramer, King Missile (the group's monicker comes from a Japanese comic book character) mutated into a quartet and had a college radio hit with "Jesus Was Way Cool" (from 1990's *The Mystical Shit*) that led to signing with Atlantic, where *The Way to Salvation* spawned two more favorites, "My Heart is a Flower" (which demolishes a sappy metaphor by carrying it to its logical extreme) and "Sex with You." The stop-start punkish riff tunes constructed by the musicians should not be underrated merely because Hall is perceived as the focus of the group, since it was actually quite collaborative. The group broke up when Atlantic dropped it, with Hall putting together The Body Has a Head with string players Sasha Forte and Jane Scarpantoni. Murdock went on to drum with the ironic country group the Wright Brothers.

what to buy: *Happy Hour* (Atlantic, 1992, prod. Kramer, Steve Watson and King Missile) contains band's best melding of music and words.

what to buy next: *The Way to Salvation* (Atlantic, 1991, prod. King Missile and Lou Giordano) covers a broad topical and attitudinal range.

what to avoid: None

the rest: *They* (Shimmy Disc, 1988) *The Mystical Shit* (Shimmy Disc, 1990) *Fluting on the Hump* (Shimmy-Disc, 1987) *King Missile* (Atlantic, 1994)

worth searching for: The various artists compilation *Broome Closet Anti-Folk Sessions* (109, 1989, prod. Roger Manning) contains five Hall poems, some later used by King Missile.

solo outings:

John S. Hall & Kramer: *Real Men* (Shimmy-Disc, 1991)

▶▶ Maggie Estep/I Love Everybody

◀◀ Bob Holman, Allan Ginsburg

Steve Holtje

King Sunny Ade

Born Sunday Adeniyi, Sept. 22, 1946 in Ohogbo, Nigeria

Guitarist-vocalist Ade is the most widely acclaimed juju musician outside of Africa and the first signed to a major international label. The term "tapestry of sound" was made for this band, with its six guitars, seven vocalists and eight percussionists, in addition to bass and keyboards. Ade arranges this orchestra into a soothing symphony that rides smooth rhythms and drifting melodies. First appearing in the 1920s, juju is a Yoruban folk music that features interplay between vocals and talking drums. I.K Cairo is the greatest juju musician to date with Chief Ebenezer Obey and Ade rivals for second place. Ade's own innovation includes adding pedal steel guitar and synthesizers to the music, making it slightly more listener-friendly to Western pop ears. His first band as a leader was the Green Spots, organized in 1966 and Ade was soon known as a guitar virtuoso with a space sound and a "shooting strings" technique of staccato chord strokes. In 1974, he started his own record label (Sunny Alade), renamed his band the African Beats and put out 40 albums over the next decade. In 1982, the group signed with Island Records, which promoted Ade as a world music star to replace the late Bob Marley. But after disappointing record sales he was dropped in 1984. Due to dissension in the ranks, Ade dropped the African Beats and reorganized the group. He's still a top international draw, and in Nigeria he regularly sells 200,000 of his releases.

what to buy: *Juju Music* (Mango, 1982, prod. Martin Meissonnier) is Ade's first international release and the one that opened the world's ears to juju. The dreamy, mesmerizing groove of "Ja Funmi" sets the tone for this exotic musical journey culled from Ade's past hits. Lightly chiming guitars, bubbling talking drums, ethereal pedal steel and Ade's soothing voice weave in and out of this delightfully different sound. *Synchro System* (Mango, 1983, prod. Meissonnier) finds the band in the same mode as the previous record, but the guitars are mixed down and the newly added synthesizer provides more sonic tricks.

what to buy next: *Live At the Hollywood Palace* (I.R.S., 1994, prod. King Sunny Ade) features the New African Beats at a 1990 show where the group kicked things off with a couple of upbeat Latin-sounding songs before moving into the polyrythmic space groove. The closer, "Talking Drum," is an absolute clinic on the instrument.

the rest: *Aura* (Mango, 1984) *The Return Of the Juju King* (Verbe, 1987) *Live Juju Live* (Rykodisc, 1988) *E Dide (Get Up)* (Mesa, 1995)

worth searching for: *Ajoo* (Makossa International, 1983, prod. King Sunny Ade) was originally released on Ade's own Sunny Alade label for the Nigerian market and displays a less flashy but satisfying side of the band.

solo outings:

Former Ade bassist Ken Okulolo's Kotoja: Sawale (Mesa, 1992)

▶▶ Segun Adewale, Kotoja, Johnny Clegg, Peter Gabriel

◀◀ IK Dairo, Tunde Nightingale

Lawrence Gabriel

King's X

Formed 1980 in Springfield, Mo.

Doug Pinnick, bass, vocals; Ty Tabor, guitar, vocals; Jerry Gaskill, drums, vocals

Initially convening as a cover band called the Edge, the trio moved to Houston and eventually hooked up with ZZ Top video producer Sam Taylor, who renamed the group King's X. Its combination of heavy metal instrumentation, Beatle-esque vocal harmonies and pro-Christian lyrics found little support at major record labels—forcing the band to issue its first record on the New Jersey-based independent Megaforce Records. Before long, the skin-tight musicianship and inventive songs began converting critics and fans alike. But King's X seemed determined to resist any easy route to success; during the metal boom the band resisted that classification, and during the boom in Christian music it avoided that tag as well. In a last-ditch attempt to break the band, Atlantic Records drafted superstar producer Brendan O'Brien (Pearl Jam) to craft its 1995 release—a matchup that produced another great album, but no hits.

what to buy: Among longtime fans, the group's sophomore album, *Gretchen Goes to Nebraska* (Megaforce, 1989, prod. King's X and Sam Taylor) is often cited as its finest, focusing its pop melodicism and hard rock musicality into a potent stew. With a fiery take on Fleetwood Mac's "Over My Head" and the supple ballad "Summertime," this record seemed to forecast a band with significant artistic strides ahead.

what to buy next: Although some will say O'Brien filed off the group's rough edges, *Dogman* (Atlantic, 1994, prod. Brendan O'Brien) presents a further refinement of the band's pop/metal sound, with the religious messages sublimated ever further in a refreshing, stripped-down sound. Still, that doesn't keep crackling midtempo cuts such as "Let's Pretend" or "Black the Sky" from rocking hard, along with a live recording of Jimi Hendrix's "Manic Depression."

what to avoid: Some bands take awhile to hit their stride, and King's X first album, *Out of the Silent Planet,* (Megaforce, 1982, prod. King's X and Sam Taylor) WOOF! show it's no different.

the rest: *Faith, Hope and Love* (Megaforce, 1990) *King's X* (Atlantic, 1992) *Ear Candy* (Atlantic, 1996)

worth searching for: One of the few bright spots on the soundtrack to the 1991 film *Bill and Ted's Bogus Journey* (Interscope/EastWest, 1991) is "Junior's Gone Wild," a contribution from King's X.

Eye and I, Follow For Now

Living Colour, Petra, the Beatles

Eric Deggans

Kingfish

See: Grateful Dead

The Kingsmen

Formed 1958 in Portland, Ore. Disbanded 1967.

Lynn Eaton, vocals, sax; Jack Ely, vocals, guitar (1958-63); Mike Mitchell, guitar; Bob Nordby, bass (1958-63); Don Gallucci, organ (1962); Gary Abbot, drums (1963-67); Norm Sundholm, bass (1963-67)

Think one name two times: "Louie Louie." What the "I Love Lucy" television series is to reruns, the Kingsmen's 1963 smash hit, recorded for just $50, is to oldies radio and shag/frat/beach parties. Both are ubiquitous; written by Richard Berry in 1956 and covered by countless bands, the Kingsmen's rendition remains the one that anyone cares about. The band landed other Top 20 hits, such as "Money" in 1964 and "The Jolly Green Giant" in 1965, all of which are captured on *The Best of the Kingsmen* (Rhino, 1991) provides a surprisingly clean sound, with even Ely's usually muffled vocals sound clearer than usual.

the rest: *On Campus* (Wand, 1965/Sundazed, 1993) *Up & Away* (Sundazed, 1993)

Patrick McCarty

Kingston Trio

Formed 1957 in San Francisco, Calif. Disbanded 1967.

Bob Shane, guitar, vocals; Nick Reynolds, guitar, vocals; Dave Guard, banjo, vocals (1957-61, died March 22, 1991); John Stewart, banjo, guitar, vocals (1961-67)

The Kingston Trio just made it look too easy, it's no wonder it was reviled by folk music colleagues who watched the group leap over them to the top of the charts. The Trio—three glib, fun-loving West Coast guys with guitars, banjos, bongos, three-part harmonies and matching striped shirts and chinos—were big stuff in the late 50s and early 60s, when five of its first six albums went to No. 1 on the Billboard charts, occupying the top spot for a total of 50 weeks. The Trio's basic sound was deceptively simple, and its albums were much better than its detractors were ready to admit. The Trio's this-business-is-easy attitude influenced many of their followers to pick up guitars and start groups of their own; when folk became rock, many of them would become stars. Guard, the most gifted, left in 1961, replaced by Stewart, who would go on to a prolific solo career.

what to buy: Best place to start is *The Kingston Trio* (Capitol Collector's Series, 1990, prod. Voyle Gilmore), 20 of their best-known tunes on one CD—including all 10 Top Ten hit singles. If you're really interested, try *The Capitol Years,* (Capitol, 1995, prod. Voyle Gilmore) an extensive four-CD reissue that favors outtakes and unreleased tracks to offer a more sympathetic look at the Trio's place in history. *New Frontier* (Capitol, 1962, prod. Voyle Gilmore), the group's finest album with Stewart, centers around the enthusiasm over John F. Kennedy's presidency.

what to buy next: *Live at the Hungry I* (Capitol, 1959, prod. Voyle Gilmore) captures a club show that includes "Zombie Jamboree,' "The Merry Minuet" and "They Call the Wind Maria," plus lots of stage patter. *At Large* (Capitol, 1959, prod. Voyle Gilmore) features Bess Hawes' "M.T.A.," Guard's "Getaway John," "The Long Black Rifle" and Jane Bowers' "Remember the Alamo." *String Along* (Capitol, 1960, prod. Voyle Gilmore) includes Tom Drake's "The Escape of Old

John Webb," Cisco Hayes and Lee Hays' "Bad Man's Blunder" and Harlan Howard's "Everglades."

what to avoid: *Once Upon a Time* (Tetragrammaton, 1969) was recorded live at Lake Tahoe near the end of the group's career in 1966, and it shows. Although the singing is fine, the jokes have gone flat and the song selection is questionable.

the rest: *The Kingston Trio* (Capitol, 1958) *Stereo Concert* (Capitol, 1959) *Here We Go Again* (Capitol, 1959) *Sold Out* (Capitol, 1960) *Something Special* (Capitol, 1962) *Make Way* (Capitol, 1961) *Goin' Places* (Capitol, 1961) *Encores* (Capitol, 1961) *Close-Up* (Capitol, 1961) *College Concert* (Capitol, 1962) *The Kingston Trio #16* (Capitol, 1963) *Sunny Side* (Capitol, 1963) *Time to Think* (Capitol, 1963) *Back in Town* (Capitol, 1964) *Nick-Bob-John* (Capitol, 1964) *Stay Awhile* (Capitol, 1965) *Somethin' Else* (Capitol, 1965) *Children of the Morning* (Capitol, 1966)

Worth Searching For: *Live at Newport,* (Vanguard, 1994, prod. Mary Katherine Aldin) recorded live at the 1959 Newport Folk Festival before a demanding East Coast audience.

Peter, Paul and Mary, Brothers Four, Chad Mitchell Trio, Limelighters, Journeymen, Serendipity Singers, New Christy Minstrels, Roger McGuinn, Bob Dylan, Simon and Garfunkel

The Weavers, Pete Seeger, Gateway Singers

see also: *John Stewart*

Leland Rucker

The Kinks

Formed 1963 in London, England

Ray Davies, vocals, guitar; Dave Davies, lead guitar, vocals; Pete Quaife, bass (1963-69); Mick Avory, drums (1963-83); John Dalton, bass (1969-77); John Gosling, keyboards (1971-78); Andy Pyle, bass (1977-79); Bob Henrit, drums (1984-present); Ian Gibbons, keyboards (1979-88); Jim Rodford, bass (1979-present)

The Kinks are the oft-forgotten group among the giants of the British Invasion. The young band, interested largely in American blues in the beginning, crashed into the charts and rock history by virtually inventing the distorted power chords of hard rock with "You Really Got Me." Yet the Kinks may have ended up contributing more through the egeliac, literate, sharply observed tunes about British everyday life and traditions gone by. The Kinks were among the first to put a sitar in a song (months before the Beatles) and to score a mini-rock opera (*Arthur*, delayed until after *Tommy*). When the original quartet fractured in the late 60s, the band continued as the pair of battling brothers backed by a long line of anonymous rhythm sections. Rediscovered by punks during the first new wave and again in the Britpop movement of the mid-90s, songwriter Ray Davies was putting the band's early days in perspective in a book, "X-Ray" and a one-man theatrical piece, "20th Century Man," even as he planned for the band's continuance.

what to buy: The band's earliest days, and most of its biggest hits, are best compiled on *The Kinks Greatest Hits.* (Rhino, 1989, prod. Shel Talmy) The buzzsaw of "All Day and All of the Night" makes way for the more insinuating "Set Me Free" and social observation of "A Well Respected Man"—all within the course of three years. A fine introduction to the other side of the Kinks has a decent starting point in *The Kinks Kronicles,* (Reprise, 1972, prod. Shel Talmy and Ray Davies) a double set that introduces Americans to the band's excellent late 60s period in a collection as quirkily anthologized as the music itself.

what to buy next: *Arthur (or the Decline and Fall of the British Empire)* (Reprise, 1969, prod. Ray Davies) is an album that remains a thrilling song cycle. The Kinks' career, like so many others', was sidetracked by bad business dealings, succinctly summarized on *Lola Versus Powerman and the Moneyground, Part One* (Reprise, 1971, prod. Ray Davies) which also gave the band arguably its biggest hit in the ingeniously sly "Lola." *Come Dancing with the Kinks* (Arista, 1986, prod. Various) collects the best of the Kinks late 70s to mid 80s work, including the hit "Come Dancing."

what to avoid: *Kinky Music: The Larry Page Orchestra Arranged by Ray Davies Plays the Music of the Kinks.* (Pye import, 1966; Rhino reissue, 1983) WOOF! Oh, boy! Early Kinks songs as elevator music!

the rest: *You Really Got Me* (Reprise, 1965) *Kinks-Size* (Reprise, 1965) *Kinda Kinks* (Reprise, 1965) *Kinks Kinkdom* (Reprise, 1965) *Kinks Kontroversey* (Reprise, 1966) *The Live Kinks* (Reprise, 1967) *Something Else* (Reprise, 1968) *The Kinks Are the Village Preservation Society* (Reprise 1968) *Muswell Hillbillies* (RCA, 1970/Rhino, 1990) *Everybody's in Showbiz* (RCA, 1972) *Preservation Act 1* (RCA, 1973) *Preservation Act 2* (RCA, 1974) *Soap Opera* (RCA 1975) *Schoolboys in Disgrace* (RCA, 1975) *Celluloid Heroes* (RCA, 1976) *Sleepwalker* (Arista, 1977) *Misfits* (Arista, 1978)

Low Budget (Arista, 1979) *One for the Road* (Arista, 1980) *Give the People What They Want* (Arista 1981) *State of Confusion* (Arista, 1983) *Word of Mouth* (Arista, 1984) *Think Visual* (MCA, 1986) *Live—The Road* (MCA, 1987) *UK Jive* (MCA, 1989) *Phobia* (Columbia, 1993)

worth searching for: *The Great Lost Kinks Album,* (Reprise, 1973, prod. Shel Talmy and Ray Davies) a kind of sequel to *Kinks Kronicles,* collects some hard-to-find songs from the great, late 60s Kinks era. *To the Bone* (Konk/Grapevine, 1994, prod. Ray Davies) is an import that finds the brothers Davies in a nostalgic mood, reviving many of their classics unplugged-style before an audience in their own studio.

solo outings:

Ray Davies: *Return to Waterloo* (Arista, 1985)

Dave Davies: *AFLI-3603* (RCA, 1980) **WOOF!** *Glamour* (RCA, 1981) *Chosen People* (Warner Bros., 1983) **WOOF!**

The Who, the Jam, Blur, Pulp

Big Bill Broonzy, The Beatles, Little Richard, Charles Dickens

Roger Catlin

Kevin Kinney

See: Drivin' N' Cryin'

Bill Kirchen

See: Commander Cody and his Lost Planet Airmen

Kiss

Formed 1972 in New York, N.Y.

Gene Simmons, bass, vocals; Paul Stanley guitar, vocals; Ace Frehley guitar, vocals (1972-81, 1996); Peter Criss, drums, vocals (1972-79, 1996); Eric Carr, drums (1980-91, died Nov. 24, 1991); Vinnie Vincent, guitar (1982-83); Mark St. John, guitar (1984); Bruce Kulick, guitar (1985-present); Eric Singer, drums (1991-present)

Complete with full make-up, cartoonish personas, and elaborate pyrotechnics that would have Michael Jackson running for something flame retardant, Kiss enjoyed phenomenon-level success during the 70s. The fire breathin', blood spittin' spectacle of the band overshadowed its often rudimentary chops, which did sharpen over the years. Kiss have always been about show biz, though, and at the height of its popularity there were Kiss dolls (worth a small fortune if you've got 'em), a TV movie (with ratings to rival Luke and Laura's wedding) and comic books to augment the regular album releases. The thumping, raging hormone party lyrics—which make David Lee Roth sound like David Thoreau—have been critically derided since day one, along with everything else about the band. Kiss, of course, has laughed all the way to the band. It's retained the enormous Kiss Army fan base (even throughout the post-Frehley/sans make-up bland years), and the original lineup's full make-up reunion tour was one of the hottest tickets of 1996.

what to buy: *Kiss Alive!* (Casablanca/Mercury, 1975, prod. Eddie Kramer) clearly reveals that Kiss is stronger in the arena than in the studio. Previously lumbering riffs turn thunderous, the bombast catching fire on soon-to-be classics such as, "Deuce," "Strutter," "Firehouse" and the anthem "Rock 'n' Roll All Night." On *Destroyer* (Casablanca/Mercury, 1976, prod. Bob Ezrin), better production captures the theatrics of the band, along with strings and a technically enhanced attack. "Detroit Rock City" is a challenging rocker in its own right, and the Criss-sung "Beth," set the mark for myriad (lesser) power ballads spewed by various hair bands during the 80s.

what to buy next: *Dressed to Kill* (Casablanca/Mercury, 1975, prod. Neil Bogart and Kiss) is the leanest and best of the early albums, nearly matching *Destroyer* in all its lewd thumping. *Love Gun* (Casablanca/Mercury, 1977. prod. Kiss and Eddie Kramer) takes a lighter tone with the same spiffy production values as *Destroyer.* Poppy jewels such as "Plaster Caster" and "Christine Sixteen" suggest Kiss has improved its songwriting.

what to avoid: *Creatures of the Night,* (Casablanca/Mercury, 1982, prod. Paul Stanley, Gene Simmons and Michael James Jackson) the first of the post-Frehley releases, marks a turn toward corporate pop-metal that gave fledgling tiger-striped, spandex wussies inspiration to buy more mousse. Most of the subsequent recordings should be approached with caution.

the rest: *Kiss* (Casablanca/Mercury, 1974) *Hotter Than Hell* (Casablanca/Mercury, 1974) *Rock and Roll Over* (Casablanca/Mercury, 1976) *Alive 2* (Casablanca, 1977) *Double Platinum* (Casablanca/Mercury, 1978) *Dynasty* (Casablanca/Mercury, 1980) *Kiss Unmasked* (Casablanca/Mercury, 1980) *Music From "The Elder"*(Casablanca/Mercury, 1981) *Lick it Up* (Mercury, 1983) *Animalize* (Mercury, 1984) *Asylum* (Mercury,

1985) *Crazy Nights* (Mercury, 1987) *Smashes, Trashes & Hits* (Mercury, 1988) *Hot in the Shade* (Mercury, 1989) *Revenge* (Mercury, 1992) *Kiss Alive III* (Mercury, 1993) *Kiss Unplugged* (Mercury, 1996) *You Wanted the Best, You Got the Best!!!* (Mercury, 1996)

worth searching for: The Japanese version of *You Wanted the Best*... includes an intriguing, lo-fi version of Frehley's "New York Groove," the best-known track for the Kiss members' solo albums.

solo outings:

Ace Frehley: *Ace Frehley* (Casablanca/Mercury, 1978) *Frehley's Comet* (Megaforce, 1987) *Frehley's Comet: Live + 1* (Megaforce, 1988) *Second Sighting* (Megaforce, 1988) *Trouble Walkin'* (Megaforce, 1989)

Peter Criss: *Peter Criss* (Casablanca/Mercury, 1978) *Criss Cat #1* (TNT, 1994) WOOF!

Gene Simmons: *Gene Simmons* (Casablanca/Mercury, 1978)

Paul Stanley: *Paul Stanley* (Casablanca/Mercury, 1978)

▶▶ Def Leppard, Poison, Misfits, Quiet Riot, Ratt, Mötley Crüe

◀◀ Lou Reed, Motörhead, the Beatles, Alice Cooper, the Crazy World of Arthur Brown

Allan Orski

Klaatu

Formed 1973 in Toronto, Canada. Disbanded 1981. Re-formed 1994.

Terry Draper, drums; Dee Long, guitar; John Woloschuk, bass

The beneficiaries of one of the most effective music rumors of the 70s, Klaatu (named for a character in the film "The Day the Earth Stood Still") achieved fleeting fame when a music critic concluded in print that the group contained one or more Beatles working together anonymously. The group's label (Capitol—the home of the Beatles) did nothing to quell the rumors, and the liner notes of the band's debut album didn't contain the musicians' names. When the public discovered the group actually consisted of Canadian session players, sales declined accordingly. The group disbanded in 1981 after four albums, but a new album was released in 1995.

what to buy: *Klaatu,* (Capitol, 1976, prod. Klaatu) the album that started the fuss. With baroque-pop arrangements and titles such as "Calling Occupants of Interplanetary Craft" and "Sub Rosa Subway," Klaatu may have shared a sense of whimsy with the Fab Four, but not much else.

what to buy next: Any Beatles album missing from your collection, but if you're determined, *Sir Army Suit,* (Capitol, 1978, prod. Klaatu) which at least has shorter, and usually less pretentious, songs.

what to avoid: The band members started putting their names on the work with *Endangered Species.* (Capitol, 1980, prod. Christopher Bond) They probably shouldn't have.

the rest: *Hope* (Capitol, 1976) *Magenta Lane* (Attic, 1981) *Klaatu/Hope* (Attic, 1992) *Sir Army Suit/Endangered Species* (Attic, 1995)

worth searching for: *Peaks,* (Attic, 1993, prod. Klaatu and Christopher Bond) a compilation of the group's best work.

▶▶ Utopia, Jellyfish

◀◀ The Beatles

Brian Mansfield

KMFDM

Formed February 29, 1984 in Paris, France

Sascha Konietzko, vocals, percussion, programming, bass; En Esch, vocals, guitar, percussion (influence has been steadily declining since 1989); Pig (Nainz Watts/Raymond Watts) vocals, bass (1984-1985, 1995); Gunter Schulz (Svet Am / Svetlana Ambrosius), guitar, bass (1990-present); Jennifer Ginsberg, vocals (1989-present); Jr. Blackmale; Mark Durantula (Mark Durante) guitar, steel guitar (1990-1992); Christine Siewert, vocals (1990-1992); Brute, album art

Industrial's first stars—KMFDM has been speculated to stand for everything from "Karl Marx Found Dead Masterbating" to the infamous pseudo-acronym, "Kill Mother Fucking Depeche Mode"—the official name has always been "Kein Mitleid Für Die Mehrheit" (No Pity For The Majority). Originally conceived by Sascha Konietzko and his friend Udo Sturm to accompany a Paris art exhibit, the first performance consisted of feedback, five bass guitars, and four Polish coal miners banging on a museum's foundations. Since its formation KMFDM has featured a constantly fluctuating line-up and ever evolving musical arrangements. While earlier recordings are mainly comprised of a sampled audio-collage laid over heavy, minimalistic drum beats, newer material often sounds closer to heavy metal. In between the two styles lies a vast landscape of fused sounds from disco, techno, hip-hop, and rap. Underlying the recordings is a good ear for a dark, throbbing beat, and an off-kilter sense of humor, politics, and sex.

what to buy: *Virus* (Wax Trax!, 1993, prod. KMFDM) ♫♫♫♫ provides a good, low priced introduction to KMFDM. Easily their strongest EP, and one of their better overall releases—the title track is an instant classic. If you're not familiar with the hard-edged sound of industrial this prelude to the band's larger collection is a necessity. *Money* (Wax Trax!, 1992, prod. KMFDM) ♫♫♫♫ captures KMFDM at their high point between beat-heavy minimalism and guitar-pounding metal in their most traditional industrial album. Although musically nothing new is explored, nobody else does this type of music with the same intensity or precision. They perfectly juxtapose dense guitar riffs with electronic noise creating a disc that works equally well on the dance floor, or in the mosh pit. *UAIOE* (Wax Trax!, 1989, prod. Paul Barkov, Lee Popa) ♫♫♫♫ provides a notion of the range KMFDM is truly capable of; a disperse fusion of musical styles from reggae, to disco, to heavy metal, glued together by a strong beat. Although the lyrics are more political than usual, instead of detracting from the music they add a weight that well compliments the feeling of the record. *Don't Blow Your Top* (Wax Trax!, 1988, prod. Adrian Sherwood) ♫♫♫♫ is the best their early work. It features a sparser sound, but crisp production and carefully chosen samples make the album worth owning.

what to buy next: *XTORT,* (Wax Trax!, 1996, prod. KMFDM) ♫♫♫♫ KMFDM's latest album returns to the *Naïve*-era with crunchy guitars, tape loops, and female vocal pads. Guest appearances from Chris Connelly, William Rieflin (Ministry, Revolting Cocks), and F.M. Einheit (Einstürzende Neubanten) among others provides a welcomed diversity to the standard KMFDM record.

what to avoid: *What Do You Know Deutschland?* (Wax Trax!, 1986, prod. KMFDM) ♫♫ is an eclectic collection of slow, simple beats and not much else. Gets boring quickly and stays there for the rest of the album.

the rest: *Angst* (Wax Trax!, 1993) ♫♫♫♫ *Naïve/Hell to Go* (Wax Trax!, 1994) ♫♫♫ *Nihil* (Wax Trax!, 1995) ♫♫♫

worth searching for: *Naïve* (Wax Trax!, 1990, prod. KMFDM) ♫♫♫♫ is one of KMFDM's best releases, unfortunately it is no longer in print due to copyright problems with the samples. There is a remixed/reworked version, but it pales in comparison to the real thing. *Opium* (Self recorded, 1985, self produced) ♫♫♫ is a self recorded promo tape made before KMFDM had a record deal—extremely rare. *Retro* (Wax Trax!, 1996, prod. KMFDM and Adrian Sherwood) ♫♫♫♫ is a promotional "best of" album and collects the top singles onto one record.

▶▶ Nine Inch Nails, My Life With the Thrill Kill Kult, KLF, Pig

◀◀ Einstürzende Neubanten, Skinny Puppy, Ministry

Bryan Lassner

The Knack

Formed 1978 in Los Angles, Calif. Disbanded 1981. Reformed 1991.

Doug Fieger, vocals, guitar; Berton Averre, guitar, vocals; Bruce Gary, drums (1978-81); Prescott Niles, bass; Billy Ward, drums (1991-present)

With all the hype the music business could conjure up—basically serving up American Beatles-style mania to the new wave audience—The Knack exploded on the scene in 1979 with one of the most auspicious first albums ever. *Get The Knack* was recorded in 11 days for just $17,000 and sold more than five million copies worldwide, going gold in 13 days and platinum in six weeks. The exuberant hit "My Sharona" sold more than five million copies as a single—making it easily the No. 1 song of that year. But audience and media reacted to the hype—as well as to the group's inaccessibility—and the descent began. The second album, ...*But The Little Girls Understand,* fell short of expectations, and The Knack—riddled by inner tensions—split up after its third album. "My Sharona" hit big a second time when it was included in the Generation X film *Reality Bites,* which inspired an unsuccessful Knack reunion during the early '90s—though the group still gets together periodically and is no doubt hoping another generation will one day get The Knack again. These days, Gary can be founding working—and even grafting drum tracks—onto Jimi Hendrix reissues, while Fieger is almost better known as the brother of Dr. Jack Kevorkian's attorney.

what to buy: *Get The Knack* (Capitol, 1979, prod. Mike Chapman) ♫♫♫♫ is a must in any pop fan's collection—albeit from a decidedly male and teenage perspective. It has "My Sharona" and "Good Girls Don't," but even the ballads—"Your Number or Your Name" and "Maybe Tonight"—are standouts.

what to buy next: ....*But The Little Girls Understand* (Capitol, 1980, prod. Mike Chapman) ♫♫♫♫ provided more of the same. Fieger wallows in more female disenchantment from the first track, "Baby Talks Dirty," but rebounds for the lusty "I Want Ya" and an energetic cover of the Kinks' "The Hardway." *Retrospec-*

tive: *The Best Of The Knack* (Capitol, 1992, prod. Various) is a short-cut to The Knack experience, with the demo version of the comeback single "Rocket o' Love" and an unreleased cover of Bruce Springsteen's "Don't Look Back."

what to avoid: *Round Trip* (Capitol, 1981, prod. Jack Douglas) [rating] is The Knack at its weakest, despite a couple of keepers like "Boys Go Crazy" (covered by The Posies in 1996) and "Another Lousy Day in Paradise."

the rest: *Serious Fun* (Charisma, 1991) [rating]

worth searching for: The original 45rpm single with the picture sleeve of "My Sharona" (Capitol, 1979) [rating], B-sided by "Let Me Out" and featuring provocative pictures of one of The Knack's female "friends."

⏩ The Plimsouls, Jellyfish, The Posies, 20-20, The Romantics

⏪ The Beatles, The Kinks, The Turtles, Herman's Hermits

John Nieman

The Knickerbockers

Formed 1964 in Bergenfield, N.J. Disbanded 1967.

Beau Charles, guitar, vocals; John Charles, bass, vocals; Buddy Randell, saxophone, vocals; Jimmy Walker, drums, vocals

The Knickerbockers were one-hit wonders with the phenomenal "Lies," a sublime rockin' pop powerhouse that almost sounded more like the Beatles than the Beatles did. If the group had never cut another track before or after, it would still deserve recognition for distilling the essence of frenzied Merseybeat succinctly and as triumphantly as they did with "Lies." So it's all the more gratifying to report that the Knickerbockers did, in fact, record several other worthy numbers, including "One Track Mind," "They Ran for Their Lives," "Just One Girl," "I Must Be Doing Something Right" and "She Said Goodbye." None of them was a big hit, and none quite ranked in the same league as "Lies," but all were remarkably engaging and crackling with an undeniable pop spark you'd swear was ignited in Liverpool rather than Jersey. (As a matter of fact, Liverpool's Swinging Blue Jeans even covered the Knickerbockers' "Rumors, Gossip, Words Untrue," though the Knicks' original version is much better.)

The Knickerbockers made two middling-to-terrible albums, but its scattered uptempo tracks were nothing short of brilliant. The accomplished mix of deadly hooks and vibrant rock 'n' roll energy in these tracks show the Knickerbockers to have been an ace power pop group, years before the term came into vogue. After the group sputtered to a halt, Walker went on to be a temporary replacement for Bill Medley in the Righteous Brothers. You'll be well served if you can find the British import *A Rave Up with . . . The Knickerbockers,* (Big Beat, 1994, prod. Jerry Fuller and Bob Irwin) [rating] a rockin' little compilation that combines the group's two albums. *Lies* (Challenge, 1966/Sundazed, 1993, prod. Jerry Fuller and Bob Irwin) [rating] is marred by five tracks of limp big-balladry, though the first five Beatley tracks rule.

Jerk and Twine Time (Challenge, 1965/Sundazed, 1993, prod. Jerry Fuller and Bob Irwin) [rating] is a horrendous coverfest, of historical interest only.

Carl Cafarelli

Knitters

See: X

David Knopfler

See: Dire Straits

Mark Knopfler

See: Dire Straits

Cub Koda

See: Brownsville Station

Kool and the Gang

Formed 1964 in Jersey City, N.J.

Robert "Kool" Bell (aka Muhammad Bayyan), bass, vocals; Ronald Bell (aka Khalis Bayyan), trumpet, sax; Dennis "D.T." Thomas, sax, flute; George "Funky George" Brown, drums; Robert "Spike" Mickens, trumpet; Charles Smith, guitar; Clifford Adams, trombone (1976-present); James "J.T." Taylor, vocals (1979-89, 1995-present); plus more than two dozen other players over the years

Although bassist Robert "Kool" Bell is the leader in name of this veteran group, it was actually his brother, Ronald Bell, who shaped the Kool and the Gang sound. After forming first as an African percussion outfit, the group changed in 1966 to the Jazziacs, influenced by the holy trinity—John Coltrane, Miles Davis and Thelonious Monk. The group played local club dates with jazz giants such as Pharoah Sanders and McCoy Tyner occasionally sitting in. Two years later, the group changed its course once again, this time to an upbeat, predominantly instrumental party-funk sound that was anchored by musical director Ronald Bell's punchy, jazz-grounded horn blasts. Calling itself the Soul Music Review, then the New Dimensions, then Kool and the Flames and finally Kool and the Gang, the group recorded a few minor singles during the late 60s and early 70s. In 1973, the group broke big with two crossover hits, "Jungle Boogie" and "Hollywood Swinging," beginning a run as one of the most successful funk outfits of the 70s and 80s. In 1979, after disco temporarily pushed its taut, jazz-informed funk off the dance floor, Kool and the Gang rebounded by adding its first lead vocalist (Taylor) and teaming up with jazz-funk producer Eumir Deodato for a more pop-oriented approach. Those moves led to two of the group's biggest songs, "Ladies Night" and "Celebration," which became a welcome-home anthem for the American hostages returned from captivity in Iran, a theme for sports teams and a staple at weddings and graduations. Although Kool and the Gang was still enjoying chart success, by the mid-80s its watered-down pop sound wore thin. In 1988, Taylor, who had become the face of Kool and the Gang, left to pursue a mildly successful solo career; he returned in 1995, but nobody seemed to notice.

what to buy: With many of the group's early albums out of print, *The Best of Kool and the Gang 1969-1976* (Mercury/Chronicles, 1993, prod. Various) is the best place to go hear the group in its pre-pop prime, as most of the key pre-Taylor tracks are included here ("Jungle Boogie," "Hollywood Swinging," etc.). The funked-up set will come as a revelation to those who only know of the group from its "Celebration" era.

what to buy next: Many of Kool and the Gang's later albums were loaded with filler, so *Everything's Kool and the Gang: Greatest Hits* (Mercury, 1988, prod. Various) is the best way to examine the most noteworthy songs from the J.T. Taylor era. Still, the music pales in comparison to the early- and mid-70s output.

the rest: *Kool and the Gang Spin Their Top Hits* (De-Lite/Mercury 1978) *Celebrate!* (De-Lite/Mercury, 1980) *Emergency* (De-Lite/Mercury, 1984) *Celebration: The Best of Kool & the Gang 1979-1987* (Mercury/Chronicles, 1994)

worth searching for: *Wild and Peaceful* (De-Lite, 1973)—out-of-print like most of the Gang's catalog—is a funky good throw-down marked by the hits "Funky Stuff" and "Hollywood Swinging."

solo outings:

J.T. Taylor: Master of the Game (MCA, 1989) *Feel the Need* (MCA, 1991) *Baby, I'm Back* (MCA, 1993)

▶▶ Digable Planets, Con Funk Shun, Living Colour, Slave, the Time, Dazz Band

◀◀ Rashaan Roland Kirk, Horace Silver, Miles Davis, Manu Dibango, Sly and the Family Stone, Mandrill, Isley Brothers, Marvin Gaye

Joshua Freedom du Lac

Al Kooper

Born Feb. 5, 1944 in Brooklyn, N.Y.

Kooper is one of those great rock 'n' roll stars many have never heard of. Consider the list of accomplishments: joining the Royal Teens ("Short Shorts") at age 15; co-writing Gary Lewis and the Playboys' No. 1 hit "This Diamond Ring;" playing the organ hook on Bob Dylan's "Like a Rolling Stone" and the French horn lick for the Rolling Stones' "You Can't Always Get What You Want;" forming the Blues Project and Blood, Sweat & Tears; and producing acts such as Lynyrd Skynyrd, the Tubes, Nils Lofgren and many others. He loves to play, write and sing, period, and the only thing that's kept Kooper from mass recognition is his own eclecticism and a reedy singing voice that's not quite the stuff of Top 40 hits. Still active today, Kooper remains an estimable talent and also a fine rock 'n' roll historian—as anyone who can scare up a copy of his 1976 memoir, "Backstage Passes." Getting him on record isn't much easier; much of Kooper's seminal work is out of print (look for the CD compilation *Al's Big Deal (Unclaimed Freight)*). The best buy at the moment is *Super Session,* (Columbia, 1968, prod. Al Kooper) a lively project that features guitar whiz Michael Bloomfield on half and Stephen Stills on the other half, subbing after the mercurial Bloomfield disappeared. *Rekooperation—A Nonverbal Scenic Selection of Soul Souvenirs* (MusicMasters, 1994, prod. Al Kooper) is enjoyable but a little stiff; the concept really comes to life on *Soul of a Man: Al Kooper Live,* (MusicMasters, 1995, prod. Al Kooper) an electric performance with guest appearances by the Blues Project, John Sebastian and former BS&T trumpeter Michael Brecker.

see also: *Blood, Sweat & Tears, the Blues Project*

Gary Graff

Peter Koppes

See: The Church

Leo Kottke

Born Sept. 11, 1945, in Athens, Ga.

Acoustic fingerpickers across the land are perpetually awed by the super-nimble guitar work of Kottke. An eclectic guitar wiz, he has developed a cult following not only for his musicianship but also for his dark humor and deadpan vocal delivery. Labeling him a folkie is too limiting a term, as he prefers jump all over the map without adhering to any one style.

what to buy: The sheer prowess Kottke displays on his traditional instrumental debut, *Six and Twelve-String Guitar,* (Takoma, 1969/Rhino 1994) makes this a must-have for anyone who takes acoustic music seriously. Kottke never stayed so close to any one particular style again. *Guitar Music* (Chrysalis, 1981, prod. Leo Kottke) is his celebrated return to solo acoustic music, with a fine turn on the Everly Brother's "All I Have to Do Is Dream" and the otherworldly "Sleepwalk."

what to buy next: On *Great Big Boy,* (Private Music, 1991, prod. Steve Berlin) guests Margo Timmins of the Cowboy Junkies and Lyle Lovett add flavor to the diversity as Kottke traipses between funkified folk and Mexican-flavored fare.

what to avoid: *That's What* (Private Music, 1990) is too muted to appeal to all but the most devoted listener. It makes for a dull spin that strays too close to New Age.

the rest: *Mudlark* (One Way, 1971/1995) *Greenhouse* (One Way, 1972/1995) *My Feet Are Smiling* (One Way, 1973/1995) *Ice Water* (One Way, 1974/1995) A Shout Toward Noon *(Private Music, 1986)* *Regards from Chuck Pink* (Private Music, 1988) *My Father's Face* (Private Music, 1989) *The Essential Leo Kottke* (Chrysalis, 1991) *Peculiaroso* (Private Music, 1993) *Live* (Private Music, 1995)

worth searching for: *Chewing Pine,* (Beat Goes On, 1975/1994) an apt title for this rootsy import collection.

Jorma Kaukonen, Edward Wright, Ry Cooder, Chris Whitley

Chet Atkins, Carl Perkins, the Rev. Gary Davis, Roy Clark

Allan Orski

Kraftwerk

Formed 1970 in Dusseldorf, Germany

Ralf Hutter, vocals, electronics; Florian Schneider, vocals, electronics; Klaus Roeder, violin, guitar; Wolfgang Flur, electronic percussion; Karl Bartos, electronic percussion

This group is to music what Bauhaus is to architecture—sterile, cold and repetitive. Kraftwerk's place in rock history is important, since it influenced a number of groups and was a progenitor of dance, techno and industrial styles. During the late 70s, the band scored disco hits with the songs "Showroom Dummies" and "Trans-Europe Express," while "Authoban" was a Top 5 hit in 1974. Since the early 80s, however, Kraftwerk's output has been sporadic.

what to buy: *Autobahn,* (Vertigo, 1975/Elektra, 1988, prod. N/A) Kraftwerk's fourth album—but first to be released in the U.S.—is its most focused. Particularly numbing is the title track, a 20-minute-plus ode to the no-speed-limit German highway. If you ever thought it would be exciting to drive on the Autobahn, this could change your mind. The rest of the album's tone is equally severe.

what to buy next: *The Mix* (Elektra, 1991) is a best-of compilation that works for your dance party.

what to avoid: *Electric Cafe* (EMI, 1986) covers tired, familiar territory already relentlessly explored with minimal expression.

the rest: *Kraftwerk* (Vertigo U.K., 1972/Elektra, 1995) *Radio-Activity* (Capitol, 1975) *Trans-Europe Express* (Capitol, 1977) *Computer World* (Warner Bros., 1981)

Tangerine Dream, the Orb, Brian Eno, David Bowie, Orbital

Phillip Glass, John Cage

Patrick McCarty

Wayne Kramer

See: MC5

Billy J. Kramer & the Dakotas

Formed 1963 in Liverpool, England. Disbanded 1967.

Billy J. Kramer (born William Howard Ashton); Mike Maxfield, guitar; Robin MacDonald, guitar; Raymond Jones, bass; Tony Mansfield, drums

Producer George Martin had no reason to doubt Beatles manager Brian Epstein when he first brought a young Billy J. and his new backup group The Dakotas into Abbey Road Studios in 1963. After all, Martin already was scoring British No. 1 hits with the last two bands Epstein had brought to his attention (Gerry & The Pacemakers and you-know-who). However, soon after putting Kramer on tape, it became apparent they certainly weren't dealing with another Paul McCartney: not only was his pitch wobbly at best, but his twee crooner's approach, not to mention his hairstyle, seem firmly rooted in another era. Still, given a steady supply of Lennon/McCartney songs (with Martin deceptively ghosting Kramer's every vocal track with a matching piano line), the Beatle magic worked its wonders long enough to provide Billy J. & the Dakotas with two years' worth of hits on both sides of the Atlantic. By 1967, however, the inevitable had taken place: the Dakotas, who often seemed acutely embarrassed performing such numbers as "Little Children," abandoned ship, resigning Karmer to a life of entertaining supper clubs, nostalgia cruises and American Beatle conventions. At least he's finally brushed his hair forward. *The Best of Billy J. Kramer* (EMI, 1991, prod. George Martin) ♪♪♪ is recommended mainly to Beatle completists, for it contains several Lennon/McCartney compositions ("Bad To Me," "From A Window") that went unrecorded elsewhere. And of course Martin's studio wizardry is remarkable throughout.

Gary Pig Gold

Lenny Kravitz

Born Leonard Albert Kravitz, May 26, 1964, in New York, N.Y.

As the son of a Jewish television producer and a black actress—the late Roxie Roker of "The Jeffersons"—Kravitz seemed assured of a career in show business, a fate compounded by high school classmates such as Slash of Guns N' Roses and Lone Justice's Maria McKee. Still, when Kravitz married "Cosby Show" actress Lisa Bonet in 1987 and announced plans to release a record, critics snickered, calling him "Mr. Bonet." But his first album, featuring Kravitz himself on nearly every instrument, silenced many naysayers; Even though his sound proved highly derivative of 60s and 70s influences, there was an unmistakable talent emerging. After collaborating with Madonna on her hit "Justify My Love" (Kravitz was later sued by Prince protege Ingrid Chavez, who claimed to have cowritten the tune, while rappers Public Enemy claimed a sample of their work used in the song was not licensed), he recorded an all-star version of the John Lennon hit "Give Peace a Chance" during the Gulf War. His own solo output veers between overt Jimi Hendrix, Curtis Mayfield and Led Zeppelin influences, selling well enough to keep him in the public eye but never enough to bring blockbuster fame.

what to buy: Although he continues to wear his influences on his sleeve, *Circus* (Virgin, 1995, prod. Lenny Kravitz) ♪♪♪½ is Kravitz's most consistent outing yet, mimicking Led Zep in the hit single "Rock and Roll Is Dead" without sacrificing the song's integrity. Elsewhere, he mines 60s and 70s soul and rock with better results than in the past, crafting an engaging, powerful rock/pop record.

what to buy next: As a blueprint of where *Circus* would eventually end up, *Are You Gonna Go My Way?* (Virgin, 1993, prod. Lenny Kravitz) ♪♪♪ is an intriguing album, fired up by the Hendrix-inspired titled track and other numbers that trace his fascination with heritage musical styles.

what to avoid: Sabotaged mostly by petulant lyrics detailing the 1991 disintegration of his marriage to Bonet, *Mama Said* (Virgin, 1991, prod. Lenny Kravitz) ♪♪½ is his most inconsistent work despite the presence of two appealing singles, "It Ain't Over 'til It's Over" and "Always on the Run." And while it's good to see him toss aside his hippie influences for psychedelic rock, here the artistic thievery is so blatant that it's hard to overlook.

the rest: *Let Love Rule* (Virgin, 1989) ♪♪½

worth searching for: Kravitz's collaboration with Madonna, *Justify My Love* (Warner Bros., 1990, prod. Lenny Kravitz) ♪♪—if only to marvel that Chavez was dumb enough to claim credit for lyrics this awful.

▶▶ Self

◀◀ Led Zeppelin, Jimi Hendrix, Living Colour

Eric Deggans

Robbie Krieger

See: The Doors

Ed Kuepper

See: The Saints

Kyuss

Formed 1989 in Palm Desert, Calif. Disbanded 1995.

Josh Homme, guitars; John Garcia, vocals; Scott Reeder, bass (1991-

New Orleans

The Best of New Orleans Rhythm & Blues, Vol. 1-2
(Rhino)

Zydeco Dynamite: The Clifton Chenier Anthology
(Rhino)

'Fess: The Professor Longhair Anthology
(Rhino)

Serious Clownin': The History of Huey "Piano" Smith and the Clowns
(Rhino, 1986)

Buckwheat's Zydeco Party
Buckwheat Zydeco (Rounder)

Gumbo
Dr. John (Atco/Atlantic)

The Wild Tchoupitoulas
(Mango)

Treacherous: A History of the Neville Brothers
(Rhino)

Lucky
The Subdudes (EastWest)

95); Alfredo Hernandez, drums (1994-95); Nick Oliveri, bass (1989-91); Brant Bjork, drums (1989-93)

Kyuss originated as a group of southern Californians who staged infamous, all-night jam sessions in the desert outside their hometown of Palm Desert. Such a venue allowed them to play as long as they wanted, whatever they wanted and, most important, as loud as they wanted. The group soon gained a loyal following, and after just one independent release, Kyuss was picked up by a major label. Often tagged heavy metal, the group has a much broader sound, incorporating a slower, bluesy edge as well as spacey, psychedelic jams. Multi-layered guitars and heavy grooves elevate Kyuss beyond the incoherent noise of most metal acts, and though the vocals are the weakest link in the band's music, the Herculean fits and starts of Homme's guitar arrangements are the guts of this quartet. Citing creative differences, the group disbanded shortly after its fourth album was released in fall 1995. Its major label debut, *Welcome to Sky Valley,* (Elektra, 1994, prod. Chris Goss and Kyuss) showcases the group's sheer force and spatial, psychedelic capabilities better than its other efforts. The first track, "Gardenia," with its deceivingly soft title, takes raw power to another level. Arranged in three movements, each comprising three songs, this album may seem somewhat pompous for a lesser-known band, but the group claimed it was just a ploy to prevent listeners from skipping tracks.

the rest: *Wretch* (Dali/Chameleon, 1991) *Blues for the Red Sun* (Dali, 1992) *And the Circus Leaves Town ...* (Elektra, 1995)

Christopher Scanlon

L.A. Guns

Formed 1987 in Los Angeles, Calif.

Tracii Guns, guitar; Phillip Lewis, vocals; Mick Cripps, guitar; Kelly Nickels, bass; Bones, drums (1992-present); Steve Riley, drums (1988-92)

Notable for reportedly requiring its potential members to have black hair, L.A. Guns began after guitarist Guns opted out of the then-burgeoning Guns N' Roses and recruited former members of Girl (Lewis) and W.A.S.P. (Riley) for his own band. Toiling in that considerable shadow, leader Guns and band produced one solid album, *L.A. Guns* (Polygram, 1988, prod. Jim Faraci), and one excellent album, *Cocked and Loaded* (Polygram, 1989, prod. Various) —the latter with a minor hit in "The Ballad of Jayne." Opening for seemingly every arena hard-rock act that came to town, the group was inevitably reduced to touring small clubs again after the poor sales of later albums.

the rest: *Hollywood Vampires* (Polydor, 1991) *Cuts* (Polydor EP, 1993) *Vicious Circle* (Polydor, 1994)

Todd Wicks

The La's /Cast

Formed 1985 in Liverpool, England. Disbanded 1992. Cast formed 1992, Liverpool England

Members (The La's): Lee Mavers, vocals, guitar; Paul Hemmings, guitar (1985-89); Cammie, guitar (1989-92); John Power, bass, vocals; John Timson, drums (1985-89); Neil Mavers, drums (1989-92); (Cast): John Power, vocals, guitar; Liam Tyson, guitar; Peter Wilkinson, bass; Keith O'Neill, drums

Rarely has a band so completely despised such a great album of theirs. The Liverpool four The La's, which nicely integrated lovely and innocent hints of classic Merseybeat, rockabilly, R&B, soul and pop so pure it was like fresh snow, spent four years recording the same LP over and over. Half a dozen big-name producers took a crack at capturing the same songs, only to find themselves in a dogfight (on the side of the label, London Records) against the band, which universally loathed each attempt. Finally, the exasperated label put together their own version of the debut LP *The La's* (Go! Discs/London, 1991, prod. Steve Lillywhite) that the band so wholly disapproved of that the members refused to have their individual names listed on the credits. Yet the public was so seduced with the 1988 pop treasure single "There She Goes," it was both included on the LP and reissued again as a new single, and the song was later the centerpiece of the movie "So I Married an Axe Murderer" (both the La's version and a cover by Boo Radleys made the soundtrack). With such irresistible material, gorgeous and cute without being sappy or maudlin (another single, "Timeless Melody" might be even better), and a golden-voiced singer in wide-eyed, good looking Lee Mavers, the La's should have been big stars. Instead the fighting with the label dragged on until the band disintegrated around 1992.

After that, wearied bassist John Power left to lead his own band, Cast, making the switch to guitar in the process. The band's album, *Allchange* (A&M, 1995, prod. John Leckie) contains many of the same elements that made La's fans swoon, and Power proves himself a capable singer. However, he lacks the highs found in Mavers' crystal voice, and the songs, though hooky, also can't quite match Mavers either. Finally, the lyrics are sometimes too ho-hum and cliched. All in all it's a promising, if too lightweight debut.

Jack Rabid

Greg Lake

See: Emerson, Lake & Palmer

Sonny Landreth

Born 1951 in Caton, Miss.

Landreth has kept alive the art of slide guitar, which was thought by some to have died with Duane Allman in the early 70s. Most people were first introduced to Landreth as the leader of the Goners, the backup group that helped John Hiatt finally get noticed with the LP *Slow Dancing* and a subsequent barnstorming tour. Landreth, who was born in Elmore James' home town and lives in Lafayette, La., is steeped in the funky-beat blues music that's indigenous to that region, though he has his own voice as a player. His sound is distinct in its thick, saturated electricity, and he's a nimble guitarist, creating interesting textures with a flurry of fingers and treating his instrument, in the grand tradition of all bluesy slide masters, as a voice. His commercial undoing may be that Landreth doesn't have a strong singing voice, but he writes songs that serve his vocal range. Both of his albums—*Outward Bound* (Zoo/Praxis, 1992, prod. R.S. Field & Sonny Landreth) and *South of I-10* (Zoo/Praxis, 1995, prod. R.S. Field & Sonny Landreth) —are worth owning not just for the six-strong pyrotechnics, but for the depth of the material.

Gil Asakawa

Ronnie Lane

See: The Faces

Mark Lanegan

See: Screaming Trees

k.d. lang

Born Kathryn Dawn Lang, Nov. 2, 1961 in Consort, Alberta, Canada

Before venturing into pop turf, lang was a true revolutionary in country music: claiming to be the reincarnation of Patsy Cline, she dug straight to the roots of country on a series of gutsy records. Nashville barely gave her the time of day—she got a similar cold-shoulder treatment from country radio—and in 1992, lang abandoned her country career and applied her gorgeous vocals to smooth torch songs and other more urbane pop styles. The wildly popular and Grammy award-winning *Ingenue* kicked off this phase of her career, which coincided with lang's coming out and becoming a spokesperson for gay and animal rights.

what to buy: *Absolute Torch and Twang* (Sire, 1989, prod. Greg Penny, Ben Mink and k.d. lang) is her best country record, ranging from spunky honky-tonk ("Three Days") to Western swing ("Full Moon of Love") to soaring ballads ("Trail of Broken Hearts").

what to buy next: lang's major label debut, *Angel With a Lariat* (Sire, 1987, prod. Dave Edmunds) mixes pure country with cowpunk. *Ingenue* (Sire, 1992, prod. Greg Penny, Ben Mink and k.d. lang) lacks the fire of most of her country discs, but her vocals are as stunning as ever on pop ballads such as "Constant Craving" and "Save Me."

what to avoid: Though it took a bit of the edge off following up *Ingenue*, lang's soundtrack for *Even Cowgirls Get the Blues* (Sire, 1994, prod. Ben Mink and k.d. lang) was an unusually disappointing trifle.

the rest: *A Truly Western Experience* (Bumstead, 1984) *Shadowland* (Sire, 1988) *All You Can Eat* (Warner Bros., 1995)

worth searching for: *Blue Sky Above Wide Plains* (Flashback, 1993), a good-sounding bootleg of lang performances in New York (1993) and Chicago (1988).

Melissa Etheridge, Mary Chapin Carpenter, Trisha Yearwood

Minnie Pearl, Patsy Cline, Julie London

Thor Christensen

Daniel Lanois

Born Sept. 19, 1951 in Gaineau, Quebec, Canada

Lanois is an artist of exceptional ambition, musical vision and lyrical depth. He is also a producer who has helmed some of the most important albums of the past two decades. While foremost a musician, he began his professional career as a producer/recording engineer at Grant Avenue Studio, which he owns with his brother. While there Lanois met ambient rock pioneer Brian Eno, and the two struck up a longstanding friendship and working relationship. Eno brought Lanois to the attention of a number of prominent artists, most notably the Irish band U2, which hired him to co-produce (with Eno) its landmark 1984 album *The Unforgettable Fire*. From there Lanois collaborated with Peter Gabriel, the Neville Brothers and Bob Dylan. During the late 80s, Lanois turned his attention to an artist of utmost importance: himself. Drawing on his French-Canadian ancestry and his love of blues and rock, he forged a unique sound that is the sum of his knowledge and a hallmark for his prodigious talents. His debut, *Acadie*, (Opal/Warner Bros., 1989, prod. Daniel Lanois) is a quiet work that showcases his dedication to his French-Canadian roots, featuring songs populated by characters who seem to have sprung direct from history. Good as it was, Lanois's second album, *For the Beauty of Wynona*, (Warner Bros., 1993, prod. Daniel Lanois) is a work of stunning majesty and emotional complexity. Drawing on elements as diverse as Cajun music, guitar rock, blues and traditional French-Canadian balladry, Lanois crafts a sound that is greater than the sum of its parts, a style that transcends musical alchemy in its seamless fusion.

David Galens

Lard

See: Ministry

Last Exit

Formed Feb. 7, 1986, in Germany and New York

Sonny Sharrock, guitar; Peter Bratzmann, saxophones and taragato; Bill Laswell, bass; Ronald Shannon Jackson, drums, vocals

This free improvisation supergroup brought together veteran leaders in their own rights: a legendary jazz noise guitarist who'd played with Miles Davis and Pharoah Sanders; a hard-blowing German saxophonist; a master conceptualist who happened to be a monster bassist; and a technically and imaginatively awesome jazz drummer who contributed significantly to records by Ornette Coleman, Albert Ayler and Cecil Taylor. Reviving the spontaneous spirit of 60s free jazz when it was at a low ebb, this group eschewed rehearsals but played with a level of intensity rarely matched.

what to buy: *The Noise of Trouble: Live in Tokyo* (Enemy, 1986 prod. N/A) ranks among the greatest concerts ever documented on tape. Drawing on two nights in October 1986 (with Japanese saxist Akira Sakata and Herbie Hancock as guests) it balances the free-for-all improvisation with actual songs and a healthy dose of blues from Sharrock and Jackson.

what to buy next: The totally improvised *Headfirst into the Flames*, (MuWorks, 1993) drawn from two 1989 concerts, is Last Exit's best purely free statement, a masterful display of creative empathy nearly as thrilling as *The Noise of Trouble* and a sonic improvement.

what to avoid: The unremitting barrage of *Last Exit*, (Enemy, 1986) the quartet's first actual release, was awe-inspiring at the time, but its muddy sound makes it no match for subsequent releases.

the rest: *Cassette Recordings 87* (Enemy/Celluloid, 1988)

worth searching for: The out-of-print *Iron Path* (Venture/Virgin, 1988, prod. Last Exit and Bill Laswell) was Last Exit's only studio album. Laswell scripts some nearly ambient moments and, conversely, a few heavy metal-like riffs. Pulsating and throbbing, it never explodes but exudes calm majesty.

▶▶ Thurston Moore and Lee Ranaldo of Sonic Youth, William Hooker, Naked City

◀◀ Albert Ayler, John Coltrane, Blind Willie Johnson

see also: *Bill Laswell/Material*

Steve Holtje

Bill Laswell /Material

Born Feb. 12, 1955 in Salem, Ill.

You can almost tell from his willingness to mix genres and defy stereotypes that Laswell grew up in Detroit, where funk and punk exist side-by-side. He's one of the busiest producers in music, not just because he's in demand (his credits include Herbie Hancock, Mick Jagger, Motörhead, Iggy Pop and scores of others) but because he's got such an overflow of ideas he needs to enact. He works steadily for a number of labels, several of them his own to varying degrees. The band Material first consisted of Laswell (an exceptional bassist), drummer Fred Maher and synthesizer/keyboardist/tape processor Michael Beinhorn working on their own or with a small coterie of fellow avant-gardists. The three found success as a production team on modern urban R&B projects, and the breadth of Material's music began increasing. When vast numbers of guest performers were brought in for 1982's *Memory Serves*, the group's future modus operandus was set; an ever-shifting array of performers has kept the group mutating, and Laswell has increased the use of world music artists over the years, particularly from Africa and Asia. Laswell also started experimenting with ambient music long before it was popular and has always pursued his own path in that area, though he's also collaborated with the most interesting members of that genre—from Peter Namlook and Terre Thaemlitz to Jah Wobble and the Orb. His ambient and techno projects incorporate a range of musics, often drawing on the bountiful vaults of his labels and completely recontextualizing the performances. He has also nurtured a stable of performers (such as Brain, Bootsy Collins and the young guitarist Buckethead). He retains a special affection for the funk heroes of his youth, in some cases giving them much-needed work and respect.

what to buy: Material's *Memory Serves* (Celluloid/Elektra Musician, 1982, prod. Material with Martin Bisi) was the group's first album to take the guest star approach to the extreme, and it worked fantastically, with the cream of New York's avant/jazz legends (Sonny Sharrock, Billy Bang, Fred Frith, Henry Threadgill, George Lewis, Charles K. Noyes, Olu Dara) concocting music unlike anything ever heard before. But the greatest moment is Laswell's unearthly combination of instrumental virtuosity and timbral imagination on "Silent Land," where he coaxes uncanny harmonics from his bass.

what to buy next: Material's *One Down* (Celluloid/Elektra, 1982, prod. Material) is Laswell at his funkiest and most commercial (the CD bonus track, "Busting Out," was a club hit). The guests range from jazzers to avant types to R&B players, but the most startling performance is "Memories," with 60s jazz great Archie Shepp playing impassioned solos and a pre-superstar Whitney Houston soaring on a performance she's never equalled on her own. Axiom Ambient's *Lost in the Translation* (Axiom, 1994, prod. Bill Laswell) is labeled "Sound Sculptures by Bill Laswell with contributions from Terre Thaemlitz, The Orb, Tetsu Inoue" and represents something of an ambient all-star team. Laswell reshapes performances from Eddie Hazel, Sharrock, Sanders, Nicky Skopelitis, Jah Wobble, Bernie Worrell, Buckethead, Collins, Ginger Baker, Liu Sola and more into abstract art music with incredible sensitivity to sonic textures.

what to avoid: Material's *Live from Soundscape* (DIW, 1991, prod. Verna Gillis) is rambling, episodic free-form improvisation with nothing more to offer than isolated moments of instrumental wizardry. Valis I's *Destruction of Syntax* (Subharmonic, year N/A, prod Bill Laswell) is a brave but flawed attempt to meld ambient and hip-hop.

the rest: Material: *Temporary Music* (Celluloid, 1981) *Red Tracks* (Red, 1985) *Seven Souls* (Virgin, 1989) *The Third Power* (Axiom, 1991) *Live in Japan* (Restless, 1993) *Hallucination Engine* (Axiom, 1994)

solo outings:

Bill Laswell: *Baselines* (Celluloid/Elektra Musician, 1983) *Hear No Evil* (Venture/Virgin, 1988)

Massacre: *Killing Time* (Celluloid, 1982)

Laswell, Ryuichi Sakamoto and Yosuke Yamashita: *Asian Games*(Verve, 1994)

SXL: *Live in Japan* (CBS/Sony Japan, 1987) *Into the Outlands* (Celluloid/Pipeline, 1988)

Deadline: *Down By Law* (Celluloid, 1985)

Arcana: *The Last Wave* (DIW, 1996)

Praxis: *Transmutation* (Mutatis Mutandis) (Axiom, 1992)

Sacrifist (Subharmonic, 1993) *Metatron* (Subharmonic, 1994)

Shango: *Shango Funk Theology* (Celluloid, 1984)

Divination: *Distill* (Submeta, 1996)

Bill Laswell & Terre Thaemlitz: *Web* (Subharmonic, year N/A)

Bill Laswell & Peter Namlook: *Psychonavigation* (Subharmonic, year N/A)

Sacred System: *Chapter One: Book of Entrance* (ROIR, 1996)

Chaos Face: *Doom Ride* (Subharmonic, year N/A)

M.J. Harris & Bill Laswell: *Somnific Flux* (Subharmonic, 1995)

Bill Laswell and Nicholas James Bullen: *Bass Terror* (Sub Rosa, 1995)

The Orb, Ben Neill, Mitchell Froom, DJ Spooky, Nona Hendryx, Arthur Baker, Golden Palominos

John Coltrane, Sonny Sharrock, Jimi Hendrix, Mad Professor, Parliament-Funkadelic/George Clinton

See also: *Last Exit*

Steve Holtje

Laswell, Ryuichi Sakamoto and Yosuke Yamashita

See: Bill Laswell

Latin Playboys

See: Los Lobos

Cyndi Lauper

Born June 20, 1953 in Queens, N.Y.

Armed with a voice that sounded like a Bronx Betty Boop and a wardrobe that looked like a thrift-store explosion, Cyndi Lauper was one of the first artists to benefit from the then-untapped power of MTV. Loopy and loveable, she possessed a sharp sense of humor and a powerful voice that could caress tender ballads ("Time After Time," "True Colors") and tear into raucous rockers ("Money Changes Everything") with a cunning combination of girlish glee and feminist gusto. Her charms were so irresistible that radio programmers didn't even notice that her 1984 hit "She-Bop" was an ode to female masturbation ("They say I'd better get a chaperone/cuz I can't stop messin' with the danger zone"). But Lauper wielded her stardom in strange ways, throwing her celebrity clout behind a rock 'n' roll revitalization of professional wrestling and choosing the ill-conceived *Vibes* as her first starring film role. Despite an impressive but commercially ignored comeback album in 1993 called *Hat Full of Stars,* she remains known as the girl who just wants to have fun.

what to buy: Produced by Rick Chertoff (who later discovered Joan Osborne) and backed by members of the Hooters, *She's So Unusual* (Portrait, 1983) is a pop treasure chest of well-chosen covers such as Jules Shear's "All Through the Night," the Brains' "Money Changes Everything," Prince's "When You Were Mine" and Robert Hazard's "Girls Just Want to Have Fun." Lauper's own "Time After Time," co-written with Hooter Rob Hyman, was certified a standard when Miles Davis covered it in 1985.

what to buy next: On *Hat Full of Stars,* (Portrait, 1993, prod. Cyndi Lauper and Junior Vasquez) Lauper grafts hip-hop rhythms, woodwinds and keyboards onto songs about child abuse ("Lies"), domestic violence ("Broken Glass"), abortion ("Sally's Pigeons," co-written with Mary Chapin Carpenter) and racial strife ("A Part Hate"), revealing a surprising maturity in insight and sound. The infectious "That's What I Think" is her best song to never reach radio.

what to avoid: The melodramatic *A Night to Remember,* (Portrait, 1989, prod. Cyndi Lauper, Lennie Petze, Phil Ramone and E.T. Thorngren) which should have been titled *An Album to Forget.*

the rest: *True Colors* (Portrait, 1986) *Twelve Deadly Cyns .... And Then Some* (Epic, 1994)

worth searching for: Before MTV, Lauper fronted a Blondie-inspired new-wave band called Blue Angel, whose self-titled debut (Polydor, 1980, prod. Roy Halee) hinted at the glass-shattering prowess to come.

Bjork

Shelley Fabares, Marlene Dietrich, Bette Midler

David Okamoto

League of Crafty Guitarists

See: Robert Fripp

Paul Leary

See: Butthole Surfers

The Leaves

Formed 1966 in Los Angeles, Calif. Disbanded 1968.

Jim Pons, bass, vocals; John Beck, guitar, vocals; Bobby Arlin, guitar, vocals; Robert Reiner, drums

This was one of the first L.A. folk-rock bands, and it was influenced as much by the British as by the burgeoning West Coast rock scene. The Leaves' strength was its harmony vocals and an alternating jangling and minor-key tone. Not remembered for penning memorable material, the group was good at emulating others' styles, culling inspiration from the Beatles, Byrds, Rolling Stones and Bob Dylan. Second only to Jimi Hendrix's rendition of "Hey Joe," the Leaves' folk/rock arrangement hit the Top 40 in 1966. That was about it; an album of weak material the next year—*Hey Joe* (MIRA, 1966/One Way, 1993 prod. Norm Ratner)

the rest: *All the Good That's Happening* (Capitol, 1967/One Way, 1994)

Patrick McCarty

Led Zeppelin

Formed 1968 in London, England. Disbanded 1980.

Jimmy Page, guitar; Robert Plant, vocals; John Paul Jones, bass, keyboards; John Bonham, drums (died Sept. 25, 1980)

Almost from the start, Led Zeppelin defined rock 'n' roll power and glory. During its prime, the quartet was rock's hottest, heaviest, highest-living player. But there was music to back it up; debatably the progenitors of heavy metal, Led Zeppelin emerged from the ashes of the Yardbirds and set sail with an unholy marriage of bloozy hard rock set to lumbering rhythms and defined by Page's state-of-the-craft guitar heroics. Plant's vocals became a rock prototype, influencing generations of singers, while Bonham's impossibly authoritative drumming was equally revered; in 1984, the British band Frankie Goes to Hollywood—whose flavor-of-the-month dance-pop was a far cry from Led Zep—sampled his trademark whomp for its hit "Relax." Knitting it all together was Jones, who proved to be one of rock's most valuable utility players.

What distinguished Led Zeppelin most was its ability to be eclectic without losing its identity; you always know a Zep song right off the bat, whether it's the primal attack of "Whole Lotta Love" or the acoustic chime of "Going to California." Throughout its 12 years together, the group used blues and rock as its base but incorporated touches of folk, funk and world music, particularly from the Middle East. Though derivative early on—Willie Dixon successfully sued the band for copyright infringement for "Whole Lotta Love"—Led Zeppelin quickly matured into a unique and distinctive outfit. And not a lick of it sounds dated. "Stairway to Heaven" is arguably the most popular rock song of all time. And it would be hard to imagine rock radio without "Rock and Roll," "Black Dog," "Kashmir" or a dozen others.

The Zep party ended in 1980, when Bonham died—choking on his own vomit in his sleep—at Page's home in Windsor, England. To their credit, the surviving trio ended the band shortly thereafter and generally stayed apart save for one-off reunions at Live Aid, the Atlantic Records 40th Anniversary concert and its induction into the Rock and Roll Hall of Fame. In 1994, however, Page and Plant began performing again as a duo, trading on the Led Zep catalog but with promises to pursue their own new music in the future.

what to buy: Led Zeppelin is one of the few rock bands that reward a random selection of its albums, but despite a bevy of boxed sets and anthologies, nothing betters the individual titles. No collection is complete without the untitled fourth album (Atlantic, 1971, prod. Jimmy Page), a uniformly exciting work that's impressive not just for its best-known cuts—"Stairway to Heaven," "Black Dog," "Rock and Roll"—but also for the bluesy "When the Levee Breaks" and the folky "Going to California." *Physical Graffiti* (Swan Song, 1975, prod. Jimmy Page) is a sprawling, double-length effort that features the enduring epic "Kashmir." *Led Zeppelin* (Atlantic, 1969, prod. Jimmy Page) and *Led Zeppelin II* (Atlantic, 1969, prod. Jimmy Page) represent an awesome output for a single year, the latter rating slightly higher due to the arresting "Whole Lotta Love."

what to buy next: There are some fans who will tell you *Houses of the Holy* (Atlantic, 1973, prod. Jimmy Page) is even better than the fourth album; it's actually a bit less consistent, though it's hard to argue with seminal tracks such as "Dancing Days," "Over the Hills and Far Away" and the reggae number "D'Yer Maker." Somewhat haphazard due to deadline pressures, *Presence* (Swan Song, 1976, prod. Jimmy Page) is the most underrated title in the Zep canon, with another engaging epic in "Achilles' Last Stand."

what to avoid: The soundtrack to the concert film of the same name, *The Song Remains the Same* (Swan Song, 1976, prod. by Jimmy Page) ♪♪ is a woeful representation of Led Zeppelin's electrifying live show. So far, there's been no legitimate release to really capture the band's concert prowess.

the rest: *Led Zeppelin III* (Atlantic, 1970) ♪♪♪♪ *In Through the Out Door* (Swan Song, 1979) ♪♪♪♪ *Coda* (Swan Song, 1982) ♪♪♪ *Led Zeppelin [Box Set]* (Atlantic, 1990) ♪♪♪♪ *Remasters* (Atlantic, 1992) ♪♪♪♪ *Led Zeppelin—Boxed Set 2* (Atlantic, 1993) ♪♪♪ *The Complete Studio Recordings* (Atlantic, 1993) ♪♪♪♪♪

worth searching for: It's likely that every Led Zeppelin performance has been bootlegged, and extreme caution should be used in delving into this overcrowded market. Representative of the best is *Trampled Underfoot* (Swingin' Pig, 1990) ♪♪♪♪♪, a two-CD set from a 1975 concert in Dallas that boast strong sound and a good, though incomplete, set of songs.

solo outings:

John Paul Jones: (with Diamanda Galas) *The Sporting Life* (Mute, 1994) ♪♪

▶▶ AC/DC, Aerosmith, Bad Company, Black Sabbath, Bonham, Alice Cooper, The Cult, Great White, Guns N'Roses, Kingdom Come, Mötley Crüe, Rush, Soundgarden, Whitesnake, Van Halen

◀◀ Willie Dixon, The Beatles, Chuck Berry, Fairport Convention, Buddy Guy, Howlin' Wolf, Robert Johnson, B.B. King, Little Richard, Joni Mitchell, Elvis Presley, The Rolling Stones, Otis Redding, Sonny Boy Williamson

see also: *Jimmy Page, Robert Plant, Page/Plant*

Gary Graff and Sarah Weber

Alvin Lee

See: Ten Years After

The Left Banke

Formed 1965 in New York, N.Y. Disbanded 1969.

Steve Martin, vocals; Michael Brown, keyboards (1966-68); Rick Brand, guitar; Tom Finn, bass; George Cameron, drums

Single-handedly responsible for the birth of the term Baroque Rock, the Left Banke was the first to graft delicate, classical-influenced melodies and instrumentation onto a standard rock beat for more than just a one-song experiment. Instead, this combination informed just about every song the group recorded. Today the Left Banke is revered by power pop fans not only for its melodic flair but also for its close harmonies and the British-flavored, achingly beautiful vocals of lead singer Martin. Generally acknowledged as the creative genius behind all this (though the band did surprisingly good work without him, too) is keyboardist-songwriter Brown; the son of violinist Harry Lookofsky (who produced pop acts such as Reparta and the Delrons under the name Hash Brown), Brown called upon his classical training to layer great countermelodies on top of already-superb melodies, embellishing it all with harpsichord and fine string arrangements. Yet it all came out as ummistakably rock 'n' roll, and the group's hits—"Walk Away Renee" and "Pretty Ballerina"—never wear out their welcome. The original band's entire recorded output—two LPS and two singles—has been collected on a 26-track single CD *There's Gonna Be a Storm: The Complete Recordings, 1966-1969.* (Mercury, 1992) ♪♪♪♪♪ Fans will also find the song "Two By Two"—a collaboration between Brown and Martin for the film "Hot Parts"—on the compilation *Mynd Excursions: A Journey Through the Vaults of Buddah and Kama Sutra* (Sequel, 1993).

see also: *Stories*

Mike Greenfield

The Lemon Pipers

Formed 1967 in Oxford, Ohio

Ivan Browne, vocals, guitar; R.G.Nave, organ, tambourine; Bill Bartlett, guitar; Steve Walmsley, bass; Bill Albaugh, drums

With their classic bubbledelic hit "Green Tambourine," a shimmering No. 1 early in 1968, the Lemon Pipers crassly mined the same candy-acid vein already being regularly visited by the likes of John Fred and the incomparable Tommy James. Unlike James, however, the Pipers had only one bona fide hit; as a result, like Mr. Fred, the group quickly vanished from the charts and reside to this day in One Hit Wonderland. A curious footnote, however: a decade after "Green Tambourine," guitarist Bartlett once again visited the Top 20 as leader of the band Ram Jam, another one-hit wonder with "Black Betty." Neither he nor his fellow Lemon Pipers have been heard from since. The first album, *Green Tambourine* (Buddah, 1968/1996) ♪♪♪ is newly available on CD, all the better to hear all the finger-cymbals and tremolo effects.

Gary Pig Gold

Lemonheads

Formed 1986 in Boston, Mass.

Evan Dando, vocals, guitar; Ben Deily, vocals, guitar, drums (1986-89); Dave Ryan, drums (1989-present); Jesse Peretz, bass (1986-89); Juliana Hatfield, bass (1991-92); Nic Dalton, bass (1992-present)

Lemonheads began life as a hardcore indie-punk outfit and snagged a major label deal after its hard 'n' fast remake of Suzanne Vega's "Luka" became a college radio hit. But the band didn't really take off until spacey "alterna-hunk" Dando took control in 1990 and began doctoring up its punk with winsome pop and folk styles. But its breakthrough didn't come via Dando; rather, it was a 1992 cover of Simon and Garfunkel's "Mrs. Robinson"—included on home video for "The Graduate"—that vaulted Lemonheads to mass popularity, though it repulsed as many boomers as it intrigued Generation Xers.

what to buy: *It's a Shame About Ray* (Atlantic, 1992, prod. The Robb Bros. and Evan Dando) is a masterful blend of gray ballads such as "My Drug Buddy" and punk-pop raveups like "Alison's Starting to Happen." A second edition added the remake of "Mrs. Robinson."

what to buy next: *Lick* (TAANG!, 1989, prod. Tom Hamilton and Terry Katzman) is the band's at its most raucous, especially on "Luka." *Come On Feel the Lemonheads* (Atlantic, 1993, prod. The Robb Bros. and Evan Dando) is a loose, experimental effort with solid songs such as "Big Gay Heart," "Being Around" and "Into Your Arms."

what to avoid: *Create Your Friends,* (TAANG!, 1989, prod. Tom Hamilton) a run-of-the-mill post-punk effort.

the rest: *Hate Your Friends* (TAANG!, 1987) *Creator* (TAANG!, 1988) *Lovey* (Atlantic, 1990)

worth searching for: The import single for "Into Your Arms," a track from *Come On Feel the Lemonheads* (Atlantic, 1993, prod. The Robb Bros. and Evan Dando) is fleshed out with interesting covers that include renditions of Cole Porter's "Miss Otis Regrets" and Buddy Holly's "Learning the Game."

▶▶ Gin Blossoms, Cracker, Everclear

◀◀ Replacements, Neil Young, Sex Pistols, Ramones

Thor Christensen

John Lennon

Born Oct. 9, 1940 in Liverpool, England. Died Dec. 8, 1980 in New York, N.Y.

An icon not only in rock 'n' roll but in all of pop culture, it's surprising how thin Lennon's post-Beatles output turned out to be. In the days when he was more in the news as a social force, his songwriting sometimes sagged. When he spent most of his days as a househusband, his songs were simply absent. Still, for the urgent familiarity of his voice and the timelessness of his best material, and, tragically, when he seemed on the verge of a return to form with the release of 1980's *Double Fantasy*, he was gunned down in front of his Manhattan apartment building. Lennon's legacy will undoubtably endure; it was his partially finished songs, after all, that led to the Beatles unexpected reunion in 1994 (with his former bandmates overdubbing his old demo tracks).

what to buy: *Plastic Ono Band* (Apple, 1970, prod. John Lennon and Phil Spector) is a searing, indelible work which has never been matched even in the days of the most confessional grunge. A collection of songs inspired by primal scream therapy of Dr. Walter Janov, Lennon's autobiographical songs about his mother (who died when he was a child), his declaration of independence from God (and the Beatles) and his lonely calls for the working class hero is a tour de force more than a quarter century later.

what to buy next: *Rock 'n' Roll* (Apple, 1975, prod. John Lennon and Phil Spector) is a splendid collection of rock favorites done in a relaxed manner by Lennon, who's in great voice. *Imagine* (Apple, 1971, prod. John Lennon and Phil Spector) contains the enduring title hymn and a dark stab at his former Beatles partner Paul McCartney in "How Do You Sleep?"

what to avoid: The early experimental albums with Yoko Ono—*Unfinished Music No. 1: Two Virgins,* (Apple, 1968, prod. John Lennon and Yoko Ono) WOOF! *Unfinished Music No. 2: Life with the Lions* (Zapple, 1969, prod. John Lennon and Yoko Ono) WOOF! and *The Wedding Album* (Apple, 1969, prod. John Lennon and Yoko Ono) WOOF! are avant garde works comprised of static, spoken word and repetition. They may have some historical interest or collectors' value—particularly the original nude cover of *Two Virgins*—but as collectors know, value goes up if the covers aren't opened. And you won't miss much if you don't open these.

the rest: *Live Peace in Toronto* (Apple, 1969) *Some Time in New York City* (Apple, 1972) *Mind Games* (Apple, 1973) *Walls and Bridges* (Apple, 1974) *Shaved Fish* (Apple,

1975) ℒℒℒℒ *Double Fantasy* (Geffen, 1980) ℒℒℒ½ *Milk and Honey* (Polydor, 1984) ℒℒ½ *The John Lennon Collection* (Capitol, 1982) ℒℒℒℒ *John Lennon Live in New York City* (Capitol, 1986) ℒℒ½ *Menlove Avenue* (Capitol, 1986) ℒℒℒ½ *Imagine: John Lennon* soundtrack (Capitol, 1988) ℒℒℒℒ *Lennon* (EMI, 1990) ℒℒℒℒ

worth searching for: Yoko Ono did release the entirety of Lennon's demo tapes on a radio series called "The Lost Lennon Tapes," which have been put on the underground market by numerous bootleg labels (there are rumors of a legitimate release in the near future). They're worth seeking out especially for "Serve Yourself"—a goof on Dylan's Jesus period—and the original version of "Free as a Bird," which was the first track Paul McCartney, Ringo Starr and George Harrison recorded for the "Beatles Anthology" series.

▶▶ Elton John, Billy Joel, Julian Lennon, Lenny Kravitz, Oasis

◀◀ Gene Vincent, Lonnie Donnegan, Buddy Holly, Chuck Berry, James Joyce

Roger Catlin

Julian Lennon

Born April 8, 1963, in Liverpool, England

"Boy, you're gonna carry that weight," Paul McCartney once sang, and although he may not have been singing about Julian Lennon then (he did that in "Hey Jude"), he couldn't have better summed up the essential dilemma of this Lennon's creative life. Using his uncanny vocal similarity to his far more talented father as his entree into the big time, Julian scored one Top 10 hit (the bouncy and infectious "Too Late For Goodbyes") and two smaller radio hits (the pretty and nostalgic but ridiculously meandering "Valotte" and the jazzy, Bowie-ish "Say You're Wrong") off his multimillion-selling debut album, *Valotte* (Atlantic, 1984, prod. Phil Ramone) ℒℒℒ But with a generally weak voice and an even less firm sense of his artistic desires and abilities, he floundered from that point, turning out a sub-par follow up in the same style (1986's *The Secret Value of Daydreaming*) and then inexplicably concocting a terrible Bowie ripoff (1989's *Mr. Jordan*), on which he vocally imitates the Thin White Duke (both of those titles are out of print). With *Help Yourself*, (Atlantic, 1991, prod. Bob Ezrin) ℒℒ he finally became himself, a mixed-up young singer with a good bit of experience making records but little knowledge gained from it.

Bob Remstein

Annie Lennox

See: Eurythmics

Let's Active

Formed 1981 in Winston-Salem, N.C. Disbanded 1988.

Mitch Easter, vocals, guitar; Faye Hunter, bass, vocals (1981-86); John Heames, bass (1988); Sara Romweber, drums (1981-84); Angie Carlson, vocals, keyboards, percussion (1986-88); Eric Marshall, drums (1986-88)

Through his Drive-In recording studio (so named because it started out in the family garage), Easter became the center of activity among the so-called "New South" bands and, when several of them moved north, their Hoboken/Manhattan friends. Low-tech but high-concept, Easter's productions were bright and poppy but left room for deeper currents, reflecting his love of 60s pop and the less pretentious of the 70s underground bands such as the revered Big Star. Let's Active (from a mangled English-language Japanese T-shirt slogan) embodied the same principles; begun as a band, by the second album it was more Easter—who most recently has toured with Velvet Crush—and occasional side people, though on his heavier swan song he returned somewhat to a band structure. His talent for fresh sounds and quirky, imaginative hooks stood out most on *Cypress/Afoot*, (I.R.S., 1989, prod. Let's Active and Don Dixon) ℒℒℒℒ which compines the first EP and LP. On the surface it can seem all similarly twinkie, but there's actually plenty of variety, and the male/female vocal split worksd well. "Blue Line" is his best chorus hook, utterly indelible.

the rest: *Big Plans for Everybody* (I.R.S., 1986) ℒℒℒ½ *Every Dog Has His Day* (I.R.S., 1988) ℒℒℒ

Steve Holtje

Level 42

Formed 1980 in London, England. Disbanded 1994.

Mark King, bass, vocals; Mike Lindup, keyboards, vocals; Phil Gould, drums (1980-1987, 1994); Boon Gould, guitar (1980-87); Alan Murphy, guitar (1987-89, died Oct. 19, 1989); Jakko Jacszyk, guitar (1991-94); Gary Husband, drums (1987-94)

Friends on the Isle of Wight, the Gould brothers (Boon and Phil are twins) and King moved to London during 1978. There they met Lindup, a friend of Phil's from college. Inspired by 70s fusion artists such as Chick Corea and Stanley Clarke, Level 42 mixed jazz, funk and rock in similar ways, with King's mighty, thumping bass sound—borrowed heavily from his idol Clarke—center stage. Although early efforts were mostly instrumental, pressure from the band's record company convinced King to start singing and writing more pop-oriented material. The group found success at home but little interest in America until 1985, when the first of its two most pop-oriented albums appeared on the charts. The hectic touring required by their newfound success proved too much for the Gould brothers, who left the band in 1987, to be replaced by former Go West guitarist Murphy (who died in 1989 of AIDS) and ex-Allan Holdsworth sideman Husband. The group remained active, but successive albums never matched the pop appeal of its mid-80s efforts and the group disbanded in 1994.

what to buy: For well-composed songs matched with funky, cohesive playing, you can't beat the band's two most successful albums, *World Machine* (Polydor, 1985, prod. Level 42 and Wally Badarou) ♪♪♪♪ and *Running in the Family.* (Polydor, 1987, Level 42 and Wally Badarou) ♪♪♪♪ Both boast quality pop tunes leavened by jaw-dropping musicianship—on *World Machine*, it's songs such as the title track and the hit single "Something About You"; on *Family*, it's the dreamy "Children Say" and funkified "Fashion Fever." The U.S. version of *World Machine* boasts two added hits from a previous album—the dance track "Hot Water" and tribal groove "The Chant Has Begun."

what to avoid: Most of the band's records after *Family* fall into a familiar rut, with the pop muse that delivered such appealing songs on its hit albums conspicuously absent. Of these, *Staring at the Sun* (Polydor, 1988, prod. Level 42, Wally Badarou and Julian Mendelsohn) WOOF! commits the greatest sin, unfolding as a totally uninteresting album assembled by a group of top-notch musicians who should have known better.

the rest: *Level 42* (Polydor, 1981) ♪♪♪ *The Pursuit of Accidents* (Polydor, 1982) ♪♪ *Standing in the Light* (Polydor, 1983) ♪♪♪♪ *True Colours* (Polydor, 1984) ♪♪♪ *A Physical Presence, Pt. 1* (Polydor, 1985) ♪♪ *A Physical Presence, Pt. 2* (Polydor, 1985) ♪♪♪♪ *Level Best* (Polydor, 1989) ♪♪♪♪ *Guaranteed* (RCA, 1992) ♪♪♪ *Forever Now* (RCA, 1994) ♪♪♪

worth searching for: The "Live at Wembley" video, shot during a triumphant four-night stand at Wembley Arena in London, captures the group at its creative best—showcasing all the best things about Level 42's sound and stage show.

▶▶ Brand New Heavies

◀◀ Chick Corea, Stanley Clarke, Return to Forever, Herbie Hancock's Headhunters

Eric Deggans

Keith Levene

See: Public Image Ltd. (PiL)

Jerry Lee Lewis

Born Sept. 29, 1935, in Ferriday, La.

Among the most arrogant men in the history of music (an achievement in itself), Lewis' saving grace has been a talent that burns as fiercely as his gun-waving personal life. Before the pills there was his first lunge at rock 'n' roll as part of the legendary Sun Records stable during the 50s. The blistering sessions that emerged—with Lewis slamming on his piano as he wailed his lyrics with a gospel-like fury—surely put him on par with Elvis Presley, though Lewis was way too hard-edged and wild-eyed for mass public acceptance. Marrying his 13-year-old cousin didn't exactly bolster his image, either; when that story broke, the blackball that ensued relegated him to country music. From the early 60s on, Lewis has been a country singer, and a great singer period when he feels like it. Since then, his day-to-day activities have been frequently more illuminating than his music. Many people visit the Graceland mansion; only Lewis has opened fire on it. Marital difficulties, perforated ulcers and the I.R.S. haven't tamed The Killer. Neither will time, as his semi-comeback in 1995 clearly affirmed.

what to buy: The 18 tracks on *Original Sun Greatest Hits* (Rhino, 1984, prod. Various) ♪♪♪♪♪ represent some of most raucous rock 'n' roll ever recorded, including the pumping "Whole Lotta Shakin' Goin' On," "Great Balls of Fire" and "Breathless." *All Killer, No Filler: The Anthology* (Rhino, 1993, prod. Various) ♪♪♪♪♪ is the single best cross-section of Lewis' career, drawing recordings from the Sun, Mercury and Elektra years and providing clear evidence of Lewis' command over rockabilly, country and rock 'n' roll. *Rare Tracks: Wild One* (Rhino, 1989, prod. Various) ♪♪♪♪♪ has "Wild One (Real Wild Child)" and the "Sail Away" duet with the supreme Charlie Rich.

what to buy next: *Killer: The Mercury Years, Vol. 1, (1963-1968)* (Mercury, 1989, prod. Various) ♪♪♪♪ *Killer: The Mercury Years, Vol. 2 (1969-1972)* (Mercury, 1989, prod. Various) ♪♪♪♪ and *Killer: The Mercury Years, Vol. 3 (1973-1977)* (Mercury, 1989, prod. Various) ♪♪♪♪ comprise an expansive overview that covers the best of the mostly country and gospel work he did during those years.

what to avoid: *The Golden Rock Hits of Jerry Lee Lewis* (Smash, 1967/1987) ✪✪ an album of remakes that seems unnecessary since he got it right the first time.

the rest: *Milestones* (Rhino, 1985) ✪✪✪✪✪ *Jerry Lee's Greatest!* (Rhino, 1961/1989) ✪✪✪✪ *20 Classic Jerry Lee Lewis Hits* (Original Sound Entertainment, 1986) ✪✪✪✪ *Killer Country* (Mercury, 1995) ✪✪✪✪ *Greatest Hits—Finest Performances* (Sun, 1995) ✪✪✪✪ *Young Blood* (Sire, 1995) ✪✪✪

worth searching for: *Jerry Lee Lewis* (Elektra, 1974) ✪✪✪✪ which shows that when given engaging material—Arthur Alexander's "Every Day I Have to Cry" and Rich's "Who Will the Next Fool Be," for instance, Lewis will rise to the occasion.

▶▶ Iggy Pop, Elton John, Billy Joel, Bruce Springsteen, Jason and the Scorchers, Kentucky HeadHunters

◀◀ Elvis Presley, Charlie Rich

Allan Orski

Gary Lewis & the Playboys

Formed 1964 in Los Angeles, Calif.

Gary Lewis, vocals, drums; Al Ramsey, guitar; John R. West, guitar; David Walker, keyboards; David Costell, bass

As if being No. 1 son of the legendary King of Comedy wasn't pressure enough, Lewis and his chums the Playboys found themselves signed to a lucrative, long-term deal with Liberty Records, performing to a nationwide audience on the Ed Sullivan Show and topping the American charts with their first-ever release (the Al Kooper-composed "This Diamond Ring"), all within the space of several weeks between Nov. 19, 1964 and Jan. 23, 1965. Just four months earlier, the band had been performing for tips at Disneyland. Such are the Cinderella tales that litter the pop world of the 60s, but of course the Playboys had more than a simple "in" to the business: without papa Jerry's considerable clout, it's hard to imagine a winsome if mediocre voice like his son's being heard much outside the family den. Nevertheless, under the watchful ear of studio ace Snuff Garrett and a roomful of the hottest session men royalties could buy (most notably arranger/keyboardist Leon Russell), the Playboys racked up an astonishing run of hits until the bubble inevitably burst in 1967. For the next several years, the fairy tale turned more than grim as Lewis found himself drafted, divorced and addicted to drugs. Things weren't much brighter insofar as his musical career was concerned either, and after several comeback attempts (his album titles of the period tell the story: *New Directions, I'm on the Right Road Now* and *Listen!*), Lewis retired from the pop scene, dazed and most definitely confused. Still, with his cheery "can-do" attitude returned and an ever-revolving lineup of Playboys at the ready, Lewis can still be heard singing his many carefully crafted hits on the Yesteryear circuit and, each and every Labor Day, on Dad's telethon. The *Legendary Masters Series* compilation (EMI, 1990, prod. Various) ✪✪✪ contains more than a dozen hits so infectiously written and performed that you can't help but crack at least half a grin, and "Time Stands Still," in which Gary for one verse does a wickedly accurate imitation of his father, is worth the price of admission alone.

Gary Pig Gold

Huey Lewis and the News

Formed 1979 in Marin County, Calif.

Huey Lewis (born Hugh Cregg III), vocals, harmonica; Chris Hayes, guitar; Johnny Colla, guitar, saxophone; Sean Hopper, keyboards; Mario Cipollina, bass (1979-95); Bill Gibson, drums

Commonly viewed as a bar band that made good, Huey Lewis and the News actually played a mere two live dates before signing a record contract. But the members mainly came from stalwart pillars of the active Marin County 70s club scene, so the impression is not without basis in fact. The band polished up the burgeoning new wave/power pop sound then coming out of England; Lewis and keyboardist Hopper had recently returned from an extended stay in that country with their band Clover, where the group recorded albums of its own and some members participated in Elvis Costello's debut, *My Aim Is True*. Although the News' second album earned the band some respectable FM airplay, it was the third release, the hit-laden *Sports*, that made Lewis and company one of the most popular American rock bands of the day—an album, ironically, that sat on a shelf for almost a year following the record label's bankruptcy.

With "Power of Love" from the *Back to the Future* soundtrack scorching up to the top of the singles charts in 1985, the News could do no wrong. Lewis' boy-next-door image played well on MTV (another irony, considering he is the son of a jazz buff father and hippie artist mother). But, live by the hit single—die by the hit single. As the band's commercial marksmanship faltered with the slightly out of character 1988 release, *Small*

World, the group fell into a popularity decline, hardly spelled by the label change and the sub-par 1991 offering, *Hard at Play*. A serendipitous a cappella radio success from a Curtis Mayfield tribute album led the band to explore obscure 60s soul songs on *Four Chords and Several Years Ago*, an album that may have helped restore some credibility to the group's tarnished luster in between lucrative private party performances and Lewis' vacations at his Montana ranch.

what to buy: Although *Sports* (Chrysalis, 1983, prod. Huey Lewis and the News) may be the obvious starting point, that multi-platinum monster's predecessor, *Picture This* (Chrysalis, 1982, prod. Huey Lewis and the News) laid out all the basic architecture to the group's forthcoming hit career.

what to buy next: Unappreciated for its quirky honesty and well rounded musicality, *Small World* (Chrysalis, 1988, prod. Huey Lewis and the News) bounced happily from the jazzy overtones of the two-part title track (illuminated by extended sax solo from Stan Getz), the New Orleans drive of "Old Antoine's" and one of the most under-appreciated tracks from the group's entire oeuvre, the Marin reggae instrumental, "Bobo Tempo," originally recorded for the soundtrack to a short film by the vocalist's mother.

what to avoid: Under pressure to produce another *Sports*, the band labored so long on *Hard at Play*, (EMI, 1991, prod. Huey Lewis and the News) the musicians managed to choke out any glimmer of life the mannered songs might have contained in the first place. Hard to Hear is more like it.

the rest: *Huey Lewis and the News* (Chrysalis, 1980) *Fore!* (Chrysalis, 1986) *Four Chords and Several Years Ago* (Elektra, 1994)

worth searching for: A European best-of, *The Heart of Rock & Roll* (Chrysalis, 1992, prod. Bill Schnee, Huey Lewis and the News) collects the singles and offers a hot live take of the customary show-closer "Workin' for a Livin'."

▶▶ Bruce Hornsby, Nick Lowe, Blues Traveler

◀◀ Clover, Brinsley Schwartz, Elvis Costello, doo-wop, Motown

Joel Selvin

Alex Lifeson

See: Rush

Gordon Lightfoot

Born Nov. 17, 1938 in Orillia, Ontario, Canada

Lightfoot is one of the few singer-songwriters who emerged during the folk music revival of the early 60s to achieve and retain recognition as a distinctive, enduring talent. Strongly influenced by Bob Dylan, Lightfoot specializes in simple yet compelling melodies and evocative lyrics about bittersweet love, the history and natural splendor of rural Canada, maritime adventures (and disasters), wanderlust and memories of happier times—all sung in Lightfoot's rich baritone voice and accompanied by expert guitar arrangements. As a songwriter, his work has been recorded by Marty Robbins ("Ribbon of Darkness"), Ian and Sylvia Tyson ("Early Morning Rain") and Peter, Paul and Mary ("For Lovin' Me"). His own hit list included 1970's "If You Could Read My Mind"—since covered by more than five dozen other artists, 1974's "Sundown" and the epic ballad of "The Wreck of the Edmund Fitzgerald."

what to buy: *Gord's Gold* (Warner/Reprise, 1975, prod. Various) is a terrific collection for which Lightfoot even rerecorded some of his pre-1970 material to good effect.

what to buy next: *Don Quixote* (Warner/Reprise, 1972, prod. Lenny Waronker) showcases Lightfoot at the height of his musical powers, from the show-stopping country stomper "Alberta Bound" (featuring superb bottleneck guitar licks by Ry Cooder) to the spare, energetic title cut and mellow pieces such as "Beautiful" and "Christian Island (Georgian Bay)." *Summertime Dream* (Warner/Reprise, 1976, prod. Lenny Waronker and Gordon Lightfoot) has "The Wreck of the Edmund Fitzgerald" and a wide variety of song styles. *If You Could Read My Mind* (Warner/Reprise, 1970, prod. Joe Wissert and Lenny Waronker) is Lightfoot's breakthrough album, marked mostly by its gentle, celestial melodies.

what to avoid: On *Endless Wire*, (Reprise, 1978, prod. Lenny Waronker and Gordon Lightfoot) Lightfoot's images are muddy, while the songs lack the strength of his earlier work.

the rest: *Lightfoot!* (United Artists, 1965) *The Way I Feel* (United Artists, 1967) *Did She Mention My Name* (United Artists, 1968) *Back Here on Earth* (United Artists, 1968) *Sunday Concert* (United Artists, 1969) *Sundown* (Warner/Reprise, 1974) *Cold on the Shoulder* (Warner/Reprise, 1975) *East of Midnight* (Warner/ Reprise, 1986) *Gord's Gold II* (Warner/Reprise, 1988) *Waiting for You* (Warner/Reprise, 1993) *Gordon Lightfoot: The United Artists Collection* (EMI, 1993)

worth searching for: The bootleg *If You Could Read My Mind: Live in Montreaux 1977* (Trade Service, 1977) includes "Edmund Fitzgerald" and others purported to be from the Montreux '77 concert. Others worth scouring used record stores for include the four albums not re-released on CD and deserving of at least 3 bones apiece—*Old Dan's Records* (Warner/Reprise, 1972), *Dream Street Rose* (Warner/Reprise, 1980), *Shadows* (Warner/Reprise, 1982) and *Salute* (Warner/Reprise)

▶▶ Nancy Griffith, James Taylor, Harry Chapin, Tracey Chapman, Janis Ian

◀◀ Woody Guthrie

James Person

The Lightning Seeds

Formed 1988 in Liverpool, England

Ian Broudie, vocals, guitar; Martin Campbell, bass; Chris Sharrock, drums; Paul Hemmings, guitar

Lightning Seeds founder Broudie began his career playing in Liverpool bands such as Big in Japan, Original Mirrors and Care before becoming a successful producer for The Fall and Echo and the Bunnymen. However, The Lightning Seeds didn't seem to develop musically the same way Broudie did; the group often comes off as the Pet Shop Boys minus the dance beats and cynicism. Still, its first album, *Cloudcuckooland* (MCA, 1989, prod. Ian Broudie) is a fine display of bouncy pop.

the rest: *Sense* (MCA, 1992) *Jollification* (Trauma/Interscope, 1994)

Anna Glen

David Lindley

Born 1944 in San Marino, Calif.

Winner of banjo and fiddle contests as a teenager, a long-time sideman to Jackson Browne through the 70s, a scraggly-haired solo artist during the 80s and a world music collaborator in the 90s, Lindley has never met a stringed instrument he didn't like. His fiddle and explosive lap steel leads ignited Browne concerts and songs (listen to "Redneck Friend" or "Running on Empty"), and his work livened albums by James Taylor (*In the Pocket*), Linda Ronstadt (*Heart Like a Wheel*), Graham Nash (*Wild Tales* and *Songs for Beginners*) and Warren Zevon (*Warren Zevon*), among others. Lindley's solo career offers a different perspective: songs, many of them familiar, but laced with a whimsical sense of humor that matched his rayon/polyester attire and eccentric faux dub reggae/chunk/Tex-Mex/pop/rock/dance style. Lindley has spent the 90s recording with Henry Kaiser in Madagascar and Norway, and touring with percussionist Hani Naser. Like Ry Cooder, the L.A. guitarist with whom he collaborates occasionally, Lindley is a musician for all seasons.

what to buy: *El Rayo-X* (Asylum, 1981, prod. Jackson Browne and Greg Ladanyi) is an album no discriminating rock lover should be without—particularly such tunes as "Mercury Blues" and "She Took Off My Romeos." *Win This Record* (Asylum, 1982, prod. David Lindley and Greg Ladanyi) is almost as good, especially the strangely prophetic "Talk to the Lawyer." *Very Greasy* (Elektra, 1988, prod. Linda Ronstadt) offers the tackiest ("Tiki Torches at Twilight") and funkiest ("Papa Was a Rolling Stone") tunes in the Lindley canon. And *World Out of Time: Henry Kaiser and David Lindley in Madagascar* (Shanachie, 1992, prod. Birger Gesthuisen and Henry Kaiser), presents a gorgeous romp with the cream of Malagasy musicians topped off with an improbably wonderful "I Fought the Law."

what to buy next: *World Out of Time Vol. 2: Henry Kaiser and David Lindley in Madagascar* (Shanachie, 1993, prod. Birger Gesthuisen and Henry Kaiser) offers more cross-cultural tomfoolery. *Mr. Dave* (WEA International, 1985, prod. David Lindley, Greg Ladanyi and Danny Kortchmar) is only slightly less fun than his other solo records.

what to avoid: His early trippy albums with the late 60s psychedelic folk group Kaleidoscope, with all the direction of a bad acid trip.

the rest: *The Sweet Sunny North: Henry Kaiser and David Lindley in Norway* (Shanachie, 1994)

worth searching for: *David Lindley and Hani Naser Live in Tokyo Playing Real Good* and *David Lindley and Hani Naser Live All Over the Place Playing Even Better!! Official Bootleg*, both self-produced with no official imprint and available only at their live shows. You haven't lived until you've heard their rendition of Jerry Lee Lewis' "The Meat Man."

▶▶ Black Crowes, Bottle Rockets, the Hooters, Chris Whitley

◀◀ Clifton Chenier, Gabby Pahinui, the Pioneers, Yellow Magic Orchestra, Ry Cooder, Duane Eddy, Ventures, Fendermen, James Burton, Huey "Piano" Smith, King Curtis, Sam the Sham and the Pharoahs

Leland Rucker

Arto Lindsay Trio

See: Ambitious Lovers

Liquorice

See: His Name is Alive

Little Eva

Born Eva Narcissus Boyd, June 29, 1945 in Bell Haven, N.C.

Little Eva is the most famous baby-sitter in pop music history. Carole King and Gerry Goffin penned "The Loco-Motion" after watching Eva dance around their house while she was watching them. They gave her a shot at singing it and Don Kirschner liked her voice enough to release it. Reaching No. 1 on both the pop and R&B charts in 1962, it became one of the great dance singles of all time. Little Eva's second single, "Keep Your Hands Off My Baby," was a hit as well, but nothing is as memorable as "The Loco-Motion." Stuck in a dance singer mode, she retired and now tours in oldies showcases. *The Best of Little Eva* (Murray Hill, 1988) and *The Loco-Motion* (Rhino, 1996) include her hits and charming misses.

Patrick McCarty

Little Feat

Formed 1969 in Los Angeles, Calif. Disbanded 1979. Reformed 1988.

Lowell George, vocals, guitar (1969-79, died 1979); Billy Payne, keyboards; Paul Barrere, vocals, guitar (1973-79, 1988-present); Roy Estrada, bass (1969-72); Kenny Gradney, bass (1972-79, 1988-present); Richard Hayward, drums; Sam Clayton, percussion (1973-79, 1988-present); Craig Fuller, vocals (1988-94); Fred Tackett, guitar (1988-present); Shaun Murphy, vocals (1994-present)

Little Feat's eclectic, groove-based rock was the vision of singer-guitarist Lowell George, a former member of the art-rock band The Factory as well as Frank Zappa's Mothers of Invention. Though it survived him in name—regrouping nine years after his death—Little Feat was an entirely different animal without him. The band's early 70s albums, however, are an enchanting combination of New Orleans grease, Nashville twang and Liverpool sparkle, often within the same song. George's lyrics display a similarly broad range, and his tenderest compositions avoid mawkishness thanks to his dry and often absurdist sense of humor. Working with an exceptional crew of players—notably the versatile Payne and fellow Zappa alum Estrada—George brought these funky, melodic tunes to life on a string of exceptional releases before breaking up the band to pursue a solo career. His debut appeared the same year he died of a heart attack that was probably brought on by his notorious substance abuse.

Little Feat reformed in 1988 with five original members, plus Tackett and Pure Prairie League vet Fuller. Its streamlined groove-pop met with greater commercial success than did its earlier, more eccentric incarnation. Like the Allman Brothers, the Neville Brothers and other kindred spirits, Little Feat's reemergence struck a chord of tenacity that no doubt reverberated with aging boomers. Meanwhile, its recycled, domesticated sound made it less threatening to the masses than George's unpredictable inventions. In addition to several successful albums, the new Little Feat appeared on some film soundtracks and guested on an album by fellow rock vet Bob Seger. Though the band's newfound status owed much to nostalgia, the legacy of George's remarkable body of work clearly lives on.

what to buy: *Dixie Chicken* (Warner Bros., 1973, prod. Lowell George) is a superb introduction to the group's smart, high-spirited rock stew, boasting delicious melodies and hip-shaking grooves. An instant party.

what to buy next: *Sailin' Shoes* (Warner Bros, 1972, prod. Ted Templeman) is a more diverse collection, but features some of George's finest songs, among them the exquisite "Willin,'" the indelible rocker "Easy to Slip" and the incandescent title track. The group's debut, simply titled *Little Feat* (Warner Bros., 1971, prod. Russ Titelman) is slightly less cohesive but boasts numerous must-have songs, particularly the ballads "I've Been the One" and "Brides of Jesus." The live collection *Waiting for Columbus* (Warner Bros., 1978, prod. Lowell George) is a veritable greatest-hits album comprised of energetic live performances.

what to avoid: *Shake Me Up* (Morgan Creek, 1991) They're still capable of cooking, but Little Feat doesn't sizzle quite as much as it should on this one.

the rest: *Feats Don't Fail Me Now* (Warner Bros., 1974) *The Last Record Album* (Warner Bros., 1975) *Time Loves a Hero* (Warner Bros., 1977) *Down on the Farm* (Warner Bros., 1979) *Hoy-Hoy!* (Warner Bros., 1981) *Let It Roll* (Warner Bros., 1988) *Representing the Mambo* (Warner Bros., 1990) *Ain't Had Enough Fun* (Zoo, 1995) *Live from Neon Park* (Zoo, 1996)

worth searching for: *As Time Goes By: The Very Best of Little*

Feat (Warner Bros., 1993, prod. Various) is a superb European sampler of Little Feat's first incarnation that has never been equalled in the U.S.

solo outings:

Lowell George: *Thanks I'll Eat It Here* (Warner Bros., 1979)

Paul Barrere: *On My Own Two Feet* (Atlantic, 1983) *If the Phone Don't Ring* (Zoo, 1995)

Elvis Costello, Emmylou Harris, Linda Ronstadt, Black Crowes, Blind Melon, Daniel Lanois

Hank Williams, the Beatles, the Byrds, Lee Dorsey, Meters, Howlin' Wolf, Muddy Waters, John Lee Hooker, Canned Heat

Simon Glickman

Little Richard

Born Richard Wayne Penniman, Dec. 5, 1935 in Macon, Ga.

The king—and the queen—of rock and roll, Little Richard drove his music with the maniacal energy of an androgynous but unambiguous raw sexuality. He blasted the path for rock and roll with his 1955 hit "Tutti Frutti," which shattered the tame tempos of the Eisenhower era. But for all his extraordinary impact, Little Richard spent something like a mere 72 hours total over in the recording studio compiling his towering legacy. He cut some sessions in a Roy Brown vein for RCA Victor during 1951-52 and did a couple of R&B sides with producer Johnny Otis on the Texas-based Duke label. But it wasn't until he hooked up with producer Bumps Blackwell in New Orleans and made "Tutti Frutti" for Specialty Records that Little Richard forever changed the course of rock and roll history.

A man as tall in life as legend, he quit show business at the height of his popularity to study for the ministry. When he returned to rock 'n' roll performances several years later in Europe, his opening acts included some band called the Beatles. Richard continues to record to this day, almost catching a comeback hit off "Great Gosh A' Mighty" from the 1986 "Down and Out in Beverly Hills" soundtrack. He has recording everything from gospel to children's records, but nothing has surpassed the handful of records he made for Specialty in the 50s.

what to buy: The current owners of the Specialty catalog have made the 25 greatest Little Richard recordings available on *The Georgia Peach* (Specialty, 1991, prod. Bumps Blackwell) and, if that isn't enough, an additional 24 lesser known pieces and alternate takes of hits on *Shag On Down By the Union Hall* (Specialty, 1996, prod. Bumps Blackwell) Blackwell) or a three-disc boxed set, *The Specialty Sessions* (Specialty, 1989, prod. Bumps Blackwell and Billy Vera) abridged from the five-disc British version.

what to avoid: Richard's gospel recordings turn up from time to time on various small labels and, although his powerful rock 'n' roll singing might lead one to reasonably suspect a great gospel singer lies beneath, Richard records deliberately tame, unexciting ballads sung without any flair or color.

the rest: *Well Alright!* (Specialty, 1970) *The Essential Little Richard* (Specialty, 1985) *18 Greatest Hits* (Rhino, 1988) *Sings the Gospel* (MCA, 1995) WOOF!

worth searching for: His 1965 Okeh Records jived-up "live" album that was actually recorded in the studio—Club Okeh, get it?—and captures the wild, extravagant personality of the man himself, along with some impossibly intense vocal performances. It was released on a budget-priced CD, *Little Richard's Greatest Hits*. (Epic, 1967/1988, prod. Larry Williams) This is one of the greatest live performances in the music's history, an under-rated masterwork that easily ranks with better known landmarks like James Brown's *Live at the Apollo* or Otis Redding's *Live in Europe*.

Paul McCartney, Otis Redding, John Fogerty, Prince, Michael Jackson

Roy Brown, Cab Calloway

Joel Selvin

Little River Band

Formed 1975 in Melbourne, Australia

Beeb Birtles, guitar, vocals (1975-83); Graham Goble, guitar, vocals (1975-92); Glenn Shorrock, vocals (1975-82, 1988-present); Roger McLachlan, bass (1975-77); Derek Pellicci, drums (1975-85, 1988-present); Rick Formosa, guitar (1975-77); David Briggs, guitar, vocals (1977-82); George McArdale, bass (1977-79); Wayne Nelson, bass, vocals (1980-present); Steve Housden, guitar (1982-present); John Farnham, vocals (1982-88); Steven Prestwich, drums (1985-88); David Hirschfelder, keyboards (1985-88); Peter Beckett, guitar (1994-present); Tony Sciuto, guitar (1994-present)

During the mid- and late-70s, Australian rock meant AC/DC (heavy), Split Enz (quirky) and—the Little River Band. To be fair, this middle-of-the-road pop group was not without its virtues: frontman Shorrock provided a prototype for the kind of singing we'd hear on Phil Collins' solo albums; harmonies were a strong suit; and with three guitarists (!) LRB could step up for the occasional guitar jam a la its first hit, "It's a Long Way There"—though nobody yelled for "Free Bird" at its concerts. Mostly, however, LRB specialized in lite rock and lush pop, at best warmly melodic ("Help Is on its Way," "Lonesome Loser"), at worst pure piffle ("Reminiscing"). Appropriately, most of what's still in print is hits collections. The single disc *Greatest Hits* (Capitol/EMI, 1982, prod. Various) ♪♪♪♪ should suffice for most. If this stuff really barbys your shrimp, go for *Reminiscing: The Twentieth Anniversary Collection,* (Rhino, 1994, prod. Various) ♪♪♪ whose two-CDs leave room for a few of the less-inspiring moments.

the rest: *Diamantina Cocktail* (Capitol/EMI, 1977/1996) ♪♪ *Worldwide Live* (Curb, 1991) ♪ *All-Time Greatest Hits* (CEMA Special Products, 1992) ♪♪♪

Gary Graff

Little Steven

Born Steven Van Zandt, November 22, 1950 in Boston, Mass.

Van Zandt made a name for himself on the Jersey shore club scene long before he was known to the world at large as Miami Steve or Little Steven. He had played in various bands during 60s and early 70s, including the early Bruce Springsteen band Steel Mill. After a stint with Southside Johnny and the Asbury Jukes, Van Zandt joined the E-Street Band in 1975, where he was dubbed Miami Steve and became an important part of Springsteen's rise to stardom, playing the role of de facto musical director for the E Street Band and co-producer in the studio. After releasing his first solo album in 1982, under the name Little Steven—and with an ace band called the Disciples of Soul—Van Zandt began to grow as a songwriter and a political artist. In 1984 he left the E Street Band and started his own solo career. Although his records have never sold well in the U.S., he did gain notoriety for his anti-apartheid single "Sun City," which he recorded with more than 50 performers including Springsteen, Bob Dylan, Pete Townshend, Lou Reed and Bono. A song that soon turned into an album and all-star concert, "Sun City" is a classic sample of Van Zandt's sound of late—heavy rhythms, driving guitars and pointed lyrics on political issues of the day.

what to buy: *Men Without Women* (EMI, 1982, prod. Miami Steve Van Zandt) ♪♪♪♪, Van Zandt's first solo effort, is a fine collection of soul-drenched rock 'n' roll that's closer to his work with the Jukes than his later efforts, with only a hint of the political tact he would take on those.

what to buy next: *Freedom—No Compromise* (EMI Manhattan, 1987, prod. Little Steven) ♪♪♪♪ By this, his third album, Van Zandt's songs carried heavier rhythms, inspired more by Prince's Minneapolis groove than by the Jersey shore rock 'n' roll swing. And even though these are mostly protest songs—including duets with Springsteen ("Native American") and Ruben Blades ("Bitter Fruit")—Van Zandt still let music drive the songs instead of the messages.

the rest: *Voice of America* (EMI, 1984) ♪♪♪

worth searching for: The hard-to-find *Revolution* (RCA, 1989, prod. Little Steven) ♪♪♪♪ continued in the hard-hitting political vein of *Freedom—No Compromise*

▶▶ Southside Johnny, Bon Jovi

◀◀ Stax, Motown, doo wop, Hank Williams, the Rolling Stones, the Yardbirds, Cream

Mike Joiner

What Album Changed Your Life?

Blue Valentine by Tom Waits was one. I was young, 12 or something, and I'd never heard music like that--the poetry, the lyrics and everything about it. It's a whole package, one whole thing. That's what amazed me about it."

Dave Matthews

Little Village

Formed 1987 in Los Angeles, Calif.

John Hiatt, vocals, guitar; Ry Cooder, guitar; Nick Lowe, vocals, bass; Jim Keltner, drums

This quartet first got together to record Hiatt's 1987 album *Bring the Family,* and the musicians enjoyed the experience so much they decided to make a go of it as a band. Unfortunately, *Little Village* (Reprise, 1992, prod. Little Village) ♪♪♪ lacks the spontaneous creative explosions you'd expect from so much songwriting and performing talent. Hiatt handles most of the singing and manages a couple of laughs on "Solar Sex Panel" and "Do You Want My Job." The rest of the album lacks personality, an odd thing for a group with so much of it, and it came out not so much like the Traveling Wilburys as a lukewarm Hiatt solo album. Little Village hasn't actually disbanded, but another record will certainly be a surprise.

see also: *John Hiatt, Nick Lowe, Ry Cooder*

Steve Knopper

Live

Formed 1985 in York, Pa.

Ed Kowalczyk, vocals, guitar; Chad Taylor, guitar, vocals; Patrick Dahlheimer, bass, vocals; Chad Gracey, drums, vocals

Straight outta York, Pa., Live is the little garage band that could. Formed when the members were wee lads of 13, the group bears the trademarks of the two most notable bands of the era in which it formed—U2 and R.E.M. Like the former, Live sports an agenda that addresses issues of the world and of the spirit. Like the latter, the band's arrangements are often circumspect. With songs extolling the wisdom of Indian philosopher J. Krishnamurti and addressing issues with utter earnestness, Live leaves itself open to charges of pretension. But the truth is, it's less preachy than U2, less precious than R.E.M., and its records are more valuable as entertainment than metaphysics. The *Four Songs* EP (Radioactive, 1991, prod. Jerry Harrison) contained signs of good things to come, most notably the anthemic "Operation Spirit," which later appeared on the debut album, *Mental Jewelry* (Radioactive, 1991, prod. Jerry Harrison) —although by then it had grown a parenthetical subtitle, "(The Tyranny of Tradition)." The first album occasionally bogs down lyrically, but it's the kind of mistakes— oversimplification, for example—that 20 year-olds are apt to make. *Throwing Copper* (Radioactive, 1994, prod. Jerry Harrison and Live) is a leap to the next level. The band still takes on the big subjects—religion, death, desperation—but it rocks rock with a newfound authority that drives the lyrics home. The hits "Selling the Drama," "I Alone" and "Lightning Crashes" are every bit as memorable as they were meaningful, a sure sign of growth for a band that may yet be honored/burdened with the tag Band of the 90s, as U2 was in the 80s.

Daniel Durchholz

Live Skull

Formed 1983 in New York, N.Y. Disbanded 1989.

Thalia Zedek, vocals (1987-89); Mark C, guitar, vocals; Tom Paine, guitar, vocals; Marnie Greenholz, bass, vocals (1983-88); Sonda Andersson, bass, vocals (1988-89); James Lo, drums (1983-87); Rich Hutchins, drums (1987-89)

Arising from the noise-rock center of the world, Manhattan's Lower East Side, Live Skull was generally overlooked outside New York despite having made two albums the equal of Sonic Youth's best. Although the focus was on guitar sounds, monolithic bass lines and Lo's tightly wound drumming, the occasional mediocrity of the various members' vocals could be distracting, so Zedek (Uzi, Dangerous Birds) was brought in and raised the band to new heights with her aggressively droning style. Greenholz and Lo left shortly after her arrival and were replaced by Andersson (ex-Rat at Rat R) and Hutchins. When lack of success eventually dissolved the band, Zedek went on to found Come. After playing in Wider, Lo turned up in Chavez.

what to buy: Zedek's peak comes on *Positraction,* (Caroline, 1989, prod. Not Listed) which includes the *Snuffer* EP (Caroline, 1988, prod. Not Listed). The guitars are sharper and less dense than on the earlier records, and the sound bludgeons more effectively.

what to buy next: The best document of the pre-Zedek band, the live *Don't Get Any On You* (Homestead, 1987, prod. Live Skull and Massive Records) is an explosion of angst punctuated by the most chilling version of "Pusherman" ever.

what to avoid: John S. Hall himself would probably tell you *Real Men* (Shimmy Disc, 1991, prod. Kramer) for while Kramer took tapes of Hall reading and, without the poet's further participation, played whatever he wanted behind him.

the rest: *Bringing Home the Bait* (Homestead, 1985) *Cloud One* (Homestead, 1986) *Dusted* (Homestead, 1987) *Chavez's Gone Glimmering* (Matador, 1995)

worth searching for: *Live Skull* EP (Massive, 1984, prod. Live Skull) shows the strength of the group's conception even at the beginning. The *Raise the Manifestation* 12" (Homestead, 1986, prod. Live Skull and Massive Records) has the only studio versions of three songs on *Don't Get Any On You*—the title song plus "Swingtime" and "Pusherman."

▶▶ Band of Susans, Come, Rein Sanction

◀◀ Joy Division, Killing Joke, Sonic Youth, Swans, Psychedelic Furs

Steve Holtje

Kerry Livgren

See: Kansas

Living Colour

Formed 1983 in Brooklyn, N.Y. Disbanded 1995.

Corey Glover, vocals; Vernon Reid, guitar; Muzz Skillings (born Manuel Skillings), bass (1983-92); William Calhoun, drums; Doug Wimbish, bass (1992-95)

Convened by Reid after stints in Ronald Shannon Jackson's Decoding Society and Defunkt, Living Colour remained a curiosity of the downtown New York rock scene until Rolling Stones frontman Mick Jagger produced a demo tape of two songs by the group in 1987. Though originally marketed as an all-black metal band, the group's brainy, politicized lyrics and razor-sharp instrumental chops showed it had much more to offer. But the MTV support that made its first album a hit never returned, and subsequent forays into subjects of racial pride and social injustice seemed to fly over the heads of many rock fans. By 1992, Skillings had left the group, replaced by former Sugarhill Gang member Doug Wimbish, and by 1995 tensions between Glover and Reid had blown the band apart for good.

what to buy: The group's sophomore record, *Time's Up* (Epic, 1990, prod. Ed Stasium) 𝄞𝄞𝄞𝄞𝄞 stakes its ground with a muscular mix of songs, from the sorta bluesy, sorta fusion vibe of "Love Rears Its Ugly Head" to the heavy metal funk of "Elvis Is Dead" and the bruising punk of the title track. One listen and it's obvious: no other band in history could have made this record.

what to buy next: Living Colour's last statement as a band, *Stain* (Epic, 1993, prod. Ron Saint Germain, Andre Betts and Living Colour) 𝄞𝄞𝄞𝄞, also turned out to be among its best, as Wimbish's bionic bass sounds prove the final link in pushing the band toward new sonic territory. Balancing almost punky rockers like "Go Away" and "Mind Your Own Business" with the tongue-in-cheek rumination "Bi" and the dreamy "Wall," the album offers a tantalizing look at what might have been.

what to avoid: Released when the band couldn't get an album together in time, the collection of live tracks and unreleased tunes that fills the six-song *Biscuits* (Epic EP, 1991, prod. Ed Stasium and Living Colour) WOOF! probably did more harm than good—exposing the public to uninspired playing and half-done compositions far below the standard set by the previous album. Sometimes, there's a reason why tracks are unreleased.

the rest: *Vivid* (Epic, 1988) 𝄞𝄞𝄞𝄞 *Pride (Greatest Hits)* (Epic, 1995) 𝄞𝄞𝄞

worth searching for: The fiery Japanese live album *Dread* (Epic, 1995) 𝄞𝄞𝄞𝄞 provides proof of Living Colour's onstage acumen.

solo outings:

Vernon Reid: Mistaken Identity (Sony 550, 1996) 𝄞𝄞𝄞

▶▶ The Fugees, Me'Shell NdegeOcello, I Mother Earth

◀◀ Jimi Hendrix, Parliament/Funkadelic, Bad Brains, Fishbone

Eric Deggans

L.L. Cool J

Born James Todd Smith, Aug. 16, 1968 in Queens, N.Y.

Hip-deep in the rap scene after a relative bought him DJ gear at the age of 9, L.L. Cool J came to the attention of then-New York University student Rick Rubin via a self-made demo sent to his dormitory. By age 13, the rapper was featured on the first release of Def Jam records—the legendary rap label Rubin co-funded with Public Enemy manager Russell Simmons and ran out of his NYU dorm. At age 16, L.L. had his first hit, a frenetic ode to his Samsonite-sized boom box called "I Can't Live Without My Radio" (also featured in the film "Krush Groove"). It's the perfect example of his rap style—upfront drum machine beats, spiced with synthesizer horn blast and scratches, with L.L.'s aggressive, adept lyrical style pushing the beat in your face. Over the next few albums, he would push his ladykilller image—his stage name, after all, stands for Ladies Love Cool James—appearing as a pinup boy for young girls and a threatening superior to other guys. After five years at the top, L.L. began to lose touch with his audience, releasing laid-back, almost experimental singles and looking ready for a hard fall. So it was a huge surprise when he bounced back with a record crafted by old school producer Marley Marl—coming back so hard, he featured one tune with insults directed at Ice-T, Kool Moe Dee and M.C. Hammer. But even as he landed roles in the films "Toys" and "The Hard Way," performed at President Bill Clinton's inauguration and became the first rapper to perform on MTV's "Unplugged," L.L. was losing his artistic way again—struggling for a way to stay hard in the face of increasingly explicit gangsta rap. Although his 1995 release has sold respectably, it's his role on the NBC sitcom "In the House" that's kept him in the public eye—a last resort for aging rap stars.

what to buy: His 1990 comeback album *Mama Said Knock You Out* (Def Jam/Columbia, 1990, prod. L.L. Cool J and Marley Marl) is the most consistent, impressive L.L. record yet. Filled with producer Marl's thumping tracks, cuts such as the hit "Boomin' System" provide a perfect soundtrack for hip hop cruising, while the funky, in-your-face groove "To Da Break a Dawn" takes on West Coast rivals with lines such as "that right/a little kick for that crap/'cause your old gym teacher ain't supposed to rap."

what to buy next: A breath of fresh air on the newly emerging rap scene, L.L.'s debut disc, *Radio* (Def Jam, 1985, prod. Rick Rubin), sets new standards in recorded hip-hop, offering tunes with recognizable verses and choruses, as well as pointed insults and muscular street jams.

what to avoid: Despite featuring one of his best singles ever—the testosterone-fueled workout "I'm Bad"—*Bigger and Deffer* (Def Jam, 1987, prod. Various) WOOF! fails to live up to its name. One reason is the sugary sweet ballad "I Need Love"; another is the uneven collection of songs that miss more often than they hit.

the rest: *Walking With a Panther* (Def Jam, 1989) *14 Shots to the Dome* (Columbia, 1993) *Mr. Smith* (Def Jam/RAL/Island, 1995)

worth searching for: The video of "Krush Groove," to see the triumphant moment when a full-of-himself L.L. walks into an office, plops his suitcase-sized jambox on the desk and belts out "I Can't Live Without My Radio."

Big Daddy Kane, the Notorious B.I.G.

Run D.M.C., Whodini, Kurtis Blow

Eric Deggans

John Lodge

See: Moody Blues

Nils Lofgren /Grin

Born June 21, 1951 in Chicago, Ill.

Always the star sideman, never the star—that pretty much sums up the career of guitar wunderkind Lofgren, who at age 17 played on Neil Young's *After the Goldrush* album and was once rumored to be a replacement candidate for Mick Taylor in the Rolling Stones. Lofgren was a member of Crazy Horse for one album and later toured with Young after playing on the album *Tonight's the Night.* As for his own work, Lofgren formed the band Grin in 1969 with Washington D.C. mates Bob Gordon (bass) and Bob Berberich (drums), later adding brother Tom Lofgren on guitar. Unfortunately, Grin never achieved the widespread recognition or critical kudos befitting its taut, melodic rock and tender ballads, and the group's legacy is tough to track these days; only *1+1* (Spindizzy, 1972, prod. David Briggs) remains in print, and luckily it's the group's best album. After Grin split up in 1974, Lofgren went on to pursue solo career marked by stellar guitar work but albums rendered wildly uneven by his weak vocals and frequently poor songwriting. His highest visibility was as a member of Bruce Springsteen's E Street band from 1984-91. Still, his last few albums are surprisingly strong, suggesting there may be hope yet for this sometimes underrated/sometimes underachieving artist.

what to buy: Lofgren's auspicious solo debut, *Nils Lofgren,* (A&M, 1975, prod. Nils Lofgren and David Briggs) is his best, featuring "Keith Don't Go," his plea to self-destructive Rolling Stones guitarist Keith Richards, as well as "Back It Up," "Rock and Roll Crook" and a version of Carole King's "Goin' Back." The 15-track *Classics Volume 13* (A&M, 1989, prod. Various) offers a generous look back at his A&M years and effectively culls the best material from those five albums.

what to buy next: After several spotty albums, *Nils* (A&M, 1979, prod. Bob Ezrin) put Lofgren back on his feet thanks to a productive writing session with Lou Reed that yielded the boxing epic "No Mercy" and the beautiful "Shine Silently." *Silver Lining* (Rykodisc, 1991, prod. Kevin McCormick and Nils Lofgren) offers Lofgren's best batch of songs in years—including the heartfelt ballad "Valentine"—and some all-star help from Springsteen, Clarence Clemons, Billy Preston and Levon Helm.

what to avoid: When Lofgren's songwriting lets him down, it's not enough for him to try and let his guitar do the talking. Those tendencies reveal themselves on several albums, most notably on *I Came to Dance* (A&M, 1977, prod. Nils Lofgren and Andy Newmark)

the rest: *Cry Tough* (A&M, 1975) *Night After Night* (A&M, 1977) *Night Fades Away* (Backstreet, 1981) *Wonderland* (Backstreet, 1983) *The Best of Nils Lofgren* (A&M,

1985) *Flip* (Columbia, 1985) *Crooked Line* (Rykodisc, 1992) *Damaged Goods* (Pure, 1995)

worth searching for: *Back It Up!!* (A&M, 1976), a promotional release of a radio concert that capitalized on Lofgren's incendiary skills as a performer—perhaps to the detriment of the studio album that was current at the time.

▶▶ Bruce Springsteen, Paul Westerberg, Eric Johnson, Stevie Ray Vaughan

◀◀ Neil Young, the Rolling Stones, Chuck Berry

Daniel Durchholz

Kenny Loggins

See: Loggins and Messina

Loggins and Messina /Kenny Loggins

Formed 1972 in Los Angeles, Calif. Disbanded 1976.

Kenny Loggins (born Jan. 7, 1948, in Everett, Wash.), guitar, vocals; Jim Messina (born Dec. 5, 1947, in Maywood, Calif.), guitar, bass, vocals

Loggins, whose claim to fame at the time was the Nitty Gritty Dirt Band's recording of his "House at Pooh Corner," was fortunate to have Messina produce his first solo album. The result, *Sittin' In,* was the first of what was to become a highly successful partnership. Messina's credentials include playing bass, assembling the material and producing Buffalo Springfield's final record, *Last Time Around* he was a founding member of Poco and remained for the group's first three superb albums. A fine technician with a great ear, Messina probably curtailed Loggins' penchant for overly sensitive mush. Together they spun out a long string of hits, including "Danny's Song," their own treatment of "House at Pooh Corner" and "Your Mama Don't Dance." On his own—following the duo's 1976 split-up—Loggins parlayed his personable image and talent into a successful, if creatively middling, solo career marked by excessively romantic songs, ultra-slick production but also numerous hits, particularly soundtrack smashes such as "Footloose," "Nobody's Fool" and "Danger Zone."

what to buy: Loggins and Messina's debut, *Sittin' In,* (Columbia, 1972, prod. Jim Messina) is their best, most fully realized recording. Practically every song is a charmer, from the tight rockin' country guitar accents on the opening track, "Nobody But You," to Loggins' sweet ballad, "Danny's Song." *On Stage* (Columbia, 1974) features an excellent backing band and a definitive, extended version of "Angry Eyes."

what to buy next: *Loggins & Messina,* (Columbia, 1972, prod. N/A) the duo's sophomore effort, has the tiresome single "Your Mama Don't Dance" but also the studio version of "Angry Eyes." Loggins' solo album *Nightwatch* (Columbia, 1978, prod. Bob James) includes the hit "Whenever I Call You Friend" (a duet with Stevie Nicks when she could still sing).

what to avoid: The duo's *Native Sons* (Columbia, 1976) WOOF! and *So Fine* (Columbia, 1975) suffer from severe lapses in songwriting originality. Loggins' *Vox Humana* (Columbia, 1985) WOOF! is so overblown and it leaves one speechless.

the rest: Loggins and Messina: *Full Sail* (Columbia, 1973) *Mother Lode* (Columbia, 1974) *Best of Friends* (Columbia, 1976) Kenny Loggins: *Keep the Fire* (Columbia, 1979) *Kenny Loggins Alive* (Columbia, 1980) *High Adventure* (Columbia, 1982) *Back to Avalon* (Columbia, 1988) *Leap of Faith* (Columbia, 1991) *Outside: From the Redwoods* (Columbia, 1993)

worth searching for: The Loggins and Messina *Star Box,* (CBS/Sony, 1989) a Japanese collection whose 20-songs offer a better overview than the domestic *Best of Friends*

▶▶ Captain and Tennille, Buckingham Nicks, Fleetwood Mac

◀◀ Simon and Garfunkel, Poco, Bread

see also: *Poco, Buffalo Springfield*

Patrick McCarty

John Lombardo

See: 10,000 Maniacs

Lone Justice /Maria McKee

Formed 1983 in Los Angeles, Calif. Disbanded 1987.

Maria Mckee (born Aug. 17, 1964 in Los Angeles), vocals, guitar; Ryan Hedgecock, guitar, vocals (1983-86); Marvin Etzioni, bass, vocals (1983-86); Don Heffington, drums (1983-86); Shayne Fontayne, guitar (1986-87); Gregg Sutton, bass (1986-87); Rudy Richman, drums (1986-87); Bruce Brody, keyboards (1986-87)

Before it was a rock 'n' roll movement, Lone Justice played rock with a countryfied twang, taking a spirited, rootsy approach that in 1985 was fresh, not trendy. With her powerful voice and eye-catching presence, it wasn't long before McKee became the group's focus—and, in fact, the group, as an entirely different group of musicians came on board for Lone Justice's second and final album. The group split up following a tour in which it opened for U2, and McKee (working with Lone Justice keyboardist Brody) took a solo path that's been nothing if not fascinating, as she's changed styles from the ethereal *Maria McKee* to the Lone Justice soundalike *You Gotta Sin to Get Saved* to the more eclectic *Life is Sweet.* Etzioni, meanwhile, has recorded some albums of his own and produced titles for Peter Case and Toad the Wet Sprocket.

what to buy: *Lone Justice* (Geffen, 1985, prod. Jimmy Iovine) ♪♪♪♪ is an exceptional debut, the arrival of a fresh new sound via exuberant performances and a tremendous batch of songs such as "East of Eden," "Sweet, Sweet Baby (I'm Falling)" and Tom Petty's "Ways to Be Wicked."

what to buy next: Lone Justice's *BBC Radio 1 Live in Concert* (Windsong, 1993) ♪♪♪½ gives a sense of Lone Justice—and particularly McKee's—strength on a concert stage. Her second solo album, *You Gotta Sin to Get Saved,* (Geffen, 1993, prod. George Drakoulias) ♪♪♪♪ is nearly as good as *Lone Justice* and features the original band's rhythm section as well as members of the Jayhawks.

what to avoid: McKee's *Life is Sweet* (Geffen, 1996, prod. Maria McKee, Bruce Brody and Mark Freegard) ♪♪ is all over the place to the point where even the force of her singing can't bring the album back into focus.

the rest: Lone Justice—*Shelter* (Geffen, 1986) ♪♪½ Maria McKee—*Maria McKee* (Geffen, 1989) ♪♪♪

solo outings:

Marvin Etzioni: The Mandolin Man (Restless, 1992) ♪♪♪

worth searching for: McKee's guest appearance for a duet on "Temple and Shine" with Etzioni on his album *Weapons of the Spirit* (Restless, 1994) ♪♪♪½

⏩ Sheryl Crow, Uncle Tupelo, the Jayhawks, Cowboy Junkies

⏪ Tom Petty and the Heartbreakers, the Byrds, the Flying Burrito Brothers, Janis Joplin, Aretha Franklin

Gary Graff

Roy Loney and the Phantom Movers

See: The Flamin' Groovies

Long Ryders

Formed 1982 in Los Angeles, Calif. Disbanded 1987.

Sid Griffin, guitar, vocals; Stephen McCarthy, guitar, vocals; Barry Shank, bass, vocals (1982); Des Brewer, bass, vocals (1983); Tom Stevens, bass, vocals (1984-87); Greg Sowders, drums

A country-influenced band coming out of the Paisley Underground scene of early 80s Southern California, the Long Ryders followed a tradition set by the late-period Byrds, the Flying Burrito Brothers and Gram Parsons. About a decade too early, the band achieved acclaim in Europe with its fresh, countryish sound, but could only attain a cult following in the U.S. outside of Los Angeles. The group broke up in 1987 but is cited as an influence on the new wave of country-styled rockers (the Jayhawks, Uncle Tupelo) that emerged during the late 80s. Only two of its albums remain in print: the rough-sounding *Native Sons* (Frontier, 1984/1993) ♪♪♪½, which is equal parts psychedelic and Bakersfield country; and the harder rocking *Two-Fisted Tales* (Island, 1987, prod. Ed Stasium) ♪♪♪♪, which features guest appearances by Los Lobos' David Hidalgo and the Peterson sisters from the Bangles. Every effort should be made to find *State Of Our Union,* (Island, 1985) ♪♪♪♪, a harbinger for what we now call Young Country.

Matt Merta

Lords of Acid

Formed 1988 in Belgium

Lady Galore (born Ruth McArdle), vocals; Nathalie Dalaet, vocals (1988-93); Lord T. Byron (born Frank Vloeberghs), bass; Sai De La Luna, keyboards, vocals; McGuinnes (born Kurt Liekens), drums; Erhan, guitar (1992-present)

Led first by Dalaet, the Lords emerged from the hot Belgian techno scene of the late 80s with the hit "I Sit on Acid," and its tawdry mix of drug subculture and unabashed sexuality established the Lords as club favorites. The first album, *Lust,* (Caroline Records, 1991, prod. Various) ♪♪♪½ expands on the singles with lusch female vocals adding a human sensuality to the electronic samples and sound machines. With *Voodoo-U,* (American Recordings, 1994, prod. Various) ♪♪½ the band makes a few changes, not only swapping lead singers and labels, but trading in the slower, mesmerizing club mix for harsh, pounding, guitar-sampled, industrial/rave music. Lady Galore screams throughout the album, ordering submission to the new sound. Songs such as "Do What You Wanna Do" emphasize the new guitar driven noise and are almost metal-esque, but the beats are still there—only they're a bit faster and denser.

Bryan Lassner

Lords of the New Church

See: Dead Boys

Los Bravos

Formed 1965 in Spain. Disbanded early 1970s.

Michael Kogel, vocals; Antonio Martinez, guitar; Miguel Luis Vicens Danus, bass; Manuel Fernandez, organ; Juan-Pablo Sanllehi, drums

During 1966, with the British invasion in retreat, one of the biggest hits in the U.S. ("Black is Back") came from Los Bravos, a rock group from the unlikely locale of Spain. In fact, it sounded more like an American group, with its brassy pop-rock arrangements and Kogel's emphatic vocals, which were tinged with an expressive tenor reminiscent of Gene Pitney's expressive tenor. "Black is Black" was a Top 5 hit here, but little else happened until the group made a minor impact with "Bring a Little Lovin'," a song written for it by Easybeats members George Young and Harry Vanda. There's nothing to be found on these shores, but the European collection, *All the Best* (prod. Various) serves up a generous 30 tracks, most of them sung in English.

Christopher Scapelliti

Los Lobos

Formed 1974 in Los Angeles, Calif.

David Hidalgo, guitar, vocals; Conrad Lozano, bass, vocals; Cesar Rosas, guitar, vocals; Louis Perez, drums, guitar, vocals; Steve Berlin, saxophone, keyboards (1984-present)

One could argue that "La Bamba" was the best thing to ever happen to Los Lobos. Not because their spunky 1987 cover of the Ritchie Valens hit gave this Los Angeles act its 15 minutes of Top 40 fame, but because fear of being labeled a Chicano version of Sha-Na-Na challenged them to put their own weird, wobbly spin on the festive fusing of blues, R&B, rockabilly and Mexican folk music that originally established them as roots-rock torchbearers. Such twangy T-Bone Burnett-produced efforts as *By the Light of the Moon* and *How Will the Wolf Survive?* introduced a tight garage band that would be happy if it never left the barrios or the bars. But in 1990, prodded by producers Larry Hirsch and Mitchell Froom, Los Lobos transformed into one of rock's most experimental acts. Fuzz, feedback, distortion and dense percussion blended with lead singer Hidalgo's soulful tenor and Froom's quirky production techniques to create the intoxicating cross-section of rhythms and textures behind "The Neighborhood" and 1992's jaw-dropping "Kiko." The band that once amazed listeners by deftly handing a variety of genres now blurs the lines so much that it's hard to figure out where it's going next. And that's something that can't be said about most roots-rock bands.

what to buy: Of its early efforts, *How Will the Wolf Survive?* (Slash/Warner Bros., 1984, prod. T-Bone Burnett and Steve Berlin) holds up the best. It's a roots-rock primer ranging from savage blues ("Don't Worry Baby") to engaging country-rock ("A Matter of Time," "Will the Wolf Survive?") and traditional Tex-Mex ("Serenata Nortena"). The band begins flexing its experimental muscles on *The Neighborhood,* (Slash/Warner Bros., 1990, prod. Larry Hirsch, Mitchell Froom and Los Lobos) a rich, riveting effort driven by guest drummer Jim Keltner and a mesmerizing mix of the band's raunchiest ("Jenny's Got a Pony," "Georgia Slop") and prettiest ("Little John of God," "Be Still") performances. All rules go out the window on *Kiko,* (Slash/Warner Bros., 1992, prod. Mitchell Froom and Los Lobos) an ambitious, atmospheric patchwork of the Beatles, Tom Waits, New Orleans jazz, country and blues that never lapses into avant garde pretension. More important, Hidalgo and Louie Perez's songs—which tackle death (the lovely "Saint Behind the Glass"), homelessness ("Angels With Dirty Faces"), child abuse ("Two Janes") and domestic violence ("Reva's House")—are their hardest hitting to date.

what to buy next: *La Pistola y El Corazon* (Slash/Warner Bros., 1988, prod. Los Lobos) is a delightful Spanish-language romp through traditional Mexican music played on accordions, nylon-string guitars, upright bass, bajo sextos and other folkloric instruments.

what to avoid: Once you break all the rules on *Kiko*, what do you do for an encore? The bluesy, noisy *Colossal Head* (Slash/Warner Bros., 1996, prod. Mitchell Froom, Tchad Blake and Los Lobos) buckles under the pressure of topping its predecessor, sounding more contrived than created.

the rest: *...And a Time to Dance* (Slash/Warner Bros., 1983) *By the Light of the Moon* (Slash/Warner Bros., 1987) *Just Another Band from East L.A.: A Collection* (Slash/Warner Bros., 1993)

worth searching for: The soundtrack to Paul Bartel's black comedy *Eating Raoul* (Varese, 1982, prod. Scot Holton and Tom Null) features the then-unknown band rampaging through "Diablo Con Vestido" (a Spanish version of "Devil With a Blue Dress").

solo outings:

Latin Playboys (Hidalgo, Perez, Mitchell Froom and Tchad Blake): *Latin Playboys* (Slash/Warner Bros., 1994, prod. Latin Playboys)

The Blazers

Ritchie Valens, Sir Douglas Quintet

David Okamoto

Loud Family

See: Game Theory

The Lounge Lizards

Formed 1979 in New York, N.Y.

John Lurie, saxophones, vocals; Evan Lurie, keyboards (1979-90); Arto Lindsay, guitar (1979-80); Dana Vicek, guitar (1980); Danny Rosen, guitar (1981); Steve Piccolo, bass (1979-81); Anton Fier, drums (1979-81); Peter Zummo, trombone (1983); Tony Garnier, bass (1983); Dougie Bowne, drums (1983-90); Roy Nathanson, saxophones (1984-90); Curtis Fowlkes, trombone (1984-90); Marc Ribot, guitar, trumpet, banjo (1984-90); Eric Sanko, drums (1984-90, 1993-present); E.J. Rodriguez, percussion (1987-90); Michael Blake, soprano and tenor saxophones (1991-present); Steven Bernstein, trumpet, cornet (1991-present); Bryan Carrott, vibraphone, marimba, timpani, (1991-92); Michele Navazio, guitar (1991-present); Dave Tronzo, slide guitar (1993-present); Danny Blume, guitar (1993-present); John Medeski, organ (1993); Oren Bloedow, bass (1991-92); Grant Calvin Weston, drums (1991-present); Billy Martin, percussion (1991-93); Jane Scarpantoni, cello (1991-present)

Once upon a time, John Lurie's self-bestowed description "fake jazz" made ironic sense, but his band long ago graduated to a warped version of the real thing, though it goes beyond jazz boundaries. The key to the band has always been not Lurie, but who's playing with him—which has taken the Lounge Lizards into the realms of rock, world musics and soul (the latter heard most clearly on the tracks credited to Lurie and arranged by Bernstein on the "Get Shorty" movie soundtrack). Lurie had earlier hooked up with director Jim Jarmusch, who not only had him score three films, but also act in "Stranger Than Paradise" and "Down By Law," where his detached presence and iconic good looks work to good noir effect. Evan Lurie, meanwhile, has a strong interest in tango; his angular, off-kilter piano style, filled with pregnant dissonances, constitutes a great deal of the Lounge Lizards' unique sound.

what to buy: *The Lounge Lizards* (EG, 1981, prod. Teo Macero) is a brilliant refraction of familiar jazz elements recontextualized. Lindsay's skronk guitar effusions and the covers of two Thelonious Monk tunes and "Harlem Nocturne" stand out.

what to buy next: *Live in Berlin 1991 Vol. 1+2,* (Intuition, 1993, prod. John Lurie) with the Bernstein-directed lineup, covers all the post-modern bases, and things get stirringly hot or cool according to the circumstance. The feeling is looser and more organic than in the earlier versions of the band, as well as more democratic.

what to avoid: Some of the compositions on *Live from the Drunken Boat* (Europa, 1983, prod. Teo Macero and John Lurie) are good, but this studio recording finds Lurie between great band lineups and not yet a strong enough player to carry the album himself.

the rest: *Live 79/81* (ROIR, 1985) *Live in Tokyo—Big Heart* (Island, 1986) *No Pain for Cakes* (Island, 1987) *Voice of CHUNK* (Lagarto, 1989) *Live in Berlin 1991 Vol. 2* (Intuition, 1995)

solo outings:

Evan Lurie: Selling Water by the Side of the River (Island, 1990) John Lurie: *Mystery Train* (RCA, 1989) *Stranger Than Paradise Soundtrack* (Enigma, 1986) *Down By Law/Variety* (Intuition/Capitol, 1987) *Get Shorty Soundtrack* (Island, 1995)

Ambitious Lovers, Jazz Passengers, Medeski Martin & Wood, Squirrel Nut Zippers, Golden Palominos, Spanish Fly

Thelonious Monk, Charles Mingus, Dollar Brand, Peter Apfelbaum's Heiroglyphics Ensemble

see also: *Ambitious Lovers*

Steve Holtje

Love and Rockets

Formed 1985 in Northampton, England

Daniel Ash, guitar and vocals; David J (born David Haskins), bass, vocals; Kevin Haskins, drums

Named after the Hernandez underground comic, this band reunites three of the four Bauhaus musicians. Ash and Haskins had spent some of the interim with Tones on Tail, while bassist J recorded two albums with the Jazz Butcher in-between solo projects. After Ash became dissatisfied with Campling and former Bauhaus frontman Peter Murphy backed out of a reunion, the three decided to form Love and Rockets. With Murphy out of the picture, the trio went on to perform varied styles from folk-rock to upbeat dance pop ("So Alive" in 1989 was the group's lone smash) to low, booming drum-based songs to ambient trance music that was a far cry their beginnings—a diversity that has made Love and Rockets always interesting and occasionally frustrating.

what to buy: *Seventh Dream of Teenage Heaven* (Beggars Banquet, 1985/1988, prod. John A. Rivers) is an odd, varied album, ranging from the booming drums in "Haunted When the Minutes Drag" to the light harmonies of "If There's a Heaven Above." *Earth Sun Moon* (Beggars Banquet/RCA, 1987, prod. Love and Rockets) is a collection of acoustic-driven songs with sweet melodies and introspective lyrics. On the solo front, two of J's albums—*Crocodile Tears and the Velvet Cosh* (Glass, 1985, prod. David J) and *On Glass* (Glass, 1986, prod. David J) show a knack for poetic and light melodies and hold up well next to the group's releases.

what to buy next: *Express* (Beggars Banquet/RCA, 1986, prod. John A. Rivers and Love and Rockets) is Love and Rockets' most upbeat album, including a cover of the Temptations' hit "Ball of Confusion." *Sweet F.A.* (American, 1996, prod. Love and Rockets) is a return to the group's beginnings, with its brooding guitars and quiet vocals.

what to avoid: *Love and Rockets.* (Beggars Banquet/RCA, 1989. prod. John Fryer and Love and Rockets) Although it yielded a Top 5 hit with "So Alive," the rest of the songs were redundant and excessive.

the rest: *Hot Trip to Heaven* (American, 1994)

worth searching for: *The Glittering Darkness* (Beggars Banquet, 1996, prod. Love and Rockets with John Fryer), an import that collects some previously unreleased tracks.

solo outings:

Daniel Ash: *Coming Down* (Beggars Banquet, 1991) *Foolish Thing Desire* (Beggars Banquet, 1992)

David J: *Etiquette of Violence* (Situation Two, 1983) *V for Vendetta* (Glass EP, 1984) *Blue Moods Turning Tail* (Glass EP, 1985) *Songs from Another Season* (Beggars Banquet/RCA, 1990) *Fingers in the Grease* (RCA, 1990) *Candy on the Cross* (MCA, 1992) *Urban Urbane* (MCA, 1992)

Ministry, Sisters of Mercy, Christian Death

Bauhaus, Tones on Tail, the Jazz Butcher, New Order, the Smiths

see also: *Bauhaus, Tones on Tail, the Jazz Butcher*

JD Cantarella

Love Spit Love (Richard Butler)

See: Psychedelic Furs

Loverboy

Formed 1979 in Calgary, Alberta, Canada. Disbanded 1988. Re-formed 1993.

Mike Reno, vocals; Paul Dean, guitar; Doug Johnson, keyboards; Matt Frenette, drums; Scott Smith, bass

Marketed at the beginning as something of a hard rock glam band, Loverboy is really a slick, mainstream lite rock group, playing anonymous arena rock that's interchangeable with any number of other early 80s outfits. Its rounded-edges approach and constant touring garnered platinum success and, presumably, enough bucks for a lifetime supply of Moosehead. Relying on party themes and driving, FM-ready singles, Loverboy enjoyed a string of hits without having to change the formula—or Reno's headband. And people wonder why punk was necessary.

what to buy: *Loverboy Classics* (Columbia, 1994, prod. Various) culls most of the more memorable hits into a fairly cohesive picture of the band's output.

what to buy next: The guitar-driven debut *Loverboy* (Columbia, 1980, prod. Bruce Fairbairn) contains the radio whopper "The Kid Is Hot Tonight," as well as the churning "Turn Me Loose." The title of *Get Lucky* (Columbia, 1981, prod. Bruce Fairbairn) 𝅘𝅥𝅮𝅘𝅥𝅮½ accurately reflects Loverboy's fortunes; this release contains the overlooked "Take Me to the Top" and the less engaging—but more successful—"Waiting for the Weekend."

what to avoid: *Wildside* (Columbia, 1987, prod. Bruce Fairbairn) WOOF! shows what happens when Reno and Dean can't come up with the hooks that camouflaged the other albums' shortcomings.

the rest: *Keep It Up* (Columbia, 1983) 𝅘𝅥𝅮𝅘𝅥𝅮 *Lovin' Every Minute of It* (Columbia, 1985) 𝅘𝅥𝅮𝅘𝅥𝅮

solo outings:

Paul Dean: Hardcore (Columbia, 1989) 𝅘𝅥𝅮𝅘𝅥𝅮

▶▶ Warrant, Poison, Skid Row

◀◀ Boston, Foreigner, Styx

Allan Orski

Lyle Lovett

Born Nov. 1, 1957 in Houston, Texas

Originally a Houston folkie, Lovett went to Nashville during the mid-80s, when alternative-leaning country acts such as Steve Earle, k.d. lang and Lovett himself could get a fair hearing. And while he did have some country hits and won a country Grammy, Nashville never could figure out what exactly was so intriguing or funny about a guy who wore an "Eraserhead" hairdo instead of a Stetson and sang Tammy Wynette's "Stand By Your Man" with a straight face. It's their loss; Lovett's albums have surveyed jazz, Texas swing, folk and country. Stylistically, he is, to use his own words, "What Hank Williams is to Neil Armstrong." But Lovett's lyrical bent—witty, ironic and sometimes unsettlingly direct—is what is most memorable about his music.

what to buy: *Pontiac* (MCA/Curb, 1987, prod. Tony Brown and Lyle Lovett) 𝅘𝅥𝅮𝅘𝅥𝅮𝅘𝅥𝅮𝅘𝅥𝅮½ Few could turn the subject matter of a wedding that ends in double murder or a surreal seagoing horseback rider to their advantage, but that's what Lovett accomplishes on "L.A. County" and "If I Had a Boat," respectively. "She's No Lady" and "She's Hot to Go" earned him charges of misogyny, but the songs are as self-deprecating as they are chauvinistic. *Lyle Lovett* (MCA/Curb, 1986, prod. Tony Brown and Lyle Lovett) 𝅘𝅥𝅮𝅘𝅥𝅮𝅘𝅥𝅮𝅘𝅥𝅮 is a spectacular debut, featuring the utterly unsentimental "God Will" and Lovett's wry reportage of nuptials held at a funeral parlor "An Acceptable Level of Ecstasy (The Wedding Song)." On *Joshua Judges Ruth* (MCA/Curb, 1992, prod. George Massenburg, Billy Williams and Lyle Lovett) 𝅘𝅥𝅮𝅘𝅥𝅮𝅘𝅥𝅮𝅘𝅥𝅮, the melancholy streak that has run through Lovett's music from the beginning nearly takes over on songs like "North Dakota" and "She's Already Made Up Her Mind," but injections of fiery gospel ("Church") and Lovett's arid wit ("Since the Last Time," which is narrated by a corpse) make the album one of his deepest and most diverse.

what to buy next: *The Road to Ensenada* (MCA/Curb, 1996, prod. Lyle Lovett and Billy Williams) 𝅘𝅥𝅮𝅘𝅥𝅮𝅘𝅥𝅮𝅘𝅥𝅮 is Lovett's most country-flavored album in a while, and while it contains plenty of upbeat humor ("That's Right (You're Not from Texas)"), it's also his most somber album, perhaps reflecting obliquely on his split with wife Julia Roberts. *Lyle Lovett and His Large Band* (MCA/Curb, 1989, prod. Tony Brown, Billy Williams and Lyle Lovett) 𝅘𝅥𝅮𝅘𝅥𝅮𝅘𝅥𝅮½ spotlights his quirkiness with a string of non-sequiturs ("Here I Am") and plays the country numbers strictly for yuks ("I Married Her Just Because She Looks Like You," "Stand By Your Man").

what to avoid: Lovett's weakest album, *I Love Everybody* (MCA/Curb, 1994, prod. Lyle Lovett and Billy Williams) 𝅘𝅥𝅮𝅘𝅥𝅮𝅘𝅥𝅮, is the musical proof of your high school football coach's imprecation that "women weaken legs." Lovett's only recording made during his brief tenure as Mr. Julia Roberts has its moments of wry humor, but it consists mostly of stale leftovers and trifles like "La to the Left" and "Penguins," which are more strange than funny.

worth searching for: The Oscar-nominated hit "You've Got a Friend in Me" 𝅘𝅥𝅮𝅘𝅥𝅮𝅘𝅥𝅮½ from the *Toy Story* soundtrack (Disney, 1995) is a boisterous duet with Randy Newman.

▶▶ Hayden, Beck

◀◀ Townes Van Zandt, Guy Clark, Ray Charles, Randy Newman

Daniel Durchholz

Lovin' Spoonful /John Sebastian

Formed 1965 in New York, N.Y. Disbanded 1968. Re-formed 1991

John Sebastian, autoharp, harmonica vocals (1965-68); Steve Boone, bass, vocals; Zal Yanovsky, guitar, vocals (1965-67); Joe Butler, drums, vocals; Jerry Yester, guitar (1967-68, 1991-present); John Marrella, drums (1991-present); Lena Yester, keyboards, guitar (1991-present)

Dressed in colorful comic-book duds, singing good-timey folk and love songs and plugged-in country blues in Greenwich Village coffee houses, the Lovin' Spoonful—named after a Mississippi John Hurt lyric—were the darlings of Greenwich Village and the country between 1965-67. (The band's early days at the Night Owl Cafe are recounted in the Mamas and the Papas' "Creeque Alley.") The Spoonful's loosey-goosey, youthful innocence and engaging folk-rock caught on like a giant happy-day smile; its first seven singles went Top 10, including "Do You Believe in Magic?" which used as its lead instrument Sebastian's electrified Appalachian autoharp, and "Summer in the City," which helped define the summer of 1966 as it rose to No. 1. The hits ended as quickly as they had begun, and Yanovsky left the group in 1967, replaced by Yester. Sebastian, who sang and wrote most of the songs, left soon afterward. With Butler as vocalist, the group managed another record, but the original spirit of the group had already dissipated.

what to buy: The Spoonful was a singles group, which means *Anthology* (Rhino, 1990, prod. Erik Jacobsen) —which includes all the hits in chronological order and enough album sides to keep everyone but the most fanatical happy—is a must-have.

what to buy next: *Hums of the Lovin' Spoonful* (Kama Sutra, 1967, prod. Erik Jacobsen) , *Do You Believe In Magic* (Kama Sutra, 1966, prod. Erik Jacobsen) and *Daydream* (Kama Sutra, 1966, prod. Erik Jacobsen) contain all the big hits. So do *Best of the Lovin' Spoonful* (Kama Sutra, 1967, prod. Erik Jacobsen) and *Best of the Lovin' Spoonful Volume 2.* (Kama Sutra, 1968, prod. Erik Jacobsen)

Sebastian, meanwhile, released some highly worthwhile solo albums. *John B. Sebastian* (Reprise/MGM, 1970, prod. Paul Rothchild) is a logical extension of Spoonful ideas along with hit, "She's a Lady." *Tarzana Kid* (Reprise, 1974, prod. Erik Jacobsen and John Sebastian) is his best solo effort, with Lowell George helping on guitar. And *I Want My Roots,* (Musicmasters, 1996, prod. Jimmy Vivino and John Sebastian) recorded with the J-Band, is a real jug-band album that reaches back to early Spoonful influences with blues legend James "Yank" Rachell as special guest.

what to avoid: *Revelation: Revolution '69,* (Kama Sutra, 1968, prod. Bob Finiz) beyond John Stewart's "Never Goin' Back," there's nothing to recommend on this leftover.

the rest: *What's Up Tiger Lily* (Kama Sutra, 1966) *You're a Big Boy Now* (Kama Sutra, 1967) *Everything Is Playing* (Kama Sutra, 1967)

worth searching for: Vinyl. Many of the masters for Spoonful recordings have long been destroyed, which makes more reissues unlikely. The only way to actually hear the group as it originally sounded is to find their records on vinyl.

solo outings:

John Sebastian: Four of Us (Reprise, 1971) *Real Live John Sebastian* (Reprise, 1972) *Welcome Back* (Reprise, 1976) *The Best of John Sebastian* (Rhino, 1989)

▶▶ Crosby, Stills and Nash, Poco, Eagles

◀◀ Mississippi John Hurt, Fred Neil, the Weavers, Rev. Gary Davis

Leland Rucker

Nick Lowe

Born March 25, 1949 in Suffolk, England

He produced groundbreaking albums for the Damned, Elvis Costello and Graham Parker, but Lowe has always been more into pranks than angst. His first American single, 1978's "So It Goes," blatantly ripped off its hook from Steely Dan's "Reeling in the Years"; he named a 1977 EP *Bowi* after David Bowie released *Low*; he put out two straightfaced paeans to the Bay City Rollers under the pseudonym Tartan Horde; and he minced no words criticizing banal pop music in his lyrics ("Do you remember Rick Astley?/He had a big fat hit/It was ghastly"). But ever since his pub-rock days in the band Brinsley Schwarz, Lowe has taken his rock 'n' roll roots very seriously, and his albums reveal a startling command of rockabilly, soul, Motown, bubblegum, country and blues. A Top 20 hit with 1979's irresistible "Cruel to Be Kind" and a media blitz following an album and tour with longtime cohorts Dave Edmunds, Terry Williams and Billy Bremner under the banner Rockpile looked to be his only commercial rewards for his efforts. Then it happened: in 1992, a Curtis Stigers cover of Lowe's "(What's So Funny 'Bout) Peace, Love and Understanding" was included on the multiplatinum soundtrack for "The Bodyguard," netting the composer a six-figure royalty check. Sometimes there is justice in the world.

what to buy: More send-up than put-down, *Pure Pop for Now People* (Columbia, 1978, prod. Nick Lowe) mocks everyone from David Bowie ("I Love the Sound of Breaking Glass") to the Jackson 5 ("Nutted by Reality"). It also showcases Lowe's perverse sense of humor by marrying innocuous 60s melodies to "Little Hitler" and "Marie Provost," about an actress whose corpse is devoured by her dog. More important, the Chuck Berry-derived "Heart of the City" and "They Called It Rock" tear

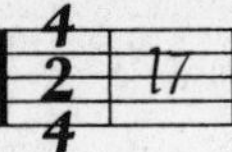

it up with a vengeance. Sex and twang are the driving forces behind the Rockpile-backed *Labour of Lust*, (Columbia, 1979, prod. Nick Lowe) ♪♪♪♪ which features such saucy rockers as "Skin Deep," "American Squirm" and Mickey Jupp's "Switchboard Susan." The 25-track *Basher: The Best of Nick Lowe* (Columbia, 1989, prod. Nick Lowe, Colin Fairley and others) ♪♪♪ gathers the essential early classics and the choice cuts from his uneven later albums, specifically "Ragin' Eyes," "Half a Boy and Half a Man" and "The Rose of England." The introspective *The Impossible Bird* (Upstart, 1994, prod. Nick Lowe and Neil Brockbank) ♪♪♪♪ is an intimate, country-flavored collection that finds Lowe confronting his personal demons and the emotional tug-of-war between love and loss. His own version of "The Beast in Me," the haunting centerpiece of Johnny Cash's *American Recordings*, is a revelation.

what to buy next: With support from Bremner and Williams, Lowe and Edmunds had been backing each other for years on their respective solo albums. So crediting *Seconds of Pleasure* (Columbia, 1980, prod. Rockpile) ♪♪♪♪ to Rockpile was merely a formality. Despite the roadhouse rock 'n' roll swagger of "You Ain't Nothin' but Fine," "Play that Fast Thing One More Time" and Chuck Berry's "Oh What a Thrill," Lowe and Edmunds' quieter Everly Brothers homages—both their own "Now and Always" and the bonus-track of covers of "When Will I Be Loved" and three other Everly hits—reveal more about their roots.

what to avoid: *Pinker and Prouder than Previous* (Columbia, 1988, prod. Nick Lowe, Colin Fairley and Dave Edmunds) ♪♪ is a throwaway compilation drawn from sessions with the Fabulous Thunderbirds, the Men They Couldn't Hang and various incarnations of Lowe's Cowboy Outfit. It screams "contractual obligation."

the rest: *Nick the Knife* (Columbia, 1982) ♪♪♪ *The Abominable Showman* (Columbia, 1983) ♪♪♪ *Nick Lowe and His Cowboy Outfit* (Columbia, 1984) ♪♪ *The Rose of England* (Columbia, 1985) ♪♪ *16 All-Time Lowes* (Demon, 1984) ♪♪♪ *Nick's Knack* (Demon, 1986) ♪♪♪ *Party of One* (Upstart, 1990) ♪♪♪

worth searching for: *The Wilderness Years* (Demon, 1991, prod. Nick Lowe), an import that collects British B-sides and rarities like "I Love My Label," a cover of Sandy Posey's "Born a Woman" (from the infamous *Bowi* EP) and "Truth Drug."

⏩ Francis Dunnery, Don Dixon, Elvis Costello, John Hiatt

⏪ Chuck Berry, the Everly Brothers, Johnny Cash, Carl Perkins

David Okamoto

L7

Formed 1985 in Los Angeles, Calif.

Suzi Gardner, vocals, guitar; Jennifer Finch, vocals, bass (1985-96); Donita Sparks, vocals, guitar; Roy Koutsky, drums (1985-90); Dee Plakas, drums (1990-present)

Direct foremothers—along with Minneapolis peers Babes in Toyland—of the "riot grrrl" movement, L7 plays lunkheaded, Black Sabbath-style heavy metal with frequently exaggerated social critiques but almost no guitar solos. The group's best songs, "Shove" and "Pretend We're Dead," have wonderful headbanging hooks and blood-curdling shrieks that eventually begat Courtney Love. To draw attention to itself, L7 does extreme things on stage—Sparks pulled a tampon out of herself and tossed it into the crowd at 1992's Reading Festival in England, for instance. Nobody can remember a punk rocker ever doing that before. Though the band doesn't come from Seattle, it recorded for that city's influential Sup Pop Records and went along literally with the "grunge" concept, showcasing outfits of rags worthy of Nirvana or the Melvins.

what to buy: *Bricks Are Heavy* (Slash, 1992, prod. Butch Vig and L7) ♪♪♪♪ is either a brilliant punk-metal album that flaunts social convention (the opening track is called "Wargasm") or a sharp satire of Black Sabbath and its legacy of bass-heavy metal bands. Either way, it works. The *Smell the Magic* EP (Sub Pop, 1991, prod. Jack Endino) ♪♪♪ whose title is a euphemism for oral sex, leads off with the pounding kiss-off single "Shove."

what to buy next: *Hungry for Stink* (Slash/Reprise, 1994, prod. L7 and G.G. Garth) ♪♪ lacks the straightforward punch of *Bricks Are Heavy*, but its highlights, including the single "Andres," rescue it from boredom.

what to avoid: The debut, *L7* (Epitaph, 1987, prod. Brett Gurewitz and L7) ♪♪, is a scratchy, angry mess, with no coherent ideas, good melodies or decipherable lyrics.

worth searching for: *The Grunge Years: A Sub Pop Compilation* (Sub Pop, 1991, prod. Various) ♪♪♪♪♪ puts "Shove" in context, along with early singles by Nirvana, Screaming Trees, the Fluid, Afghan Whigs and Babes in Toyland.

⏩ Hole, Alanis Morrissette, Bikini Kill, Bratmobile, Pearl Jam

⏪ Black Sabbath, Iggy Pop, Sex Pistols, Holly and the Italians, X, Babes in Toyland, Nirvana, Motörhead

Steve Knopper

Lulu

Born Marie McDonald McLaughlin Lawrie in 1949 in Lennox Castle, Scotland

The raspy-voiced white lass from the suburbs of Glasgow got her stage name when an early manager, blown away by her 14-year-old pipes, exclaimed "That girl is one lulu of a singer!" And so it was as Lulu that she went on to crack the English charts from 1964 through the early 70s with fine and rowdy R&B singles performed and produced in the spirit of Dusty Springfield and Aretha Franklin. The peak of Lulu's career came in 1967 when she soared to the top of the U.S. charts with the theme from "To Sir with Love," a movie in which she also starred. By decade's end, her music had become passé, although an attempted comeback in 1973 resulted in covers of several David Bowie songs performed with and co-produced by Bowie. *Something to Shout About* (Decca, 1965, prod. Micky Most) is a 20-song compilation of her earliest hits, including her raucous debut recording of the Isley Brother's rave-up "Shout," "I'll Come Running Over" (featuring Jimmy Page on guitar) and "Here Comes the Night," which would become a hit for Van Morrison's Them. For a broader retrospective, pick up *From Crayons to Perfume: The Best of Lulu,* (Rhino, 1994, prod. Various) which includes the hits, some B-sides and the Bowie covers.

Christopher Scapelliti

Luna

Formed 1991 in New York, N.Y.

Dean Wareham, guitar and vocals; Sean Eden, guitar (1993-present); Justin Harwood, bass; Stanley Demeski, drums

Wareham formed Luna after the break-up of his band Galaxie 500, which was a college radio favorite. To complete the band, Wareham enlisted former Feelies drummer Demeski and bassist Harwood of the Chills. Luna plays a form of understated, enigmatic rock that goes beyond lo-fi, complementing Wareham's wry lyrics with a masterful weaving of guitars and the band's fluid ensemble playing. Comparisons to to the Velvet Underground are unending, and Lou Reed invited to the group to open the VU's 1993 European reunion tour and his own 1996 solo tour. *Lunapark,* (Elektra, 1992, prod. Fred Maher) the group's debut album, is comprised of the leisurely melodic tunes, soft-voiced vocals and ironic humor that give Luna its subtle edge. *Bewitched* (Elektra, 1994, prod. Victor Vugt and Luna) reaches an even greater level of understatement, with the late VU guitarist Sterling Morrison on two highlight tracks, "Friendly Advice" and "Great Jones Street." Tom Verlaine of Television guests on *Penthouse,* (Elektra, 1995, prod. Luna with Pat McCarthy and Mario Salvati) a magical and melancholy album with delicate mellotron and theremin sounds coloring the soft understatedness. The six-song *Luna,* (Number 6 EP, 1996) is the group's most recent offering and doesn't change course form its predecessors.

Kim Forster and Anna Glen

Evan Lurie

See: The Lounge Lizards

John Lurie

See: The Lounge Lizards

Luscious Jackson

Formed 1992 in New York, N.Y.

Jill Cunniff, bass; Gabrielle Glaser, guitar; Vivian Trimble, keyboards; Kate Schellenbach, drums

Named after a sports announcer's mispronunciation of NBA star Lucius Jackson's name, this group began with friends Cunniff and Glaser; Trimble and Schellenbach joined during the making of the debut EP. Schellenbach drummed in an early version of the Beastie Boys (as well as with Lunachicks and Wench), while Trimble has worked with dance companies on the N.Y. music scene. The group's style suggests an all-female take on the funky sound of the Beastie Boys' *Check Your Head.*

what to buy: *In Search of Manny* (Grand Royal/Capitol EP, 1992, prod. not listed) is a seductively catchy 24-minute, seven-track EP that blends girl group pop, hip-hop rhythms and smooth urban attitude into a unique stew.

the rest: *Natural Ingredient* (Grand Royal/Capitol, 1994, prod. Jill Cunniff, Gabrielle Glaser and Tony Mangurian)

Steve Holtje

Lush

Formed 1988, London, England

Miki Berenyi, guitar, vocals; Emma Anderson, guitar, vocals; Chris Acland, drums; Philip King bass (1992-present); Steve Rippon, bass (1988-92)

Weaving otherworldly harmonies with blurred guitar chords,

Lush set a new course for sonic adventure in the British music scene. The group's impeccable string of early singles provided the missing link between the Cocteau Twins and the Beach Boys, between My Bloody Valentine and Phil Spector's 60s girl groups; Lush essentially put a face and some personality to England's blossoming dreampop genre—including a main stage spot on the 1992 Lollapalooza festival—before moving on to a harder-edged sound on its later albums.

what to buy: Lush's debut album *Gala* (4AD/Reprise, 1990, prod. Tim Friese-Greene, Robin Guthrie, Lush and John Fryer) compiled two early EPs of astral, ambient pop. Among its stellar tracks were the unforgettable "De-luxe" and "Sweetness and Light." The equally radiant *Spooky* (4AD/Reprise, 1992, prod. Robin Guthrie) captured a worldwide audience, luring listeners with its layers of soothing guitars, cherubic voices and convincing songs such as "Fantasy" and "Untogether."

what to buy next: Even though Lush excelled in the dreampop genre, *Lovelife* (4AD/Reprise, 1996, prod. Pete Bartlett and Lush) showed that the group was equally adept at crunchy new wave ("Ladykillers") and elegiac ballads ("Olympia").

what to avoid: *Split* (4AD/Reprise, 1994, prod. Mike Hedges and Lush) found the band in a creative wilderness, struggling to balance its opulent melodies with a punkier edge that was emerging in its sound.

worth searching for: Either of the original British EPs, *Sear* (Nesak, 1989) and *Mad Love* (Nesak, 1990), though *Gala* makes them of interest to collectors only.

▶▶ Slowdive, Medicine, The Cranes

◀◀ Cocteau Twins, Phil Spector, My Bloody Valentine, the Beach Boys

Aidin Vaziri

Luxuria

See: Magazine

Annabella Lwin

See: Bow Wow Wow

Frankie Lymon and the Teenagers

Formed 1955 in New York, N.Y. Disbanded 1956. Reunited 1965.

Frankie Lymon (born Sept. 30, 1942 in New York, N.Y. Died Feb. 28, 1968), lead vocals; Joe Negroni, baritone vocals; Herman Santiago, first tenor vocals; Jimmy Merchant, second tenor vocals

One of the sweetest voices in all of doo-wop, 13-year-old Lymon brought the Teenagers massive acclaim with the 1956 smash "Why Do Fools Fall in Love?" An enduring paean that has not aged one whit, it showcased Lymon's wise-beyond-his-years delivery, thus spawning a number of kid groups and influencing legions of later superstars such as Michael Jackson, Smokey Robinson, Marvin Gaye and Diana Ross. That was about all she wrote, as Lymon soon left for a disappointing solo career hampered by drug addiction, which killed him at age 26. Nasty legal battles among surviving band members over authorship of the hit and over his estate cast a greedy shadow over an already tragic tale. *The Best of Frankie Lymon and the Teenagers* (Rhino, 1990) offers classic New York doo-wop and has all the essential songs recorded by the child prodigy. *At the London Palladium* (Collectables, 1991) captures a performance in front of an ecstatically excited crowd, while *Complete Recordings* (Bear Family) is a five-disc import set for hard-core collectors.

Allan Orski

George Lynch

See: Dokken

Lynch Mob

See: Dokken

Frida Lyngstad

See: ABBA

Jeff Lynne

See: Electric Light Orchestra

Lynyrd Skynyrd

Formed 1965 in Jacksonville, Fla. Disbanded 1977. Re-formed 1987.

Ronnie Van Zant, vocals (died Oct. 20, 1977); Gary Rossington, guitar; Allen Collins, guitar (died Jan. 23, 1990); Ed King, guitar (1973-75. 1987-93); Billy Powell, keyboards; Leon Wilkeson, bass; Bob Burns, drums (1965-74); Artimus Pyle, drums (1974-1991); Steve Gaines, guitar (1976-77, died Oct. 20, 1977); Johnny Van Zant, vocals (1987-present), Randall Hall, guitar, (1991-93); Custer, drums (1991-present); Hughie Thomasson, guitar (1996)

Lynyrd Skynyrd was the most commercially successful, critically acclaimed and hardest rocking of the Allman Brothers-influenced Southern rock bands to emerge during the early 70s. With fierce regional pride, the Florida natives always evinced tremendous creativity and originality, mixing Allmanesque guitar harmonies with crunchy Stones-style rhythms and overdriven, Cream-influenced distortion. At the heart of the band's sound was a three-guitar juggernaut of Rossington, King (later Gaines) and Collins, as well as the forceful presence of vocalist Van Zant, who successfully combined a country voice with heavy metal swagger. And while some of its Southern Rock peers went over the edge into boogie excess, Skynyrd never did, in large part because—in addition to being a ferocious live band—its members wrote great songs, including "Sweet Home Alabama," "Gimme Three Steps," "What's Your Name" and the seminal guitar orgy "Free Bird." After a short dry spell, the band was reenergized by the 1976 addition of the phenomenally talented guitarist Gaines, who infused the band with new energy that lead to its finest album, *Street Survivors* But before Lynyrd Skynyrd could reap the fruits of its second coming, its charter plane crashed into a Mississippi swamp, killing Van Zant and Gaines and two others, and seriously injuring the other members. The group re-formed during the late 80s, with Van Zant's brother Johnny taking over as a vocalist.

what to buy: It doesn't get much better than *Street Survivors,* (MCA, 1977, prod. Lynyrd Skynyrd, Jimmy Johnson and Tim Smith) a molten slab of fiery three-guitar Southern rock with just the right amount of country and a fantastic collection of songs—including "You Got That Right," "That Smell" and "What's Your Name." *One More From the Road* (MCA, 1977, prod. Tom Dowd) is an awesome live document and includes the famous "What song is it you want to hear?!" "Freeee-bird!!!" dialogue. *Pronounced 'leh-nerd' skin'-nerd* (MCA, 1973, prod. Al Kooper) introduced the band with a bang, though it's occasionally weighed down by Kooper's excessive production. The three-CD *Lynyrd Skynyrd* (MCA, 1991, comp. Ron O'Brien and Andy McKaie) is everything a boxed set should be; it's not over-stuffed, and it features all the essential tracks as well as a host of previously unreleased material, most of which is actually good—including the demo of "Free Bird."

what to buy next: Both *Second Helping* (MCA, 1974, prod. Al Kooper) and *Nuthin' Fancy* (MCA, 1975, Al Kooper) follow the same path as the band's debut. The former includes "Sweet Home Alabama," "Don't Ask Me No Questions," "Call Me the Breeze" and "The Needle and the Spoon," classics all, while the latter includes "Saturday Night Special" and the surprisingly introspective "Am I Losin.' " *Gold & Platinum* (MCA, 1979, prod. Various) is thorough greatest hits collection with an annoying lack of notes or credits.

what to avoid: The band was sounding a little strained and creatively dry by *Gimme Back My Bullets* (MCA, 1976, prod. Tom Dowd), its fourth album in as many years. *Lynyrd Skynyrd 1991* (Atlantic, 1991, prod. Tom Dowd) was an outright embarrassment.

the rest: *Skynyrd's First and...Last* (MCA, 1978) *Best of the Rest* (MCA, 1986) *Legend* (MCA, 1987) *Southern by the Grace of God* (MCA, 1988) *Skynyrd's Innyrds* (MCA, 1989) *The Last Rebel* (Atlantic, 1992) *Endangered Species* (Capricorn, 1994)

worth searching for: *The King Biscuit Flower Hour Presents Lynyrd Skynyrd* (King Biscuit Flower Hour Records, 1995) was mistakenly released and quickly re-called, making this 1975 concert broadcast a collector's item.

solo outings:

Johnny Van Zant: Brickyard Road (Atlantic, 1990) The Johnny Van Zant Collection (Polydor, 1994)

Rossington Collins Band: Anytime, Anyplace Anywhere (MCA, 1980)

Molly Hatchet, Metallica, the Black Crowes, .38 Special, Zakk Wylde

The Allman Brothers Band, Cream, Led Zeppelin, the Rolling Stones, the Yardbirds

Alan Paul

The Lyres

Formed 1983 in Boston, Mass.

Jeff Connolly, vocals, keyboards; Rick Coraccio, bass (1983-88, 1993-94); Paul Murphy, drums (1983-86, 1993-94); Danny McCormack, guitar (1983-86); John Bernardo, drums (1986); Matt Miklos, bass (1988); John Smith, drums (1988); Richard Carmal Jr., guitar; Jack Hickey, guitar, harmonica (1988-94)

The keepers of the garage-rock flame in Boston, the Lyres formed as a vehicle for organist/singer Connolly (formerly of DMZ) to pursue his quest for the perfect garage sound. He has kept his pursuit up well into the 90s, putting out occasional releases to a cult audience.

What Album Changed Your Life?

"Every single Bob Dylan album did something for me--Highway 61 Revisited, Blonde on Blonde, all of them. I think each one of his records gave me what I needed at the time, especially in the 60s. I can't tell you exactly what 'Desolation Row' meant or what he meant in 'Like a Rolling Stone,' but it didn't matter. Bob Dylan just had a way of speaking for you; I felt less estranged, less like a stranger in the world."

Patti Smith

what to buy: *On Fyre,* (Ace of Hearts, 1984, prod. Richard W. Harte) ♪♪♪ which brought the Lyres as close to national prominence as they'd ever come when heavy local airplay of "Don't Give It Up Now" prompted a positive review in Rolling Stone. The album is a minor classic for garage-rock aficionados.

what to buy next: *Some Lyres* (Taang!, 1994, prod. Jeff Connolly and Richard W. Harte) ♪♪♪ is a career retrospective, imaginatively packaged as a satire of the Rolling Stones' *Some Girls.*

what to avoid: *A Promise Is a Promise + 9 Bonus/Live Europe,* (Ace of Hearts, 1988, prod. Richard W. Harte) ♪♪ which is burdened by its lo-fi live tracks.

the rest: *Lyres Lyres* (Ace of Hearts, 1986) ♪♪♪ *Live at Continental* (Ace of Hearts, 1987) ♪♪ *Lyres Live 1983: Let's Have a Party!* (Ace of Hearts, 1989) ♪♪ *Nobody But Lyres* (Taang!, 1992) ♪♪ *Happy Now* (Taang!, 1993) ♪♪ *Those Lyres* (Norton, 1995) ♪♪

worth searching for: The cassette version of *On Fyre,* which includes eight bonus tracks. So does the French CD on the New Rose label. Contains "She Pays the Rent," one of Connolly's most accessible 60s rewrites.

▶▶ Del Fuegos

◀◀ The Kinks, the Standells, the Shadows of Knight, ? and the Mysterians

Brian Mansfield

Kirsty MacColl

Born Oct. 10, 1959 in London, England

The daughter of Brit folkie Ewan MacColl (writer of "The First Time Ever I Saw Your Face") has had a long string of hit singles in England but has never gone beyond a cult following in the U.S. despite her distinctive voice. A songwriter with a knack for organic melodies and clever turns of phrase, she may have handicapped herself commercially by being adept at so many styles, from country and rockabilly to alternative, dance-pop and even the suave Latin arrangement of "My Affair." She also has a good ear for other people's material and has done wonderful covers of the Smiths' "You Just Haven't Earned It Yet Baby," the Kinks' "Days," Billy Bragg's "A New England," Lou Reed's "Perfect Day" (a duet with Lemonheads' Evan Dando) and Cole Porter's "Miss Otis Regrets" (with the Pogues, originally on the Red, Hot & Blue AIDS benefit album). After appearing in 1979 on Stiff with her first single, "They Don't Know" (later a hit for Tracey Ullman), she made *Desperate Character* for Polydor (never released in the U.S.) in 1981 but had the follow-up rejected. She was hardly unheard-from, however, since her vocal talents were in demand and she did sessions with the Rolling Stones and Van Morrison, among others. Her 1984 marriage to Steve Lillywhite, a producer noted for the shimmering guitar sounds heard on albums by U2 and others, eventually led to him producing her 1989 and 1991 comeback albums. (They later split up.) During the time between her Polydor and Charisma albums, she apparently become more politicized (dare we speculate that Billy Bragg may have had something to do with that?), and several Charisma tracks tackle reactionary British Prime Minister Margaret Thatcher, poverty and the like, though MacColl's focus remains interpersonal relationships.

what to buy: *Titanic Days* (I.R.S., 1993, prod. Various) ♪♪♪♪ is janglier and sunnier than the Lillywhite productions, with a bittersweet tone typified by "Soho Square." The Lillywhite-produced "Angel" boasts a mutant dub/hip-hop beat supporting MacColl's ethereal vocals. That was as close as the album came to a hit, but every track is strong, with many pretty string arrangements suggesting MacColl's calling is as a sophisticated chanteuse.

what to buy next: *Electric Landlady* (Charisma/I.R.S, 1991, prod. Steve Lillywhite) is MacColl at her most eclectic, featuring the moody, almost funky "Walking Down Madison" (co-written with Smiths' guitarist Johnny Marr, a frequent collaborator) and "My Affair."

the rest: *Kite* (Charisma/I.R.S., 1989) *Galore* (I.R.S., 1995)

worth searching for: The out-of-print import *Desperate Character* (Polydor, 1981), an estimable start that features early gems ("They Don't Know," "There's a Guy Works Down the Chip Shop Swears He's Elvis") and some fine guitar contributions from Rockpile's Billy Bremner.

▶▶ Billy Bragg, Tracey Ullman, (garbage singer)

◀◀ Patsy Cline, Pretenders, Rockpile, Smiths, Billy Bragg, Elvis Costello

Steve Holtje

The Maccoys

See: Rick Derringer

Shane Macgowan & the Popes

See: The Pogues

Ashley MacIsaac

Born February 24, 1975 in Creignish, Cape Breton, Nova Scotia, Canada

Young Ashley MacIsaac's success in the music industry shouldn't come as much of a surprise. The teenage fiddle phenomenon has been exposed to music all his life—his father, a fiddle player, would play around the house, and Ashley himself got a rather early start learning to stepdance at age 5 and beginning formal fiddle instruction at the tender age of 9. He began touring Canada as well as U.S. cities such as Detroit and Boston by the time he was 13 and has filled venues ranging from local Cape Breton sites to New York's Carnegie Hall. The term "prodigy" come to mind? MacIsaac has won numerous awards including, Best Live Act at the 1995 East Coast Music Awards, and Best New Solo Artist and Best Roots and Traditional Album-Solo at the 1996 Juno Awards. He was the subject of a major label feeding frenzy while still in his teens, with his major label debut, *How Are You Today?* (A&M, 1995, prod. N/A) receiving critical and commercial acclaim. This album, which sold more than 50,000 copies in three weeks, reflects both his Celtic/Canadian heritage and his youthful exhuberance in its driving, agressive instrumentation. A perfect, if unlikely combination of ancient celtic folk songs with modern rock arrangements and attitude. Keep your eyes and ears open as MacIsaac is certainly just scratching the surface of a wealth of talent.

the rest: *Close To the Floor* (Independent, 1992) *A Cape Breton Christmas* (Independent, 1993)

▶▶ He's only 19, give him time

◀◀ The Chieftains

Christopher Scanlon

Jeep Macnichol

See: The Samples

Madonna

Born Madonna Louise Veronica Ciccone, Aug. 16, 1958, Bay City, Mich.

Madonna's career began as another cute blonde singer making electronic dance music in the 80s. Then she began to wield her amazing talent—for business and marketing as well as music—and wound up, along with Michael Jackson, as the biggest pop star since Elvis Presley. Her early hits were innocent throwaways ("Everybody," "Holiday"), promoted by titillating videos of a scantily clad Madonna dancing hither and yon. She even parlayed her videocentricity into a co-starring role in the hit film "Desperately Seeking Susan." But once she lured the masses, Madonna began spewing messages. With every record she changed costumes and, like David Bowie in the early 70s, personas. MTV followed her every move, whether she was challenging moral conventions in "Papa Don't Preach," sexual mores in "Like a Virgin" or religious sensibilities with "Like a Prayer." (She gained a quick foothold in the tabloids, too, by marrying and quickly divorcing hot-tempered actor Sean Penn, then having affairs with—depending who you believe—Warren Beatty, and basketball players Charles Barkley and Dennis Rodman.) Her videos, at the time, were consistently more outrageous than her songs, which remained impeccably crafted and well-sung dance music. As she grew older, Madonna turned into a self-contained entertainment industry, producing a tour documentary called "Truth or Dare" and a photo book called "Sex" that shocked millions—though maybe more for the naked pictures of Vanilla Ice than anything else. She began her own label, Maverick, which scored hits with Candlebox and Alanis Morrissette. Unlike her contemporaries,

Prince and Michael Jackson, Madonna has always managed to stay ahead of the pop curve—embracing gay and club cultures so as to be a leader in bringing them to the mainstream, rather than a follow. In 1996, she starred in the film version of "Evita" and decided to have a baby—though not to marry again.

what to buy: *The Immaculate Collection* (Sire, 1990, prod. Various) saves you the trouble of compiling all Madonna's singles among her inconsistent albums. *Like a Virgin,* (Sire, 1984, prod. Nile Rodgers) *True Blue* (Sire, 1986, prod. Madonna, Patrick Leonard and Stephen Bray) and *Like a Prayer* (Sire, 1989, prod. Madonna, Patrick Leonard, Stephen Bray and Prince) are the best of her studio albums, though in retrospect the electronic touches don't sound as good as they did during the 80s.

what to buy next: *Erotica* (Maverick, 1992, prod. Madonna and Shep Pettibone) is Madonna's foray into the world of hypnotic ambient-techno music, and as an added bonus features her sucking on somebody's toe on the back cover. A collection of Madonna's ballads, *Something to Remember,* (Maverick/Sire, 1995, prod. Various) includes two new songs and two versions of her trancey take on "I Want You," originally recorded for the Marvin Gaye tribute album *Inner City Blues.*

what to avoid: As if the movie wasn't painful enough, *Who's That Girl* (Sire, 1987, prod. Various) is an embarrassment for such an ambitious artist.

the rest: *Madonna* (Sire, 1983) *You Can Dance* (Sire, 1987); *I'm Breathless* (Sire, 1990) *Bedtime Stories* (Maverick, 1994)

worth searching for: Sonic Youth's bizarre and hilarious send-up of (mostly) Madonna tunes, *The Whitey Album,* (Blast First, 1989, prod. Ciccone Youth) credited to Ciccone Youth, a sly parody of Madonna's surname.

▶▶ Terence Trent D'Arby, Whitney Houston, TLC, En Vogue, Celine Dion, Alanis Morrissette

◀◀ Donna Summer, the Crystals, Tina Turner, Cyndi Lauper, Aretha Franklin, Billie Holiday, Elvis Presley, Michael Jackson

Tracey Birkenhauer and Steve Knopper

Magazine

Formed 1977 in Manchester, England. Disbanded 1981.

Howard Devoto, vocals; John McGeoch, guitar (1977-79); Barry Adamson, bass; Dave Formula, keyboards; Martin Jackson, drums (1977-78); John Doyle, drums (1978-81); Robin Simon, guitar (1979-80); Ben Mandelson, guitar (1980)

Magazine's arty, cerebral post-punk earned a cult following thanks in large part to singer-lyricist Devoto's prodigious wit and the gifted band's utter refusal to honor musical boundaries. A founding member of punk/new-wave innovators the Buzzcocks, Devoto co-wrote several songs with that band's leader Pete Shelley; one of these, "Shot By Both Sides," became an early Magazine favorite. Balancing punk's manic energy and questioning attitude with frosty keyboard textures and funky grooves, however, Magazine quickly set themselves apart from the pack. By the release of its third LP, *The Correct Use of Soap,* the band had moved in a poppier direction; though a bit of airplay widened its audience, Magazine dissolved in 1981. Guitarist McGeoch, who departed for greater fame with Siouxie and the Banshees in 1980, also played with Formula and Adamson in the successful synth-pop band Visage. Devoto released a solo album and subsequently formed a new band, Luxuria, with guitarist Noko; this effort, though periodically impressive, lacked the powerful gestalt of Magazine. Adamson played with Nick Cave and the Bad Seeds and released a string of eclectic solo albums. In the ensuing years, Magazine's influence on a number of younger artists has become even more apparent.

what to buy: The Magazine retrospective *Rays and Hail, 1978-81* (Virgin, 1987, prod. Various) collects the band's essential tracks.

what to buy next: Fans of the earlier, harder material will gravitate toward Magazine's debut, *Real Life,* (Virigin, 1978, prod. John Leckie) while those who enjoy the more melodic songs are likely prefer *The Correct Use of Soap* (Virgin, 1980, prod. Martin Hannett)

what to avoid: Devoto's solo album *Jerky Versions of the Dream* (I.R.S., 1983, prod. Howard Devoto and Greg Walsh) shows flashes of wit but suffers, in large part, from musical anemia.

the rest: *Secondhand Daylight* (Virgin, 1979) *Play* (I.R.S., 1981) *Magic, Murder and the Weather* (I.R.S., 1982) *After the Fact* (I.R.S., 1982) *Scree (Rarities, 1978-81)* (Blue Plate, 1991)

worth searching for: A furious live version of *The Correct Use of Soap's* "Model Worker" on the film soundtrack *Urgh! A Music War* (I.R.S., 1981, prod. various)

solo outings:

Luxuria (Devoto): Unanswerable Lust (I.R.S., 1985) *Beast Box* (I.R.S., 1987)

Visage (McGeoch and Adamanson): Visage (Polydor, 1980) *The Anvil* (Polydor, 1982) *Fade to Grey—The Singles Collection* (Polydor, 1983) *Beat Boy* (Polydor, 1984)

Barry Adamson: Moss Side Story (Mute, 1989) *Delusion* soundtrack (Mute, 1991) *Soul Murder* (Mute, 1992) *The Negro Inside Me* (Mute, 1993)

▶▶ Radiohead, The Negro Problem

◀◀ Sex Pistols, Buzzcocks, Captain Beefheart, Sly and the Family Stone, Franz Kafka, Fyodor Dosotevsky

see also: *Siouxsi and the Banshees, Nick Cave*

Simon Glickman

Magnapop

Formed 1987 in Athens, Ga.

Linda Hopper, vocals; Ruthie Morris, guitar; Shannon Mulvaney, bass; David McNair, drums (1987-95); Mark Posgay (1996-present)

Magnapop's edgy alternative pop is distinguished by Morris' economically powerful guitar work and Hopper's affectless vocals, and by driving rhythms that propel the sweet-and-sour tension of the melodies. But the band first courted attention with its high-profile producers—R.E.M.'s Michael Stipe, a fellow Athenian, on *Play It Again* (Play it Again Sam, 1992) and Bob Mould of Hüsker Dü and Sugar on *Hot Boxing* (Priority, 1994) The latter courted favorable word-of-mouth, generating expectations for *Rubbing Won't Help,* (Priority, 1996, prod. Geza X) which showed the band moving in a poppier direction and gaining some radio airplay.

Simon Glickman

Taj Mahal

Born Henry Sainte Claire Fredricks, May 17, 1942 in New York, N.Y.

Singer-instrumentalist Taj Mahal emerged during the mid-60s as a bluesman in the tradition of Mississippi John Hurt and Sleepy John Estes. He's always held onto the blues as his root, but over the years he's added reggae, calypso, African and pop elements. Taj has a powerful gospel voice and vocal timing that alternately drags out notes and then squeezes many into a short space. His Caribbean forays sometimes evidence a beautiful blending of acoustic fingerpicking, soprano saxophone and steel pan playing. Taj's shows usually include a solo set even when he has a band, and these portions range through a cappella singing to accompanying himself on pennywhistle, kalimba, handclaps, guitar, conch shell, banjo, harmonica, piano and more.

what to buy: Which Taj Mahal do you want? For the bluesman, try the double-length *Giant Step/De Ole Folks At Home* (Columbia, 1969, prod. David Rubinson) covers the country and urban sides. *Giant Step* features Taj backed by bass, drums and guitar doing his unique takes on standards such as "Good Morning Little Schoolgirl" and his own songs. *De Ole Folks*... is Taj acoustic and alone on a series of work songs, blues and rags; "Fishin' Blues" and "Annie's Lover" are exquisite. On the Caribbean side, *Mo' Roots* (Columbia, 1974, prod. Taj Mahal) marks a revelatory change in his music. From "Johnny Too Bad," through "Cajun Waltz" and "Clara (St. Kitts Woman)" each song drips with genuine island charm.

what to buy next: The 1966-71 years are well represented on *The Taj Mahal Anthology,* (Columbia, 1977, prod. David Rubinson) which caters to the blues crowd. *World Music* (Columbia, 1993, prod. Various) has most of the *Mo' Roots* album with a few other West Indian revelations.

what to avoid: *Taj* (Gramavision, 1986, prod. Taj Mahal) has Taj all slicked up for the pop market. And he doesn't slick up well.

the rest: *The Natch'l Blues* (Columbia, 1969) *Happy Just To Be Like I Am* (Columbia, 1971) *The Real Thing* (Columbia, 1971) *Recycling the Blues (and Other Related Stuff)* (Columbia, 1972) *Oooh So Good 'n' Blues* (Columbia, 1973) *Satisfied 'n' Tickled Too* (Columbia, 1976) *Music Fuh Ya'* (Warner Bros., 1977) *Mule Bone* (Gramavision, 1991) *Taj's Blues* (Legacy, 1992) *Dancing the Blues* (Private Music, 1993) *Phantom Blues* (Private Music, 1996)

worth searching for: There's proof that Taj is still worth listening to on *Like Never Before,* (Private Music, 1991, prod. Skip Drinkwater) with the real R&B of "Don't Call Us" and the boogie woogie of "Big Legged Mamas Are Back In Style."

▶▶ Keb' Mo, Vinx

◀◀ Sleepy John Estes, Mississippi John Hurt

Lawrence Gabriel

Major Lance

Born April 4, 1941 Chicago, IL. Died Sept. 3, 1994, Decatur, Ga.

Growing up in Chicago with fellow stars-to-be Curtis Mayfield and Jerry Butler (they all went to the same high school), this slim, handsome R&B singer parlayed a job as a dancer on a local TV show into a single deal on Mercury. The Mayfield-penned songs didn't take off, but three years later, Lance's smooth, caressing voice began making him a regular presence on the R&B charts. He specialized in mid-tempo plaints ("Crying in the Rain," "Gotta Right to Cry," "It Ain't No Use," "Ain't It a Shame," "I'm So Lost," "You Don't Want Me No More") with an undercurrent of happy buoyancy. His biggest hit by far (Billboard Pop Chart #5, 1963), and one of the greatest R&B songs ever, was Mayfield's "Um, Um, Um, Um, Um, Um," the story of a man so overwhelmed that the title was all he could say. Mayfield's "The Monkey Time," a jumping party tune, charted almost as high (Pop #8, 1963). After some label hopping, Lance's luck ran out, and he was convicted in 1978 of selling cocaine. He returned to performing after his release in 1982 and died of heart failure at age 55. The two-CD compilation *Everybody Loves a Good Time!* (Legacy/Epic, 1995, prod. Carl Davis, others) is currently Lance's only domestically available album. Since he was primarily a singles artist, its 40 tracks do justice to his peak period with Okeh Records (1962-68), with all six of his pop hits and five previously unreleased tracks.

Steve Holtje

Yngwie Malmsteen

Born June 30, 1963 in Stockholm, Sweden

By age 21, Malmsteen had the rock world praising his blazing speed and impressive dexterity—even if his greatest admirers tended to overlook a certain absence of feeling. Yngwie (which means "young viking chief") received his first guitar at 5, but it took a 1970 Jimi Hendrix TV special to make him pick it up. He moved to California in 1983—thanks to the patronage of *Guitar Player* editor Mike Varney, who had heard a Malmsteen demo tape—and quickly established himself as a successor in the lineage of Edward Van Halen and Randy Rhodes. Malmsteen first joined the group Steeler, then recorded two albums with Alcatrazz before moving on to greater notoriety as a solo act. His sales don't approach the levels of many of his colleagues, but Malmsteen remains undeterred, plying his particular brand of guitar pyrotechnics for anyone who will listen.

what to buy: Malmsteen's debut, *Rising Force*, (Polydor, 1984, prod. Yngwie Malmsteen) is a call to arm, a non-stop barrage of technique blazing over the leaden drumming of ex-Jethro Tuller Barriemore Barlow. The birth of a guitar master. *Odyssey* (Polydor, 1988, prod. Jeff Glixman) signaled his return after a serious car accident, and with the help of former Rainbow singer Joe Lynn Turner, it's his most successful to date.

what to buy next: *The Yngwie Malmsteen Collection*, (Polygram, 1992, prod. Various) a good sampler that's not quite as satisfying as the other albums.

what to avoid: *Live in Leningrad: Trial by Fire* (Polydor, 1992) WOOF! one of the most pompous and indulgent hard rock displays this side of Spinal Tap.

the rest: *Marching Out* (Polydor, 1985) *Trilogy* (Polydor, 1986) *Eclipse* (Polydor, 1990) *Fire and Ice* (Elektra, 1992) *The Seventh Sign* (CMC International, 1994) *Magnum Opus* (Viceroy/Architect Music, 1995) (with Alcatrazz): *No Parole for Rock & Roll* (RCA/Rockshire/Grand Slamm, 1983) *Live Sentence* (Grand Slamm, 1983)

worth searching for: *Steeler* (Shrapnel, 1983, prod. Mike Varney) , Malmsteen's first recorded work on these shorts that caused an underground sensation.

Jennifer Batten, "Dimebag" Darrell Abbott (Pantera), Zakk Wylde, Slash

Ritchie Blackmore, Jimi Hendrix, Bach, Beethoven, Vivaldi, Paganini, Steve Hillage

Sarah Weber

The Mamas and the Papas

Formed 1965 in New York, N.Y. Disbanded 1968. Reunited 1971, 1981.

John Phillips, vocals, guitar; Dennis Doherty, vocals; Michelle Phillips (born Holly Michelle Gilliam), vocals; Cass Elliot, vocals (died July 29, 1974); Mackenzie Phillips, vocals (1981-present); Elaine "Spanky" McFarlane, vocals (1981-present)

It's ironic that the original vision for the what was to become the Mamas and Papas was a New York folk act named the Journeymen, since the Mamas and Papas were second only to the Beach Boys in celebrating with glorious harmonies the free-wheeling California lifestyle of fun and romance. Beginning in 1966, the hits rolled in like a Pacific coast surf: "California Dreamin'," "Monday, Monday," "I Saw Her Again," "Look Through My Window," "Dedicated to the One I Love" and "Creeque Alley." Just as quickly, the sun set on the group's career. Most recently John and Michelle Phillips published their confessional memoirs, while John Phillips and Doherty stage occasional tours with a new version of the Mamas and the Papas featuring Phillips' daugther Mackenzie and McFarlane, formerly of Spanky & Our Gang.

what to buy: *Creeque Alley: The History of the Mamas and Papas* (MCA, 1991) is a comprehensive two-disc set that includes all the hits and good selections from their albums, plus earlier work from the Mugwumps and Elliot's group Cass and the Big Three.

what to buy next: *If You Can Believe Your Eyes and Ears* (Dunhill/MCA, 1966) and *Deliver* (Dunhill/MCA, 1967) contain sparkling harmonies, superb arrangements and terrific songs.

what to avoid: *People Like Us* (Dunhill/MCA, 1971) is devoid of any redeeming value. *16 of Their Greatest Hits* (Dunhill/MCA, 1969) is plauged by terrible digital transfers. For a few bucks more, buy the definitive *Creeque Alley*.

the rest: *Monterey International Pop Festival* (One Way, 1969)

worth searching for: John Phillips' *John the Wolfking of L.A.* (Dunhill, 1969) His eclectic solo debut provides some inspiring moments, uneven songwriting and quirky indulgences. Given his past writing style, it's a true oddity.

▶▶ The Manhattan Transfer, Wilson Phillips

◀◀ Rick Nelson, the Weavers, the Everly Brothers, the Beatles

Patrick McCarty

Manic Street Preachers

Formed 1990 in Cardiff, Wales

James Dean Bradfield, guitar; Sean Moore, drummer; Nicky Wire, bass; Richey Edwards, guitar

Despite its loud politics and punk image, the Manic Street Preachers played a soft brand of hard rock. Achieving some success in England, the group was mostly ignored in America. The band's legend rests not on music but on the disappearance of guitarist Edwards—who had a history of depression and self-mutilation—before a major U.K. tour in 1995. His car was found, but Edwards is still missing. *Holy Bible*, (CBS U.K., 1994, prod. Steve Brown) the last album before Edward's disappearance, is the band's strongest, with songs that are angry, political and, most importantly, well-written. Afterwards, bassist Nicky Wire became the group's primary songwriter, introducing a lusher, less political style.

the rest: *Generation Terrorists* (Columbia, 1992) *Gold Against The Soul* (Columbia, 1993) *Everything Must Go* (Columbia, 1996)

Anna Blen

Aimee Mann

Born Aug. 19, 1960 in Richmond, Va.

The bassist and vocalist for the now-defunct 'Til Tuesday, Aimee Mann has in recent years distinguished herself as a songwriter of formidable talent, much along the lines of Chrissie Hynde and Elvis Costello. Foregoing the synth-laden pop of her former band, Mann's albums are sonically adventurous affairs that blend catchy melodies with eloquent and dryly humorous observations of relationships and vulnerability. Much credit is due to Jon Brion, Mann's producer and a multi-instrumentalist who performs much of the material. A perennial darling of both critics and songwriters (including Squeeze's Chris Difford and Glenn Tilbrook), Mann has shown remarkable creative growth over her first two albums and is definitely an artist to keep an eye on.

what to buy: Packed end to end with instantly memorable melodies, *I'm with Stupid* (Geffen Records, 1995, prod. Jon Brion) is simply one of the best pop albums to come out in years. From power-distortion rockers like "Superball" and "Choice in the Matter" to gorgeous ballads like "Amateur" and "Ray," Mann shows a talent for crafting delectable pop candy that occasionally bites back.

what to buy next: *Whatever* (Imago, 1993, prod. Jon Brion) is brighter and more pop-oriented than its successor. While nothing here is particularly ground breaking, there are numerous standouts, including "I Should've Known," "Fifty Years After the Fair" and "Could've Been Anyone."

worth searching for: The *Say Anything* EP (Imago, 1993, prod. Jon Brion) offers up an acoustic version of "Say Anything" (from *Whatever*) and adds on Mann's capable cover of the Badfinger hit "Baby Blue" and the previously unreleased "Jimmy Hoffa Jokes."

▶▶ Crowded House, Jules Shear, Sam Phillips, Juliana Hatfield, Michael Penn

◀◀ The Beatles, The Byrds, Elvis Costello, The Pretenders, Squeeze

see also: *'Til Tuesday*

Christopher Scapelliti

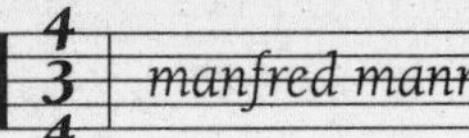

Manfred Mann /Manfred Mann's Earth Band

Manfred Mann (1964-67): Manfred Mann, keyboards; Paul Jones, vocals, harmonica (1964-66); Mike Hugg, drums; Michael Vickers, guitar (1964-65); Tom McGuinness, bass, guitar; Jack Bruce, bass (1965-66); Klaus Voorman, bass (1967); Michael D'Abo, vocals (1967). Earth Band (1971-80): Manfred Mann; Mick Rogers, vocals, guitar (1971-74); Colin Pattenden, bass (1971-76); Chris Slade, drums (1976-78); Chris Thompson, vocals, guitar (1976-80); Geoff Britton, drums (1979); Dave Flett, guitar (1976-78); Pat King, bass (1978-80); Steve Waller, guitar (1979-80); John Lingwood, drums (1980)

Under the calculating eyes of the jazz- and blues-trained Mann, the band bearing his name first surfaced with trash pop in the early 60s ("Do Wah Diddy") for the sole purpose of selling records. Although he had a good belter in Jones, Mann then employed D'Abo, a lesser talent notable mostly for writing the lovely "Handbags and Gladrags," which Rod Stewart later nailed. Mann then disbanded the group for lackluster jazz excursions before forming the Earth Band and pursuing heavier art-rock ambitions. The group had considerable success with re-makes of Bruce Springsteen's "Blinded by the Light" and "Spirit in the Night;" alas, the band did not repeat those successes, and Mann finally put a wedge in the revolving door of band members and called it a day in 1980, to pursue his lofty ambitions on his own. Reports of a new Earth Band began surfacing in Britain during 1996, however.

what to buy: *Best of—The Definitive Collection* (EMI, 1992, prod. Various) is for fans of the early pop material such as the durable "Do Wah Diddy," along with first versions of "Pretty Flamingos" (covered to greater effect by Stewart) and "My Little Red Book."

what to buy next: *The Best of Manfred Mann's Earth Band* (Warner Archives, 1996, prod. Various) highlights Mann's elaborate cover versions during the 70s, ranging from nifty ("Blinded by the Light") to ponderous ("Quit Your Low Down Ways"), and revealing his continued dependence on Dylan material. It includes one last stab at a Springsteen overhaul, "For You," which has little of the charm of Greg Kihn's version.

what to avoid: The Earth Band's catalog has been recently reissued by Twinbrook Music, but unless the extravagant reworkings that make up the above compilation leave you crying out for more, stay away.

the rest: *The Manfred Mann Album/The Five Faces of Manfred Mann* (Ascot, 1964/EMI, 1996) *The Roaring Silence* (Warner Bros., 1976) *The Best of the Fontana Years* (Fontana, 1994)

solo outings:

Manfred Mann: Plains Music (Priority Music, 1991)

Emerson, Lake and Palmer, Asia

Lonnie Donegan, the Beatles, Bob Dylan, Bruce Springsteen

Allan Orski

Marilyn Manson

Formed 1990 in Ft. Lauderdale, Fla.

Mr. Manson, vocals; Daisy Berkowitz, guitar; Madonna Wayne Gacy, keyboards; Gidget Gein, bass (1990-93); Twiggy Ramirez, bass (1993-present); Sara Lee Lucas, drums (1991-95); Ginger Fish, drums (1995-present)

Flaunting a circus horror show-meets-gothic dominatrix vibe, Marilyn Manson's initial claim to fame was its live shows, which feature lots of 90s-style headbanging with touches of Alice Cooper-style theatrics. Discovered by nine inch nails guru Trent Reznor and signed to his nothing label, the band benefited from his production help and guitar playing on its first album, *Portrait of an American Family.* (Interscope/nothing, 1994, prod. Trent Reznor and Mr. Manson) Touring with nine inch nails offered tremendous exposure, but it was a gothic/industrial remake of Eurythmics' "Sweet Dreams" from *Smells Like Children* (Interscope/nothing, 1995. prod. by Marilyn Manson and Trent Reznor) that snared radio and mainstream attention. Its members bearing stage names combining famous women with serial killers, Marilyn Manson explores the seamy underbelly of American life and pop culture with an eye toward the shocking and absurd.

Eric Deggans

Phil Manzanera /801

Born Phillip Targett-Adams on Jan. 31, 1951, in London, England

Manzanera played experimental music in a rock band called Quiet Sun before Bryan Ferry asked him to join Roxy Music, where Manzanera's frantic, angular guitar lines became a hallmark. By the time the group disbanded after *Avalon* in 1982, Manzanera's guitar playing had become less abstract and more lyrical. Though he had been active in outside projects while Roxy was together, his post-Roxy life freed the South American-raised guitarist to explore any number of directions, from free-form jazz to Latin-flavored progressive rock.

what to buy: A surprising number of Manzanera's daring and occasionally dull solo efforts, including collaborations with Roxy Music reedman Andy Mackay and his avant-garde supergroup 801, are available on CD. But none encapsulates the guitarists' vast stylistic range, not to mention his six-string daring, more than *The Manzanera Collection* (Caroline, 1992, prod. Various) which touches upon the many stepstones of his career. It offers some of his best recorded work, including the group 801's breathtaking live version of the Beatles' "Tomorrow Never Knows."

what to buy next: *Diamond Head,* (Editions E.G., 1975, prod. Ray Manzanera) a solo recording while Roxy was still active, features most of the band's players plus all of Quiet Sun and Robert Wyatt. Those are dispirate talents, but Manzanera's fluid playing holds it all together.

what to avoid: *Listen Now,* (Editions E.G., 1977) recorded with the side band 801 (including Quiet Sun bassist Bill MacCormick) is a rote letdown—particularly after its exciting predecessor, the out of print *801 Live.*

the rest: *K-Scope* (Editions E.G., 1978) Primitive Guitars *(Editions E.G., 1982)* Guitarissimo *(Editions E.G., 1986)* Christmas: The Players *(with Andy Mackay) (Rykodisc, 1986)* Crack the Whip *(with Andy Mackay) (Relativity, date N/A)* Up in Smoke *(with Andy Mackay) (Relativity, date N/A)* Mato Grosso *(with Sergio Dias) (Black Sun/Celestial Harmonies, date N/A)*

worth searching for: The aforementioned *801 Live* (Editions E.G./Polydor, 1976/1982, prod. N/A) is an electrifying live album with Brian Eno sitting in to perform his "Baby's on Fire."

Andy Taylor (Duran Duran), Adrian Belew

Charlie Christian, Charles Mingus, Edgar Varese

see also: *Roxy Music*

Doug Pullen and Gary Graff

Ray Manzarek

See: The Doors

Teena Marie

Born Mary Christine Brockert March 5, 1957, in Santa Monica, Calif.

With a family full of music lovers supporting her, young Mary Brockert began performing at age eight, eventually taking her nickname—Teena Marie—as her stage name. While in college, she was spotted by Motown Records chief Berry Gordy and signed to the label; as legend goes, R&B superstar Rick James heard her singing in a studio and offered to produce her first record. Before long, the industry and fans were buzzing about this white girl who could sing funk and soul with convincing passion. From 1979-81, she found success with Motown and James, gradually taking over more of her own songwriting and production responsibility as she became the most successful white artist ever to work at Motown. Moving to Epic Records during the early 80s after a royalty dispute with Motown, Marie truly spread her creative wings, refining the rock/funk mix alongside Prince, Cameo and James were successfully spreading while adding her own unique touches. Enjoying her biggest hit in the 1984 single "Lovergirl," Marie crossed into the pop territory that Mariah Carey would later stumble into. But it was a success she would never duplicate again. Releasing a series of ever more ambitious albums that failed to find an audience, she lost her record deal in 1991.

what to buy: *Starchild* (Epic, 1984, prod. Teena Marie) balances Marie's talents as a multi-instrumentalist, producer and performer, offering "Lovergirl" and a touching tribute to Marvin Gaye ("My Dear Mr. Gaye"). Marie's records for Motown had a different flavor, shaped less by the Minneapolis influence of Prince than by the grittier Detroit-bred funk of her mentor James. The best album from this period is *It Must Be Magic,* (Motown, 1981, prod. Teena Marie) on which she experiments with Latin-tinged numbers such as "Portuguese Love" and straight-up funk grooves like "Square Biz."

what to buy next: Because no one's yet waded through the legal morass involved in Marie's united Motown and Epic material, you'll have to buy two greatest-hits packages to get her best. Motown's *Greatest Hits* (Motown, 1985, prod. Various) features the James-penned smash "I'm a Sucker for Your Love"—Marie's breakthrough single—along with the surprise disco smash "Behind the Groove." Epic's *Greatest Hits* (Epic, 1991, prod. Teena Marie) boasts her less impressive post-Motown work.

what to avoid: Coming after the powerhouse success of *Starchild,* the ambitious experimental funk of *Emerald City* (Epic, 1986, prod. Teena Marie) WOOF! seems like a jagged left turn, offering a host of rock- and jazz-influenced compositions that fell on deaf ears.

the rest: *Wild and Peaceful* (Motown, 1979) *Lady T.* (Motown, 1980) *Irons in the Fire* (Motown, 1980) *Robbery* (Epic, 1983) *Naked to the World* (Epic, 1988) *Ivory* (Epic, 1990)

worth searching for: Any audio or video tape of Marie's performance during "Sinbad's Summer Jam," a funk tribute organized by comedian Sinbad and broadcast on HBO.

▶▶ Mariah Carey, Lisa Stansfield, Madonna, Wendy & Lisa

◀◀ Aretha Franklin, Rick James, Prince

Eric Deggans

Marillion /Fish

Formed 1979 in London, England

Steve Rothery, guitars; Mick Pointer, drums (1979-83); Fish (born Derek William Dick), vocals (1980-88); Mark Kelly, keyboards, vocals (1981–present); Pete Trewavas, bass, vocals (1982–present); Ian Mosely, drums (1984–present); Steve Hogarth, vocals, keyboards (1989–present)

Taking its name by shortening the title of the J.R.R. Tolkien book "The Silmarillion," Marillion became known for its dramatic art rock presentations, both in concert and on record. Carrying the torch of theatrical progressive music that was abandoned by Genesis after Peter Gabriel left, Marillion made its name with their lengthy, orchestral opuses and spectacle-driven live shows. Fish, a six-foot-six behemoth, clearly emulated Gabriel in both his vocal styling and early stage antics (like Gabriel, he took to wearing face paint for performances). But while the music often evokes Genesis, Marillion managed to carve its own signature sound into the art rock mantle. By the late 80s it was one of the most popular touring acts in the United Kingdom. Internal discord prompted Fish's departure in 1988, which left a substantial vacuum that the remaining band members were hard-pressed to fill. Hogarth proved to be the ideal choice in that he embodied many of Fish's best theatrical qualities, was a strong singer and, perhaps most importantly, sounded nothing like his precursor, thus avoiding backlash for hiring a sound-a-like. Hogarth's arrival marked a gradual shift from the band's Genesis-heavy sound to a leaner template that is still firmly rooted in progressive rock. For his part, Fish led many loyal fans to his solo career, which has flourished in the U.K. but—like Marillion itself—has yet to transcend cult boundaries in America.

what to buy: A record from each vocalist's era is suggested. The album that best defines Fish's tenure with the band is *Misplaced Childhood,* (Capitol, 1985, prod. Chris Kimsey) which gave Marillion their sole U.S. hit, "Kayleigh." Influenced by Gabriel-era Genesis, this is a concept album that draws heavily from Fish's personal history (as the bulk of his material does). In true art rock fashion, the songs segue into one another, creating an extended mood piece in multiple parts. Hogarth's debut, *Season's End,* (Capitol, 1989, prod. Nick Davis and Marillion) retains the band's sense of drama and dynamics, with lengthy songs that start slow and quiet and gradually build to operatic crescendos. Hogarth's more polished vocals, however, clearly set him apart from Fish's raw energy and emotional immediacy.

what to buy next: Fish's final Marillion studio album, *Clutching at Straws,* (Capitol, 1987, prod. Chris Kimsey and Marillion) is a good companion piece to *Misplaced Childhood*, following the chronology of its predecessor by picking up with reflections of Fish's adult life—primarily on his love/hate relationship with alcohol. Marillion's latter-day concept album, *Afraid of Sunlight,* (I.R.S./El Dorado, 1995, prod. Dave Meegan and Marillion) illustrates the extent to which its sound has evolved since Hogarth came on board in 1988. The theme is the toll of celebrity status, with particular attention paid to Elvis Presley, Brian Wilson, John Lennon and O. J. Simpson. The songs "King," "Out of This World" and "Afraid of Sunrise" still bear elements of Marillion's trademark sound, but other cuts explore new territory; "Cannibal Surf Babe" combines Beach Boys-style vocals with a menacing techno beat for an effect that is quite different from anything the band has previously done.

what to avoid: *Holidays in Eden,* (Capitol, 1991, prod. Chris Neil) Hogarth's second outing with Marillion, is something of a hit or miss affair—with a good dose of "miss" taking the spotlight.

the rest: *Script for a Jester's Tear* (Capitol, 1983) *Fugazi* (Capitol, 1984) *Brief Encounter* (Capitol EP, 1986) *B'Sides Themselves* (Capitol, 1988) *The Thieving Magpie (La Gazza Ladra)* (Capitol, 1988) *Brave* (I.R.S./El Dorado, 1994)

worth searching for: Frustratingly, Fish's solo albums are only available as imports. Most are worthwhile and illustrate the singer's creative growth in his years after Marillion, particularly in his broadened lyrical approach and introduction of new music forms. His catalog is well represented by his solo debut, *Virgil in a Wilderness of Mirrors* (EMI, 1989, prod. Fish) and the dual releases *Yin* and *Yang* (both Dick Bros. Records, 1995, prod. Fish) An early Marillion live album, *Real to Reel*, (EMI, 1984) is also worth searching out.

▶▶ Dream Theatre, Dramarama, Queensryche

◀◀ Genesis, Yes, Emerson, Lake & Palmer, King Crimson, Moody Blues

Dave Galens

Bob Marley and the Wailers

Formed 1963 as the Wailin' Wailers in Kingston, Jamaica

Robert Nesta Marley, vocals, guitar (died May 11, 1981 in Miami, Fla.); Peter Tosh (born Winston Hubert McIntosh), vocals, keyboards, guitar (1963-73, died Sept. 11, 1987 in Barbican, St. Andrew, Jamaica); Bunny Wailer (born Neville O'Reilly Livingstone), vocals (1963-73); Rita Marley, vocals (1973-81); Judy Mowatt, vocals (1973-81); Marcia Griffiths, vocals (1973-81); Carlton Barrett, drums (1963-81); Ashton Barrett, bass (1963-81); Touter, keyboards (1972-74); Tyrone Downie, keyboards (1975-81); Al Anderson, guitar (1972-81); Alvin Patterson, percussion (1972-81); Julian "Junior" Marvin, guitar (1972-81); Earl "Wire" Lindo, keyboards (1978-81); Earl Smith, guitar (1974-76)

Marley's is the one name most associated with reggae worldwide, though the original Wailin' Wailers was a more-or-less equal partnership between him, Tosh and Wailer. The Wailers were a moderately successful harmony singing group in Jamaica when they signed with Island records in 1972. The two seminal albums, *Catch A Fire* and *Burnin'* put reggae and rastas, Jamaica and ganja on the international music map with their hard-edged music and uncompromising, socially and spiritually conscious lyrics. When the trio broke up in 1973, Marley took over, added the I-Threes as background singers and embraced a more rock-oriented sound. Marley's raw charisma and brilliant songwriting led to international superstar status no other reggae musician has equalled, though his biggest hit would come in another's hands—Eric Clapton's 1973 cover of "I Shot the Sheriff." Marley became the revolutionary standard bearer rock musicians of the 60s had been. He was given he United Nations Peace Medal in 1978, the same year he coaxed feuding Jamaican presidential candidates to join hands on stage at a concert. Marley died of cancer in 1981, at age 36.

what to buy: *Burnin'* (Island, 1973, prod. Chris Blackwell and the Wailers) features the Wailers' classic harmonies on some of their best material; "Get Up, Stand Up," "I Shot the Sheriff" and "Burnin' and Lootin' " took the world by storm. *Legend* (Tuff Gong/Island, 1984, prod. Various) is a tightly compiled greatest hits set with "No Woman No Cry," "Is This Love" and the lovely acoustic "Redemption Song."

what to buy next: *Babylon By Bus* (Island, 1978 prod. Blackwell and Jack Nuber) captures the Marley charisma at various concerts over a three-year period, particularly on a killer version of "War."

what to avoid: It's not actually bad, but *Kaya* (Island, 1978, prod. Bob Marley and the Wailers) is comprised of some of Marley's most forgettable tunes, except for "Easy Skanking" and "Is This Love."

the rest: *Natty Dread* (Island, 1974) *Live* (Island, 1975) *Rastaman Vibration* (Island, 1976) *Exodus* (Island, 1977) *Survival* (Island, 1979) *Uprising* (Island, 1980) *Confrontation* (Island, 1983) *Rebel Music* (Island, 1986) *Talkin' Blues* (Tuff Gong/Island, 1991) *One Love* (Heartbeat, 1991) *Songs of Freedom* (Tuff Gong/Island, 1992) *Natural Mystic* (Tuff Gong/Island, 1995)

worth searching for: *The Birth of a Legend* (Calla, 1976, prod. C.S. Dodd) features some of the Wailers' 60s work at the legendary Studio One, including the 1964 Jamaican hit "Simmer Down."

▶▶ Ziggy Marley and the Melody Makers, UB40, English Beat, Lucky Dube

◀◀ Skatalites, Desmond Dekker

Lawrence Gabriel

Ziggy Marley & the Melody Makers

Formed 1979 in Kingston, Jamaica

David "Ziggy" Marley, vocals, guitar; Stephen Marley, vocals, percussion; Cedella Marley, vocals; Sharon Marley Prendergast, vocals

Bearing a striking resemblance, both physically and vocally, to his father—reggae icon Bob Marley—has likely been as much a burden as a boone to Ziggy Marley. But he's borne up under it amazingly well, leading a group that includes his brother and two sisters. Their father wrote and produced a single for the group, "Children Playing in the Streets," but the Melody Makers' first two albums suffered from the group's general lack of seasoning and from their record company's focus on making Ziggy a solo star. After moving to Virgin, Ziggy was still out front, but his family's influence and contributions grew on each successive album. While the group leans decidedly towards the pop side of reggae—with considerable influence from American R&B and hip-hop, its lyrics continue in the vein of their late father; cautionary, righteous, but ever optimistic.

what to buy: *Conscious Party* (Virgin, 1988, prod. Chris Frantz and Tina Weymouth) fulfills both parts of its title, with lyrics extolling Rastafarianism and liberation, and grooves that just won't quit. Give credit also to Talking Heads Weymouth and Frantz, whose production makes the group's songs *Jahmakya* (Virgin, 1991, prod. by the Melody Makers and Glenn Rosenstein) is perhaps the groups first truly mature album, with a nod to reggae's past but with an eye more on creating a sound of its own by incorporating riddim-heavy hip-hop and dancehall influences, with a harder rock edge to boot. *Free Like We Want 2 B* (Virgin, 1995, prod. the Melody Makers) finds the rest of the family's involvement at an all-time high; Cedella and Sharon (along with Erica Newell) take the lead on "Today," whole Stephen steps to the fore on a number of tunes.

what to buy next: *One Bright Day* (Virgin, 1989, prod. Ziggy Marley, Glenn Rosenstein, Chris Frantz and Tina Weymouth) hits many of the same targets as *Conscious Party,* but without the same impact. Similarly, *Joy and Blues,* (Virgin, 1993, prod. Ziggy Marley and the Melody Makers) benefits from the advances of *Jahmakya* but doesn't push much beyond.

the rest: *Time Has Come...The Best of Ziggy Marley & the Melody Makers* (EMI America, 1988, prod. Various)

worth searching for: Die-hard fans or collectors can scour the racks for the original Melody Makers releases: *Children Playing* (EMI America, 1984, prod. Steve Levine) *Play the Game Right* (EMI America, 1985, prod. Various) and *Hey World* (EMI America, 1986, prod. Various)

Fugees, Spearhead, Big Mountain

Bob Marley, the Wailers, the Jacksons, New Edition, Earth, Wind and Fire

Daniel Durchholz

Steve Marriott

See: Humble Pie

Chris Mars

See: The Replacements

Martha and the Vandellas

Formed 1962 in Detroit, Mich.

Martha Reeves, lead vocals; Annette Beard, vocals (1962-63); Rosalind Ashford, vocals (1962-69); Betty Kelly, vocals (1963-67); Lois Reeves, vocals (1967-73); Sandra Tilley, vocals (1969-73)

A more emotionally forthright alternative to their chief rivals, The Supremes, the Vandellas were led by Reeves' no-nonsense vocals, making it one of the toughest sounding girl groups of the 60s. Possessing an earthy soulfulness and a street-sass charm, the group recorded a string of propulsive dance hits ("Heatwave," "Dancin' in the Streets," "Quicksand") that stand among some of Motown's finest achievements. Reeves locked horns with Motown and left for a solo career in 1974, though she still performs with different combinations of Vandellas, including Beard and Ashton.

what to buy: *Motown Milestones* (Motown, 1995, prod. Various) is condensed, definitive and cheap, an 18-track collection with all the essential hits—including "Jimmy Mack," "Nowhere to Run," "Heatwave" and "Dancin' in the Streets."

what to buy next: *Live Wire! The Singles 1962-1972.* (Motown, 1993, prod. Various) An excellent two-disc package that has numerous B-sides and non-hit singles in addition to the obvious hits.

what to avoid: *Motown Superstar Series, Vol. 2* (Motown, 1981, prod. Various) is a skimpy 11-track sampler.

the rest: *Heatwave* (Motown, 1963) *Come and Get These Memories* (Motown, 1994/1963) *Greatest Hits* (Motown, 1966)

worth searching for: *Martha Reeves: The Collection* (Object Enterprises, 1986) gathers some of her later, though inferior, material.

The Supremes, the Pointer Sisters, Salt-N-Pepa, TLC

Della Reese

Allan Orski

John Martyn

Born 1948 in Glasgow, Scotland

This singer's husky baritone evokes a huge and sentimental heart. His first recording, *London Conversation,* in 1968, was mostly acoustic; the arrangements were folk-oriented, and the spirit was unabashedly romantic and optimistic. While romantic sentiment remained a focus, optimism could run in short supply. Still, it's a wonder that more people are not aware of Martyn; his strengths include an unusual ear for arranging, finely constructed songs, first-rate lyrics and a compelling voice. His early use of an echoplex (an analog tape loop device) to create cascading and repeating rhythmic and melodic lines was groundbreaking, particularly on *Solid Air* and the title track. Instead of pyrotechnic guitar displays, Martyn embraces an understated style that makes his songs all the more profound. Some of his best moments are during his love songs, which flow like gentle persuasions; "Bless the Weather," "Head and Heart," "Don't Want to Know," "Sweet Little Mystery," "May You Never" and "Couldn't Love You More" are packed with emotion. Although at times he may wear his heart on his sleeve, there is no posturing or indulgence. Sincerity, integrity and originality are fundamental elements in Martyn's work.

what to buy: *Sweet Little Mysteries: The Island Anthology* (Island, 1994, prod. Various) ♪♪♪♪♪ offers most of his memorable work and terrific overview of Martyn's styles and technique.

what to buy next: *No Little Boy* (Mesa/Bluemoon, 1993, prod.Matt Butler) ♪♪♪♪½ comprises 15 newly rendered versions of some of Martyn's best work. It is an unusual project for a performer to re-record his own material, but it's a blessing that Martyn did. These in no way supplant the originals; instead, these are rich and generous re-enactments arranged with a slightly different slant. It's so good that you really can't have one without the other.

what to avoid: *Piece By Piece* (Island, 1986) ♪♪♪ has all of Martyn's usual virtues, but the results are a bit more comfortable than dynamic.

the rest: *Grace and Danger* (Antilles, 1980) ♪♪♪♪ *BBC Radio One* Windsong, 1986/1993) ♪♪♪ *The Apprentice* (Off Beat, 1993) ♪♪♪ *Cooltide* (Off Beat, 1993) ♪♪♪

worth searching for: The out-of-print titles *Solid Air* (Island, 1973) and *Bless the Weather* (Island, 1971), the former for its guitar technique and the latter for its luxurious, jazzy overtones.

▶▶ Eric Clapton, Phil Collins, Robert Palmer, Richard Thompson

◀◀ Tim Hardin, Billie Holiday, Louis Armstrong, Harold Arlen

Patrick McCarty

Richard Marx

Born Sept. 16, 1963 in Chicago, Ill.

Earnest pop craftsmanship isn't necessarily a crime, but sometimes it just doesn't hold up to serious scrutiny or over time. We give you Marx—a guy with a pleasant, mellow image, a bit of a rock 'n' roll jones and a touch for sweeping, romantic balladry. He broke into the business singing backup for Lionel Richie hits (including "All Night Long (All Night)") and writing for Chicago and Kenny Rogers before beginning his own recording career—one that would see numerous smash hits ("Satisfied," "Hold On to the Nights," "Right Here Waiting") that are still waiting for their resurrection in the 80s nostalgia boom. His best outing remains his first, *Richard Marx,* (EMI Manhattan, 1987, prod. David Cole and Richard Marx) ♪♪♪ which is driven by the palpable exuberance of a man finally making his own music—something that comes through on the hits "Should've Known Better" and the Eagles soundalike "Don't Mean Nothing," with Joe Walsh playing slide guitar and Eagles Randy Meisner and Timothy B. Schmit singing backup. After that, Marx churned out nothing more than overly slick piffle.

the rest: *Repeat Offender* (EMI, 1989) ♪♪ *Rush Street* (Capitol/EMI, 1991) ♪♪ *Paid Vacation* (Capitol/EMI, 1994) WOOF!

Gary Graff

Mary Jane Girls

See: Rick James

J Mascis

See: Dinosaur Jr.

Dave Mason

Born May 10, 1946, in Worchester, England

An excellent guitarist with a smoothly distinctive voice that has just enough strain to suggest emotional intensity, Mason quit Traffic in 1968 (returning briefly in 1971) and eventually moved to California. After hooking up with Delaney & Bonnie for their

1969 tour, he went into the studio the next year with them, fellow tour member Leon Russell, Traffic drummer Jim Capaldi and others and made by far his best album, *Alone Together.* The same year he made a forgettable duet album with Cass Elliot of the Mamas and the Papas; in 1971 he appeared in George Harrison's benefit Concert for Bangladesh. But he did little to build on the success of *Alone Together* aside from touring with his crack quartet. Switching to Columbia, his albums appeared more regularly, but the music was so mellow that it left little impression even when it was well done. Despite several catchy tuns on *Let It Flow*, his style had come to seem irrelevant, and in the 80s he could be heard singing in Miller beer commercials. Mason continued touring but has released just one album of new material since 1980. In 1994 he joined the revolving cast of the post-Buckingham/Nicks Fleetwood Mac, joining Delaney & Bonnie's daughter Bekka and performing on the 1995 album *Time*, which includes two songs he co-wrote.

what to buy: *Alone Together* (Blue Thumb, 1970, prod. Tommy Li Puma and Dave Mason) is a bit deficient in the lyric department (always a Mason problem) but offers music so perfect that here, for once, that shortcoming can be overlooked. There's more forward momentum here than on all his Columbia work combined.

what to buy next: Some of Mason's Columbia albums are decent, but *Long Lost Friend: The Best of Dave Mason* (Columbia Legacy, 1995, prod. Various) contains all the high points you'll need.

what to avoid: *The Best of Dave Mason* (Blue Thumb, 1973, prod. Li Puma, Mason) is a shameless rehash of far too much of *Alone Together* when what's really needed is *Headkeeper* and *Dave Mason Is Alive* combined on one CD (they'd fit easily).

the rest: *Dave Mason & Cass Elliot* (Blue Thumb, 1971) *It's Like You Never Left* (Columbia, 1973) *Dave Mason* (Columbia, 1974) *Split Coconut* (Columbia, 1975) *Certified Live* (Columbia, 1976) *Let It Flow* (Columbia, 1977) *Mariposa de Oro* (Columbia, 1978) *Old Crest on a New Wave* (Columbia, 1980) *Two Hearts* (MCA/Voyager, 1988)

worth searching for: The half-studio half-live *Headkeeper* (Blue Thumb, 1972, prod. Tommy Li Puma, Mason) and *Dave Mason Is Alive,* (Blue Thumb, 1972, prod. Li Puma, Mason) may be a bit redundant, but Mark Jordan's electric piano work and Mason's electric guitar solos are very sharp, and both versions of Mason's Traffic classic "Feelin' Alright" cook.

▶▶ Joe Cocker, Delaney & Bonnie

◀◀ The Beatles, Jimi Hendrix, Stephen Stills, Eric Clapton

see also: *Traffic, Delaney & Bonnie*

Steve Holtje

Nick Mason

See: Pink Floyd

Massacre

See: Bill Laswell

Material

See: Bill Laswell

Material Issue

Formed July 4, 1986, in Chicago, Ill.

Jim Ellison, guitar, vocals (died June 20, 1996); Ted Ansani, bass; Mike Zelenko, drums

Material Issue is a Chicago power-pop trio in the tradition of such heartland bands as Cheap Trick and the Shoes. With songs characterized by a devotion to tight harmonies and girls, the group became one of the premiere power-pop bands of the 90s but hasn't grown its audience outside that circle. The group likely ended when frontman and chief songwriter Ellison committed suicide in June 1996.

what to buy: If you like one Material Issue record, you'll probably like 'em all, but *Destination Universe,* (Mercury, 1992, prod. Material Issue and Jeff Murphy) the group's second album, contains its finest moment, the near-hit "What Girls Want," which more likely is what Ellison wished girls wanted ("love, drugs, sex and affection ... Rod Stewart's hair and Keith Richards' stagger").

what to buy next: Material Issue's major label debut, *International Pop Overthrow* (Mercury, 1991, prod. Material Issue and Jeff Murphy) occasionally comes close to revolution promised in the title, but there's something of a traditionalist bent when four songs feature girls' names in the titles (i.e., "Valerie Loves Me," "Renee Remains the Same").

what to avoid: *Freak City Soundtrack* (Mercury, 1994, prod. Mike Chapman) doesn't quite measure up to the group's first two albums, despite assistance from former Sweet producer Chapman. Sometimes it sounds as though the trio is going for the big-success sounds of other power-pop acts such as the Gin Blossoms. Guitarists Rick Nielsen (Cheap Trick) and Gilby Clarke (Guns N' Roses) guest.

the rest: *Material Issue* (Big Block/Landmind, 1987)

worth searching for: This trio has contributed fun covers to a number of compilations, among them Sweet's "Little Willy" on *20 Explosive Dynamic Super Smash Hit Explosions!* (Pravda, 1991, prod. Phil Bonnet) and "The Tra La La Song (One Banana, Two Banana)" with Liz Phair on *Saturday Morning Cartoon's Greatest Hits* (MCA, 1995, prod. Material Issue and Jeff Murphy)

Sweet, the Hollies, Big Star

Brian Mansfield

Dave Matthews Band

Formed 1991 in Charlottesville, N.C.

Dave Matthews, vocals, acoustic guitars; Boyd Tinsley, violin; LeRoi Moore, saxophone; Stefan Lessard, bass; Carter Beauford, drums

Among the bands poised to become "the next Grateful Dead" following the 1995 the death of Jerry Garcia, the Dave Matthews Band (DMB) had already shown it could stand on its own with the independently released live album *Remember Two Things* (Bama Rags, 1993, prod. John Alagia) and with its debut studio album, the multi-million selling *Under the Table and Dreaming.* (RCA, 1994, prod. Steve Lillywhite) Blending the sensibilities of world beat, jazz, folk and pop—as well as fierce jamming skills—DMB scored a string of hits that included the sweet, acoustic "Satellite," the funk-driven "What Would You Say" and the sprightly "Ants Marching." Matthews shares his sexier and darker side on the follow-up, *Crash.* (RCA, 1996, prod. Steve Lillywhite) Louder and more aggressive, *Crash* swerves through a collage of country, funk and pop before closing with "Proudest Monkey," an ode to Matthews start as a bartender in Charlottesville, Va.

Christina Fuoco

Eric Matthews

Born 1970 in Gresham, Ore.

Matthews lives in the Pacific Northwest and records for Sub Pop Records, but sounds nothing at all like the stereotype that implies. A classically trained trumpet player, Matthews is instead an old-school pop craftsman of the highest order. He first gained notice as half of the duo Cardinal with Richard Davies, former leader of the Australian band the Moles. The one album they made together,*Cardinal,* (Flydaddy, 1994, prod. Not Listed) was a well-wrought pop record. But that was just a warm-up for Matthews' incredible solo debut, *It's Heavy in Here.* (Subpop, 1995, prod. Eric Matthews) Picking up where the Beatles' "Penny Lane" left off, Matthews evokes the golden age of mid-60s English rock, when pop and psychedelia were beginning to mingle. The album's 14 songs have dry, spare arrangements, with each instrument clearly defined and hooks that just won't quit. Matthews' muted trumpet is the perfect embellishment to his own languid croon, and the multi-instrumental contributions from ex-Jellyfish guitarist Jason Falkner are likewise impeccable. Except for some of the lyrics' hippie-dippie psychobabble ("Trip out on long lost time" and so forth), *It's Heavy in Here* is just about flawless.

David Menconi

Matthews Southern Comfort

See: Iain Matthews

Iain Matthews /Matthews Southern Comfort/Plainsong/Hamilton's Pool

Born Iain Matthew MacDonald, June 16, 1946 in Lincolnshire, England

Matthews has had two careers, really. The first began during the late 60s when he co-founded the influential British folk group Fairport Convention. He left Fairport after two records and in 1970 started Matthews Southern Comfort, which recorded three albums and had a Top 40 hit with Joni Mitchell's "Woodstock" (a year after Crosby, Stills & Nash's version had charted). In 1971, Matthews embarked on a moderately successful and quite prolific solo career as a singer (and occasional songwriter) of easygoing folk/country-pop songs; he released 10 albums in 10 years, plus a couple with the singers' collective Plainsong. Matthews then vanished from the record bins for eight years, though he spent some time in Seattle playing in a band called Hi-Fi with David Surkamp. His second career began in 1988 with the release of *Walking A Changing Line,* an album of Jules Shear covers that was Windham Hill's first all-vocal project. Counting various retrospectives and live collections, Matthews has released an amazing 12 records since then, including a new disc with a reunited Plainsong and a one-off with a band called Hamilton's Pool (named after a swimming hole just outside Austin, Texas, where Matthews has lived since 1990).

what to buy: CD retrospective collections have been a welcome development for both Matthews and his fans, as his extensive 70s catalog is rather spotty in quality. *The Soul Of Many Places: The Elektra Years, 1972-1974* (Elektra, 1993, prod. Iain Matthews, Michael Nesmith and Sandy Roberton) gathers the best tracks from what was probably his strongest artistic period; included are richly melodic covers of classics such as Tom Waits' "Ol' 55" and Jesse Winchester's "Biloxi," as well as Matthews' own hauntingly beautiful "For the Second Time" and "You Fell Through My Mind." Documenting the best tracks from a slightly earlier period in his career is *The Best of Matthews Southern Comfort* (MCA, 1992, prod. Various) As for actual albums, his most recent efforts are his best; their cohesiveness reveals a significant artistic growth from the hit-and-miss nature of his 70s records. Particularly strong is *The Dark Ride* (Watermelon, 1994, prod. Mark Hallman) a close second is *Skeleton Keys* (Mesa, 1992, prod. Mark Hallman)

what to buy next: *Walking A Changing Line* (Windham Hill, 1988, prod. Mark Hallman) is an intriguing attempt to bring mainstream accessibility to the brilliant pop songs of Jules Shear, though the record didn't quite live up to its potential. Also of interest to serious fans are four collections of demos and live tracks from throughout Matthews' career: *Orphans and Outcasts Vol. I: Demos 1969-1979* (Dirty Linen, 1991) *Orphans and Outcasts Vol. II: Demos 1981-1989* (Dirty Linen, 1993) *Intimate Wash* (Perfect Pitch, 1993) and *Camouflage* (Perfect Pitch, 1996)

what to avoid: *Stealin' Home* (Mushroom, 1978) contains "Shake It," Matthews' highest-charting hit single to date, but that song is also one of the shallowest things he's ever recorded and is indicative of the lack of creativity in his late 70s work—which likely led to his extended sabbatical during the 80s.

the rest: *If You Saw Thro' My Eyes* (Vertigo, 1971) *Tigers Will Survive* (Vertigo, 1972) *Valley Hi* (Elektra, 1973) *Some Days You Eat The Bear And Some Days The Bear Eats You* (Elektra, 1974) *Journeys From Gospel Oak* (Mooncrest, 1974) *Go For Broke* (Columbia, 1976) *Hit And Run* (Columbia, 1977) *Siamese Friends* (Mushroom, 1979) *Spot Of Interference* (RSO, 1980) *Pure And Crooked* (Gold Castle, 1990) Matthews Southern Comfort—*Matthews Southern Comfort* (Sire, 1970) *Second Spring* (Decca, 1970) *Later That Same Year* (Decca, 1970) Plainsong: *In Search Of Amelia Earhart* (Elektra, 1972) *Plainsong II* (Elektra, 1972) *Dark Side Of The Room* (Mesa, 1993) Hamilton's Pool: *Return To Zero* (Watermelon, 1995) God Looked Down (Watermelon, 1996) not available for rating

see also: *Fairport Convention*

▶▶ Seals & Crofts, England Dan & John Ford Coley, America

◀◀ Simon & Garfunkel, Peter & Gordon, Jimmy Webb

Peter Blackstock

Brian May

See: Queen

John Mayall

Born Nov. 29, 1933, in Macclesfield, England

Two truths about singer-harmonica player John Mayall: He's a survivor, and he's got a keen ear for talent. Mayall was a seminal force in the early British blues scene that produced so many great and influential artists, most notably Eric Clapton. Ol' Slow Hand was working construction after leaving the Yardbirds, a young British rock band that was just starting to have commercial success, when Mayall made him one of his Bluesbreakers, in which Clapton really established his name as one of the preeminent guitarists on the scene. Mayall fronted the Bluesbreakers until the 80s, and the roster of artists who passed through the group reads like a who's who of British blues-rock: Mick Taylor (Rolling Stones); John McVie, Mick Fleetwood and Peter Green (Fleetwood Mac); Colin Allen; Jimmy McCulloch (Wings); Jack Bruce (Cream); journeyman Aynsley Dunbar; and countless others. Mayall is considered one of the fathers of the 60s British blues movement, but, unlike his peer, the late Alexis Korner, Mayall was able to make it beyond the small clubs to become a star, releasing some of the most consistent, faithful blues records on either side of the Atlantic. Mayall's longevity—he's still recording and touring and discovering new talent well into his 60s—is attributable largely to his ability to redefine the blues, finding new and challenging ways to interpret and expand the American music he loves so dearly.

what to buy: If ever an artist cried out for a box set, Mayall's him. But there is no such thing, so you're better off checking out a few albums that represent important phases in Mayall's career. *Bluesbreakers—John Mayall with Eric Clapton* (Deram, 1966, prod. Mike Vernon) captures the legendary singer and guitarist in one of their earliest and grittiest phases (there's a more expensive Mobile Fidelity gold disc version that offers improved sound; the recordings are pretty raw). *The Turning Point* (Deram, 1969, prod. John Mayall) is an all-acoustic affair (no drums, even) that included his harmonica showcase "Room to Move." *Archives to Eighties* (Deram, 1988, prod. John Mayall) is an unusual and successful late 80s restoration of his 1971 *Back to the Roots* album, which featured Clapton and Taylor. Mayall spruced up the drums, added some new material and essentially came up with a new and fresh-sounding record.

what to buy next: The mid-70s to 80s were mostly fallow for Mayall, who had fallen out of favor with blues and rock fans. But he hung in there and in 1990 came up with one of the most assured and eloquent sets of blues-rock in his career. *A Sense of Place* (Island, 1990, prod. R.S. Field) is a little more slick than his fans are used to, but Mayall's wizened vocals and smart song selection proved that the blues don't have to be raw or formulaic.

what to avoid: *Behind the Iron Curtain* (GNP/Crescendo, 1985) is a good idea—it was recorded in Hungary—but not a particularly thrilling or memorable live album.

the rest: *A Hard Road* (Deram, 1967) *Crusade* (Deram, 1967) *Raw Blues* (Polydor, 1967) *Diary of a Band, Vol. 1* (London, 1968) *Diary of a Band, Vol. 2* (London, 1968) *Blues Alone* (Deram, 1968) *Bare Wires* (Rebound, 1968) *Blues From Laurel Canyon* (Deram, 1968) *Looking Back* (Deram, 1968) *Empty Rooms* (Polydor, 1969) *USA Union* (Polydor, 1970) *Memories* (Polydor, 1971) *Jazz Blues Fusion* (Polydor, 1972) *Thru the Years* (Deram, 1972) *New Year, New Band, New Company*MDBR *(One Way, 1975)* Notice to Appear *(One Way, 1976)* The Last of the British Blues *(One Way, 1978)* Primal Solos *(Deram, 1988)* A Banquet of Blues *(One Way, 1976)* Lots of People *(One Way, 1977)* A Hard Core Package *(One Way, 1977)* Return of John Mayall *(Aim, 1982)* Chicago Line *(Island, 1988)* John Mayall: London Blues, 1964-1969 *(Polydor, 1992)* John Mayall: Room to Move, 1969-74 *(Polydor, 1992)* Wake Up Call *(Silvertone, 1993)* Cross Country Blues, *(One Way, 1994)* The 1982 Reunion Concert *(One Way, 1994)* Spinning Coin *(Silvertone, 1995)*

worth searching for: Mayall's first album, *John Mayall Plays John Mayall* (Decca, 1965) was released in England but never made it to these shores, except as an import.

10 Blues Albums Every Rock Fan Should Own

Showdown
Albert Collins, Robert Cray and Johnny Copeland (Alligator, 1985)

The Ultimate Collection 1948-90
John Lee Hooker (Rhino, 1991)

The Sky is Crying: The History of Elmore James
(Rhino, 1993)

Thursday Night in San Francisco
Albert King (Stax, 1990)

Live at the Regal
B.B. King (MCA, 1971)

West Side Soul
Magic Sam (Delmark, 1968)

Blues of the Month Club
Joe Louis Walker (Verve, 1995)

T-Bone Blues
T-bone Walker (Atlantic, 1959)

Best of Muddy Waters
(Chess/MCA, 1987)

Moanin in the Moonlight/Howlin' Wolf
Howlin' Wolf (Chess/MCA, 1964)

▶▶ The Rolling Stones, Savoy Brown, Foghat, the Fabulous Thunderbirds, Blues Traveler

◀◀ Muddy Waters, Little Walter, Howlin' Wolf

see also: *Eric Clapton, the Rolling Stones, Cream, the Yardbirds*

Doug Pullen

Curtis Mayfield /The Impressions

Formed 1957 in Chicago, Ill.

Curtis Mayfield (born June 3, 1942, in Chicago, Ill.) guitar, vocals, mu-

sical director (1957-1970); Jerry Butler, vocals (1957-59); Arthur Brooks, vocals (1957-61); Richard Brooks, vocals (1957-61); Sam Gooden, vocals; Fred Cash, vocal (1958-present); Leroy Hutson, vocals (1970-73); Reggie Torrian, vocals (1973-present); Ralph Johnson, vocals (1973-80); Nate Evans, vocals (1980-present)

Mayfield got his chance to lead the Impressions and made the best of it when Butler left the group in 1959 after a handful of hits such as "For Your Precious Love." Mayfield's songwriting, engaging vocals and spare arrangements led the group to an early and mid-60s peak with hits such as "Gypsy Woman" and "I'm So Proud." Unlike many soul artists during the early part of the decade, Mayfield's themes embraced civil rights sentiments; "People Get Ready" and "Choice of Colors" set a musical agenda long before its artists forced Motown to address social issues. Mayfield started his own Curtom label in 1968 for Impressions releases and wrote hits for Major Lance, Jerry Butler and others. He left the Impressions for a solo career in 1970, though he continued to manage the group, and reached the height of fame with his score for the 1972 movie "Superfly"—a gritty souladelic tour de force that yielded the hits "Freddy's Dead," "Pusherman" and the title track. Mayfield even performed in the movie as the leader of a local bar band. Though he began to lose form in the mid-70s, Mayfield stands as a giant of soul music as a songwriter, singer, arranger, producer and label owner. His performing career ended tragically in 1990, when some stage lights fell on him and left him a quadriplegic.

what to buy: Mayfield was never better than on *Superfly,* (Curtom, 1972, prod. Curtis Mayfield) 🦴🦴🦴🦴🦴 where his falsetto cut through visions of ghetto life like a stiletto blade in a street fight. The wah-wah guitar that drives through this album is exemplary proto-funk. His Impressions' tenure—as well as some of his solo highlights, are captured on *Curtis Mayfield and the Impressions: The Anthology 1961-1977,* (MCA, 1992, prod. Various) 🦴🦴🦴🦴½

what to buy next: The three-disc boxed set *People Get Ready* (Rhino, 1996, prod. Various) 🦴🦴🦴🦴🦴 covers the whole spectrum, from the Impressions to 70s hits such as "Kung Fu" and "Billy Jack." The liner notes include reflections from proteges such as Stevie Wonder, Don Cornelius and George Clinton, in addition to an interview with Mayfield.

what to avoid: Taking on longer forms and conceptual compositions didn't serve Mayfield well on *There's No Place Like America Today,* (Curtom, 1975, prod. Curtis Mayfield) 🦴🦴½ which features preachy raps on themes not conducive to partying.

the rest: *The Impressions Greatest Hits* (MCA, 1965) 🦴🦴🦴🦴 *Groots* (1971, Curtom) 🦴🦴🦴🦴 *Curtis In Chicago* (Charly, 1973) 🦴🦴🦴 *Of All Time* (Curtom, 1974) 🦴🦴🦴🦴 *Do It All Night* (Curtom, 1978) 🦴🦴🦴½ *Living Legend: Heartbeat* (Curtom, 1979, prod. Various) 🦴🦴🦴🦴 (1995, Curtom) 🦴🦴🦴🦴 *Curtis Mayfield's Chicago Soul* (Legacy, 1995) 🦴🦴🦴🦴

worth searching for: *Heartbeat* (Curtom, 1979, prod. Various) 🦴🦴🦴🦴 finds Mayfield in a disco mode with dance floor grooves such as "Tell Me, Tell Me (How Ya Like To Be Loved)."

solo outings:

Jerry Butler: The Best of Jerry Butler (Rhino, 1987) 🦴🦴🦴🦴

⏩ Seal, Maxwell, D'Angelo, Tony Rich

⏪ The Drifters, the Soul Stirrers

Lawrence Gabriel

Mazzy Star

Formed 1989 in Los Angeles, Calif.

David Roback, guitar; Hope Sandoval, vocals

Formed by former Rain Parade member Roback and Sandoval of Going Home, Mazzy Star has a psychedelic, folk sound. *She Hangs Brightly* (Capitol, 1990, prod. David Roback) 🦴🦴🦴 is a collection of slow, dreamy songs characterized by Sandoval's detached, cold delivery. *So Tonight That I Might See* (Capitol, 1993, prod. David Roback) 🦴🦴🦴🦴 is better, with a warmer, otherwordly quality and the beautiful hit "Fade Into You."

Anna Glen

MC 900 Foot Jesus

Formed 1988 in Dallas, Texas

Mark Griffin; DJ Zero, mixer

MC 900 Foot Jesus, named for the vision Oral Roberts claimed to have had, started as the brainchild of record store clerk Griffin. While working at one of Dallas' best-known independent stores, Griffin started collaborating with local mixer DJ Zero, combining his own interest in the avant-garde post-industrial music of the time with Zero's rap and hip-hop interests. What resulted was one of the first bands to consolidate these two forms of music into something entirely new. Quickly signed to the respectable Canadian Nettwerk Records, Griffin and Zero started releasing singles that were instant club hits. Griffin and Zero later parted ways, but his impact on Griffin's musical sensibilities is still felt on the most recent releases. Streetwise and cocky, MC900 Foot Jesus combines the best elements from Front 242 and Skinny Puppy with Public Enemy and Boo-Ya Tribe; while not technically prone to the American form of rap, Griffin could easily pass as European. His vocals have a quirky narrative style that can sound like a disembodied voice or someone screaming. Griffin rarely sings in the traditional sense; he just talks to you over thumping music. While the band's first effort, *To Hell with the Lid Off*, (Nettwerk/IRS, 1989) lacks a range of style and leaves the listener feeling like he or she should be in a club to enjoy it, Griffin begins coming into his own on *Welcome to My Dream* (Nettwerk/IRS, 1991) The album displays more dynamics and proves Griffin is a competent songwriter—particularly on the eerie "While the City Sleeps," a narrative that tracks the nightly rounds of an arsonist. Griffin shows off his comical prowess on *One Step Ahead of the Spider*, (Nettwerk/IRS, 1994) his twisted sarcasm is especially keen on "If I Only Had a Brain." For more MC900 Foot Jesus, check the import bins; remixes, EPs and singles are available as Canadian and British imports only.

Tim Davis

Paul McCartney /Wings

Born June 18, 1942, Liverpool, England

Wings (1971-81): Denny Laine, guitar, vocals, Linda McCartney, keyboards, vocals; Denny Seiwell, drums (1971-73); Henry McCullough, guitar (1972-73); Geoff Britton, drums (1974); Joe English, drums (1974-76); Jimmy McCulloch, guitar (1974-76); Laurence Juber, guitar, vocals, 1978-81); Steve Holly, drums (1978-81)

The most steadily active former Beatle, McCartney also seems the most frustrated at his inability to consistently top the group that gave him his fame, although he has most certainly been the most commercially successful on his own. As the Beatle who officially announced the breakup of the band as a way to plug his first solo album, he was the first to benefit from the fallout (although all the other band members by then had released solo turns). While *McCartney* was an interesting notebook of leftover Beatles ditties (some of which the band had considered), he hoped to lose himself in the anonymity of the band Wings, which had its ups and down but was never considered anything but a McCartney project. Because its hit singles were almost always upbeat, fluff, he was dismissed as the airhead yin to John Lennon's more serious and politicized yang. Disbanded in 1981, Wings made way for some spectacular McCartney flops, including a film ("Give My Regards to Broad Street") and a financial slip (he saw his two-time duet partner Michael Jackson buy the rights to the Beatles publishing from under him). McCartney buckled down and even met a co-writer for the first time in Elvis Costello to bolster a pair of albums in the late 80s and early 90s, which formed the basis for two successful world tours that saw him embracing more and more Beatles material. By 1991, he even tried his hand at classical music in the "Liverpool Oratorio" which, because of his fame, at least got performed quite a bit for a new piece of serious music.

what to buy: Wings' *Band on the Run* (Apple, 1974, prod. Paul McCartney) was the best conceived, least embarrassing album of McCartney's solo career. With just he, Linda and Laine comprising the band, it was recorded in Nigeria, where the rhythms helped give the tunes a sunny disposition. *Choba B CCCP - The Russian Album* (Melodiya, 1988/Capitol, 1991, prod. Paul McCartney) is a freewheeling album of American rock oldies that's as relaxed as McCartney has ever sounded since the Beatles split.

what to buy next: *McCartney* (Apple, 1970, prod. Paul McCartney) is an intriguing notebook of works in progress—some of which, including "Maybe I'm Amazed" turned out to be among his more fully realized post-Beatles tunes. *Ram* (Apple, 1971, prod. Paul and Linda McCartney) is credited to Paul and Linda McCartney, so you'll have to discount "Queen of the Kitchen" to accept more fully formed pop tunes from the hubby. Fluff, sure, but darn catchy fluff. *Flowers in the Dirt* (Capitol, 1989, prod. Various) showed a serious intent—as well as some of the first fruits of his collaborations with Costello—that signaled a near-return to form.

what to avoid: It's a battle, but *Press to Play*, (Capitol, 1986, prod. Paul McCartney and Hugh Padgham) **WOOF!** without a single hit, was probably the low point.

the rest: *McCartney II* (Columbia, 1980) *Tug of War* (Columbia, 1982) *Pipes of Peace* (Columbia, 1983) *Give My Regards to Broad Street* (Columbia, 1984) *All The Best* (Capitol, 1987) *Tripping the Live Fantastic* (Capitol, 1990) *Tripping the Live Fantastic—Highlights!* (Capitol, 1990) *Liverpool Oratorio* (EMI Classics, 1991, prod. John Fraser) *Off the Ground* (Capitol, 1993) *Paul is Live* (Capitol, 1993) (with Wings): *Wild Life* (Apple, 1971) *Red Rose Speedway* (Apple, 1973) *Venus and Mars* (Capitol, 1975) *Wings at the Speed of Sound* (Capitol, 1976) *Wings Over America* (Capitol, 1976) *London Town* (Capitol, 1978)

𝄞𝄞 *Wings Greatest* (Capitol, 1978) 𝄞𝄞𝄞 *Back to the Egg* (Columbia, 1979) 𝄞

worth searching for: *Unplugged*, (Capitol, 1991, prod. Paul McCartney and Geoff Emerick) 𝄞𝄞𝄞 a limited edition album meant to fend off bootleggers. It has some wonderful renditions of McCartney's best material.

⏩ Oasis, Blur, Jellyfish

⏪ Fats Domino, Jim Mac Jazz Band, Eddie Cochran, Buddy Holly, Elvis Presley, George and Ira Gershwin, Sammy Cahn

Roger Catlin

Kathy McCarty /Glass Eye

Formed 1983 in Austin, Texas. Disbanded 1993.

Kathy McCarty (born Feb. 1, 1961 in Stamford, Conn.), vocals, guitar; Brian Beattie, bass; Scott Marcus, drums (1985-86, 1989-93); Stella Weir, vocals, keyboards 1985-86, 1989-93); Dave Cameron, drums, (1986-89); Sheri Lane, vocals, keyboards, (1986-89)

McCarty, a terrific guitarist who seems to hear melodies slightly more bent than other musicians, was the heart of the Austin, Texas, indie band Glass Eye. The band was deliberately skronky—fretless bassist Beattie set typically bizarre, hard-to-follow rhythms—and never managed to build more than a loyal cult following in Austin despite some terrificly twisted pop songs, including "Christine." At one point, singer-songwriter Daniel Johnston went to a show, gave McCarty a tape of his *Hi, How Are You* album and begged to open concerts for them. The connection led to much creative respect between Johnston and McCarty, and after Glass Eye broke up in 1993, the singer-songwriter put out a masterpiece comprised of Johnston's songs.

what to buy: McCarty's brilliant *Dead Dog's Eyeball* (Bar/None, 1994, prod. Brian Beattie and Kathy McCarty) 𝄞𝄞𝄞𝄞 tools Johnston's "Sorry Entertainer," "Like a Monkey in a Zoo" "Rocket Ship" and "Hey Joe" so that they sound purely rocking instead of purely eccentric.

what to buy next: The best Glass Eye albums, *Bent by Nature* (Bar/None-Restless, 1988, prod. Brian Beattie) 𝄞𝄞𝄞 and *Christine*. (Bar/None-Restless EP, 1989, prod. Brian Beattie) 𝄞𝄞𝄞 Both are the works of a retooled band and that employs a (decently) straightforward rock attack.

what to avoid: The *Marlo* EP (No label, 1985) 𝄞𝄞 shows the band, while talented, still trying to come up with a sound and meandering behind McCarty's then-unfocused voice.

the rest: *Hello Young Lovers* (Bar/None-Restless, 1989) 𝄞𝄞

worth searching for: *Sorry Entertainer* (Bar/None EP, 1995, prod. Various) 𝄞𝄞𝄞 includes a couple of the best tracks from "Dead Dog's Eyeball" and the unreleased Glass Eye track "Exodus Song."

⏩ Yo La Tengo, Dead Milkmen

⏪ Daniel Johnston, Minutemen, Raincoats, Robyn Hitchcock, Sonic Youth, Talking Heads

Steve Knopper

Scott McCaughey

See: Young Fresh Fellows

Country Joe McDonald

See: Country Joe and the Fish

Michael McDonald

See: The Doobie Brothers

John McEuen

See: Nitty Gritty Dirt Band

MC5

Formed 1965 in Lincoln Park, Mich. Disbanded 1972.

Rob Tyner (died Sept. 17, 1991), vocals; Wayne Kramer, guitar; Fred "Sonic" Smith (died Nov. 4, 1994), guitar; Michael Davis, bass; Dennis Thompson, drums

The MC5 were so concerned with social revolution—although it was never entirely clear what they were revolting for—that it forgot to follow through with the musical revolution. For a while, the band's rock 'n' roll was as explosive as its Detroit-area brethren, including Bob Seger's early punk experiments (don't laugh), Ted Nugent's rambling metallic guitar and Iggy Pop's onstage self-destruction. The MC5's social figurehead was White Panther John Sinclair, who was always screaming about something, but the band was best known for its enduring anthem, "Kick Out the Jams," which even today has the power to make young people run amok in a room full of speakers. After that, the band's work is much more sporadic—the rest of the album *Kick Out the Jams* is incoherent and spacey. *Back in the U.S.A.* is much more interesting, if far under-produced, with 50s-style Chuck Berry rock 'n' roll and compact guitar solos that later inspired Television, Richard Hell, the Sex Pistols, X and Black Flag. Where the punks picked up on the Velvet Underground and the Stooges' overall social-musical legacy, the MC5's meager contributions were one amazing song and a couple of impressive guitar solos. After the group broke up, Tyner became a songwriter and photographer before dying of a heart attack. Smith toured briefly with Iggy Pop before forming his own band, Sonics Rendezvous and marrying punk songstress Patti Smith; he died in 1994 from heart failure. Kramer, who spent some time in prison for cocaine dealing, resumed his career in 1995, with powerful multi-sourced rock that both recalls and steps beyond the work of his old band.

what to buy: *Back in the U.S.A.* (Atlantic, 1970/Rhino, 1992, prod. Jon Landau) sounds tinny and bassless, but its rehashing of Elvis Presley and Chuck Berry sensibilities and its theme of "Teenage Lust" is wonderful in its simplicity.

what to buy next: *Kick Out the Jams* (Elektra, 1969, prod. Jac Holzman and Bruce Botnick) is worth buying for the title track, "Ramblin' Rose" and "Motor City Is Burning," three key songs in the big-guitar-riff Detroit hard-rock tradition.

what to avoid: *High Time* (Atlantic, 1971/Rhino, 1992, prod. MC5 and Geoffrey Haslam) contains "Poison" and a few other too-long, unmemorable pre-metal songs.

worth searching for: The *Babes In Arms* cassette (ROIR, 1983, prod. Various) is a winning hodgepodge that contains "Kick Out the Jams," some best-of stuff from the three studio albums and a few live tracks.

solo outings:

***Wayne Kramer:** The Hard Stuff* (Epitaph, 1995) *Dangerous Madness* (Epitaph, 1996)

▶▶ Modern Lovers, Alice Cooper, the Sex Pistols, Black Flag, Bad Brains, Presidents of the United States of America, Kiss, Rollins Band, Motörhead, Metallica, Slayer, Guns N' Roses

◀◀ The Rolling Stones, the Velvet Underground, the Stooges, Bob Seger, the Amboy Dukes, Chuck Berry, the New York Dolls, Mitch Ryder & the Detroit Wheels, John Coltrane

Steve Knopper

Kate and Ann McGarrigle

Born 1944 (Kate) and 1946 (Anna) in St. Sauveur, Montreal, Canada

These Canadian sisters gained critical attention with their mid-70s releases because they played a perfectly pitched type of folksy music that combined their beautifully trilling vocals with a wide-eyed sensual purity that was downright refreshing at a time when punk rock was fermenting (the Patti Smith Group's debut came out the same year as the McGarrigles'), FM radio album rock was bottoming out and rock was becoming a pop commodity. As an antidote, here were two intelligent, whimsical and decidedly quirky women who wrote often-witty, often-wrenching songs that shot straight for the heartstrings without a hint of cheap hamming. In fact, it was songwriting that snared the McGarrigles their record deal after Maria Muldaur recorded "Work Song" and Linda Ronstadt covered "Heart Like a Wheel." Unfortunately, their own records—liberally laced with the wheezy, evocative fiddles and accordions of their French-Canadian culture (and songs sung in French)—never were meant to be huge hits. After a couple of fabulous efforts, the songwriting was obscured in efforts to "produce" them for better commercial advantage. But those efforts failed, of course, and the McGarrigles disappeared from the scene for the better part of a decade (a couple of their albums are out of print and have not been re-released on CD; *French Record* collects all the songs over their discography recorded in French). Their 1990 "comeback" release, *Heartbeats Accelerating,* was a beautiful, though emotionally downbeat, return. Fans are still waiting for the next chapter.

what to buy: *Dancer with Bruised Knees* (Hannibal, 1977, prod. Joe Boyd) remains a thrilling recorded moment that transcends its period despite (or because of) its fearless use of goofy sonic elements, from a cornball voice-over on the opening title track to oompah music. Country, gospel and rock all come into play, and songs such as "No Biscuit Blues," "Be My Baby," "Kitty Come Home" are all indelible melodies written with the very rare combination of smart, funny and touching lyrics.

what to buy next: *Kate & Anna McGarrigle* (Hannibal, 1975, prod. Joe Boyd) got rave reviews upon its release, but its songs don't have the timeless ring that the material on *Dancer* does. But it's a startling record for its time, featuring "Heat Like a Wheel" and a lively take of Loudon Wainwright III's hilarious "Swimming Song" (Kate was married to Wainwright).

the rest: *French Record* (Hannibal, 1980) *Heartbeats Accelerating* (Private Music, 1990)

The Roches, Iris DeMent, Nanci Griffith

Carter Family, Joni Mitchell, Maria Muldaur

Gil Asakawa

McGuinn, Clark and Hillman

See: The Byrds

Barry McGuire

Born Oct. 15, 1935, in Oklahoma City, Okla.

The folk-rock protest hit "Eve of Destruction" earned McGuire his first and only hit in 1965. A Dylan knockoff, the song featured McGuire trumpeting the certain doom that awaited us all. Trouble is, the apocalypse only comes ... what, once? That didn't leave much for an encore, and he sank into drug addiction before emerging as a born-again Christian singer during the 70s. Besides "Eve," *The Barry McGuire Anthology* (One Way, 1994, comp. Terry Wachsmuth) contains a number of predictable Dylan covers. And with titles such as "Why Not Stop & Dig it While You Can?" it's probably more McGuire than you need to know.

Allan Orski

Maria McKee

See: Lone Justice

Sarah McLachlan

Born Jan. 28, 1968 Halifax, Nova Scotia, Canada

Sarah McLachlan, grew up in Halifax, Nova Scotia, studying classical guitar and piano. At the age of 17, Nettwerk Records took notice—particularly of her stunning, dramatic vocals that tiptoe between her normal range, a throaty push and a soprano falsetto (kind of like Enya without sounding too New Agey). McLachlan mixes that with an ethereal combination of layered guitars, keyboards and ambient percussion, while her lyrics create almost visual images out of feelings and emtions. It's a unique sound that's allowed McLachlan to stand apart from the scores of female singers that long-negligent labels brought to the pop mainstream during the mid-90s. Her second album, *Solace,* (Arista/Nettwerk, 1991, prod. Pierre Marchand) is the deepest and most mesmerizing of her three releases, from the ambient-Celtic-folk mix of "Drawn to the Rhythm" to the gutsy guitar drive of "Into the Fire." *Fumbling Towards Ecstasy* (Arista/Nettwerk, 1993, prod. Pierre Marchand) adds some dance rhythms, drum machines and a more straightforward pop tone to the songs, while *Touch* (Arista/Nettwerk, 1988, prod. Greg Reely) —despite gems such as "Vox" and "Ben's Song"—is definitely the work of a 20-year-old who hasn't quite caught her stride yet. *Live* (Arista/Nettwerk, 1992) covers mostly "Solace" songs and shows McLachlan can replicate all the textures and layers of her studio albums onstage. Multimedia fans should check out *The Freedom Sessions,* (Arista/Nettwerk, 1994) an eight-song EP featuring alternate versions of her songs, a cover of Tom Waits' "Ol' 55" and CD-ROM footage of interviews, videos and concerts.

Joshua Zarov

Ian McLaglan

See: The Faces

Malcolm McLaren

Born Jan. 22, 1946, in London, England

Known more for his canny opportunist posturing as the Sex Pistols' manager than for his musical contributions, McClaren manipulated several less controversial acts (Adam and the Ants, Bow Wow Wow) before taking matters into his own non-musical but foxy hands. He has since exploited the marketplace numerous times to varying degrees of success, but never without the stamp of his looming presence. *Fans* (Island, 1984, prod. Various) melds opera with rap in an unholy but clever union, particularly his nutso take on "Madam Butterfly." *Duck Rock* (Island, 1984, prod. Trevor Horn) takes hip-hop and African music to novel "heights" in the dance-junk of "Buffalo Gals" and "Double Dutch;" of course, he didn't give proper credit to his sources, further tainting his charlatan image.

the rest: *Paris* (Island, 1984) *Waltz Darling* (Epic, 1989)

Allan Orski

Pat McLaughlin

Born Sept. 28, 1950 in Waterloo, Iowa

Southern white soul has seldom sounded this good. McLaughlin, a Nashville-based singer-songwriter, can bring to mind Van Morrison and Aaron Neville with his emotional voice, and John Hiatt with his smart songs. He even had a kickass band for the debut record and tour, which featured former Rockpile guitarist Billy Bremner. Capitol signed him with all the fanfare of a star-to-be, and *Pat McLaughlin* (Capitol, 1988, prod. Mitchell Froom) delivers the goods with some of his best songs and most soulful singing.

The label couldn't promote him well after the debut, though, and McLaughlin almost fell victim to the dreaded record-industry purgatory syndrome. The label wouldn't let him release his follow-up, *Get Out and Stay Out* (dos/Capitol, 1995, prod. Mitchell Froom) —which finally came out in 1995, although early copies had been sent to some critics on cassette for a mostly favorable word of mouth. It took six years before McLaughlin could extricate himself from the label machinery and allow an Austin indie label, Dos, released his second (really third) album, *Unglued* (dos, 1994, prod. Ben Keith), a good but flawed effort that could be chalked up to his years of label woes. Most recently McLaughlin has been writing songs and performing in an informal group calling itself Tiny Town, with members of the subdudes.

Gil Asakawa

Don McLean

Born Oct. 2, 1945 in New Rochelle, N.Y.

One song does not a career make, but McLean's "American Pie" was such a phenomenon in 1972 that it remains a popular culture touchstone—which is good for the royalty statements but isn't necessarily healthy for the career. Ask someone to name another McLean song, and the clued-in few might recall "Vincent." And far fewer will come up with any of the plaintive, folky titles from before and after "American Pie." For better or worse, McClean—who had worked with Pete Seeger and wrote a hit for Perry Como ("And I Love You So")—is forever tied to his eight and a half minute tale of personal doubts and musical redemption in the face of Buddy Holly's death.

what to buy: *Favorites and Rarities* (EMI, 1992, prod. Various) is the collection that makes the case that there's more to McLean than "American Pie." Anyone who's derived some enjoyment from that song over the years can thank McLean by giving a fair hearing to the rest of his story.

what to avoid: Lesser collections of his work, such as the skimpy *American Pie and Other Hits* (CEMA Special Products, 1992/1994, prod. Various) **WOOF!**

the rest: *American Pie* (United Artists/EMI America, 1971) *The Best of Don McLean* (EMI, 1988) *Headroom* (Curb, 1991) *Christmas* (Curb, 1991) *The River of Love* (CPI/Curb, 1995)

worth searching for: McLean's debut, *Tapestry*, (United Artists, 1970) is long out of print but is as fine a collection of gentle, folk-tinged songs as the more celebrated *American Pie* album.

▶▶ James McMurtry, Garth Brooks, Jewel

◀◀ Pete Seeger, Bob Dylan, Phil Ochs, Tim Hardin, Roger Whittaker

Gary Graff

Grant McLennan /Jack Frost

Born Feb. 12, 1957 in Rock Hampton, Australia

During the late 70s, McLennan formed the Go-Betweens with fellow Brisbane University student Robert Forster. Inspired by the poetry of Bob Dylan and the energy of punk, the pair sought to draw on both—thus, the Go-Betweens. After a half-dozen albums that were critically acclaimed but sold poorly, the band split, and McLennan brought his gift for tuneful, melodious pop to his solo career. Recording first as G.W. McLennan, the singer debuted with *Watershed*, (Beggars Banquet/RCA, prod. Dave Dobbyn) an album that is slightly marred by an ill-advised venture into dance/funk territory. *Fireboy* (Beggars Banquet/ADA, 1993, prod. Dave Dobbyn) brings McLennan back to what he does best. But both of those efforts were neutralized by poor distribution. McLennan's third effort, *Horsebreaker Star* (Beggars Banquet, 1995, prod. John Keane) presents the best work of his career—sunny pop melodies, nicely undercut by lyrics reflecting complex emotional situations. Recorded in Athens, Ga., with a backing band McLennan had never met, *Horsebreaker Star* sounds like an album made by musicians who'd been mates for years. (Note: the import version of the album is a two-disc set with 25 tracks). McLennan has also recorded two albums with the Church's Steve Kilbey under the name Jack Frost. Both *Jack Frost* (Arista, 1991, prod. Steve Kilbey) and *Snow Job* (Beggars Banquet, 1996, prod. Steve Kilbey) feature ethereal, experimental pop that is closer to the Church than the Go-Betweens.

see also: *The Go-Betweens*

Dan Durchholz

James McMurtry

Born in 1962 in Fort Worth, Texas

Son of the Lonesome Dove novelist and a university English

professor, you'd expect McMurtry to have a respect for the delicacies of language. And he doesn't disappoint. With three albums to his credit, McMurtry is gaining notice as a fine narrative songwriter, spinning ironic tales of small-town boredom, vagabond loners and lovers, the weight of the past and the illusions of memory in a style that's spare but finely etched. He sings in a detached world-weary monotone reminiscent of another deadpan non-singer, Lou Reed, and plays guitar with a subtle passion. McMurtry learned to play guitar at seven and after taking courses at the University of Arizona, he began to see the instrument as his meal-ticket, soloing at a local beer garden during happy hour. "I could sort of sing, but I decided I would really play," he says. "In those days, I wanted to be a major flat picker like David Bromberg and Doc Watson. That was before I figured out I didn't really have the speed. I'm more an endurance guitarist." In 1987, he was one of the winners of the prestigious New Folk contest that is part of the Kerrville Folk Festival. When dad Larry and John Mellencamp collaborated on the screenplay for the film "Falling from Grace," Larry passed a tape of James's music to Mellencamp, who was impressed enough to volunteer his services as producer. Co-produced by Mellencamp band members Michael Wanchic and Larry Crane, that album was released to critical acclaim, leading to a second Mellencamp-sponsored set.

what to buy: McMurtry's debut *Too Long in the Wasteland* (1989, Columbia, prod. John

Mellencamp) ♪♪♪♪ is a compelling collection of short stories set to song, highlighted by the title cut, "Paint by Numbers," and I'm Not from Here."

what to buy next: *Where'd You Hide the Body* (1995, Columbia, prod. Don Dixon) ♪♪♪♪ is a more electric, broader album with one great song ("Levelland") supported by 12 other substantial tunes. Also available is a video compilation of the album directed by a variety of USC and CalArts film students.

the rest: *Candyland* (1992, Columbia, prod. Michael Wanchic) ♪♪♪

◀◀ Lou Reed, Bruce Springsteen

Martin Connors

Christine McVie

See: Fleetwood Mac

Meat Loaf

Born Marvin Lee Aday, Sept. 27, 1951, in Dallas, Texas

At a time when rock 'n' roll had reached its bloated, bloodless nadir with the unholy trilogy of Styx, Kansas and Supertramp, Meat Loaf and songwriter Jim Steinman screamed onto the charts with 1977's *Bat Out of Hell*. Fueled by shameless bombast and backseat bravado, they offered emotion-starved, hormone-driven teenagers salvation in the form of operatic, Springsteen-derived mini-dramas. The new-wave movement would soon render their Wagnerian excess moot, but for one glorious summer the motorcycle-riding cult hero from "The Rocky Horror Picture Show"—who's previous credit was an album with future Bob Seger/Little Feat singer Shaun Murphy on Motown—tapped into what it was like to be clumsy, young and in lust. A fallout with Steinman resulted in the longest sophomore jinx in rock history, which found Meat Loaf floundering from pseudo-Steinman copycats to heavy-metal posing until the duo reunited for 1993's multi-platinum "Bat Out of Hell II: Back Into Hell." He continues to be a great voice in search of a vision.

what to buy: *Bat Out of Hell,* (Epic, 1977, prod. Todd Rundgren) ♪♪♪ featuring such sweat-soaked anthems as "Paradise By the Dashboard Light," "You Took the Words Right Out of My Mouth" and "Two Out of Three Ain't Bad," holds up remarkably well. Audiophiles may want to splurge on the gold Master Sound reissue, which indeed adds some much-needed definition to Todd Rundgren's dense production. *Bat Out of Hell II* (MCA, 1993, prod. Jim Steinman) ♪♪♪ ably mimics its predecessor's sound and fury, albeit with long-winded song titles like "Objects in the Rear View Mirror May Appear Closer Than They Are" and "I'd Do Anything For Love (But I Won't Do That)."

what to buy next: Rebounding from legal woes and throat problems, Meat Loaf dusted off eight early Steinman compositions for the passable *Dead Ringer,* (Epic, 1981, prod. Jimmy Iovine and Jim Steinman) ♪♪♪ including "Read 'Em and Weep" (later a Steinman-produced hit for Barry Manilow) and the title track (a duet with Cher, who's no Ellen Foley).

what to avoid: *Welcome to the Neighborhood* (MCA, 1996, prod. Ron Nevison, Sammy Hagar, Steven Van Zandt and Meat Loaf) **WOOF!** finds Meat Loaf again abandoned by Steinman and turning to hook-for-hire song doctors like Diane Warren. The results are such lunkheaded pop-metal anthems as "I'd Lie For You (And That's the Truth)" and "Where the Rubber Meets the Road," which is about safe sex (really). When the best song on the disc is written by Sammy Hagar, you know you're in trouble.

the rest: *Midnight at the Lost and Found* (Epic, 1983) *Bad Attitude* (RCA, 1984) *Blind Before I Stop* (Atlantic, 1986) *Hits Out of Hell* (Epic, 1994)

worth searching for: *Bad For Good* (Epic,1981), Jim Steinman's solo debut, is the original sequel to *Bat Out of Hell.* Made up of the songs and arrangements originally written for Meat Loaf before he broke off his partnership with Steinman, this album is hampered by some of the most dreadful lead vocals ever committed to tape. But the teen angst is palpable.

Bon Jovi

Bruce Springsteen, Phil Spector, Richard Wagner

David Okamoto

Meat Puppets

Formed 1980 in Phoenix, Ariz.

Curt Kirkwood, guitar, vocals; Cris Kirkwood, bass, vocals; Derrick Bostrom, drums

Many only know this trio's music from Nirvana's "MTV Unplugged" session (the Meat Puppets guested and the CD has three of their songs) and from covers by Minutemen/fIREHOSE. Its members' penchant for trading instruments for endearingly sloppy, feedback-drenched concert finales typifies the group's spirited aesthetic. Having come from the punk scene but soon incorporating country twang, psychedelia and heavy guitar, the group's punk days now are long behind it, as is any apparent urge to try something new. Still, the Puppets are consistently entertaining and unusual—imagine an alternative Blue Oyster Cult, with fat, dark, rumbling guitar riffs. Curt Kirkwood's inimitable vocals make even the most minimal melodies sound catchy; similarly, his lyrics say a lot with simple means and images. That's harder than it seems.

what to buy: *Up On the Sun* (SST, 1985) is a conceptual shock and a musical tonic, with a totally warped slacker interpretation of the Byrds' interpretation of country at its center.

what to buy next: *Too High to Die* (London, 1994, prod. Paul Leary and Meat Puppets) is the best of the group's major-label albums.

what to avoid: *Huevos* (SST, 1987) Apparently it's inevitable; every rock 'n' roll trio tries to sound like ZZ Top at one point or another.

the rest: *In a Car EP* (World Imitation/SST, 1981) *Meat Puppets* (SST, 1982) *II* (SST, 1983) *Out My Way* EP (SST, 1986) *Mirage* (SST, 1987) *Monsters* (SST, 1989) *No Strings Attached* (SST, 1990) *Forbidden Places* (London, 1991) *No Joke!* (London, 1995)

Overwhelming Colorfast, Nirvana

Black Flag, Byrds, Buck Owens, Captain Beefheart, Blue Oyster Cult, ZZ Top

Steve Holtje

Joe Meek

Born April 5, 1929, in Gloucetershire, England. Died Feb. 3, 1967, in London, England.

Britain's first independent producer, a believer in the occult, was not above holding seances in the recording studio to summon the assistance from beyond the veil of his leading inspiration, Buddy Holly. When he killed himself after murdering his landlady—on the anniversary of Holly's death—Meek assured his place in rock 'n' roll annals, even though his impact in the U.S. was limited to the 1963 No. 1 hit by the Tornadoes, "Telstar," and another modest British Invasion chart entry, "Have I the Right" by the Honeycombs. An engineer trained in the Royal Air Force, Meek helped bring Britain's nascent recording industry into the modern age. His productions employed rudimentary sound effects, celestial choirs and majestic melodies to evoke worlds from beyond. Eccentric and inventive, Meek made more of a mark with hit records by artists unknown on the other side of the Atlantic such, as John Leyton, Mike Berry, Heinz and others. In England, Meek has been the subject of a biography, a remarkable BBC documentary, as well as several reissues devoted to his recordings. A 20-track collection of Meek's work was released in this country, *It's Hard To Believe It: The Amazing World of Joe Meek,* (Razor and Tie, 1995) that encompasses his best-known independent productions. Those fascinated by the sound and story of Meek's career should look for two British imports—*The Joe Meek Story: The Pye Years* (Sequel, 1991) and *The Joe Meek Story* (Decca, 1977)—which offers even more exhaustive looks at recordings he made for two of the three British labels with which he customarily worked.

Joel Selvin

Mega City Four

Formed 1988 in Farnborough, England

Wiz, guitar/vocals; Danny Brown, guitar; Gerry Bryant, bass; Chris Jones, drums

Led by first-rate singer/songwriter/guitarist Wiz, Mega City Four—which has had the same lineup for the near-decade it's existed—has kept up an admirable standard of superb consistency over five studio albums plus a blizzard of non-LP singles and EPs. Known around its native England for excessive, non-stop tours in a beat-up van (thus the title of their 1989 debut LP *Tranzophobia*) this Farnborough foursome skirted the punk scene despite the original releases' scruffy, raw assault. This was managed thanks to the melodic pop sensibility it established early on, and as the band matured, it's managed to temper the attack with no loss of power. More recent work has shown a decided influence of American 80s bands that made a similar progression, such as The Replacements, and Husker Du (the latter the Megas covered on its live LP). This progression briefly resulted in English chart success for the group in 1992, but when the fashion there turned to Oasis and Blur, the group comfortably returned to the clubs and garages from whence it sprang and even redoubled its intensity on its most recent LP.

what to buy: The Megas transformation is best heard on the magnificent *Sebastopol Rd.*, (Big Life/Caroline, 1992, prod. Jessica Corcoran) with its well-rounded variety and non-stop dramatic moments. The glistening "Scared of Cats," the searing disquiet of "Prague," and the pulsing "Ticket Collector" run afoul of the gentle nature of Wiz's empathy, despite the pounding rhythm section. This is a tense, taut, pop mini-masterpiece, with great romantic words from one of the world's best relationship-oriented lyricists. It's also the Megas only album released in the U.S. For those who want the more mainlined stuff, *Terribly Sorry Bob* (Decoy Records U.K., 1991, prod. Various) is a knockout compilation of all 12 non-LP songs from the group's earliest singles/EPs. This hot document is one hot speedy-pop, hook-collision after another; don't miss "Finish." *Magic Bullets* (Big Life, 1993, prod. Chris Potter) is barely a fall-off from *Sebastopol Rd.'s* brilliance; any LP that includes the punishing single "Iron Sky" is reason enough for purchase, but there are plenty of other hummable gifts, such as the kick-starting opener "Perfect Circle," the also-vicious "Enemy Skies," and the quiet passion of "Speck."

what to buy next: It's hard to go wrong with the naive but energetic, souped-up smacking that is the second LP, *Who Cares Wins* (Decoy U.K., 1990, prod. Iain Burgess) Although the production mix is too muddy, there's plenty of stinging zingers, such as the slam-bang "Me Not You," the tangy charm of "Messenger" and the great harmonies and hooks of "Who Cares?" The band's latest, *Soulscraper* (Fire Records U.K., 1996, prod. Chris Potter) is its most abrasive outing in six years. Once again, Wiz's pen is as sharp as ever despite a three-year layoff, as evidenced by the bopping singles "Android Dreams," "Skidding" and "Superstar." Rocks off!

what to avoid: The first LP, *Tranzophobia* (Decoy Records U.K., 1989, prod. Iain Burgess) is actually not that bad; it's just too rough in spots and overshadowed as a document of the young Megas by *Terribly Sorry Bob*

the rest: *Inspiringly Titled The Live Album* (Big Life U.K., 1992) *The Peel Sessions* (Strange Fruit U.K., 1993)

The Doughboys, Les Thugs, Leatherface

Replacements, Husker Du, Buzzcocks

Jack Rabid

Megadeth

Formed in 1983 in Los Angeles, Calif.

Dave Mustaine, guitar, vocals; David Ellefson, bass; Chris Poland, guitar (1983-86); Gars Samuelson, drums (1983-86); Jeff Young, guitar (1986-88); Chuck Behler, drums (1986-88); Marty Friedman, guitar (1988-present); Nick Menza, drums (1988-present)

Named for the military term for nuclear war casualties, Megadeth has been laying out arenas full of fans with tactical speed-metal strikes since leader Mustaine was kicked out of Metallica during its early days. And just as that band has balanced its thrash-intensive, chops-heavy attack with measured, radio-ready hard-rock, so has Mustaine, and massive popularity has been the reward for both acts, albeit on a significantly smaller scale for Megadeth. A notorious attitude problem, Mustaine was ousted from Metallica in a power struggle over control of the band and, allegedly, his out-of-control drug use. Mustaine's abuse of drugs, including heroin, continued until he was arrested for impaired driving in 1990. He cleaned up with the help of a 12-step program and apparently has stayed straight ever since, though his misbehavior got the band bounced from an opening slot on Aerosmith's 1993 tour. But then, among metal's devoted fans, repentance is rarely seen as a virtue.

what to buy: It may pain longtime fans to read, but *Youthanasia* (Capitol, 1994MDBR, prod. Dave Mustaine and Max Norman) is Megadeth's best overall album. With its slower tempos, polished production and conventional song structures, the album moved the band into the big leagues. *Rust in Peace,* (Combat/Capitol, 1990, prod. Dave Mustaine and Mike Clink) the band's first sober effort, plays Mustaine's guitar off that of Friedman and jazz-schooled drummer Menza, allowing the fusion influenced brand of metal envisioned by Mustaine from the very start.

what to buy next: Like its predecessor *Rust in Peace*, *Countdown to Extinction* (Combat/Capitol, 1992MDBR, prod. Dave Mustaine and Max Norman) features Megadeth's by-now trademark instrumental twists, but doesn't shy away from headbanging heaviness. The best of the band's early phase, *So Far, So Good...So What!* (Capitol, 1988, prod. Paul Lani and Dave Mustaine) cuts to the bone with Mustaine's razor-sharp guitar and double-time rhythms.

what to avoid: *Peace Sells...But Who's Buying?* (Combat/Capitol, 1986, prod. Dave Mustaine and Randy Burns) has the fury, but the band seems to be treading water here.

the rest: *Killing Is My Business...and Business Is Good!* (Combat, 1985) *Hidden Treasures* (Capitol, 1995)

worth searching for: *Maximum Megadeth*, (Capitol, 1991, prod. Various) an eight-song promotional sampler with live versions of "Hangar 18" and the Sex Pistols' "Anarchy in the U.K."

White Zombie, Pantera, Entombed, Corrosion of Conformity

Black Sabbath, Iron Maiden, the Dead Boys, the Sex Pistols

see also: *Metallica*

Daniel Durchholz

Randy Meisner

See: The Eagles

Mekons

Formed 1977 in Leeds, England

Jon Langford, guitar, vocals, drums; Tom Greenhalgh, guitar, vocals; Kevin Lycett, guitar (1977-83); Mark White, vocals (1977-83); Sally Timms, vocals (1985-present); Rico Bell, accordion, vocals (1985-present); Steve Goulding, drums (1985-present); Dick Taylor, guitar (1985-91); Brendan Crocker, guitar (1985-91); Lu Edmonds, bass (1985-91); Susie Honeyman, violin (1985-present); Sarah Corina, bass (1994-present)

The Mekons just may be the last, and certainly longest lasting, punk band remaining, not because they play exclusively punk music (on the contrary, the group has embraced numerous styles, from country to dub reggae) but in the sense that punk is an attitude, an ethic and a way of defining one's place in the world. The band's first single "Never Been in a Riot," gored the Clash's sacred cow, "White Riot," and the Mekons have been pursuing a singularly contrary path ever since, undeterred by a constant state of near poverty, abysmal relations with a series of record companies and frequent lineup changes. In directing the band through a bewildering variety of incarnations, core members Langford, Greenhalgh and Timms have retained their fondness for biting humor, socialist politics and buoyant live performances. Almost in spite of themselves, the Mekons have become the most celebrated underground rock band of the last 20 years.

what to buy: *Fear and Whiskey*, (Sin U.K., 1985) also contained in its entirety in the more expansive mid-period compilation *Original Sin*, (Sin-Twin/Tone, 1989, prod. The Mekons and Tony Bonner) is the Mekons' bleary, back-against-the-wall attempt to play honky-tonk music as Hank Williams and Ernest Tubb once did. It fails, of course, but comes up with a rustic sound just as passionate and moving. Ground down by the twin boot of Reagan-Thatcher oppression, the 3 a.m. voices of Greenhalgh, Langford and the rest sound like the last stand of the dispossessed. In *The Mekons Rock 'n' Roll*, (Twin/Tone-A&M, 1989, prod. The Mekons and Ian Caple) the subject is Rock 'n' Roll Inc. itself, and the music roars with an energy and vigor not heard on any Mekons record. "Memphis, Egypt," for example, takes its cues from Motorhead, and "Blow Your Tuneless Trumpet" razzes "Dublin messiah" Bono.

what to buy next: *The Edge of the World* (Sin U.K., 1986 prod. The Mekons and Tony Bonner) is nearly the mutant-country equal of *Fear and Whiskey* and introduces the subversively pure and melodious voice of Timms to the Mekons' arsenal. *The Curse of the Mekons* (Blast First U.K., 1991, prod. The Mekons and Ian Caple) sustains the band's touch for diversity, touching on Cajun, country, Stonesy rock and country-swing rhythms, with plenty of defiant attitude in the aftermath of the group's short-lived major-label deal with A&M Records.

what to avoid: *The Quality of Mercy is Not Strnen*, (Virgin U.K., 1979/Blue Plate, 1990) the band's debut, has its moments of comic relief but musically is pretty much unlistenable, even by the loose standards of punk.

the rest: *Devils Rats and Piggies a Special Message from Godzilla* (Red Rhino U.K., 1980) *It Falleth Like Gentle Rain From Heaven—The Mekons Story* (Feel Good All Over, 1982) *Honky Tonkin'* (Sin-Twin/Tone, 1987) *So Good It*

Hurts (Twin/Tone, 1988) *F.U.N. 90* (Twin/Tone-A&M EP, 1990) *Wicked Midnight* (Loud Music EP, 1992) ♥ *Mekons* (Quarterstick, 1993) *Millionaire* (Quarterstick EP, 1993) *Retreat From Memphis* (Quarterstick, 1994) Mekons with Kathy Acker: *Pussy, King of the Pirates* (Quarterstick, 1996)

worth searching for: *New York,* (ROIR, 1987) initially available on cassette only, is an almost too-accurate account of one of the band's typically raucous tours, the mood nailed by a boozy spin through The Band's "The Shape I'm In."

▶▶ The Pogues, the Palace Brothers, the Ex, the Handsome Family

◀◀ The Band, Johnny Cash, Hank Williams, Ernest Tubb, Sex Pistols

Greg Kot

Melanie

Born Melanie Safka, Feb. 3, 1947 in Queens, N.Y.

A guitar-wielding flower child with a sultry rasp of a voice, Melanie combined the winsome folk of late-60s Joni Mitchell with the folk-naif girlishness of England's Mary Hopkin. Somehow, she managed to crack the mainstream in a way neither of those artists did. From 1969-71, Melanie landed on pop charts both at home and abroad, establishing herself in the vein of other nonpolitical folk artists (Donovan, John Sebastian) with pleasant sing-alongs such as "What Have They Done to My Song, Ma?" and the chart-topping "Brand New Key." Her music has enjoyed an element of crossover success thanks to covers by Barbra Streisand, Ray Charles and Mel Torme, among others. Comebacks during late 80s and again in the mid-90s showed she hasn't lost her audience or her touch. She remains a sophisticated songwriter of humane and healing themes.

what to buy: *The Best of Melanie* (Rhino, 1990, prod. Various) is certainly the right choice to make. The 18 tracks include all six of her Top 40 hits, as well as her compelling cover of the Rolling Stones' classic "Ruby Tuesday."

what to buy next: *Candles in the Rain* (Buddah, 1970, prod. Hank Hoffman) is Melanie's premiere album, featuring deft and inspired songwriting ("Lay Down," "Ruby Tuesday," "What Have They Done To My Song, Ma?") and glorious backup vocals from the gospel chorus (and Buddah labelmates) the Edwin Hawkins Singers.

what to avoid: Melanie tried to shed her girlish image on *Ballroom Streets,* (RCA/Rhino, 1979) and while the songs are more sophisticated than on previous efforts, nothing here is as strong as her early hits.

the rest: *Leftover Wine* (Buddah/One Way, 1970) *Freedom Knows My Name* (Lonestars, 1993)

worth searching for: *Gather Me,* (Neighborhood, 1971, prod. Peter Schekeryk) the first release on the label founded by Melanie and husband Schekeryk, was a winning effort that housed "Brand New Key" and the equally wonderful "Ring the Living Bell."

▶▶ Olivia Newton-John, Alanis Morissette, Jewel

◀◀ Joan Baez, Odetta, the Ronettes, Dusty Springfield

Christopher Scapelliti

John Mellencamp

Born Oct. 7, 1951 in Seymour, Ind..

Mellencamp is often dismissed as a bantamweight Bruce Springsteen. He too writes guitar-based rock songs about the shattered dreams of America's common folk, but just because Springsteen does a similar job better is no reason to knock Mellencamp. Rebounding from some dismal early recordings under the stage name Johnny Cougar, Mellencamp began in the early 80s to make music that was thoughtful and rollicking, with his Midwest sensibility decidedly on his sleeve. Mellencamp has also displayed broad musical ambitions, going rootsy in the mid-80s—well before the so-called No Depression movement hit—and embracing dance rhythms during the 90s. He joined forces with Willie Nelson and Neil Young to launch the Farm Aid concerts during the mid-80s and tried his hand at record producing (for Mitch Ryder and James McMurtry) and film acting and directing (1992's "Falling From Grace"). Mellencamp suffered a minor heart attack in 1994, but a few months later he was back onstage, playing clandestine club shows and—surely to his doctors' disapproval—chain-smoking cigarettes.

what to buy: Mellencamp's experiment in Appalachian garage-rock, *The Lonesome Jubilee,* (Mercury, 1987, prod. John Mellencamp and Don Gehman) produced some of his most durable songs ("Paper in Fire," "Check It Out," "Cherry Bomb"). The earlier *Scarecrow* (Riva, 1985, prod. John Mellencamp and Don Gehman) mixed protest songs ("Rain on the Scarecrow") with lighter but equally soulful fare such as "R.O.C.K. in the U.S.A" and "Rumbleseat."

what to buy next: *Uh-huh* (Riva, 1983, prod. John Mellencamp and Don Gehman) finds the singer in full Stones-inspired glory ("Pink Houses," "The Authority Song"). *American Fool* (Riva, 1982, prod. John Mellencamp and Don Gehman) was an eloquent throat-clearing, buoyed by a pair of great pop singles—"Hurt So Good" and "Jack and Diane"—that established the then-John Cougar's star in the pop pantheon.

what to avoid: *Chestnut Street Incident* (Mainman/MCA, 1976; Rhino, 1986, prod. John Cougar), a dead-end collection of cover songs.

the rest: *A Biography* (Riva UK, 1978) *John Cougar* (Riva, 1979) *Nothin' Matters and What If It Did* (Riva, 1980) *Big Daddy* (Mercury, 1989) *Whenever We Wanted* (Mercury, 1991) *Human Wheels* (Mercury, 1993) *Dance Naked* (Mercury, 1994) *Mr. Happy Go Lucky* (Mercury, 1996)

worth searching for: A promotional-only issue of *Dance Naked* (Mercury, 1994) in book form that featured a second CD of 18 Mellencamp hits.

▶▶ Michael McDermott, Uncle Tupelo, James McMurtry

◀◀ Rolling Stones, James Brown, Mitch Ryder and the Detroit Wheels, Van Morrison, Humble Pie

Thor Christensen

Men at Work

Formed 1979 in Melbourne, Australia. Disbanded 1985.

Colin Hay, vocals, guitar; Ron Strykert, guitar, vocals; Jerry Speiser, drums, vocals (1979-84); Greg Ham, winds, keyboards, vocals; John Rees, bass, vocals (1979-84)

The Scottish-born Hay moved to Australia as a teenager and perfected his guitar skills by performing original work in pubs and universities. In 1978 he met Strykert, and the next year Men at Work was formed. Mixing engaging lyrics and solid guitar playing with melodic pop-synth and a touch of horns proved to be a winning combination. Arriving at the hub of the 80's New Wave revolution, combined with the exotic nature of the Australian band (and America's growing infatuation with the land down under) propelled Men at Work to a series of consecutive No. 1 hits. The first album, *Business as Usual* (Columbia, 1981, prod. Peter Mclan) quickly went multi-platinum, becoming a huge international success, earning the group a Best New Artist Grammy and spawning the hits "Who Can It Be Now" and "Down Under." The next album, *Cargo,* (Columbia, 1993, prod. Peter Mclan) comes in just a shade behind and contains the hit single "It's a Mistake." *Contraband: The Best of Men at Work* (Columbia/Legacy, 1995, prod. Various) is all you really need to own; it has the hits from the first two albums, as well as some overlooked songs, such as "Hard Luck Story," from the out-of-print third album, *Two of Hearts.*

Bryan Lassner

Men Without Hats

Formed 1980 in Montreal, Quebec, Canada

Ivan Doroschuk, vocals; Stefan Doroschuk, guitar; Colin Doroschuk, keyboards; Allan McCarthy, drums

Men Without Hats' first single was "The Safety Dance," which hit No. 3 in 1983. Its repetitive octave-interval synth riff stuck itself into pop consciousness like a lawn dart; only the Knack's "My Sharona" had the same madness-inducing jumpy repetition. And also like the Knack, Men Without Hats would fail to expand on its initial success. Bound up by serious artistic ambitions, the group's novelty pop songs often suffered from delusions of grandeur, making them a lot less fun than "The Safety Dance." The band made some headway in 1987 with "Pop Goes the World," a weightlessly engaging ditty that has a fair amount of charm. But the band's career was all but over by the early 90s. *Collection* (Oglio, 1996, prod. Various) offers the group's two hits and its more listenable fare, such as "I Got the Message," and "I Like," revealing that underneath the pomposity were a few pop songs with more enduring qualities than "The Safety Dance."

Allan Orski

Natalie Merchant

See: 10,000 Maniacs

Freddie Mercury

See: Queen

Mercy Seat

See: Violent Femmes

The Merry-Go-Round /Emitt Rhodes

Formed Hawthorne, California, 1965. Disbanded 1969.

Emitt Rhodes, vocals, guitar (born 1950, Hawthorne, Calif.); Gary Kato, guitar, vocals; Bill Rhinehart, bass; Joel Larson, drums

Perhaps America's best-ever response to the kind of melodic magic wrought by the Beatles came from this California quartet and, later, from Rhodes as a solo act. At the tender age of 16, Rhodes formed the Merry-Go-Round, whose one album and two additional 45s feature sprightly melodies and Rhodes' English-inflected singing backed by winning harmonies, a crunchy guitar attack and Paul McCartneyesque bass work. The highlights can be found on *The Best of The Merry-Go-Round*. (Rhino, 1985, prod. Larry Marks) After disbanding the group, Rhodes resurfaced as a solo act for three albums on Dunhill, producing, playing every instrument and singing every vocal—just like his greatest influence, McCartney, did on his debut solo album. Many of these tracks feature nice keyboard underpinnings as well as the standard guitar backing. *Listen, Listen: The Best of Emitt Rhodes* (Varese Sarabande, 1995, comp. Cary Mansfield and Michael Amicone) does a good job of compiling the best of those albums plus key Merry-Go-Round tracks. The straight reissue of his first solo LP, *Emitt Rhodes* (Dunhill, 1970/One Way, 1993, prod. Emitt Rhodes and Harvey Bruce) is also good, with mostly sunny, upbeat tunes such as "Fresh As a Daisy" and "Live Till You Die." Sadly, Rhodes disappeared from view after 1973, recording only for his personal pleasure in his garage studio.

Mike Greenfield

Jim Messina

See: Poco

Metallica

Formed 1981 in Los Angeles, Calif.

James Hetfield, guitar, vocals; Lars Ulrich, drums; Dave Mustaine, guitar (1981-83); Ron McGovney, bass (1981-83); Kirk Hammett, guitar (1983-present); Cliff Burton, bass (1983-86, died Sept. 27, 1986); Jason Newsted, bass (1986-present)

A monster band whose ferocious attack defined a new brand of heavy metal during the 80s, Metallica is the closest thing this generation has to a Led Zeppelin. Integrity is the key here; Metallica has always flown a flag of no-compromise, which meant that when the rock 'n' roll mainstream (including radio) finally embraced the group during the early 90s, it was a strong bond built gradually by years of relentless touring and literally headbanging away at every corner of the globe to be heard. The group takes its sonic sledgehammer—replete with stop-start dynamics, doomy ambience and leaden rhythms—from both British metal bands and punk rockers, though it certainly dresses up any lessons taken from the latter in a hellish, heavier sonic garb than you'll generally hear at CBGB. When Hammett and Burton joined Metallica in 1983—the former replacing Mustaine, who went on to form Megadeth—the group's sound coalesced. Since then it's only been refined, but strictly on Metallica's terms. That its last two albums—*Metallica* and *Load*—have turned the group into an arena-filling rock radio favorite (and the headliner of the 1996 Lollapalooza tour!) is merely a sign that the audience has met the band half-way, which is the way many a lasting musical relationship has been created.

what to buy: *Metallica* (Elektra, 1991, prod. Bob Rock, James Hetfield and Lars Ulrich) is an exceptional hard rock album, retaining the sinister, subversive edge that won the group its underground following amidst considerable growth in craft. "Enter Sandman" and "Sad But True" are pulverizing, but "Nothing Else Matters" is disarmingly pretty and melodic. Metallica really hit stride with the aptly titled *Ride the Lightning*, (Elektra, 1984, prod. Mark Whittaker) a sizzling, electrifying assault that contains continuing concert favorites such as "For Whom the Bell Tolls," "Fade to Black" and "Creeping Death."

what to buy next: *Master of Puppets* (Elektra, 1986, prod. Flemming Rasmussen and Metallica) refined *Ride the Lightning's* ground-shaking dynamics and was the group's first million-seller. *Live Shit: Binge & Purge* (Elektra, 1993, prod. James Hetfield and Lars Ulrich) is an over-the-top live box set—three CDs, three videos, a book and a stencil of the band's scary guy mascot. Know what? Metallica is such a tremendous live act it's worth it. *Load* (Elektra, 1996, prod. Bob Rock, James Hetfield and Lars Ulrich) is darker than *Metallica* and finds the band trying on a few of the sonic stances introduced by so-called alternative rockers after *Metallica* was released.

what to avoid: *...And Justice For All* (Elektra, 1988, prod. Flemming Rasmussen) is conceptually sound, but the production is too dense and murky to give the songs their due.

the rest: *Kill 'Em All* (Megaforce, 1983/Elektra, 1987)

worth searching for: *The $9.98 CD—Garage Days Revisited* (Elektra EP, 1987, prod. Metallica) is a spirited collection of covers of songs by influences and friends such as the Misfits and Killing Joke. It marks Newsted's first work with the band and is sadly out of print.

Megadeth, Danzig, Slayer

◀◀ Black Sabbath, Iron Maiden, Queen, the Misfits, Killing Joke, the Sex Pistols

see also: *Megadeth*

Gary Graff

The Meters

Formed 1967 in New Orleans, La. Disbanded 1977. Re-formed 1990.

Art Neville, keyboards, vocals; Leo Nocentelli, guitar; George Porter, Jr., bass; Zig Modeliste, drums (1967-77); Cyril Neville, percussion, vocals (1975-77); David Russell Baptiste, drums (1990-present)

The Meters cooked up some of the most intoxicating grooves in funk history of funk, adding the flavor of the syncopated rhythms from the group's hometown, New Orleans. Under the leadership of organist Neville—overseen by impressario Allen Toussaint—the quartet assembled during the late 60s as the house band for Toussaint's and Marshall Sehorn's label, Josie. Between studio sessions for a panoply of New Orleans soul artists and grueling live work, the Meters honed a funky chemistry that surfaced most distinctively on the instrumental tracks the group cut toward the end of the decade. A few of these recordings became R&B hits, notably "Sophisticated Cissy," "Cissy Strut," "Looka-Py-Py" and "Chicken Strut." After signing with Reprise during the early 70s, the Meters moved into rock-soul territory, with vocals provided by Neville. While none of the band's albums achieved the success of its leaner 60s instrumentals, the Meters have been widely influential and frequently sampled, with a track record of backing up other acts such as Dr. John, Paul McCartney and Wings, the Pointer Sisters and Robert Palmer. The band broke up in 1977 but have reunited in different configurations into the 90s; legal disputes involving the name of the band the rights to their recordings were mostly resolved by the middle of that decade. Neville moonlights in the Neville Brothers, a troupe that has enjoyed some of the commercial success that The Meters never found.

what to buy: The two-CD anthology *Funkify Your Life* (Rhino, 1995, prod. Various) collects most of the group's important tracks, with one disc devoted to its work for Josie and the other sifting the wheat of the Reprise years from the substantial chaff.

what to buy next: The best album-length collection of instrumentals, *Looka Py-Py* (Josie, 1969/Rounder, 1990, prod. Allen Toussaint and Marshall Sehorn) captures the band at its grooving peak.

what to avoid: The band's first farewell album, *New Directions* (Reprise, 1977, prod. David Rubinson and Friends) dilutes its greasy funk with soggy rock tropes and is a far cry from the economy of its best work.

the rest: *The Meters* (Josie, 1969) *Struttin'* (Josie, 1970) *Cabbage Alley* (Reprise, 1972) *Fire on the Bayou* (Reprise, 1975) *Trick Bag* (Reprise, 1976) *Good Old Funky Music* (Rounder, 1990) *Funky Miracle* (Charly, 1991) *The Meters Jam* (Rounder, 1992) *Uptown Rulers: The Meters Live on the Queen Mary* (Rounder, 1992)

worth searching for: The hard-to-find *Rejuvenation* (Reprise, 1974, prod. Allen Toussaint and the Meters) has a few vital tracks that didn't make it to the Rhino anthology.

▶▶ Parliament-Funkadelic, the Neville Brothers, Prince, Red Hot Chili Peppers, Beastie Boys, De La Soul

◀◀ James Brown, Booker T. and the MGs, Allen Toussaint

see also: *The Neville Brothers*

Simon Glickman

Miami Sound Machine

See: Gloria Estefan

George Michael /Wham!

Formed 1981 in London, England. Disbanded 1986.

George Michael (born Georgios Kyriacos Panayiotou, June 25, 1963 in London, England), vocals; Andrew Ridgely, vocals, guitar

When lightweight British pop bands began storming the American charts during the early-80s, it was Michael's talent that set Wham! apart from its competition. In a glut of synthesizers and hairstyles, it was the songs the honey-voiced singer authored for Wham!'s brief string of albums that gave the duo's music uncommon appeal, with a sound that clinched the American R&B tradition and set it to a contemporary pop beat. Wham!'s exhaustive success caused Michael to disband the group at the height of its popularity in 1986 and head out on a solo career that proved initially more lustrous though has since bogged down in high-minded denouncements of pop music marketing and an unsuccessful lawsuit against his old record company.

what to buy: Michael did not come into his creative prime until *Listen Without Prejudice: Vol. 1,* (Columbia, 1990, prod. George

What Album Changed Your Life?

"Peter Gabriel's Security. I was 16 years old, and that was sort of the first record I ever heard with the kind of music I could think of myself doing. It was more the feelings it evoked. I thought 'I want to make music like this, music that makes people feel like this.'"

Sarah McLachlan

Michael) ⚐⚐⚐⚐ an album filled with melancholy lyrics and lush, soaring melodies that recalled the great pop and soul hits of the 60s. As Michael's commanding artistic statement, it gave the former teen idol uncharacteristic depth, inspiring comparisons to everyone from Stevie Wonder to Elton John.

what to buy next: Michael's solo debut, *Faith*, (Columbia, 1987, prod. George Michael) ⚐⚐⚐⚐ sold nearly 15 million copies worldwide and It also represented an artistic leap from the pre-fab pop of Wham!, balancing soulful ballads ("Kissing a Fool") with hard-hitting dance numbers ("Monkey," "I Want Your Sex").

what to avoid: Michael's talentless Wham! partner Andrew Ridgely made a dismal attempt at a solo singing career with *Son of Albert*, (Epic, 1990) WOOF! which deservingly slipped through the cracks unnoticed.

the rest: George Michael: *Older* (DreamWorks, 1996) ⚐⚐⚐⚐ Wham!: *Fantastic* (Columbia, 1983) ⚐⚐⚐ *Make It Big!* (Columbia, 1984) ⚐⚐ *Music from the Edge of Heaven* (Columbia, 1986) ⚐⚐⚐

worth searching for: Paying tribute to Queen's legendary late singer Freddy Mercury, Michael joined the British group onstage at Wembley with special guest Lisa Stansfield. The resulting EP, *Five Live*, (Hollywood, 1992) ⚐⚐⚐⚐ features several remarkable covers by the assemblage, including a take on Seal's "Killer."

▶▶ Seal, Take That, Babyface

◀◀ Elton John, Aretha Franklin, Stevie Wonder

Aidin Vaziri

Lee Michaels

Born Nov. 24, 1945, Los Angeles, Calif.

Michaels' organ-heavy soul-rock was an anomaly in guitar-happy California during the mid-60s. Michaels worked with a number of inconsequential bands until moving to San Francisco in 1965 and coming under the influence of the Jefferson Airplane (Michaels had formerly worked with Airplane drummer John Barbata). A talented producer, Michaels became enamored of overdubbing and began playing all the instruments on his records shortly after garnering a contract. His eponymous third album, a jam between Michaels and drummer Frosty (Bartholomew Eugene Smith-Frost), gave Michaels his first large-scale public notice, and he remained a draw for the next few years, scoring a major hit, "Do You Know What I Mean?" off *5th*. (A&M, 1971, prod. Lee Michaels) ⚐⚐⚐⚐ When Michaels lost drummer Keith Knudsen to the Doobie Brothers in 1973, he retired for a short while before returning to a lower rung on the rock ladder. Most of what you want to hear from him can be found on *The Lee Michaels Collection*. (Rhino, 1992) ⚐⚐⚐⚐

Larry Gabriel

Midnight Oil

Formed 1976 in Sydney, Australia

Peter Garrett, vocals; Jim Mogine, guitar, keyboards; Rob Hirst, drums; Martin Rotsey, guitar; Andrew "Bear" James, bass, (1976-79); Peter Gifford, bass (1979-87); Bones Hillman, bass (1990-present)

A muscular outfit with a burning social conscience, the Oils honed its chops in the Sydney pubs, where its incendiary live act has long been revered. The towering, shaven-headed Garrett—who holds a law degree and has run for public office in Australia—delivers the band's political messages with raging force, matched by Mogine's inventive hard-nosed melodies and Hirst's impassioned pounding. The band's creative peak during the 80s led to a fuller sound and a decidedly lower key urgency. Whether standing up for aboriginal Australians rights, nuclear disarmament or simply blasting away at suburban complacency, the Oils have maintained an individualistic integrity while achieving mainstream acceptability

what to buy: *10,9,8,7,6,5,4,3,2,1* (Columbia, 1983, prod Nick Launay and Midnight Oil) ⚐⚐⚐⚐ matches the band's intensity with its strongest (and most articulate) set of songs to date. Starting with the slow burn of "Outside World," the bone-rattling "Only the Strong" follows like a leer jet whipping through your back yard. And that's just the first two songs. To glimpse the thunder of its live shows, *Scream in Blue* (Columbia, 1992, prod. Midnight Oil and Keith Walker) ♪♪♪♪ provide a raw (and random) selection that includes fierce versions of many lesser known songs such as "Brave Faces" and "Progress," as well as "Read About It" and "Only the Strong." *Head Injuries* (Columbia, 1978, prod. Leszek J. Karski) ♪♪♪♪ is the band's best pre-*10,9,8...* work. The pure, lean muscle of "Cold, Cold Change" and "Back on the Borderline" are prime examples of its formative years

what to buy next: *Red Sails in the Sunset* (Columbia, 1985, prod. Nick Launay and Midnight Oil) ♪♪♪♪ finds the band at its most ambitious, welding funk and dense atmospheric keyboards to its hard rock roots. *Blue Sky Mining* (Columbia, 1990, prod. Warren Livesey and Midnight Oil) ♪♪♪♪ doesn't quite reach previous levels, but the tuneful title track, "King of the Mountain" and "Forgotten Years" make up for the lulls.

what to avoid: *Earth and Sun and Moon* (Columbia, 1993, prod. Nick Launay and Midnight Oil) ♪♪ is an ill-conceived attempt to return to the Oils' early rawness. Short on decent material, it sounds forced and redundant.

the rest: *Midnight Oil* (Aus. Powderworks, 1978/Columbia, 1990) ♪♪ *Bird Noises* (Aus. Powderworks EP, 1979/Columbia EP, 1990) ♪♪♪ *Species Deceases* (Aus. CBS EP, 1985/Columbia EP, 1990) ♪♪♪♪ *Place Without a Postcard* (Aus. CBS, 1981/Columbia 1990) ♪♪♪♪ *Diesel and Dust* (Columbia, 1987) ♪♪♪

worth searching for: *The Green Disc*, (Columbia, 1989, prod. Various) ♪♪♪♪ an exceptional—but promotion-only—retrospective that features hits, remixes and unreleased tracks.

▶▶ Love and Rockets, Inxs, silverchair

◀◀ The Clash, the Easybeats, Split Enz

Allan Orski

Mike & the Mechanics

See: Genesis

Milla

Born Milla Jovovich, Dec. 17, 1975 in Kiev, Ukraine

When they start handing out record contracts to fashion models, conventional wisdom dictates that you head for the hills. Not this time. Ukranian-born, L.A.-reared Milla Jovovich is as capable a lyricist as one could hope to find in an 18-year-old girl—dreamy and slightly schoolgirlish, perhaps, but look what those attributes have done for a grizzled vet like Tori Amos. On the ambitiously titled *The Divine Comedy*, (SBK/ERG, 1994, prod. Rupert Hine, Richard Feldman and Mark Holden) ♪♪♪♪ Milla's delicate vocals are surrounded by an intriguing soundscape of gently burbling keyboards, cascading acoustic guitars and more exotic instruments such as harmonium and kalimba. Milla hardly reinvents the wheel, but songs such as "It's Your Life" and "The Alien Song (for those who listen)" could mark the beginning of a new genre: Call it New Waif.

Daniel Durchholz

Steve Miller

Born Oct. 5, 1943 in Milwaukee, Wisc.

Throughout his prolific and protean journeyman career, Miller has braided together polished pop-rock, straight-ahead blues and acoustic-flavored pop. Widely regarded as Top 40 stooge whose 70s hits remain a staple of classic rock radio twenty years later, Miller—usually performing under the Steve Miller Band moniker—has actually made rewarding forays into a broad array of musical styles, displaying a depth and prowess often nothing short of astonishing. His father was a fanatical music buff with a tape recorder and Les Paul, T-Bone Walker and Charles Mingus all held sessions in the Miller living room. His first high school band in Dallas also included schoolmate Boz Scaggs and backed up visiting r&b stars at local clubs like Jimmy Reed.

Miller left college to pursue a musical career in the Chicago blues realm, where he recorded an unreleased album with the Goldberg-Miller Blues Band. He found his real starting place several years later in the burgeoning San Francisco rock scene. His band appeared at the historic 1967 Monterey Pop Festival and signed to record for Capitol records, an association that lasted more than a quarter-century. While Miller's early albums made him an underground radio favorite, Miller finally found the pop chart stroke in 1973 with *The Joker*; subsequent albums *Fly Like An Eagle* and *Book Of Dreams* made Miller one of the top attractions of the day. Although the gleaming hits gave Miller his Top 40 hack reputation, he was still capable of turning out a soulful jazz experiment like *Born 2B Blue* or a solid blues outing like *Living In the 20th Century*. He *is* Maurice, the Gangster, the Space Cowboy, Stevie "Guitar" Miller—the musician of many faces.

what to buy: His second greatest hits album, *The Best Of the Steve Miller Band 1974-1978*, (Capitol, 1978, prod. Steve Miller) has stayed on the best-seller lists since its release. But *Fly Like An Eagle* (Capitol, 1976, prod. Steve Miller) contains the best single all-around look at his great gifts.

what to buy next: Samples of his first six albums cover a broad territory, but *Best of 1968-1973* (Capitol, 1990, prod. Various) provides a quick, albeit spotty retrospective of his development. *Book Of Dreams* (Capitol, 1977, prod. Steve Miller) was actually recorded at the same sessions as *Fly Like An Eagle* and released a year later.

what to avoid: Miller remixed and edited many of the tracks on the three-CD collection, *Box Set* (Capitol, 1994, prod. Various), without broadening the set's viewpoint beyond much more than a greatest hits on steroids.

the rest: *Sailor* (Capitol, 1969) *Your Saving Grace* (Capitol, 1970) *Anthology* (Capitol, 1972) *The Joker* (Capitol, 1973) *Abracadabra* (Capitol, 1982) *Circle Of Love* (Capitol, 1981) *Steve Miller Band Live* (Capitol, 1983) *Italian X-Rays* (Capitol, 1984) *Living In the 20th Century* (Capitol, 1986) *Born 2B Blue* (Capitol, 1988) *Wide River* (Polydor, 1993)

worth searching for: The Miller band's debut album, *Children Of the Future* (Capitol, 1969, prod. Glyn Johns) is a bluesey Beatlesque undiscovered gem that was briefly available on compact disc.

▶▶ Omar and the Howlers, Blues Traveler, Spin Doctors, Big Head Todd and the Monsters

◀◀ Jimmy Reed, The Beatles, Cream

see also: *Boz Scaggs*

Joel Selvin

Milli Vanilli

Formed 1988 in Munich, Germany

Rob Pilatus and Fabrice Morvan

Milli Vanilli almost went down in pop history as one of the most successful—albeit artistically insignificant—groups of the video era. Instead, the duo has become the biggest punchline in pop. After scoring five Top 5 hits (including the consecutive No. 1's, "Baby Don't Forget My Number," "Girl I'm Gonna Miss You" and "Blame It On the Rain"); selling more than 7 million copies of its debut album, *Girl You Know It's True* (Arista, 1989, prod. Frank Farian) WOOF!, and capturing a Grammy for Best New Artist Grammy, it was discovered that Pilatus and Morvan revealed that they hadn't sung a single note on their record. Instead, the vocals were handled by Charles Shaw, John Davis and Brad Howe. But Milli Vanilli mastermind Farian—the German producer known for his work with Boney M—wanted an attractive look to go with his lightweight dance-pop, so he hired former breakdancers Pilatus (from Munich) and Morvan (from Paris) to become the faces of Milli Vanilli. The dreadlocked, bare-chested men, who had met at a Los Angeles club during the mid-80s, appeared on the album cover, in videos and on stage (lip-synching, of course) and were described by the New York Times as "exotically sexy." The group also conducted interviews as Milli Vanilli, with Pilatus telling a writer at one point: "Musically, we are more talented than any Bob Dylan. We are more talented than Paul McCartney, Mick Jagger...I'm the new Elvis." Following the revelations that they weren't quite ready to build their own Gracelands, Pilatus and Morvan were stripped of their Grammy, while their record company was ordered to give partial refunds to anybody who bought Milli Vanilli recordings or attended concerts believing that the duo was actually singing. Ironically, after Pilatus and Morvan sang a capella at a press conference, a voice coach said the duo sounded better than the men who actually were recorded. In 1991, a despondent Pilatus attempted suicide; five years later, he was charged on eight counts of allegedly attacking and threatening two people in separate incidents. Under court order, he later entered a drug treatment facility.

the rest: *Quick Moves: The Remix Album* (Arista, 1990) *Rob and Fab* (Taj, 1993) WOOF!

Joshua Freedom du Lac

Ministry

Formed 1981 in Chicago, Ill.

Al Jourgensen, vocals, guitar, keyboards; Lamont Welton, bass (1981-82); Paul Barker, bass, programming (1986-present); Stevo, drums (1981-82); Stephen George, drums (1982-86); William Rieflin, drums (1986-present); Roland Barker, keyboards (1986-present); Mike Scaccia, guitar (1990-present)

nine inch nails might sell more records, but the Al Jourgensen-led Ministry is the most influential American industrial-rock band. The group's 1983 debut, *With Sympathy*, was a forgettable exercise in synth-driven Europop, complete with fake British accents, but by the mid-80s, Jourgensen and Paul Barker, his chief collaborator, had cooked up a brave new sound, fusing menacing guitar-punk with harsh vocals and factory style rhythms pioneered by European acts such as Einsturzende Neubauten. Ministry defined industrial rock in the U.S. with albums such as *The Land of Rape and Honey* and *The Mind is a Terrible Thing to Taste* Though unquestionably on the cutting edge, the group muscled onto the pop charts with its 1992 album *Psalm 69* and stole the show on that summer's Lollapalooza tour. Meanwhile, Jourgensen and Barker have dabbled in countless projects outside of Ministry, most notably the Revolting Cocks but also 1,000 Homo DJs, Lard (with the Dead Kennedys' Jello Biafra), Pigface, Pailhead (with Fugazi/Minor Threat's Ian MacKaye) and Lead Into Gold.

what to buy: *The Land of Rape and Honey* (Sire, 1988, prod. Hypo Luxa and Hermes Pan (Al Jourgensen and Paul Barker)) is Ministry's most harrowing journey into the sonic apocalypse, featuring the hypnotic scream-fest "Stigmata."

what to buy next: *The Mind is a Terrible Thing to Taste* (Sire, 1989, prod. Hypo Luxa and Hermes Pan) walks the same path of horrific guitar-punk as *Rape and Honey*, though, as a successor, it doesn't sound quite as groundbreaking. The more experimental *Psalm 69: The Way to Succeed and the Way to Suck Eggs* (Sire, 1992, prod. Hypo Luxa and Hermes Pan) boasts "Jesus Built My Hotrod," a brilliant duet with Butthole Surfer Gibby Haynes.

what to avoid: *Twelve Inch Singles, 1981-1984,* (Wax Trax!, 1987, prod. N/A) a spotty collection of dance remixes from the band's early days.

the rest: *With Sympathy* (Wax Trax!/Arista, 1983) *Twitch* (Sire, 1986) *In Case You Didn't Feel Like Showing Up* (Sire EP, 1990) Filth Pig (Warner Bros., 1996)

worth searching for: The unintentionally amusing debut EP, *Cold Life,* (Wax Trax!, 1981) which casts the band as a Human League wanna-be.

solo outings:

Revolting Cocks *Big Sexy Land* (Wax Trax!, 1986) *You Goddamned Son of a Bitch* (Wax Trax!, 1988) *Beers, Steers & Queers* (Wax Trax!, 1990) *Linger Ficken' Good...And Other Barnyard Oddities* (Sire, 1993)

Lard *Power of Lard* (Alternative Tentacles, 1989) *The Last Temptation* (Alternative Tentacles, 1990);

Pailhead *Trait* (Wax Trax! EP, 1988)

▶▶ nine inch nails, KMFDM, Filter, Gravity Kills

◀◀ Einsturzende Neubauten, Cabaret Voltaire, Throbbing Gristle, the Sex Pistols

Thor Christensen

Minor Threat

Formed 1980 in Washington, D.C. Disbanded 1983.

Ian MacKaye, vocals; Lyle Preslar, guitar; Brian Baker, bass, guitar; Steve Hansgen, bass (1982-83); Jeff Nelson, drums

Behind its D.C. mentors, the pre-Rasta Bad Brains, Minor Threat was easily the second best thrash band of all time in that peculiar genre of already-fast punk sped up to hyper-warp speeds. Singer MacKaye and drummer Nelson launched the now-fabled, still prospering independent label Dischord with the their preceding band, the Teen Idles, but the raspy Idles were quickly overshadowed by this teen-powerhouse. Sometime after Minor Threat's demise, what little the group managed to release was culled together on one handy CD. Entitled *Complete* (Dischord, 1987, prod. Minor Threat), the force of this jagged juggernaut is still fierce. MacKaye's fervor and eyes-open passion approach that of a preacher's, but with a snarl instead of a smile. Railing against the violent, the cement-headed, the drug-dependent, basic hypocrisy and two-facedness, the man/boy is a human dynamo of rage, sarcasm, morals and liberating spirit, the howl of the young who want something better (a vision he still perpetuates, a decade and a half later, as a member of Fugazi). This ungodly performance is backed up by some of the most searing rock imaginable, so blistering and raw and sped up it's as if your 45 rpm record is playing at 78 without sounding like the Chipmunks. Such lacerating blips as "Minor Threat," "Bottled Violence," "Guilty of Being White" "Out of Step" and a cover of Wire's "12XU" are awe-striking in their pure, uncut speed and fury. Even when Minor Threat tempers the tempos on the second half (from 1983's *Out of Step* EP), the force remains a rocket, though with more sing-a-long results; listen to "Cashing In," and the surprising take on the Standells' mid-60s classic "Good Guys Don't Wear White." A kick in the ass that also kicked serious butt over the unwashed masses of international hardcore shouters/thrashers that followed in their wake. Besides Fugazi, Minor Threats members also went on to work in bands such as Bad Religion, Dag Nasty, the Meatmen, Egg Hunt and Embrace.

see also: *Fugazi, Bad Religion*

Jack Rabid

The Minus Five

See: Young Fresh Fellows

Minutemen

See: fIREHOSE

The Misfits

Formed 1977 in New Jersey. Disbanded 1983.

Glenn Danzig, vocals, electric piano; Jerry Caiafa, bass; Manny, drums (1977-78); Frank Licata, guitar (1978); Jim Catania, drums (1978-79); Bobby Steele, guitar (1979); Joey Image, drums, (1979); P.C. Doyle, guitar (1979-83); Arthur Googy, drums (1979-83); Robo, drums (1983)

If you outgrow Kiss seeking the darker underbelly of rock, The Misfits will pound you straight through the midnight hour. With an evil glee, the group emerged in New York clubs playing fast and brutal punk, complete with ghoulish make-up and lyrics that splatter like aural horror flicks. What sets The Misfits apart is Danzig's articulate and tuneful bellowing and an undercurrent of humor in their perverted 50s-style attack. The band broke up 1983, becoming an influential force on American hardcore. Danzig went on to form the short-lived Samhain and then the current MTV darling that bears his surname.

what to buy: *Walk Among Us* (Ruby, 1982) ♫♫♫♫ The definitive and highly sought-after album (before Ruby re-issued it in 1988) contains the classics "Vampira" and "Mommy, Can I Go Out and Kill Tonight?" It's offensive, ugly and indespensable. *Misfits* (Plan 9, 1986) ♫♫♫♫ packs most of the essential tracks into a melodic roar. *Legacy of Brutality* (Caroline, 1985) ♫♫♫½ compiles, with a few missteps, some of the band's early recordings and excellent outtakes—notably the bossa nova "Angelfuck" and "She."

what to buy next: *Misfits Box* (Caroline, 1996) ♫♫♫♫ slams together virtually everything the band recorded into a four-CDs housed in a coffin-shaped box. Pricey, but a demonic Christmas present for the completists.

what to avoid: *Earth A.D./Wolfsblood* (Plan 9, 1982) ♫♫ finds the band attempting to conform to hardcore with stiff and tuneless results.

the rest: *Misfits 2* (Caroline, 1995) ♫♫♫

worth searching for: *Evil Live* (Plan 9, 1982), an out-of-print concert souvenir that captures their live thunder shortly after the release of *Walk Among Us*

▶▶ Samhain, Danzig, Guns 'n' Roses, Sepultura, Slayer

◀◀ The Ramones, The Damned, Kiss

see also: *Danzig*

Allan Orski

Missing Persons /Polytown/Patrick O'Hearn

Formed 1980 in Los Angeles, Calif. Disbanded 1986.

Dale Bozzio, vocals; Warren Cuccurullo, guitar; Patrick O'Hearn, bass; Chuck Wild, keyboards; Terry Bozzio, drums

Whether you love or hate the music of Frank Zappa, you can't deny his knack for assembling talented backup musicians. One of Zappa's most accomplished ensembles—the Bozzios, O'-Hearn and Cuccurullo—went on to form Missing Persons, whose poppy New Wave, marked by Dale Bozzio's hiccup-riddled Kewpie doll vocals, was a far cry from Zappa's avant rock madness. At this point, little of the group's work remains in print. *The Best of Missing Persons* (Capitol, 1987, prod. Various) ♫♫♫½ is a good starting point, with most of the band's singles ("Words," "Destination Unknown," "Walking in L.A.,") and some of its better album tracks ("Mental Hopscotch", "I Can't Think About Dancin'"). *Spring Session M* (Capitol, 1982/One Way, 1995, prod. Ken Scott) ♫♫♫ is entertaining but decidedly weaker.

solo outings:

Terry Bozzio (with Polytown) Polytown (CMP Karakter, 1994) ♫♫♫½

Patrick O'Hearn Ancient Dreams (BMG, 1985) ♫♫♫♫ *Between Twc Worlds* (BMG, 1987) ♫♫♫½ *Rivers Gonna Rise* (BMG, 1988) ♫ *El Dorado* (BMG, 1989) ♫♫♫½ *Indigo* (BMG, 1991) ♫♫♫½ *Private Music* (BMG, 1992) ♫♫♫ *Trust* (Deep Cave, 1995) ♫♫ *Metaphor* (Deep Cave, 1996) ♫♫

see also: *Frank Zappa, Duran Duran (Cuccurullo), Jeff Beck (Terry Bozzio)*

Brandon Trenz

Mission of Burma

Formed 1979 in Boston, Mass. Disbanded 1983

Clint Conley, bass, vocals, percussion; Roger Miller, guitar, vocals, piano, trumpet, percussion; Peter Prescott, drums, vocals, percussion; Martin Swope, tape manipulations, loops, percussion

The best punk band to ever come from Boston, and maybe the most important Beantown band of any genre, Mission of Burma had a fruitful, extremely loud existence that lasted until 1983, when Miller's severe hearing damage forced him to stop playing. "Academy Fight Song," MoB's first single, has frequently been covered, most notably by R.E.M., and "That's When I

Reach for My Revolver" is one of the three greatest alternative rock songs ever. The band was formed by Miller, who had moved to Boston from Ann Arbor, Mich., in 1978, when he and Conley quit Moving Parts. The relentlessly clanging guitars and the throbbing bass set a standard for intense, dense rock that many bands since have aspired to. The band's final hometown show in 1983 was filmed, and though "Live at the Bradford" (Atavistic) barely breaks the half-hour mark, it's a worthwhile document. Prescott went on to form Volcano Suns and, in the 90s, Kustomized. Miller and Swope stayed together in Birdsongs of the Mesozoic. Miller also released a large quantity of work under his own name and with his group No Man, as well as childhood recordings under the name M-3. Conley produced the first Yo La Tengo album and then left the music industry. *Mission of Burma* (Rykodisc, 1988, prod. Richard W. Harte) is a magnificently generous (80 minutes) CD compilation that has "Academy Fight Song," all of the seminal EP *Signals, Calls, and Marches* (Ace of Hearts EP, 1981, prod. Richard W. Harte) and the group's only studio LP, *Vs.* (Ace of Hearts, 1982, prod. Richard W. Harte) Nobody can understand punk without this CD.

the rest: *The Horrible Truth About Burma* (Ace of Hearts, 1985) *Let There Be Burma* (Taang!, 1990)

Steve Holtje

Mr. Big

Formed 1988 in Los Angeles, Calif.

Eric Martin, vocals; Paul Gilbert, guitar; Billy Sheehan, bass; Pat Torpey, drums

When Mr. Big came together during the late 80s, each of its members had done time on the hard rock/lite metal circuit with varying amounts of commercial success (Sheehan was a noted bassist who played for a newly solo David Lee Roth). Swearing allegiance to 70s blues-rock (such as the Free song from whence the band took its name), Mr. Big's first videos and concerts nevertheless showcased flourescent guitars, flashy shredding and guitar and bass solos played with electric drills (which eventually led to a Makita power tool sponsorship). The band's brief moment in the spotlight came when the 1991 power ballad, "To Be With You," hit big, taking the parent album *Lean Into It* (Atlantic, 1991, prod. Keith Olsen), to platinum status. After that blip, however, Mr. Big's impact has been untrackable, and nowadays the band spends its time cultivating its popularity in Japan and other overseas markets.

the rest: *Mr. Big* (Atlantic, 1989) *Bump Ahead* (Atlantic, 1993) *Hey Man* (Atlantic, 1996)

Todd Wicks

Mr. Bungle

See: Faith No More

Mr. Mister

Formed 1982 in Los Angeles, Calif. Disbanded 1988.

Richard Page, bass, vocals; Steve George, keyboards; Steve Farris, guitar; Pat Mastelotto, drums

Enjoying pop success that seemed to come from nowhere during the mid-80s, Mr. Mister actually began as the vision of Page and George, experienced songwriters who had crafted hits for acts such as John Parr and REO Speedwagon. Eager to grab a bit of the spotlight for themselves, they recruited two other session aces to round out the band and concentrated on writing hits for themselves. The group's sophomore effort, *Welcome to the Real World*, (RCA, 1985, prod. Mr. Mister and Phil DeVilliers) is all that remains in print, boasting massive, semi-spiritual hits such as the atmospheric ballad "Broken Wings" and "Kyrie." Despite selling millions of copies of that album, Mr. Mister flopped on its next outing as its particular brand of synth-pop faded from view. After the group disbanded, Page turned down offers to join both Toto and Chicago.

Eric Deggans

Joni Mitchell

Born Roberta Joan Anderson, November 1943 in Fort Macleod, Alta., Canada

Mitchell is one of the most influential singer-songwriters to emerge from the late 60s folk-rock scene, a poet on par with Bob Dylan. As a child, Joan Anderson took piano lessons in Saskatoon, Canada, and as a teenager taught herself to play ukelele and later guitar so she could entertain at parties. She first gained notice as a songwriter when Judy Collins turned her song "Both Sides Now" into a Top 10 hit in 1968. That same year, Mitchell's debut album was released to critical acclaim, and the rapid succession of albums that followed peaked with the classic *Court and Spark* During the mid-70s, Mitchell shifted gears, dropped the angst angel image and stretched out for experimentations in electronic and ethnic music and collaborations with jazz players such as Tom Scott and the legendary Charles Mingus. Though she releases albums infrequently—she also pursues an active career as a painter—Mitchell remains a vital and ambitious artist; her latest effort, 1995's *Turbulent Indigo*, captured two Grammy Awards.

what to buy: *Court and Spark* (Asylum, 1974, prod. Joni Mitchell) remains Mitchell's top achievement, a melding of pop and jazz stylings that netted multiple Grammy nominations and the hit singles "Help Me" and "Free Man in Paris". *Turbulent Indigo* (Warner Bros., 1994, prod. Joni Mitchell and Larry Klein) is an evocative collection of songs that sounds both modern and timeless. With its all-star guest list—including Stephen Stills and James Taylor—*Blue* (Reprise, 1971, prod. Joni Mitchell) is a frank and revealing work, as well as one of Mitchell's finest singing performances.

what to buy next: *Ladies of the Canyon* (Reprise, 1971, prod. Joni Mitchell) houses the Mitchell standards "Big Yellow Taxi," "Woodstock" and "The Circle Game." *For the Roses* (Asylum, 1972, prod. Joni Mitchell) was Mitchell's first gold album and includes her first Top 40 hit "You Turn Me On, I'm a Radio." *The Hissing of Summer Lawns* (Asylum, 1975, prod. Joni Mitchell) continues to explore jazzy and impressionistic song veins using the same all-star jazz aces who worked on *Court and Spark*

what to avoid: The guest-laden (Billy Idol?) *Chalk Mark in a Rain Storm* (Geffen, 1988, prod. Joni Mitchell and Larry Klein) is a surprisingly slight effort, musically bland and lyrically weak.

the rest: *Joni Mitchell* (Reprise, 1968) *Clouds* (Reprise, 1969) *Miles of Aisles* (Asylum, 1974) *Hejira* (Asylum, 1975); *Don Juan's Reckless Daughter* (Asylum, 1977) *Mingus* (Asylum, 1979) *Shadows and Light* (Asylum, 1980) *Wild Things Run Fast* (Geffen, 1982) *Dog Eat Dog* (Geffen, 1985) *Night Ride Home* (Geffen, 1991)

worth searching for: *Just Ice* (KTS, 1994) a digital bootleg recording of a rare Mitchell performance in Toronto after *Turbulent Indigo's release.*

Tori Amos, Tracey Bonham, Shawn Colvin, Milla Jovovich, Jewel, Alannis Morisette, Sarah MacLachlan, Prince, Seal

Crosby, Stills & Nash, James Taylor, Motown, Charles Mingus, John Coltrane, Dizzy Gillespie

Hilary Weber

Moby

Born Richard Melville Hall, Sept. 11, 1965 in Darien, Conn.

Although Moby (a distant relative of "Moby Dick" author Herman Melville) is one of techno's brightest stars, he works outside of techno conventions. He's emerged from the studio to put a face with his music in an otherwise anonymous genre. He's frowned upon drug and alcohol consumption while working in a community in which Ecstacy is all the rave. And he's exploded far beyond the sonic boundaries of techno, boldly folding elements of other genres into his cathartic recordings. A born-again Christian who used to play in a hardcore punk band—then worked as a New York club DJ, spinning records for the likes of Run-D.M.C. and Cher—Moby refuses to preach to the converted. Instead, the self-contained studio whiz passionately challenges with his strong ideals and intense, three-dimensional music, which contains uplifting messages of faith and strong elements of spirituality.

what to buy: Although you'll find it filed under techno, the masterful *Everything Is Wrong* (1995, Elektra, prod. Moby) is free from lyrical and musical constraints, incorporating elements of classical, reggae, gospel, hip-hop, funk, industrial, disco and punk into its restless but cleansing fold. As always, Moby handles almost all of the writing, composing, producing, instrumentation, programming and engineering, although several disco divas and a dance-hall toaster share much of the vocal load. The hyper "Feeling So Real" and "Everytime You Touch Me," and the ambient, album-closing "When It's Cold I'd Like to Die" are standouts.

what to buy next: *Move*, (Elektra EP, 1993, prod. Moby) which features the moving "Unloved Symphony," provides a sneak preview of the ground Moby covers on *Everything Is Wrong.*

the rest: *Moby* (Instinct, 1992) *Early Underground* (Instinct, 1993) *Ambient* (Instinct, 1993)

Tricky, Goldie, Aphex Twin

Brian Eno, Arvo Part, Tangerine Dream, Donna Summer, Bad Brains, the Orb, Saint Etienne

Joshua Freedom du Lac

Moby Grape

Formed 1966 in San Francisco, Calif.

Skip Spence, guitar, vocals (1966-68); Jerry Miller, guitar, vocals;

Peter Lewis, guitar, vocals; Bob Mosley, bass, vocals; Don Stevenson, drums, vocals

Though the Dead, the Airplane and Big Brother are the groups synonymous with the Summer of Love, no finer record emerged from San Francisco in 1967 than *Moby Grape.* Spearheaded by a three-guitar frontline, tight harmonies and a more propulsive sound than their Bay Area brethren, the Grape mixed equal parts rock, psychedelia, country-funk and folk on their superb debut. They seemed a band destined for great things; everyone could write, everyone had chops and they all could sing—from Bob Mosely's gravely white soul to the hauntingly plaintive Peter Lewis. Yet, by their second album, ego and excess were beginning to show. *Wow* was a double LP, with one record ("Grape Jam") consisting entirely of aimless studio jammming. Within three years, the group was hopelessly and weirdly splintered—Mosely left to enlist in the Marines (!!), Skip Spence was in Bellevue and the rest were wandering through the wreckage, never to recapture the promise of their fine first album.

what to buy: Perhaps the only Moby Grape you'll ever need to own, *Vintage: Very Best* (Columbia/Legacy, 1993, prod. Various) ♪♪♪♪ is a well-packaged two-CD retrospective that includes the entire debut album as well as a strong selection of late 60's material along with unreleased demos, outtakes and live performances. If, understandably, you'd prefer the debut album alone, *Moby Grape* (San Francisco Sound, 1994, prod. David Rubinson) ♪♪♪♪ is available on a single CD.

what to buy next: *Wow/Grape Jam* (San Francisco Sound, 1994, prod. David Rubinson) ♪♪♪ is the band's overblown sophomore release, with a few gems among the over-ambitious misses—plus the lackluster set of studio jams. Only available on vinyl as of this writing, *Moby Grape '69* (Columbia, 1969, prod. David Rubinson) ♪♪♪ is the best of the later records, notably for some fine songs by Peter Lewis.

what to avoid: *Moby Grape '83,* (San Francisco Sound, 1983, prod. David Robinson) ♪♪ a far from successful reunion. For fanatics only.

the rest: *Truly Fine Citizen* (Columbia, 1969) ♪♪ *20 Granite Creek* (Reprise, 1971) ♪♪♪ *Live Grape* (Escape, 1978) ♪♪

worth searching for: During the late 70's, Mosley formed a band called "The Ducks," who backed up Neil Young on a brief but notorious back-to-the-bars tour of California. Look for the bootlegs.

solo outings:

Skip Spence Oar (Columbia, 1969) ♪♪♪

Bob Mosley Bob Mosley (Warner Bros., 1972) ♪

▶▶ Gin Blossoms, Golden Smog, Wilco

◀◀ The Byrds, Buffalo Springfield, Jefferson Airplane, The Beatles

Doug Pippin

Modern English

Formed in 1979 in Colchester, England. Disbanded 1991. Reformed 1995

Robbie Grey, vocals; Richard Brown, drums (1979-84); Gary McDowell, guitar; Michael Conroy, bass; Stephen Walker, keyboards (1979-84); Aaron Davidson, keyboards, guitar, vocals (1984-91). Current lineup—Grey; Ted Mason, guitars, keyboards; Matthew Shipley, keyboards; Nicholas Denton, bass; Robbie Brian, drummer

Modern English, comprised of self-taught musicians, played a psychedelic revival style of new wave. Falling into the "bands with weird haircuts" category, its biggest contribution was a memorable song called "I Melt With You" from its sophomore effort, *After The Snow,* (Sire, 1983, prod. Hugh Jones) ♪♪♪♪ which the band has milked for a reunion in the midst of the mid-90s wave of 80s nostalgia.

the rest: *Mesh And Lace* (4AD, 1980) ♪♪♪ *Richochet Days* (Sire, 1984) ♪♪♪ *Stop Start* (Sire, 1985) ♪♪♪ *Pillow Lips* (TVT, 1991) ♪♪♪ *Everything's Mad* (Imago, 1996) ♪♪♪♪

Anna Glen

Mojave 3

See: Slowdive

Eddie Money

Born Edward Mahoney, March 21, 1949 in Brooklyn, N.Y.

For straight-ahead, shot-and-a-beer barroom rock 'n' roll, it's hard to do better than Money's 1977 debut album and a few other assorted moments from his career. The son of a police officer, Money attended the New York Police Academy himself but was more interested in the rock he was playing at night. He dropped out of cop school and headed to the Bay Area where, with help from promoter Bill Graham, Money began his music career as an affable palooka with a knack for irresistible hits such as "Two Tickets to Paradise" and "Baby Hold On." But since the Money's partnership with guitarist and chief foil Jimmy Lyon splintered during the early 80s, he's floundered, with the occasional hit—such as "Take Me Home Tonight (Be My Baby)," a Top 5 hit in 1986—rising out of a wealth of tepid and forgettable material.

what to buy: *Eddie Money* (Columbia, 1977, prod. Bruce Botnick) 🦴🦴🦴½ is a fine debut that remains Money's strongest entry, buoyed by the hits ("Two Tickets to Paradise," "Baby Hold On") and other fine tracks such as his cover of the Miracles' "You've Really Got a Hold On Me."

what to buy next: *Life For the Taking* (Columbia, 1978, prod. Bruce Botnick) 🦴🦴🦴 and *Playing for Keeps* (Columbia, 1980, prod. Ron Nevison) 🦴🦴🦴 are solid, rocking efforts whose key songs—"Gimme Some Water," "Rock and Roll the Place," "Trinidad," "Get a Move On"—still hold up. *Greatest Hits: Sound of Money* (Columbia, 1989, prod. Various) 🦴🦴🦴½ is a reasonable best-off whose three new songs should have been canned in favor of better songs form his albums.

what to avoid: *Unplug it In.* (Columbia EP, 1992) **WOOF!** The unplugged format benefits some artists, but Money isn't one of them.

the rest: *No Control* (Columbia, 1982) 🦴🦴🦴 *Where's the Party?* (Columbia, 1983) 🦴🦴 *Can't Hold Back* (Columbia, 1986) 🦴🦴½ *Nothing to Lose* (Columbia, 1988) 🦴 *Right Here* (Columbia, 91) 🦴 *Love and Money* (Wolfgang, 1995) 🦴🦴

▶▶ Michael Bolton, Jon Secada, Peter Cetera, John Mellencamp, Bryan Adams

◀◀ Sam Cooke, Chuck Berry, Elvis Presley, Rod Stewart, Eric Burdon (Animals), Motown, Stax

Gary Graff

The Monkees

Formed 1965 in Los Angeles, Calif. Disbanded 1970. Reunited 1986-89, 1996.

David Jones, vocals; Mickey Dolenz, vocals, drums; Mike Nesmith, vocals, guitar (1965-69); Peter Tork, bass, guitar, vocals (1965-69, 1989-present)

From the Fab Four to the prefab four. The Monkees didn't form; the band was made—in this case for an American TV show inspired by the Beatles' film "A Hard Day's Night" (among the auditions' more famous rejects were Stephen Stills and Three Dog Night's Danny Hutton). The show retained the movie's zaniness and even went a step or two further into a plotless kind of creative anarchy. Musically, however, the Monkees played tightly constructed, Brill Building-style pop overseen by music biz mogul Don Kirshner. It worked; with songs written by Neil Diamond, and the team of Gerry Goffin and Carole King, among others, the Monkees were a chart and radio fixture with "Last Train to Clarksville," "Pleasant Valley Sunday," "I'm a Believer" and "Daydream Believer." The group even enjoyed a bit of influence on the punk scene with "(I'm Not Your) Steppin' Stone," a particular favorite of the Sex Pistols. The hits stopped coming—at least in droves—about the time the group wrested creative control for itself. After the TV show was canceled in 1968, the Monkees tried a movie, the trippy and largely unwatchable "Head," and slowly splintered—Tork leaving first, then Nesmith. But when MTV started airing episodes of the TV show again in 1986, the Monkees (sans Nesmith) were back, and the revival repeats itself periodically.

what to buy: *The Monkees Greatest Hits* (Rhino, 1995, prod. Various) 🦴🦴🦴🦴🦴 is a 20-song confection of timeless pop hits—something nobody with an ounce of hipness could have expected of the Monkees at the time.

what to buy next: This is a bit problematic—how much more do you want than the hits? But try the soundtrack to "Head" (Colgems, 1968/Rhino, 1994, prod. Various) 🦴🦴🦴 a trippy little souvenir of the times which features poetry, dialogue from the film and guest appearances by Neil Young, Leon Russell and Ry Cooder. *Barrel Full of Monkees: Monkees for Kids* (Kid Rhino, 1996, prod. Various) 🦴🦴🦴 is considerably more listenable than a Barney tape.

what to avoid: The three-volume series *Missing Links* (Rhino, 1988, 1989 and 1996, prod. Bill Inglot and Andrew Sandoval) 🦴 The Monkees made some terrific singles, but it wasn't a band whose vault is filled with treasures.

the rest: *The Monkees* (Colgems, 1966/Rhino, 1994) 🦴🦴🦴 *More of the Monkees* (Colgems, 1967/Rhino, 1994) 🦴🦴🦴 *Headquarters* (Colgems, 1967/Rhino, 1995) 🦴🦴½ *Pices, Aquarius, Capricorn & Jones, Ltd.* (Colgems, 1967/Rhino, 1995) 🦴🦴🦴 *The Birds, the Bees and the Monkees* (Colgems, 1968/Rhino, 1994) 🦴🦴½ *Instant Replay* (Colgems, 1969/Rhino, 1995) 🦴🦴 *The Monkees Present* (Colgems, 1969/Rhino, 1994) 🦴🦴 *Changes* (Colgems, 1970/Rhino, 1994) 🦴 *Live 1967* (Rhino, 1987) 🦴🦴 *Pool It* (Rhino, 1987/1995) 🦴🦴 *Listen to the Band* (Rhino, 1991) 🦴🦴🦴½

worth searching for: Videotapes from the Monkees' TV shows. They're out there, including a lavish (and expensive) boxed set from Rhino.

solo outings:

Dolenz and Jones (with Tommy Boyce and Bobby Hart): *Concert in Japan* (Varese Sarabande, 1996) 🦴🦴

Mike Nesmith: And the Hits Just Keep Comin' (Rio, 1972/1995)

▶▶ The Partridge Family, the Archies, Josie & the Pussycats, Big Star, the Sex Pistols, the Go-Go's

◀◀ The Beatles, Herman's Hermits, the Hollies

Gary Graff

Monks of Doom

See: Camper Van Beethoven

Moody Blues /Justin Hayward and John Lodge/Mike Pinder

Formed 1964 in Birmingham, England. Disbanded 1974. Re-formed 1978.

Justin Hayward, vocals, guitar (1966-present); John Lodge, vocals, bass (1966-present); Ray Thomas, vocals, flute; Graeme Edge, drums; Mike Pinder, keyboards (1964-78); Patrick Moraz, keyboards (1978-89); Denny Laine, vocals, guitar (1964-66); Clint Warwick, bass, vocals (1964-66)

One of the longest-living bands to emerge during the 60s, the Moody Blues quickly departed from its original blues orientation to adopt the "cosmic" style for which it's best known. The band's work is strongly melodic, ranging from meditative mood pieces ("Isn't Life Strange," "Legend of a Mind") to driving rock ("Ride My See Saw," "I'm Just a Singer (In a Rock and Roll Band)"), with lyrics that ponder questions of existence, the nature of reality and other Big Questions. The group has enjoyed two periods of great success, one during the late 60s and early 70s, the other during the late 70s and early 80s with a string of more straightforward hits such as "Your Wildest Dreams" and "I Know You're Out There Somewhere." The Moodies' latest tact is augmenting its summer amphitheater shows with symphony orchestras, hearkening back to the early days of the Hayward-Lodge lineup.

what to buy: *Days of Future Passed* (Deram/Polydor, 1967, prod. Hugh Mendl, Tony Clarke and Michael Dacre-Barclay) is one of the earliest collaborations between rock band and orchestra, a flowing, conceptual piece that houses the hits "Nights in White Satin" and "Forever Afternoon (Tuesday?)." *Seventh Sojourn* (Threshold, 1972, prod. Tony Clarke) is one of the Moodies' most consistent albums and its last before an extended hiatus. *This Is the Moody Blues* (Polydor, 1974, prod. Various) is a good compilation of the group's 1967-72 peak.

what to buy next: *On the Threshold of a Dream* (Deram/Polydor, 1969, prod. Tony Clarke) prominently features the band's signature Mellotron sound, while *Every Good Boy Deserves Favour* (Polydor, 1971, prod. Tony Clarke) features some of its best songs, including "Emily's Song" and the upbeat "The Story in Your Eyes." Devotees will have a ball with *Time Traveller,* (Polydor, 1994, prod. Various) an extensive and comprehensive box set; the more modest *Greatest Hits* (PolyGram, 1989, prod. Various) should suffice for those seeking a simple sampler.

what to avoid: *The Present* (Polydor, 1983) is mediocre at best, with nothing new to offer even die-hard fans.

the rest: *In Search of the Lost Chord* (Deram/Polydor, 1968) *To Our Children's Children's Children* (Polydor, 1969) *Question of Balance* (Polydor, 1970) *Caught Live + 5* (PolyGram, 1977) *Octave* (Polydor, 1978) *Long Distance Voyager* (Polydor, 1981) *The Other Side of Life* (Polydor, 1986) *Sur la Mer* (PolyGram, 1988) *Keys of the Kingdom* (PolyGram, 1991) *A Night at Red Rocks with the Colorado Symphony Orchestra* (Polydor, 1993)

worth searching for: The import *The Magnificent Moodies* (London, 1965/Polydor,1989) showcases the earliest edition of the band. *Prelude* (Polydor, 1987) is another import compilation and includes some "lost" tracks and B-sides.

solo outings:

Justin Hayward: *Night Flight* (Deram/PolyGram, 1980)

Justin Hayward and John Lodge: *Blue Jays* (Threshold/Polydor, 1975)

Michael Pinder: *The Promise* (Threshold, 1975) *Off the Shelf* (Higher and Higher, 1993) *Among the Stars* (One Step, 1995)

▶▶ Electric Light Orchestra, Genesis, Yes, Barclay James Harvest, Fairport Convention

◀◀ Buddy Holly, Elvis Presley, the Beatles, Motown

Polly Vedder

Keith Moon

See: The Who

Gary Moore

Born April 4, 1952 in Belfast, Ireland

A lively, energetic guitar player, Moore served stints in Coliseum and Thin Lizzy—during the latter's mid-70s *Jailbreak* peak—before following his own path. He stumbled at first, chasing rock radio with a series of plodding, occasionally contrived albums. But during the late 80s Moore got the blues, and since then, all has been well. Moore isn't necessarily about flash, so you have to pay attention to hear his subtle mix of rhythm and lead elements. He's also good for a few hot guests on each album, ranging from blues heroes such as B.B. King and Albert Collins to heavy metal icon Ozzy Osbourne.

what to buy: *Still Got the Blues* (Charisma, 1990, prod. Gary Moore) commands an immediate re-assessment of Moore's place in the rock pantheon, with guest appearances by Albert King and Albert Collins and Moore's best-known track, "Oh Pretty Woman." He also helmed *Blues For Greeny,* (Charisma, 1996, prod. Gary Moore and Ian Taylor) an album of deftly played early Fleetwood Mac covers in tribute to that band's troubled founder Peter Green.

what to buy next: Moore can cut a commanding live figure, though that aspect of his talents has never been captured adequately on record. *Blues Alive* (Virgin, 1993, prod. Gary Moore and Ian Taylor) is the best of his concert albums, with estimable—though not quite transcendent—versions of blues staples such as "The Sky is Crying," "Further On Up the Road" and "Walking By Myself."

what to avoid: *Wild Frontier,* (Virgin, 1987, prod. Gary Moore and Peter Collins) one of those early albums that shows for a hard rocker, Moore is a pretty good blues player.

the rest: *We Want Moore* (Virgin, 1986/1989) *After the War* (Virgin, 1989) *Rockin' Every Night: Live in Japan* (Virgin, 1989) *Still Got the Blues* (Charisma, 1990) *Dirty Fingers* (Roadrunner, 1990) *After Hours* (Charisma, 1992) *The Early Years* (WTG, 1992) *G Force* (Roadrunner, 1992) *Live at the Marquee* (Griffin, 1994) *Ballads + Blues 1982-1994* (Charisma, 1995)

worth searching for: There's a plethora of Moore guest appearances in the record racks. Check out his licks on "If Trouble Was Money" from the Albert Collins best-of *Collins Mix* (Pointblank, 1993) or his solo on "She's My Baby" from the Traveling Wilburys' *Vol. III* (Warner Bros., 1990)

Stevie Ray Vaughan, Randy Rhoads, Metallica, Colin James, Kenny Wayne Shepherd

Fleetwood Mac, John Mayall's Bluesbreakers, Elmore James, B.B. King, Albert Collins, Hubert Sumlin

see also: *Thin Lizzy*

Gary Graff

Thurston Moore

See: Sonic Youth

Ikue Ile Mori

See: DNA

Alanis Morissette

Born June 1, 1974 in Ottawa, Canada

Americans may think that Morissette came out of nowhere. But Canadians know that she came from worse than that. Her first two albums, *Alanis* (MCA Canada, 1991, prod. Leslie Howe) and *Now is the Time,* (MCA Canada, 1992, prod. Leslie Howe) were recorded in her teens and only ever available in her home country; they're now strenuously deleted worldwide. Collectively, they earned her a reputation as the Tiffany of Canada. Her multi-million-selling, chart-topping, Grammy/Juno/Brits Award-winning international debut, *Jagged Little Pill* (Maverick, 1995, prod. Glen Ballard), is quite a different story. With producer and co-writer Ballard, she's crafted a pensive but volatile persona and a sound that's very attentive to current music but fertile with its own ideas. Her graft of haggard, Dylan-esque harmonica to grunge-era guitars sets up a generational dialogue which reflects with witty irony on the simple style-recycling of her peers. Her continuation of the demonic-possession vocal tradition of Buffy Sainte-Marie and Sinead O'Connor stands out refreshingly in an age of monotone alterna-rock grumblers, though her singing can tend toward affect in the studio and benefits from the rawness and spontaneity of live performance. Ballard's production makes too frequent use of the stop-short, a cappella ending, but is satisfyingly gimmick-free otherwise, particularly in the power-folk atmospherics of "Right Through You" and "Forgiven."

Adam McGovern

Morphine

Formed 1992 in Boston, Mass.

Mark Sandman, two-string slide bass, vocals; Dana Colley, baritone saxophone; Billy Conway, drums

Morphine could easily be dismissed as a gimmick—a rock band with no guitar—were it not for the musician's skills as musicians and their ability to craft great songs from sparse resources. What makes the band's minimalist formula click is each member's keen understanding of his role: Sandman writes insidiously catchy songs that he injects with propulsively cool bass lines (think the "Peter Gunn Theme" on peyote) and a sly vocal style; Conway's drumming is a rock solid anchor; and, most importantly, Colley's sax (or saxes; he occasionally plays two at a time) writhes and slithers with sleazy delight. You never miss the guitar. Morphine has had continued success with this formula; each of its three records sounds fresh, inventive and addictively cool. *Yes* (Rykodisc, 1995, prod. Mark Sandman and Paul Q. Kolderie) ₰₰₰₰ is the best so far, boasting a lexicon of alluring riffs riding beneath Sandman's detached vocals. The best songs on the disk ("Honey White," "All Your Way" and "Super Sex") achieve an infectious hybrid of rock and seedy strip club jazz that perfectly conveys Sandman's world-weary lyrics which accept that the world is full of treachery, infidelity and dangerous sexual curves and, like a New Orleans funeral, finds reason to celebrate anyway.

the rest: *Cure for Pain* (Rykodisc, 1993) ₰₰₰♪ *Good* (Rykodisc, 1992) ₰₰₰

Dave Galens

Van Morrison

Born August 31, 1945 in Belfast, Ireland

More than anyone's except maybe Jerry Lee Lewis or Little Richard, the mercurial music of Morrison explores that most elusive of dichotomies: the tension between the sacred and the profane, the spiritual and the worldly, sex and chastity. Alternatingly pious and lascivious, Morrison's best albums explore that most tenuous and volatile of life's conflicts. He has lurched all over the emotional and musical landscape in his search. As a teen-ager in Them, Morrison screamed lustily, emulating hard-bitten American bluesmen and scoring hits with the proto-rock/blues of "Baby, Please Don't Go" and his own "Gloria," still a garage-band mainstay. After the pop-heavy (but controversial) "Brown-Eyed Girl," which revealed a seemingly endless capacity for hit records, Morrison's first real solo record, *Astral Weeks,* veered away from the mainstream, introducing an inquisitive, introspective and self-absorbed obsession with folk/jazz, all banging acoustic guitars, strings, impressionistic lyrics and a grunting, growling scat that would differentiate his voice from all others. He embraced the poetry and mysticism of William Blake and William Butler Yeats with the same enthusiasm as the lyrics of Jackie Wilson or Huddie Ledbetter. His early solo records for Warner Bros., especially the warm country/soul of *Moondance, His Band and Street Choir, Tupelo Honey* and *St. Dominic's Preview* reflect the rural hippie aesthetic of the period and his Woodstock, N.Y., surroundings. After a brief hiatus between 1974-77, his later Warners albums seemed to tilt further in favor of the mystic and spiritual, most notably on *Beautiful Vision* and *Into the Music.* Since moving to Polydor in the mid-80s, Morrison's music has matured even more but has retained—some would probably say re*gained*—its edge. For all his accomplishments and influence, Morrison remains something of a (large) cult artist, and his aversion to show business mechanisms has been well-documented. Eschewing fashion in favor of his muse, wherever it takes him, Morrison displays a rare honesty, tenacity and willingness for growth and exploration without consideration for commercial trends or fashion. It can be a bumpy ride at times, but none of his albums have been completely without merit. Morrison seems forever trapped at the junction of the path of righteousness and the highway to hell, and he's brought us along as he makes up his mind which way he's heading. It's a trip well worth taking.

what to buy: Choosing the best from someone as prolific and challenging as Morrison is difficult at best, but his first three solo records are absolute musts. *Astral Weeks* (Warner Bros., 1968, prod. Lewis Merenstein) ₰₰₰₰₰ is a song cycle that sounds like a concept album, even if it isn't, as it meanders through the alleys and back streets of London's pre-punk Notting Hill Gate with sleazy eccentrics like the unforgettable icon "Madame George." *Moondance* (Warner Bros., 1970, prod. Van Morrison) ₰₰₰₰₰ and *Van Morrison His Band and the Street Choir* (Warner Bros., 1970, prod. Van Morrison) ₰₰₰₰♪ would have made an extraordinary double album, with numerous youthful examples of the Morrison acoustic soul magic including "Into the Mystic," "Caravan," "Crazy Love," "Domino," "Blue Money" and "Call Me Up in Dreamland." *Hymns to the Silence,* (Polydor, 1991, prod. Van Morrison) ₰₰₰₰ a lengthy double set, is one of his more recent triumphs. Disc one, with a couple of wry show-biz rants ("Professional Jealousy" and "Why Must I Always Explain") and a masterful version of "I Can't Stop Loving You," is especially listenable.

what to buy next: *St. Dominic's Preview,* (Warner Brothers, 1972, prod. Van Morrison and Ted Templeman) ₰₰₰₰ with wonderful songs such as "Jackie Wilson Said (I'm in Heaven When You Smile)," "Almost Independence Day" and the epochal "Listen to the Lion." *Irish Heartbeat,* (Mercury, 1988, prod. Van Morrison and Paddy Maloney) a collaboration with the Chieftains, is an inspired collection of traditional music. *A Night in San Francisco* (Polydor, 1994, prod. Van Morrison) is a two-disc extended live set that does justice to his current high-energy, big-band performances and includes amazing medleys that place his music in context. *Too Long in Exile* (Polydor, 1993, prod. Van Morrison) finds a loose Morrison in a bluesy mood, relaxing on alto saxophone, electric guitar and harmonica and reprising "Gloria" for his middle age. Neophytes can't go wrong with *The Best of Van Morrison* (Polydor, 1990, prod. Various) and *The Best of Van Morrison Vol. 2,* (Polydor, 1993, prod. Various) with 35 distinct tracks between them that will have to do until the inevitable boxed set comes along.

what to avoid: *Inarticulate Speech of the Heart* (Warner Brothers, 1983, prod. Van Morrison) is as confusing as the title implies, synthesized New Age blather was, not surprisingly, his last record for Warner Brothers.

the rest: (with Georgie Fame): *How Long Has This Been Going On* (Verve, 1996) *Blowin' Your Mind* (Bang, 1967) *Best of Van Morrison* (Bang, 1970) *Tupelo Honey* (Warner Bros., 1971) *T.B. Sheets* (Bang, 1972) *Hard Nose the Highway* (Warner Bros., 1973) *It's Too Late to Stop Now* (Warner Bros., 1974) *Veedon Fleece* (Warner Bros., 1974) *A Period of Transition* (Warner Bros., 1977) *Wavelength* (Warner Bros., 1978) *Into the Music* (Warner Bros., 1979) *Common One* (Warner Bros., 1980) *Beautiful Vison* (Warner Bros., 1982) *A Sense of Wonder* (Mercury, 1985) *Live at the Grand Opera House Belfast* (Mercury, 1985) *No Guru, No Method, No Teacher* (Mercury, 1986) *Poetic Champions Compose* (Mercury, 1989) *Avalon Sunset* (Mercury, 1989) *Enlightenment* (Mercury, 1990) *Bang Masters* (Epic, 1991) *Days Like This* (Polydor, 1995) (with Them): *Them* (Parrot/Decca, 1965) *Them Again* (Parrot/Decca, 1966) *Them Featuring Van Morrison* (Parrot/London, 1972)

worth searching for: Morrison's infrequent live sets are generally considered the best way to experience the Belfast Cowboy, as witnessed by his three excellent, authorized live albums. There are literally dozens more available in bootleg form, and since Morrison rarely does the same show twice, many of them are worth the effort. *Can You Feel the Silence?,* (Great Dane) a 1982 show with a great Morrison rant about "Idiot Wind" that tries to explain why he's playing at a rock festival. *Van Morrison Gets His Chance to Wail Vols. 1 & 2* (Gold Standard) puts you in the studio during 1969-71, with Van on acoustic guitar as he works out demo versions of "Ballerina," "Domino," "And It Stoned Me," "Wild Night," "Caravan" and many more.

Counting Crows, Graham Parker & the Rumour, Dexy's Midnight Runners, Sinead O'Connor, U2, the Band, Elvis Costello, Rod Stewart, Mark Knopfler, Bob Seger, John Mellencamp, Bruce Springsteen, Joan Armatrading, Rickie Lee Jones

Sonny Boy Williamson, Leadbelly, Muddy Waters, John Lee Hooker, Sam Cooke, Slim Harpo, Solomon Burke, James Brown, Ray Charles, Sonny Terry and Brownie McGhee, Jackie Wilson, Bo Diddley, Curtis Mayfield and the Impressions, Johnny and the Pirates, Alexis Korner, Mose Allison, Bob Dylan

Leland Rucker

Morrissey

Born Stephen Patrick Morrissey, May 22, 1959 in Manchester, England

As lead singer of the Smiths, Morrissey became an icon for a legion of mournful followers. Blending angst with humor, homoerotic swagger with impenetrable attitude, Morrissey carried the Smiths out of the underground and into worldwide alternative music stardom. Releasing a small load of influential albums, the group disintegrated in 1987 after only five years together, but the road had already been paved for Morrissey's solo career; he released his debut album, *Viva Hate*, the following year. But despite his prolific outpouring of singles and albums, his post-Smiths work rarely came close to either the majesty or innovation of his former band. Many of his critics even suggest that he has turned into a caricature of his former self; even though he has scored an occasional hit single, his career has been on a steady decline—both artistically and commercially—in recent years.

what to buy: Hot on the heels of the Smiths' death, *Viva Hate* (Sire, 1988, prod. Stephen Street) does not drift too far from the group's well-established formula. While lacking the sonic finesse of guitarist Johnny Marr, it still contains some classic Morrissey intellect, particularly on standout tracks such as "Everyday Is Like Sunday" and "Suedehead."

what to buy next: *Bona Drag,* (Sire, 1990, prod. Clive Langer and Stephen Street) a collection of singles, similarly showcased some of Morrissey's finest moments as a solo artist—including the indispensable "Interesting Drug" and "November Spawned A Monster," which come close to capturing the walloping grandeur of the Smiths.

what to avoid: Morrissey's creative flame went out fast after he left the Smiths. Rather than pushing his work into new terrain, he fell into a tired groove on insipid offerings such as *Kill Uncle* (Sire, 1991, prod. Clive Langer) and *Southpaw Grammar* (Sire, 1995, prod. Steve Lillywhite) Both discs were colorless takes on the former Morrissey sound.

the rest: *Your Arsenal* (Sire, 1992) *Vauxhall & I* (Sire, 1994) *World Of Morrissey* (Sire, 1995)

worth searching for: *Beethoven Was Deaf* (EMI, 1993) a British live album recorded with one of his strongest bands cranking through 16 songs from throughout his solo career.

⏩ The La's, the Sundays, James, Judybats

⏪ David Bowie, Lou Reed, the Kinks, the Velvet Underground, the New York Dolls

Aidin Varizin

Steve Morse

See: Dixie Dregs

Bob Mosley

See: Moby Grape

Motörhead

Formed 1975 in London, England

Lemmy Kilmister, vocals, bass; "Fast" Eddie Clark, guitar (1975-82); Phil "Philthy Animal" Taylor, drums (1977-83, 1991); Brian Robertson, guitar (1982-83); Mick "Wurzel" Burston, guitar (1983-96); Pete Gill, drums (1983-91); Mikkey Dee, drums (1991-present)

Yeah, they play the same three-chord rock song over and over until your head snaps off, flies onto the stage and rolls into the bass drum with a dull thud. Yeah, Lemmy's voice sounds like somebody crammed 27 cigarettes into his mouth and lit them while he sings. Yeah, they've been doing this the exact same way (give or take a few personnel changes) for more than two decades. If not for Motrhead puts out today, is a necessary glob of phlegm hoarked into the music industry. Heavy metal has always flirted with daintiness and pretty-boy showmanship, but Motörhead hits as "the Lemmys." Now, *that's* love.

what to buy: *No Sleep 'Til Hammersmith* (Mercury, 1981/Roadracer Revisited, 1992, prod. Vic Maile) is the consummate fist-pounding, neighbor-annoying, speaker-exploding, normality-disturbing metal record, capturing the band in full peak live, with versions of "Ace of Spades," "Iron Horse," "Overkill" and "Metropolis." *No Remorse* (Bronze, 1984/Roadracer Revisited, 1990, prod. Various) advertises itself as "the ultimate Motörhead *(Chiswick U.K., 1977/Roadracer Revisited, 1990, prod. Speedy Keen)*, Overkill *(Bronze U.K., 1979/Roadracer Revisited, 1992, prod. Jimmy Miller)* *and* 1916 *(WTG/Sony, 1992, prod. Peter Solley)* *all amplify the Motörhead experience.* 1916 *includes Lemmy's slow, riveting, guitarless anti-war title track.*

what to avoid: Despite a good cover of Ted Nugent's "Cat Scratch Fever," *March or Die* (WTG/Sony, 1992, prod. Peter Solley) is part of the band's slide into boring old age.

the rest: *Bomber* (Bronze, U.K. 1979/Roadracer Revisited, 1992); *Iron Fist* (Mercury, 1982/Roadracer Revisited, 1990) *Orgasmatron* (GWR/Profile, 1986) *Rock'n'Roll* (GWR/Profile, 1987) *No Sleep at All* (Enigma, 1988/Roadracer Revisited, 1992) *All the Aces* (Roadracer Revisited, 1992) *On Parole* (1980/Cleopatra, 1992 *The Best of Motrhead doing Elvis Presley to sound, on the British fundraising album* The Last Temptation of Elvis *(New Musical Express, 1990). Classic liner note: "If you bumped into Elvis this very day, what would be your immediate reaction?" Lemmy: "I would be astounded, and I would say, 'Elvis, I'm astounded!'"*

⏩ Metallica, Megadeth, Slayer, Anthrax, Soundgarden, Ministry, Bad Religion, Guns N' Roses, Body Count

⏪ Ted Nugent, MC5, Ramones, Who, Iggy Pop, Count Five, Yardbirds, Alice Cooper, Black Sabbath

Steve Knopper

The Motels

Formed 1972 in Berkeley, Calif. Disbanded 1986.

Martha Davis, vocals; Dean Chamberlain, guitar (1972-75); Richard D'Andrea, bass (1972-76); Michael Goodroe, bass (1976-86); Marty Jourard, saxophone, keyboards (1976-86); Brian Glascock, drums (1976-86); Jeff Jourard, guitar (1976-79); Tim McGovern, guitar (1979-81); Guy Perry, guitar (1980-86); Scott Thurston, guitar, keyboards (1982-86)

The Motels hovered in L.A. for a decade, sifting through numerous band members before ever releasing a record. In addition to being among the first of the West Coast's New Wave groups, the band boasted the dramatic vocals of Davis, evolving into a critically lauded, if only modestly successful, group. The group's main stab at pop mainstream came with the melancholy hit "Only the Lonely" in 1982. Public indifference, constantly shifting personnel and Davis' own health issues all factored into the band's demise in the mid-80s. *The Motels* (Capitol/EMI, 1979/1996, prod. Various) is the band's appealingly raw debut, while *No Vacancy: Best of the Motels* (Capitol/EMI, 1990, prod. Various) is a tidy summation of the best of the band's largely unrecognized career.

Allan Orski

Mother Love Bone

See: Pearl Jam

Mother's Finest

Formed late 60s in Chicago, Ill. Disbanded 1983. Re-formed 1989.

Joyce Kennedy, vocals; Garry Moore (a.k.a., Moses Mo), guitar; Glenn Murdock, vocals; Jerry Seay (a.k.a.,Wizzard), bass; Barry Borden (a.k.a., B.B. Queen), drums; Mike Keck, keyboards

Starting in Chicago, Mother's Finest perfected its potent blend of funk and rock in Atlanta, Ga., home of seminal funk outfit Cameo. Though renown for incendiary live shows and the Chaka Khan-style power of vocalist Joyce Kennedy, the band was never able to harness that formula on record, coming closest in its concert album, *Live* (Epic, 1979, prod. not listed) —which melded old-school soul vocals to a riff-laden, bombastic live sound. In the studio, record companies kept trying to turn the band into the next K.C. & Sunshine Band or the next Rufus, refusing or unwilling to let MF claim its status as one of the first modern-day funk/rock groups. Despite the success of the sultry ballad "Love Changes" the band broke up in 1983, with Kennedy moving on to a solo career and drummer Barry Borden playing with Molly Hatchet. Though the group re-formed in 1989, they found the same problems in reaching audiences, prompting the irreverent title of its most recent album *Black Radio Won't Play This* (RCA, 1992, prod. Thom Panunzio)

the rest: *Another Mother Further* (Columbia, 1977) *Mother Factor* (Columbia, 1978/1989)

Eric Deggans

Mötley Crüe /Vince Neil

Formed 1981 in Los Angeles, Calif.

Tommy Lee, drums, vocals; Mick Mars, guitar, vocals; Vince Neil, vocals (1981-92); Nikki Sixx (born Frank Carlton Serafino Ferranno), bass, piano, vocals; John Corabi, vocals, guitar (1992-present)

One of the leaders of the "hair metal" movement that dominated MTV and magazine covers briefly during the 80s, Mötley Crüe had several big hits with its hard rock songs and soupy ballads. The band carefully crafted a decadent outlaw image and took concert excess to unprecedented heights, and by the original lineup's last studio album, *Dr. Feelgood,* it was a decent hard-rock outfit with an OK pop sense. But in the early 90s, when Nirvana changed the hard rock marketplace, Mötley Crüe began to sound out of vogue. Neil fared the worst, getting fired, putting out a stinker solo album and filing a (still unresolved) $5 million wrongful termination lawsuit. Lee did better, rebounding from a failed marriage with "Melrose Place" star Heather Locklear by marrying and starting a family with the buxom "Baywatch" bombshell Pamela Anderson.

what to buy: *Dr. Feelgood* (Elektra, 1989, prod. Bob Rock) was a No. 1 album, featuring the hits "Kickstart My Heart" and "Same Ol' Situation (S.O.S.)." The career retrospective *Decade of Decadence—'81-'91* (Elektra, 1991, prod. Various) does a good job of showcasing the band's strengths and avoiding its weaknesses.

what to buy next: *Theater of Pain* (Elektra, 1985, prod. Tom Werman) has the Crüe's hit remake of Brownsville Station's "Smokin' in the Boys' Room" as well as "Home Sweet Home," the hit that kicked open the doors for the power ballad—certainly a dubious achievement.

what to avoid: The post-Neil *Mötley Crüe* (Elektra, 1994, prod. Bob Rock) is a desperate, failed stab to regain the band's former foothold in the hard rock marketplace.

the rest: *Too Fast For Love* (Elektra, 1981) *Shout at the Devil* (Elektra, 1983) *Girls, Girls, Girls* (Elektra, 1987)

solo outings:

Vince Neil Exposed (Elektra, 1993) *Carved in Stone* (Warner Bros., 1995)

▶▶ Warrant, Ratt, Ugly Kid Joe, Guns N' Roses

Black Sabbath, Foreigner, Alice Cooper, Boston, Kansas, Kiss, Cheap Trick

Tracey Birkenhauer and Steve Knopper

Motown

Berry Gordy, Jr., was writing songs for Jackie Wilson ("Reet Petite," "To Be Loved") and came to realize he probably wasn't making the kind of money he should for the hits. His answer; start his own record company. So with a loan of $800 from his family, Gordy launched the Motown empire in 1959 with the appropriately titled Barrett Strong single "Money (That's What I Want)." That's what Motown got, too, as the company went through the roof during the 60s with an unstoppable string of hits by the likes of Smokey Robinson and the Miracles, Martha & the Vandellas, the Marvelettes, Mary Wells, the Supremes, the Temptations, the Four Tops, Marvin Gaye, Stevie Wonder, Jr. Walker and the All Stars—a veritable hall of fame of popular music. And that's not counting other groups, such as the Spinners, the Isley Brothers and Gladys Knight & the Pips, that schooled at Motown on their way to bigger things; heck, Motown even had Neil Young for a minute, in a group called the Mynah Birds, as well as Meat Loaf's first recording. Coming as the Civil Rights movement was kicking into gear, Motown gave voice to the hopes and aspirations of black Americans at a crucial time, and while the company always treaded lightly in the political arena, it did release such crucial statements as Marvin Gaye's *What's Going On*, Edwin Starr's hit "War" and the Temptations' "Message From a Black Man," as well as releasing recordings of the Rev. Martin Luther King Jr.'s speeches. Gordy withstood charges of inequitable promotion and financial mismanagement—though several of his acts went elsewhere over the years—and he eventually set his sights on the show biz empire and moved Motown to Los Angeles during the 70s, where it got into the movie business ("Lady Sings the Blues," "Mahogany," "The Wiz"). Recent years have seen its cadre of hitmakers diminish (Boyz II Men is the leading light these days.) Still, Motown remains a formidable brand name, with a burgeoning back catalog and a restaurant chain, the Motown Cafe.

what to buy: *Hitsville U.S.A.: The Motown Singles Collection 1959-1971* (Motown, 1992) is a supreme (ar, ar) four-CD anthology of all the label's seminal hits, featuring not only the obvious superstars but also important pieces of the Motown picture such as Barrett Strong, the Contours, the early Spinners and the Velvellettes. *Hitsville U.S.A., Vol. 2: The Motown Singles Collection 1972-1992*, (Motown, 1993) another four-CD set, is just a touch less essential; the first couple of discs are as non-stop great as its predecessor, but the rest of the set—like the label itself—gets a little thin as it goes on. *Every Great Motown Song, Vol. 1: The 1960's Every* (Motown, 1986) and *Great Motown Song, Vol. 2: The 1970's* (Motown, 84) overlap the box sets but are great to toss on for parties.

what to buy next: The catalogs of many Motown B-tier acts have been given short-shrift, but any of these collections should be included in a thorough Motown collection: the Marvelettes' *Motown Milestones* (Motown, 1995) or *Deliver: The Singles 1961-71* (Motown, 1993) the Contours' *Do You Love Me* (Motown, 1962/1988) Kim Weston's *Greatest Hits & Rare Classics* (Motown, 1991) Edwin Starr's *Motown Legends* (ESX, 1994) Also, the label's *Motown Year by Year: The Sound of Young America* series—12 individual volumes released during 1995, each in the to range—combines hits with rarities for a solid historical overview.

what to avoid: The three-part *Baddest Love James*, series (Motown, 1996) proof that you *can* have too much of a good thing.

worth searching for: The out-of-print two-volume set *20 Hard to Find Motown Classics*, (Motown, 1986) which gathers hits by some of those Motowners (Shorty Long, Barbara Randolph, the Elgins, R. Dean Taylor) that have fallen between the cracks.

Gary Graff

What Album Changed Your Life?

"Blue Valentine by Tom Waits was one. I was young, like 12 or something. I was a little kid, and I had never heard music like that--the poetry, the lyrics, everything about it. It was a whole package--one unified thing. That's what amazed that album. That music was speaking to me."

Tommy Shaw (Styx, Damn Yankees)

Mott the Hoople

Formed 1968 in Hereford, England. Disbanded 1977.

Stan Tippens, vocals (1968); Ian Hunter, vocal, piano, guitar (1969-74); Mick Ralphs, guitar, vocals (1969-73); Overend Pete Watts, bass; Dale "Buffin" Griffin, drums; Verden Allen, organ, vocals (1969-73); Ariel Bender, guitar, vocals (1973-74); Morgan Fisher, keyboards (1973-77); Mick Ronson, guitar (1974); Ray Major, guitar (1975-77); Nigel Benjamin, vocals (1975-77)

Mott the Hoople, at least at the beginning, was a somewhat plodding, English Bob Dylan/Rolling Stones clone. Its early efforts on Atlantic went nowhere, and it wasn't until David Bowie wrote "All the Young Dudes," which became Mott's only American hit, that the group enjoyed some mid-level success. The only problem was that although the single (and corresponding album) became cornerstones of the glitter/glam-rock scene, the Hooples themselves weren't Dudes. Still, the band's killer live shows (check their onstage version of Little Richard's "Keep a Knockin' " on *Wildlife*) took it a long way, and Hunter was inspired to his best songwriting before Ralphs left to form Bad Company and Mott ran out of gas. Mott is now fondly remembered for some great songs ("All the Way From Memphis," "Ballad of Mott the Hoople" "Roll Away the Stone") and as the great 70s band that might have been. Its music provides a solid link from the 60s to the punk movement that was gathering steam just as Mott broke down.

what to buy: Even if he hated to be involved, the last album with Ralphs— *Mott* (Columbia, 1973, prod. Mott the Hoople) —is a splendid example of crunching, post-Bowie British rock. *The Ballad of Mott: A Retrospective* (Columbia Legacy, 1993, prod. Various) is two-disc compilation that gathers all the best Columbia recordings but goes light on the Atlantic albums. *Mott the Hoople* (Atlantic, 1969, prod. Guy Stevens) is a wild, eclectic debut with outlandish covers of Doug Sahm ("At the Crossroads"), Sonny Bono ("Laugh at Me"), the Kinks ("You Really Got Me") and the band's own outrageous Dylan and Stones tributes, "Backsliding Fearlessly" and "Rock 'n' Roll Queen."

what to buy next: *All the Young Dudes* (Columbia, 1972, prod. David Bowie) , though to be orientationally accurate, it could have been called "All the Wrong Dudes. *Backsliding Fearlessly: The Early Years* (Rhino, 1994, prod. Various) provides a good sampling of Mott's Atlantic output. *The Hoople* (Columbia, 1974/1990, prod. Ian Hunter, Dale Griffin and Overend Watts) is the final album with Hunter.

what to avoid: Hardcore fans might disagree, but except for "Walking With a Mountain," *Mad Shadows* (Atlantic, 1970, prod. Guy Stevens) is a muddy, unintelligible mess, the sound of a band backsliding fearfully.

the rest: *Wildlife* (Atlantic, 1971) *Brain Capers*(Atlantic, 1972) *Mott the Hoople Live* (1974, Columbia, 1989) *Drive On* (Columbia, 1975) *Shouting and Pointing* (Columbia, 1976) *Greatest Hits* (Columbia, 1976)

worth searching for: Hunter's diary of Mott's 1972 American tour, "Reflections of a Rock Star" (Flash Books, London, 1976) is as fascinating as it is rare, breaking down the myths of rock stardom as it shows the day-to-day inner workings of a rock 'n' roll tour. Musically, the bootleg *Hoopling Furiously* (Hiwatt) surveys a series of early live performances that catch Mott making an enjoyably spirited racket.

▶▶ The Clash, Generation X, Sex Pistols

◀◀ Little Richard, Bob Dylan, Rolling Stones, Sir Douglas Quintet

see also: *Ian Hunter*

Leland Rucker

Bob Mould /Sugar

Born Oct. 12, 1960, in Malone, N.Y.

Sugar (1992-95): Mould, vocals and guitars; David Barbe, bass; Malcolm Travis, drums

Though Mould has never had anything close to a hit single, he is the most recognizable and successful ex-member of the great Minneapolis punk trio Hüsker Dü. A brilliant pop melody writer, the singer-guitarist probably could be a solo superstar in the age of big-bucks alternative music if he weren't so (deservedly) suspicious of fame and the music industry. Instead, he deliberately writes cryptic songs and produces albums on which the bass is hard to hear and the treble is fuzzy and jagged. Yet the melodies usually grow into irresistible songs no matter what he does with them. Mould left Hüsker Dü in early 1988; his first solo albums were downbeat and overly confessional, sort of like Hüsker Dü's "Candy Apple Gray." The trio Sugar, like Hüsker Dü, filtered Mould's raw emotions through an old-fashioned rock 'n' roll lens of loud, fun guitars. That band ended in 1995, when Mould and other band members, surprisingly enough, had a disagreement about pursuing fame.

what to buy: Sugar's *Copper Blue* (Rykodisc, 1992, prod. Bob

Mould and Lou Giordano) at first sounds like a scratchy racket, with Mould's nasally voice matching the guitars' exaggeratedly high pitch. Eventually, the tightly controlled tunes grab you, particularly the melancholy "If I Can't Change Your Mind" and the pleasantly schizoid "A Good Idea." Despite Mould's aversion to fame, the trio's *File Under: Easy Listening,* (Rykodisc, 1994, prod. Bob Mould) is the purest pop record of his career. Bubblegum tunes such as "Your Favorite Thing" and "Believe What You're Saying" came dangerously close to making the band alternative-rock MTV heroes.

what to buy next: Mould's first post-Sugar album, *Bob Mould,* (Rykodisc, 1996, prod. Bob Mould) is wholly suspicious of contemporary post-punk; it includes the self-explanatory "I Hate Alternative Rock" and "Egoverride," which deals with being "burned out in the galaxy." Sugar's *Besides* (Rykodisc, 1995, prod. Bob Mould and Nick Giordano) is a relaxed and fun collection of studio outtakes and live recordings, including a stellar version of the Who's "Armenia City in the Sky."

what to avoid: Mould's second album, *Black Sheets of Rain,* (Virgin, 1990, prod. Bob Mould) endures mostly for its college-radio hit "It's Too Late," but it's neither coherent nor focused.

the rest: Mould's *Workbook* (Virgin, 1989) *Poison Years* (Virgin, 1994, prod. Mould)

worth searching for: Sugar's *Beaster* (Rykodisc EP, 1993, prod. Bob Mould and Nick Giordano) contains longer, angrier songs and more repetitive choruses and solos than *Copper Blue* it peaks with "JC Auto," which melts down images of cars and Jesus Christ into one wonderfully traditional rock 'n' roll song.

▶▶ Nirvana, the Pixies, the Breeders, the Offspring, Boo Radleys, Medicine, Magnapop

◀◀ Hüsker Dü, Ramones, Richard Thompson, Sex Pistols, Minutemen, Television.

see also: *Hüsker Dü*

Steve Knopper

Mountain

Formed 1969 in New York N.Y. Disbanded 1972. Re-formed 1974-76 and in 1985.

Leslie West (born Leslie Weinstein), guitar vocals; Felix Pappalardi, bass, vocals (died April 17, 1983); N.D. Smart, drums (1969); Steve Knight, organ (1970-71), Corky Laing, drums (1970-72, 1985-present); Alan Schwartzberg, drums (1974-76); Mark Clarke, bass (1974-present)

A heavin', sweatin' beast was Mountain. with is ham-fisted pounding submerged in barnyard sludge. A brute strength trio led by former Cream producer Felix Pappalardi and the mammoth Leslie West, Mountain shook the foundations with heavy rock excess and greasy jams. The lumbering cowbell-rocker "Mississippi Queen" started the 70s off with a whomp, and it's been a sweatshop of hard, grungey guitar noise ever since. The group has broken up and regrouped many times—West and Laing even hooked up with Cream's Jack Bruce at one point—but the seminal lineup was destroyed in 1983 when Pappalardi was shot and killed by his wife. Although the group performs occasionally, West can be heard more often as a guest on Howard Stern's morning radio show.

what to buy: The anthology *Over the Top* (Columbia, 1995, prod. Various) is a bulging monument much like the band itself. The album stuffs two-discs worth of thumping rock and endless solos into a package of lowbrow glory. It also contains "Dreams of Milk and Honey" from West's deleted 1969 solo debut.

what to buy next: *Mountain Climbing!* (Columbia/Legacy, 1970, prod. Felix Pappalardi) is the group's first and best album, containing "Mississippi Queen."

what to avoid: *Twin Peaks* (Columbia, 1973/1989, prod. Felix Pappalardi) is a sprawling two-disc set that runs out of steam early on.

the rest: *Nantucket Sleighride* (Columbia/Legacy, 1971/1992) *Flowers of Evil* (Columbia/Legacy, 1972/1996) *Best of Mountain* (Columbia, 1973/1989) *Go for Your Life* (Scotti Bros., 1986)

worth searching for: Leslie West's solo debut *Mountain,* (Windfall, 1969/Columbia, 1996, prod. Felix Pappalardi) the wailing precursor to what would become the Mountain sound. The albums West and Laing recorded with Jack Bruce—*Why Dontcha* (Columbia, 1972) and *Whatever Turns You On* (Columbia, 1973)—have been deleted, but Mountain fans should enjoy the addition of Bruce's manic elegance.

solo outings:

Leslie West Dodgin' the Dirt (Blues Bureau International, 1993)

▶▶ Black Sabbath, Uriah Heep, Nazareth, AC/DC

◀◀ Cream, the Jimi Hendrix Experience

Allan Orski

The Move /Roy Wood/Wizzard

Formed 1966 in Birmingham, England. Disbanded 1972.

Roy Wood (born Ulysses Adrian Wood), guitar, vocals; Bev Bevan, drums, vocals; Jeff Lynne, guitar, keyboards, vocals (1970-72); Carl Wayne, vocals (1966-70); Trevor Burton, guitar, bass, vocals (1966-69); Chris "Ace" Kefford, bass, vocals (1966-68); Rick Price, bass, vocals (1969-71)

The Move was an early pioneer in the art of power pop. Though the group followed in the footsteps of the Beatles and Beach Boys by combining riff-rock with choirboy harmonies, its work clearly influenced much of the glam and pomp-rock that followed in its wake. Leader Wood, a gifted songwriter, shared the reins in the group's final incarnation with the similarly talented Lynne, who would go on to form the far more successful Electric Light Orchestra. Wood, meanwhile, joined ELO briefly before moving on to a series of eccentric recordings with his band Wizzard and as a solo act. Wood's ambition showed in the use of classical motifs in the earliest works, which he integrated with English psychedelia, lush chamber-pop and thundering proto-metallic riffs. Lynne's influence took the Move in more of a symphonic power-pop direction, though this, too, was part of Wood's repertoire. Lynne has since become a preeminent producer, most famously with the Traveling Wilburys and as an engine in the ghostly "reunion" during the mid-90ss. Wood has traveled more obscure roads but announced in the mid-90s that he was starting his own record label, Woody, and projected the release of a live album.

what to buy: *Shazam* (A&M, 1970, prod. Roy Wood) shows the band in all its eclectic glory, from incandescent folk-pop to full-blown pomp.

what to buy next: *The Collection/The Collector's Series (1967-70)* (Castle Communications, 1986, prod. Roy Wood and Jeff Lynne) captures a range of delectable, most early, highlights. Meanwhile, *Great Move! The Best of the Move* (EMI, 1994, comp. Ron Furmanek) emphasizes the finest late work.

what to avoid: Wood's *Boulders,*(United Artists, 1973, prod. Roy Wood) has one or two lovely moments but for the most part chronicles his artistic scizophrenia, careening from pretense to adolescent retro-rock. Wood played, arranged and sang everything on the record. He clearly needed a hand.

the rest: The Move: *The Move* (Regal Zonophone, 1968) *Something Else* (Regal Zonophone, 1968) *Looking On* (Capitol, 1971) *Message from the Country* (Harvest, 1972) *Split Ends* (United Artists, 1972) *The Best of the Move* (A&M, 1974) *Shines On* (A&M, 1979) *Black Country Rock* (Gold Standard, 1993) *BBC Sessions* (Band of Joy, 1995)

solo outings:

Roy Wood Wizzard's Brew (Harvest, 1973) *See My Baby Jive* (Warner Bros., 1974) *Introducing Eddie and the Falcons* (Warner Bros., 1974) *Mustard* (Jet, 1975) *Super Active Wizzo* (Warner Bros., 1977) *On the Road Again* (Warner Bros., 1979)

worth searching for: *You Can Dance the Rock 'n' Roll: The Roy Wood Years 1971-73,* (EMI/Harvest, 1989, prod. Roy Wood and Jeff Lynne) a strong import overview of Wood's work with the Move, ELO, Wizzard and on his own.

David Bowie, T. Rex, Queen, Cheap Trick, ELO, Elvis Costello, Posies, Jellyfish, Teenage Fan Club

Beatles, Beach Boys, Kinks, Stax, Motown, Bach, Donovan

Simon Glickman

Alison Moyet /Yaz/Yazoo

Born Genevieve Alison-Jane Moyet June 18, 1961 in Basildon, Essex, England

Yaz (Yazoo in England)—singer Moyet and Depeche Mode refugee Vince Clark on keyboards—made an argument for synthesizer music with its remarkably emotional pop created in the often vacuous techno landscapes of the early 80s. Much of the duo's vibrancy belonged to Moyet's rich, passionate voice, a sultry blend of R&B and nervy energy. Her singing, matched with Clarke's quirky keyboard pop, lifted the group's songs to a more resonant level above many of their peers. After only a year and a half with Yaz, Clarke went on to form Erasure, while Moyet carved out a successful solo career that has seen her moving quickly into American mainstream.

what to buy: Yaz' *You and Me Both,* (Sire, 1983) the group's second and last release, is a romantic overture of defiance and desperation with a little joyous bounce thrown in to lighten the load. Moyet has yet to come up with material as strong as "Nobody's Diary," "Good Times" and "Walk Away From Love." Moyet's *Hoodoo* (Columbia, 1991, prod. Pete Glenister) was a commercial flop, but its diversity creates a better stage for her blazing honesty than any of her previous solo efforts.

what to buy next: Yaz' *Upstairs at Eric's* (Sire, 1982, prod. E.C. Radcliffe and Yaz) is the group's ambitious and experimental debut that hits sonic warm spots ("Only You" and "Don't Go") as well as horrendous left-field ditches ("I Before E Except After C").

what to avoid: Moyet's *Raindancing* (Columbia, 1987, prod. Jimmy Iovine) is smothered by formula pop production. And titles such as "I Grow Weak in the Presence of Beauty" add insult to injury.

the rest: Moyet: *Alf* (Columbia, 1984) *Essex* (Columbia, 1994) *Singles* (Columbia, 1995)

▶▶ Erasure, Blue Nile, Eurythmics, Annie Lennox

◀◀ Depeche Mode, Kraftwerk, Joy Division

see also: *Erasure*

Allan Orski

Mudhoney

Formed 1988 in Seattle, Wash.

Mark Arm, vocals, guitar; Steve Turner, guitar, vocals; Matt Lukin, bass; Dan Peters, drums

Mudhoney's summer of '88 debut single, "Touch Me, I'm Sick," was the first and most elegant signature song of what came to be called grunge. Formed in the ashes of seminal Sub Pop act Green River (most of whom became Mother Love Bone, some of whom then became Pearl Jam), Mudhoney were the first Seattle band to fuse down-and-dirty punk with a peculiar pop instinct *and* attract an international audience doing it. Named for a Russ Meyer film, Mudhoney was the first standard-bearer for the Seattle scene; its debut EP, "Superfuzz Bigmuff" (named for two inexpensive effects pedals they favored, or so the story goes) attracted the "grunge" tag, while the group's spectacularly passionate live shows first won over the fickle British press. Despite considerable financial inducements, Mudhoney has stayed true to its anti-corporate roots long after their contemporaries had cashed in. When Mudhoney signed to Reprise in 1992, the Seattle gold rush was clearly over. It was also one of many bands to have benefited from the efficient and sympathetic production of Jack Endino.

what to buy: *Superfuzz Bigmuff* (Sub Pop, 1988, prod. Jack Endino) has been repackaged with Mudhoney's first two epic singles—"Touch Me, I'm Sick" and "You Got It (Keep It Outta My Face)"—and remains the benchmark by which all future releases might be judged. Here they are at their unequaled best: snide, angry, catchy, brooding, very, very loud, and utterly committed. The most recent release, *My Brother the Cow* (Reprise, 1995, prod. Jack Endino and Mudhoney) is a canny, muscular return to form, though its popularity had long since been eclipsed by second- and third-generation grunge imitators.

what to buy next: It's hard to argue against Mudhoney's self-titled debut long-player (Sub Pop, 1989, prod. Jack Endino), for it's full of vim and vigor and classic songs like "This Gift" and "Here Comes Sickness." Like most Mudhoney records, it is better approached as a collection of singles than as a suite of thematically connected songs.

what to avoid: The seven-song *Five Dollar Bob's Mock Cooter Stew* (Reprise, 1993, prod. Kurdt Bloch and Mudhoney) can only be explained by the need to keep product in the pipeline. It is as passionless and unfocused a record as a proud band could make, and is little more than a collection of released and unreleased B-sides.

the rest: *Every Good Boy Deserves Fudge* (Sub Pop, 1991) *Piece of Cake* (Reprise, 1992).

worth searching for: *Mudhoney* (Reprise, 1993) is an eight-song live promotional CD recorded during the filming of the movie *Hype* at the Oddfellows Hall in Seattle. It's a solid performance—a bit more restrained and professional than they managed when younger, but several of the songs are unique to this release, and it's a good barometer of how stunning the band could be on a good night.

▶▶ Nirvana, Tad, Jon Spencer Blues Explosion

◀◀ The Stooges, Billy Childish, The Ramones, Green River

Grant Alden

The Muffs

Formed 1991, Los Angeles, Calif.

Kim Shattuck, vocals and guitar; Ronnie Barnett, bass; Roy McDonald, drums; Melanie Vammen, guitar (1991-94); Cris Crass, drums (1991-94)

A poster child for laryngitis, Kim Shattuck left her mediocre underground 80s band the Pandoras to create the Muffs in 1991. Their concept is simple—loud guitars, irresistible melodies and lots of high-pitched, Courtney Love-style shrieking. When they're on, the Muffs can match the concise power and humor of the Ramones. When they're off, they sound like a few punks making a hideous cacophony.

what to buy: *The Muffs* (Warner Bros., 1991, prod. Rob Cavallo, David Katznelson and the Muffs) ♪♪♪♪ is a glorious collection of catchy kiss-offs—on "Lucky Guy," "Better Than Me," "Big Mouth" and "Stupid Jerk," Shattuck sounds like she wants to bash the entire male gender with her big guitar and extremely big voice.

what to buy next: *Blonder and Blonder* (Warner Bros., 1995, prod. Rob Cavallo and the Muffs) ♪♪♪, which features the band reconfigured into a trio (without Vammen and with a new drummer) has a couple of nice tracks in "Oh Nina" and "Red Eyed Troll." But Shattuck's screeches are starting to wear thin, especially without the spirit of the debut.

what to avoid: Anything by The Pandoras, an ultra-horny mid-80s band led by singer-guitarist Paula Pierce, who put out two albums, two EPs and a live disc but are mostly notable for siring Kim Shattuck.

worth searching for: The Muffized version of Kim Wilde's 1981 suburbia electro-hit "Kids of America," on the *Clueless* soundtrack (Capitol, 1995, prod. Various) ♪♪

▶▶ Hole, Green Day, Offspring, NOFX

◀◀ Ramones, Joan Jett, L7, Bad Religion

Steve Knopper

Maria Muldaur

Born Maria Grazia Rosa Domenica d'Amato, Sept. 10, 1943, in New York, N.Y.

Muldaur's delightfully clear voice rang out on the 1973 hit "Midnight At the Oasis," which is pretty much the extent of her widespread fame but, luckily, not the end of her excellent recording career. Muldaur has been singing since the late 50s, starting with a hometown girl group and then graduating to the folk scene, where she sang in the Even Dozen Jug Band (with John Sebastian), the Jim Kweskin Jug Band (where she met her husband, Geoff Muldaur) and, later, with Dan Hicks. She went on her own in 1972 and has been in and out of the public eye ever since, including a stint as a stage actress and gospel music produced after she became a born-again Christian. Her country and blues repertoire has held her in good stead, and her albums have always enjoyed top sidemen and guests such as Dr. John, Paul Butterfield, Linda Rondstadt, Lowell George, Harry "Sweets" Edison, Milt Holland and Doc and Merle Watson. The Muldaurs divorced in 1972; their daughter, Jenni, released her own album during 1993.

what to buy: Muldaur's been around for more than three decades, and her experience shows on *Louisiana Love Call,* (Black Top, 1993, prod. Hammond Scott) ♪♪♪♪ where she takes her sweet voice on a trip through bayou country. This isn't zydeco, but the soulful rhythms and harmonies are pure Louisiana, with Dr. John and a couple of Neville brothers guesting to make sure it's authentic. *Waitress In a Donut Shop* (Warner Bros., 1974, prod. Joe Boyd and Lenny Waronker) ♪♪♪♪ contains the country funk "I'm A Woman" and the jazzy "Squeeze Me." Every tune on this album sparkles, including the country of "Cool River" and a tour south of the border with "Gringo En Mexico."

what to buy next: The public took big notice of *Maria Muldaur,* (Warner Bros., 1973, prod. Joe Boyd and Lenny Waronker) ♪♪♪ which isn't a terribly coherent package though it does contain "Midnight At the Oasis" and an equally stellar cast of guests.

what to avoid: The slight *Sweet Harmony* (Warner Bros., 1976) ♪♪ just kind of drifted away, as Muldaur was threatening to do herself at the time.

the rest: *Meet Me At Midnite* (Black Top, 1994) ♪♪♪

worth searching for: For some fun, check out the out-of-print *Jim Kweskin and the Jug Band's Greatest Hits* (Vanguard, 1970, prod. Maynard Solomon), ♪♪♪♪ which finds Muldaur laughing, singing, playing fiddle and just having a good time with the boys.

▶▶ Linda Ronstadt, Alison Krauss, Sheryl Crow, Mary-Chapin Carpenter

◀◀ The Weavers

Lawrence Gabriel

Elliot Murphy

Born March, 16, 1949 in Garden City, N.Y.

Hemingway said no man who ever wrote anything of value left his country to work his craft. Murphy, one of the more gifted practitioners of heartland rock to ever labor under the "new Dylan" tag, is the contradiction to refute such a claim. Due to a grievous lack of attention in the U.S., Murphy now resides in the more welcoming environs of Paris. While there is woefully little available from his 23-year recording career, you can find

Party Girl, Broken Poets (Dejadisc, 1984, prod. Elliot Murphy and Ernie Brooks) ♪♪♪, a solid introduction to his literate storytelling. *Selling the Gold* (Dejadisc, 1996, prod. Djoum and Elliot Murphy) ♪♪♪♪ is an even better example of his mature subtlety. Without resorting to the bombast of Bruce Springsteen or the simplistic immediacy of John Mellencamp (both of whom are ardent Murphy fans), he nonetheless continues to craft songs of remarkable intellectual depth while retaining and a journeyman's stance. All of which probably ensures continued obscurity.

Allan Orski

Peter Murphy /Dali's Car

Born July 11, 1957 in Northampton, England

Murphy began his career as the singer of the seminal gothic band Bauhaus. Upon that band's break-up in 1983, he joined forces with former Japan member Mick Karn in the group Dali's Car, releasing just one album before going solo. Murphy initially clung to Bauhaus' moody, gloomy approach, and it wasn't until his sophomore effort (*Love Hysteria*) that he found his own way and began to separate himself from that sound. He learned to control his voice, allowing him to sing a rich range of sensual melodies that were backed by dense, layered instrumental attacks.

what to buy: *Love Hysteria* (Beggars Banquet, 1988, prod. Simon Rogers) ♪♪♪♪♪ is where Murphy realizes he is no longer part of Bauhaus. His upbeat, moving melodies and smooth vocals delicately lure the ear into the music.

what to buy next: *Cascade* (Beggars Banquet/Atlantic, 1995, prod. Pascal Gabriel) ♪♪♪♪ finds a refreshed Murphy singing dramatic with catchy melodies.

what to avoid: *Deep* (Beggars Banquet/RCA, 1990, prod. Simon Rogers) ♪♪ laced Murphy's flare and brought him into adult contemporary radio and easy listening.

the rest: *Should the World Fail to Fall Apart* (Beggars Banquet, 1986) ♪♪♪♪ *Holy Smoke* (Beggars Banquet, 1992) ♪♪♪♪

worth searching for: The lone Dali's Car effort, *The Waking Hour* (Paradox/Beggars Banquet, 1984) ♪♪♪♪ is sonically close to Japan, though it never quite reaches that group's heights.

▶▶ David Sylvian, Edwyn Collins

◀◀ John Cale, David Bowie, Bryan Ferry, Japan

see also: *Bauhaus*

JD Cantarella

The Music Explosion

Formed mid-1960s in Ohio. Disbanded 1969.

Jamie Lyons, vocals, guitar, trombone; Don Tudor Atkins, guitar; Rick Nesta, guitar; Butch (Burton) Stahl, bass, organ; Bob Avery, drums, harmonica

Sounding like a polished version of ? and the Mysterians—it covered "96 Tears" on its first album—this one-hit Ohio garage band reached No. 2 in 1967 with "Little Bit O' Soul," a gutsy R&B number with a hooky bass-organ riff. Lyons sneered out his vocals in what sounds like an earnest tribute to Mick Jagger, but whatever personality the group may have had was subverted by producers Jeff Katz and Jerry Kasenetz, who would go on to create successful bubblegum acts such as the 1910 Fruitgum Co. and the Ohio Express. *Anthology* (One Way, 1995, prod. Elliot Cheprut, Jerry Kasenetz and Jeff Katz) ♪♪ is an interesting retro-punk artifact that effectively pulls together the bulk of the Music Explosion's meager catalog; little of the material stands up today, but some of it ("Little Bit O' Soul," "I See the Light," "96 Tears" and "Sunshine Games") is just offbeat enough to be interesting.

Christopher Scapelliti

My Bloody Valentine

Formed 1984 in Dublin, Ireland

Kevin Shields, vocals, guitars; Colm O'Ciosoig, drums,; Tina, keyboards (1984-85); Dave Conway, vocals (1984-87); Deb Googe (1986-present), bass; Belinda Butcher, guitar, vocals (1987- present)

As far as most pop music pundits are concerned, My Bloody Valentine—whose name is derived from a B-grade Canadian horror film—redefined rock music. Following the addition of Butcher's haunting vocals, the group's 1988 debut album, *Isn't Anything*, and its follow-up, 1991's *Loveless*, presented a sound that was fresh and distinctive. Using feedback, tape loops, flutes, pianos, distortion and drums, and a variety of skewed production techniques, My Bloody Valentine earned acclaim not only for its warped sound collages but also for its captivating songs. This quest for innovation has a price, though; The recording of *Loveless* took three years, cost as much as

$500,000 and nearly bankrupted the band's British label, Creation Records.

what to buy: On *Loveless,* (Sire, 1991, prod. Kevin Shields) the band perfected its melodic noise pop with richly textured music that's loud and noisy, yet never harsh or abrasive. The closing track, "Soon," "sets a new standard for pop," according to Brian Eno. *Glider*(Creation/Sire EP, 1991, prod. Kevin Shields and My Bloody Valentine) contains "Soon," as well as three other songs that aren't as ethereal as *Loveless*—making it perhaps an even better starting point.

what to buy next: *Isn't Anything* (Creation/Relativity, 1988, prod. My Bloody Valentine) isn't quite as fully realized as *Loveless*, but it's still mesmerizing—sort of like grunge with eerie overtones. *Tremolo* (Creation/Sire EP, 1991, prod. My Bloody Valentine) offers some of the group's most noisy and experimental songs, each loaded with distortion, tape loops and re-engineering touches.

what to avoid: Lacking Butcher's vocals and the complex, organic feel of the later releases, *This Is Your Bloody Valentine* (Tycoon EP, 1985/Dosier EP, 1991, prod. My Bloody Valentine) is a basic, bland rock set. Stick to the more recent records.

worth searching for: *Ecstasy and Wine,* (Lazy EP, 1989, prod. My Bloody Valentine) an out of print EP that finds the group making more strides towards its signature sound.

Seefeel, Slowdive, Chapterhouse, Lush, Ride, Curve

Beatles, Brian Eno, Cocteau Twins, Sonic Youth, Philip Glass

Aidin Varizi and Bryan Lassner

My Life with the Thrill Kill Kult

Formed 1987 in Chicago, Ill.

Groovie Mann (born Frank Nardiello), vocals; Buzz McCoy (born Marston Daley) vocals, guitar; Levi Levi (born Charles Levi), bass (1991-present); Buck Ryder (born Thomas Thorn), keyboards, samples (1987-93); Otto Mattix, drums (1987-93); Trash K., guitars (1994); Dick Furry, drums (1995-present); Wolfgang Dodge, horns (1995). The Bomb Gang Girlz: Kitty Killdare (born Laura Gomel), keyboards, vocals (1987-95); Jacky Blacque (born Rachel Hollingsworth), vocals; Rhond "Pickles" Bond, vocals; Beat Mistress, drums; Cinderella Pussie, vocals (?-1995); Linda Lunch, vocals; Arena Rock (born Carmen Marusich), vocals (1995-present); Sekret DeZyre, vocals (1990-95)

In 1987 Nardielo and Daley approached Dannie Flesher of Wax Trax! records with an idea to create a B-horror movie, entitled "My Life with the Thrill Kill Kult." The project almost got underway, and the two even went as far as to record a soundtrack to the film that subsequently became the group's first EP (the film is long forgotten). Incorporating an array of musicians and an ever-changing line-up of female singers (known collectively as the Bomb Gang Girlz), Thrill Kill Kult (TKK) has always sounded just like it originally intended, a kitschy horror movie soundtrack. Even though the band has never made a movie, the music has been used in several motion pictures, and the group generously samples from a wide variety of cult films and television shows.

what to buy: TKK's first outings contain an industrial edge, culminating with *Confessions of a Knife* (Wax Trax!, 1990, prod. Buzz McCoy) which combines glam, metal and industrial touches with an electro-dance groove. With the release of *Sexplosion!,* (Interscope, 1991, prod. Buzz McCoy) TKK changes not only the labels, but also sounds, becoming even more dance oriented and less harsh. The album launched a club and underground hit, "Sex On Wheels."

what to buy next: For fans of the Wax Trax! era, TKK's original outing, *I See Good Spirits and I See Bad Spirits* (Wax Trax! 1988, prod. Buzz McCoy) is sure to please; Satan and samples abound, thrown in with a good mix of disco and an industrial backbone. *13 Above the Night* (Interscope, 1994, prod. Buzz McCoy) follows *Sexplosion!'s* decent into disco-glam, softening the tinge of distortion that remains.

what to avoid: *Hit and Run Holiday* (Interscope Records, 1995, prod. Buzz McCoy) is TKK's most dance-oriented album to date, and its most tempered, with relatively subdued guitar and vocal distortion.

the rest: *Kooler Than Jesus* (Wax Trax!, 1989)

solo outings:

Electric Hellfire Club (Buck Ryder and Otto Mattix): Burn Baby Burn (Cleopatra, 1993) *Kiss the Goat* (Cleopatra, 1995)

Pigface, Electric Hellfire Club, Ministry, Luc Van Acker, KMFDM, Lords of Acid, Meat Beat Manifesto

Big Stick, Death in June, Legendary Pink Dots

Bryan Lassner

Mystery Machine

Formed in Chilliwack, British Columbia, Canada

Luke Rogalsky, guitar and vocals; Bean, guitar; Shane Ward, bass; Jordan Pratt, drums and backing vocals

With its two albums, Mystery Machine has gradually won attention for its intricate, guitar heavy hard rock—the kind of modern style that can appeal to both the alternative and headbanger crowds. The quartet's debut, *Glazed* (Nettwerk, 1993), received minimal attention in the U.S. but won underground converts on the strength of songs such as "Valley Song." Its successor, *10 Speed* (Nettwerk, 1995, prod. Glen Reely, Ken Lomas and Chris Shaw). courted radio play thanks to a more mature sound, one that mixes strong melodies with hypnotizing, chaotic riffs that create a swirling, almost tranquilizing effect.

Kim Forster

Naked Eyes

Formed 1982 in London, England. Disbanded 1984.

Pete Byrne, vocals; Rob Fisher, keyboards

A featherweight addition to the early 80s MTV electro-pop scourge, Naked Eyes is one of the many indistinguishable airy duos that swept across the airwaves. Like the rest, it had one song in it ("Promises, Promises") and a cover (R.B. Greaves' 1970 hit "Always Something There to Remind Me") before it chirped right off the charts. If the latter carries any worth at all, it is to turn listeners back to Dionne Warwick's chiming original. Both *The Best of Naked Eyes* (EMI, 1991, prod. Various) and *Promises, Promises: the Very Best of Naked Eyes* (EMI, 1994, prod. Various) offer pretty much the same mix, although the more recent disc presents a slightly fuller picture.

Allan Orski

Peter Namlook & Bill Laswell

See: Bill Laswell

Johnette Napolitano

See: Concrete Blonde

Steve Nardella

Born June 26, 1948 in Providence, R.I.

This no-nonsense roots rocker-bluesman moved to Ann Arbor, Mich., during the early 70s and gained prominence at the legendary 1972 Ann Arbor Blues & Jazz Festival, playing guitar and harmonica in the Boogie Brothers band he formed with drummer Fran Christina (later of Roomful of Blues and the Fabulous Thunderbirds) and guitarist John Nicholas. An excellent session band, the group was frequently called to back up a who's who of blues legends when tours brought them to town. Nardella later formed the popular local band the Silvertones with fellow Ann Arbor guitar slinger George Bedard. With his quick-fingered guitar work, expressive harmonica playing and working man's wail, Nardella has been a stalwart of the Midwestern rock and blues scene for a quarter-century. He has only one CD to date, *Daddy Rollin' Stone,* (Schoolkids, 1993, Henry Weck and Steve Nardella) an exceptional outing that showcases Nardella's rockabilly-tinged vocals and Chuck Berry-styled guitar licks.

see also: *George Bedard*

William Hanson

Graham Nash

See: Crosby, Stills and Nash

Nazareth

Formed 1968 in Dunfermline, Scotland

Dan McCafferty, vocals; Manny Charlton, guitar (1968-90); Darrel Sweet, drums; Pete Agnew, bass; Zal Cleminson, guitar (1978-80); Billy Rankin, guitar, keyboards (1981-83, 1990-present); John Locke, keyboards (1981-82)

Like a boot slamming on a hardwood floor, Nazareth crunched up their rock and spit it out with a pretty good thwack. While not overly creative, the group did rework a surprising selection of cover material (songs by Bob Dylan, Joni Mitchell and Woody Guthrie). Purging the songs of their rustic beauty—the grinding version of the Everly Brothers' "Love Hurts" being the most famous example—the Scots gave 'em a solid stomp, while McCafferty's rip-saw vocals shredded everything in sight without apology. After middling through the 80s without a U.S. label (spending its time in Canada and Europe), Nazareth returned to the States in '93 with its thumping style still intact.

what to buy: Since most of its albums are spotty, *Greatest Hits* (A&M, 1996, prod. Various, a distillation of their best material digitally remastered, is a handy intro.

what to buy next: *Hair of the Dog* (A&M, 1975, prod. Manny

Charlton) is the group's most consistent album, with "Love Hurts" and the relentlessly nasty title track.

what to avoid: *Razamanaz* (A&M, 1973/1994, prod. Roger Glover) demonstrates that plodding around without a good tune is just plodding around.

the rest: *Hot Tracks* (A&M, 1977) *Classics Vol. 16* (A&M, 1987) *No Jive* (Griffin, 1995/1993) *Singles Collection* (Griffin, 1994) *Early Years* (Griffin, 1995) *Snaz Live* (Griffin, 1981/1995)

Mötley Crüe, Krokus

Led Zeppelin, Mountain, Deep Purple, Sensational Alex Harvey Band

Allan Orski

Me'Shell Ndegeocello

Born late 1960s, in Berlin, Germany

Bassist and singer-songwriter Ndegeocello (her last name, pronounced "N-day-gay-o-chello," means "Free as a Bird" in Swahili) is a jazz-trained virtuoso raised in Washington D.C. amidst the burgeoning go-go scene. She worked as a session player for singer Caron Wheeler, fusion drum hero Lenny White and others, was invited to audition for Living Colour and served as the musical director for Arrested Development's appearance on TV's "Saturday Night Live." But she first garnered public attention with her impressive debut album, *Plantation Lullabies,* (Maverick, 1993, prod. Bob Power, Andre Betts and David Gamson) which suggested that she was a serious contender in the old-school soul department. Her tough, emotionally direct songs and arrangements, go-for-broke fretwork and low, affectless vocals were a marked departure for black female performers at the time—as were her shaved head and professed bisexuality. The album earned a couple of Grammy nominations, as did her breakthrough duet with John Mellencamp on his cover of Van Morrison's "Wild Night." Ndegeocello returned to the studio to produce the daring follow-up *Peace Beyond Passion.* (Maverick, 1996, prod. David Gamson) With its bold use of Biblical themes and hot-button language about sexuality and race, the album immediately generated controversy at radio and in the press. But she drapes her hard-hitting themes in exquisite, driving soul arrangements that recall some of the most poignant black music of the 70s.

Simon Glickman

Fred Neil

Born 1937 in St. Petersburg, Fla.

If you've seen the movie "Midnight Cowboy," you're familiar with the highlight of Neil's career. He wrote the song "Everybody's Talkin'," which was performed by Harry Nilsson on the soundtrack. Unfortunately, this was as close as Neil would come to reaching a broad audience. He became a fixture on the Greenwich Village folk club scene during the early 60's, and his laid-back 12-string guitar style and his singing voice, which slipped effortlessly from a mellow tenor to a haunting baritone, influenced everyone from Bob Dylan to Tim Buckley to John Sebastian. After recording four albums from 1965-71, Neil retreated to his home in Florida, where, by all accounts, he lives in virtual seclusion. Neil's recorded output is spotty, but this cult figure really shone on his second release; moody and introspective, *Fred Neil* (Capitol, 1966, prod. Nik Venet) is highlighted by the dreamlike "The Dolphins" and Neil's own version of "Everybody's Talkin'."

the rest: *Bleecker and McDougal* (Elektra, 1965) *Other Side of This Life* (Capitol, 1971)

Dan Weber

Vince Neil

See: Mötley Crüe

Nelson

Formed 1988 in Los Angeles, Calif.

Matthew Nelson, vocals, bass; Gunnar Nelson, vocals, guitar

With a rock star father (teen idol Ricky Nelson) and blonde, blue-eyed hunky good looks, the Nelson twins jumped onto the pop-metal bandwagon in 1990. Musically active as children, the pair had once recorded a song in a pro studio (courtesy of Dad) with the Pointer Sisters singing back up. They kicked around in metal bands throughout the 80s, positioning themselves perfectly for teen idol success in 1990 with the release of *After the Rain,* (Geffen, 1990, prod. David Thoener, Mark Tanner) which housed a No. 1 single, "(Can't Live Without Your) Love and Affection." Of course, the downturn in metal soon after their debut cast their future in doubt, delaying by four years their follow-up album—*Because They Can* (Geffen, 1995, prod. Tanner) —and ensuring no one would care when it finally was released.

Eric Deggans

Rick Nelson

Born Eric Hilliard Nelson, May 8, 1940 in Teaneck, N.J. Died Dec. 31, 1985 in DeKalb, Texas

Unjustly maligned as a pretty boy teen idol, Nelson actually made records in his early days that rivaled his more "authentic" counterparts in Memphis. He didn't live long enough to receive the recognition he deserved as one of rock 'n' roll's early greats, but he never stopped rocking. He died, in fact, when his plane literally went down in flames on his way to yet another in an endless stream of one-nighters, churning out the oldies for an audience of middle-aged housewives who remembered the adorable, wise-cracking scion of TV's "Ozzie and Harriet."

what to buy: His string of hit singles pioneering the California rockabilly sound have been commemorated on two worthwhile discs. *Ricky Nelson: The Legendary Masters Series* (EMI, 1990, prod. Various) showcases the spare, Memphis-influenced rock 'n' roll of his early recordings, with guitarist James Burton adding to the instrument's vocabulary on virtually every new side. The subsequent singles, including more pop-oriented pieces like Gene Pitney's "Hello Mary Lou," Jerry Fuller's "Travelin' Man" and Dave Burgess' "Everlovin'," have been compiled on *The Best Of Rick Nelson (Volume 2)* (EMI, 1991, prod. Various)

what to buy next: Nelson's slow decline into middle-of-the-road 60s pop-rock and eventual resuscitation with the 1972 hit, "Garden Party," is chronicled on *The Best Of Rick Nelson 1963-1975* (Decca/MCA, 1990, prod. Various)

what to avoid: At his most confused, Nelson did a mundane album with Hollywood producer Keith Olsen (Fleetwood Mac, Foreigner), an entirely misguided unreleased project with producer Al Kooper and a relatively refreshing return to his rockabilly roots recorded in Memphis, also unreleased. Bits of these are commemorated on *Stay Young: The Epic Recordings* (Epic/Legacy, 1993, prod. Various)

the rest: "All My Best" (Silver Eagle 1986) *Live 1983-1985* (Rhino, 1989)

worth searching for: Both of his first country experiments, compiled on *Rick Nelson: Country Music* (The Entertainers, 1994, prod. J. Haskell), and his influential Hollywood country-rock of the late 60s, *Rick Nelson and the Stone Canyon Band 1969-1976* (Edsel, 1995, prod. Various), have been released by European labels. Also, a vinyl version of his third album, *Ricky Sings Again* (Imperial, 1958, prod. J. Haskell), is one of the great, unheralded rock and roll albums of the 50s, easily the match of the best of more highly regarded contemporaries like Eddie Cochran, Gene Vincent or Buddy Holly.

The Eagles, Fleetwood Mac, Nelson

Carl Perkins, Elvis Presley, Dale Hawkins

Joel Selvin

Mike Nesmith

See: The Monkees

Aaron Neville

See: Neville Brothers

Art Neville

See: Neville Brothers

Charles Neville

See: Neville Brothers

Cyril Neville

See: Neville Brothers

Neville Brothers

Formed 1977 in New Orleans, La.

Art Neville, keyboards, vocals; Charles Neville, saxophone, vocals, percussion; Aaron Neville, vocals, percussion; Cyril Neville, percussion, vocals

The Neville Brothers formed in New Orleans in 1977, though various incarnations of the group had been performing and recording since the early 60s. Indeed, keyboardist Art Neville formed his first band, The Hawketts, in the preceding decade and later achieved some success with the soul/funk quartet The Meters, which had backed up brother Aaron on his solo sides and on some records made under the Neville Sounds moniker. The group's debut as the Neville Brothers came out in 1978, after the brothers had gotten together with their uncle George "Big Chief Jolly" Landry on his *Wild Tchoupitoulas* proect. The Nevilles' following increased during the 80s, mostly on the strength of the group's firey live shows. Aaron's success both as a solo artist and in a series of high-profile, Grammy winning duets with pop singer Linda Ronstadt and country singer Trisha Yearwood earned the group a larger following. Its upbeat, grooving, often syncopated soul and Mardi Gras vibe owe much to the Meters, though the Nevilles streamlined the sound with pop and, of course, Aaron's sweet, soaring pipes.

what to buy: *Treacherous: A History of the Neville Brothers* (Rhino, 1988, prod. Various) ♫♫♫♫ is, hands-down, the best collection of the group's strongest work.

what to buy next: *Yellow Moon* (A&M, 1989, prod. Daniel Lanois) ♫♫♫♪ is an impressive, mature album that boasts a kinetic rendition of Link Wray's "Fire and Brimstone."

what to avoid: Aaron's *Soulful Christmas*, (A&M, 1993, prod. Steve Lindsey) ♫♫ on which the fine singer makes lite R&B mush of over-recorded seasonal favorites.

the rest: *The Neville Brothers* (Capitol, 1978) ♫♫♫ *Fiyo on the Bayou* (A&M, 1981) ♫♫♫♪ *Neville-Ization* (Black Top, 1984) ♫♫♫♪ *Live at Tipitina's* (Spindletop, 1985) ♫♫♫ *Uptown* (EMI America, 1987) ♫♫♪ *Brother's Keeper* (A&M, 1990) ♫♫♫ *Treacherous Too!* (Rhino, 1991) ♫♫♫♪ *Family Groove* (A&M, 1992) ♫♫♪ *Live on Planet Earth* (A&M, 1994) ♫♫♪ *Mitakuye Oyasin Oyasin (All My Relations)* (A&M, 1996) ♫♫♫♪

worth searching for: *The Wild Tchoupitoulas* (Island, 1976, prod. Allen Toussaint and Marshal Sehorn) ♫♫♫♪ the Nevilles' soulful collaboration with its older realatives, mines a soulful vein of Louisiana musical history.

solo outings:

Aaron Neville *Greatest Hits* (Curb, 1990) ♫♫♫♪ *My Greatest Gift* (Rounder, 1991) ♫♫♫♪ *Warm Your Heart* (A&M, 1991) ♫♫ *The Grand Tour* (A&M, 1993) ♫♫ *The Tattooed Heart* (A&M, 1995) ♫♫♪

Art Neville *His Specialty Recordings, 1956-58* (Specialty, 1992) ♫♫♫♪ *That Old Time Rock 'n' Roll* (Specialty, 1993) ♫♫♪

Cyril Neville *Fire This Time* (Iguana, 1995) ♫♫♫

Charles Neville (with Songcatchers) *Moving in Color* (A&M, 1994) ♫♫♫♫

▶▶ Daniel Lanois, Elton John, Black Crowes, Angelo and Boyz II Men

◀◀ Gospel, Professor Longhair, Ray Charles, Lee Dorsey, Meters

Simon Glickman

New Edition

Formed 1981 in Boston, Mass.

Ralph Tresvant, vocals; Ronnie DeVoe, vocals; Michael Bivins, vocals; Ricky Bell, vocals; Bobby Brown, vocals (1981-88); Johnny Gill, vocals (1988-present)

Bound by friendships forged growing up in one of Boston's more notorious ghettos, New Edition hit the road to stardom when producer/manager Maurice Starr caught the vocal quartet performing at one of his talent shows. Crafting a sound much like an 80s update of the classic Jackson 5 singles, Starr packaged the group around Tresvant's eerily high, Michael Jackson-style lead vocals, producing hits on the R&B charts from their first two records. In 1984, the group dumped Starr as manager/producer/Svengali, two years before Bobby Brown left for an uneven solo career. The group floundered for a few years, until Stacy Lattisaw protege Gill replaced Brown and the group enlisted Janet Jackson producers James "Jimmy Jam" Harris III and Terry Lewis to handle its comeback record, which hinted at the mixture of soul power and hip-hop flavor (also called New Jack Swing) that would fuel each member's future solo success. After a successful fifth record, the group splintered, with Gill, Tresvant and Brown all scoring major solo hits by riding the New Jack wave, while DeVoe, Bivins and Bell joined forces in Bell Biv Devoe. But the quickly-changing face of contemporary R&B made New Edition's late 80s schtick passe, forcing all of the band members to team up for yet another comeback project in 1996.

what to buy: As a group, New Edition's *Heart Break* (MCA, 1989, prod. James "Jimmy Jam" Harris III and Lewis) ♫♫♫♪ exposes the entertaining and aggressive urban vocal quartet that was hiding in the fledgling group's poppier early album. Presaging by years the fusion of hip-hop techniques with traditional R&B styles, the album emphasizes lush, percolating soundscapes while giving the best singers in the band—Gill and Tresvant—plenty of room to strut their stuff. On the solo tip, the albums that best took advantage of the New Jack explosion were Brown's *Don't Be Cruel* (MCA, 1988, prod. Various) ♫♫♫♪ and Bell Biv DeVoe's percolating *Poison* (MCA, 1990, prod. Various) ♫♫♫♪—each chock full of hits that moved the music forward.

what to buy next: As the only record that jams together both their Jackson 5 and New Jack periods, *Greatest Hits, Vol. 1* (MCA, 1991, prod. Various) ♫♫♫ offers every notable single from the group's five albums, including "Cool It Now," "If It Isn't Love" and a new cut, "Boys To Men," that provided a name for a Philadelphia group Bivins would go on to produce. Gill's first solo outing, *Johnny Gill* (Motown, 1990, prod. Various) 𝅘𝅥𝅘𝅥𝅘𝅥 ekes out a few hits—"My, My My" and "Fairweather Friend"—while showcasing the singer's gritty, soulful vocals.

what to avoid: New Edition's cover of 50s and 60s hits, *Under the Blue Moon* (MCA, 1986, prod. Freddie Perrin) **WOOF!** is an exercise in endurance. Just listen to them try to hit the low notes in "Duke of Earl." On the solo front, no New Edition alumnus has yet produced an effort as embarrassing as Brown's toothless solo debut *King of Stage,* (MCA, 1987, prod. Larry Blackmon) **WOOF!** a record so generically boring, it's hard to imagine how he had the chance to do *Don't Be Cruel*

the rest: *Candy Girl* (Streetwise, 1983) 𝅘𝅥𝅘𝅥𝅘𝅥 *New Edition* (MCA, 1984) 𝅘𝅥𝅘𝅥𝅗𝅥 *Christmas All Over the World* (MCA, 1985) 𝅘𝅥𝅘𝅥 *All For Love* (MCA, 1985) 𝅘𝅥𝅘𝅥𝅗𝅥

solo outings:

Bobby Brown *Dance!...Ya Know It!* (MCA, 1990) 𝅘𝅥𝅘𝅥𝅘𝅥 *Bobby* (MCA, 1992) 𝅘𝅥𝅘𝅥𝅗𝅥

Johnny Gill *Perfect Combination* (Cotillion, 1983) 𝅘𝅥𝅘𝅥𝅗𝅥 *Chemistry* (Atlantic, 1985) 𝅘𝅥𝅘𝅥𝅗𝅥 *Provocative* (Motown, 1993) 𝅘𝅥𝅘𝅥𝅘𝅥

Ralph Tresvant *Ralph Tresvant* (MCA, 1990) 𝅘𝅥𝅘𝅥𝅗𝅥 *It's Goin' Down* (MCA, 1993) 𝅘𝅥𝅘𝅥

Bell Biv DeVoe *WBBD-Bootcity!* (MCA, 1991) 𝅘𝅥𝅘𝅥𝅘𝅥 *Hootie Mack* (MCA, 1993) 𝅘𝅥𝅘𝅥𝅗𝅥

worth searching for: To actually see the transformation of New Edition from a bunch of parachute pants-wearing, Jheri curl-sporting pre-teens to self-assured, hip hop-influenced young men, consult the video anthology "Past To Present," which boasts clips from throughout the group's career.

⏩ H-Town, Solo, New Kids on the Block

⏪ Jackson 5, Four Tops, Cameo, The Time, Janet Jackson

Eric Deggans

New Kids on the Block

Formed 1985 in Boston, Mass. Disbanded 1994.

Jordan Knight, vocals; Donnie Wahlberg, vocals; Joe McIntyre, vocals; Danny Wood, vocals; Jon Knight, vocals

There was no middle ground with teen sensations New Kids on the Block during the late 80s and early 90s: You either loved 'em or hated 'em. And although prepubescent girls seemed to be the only ones who loved them, that was apparently enough. At its peak, the ubiquitous New Kids had their own line of Hasbro dolls and were named the world's highest-paid entertainers by Forbes, earning $115 million in 1990 and 1991. More a marketing ploy than a musical force, the group was formed and controlled by writer-producer-manager Maurice Starr, who wanted to replace his suddenly departed black teen group, New Edition, with a similar group that would appeal to a broader (read: white) audience. One of his original recruits was Mark Wahlberg, who later decided to pursue a career in rap as Marky Mark instead. However, Wahlberg's brother, Donnie, signed up and was eventually joined by three of his schoolmates (Wood and the Knight brothers) plus McIntyre. The group, which was originally called Nynuk, broke through in 1988 with its chart-topping second album, *Hangin' Tough,* winning over legions of adoring, squealing teenyboppers through boyish looks and hook-laden, R&B-influenced, bubble-gum pop. Its 1990 tour was one of the biggest-grossing in the history of the concert business, bringing in $74.1 million, but the group was greeted with hard skepticism and intense loathing by nearly everybody over the age of 15, particularly pop critics. During the Milli Vanilli scandal, a disgruntled associate producer for the New Kids accused the group of similar fraudulent practices, saying that Starr and his brother did most of the singing on the New Kids' albums. The group eventually appeared on "The Arsenio Hall Show" to sing a capella and prove its detractor wrong. After a four-year hiatus from studio work and a split with Starr, the group attempted to reposition itself in 1994 as tougher and more mature, appearing with facial hair and a changed name, NKOTB. But New Kids simply could not shake the past (Hey, whatever they call themselves, they're still L-A-M-E, said David Letterman) and broke up later that year.

what to buy: Although it sounds grossly dated now, if you must see what the New Kids fuss was about, the breakthrough *Hangin' Tough* (Columbia, 1988, prod. Maurice Starr) 𝅘𝅥𝅘𝅥 is the best place to go with its abundance of hits, including the innocent teen ballads "I'll Be Loving You (Forever)" and "Please Don't Go Girl" and the quasi-funk title track, as well as "You Got It (The Right Stuff)" and "Cover Girl."

what to buy next: Hip-hop-informed New Jack production values and tight, layered harmonies make *Face the Music* (Columbia, 1994, prod. Teddy Riley, Donnie Wahlberg, Narada Michael Walden and Walter Afanasieff) 𝅘𝅥𝅘𝅥𝅘𝅥 the most current and vibrant-sounding album in the New Kids catalog, although the group's street-style stance is a bit tough to digest after three albums of sugar-sweet pop.

What to Avoid: *New Kids on the Block* (Columbia, 1986) *Merry, Merry Christmas* (Columbia, 1989) WOOF! *Step By Step* (Columbia, 1990) *No More Games: The Remix Album* (Columbia, 1990)

▶▶ Milli Vanilli, Marky Mark

◀◀ New Edition, Bay City Rollers, the Jackson Five

Joshua Freedom duLac

New Order

Formed 1980 in Manchester, England

Bernard Sumner (born Bernard Albrecht), guitar, vocals; Peter Hook, bass, vocals; Stephen Morris, percussion; Gillian Gilbert, keyboards, vocals

New Order rose out of the ashes of Joy Division after that group's frontman Ian Curtis took his own life. The remaining members—Sumner, Hook and Morris—brought in keyboardist Gilbert and went on to become one of the most pivotal synth-based pop bands of the 80s. Casting away Joy Division's dark overtones, the new group instead embraced disco rhythms and forward-thinking ideals while maintaining an astute sense of emotional alienation. Where Joy Division provided the morbid missing link between the Doors and Nirvana, New Order was all about living for the thrill of the moment—and in the process paved the way for the U.K.'s current techno scene. Most of its singles—from "Age of Consent" to "Bizarre Love Triangle" to "Regret"—remain staples at dance clubs, while the individual musicians have also pursued a variety of side projects.

what to buy: The bulk of New Order's best songs were released as singles, which makes both *(The Best of) New Order* (Qwest, 1995, prod. Various) and the more eclectic *Substance 1987* (Qwest, 1987, prod. Various) ideal packages for neophytes. For the more discriminating ear, however, New Order's second album, *Power, Corruption and Lies* (Qwest, 1983, prod. Martin Hannet and New Order) represents the perfect embodiment of the group's original sound, linking Joy Division's dark power with the new group's experimental ambitions.

what to buy next: New Order's debut album, *Movement*, (Factory/Rough Trade, 1981, New Order) laid the blueprint for the group's innovative sound, making it one of the most pivotal records of the 80s. *Technique* (Qwest, 1989 prod. New Order) is the group's most melodic album to date, mixing contemporary club rhythms with acoustic guitars and Hook's exquisite bass lines.

what to avoid: On its forth album, *Brotherhood*, (Qwest, 1986, prod. New Order) it sounded like New Order had run out of ideas, despite the indispensable "Bizarre Love Triangle" single.

the rest: *Low-Life* (Qwest, 1985) *Republic* (Qwest, 1993)

worth searching for: *BBC Radio 1 Live In Concert* (Windsong, 1992, prod. Pete Ritzema) features rough renditions of such New Order classics as "Touched By The Hand of God" and "Perfect Kiss." The sound quality and song selection are both excellent.

solo outings:

Peter Hook (with Revenge) One True Passion (Capitol, 1990)

The Other Two (Stephen Morris, Gillian Gilbert) The Other Two and You (Qwest, 1992) WOOF!

▶▶ Pet Shop Boys, Underworld, the Cure, Stone Roses, Charlatans U.K.

◀◀ Kraftwerk, Sylvester, Brian Eno, Velvet Underground, Love, Joy Division.

see also: *Joy Division, Electronic*

Aidin Vaziri

New Riders of the Purple Sage

Formed 1969 in Marin County, Calif.

John Dawson, guitar, vocals; David Nelson, guitar, vocals; Jerry Garcia, pedal steel guitar (1969-71); Mickey Hart, drums (1969-70); Phil Lesh, bass (1969-70); Spencer Dryden, drums (1970); Dave Torbert, bass (1970-74); Buddy Cage, pedal steel guitar (1971-82); Skip Battin, bass (1974-76); Stephen Love, bass (1976-82); Allen Kemp, guitar (1977-85); Rusty Gauthier, guitar, violin, fiddle, mandolin, dobro (1982); Gary Vogensen, vocals, guitar (1985-93), Evan Morgan, guitar (1993)

This group began as a busman's holiday by Garcia and other members of the Grateful Dead, John Dawson and David Nelson. Initially, it played traditional country-western, but with a distinct rock attitude. Fine playing and strong songwriting marked its debut. Over time, the band was hurt by frequent changes in support players, unsteady songwriting and a fuzzy focus; country, rock, pop and R&B filtered through the albums unchecked. Sometimes the group toured with only a couple of members and picked up players from the town it was performing in. This resulted in some atrocious concerts; it also points to a serious disdain for fans.

what to buy: By the time of the band's first and best recording, *New Riders of the Purple Sage,* (Columbia, 1971, prod. New Riders of the Purple Sage) Garcia was the only Dead musician left. He exited after this recording, but contributed to other albums.

what to buy next: The band's biggest commercial success came with *Adventures of Panama Red* (Columbia, 1973) With lovelorn, down-on-their-luck cowboys and wheeling-and-dealing dopers, the band cultivated a stance as it's-good-to-be-bad hippie outlaws. First-rate musicianship could overcome inherent confusion over material; some recordings were barbed-wire tight, while others needed mending.

what to avoid: *New Riders with Skip Battin* (One Way) WOOF!, from one of the group's weaker periods.

the rest: Powerglide *(Columbia, 1972/Legacy, 1996)* Marin County Line *(MCA/One Way, 1978)* Before Time Began *(Relix, 1986)* Vintage New Riders of the Purple Sage *(Relix, 1987)* Live On Stage *(Relix)* Live in Japan *(Relix, 1994)*

Eagles, Ozark Mountain Daredevils, Marshall Tucker Band

Flying Burrito Brothers, Seatrain, the Byrds with Gram Parsons, Gene Clark

Patrick McCarty

New York Dolls /Johnny Thunders

Formed 1971, New York, N.Y. Disbanded 1977.

David Johansen, vocals (1971-75); Johnny Thunders (born John Anthony Genzale) guitar (1971-75, died April 23, 1991); Arthur Kane, bass (1971-75); Sylvain Sylvain (born Syl Mizrahi), guitar (1974-77); Jerry Nolan, drums (1972-1974, died Jan. 14, 1992); Billy Murcia, drums (1971-72, died Nov. 6, 1972); Rick Rivets, guitar (1971-72)

The visual prototype for many 80s metal bands, the tremendously influential New York Dolls started off acting and sounding like a second-rate Rolling Stones. In glam makeup and nearly full drag, the group came to prominence in the tumultuous New York pre-punk club scene of the mid-70s via venues such as Max's Kansas City. Though revered by the music press, the band's actual lifespan was fairly short: two unsuccessful albums and a brief, turbulent period with future Sex Pistols (mis)handler Malcom McLaren as its manager—after which the Dolls split up. Johansen reinvented himself during the 80s as hambone party boy Buster Poindexter and took small roles in several films; he still records occasional solo albums. Thunders, a notorious junkie, developed cult status as Keith Richards-styled living zombie, and continued to play and record—with and without backing band the Heartbreakers—up until his drug overdose in 1991. He remains a rock legend more for his abusive habit than any great musical legacy. Drummer Nolan died of a stroke soon after. Like the Pistols, whom they greatly influenced, there are endless Dolls bootlegs and live shows circulated by succeeding generations of fans who weren't around to see the real thing.

what to buy: *New York Dolls* (Mercury, 1973, prod. Todd Rundgren) perfectly captures the group's tongue-in-cheek mix of glam guitar swagger and bleak NYC realism.

the rest: *Too Much Too Soon* (Mercury, 1974) *Lipstick Killers* (ROIR, 1981/1990) *Red Patent Leather* (Restless, 1984) *Rock 'n' Roll* (Mercury, 1994)

worth searching for: *Paris Burning* (Skydog, 1974) a live set that does the band better than the flawed, late-career *Red Patent Leather.*

The Sex Pistols, Guns N' Roses, D Generation

The Rolling Stones, David Bowie, the Stooges

see also: *David Johansen*

Todd Wicks

Randy Newman

Born Nov. 28, 1943 in New Orleans, La.

Swaggering onto the scene like Jonathan Swift at a Bourbon Street piano bar, Newman thrives on misinterpretation. His biggest hit, 1977's "Short People," drew protests from diminutive listeners who didn't realize he was attacking a larger target—prejudice in general. He sometimes takes on the personae of apartheid-supporting South Africans ("Christmas in Capetown"), insecure gay bashers ("Half a Man"), Southern bigots ("Rednecks") and right-wing conservatives ("Roll With the Punches") to get his points across. The ultimate irony is that despite his perennial cult-hero status, Newman's wry blend of Tin Pan Alley pop, ragtime and Crescent City R&B has won over Madison Avenue and Hollywood: he's licensed his songs for commercial jingles ("I Love L.A." for Nike, "I Love to See You Smile" for Colgate), penned soundtracks for "Ragtime," "The Natural" and "Avalon" and dueted with Lyle Lovett on the catchy theme for 1995's "Toy Story." His albums barely

What Album Changed Your Life?

"The Who's Live at Leeds, when I was a kid, because you could hear the bass. I didn't know what bass was...but on Live at Leeds, you could really hear that bass. That record--it wasn't a record actually; it was an 8-track--was just a mind-blower, a really intense record for me."

Mike Watt (the Minutemen, fIREHOSE, Porno For Pyros)

trickle out—between 1979 and 1996, he's released all of four discs—but he hasn't lost his satirical edge or ambitious flair: 1995's *Randy Newman's Faust* is a twisted musical-theater adaptation of Johann Wolfgang von Goethe's classic set in South Bend, Ind. The Lord is played by James Taylor, the Devil, of course, by Newman.

what to buy: Newman wedges his tongue into his cheek on the gloriously sardonic *Sail Away* (Reprise, 1972, prod. Russ Titelman and Lenny Waronker) ♪♪♪♪♪ as he entices slaves to America like a sideshow huckster ("Sail Away"), celebrates the polluted Cuyahoga River like it was Walden Pond ("Burn On") and advocates dropping the Big One ("Political Science"). *Good Old Boys*, (Reprise, 1974, prod. Russ Titelman and Lenny Waronker) ♪♪♪♪♪ a rollicking concept album about the South, is celebrated for skewering redneck ignorance but "Louisiana 1927," "A Wedding in Cherokee County" and "Marie" garner their emotional clout from Newman's sympathetic narrative eye. The engaging *Land of Dreams* (Reprise, 1988, prod. Mark Knopfler, James Newton Howard, Tommy LiPuma and Jeff Lynne) ♪♪♪♪ opens with three autobiographical numbers about his New Orleans childhood and ends with "I Want You to Hurt Like I Do," his chilling answer to "We Are the World."

what to buy next: *Trouble in Paradise* (Reprise,1983, prod. Russ Titelman and Lenny Waronker) ♪♪♪♪ is often dismissed as the album that spawned "I Love L.A." But digging deeper uncovers such gems as "Miami," the scathing "Christmas in Capetown" and "My Life Is Good," in which a cocky Newman brags about Bruce Springsteen asking him "How would you like to be the Boss for a while?"

what to avoid: The pinched production and bloated orchestrations of *Randy Newman* (Reprise, 1968, prod. Lenny Waronker and Van Dyke Parks) ♪♪ make for a tough listen, even with "Davy the Fat Boy" and "I Think It's Going to Rain Today."

the rest: *12 Songs* (Reprise, 1970) ♪♪♪♪ *Randy Newman Live* (Reprise, 1971) ♪♪♪ *Little Criminals* (Reprise, 1977) ♪♪♪♪ *Born Again* (Reprise, 1979) ♪♪♪ *Randy Newman's Faust* (Reprise, 1995) ♪♪♪

worth searching for: For timid beginners, the German-made *Lonely at the Top* (WEA International, 1987, prod. Lenny Waronker, Russ Titelman and Van Dyke Parks) ♪♪♪♪ is a 22-track best-of collection that mixes sarcastic favorites like "Rednecks" and "Short People" with such lovely ballads as "Marie," "I Think It's Going To Rain Today" and "Living Without You." It's an impressive portrait, though hardly a complete picture.

▶▶ Lyle Lovett, Timbuk 3

◀◀ Stephen Foster, uncles Lionel and Alfred Newman, George and Ira Gershwin, Fats Domino

David Okamoto

Olivia Newton-John

Born Sept. 26, 1948 in Cambridge, England

Newton-John had all the tools for pop star perfection—good looks, a good voice and perk to spare. Somebody saw that when she was 16; she won a talent contest in Australia (where she was living at the time) and was sent to England to make her mark. She wasn't always the aerobicized pop diva we came to know during the 80s; in fact, her first hit was a sweetened-up remake of Bob Dylan's "If Not For You," while in England she also scored with re-makes of George Harrison's "What is Life" and John Denver's "Take Me Home Country Roads." She even used her supple tones to mine the country market for awhile, though she caused a stir when she was named the Country Music Association's Female Vocalist of the Year in 1974. Well, if folks were going to get sassy with her, Newton-John could get sassy right back. Following her starring role in the film "Grease," she put out two albums—*Totally Hot* and *Physical*—that let her body do the talking right around the time music videos were starting to take hold in the U.S. There were more films and more hits, though Newton-John did slow down after marrying actor Matt Lattanzi and giving birth to a daughter.

During the early 90s, just after the release of a new greatest hits collection, Newton-John was diagnosed with breast cancer, for which she was successfully treated.

what to buy: Singles are her stock in trade, so *Back to Basics: The Essential Collection 1971-1992* (Geffen, 1992, prod. Various) is a good place to start, though it would be much better if the brand new songs were removed to make room for neglected hits such as "If Not For You."

what to buy next: It was a sales bust, but *The Rumour* (MCA, 1988/1993, prod. Davitt Sigerson) was a daring, uncommercial twist for Newton-John, who worked with different textures as well as an inspired group of guests that included Elton John, Paulinho Da Costa and rock troubadour David Baerwald.

what to avoid: *Physical* (MCA, 1981, prod. John Farrar) **WOOF!** was huge. But it stinks.

the rest: *Have You Ever Been Mellow* (Griffin, 1975/1995) *Come on Over* (MCA, 1976) *Making a Good Thing Better* (MCA, 1977/1990) *Greatest Hits, Vol. 2* (MCA, 1982) *Soul Kiss* (MCA, 1985/1993) *Warm and Tender* (Geffen, 1989)

worth searching for: The out-of-print *Greatest Hits* (MCA, 1977) which has the crucial—and far more palatable—early hits.

▶▶ Debbie Gibson, Tiffany, Kylie Minogue

◀◀ Sandra Dee, Lulu, Cilla Black

Gary Graff

Stevie Nicks

Born May 6, 1948, in Phoenix, Ariz.

As the tensions in Fleetwood Mac escalated, Nicks went solo and scored big. Her dramatic vocals, openly vulnerable lyrics and fantasy images spoke directly to young women. Nicks imagines herself a good witch, and . . . she writes with lots of . . . ellipses. Nicks started her career in a duo with Lindsay Buckingham, and has always preferred collaborations. During her solo career, she has worked with Tom Petty (including a cover of "Needles & Pins" released under his name) and his guitarist Mike Campbell, Don Henley, Prince and Jon Bon Jovi.

what to buy: Nicks's first and best solo album, *Bella Donna,* (Modern, 1981, prod. Jimmie Iovine) had successful duets with Tom Petty ("Stop Draggin' My Heart Around") and Don Henley ("Leather and Lace") and no weak tracks. Waddy Wachtel (guitar) and Benmont Tench and Roy Bittan (keyboards) put fire in the arrangements.

what to buy next: *Time Space—The Best of Stevie Nicks* (Modern, 1991, prod. Various) is missing three of her Top 40 hits, and there's room for them, but there are also three new tracks and Nicks's comments on every song.

what to avoid: *The Other Side of the Mirror.* (Modern, 1989, prod. Rupert Hine) This time, the house landed on the Good Witch.

the rest: *The Wild Heart* (Modern, 1983) *Rock a Little* (Modern, 1985) *Street Angel* (Modern, 1994)

▶▶ Tori Amos, Toni Childs

◀◀ Melanie, Janis Ian

see also: *Fleetwood Mac, Lindsey Buckingham*

Steve Holtje

Nico

See: Velvet Underground

Tim Nielsen

See: Drivin' N' Cryin'

Harry Nilsson

Born June 15, 1941 in Brooklyn, N.Y. Died January 15, 1994 in Agoura Hills, Calif.

Nilsson was both a remarkable singer and a gifted songwriter. It was the latter talent that launched his career during the mid-60s; bands such as Three Dog Night scored hits with his songs, which helped him embark on his own recording career. His supple voice—which could handle mellow, swing-influenced ballads and soaring rock anthems with equal facility—was given full rein, as were his more eclectic instincts as a composer. He achieved mainstream success with his version of "Everybody's Talkin'," the theme from the hit film "Midnight Cowboy," and scored massive hits with the humorous original "Coconut" and Badfinger's ultimate power-ballad "Without You." He also wrote songs for the cartoon musical "The Point," which became a success with help from the single "Me and My Arrow." Nilsson composed other music for film and television, notably the theme from the series "The Courtship of Eddie's Father," which he also performed over the show's opening credits. He rarely performed live, however, and never toured in support of his recordings. He followed a decidedly idiosyncratic career path, recording standards, making mock-horror films with Ringo Starr and drinking quite a lot with John Lennon. Unfortunately, Nilsson's voice was damaged along the way, and he lost his exquisite falsetto—apparently from booze. Lennon's murder in 1980 made Nilsson an outspoken advocate of gun control; he recorded very little during that decade, however. After his own death from heart disease in 1994, he was the subject of an all-star tribute album that demonstrated his profound influence on pop.

what to buy: The two-disc anthology *Personal Best* (RCA, 1995, prod. Various) is a stunning treasury of Nilsson's achievements as both vocalist and songwriter. In addition to boasting his best-known moments, the compilation features many obscure gems.

what to buy next: *Nilsson Schmilsson* (RCA, 1971, prod. Richard Perry) is a fine mix of hits and lesser-known delights.

what to avoid: *Son of Dracula* (RCA, 1974, prod. Nilsson and Ringo Starr) may have been fun to make, but its blend of songs (mostly recycled from other albums), stoned dialogue and incidental music from this dog of a movie will try the patience of most listeners.

the rest: *Pandemonium Shadow Show* (RCA, 1967) *Spotlight on Nilsson* (RCA, 1967) *True One* (RCA, 1967) *Aerial Ballet* (RCA, 1968) *Nilsson Sings Newman* (RCA, 1970) *The Point* (RCA, 1971) *Aerial Pandemonium Ballet* (RCA, 1971) *Son of Schmilsson* (RCA, 1972) *Songwriter* (RCA, 1972) *A Little Touch of Schmilsson in the Night* (RCA, 1973) *Pussy Cats* (with John Lennon) (RCA, 1974) *Sandman* (RCA, 1975) *That's the Way It Is* (RCA, 1976) *Knilsson* (RCA, 1977) *Nilsson's Greatest Music* (RCA, 1978) *A Touch More Schmilsson in the Night* (RCA, 1988)

worth searching for: *Harry* (RCA, 1969, prod. Nilsson and Rick Jarrard) is gentler and more nostalgic, but contains some of his very best early work.

▶▶ Marshall Crenshaw, Aimee Mann, Gin Blossoms, Jellyfish, The Posies, Semisonic, Jennifer Trynin

◀◀ Cole Porter, Gershwin, Hank Williams, Little Richard, the Beatles, Beach Boys, Burt Bacharach, Randy Newman, Van Dyke Parks

Simon Glickman

Nine Inch Nails

Formed 1987 in Cleveland, Ohio

Trent Reznor (born May 17, 1965 in Mercer, Pa.), vocals, guitar, bass, drums, electronics, computers. Other members include: Robin Finck, guitar; Danny Lohner, keyboards, guitar, bass; Charlie Clouser, keyboards; Chris Vrenna, drums

In the early 90s, as the so-called Generation X was starting to gain a media identity as a consumer group of alienated, jobless slackers, Reznor's nine inch nails came out with the perfect soundtrack of anger and angst. Originally a hard dance band, NIN built a huge underground buzz by gradually injecting its debut, *Pretty Hate Machine,* into gloomy nightclubs all over the world. Though Reznor's problems with his original record label, TVT, prevented a timely releases of a follow-up, the long-haired young scientist-type gained a cult following that eventually earned NIN a spot on the first Lollapalooza tour. By then, fans and critics were crediting him as the most artistically consistent innovator of hardcore, loud, throbbing "industrial" music, at the head of a pack that also included Ministry, Skinny Puppy and KMFDM. After that, it was only a matter of time before Reznor became a huge alternative-rock superstar, coating himself with mud for Woodstock '94 and scoring of huge MTV and radio hits.

what to buy: *Pretty Hate Machine* (TVT, 1989, prod. Trent Reznor) is most notable for the terrific angry single, "Head Like a Hole." The rest was originally intended to sound like a harsh factory of metallic objects slamming into each other, but several years later it sounds (agreeably) goofy.

what to buy next: *The Downward Spiral* (TVT/Interscope, 1994, prod. Trent Reznor) took five years to create, but its catchy (yes, catchy) hits "Closer," "Piggy" and "Hurt" helped create the alternative-rock radio format as we know it.

what to avoid: *Fixed* (nothing/TVT/Interscope, 1992, prod. Various) is a bunch of inconsequential remixes from the *Broken* EP.

the rest: *Broken (EP)* (nothing/TVT/Interscope, 1992, prod.Trent Reznor) *Further Down the Spiral* (TVT/Interscope, 1995, prod. various)

worth searching for: The soundtrack to "Natural Born Killers" (nothing/Interscope, 1994, prod. Trent Reznor) has new NIN remixes and artfully stews up bits of violent movie dialogue with harsh industrial music and a couple of folk songs.

▶▶ Filter, Rage Against the Machine, KMFDM, White Zombie

⏪ Butthole Surfers, Ministry, Black Sabbath, Motorhead, Can, Kraftwerk

Tracey Birkenhauer and Steve Knopper

Nirvana

Formed 1987, Aberdeen, Wash.

Kurt Cobain, vocals and guitar (d. April 5, 1994); Krist Novoselic, bass; Jason Everman, guitar (1987-89); Chad Channing, drums (1987-90); Dave Grohl, drums (1990-94); Pat Smear, guitar (1993-94)

Millions of music fans were shocked to pick up *Billboard* magazine one morning in early 1992 to read that Nirvana, a rattily dressed group of anti-authority Seattle kids who made shrieking punk rock, had the number one album in the country. But it wasn't so surprising: singer-songwriter Cobain, despite his hollering and cryptic angst lyrics, had a Paul McCartney-level knack for catchy melodies. And the band's breakthrough album, *Nevermind*, used Butch Vig's crisp, big production to build an inviting rock 'n' roll sound that dragged raw punk rock into the mainstream. Cobain's songs, backed with the stellar rhythm section of Grohl and Krist Novoselic, were downbeat and confusing and struck a chord with a generation disgusted with baby boomers, happy hippies and classic-rock radio. The band ushered in the oxymoronic "grunge fashion" movement, paved the way for mass acceptance of Pearl Jam and Stone Temple Pilots and was an icon for what became "alternative music" and "modern-rock radio." But the troubled 27-year-old Cobain handled his success poorly and shot himself to death in his Seattle home in 1994. Grohl formed the Foo Fighters, Novoselic turned to grassroots political activism and Cobain's wife, the equally angst-ridden Courtney Love of the group Hole, became a love-her-or-hate-her rock star in her own right.

what to buy: The opening chords of "Smells Like Teen Spirit," the trailblazing single and video from *Nevermind* (DGC, 1991, prod. Butch Vig) 🦴🦴🦴🦴🦴, have become as gratifyingly familiar as the whoooos in the Beatles' "She Loves You" or the stuttering in The Who's "My Generation." The album also contained the guitar-rock gems "Lithium," "Polly," "Come As You Are" and "Territorial Pissings." The follow-up, *In Utero* (DGC, 1993, prod. Steve Albini) 🦴🦴🦴🦴 reflects Cobain's maturing songwriting style ("All Apologies," "Pennyroyal Tea") but also his indulgences with unlistenable noise. The band's postmortem, *MTV Unplugged in New York* (DGC, 1994, prod. Scott Litt and Nirvana) 🦴🦴🦴🦴 showcases Cobain with his mojo hand in the Leadbelly blues "Where Did You Sleep Last Night?" and intense, slow versions of Nirvana, Meat Puppets and David Bowie songs.

what to buy next: *Bleach* (Sub Pop, 1989, no production credit; prod. by Jack Endino) 🦴🦴🦴 is the raw, unfocused sound of a band coming together. The inconsistent *Incesticide* (DGC, 1992, prod. Various) 🦴🦴🦴 outtakes collection contains the wonderful cover of the Vaselines' "Molly's Lips" plus the originals "Dive" and "Sliver."

the rest: *Blew (EP)* (Tupelo, 1989) 🦴🦴🦴 *From the Muddy Banks of the Wishkah* (Geffen, 1996) not available for rating

worth searching for: *Rare Tracks Vol. II* 🦴🦴🦴🦴 a bootleg with two versions of "Smells Like Teen Spirit," including one with the Red Hot Chili Peppers' Flea on trumpet, plus the Who's "Baba O'Riley" and an irritating, unfocused, moaning duet, "It's Closing Soon," by Cobain and Love.

solo outings:

Dave Grohl Foo Fighters (Capitol, 1995) 🦴🦴🦴🦴

⏩ Pearl Jam, Stone Temple Pilots, Bush, Everclear, Presidents of the United States of America

⏪ David Bowie, the Who, Cheap Trick, The Melvins, Leadbelly, Husker Du, Sonic Youth, Replacements, Flipper, Vaselines, Raincoats

Steve Knopper

Nitty Gritty Dirt Band

Formed 1966 in Long Beach, Calif.

Jeff Hanna, vocals, guitar; Jimmie Fadden, vocals, drums; Les Thompson, vocals, mandolin (1966-73); Bruce Kunkel, guitar, violin, vocals (1966-67); Ralph Barr, guitar, clarinet, vocals (1966-68); Jackson Browne, guitar, vocals (1966); John McEuen, banjo, guitar, fiddle, (1967-86); Chris Darrow, guitar, fiddle (1968); Jimmy Ibbotson, bass, vocals (1969-76, 1983-present); John Cable, guitar, bass, vocals (1976-77); Jackie Clark, bass, guitar (1976-77); Michael Buono, drums (1976-77); Bob Carpenter, keyboards, vocals (1979-present); Al Garth, saxophone, violin (1978-82); Richard Hathaway, bass (1978-82); Merle Brigante, drums (1978-79); Vic Mastriani, drums (1980-82); Michael Gardner, bass (1980-82); Bernie Leadon, guitar, banjo (1987-88)

The Nitty Gritty Dirt Band was the group that introduced many second-generation rock-and-rollers to music outside of the bubblegum pop that AM Top 40 radio served during the late 60s and early 70s. With hits such as "Mr. Bojangles" (written by

Jerry Jeff Walker), the NGDB lead interested fans to other singer-songwriters and the country-rock scene. Its sprawling, landmark 1972 three-record set, "Will the Circle Be Unbroken" brought unadulterated folk and roots country stars to rock fans' ears. The collection was a generational gathering of traditional musicians from Mother Maybelle Carter and Doc Watson to Opry founders Roy Acuff and Merle Travis, with the long-haired Dirt Band members playing backup and proving they listened to a wider range of music than many of their fans.

That catholic stylistic sense came from the band's roots in the halcyon L.A. folk-rock scene of the mid-60s. The NGDB first formed as a jug-band. When multi-instrumentalist John McEuen joined, the core group was set for most of the rest of its career. Its records at various times were more rock than country (the 1975 "Dream" LP even included a spacey banjo opus that sounded like Pink Floyd for hillbillies), but by the 80s, with myriad personnel changes and a stint officially calling themselves "The Dirt Band," the core members settled in as something of a country-music institution; their music hadn't changed, but in the post-punk era, twangy music found itself unhip and relegated to country radio. Although it wasn't as much of a revelation the second time around, the Dirt Band also released an updated version of "Circle" in 1989, a songfest featuring some of the original legends (Roy Scuff, Earl Scruggs) as well as the new Nashville set (Rosanne Cash, John Hiatt, Emmylou Harris, Bruce Hornsby). Now in its 30th year, the band is without a major label deal for the first time ever, but it's still a staple on the road and seems far from quitting.

what to buy: *Will the Circle Be Unbroken* (Liberty, 1972, prod. William E. McEuen) is the hands-down must-own release by the NGDB, although it's not as much a reflection of the band's own music as it is a testament to its roots. The music was already old by then but sounded fresh in this context. And it hasn't aged in the quarter-century since.

what to buy next: *Uncle Charlie and His Dog Teddy* (Liberty, 1970, prod. William E. McEuen) includes the group's biggest hit, "Mr. Bojangles," as well as a minor-hit version of Michael Nesmith's great "Some of Shelley's Blues" (recently covered by the Continental Drifters) that's typical of its hippie eclecticism. The mid-career three-LP compilation *Dirt, Silver & Gold* (United Artists, 1976, prod. Various) collects the good stuff and filters out the dross.

the rest: *Nitty Gritty Dirt Band* (Liberty, 1967) *Ricochet* (Liberty, 1967) *Rare Junk* (Liberty, 1968) *Alive* (Liberty, 1968) *All the Good Times* (Liberty, 1971) *Stars and Stripes Forever* (Liberty, 1971) *Dream* (United Artists, 1975) *Wild Nights* (United Artists, 1978) *An American Dream (United Artists, 1979)* Make a Little Magic *(United Artists, 1980)* Jealousy *(Liberty, 1981)* Let's Go *(Liberty, 1983)* Plain Dirt Fashion *(Warner Bros., 1984)* Partners, Brothers and Friends *(Warner Bros., 1985)* Twenty Years of Dirt *(Warner Bros., 1986)* Hold On *(Warner Bros., 1987)* Workin' Band *(Warner Bros., 1988)* More Great Dirt *(Warner Bros., 1989)* The Rest of the Dream *(MCA, 1990)* Live Two Five *(Capitol Nashville, 1991)* Not Fade Away *(Liberty, 1992)* Acoustic *(Liberty, 1994)*.

solo outings:

John McEuen *John McEuen* (Warner Bros. 1988) *String Wizards* (Vanguard, 1992) *String Wizards II* (Vanguard, 1993) *The Wild West* (soundtrack) (Aspen Recording Society, 1993).

Jimmy Ibbotson *Wild Jimbos* (MCA, 1991) *Wild Jimbos Two* (Resounding Records, 1993).

Rodney Crowell, Rosanne Cash, Foster & Lloyd, Travis Tritt, Hank Williams Jr., Michelle Shocked, Uncle Tupelo

Carter Family, Weavers, Buddy Holly, Jim Kweskin Jug Band, The Byrds

Gil Asakawa

Mojo Nixon

Born Neill Kirby McMillan Jr., Aug. 2, 1957 in Chapel Hill, N.C.

Poking holes in stuffy celebrities and chiding right-wing zealots, Mojo Nixon mashes blues, folk, rock, punk, soul and country into a steamy stew and serves it up with a rabble-rousing yelp that is part Howlin' Wolf, part Wolfman Jack, part late-night used-car salesman. 1987's "Elvis is Everywhere," a back-handed tribute to the King, got him on radio, talk shows and MTV. But he has earned his reputation as the guardian of rock 'n' roll's lunatic fringe with such biting music-industry diatribes as "Stuffin' Martha's Muffin" (a serenade for former MTV VJ Martha Quinn), "Don Henley Must Die" ("He's a tortured artist/used to be in the Eagles/now he whines like a wounded beagle") and "Don't Want No Foo Foo Haircut on My Head." After three duo projects with washboard-toting partner Skid Roper, Nixon started recording with a full band in 1990, achieving a hard-nosed balance between the musical and the maniacal. In between his politically incorrect collaborations with Jello Biafra (which reached a tasteless nadir with 1993's "Will the

Fetus Be Aborted"), he has contributed to a spate of tribute albums honoring everyone from Led Zeppelin to the Sonics.

what to buy: John Doe, the late Country Dick Montana, Bill Davis and Eric Ambel provide the muscle power on *Otis* (I.R.S., 1990, prod. Jim Dickinson). Not only is this Nixon's most savage album, it's also his most consistent, thanks to "Destroy All Lawyers," "You Can Dress 'Em Up (But You Can't Take 'Em Out)" and "Don Henley Must Die." *Root Hog or Die* (I.R.S., 1989, prod. Jim Dickinson), his swan song with Skid Roper, ups the ante on outrageousness with the James Brown-style "Louisiana Liplock" and the riotous lawsuit-waiting-to-happen "Debbie Gibson Is Pregnant With My Two-Headed Love Child." *Bo-Day-Shus!* (I.R.S., 1987, prod. Ron Goudie) offers "Elvis Is Everywhere," "Gin Guzzlin' Frenzy," "Don't Want No Foo-Foo Haircut on My Head" and the surprisingly touching "Wide Open."

what to buy next: The CD reissue of Nixon and Roper's second album, *Frenzy* (I.R.S., 1986, prod. Ron Goudie), combines such hilarious rants as "Where the Hell's My Money?", "I Hate Banks" and a cover of Alice Cooper's "Be My Lover," along with six tracks from 1986's "Get Out of My Way" EP—including "Burn Down the Malls" and the yuletide chestnut "Son of Santa."

what to avoid: *Mojo Nixon and Skid Roper* (I.R.S., 1985, prod. Ron Goudie) captures the duo in their primal stage, flailing away with testosterone-fueled tantrums like "Jesus at McDonald's," "Mushroom Maniac" and a barely recognizable cover of Bruce Springsteen's obscure "The Big Payback" (the European B-side of his "Open All Night").

the rest: : *Horny Holidays* (Triple X, 1992), *Whereabouts Unknown* (Ripe and Ready, 1995)

worth searching for: *20 Explosive Dynamic Super Smash Hit Explosions* (Pravda, 1991, prod. Various), a various-artists tribute to K-tel, ends with Nixon's warped remake of Kenny Rogers and the First Edition's "Just Dropped In (To See What Condition My Condition Was In)."

▶▶ Reverend Billy C. Wirtz

◀◀ Howlin' Wolf, Foghorn Leghorn, James Brown, Jerry Lee Lewis

David Okamoto

Nova Mob

See: Hüsker Dü

NRBQ

Formed 1967 in Miami, Fla.

Terry Adams, piano, vocals; Joey Spampinato, bass, vocals; Steve Ferguson, guitar (1967-71); Frankie Gadler, vocals (1967-72); Tom Staley, drums (1967-74); Al Anderson, guitar, vocals (1971-94); Tom Ardolino, drums (1974 to present); Johnny Spampinato, guitar (1994 to present)

In the liner notes to NRBQ's 1990 retrospective *Peek-a-Boo*, Mark Rowland writes: "Pop music fans generally divide into two camps regarding NRBQ—those who consider them among the great bands of the last two decades, and those who have not yet heard them play." Rowland is right: NRBQ may be the best band you've never heard. The name is an acronym for the New Rhythm and Blues Quartet (Quintet when it formed)—although rhythm and blues are just two of the myriad elements that make up its sound. The band's foundation is one of roots-influenced rock with a hearty helping of boogie-woogie ladled on top. Those familiar with NRBQ's eclectic ways, however, know that the band is just as likely to break midsong into free-form jazz, execute an irresistible Motown shuffle or toss off a letter-perfect country ballad. With lesser outfits, this merry genre-hopping could merely be construed as showing off—a trait at which, granted, NRBQ is quite adept. But the band's encyclopedic knowledge of music styles is most often applied to the delivery of their material. NRBQ have always been about good songs; the fact that they are played with witty irreverence and blinding chops only intensifies their power. While numerous musicians populated the band prior to 1974, the lineup that came together in that year—Anderson, Adams, Ardolino and Joey Spampinato—is generally considered the definitive NRBQ.

what to buy: *Peek-a-Boo* (Rhino, 1990, comp. Bill Inglot) is a superb collection of material from NRBQ's first 20 years of recordings. The two-disc set offers prime examples of the band's keen understanding of musical idioms as well as their dedication to fine pop craftsmanship. Standout cuts include the good-time rock 'n' roll of "Flat Foot Flewzy," "RC Cola and a Moon Pie," and "Me and the Boys," which sit comfortably alongside such goofy workouts as "Captain Lou" (with professional wrestling legend Captain Lou Albano contributing enthusiastically atonal vocals) and "Here Comes Terry."

what to buy next: *Message for the Mess Age* (Rykodisc, 1994, prod. Terry Adams and Joey Spampinato) is another stellar outing from NRBQ and shows the band only improving with age as it sails beyond the quarter century mark. There's not a lot of new ground plowed here (the band's previous excursions have left very little uncharted territory), but the material and playing are so good that stylistic freshness isn't really an issue.

the rest: *Scraps* (Kama Sutra, 1972/Red Rooster-Rounder, 1982) *Workshop* (Kama Sutra, 1973/Red Rooster-Rounder, 1982) *All Hopped Up* (Red Rooster/Rounder, 1977) *At Yankee Stadium* (Mercury, 1978/1988) *Kick Me Hard* (Red Rooster/Rounder, 1979/1990) *Grooves in Orbit* (Bearsville, 1983; Bearsville/Rhino, 1990) *Tapdancin' Bats* (Rounder, 1983; Red Rooster/Rounder, 1990) *God Bless Us All* (Rounder, 1988) *Wild Weekend* (Virgin, 1989) *Honest Dollar* (Rykodisc, 1992)

worth searching for: NRBQ's early albums on Columbia unfortunately fell out of circulation within a few years of their release. *NRBQ* (Columbia, 1969) is an audacious melding that runs from Eddie Cochran's "C'mon Everybody" to Sun Ra's "Rocket Number 9." Carl Perkins, meanwhile, guest on *Boppin' the Blues* (Columbia, 1970).

solo outings:

Steve Ferguson Jack Salmon and Derby Sauce (Schoolkids, 1993) *Mama U-Seapa* (Schoolkids, 1995)

Al Anderson Party Favors (Twin/Tone, 1988)

Terry Adams Terrible (New World, 1995)

▶▶ Steely Dan, Uncle Tupelo, Blue Rodeo, the Jayhawks, Golden Smog

◀◀ The Beatles, Chuck Berry, Eddie Cochran, Little Richard, Jerry Lee Lewis, the Everly Brothers, Carl Perkins, Elvis Presley, the Rolling Stones, Duane Eddy, Johnny Cash, Hank Williams, Sr., Cecil Taylor, Thelonius Monk, Charlie Christian, Spike Jones

Dave Galens

Ted Nugent

Born Dec. 13, 1948, Detroit, Mich.

Though it may seem that Nugent was raised by wolves, he's really just a guy who loves bow-hunting as much as guns, girls, and guitars. Nugent first made waves with his searing, psychedelic guitar wailing on "Journey to the Center of Your Mind" by his first big band, the Amboy Dukes. But the Motor City Madman raised bombast to a fine art during the 70s after he broke up the Dukes to go solo. Known for his squawking lead guitar work, outrageous stage antics and songs that reveled in macho bravado and blatant sexual imagery, Nugent was one of the most popular hard rock acts in the U.S. during the mid- and late-70s. Though his commercial fortunes have flagged since then, Nugent's managed to survive in the ever-changing wilds of rock 'n' roll while developing side careers as a guitarist with the popular DamnYankees group and as a hunting advocate, merchandiser, publisher, activist and aspiring radio talk show host.

what to buy: With its air-raid guitars and urgent sexual suggestiveness, *Cat Scratch Fever* (Epic, 1977, prod. Tom Werman) captures the Nuge in all his outrageous, piledriving, crotch rock glory. He's at the top of his game as both a writer and a player.

what to buy next: Nugent's recorded output has been pretty spotty since his late 70s glory days, and most of what he's released since then has been pretty weak. It's surprising, then, to hear him put it all together again nearly 20 years later on *Spirit of the Wild.* (Atlantic, 1994, prod. Ted Nugent) It's his first album that balances his love of the outdoors with his love of the indoors (i.e. the bedroom) and includes "Fred Bear," a sincere tribute to the legendary hunter. *Out of Control* (Epic/Legacy, 1993, prod. Various) is a two-CD box set that encapsulates Nugent's career from his first recordings with the Amboy Dukes.

what to avoid: All of his work with Atlantic during the 80s was tepid, formulaic stuff—a retread of his earlier successes, but audience had moved on. The worst of the lot is *Nugent* (Atlantic, 1982, prod. Ted Nugent)

the rest: (with the Amboy Dukes): *Journey to the Center of Your Mind* (Mainstream, 1968) *Call of the Wild* (Discreet, 1972) Solo: *Ted Nugent* (Epic, 1975) *Free For All* (Epic, 1976) *Double Live Gonzo* (Epic, 1977) *Weekend Warriors* (Epic, 1978) *State of Shock* (Epic, 1979) *Scream Dream* (Epic, 1980) *Intensities in Ten Cities* (Epic, 1980) *Great Gonzos! The Best of Ted Nugent* (Epic, 1980) *Penetrator* (Atlantic, 1984) *Little Miss Dangerous* (Atlantic, 1986) *If You Can't Lick 'Em ... Lick 'Em* (Atlantic, 1988)

worth searching for: The vast bulk of the Amboy Dukes' catalog is out of print, and it's as varied in quality as Nugent's solo work. *Survival of the Fittest* (Polydor, 1971) and *Tooth, Fang and Claw*(Discreet, 1973) come closest to approximating what would become the Nugent solo sound.

▶▶ Aerosmith, Jackyl, Cry of Love

◀◀ Duane Eddy, Chuck Berry, Jimi Hendrix

Doug Pullen

Gary Numan

Born Gary Anthony James Webb, March 8, 1958, in Hammersmith, London, England

First appearing on the scene in 1978 under the name Tubeway Army, Numan was a sight to behold. With his glum, robotic appearance, staring eyes and synthesizer music, he popularized robots and inspired a cult that exists to this day. He has released many albums and in the course of time has changed his image from a cold machine operator to a debonair man about town. After establishing the first synth-pop hits of the era (especially "Cars"), he began to pursue his other passion, flying planes. In 1982, Numan attempted to fly around the world in his light aircraft; he was arrested in India on suspicion of spying, charges that were later drop but, in the meantime, enhanced his image Numan still flies planes and records albums, and he continues to enjoy a legion of die-hard fans.

what to buy: *The Pleasure Principle* (Atco, 1979, prod. Numan) is the first album he released under his own name and is Numan at his best in the electronic pop realm. *Telekon* (Atco, 1980, prod. Gary Numan) features guitars for the first time and thereby creates intriguing new musical textures.

what to buy next: *Exhibition* (Beggars Banquet, 1987, prod. Gary Numan) is a compilation of his classic singles as well as some live tracks. *Replicas* (Atco, 1979, prod. Gary Numan) features the hit song "Are Friends Electric."

what to avoid: *First Album,* (Atco, 1978, prod. Gary Numan) a messy Tubeway Army effort on which Numan was still forming what would become his signature sound.

the rest: *Dance* (Atco, 1981) *Living Ornaments '79* (Beggar's Banquet, 1981) Living Ornaments *80* (Beggars Banquet, 1981) *I Assassin* (Atco, 1982) *Warriors* (Beggars Banquet, 1983) *The Plan* (Beggars Banquet, 1984) *The Other Side of Gary Numan* (Receiver, 1992) *Here I Am* (Receiver, 1994)

worth searching for: Numan's batch of self-produced albums on his own label—*Berserker,* (Numa, 1984) *White Noise—Live,* (Numa, 1985) *The Fury,* (Numa, 1985) *Strange Charm,* (Numa, 1986) *1978-1979, Vols. 2 & 3* (Numa, 1985) and *Sacrifice* (Numa, 1994) —are scattershot but make him look like the most prolific, self-contained artist this side of Prince.

Underworld, Orbital, The Orb, Deee-Lite

Kraftwerk, Brian Eno, David Bowie

Anna Glen

Laura Nyro

Born Laura Nigro, Oct. 18, 1947 in the Bronx, N.Y.

One of the best and brightest songwriters of the late 60s, Nyro is essential listening for anyone seeking out the roots of rock's singer-songwriter movement. Nyro was a mere 18 years old when she recorded her first album, *More Than a New Discovery,* a remarkable debut that showcased her prodigious musical talent and gutsy, swooping voice. Throughout a 30-year career, Nyro has written and released a sterling catalog of angst-bearing, confessional music inflected with R&B, soul and gospel touches. While she has had only one recording reach the Top 100 (her cover of the Drifters' "Up on the Roof" in 1970), her own songs have been major hits for artists such as Barbra Streisand ("Stoney End"), the 5th Dimension ("Wedding Bell Blues"), Blood, Sweat & Tears ("And When I Die") and Three Dog Night ("Eli's Coming"). With her 1971 album *Gonna Take a Miracle,* Nyro became one of the first rock-era songwriters to release an album of cover material in tribute to past mentors. While her output has slowed over the years, her material remains something to look forward to.

what to buy: Basically a re-release of Nyro's 1966 debut album, *The First Songs* (Columbia, 1973, prod. Milton Okun) is a remarkable debut from an 18-year-old woman whose wisdom, voice and talent belie her years. Featuring numerous songs that later became hits for other artists ("Wedding Bell Blues," "And When I Die," "Flim Flam Man" and "Stoney End"), the album spins out a continuous stream of first-class, introspective music. Another bona fide classic. *New York Tendaberry* (Columbia, 1969, prod. Laura Nyro and Roy Halee) is the culmination of the style Nyro began developing on her debut, a dramatic *noir* journey through love and its loss. Supporting her expressive vocal work with piano and delicate instrumental accompaniment, Nyro explores a vast spectrum of human emotions with music that memorably touches the core of expression.

what to buy next: *Eli & the 13th Confession* (Sony, 1968, prod. Charlie Calello and Laura Nyro) is a mini-progression from *The First Songs.* Nyro is more soulful and more introspective, presenting a stellar collection of memorable songs that range from R&B ("Stoned Soul Picnic") to gospel ("Poverty Train") and powerful ballads ("Lonely Women"). Nyro changed the pace on her fourth album, *Gonna Take a Miracle,* (Sony, 1971, prod. Gamble & Huff) teaming with soul-funk group Labelle for joyful and inspired readings of 1960s R&B hits such as "Jimmy Mack," "Spanish Harlem" and "Nowhere to Run."

what to avoid: Although Nyro's work can never be considered weak, *Mother's Spiritual* (Line, 1984, prod. Laura Nyro) 🎧🎧 is not among her best works. The urgent passion of her earlier music is replaced here by a cooler, more politically attuned sensibility that's respectable but not compelling.

the rest: *Smile* (Sony, 1976, prods. Charlie Calello and Laura Nyro) 🎧🎧🎧 *Live at the Bottom Line* (Cypress, 1990) 🎧🎧🎧 *Walk the Dog & Light the Light* (Columbia, 1993, prod.) 🎧🎧🎧

worth searching for: At the height of Nyro's comeback during the late 70s, Columbia Records planned a double LP of Nyro performing her greatest hits in concert with an all-star lineup. By the time the album was released as *Season of Lights*, (Columbia, 1977) 🎧🎧🎧🎧 it had been trimmed back to a single live LP featuring 10 songs that had been significantly rearranged from their studio versions. The two-album set can be found on bootleg.

▶▶ Todd Rundgren, Barbra Streisand, Carole King, the 5th Dimension, Blood, Sweat & Tears, Randy Newman, Rickie Lee Jones, Carly Simon, Chaka Kahn, Des'ree, Alanis Morissette

◀◀ Joan Baez, Leonard Cohen, Bob Dylan, Labelle, Carole King, Judy Collins, Joni Mitchell, Aretha Franklin

Christopher Scapelliti

The O'Jays

Formed 1958, in Canton, Ohio

Bobby Massey, vocals (1958-72); Walter Williams, vocals; Eddie Levert, vocals; Bill Isles, vocals (1958-65); William Powell, vocals (1958-76); Sammy Strain, vocals (1976-91); Nathaniel Best, vocals (1991-93)

Arguably the pre-eminent vocal group of Philly soul—along with the Spinners—the Ohio trio released a string of danceable yet socially conscious songs during its peak years (1972-78), culminating in eight No. 1 singles. They featured smooth, communal harmonies augmented by Levert's impassioned growls, driven by the high-powered production gloss of Gamble and Huff. Unlike many of its peers, the O'Jays have remained largely intact, releasing engaging albums throughout the 80s and into the 90s—touring often with Levert's sons Gerald and Sean and their group, Levert.

what to buy: *Backstabbers* (Epic/Legacy, 1972/1976, prod. Kenny Gamble and Leon Huff) 🎧🎧🎧🎧🎧 is the O'Jays best album, a searing and complex document of groove-laced R&B that set a new mark for other soul groups. *Love Train: The Best of The O'Jays* (Epic/Legacy, 1994, prod. Kenny Gamble and Leon Huff) 🎧🎧🎧🎧🎧 is a concise but meaty intro for the uninitiated. Several of the inspirational singles, culled from the glory years, are here, making for a barrel-chested soundtrack of Philly soul.

what to buy next: *Give the People What They Want* (Epic/Legacy, 1995, prod. Kenny Gamble and Leon Huff) 🎧🎧🎧🎧 delivers a street-shuffle of 11 politically minded tracks from the 70s.

what to avoid: *Serious* (EMI America, 1989) 🎧🎧 has its moments, the dabbling with New Jack styles sounds out of place.

the rest: *In Philadelphia* (Epic/Legacy, 1969/1994) 🎧🎧🎧▽ *Ship Ahoy* (Philadelphia International, 1973) 🎧🎧🎧🎧 *Survival* (Columbia, 1975) 🎧🎧🎧🎧 *Family Reunion* (Philadelphia International, 1975) 🎧🎧🎧 *Message in the Music* (The Right Stuff, 1976/1993) 🎧🎧🎧 *So Full of Love* (The Right Stuff, 1978/1993) 🎧🎧🎧 *Collector's Item* (Philadelphia International, 1978/1989) 🎧🎧🎧▽ *Love Fever* (CEMA Special Products, 1985) 🎧🎧🎧 *Greatest Hits* (Columbia, 1989); 🎧🎧🎧 *Home for Christmas* (EMI America, 1991) 🎧🎧 *Emotionally Yours* (EMI America, 1991) 🎧🎧🎧 *Heartbreaker* (EMI America, 1993) 🎧🎧🎧 *From The Beginning* (MCA Special Products, 1994) 🎧🎧🎧🎧 *Let Me Make Love to You* (Epic/Legacy, 1995) 🎧🎧🎧🎧

▶▶ Levert, Isley Jasper Isley, Boyz II Men, Keith Sweat, New Edition

◀◀ The Mascots, the Drifters, Sam Cooke, Jackie Wilson

Allan Orski

Oasis

Formed 1991 in Manchester, England

Liam Gallagher, vocals; Noel Gallagher, guitar, vocals; Paul "Bonehead" Arthurs, guitar; Paul "Guigsy" McGuigan, bass; Tony McCarroll, drums (1991-94); Alan White, drums (1994-present)

Oasis' debut album, *Definitely Maybe* (Epic, 1994, prod. Oasis and Mark Coyle) 🎧🎧🎧🎧 started it all. It was the fastest selling debut album in British history and made a favorable first impression in America, going gold in a country whose interest in British bands had cooled. The group had more than music going for it; its wanton attitude rarely failed to inspire scandal, as the Gallagher brothers (Noel's the elder) made headlines for their public punch-ups, their brags of excessive drug use and their unabashed rivalries with other British bands—particularly Blur.

Nevertheless, the group transcended its outrageous reputation with an unassuming blend of gritty, melodic guitar pop of

(What's The Story?) Morning Glory. (Epic, 1995, prod. Owen Morris and Noel Gallagher) Over its 12 tracks, Oasis swaggers through a collection of songs built on familiar melodies, lending them an unmistakably caustic edge of sheer attitude. Like *Definitely Maybe*, it's a gorgeous mess that draws on a Britpop who's who of influences that includes the Beatles, the Small Faces, T. Rex, Status Quo and David Bowie, among others.

Aidin Vaziri

Oblivious

See: Holly Vincent

Ric Ocasek

See: The Cars

Billy Ocean

Born Leslie Sebastian Charles on Jan. 21, 1950, in Trinidad

Ocean was a hitmaker in England before he landed on U.S. shores in 1984 with his Top 10 single "Caribbean Queen (No More Love on the Run)." It began an impressive run as he garnered six more Top 10 hits during the next four years. His albums are best remembered for their hits, however, not for the adjoining tracks. That's a pity, since Ocean produced some seamless recordings, deftly incorporating soul, pop and dance material into each. His knack for crossover success made him a bigger star in pop than R&B, but in the 90s he seems to have pulled a disappearing act. With his talent and soulful, expressive voice, don't count him out. Meanwhile, get his *Greatest Hits* (Jive, 1989, prod. Various), which includes all of them—his lovely and passionate ballad "What Is the Color of Love," his pumped-up dance track "Get Outta My Dreams, Get into My Car" and his huge soundtrack hit "When the Going Gets Tough, the Tough Get Going," plus a couple of new tracks.

the rest: *Nights (Feel Like Getting Down)* (Epic, 1981) *Suddenly* (Jive, 1984) *Love Zone* (Jive, 1986) *Tear Down These Walls* (Jive, 1988)

Patrick McCarty

Maura O'Connell

Born Sept. 16, 1958, in Ennis, County Clare, Ireland

O'Connell is a quality example of singer as freewheeling interpreter, unfettered by any genre in particular. Her soulful eclecticism is only fitting in an Irish-born artist who scored her first big musical successes by recording pop albums in Nashville.

After starting out singing in clubs for Galway college kids, O'Connell hooked up with the traditional group De Danann for two years. She split in 1983, trekking to Nashville on her manager's advice to record three solo albums that became huge hits in her home country.

O'Connell's signing to the Warner Bros. sparked a string of meticulously produced albums distinguished by her warm, flexible mezzo and adventuresome song selections from John Hiatt, Tom Waits and Shawn Colvin, mixed with second looks at Tin Pan Alley and John Lennon and Paul McCartney). The efforts earned critical raves but modest U.S. sales. Her incandescent live performances have solidified her audience in the U.S., while her star status in Ireland remains assured. Still, Warner Bros. opted not to renew her contract in 1994, so O'Connell launched her own Permanent Records for her most recent album, *Stories,* which was released through Hannibal/Rykodisc in 1995.

what to buy: *Helpless Heart (Warner Bros., 1989, prod. Bela Fleck) probably is the closest O'Connell has flirted with country, but Fleck's thoughtful arrangements deftly blend bluegrass and mountain influences with traditional Irish touches—and in "You'll Never Know," O'Connell demonstrates her authority with standards.*

what to buy next: The smokier *A Real Life Story* (Warner Bros., 1991, prod. Greg Penny) continues O'Connell's great sense of song selection for grownups, with such meaty items as Hiatt's "When We Ran" and Hugh Prestwood's "A Family Tie" —a wrenching, ambivalent look at an alcoholic husband.

what to avoid: You won't get burned with any of O'Connell's stuff—it's all at least interesting—but you can skip some of the efforts, such as the folky, low-key *Just In Time* (Philo, 1988, prod. Bela Fleck) until after you've bought the Warner Bros. albums.

the rest: (with De Danann): *The Star-Spangled Molly* (Shanachie Records, 1981) *Maura O'Connell* (Third Floor Music, 1983) *Blue Is the Colour of Hope* (Warner Bros., 1992) *Stories* (Hannibal Records, 1995)

worth searching for: *A Woman's Heart,* (Dara, 1992, prod. Various) a collection of work by Irish female singers that includes O'Connell's "Trouble in the Fields" and "Western Highway."

Mary Black, Mary Coughlan, Delores O'Riordan (the Cranberries)

Bonnie Raitt, Little Feat

Elizabeth Lynch

Sinead O'Connor

Born December 8, 1966 in Glenagerry, Co. Dublin, Ireland

Sinead O'Connor may yet turn out to be a great artist. For sure, she's an emotional, experimental artist with an innate sense of drama. And she's clearly Irish. She's had problems with the Pope, maybe smoked too much dope, became overly self-indulgent, attempted to regain her focus, and is still self-absorbed and self-pitying to the point where listener reference points are sometimes hard to come by. Regardless, she's a compelling artist who figures that she's serving the truth and who at some point is likely to create an album better than the first two releases, which are terrific. The third of four children, her parents separated when she was quite young. According to O'Connor, her mother was a very violent woman, physically and emotionally abusing her family. O'Connor blames the Catholic Church for the circumstances of her childhood, believing that that institution, central to life in Ireland, condones child abuse and has, for several centuries, conspired with the English to take away Irish rights. Hence, her take on the Pope, which culminated in the infamous "Saturday Night Live" incident, in which O'Connor, upon finishing her number, ripped apart a photograph of Pope John Paul. The abusive relationship with her mother is also the source of many of her songs, as she continues to work out the relationship in public. Escaping through music and blessed with a powerful soprano, O'Connor made her recording debut in 1983 with vocals on the single, "Take My Hand," by the Irish group In Tua Nua. That single also served to introduce her to fiddler Steve Wickham, later of the Waterboys, who would reunite with her on the standout cut from *I Do Not Want What I Haven't Got,* "I Am Stretched on Your Grave." O'-Connor has four albums to her credit, and continues to assist a wide variety of other artists, lending her pipes to recordings by everyone from Jah Wobble to Willie Nelson.

what to buy: *I Do Not Want What I Haven't Got* (Chrysalis, 1990, prod. Sinead O'Connor) ♪♪♪♪♪ is O'Connor's second album, and better by degrees than the masterful debut. Her vocals are assured and powerful, the songwriting is tight and exploratory, and the production is top-notch. Conceptually, the album evokes a sense of deep spirituality, of characters searching for a god while dealing with the joy and despair of relationships. A great break-up album.

what to buy next: Somewhat pretentious but riveting, *The Lion and the Cobra* (Chrysalis, 1987, prod. Sinead O'Connor) ♪♪♪♪ is as self-assured a debut as you're likely to find. Songs range from the sexy funk of "I Want Your (Hands on Me)" to the Enya-assisted Celtic elegy, "Never Get Old."

what to avoid: On *Am I Not Your Girl?* (Chrysalis, 1992, prod. Phil Ramone) ♪♪ O'Connor employs an orchestra of 47 musicians to cover classic big-band songs. Unfortunately, it doesn't work.

the rest: Universal Mother (Chrysalis, 1994) ♪♪♪

worth searching for: O'Connor has released a bunch of CD, seven-inch, and 12-inch singles containing scorching club remixes and/or unreleased songs. Many of these are imports and for fans, well worth seeking, including a fairly naughty duet with Karen Finley on "Jump in the River" and the remixes of "Stretched on Your Grave" on the UK single release of *The Emperor's New Clothes.* O'Connor makes appearances on other compilation and artist releases, including a standout on the Van Morrison tribute "No Prima Donna," a duet with Shane MacGowan on "Haunted" from his solo album, *The Snake,* and arresting vocals on The Chieftains *Long Black Veil.* She closed the film, "In the Name of the Father," with "You Made Me the Thief of Your Heart," released on the soundtrack and as a single. Two live concert videos exist as well, "The Value of Ignorance" (1989) and "The Year of the Horse (1991). For a complete list of recordings, check Marcel Bobbink's web site at http://www.engr.ukans.edu/~jrussell/music/sinead/disc.html.

The Cranberries

Enya, Clannad, In Tua Nua

Martin Connors

The Offspring

Formed 1986 in Orange County, Calif.

Brian "Dexter" Holland, vocals, guitar; Ron Welty, drums; Greg Kriesel, bass; Kevin Wasserman (a.k.a., Noodles), guitar

Toiling away in the punk rock underground for years, it took the Offspring nearly a decade to make its mark via a combination of edgy rock and catchy tunes to make a mark. Though produced by punk stalwart Thom Wilson (Dead Kennedys, The Vandals), *The Offspring* (Nemesis, 1989/Nitro-Epitaph, 1995) ♪♪ didn't do much. It took *Ignition* (Epitaph, 1993, prod. by Thom

Wilson) to take off in the punk underground—particularly with the skateboarding crowd—selling a respectable 50,000 or so copies. The Offspring's appropriately titled *Smash* (Epitaph, 1994, prod. Thom Wilson) sold several million copies and succeeded mostly on the strength of tunes that weren't punk, including the Nirvana-influenced "Come Out and Play" and the grungey-sounding teen anthem "Self Esteem." Though the band chose to hang with its independent label for years, in 1996 it announced a deal with Columbia Records—for an advance reported in the millions of dollars—citing conflicts with Epitaph owner Brett Gurewitz (a former guitarist with punk stalwarts Bad Religion).

Eric Deggans

Patrick O'Hearn

See: Missing Persons

The Ohio Express

Formed 1966 in Mansfield, Ohio

Joey Levine, vocals; Doug Grassel, guitar; Dale Powers, guitar; Jim Pfayler, keyboards; Dean Kastran, bass; Tim Corwin, drums

Create a vacuum and something must fill it, goes the Law of the Universe. So as popular music started becoming somewhat grown-up and sophisticated circa *Sgt. Pepper's Lonely Hearts Club Band,* a definite hole appeared where once had thrived such happy-go-lucky popsters as Herman's Hermits and the Dave Clark Five. Realizing as much, the savvy production team of Jerry Kasenetz and Jeff Katz decided to fill this hole with something called they called bubblegum, and soon enlisted singer Levine to front not one, but *two* groups for Buddah Records. While one, the 1910 Fruitgum Company, was basically a studio concoction, the Ohio Express had a life of its own prior to Kasenetz-Katz, already having recorded several garage-rock gems on the Cameo label ("Beg, Borrow and Steal" actually charted at No. 29). But it was the terrifically gummy "Yummy Yummy Yummy" and its ultra-sticky follow-up, "Chewy Chewy," for which the Ohio Express will forever be remembered. It's interesting to note that Joey Levine's voice sold more records during 1968 than Mick Jagger's did. Food for thought—just remember to spit out that gum first. *Golden Classics* (Collectables, 1994, prod. Various) says it all, and could very well lead entire new generations to ponder the possible aural-sexual innuendoes within the "Yummy Yummy Yummy" lyrics.

Gary Pig Gold

Ohio Players

Formed 1969 in Dayton, Ohio

Leroy "Sugar" Bonner, guitar, vocals; James "Diamond" Williams, drums, percussion; Marvin Pierce, trumpet; Billy Beck, keyboards; Clarence Satchell, saxes; Marshall Jones, bass; Ralph "Pee Wee" Middlebrooks, trumpet

Created as an instrumental group, the Players started as the Ohio Untouchables before lucking into a stint backing the Falcons (featuring lead singer Wilson Pickett) in 1962. Though they were recording on their own that year, it took until the early 70s for the band to make a dent—fusing hardcore funk sensibility with Sly Stone-style groove adventures to create ambitious jams such as "Funky Worm." Once the group moved from the Westbound label to Mercury, its hit-making career began in earnest. Chart-toppers such as "Fire," "Skin Tight" and "Love Rollercoaster" came during the mid-70s, along with a string of outrageous album covers featuring scantily clad women (one draped in honey for the album *Honey*) that elicited a bit of outage—and certainly didn't hurt at sales counters. But as disco began to push out the classic funk bands, the Players' albums became increasingly more predictable. Hoping to ride out the disco craze, the group attempted to change is sound to meet the new commercial priorities but only succeeded in stifling its career—a decision from which the group has yet to rebound.

what to buy: *Ohio Players Gold* (Mercury, 1976, prod. the Ohio Players) compiles tracks from the band's most successful and best-constructed records—*Skin Tight, Fire* and *Honey*—including unforgettable hits such as "Sweet Sticky Thing" and the ballad "I Want to Be Free."

what to buy next: *Skin Tight* (Mercury, 1974, prod. the Ohio Players) and *Honey* (Mercury, 1975, prod. the Ohio Players) are each chock full of nasty funk grooves and slick, emotive soul ballads.

what to avoid: *Jass-Ay-La-Dee* (Mercury, 1978, prod. the Ohio Players) WOOF! was the worst album in the group's string of late 70s mishaps, filled with uninspired songs and shameless trend-hopping to compete with disco.

the rest: *Pain* (Westbound, 1972) *Ecstasy* (Westbound, 1973) *Pleasure* (Westbound, 1973) *Climax* (Westbound, 1984) *Rattlesnake* (Westbound, 1975) *Contradiction* (Mercury, 1976) *Angel* (Mercury, 1977) *Mr. Mean* (Mercury, 1977) *Ohio Players* (Trip, 1977) *Tenderness* (Boardwalk, 1981) *Funk On Fire: The Mercury An-*

thology (Mercury, 1995) *Old School* (Intersound, 1996)

worth searching for: The Players backing Wilson Pickett and the Falcons on that group's seminal recording "I Found a Love," which kicks off the Pickett compilation *A Man and a Half* (Rhino/Atlantic & Atco Remasters, prod. Various)

Cameo, Guy, the Time, Prince

Sly & the Family Stone, the Bar Kays, the Isley Brothers

Eric Deggans

Oingo Boingo /Danny Elfman

Formed 1979 in Los Angeles, Calif. Disbanded 1995.

Danny Elfman, vocals, guitar; Steve Bartek, guitar; Kerry Katch, bass (1979-83); Rich Gibbs, keyboards (1979-83); Johnny "Vatos" Hernandez, drums; Sam Phipps, tenor sax; Leon Schneiderman, baritone sax; Dale Turner, trumpet, trombone; John Avila, bass, vocals (1983-95)

Oingo Boingo started out during the late 70s as a New Wave outfit with a keen sense of humor—resulting in some awfully quirky music—and a truly impressive horn section. California crowds loved the band and the rest of the country, except for a few college students, thought little of Oingo Boingo. Main song man Elfman has captured critical acclaim for his side projects, soundtracks to films such as "Batman," "Edward Scissorhands" and "The Nightmare Before Christmas," as well as the theme to "The Simpsons" television show. After 16 years of trying to make its mark with little to show except a cult following and one semi-hit, "Dead Man's Party," the group decided to pack it in after its traditional 1995 Halloween blowout in Los Angeles.

what to buy: *Dead Man's Party* (MCA, 1985) is a solid example of how effective and creative this band can be when focused. The title song, a toe-tapping classic, created a small buzz when the band appeared in the Rodney Dangerfield movie, "Back to School."

what to buy next: *Only A Lad,* (A&M, 1981) Oingo Boing's first full-length album, is raw, irreverent and all the more charming for it.

what to avoid: *Boingo (As Boingo)* (Giant, 1994, prod. John Avila, Steve Bartek, and Danny Elfman) **WOOF!** Shortened name, shortened interest in project, shortened list of worthwhile songs.

the rest: *Nothing to Fear* (A&M, 1982) *Good For Your Soul* (A&M, 1983) *BOI-NGO* (MCA, 1987) *Boingo Alive: Celebration of a Decade 1979-1988* (MCA, 1988) *Skeletons in the Closet: The Best of Oingo Boingo* (A&M, 1988) *Dark at the End of the Tunnel* (MCA, 1990) *Best O' Boingo* (A&M, 1991) *Farewell* (A&M, 1996)

worth searching for: *Boingo Jr.* (MCA, 1988, prod. Danny Elfman, Steve Bartek and John Avila) is a promotional sampler from the *Boingo Alive* album, a good collector's piece and not a bad distillation of the album.

solo outings:

Danny Elfman Music For a Darkened Theatre (MCA, 1990)

No Doubt, Mighty Mighty Bosstones, Presidents of the United States of America

Devo, XTC, Frank Zappa, Madness

Chris Newburg

Ken Okulolo

See: King Sunny Ade

Yoko Ono

Born Feb. 18, 1933, in Tokyo, Japan

Much villified but rarely understood, Ono already was an important artist in the Fluxus movement (for her music, film and conceptual/performance art) before she met John Lennon; in fact, they met at an exhibit of her work, which was largely conceptual and interactive. As a musician, her disregard for accepted rock practices, complete openness to experimentation and awareness of avant-garde theories and examples such as John Cage's music made her ahead of her time. Sometimes during the 80s, when she was flirting more seriously with the pop mainstream, her unwillingness to mediate her sentiment resulted in sappy songs, but they were often beautiful sappy songs, a surprise to those who had filed her away under "unlistenable noise." Granted, the only thing close-minded rock fans might appreciate about the couple's first release, *Unfinished Music No. 1. Two Virgins* filled as it is with lo-fi tape recordings of music (and musique concrete) more concerned with sounds than structure, much less harmony or melody—are the nude photos, front and back. The title itself was significant; not only did they feel reborn emotionally, each was a virgin in the other's musical universe. In addition to the work issued under her own name—which sometimes included Lennon, most often on guitar—the couple issued several dually credited albums that were divided evenly between Lennon's music and Ono's. Here, discussion and ratings of the latter albums will only examine her contributions—a slight compensatation for the long history of the opposite being the case.

what to buy: *Onobox* (Ryko, 1992) is a pricey six-CD set that, in design, must be the most beautiful box set ever produced. It contains brief liner notes by Ono for each volume and a booklet with oodles of photos, an extensive essay by critic Robert Palmer and a complete discography. All of her work deserves to be released on CD, but for now this set—which covers her career from 1968 until the present and includes an entire previously unreleased album—must do. The first two CDs contain some of Lennon's most adventurous, far-out guitar playing—and Eric Clapton's, too.

what to buy next: *Season of Glass* (Geffen, 1981, prod. Yoko Ono and Phil Spector) can be seen as a reaction to Lennon's soul-shattering death. The sheer existential terror of "No No No" and the bottomless despair of "I Don't Know Why" are balanced by the touching "Nobody Sees Me Like You Do." This album and the single "Walking on Thin Ice" are her greatest achievements in song. *Yoko Ono/IMA's Rising* (Capitol, 1996, prod. Yoko Ono and Rob Stevens) is a triumphant return to her more avant-garde, "outside" singing style, accompanied by her son (with John) Sean's band.

what to avoid: Ono's *It's Alright (I See Rainbows)* (Polydor, 1983, prod. Yoko Ono) and *Starpeace* (Polydor, 1985, prod. Bill Laswell and Yoko Ono) are studio hackwork and pop pablum.

the rest: *Unfinished Music No. 2. Life with the Lions* (Zapple, 1969) *Wedding Album* (Apple/Capitol, 1969) *Approximately Infinite Universe*(Apple/Capitol, 1973) *Walking on Thin Ice* (Ryko, 1992) *New York Rock* cast recording (Capitol, 1995) WOOF! Ono and Lennon: *Live Peace in Toronto* (Apple/Capitol, 1969) *Some Time in New York City* (Apple/Capitol, 1972) *Double Fantasy* (Geffen, 1980) *Milk and Honey* (Polydor, 1984)

worth searching for: Far too little of Ono's *Fly* (Apple/Capitol, 1971, prod. Yoko Ono and John Lennon) made it onto *Onobox;* more ridiculous than the omissions is the shrinking of "Airmale" (10:40), "You" (9:00) and "Fly" (22:53) down to a 2:32 medley. This double LP contains some of her most intense longform improvisation and should be heard.

Patty Waters, Diamanda Galas, Lene Lovich, Shonen Knife, B-52s, Nina Hagen, Death of Samantha, Cibo Matto

John Cage, LaMonte Young, Albert Ayler, Cathy Berberian

Steve Holtje

Opal

See: The Dream Syndicate

The Orb

Formed 1989 in London, England

(Dr.) Alex Patterson, engineering; Thrash (Chris Weston), engineering

Labeled as everything from the Pink Floyd of the 90's to new Brian Eno, The Orb have managed to break from their influences and create their own new musical genre, ambient-house. Originally intended to calm ravers after a hectic night of partying, the music has the paradoxical ability to mellow people out while at the same time inspiring them to dance. In the tradition of dub, The Orb uses pre-existing music and sound to create new ethereal melodies. While many have acussed them of being nothing more than high-concept, no-substance, rip-off artists, The Orb don't merely copy, they originate new ways of using sound to define music. For The Orb samples of book pages being turned can be morphed into hi-hat cymbols, while the sound of a coin dropping can be looped and manipulated to become a bass drum.

what to buy: *U.F.Orb* (Big Life, 1992, prod. Steve Hillage and the Orb) is a masterpiece of ambient sounds. The Orb takes you on a trip around the globe, into space, and back. Vocal samples are more played down than in their earlier releases, alowing the record to encircle and wrap you up in it's sonic textures. At times the music can become all engrossing as it drenches you in wave after wave of lush noise; or it can conversely become a soothing background, lulling away behind your conscious mind.

what to buy next: *Adventures Beyond UltraWorld* (Big Life, 1991, prod. Steve Hillage, Jimmy Cauty, Youth, Baku) is The Orb's first full length album. More traditional techno than later releases, and a greater dependance on electronic sounds, give this record a spacier feel. Vocal samples are more widely used, often to hilarious results, but the enthralling multi-layered music still predominates. *Orbus Terrarum* (Island, 1995, prod. the Orb and Thomas Fehlmann) comes from the opposite direction of the space-noodlings on *Ultraworld* incorporating a variety of engineered nature sounds into the music, but it doesn't matter if The Orb are making music on the dark side of the moon or this side of terra firma, they always capture the escense of a place in spellbinding aural mastery.

the rest: *Live 93* (Island, 1993, prod. the Orb) is a double album collection of live shows. Live shows of sampled music? That's right, its an odd concept but The Orb manages to pull it off. *Aubrey Mixes: Ultraworld Excursions* (Carolione, 1992, prod. Orb) a well spun collection of remixes from *Adventures Beyond UltraWorld.*

Orbital, Skylab, Chemical Brothers, Vapoursapce, The Future Sound of London

Brian Eno, Kraftwerk, Fripp, Pink Floyd, Mad Proffesor, KLF, Justified Ancients of Mumu

Bryan Lassner

Roy Orbison

Born April 23, 1936, in Vernon, Texas. Died Dec. 6, 1988, in Hendersonville, Tenn.

Perhaps the greatest pure singer that rock 'n' roll has produced, Orbison brought an unsurpassed sense of melodrama and angst to the music that has had a huge influence on other performers. A native of Texas, Orbison began singing country and rockabilly music but found that the styles weren't particularly suited to his tremendous tenor voice, which seemed to have no upper limit. Orbison recorded for Sun Records during the 50s and then RCA, but he didn't achieve fame until he signed with Monument in 1960 and began working with producer Fred Foster. Together, they made records that were miniature pop operas—"Only the Lonely (Know How I Feel)," "Running Scared," "Crying" et al. He also recorded for MGM, Mercury, Elektra and Virgin. Orbison's 1987 induction into the Rock and Roll Hall of Fame—as well as membership in the superstar group the Traveling Wilburys (with Bob Dylan, George Harrison, Tom Petty and Jeff Lynne)—helped spark a career revival: he was finishing *Mystery Girl*, his first album of new material in a decade, when he died at his Tennessee home.

what to buy: Take your choice of three worthwhile anthologies. *The Legendary Roy Orbison* (CBS Special Products, 1990, prod. Various) is a three-disc box set that outshines all other Orbison collections, but *For the Lonely: A Roy Orbison Anthology, 1956-1964* (Rhino, 1988, prod. Fred Foster and Sam Phillips) or *The All-Time Greatest Hits of Roy Orbison* (Monument, 1972, prod. Fred Foster) will do just fine as a starter set.

what to buy next: *Roy Orbison and Friends: a Black and White Night Live* (Virgin, 1989, prod. T-Bone Burnett) is an excellent concert document recorded for an HBO film and featuring guest performances by Bruce Springsteen, k.d. lang and others. *Mystery Girl* (Virgin, 1989, prod. Various) shows how other performers, such as U2's Bono and the Electric Light Orchestra's Jeff Lynne, viewed his music.

what to avoid: *The RCA Days* (RCA, 1988, prod. Chet Atkins) and *Little Richard/Roy Orbison* (RCA, 1990, prod. Chet Atkins) cull material from Orbison's time with RCA in Nashville, among the least successful recordings (artistically and commercially) of his career. And if you buy *In Dreams: The Greatest Hits*, (Virgin, 1987, prod. T-Bone Burnett) know what you're getting; these are re-recordings of Orbison's big songs, inspired by a new version of "In Dreams" for the film "Blue Velvet." They're quite good as these things go, but they're not the originals.

the rest: *Laminar Flow* (Elektra, 1979) *Class of '55* (with Johnny Cash, Carl Perkins and Jerry Lee Lewis) (America/Smash, 1986) *Interviews From the Class of '55 Recording Sessions* (America/Smash, 1986) *For the Lonely: 18 Greatest Hits* (Rhino, 1988) *The Sun Years* (Rhino, 1989) *The Classic Roy Orbison (1965-1968)* (Rhino, 1989) *King of Hearts* (Virgin, 1992)

worth searching for: *The Sun Story*, (Rhino, 1987) a sampler of Sun's glory days that prominently features early Orbison hits such as "Ooby Dooby" and "Devil Doll."

Chris Isaak, Bruce Springsteen, the Mavericks

Elvis Presley, Hank Williams

see also: *The Traveling Wilburys*

Brian Mansfield

Orbital

Formed 1987 in Kent, England

Paul Hartnoll, keyboards; Phil Hartnoll, keyboards

Named after a dreaded stretch of motorway in their native England, by 1990 Orbital would make its grand entrance into the international electronic dance music arena with the debut single "Chime," recorded on home equipment. Built on minimal loops and a subtle (yet memorable) bass line, its impact demonstrated the triumph and proficiency of the bedroom musician, in turn sparking the creativity of a wave of new, young, British electronic upstarts with their own homegrown—and low-priced—creations. Orbital's willingness to incorporate any number of disparate musical sources as sampling fodder (anything from ABC to the Butthole Surfers, classical music to Crass), paired with the Hartnolls' unique musical sensibility in sound synthesis, has earned them a signature "Orbital sound." This recognizability has garnered praise and remix work for Madonna, Meat Beat Manifesto, Yellow Magic Orchestra and Queen Latifah, among others. Having routinely played the English festival circuit, Orbital was one of the few electronic acts invited to perform at the Woodstock '94. With four albums and numerous singles and EPs behind them, the Hartnoll brothers stand as seasoned veterans in techno's fleeting history.

what to buy: Orbital's first two albums are self-titled, but referred to by their colors; the "green" debut, *Orbital* (ffrr/London, 1992, prod. Paul and Phil Hartnoll) ♪♪♪♪ contains the early rave anthems that won the band international repute ("Satan," "Chime" and "Midnight") plus Moby's remix of "Speed Freak." The "brown" *Orbital* (ffrr/London, 1993, prod. Paul and Phil Hartnoll) ♪♪♪♪ is a more varied and experimental affair, containing the club hits "Impact," "Halcyon + On + On + On" (a variation on an earlier, rare single) and the two-part opus "Lush."

what to buy next: *Diversions* (ffrr/London, 1994, prod. Paul and Phil Hartnoll) ♪♪♪ is an excellent opportunity for non-vinyl collecting enthusiasts to sample some of the "brown" *Orbital's* remixes (previously available only on DJ-oriented 12-inch singles) alongside excerpts from the duo's John Peel Sessions and unreleased bonus tracks. *Snivilisation* (ffrr/London, 1994, prod. Paul and Phil Hartnoll) ♪♪♪ seems to be the album that splits most Orbital fans down the middle as the Hartnoll brothers take their most adventurous foray outside of their expected sound. While it may disappoint some upon initial listen, it takes a few plays to discover the diamonds, such as the piano-driven "Kein Trink Wasser" or the neo-jungle rhythms of "Are We Here?"

the rest: *In Sides* (ffrr/London, 1996) ♪♪♪

worth searching for: Orbital's rare singles and EPs contain some dazzling tracks unavailable elsewhere, many of which capture the true charm of the band. One the best is *Midnight* (ffrr/London U.K., 1991, prod. Paul and Phil Hartnoll).

⏩ Pressure of Speech, Drum Club

⏪ The Archies, Kate Bush, Crass, Dead Kennedys, Kraftwerk, Tangerine Dream

Tamara Palmer

What Album Changed Your Life?

"The obvious one that springs to mind is Sgt. Pepper's Lonely Hearts Club Band. I was at boarding school, and it was such a big deal that one of the boys was sent to town to buy this record. He came back and 150-200 boys sat around the assembly hall and listened to that record twice without saying a word. That was the degree of unity the Beatles produced amongst people. I'll never forget it."

Tim Finn (Split Enz, Crowded House, Finn Brothers)

Orchestral Manoeuvres in the Dark

Formed 1978 in Liverpool, England

Paul David Humphreys, keyboards, percussion, vocals (1978-86); Andy McCluskey (born George Andrew McCluskey), bass, keyboards, vocals; Malcolm Holmes, drums (1980-86); Michael Douglas, keyboards; Dave Hughes, tape editing (1978-80); Martin Hansley Cooper, saxophone (1980-86)

Starting out as a slick synth-pop outfit, OMD was inventive and versatile enough to abandon its sparkling techno sound in favor of more natural instrumentation and, eventually, progressive experimentation. Core members Humphreys and McCluskey began performing together in school, creating their own four-track tapes and eventually adding drummer Holmes.

Throughout the group's early years, the presence of a live drummer helped to warm up OMD's techno sound and give the group some distinction among the many synthesizer-driven bands of the period. Other members came and left as the group progressed first into soundscape experiments (*Architecture & Morality*) and later into rhythm-heavy dance music (*Junk Culture*) and mainstream pop (*Crush*). A mass exodus in 1986 left McCluskey alone to create a new incarnation of OMD. Most of the albums since that period have been tepid though not wholly unenjoyable rehashings of his group's previous efforts.

what to buy: *The Best of OMD* (Virgin/A&M, 1988, prod. Various) is a handy guide to the many stages and sounds of OMD's long and varied career. Featuring 14 A-sides, the album gleans the choice bits from the group's synth periods ("Enola Gay," "Messages"), dance tracks ("Tesla Girls," "Locomotion"), and mainstream romance singles ("If You Leave," "So In Love"). Start here and decide what you like before digging in too deeply.

what to buy next: *Architecture & Morality* (Virgin/Epic, 1981, prod. Mike Howlett) finds OMD pursuing techno-pop dance music but with an emphasis on natural sounds rather than electronic gimmickry. The standouts are "Souvenir" and a cover of Leonard Cohen's gem "Joan of Arc." *Junk Culture* (Virgin/A&M, 1984, prod. Brian Tench) hones the sound OMD began creating on *Architecture & Morality,* giving it a denser rhythm layer and stronger melodies.

what to avoid: *Dazzle Ships* (Virgin/Epic, 1983, prod. Rhett Davies) eschews songwriting for found-tape sampling and technological doodling. Despite some fine atmospherics, the album has little going for it, and only two tracks, "Genetic Engineering" and "Radio Waves" have any lasting appeal.

the rest: *Orchestral Manoeuvres in the Dark* (Virgin, 1980) *Organisation* (Virgin, 1980) *Crush* (Virgin/A&M, 1985) *Sugar Tax* (Virgin, 1991) *Liberator* (Virgin, 1993)

worth searching for: Although widely panned in Britain, *The Pacific Age* (A&M, 1986) did quite well in the United States; surprisingly, it's no longer available on CD. OMD scored with the hits "(Forever) Live & Die" and "We Love You," but the most interesting nugget here is "Southern," featuring snippets of Martin Luther King Jr. speeches played over an instrumental bed.

Duran Duran, Human League, Talk Talk, ABC, A Flock of Seagulls, Gary Numan, Soft Cell, Spandau Ballet, Arcadia, the Buggles

David Bowie, Roxy Music, Ultravox

Christopher Scapelliti

Ben Orr

See: The Cars

Joan Osborne

Born July 8, 1965, in Louisville, Ky.

The hit "One of Us" made Osborne a household name thanks to its four Grammy nominations. Ironically, it's the one original tune on her major label debut, *Relish,* that was written by someone else (Eric Bazilian of the Hooters), and its innocence is atypical of her dark, soulful, yet intelligent style. *Relish* (Blue Gorilla/Mercury, 1995, produced by Rick Chertoff) has plenty of other great songs: the eerie "Pensacola," the forcefully soulful "Ladder," the spooky, surreal "Spider Web," the gorgeous "Lumina" and a cover of Bob Dylan's "Man in the Long Black Coat." As of this writing, Mercury was planning to combine Osborne's two independent releases—*Soul Show* (Womanly Hips, 1991) and *Blue Million Miles* (Swimming Pool Blue 9330102 EP, 1993)—for single CD re-release.

Steve Holtje

Ozzy Osbourne

Born Dec. 3, 1948 in Birmingham, England

Osbourne's descent into self-parody after leaving the seminal thundering of Black Sabbath for the solo path has been painful to witness. At the beginning, the classically founded guitar work of Randy Rhoads fueled Osbourne to produce some inspired material that equals Sabbath's in places. Rhoads' untimely death in a 1982 plane crash put the brakes on Osbourne's momentum, and since then the revolving door of axemen (getting younger every year) has led him to rely on hambone antics, battles with the religious right and the oldest ploy in the book—a retirement that's quickly rescinded—to court the spotlight. Still, he has his audience, which seems perfectly happy to board the "Crazy Train" now and again even if the conductor's abilities have diminished to the point where he's singing songs about TV lawyer Perry Mason.

what to buy: *Tribute* (Epic, 1987, prod. Max Norman), a blazing live set showcasing the Rhoads' wicked virtuosity and the inspired performances it prodded from Osbourne. *Blizzard of Ozz,* (Jet/Epic, 1981, prod. Ozzy Osbourne, Bob Daisly, Lee Kerslake and Randy Rhoads) Osbourne's solo debut, introduces the disciplined attack of Rhoads plus blowtorchers such as "Crazy Train" and the anti-alcohol paean "Suicide Solution" which has been wrongly accused of precipitating three suicides.

what to buy next: *Diary of a Madman* (Jet/Epic, 1981, prod. Ozzy Osbourne, Randy Rhoads and Max Norman) which, despite its goofy cover, show signs of artistic growth in "You Can't Kill Rock 'n' Roll" and the rollicking "Flying High Again." *No More Tears* (Epic, 1991, prod. Duane Baron and John Purdell) finds Osbourne writing songs with Motorhead's Lemmy Kilmister. It's a promising return to form that contains one of his best ballads, "Mama, I'm Coming Home."

what to avoid: *No Rest for the Wicked,* (Epic, 1989, prod Keith Olsen and Roy Thomas Baker) faux horror that indicates Osbourne is ripe for some rest himself.

the rest: *Speak of the Devil* (Jet/Epic, 1982) *Bark at the Moon* (CBS Associated/Epic, 1983) *Just Say Ozzy* (CBS Associated/Epic, 1990) *Live & Loud* (Epic, 1992) *Ozzmosis* (Epic, 1996)

worth searching for: Osbourne's duet with Miss Piggy on "Born to Be Wild" from *Kermit Unplugged* (Jim Henson Records, 1994, prod. Robert Kraft and John Boylan) Reliable reports say he didn't take a bite out of the pig.

▶▶ Danzig, W.A.S.P., White Zombie

◀◀ Black Sabbath, Alice Cooper, the Tubes

see also: *Black Sabbath*

Allan Orski

The Other Two

See: New Order

The Outfield

Formed 1983 in London, England

Tony Lewis, vocals, bass; John Spinks, guitar, keyboard, vocals; Alan Jackman, drums

This smooth power trio achieved its goal—making hits—and managed to stick it out over four albums. Lewis' high-pitched voice (which sounds a lot like the guys from Boston and Styx, only more New Wave) and some great catchy tunes, including "For You," were perfect for the radio. Plus, the group's slick outfits and slightly shaggy demeanor fit MTV pretty well.

what to buy: *Bangin'* (Columbia, 1987, prod. William Wittman) and *Play Deep,* (Columbia, 1985, prod. William Wittman) the trio's first two albums, were the sounds of a confident pop band ready for the radio, but we're not talking the Velvet Underground here.

what to buy next: *Diamond Days* (MCA, 1990, prod. John Spinks and David Leonard) has "For You" and a pretty fun novelty song in "John Lennon."

what to avoid: By *Rockeye,* (MCA, 1992, prod. John Spinks) the group had lost its hitmaking momentum.

the rest: *Voices of Babylon* (Columbia, 1989) *Playing the Field* (Columbia Special Products, 1993)

▶▶ Hootie and the Blowfish, Bush, Rembrandts

◀◀ Scorpions, Alarm, U2, Boston, Styx

Tracey Birkenhauer and Steve Knopper

The Outlaws

Formed 1974 in Tampa, Fla. Disbanded 1995.

Hughie Thomasson, guitar; Billy Jones, guitar (1974-1981, died 1995); Henry Paul, rhythm guitar, vocals (1974-1977, 1983-86); Monte Yoho, drums (1974-1980); Frank O'Keefe, bass (1974-1977, died 1995); Harvey Arnold, bass (1977-1979); Freddy Salem, guitar (1978-79); David Dix, drums (1977-95); Rick Cua, bass (1979-); Chris Hicks, guitar (1983-95); Jeff Howell, drums (1983-95); Barry Borden, bass (1983-95); Timothy Cake, guitar, vocals

One of the last of the Southern boogie bands to get a record deal during the early 70s, the Outlaws often appeared to exist because Southern deejays could program only so much Lynyrd Skynyrd and Marshall Tucker. They developed a good reputation for their live, three-guitar jams, which could go on for 20 minutes, but 1975's "There Goes Another Love Song" would be their only original Top 40 hit. Eventually the group became a stopping point for musicians who wanted Southern rock credentials, and some Outlaws alumni went on to respectable careers: bassist Rick Cua became a contemporary Christian artist, and Henry Paul formed the platinum-selling country band BlackHawk. Thomasson now plays guitar with Lynyrd Skynyrd.

what to buy: Though many of their songs topped six minutes, the Outlaws were basically a singles band for Southern AOR radio, so *Greatest Hits of the Outlaws: High Tides Forever* (Arista, 1982, prod. various) adequately represents the band's output. Only eight tracks long, "High Tides Forever" still captures the Outlaws' best stuff—"There Goes Another Love Song," the "Free Bird"-wannabe "Green Grass & High Tides" and a live rendition of "(Ghost) Riders in the Sky."

what to buy next: The Outlaws were a fairly consistent band, at least until relegated to the Southern-rock oldies circuit, so any album's as good as another. But the best is probably *Outlaws*, (Arista, 1975, prod. Paul Rothchild) ♪♪♪ recorded when the group still seemed like it might develop into something more than just another boogie band.

what to avoid: *Hittin' the Road—Live!* (Blues Bureau, 1993, prod. Mickey Mulcahy and Hughie Thomasson) ♪♪ is retread Southern rock only for those needing a memento of their red-neck youth.

the rest: *Lady in Waiting* (Arista, 1976) ♪♪♪ *Bring It Back Alive* (Arista, 1978) ♪♪♪ *Hurry Sundown* (Arista/Collector's Pipeline, 1977) ♪♪♪ *Playin' to Win* (Arista, 1978) ♪♪♪ *In the Eye of the Storm* (Stodys. 1979) ♪♪ *Ghost Riders in the Sky* (Arista/Collector's Pipeline, 1980) ♪♪♪ *Los Hombres Malo* (Arista, 1982) ♪♪ *Soldiers of Fortune* (Pasha, 1986) ♪♪

solo outings:

Henry Paul Grey Ghost (Atlantic, 1979) ♪♪ *Feel the Heat* (Atlantic, 1980) ♪♪ *Anytime* (Atlantic, 1981) ♪♪

▶▶ The Henry Paul Band, BlackHawk, Georgia Satellites, Screaming Trees

◀◀ Poco, Eagles, the Allman Brothers Band

Brian Mansfield

The Outsiders

Formed 1965 in Cleveland, Ohio. Disbanded 1968.

Tom King, guitar; Sonny Geraci, vocals; Bill Bruno, lead guitar; Merdin Madsen, bass; Ricky Baker, drums

Better than the average garage band from that era, The Outsiders were formed by King with an eye on the charts. Signed by Capitol in early 1966, the Outsiders sold more than 600,000 copies of its first single "Time Won't Let Me" by April. That summer, the Outsiders reached No. 1 again with "Girl in Love." With such quick success, the Outsiders seemed destined for more. They hit again with "Respectable," but then the capricious winds of pop blew them into obscurity. Lead singer Geraci later formed Climax, landing such hits as "Precious and Few" and "Life and Breath." *Capitol Collectors Series: The Outsiders* (Capitol, 1991) ♪♪♪♪ shows the band was more than a hit-making machine. Through four albums, one of which was a live recording, the Outsiders put together generally cohesive recordings that ran deeper than the singles. *The Best of the Outsiders (1965-1968)* (Rhino, 1986) ♪♪♪ also offers a good selection, but not nearly as comprehensive as the Capitol set.

Patrick McCarty

The Oyster Band

Formed in 1981 in England

John Jones, lead vocals, melodeon, accordian, piano; Ian "Chopper" Kearey, bass, cello, tiple, vocals; Ian Telfer, fiddle, viola, tenor concertina; Russell Lax (Lee), drums, percussion, hammer, vocals; Alan Prosser, guitar, banjo, mandolin, violin, vocals; Cathy LeSurf, vocals (1981); Chris Taylor (1981-1984)

The Oyster Band is a one-of-a-kind punk band of master musicians leaning on Celtic and English dance traditions while rocking harder than most of the mainstream. Criminally underappreciated, the band explores the political and personal landscape with intensity and consistency, generating high-spirited power-folk led by the assertive vocals of Welshman John Jones and the incisive electric fiddle of Telfer. The Oysters are frequently transcendent on disc, though no release has ever approached the band's incendiary live performance. The Oyster Band had its genesis in two bands, the Whitstable Oyster Co. Ceilidh Band (later the Oyster Celidh Band), which first took the stage in 1975, and Fiddler's Dram, founded in 1972 by violinist David Arbus, known for his work with East of Eden and The Who. Fiddler's Dram, then consisting of Prosser, Telfer, Taylor and LeSurf, made an album, "To See the Play," notable for a "posthumous" hit novelty single in 1979, "Day Trip to Bangor," forcing the band to make another album, where they were joined by Kearey, among others. Meanwhile, much of Fiddler's Dram enjoyed a parallel existence in The Oyster Ceilidh Band, with LeSurf, Prosser, Kearey, Telfer, and Taylor joining Jones on the dancehall circuit. In 1981, the band dropped "Ceilidh" from its name, LeSurf departed, and The Oyster Band became essentially the unit that exists today. The Oysters have occasionally collaborated with English folk singer June Tabor.

what to buy: *Ride* (Polygram, 1989, prod. Dave Young) ♪♪♪♪♪ comes closest to the glorious assault of their live show. Cuts range from the rollicking "New York Girls" to the pensive "This Year, Next Year," closing with the itchy fiddle cover of New Order's "Love Vigilantes." *The Shouting End of Life* (Cooking Vinyl, 1995, prod. Pat Collier) ♪♪♪♪ is led by the fiddle and guitar pyrotechnics of "Blood-Red Roses" and a pulsating reworking of Bruce Cockburn's "Lovers in a Dangerous Time." *Deserters* (Ryko, 1992, Prod. John Ravenhall) ♪♪♪♪ is a hard-edged beauty that includes the reeling "All That Way for This" and the working class anthem "Fiddle or a Gun."

what to buy next: The band's one full-fledged experiment with June Tabor, *Freedom and Rain* (1990, Rykodisc, prod. by The Oyster Band) is an atmospheric near-masterpiece that includes tunes by Shane McGowan, Richard Thompson, and Billy Bragg.

what to avoid: Though a poor Oyster recording is not to be had, *Little Rock to Leipzig* (1991, Rykodisc, prod. The Oyster Band and Dave Young) is a less compelling collection of studio and live odds and ends best left to die-hard fans.

the rest: Several early Oyster recordings were released on the band's own Pukka label, and are not readily available: *English Rock 'n' Roll—The Early Years 1800-1850 Lie Back and Think of England 20 Golden Tie Slackeners Liberty Hall* More attainable: *Step Outside* (1986, Cooking Vinyl) *Wild Blue Yonder* (1987, Cooking Vinyl) *Holy Bandits* (1993, Rykodisc)

worth searching for: The CD-single *Cry Cry* (1994, Rykodisc) from the Holy Bandits album includes three previously unreleased tunes, including an astonishing "Star of the County Down."

⏩ The Pogues, Spirit of the West

⏪ Fairport Convention, Pentangle, The Clash

Martin Connors

Jimmy Page

Born James Patrick Page, Jan. 9, 1944 in Heston Middlesex, England

With stints in the Yardbirds and Led Zeppelin, legendary fretmaster Page is one of rock's all-time guitar heroes. A self-taught musician, Page established his name when he was just 17 and was playing with Neil Christian and the Crusaders. The guitar ace with the choirboy's face was definitely a superstar, and every aspiring guitarist in the city checked him out regularly. By the time he joined the Yardbirds in 1966, Page was a super-sessioneer (the Kinks, Herman's Hermits, Donovan), a veteran arranger and a pioneering producer of avant-rock techniques.

He formed Led Zeppelin from the ashes of the Yardbirds in 1968 and achieved world rock 'n' roll domination for the next 12 years. Afterward, Page soldiered on to various short-lived projects, including The Firm with former Free/Bad Company singer Paul Rodgers, a solo album and a collaboration with former Deep Purple/Whitesnake singer David Coverdale—before reuniting with Led Zeppelin singer Robert Plant for an album, MTV special and world tour.

what to buy: *The Firm,* (Atlantic, 1985, prod. Jimmy Page and Paul Rodgers) offered bone-crunching riff rock that recalled Bad Company more than Led Zeppelin. Page's solo effort, *Outrider,* (Geffen, 1988, prod. Jimmy Page) is pure ear candy that features Jason Bonham (son of Led Zep skinpounder John Bonham) on drums and a guest shot by Plant.

what to buy next: *Coverdale/Page,* (Geffen, 1993, prod. David Coverdale, Jimmy Page and Mike Fraser) a collaboration that lets Page's searing guitar work shine above his large-haired partner's vocals.

what to avoid: *Death Wish II,* (Swan Song, 1982, prod. Jimmy Page) a soundtrack that's only for fans of ambient guitar excursions.

the rest: (with The Firm) *Mean Business* (Atlantic, 1986)

worth searching for: Import collections of Page's session work, including *Session Man, Vol. 2* (Bomp!, 1991, prod. Various) and *Jimmy's Back Pages: The Early Years* (Sony, 1992, comp. Doug Wygal)

⏩ Eddie Van Halen, Brian May, Alex Lifeson, Slash

⏪ Willie Dixon, Albert King, Howlin' Wolf, Muddy Waters, Eric Clapton, Jimi Hendrix

see also: *Led Zeppelin, Page/Plant*

Sarah Weber

Page/Plant

Formed 1994 in London, England

After years of squabbling, Led Zeppelin principals Jimmy Page and Robert Plant decided to get back together for an extended series of projects that included an MTV special, an album and a concert tour—as well as the promise of continued work together. The album, *No Quarter: Jimmy Page & Robert Plant Unledded* (Atlantic, 1994, prod. Jimmy Page) finds the duo charting some new sonic territory—delving deeply in the World Music realm—as well as re-arranging some of Led Zeppelin's most challenging material. The set's highlight is a killer, orchestrated rendition of "Kashmir."

see also: *Led Zeppelin, Jimmy Page, Robert Plant*

Sarah Weber

Pailhead

See: Ministry

Pale Saints

Formed in 1987 in Leeds, England

Chris Cooper, drums, percussion; Ian Masters, guitar; Graeme Naysmith, guitar; Meriel Barham, vocals, guitar (1990-present); Colleen Browne, bass (1994-present)

Falling into the same vein of music as Lush and My Bloody Valentines, Pale Saints play an ethereal, jangly pop style of music. It's best displayed on *In Ribbons* (4AD, 1992, prod. Hugh Jones), which highlights Barham's pretty vocals and Master's strongest collection of songs.

the rest: *Comforts of Madness* (4AD, 1990) *Slow Buildings* (4AD/Warner Brothers)

Anna Glen

Palm Fabric Orchestra

See: Poi Dog Pondering

Robert Palmer

Born Alan Palmer, Jan. 19, 1949 in Bately, England

Not to be confused with the rock critic of the same name, this Robert Palmer started off in a series of forgettable British groups before going solo during the mid-70s. With a knack for picking the right cover tunes and an intriguing mix of rootsy, soul-tinged, Caribbean-influenced rock compositions (early albums featured members of the Meters and Toots & the Maytals), Palmer carved out a healthy niche as an eclectic, progressive pop artist. Still, it wasn't until his brief stint with supergroup the Power Station—which featured members of Duran Duran and Chic—that the singer became a bona fide pop star. Leaving the group after one record (his refusal to tour was the reported stumbling block), Palmer snagged the group's production team for his own work, rafting a metallized rock/soul sound that brought his biggest solo hits yet. But an unfortunate turn toward the Tin Pan Alley standards of his youth brought commercial disaster—a fate from which he has yet to recover.

what to buy: As one of the few Palmer albums that doesn't sabotage its great material with equally confusing and eclectic indulgences, *Secrets* (Island, 1979, prod. Robert Palmer) contains classics such as his rocking cover of Moon Martin's "Bad Case of Lovin' You (Doctor, Doctor)" along with a sensitive, soulful take on Todd Rundgren's "Can We Still Be Friends?" Almost as impressive is his solo debut, *Sneakin' Sally Through The Alley* (Island, 1974, prod. Steve Smith) Featuring the Allen Toussaint-written title cut backing by both Little Feat and The Meters, the record is about as close to New Orleans soul as any British guy will ever get.

what to buy next: For a consistently engaging taste of his 80s pop star incarnation, no album touches all the bases better than his breakthrough, *Riptide* (Island, 1986, prod. Bernard Edwards) With a well-crafted, edgy production style courtesy of Power Station mate Edwards, and with songs ranging from the hormone-addled hit "Addicted to Love" to a synthesizer-laden remake of the blues tune "Trick Bag," Palmer turns in his most creative, confident album in years. To sample the best of his 70s and early 80s work, the hits collection *Addictions, Volume Two* (Island, 1992, prod. Various) isolates highlights such as his inspired cover of The System's funky "You Are In My System" and the dreamy, reggae-tinged ballad "Every Kind of People."

what to avoid: As a tribute to the jazzy pop standards of the 40s, *Ridin' High* (EMI, 1992, prod. Teo Maceo and Robert Palmer) WOOF! falls flat—mostly due to Palmer's emotionless, bionic delivery.

the rest: *Pressure Drop* (Island, 1975) *Some People Can Do What They Like* (Island, 1976) *Double Fun* (Island, 1978) *Clues* (Island, 1980) *Maybe It's Live* (Island, 1982) *Pride* (Island, 1983) *Heavy Nova* (EMI, 1988) *Addictions, Volume One* (Island, 1989) *Don't Explain* (EMI America, 1990) WOOF! *Honey* (EMI America, 1994)

worth searching for: *Simply Palmer* (EMI, 1988), a promotional interview CD that has a smooth, suave James Bond quality.

▶▶ Toto, Mr. Mister

◀◀ James Brown, Wilson Pickett, Tony Bennett, Mel Torme, Billie Holiday, Nina Simone, Ronald Isley

Eric Deggans

The Pandoras

Formed 1983, Los Angeles, Calif. Disbanded 1991.

Paula Pierce, vocals, guitar (died 1991); Casey, drums (1983-84); Bambi Conway, bass, vocals (1983-84); Gwynne Kelly, organ, vocals (1983-84); Karen Blankfield, drums, vocals (1984-87); Julie

Patchouli, bass, vocals (1984-85); Melanie Vammen, organ, vocals (1984-91); Kim Shattuck, bass, vocals (1985-91); Rita D'Albert, guitar, vocals (1988-91); Sheri Kaplan, drums, vocals (1988-91)

The Pandoras were the only all-female group to achieve any notoriety during the mid-80s psychedelic/garage-punk revival, an insular scene dominated by male acts imitating the Sonics and the Chocolate Watch Band, desperately seeking to convince you that it was 1966 and this was the now sound. Although the Pandoras were notoriously willing to trade on the their gender, the group was ultimately memorable because it delivered the goods; at its best, the Pandoras were one of the few neo-garage groups to transcend novelty value and rock 'n' roll as convincingly and as engagingly as its Nuggets/Pebbles-enshrined heroes. The group ended when Pierce passed away in 1991. Shattuck went on to form the Muffs, initially with Vammen in tow.

what to buy: The first incarnation of the Pandoras recorded *It's About Time,* (Voxx, 1984/Rhino, 1993, prod. Greg Shaw, Gary Stern and Bill Inglot) a growling, grungy slab of garage-bred rock 'n' roll with a belligerent pop sensibility. The expanded reissue adds non-LP tracks.

what to avoid: *Rock Hard* (Restless, 1988, prod. Stevie Salas) proves that leering, single-entendre odes to sexual prowess and primal horniness are no more palatable when offered by, y'know, gurls. The live album, *Live Nymphomania,* (Restless, 1989) WOOF! is worse.

Hole, 4 Non-Blondes, Babes in Toyland, Lunachicks

The Sonics, the Standells, the Rolling Stones, Them, the Pretty Things, the Chocolate Watch Band, the Kinks

see also: *the Muffs*

Carl Cafarelli

Pantera

Formed 1982 in Arlington, Texas

Terrence Lee, vocals (1982-87); Philip Anselmo, vocals (1987-present); "Dimebag" (formerly "Diamond") Darrell Abbott, guitars; Vinnie Paul Abbott, drums; Rex "Rocker" Brown, bass

Starting out as 80s glam rockers, Pantera hit big when it lost the glitter and found the tattoo parlor. With four independent releases behind it, the band collected an underground following encompassing the punk and metal crowds with the release of *Cowboys From Hell* in 1990. Pantera's full-on but melodic aural assault of power chords, slow grooves and growling vocals turned the band into million-sellers, while its live performances show no mercy to the audience with a deafening onslaught of volume that acts as a soundtrack for Anselmo, who stalks the stage like an animal ready to pounce on its prey.

what to buy: *Vulgar Display of Power* (EastWest, 1992, prod. Terry Date and Vinnie Paul Abbott) is an impressive display of machine-gun power chords, crafty guitar work and double bass drum rhythms. The infectious, anthemic song "Walk" is the standout track

what to buy next: *The Great Southern Trendkill* (EastWest, 1996, prod. Terry Date and Vinnie Paul Abbott) musically takes an even more brutal approach. Anselmo's furious vocals on the title track open the album as it continues through to the hypnotic groove of "Drag The Waters," the morose (in terms of Pantera) "10's," the somber "Suicide Note Pt. 1" and its inflammatory partner "Suicide Note Pt. 2."

the rest: *Cowboys From Hell* (Atco, 1990) *Far Beyond Driven* (EastWest, 1994)

worth searching for: Although out of print—and a far cry from what Pantera sounds like now—the horrific glam-rock albums *Metal Magic,* (Metal Magic, 1984, prod. Vinnie Paul Abbott) *Projects in the Jungle* (Metal Magic, prod. Vinnie Paul Abbott) *I Am The Night* (Metal Magic, prod. Vinnie Paul Abbott) and *Power Metal* (Metal Magic, 1988, prod. Vinnie Paul Abbott) are amusing to listen to just to see how far the band has come.

solo outings:

Phil Anselmo (with Down) Nola (Elektra, 1995)

Clutch, Prong

Black Sabbath, Metallica, Suicidal Tendencies

Christina Fuoco

Graham Parker /Graham Parker & The Rumor

Born 1950 in East London, England

(The Rumor, 1977-81): Graham Parker, guitar, harmonica and vocals; Brinsley Schwarz, guitar; Martin Belmont, guitar; Bob Andrews, keyboards; Andrew Bodnar, bass; Stephen Goulding, drums

Although he seldom gets the credit for it, Graham Parker blazed the trail for punk rock. With his acerbic lyrics, caustic vocals and angry young man stance, Parker bridged the gap between raucous pub rock and punk, creating a prototype for the likes of fellow Brits Joe Jackson and Elvis Costello. At a time when British music had been polarized into Fairport Convention neofolkies and artsy glam acts such as Roxy Music and Sweet, Parker reminded everyone that rock 'n' roll was always, first and foremost, a personal thing. Against a high-octane blend of R&B, soul and Dylanesque cynicism, Parker churned out memorable attacks against former lovers, hipster poseurs and record company suits. Little has changed in Parker's music over the years; although his recent songs tend toward more mature themes of marriage and family, his passion, as always, comes through loud and strong.

what to buy: *Passion Is No Ordinary Word: The Graham Parker Anthology, 1976-1991* (Rhino, 1993, prod. Various) is a terrific introduction to Parker's lengthy career. In addition to pulling the critical cuts from Parker's stronger albums, the compilation culls gems such as "Temporary Beauty," "Life Gets Better" and "Little Miss Understanding" from otherwise mediocre albums and adds the previously unavailable single "Mercury Poisoning."

what to buy next: The touchstone for every British singer-songwriter to come, *Howlin' Wind* (Polygram, 1976, prod. Nick Lowe) demonstrates a breathtaking range of styles and emotions. Parker shows equal parts venom and sensitivity throughout on the finger-snapping R&B number "White Honey," the vitriolic "Back to Schooldays" and the haunting "Don't Ask Me Questions." A classic album. *The Mona Lisa's Sister* (RCA, 1988, prod. Graham Parker and Brinsley Schwarz) shows Parker older, wiser and in peak form. Backed by Schwarz and former members of Rockpile, Parker delivers a smooth collection of masterful R&B ("Under the Mask of Happiness"), soul ("The Girl Isn't Ready") and folk ("Blue Highways").

what to avoid: Anxious to get out of his contract with Mercury, Parker released *The Parkerilla*, (Mercury, 1978, prod. Robert John "Mutt" Lange), three sides of live material plus a second studio version of "Don't Ask Me Questions." Despite strong performances, there's nothing here that isn't better covered on the studio releases.

the rest: *Stick to Me* (Polygram, 1977) *Squeezing Out Sparks* (Arista, 1987) *The Up Escalator* (Arista/Razor & Tie, 1980) *Another Grey Area* (Arista/Razor & Tie, 1982) *The Real Macaw* (Arista/Razor & Tie, 1983) *Steady Nerves* (Elektra, 1985) *Live! Alone in America* (RCA, 1989) *Human Soul* (RCA, 1989) *Pumpin' It Out* (Phonogram, 1990) *Struck by Lightning* (RCA, 1991) *The Best of Graham Parker & the Rumor* (Vertigo, 1992) *The Best of Graham Parker 1988-1991* (RCA,1992) *Burning Questions* (Demon, 1992) *Live Alone! Discovering Japan* (Demon, 1993) *Live on the Test* (Windsong, 1994) *12 Haunted Episodes* (Razor & Tie, 1995)

worth searching for: *Energetic* (Kisses Deluxe, prod. Ron Wolfe) is a live bootleg emanating from Parker's 1979 gig at San Francisco's Old Waldorf. Recorded by Arista when Parker and the Rumor were sonically at their toughest and leanest, about half the tracks here were also released on the promotion-only LP *Live Sparks* (Arista, 1979, prod. Ron Wolfe). Cuts such as "Passion is No Ordinary Word," "Protection" and "I Want You Back (Alive)" are worthy reminders that, in concert, Parker and the Rumor were a force to be reckoned with.

Rockpile, Dave Edmunds, Brinsley Schwarz, Nick Lowe, Elvis Costello, Joe Jackson, The Jam, Tom Petty, The Pretenders, John Hiatt, Billy Bragg, John Wesley Harding, Frank Black

Sam Cooke, Dion, Bob Dylan, Van Morrison, Motown, Bruce Springsteen

Christopher Scapelliti

Maceo Parker

Born Feb. 14, 1943 in Kinston, N.C.

The public became aware of funk-jazz saxophonist Parker when he joined James Brown's band during the mid-60s. His sympathetic ear and playing—rhythms, accents and countermelodies to Brown's voice—was instrumental in defining the JB sound on tunes such as "It's a Man's, Man's, Man's World," "Money Won't Change You" and "Say It Loud." Along with trombonist Fred Wesley, Parker helped develop the choppy horn section style that was more rhythmic than melodic and powerfully in sync. The JB's stepped out on their own in 1972 with *Food For Thought*, an album regularly sampled by modern rappers. Parker and Wesley switched to the P-Funk Mob in 1975 and helped define that group's sound during its hottest years. Parker still works with George Clinton and in recent years has recorded jazz-funk albums as a bandleader himself.

what to buy: Parker's been around a long time and played all kinds of stuff, but deep down it's the music on *Mo' Roots* (Verve, 1991 prod. Steve Meyner and Maceo Parker) that's in his heart—a little jazz, a little soul, a little gospel and the eight-minute "Chicken," which bumps along on a bass line while the horns stretch out with the groove. *Roots Revisited* (Verve, 1990 prod. Steve Meyner and Maceo Parker) hangs with some jazzy arrangements and the seldom-heard Charles Mingus piece "Better Get Hit In Your Soul." A nice reading of the Impressions' "People Get Ready" shows the soulful side of the package.

what to buy next: *Life On Planet Groove* (Verve, 1992, prod. Steve Meyner and Maceo Parker) gets a little more modern and into stretchy funk, but "Shake Everything You've Got" is 16 minutes of solosists taking it to the limit.

what to avoid: *For All the King's Men* (4th and Broadway/Island, 1990, prod. Bill Laswell and Bootsy Collins) is all P-Funked up and has little identity outside that arena.

worth searching for: *Southern Exposure* (Novus, 1994, prod. Stephen Meyner and Maceo Parker) features Parker, along with the Rebirth Brass Band and the Meters, serving up a big helping of Crescent City funk.

▶▶ The Brecker Brothers, Tower of Power, Clarence Clemons

◀◀ Ray Charles, John Coltrane, Charlie Parker

Lawrence Gabriel

Van Dyke Parks

Born January 3, 1943 in Hattiesburg, Miss.

This idiosyncratic songwriter and arranger first achieved recognition for his work with Beach Boy Brian Wilson on the abortive but now legendary *Smile* project. Steeped in jazz and early American songcraft, Parks' solo work is dense and complex, utilizing everything from calypso to chamber pop to Ragtime in the service of his frequently ironic meditations on American and other cultures. Parks was born in Mississippi but grew up in Los Angeles; classically trained on piano, he worked as an actor during his adolescence but moved into pop music later. Besides writing his own songs, he worked as a producer (for acts such as Harper's Bizarre) and a session pianist. Though Parks' own albums have been few and far between, each one has been the subject of intense scrutiny by rock writers, and most have been lavished with praise. None of the albums has sold well in the U.S., though Parks is a relatively big seller in Japan. In between albums, he has worked steadily as a composer, arranger and session musician—and in 1995 he worked again with Wilson on the *Orange Crate Cart* album.

what to buy: Parks' debut, *Song Cycle* (Warner Bros., 1967, prod. Lenny Waronker) is a worthy introduction to his weird world. Dreamily symphonic, it remains as unclassifiable and startling as it was when it came out.

what to buy next: *Jump* (Warner Bros., 1984, prod. Steve Goldman) is Parks' acclaimed evocation of the storybook South, as filtered through the Brer Rabbit stories.

what to avoid: Despite good intentions and some beautiful passages, Parks' reunion with Wilson on *Orange Crate Art* (Warner Bros., 1995, prod. Van Dyke Parks) is less memorable from a musical standpoint than one might have hoped.

the rest: *Clang of the Yankee Reaper* (Warner Bros., 1975)
Tokyo Rose (Warner Bros., 1989)

worth searching for: On his sophomore effort, *Discover America,* (Warner Bros., 1972, prod. Kirby Johnson) Parks finds America...in the Caribbean. The album boasts lovely, languid renditions of great songs such as Little Feat's "Sailing Shoes."

▶▶ Victoria Williams, Eric Matthews, Richard Davies, Medicine, The Negro Problem, High Llamas, Witch Hazel

◀◀ Stephen Foster, Leadbelly, Tin Pan Alley, Trinidadian music, Phil Spector

see also: *Brian Wilson*

Simon Glickman

Parliament-Funkadelic

See: George Clinton

Alan Parsons /Alan Parsons Project

Born 1949 in England

As one of the engineers on the Beatles' *Abbey Road* album and Pink Floyd's *The Dark Side of the Moon,* Parsons ranks as studio rat supreme. So it was little surprise when, in 1975, he decided to make his own musical expression a studio-based venture. Operated with colleague Eric Woolfson, the Alan Parsons Project became a sonic pop lab, with musicians and singers constantly changing as the two engineers toiled to create perfec sonic experience. It made for great headphone music which, in the 70s, went a long way. But as mass tastes veered away from such sterile endeavors, the Parsons Project's commercial fortunes declined—and so did the quality of the product, degenerating into New Agey fluff. By the time Parsons finally decided to take his project on the road during the early 90s, it was well beyond the point where it mattered.

what to buy: *I Robot* (Arista, 1977, prod. Alan Parsons) is the penultimate Parsons Project album. In hindsight it's a little thin on songs, though the hit single "I Wouldn't Want to Be Like You," "Some Other Time" and "Breakdown" made for a strong early album set. But put the headphones on while you're listening, and you'll understand why it worked.

what to buy next: Either Parsons hits collection—*The Best of the Alan Parsons Project* (Arista, 1983, prod. Alan Pasons) or *The Best of the Alan Parsons Project Vol. 2* (Arista, 1987, prod. Alan Parsons) —glean the best tracks off the assorted albums. Of the individual efforts, *Tales of Mystery and Imagination—Edgar Allan Poe* (20th Century, 1976/Arista, 1987, prod. Alan Parsons) and *The Turn of a Friendly Card* (Arista, 1980, prod. Alan Parsons) are the most thematically cohesive.

what to avoid: *Try Anything Once* (Arista, 1993, prod. Alan Parsons) WOOF! has neither thematic unity nor good individual songs to carry it.

the rest: *Pyramid* (Arista, 1978) *Eve* (Arista, 1979) *Eye in the Sky* (Arista, 1982) *Ammonia Avenue* (Arista, 1984/1991) *Vulture Culture* (Arista, 1984) *Stereotomy* (Arista, 1985/1991) *Gaudi* (Arista, 1987/1991) *Very Best—Live* (RCA Victor, 1995)

worth searching for: Parsons' approach lends itself well to film music. He recorded a compelling theme and song, "Voyager," for the soundtrack to *Ice Castles* (Arista, 1979/1990)

▶▶ Manfred Mann's Earth Band, Donna Summer, M, Queen

◀◀ Pink Floyd, Tangerine Dream, Wings

Gary Graff

Gram Parsons

Born Cecil Ingram Connor, Nov. 5, 1946 in Winterhaven, Fla. Died Sept. 19, 1973 in Joshua Tree, Calif.

A Harvard dropout who played with both the Byrds and the Flying Burrito Brothers before going solo, Parsons gave rock 'n' roll a country martyr it could claim as its own. Parsons serves much the same function for 90s "alternative country" acts like Son Volt and the Jayhawks that Hank Williams serves for mainstream country—he drank too much, wrote sad songs and died before he hit 30. Parsons's storytelling gift is enhanced by his tragic legend, and it didn't hurt that he helped introduce Emmylou Harris to the music world. When he died, his road manager and a friend stole his body, cremated it and scattered the ashes at Cap Rock, a California national monument.

what to buy: *G.P./Grievous Angel* (Reprise, 1990, prod. Gram Parsons and Rick Grech) is a twofer classic that combines Parsons' two solo albums. California country-rock doesn't come more influential than this.

what to buy next: *Sleepless Nights,* (A&M, 1976, prod. Various) a posthumous release, was compiled from solo material and tracks from Parsons' days with the Flying Burrito Brothers.

the rest: *G.P.* (Reprise, 1973) *Grievous Angel* (Reprise, 1974) *Gram Parsons and the Fallen Angels Live* (Sierra, 1992)

worth searching for: *Safe at Home* (Shiloh, 1968) an early record with the International Submarine Band that shows the direction Parsons would travel. Also, *Warm Evenings, Pale Mornings, Bottled Blues* (Raven, 1995), an Australian compliation.

▶▶ Emmylou Harris, The Eagles, The Jayhawks, Uncle Tupelo, Wilco, Son Volt, the Bottle Rockets

◀◀ Hank Williams, Merle Haggard, Elvis Presley, The Byrds

see also: *The Byrds, The Flying Burrito Brothers*

Brian Mansfield

Andy Partridge

See: XTC

Passengers

Brian Eno, Bono, Adam Clayton, Larry Mullen Jr., Luciano Pavarotti, Holi, Howie B, Craig Armstrong, Paul Barrett, Des Broadbery, David Herbert, Holger Zschenderlein

Passengers is what U2 would sound like if Brian Eno were fully at the helm, as opposed to being a sounding board and creative foil for Bono and the Edge. Consisting mainly of moody ambient soundscapes, *Passengers: Original Soundtracks 1* (Island, 1995, prod. Brian Eno) contains a few vocal tracks—notably "Miss Sarajevo," on which the level of pathos is driven to literally operatic heights by none other than Pavarotti. Bono's Elvis obsession reaches a new low on the downright silly "Elvis Ate America," but heck, what are side projects for, anyway?

see also: *Brian Eno, U2, Skylab*

Daniel Durchholz

Henry Paul

See: The Outlaws

Pavement

Formed 1989 in Stockton, Calif.

S.M. (Steve Malkums), vocals, guitar; Spiral Stairs (Scott Kannberg), vocals, guitar; Gary Young, drums (1989-1992); Steve West, drums (1992-present); Bob Nastanovich, percussion (1992-present); Mark Ibold, bass (1992-present)

Pavement exploded onto the indie rock scene in 1992 with the huge press surrounding their debut LP—which consisted of mutating guitars, low-fi bursts of noise, and slacker lyrics that floored fans with their intensity and feeling. Critics were equally blown away by Pavement's solid instrumental grasp and their uncanny ability to recall the greatness of the Velvet Underground while maintaining a distinctly dark, yet beautiful sound of their own. Later records mellowed out the low-fi noise to create more accessible music, but they still contain the key features that make Pavement a great band.

what to buy: *Slanted and Enchanted* (Matador, 1992, Pavement) ♫♫♫♫♫ is the rare album that not only lives up to all the hype but actually surpasses it. The music features overwhelming amounts of low-fi noise that brings up images of magnificence only to be slowly and unexpectedly replaced by upbeat garage-pop. This album is a treasure chest of surprises; every listen brings something unheard and equally enchanting.

what to buy next: *Crooked Rain, Crooked Rain* (Matador, 1994, prod. Pavement) ♫♫♫♫ tones down the bursts of noise and features cleaner production values. Decepitvely more radio friendly—"Cut Your Hair" received some time on MTV—*Crooked Rain* actually hides a more cynical feeling behind it's easier to listen to exterior. *Wowee Zowee* (Matador, 1996, prod. Pavement) ♫♫♫♫ continues Pavement's dark foray into their own dissonant brand of pop-rock—a solid follow up to *Crooked Rain*. *Westing (By Musket and Sextant)* (Drag City, 1993, prod. Pavement) ♫♫♫♫ collects early vinyl singles onto one disc. Returns to low-fi while evoking fond memories of the great garage bands.

the rest: *Watery Domestic* (Matador, 1992) ♫♫♫½ *Pacific Trim* (Matador, 1996) ♫♫♫½

▶▶ Guided By Voices, The Silver Jews, Free Kitten

◀◀ The Fall, The Velvet Underground, Iggy Pop, Sonic Youth, Hüsker Dü

Bryan Lassner

Freda Payne

Born Sept. 19, 1945, in Detroit, Mich.

Before she struck gold with soul, Payne studied voice, piano and ballet. She sang in the chorus of a Pearl Bailey show and toured with Duke Ellington's band as a jazz singer and with Quincy Jones—a sophisticated early career for a woman who smoked the charts in 1970 with her passionate urgency and longing on "Band of Gold." One of the most memorable soul tracks from the 70s, it launched an R&B career that was curiously brief. In the hands of legendary songwriters and producers Holland-Dozier-Holland, Payne had the material, sound and backing to have a long run on the charts. But she had only a handful of hits ("Deeper and Deeper," "Cherish What Is Dear to You (While It's Near to You)," "Joy" and an anti-Vietnam War single, "Bring the Boys Back Home.") *Greatest Hits* (HDH, 1991) ♫♫♫♫ has all of them and a fine sampling of her other material.

Patrick McCarty

Pearl Jam /Mother Love Bone/Green River

Formed 1991 in Seattle, Wash.

Eddie Vedder, vocals, guitar; Stone Gossard, guitar; Mike McCready, guitar; Jeff Ament, bass; Dave Krusen, drums (1991); Dave Abbruzzese, drums (1991-94); Jack Irons, drums (1994-present)

Seattle's Pearl Jam broke through the door Nirvana and Soundgarden kicked open as part of the much-ballyhooed "grunge" wave of the early 90s. Fronted by charismatic singer Vedder—who swooped from mopey mumble to feral wail, and whose good looks and apparent integrity quickly made him a reluctant media darling—the group's sonic attack owed much to the arena rock of the 70s, though with a goodly dose of post-punk attitude and the requisite 90s angst. The group formed after Mother Love Bone members Ament and Gossard—bereft by the death of their band's singer Andrew Wood—recorded the *Temple of the Dog* album with Soundgarden's Chris Cornell and Matt Cameron, local guitar-slinger McCready and, at the last moment, Vedder. Vedder, then in San Diego, sent the band a homemade tape of himself singing lyrics over its instrumental demos (ironically, at the behest of Irons); the chemistry was immediate and remains intact. Outspoken on a number of political issues, the band earned points with fans—but ultimately spun its wheels—for its quixotic but highly publicized battle with the ticket agency TicketMaster, which the band felt charged extortionate surcharges. The band has also backed rock legend Neil Young several times, notably on his 1995 album *Mirror Ball.*

what to buy: *Ten* (Epic, 1991, prod. Pearl Jam and Rick Parashar) 🎧🎧🎧🎧 remains the band's finest collection of songs, several of which—notably "Jeremy," "Alive" and "Evenflow"—were smashes on both radio and MTV. A good, loud rock record with some emotional depth. *Temple of the Dog* (A&M, 1991, prod. Rick Parashar and Temple of the Dog) 🎧🎧🎧🎧 is every bit as good, and, written as it was on the heels of their friend's death, is a good bit more emotionally empowered.

what to buy next: *Vs.* (Epic, 1993, prod. Brendan O'Brien and Pearl Jam) 🎧🎧🎧½ is a worthy follow-up that made the band even bigger thanks to the crossover success of the single "Daughter." *Merkin Ball* (Epic, EP, prod. Brendan O'Brien and Pearl Jam) 🎧🎧🎧 contains two songs, "I Got Id" and "Long Road," recorded during Young's *Mirror Ball* sessions. Vedder re-recorded the latter for the "Dead Man Walking" movie soundtrack. Considering Pearl Jam's phenomenal success, fans might find it illuminating to touch on the bands that came before it. Green River output—angrier, punkier and more raw than Pearl Jam—is summarized on the compilation *Dry As A Bone/Rehab Doll* (Sub Pop, 1990, prod. Jack Endino and Bruce Calder) 🎧🎧🎧 Mother Love Bone's album, *Apple,* and another half-dozen stray tracks comprise *Mother Love Bone* (PolyGram, 1992, prod. Tarry Date and Mother Love Bone) 🎧🎧🎧

what to avoid: *Vitology* (Epic, 1994; prod. Brendan O'Brien and Pearl Jam) 🎧½ contains a couple of compositions that are identifiable as songs—two are actually decent—and a great deal of self-indulgent murk.

the rest: *No Code* (Epic, 1996) 🎧🎧½

worth searching for: The CD-5 for "Dissident" (Epic, 1994, prod. Brendan O'Brien and Pearl Jam) 🎧🎧🎧🎧 kicked off a three-CD series of tracks recorded during a live radio broadcast from Atlanta—the only way other than the bootleg market to acquire a Pearl Jam live album.

solo outings:

Brad (Stone Gossard): *Shame* (Epic, 1993) 🎧🎧½

Three Fish (Jeff Ament): *Three Fish* (Epic, 1996) 🎧🎧🎧

⏩ Stone Temple Pilots, Bush, silverchair

⏪ Led Zeppelin, Black Sabbath, Beatles, the Allman Brothers Band

see also: *Neil Young*

Grant Alden and Simon Glickman

Neil Peart

See: Rush

Ann Peebles

Born April 27, 1947, in St. Louis, Mo.

Often overlooked in the vast shadow of Al Green's success, Peebles' seven albums for Memphis-based Hi Records contain some of the finest music of the 70s soul era. Like Green, Peebles' records were produced and arranged by Willie Mitchell, and they featured the same superb Hi Records house band. But while Green sang of "Love and Happiness," Peebles mined a darker vein of bitter loss, betrayal and regret with tunes such as "I'm Gonna Tear Your Playhouse Down" and "Feel Like Breakin' Up Somebody's Home." And Mitchell's musical arrangements for Peebles were sparer, more intimate—emotionally attuned to a voice soaked in longing and pain. Her high point came with the 1974 album *I Can't Stand The Rain* and its oft-covered title tune. During the late 70s, she abruptly retired from music to raise a family, though she was coaxed back into a Memphis studio for an excellent 1992 comeback record, *Full Time Love*

what to buy: *Ann Peebles' Greatest Hits* (MCA, 19??, prod. Willie Mitchell) 🎧🎧🎧🎧 is the only existing domestic-released overview of Peebles' Hi Records years. Containing all the essential hits, it's the place to start. Anyone who loves classic soul should own a copy of *I Can't Stand The Rain* (Hi/The Right Stuff, 1973, prod. Willie Mitchell) 🎧🎧🎧🎧

what to buy next: *Full Time Love* (Bullseye Blues, 1992, prod. Ron Levy) 🎧🎧🎧 is Peebles' long-overdue return to the studio, backed by many of the original Hi Records studio musicians. Despite the absence of Mitchell's guiding hand, its high points (such as a brilliant version of Delbert McClinton's "Read Me My Rights") reach the level of her finest Hi recordings.

the rest: *Part Time Love* (Hi/The Right Stuff, 1971) 🎧🎧🎧½ *Straight From The Heart* (Hi/The Right Stuff, 1971) 🎧🎧🎧½

worth searching for: Most of Peebles' original Hi albums are only available now as imports. Look for *If This Is Heaven.* (Hi U.K., 1978, prod. Willie Mitchell)

▶▶ Toni Braxton, Annie Lennox, Otis Clay

◀◀ Mahalia Jackson, Aretha Franklin, Sam Cooke

Doug Pippin

Michael Penn

Born Aug. 1, 1958, New York, N.Y.

To say that Penn has show business in his blood is to state the obvious: his father is actor/director Leo Penn, his mother actress Eileen Ryan, his brothers Sean and Christopher, and Madonna was his former sister-in-law. And while he may have gotten his first big break singing on a "Saturday Night Live" episode hosted by Sean, Michael's songwriting skills hold up under the scrutiny his famous family may have initially attracted. On his debut album, *March* (RCA, 1989, prod. Tony Berg), Penn shows a gift for melodious popcraft, though his lyrics tend toward the willfully obscure. Die-hard fans, no doubt, are out there still trying to figure out the meaning of Penn's hit "No Myth," as well as the equally cryptic but listenable tunes "This & That" and "Cupid's Got a Brand New Gun." Of special note on "March" are the contributions of Penn's keyboardist Patrick Warren, whose manipulation of the Chamberlain, an arcane Mellotron-like instrument, gives many of Penn's songs their distinctive sound. The follow-up album *Free For All* (RCA, 1992, prod. Tony Berg and Michael Penn) was nearly as fine an effort, but failed to attract much attention.

Daniel Durchholz

Pentangle

Formed 1967 in England. Disbanded 1973. Re-formed 1983.

Bert Jansch, guitar, vocals; Jacqui McShee, vocals; Terry Cox, drums, percussion (1967-73, 1983-89); John Renbourne, guitar, vocals, sitar (1967-73, 1983-85), vocals, sitar; Danny Thompson, bass (1967-73, 1983-85); Mike Piggott, guitar (1985-89); Nigel Portman-Smith, bass (1985-89); Gerry Conway, drums (1990-present); Peter Kirtley, guitar (1990-present)

Pentangle plays an elegant hybrid of Celtic, folk, jazz and blues. Instrumentally seamless, lyrical, introspective and consistently arresting, it was one of the finest groups signed in the heady days of late 60s pop and rock. Guitarists Jansch and Renbourne conveyed a delicate, easy-going rapport, while McShee's crystalline vocals compelled with a quiet urgency and the rhythm section of Thompson and Cox was pinpoint and articulate. The band members have done a considerable amount of work outside Pentangle, and the current group is led by Jansch and McShee.

what to buy: There isn't a false step in Pentangle's brief career, though the great albums are available only on import (see Worth Searching For). *Basket of Light* (Reprise/Transatlantic, 1969) is perhaps the most commercially successful effort, yielding two modest hits in the U.K., "Once I Had a Sweetheart" and "Sally Free and Easy."

what to buy next: *Early Classics* (Shanachie, 1992, prod. Various) is a good overview, but the flow and segues from the original recordings are missed.

what to avoid: *Open the Door* (Varrick, 1985, reissued Shanachie, 1985) is a disappointing return after a lengthy absence and holds none of the magic of the early recordings.

the rest: *In the Round* (Varrick, 1986) *So Early in the Spring* (Green Linnet, 1990) *Think of Tomorrow* (Green Linnet, 1991) *People on the Highway (1968-1971)* (Transatlantic, 1992/94)

worth searching for: *The Pentangle,* (Reprise, 1968) is a double album that explores most of the themes on subsequent releases. *Cruel Sister* (Reprise, 1971) introduced electric guitars into the group's arrangements; understated and flowing, its focus is more exclusive of Celtic folk. Both are available as imports on Germany's Line label.

▶▶ Nick Drake, John Martyn, Clannad, the Corrs

◀◀ British folk, Miles Davis, Charlie Parker, Duke Ellington

Patrick McCarty

Pere Ubu

Formed 1975 in Cleveland, Ohio. Disbanded 1982. Re-formed 1987.

David Thomas, aka Crocus Behemoth, vocals; Tom Herman, guitar (1975-79, 1995-present); Peter Laughner, guitar (1975-77); Tim Wright, bass (1975-78); Allen Ravenstine, synthesizer (1975-89); Scott Krauss, drums (1975-82, 1985-95); Tony Maimone, bass (1978-1993); Mayo Thompson, guitar, vocals (1979-85); Anton Fier, drums (1982-85); Jim Jones, guitar (1985-present); Chris Cutler, drums (1985-1989); Eric Drew Feldman, synthesizer (1989-1991); Garo Yellin, cello (1993-95); Michele Temple, bass (1993-present); Robert Wheeler, synthesizer (1995-present); Steven Mehlman, drums (1995-present)

Pere Ubu — named after the hero in the French absurdist play

"Ubu Roi," by Alfred Jarry — released a classic debut single, "30 Seconds Over Tokyo/Heart of Darkness," that prefigured punk rock, then quickly moved on to the more enigmatic terrain staked out by Ravenstine's synthesizer gurgles and Thomas' wheezing, wailing vocals. The group dubbed its synthesis of punk and art-rock "avant-garage," and its early albums were enormously influential, darkly powerful works that barely made a ripple commercially. Ubu disbanded in 1982, only to regroup five years later to pursue a more direct emotional and musical language. "Where do the broken-hearted park their cars?" Thomas asked. By 1995, the group had virtually been remade, with Thomas the sole constant, and began returning to the oblique soundscapes of its '70s albums.

what to buy: *The Modern Dance* (Rough Trade, 1978, prod. Pere Ubu and Ken Hamann) inspired impressionable would-be alt-rockers by the hundreds with Ubu teetering between the hard-rocking perfection of "Non-Alignment Pact" and wiggy noise experiments. *Dub Housing* (Rough Trade, 1978, prod. Pere Ubu and Ken Hamann) is among the most fully realized — and abrasive — post-punk discs ever made, featuring the noise-rock masterpiece "Codex." More instantly accessible to students of punk history is *Terminal Tower: An Archival Collection* (Twin/Tone, 1985, prod. Pere Ubu, Ken Hamann and Paul Hamann), which collects the essential early singles including "Heart of Darkness," "Final Solution" and "30 Seconds Over Tokyo." Of the band's comeback discs, *Cloudland* (Fontana, 1989, prod. Stephen Hague, Paul Hamann, Dave Meegan, Daniel Miller and Rico Conning), is the most ravishing approximation of pop, especially "Waiting for Mary" and "Bus Called Happiness."

what to buy next: *The Tenement Year* (Enigma-Mercury, 1988, prod. Pere Ubu and Paul Hamann) bridges the gap between the band's more experimental first phase and the more accessible sound of *Cloudland One Man Drives While the Other Man Screams* (Rough Trade, 1989, prod. Paul Hamann) offers a live overview of the band's 1978-81 period.

the rest: *New Picnic Time* (Rough Trade, 1979) *The Art of Walking* (Rough Trade, 1981) *390 Degrees of Simulated Stereo* (Rough Trade, 1981) *Songs of the Bailing Man* (Rough Trade, 1982) *Worlds in Collision* (Fontana, 1991) *Story of My Life* (Imago, 1993) *Ray Gun Suitcase* (Tim Kerr, 1995)

worth searching for: The limited edition "The Hearpen Singles" (Tim Kerr Records, 1995, prod. Various), which includes vinyl versions of four early singles—including "30 Seconds Over Tokyo," "Final Solution," "Street Waves" and "The Modern Dance"—with original artwork.

Pixies, Big Black, R.E.M., Husker Du

Stooges, Red Crayola, Can, Henry Cow, Captain Beefheart

Greg Kot

Carl Perkins

Born April 9, 1932 in Tiptonville, Tenn.

Like Bill Haley, his career often boils down to one record—the redoubtable "Blue Suede Shoes"—but Carl Perkins, even more than Elvis, served as a role model for aspiring rockabilly kings. A badly timed car crash on his way to become the second rock 'n' roller ever to appear on the Ed Sullivan show interrupted his career at a crucial juncture, but Perkins churned out a slew of classic sides for Sun Records, a body of work that stands like a mountain in the tiny realm of authentic rockabilly. Like many others, Perkins was a country singer who heard the clarion call of rock 'n' roll on the first Presley record and headed straight for 706 Union Ave. in Memphis to sign up with the suddenly ascendant Sun label. When Sun owner Sam Phillips sold Presley's contract to RCA Victor, he did so under the assumption that he had in Perkins another guy as good as Presley—and maybe even a little better because this one wrote his own songs. But Perkins never followed "Blue Suede Shoes"—his version actually beat Presley's RCA debut, "Heartbreak Hotel," into the Top 10—with anything remotely of that impact. He spent the rest of his career making records that hewed closely to his original artistic vision, while the pop music world quickly left rockabilly—and Perkins—behind. But proof of his enduring legacy could be found in the plans for a 1996 tribute album that included recordings by such admirers as Paul McCartney, George Harrison, John Fogerty, Ringo Starr, Paul Simon, Tom Petty and others.

what to buy: His *Original Sun Greatest Hits* (Rhino, 1986, prod. Various) eloquently makes the case for Perkins as one of rock 'n' roll's greats. The wealth of material he cut in the few short years at Sun runs far deeper than just "Blue Suede Shoes."

what to buy next: Perkins continued to record in the same style for years, without much commercial success, for the Columbia label alongside his Sun compatriot Johnny Cash. *Restless: The Columbia Recordings* (Columbia/Legacy, 1992, prod. Various) chronicles the second decade of Perkins recordings, kind of like rockabilly in exile.

what to avoid: The chintzy *Best Of Carl Perkins* (Curb, 1993), a 10-song rip-off featuring re-recordings of "Blue Suede Shoes" and lesser-known pieces.

the rest: *Jive After Five* (Rhino, 1991) *Carl Perkins and NRBQ: Boppin' the Blues* (Columbia, 1970) *Friends, Family and Legends* (Platinum Records Int., 1992)

worth searching for: The obscure *Carl Perkins On Top* (Columbia, 1969, prod. B. Denny) contains a rare, unreissued track, "Champagne, Illinois," that Perkins co-wrote with Bob Dylan.

▶▶ Ricky Nelson, the Beatles, John Fogerty, the Stray Cats

◀◀ Ernest Tubb, Muddy Waters, Elvis Presley

Joel Selvin

Joe Perry Project

See: Aerosmith

Steve Perry

See: Journey

Pet Shop Boys

Formed in 1983 in London, England

Neil Tennant, vocals; Chris Lowe, instruments

Ex-music journalist Tennant and former architecture student Lowe met and discovered they had a mutual love for Euro-disco and pop. The Pet Shop Boys were born and quickly found a successful formula for their music—sardonic lyrics with hypnotic synthesizer melodies and infectious beats, which led to a parade of hits in the U.K. (though somewhat fewer in the U.S.). The duo still reigns in an area where bands such as the Human League once reigned supreme. They maintain a low profile, seeming unemotional and scheming, with an intuitive sense for blending the artistically subversive and commercially populist. Besides their own music, Tennant and Lowe also lent their skills to diva Liza Minnelli's album *Results* (Epic, 1989).

what to buy: *Discography: The Complete Singles Collection* (EMI, 1991, prod. Various) provides ample evidence of the Pet Shop Boys' fine songwriting and musical sophistication. *Very* (ERG, 1993, prod. Pet Shop Boys) achieves an effective balance between happiness and melancholy.

what to buy next: *Please* (EMI, 1986, prod. Stephen Hague) features the hit singles "West End Girls," "Opportunities (Let's Make Lots of Money)," "Love Comes Quickly" and "Suburbia." *Actually* (Parlophone, 1987, prod. Various) includes Tennant's duet with Dusty Springfield on "What Have I Done to Deserve This," "It's A Sin" and a cover of Elvis Presley's "Always On My Mind."

what to avoid: *Disco* (EMI, 1986, prod. Various) and *Disco 2* (Capitol, 1994, prod. Pet Shop Boys and Harold Faltermeyer) are a pair of tedious remix albums.

the rest: *Behavior* (EMI America, 1990) *Introspective* (EMI America, 1988) *Alternative* (EMI, 1995)

worth searching for: The special edition of *Very* in a textured, orange jewel box. A nice way to own one of the essential titles.

▶▶ Electronic

◀◀ Human League, New Order, The Smiths, Kraftwerk

Anna Glen

Peter and Gordon

Formed 1963 in London, England

Peter Asher, vocals, guitar (born June 22, 1944 in London, England); Gordon Waller, vocals, guitar (born June 4, 1945 in Braemar, Scotland)

This duo crested the first wave of the mid-60s British Invasion. More folk-pop in style, Peter and Gordon's string of hits includes "I Don't Want to See You Again," "I Go to Pieces," "Woman" and "Lady Godiva," all showing off the duo's fine harmonies and charm to spare. The duo called it quits in 1968, and Asher went into the business side of music, handling a luminous roster that includes James Taylor, Linda Ronstadt and 10,000 Maniacs. *The Best of Peter & Gordon* (Rhino 1991, comp. Bill Inglot) is a terrific compilation showcasing top-notch production, Beatlesque arrangements and memorable songs.

Patrick McCarty

Tom Petty and the Heartbreakers

Formed 1975 in Los Angeles, Calif.

Tom Petty (born Oct. 20, 1952 in Gainseville, Fla.), vocals, guitar, keyboards: Mike Campbell, guitar; Benmont Tench, keyboards; Ron Blair, bass (1875-82); Howie Epstein, bass, guitar, vocals (1982-present); Stan Lynch, drums (1975-94); Steve Ferrone, drums (1994-present)

What Album Changed Your Life?

"I think it's Down There on the Ground by Wes Montgomery. That's such a good guitar record; it's moody and just evoked something in me when I was really starting to see that there was something out there. I was living at my parent's house in Alabama, and this music--remember Steve Martin in The Jerk? That's what I was like when I heard that album. That music was speaking to me."

Tommy Shaw (Styx, Damn Yankees)

If a prototype for a cool rock 'n' roll star were ever drawn up, chances are it would look a lot like Petty. He's a bit of a hippie *and* a bit of a punk; the leather-jacketed look of his first album cover looked New Wave, but the songs showed plenty of reverence for his forebears (particularly the jangly guitar sound of the Byrds) while retaining a decidedly modern sensibility. He's equal parts Southern and urbane. Petty is undeniably mainstream, but he's no star-machine conformist: after the giant MCA conglomerate swallowed his original label, Petty held back what would be his breakthrough album, *Damn the Torpedoes*, until he renegotiated an unacceptable deal; and he fought his new label when it wanted to release the follow-up, *Hard Promises*, for $1 more than what was then the standard list price. Ultimately, Petty wins with songs—tuneful, catchy, hard-hitting—and one of the best bands in the business. The Heartbreakers have their roots in Mudcrutch, a Gainesville band they brought west to Los Angeles. The migration was at first unsuccessful and the group split up, but when Campbell and Tench began working with Blair and Lynch, Petty roped them in to become the Heartbreakers. It's been a trying two decades—replete with personnel changes and the unsettling specter of Petty's solo ambitions—but the group has bent and grown together, incorporating mature, rootsy flavorings while still maintaining a admirable cross-generational appeal. And if you ever worry that Petty is losing his adolescent outlook, he comes up with a song like "You Don't Know How it Feels," with its decidedly un-adult "let's roll another joint" sentiments.

what to buy: *Damn the Torpedoes* (Backstreet, 1979, prod. Tom Petty and Jimmy Iovine) ♪♪♪♪♪ bursts forth with all the pent-up energy of Petty's corporate fight prior to its release. "Don't Do Me Like That"—actually a holdover form the old Mudcrutch days—the ferocious "Refugee," the yearning "Even the Losers" and the unapologetically smug "Here Comes My Girl" all sound great coming out of the radio today. *Hard Promises* (Backstreet, 1981, prod. Tom Petty and Jimmy Iovine) ♪♪♪♪♪ is just as good if maybe a touch more mature. "The Waiting" is a winning testament to faith and love, while "Insider"—a duet with Stevie Nicks—is a real heartstring-tugger. Petty's first solo album, *Full Moon Fever*, (MCA, 1989, prod. Jeff Lynne, Tom Petty and Mike Campbell) ♪♪♪♪½ counters its acoustic trappings with the feisty lyrics of "I Won't Back Down" and "Yer So Bad," while "Runnin' Down a Dream" is one of the best rockers he's ever recorded. *Greatest Hits* (MCA, 1993, prod. Various) ♪♪♪♪½ is a generous (18 songs), career-spanning collection that makes a case for Petty's spot in the upper echelon of rock songwriting.

what to buy next: Splurge for *Playback*, (MCA, 1995, prod. Various) ♪♪♪♪½ a whopping five-volume box set that's well worth the price. The first volume alone is crammed with some of the best rock America has to offer, while the voluminous collection of rarities are unusually strong. For individual albums, you can't miss with *You're Gonna Get It*, (Shelter/Gone Gator, 1978, prod. Denny Cordell, Noah Shark and Tom Petty) ♪♪♪♪ the semi-concept album *Southern Accents* (MCA, 1985, prod. Various) ♪♪♪♪ or the under-appreciated *Let Me Up (I've Had Enough)* (MCA, 1987, prod. Tom Petty and Mike Campbell) ♪♪♪½.

what to avoid: There's hardly a clunker in Petty's catalog, but his second solo album, *Wildflowers* (Warner Bros., 1994, prod. Rick Rubin, Tom Petty and Mike Campbell), ♪♪½ is an unusually soft and unfocused work.

the rest: *Tom Petty and the Heartbreakers* (Shelter/Gone Gator, 1976) ♪♪♪ *Pack Up the Plantation* (MCA, 1985) ♪♪♪½ *Into the Great Wide Open* (MCA, 1991) ♪♪½

worth searching for: *Breakdown* (Seagull) and *Straight Into Darkness* (Swingin' Pig) are among the several bootlegs that chronicle the Heartbreakers' raucous live show better than the legitimately released *Pack up the Plantation*.

▶▶ The Plimsouls, Phil Seymour, Georgia Satellites, Pearl Jam, the Wallflowers

The Byrds, Chuck Berry, Del Shannon, Bob Dylan, The Kingsmen, The Outsiders

see also: *The Traveling Wilburys*

Gary Graff

Liz Phair

Born Elizabeth Clark Phair, April 17, 1967 in New Haven, Conn.

The Chicago singer-songwriter's out-of-nowhere debut, *Exile in Guyville*, caught critics' attention for its blunt sexuality, its cryptic but pointed analysis of relationships and its simplistic, barely produced but rocking sound. Phair bared her nipples (partially) on the cover and delighted in saying the F-word, for which she got a lot of press. The album is more compelling, though, because it seizes stereotypical rock machismo and spits it back from a woman's perspective. It's intended as a song-by-song response to the Rolling Stones' classic *Exile on Main Street*, and if you actually take the nerdy step of making a tape alternating the two albums' songs, Phair's social critique of traditional rock becomes interesting and subversive. Also the tunes are damned catchy. Phair's follow-up had its moments, and the modern-rock radio and MTV hit "Supernova" gave her some cash flow, but the much happier album earned more mixed reviews.

what to buy: *Exile in Guyville* (Matador, 1993, prod. Brad Wood and Liz Phair) ♪♪♪♪♪ won the annual Village Voice Pazz & Jop critics' poll. Its best songs, the Stones-grooved "6'1"," the lonely "Fuck and Run" and the buoyant "Soap Star Joe," validate the critical hype.

what to buy next: *Whip-smart* (Matador/Atlantic, 1994, prod. Brad Wood and Liz Phair) ♪♪♪ isn't a sophomore slump, but the tunes aren't quite as memorable—although "Cinco De Mayo" and "Jealousy" were underrecognized.

what to avoid: The eight-song EP *Juvenalia* (Matador, 1995, prod. Various) ♪♪ contains a boring novelty version (with the Chicago power-pop band Material Issue) of the Vapors' racist hit "Turning Japanese" as well as several songs from Phair's pre-*Guyville* debut, the impossible-to-find Girlysound indie tapes, which don't wear well.

worth searching for: *Secretly Timid* (Empire, 1996) ♪♪ a bootleg compilation of her underwhelming Girlysound releases, which provides insight if not much enjoyment.

Alanis Morissette, Ben Lee, Jennifer Trynin, Tracy Bonham

Rolling Stones, Patti Smith, Suzanne Vega, Urge Overkill, Smashing Pumpkins

Steve Knopper

Phantom, Rocker and Slick

See: Stray Cats

Chynna Phillips

See: Wilson Phillips

Sam Phillips

Born Leslie Phillips, 1962 in Los Angeles, Calif.

Phillips walks the line between teenage heartache and womanly wisdom. Sporting a throaty and girlishly seductive voice, she sings familiar lines about strained and failed relationships. What separates her from the dross is her ability to write exacting phrases that cut to the heart of the matter, as well as lovely poetic couplets that lend a surprisingly different perspective on familiar emotions. Phillips began her musical career in 1984 as a Christian rock artist performing under her given name. Under the guidance of her husband and producer, T Bone Burnett, she switched to secular music in 1988. Since then, Phillips has cultivated a sound that shows the strong influence of the Beatles. Her albums are sprightly pop affairs laden with bright guitars and dark atmospherics, a compelling combination that works particularly well with her woman-child persona.

what to buy: *The Indescribable Wow* (Virgin, 1988, prod. T Bone Burnett) ♪♪♪♪♪ is Phillips' stunning secular debut recording. It's the most varied album of her career, offering 60s-influenced pop and lush, heart-wrenching ballads. Many of the tracks here are among Phillips' best work, including "What You Don't Want to Hear," "I Don't Know How to Say Good-bye to You" and "What Do I Do?"

what to buy next: *Martinis & Bikinis* (Virgin, 1994, prod. T-Bone Burnett and Colin Moulding) ♪♪♪♪ shows Phillips emerging as a distinctive songwriter. Despite the obvious Beatles influence here, Phillips imbues the songs with her own pop sensibilities and an original and poetic voice. *Omnipop (It's Only a Flesh Wound, Lambchop)* (Virgin, 1996, prod. T-Bone Burnett) ♪♪♪♪ is a sly and eclectic change-of-pace that revels in its funk to punk to ska to trippy psychedelia. It's nothing we were expecting, which makes it all the better.

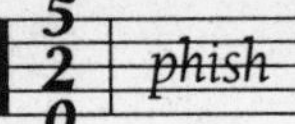

what to avoid: Phillips strays from her pop roots on *Cruel Inventions,* (Virgin, 1991, prod. T-Bone Burnett) and while the results aren't bad, they aren't nearly as stunning as her earlier and later albums. Of the 10 tracks, only a few make the grade ("Tripping Over Gravity," "Where the Colors Don't Go" and "Standing Still") If you must have it all, those cuts will make the album a necessary addition to your collection.

the rest: (As Leslie Phillips): *Recollection* (Myrhh, 1987)

worth searching for: *The Turning* (Myrhh, 1987, prod. Burnett) is Phillips' last album of Christian rock and offers a fascinating look at the singer at the height of her pre-secular career. She fills the tracks with lots of guitars and synthesizers, coming up with a sound not unlike the Eurythmics or, for that matter, Pat Benatar. Although out of print, this album and Phillips' other Christian albums, *Beyond Saturday Night* (Myrhh, 1984) and *Black and White in a Grey World* (Myrhh, 1985), can still be found frequently in Christian bookstores.

Stevie Nicks, Suzanne Vega, Crowded House, Aimee Mann, Juliana Hatfield, Joan Osborne

Bob Dylan, the Beatles, Elvis Costello, Squeeze, the Pretenders, T Bone Burnett, John Hiatt, Fleetwood Mac

Christopher Scapelliti

Phish

Formed 1983 in Burlington, Vt.

Page McConnell, piano, organ, vocals; Trey Anastasio, guitars, vocals; Jon Fishman, drums; Mike Gordon, bass, mandolin, vocals

Now that the Grateful Dead has jammed its last, the race is on to decide which band stands to inherit the Dead's moveable feast of freaks hooked on songs that are little more than excuses to tune in, turn on (optional, of course) and soak up the universe's seemingly limitless supply of grooves. Like the Dead, Phish draws on genres as various as rock, jazz, bluegrass and country, and still like the Dead, the songs are brilliant in their inventiveness one moment and mightily vexing the next. Still, Phish lives for the stage, and the group's studio albums have sometimes phloundered in attempts to recreate the concert vibe. One final comparison to the Dead: Like Jerry & Co., Phish, whose songs tend to meander sometimes for half an hour, has survived and, yes, phlourished, utterly without radio support. Indeed, Phish has been among the vanguard of 90s DIY music marketing, utilizing mailing lists, hotlines and web sites to bolster its devoted following.

what to buy: *A Picture of Nectar* (Elektra, 1992, prod. Phish) is the album on which Phish phights its worst tendencies and wins. The songs are not the band's strongest, perhaps, but the jams are reined in enough to serve instead of shine on their own. The album is stylistically varied as well: "The Landlady" and "Stash" are sparked by subtle Latin touches, while country, cocktail jazz and funk creep in on "Magilla," "Poor Heart" and "Llama," respectively. *A Live One* (Elektra, 1995, prod. Phish) offers justification for Phish phanatics who insist that you gotta see 'em live. With a dozen songs spread over two CDS, the group stretches out without apology, particularly on "Tweezer," which crosses the half-hour mark.

what to buy next: One of the band's earlier efforts, *Lawn Boy* (Absolute A Go Go, 1990/Elektra, 1992, prod. Phish) shows off an appealing sense of humor on the title track, "Bathtub Gin" and "Run Like an Antelope." Two additional strong numbers, "The Squirming Coil" and "Bouncing Around the Room" remain in the group's live repertoire.

what to avoid: *(Hoist)* (Elektra, 1994, prod. Paul Fox) finds the group out of its element, proffering stilted studio constructions in place of its usual road-tested material. "Julius" and "Scent of a Mule" are worth a listen, and the guest list is impressive: Alison Krauss, Bela Fleck, the Tower of Power Horns. But overall, *Hoist* is Phish's least-distinguished album.

the rest: *Junta* (1988/Elektra, 1992) *Lawn Boy Rift* (Elektra, 1993) (with the Dude of Life) : *Crimes of the Mind* (Elektra, 1994)

solo outings:

Trey Anastasio Surrender to the Air (Elektra, 1996)

worth searching for: Phish bootlegs. Any show you want, someone's taped it. Hit the Internet and make your requests.

Spin Doctors, Blues Traveler

The Grateful Dead, Frank Zappa, Sun Ra

Daniel Durchholz

Phranc

Born Susan Gottlieb, August 28, 1957 in Santa Monica, Calif.

Of all the Jewish lesbian folksingers who emerged from the L.A. underground scene, Phranc is probably the best-known. Balancing trenchant political and social commentary with nutty, sweet-natured humor, she writes point-blank folk tunes with a surprising bite. Influenced by traditional Jewish songs, show tunes and such gifted folk farceurs as Allen Sherman, she began playing guitar as a child and was soon entertaining family and friends with her own approach. The unlikely combination of lesbian separatist politics and the male-dominated punk scene, however, helped form her adult identity as a songwriter. After a stint with the seminal underground bands Nervous Gender and Catholic Discipline, she decided to go solo. Opening for punk bands in L.A. clubs, she soon tamed the most unruly crowds with the sheer emotional directness—and wit—of her songs, which she peformed on acoustic guitar. She released a string of albums during the 80s and 90s; despite remaining for the most part a cult artist, Phranc has earned a bit of press and toured as the opener for such like-minded bands as The Smiths. A die-hard Neil Diamond fan, she put on a one-woman revue during which she performed a set of his in "male drag." Any of her releases—*I Enjoy Being a Girl,* (Island, 1989) *Folksinger,* (Island, 1985) *Positively Phranc* (Island, 1991) and *Goofyfoot* (Kill Rock Stars EP, 1995) —offer a fine portal into her distinctive universe.

Simon Glickman

Wilson Pickett

Born March 18, 1941, in Prattville, Ala.

Among all of soul music's throat-shredding testifiers, none could match Pickett. From his earliest recordings as lead vocalist with the Falcons, Pickett's voice was unmistakable in its sheer, unsettling power. But until he was sent off to Memphis in 1965 by Atlantic Records, Pickett had not found the right instrumental backing for chart success. He most definitely found it there; using musicians from the Stax house band and from Muscle Shoals, Pickett unleashed a string of incomparable soul classics—"Mustang Sally," "In The Midnight Hour" and "Funky Broadway" among them. His combination of gospel urgency and sexual swagger earned him the nickname "The Wicked Pickett," as his singles ruled the dance floor. But despite a career-reviving stint with Gamble and Huff's slicker Philadelphia sound during the early 70's, the hits soon stopped coming. Though the wicked side of Pickett gets him more press these days than his music (he has a fondness for guns, it seems), he still stands as one of the soul era's greatest vocalists.

what to buy: Pickett's best has been thoroughly and admirably documented on the two-CD set *Wilson Pickett: A Man And A Half* (Rhino/Atlantic, 1992, prod. Various) Beginning in 1961 with Pickett's vocalizing on "I Found A Love" by The Falcons, this collection offers the comprehensive journey through the Atlantic years, the Philadelphia sides and culminates with a live 1971 performance of "Funky Broadway" from a show in Ghana. And there are a few unreleased songs, alternate versions and rare live cuts along the way. If you just want the hits and nothing more, *The Very Best Of Wilson Pickett* (Rhino, 1993, prod. Various) is where to find them on one tight CD.

what to buy next: Of the earlier Atlantic albums available on CD, *The Exciting Wilson Pickett* (Atlantic, 1966, prod. Jerry Wexler) and *The Sound of Wilson Pickett* (Atlantic, 1967, prod. Tom Dowd) are the best. *Wilson Pickett In Philadelphia* (Atlantic, 1970, prod. Gamble & Huff) is the great soul shouter's final outstanding album.

what to avoid: *Mr. Magic Man* (RCA, 1973) the voice is still there, but this is the beginning of Pickett's slide into uninspired mediocrity.

the rest: *In The Midnight Hour* (Atlantic, 1965) *Wicked Pickett* (Atlantic, 1966) *Wilson Pickett's Greatest Hits* (Atlantic, 1973)

worth searching for: *American Soul Man* (Motown, 1987), a brief stop at the legendary Detroit R&B label that finds Pickett in good voice—perhaps inspired by the hallowed surroundings.

▶▶ Bobby Womack, Teddy Pendergrass, The Commitments

◀◀ The Swan Silvertones, The Soul Stirrers, Hank Ballard & The Midnighters

Doug Pippin

Michael Pinder

See: Moody Blues

Pink Floyd

Formed 1965 in London, England

Roger Keith (Syd) Barrett, guitar and vocals (1965-69); David Gilmour, guitar and vocals (1968-present); Nick Mason, drums; Roger Waters, bass and vocals (1965-84); Richard Wright (1965-82, 1987-present)

Syd Barrett named Pink Floyd for two bluesmen—Pink Anderson and Floyd Council—but the closest the band came to the blues was the demeanor of its lyrics. The Floyd was among the first of Britain's post-"Sgt. Pepper's" groups, riding the psychedelic pop wave with hits such as "Arnold Layne" and "See

Emily Play" before evolving into the more space-age, tripped-out fury of "Astronomy Domine" and "Interstellar Overdrive." Barrett tripped himself out of the band before long, and the Floyd evolved yet again into a more ethereal, ambient style that was enhanced by the group's high-tech, multi-media stage shows.

The zenith of this was *Dark Side of the Moon,* one of rock's most original and durable epics. Driven by Waters' bleak lyrical outlook, each succeeding album was a thematic work, examining insanity, fascism, societal decay and other social and political issues. *The Final Cut* was largely a Waters solo album, after which he decided Pink Floyd was over. But the other Floyds, particularly Gilmour, weren't quite ready to pack it in, and they continued—fending off Waters' legal and verbal attacks while packing stadiums around the world. The rift hadn't healed by the time Pink Floyd was inducted into the Rock and Roll Hall of Fame in 1996 (Waters didn't show), but rest assured that all concerned are benefiting handsomely from the group's continuing activity.

what to buy: *Dark Side of the Moon* (Harvest, 1973, prod. Pink Floyd) is the essential piece, a seamless and inventive song cycle bolstered by a three-dimensional soundscape of instruments and special effects—not to mention some first-rate songs like "Money," "Us and Them" and "Time." *Wish You Were Here* (Columbia, 1975, prod. Pink Floyd) is just as good and a touch more organic, highlighted by the extended piece "Shine On You Crazy Diamond." *The Wall* (Columbia, 1979, prod. Waters, Gilmour, Bob Ezrin) is another masterful concept piece that, despite its length, housed more solid songs such as "Comfortably Numb," "Goodbye Blue Sky" and Pink Floyd's biggest hit, "Another Brick in the Wall (Part II)." No collection is complete without a piece of Pink Floyd's early days, and *The Piper at the Gates of Dawn* (Capitol, 1967, prod. Norman Smith) fits the bill, even if it now sounds a bit dated.

what to buy next: *Meddle* (Harvest, 1971, prod. Pink Floyd) captures Pink Floyd at a crucial, formative juncture just before *Dark Side's* breakthrough. *Works,* (Capitol, 1983, prod. Various) is a useful collection of early singles and album tracks. *The Division Bell* (Columbia, 1994, prod. Gilmour, Ezrin) shows that the post-Waters Pink Floyd still has something to offer.

what to avoid: *A Collection of Great Dance Songs* (Columbia, 1981, prod. Various) is a misbegotten compilation that's only worthwhile for the wonderfully ironic title.

the rest: *A Saucerful of Secrets* (Harvest, 1968); *Tonite Let's All Make Love in London* soundtrack (Columbia, 1968); *Ummagumma* (Harvest, 1969); *More* soundtrack (Harvest, 1969); *Atom Heart Mother* (Harvest, 1970); *Relics* (Harvest, 1971); *Obscured by Clouds* soundtrack (Harvest, 1972); *Animals* (Columbia, 1977); *The Final Cut* (Columbia, 1983); *A Momentary Lapse of Reason* (Columbia, 1987); *Delicate Sound of Thunder* (Columbia, 1988); *Pulse* (Columbia, 1995).

worth searching for: *Shine On* (Columbia, 1992) is as lavish—and expensive—as box sets come. Eight of Pink Floyd's titles are included, as well as an extra disc of early singles and a hardcover book. An easy way to attain an instant Pink Floyd collection.

solo outings:

David Gilmour *David Gilmour* (Columbia, 1978) *About Face* (Columbia, 1984)

Nick Mason *Nick Mason's Fictitious Sports* (Columbia, 1981) *Profiles* (Columbia, 1985)

Roger Waters *The Pros and Cons of Hitch Hiking* (Columbia, 1984) *Radio K.A.O.S.* (Columbia, 1987) *The Wall: Live in Berlin* (Mercury, 1990) *Amused to Death* (Columbia, 1992)

Richard Wright *Wet Dream' (Harvest, 1978)* Identity *(Harvest, 1984)*

▶▶ Genesis, Roxy Music, Kansas, Focus, The Orb, Orbital

◀◀ Early British blues and jazz, the Beatles, the Beach Boys

see also: Syd Barrett

Gary Graff

Gene Pitney

Born Feb. 17, 1941, in Hartford, Conn.

Pitney had some huge hits during the early 60s, thanks to a vibrant but pained tenor that could give the hearstrings a pretty good tug. Unlike many pop singers of his day, Pitney wrote many of his own songs, established his own record company (Musicor) and worked easily in a variety of styles and with a diversity of artists, including songwriters Burt Bacharach and Hal David (who wrote his wrenching hit "Only Love Can Break a Heart"), the Rolling Stones and George Jones. Pitney was much bigger in Europe than in the U.S., so he concentrated his recording and touring efforts there by the mid-60s. The resilient singer had a No. 1 hit in the U.K. as recently as 1988 ("Something Gotten Hold of My Heart," a collaboration with Marc Almond) and made a triumphant return to the U.S. in 1993 with a sold-out show at Carnegie Hall. Mostly a singles artist, Pitney has wracked up more than 20 hits during his career.

what to buy: There is no definitive Pitney collection that deftly covers the singer's long and varied career. The one that comes closest is *More Greatest Hits,* (Varese Vintage, 1995, prod. Various) ♪♪♪ which rounds up 19 re-mastered versions of Pitney's biggest hits, including "Town Without Pity," "(The Man Who Shot) Liberty Valance," "Only Love Can Break a Heart" and the more recent "Something's Gotten Hold of My Heart."

what to buy next: *Anthology (1961-1968)* (Rhino, 1991, prod. Various) ♪♪♪ sums up his most prolific period, the 60s, with the obvious hits but also Pitney's versions of hits he wrote for other artists, including Ricky Nelson's "Hello Mary Lou."

what to avoid: With just 10 songs, *Greatest Hits* (Curb, 1995, prod. Various) ♪♪ is far too skimpy, particularly compared to what else is available.

the rest: *Best of Gene Pitney* (K-Tel International, 1991) ♪♪ *Best of Gene Pitney* (Laserlight Digital, 1995) ♪♪ *Best of Gene Pitney* (Delta, date N/A) ♪♪ *Great Gene Pitney* (Goldies, date N/A) ♪♪ *Greatest Hits* (Evergreen, date N/A) ♪♪ *Greatest Hits Vol. 1 and 2* (Eclipse, date N/A) ♪♪ *His Golden Classics* (Collectables, date N/A) ♪♪ *The Collection* (Griffin, date N/A) ♪♪ *The Great Recordings* (Tomato, date N/A) ♪♪

⏩ Soft Cell, Chris Isaak

⏪ George Jones, Johnny Ray

Doug Pullen

The Pixies

Formed 1986 in Boston, Mass. Disbanded 1993.

Black Francis, a.k.a. Frank Black (born Charles Michael Kitteridge Thompson IV), guitar and vocals; Kim Deal (a.k.a. Mrs. John Murphy), bass and vocals; Joey Santiago, lead guitar; David Lovering, drums

At a time when rock's more subversive talents (chief among them, Elvis Costello and Joe Jackson) had been declawed, defanged and preened for mainstream acceptance, the Pixies embraced the raucous chaos at rock's very core: squealing guitars, passable musicianship, sly humor and disturbingly sodomistic lyrics. As a result, the group brought lively unpredictability to a genre homogenized by commercial interests, giving new hope to the musically disenfranchised. (Nirvana, for example, cited the Pixies as an influence.) As the group's main songwriter, Francis crafted short, punchy songs that alternate the noisy anarchy of thrash punk with the melodicism of surf-rock and pop. His lyrics (which frequently incorporate Spanish) are a ride down a decaying Route 66—a cultural malaise of sex, religion, and mutilation that speaks reams about the growing fragmentation of America, always earning a wry smile for the effort.

Signed by Britain's alternative label 4AD in 1987, the Pixies became a favorite of the college circuit, eventually scoring a minor hit in 1989 with the single "Here Comes Your Man." With its final album, 1991's *Trompe Le Monde,*the band was looking more and more like a solo project for Francis, and in early 1993 its members split. Francis went solo three months later under the name Frank Black, Lovering joined Cracker and Deal threw her efforts into her side band, the Breeders.

what to buy: A mini-album born out of eight demos financed by Francis' father, *Come on Pilgrim* (4AD/Rough Trade, 1988, prod. Gary Smith) ♪♪♪♪♪ is a bold debut that put the Pixies firmly on its own terra firma. "Ed is Dead" and "The Holiday Song" are headshakingly hooky, while "Isla de Encanta" and "Vamos" are hip little gems fueled by potent rhythms and Francis' effective (and humorous) employment of Spanish. The Pixies' third album, *Doolittle* (4AD/Elektra, 1989, prod. Gil Norton) ♪♪♪♪ is as close to mainstream as the group ever got. Producer Norton smoothed out the band's rough edges and endearing inconsistencies to craft an album that's never quite punk, never quite pop. Frenetic rants like "Debaser" and "Monkey Gone to Heaven" serve up infectious choruses, while seemingly innocuous tunes like "Here Comes Your Man" and "La La Love You" show Francis' finely tuned schizophrenic pop sensibilities present and accounted for.

what to buy next: *Surfer Rosa* (4AD/Rough Trade, 1988, prod. Steve Albini) ♪♪♪♪ is a free-for-all of thrashing punk and innovative pop that still sounds fresh today. Tracks like Deal's "Gigantic" and Francis' "Bone Machine" harness a manic energy that delights time and time again. (Note: The import version adds the eight tracks from *Come On Pilgrim.*)

what to avoid: *Bossa Nova* (4AD/Elektra, 1990, prod. Gil Norton) is a surprisingly lackluster followup to the brilliance of "Doolittle," a smug bit of self-indulgence that just sounds bad.

the rest: *Trompe Le Monde* (4AD/Elektra, 1993) ♪♪

worth searching for: The Japanese version of "Trompe Le

Monde," which adds four live tracks —"Bone Machine," "Cactus," "Debaser" and "Gouge Away."

solo outings:

Kim Deal: (with the Breeders) Pod (4AD/Elektra, 1990) *Safari (4AD/Elektra, 1991)* *Last Splash (4AD/Elektra, 1993)* *(with The Amps) Pacer (Elektra, 1995)*

▶▶ Dinosaur Jr., The Feelies, The Flaming Lips, My Bloody Valentine, Nirvana, Sonic Youth, Throwing Muses, Belly, Weezer, The Lemonheads, The Sugarcubes, Husker Du

◀◀ Dick Dale & His Del-Tones, the Ventures, The Velvet Underground, Iggy Pop, The Ramones

see also: *Frank Black, Cracker*

Christopher Scapelliti

Pizzicato Five

Formed 1984, Tokyo, Japan

Yasuharu Konishi composer/concept; Maki Nomiya, vocals, style (1991-present); K-Taro Takanami, composer/concept (1984-95)

This Japanese duo is really more of a conceptual-art piece-in-progress than a rock band. Konishi formed P5 in the mid-80s as an outlet for his fascination with Western pop (especially 70s soul music), sampling snatches of music and creating whacked-out sound collages for dance-crazed Tokyo-ites. He met his perfect visual foil in Nomiya, whose jones for high fashion and low culture includes a dizzying number of costume changes during the group's rare performances. America was finally introduced to P5's filtered view of America through an indie label, Matador, which released a compilation of Japanese hits, *Made in USA*, in 1994. Matador's major-label mentors, Atlantic, helped give the next year's CD, *The Sound of Music By...* a bigger push, as well as getting it placed in the documentary about fashion designer Isaac Mizrahi.

Give the group a cursory listen and you'll swear you've heard all their music before—probably during the 70s—but upon closer listening, you'll find the songs are all original, even if they evoke another time and place. The group's cultural pilfering doesn't just stop at musical references and retro clothing; each release is a conceptual art piece in itself, with extravagant packaging and chatchkas like a "Carte Pizzicato" club member card enclosed with the second U.S. release. (The Japanese version of P5 releases are even more complex in their packaging.)

what to buy: *Made in USA* (Matador, 1994, prod. Pizzicato Five) *The Sound of Music By Pizzicato Five* (Matador/Atlantic, 1995, prod. Pizzicato Five)

worth searching for: Any of the many Japanese import singles and albums, including *Overdose* (Triad/Nippon Columbia, 1994, prod. Pizzicato Five), which includes the Japanese version of "Happy Sad." Also, the U.S. CD-single of *Happy Sad* (Matador/Atlantic, 1995) includes both the English "Single Mix" and Japanese "Hot Wax Mix" versions of the song.

▶▶ Dee-Lite, St. Etienne, Esquivel

◀◀ Esquivel, James Bond movie themes, Sly & the Family Stone, disco

Gil Asakawa

Plainsong

See: Iain Matthews

Robert Plant

Born Robert Anthony Plant, Aug. 20, 1948, in Bromwich, Staffordshire, England

Plant left home at 16, released a couple of singles and went through the ranks of such colorful local bands as The New Memphis Bluesbreakers, The Crawling King Snakes, Black Snake Moan, The Banned, The Delta Blues Band and the Band of Joy, the latter featuring future Led Zeppelin drummer John Bonham. Yardbirds guitar star Jimmy Page was looking for a frontman for his new band and turned up at a Hobbstweedle gig one night in 1968. Page was immediately knocked out by the 20-year-old singer's good looks and sexually charged singing. And for the next 12 years, as Led Zeppelin's lead singer, Plant embodied rock's Golden God fantasy and fashioned a prototypical look for hard rock singers, from his poses to his testosterone-fueled cries of "Baby, baby, bay-beeee!" After Led Zeppelin splintered, Plant launched the most ambitious of all Led Zeppelin solo careers, exploring a variety of new musical directions—World Music, ambient pop, rockabilly—without ever leaving his Zep-style pomp. He also regularly tested the Led Zep waters, reuniting with Page and John Paul Jones for one-off gigs or sampling the group's music in his songs. In 1994, he made the plunge and got back together with Page for an extended reunion.

what to buy: Teaming with guitarist Robbie Blunt, a childhood friend, Plant began his solo career with *Pictures at Eleven*, (Swan Song, 1982, prod. Robert Plant) an album that rocks hard but also pursues some of the same ambient directions of later Led Zeppelin albums. His next album, *Principle of Moments* (Es Paranza, 1983, prod. Robert Plant, Benji Lefevre and Pat Moran), offered more of a departure by way of moody, textured tracks such as "Big Log" and "In the Mood."

what to buy next: *Now and Zen* (Es Paranza, 1989, prod. Robert Plant, Tim Palmer and Phil Johnstone) found Plant re-embracing his Led Zep roots after determinedly straying from them for several years. He samples some Zep pieces on "Tall Cool One," while Page solos on that song and on "Heaven Knows." *The Honeydrippers, Volume One* (Es Paranza, 1984) is a spirited five-song oldies workout that features Page and Jeff Beck on guitar

what to avoid: The socially conscious *Fate of Nations* (Es Paranza, 1993, prod. Chris Hughes and Robert Plant) is an inconsistent outing, the weakest of Plant's strong solo career.

the rest: *Shaken 'N' Stirred* (Es Paranza, 1985) *Manic Nirvana* (Es Paranza, 1990)

worth searching for: The vinyl 12-inch single for "Burning Down One Side" (Swan Song, 1982, prod. Robert Plant) from *Pictures at Eleven* features the non-album track "Far Post," a fine song that's well worth owning.

▶▶ David Coverdale, Axl Rose, Vince Neil, Bret Michaels

◀◀ Donovan, Tim Hardin, Little Richard, Keith Relf, Muddy Waters, Howlin' Wolf

see also: *Led Zeppelin, Page/Plant*

Sarah Weber

The Platters

Formed 1953 in Los Angeles, Calif.

Tony Williams, lead vocals (1953-60); David Lynch, tenor vocals; Herbert Reed, bass, vocals; Alex Hodge (1953-54), baritone, vocals; Zola Taylor, contralto vocals (1954-61); Paul Robi, baritone vocals (1955-62); Sonny Turner, lead vocals (1961-65); Nate Nelson, baritone vocals (1962-65); Sandra Dawn, contralto vocals (1962-65)

From 1955-60, few vocal groups could touch the Platters' crossover appeal. Featuring Williams' heart-rending lead vocals, the group had several smash hits which are now inarguable classics of the genre. "Only You," "The Great Pretender" and "Smoke Gets in Your Eyes" remain piercing examples of head-over-heels romantic R&B. Williams' total emotional immersion in the material is nothing less than overwhelming. As the 60s wore on, numerous member changes effectively stalled the former hit-makers. The 70s were marked by court battles over ownership of the group's name; the rights are now held by Robi's widow. The group was inducted into the Rock and Roll Hall of Fame in 1990..

what to buy: *The Very Best of the Platters* (Mercury, 1991, comp. Bill Levenson) hits the highlights from these tremulous masters of melodrama in a single-disc package. It's the perfect introduction.

what to buy next: *The Magic Touch—An Anthology* (Mercury, 1991, comp. Harry Weinger) is a more complete two-disc set that includes many lesser-known tracks, making it a more definitive album for those already acquainted.

what to avoid: *Greatest Hits Vol. 2*, (Curb Records, 1996, prod. Various) a skimpy collection devoid of the biggest hits.

the rest: *Christmas With The Platters* (Mercury, 1994) *Greatest Hits* (Special Music Company, date N/A) *The Platters* (King, date N/A) *Golden Hits Collection* (Pickwick, 1993) *The Musicor Years* (Kent, 1994)

worth searching for: *Four Platters and One Lovely Dish*, (Bear Family, 1994, prod. Various) a typical whole-hog, nine-disc set that should appeal to the ultra-completists.

▶▶ New Edition, Boyz II Men, Huey Lewis & the News

◀◀ the Ink Spots, Bobby Bland

Allan Orski

PM Dawn

Formed 1990 in Jersey City, N.J.

Prince Be (born Attrell Cordes); DJ Minutemix (born Jarrett Cordes)

"Reality Used to Be a Friend of Mine" is the anthem that put PM Dawn on the map; it could also serve as a label for the duo's metaphysical raps and musings. Some take its hippy dippy attitude as an influence from De La Soul, which has since taken on a more hardcore image. But in music, the tent is big, and the otherworldly excursions of PM Dawn add another spoke to the wheel. Paradoxically, PM Dawn broke in during the height of gangsta rap with *Of the Heart, of the Soul and the Cross: The Utopian Experience* (Gee Street/Island, 1991, prod. PM Dawn) with its 60s pop samples and Prince Be's crooning bona fide soul between throwing down rhymes. *The Bliss Album...?* (Gee Street/Island, 1993, prod. PM Dawn) proves inspired musicianship, whatever the genre, though "Beyond Infi-

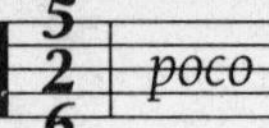

nite Affections" and "Nocturnal Is in the House" prove the duo can throw down when the challenge rises. But the poppish psychedelia wears thin on *Jesus Wept*, (Gee Street/Island, 1995, prod. PM Dawn) ♪♪♪ even though "My Personal Gravity" hit airwaves with its haunting "What could be lonely 'bout you?" line.

Lawrence Gabriel

Poco

Formed 1968 in Los Angeles, Calif.

Rusty Young, pedal steel, vocals (1968-84, 1989-present); Richie Furay, guitar, vocals (1968-73, 1989-91); Jim Messina, guitar, vocals, 1968-70, 1989-91); Randy Meisner, bass, vocals, (1968-69, 1989-91); Timothy B. Schmit, bass, vocals (1969-77); George Grantham, drums, vocals (1968-77); Paul Cotton, guitar, vocals, 1970-84; Steve Chapman, drums (1977-84); Kim Bullard, keyboards, (1977-84); Charlie Harrison, bass (1977-84)

Of all the original groups that tried to combine rock and country music in the wake of the Byrds' *Sweethearts of the Rodeo* album, Poco went farthest in creating a new kind of sound. Instead of just singing with a twang and adding pedal steel (they did those, too), Poco's members incorporated elements of bluegrass music but sang with a high-pitched fever that was matched by the group's electric performances, both on record and on stage. These guys just never sounded like a mere folk-rock band (except for in its later, more commercial years). Founded by former Buffalo Springfield members Messina and Furay, the group recruited several Colorado musicians—Meisner (who left before the first album came out), pedal steel specialist Young (who brought a rock mentality to what was still considered a country instrument) and Grantham—and cut loose for a handful of breathless albums before attrition and a changing radio climate tamed the sound.

Meisner was the first out, joining Rick Nelson's band, then Linda Ronstadt's, then the Eagles (he was replaced by Schmit, who later left to replace Meisner again, in the Eagles). Messina followed his muse to a successful duo career with Kenny Loggins. Furay left to form a "supergroup," the Souther Hillman Furay Band, and now is a pastor in Boulder, Colo. Latter-day releases under Rusty Young's leadership are likable pop albums, with big production touches including horns and synthesizer strings on hits such as "Heart of the Night," "Keep on Tryin'" and "Crazy Love." Watch for Young's new career as one of the co-leaders of Sky Kings, a new group featuring Bill Lloyd and John Cowan. The original Poco lineup reformed in 1989 for the *Legacy* recording and tour.

what to buy: The group's purity of vision is still clear as a bell, 25 years later, on *Poco* (Epic, 1970, prod. Jim Messina) ♪♪♪♪. The album's sound is driven by Furay's cutting tenor, which gives the record a sonic edge that other country rockers didn't have. Even the harmonies are unbelievably high. But the music rocks (and also gets churchy when it needs to), and makes cool use of Young's pedal steel without ever sounding like a rock imitation of country music. *Deliverin'* (Epic, 1971, prod. Jim Messina) ♪♪♪♪ is the live flipside and shows how powerful a live group Poco was, even at its start.

what to buy next: *The Very Best of Poco* (Epic, 1975, prod. Various) ♪♪♪♪ is a good choice—a non-stop fun-fest and a great overview of Poco's strengths up to mid-career. As for Poco's later work, after *Rose of Cimarron* (ABC, 1976, prod. Poco and Mark Harman) ♪♪♪ the band sounded increasingly more pedestrian and middle-of-the-road despite its original uniqueness. Then again, this is the period when the big hits came—go figure. *Crazy Loving, The Best of Poco 1975-1982* (MCA, 1989, prod. Various) ♪♪♪ is a lean, no-fat collection of those pop chartmakers.

what to avoid: *Legacy* (RCA, 1989, prod. David Cole) was a calculated move at reigniting the fan base with an reunion of original members, but the music was so cynically aimed at middle-of-the-road radio. One of the hits (there were two) was co-written by lame-o rocker Richard Marx.

the rest: *Pickin' Up the Pieces* (Epic, 1969) ♪♪♪ *From the Inside* (Epic, 1971) ♪♪♪ *A Good Feelin' To Know* (Epic, 1972) ♪♪♪ *Crazy Eyes* (Epic, 1973) ♪♪♪ *Seven* (Epic, 1974) ♪♪♪ *Cantamos* (Epic, 1974) ♪♪♪ *Head Over Heels* (Epic, 1975) ♪♪♪ *Live* (Epic, 1976) ♪♪ *Indian Summer* (ABC, 1977) ♪♪♪ *Legend* (ABC, 1978) ♪♪ *Under the Gun* (MCA, 1980) ♪♪ *Blue and Gray* (MCA, 1981) ♪♪ *Cowboys and Englishmen* (MCA, 1982) ♪♪ *Ghost Town* (Atlantic, 1982) ♪♪ *Inamorata* (Atlantic, 1984) ♪♪ *The Forgotten Trail 1969-1974* (double-CD collection) (Epic/Legacy, 1990, prod. Various).

worth searching for: The CD single for "Call It Love" (RCA, 1989, prod. David Cole) ♪♪, not so much for the fairly pedestrian song but for the arresting, fold-out graphics that feature a cut-out of the Poco horse emblem on the cover.

solo outings:

Richie Furay (with Souther, Hillman, Furay Band) *The Souther, Hillman, Furay Band* (Asylum, 1974) ♪♪♪, *Trouble in Paradise* (Asylum, 1975) ♪♪♪ (with Richie Furay Band) *I've Got a Reason* (Asylum, 1976) ♪♪

Jim Messina *Oasis* (Columbia 1979) *Messina* (Warner Bros., 1981)

Rusty Young: (with the Sky Kings) *The Sky Kings (Warner/Reprise, 1996)*

New Grass Revival, Foster & Lloyd, Alison Krauss & Union Station, Uncle Tupelo, Son Volt, Wilco

Flatt & Scruggs, Everly Brothers, the Byrds, Flying Burrito Brothers, Buffalo Springfield

see also: *The Eagles, Loggins and Messina*

Gil Asakawa

The Pogues /Shane MacGowan and The Popes

Formed 1982 in London, England

Peter "Spider" Stacy, vocals, pennywhistle; Jeremy "Jem" Finger, banjo, guitar; Shane MacGowan, vocals (1982-91); Joe Strummer, vocals, guitar, (1991-93); James Fearnley, accordion (1982-93); James McNally, accordion (1993-present); Philip Chevron, guitar (1984-93); Jamie Clarke, guitar (1993-present); Andrew Ranken, drums; Cait O'Riordan, bass (1982-86); Darryl Hunt (1986-present)

The Pogues inject the bile of punk rock into traditional Celtic folk music. And at its best—with the brilliant gutter-poet Shane MacGowan on lead vocals—the band was one of England's most original rock acts. But MacGowan, a career alcoholic, became increasingly unstable and left the band in 1991. With Stacy now handling lead vocals, the Pogues are a decent Celtic rock outfit, but hardly the revolutionary group it was in the past.

what to buy: *Rum, Sodomy & the Lash* (MCA, 1985, prod. Elvis Costello) is MacGowan and the Pogues at the group's peak, thrashing through punk workouts such as "The Sock Bed of Cuchulainn" and switching easily into ballads like "And the Band Played Waltzing Matilda."

what to buy next: MacGowan was still in fine form on *If I Should Fall From Grace With God,* (Island, 1988, prod. Steve Lillywhite) especially his brawling duet with Kirsty MacColl on "Fairy tale of New York." But you could practically smell the whiskey in his slurred vocals on *Peace and Love* (Island, 1989, prod. Steve Lillywhite), a still-strong effort that foreshadowed a downhill stumble to follow.

what to avoid: *Pogue Mahone,* (Mesa, 1995, prod. Steve Brown) a pleasant but all-too-safe post-MacGowan effort.

the rest: *Red Roses For Me* (Enigma, 1984) *Poguetry in Motion* (MCA EP, 1986) *Hell's Ditch* (Island, 1990) *Yeah, Yeah, Yeah, Yeah* (Island, 1990) *Essential Pogues* (Island, 1991) *Waiting for Herb* (Chameleon, 1993)

worth searching for: The soundtrack for "Straight to Hell" (Enigma Classics, 1987), which features the Pogues version of Ennio Morricone's theme for "The Good, the Bad and the Ugly" as well as the traditional "Danny Boy."

solo outings:

Shane MacGowan & the Popes *The Snake* (ZTT/Warner Bros., 1995)

The Drovers, the Levellers, the Cranberries

The Clancy Brothers, the Clash, the Chieftains, the Sex Pistols

Thor Christensen

Poi Dog Pondering

Formed 1984 Wai Ki Ki, Hawaii

Frank Orrall, guitar, vocals; Dave "Max" Crawford, keyboards, trumpet, accordion; Susan Voeltz, violin; Brigid Murphy (saxophone); Dag Julan, guitar.

The first question everyone asks is "Where did the name come from?" The answer; from the Hawaiian food Poi, a sort of regional fruit staple—kind of like mashed potatoes on the mainland. The term "Poi Dog" is a Hawaiian slang term for mixed breed or mutt. Seeing themselves as a bit of a thinking mixed-breed of musicians, Poi Dog Pondering was the perfect name. The group kicked around for several years as a street band in Hawaii before attacking the rest of the country. On the way, they picked up new members in California and Austin, until they eventually ended up in New York. There, they signed a deal with Texas Hotel records and were quickly picked up by Columbia. After three albums and an EP, Columbia dropped the band and PDP created its own record company, Pomegranate.

Its lineup over the years has included more than 30 different musicians, and the sound has remained an exciting combination of roots rock, world music, techno-dance and disco blended with classically styled arrangements. PDP is more of a modern rock orchestral troupe (with a horn section, strings, keyboards, guitars, bass, drums, percussionists and soulful background vocals) than a conventional rock band. Its lyrical content may be as simple as what's for breakfast and the joys of walking, or as complex as the embracing of one's mortality and the beauty of love. While so many ingredients could convolute a band, PDP succeeds brilliantly.

What toBuy: *Volo Volo* (Columbia, 1992, prod. Various), their third and final full-length record with Columbia, best displays the full extent of this band's talents and is wonderfully team-produced by Orall, ex-Talking Head Jerry Harrison and many others. "Lackluster" and "Jack Ass Ginger" showcase their strong horn section and funky bass lines for a contagiously fun and danceable side, while songs like "Collarbone" showcase Voeltz's amazingly haunting violin layered over a light acoustic guitar and keyboards.

what to buy next: The debut album, *Poi Dog Pondering* (Columbia Records 1989, prod. Poi Dog Pondering and Mike Stewart), captures the PDP energy and fun before the big-time producers really got involved. "Wood Guitar" displays their louder, rocking side, while "Pulling Touch" is quite possibly their most beautiful and perfect song.

what to avoid: *Pomegranate* (Pomegranate, 1995, prod. Frank Orrall, Martin Stebbing and Poi Dog Pondering.). Since they re-located to Chicago in the early 90's, PDP performed and experimented in small clubs, adding a bit of disco as well as some classically arranged strings to the already stellar repertoire. The response to the new music performed live was more than enthusiastic, but the album is a disappointment. The production is flat, burying great guitar hooks and dramatic drum sweeps while turning up the hokey saxophone solo's reminiscent of Kenny G.

the rest: *Wishing like a Mountain and Thinking like the Sea* (Columbia, 1990, prod. Poi Dog Pondering & Mike Stewart)

worth searching for: The out-of-print *Fruitless* (Columbia EP, 1990), which contains an amazing cover of New Order's "Love Vigilantes" that's alone worth the search, as well as live versions of "Wood Guitar" and "Falling."

solo outings:

Palm Fabric Orchestra Vague Gropings in the Slip Stream (Carrot Top Records 1994, prod. Frank Orrall)

Future References: Rusted Root, Dave Matthews Band

Roots: Talking Heads, Van Morrison, The Pogues, The Waterboys, Paul Simon

Joshua Zarov

Poison

Formed 1983 in Harrisburg, Pa.

Bret Michaels (born Bret Michael Sychak), vocals, guitar; Matt Smith, guitar (1983-85); Bobby Dall (born Robert Kuy Kendall), bass, vocals; Rikki Rockett (born Richard Ream), drums; C.C. Deville (born Bruce Anthony Johannesson), guitar, vocals (1985-92); Richie Kotzen, guitar (1992-93); Blues Saraceno, guitar (1992)

The title of Poison's debut, *Look What the Cat Dragged In*, summed up the attitude of this makeup-wearing, hairspray loving 80s pop-metal band. Michaels, underneath his long, blonde, Motley Crue-like hair, was an equally charismatic and cynical frontman who carried his band to the top of the pop charts. Poison had many massive '80s hits, including the power ballad "Every Rose Has Its Thorn," which hit No. 1 in 1988, and "Unskinny Bop," No. 3 in 1990. But, like all the other hair metal bands, Poison found itself without an audience during the early 90s and, despite a desperate shift of personnel, faded into trivia.

what to buy: *Look What the Cat Dragged In* (Capitol, 1986, prod. Ric Browde) sold 3 million copies with the strength of hits such as "Talk Dirty to Me," "I Want Action" and "I Won't Forget You."

what to avoid: *Open Up and Say . . . Ahh!* (Enigma/Capitol, 1988, prod. Tom Werman) is a rehash of Poison's debut.

the rest: *Flesh and Blood* (Enigma/Capitol, 1990) *Swallow This Live* (Capitol, 1991) *Native Tongue* (Capitol, 1993)

▶▶ Winger, Warrant, Ratt, Cry of Love

◀◀ AC/DC, Kiss, Kansas, Journey

Tracey Birkenhauer and Steve Knopper

The Police

Formed 1977 in London, England. Disbanded 1984.

Sting (born Gordon Sumner), bass, vocals, saxophone, keyboards; Stewart Copeland, drums; Henri Pandovani, guitar (1977); Andy Summers (born Andrew Somers), guitar

Though they arrived amid the fury of England's punk revolution, the members of the Police, while not actual punks themselves, played them on TV. By bleaching their hair so they could appear in a bubblegum commercial, the band may have called its credibility into question from the very beginning, but the fact is, their ability to write songs and actually play their instruments wouldn't have curried much favor in the D.I.Y. era anyway. With musical pasts ranging from jazz (Sting) to prog-rock (Copeland) to all manner of session work (Summers), the Police focused on white reggae (*Reggetta de Blanc* as their second album's title proclaimed), coating it with a pop sheen that soon enough brought to world to their punky reggae party. Sting's middle-to-highbrow lyrics included some serious pretensions—namechecking novelist Vladimir Nabokov here, attempting to explain Jungian concepts there. But give the guy credit: if he helped sell a few extra copies of "Lolita" or "Psychology of the Unconscious," then so much the better.

what to buy: The group's best album over-all was also its swan song. *Synchronicity* (A&M, 1983, prod. Hugh Padgham and the Police) contains the seamless hit "Every Breath You Take," a song about control that was subtle enough to be mistaken for a love ditty. "King of Pain" laid bare Sting's martyr complex, and "Tea in the Sahara" revealed him to be a man of wealth and taste. But "Synchronicity" is the band's strongest statement, full of exotic elements but played with utter assurance. Alas, the same creative friction that drove them to new heights split them apart in the wake of the album's massive success. *Zenyatta Mondatta* (A&M, 1980, prod. the Police and Nigel Gray) is the album on which the Police's grasp finally matched its outsized reach. "Don't Stand So Close to Me," and the nonsensical "De Do Do Do, De Da Da Da" turned the group more toward pop, while "Driven to Tears" kept an eye on world events and "When the World is Running Down, You Make the Best of What's Still Around" somehow works the topic of entropy into a love song. If you can only afford to buy one Police album, though, let it be *Every Breath You Take: The Singles* (A&M, 1986, prod. Various) which covers the territory as well as one disc will allow, though it's docked 1 bone for its pointless remake of "Don't Stand So Close to Me."

what to buy next: For those with plenty of money and a weekend to kill, the four-CD *Message in a Box: The Complete Recordings* (A&M, 1993, prod. Various) offers just what it's title indicates—the whole of the bands oeuvre in one package. The rarities are pretty spare, though, and don't offer enough additional insight into the band to justify the purchase to someone who owns the individual albums. On *Regatta de Blanc* (A&M, 1979, prod. the Police and Nigel Gray) you can hear Sting's songwriting take a leap forward the moment his self-pity turns to empathy in "Message in a Bottle." The album also contains the equally fine "Bring on the Night" and "Walking on the Moon." *Ghost in the Machine* (A&M, 1981, prod. the Police and Hugh Padgham) contains the band's most ebullient single, "Every Little Thing She Does is Magic," as other songs survey themes of media overload ("Too Much Information") and future shock ("Demolition Man") over an increasingly complex instrumental attack.

the rest: *Outlandos d'Amour* (A&M, 1978) *The Police Live!* (A&M, 1995)

worth searching for: The two-volume bootleg *Live in Melbourne* (Golden Stars, 1990) captures a fiery 1981 show during a tour that found the Police enthusiastically embracing its newfound arena-sized popularity.

▶▶ Wang Chung, Men at Work, The Samples, Rancid, Goldfinger

◀◀ Bob Marley, the Beatles, Miles Davis, Wayne Shorter

see also: *Andy Summers, Sting, Stewart Copeland*

By Daniel Durchholz

Robert Pollard

See: Guided by Voices

Polytown

See: Japan; Missing Persons

Iggy Pop /The Stooges

Formed 1967 in Ann Arbor, Mich. Disbanded 1971, Re-formed 1972. Disbanded 1974.

Iggy Pop (born James Jewel Osterberg, April 21, 1947 in Ypsilanti, Mich.), vocals; Ron Asheton, guitar, bass; Dave Alexander, bass (1967-70, died Feb. 10, 1975); Scott Asheton, drums; James Williamson, guitar (1970-74); Scott Thurston, bass, keyboards (1973-74)

We can only marvel at the sheer resilience Iggy has displayed over the years. Like the Rolling Stones' Keith Richards, Iggy has done enough drugs and engaged in enough self-destructive behavior to wipe out a squadron of lesser pop stars—maybe more, since Richards never spread peanut butter all over himself or rolled around in broken glass onstage. Whatever the case, Iggy keeps at it, and even now he cuts a lean, sinewy figure who, in his music, never seems to have trouble finding something to be angry about or finding a girl to chase. Raised in a trailer park, Iggy was inspired to pursue rock 'n' roll after attending a Doors concert and formed the Stooges in time for the group to debut, appropriately enough, on Halloween night, 1967. The Stooges will forever be intertwined with fellow Ann Arborites the MC5 as punk rock forebears, and the rock community of the late 60s—with its plethora of love beads and flower power—had neither seen nor heard anything like the Stooges' primal roar and songs about raw power and wanting to be your dog. It wasn't just outrage that made the Stooges legendary, though; it was the sheer, brutal force of its rock, driven not only by Williamson and Ron Asheton's raging guitars but also by the Scott Asheton's drumming, a combination of rock quarry thud and soulful swing that owed more than a little to the music being made at Motown Records in nearby Detroit. The Stooges lasted just long enough to record some amazing rock 'n' roll albums and secure its legacy, and a year doesn't go by when there isn't some discussion about a reunion. Iggy's solo career, on the other hand, has been more fitful; excepting the electrifying 1977 double dip of *The Idiot* and *Lust For Life*, he's never really approached the Stooges' level of fury. More worrisome is how he flirts with becoming a caricature, playing to an image of rather than fully exercising his artistry. He never quite reaches that point, and there's always something on his albums—and certainly in his live shows—that brings you back for more. But at the same time, there's something both invigorating and disconcerting about hearing one of rock's most revered personalities sing about chasing girls in the most base and sophomoric terms.

what to buy: Consider this a grand slam of primal punk rock power. The Stooges' *Fun House* (Elektra, 1970/1987, prod. Dan Galluci) and *Raw Power* (Columbia, 1972/1988, prod. David Bowie) are molten slamfests that are essential touchstones for every form of aggressive rock that came after—from 70s heavy metal to punk to speed metal and thrash. Lots of blitzkrieg, but no bop. (Nike used the song "Search and Destroy" from *Raw Power* during its commercials for the 1996 summer Olympics.) On the solo front, 1977 wasn't only a good year for British punk; Iggy's *The Idiot* (RCA, 1977/Virgin, 1990, prod. David Bowie) and *Lust For Life* (RCA, 1977/Virgin, 1990, prod. the Bewlay Brothers) are seminal works, capturing the energetic magic of the Stooges but incorporating some dynamic sophistication courtesy of Bowie's influence.

what to buy next: *The Stooges* (Elektra, 1968/1988, prod. John Cale) is inconsistent and a bit rough (in the bad sense), but you've got to have songs such as "1969," "I Wanna Be Your Dog" and "No Fun" in the collection. Iggy's *Brick by Brick* (Virgin, 1990, prod. Don Was) was considered too soft by some; that's a mistake, because it conveys the broadest range of emotions he's ever set on record, in some of the most tuneful settings as well.

what to avoid: Iggy's *Zombie Birdhouse* (I.R.S., 1982/1992, prod. Chris Stein) represents a noble effort by Blondie guitarist Stein to put the singer in some new sonic settings, but he never quite warms to them and, consequently, the album sounds forced.

the rest: Iggy Pop: *TV Eye* (RCA, 1978/Virgin, 1994) *Blah, Blah, Blah* (A&M, 1986) *American Caesar* (Virgin, 1993) *Naughty Little Doggie* (Virgin, 1996)

worth searching for: The Stooges' final concert in 1974 is enshrined on the import *Metallic 2 X KO*, (Skydog, date N/A) a rough-sounding recording that still conveys the band's anarchic zeal. *Rough Power* (Bomp, 1996) is the legitimate release of the long-bootlegged alternate version of *Raw Power*, which replaces Bowie's softer mix with a more in-your-face dynamic.

Ramones, the Sex Pistols, the Damned, Black Flag, the Misfits, Metallica, Danzig

The Doors, the Animals, Mitch Ryder & the Detroit Wheels, the Rolling Stones, Motown

Gary Graff

Porno for Pyros

Formed 1991 in Los Angeles, Calif.

Perry Farrell, vocals, percussion, samples, keyboards; Peter DiStefano, guitar; Paul Stephen Perkins, drums; Martyn LeNoble, bass (1991-96); Mike Watt, bass (1996)

In a city choking on bands eager to find that consummate union of funk and metal during the late 80s, it Farrell's eccentric vision that set Jane's Addiction apart from its competition. But Jane's Addiction's mounting popularity caused Farrell to disband the group in 1991—just after he launched the Lollapalooza tour—and start up Porno For Pyros. The new group left Farrell open to new sonic experimentation, set against soul-searching revelations, loose-limbed grooves and cosmic city and surf themes. Unfortunately, *Porno For Pyros* (Warner Bros., 1993, prod. Perry Farrell and Matt Hyde) left a lot to be desired; following Jane's superlative string of albums, the record came across as an unfinished sketchbook of ideas, filled with Farrell's mercurial warbling and a hyper kinetic soundtrack that never quite clicked. The second album, *Good God's Urge*,

(Warner Bros., 1996, prod. Perry Farrell, Thomas Johnson and Matt Hyde) attained Farrell's ideal union of jagged rock songs and exotic textures. In songs such as the soaring "Porpoise Head," the whimsical "Tahitian Moon" and the forlorn "Wishing Well," the band conjured up a majestic, oceanic rush of melody and feeling.

see also: *Jane's Addiction*

Aidin Vaziri

Portastic

See: Superchunk

Portishead

Formed 1991 in Bristol, England

Geoff Barrow, programming, keyboards; Beth Gibbons, vocals.

Part of the Bristol posse that includes Massive Attack, Portishead came about when producer Barrow met local cover-band veteran Gibbons at the unemployment office. Their collaboration has produced one of the most innovative and compelling sounds of the 90s. Combining dub and hip-hop beats, haunting, atmospheric melodies and the melanchly vocals of Gibbons, Portishead's debut album *Dummy* (Go!Discs/London, 1994, prod. Portishead and Adrian Utley) sounds like a soundtrack to a 60s suspense film updated with a hip-hop beat.

Anna Glen

The Posies

Formed 1988 in Seattle, Wash.

Ken Stringfellow guitar, vocals; Jon Auer guitar, vocals; Rick Roberts, bass (1988-91); Michael Musburger, drums (1988-94); Dave Fox, bass (1992-94); Brian Young, drums (1994-present); Joe "Bass" Howard, bass (1994-present)

Formed by childhood friends, the Posies recorded first in Auer's father's house, a tape that eventually became the independent release *Failure.* (Pop Llama, 1988 prod. Jon Auer and Ken Stringfellow) Strong local sales and good reviews started a bidding war, and the Posies wound up with DGC for its major label debut *Dear 23.* (DGC, 1990 prod. John Leckie) Still the definitive release in the band's canon, it set the foundation for the Posies' brand of power pop—rich harmonies and sharp arrangements played off of raunchy guitar parts with big hooks, all gleaned from heroes such as the Beatles, Cheap Trick, the Hollies and the Move. Its subsequent releases—*Frosting On The Beater* (DGC, 1993, prod Don Fleming) and *Amazing Disgrace* (DGC, 1996, prod. Nick Launey) —have continued in the same vein, while Auer and Stringfellow distinguished themselves as part of a reunited Big Star, performing and recording with Alex Chilton and Jody Stephens.

see also: *Big Star*

John Nieman

The Power Station

See: Duran Duran

Johnny Powers

Born John Pavlick, May 25, 1938, in Utica, Mich.

Detroit's most well-known rockabilly artist, Powers rose to regional fame during the 50s, recording for several labels—including the local companies Fortune and Fox, where Powers had his trademark hit "Long Blond Hair." From there, Powers moved to the legendary Sun Records, where he released two singles (including the sublime "With Your Love, With Your Kiss") and soon after made history as the first white artist signed to Motown. As his popularity waned, Powers moved to the producer's chair, where he worked with mostly obscure artists through the 70s. However, as with many lesser-known American rockabilly treasures, European interest prompted a return to the stage, and after several tours overseas, Powers began concentrating on the American market once again with the release of the fiery *New Spark (For an Old Flame* (Schoolkids, 1994, prod. Johnny Powers, George Clinton and Steve Bergman) —which features a guest appearance from fellow Michigander George Clinton—and a career retrospective *Long Blond Hair.* (Norton, 1992, prod. Various)

Todd Wicks

Praxis

See: Bill Laswell

Prefab Sprout

Formed 1980 in Newcastle, England

Paddy McAloon, lead vocals, guitar; Martin McAloon, bass; Wendy Smith, vocals, percussion (1981-present); Neil Conti, drums (1985-present)

Those people impressed by heavy guitars and raw, intense emotions can go ahead and flip the page. Do it now, because the music and lyrics of this matchless British quartet aim at unraveling the subtleties of romance, guilt, and aspiration, often with a dry sense of humor. Imagine Elvis Costello with less attitude and a better melodic gift, or a weirder Aztec Camera, and you've got a general idea of Prefab's approach. Frontman/mastermind McAloon has rarely targeted his songs at a particular radio format, and the band has never toured the States, so its following remains limited here. In Britain, though, McAloon is revered as a unique songwriter—on the level of, say, a Tom Waits—and the group's last studio album, 1990's *Jordan: The Comeback*, was nominated for the British equivalent of a Grammy. The band's 1984 debut, *Swoon*, established it as an offbeat, jazzy sort of pop outfit, but it was the followup, *Two Wheels Good* (called *Steve McQueen* in the U.K.), which showed what they were capable of. For the past five years, McAloon has been lying low and experimenting with different musical concepts. Expect a new album soon, but don't even try to predict what it'll sound like. "This world needs its dreamers/May they never wake up," sings McAloon in "Cars and Girls." Hear, hear.

what to buy: Brilliantly conceived and executed, *Two Wheels Good* (Kitchenware/Epic, 1985, prod. Thomas Dolby) easily ranks as the band's crowning achievement. McAloon serves up his best set of tunes here, as well as his most dynamic vocal performances, but it is Dolby who provides the extra spark, supplying unusual synth parts that often add just the right touch to these songs of love and regret. Nineteen songs long and divided into four essentially unrelated thematic segments, *Jordan: The Comeback* (Kitchenware/Epic, 1990, prod. Thomas Dolby) certainly can be criticized for being sprawling and uneven, yet it features a wide variety of impressive songs. The most moving cuts come near the end, especially the gospel-influenced "One of the Broken" (with McAloon providing the voice of God!) and the upbeat, yet strangely haunting "Doo-Wop in Harlem" (dedicated to McAloon's late father).

what to buy next: The group's full-length debut, *Swoon* (Kitchenware/Epic, 1984, prod. David Brewis and Prefab Sprout) was a revelation at the time of its release. Jazzy, poetic, and utterly weird without being off-putting, the album features a tribute to chess champion Bobby Fischer ("Cue Fanfare"), and a coolly devastating confession of jealousy ("Cruel"). Although it leaves out too much of *Swoon* in favor of too much of *Langley Park* (and skips many of the best numbers from *Jordan*), *The Best of Prefab Sprout: A Life of Surprises* (Epic, 1992, prod. Various) is a worthy overview of the band's more immediate tunes.

what to avoid: Overproduced and synth-heavy, *From Langley Park to Memphis* (Kitchenware/Epic, 1988, prod. Various) is the least representative Prefab release. Its best songs can be heard on *Life of Surprises*

the rest: *Lions in My Own Garden* (Kitchenware EP, 1983)

worth searching for: Recorded just after *Two Wheels Good*, *Protest Songs* (Kitchenware, 1989, prod. Paddy McAloon) never was released in the U.S., and only saw release in the U.K. after "Langley Park" came out. Though the production is a bit plain, the disc shows an odder side of the band.

Everything But the Girl, Deacon Blue, Lloyd Cole, Gavin Friday

Aztec Camera, Steely Dan, Frank Sinatra, Antonio Carlos Jobim

Bob Remstein

Presence

See: The Cure

The Presidents of the United States of America

Formed 1991 in Seattle, Wash.

Chris Ballew, vocals, two-string basitar; Dave Dederer, three-string guitbass, vocals; Jason Finn, drums, vocals

Just as the Knack provided a pure pop answer to the first wave of punk, so too do the Presidents of the United States of America have a response to the triumph of alternative rock. Understandably tagged by some as a novelty band, the Presidents display a sense of fun and lyrical guile that holds up to repeated listenings—a few, anyway. On the self-titled debut, *Presidents of the United States of America* (Columbia, 1995, prod. Chris Ballew, Dave Dederer and Conrad Uno) the group tosses off a few funny lines and then drive them deep into your cerebrum with repeated choruses and irresistible melodies. There's the nonsensical hit "Lump," plus a string of songs ("Kitty," "Peaches," "Boll Weevil") which turn the mundane into three-chord art. The throwaway cover of the MC5's "Kick Out the Jams" ultimately reveals the trio to be lightweights, but the album is harmless fun for the whole family. Anything wrong with that?

By Daniel Durchholz

Elvis Presley

Born Elvis Aron Presley, Jan. 8, 1935, in East Tupelo, Miss. Died Aug. 16, 1977.

People sometimes forget that Presley—king of rock 'n' roll, movie star, tragic symbol of garish excess, paragon of moral decay, one of the best-selling pop artists of all time, even a pop-culture Christ figure—actually was talented. Whether or not he invented rock 'n' roll by linking, as myth recalls, white country music and black R&B, he had an innate command of the stage and audience, and he was a terrific singer and interpreter. Born to a poor Southern couple, Vernon and Gladys, Presley's future might have been to meet a pretty girl, marry her, possibly graduate from high school and fix plumbing or drive a truck for the rest of his life. But his instincts and ambition wouldn't let him go in that direction, even after his parents upgraded their lifestyle slightly and moved to Memphis. Beginning in high school, the shy boy began greasing his hair into a tall pompadour, wearing long sideburns and choosing his outlandish outfits carefully in pinks, blacks and whites. Peers thought he was nuts. He was eventually vindicated; after he hung around the downtown Sun Records studio for a year, confident entrepreneur and record producer Sam Phillips saw an intangible quality in Presley and set him up for a session. (Phillips, a longtime recorder of black bluesmen and minor R&B stars, from Junior Parker to Rufus Thomas, had long predicted that if he could get a white boy with "the Negro look and the Negro feel" to sing black music, he would make a million dollars. That turned out to be a significant understatement.) With hungry session musicians Scotty Moore on guitar and Bill Black on upright bass, the trio performed take after take until, while fooling around, they came up with reworked versions of Arthur (Big Boy) Crudup's "That's All Right (Mama)" and Bill Monroe's "Blue Moon of Kentucky." They were fast and smooth, and they sounded like nothing anybody had ever heard. An excited Phillips dropped the cuts off to famous Memphis DJ Dewey Phillips, who played "That's All Right (Mama)" countless times in a row, thus creating Presley's first buzz.

For the subsequent two decades, Presley's career moved so fast that he—and his friends and family, who were simultaneously excited and suspicious—could barely keep up. "The Colonel," brilliant opportunist and Hank Snow manager Tom Parker, took the young singer under his wing and autocratically began navigating Presley's career trajectory. Parker immediately negotiated a deal with RCA Records, with whom Presley remained for the rest of his recording career. As Presley began performing more and more unprecedentedly great concerts, attracting teenage girls by the truckload to scream their heads off, his legend started to grow well beyond one-hit wonder level. Then came a rash of tremendous singles: "Hound Dog," "Don't Be Cruel," "Love Me Tender," "All Shook Up" and the classic hits written by the now-legendary pop songwriting duo Leiber and Stoller, including "Jailhouse Rock." Over at Sun, Phillips trotted out Carl Perkins, Roy Orbison and Johnny Cash in Presley's huge rockabilly wake. Gene Vincent, Eddie Cochran, Buddy Holly and Richie Valens were waiting in the wings. The King bought a pink Cadillac for his mother, many more Cadillacs for himself and, in 1957, Graceland, a former Memphis church he converted into a mansion. Everything was going perfectly until Presley was inducted into the Army in 1958; shortly after that, a plane carrying Holly and Valens crashed—that was, as Don McLean later lamented, "the day the music died."

What Album Changed Your Life?

"I think maybe it was Singles Going Steady by the Buzzcocks. That really made me think I could sort of write my own songs and have my own band."

David Lowery (Cracker, Camper Van Beethoven)

But despite all this and the eventual onslaught of Bob Dylan, the Beach Boys and the Beatles, Presley never went away. He was rock's first "careerist," continuing to release hits ("Little Sister," "It's Now or Never," "Can't Help Falling in Love," "Return to Sender" and "Bossa Nova Baby") through the 60s. In that decade of hippies, the Vietnam War and baby boom counter-culture, Presley focused on innocent movies (and soundtracks), starring in total throwaways such as "It Happened at the World's Fair," "Frankie and Johnny" and "Girl Happy," and energetic dance flicks such as "Blue Hawaii" and "Clambake." (All Presley's movies, frequently replayed on late-night television and Nickelodeon channels, have become cult classics.) By the 70s, Graceland had become famous for its lavish Jungle Room (full of green Astroturf, loud velvet paintings and three television sets) and Presley gradually creating an isolationist world for himself and a close circle of friends and relatives. His 1968 television concert, recorded shortly after he and wife Priscilla had their child, Lisa Marie, was a tremendous comeback, an explosive show with a smash soundtrack. But Presley inevitably drifted toward Las Vegas, gained much weight and became a parody of himself. Not a total parody, though—some of Presley's late 60s and 70s songs, including "In the Ghetto," "Suspicious Minds" and the underrated "Burning Love," were explosive and funky. Presley had become more famous for his lifestyle, obesity and white-fringed costumes than he previously had been for his music. Legions of imitators stepped up to create a bizarre and enduring cottage industry in Vegas, Memphis and elsewhere. On Aug. 12, 1977, his three bodyguards put out a book ("Elvis: What Happened?") about Presley's rumored drug abuse and gun obsessions.

Racked with fear and insecurity, Presley died in his Graceland bathroom. Though the cause of death has been frequently disputed, the most reliable diagnosis lists drug-related heart failure, advanced arteriosclerosis and enlargement of the liver. Presley left behind his daughter, heir to the $100-million Graceland mansion and its 675,000 annual visits from tourists; a manager, Parker, who said upon Presley's death that he would "go right on managing him"; 94 gold singles; 40 gold albums; $180 million in movie grosses; millions more in merchandise sales, and, perhaps most important, the entire pop music industry (rock 'n' roll in particular) as his legacy. Some performers have hated him—including the punks, who not-so-coincidentally began to rise the year of his death, and rappers such as Public Enemy, who ripped him as a racist in "Fight the Power." Some have honored him, including follower Mojo Nixon, whose hilarious song "Elvis Is Everywhere" is the finest of many Presley tribute songs, and Grant Lee Buffalo, who rescued "Burning Love" from the schlock pile and turned it back into the desperate, wanton love song it deserves to be. Some have said the King is still alive—for a while, during the late 80s, shoppers in Kalamazoo, Mich., and elsewhere insisted they saw him in a grocery store. It's possible that, centuries from now, when the rest of American pop culture has decayed and disappeared, the King's velvet image will remain.

what to buy: RCA's three five-disc box sets were a godsend, because without them it was impossible to navigate the record store binfuls of studio albums and greatest-hits collections for the essential stuff. Start with *Elvis—The King of Rock 'n' Roll—The Complete 50's Masters,* (RCA, 1992, comp. Ernst Mikael Jorgensen and Roger Semon) and hear the young truck driver transform from raw talent in the early hits "Blue Moon of Kentucky" and "That's All Right" to accomplished showman in "Jailhouse Rock" and "Love Me Tender." Next stop: *From Nashville to Memphis: The Essential 60's Masters I* (RCA, 1994, comp. Ernst Mikael Jorgensen and Roger Semon) proves that despite the Beatles and his late 50s stint in the Army, Presley was still a vital performer; "Little Sister," "Suspicious Minds," "In the Ghetto" and "Fever" are among the transcendental tracks. *Walk a Mile in My Shoes: The Essential '70s Masters* (RCA, 1995, comp. Ernst Mikael Jorgensen and Roger Semon) and *Command Performances: The Essential 60s Masters II* (RCA, 1995, comp. Ernst Mikael Joregensen and Roger Semon) compile the best live tracks and soundtrack songs and eliminate most of the chaff. *The Complete Sun Sessions* (RCA, 1987, prod. Sam Phillips) is mostly revisited on the first box set, but it contains the fascinating sound of Elvis, Moore, Black and producer Phillips inventing rock 'n' roll in the Sun Records studio; "Milkcow Blues Boogie" finds Elvis stopping a slow blues song, announcing "that don't MOVE me" and proceeding to change it before our ears into something completely different.

what to buy next: The boxes don't necessarily preclude Presley's individual titles. Many are worthwhile, but these are the first to check out: *Loving You,* (RCA, 1957, prod. Elvis Presley and Hal Wallis) the first Elvis movie soundtrack; *His Hand In Mine,* (RCA, 1960, prod. Elvis Presley) a gospel album that initially confused the record company; *Elvis NBC-TV Special,* (RCA, 1968, prod. Steve Binder) the master's triumphant return to television when everybody thought he was washed up; *From Elvis in Memphis,* (RCA, 1969, prod. Felton Jarvis and Chips Moman) another triumphant return, this time to where he began his career; *Elvis Country,* (RCA, 1971, prod. Felton Jarvis and Steve Sholes) proof that the 70s Elvis wasn't just a fat druggie awaiting death; *Burning Love,* (RCA Camden, 1972, prod. Various) whose title track still sounds surprisingly fresh and vital; and *The Million Dollar Quartet,* (RCA, 1990, prod. Sam Phillips) which features Presley, Jerry Lee Lewis and Carl Perkins (plus a no-show Johnny Cash), sharing classic 50s rockabilly hits with spontaneity, style and fun.

what to avoid: Most of Presley's schlock, which became almost as famous as his great stuff, was in either the bad-live-performance or icky-movie soundtrack categories. His bad live albums were most prominent during the 70s, including *As Recorded at Madison Square Garden,* (RCA, 1972, prod. Felton Jarvis) *Recorded Live on Stage in Memphis,* (RCA, 1974, prod. Felton Jarvis) *Having Fun With Elvis on Stage* (RCA, 1974) (just the King making bad jokes), *Elvis In Concert* (RCA, 1977, prod. Don Wardell) and *Elvis on Stage.* (RCA, 1977) Of the soundtracks, stay away from *Fun in Acapulco,* (RCA, 1963, prod. Elvis Presley) *Live A Little, Love a Little/Charro!/The Trouble With Girls/Change of Habit,* (RCA, 1995, comp. Ernst Mikael Jorgensen and Roger Semon) *Girl Happy/Harum Scarum* (RCA, 1965/1995, prod. Elvis Presley) and *Frankie and Johnny/Paradise, Hawaiian Style.* (RCA, 1966/1994, prod. Elvis Presley) Also gloriously bad are *Interviews and Memories of: The Sun Years,* (Sun, 1977, prod. Sam Phillips) *From Elvis Presley Boulevard, Memphis, Tennessee,* (RCA, 1976, prod. Crumpacker) both volumes of *Our Memories of Elvis,* (RCA, 1979, prod. Various) *I Was the One* (RCA, 1983, prod. Various) and *The Elvis Presley Interview Record: An Audio Self-Portrait.* (RCA, 1984) Also, stay away from *It's Now or Never: The Tribute to Elvis,* (Mercury, 1994, prod. Various) which does have fan Dwight Yoakam but unfortunately has loser hacks Michael Bolton, Travis Tritt and Wet Wet Wet as well.

the rest: Elvis Presley *(RCA, 1956)* Elvis *(RCA, 1956)* Elvis' Christmas Album *(RCA, 1957)* *King Creole* (RCA, 1958) *Elvis' Golden Records, Vol. I* (RCA, 1958) *For LP Fans Only* (RCA, 1959) *A Date With Elvis* (RCA, 1959) *Elvis Is Back!* (RCA, 1960) *G.I. Blues* (RCA, 1960) *50,000,000 Elvis Fans Can't Be Wrong: Elvis' Golden Records, Vol. 2* (RCA, 1960) *Something for Everybody* (RCA, 1961) *Blue Hawaii* (RCA, 1961) *Pot Luck* (RCA, 1962) *Girls! Girls! Girls!* (RCA, 1962) *It Happened at the World's Fair* (RCA, 1963) *Elvis' Golden Records, Vol. 3* (RCA, 1963) *Elvis for Everyone* (RCA, 1965) *Spinout* (RCA, 1966) *Double Trouble* (RCA, 1967) *How Great Thou Art* (RCA, 1967 *Speedway* (RCA, 1968) *Elvis' Golden Records, Vol. 4* (RCA, 1968) *Elvis Sings Hits from His Movies* (RCA, 1969) *From Memphis to Vegas/From Vegas to Memphis* (RCA, 1969) *Back in Memphis* (RCA, 1970) *That's the Way It Is* (RCA, 1970) *Almost In Love* (RCA, 1970) *On Stage—February 1970* (RCA, 1970) *World Wide 50 Gold Award Hits, Vol. 1, Nos.1-4* (RCA, 1970-71, prod. Various) *Elvis in Person at the International Hotel, Las Vegas* (RCA, 1970) *I Got Lucky* (RCA, 1971) *You'll Never Walk Alone* (RCA, 1971) *Love Letters From Elvis* (RCA, 1971) *C'mon Everybody* (RCA, 1971) *Elvis* (RCA, 1971) *Elvis Sings the Wonderful World of Christmas* (RCA, 1971) *He Touched Me* (RCA, 1972) *Elvis Now* (RCA, 1972) *Separate Ways* (RCA, 1973) *Elvis: Raised on Rock/For Ol' Times Sake* (RCA, 1973) *Aloha From Hawaii* (RCA, 1973) *A Legendary Performer: Volume 1* (RCA, 1974) *Let's Be Friends* (RCA, 1975) *Promised Land* (RCA, 1975) *Pure Gold* (RCA, 1975) *A Legendary Performer: Volume 2* (RCA, 1976) *Welcome to My World* (RCA, 1977) *Moody Blue* (RCA, 1977) *The Elvis Tapes* (Redwood, 1977) *He Walks Beside Me* (RCA, 1978) *A Canadian Tribute* (RCA, 1978) *Elvis Sings for Children and Grownups Too!* (RCA, 1978) *A Legendary Performer: Volume 3* (RCA, 1978) *Elvis Aron Presley* (RCA, 1980) *This is Elvis* (RCA, 1981) *Elvis: The Hillbilly Cat* (The Music Works, 1982) *Elvis: The First Live Recordings* (The Music Works, 1982) *Memories of Christmas* (RCA, 1982) *A Legendary Performer: Volume 4* (RCA, 1983) *Elvis—A Golden Celebration* (RCA, 1984) *Elvis' Gold Records, Vol. 5* (RCA, 1984) *Reconsider Baby* (RCA, 1985) *A Valentine Gift for You* (RCA, 1985) *Always On My Mind* (RCA, 1985) *Return of the Rocker* (RCA, 1986) *The Memphis Record* (RCA, 1987) *The Number One Hits* (RCA, 1987) *Essential Elvis* (RCA, 1988) *Stereo '57 (Essential Elvis, Volume 2)* (RCA, 1988) *Elvis in Nashville* (RCA, 1988) *The Alternate Aloha* (RCA, 1988) *50 World Wide Gold Award Hits, Volume 1, Parts 1 and 2* (RCA, 1988) *The Top Ten Hits* (RCA, 1988) *Known Only to Him: Elvis Gospel, 1957-1971* (RCA, 1989) *The Great Performances* (RCA, 1990) *The Lost Album* (RCA, 1990) *The Great Performances (RCA, 1990)* Elvis Presley Sings Leiber & Stoller *(RCA, 1991)* Viva Las Vegas/Roustabout *(RCA, 1993)* The Essential Elvis, Vol. 3 *(RCA, 1991)* Amazing Grace: His Greatest Sacred Performances *(RCA, 1994)* Kissin' Cousins/Clambake/Stay Away, Joe *(RCA, 1994)* Flaming Star/Wild in the Country/Follow That Dream, *(RCA, 1995)*

worth searching for: Great songs about Elvis: "Elvis Is Dead" by Living Colour; "Elvis Is Everywhere" by Mojo Nixon; "My Boy Elvis," by Janis Martin; "Galway to Graceland" by Richard Thompson; "Elvis Ate America" by U2/Brian Eno as the Passengers; "Little Sister" by Dwight Yoakam; "Johnny Bye Bye" by Bruce Springsteen. Also, the entire soundtrack of "Honeymoon in Vegas" (Epic, 1992, prod. Peter Afterman and Glen Brunman) despite the lifeless carbon-copy Billy Joel versions of "All Shook Up" and "Heartbreak Hotel." Finally, one great disc of Elvis songs: the British import *The Last Temptation of Elvis* (New Musical Express, 1990, executive prod. Roy Carr) has Motörhead's Lemmy doing "Blue Suede Shoes," Springsteen doing "Viva Las Vegas," the Jesus and Mary Chain demolishing "Guitar Man" and Cath Carroll and legendary weirdo punk-noise producer Steve Albini deconstructing "King Creole."

Buddy Holly, Carl Perkins, Roy Orbison, Beatles, Johnny Cash, Bob Dylan, Beach Boys, Janis Martin, Bruce Springsteen, Billy Joel, Mojo Nixon, Dwight Yoakam, the Band, the Blasters, Elvis Hitler, Elvis Costello, U2, Stray Cats, Living Colour, Public Enemy (we should have just listed everybody...)

Bill Monroe, Hank Snow, Arthur (Big Boy) Crudup, Little Richard, Chuck Berry, Lowell Fulson, Big Mama Thornton, Frank Sinatra, Hank Williams Sr., Roy Brown, Carter Family, Jimmie Rodgers, the Ink Spots, Eddy Arnold

Steve Knopper

Billy Preston

Born Sept. 9, 1946 in Houston, Texas

Best known for his distinctive bluesy keyboard work on the Beatles' *Let It Be* album, Preston had already established himself on the gospel and R&B circuits before George Harrison pulled him into the Fab Four's fracturous recording sessions in 1969. A child prodigy, Preston played organ for gospel queen Mahalia Jackson and landed a role playing songwriter W.C. Handy as a boy in the movie "St. Louis Blues" (1958). (Nat King Cole played the adult Handy.) Throughout the early 60s, Preston toured with Little Richard and Sam Cooke in Europe, where he first met the Beatles at Hamburg's Star Club. A spot as a backup musician on Britain's "Shindig" TV music program landed him a gig touring the continent with Ray Charles; On that tour, he again met up with Harrison, who promptly signed him to the Beatle's Apple label. Next to Badfinger, Preston was the best-known and most prolific artist in Apple's stable, and he was the only artist to receive a performance credit with the Beatles (the "Get Back" single is credited to "The Beatles with Billy Preston"). After the Beatles broke up, Preston worked with John Lennon on a number of his Plastic Ono Band albums and also recorded with Ringo Starr and Harrison. He performed at Harrison's Concert for Bangladesh in 1971, where his was among the concert's standout performances. Throughout the 70s Preston enjoyed a string of hit singles ("Will It Go 'Round in Circles," "Outa-Space") while backing up such top acts as the Rolling Stones and Aretha Franklin. Preston continues to write and record, dividing his energies between gospel and secular recordings. Among rock keyboardists, he is an original, a true living legend. *The Best of Billy Preston* (A&M, 1988, prod. Billy Preston and George Martin) is an excellent retrospective of Preston's solo work, with all his pop hits along with the with the moving gospel-rocker "That's The Way God Planned It," originally recorded for Apple. *Encouraging Words* (Apple, 1970, prod. George Harrison and Billy Preston) is a vintage gem from the vaults. Preston tackles the Beatles' "I've Got a Feeling" and the Harrison songs "My Sweet Lord" and "All Things Must Pass" in his own impeccable style. *Minister of Music* (Pepper Co. Music Group, 1995) shows Preston's roots are still firmly planted in church. These 12 songs of praise kick up as many thrills and as much excitement as anything else in Preston's catalog.

Christopher Scapelliti

The Pretenders

Formed 1978 in London, England

Chrissie Hynde, vocals, guitar; James Honeyman-Scott, guitar, vocals (1978-82, died June 16, 1982); Pete Farndon, bass, vocals (1978-82, died April 14, 1983); Martin Chambers, drums, vocals (1978-84, 1993-present); Robbie McIntosh, guitar, vocals (1983-87); Malcolm Foster, bass, vocals (1983-84, 1987, 1990); T.M. Stevens, bass (1986-87); Blair Cunningham, drums (1986-90); Billy Bremner, guitar, vocals (1990); Dominic Miller, guitar (1990); John McKenzie, bass (1990); Adam Seymour, guitar, vocals (1995-present); Andy Hobson, bass, vocals (1995-present)

The Pretenders have always been Hynde's band; even at its most democratic—the short period when the original lineup was together—it was clear that the expatriate Akron native called the shots and set the tone. The Pretenders emerged from London's late 70s punk scene (Hynde even worked for Sex Pistols impresario Malcolm McLaren), but the music it put forth on its debut record was markedly different from its contemporaries. While Hynde's sneering, leather-clad image made it clear that she was no boy-toy, her music was far removed from punk's atonal anger. She was, instead, something altogether new on the pop horizon: a tough, independent woman who was nevertheless unafraid to show that she possessed both a rational mind and human tenderness. The early Pretenders were skilled players whose capabilities encompassed punk aggression and deft pop melodicism; their music was rugged, tuneful and, with Hynde's punk chanteuse image, widely accessible. The group managed to retain punk credentials while simultaneously appealing to pop radio.

By 1982, however, dissension and deaths had fractured the

original Pretenders, and the group's membership became volatile, making subsequent albums little more than Hynde solo efforts.

But with 1994's *Last of the Independents* found Hynde more interested in a more stable band format, and the Pretenders regained some of the unique energy and interplay of its early years.

what to buy: *The Pretenders* (Sire, 1980, prod. Chris Thomas) is a tour de force of sharp playing and writing, with a range that covers the tough slam of "Tattooed Love Boys" and "Precious," the melodic delights of "Brass in Pocket" and "Mystery Achievement," and the subtle beauty of "Kid" and "Stop Your Sobbing."

what to buy next: Formed from the ashes of Honeyman-Scott's and Farndon's deaths, the band that came together to record *Learning to Crawl* (Sire, 1984, prod. Chris Thomas) was the closest Hynde would get to the essence of her original lineup. In guitarist McIntosh, she found a spiritual and ideological descendent of Honeyman-Scott, a guitarist with a gift for melody and sharp accompaniment, while the material showcases Hynde's growing facility with the songwriting craft. *Singles* (Sire, 1987, prod. Various) is testament to the body of first-rate music Hynde and her collaborators have produced over the years.

what to avoid: *Packed!* (Sire, 1990, prod. Chrissie Hynde) —a mundane workout of themes that she exercised better on previous albums—brutally highlights Hynde's need for strong musical accompaniment.

the rest: *Pretenders II* (Sire, 1981) *Extended Play (Sire EP, 1981)* Get Close *(Sire, 1986)* Last of the Independents *(Sire, 1994)* The Isle of View *(Warner Bros., 1995)*

worth searching for: Pretenders historians and completists will want to look for Hynde's early material. She worked with a band called the Berk Brothers and also recorded a single under the name Moors Murders—a challenging quest, to be sure.

▶▶ Divinyls, Nick Lowe, Rockpile, Scandal/Patti Smyth, Alanis Morrisette, Elastica

◀◀ The Kinks, The Byrds, the Beatles, Patti Smith, Suzi Quatro, the Who, Jimi Hendrix, Elvis Costello, Nick Lowe

David Galens

Pretty Things

Formed 1963 in London, England. Disbanded 1976.

Phil May, vocals, harmonica; Dick Taylor, guitar (1963-69); Brian Pendleton, guitar(1963-66); John Stax, bass (1963-66); Viv Prince, drums (1963-65); Skip Alan, drums (1965-68, 1970-76); Wally Allen, bass (1966-70); John Povey, keyboards (1966-76); John Alder, drums (1968-70); Victor Unitt, guitar (1969-70); Peter Tolson, guitar (1970-76); Stuart Brooks, bass (1971-73); Gordon Edwards, keyboards, guitar, bass (1974-76); Jack Green, bass (1975-76)

Pretty Things was one of those unfortunate, talented bands that garnered heaps of critical praise but never quite caught on with the buying public—particularly not in the U.S. The schizophrenic reception to its work helps explain the long list of musicians who have passed through the group as well as the abrupt changes in musical direction during the band's 12-year career. Led by May and Taylor, Pretty Things started out as R&B roots rockers along the lines of the early Rolling Stones. (Not surprising, since Taylor was the original Stones bassist.) This period is well chronicled by *Get a Buzz—The Best of the Fontana Years* (Fontana, 1982, prod. Various) During the late 60s, frustrated by its inability to break through in the U.S., the band switched gears, entering the world of psychedelia and progressive rock. The major achievement of this period was the out-of-print *S.F. Sorrow*, which in 1968 was the first rock opera and both a precursor to and influence on the Who's *Tommy* Entering the 70s, Taylor was gone and May led a more straight-ahead, album-rock version of Pretty Things; again, its best work from this period —1974's *Silk Torpedo*—is out of print.

Gary Plochinksi

Alan Price

See: The Animals

Primal Scream

Formed 1986 in Scotland

Bobby Gillespe, vocals; Denise Johnson, vocals; Robert Young, guitar; Andrew Innes, guitar; Martin Duffy, keyboard; David Hood, bass; Roger Hawkins, drums

Contrary to popular opinion, Primal Scream has not preyed on the past; it's helped create the future. Although the Scottish group's string of hits—ranging from the trance-dance "Loaded" to the communal, celebratory romp "Come Together"—inevitably brought on comparisons to everyone from the Rolling

Stones to T. Rex to Sly & the Family Stone, the band's sound was definitely a product of the times. Primal Scream's freewheeling, Ecstasy-inspired attitude often gained the band association with England's once-thriving rave scene, which also bred the likes of the Stone Roses, Happy Mondays, Inspiral Carpets and the Charlatans. But its music definitely set the group apart from the pack: mixing a blues/gospel pace with modern technology, it created an effervescent pop previously unheard. Primal Scream's third album, *Screamadelica,* (Sire, 1991, prod. Various) is the one to hear, an album that solidifies the band's identity and traces its remarkable creative history—which can best be described as 60s-influenced, slick, melodic and slightly psychedelic. The album covers a spectrum of styles: "Slip Inside This House" is an acid-soaked rocker; "Damaged" is an enchanting lullaby about love gone bad; and "Higher Than The Sun" is an ambient killer. All in all, an enthralling mix.

the rest: *Sonic Flower Groove* (Creation, 1987) *Primal Scream* (Creation, 1989) *Give Out But Don't Give Up* (Sire, 1994)

Aidin Vaziri

Primus /Sausage

Formed 1984 in San Francisco, Calif.

Les Claypool, vocals and bass; Larry LaLonde, guitar (1989–present); Todd Huth, guitar (1984-89); Tim "Herb" Alexander, drums

Primus' bizarre musical vision has two elements: great technical playing, with a thrash-funk rhythm section that emulates Rush's machine-like perfection; and a sense of humor that's often purely goofy but sometimes sophisticated enough to impress singer-songwriter Tom Waits. Claypool struts on stage like he's auditioning for Monty Python's "Ministry of Silly Walks," sings in a clipped cartoonish voice and writes songs about tragic race car drivers, weird fishermen and big brown beavers. The songs almost always move aside for long, spacey jams, in which Claypool (who once auditioned for Metallica) shuts off the funk and plays up his chops. The band, whose legions of fans perversely shout "Primus sucks!" scored several terrific concert slots during the early 90s, opening for Jane's Addiction, the Public Enemy-Anthrax tour and U2's Zoo TV Tour, as well as headlining Lollapalooza '93—all of which helped push the band onto alternative radio playlists.

what to buy: *Sailing the Seas of Cheese* (Interscope, 1991, prod. Primus) is an eccentric masterpiece, with the hilariously tragic "Jerry Was a Race Car Driver." On the band's one true classic song, "Tommy the Cat," Tom Waits sings the demented cat's part.

what to buy next: *Tales from the Punch Bowl* (Interscope, 1995, prod. Primus) contains Primus' biggest hit single, the not-so-subtle "Wynona's Big Brown Beaver." *Pork Soda* (Interscope, 1993, prod. Primus) was the big breakthrough, hitting No. 7 the same summer the band headlined the Lollapalooza tour.

what to avoid: *Riddles Are Abound Tonight,* (Interscope, 1994, prod. Sausage) a side project by the group Sausage (Claypool, original Primus guitarist Huth and drummer Jay Lane) has all the technical prowess with none of Primus' endearing whimsy.

the rest: *Suck on This* (Prawn Song, 1989) *Frizzle Fry* (Caroline, 1990)

worth searching for: Waits' apocalyptic single "Earth Died Screaming," off his 1992 album *Bone Machine,* (Island, 1992, prod. Tom Waits) has Claypool returning the "Tommy the Cat" favor with sharp, focused bass playing.

▶▶ Presidents of the United States of America, Rage Against the Machine

◀◀ Talking Heads, Rush, Tom Waits, Dead Milkmen, Metallica, Red Hot Chili Peppers, the Residents

Steve Knopper

Prince

Born Prince Roger Nelson, June 7, 1958, in Minneapolis, Minn.

No matter what you call him—Prince, The Artist Formerly Known As Prince, or that unpronounceable symbol that he goes by of late—there's no denying his stature as one of the most influential dance/funk artists in the history of popular music. Named after his father's jazz trio, Prince didn't attract much more than a cult following until after his fifth album, "1999," was released in 1982, earning him Rock Artist of the Year honors from "Rolling Stone." The semi-autobiographical movie "Purple Rain" and its soundtrack propelled Prince to the top of the charts and exposed one of music's best-kept secrets to the world. Frequently laced with sexually explicit lyrics and religious overtones, the sound of Prince encompasses a wide range of musical genres—pop, rock, dance, funk, soul, gospel, jazz, rap, world music, and more. The ability of "His Royal Bad-ness" to mesh these many styles into his own unique sound is truly remarkable. Dubbed a musical genius by many, Prince writes all his own material, plays all the instruments on many of his albums, and has never been produced by anyone but himself.

what to buy: *Sign O' the Times* (Paisley Park/Warner Brothers, 1987, prod. Prince) ♪♪♪♪♪ is a masterpiece that leads the listener on an incredible journey through the world according to Prince. This double-disc set is Prince at his diverse best and showcases his amazing range as an instrumentalist and singer. *1999* (Warner Brothers, 1982, prod. Prince) ♪♪♪♪♪ gave rockdom its first taste of Prince with the title track and "Little Red Corvette." It's a masterful mix of pop, rock, and funk, and was Prince's breakthrough project. *Dirty Mind* (Warner Brothers, 1980, prod. Prince) ♪♪♪♪♪ is perhaps the definitive funk/rock album (with a nasty theme) and contains the classics "When You Were Mine," "Uptown," and "Partyup." *Purple Rain* (Warner Brothers, 1984, prod. Prince) ♪♪♪♪½ may be a bit too mainstream for some (it was #1 for 24 weeks), but this album put Prince over the top, and it's loaded with great dance/pop songs.

what to buy next: *The Hits/The B-Sides* (Paisley Park/Warner Brothers, 1993, prod. Prince) ♪♪♪♪½is chock full of hits, though they do lose some of their luster when listened to out of their original context. Nevertheless, this is the only album that contains such legendary Prince B-sides as "Erotic City," "Gotta Stop (Messin' About)," and "How Come U Don't Call Me Anymore." *Parade (Music from the Motion Picture 'Under the Cherry Moon')* (Paisley Park/Warner Brothers, 1986, prod. Prince) ♪♪♪♪ is often dismissed as a failure, due largely in part to the lack of success of its companion movie. While "Kiss" may be its most familiar track, it contains other great songs—"Girls & Boys," "Mountains," "Anotherloverholenyohead," and the haunting "Sometimes It Snows In April"—that were inexplicably left off the hits packages.

what to avoid: Prince was handpicked to do the *Batman Motion Picture Soundtrack* (Warner Brothers, 1989, prod. Prince) **WOOF!** by one of the film's stars (and Prince fan), Jack Nicholson. That's one phone call Prince should've never answered. A couple of cuts ("The Future," "Partyman") aren't half bad, but the album as a whole is Prince's worst effort to date.

the rest: *For You,*(Warner Brothers, 1978, prod. Prince) ♪♪½ *Prince,* (Warner Brothers, 1979, prod. Prince) ♪♪♪♪ *Controversy,* (Warner Brothers, 1981, prod. Prince) ♪♪♪♪ *Around the World In a Day,* (Paisley Park/Warner Brothers, 1985, prod. Prince) ♪♪♪♪ *The Black Album,* (Warner Brothers, 1994, prod. Prince) (recorded in 1987 and originally available only as a bootleg) ♪♪½ *Lovesexy,* (Paisley Park/Warner Brothers, 1988, prod. Prince) ♪♪♪ (with others) *Music from 'Graffiti Bridge',* (Paisley Park/Warner Brothers, 1990, prod. Prince) ♪♪ *Diamonds and Pearls,* (Paisley Park/Warner Brothers, 1991, prod. Prince) ♪♪♪½ *Love Symbol Album,* (Paisley Park/Warner Brothers, 1992, prod. Prince) ♪♪♪ *The Hits 1,* (Paisley Park/Warner Brothers, 1993, prod. Prince) ♪♪♪♪½ *The Hits 2,* (Paisley Park/Warner Brothers, 1993, prod. Prince) ♪♪♪♪½ *Come,* (Warner Brothers, 1994, prod. Prince) ♪½ *The Gold Experience* (NPG/Warner Brothers, 1995, prod. Prince) ♪♪½ (with others) *'Girl 6' Motion Picture Soundtrack* (Warner Brothers, 1996, prod. Prince) ♪♪♪½ *Chaos & Disorder* (Warner Brothers, 1996, prod. Prince) ♪♪

worth searching for: *The White Album,* (Neutral Zone, 1989, prod. Prince) ♪♪♪♪♪ a bootleg live CD recorded in Germany in 1988, is 71 minutes of no-holds-barred funk, made even better by its surprisingly fine sound quality.

▶▶ The Time, Vanity 6, and virtually every dance/funk artist of the 1980s

◀◀ Carlos Santana, Sly and the Family Stone, Jimi Hendrix, James Brown, The Beatles, The Rolling Stones

Dean Dauphinais

John Prine

Born Oct. 10, 1946 in Maywood, Ill.

One of the first to be strapped as "the new Dylan," Prine is one of the few to actually outgrow the tag and become a distinct, trenchant songwriting voice. Mostly because of his admittedly limited guitar skills, Prine often gets lumped in the folkie/singer/songwriter genre, but as anyone who has ever listened carefully or heard him play with a band knows, he has the heart and soul of a rock 'n'roller. His 1971 self-titled debut alone includes astonishing songs like: "Sam Stone," the first Vietnam protest song to examine the war's effect on soldiers' lives; an homage to the elderly wryly titled "Hello in There;" "Donald and Lydia," a touching ode to masturbation; the wicked social satire "Spanish Pipedream" with the oft-repeated chorus, "Blow up your TV/Throw away your paper;" and "Angel From Montgomery," a longtime Bonnie Raitt staple.

Major labels gave up on Prine, which led to him to start his own Oh Boy Records during the early 80s. These days his edge, sharp eye for detail and feel for simple melodies, common language and popular culture seems, if anything, more intact—and he's even more effective in concert. His songs have been recorded by many diverse artists, including Joan Baez, Bette Midler, the Everly Brothers and Cowboy Junkies, but more importantly, Prine's influence can be heard whenever guitars are played on streets and living rooms around the world.

what to buy: *John Prine,* (Atlantic, 1971, prod. Arif Mardin) with its raw, harrowing, sometimes goofy tales of life. *The Missing Years,* (Oh Boy, 1991, prod. Howie Epstein), offers the same kind of world-view undaunted by middle age. *Bruised Orange* (Asylum/Oh Boy, 1978, prod. Steve Goodman), offers Goodman's inspired arrangements. *John Prine Live* (Oh Boy, 1988, prod. John Prine, Dan Einstein and Jim Rooney), includes the stories and onstage charisma that's missing on his studio albums.

what to buy next: *Storm Windows* (Asylum, 1980, prod. Barry Beckett) offers Prine's best sound, courtesy of producer Beckett. *Aimless Love,* (Oh Boy, 1984, prod. Prine and Jim Rooney) is a pleasant, country-flavored record. *Great Days,* (Rhino, 1993, prod. Various) is as good a collection you'll find, with all albums represented.

what to avoid: *Common Sense,* (Atlantic, 1975, prod. Steve Cropper) is a classic example of mismatching producer and artist. The songs, and there are some good ones, often sound incomplete, and Prine sounds out of breath at the end of every one.

the rest: *Sweet Revenge* (Atlantic, 1973) *Prime Prine* (Atlantic, 1976) *German Afternoons* (Oh Boy, 1988,) *A John Prine Christmas* (Oh Boy, 1993) *Lost Dogs and Mixed Blessings* (Oh Boy, 1995).

worth searching for: *Pink Cadillac,* (Asylum/Oh Boy, 1979, prod. Knox Phillips and Jerry Phillips), on which a primal Prine draws a strange energy and vibe from Sam Phillips' kids in the famous Sun Studios.

▶▶ Nanci Griffith, Iris Dement, Cowboy Junkies

◀◀ The Carter Family, Hank Williams, Chuck Berry, Jerry Lee Lewis, Bob Dylan

Leland Rucker

The Proclaimers

Formed 1983 in Edinburgh, Scotland

Craig Reid, vocals; Charlie Reid, guitar, vocals

A couple of geeky brothers with bizarre rockabilly haircuts, Buddy Holly glasses and Schwarzenegger-like voices (not to be confused with the Jesus & Mary Chain's Reid brothers), the Proclaimers wrote some incredibly melodic post-post-New Wave tunes during the 80s. They immediately hit the charts in England and Australia, but it took the 1993 film "Benny and Joon," whose soundtrack contained the duo's best-known song "I'm Gonna Be (500 Miles)," to really make them American one-hit wonders. Their *Hit the Highway* album was disconcertingly religious, but there's no denying the Reids' crisp pop talent.

what to buy: *Sunshine on Leith,* (Chrysalis, 1988, prod. Pete Wingfield) the original home of "I'm Gonna Be (500 Miles)," offers the best evidence of the Proclaimers' strong melodic skills.

what to buy next: *This is the Story,* (Chrysalis, 1987, prod. John Williams) a collection of acoustic tunes, produced the No. 3 U.K. single "Letter to America."

what to avoid: *Hit the Highway* (Chrysalis, 1994, prod. Pete Wingfield) was a gospel album, and a way-too-preachy one at that.

the rest: *King of the Road* (Chrysalis EP, 1990)

worth searching for: The *Benny and Joon*soundtrack (BMG, 1993, prod. Various) provided the band's belated breakthrough; though beyond two versions of the "I Wanna Be..." hit, the rest is a bland movie score.

▶▶ Lowen and Navarro, Jackopierce, Green Day

◀◀ Everly Brothers, Buddy Holly, Tom Robinson Band, Romantics, Buzzcocks, Plimsouls

Tracey Birkenhauer and Steve Knopper

Procol Harum

Formed 1966 in London, England. Disbanded 1977. Reunited 1991.

Gary Brooker, piano, vocals; Keith Reid, lyrics; Matthew Fisher, organ, vocals (1966-70, 1991); Dave Knights, bass (1966-70); Ray Royer, guitar (1966-67); Bobby Harrison, drums (1966-67); Robin Trower, guitar (1967-71, 1991); B.J. Wilson drums, (1967-77, died 1989); Chris Copping, bass, organ (1970-77); Dave Ball, guitar (1971-72); Alan Cartwright, bass (1971-76); Mick Grabham, guitar (1972-77); Pete Solley, organ (1976-77); Dave Bronze, bass (1991); Mark Brzezicki, drums (1991)

From the ashes of the Paramounts, a commercially unsuccessful British R&B band, rose Procol Harum, which established itself early with the single "A Whiter Shade of Pale." Unlike other "progressive" rock bands of the time, Procol Harum didn't use string arrangements and classical melodies to disguise the fact that it couldn't write or as a way to seem more important than it was. On the contrary, Procol Harum wrote concise pop songs that were magnificent, beautiful, haunting, mysterious and hummable. Brooker and Reid are obvious choices when discussing what made Procol Harum tick, but Wilson is possibly one of the most underrated drummers ever (slightly less manic than Keith Moon and far more stylish), and the many guitarists who played with the band (Trower went on to huge success as a solo act) all provided flash and taste. Things tended to sound bombastic or pretentious at times, but you always got the feeling that the band was winking at you all the while. For example, is "A Salty Dog" a sailing song or is it the story of conception? Only Reid knows for sure. But Procol Harum ran out of inspiration a couple of albums before it quit recording for the first time (the group reunited in 1991). Brooker, Reid and Fisher have recorded and toured together recently, and much of the magic has returned with them.

what to buy: *A Salty Dog* (A&M, 1969, prod. Matthew Fisher) has the title song, "So Much Between Us," Fisher's "Boredom" and probably the strangest drinking song ever recorded, "The Devil Came from Kansas."

what to buy next: *Grand Hotel* (Chrysalis, 1973, prod. Chris Thomas) Powerful production, good songs, great guitar solos and some wonderful counterpoint singing on "Fires Which Burn Brightly" make for a surprising and consistently fine album.

what to avoid: On *Something Magic,* (Chrysalis, 1977, prod. Procol Harum, Ron and Howie Albert) the band sounds too tired to do anything but go for the formula and hope for the best. It didn't work, and the band broke up shortly after.

the rest: *A Whiter Shade of Pale* (A&M, 1967) *Shine On Brightly* (A&M, 1968) *Home* (A&M, 1970) *Broken Barricades* (A&M, 1971) *Procol Harum in Concert with the Edmonton Symphony Orchestra* (Chrysalis, 1972) *Exotic Birds and Fruit* (Chrysalis, 1974) *Procol's 9th* (Chrysalis, 1975) *The Best of Procol Harum* (A&M, 1972) *The Prodigal Stranger* (Zoo, 1991)

solo outings:

Gary Brooker *No More Fear of Flying* (Chrysalis, 1979) *Lead Me to the Water* (Polygram, 1982) *Echoes in the Night* (Polygram, 1984)

Matthew Fisher *I'll Be There* (RCA, 1974) *Matthew Fisher* (A&M, 1980)

worth searching for: Fisher's first solo outing, *Journey's End,* (RCA, 1973) is a neat collection of pop tunes—not at all what you might expect after hearing the band's work.

▶▶ Electric Light Orchestra, Genesis, Kansas

◀◀ J.S. Bach, the Shangri-Las

see also: *Robin Trower*

Shane Faubert

Professor Longhair

Born Henry Roeland "Roy" Byrd, December 19, 1918, in Bogalusa, La. Died January 30, 1980 in New Orleans, La.

Professor Longhair's music is important to a number of musical genres, not the least of which are rock 'n' roll, calypso, zydeco and the New Orleans R&B with which he is most often associated. A piano player and singer of profound talent and innovative technique, 'Fess (as he was often called) has been cited by a number of prominent musicians, including Fats Domino, Dr. John, Allen Toussaint, Art Neville and Huey "Piano" Smith, as a primary influence on their playing. Raised in New Orleans, 'Fess was a sponge for the city's diverse culture and rich musical heritage, especially the prevalent sounds of boogie woogie, blues and calypso. His musical gumbo is best defined in his piano playing—a style often referred to as "rhumba-boogie," driven by propulsive left hand rhythms and intricate right hand chording. In addition to his piano playing, 'Fess was a gifted singer with a wide and idiosyncratic range; whoops, hollers, whistles, high screeches and low growls were all in his repertoire. Though suffused with his ripe sense of humor, his vocals ran the gamut from heartsick longing to predatory sexuality to pure unbridled joy. Despite having more than enough talent to strike it rich during rock's gold rush years of the 50s, a combination of mismanagement and his reluctance to tour extensively prevented the 'Fess' ascendancy to stardom. As a result, many of his proteges, notably Domino, surged ahead of him in popularity, and until his "rediscovery" in 1971, Longhair worked as a janitor and was frequently destitute. Popular support notwithstanding, Professor Longhair's contributions to rock are now deemed irreplaceable, and he is today considered a cornerstone of New Orleans's rich musical tableau.

what to buy: Originally released in France, *Rock 'n' Roll Gumbo* (Barclay, 1974/Dancing Cat, 1985, prod. Philippe Rault, George Winston, Steve Hodge and Frosty Horton) is a veritable primer on Longhair's style. Recorded in three days in 'Fess's birthplace of Bogalusa, La., the album features a number of his regular sidemen (who, in the manner of James Brown's band, played *exactly* what the Professor told them to play) and legendary blues guitarist Clarence "Gatemouth" Brown. The tracks offer a sampling from across Longhair's career and include many Crescent City classics—"Rockin' Pneumonia," "Rum and Coke," "Tipitina," "Hey Now Baby." *Rock 'n' Roll Gumbo* epitomizes Longhair's contributions and expertly conveys the exhilaration that music brought to his life.

what to buy next: It's equally important to recognize the genesis of 'Fess' career, and *Mardi Gras in New Orleans* (Nighthawk, 1981, prod. not listed) collects 'Fess's crucial recordings from the late '40s and early 50s, including "She Ain't Got No Hair," "Professor Longhair's Boogie" and the original versions of the title track and "Tipitina." The sound quality is less than desirable, but the fire of the performances is unforgettable.

what to avoid: Beware of cheap compilations from off-brand labels; the quality is almost always poor.

the rest: *New Orleans Piano* (Blues Originals, Vol. 2) (Atlantic, 1989) *Crawfish Fiesta* (Alligator, 1980) *The Last Mardi Gras* (Atlantic, 1982) *Houseparty New Orleans Style* (Rounder, 1987) *'Fess: The Professor Longhair Anthology* (Rhino, 1993)

worth searching for: A live recording from 1975, *Live on the Queen Mary,* (Harvest, 1978, prod. not listed) is scarce, but persistent hunters should find it with moderate effort. The album features 'Fess performing at a gala party hosted by Paul McCartney aboard the Queen Mary luxury liner.

Fats Domino, Dr. John, Allen Toussaint, Art Neville (and the Neville Brothers), Huey "Piano" Smith, Little Richard, Jerry Lee Lewis, Elvis Presley, James Booker, Bruce Hornsby, Jason D. Williams

Albert Ammons, Meade Lux Lewis, Big Maceo, Pete Johnson, Jimmy Yancey

David Galens

Prong

Formed 1986 in New York, N.Y.

Tommy Victor, vocals, guitar; Ted Parsons, drums; Mike Kirkland, bass, vocals (1986-90); Troy Gregory, bass, vocals (1991-93); Paul Raven, bass (1993-present)

Brutal and uncompromising, Prong is the rare case of a band starting in the underground and then letting its sound get *harder* when it signs with a major label. The group was put together by guitarist Victor, who mixed sound at CBGB before deciding to get his own band together. He took a New York brand of thrash and stripped it to its essence—just the song structures and a lot of noise made by the three instrumentalists, but all in service of the tune rather than for shows of speedy virtuosity.

what to buy: *Beg to Differ* (Epic, 1990, prod. Mark Dodson and Prong) is the major label debut that caught everyone off guard. Rather than soften its sound, Prong cranks it up yet another notch, making an almost industrial kind of racket.

what to buy next: *Rude Awakening* (Epic, 1996, Terry Date and Tommy Victor) imports pal Charlie Clauser from nine inch nails to add keyboards and sampling for an extra layer of density in Prong's already harsh attack.

what to avoid: *Primitive Origins* (Mr. Bear/Sound League, 1987) is invigorating but indistinct from the rest of the thrash pack.

the rest: *Force Fed* (In-Effect, 1989) *Prove You Wrong* (Epic, 1991) *Whose Fist is This Anyway?* (Epic, 1993) *Cleansing* (Epic, 1993)

nine inch nails, Pantera, White Zombie, Body Count

Black Flag, Metallica, Megadeth, Living Colour

Gary Graff

Chuck Prophet IV

See: Green on Red

The Psychedelic Furs /Richard Butler (Love Spit Love)

Formed 1978 in London, England. Disbanded 1991.

Richard Butler, vocals; Tim Butler, bass; Duncan Kilburn, sax (1978-81); Mars Williams, horns, saxes (1984-88); Roger Morris, guitar (1978-81); John Ashton, guitar; Knox Chandler, guitar, cello (1989-91); Vince Ely, drums (1979-82, 1987-90); Phil Calvert, drums (1982-83); Paul Garisto, drums (1984-87); Don Yallech, drums (1990-91)

With his ragged, raspy voice, Richard Butler sounded like the prototypical punk, and his band did come from that background. But by the time the group disbanded 13 years later, it had garnered glossy pop hits and been popular in dance clubs—yet with that voice up front, it rarely sounded compromised. The debut recordings were fairly dirgy, but in a catchy way; BBC DJ John Peel played them, and the group was signed by Columbia. It would prove to be popular in its native country but continually have trouble breaking through in the U.S., though often coming tantilizingly close. For instance, a Furs song was the inspiration for John Hughes' film "Pretty in Pink" and was re-recorded for its soundtrack; Hughes was the most American of 80s directors, yet the single peaked at No. 41. The group moved to America and recorded its third album, *Forever Now*, with Todd Rundgren and actually found itself with a gold record and a hit, "Love My Way." Ultimately, the dancey "Heartbreak Beat," from the otherwise uninteresting *Midnight to Midnight*, was the only Top 40 hit the band ever had here. It was all downhill from there, with apparent confusion among band members as to just what they wanted to sound like and represent. Three years after the band was dissolved, Butler was trying to duplicate its rock sound with a new band, Love Spit Love, which went nowhere.

what to buy: *Talk Talk Talk* (Columbia, 1981, Steve Lillywhite) 🦴🦴🦴🦴½ moves the bleakness of the debut into mainstream territory without compromising. *Forever Now* (Columbia, 1982, prod. Todd Rundgren) 🦴🦴🦴🦴½ is positively Beatlesque (Rundgren's doing, of course) in its production effects.

what to buy next: *The Psychedelic Furs* (Columbia, 1980, prod. Various) 🦴🦴🦴🦴 is one of the bleakest documents of the punk era to have actual melodies and hooks—droning yet shiny, and gloriously unnerving. *Mirror Moves* (Columbia, 1984, prod. Keith Forsey) 🦴🦴🦴🦴 is the most pop-melodic Furs, with "The Ghost in You," "Heaven," and "High Wire Days."

what to avoid: *World Outside* (Columbia, 1991, prod. Stephen Street and Psychedelic Furs) 🦴 is exhausted of new ideas, and the desperate-for-a-hit production makes the sound annoying.

the rest: *Midnight to Midnight* (Columbia, 1987) 🦴🦴 *All of This and Nothing* (Columbia, 1988) 🦴🦴🦴🦴 *Book of Days* (Columbia, 1989) 🦴🦴

solo outings:

Richard Butler *Love Spit Love* (Imago, 1994) 🦴🦴

▶▶ Sisters of Mercy, Live Skull

◀◀ Velvet Underground, Beatles, Joy Division

Steve Holtje

Public Enemy

Formed 1982, Long Island, N.Y.

Chuck D. (Carlton Ridenhour), vocals; Flavor Flav (William Drayton), vocals; Terminator X (Norman Lee Rogers), DJ; Professor Griff (Richard Griffin), minister of information (1985-89)

Public Enemy seized the still-young hip-hop genre and transformed it from lighthearted, braggy dance music to a politically potent bullhorn news broadcast. Leader Chuck D.'s voice, always the equivalent of yelling "fire!" at a crowded concert, dismissed Elvis Presley as a racist, attacked Hollywood as patronizing and encouraged revolution. He was often brilliant but, as egotistical visionaries are wont to do, often shot himself in the foot. He embraced the anti-Semitic Nation of Islam Minister Louis Farrakhan; hired, apologized for and reluctantly fired the even more anti-Semitic "minister of information" Professor Griff; and his lyrics distorted Biblical passages to hold Jews responsible for Christ's crucifixion. The flip-side was Public Enemy's songs: Chuck D's voice, augmented by sidekick Flavor Flav's high-pitched "Yeeeeehhh booooyyyyyys" and DJ Terminator X's complex collage of funk samples, was as powerful as Johnny Rotten or Mick Jagger (but maybe not Howlin' Wolf) ever were. Public Enemy bestowed upon rap a political conscience and, more importantly, gave hip-hop music and culture a soul.

what to buy: *It Takes a Nation of Millions to Hold Us Back* (Def Jam, 1988, prod. Hank Shocklee and Carly Ryder) 🦴🦴🦴🦴🦴 is the definitive political rap album, establishing Public Enemy's underground power with "Bring the Noise," the anti-media "Don't Believe the Hype" and the searing funk grooves of "She Watch Channel Zero" and "Black Steel (In the Hour of Chaos)." The follow-up, *Fear of a Black Planet*, (Def Jam, 1990, prod. the Bomb Squad (Hank Shocklee, Carl Ryder, Eric (Vietnam) Sadler and Keith Shocklee)) 🦴🦴🦴🦴 has more filler, but "Fight the Power" (originally heard in Spike Lee's film "Do the Right Thing"), "Who Stole the Soul?" and "Welcome to the Terrordome" are some of the most forceful songs ever recorded. *Muse Sick-N-Hour Mess Age*, (Def Jam, 1994, prod. Bomb Squad Production) 🦴🦴🦴½ with the wise-old-soul hit "Give It Up," was tremendously underrated.

what to buy next: *Yo! Bum Rush the Show*, (Def Jam, 1987, prod. Hank Shocklee, Bill Stephney, others) 🦴🦴🦴 the first album, is not as complex as later stuff but it contains the buzzing battle cry "Public Enemy No. 1." *Apocalypse '91 ... The Enemy Strikes Black* (Def Jam, 1991, prod. Stuart Robertz, Cerwin (C-Dawg) Depper, Gary G-Wiz, the JBL) meanders with moral messages about the evils of drinking alcohol, but it's worth the price for the Public Enemy-Anthrax metal-rap collaboration "Bring the Noise."

what to avoid: Professor Griff's morally irritating solo albums *Pawns in the Game* (Luke Records, 1990) ♪ and *Kao's II Wiz*7*Dome* (Luke, 1991) WOOF!.

the rest: *Greatest Misses* (Def Jam, 1992) ♪♪

worth searching for: Chuck D.'s brilliant improvised reading of the Charles Mingus poem "Gunslinging Bird (Or If Charlie Parker Were a Gunslinger, There'd Be a Whole Lot of Dead Copycats)," on the Mingus tribute, *Weird Nightmare: Meditations on Mingus* (Columbia, 1992, prod. Hal Willner) ♪♪♪♪

solo outings:

Terminator X *Terminator X and the Valley of the Jeep Beets* (RAL, 1991) ♪♪♪ *Terminator X and the Godfathers of Threatt: Super Bad* (RAL, 1994) ♪♪.

▶▶ Rage Against the Machine, Geto Boys, Boo-Yaa T.R.I.B.E, Tricky

◀◀ James Brown, Gil Scott-Heron, Last Poets, Kurtis Blow, Boogie Down Productions, Anthrax

Steve Knopper

Public Image Ltd. (PiL)

Formed 1978 in London, England. Disbanded 1993.

John Lydon, vocals; Keith Levene, guitar (1978-83); Jah Wobble (born John Wordle), bass (1978-81); Jim Walker, drums (1978-79); Richard Dudanski, drums (1979); Martin Atkins, drums (1979-80); John McGeogh, guitar (1987-92); Lu Edmonds, keyboards, guitar (1987-92); Alan Dias, bass (1987-92); Bruce Smith, drums (1987-92)

When the Sex Pistols self-destructed, Johnny Rotten reverted to John Lydon and, with Public Image Ltd., set off on a renewed run of envelope-pushing music from which he's only recently retreated—while the rest of the world catches up. (Suffice it to say, he still has some time.) Known for its offbeat packaging, its industry-mocking presentation and the occasional violent outbursts by uncomprehending concert audiences, as well as for its groundbreaking music, PiL was subversive in a way more subtle and perhaps more durable than that of the Pistols themselves. Early versions of the band included avant-guitarist Levene, drummer Atkins (of later Brian Brain and Pigface fame) and bassist Wobble, who'd been vetoed as a Sex Pistol by that band's guitarist and drummer for his allegedly physical brand of conflict resolution. Dissension after PiL's first U.S. tour in 1980 began its attrition into a Lydon solo project, and in 1993 he deactivated the band, releasing a dance single with Leftfield that year and publishing his autobiography "Rotten: No Irish—No Blacks—No Dogs" the next. With a Mountain Dew commercial and the recent Sex Pistols reunion tour preceding a planned late-'96 solo album, Lydon seems to have come full-circle to PiL's satirical early claim to be a corporation and not a band. Of course, his last revival of Pistols material (on the mid-80s concert trail) preceded his last great album (1986's *Album*). If that's any indication, then, to contradict one of his favorite lyrical themes, there are better days ahead.

what to buy: The band's two best albums are at either end of the pop-to-alternative spectrum. PiL's masterwork, *Second Edition* (Virgin, 1979, prod. PiL) ♪♪♪♪♪ is a fascinating album of deconstructed rock music that intersects dance grooves, ambient structures and noise guitar in a way hard to imagine in the stylistically sectarian 70s. The album's sound is improvisational but remarkably cohesive, disintegrating and rebuilding before your ears, while Lydon channels a variety of song-specific voices which don't lead the band so much as haunt it. At the opposite extreme, *Album* (Elektra, 1986, prod. Bill Laswell and John Lydon) ♪♪♪♪♪ ferociously updated the Pistols' sound, filtered through the mainstream techniques of the time. It surrounded some of the typical experiments in ranting polyphony ("Rise," "Round") with mid-80s metal and synth-pop accents and an ironically corporate package (also titled Cassette and Compact Disc for the appropriate formats), but it was the sound of Reagan-era complacency being blown up from the inside.

what to buy next: The debut, *First Issue*, (Virgin, 1978, prod. PiL) ♪♪♪♪ adds a novel, mournful strain to post-Pistols punk, while moving toward the band's mature style. *Paris au Printemps* Virgin, 1980, prod. PiL) ♪♪♪♪ convincingly adapts the band's spontaneity and sense of mischief to the concert setting. *The Greatest Hits So Far* (Virgin, 1990, prod. Various) ♪♪♪♪ is a solid sampling that traces PiL's evolution from punk energy to pop sheen.

what to avoid: The nondescript *Live in Tokyo* (Elektra, 1983, prod. PiL) ♪ is inessential and only for die-hards.

the rest: *The Flowers of Romance* Warner Bros., 1981) ♪♪♪ *This is What You Want ... This is What You Get* Elektra, 1984) ♪♪♪ *Happy?* Virgin, 1987) ♪♪♪ *9* Virgin, 1989) ♪♪ *That What is Not* Virgin, 1992) ♪♪

worth searching for: *Metal Box* (Virgin U.K., 1979, prod. PiL) is the original import version of *Second Edition* It came as three vinyl discs in a round metal canister. Also, the imported version of *Flowers of Romance* (Virgin U.K., 1981, prod. PiL) offers three additional songs not found on other albums.

solo outings:

Keith Levene *Violent Opposition* (Rykodisc, 1989)

Jah Wobble *Legend Lives On* (Blue Plate, 1990) *Without Judgement* (Restless, 1994) (with Brian Eno): *Spinner* (Gyroscope, 1995) *Heaven and Earth* (Island, 1996)

Jah Wobble's Invaders Of The Heart *Rising Above Bedlam* (Atlantic, 1992) *Take Me To God* (Island, 1994)

▶▶ Glenn Branca, U2

◀◀ Yoko Ono, Sex Pistols, psychedelic rock

see also: *Sex Pistols*

Adam McGovern and Anna Glen

Gary Puckett & the Union Gap

Formed 1967 in San Diego, Calif. Disbanded 1971.

Gary Puckett, vocals; Dwight Bement, tenor sax; Kerry Chater, bass; Gary Withem, keyboards; Paul Wheatbread, drums

Suited up in mock Civil War regimental finery, the San Diego-based Gary Puckett & the Union Gap honed a power-pop formula of earnest love songs performed with full-throttle brass and string arrangements. (Imagine Blood, Sweat & Tears performing endless variations on "You've Made Me So Very Happy.") For all their beseeching quality, the songs were well-served by Puckett's full-bodied vocals, which served to amplify the music's soaring, easy-listening nature. From 1967-68, the group scored a string of hit tunes about young girls ("Young Girl"), young girls becoming young women ("This Girl is a Woman Now") and young women with cheating on their minds ("Woman Woman"). It's more than one man could take, but Puckett made it easy to swallow, with memorable melodies and a golden voice. *Looking Glass* (Sony, 1992, prod. Various) is a 20-track retrospective that pulls out the Puckett plums ("Lady Willpower," "Over You," plus the aforementioned hits) and for good measure adds on his solo work (a cover of Paul Simon's "Keep the Customer Satisfied").

Christopher Scapelliti

Pulp

Formed 1980 in Sheffield, England

Jarvis Cocker, vocals; Russell Senior, guitar, violin; Steve Mackey, bass; Candida Doyle, keyboards; Nick Banks, drums; Mark Webber, guitar, keyboards

Formed nearly 16 years ago—but only a presence in the U.S. since 1994—Pulp's music is synth/pop in the tradition of Roxy Music and David Bowie. Nerdish lead singer Cocker's lyrics chronicle the lives of everyday people from an outsider's perspective. *His 'n' Hers* (Island, 1994, prod. Ed Buller) produced a hit single in the U.K., "Do You Remember The First Time?" On *Different Class* (Island, 1995, prod. Chris Thomas), songs such as "Common People," "I Spy" and "Sorted For E's and Wizz" display Pulp's epic crescendos and wry lyrics.

Anna Glen

Pure Prairie League

Formed 1971 in Cincinnati, Ohio. Disbanded 1988.

Craig Fuller, vocals, guitars (1971-75, 1985-88); George Powell, guitars, vocals (1971-77); Jim Lanham, bass, vocals (1971-72); Jim Caughlan, drums (1971-72); John David Call, steel guitar (1971-75); Michael Connor, keyboards (1972-88); Michael Reilly, bass, vocals (1972-88); Billy Hinds, drummer (1972-88); Larry Goshorn, guitar (1975-77); Timmy Goshorn, steel guitar (1975-77); Vince Gill, guitar, vocals (1978-81); Patrick Bolin, woodwinds (1979-80); Jeff Wilson, guitar, vocals (1980-88); Gary Burr, vocals (1981-85)

Pure Prairie League, which took its name from a women's temperance group in an Errol Flynn movie, was a Cincinnati country-rock group that drew influences from the California sounds of the Flying Burrito Brothers as well as from the local regions' bluegrass. Neither of the group's first two albums, *Pure Prairie League* or *Bustin' Out,* did well upon their release in 1972, prompting RCA to drop the group. Fuller, having draft problems, left the band (Gerald Ford eventually pardoned him). Two years later, "Amie" began receiving national airplay, leaving the group in the unenviable position of having a hit and no frontman. RCA re-signed a revamped group, which continued evolving into the 80s and eventually featured a young Vince Gill on the group's only Top 10 hit, 1980's "Let Me Love You Tonight." Fuller went on to form American Flyer and front a post-Lowell George version of Little Feat before rejoining PPL in 1985.

what to buy: At the time of its release, *Bustin' Out* (RCA, 1972, prod. Robert Alan Ringe) didn't quite seem to be either rock or country but rather a blend of the better parts of both.

Fuller wrote and sang gentle pop-rock songs, which were accented by steel guitar and a largely acoustic background. The "Falling in and Out of Love/Amie" medley that appears here became an FM radio hit before "Amie" turned into a Top 40 single on its own, suggesting possibilities to an entire generation of future country singers. Mick Ronson of David Bowie's Spiders From Mars contributed string arrangements.

what to buy next: Fuller left PPL before the group made *Two Lane Highway,* (RCA, 1975, prod. John Boylan) so the songwriting suffers. But this album showcases the group's country licks, particularly on the concert favorite "Pickin' to Beat the Devil." Even though *Best of Pure Praire League* (Mercury, 1995, prod. various) sequences the "Falling In and Out of Love/Amie" medley backwards and favors the band's Mercury days over its better RCA material, the compilation is still the only place to get "Amie" and "Let Me Love You Tonight" on the same disc.

what to avoid: Pure Prairie League hasn't been well served by best-of compilations, partially because the group's two biggest hits came five years apart for different labels. Those singles aside, the band's albums are fairly consistent, *Dance* (RCA, 1976, prod. Alan Abrahams) being the weakest album from the early period and *Something in the Night* (Mercury, 1981, prod. Rob Fraboni) the weakest from the latter.

the rest: *Pure Prairie League* (RCA, 1972) *If the Shoe Fits* (RCA, 1976) *Just Fly* (RCA) *Live! Takin' the Stage* (RCA, 1977) *Firin' Up* (Mercury, 1980) *Let Me Love You Tonight* (PolyGram Special Products, 1971) *Mementos: 1971-1987* (Rushmore Productions, 1987) *"Amie" and Other Hits* (RCA, 1990)

Vince Gill, Little Feat, Garth Brooks, Clint Black

The Byrds, Flying Burrito Brothers, Creedence Clearwater Revival

see also: *Little Feat*

Brian Mansfield

Jimmy Pursey

See: Sham 69

Pursuit of Happiness

Formed 1986 in Edmonton, Alberta, Canada

Moe Berg, vocals, guitar; Dave Gilby, drums; Kris Abbot, guitar, vocals; John Sinclair, bass (1988-90); Leslie Stanwyck, vocals (1988-90); Brad Barker, bass, vocals (1990–present); Rachel Oldfield, vocals (1993-95); Jenny Foster, vocals (1995–present)

The Pursuit of Happiness (or TPOH for short) is that rare band that delivers visceral and cerebral pleasures in equal doses. Its sound is deceptively simple, with chunky guitars and vigorously solid drums buttressing irresistible pop melodies. The appeal is heightened by sharp arrangements that make adroit use of the group's two female singers; their innocently sweet harmonies render a poignant counter to Berg's everyman vocals. The result is music that is both reassuringly familiar and invitingly fresh. To its further credit, TPOH execute this highly accessible style with a bare minimum of cliche. What truly separates TPOH from other rock bands, however, is Moe's songwriting. His relationship songs offers a bracing hit of reality; Berg has the courage to confront listeners with the bald truth that real romance is rarely perfect and that most people *do* look silly having sex. Berg is well aware when his libido plunges him into typical male behavior, and he's intelligent enough to seek alternative methods of relief. It's fortunate for rock music that one of those methods is his great songwriting.

what to buy: While all four of TPOH's releases boast remarkable consistency, *One Sided Story* (Chrysalis, 1990, prod. Todd Rundgren) stands out for Berg's exceptionally strong writing and the band's no-nonsense delivery. "Two Girls in One" and "Food"—which likens intestinal appetite with sexual appetite—brilliantly showcase Berg's sense of humor while "Shave Your Legs" depicts a challenged romance that, while far from storybook, nevertheless finds a redeeming emotional core.

what to buy next: *Love Junk* (Chrysalis, 1988, prod. Todd Rundgren) is TPOH's major label debut and bears the group's major hit, the humorous "I'm an Adult Now." And the single is far from the best the album has to offer.

the rest: *The Downward Road* (Mercury, 1993) *Where's the Bone?* (Iron Music Group, 1995)

worth searching for: TPOH's first album, an independent release that contains the original versions of "I'm an Adult Now" and "Killed by Love," is difficult to find in the U.S. but can be obtained from the group's fan club, Loveslaves of TPOH (253 College St., Box 127, Toronto, Ontario M5T 1R5, Canada).

The Breeders, Veruca Salt, the Pixies

Todd Rundgren, Television

Dave Galens

Quarterflash

Formed 1980 in Portland, Ore.

Rindy Ross, vocals, sax; Marv Ross, vocals, guitar; Jack Charles, vocals, guitar; Rick DiGiallonardo, keyboards; Brian Willis, drums; Rick Gooch, bass

Quarterflash made its break fast; its debut *Quarterflash* (Geffen, 1981, prod. John Boylan) ♪♪♪ went platinum thanks to Rindy Ross' sultry to plaintive vocals and sax work on the hits "Harden My Heart" and "Find Another Fool." The band's other two albums *Take Another Picture* and *Back Into Blue* are out of print.

Patrick McCarty

Suzi Quatro

Born June 3, 1950, in Detroit, Mich.

Although best known in the U.S. from her role as Leather Tuscadero on TV's "Happy Days," and from "Stumblin' In"—the sappy duet with Chris Norman that was her only American Top 40 hit—Quatro is a major star in her adopted U.K. home. More importantly, she was the first female rock 'n' roller to rock as hard as the big boys, an androgynous tough girl wrapped in tight leather and wielding a dangerous-looking bass guitar. Quatro's mid-70s British hits were fashioned in the image of the Sweet (Sweet auteurs Mike Chapman and Nicky Chinn wrote and produced most of her early singles), propelled by teenage-rampage hooks and a plodding, clunky charm. It was formula stuff, not all that dissimilar to what Slade, Mud, Hello, T. Rex, Gary Glitter and scads of other glam/glitter Brits were pounding out at the time, but it was a goofy, catchy formula. Quatro's gender-bending stance may have seemed a novelty at first, but its groundbreaking effect was nothing short of revelatory, perhaps even revolutionary. By the mere act of rocking out on her own aggressive terms, Quatro served as an inspiration to any girl who would ever reject the idea of just becoming the rock star's girlfriend, and instead embrace the idea of becoming the rock star herself. Just ask Joan Jett.

The Wild One: Classic Quatro (Razor & Tie, 1996, prod. Various) ♪♪♪ is all the Quatro most folks will ever need. Its 20 tracks include a fair amount of drek (including the ever-limp "Stumblin' In"), but its sins are fully redeemed by the American debut of Quatro's best track, the terrific "Tear Me Apart." Steer clear of *Your Mama Won't Like Me*, (Arista, 1975, prod. Mike Chapman and Nicky Chinn) ♪ a simply horrid stab at fake funk.

Carl Cafarelli

Queen

Formed 1971 in England. Disbanded 1991.

Freddie Mercury, (born Frederick Bulsara) vocals, piano (died Nov. 24, 1991); Brian May, guitar, vocals; John Deacon, bass; Roger Meddows Taylor, drums, vocals

When you think of great rock 'n' roll harmony groups, the Beach Boys or some doo-wop outfits spring to mind. Unless you're a Queen fan. The quartet's unique sound blended glam-rock, heavy metal, disco rhythms and intricate vocal harmonies inspired more by opera and show-tunes than by classic doo-wop or the call-and-response technique most rock bands incorporate. Although it would take until its third album before the Queen sound fully developed, its live act was a hit from the start. Led by one of rocks most outrageous frontmen (Mercury) and anchored by soaring guitar work by May, Queen's concerts rank among some of rock's finest. The group's pomp and bombast won it a worldwide audience, but its U.S. success dwindled during late 80s. In 1991, Mercury died from AIDS, and while the surviving trio has staged a memorial concert and released an album of material culled from Mercury's final sessions—they have no plans to continue on as Queen.

what to buy: No collection its complete without *A Night at the Opera* (Elektra, 1975, prod. Roy Thomas Baker and Queen) ♪♪♪♪ and *A Day at the Races* (Elektra, 1976, prod. Queen) ♪♪♪♪ From heavy metal powerhouses to operatic ballads, Queen fills these albums with every sound imaginable, including kazoos and ukulele, without even using synthesizers. In fact, each of these albums features one of the band's operatic opuses—the seminal "Bohemian Rhapsody" from *A Night at the Opera* and "Somebody to Love" from *A Day At The Races*

what to buy next: *News of the World* (Elektra, 1977, prod. Queen and Mike Stone) ♪♪♪♪ is as entertaining an album as *Opera* or *Races*. It finds the group moving into the safer regions of rock, marking something of an end to Queen's most adventurous period. *Live Killers* (Elektra, 1979, prod. Queen) ♪♪♪♪ features a feisty collection of performances and serves as a pleasant relic from one of rock's great live acts, while *Greatest Hits* (Hollywood, 1992) ♪♪♪♪ gathers the appropriate singles.

what to avoid: *Flash Gordon*. soundtrack (Elektra, 1980, Brian May and Mack) **WOOF!** The only redeeming thing to say about this soundtrack is the movie of the same name based on comic strip hero "Flash Gordon" deserves nothing better.

the rest: *Queen* (Elektra, 1973) ♪♪♪ *Queen II* (Elektra, 1974)

What Album Changed Your Life?

"I think Rubber Soul was the first one that never left my turntable for months. It was basically an acoustic Beatles album, an acoustic rock 'n' roll album. I was a kid, but that was when I started to notice the Beatles' arranging ability, how they put a song together. Ultimately I saw the possibilities of what could be done, in a primitive sense because I was just learning how to play. All of a sudden I realized how much I didn't know."

Bill Morrissey

Sheer Heart Attack (Elektra, 1973) *Jazz* (Elektra, 1978) *The Game* (Elektra, 1980) *Greatest Hits* (Elektra, 1981, prod. Various) *Hot Space* (Elektra, 1982) *The Works* (Capitol) *A Kind of Magic* (Capitol, 1986) *The Miracle* (Capitol, 1989) *Innuendo* (Hollywood, 1991) *Classic Queen* (Hollywood, 1992) *Live at Wembley '86* (Hollywood, 1992) *Greatest Hits* (Hollywood, 1992) *Five Live* (With George Michael and Lisa Stansfield) (Hollywood EP, 1992); *Queen at the BBC* (Hollywood, 1995) *Made in Heaven* (Hollywood, 1995)

worth searching for: The promo-only four-volume *Queen Rocks* sampler series, a nicely packaged 20th anniversary set that heralded the group's signing to Hollywood Records.

solo outings:

Freddie Mercury *Mr. Bad Guy* (Columbia, 1985) *Barcelona* (with Montserrat Cabelle) (Hollywood, 1987) *The Great Pretender* (Hollywood, 1992)

Brian May *Star Fleet Project* (Capitol EP, 1983) *Back to the Light* (Hollywood, 1993)

Roger Taylor *Fun in Space* (Elektra, 1981) *Strange Frontier* (Capitol, 1984)

Def Leppard, Oasis, Guns N' Roses, George Michael, Annie Lennox, "Wayne's World"

Led Zeppelin, David Bowie, Mott the Hoople, Liza Minnelli, Maria Callas

Mike Joiner

Queensryche

Formed 1981 in Bellevue, Wash.

Geoff Tate, vocals; Chris DeGarmo, guitar; Michael Wilton, guitar; Eddie Jackson, bass; Scott Rockenfield, drums

This Seattle band; with its art rock pretensions and heavy metal thunder, came along as Kansas, Boston, Styx and other 70s American progressive rock bands were faltering or disbanding. Formed by guitarists DeGarmo and Wilton, the group skipped the bars and concentrated on writing songs and developing a concert-level stage show. Its first EP, *Queen of Reich*, won a contract with EMI America, which reissued the album in an expanded version as Queensryche's self-titled debut in 1983. A cult favorite for several years, the group finally broke through commercially with the Top 10 hit and video "Silent Lucidity" from its 1990 album, *Empire*.

what to buy: *Empire* (EMI, 1990, prod. Peter Collins) moved away from the conceptual approach of previous albums and worked as a flowing collection of arty hard rock, from the pounding to the poignant. The centerpiece is "Silent Lucidity," the Seattle group's answer to "Dust in the Wind."

what to buy next: *Operation: Mindcrime* (EMI Manhattan, 1988, prod. Peter Collins) a smart—and fast—concept album about censorship and mind control.

what to avoid: *Queensryche*, (EMI, 1983, prod. Queensryche and Neil Keram) an inauspicious debut.

the rest: *The Warning* (EMI, 1984) *Rage for Order* (EMI, 1986) *Operation: Livecrime* (EMI, 1991) *Promised Land* (EMI, 1994)

Pearl Jam, Alice in Chains

Kansas, Styx, Pink Floyd

Doug Pullen

? and the Mysterians

Formed 1962 in Flint, Mich. Disbanded 1968.

? (Question Mark), vocals; Larry Borjas, guitar; Robert Balderrama, guitar; Frankie Rodriguez, keyboards; Frank Lugo, bass; Robert Martinez, drums (replaced by Edward Serrato)

The personification of one-hit wonders, this mysterious Michigan group, made up of the sons of migrant farm workers, contributed one of the consummate garage rock anthems of the 60s, "96 Tears," which was recorded in a basement studio in Bay City, Mich. It featured a cheesy, repetitive organ line (often attributed to a Farfisa, but in actuality it was a Vox Continental) and the emphatic, embittered vocals of the band's enigmatic singer). It became a regional hit in Flint and Detroit, then was picked up by Cameo records and topped the charts in 1966. The band (which at one point included future Grand Funk Railroad bassist Mel Shacher) released two albums and disappeared, though its singer, ?, who legally changed his name and never allows himself to be photographed without his trademark sunglasses, has kept the band alive and makes occasional appearances. "96 Tears" is credited to a Rudy Martinez, though nobody has acknowleged whether that's ?'s real name or not. He signed away the publishing rights to those songs years ago. The company that owns "96 Tears" has allowed other artists, including Aretha Franklin, to record the song, and allowed its use on various compilations, but has not reissued either of the Mysterians' albums—*96 Tears* and *Action*—on CD. All that's available is *96 Tears Forever: The Dallas Reunion Tapes*, (ROIR, 1984) an almost a bootleg-quality live album, featuring ? and a new group of Mysterians. The live version of the song also is available on the compilation *Ten ROIR Years*

Doug Pullen

Quicksilver Messenger Service

Formed 1965 in San Francisco, Calif. Disbanded 1975. Re-formed 1987 Disbanded again in 1988

Gary Duncan, guitar, vocals (1965-69, 1970-75, 1987-88); John Cipollina (died May 29, 1989), guitar (1965-71); David Freiberg, bass, vocals (1969-71); Greg Elmore, drums; Jim Murray, harmonica, vocals (1965-67); Nicky Hopkins, keyboards (1969-70); Dino Valente (born Chester Powers), vocals (1970-75); Mark Naftalin, keyboards (1971); Mark Ryan, bass (1971-73); Chuck Steales, keyboards (1971-73); Sammy Piazza, drums (1987-88); W. Michael Lewis, keyboards (1987-88)

Little remembered these days, the Quicksilver, on any given night, could easily surpass better-known peers from the San Francisco rock scene like the Jefferson Airplane or the Grateful Dead. Stacking harmony vocals on top of a charging guitar-driven sound, Quicksilver transformed the band's signature folk-rock material into high-flying electrical improvisations that transported audiences at the Fillmore and Avalon Ballrooms into other realms. Once persuasive vocalist Valente joined the ranks, the band managed a couple of radio hits ("Fresh Air," "What About Me"), but it is the Quicksilver of the band's first two albums that really left its mark on the San Francisco scene.

what to buy: The first two albums say it all; *Quicksilver Messenger Service* (Capitol, 1968, prod. Nick Gravenites, Harvey Brooks and Pete Welding) and *Happy Trails* (Capitol, 1969) —especially the side-long version of "Who Do You Love" on the second album, which was edited *down* to 25 minutes.

what to buy next: A two-disc retrospective, *Sons Of Mercury 1968-1975* (Rhino, 1991, prod. Various), lends a complete overview of the band's checkered career, including some rare early material and a second CD that does little more than chronicle the band's decline.

what to avoid: Guitarist Gary Duncan reprised the band name for a hapless, heavy metal solo album, *Peace By Piece* (EMI, 1987, prod. Gary Duncan, Sammy Piazza and Bob Ohlsson) **WOOF!**

the rest: *Shady Grove* (Capitol, 1970/One Way, 1995) *Just For Love* (Capitol, 1970/One Way, 1995) *What About Me* (Capitol, 1971/One Way, 1995) *Quicksilver* (Capitol, 1971/One Way, 1995) *Comin' Thru* (Capitol, 1972/One Way, 1995)

solo outings:

Dino Valente *Dino Valente* (Epic, 1968)

John Cipollina *Copperhead* (Columbia, 1973)

Copperhead, Man, Blues Traveler

Righteous Brothers, Buffy St. Marie, The Charlatans

Joel Selvin

Quiet Riot

Formed 1975, Burbank, Calif. Disbanded 1987. Re-formed 1990.

Kevin DuBrow, vocals (1975-87, 1990-present); Randy Rhoads, guitar (1975-77, died March 19, 1982); Kelly Garni, bass (1975-76); Drew Forsyth, drums (1975-77); Drew Cavazo, guitar (1977-87, 1990-present); Rudy Sarzo, bass (1978-83); Frankie Banali, drums (1978-87);

Chuck Wright, bass (1984-85); Paul Shortino, vocals (1986-87); Sean McNabb, bass (1986-87); Kenny Hillary, bass (1990-present); Bobby Rondinelli, drums (1990-present)

A quick blip on the pop charts, Quiet Riot helped usher in the mid-80s era of the heavy metal hair bands with its smash cover of Slade's "Cum on Feel the Noize." But the real noteworthy aspect of the band's career is that it was an early stop for guitarist Rhoads, who went on to trend-setting glory at Ozzy Osbourne's side until his death in a 1982 plane crash. Quiet Riot, meanwhile, never equalled its initial success—despite another Slade cover, "Mama Weer All Crazee Now"—and by 1984 its popularity was already on the slide. Frontman DuBrow was axed in one of rock's nastier bootings, and the group floundered before taking him back in 1990. Now it flounders on a hard rock club circuit that makes Spinal Tap's itinerary look glamorous.

what to buy: *Metal Health* (Pasha, 1983, prod. Spencer Proffer) is Quiet Riot's big moment, spirited and dispensable trash-metal, highlighted by "Cum on Feel the Noize."

what to buy next: *The Randy Rhoads Years* (Rhino, 1993) lets Rhoads fans—and they are a legion—take a listen to his formative years before hooking up with Osbourne. *Winners Take All* (Columbia Special Products, 1993, prod. Various) is a compact best-of, probably all the Quiet Riot you'll need.

what to avoid: *Terrified* (Moonstone, 1993) Absolute junk, like most of the post-*Metal Health* releases.

the rest: *Condition Critical* (Pasha, 1984) *QR III* (Pasha, 1986) *QR* (Pasha, 1988) *Down to the Bone* (Kamikaze Records, 1995) *Best of* (Pasha, 1996)

▶▶ Winger, Dokken, Ratt

◀◀ Slade, Kiss, Van Halen

Allan Orski

Robert Quine

Born Dec. 30, 1942, in Akron, Ohio

After giving up bands in favor of a law career, Quine reversed his decision after meeting Tom Verlaine and Richard Hell. With Hell & the Voidoids, Quine's abstract, jagged guitar lines had a major influence on the sound of punk; among his influences were early rockabilly, mid-70s Miles Davis records and Lou Reed's Velvet Underground work, all of which he distilled into a flexible, versatile style. Quine subsequently joined Lou Reed's band. With fellow guitarist Jody Harris (Raybeats, Contortions), he made *Escape*, (Lust/Unlust, 1981, prod. Jody Harris and Robert Quine) on which they share bass and electronic percussion duties for a stylistically varied, mildly experimental album. With Lou Reed bandmate Fred Maher, Quine made the more abstract *Basic* (EG, 1984, prod. Robert Quine and Fred Maher) Having mostly abandoning touring, Quine's session work kept him on the periphery of public recognition, most notably for his contributions to several successful Matthew Sweet albums.

Steve Holtje

Trevor Rabin

See: Yes

Radiohead

Formed 1991, Oxford, England

Thom Yorke, piano, guitar and vocals; Jon Greenwood, guitar, organ, recorder, synthesizer and keyboards; Ed O'Brien, guitar; Colin Greenwood, bass; Phil Selway, drums.

Radiohead broke in America on the strength of a self-loathing anthem called "Creep." Recorded spontaneously in one take and included as the opening cut on its debut album, *Pablo Honey* (Capitol, 1993, prod. Sean Slade/Paul Q. Kolderie), the song's undeniable charms made it clear that this group was different from the usual U.K. hype-driven fluff. In fact, no one in Britain even acknowledged Radiohead until the group had already conquered the U.S. charts. While the English music tabloids were trying to shove fey groups like Suede and Verve down American throats, Radiohead snuck out and ahead of the ranks by mixing sensitive Britpop jangle with hormone-induced American grunge. Ripe with ambition, *Pablo Honey*, showed that Radiohead had the chops for greatness. Its successor, *The Bends* (Capitol, 1995, prod. John Leckie) is unblinkingly charged, exasperatingly beautiful, full of graceful crevices, glorious melodies and ambitious musical flex.

Aidin Vaziri

Gerry Rafferty

See: Stealers Wheel

Rage Against the Machine

Formed 1991 in Los Angeles, Calif.

Zack de la Rocha, vocals; Tom Morello, guitar; Tim Bob Commerford, bass; Brad Wilk, drums

Who says that the revolution will not be televised? Rage Against the Machine has managed to get its fiery brand of revolutionary metal-funk-rap all over MTV (not to mention alternative radio), making the dynamic quartet the most-popular politically charged group in pop since Public Enemy. Led by militant spit-fire singer de la Rocha and Harvard-educated guitarist Morello—the son of an American anti-censorship activist school teacher and a Mau Mau revolutionary from Kenya—the group pounds the status quo with angry lyrics, thunderous riffs and crushing rhythms, taking on big business, oppressive governments, state corruption, racism, right-wing hatred, police brutality, media manipulation, domestic decay and inner-city violence. The uncompromising group also throws its intense support behind controversial causes (the Zapatista movement in the Chiapas state of Mexico) and figures (Leonard Peltier, Mumia Abu-Jamal). Rage put a photo of Che Guevara on the cover of an import single and included a picture of a Buddhist monk burning himself to death to protest the American invasion of Vietnam on its self-titled debut. Rage has also been known to stage benefit concerts at de la Rocha's house (for the Chiapas) and to stand naked in front of 40,000 (at Lollapalooza) to protest censorship. Morello, who once worked for U.S. Sen. Alan Cranston, is even writing a collection of 25 short biographies of figures such as Malcolm X, who often are overlooked in U.S. history books.

what to buy: With its visceral guitar attack, thunderous rhythms and furious social commentary, *Rage Against the Machine* (Epic, 1992, prod. Rage Against the Machine and Gggarth) is equal parts Black Sabbath and Public Enemy, with a dash of Sly Stone funk thrown in for good-rocking measure. Of course, while the lyrics are full of sociopolitical relevance, the mesmerizing grooves of such standouts as "Killing in the Name" and "Bullet In the Head" are probably what earned the band most of its fans.

what to buy next: As improbable as it may seem to anybody who's seen Rage live, the thick, raw, frenzied churning *Evil Empire* (Epic, 1996, prod. Brendan O'Brien and Rage Against the Machine) manages to capture the intensity of the group's explosive performances. Morello's wah-wah guitar break on "Bulls on Parade,"a rant against government misspending, steals the show.

worth searching for: In 1996, the band issued a vinyl 7-inch since to fan-club members featuring an intense live version of "Bombtrack" (from a BBC performance). The spit-fire B-side cover of "Fuck Tha Police" (recorded at a benefit concert for Mumia Abu-Jamal) is exceptional.

▶▶ Deftones, Korn, Salmon

◀◀ MC5, Clash, Ice Cube, Public Enemy, Black Sabbath, Body Count, Minor Threat, Youth of Today, Led Zeppelin, Beastie Boys, the Sex Pistols, Red Hot Chili Peppers, Fugazi

Aidin Vaziri

The Rain Parade

Formed 1982 in Los Angeles, Calif. Disbanded 1985.

David Roback, vocals, guitar, percussion (1982-84); Steven Roback, vocals, bass; Matthew Piucci, vocals, guitar, sitar; Will Glenn, keyboards, violin; John Thoman, guitar, vocals (1984-85); Eddie Kalwa, drums (1982-84); Mark Marcum, drums (1984-85)

Perhaps the "paisley underground" band that hewed closest to the perceived influences of the scene, the Rain Parade was formed by the Roback brothers and signed by Enigma on the strength of the self-issued first single, the Byrdsy "What's She Done to Your Mind?" The debut album, *Emergency Third Rail Power Trip*, and the following EP, *Explosions in the Glass Palace*, are combined on one CD (Enigma, 1983-84, prod. David Roback, the Rain Parade and Jim Hill) which is the group's only in-print material. Besides the Byrds, obvious influences are Buffalo Springfield (especially Neil Young's guitar style), Love, Big Star, *Revolver*-era Beatles and Syd Barrett-era Pink Floyd. The overall mood is quite subdued, with the EP's last two tracks (the quiet "Broken Horse," the spacey "No Easy Way Down") standing out the most.

see also: *Dream Syndicate, Mazzy Star*

Steve Holtje

Rain Tree Crow

See: Japan

Rainbow

Formed 1975 in Los Angeles, Calif. Disbanded 1984. Reformed 1995.

Ritchie Blackmore, guitar; Ronnie James Dio, vocals (1975-78); Craig Gruber, bass (1975); Mickey Lee Soule, keyboards (1975); Gary Driscoll, drums (1975); Jimmy Bain, bass (1975-77); Tony Carey, keyboards (1975-77); Cozy Powell, drums (1975-80); Bob Daisley, bass (1977-78); David Stone, keyboards (1977-78); Graham Bonnett, vocals

(1979-80); Roger Glover, bass (1979-84); Don Airey, keyboards (1979-81); Joe Lynn Turner, vocals (1980-84); Bob Rondinellie, drums (1980-84); David Rosenthal, keyboards (1981-84); Dookie White, vocals (1995-present); Chuck Berge, drums (1995-present); Greg Smith, bass (1995-present); Paul Morris, keyboards (1995-present); Candice Night, vocals (1995-present)

Fed up with the group dynamic in Deep Purple—mostly the other members' desire for democracy—fabulously tempermental guitarist Blackmore put together Rainbow as an outlet for his classically based, virtuostic brand of bombast. He initially recruited the little-known band Elf, scoring a captivating frontman in singer Dio. The second version of Rainbow—with powerhouse drummer Powell—was Blackmore's best, a group of solid players that could pull off the kind of extended pieces Blackmore wanted to perform (without, of course, getting in the guitarist's way). Over the years, Blackmore's temperament made Rainbow something of a musician's lab, even a launching pad for a few careers, such as singers Bonnett and Turner. Rainbow had its greatest commercial success after Deep Purple bassist Glover joined the fold and took over production chores, and while the group was put on ice for Purple's mid-80s reunion, Blackmore re-activated it after he left the band again a decade later.

what to buy: Rainbow's best lineup, its second, recorded just one studio album, *Rainbow Rising.* (Polydor, 1976, prod. Martin Birch) ♪♪♪♪ With extended pieces such as "Stargazer" and "A Light in the Black," it's the definitive representation of Blackmore's ambitions. *Live in Europe* (Mausoleum Classix, 1996, exec. prod. Steve Ship, Barry Ehrmann and Evert Wilbrink) ♪♪♪♪ captures the same lineup onstage in 1976, stretching out even further on "Mistreated," "Catch the Rainbow" and the Yardbirds' "Still I'm Sad."

what to buy next: *The Best of Rainbow* (Polydor, 1981, prod. Various), ♪♪♪♪ a good sampling of the band's prime material, with the focus rightly on the Dio years.

what to avoid: *Down to Earth* (Oyster/Polydor, 1979, prod. Roger Glover) ♪, Bonnet's sole effort as Rainbow frontman, is a tepid collection that particularly misses Dio's power as a singer.

the rest: *Ritchie Blackmore's Rainbow* (Polygram, 1975) ♪♪♪ *Onstage* (Oyster/Polydor, 1977) ♪♪ *Long Live Rock 'n' Roll* (Oyster/Polydor, 1978) ♪♪♪ *Difficult to Cure* (Polydor, 1981) ♪♪ *Jealous Lover* (Polydor, 1981) ♪♪ *Straight Between the Eyes* (Mercury, 1982) ♪♪♪ *Bent Out of Shape* (Mercury, 1982) ♪♪ *Final Vinyl* (Mercury, 1986) ♪♪♪ *Stranger in Us All* (BMG, 1995) ♪♪♪

worth searching for: *Live in Tokyo '84*, a Japanese laser disc of what turned out to be Rainbow's temporary farewell. The Tokyo Symphony Orchestra is on hand for a particularly rousing version of "Difficult to Cure" that leads into Beethoven's Ninth Symphony.

▶▶ Accept, Metallica, Alcatrazz, Dokken

◀◀ Deep Purple, Jeff Beck Group, Yardbirds, Ludwig Van Beethoven, Richard Wagner

see also: *Deep Purple, Dio*

Gary Graff

Bonnie Raitt

Born Nov. 8, 1949 in Los Angeles, Calif.

There are two Raitt stories—one in the bottle and one out. From the late 60s to the early 80s, the Quaker-raised, Radcliffe-educated daughter of Broadway star John Raitt was a blues mama who learned her craft at the feet of John Lee Hooker, Mississippi Fred McDowell and Sippie Wallace. They taught her to play hard and true—and to party hard, too. Raitt made good on their lessons, turning out songs that mined blues, pop and folk while developing a distinctive, stinging slide guitar style and an aching, honest vocal delivery. An exceptional cover of Del Shannon's "Runaway" unjustly defined the first phase of her career, though Raitt also proved herself a performer of rare conscious, joining kindred spirits such as Jackson Browne and James Taylor at various benefits and rallies. It was after being dropped by Warner Bros. in 1983 that Raitt decide to clean up, dry out and, essentially, start over again. Her 1986 release *Nine Lives* revealed a smoother pop style that retained just enough blues touches to make it work; it sold more than four million copies and started a string of Grammy victories that made Raitt—who married actor Michael O'Keefe in 1991—the darling of her peers as well as of the mainstream audience. She's explored other styles on subsequent releases, though never straying too far from the proven sound. And in 1995, Fender made her the first female guitarist to have an instrument named after her, with royalties funding a program to provide guitars and music lessons to inner city youths.

what to buy: Smooth, assured and forthright, *Nine Lives* (Capitol, 1986, prod. Don Was) ♪♪♪♪ is a mature and celebratory effort in which Raitt unveils her new sound and sings with depth and feeling about the tribulations of the past; she even makes Jerry Williams' "I Will Not Be Denied" sound like one of her own songs. *The Bonnie Raitt Collection* (Warner Bros., 1990, prod. Various) is her old label's cash in on *Nine Lives'* success, but it's a terrific overview anyway, featuring previously unreleased live duets with Wallace ("Woman Be Wise") and John Prine ("Angel From Montgomery").

what to buy next: *Give it Up* (Warner Bros., 1973, prod. Michael Cuscuna) is the best of Raitt's Warners albums, a corker that blasts open with her own "Give it Up or Let Me Go" and continues through an inspired collection of originals and covers. *Luck of the Draw* (Capitol, 1991, prod. Don Was and Bonnie Raitt) finds the Raitt of *Nick of Time* exuberantly in love and ready to tell the world about it on "Something to Talk About" and her burning duet with Delbert McClinton, "Good Man, Good Woman."

what to avoid: *Home Plate* (Warner Bros., 1975, prod. Paul D. Rothchild) is a weak and ill-conceived attempt to take Raitt in a country direction—and it strikes out.

the rest: *Bonnie Raitt* (Warner Bros., 1971) *Takin' My Time* (Warner Bros., 1973) *Streetlights* (Warner Bros., 1974) *Sweet Forgiveness* (Warner Bros., 1977) *The Glow* (Warner Bros., 1979) *Green Light* (Warner Bros., 1982) *Longing in Their Hearts* (Capitol, 1994) *Road Tested* (Capitol, 1995)

worth searching for: Raitt's ubiquitous guest shots on her friends albums have resulted in some fine music. Her Grammy winning duet with Hooker on "In the Mood" from his album *The Healer* (Chameleon, 1989, prod. Roy Rogers) is definitive, while her contributions to her father's *Broadway Legend* (Angel, 1995) are sweet.

▶▶ Pat Benatar, Melissa Etheridge, Melissa Ferrick, Sheryl Crow, Joan Osborne

◀◀ Howlin' Wolf, Muddy Waters, Sippie Wallace, Mississippi Fred McDowell, John Lee Hooker, Odetta, Joan Baez

Gary Graff

Dee Dee Ramone

See: The Ramones

The Ramones

Formed 1974 in Queens, N.Y.

Joey Ramone (born Jeffrey Hyman), lead vocals; Johnny Ramone (born John Cummings), guitar; Dee Dee Ramone (born Douglas Colvin), bass (1974-89); C.J. Ramone (born Christopher Ward), bass (1989-present); Tommy Ramone (born Tommy Erdelyi), drums (1974-77); Marky Ramone (born Marc Bell), drums (1977-83, 1987-present); Richie Ramone (born Richard Reinhardt), drums (1983-1987).

Back in their gabba-gabba-heyday, the Ramones were championed as living, leather-jacketed cartoon characters, a punk band to be adored but not taken seriously. And given the subject matter of such fast, furious two-minute anthems as "Now I Wanna Sniff Some Glue," "Teenage Lobotomy" and "Beat on the Brat," even that might be giving them too much credit. But what the safety pin crowd loved about the band—its relentless tenacity and ability to play 30 songs in an hour—would have worn thin before you could say "1-2-3-4!" if not for the fact that hidden under the power chords was a genuine affection for such 60s icons as Beach Boys, the Trashmen and the Searchers. As punk waned, the Ramones matured—that is, they learned a couple more chords, extended their songs beyond two minutes and started writing about topics other than girls and mental disorders (a topic they officially exhausted with 1983's "Everytime I Eat Vegetables It Makes Me Think of You"). But their subsequent records have run all over the map, from the Phil Spector-produced grandeur of *End of the Century* to the headbanging speed metal of *Halfway to Sanity* to the 60s covers of *Acid Eaters* In 1995, they announced their impending break-up but were still touring a year later, though they claimed their 1996 Lollapalooza jaunt would indeed mark the end.

what to buy: The first two albums, *The Ramones* (Sire, 1976, prod. Craig Leon) and *Leave Home*, (Sire, 1977, prod. Tony Bongiovi and Tommy Erdelyi) are compiled as *All The Stuff (And More) - Vol. 1* (Sire, 1990). But the group's pop roots begin to show on *Rocket to Russia* (Sire, 1977, prod. Tony Bongiovi and Tommy Erdelyi) and *Road to Ruin* (Sire, 1978, prod. Tommy Erdelyi and Ed Stasium) —compiled on volume two of *All the Stuff*—making it the best place to start, if only for Joey's yearning vocal on the Searchers' "Needles and Pins," the convincing country-rock of "Questioningly" and the fist-pumping guitar attack of "I Wanna Be Sedated" and "I Just Want to Have Something to Do."

what to buy next: Former 10cc member Graham Gouldman helms *Pleasant Dreams*, (Sire, 1981) which turns out to be a protest album driven by the metallic crunch of "We Want the Airwaves," "This Business Is Killing Me" and "The KKK Took My Baby Away."

what to avoid: *Halfway to Sanity* (Sire, 1987, prod. the Ramones and Daniel Rey), one of several veerings into hardcore punk and metal, offers all of the volume and none of the charm of its predecessors.

the rest: *It's Alive* (Sire, 1979) *End of the Century* (Sire, 1980) *Subterranean Jungle* (Sire, 1983) *Too Tough to Die* (Sire, 1984) *Animal Boy* (Sire, 1986) *Brain Drain* (Sire, 1989) *Ramones Mania* (Sire, 1989) *Loco Live* (Sire, 1991) *Mondo Bizarro* (Radioactive, 1992) *Acid Eaters* (Radioactive, 1994) *Adios Amigos* (Radioactive, 1995) *Greatest Hits Live* (Radioactive, 1996)

worth searching for: The first-run vinyl pressings of *Leave Home* (Sire, 1977) contain "Carbona Not Glue," which was removed from subsequent pressings after a threatened lawsuit.

solo outings:

Dee Dee Ramone (as Dee Dee King) Standing in the Spotlight (Sire, 1987)

▶▶ Pansy Division, Green Day, Shonen Knife

◀◀ The Trashmen, the Beach Boys, Phil Spector

David Okamoto

Willis Alan Ramsey

Born March 5, 1951, in Birmingham, Ala.

Wielding more influence than the meager sales of his one album would indicate, Ramsey is seen today as a genuine forbear to the progressive country scene that has grown up around Austin, Texas, during the past two decades. *Willis Alan Ramsey* (Shelter, 1972/DCC Compact Classics, 1990, prod. Denny Cordell and Willis Alan Ramsey) is an acoustic-based collection of narrative country/folk tunes that became known mostly via versions of its songs by Leon Russell, Jimmy Buffett and America. Ramsey's best-known song, "Muskrat Love," was a No. 4 hit for the Captain & Tennille in 1976. There have been rumors of a new Ramsey album, but thus far none has appeared.

Daniel Durchholz

Lee Ranaldo

See: Sonic Youth

Rancid

Formed 1991 in Marin County, Calif.

Tim Armstrong, guitar, vocals; Matt Freeman, bass, vocals; Brett Reed, drums, backing vocals; Lars Fredericksen, guitar, vocals (1994-present)

Emerging as the next big thing during the mid-90s new-punk media craze, Rancid blends 70s punk and ska and 80s hardcore into an energized (and rote) flurry of tough, taut dynamics. The group emerged with a strong pedigree; Armstrong and Freeman hail from the acclaimed Bay Area group Operation Ivy, while Fredericksen spent some time in a latter day version of the U.K. subs. With its mohawk haircuts and strident lyrical themes, Rancid has the familiar feel of the Clash—a comparison that both rattles and flatters the band members. The group did earn credibility points by staying with its independent label, Epitaph, in the face of an intense major label bidding wars, and in 1996 played on the Lollapalooza main stage. Its third album, *...And Out Come the Wolves,* (Epitaph, 1995, prod. Jerry Finn and Rancid) is group's most fully realized so far, as the group tears through hardcore, ska and 70s-styled punk anthems with appealing abandon. The handful of catchy pounders that highlight the album—"Lock, Step, & Gone," "Ruby Soho" and "Time Bomb" —are tasty, if a bit disposable.

the rest: *Rancid* (Epitaph, 1993) *Let's Go* (Epitaph, 1994)

Allan Orski

Rare Earth

Formed 1964 as the Sunliners in Detroit, Mich. Disbanded 1983. Reformed late 80s.

Gil Bridges, reeds, vocals (1964-78); Pete Rivera (born Pete Hoorelbeke), drums, vocals (1964-74, 1977-78); John Persh, bass, trombone, vocals (1964-72); Rod Richards, guitars, vocals (1969-70); Kenny James, keyboards (1969-70); Ray Monette, guitar (1971-76, 1978); Mark Olson, keyboards (1970-); Ed Guzman, percussion (1970-78, died July 29, 1993); Mark Olson, keyboards, vocals (1971-74, 1978); Michael Urso, bass, vocals (1972-74, 1977-78); Roger McBride, bass, vocals (1975-76); Gabriel Katona, keyboards, vocals (1975); Jerry LaCroix, vocals, reeds (1975-76); Barry Eugene Frost, percussion (1975); Paul Warren, guitar, vocals (1975); Frank Westerbrook, keyboards (1976); Ron Fransen, keyboards (1977); Daniel Ferguson, guitar (1977)

For a long time Motown played around with rock 'n' roll, dabbling—with the Neil Young/Rick James-led Mynah Birds, for instance—but never really making a move until the label signed Rare Earth in 1968. Ironically, the group's first big hit was a remake of the Temptations' "Get Ready" in 1970; it was a workmanlike cover, but it was wholly unrepresentative of Rare Earth's original material, which blended touches of jazz and psychedelic pop. Crammed into the Motown machine, where its songs came from staff songwriters, Rare Earth fit somewhere between Parliament and Blood, Sweat & Tears, which made it a hard sell for any company much less a label whose primary experience had been in the R&B and pop markets and was a virtual stranger to the newer—and growing—rock community. Rare Earth did hit the Top 20 again with "I Just Want to Celebrate" and "Hey Big Brother," both driven by soulful vocal chorales.

But the group never really hit the mainstream in a big way, which has as much to do with the woozy focus of its music as it does with Motown's unfamiliarity with rock. Rare Earth is still around however, led by Bridges and Monette and enjoying particular favor in Europe.

what to buy: With 20 tracks, *Greatest Hits and Rare Classics* (Motown, 1991, prod. Various) is a good introduction to this group's varied body of work.

what to buy next: If *Greatest Hits* really grabs you, go for the two-CD *Anthology,* (Motown, 1995, prod. Various) which is diffuse but also provides a sonic smorgasbord for the various sounds being made in pop music as the 60s became the 70s.

what to avoid: *Earth Time: The Essential Rare Earth* (Motown, 1994, prod. Various) a misleadingly titled collection marked by long, ponderous live cuts and the unfair sense that these guys couldn't play a tightly constructed song.

the rest: *Get Ready* (Rare Earth/Motown, 1969) *Ecology* (Rare Earth/Motown, 1970) *In Concert* (Rare Earth, 1971/Motown, 1989) *Different World* (Koch International, 1993)

▶▶ The Commodores, Was (Not Was), Funkadelic

◀◀ The Temptations, Pink Floyd, Procol Harum, Sly & the Family Stone

Gary Graff

The Rascals

See: The Young Rascals

The Raspberries

Formed 1970 in Cleveland, Ohio. Disbanded 1975.

Eric Carmen, keyboards, bass, guitar; Wally Bryson, guitar; Dave Smalley, bass, guitar (1970-73); Jim Bonfanti, drums (1970-73); Scott McCarl, bass (1974-75); Michael McBride, drums (1974-75)

Miscast throughout its career as a lightweight singles band, the Raspberries have since gained a rightful place as one of the true pioneers of power pop. Forming in Cleveland from the ashes of local phenoms The Choir and Cyrus Erie, the Raspberries were propelled by Eric Carmen's McCartney-esque songwriting and featured some of the most powerful pop you'd ever want to hear. With producer Jimmy Ienner leading the way, the Raspberries recorded output is filled with soaring ballads and rock 'n' roll treasures. There were some conflicts between Carmen's teen idol poses and Bryson's harder rock leanings, and the Raspberries fourth album, *Starting Over,* found to new Berries in the place of Smalley and Bonfanti. The new personnel didn't ease the tension, and the Raspberries called it quits in 1975. Carmen went on to a solo career marked by soft rock hits such as "All By Myself" and "Hungry Eyes." But with power pop classics such as "Go All The Way", "Tonight" and "Overnight Sensation (Hit Record)" waiting to be re-discovered, the Raspberries will continue to be one of the most influential pop bands to come out of the post-Beatle 70s. That makes the lack of Raspberries product on U.S. shelves all the more tragic. *Capitol Collectors Series* (Capitol, 1991, prod. Jimmy Ienner) is certainly enjoyable—and essential, with 20 songs that cover all the hits and the good album tracks. But you'll be doing yourself a real favor to scare up *The Raspberries—Power Pop Volume 1* (RPM, 1996, prod. Jimmy Ienner) and *The Raspberries—Power Pop Volume 2,* (RPM, 1996, prod. Jimmy Ienner) import sets that each house two of the original albums plus extensive liner notes and song commentary from the band members.

the rest: *Greatest Hits* (Capitol/EMI, 1995)

solo outings:

Eric Carmen Eric Carmen (Arista, 1975/Rhino, 1992) *The Best of Eric Carmen* (Arista, 1988)

Keith Klingensmith

Ratt

Formed 1981 in Los Angeles, Calif. Disbanded 1992.

Bobby Blotzer, drums; Juan Croucier, bass; Robbin Crosby, guitar; Warren De Martini, guitar; Stephen Pearcy, vocals

Riding the 80s wave of pop-metal, Ratt spent more time mimicking Led Zeppelin licks than developing a Motley Crue-like fake rebelliousness or a Poison-like cynicism. This was hardly the high road. Ratt's biggest hit, the high MTV-rotated "Round and Round," gave the musicians some money but wasn't exactly an enduring contribution to American music history. Ratt broke up in 1992, after Pearcy quit the band.

what to buy: *Ratt and Roll 8191,* (Atlantic, 1991, prod. Various) is a dubious greatest-hits package, showcasing Ratt as little more than a second-rate Aerosmith (or a fourth-rate Rolling Stones).

what to buy next: *Out of the Cellar,* (Atlantic, 1984, prod. Beau Hill) which contains "Round and Round," and *Invasion of Your Privacy* (Atlantic, 1985, prod. Beau Hill) both hit the Top 10 and were two of the band's four platinum albums.

what to avoid: *Detonator* (Atlantic, 1990, prod. Sir Arthur Payson) showed that Ratt had worn out its musical welcome by the turn of the decade.

the rest: *Ratt* (Time Coast, 1983) *Dancing Undercover* (Atlantic, 1986) *Reach for the Sky* (Atlantic, 1988)

▶▶ Meat Loaf (part II), Ugly Kid Joe, Skid Row

◀◀ Aerosmith, the Rolling Stones, Alice Cooper, Kiss, Styx, Journey

Tracey Birkenhauer and Steve Knopper

Johnnie Ray

Born Jan. 10, 1927, in Dallas, Ore. Died Feb. 24, 1990, in Los Angeles, Calif.

Something less than the missing link between Frank Sinatra and Elvis Presley, but something more than another Italianate 50s pop crooner, Ray inhabited a space all his own in the pre-rock 'n' roll pop music universe. His near-hysterical signature melodrama, "Cry," seemed to presage the raw emotionalism of rock 'n' roll, although Ray himself remained true to the supper club esthetics that the advent of rock 'n' roll overturned. He emerged from Detroit's Flame Showbar, where he performed alongside black R&B acts, to be signed by Columbia Records in 1951. His first release, "Whiskey and Gin," was a raucous noise, with Ray accompanying himself on piano. But it was his second single, "Cry/The Little White Cloud That Cried," that blasted Ray into a full-fledged phenomenon. He continued to cut hits through the 50s, including many tunes originally associated with black artists ("Such a Night," "Walkin' In the Rain"). But changing musical styles and his own personal problems led to a decline he never reversed. In his extraordinary Ray biography, "Cry: The Johnnie Ray Story" (Barricade Books, 1994), author Jonny Whiteside paints a portrait of a man haunted by a troubled extramarital affair with columnist Dorothy Kilgallen, his own homosexuality, deafness, drugs and alcohol—making Ray sound like the ultimate victim of his own dark and desolate songs.

what to buy: The standard compilation, *16 Most Requested Songs,* (Columbia/Legacy, 1991, prod. Various) covers Ray's glory years as one of Columbia's leading record-sellers.

what to buy next: The German reissue specialists Bear Family unearthed a live 1954 recording, *Live At the Palladium,* (Bear Family, 1993) that documents the feverish ecstasy Ray could provoke at the height of his powers.

what to avoid: Most of Ray's Columbia Records album were dull, lifeless affairs, built on lightweight filler. And *Johnnie Ray's Greatest Hits* (Columbia, 1958, prod. Various) unfortunately was not well mastered when transferred to compact disc.

the rest: *Cry* (Bear Family, 1990)

worth searching for: His first Columbia album, *Johnnie Ray,* (Columbia, 1952) was an eight-song, 10-inch record that qualifies as the most consistent collection of his career.

▶▶ Tom Jones, Anthony Newley, Dexy's Midnight Runners

◀◀ Billie Holiday, Frankie Laine, Ivory Joe Hunter

Joel Selvin

Chris Rea

Born March 4, 1951, in Middlesbrough, England

Kind of a Mark Knopfler for mellow adult listeners, Rea is a fine guitarist with an inclination toward bluesy slide textures. With his smoky baritone voice, he could have been the poor man's Leonard Cohen, but his musical tastes run too much toward bouncy pop and his lyrics toward wistful sentimentality. Still, he's had a lengthy career in the U.K., and his success shows no signs of abating just yet. He scored his biggest U.S. hit with his debut single back in 1978, the lightly cha-cha infused "Fool (If You Think It's Over)." After a few years of stiffs, he finally started receiving acclaim again with some of his mid-80s releases. A collection of those tunes was re-recorded for 1988's *New Light From Old Windows*, with the slinky "On the Beach" (kind of like Bryan Ferry singing a Sade number while on summer vacation) being the most memorable. More recently, he's alternated between moodier stuff that begs to be taken seriously and synthy pop-rockers that beg the question, why?

what to buy: *The Road to Hell* (Atco, 1989, prod. Chris Rea and Jon Kelly) ♪♪♪♪ is a darker semi-concept album, with the wry title track offering a deadpan deconstruction of yuppie mores. Lighter but no less compelling, *Auberge* (Atco, 1991, prod. Jon Kelly) ♪♪♪♪ finds Rea in a hazy mood, and waxing particularly elegant on "Heaven" and "Looking For the Summer."

what to buy next: *The Best of Chris Rea* (EastWest America, 1994, prod. Chris Rea and Jon Kelly) ♪♪♪ not only includes "Fool" and "On the Beach," it also contains "If You Were Me," the warm pairing between Rea and Elton John found originally on John's otherwise awful *Duets* album.

what to avoid: Perky and occasionally irritating, *Espresso Logic* (EastWest America, 1993, prod. Chris Rea) ♪♪ lacks the charm that makes Rea's better work worth hearing.

the rest: *New Light From Old Windows* (Geffen, 1988, prod. Jon Kelly) ♪♪♪

▶▶ Del Amitri, Curtis Stigers

◀◀ Dire Straits, Robert Palmer, Gerry Rafferty, Neil Diamond

Bob Remstein

Eddi Reader

See: Fairground Attraction

Recoil

See: Depeche Mode

The Records

Formed 1978 in England. Disbanded 1982.

John Wicks, vocals, guitar; Huw Gower, guitar, vocals, harmonica (1978-79); Jude Cole, guitar, vocals (1980); Dave Whelan, lead guitar (1982); Chris Gent, lead vocals (1982); Phil Brown, bass, vocals; Will Birch, drums, vocals

The Records were noted for cool harmonies and irresistible hooks, as exemplified on "Starry Eyes"—by far the best-known Records record (though the Searchers successfully covered "Hearts in Her Eyes"). Wicks and Birch (who later became a music critic) were the main songwriters and consistently honored the pop-rock verities. After the first album, Gower quit, later serving time in David Johansen's band and putting out a solo EP. American Jude Cole replaced him on the second album and then also quit, putting out two bland records. The Records' final lineup lasted long enough to record a so-so swan song. The group surprisingly reunited in 1990 to record "Darlin'" for the Beach Boys tribute *Smiles, Vibes, & Harmony.* With everything else out of print, *Smashes, Crashes, and Near Misses* (Blue Plate/Caroline, 1995, prod. Various) ♪♪♪♪♪ collects this underrated band's many gems as intelligently and thoroughly as possible on one CD, leading off with "Starry Eyes." The first two albums, by far their best, are each represented by seven out of ten cuts, and this group never recorded a bad song. Most stops to a used record store, meanwhile, should be able to scare up copies of *The Records* (Virgin, 1979, prod. Various) ♪♪♪♪♪ and *Crashes* (Virgin, 1980, prod. Craig Leon and Mick Glossop) ♪♪♪♪ for the six songs not on the collection. *Music on Both Sides* (Virgin, 1982, prod. Will Birch) ♪♪♪ has a few worthy tracks left off the compilation.

see also: *Jude Cole*

Steve Holtje

Red Hot Chili Peppers

Formed 1983 in Hollywood, Calif.

Flea, (born Michael Balzary), bass, vocals; Jack Irons, drums (1983-88); Anthony Kiedis, vocals; Hillel Slovak, guitar (1983-88, died June 25, 1988 in Los Angeles, Calif.); Chad Smith, drums (1989-present); Jack Sherman, guitar (1983-85); Cliff Martinez, drums (1983-85); John Frusciante, guitar (1989-1992); Jesse Tobias, guitar (1993); Dave Navarro, guitar (1993-present)

The Red Hot Chili Peppers began as post-punk novelties, like less funny, more funky Dead Milkmen. The group was best known for lunkheaded stunts like posing with socks on their private parts and lampooning the cover of the Beatles' *Abbey Road.* Gradually, thanks to tattooed, crewcutted underwear exhibitionist bassist Flea's growing technical skill, it became a legitimate band of good songwriters and accomplished musicians; Flea's bass, derived from a lifetime of listening to old P-Funk records, gave the funny songs a killer bottom, which was nurtured when the group scored a coup and hired George Clinton himself as an early producer. Through perseverance—including numerous personnel changes and over coming tragedies such as original guitarist Slovak's death and Kiedis' drug addiction—novelties gave way to hits, first with the 1989 singles "Knock Me Down" and a cover of Stevie Wonder's "Higher Ground," then with the breakthrough 1991 album *BloodSugarSexMagik*. By 1992, the Chili Peppers were one of the world's most popular rock bands, headlining Lollapalooza, dominating MTV and helping create alternative-rock radio. Though its music became more serious—the smash "Under the Bridge" was a heroin-hazed walk through the big city—the musicians continued to undress onstage and performed at Woodstock '94 with giant light bulbs on their heads. The Peppers lineup finally seems settled with the addition ex-Jane's Addiction guitarist Navarro, but its latest album, *One Hot Minute,* sounds disconcertingly like the Doobie Brothers.

what to buy: Clocking in at more than 75 minutes, *BloodSugarSexMagik* (Warner Bros., 1991, prod. Rick Rubin) is far too long and has plenty of filler, but if you wade towards "Under the Bridge" and the wonderful first single "Give It Away," it's an essential part of a modern rock record collection. *What Hits!?* (EMI, 1992, prod. Various) completes a non-fanatic's essential collection; it summarizes the band's career up to *BloodSugarSexMagik* and includes "Taste the Pain," "If You Want me to Stay" and "Higher Ground."

what to buy next: *Mother's Milk* (EMI, 1989, prod. Michael Beinhorn) is a great transition album, with good jokes ("Magic Johnson"), strong funk ("Higher Ground" and Jimi Hendrix' "Fire") and powerful punk ("Nobody Weird Like Me"). Of the pre-superstar albums, *Freaky Styley* (EMI, 1985, prod. George Clinton) is the funniest and most charming.

what to avoid: *Out in L.A.* (EMI, 1994, prod. Tom Cartwright and Vincent M. Vero) is a hodgepodge of nasty remixes.

the rest: *The Red Hot Chili Peppers* (EMI, 1984) *The Uplift Mofo Party Plan* (EMI, 1987) *Abbey Road* (EMI EP, 1988) *One Hot Minute* (Warner Bros., 1995) *Abbey Road* (EMI EP, 1988, prod. various)

solo outings:

John Frusciante To Clara (American, 1994)

▶▶ Primus, Rage Against the Machine, Fishbone, Anthrax, Onyx, Body Count, Pearl Jam

◀◀ Parliament-Funkadelic, Stevie Wonder, Jimi Hendrix, Sex Pistols, Minutemen, Flipper

Tracey Birkenhauer and Steve Knopper

Red House Painters

Formed 1989 in San Francisco, Calif.

Mark Kozelek, vocals, guitar; Gordon Mack, guitar (1989-95); Jerry Vessel, bass; Anthony Koutsos, drums, Phil Carney, guitar.

Red House Painters was the brainchild of frontman Kozelek, who formed the group after moving to San Francisco from Massillon, Ohio. Within a year, the band was playing local venues on a regular basis and creating a considerable buzz. One of the people turned on by the Red House Painters' downhearted sound was Mark Eitzel, then a member of American Music Club. He enthusiastically peddled the group's demo tape to various record companies, including Ivo Watts-Russell at the prestigious 4AD label. Watts-Russell signed Red House Painters, selected six tracks from their demo and released it as the band's debut album, *Down Colorful Hill,* in 1992. This set off a tide of critical acclaim for the group. Although its sound was too unwieldy for radio, the group quickly built up a loyal cult following, sealed with the release of their 1993 eponymous double album, and its companion disc of outtakes released a few months later. Red House Painters released an EP covering Kiss' "Shock Me" in 1994, then their final album for 4AD in 1995, *Ocean Beach.* After a bout of creative differences with the label, the group bowed out of its deal and signed with filmmaker John Hughes' newly-developed Supreme Recordings for its more rock-oriented 1996 release, *Songs for a Blue Guitar.*

what to buy: *Red House Painters (Rollercoaster),* (4AD, 1993, prod. Mark Kozelek) the group's double album-length debut, is all about painfully intricate melodies and lyrics. It's a magnificent experiment in stretching out a three-minute pop song into a 75-minute monument that punctuates every chord, word and beat with mesmerizing desolation. On "Rollercoaster," Kozelek recalls the sights, smell and abandon of being a kid in an amusement park; on "Mother," he relives an age when his mother would brush his hair, clean his belly button and breathe unrivaled love. In other words, the singer ached for a world free of adulthood constraints—broken hearts, sexual hang-ups, relationships, etc. *Red House Painters (Bridge),* (4AD, 1993, prod. Mark Kozelek) the companion piece of tracks that did not fit the mood of the double-album, continues in the same vein. Released only a few months after its predecessor, it contained such poignant songs as "Evil," "Blindfold" and an aching cover of Paul Simon's "I Am a Rock."

what to buy next: *Down Colorful Hill,* (4AD EP, 1992, prod. Mark Kozelek) the Red House Painters' majestic debut, includes such striking songs as "24" and "Japanese to English." *Ocean Beach* (4AD, 1995, prod. Mark Kozelek) finds a tighter, more grounded group offering irresistible cuts such as "Summer Dress" and "Brockwell Park."

the rest: *Shock Me* (4AD, 1994) *Songs for a Blue Guitar* (Supreme, 1996)

Jeff Buckley, Spain, Mark Eitzel

Leonard Cohen, Nick Drake, Tim Buckley, Velvet Underground

Aidin Vaziri

Red Rockers

Formed early 80s in New Orleans, La. Disbanded 1985.

John Griffith, vocals, guitar, piano; Darren Hill, bass; Jim Reilly, drums; James Singletary, guitar (until 1983); Shawn Paddock, guitar (until 1984)

This early post-punk outfit didn't have the teeth or the depth to tear into anything really meaningful. It did, however, release one solid album and a near-great single ("China") before returning to inadequate stabs at importance. *Good as Gold/Schizophrenic Circus* (Oglio Records, 1995, prod. Various) reissues both albums in their entirety. At best, as on "China," the Rockers reveal themselves to be sturdy craftsmen capable of engagingly melodic pulls. At worst, the band is like reheated Clash leftovers: bland and mushy. The reissue illustrates both sides.

Allan Orski

Redd Kross

Formed 1978 in Hawthorne, Calif.

Jeff McDonald, vocals, guitar; Steve McDonald, vocals, bass; Greg Hetson, guitar (1978-82); Ron Reyes, drums (1978-82); Gere Fennelly, keyboards (1993-present), Eddie Kurdziel, guitar (1993-present), Brian Reitzell, drums (1993-present)

Originally named the Tourists, then Red Cross, L.A.'s Redd Kross pioneered punk-fueled power-pop long before Green Day and others turned the formula into mainstream success. Formed around the nucelus of the brothers McDonald, the band began plying its trade on the L.A. punk scene at the end of the 70s; its first gig was opening for hardcore heroes Black Flag, and with a partisan in hip local DJ Rodney Bingenheimer, Redd Kross became a staple on the scene. Over the years, the McDonalds' pop instincts have sharpened; influenced equally by good-time punk rock of the Ramones and the Carpenters' aching melodicism, Redd Kross fashioned a delectable pop hybrid of chainsaw guitars and choirboy vocal harmonies blend with remarkable ease. The McDonalds have dabbled in everything from metal to adult contemporary without losing their signature sound. After releasing a handful of highly acclaimed indie albums, the band signed to Atlantic in 1990, only to returneto an indie when fame continued to elude them. Though they have yet to achieve the success that their acolytes have seen, Redd Kross has stayed true to its fun-loving vision and remains an important influence on 90s alternative rock.

what to buy: *Phaseshifter* (This Way Up, 1993, prod. Redd Kross) is a heady confection of uptempo rock and lovely, well-crafted pop, largely eschewing the adolescent fury of its earlier work.

what to buy next: *Neurotica* (Big Time, 1987, prod. Redd Kross) blends power-pop and psychedelia to splendid effect.

what to avoid: *Born Innocent* (Frontier, 1986, prod. Redd Kross) his its share of fine moments but is the least consistent album the band has crafted.

the rest: *Red Cross* (Posh Boy, 1980) *Teen Babes from Monsanto* (Enigma, 1984) *Third Eye* (Atlantic, 1990)

worth searching for: *The Siren,* (Posh Boy, 1980, prod. Various) a three-band sampler album that includes a half-dozen songs from the fledgling Red Cross—when Steven McDonald was all of 13 years old.

Jellyfish, Teenage Fanclub, Lemonheads, Stone Temple Pilots, Green Day

Beatles, Beach Boys, Phil Spector, Carpenters, Cheap Trick, KISS, Raspberries, Ramones

Simon Glickman

Otis Redding

Born Sept. 9,1941, in Dawson, Ga. Died Dec. 10, 1967, in Madison, Wisc.

Because of his more organic approach to 60s soul, Redding's music has endured—and even deepened—in the years since his death in an airplane crash at age 26. The prince of Memphis soul has blossomed into something only hinted at in his final recording, "(Sittin' On) The Dock of the Bay," made only three days before he died. He might not have bothered to learn all the lyrics to a song before recording—the most glaring example is his version of the Rolling Stones' "(I Can't Get No) Satisfaction"—but close scrutiny of his live recordings or the available outtakes indicate it was exactly this spirit of improvisation, this enthusiasm for creativity, that illuminated his work. From his earliest Little Richard-inspired efforts to the enormous body of work he compiled in four short years at Memphis' Stax/Volt, Redding dominated whatever he recorded with a vivid vision of himself; warm and whimsical, cornpone and secretly wise.

what to buy: With ace Atlantic engineer Tom Dowd at the board, *Otis Blue* (Stax, 1965, prod. Jim Stewart) featured a slightly richer sound that, coupled with the single finest selection of songs of any Redding album, made this one of the greatest soul albums of its era. *The Very Best of Otis Redding* (Rhino, 1992, prod. Various) is a terrific compilation of the essential material.

what to buy next: The evergreen *Live in Europe,* (Stax, 1967, prod. Jim Stewart) with Dowd at the controls again, commemorates Redding's power as a galvanizing live performer on one of the most historic live albums ever.

what to avoid: Although compelling in its unvarnished honesty, *Good to Me* (Stax, 1993, prod. Al Jackson Jr.) is not a very good album. Composed of scraps left over from *Live at the Whiskey* and featuring Redding's unskilled—and undoubtedly underpaid—road band stumbling through his command, this is the least interesting of his many live recordings.

the rest: *Pain in My Heart* (Stax, 1965) *The Great Otis Redding Sings Soul Ballads* (Stax, 1965) *The Soul Album* (Stax, 1966) *The Otis Redding Dictionary of Soul* (Stax, 1966) (with Carla Thomas) *King and Queen* (Stax, 1967) *The Dock of the Bay* (Stax, 1968) *In Person at the Whiskey a Go Go* (Stax, 1968) *The Immortal Otis Redding* (Stax, 1968) *Love Man* (Atco, 1970) *Tell the Truth* (Atco, 1970) *Remember Me* (Stax, 1992) *The Very Best of Otis Redding, Vol. 2* (Rhino, 1995)

worth searching for: The three-disc box, *The Otis Redding Story,* (Atlantic, 1987, prod. Various) also released in a six-LP edition, was replaced—but not improved upon—by a pricey, four-disc box, *Otis! The Definitive Otis Redding* (Rhino, 1993, prod. Various)

▶▶ Al Green, Janis Joplin, Mick Jagger

◀◀ Little Richard, Sam Cooke, Solomon Burke

Joel Selvin

Lou Reed

Born Louis Firbank, March 2, 1942 in Brooklyn, N.Y.

Reed's place in the rock pantheon rests primarily on his role in guiding the commercially ignored but enormously influential Velvet Underground from 1965-70. But his post-VU career, though dizzyingly erratic, contains several notable albums. After quitting the Velvets, he re-emerged as a solo act in England, where he was adopted by admirers such as David Bowie, who produced and performed on his breakthrough hit, "Walk on the Wild Side," and Mott the Hoople, who covered Reed's Velvets classic, "Sweet Jane." Later, he would be embraced by the likes of Johnny Rotten and Patti Smith as the godfather of punk, Nooo Yawk division.

Throughout the 70s, Reed flirted with self-parody, as his records veered wildly from blatant pop compromises to scarifying song cycles to perverse noise experiments. At the onset of the 80s, he recruited his best post-Velvets band, including guitarist Robert Quine and bassist Fernando Saunders, and uncorked a handful of brilliant ensemble albums. By the 90s he was releasing album-long song cycles such as *New York* and *Magic and Loss* that approached the level of his Velvets work.

what to buy: *The Blue Mask* (RCA, 1982, prod. Lou Reed and Sean Fullan) combines delicate melodicism and raging rock, stoked by Quine's incendiary guitar on "Waves of Fear" and Saunders' beautifully buoyant bass on "My House," a tender tribute to the late poet and Reed mentor Delmore Schwartz. *New York* (Sire, 1989, prod. Lou Reed and Fred Maher) examines a city's moral and spiritual decay in one of Reed's most bluntly political and pissed-off works. *Magic and Loss* (Sire, 1991, prod. Lou Reed and Mike Rathke) is more subdued, but it's a magnificently moving meditation on dealing with a loved one's death.

what to buy next: *Berlin* (RCA, 1973, prod. Bob Ezrin) is a jarring song cycle about a modern day Romeo and Juliet—that is if Romeo were a pusher and Juliet a masochist. Hide the razor blades, but it's among Reed's most fully realized works. *Street Hassle* (Arista, 1978, prod. Reed and Richard Robinson) is the "Mean Streets" of rock; the three-part title track is a brilliant drama of drugs, degradation and redemption. *The Bells* (Arista, 1979, prod. Lou Reed) is among Reed's most underrated releases, with a jazz-oriented backing cast, including Don Cherry, and eloquent, affirming lyrics. *New Sensations* (RCA, 1984, prod. Lou Reed and John Jansen) noses out *Transformer* as the most enduring and least contrived of Reed's pop-oriented discs. *Between Thought and Expression: The Lou Reed Anthology* (RCA, 1992, prod. Various) is a solid three-CD overview.

what to avoid: The spin cycle of a washing machine has more melodic variation than the electronic drone that was *Metal Machine Music* (RCA, 1975, prod. Lou Reed) WOOF!.

the rest: *Lou Reed* (RCA, 1972) *Transformer* (RCA, 1972) *Rock 'N' Roll Animal* (RCA, 1974) *Sally Can't Dance* (RCA, 1974) ; *Lou Reed Live* (RCA, 1975) *Coney Island Baby* (RCA, 1976) *Rock and Roll Heart* (RCA, 1976) *Walk on the Wild Side: The Best of Lou Reed* (RCA, 1977) *Live Take No Prisoners* (Arista, 1978) *Growing Up in Public* (Arista, 1980) *Rock and Roll Diary 1967-1980* (Arista, 1980) *Legendary Hearts* (RCA, 1983) *City Lights: Classic Performances* (Arista, 1985) *Mistrial* (RCA, 1986) *Songs For Drella* (with John Cale) (Sire, 1990) *Set the Twilight Reeling* (Sire, 1996)

worth searching for: *Live in Italy* (RCA, 1984,) is an import title featuring Reed with Quine, Saunders and drummer Fred Maher ripping through a career-spanning series of classics, from "Satellite of Love" to an incendiary "White Light/White Heat."

▶▶ Patti Smith, Kurt Cobain, Ian Hunter, R.E.M., Nick Cave

◀◀ Andy Warhol, Ornette Coleman, Don Cherry, Bob Dylan, Doc Pomus

Greg Kot

The Reegs

See: Chameleons

Vernon Reid

See: Living Colour

R.E.M.

Formed 1980 in Athens, Ga.

Michael Stipe (b. John Michael Stipe), vocals; Peter Buck, guitar; Mike Mills, bass and vocals; Bill Berry, drums

In the early 80s, R.E.M. created the new Southern rock—ringing guitars, punky rhythms and oblique, indecipherable vocals. By the end of the decade these erstwhile underground heroes were headlining arenas, a mainstream incision accomplished virtually without artistic compromise. Perhaps the only notable shift in the band's sound was the more pronounced clarity of Stipe's vocals and lyrics, which coincided with his emergence as a political activist. It even could be argued that R.E.M. has actually gotten better and more adventurous the longer it has remained in the game. During the early 90s, the band quit touring and cranked out three of its finest albums and its biggest hit, "Losing My Religion" (from the 1991 *Out of Time* album), before returning to the arenas with newfound purpose in 1995.

what to buy: The band's full-length debut, *Murmur* (IRS, 1983, prod. Mitch Easter), , remains one of the prototypical college-rock albums of the 80s. It insinuates rather than bludgeons, yet also manages to avoid sounding wimpy. Which is to say it rocks hard enough to keep a frat party in full swing, but layers on the melancholy atmosphere and oblique lyricism so thick that a moody sophomore could spent an entire semester plumbing its murky depths. The band's second masterpiece is *Automatic for the People* (Warner Bros., 1993, prod. Scott Litt and R.E.M.) , a uniformly downcast, but emotionally transcendent meditation on death and loss. *Document* (IRS, 1987, prod. Scott Litt and R.E.M.) is the band's hardest-rocking disc; Litt introduces a new punch and clarity that presages the jump to arenas. *Out of Time* (Warner Bros., 1991, prod. Scott Litt and R.E.M.) is a sprawling, brilliantly executed tour of pop styles, with the classic "Losing My Religion" as its centerpiece.

what to buy next: *Monster* (Warner Bros., 1994, prod. Scott Litt and R.E.M.) is a bombastically entertaining homage to early 70s glam-rock and finds Stipe cleverly trying on a variety of vocal personas.

what to avoid: *Dead Letter Office* (IRS, 1987, prod. Various) is a batch of B-sides and rarities of interest only to hard-core collectors, redeemed partially by the inclusion of the 1982 *Chronic Town* EP.

the rest: *Reckoning* (IRS, 1984) *Reconstruction of the Fables* (IRS, 1985) *Life's Rich Pageant* (IRS, 1986) *Eponymous* (IRS, 1988) *Green* (Warner Bros., 1988) *New Adventures in Hi-Fi* (Warner Bros., 1996)

worth searching for: The *Chronic Town* EP (IRS, 1982, prod. Mitch Easter and R.E.M.) without the deadweight of *Dead Letter Office.*

▶▶ Gin Blossoms, Hootie and the Blowfish, Toad the Wet Sprocket, For Squirrels, Drivin' N' Cryin'

◀◀ Patti Smith, Soft Boys, New York Dolls, Wire, Pere Ubu, Television, Velvet Underground

see also: *Hindu Love Gods*

Greg Kot

The Rembrandts

Formed 1990 in Los Angeles, Calif.

Phil Solem, vocals, guitar, banjo, piano, synthesizer, percussion, bass; Danny Wilde, vocals, bass, guitar, mandolin, harmonica, synthesizer

There is an unfortunate possibility that the Rembrandts may one day be remembered (inaccurately) as one-hit wonders for "I'll Be There For You," the massively successful theme song to the popular TV sitcom "Friends." "I'll Be There For You" is a winning radio-ready track, whose ad-jingle exuberance and Monkees-derived virtues virtually guaranteed it would be played over and over again. Nonetheless, it would be a shame to see the Rembrandts' ultimate legacy reduced to just that song. Solem and Wilde's partnership goes back to the early 80s and the L.A. pop band Great Buildings, whose one LP—*Great Buildings* (Columbia, 1981, prod. Ed E. Thacker and John Boylan) —is a gem worth seeking. Wilde did some solo albums—often enlisting the aid of Solem—and the pair officially resurfaced at the start of the 90s as the Rembrandts, a pop duo drawing recognizable inspiration from the Beatles and the Everly Brothers. *The Rembrandts* (Atco, 1990, prod. the Rembrandts) is a casual, easygoing affair, with hidden hooks and gorgeous vocals. *Untitled* (Atco, 1992, prod. the Rembrandts) breaks no new ground but is cast in the same agreeable pop image as the debut. *LP* (EastWest, 1995, prod. Don Smith) is a touch heavier, mixing heartache and harmony but not scrimping on the hooks. And there are lots of songs on *LP* as good as "I'll Be There For You."

Carl Cafarelli

Renaissance

Formed 1969 in Surrey, England. Disbanded 1987.

Keith Relf, vocals (1967-69); Jim McCarty, drums (1967-69); Jane Relf, vocals (1967-69); John Hawken, keyboards (1967-69); Louis Cennamo, bass (1967-69); Rob Hendry, guitar (1969-72); Annie Haslam, vocals (1969-87); Michael Dunford, guitar (1972-87); Jon Camp, bass (1969-87); John Tout, keyboards (1969-79); Terry Sullivan, drums, percussion (1969-79); Peter Gosling, keyboards (1979-87), Peter Barron, drums (1979-87)

Started by former Yardbirds Relf and McCarty, Renaissance was completely overhauled after its self-titled 1969 album. Unsatisfied with their venture, Relf, McCarty and the other founding members left and the lineup had completely changed by the time *Prologue* was issued in 1971. That decade, when progressive and art rock thrived, suited the group, which blended classical, pop, folk and subtle jazz influences into an almost symphonic form of pop music. It found favor in the U.S., but not much interest abroad, including its native England. Renaissance broke up in 1987, its lush style of music pushed aside by the new punk generation. Haslam resurfaced as a solo artist. Most of the group's material is out of print; fortunately, its home label, Sire, issued some of the group's best-known material—including "Mother Russia," "Ashes Are Burning" and its ambitious "Scheherazade" interpretation—into a two-part CD compilation called *1001 Nights—Vol. 1* and *Vol. 2* (Sire, 1990, prod. Various) Two individual albums, *Ashes Are Burning* (Elektra/One Way, 1973, prod. Dick Plant) and *Prologue* (Elektra/One Way, 1972, prod. Miles Copeland, Renaissance) are available, but hard to find.

Doug Pullen

The Rentals

See: Weezer

REO Speedwagon

Formed 1969 in Champaign, Ill.

Terry Luttrell, vocals (1969-71); Kevin Cronin, vocals (1972, 1976-present); Mike Murphy, vocals (1973-75); Gary Richrath, guitar (1969-90); Dave Amato, guitar (1990-present); Neal Doughty, keyboards; Jesse Harms, keyboards (1990-91); Gregg Philbin, bass (1969-77); Bruce Hall, bass (1978-present); Alan Gratzer, drums (1969-90); Bryan Hitt, drums (1990-present)

Formed in 1969 by college roommates Doughty and Gratzer, REO Speedwagon evolved from a moderately successful country-rock band to an immensely successful arena rock band to a perennial participant on the 70s nostalgia summer concert circuit. Fraught with personality conflicts, the band's ever-changing lineup finally stabilized in 1978 with Cronin, Richrath, Doughty, Hall and Gratzer; it was this incarnation that produced the band's first big seller, *You Can Tune a Piano but You Can't Tuna Fish*, as well as its hit-laden, multi-million selling mainstream breakthrough *Hi Infidelity* But after another smash album with *Wheels are Turnin'*, the tenuous peace that had existed between band members began to crumble, as did its sales. Though it continues to release albums, REO mostly serves to play "Ridin' the Storm Out" and "Keep on Loving You" for the same crowds that have worn out their *Boston* and *Frampton Comes Alive* album.

what to buy: Though anyone owning a radio in 1981 may have gotten their fill of *Hi Infidelity,* (Epic, 1981, prod. Kevin Cronin, Gary Richrath and Kevin Beamish) the album still reigns as REO's best effort. While the sappy ballad "Keep On Loving You" sounds a bit dated, most of the album reflect's Richrath and Cronin's ability to weave country, rock and pop into an eminently listenable collection of tunes.

what to buy next: *You Can Tune A Piano, But You Can't Tuna Fish* (Epic, 1978, prod. Kevin Cronin, Gary Richrath and Paul Grupp) and *Wheels Are Turnin'* (Epic, 1985, prod. Kevin Cronin, Gary Richrath and Alan Gratzer) offer a similar brand of feel-good arena rock, though the latter displays both more maturity and a willingness to stray a bit from the proven pop formula.

what to avoid: Though the title track is one of REO's seminal tunes, *Ridin' the Storm Out* (Epic, 1973, prod. John Stronach, Gary Richrath and John Henning) WOOF! originally featured Cronin on vocals, but partway through recording he was replaced by the soporific Mike Murphy (prompting an 11th-hour album cover reshoot). The last-minute replacement transformed what would have been merely a dull album into a slipshod embarrassment.

the rest: *REO Speedwagon* (Epic, 1971) *R.E.O./T.W.O.* (Epic, 1972) *Lost in a Dream* (Epic, 1974) *This Time We Mean It* (Epic, 1975) *R.E.O. (C.O.W.)* (Epic, 1976) *Live: You Get What You Play For* (Epic, 1977) *Nine Lives* (Epic, 1979) *A Decade of Rock and Roll* (Epic, 1980) *Good Trouble* (Epic, 1983) *Life as We Know It* (Epic, 1987) *The Hits* (Epic, 1988) *The Earth, a Small Man, His Dog and A Chicken* (Epic, 1990) *The Second Decade of Rock and Roll* (Epic, 1991) *Building the Bridge* (Castle, 1996) *Building the Bridge* (Castle, 1996)

solo outings:

Gary Richrath *Richrath* (GNP/Crescendo, 1992)

▶▶ Mr. Mister, Eddie Money, Kenny Loggins, Boston, Journey, Starcastle

◀◀ Allman Brothers Band, the Beatles, Creedence Clearwater Revival, Chuck Berry

Brandon Trenz

What Album Changed Your Life?

"I loved Shirley Horn's Here's to Life. When she sings, it's like she's giving a blessing. She never sings a blue note, never sings too much. Not one note is out of place or wasted."

Mark Eitzel

The Replacements

Formed 1981 in Minneapolis, Minn. Disbanded 1991

Paul Westerberg, guitar, vocals; Bob Stinson, guitar 1980-86 (died Feb. 15, 1995); Tommy Stinson, bass, vocals; Chris Mars, drums; Slim Dunlap, guitar (1987-91)

The Replacements were widely known for their drunken antics and unpredictable live shows, which ranged from the sublime to the ridiculous—often within the same song. But what set the band apart from its fellows in the burgeoning early-80s modern rock scene was its ability to balance scorching rockers featuring Bob Stinson's crash and burn guitar with Westerberg's aching, vulnerable ballads like "Sixteen Blue," "Unsatisfied" and "Here Comes A Regular." It seemed for a time that the band that would lead the underground into the mainstream; they were among the first alternative bands to sign with a major label, leaving Twin/Tone for Sire in 1985—a full three years before their underground rivals R.E.M. hitched their wagon to Warner Bros. But the band could never quite maintain the same level of consistency, and its members drifted apart without ever becoming household names. Which isn't to say the band didn't leave a mark; its melding of punk aggression and pop hooks became a touchstone for legions of alternative bands. Kurt Cobain, for one, was a major acolyte, taking much of his frayed flannel vulnerability, as well as the pained, nicotine and vinegar singing, from Westerberg. And the Goo Goo Dolls hit pay dirt in 1996 after years of building on a heavily Replacements oriented sound.

what to buy: Without a doubt, three albums represent the peak Replacements. *Let It Be* (Twin/Tone, 1984, prod. Steve Fjelstad, Paul Westerberg and Peter Jesperson) is an uneven album, and several songs are almost unlistenable. But the high points are fantastic: "I Will Dare," "Unsatisfied," "Sixteen Blue" and "Answering Machine" are as good as 80s indie rock got. The high points of *Tim* (Sire, 1985, prod. Tommy Erdelyi) are almost as good, and it's a more even album, the perfect realization of the band's ballad/rocker yin-yang. *Pleased To Meet Me* (Sire, 1987, prod. Jim Dickinson) is also top-notch, arguably the band's finest, but Bob Stinson's careening, over-the-top guitar leads are sorely missed in some spots.

what to buy next: Both of Westerberg's solo albums, *14 Songs* (Sire, 1993, prod. Matt Wallace & Paul Westerberg) and *Eventually* (Sire, 1996, prod. Paul Westerberg, Lou Giordano and Brendan O'Brien) are somewhat uneven, but both also feature some of Westerberg's finest writing. You won't go wrong with either.

what to avoid: The band's final two outings are both pretty dispirited affairs. *Don't Tell a Soul* (Sire, 1989, prod. Matt Wallace and The Replacements) is a lackluster attempt to score a pop hit, while *All Shook Down* (Sire, 1990, prod. Scott Litt and Paul Westerberg) is essentially a Westerberg solo album—one which isn't nearly as strong as what has followed.

the rest: *Sorry Ma, Forgot To Take Out the Trash* (Twin/Tone, 1981) *The Replacements Stink* (Twin/Tone, 1982) *Hootenany* (Twin/Tone, 1983)

solo outings:

Slim Dunlap *The Old New Me* (Medium Cool, 1983)

Tommy Stinson (with Bash and Pop) *Friday Night is Killing Me* (Reprise, 1983) (with Perfect): *When Squirrels Play Chicken* (Medium Cool, 1996)

Chris Mars *Horseshoes and Hand Grenades* (Smash, 1992) *75% Less Fat* (Smash, 1993) *Tenterhooks* (Bar/None, 1995)

worth searching for: *Live Inconcerated* (Sire, 1989) is a promotional only sampling of the Replacements' live show. Its five songs are a bit brief, but it'll certainly whet your appetite for some full-length bootlegs.

▶▶ Nirvana, Goo Goo Dolls, Wilco, Soul Asylum, Cracker

◀◀ Big Star, Sex Pistols, Faces, Kinks, Black Flag, Ramones

Alan Paul

The Replicants

See: Tool

The Residents

Formed 1970 in San Francisco, Calif.

Members Unknown

We may never encounter another musical force quite like the Residents, a band that somehow has sustained a career of more than 25 years built on aural experimentation, enigmatic visuals and a series of myths that has followed it through every stage of its career. The band's personnel has always been a closely guarded secret, which leaves us with the music, intermittent live performances and some willfully obscure liner notes from which to glean clues. The Residents' first full-length release, *Meet the Residents,* (Ralph, 1974, prod. the Residents) laid the groundwork for what was to come: nightmarish nursery-rhyme word play "sung" over sound collages, sometimes based on familiar melodies. Imagine a twisted, funny, extreme and musically coherent "Revolution #9," and you get the idea. The band's sound has changed through the years, possibly due to new personnel, but it has always managed to be interesting, inspired and technologically advanced. Three of the most recent outings are re-worked soundtracks to interactive CD-ROMs. All of the band's recordings are self-produced.

what to buy: *The Commercial Album* (Ralph, 1980/ESD, 1988, prod. The Residents) is a great place to start. The ESD reissue adds 10 bonus tracks to the original 40.

what to buy next: For early craziness, try *The Residents Present the Third Reich and Roll.* (Ralph, 1975/ESD, 1988, prod. The Residents) Again, the ESD reissue has bonus tracks, this time four. The more musically accessible and emotionally intense later-period Residents are showcased on *The King and Eye* (Enigma, 1988, prod. The Residents)

what to avoid: *Heaven?* (Rykodisc, 1986, prod. The Residents) and *Hell!* (Rykodisc, 1986, prod. The Residents) consist of material from various albums. While the songs on both are good choices, they are decidedly less powerful out of context. Also skip the "God in Three Persons" soundtrack (Torso, 1987) the music just doesn't make it on its own.

the rest: *Fingerprince* (Ralph, 1977) *Not Available* (Ralph, 1978) *Duckstab/Buster & Glen* (Ralph, 1978) *Eskimo* (Ralph, 1979) *Mark of the Mole* (Ralph, 1981) *The Tunes of Two Cities* (Ralph, 1982) *Intermission* (Ralph, 1983) *The Mole Show* (Ralph, 1983) *Residue of the Residents* (Ralph, 1983) *George & Jones* (Ralph, 1984) *What Happened to Vileness Fats?* (Ralph, 1984) *The Big Bubble* (Ralph, 1985) *Stars and Hank Forever* (Ralph, 1986) *13th Anniversary Show—Live in Japan* (Ralph, 1986) *The Mole Show Live in Holland* (ESD, 1988) *Liver Music* (U-WEB, 1990) *Cube E Live in Holland* (Enigma, 1990) *Daydream B-Liver* (U-WEB,

1990) *Freak Show,* (Official Products, 1991) *Our Finest Flowers* (Ralph, 1992) *Gingerbread Man* (Ralph, 1992) "Hunters" soundtrack (Milan, 1995)

▶▶ Primus, Half Japanese

◀◀ The Beatles, Captain Beefheart, Edgar Varese

Shane Faubert

Paul Revere & the Raiders

Formed 1960 in Portland, Ore.

Paul Revere, keyboards; Mark Lindsay, vocals, saxophone (1960-75, 1976); Drake Levin, guitar (1960-66); Mike "Doc" Holiday, bass; Mike "Smitty" Smith, drums (1960-67, 1971-present); Phil "Fang" Volk, bass (1960-67); Jim "Harpo" Valley (1966-67), guitar; Joe Correro Jr., drums (1967-71); Charlie Coe, bass (1967-68); Freddy Weller, guitar (1967-73); Keith Allison, bass (1968-75); Omar Martinez, vocals (1971-present); Robert Woolley, guitar (1971-present)

The Raiders were among the founders and architects of the early Pacific Northwest rock scene and released the first rock arrangement of the perennial classic "Louie Louie," recorded Columbia Records' first-ever million-selling rock LP and was the first rock band to star in a hit television series—yet it's remembered today mostly for the red, white and blue Revolutionary War costumes the musicians stubbornly wore on stage throughout the entire 60s. Well, hopefully enough time has now passed—and the sight of oddly attired rock groups singing on TV has become common enough—that the Raiders can finally begin to be appreciated solely for the abundance of great music the band wrote and recorded during its spectacular reign: 15 albums and just about as many Top 20 hits between 1965-71, which puts it right up there with the Beatles, the Beach Boys, the Rolling Stones and the Supremes in terms of sales. So there! The story really began when Lindsay Revere's already locally thriving show band, the Downbeats, in 1959, but it was not until the mid-60s, after Dick Clark had cast them in his daily "Where The Action Is" series and Columbia had assigned hot young staff producer Terry Melcher to record them, that the Raiders finally hit pay-dirt. "Steppin' Out", "Just Like Me," "Kicks" (an anti-drug song, highly unusual for the time), "Hungry," "Good Thing" and "Him Or Me," Top 10 hits one and all, remain among the best examples of American hard pop you'll ever hear, and even after Melcher's departure Lindsay continued to write and produce hits for the band, ranging from the innovative bubblegum of "Mr. Sun Mr. Moon" to the Led Zeppelin-like "Just Seventeen." Yet it wasn't until '71 that the band released its biggest seller and only No. 1 smash, "Indian Reservation," which was ironically its final hit. Four years later, Lindsay finally hung up his colonial headgear, but a staunchly determined Revere still fronts new bands of Raiders to this day, still wears his high-boots and tights, and still insists his "Louie Louie" is not only the first, but the best.

what to buy: *The Essential Ride, '63-'67* (Columbia Legacy, 1995, prod. Various) presents a carefully chosen, lovingly annotated 20-song collection of hits, album tracks and rarities, including the unreleased gastro-sexual tub-fest "Crisco Party" (listeners under the age of 17 should be accompanied by an adult for this track).

what to buy next: *The Legend Of Paul Revere* (Columbia Legacy, 1990, prod. Various) is a more in-depth, double-disc overview that also contains examples of the band's more R&B-flavored pre-Columbia recordings.

worth searching for: *A Christmas Present—And Past* (Columbia, 1967, prod. Terry Melcher) proves that the Beatles weren't the only rock stars creating chemically induced seasonal greetings for their unsuspecting fans every December.

▶▶ The Monkees, Pat Benatar, John Mellencamp, Bruce Springsteen.

◀◀ Little Richard, Jerry Lee Lewis, Spike Jones.

Gary Pig Gold

The Reverend Horton Heat

Born Jim Heath (date not available) in Corpus Cristi, Texas

The Reverend Horton Heat does not play barn-dance rockabilly—he's more likely to set the barn on fire. With his vicious guitar leads and hopped-up vocals, plus the relentless rhythm attack of Jimbo on stand-up bass and Taz on drums, this not-so-religious figure delivers his music like a preacher delivers his sermon: with conviction. Best of all, it's easy to be converted. *Smoke 'Em If You Got 'Em* (Sub Pop, 1990, prod. Rev. Horton Heat) is Heat's hottest offering; songs such as "Bad Reputation" and "Baby You Know Who" hook up danceable, minor-key rockabilly licks with R-rated suggestiveness. "Marijuana" and "Psychobilly Freakout" show off the Reverend's aptitude for a good novelty tune. *The Full-Custom Gospel Sounds of The Reverend Horton Heat* (Sub Pop, 1993, prod. Gibby Haynes) rocks even harder with "Big Little Baby" and "Wiggle Stick," but suffers at times from going too far over the top. *Liquor in the Front* (Interscope,1994, prod. Al Jourgensen) is a classic example of heavy-handed production taking a band in the wrong direction; in this case, into thrash metal closer to Ministry than the Reverend's original punkabilly intent.

Dan Weber

Revolting Cocks

See: Ministry

Emitt Rhodes

See: the Merry-Go-Round

Marc Ribot

Born May 21, 1954 in Newark, N.J.

This mainstay of the Downtown New York scene and former Lounge Lizard is a versatile, inventive guitarist heard frequently and often extensively on albums by Elvis Costello, Tom Waits, Marianne Faithfull, Allen Ginsburg, David Sanborn, T-Bone Burnett and many more. Ribot also he played in a group called the Real Tones, which specialized in backing band-less performers such as Wilson Pickett, Solomon Burke and Chuck Berry. Ribot's own albums add E-flat horn, piano and vocals to his toolbox, covering even more stylistic territory than suggested by the above list, yet always in distinctive fashion. Representative of the younger avant-garde that refuses to exclude pop materials, he skews familiar tunes and styles into non-Euclidean shapes, and makes outre techniques listener-friendly.

what to buy: *Rootless Cosmopolitans* (Island, 1990, prod. Arthur Moorhead) mixes shockingly deconstructed covers—sometimes wry, sometimes oddly beautiful—of Sammy Cahn's "I Should Care," Jimi Hendrix's "The Wind Cries Mary," George Harrison's "While My Guitar Gently Weeps" and Duke Ellington's "Mood Indigo" with Ribot originals positing a fresh, unique amalgam of jazz, rock and avant-garde that has nothing to do with fusion.

what to buy next: *Shrek* (Avant, 1994, prod. Marc Anthony Thompson and Marc Ribot) is mostly performed by Ribot's group of that name, which here includes Soul Coughing bassist Sebastian Steinberg. Closing with Albert Ayler's "Bells," this instrumental record is more consistently abstract than the above album.

the rest: *Subsonic 1* (Subsonic/Sub Rosa, 1994) *The Book of Heads* (Tzadik, 1995) *Don't Blame Me* (DIW, 1995)

worth searching for: The import *Requiem for What's His Name* (Les Disques du Crepuscule, 1992, prod. Kirk Yano and Marc Ribot) is along the same lines as Ribot's debut but slightly more self-assured.

▶▶ Brad Schoeppach (Babkas, Paradox Trio), David Tronzo, Danny Blume (Liminal)

◀◀ Derek Bailey, Jimi Hendrix, Eugene Chadbourne, Arto Lindsay, Fred Frith, Frantz Casseus, John Zorn, Bill Frisell, Captain Beefheart

see also: *Tom Waits, Elvis Costello*

Steve Holtje

Cliff Richard

Born Harry Rodger Webb, Oct. 14, 1940 n Lucknow, India

Richard has always been big in Britain—the empire's Elvis, if you will. He's had more hits in Britain than anyone but Elvis Presley, for that matter, and these days he even holds his own alongside more contemporary (and dare we say trendy?) hitmakers such as Oasis and Blur. In America? Hey, we *have* Elvis (or had him, at least). Richard has never meant much over here—even during his early 60s heyday when he was backed by the Shadows. In the U.S. he's had all of nine singles in the Top 40, two of them duets with Olivia Newton-John ("A Little in Love" and "Daddy's Home"). *The Cliff Richard Collection* (Razor & Tie, 1994, prod. Various) is all you'll find in the racks on these shores, and it's a pretty skimpy representation. For the real story, check out any number of import hits sets.

Gary Graff

Keith Richards

Born Nov. 18, 1943, in Dartford, England

The Rolling Stones guitarist's solo retaliations to Mick Jagger's mid-80s "defection" proves once and for all which one of the Glimmer Twins has the piss and vinegar—in case anyone still wondered. Richards' solo work is a raw, sloppy free-for-all that would barely qualify as demo for some rock acts. And Richard's voice, never a honey bear, is now a ravaged strep-throat croak. But if the Stones could still clang and rattle with such disheveled grace, we'd still think it was the greatest rock 'n' roll band in the world. *Talk Is Cheap* (Virgin, 1988, prod. Keith Richards and Steve Jordan) features "Take it So Hard" and a grooving rhythm section of Jordan and Charley Drayton. *Live at the Hollywood Palladium* (Virgin, 1991, prod. Keith Richards, Steve Jordan and Don Smith) takes the virtues of

Talk is Cheap to stage, where Richards' backup band, The X-pensive Winos, rocks with ragged glory. *Main Offender* (Virgin, 1992, prod. Keith Richards, Steve Jordan and Waddy Watchtel) continues in the same vein as the debut, highlighted by "Wicked as it Seems," and the swinging "Eileen." The latter is also available on a CD single (Virgin, 1993) that carries live tracks and a previously unreleased version of "Key to the Highway."

see also: *The Rolling Stones*

Allan Orski

Lionel Richie

See: The Commodores

Jonathan Richman

Born 1951 in Boston, Mass.

If you thought Ronald Reagan's leap from the movie screen to the White House was a stunner, consider Richman's left-turn from underappreciated father of punk rock to heel-clicking, soul-baring hopeful romantic. As the leader of an early -70s Boston bar band called the Modern Lovers—which also featured future Talking Heads keyboardist Jerry Harrison and future Cars drummer David Robinson—Richman created a brooding, Velvet Underground-derived sound that yielded such influential three-chord classics as "Roadrunner" and "Pablo Picasso." But even back then he wasn't afraid to express his deepest feelings and darkest fears, an unflinching honesty that pervades his work to this day—even though he's now funneling those emotions through stripped-down 50s-and 60s-inspired ditties that range from offbeat covers (Bette Midler's "The Rose," the theme from "Moulin Rouge") to disarming paeans to awkward slow dancing ("They're Not Tryin' on the Dance Floor") and dressing down for a date ("Everyday Clothes"). Cynics dismiss him as childish and self-consciously cute, but they haven't been paying attention since the days of "I'm a Little Dinosaur" and "Hey There Little Insect." Richman's world is full of treasured moments and small pleasures, where growth is measured in wrinkles, not milestones, and where true love is still a quest, not an anachronism.

what to buy: Mopey and minimalistic, *Modern Lovers* (Beserkley/Rhino, 1975, prod. John Cale) is the album that launched a thousand garage bands with "Roadrunner," "Pablo Picasso" and "She Cracked." The mostly acoustic *Back In Your Life* (Beserkley, 1979, prod. Matthew King Kaufman, Glen Kolotkin and Kenny Laguna) contains both his silliest ("I'm Nature's Mosquito," "Party in the Woods Tonight") and most sublime ("Affection," "Back in Your Life") material. The title track contains what may be the single-best line about the passage of time ever written: "What once was a puppy is now a dog/and what was once was a piglet is now a hog." *Jonathan Sings!* (Sire, 1983, prod. Peter Bernstein) marks an important transition as Richman learns how to celebrate life and love from an adult's perspective and a child's heart. "This Kind of Music," which champions rock 'n' roll as something to be felt and not merely heard, and "The Neighbors," about not letting other people control your life, are as empowering as they are entertaining. *I, Jonathan* (Rounder, 1992, prod. Brennan Totten) is the most consistent of the recent work, although it would be worth the price just for the uplifting "A Higher Power" and the funky "I Was Dancing in the Lesbian Bar."

what to buy next: *Jonathan Goes Country* (Rounder, 1990, prod. Lou Whitney and D. Clinton Thompson) unites Richman with the Missouri bar band the Skeletons. "Since She Started to Ride," "Reno" and an instrumental version of Skeeter Davis' "I Can't Stay Mad at You" lock into a tight, twangy bar-band groove. But the highlight is Richman's tender cover of "Man Walks Among Us," Marty Robbins' cautionary tale about urban sprawl.

what to avoid: The self-indulgent, sonically anemic *Jonathan Richman* (Rounder, 1989, prod. Brennan Totten) contains some great tunes—Ronnie Dawson's "Action Packed" and Richman's "Everyday Clothes"—but they're drowned out by droning instrumentals, foreign-language ditties and a painful spoken-word number called "I Eat With Gusto, Damn! You Bet."

the rest: With the Modern Lovers: *Modern Lovers Live* (Beserkley/Rhino, 1977) *Jonathan Richman and the Modern Lovers* (Beserkley, 1977) *Rock 'n' Roll With the Modern Lovers* (Beserkley/Rhino, 1977) *Modern Lovers 88* (Rounder, 1988) *Precise Modern Lovers Order* (Rounder, 1994) Solo: *Rockin' and Romance* (Twin Tone, 1985) *It's Time For Jonathan Richman* (Upside, 1986) *The Beserkley Years* (Rhino, 1987) *Jonathan, Te Vas a Emocionar* (Rounder, 1984) *You Must Ask the Heart* (Rounder, 1995)

worth searching for: *Chartbusters: The Best of Beserkley 1975-1978* (Rhino, 1986, prod. Matthew King Kaufman and Glen Kolotkin), a reissue of the 1975 compilation of rare tracks by labelmates the Rubinoos, Greg Kihn and Earth Quake, contains four Richman rarities: "The New Teller," a joyful rocker about his crush on a bank teller; a heartfelt cover of the Showmen's "It Will Stand"; "Government Center;" and a bouncier, post-John Cale rendition of "Roadrunner."

▶▶ Poi Dog Pondering, Ben Lee, Beck

◀◀ Velvet Underground, Chuck Berry, the Ventures

David Okamoto

Gary Richrath

See: Reo Speedwagon

Ride

Formed 1988 in Oxford, England. Disbanded 1995.

Mark Gardener, vocals, guitar; Andy Bell, vocals, guitar; Steve Queralt, bass; Laurence Colbert, drums

After launching its career as the voice of England's blank generation (i.e. the so-called "shoe gazers"), the Oxford quartet went through some interesting changes. From the shiftless sonic layers of feedback on 1990's *Smile* EP to the assured pop bite of 1992's *Going Blank Again*" to 1994's rootsy *Carnival of Light*, Ride rarely treaded the same ground twice. But as the music became more disparate, so did the band members' individual interests. Ride had split up by the time 1995's *Tarantula* was completed, though hearing a band falling apart at the seams still made for engaging listening.

what to buy: *Nowhere* (Sire/Reprise, 1990, prod. Marc Waterman) ♪♪♪♪ is a sonic monster, using layers of guitars, wispy vocals and hard-hitting drums to help re-define British rock at the outset of the decade. The decidedly American rock vibe of *Carnival of Light* (Sire/Reprise, 1994, prod. John Leckie) ♪♪♪♪ shows that Ride was more than a one-trick pony.

what to buy next: *Going Blank Again* (Sire/Reprise, 1992, prod. Ride and Alan Moulder) ♪♪♪ contains Ride's most pop-oriented and accessible batch of songs, particularly the single "Twisterella."

what to avoid: *Smile* (Sire/Reprise, 1990, prod. Ride) ♪♪ which combines two filler-laden EPs for a less-than-overwhelming introduction to U.S. audiences.

the rest: *Tarantula* (Sire, 1996) ♪♪

worth searching for: *Live Light* (Mutiny, 1995) ♪♪♪ is an sanctioned bootleg released during the awkward interim between *Carnival of Light* and *Tarantula* The sound quality is superlative, as is the comprehensive selection of songs.

▶▶ Revolver, Rosemary's, Chapterhouse

◀◀ Jesus & Mary Chain, Echo & the Bunnymen, My Bloody Valentine, the House of Love

Aidin Vaziri

Stan Ridgway

See: Wall of Voodoo

Will Rigby

See: the dB's

Righteous Brothers

Formed 1962 in Los Angeles, Calif. Disbanded 1968. Subsequent reunions in 1974 and throughout the 80s and 90s.

Bill Medley (born Sept. 19, 1940 in Santa Ana, Calif.), vocals; Bobby Hatfield, (born Aug. 10, 1940 in Beaver Dam, Wis.), vocals

The archetypal blue-eyed soul team, the Righteous Brothers churned out a steady procession of classic rock 'n' roll—with "Little Latin Lupe Lu" at the apex—long before even meeting Wagnerian producer Phil Spector, who assured the duo pop immortality on their first collaboration, the epochal 1965 No. 1 hit, "You've Lost That Lovin' Feelin'." By matching Medley's oozing baritone with Hatfield's ecstatic tenor, the pair could generate sparks with furious, almost intuitive vocal tradeoffs. And after splitting with Spector after a string of massive hits, with Medley at the helm, the Brothers proved they learned their lessons well, etching a pop-perfect re-creation of the Spector sound, "(You're My) Soul and Inspiration," which also hit No. 1. After splitting up and re-forming—on a guest appearance on the Sonny and Cher TV show, no less—the Righteous Brothers returned to the Top 5 in 1974 with "Rock 'n' Roll Heaven," a relatively cheesy piece of formula radio fodder fashioned for them by the songwriting-production team of Dennis Lambert and Brian Potter, who were experiencing similar Top 40 successes at the time with the Four Tops and the Tavares. The re-emergence of the Spector-produced "Unchained Melody" on the 1990 soundtrack of "Ghost" led to yet another re-formation (Medley, in the meantime, scored a No. 1 hit on a duet with Jennifer Warnes with "(I've Had) The Time Of My Life" from the "Dirty Dancing" soundtrack), leaving the pair headlining oldies shows and casino main rooms with a slickly produced act honed to a fare-thee-well over four decades of performing.

what to buy: Released in the wake of the "Ghost" soundtrack,

Unchained Melody: The Very Best Of the Righteous Brothers (PolyGram, 1990, prod. Various) 𝄞𝄞𝄞𝄞 covers the basics of the group's hit repertoire with little chaff amidst the wheat.

what to buy next: Before linking up with Spector, Medley and Hatfield combined on a succession of rollicking R&B-influenced sides collected on *The Moonglow Years* (PolyGram, 1991, prod. Various) 𝄞𝄞𝄞

what to avoid: The two-disc *Anthology: 1962-1974* (Rhino, 1989, prod. Various) 𝄞𝄞𝄞𝄞 contains more Righteous Brothers than is probably useful. The second disc is almost gratuitous, but the 16-track first disc thoroughly covers the duo's frat rock classics on the Moonglow label and culminates with five Spector epics.

the rest: *The Best Of the Righteous Brothers* (Curb 1993) 𝄞𝄞 *The Best Of the Righteous Brothers, Vol. 2* (Curb 1993) 𝄞

worth searching for: *Some Blue-Eyed Soul,* (Moonglow, 1964) 𝄞𝄞𝄞 the deepest and most consistent of the individual albums from the duo's peak period.

▶▶ The Walker Brothers, Hall and Oates

◀◀ Don and Dewey, Ray Charles

Joel Selvin

Jason Ringenberg

See: Jason and the Scorchers

Rising Sons

Formed 1964 in Los Angeles, Calif. Disbanded 1966

Taj Mahal, vocals, harmonica, guitar, piano; Ry Cooder, vocals, guitar, mandolin, dobro; Jesse Lee Kincaid, vocals, guitar; Gary Marker, bass; Ed Cassidy, drums (1964-65), Kevin Kelley, drums (1965-66)

Contrary to what another reference says, this legendary band, though commercially ill-fated, didn't break up before recording and actually released a single in February 1966 ("The Devil's Got My Woman"/"Candy Man") that's included on the archival album—MDULRising SonsMDNM (Columbia Legacy, 1992, prod. Terry Melcher) 𝄞𝄞𝄞—issued a quarter-century after the fact. The mix of Kincaid's original pop songs (as well as Dylan's "Walkin' Down the Line" and Goffin/King's "Take a Giant Step") and country blues covers was too far ahead of its time for the label to sell, and the band broke up in 1966 without having issued anything but that one single. Beyond the obvious subsequent successes of Taj Mahal and Cooder, original drummer Cassidy (apparently not on the issued recordings) went on to co-found Spirit, while his replacement Kelley later spent time as a Byrd. Kincaid made some singles for Capitol, and Marker's jazz-rock band Fusion put out an album on Atco.

Steve Holtje

Brian Ritchie

See: Violent Femmes

Johnny Rivers

Born John Ramistella on Nov. 7, 1942, in New York, N.Y.

Named by Alan Freed and raised in Baton Rouge, La., Rivers arrived in Los Angeles in 1960 and worked as a record producer and writer before becoming a star as a regular at the Whisky A Go Go in 1963 during its discotheque incarnation. His version of Chuck Berry's "Memphis" and his debut album, recorded "live, very live," became one of 1964's biggest sellers, no mean feat during the first year of the British Invasion. He showed great taste in musicians, employing only the best of L.A. (Lou Adler as producer and bassist Joe Osborn, drummer Hal Blaine and keyboardist Larry Knechtel before they became known as one of rock's master rhythm sections). But Rivers' lasting gift is his taste in songs and writers across the spectrum; Chuck Berry, Sam Cooke, Arthur Alexander, Willie Dixon, Pete Seeger, P.F. Sloan, Jimmy Webb (Rivers discovered him), Holland/Dozier/Holland, Gene Vincent, Van Morrison—Rivers had hits with songs by all of them. With Adler, Rivers founded Dunhill Records, which helped establish Los Angeles as a recording center and was home to the Mamas and the Papas, Barry McGuire, Scott McKenzie, Steppenwolf and the Grass Roots. For his own Soul City Records, Rivers produced the Fifth Dimension's "Up, Up and Away." The hits stopped around 1973, and Rivers emerged again in the 80s as a born-again gospel singer.

what to buy: *The Johnny Rivers Anthology: 1964-1977*, (Rhino, 1991, prod. Lou Adler, Johnny Rivers and Bill Inglot) 𝄞𝄞𝄞𝄞 a two-disc collection that includes everything you need—all the hits, a few surprises and a nice booklet that analyzes Rivers' 13-year chart run.

what to buy next: *Johnny Rivers at the Whiskey A Go Go* (Imperial, 1964, prod. Lou Adler) 𝄞𝄞𝄞𝄞 features tight arrangements and the introduction of Hal Blaine, one of rock's all-time great drummers, who struts his stuff in this trio setting. On *Changes/Rewind* (Imperial, 1966-67/1992, prod. Lou Adler) we hear Rivers, affected by the major changes in music trading in the suit-and-tie of the Whiskey days for beads and leather. His music turned introspective on these two albums, packaged on CD as a two-fer.

what to avoid: Take your pick of the repetitive sequels to the *Whiskey* debut: *Here We A Go Go Again* (Imperial, 1964, prod. Lou Adler) *Johnny Rivers in ActionMDBR* (Imperial, 1965, prod. Lou Adler) *Meanwhile Back at the Whiskey* (Imperial, 1965, prod. Lou Adler)

the rest: *Johnny Rivers Rocks the Folk* (Imperial, 1965) *Realization* (Imperial, 1968) *A Touch of Gold* (Imperial, 1969) *Slim Slo Slider* (Imperial, 1970) *Homegrown* (United Artists, 1971) *L.A. Reggae* (United Artists, 1972) *Blue Suede Shoes* (United Artists, 1973) *Road* (United Artists, 1974) *New Lovers and Old Friends* (Epic, 1975) *Wild Night* (United Artists, 1976) *Outside Help* (Soul City, 1977)

worth searching for: For *Johnny Rivers Greatest Hits,* (MCA, 1985, prod. Johnny Rivers) Rivers re-recorded versions of nine early hits, including "Secret Agent Man" and especially "Summer Rain," without the cloying arrangement of the original single).

Tom Petty & the Heartbreakers, John Mellencamp, Doobie Brothers, Bob Seger

Chuck Berry, Jimmy Reed, Dick Holler, Jimmy Clanton, Elvis Presley, Jerry Lee Lewis, Trini Lopez, Mose Allison

Leland Rucker

Rick Roberts

See: Firefall

Smokey Robinson and the Miracles

Formed 1957 in Detroit, Mich.

William "Smokey" Robinson (born Feb. 19, 1940 in Detroit, Mich.), vocals (1957-72); Ronnie White, vocals (died August 26, 1995 in Detroit, Mich); Bobby Rogers, vocals; Warren "Pete" Moore, vocals; Claudette Rogers, vocals (1957-64); William Griffin, vocals

Berry Gordy, Jr., owned Motown, but Robinson was the label's king. A singer and songwriter who befriended Gordy during the late 50s, Robinson was Motown's go-to guy. He wrote the label's first No. 1 pop hit, "My Guy" for Mary Wells, and its biggest, "My Girl" for the Temptations. Sensing a theme here? As an artist, Robinson wrote and performed some of the sweetest and most poetic loves songs in pop music history. No less than Bob Dylan called him "America's greatest living poet," and the British band ABC celebrated Robinson in song with "When Smokey Sings." In his prime, Robinson was able to convey passion, pain, longing and any other emotion with just a few words and his own flexible vocals—particularly his ability to sweep into an ear-clutching falsetto. The Miracles were no simple backup group, either; the others—particularly White (who co-wrote "My Girl") and Bobby Rogers—served as creative foils, while Robinson and Claudette Rogers were married for nearly 25 years. On his own, Robinson coined a whole new pop music genre—the pillow-talk "Quiet Storm"—though his hits have become considerably more sporadic. He actually left Motown during the early 90s, though he remains an occasional ambassador for the label.

what to buy: *Anthology: The Best of Smokey Robinson & the Miracles* (Motown, 1995, prod. Smokey Robinson) is a marvelous two-CD distillation that has all the hits—"Ooo Baby Baby," "Going to a Go-Go," "I Second That Emotion," "The Tears of a Clown"—plus some important album tracks. *A Quiet Storm* (Motown, 1975/1989, prod. Smokey Robinson) is a landmark solo album, a sexy, whispery affair that launched a whole new realm of music.

what to buy next: *The 35th Anniversary Collection* (Motown, 1994, prod. Various) While some of the other Motown box sets have their share of filler, this one reminds us that with a talent like Robinson on board, it's not hard to have four discs worth of wonderful music (including selections from his solo career and from the post-Smokey Miracles). Robinson's *One Heartbeat* (Motown, 1987, prod. Various) is another fine solo album, a return to form after several fallow years with the hits "Just to See Her" and the title track.

what to avoid: *Motown Superstar Series Volume 18* (Motown, date N/A) is, in this case, a useless redundancy.

the rest: Smokey Robinson and the Miracles—*Cookin' With the Miracles* (Motown, 1962/1994) *Christmas With the Miracles* (Motown, 1963) *Going to a Go-Go* (Motown, 1965) *Greatest Hits, Vol. II* (Motown, 1968) *The Season For Miracles* (Motown, 1970) *The Tears of a Clown* (Motown, 1970) *Whatever Makes You Happy: More of the Best* (Rhino, 1993) *Motown Legends: The Ballad Album* (ESX, 1994) Smokey Robinson—*Blame it On Love & All the Great Hits* (Motown, 1983/1990) *Double Good Every-*

thing (SBK/EMI, 1991) ♪♪♪ *Cruisin'—Being With You* (ESX, 1995) ♪♪♪♪

worth searching for: Here's a true mark of Robinson's talents; his vocal on "We've Saved the Best for Last" actually makes a Kenny G album worth buying (*Silhouette* (Arista, 1988)

▶▶ Paul McCartney, Michael Jackson, Terence Trent D'Arby, Babyface

◀◀ Jackie Wilson, Clyde McPhatter, Sam Cooke

Gary Graff

Tom Robinson Band /Sector 27

Tom Robinson Band—Formed 1977 in London, England. Disbanded 1979 Sector 27—Formed 1979 in London, England. Disbanded 1980.

Tom Robinson (born 1951 in Cambridge, England), vocals, bass; Danny Kustow, vocals, guitar; Mark Ambler, keyboards (1977-79); Brian "Dolphin" Taylor, drums (1977-79); Ian Parker, keyboards (1979); Preston Heyman, drums (1979). Sector 27: Tom Robinson, vocals, guitar; Jo Burt, bass; Stevie B., guitar; Derek Quinton, drums

Though he got more attention for being openly gay and proudly singing his subversive song "Glad to Be Gay," Robinson's explosive band contributed to the rich new wave movement that rose in the Sex Pistols' wake. TRB's U.K. hit "2-4-6-8 Motorway" is among the finest driving songs ever recorded, and Robinson's explicit politics gave his songs a social punch. Like much of the flag-waving punks, Robinson's muse eventually dissolved, and he spent the rest of his career behind the scenes. He still puts out an album now and then, and he still contributes to gay rights and anti-AIDS causes, but he now has a young son and a relationship with a woman. Robinson touchingly acknowledged the changes in his life, and the death of punk, in the 1994 song "Days."

what to buy: The American version of the TRB debut, *Power in the Darkness* (Harvest, 1978/Razor & Tie, 1993, prod. Chris Thomas) ♪♪♪♪, captures the group's early spirit and includes the first single, "2-4-6-8 Motorway."

what to buy next: The band's more polished followup, *TRB Two* (Harvest, 1979/Razor & Tie, 1993, prod. Todd Rundgren) ♪♪♪ contains a duet with Peter Gabriel, which became a small U.K. hit. Sector 27's only record, *Sector 27* (I.R.S., 1980, prod. Steve Lillywhite) ♪♪♪, isn't quite as good as Robinson's former band incarnation, but it works out O.K.

what to avoid: Robinson's string of solo records, many released only outside the U.S.—including *Hope and Glory* (Geffen, 1984, prod. Robin Millar and Tom Robinson) ♪♪—are close to pointless.

the rest: *North by Northwest* (I.R.S., 1982) ♪♪♪ *Love Over Rage* (Rhythm Safari, 1994) ♪♪♪

worth searching for: Most people bought *The Secret Policeman's Ball* (Island, 1980, prod. Martin Lewis) ♪♪♪ to hear Pete Townshend play Who songs as an acoustic solo act. But Robinson sneaks in two wonderful performances—his strident-and-powerful "Glad to Be Gay" and his wistful "1967 (So Long Ago)."

▶▶ Elvis Costello, John Wesley Harding, Pansy Division, Me'Shell Ndegeocello

◀◀ The Kinks, the Who, Todd Rundgren, Bob Dylan

Steve Knopper

The Roches

Formed in December 1976, Greenwich Village, N.Y.

Maggie Roche, guitar, keyboards and vocals; Terre Roche, guitar and vocals; Suzzy Roche, guitar and vocals

Graduates of the Greenwich Village folk scene, Maggie, Terre and Suzzy Roche stood out like crewcuts at a Grateful Dead concert when they released their self-titled debut in 1979: folk was dead, punk was threatening and the idea of three sisters harmonizing around acoustic guitars was hardly hip. Yet, their songwriting was filled with quirky humor, and their voices purposely didn't weave so much as collide, flirting with atonalism and eschewing traditional rules of harmony singing. Alternately pretty ("The Married Men"), powerful ("The Hallelujah Chorus") and punishing ("Bobby's Song"), their unison sound was so daring and distinctive that the trio spent the better part of a decade harnessing its force and fighting with record companies over the best direction to follow. Such recent albums as *A Dove* and *Can We Go Home Now?* show they've finally won both battles.

what to buy: A clarion-calling card if there ever was one, *The Roches* (Warner Bros., 1979, prod. Robert Fripp) ♪♪♪♪ is a mesmerizing acoustic showcase framed around such striking compositions as "Hammond Song," "Married Men" and the giddy "Mr. Sellack." The immediacy and intimacy of Fripp's "audio verite" production captures every nuance from breathing sounds to the squeaks of sliding fingers on the frets. The sisters' relentless quest to weave pop elements and band arrangements around their harmonies is finally fulfilled on *A Dove* (MCA, 1992, prod. Stewart Lerman). *Keep on Doing* (Warner Bros., 1982, prod. Robert Fripp) includes their stunning a cappella version of "The Hallelujah Chorus" and the strange but endearing "The Largest Elizabeth in the World."

what to buy next: *Nurds* (Warner Bros., 1980, prod. Roy Halee) is a brave attempt to shoehorn them into the new-wave movement with such oddities as "Bobby's Girl," "The Boat Family" and the hysterically self-depreciating "Death of Suzzy Roche."

what to avoid: *No Trespassing* (Rhino, 1986, prod. Joe Terry, Andy Bloch and the Roches) WOOF! is a lifeless four-song EP recorded after the trio split from Warner Bros.

the rest: *Another World* (Warner Bros., 1985) *Speak* (MCA, 1989) *We Three Kings* (Rykodisc, 1990) *Will You Be My Friend*, a children's album (Baby Boom, 1994) *Can We Go Home Now* (Rykodisc, 1995)

worth searching for: *Seductive Reasoning* (Columbia, 1975, prod. Paul Simon and Paul Samwell-Smith), a pre-Suzzy album co-produced by Simon after Maggie and Terre backed him on "There Goes Rhymin' Simon."

The Murmurs, The Story

Madrigal singing, Simon and Garfunkel, Kate and Anna McGarrigle

David Okamoto

Lee Rocker's Big Blue

See: Stray Cats

Rocket from the Crypt

Formed 1989 in San Diego, Calif.

Speedo (born John Reis) vocals, guitars; Petey X, bass, vocals; N.D., guitar; Atom, drums; Apollo 9, saxophone (1991-present); J.C. 2000, trumpet (1995-present)

Primarily a 7" singles factory (16 between 1991-96), Rocket from the Crypt is a band that abuses rock cliches by masterfully blending punk energy with mainstream accessibility. Its Phil Spector wall-of-sound-on-crack production fused with 60s garage gutters and Famous Flames-ish horn attacks has turned Rocket into San Diego's undisputed rock 'n' roll royalty. Named by band leader Speedo as a tribute to Rocket from the Tombs (the late 70s Cleveland band that evolved into Pere Ubu), Rocket's prodigious output of West Coast sonic soul has brought fun and chicanery back to 90s alterna-rock.

what to buy: *All Systems Go* (Headhunter/Cargo, 1993, prod. John Reis) unwittingly is the definitive Rocket. Originally a compilation of B-sides and studio out-takes intended as a Japanese-only tour release, copies were quickly smuggled back into the U.S. (at $30 a pop!), forcing the band to re-issue it here. More complete and, where necessary, re-recorded, the domestic version of *All Systems Go* captures the raw, hook-laden Rocket without the studio polish, and it saves one from the maddening task of trying to accumulate the original (and essential) vinyl.

what to buy next: *Circa: Now!* (Headhunter, 1992/Interscope, 1993 prod. John Reis) offers a more fully fleshed-out Rocket sound to complement its silvery riffs and singsongy chants.

what to avoid: *Gold* one-sided single (Drunken Fish, 1992, prod. John Reis) WOOF! is pure dreck—a sham, actually. Fans of Lou Reed's grating *Metal Machine Music* might appreciate the grin, but don't bother.

the rest: *Paint As Fragrance* (Headhunter, 1991) *Scream, Dracula, Scream!* (Interscope, 1995) *The State of Art Is on Fire* (Sympathy For The Record Industry, 1995)

worth searching for: The LP only *Hot Charity* (Perfect Sound, 1995, prod. John Reis) was limited to 5,000 red vinyl copies and introduces J.C. 2000 and his rocking trumpet.

Lucy's Fur Coat, Back Off Cupids

The Beatles, Black Flag, Graham Parker, Ramones

Jim Cummer

Rockpile

See: Dave Edmunds

Tommy Roe

Born 1942 in Atlanta, Ga.

Best known as one of bubblegum music's biggest hit makers, Roe began his recording career as a rocker in the same mold as Buddy Holly. During the early 60s, Roe cut a number of top-notch R&B tunes, including the 1962 chart-topper "Sheila" (a song much like Holly's "Peggy Sue"), "Stagger Lee" and "Everybody." As R&B fell behind pop, Roe switched to bubblegum, scoring hits in 1966 with "Sweet Pea" and "Hooray for Hazel."

His smash was "Dizzy," a transatlantic hit in 1969. Like other teenybopper idols of the period, Roe switched to country music in the early bloom of the 70s and eventually became a staple of the oldies circuit. *Tommy Roe's Greatest Hits* (MCA, 1993, prod. Bill Inglot) ♫♫♫ is the best of the Roe anthologies, offering 18 hits (including "Sheila," "Hooray for Hazel," "Dizzy" and "Stagger Lee") and excellent liner notes.

the rest: *The Best of Tommy Roe* (Curb, 1990) ♫♫ *Tommy Roe's Greatest Hits* (Curb, 1994) ♫♫

Christopher Scapelliti

Rolling Stones

Formed 1962 in London, England

Mick Jagger (born Michael Phillip Jagger), vocals, guitar; Keith Richards, guitar, vocals; Brian Jones (born Lewis Brian Hopkins-Jones), guitar (1962-69, died 1969); Bill Wyman (born William Perks), bass (1962-94); Charlie Watts, drums; Mick Taylor, guitar (1969-74); Ronnie Wood, guitar (1974-present); Daryl Jones, bass (1994-present)

In its first decade, the Stones defined the classic rock lineup—two guitars, bass, drums and a little red rooster crowing out front—and created the enduring standard for how it should sound. The Stones never were much for innovation; the group's more experimental tracks and albums sounded instantly contrived and dated. Instead they were expert at synthesis: Chicago blues, hard country music, a bit of Motown (and, later, Stax), played with a raw sexuality that freely appropriated from black performers such as James Brown and Tina Turner. They affirmed the primacy of the electric guitar as Richards succeeded Chuck Berry as rock's primary riff-meister. Richards and Jagger (aka The Glimmer Twins) wrote classic melodies and pithy, unsentimental and frequently just plain cruel lyrics that were the equal of their 60s rivals Bob Dylan and the Beatles. And the group's rhythm section, anchored by the peerless Watts, made it all swing like nobody's business. Only problem is, the Stones kept the money machine in motion long after their artistic drive waned. Like their blues heroes, the Stones entered their 50s still singing about their overworked mojos and cranking out competent product that bespoke professionalism rather than inspiration.

what to buy: *Aftermath* (Abkco, 1966, prod. Andrew Loog Oldham) ♫♫♫♫♫ marked the entry of these erstwhile blues traditionalists into the album-rock pantheon alongside Dylan and the Beatles, with its canny use of sitar, marimba and dulcimer (all performed by Brian Jones) to augment Jagger's multifaceted star turn as a vocalist on "Paint It Black," "Lady Jane" and "Under My Thumb." The weakest cuts on *Beggars Banquet* (Abkco, 1968, prod. Jimmy Miller) ♫♫♫♫½ are its best known: "Street Fighting Man" offers a rare political commentary that is musically stirring but lyrically ambivalent; and "Sympathy for the Devil" finds Jagger pandering to the group's bad-boy image. Otherwise, the disc is a tour de force of acoustic-tinged savagery and slumming sexuality, particularly the gleefully flippant "Stray Cat Blues." *Let It Bleed* (Abkco, 1969, prod. Jimmy Miller) ♫♫♫♫♫ slams the door on the 60s with such harrowing anthems as "Gimme Shelter" and "You Can't Always Get What You Want." *Exile on Main Street* (Virgin, 1972, prod. Jimmy Miller) ♫♫♫♫♫ got some bum reviews when first issued for its muddy sound and decadent atmospherics. It's now rightly hailed as a masterpiece, and from the passionate yearning of the gospel-tinged "Let It Loose" to the demon fury of "Rip This Joint," it remains a towering survey of the Stones as they reinvent their influences.

what to buy next: *Big Hits/High Tide and Green Grass* (Abkco, 1966, prod. Andrew Loog Oldham) ♫♫♫♫♫ is an impeccable 12-cut summary of the Stones' pre-*Aftermath* singles; of the hits collections, it's surpassed only by the pricey but worth-it box set, *The Singles Collection*, (Abkco, 1989, prod. Various) ♫♫♫♫♫ which documents the band's first and best decade of music-making. *Sticky Fingers* (Virgin, 1971, prod. Jimmy Miller) ♫♫♫♫½ has the most famous cover art of any Stones album (Andy Warhol's zippered crotch shot) and—"Brown Sugar" excepted—among the most darkly weary music. But amid the druggy drama, the luminous beauty of "Sway" and "Moonlight Mile" is redemptive. *Some Girls* (Virgin, 1978, prod. The Glimmer Twins) ♫♫♫♫ is the last gasp of greatness, with Richards' "Before They Make Me Run" serving as what should have been a fitting epitaph: "See my tail lights fading/Not a dry eye in the house." Those who insist on owning something from the latter-day, Steel Wheelchairs-era Stones should head straight for *Stripped* (Virgin, 1995, prod. Don Was and The Glimmer Twins) ♫♫♫½, the first live album by the group that isn't superfluous, with its revelatory "unplugged" treatment of several classic tracks compensating for a tepid cover of Dylan's "Like a Rolling Stone."

what to avoid: Before *Stripped*, the Stones released five live albums, all of them stiffs. None offer tracks that improve upon the studio originals, including: *Got Live if You Want It* (Abkco, 1966, prod. Andrew Loog Oldham) ♫ the overrated *Get Yer Ya's-Ya's Out* (Abkco, 1970, prod. Glyn Johns and the Rolling Stones) ♫♫ *Love You Live* (Rolling Stones, 1977, prod. The Glimmer

Twins) *Still Life* (Rolling Stones, 1982, prod. The Glimmer Twins) and *Flashpoint.* (Rolling Stones, 1991, prod. Chris Kimsey and Glimmer Twins)

the rest: *The Rolling Stones: England's Newest Hit Makers* (Abkco, 1964) *12 X 5* (Abkco, 1964) *The Rolling Stones, Now!* (Abkco, 1965) *Out of Our Heads* (Abkco, 1965) *December's Children* (Abkco, 1965) *Between the Buttons* (Abkco, 1967) *Flowers* (Abkco, 1967) *Their Satanic Majesties Request* (Abkco, 1967) *Through the Past Darkly (Big Hits, Vol. 2)* (Abkco, 1968) *Hot Rocks 1964-71* (Abkco, 1972) *More Hot Rocks: Big Hits and Fazed Cookies* (Abkco, 1973) *Goats Head Soup* (Virgin, 1973) *It's Only Rock 'n' Roll* (Virgin, 1974) *Made in the Shade* (Virgin, 1975) *Black and Blue* (Virgin, 1976) *Emotional Rescue* (Virgin, 1980) *Sucking in the Seventies* (Rolling Stones, 1981) *Tattoo You* (Virgin, 1981) *Undercover* (Rolling Stones, 1983) *Rewind (1971-84)* (Rolling Stones, 1984) *Dirty Work* (Rolling Stones, 1986) *Steel Wheels* (Rolling Stones, 1989) *Voodoo Lounge* (Virgin, 1994)

worth searching for: *Jump Back: The Best of the Rolling Stones* (Virgin, 1993, prod. Various), a sparkling sounding (20-bit mastered) U.K. compilation spanning 1971-93, with exceptional liner notes.

New York Dolls, Aerosmith, Guns N' Roses, Black Crowes

Willie Dixon, Muddy Waters, Chuck Berry, Buddy Holly, Sam Cooke, the Beatles

Greg Kot

Henry Rollins

Born Henry Garfield on Feb. 13, 1961, in Washington, D.C.

Rollins is a one-man industry, simultaneously the leader of a highly respected alternative rock band, actor, author, tireless spoken word performer, publisher and executive of two record labels. The product of a broken home, Rollins musically started out in D.C.'s SOA, came to prominence and maturity in Black Flag (which he joined at the age of 20), and began leading his Rollins Band (drummer Simeon Cain, guitarist Chris Haskett and bassists Andrew Weiss and later Melvin Gibbs) after Black Flag broke up in 1986. The ensemble melded punk and heavy metal in a way that infuriated some punk purists but which prophetically turned out to be the commercial future of alternative rock. (Mix engineer Theo van Eenbergen, later known as Theo Van Rock, is considered a fifth member of the group.) Rollins' spoken word career has become as important as his music; he began publishing his writings through his book company, 2.13.61, which has issued more than a dozen of his books plus work by Exene Cervenka, Hubert Selby, Nick Cave and more. His no-BS attitude also has made him a popular guest writer for such magazines as Details and Spin. The external image—multiple tattoos, including a massive sun face covering his back; body pumped up from weightlifting; scowling visage; black shorts and black T-shirt—certainly reflects genuine aspects of his personality but hardly tells the whole story. He listens to music across a broad spectrum, from John Lee Hooker to John Coltrane. He uses most of his money to make available neglected music he loves via his labels Infinite Zero, a collaboration with Rick Rubin, and 213CD, the sonic arm of his publishing company.

what to buy: *Weight* (Imago, 1994, prod. Theo Van Rock) became the Rollins Band's biggest seller on the strength of the sardonic "Liar" and its amusing video, but "Disconnect" is the best track, typical of Rollins's elevated self-analysis. *Do It* (Texas Hotel, 1988, prod. Ian MacKaye and Theo van Eenbergen) has three good outtakes from *Life Time*—including the cover of the Pink Fairies' title cut—and 12 hot live tracks from a 1987 European tour that improve on the studio versions. The best version of the desolately alienated "Lonely" is the touchstone of Rollins' indie period. The double spoken word CD *Human Butt* (1/4 Stick/Touch & Go, 1992) finds Rollins weaving long stories drawn from his life, by turns hilarious and poignant—a real, complex, compassionate human being eloquently expressing simple truths.

what to buy next: *The End of Silence* (Imago, 1992, prod. Andy Wallace) captures the power and passion of the band's epochal performances on the first Lollapalooza Tour. "Low Self Opinion" is the pinnacle of a cleaner, sometimes more intricate and more constructive approach that retains the old power. *The Boxed Life* (Imago, 1992) positions Rollins as a stand-up comedian, with funny stories and astute observations concentrating on the nomadic existence of touring. *Everything* (2.13.61, 1996) matches some of Rollins' most intense, best-written spoken word material with occasional musical accompaniment by free jazz greats Charles Gayle (tenor sax, piano) and Rashied Ali (drums).

what to avoid: With all the live Rollins Band music available, *Turned On* (1/4 Stick/Touch & Go, 1990, prod. not listed) is unnecessary. The sound is not as good as elsewhere, and there's no CD indexing—just one long track for 15 songs. Also avoid *Fast Food for Thought*, (Chrysalis EP, 1990, prod. Andrew Weiss and Theo Van Rock) 🦴🦴 a numbing enteprise by Wartime, a duo comprised of Rollins and Weiss.

the rest: *Hot Animal Machine* (Texas Hotel, 1987) 🦴🦴🦴 *Life Time* (Texas Hotel, 1988) 🦴🦴🦴 *Hard Volume* (Texas Hotel, 1989) 🦴🦴🦴 Spoken word—*Big Ugly Mouth* (Texas Hotel, 1987) 🦴🦴🦴 *Sweat Box* (Texas Hotel, 1989) 🦴🦴🦴 *Deep Throat* (1/4 Stick, 1992) 🦴🦴🦴🦴 *Live at McCabe's* (1/4 Stick/Touch & Go, 1993) 🦴🦴🦴 *Get in the Van* (Time Warner Audio Books, 1994) 🦴🦴

worth searching for: A limited edition of *Weight* that comes packaged in a round tin designed like a weight.

⏩ Pearl Jam, Soundgarden

⏪ Led Zeppelin, Black Sabbath, Bad Brains, Charles Bukowski

see also: *Black Flag*

Steve Holtje

The Romantics

Formed 1977 in Detroit, Mich.

Wally Palmar, guitar, vocals; Mike Skill, guitar, bass, vocals (1977-81, 1985-present); Richard Cole, bass, vocals (1977-85); Jimmy Marinos, drums, vocals (1977-83, 1995-present); Coz Canler, guitar (1977-83); David Patratos, drums (1983-89); Clem Burke, drums (1989)

The Romantics summed up New Wave fashion with signature matching suits and skinny ties, and New Wave music with the incredibly infectious singles such as "What I Like About You" and "Talking in Your Sleep." The group's hits are perfectly disposable pop songs, built on classic rock 'n' roll major chords that rehash "Gloria" and "Louie Louie" with grand enthusiasm. Though "What I Like About You" hit just No. 49 when it came out in 1980, it has been played endlessly at school dances and sports arenas, and on Budweiser commercials and HBO movies. The band went to court during the mid-90s to win ownership of its songs and—re-united with original singer-drummer Marinos—planned another round of recording.

what to buy: *The Romantics* (Nemperor, 1980, prod. Peter Solley) 🦴🦴🦴🦴 contains the big hit (you know the title by now) and a bunch of other explosive, fun pop singles. *National Breakout* (Nemperor, 1980, prod. Peter Solley) 🦴🦴🦴 is more of the same—almost as good—with "Tomboy" and "Stone Pony" as standouts.

what to buy next: *What I Like About You (And Other Romantic Hits)* (Epic Associated, 1990, prod. Various) contains—guess what?—and a bunch of other pop tarts, though at 10 songs it's a bit skimpy.

what to avoid: *Strictly Personal* (Nemperor/Epic, 1981, prod. Mike Stone) 🦴🦴 is the band's major misstep, trading the explosive Kingsmen-like garage-pop for bland, overproduced schlock.

the rest: *In Heat* (Nemperor, 1983) 🦴🦴🦴 *Rhythm Romance* (Nemperor, 1985) 🦴🦴🦴 *Made in Detroit* (Westbound EP, 1993) 🦴🦴🦴

worth searching for: For the proper context, try *Shake It Up!: American Power Pop II, (1978-80)* (Rhino, 1993, prod. Gary Stewart) 🦴🦴🦴🦴 which has you-know-what plus "Tell It to Carrie" alongside songs by the Shoes, Plimsouls, Holly and the Italians, 20/20, the Beat and others kindred spirits.

⏩ Green Day, the Offspring, the Proclaimers, the Plimsouls, the Shoes

⏪ The Kingsmen, Them, the Easybeats, the Buzzcocks, Rockpile, the Monkees, the Beatles

Tracey Birkenhauer and Steve Knopper

Romeo Void

Formed 1979 in San Francisco, Calif. Disbanded 1985

Debora Iyall, vocals; Frank Zincavage, bass; Peter Woods, guitar; Jay Derrah, drums (1979-80); John Stench, drums (1980-1981); Larry Carter, drums (1981-1984); Ben Bossi, saxophone

Romeo Void whomped across the post-punk landscape with a wailing sax, a dark dance beat and Iyall's detached talk-singing. Vacant love was the main thrust of her songs, which gave some relief to the more vacuous and hollow areas of New Wave. The crashing emptiness in the lyrics of 1981's "Never Say Never" ("I might like you better if we slept together") sound like they could have lifted from one of Bret Easton Ellis' despairing novels. The group's only chart hit was the slippery pop of "A Girl in Trouble (Is a Temporary Thing)" in 1984; that and the best of the group's output, can be found on the band's sole remaining title, the compilation *Warm, in Your Coat* (Columbia, 1992, prod. Various) 🦴🦴🦴.

Allan Orski

Mick Ronson

Born 1946 in Hull, England. Died April 30, 1993, London, England

The author of three little-known solo albums, Mick Ronson was also a silent partner in some of rock's finest moments and a guitar hero whose mix of virtuosity and economy was alien to many others more famous and flashy. He was the musical director for David Bowie's Ziggy Stardust period (1972-74), co-creating the sound that first brought Bowie superstardom. He also earned his stripes co-producing Lou Reed's 1972 album *Transformer*, joining Bob Dylan's eclectic Rolling Thunder Revue tour in 1975, collaborating with Ian Hunter through 1989's *Y U I Orta* and producing Morrissey's *Your Arsenal* in 1992. When diagnosed with liver cancer in 1991, Ronson had embarked on an all-star solo project which turned out to be his own posthumous tribute album, *Heaven and Hull*. A musician's musician, Ronson worked until his death, facing the future and not just the end.

Play Don't Worry RCA, 1975, prod. Mick Ronson) is Ronson's most cohesive, assured and individual album. It holds up as a prime example of the glam genre, and features some forward-looking machine sonics and clean-but-full production. His debut, *Slaughter on 10th Ave.*, (RCA, 1974, prod. Mick Ronson) is ambitious but random, though finely produced, arranged and played. The lost glam-rock classic "Only After Dark" still holds up, as do the lean, atonal jams of "Pleasure Man." (The first two albums can be found, with some searching, on the two-disc set *Only After Dark* (Griffin, 1995) .) The posthumous *Heaven and Hull* (Epic, 1994, exec. prod. Suzanne Ronson, Sam Lederman and Steve Popovich) is solidly crafted but seldom dynamic. Chrissie Hynde fans will want her tour-de-force guest vocal on "Trouble With Me," and "Colour Me" is a prize of dexterous fretwork, inventively verse-heavy pop-drone structure and Prince-inspired choral vocal.

see also: *David Bowie, Ian Hunter, Morrissey*

Adam McGovern

Linda Ronstadt

Born July 15, 1946, in Tucson, Ariz.

Any assessment of Ronstadt stands or falls on how strongly you feel about songwriting as an artistic credential. Ronstadt's not a writer; rather, she interprets other's songs—often in tones so distinctive and authoritative that they sound like they're her own.

The profound influence of Ronstadt's singing mandates a place for her, along with Emmylou Harris, as a major voice in the 70s fusion of country and rock. But where Harris leaned toward country's mountain and bluegrass traditions, Ronstadt mined the throbbing, emotional territory once owned by Patsy Cline. In doing so, she established a model for any number of subsequent pop-rock belters.

Ronstadt arrived in Los Angeles at the end of the 60s as singer for the Stone Poneys, scoring her first chart success with 1967's "Different Drum" before the group broke up. Ronstadt eventually emerged as princess of the California rock mafia that included the Eagles, John David Souther and Jackson Browne—sealing her ascension with the No. 1 hit "You're No Good" in 1974. But as the decade moved on, so would Ronstadt, and succeeding years have found her acting on Broadway ("Pirates of Penzance"), recording mariachi music, playing pop standards with the late Nelson Riddle and his orchestra, dueting with New Orleans' angel-voiced Aaron Neville and, most recently, recasting rock standards as lullabies. With the occasional exception, the hits are mostly in the past, but Ronstadt does enjoy a body of work that speaks of considerable artistic ambition.

what to buy: *Heart Like a Wheel* (Capitol, 1974, prod. Peter Asher) and *Prisoner in Disguise (Asylum, 1975, prod. Peter Asher) exemplify Asher's influential production style and Ronstadt's emotional brand of country-rock. In the poignant title tunes, memorable duets with Harris and carefully chosen remakes (such as Smokey Robinson and the Miracles' "Tracks of My Tears"), Ronstadt successfully walks the line dividing sadness from sappiness. Some of Ronstadt's best singing of the 80s is on the country-traditional* Trio, *(Warner Bros. 1987, prod. George Massenburg) with Harris and Dolly Parton.*

what to buy next: *Hasten Down the Wind* (Asylum, 1976, prod. Peter Asher) completes the 70s trio of Ronstadt/Asher mega-successes and spotlights excellent songwriting by Karla Bonoff and Warren Zevon.

Ronstadt is not a definitive artist in either big-band sound or mariachi folk, but her experiments are honorable introductions to those genres. *For Sentimental Reasons* (Asylum, 1984, prod. Peter Asher) is the best of the Riddle records; *Canciones de Mi Padre* (Asylum, 1987, prod. Peter Asher and Ruben Fuentes) pays homage to the vibrant art of such singers as Lola Beltran.

Those interested in pre-Asher Ronstadt should seek out *A Ret-*

rospective (Capitol, 1977, prod. Various), which collects the best of her early output.

what to avoid: *Mad Love* (Asylum, 1980, prod. Peter Asher), an ill-advised foray into tough-posturing punk, on which she sounds like the Girls' Citizenship club president trying to smoke her first joint—and swallowing instead of inhaling.

the rest: with the Stone Poneys: *Stone Poneys* (Capitol, 1967/1995) *Evergreen Vol. 2* (Capitol, 1967) *Stone Poneys and Friends, Vol. III* (Capitol, 1995) solo: *Hand Sown Home Grown* (Capitol/EMI, 1969) *Silk Purse* (Capitol, 1970) *Linda Ronstadt* (Capitol, 1972) *Don't Cry Now* (Capitol, 1973) *Greatest Hits Vol. I* (Asylum, 1975) *Simple Dreams* (Asylum, 1977) *Living in the USA* (Asylum, 1978) *Greatest Hits Vol. 2* (Asylum, 1980) *Get Closer* (Asylum, 1982) *What's New* (Asylum, 1983) *Lush Life* (Asylum, 1984) *'Round Midnight: The Nelson Riddle Sessions* (Elektra, 1986) (with Aaron Neville); *Cry Like a Rinstorm, Howl Like the Wind* (Elektra, 1989) *Mas Canciones* (Elektra, 1991) *Frenesi* (Elektra, 1992); *Winter Light* (Elektra, 1993) *Dedicated to the One I Love* (Elektra, 1996)

worth searching for: Ronstadt has made myriad guest appearances on an assortment of albums. Two of the most interesting (and varied): Philip Glass' *1000 Airplanes* (Virgin Classics, 1989), on which her singing humanizes Glass' ethereal minimalism; and *Kermit Unplugged* (Jim Henson Records, 1994), on which she and the frog duet on "All I Have to Do Is Dream"

▶▶ Trisha Yearwood, Celine Dion, Rosanne Cash

◀◀ Patsy Cline, Elvis Presley, Lola Beltran

Elizabeth Lynch

Diana Ross

Born March 26, 1944 in Detroit, Mich.

Smokey Robinson was the king of Motown, and Ross was the label's queen. As the focal point of the Supremes, her delicate features, doe-eyed expressions and clear—if sometimes thin—vocals became symbols for the company's desired image of sophistication and glamour. Motown lore is filled with trash talk about Ross: ego, ambition, *espirit de Me.* And when you read her self-celebratory autobiography, "Secrets of a Sparrow," or look at the photo of magazine covers she's graced in the booklet for *The Ultimate Collection*, it does seem that modesty is not among Ross' virtues. But she must be given her due as a distinctive talent, with a drive that established her star not only in music but also in movies ("Lady Sings the Blues," "Mahogany"). She left Motown to record for RCA in 1981, but eight years later she was back "home," and whatever is said about her it's certain that no one would be talking unless she was a star.

what to buy: With only six of its 20 songs overlapping with Supremes anthologies, *The Ultimate Collection* (Motown, 1994, prod. Various) is a good way to sample Ross' solo career, from the epic schmaltz of "Ain't No Mountain High Enough" to heartfelt ode to Marvin Gaye, "Missing You." *Diana* (Motown, 1980, prod. Nile Rogers) was a smart move forward, bringing in Chic's Nile Rogers and Bernard Edwards to modernize Ross' sound and launch two of her biggest solo hits, "Upside Down" and "I'm Coming Out."

what to buy next: *Diana & Marvin* (Motown, 1973, prod. Hal Davis) is a pleasant summit from two of Motown's brightest lights that was reportedly driven by some real sparks (of anger) in the studio.

what to avoid: The box set *Forever Diana* (Motown, 1993, prod. Various) is a padded vanity project that was initially withdrawn from sale due its poor sound quality (which was corrected upon reissue).

the rest: *Lady Sings the Blues* (Motown, 1972) *Touch Me in the Morning* (Motown, 1973) *Ain't No Mountain High Enough* (Motown 1979/1989) *The Boss* (Motown, 1979) *Anthology* (Motown, 1986) *Diana's Duets* (Motown, date N/A) *Diana Ross* (Motown, 1989) *Live at Caesar's Palace* (Motown, 1990) *All the Great Hits* (Motown, 1991) *An Evening With Diana Ross* (Motown, 1991) *The Force Behind the Power* (Motown, 1991) *Diana Ross' Greatest Hits* (Motown, 1991) *Stolen Moments: The Lady Sings Jazz & Blues* (Motown, 1993) *Extended—The Remixes* (Motown, 1994) *Take Me Higher* (Motown, 1995)

worth searching for: Diana, Placido and Jose? That's Domingo and Carreras to you non-opera buffs, making for a classy kind of Supremes on *Christmas in Vienna* (Sony Classical, 1993)

▶▶ Donna Summer, Cher, Dionne Warwick, Brandy

◀◀ Billie Holiday, Ella Fitzgerald, Smokey Robinson

Gary Graff

What Album Changed Your Life?

"I think The Times They Are a-Changin' was the most life-altering for me. It was the first time I had ever heard folk music from a modern perspective, talking about issues of today. I decided not to get the new Beatles record immediately but to get the new Bob Dylan record instead."

Bonnie Raitt

Rossington Collins Band

See: Lynyrd Skynyrd

David Lee Roth

See: Van Halen

Roxette

Formed 1986 in Sweden

Marie Fredriksson, vocals; Per Gessle, guitar, vocals

As Sweden's hottest musical export since ABBA, Roxette has developed a worldwide fan base via its success in America. Gessle, a member of popular Scandinavian rocker group Gyllene Tider, first used the name Roxette on a 1984 record by his band, which aspired to crack the more lucrative U.S. market. The gambit failed, but former ABBA manager Thomas Johannson suggested Gessle team with vocalist Fredriksson for a record under the same name in 1986. Although that album was only released in Sweden and Canada, the next album in 1988 brought blockbuster sales in America—fueled both by hit singles such as "The Look" and "It Must Have Been Love," the latter on the soundtrack for the film "Pretty Woman." Combining catchy pop/rock tunes with a New Wave-influenced image, the pair enjoyed a string of hits: "Dressed for Success," "Dangerous" and "Joyride." The onset of modern rock during the early 90s spelled doom for the group's commercial ambitions in the U.S., though it continues to crank out the hits overseas.

what to buy: Grounding catchy pop melodies in the spirit of classic rock and New Wave, Roxette's giddy hits connected with the tenor of the late 80s on *Look Sharp*, (EMI, 1988, prod. Clarence Ofwerman) 𝅘𝅥𝅘𝅥𝅘𝅥𝅘𝅥 which veers effortlessly from rockers such as "The Look" to soaring ballads such as "Listen to Your Heart" and perky, percolating pop such as "Dressed for Success."

what to buy next: As a further refinement of the formula that conquered the world, *Joyride* (EMI, 1991, prod. Clarence Ofwerman and Anders Herlin) 𝅘𝅥𝅘𝅥𝅘𝅥 is the perfect Roxette follow-up. Songs such as "Knock on Every Door" and "Watercolors in the Rain" pick up exactly where the last album left off.

what to avoid: A confusing collage of live performances and new studio material, *Tourism: Songs from Studios, Stages, Hotel Rooms and Other Strange Places* (EMI, 1992, prod. Clarence Ofwerman) WOOF!, proves a directionless mishmash. And hearing thousands of fans sing along to hits such as "It Must Have Been Love" highlights just how lunkheaded Gessle's lyrics can be.

worth searching for: *Greatest Hits: Don't Bore Us, Get to the Chorus*, (EMI, 1995) 𝅘𝅥𝅘𝅥𝅘𝅥 an import collection that features the new-look Roxette—Gessle bleached blond and Fredriksson sporting a Susan Powter-style buzz cut.

▶▶ Ace of Base

◀◀ Eurythmics, the Beatles

Eric Deggans

Roxy Music

Formed 1971 in London, England. Disbanded 1983.

Bryan Ferry, vocals and keyboards; Andy Mackay, saxophone and oboe; Brian Eno (b. Brian Peter George St. John le Baptiste de la Salle Eno), synthesizers and treatments (1971-73); Dexter Lloyd, drums (1971); Roger Bunn, guitar (1971); Graham Simpson, bass (1971-72); Paul Thompson, drums (1971-80); David O'List, guitar (1972); Phil Manzanara (b. Philip Targett-Adams), guitar (1972-83); Rik Kenton, bass (1972); John Porter, bass (1972); Sal Maida, bass (1972-73); John Gustafson, bass (1972-75); Eddie Jobson, violin, synthesizer (1973-78); John Wetton, bass (1975-76); Rick Wills, bass (1976-78); Gary Tibbs, bass (1978); David Skinner, keyboards (1978-83); Paul Carrack, keyboards (1978-80); Alan Spenner, bass (1978-83); Andy Newmark, drums (1980-83)

Roxy Music's sense of style—by turns effete, subversive, sexy and confounding—was exceeded only by its brilliance as one of the 70s finest art-rock bands. It featured inventive instrumentalists in Mackay and Manzanara, and two bonafide musical visionaries in Ferry and Eno, whose brief, tumultuous and enormously influential collaboration was reminiscent of the sparks generated by Lou Reed and John Cale in the Velvet Underground. Roxy never achieved commercial success in America on par with its artistic achievement, in part because of its genre- and gender-bending cool and wicked humor (Ferry at times sang like a tremulous lounge crooner, and his lyrical obsession with unrequited love/lust extended in an least one instance to a blow-up doll on "In Every Dream Home a Heartache"). The group burnished some of those edges after a brief hiatus in the mid-70s, and it scored a few unremarkable hits before calling it quits in 1983.

what to buy: *Siren* (EG/Reprise, 1975, prod. Chris Thomas) is the ultimate synthesis of the group's arty experimentation and adroit, wide-ranging pop instincts. Ferry cruises the land of one-night stands with equal parts fascination and revulsion, and the epiphanies are numerous: "Both Ends Burning," "Just Another High," "Love is the Drug," "Sentimental Fool."

what to buy next: *Roxy Music* (EG/Reprise, 1972, prod. Peter Sinfield) introduced a twisted pop fabulousness to the U.K. music scene that would resonate for decades. *For Your Pleasure* (EG/Reprise, 1973, prod. Chris Thomas and John Anthony), the second and final Ferry-Eno collaboration, is weirder still, and nearly as good. *Stranded* (EG/Reprise, 1973, prod. Chris Thomas) is a showcase for Ferry's increasingly theatrical vocals. *Avalon* (Warner Bros., 1982, Rhett Davies and Roxy Music) sounds like a new age album in comparison to the early stuff, but Ferry's nuanced vocal performance and the shimmering, sculpted beauty of the arrangements are undeniable.

what to avoid: *The High Road* (Warner Bros. EP, 1983, prod. Rhett Davies and Roxy Music) finds the band sounding stiff and glossy near the end of its life, redeemed only by a strangely moving cover of John Lennon's "Jealous Guy."

the rest: *Country Life* (EG/Reprise, 1974) *Viva!* (EG/Reprise, 1976) *Greatest Hits* (EG/Reprise, 1977) *Manifesto* (EG/Reprise, 1979) *Flesh + Blood* (EG/Reprise, 1980) *The Atlantic Years* (Atco, 1983) *Street Life: 20 Greatest Hits* (Reprise, 1989) *Heart Still Beating* (EG/Reprise, 1990)

worth searching for: *The Thrill of It All* (Virgin U.K., 1995, prod. Various) is a four-CD set from Britain that covers plenty of ground, though it doesn't replace the most essential individual albums.

New York Dolls, Adam and the Ants, Duran Duran, Cars, ABC, Combustible Edison

Velvet Underground, Brecht-Weill, Humphrey Bogart, King Crimson, Billie Holiday

see also: *Bryan Ferry*

Greg Kot

Royal Crescent Mob

Formed 1985 in Columbus, Ohio. Disbanded 1994.

David Ellison, lead vocals, harmonica; B, guitar, vocals; Harold Chichester, bass, vocals; Billy Schwers, drums (1985); Carlton Smith, drums (1986-94)

This band garnered critical acclaim for combining dirty rock guitar and a funky backbeat. Ellison was fond of pointing out that he mowed the lawn of the Ohio Players' Leroy (Sugar) Bonner while growing up and absorbed both funk and punk. The band was put together from the pieces of two groups competing in a local battle of the bands, so they could better use the contest prize: studio time. After two small releases, the band was signed by Sire records. But its producers on Sire, Richard Gottehrer and Eric Calvi, were not well suited to funk and whitewashed the proceedings. Despite critical appreciation, record sales were disappointing, and Sire did not keep the group. Royal Crescent Mob, always hot live, continued gigging and put out a 1992 concert recording, *Destruction 13*, on its own Mobco imprint. The band then retreated to its hometown, playing within driving range on weekends, and managed to put out a final album before Chichester left to spend more time with his family, which ultimately ended the band's run. Chicester later showed up in Howlin' Maggie, playing in a related but inferior style.

what to buy: *Omerta* (Moving Target, 1987, prod. Jonathon Myner, Royal Crescent Mob and Montie Temple) is by far the band's best work, with "Get on the Bus" and covers of "Fire" and "The Big Payback." Funky, hard-driving, showing no mercy, it's the must-own album. Fortunately, it was reissued on CD just before the band's demise.

what to avoid: *Midnight Rose's* (Sire, 1991, prod. Eric Calvi) has a few funky tracks, but largely sounds like Calvi was aiming for too heavy and dense of a sound.

the rest: *Spin the World* (Sire, 1989)

worth searching for: Funky but hard to find collections such as *Good Lucky Killer*, (Enemy, 1993, prod. Royal Crescent Mob and Montie Temple) *Something New, Old and Borrowed* (Moving Target, 1988) and the live *13 Destruction* (Mobco, 1992, prod. Royal Crescent Mob and Montie Temple)

solo outings:

Howling Maggie (Harold Chichester) Honeysuckle Strange (Columbia, 1996)

▶▶ Infectious Grooves, Mind Funk

◀◀ Ohio Players, James Brown, the Stooges, the Dead Kennedys

Steve Holtje

The Rubinoos

Formed in 1973 in San Francisco, Calif.

Jon Rubin, vocals, guitar; Donn Spindt, drums; Royse Ader, bass; Tommy Dunbar, guitars, keyboards, vocals

There were the Archies, the 1910 Fruitgum Co. and the DeFranco Family—but bubblegum rarely got sweeter, stickier and unabashedly more goo-goo-eyed than the three-minute outbursts of puppy love songs and schoolboy rock practiced by the Rubinoos. Signed to the maverick Beserkley label—home of Greg Kihn and Jonathan Richman—the Rubinoos debuted with the cheesy but cheerful *Rubinoos* (Berserkley, 1977, prod. Matthew King Kaufman, Glen Kolotkin and Gary Phillips) . Highlights included a wicked Who parody called "Rock and Roll Is Dead" and a heartfelt cover of Tommy James' "I Think We're Alone Now" that rivaled the original and actually grazed the Top 40. But the short-lived quartet's footnote contribution to the power-pop pantheon was the Raspberries-influenced *Back to the Drawing Board* (Beserkley, 1979, prod. Matthew King Kaufman and Gary Phillips) , a luscious collection of harmony-laden, heel-clicking anthems like "Operator," "Promise Me," "Fallin' in Love" and the irresistible "I Wanna Be Your Boyfriend." The sugar-coated, Stridex-scented sentiments may make your teeth ache, but your heart will never feel so young.

the rest: *Party of Two* (Warner Bros., 1983) *Basement Tapes* (One Way, 1993) *Garage Sale* (Big Deal, 1994)

David Okamoto

Jimmy & David Ruffin

See: The Temptations

Rufus /Chaka Khan

Born Yvette Marie Stevens, March 22, 1953 in Great Lakes, Ill.

Rufus (formed 1970 in Chicago, Ill. Disbanded 1983.): Chaka Khan, vocals (1970-83); Kevin Murphy, keyboards; Ron Stockard, guitar (1970-1973); Tony Maiden, guitar (1973-83); Al Siner, bass (1970-73); Bobby Watson, bass (1973-83); Dennis Belfield, keyboards (1970-73), Nate Morgan, keyboards (1973-77); David "Hawk" Wolinski, keyboards (1977-83); Andre Fisher, drums (1970-78), John "J.R." Robinson, drums (1978-83)

Dedicated to a career as a singer by her teens, a young Chaka Khan (a stage name reportedly developed while working with the Black Panther Party during the 60s) kicked around Chicago-area clubs, eventually hooking up with a Top 40 band called Ask Rufus. Before long, Khan's spellbinding vocals convinced the group to head west and audition for ABC Records in Los Angeles. By 1973, the group had released its first record, though it wasn't until the band's second album—featuring the smash "Tell Me Something Good," written by Stevie Wonder specifically for Khan—that Rufus joined the R&B elite. Featuring a whipcrack, funky backing band of whiz players and Khan's incendiary voice, Rufus ruled the R&B charts for years, with the singer eventually getting top billing, then striking out on her own during the late 70s. Khan kept recording with the band until 1983, eventually leaving the group for good (it broke up shortly afterwards) to concentrate on her own solo releases—often mesmerizing collections of soulful dance-pop and contemporary jazz selections, pieced together by the industry's most talented producers. But R&B's turn toward youthful, hip hop-influenced divas pulled the commercial rug out from under the singer, relegating Khan's efforts to occasional appearances on other artists' albums and film soundtracks.

what to buy: In a catalog that spans some 15 albums, the high points are many. As a band, Rufus connected with R&B history on *Rags to Rufus* (ABC, 1974/ MCA, 1990, prod. Bob Monaco and Rufus) the album with "Tell Me Something Good" and the Ray Parker Jr-penned classic workout "You Got the Love." The follow up, *Rufus Featuring Chaka Khan,* (ABC, 1975/MCA, 1990, prod. Rufus) was almost as good, boasting ear candy such as the simmering "Sweet Thing" and boisterous "Dance With Me." On her own, Khan scored with *Chaka Khan,* (Warner Bros., 1982, prod. Arif Mardin) a collection of high-quality, well-produced tunes topped with astounding vocals—including the ballad "Got to Be There" and jazzy excursion "Be Bop Medley" *I Feel For You* (Warner Bros.,

1984, prod. Arif Mardin) adds a heavy synthesizer and DJ touch, from the hit title track to a stratospheric remake of Gary Wright's "Love Is Alive."

what to avoid: As good as Rufus and Khan were at crafting hit singles, consistent albums were never their strong suit. Together, their worst effort still in print is probably *Stompin' at the Savoy* (Warner Bros., 1983, prod. Russ Titleman) WOOF! an uninspiring collection of live performances and studio cuts redeemed only by the inventive, last-gasp hit "Ain't Nobody."

the rest: Rufus: *Rufus* (ABC, 1973) *Rufusized* (ABC, 1974/MCA, 1990) *Ask Rufus* (ABC, 1977) *Street Player* (ABC, 1978) *Numbers* (ABC, 1979) *Masterjam* (MCA, 1979) Chaka Khan: *Chaka* (Warner Bros., 1979) *Naughty* (Warner Bros., 1980) *What 'Cha Gonna Do For Me?* (Warner Bros., 1981) *Destiny* (Warner Bros., 1986) *C.K.* (Warner Bros., 1988) *Life Is a Dance (The Remix Project)* (Warner Bros., 1989) *The Woman I Am* (Warner Bros., 1992)

worth searching for: Khan's dynamic backing vocal on Steve Winwood's 1996 smash, "Higher Love," available on several of his albums.

▶▶ Mary J. Blige, Faith Evans, Monica

◀◀ Betty Carter, Aretha Franklin, Gladys Knight

Eric Deggans

Run-D.M.C.

Formed 1981 in Hollis, Queens, N.Y.

Run (born Joseph Simmons), vocals; D.M.C. (born Darryl McDaniels), vocals; Jam Master Jay (born Jason Mizell), turntables, programming

No group was more responsible for taking hip-hop into the pop culture mainstream than Run-D.M.C. The trio did it with a canny mixture of streetwise image (a casual, jock-inspired look and attitude known as "b-boy"), clever, conversational wordplay and, most of all, stripped-down beats that drew as much on hard rock as funk. On its 1984 self-titled debut album, Run-D.M.C. established its signature sound; nothing in rap sounded quiet so hard and minimalist as "Sucker M.C.'s" and "It's Like That," reprised from the trio's groundbreaking 1983 single. The debut also introduced the wailing, P-Funk-like guitar of Eddie Martinez, who returned on the title track of the 1985 album, *King of Rock*—a boast the group would make good on the next year. That's when Aerosmith's Steven Tyler and Joe Perry collaborated with the rappers on a remake of Aerosmith's cock-rock standard "Walk This Way," a team-up that launched Aerosmith's comeback and, as the cornerstone of the multimillion-selling *Raising Hell* album, established Run-D.M.C. as an arena act. Unfortunately, the group's attempt to expand its success with a 1988 movie and album of the same name, *Tougher Than Leather,* bombed, and the increasing political militancy and verbal explicitness of a new breed of hip-hop groups eventually made Run-D.M.C. sound quaint and dated.

what to buy: *Raising Hell* (Profile, 1986, prod. Russell Simmons and Rick Rubin) has its thin moments, but the initial burst of "Peter Piper," "It's Tricky," "My Adidas" and "Walk This Way" is as powerful an opening sequence as you'll find on any rap or rock record of the 80s. While *Raising Hell* is as much a cultural milestone as a musical one, the aural pleasures are packed wall to wall on the thumping *Together Forever: Greatest Hits 1983-1991.* (Profile, 1991, prod. Various)

what to buy next: The debut, *Run-D.M.C.* (Profile, 1984, prod. Russell Simmons and Larry Smith) is another milestone, the first true hip-hop album—though it may sound a tad too stripped-down and insular to rap non-believers. With its minimal but meaty rhythms and strident vocal cadences, even the tracks without electric guitar still rock.

what to avoid: *Back From Hell* (Profile, 1990, Run-D.M.C. and Jam Master Jay) is a transparent attempt to keep up with foul-mouthed gangsta rappers. For the first time, the group is chasing trends rather than starting them.

the rest: *King of Rock* (Profile, 1985); *Tougher Than Leather* (Profile, 1988); *Down With the King* (Profile, 1993)

worth searching for: The debut 12-inch single, "It's Like That/Sucker M.C.'s" (Profile, 1983, prod. Russell Simmons and Larry Smith) is a hip-hop classic, with an extended mix of "It's Like That" and instrumental versions of both tracks perfect for your own karaoke party.

▶▶ Public Enemy, N.W.A., the Beastie Boys, Rage Against the Machine

◀◀ Grandmaster Flash, Parliament-Funkadelic, James Brown, Afrika Bambaataa, Kool DJ Herc, Queen, Aerosmith

Greg Kot

The Runaways

Formed 1975 in Los Angeles, Calif. Disbanded 1979.

Joan Jett, guitar, vocals; Sandy West, drums; Micki Steele, bass, vo-

cals (1975); Cherie Currie, vocals (1975-77); Lita Ford, guitar (1975-79); Jackie Fox, bass (1975-77); Vickie Blue, bass (1977-79)

Launched as manager Kim Fowley's jailbait fantasy of lingerie and leather-clad vixens, the Runaways never took hold anywhere except in Japan. The band's lasting contribution is not its brand of hyped-up shriek rock but rather its role as a forebear to girl groups such as the Go-Go's and the Bangles—as well as a launching pad for Jett's solo career (and, to a lesser extent, Ford's).

what to buy: *Best of the Runaways* (Mercury, 1982/1987, prod. Kim Fowley) ♪♪♪ culls the best from the group's two albums. The signature blast of "Cherry Bomb" from their debut typifies the crass, barely legal sex appeal Fowley was after.

what to buy next: *Queens of Noise,* (Mercury, 1977/Collectors Pipeline, 1994, prod. Kim Fowley) ♪♪♪ the Runaways' second album, is a touch better than the debut thanks to Jett exerting a little more control.

what to avoid: *The Runaways,* (Mercury, 1976/Collectors Pipeline, 1994, prod. Kim Fowley) ♪ a dead end of a debut that's insulting in its blatant titillation.

the rest: *Little Girls Lost* (Rhino Records, 1981) ♪♪ *Neon Angels* (Polygram Special Products) ♪♪

worth searching for: The spirited import *Live in Japan* (Mercury, 1977, prod. Kent J. Smythe and the Runaways) ♪♪♪ shows that every band can find an audience.

▶▶ The Go-Gos, the Bangles, L7

◀◀ T. Rex, Slade, Suzi Quatro

see also: *Joan Jett, Lita Ford*

Allan Orski

Todd Rundgren /Utopia

Born June 22, 1948 in Upper Darby, Pa.

(Utopia): Todd Rundgren, guitars, vocals; John Siegler, bass, cello (1974-76); Kasim Sulton, bass, vocals (1977-1985); Mark "Moogy" Klingman, keyboards (1974-76); Ralph Shuckett, keyboards (1974-76); M. Frog Labat, synthesizers (1974); Roger Powell, keyboards, vocals (1975-85); Kevin Ellman, drums (1974); John Wilcox, drums, vocals (1975-85)

As pretentious as it sounds, Renaissance Man may be the most accurate description befitting Rundgren. A musician, songwriter, producer and techno-dabbler, Rundgren is the da Vinci of rock 'n' roll, having left no corner of the music industry untouched. From his early work with the Nazz (1968-1970), Rundgren showed a tremendous melodic gift and an ability to craft a sophisticated sound fused from various genres. While his music ranges from Beatles-influenced pop to Hendrix-inspired rock and Philadelphia soul, he retains a gift for honest sentiment, inspiring lyrics and laconic wit throughout his ample body of work. Proficient on no end of instruments, Rundgren has frequently displayed his ample chops by performing all vocals and instruments on some of his albums (well before digital sampling was possible). His adventurous use of synthesizers during the early 70s helped to usher that instrument into widespread use in popular music, and while at times he could use it to the point of distraction, he also showed what was possible. If his musical dexterity has at times bordered on grandstanding, it has also clearly inspired many artists, most notably Prince, to follow suit. As a producer, Rundgren can be most likened to Phil Spector: brilliant, innovative and at times wildly erratic. Despite his self-indulgent tendencies with such acts as the Patti Smith Group, Hall & Oates, Grand Funk Railroad and XTC, he has more often than not helped musicians score chart hits (most notably Meatloaf's mega-hit *Bat Out of Hell*). With the advent of digital recording techniques in the late 70s, Rundgren began breaking new ground in music technology, producing some of the most advanced rock videos and exploring new possibilities in digital technology with interactive CD-ROMs (such as his 1993 release, *No World Order*) Beginning in 1975, Rundgren began releasing a number of albums in the progressive-rock mode with his band Utopia; despite his best efforts to blend in, Rundgren's character permeates the band's catalog, making it at times indistinguishable from his solo work.

what to buy: Roundly considered one of rock's more important albums, the double-CD extravaganza *Something/Anything?* (Bearsville/Rhino, 1972, prod. Todd Rundgren) ♪♪♪♪♪ is a landmark work, filled with lovely pop confection, pristine production and a lighthearted sense of humor. Rundgren performs and sings the first three-quarters of the album, a nervy feat that's still breathtaking to behold. Those looking for the hits will find them here ("I Saw the Light," "It Wouldn't Have Made Any Difference," "Hello, It's Me") along with a host of stellar though lesser-known treasures ("Torch Song" and "Breathless"). Rundgren's follow-up effort, *A Wizard, A True Star,* (Bearsville/Rhino, 1973, prod. Todd Rundgren) ♪♪♪♪♪ is a fascinating sonic collage that skews his pop-star image 180 degrees. Opening with a dizzying 30-minute medley of short songs and musical skits, the album catches its breath midway, relaxing into the Philly soul number "Sometimes I Don't Know What to Feel," a clever medley of 60s tunes and the hit anthem "Just One Victory." Rundgren never hit the mark so solidly again until *Nearly Human* (Warner Bros., 1989, prod. Todd Rundgren) Sliding into the soul groove he knows so well, Rundgren turns in an emotional and inspiring effort. Although none of the songs here are as well known as his earlier hits, a few of them—"The Want of a Nail," "The Waiting Game" and "Parallel Lines"—are among his best work.

what to buy next: The double CD *Anthology (1968-1985)* (Rhino, 1989, prod. Various) is a tidy retrospective of Rundgren's career dating back to his days with the Nazz. Rhino does a first-class job here, compiling and remastering all the essential Rundgren tunes from a nearly 20-year period, among them "A Dream Goes on Forever," "Love of the Common Man," "Can We Still Be Friends?" and "Bang the Drum All Day."

what to avoid: The interactive CD (CD-I) *No World Order* (Forward/Rhino, 1993, prod. Todd Rundgren) is an intriguing idea that never quite takes off. Rundgren offers some four hours of musical snippets for listeners to manufacture into new songs via their CD-I. For those without the required hardware, the disk includes 10 lackluster dance tracks on which Rundgren ventures unsuccessfully into rap. *No World Order Lite* (Forward/Rhino, 1994) WOOF! excludes the interactive element and, with it, what little enjoyment it offered.

the rest: *Runt* (Bearsville/Rhino, 1970) *The Ballad of Todd Rundgren* (Bearsville/Rhino, 1971) *Todd* (Bearsville/Rhino, 1974) *Initiation* (Bearsville/Rhino, 1975) *Faithful* (Bearsville/Rhino, 1976) *Hermit of Mink Hollow* (Bearsville/Rhino, 1978) *Back to the Bars* (Bearsville/Rhino, 1978) *Healing* (Bearsville/Rhino, 1981) *The Ever Popular Tortured Artist Effect* (Bearsville/Rhino, 1983) *A Cappella* (Warner Bros./Rhino, 1985) *2nd Wind* (Bearsville/Rhino, 1991) *The Best of Todd Rundgren* (Rhino, 1994) *Individualist* (Digital Entertainment Enhanced CD, 1995)

Utopia: *Todd Rundgren's Utopia* (Bearsville/Rhino, 1974) *Another Live* (Bearsville/Rhino, 1975) *RA* (Bearsville/Rhino, 1977) *Oops! Wrong Planet* (Bearsville/Rhino, 1977) *Deface the Music* (Bearsville/Rhino, 1980) *Adventures in Utopia* (Bearsville/Rhino, 1980) *Utopia* (Network/Rhino, 1982) *Swing to the Right* (Bearsville/Rhino, 1982) *Anthology 1974-1985* (Rhino, 1989) *Oblivion, P.O.V. & Some Trivia* (Rhino, 1986)

worth searching for: If there is a Holy Grail for Rundgren fans, it is the alternate release of his solo debut, *Runt* (Ampex, 1970, prod. Todd Rundgren) Although the covers and track listing are identical to the more commonly found release, the rare *Runt* features numerous differences, including a complete version of "Baby Let's Swing," an unlisted and haunting track called "Say No More," and an early recording of "Hope I'm Around," a later version of which appeared on *The Ballad of Todd Rundgren*

Electric Light Orchestra, Meat Loaf, Hall & Oates, The Tubes, Queen, XTC, Prince, Madonna

The Beach Boys, The Beatles, Jimi Hendrix, Stevie Wonder, The Move, Motown, Doo-Wop

Christopher Scapelliti

Rush

Formed 1969, Toronto, Canada

Geddy Lee (b. Gary Lee Weinrib), bass, vocals, keyboards; Alex Lifeson (b. Alex Zivojinovich), guitar; Neil Peart, drums (1974-present); John Rutsey, drums (1969-74)

Starting out as a flashy, power chord slinging hard rock trio, Rush gradually moved into egghead territory—first with the addition of Peart's Ayn Rand-inspired lyrics, then with the introduction of keyboards, which resulted in a sonic straddle of the metal and progressive rock lines. Remaining intact for 22 years, Rush has become something of a rite of passage band, celebrated by successive generations for its instrumental prowess and state-of-the-art stage performances. Modern rockers such as Primus regularly sing Rush's praises, giving the trio a hip credential most of its 70s counterparts lack.

what to buy: *Chronicles* (Anthem/Mercury, 1990, prod. Various) is a solid two-CD anthology that allows for sampling without having to wade through individual albums whose concepts are often ponderous and oblique. *All the World's a Stage* (Mercury, 1976, prod. Rush and Terry Brown) is the first and best of Rush's three live albums, an energetic outing that (fortunately) focuses more on punch than intellect. *Moving Pictures* (Mercury, 1981, prod. Rush and Terry Brown) is the most consistent of the studio sets, featuring some of Rush's most memorable songs ("Tom Sawyer," "Limelight") and most ambitious instrumental excursions ("YYZ," "Red Barchetta").

what to buy next: *Permanent Waves* (Mercury, 1980, prod.

Rush and Terry Brown) is on a par with *Moving Pictures* and includes the seminal Rush radio hits "Spirit of Radio" and "Freewill." *2112* (Mercury, 1976, prod. Rush and Terry Brown) houses the sidelong title suite. *Presto* (Anthem/Atlantic, 1989), on wish Rush switched labels, showcases a more spacious, organic approach.

what to avoid: *Grace Under Pressure* (Mercury, 1984, prod. Rush and Peter Henderson) is an unusually stiff and graceless entry in the Rush catalog.

the rest: *Rush* (Mercury, 1974) *Fly By Night* (Mercury, 1975) *Caress of Steel* (Mercury, 1975) *A Farewell to Kings* (Mercury, 1977) *Hemispheres* (Mercury, 1978) *Exit...Stage Left* (Mercury, 1981) *Signals* (Mercury, 1982) *Power Windows* (Mercury, 1985) *Hold Your Fire* (Mercury, 1987) *A Show of Hands* (Atlantic/Anthem, 1989) *Roll the Bones* (Atlantic/Anthem, 1991) *Counterparts* (Atlantic/Anthem, 1993) *Test for Echo (ECD)* (Atlantic, 1996) not available for rating

worth searching for: *Rush Profiled* (Atlantic/Anthem 1990) a promotional interview CD that finds the three musicians in an expansive and reflective mood as they switch labels after 15 years with Mercury.

solo outings:

Alex Lifeson *Victor* (Atlantic/Anthem, 1996)

Neil Peart *Burning For Buddy: A Tribute to the Music of Buddy Rich* (Atlantic/Anthem, 1994)

Triumph, Primus, Zebra.

Led Zeppelin, Yes, King Crimson, The Move, The Guess Who, Buddy Rich

Gary Graff

Leon Russell

Born April 2, 1941, in Lawton, Okla.

In addition to his idiosyncratic solo career of swampy blues-gospel, Russell has an amazing resume as a session player on Phil Spector's masterpieces along with guest spots for Joe Cocker, Bob Dylan and Jerry Lee Lewis, a touring gig with the Rolling Stones and his own label, the now-defunct Shelter Records. Subsequently, his own work has been covered by various artists, and "A Song For You" has become a piano bar standard. With his menacing stare and cheese-grater voice, Russell's originals may be a bit rough for the timid, but his material has a strong individuality that warrants a listen.

what to buy: His major label debut album, *Leon Russell,* (Shelter-A&M, 1970/The Right Stuff, 1995, prod. Denny Cordell and Leon Russell) contains many of his best songs, including "Delta Lady," "A Song for You" and "Shoot Out at the Plantation." The reissue adds a bizarre take of Dylan's "Masters of War" sung to the tune of "The Star-Spangled Banner." *Leon Russell and the Shelter People* (Shelter, 1971/The Right Stuff, 1995, prod. Denny Cordell and Leon Russell) is a rollicking follow-up of backyard blues and well-chosen covers.

what to buy next: On *Hank Wilson's Back!,* (Shelter, 1973/The Right Stuff, 1995, prod. Various) Russell predates The The's Matt Johnson by 20-odd years with a joyously executed tribute to the country master. *Carny* (Shelter, 1972/The Right Stuff, 1995, prod. Denny Cordell and Leon Russell) is his biggest seller thanks to the ubiquitous single "Tightrope."

what to avoid: *Anything Can Happen* (Virgin, 1992, prod. Bruce Hornsby) is an unheralded comeback. Despite Hornsby's presence, much of the material feels like a car stalling uphill.

the rest: *Asylum Choir* (Shelter, 1971/The Right Stuff, 1995) *Leon Live* (Shelter, 1973/The Right Stuff, 1996) *Stop All That Jazz* (Shelter, 1994/The Right Stuff, 1995)

worth searching for: His debut, *Look Inside the Asylum Choir,* (Smash, 1968) which was good enough to attract admirers such as Delaney and Bonnie and Joe Cocker to Russell's camp.

Richie Havens, Bruce Hornsby

Bob Dylan, Clarence "Gatemouth" Brown, J.J Cale

Allan Orski

Mike Rutherford

See: Genesis

Paul Rutherford

See: Frankie Goes to Hollywood

The Rutles

Formed 1978 in England

Neil Innes, guitar, keyboards, vocals; Ollie Halsall, guitar, keyboards, vocals; Ricky Fataar, guitar, bass, sitar, tabla, vocals; Andy Brown, bass; John Halsey, drums, vocals

As Beatles parodies go, none have been as good-naturedly hilarious, dead-on accurate or tuneful as the Rutles. The group originated from an idea by Monty Python troupe member Eric Idle, who recruited British musician/songwriter (and ex-Bonzo Dog Band member) Innes to perform his Beatles sound-alike song "I Must Be in Love" for a Python TV skit. The sketch went down well enough that Idle decided to pursue a full-length TV "documentary" (titled "All You Need Is Cash") chronicling the rise and fall of the Rutles, a.k.a. the Prefab Four. Innes played "Ron Nasty" (John Lennon), Fataar portrayed "Stig O'Hara" (George Harrison) and Halsey appeared as "Barry Wom" (Ringo Starr). Although he plays no instruments on the soundtrack, Idle portrayed the Paul McCartney character "Dirk McQuickley" in the film. Basically a soundtrack from Idle's movie, *The Rutles* (WEA/Atlantic/Rhino, 1978, prod. Neil Innes) presents Innes' 20 terrific send-ups of key songs from the Beatles' career, including "Hold My Hand" ("All My Loving"), "Doubleback Alley" ("Penny Lane") and "Piggy in the Middle" ("I Am the Walrus"). At least half the fun is listening for the original sources within the Rutles' parodies. Vinyl owners note: The CD version includes six worthwhile bonus tracks from the movie. Collectors may also want to look for the out-of-print CD *Rutles Highway Revisited* (Shimmy Disc, 1990, prod. Various), a "tribute" album containing the 20 Rutles tracks performed by Syd Straw, Marc Ribot, and Shonen Knife, among others. In 1996, Innes re-grouped the Rutles, sans Idle, for a new album of "vintage, unreleased" music from the band's heyday.

Christopher Scapelliti

Mitch Ryder

Born William Levise, Jr., Feb. 26, 1945 in Hamtramck, Mich.

Ryder's music of the mid-60s was the *other* Motown sound—the sound of the auto plants, the shot-and-a-beer bars, the raucous, industrial, violent roots of his hometown. He never conveyed it better than he did with the Detroit Wheels, a band driven by one of the great drummers in rock 'n' roll history (Johnny "Bee" Badanjek) and given spice by the lethal guitar licks of Jimmy McCarty. Ryder and the Wheels cranked out two years of hits—"Jenny Take a Ride!," "Little Latin Lupe Lu," "Shake a Tail Feather," the "Devil With a Blue Dress On/Good Golly Miss Molly" medley (an encore favorite of Bruce Springsteen and the E Street Band)—before producer Bob Crewe convinced him to go solo in 1967. The move met with limited success, but Ryder caught the fire once again when he, Badanjek and McCarty reunited for one album as Detroit. Since then, Ryder has made his living touring Europe, particularly Germany, and releasing records in Europe with only occasional attempts to crack the U.S. market again. His 1994 album *Rite of Passage* featured the song "Mercy," which voiced support for assisted suicide advocate Dr. Jack Kevorkian.

what to buy: *Rev Up: The Best of Mitch Ryder and the Detroit Wheels* (Rhino, 1989, prod. Various) is a generous (21 tracks) must-have that surveys not only the Wheels' best but also highlights from Ryder's solo career and from Detroit. The original *Breakout!!!* (New Voice, 1966/Sundazed, 1993, prod. Bob Crew) lives up to its multiple exclamation points.

what to buy next: *Sock It to Me!* (New Voice, 1967/Sundazed, 1993, prod. Bob Crewe) is another four-on-the-floor blowout; the re-issue betters it with some singles that weren't on the original album. *Detroit with Mitch Ryder* (Paramount, 1971/MCA, 1987) boasts considerable hard rock muscle heard in the pumped-up treatment of the Velvet Underground's "Rock and Roll."

what to avoid: *The Rockin' Hits*, (Special Music, 1993, prod. Bob Crewe) a collection that pales in comparison to *Rev Up*

the rest: *Take a Ride* (New Voice, 1966/Sundazed, 1993, prod. Bob Crewe) *All Hits!* (Sundazed, 1994) *Devil With the Blue Dress On* (Rhino, 1995)

worth searching for: At this point, Ryder has released more albums in Europe than he has in the U.S. The most interesting is one that actually did come out here. *Never Kick a Sleeping Dog* (Riva, 1983/Line, 1987, prod. John Mellencamp) was longtime fan Mellencamp's noble effort to give Ryder another shot in the U.S., and the producer's spare, energetic aesthetic worked well on a cover of Prince's "When You Were Mine" as well as originals such as "The Thrill of It All," "Code Dancing" and "B.I.G.T.I.M.E."

▶▶ John Mellencamp, Bruce Springsteen, the Rockets, the Iron City Houserockers

◀◀ Big Joe Turner, Little Richard, Gary U.S. Bonds, Jackie Wilson

Gary Graff

Sacred System

See: Bill Laswell

Sade

Born Helen Folsade Adu, Jan. 16, 1959 in Lagos, Nigeria

Reared as the daughter of an African father and English mother,

Sade made a minor name for herself as a clothes designer during the 1980s before turning heads in London as lead singer for the jazz-funk band Pride. Joined by keyboardist Andrew Hale, bassist Paul Denman and guitarist/saxophonist Stuart Matthewman, Sade organized her own self-named band in 1984, eventually forging a mix of cool-school jazz and smoldering funk that brought the group to worldwide attention. Though critics have often focused on Sade herself—a coffee-colored beauty with a fashion model's face and jazzy, delicate vocal chops—the publicity-shy singer has always insisted that Sade be viewed as a band. And while some have found the group's laid-back instrumental mix a bit boring, its signature sound has garnered a wide and loyal fan base.

what to buy: It's not until her second album, *Promise*, (Portrait, 1986, prod. Robin Millar and Sade) 🦴🦴🦴🦴 that Sade begins to live up to the promise of her own jazz/pop/soul sound. Veering from the percolating hit "The Sweetest Taboo" to the jazzy minor-chord lament "Mr. Wrong" and the semi-funky, lounge-tinged workout "Never as Good as the First Time," the singer's detached cool mixes with her crack backing band to bring some truly inspired moments. Coming back after a four-year layoff, Sade added 90s-style reggae touches for her best effort yet, *Love Deluxe*, (Epic, 1992. prod. Sade) 🦴🦴🦴🦴½ a heady mix of tunes fueled by the burning, sensual grooves "No Ordinary Love" and "Cherish the Day."

what to buy next: *The Best of Sade*, (Epic, 1994, prod. Various) 🦴🦴🦴🦴 a smart collection of the key tracks from her four albums.

what to avoid: Though Sade's debut, *Diamond Life* (Portrait, 1985, prod. Robin Millar) 🦴🦴½ made a splash by introducing the world to her jazz-influenced ice-queen persona, the songs here are a little too restrained—excepting the hit single "Smooth Operator."

the rest: *Stronger Than Pride* (Epic, 1988) 🦴🦴🦴½

worth searching for: The promotional only *Interview Deluxe* (Epic, 1992) brings a bit of insight from the interview-shy Sade.

⏩ Des'ree, Me'Shell Ndeg'eocello

⏪ Nina Simone, Billie Holiday, Marvin Gaye

Eric Deggans

Greg Sage

See: Wipers

Douglas Sahm

See: Sir Douglas Quintet

St. Etienne

Formed 1990 in Croydon, England

Bob Stanley, keyboards, programming; Pete Wiggs, keyboards, programming; Sarah Cracknell (1991-present), vocals

Disillusioned with the state of pop records, Stanley—who at the time was writing for Britian's Melody Maker magazine—teamed up with school-mate Wiggs to form St. Etienne, intending to show people how to do pop right. Their stated goal was to incorporate the feeling of the fantasy-happy 60s and 70s into pop songs that nonetheless felt current. Originally intending to write for specific individuals instead of having one constant singer, St. Etienne's first singles include vocals from Kyle Minouge, Shara Nelson and Mora Lambert. Cracknell became a permanent member after the release of the first album, *Foxbase Alpha*. With a new album every other year and a frantic release of singles in-between, St. Etienne has quickly risen to the forefront of Britpop.

what to buy: *Foxbase Alpha* (Warner Bros., 1991, prod. Bob Stanley and Pete Wiggs) 🦴🦴🦴🦴 at first sounds familiar because St. Etienne draws from a vast collection of pop sources. But the album quickly becomes unique because of the special way the group effortlessly combines those many influences, blending warmer sounds and samples with its electronic orientation. *So Tough*, (Warner Bros., 1993, prod. St. Etienne) 🦴🦴🦴🦴½ continues the foray into techno/synth pop, and although the band seems to follow the popular dance whims of the moment, it consistently values musical expertise over trendy stylings. *So Tough* also contains its biggest hit (though probably not one of its best songs), "You're in a Bad Way."

what to buy next: The third album, *Tiger Bay*, (Warner Bros., 1995, prod. St. Etienne) 🦴🦴🦴🦴 is a bit of a departure from the previous releases, experimenting with folk songs laid out on techno and other electronic beats. Its a bit darker than its predecessors, though U.S. fans might want to look into the British version since Warner Bros. slightly altered the format of *Tiger Bay* in the U.S. to make it more "American sounding" and, in the process, removed a few good tracks.

worth searching for: St. Etienne releases a large number of singles and remixes in England, often containing some of its finest work. The import compilation album, *Too Young to Die* (Heavenly, 1995, prod. St. Etienne) 🦴🦴🦴🦴🦴 features the best singles from all three albums, as well as two extra tracks, including the hit "He's On the Phone."

solo outings:

Cola Boy (Stanley and Wiggs) 7 Ways to Love (Arista, 1991) *He is Cola* (Arista, 1991)

▶▶ Boo Radleys, Shara Nelson, the Charlatans

◀◀ The Fall, the Jam, Neil Young, Bee Gees, Adam Ant, ABBA, the Monkeys

Bryan Lassner

The Saints

Formed 1973 in Brisbane, Australia

Chris Bailey, vocals, guitar; Ed Kuepper, guitar (1973-78); Ivor Hay, drums (1973-78, 1980, 1986); Kym Bradshaw, bass (1973-76); Algy Ward, bass (1977-78); Barrington, guitar (1979-81, 1985-88); Janine Hall, bass (1979-84); Mark Birmingham, drums (1979-81); Ian Shedden, drums (1981-85, 1987-88); Archie Larizza bass (1986-88)

"Rock music of the 70s was changed by three bands—The Sex Pistols, The Ramones and The Saints," according to Sir Bob Geldof. The world now realizes that the once-reviled Pistols and the marginalized Ramones left behind crucial, trailblazing work that inspired thousands of young people to buy instruments and play, and spawned true musical revolutions in their respective countries. But too many still are not aware that the Saints did likewise, not only in its native Australia (mostly), but abroad as well—where most of the Saints' albums are available. In fact, along with countrymen Radio Birdman, The Saints were totally unprecedented in its continent—whereas The Pistols and Ramones quickly found supportive scenes they could thrive in. During The Saints' first four years, the group encountered total resistance—from clubowners to labels to fans—before the worldwide punk explosion recognized its fiery genius; and even then, the group had to move to England in 1977, where it had one Top 40 hit with "This Perfect Day." The three albums the original incarnation made are classic rock records, with great variety; the third, *Prehistoric Sounds*, is not even faintly a punk record. Even without inflammatory lyrics, The Saints managed to threaten the status quo (and Status Quo) just as much. And even when incredible singer Bailey co-opted the Saints name for himself with an entirely different lineup, he released from 1980-1988 four superb—if totally different—rock albums and one final so-so one. Bailey has since retreated to a series of also-excellent solo albums. So has original guitarist and songwriter extraordinaire Kuepper, who returned to Australia in 1978 and formed The Laughing Clowns—one of the most uncompromising bands of the early 80s, an ensemble that is spoken of in awed whispers Down Under to this day thanks to his use of jazz structures and soul horns. Kuepper's solo career began in 1985, and his nine solo LPs are what he does best: solid and soulful rock with an emphasis on his guitar talents and songwriting abilities.

what to buy: *Eternally Yours* (Sire, 1978, prod. Chris Bailey and Ed Kuepper) picks up on every rock 'n' roll influence of the genre's first 20 years and ups the throttle considerably to absolutely torch a series of knockout songs. In addition to the crushing hit "This Perfect Day," the album is particularly remembered for the first "punk with Stax horns" experiment-with god-like results-on its opening track, "Know Your Product." Punk historians and all fans of the dirtiest rock sounds marvel over the sheer grit and determination of the band's rough debut, *(I'm) Stranded* (Sire, 1977, prod. Rod Coe) Originally intended as merely a demo—and two of its songs were greatly bettered when re-recorded properly for a 7" EP called "1-2-3-4"—it's still so blistering, uncompromising and raw that it's a bit of a purist statement of intent and is punishing as all get out. *All Fool's Day* (TVT, 1987, prod. Hugh Jones) by the Bailey-led Saints, finds a singer/songwriter at the height of his powers. The opening "Just Like Fire Would" even matches the multi-instrumental prowess of "Ghost Ships," and Jones' production positively crackles.

what to buy next: The final record of the Kuepper-era Saints, *Prehistoric Sounds* (EMI U.K., 1978, prod. by Chris Bailey and Ed Kuepper) was a brave post-punk album for its time, the first indication of where Bailey would take the band without his original guitar player. Stacks of horns dominate whole sides, on a mixture of soul-raveups and rockers with terrific lyrics. A cover of Otis Redding's "Security" fits in particularly well with this swinging Saints. As for the rest of the Bailey oeuvr, *Out in the Jungle* (New Rose Records France, 1982, prod. Ricardo Mentalban (Bailey)) is the most outright simple rock 'n' roll record he attempted, with The Damned's Brian James even guesting on "Animal" and "Out of Sight." *The Monkey Puzzle* (New Rose Records France, 1981, prod. by Chris Bailey) is a similar record with more dense production and less economical playing. Finally, fans of the early Bailey-Kuepper Saints are well served by the compilation *Scarce Saints*, (Raven Records Australia, 1989, prod. Chris Bailey and Ed Kuepper) which culls together the quality B-sides and EP tracks of this halcyon legend and adds a bunch of smoking live tracks.

what to avoid: *Prodigal Son* (TVT Records, 1988, prod. Chris Bailey), the last true album of Bailey Saints, does its best to tear down some typically wonderful songs in uncharacteristic, overblown production.

the rest: *Paralytic Tonight, Dublin Tomorrow* (New Rose Records France EP, 1979) *Prehistoric Songs* (Harvest France, 1981) *Live in a Mud Hut* (New Rose Records France, 1985) *Best of the Saints* (Razor Records Australia, 1986) *Box Set* (Mushroom Australia, 1989) *The New Rose Years* (Fan Club Records France, 1989) *Songs of Salvation 1976-1988* (Raven Records Australia, 1991) *Permanent Revolution* (Mushroom Records Australia, 1991) *The Most Primitive Band in the World, Live '74* (Restless Records, 1995)

worth searching for: Bailey's Saints' *A Little Madness to be Free* (New Rose Records France, 1984, prod. Chris Bailey) is the penultimate work of the post-Kuepper era. Still working with heavy guitars, the more reflective, bluesy Bailey washes in whole oceans of strings, barking brass, and an bleakly romantic worldview. The icy chill that storms through the tour-de-force "Ghost Ships" is just the final thought of an LP that also encompasses the neo-New Orleans jump of "Imagination" and the beautiful, turgid horror of "The Hour." Remarkable.

solo outings:

Chris Bailey *Casablanca* (New Rose Records France, 1983) *What We Did on Our Holidays* (New Rose France, 1984) *Demons* (Mushroom Records Australia, 1991) *Savage Entertainment* (New Rose Records France, 1992) *54 Days at Sea* (Mushroom Records U.K., 1994)

Ed Kuepper *Electrical Storm* (Hot Records Australia, 1986) *Rooms of the Magnificent* (Hot Records Australia, 1987) *Everybody's Got To* (Capitol Records, 1989) *Today Wonder* (Rattlesnake Records Germany 1990) *Honey Steel's Gold* (Restless Records, 1982) *Black Ticket Day* (Hot Records Australia, 1992) *Serene Machine* (Hot Records Australia, 1993) *Character Assassination* (Restless Records, 1994) *The Butterfly Net* (Restless Records, 1994) *A King in the Kindness Room* (Hot Records Australia, 1995) *I Was a Mail Order Bridegroom* (Hot Records Australia, 1995) *Exotic Mail Order Moods* (Hot Records Australia, 1995) *Sings His Greatest Hits For You* (Hot Records Australia, 1995)

Celibate Rifles, Leaving Trains, White Flag

Eddie Cochran, Easybeats, Pretty Things

Jack Rabid

Ryuichi Sakamoto

Born Jan. 17, 1952 in Nakano, Japan

Along with Peter Gabriel and Brian Eno, Ryuichi Sakamoto occupies an extremely rare position in the world of contemporary popular music: that of a world-class artist who has created a unique, truly global form of music and whose every move is viewed with excitement and trepidation by fans all over the planet. Schooled in Western classical music but influenced by both Japanese music and Western pop, Sakamoto is an international leader in the melding of synth-pop and dance music with folk elements from not only Japan but also Africa, Brazil, India and even (gulp) North America. After an initial solo album in 1978 (*Thousand Knives*), the keyboardist-composer formed the Yellow Magic Orchestra or YMO with drummer-vocalist Yukihiro Takahashi and bassist-producer Harry Hosono. The three proceeded to take Japan by storm with their arty and sometimes downright silly disco-ish synth-pop. Sakamoto left the trio in 1983 and immediately placed himself squarely on the map with his lovely, synth-inflected score to the film "Merry Christmas, Mr. Lawrence," the first of close to a dozen such works. In 1984, he took the first step toward the extraordinary synthesis of styles that now characterizes his music, releasing *Illustrated Musical Encyclopedia.* By 1987's *Neo Geo*, he had developed his concept to a level that still stands as a benchmark for world-music fusion, and a year later his portion of the score to Bernardo Bertolucci's "The Last Emperor" won him both an Oscar and a Grammy for best motion picture soundtrack. Since then he has furthered both his pop and film-scoring careers, honing the advancements of *Neo Geo* on *Heartbeat* and reworking themes from his scores on *Playing the Orchestra* and the chamber-music album *1996.* Given his interest in using technology to serve the creative process, one can probably expect to see Sakamoto moving further into the burgeoning multimedia scene. No matter where his interests lead him, however, he will most certainly continue to produce quirky, dazzling, beautiful and ultimately meaningful music of real lasting value.

what to buy: From start to finish, *Neo Geo* (Epic, 1987, prod.

Bill Laswell and Ryuichi Sakamoto) is a knockout. Framed by gentle, Satie-like instrumental pieces, the album shifts through Okinawan/hip-hop combinations, rocketing dance-funk and cool 'n' jazzy alternative rock ("Risky," sung by collaborator Iggy Pop). Of his soundtracks, "Merry Christmas, Mr. Lawrence" (London/Milan, 1983) is the best starting point, as the main theme illustrates his singular ability to mix Asian modality with a rather French, impressionistic style of classical music.

what to buy next: *Heartbeat* (Virgin, 1991, prod. Ryuichi Sakamoto and David Sylvian) is in many ways a more listenable affair than *Neo Geo*, although it seems more of a stylistic grab bag. Still, no matter what genres he dances through, Sakamoto's composing, arranging and producing skills are in tip-top form here. Although the best-known cut from *Illustrated Musical Encyclopedia* (Midi, 1984) is the bouncy Thomas Dolby collaboration, "Field Work," it doesn't begin to reveal the cross-cultural wonders hidden within this disc, which ties together big-band jazz lines, Asian beats, rugged classical passages, light funk, and Japanese and Brazilian motifs.

what to avoid: Because Sakamoto has never been much of a singer, he (like Carlos Santana) has often been at the mercy of the vocalists with whom he's collaborated. On *Media Bahn Live* (Midi, 1986, prod. Ryuichi Sakamoto) he depends on Bernard Fowler to carry most of the melodies, and Fowler is little more than a middle-of-the-road R&B singer. Even the band seems rather stiff on this dismissable double-album.

the rest: *Thousand Knives* (Alfa, 1978) *Miraiha Yaro* (Midi, 1985) "The Last Emperor" soundtrack (with David Byrne and Cong Su) (Virgin, 1988) "A Handmaid's Tale" soundtrack (GNP Crescendo, 1989) *Beauty* (Virgin, 1990, prod. Ryuichi Sakamoto) "The Sheltering Sky" soundtrack (Virgin, 1991) "High Heels" soundtrack (Island, 1992) "Little Buddha" soundtrack (Milan, 1993) *Asian Games* (with Yosuke Yamashita and Bill Laswell) (Verve, 1993, prod. Bill Laswell) *Sweet Revenge* (Elektra, 1994, prod. Ryuichi Sakamoto) *1996* (Milan, 1996, prod. Ryuichi Sakamoto)

worth searching for: *Playing the Orchestra* (Virgin, 1988, prod. Aki Ikuta and Ryuichi Sakamoto) features a suite of material from the score to "Merry Christmas, Mr. Lawrence" and one from "The Last Emperor" performed live by an orchestra. The music is gripping, poignant and marvelously played. Rarity seekers may want to search for the special promo-only boxed version of this album, which includes an extra three-song CD-single highlighted by an orchestral version of "Before Long," the opening cut from *Neo Geo*

Pizzicato 5, Deee-Lite, Soul Coughing

Brian Eno, Bill Nelson, Prince, David Byrne, Material, Sergio Mendes, Erik Satie, Maurice Ravel, Japanese, African and Arabian folk music

Bob Remstein

Walter Salas-Humara

See: The Silos

Sam and Dave

Sam Moore (born Oct. 12, 1935 in Miami, Fla.), vocals; Dave Prater (born May 9, 1937 in Ocilla, Ga. Died April 9, 1988 in Atlanta, Ga.), vocals

Soul men indeed, Sam and Dave could trade vocals with both ease and urgency that seemed almost instinctive. Using the call-and-response technique that harkened back to both their beginnings as gospel singers, Prater and Moore slipped around each other's vocal lines like cracking bullwhips. Their Stax/Volt recordings, largely written and produced by the team of Isaac Hayes and David Porter, rank with the finest works in the field, records that have been covered by as disparate a group of artists as Elvis Costello, the Fabulous Thunderbirds, Tom Jones and Carl Wilson of the Beach Boys. They first paired in 1961 and recorded several unsuccessful singles for the Roulette label before producer Jerry Wexler of Atlantic Records signed them and put the duo in the bosom of Memphis soul. There, Hayes and Porter supervised a string of hit singles beginning with the timeless "Hold On I'm Coming," one of the definitive records of 60s soul and a title allegedly inspired by songwriter Hayes' response to repeated calls that he return to a session from the bathroom. After Stax folded its tent, the duo continued to record for Atlantic, without much success, under a procession of different producers—notably Wexler and Tom Dowd and Miami's Brad Shapiro and Dave Crawford. Personal conflicts led to a split in 1970; they reunited a number of times, but nothing they ever did again on their own or as a team matched the incendiary force of their Stax/Volt recordings. Prater died in a 1988 car crash, after the Blues Brothers' hit version of their "Soul Man" reignited interest in their work. Moore continued to ply his trade, notably singing harmonies on the 1992 Bruce

Springsteen album *Human Touch,* a 1994 duet with Conway Twitty on the country and soul collaboration *Rhythm Country and Blues* and live with John Fogerty at the 1995 Concert for the Rock and Roll Hall of Fame in Cleveland.

what to buy: The double-disc retrospective *Sweat 'N' Soul: Anthology 1965-1971* (Rhino, 1993, prod. Various) combines all the duo's famed highspots with rewarding gems plucked from the dusty corners of their estimable body of work.

what to buy next: All the original Stax albums boast non-single tracks steeped in that greasy fatback sound of Memphis soul, but *Soul Men* (Stax, 1967, prod. Isaac Hayes and David Porter) holds a slight edge with such cuts as "Broke Down Piece of Man" (later covered by Southside Johnny and the Asbury Jukes), "May I Baby" and their delicious take on the Everly Brothers' "Let It Be Me."

what to avoid: Moore remade the duo's signature tune as the title track for the soundtrack to the 1987 movie, "Soul Man," with—of all people—Lou Reed. The intended irony falls somewhat flat.

the rest: *Hold On I'm Coming* (Stax, 1966) *Double Dynamite* (Stax, 1966) *I Thank You* (Stax, 1968) *The Very Best of Sam & Dave* (Rhino, 1995)

worth searching for: *The Stax/Volt Revue Volume One—Live in London* (Stax, 1967, prod. Jim Stewart) contains a spellbinding live version of their drop-dead soul ballad, "When Something Is Wrong with My Baby," alongside another pair of Sam and Dave performances, not to mention cuts by Otis Redding, Booker T. and the Gs, Eddie Floyd and others.

▶▶ The Righteous Brothers, the Blues Brothers, Bruce Springsteen, Elvis Costello, the Fabulous Thunderbirds

◀◀ Sam Cooke, Jackie Wilson, Sims Twins

Joel Selvin

Samhain

See: Danzig

The Samples

Formed 1987 in Boulder, Colo.

Sean Kelly, vocals, guitar; Andy Sheldon, bass, vocals; Jeep MacNichol, drums, vocals; Al Laughlin, keyboards, vocals; Charles Hambleton, guitar (1987-91)

In an odd twist, The Samples started with a major label deal with Arista then switched to the small indie W.A.R.? (What Are Records?). But this backwards career path worked, since the band's frequent touring slowly built a solid grassroots following, especially in college towns. Named for the band's early survival technique of making meals from free supermarket samples, the group offer airy, jazzy pop, a singer who sounds eerily like Sting, sincere lyrics and CDs that come packaged in environmentally friendly cardboard.

what to buy: The Samples' recordings have a certain similarity to them, but *Underwater People* (W.A.R.?, 1992, prod. Jim Scott and the Samples) —a collection of demos, live tracks and leftovers from an aborted second album—rises above the rest with lots of energetic reggae rhythms and more consistent songwriting, as well as a guest shot from Branford Marsalis.

what to buy next: *No Room* (W.A.R.?, 1992, prod. Jim Scott) is a solid effort with a spacious, jazzy feel and strong songs.

what to avoid: *The Last Drag* (W.A.R.?, 1993, prod. Marc DeSisto and the Samples) is indeed a drag due to plodding, mediocre songs.

the rest: *The Samples* (Arista/W.A.R.?, 1990) *Autopilot* (W.A.R.?, 1994) *Still Water* (W.A.R.?, 1994) *Outpost* (W.A.R.?, 1996)

worth searching for: Before *No Room*, the Samples recorded *The Sigma Album*. It went unreleased, though it's available via bootlegs. And some of the tracks appear on "Underwater People."

solo outings:

Sean Kelly Light House Rocket (W.A.R., 1995)

Jeep MacNichol With A Fist (W.A.R., 1996)

Andy Shelton's (with Hazard MDBR): Science Fiction (W.A.R.?, 1996)

▶▶ The Why Store, Ugly Americans

◀◀ The Police, Bob Marley, The Grateful Dead

Jill Hamilton

Sand Rubies

See: The Sidewinders

Santana /Carlos Santana

Formed 1967 in San Francisco, Calif.

Carlos Santana (born July 20, 1947 in Autlan de Navarro, Mexico), Gregg Rollie, organ, vocals; David Brown, bass; Michael Shrieve, drums; Jose "Chepito" Areas, timbales; Michael Carabello, congas

Unknowns who took Woodstock by storm—literally, since the band played during a downpour—if Santana stopped recording after the band's third album, their legacy would still be secure. But guitarist Carlos Santana continued to ply the group's trademark Latin-tinged rock sound to increasingly lesser effect over the next three decades, using an uncountable array of players and even regrouping with the original band members in 1988 in an attempt to recapture the majestic magic of those early days. His piercing, stinging guitar set against the roiling clatter of Latin percussion led the attack; when future Journey lead guitarist Neal Schon joined the band for the third album, his bluesy fusillades gave guitarist Santana a latticework to play against. Although he recorded umpteen albums, in a wide variety of variations of the basic formula, Santana never again equaled the power and sweep of those first three albums.

what to buy: The sound quality on the still-sparkling debut, *Santana* (Columbia, 1969, prod. Brent Dangerfield), may leave something to be desired, but nobody can argue with "Evil Ways" or "Jingo." By the time the group recorded *Abraxas,* (Columbia, 1970, prod. Fred Catero) even that modest insufficiency was removed (the Mobile Fidelity Sound Lab Ultradisc is worth the extra fare). For the third album, the band brought in additional percussion, Schon on guitar, the Tower of Power horns and romped through a walloping *Santana III* (Columbia, 1971, prod. Santana) that proved to be the swan song of the original band.

what to buy next: For the subsequent quarter-century, Carlos Santana has only once come close to duplicating the grand passion of those first three classics. *Havana Moon'* (Columbia, 1983, prod. Jerry Wexler) displayed an entirely different sound, backed by the then-obscure Fabulous Thunderbirds with the Tower of Power horns and Booker T. Jones on organ, all produced by wizened Wexler (Ray Charles, Aretha Franklin).

what to avoid: The so-called *Lotus* (Columbia, 1973, prod. New Santana Band) WOOF! album, a three-record set recorded live in Japan but unreleased in this country for nearly 20 years, is the guru guitarist's jazz-fusion conceit at its highest.

the rest: *Carvanserai* (Columbia 1972) *Welcome* (Columbia 1973) *Greatest Hits* (Columbia 1974 *Borboletta* (Columbia 1974), *Amigos* (Columbia 1976) *Festival* (Columbia 1977) *Moonflower* (Columbia 1977) *Inner Secrets* (Columbia 1978) *Marathon* (Columbia 1979) *Zebop!* (Columbia 1981) *Shango* (Columbia 1982) WOOF! *Beyond Appearances* (Columbia 1985) *Freedom* (Columbia 1987) WOOF! *Viva Santana!* (Columbia 1988) *Spirits Dancing In the Flesh* (Columbia 1990) *Milagro* (Polydor, 1992) Carlos Santana solo: *Love, Devotion and Surrender* (with Mahavishnu John McLaughlin) (Columbia, 1973) *Illuminations* (with Turiya Alice Coltrane) Columbia, 1974) WOOF! *Oneness, Silver Dreams—Golden Reality* (Columbia, 1979) WOOF! *The Swing of Delight* (Columbia, 1980) *Blues for Salvador* (Columbia, 1987) *Sacred Fire: Live in South America* (Polydor, 1993) *Brothers* (Island, 1994) *Dance of the Rainbow Serpent* (Columbia, 1995)

worth searching for: The only time the most ferocious Santana band ever performed the Miles Davis classic, "In a Silent Way," happened to also turn out to be the final time the illustrious lineup played together, closing night at the Fillmore West in 1971. Ironically, this serene benediction was recorded live and included on the boxed set, *Fillmore: The Last Days* (Epic/Legacy, 1972)

▶▶ Malo, Azteca, Journey

◀◀ Willie Bobo, Tito Puente, Olatunji, John Coltrane, Miles Davis, Peter Green

Joel Selvin

Joe Satriani

Born July 15, 1957 in Carle Place, N.Y.

Satriani's six-string wizardry leaves guitar fans gasping for breath, but he's also one of the few rock instrumentalists who has cracked the mainstream charts. That's because the former guitar teacher, whose pupils included Steve Vai and Metallica's Kirk Hammett, never neglects melody or arrangement when he puts his jaw-dropping technique to work. A guitar *player,* Satriani gave lessons and sold his own recordings through ads in guitar magazines until Vai, who by then was playing with David Lee Roth's band, persuaded Relativity Records to sign his former instructor. Satriani's first recording with Relativity produced the platinum-selling hit *Surfing With the Alien* and landed him a spot in Mick Jagger's solo band. Satriani is undeniably one of rock's quickest, most creative guitarists; his imagination sometimes takes him to the outer limits—as seen on songs with titles such as "The Mystical Potato Head Groove

Thing" and "Luminous Flesh Giants." But he can pluck, whammy, hammer or tap his way through a maelstrom of metal, blues, boogie or funk, then squeeze the most delicate and emotional notes out of his Ibanez. Satriani's vocals and harmonica, which he began adding on 1989's *Flying in a Blue Dream*, are adequate but unexceptional.

what to buy: The lightning-fast electric guitars, futuristic tones and inventive rhythms of *Flying in a Blue Dream* (Relativity, 1989, prod. Joe Satriani and John Cuniberti) make it mandatory for all axe-aholics who revere the Mount Rushmore of Hendrix, Page, Clapton and Beck. It's hard-driving but not overly heavy as Satch struts his stuff on "Back to Shalla-Bal" and "Can't Slow Down."

what to buy next: *Surfing With the Alien* (Relativity, 1987, prod. Joe Satriani and John Cuniberti) opens with swooshing jet guitars on the title cut and keeps the afterburners red-hot, hitting a sonic boom on the explosive "Satch Boogie." One complaint: the 10 instrumentals measure up to a relatively paltry 37 minutes. *Satriani* (Relativity, 1995, prod. Glyn Johns) comes through as a delayed sequel to *Flying in a Blue Dream*, showing the same brilliant technique but no new vision.

what to avoid: Though Satriani hasn't released a loser yet, *Not of This Earth* (Relativity, 1986) tread a bit too much of the same ground as *Surfing With the Alien*

the rest: *Dreaming #11* (Relativity EP, 1988) *The Extremist* (Relativity, 1992) *Time Machine* (Relativity, 1993)

worth searching for: *Joe Satriani*, (Rubina EP, 1984) the guitarist's low-budget debut EP, is out of print but not impossible to find.

Steve Vai, Metallica, Megadeth, Pantera

Jimmy Page, Jeff Beck, Pat Metheny, Jimi Hendrix, Johnny Winter

David Yonke

Sausage

See: Primus

Savoy Brown

Formed 1966 in London, England

Kim Simmonds, guitar, vocals; Bruce Portius, vocals (1966-68); Martin Stone, guitar (1966-68); Ray Chappell, bass (1966-68); Leo Manning, drums (1966-68); Bob Hall, keyboards (1968-70); Chris Youlden, vocals (1968-70); "Lonesome" Dave Peverett, guitar (1968-70); Rivers Jobe, bass (1968); Roger Earl, drums (1968-70); Tony Stevens, bass (1968-70); Paul Raymond, keyboards (1971-75); Dave Walker, vocals (1971-73); Dave Bidwell, drums (1971-73); Andy Pyle, bass (1973); Andy Silvester, bass (1971-72); Jackie Lynton, vocals (1973); Ron Berg, drums (1973); Eric Dillon, drums (1974); Stan Webb, guitar, vocals (1974); Miller Anderson, guitar, vocals (1974); Jimmy Leverton, bass (1974); Ian Ellis, bass (1976-78); Tom Farnell, drums (1975-78); plus others

Simmonds was something of a poor man's John Mayall. A blues rocker propelled by a rocking ragged back beat, he had an affinity for replacing musicians seemingly as frequently as he filled up his car. Unlike Mayall, most of Simmonds supporting cast faded into obscurity—the important exceptions being Peverett, Earl and Stevens, who formed Foghat, an even more high octane blues and boogie rock band. Youlden, a masterful baritone blues singer, pursued a solo career, and others found their own niche. Simmonds has certainly suffered for the changeovers; Savoy Brown has never achieved the level of fame, particularly in the U.S., that many of its contemporaries enjoyed. But Simmonds has a strong work ethic, and he keeps Savoy Brown on the road in whatever incarnation he can put together at the moment.

what to buy: Youlden sang on four albums including Savoy Brown's finest, *Raw Sienna*, (Deram, 1970, prod. Kim Simmonds and Chris Youlden) his voice carrying the day on tunes such as "Stay While the Night Is Young," "Needle and Spoon," "I'm Crying" and "When I Was a Young Boy." *The Savoy Brown Collection: 1967-1978* (Deram/Chronicles, 1993, prod. Various) culls the best from 14 albums for a terrific overview, but you still need the seminal *Raw Sienna*.

what to buy next: *Blue Matter* (Deram, 1968, prod. Mike Vernon) is almost as good as *Raw Sienna* but lacks the ultra-tight focus and verve of that album. *Hellbound Train* (Deram, 1972/1991, prod. Neil Slaven) further stretches Simmonds' blues bonds as he heads for a flashier rock and boogie sound. *Lion's Share* (Deram 1973/1992, prod. Neil Slaven) pulls together some tight and memorable songs, leaning more towards hard rock than boogie.

what to avoid: Once he succumbed to pyrotechnic guitar flash, his recordings became indistinguishable and boring. Stay away from *Kings of Boogie* (GNP Crescendo, 1989) **WOOF!** *Live and Kickin'* (GNP Crescendo, 1990) and *Make Me Sweat*. (GNP Crescendo, 1988) **WOOF!**

worth searching for: *Getting to the Point* (Dream, 1968, prod. Mike Vernon) ♪♪♪ is another first-rate early effort that's well worth hearing.

▶▶ Foghat, ZZ Top, the Allman Brothers Band, the Nighthawks, the Fabulous Thunderbirds, George Thorogood and the Destroyers

◀◀ John Lee Hooker, the Yardbirds, John Mayall's Bluesbrakers

see also: *Foghat*

Patrick McCarty

Boz Scaggs

Born William Royce Scaggs, June 8, 1944 in Ohio

Before he started making hits during the 70s as a sophisticated, soulful crooner, Scaggs was a cohort of Steve Miller, who he met at St. Mark's Preparatory School in Dallas during in the late 50s. Both attended the University of Wisconsin, then separated when Scaggs moved to England during the mid-60s. Returning to San Francisco in 1967, Scaggs hooked up with the Steve Miller Band for two albums of psychedelic blues before the singer-guitarist decided to go solo. His debut, *Boz Scaggs*, was co-produced by Rolling Stone magazine publisher Jann Wenner and features one of Duane Allman's seminal solos on "Loan Me a Dime." Gradually eschewing rockers for ballads, Scaggs began working with the cream of L.A.'s studio crop and fashioned a slick, Teflon soul sound that hit its peak with *Silk Degrees*, a five-million seller that made him one of pop's hottest commodities during the mid-70s. During the past 16 years, however, he's spent more time nurturing his Bay Area club, Slim's, than making music; he's only released two albums, returning to the bluesier tenor of his early solo recordings.

what to buy: *Silk Degrees* (Columbia, 1976, prod. Joe Wissert) ♪♪♪♪ shines with the laid-back cool elegance of "Lowdown" and the chugging "Lido Shuffle." The Muscle Shoals house band provides hot backing on the rootsy debut *Boz Scaggs* (Atlantic, 1969/1988, prod. Boz Scaggs, Jann Wenner and Marlin Greene) ♪♪♪♪ and Allman's slide guitar on "Loan Me a Dime" is a seminal moment in rock history.

what to buy next: *Some Change* (Virgin, 1994, prod. Boz Scaggs and Ricky Fataar) ♪♪♪ is a sincere comeback that has a down-home comfort. Scaggs sounds assured and inspired, and Booker T. Jones on the organ doesn't hurt, either.

What Album Changed Your Life?

"It had to be Adam and the Ants' Kings of the Wild Frontier. It was such great music; every song was cool. And Adam Ant had that look, created a whole thing there. There was a lot of stuff that people thought was sort of tacky or whatever, but it really hit me."

Donovan Leitch (Nancy Boy)

what to avoid: *Other Roads,* (Columbia, 1988, prod. Bill Schnee and Stewart Levine) ♪♪ which came after an eight-year hiatus, is so anti-climatic it makes you wonder if he shouldn't stick to running his restaurant.

the rest: *Hits* (Columbia, 1980) ♪♪♪ *Down Two Then Left* (Columbia, 1977) ♪♪ *Slow Dancer* (Columbia, 1974) ♪♪ *Hits!* (Columbia, 1980) ♪♪♪

worth searching for: The out-of-print *My Time* (Columbia, 1972) ♪♪♪♪ features the last of Scagg's rockers, "Full-Lock Power Slide" and "Dinah Flo"—pretty charged-up stuff, considering what the next 20 years would hold.

▶▶ Phil Collins, Huey Lewis & the News, Michael Bolton, Tony Rich

◀◀ Lightnin' Hopkins, Lou Rawls, Dan Penn, Steve Miller Band, Motown

Allan Orski

Scandal

See: Patty Smyth

Peter Scherer

See: Ambitious Lovers

Timothy Schmit

See: The Eagles

Neal Schon

See: Journey

School of Fish /Josh Clayton-Felt

Formed 1990 in Los Angeles, Calif. Disbanded 1993.

Josh Clayton-Felt, vocals, guitar; Michael Ward, guitar, vocals; Dominic Nardini, bass; MP, drums

In 1991, School of Fish was set to conquer the world. With an electrifying alternative radio hit in "Three Strange Days" from a debut album *School of Fish* (Capitol, 1991, prod. John Porter) that paired strong songwriting with innovative playing, the group appeared to be indestructible. Unfortunately, School of Fish's second and final release, *Human Cannonball,* (Capitol, 1993, prod. Matt Wallace and School of Fish) was burdened by lackluster songs lost in layers of ringing feedback and a mess of haphazard ideas. Clayton-Felt, at least, redeemed himself with the smart songwriting and sharp bit of his solo debut, *Inarticulate Nature Boy.* (A&M, 1996, prod. Josh Clayton-Felt and Matt Wallace)

Aidin Vaziri

Brinsley Schwarz

Formed 1970 in London, England. Disbanded 1975.

Brinsley Schwarz, guitar, vocals; Nick Lowe, bass, vocals; Billy Rankin, drums; Bob Andrews, keyboards, vocals; Ian Gomm, guitar (1970-74)

Historically speaking, Brinsley Schwarz is a known entity in the U.S. mainly due to several of the band's members' later success—and, indirectly, the originators of the future Elvis Costello hit "(What's So funny 'Bout) Peace, Love and Understanding." Schwarz and Andrews were part of Graham Parker's Rumour, while Lowe built a respectable solo career; he and Gomm co-wrote Lowe's biggest hit "Cruel to be Kind." Eschewing the post-Woodstock acid hangovers in favor of a basic, roots-oriented pub-rock, Schwarz was out of step with most early 70s rock trends. Although its country tinged party rock won a solid fan base in England, they never broke in the U.S. Still, any fan of late 70s and early 80s New Wave would do well to hunt down the imports *Please Dont Ever Change,* (Edsel, 1993) *Silver Pistol* (Edsel, 1993) or the British collection *Surrender to the Rhythm* (EMI, 1991)

Allan Orski

Scorpions

Formed 1971 in Hanover, Germany

Klaus Meine, vocals; Michel Schenker (1971-73, 1978-79), guitar; Rudolf Schenker, guitar; Lother Heimberg, bass (1971-73); Jurgen Rosenthal, drums (1971-73); Francis Buccholz, bass (1973-93); Wolfgang Dziony, drums (1973-76); Ulrich Rother, guitar (1973-78); Rudy Lenners, drums (1976-77); Herman Rarebell, drums (1977-present); Matthias Jabs, guitar (1978-present); Ralph Rieckermann, bass (1993-present)

The members of Scorpions have long contended that prior to 1980, its record companies wouldn't fork over the bucks to help the group tour in the U.S., therefore rendering the hard rock band obscure on these shores even as it won a following in Europe. That may have been the group's benefit in the long run; when it finally began touring in the U.S., Scorpions roared forth with a fully finished sound, honed and polished by the band and its longtime producer Dieter Dierks. It was slick but not Teflon, mixing crunch and melody in a recipe that was perfect for the 80s pop-metal market. Scorpions delivered the goods with raging rockers such as "Rock You Like a Hurricane" and "No One Like You," as well as Bic-lighter power ballads like "Still Loving You" and "You Give Me All I Need." Always a part of the various Monsters of Rock festivals, Scorpions has been more like Rodan than Godzilla. Then again, this group is still around, and where's Guns N' Roses?

what to buy: *Love at First Sting* (Mercury, 1984, prod. Dieter Dierks) is Scorpions' best, the full realization of its sound in a powerful, radio-friendly package. *Best of Rockers 'n' Ballads* (Mercury, 1989, prod. Dieter Dierks and Bruce Fairbairn) fills the gaps with hits from the rest of the band's 80s albums.

what to buy next: *Hot + Heavy* (RCA, 1993, prod. Dieter Dierks and Scorpions) offers up tracks from the 70s, when the Scorpions were a decidedly underground attraction in the U.S. For that matter, metal fans might want to check out the group's debut, *Lonesome Crow,* (Brain, 1972/Rhino, 1989, prod. Conny Plank) which features Michel Schenker during his short tenure with Scorpions, before he went off to join UFO.

what to avoid: *Live Bites (1988-1995)* (Mercury, 1995, prod. N/A) suffers for being the second live album in a decade, without enough top shelf songs to support it.

the rest: *In Trance* (RCA, 1976/1991) *Tokyo Tapes* (RCA 1979/1993) *Love Drive* (Mercury, 1979) *Animal Magnetism* (Mercury, 1980) *Blackout* (Mercury, 1982) *Best of*

Scorpions, Vol. 2 (RCA, 1984/1992) *World Wide Live* (Mercury, 1985) *Savage Amusement* (Mercury, 1987) *Crazy World* (Mercury, 1990) *Feel the Heat* (Mercury, 1993) *Pure Instinct* (Atlantic, 1996)

worth searching for: When former Pink Floyder Roger Waters staged an all-star performance of *The Wall* to celebrate the fall of the Berlin Wall, he invited Scorpions to open the show. The group's celebratory version of "In the Flesh?" is captured on *The Wall Live in Berlin* (Mercury, 1990, prod. Nick Griffiths and Roger Waters)

Metallica, Dokken, Def Leppard, Warrant, Spinal Tap

The Beatles, the Rolling Stones, the Kinks, the Who

Gary Graff

Screaming Blue Messiahs

Formed 1984 in Great Britain

At their best, the Messiahs bristled with a punk energy unmatched by anyone this side of The Clash. Frontman Bill Carter seeths—howling, mumbling and ranting above his jagged guitar slashes and the group's psycho-punk attack. The Messiahs stopped screaming too soon, however, splitting up shortly after their third album. Sadly, the catalog is out of print, making all three offerings— *Gun-Shy,* (Elektra, 1986) *Bikini Red,* (Elektra, 1987) *Totally Religious* (Elektra, 1989) —a collective Worth Searching For.

Allan Orski

Screaming Trees

Formed 1984 in Ellensburg, Wash.

Mark Lanegan, vocals; Gary Lee Conner, guitars, backing vocals; Van Conner, bass, backing vocals; Barrett Martin, drums (1992-present); Mark Pickerel, drums (1984-1992)

Ellensburg, Wash., is a small college and cow town slightly east of the mythical Twin Peaks in the Cascade Mountains. In such a place young men with musical tastes at all removed from what is played on the local radio station are compelled to hang out together, if only for protection. Screaming Trees, originally formed as the Explosive Generation (in which guise they played new wave covers) were intended to be a punk band, in which incarnation none of the original members played the instrument they finally settled on. Instead they found a neo-psychedelic voice—the middle ground of their myriad prog and punk instincts—which they explored prolifically during the initial stages of their career, frequently aided by producer Steve Fisk (Pell Mell, Pigeonhed).

The Trees were one of the first Northwest underground bands to sign with a national label (SST, at the time a dominant indie), and then had more in common with the Olympia scene (Beat Happening, with whom they recorded an early EP) and Portland, Ore.'s Wipers than with the harder punk-metal sounds evolving in Seattle. In the end, they, too, were swept up in the grunge signing frenzy; by dint of the "Singles" soundtrack, tighter song-craft, and a more self-assured lead singer, the Trees at last dented the charts with *Sweet Oblivion* Perhaps coincidentally this was the first recording to feature Barrett Martin, late of Skin Yard, on drums. Throughout, Lee Conner's guitars have given the band a distinctive, swirling sound.

what to buy: *Sweet Oblivion* (Epic, 1992, prod. Don Fleming) is the first record in years to feature songwriting from the band as an ensemble, rather than as individuals. Bolstered by the critical success of his first solo album, Lanegan's vocals are confident and no longer compete for space in the mix with Lee's guitar. "Nearly Lost You" became the hit single off the hit "Singles" soundtrack, but "Dollar Bill," and "Butterfly" are equally vibrant pop songs, with Lanegan's deep vocals playing hard and sad against keening guitars. Their second full-length *Even If And Especially When* (SST, 1987, prod. Steve Fisk and Screaming Trees) is full of raw enthusiasm, innocently complicated musical structures, and, as announced by the opener "Transfiguration," an alienated view of life. *Buzz Factory* (SST, 1989, prod. Jack Endino and Screaming Trees) is the best-known of their indie releases, but the songs are less spontaneous and energetic, having been recorded twice. *Buzz Factory* was originally recorded as a double-LP, with Donna Dresch on bass; Dresch left for Dinosaur Jr.—and, now, Team Dresch—and Van rejoined the band.

what to buy next: *Invisible Lantern* (SST, 1988, prod. Steve Fisk and Screaming Trees) and the *Change Has Come* EP (Sub Pop, 1990, prod. Steve Fisk, Jack Endino and Screaming Trees) are fine frolics through the Trees' woody world. *Anthology* (SST, 1992, prod. Various) is a two-disc compilation of their years in the indie world.

what to avoid: Sometimes everybody tries just too hard and the stakes are just too high. *Uncle Anesthesia* (Epic, 1991, prod. Terry Date and Chris Cornell) came at the height of the grunge frenzy. Produced by Date, better known for his work with metal bands, and Soundgarden singer Cornell, *Uncle*

Anesthesia is stiff and awkward, and the band play for the first time as if it were aware of a potential audience.

the rest: *Clairvoyance* (Velvetone, 1986) 𝄞𝄞𝄞 *Other World* (SST, 1988) 𝄞𝄞 *Beat Happening/Screaming Trees* (Homestead EP, 1988) 𝄞𝄞 *Something About Today* (Epic EP, 1990) 𝄞𝄞𝄞 *Dirt* (Epic, 1996).

worth searching for: A sterling cover of the Youngbloods' "Darkness Darkness" on the *True Lies* soundtrack (Lightstorm Music/Epic, 1994, prod. John Agnello) 𝄞𝄞𝄞𝄞 is all that remains of the initial sessions for the Trees' 1996 release. It's an odd soundtrack—a few pop songs and a long batch of incidental music (and nobody's exactly sure where in the movie the song might have been heard, anyway)—but this one number is quite spectacular.

solo outings:

Mark Lanegan: The Winding Sheet (Sub Pop, 1990) 𝄞𝄞𝄞𝄞 *Whiskey For the Holy Ghost* (Sub Pop, 1993) 𝄞𝄞𝄞𝄞𝄞

Gary Lee Conner (with The Purple Outside): Mystery Lane (New Alliance, 1990) 𝄞𝄞𝄞

Van Conner (with Solomon Grundy) Solomon Grundy (New Alliance, 1990) 𝄞𝄞𝄞𝄞

▶▶ Luna, Darkside

◀◀ Love, Leonard Cohen, Lee Hazelwood, Spirit

Grant Alden

Scritti Politti

Formed 1977 in Leeds, England

Green Gartside, vocals, guitar, keyboards; Nial Jinks, bass; Tom Morley, drums; David Gamson, keyboards; Fred Maher, drums

Few bands have changed identity so dramatically as Scritti Politti. Starting out as an avant-garde rock band in the post-punk mold, the group recorded a handful of singles that were heavy on scratchy guitar, weird tempo changes and situational lyrics. After frontman Green (as he is largely known) suffered from a heart ailment and took some time off to recover and write, the band's focus turned toward soul-influenced pop. By the mid-80s, Green and his partner Gamson were penning songs for such R&B and Adult Contemporary heavyweights as Chaka Khan and Al Jarreau; even jazz legend Miles Davis covered one of their compositions.

A couple of bubbly pop records made the band a presence in 80s dance clubs, after which the reclusive Green once again submerged, returning to assemble a series of soul covers with such reggae artists as Shabba Ranks and Sweetie Irie.

what to buy: *Cupid & Psyche '85* (Warner Bros., 1985, prod. Green Gartside and David Gamson) 𝄞𝄞𝄞𝄞 is an effervescent collection of dance pop tunes. Though Green's wispy vocals can be terribly cloying, the strength of the material wins out.

what to avoid: *Provision* (Warner Bros., 1988, prod. Green and Gamson) 𝄞𝄞 is the less-than-illustrious follow-up to *Cupid* it boasts a couple of strong tracks but generally falls flat.

the rest: *The Peel Sessions* (Rough Trade, 1979) 𝄞𝄞𝄞 *Songs to Remember* (Rough Trade, 1982) 𝄞𝄞𝄞

Worth Seeking Out: *4 A Sides* (St. Pancras/Rough Trade EP, 1979, prod. Various) 𝄞𝄞𝄞𝄞 is a smashing example of the group's idiosyncratic but compelling early work—a completely different animal from its better-known, squeaky-clean pop, reminiscent of fellow Leeds post-punkers Gang of Four but with a more developed melodic sense and off-kilter arrangements.

▶▶ Ace of Base, Madonna, Pet Shop Boys

◀◀ Beatles, Gang of Four, the Fall, Al Green, Motown, Kraftwerk

Simon Glickman

Seal

Born Sealhenry Samuel, Feb. 19, 1963 in Paddington, England

Seal strikes an imposing figure—six-foot-plus, shaved head, odd facial scars, swathed in black leather. His music is only slightly less imposing, mixing Seal's sweet voice, Trevor Horn's impeccable production and a blend of polyrhythmic dance rhythms and soaring melodies for something close to pop perfection. Like Peter Gabriel, he's titled each of his two albums *Seal* The infectious single "Crazy" was the calling card for the first *Seal*, (ZTT/Sire, 1991, prod. Trevor Horn) 𝄞𝄞𝄞𝄞𝄞 a wholly splendid effort in which every song carries weight and significance. The second *Seal* (ZTT/Sire, 1994, prod. Trevor Horn) 𝄞𝄞𝄞𝄞 shows songwriting maturity, with tunes that are mellower and a bit deeper. The single "Kiss From A Rose," used in the film "Batman Forever," was a worldwide smash. Worth hunting down is *The Acoustic Session*, (ZTT/Sire, 1991, prod. Dick Meanie) 𝄞𝄞𝄞𝄞 a promotional CD that features wonderfully stripped-down reinterpretations of songs from his debut.

Aidin Vaziri

Seals and Crofts

Formed 1969 in Los Angeles, Calif.

Jim Seals, vocals, guitar, saxophone, fiddle; Dash Crofts (born Darnell Crofts), vocals, mandolin, keyboards, guitar, drums

Seals and Crofts are both Texas natives who met on the club circuit during the 50s. They both wound up playing in the Champs ("Tequila") and later moved to Los Angeles, where they worked sessions, formed bands and finally settled into working as a duo. Devout followers of the Baha'i faith, they scored a recording contract in 1971 and were on radio in short order with seminal soft rock hits such as "Summer Breeze," "Hummingbird," "Diamond Girl" and the high school yearbook special "We May Never Pass This Way Again." You'll find them all on *Greatest Hits,* (Warner Bros., 1975, prod. Louie Shelton) a collection of tuneful, sturdy melodies. The duo's fourth album, *Summer Breeze,* (Warner Bros., 1972/1994, prod. Louie Shelton) is also available but is wholly inessential. These days, Seals and Crofts rarely play together; the former farms coffee in Costa Rica, while the latter was last seen around Nashville.

Gary Graff

Seam

Formed 1990 in Chapel Hill, N.C.

Sooyoung Park, guitar, vocals; Lexi Mitchell, bass (1990-94); Mac McCaughan, drums (1990-92); Bob Rising, drums (1992-93); Craig White, guitar (1992-93); Chris Manfrin, drums (1993-present); Reg Shrader, guitar (1993-present); William Shin, bass (1994-present)

Seam's initial lineup was responsible for *Headsparks* (Homestead, 1992, prod. Jerry Kee), which established the brooding, melancholy sound that became the band's trademark—and a style it would maintain despite numberous personnel changes in a relatively short period. After McCaughan left to concentrate on his other band, Superchunk, Seam relocated to Chicago and signed with Touch & Go Records. *The Problem With Me* (Touch & Go, 1993, prod. Brad Wood) is a bit more optimistic than *Headsparks*, but it's still characterisitcally grim. *Are You Driving Me Crazy* (Touch & Go, 1995, prod. Brad Wood) came after another full re-haul of the Seam lineup, with Park and his new chorts still holding firm to the languid, contemplative music Seam began making five years before.

Kim Forster

The Searchers

Formed 1961 in Liverpool, England

Mike Pender (born Mike Prendergast), guitar, vocals (1961-85); John McNally, guitar, vocals; Tony Jackson, bass, vocals (1961-64); Chris Curtis, drums, vocals (1961-66); Frank Allen, bass, vocals (1964-); John Blunt, drums (1966-68); Billy Adamson, drums, 1968-present); Spencer James, guitar, vocals (1985-present)

Remembered by most Americans as a Top 40 group with a few hits—especially "Needles and Pins"—the Searchers were somewhat more successful in Britain. But listeners on either side of the Atlantic generally don't give the band all the credit it deserves an influence on more highly-regarded bands that came later—particularly the Byrds, whose vocal sound was partially modeled after the Searchers. The Searchers' electrified a folk song ("What Have They Done To the Rain") came out several months before the Byrds released "Mr. Tambourine Man." Always a tight and very professional band, the Searchers' guitars rang out nicely and its vocals were crystal-clear. Perhaps its relatively scant output of original songs (though the group picked some great ones to cover) and lack of a clearly-defined image have kept it out of the ranks of more highly-esteemed 60s rockers, anyone who takes a listen will walk away impressed with how forward looking the band was. There are two choices for the curious these days. *The Best of The Searchers* (Rhino, 1988, prod. Various) covers all the necessary bases, as well as its exceptional cover of Jackie de-Shannon's "Each Time." For the more adventurous, there's *The Searchers 30th Anniversary Collection,* (Sequel, 1992, prod. Various) a 3-CD set that comprises all of the hit singles, prime LP tracks, and a generous selection of rarities.

Mike Greenfield

Sebadoh

Formed 1987, Amherst, Mass.

Lou Barlow, vocals and guitars; Eric Gaffney, percussion (1987-93); Jason Loewenstein, bass (1989-present); Bob Fay, drums (1990-present)

Getting fired from Dinosaur Jr. was the most creatively lucrative thing Lou Barlow ever did. The singer-guitarist, long frustrated with J Mascis' control obsession, collaborated with his friend Gaffney in 1987 on a folky, poorly produced demo tape called *Weed Forestin.* The songs were all short, mostly catchy and wrapped in spontaneous noise distortions that sometimes made them more powerful and sometimes made them incomprehensible. For a while, Dinosaur Jr. brought Sebadoh tapes to concerts and packaged them to fans with the latest Dinosaur albums. Then Mascis dumped Barlow, who weathered various Sebadoh personnel changes (Gaffney left and returned several times before exiting for good in 1993), and let his project gradually ferment into a great rock 'n' roll band. Beginning with *Sebadoh III,* a wonderfully unfocused mix of folk, rock and pop, the trio started a streak of records so great it had to spin off two entirely new bands. The Folk Implosion, and its expanded alter-ego, the Deluxx Folk Implosion, helped cement Barlow's legend as the leader of the "lo-fi" production trend that inspired Liz Phair producer Brad Wood, among several others.

what to buy: *Sebadoh III* (Homestead, 1991) and *Bakesale,* (Sub Pop, 1994, recorded by Tim O'Heir) gut the '90s big-guitar alternative-rock trends by writing good songs but recording them in the sloppiest possible way. *Sebadoh vs. Helmet* (20/20, 1992) and *Smash Your Head on the Punk Rock* (Sub Pop, 1992) are explosive punk records that pay homage to Flipper and Husker Du.

what to buy next: At 41 songs, *Freed Weed* (Homestead, 1990, prod. Barlow) is hard to pore through, but it compiles the band's first two tapes, *Freed Man* (Homestead, 1989, prod. Barlow) and *Weed Forestin.* (Homestead, 1990, prod. Barlow)

what to avoid: The live album ... *In Tokyo* (Bolide, 1995) is full of irony and sneering punk-rock pyrotechnics, but it's not much fun to listen to.

the rest: *Rocking the Forest* (20/20, 1992) *Bubble & Scrape* (Sub Pop, 1993) and *Four Song CD* (Domino, 1994) *Harmacy* (Sub Pop, 1996) not available for rating

worth searching for: The Folk Implosion was the big story on the *Kids,* soundtrack (London/Polygram, 1995, prod. Various) when "Natural One" became a much bigger hit than any single Dinosaur Jr. ever released. The soundtrack, in addition to nine songs by the Folk Implosion, Deluxx Folk Implosion and Sebadoh, contains tracks by Daniel Johnston and Slint.

Liz Phair, Superchunk, Nirvana, Smashing Pumpkins

Flipper, Husker Du, Sex Pistols, Dinosaur Jr., Replacements, Minutemen, Velvet Underground, Stooges, Neil Young

Steve Knopper

John Sebastian

See: Lovin' Spoonful

Secret Affair

Formed 1978 in London, England. Disbanded 1982.

Ian Page, vocals, trumpet; Dave Cairns, guitar; Dave Winthrop, sax; Dennis Smith, bass; Seb Shelton, drums

During the fall of 1978, while punk was in its middle stages, a neo-mod revival occurred in London's West End. Secret Affair embodied this revival with its skinhead following and its commitment to 60s soul-influenced mod music. With Fred Perry shirts and Lambrettas, the mods had a new group that was different from The Jam and The Small Faces. Secret Affair announced it was a "Time For Action" on *Glory Boys* (named after the skinhead following) (Sire, 1980, prod. Dave Cairns and Ian Page) "Let Your Heart Dance" and their cover of "Going To A Go-Go" from that album were danceable tracks with a Motown beat and that English touch. *Behind Closed Doors* (Sire, 1980, prod. Dave Cairns and Ian Page) is musically tighter but misses the enthusiasm of the first album.

Anna Glen

Sector 27

See: Tom Robinson Band

The Seeds

Formed 1965 in Los Angeles, Calif. Disbanded 1970.

Sky Saxon (born Richard Marsh), vocals; John Savage, guitar; Daryl Hooper, keyboards; Rick Andridge, drums

A garage band with a psychedelic punk attitude, the Seeds made an impact with cheesy-sounding instruments and the long, annoying whine of Saxon; ultimately, when it came to skills, the Seeds were low on the food chain. The group is best remembered for its 1967 hit "Pushin' Too Hard," after which it had little success for its succession of soundalike songs. That's not to say the band didn't experiment; in 1969 it released a blues album *Full Spoon of Seedy Blues*. But as the psychedelic movement was making way for blues-based hard rock bands, the Seeds' limitations became more obvious, leading to diminishing record sales, smaller audiences and, ultimately a breakup—though Saxon still periodically trots out a new version of the Seeds.

what to buy: *Future* (Crescendo, 1967, prod. Marcus Tybalt) is the pinnacle of the Seeds' enchantment with psychedelic music, a true time warp with "March of the Flower Children," "Travel with Your Mind" and "Where Is the Entranceway to Play," as well as the hit "Thousand Shadows."

what to buy next: *Seeds* (GNP Crescendo, 1966) includes the first two albums, *The Seeds* and *Web of Sound*. The band's best-remembered hits are here.

what to avoid: *A Full Spoon of Seedy Blues* (GNP Crescendo, 1969) WOOF! is dismal stuff from a band that should have never played the blues.

the rest: *Raw & Alive: Merlin's Music Box* (GNP Crescendo, 1968) *Fallin' Of the Edge* (GNP Crescendo, 1977)

▶▶ Soul Asylum, the Replacements, Green River, Dukes of the Stratosphere

◀◀ The Rolling Stones, Shadows of Knight, the Yardbirds, the Standells, the Electric Prunes

Patrick McCarty

Jonathan Segel

See: Camper Van Beethoven

Bob Seger

Born May 6, 1945 in Detroit, Mich.

Seger is the consummate Midwestern rocker—earnest but (mostly) apolitical, sentimental but not maudlin and creatively steeped in soul, country and pounding rock 'n' roll. His songs are honest and occasionally philosophical musings, remembrances of backseat maneuvers ("Night Moves," "Brave Strangers"), working on the line ("Making Thunderbirds") and struggling for perspective ("Hollywood Nights," "Against the Wind"). Raised in Ann Arbor, Seger is indelibly marked by the departure of his father, who abandoned the family when his youngest son was 12, and by the near-poverty conditions he grew up in. Seger's songs are the paeans of an outsider, the "Beautiful Loser" he started singing about in 1975; even after he became successful, Seger retained a shiftless spirit, the hallmark of the insecure and distrustful who, as he sings, will "always be running against the wind." Only on his most recent albums, *The Fire Inside* and *It's a Mystery*, has Seger revealed any sense of comfort, singing warmly about his wife and children—but also taking sharp aim at the violent and capricious elements of society that he fears can undermine his family's well being. A little wariness makes for great songs, of course, and Seger has written them by the bushel—dating back to the 1966 street narrative "East Side Story" and the late 60s frat party favorites "Ramblin' Gamblin' Man" and "Heavy Music." And when Seger and his Silver Bullet Band get cooking, they're—still—as formidable a rock 'n' roll outfit as you'll find treading the boards.

what to buy: Maybe it was the bicentennial, but 1976 was a great year for Seger. First, *Live Bullet* (Capitol, 1976, prod. Bob Seger and Punch Andrews) showed the world what the middling production of Seger's eight prior albums couldn't; that he could rock with a fury to match anyone in rock's upper echelon. Playing in front of the partisan hometown brethren at Detroit's Cobo Arena, Seger and the Silver Bullet Band delivered a storming barn-burner of a show that—thanks to some radio play for "Katmandu"—finally made the rest of the country notice. Then he delivered *Night Moves*, (Capitol, 1976, prod. Bob Seger, Punch Andrews, Jack Richardson and the Muscle Shoals Rhythm Section) a masterful collection of songs that retains the energy of *Live Bullet*—particularly on the ferocious rockers "The Fire Down Below," "Sunspot Baby" and "Rock and Roll Never Forgets." Recorded with a trimmed-down Silver Bullet Band, *The Distance* (Capitol, 1972, prod. Jimmy Iovine) is a loosely themed collection of soaring affirmations, with Seger exulting in triumphing over adversity in "Roll Me Away," "Little Victories" and "Even Now."

what to buy next: *Stranger in Town* (Capitol, 1978, prod. Bob Seger, Punch Andrews and the Muscle Shoals Rhythm Section) and *Against the Wind* (Capitol, 1980, prod. Bob Seger, Punch Andrews and the Muscle Shoals Rhythm Section) are of a piece, cementing the mass success grasped by *Night Moves* without really advancing the craft. Despite a couple of rockers that remain concert favorites ("The Horizontal Bop," "Betty Lou's Gettin' Out Tonight"), *Against the Wind* is a notably softer album, marked by medium tempo hits such as "Fire Lake," "You'll Accomp'ny Me" and the title track.

what to avoid: Despite a bunch of terrific songs, the single-volume *Greatest Hits* (Capitol, 1994, prod. Various) is really a slight overview of Seger's career. He deserves better.

the rest: *Ramblin' Gamblin' Man* (Capitol, 1969) *Noah* (Capitol, 1969) *Mongrel* (Capitol, 1970) *Smokin' O.P.'s* (Capitol, 1972) *Back in '72* (Capitol, 1973) *Seven* (Capitol, 1974) *Beautiful Loser* (Capitol, 1975) *Nine Tonight* (Capitol, 1981) *Like a Rock* (Capitol, 1986) *The Fire Inside* (Capitol, 1991) *It's a Mystery* (Capitol, 1995)

worth searching for: *The Silver Seger Sampler*, (Capitol, 1993, prod. Various) a six-song promotional release containing some of the cream from Seger's pre-*Live Bullet* albums.

- The Eagles (Glenn Frey), Bruce Springsteen, John Mellencamp, Michael Stanley, Garth Brooks
- Van Morrison, Wilson Pickett, Chuck Berry, John Fogerty, Hank Williams, Bob Dylan, Rodney Crowell

Gary Graff

Selecter

Formed 1979 in Coventry, England. Disbanded 1982. Re-formed 1992.

Noel Davies, guitar; Charley Anderson, bass (1979-81); Pauline Black, vocals; Charley "H" Bembridge, drums (1979-81); Compton Amanor, guitar (1979-81); Arthur Hendrickson, vocals (1979-81); Desmond Brown, keyboards (1979-81); Perry Melius, drums (1992-present); Martin Stewart, keyboards (1992-present); Nick Welsh, bass (1992-present)

In an effort to get its ska brew heard, Selecter started its own company, 2-Tone, a label that had considerable success with kindred spirits such as the Specials. Like most of its ska-revivalist peers, Selecter focused mainly on brittle and propulsive tunes with a political edge, highlighted by the jumpy drama of Black's vocals. Selecter wrongly played second fiddle as England embraced the Specials and Madness. Black and Davies regrouped in 1992 to no greater recognition—just a bit too early for the new ska movement in the U.S. *Selected Selecter Selections* (Chrysalis Records, 1989, prod. Errol Ross) is a potent reminder of the band's best work, culled from its first two albums (*Too Much Pressure* and *Celebrate the Bullet*), and selections such as "Too Much Pressure," "Murder," "On My Radio," "Three Minute Hero" and "Celebrate the Bullet" all reveal, again, that Selecter was indeed an unjustly neglected part of the early 80s ska scene.

the rest: *Out on the Streets* (Triple X Records, 1992) *The Happy Album* (Triple X Records, 1994)

Allan Orski

Bettie Serveert

Formed 1986 in Amsterdam, Holland

Carol van Dijk, guitar, vocals; Peter Visser, guitar; Herman Bunskoeke, bass; Berend Dubbe, drums

Though formed in 1986, Bettie Serveert took a back seat to the Dutch band De Artsen—which included Visser and Bunskoeke—until that band broke up in 1991. The re-energized quartet band recorded a seven-song demo in 1992 and quickly signed with Matador Records. Bettie Serveert's first release, *Palomine,* (Matador, 1992, prod. Bettie Serveert, Edwin Heath and Frans Hagenaars) combined jangling acoustic guitar with heavy electric riffs and snappy rhythms for a fresh, frenetic sound that gained immediate attention from modern rock radio. "Kid's Allright" introduced the group's heavier side, while "Tomboy" displayed a lighter, more hummable touch. van Dijk, meanwhile, showed her mettle as a singer on the title track and "Brain-Tag." *Lamprey,* (Matador, 1995, prod. Frans Hagenaars, Bettie Serveert and Wayne Lorenz) bears close resemblance to *Palomine* but, with the first album's element of surprise gone, it's neither as invigorating nor as successful.

Kim Forster

Brian Setzer

See: Stray Cats

The Sex Pistols

Formed 1975 in London, England. Disbanded 1978. Reformed 1996.

Johnny Rotten (born John Lydon), vocals; Glen Matlock, bass (1975-77, 1996); Sid Vicious (born Simon Ritchie), bass (1977, died 1979); Steve Jones, guitar; Paul Cook, drums

The band that defined the punk rock revolution, the Sex Pistols thrived on a notorious reputation culled by angry, irreverent songs (a blitz-speed "God Save the Queen" doesn't endear you to most British folks) and outrageous on- and off-stage antics, many manipulated by the group's manager-of-sorts, Malcolm McLaren. Though only teenagers when they formed, the Pistols almost single-handedly launched the punk movement in Britain and opened the door for New Wave; like the Ramones before them, the Sex Pistols told disaffected youth that you could indeed pick up a guitar and, without technical prowess, just start bashing it to make a valid noise. Reacting to the complacency of dinosaur rock bands and bland popular music, the group set out to shock and antagonize people out of their musical apathy. Taking on subjects such as the royal family, anarchy and corporate irresponsibility—as well as giving voice to the rising mood of hopelessness Lydon sensed in his country—the Pistols' were raw, angry, violent and alive. Unfortunately, the Sex Pistols were destined to be short-lived. The group broke up following a dismal and unorganized U.S. tour in 1978; its members went on to an assortment of solo projects—Lydon's Public Image Ltd. being the most durable—and Vicious died of a drug overdose in 1979 after being arrested for the murder of his girlfriend. But in 1996, amidst cynicism and accusations of sellout—which the group readily fessed up to—the Sex Pistols announced they would reform and tour with original bass player Matlock.

what to buy: *Never Mind The Bollocks Here's The Sex Pistols* (Warner Bros., 1977, prod. Chris Thomas) ♪♪♪♪♪ was the great punk rock wake-up call whose resonance still echoes in the modern rock community.

what to buy next: *The Great Rock & Roll Swindle* (Warner Bros., 1979, prod. Various), ♪♪♪♪ from the crappy movie of the same name, is filled with muddled garbage but just enough noteworthy live and studio cuts to make it a worthwhile addendum to "Bollocks."

what to avoid: *Better Live Than Dead* (Restless, 1988) ♪♪ is interesting for its energetic performance and selection of covers (the Who's "Substitute," the Monkees' "Stepping Stone"), but the poor fidelity is grating.

the rest: *The Swindle Continues* (Restless, 1988, prod. Various) ♪♪♪ *Live at Chelmsford Top Security Prison* (Restless, 1990) ♪♪♪♪

worth searching for: *Kiss This* (Virgin, 1992, prod. Various) ♪♪♪♪♪, a U.K. compilation that should be, for most, a one-stop Pistols collection.

solo outings:

Steve Jones: Mercy (Gold Mountain/MCA, 1987) ♪♪ *Fire and Gasoline* (Gold Mountain/MCA, 1989) ♪ (with Chequered Past) *Chequered Past* (EMI, 1984) ♪♪

Malcolm McLaren: Duck Rock (Island, 1983) ♪♪ *Would Ya LIke More Scratchin'?* (Island, 1984) ♪ *Fans* (Island, 1984) ♪♪♪♪ *Swamp Thing* (Island, 1985) ♪ *Waltz Darling* (Epic, 1989) ♪ *Round the Outside! Round the Outside!* (Virgin, 1990) ♪♪♪ *Paris* (Gee Street/Island, 1995) ♪♪

▶▶ Black Flag, Minutemen, Nirvana, Green Day, any band that operates under the punk umbrella

◀◀ Ramones, The Who, The Monkees

see also: *Public Image Ltd.*

Anna Glen and Gary Graff

Charlie Sexton

Born Aug. 11, 1968, San Antonio, Texas

A guitar phenom from an early age, this San Antonio and Austin product was touring with fellow Texan Joe Ely's band at age 13. He won a recording contract two years later, hobnobbing with the likes of Bob Dylan and Keith Richards. Sexton de-emphasized his guitar prowess for a pouty, prettyboy look (with a faux British accent to boot) for his debut album, released when he was 17. It was a hit, but a second album flopped. Sexton dropped the glam-rock facade to join the late Stevie Ray Vaughan's rhythm section in Arc Angels, a gutsy blues rock band released one album and toured extensively, but broke up soon after. A more mature and focused Sexton convened a new band and began performing and writing more strong, autobiographical materal—sometimes with help from the enigmatic songwriter Tonio K. *Under the Wishing Tree* (MCA, 1995, prod. Malcolm Burn and Charlie Sexton) ♪♪♪ finds Sextion purging some personal demons and making the kind of big, open, rangey roots rock that fits his lyrical motifs.

the rest: *Pictures for Pleasure* (MCA, 1985) ♪ *Charlie Sexton* (MCA, 1985) ♪

see also: *Arc Angels*

Doug Pullen

Phil Seymour

See: Dwight Twilley

Sham 69

Formed 1977 in Hersham (London), England. Disbanded 1981.

Jimmy Pursey, vocals; Dave Parsons, guitar; Dave "Kermit" Treganna bass; Albie "Slider" Maskell drums (1977); Mark "Dodie" Cain drums (1978-79); Ricky Goldstein, drums (1980)

Of all the late 70s original U.K. punk legends, none was more maligned (and more beloved by a "Sham Army" of fans) than Sham 69. Like its equally great and also roundly dismissed contemporaries The U.K. Subs, Sham's crime was to take the intellectual edge out of this once vibrant movement, bringing the music down to the level of the average kid concert-goer, complete with football-stadium-style chants for all to sing along. In this sense, the group completely anticipated the coming 80s hardcore explosion, particularly the American branch (Note that Ian MacKaye and Henry Rollins migrated all the way to New York to attend the two '79 East Coast Sham shows, before singing for Minor Threat—and Fugazi—and Black Flag), but in so doing, traded industry respect and credibility for simplistic and crude, yet honestly affecting and enduring, punk. Those purchasing Dojo Records' reissues of the first four albums (only the spotty debut *Tell Us the Truth* enjoyed an American release back then) will be struck by the band's saving graces, the kind that inspired such a loyal, albeit thuggish (and exclusive) audience that the band racked up seven U.K. Top 40 singles (including three Top 10s) in those first three years. For a bunch of bellowing, braying Joes, there was no denying that motormouth man-of-the-people singer Pursey was a hardworking, committed and charismatic leader, and that sidekick Parsons came up with effective guitar riffs, making them more than just punks becoming popular after the original innovators left the scene. Sham 69 has reunited periodically, but without the notoriety of its original incarnation.

what to buy: 1980's swan song *The Game* (Dojo, 1996, prod. Jimmy Pursey and Pete Wilson) sent Sham out in a blaze of surprising glory with its most convincing and workmanlike album, punctuated by a hot single "Give a Dog a Bone." 1978's *That's Life*, (Dojo, 1996, prod. Jimmy Pursey and Pete Wilson) the first punk-rock concept LP (a day in the life of a working class teen, complete with a pub fight over a girl) is not quite The Kinks but still succeeds thanks to the abundance of big hooks in "Leave Me Alone," "That's Life" and the U.K. hit "Hurry Up Harry."

what to buy next: On 1979's *Hersham Boys* (Dojo, 1996, prod. Jimmy Pursey and Pete Wilson), the group stepped away from the narrow dictates of its violent crowd by donning cowboy gear for a country-western homage, along with a tribute to James Dean, ("Lost on Highway 46") and solidly covering The Yardbirds' "You're a Better Man Than I." 1978's *Tell Us the Truth* (Dojo, 1996, prod. by Jimmy Pursey and Pete Wilson) is too formulaic, which made many miss their later improvement, though it has some good moments such as the oft-covered "Borstal Breakout."

what to avoid: If ever there was a band that shouldn't have attempted a comeback, it was Sham 69. Though admirable in intent, the new direction it hit upon—a crap rap/boogie/metal/dance trip without edge—*Volunteer* (Legacy U.K., 1988, prod. Jimmy Pursey) WOOF! was just awful.

the rest: *The First, Best, and Last* (Polydor U.K., 1980) *Angels With Dirty Faces: The Best of Sham 69* (Receiver U.K., 1986) *Live and Loud! Volume 2* (Link U.K., 1988) *Sham's Last Stand* (Link U.K., 1989) *Live at the Roxy* (Receiver U.K., 1990) *Rare and Unreleased* (Limited Edition U.K., 1991)

worth searching for: *Live and Loud!* (Link U.K., 1987) is a scorching concert LP recorded in 1979 that proves the band was far better than its reputation and was in fact a hot group of musicians by the end of its tenure.

solo outings:

Jimmy Pursey: Imagination Camouflage (Polydor U.K., 1980) *Alien Orphan* (Epic U.K. 1982) *Revenge is Not the Password* (Turbo U.K., 1983) *The Lord Divides* (Eskimo Green U.K., 1983)

▶▶ Minor Threat, Cockney Rejects, Angelic Upstarts

◀◀ Sex Pistols, Chelsea, Yardbirds

see also: *Lords of the New Church*

Jack Rabid

Shango

See: Bill Laswell

Del Shannon

Born Dec. 30, 1939 in Coopersville, Mich. Died Feb. 8, 1990 in Santa Clarita, Calif.

Exhibit A of pre-British Invasion American rock 'n' roll. While rock historians would have you believe that everyone was just piddling around before the Fab Four arrived, Shannon was releasing seething and imaginative music ("Runaway," "Little Town Flirt," "Hey! Little Girl") as early as 1961. Along with Roy Orbison, he is virtually the first U.S. artist to write dark, paranoid love songs that offered no light at the end of the tunnel. Focusing on aggressive, minor key verses that shifted dramatically to major key choruses, Shannon seemed incapable of playing with anything less than gripping urgency. A versatile singer, he leapt to falsetto with startling effect and stayed on the charts throughout the first half of the 60s. But in a grievous effort to mold him into a teen idol, the production team at Liberty Records all but snuffed out his career. Suffering from alcoholism and depression, he nonetheless made several attempts to return to music during the late 70s and early 80s, some with the help of Tom Petty. Shannon was a candidate to replace Orbison in the Traveling Wilburys at the time of his suicide in 90.

what to buy: *Greatest Hits* (Rhino, 1990, prod. Various) is a riveting compilation of Shannon's teen heartbreak tragedies, with his signature smash "Runaway" along with nearly everything else. "Hats off to Larry," "Stranger in Town," "Keep Searchin' (We'll Follow the Sun)" and a kicking rendition of the Beatles "From Me to You."

what to buy next: The posthumous *Rock On* (Gone Gator/MCA Records, 1991, prod. Jeff Lynne and Mike Campbell) ♫♫♫ is a competent return to form with various members of Tom Petty's Heartbreakers lending strong support.

what to avoid: *Greatest Hits* (Curb, 1996, prod. Harry Balk) ♫♫ is skimpier than Rhino compilation, so why bother?

the rest: *Sings Hank William's* (Rhino, 1990) ♫♫♫

worth searching for: The out-of-print *Drop Down and Get Me* (Elektra, 1981, prod. Tom Petty) ♫♫♫ is the first Petty-induced comeback attempt and runs closer to country than to his 60s rock.

▶▶ Bruce Springsteen, Tom Petty, Bonnie Raitt, Dwight Twilley

◀◀ Roy Orbison, Bill Haley, Buddy Holly, Bobby Freeman

Allan Orski

Feargal Sharkey

See: The Undertones

Dave Sharp

See: The Alarm

Garrett Shavlik

See: The Fluid

Sandie Shaw

Born Sandra Goodrich, 1947 in Dagenham, England

Shaw's career divides neatly into two periods: that of the cool London Swinging Girl of the 60s who sang her way through a string of No. 1 songs, and that of the cool 80s chanteuse who briefly returned to fame with tasteful renditions of songs by the Smiths and Lloyd Cole. From 1964-967, Shaw epitomized the London sound on hit records like "Long Live Love" and "There's Always Something There to Remind Me." "Puppet on a String," her entry in the 1967 Eurovision Song Contest, also went No. 1, resulting in endless European imitations of her unique pop style. Shaw disappeared in the late 1960s to raise a family with British fashion designer Jeff Banks, but she returned to the spotlight with a guest appearance on Heaven 17's *Music of Quality and Distinction* (1981). Her career got a minor boost from the Smiths when Morrissey, a longtime fan, brought Shaw in to sing lead vocals on reprised versions of his group's hits "Hand in Glove" and "I Don't Owe You Anything." Shaw continued collaborating with contemporary artists throughout the 80s although her output had thinned out considerably by the end of the decade.

what to buy: *Collection* (Castle, 1991, prod. Various) ♫♫♫♫ is a fairly comprehensive retrospective, from the early hits to her collaborations with the Smiths. An excellent introduction to one of Britain's original pop singers.

what to buy next: *Reviewing The Situation* (RPM, 1996, prod. Various) ♫♫♫♫ is an excellent reissue compiled with Shaw's assistance and featuring elaborate packaging, including photos and extensive liner notes. The compilation couples her last album of the 60s with five contemporary singles. Shaw tackles songs by the Rolling Stones, Bob Dylan and even Led Zeppelin, and while not all the results are flattering, she shines on the bulk of the material. *The Sandie Shaw Supplement* (RPM, 1996, prod. Various) ♫♫♫ is the reissue of her 1968 album of the same name, featuring songs performed during Shaw's six-week BBC TV series that same year. The selections read like a cross-section of greatest hits from the day, including Simon & Garfunkel's "Homeward Bound" and "Scarborough Fair," the Rolling Stones' "Satisfaction" and the Mary Hopkin hit "Those Were The Days." Like all the RPM reissues of Shaw's work, *Supplement* features deluxe packaging and a good eye for historical detail.

what to avoid: After a long absence from the music scene and before recording with the Smiths, Shaw privately released *Choose Life* (RPM, 1996, prod. Sandie Shaw) ♫♫ as a limited-edition album on her own label. Although her voice is in excellent form, Shaw's choice of material lacks focus and her themes of mysticism and empowerment, while worthy, come off as strident and forced.

the rest: *Sandie/Me* (See for Miles, 1996) ♫♫♫ *Long Live Love* (Sequel, 1996) ♫♫♫ *Love Me, Please, Love Me* (RPM, 1996) ♫♫

worth searching for: *64/67 Complete Sandie Shaw Set* (Sequel, 1994, prod. Various) ♫♫♫♫ is an excellent but hard-to-find, double-disc set featuring all of Shaw's essential 1960s hits plus minor chart entries. The definitive portrait of London's Swinging Girl vocalist.

⏩ Petula Clark, Marianne Faithfull, Nico, Mary Hopkin, the Smiths

⏪ Cilla Black, Dusty Springfield, Dionne Warwick

Christopher Scapelliti

Tommy Shaw

See: Styx

Jules Shear

Born March 7, 1952 in Pittsburgh, Penn.

Like John Hiatt, Shear's songs are more familiar to the masses than his name, thanks to the Bangles ("If She Knew What She Wants"), Cyndi Lauper ("All Through the Night") and Alison Moyet ("Whispering Your Name"). After false starts as a member of L.A.'s woefully misnamed Funky Kings (a laid-back sextet featuring ex-Eagle Jack Tempchin) and the leader of the New Wave act Jules and the Polar Bears, Shear hit his stride as a songwriter with such superb solo albums as 1983's Todd Rundgren-produced *Watch Dog* and 1985's *The Eternal Return* His passionate, nasal singing is an acquired taste, but his knack for expressing complex emotions within simple song structures laced with 60s-inspired melodies, jangling guitars and heavenly harmonies has resulted in an impressive catalog overflowing with small but significant treasures. Footnote: he was the original host and brainstormer behind "MTV Unplugged."

what to buy: *Watch Dog* (EMI, 1983, prod. Todd Rundgren) 🦴🦴🦴🦴 drapes such edgy love songs as "Whispering Your Name," "Never Fall" and "All Through the Night" against Rundgren's dense, swirling sonic pastiche of textures drawn from the Beatles and Roy Orbison. *The Eternal Return* (EMI, 1985, prod. Jules Shear and Bill Drescher) 🦴🦴🦴½ layers on the synthesizers, but nothing can obscure the irresistible charms of "Memories Burn Hard," "If She Knew What She Wants" and the blue-eyed soul of "Steady" (co-written with Lauper). Tougher guitars and tasteful keyboards bring a fuller sound to *The Great Puzzle*, (Polydor, 1992, prod. Jules Shear and Stewart Lerman) 🦴🦴🦴½ which is highlighted by "The Sad Sound of the Wind" and the Lovin' Spoonful-influenced "The Mystery's All Mine." The first pressing was packaged with a bonus CD titled *Unplug This*, featuring acoustic versions of "If She Knew What She Wants," "All Through the Night" and six others.

what to buy next: *Horse of a Different Color: The Jules Shear Collection* (Razor and Tie, 1993, prod. Various) 🦴🦴🦴 samples his solo career and short-lived stints with the Funky Kings, Jules and the Polar Bears and Reckless Sleepers. The majestic "If We Never Meet Again," recorded with the Sleepers and covered by ex-Byrd Roger McGuinn, is one of the most touching songs about faith and devotion ever written.

what to avoid: For all the critical accolades, Jules and the Polar Bears' *Got No Breeding* (Columbia, 1978, prod. Larry Hirsch and Stephen Hague) 🦴🦴 and *Fenetiks* (Columbia, 1979, prod. Stephen Hague and Jules Shear) 🦴🦴 sound distressingly dated, the work of a maturing artist reaching for notes out of his range and straining for new-wave credibility.

the rest: *Demo-Itis* (Enigma, 1987) 🦴🦴½ *The Third Party* (I.R.S., 1989) 🦴🦴🦴 *Healing Bones* (Island, 1994) 🦴🦴🦴

worth searching for: Long before tribute albums were cool, Ian Matthews covered 12 Shear compositions on *Walking a Changing Line: The Songs of Jules Shear* (Windham Hill, 1988, prod. Ian Mathews and Mark Hallman) 🦴🦴🦴½ His crisp tenor brings out the elegance of "Standing Still," "Following Every Finger" and "On Squirrel Hill."

⏩ Jonny Polonsky, Frank Black, Goo Goo Dolls

⏪ The Beatles, the Byrds, Roy Orbison

David Okamoto

Sheila E.

Born Sheila Escovedo, Dec. 17, 1957 in Oakland, Calif.

A featured performer in father Pete Escovedo's renown Latin-jazz band Azteca before she was old enough to drive, Sheila E. had a growing career as a percussionist/backing vocalist for stars such as Lionel Richie, Diana Ross and George Duke before Prince "discovered" her in 1983. Recruiting her to sing on his 1984 hit "Erotic City," he also produced her solo debut the same year—building an album so grounded in his own sounds that Escovedo sounded like a guest star on her own record. And when she took control of her own sonic destiny in 1987, there wasn't much to replace his vision. A short stint as drummer for Prince's backing band during the late 80s did little to establish her solo career, and when she finally released a solo album worthy of her talents in 1991, persistent health problems kept her from promoting it to anyone who would care.

what to buy: As a showcase for her full range of talent—songwriting, producing, playing and singing—*Sex Cymbal* (Warner Bros., 1991, prod. Sheila E. and Peter Michael Escovedo) 🦴🦴🦴🦴 stands as Sheila E.'s most arresting and underrated effort. Featuring thickly layered funk in "Loverboy," the title track's danceable pop, the slick ballad "Heaven" and various percussion jams, this record is her most complete individual statement as a solo artist.

what to buy next: Her solo debut, *The Glamorous Life* (Warner Bros., 1984, prod. Sheila E. and the Starr Company) introduced the Prince-derived, bodacious babe-behind-the-timbales persona fans knew best—buoyed by the sax-laden dance groove of the title track.

what to avoid: Though it boasts a standout track in the ballad "Hold Me," the rest of Sheila E's self-titled third album (Paisley Park, 1987, prod. Sheila E. and David Z.) WOOF! is lifeless, directionless filler.

the rest: *Romance 1600* (Paisley Park, 1985)

worth searching for: Captured in a live homecoming performance shortly after the release of "Romance 1600," Sheila E and her crack backing band shine in the concert video "A Glamorous Life."

Crystal Taliefero, Me'Shell NdegeOcello, Dionne Farris

Prince, Santana, Tito Puente, Azteca

Eric Deggans

Pete Shelley

See: Buzzcocks

Michelle Shocked

Born Michelle Johnston, Feb. 24, 1962 in Dallas, Texas

Discovered playing around a campfire in 1986 at Texas' legendary Kerrville Folk Festival, Shocked became an instant overseas sensation after a Walkman-recorded tape of her performances got released on London's Cooking Vinyl Records. When she concentrates on her music, the gifted and outspoken Shocked can be a captivating storyteller with a sassy, soulful voice and an endearing blend of East Texas charm and East Coast street savvy. However, in concert and in interviews, she sometimes tries too hard to live up to her stage name, spouting her passionate but clumsily articulated left-wing politics and toying with the volatile combination of good intentions and questionable judgment. In 1991 she proposed posing in blackface on the cover of *Arkansas Traveler* to drive home the belabored point that black musicians have been robbed of their legacy by white artists. It was the crowning thorn in a stormy eight-year tenure with Mercury Records, which ended in 1996 after she filed suit against the company citing the 13th Amendment—the abolition of slavery.

what to buy: Poignant and pointed, *Short Sharp Shocked* (Mercury, 1988, prod. Pete Anderson) blends rustic reminisces about her Texas childhood with chugging country-rockers and the Dylanesque "Anchorage," which remains her most touching and timeless song. *Arkansas Traveler* (Mercury, 1991, prod. Michelle Shocked) is an ambitious project—recorded around the world with Pops Staples, Taj Mahal, Clarence Gatemouth Brown and members of Hothouse Flowers and Uncle Tupelo—that got overshadowed by Shocked's ham-handed indictments of blackfaced minstrels. Years later, after the controversy has died down, it's easier to appreciate the album's musical strengths, particularly a delicate duet with Alison Krauss on "Prodigal Daughter (Cotton Eyed Joe)" and a rousing rewrite of the Pretenders' "Back on the Chain Gang" called "Come a Long Way."

what to buy next: *The Texas Campfire Tapes* (Mercury, 1986, prod. Pete Lawrence) contains the now-mythical Kerrville recordings, complete with crickets chirping and low-fidelity sound. Three songs—"Fogtown," "Don't You Mess Around With My Little Sister" and "The Secret to a Long Life"—would be rerecorded on later albums.

what to avoid: *Captain Swing* (Mercury, 1989, prod. Pete Anderson) has its nostalgic charms, but much of the material crosses the line between lighthearted and lightweight.

worth searching for: Since leaving Mercury, Shocked has been recording limited-edition CDs in her New Orleans home and selling them exclusively at her shows. *Kind Hearted Woman* (1994) is a solo electric guitar collection. *Artists Make Lousy Slaves* (1996) is a direct-to-DAT effort that finds her sharing lead vocals with Fiachna O'Braonain of Hothouse Flowers and includes the jaunty "Laundry Day" and an a cappella reading of "The Water is Wide."

Liz Phair, Ani DiFranco

Guy Clark, Woody Guthrie, Jean Ritchie

David Okamoto

Shoes

Formed 1974 in Zion, Ill.

Jeff Murphy, vocals, guitar, keyboards, perc.; John Murphy, vocals,

bass, guitar, keyboards, perc.; Gary Klebe, vocals, guitars, keyboards, perc.; Skip Meyer, drums

In the mid-70s, in the middle-of-nowhere town of Zion, Ill., Shoes took the Beatles' blueprint and built its own model of pure pop on it. The four musicians taught themselves how to play as they wrote songs, practically guaranteeing a fresh approach. Unlike so-called skinny-tie bands that took New Wave shortcuts (and haircuts) by replicating Beatles harmonies with a retro cynicism, Shoes' sound meshed hard guitars and soft harmonies—a commercially promising middle ground between Big Star and Boston. The lyrics sidestepped cliches, reflecting the heartbreak and anger of lost romance, deftly making art out of therapy.

what to buy: Musically, Shoes' albums vary little; this is not a band that tries on new styles with each album. For the value conscious, *Present Tense/Tongue Twister* (Elektra, 1979 and 1981/Black Vinyl, 1988, prod. Mike Stone/Richard Dashut) 🦴🦴🦴🦴½ combines two of the very best titles. *Propeller,* (Black Vinyl Records, 1995, prod. Shoes) 🦴🦴🦴🦴½ and the darker, more ethereal *Black Vinyl Shoes* (Black Vinyl, 1978/1994, prod. Shoes) are also landmark pop works.

what to buy next: *Boomerang/Shoes on Ice* (Elektra, 1982/Black Vinyl, 1990, prod. Shoes) 🦴🦴🦴🦴 is another solid two-fer, the second part recorded live at the Zion Ice Arena (get it?). *Fret Buzz* (Black Vinyl, 1996) 🦴🦴🦴🦴 is a good live album (with much better fidelity than *Shoes on Ice*), while *Shoes' Best* (Black Vinyl, 1987) 🦴🦴🦴🦴 provides a fine, if overly long, overview.

what to avoid: The rare *Un dans Versailles* (no label, 1975, prod. Shoes) 🦴🦴 is an early 4-track recording that contains no imput from Klebe. It's a raw, nascent work that shows how far the band has come and how quickly the group grew.

the rest: *Silhouette* (Demon, 1984/Black Vinyl, 1991) 🦴🦴🦴🦴

worth searching for: A great bit of ethereal hard-pop, "Like I Told You," appears only on the cassette *Trouser Press Presents the Best of America Underground* (ROIR, 1983).

⏩ Material Issue, Urge Overkill, the Figgs

⏪ The Beatles, the Raspberries, Badfinger, Grin

Jordan Oakes

Shonen Knife

Formed 1982 in Osaka, Japan

Naoko (AKA Nancy) Yamano, vocal, guitar; Michie Nakatani, vocals, bass; Atsuko Yamano, drums, vocals

This Japanese trio distills the DIY spirit of punk across the generations—not just the Buzzcocks, Ramones and XTC, but also the early Beatles. Naoko writes most of its songs, Michie writes a few and Atsuko (Naoko's sister) designs the group's trademark pop-Mondrianesque clothes. Unlike the vast majority of Japanese bands, Shonen Knife isn't prepackaged and—even more shocking—is from Osaka, not Tokyo (its original Japanese label, Zero, is based in Kyoto). The utterly unironic songs gained the three women cult status in Los Angeles, resulting in a two-LP tribute album, *Every Band Has a Shonen Knife Who Loves Them,* (Gasatanka/Giant, 1989, prod. Various) with Sonic Youth and other underground groups. And for that matter, California bubblegum punks Redd Kross put their ode "Shonen Knife" on 1990's *Third Eye.* (The name, by the way, basically means "toy knife" ("shonen" translates as "little boy"). The first three Knife albums and some EP tracks were repackaged for America on the two 1990 Gasatanka releases listed below, after which the Japanese and American releases are more or less parallel, aside from some language differences. A U.K. tour with Nirvana in 1991 and some small U.S. excursions spread the group's name enough that Virgin began issuing its albums here, allowing the trio to afford higher production values and more studio time.

what to buy: *Let's Knife* (Virgin, 1992, prod. Shonen Knife) 🦴🦴🦴½ features many of the group's best songs redone at a level of genuine competence, but they're just as charming and tuneful and pop-iconic as ever.

what to buy next: On *Rock Animals,* (Virgin, 1993, prod. Page Porrazzo and Shonen Knife) 🦴🦴🦴 the trio stops recycling its old material, coming up with simple, often sitarish guitar riffs (punk has mostly been dropped in favor of 60s pop), while the lyrical focus on fauna and flora are surreal enough to forgive the stolid drumming.

what to avoid: *Pretty Little Baka Guy + Live in Japan* (Gasatanka/Rockville, 1990) 🦴🦴 isn't bad, but it's the least necessary of the group's output.

the rest: *Shonen Knife* (Gasatanka/Rockville, 1990) 🦴🦴½ *712* (Gasatanka/Rockville, 1991) 🦴🦴 *The Birds & the B-sides* (Virgin, 1996) 🦴🦴½

⏩ Boredoms, Nirvana, Redd Kross

⏪ The Beatles, the Byrds, the Beach Boys, the Ramones, XTC, the Buzzcocks

Steve Holtje

Shriekback

See: Gang of Four

Jane Siberry

Born Oct. 12, 1955 in Toronto, Canada

Although every one of her albums have their shortcomings, this Canadian singer/songwriter/experimental artiste is an utterly unique figure whose importance should not be underestimated. Siberry has always been an innovative arranger and composer, using breathy vocal clusters and a wide vibrato, and often ending melodic lines on a dissonant note to create alluring, off-putting or comical effects. Sometimes shrill, sometimes self-indulgent, her work is consistently original, frequently demanding several listens to be comprehended fully. When she released *Maria*, an odd jaunt into concept-heavy jazziness, Reprise thanked her by dropping her from the label in early 1996; Siberry turned around and started her own label, Sheeba, kicking things off with *Teenager*, on which she recorded a series of the first songs she ever wrote. Once again, she was carving out her own path; expect more of the (not the) same from her.

what to buy: *When I Was a Boy* (Reprise, 1993, prod. Jane Siberry, Brian Eno and Michael Brook) is in some ways her most straightforward effort, and yet it ranges from Peter Gabriel-like lushness to cuts that make use of hip-hop and operatic ideas. Heartbreak seems to have been her inspiration; she makes it seem like the off-ramp into heaven.

what to buy next: With its Linn drums and thin keyboard sounds, *No Borders Here* (Duke Street/Open Air, 1984, prod. Jo Goldsmith/Kerry Crawford and Jane Siberry/John Switzer) sounds a bit dated now, but it's still mighty involving, with the lovely, sardonic "I Muse Aloud," the half-whimsical, half-spooky "Dancing Class" and the extended revenge fantasy of "Mimi on the Beach." *Bound By the Beauty* (Duke Street/Reprise, 1989, prod. Jane Siberry and John Switzer) marked a turning point for Siberry away from the near prog-rock of its immediate predecessors. The Latin touches may remind some of later k.d. lang.

what to avoid: *The Speckless Sky*, (Duke Street/Open Air, 1985, prod. Jane Siberry and John Switzer) not an awful record but certainly not the first one to purchase.

the rest: *The Walking* (Duke Street/Reprise, 1987, prod. Jane Siberry and John Switzer) *Maria* (Reprise, 1995, prod. Jane Siberry) *Teenager* (Sheeba, 1996)

worth searching for: Siberry's debut, *Jane Siberry*, (Can. Street, 1981/ESD, 1991) finds her already in impressive command of the wryly humorous side of her sound.

▶ Sarah McLachlan, the Story, the Innocence Mission

◀ Kate Bush, Laurie Anderson, Joni Mitchell

Bob Remstein

The Sidewinders /Sand Rubies

Formed 1985 in Tuscon, Ariz.

David Slutes, vocals, guitar; Rich Hopkins, guitar; Mark Perrodin, bass; Andrea Curtis, drums, vocals (1987-89); Diane Padilla, drums (1989); Bruce Hapler, drums (1990)

Even when Neil Young was floundering during the mid-80s, bands bearing his stamp kept popping up—such as the Sidewinders, an Arizona quartet who pick up where Crazy Horse leaves off. They very quietly dropped a great little record right out of the box with the full-length debut *Witch Doctor*, (Mammoth/RCA, 1989, prod. Rich Hopkins and David Slutes) which is full of anthemic-sounding buzzsaw originals that stick ("What She Said," "What Am I Supposed to Do?"), as well as a terrific cover of Neil Diamond's "Solitary Man." *Auntie Ramos' Pool Hall* (Mammoth/RCA, 1990, prod. Rich Hopkins and David Slutes) is a decent riff-rock record that comes up a bit short on material. Unfortunately, the band ran into heinous legal difficulties right about then, losing its name to a similarly monikered cover band from North Carolina. Hopkins and Slutes emerged as a duo with a new name on the eponymous *Sand Rubies* (Atlas/Polygram, 1993, prod. Various) which, given all the different producers and lineups, it's no surprise that the album is a patchwork that doesn't quite hang together.

David Menconi

Dick Siegel

Born Dec. 28, 1948 in Newark, N.J.

A veteran of several semi-successful Midwest bands during the 70s and 80s (most notably Siegel Schwal), Siegel didn't really hit his stride until he went solo during the mid 70s. His work is based on folk music, but the folk is taken uptown and uptempo with a big jolt of finger-snapping jive. His songs have an old-fashioned feel—his venues are "joints," and they're usually "jumpin'." Lyrically, Siegel sticks with the simple subjects like listening to a favorite band or the joys of eating breakfast at a

What Album Changed Your Life?

"As nobody that I knew prior to 1963 wrote songs with their brain in gear, it would have the be a Bob Dylan record--probably (The Times They are a-Changin'). I loved (The Freewheelin' Bob Dylan), but I thought it was a bit fluffy. This was quite a long time after I was exposed to John Lee Hooker and Lightnin' Hopkins, but I think that for me, Dylan is the fulcrum of modern music."

Pete Townshend

favored Ann Arbor, Mich., hangout. In 1992 he won a New Folk award at the Kerrville Folk Festival and has since become a popular fixture on the folk circuit.

what to buy: Siegel first released *Snap!* (Schoolkids Records, 1992, prod. Neil Scott and Dick Siegel) ♪♪♪♪ on his own tiny Boo-Kay records in 1980, but it wasn't until its re-release over a decade later that the record found a wider audience for its jazzy, swing sound.

what to buy next: On *Angels Aweigh,* (Schoolkids, 1994, prod. Paul Pearcy and Dick Siegel) ♪♪♪♪ Siegel loses some of the jazziness and puts the emphasis on a gentler folk sound.

what to avoid: Siegel's turn with 80's party band Tracy Lee and the Leonards on the cassette-only *Tomorrow Morning* (Schoolkids Records, 1993, prod. Dick Siegel, George Bedard and Greg Ward) ♪ sounds dated now.

worth searching for: During the 80s, Siegel made a compilation of his live performances with his band the Ministers of Melody on the cassette-only *Dick Siegel Live* (Boo-Kay, 1984, prod. Dick Siegel) ♪♪♪

▶▶ Townes Van Zandt, Mark Eitzel, John Doe (X)

◀◀ Dr. John, Bob Dylan

Jill Hamilton

The Silos /Vulgar Boatmen/Walter Salas-Humara

Formed 1985 in New York City, N.Y.

The Silos—Bob Rupe, guitar, vocals (1985-91); Walter Salas-Humara, guitar, vocals; Mary Rowell, violin (1985-90, 1991-present). Vulgar Boatmen—Salas-Humara; Robert Ray, guitar, vocals; Dale Lawrence, guitar, vocals

As musicians in Florida—Salas-Humara in Gainesville, Rupe in Ft. Lauderdale—the two musicians took a defiantly independent route to distributing the unadorned country-tinged pop sound of their separate bands. The two left their bands and moved to New York within six months of each other, and in 1985 they put together the Silos, continuing their independent course until the major lables came courting—which led to a short-lived and unpleasant experience with RCA and the Silos' eventual return to the proud ranks of the independents.

what to buy: The offhand, ramshackle recklessness of the Silos' *Susan Across the Ocean* (Watermelon, 1994, prod. Walter Salas-Humara and David McNair) ♪♪♪♪ is beguiling, with choice covers such as "Let's Take Some Drugs and Drive Around" fitting alongside the group's originals.

what to buy next: The Boatmen's *You and Your Sister* (Safe House, prod. Walter Salas-Humara) ♪♪♪♪ is a sterling debut of winsome melodic hooks and jittery charm ("Fallen Down," "Drive Somehwere"), introducing the songwriting talents of Ray and Lawrence. The Silos/Salas-Humara release *Ask the Dust* (Watermelon, 1995, prod. Walter Salas-Humara) ♪♪♪♪ is a generous sampler of early solo recordings and previously unreleased Silos work, many of which were originally recorded at friends' lofts and other intimate locales, which lends an organic immediacy to the album.

what to avoid: Salas-Humara's solo album *Radar,* (Watermelon, 1995, prod. Walter Salas-Humara) ♪♪♪ on which the fuller, harsher waves of dischord overtake his melodic sensibilities. As this is a significantly different record from anything else in his catalogue, it's not the place to start.

the rest: The Silos—*Cuba* (Watermelon, 1987) ♪♪♪♪ *Hasta La Victoria!* (Watermelon, 1992) ♪♪♪♪

worth searching for: *The Silos,* (RCA, 1990) ♪♪♪♪ the band's out-of-print major label debut, is engaging even though it sacrifices none of the lean pull of its earlier work. The Boatmen's *Please Panic* (Safe House, 1992, prod. Jonathon Isley and

Robert Ray) is arguably a stronger and better sounding record than *You and Your Sister*, with the Boatmen's light touch zeroeing in like a homing pidgeon.

Beat Happening, Uncle Tupelo, Son Volt, Wilco

Buddy Holly, Johnny Cash, Waylon Jennings, Buffalo Springfield

Allan Orski

Gene Simmons

See: Kiss

Patrick Simmons

See: The Doobie Brothers

Simon and Garfunkel

Formed 1956 in New York, N.Y. Broke up in 1970.

Paul Simon, vocals, guitar; Art Garfunkel, vocals

Never mind that their first hit happened after they had broken up a second time; Simon and Garfunkel proved one of the most durable of the folk groups of the 60s—and all-time. Boyhood friends who had a minor hit ("Hey, Schoolgirl") in 1957 as Tom and Jerry, they recorded on and off, including a folk album, *Wednesday Morning, 3 A.M.*, in 1964 before Simon headed off to England. It might have ended there, but for producer Tom Wilson; the rock backing that he added to "The Sounds of Silence" sounds more forced and intrusive today than it did back then, but it proved perfect radio fare for the mid-'60s alongside the chiming guitars of the Byrds' "Turn, Turn, Turn" and the Beatles' "We Can Work It Out."

Simon returned and came up with literate, ambitious songs like "Homeward Bound," "I Am a Rock," "The Dangling Conversation," "The Boxer" and "Mrs. Robinson"—the latter a massive hit in the soundtrack for "The Graduate." Those, with equally ambitious production, became some of the era's biggest hits and threaded together the folk/protest movement of the early '60s, Simon's earlier Brill Building apprenticeship and the burgeoning singer/songwriter movement. If his confessional lyrics often seemed pretentiously literary (see "Richard Cory") and were considered sophomoric tripe by some critics, they were also seen as poetry by the baby boom generation entering college. In fact, Simon's lyrics often found their way into college literature and poetry courses.

The obvious disparity in the act—Simon was musically adept, wrote the songs and sang most of them; Garfunkel played no instrument, sang harmony and occasional lead—resulted in their parting while they were at a creative and commercial peak with *Bridge Over Troubled Water*, their most successful album and, with the title track (their last No. 1) Garfunkel's best moment. Garfunkel went on to films ("Catch-22," "Carnal Knowledge") and a part-time recording career. Simon began a more successful solo career. They have collaborated occasionally since then, including a massive reunion concert in New York's Central Park during 1981. After Simon and Garfunkel, any nerd with a sensitive lyric, a few guitar moves and a friend singing would become fair game for the pop market.

what to buy: *Bookends* (Columbia, 1968, prod. Simon, Garfunkel and Roy Halee), holds together like a concept album, with the film hit "Mrs. Robinson" crassly tacked on at the end. *Parsley, Sage, Rosemary and Thyme* (Columbia, 1966, prod. Bob Johnston), is their real first album together as S&G. *Bridge Over Troubled Water* (Columbia, 1970, prod. Simon, Garfunkel and Roy Halee), is considered their masterpiece, though today it sounds overproduced.

what to buy next: *Sounds of Silence* (Columbia, 1966, prod. Bob Johnston), is basically an electric reworking of *The Paul Simon Songbook* (CBS UK, 1965), adding the electrified "Sounds of Silence."

what to avoid: *The Graduate* (Columbia, 1968, prod. Teo Macero) Yes, it was an important soundtrack; no, it doesn't have anything new on it except "Mrs. Robinson." *The Concert in Central Park*, (Warner Bros., 1982, prod. Simon, Garfunkel, Roy Halee and Phil Ramone) is a too-late attempt to recapture the magic.

the rest: *Wednesday Morning, 3 A.M.* (Columbia, 1966) *Greatest Hits* (Columbia, 1972)

worth searching for: *Collected Works* (Columbia, 1990, prod. Various) combines all the studio albums on three compact discs.

James Taylor, George Harrison, Jim Croce, Jackson Browne, Mary Chapin Carpenter, Joe Henry, Sheryl Crow

Pete Seeger, Weavers, Peter, Paul and Mary, Bob Dylan, Kingston Trio, Beach Boys, Everly Brothers

Leland Rucker

Carly Simon

Born June 25, 1945, in New York, N.Y.

Simon's career began more than 30 years ago when she dueted with her sister, Lucy, on "Winken Blinken and Nod," a modest hit on the Kapp label. After a couple of false starts, Simon—whose father co-founded the Simon & Schuster publishing house and who was married to James Taylor between 1972-73—landed a deal with Elektra and her self-titled debut was released in 1971, and since then she has released 23 albums. Her warm, often vulnerable-sounding vocals share romantic intimacies, child-like wonders and bold observations. Though she's released a continuous stream of recordings, the 70s remain her most-accomplished decade; part of her appeal, as well as a problem, is that no one knows quite what to expect from one recording to the next—an artistically bold approach but one that hasn't helped Simon build a loyal, dependable audience. Her spotty *Hotcakes* album is a case in point; she scored a hit with the bouyant "Mockingbird" (a duet with Taylor), but it was her more introspective and heartfelt songs such as "Haven't Got Time for the Pain" that rang the truest.

what to buy: Simon's first three albums remain her best. *No Secrets* (Elektra, 1972, prod. Richard Perry) is forthright, passionate and wonderfully outspoken, particularly on the great put-down classic "You're So Vain." Her debut, *Carly Simon,* (Elektra, 1971, prod. Eddie Kramer) is a fine melding of rock, pop, blues, country and ballads. She landed a deserved Top 10 with the lead track, "That's the Way I Always Heard It Should Be." *Anticipation* (Elektra, 1971, prod. Paul Samwell-Smith) is not as varied and lacks the instrumental depth of Simon's debut, but her vocals carry the album in an increasingly confident and at times confidential manner.

what to buy next: *Coming Around Again* (Arista, 1987, prod. Various) is a mature, confident work with hits in the title track, "All I Want Is You" and "Give Me All Night." *Letters Never Sent* (Arista, 1994, prod. N/A) takes an interesting concept—notes and letters that Simon has stashed away—and turns it into a rich, personal musical outing.

what to avoid: Simon's to attempts to cover American popular standards generally wind up in failure. Though her heart may be in *Torch* (Warner Bros., 1981) **WOOF!** and *My Romance* (Arista, 1990) **WOOF!** her pipes and tone are incompatible, so removed from the high quality of the real thing as to be an embarrassment.

the rest: *Hotcakes* (Elektra, 1974) *Playing Possum* (Elektra, 1974) *The Best of Carly Simon* (Elektra, 1975) *Another Passenger* (Elektra, 1976) *Boys in the Trees* (Elektra, 1978) *Spy* (Elektra, 1979) *Come Upstairs* (Elektra, 1980) *Hello Big Man* (Warner Bros., 1983) *Spoiled Girl* (Epic, 1985) **WOOF!** *Heartburn* soundtrack (Arista, 1986) *Working Girl* soundtrack (Arista, 1988) *Greatest Hits Live* (Arista, 1988) *Have You Seen Me Lately* (Arista, 1990) *Postcards From the Edge* soundtrack (Arista, 1990) *This is My Life* soundtrack (Qwest, 1992) *Clouds In My Coffee: 1965-1995* (Arista, 1995)

▶▶ Melissa Manchester, Olivia Newton-John, Helen Reddy, Yvonne Elliman

◀◀ James Taylor, Cat Stevens, Joni Mitchell, Carole King, Laura Nyro, Judy Collins, William Butler Yeats

Patrick McCarty

Paul Simon

Born Oct. 13, 1941 in Newark, N.J.

Riding high on the success of Simon and Garfunkel's "Bridge Over Troubled Water"—the duo's last gasp—Simon began strong as a solo artist, churning out five hits from his first three albums before cooling off. His attempt at a movie about the life of a touring rock act ("One Trick Pony") flopped, and his 1983 *Hearts and Bones*—which started as a reunion album with Garfunkel—is still his worst-seller. In 1986 he took a chance, recording with South African musicians and then adding his own lyrics to the instrumental tracks. The resulting collaboration, *Graceland*, became one of the most influential albums of the 80s, exposing African music to American mainstream audiences like never before. Since then, he has recorded only one studio album, *The Rhythm of the Saints*, a less-successful attempt to fuse Brazilian music and his lyrics. Still, he remains one of the rock era's most accomplished and ambitious artists.

what to buy: *Graceland,* (Warner Bros., 1986, prod. Paul Simon) is an amazing comeback and still the best collaboration between a Western songwriter and African musicians. *Paul Simon* (Warner Bros., 1972, prod. Paul Simon and Roy Halee) picks up the world music groove—which he lightly pursued with Garfunkel—on the hits "Mother and Child Reunion" and "Me and Julio Down By the Schoolyard."

what to buy next: *Live Rhymin,'* (Columbia, 1974, prod. Phil Ramone) a well-recorded live set that featured the Dixie Hummingbirds singing backup and the Peruvian folk troupe Urubamba. *Still Crazy After All These Years* (Warner Bros. 1975, prod. Paul Simon) features classy songs caught in a rich, 70s-styled production.

what to avoid: *Hearts and Bones* (Warner Bros., 1983, prod. Paul Simon, Russ Titelman, Roy Halee and Lenny Waronker), contains one great song ("The Late Great Johnny Ace") but also features selections such as "When Numbers Get Serious" and "Cars Are Cars," which are as silly as their titles imply.

the rest: *There Goes Rhymin' Simon* (Columbia, 1973) *Greatest Hits, Etc.* (Columbia, 1977) *One Trick Pony* (Warner Bros., 1980) *Negotiations and Love Songs* (Warner Bros., 1988) *The Rhythm of the Saints* (Warner Bros., 1990) *Paul Simon's Concert in the Park* (Warner Bros., 1991) *Paul Simon 1964/1993* (Warner Bros., 1993)

worth searching for: *Paul Simon: The Collection* (Warner Bros., 1991), a three-volume Japanese set that includes a selection of Simon's hits, a live set from his "Graceland" tour and an interview.

James Taylor, George Harrison, Jim Croce, Jackson Browne, Mary Chapin Carpenter, Joe Henry, Sheryl Crow

Pete Seeger, Weavers, Peter, Paul and Mary, Bob Dylan, Kingston Trio, Beach Boys, Everly Brothers

Leland Rucker

Simple Minds

Formed 1977 in Glasgow, Scotland

Jim Kerr, vocals; Charlie Burchill, guitar, keyboards; Duncan Barnwell, guitar (1977-78); Mick McNeil, keyboards; Tony Donald, bass (1977-78); Derek Forbes, bass (1978-84); Brian McGee, drums (1977-80); Kenny Hyslop, drums (1980); Mike Ogletree, drums (1980-82); Mel Gaynor, drums (1982-); Michael McNeil, keyboards (1977-89); John Giblin, bass (1984-89); Robin Clark, vocals (1984-89); Sue Hadjopoulos, percussion (1984-89); Peter Vitesse, keyboards (1989-93)

Simple Minds sprung out of the English punk scene of the late 70s, but it was a punk band with good musical skills. The band originally started with Kerr and Burchill as Johnny and The Self Abusers with a 7-inch single featuring the tracks "Saints And Sinners" and "Dead Vandals." While the first album, *Life In A Day,* proved to be more influenced by psychedelic pop, the band's roots were firmly entrenched in a post-punk feel, even before punk had died. Simple Minds rode through many phases—including industrial, New Wave, the short-lived New Romantic movement and heartily into arena rock of the mid-80s thanks to the massive hit "Don't You (Forget About Me)" from the film "The Breakfast Club." It wasn't until the early 90s that the band—by this point a duo—found its own groove. The band moved into new territory, really only navigated by the likes of Peter Gabriel and a handful of others, with a slant toward World Music and influences from early Celtic folk songs.

what to buy: *New Gold Dream* (Virgin/A&M, 1983, prod. Peter Welsh) is as solid a post-New Wave album as you can find. Ranging from gloomy to introspective, the one word that seems to best describe this record is grandiose. The sound of the recording, even on vinyl, has the ability to fill a room with a glow.

what to buy next: *Glittering Prize* (A&M, 1993, prod. Various) is a safe bet. It's a rather impressive singles collection that offers a nice overview of the band's history, although it's rather stunted in that it doesn't include but one song prior to *New Gold Dream Sparkle In The Rain,* (Virgin/A&M, 1984, prod. Peter Welsh) was the band's stylistic follow-up to *New Gold Dream.* Showing a smarter but less open sound than previous efforts, this record has moments where it almost rocks. The second half (second *side* in the old days) showed the band's experimental side, with instrumentals and a Lou Reed cover ("Street Hassle"). The modern side of Simple Minds is revealed on *Good News From The Next World* (Virgin, 1995, prod. Keith Forsey and Simple Minds) which, while not as good as the mid-80s material, makes an effort to recapture that vibe. Hitting the charts with "She's A River," the album goes a long way toward returning the band to the limelight.

what to avoid: *Real Life* (A&M, 1991, prod. Stephen Lipsey) showed the band trying to live up to the commercial success of the massive *Once Upon A Time* and falling flat.

the rest: *Life In A Day* (Virgin, 1979) *Real to Real Cacophony* (Virgin, 1980) *Empires And Dance* (Virgin, 1980) *Sons And Fascination/Sister Feelings Call* (Virgin, 1981) *Once Upon A Time* (A&M, 1985) *Live In The City Of Lights* (A&M, 1987) *Street Fighting Years* (A&M, 1989)

The Call, U2, Jars Of Clay, Zerra One, Tears For Fears

Roxy Music, Peter Gabriel, Genesis, King Crimson

Tim Davis

Simply Red

Formed 1982 in Manchester, England

Mick Hucknall, vocals; Sylvan Richardson, guitar (1985-89); Fritz

McIntyre, keyboards; Tony Bowers, bass; Chris Joyce, drums; Tim Kellett, horns, keyboards; Aziz Ibrahim, guitar (1989-91); Ian Kirkham, sax (1989)

With its polished commercial soul sound and R&B riffs, Simply Red was a fresh-sounding new force when it landed in the U.S. during the 80s. Lead singer and band leader Hucknall, who sang in punk bands during the late 70s and early 80s, was the key to this success, singing in a plaintive high tenor that evokes yearning and loss and has just enough texture to make it interesting. It continues to provide a good counter to the band's slick and slightly tame arrangements, which have worked for the occasional hit—"Holding Back the Years" in 1985 and with its cover of Harold Melvin and the Blue Notes' "If You Don't Know Me by Now" four years later.

what to buy: *Picture Book*, (Elektra, 1985, prod. Stewart Levine) ♪♪♪♪ the band's debut, was a revelation that showcased Richardson's classical background brought and Hucknall's tremendously emotional singing. The result is Stax/Volt meets Philly soul and two of the year's best singles in "Holding Back the Years" and the group's rendition of "Money$ Too Tight to Mention."

what to buy next: After some middling releases in-between, *Stars* (EastWest, 1991) is Simply Red's strongest album since its debut.

what to avoid: Coming after such a stellar debut, *Men & Women* (Elektra, 1987, prod. Alex Sadkin) ♪♪ is a significant sophomore slump—even though Hucknall had Motow great Lamont Dozier as a collaborator.

the rest: *A New Flame* (Elektra, 1989) ♪♪♪ *Life* (EastWest, 1995) ♪♪♪

▶▶ Lisa Stansfield, Rick Astley, the Committments

◀◀ Bobby Purify, Smokey Robinson, the Dells, Harold Melvin and the Blue Notes

Patrick McCarty

Nancy Sinatra

Born June 8, 1940 in Jersey City, N.J.

It's unlikely Nancy Sinatra would have enjoyed much of a music career were it not for her famous father. Sporting a set of average-sounding pipes, she passed muster on a slew of uneven albums that today play like deliciously kitschy novelties. With producer Lee Hazelwood, Sinatra found success, first in tough, sex-kitten "go-go" music (typified by her 1966 hit "These Boots Are Made for Walkin'") and later on a string of bizarre modern Western tunes penned by Hazelwood. Whatever one makes of her singing, Sinatra's musical backing (including Hal Blaine, James Burton, and Larry Knechtel) was impeccable, and her lightweight pop was masterfully performed. Without exception, Sinatra's albums follow a prescribed formula: a hit title track, a few adequate remakes of contemporary hits and a whole passal of Hazelwood's disquieting country-western songs. *Hit Years* (WEA/Atlantic/Rhino, 1986, prod. Lee Hazelwood) ♪♪♪♪ is the album to own, containing all of Sinatra's solo hits, her duets with dad, plus the best of her output with Hazelwood ("Some Velvet Morning," "Sugar Town" and the head-bobbin' truckin' song "Jackson").

the rest: *Boots* (Reprise/Sundazed, 1966) ♪♪ *How Does That Grab You?* (Sundazed, 1966) ♪♪ *Nancy in London* (Reprise/Sundazed, 1966) ♪♪ *Sugar* (Sundazed, 1967) ♪

Christopher Scapelliti

Siouxsie and the Banshees

Formed 1976 in London, England. Disbanded 1996.

Siouxsie Sioux (born Susan Dallion), vocals; Steve Severin, bass; Marco Pirroni, guitar (1976-77); Peter Fenton, guitar (1977); John McKay, guitar, 1977-79); Robert Smith, guitar (1979-80, 1983-84); John McGeoch, guitar (1980-83); John Carruthers, guitar (1984-87); Jon Klein, guitar (1987-96); Sid Vicious, drums (1976-77); Kenny Morris, drums (1977-79); Budgie, drums (1979-96); Martin McCarrick, cello, keyboards (1987-96)

The spiritual godmother of Gothic rock, Siouxsie Sioux was a British punk fan who turned her admiration into action, forming the Banshees for a 1976 English punk festival, with future Sex Pistols bassist Vicious on drums. Group membership changed frequently, particularly in the guitar position, which has included Marco Pirroni (later of Adam and the Ants) and Robert Smith (the Cure founder, who appeared on *Hyaena* and the live *Nocturne*). Originally a punk band with arty pretensions, the Banshees gradually evolved into a more dance-oriented group. But the group's lofty status among the future alternative crowd rarely translated into mainstream success in the United States, but its egos and record sales got a big boost by its inclusion on the first Lollapalooza tour in 1991. Sioux, who dabbled with a side project called The Creatures in the 1980s, broke up the Banshees in 1996; she and Budgie, her husband, plan to continue their side project, The Creatures.

what to buy: Most of the band's albums sound dated now, but the second hits collection, *Twice Upon a Time—The Singles,* (Geffen, 1992, prod. Various) at least displays a clarity of vision and conviction that runs through the group's groovy Gothic-art-punk rock. This set rounds up singles released between 1981-92, after the band signed with Geffen.

what to buy next: Some of the crude punk trappings had worn off by the time the Banshees released *Juju,* (Geffen, prod. the Banshees/Nigel Gray) a dark, mysterious, sometimes sensual record that combined Sioux's pained lyrics with smartly evocative grooves.

what to avoid: The live album *Nocturne* (Geffen, 1983, prod. Siouxsie and the Banshees) was recorded during one of Smith's tenures in the band but isn't compelling beyond that.

the rest: *The Scream* (Polydor, 1978/Geffen, 1992) *Kaleidoscope* (PVC, 1980/Geffen,MDBR *1992)* Once Upon a Time: The Singles *(PVC, 1981/Geffen, 1984)* A Kiss in the Dreamhouse *(Polydor U.K., 1982/Geffen, 1984)* Hyaena *(Geffen, 1984)* Tinderbox *(Geffen, 1986)* Though the Looking Glass *(Geffen, 1987)* Peepshow *(Geffen, 1988)* The Peel Sessions *(Strange Fruit, 1991)* Superstition *(Geffen, 1991)* The Rapture *(Geffen, 1995)*

worth searching for: The British CD-5 single for "Cities in Dust" from the *Tinderbox* album, which features five extra non-album songs.

▶▶ The Cure, Alanis Morissette, Hole

◀◀ the Sex Pistols, New York Dolls, Ramones

Doug Pullen

Sir Douglas Quintet /Doug Sahm

Formed 1964 in California. Disbanded 1972. Re-formed 1994.

Doug Sahm, guitar, vocals; Augie Meyers, organ, vocals; Francisco Moran, saxophone; Harvey Kagan, bass; Johnny Perez, drums

Although it was Meyer's organ that would distinguish the unique sound of the Sir Douglas Quintet's hits, the group was the brainchild of San Antonio, Texas-born and original cosmic cowboy Sahm, who has kept the name going on and off in various incarnations. A steel guitar prodigy—he was placed on Hank Williams Sr.'s lap just before Williams died—Sahm began performing as Little Doug Sahm at age 6. In 1964, after moving to California and recruiting Meyers, Sahm started the quintet. Although the music of the group's first big single, "She's About a Mover," produced by Cajun wildman Huey Meaux, was a mixed bag of border conjunto and San Francisco psychedelia (especially Meyer's primal organ licks), the long hair and quasi-royal name had many thinking the quintet hailed from England. The band had one more hit, 1969's "Mendocino," before Sahm began a fascinating, checkered solo career that has included recordings with Bob Dylan, Dr. John, Flaco Jimenez, David (Fathead) Newman, Yusef Lateef and most recently with Freddie Fender, Jimenez and Meyer as the Texas Tornados. Sahm's wry blend of rock, country, conjunto, soul and horn-based R&B has grown even better with age, and he remains an understated master of stringed instruments. In fact, a couple of Sahm's latest albums are among his best, and the old stuff sounds more revolutionary than it did when it was released. Sahm, in whatever incarnation, represents Texas music at its finest.

what to buy: Two recent solo albums capture the heady ambience of Sahm's amalgam. *Juke Box Music* (Antone's, 1988, prod. Doug Sahm) offers a refreshing set of pure Texas soul classics, including Sahm's unforgettably tasty cover of Little Sunny's "Talk to Me." *The Last Real Texas Blues Band* (Antone's, 1994, prod. Doug Sahm and Derek O'Brien) forms a perfect bookend, reprising the R&B of the big horn bands that Sahm chewed up in San Antonio in the 50s, recorded live with a fine big band at Antone's, one of Sahm's favorite Austin haunts. *Best of Doug Sahm and the Sir Douglas Quintet* (Mercury, 1990, prod. Doug Sahm) has 22 tracks that fill in many of the gaps in Sahm's canon before the Antone's discs.

what to buy next: *Best of Doug Sahm and Friends: Atlantic Sessions,* (Rhino, 1992) an eclectic selection from Sahm's two early 70s Atlantic albums. It includes Sahm's collaborations with Dylan.

what to avoid: *Daydreaming at Midnight,* (Elektra, 1994, prod. Doug Sahm and Doug Clifford) a recent heavy-metal version of the Quintet with Sahm's son Shawn on second guitar.

the rest: *Amos Garrett, Doug Sahm, Gene Taylor* (Rykodisc, 1989)

worth searching for: You can't go wrong with most of the quintet's long-out-of-print vinyl albums, especially *Honkey Blues,* (Smash, 1968)

▶▶ Sam the Sham and the Pharoahs, ? and the Mysterians, Mouse and the Traps, Creedence Clearwater Revival, Joe (King) Carrasco and the Crowns, Elvis Costello and the Attractions, Uncle Tupelo

◄◄ Hank Williams, Freddie Fender, Santiago Jimenez Sr., Little Sunny and the Skyliners, T-Bone Walker, Junior Parker, Bobby (Blue) Bland, Howlin, Wolf, Jimmy Reed

see also: *Texas Tornadoes*

Leland Rucker

The Skeletons /The Morells

The Skeletons (1979-present)—Lou Whitney, bass, vocals; D. Clinton Thompson, guitar, vocals; Bobby Lloyd Hicks, drums, vocals; Randle Chowning, guitar, harmonica, vocals (1979); Nick Sibley, keyboards, guitar, harmonica, vocals (1979-88); Joe Terry, keyboards, vocals (1988, 1990-present); Kelly Brown, keyboards, vocals (1990-present). The Morells (1980-87)—Whitney; Thompson; Maralie, keyboards, vocals; Ron Gremp, drums, vocals; Joe Terry, keyboard, vocals (1983-87)

Purveyors of roots rock in nearly all its myriad guises, the Skeletons and Morells—different expressions of the same sensibility—are the greatest bar bands you never heard. Its members have assimilated an astounding array of influences—rockabilly, country, R&B, beach music, frat rock and Phil Spector are all in there someplace—for an eclecticism that may be too clever for their own good. The Skeletons formed from the ashes of the Original Symptoms, then took a hiatus when Whitney, Thompson and Hicks backed Steve Forbert for a spell. Whitney and Thompson then chose to start the Morells before re-activating the Skeletons during the late 80s. The Skeletons continue to work on their own and as a popular backing band for other artists; most recently the group co-produced and backed Syd Straw on her latest album, *War and Peace.* The Morells' *Shake and Push* (Borrowed Records, 1982/East Side Digital, 1989, prod. the Morells) ♪♪♪♪♪ is an absolute masterpiece of what was not yet called roots rock. Drawing on obscure sources from across the musical spectrum, *Shake and Push* is a rockin' dance-floor delight with lots of wry humor in the fitness ode "Gettin' in Shape," "Bumble Boogie," "Beatnik" and a cover of the Maddox Brothers and Rose's hilarious "Ugly and Slouchy." The Skeletons' *In the Flesh!* (East Side Digital, 1991, prod. the Skeletons) ♪♪♪♪ collects terrific early singles such as Whitney's brilliant "Trans Am," Sibley's nuclear-age warning "Sour Snow," and a rocked-up version of Peter, Paul & Mary's "Very Last Day." *Waiting* (Alias, 1993, prod. the Skeletons) ♪♪♪♪ puts more emphasis on originals such as Thompson's pop gem "Downtown" and Terry's 12-step anthem "Things We Need," though the wild selection of covers—the Easybeats' "St. Louis," the Beach Boys' obscurity "How She Boogalooed It," a funk version of Waylon Jennings' "Only Daddy That'll Walk the Line"—are a hoot.

By Daniel Durchholz

Skid Row

Formed 1986 in New Jersey

Matt Fallon, vocals (1986-87); Dave "Snake" Sabo, guitar; Scotti Hill, guitar; Rachel Bolan, bass; Rob Affuso, drums; Sebastian Bach (born Sebastian Bierk), vocals (1987-present)

Owing its success first to Bon Jovi and then to MTV, Skid Row's derivative success didn't last long. Signing Bon Jovi's original guitarist proved to be one of the band's smartest moves, since it gave it the chance to open for the hugely popular band in 1989. After a few hits from the first album—including MTV's embrace of "Youth Gone Wild"—and a lucrative spot opening a tour for Guns N' Roses, the band plummeted into obscurity, making headlines more for Bach's homophobic statements and rowdy antics than for any alleged musical gifts.

what to buy: *Skid Row* (Atlantic, 1989, prod. Michael Wagener) ♪♪ is the apex of Skid Row's existence, selling 4 million copies thanks to Bach's more-operatic-than-Bon Jovi voice and a Guns N' Roses-inspired bad-boy image.

what to buy next: The *B-Sides Ourselves* (Atlantic EP, 1992, prod. Skid Row) ♪♪♪ is the band's most interesting album, playing up its punk fascination with covers of the Ramones' "Psycho Therapy" and Jimi Hendrix' "Little Wing."

what to avoid: By *Subhuman Race* (Atlantic, 1995, prod. Randy Staub) ♪ the band's commercial health mercifully took a turn for the worst.

the rest: *Slave to the Grind* (Atlantic, 1991) ♪♪

►► Ugly Kid Joe, Bush, Alanis Morrissette

◄◄ Poison, Bon Jovi, Warrant, Motley Crue, Guns N' Roses, Ramones, Jimi Hendrix, Sex Pistols

Tracy Birkenhauer and Steve Knopper

Skinny Puppy

Formed 1983 in Vancouver, British Columbia, Canada

cEVIN Key, percussion; Nivek Ogre, vocals; Wilhelm Schroeder, keyboards (1985-86); Dwayne Goettel (1986-95, died Aug. 23, 1995)

Skinny Puppy was born out of the dark imaginations of cEVIN Key (yes, that's how he spells it) and Ogre, who discovered that they shared a taste for bizzare, eerie music and films. The band pioneered a brand of industrial music that used electronics and samples to create not only music but also a mood—usually dark and menacing. Sometimes criticized for borrowing too much from forefathers such as Cabaret Voltaire and Throbbing Gristle, Skinny Puppy has nonetheless left its own stamp on terror-industrial/dance music. The group's mix of thunderous percussion, howling vocals, distorted lyrics and seering electronics results in a generally brutal sound that was picked up by such contemporary mainstream bands as Ministry and nine inch nails.

what to buy: *VIVI SectVI* (Nettwerk, 1988, prod. David Ogilvie and cEVIN Key) ♪♪♪♪ is the most listenable, danceable and satisfying of Skinny Puppy's albums—as well as an overtly political record that attacks crimes against humanity, animals and the world at large. *ain't it dead yet?* (Nettwerk, 1991, prod. David Ogilvie and cEVIN Key) ♪♪♪♪ is a live recording of a ferocious 1989 show at the Toronto Concert Hall that was also released on video. The distorted Barbra Streisand samples that open the show are a nice touch.

what to buy next: *Cleanse Fold and Manipulate,* (Nettwerk, 1987, prod. David Ogilvie and cEVIN Key) ♪♪♪½ Skinny Puppy's third full-length release, was the first full realization of the band's horrific, sonic assault—the first that actually sounds as scary as they want it to. *Too Dark Park* (Nettwerk, 1990, prod. David Ogilvie and cEVIN Key) ♪♪♪ is a dense, bass-heavy album with a richer sound and lyrics that paint a more dismal than usual vision of an apocalyptic, decaying world. *Rabies* (Nettwerk, 1989, prod. David Ogilvie, cEVIN Key and Al Jourgensen) ♪♪♪ is distinguished only by the powerful presence of Ministry's Al Jourgensen, whose thunderous guitar, angry vocals and expert production add a bone to its rating.

what to avoid: *Last Rites* (Nettwerk, 1992, prod. David Ogilvie and cEVIN Key) ♪♪ was recorded just before the band temporarily broke-up and the lack of originality and enthusiasm comes through loud and clear.

the rest: *Bites* (Nettwerk, 1985) ♪♪½ *Mind: The Perpetual Intercourse* (Nettwerk, 1986) ♪♪½ *12 Inch Anthology* (Nettwerk, 1990) ♪♪½

▶▶ Ministry, nine inch nails, Marilyn Manson

◀◀ Cabaret Voltaire, Chrome, Throbbing Gristle

Christopher Scanlon

Slade

Formed 1966 in Wolverhapton, England

Noddy Holder, vocals, guitar; Dave Hill, guitar; Jimmy Lea, bass, piano; Don Powell, drums.

Wildy successful in its homeland during the 70s, Slade pulverized cheesy glam rock into tight anthems of simplistic power chords and thumping backbeats. The band's in-your-face approach and Holder's raw vocals provided an influence for a number of hard and punk rockers that came in its wake. With deliberately misspelled song titles that nodded to its working class roots, Slade's hits such as "Cum On Feel the Noize" and "Mama Weer All Crazee Now" became cornerstones of the glam rock movement and were given second lives when covered by Quiet Riot during the 80s—which allowed Slade an opportunity for its own U.S. hits with "Run Runaway" and "My Oh My." Inexplicably, nothing remains available stateside, although Slade continues its trash rock career across the pond. It's well worth looking for the compilation *Sladest* (Polydor, 1973) ♪♪♪♪ and *Keep Your Hands Off My Power Supply* (CBS, 1984) ♪♪♪

Allan Orski

Slash's Snakepit

See: Guns N' Roses

Slayer

Formed 1982 in Los Angeles, Calif.

Tom Araya, bass, vocals; Jeff Hanneman, guitar; Kerry King, guitar; Dave Lombardo, drums (1982-92); Paul Bostaph, drums (1992-present)

The albums are called *Reign in Blood* and *Hell Awaits.* There are songs with titles such as "Die by the Sword," "The Antichrist" and "Serenity in Murder." Clearly it's not the Carpenters we're talking about here. Slayer is your parent's worst nightmare for the 90s—brutal music, brutal subject matter (death, serial killers, death, Satanism, death), brutal imagery. This is dark, mean and humorless stuff, played at breakneck speed with the same kind of on-a-dime dynamics practiced by early speed metal scene mates Metallica and Megadeth. Unlike those bands, however, Slayer has little chance—or desire—of slipping itself into the pop culture mainstream, though its audience remains a sizable, arena-filling cult. Now *that's* scary.

what to buy: For the timid, might we suggest *Haunting the Chapel,* (Metal Blade EP, 1993) ♪♪♪ a nugget-sized portion of

Slayer music that gives a clear indication of what awaits on the full-length albums. An all-star production team makes *Seasons in the Abyss* (Def American, 1990, prod. Rick Rubin and Andy Wallace) Slayer's best sounding album, with crackling sonics to support the band's aural assault.

what to buy next: *Divine Intervention* (American, 1994, prod. Slayer) is a slightly—ever so slightly—more accessible outing, with the tempos slowed down just a tad and songs that veer away from the horrific to take on the occasional issue, such as "SS-3's" indictment of war criminals.

what to avoid: The debut *Show No Mercy,* (Metal Blade, 1983/1994, prod. Slayer) a spirited but not ready for prime time outing.

the rest: *Live Undead* (Metal Blade, 1984/1994) *Hell Awaits* (Metal Blade, 1985/1994) *Reign in Blood* (Def Jam, 1985) *South of Heaven* (Def Jam, 1988) *Decade of Aggression Live* (Def American, 1991) *Undisputed Attitude* (American, 1996)

worth searching for: The sampler *Metal Massacre III* (Metal Blade, 1983) which features Slayer's auspicious debut, "Aggressive Perfector."

Cannibal Corpse, Sepultura, Entombed

Black Sabbath, Deep Purple, the Minutemen

Gary Graff

Percy Sledge

Born Nov. 25, 1940, in Leighton, Ala.

The diminutive former boxer with the huge voice will forever be remembered for his 1966 hit "When a Man Loves a Woman," a majestic ballad that still moves the soul, regardless of how many weddings you've heard it at. While Sledge never pretended to possess the uptempo, bone-rattling excitement of more celebrated peers such as Otis Redding or Sam and Dave, he was virtually unchallenged when it came to ballads, heartbreakers in particular. Sledge hit the mark, and the charts, many times during the late 60s with weepers marked by his warm, expressive vocal delivery. With 22 tracks, *It Tears Me Up: The Best of Percy Sledge* (Rhino, 1992, prod. Quin Ivy and Marlin Greene) offers the most comprehensive collection on the market, covering all his great tear-jerkers from 1966-71, including his carefully executed renditions of "The Dark End of the Street," "Love Me Tender," and "Try a Little Tenderness." Sledge, his timbre undiminished, returned after a 21-year absence with *Blue Night,* (Pointblank, 1994, prod. Saul Davis and Barry Goldberg) which features top-notch material and help from old hands such as Steve Cropper, Bobby Womack and former Rolling Stone Mick Taylor; Rising to the level of his surroundings, his performance is emotionally centered and nothing less than inspiring.

the rest: *The Best of Percy Sledge* (Atlantic, 1969/1989) *The Ultimate Collection: When A Man Loves a Woman* (Atlantic, 1987) *Greatest Hits: When A Man Loves a Woman* (Hollywood/Rounder) *Best of* (Curb, 1996)

Allan Orski

Sleeper

Formed 1993 in London, England

Louise Wener, vocals, guitar; Jon Stewart, guitar; Diid Osman, bass; Andy McClure, drums

Wener and Stewart decided to start their own band after meeting at Manchester University. Frustrated with the tight-knit, P.C. attitudes of the local music scene, they moved to London and formed Sleeper—a forum for Wener's outspoken views on feminism and sex, delivered within bright, pop-rock tunes. Sleeper's debut, *Smart* (Arista, 1995, prod. Sleeper, Paul Corkett and Ian Broudie) covers the complexities of relationships with a cynical twist. *The It Girl* (Arista, 1996, prod. Stephen Street) goes over the same territory but with lyrics that are more introspective, less cynical and boasting a greater sense of humor.

Anna Glen

Grace Slick

See: Jefferson Airplane

The Slits

Formed 1976 in London, England. Disbanded 1982.

Arri Up, vocals; Palmolive, drums (1976-78); Kate Korus, guitar (1976); Viv Albertine, guitar (1977-81); Tessa Pollott, bass (1977-81); Budgie, drums (1978-79)

In the early days of punk, encouraged by friends like The Clash's Joe Strummer and Mick Jones, The Slits formed with former Flowers of Romance members Albertine and Palmolive, and with Up—fresh out of German boarding school at the ripe age of 14. Armed with a raucous and chaotic attitude, The Slits played its first gig on the 1977 White Riot tour with the Buzzcocks, Subway Sect and The Clash. The dub-influenced *Cut* (Antilles, 1978, prod. Dennis Bovell) ♪♪♪ is a more sophisticated than anarchic, probably owing more to reggae dubmaster Bovell's production. It remains their sole record released in the U.S.

Anna Glen

Sloan

Formed 1991 in Nova Scotia, Canada

Jay Ferguson, guitars, vocals; Chris Murphy, bass, vocals; Patrick Pentland, guitars, vocals; Andrew Scott, drums, vocals

Sloan's brand of pop sounds at times like a science experiment gone wrong and at other times so sugary-sweet it makes your molars ache. Either way you can't go wrong. This Great White North foursome has released three full-length albums and an EP, and while perfectly accessible guitar pop is Sloan's game, the buying public hasn't quite played along. Lost in the Geffen Records' power packed early 90s roster (Nirvana, Guns N' Roses, Counting Crows), Sloan's slow sales ended its brief American major label experience. But the band sounds absolutely liberated on its latest album, *One Chord to Another,* (Murder Records, 1996, prod. Sloan) ♪♪♪♪ a work of exuberant pop and mature style that renders everything else in its catalog almost irrelevant. Sloan takes listeners on a musical trip through decades of pop music from the Who-sounding "Anyone Whose Anyone" to the almost Chicago-styled "Everything You've Done Wrong."

the rest: *Peppermint* (Murder EP, 1992) ♪♪ *Smeared* (Geffen, 1992) ♪♪♪ *Twice Removed* (Geffen, 1994) ♪♪♪

Chris Richards

Slowdive /Mojave 3

Formed 1989 in Reading, Britain

Slowdive (1989-94): Rachel Goswell, vocals, guitar; Nick Chaplin, bass; Neil Halstead, vocals, guitar; Ian McCutcheon, drums (1994-present); Christian Saville, guitar; Simon Scott, drums (1989-94); Mojave 3 (1995-present): Goswell, Halstead, McCutcheon

Started as a noise-tinged My Bloody Valentine/Sonic Youth clone by school friends Halstead and Goswell, Slowdive did not take long to evolve into its own wondrous entity. Taking the inventive aesthetics of its progenitors, Slowdive quickly gained acclaim in Britain as a moving force of the so-called dream-pop pack, alongside bands such as Chapterhouse, Ride and the Pale Saints. When the fickle British audience cooled to that sound, however, Slowdive took a dive, trying in vein to re-invent itself as an ambient outfit. The group fizzled to an end, while Halstead, Goswell and drummer McCutcheon breathed new life into their music-making in the new band Mojave 3.

what to buy: Slowdive's debut album, *Just For A Day* (Creation/SBK, 1991, prod. Chris Hufford and Neil Halstead) ♪♪♪♪♪ was the definitive dreampop record, channeling droning guitars, lush melodies and velvety textures into an astral musical mix.

what to buy next: Mojave 3's debut, *Ask Me Tomorrow* (4AD, 1996, prod. Paul Tipler and Mojave 3) ♪♪♪♪ casts away Slowdive's daydreaming ways in favor of stirring up the sum and substance of languid pop greats such as Neil Young, Leonard Cohen and Lee Hazlewood.

what to avoid: The U.K.-only *Pygmalion,* (Creation, 1994, prod. Slowdive) ♪♪ a tired and bleary album that got the band dropped from its record label.

the rest: *Souvlaki* (Creation/SBK, 1994, Slowdive) ♪♪♪

▶▶ Medicine, Garbage, Saint Etienne

◀◀ Cocteau Twins, The Byrds, My Bloody Valentine, Lee Hazlewood, Brian Eno

Aidin Vaziri

Sly & Robbie

See: Black Uhuru

Sly and the Family Stone

Formed 1967 in San Francisco, Calif.

Sly Stone (born Sylvester Stewart), keyboards, guitar, vocals; Freddie Stone, guitar, vocals; Larry Graham, bass, vocals (1967-72); Rosie Stone, keyboards, vocals; Greg Errico, drums (1967-72); Jerry Martini, saxophone; Cynthia Robinson, trumpet

Sly Stone dragged black music into the modern era. He bridged the worlds of traditional rhythm and blues and the new '60s rock sound with a dazzling amalgam of rock, soul and gospel, and music was never the same again. By the time Sly and his Family Stone burst onto the radio with the 1968 hit, "Dance To the Music," the bandleader had already amassed an extraordinary background in music. His recording career dates back to a childhood 78 RPM gospel record he made with his family, the Stewart Family Four, and he notched a regional doo-wop hit before he was out of high school in Vallejo, Calif. As a disc jockey, he was the fastest talking, jivingest spieler on two Bay Area soul stations. As a house producer for San Francisco-based Autumn Records, he supervised hit records by Bobby Freeman ("C'mon and Swim"), the Beau Brummels ("Laugh Laugh") and an assortment of lesser knowns like the Great Society, which featured a young, pre-Airplane Grace Slick. But with the Family Stone—the rich, throbbing thump-and-pluck bass of Larry Graham, colorful contrapuntal vocal harmonies and sassy, brassy, downright uppity sloganeering songs—Sly led his band to the mountain of Woodstock and beyond before succumbing to massive drug abuse and titanic flights of ego. One of the most talented musicians to ever tackle the soul scene, Stone himself was reduced to a cocaine ravaged wraith, a fugitive from justice for several years during the late 80s. But his vast influence becomes only more pervasive as the years pass.

what to buy: The band's fourth album, *Stand!* (Epic, 1969, prod. Sly Stone) remains Stone's towering achievement, an album by turns militant ("Don't Call Me Nigger, Whitey"), paranoid ("Somebody's Watching You") and inspirational ("Everyday People," "You Can Make It If You Try").

what to buy next: Although the band's record label has done an abysmal job of introducing the full body of work to the digital domain, the unheralded first three albums—*A Whole New Thing*, (Epic, 1967, prod. Sly Stone) *Life* (Epic 1968) and *Dance To the Music* (Epic, 1968, prod. Sly Stone) —have been made available with previously unreleased bonus tracks. His epic, angry and sarcastic masterpiece, *There's a Riot Goin' On*, (Epic, 1971, prod. Sylvester Stewart) is a bitter, snarling diatribe that presaged his downfall.

the rest: *Greatest Hits* (Epic 1970) *Anthology* (Epic, 1981)

worth searching for: A collection of largely unreleased Autumn Records solo recordings and productions, *Precious Stone: In the Studio With Sly Stone 1963-1965* (Ace, 1994, prod. Sly Stone) was released in England, where his 1972 album, *Fresh* (Edsel, 1987, prod. Sly Stone) is also available. In used record stores, it is still possible to find the Billy Preston album, *The Wildest Organ In Town* (Capitol, 1966, prod. Steve Douglas) with Sly playing piano and the original version of what later became the Sly and the Family Stone standard, "I Want To Take You Higher."

▶▶ Temptations, Stevie Wonder, Miles Davis, Funkadelic, Prince, Red Hot Chili Peppers

◀◀ Otis Redding, Lenny Bruce, Swan Silvertones

Joel Selvin

The Small Faces

See: The Faces

Smashing Pumpkins

Formed 1989 in Chicago, Ill.

Billy Corgan, vocals, guitar; James Iha, guitar; D'arcy Wretzky, bass, vocals; Jimmy Chamberlin, drums (1989-96)

The Smashing Pumpkins were among the first groups to dive through the alternative-rock portal Nirvana opened during the early 90s. Then, after Kurt Cobain died and Nirvana broke up, the Pumpkins found themselves de facto leaders of a popular youth culture hungry for loud guitars and unhappy anthems. In his songs, singer-songwriter Corgan sometimes whines like a spoiled brat and other times screeches in an exhilarating complement to Iha's grunge noise. Racked with personal problems almost from the beginning—most notably over Corgan's tight-fisted control and Chamberlin's reported drug use—the Pumpkins held together and wound up co-headlining the third+ Lollapalooza tour. The Technicolor videos for "Today" and "Cherub Rock" resulted in smash hits and shot 1993's *Siamese Dream* album well past platinum. For an encore, Corgan drew from such reviled rock sources as Emerson, Lake and Palmer and Boston to come up with a double-disc concept album titled *Melon Collie and the Infinite Sadness* Despite a couple of irritating art-rock indulgences, including a concept about a boy growing up, the songs "Bullet and Butterfly Wings" and "1979" were forceful and strong. But near the start of the band's North American tour to support the album, touring keyboardist Jonathan Melvoin died in July 1996 after an alleged heroin overdose in his New York City hotel room. Shortly thereafter, the band fired drummer Chamberlin, who had been in the same room and was arrested for heroin possession. The band has vowed to continue touring and recording.

what to buy: *Siamese Dream* (Virgin, 1993, prod. Butch Vig and Billy Corgan) is the (sometimes overwrought) sound of a maniac shrieking his discontent to the sound of sympathetic grunge guitars. When Corgan sings, "Today is the greatest day I've ever known," you wonder if maybe he just murdered or ate somebody. *Melon Collie and the Infinite Sadness* (Virgin, 1995, prod. Flood, Alan Moulder and Billy Corgan) is irritating only if you can't stand "concept albums" in any form; otherwise, it's a decent record with lots of angst and Corgan believably shrieking that he's a rat in a cage.

what to buy next: *Gish* (Caroline, 1991/Virgin, 1994, prod. Butch Vig) is a good record, but its 60s garage-band sound gave few hints that the Pumpkins would turn to 70s hard and art-rock for later inspiration.

the rest: *Pisces Iscariot* (Virgin, 1994)

worth searching for: The Pumpkins, like R.E.M. and Bruce Springsteen, are generous about doling outtakes and obscure studio experiments to their fans. Among the best of these are *Zero* (Virgin EP, 1995) and *Tonight, Tonight,* (Virgin EP, 1996) two generous "singles" loaded with extra tracks that didn't appear on *Melon Collie*

Bush, Sponge, Alanis Morissette, Dig, Tripping Daisy, silverchair, Stone Temple Pilots

Nirvana, Black Sabbath, Kiss, Boston, Pixies, Velvet Underground, Cheap Trick, Soundgarden

Steve Knopper

Curt Smith

See: Tears for Fears

Darden Smith

Born 1962 in Brenham, Texas.

A veteran of the fertile early-80s Austin scene that also spawned Lyle Lovett and Nanci Griffith, Smith is a pop craftsman with a folk singer's eye for detail and ear for the truth. In concert, he can be both elegant and electrifying, prefacing his songs with wry parables and often jumping offstage to serenade fans row by row. That rousing attitude translates to his uplifting music, which evokes a reflective, philosophical warmth that is poetic but never preachy, gung-ho but rarely giddy in his quest for true love and redemption. Hometown fans rightly revere *Native Soil* (Watermelon, 1986, prod. Darden Smith and Larry Seyer) for its touching country-folk vignettes such as "Two Dollar Novels" and "Painter's Song," as well as harmony help from Griffith and Lovett. But Smith's most affecting hybrid of farm-boy dreams and city-boy polish is *Trouble No More,* (Columbia, 1990, prod. Darden Smith, Martin Lascelles and Pete Anderson) which utilizes gospel, country, folk and pop as disarmingly bouncy backdrops for touching narratives about everything from heel-clicking lovers ("Frankie and Sue") to disillusioned Vietnam vets ("Johnny Was a Lucky One").

the rest: *Darden Smith* (Epic, 1988) *Evidence* (with Boo Hewerdine) (Compass, 1989) *Little Victories* (Chaos/Columbia, 1993)

David Okamoto

Kendra Smith

See: The Dream Syndicate

Patti Smith /Patti Smith Group

Formed 1976 in New York, N.Y. Disbanded, 1979.

Patti Smith (born 1946 in Chicago, Ill.), vocals and guitar; Lenny Kaye, guitar, bass and vocals; Ivan Kral, bass, guitar, vocals; Richard Sohl, keyboards (died June 3, 1990 on Long Island, N.Y.); Bruce Brody, keyboards (1978); Jay Dee Daugherty, drums

Like the great rock poets before her, Smith writes music that is defiantly original and emotionally raw; what makes her stand out from the meager pack is her bare aggression. Smith was already an established poet, playwright and music critic when she entered New York's underground music scene during the mid-70s. In short course, she became the underground's figurehead, and her trademarks—poetic ramblings, vocal wailings and sonic distortion—became the sound of the movement. With its passionate rage, rudimentary musicianship and audio verite production, Smith's 1975 debut album, *Horses,* established the protocol that punk music would follow when it emerged two years later. Ironically, Smith and her band (galvanized on subsequent albums as the Patti Smith Group) had tightened up their performances and expanded their sonic palette by the time punk came along. Although Smith served to inspire the likes of Michael Stipe and U2, her own band eventually peaked out. In 1979 she took a lengthy sabbatical and settled in suburban Detroit to raise a family with ex-MC5 guitarist Fred "Sonic" Smith, who died in 1995. Her recent albums show a more resolved and peaceful artist at work. But the music, as always, comes from the heart and hits you right in the gut. (Note: In 1996, Arista released re-mastered versions of Smith's albums, filled out with bonus tracks.)

what to buy: Smith's debut album, *Horses,* (Arista, 1995, prod.

John Cale) ✪✪✪✪ is required listening for anyone interested in her music—or in the evolution of rock music into the genres of punk and grunge. From the album's opening refrain ("Jesus died for somebody's sins, but not mine"), Smith creates an edgy and disconcerting standoff between artistic expression and listener expectations that's troubling even today. Tracks such as "Redondo Beach" and "Free Money" still stand up quite nicely. Her second effort, *Radio Ethiopia,* (Arista, 1976, prod. Jack Douglas) ✪✪✪✪ hits a friendly balance between the idiosyncrasies of *Horses* and her later, more commercialized releases. The band is tighter, the arrangements are strong and the songs—in particular "Ask the Angels," "Pumping (My Heart)," "Poppies" and "Distant Fingers"—show how quickly Smith made the leap from punk poet to accomplished songwriter.

what to buy next: The union of Patti Smith Group and rock producer Jimmy Iovine resulted in *Easter,* (Arista, 1978,) ✪✪✪ a swaggering rock album that only begins to border on strident overconfidence. Although songs such as "Till Victory," "Ghost Dance" and "We Three" rehash some of the group's earlier (and better) efforts, the album earns high points for the gorgeous Top 20 hit "Because the Night" (co-written with Bruce Springsteen).

what to avoid: If it's hard to imagine a boring Patti Smith album, take a listen to *Wave.* (Arista, 1979, prod. Todd Rundgren) ✪ The band sounds dispirited, and Rundgren's production is a loathsome distraction. While "Frederick" and "Dancing Barefoot" are among the best songs Smith has written, the rest of the material suggests her passion had shifted from her art to her marriage.

the rest: *Dream of Life* (Arista, 1988) ✪✪✪ *Gone Again* (Arista, 1996) ✪✪✪ *The Patti Smith Masters: The Collective Works* (Arista, 1996) ✪✪✪✪

worth searching for: *Live in Paris* (Golden Stars-Italy, 1978) ✪✪✪ is a well-recorded bootleg that presents the Patti Smith Group in peak form. In addition to offering a wealth of the band's best cuts—"Ask the Angels," "Till Victory," "Because the Night"—the CD tacks on three *Horses*-era television performances from "The Mike Douglas Show" along with a 1978 performance of "I Was Working Real Hard" from NBC's "The Today Show."

▶▶ Lou Reed, John Cale, Iggy Pop, Television, Bruce Springsteen, The Pretenders, Television, Marianne Faithfull, R.E.M., the Sugarcubes, Bjork, Nirvana, Hole, P.J. Harvey, Liz Phair, Alanis Morissette, Yoko Ono

◀◀ Bob Dylan, the Rolling Stones, the Velvet Underground, Nico, the Doors, Jimi Hendrix, Joni Mitchell, Leonard Cohen, Plastic Ono Band, Iggy & the Stooges

Christopher Scapelliti

Smithereens

Formed 1980 in Carteret, N.J.

Pat DiNizio, guitar, vocals; Jim Babjak, guitar, vocals; Dennis Diken, drums, vocals; Mike Mesaros, bass, vocals

Smithereens play latter-day British Invasion pop with a decidedly American garage band edge. While it's not hard to pick out the Beatles and Kinks references in their tunes, the Smithereens can also roar with the force of the Stooges. That effortless balance of noise and melody makes the group one of America's best post-punk outfits, though the mass audience seems to have noticed only on all-too-rare occasions.

what to buy: *Especially For You* (Enigma, 1986, prod. Don Dixon) ✪✪✪✪ contains the brooding-pop gems "Blood and Roses" and "Behind the Wall of Sleep." *Blown to Smithereens: The Best of the Smithereens* (Capitol, 1995, prod. Various) ✪✪✪✪ shows what a great singles band the group is with an absolutely awesome parade of should-have-been radio smashes.

what to buy next: *Green Thoughts* (Capitol, 1988, prod. Don Dixon) ✪✪✪✪ is the band's second full-length LP, filled with near-perfect downer pop tunes such as "Only a Memory" and "Drown In My Own Tears."

the rest: *Beauty and Sadness* (Enigma EP, 1983) ✪✪✪ *Smithereens Live* (Restless EP, 1987) ✪✪✪ *11* (Capitol, 1990) ✪✪✪ *Blow Up* (Capitol, 1991) ✪✪✪✪ *Date with the Smithereens* (RCA, 1994) ✪✪✪

worth searching for: The British CD-5 for "Top of the Pops" (Capitol, 1991, prod. Various) which includes covers of "One After 909," "Shakin' All Over" and the "MTV Unplugged" version of the hit "A Girl Like You."

▶▶ Better Than Ezra, Weezer, Muzzle

◀◀ Beatles, Kinks, Beach Boys, Hollies, Black Sabbath

Thor Christensen

The Smiths

Formed 1983 in Manchester, England. Disbanded 1987.

Morrissey (born Stephen Patrick Morrissey), vocals; Johnny Marr (born John Maher), guitar; Andy Rourke, bass; Mike Joyce, drums; Craig Gannon, guitar (1985-87)

The Smiths excelled in bucking trends. While the rest of England was infatuated with new wave synthesizer pop and other transient movements at the outset of the 80s, the Smiths came along with a more traditional guitar sound that seemed eerily out of place. But its songs, bolstered by Marr's exquisite guitar playing and Morrissey's sharp lyrics, were so enchanting that the group didn't really need to fit in. Embracing poetry and a sound reminiscent of 60s beat groups, the Smiths laid the groundwork for modern alternative rock. Morrissey's contemplative lyrics brought the group a die-hard cluster of fans who connected with his tales of torment and loneliness. In its four years together, the group released an abundance of original material in various formats, all of it consistently solid before the Smiths broke up just prior to the release of its last album, *Strangeways Here We Come.* Morrissey went on to a fruitful solo career, while Marr played with The The, Bryan Ferry and the Pretenders before making Electronic—originally a side project for him and New Order's Bernard Sumner—a full-time endeavor. Rourke and Joyce joined Sinead O'Connor's band, and Joyce later sat in with the reunited Buzzcocks.

what to buy: *The Queen Is Dead* (Sire, 1986, prod. John Porter, Johnny Marr and Morrissey) represents the Smiths' artistic peak, blending an impeccable set of songs with Morrissey exceptional wit and Marr's most accomplished guitar playing. Its highlights include "The Boy With the Thorn in His Side" and the stirring "There Is a Light That Never Goes Out." The Smiths' first two albums, *The Smiths* (Sire, 1984, prod. John Porter) and *Hatful of Hollow,* (Rough Trade, 1984, John Porter) are important because they capture the group as it develops its sound—a heady mix of Byrdsy jangle, gritty glam and old school British pop—along with seminal songs such as "How Soon Is Now?," "This Charming Man" and "Hand in Glove."

what to buy next: You really can't go wrong with the two-part Smiths greatest hits collections, *Bestè I* (Sire, 1992, prod. Various) and *Bestè II* (Sire, 1992, prod. Various) While not as cohesive as the group's proper albums, they are great testament to the Smiths' fantastic vision.

what to avoid: *Rank* (Sire, 1988, prod. Pete Dauncey) a posthumous live release recorded a bit too late to capture the Smiths in peak form.

the rest: *Hatful of Hollow* (Rough Trade, 1984/Sire, 1993) *Meat Is Murder* (Sire, 1985) *Louder Than Bombs* (Sire, 1987) *Strangeways Here We Come* (Sire, 1987) *Singles,* (Sire, 1995)

worth searching for: The Japanese EP for "This Charming Man" (WEA, 1992, prod. Various) which includes seven surprisingly decent versions of the songs plus the B-sides from the song's original 1983 release.

solo recordings: Johnny Marr (with Electronic): *Electronic* (Sire, 1992)

Jeff Buckley, Ride, the Sundays, the Stone Roses, Oasis, James

David Bowie, Roxy Music, The Jam, Nico, New York Dolls

see also: *Morrissey, New Order, The The*

Aidin Vaziri

Patty Smyth /Scandal

Born June 26, 1957 in New York, N.Y.

Scandal members: Patty Smyth, vocals; Zachary Smith, guitar; Keith Mack, guitar; Ivan Elias, bass; Frankie LaRocka (1982-83), drums; Thommy Price (1983-4), drums

Built around the core of Smyth and Smith, and with studio musicians augmenting the group, Scandal rode a video showcasing Smyth's girl-next-door good looks into the middle of the charts with "Goodbye to You," one of the earliest MTV-propelled hits, in 1982. It made the debut EP Columbia's bestseller in that format, ironically conceived as a way of selling less commercial music (such as the Clash) in a cheaper package. LaRocka left for an A&R position, and the group fell apart after releasing its only full-length album. Smyth went on to a more successful solo career, though one that seems built around her relationships. In the mid-80s, Smyth married rocker Richard Hell and had a daughter with him; during the mid-90s she became tennis star John McEnroe's girlfriend and sometimes sang in his ad-hoc performances (he plays guitar; one jam included fellow tennis pro Jim Courier on drums). Through it all, her unabashed pop style has offered catchy nuggets, with her voice—and a native New Yorker's don't-mess-with-me image—carrying the less memorable moments.

what to buy: *Patty Smyth* (MCA, 1992, prod. Roy Bittan) was a hit on the strength of the anthemic Billboard #2 smash "Sometimes Love Just Ain't Enough," a duet with Don Henley that, like several other tracks here, Smyth co-wrote with gun-for-hire and brief Styx member Glen Burtnik. Springsteen keyboardist Bittan, who also plays on the album, fortunately can't smooth the rough edges off Smyth's voice, he but polishes everything else—though some numbers ("My Town") have a tougher impact and "River of Love" is almost funky.

what to buy next: The five-song EP *Scandal* (Columbia, 1982, prod. Vini Poncia) contained two hits, "Goodbye to You" and "Love's Got a Line on You." Smyth's *Never Enough* (Columbia, 1987, prod. Rick Chertoff and William Wittman) contains an effective version of Tom Waits's "Downtown Train" (three years before Rod Stewart covered it). As with many Chertoff productions, Hooters Rob Hyman and Eric Bazilian have songwriting input and play extensively. Some of the synthesizer sounds here have dated, but guitar riffs power most of the refrains.

the rest: Scandal: *The Warrior* (Columbia, 1984)

Sheryl Crow, Alanis Morrissette, Joan Osborne, Magnapop, Garbage

Pat Benatar, Bonnie Raitt

Steve Holtje

Phoebe Snow

Born July 17, 1952 in New York City, N.Y.

The purity of Snow's singing has always been disarming; a rich contralto with seemingly limitless versatility, she has never received the proper due her talents command (with the possible exception of her 1974 hit "Poetry Man"). The problem has always been focus—where and how to house her fluid chops; similarly, poor production, nasty label relations and her own (admirable) decision to provide home care for her autistic daughter have seriously hampered her commercial viability. From her jazzy-folk beginnings during the 70s to her solid return in 1989, Snow has been an undeniable talent in search of a worthy surroundings. She is currently without a record deal.

what to buy: *Phoebe Snow* (Right Stuff, 1974/1995, prod. Dino Airali) is an auspicious coffee house folk debut that reveals an emotional assuredness underneath her considerable vocal range. It contains "Poetry Man," as well as the gutsy "Harpo's Blues" and an interesting cover of Sam Cooke's "Good Times."

what to buy next: Snow's emotional urgency in the title track of *Something Real* (Elektra, 1989, prod. Rob Fraboni and Ricky Fataar) makes the album worth buying, and there's lots of other top-shelf material besides.

what to avoid: Because she's not a hit machine, *The Best of Phoebe Snow* (Columbia, 1981, prod. Various) is a brief collection that's ultimately short-sighted and unrevealing.

the rest: *Never Letting Go* (Columbia, 1978/1990); *It Looks Like Snow* (Columbia, 1976/1989); *Second Childhood* (Columbia, 1976/1988)

worth searching for: *Against the Grain* (Columbia, 1978, prod. ??) is a bit slick but boasts a strong version of Paul McCartney's "Every Night." On *Rock Away,* (Atlantic, 1981) Snow tries her hand at rock, covering everything from "Gasoline Alley" to Dylan's "I Believe in You."

Dar Williams, Suzanne Vega, Tracy Chapman

Joni Mitchell, Sandy Denny, Laura Nyro

Allan Orski

Jill Sobule

Born Jan. 16, 1959, in Denver, Colo.

Sobule's family is full of storied characters; there was, for example, the grandfather who was one of Jack Dempsey's sparring partner. But none may be as storied as Sobule, who got an electric guitar when she was in sixth grade and soon began writing her own songs. Her first album, on which she sang serious relationship songs, went nowhere, and her follow-up album, produced by Joe Jackson, was rejected by MCA and never issued. It wasn't until she let loose her humor that she broke through. "I Kissed a Girl" garnered attention not only with its subject but also by its wit. Despite Sobule's girlish voice, wacky persona and tendency to lightweight pop, she showed a keen sense of irony.

what to buy: *Jill Sobule* (Lava/Atlantic, 1995, prod. Brad Jones and Robin Eaton) contains not only "I Kissed a Girl" but also the hilarious "Good Person Inside" and "Supermodel" from the soundtrack to the movie "Clueless."

the rest: *Things Here Are Different* (MCA, 1990)

Steve Holtje

Social Distortion

Formed 1979, Fullerton, Calif.

Mike Ness, vocals and guitar; Dennis Danell, guitar; Brent Liles, bass (1979-88); Derek O'Brien, vocals, drums (1979-88); Chris Reece, drums (1988-1996); Chuck Biscuits, drums (1996-present); John Maurer, bass (1988-present); Chuck Biscuits, drums (1996-present)

Mike Ness and his rebel-rock pals, like so many suburban Los Angeles teens in the late-70s, picked up guitars and learned how to rock with them. At first, they rehashed Clash-Sex Pistols-X chords with youthful exuberance. Then they hit a creative wall until Ness discovered country music and figured out how to write good songs. By 1990, the tattooed, Elvis-haircutted Ness was heavily into Johnny Cash and making music that predated (with the Mekons, among others) the country-punk fusion that led indirectly to Uncle Tupelo, Wilco and Son Volt. A couple of early-90s college-radio hits gave Social D a spot opening for Neil Young and Sonic Youth in a high-profile arena tour, and Ness' skills steadily improved after that.

what to buy: *Social Distortion* (Epic, 1990, prod. Dave Jerden) ♪♪♪♪ has a killer version of Cash's "Ring of Fire" plus the enduring college-radio hits "Ball and Chain" and "Story of My Life." The debut *Mommy's Little Monster* (Time Bomb Recordings, 1982, prod. Chaz Ramirez with Social Distortion) ♪♪♪♪ is all smash and thrash, and the nine songs are over before you know it.

what to buy next: *Somewhere Between Heaven and Hell* (Epic, 1992, prod. Dave Jerden) ♪♪♪½ sacrifices some of Social Distortion's sloppy firepower but adds a nice dimension of lonely-loser country music.

the rest: *Prison Bound* (Sticky Fingers Records, 1988) ♪♪ *White Light, White Heat, White Trash* (Epic, 1996) not available for rating

worth searching for: The promotional CD for the single "Story of My Life," (Epic, 1990) ♪♪♪♪ includes two versions of the track plus four energetic live recordings.

▷▷ Jason and the Scorchers, Uncle Tupelo, Wilco, Son Volt.

◁◁ Ramones, X, Avengers, Johnny Cash, Carl Perkins.

Steve Knopper

The Soft Boys

Formed 1976 in Cambridge, England. Disbanded 1981

Robyn Hitchcock vocals, guitar; Alan Davies guitar, vocals (1976-77); Kimberly Rew guitar, vocals (1977-81); Morris Windsor drums, vocals; Andy Metcalfe bass, vocals (1976-79); Matthew Seligman bass, vocals (1979-81)

Formed in the midst of a folk boom in Cambridge (which immediately preceded punk and new wave), the Soft Boys featured the surreal and psychedelic songwriting of Robyn Hitchcock (twin muses: Syd Barrett and Bob Dylan), and the blazing guitar prowess of Kimberly Rew (who went on to Katrina & the Waves, among others). It was not an altogether happy marriage of sensibilities and was certainly commercially unrewarding—not to mention utterly out of step with the surrounding music scene by the time their records finally came out. The Soft Boys' discography is filled with mysterious singles, EPs, repackages, live fan club cassettes and other oddments.

what to buy: *Underwater Moonlight* (Armageddon, 1980/Rykodisc, 1992, prod. Pat Collier) ♪♪♪♪½ was the Soft Boys' last gasp. The band was in trouble, knew it and agreed simply to cooperate long enough to make one good record before calling it a day. Instead, they managed a minor masterpiece. Recorded for 600 British pounds on the fly, it includes such pop classics as "I Wanna Destroy You," "Kingdom of Love" and the title track.

what to buy next: The course of least resistance leads to the two-disc compilation *The Soft Boys 1976-81*, (Rykodisc, 1993) ♪♪♪♪ which neatly compiles an assortment of tracks from the Soft Boys' three long-players, rarities, unreleased tracks, obscurities, etc. It's a cagey enough collection—and Hitchcock's songwriting is strong enough—to make for a fine summary.

What Album Changed Your Life?

"I always go back to Beggar's Banquet by the Stones. There's a little bit of everything on there, and some of Mick Jagger's best lyrics ever. It surprises me after years of listening to it how a song like 'Street Fighting Man' sounds so heavy, and it's mostly acoustic guitars!"

Joey Mazzola (Sponge)

what to avoid: Why would you want to?

the rest: *A Can of Bees* (Two Crabs, 1979/Rykodisc, 1992) *Invisible Hits* (Armageddon, 1983/Rykodisc, 1992)

worth searching for: Nah, leave the rest of 'em be. If Hitchcock didn't put tracks on the Ryko reissues, there's probably a good reason for that.

Robyn Hitchcock & the Egyptians, Katrina & the Waves, R.E.M.

John Lennon, Syd Barrett, Bob Dylan

Grant Alden

Soft Machine

Formed 1966 in Canterbury, England

Mike Ratledge, keyboards (1966-76); Robert Wyatt, drums, vocals (1966-71); Kevin Ayers, guitar, vocals, bass (1966-69); David Allen, guitar, vocals (1966-67); Hugh Hopper, bass, guitar (1968-73). Other members: Larry Nolan, guitar; Elton Dean, sax; Marc Charig, trumpet; Nick Evans, trombones; Lyn Dobson, flute, sax; Rob Spall, violin; Phil Howard, drums; John Marshall, drums; Karl Jenkins, sax, keyboards; Roy Babbington, bass; Allan Holdsworth, guitar; John Etheridge, guitar; Alan Wakeman, sax; Steve Cook, bass; Jack Bruce, bass, vocals; Dick Morisey, sax; Alan Parker, guitar; Ray Warleigh, sax; Dave Macrae, keyboards

Soft Machine was a band to catch in its early days, since the band's revolving door was spinning from the get-go. Before the self-titled debut, original guitarist Allen had left to form the trippy, evolving group Gong. After the first album, vocalist and bassist Ayers quit, taking with him a fine sense of absurd humor. At least vocalist-drummer Wyatt hung around for a few years, though it would be keyboardist Ratledge whose vision would guide the band longer than any of his cohorts. Blending snippets of pop, jazz, rock and just plain weirdness throughout its music, Soft Machine offered sonic adventure with every new bar of notes—which delighted bolder listeners and confused the more timid. In that way, Soft Machine's constantly in-flux line-up works to the group's benefit, bringing new ideas into a system that can't wait to try them.

what to buy: Saxophonist Elton Dean, trumpeter Marc Charig, flutist/saxophonist Lyn Dobson and violinist Rob Spall joined for *Third*, (Columbia, 1970/1991) a double album with one composition per side—well before Yes came forth with *Tales From Topographic Oceans* Wyatt's equally ethereal and dramatic composition "Moon in June" is a must for any serious popular music collection.

what to buy next: *The Soft Machine* (Probe, 1968/One Way, 1993) and *The Soft Machine, Volume Two* (Columbia, 1969/One Way, 1993) each boast quirky charm and a fistful of music styles to create floating, Alice in Wonderland style pastiches.

what to avoid: *Fifth*, (Columbia, 1972/One Way, 1993) *Sixth* (Columbia, 1973/One Way, 1995) and *Seventh* (Columbia, 1974/One Way, 1995) are burdened by uncommitted, journeyman musicians and pale against the ground-breaking *Third.*

the rest: *Fourth* (Columbia, 1971/One Way, 1993) *Land of Cockayne* (EMI, 1981/One Way, 1996) *Peel Sessions* (Dutch East India, 1991) *BBC Live* (Windsong, 1993) *Live in France* (One Way, 1995)

worth searching for: *The Soft Machine* and *Volume Two* combined on a single two-fer CD (Big Beat, 1989) makes for some wonderful, uninterrputed listening.

Sting, Kansas, Steely Dan

Pink Floyd, Miles Davis, Ornette Coleman

see also: *Robert Wyatt*

Patrick McCarty

Jimmy Somerville

See: Bronski Beat

Son Volt

Formed 1994 along the Mississippi River

Jay Farrar, vocals, guitar; Jim Boquist, bass, vocals; Mike Heidorn, drums; Dave Boquist, guitar, fiddle, banjo, lap steel

After splitting from Uncle Tupelo in 1994, Farrar formed this unit, which, in terms of geography, must be as extreme a representation of middle America as exists. While forming the band, Farrar lived in New Orleans (he's since moved to St. Louis), Heidorn (Tupelo's original drummer) in Belleville, Ill., and the Boquist brothers in Minneapolis. Because Farrar wrote the songs for *Trace* (Warner Bros., 1995, prod. Brian Paulson and Son Volt) during long, searching sojourns up and down the highways along the Mississippi River; because he's so inclined anyway, the album accurately reflects the countryside that inspired it. Though lyrically obtuse, Farrar's tunes hit home hard, particularly the hard-country/folk numbers "Windfall" and "Tear Stained Eye," and the slashing rockers "Drown" and "Loose String."

see also: *Uncle Tupelo, Wilco*

Daniel Durchholz

Sonic Youth /Thurston Moore/Lee Ranaldo/ Ciccone Youth/Bewitched

Formed 1981 in New York, N.Y.

Thurston Moore, vocals, guitar; Kim Gordon, vocals, bass; Lee Ranaldo, guitar; Richard Edson, drums (1981-82); Jim Sclavunos, drums (1982-83); Bob Bert, drums (1983-85); Steve Shelley, drums (1985-present)

One of the most innovative, inconsistent, influential, annoying, cathartic and frustrating groups in rock history, Sonic Youth has spent 15 years exploring guitar sounds and ways to confuse the public (and critics). Along the way, it has made some of the most intensely dark yet ecstatic and accessible albums to come out of the pop underground. Moore and Ranaldo met while playing in one of avant-gardist Glenn Branca's multiple-guitar ensembles (Sonic Youth's first two efforts initially came out on Branca's label). Ranaldo's love of pure sound in its infinite variety combined with Moore's rudimentary songcraft for a sound that extended the experiments of the New York No Wave scene into somewhat more accessible (if still uncompromised) rock territory. Gradually combining the members' varying musical impulses more coherently, the group hit its stride in 1986-88 when, having settled on Shelley as drummer, it made the great indie trilogy of *Evol, Sister* and *Daydream Nation* Its signing to DGC was supposed to open mainstream doors for the underground, though that breakthrough was achieved not by the group but rather by a band Moore and company touted highly to Geffen: Nirvana. The members of Sonic Youth are so relentlessly hip that there's been a constant backlash against them ever since SY joined the major-label ranks, but their work—with the band and with myriad outside projects—has remained rewarding, even if it's returned to more erratic expression (probably deliberately).

what to buy: *Sister* (SST, 1987, prod. Sonic Youth) combines a great vocabulary of guitar sounds, a modicum of avant daring and the most memorable songs of SY's career ("Schizophrenia," "Catholic Block," "Hot Wire My Heart"). *Daydream Nation,* (Blast First/Enigma, 1988, prod. Sonic Youth and Nicholas Sansano) a sprawling 71-minute album, consolidated the group's many innovations within a consistent mood. The glinting walls of guitar produces an unmatched spooky edge.

what to buy next: *Evol* (SST, 1986, prod. Sonic Youth and Martin Bisi) is the first SY album with no failed experiments, its dreamlike mood haunting and disturbing. *Washing Machine* (DGC, 1995, prod. Sonic Youth and John Siket) explores the nuances within SY's ample niche, cohering better than other 90s SY albums. The 1986 soundtrack to the indie film *Made in USA* (Rhino, 1995, prod. Sonic Youth) includes much that was dropped in the final edit of the movie. The short, often instrumental cues provide a surprisingly good setting in which to appreciate the textures that make this band great.

what to avoid: The debut *Sonic Youth* (Neutral EP, 1982/SST, 1987, prod. Sonic Youth) gets points for trying something new, but its mechanical processes and clunky rhythms pale compared to future works. *The Whitey Album,* (Blast First/Enigma, 1988, prod. Ciccone Youth) WOOF! SY's sole full-length album as Ciccone Youth, includes a massive amount of shamelessly pointless goofing around.

the rest: *Sonic Death: Sonic Youth Live* (Ecstatic Peace, 1984/SST, 1988) *Bad Moon Rising* (Homestead, 1985) *Death Valley '69* (Homestead EP, 1985) The Master-Dik *(SST EP, 1988)* *Goo* (DGC, 1990) *Dirty Boots* (DGC EP, 1991) *Dirty* (DGC, 1992) *TV Shit* (Ecstatic Peace EP, 1993) *Screaming Fields of Sonic Love* (Geffen, 1994) *Experimental Jet Set, Trash and No Star* (DGC, 1994) *Confusion Is Sex/Kill Yr. Idols* (Geffen, 1994)

solo outings:

Ciccone Youth (Sonic Youth): *Into the Groove(y)/Burnin' Up* 12 (Blast First, 1986)

Thurston Moore: *Psychic Hearts* (DGC, 1995)

Lee Ranaldo: *From Here to Infinity* (SST, 1987) *Envisioning* (Knitting Factory Works, 1994) *East Jesus* (Atavistic, 1995, prod. Not listed)

Bewitched (Bert): *Brain Eraser* (No.6/Rough Trade, 1990)

▶▶ Live Skull, Nirvana, Sloan, Hole, Neil Young

◀◀ DNA, Television, Richard Hell & the Voidoids, Sonny

Sharrock, Sun Ra, John Coltrane, Glenn Branca, Rhys Chatham, Einsturzende Neubauten, Velvet Underground

Steve Holtje

Sonny and Cher /Cher

Born Salvatore Bono on Feb. 16, 1935, in Detroit, Mich. Born Cherilyn Sarkasian La Pier on May 20, 1946, in El Centro, Calif.

Sonny and Cher met while working for producer Phil Spector. She was a 19-year-old backup singer; he was a glorified go-fer with a variety of dubious accomplishments. They recorded a couple of singles under the name Caesar and Cleo but only started to click when, as Sonny and Cher, they scored a modest regional hit with "Baby Don't Go." After a switch to Atco Records and the No. 1 hit "I Got You Babe," Sonny and Cher became the Ozzie and Harriet of the Flower Power set, invariably garbed in mod rags. Bono cut Spectorian duo records for one label and even tossed off one immortal protest record of his own, "Laugh at Me," after being asked to leave a restaurant because he wasn't wearing a tie. Cher did solo records for Liberty (notably "Bang Bang"). Their decline from Top 40 popularity may have been inevitable, but their 70s resurrection as a kind of Louis Prima-Keely Smith comedic pop vocal team could hardly have been predicted. With a top-rated weekly TV program and a series of hit records produced by the sage veteran Snuff Garrett (Bobby Vee, Gary Lewis and the Playboys), Sonny and Cher were back entertaining the parents of the people who only a few years before were buying their records. In the wake of their divorce, personal and professional, Cher established herself as one of Hollywood's leading ladies. Music dropped to little more than a sideline for her; in fact, her albums became more noteworthy for fleshy covers than the music inside. Bono, meanwhile, opened a restaurant and entered politics in sleepy Palm Springs, which he currently represents as a congressman. Their mentor, Phil Spector, likely remains amused at the turn of events.

what to buy: Because of the number of different labels involved, no single set comprehensively covers the career of Sonny and Cher, but *The Beat Goes On* (Atco, 1991, prod. Sonny Bono) covers their most fruitful period.

what to buy next: The double-CD set, *All I Ever Need Is You: The Kapp/MCA Anthology,* (MCA, 1995, prod. various) may be rather more Sonny and Cher from their TV years than anyone truly needs.

what to avoid: On the other hand, there is an abundance of mediocre recordings in their *oeuvre* Take your pick: *Allman and Woman* (Capricorn, 1976), a bizarre collaboration between Cher and her second husband, Gregg Allman (of *those* Allmans) and any of the Kapp/Uni albums with one of the hit songs in the title—*Gypsies, Tramps and Thieves* (MCA, 1971) *All I Ever Need Is You* (MCA, 1972) *Half Breed* (MCA, 1973) or her disco-era excesses, currently collected on one convenient set, *The Casablanca Years* (Polydor, 1996) WOOF!

the rest: *All I Really Want to Do/The Sonny Side of Cher* (EMI, 1992) Cher—*Bang Bang and Other Hits* (Capitol Special Products, 1992) *Cher* (Geffen, 1987) *Heart of Stone* (Geffen, 1989) *It's a Man's Man's World* (Geffen, 1996)

worth searching for: Two bonafide Phil Spector-produced singles productions, both collector's items, feature Cher as lead vocalist—"Ringo I Love You" by Bobbie Jo Mason (Annette, 1964), her first record, and "A Love Like Yours," (Warner Spector, 1975) a duet with Harry Nilsson.

ABBA, the Captain and Tennille, Madonna

Louis Prima and Keely Smith, Phil Spector

Joel Selvin

Sons of Champlin

Formed 1965 Marin Co., Calif. Disbanded 1978

Bill Champlin, vocals, guitar, keyboards; Terry Haggerty, guitar; Geoff Palmer, vibes, saxophone; David Shallock, bass (1972-1977); James Preston, drums (1972-1979)

Little known outside the San Francisco music scene, the Sons was widely regarded in that provincial circle as the most accomplished set of musicians around. Champlin, a triple-threat vocalist-keyboardist-guitarist, went on to write two Grammy-winning R&B songs ("After the Love Is Gone" for Earth, Wind & Fire and "Turn Your Love Around" for George Benson) after he finally gave up, left the band and moved to Los Angeles, where he eventually joined multi-platinum popsters Chicago. But this band of staunch hippies, who released a debut album without either a photo of the group or any musicians' names, left behind some stunning, soul-infused acid rock, unmatched by many more famous groups of the era.

what to buy: The double-record set that introduced the band to an unsuspecting and, ultimately, unsympathetic world, *Loosen Up Naturally* (Capitol, 1969/One Way, 1995, prod. Sons of Champlin) was finally released in its entirety on CD, after

Capitol, the band's old label, put together a budget-priced compilation, *The Best Of the Sons Of Champlin* (Capitol, 1993, prod. Various), drawing from the first three albums.

what to avoid: Bill Champlin solo albums.

worth searching for: In the band's second incarnation, the Sons allowed Hollywood producer Keith Olsen to distill the group's often uncontrollable instincts into a svelte, sonically superb package, *Circle Filled With Love,* (Ariola America, 1976) that actually launched a Top 50 hit, "Hold On." *Seeds and Stems* (1970) was a private pressing of around 500 copies of demos highly prized by aficionados. Also, the Sons made Capitol send out a free 7-inch 33 1/3 rpm disc of "Jesus is Coming"—a track Capitol insisted be deleted from the debut album—to anyone who wrote in.

▶▶ Chicago, Tower of Power, Lee Ritenour (Champlin's vocal on the Stevie Wonder song, "Isn't She Lovely")

◀◀ Lou Rawls, Bobby Bland, Johnny Smith

Joel Selvin

Soul Asylum

Formed 1981 in Minneapolis, Minn.

Dave Pirner, vocals, guitar, piano, sax, drums; Dan Murphy, guitar, vocals; Karl Mueller, vocals, bass; Pat Morley, drums (1984-85); Grant Young, drums (1985-94); Sterling Campbell, drums (1995-present)

Starting as the teenage punk band Loud Fast Rules, Soul Asylum's mid-80s incorporation of country into its sound helped set it apart from hometown heroes Husker Du (whose Bob Mould produced Soul Asylum's first two albums) and the Replacements. Pirner, who began as the group's drummer, was frontman by the time of the debut. Writing the vast majority of the group's material (Murphy contributes a song occasionally), he set the tone for the group's image as passionate, rowdy losers hiding a sensitive side on masterpieces such as "Never Really Been" (from *Made to Be Broken*). Frequent touring honed the band into a powerful force, just sloppy enough to avoid slickness. Its years on the Minneapolis label Twin/Tone, which eventually entered into a distribution deal with A&M, brought the band critical and underground respect but little commercial success. Switching to Columbia certainly changed that, with Pirner's sappy ballad "Runaway Train" reaching #5 on Billboard's pop chart and the album *Grave Dancers Union* breaking the platinum sales barrier. The band became ubiquitous, with Pirner (now sporting dreadlocks) making the gossip pages by dating Winona Ryder for several years. That symbolized for many old fans of the group how mainstream it had become, smoothing out the group's rough edges, though its live appearances remain exciting. Murphy and Pirner's work with the side group Golden Smog album is more interesting than anything on *Grave Dancers'* follow-up, *Let Your Dim Light Shine.* Pirner also sang on one of the *Backbeat* film soundtracks).

what to buy: Soul Asylum's second album, *Made to Be Broken,* (Twin/Tone, 1986, prod. Bob Mould) was a huge leap forward, with improved production and more pointed songs. Pirner's country music interests surfaced here (usually tinging rather than transforming the songs) and made for some of the most memorable tracks. "Ship of Fools," "Can't Go Back," the punky "Whoa!", "New Feelings," and the emotional "Never Really Been" are the work of a masterful songwriter. *Hang Time* (Twin/Tone /A&M, 1988, prod. Lenny Kaye and Ed Stasium) put major-label dollars to good use with sparkling production that honed the group's strengths rather than glossing them over. Though the sound's clear, there's an edge to the music, and "Endless Farewell" shows Pirner can do heartwrenching ballads without losing his edge. Murphy's "Cartoon" is another highlight and suggests Pirner's not the only appreciator of country twang.

what to buy next: *Grave Dancers Union* (Columbia, 1993, prod. Michael Beinhorn) may have the group's first hit, "Runaway Train," but there's a loss of identity here: "April Fool" could be Kiss, and "Sun Maid" is just plain wimpy. Enough of the old sound remains ("Somebody to Shove," "Growing into You") to save it.

what to avoid: *Let Your Dim Light Shine* (Columbia, 1995, prod. Butch Vig and Soul Asylum) is even more mainstream than its predecessor; worse, it sounds formulaic and tired.

the rest: *What You Will, Clarence...Karl Sold the Truck* (Twin/Tone, 1984) *While You Were Out* (Twin/Tone, 1986) *Clam Dip & Other Delights* (Twin/Tone EP, 1989) *Soul Asylum and the Horse They Rode in On* (Twin/Tone/ A&M, 1990) *Runaway Train* (Columbia EP, 1993)

worth searching for: The "Standing in the Doorway"/James at 16" (Heavy Medley) 12" (Twin/Tone/ A&M, 1988) is a must-own for the B-side's unbelievably eclectic live medley of songs by Prince, Buffalo Springfield, the Velvet Underground, Wild Cherry, Ted Nugent, the Bee Gees and others.

▶▶ Afghan Whigs, Gin Blossoms, Dharma Bums

⏪ Hüsker Dü, Replacements, Buck Owens, Rolling Stones

Steve Holtje

The Soul Survivors

Formed 1966 in New York, N.Y. Disbanded 1970. Re-united 1974.

Kenneth Jeremiah, vocals; Richard Ingui, vocals; Charles Ingui, vocals; Paul Venturini, organ; Edward Leonetti, guitar; Joey Forigone, drums

The Soul Survivors had only one hit, but it was a big one. In 1967, "Expressway to Your Heart" reached the Top 5 on both the pop and R&B charts. But *When The Whistle Blows Anything Goes* (Collectables,1993) 🦴 points to the weaknesses of the group; the Soul Survivors couldn't write and, except for the one hit, made poor song selections. Better to find "Expressway" on an good oldies collection.

Patrick McCarty

Soundgarden

Formed 1984 in Seattle, Wash.

Chris Cornell, vocals, guitar; Kim Thayil, guitar; Scott Sundquist, drums, (1985-86); Matt Cameron, drums (1986-present); Hiro Yamamoto, bass (1984-89); Jason Everman, bass (1989-90); Ben Shepherd (b. Hunter Shepherd), bass (1990-present)

The members of Soundgarden grouse about being regarded as a metal band, and they have a point. After all, they played an important role in creating the 90s Seattle scene of grunge and alternative rock, and their EP *Screaming Life* was the very first release on the Sub Pop label, which eventually brought the Seattle sound to the world. Plus, much of their hard rock bluster was tongue-in-cheek, even if their audience didn't necessarily notice. But like Blue Öyster Cult a generation before them, what began as an ironic comment on metal became the thing itself. Soundgarden's intelligence kept the quality of their music from descending to metal's cliched excess. Unabashedly Zeppelinesque, Cornell's keening vocals reach operatic heights, slicing through the wall-o-sludge guitar cranked out by Thayil. Their roots may have been as much in punk as in 70s AOR, but Soundgarden made it safe for Seattlites and their fellow grungesters everywhere to shake their hair down in their face and rock out.

what to buy: *Superunknown.* (A&M, 1994, prod. Michael Beinhorn and Soundgarden) 🦴🦴🦴🦴🦴 From the apocalyptic "Black Hole Sun" to the contemplative "Fell on Black Days," to the downright desperate "The Day I Tried to Live," *Superunknown* is lyrically complex and packs the sonic wallop of a tsunami. It's the best hard rock album of the 90s. The follow-up, *Down on the Upside* (A&M, 1996, prod. Soundgarden and Adam Kasper) 🦴🦴🦴🦴 further refines the band's attack, featuring shimmering pop-metal ("Pretty Noose"), Ramones-inspired punk ("Ty Cobb") and Lennonesque psychedelia ("Blow Up the Outside World"). *Badmotorfinger* (A&M, 1991, prod. Terry Date and Soundgarden) 🦴🦴🦴🦴 is the album on which the band truly found it's voice. Songs like "Rusty Cage," "Jesus Christ Pose" and "Outshined" feature well-tempered hard rock and razor-sharp lyrics.

what to buy next: *Louder Than Love* (A&M, 1989, prod. Terry Date and Soundgarden) 🦴🦴🦴🦴 convincingly updates 70s hard rock, but the band's sense of irony is subtle enough that not everyone got the joke of macho anthems like "Big Dumb Sex."

what to avoid: The individual EPs *Screaming Life* (Sub Pop EP, 1987) 🦴🦴🦴 and *Fopp* (Sub Pop EP, 1988) 🦴🦴🦴 were combined by Sub Pop in 1990 for a more value efficient single disc.

the rest: *Ultramega OK* (SST, 1988) 🦴🦴🦴

worth searching for: *Alive in the Superunknown* (A&M, 1995) 🦴🦴🦴🦴 is a multimedia CD-Plus featuring tracks and videos from *Superunknown* and unreleased material.

solo outings:

Ben Shepherd and Matt Cameron (with Hater) Hater (A&M, 1993) 🦴🦴

⏩ Alice in Chains, Screaming Trees, Mudhoney, Pearl Jam, Bush, silverfish

⏪ Led Zeppelin, Black Sabbath, Killing Joke, The Melvins

see also: *Hater, Temple of the Dog*

Daniel Durchholz

The Soup Dragons

Formed 1985 in Belshill, Scotland

Sean Dickson, vocals; Jim McCullouch, guitar (1985-94); Sushil Dade, bass (1985-94); Paul Quinn, drums (1985-94)

This mid-80s punk/pop band had little to no success during the early years with its edgy guitar albums. But thanks to the late 80s success of its Manchester chums Happy Mondays and Stone Roses, the Soup Dragons found its talents were in infusing funky rhythms with psychedelic, 60s-style guitars. The band's success was short-lived, and its most memorable recorded work was the remake of The Rolling Stones' "I'm Free."

what to buy: *Love God* (Big Life/Mercury 1990) is the Generation X handbook to what the Manchester sound is all about. It contains the megga smash "I'm Free," complete with a raggae-rap segment by Jamaican artist Junior Reid and a gospel choir that's a nice touch.

what to buy next: *Hot Wired* (Big Life/Mercury 1992) is spotty but worthwhile for "Divine Thing." Imagine "I'm Free" with different words; the potential is limitless.

what to avoid: *Hydrophone* (Raw T.V./Mercury 1994) A pretentious lead singer thinks the way to bring back the hipness is to fire the entire band and do it himself. Wrong.

the rest: *Hang Ten* (Sire 1987)

Jesus Jones, Happy Mondays, Charlatans U.K., Stone Roses

Procol Harum, the Rolling Stones, Pretty Things, Thompson Twins

Chris Newberg

Joe South

Born Feb. 28, 1940, in Atlanta, Ga.

South's career began as a session guitarist for country, soul and pop acts. He performed on Bob Dylan's *Blonde on Blonde* and in recent years recorded with ex-Georgia Satellite Dan Baird. After turning his attention to songwriting, South scored hits with "Hush," "Down in the Boondocks," "Walk a Mile in My Shoes" and "Rose Garden," and he won a Grammy for "Games People Play." During the early 70s, he began performing his own songs, though they haven't been as successful for him as they were for other artists. Still, the heart of this fine musician and arranger's career can —and should—be heard on *The Best of Joe South* (Rhino, 1990, prod. Joe South)

Patrick McCarty

Southside Johnny & the Asbury Jukes

Formed 1974 in Asbury Park, N.J.

Southside Johnny (born John Lyon, Dec. 4, 1948, Neptune, N.J.), vocals, harmonica; Billy Rush, guitar (1974-85); Kevin Kavanaugh, keyboards; Al Berger, bass (1974-80); Kenny Pentifallo, drums (1974-77); Carlo Novi, tenor sax (1974-77); Eddie Manion, baritone sax (1974-82); Tony Palligrosi, trumpet (1974-78); Ricky Gazda, trumpet (1974-82); Richie (La Bamba) Rosenberg, trombone (1974-82); Steve Becker, drums (1977-91); Bob Muckin, trumpet (1978-80); Stan Harrison, tenor sax (1978-80); Joel Gramolini, guitar (1979-82); Gene Boccia, bass (1980-85); Mike Spencer, trumpet (1980-82); Joey Stann, baritone & tenor sax (1980-82, 1986-91); Rusty Cloud, keyboards (1983-present); Mark Pender, trumpet (1983-86); Al Torrente, trumpet (1983-85); Bobby Ferrel, trombone (1983-86); Frank Elmo, saxophone (1983-86, 1991); George L. Ruiz, bass (1986); Bobby Bandiera, guitar (1986-present); Barry Danielian, trumpet; Dan Levine, trombone; Jerry Vivino Jr., tenor sax

Southside Johnny & the Asbury Jukes came out of same Asbury Park, N.J., scene that produced Bruce Springsteen, and at roughiy the same time. In fact, the group's leader, Southside Johnny Lyon, and Springsteen occasionally played in the same bands during the early 70s. But where Springsteen leaned toward 50s rock and Phil Spector records, Lyon preferred urban blues and horn-band R&B, leading him to form the Jukes. Lyon is an excellent, gravel-voiced white-soul singer, but the Springsteen connection has been a double-edged sword. Springsteen has written much of the Jukes' best-known material ("Hearts of Stone," "The Fever"), which has gained the group fans while creating a shadow from which it's not been able to emerge. And when the group has abandoned the Springsteen connection (as on 1979's *The Jukes*, when guitarist Rush became the primary songwriter), it has faltered. But it remains a great band in the New Jersey R&B/rock vein, if more limited in appeal than their more famous colleague.

what to buy: *Havin' a Party With Southside Johnny* (Epic, 1979, prod. Miami Steve) is a solid, if a bit skimpy, hits collection with an added live recording of Sam Cooke's "Havin' a Party." It's a great white-soul, horn-band album that features tunes by Springsteen and cameos by Ronnie Spector and Lee Dorsey.

what to buy next: *Better Days* (Impact, 1991, prod. Little Steven) finds Southside Johnny making his peace with his place in New Jersey music—and with Springsteen's shadow—reuniting with the Miami Horns for one of his toughest, most exciting albums. Little Steven returned to the production board, and Springsteen and Jon Bon Jovi contributed guest vocals. *Live/Reach Up and Touch the Sky* (Epic, 1981, prod. John Lyon and Stephan Galfas) shows the band in its natural element.

what to avoid: *Trash It Up* (Mirage, 1983, prod. Nile Rogers) totally removes Southside from his Jersey bar roots and places him in some parallel MTV-spawned R&B universe. Instead of sounding passionate, he sounds merely lascivious.

the rest: *I Don't Want to Go Home* (Epic, 1976) *This Time It's for Real* (Epic, 1977) *Hearts of Stone* (Epic, 1978) *The Jukes* (Mercury, 1979) *The Best of Southside Johnny and the Asbury Jukes* (Epic/Legacy, 1992) *The Very Best of Southside Johnny & the Asbury Jukes* (Columbia, 1993) *All I Want Is Everything: The Best of Southside Johnny & the Asbury Jukes* (Rhino, 1993) *Jukes Live at the Bottom Line* (Image, 1996)

worth searching for: *At Least We Got Shoes* (Atlantic, 1986, prod. John Lyon and John Rollo) contains a marvelous rendition of "I Only Want to Be With You."

▶▶ Little Steven & the Disciples of Soul, Jack Mack & the Heart Attack, Iron City Houserockers

◀◀ Bruce Springsteen, the Coasters, the Drifters, Gary U.S. Bonds, James Brown, Wilson Pickett

Brian Mansfield

Spandau Ballet

Formed 1980 in London, England. Disbanded 1990.

Tony Hadley, vocals; Gary Kemp, guitars; Martin Kemp, bass; Steve Norman, saxophones; John Keeble, drums

Starting out as one of the many New Romantic bands to emerge from England's late New Wave scene, this glossy, puffy pop group (which, according to some, took its name from an expression used to describe the paroxysmic flailings of a person's body as they were being gassed in a Nazi concentration camp) eventually made its mark as an overheated MOR outfit before quickly burning out and then slowly disintegrating throughout the course of the 80s. Little remains available. The quintet hit it big worldwide with the title track of its third album, *True.* (Chrysalis, 1983, prod. Tony Swain, Steve Jolley and Spandau Ballet) Here, the group was recast as a proto-lounge band, only with none of the needed irony. Granted, "Lifeline" and "Gold" were decent enough attempts at funky pop lite, and "True" did ultimately serve as the basis for P.M. Dawn's rap-lite breakthrough "Set Adrift on Memory Bliss" in 1991. But the group has to answer for its role as prototypes for mellow bellowers King and Cutting Crew, and even Spandau's better material always seemed false and unabashedly annoying. For diehards, there's always *The Singles Collection,* (Chrysalis, 1985, prod. Various) but let's just say there's not much there to collect.

Bob Remstein

Spanic Boys

Formed 1987 in Milwaukee, Wis.

Ian Spanic, vocals, guitar; Tom Spanic, vocals, guitar; Mike Fredrickson, bass (1987-93); Teddy Freese, drums (1987-91); Paul Schroeder, bass (1993-present); Curt Lefevre, drums (1991-present)

Best known as the band that replaced Sinead O'Connor when she refused to perform on "Saturday Night Live" with host Andrew (Dice) Clay in 1990, the Spanic Boys know exactly how to rock. The father-and-son team—both wearing horn-rimmed glasses goofier than Buddy Holly's—rehashes rockabilly and other roots music, but adds wailing, raging guitars that would fit on some Metallica songs. Tom, the elder Spanic, played in rock 'n' roll cover bands during the 60s, then taught guitar lessons for two decades before forming the band with his son in early 1987. Though the Boys have never produced a follow-up as powerful as the debut or *Strange World,* they deserve far more commercial attention than they've received.

what to buy: *Strange World* (Rounder, 1991, prod. Ian Spanic and Mike Hoffman) is a wonderfully catchy mix of sharp rockabilly rhythms, spooky harmonies and fierce guitar playing. *Spanic Boys* (Rounder, 1990, prod. Scott Billington) is an out-of-nowhere update of Everly Brothers harmonies and 50s-style rock 'n' roll songwriting.

what to buy next: *Dream Your Life* (Rounder, 1992, prod. Ian Spanic and Mike Hoffman) has "That Train" and a few other stomping songs, but it's not as explosive as *Strange World* or the debut.

the rest: Spanic Family, *Family Album* (ESD, 1994)

worth searching for: *Early Spanic Boys,* (Rounder, 1992, prod. Mike Hoffman) a reissue of the band's tiny-label debut, showcases its developing Buddy Holly and Chet Atkins influence.

▶▶ Blazers, Wayne Hancock, Rosie Flores, Big Sandy and the Fly-Rite Boys

◀◀ Buddy Holly, Chet Atkins, Elvis Presley, Everly Brothers, Jimi Hendrix, Richie Valens, X, Los Lobos

Steve Knopper

Sparks

Formed 1971 in Los Angeles, Calif.

Russell Mael, vocals; Ron Mael, keyboards

Brothers Ron and Russell Mael are half musical act, half comic duo. In that respect, they could almost be a pop-rock incarnation of Gilbert and Sullivan. Between Ron's operatic near-falsetto and Russell's deft and comic keyboard flourishes, the two have created their own niche in the music industry, in which excellent keyboard-pop music melds seemlessly with humorously insightful lyrics. The duo (including an ever-changing backup band) made a significant impact in England during the mid-70s with the singles "This Town Ain't Big Enough for the Both of Us" and "Amateur Hour." Success has been more elusive in its homeland, where the bulk of the group's largely terrific body of work is now out of print.

what to buy: *Profile: The Ultimate Sparks Collection* (Rhino, 1991, prod. Various) is certainly the best Sparks album available at this time. The generous double-CD package offers all the group's best material, including "This Town Ain't Big Enough for the Both of Us," "Amateur Hour," "Hasta Manana, Monsieur," "Big Boy," "Cool Places" (which features the Go-Go's Jane Wiedlin) and "Change."

what to buy next: *Angst in My Pants* (Atlantic, 1982, prod. Mack) marks the point in Sparks' history when both music and lyrics achieved an equal measure of cleverness. The album contains some of the best songs from the group's middle period, including "Eaten by the Monster of Love," "Mickey Mouse" (a bizarre tribute to the Disney gang) and "Moustache" (a history of brother Ron's facial hair). In a terrific return to form, the Mael brothers bounced back from nowhere with *Gratuitous Sax and Senseless Violins* (Logic Records, 1995, prod. Sparks) perhaps the best album from the duo since "Angst," and, indeed, the album is reminiscent of the group's earliest and most inventive work.

what to avoid: *Sparks in Outer Space* (Atlantic, 1983, prod. Ron and Russell Mael) is too self-consciously cute, and the songs are less inventive—though "Cool Places" did sneak into the Top 50.

worth searching for: *Kimono My House,* (Island, 1974) one of the best of Sparks' early albums, though it was way too quirky for the times.

▶▶ The B-52's, Talking Heads

◀◀ Captain Beefheart, Frank Zappa, Todd Rundgren, Commander Cody

Christopher Scapelliti

Spearhead

See: Disposable Heroes of Hiphoprisy

The Specials

Formed 1977 in Coventry, England. Disbanded 1981. Re-formed 1994.

Jerry Dammers, keyboards (1977-81); Lynval Golding, guitar; "Sir" Horace Panter, bass; Terry Hall, vocals (1978-81); Neville Staples, vocals, percussion; Roddy "Radiation" Byers, guitar; Siverton, drums (1977-78); John Bradbury, drums (1979-81); Mark Adams, keyboards, vocals (1994-present); Adam Birch, horns (1994-present); Aitch Hyatt, drums (1994-present)

A ska revival group, the Specials were the showpiece band of the U.K.'s short-lived two-tone movement of the late 70s and early 80s. Two-tone referred to the racially mixed groups that formed partly as a reaction to emerging skinhead racial violence in England. Evolving from various bands known as Coventry, the Coventry Specials and the Specials AKA, the group had a number of U.K. singles and EP hits with their bouncy, party-friendly ska songs. *The Specials* (Chrysalis, 1979, prod. Elvis Costello) is the peak, with party favorites such as "A Message to You, Rudy," "Monkey Man," "Gangsters" and "Too Much, Too Young." *More Specials,* (Chrysalis, 1980, prod. Jerry Dammers and Dave Jordan) the follow-up effort, lost the beat as they veered into lounge music. The best set in print is *Singles Collection* (Capitol, 1991, prod. Various) which includes "Ghost Town" and "Free Nelson Mandela," two of the group's best songs. The band shattered in 1981, when Staples, Hall and Golding formed Fun Boy Three, Byers formed Roddy Radiation & the Tearjerkers and Dammers led a revamped Specials AKA. The Specials regrouped in 1994, and *Today's Specials* (Virgin, 1996, prod. various) gets back on the ska track with a number of covers—particularly a scorching version of "Take Five"—but doesn't quite match the unbridled exuberance of the first album.

see also: *Fun Boy Three*

Lawrence Gabriel

Phil Spector

Born Dec. 24, 1940 Bronx, N.Y.

The trademark mulched sound of Spector's glorious productions—borrowed equally from Frank Guida and Leiber and Stoller—didn't survive the transfer into the digital domain with all their majesty intact. But his landmark work, probably best heard on the original 45's, commands an incomparable position in the realm of rock's history. His story is well known and, in fact, reads like fiction—the high school senior who wrote a No. 1 record (the Teddy Bears' "To Know Him is to Love Him") from his father's epitaph and "retired" at age 25 to live the life of a reclusive Beverly Hills millionaire, only to return to the studio to re-mix the tapes from the Beatles' arduous *Let it Be* sessions. Spector was rock's ultimate *auteur,* a visionary—and a notorious eccentric, to be kind—who imprinted his artistic signature so thoroughly on the records he made in the early 60s for his own Philles Records that they are universally known as Phil Spector records and not by the name of the titular artists—who, by the way, included Gene Pitney, the Crystals, the Ronettes, Darlene Love and the Righteous Brothers' "You've Lost That Lovin' Feelin'." Virtually every musician who stepped into a recording studio in his wake owes Spector a debt.

what to buy: Spector personally oversaw the production of the four-disc boxed set *Back To Mono (1958-1969),* (Abkco, 1991, prod. Phil Spector) ✪✪✪✪ so he has nobody else to blame for the indifferent, cloudy digital transfers of his masterpieces. In addition to his brilliant 1963 Christmas album, included on its own disc, the set spans his entire career—from "To Know Him Is To Love Him" to Tina Turner's "River Deep-Mountain High" and a selection of rare and unissued latter-era studio experiments.

what to buy next: Some of the invdividual albums Spector produced are well worth owning, both for the musical content as well as for the sonic virtues. Among them: George Harrison's *All Things Must Pass* (Apple, 1970); John Lennon's *Imagine* (Apple, 1971); Leonard Cohen's *Death of a Ladies' Man* (Columbia, 1977) and the Ramones' *End of the Century* (Sire, 1980). (See individual entries for ratings.) Most recently, he produced sessions for Canadian chanteuse Celine Dione that she chose not to use, so Spector keeps threatening to put out *his* version of the album.

worth searching for: Spector so carefully rewrites his own history, he breezes through his wilderness years hitting just a few successful highpoints. But a Japanese import, *Twist and Shout,* (WEA, 1989, prod. Phil Spector) ✪✪✪ collects 12 early productions he did for Atlantic Records that capture the artist in transition. They aren't uniformly great records, but the original singles are so hard to find, this set offers an unparalleled glimpse of the young Spector.

▶▶ Beach Boys, The Beatles, the Ramones, U2, Steve Lillywhite

◀◀ Gary U.S. Bonds, the Drifters, Frankie Lymon and the Teenagers

Joel Selvin and Gary Graff

Skip Spence

See: Moby Grape

Jon Spencer Blues Explosion

Formed 1991 in New York, N.Y.

Jon Spencer, vocals, guitar; Judah Bauer, guitar; Russell Simins, drums

A clever white guy from New England who attended Brown University and is obsessed with dischordant noise and low-fi recording techniques, Spencer would be a prototypical indie-rocker if it weren't for his obsession with the perverted, oily side of the blues. While his previous band, Pussy Galore, made noisy and offensive sleaze-rock, Spencer's Blues Explosion makes noisy and compellingly chaotic sleaze-blues that matches a perverted, amped-up two-guitar boogie crunch with a punch-drunk vocal delivery. Sounding at once urgent and kitschy, Spencer is a combustible, idiosyncratic showman whose crude playing and singing is unpredictable and, therefore, exciting. By no means a blues trio, the Blues Explosion did close the gap between its ironic, postmodern music and the blues when it backed R.L. Burnside on the elderly bluesman's fascinating *A Ass Pocket of Whiskey* (Matador, 1996, prod. Bruce Watson) ✪✪✪✪ Significantly less interesting are Spencer's contributions to wife Christina Martinez's band, Boss Hog.

what to buy: On the fierce and sludgy *Orange,* (Matador, 1994, prod. Jon Spencer and Jim Waters) ✪✪✪✪ the Blues Explosion finally (and thankfully) grasps the notion of song structure, making it the most accessible Blues Explosion album yet. However, lyrically, it's still often difficult to figure out exactly what Spencer is so hopped-up about.

what to buy next: *Experimental Remixes* (Matador, 1995, prod. Various) ✪✪✪✪ features dueling versions of "Greyhound" by techno auteur Moby and Wu-Tang Clan's Genius (with a menacing rap by the Wu's Killah Priest), as well as a double dip of "Flavor" by Beck, Beasties Boy Mike D and Beasties producer Mario Caldato Jr. The boot-stompin' *Extra Width* (Matador,

1993, prod. Spencer) ♪♪♪♪ isn't quite as structured as *Orange*, but it does show the trio finally finding its bearings, not to mention a funky undertone on the breakthrough "Afro."

what to avoid: Mo Width *(Au-Go-Go, 1994)* ♪♪ *isn't terrible, but it's hard for anything coming out between* Extra Width *and* Orange *to compete.*

The Rest: Jon Spencer Blues Explosion *(Caroline, 1992)* ♪♪♪♪
Crypt Style *(Crypt, 1993)* ♪♪♪

▶▶ Big Ass Truck, Beck

◀◀ Hound Dog Taylor, Elvis Presley, Cramps, Jerry Lee Lewis, Johnny Burnette, Stooges, Gibson Brothers, Stax/Volt, James Brown

Joshua Freedom du Lac

Spin Doctors

Formed 1988 in New York, N.Y.

Chris Barron (born Christopher Barron Gross), vocals; Aaron Comess, drums; Mark Burton White, bass; Eric Schenkman, guitar (1988-94); Anthony Krizan, guitar, vocals (1994-present)

Borne from the same fertile New York City blues-rock scene that also produced Joan Osborne and Blues Traveler (whose members went to the same Princeton, N.J., high school as Barron), Spin Doctors built its reputation as a tireless live band that jammed to a funky, elastic groove while rubber-boned frontman Barron bounced up and down reciting his sometimes catchy, sometimes quizzical lyrics. Despite the members' instrumental prowess, it was a tightly written hit single, "Little Miss Can't Be Wrong" that broke the band nationally. The group has been unable to repeat that accomplishment on subsequent albums, and Barron's lyrics have grown prolix. Spin Doctors have been compared to the Grateful Dead for its extended live jams and for its dedicated audience, which often follows them around the country. But maybe the real similarity is that, as with Deadheads and the Dead, dyed-in-the-wool Spin Docs fans should NOT—repeat SHOULD NOT—listen to the band after they've run out of dope. A rude awakening awaits.

what to buy: *Pocket Full of Kryptonite* (Epic, 1991, prod. Spin Doctors, Peter Denenberg and Frankie LaRocka) ♪♪♪♪ shows off both sides of the band. Its instrumental attack if varied, and what jamming goes on is well thought out and executed. The album also contains the band's two best and most concise singles, "Two Princes" and "Little Miss Can't Be Wrong." The latter song sounds so much like a Steve Miller Band smasheroo, it should have been titled "Little Miss Can't Miss"—despite its misogynistic lyric directed at Barron's former stepmother.

what to buy next: The concert recording *Homebelly Groove* (Epic, 1992, prod. Peter Denenberg, Aaron Comess, Eric Schenkman, Frankie LaRocka and Spin Doctors) ♪♪♪ bears witness to Spin Doctors' appeal as a live act. The emphasis is squarely on jamming, with Schenkman's guitar leading the way and some impressive rhythmic interplay between Comess and White. This release adds a handful of new and previously unreleased tracks to the 1990 *Up For Grabs* EP, including a live version of "Little Miss Can't Be Wrong."

what to avoid: *Turn It Upside Down* (Epic, 1994, prod. Frankie LaRocka) WOOF! is the very definition of a sophomore slump; it makes all the same moves as *Pocket Full of Kryptonite*, only not half as well. The downward spiral continues with *You've Got to Believe in Something* (Epic, 1996, prod. Danny Kortchmar and Peter Denenberg) which features moronically pseudopoetic lyrics ("Riches and the roads bring brigands hither...") and even less musical oomph than *Turn It Upside Down*

worth searching for: Fanatics and collectors may want to search used CD bins for the now deleted original version of *Up for Grabs*, (Epic EP, 1990) ♪♪♪ just so they can say they knew 'em when.

▶▶ Screaming Cheetah Wheelies, the Why Store, Ugly Americans

◀◀ The Grateful Dead, the Steve Miller Band, Parliament-Funkadelic, Blues Traveler

Daniel Durchholz

Spinal Tap

Formed 1984 in Los Angeles, Calif.

David St. Hubbins (Michael McKeon), vocals/guitar; Nigel Tufnel (Christopher Guest), guitar/vocals; Derek Smalls (Harry Shearer), bass

Spinal Tap is really two bands: the fictional heavy metal dinosaurs featured in director Rob Reiner's brilliant 1984 rockumentary satire "This is Spinal Tap," and the film's writers/actors who wrote and performed the music for the film's soundtrack and one other album. "This is Spinal Tap" documented the waning years of a British hard rock outfit that never quite made it over the course of two decades, numerous name changes, dozens of albums with titles such as *Brain Hammer, Shark Sandwich, Intravenus de Milo* and *The Sun Never Sweats*, and a succession of drummers, all of whom seem to die under mysterious circumstances (including one who choked on vomit—somebody else's—and several who spontaneously combusted). It's all great fun, and occasionally all too accurate to real-life music industry experiences. The *This is Spinal Tap* soundtrack (Polydor, 1984, prod. Spinal Tap) contains passable musicianship and hilarious metal send-ups such as "Sex Farm," "Hell Hole" and "Big Bottom" ("The bigger the cushion/The better the pushin' "), as well as the psychedelic "(Listen to the) Flower People." But *Break Like the Wind* (MCA, 1992, prod. Danny Kortchmar) showed that the joke wasn't as funny the second time around, despite guest shots by Jeff Beck, Joe Satriani, Cher and Guns N' Roses' Slash

Brandon Trenz

The Spinners

Formed 1957 in Detroit, Mich.

Bobbie Smith, tenor vocals; Pervis Jackson, bass vocals; Henry Fambrough, baritone vocals; Billy Henderson, tenor-baritone vocals; George Dixon, tenor vocals (1957-62); Edgar Edwards, tenor vocals (1962-66); G.C. Cameron, tenor vocals (1967-72); Phillipe Wynne, tenor vocals (1972-77, died July 13, 1984); John Edwards, tenor vocals (1977-present)

The Spinners' easy soul is so eminently likable and immediate it's easy to take the group for granted. The singers spent most of the 60s spinning their wheels at Motown, but the group hit gold with a move to Atlantic and the patronage of producer Thom Bell in 1972. Bell crafted breathtakingly smooth songs which the Spinners nailed in performance, culminating in 17 charted singles and five gold albums—figures that rivaled the group's chief counterparts of Philly soul, the O'Jays. Flanked by sweet harmonies and deceptively simple strings and brass, newcomer Wynne—gruff yet sensitive, versatile yet controlled—was one of the best soul singers of the 70s. Wynne left for a solo career in 1977 and died of a heart attack onstage seven years later. Although Edwards is a strong frontman, Bell was only able to channel the new blood into one more hit in 1979. But the Spinners clearly have enough material to fill the shows the group continues to play on the oldies circuit.

what to buy: The hit parade began with *Spinners* (Rhino, 1973/1995, prod. Thom Bell) with the buoyant likes of "I'll be Around," "One of a Kind (Love Affair)," "Ghetto Child" and "Could it be I'm Falling in Love." *Pick of the Litter* (Rhino, 1975/1995, prod. Thom Bell) is the most fully conceptualized Spinners album, containing the group's best song, "Games People Play."

what to buy next: *One of a Kind Love Affair: The Anthology* (Rhino Records, 1991, prod. Various) brilliantly seams the group's best work together on a two-disc, 30-track whopper. In addition to the obvious, it also includes the pre-Wynne hit "It's a Shame" (featuring the long-forgotten G.C. Cameron's shining moment) as well as later disco pop-offs such as "The Rubberband Man." On *Mighty Love*, (Rhino, 1975/1995, prod. Thom Bell) Wynne stakes his claim as the decade's most exciting soul man, particularly with his blissful, extemporaneous vocal on the title track.

what to avoid: The 13-track *Best of The Spinners* (Rebound Records, 1994, prod. Howard Smiley) hardly realizes the scope of the group's work and is skimpy in comparison to *One of a Kind Love Affair*

the rest: *Best of the Spinners* (Rhino, 1978/1986) *Dancin' and Lovin'* (Rhino, 1979/1992) *Best of the Spinners* (Motown, 1988) *Down to Business* (Volt, 1989) *New and Improved* (Rhino, 1995)

worth searching for: The out-of-print *Spinners Live* (Atlantic, 1975) showed the group could do it onstage, too.

The Trammps, Maze, the Dazz Band

Smokey Robinson and the Miracles, the Temptations, the Drifters, the O'Jays, Major Lance

Allan Orski

Spirit

Formed 1969, Los Angeles, Calif.

Randy California (b. Randy Wolfe), vocals, guitar (1967-70, 1974-present); Ed Cassidy, drums (1967-present); Jay Ferguson (b. John Ferguson), vocals, guitar, keyboards (1967-70, 1984); John Locke, keyboards, vocals (1967-72, 1976-77, 1984); Mark Andes, bass, vocals (1967-70, 1976-77, 1984); Chris Staehely, vocals, guitar (1970-74); Al Staehely, bass, vocals (1970-74); Matt Andes, guitar (1976-77); Larry Knight, bass (1977-present)

Spirit was very much a band of its time, that being the psychedelic late 60s. All of the original members encountered each other in and around Los Angeles before settling into the group; Cassidy, Spirit's oldest member by at least 25 years, was California's stepfather. Though its musical scope was impressive—

mixing rock, blues, jazz and country in a trippy stew—Spirit was a second division fixture at best, though it did produce one enduring hit in "I Got a Line on You." Numerous personnel changes led to an original lineup reunion in 1984. Andes and Ferguson co-founded the band Jo Jo Gunne; Andes moved on to Firefall and Heart, while Ferguson had a couple of solo hits ("Thunder Island," "Shakedown Cruise"). These days California and Cassidy keep Spirit on the oldies circuit with a revolving series of bassists.

what to buy: *The Twelve Dreams of Dr. Sardonicus* (Epic, 1970, David Briggs, prod.) was Spirit's crowning moment and one of era's great underrated albums. Loosely conceptual, it housed songs that were Spirit's prettiest ("Nature's Way"), funkiest ("Mr. Skin") and hippiest ("Animal Zoo," "Nothin' to Hide"). Rather than dated, it still sounds fresh today.

what to buy next: Everyone needs to own "I Got a Line on You" in some form. The best is probably *Time Circle, (1968-1972)* (Epic/Legacy, 1991, prod. Bob Irwin) a double-length compilation of music from Spirit's first four albums. Some of the 41 songs haven't aged as well as "Line" or the "Sardonicus" material, but it's still better than any of the individual albums.

what to avoid: *The Adventures of Kaptain Kopter & Commander Cassidy in Potatoland* (Rhino, 1981, prod. Randy California). WOOF! You need more explanation than the title?

the rest: *Spirit* (Ode, 1968) *The Family That Plays Together* (Ode, 1968) *Clear* (Ode, 1969) *Feedback* (Epic, 1972) *The Best of Spirit* (Epic, 1973) *Spirit of '76* (Mercury, 1975) *Son of Spirit* (Mercury, 1975) *Farther Along,* (Mercury, 1976) *Future Games* (Mercury, 1977) *Spirit of '84* (Mercury, 1984) *Rapture in the Chambers* (I.R.S., 1989) *Tent of Miracles* (Dolphin/Caroline, 1990)

worth searching for: *Live Spirit* (Potato, 1979, prod. Randy California) offers an inspired trio performance with an additional verse in "Nature's Way" and expanded versions of "Looking Down" and "All the Same."

solo outings:

Randy California *Kaptain Kopter & the Fabulous Twirlybirds* (Epic, 1972) *Euro-American* (Beggars Banquet, 1982) *Shattered Dreams* (Line, 1987)

Jo Jo Gunne (Ferguson and Andes) *Jo Jo Gunne* (Asylum, 1972) *Bite Down Hard* (Asylum, 1973) *Jumping the Gunne* (Asylum, 1973) WOOF! *So...Where's the Snow?* (Asylum, 1974)

Jay Ferguson *All Alone in the End Zone* (Asylum, 1976) *Thunder Island* (Asylum, 1977) *Real Life Ain't This Way (Asylum, 1979)* White Noise *(Capitol, 1982)*

Jo Jo Gunne (Ferguson and Andes), Firefall, Heart (Andes)

The Weavers, Gerry Mulligan, Thelonious Monk, Rising Sons, Jimi Hendrix

see also: *Heart, Firefall*

Gary Graff

Split Enz /Tim Finn/Finn Brothers/Alt

Formed 1972 in Auckland, New Zealand

Tim Finn, vocals (1972-83); Phil Judd, guitars, vocals (1972-77); Eddie Rayner, keyboards; Malcolm Green, drums (1972-82); Noel Crombie, percussion, drums (1972-84); Phil Chunn, bass (1974-77); Nigel Griggs, bass (1977-84); Neil Finn, guitar, lead vocals (1977-84); Paul Hester, drums (1984)

Split Enz's history begins with the band's art school genesis in 1972. Not quite fitting into the burgeoning punk scene of the mid-70s, the band did little to distinguish itself. But in 1977, following the departure of co-founder Judd, singer Tim Finn brought his younger brother Neil aboard as the band's guitarist and second vocalist, thus beginning Split Enz's most commercially fruitful period. Where the band had previously explored odd song structures and artistic indulgences, Neil's influence added a leaner pop sensibility to the mix. With the release of the 1980 album *True Colors*, Split Enz achieved a balance between its past quirks and an increasing talent for hooks that brought the group to the fore of the New Wave movement bubbling up in punk's wake. Tim Finn left the group for a solo career in 1983, and in the early 90s he formed the group Alt with Liam O'Maonlai from Hothouse Flowers and Irish recording star Andy White. Split Enz split up a year later, and Neil Finn led the group Crowded House—which included Tim on its excellent album *Woodface* In 1994, the brothers reunited as the Finn Brothers in the U.S. and as Finn everywhere else.

what to buy: Regrettably, almost all of the Split Enz catalog has been deleted in the U.S.—a pity given the quality that its best albums displayed. Of the remaining choices, the retrospective *History Never Repeats* (A&M, 1987, prod. Various) is the most representative of the band's range. The collection focuses on the more pop-friendly material in the band's ouevre, and, as a result, Neil Finn's material gets a greater proportion of the spotlight than it did on the group's albums.

what to buy next: The only other Split Enz album that is available domestically is its landmark *True Colors*, (A&M, 1980, prod. David Tickle) which saw the first flourish of Neil's pop sensibility (the hit "I Got You"), while Tim still managed to infuse the album with plenty of nervous, arty energy ("Shark Attack"). *Finn Brothers* (Discovery, 1996, prod. Tchad Blake, Neil Finn and Tim Finn) is an excellent showcase for the brothers' love of close harmony singing and catchy melodies. It's an engaging and often quirky album that sounds at once familiar but nothing like anything they've done in the past.

what to avoid: Tim Finn's solo album *Big Canoe* (Virgin, 1988, prod. Nick Launay) is an unruly, self-indulgent mess, missing his characteristic knack for melody.

worth searching for: With so much of the Split Enz catalog available on import only, there are lots of choices here. *Waiata*, (A&M, 1981, prod. David Tickle) featuring the stellar Neil Finn compositions "One Step Ahead" and "History Never Repeats," is particularly worth the hunt.

solo outings:

Tim Finn: Tim Finn (Capitol, 1989) *Before and After* (Capitol, 1993) (with Alt) *Altitude* (Cooking Vinyl, 1995)

▶▶ Phil Keaggv, Schnell Fenster, That Petrol Emotion, Boom Crash Opera, Crowded House

◀◀ Roxy Music, David Bowie, the Beatles

see also: *Crowded House*

Dave Galens

Sponge

Formed 1993 in Detroit, Mich.

Vinnie Dombroski, vocals; Mike Cross, guitar; Joey Mazzola, guitar; Tim Cross, bass; Jimmy Paluzzi, drums (1993-95); Charlie Grover, drums (1995-present)

Blending glam attitude and traditional blue collar Detroit rock, Sponge is no overnight sensation. Most of the band members sharpened their teeth in Loudhouse, which was dropped by Virgin Records after one album. The bad news fiercely motivated Dombroski and the Cross brothers into creating and succeeding with Sponge—an attitude reflected in songs such as "Plowed" and "Rainin' " off its debut *Rotting Pinata*. (Work, 1994, prod. Sponge and Tim Patalan) But it's the follow-up, *Wax Ecstatic*, (Columbia, 1996, prod. Sponge and Tim Patalan) that really has the goods, with grinding guitars, relentlessly hook-laden lyrics and melodies, and Dombroski's raw vocals fill the 10-song album originally meant to be a concept album about a drag queen.

Christina Fuoco

The Spongetones

Formed circa 1980 in Charlotte, N.C.

Jamie Hoover, vocals, guitar, bass, mandolin,recorder, harmonica; Steve Stoeckel, vocals, bass, guitar; Rob Thorne, drums, percussion; Patrick Walters, vocals, keyboard, guitar, harmonica, dulcimer

The early Beatles reborn, or merely an incredible simulation (or maybe Klaatu in disguise)? Dismissed by some as too slavishly derivative of the Fab Four , the Spongetones have delighted discerning pop fans with avowedly Beatlesque hooks 'n' harmonies. The group's earliest efforts were engaging pastiches of *Beatles '65*—much like the Rutles played straight—with each tune a familiar-sounding rummage through the British Invasion songbook. While it's certainly fun playing name-that-tune, the appeal of the Spongetones' recordings lies not in where the group nicks its hooks and melodies, but in the self-assured manner in which it assembles such thefts into appealing new pop confections. Later recordings have downplayed the Mersey factor but have generally retained an unspoiled, irresistible pop charm.

what to buy: *Beat & Torn* (Black Vinyl, 1994, prod. Jamie Hoover) combines the group's first two releases, *Beat Music* (Ripete, 1982) and *Torn Apart*, (Ripete, 1984) on one CD, along with a bonus song; that means 19 tracks of heart-stopping ersatz Mersey beat, performed with a sense of gusto and accomplishment that makes the music's second-hand roots an irrelevant point. *Oh Yeah!* (Black Vinyl, 1991, prod. Jamie Hoover) assimilates the Spongetones' influences into a brilliant work that's still beholden to the Beatles, but less slavish in its devotion.

what to buy next: *On* For Textural Drone Thing, *(Black Vinyl, 1995, prod. Jamie Hoover) the Spongetones cut back on the Beatlemania moves in an attempt to forge a new group identity. The result lacks the immediate rush of the group's faux Liverpudlian material, but succeeds in the easy-going pop style familiar to fans of Marshall Crenshaw.*

what to avoid: Recorded without participation from Stoeckel, *Where-Ever-Land* (Triapore, 1987, prod. Jamie Hoover and Don

Dixon) was the group's first attempt to get away from imitation Britboom, a stumble despite the superior tracks "Anna" and "Talk to the Girl."

worth searching for: The Spongetones have contributed worthwhile non-album tracks to a few sampler albums, including "Christmasland" on *Yuletunes,* (Black Vinyl, 1991, prod. Various) "Skinny" on *Yellow Pills, Volume One* (Big Deal, 1993, prod. Various) and "Eyedoan Geddit" to *Hit the Hay, Volume 2.* (Sound Asleep, 1996, prod. Various)

solo outings:

Jamie Hoover Coupons, Questions and Comments (Triapore, 1990)

Marshall Crenshaw, JellyfishRewind: The Beatles, the Hollies, the Knickerbockers, the Searchers, the Dave Clark Five

Carl Cafarelli

Dusty Springfield

Born Mary O'Brien on April 16, 1939, in London, England

Springfield's remarkable range allows her to invest everything from baroque pop to Southern soul with nuance and grit. Though possessed of extraordinary power—when she belts, the hairs on the back of your neck are likely to give her a standing ovation—she shows in her finest work great restraint and vulnerability. And despite her prodigious technical abilities, she makes it seem easy. She emerged during the early 60s with the Lana Sisters, and then moved on to the folk group the Springfields, which featured her brother and was best known for such hit songs as "Silver Threads and Golden Needles." Springfield embarked on a solo career after the group broke up in 1963 and was soon making waves with her clarion interpretations of both pop and R&B numbers. She continued scoring hits through the 60s with everything from gutsy soul tracks ("I Only Want to Be with You") to Burt Bacharach and Hal David's "I Just Don't Know What to Do with Myself." She went for a slightly saucier sound as the decade progressed, typified by the gritty, soul-inflected hit "Son of a Preacher Man." After lying low during most of the 70s, she returned to the charts in 1987 as the singer on "What Have I Done to Deserve This" by ironic synth-popsters the Pet Shop Boys. She was last spotted in Nashville recording her 1995 album, *A Very Fine Love.*

what to buy: *Dusty in Memphis* (Atlantic, 1969, prod. Jerry Wexler, Arif Mardin and Tom Dowd) is a perfect marriage of singer and material for an incandescent moment in pop history. Springfield's every aching syllable is perfection.

what to buy next: *Golden Hits* (Philips, 1966, prod. various) is a reasonable, if spotty, retrospective that concentrates mostly on her giddy Brill Building tunes.

what to avoid: *It Begins Again* (United Artists, 1978, prod. Roy Thomas Baker) is an ill-advised attempt to modernize the singer.

the rest: *The Dusty Springfield Album* (Philips, 1964) *You Don't Have to Say You Love Me* (Philips, 1966) *Look of Love* (Philips, 1967) *Stay Awhile* (Mercury, 1968) *A Brand New Me* (Atlantic, 1970) *For You, Love, Dusty* (Philips, 1971) *Cameo* (Dunhill, 1973) *Living Without Your Love* (Mercury, 1979) *White Heat* (Casablanca, 1982) *Reputation* (Casablanca, 1990) *A Very Fine Love* (Columbia, 1995)

worth searching for: *The Silver Collection,* (Philips, 1988, prod. Various) an import collection that is the final word on all Springfield compilations.

Blondie, Chrissie Hynde, Elvis Costello, Pet Shop Boys, Echobelly

Aretha Franklin, Diana Ross, Fontella Bass, Leslie Gore, Sandy Denny, Lulu

Simon Glickman

Springhouse

Formed 1988 in New York, N.Y. Disbanded 1993.

Mitch Friedland, guitar, vocals, hammer dulcimer; Jack Rabid (born Paul Corradi), drums, vocals; Larry Heinemann, bass, guitar, Chapman Stick, mandolin, backing vocals

Springhouse combined the talents of Blue Man Group music director Heinemann, punk drummer and music critic (and MusicHound contributor) Jack Rabid, formerly of Even Worse, and a guitar sound-obsessed ambulance driver, Friedland. The group became a downtown Manhattan favorite thanks to opening slots with British bands championed by Rabid in his long-running fanzine, the Big Takeover. Those bands' fans were exactly the audience most likely to appreciate Springhouse's pastel-tinted sound, akin to some British "shoegazer" bands. Friedland constructed shimmering walls of tintinnabulation by running his gut-strung acoustic guitar through effects boxes and then singing over it in the prototypical voice of understated angst. Underpinning his work were Rabid's sophisticated,

What Album Changed Your Life?

"When I was a teenager and just staring to play guitar, I got Aerosmith's Toys in the Attic. I listened to it and learned how to play the stuff they were playing. It was my first real hard rock album, so I identified with that. I can listen to it today and it's still one of my favorite Aerosmith records."

Mike Cross (Sponge)

punky drumming and Heinemann's elastic bass. After releasing an indie single, the group signed with Caroline and released a debut that did moderately well thanks to a little MTV play. Ironically, the rise of alternative music crowded out the band's sophomore effort. The group experienced a disastrous cross-country tour in early 1993—its equipment was stolen and its van was damaged so badly in the robbery that it couldn't be driven and, as a result, shows were cancelled. If that weren't bad enough, its record company dropped it. So the group chose to disband.

what to buy: On *Postcards from the Arctic,* (Caroline, 1993, prod. Joe Chiccarelli) ♪♪♪♪♪ the best song among many great slices of atmospheric, melodic pop is "Alley Park," aka "Twilight." And twilight symbolizes the overall mood—a thoughtful, almost painfully beautiful sound enveloping lyrics about finding one's place in this world.

the rest: *Land Falls* (Caroline, 1991) ♪♪♪♪ *Eskimo* (Caroline EP, 1991) ♪♪♪♪

Steve Holtje

Bruce Springsteen /Bruce Springsteen and The E Street Band

Born Sept. 23, 1949 in Freehold, N.J.

E Street Band: Clarence Clemons, saxophone, vocals (1972-89); Garry Tallent, bass (1972-89); Danny Federici, keyboards (1972-89); Vini "Mad Dog" Lopez, drums (1972-73); Ernest "Boom" Carter, drums (1973-74); David Sancious, keyboards (1972-74); Max Weinberg, drums (1974-89); Roy Bittan, keyboards (1972-89); "Miami" Steve Van Zandt, guitar, vocals (1975-84); Nils Lofgren, guitar, vocals (1984-89); Patti Scialfa, vocals, guitar (1984-89)

Springsteen didn't set out to be the new Bob Dylan or the future of rock 'n' roll or any of the other hyperbole attached to him when he began recording during the early 70s. He was, in fact, a prototypical Jersey shore rocker—big guitars and bouncy tunes with at least a little bit o' soul—who also had an appreciation for poetry and the great, sweeping narratives of American literature; Springsteen understood the art in "The Grapes of Wrath," in "Like a Rolling Stone," and in "Louie, Louie," and he funneled those sensibilities into his own body of work. Besides the new Dylan tag, Springsteen also survived having his picture appear simultaneously on the cover of Time and Newsweek, being used as a crass campaign tool by Ronald Reagan and a troubled (and short) first marriage that ended amidst papparazzi photos of his affair with current wife Patti Scialfa. That's a testament to the credibility of his music—with and without the E Street Band—which has proven more durable than the transient aspects of image-building and marketability. Springsteen's common man touch never stood in the way of strong, vivid writing; "Baby this town rips the bones from your back" is a killer image, and Springsteen has dozens of 'em. Springsteen made a name for himself during the 70s as the ultimate bar-rocker on a big stage, but there's been considerable growth and stylistic diversions that have been fascinating to witness, from his full-on embrace of big, stadium rock on *Born in the U.S.A.* to the stripped-down, folky orientation of *Nebraska* and *The Ghost of Tom Joad* to the more personal ruminations of *Lucky Town*. Through it all, Springsteen has upheld the notion of rock 'n' roll as spiritual salvation, something that can help you through the worst of times and celebrate the best. He's a True Believer who's been able to convey that faith both on record and onstage.

what to buy: Springsteen hit a prolific creative peak between 1975-80, turning out three seminal albums and a wealth of castoffs that—as myriad bootlegs attest—were of equally high quality. *Born to Run* (Columbia, 1975, prod. Bruce Springsteen, Jon Landau and Mike Appel) ♪♪♪♪♪ mines themes of escapism (the title track, "Thunder Road") and nostalgia ("Backstreets"), and delivers a rare four-on-the-floor love song in "She's the One" and an epic street tale in "Jungleland." Coming after a long legal battle to extricate himself from a management deal,

Darkness on the Edge of Town (Columbia, 1978, prod. Bruce Springsteen and Jon Landau) is indeed darker but not without redemptive hope in songs such as "Badlands" and "The Promised Land." This may well be Springsteen's best batch of songs, though the production is criminally flat. *The River* (Columbia, 1980, prod. Bruce Springsteen, Jon Landau and Steve Van Zandt) is a sprawling, double-length collection that sweeps from the frat rock of "Sherry Darling" and "Cadillac Ranch" to the more somber "Independence Day" and "The Price You Pay" to the endlessly moving title track. An epic aural journey. Fifteen years later, Springsteen's spare, folky *The Ghost of Tom Joad* (Columbia, 1995, prod. Bruce Springsteen and Chuck Plotkin) finds him examining many of the same themes—namely the state of the American Dream and where it's left ordinary Joes and Janes—in hushed and vividly cinematic narratives.

what to buy next: *The Wild, the Innocent and the E Street Shuffle* (Columbia, 1973, prod. Mike Appel and Jim Cretecos) is loose and expansive, with Springsteen and the original E Streeters really stretching out on "Kitty's Back" and the seminal "Rosalita (Come Out Tonight)." The multi-million selling magnitude of *Born in the U.S.A.* (Columbia, 1984, prod. Bruce Springsteen, Jon Landau, Chuck Plotkin and Steve Van Zandt) sometimes obscures the disturbing vision that exists within this crafted, radio-friendly batch of songs. *Lucky Town* (Columbia, 1992, prod. Bruce Springsteen, Jon Landau and Chuck Plotkin) came out as a twin to the poppier *Human Touch,* but this one digs deeper into Springsteen's emotional revitalization following his divorce and subsequent marriage to Scialfa.

what to avoid: On his debut, *Greetings from Asbury Park, N.J.* ,(Columbia, 1973, prod. Mike Appel and Jim Cretecos) Columbia thought it had a troubadour, not a rocker, and this set sounds more stiff and mannered each passing year.

the rest: *Nebraska* (Columbia, 1982) *Live, 1975-1985* (Columbia, 1986) *Tunnel of Love* (Columbia, 1987) *Human Touch* (Columbia, 1992) *Greatest Hits* (Columbia, 1994)

worth searching for: Along with the Beatles, Bob Dylan and Prince, Springsteen is one of rock's most bootlegged artists. There are lots of worthwhile titles, but two live releases stand out: *The Saint, The Incident & the Main Point Shuffle,* (Great Dane, 1990) from a 1975 show that features violinist Suki Lahav, an E Street short-timer; and the three-disc *Piece De Resistance,* (Great Dane, 1990) the best of many radio broadcasts during Springsteen's 1978 tour. Also worthwhile is *The Early Years,* (Early, 1994, prod. Mike Appel and Jim Cretecos) a legitimate collection of early recordings and demos that slipped out overseas before Springsteen put the legal clamps on it.

solo outings:

Clarence Clemons Peacemaker (Zoo, 1995)

▶▶ Bryan Adams, John Mellencamp, John Cafferty, Will T. Massey, Melissa Etheridge

◀◀ Roy Orbison, Chuck Berry, Bob Dylan, Van Morrison, Creedence Clearwater Revival

see also: *Nils Lofgren, Little Steven*

Gary Graff

Squeeze /Difford and Tilbrook/Jools Holland

Formed 1974 in London, England. Disbanded 1982. Re-formed 1985.

Chris Difford, guitar, vocals; Glenn Tilbrook, guitar, vocals; Julian (Jools) Holland, keyboards, vocals (1974-80, 1985-90); Harry Kakoulli, bass (1974-79); Gilson Lavis, drums (1974-93); John Bentley, bass (1979-82); Paul Carrack, vocals, keyboards (1981-82, 1993); Don Snow, keyboards, vocals (1982, 1995-present as John Savannah); Keith Wilkinson, bass, vocals (1985-present); Andy Metcalfe, keyboards (1985-90); Matt Irving, keyboards, accordion (1985-90); Pete Thomas, drums (1993); Kevin Wilkinson, drums (1995-present)

Lousy promotion, comparisons to the Beatles and regular lineup changes have kept this plucky bunch at cult status in the U.S., but to their fans, music critics and fellow musicians, Squeeze was one of the most important bands to emerge from the British New Wave scene of the early 80s. The songwriting duo of Difford (lyrics) and Tilbrook (music) have been crafting sublime music together for nearly 25 years; they've often been mentioned in the same breath as Lennon-McCartney and Gilbert and Sullivan. Unsettled by such lofty comparisons and the constant turnover of keyboardists, Difford and Tilbrook folded up the tent in 1982 to pursue a career as a duo. They restarted Squeeze's engines in 1985, and the band has been rolling along ever since. Through all the ups and downs, Difford and Tilbrook have remained remarkably loyal to each other, and their place in pop history is secure.

what to buy: *Argybargy* (A&M, 1980, prod. John Wood and

Squeeze) features clever, driving pop songs such as "Pulling Mussels From the Shell" and "If I Didn't Love You," which showcase Holland's considerable piano skills, Difford's wordsmithery and Tilbrook's meaty guitar hooks. The equally impressive and Beatlesque *East Side Story* (A&M, 1981, prod. Roger Bechirian, Elvis Costello and Dave Edmunds) was the band's breakthrough album Stateside, with a broad pop style embraced country and classical undertones—as well as ace songs such as "Tempted," "In Quintessence" and "Piccadilly," a masterful pop portrait of London life. *Singles—45's and Under* (A&M, 1982, prod. Various) offers a classy dollop of the band's early years.

what to buy next: *Sweets From A Stranger* (A&M, 1982, prod. Squeeze and Phil McDonald) is another finely crafted pop album that contains the enduring fan favorites "Black Coffee In Bed" (with background vocals by Costello and Paul Young).

what to avoid: *Frank* (A&M, 1989, prod. Eric (E.T.) Thorngren and Glenn Tilbrook) isn't one of Difford's best efforts lyrically, and his voice is pressed to its limit during his lead vocals on "Slaughtered, Gutted and Heartbroken" and "Love Circles."

the rest: *U.K. Squeeze* (A&M, 1978) *Cool For Cats* (A&M, 1979) *Babylon And On* (A&M, 1987) *Classics Volume 25* (A&M, 1988) *A Round And A Bout* (I.R.S., 1990) *Play* (Reprise, 1990) *Some Fantastic Place* (A&M, 1993) *Ridiculous* (I.R.S., 1996)

worth searching for: *Cosi Fan Tutti Frutti,* (A&M, 1985) the reformed band's lush, complex comeback, features the haunting "Last Time Forever" and Motown-influenced "Hits of the Year."

solo outings:

Difford and Tilbrook *Difford & Tilbrook* (A&M, 1984)

Jools Holland *A World of His Own* (I.R.S., 1990) *The A-Z of the Piano* (Bugle, 1993)

Gin Blossoms, Crowded House, the Odds, Del Amitri

Roots: the Beatles, Motown, 10CC, Todd Rundgren

see also: *Paul Carrack*

William Hanson

Billy Squier

Born May 12, 1950 in Wellesley Hills, Mass.

Squier's blown-dry shag and rock star good looks, coupled with semi-aggressive thumpers of macho lust, eventually computed to national success during the early 80s with slickly produced rock radio favorites such as "Everybody Wants You," "The Stroke" and "My Kinda Lover." Although he recoiled from the teen idol popularity that ensued, subsequent recordings (and videos) did little to dissuade his beef-boy image. Resolutely sticking to a sexist one-two grind, he pushed his horny Telecaster against the increasingly politically correct climate while record sales dropped in proportion. His recent recordings also reveal cranky rockers that lack the melodic hooks that redeem his early material—though, to his credit, he's refused to latch onto the 70s/80s retro tours that trot out on the road every summer.

what to buy: *Don't Say No* (Capitol/EMI, 1981, prod. Mack and Billy Squier) is unquestionably his finest moment as well as his commercial breakthrough, with the not-so-subtle wordplay of "The Stroke" and enduring radio faves such as "Lonely is the Night," "In the Dark" and "My Kinda Lover." *The Best of Billy Squier: 16 Strokes* (Capitol/EMI, 1995, prod. Various) is the most economical overview available, though it curiously omits "Lonely is the Night."

what to buy next: *Reach for the Sky: The Anthology* (Polygram, 1996, prod. Various) rewards those with more than a passing interest with a good chunk of material from out-of-print albums as well as two tracks from his fledgling band, Piper. Even so, a 41-year-old man jerking around with nonsense such as "She Goes Down" is just plain sad, not to mention creepy.

what to avoid: The sophomoric pitfalls of *Here and Now* (Capitol/EMI Records, 1989, prod. Godfrey Diamond and Billy Squier) are summed up by song titles such as "Rock Out/Punch Somebody" sum it up. It's redeemed slightly by "Don't Say You Love Me," but it's hard to mess up a Bo Diddley beat.

the rest: *Emotions in Motion* (Capitol/EMI, 1982)

worth searching for: *Enough is Enough,* (Capitol, 1986) now out-of-print, features a guest appearance from Queen's Freddie Mercury as well as "Love is the Hero" and "Lady With a Tenor Sax," Squier's best songs since *Don't Say No*

Bon Jovi, Def Leppard, Winger, Dokken, Quiet Riot

Kiss, Led Zeppelin, Rick Springfield, Queen

Allan Orski

Chris Squire

See: Yes

The Standells

Formed 1964 in Los Angeles, Calif. Disbanded 1967.

Dick Dodd, drums, vocals; Larry Tamblyn, organ, vocals; Tony Valentino, guitar, vocals; Gary Lane, bass, vocals (1964-66); Dave Burke, bass, vocals (1966); John Fleck, bass, vocals (1966-67)

Beloved TV personality Herman Munster said it best: "I'm going to sleep a lot easier tonight knowing that the future of America is in the hands of fine young men like the Standells." What a testimonial! The Standells were the definitive American punk band of the 60s; never mind that they'd started out as just another L.A. teen cover act, or that Dodd had been a Mouseketeer on TV's Mickey Mouse Club (or that Tamblyn's brother Russ played Riff in "West Side Story"). On record, these guys projected themselves as the American Rolling Stones, seething with attitude and daring you to tempt their wrath. The confidant swagger of "Dirty Water" scored a No. 11 hit single and a permanent entry in the Punk Rock Hall O' Fame. No other big hits followed, but equally sneering efforts such as "Why Pick on Me," "Sometimes Good Guys Don't Wear White," the salacious "Try It," "Riot On Sunset Strip," "Have You Ever Spent the Night in Jail" and "Rari," the ferocious punk B-side of "Dirty Water," ensure the Standells a place in the heart of anyone with a chip on his shoulder and a song in his heart. *Best of the Standells* (Rhino, 1989, prod. Ed Cobb and Sonny Bono) collects all of the essential Standells sides in one package, and packs the most potent punch of any Standells disc. For the more serious fan, the four original Standells albums are available. Avoid *The Hot Ones,* (Tower, 1966/Sundazed, 1994, prod. Ed Cobb) an ill-advised collection of then-contemporary covers, but *Dirty Water,* (Tower, 1966/Sundazed, 1994, prod. Ed Cobb) *Why Pick on Me* (Tower, 1966/Sundazed, 1994, prod. Ed Cobb) and *Try It* (Tower, 1967/Sundazed, 1994 prod. Ed Cobb) are well worthwhile.

Carl Cafarelli

Paul Stanley

See: Kiss

Lisa Stansfield

Born April 11, 1966 in Rochdale, England

Stansfield had all the makings of another teen diva, coming up through the talent contest and TV show ranks. But her tastes ran not towards pop but to soul, which isn't surprising considering that she hung around R&B-loving Manchester quite a bit. She started out in a group called Blue Zone with former schoolmates Andy Morris and Ian Devaney; the group—or, rather, Stansfield's—break came when the British production team Coldcut recorded its "People Hold On," which became a Top 20 hit. Arista Records signed Stansfield, and Morris and Devaney stayed on as her producers, songwriters and backing musicians. Her debut, *Affection* (Arista, 1989, prod. Ian Devaney and Andy Morris) was a deserving smash, lush, sultry and buoyant all at the same time. The songs—including the hits "All Around the World" and "You Can't Deny It"—are deft pop confections, and Stansfield's performance is absolutely outstanding. Unfortunately, the trio hasn't come up with anything of the same caliber since.

the rest: *Real Love* (Arista, 1991) *So Natural* (Arista, 1993)

Gary Graff

The Staple Singers

Formed 1953 in Chicago, Ill.

Roebuck "Pops" Staples, vocals, guitar; Mavis Staples, vocals; Cleo Staples, vocals; Pervis Staples, vocals (1953-71); Yvonne Staples, vocals (1966-present)

The Staple Singers began as a gospel group founded by parents Pops and Oceola Staples, who migrated to Chicago from Mississippi during the early 40s. Enlisting their two older daughters and one son, they began performing in church and, during the 50s, started recording for the Vee-Jay label. Youngest daughter Yvonne joined during the 60s, and the Staples became one of the country's most beloved Southern-style gospel ensembles. The family edged into non-religious pop as the 60s rolled on, then turned into a mainstream soul act upon signing to the legendary Stax label. Their churchy testifying worked perfectly against the backdrop of the funky soul that Stax provided—scoring hits such as "Respect Yourself" and "I'll Take You There"—though many in the gospel world never forgave the group for giving in to the temptations of secular music. What these purists failed to recognize is that the Staples' spiritual message was a powerfully uplifting force on black radio. While the Staples' hits continue to be sampled by hip-hop artists, Pop and Mavis (who collaborated with Prince during the late 80s) continue to pursue solo interests.

what to buy: *The Best of the Staple Singers* (Stax, 1986, prod. Al Bell) features most of their most familiar tracks in a good-vibes marathon.

what to buy next: The group's gospel side is faithfully anthologized on *Chronicle.* (Fantasy, 1985, prod. Various) 🦴🦴🦴🦴

what to avoid: *This Time Around* (Stax, 1981) 🦴🦴 finds the group sounding uncharacteristically tired and musically moribund.

the rest: *Make You Happy* (Epic, 1965) 🦴🦴🦴 *Amen!* (Epic, 1965) 🦴🦴🦴 *Freedom Highway* (Epic, 1965) 🦴🦴🦴½ *For What It's Worth* (Epic, 1967) 🦴🦴🦴½ *Soul Folk in Action* (Stax, 1968) 🦴🦴🦴 *We'll Get Over* (Stax, 1968) 🦴🦴🦴 *Staple Swingers* (Stax, 1971) 🦴🦴🦴 *Heavy Makes You Happy* (Stax, 1971) 🦴🦴🦴 *Be Altitude: Respect Yourself* (Stax, 1972) 🦴🦴🦴½ *Be What You Are* (Stax, 1973) 🦴🦴🦴 *City in the Sky* (Stax, 1974) 🦴🦴🦴 *Pass It On* (Warner Bros., 1976) 🦴🦴🦴 *Family Tree* (Warner Bros., 1977) 🦴🦴🦴 *Unlock Your Mind* (Warner Bros., 1979) 🦴🦴🦴 *Turning Point* (Private I, 1984) 🦴🦴½ *Are You Ready* (Private I, 1985) 🦴🦴½ *The Staple Singers* (Stax, 1992) 🦴🦴🦴½

worth searching for: *Let's Do It Again* (Curtom, 1975, prod. Curtis Mayfield) 🦴🦴🦴½ is worth owning just for its gorgeously sexy title track.

solo outings:

Mavis Staples Mavis Staples (Stax, 1969) 🦴🦴🦴 *Only For the Lonely* (Stax, 1976) 🦴🦴🦴 *A Piece of the Action* (Curtom, 1976) 🦴🦴🦴 *Oh, What a Feeling* (Warner Bros., 1979) 🦴🦴🦴 *Time Waits for No One* (Paisley Park, 1989) 🦴🦴½ *The Voice* (Paisley Park, 1993) 🦴🦴🦴

Pops Staples Peace to the Neighborhood (Pointblank/Charisma, 1992) 🦴🦴½ *Father, Father* (Pointblank/Charisma, 1994) 🦴🦴🦴

▶▶ Salt-n-Pepa, Madonna, Prince, Talking Heads, Spearhead, Arrested Development, Me'Shell Ndegeocello

◀◀ Charley Patton, Howlin' Wolf, Ray Charles, Mahalia Jackson, the Impressions, Aretha Franklin, Sam Cooke

Simon Glickman

Mavis Staples

See: The Staple Singers

Pops Staples

See: The Staple Singers

Edwin Starr

Born Jan. 21, 1942, in Nashville, Tenn.

Starr never really achieved a consistent string of R&B hits (or albums, for that matter), but when you cut a single as cataclysmic as "War," it doesn't really matter, does it? With his guttural shout, Starr's voice rose above all others on the 1970 protest anthem, a heaving ground-shaker and easily the most visceral thing ever to come out of Motown. Prior to that, he charted with "25 Miles," which was nearly as good. Most of Starr's material doesn't pack the same wallop as "War," which means that, at worst, he's merely energetic. *Motown Legends: War-Twenty Five Miles* (Essx Enterainment, 1994, comp. Diane Haig) 🦴🦴🦴½ has the edge for containing material from his long-deleted first album in addition to "War" and "25 Miles." *Motown Superstars Series, Vol. 3* (Motown Records, 1980, prod. Various) 🦴🦴🦴 is rote in comparison.

Allan Orski

Ringo Starr

Born Richard Starkey, July 7, 1940 in Liverpool, England

One of the best rock 'n' roll drummers ever, a most engaging show business personality, or one of the luckiest men on earth? There seems no easy way to categorize the Beatles' little drummer boy, and even a superficial gaze over his long and spotty post-Fab career confirms that Ringo perhaps, in struggling to be all things to all people, ultimately turns out disappointing us all— and possibly himself as well. Hindsight confirms he *was* a great drummer (session tapes from the Beatle years reveal Starr to be both as creative on his instrument as the rest of the band and as consistent in his time-keeping as a metronome), and while he may pose no immediate threat to Tony Bennett, his vocal abilities, when set against a sympathetic back-drop, can be pleasant enough. For his first album, *Sentimental Journey,* (1970) producer George Martin helped the soon-to-be-ex-Beatle record a dozen standards from the 40s and 50s (apparently as a present for Ringo's mum). A country LP cut in Nashville with the cream of Music City's session men (including D.J. Fontana from Elvis Presley's original band on drums, not Ringo) was followed by two strong singles produced by George Harrison, "It Don't Come Easy" and "Back Off Boogaloo," both of which were deserving Top 10 hits. In 1973, producer Richard Perry surrounded Ringo with an all-star cast, including all three ex-Beatles, and the *Ringo* album became the drummer's biggest-ever sales success, spawning three hit singles. Since then, however, ill-advised attempts to repeat this once-winning formula have resulted in a steadily decreasing quality of both material and execution—not to mention sales. Today, he lugs various editions of B-level rockers on the road with him under the moniker of "The All-Starr Band," but what worked so easily in 1973 doesn't seem to apply to today's marketplace. Still, the man remains a perennial favorite amongst graying boomers and their children everywhere, and so long as he continues riding the Yellow Submarine of nostalgia, Starr will continue to get by—with a little help from his friends, that is.

what to buy: Were Ringo's wonderful *Beaucoups Of Blues* (Apple, 1970, prod. by Pete Drake) released today, it would no doubt fit in quite nicely amongst the genial syrup which passes for modern-day country music—though Ringo possesses far more charm and personality than a barnful of Alan Jacksons. *Blast From Your Past* (Apple, 1975/Capitol , prod. Various) amply chronicles Ringo's glory days of mid-70s chart-toppers. And yes, John, Paul and George pop up all over the place.

what to buy next: The million-selling *Ringo* album (Apple, 1973/Capitol, 1991, prod. Richard Perry) is recommended for those who like their rock 'n' roll Hollywood-style. It includes Ringo's, uh, theme song—"I'm the Greatest," one of the most sarcastic songs John Lennon ever wrote. The CD reissue adds "It Don't Come Easy" and some other tracks to make it almost a de facto best-of itself.

what to avoid: Either *Ringo Starr & His All-Starr Band* (Rykodisc, 1990) **WOOF!** or *Live From Montreux Vol. 2*, (Rykodisc, 1993) **WOOF!** the audio equivalent of a rock 'n' roll old folks' home (Burton Cummings? Nils Lofgren?? Timothy B. Schmit?!!).

the rest: *Sentimental Journey* (Apple, 1970/Capitol, 1995) *Goodnight Vienna* (Apple, 1974/Capitol, 1993) *Ringo's Rotogravure* (Atlantic, 1976/1992) *Ringo the 4th* (Atlantic, 1977/1992) *Bad Boy* (Columbia, 1981/1991) *Old Wave* (RCA Canada, 1983/Capitol/Right Stuff, 1994) *Starr Struck: The Best of Ringo Starr, Volume 2* (Rhino, 1989) *Stop and Smell the Roses* (Capitol, 1994) *Time Takes Time* (Private Music, 1992)

worth searching for: The soundtrack from "Magic Christian Music" (Commonwealth-United, 1969) —deleted shortly after its issue to avoid confusion with the Badfinger album of the same name—contains some of Ringo's dialogue from the film dubbed over background music.

Micky Dolenz, Phil Collins

Roy Rogers, Anthony Newley

Gary Pig Gold

Stealers Wheel /Gerry Rafferty

Formed 1972 in London, England. Disbanded 1975.

Gerry Rafferty (born April 16, 1947 in Paisley, Scotland), guitar, vocals (1973-75); Joe Egan, keyboards, vocals (1973-75); Paul Pilnick, guitar (1973); Tony Williams, bass (1973); Rod Coombes, drums, vocals (1973); Joe Jammer, guitar (1974-75); Gary Taylor, bass (1974-75); Andrew Steele, drums (1974-75); Bernie Holland, guitar (1975); Dave Wintour, bass (1975)

A couple of Scottish guys (Egan and Rafferty) with a penchant for writing plaintive folk/pop songs somehow wound up in the studio with Leiber and Stoller (the team behind the Coasters) producing. The result was *Stealers Wheel*, one of the great debut albums of the 70s, with its hit single, "Stuck in the Middle With You." The combination of Beatles-esque harmonies, slightly off-kilter production and heartfelt melodies served the band well artistically and critically, but it wasn't quite enough to enable Egan and Rafferty to weather personality and management problems. All three Stealers Wheel albums are worth seeking out; along with Badfinger, Big Star, the Hollies and others, the band kept a certain style of British pop songwriting alive at a time when most others (most notably the Beatles) had abandoned the form.

what to buy: Start with *Stealers Wheel* (A&M, 1974, prod. Lieber and Stoller) and Rafferty's *City to City*, (United Artists, 1974, prod. Hugh Murphy and Gerry Rafferty) which includes the huge hit "Baker Street."

what to buy next: Rafferty's *Can I Have My Money Back* (Blue Thumb, 1971, prod. Hugh Murphy and Gerry Rafferty) has considerable talents as a songwriter and singer already in evidence. The title song in particular is lots of fun.

what to avoid: *Gerry Rafferty* (Visa, 1974, prod. Bill Leader) is a compilation of tracks recorded when Rafferty was in the Humblebums with Billy Conolly. Some good songs, but not as sure-footed as his later work.

the rest: *Right or Wrong* (A&M, 1975)

solo outings:

Gerry Rafferty Night Owl (U/A, 1979) *Snakes and Ladders* (U/A, 1980)

worth searching for: The single version of Stealers Wheel's "Everyone's Agreed That Everything Will Turn Out Fine" was originally recorded with an arrangement reminiscent of "Stuck in the Middle" and is far superior to the version recorded for *Ferguslie Park* (A&M, 1973, prod. Leiber and Stoller)

The Proclaimers

Everly Brothers, the Beatles, the Hollies

Shane Faubert

Steely Dan

Formed 1972, Los Angeles, Calif.

Walter Becker, bass, guitar and vocals; Donald Fagen, vocals and keyboards; Jim Hodder, drums 1972-74 (d. June 5, 1990); Denny Dias, guitar 1972-79); David Palmer, vocals (1972-73); Jeff "Skunk" Baxter, guitar 1972-75; Michael McDonald, vocals and keyboards (1974-75).

Steely Dan was one of rock's first "projects"—a group in name only. Becker and Fagen, friends at Bard College in upstate New York during the late 60s, shared a fondness for jazz, blues, pop, r&b and beatnik culture. They brought all this to Steely Dan, named after the talking dildo in William Burrough's *Naked Lunch.* From the get-go, Steely Dan's brand of rock was more sophisticated than most, blending catchy hooks with jazz chordings and tricky instrumental arrangements. As band members gradually departed—many of them frustrated by their leaders' reluctance to tour— Becker and Fagen's chief cohort became producer Gary Katz; employing dozens of session musicians, they steered Steely Dan's sound more towards jazz, and set standards for sonic perfectionism along the way. Becker and Fagen parted company during the early 80s but began working together again during the early 90s. Ironically, Steely Dan came back via tours and a live album, while Becker and Fagen kept their studio collaborations to each other's solo albums.

what to buy: For as sophisticated as Steely Dan became, it never really beat its debut effort, *Can't Buy a Thrill* (ABC, 1972, prod. Becker, Fagen and Katz) Becker and Fagen showed a clear gift for pop melodicism with instantly memorable tracks such as "Do it Again," "Dirty Work," "Midnight Cruiser" and "Brooklyn." Elliot Randall's guitar solos on "Reelin' in the Years" would be worth the price of admission alone. *Aja* (ABC, 1977, prod. Becker, Fagen and Katz) had songs that were just as infectious ("Peg," "Black Cow") but also showcased expansive moments such as the title track and "Deacon Blue." *Pretzel Logic* (ABC, 1974, prod. Becker, Fagen and Katz) has some of Steely Dan's best songs ("Rikki Don't Lose That Number," "Any Major Dude Will Tell You") as well as early steps towards jazz fusion such as "Parker's Band" and the title track.

what to buy next: The four-volume *Citizen Steely Dan* (MCA, 1993) packages the group's seven albums plus a couple of rarities. If you're hooked by the essential recordings, it's worth having the entire oeuvre.

what to avoid: Despite a couple of fine songs ("Hey Nineteen," "Time Out of Mind"), the stiff and tired *Gaucho* (MCA, 1980, prod. Becker, Fagen and Katz) shows why Becker and Fagen brought the curtain down on Steely Dan after this album.

the rest: *You Got to Walk it Like You Talk It* (Spark soundtrack, 1971) *Countdown to Ecstasy (MCA, 1973)* Katy Lied *(MCA, 1975)* The Royal Scam *(MCA, 1976)* Greatest Hits *(MCA, 1978)* Steely Dan Gold *(MCA, 1982)* Live *(Giant, 1995)*

worth searching for: *Catalyst* (Thunderbolt, 1994) is a sterling sounding, two-CD British import of early Becker and Fagen recordings between 1968-71. Includes early versions of "Brooklyn," "Parker's Band" and "Barrytown."

solo outings:

Walter Becker *11 Tracks of Whack* (Giant, 1994)

Donald Fagen: See separate entry

Rickie Lee Jones, Deacon Blue, China Crisis

Stax-Volt, Duke Ellington, Charlie Parker, B.B. King

Gary Graff

Steppenwolf

Formed 1967 in Los Angeles, Calif. Disbanded 1972. Reformed 1974-76, 1980.

John Kay (born Joachim F. Krauledat), vocals, guitar; Jerry Edmonton (born Jerry McCrohan), drums (to 1976, died 1993); Goldy McJohn (born John Goadsby),organ (to 1975); Michael Monarch, guitar (1967-69); Rushton Moreve, bass (1967-68, died 1991); John Russell Morgan, bass (1968-69); Larry Byrom, guitar (1969-71); Nick St. Nicholas (born Klaus Karl Kassbaum), bass (1969); George Biondi, bass (1969-72, 1974-76); Kent Henry, guitar (1971-72); Bobby Cochran, guitar (1974-76); Andy Chapin, keyboards (1975); Wayne Cook, keyboards (1975-76)

If they wore flowers in their hair in San Francisco during the late 60s, Steppenwolf countered from Los Angeles with denim, leather, dark shades and the biker anthem "Born to Be Wild." Used to great effect in the film "Easy Rider," that song alone insured Steppenwolf a place in rock history. Steppenwolf began as the Sparrows, which united folk singer Kay—an East German native who emigrated to Canada in 1958 and later moved to Southern California—with former members of the Mynah Birds, the Toronto group that was led by Neil Young and Rick James. The Sparrows recorded an early version the Steppenwolf hit "The Pusher;" after the band split up, producer Gabriel Mekler prevailed upon Kay to reunite the players and christened the aggregate Steppenwolf, after the Herman Hesse novel. For five years, Steppenwolf cranked out an agreeable blend of hard rock and psychedelia, following "Born to Be Wild"—written by Edmonton's brother Dennis (under the moniker Mars Bonfire)—with "The Pusher," "Magic Capret Ride," "Rock Me" and "Hey Lawdy Mama." Kay's lyrics were pointedly political, producing one entire album—1969's *Monster*—of social commentary. The group split up in 1972, and subsequent incarnations haven't been nearly as successful, though "Born to be Wild" still gets 'em on their feet at the summer amphitheater oldies shows.

what to buy: The concise, well-annotated *Born to Be Wild: A Retrospective 1996-1990* (MCA, 1991, comp. Andy McKaie) renders almost everything else in the catalog unnecessary. Opening with a taste of The Sparrows and closing with "The Wall," Kay's reflection on the dismantling of the Berlin Wall, it's the Steppenwolf story in a satisfying nutshell.

what to buy next: *Tighten Up Your Wig: The Best of John Kay & Sparrow* (Columbia Legacy, 1993, comp. Bob Irwin) suffers for its fodder, but the collection does provide an insightful look at the strains of folk, blues and rock that became the sound not only of Steppenwolf but also of one segment of the late 60s rock community. Similarly, *Monster* (Dunhill, 1969, prod. Gabriel Mekler) is a dated but fascinating period piece that captures the counter-culture political sensibility.

what to avoid: Such latter day Steppenwolf albums as *Rock 'n' Roll Rebels* (Quil, 1987, prod. John Kay, Michael Wilk and Rocket Ritchotte) and *Rise and Shine* (I.R.S., 1990, prod. John Kay, Michael Wilk, Rocket Ritchotte), which miss the character and energy of the original band.

the rest: *Steppenwolf* (Dunhill, 1968) *Steppenwolf the Second* (Dunhill, 1968) *Early Steppenwolf* (Dunhill, 1969) *Steppenwolf at Your Birthday Party* (Dunhill, 1969) *Steppenwolf Live* (Dunhill, 1970) *Steppenwolf 7* (Dunhill, 1970) *Steppenwolf Gold* (Dunhill, 1971) *For Ladies Only* (Dunhill, 1971) *Rest in Peace* (Dunhill, 1972) *16 Greatest Hits* (Dunhill, 1973) *Slow Flux* (Mums, 1974) *Hour of the Wolf* (Epic, 1975) *Skullduggery* (Epic, 1976) *Reborn to be Wild* (Epic, 1977) *Wolftracks* (Allegiance, 1982) *Paradox* (Attic, 1984) *Live at 25* (ERA, 1994) *Feed the Fire* (Winter Harvest, 1996)

worth searching for: Kay's autobiography, "Magic Carpet Ride" (Quarry Press, 1994), co-written with John Einarson, gives the skinny on the band and the 60s L.A. rock scene.

solo outings:

John Kay Forgotten Songs and Unsung Heroes (Dunhill, 1972) *My Sportin' Life* (Dunhill, 1972) *All in Good Time* (Mercury, 1978) *Lone Steppenwolf* (MCA, 1987)

▶▶ Led Zeppelin, Blue Oyster Cult, Kiss, Boston

◀◀ Sonny Boy Williamson, Chuck Berry, The Animals, Bob Dylan, Pete Seeger, the Yardbirds

Gary Graff

Stereolab

Formed 1991 in London, England

Tim Gane, guitar, bass, keyboards, percussion; Laetitia Sadier, vocals, percussion, keyboards; Martin Kean, bass (1990-92); Joe Dilworth, drums (1990-92); Gina Morris, vocals (1990-92); Mary Hansen, vocals, guitar, keyboards, percussion (1993-present); Sean O'Hagan, keyboards, bass (1993-present); Duncan Brown, bass (1993-96); Andy Ramsay, drums (1993-present); Katharine Gifford, keyboards, vocals (1994); Morgane Lhote, keyboards (1995-present); Richard Harrison, bass (1996)

The 90s aren't about formal innovation in rock so much as evermore refined recombinations of the past. Stereolab was ahead of the pack in looking beyond traditional rock sources for inspiration, plundering the cut-out bins for Moog (and mood) music, lounge combos, novelty numbers and even stereo equipment-testing records. Stereolab's albums — essentially the work of London underground rocker Gane, French chanteuse Sadier and an army of vintage synthesizers and organs — meld insidiously catchy pop melodies, avant-garde electronics, Caribbean textures and cheesy sound effects into percolating songs that shouldn't work but somehow do. This unlikely pastiche is summed up in the title of one of the group's EPs—*John Cage Bubblegum.* Striking a balance between the cerebral and the silly, the synthetic and organic, Stereolab anticipated the lounge and post-rock scenes that have sprung up in the rock underground, but has made pop music durable enough to outlast them both.

what to buy: *Transient Random-Noise Bursts With Announcements* (Elektra, 1993, prod. Phil Wright) is an ungainly title for an album that glides effortlessly on a bed of electronic rhythms worthy of early 70s Kraut-rockers Neu! or percolates with a sensuality worthy of Antonio Carlos Jobim. Sadier's lulling, lilting French-accented vocals keep the melodic hooks flowing, but it's the group's command of the groove, particularly on the 18-minute "Jenny Ondioline," that makes this a trance-pop milestone.

what to buy next: *Switched on Stereolab* (Slumberland, 1992, prod. Stereolab) collects the early, highly addictive singles from the group's Duophonic label. *Emperor Tomato Ketchup* (Elektra, 1996, prod. Paul Tipler, John McEntire and Stereolab) is the band's deepest excursion yet into analog-synthesizer esoterica, without skimping on the melodic allure.

the rest: *Peng!* (Too Pure, 1992) *Low Fi* (Too Pure EP, 1993) *Space Age Batchelor Pad Music* (Too Pure EP, 1993) *Crumb Duck* (Clawfist EP, 1993) *Mars Audiac Quintet* (Elektra, 1994)

worth searching for: The self-produced *Music For the Amorphous Study Center* (Duophonic, 1995) is one of numerous import EPs, this for an exhibit by artist Charles Long. It introduces live strings to the Stereolab studio machinery.

Tortoise, Ui, Trans Am, Cornershop, Cardigans

Martin Denny, Neu!, Throbbing Gristle, Brian Wilson, the Velvet Underground, Brazil-pop

Greg Kot

Cat Stevens

Born Steven Demetri Georgiou, July 21, 1947 in London, England

Despite immensely popular folk-rock songs that have become international standards, Stevens is the pop star who didn't want to be a pop star. In 1966, just a year after he started performing professionally, he had his first hit; by 1968, he was semi-retired with tuberculosis. Stevens was turned off by the pop star life, and when he resurfaced in 1970 with *Mona Bone Jakon*, the music was more developed and the lyrics more mature and sensitive. Stevens' fame grew during the next few years, as the music became more orchestrated and spiritually concerned. By 1973, Stevens was even more reclusive; he moved to Brazil as a tax exile and donated the savings to charities. This pattern followed through the 70s as his record sales eventually flagged. A devout muslim by 1979, Stevens changed his name to Yusef Islam and retired from music; he stirred controversy in 1989 by endorsing the Ayatolla Khomeini's decree that "The Satanic Verses" author Salman Rushdie deserved to die for alleged blasphemies in the book. He has since reversed that position.

what to buy: Even though he'd had a few hits, *Tea for the Tillerman* (A&M, 1971, prod. Paul Samwell-Smith) blasted Stevens into international superstardom. "Wild World," "Father and Son," "Where Do the Children Play," "Hard Headed Woman" and others made Stevens an album-rock radio staple. The album's cartoon cover art and the innocence expressed in the songs were perfect for the flower child ethos. *Teaser and the Firecat* (A&M, 1971, prod. Paul Samwell-Smith) is almost as good, particularly the (then) side two combination of "Morning Has Broken," "Bitterblue," "Moonshadow" and "Peace Train."

what to buy next: *Foreigner* (A&M, 1973, prod. Cat Stevens) offers a taste of the more orchestral side of Stevens' music. The composition "Foreigner Suite" is a complex long form that veers away from lyrics and displays his talent as a musician. *Classics—Vol. 24* (A&M, 1987, prod. Various) is an aptly titled hits collection, including songs he recorded for the dark cult comedy "Harold and Maude."

what to avoid: *Izitso* (A&M, 1977, prod. Cat Stevens and Dave Kershenbaum) delves into electronics to little avail, though there are some revealing personal tales on a couple of songs.

the rest: *New Masters* (Deram, 1967) *Mona Bone Jakon* (A&M, 1970) *Very Young and Early Songs* (Deram, 1972) *Catch Bull at Four* (A&M, 1973) *Buddah and the Chocolate Box* (A&M, 1974) *Greatest Hits* (A&M, 1975) *Numbers* (A&M, 1976) *Back to Earth* (A&M, 1979)

worth searching for: *Matthew and Son* (Deram, 1967) provides an early earful of the straight folk sound of one guy with a guitar and a song to sing.

Jackson Browne, James Taylor, Joe Henry, 10,000 Maniacs

Bob Dylan, Paul Simon

Lawrence Gabriel

Al Stewart

Born Sept. 5, 1946, in Glasgow, Scotland

With his cerebral lyrics, light vocal delivery and understated guitar work, Stewart was something of an antidote for the disco crazed 70s. His recordings were pleasant-sounding excursions that delved into such unusual topics as Nostradamus. With roots in folk and arid vocals, Stewart needed somebody to push him over the top. Who better than the over-the-top producer himself, Alan Parsons? Each complemented the other: Stewart sang with greater confidence and had lush multi-tracked layers of sound backing him, while Parsons was limited to the amount of sound he could produce lest he squash Stewart's sensitive sensibilities. Despite a few hits—"Year of the Cat," "Song on the Radio," "Time Passages"—Stewart's older material doesn't time travel well. But he continues to make new music that's gripping and forward looking.

what to buy: *Between the Wars* (Messa/Bluemoon, 1995, prod. Al Stewart and Laurence Juber) is a terrific album that doesn't sound much like old Stewart. He and guitarist Juber fashion 13 songs that conjure up musical memories of '30's swing-time Paris, with looser arrangements and a full backing band that includes bass, drums, strings, reeds and percussion.

what to buy next: *The Best of Al Stewart* (Arista, 1988, prod. Various) is a 13-track thumbnail sketch of his work with Parsons and others. It includes material from *Year of the Cat, Time Passages, 24 Carrots* and the rest of his most well-known, if not well-work, periods.

what to avoid: The thematic bent of *Russians and Americans* (Passport, 1984/Mesa-Bluemoon, 1994) is a noble concept, but it ends up interfering with the album's musical flow.

the rest: *Past, Present and Future* (Columbia, 1974/Rhino, 1992) *Modern Times* (Janus, 1975/Rhino, 1992) *Year of the Cat* (Arista, 1976) *Time Passages* (Arista, 1978) *24 Carrots* (Arista, 1980/Razor & Tie, 1993) *Rhymes in Rooms* (Messa/Blue Moon, 1992) *Famous Last Words* (Mesa/Bluemoon, 1994)

worth searching for: Stewart was more of a lovelorn folkie when he recorded *Orange,* (Columbia, 1972/Beat Goes On, 1993) but guests Rick Wakeman and Brinsley Schwarz brought some muscle to his muse.

Sting, Rupert Holmes, Nick Gilder

Donovan, Bob Dylan, King Crimson, Alan Parson Project

Patrick McCarty and Gary Graff

Dave Stewart

See: Eurythmics

John Stewart

Born Sept. 5, 1939 in San Diego, Calif.

Stewart took a giant step upon leaving the Kingston Trio in 1967. His first album, *California Bloodlines*, recorded at the same time as Bob Dylan's *Nashville Skyline* with many of the same musicians, became a classic and set the foundation for his lengthy solo career. Working from the enthusiasm of the Kennedy years (with the Trio, he wrote "New Frontier" for John F. Kennedy, and the songs he wrote while traveling with the 1968 Robert Kennedy presidential campaign are a continuing thread through his albums for the next decade), Stewart wrote with a liberal's unabashed love of country, good humor and compassion for the less fortunate. He bounced from label to label through 1980, with only the strangely ironic "Gold," recorded for RSO—a label that marketed him alongside the Bee Gees and "Saturday Night Fever"—as his only real hit. Many of his songs have been recorded by others, the most famous being the Monkees' 1967 smash "Daydream Believer." Stewart's later albums, on small labels and often for his own Homecoming imprint, continue in the same vein, although he has favored a more synthesized approach to recording. Though his optimism wavered and his images turned more impressionistic over the decades, Stewart remains a durable songwriter and formidable songwriter.

what to buy: Stewart's early albums are available on compact disc mostly in European import configurations. The best is still *California Bloodlines/Willard Minus 2,* (Bear Family, 1989, prod. Nick Venet) written in 1968 while Stewart traveled with the Robert Kennedy campaign? It captures the yin and yang of that period as well as anything. Now packaged with its equally charismatic 1970 follow-up *Willard* on one CD, it's an incredible bargain even at import prices. *The Complete Phoenix Concerts* (Capitol, 1974/Bear Family, 1990, prod. Nick Venet) is a superb live recording with one of Stewart's best ensembles. *Bullets in the Hourglass* (Shanachie, 1992, prod. John Hoke and John Stewart) shows the ever-widening direction and more impressionistic imagery of his recent songwriting.

what to buy next: *Airdream Believer* (Shanachie, 1995, prod. John Stewart) includes several new songs and a retrospective that even reaches back into his Trio days, including the pre-rap "The Rev. Mr. Black." *Secret Tapes '86* (Homecoming, 1986, prod. John Stewart) includes medleys of some old favorites and strong songs such as "Justiceville" and "Unchained Beast." *Lonesome Picker Rides Again* (Warner Bros., 1971, prod. Michael Stewart) and *Sunstorm* (Warner Bros., 1972, prod. Michael Stewart) are both strong Americana song collections in the manner of *California Bloodlines* that got lost in the shuffle.

what to avoid: *Dream Babies Go Hollywood* (RSO, 1980, prod. John Stewart) On the heels of "Gold," RSO pushed for another *Bombs Away Dream Babies*, and Stewart came up with this attempt to retain some dignity while going Hollywood. That he failed was perhaps best for the label and Stewart.

the rest: *American Originals* (Capitol, 1992) *Bombs Away Dream Babies* (RSO, 1979/Razor & Tie, 1993) *Cannons in the Rain/Wingless Angels* (Capitol, 1973, 1975/Bear Family, 1990) *Chilly Winds* (Folk Era) *John Stewart In Concert* (RCA, 1980) *Fire in the Wind* (RSO, 1977) *Blondes* (Allegiance, 1982) *Trancas* (Affordable Dreams, 1984) *The Gathering* (Homecoming, 1984) *Centennial* (Homecoming, 1984) *Punch the Big Guy* (Shanachie, 1987) *Secret Tapes II* (Homecoming, 1987) (with Buffy Ford): *Signals Through the Glass* (Capitol, 1968) *The Essential John and Buffy* (Feegie, 1994) (with Nick Reynolds): *Revenge of the Budgie* (Takoma, 1983) *Trio Years* (Homecoming, 1986) (with the Cumberland Three): *Songs of the Civil War* (Rhino, 1991)

worth searching for: *The Last Campaign,* (Homecoming, 1985, prod. John Stewart) gathers together some songs written in the 60s, specifically about the Robert Kennedy campaign, most of which had ended up as pieces of other albums. *Neon Beach* (Homecoming, 1990, prod. John Stewart) is a ragged, exciting live tape with a rock band that includes some classic 80s songs and weird, yet affecting, covers —"Lady Came From Baltimore," "Shake, Rattle and Roll," even Paul Simon's "The Boy in the Bubble."

▶▶ Lindsey Buckingham, Beat Farmers

◀◀ Cumberland Three, Kingston Trio, Dave Guard

Leland Rucker

Rod Stewart

Born Jan. 10, 1945 in London, England

Former frontman for the Jeff Beck Group and Faces, Rod Stewart has been written off so many times that rock critics could use him as a tax deduction. Granted, consistency has never been his forte: even *Foolish Behaviour, Tonight I'm Yours* and *A Night on the Town*—his best, hardest-rocking albums since his early-70s heyday with the Faces—were uneven, reneging on the promise of his classic 1972 album title, *Never a Dull Moment*. But "Maggie May," "You Wear It Well" and "Stay With Me" still sound great on classic-rock radio and even in middle age, that soulful howl can wring emotion from the sappiest of love songs. Credit Stewart's longevity to a thrilling live show (save for his yawn-inducing 1996 tour that inexplicably found him performing his hits in chronological order) and an impeccable taste in cover songs that over the years has included Eddie Cochran's "Cut Across Shorty," Bobby Womack's "It's All Over Now," Jimi Hendrix's "Angel," Cat Stevens' "The First Cut Is the Deepest," Tom Waits' "Downtown Train" and the Blue Nile's "Downtown Lights."

what to buy: *Every Picture Tells a Story* (Mercury, 1971, prod. Stewart) and *Never a Dull Moment* (Mercury, 1972, prod. Stewart) make up one of the most overwhelming one-two punches in rock history. Acoustic guitars, mandolins, organs and drums collide with Stewart's potent, scruffy, pipes. Gloriously reckless but never sloppy.

what to buy next: *The Rod Stewart Album* (Mercury, 1969, prod. Lou Reizner) offers a formative glimpse at his songwriting ("An Old Raincoat Won't Ever Let You Down") and interpretive (the Rolling Stones' "Street Fighting Man," Michael D'Abo's "Handbags and Gladrags") prowess. *A Night on the Town* (Warner Bros., 1976, prod. Tom Dowd) plays to his strengths as a balladeer ("Tonight's the Night," "The First Cut Is the Deepest") and barroom rocker ("The Balltrap," "The Wild Side of Life"). *Absolutely Live* (Warner Bros., 1982, prod. Rod Stewart) is a sweat-soaked document of one of his strongest post-Faces tours, with roof-raising versions of "Hot Legs," Chuck Berry's "Sweet Little Rock 'n' Roller" and a smoking medley of "Little Queenie" and "She Won't Dance With Me."

what to avoid: *Body Wishes* (Warner Bros, 1983, prod. Rod Stewart and Tom Dowd) WOOF!, a wimpy, synthesizer-drowned album notable only for its utter lack of artistic relevance. The hit was "Baby Jane" if that tells you anything.

the rest: *Gasoline Alley* (Mercury, 1970) *Smiler* (Mercury, 1974) *Sing It Again Rod* (Mercury, 1972) *Atlantic Crossing* (Warner Bros., 1975) *Footloose and Fancy Free* (Warner Bros., 1977) *Blondes Have More Fun* (Warner Bros., 1978) *Greatest Hits* (Warner Bros., 1979) *Foolish Behaviour* (Warner Bros., 1980) *Tonight I'm Yours* (Warner Bros., 1981) *Camouflage* (Warner Bros., 1984)

Rod Stewart (Warner Bros., 1986) *Out of Order* (Warner Bros., 1988) *Storyteller: The Complete Anthology 1964-1990* (Warner Bros., 1989) *Downtown Train: Selections From Storyteller* (Warner Bros., 1990) *Vagabond Heart* (Warner Bros., 1991) *The Mercury Anthology* (Polydor, 1992) *Unplugged .... and Seated* (Warner Bros. , 1993) *A Spanner in the Works* (Warner Bros., 1995)

Worth Seeking Out: The European import *Lead Vocalist* (Warner Bros., 1993, prod. Various) that mixes hits with five tracks from an aborted Trevor Horn-produced album, including covers of Stevie Nicks' "Stand Back" and the Stones' "Ruby Tuesday."

Dan Baird, Black Crowes, Bash and Pop

Sam Cooke, Otis Redding

David Okamoto

Stephen Stills

See: Crosby, Stills and Nash

Sting

Born Gordon Matthew Sumner, Oct. 2, 1951 in Newcastle, England

For all the rending of garments and tearing of hair that accompanied Sting's hiring of an all-black jazz band to back him on his solo debut, *The Dream of the Blue Turtles*, you'd think it would be remembered that Sting began his career playing jazz in the pubs of his native Newcastle. And for someone who crossed as many musical boundaries as he did with the Police, charges of cultural imperialism are absolutely absurd. Indeed, *Blue Turtles* wasn't that much of a departure from his earlier music—a little reggae here, a little jazz there, and solid pop melodies throughout. Lyrically, Sting has always had much to answer for, invoking mythological beasties and occasionally slipping into a foreign tongue. But give him this much—few pop stars have taken as many risks and have scored as many hits with such challenging material. Sting has always been willing to stick his neck out far enough for his critics to chop it off. His albums are consistently marked by intelligence, wit, political savvy and, yes, an intense fascination with the importance of being Sting. So sue him already—but not without giving his albums a fair listen.

what to buy: An obvious place to start is *Fields of Gold: The Best of Sting 1984-1994* (A&M, 1994, prod. Various) a 14-song compilation that hits the highlights of his solo career and includes the new songs "When We Dance" and "This Cowboy Song." Recording a live album after only one studio effort was a bold move, but *Bring on the Night* (A&M, 1986, prod. Kim Turner and Sting) offers ample justification, with expansive versions of songs from *Blue Turtles* plus some well-chosen and re-worked Police selections. Further, *Bring on the Night* offers a more accurate portrait of Sting's jazz-oriented group than does his debut. Dauntingly verbose, *..Nothing Like the Sun* (A&M, 1987, prod. Neil Dorfsman and Sting) scores on the basis of its joyous polyrhythmic groove, thanks in large part to drummer Manu Katche. Dedicated to Sting's late father, *The Soul Cages* (A&M, 1991, prod. Hugh Padgham and Sting) is an extraordinarily moving album and his most emotionally rewarding work, filled with autobiographical details and provocative (for pop music) philosophy.

what to buy next: *The Dream of the Blue Turtles* (A&M, 1985, prod. Sting and Pete Smith) offers a departure from Sting's work with the Police, though not as radical a one as the makeup of his band might indicate. The album opening "If You Love Somebody Set Them Free" is a curious sentiment coming from the man who wrote the smash "Every Breath You Take"; "Fortress Around Your Heart," the album's closer, is more on the same beam. Showing less ambition than the albums that preceded it, but no less quality or style, *Ten Summoner's Tales* (A&M, 1993, prod. Hugh Padgham and Sting) features 11—ha,ha—pop songs that entertain more and preach less than is usual for Sting. As musically accomplished as anything he's done, yet slightly less fun for its relentless sobriety, *Mercury Falling* (A&M, 1996, prod. Hugh Padgham and Sting) contains one grim tale after another, though the album is redeemed with the hopeful "Let Your Soul Be Your Pilot" and the sly "All Four Seasons in One Day."

worth searching for: From the same sessions that produced *..Nothing Like the Sun, Nada Como el Sol* (A&M EP, 1991, prod. Neil Dorfsman and Sting) offers Spanish-language versions of "We'll Be Together," "Little Wing" and "Fragile," plus a version of "Fragile" sung in Portuguese.

The Samples, Peter Himmelman, Dave Matthews Band

Gilberto Gil, Gil Evans, Bob Marley, the Beatles

Daniel Durchholz

Stone Roses

Formed 1985 in Manchester, England

Ian Brown, vocals; John Squire, guitar (1985-96); Andy Couzens, guitar (1985-87); Pete Garner, bass (1985-87); Gary "Mani" Mounfield, bass (1987-present); Alan "Reni" Wren, drums (1985-95)

Formed out of the dubious ashes of a Clash-copy band, The Patrol, and an equally sketchy mod-revival act English Rose, this quartet nevertheless went on to become the biggest band to hit England during the late 80s, a phenomenon so fast and so unprecedented, it went from playing small clubs to selling out an entire island (just under 100,000), namely Spike Island, in the space of a year. Considering how patchy its earliest singles were, the band's debut *The Stone Roses* (Silvertone, 1989, prod. John Leckie) is a shocking LP, as close to perfection as stylish, edgy English pop gets. Songs that had seemed ordinary in original (later bootlegged) demos became minor wonder-rockets, a mixture of styles segueing beautifully thanks to Leckie's mellifluous production, so flawless it's as if the producer was playing a violin. Right from the opening, dramatic moments of the anthemic "I Wanna Be Adored," through to the vaguely funk/Hendrix psychedelic groove of "I Am the Resurrection," going from grandiose pop to backwards-tape-looped melanges, this LP weaves an atmospheric spell without ever sounding nostalgic.

But Stone Roses failed to catch on in America because the band failed to play a single date here in support of it, even canceling what dates were booked. Instead, it sued its way out of its record contract, and the protracted legal fight resulted in a five-year vacation between LPs. In between, two decent B-sides albums were issued, *Turns to Stone* (Silvertone, 1992, prod. John Leckie and Peter Hook) and the more generous *The Complete Stone Roses.* (Silvertone, 1995, prod. John Leckie and Peter Hook) By the time the Roses convened to record a proper follow-up for new label Geffen, the air had exited the balloon. *Second Coming* (Geffen, 1994, prod. Simon Dawson and Paul Schroeder) showed the band still had plenty of aplomb, but it's easy to see why an exasperated Leckie, the original producer, walked off in a huff. The LP is nothing more than bombastic, overblown, tired rockisms, with Squire reduced to ripping of Jimmy Page's Led Zeppelin licks on top of way-too-long dance jams crying out for an editor. Not surprisingly, drummer Reni followed Leckie's lead and walked before the world tour to promote it. A year later, Squire also bolted, leaving the group still surviving, but in ruins.

Jack Rabid

Stone Temple Pilots

Formed as Mighty Joe Young, 1987 in San Diego, Calif.

Scott Weiland, vocals; Dean DeLeo, guitar; Robert DeLeo, bass; Eric Kretz, drums

Alternarock's favorite whipping boy, Stone Temple Pilots has gotten a bad rap, plain and simple. Damned for its success and for its sonic similarity to Seattle grungesters Soundgarden, Alice in Chains and Pearl Jam, STP can't win with critics. So the band has taken its case straight to the people, who have made each of STP's three albums—each one better than its predecessor—platinum-plus affairs. And as for the latter charge, anyone who does the math can see that STP, Alice and Pearl Jam are roughly contemporaries, and that it's nigh unto impossible that the group ripped off its sound from anyone except the same folks as Alice and Pearl Jam—that is, purveyors of 70s rock and 80s punk, from Led Zeppelin to Black Flag, et al. So sue STP for its hooky, concise alternametal if you want—it'll never hold up in court. The group's debut, *Core* (Atlantic, 1992, prod. Brendan O'Brien) scored with the grim "Creep," stirred controversy with "Sex Type Thing"—a song about date rape told from a seemingly unironic, first-person point of view—and otherwise delivered heavy, arena-ready anthems such as "Plush" and "Wicked Garden." The follow-up, *Purple,* (Atlantic, 1994, prod. Brendan O'Brien) was equally reviled by critics, but fans rallied around it, and why not? Little had changed—Weiland's lyrics were still downcast, the arrangements remained tight. "Vasoline," "Interstate Love Song" and the acoustic "Pretty Penny" are the standout tracks. *Tiny Music...Songs From the Vatican Gift Shop* (Atlantic, 1996, prod. Brendan O'Brien) lessens the metallic grind (still evident in "Trippin' on the Hole in a Paper Heart" and "Big Bang Baby") in favor of a lighter touch; "Lady Picture Show," for example, is downright Beatlesque, while "And So I Know" finds Weiland crooning over some smooth cocktail jazz. As of this writing, the group's future is suspect after Weiland's arrest for cocaine and heroin possession and subsequent, court-ordered rehab that forced STP into inactivity.

Daniel Durchholz

The Stooges

See: Iggy Pop

Stories

Formed 1971 in New York, N.Y. Disbanded 1975.

Michael Brown (born Michael Lookofsky), keyboards (1971-73); Ian Lloyd (born Ian Buoncocglio), vocals, bass; Steve Love, guitar, vocals; Bryan Madey, drums, vocals (1971-75); Kenny Aaronson, bass (1971-75); Ken Bichel, keyboards (1971-75); Rick Ranno, drums (1974-75)

After the dissolution of the Left Banke and his stint as songwriter for the group Montage, keyboardist/songwriter Brown's co-founded Stories. Lead singer Lloyd's raspy, Rod Stewart-like vocals don't complement Brown's melodic compositions quite as well as Steve Martin's in the Banke, but Stories still managed to produce two enjoyable albums. *Stories* (Kama Sutra, 1972) ♪♪♪♪ is out of print but worth searching for thanks to the unlikely Top 40 hit "I'm Coming Home" as well as strong tracks such as "Hello People," "Step Back" and "Take Cover." The second LP, *About Us,* (Kama Sutra, 1973/Original Buddah Classics, 1996) ♪♪♪♪♪ put Stories over the top with its No. 1 cover of Hot Chocolate's "Brother Louie" which was actually released as a single and appended to the album when it hit big, which was after Brown left the group.

see also: *The Left Banke*

Mike Greenfield

Stormtroopers of Death

See: Anthrax

The Strangeloves

Formed 1964 in New York, N.Y.

Bob Feldman, Jerry Goldstein and Richard Gottehrer, all vocalists

During the summer of '64, the songwriting team of Feldman, Goldstein and Gottehrer was in trouble. They'd had a string of hits—not the least of which was the Angels' teen classic "My Boyfriend's Back"—during the Brill Building pop era, the last vestiges of the Tin Pan Alley days of songwriters. But the Beatles had arrived in New York that February, and the mop-topped sensations had re-written the rules. Record companies were only interested in acts that write their own material—especially if the act came with British accents. So the trio invented Brit-accented alter-egos as a goof, calling themselves the Strangeloves—Miles, Niles and Giles Strangeloves, that is, brothers from Australia, because Feldman's lousy British accent might have given them away, and who would know from Australia? They wore a hodgepodge of tribal costumes from several continents and beat out variations of the primitive Bo Diddley Beat on drums supplied by a friend, the acclaimed African percussionist Olatunji. They went on the TV show "Hullabaloo" and faked their way through a performance, like some sort of primal Milli Vanilli. The wonder of it was that a couple of the trio's phony Brit-Invasion singles—"I Want Candy" and "Night Time"—were kicking rock songs and became staples of garage-bands everywhere. *I Want Candy* (Bang, 1965/Legacy, 1995, prod. Bob Feldman, Jerry Goldman and Richard Gottehrer) ♪♪♪♪ is glorious and twisted document of the British Invasion era; the songs sound fresh—and still convincingly British—and the beats are as big as they could be. The album also includes the original Strangeloves' version of "Hang on Sloopy," later recorded by the McCoys, a band led by the trio's discovery—guitarist Rick Zheringer (ne Derringer). One the Strangeloves the masquerade was over, the FGG songwriting and production team returned to what it knew best: finding talent and recording great songs (Gottehrer went on to produce some of the best music of the punk era, Blondie's early tracks).

Gil Asakawa

The Stranglers

Formed 1974 in Guilford, England

Hugh Cornwell, guitar, vocals (1974-90); Dave Greenfield, keyboards; Jet Black (born Brian Duffy), drums (1974-93); Jean-Jacques Burnel, bass; John Ellis, guitar (1990-present); Paul Roberts, vocals (1990-present); Tikake Tobe, drums (1993-present)

Credibility and respect was in short supply for the Stranglers. Positioning itself in the punk bad-boy mode, it found moderate success in England and Europe with hits such as "Something Better Change," "Peaches," "No More Heroes," "Nice 'n' Sleazy," "Golden Brown" and "Skin Deep." But America ignored the Stranglers; the band had a good name and an appropriately insufferable punk attitude, but little to no compelling material. From punk to some arty miscues and desperate grabs at other songwriters' material, the Stranglers became bad boys to whom no one paid any attention. In some ways the band was ahead of its time, in that such early Stranglers' songs as "Peaches" were refused airplay because of crude lyrics. Ultimately, the Stranglers' success was more due to hype than talent—nothing new for the pop business, but this band made quite a long run of it.

what to buy: *Dreamtime* (Epic, 1986) ♪♪♪ departed from the typical buzz and grind. With its haunting keyboard beds and soft edges, it could well have been from a different group.

what to buy next: *The Stranglers' Greatest Hits* (Epic, 1991) ♪♪ offers a reasonable overview of what the group did have to offer.

what to avoid: The big record company push on the lumbering *Feline* (Epic, 1982/1991) ♪♪ left lots of folks wondering what the fuss was about.

the rest: *Aural Sculpture* (Epic, 1984) *10* (Epic, 1990)

what to avoid: *All Live All of the Night* (Epic, 1988) **WOOF!** brings us a night of egocentric posturing, miserable covers and a noisy exit.

Sonic Youth, L7, Green Day, Daniel Lanois

The Doors, the Kinks, the Rolling Stones, Richard Hell and the Voidoids

Patrick McCarty

Syd Straw

The gifted singer Straw honed her chops on the New York alternative rock scene during the 80s, guesting on recordings by Golden Palominos, the dBs and many others. Her voice is powerful and mellifluous, but it can also be soft and vulnerable, with a pronounced drawl that isn't traceable to her geographic origins. Though Straw's songwriting has been somewhat uneven, her best compositions, which tend toward folky jangle-pop, have both depth and quirk. Her debut album *Surprise* (Virgin, 1989, prod. Syd Straw) features guest appearances by a large roster of friends and collaborators, notably Richard Thompson, Michael Stipe, Bernie Worrell, dB Peter Holsapple, Van Dyke Parks and Peter Blegvad. After this album tanked, Straw continued singing on other people's records and even rented out her pipes for a beer commercial—it was one of the most strangely emotional jingles ever to air on radio—but ultimately landed another deal. Her sophomore release, *War and Peace* (Capricorn, 1996, prod. Syd Straw) was recorded with the sturdy accompaniment of the Skeletons.

see also: *The Golden Palominos*

Simon Glickman

The Strawberry Alarm Clock

Formed 1967 in Santa Barbara, Calif. Disbanded 1971.

Ed King, guitar, vocals; Lee Freeman, guitar, bass, horns, drums, vocals; Mark Weitz, keyboards; Gary Lovetro, bass, vocals (1967-68); George Bunnel, bass (1967-69); Randy Seol, drums, vocals (1967-69); Jimmy Pitman, guitar, vocals (1969-70); Gene Gunnels, drums (1969-71); Paul Marshall, guitar, vocals (1970-71)

With flowers, beads and hippie dreams, the Strawberry Alarm Clock tapped into a psychedelic vein with the album and hit single "Incense and Peppermints." Better-than-average arrangements and proficient instrumentation—guitarist King went on to join Lynyrd Skynyrd—helped make up for such ludicrous songs as "Strawberries Mean Love." *Anthology: Strawberry Alarm Clock* (One Way, 1993, comp. prod. Steve Bartek) makes for an easy, if dated, listen.

Patrick McCarty

The Strawbs /Dave Cousins

Formed as the Strawberry Hill Boys, 1967 in Leicester, England. Disbanded late 1979. Reformed 1983.

David Cousins, vocals, guitar; Tony Hooper, guitar, vocals (1967-72, 1983-present); Dave Lambert, guitar (1972-79); Arthur Philips, mandolin (1967-68); Ron Chesterman, bass (1968-69); John Ford, bass (1969-73, 1983-present); Chas Cronk, bass (1974-79); Sandy Denny (1968); Rick Wakeman, keyboards (1969-71); Blue Weaver, keyboards (1971-73, 1983-present); John Hawkin, keyboards (1974-79); Richard Hudson, drums (1969-73, 1983-present); Rod Coombes, drums (1974-79); Brian Willoughby, guitar (1979, 1983-present); Rod Demick, bass (1985-present); Chris Parren, keyboards (1985-present)

Eclectic and often changing, the Strawbs started out as folkies (the Strawberry Hill Boys) during the mid-60s and metamorphosed into a strong folk-rock-progressive band. While a constantly changing stream of musicians has passed through the group—including keyboard wizard Wakeman, later of Yes, and pop-rock duo Hudson-Ford—its constant has always been singer-songwriter-guitarist Cousins. His voice isn't for all tastes—the sound lies somewhere between Jethro Tull's Ian Anderson and Bob Dylan—but as a folk instrument it's more than adequate to convey a wide range of viewpoints and emotions. His lyrics, often taking either a personal or a bardic, folk tale tack, encompass satirical jabs at society, organized labor and religion; searching treatments of life, death, spirituality and ethical problems; lullabies; and love songs ranging from earthy to humorous to lush. The music ranges from a consciously ancient sound to straight-ahead rock 'n' roll—variously intimate, folky or grand. Moody Blues fans may find Strawbs to be kindred spirits. Various members of the group, including Cousins, Wakeman, Hudson-Ford and Lambert, released independent projects either during or outside their time with Strawbs.

what to buy: *From the Witchwood* (A&M, 1971, prod. Tony Visconti) from the Strawbs' "ancient music" period features lush harmonies on traditional-style ballads with a semi-medieval lyric setting as well as more contemporary folk-rock arrangements played on dulcimer, harpsichord, recorder, banjo, sitar and autoharp in addition to rock instruments.

what to buy next: *A Choice Selection of Strawbs* (A&M, 1992, prod. Various) 𝄞𝄞𝄞𝄞 has much of the group's best out-of-print material. *Greatest Hits Live!* (Road Goes On Forever, 1993) 𝄞𝄞𝄞 captures the best of the band's long history in a concert setting.

the rest: *Preserves Uncanned* (Road Goes On Forever, 1991); *Sandy Denny and The Strawbs* (Hannibal, 1991) 𝄞𝄞𝄞▽ *Heartbreak Hill* (Road Goes On Forever, 1995) 𝄞𝄞𝄞𝄞

worth searching for: *Bursting at the Seams,* (A&M, 1973, prod. Strawbs) 𝄞𝄞𝄞𝄞 a Germany import of one of the Strawbs' most accessible albums, which features the hits "Lay Down" and "Part of the Union" (a satirical look at the inordinate power of British labcr unions). Although the sound ventures into Eastern European ethnic ground in one song and retains some of the lushness of the group's earlier work, the album has a generally more contemporary feel.

solo outings:

Dave Cousins: The Bridge (Road Goes On Forever, 1994); (with Brian Willoughby) *Old School Songs* (Road Goes On Forever, 1979)

▶▶ Fairport Convention, Alan Parsons Project, Jethro Tull

◀◀ The Weavers, Bob Dylan, the Beatles, the Hollies

Polly Vedder

Stray Cats /Brian Setzer, Lee Rocker's Big Blue

Formed 1979 in Massapequa, N.Y.

Brian Setzer, vocals, guitar; Lee Rocker (born Lee Drucker), upright bass, vocals; Slim Jim Phantom (born Jim McDonell), drums

A definite anomaly in the synth-heavy early 80s, the pompadoured, tattooed and bowling-shirted Stray Cats can be credited with introducing rockabilly to a whole new audience. After scuffling around the New York scene, the band moved to the more rockabilly-receptive England, where it enjoyed the patronage of Dave Edmunds, who produced its first two albums. Returning to the U.S. in 1982—after opening some shows on the Rolling Stones 1981 tour—the Cats scratched the U.S. with hits such as "Rock This Town" and "Stray Cat Strut." Suddenly teenagers who wouldn't even think about buying an old Elvis Presley record were interested in a sound that was more akin to their parents' generation than their own. The Cats' popularity quickly faded, however, and while the group hasn't disbanded, it gets together only sporadically while its members pursue their own interests—Setzer crooning big band standards and the odd Stray Cats tune with the 16-piece Brian Setzer orchestra, Rocker with the more traditional rockabilly outfit Big Blue, whose first album featured Presley guitarist Scotty Moore.

What Album Changed Your Life?

"I guess Meet the Beatles. That got me started thinking about being more involved in music. It just sucked me right in, and I wanted to be involved in everything about it--the attitude and how they got a different sound for that recording than anything I'd ever heard before."

Shaun Murphy (Little Feat)

what to buy: *Built For Speed* (EMI America, 1982, prod. Dave Edmunds) 𝄞𝄞𝄞𝄞 compiles the best of the Stray Cats two British releases for a powerhouse introduction.

what to buy next: The unjustly ignored *Blast Off* (EMI America, 1989, prod. Dave Edmunds) 𝄞𝄞𝄞𝄞 is a corker, with nine exhilarating rockabilly workouts and an anthemic, swinging closer, "Nine Lives." Of the solo albums, Setzer's rowdy *Live Nude Guitars* (EMI Manhattan, 1988, prod. Various) 𝄞𝄞𝄞▽ comes closest to the Stray Cats' spirit and energy level.

what to avoid: *Rock Therapy* (EMI, 1986, prod. Stray Cats) 𝄞𝄞 finds Setzer and Co. staying true to their sound but so desperate for a comeback that the songwriting is flawed and the performances tentative.

the rest: *Rant 'n' Rave* (EMI America, 1983) 𝄞𝄞𝄞 *Rock This Town: The Best of the Stray Cats* (EMI America, 1989) 𝄞𝄞 *Choo Choo Hot Fish* (JRS/Great Pyramid, 1992) 𝄞𝄞𝄞▽ *Greatest Hits* (Curb, 1992) 𝄞

worth searching for: *Original Cool,* (Griffin Music, 1993, prod. Stray Cats and Jeff "Skunk" Baxter) a Japanese import of the still-kicking Cats blazing through fifteen rockabilly and early rock standards.

solo outings:

Brian Setzer *The Knife Feels Like Justice* (EMI, 1986) *The Brian Setzer Orchestra* (Hollywood, 1994) *Guitar Slinger* (Interscope, 1996)

Phantom, Rocker and Slick *Phantom, Rocker and Slick* (EMI America, 1985) *Cover Girl* (EMI America, 1986)

Lee Rocker's Big Blue *Lee Rocker's Big Blue* (Black Top, 1994)

▶▶ Uncle Tupelo, Bottle Rockets, Royal Crown Revue

◀◀ Eddie Cochran, Gene Vincent, Elvis Presley

Todd Wicks

Keith Streng

See: The Fleshtones

Joe Strummer

See: The Clash

Dan Stuart

See: Green on Red

Style Council

Formed 1983 in London, England. Disbanded 1989.

Paul Weller, guitar, bass, keyboards, vocals; Mick Talbot, keyboards, vocals; Dee C. Lee, vocals (1986-89)

If the Jam's punk-rock roots were too confining for Paul Weller's expanding musical interests, the Style Council gave him an open door to unrestricted excess. Backed by an army of jazz and funk session musicians, Weller and keyboardist Mick Talbot (formerly of the Merton Parkas and Dexy's Midnight Runners) fused R&B, soul, funk and jazz, straining it all through European elitism and Weller's growing leftist political ideologies. While the music was highly polished and sophisticated, it could be wildly pretentious and slick as well, produced at times with layered synth brass and drum machines. Nevertheless, the Style Council demonstrated what could be done with a palette of divergent styles, setting a trend that was echoed in the work of other former punk artists, including the Clash's Mick Jones (in Big Audio Dynamite) and Bow Wow Wow's Matthew Ashman (in Chiefs of Relief). By 1988, the Style Council was tripping over its own self-importance, and, as slipping album sales indicated, no one really cared anymore. Weller wisely abandoned the project, married vocalist Dee C. Lee, and, following a lengthy sabbatical, launched a successful solo career.

what to buy: Of the Style Council's albums, *Our Favourite Shop* (Polydor, 1985, prod. Peter Wilson and Paul Weller) is more consistent than anything that preceded it and more optimistic than anything that would follow it. (Weller admits he lost interest in the band after this release.) For once the group's varied styles worked together in a surprisingly coherent mix of funk ("The Lodgers"), soul ("Shout to the Top") and classic instrumentation ("A Stone's Throw Away"). [Note: This album was also released as *Internationalists* (Geffen, 1985) with a different cover, alternate mixes and a slightly revised track list. It is currently not available on CD.]

what to buy next: As greatest hits offerings go, *The Style Council Collection* (Polydor, 1996, prod. Peter Wilson and Paul Weller) is just about perfect, emphasizing the band's early hits ("Speak Like A Child," "Long Hot Summer," "My Ever Changing Moods") and tossing in several excellent non-LP tracks ("It Just Came to Pieces in My Hands," "Ghosts of Dachau") for good measure. Oddly, some of the Style Council's best work appeared not on albums but on singles and EPs. *Here's Some That Got Away* (Pony Canyon, 1994, prod. Peter Wilson and Paul Weller) serves them up on one fine disc. Among the treats are the lovely and wistful "The Piccadilly Trail" and Talbot's rousing instrumental "Party Chambers."

what to avoid: Weller's disgust with everything (including the Style Council) comes across loud and clear on *Confessions of a Pop Group* (Polydor, 1988, prod. Peter Wilson and Paul Weller). Opening with a toilet flush, the album wearily concludes with a 10-minute orchestral suite, complete with doo-wop chorus.

the rest: *Cafe Bleu* (Polydor, 1984) *My Ever Changing Moods* (Geffen, 1984) features a different cover, alternate mixes, and slightly revised track list. Currently not available on CD. *Live! The Style Council, Home & Abroad* (Polydor, 1986); *The Singular Adventures of the Style Council (Greatest Hits Vol. 1)* (Polydor, 1989)

worth searching for: The seven-song CD *Introducing the Style Council* (Polydor, 1983, prod. Peter Wilson & Paul Weller) brims with enthusiasm and breezy soul. Standouts include the group's debut single, "Speak Like a Child," the moody hit "Long Hot Summer" and an excellent alternate version of "The Paris Match."

▶▶ Big Audio Dynamite, Chiefs of Relief, Everything But the Girl, Communards, US3, Guru

◀◀ Curtis Mayfield, Marvin Gaye, Steely Dan, Modern Jazz Quartet, Dexter Gordon

see also: *The Jam, Paul Weller*

Christopher Scapelliti

Styx

Formed 1963 in Chicago, Ill. Disbanded 1984. Re-formed in 1990 and 1996.

Dennis DeYoung, vocals, keyboards; James Young, guitar, vocals (1970-present); Tom Naridni, guitar (1963-69); John Curulewski, guitar (1969-74); Chuck Panozzo, bass; John Panozzo, drums (1963-94; died July 17, 1996); Tommy Shaw, guitar, vocals (1974-84, 1996-present); Glen Burtnik, guitar, vocals (1990)

Styx took its name from the mythical river to hades, and more than a few critics have equated the group's music with a journey in that direction. Styx' response? Keep paddling, guys. A 1979 Gallup poll named Styx the favorite rock band among the 13- to 18-year-old set, which the group fed throughout the late 70s and early 80s with a string of hits that combined elements of Midwestern hard rock, British art rock and lush melodicism that would make Barry Manilow proud—a wide sweep from the grind of "Renegade" to the sap of "Babe" and "The Best of Times" to the downright silliness of "Mr. Roboto." Styx scored its hit in 1974 with "Lady" (a song which had actually come out two years prior), but it was 1977's loosely conceptual *The Grand Illusion* that put the group over the top and began a string of commercial successes that didn't stop until Styx splintered in 1984, following another bloated conceptual work, *Kilroy Was Here* The subsequent reunions have produced little music of new consequence, though Styx' 1996 summer tour with Kansas was one of the season's hottest tickets.

what to buy: Save yourself the individual albums and go straight for *Styx Greatest Hits,* (A&M, 1995, prod. Styx and Dennis DeYoung) a replay of late 70s rock radio. The only downside is that the group had to re-record "Lady" rather than include the original version, which was recorded for another label.

what to buy next: *Styx Greatest Hits, Part 2* (A&M, 1996, prod. Styx and Dennis DeYoung) is the best of the rest, with two new songs that don't add much to the story. *Pieces of Eight* (A&M, 1978, prod. Styx) is the best of the individual albums, with durable rockers such as "Renegade" and "Blue Collar Man (Long Nights)."

what to avoid: *Kilroy Was Here.* (A&M, 1983, prod. Styx) WOOF! Two words: "Mr. Roboto."

the rest: *Styx* (Wooden Nickel/RCA, 1972) *Styx II* (Wooden Nickel/RCA, 1973) *The Serpent Is Rising* (Wooden Nickel/RCA, 1973) *Man of Miracles* (Wooden Nickel/RCA, 1974) *Equinox* (A&M, 1975) *Crystal Ball* (A&M, 1976) *The Grand Illusion* (A&M, 1977) *Cornerstone* (A&M, 1979) *The Best of Styx* (RCA, 1980) *Paradise Theater* (A&M, 1981) *Caught in the Act—Live* (A&M, 1984) *Edge of the Century* (A&M, 1990)

worth searching for: *Radio-Made Hits 1975-1991,* (A&M, 1991, prod. Styx and Dennis DeYoung) a promotion-only sampler that includes the original "Lady" and most of the big hits—though it does have three selections from the lackluster *Edge of the Century*

solo outings:

Dennis DeYoung *Desert Moon* (A&M, 1984) *Back to the World* (A&M, 1986) *Boomchild* (A&M, 1988) *10 on Broadway* (Atlantic, 1994)

Tommy Shaw *Girls With Guns* (A&M, 1984) *What If* (A&M, 1985)

James Young (with Jan Hammer) *City Slickers* (Whitehouse, 1985/1995) *Raised By Wolves* (Absolute/Whitehouse, 1995)

▶▶ A Flock of Seagulls, Starcastle, Asia, Smashing Pumpkins, The Cure, Depeche Mode

◀◀ The Beatles, Yes, Chicago

see also: *Damn Yankees (Shaw)*

Gary Graff

The Subdudes

Formed in 1987 in New Orleans, La.

John Magnie, keyboards, accordion, vocals; Tommy Malone, guitar, vocals; Johnny Ray Allen, bass, vocals; Steve Amedee, percussion

The subdudes play music that's both simple and pure in its roots, but also hybridized with a pragmatic, non-purist's sense of style. Like the group's percussive gimmick—Amedee pounds his funky multi-rhythms on a tambourine, not a full drum set—the group is willing to try, and use, whatever works. But the music's essential purity comes from its deep base in New Orleans funk and R&B; Malone's understated, bluesy guitar playing, and the soulful vocal interplay between Malone and Magnie, which recall nothing if not The Band in its glory days. Like The Band, the 'dudes have known each other so long they play almost intuitively with each other. Malone, Allen and Amedee all grew up together in the upriver town of Edgard, La., before running off to New Orleans, eventually playing in a group called the Continental Drifters (now headed by Peter Holsapple). Magnie, a Colorado native, relocated to New Orleans during the 70s, attracted by the city's indigenously funky piano-playing. The subdudes formed out of necessity: Magnie played a regular Tuesday solo gig at Tipitina's, and the only way the rest could sit in was as an acoustic outfit. Hence Amedee's tambourine and Malone's acoustic guitar, which he plays more often than not. To escape the then-oppressive Crescent City music scene, which required cover material from bands instead of original songs, the band moved as a unit, families and all, to northern Colorado in late '87 and began tearing up the Denver area club scene with its acoustic-based grooves and original songs that already sounded like timeless R&B classics. Every album still includes a couple of these classic-sounding songs, but the group's live show is what makes converts out of skeptics, partly because producers have found it hard to capture the enormous live sound of the tambourine on tape. The band added touring member and studio session guitarist Willie Williams in 1994 as an unofficial member.

what to buy: *the subdudes*, (Atlantic, 1989, prod. Don Gehman) the group's debut, includes some of its best songs to date and staples of its live shows: "Light in Your Eyes," "Got You on His Mind" and "Need Somebody." *Annunciation* (High Street, 1994, prod. the subdudes, Keith Keller and Glyn Johns) is the best-produced of the 'dudes' albums, featuring strong songs and passionate, churchy performances.

what to buy next: *Primitive Streak* (1996, High Street, prod. Clark Vreeland) finds the band finding its feet as a recording group, with balanced studio performances but some weaker songs. Malone's "Carved in Stone" is a beautiful tribute to a deceased friend.

the rest: *Lucky* (EastWest, 1991)

Continental Drifters

The Band, Eric Clapton, Neville Brothers, Wild Tchoupitoulas, Earl King, Bonnie Raitt

Gil Asakawa

Suede

Formed 1990 in London, England

Brett Anderson, vocals; Bernard Butler, guitar, keyboards (1990-94); Justine Frishmann guitar, (1990-91); Richard Oakes, guitar (1994-present); Mat Osman, bass; Simon Gilbert, drums

Launched by an obnoxious barrage of U.K. music-press hype then unprecedented (but later matched by Blur and Oasis), this quartet sounded so much like early 70s *The Man Who Sold the World* David Bowie—an influence the group at least owned up to—that it was quickly introduced to the him for a master/pupil interview in one music magazine. Add in decided punk influences and hints of The Smiths, T-Rex/New York Dolls camp-glam, and this decidedly sassy group more or less ushered in the "Britpop" movement that later almost eclipsed it. Underneath the worn-on-the-sleeve influences, however, the debut LP *Suede* (Columbia, 1993, prod. Ed Buller) displays a rich world of inventive tunes and textures, thanks to Butler's masterful guitar—a true heir to Mick Ronson and The Stone Roses' John Squire—over which Anderson plays his ribald, funny and strangely touching lyrics (several homoerotic, though Anderson himself is straight). Given the fickle mantle of English stardom, Suede rose to the challenge on the breakthrough second LP *Dog Man Star*, (Columbia, 1994, prod. by Ed Buller) which advances the band to Bowie's *Alladin Sane* but otherwise shucks the more obvious influences in favor of expanding on them. It remains to be seen where a third LP will take Suede without the defected prime-songwriter Butler; its survival of the departure of original second guitarist Frishmann—who proved herself a considerable talent in her own right by forming and leading Elastica—suggests it will continue to prosper.

see also: *Elastica*

Jack Rabid

Sugar

See: Bob Mould

Sugarcubes

See: Bjork

Suicidal Tendencies

Formed early 1980s in Venice, Calif. Disbanded 1996.

Mike "Cyko Mico" Muir, vocals; Grant Estes, guitar (1983-96); Louiche Mayorga, bass (1983-87); Mike Clark, guitar; Rocky George, guitar (1987-94); Robert Trujillo, bass (1992-94); R.J. Herrara, drums (1987); Jimmy Degrasso, drums; Amery Smith, drums (1983)

This band rumbled out of the West Coast hardcore environment with potent and expressive punk. Spearheaded mainly by Muir, a forceful singer, Suicidal Tendencies released one of the best hardcore debuts in 1983. As the 80s metal bell tolled, the genre attracted status-seeking bands such as Suicidal Tendencies. The band gradually abandoned its hardcore roots for a far less imaginative form of heavy metal, with Muir picking up the handle "Cyco Miko" along the way. Black Flag this band is not.

what to buy: *Suicidal Tendencies* (Frontier Records, 1983/1993, prod. Glen E. Friedman) A rushing debut of articulate isolation, detachment and alienation in a galloping but clean hard-core setting. The half-hilarious, half-unsettling "Institutionalized" and "Suicide's an Alternative" give the album a tempo-shifting recklessness.

what to buy next: On *Join the Army,* (Caroline, 1987, prod. Lester Claypool) the swing to metal already had begun, though the band still cultivated the skate-punk image. Muir's hardened vocals and the warp-speed punk peel off into the netherworld between hard-core and heavy metal.

what to avoid: The raging but formless *Suicidal for Life* (Epic, 1994, prod. Paul Northfield) features Cyco Miko bellowing like a football lineman in a steroid rage.

the rest: *How Will I Laugh Tomorrow When I Can't Even Smile Today* (Epic, 1988) *Feel Like Shit ... Deja Vu/Controlled by Hatred* (Epic, 1989) *Lights ...Camera ... Revolution* (Epic, 1990) *The Art of Rebellion* (Epic, 1992) *Still Cyco After All These Years* (Epic, 1993)

solo outings:

Infectious Grooves (Muir and Trujillo) *The Plague That Makes Your Booty Move ... It's the Infectious Groove* (Epic, 1991) *Sarsippius' Ark* (Epic, 1993) *Groove Family Cyco* (550, 1994)

Anthrax, Faith No More, Corrosion of Conformity

Back Flag, D.R.I.

Allan Orski

The Suicide Machines

Formed 1991 in Redford, Mich.

Jason Navarro, vocals; Dan "Suicide Machine" Lukacinsky, guitars, vocals; Derek Grant, drums, vocals, keyboards; Royce Nunley, bass, backing vocals

The Suicide Machines' first gig, opening for the Mighty Mighty Bosstones in 1992, was an absolutely appropriate beginning. The foursome—once known as Jack Kevorkian and the Suicide Machines—honed its frenetic, adrenalized power-punk/ska skills supporting acts such as Rancid. A split CD with California's the Rudiments *Skank for Brains* (Dill, 1995, prod. Dan Lukacisnky, Derek Grant and Steve Presti) spawned the Detroit radio hit "New Girl," which piqued the attention of major labels. The Suicide Machines captured that sound on its debut full-length CD *Destruction by Definition,* (Hollywood, 1996, prod. Julian Raymond and Phil Kaffel) a collection of songs about youth angst, broken relationships and the horror of murdered peers.

Christina Fuoco

Jeff Sullivan

See: Drivin' N' Cryin'

Donna Summer

Born Donna Gaines, Dec. 31, 1948 in Boston, Mass.

Disco had a queen, and it was Summer. Nurtured in church choirs and in theater troupes, Summer—in cahoots with producers Giorgio Moroder and Pete Bellote—delivered a breathless, orgasmic performance on "Love to Love You Baby" that stirred loins on dance floors around the world in 1975 and eventually scaled the pop charts. That was the start of something big, as Summer reeled off a five-year string of club and radio hits ("I Feel Love," "Last Dance," an epic rendition of Jimmy Webb's dynamically twisted "MacArthur Park"). But Summer and her producers were savvy enough to follow the trends; as disco ebbed at the end of the 70s, she moved subtley into dance rock on albums such as *Bad Girls* and *The Wanderer* and continued to broaden her reach and embrace her born-again faith (she won a Grammy for Best Inspirational Vocal in 1984)—even though the hits slowed and eventually stopped during the 80s. Summer hasn't necessarily given up, but when you see her perform these days it's little more than a trip down a polyester memory lane.

what to buy: The compact, 18-song *Endless Summer: Donna Summer's Greatest Hits* (Mercury/Casablanca, 1984, prod. Various) ♪♪♪♪½ is a nonstop treat of pleasures—guilty in some cases, but well worth having in the collection.

what to buy next: *Bad Girls* (Mercury/Casablanca, 1979, prod. Giorgio Moroder and Pete Bellote) ♪♪♪♪ added rock to Summer's dance-oriented palette via the title track and the wonderful "Hot Stuff." *The Wanderer* (Geffen, 1980/Casablanca-Mercury, 1994, prod. Giorgio Moroder and Pete Belotte) ♪♪♪♪ branches out even further, with contributions from Jeff Beck and Billy Idol. *The Donna Summer Anthology* (Casablanca/Chronicles, 1993, prod. Various) ♪♪♪♪ offers a broader sampling than *Endless Summer.*

what to avoid: *Another Place and Time* (Atlantic, 1989, prod. Stock, Aitken and Waterman) ♪ is bland and soulless, diluting Summer's powerful presence in the antiseptic arrangements that are the British production trio's stock in trade.

the rest: *Love to Love You Baby* (Mercury/Casablanca, 1975/1992) ♪♪½ *A Love Trilogy* (Mercury/Casablanca, 1976/1992) ♪♪ *The Four Seasons of Love* (Mercury/Casablanca, 1976/1991) ♪♪ *I Remember Yesterday* (Mercury/Casablanca, 1977/1991) ♪♪ *Once Upon a Time* (Mercury/Casablanca, 1977/1991) ♪½ *Live and More* (Mercury/Casablanca, 1978/1990) ♪♪ *On the Radio: Greatest Hits* (Mercury/Casablanca, 1979) ♪♪♪½ *Walk Away: Collector's Edition* (Mercury/Casablanca, 1982) ♪♪♪½ *Donna Summer* (Geffen, 1982/Mercury-Casablanca, 1994) ♪♪♪½ *She Works Hard for the Money* (Mercury, 1983) ♪♪♪ *Cats Without Claws* (Geffen/Mercury, 1984) ♪♪ *All Systems Go* (Mercury/ Casablanca, 1987) ♪♪ *Dance Collection* (Mercury/ Casablanca, 1987) ♪♪♪½ *Mistaken Identity* (Atlantic, 1991) ♪½ *Christmas Spirit* (Mercury, 1994) ♪♪♪

worth searching for: Summer has made lots of guest appearances, ranging from the ridiculous—Kiss' *Gene Simmons* (Mercury, 1978) ♪♪—to her sublime vocals on Brooklyn Dreams' *The Music, Harmony and Rhythm* (Mercury/Casablanca, 1996) ♪♪♪½

▶▶ Irene Cara, Grace Jones, Madonna, Paula Abdul, Taylor Dayne

◀◀ Mahalia Jackson, Aretha Franklin, Nico, Kraftwerk, Gloria Gaynor

Gary Graff

Andy Summers

Born Andrew Sommers, Dec. 31, 1942, in Blackpool, England

A well-known professional who'd worked with Eric Burdon's Animals and Neil Sedaka, Summers was recruited by drummer Stewart Copeland and bassist Sting to add instrumental heft with founding guitarist Henry Padovani in the then-fledgling group, the Police. Soon, Padovani was gone, jettisoned to make room for Summers' flights of echo-laden guitar noise and sideways tonal excursions. Like Copeland, Summers grew frustrated with frontman Sting's control jones, venting his songwriting work in collaborations with art-rock guitar king Robert Fripp during the early 80s. After the Police went on indefinite hiatus in 1985, Summers released a number of solo records that veer from experimental rock guitar bombast to unconventional jazz-fusion work.

what to buy: A master of many styles of playing, Summers suffers from two weaknesses as a recording artist—an amazing inability to write good material and an annoying habit of down playing his own instrumental talents. His best solo outing, *Charming Snakes,* (Private Music, 1990, prod. Andy Summers and David Hentschel) ♪♪♪♪ diminishes both of those faults. Featuring such August sidemen as Herbie Hancock, Bill Evans and the Sting-man himself, this record marks Summers' first and best turn from ambient rock guitar noise to artful jazz fusion.

what to buy next: For fans of great guitar playing, there's few better records than Summers' collaboration with Robert Fripp, *I Advance Masked.* (A&M, 1982, prod. Robert Fripp and Andy Summers) ♪♪♪½ While Summers leaps off melodic cliffs Fripp dare not approach, Fripp's echo-drenched fretwork provides the perfect bedrock for his partner's sonic flights.

what to avoid: There's nothing more tedious than a bad jazz/rock fusion record—which is Summers' first post-Police outing, *XYZ,* (MCA, 1987, prod. Andy Summers) WOOF! a boring mishmash of tired themes and conventionally unconventional playing.

the rest: *Mysterious Barricades* (Private Music, 1988) ♪♪♪ *The Golden Wire* (Private Music, 1989) ♪♪♪½ *World Gone Strange* (Private Music, 1991) ♪♪♪½ *Synaesthesia* (CMP, 1995) ♪♪½ (with Robert Fripp): *Bewitched* (A&M, 1984) ♪♪½ (with John Etheridge): *Invisible Threads* (Mesa/Blue Moon, 1993) ♪♪♪

worth searching for: Back in the days when Sting would let someone else from the band intrude on his creative vision, Summers composed a love poem for a blow-up doll, dutifully inserted in the punky workout "Be My Girl" from the Police's first album, *Outlandos D'Amor.* Hearing him describe the object of his affection in a thick cockney accent is worth the price of admission.

▶▶ Adrian Belew, Steve Farris (Mr. Mister), the Samples

◀◀ Steve Howe, Allan Holdsworth, Syd Barrett, David Gilmour

Eric Deggans

Sun Ra

Born Herman Blount, May 22, 1914, in Birmingham, Ala. Died May 30, 1993 in Birmingham, Ala.

Sun Ra went to Saturn long before P-Funk's Mothership was ever seen on the horizon. His freaky clothes and outlandish chants set the orbit that George Clinton eventually followed. Ra's early years playing around Chicago and with the Fletcher Henderson Orchestra were undistinguished. He didn't take off until the mid-50s, when he renamed himself Sun Ra and assembled his Arkestra—an assemblage that would include more than 100 members, including saxophonist John Gilmore, reeds specialist Laurdine "Pat" Patrick, bassist Ronald Boykins and vocalist June Tyson. Ra's work breaks roughly into three periods: big band/hard bop exotica during the 50s; outer and outer free jazz in the 60s; and swing from the mid-70s until his death. The free music rode on a bedrock of rhythms borrowed from Latin and African music and spacey melodies. During the late 60s, the band freaked out with colorful costumes, and even drew attention from hippie rock crowd, playing major festivals all over the world. Ra's free music pre-dated Ornette Coleman and Cecil Taylor, and his return to swing beat the 80s traditionalist movement spearheaded by Wynton Marsalis. Ra is also distinguished for having maintained a big band throughout the rock era.

what to buy: *The Magic City* (Evidence, 1965, prod. Infinity Inc. and Alton Abraham) is a high point for Ra—and for anyone else. Its mysterious ebbs and flows slowly build to musical tidal waves with eerie synthesizer work, agitated piano and exultant saxophone solos. *Mayan Temples,* (Black Saint, 1990, prod. Giovanni Bonandrina) one of Ra's final studio albums, is fine summation of his late period, mixing up standards ("Alone Together"), big band exotica and one long, exploratory piece. Included is wonderful reading of "El Is the Sound of Joy," which prefigured John Coltrane's "Giant Steps."

what to buy next: *Live at Pitt-Inn* (DIW, 1988, prod. Kohei Kawakami) gives a balanced look at the swing and free work of the late era.

the rest: Sun Ra made over 500 albums, the best being: *Sun Song* (Delmark, 1956) *Jazz in Silhouette* (Evidence, 1958) *The Nubians of Plutonia* (Saturn, 1959) *Atlantis* (Impulse, 1960) *The Magic City* (Evidence, 1965) *Pictures of Infinity* (Black Lion, 1968) *Solar Myth Approach* (Affinity, 1970) *Space Is the Place* (Evidence, 1972) *St. Louis Blues* (Evidence, 1977) *Unity* (Horo, 1977) *Visions* (Steeplechase, 1978) *Strange Celestial Road* (Rounder, 1980) *Reflections in Blue* (Black Saint, 1986) *Out There a Minute* (Enigma, 1990) *Somewhere Else* (Rounder, 1993)

worth searching for: *The Night of the Purple Moon* (El Saturn, 1970, prod. Infinity Inc and T.T. Mims) is an oddball release with Gilmore mostly on drums, Stafford James on electric bass and Ra playing mostly the briefly marketed roksichord, a clavinet-like instrument. It includes the wonderful "Love in Outerspace."

▶▶ Art Ensemble of Chicago, Michael Ray and the Cosmic Krewe, George Clinton/Parliament/Funkadelic, Phish

◀◀ Fletcher Henderson, Duke Ellington

Lawrence Gabriel

The Sundays

Formed 1987 in London, England

David Gavurin, guitar; Harriet Wheeler, vocals; Paul Brindley, bass; Patrick Hannan, drums

The Sundays is an alternative band before it was a marketing term or radio format. Emerging during the late 80s, just a shade before the Lollapalooza generation became mass consumers, the group scored a minor hit with its debut single—an enchanting tune about bittersweet love called "Here's Where the Story Ends"—and bounced around in the college album charts with its debut album, *Reading, Writing and Arithmetic,* (DGC, 1989, prod. The Sundays and Ray Shulman) a jangly, sweet and invigorating effort that blends melancholy moods with uplifting melodies. *Blind* (DGC, 1992, prod. David Gavurin, Harriet Wheeler and Dave Anderson) is just as exquisite as its predecessor, though it's slightly more downhearted. It includes a fine cover of the Rolling Stones' "Wild Horses," as well as stellar originals such as "Love" and "Blood on My Hands." Unfortunately, the Sundays never achieved the success it deserves, while superficial soundalikes such as the Cranberries have gone on to conquer the pop charts.

Aidin Varizi

Superchunk

Formed 1989 in Chapel Hill, N.C.

Mac McCaughan, guitar, vocals; Jack McCook, guitar (1989-91); Jim Wilbur, guitar (1991-present); Laura Ballance, bass; Jon Wurster, drums (1991-present); Chuck Garrison, drums (1989-91)

Occasionally likened to a happier Nirvana, Superchunk combines old school 80's punk (i.e., The Buzzcocks and Hüsker Dü) with pop melodies. The band manages to remain an important indie band, and the only thing that separates Superchunk from "Alternative Nation" stardom is the band's fear of major labels; thus the group formed its own record company, Merge, when former distributors were purchased by a conglomerate. While the group isn't breaking any new ground and the music may be somewhat static, Superchunk still scores with authentic, high-energy and hard rocking tales of suburban angst.

what to buy: *Tossing Seeds: Singles 89-91* (Merge, 1992, prod. Superchunk) is a compilation of 19 tracks that highlight what Superchunk does best: create good, fast, hard-hitting hooks and songs. The music does seem to blend together after awhile, but *Tossing Seeds* highlights the transition from noisy garage band to a tight pop/punk ensemble. *On The Mouth* (Matador, 1992, prod. Superchunk) catches Superchunk at one of its best and most accessible periods; the sound is starting to get cleaned up, though it retains its garage-inspired immediacy and rawness.

what to buy next: *No Pocky for Kitty* (Matador, 1991, prod. Superchunk) is a solid album with a number of good punk anthems, catching Superchunk in transition from its noisy music phase and starting to sound more song oriented. *Incidental Music 1991-1995* (Merge, 1995, prod. Superchunk) is a collection of rare singles and B-sides from the group's later, more accessible period.

what to avoid: With its crisper sound, *Here's Where the Strings Come In* (Merge, 1995, prod. Superchunk) sounds a bit watered down and less vital than its predecessors.

the rest: *Foolish* (Merge, 1995) *Superchunk* (Matador, 1990)

worth searching for: Superchunk's split seven-inch single entitled, *She Cracked* (Honey Bear, 1995, prod. Superchunk) shares the vinyl with another indie fave, Tsunami.

solo outings:

Portastatic (Mac McCaughan) I Hope Your Heart Is Not Brittle (Merge, 1993, prod. Mac McCaughan)

Polvo, Tsunami, Helium

Hüsker Dü, the Buzzcocks, the Sex Pistols, the Ramones

Bryan Lassner

Supergrass

Formed 1993 in Oxford, England

Gaz Coombes, vocals, guitar; Mickey Quinn, bass; Danny Goffey, drums

Supergrass released its *I Should Coco* (Parlophone, 1995, prod. Sam Williams) amid the Britpop fever that continues to engage Britain. The trio's brand of alternative pop, characterized by fast guitar hooks and infectious melodies, is original and energetic—and borrows freely from groups as diverse as The Buzzcocks, The Who, The Beatles and The Undertones.

Anna Glen

Supertramp

Formed 1969 in London, England. Disbanded 1989.

Rick Davies, keyboards, vocals; Roger Hodgson, guitar, keyboards, vocals (1969-83); Richard Palmer, guitar (1969-70); Bob Miller, drums (1969-70); Dave Winthrop, saxophone, (1970-74); Frank Farrell, bass (1970-74); Kevin Currie, drums (1970-74); Bob C. Benberg, drums (1974-89); John Anthony Helliwell, saxophone, reeds, vocals (1975-89); Dougie Thompson, bass (1975-89)

Thanks to the financial support of a young, eccentric Dutch millionaire, Supertramp was able to muddle through the first few years of its existence pursuing a ponderous, art/rock sound. After its first two records went virtually unnoticed, the group's patron withdrew his backing forcing Davies and Hodgson to come up with something more appealing in order to keep the band alive. They recruited a new line-up and created the tightly produced, high-voiced, sax-and-keyboard-dominated pop style that became Supertramp's trademark. After four successful records with this formula, culminating in the platinum-selling *Breakfast in America*, the band changed directions yet again, this time to a more R&B flavored sound. This move cost them most of their following, as well as Hodgson, who left to pursue a short-lived solo career. After Hodgson left, the band put out two more undistinguished efforts before calling it quits.

what to buy: *Crime of the Century* (A&M, 1974, prod. Ken Scott and Supertramp) ♪♪♪♪ is worth owning if only for the piano solo on "School." This is the album where the band first put its sound together, and it remains its best, with other highlights such as "Bloody Well Right" and "Dreamer." *Crisis? What Crisis?* (A&M, 1975, prod. Ken Scott and Supertramp) ♪♪♪♪ was a strong follow-up, from the jangly guitars on "Sister Moonshine" to the final lilting chords of "Two of Us"—as well as lots of first-rate work that was never subjected to radio overkill.

what to buy next: *Breakfast in America* (A&M, 1979, prod. Supertramp and Peter Henderson) ♪♪♪½ was the band's biggest success—with hits such as "The Logical Song," "Take the Long Way Home" and the title track—and probably the album that most casual fans would label their favorite. *Even in the Quietest Moments* (A&M, 1977, prod. Supertramp) ♪♪♪ is another compelling effort that occasionally offers a taste of the bands art/rock beginnings.

what to avoid: The band's first two albums—*Supertramp* (A&M, 1970, prod. Supertramp) ½ and *Indelibly Stamped,* (A&M, 1971, prod. Supertramp) ½ which, like so much early 70s art/rock, were neither art nor rock.

the rest: *Paris* (A&M, 1980) ♪♪♪ *Famous Last Words* (A&M, 1982) ♪♪ *Brother, Where You Bound* (A&M, 1985) ♪½ *Free as a Bird* (A&M, 1987) ♪½ *Classics, Volume 9* (A&M, 1987) ♪♪♪½

worth searching for: Though Supertramp couldn't really cut it in the studio after Hodgson left, the import-only *Supertramp Live '88* (A&M, 1988, prod. Rick Davies and Norman Hall) ♪♪♪ still had something to offer in concert.

solo outings:

Roger Hodgson In the Eye of the Storm (A&M, 1984) ♪♪ *Hai Hai* (A&M, 1987) ♪½

▶▶ Jellyfish, The Judybats

◀◀ Willie Dixon, The Beatles, Dusty Springfield

Gary Plochinski

The Supremes

Formed 1959 as the Primettes in Detroit, Mich.

Diana (Diane) Ross, vocals (1959-69); Florence Ballard, vocals (1959-67); Mary Wilson, vocals; Betty McGlown, vocals (1959-60); Barbara Martin, vocals (1960-63); Cindy Birdsong, vocals (1967-71, 1974-76); Jean Terrell, vocals (1970-74); Lynda Laurence, vocals (1972-74); Scherrie Payne, vocals (1974-77); Susaye Greene, vocals (1976-77)

The Supremes were as much about sugary pop confection and image as about R&B; they were Berry Gordy, Jr.'s ticket to the Copacabana and other mainstream trappings he craved, which (along with his romance with Ross) helps explain why they were the most successful of Motown's female vocal groups. It's hard to overstate the magic of Holland-Dozier-Holland's hits and, to a slightly lesser extent, Ross' dynamic and striking lead vocals. Balancing choreographed stage glamour with alternatingly cool and flirty coyness, the Supremes' sweet vocals epitomized the everyone-welcome crossover nature of the Motown sound. Along with the Beatles, the Supremes defined Top 40 pop during the 60s. But after Ross' departure for a career as a solo artist and movie star, the Supremes were placed on Motown's back burner; the gradual departure of Holland-Dozier-Holland's songs and the label's decreased support left the group floundering until it folded in 1977, though Wilson continues to tour using the Supremes moniker.

what to buy: *Anthology* (Motown, 1970, prod. Various) ♪♪♪♪½ contains every single Motown hit the group recorded—an awesome display of timeless music making that's still amazing to behold.

what to buy next: *Greatest Hits and Rare Classics* (Motown, prod. Various) ♪♪♪♪ is an informative supplement to *Anthology* for those interested in the post-Ross years.

what to avoid: *The Best of The Supremes & The Four Tops* (Motown, 1991, prod. Various) ♪♪ is a skimpy compilation that sells both groups short.

the rest: *Merry Christmas* (Motown, 1965) ♪♪½ *The Supremes Sing Country, Western & Pop* (Motown, 1965/1994) ♪♪ *I Hear a Symphony* (Motown, 1966) ♪♪♪ *Supremes A-Go-Go* (Motown Records, 1966/1989) ♪♪♪½ *Reflections* (Motown, 1968/1991) ♪♪♪ *Great Songs & Performances That Inspired Motown 25* (Motown, 1983/1991) ♪♪½ *Greatest Hits, Vol. I* (Motown, 1986) ♪♪♪ *Greatest Hits, Vol. II* (Motown, date N/A) ♪♪♪ *Greatest Hits, Vol. III* (Motown, 1991) ♪♪½ *Motown Superstar Series, Vol. 1* (Motown, date N/A) ♪♪♪½ *Live at London's Talk of the Town* (Motown, date N/A) ♪♪♪ *Captured Live On Stage* (Motown, date N/A) ♪♪♪ *Every Great #1 Hit* (Motown, date N/A) ♪♪♪♪ *Motown Legends: Stoned Love* (ESX Entertainment, 1995) ♪♪½

worth searching for: *Where Did Our Love Go,* (Motown, 1964) ♪♪♪½ the trio's sophomore effort and one of Ross' great prevanity showcases.

▶▶ The J. Geils Band, Bananarama, the Go-Go's

◀◀ The Shangri-las, the Chiffons

see also: *Diana Ross*

Allan Orski

Surf Music

During the late 50s and early 60s, just before John F. Kennedy was assassinated, everybody was (seemingly) having fun. On California beaches, anyhow. The first major surf character was Dick Dale (born Richard Monsour), who approximated the crashing sound of a tidal wave on his guitar. Dale, with the early-60s hits "Let's Go Trippin'" and "Misirlou," stole a bit of funky country style from Link Wray and Duane Eddy and a lot of fun-loving teen attitude from Chuck Berry and invented a fingernails-down-the-fretboard style that could explode and shiver at will. Soon the beaches of Malibu were filled with surfboards, bikinis, hot rods and ... guitars. Not only that, but rockers-to-be in such non-surfing fiefdoms as New York City and Boulder, Colo., were listening to the sounds and deciding they could make surf music their own way.

The most famous surf offspring was, of course, the Beach Boys, who drew from Berry, doo-wop and the blues to make "Surfin' U.S.A.," "Fun Fun Fun," "California Girls," "In My Room" and the rest. Also breaking out were Jan & Dean ("Drag City"), the Trashmen ("The Bird"), the Ventures ("Diamond Head"), the Chantays ("Pipeline"), the Surfaris ("Wipe Out"), the Astronauts ("Baja") and countless underground ("undersand"?) bands that picked up guitars and tried to rock—similar to the phenomenon of the 60s garage bands. The obscure surf rockers, too, put out some wonderful records, often hilarious in the most campy possibly way: the Del-Vettes' "Ram Charger," Brian Lord's "The Big Surfer," the Honeys' "Shoot the Curl," the Tradewinds' "New York's a Lonely Town" and Eddie & the Showmen's "Mr. Rebel," to name just a few.

It all wiped out after the Beach Boys lost their hegemonic battle for creative superiority with the Beatles. After the Boys' landmark 1966 album "Pet Sounds," surf-rockers' days in the sun were numbered. It wasn't until the late 70s, when punks recaptured some of its sounds, that surf returned to anything beyond oldies stations. During the early 90s, such bands as Laika and the Cosmonauts, the Mermen, Man ... Or Astroman? and Dale himself picked up the long-snuffed torch.

what to buy: The four-disc *Cowabunga!* (Rhino, 1996, prod. Various) set, with 82 songs and samplings of most of the aforementioned bands' repertoire, is the most comprehensive and well-packaged surf collection to date. Other good compilations include: *Wild City* (Capitol, 1991, prod. Various) *Drag City* (Capitol, 1991, prod. Various) *Pebbles, Vol. 4: Surf N Tunes!* (Archive International, 1992, prod. Various) *Rock Instrumental Classics, Vol. 5: Surf* (Rhino, 1994, prod. Gary Stewart, James Austin and David McLees)

what to buy next: An assortment of collections from indvidual surf practitioners that are diverse and fascinating, if spotty, The Honeys' *Collectors Series* (Capitol, 1992, prod. Ron Furmanek) showcases an all-girl surf band who were 60s pals of Beach Boy Brian Wilson (and featured his first wife, Marilyn). The Ventures' *Ventures in Space* (Dolton, 1964/EMI, 1992, reissue prod. Ron Furmanek) and *Play Telstar—the Lonely Bull and Others* (Dolton, 1963/EMI, 1992, reissue prod. Ron Furmanek) offer spacey, explosively performed psychedelic instrumentals that influenced the Who's Keith Moon, among many others. *Surfin' Bird* (Soma, 1964/Sundazed, 1995, prod. Bob Irwin) is a surprisingly fresh argument that the Trashmen were more talented than their novelty place in rock history. Jan & Dean, whose tragedy-filled career is documented in the 70s movie "Deadman's Curve," were Beach Boys' imitators, but good ones, showcased best on *The Little Old Lady From Pasadena* (Liberty, 1964/EMI, 1992, reissue prod. Ron Furmanek)

▶▶ Some of the best contemporary surf music can be heard on: Man Or Astro-Man?'s *Is It Man ... Or Astro-Man?* (Estrus, 1993, prod. Jim Marrer and Birdstuff) and Laika and the Cosmonauts' straight-outta-Finland *The Amazing Colossal Band* (Upstart, 1994, prod. Laika and the Cosmonauts)

see also: *The Beach Boys, Dick Dale*

Steve Knopper

Matthew Sweet

Born Oct. 6, 1964 in Lincoln, Neb.

Sweet (yes, it's his real name) came out of the Athens, Ga. scene and was first heard on EPs by Oh-OK (with Linda Stipe, Michael's sister) and Buzz of Delight. A masterful songwriter and talented multi-instrumentalist ironically known for the superb performances of his sidemen (especially guitarists Robert Quine and Richard Lloyd), Sweet was dropped by Columbia and then A&M after fine albums attracted little attention. But when

A&M declined his third album, *Girlfriend,* Zoo picked it up and it rocketed onto the charts on the strength of the Japanese animation video for the song "Divine Intervention." The best songwriting and most Beatlesque production of his career didn't hurt either, and it could be that the tuneful success of *Girlfriend* (full of classic rock verities) paved the way for the acceptance of the like-minded rock melodists such as Gin Blossoms and Goo Goo Dolls. However, Sweet's creativity has subsequently been infected by a slight sense of formula and routine; he still sounds good, but he's not advancing.

what to buy: If Sweet never again equals *Girlfriend,* (Zoo, 1991, prod. Fred Maher and Matthew Sweet) ♪♪♪♪♪ it's nothing to be ashamed of. It's that good. Lloyd's trademark freak-out solos on "Divine Intervention" followed by the wistful "I've Been Waiting" set the album's tone of alternating guitar aggression with twangy ballads, while Sweet overdubs angelic harmonies all over the place.

what to buy next: *Earth* (A&M, 1989, prod. Fred Maher, David M. Allen and Matthew Sweet) ♪♪♪♪ has a slightly lusher pop sound than *Girlfriend*, but with hooks galore and enough crunch ("Underground" and "The Alcohol Talking") to not cloy. Members of Trip Shakespeare add rich harmony vocals to a batch of Sweet's most poignant tunes, and Quine, Lloyd, and Gary Lucas contribute scintillating guitar work.

what to avoid: *Inside* (Columbia, 1986) ♪♪ was good for a debut but is slick and bland compared to Sweet's later work.

the rest: *Altered Beast* (Zoo, 1993) ♪♪♪♪ *100% Fun* (Zoo, 1995) ♪♪♪

worth searching for: The 13-track, promo-only *Goodfriend* (Zoo, 1992) ♪♪♪♪ has live, radio and home recordings. Mostly it focuses on *Girlfriend* material, but there's also an early version of Altered Beast's "Someone to Pull the Trigger" as well as superb covers of Neil Young's "Cortez the Killer" (with the Indigo Girls) and John Lennon's "Isolation." The seven-song EP *Son of Altered Beast* (Zoo, 1994) ♪♪♪♪ has five live tracks (including another Neil Young tune, "Don't Cry No Tears").

▶▶ Velvet Crush, Teenage Fanclub

◀◀ Beatles, Raspberries, Neil Young, Television, dB's

Steve Holtje

Rachel Sweet

Born 1963 in Akron, Ohio

Growing up in summer stock productions, Sweet had been discovered many times as a child. When she was 12, she released her debut album *Fool Around* (Stiff/Columbia, 1978, prod. Liam Sternberg) ♪♪♪—bubblegum pop (what else can you be at 12?) at a time when the punk and mod scenes were thriving. Ironically, it remains the best thing she did, save for the title song of John Waters' 1988 film "Hairspray."

the rest: *Protect The Innocent* (Stiff/Columbia, 1980) ♪♪♪ *..And Then He Kissed Me* (Columbia, 1981) ♪♪♪ *Blame It On Love* (Columbia, 1982) ♪♪♪

Anna Glen

The Sweet

Formed 1968 in London, England. Disbanded 1981.

Brian Connolly, vocals; Mick Tucker, drums, vocals; Andy Scott, guitar, keyboards, vocals; Steve Priest, bass, vocals

As catchy as they were stupid, the Sweet's hits led the raunchy, glam cheese pack during the 70s. Developed as a bubblegum teenybopper sensation by British producers Nicky Chinn and Mike Chapman (who wrote most of the group's biggest hits), the Sweet charted with insistent, trashy singles such as "Little Willy," "Blockbuster" and "Ballroom Blitz," all of which make for guilty pleasures. Fueled by fat power chords, nitro-vocals and bone-snappingly crisp production (often covering the group's musical slightness)—not to mention obvious, crude lyrics—these coiffed-haired pretty boys were just obnoxious enough to offend your mother but safe enough to cultivate a mass success. And there are certainly enough modern rockers whose teenybopper years were spent with the band to acknowledge it as something of an influence. Apparently there may have been a real band lurking in there somewhere, as some of its own material—such as its biggest hit, "Fox on the Run"—stands up to Chinn-Chapman's. With the individual albums long out of print, *The Best of Sweet* (Capitol, 1992, prod. Various) ♪♪♪♪ packs all the Sweet you'd ever want to hear onto a 16-track set.

Allan Orski

Swervedriver

Formed 1988 in Oxford, England

Adam Franklin, vocals, guitar; Jim Hartridge, guitar; Adi Vines, bass (1988-92); Steve George, bass, vocals (1992-present); Graham Bonnar, drums (1988-91); Danny, drums (1991-92); Jez, drums (1991-present)

Few groups that aren't metal bands are as beautifully punishing as Swervedriver. Combining the heaviness of that genre with the smack-slap attack of punk, the hiss of hardcore, the dreamy soundscapes of shoegaze, the pop smarts of Britpop (The Who seem to be a large influence) and the simple, vaguely psychedelic jams of The Stooges (another major checkpoint here), Swervedriver lash, with edge, but in the most laconic blast of heat imaginable. Toss in lyrics obsessed with cars (and motorbikes), science fiction and film noir cinema, and you have one of the more intriguing groups Britain has produced during the 90s. Perhaps *Raise* (A&M, 1991, prod. Swervedriver) is a bit ragtag—it was made up of a number of different sessions that produced the earliest EPs—but the main tracks ("Son of Mustang Ford," "Rave Down," "Sandblasted") remain some of the band's signature power-moments. A new rhythm section improved things on the smashing *Mezcal Head* (A&M, 1993, prod. Alan Moulder and Swervedriver) an album of pure, adrenalized, souped-up rock complete with the deceptive, harsh hooks of "Duel" and "Blowin' Cool." Sadly, Swervedriver's best album, *Ejector Seat Reservation* (Creation U.K., 1995, prod. Swervedriver and Alan Moulder) wasn't released in the U.S. but that hopefully won't happen again now that the band is signed to Geffen.

Jack Rabid

The Swinging Blue Jeans

Formed 1958 in Liverpool, England

Ray Ennis, vocals, guitar; Ralph Ellis, guitar; Les Braid, bass; Norman Kuhlke, drums; Terry Sylvester, guitar

Back when Messrs. Lennon, McCartney and Harrison were still skiffling their way around local talent contests, the Swinging Blue Jeans (though admittedly an early "trad-jazz" incarnation, complete with banjoist Paul Moss) were already headlining at Liverpool's legendary Cavern Club. By 1963, the Blue Jeans were right up at the top of the U.K. charts alongside those Beatles, and the following year had successfully invaded America as well. Perhaps what ultimately lead the band down the road to obscurity—along with practically every other non-Beatle combo from Liverpool—was the lack of in-house songwriting ability: its several hits ("The Hippy Hippy Shake," "Good Golly Miss Molly" and "You're No Good") were all competent, if unspectacular covers of stage-tested chestnuts, which is not the way to ensure a lasting recording career. As a result, they've spent the past three decades back on the club circuit, happily playing their "Shaking" medley at European pubs and resort clubs. *Hippy Hippy Shake: The Definitive Collection* (EMI, 1993, prod. Walter J. Ridley) demonstrates, if nothing else, what a powerhouse unit these guys must've been back at the Cavern. Keen students of Merseybeat can hear, in the latter material, the first tentative strummings of Hollie-to-be Terry Sylvester.

Gary Pig Gold

SXL

See: Bill Laswell

David Sylvian

Born David Batt, Feb. 23, 1958 in Beckenham Kent, England

While his former band, Japan, was a largely collaborative effort, Sylvian is generally regarded as the group's primary creative force. This is borne out by Sylvian's solo career, which is easily the most successful and diverse of the post-Japan projects. Despite the fact that all of his solo albums feature significant contributions from Japan drummer Steve Jansen and keyboardist Richard Barbieri, Sylvian's catalog boasts a stamp that is singular and distinctive. His first solo album, *Brilliant Trees*, has lingering elements of Japan's trademark Eastern sound but is more focused on introducing jazz overtones and lusher acoustic instruments. Contributions from notable musicians such as Ryuichi Sakamoto, Robert Fripp and former Bebop Deluxe guitarist Bill Nelson made Sylvian's subsequent outings even more discrete.

what to buy: Two Sylvian albums do a nice job of illustrating the primary thrusts of his solo career. *Secrets of the Beehive* (Virgin, 1987, prod. David Sylvian) showcases his contemplative side with sumptuous mood pieces buoyed by rich acoustic tones, luxurious string arrangements and Sylvian's rich vocals. (Note: later editions of the album omit "Forbidden Colors," Sylvian's collaboration with Sakamoto.) Partnering with seminal art rock guitarist Fripp (King Crimson, League of Crafty Guitarists), Sylvian shifted gears with the release of the more aggressive *The First Day* (Virgin, 1993, prod. Robert Fripp and David Sylvian) A true collaboration, the album successfully grafts Fripp's angular guitar style to Sylvian's mellifluous vocals and ambient inclinations for a work that is both driving and ethereal, at times recalling middle period King Crimson.

what to buy next: *Gone to Earth* (Virgin, 1986, prod. David Sylvian and Steve Nye) is really two releases in one. The first half of the recording features vocals and the significant guitar work of Nelson and Fripp; this material, particularly "Taking the Veil" and the title track, offer a transitional view of Sylvian as he moves from Japan toward the quieter sounds he pursued on *Secrets of the Beehive.* The second half of the album is comprised of instrumental mood pieces that draw heavily from Brian Eno's atmospheric canon for songs that create a dreamlike tapestry that is simultaneously soothing and eerie. (Note: The CD version of the album excises half the instrumental tracks.)

what to avoid: *Plight and Premonition* (Virgin, 1988, prod. David Sylvian and Holger Czukay) ♪½ is the first of two nearly identical collaborations that Sylvian undertook with former Can bassist Holger Czukay, and, if a distinction can be made, is the worst of the two. Like the most insipid New Age music, the instrumentals on this album are vacuous and without direction.

the rest: *Brilliant Trees* (Virgin, 1984) ♪♪♪½ (with Czukay): *Flux and Mutability* (Virgin, 1989) ♪♪

worth searching for: *Damage,* (Virgin, 1994, prod. David Sylvian and Robert Fripp) ♪♪♪♪ a limited-edition import, is a live recording of the tour that Sylvian and Fripp undertook in support of *The First Day* and is well worth hearing. If you're looking for the definitive Sylvian collection, *Weatherbox* (Virgin, 1989) ♪♪♪♪ is the ticket; now out of print, the boxed set contains all of Sylvian's full length albums, his two EPs—*Alchemy, An Index of Possibilities* and *Words with the Shaman*—and, for the first time on CD in the U.S., the complete instrumental half of *Gone to Earth.*

▶▶ Holger Czukay, Bill Nelson/Bebop Deluxe, Depeche Mode, Moby, Aphex Twin

◀◀ Bryan Ferry/Roxy Music, Brian Eno, David Bowie, King Crimson, Can, Gong

see also: *Japan*

Dave Galens

Sylvian & Fripp

See: Robert Fripp

T. Rex

Formed 1967 in London, England. Disbanded 1975.

Marc Bolan (born Mark Feld), vocals, guitar (died Sept. 16, 1977); Steve Peregrine Took, drums, bass, percussion, vocals (1967-69); Mickey Finn, guitar, percussion, vocals

Along with David Bowie, no act symbolizes 70s glam rock better than Bolan and T. Rex. Begun as Tyrannosaurus Rex, Bolan's acoustic strumming and whispered nonsense lyrics about wizards, dragons and other mystical topics became popular with a hippie audience in England. However, the band didn't come into its own until Bolan plugged in; with a full group behind him (and the moniker shortened to T. Rex) he recorded the masterful *Electric Warrior* and its international hit, "Bang a Gong (Get It On)." With his curly hair and impish demeanor, Bolan inspired a fanatical following documented by Ringo Starr in the film "Born to Boogie." Other U.K. hits—"Telegram Sam," "The Groover"—didn't make much sense lyrically but were highly addictive glitter goodies. Beyond "Bang a Gong," American success eluded Bolan, and after a few more stellar albums he slipped into making watery, synth-dominated disco which showcased girlfriend Gloria Jones. Bolan eventually got his own British TV series, titled "Marc," which introduced several New Wave acts to the nation as well as showcasing his own music—often on ridiculously lavish sets. On the eve of a supposed comeback in 1977, Bolan died when his car, driven by Jones, hit a tree. Dozens of posthumous best-ofs and compilations of unreleased material have been released, and caution is urged when building a collection.

what to buy: *Electric Warrior* (Reprise, 1971, prod. Tony Visconti) ♪♪♪♪ remains T. Rex' seminal work—saucy, playful and filled with A-material such as "Bang a Gong," "Jeepster" and "Rip Off."

what to buy next: The slightly more restrained *The Slider* (Reprise, 1972/Relativity, 1989 prod. Tony Visconti) ♪♪♪♪ came at a time when even Bolan's lesser songs were brilliant. A glam-rock superstar at his peak.

what to avoid: *Dandy in the Underworld* (EMI, 1977/Relativity, 1989, prod. Marc Bolan) ♪ has frustrating flashes of excitement among the trash that makes Bolan's downfall even more disappointing.

the rest: *Zinc Alloy and the Hidden Riders of Tomorrow* (EMI, 1974/Relativity, 1989) ♪♪½ *Zip Gun Boogie* (EMI, 1975/Relativity, 1989) ♪♪ *Tanx* (EMI, 1973/Relativity, 1989) ♪♪♪½ *Futuristic Dragon* (EMI, 1976/Relativity, 1989) ♪♪ *BBC Live* (Windsong, 1993) ♪♪♪

worth searching for: *The Essential Collection,*(PolyGram TV, 1995, prod. Various) ♪♪♪♪♪ a 24-track best-of that serves as a fine introduction *and* is the only compilation that has "Get It On" *and* the group's later hits.

⏩ The Replacements, Soup Dragons, Love and Rockets

⏪ David Bowie, Gary Glitter

Todd Wicks

Talk Talk

Formed 1981 in London, England

Mark Hollis, vocals, keyboards; Simon Brenner, keyboards; Paul Webb, bass; Lee Harris, drums

You couldn't swing a stick in the early 80s without whacking a slick pretty boy synth-pop outfit, and you wouldn't have to swing very long before connecting with Talk Talk. Not content as foppish new wavers, the band soon ditched the echoing angst in favor of art-rock that led to experimental ambiance whose lack of texture or inspiration led to its eventual demise. *Natural History: The Very Best of Talk Talk* (EMI, 1990, prod. Rhett Davis and Tim Friese-Greene) ♪♪♪ contains its best song, "Talk Talk," which gave the band a promising future in 1982. But those hopes rapidly diminished as a misguided Roxy Music/Brian Eno fixation took over.

the rest: *It's My Life* (EMI America, 1984) ♪♪ *Laughing Stock* (Polydor, 1991) ♪♪

Allan Orski

Talking Heads /Jerry Harrison/Tom Tom Club

Formed 1975 in New York, N.Y.

David Byrne, vocals, guitar; Chris Frantz, drums; Tina Weymouth, bass; Jerry Harrison, keyboards, guitar, vocals (1977-present)

This is what happens at art school, when you bring together high thinkers with a taste for forms that lean towards the baser instincts. Talking Heads specialize in colliding sensibilities, cutting a wide swath from cheesey pop to African rhythms, punk to funk, and bringing them all together around the quirky high tenor of frontman Byrne. Initiated at the Rhode Island School of Design, where Byrne and Frantz met, Talking Heads was one of the most original sounding bands to play the burgeoning scene at New York's CBGB during the mid-70s; not the Ramones or Blondie or Television, the group was much more spare and halting in its delivery, kind of like the tentative younger siblings trying to step into the older brothers' football game. The sound got a little more meat after former Modern Lover Harrison joined the band, and Talking Heads set out on a stylistic journey that delivered 15 years of some of pop's most original and tuneful music—dropping into the mass consciousness just once, with the roiling 1983 hit "Burning Down the House." Byrne's ambitions in theater, film and photography rendered the band inactive since 1992, but it's never officially called it quits; though Byrne says he's out, Harrison, Weymouth and Franz re-grouped in 1996 to record an album with guest vocalists; they also planned to hit the road with former Concrete Blonde singer Johnette Napolitano handling vocals. Harrison, meanwhile, has also become an in-demand producer, working with BoDeans, Live and the Verve Pipe.

what to buy: In three consecutive years (1978-80), Talking Heads—along with producer Brian Eno—released three remarkable albums of incredible growth and adventure. *More Songs About Buildings and Food* (Sire, 1978, prod. Brian Eno and Talking Heads) ♪♪♪♪½ was firmly rooted in pop but added World Music touches and electronic sound experiments; it also got the band some radio play with its cover of Al Green's "Take Me to the River." *Fear of Music* (Sire, 1979, prod. Brian Eno and Talking Heads) ♪♪♪♪½ was darker and denser, employing more polyrhythms to drive the chanted vocals of "I Zimbra" and Byrne's apocalyptic visions in "Life During Wartime." *Remain in Light* (Sire, 1980, prod. Brian Eno) ♪♪♪♪♪ brought everything to a tightly focused peak, resulting in a groove-driven group of songs so powerful they explode from the speakers.

what to buy next: Apart from Eno, *Speaking in Tongues* (Sire, 1983, prod. Talking Heads) ♪♪♪♪ takes the spirit of *Remain in Light* in a slightly more straightforward direction, capping a bold era with the percolating "Burning Down the House" and the delicately sweet "This Must Be the Place (Naive Melody)." *Popular Favorites 1976-1992: Sand in the Vaseline* (Sire, 1992, prod. Various) ♪♪♪♪ is an exemplary two-disc retrospective, with the best songs from those four landmark albums plus the highlights from the rest of the group's catalog.

what to avoid: *True Stories* (Sire, 1986, prod. Talking Heads) ♪♪♪ was hampered by dual agendas, since it also served as a de facto soundtrack album for the Byrne-directed movie of the same name. But lots of bands would love to have something this good as their least-essential offering.

the rest: *Talking Heads 77* (Sire, 1977) ♪♪♪½ *Stop Making Sense* (Sire, 1984) ♪♪♪♪ *Little Creatures* (Sire, 1985) ♪♪♪½ *Naked* (Sire, 1988) ♪♪♪½

worth searching for: *The Name of This Band Is Talking Heads* (Sire, 1982, prod. Talking Heads) is an innovative, career-spanning (to that point) live album that shows the development of the Heads' stage prowess. It has yet to appear on CD.

solo outings:

Tom Tom Club (Frantz and Weymouth) Tom Tom Club (Sire, 1981) *Close to the Bone* (Sire, 1983) *Boom Boom Chi Boom Boom* (Sire, 1989) *Dark Sneak Love Action* (Sire, 1992)

Jerry Harrison The Red and the Black (Sire, 1981) *Casual Gods* (Sire, 1988) *Walk on Water* (Sire, 1990)

R.E.M., Big Audio Dynamite, Blancmange, Love and Rockets, Rusted Root

Ramones, Modern Lovers, Mothers of Invention, John Cage, Parliament-Funkadelic

see also: *David Byrne*

Gary Graff

Tangerine Dream

Formed 1967 in Germany

Edgar Froese, synthesizer, bass, guitars; Volker Hombach, flute, violin (1967-69); Kurt Herkenburg (1967-69); Lance Hapshash, drums (1967-68); Charlie Prince (1967-69); Sven Ake Johannson (1968-69); Klaus Schulze, drums, keyboards (1969-70); Conrad Schnitzler, flute (1969-70); Steve Schroyder, organ (1971-73); Christoph Franke, synthesizer, keyboards (1971-88); Peter Baumann (1972-77); Steve Jollieffe (1978); Klaus Krieger (1978-79); Johannes Schmoelling (1980-86); Paul Haslinger (1985-90); Paul Wdephul (1988); Jerome Froese (1989-present); Zlatko Perica, guitar (1992-94); Unda Spa, keyboards, saxophone (1993-94)

The influence Tangerine Dream has had upon modern music cannot be overstated; everything from pop to modern movie scores have all been influenced by Tangerine Dream. They practically invented new age and ambient music, and synth-pop groups like Kraftwerk and Devo are direct descendants—anyone who uses electronic instruments to create music owns some debt to Tangerine Dream. For a concept band their range is massive: early material can sound like anything from textured space odysseys to synthesized classical music, while recent albums explore a variety of music from structured pop songs to cutting-edge techno. No matter what the sound, Tangerine Dream has always understood how to manipulate their instruments to the fullest degree and that's why after almost 30 years they can still craft well-made, innovative records.

what to buy: *Dream Sequence* (Virgin, 1984, prod. Edgar Froese) is a 19 track, two-disc compilation of the best excerpts and songs Tangerine Dream has to offer; a good introduction to vast library of albums. *Rubycon* (Virgin, 1975, prod. Tangerine Dream) is a 35 minute masterpiece of sonic layers; it offers a thick blanket of sound that's as complex as any classical symphony, and rich enough to find new enjoyment with every listen. *Optical Race* (Atlantic, 1989, prod. Edgar Froese, Paul Haslinger) is Tangerine Dream's strongest contemporary styled album, featuring an updated sound that switches between rock and new age jazz. More traditional instruments and song structures are also used, but the signature Tangerine Dream sound remains intact. *Dream Mixes* (Miramar, 1995, prod. Edgar Froese) proves that Tangerine Dream can still keep up with modern electronic music. This collection remixes classic songs and updates them with a house beat, but these tracks are more than the standard techno beat, they have rhythm and feeling that's lacking in most dance music. *Dream Music: The Movie Music of Tangerine Dream* (Silva America, 1992, prod. Tangerine Dream) compiles some of the songs that made them so popular in the 80s when they were one of the most prolific bands in Hollywood. This is the music from which most people remember Tangerine Dream.

what to buy next: *Tangents: 1973-1983*, (Virgin, 1994, prod. Tangerine Dream) coming in at just under 60 tracks, is the new collector's dream—all of the great early electronic works are here from the most experimental and innovative period in Tangerine Dream history. *Ricochet* (Virgin, 1976, prod. Tangerine Dream) is a live album that is on par with the sequencer masterpiece *Rubycon*—proves electronic music is not just for studio work. *Hyperborea* (Virgin, 1983, prod. Edgar Froese) explores the classical influences on the band—baroque to Celtic music is emulated in new age style. *Zeit* (Relativity, 1972, prod. Tangerine Dream) is the best of the early explorations into space-age ambient music—beautiful to listen to as all the notes seamlessly flow into one another.

what to avoid: *Shy People* (Atlantic, 1987, prod. Tangerine Dream) and *Near Dark* (Varese Saraban, 1987, prod. Tangerine Dream) are two soundtracks that never should have been released to the public. Extremely short production schedules and pathetic use of vocals bury these two albums.

What Album Changed Your Life?

"Something that touched my soul was an album that Howard Tate, a blues singer, did called Get it While You Can. His voice touched my soul like nothing else ever did. It really moved me. I tried to use him as a base for my vocal style, him and Aretha Franklin."

Mark Farner (Grand Funk Railroad)

the rest: *Electronic Meditation* (Relativity, 1970) ♪♪♪ *Alpha Centari* (Relativity, 1971) ♪♪♪ *Atem* (Relativity, 1973) ♪♪♪ *Green Desert* (Relativity, 1973) ♪♪♪ *Paedra* (Virgin, 1974) ♪♪♪♪ *Stratosfear* (Virgin, 1977) ♪♪♪♪ *Sorcerer* (MCA, 1977) ♪♪♪ *Encore* (Virgin, 1977) ♪♪♪♪ *Cyclone* (Virgin, 1978) ♪♪♪ *Force Majeure* (Virgin, 1979) ♪♪♪♪ *Tangerine Dream: 1970-1980* (Virgin, 1980) ♪♪♪♪ *Tangram* (Blue Plate, 1980) ♪♪♪ *Quichotte - Live East Berlin '80* (Virgin, 1980) ♪♪♪ *Exit* (Elektra, 1981) ♪♪♪ *Theif* (Asylum, 1981) ♪♪♪ *White Eagle* (American Gramaphone, 1982) ♪♪♪♪ *Logos - Live at the Dominion* (A&M, 1982) ♪♪♪♪ *Wavelength* (Varese Saraban, 1983) ♪♪♪ *Risky Buisiness* (Virgin, 1983) ♪♪♪ *Poland* (Combat, 1983) ♪♪♪ *Firestarter* (Varese Saraban, 1984) ♪♪♪ *Flashpoint* (One Way, 1984) ♪♪♪ *Le Park* (Relativity, 1985) ♪♪♪♪♪ *Heartbreakers* (Virgin, 1985) ♪♪♪ *In the Begining* (1986) ♪♪♪♪ *Legend* (MCA, 1986) ♪♪ *Underwater Sunlight* (1986) ♪♪♪ *Pergamon - Live at the Palast* (Caroline, 1986) ♪♪♪ *Tyger* (Relativity, 1987) ♪♪ *Collection* (A&M, 1987) ♪♪♪♪ *Three O'Clock High* (Atlantic, 1997) ♪♪ *Deadly Care* (Silva America, 1987) ♪♪ *Live Miles* (Caroline, 1988) ♪♪♪ *Optical Race* (Private Music, 1988) ♪♪♪ *Miracle Mile* (Private Music, 1989) ♪♪♪ *The Best of Tangerine Dream!* (Jive, 1989) ♪♪♪ *Destination Berlin* (American Gramaphone, 1989) ♪♪♪ *Melrose* (Private Music, 1990) ♪♪♪ *Dead Solid Perfect* (Silva Screen, 1990) ♪♪ *The Man Inside* (1991) ♪♪♪ *From Dawn 'til Dusk - Tangerine Dream 1973-1988* (1991) ♪♪♪♪ *Canyon Dreams* (1991) ♪♪♪ *The Park Is Mine* (Silva America, 1991) ♪♪♪ *Rockoon* (Miramar, 1992) ♪♪♪ *Deadly Care* (Silva America, 1992) ♪♪♪ *The Private Music of Tangerine Dream* (Private Music, 1992) ♪♪♪ *220 Volts Live* (Miramar, 1993) ♪♪♪ *Turn of the Tides* (Miramar, 1994) ♪♪♪ *Tyranny of Beauty* (Miramar, 1995) ♪♪♪ *Dream Music 2* (Silva America, 1995) ♪♪♪♪

⏩ Brian Eno, Kraftwerk, New Order, Dancing Fantasy, Software, Devo

⏪ Klaus Schulze

Bryan Lassner

Tar

Formed in Chicago, Ill.

John Mohr, guitar, vocals; Mark Zablocki, guitar, e-bow; Tom Zaluckyi, bass, guitar; Mike Greenlees, drums

With its pummeling two-guitar attack, Tar was long one of Chicago's finest bands and something of an underground secret. Mohr's vocals are hardly melodic, but he's not just a shouter; he shows a fine sense of dynamic contrast reflected in the band's music. That and the unhackneyed chord progressions keep the rather basic ingredients from growing overly repetitious. Slowly building structures make this group a slightly more complex Chicago version of Mission of Burma.

what to buy: If there was ever an album made to be played loud, *Clincher* (Touch and Go EP, 1993, prod. Brad Wood, Tar) ♪♪♪♪ is it. A monolithic block of sound, its parts can't be differentiated unless you turn the volume way up. The quartet's sound on *Over and Out* (Touch and Go, 1995, prod. not listed) ♪♪♪♪ is stripped down compared to earlier efforts, with a new, menacing darkness that occasionally resembles Sonic Youth.

the rest: *Handsome* (Amphetamine Reptile EP, 1989) ♪♪♪ *Roundhouse* (Amphetamine Reptile, 1990) ♪♪♪ *Toast* (Touch & Go, 1993) ♪♪♪

Steve Holtje

Tar Babies

Formed 1982 in Madison, Wis.

Bucky Pope, guitars, vocals; Daniel Bitney, drums, piano, vocals; Robin Davies, bass, vocals; Steve Lewis, bass (1988-92); Tony Jarvis, alto sax, clarinet, flute, guitar, vocals, piano (1987-88); Bobby Vienneau, guitar (1991-92)

On this band's final album is this declaration: "God grant us the blissfulness to change the things we want, blow up the things we can't, and the money to cover the difference." You'd feel like that, too, if you had pioneered the intersection of funk, punk and heavy guitar, only to see lesser bands get rich off the style. The Tar Babies are like a funky 90s version of the Voidoids, thanks to Robert Quine-like snarling guitar lines and some stuffy-nosed, half-spoken vocals.

what to buy: *Fried Milk* (SST, 1987, prod. Robin Davies) has 19 tracks (averaging two minutes apiece) of the funkiest punk ever committed to vinyl.

the rest: *Face the Music* (Bone Air EP, 1982) *Respect Your Nightmares* (Bone Air/Paradise, 1985) *No Contest* (SST, 1988, prod. Not listed) *Honey Bubble* (SST, 1989) *Death Trip* (Sonic Noise, 1992)

Steve Holtje

Andy Taylor

See: Duran Duran

James Taylor

Born March 12, 1948 in Boston, Mass.

Regardless of what he says in the song "Steamroller," of the many things that Taylor is, has been, or may someday be, a "churnin' urn of burnin' funk" is not one of them. Perhaps the dictionary definition of the sensitive male singer/songwriter, Taylor's confessional odes and gentle, folk-inflected R&B covers to this day make whole amphitheaters full of boomers swoon. One of the Beatles' initial signings to Apple Records, Taylor ushered in an era of—depending on your point of view—ruthless self-examination or hopeless navel-gazing. It's telling that he actually began his career as a songwriter after checking himself into a mental institution. Songs such as "Fire and Rain" were the result, but Taylor (who was once married to singer Carly Simon) actually had greater success covering the work of others, notably Carole King's "You've Got a Friend." Once a dependable hitmaker, if an erratic songwriter, Taylor has for the most part vanished from the scene, save for semi-annual summer tours, political campaigns and public-television pledge drives. If that doesn't sum up the mellow music of the 70s, what does?

what to buy: *Greatest Hits* (Warner Bros., 1976, prod. Various) would seem the natural place to start, but "Carolina in My Mind" and "Something in the Way She Moves" are re-recorded versions, not the originals. If you're looking for Taylor's best single album, you have to go all the way back to *Sweet Baby James,* (Warner Bros., 1970, prod. Peter Asher) which contains a number of songs that became his fans' favorites, including the title track, "Fire and Rain," "Country Road" and "Steamroller Blues"—Taylor's own personal "Freebird." Since Taylor lacks a hits collection that covers his entire career—excepting the import *Classic Songs (Live)* (Columbia, 1993, prod. Don Grolnick and George Massenburg) has to do. All the requisite songs are here, but Taylor's performance is disappointingly subdued. (The set is also available in an abridged one-disc version, *Best Live.* (Columbia, 1994, prod. Don Grolnick & George Massenberg)

what to buy next: Taylor's debut, *James Taylor* (Apple, 1969, prod. Peter Asher) lets you feel his pain as he helps establish the singer/songwriter genre with "Rainy Day Man," "Carolina in My Mind" and "Something in the Way She Moves," as well as the upbeat "Knockin' Around the Zoo." *Gorilla* (Warner Bros., 1975, prod. Lenny Waronker and Russ Titelman) was Taylor's comeback album after a self-imposed exile during the early 70s; it contains the delightful original "Mexico" but also eased Taylor's transition from confessional singer/songwriter to craftsmanlike cover man with Marvin Gaye's "How Sweet It Is (To Be Loved by You)." One of his better mid-period albums, *J.T.* (Columbia, 1979, prod. Peter Asher) includes the sunny hit "Your Smiling Face," the requisite R&B cover "Handy Man" and the charming "Secret o' Life," plus "Bartender's Blues," which Taylor wrote for George Jones. More recently, *New Moon Shine* (Columbia, 1991, prod. Danny Kortchmar and Don Grolnick) offers Taylor's sharpest and most relevant set of lyrics in some time, notably on "Slap Leather" and "Shed a Little Light."

what to avoid: *Never Die Young* (Columbia, 1988, prod. Don Grolnick) is a slight collection, even by Taylor's sometimes lightweight standards.

the rest: *Mud Slide Slim and the Blue Horizon* (Warner Bros., 1971) *One Man Dog* (Warner Bros., 1972) *Walking Man* (Warner Bros., 1974) *In the Pocket* (Warner Bros., 1976) *Flag* (Columbia, 1979) *Dad Loves His Work* (Columbia, 1981) *That's Why I'm Here* (Columbia, 1985) *Never Die Young* (Columbia, 1988)

worth searching for: *James Taylor and the Original Flying Machine 1967* (Euphoria, 1971) is an interesting curio which contains demos—studio chatter included—of "Night Owl," "Rainy Day Man" and "Brighten Your Night With My Day" that Taylor and guitarist Danny Kortchmar recorded in 1967. The seven-song album saw the light of day only after Taylor hit pay dirt elsewhere.

⏩ Jackson Browne, Garth Brooks

⏪ Simon & Garfunkel, Bob Dylan, Carole King, the Beatles

Daniel Durchholz

Roger Taylor

See: Queen

Tears for Fears

Formed 1982 in Bath, England

Roland Orzabal (born Roland Jaime Orzabal de la Quintana), guitar, vocals, keyboards; Curt Smith, bass, vocals, keyboards (1982-92)

Bonded by early friendship, tough childhoods and an interest in psychotherapist Arthur Janov's primal scream therapy, Orzabal and Smith founded Tears for Fears in an effort to give Janov's concepts a musical voice. Though their sound began as a typically overwrought blend of New Wave synthesizers and despondent British nilhism, later albums reveal a knack for songcraft and textured, complex arrangements that brought swift commercial success. Unfortunately, creative differences forced Smith out of the band during the early 90s, allowing Orzabal to craft increasingly self-absorbed and pointless albums that, not surprisingly, have reached fewer and fewer fans.

what to buy: Combining flawless, forward-looking pop tunes with innovative production and accomplished musicianship, *Songs From the Big Chair* (Mercury, 1985, prod. Chris Hughes) provided the group's commercial breakthrough. From the drum machine-fueled hit "Shout" to the percolating, dreamy vibe of "Everybody Wants to Rule the World" and the mechanized, percussive "Mothers Talk," the album proved a perfect blend of inspired songwriting and creative arrangements. The next effort, *The Seeds of Love* (Mercury, 1989, prod. David Bascombe and Tears for Fears) enlarged the band's vision to an epic canvas, with help from a veritable army of support players that included Oleta Adams and Phil Collins. The inspired Beatles update "Sowing the Seeds of Love" referenced the best of 60s psychedelic pop without resorting to empty mimicry, while the atmospheric "Woman in Chains" and expansive rock/gospel workout "Badman's Song" affixed Adams' spine-tingling vocals to even better melodies.

what to avoid: Despite two interesting songs—"Pale Shelter" and "Mad World"—the group's debut, *The Hurting* (Mercury, 1983, prod. Chris Hughes and Ross Cullum) is mostly a tired, formulaic melding of pop angst and dated keyboard sounds.

the rest: *Tears Roll Down (Greatest Hits, 1982-1992)* (Mercury, 1992) *Elemental* (Mercury, 1993) *Raoul and the Kings of Spain* (Epic, 1995)

worth searching for: The import CD-5 for *Laid So Low (Tears Roll Down)* (Mercury/Fontana, 1992) includes two new songs that signaled the transition into the Smith-less Tears.

solo outings:

Curt Smith Soul On Board (Mercury, 1993)

▶▶ Oleta Adams

◀◀ The Beatles, Bauhaus, Kraftwerk

Eric Deggans

Teenage Fanclub

Formed 1989 in Glasgow, Scotland

Norman Blake, guitars, vocals; Raymond McGinley, guitar, vocals; Gerard Love, bass, vocals; Francis MacDonald, drums (1989-90); Brendan O'Hare, drums (1990-94); Paul Quinn, drums (1994-present)

Listen to Teenage Fanclub for 15 seconds and it's obvious these guys are huge fans of Alex Chilton and Neil Young (not to mention the Beach Boys and the Beatles). But the quartet is much greater than the sum of its influences; carrying the best of 60s-rock styles into the noisy 90s, Teenage Fanclub's distorted punk-pop tunes are nothing short of intoxicating. *Bandwagonesque* (DGC, 1991, prod. Don Fleming, Paul Chisholm and Teenage Fanclub) was greeted as Album of the Year by Spin magazine, and while that might be pushing it (after all, Nirvana's *Nevermind* also came out in '91), the album *is* a brilliant melange of post-punk guitar gauze and classic pop melodies, particularly *The Concept.*

the rest: *A Catholic Education* (Matador, 1990) *Thirteen* (DGC, 1993) *Grand Prix* (DGC, 1995)

Thor Christensen

Television

Formed 1973 in New York, N.Y. Disbanded, 1978. Re-formed 1991. Disbanded, 1993.

Tom Verlaine, guitar, vocals; Richard Lloyd, guitar; Billy Ficca, drums; Richard Hell, bass (1973-75); Fred Smith, bass (1975-78, 1991-93)

Despite a marked lack of commercial success, the two albums Television recorded for Elektra Records during the late 70s are among the most important and influential of the post-punk era. While Television was born to the punk scene, it quickly set itself apart with a successful combination of intellectual lyrical themes and stunningly creative musical applications. Television appropriated the intensity and raw energy of punk, the introspective lyrical style of the city's thriving poetry community and sense of musical freedom enjoyed by the jazz scene. Unlike most rock bands, Television eschewed a blues foundation, resulting in a loud, guitar-based sound that was complex and often beautifully lyrical, with balanced measures of improvisation and painstaking structure. The result was music that matched art rock's intricacy and invention and yet retained the accessibility and immediate pleasures of the best garage rock: manna for the thinking guitar freak. Unfortunately, the band's skill at music was accompanied by strong personalities that often clashed. It disbanded after the release of its second album, reuniting in 1991 for an album and tour before the old problems surfaced and split the group up again.

what to buy: *Marquee Moon* (Elektra, 1977, prod. Andy Johns and Tom Verlaine) is Television's undisputed masterpiece and a landmark in modern rock. Verlaine and Lloyd achieve guitar nirvana; drawing on the Allman Brothers technique of harmonized guitar lines, the guitarists limn songs such as "See No Evil" and "Torn Curtain" with delicate melodic passages that soothe the angular attack of the rhythm parts and countermelody the vocals. *Marquee Moon* manages to simultaneously evoke the influence of mediative acts such as the Velvet Underground and Talking Heads and the aggressive virtuosity and arranging skills of bands like the Allmans and Led Zeppelin.

what to buy next: *Adventure* (Elektra, 1978, prod. John Jansen and Tom Verlaine) is an over-produced, watered-down version of *Marquee Moon* that still manages to be brilliant and commanding.

what to avoid: Released four years after the band broke up, *The Blow Up*, (ROIR, 1982, prod. not listed) attempts to provide some kind of insight into Television's volatile live shows. Recorded live at the band's New York base, CBGB, the albums poor sound quality makes it only of interest for diehard Television/Verlaine fans.

the rest: *Television* (Capitol, 1992)

worth searching for: There are two early Television recordings that predate *Marquee Moon* and are worthwhile as precursors to that opus: the single, "Little Johnny Jewel" (Ork, 1976) and the British EP *Television* (Stiff, 1976)

solo outings:

Tom Verlaine: *Tom Verlaine* (Elektra, 1979) *Dreamtime* (Warner Bros., 1981) *Words from the Front* (Warner Bros., 1982) *Cover* (Warner Bros., 1984) *Flashlight* (I.R.S., 1987) *Warm and Cool* (Rykodisc, 1992)

Matthew Sweet, the Heartbreakers, Robyn Hitchcock/Soft Boys, Blondie, the Pixies, Sonic Youth, R.E.M., the Feelies, XTC, Eleventh Dream Day, My Bloody Valentine, the Breeders, the Cars, Durutti Column, Material Issue, Posies, Game Theory, Urge Overkill, the dBs, Big Star

Bob Dylan, Roky Erikson, the Velvet Underground, Neil Young, Allman Brothers Band, Led Zeppelin, Beach Boys, David Bowie, John Coltrane, Charlie Parker, Miles Davis

Dave Galens

The Temptations

Formed 1961 in Detroit, Mich.

Otis Williams (born Otis Miles), vocals; Eddie Kendricks, vocals (1961-72, died Oct. 5, 1992); Paul Williams, vocals (1971-72, died Aug. 17, 1973); Melvin Franklin (born David English), vocals (1971-95, died Feb. 23, 1995); Elbridge Bryant, vocals (1961-63); David Ruffin, vocals (1963-68, died June 1, 1991); Dennis Edwards, vocals (1968-77, 1979-83, 1986-87); Ricky Owens, vocals (1972); Damon Harris, vocals (1972-75); Richard Street, vocals (1972-93); Glenn Leonard, vocals (1975-83); Louis Price, vocals (1977-79); Ron Tyson, vocals (1983-present); Ali Ollie Woodson, vocals (1983-86, 1987-present); Theo Peoples, vocals (1993-present); Ray Davis, vocals (1995-present)

With respect to the Four Tops—who deserve much credit for their longevity and wonderful body of work—the Temptations are *it* when it comes to Motown male vocal groups. The visceral power of the Tempts' five voices combined with its high-stepping stage show (a cross between the Tops' smooth 'n' natural and the Contours' chaos) super-charged the vocal group model to another level; when you hear "Get Ready," it's not just a song—it's a command. The Tempts' history is both blessed and cursed. It's been blessed with some otherwordly lead singers (Paul Williams, Ruffin, Kendricks, Edwards) and some of Motown's top producers and writers (Smokey Robinson, Norman Whitfield). The group has had some luck, too; Robinson and Ronnie White could have kept "My Girl" for their own group, the Miracles. But the Tempts' dominance came with a price; four members are dead from tragic circumstances (suicide, drug OD, lung cancer, a brain seizure). Otis Williams, the band's biographer, is the sole founding member left, but he's been carrying the torch through decades of internal squabbling and ego battles. The Temptations of today surely aren't on a par with the classic lineup of the 60s, but the incredible battery of songs—"The Way You Do the Things You Do," "Girl (Why You Wanna Make Me Blue)," "Ain't Too Proud to Beg," "I Wish it Would Rain," "Cloud Nine," "Just My Imagination (Running Away With Me)"—usually will out.

what to buy: *The Temptations Anthology* (Motown, 1995, prod. Various) packs 46 hits onto two CDs, with not a bad note to be found.

what to buy next: A more total—and worthwhile—immersion can be made with *Emperors of Soul,* (Motown, 1995, prod. Various) a regally titled box set that, at five discs, needs to be considered before purchase. *One by One* (Motown, 1995, prod. Various) offers a well-chosen collection of solo recordings by Kendricks, Ruffin, Edwards and Paul Williams. *The Temptations Sing Smokey* (Motown, 1965/1989, prod. Smokey Robinson) is a nicely conceived collaboration between the Tempts and one of the group's chief patrons.

what to avoid: After all that great music, it's hard to swallow *For Lovers Only* (Motown, 1995, prod. Richard Perry) and its lush covers of "Some Enchanted Evening," "Night and Day" and "You Send Me."

the rest: *Meet the Temptations* (Motown, 1964/1992) *The Temptin' Temptations* (Motown, 1965/1990) *Gettin' Ready* (Motown, 1966/1989) *Greatest Hits, Vol. 1* (Motown, 1966) *In a Mellow Mood* (Motown, 1967/1969) *I Wish It Would Rain* (Motown, 1968) *Cloud Nine* (Motown, 1969) *Psychedelic Shack* (Motown, 1970/1989) *Puzzle People* (Motown, 1970/1989) *Christmas Card* (Motown, 1970/1989) *Give Love at Christmas* (Motown, date N/A) *Greatest Hits, Vol. II* (Motown, 1970) *Sky's the Limit* (Motown, 1971/1990) *All Directions* (Motown, 1972) *Masterpiece* (Motown, 1973/1989) *A Song for You* (Motown, 1975) *All the Million Sellers* (Motown, 1981) *Reunion* (Motown, 1982) *Great Songs & Performances That Inspired Motown 25* (Motown, 1983) *Truly for You* (Motown, 1984/1989) *To Be Continued* (Motown, 1986) *Special* (Motown, 1989) *Milestone* (Motown, 1991) *Hum Along and Dance: More of the Best (1963-1974)* (Rhino, 1993) *Motown Legends: My Girl—(I Know) I'm Losing You* (ESX, 1994) *Motown Legends: Just My Imagination—Beauty Is Only Skin Deep* (ESX, 1994)

worth searching for: *Temptations Live!* (Motown, 1967) You may not be able to see 'em, but the Tempts' voices convey enough of the show's excitement to compensate.

solo outings:

Eddie Kendricks *People Hold On* (Motown, 1972/1991) *At His Best* (Motown, 1990)

David Ruffin *At His Best* (Motown, 1991)

Jimmy & David Ruffin *Motown Superstar Series Volume 8* (Motown, date N/A)

The Jackson 5, the Commodores, the Ohio Players, Maze

The Soul Stirrers, the Falcons, the Drifters

Gary Graff

10cc

Formed 1972 in London, England. Disbanded 1982. Reformed 1991.

Lol Creme, guitars, keyboards, vocals (1972-76); Kevin Godley, drums, vocals (1972-76); Graham Gouldman, guitars, keyboards, vocals; Eric Stewart, guitars, keyboards, vocals; Paul Burgess, drums (1976-77); Rick Fenn, guitars, vocals (1977-82); Tony O'Malley, keyboards (1977-82); Stuart Tosh, drums, vocals (1977-82)

Taking its name from the average volume of fluid produced by a certain procreative act, 10cc's chief tools were witty lyrics, hooky song writing and tight harmonies. When the group was able to avoid a certain proclivity towards sappiness, it produced some of the more distinctive pop of the middle 70s. 10cc hit the charts quickly in its native England, but U.S. recognition didn't come until 1975's "I'm Not in Love" became a pillow talk smash. Unfortunately, 10cc followed this success with only one more album before splitting into two camps: Godley and Creme recorded as a duo and directed some groundbreaking music videos, scoring their own hit with 1985's "Cry"; while Graham and Eric kept the 10CC moniker alive. But neither fragment lived up to the commercial or artistic promise of the foursome.

what to buy: The fact that it contains the biggest hit isn't the only reason to grab *The Original Soundtrack* (Polygram, 1975, prod. 10cc) A solid effort top to bottom, it showcases the band at its literate best, including "The Second Sitting for the Last Supper" and the quirkily metaphorical "Life Is a Minestrone" *Two Classic Albums by 10cc* (DCC Compact Classics, 1990, prod. 10cc) puts the band's first two records—*10cc* and *Sheet Music* — on a single CD containing the U.K. hits "Rubber Bullets," "The Wall Street Shuffle" and "Silly Love."

what to buy next: *How Dare You* (Polygram, 1976, prod. 10cc) was the last effort by the complete band. There isn't a standout track, but it holds its own with the essential titles.

what to avoid: Virtually everything else, but particularly *10cc in Concert,* (King Biscuit Flower Hour Records, 1995) a live radio from 1975 which proves that the band's complex vocal arrangements were best kept to the safe confines of the studio.

the rest: *Deceptive Bends* (Polygram, 1977) *Mirror, Mirror* (Critique, 1995)

worth searching for: *Greatest Hits, 1972-78* (Mercury, 1979, prod. 10cc) Not as good as *The Original Soundtrack* but still a worthwhile toe-dipper for the novice.

Barenaked Ladies, They Might Be Giants

Beach Boys, Hollies, Badfinger, The Beatles

Gary Plochinski

10,000 Maniacs /Natalie Merchant

Formed 1981 in Jamestown, N.Y.

Natalie Merchant (born Oct. 26, 1963 in Jamestown), vocals (1981-93); Mary Ramsey, vocals (1995-present); John Lombardo, guitar (1981-86, 1995-present); Robert Buck, guitar; Steven Gustafson, bass; Dennis Drew, keyboards; Jerry Augustyniak, drums

Rarely in rock history has there been a band more woefully misnamed than 10,000 Maniacs. Starting out as a reggae-influenced dance band mixing originals with everything from the Andrews Sisters' "Rum and Coke" to obscure Roxy Music and Gang of Four covers, the group eventually jelled into a melodic, politically minded folk-pop act that brought a refreshing dose of depth and discipline to the mid-80s college-rock scene. Lead singer Merchant, always the visual focus with her giddy spins, sang with a soothing, seductive clarity that softened her commentaries on alcoholism ("Don't Talk"), poverty ("Dust Bowl") and media pandering ("Candy Everybody Wants"). That precarious balance shifted on 1992's *Our Time in Eden* as Merchant's heavy-handed lyrics weighed down the band's denser, more-brooding sound. Her 1993 departure to launch a solo career suggested that she would move in a different direction, but her pensive *Tigerlily* is surprisingly similar to her Maniacs work, even though her live performances were sparked by energetic romps through Aretha Franklin's "Baby I Love You" and the Rolling Stones' "Sympathy for the Devil." The group continues without her, drafting violinist-vocalist Mary Ramsey and original Maniacs guitarist John Lombardo, who had recorded two albums for Rykodisc as John and Mary.

what to buy: Despite such heavy-handed topics as child abuse ("What the Matter Here?"), war ("Gun Shy"), alcoholism ("Don't Talk") and illiteracy ("The Cherry Tree"), *In My Tribe* (Elektra, 1987, prod. Peter Asher) is surprisingly melodic and upbeat. Driven more by resilience than resignation, the songs gain impact from Merchant's ability to put a face on her platforms, telling compelling stories rather than just telling us what to think. Original pressings contained a cover of Cat Stevens' "Peace Train" that was removed at the band's request after the author, a devout Muslim, put a bounty on the head of "The Satanic Verses" author Salman Rushdie.

what to buy next: *The Wishing Chair,* (Elektra, 1985, prod. Joe Boyd) the band's major-label debut, foreshadows Merchant's socio-political concerns but also exudes an infectious innocence on "Can't Ignore the Train" and "Back o' the Moon."

what to avoid: *Hope Chest* (Elektra, 1990, prod. Albert Garzon and 10,000 Maniacs) is a remixed compilation of the band's sonically anemic indie releases —1982's *Human Conflict No. 5* EP and 1983's *Secrets of the I Ching*—which find them zig-zagging from reggae to pop to punk.

the rest: *Blind Man's Zoo* (Elektra, 1989) *Our Time in Eden* (Elektra, 1992) *MTV Unplugged* (Elektra, 1993)

worth searching for: The CD single for "Few and Far Between" (Elektra, 1993) sports non-LP live duets with Michael Stipe on Lulu's "To Sir With Love" and David Byrne on Iris DeMent's "Let the Mystery Be."

solo outings:

Natalie Merchant *Tigerlily* (Elektra, 1995)

John Lombardo (with John and Mary) *Victory Gardens* (Rykodisc, 1991) *The Weedkiller's Daughter* (Rykodisc, 1993)

John and Mary, the Nields

R.E.M., Fairport Convention, Patti Smith, Bob Marley

David Okamoto

Ten Years After

Formed 1967 in Nottingham, England. Disbanded 1974. Reunited 1989.

Alvin Lee, guitar, vocals; Chick Churchill, keyboards; Leo Lyons, bass; Ric Lee, drums

Before there was "Stairway to Heaven" or "Free Bird," Ten Years After held the Bic lighter-inducing crown for "I'm Going Home," a crunching, bruising blues-rocker that lit up the Woodstock festival in a 13-minute version that featured seemingly endless (and if you were on acid, it probably was) improvised riffing by Alvin Lee. Playing electrifying blues at a peace 'n' love gathering is kind of the way TYA does things; it'll crank up the volume with something like "Baby Let Me Rock 'n' Roll You," but then the group will glide into something fuzzy and trippy like its biggest hit, "I'd Love to Change the World." Always a workhorse, Lee has kept playing with his own band, though he did bring TYA together for an album and tour in 1989.

what to buy: *Cricklewood Green* (Deram, 1970, prod. Ten Years After) is the group's most mature and varied effort, striding from the bravado of "Love Like a Man" through the psychedilia of "50,000 Miles Beneath My Brain" to the almost jazzy swing of "Me and My Baby."

what to buy next: *Essential Ten Years After* (Chrysalis, 1991, prod. Various) gets you most of what you'd want—with a nicely annotated booklet, too—although it leaves some good tracks off and includes a live rendition of "I'm Going Home" recorded somewhere other than Woodstock.

what to avoid: Take your pick of a fair share of leaden, same-sounding albums—a category that holds both *Stonehenge* (Deram, 1969, prod. Mike Vernon) or *Watt* (Deram/Chrysalis, 1970, prod. Chris Wright)

the rest: *Undead* (Deram, 1968) *A Space in Time* (Columbia, 1971/Chrysalis, 1989) *Greatest Hits* (Deram, date N/A) *Rock and Roll Music to the World* (Columbia, 1972/Chrysalis, 1989) *Recorded Live* (Columbia, 1973/Chrysalis, 1989) *Live at Reading* (Dutch East India, 1983) *Collection* (Griffin, 1994)

worth searching for: What else—"I'm Going Home" live at Woodstock, either via one of the Woodstick albums or on the out-of-print TYA collection *Universal* (Chrysalis, 1987)

solo outings:

Alvin Lee Zoom (Viceroy, 1992) *Nineteen Ninety Four* (Thunderbolt, 1993) *I Hear You Rockin'* (Viceroy, 1994) *Pure Blues* (EMI, 1995) *Live in Vienna* (Viceroy, 1996)

▶▶ George Thorogood and the Destroyers, Molly Hatchet, Stevie Ray Vaughan

◀◀ John Lee Hooker, John Mayall's Bluesbreakers, Jimi Hendrix

Gary Graff

Terminator X

See: Public Enemy

Tesla

Formed 1984 in Sacramento, Calif. Disbanded 1996.

Jeff Keith, vocals; Tommy Skeoch, guitar (1984-95); Frank Hannon, guitar; Brian Wheat, bass; Troy Luccketta, drums

Although it was labeled a hair-metal band, Tesla had more in common with the unadorned, workmanlike 70s classic rock of Led Zeppelin and Aerosmith than the slick, processed pop-metal of Whitesnake, Poison and Ratt. And it scores a point or two for naming itself after the groundbreaking but little-known scientist Nikola Tesla. One of the most faceless million-selling bands to come out of the 80s hard rock scene, Tesla's vigorous, big-bottomed music had a fierce rock 'n' roll energy and demonstrated a studied sense of 70s-style rock dynamics. But it lacked both the flamboyance and cutting-edge style of the most popular 80s rock. As such, the band's melodic, blues-influenced output has held up better than that of most of its less-than-conservative contemporaries. Called City Kidd at first, the five-piece band was one of the first rock groups to record an acoustic album. Its 1990 hit release, *Five Man Acoustical Jam* anticipated the MTV Unplugged trend. After sales of its next two albums sagged and guitarist Skeoch was kicked out for drug addiction, Tesla released a greatest-hits album in 1995 that included the only song it ever recorded as a four-piece, the new "Steppin' Over." The following year, the band broke up.

what to buy: While the ballad "Love Song" was the album's big hit, *The Great Radio Controversy* (Geffen, 1988, prod. Steve Thompson and Michael Barbiero) is highlighted by the backwater-flavored swagger of "Heaven's Trail (No Way Out)," the piano-flavored "Lazy Days, Crazy Nights" and the winsome "Paradise."

what to buy next: The unplugged *Five Man Acoustical Jam* (Geffen, 1990, prod. Dan McClendon) features a wide array of covers—the Five Man Electrical Band's "Signs," Credence

Clearwater Revival's "Lodi," the Grateful Dead's "Truckin'" plus reworked originals including the hit "Modern Day Cowboy."

what to avoid: *Bust a Nut* (Geffen, 1994, prod. Terry Thomas) Bland, tasteless corporate rock—and a lousy title to boot.

the rest: *Mechanical Resonance* (Geffen, 1986) *Psychotic Supper* (Geffen, 1991) *Time's Makin' Changes: The Best of Tesla* (Geffen, 1995)

worth searching for: *Electric, Acoustic and Psychotic*, (Geffen, 1992, prod. Various) a 12-song promotional sampler from the fist four albums that makes a nice collector's piece.

Poison, Guns N' Roses

Queen, Led Zeppelin, Rolling Stones, Aerosmith, Def Leppard, AC/DC, Rush

Joshua Freedom du Lac

Texas

Formed 1987 in Glasgow, Scotland

Sharleen Spiteri, vocals, guitar; Ally McErlaine, guitar; John McElhone, bass; Stuart Kerr, drums, vocals

Don't expect any roots music from this band; Texas has as much to do with the moody textures and boxed-in sound of Scottish 80s pop/rock as it does with the sort of open desert blues-rock that the name would suggest. Its debut, *Southside* (Mercury, 1989, prod. Tim Palmer) is still the best starting point, with the strongest set of songs. Spiteri was already in fine voice by this point, sounding like a more contained Bonnie Raitt/Linda Ronstadt hybrid, and the then 19-year-old McErlaine had already developed quite a hang for the slide guitar. "I Don't Need a Lover" is a solid single, with a tight beat and technopop production reminiscent of Eurythmics. *Mothers Heaven* (Mercury, 1991, prod. Tim Palmer) was more of the same, but with fewer songs to recommend, while *Ricks Road* (Mercury, 1994, prod. Paul Fox) marked a bit of a comeback, with the semi-hit "So-Called Friend" serving as a looser sequel to "I Don't Need a Lover." All in all, a pleasant but hardly essential outfit.

Bob Remstein

The Texas Tornados

Formed 1988 in San Francisco, Calif.

Doug Sahm, vocal, guitar; Augie Meyers, vocal, organ; Flaco Jiminez, vocal, accordion; Freddy Fender, vocal (1988-present)

Grizzled old veterans of rock and Tejano, the Texas Tornados are a bona fide Tex Mex supergroup. Sahm and Meyers were key member of the Sir Douglas Quintet, Fender had smash country hits during the 70s and Jimenez comes from a noted family of deeply Mexican accordionists. The quartet first got together for a jam session in San Francisco, and things grew from there. Together they play a bouncy, good-time country music with plenty of Mexican and a little rock. The group has worked sporadically, but it's managed to win a Grammy Award and score a couple more nominations. The debut, *Texas Tornados*, (Reprise, 1990, prod. Bill Halverson) puts it all on the table; Flaco's accordion work imprints most of the record while the foursome trade off lead vocals. Fender is his honey-dripping best on "A Man Can Cry." There's no drop-off on *Zone of Our Own* (Reprise, 1991, prod. Bill Halverson and the Texas Tornados) and *Hangin' On by a Thread*, (Reprise, 1992, prod. Halverson and the Texas Tornados) which shows an ability to pick rarely heard chestnuts ("To Ramona") and render them in heart-stopping beauty. *4 Aces* (Reprise, 1996, prod. Jim Dickinson) brings in Big Star cohort Dickinson for a slightly poppier sound, but that doesn't undermine the Tornados' wonderfully rootsy and easygoing allure.

see also: *Sir Douglas Quintet, Freddy Fender*

Lawrence Gabriel

Terre Thaemlitz & Bill Laswell

See: Bill Laswell

that dog.

Formed 1990 in Los Angeles, Calif.

Anna Waronker, guitar, vocals; Petra Haden, violin, vocals; Rachel Haden, bass, vocals; Tony Maxwell, drums, acoustic guitar, piano, percussion

that dog.'s sweet-and-sour harmonies and use of violin over crashing punk rock immediately set the group apart from the indie-rock pack. Lead singer Waronker is the daughter of record biz legend Lenny Waronker, while the Hadens are the offspring of famed jazz bassist Charlie Haden. Yet their lineage gave no indication of the twisted pop their band would create. While its low-key debut *that dog.* (DGC, 1994, prod. that dog.) contained a few interesting tunes, it showed a band just coming into focus. After considerable touring, the group demonstrated true growth on *Totally Crushed Out*, (DGC, 1995, prod. that dog.) which is filled with intriguing melodies, bitter lyrics

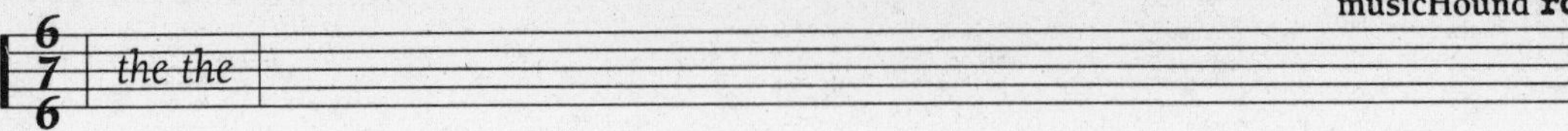

about love and loss, and more wild harmonies. Also check out the group's radical reworking of Maria Muldaur's mellow-rock classic "Midnight at the Oasis" on the anthology *Spirit of '73: Rock for Choice.* (Sony, 1995, prod. Various)

Simon Glickman

The The

Formed 1980 in London, England

Matt Johnson's The The originally started out as a studio project with no real band, though he would shortly begin using other players. The group's early-80s ties to the 4AD labels, which released the group's early singles and first album, were enough to give Johnson the inspiration and acclaim he needed to progress to the next level. The keystone for The The has always been Johnson's lyrics; fancying himself a philosopher, Johnson writes songs that transcend the immediate meaning and pursue loftier topics—often railing against the evils of mankind. The key to dealing with The The's records is to always expect the unexpected; just when a song feels comfortable, it takes a massive twist either musically or lyrically. Johnson's songs generally pursue an alternative rock-pop course, but he likes to flavor them with touches of dance, blues, jazz and psychedelia. An enormously talented musician and songwriter, Johnson has been party to a number of side projects throughout his career as well as attracting top notch musicians to his stable. Cohorts have included Johnny Marr of the Smiths and Neneh Cherry. He has even tried his hand at film, creating a series of connected videos for the songs on the *Infected* album and linking them together into a critically acclaimed movie.

what to buy: *Mind Bomb* (Epic, 1989, prod. Wayne Livesey, Rolli Mossiman and Matt Johnson) shows a much darker side of Johnson (partly influenced by producer Rolli Mossiman of the Swans), with songs that present a philosophical treatise on the state of man and religion. The album features a stunningly beautiful duet with Sinead O'Connor on "Kingdom of Rain" and also finds Johnson reaching into more experimental rhythmic patterns from Africa and the Middle East.

what to buy next: *Infected* (Epic, 1986, Wayne Livesey and Matt Johnson) is a rare treat, a pretentious concept album about good vs. evil loaded with pop nuggets that consistently entertain.

what to avoid: While entertaining as a novelty album, *Hanky Panky* (Epic, 1995, Matt Johnson and Bruce Lampcov) —Johnson's collection of Hank Williams covers—is not for the faint of heart. His versions are certainly unique, but the album doesn't measure up to any of the band's previous efforts.

the rest: *Burning Blue Soul* (4AD, 1982) *Soul Mining* (Epic, 1983) *Dusk* (Epic, 1993)

worth searching for: *The The vs. The World* (Epic, 1989, prod. Various) a wonderful promotional compilation of songs from *Soul Mining, Infected* and *Mind Bomb.*

▶▶ Echo and the Bunnymen, the Smiths, XTC

◀◀ Hank Williams, Julian Cope, Teardrop Explodes, the Doors, Pink Floyd

Tim Davis

Them

Formed 1963 in Belfast, Northern Ireland. Disbanded 1966.

Van Morrison, vocals; Billy Harrison, guitar; Alan Henderson, bass; Ronnie Millings, drums

Them was a bruising R&B unit, featuring the gruff vocals of a young Morrison. Its brief recording career (three years) spawned few singles, but Morrison's fierce passion and the raw power of the hits left a more significant impression in the U.S. than many of the other British Invasion acts with whom they were grouped. The classic "Gloria" remains its defining moment—just three chords and feral growls, but its mark can be felt not only in its stomping performance but also in the innumerable cover versions that have surfaced since then (not counting every garage and bar band that peels through the song at a moment's notice). The group's catalog is woefully underrepresented; *Them Featuring Van Morrison* (Deram, 1965, prod. Various) is the only compilation currently available, and while it's by no means complete, it does contain its best-known work, including "Gloria" and the crashing "Mystic Eyes," as well as the searing "Baby, Please Don't Go" (on which Jimmy Page reportedly supplied the fiery solo).

see also: *Van Morrison*

Allan Orski

Therapy?

Formed 1989 in Belfast, Ireland

Fyfe Ewing, drums (1989-96); Andrew James Cairns, vocals, guitar; Michael McKeegan, bass; Graham Hopkins, drums (1996-present); Martin McCarrick, guitar (1996-present)

This Irish band effectively mixes headbanging thrash-metal rhythms with Alice In Chains-style downbeat vocals and catchy, chanting choruses. "I've got nothing to do, 'cept hang around and get screwed up on you." Cairns sings on "Screamager," Therapy?'s best song—which almost became a radio hit. His lyrics deal with religious depression, psychoses, liars and sexual frustration, which, content-wise, puts Therapy? among Nirvana, Slayer, Metallica and Black Sabbath in the gloomy rock club.

what to buy: *Troublegum* (A&M, 1994, prod. Chris Sheldon) ♪♪♪ contains "Screamager" and is a strong, tight sampling of the band's heavy-guitar sound and tortured words.

what to buy next: *Nurse* (A&M, 1993, prod. Harvey Birrell) ♪♪♪ occasionally gels as well as *Troublegum*, but Therapy? hadn't yet effectively honed its sound. The compilation *Caucasian Psychosis* (Quarterstick, 1992, prod. Mudd, Therapy?, Harvey Birrell and John Loder) ♪♪♪ comprises two early EPs and a single.

what to avoid: *Hats Off to the Insane* (A&M EP, 1993, prod. Chris Sheldon and Therapy?) ♪♪ sounds like any other Soundgarden wannabe, just characterless metal and angst-ridden screaming.

the rest: *Nurse* (A&M, 1993) ♪♪ *Teethgrinder* (A&M, 1992) ♪♪ *Infernal Love* (A&M, 1996) ♪♪♪

worth searching for: The band backs Ozzy Osbourne on a terrific version of Black Sabbath's "Iron Man" on *Nativity In Black: A Tribute to Black Sabbath* (Columbia, 1994) ♪♪♪

▶▶ Bush, Stone Temple Pilots, Gravity Kills, Type O Negative, White Zombie, Biohazard

◀◀ Soundgarden, Black Sabbath, Nirvana, Metallica, Slayer, Alice In Chains, Faith No More

Steve Knopper

They Might Be Giants

Formed 1984 in Brooklyn, N.Y.

John Linnell, accordion, keyboards, vocals; John Flansburgh, guitar, bass, vocals; Tony Maimone, bass (1992-95); Brian Doherty, drums (1992-present); Graham Maby, bass (1996-present); Eric Schermerhorn, guitar (1996-present)

Quirky doesn't begin to describe the manic inventions of They Might Be Giants. The band started out as a cabaret-style duo, deconstructing pop songs with accordion breaks, witty, hyper-referential lyrics and a gift for melody that kept them from lapsing into mere parody. After a couple of well-regarded indie albums, the group signed with Elektra and became increasingly adventuresome (and mature) in its approach. By 1992 the original duo had fleshed out the group, adding Pere Ubu alum Maimone and drummer Doherty to the fold. Linnell and Flansburgh took time off to pursue solo projects during the mid-90s, while a Giants collection called *Superfueled Freaksickle*, meanwhile, was slated for release during 1997.

Some listeners will find the group's penchant for the absurd—not to mention its generally nasal, geeky vocals—insurmountable. But those with a disposition for silliness will be in hog heaven. And its melodies are often surprisingly moving; thus the paradoxical experience of weeping to a song that goes "Have a nice day/you want it when?" (from *Lincoln*'s "Snowball in Hell").

what to buy: *Apollo 18* (Elektra, 1992, prod. They Might Be Giants) ♪♪♪♪ is a startling, sprawling collection. In addition to a fine array of typically warped compositions, there are microscopic song fragments called "Fingertips" designed to take full advantage of your CD player's "shuffle" mode.

what to buy next: Purists generally prefer the earlier and less slick *Lincoln*, (Bar/None, 1989, prod. Bill Krauss) ♪♪♪♪ which boasts the mind-bogglingly great "Ana Ng."

what to avoid: If you have to avoid one (and don't!), put *John Henry* (Elektra, 1994, prod. Paul Fox) ♪♪♪ at the bottom of your Giants shopping list. It isn't quite as strong as their other work, though it does contain a handful of splendid tracks.

the rest: *They Might Be Giants* (Bar/None, 1986) ♪♪♪♪ *Flood* (Elektra, 1990) ♪♪♪♪ *Micellaneous T* (Elektra, 1991) ♪♪♪

worth searching for: *Don't Let's Start,* (One Little Indian, 1989) ♪♪♪ a British rarities collection that features a few gems from B-sides and other sources.

▶▶ Ben Folds Five, The Negro Problem, Barenaked Ladies

◀◀ Tin Pan Alley, the Beatles, the Beach Boys, Burt Bacharach, Monty Python, Spinal Tap, Frank Zappa, the dBs

Simon Glickman

Thin Lizzy

Formed 1970 in Dublin, Ireland. Disbanded 1983.

Phil Lynott, vocals, bass (died Jan. 4, 1986); Brian Downey, drums; Eric Bell, guitar (1970-73); Gary Moore, guitar (1974, 1977-78); Andy

Gee, guitar (1974); John Cann, guitar (1974); Scott Gorham, guitar, vocals (1974-83); Brian Robertson, guitar, vocals (1974-77); Midge Ure, guitar (1979); Snowy White, guitar (1980-82); Darren Wharton, keyboards (1981-83); John Sykes, guitar (1982-83)

Driven by the underrated Lynott—a wonderfully literate songwriter—Thin Lizzy is best remembered for its carefully constructed melodic dual guitar leads and Lynott's throaty, soulful vocals. The scope of Lynott's ambition led to vaguely thematic albums, alternating between macho pounders and soaring, working-class ballads. Highly romanticized and often insightful writing mixed too often with pretentious, obtuse male bonding, and the band failed to break through to a higher level of stardom and broke up in 1983. After recording a solo album and publishing two books of poetry, Lynott suffered a drug overdose that led to fatal bouts of pneumonia and heart failure in 1986. A Lynott/Thin Lizzy tribute concert was held in 1995—with Henry Rollins and others joining surviving band members—with an album of the show expected to be released at some point.

what to buy: On *Jailbreak,* (Mercury, 1976, prod. John Alcock) ♪♪♪♪ Lynott's sensitivity and swagger gel like shots and beers with his strongest set of tunes—notably, "The Boys Are Back in Town," a violent summertime paean to male camaraderie. *Dedication: The Very Best of Thin Lizzy* (Polygram, 1991, prod. Various) ♪♪♪♪ offers a streamlined view of the band's pub punch, starting with its first hit, "Whiskey in the Jar," through to the final three albums on Warner Bros., which are now unavailable.

what to buy next: *Live and Dangerous* (Warner Bros., 1978, prod. Thin Lizzy and Tony Visconti) ♪♪♪♪ is a bare-knuckled tour de force that's arguably the best showcase for the band's power. Swirling guitars, Lynott's thick delivery and a tight rhythm section illuminate even the obscure tunes.

what to avoid: *Thin Lizzy* (Mercury, 1971, prod. Scott English and Nick Tauber) ♪ is buried in mystical murk with titles such as "The Friendly Ranger at Clontarf Castle"—a rambling mess that offers few hints of things to come.

the rest: *Shades of a Blue Orphanage* (Mercury, 1972) ♪ *Vagabonds of the Western World* (Mercury, 1973) ♪♪ *Night Life* (Mercury, 1974) ♪♪♪ *Fighting* (Mercury, 1975) ♪♪♪ *Johnny the Fox* (Mercury, 1976) ♪♪♪½ *Bad Reputation* (Mercury, 1977) ♪♪♪½

worth searching for: *Solo in Soho,* (Warner Bros, 1980) ♪♪ Lynott's only solo effort, is spotty but contains "Ode to a Black Man," which ranks with the best songs he wrote for the band.

⏩ Graham Parker, Metallica, Bon Jovi

⏪ Van Morrison, Bob Seger

Allan Orski

.38 Special

Formed 1974 in Jacksonville, Fla.

Donnie Van Zant, vocals; Don Barnes, guitar, vocals (1975-87, 1992-present); Jeff Carlisi, guitar; Ken Lyons, bass (1975-78); Jack Grondin, drums (1974-75); Steve Brookins, drums (1975-87); Larry Junstrom, bass, guitar, (1978-present); Danny Chauncey, guitar (1987-present); Max Carl, drums (1987-91); Scott Hoffman, drums (1991-present), Bobby Capps, keyboards (1991-present)

.38 Special worked for years in the shadow of Southern rock giants Lynyrd Skynyrd. (Van Zant, the group's frontman, was the younger brother of Skynyrd's Ronnie Van Zant.) In fact, the group didn't have a Top 40 hit until 1980, well after Southern rock had peaked. But once it hit with "Hold On Loosely," .38 Special became the top Southern rock act of the decade, with three consecutive platinum albums. The band achieved this by turning its Southern boogie roots into an accessible pop formula for radio. Where other bands played loose jams, .38 Special was tight; instead of being dominated by guitar solos, .38 Special lived and died by the hooky chorus. It wasn't Lynyrd Skynyrd, by any standards, but, then again, it wasn't intended to be.

what to buy: *Flashback* (A&M, 1987, prod. Various) ♪♪♪♪ celebrates the fact that .38 Special was one of the best singles bands of the early and mid-80s, evolving from rough-hewn anthems such as "Rockin' Into the Night" to melodic masterpieces like "If I'd Been the One" and "Caught Up in You."

what to buy next: *Tour de Force* (A&M, 1983, prod. Rodney Mills, Don Barnes and Jeff Carlisi) ♪♪♪ is, start to finish, the most consistent of the band's albums, containing the singles "If I'd Been the One" and "Back Where You Belong."

what to avoid: *Bone Against Steel* (Charisma, 1991, prod. Rodney Mills) ♪♪ If you have to choose between underdeveloped Southern power and an overworked formula for radio success, choose the former. This is the latter.

the rest: *Rockin' Into the Night* (A&M, 1979) ♪♪½ *Wild Eyed Southern Boys* (A&M, 1981) ♪♪½ *Special Forces* (A&M, 1982) ♪♪½ *Strength in Numbers* (A&M, 1986) ♪♪ *Rock & Roll Strategy* (A&M, 1988) ♪♪

worth searching for: *38 Special at the Rainbow Music Hall,* (A&M, 1980, prod. Rodney Mills) a promotional vinyl release that features four songs performed live in Denver.

Garth Brooks, Travis Tritt, the Mavericks

The Allman Brothers Band, Lynyrd Skynyrd, Molly Hatchett, the Beatles

Brian Mansfield

This Mortal Coil

Formed in 1984 in London, England

This Mortal Coil is a rare thing in the music world, the whole being greater than sum of its parts. Normally these supergroup confabs are nothing more than an attempt to bring in a few extra bucks with name-brand recognition—and with the end product being marginal at best. In the case of TMC, none of the featured members truly has an enormous presence in the music world to begin with. Their unifying factor is that they are all part of Ivo Watts Russell's vision for what modern music should sound like. Being on 4AD Records is the only thing needed to join This Mortal Coil for most—the lineup features members of the Cocteau Twins, Dead Can Dance, Colourbox, the Wolfgang Press, Modern English, the Pixies, Throwing Muses, the Breeders—and a few minor-league studio musicians who frequent 4AD studio sessions for the aforementioned bands. The only artists of note who contribute significantly to the projects are Dominic Appleton of Breathless, an English band that sells thousands of records in Italy, Gordon Sharp of Cindytalk and, most notably, the Buzzcocks' Howard Devoto. This "all-star" lineup formed as a one-off project conceived by Russell, who writes plays and acts as producer to some extent on each of the band's albums. While no real departure is found from the usual murky 4AD fare, the records are noteworthy simply because of the quality of each album; if you like the Cocteau Twins and Dead Can Dance, you will love TMC. The project allows the band members to cross-pollinate and experiment away from their usual surroundings, and the musicians clearly fee liberated in the TMC fold—as evidenced by wild covers such as Tim Buckley's "Song to the Siren," Big Star's "Kangaroo" and the Talking Heads' "Drugs," all done in the inimitable 4AD style. For lush atmospheres and moody, gothic style arrangements, very little competes with the quality and consistency of TMC.

what to buy: Strong from start to finish, *Filigree & Shadow* (4AD, 1986, prod. Ivo Watts Russell) is a double album that more than makes up for its extra cost by being a true work of art. While not as traditionally stylized as the band's first effort, it shows TMC actually coming into its own as a band, rather than a studio project of label mates. Weighing in at 74 minutes, it's long enough to be a good candlelight dinner record.

the rest: *It'll End in Tears* (4AD, 1984) *Blood* (4AD, 1991) *Box Set* (4AD, 1993)

worth searching for: A self-titled promotional-only album (4AD, 1993) released to introduce the U.S. to the band's material when 4AD opened an American office and prepared to release a TMC box set, The 12-song sampler culls tracks from all three of the band's albums and a contribution to a 4AD compilation album.

Cocteau Twins, Dead Can Dance, Wolfgang Press, Colourbox, Pixies

Bauhaus, Breathless, Modern English, Legendary Pink Dots

Tim Davis

Mickey Thomas

See: Jefferson Starship

Richard Thompson /Linda Thompson/Richard and Linda Thompson

Richard Thompson (born April 3, 1949, in London, England), vocals, guitar; Linda Thompson, vocals

Richard Thompson was an original member of the innovative folk-rock band Fairport Convention and has in the intervening years carved out a niche as a supremely gifted songwriter and guitarist. With his deep, burnished vocals and generally dark songs, he has modernized the British folk idiom in several ways; his expressive, often baroque fretwork joins a number of different traditions—imagine a Celtic Hendrix in Morocco—and has hugely influenced Mark Knopfler of Dire Straits, among many others. Thompson met Linda Peters while working with the group Bunch, a loose aggregation of Fairport alumni; they married during the early 70s, converted to Islam in 1974 and divorced in 1982 (Richard subsequently married Nancy Covey). Richard began his solo career first, with 1972's *Henry the Human Fly,* then joined forces with Linda for some of the most emotionally bare music ever produced in the pop idiom. After they split up, Richard re-activated his solo career, worked with avant-gardists Fred Frith, Henry Kaiser and John French, was a busy gun-for-hire (Nick Drake, J.J. Cale, Robert Plant, Bonnie Raitt, Crowded House, Suzanne Vega, the Golden Palominos, Syd Straw) and wielded enough influenced to inspire a 1994 tribute album featuring a bevy of cutting-edge acts. Linda moved into theater before releasing a solo album in 1985 and a retrospective in 1996.

what to buy: The couple's *Shoot Out the Lights* (Hannibal, 1982, prod. Joe Boyd)—whose release barely preceded their divorce—is a devastating, virtually flawless set of performances and the last of their collaborations. Their first release, *I Want to See the Bright Lights Tonight,* (Hannibal, 1974/Rykodisc, 1991, prod. Richard Thompson and John Wood) is a equally gripping and somewhat happier dialogue. Richard's *Rumour and Sigh* (Capitol, 1991, prod. Mitchell Froom) is his personal masterpiece, highlighted by the ironic "I Feel So Good" and the updated Irish ballad "1952 Vincent Black Lightning."

what to buy next: Richard's best solo work is collected in the hefty but consistently engaging three-disc set *Watching the Dark: The History of Richard Thompson.* (Rykodisc/Hannibal, 1993, prod. Various) Linda's *Dreams Fly Away* (Rykodisc/Hannibal, 1996, prod. Various) is a 20-track overview of her career, from before Richard to her post-divorce work.

what to avoid: *Richard Thompson Live! (More or Less),* (Island, 1977, prod. Joe Boyd) was originally paired with *I Want to See the Bright Lights Tonight* as a double album—but didn't deserve to be.

the rest: Richard Thompson: *Henry the Human Fly* (Warner Bros., 1972/Rykodisc-Hannibal, 1991) *(Guitar, Vocal)* (Island, 1976/Rykodisc-Hannibal, 1991) *Strict Tempo!* (Hannibal, 1981) *Hand of Kindness* (Hannibal, 1983/Rykodisc-Hannibal, 1991) *Small Town Romance* (Hannibal, 1984) *Across a Crowded Room* (Polydor, 1985) *Daring Adventures* (Polydor, 1986) *Amnesia* (Capitol, 1988) *Mirror Blue* (Capitol, 1994) *You? Me? Us?* (Capitol, 1996) Richard and Linda Thompson: *Hokey Pokey* (Hannibal, 1975/Rykodisc-Hannibal, 1991) *Pour Down Like Silver* (Hannibal, 1975/Rykodisc-Hannibal, 1991) *First Light* (Carthage, 1978/Rykodisc, 1992) *Sunnyvista* (Carthage, 1979/Rykodisc, 1992) Linda Thompson: *One Clear Moment* (Warner Bros., 1978) French, Frith, Kaiser and Thompson: *Live, Love, Larf & Loaf* (Rhino, 1987) *Invisible Means* (Windham Hill, 1990)

worth searching for: *Lonely Hearts,* (Silver Rarities, 1995) a wonderful two-disc bootleg set that captures Richard and Linda performances from 1981 and 1982, with a few Fairporters guesting on the latter.

Dire Straits, Elvis Costello, Jeff Buckley, Womack & Womack

Wes Montgomery, Django Rheinhardt, Jimi Hendrix, Fairport Convention, Nick Drake, Van Morrison, Bob Dylan

Simon Glickman and Gary Graff

Thompson Twins /Babble

Formed 1977 in Chesterfield, England

Thompson Twins (1977-92): Tom Bailey, vocals, keyboards, guitar; John Roog (1977-82), guitar; Pete Dodd, guitar (1977-82); Chris Bell, drums (1977-82); Alannah Currie, percussion, saxophone, vocals (1981-92); Joe Leeway, percussion, vocals (1982-86); Matthew Seligman, bass (1981-82). Babble (1993-present): Bailey, Currie

With their MTV-ready haircuts and bouncy synth-pop, the Thompson Twins hit big in the early 80s—after spending its earliest years as a kind of tribal collective formed in London's squatter culture. Its 15 minutes of fame came via the hit 1984 album *Into the Gap*, a commercial zenith the Twins would never again hit. By 1986, the group was down to the husband-wife duo of Bailey and Currie; they soldiered on for a few years, pursuing exotic and rhythmic music until they finally decided the Thompson Twins moniker (which came from a British cartoon) was an albatross. Jettisoning it, they continue to record as Babble, plowing wholeheartedly into Eastern-oriented ambient styles.

what to buy: The synth sounds on *Into the Gap* (Arista, 1984, prod. Alex Sadkin and Tom Bailey) are a bit dated today, but in a charming way, and the hits—"Hold Me Now," "Sister of Mercy," "You Take Me Up"—still sound great.

what to buy next: Babble is a compelling new venture for Bailey and Currie, but an acquired taste for those hooked by the Thompson Twins' more accessible pop fare. Either *The Stone* (Reprise, 1994, prod. Alannah Currie and Tom Bailey) or *Ether* (Reprise, 1996, prod. Tom Bailey, Alannah Currie and

Keith Fernley) reward repeated listenings with their deep grooves and subtle melodicism.

what to avoid: The bulk of the Thompson Twins' catalog is out of print, and the remix collection *Greatest Mixes: Best of the Thomson Twins* (Arista, 1988, prod. Various) is an inadequate—and misleadingly titled—representation of the group's work.

the rest: *Big Trash* (Warner Bros., 1989) *Queer* (Warner Bros., 1991)

worth searching for: A British import, *The Greatest Hits,* (Stylus Music, 1990, prod. Various) is that collection that the U.S. lacks.

▶▶ Depeche Mode, Neneh Cherry, Howard Jones, Thomas Dolby

◀◀ David Bowie, Roxy Music, Talking Heads

Gary Graff and Allan Orski

George Thorogood and the Destroyers

Formed 1973 in Wilmington, Del.

George Thorogood, guitar, vocals; Michael Lenn, bass (1973-75); Jeff Simon, drums; Billy Blough, bass (1975-present); Hank Carter, saxophone (1980-present)

Thorogood blew a breath of fresh air into the studied poses of the New Wave era with a blast of unexpurgated, unrepentant blues and boogie on a series of albums for the tiny independent label, Rounder Records of Boston. His faithful, frankly derivative attack on blues classics made up in splashy conviction and hard-wrought passion what it lacked in originality. As Thorogood caught fire with radio and the public, he honed his approach, supplying himself with effective originals alongside the vintage R&B numbers, and emphasized the boogie side of his mix somewhat more heavily. But in general, Thorogood has remained true to his initial vision after more than 20 years of recording.

what to buy: His breathtaking debut album, *George Thorogood and the Destroyers,* (Rounder, 1975, prod. J. Nagy) retains its fresh, ferocious feel, as Thorogood introduces a style that would remain constant—blues, boogie and lots of slashing slide guitar.

what to buy next: *The Baddest of George Thorogood and the Destroyers* (EMI, 1992, prod. Terry Manning and the Delaware Destroyers) contains only one track from that original release and collects the highlights of his dozen subsequent albums.

what to avoid: His 1974 demo recordings, when the band was unformed and Thorogood himself rather green, found their way into release as *Better Than the Rest,* (MCA, 1979, prod. D. Lipman) without any hint that these were early experiments by the then-popular guitarist. Tsk, tsk.

the rest: *Move It On Over* (Rounder, 1978) *More George Thorogood and the Destroyers* (Rounder, 1980) *Bad to the Bone* (EMI, 1982) *Maverick* (EMI, 1985) *Live* (EMI, 1986) *Born to Be Bad* (EMI, 1988) *Boogie People* (EMI, 1991) *Haircut* (EMI, 1993)

worth searching for: *Greatest Hits,* (Rounder, 1988, prod. Various) a Japanese import that provides a good summation of his Rounder years.

▶▶ The Nighthawks, the Fabulous Thunderbirds, the Black Crowes

◀◀ John Lee Hooker, Bo Diddley, Chuck Berry, Duane Eddy

Joel Selvin

Three Dog Night

Formed 1967 in Los Angeles, Calif. Disbanded 1977. Re-formed 1981.

Danny Hutton, vocals (1967-76, 1981-present; Chuck Negron, vocals (1967-77, 1981-83); Cory Wells, vocals; Mike Allsup, guitar (1967-76); Jimmy Greenspoon, keyboards; Joe Schermie, bass (1967-73); Jack Ryland, bass (1973)-76); Floyd Sneed, drums (1967-76); Skip Konte, keyboards (1973-76); Jay Gruska, vocals (1976-77)

Three Dog Night was a hit-making machine. From 1969-75, the group charted more than 20 times thanks to terrific lead vocals and harmonies, a keen ear for selecting good songs by great songwriters and an ability to arrange these songs in a dynamic fashion. A full-fledged seven-piece band, Three Dog Night began as a group of rockers with strong soul and R&B influences; initially the band was as comfortable covering Otis Redding's "Try a Little Tenderness" as Argent guitarist Russ Ballard's "Liar." In so doing, Three Dog Night aided the careers of such songwriters as Randy Newman, Elton John, Bernie Taupin and Harry Nilsson, to name a very few. What made the group immensely popular also cost it credibility in the burgeoning underground radio market, however. But it was a respect the band could forgo, as 10 of its albums sold more than a million copies each. The hits wound down in the mid-70s, and these days Hutton and Wells keep the band out on the oldies circuit.

what to buy: *Celebrate: The Three Dog Night Story 1965-1975* (MCA, 1993, prod. Various) has all the hits, plus the better album stuff and two previously unreleased tracks. It's an interesting listen as Three Dog Night grows into its own, at first fumbling but then clicking with precision.

what to buy next: *Harmony* (Dunhill, 1971/MCA Special Products 1994, prod. Richard Podolor) is the group's best studio effort, with the early hits "Old Fashioned Love Song," "Family of Man" and Hoyt Axton's "Never Been to Spain."

what to avoid: *Joy to the World: Their Greatest Hits* (Dunhill, 1974/MCA, 1989) is burdened by haphazard digital transfers makes for a dull to aggravating listening experience. *Captured Live at the Forum* (Dunhill, 1969/MCA, 1989) is not a compelling live performance and does little to enhance the original studio versions.

the rest: *Naturally* (Dunhill, 1970/MCA Special Products, 1989) *Seven Separate Fools* (Dunhill, 1972/MCA Special Products, 1989) *Cyan* (Dunhill, 1973/MCA, 1990) *Hard Labor* (Dunhill, 1974/MCA, 1990) *Best of* (MCA, 1982)

worth searching for: *Around the World With Three Dog Night* (Dunhill, 1973) is a better-sounding concert document than the *Captured Live at the Forum* set.

▶▶ America, Bo Donaldson & the Heywoods, Paper Lace

◀◀ Otis Redding, Laura Nyro, the Four Tops, the Beatles

Patrick McCarty and Gary Graff

Three Fish

See: Pearl Jam

Throwing Muses

Formed 1980 in Newport, R.I.

Kristin Hersh, vocals, guitar; Tanya Donelly, vocals, guitar (1980-92); David Narcizo, drums; Elaine Adamedes, bass (1980-86); Leslie Langston, bass (1986-91, 1992-94); Fred Abong, bass (1991-92); Bernard Georges, bass (1994-present)

Hersh and Donelly, stepsisters inspired by punk and turned off by corny 80s new wave, built a noisy sound out of fuzzy guitars and high-pitched, dreamy vocals. At their peak, the Hersh-Donelly duo produced a raw tension—Donelly liked catchy pop songs, Hersh was more into confessional singer-songwriting and Led Zeppelin-style heavy metal that made the band's sound thick and potently jagged. The Muses' early albums, notably the self-titled debut and *Hunkpapa,* lurch from soft folk to roaring rock and take in some reggae and waltz rhythms along the way. Eventually, the team unraveled; *The Real Ramona* is the sound of two strong personalities tugging against each other, but it lacks any central vision or coherence. Donelly—who was already working in a side band, the Breeders—left to form Belly, a more straightforward guitar-pop band. Hersh kept Throwing Muses a trio and put out one gloomy folk-rock solo album.

what to buy: *Hunkpapa* (Sire, 1989, prod. Gary Smith) echoes the Beatles in its give-and-take between raw, screeching punk and glorious little melodies. The hard-to-find debut, *Throwing Muses,* (4AD, 1986, prod. Gil Norton) is the fresh sound of energetic young women trying all kinds of (mostly noisy) combinations before coming up with their own musical identity. On *Limbo,* (Rykodisc, 1996, prod. Throwing Muses) Hersh often sounds like she's come around to Donelly's way of thinking; it's the most melodic Muses' collection yet, still deeply personal and tortured but with a greater range of moods and an agreeably spare instrumental approach.

what to buy next: Hersh's solo album, *Hips and Makers* (Sire, 1994, prod. Lenny Kaye, Kristen Hersh and Steve Rizzo) lacks Donelly's Paul McCartney that always supplemented Hersh's John Lennon so nicely; despite some good spooky lyric-writing, it can often be a downer.

what to avoid: Hersh's pretentions become tedious on her *Strings,* EP (Sire, 1994) which actually includes a Led Zeppelin song arranged with cello and violins.

the rest: *House Tornado* (Sire, 1988) *The Real Ramona* (Sire, 1991) *Red Heaven* (Sire, 1992) *University* (Sire, 1995)

worth searching for: *The Fat Skier* (Sire EP, 1987, prod. Mark Van Hecke) and *Chains Changed* (4AD EP, 1987) are less meandering, harder-rocking portraits of the Muses in the careening-genre stage of their career.

▶▶ The Breeders, the Pixies, Belly, PJ Harvey, Voice of the Beehive, Veruca Salt, Sebadoh, Superchunk, Buffalo Tom

◀◀ The Beatles, Siouxsie and the Banshees, X-Ray Spex,

the Sex Pistols, the Modern Lovers, Led Zeppelin, Joni Mitchell, the Velvet Underground, Sonic Youth

Steve Knopper

Thunderclap Newman

Formed 1969 in London, England. Disbanded 1970.

Pete Townshend, bass; Speedy Keen, vocals, drums; Jimmy McCulloch, guitar (died Sept. 27, 1979); Andy Newman, keyboards

This quartet was one of the stranger yet more satisfying one-shot wonders of the early 70s. In a loose union, Townshend gathered Who friend Keen, a teenage McCulloch and postal clerk Newman to make one album, *Hollywood Dream.* (Track, 1970/Polygram, 1991, prod. Pete Townshend) ♪♪♪♪ The album contains the previously released single "Something in the Air," a sweet call for togetherness that was most recently covered by Tom Petty. The band was worlds away from Townshend's guitar-smashing fury in the Who, and it dissolved quickly. Keen released a couple of solo albums, while McCulloch went on to play in Wings before OD'ing in 1979.

see also: *The Who, Paul McCartney/Wings*

Allan Orski

Johnny Thunders

See: New York Dolls

'Til Tuesday

Formed 1984 in Boston, Mass. Disbanded 1988.

Aimee Mann, bass, acoustic guitar, and vocals; Michael Hausman, drums and percussion; Robert Holmes, guitars, background vocals; Joey Pesce, keyboards and background vocals 1984-87; Michael Montes, keyboards 1987-88

'Til Tuesday most likely would be long forgotten if it weren't for the solo career of its frontwoman, Aimee Mann. A synth-pop quartet of average talent, 'Til Tuesday was blessed with Mann's gift for writing engaging melodies and sophisticated lyrics. The group scored a mega-hit early on with the single "Voices Carry" and then promptly joined the rank and file of one-hit wonders. Despite Mann's obvious talents, the songs on all of the band's three albums are swamped by what was for the mid-1980s formulaic production: shimmering synths and stadium-size reverb. While critics praised the group and luminaries like Elvis Costello gave creative input, 'Til Tuesday was largely ignored by its label and broke up shortly after releasing its third album.

What Album Changed Your Life?

"I grew up on R.E.M.; if they weren't a band, I probably wouldn't have picked up an instrument to play music. They're the closest to my heart, the second record (Reckoning) in particular. I'd heard about Murmur and stuff like that when they started coming out, but it hadn't struck me yet. I bought the second one after I saw the video for 'So. Central Rain' and everything about it felt like...wow! I put that record on and feel better every time I hear it."

Ruthie Morris (Magnapop)

what to buy: Music and production never melded better for 'Til Tuesday than on *Welcome Home.* (Epic, 1986, prod. Rhett Davies) ♪♪♪ The group spins out tasteful confections that include "What About Love," "On Sunday" and the song that should have been a hit, "Sleeping and Waking."

what to buy next: Davies' production was decidedly wrong for *Everything's Different Now,* (Epic, 1988) ♪♪♪ an effort made worthy by its mature songwriting and confident vocal work. Penned by Mann and songwriter/former "MTV Unplugged" host Jules Shear, the album chronicles the couple's relationship and breakup through such gems as "J for Jules," "Limits to Love," and the bouncy title track. Notable among the tunes is "The Other End (of the Telescope)," written by Mann and Elvis Costello and featuring supporting vocals from the latter.

the rest: *Voices Carry* (Epic, 1985) ♪♪

▶▶ Crowded House, Jules Shear, Sam Phillips, Juliana Hatfield

The Beatles, The Byrds, Elvis Costello, The Pretenders, Squeeze

see also: *Aimee Mann*

Christopher Scapelliti

Timbuk 3

Formed 1978 in Madison, Wisc.

Pat MacDonald, vocals, guitar, harmonica, bass; Barbara Kooyman MacDonald, vocals, guitar, harmonica, violin, mandolin; Wally Ingram, drums (1991-present); Courtney Audain, bass (1991-present)

Ever since their bluesy anti-nuclear diatribe "The Future's So Bright, I Gotta Wear Shades" was adopted as a yuppie-lifestyle anthem in 1986, this Austin, Texas-based husband-wife duo has been thwarted by the Randy Newman Principle: if you use tongue-in-cheek humor to get under the skin, you'll wind up going over the heads of most listeners. Their compelling blend of hypnotic rhythms, clever wordplay, stinging guitars and sweet-and-sour harmonies helped them score big on college radio with underdog-championing commentaries on homelessness ("Dirty Dirty Rice"), the religious right ("Prey"), jingoism ("National Holiday") and shallow values ("Hairstyles and Attitudes"). Once relying on a beatbox for backing, Timbuk 3 expanded to a four-piece band on its last two albums, but the MacDonalds still frequently perform as a duo. Even though repeat commercial success continues to elude them, Timbuk 3 clings to their values and have so far refused the relentless offers to sell the rights to "The Future's So Bright" for commercial jingles touting everything from toothpaste to sunglasses.

what to buy: The MacDonalds' bluesy cynicism runs rampant through *Greetings From Timbuk 3*, (I.R.S., 1986, prod. Dennis Herring) ♪♪♪♪ the launchpad of such college favorites as "The Future's So Bright," "Life Is Hard" and "Just Another Movie." *Eden Alley* (I.R.S., 1988, prod. Dennis Herring) ♪♪♪♪ broadens their musical base and expands their targets to include "Sample the Dog" (which predicted technology's chilling effect on education and the arts), the ska-flavored "Too Much Sex, Not Enough Affection" and a reggae-tinged hymn of devotion called "A Sinful Life." *Edge of Allegiance* (I.R.S., 1989, prod. Denardo Coleman and Timbuk 3) ♪♪♪♪ boasts some of Pat MacDonald's darkest compositions, including "Standard White Jesus," "Daddy's Down in the Mine," "B-Side of Life" and "Acid Rain."

what to buy next: *Espace Ornano* (Watermelon, 1993, prod. Timbuk 3) ♪♪♪ is a live band album recorded in France that mixes longtime favorites like "Tarzan Was a Bluesman" and "Reckless Driver" with the previously unreleased "Rage of Angels," "Throw Down Gun" and "Bleeding Heart."

what to avoid: *Looks Like Dark to Me*, (Windham Hill, 1994, prod. Timbuk 3) ♪♪ a stopgap EP with alternate versions of two songs found on "A Hundred Lovers," a spooky rearrangement of "The Future's So Bright" and a bland cover of Steppenwolf's "Born to Be Wild."

the rest: *Big Shot in the Dark* (I.R.S., 1991) ♪♪♪ *Field Guide: Some of the Best of Timbuk 3* (I.R.S., 1992) ♪♪♪ *A Hundred Lovers* (Windham Hill, 1995) ♪♪♪

worth searching for: Pat MacDonald wrote lyrics and sang harmony vocals on Brazilian singer Marina Lima's *A Tug on the Line* (World Pacific/Blue Note, 1994, prod. Joao Augusto).

Mary Lou Lord, Lisa Loeb, Penelope Houston, Luscious Jackson

Muddy Waters, Talking Heads, Leonard Cohen, Jim Kweskin Jug Band

David Okamoto

The Time

Formed 1981 in Minneapolis, Minn. Disbanded 1984. Re-formed in 1990 and in 1995.

Morris Day, vocals; Jesse Johnson, guitars, vocals; Jellybean Johnson, drums; Terry Lewis, bass (1981-83, 1990); James "Jimmy Jam" Harris III, keyboards (1981-83, 1990); Monte Moir, keyboards (1981-83, 1990, 1995); Gerry Hubbard, bass (1983-84); Paul "St. Paul" Peterson, keyboards, vocals (1983-84); Mark Cardenas, keyboards (1983-84)

Originally formed as a convenient home for Prince songs too conventionally funky for the diminutive funk master's own records, The Time grew into the ultimate R&B party band—also becoming the most successful spin-off from the Minneapolis-based wunderkind's stable of mid-80s acts. Though its 1981 debut album features a band on the cover, it was actually recorded entirely by Prince and Day. Eventually, Minneapolis' hottest funk band was recruited to back Day, and The Time was born. By its second album—also bearing the heavy sonic stamp of its producer Jaime Starr, a.k.a. Prince—the band's roles had solidified, offering forward-looking funk jams knit together by electric synthesizer licks and Day's own class-clowning, party animal image. Unfortunately, efforts by Harris and Lewis to produce other artists got them forced out of the group (they went on to produce hits for Janet Jackson, the Human

League and many others), followed shortly by Moir. The remaining band, showcased in Prince's breakthrough "Purple Rain" movie, had nonetheless lost its magic. Regrouping in 1990 after a six-year hiatus—for another Prince film, "Graffiti Bride," the classic lineup found modern production techniques couldn't make up for a lack of passion. The latest incarnation has yet to produce an album.

what to buy: Every so often, a band manages to bring its creative best at a time when the world is perfectly poised to hear it. For The Time, *What Time Is It?* (Warner Bros., 1982, prod. Jamie Starr) [5 bones] is that record. Tracks such as "777-9311" and "Wild and Loose" meld incendiary funk playing with the band's image as slick-suited, perfectly coiffed party dogs, while the ballad "Gigolos Get Lonely Too" show they can work a slow-jam to death as well.

what to avoid: Besides the mostly forgettable solo stuff cranked out by the individual members, *Ice Cream Castle* (Warner Bros., 1984, prod. Prince and Morris Day) **WOOF!** is a popified rehash of the band's vibe, built around the two songs featured in the "Purple Rain" movie—"Jungle Love" and "The Bird." Though this album won the band lots of new fans, those who'd been around from the early days knew it was the beginning of the end.

the rest: *The Time* (Warner Bros., 1981) [3 bones] *Pandemonium* (Reprise, 1990) [3 bones]

worth searching for: A slick promotional piece for *Pandemonium* that includes a digital clock in the packaging (The Time—get it?). A fun way to own an otherwise mediocre album.

solo outings:

Morris Day *Color of Success* (Warnes Bros., 1985) [2 bones] *Daydreaming* (Warner Bros., 1987) [2 bones]

Jesse Johnson *Jesse Johnson's Revue* (A&M, 1985) [3½ bones] *Shockadelica* (A&M, 1986) [3 bones] *Every Shade of Love* (A&M, 1988) [3 bones]

▶▶ Chuckii Booker, Tony Toni Tone, The Wooten Brothers

◀◀ James Brown, Prince, Parliament/Funkedelic, Ohio Players

Eric Deggans

The Tindersticks

Formed 1992 in London, England

Stuart Staples, vocals, guitar; Neil Fraser, guitar, zither; David Boulter, keyboards, organ; Al Macauley, drums; Mark Colwill, bass; Dickon Hinchliffe, guitar, violin

The Tindersticks quietly released a series of singles in late 1992. They quickly sold by word of mouth, and the slow rise yielded nearly unanimous critical acclaim by the time the group released *Tindersticks.* (Bar/None, 1993, prod. Ian Caple and The Tindersticks) [5 bones] Fronted by Staples' sultry, world-weary vocals, the group produces evocative, atmospheric, dark-hued and gorgeous music, with extensive use of strings and woodwinds. *Tindersticks* (London International, 1995, prod. Ian Caple and The Tindersticks) [5 bones] retains the lush, enigmatic quality of the first, but the songs have a broader sound.

Anna Glen

Toad the Wet Sprocket

Formed 1988 in Santa Barbara, Calif.

Glen Phillips, vocals, guitars; Todd Nichols, guitars; Dean Dinning, bass, keyboards, backing vocals; Randy Guss, drums

Folk-style songwriting with a toe-tapping guitar-pop beat, Toad the Wet Sprocket is one of the few bands that successfully used early R.E.M. as a base and created a sound of its own. Formed by childhood friends, Toad began as a college band but moved up to the major league after the release of the beautifully melodic album *fear.* A laudable live band, Toad also enjoys a warm—and hardly harmful—relationship with Hootie and the Blowfish; the two bands have toured together, and Phillips lent his hand to Hootie's second album.

what to buy: *fear* (Columbia, 1991, prod. Gavin MacKillop) [4 bones] is as perfect as an album can get. A poet laureate of the modern pop scene, Phillips sings his lyrics with equal amounts of grace and unleashed emotion. "I Will Not Take These Things for Granted," "Before You Were Born" and the shimmering mandolin in "Walk on the Ocean" are the highlights of the album.

what to buy next: *Dulcinea* (Columbia, 1994, prod. Gavin MacKillop) [3½ bones] is even poppier than previous releases. The singles "Fly From Heaven," "Something's Always Wrong" and "Fall Down" are tasty, well-crafted songs, but the gems of the album are "Stupid" and "Nanci," the latter a sing-around-the-campfire folk ode to Nanci Griffith and Loretta Lynn.

what to avoid: With the exception of "Good Intentions," it's easy to see why the songs on *In Light Syrup* (Columbia, 1995, prod. Various) ℰℰℰ were either not used or consigned to B-sides and movie soundtracks.

the rest: *Bread and Circus* (Columbia, 1989) ℰℰℰ *Pale* (Columbia, 1990) ℰℰℰ

worth searching for: The sweet-tempered *Acoustic Dance Party* (Columbia EP, 1994, prod. Toad the Wet Sprocket ℰℰℰℰ a five-song CD sold at Toad concerts that offers a nibble of the band's outstanding live shows.

▶▶ Hootie and the Blowfish, The Verve Pipe, Gin Blossoms, Better Than Ezra

◀◀ R.E.M., Nanci Griffith, The Beatles, Crosby, Stills and Nash

Christina Fuoco

Toenut

See: Drivin' N' Cryin'

Tom Tom Club

See: Talking Heads

Tones on Tail

Formed 1981 in Northhampton, England. Disbanded 1984.

Daniel Ash, vocals and guitar; Glen Campling, bass; Kevin Haskins, drums

Tones on Tail began in 1981 as a Bauhaus side project for Ash and roadie Glen Campling; after Bauhaus split in 1983, Haskins joined as drummer. Tones on Tail was completely different than its parent band, with a poppier and more modern feel in contrast to Bauhaus' gloomy Gothic sound. Tones' only proper release, *The Album Pop,* (Vertigo/Polygram, 1984, prod. Tones on Tail) ℰℰℰℰℰ sounds genuinely contemporary, giving Ash the kind of free creative rein he didn't have in Bauhaus. The single "Go!" hit big in U.S. dance clubs. Tones on Tail ended after a U.S. tour in 1984, as Ash and Haskins were preparing to step into Love and Rockets. The subsequent releases have been repackagings of EPs, B-sides and other material around a core of songs from *The Album Pop.*

the rest: *Tones on Tail* (Situation Two, 1985) ℰℰℰ *Night Music* (Beggars Banquet, 1987) ℰℰℰℰ *Tones on Tail* (Beggars Banquet, 1990) ℰℰℰℰ

see also: *Bauhaus, Love and Rockets*

JD Cantarella

Too Much Joy

Formed 1983 in Scarsdale, N.Y.

Tim Quirk, vocals; Jay Blumenfield, guitar, vocals; Sandy Smallens, bass, vocals (1983-93); Tommy Vinton, drums; William Wittman, bass, vocals (1993-present)

Quirk is a genuinely funny guy, which is a good thing for a rock 'n' roll band—except for those occasions when he's not funny. Too Much Joy's first two or three albums are hilarious; Quirk's clever, simple knack with words produces such descriptions as "People wore dumb hats/and they fell in love," about the year 1964. His wonderfully weird lyrics drop the names Genghis Khan, Edgar Allen Poe, Red Riding Hood, the Mekons, the Clash ("Hugo" deservedly lampoons "Combat Rock") and all long-haired guys from England. It helps that behind Vinton's Keith Moon-like drumming, the band backs up Quirk's sarcastic musings with loud, explosive rock 'n' roll. Alas, Too Much has never received the attention it deserves—despite inspired stunts like following up the 2 Live Crew's famous arrest by playing the controversial rap song "Me So Horny" in Florida and getting arrested for it, too. After business problems with Giant Records, which never figured out how to market the band, Too Much Joy wandered around labelless before putting out a lukewarm return, *..Finally,* in 1996.

what to buy: *Son of Sam I Am* (Alias, 1988/Giant-Warner Bros., 1990, prod. Michael James) ℰℰℰℰ is the definitive Too Much Joy album, with the classic "Hugo" and 15 funny songs that never get old. Some critics said the band finally lost its edge on *Mutiny,* (Giant-Warner Bros., 1992, prod. William Wittman) ℰℰℰℰ but they weren't listening carefully enough. With a snappy, rewritten version of the Records' "Starry Eyes" and a tremendous femme-fatale song, "Donna Everywhere," the album should have made at least a commercial blip.

what to buy next: *Cereal Killers* (Alias/Giant-Warner Bros., 1991, prod. Paul Fox) ℰℰℰ is more notable for its jokes (a parody of the TV ad "King of Beers," among them) than its music, but it's still fun listening.

what to avoid: On *.. Finally,* (Discovery, 1996, prod. William Wittman) ℰℰ Quirk downplays humor for rebellious introspection—like James Taylor fronting a punk band or something.

worth searching for: The debut, *Green Eggs and Crack,* (Stonegarden, 1987, prod. Al Hemburger and Too Much Joy) ℰℰℰ is hard to find, but it's full of electric tunes and songs about James Dean.

▶▶ The Presidents of the United States of America, Cracker, Weezer

◀◀ The Who, the Clash, the Records, Tom Petty, Dead Milkmen

Steve Knopper

Tool /The Replicants

Formed 1986 in Los Angeles, Calif.

Maynard James Keenan, vocals; Adam Jones, guitar; Paul D'Amour, bass (1986-95); Justin Chancellor, bass (1995-present); Danny Carey, drums

Tool's hard, raw rock assault began with the EP *Opiate* (Zoo, 1992, prod. Sylvia Massy, Steve Hansgen and Tool), which hinted toward the dark, horror film-like spirit of its debut full-length *Undertow.* (Zoo, 1993, prod. Sylvia Massy and Tool) A rape victim tells a gritty tale of physical retribution in "Prison Sex," a song that ironically became a hit in alternative dance clubs. During the long delay in following *Undertow,* bassist D'Amour hooked up with members of Failure to form the Replicants in 1995 and left during the making of its self-titled debut *The Replicants.* (Zoo, 1995, prod. Replicants) *Replicants* offers an acerbic assortment of covers, including guest vocalist Keenan's take on Wings' "Silly Love Songs."

the rest: *AEnima* (Zoo, 1996) not available for rating

Christina Fuoco

Tortoise

Formed 1991 in Chicago, Ill.

Doug McCombs, bass, lap steel; John Herndon, drums, vibraphone, keyboards; John McEntire, drums, keyboards, marimba, programming (1992-present); Bundy K. Brown, bass (1992-95); Dan Bitney, percussion, keyboards, bass, programming (1994-present); Dave Pajo, bass, guitar (1995-present)

Begun as a side project by McCombs and Herndon, Tortoise evolved into a veritable indie-rock all-star band of Chicago musicians representing notable outfits such as Eleventh Dream Day, the Poster Children, the Sea and Cake, Gastr del Sol and Slint. The quintet, which at first may have appeared to be an esoteric indulgence with its guitarless, double-bass lineup and all-instrumental compositions, emerged as a leading light in the mid-90s post-rock wave, in which bands formed by rock musicians looked to non-rock sources for inspiration. Following a pair of singles, the debut album, *Tortoise,* (Thrill Jockey, 1994, prod. John McEntire) established the group's vocabulary: a blend of fusion jazz, progressive rock, dub reggae and avant-garde electronic music in which melody is on equal footing with texture, mood and dynamics, and in which linear song structure is not a concern. A handful of the tracks on the debut were remixed on *Rhythms, Resolutions and Clusters.* EP (Thrill Jockey, 1995, prod. Various) The studio-as-instrument aesthetic was fully realized on the 21-minute "Djed" that opens *Millions Now Living Will Never Die,* (Thrill Jockey, 1996. prod. John McEntire) in which the band creates mood music that refuses to be shoved into the background.

see also: *Eleventh Dream Day*

Greg Kot

Toto

Formed 1976 in Los Angeles, Calif.

David Paich, keyboards, vocals; Steve Lukather, guitar, vocals; Steve Porcaro, keyboards (1976-86); Jeff Porcaro, drums, percussion (1976-92, died Aug. 5, 1992); David Hungate, bass (1976-83); Michael Porcaro, bass (1983-present); Simon Phillips, drums (1993-present); Bobby Kimball, vocals (1976-84); Fergie Fredericksen, vocals (1984-86); Joseph Williams, vocals (1986-90); Jean-Michel Byron, vocals (1990-92)

Based around a core of high school buddies who eventually became Los Angeles' hottest 70s and 80s-era session musicians—Paich, Lukather and the Porcaro brothers—Toto emerged as an instrumentally slick, endlessly evolving rock band whose soft side scored big with the adult contemporary audience. Starting out as a group of hopeful rockers—the band formed while cutting tracks for Boz Scaggs' "Silk Degrees"—the group started strong but really wet through the roof when it won six Grammys for its 1982 album *Toto IV.* But success took its toll, bringing an endless string of lead singers that kept the group off-balance, unable to assemble more than two or three quality tunes for any one album. By 1993, the band gave up, installing Lukather as lead singer and chief songwriter and developing a Bon Jovi-ish rock sound just as the grunge revolution made that style passe. Founding drummer Jeff Porcaro's 1992 death prompted the band to recruit studio whiz Phillips for the drum chair—but by then, Toto's popularity had shifted to Japan and Europe, the only places where a post-punk disdain for its well-crafted sound hadn't made the group irrelevant.

what to buy: Few Toto records offer more than a couple of good cuts among an album's worth of seamless playing, which is why the debut record, *Toto,* (Columbia, 1978, prod. Toto) stands out. Offering a range of material, from the AOR hit "Hold the Line" to the urban radio single "Georgy Porgy" (with R&B diva Cheryl Lynn helping out on vocals), this record is the band's most consistent.

what to buy next: It took the slick rock/pop of *Toto IV* (Columbia, 1982, prod. Toto) to put Toto over the top, with five hits and the six Grammy awards. But even as well-produced, middle-of-the-road tunes like "Rosanna," "Africa" and "I Won't Hold You Back" were creating a new niche for easygoing rockers, their seamless sound was becoming less and less popular. *Past to Present 1977-1990* (Columbia, 1990, prod. Various) fails as a retrospective—missing several cool tunes never released as singles—but remains the best way to get the wheat without the chaff.

what to avoid: *Kingdom of Desire* (Combat, 1993, prod. Toto and Danny Kortchmar) **WOOF!** stands as the worst Toto album ever—no mean feat. It's primarily an ego-stroking showcase for Lukather, who gets to strut his limited vocal range and limited songwriting chops in a metal-tinged setting that emphasizes his guitar playing. Great for chasing stray cats out of your yard.

the rest: *Hydra* (Columbia, 1979) *Turn Back* (Columbia, 1981) *Isolation* (Columbia, 1984) *Fahrenheit* (Columbia, 1986) *The Seventh One* (Columbia, 1988) *Tambu* (Legacy, 1996)

worth searching for: Numerous albums—by the likes of Scaggs, Pink Floyd, Steely Dan, Bruce Springsteen, Earth Wind & Fire and others—that feature the session contributions of Toto's core members.

⏩ The Tubes, Mr. Mister

⏪ The Shadows, Jimi Hendrix, The Beatles

Eric Deggans

Allen Toussaint

Born Jan. 14, 1938 in New Orleans, La.

Through the course of his five-decade career, outside influences never interfered with the basic integrity of Toussaint's brilliant, evocative productions and songwriting. Deeply rooted in the traditional jazz and parade rhythms of his native New Orleans, Toussaint's music evolved and grew based on his own artistic premises. He rarely leaves New Orleans, which is why artists as distinguished as The Band and Paul McCartney have traveled to him to have Toussaint's help making records. His productions have ranged from 70s hits with Dr. John and Labelle to minor masterpieces by a galaxy of homegrown New Orleans R&B stars such as Irma Thomas, Ernie K-Doe, Lee Dorsey, Chris Kenner, the Meters and virtually anyone who mattered after Fats Domino on that city's rich and colorful scene. But Toussaint's own recordings have been quizzical affairs, undermined by his own insecurities as a vocalist—though Bonnie Raitt, Esther Phillips, Boz Scaggs and others have recorded songs off his solo albums. But his solid sense of craftsmanship, along with his slightly florid but mellifluous piano playing, always informed his own records with a scrupulous sense of purpose and powerful musicality.

what to buy: His lack of commercial success as a recording artist has left his infrequent solo outings largely out of print and difficult to find, so most people will have to make do with *The Allen Toussaint Collection,* (Reprise, 1991, prod. Various) a selection drawn from solo albums recorded between 1970-78.

what to buy next: *Connected* (NYNO, 1996, prod. Allen Toussaint) shows that Toussaint hasn't lost his elegant touch after all these years.

what to avoid: His instrumental debut, *The Wild Sound of New Orleans* (RCA 1957), which has been released on European CDs, may have yielded the hit—"Java," for Al Hirt—but is largely an uninteresting—if jaunty—exercise in Longhairish pianistics.

worth searching for: *Southern Nights* (Reprise, 1975, prod. Allen Toussaint and M. Sehorn) is a marvel, his vocals bathed in shimmering effects, the supple majesty of the production lighting each of the intricately wrought compositions. His first two solo albums, *From a Whisper to a Scream* (Scepter, 1970, prod. Allen Toussaint and C. Greene) and *Life, Love and Happiness,* (Reprise, 1972, prod. A. Toussaint) have been released on CD in Europe.

⏩ Neville Brothers, Boz Scaggs

⏪ Professor Longhair, Fats Domino

Joel Selvin

Tower of Power

Formed 1968 in Oakland, Calif.

Rufus Miller, vocals (1969-70); Rick Stevens, vocals (1970-72); Lenny Williams, vocals (1973-75); Hubert Tubbs, vocals (1975-76); Edward

McGee, vocals (1976); Michael Jeffries, vocals (1977-79); Ellis Hall, vocals, keyboards, guitar (1987-present); Tom Bowes, vocals (1991-94); Brent Carter, vocals (1995-present); Emilio Castillo, alto sax, tenor sax, vocals; Greg Adams, trumpet, flugelhorn, vocals (1968-93); Lenny Pickett, reeds, vocals (1973-79); Steve Kupka, baritone sax, oboe, English horn, vocals; Skip Mesquite, tenor sax, flute, vocals (1968-72); Richard Elliot, alto sax, tenor sax, lyricon (1987); David Mann, sax (1994-present); David Padron, trumpet (1968-70); Mic Gillette, brass, vocals (1970-79); Lee Thornburg, brass, vocals (1987-93); Barry Danielian, trumpet, flugelhorn (1995-present); Bill Churchill, trumpet, flugelhorn, trombone (1995-present); Jay Spell, keyboards (1972); Chester Thompson, keyboards, vocals (1973-79); Nick Milo, keyboards (1991-present); Willie Fulton, guitar, vocals (1968-72, 1987); Bruce Conte, guitar, vocals (1973-78); Danny Hoefer, guitar (1979); Carmen Grillo, guitar, vocals (1991- present); Francis Rocco Prestia, bass (1968-76, 1991-present); Victor Conte, bass (1978); Vito San Filippo, bass, vocals (1979); Dave Garibaldi, drums, vibes, vocals (1968-76, 1979); Brent Byars, percussion (1972-74); David Bartlett, drums (1975); Ronnie Beck, drums, vocals (1976-78); Mick Mestek, drums (1987); Russ McKinnon, drums, piano (1991-93); Herman Matthews, drums (1995-present)

When Lenny Williams was its florid lead vocalist, Tower of Power was in the first rank of funk, artistically and commercially. Even without him, its funky rhythm section and tight, jazzy horns are always worth hearing. Throughout the group's many personnel changes, most of the horn section has been constant; however, its best-known member, Lenny Pickett, went to New York, joined the "Saturday Night Live" band and worked with avant-garde musicians, though as a guest he took five solos on 1993's *T.O.P.*, the pinnacle of the group's comeback. TOP's horn sound was especially distinctive thanks to Steve Kupka's use of baritone sax for a fat low end, and the arrangements at their best emphasized intricately interlocking parts. The horn section found itself an in-demand brand-name entity, spicing up countless sessions by bands across the rock and R&B spectrums—including Huey Lewis & the News and the Rolling Stones. During the dark decade of the 80s, in fact, the group practically disbanded while the horns worked more away from the band than with it. The challenge for T.O.P. has always been to retain its trademark sound yet stay up-to-date, a challenge that has been met with varying degrees of success during the past two decades. Throughout all the ups and downs, however, TOP has been a thrilling live band with a huge repertoire of classic funk to sustain it.

what to buy: *Urban Renewal* (Warner Bros., 1975, prod. Emilio Castillo and TOP) has the amazingly tight rhythm section interplay among Thompson, Conte, Prestia and Bartlett that makes "Maybe It'll Rub Off," "Give Me the Proof," "Only So Much Oil in the Ground" and "It's Not the Crime" so funky they hurt. Williams' fervid singing is front and center on the ballads "I Won't Leave Unless You Want Me To" and "Willing to Learn."

what to buy next: *Tower of Power* (Warner Bros., 1973) contains "What Is Hip?" and the ultra-funky "Soul Vaccination." *Back to Oakland* (Warner Bros., 1974, prod. N/A) offers "Don't Change Horses (In the Middle of a Stream)." Both albums feature Williams on vocals.

what to avoid: *Ain't Nothin' Stoppin' Us Now* (Columbia, 1976, prod. Emilio Castillo and TOP) has dated production along with the annoying vibrato and thin voice of McGee, who oozes insincerity. *Power* (Cypress/A&M, 1987, prod. Emilio Castillo and Ellis Hall) fails not only because Ellis Hall is a forced, unsoulful singer, but also because there's too much unidiomatic synthesizer and formulaic arranging.

the rest: *East Bay Grease* (San Francisco/Atlantic, 1971) *Bump City* (Warner Bros., 1972) *In the Slot* (Warner Bros., 1975) *Live in Living Color* (Warner Bros., 1976) *We Came to Play!* (Columbia, 1978) *Back on the Streets* (Columbia, 1979) *Direct* (Sheffield Lab, 1981) *Monster on a Leash* (Epic, 1991) *T.O.P.* (Epic, 1993) *Souled Out* (Epic, 1995)

worth searching for: Huey Lewis & the News' albums *Picture This* (Chrysalis, 1982) and *Fore!* (Chrysalis, 1986) testify to the supple versatility of the TOP horns as the shift gears into a pop format.

▶▶ Cameo, Uptown Horns, Incognito, Weapon of Choice

◀◀ Stan Kenton, James Brown, Sam & Dave, Otis Redding, Sly & the Family Stone

Steve Holtje

Pete Townshend

Born Peter Dennis Blandford Townshend, May 19, 1945 in London, England

One of rock's premiere architects, and one of its major theoreticians—on his own and as the leader of the Who—Townshend's solo career has often suggested he's too smart for his own good. On his own, his material is often the equal of his Who songs but are increasingly bogged down in conceptual trappings that need further fleshing out. Townshend, of course, is the one who penned the now-infamous line "Hope I die before I get old," and his albums often address his ever-changing feelings on the relationship between rock and maturity. Some of the songs on *Empty Glass* in particular bespeak something of a mid-life crisis, and his most recent conceptual piece, *Psychoderelict,* concerns the tribulations of a washed-up rock star; it hits a little too close to home for comfort. On *Empty Glass*, Townshend proved he could respond when he feels he's been challenged as a spokesman for rock and roll, but most often, his solo work is at its best when he simply relaxes and delves into what truly interests him. Still, Townshend's ambitions have always been outsized, so much so that in recent years rock 'n' roll by itself couldn't contain them. He has also published "Horse's Neck," a book of short fiction, worked as a editor at the London publishing house Faber and Faber, and helped turn the Who's rock opera *Tommy* into a Tony-winning Broadway hit. His interest in the album as the proper format for his work seems to have waned, but he remains an artist that nearly everyone in rock and roll has either emulated him and rejected him, or rejected and then emulated.

what to buy: *Rough Mix* (with Ronnie Lane) (MCA, 1977/Atco, 1983, prod. Glyn Johns) is the model of what a solo album from a member of a superstar act should be. The atmosphere is easy and assured, the host and his guests (in this case, the Faces' Ronnie Lane, Rolling Stone Charlie Watts and Eric Clapton) step out of their familiar roles, and the songs are great. *Empty Glass,* (Atco, 1980, prod. Chris Thomas) on the other hand, is quite in the opposite direction. An attempt to reconcile with the punks that abhorred him, the roaring, homoerotic "Rough Boys" finds Townshend leaping into the breach with abandon. Similarly, "Jules and Jim" angrily answers his critics. The hit single "Let My Love Open the Door" and "A Little Is Enough" return to more familiar territory, but they would have made terrific Who songs. *The Best of Pete Townshend: Coolwalkingsmoothtalkingstraightsmokingfirestoking* (Atlantic, 1996, prod. Various) provides a useful thumbnail sketch of Townshend's solo career, but performs a real service in gathering up songs such as "Slit Skirts," "English Boy" and "Face the Face" from Townshend's less listenable albums.

what to buy next: *Who Came First* (Decca, 1972/Rykodisc, 1993, prod. Pete Townshend) is not the star trip you'd imagine from the guitarist and theoretician from (at the time) the world's biggest band. It's a collection of odds and sods (sorry) in which Townshend occasionally turns lead vocals over to Ronnie Lane and Billy Nichols, sets other people's poems to music and even performs his guru's favorite Jim Reeves tune. The highlights are "Pure & Easy" and "Let's See Action" from the Who's abandoned "Lifehouse" project. The Rykodisc reissue offers six bonus tracks. Who obsessives will likely want both *Scoop* (Atco, 1983, prod. Spike) and *Another Scoop,* (Atco, 1987, prod. Pete Townshend and Spike) which comprise many of Townshend's demos and early song sketches for an intriguing glimpse into the creative process.

what to avoid: Despite the presences of good songs such as "Slit Skirts" and "Stardom in Action," most of *All the Best Cowboys Have Chinese Eyes* (Atco, 1982, prod. Chris Thomas) is simply impenetrable.

the rest: *White City—A Novel* (Atco, 1985) *Pete Townshend's Deep End Live!* (Atco, 1986) *The Iron Man* (Atco, 1989) *Psychoderelict* (Atlantic, 1993) WOOF! *Psychoderelict: Music Only* (Atlantic, 1993)

worth searching for: For fans with deep pockets and great contacts, look for the limited-edition, privately issued albums *Happy Birthday* (1970) and *I Am* (1971). Both are tributes to Townshend's guru, Meher Baba, and contain some tracks eventually used on *Who Came First*

U2, Paul Weller, Kurt Cobain, Eddie Vedder

Sonny Boy Williamson, Meher Baba, the Rolling Stones, Stephen Sondheim

Daniel Durchholz

Traffic

Formed 1967 in Berkshire, England. Disbanded 1974. Re-formed 1994.

Steve Winwood, vocals, guitar, keyboards; Jim Capaldi, drums, vocals; Chris Wood, reeds (died July 12, 1983); Dave Mason, guitar, vocals (1967-68, 1971); Rick Grech, bass (1970-71); Jim Gordon, drums (1971); Reebop Kwaku Baah, percussion (1971-73); Roger Hawkins, drums (1971-73); David Hood, bass (1971-73); Rosco Gee, bass (1973-74, 1994)

Winwood was already famous as Little Stevie Winwood, the child prodigy of "Gimme Some Lovin'," before he left the Spencer Davis Group in search of something more mature and foreward looking. He, Capaldi, Wood and Mason retired to a rural cottage to craft the Traffic sound, a blend of rock, psychedelia, blues, r&b and folk that was wholly unique for the time but also completely in step with the adventurous spirit of the times. The group enjoyed instant radio success with "Paper Sun," but it was the winding, textured "Dear Mr. Fantasy" and "Heaven Is in Your Mind" that were harbingers of things to come as Traffic explored different arranging and instrumental sensibilities. It was a volatile outfit, changing membership and even taking a mid-term hiatus—during which Winwood played in the supergroup Blind Faith—before recording the masterful *John Barleycorn Must Die*. Ultimately, Traffic assembled a broad musical palette from which other bands would draw inspiration for decades to follow. The recent reunion of Winwood and Capaldi didn't produce any new music of note, but it was good to hear them play "40,000 Headmen," "Feelin' Alright" and "Low Spark of High-Heeled Boys" again.

what to buy: *John Barleycorn Must Die* (United Artists, 1970/Island, 1987, prod. Steve Winwood and Chris Blackwell) is an exceptionally cohesive piece, tapping into the acoustic vibe of the time but still offering plenty of bite in "Freedom Rider," "Glad" and the wonderful "Empty Pages." The excellent retrospective *Smiling Phases* (Island, 1991, prod. Various) contains every crucial track and serves as the best guide for subsequent album purchases.

what to buy next: The epic title track alone makes *The Low Spark of High-Heeled Boys* (United Artists, 1971/Island, 1987, prod. Steve Winwood) worthwhile, but it's just one of several aces as Traffic sets out on a new, more expansive musical path.

what to avoid: *Welcome to the Canteen* (United Artists, 1971/Island, 1988, prod. Jimmy Miller) is a tepid live album that contains a particularly vapid version of "Gimme Some Lovin'."

the rest: *Mr. Fantasy* (United Artists, 1968/Island, 1987) *Traffic* (United Artists, 1968/Island, 1987) *Last Exit* (United Artists, 1969/Island, 1988) *Shoot Out at the Fantasy Factory* (United Artists, 1973/Island, 1988) *Traffic on the Road* (United Artists, 1973/Island, 1988) *When the Eagle Flies* (Asylum, 1974) *Far From Home* (Virgin, 1994)

worth searching for: *The Perfumed Garden,* (Gold Standard, 1994) a bootleg of early BBC performances in exceptionally strong sound quality.

▶▶ Steely Dan, Fleetwood Mac, the Grateful Dead, Toad the Wet Sprocket, the Tragically Hip

◀◀ Ray Charles, the Spencer Davis Group, the Beatles, Procol Harum, the Zombies, Fairport Convention

see also: *Steve Winwood, the Spencer Davis Group, Blind Faith*

Gary Graff

The Tragically Hip

Formed 1986 in Kingston, Ontario, Canada

Gordon Downie, vocals; Paul Langlois, guitar; Bobby Baker, guitar; Gord Sinclair, bass; Johnny Fay, drums

The members of the Tragically Hip were high school friends prior to forming the band in 1986. Since the beginning, the Hip has been a Canadian favorite, filling arenas and regularly earning its country's gold and platinum awards; it's only gotten more popular as its sound has evolved from bluesy, guitar-driven rock to more textured and ambient—but equally energetic fare. No matter the direction, singer Downie's yearning, experessive vocals are the band's calling chard, a distinctive characteristic that gives the Hip an identity in much the same way Bono and Michael Stipe help define U2 and R.E.M., respectively. The U.S. pop audience has yet to really embrace the Hip, but in this case, it's their loss.

what to buy: *Road Apples* (MCA, 1991, prod. Don Smith) is the Hip's finest release to date, a stirring collection of straightforward, blues-inspired rock exemplified by "Little Bones," "The Luxury" and "Three Pistols." It's predecessor, *Up to Here*, (MCA, 1989, prod. Don Smith) is another strong and straight-ahead work, housing such favorites as "Blow at High Dough" and "New Orleans Is Sinking."

what to buy next: *Fully Completely* (MCA, 1993, prod. Chris Tsangarides) follows the Hip as it moves forward, striving for and achieving a more intimate recording than its predecessors, with more varied musical approaches—from the edgy rock of "Courage" to the gentle acoustic feel of "Wheat Kings"—to Downie's masterful stream of consciousness lyrics on songs such as "Fifty Mission Cap."

the rest: *The Tragically Hip* (MCA, 1987) *Day For Night* (MCA, 1994, prod. Mark Howard and The Tragically Hip with Mark Vreeken) *Trouble at the Hen House* (Atlantic, 1996, prod. The Tragically Hip and Mark Vreeken)

▶▶ Live, Our Lady Peace

◀◀ Neil Young, Joni Mitchell, Gordon Lightfoot, the Rolling Stones, the Yardbirds, The Band

Kim Forster

Translator

Formed 1979 in Los Angeles, Calif. Disbanded 1986.

Steve Barton, vocals, guitar; Robert Darlington, vocals, guitar; Larry Decker, bass; David Scheff, drums

This is one of the best guitar pop bands nobody heard during the 80s. Although the band never had a hit or made much of a ripple outside the Bay Area in its time, it has been the subject of numerous anthologies, which may be evidence enough of the music's durability. What keeps resurfacing is the before-its-time alternative jangle and tuneful pop smarts held aloft by sharp emotional insistence. Translator's most striking song—"Everywhere That I'm Not," written the day after John Lennon's assassination—is a riveting lament that certainly beats the pants off Elton John's "Empty Garden" gurglings. *Everywhere That We Were: The Best of Translator* (Columbia/Legacy, 1996, prod. Various) 𝅘𝅥𝅘𝅥𝅘𝅥𝅘𝅥 rounds up 17 memorable tracks, including the band's signature song as well as "Oh Lazurus" and "Everywhere"; both boast similarly strong melody lines and are nearly as gripping. *Translation* (Oglio Records, 1995, prod. Various) 𝅘𝅥𝅘𝅥𝅘𝅥𝅗𝅥 is docked a half bone for having slightly fewer tunes and less extensive liner notes, but it does have a number of tracks not included on the Columbia compilation.

Allan Orski

The Traveling Wilburys

Bob Dylan, vocals, guitar; George Harrison, vocals, guitar; Roy Orbison, vocals, guitar (died Dec. 6, 1988); Tom Petty, vocals, guitar, bass; Jeff Lynne, vocals, guitar, bass, keyboards; Jim Keltner, drums

Checking their egos at the door, the superstar lineup of the Wilburys surprised everyone with the status-shedding of their debut. Reveling in the "anonymity" of adopted surnames (Otis Wilbury, Nelson Wilbury, etc.), each member turns in stronger performances here than in some of their solo fare. Orbison is unearthly, Petty is jocular and Dylan whips out the most playful lyrics he's penned in years. *Traveling Wilburys Vol. 1* (Warner Bros., 1988, prod. Otis and Lucky Wilbury) 𝅘𝅥𝅘𝅥𝅘𝅥𝅗𝅥 is a welcome delight. *Traveling Wilburys Vol. 3* (Warner Bros., 1990, prod. Spike and Clayton Wilbury) 𝅘𝅥𝅘𝅥 is like eating too much dessert—tasty at first, but you'll feel bloated and woozy later. Orbison's sudden death after the first album certainly dampened the proceedings, and the remaining members summon up none of the off-the-cuff looseness that made *Vol. 1* so charming. The dour set is redeemed only by Dylan's singing, his most free since *Slow Train Coming* in 1979. Meanwhile, rumors persist about another Wilburys project in the future.

Allan Orski

Ralph Tresvant

See: New Edition

Trip Shakespeare

Disbanded 1991

Elaine Harris, drums; John Munson, bass, vocals; Dan Wilson, guitar, piano, vocals; Matt Wilson, guitar, piano, vocals

More people have probably heard Trip Shakespeare's backing vocals on Matthew Sweet's *Earth* than have heard the group's own albums. Matt Wilson's quirky, often whimsical songs are built on 70s psychedelia in an energetic, pop-minded way. Originally a trio, Trip Shakespeare was augmented by Wilson's brother Dan, who enriched the harmonies. Harris gleaned her distinctive drum style from the Velvet Underground's Moe Tucker style; she also distinguished herself by drumming standing, not sitting, behind the kit on a stool. The band broke up when A&M dropped it, releasing an EP of six well-chosen covers as a farewell.

what to buy: *Across the Universe* (A&M, 1990, prod. Fred Maher and Trip Shakespeare) 𝅘𝅥𝅘𝅥𝅘𝅥𝅘𝅥𝅗𝅥 gained considerable polish from having a major-label recording budget but without losing its eccentricities. The result sounds like Jefferson Airplane played by a jangly new wave guitar-pop band. The sophomore album *Are You Shakespearienced* (Clean, 1989, prod. Trip Shakespeare) 𝅘𝅥𝅘𝅥𝅘𝅥𝅘𝅥 has some of Matt Wilson's best songs, including "Two Wheeler, Four Wheeler," with sparer production.

the rest: *Applehead Man* (Clean, 1988) 𝅘𝅥𝅘𝅥𝅗𝅥 *Lulu* (A&M, 1991) 𝅘𝅥𝅘𝅥𝅘𝅥𝅗𝅥 *Volt* (Black Hole/Clean, 1992) 𝅘𝅥𝅘𝅥𝅘𝅥 *The Crane* (A&M EP, 1990) 𝅘𝅥𝅘𝅥𝅘𝅥

Steve Holtje

The Troggs

Formed 1965 in Andover, England

Reg Presley, vocals; Chris Britton, lead guitar; Peter Staples, bass (1965-69); Ronnie Bond, drums (1965-92); Tony Murray, bass (1972-76); Colin Fletcher, guitar; Peter Lucas, bass (1976-present); Dave Maggs, drums (1976-present)

The Troggs stood out from most of the British Invasion bands with its total lack of pretension; the group made a crude thumping so devoid of art that it's not unreasonable to view the band as an embryonic forerunner to the late 70s punk explosion. Its classic "Wild Thing"—perhaps the fundamental non-singin', garage-rockin' anthem of the '60s—shot the group to rock 'n' roll immortality. Although its commercial success was brief, the Troggs have soldiered on through the decades and remain a popular attraction in England, though in 1992 it recorded *Athens Andover* with members of R.E.M. *Archeology* (Fontana/Chronicles, 1992, prod. Various) gives the band its due with 52 tracks comprising the lewd, crude anthems as well as the group's excursions into hard pop and flowery ballads. Obscurities and B-sides are thrown in as well, making this their definitive statement.

the rest: *Live at Max's Kansas City* (Griffin, date N/A) *Athens Andover* (Rhino, 1992) *Best of the Troggs* (Fontana, 1994)

Allan Orski

Robin Trower

Born March 9, 1945 in London, England

Procol Harum may be remembered mostly for its ruminative chamber pop, but within the band seethed the roiling guitar ambitions of longtime blues devotee Trower. Hooked by Jimi Hendrix' sonic pyrotechnics, Trower began to assert himself more in the band—check out "Whiskey Train" on Procol's *Home* — and finally decided to step out on his own after 1971's *Broken Barricades*. On his own, Trower first specialized in distorted electric blues that came so close to the Hendrix model—right down to bassist Jimmy Dewar's husky vocals—that it was at once skillful and derivative. Ultimately, when the songs were good ("Day of the Eagle," "Too Rolling Stoned," "Alethea"), the skill won out. There's been a journeyman nature to much of Trower's solo career, including a brief early 80s collaboration with Cream's Jack Bruce and participation in the 1991 Procol Harum reunion. These days you're most likely to find Trower doing session work (most notably for Bryan Ferry) and playing the blues, hewing a bit closer to the original root but never leaving those lightning-fast Hendrix riffs too far behind.

what to buy: *Bridge of Sighs* (Chrysalis, 1974/1985, prod. Matthew Fisher) is the epochal Trower album, with his best batch of songs ("Day of the Eagle," "Too Rolling Stoned," "Lady Love," the title track) and empathetic backing from Dewar and drummer Reggie Isadore. *BBC Radio 1 Live in Concert* (Griffin, 1995, prod. Jeff Griffin) and *The King Biscuit Flower Hour Presents Robin Trower* (King Biscuit, 1996) are solid concert documents—the latter with some funkier touches—on which Trower stretches out into longer, even more Hendrixian solos.

what to buy next: *Essential Robin Trower* (Chrysalis, 1991, prod. Various) is a good sampling of his first eight albums, though the absence of "Day of the Eagle" really weakens the set.

what to avoid: *Passion*, (GNP/Crescendo, 1987, prod. Neil Norman) a transitional album that is often just the opposite of its title.

the rest: *Truce* (with Jack Bruce) (Chrysalis, 1982/One Way, 1981) *No Stopping Anytime* (with Bruce) (Chrysalis, 1989/Rodolphe Opera Viva, 1989) *20th Century Blues* (V12, 1994)

worth searching for: *The Robin Trower Portfolio*, (Chrysalis, 1987) a British import anthology that bests its U.S. counterpart, though the CD version lopped off the live tracks that were part of the original double-LP.

Steve Vai, Joe Satriani, Eric Johnson, Vernon Reid

Jimi Hendrix, Jimmy Page, Robert Johnson

see also: *Procol Harum*

Gary Graff

Tsunami

Formed 1990 in Arlington, Va.

Jenny Toomey, vocals, guitars; Kristin Thomson, guitars, vocals; Andrew Webster, bass, vocals; John Palmer, drums

One of the major leaders in the indie rock movement, Tsunami has worked with practically every respected band in the scene: Superchunk, Velocity Girl, Jawbox, Seaweed and, of course, spiritual leader Fugazi. In true indie spirit, Toomey and Thomson not only lead the band but run their own record label and produce all of their label-mates' albums. In her spare time, Toomey shows up in a number of other bands, including Liquorice and Grenadine. Like many indie acts Tsunami began by releasing a tidal wave of seven-inch records and compilation singles before plunging into full-length albums. *Deep End* (Simple Machines, 1992) is Tsunami's first full-length album, a danceable disc that showcases the group's ability to create an instantly catchy tune while still remaining musically complex. *The Heart's Tremolo* (Simple Machines, 1994, prod. Brian Paulson) boasts even more complex and lyrically intriguing songs, combined with a darker mood. *World Tour and Other Destinations* (Simple Machines, 1995) puts together the huge collection of Tsunami's singles and seven-inch recordings onto one convenient album, providing a musical time line that displays not only Tsunami's musical range but also the steady maturation of an excellent band.

Bryan Lassner

The Tubes

Formed 1972 in San Francisco, Calif. Disbanded 1988. Re-formed 1993.

Fee Waybill, vocals; Bill Spooner, guitar (1972-88); Roger Steen, guitar; Vince Welnick, keyboards (1972-88); Michael Cotten, keyboards (1972-88); Prairie Prince, drums; Rick Anderson, bass; Re Styles, vocals (1972-88); Gary Cambra, keyboards (1993-present); Jennifer McFee, vocals (1993-present); Amy French, vocals (1993-present)

From the mid-70s through the early 80s, the Tubes peddled an elaborate live show that gave the group's proto-metal lumberings a theatrical infamy. As its albums whiffed one right after the other, the band chiseled off the satirical excess for MTV, recording a series of radio friendly pop-rockers during the early 80s ("Talk to Ya Later," "She's a Beauty") that achieved their goal. But the success was short-lived, and the group faded away, though it still pops up for occasional appearances of frontman Waybill's alter ego Quay Lewd.

what to buy: *The Best of the Tubes* (Capitol/EMI Records, 1992, prod. Various) covers most of the Tubes' music you'll need to hear, including the undeniably catchy mainstream pop breakthroughs as well as a plundering of Curtis Mayfield's "The Monkey Time" which probably had oodles of old-school soul men flipping in their graves.

what to buy next: The band's debut, *The Tubes,* (A&M Records, 1975, prod. Al Kooper) contains the mocking metal anti-anthem "White Punks on Dope" and the lesser known (but gleefully crude) "Mondo Bondage."

what to avoid: On *Remote Control,* (A&M, 1979/1988, prod. Todd Rundgren) even Rundgren's skills couldn't redeem the melodic monotony.

the rest: *Best of the Tubes* (CEMA Special Products, 1992)

worth searching for: *What Do You Want From Live?* (A&M, 1978, prod. Peter Henderson and Rikki Farr) documents the group's stage antics, many of which are lost in an audio-only format. *Outside/Inside* (Capitol, 1983, prod. David Foster and the Tubes) is the most listenable studio album, with "She's a Beauty," "The Monkey Time" and "Out of the Business."

Meat Loaf, Pet Shop Boys

 New York Dolls, Kiss, Frank Zappa

Allan Orski

Maureen Tucker

See: Velvet Underground

Marshall Tucker Band

Formed 1971 in Spartanburg, S.C.

Toy Caldwell, guitar, vocals (1971-83, died Feb. 23, 1994); Doug Gray, vocals; George McCorkle, guitar (1971-83); Paul Riddle, drums (1971-83); Jerry Eubanks, reeds, keyboards, vocals; Tommy Caldwell, bass, vocals (1971-80, died April 28, 1980); Frank Wilkie, bass (1980-83); Rusty Milner, guitar (1983-present); Tim Lawter, bass (1983-present)

Marshall Tucker is a unique entity in Southern rock; the group could boogie with the rest of them, but it also had a jazzier sensibility that gave Gray's flutes and saxophones a birth along side the dueling guitars. The group was also a little more Southern, with a bit more twang in its sound than compatriots such as the Allman Brothers Band and Lynyrd Skynyrd; Waylon Jennings was even able to turn MTB's first hit, "Can't You See," into a country hit for himself in 1976. The group's heyday came during the mid-70s; it was never the same after the 1983 schism that took three of the original members—including the indispensible Toy Caldwell—out of the picture. You'll still find Marshall Tucker trucking itself out on the road, though, stretching hits such as "24 Hours at a Time" to just about that length.

what to buy: With a series of generally interchangeable albums, it's the comprehensive *The Best of the Marshall Tucker Band: The Capricorn Years* (Era, 1995, prod. Various) that gives the band its due, though it chooses the occasional life track over the preferable studio version.

what to buy next: Though the biggest hits are on other albums, *Searchin' for a Rainbow* (Capricorn/AJK, 1975, prod. Paul Hornsby) is the group's most consistent outing.

what to avoid: The criminally skimpy *Greatest Hits* (Capricorn, 1978/AJK, 1989, prod. Paul Hornsby) offers just eight selections from the group's 1972-77 heyday.

the rest: *The Marshall Tucker Band* (Capricorn, 1973/AJK, 1988) *A New Life* (Capricorn, 1974/AJK, 1988) *Where We All Belong* (Capricorn, 1974/AJK, 1988) *Long, Hard Ride* (Capricorn, 1976/AJK, 1988) *Carolina Dreams* (Capricorn,

1977/AJK, 1988) *Southern Spirit* (Cabin Fever, 1990) *Still Smokin'* (Cabin Fever, 1992) *Walk Outside the Lines* (Cabin Fever, 1993)

worth searching for: The out-of-print *Dedicated* (Warner Bros., 1981) finds the band, deeply moved by Tommy Caldwell's death, delving deeper into the country side of its sound.

Sea Level, Atlanta Rhythm Section, Black Crowes

Allman Brothers Band, Waylon Jennings, Johnny Cash, the Grateful Dead

Gary Graff

Big Joe Turner

Born Joe Vernon Turner on May 18, 1911, in Kansas City, Mo.; Died Nov. 24, 1985, in Los Angeles, Calif.

When Atlantic Records signed Turner in 1952, he was the first top artist to be associated with the fledgling R&B company. The Atlantic partners knew Turner well from the minor boogie-woogie craze the barrel-chested vocalist stirred in New York during the early 40s with pianist Pete Johnson. In fact, Turner was probably deemed past his commercial prime at the time, although he went on to make his greatest records with Atlantic during the 50s. Turner was the last bastion of the Kansas City school of blues shouting, a relaxed, easy moaning style, swung with a voice that sounded like it came from the bottom of a well. He was an unlikely teenage rock 'n' roll star, but after Bill Haley transformed Turner's "Shake, Rattle and Roll" into a rock evergreen—recorded subsequently by everyone from Elvis Presley to Huey Lewis and the News—Turner himself followed Haley into the Top 40 with "Corinna Corrina" in 1956. At the same time, Atlantic showed good taste by reteaming Turner and pianist Johnson for an album, *The Boss of the Blues*, now recognized as a classic.

what to buy: It took a three-disc retrospective to encompass the breadth of Turner's almost 50 years of recording. *Big, Bad & Blue: The Big Joe Turner Anthology* (Rhino, 1994, prod. Various) runs from his 1939 sessions with pianist Johnson through a 1983 date with jump band revivalists Roomful of Blues.

what to buy next: While he was touring on package rock 'n' roll tours with the teen heartthrobs of the day, Turner took time to recreate the classic Kansas City jazz sound of his youth on *The Boss of the Blues*, (Atlantic, 1956, prod. Neshui Ertegun and Jerry Wexler) an utterly magnificent chapter in American music.

what to avoid: Turner recorded extensively in the 80s, often with indifferent results, and was not at his best in the informal, jazz-like settings he received on *Stormy Monday* (Pablo, 1976)

the rest: *I've Been to Kansas City* (Decca, 1990) *Every Day in the Week* (Decca, 1993) *Tell Me Pretty Baby* (Arhoolie, 1992) *Jumpin' with Joe: The Complete Aladdin & Imperial Recordings* (EMI, 1993) *Rhythm and Blues Years* (Atlantic, 1988) *Big Joe Rides Again* (Atlantic, 1959)

worth searching for: The rollicking backdrop provided by relative youngsters Roomful of Blues made *Blues Train* (Muse, 1983, prod. Doc Pomus and Bob Porter) one of the most satisfying Turner outings since he left Atlantic 20 years earlier.

James Brown, Chuck Berry, Little Richard, Mick Jagger, Otis Redding, Sam and Dave, Bruce Springsteen

Jimmy Rushing

Joel Selvin

Ike and Tina Turner

Ike Turner (born Izear Luster Turner, Nov. 5, 1931, in Clarksdale, Miss.); Tina Turner (born Annie Mae Bullock, Nov. 26, 1938, in Nutbush, Tenn.)

Considering the dramatic saga behind Tina Turner's escape from an abusive relationship with husband Ike, it's not surprising that the duo's role as seminal rock 'n' roll pioneers is sometimes obscured. Ike first came to prominence as leader of the Kings of Rhythm, a group that recorded "Rocket 88"—a tune widely cited as the first rock 'n' roll tune—in 1951 at Sun Studios. Taking the Kings of Rhythm on the club circuit, Ike met Tina at an East St. Louis, Ill. club and eventually she convinced him to let her sing with the band. In 1956, she became a sometimes member, moving into full-time and eventually marrying Ike. When a singer failed to show for a session in 1960, Tina sang lead vocals on the band's first hit, "A Fool in Love." Ike decided to focus the show on Tina after that, hiring a trio of backing singers and creating the Ike and Tina Turner Revue, a roaring R&B act that delivered killer covers of rock tunes such as "Proud Mary" and "Come Together." The Rolling Stones invited the Turner Revue to open its 1969 North American tour, while Phil Spector wooed Tina for her first solo hit, "River Deep, Mountain High." But the beatings Tina received from Ike and his escalating drug use eventually prompted her to leave him in 1976, sneaking away with just 36 cents in her pocket. Although Tina's comeback was rocky at first, her friendship with members of British synth-popsters Heaven 17 led to a cover of Al Green's "Let's Stay Together" that launched her new solo career. With help from other friends—Bryan Adams, Eric Clapton, Robert Cray, David Bowie—Tina Turner's star rose higher than ever during the 80s, as she released hit after hit and became an MTV staple. Her autobiography, "I, Tina," detailed her years with Ike and was the main source for the feature film "What's Love Got to Do With It." Meanwhile, Ike's continuing drug problems led to a short prison stay, damaging his already-ugly reputation further.

what to buy: For an accurate take on the arc of this amazing duo's career, the greatest-hits collection *Proud Mary: The Best of Ike and Tina Turner* (EMI International, 1991, prod. Various) pulls together seminal cuts such as "A Fool in Love" and Tina's rendition of "The Acid Queen" for the Who's film versions of "Tommy." Fortified by impressive liner notes, this collection is a must for any fan seeking a full history. On her own, Tina's best outing remains her solo debut, *Private Dancer,* (Capitol, 1984, prod. Various) which bounds effortlessly from the midtempo hit "What's Love Got to Do With It?" to the Mark Knopfler-penned title track and the rocking "Better Be Good to Me."

what to buy next: As their most successful album, Ike and Tina's *Workin' Together* (Liberty, 1970, prod. Ike Turner) contains their breakthrough hit "Proud Mary," along with tasty nuggets of the group's R&B/early rock sound—including a masterful cover of "Ooh Poo Pah Doo." For the soundtrack to the "What's Love Got to Do With It" film, (Virgin/EMI, 1993, prod. Various) Tina re-records some of the classic Ike and Tina cuts with a better band and better production. Although some later hits are here, updated versions of tunes such as "A Fool in Love," "Nutbush City Limits" and "Rock Me Baby" are the real reason to get this one.

what to avoid: Marrying Tina's earthy, powerful vocals with producer Phil Spector's wall of sound proved a deadly, misguided combination, sinking half the material on *River Deep, Mountain High.* (A&M, 1969, prod. Phil Spector and Ike Turner) It's no wonder that, when the record failed to do well in the U.S., Spector went into a three-year seclusion. On her own, Tina loses more of her distinctive soul flair and rock energy with every record, sublimating those distinctive qualities in favor of a generic pop appeal. Small wonder that her last proper solo record, *Foreign Affair,* (Capitol, 1989, prod. Tina Turner and Dan Hartman) WOOF! proves the worst—just a bunch of generic pop tunes linked solely by Tina's vocals.

the rest: *Ike and Tina Turner—Live! The Ike and Tina Turner Show* (Warner Bros., 1965) *Outta Season* (Blue Thumb, 1969) *In Person* (Minit, 1969) *The Hunter* (Blue Thumb, 1969) *Come Together* (Liberty, 1970) *Live at Carnegie Hall/What You Hear Is What You Get* (United Artists, 1971) *Nuff Said* (United Artists, 1971) *Feel Good* (United Artists, 1972) *Nutbush City Limits* (United Artists, 1973) *Very Best Of* (United Artists, 1976) *Delilah's Power* (United Artists, 1977) *Get Back* (United Artists, 1985). Tina Turner: *Break Every Rule* (Capitol, 1986) *Tina Live in Europe* (Capitol, 1988) *Simply the Best* (Capitol, 1991) *Collected Recordings: 60s to 90s* (Capitol, 1994) Ike Turner: *Blues Roots* (United Artists, 1972); *I'm Tore Up* (Red Lightning, 1978) *I Like Ike! The Best of Ike Turner* (Rhino, 1994).

worth searching for: "I, Tina," Tina's spellbinding autobiography, is a must-read. And she narrates the book-on-tape version herself.

▶▶ Nona Hendryx, Chaka Khan, Donna Summer

◀◀ Bessie Smith, Big Mama Thornton

Eric Deggans

The Turtles /Flo & Eddie

Formed 1963, Inglewood, Calif. Disbanded 1970.

Mark Volman, vocals, guitar, saxophone; Howard Kaylan, vocals; Al Nichol, guitar; Chuck Portz, bass; Donald Ray Murray, drums; Chip Douglas, Jim Pons, bass; John Seiter, John Barbata, drums

What ultimately prevented this extremely talented band from receiving the success and recognition it so richly deserved, and fought its entire career to obtain, was a basic confusion amongst the band's record company, its audiences worldwide and the band-members themselves. Were the Turtles merely a happy-go-lucky, witless pop group capable of producing Top 10 hits at the drop of a hat and innocuous enough to procure an invitation to entertain at the Nixon White House? Or was it a seriously visionary group of musicians dedicated to pushing the frontiers of mid-60s rock as far out there as possible? (One listen to tracks such as "Sound Asleep" and "Grim Reaper of Love" prove they had few equals in the recording studio at the time). Well, it tried to be both — this musical schizophrenia best illustrated on its classic *Battle of the Bands* album, where in 12 songs it skillfully adopted the stylistically dissimilar personas of *12* different "Turtles"— but after nine Top 40 hits in less than four years, the Turtles just couldn't shake the teenybop tag. To this day, "Happy Together," "She'd Rather Be With

Me" and "Elenore" remain staples of oldies radio, and whenever group leaders Volman and Kaylan step on stage—whether with their latest batch of Turtles or under the guise of their acid-fractured alter-egos Flo & Eddie—it's the hits, and nothing but the hits, everyone's come to hear. But what the group may be lacking in respect, it continues to more than make up for with buckets full of happy, self-deflationary, rockin' good fun. Should we ever ask for more?

what to buy: The *20 Greatest Hits* (Rhino, 1984, prod. Various) contains all the hits and some of the misses, though with music as varied as the Turtles', the misses often reign supreme. The aforementioned *Battle of the Bands,* (White Whale, 1968/Sundazed, 1995, prod. Chip Douglas and the Turtles) with tracks such as "I'm Chief Kamanawanalea (We're The Royal Macadamia Nuts)" practically beats *Sgt. Pepper's* at its own game.

what to buy next: The Crossfires' *Out of Control* (Sundazed, 1995, comp. Mark Volman and Howard Kaylan) is actually the pre-Turtles in a surf-rockin' incarnation, though even this early on, the insanity was rearing its head ("Santa and the Sidewalk Surfer"). And for those who just *can't* stop, the five (!) disc *30 Years of Rock 'n' Roll,* (Laserlight, 1994, prod. Various) lovingly compiled and annotated by Volman and Kaylan themselves, proves that if the Beach Boys and Byrds merit the box-set treatment, then surely do The Turtles!

the rest: *Turtle Wax* (Rhino, 1988) *Captured Live* (Rhino, 1992) *Best of* (Rhino, 1995) *Love Songs* (Rhino, 1995) *It Ain't Me Babe* (White Whale, 1965; Sundazed, 1995) *You Baby* (White Whale, 1966/Sundazed, 1995) *Happy Together* (White Whale, 1967/Sundazed, 1995)

worth searching for: *Turtle Soup* (White Whale, 1969, prod. Ray Davies) was the band's last original release, and a rare outside production job for the head Kink.

▶▶ Cheap Trick, Barnes & Barnes, the Evaporators

◀◀ The Mothers of Invention, Stan Freberg, The Four Preps

Gary Pig Gold

Tommy Tutone

Tommy Heath, vocals; Jim Keller, guitar

This duo first surfaced with "Angel Say No" in 1980, but it was 1981's indelible "867-5309/Jenny" that earned Heath and Keller their footnote in pop history, at the same time spawning innumerable crank calls to the title number. The obsessive ditty opens with a guy so immobilized with passion for a girl whose name and number he got off a wall—a girl he's never met, mind you—that he can only sit by the phone in torment. What happens next is anybody's guess, but it probably involves stalking. As the group's albums are deleted, the best compilation to find it is on *Just Can't Get Enough: New Wave Hits of the '80s Vol. 5.* (Rhino, 1994, comp. David McLees and Andrew Sandoval)

Allan Orski

20/20

Formed 1977 in Los Angeles, Calif. Disbanded 1983 Re-formed 1995.

Steve Allen, vocals, guitar; Ron Flynt, vocals, bass, keyboards; Mike Gallo, drums (1977-79); Chris Silagyi, vocals, guitar, synthesizer (1979-81); Joel Turrisi, drums (1979-81); Dean Korth, drums (1982-83); Keith Clark, drums (1983); Bill Belknap, drums (1995-present)

Neither hitmaker nor massive seller, 20/20 is a mere footnote in the rock history books. But its legend looms large in the world of power pop, where its first two Beatles-influenced albums should appear on any short list of albums that define the form. Incorporating all the tools on the popcraft workbench—buzzing guitars, three-part harmonies and energy to spare—20/20 was a breath of fresh air during the days of disco. But pop songs were a hard sell during the late 70s and early 80s, and 20/20 called it quits in 1983. When artists such as Matthew Sweet showed the 90s to be much more pop friendly, though, and Ron Flynt and Steve Allen decided to reunite and give 20/20 another shot.

what to buy: 20/20's debut album, *20/20,* (Portrait/Epic, 1979, prod. Earle Mankey) is practically a power pop primer. Tracks such as "Yellow Pills," "Remember The Lightning" and "Jet Lag" stand among the best of the era. Its successor, *Look Out,* (Portrait/CBS, 1981, prod. Richard Podolor) while not as drop-dead great as the first, features some of 20/20's strongest songs: "Nuclear Boy," one of the great lost singles of the early 80s, and the simply perfect "The Night I Heard a Scream." Both titles have been re-issued on a single CD *20/20, Look Out!* (Oglio, 1995)

what to buy next: Time off seems to have mellowed 20/20 on its latest, *4 Day Tornado,* (Oglio, 1995, prod. 20/20) but the album proves this trio still has the basic stuff that earned 20/20 its reputation.

what to avoid: After *Look Out,* 20/20 released an independent album called *Sex Trap,* which was a significant let-down from the first two albums. The songs are stripped down to shells and sound more like a collection of luke-warm demos.

What Album Changed Your Life?

I was living with some bluegrass musicians at the time, in Santa Cruz. One of the guys put this record on while he was cooking Sunday breakfast. I was in the bathroom, cleaning up the bathtub, real Sunday morning stuff. I heard the first tune on the first side, "Dream of the Miner's Child," and this tune came on and I don't know what happened, but it went straight to my blood. I know I'd heard Bill Monroe before that, but for whatever reason, I was fully primed and ready to absorb the stuff. My main reaction was 'Oh! This is the stuff I was meant to play.'"

Gillian Welch

worth searching for: 20/20 contributed a terrific song, "Drive," to the sampler *Waves* (Bomp, 1979)

Adam Schmitt, Tommy Keene, Martin Luther Lennon, Matthew Sweet

The Beatles, the Raspberries, Dwight Twilley Band

Keith Klingensmith

Dwight Twilley /Dwight Twilley Band/Phil Seymour

Formed 1973 in Tulsa, Okla. Disbanded 1973.

Dwight Twilley (born June 6, 1951 in Tulsa, Okla.), guitar, vocals; Phil Seymour, bass, drums, vocals (died Aug. 17, 1993); Roger Lynn, bass, keyboards; Bill Pitron IV, guitar

Twilley was one of the first singer-songwriters to crawl from the disco demolition and arena rock stiffness of the 70s. Twilley and Seymour, his partner in crime, set out to preserve guitar pop in the mid-70s with the now out-of-print album *Sincerely* (1976) and *Twilley Don't Mind* (1977), seminal works that combined Twilley's straightforward, Tom Petty-style rock and Seymour's sweeter pop sensibilities. After the second Twilley Band album, Seymour split and Twilley went on to record three somewhat mediocre solo albums. Each of their work is represented these days by anthologies. Twilley's *XXI* (The Right Stuff, 1996, prod. Various) is a comprehensive anthology of his band and solo work, featuring the cult power pop hits "I'm on Fire," "Looking for the Magic" and the 1982 Top 20 solo hit "Girls" (which features Petty on vocals). The Seymour collection *Precious to Me* (The Right Stuff, 1996, prod. Various) gathers songs from the Twilley Band, his own solo albums as well as the previously unreleased Petty tune "Save Me."

Chris Richards

Twisted Sister

Formed 1973 in Ho-Ho-Kus, N.J.

Dee Snyder, vocals; Jay Jay French (born John Segall), guitar; Mark "The Animal" Mendoza, bass; Eddie Ojeda, guitar; Tony Petri, drums (1973-81); A.J. Pero, drums (1982-86); Joe Franco, drums (1987)

Taking nothing from the New York Dolls except the rouge, Twisted Sister was like a screaming-gasp-of-the-70s bar band, bird-flipping metal mediocrity that capitalized on MTV's willingness to showcase its outrageously obnoxious appearance. Nuclear meltdown makeovers notwithstanding, the band's grade-school mentality masked a lack of true hard-rock aggressiveness; those who questioned such half-baked rock were bitten in the face, which says more than "I Wanna Rock" ever did. *Big Hits and Nasty Cuts: The Best of Twisted Sister* (Atlantic, 1992, prod. Various) chronicles the Alice Cooper-wannabe wall of smeared mascara starting with the early "Shoot 'Em Down" and continuing through the attempted anthems "I Am (I'm Me)" and "You Can't Stop Rock 'n' Roll."

the rest: *You Can't Stop Rock 'n' Roll* (Atlantic, 1983/1990) *Stay Hungry* (Atlantic, 1984) *Live* (CMC, 1994)

Allan Orski

Type O Negative

Formed 1991 in Brooklyn, N.Y.

Peter Steele, vocals, bass; Josh Silver, keyboards; Kenny Hickey, guitar; Sal Abruscato, drums (1991-93); John Kelly, drums (1993-present)

Any death-rock band can sing about despair, ingest blood and taunt religious icons, but how many can do a cover of a Seals and Crofts tune? Type O Negative can; it turned "Summer Breeze" into a haunting horror story. The twisted, talented and unpredictable quartet is led by Steele, a former heavy-equipment operator for the City of New York, a former member of Carnivore and the band's chief songwriter. Type O Negative creates slickly orchestrated gothic metal from the dark side, featuring layered keyboards, slashing guitars and Steele's ominously slow, brooding vocals. The music is embellished with background nuances, including bubbling liquids, heavy breathing and sobbing women. *Bloody Kisses* (Roadrunner, 1993, prod. Peter Steele and Josh Silver) is positively evil but sonically compelling gloom-and-doom metal with actual melodies, intriguingly theatrical arrangements and superb production techniques that include allusions to the Beatles and M.C. Hammer.

the rest: *Slow, Deep, and Hard* (Roadrunner, 1991) *Origin of the Feces* (Roadrunner EP, 1992) **WOOF!** *October Rust* (Roadrunner, 1996) not available for rating

David Yonke

UB40

Formed 1978 in Birmingham, England

Ali Campbell, guitar and vocals; Robin Campbell, lead guitar; Astro, vocals; Earl Falconer, bass; Mickey Virtue, keyboards; Brian Travers, saxophone; James Brown, drums; Norman Hassan, percussion

UB40 widened the audience for reggae by blending the rhythm-heavy, traditional, Caribbean music with a British pop sensibility. Taking its name from the English unemployment form, (something with which the eight band members were quite familiar), UB40 received its first major exposure opening for the Pretenders on that band's first U.S. tour. UB40 rapidly became a college radio favorite, and its 1983 rendition of Neil Diamond's "Red, Red Wine" scored with the masses. Socially conscious on and off record, UB40 was particularly proud to be one of the first Western acts to perform in the Soviet Union. With its lineup remarkably intact, the band enjoys a true worldwide following, taking its typical tours to no less than six continents. One tip: you can find UB40's albums in the reggae rather than the pop sections in more than a few record stores.

what to buy: Sitting squarely in the middle of the discography, the self-titled *UB40* (Virgin, 1988, prod. UB40) finds the band at a career peak with pointed songs such as "Come Out to Play", "Where Did I Go Wrong" and "Breakfast in Bed," a duet with early benefactor Chrissie Hynde of the Pretenders. The band's first album, *Signing Off* (Virgin, 1980/1994, prod. Roy Falconer, Bob Lamb and UB40), features the first U.K. hit, "King" as well as the standouts "Food for Thought" and "Tyler." *Labour of Love* (Virgin, 1983, prod. Roy Falconer and UB40) showcases the band applying its reggae-pop flavoring to 10 covers, including "Red, Red Wine" and "Please Don't Make Me Cry."

what to buy next: Two strong, simultaneously released best-of compilations—*Volume One* (Virgin, 1995, prod. Various) features earlier, edgier work, while *Volume Two* (Virgin, 1995, prod. UB40) features more radio-friendly fare from the near past.

what to avoid: *Little Baggaridm* (A&M EP, 1985, prod. Ray Falconer and UB40), an unsatisfying winnowing of the *Baggaridm* album that went unreleased in the U.S.

the rest: *Present Arms* (Virgin, 1981/1992) *Present Arms in Dub* (A&M, 1981) *Live* (Virgin, 1983) *1980-83* (A&M, 1983) *Geoffrey Morgan* (A&M/Virgin, 1984) *Rat in the Kitchen* (A&M/Virgin, 1986) *CCCP—Live in Moscow* (A&M, 1987) *Labour of Love II* (Virgin, 1989) *Promises and Lies* (Virgin, 1993)

worth searching for: The import *Best of UB40, Volume 1* (Virgin U.K., 1987), a thorough representation of the group's prime period.

solo outings:

Ali Campbell Big Love (Virgin, 1995)

Rancid, Big Mountain, Chrissie Hynde

Bob Marley, Gregory Isaacs, Bim Sherman

Gary Plochinski

Tracey Ullman

Born December 30, 1959 in Slough, Berkshire, England

As a multifaceted actress and comedian, Ullman is known for her ability to take on myriad personalities, nailing each one with a startling degree of nuance and individual quirks. During her brief singing career, Ullman took on the role of a singer in the classic girl-group mold, though most of her material was drawn from more contemporary sources such as Blondie ("(I'm Always Touched By Your) Presence Dear"), Madness ("My Guy") and Reunion ("(Life is a Rock) But the Radio Rolled Me").

Her finest moment on her debut album, *You Broke My Heart in 17 Places* (Stiff/MCA, 1983, prod. Peter Collins) is Kirsty MacColl's chiming "They Don't Know," which became a Top 10 hit in America. A second album, *You Caught Me Out,* (Stiff/MCA, 1984, prod. Peter Collins) failed to gain as much notoriety. Ullman stopped recording after her film and TV career took off, but *The Best of Tracey Ullman* (Rhino, 1992, prod. Peter Collins) compiles the entire first album along with selected tracks from the second, plus a few B-sides.

Daniel Durchholz

James Blood Ulmer

Born Feb. 2, 1942, in St. Matthews, S.C.

Free-funk jazzman Blood Ulmer has one of the most distinctive guitar sounds in music today; his sharp, staccato attack alternates flurries of notes with raw chord tones and distortions. Starting out in 1959, Ulmer was a journeyman when a mid-70s meeting with Ornette Coleman converted him to the harmolodic school of free jazz and subsequent pairings with such players as Arthur Blythe, Ronald Shannon Jackson and David Murray. Ulmer adds his rough vocal skills to the more blues and rock-oriented records, though these generally don't stand up as strongly as his harmolodic forays—which lately have been made under the name Music Revelation Ensemble.

what to buy: A series of duets with lead hornmen lifts the Music Revelation Ensemble's *In the Name of...* (DIW, 1994, prod. James Blood Ulmer and Kazanori Sugiyema) with its odd stretched-out melodies and Ulmer's slash-and-run chording. Ulmer steps into the rock arena with *Blues Preacher* (DIW, 1994, prod. James Blood Ulmer) and, aside from his unengaging vocal style, pulls it of with elan. "Cheering" is a slow groove on which he shows off some Hendrix chops.

what to buy next: *Revealing* (In + Out, 1990, prod. James Blood Ulmer) is a compilation of earlier tapes, but it cooks in a jazzy vein as Ulmer's splashes around the musical water with saxophonist George Adams.

what to avoid: *The Blues Allnight* (In + Out, 1995, prod. James Blood Ulmer and Frank Kleinschmidt) aims high and misses the mark as far as the blues is concerned. Again, Ulmer's voice grates on the nerves.

the rest: *America—Do You Remember the Love?* (Blue Note, 1987) *Electric Jazz* (DIW, 1990) *Blues in the East* (Axiom, 1994)

worth searching for: When Ulmer heads outside, he's at his best, and *Music Revelation Ensemble* (DIW, 1988, prod. James Blood Ulmer) finds him grinding, cutting and exploring beyond the horizon.

Jon Butcher, Helmet, Jon Spencer Blues Explosion

Jimi Hendrix, Ornette Coleman

Lawrence Gabriel

Peter Ulrich

See: Dead Can Dance

Ultravox

Formed 1973 in London, England. Disbanded 1987.

John Foxx (born Dennis Leigh), vocals, synthesizers (1973-79); Steve Shears, keyboards, vocals (1973-77); Billy Currie, keyboards, synthesizers, violin; Chris Cross (born Christopher Allen), bass; Warren Cann, drums (1973-86); Robin Simon, guitar (1978-79); Midge Ure (born James Ure) guitar, vocals (1980-87); Mark Brzezicki, drums (1986-87)

Ultravox was one of the first New Wave bands to let synthesizers dominate its arrangements, though when Ure came on board he not only brought guitar back into the mix but also gave the group a poppier, more accessible flavor. Ultravox landed numerous hits and top-selling albums in Britain, but never quite hit stride in the U.S. More's the pity, since the band recorded some imaginative and fresh-sounding material. *If I Was: The Very Best of Midge Ure & Ultravox* (Chrysalis, 1993, prod. Various) is a comprehensive, solid selection of hits, though Ure's voice might wear you out.

the rest: *Systems of Romance* (Antilles, 1978) *Three Into One* (Antilles, 1980) *The Collection* (Chrysalis, 1986)

Patrick McCarty

Uncle Tupelo

Formed 1987 in Belleville, Ill. Disbanded 1994

Jeff Tweedy, vocals, guitar, bass; Jay Farrar, vocals, guitar, banjo, harmonica, mandolin; Mike Heidorn, drums (1987-1992); Bill Belzer, drums (1992); Ken Coomer, drums (1992-94); John Stirratt, bass; Max Johnston, banjo, fiddle, mandolin, steel guitar (1993-94)

Like many important bands before them, Uncle Tupelo's reputation spread fastest after their breakup, and their influence far outdistanced the number of units sold, to the point where they are now seen by some as the Rosetta stone of the alternative/roots/country movement sometimes called "No Depression" after their debut album. Rising from the factory- and farm-belt community of Belleville, Ill. (near St. Louis), the band drew equally on hard-core country and hardcore punk. Songwriting chores were split between Farrar, whose tunes are oblique and wistful, and Tweedy, who speaks more directly but is no less profound in describing the pair's favorite subject—small-town ennui. Just as the band was gaining steam with new members, a major-label contract and *Anodyne*, their best album, Farrar left the band in 1994 and went on to form Son Volt with Heidorn. Tupelo, with Tweedy at the helm, became known as Wilco.

what to buy: *Anodyne* (Sire/Reprise, 1993, prod. Brian Paulson) ♪♪♪♪½ is the group's swan song, but also it's finest hour. Alternating between yearning, hard-bitten country-folk ("Slate," "Anodyne") and careening rockers ("The Long Cut," "We've Been Had"), it epitomizes the sound, pacing and texture of Tupelo's memorable live shows.

what to buy next: The group's first two albums, *No Depression* (Rockville, 1990, prod. Paul Kolderie and Sean Slade) ♪♪♪½ and *Still Feel Gone* (Rockville, 1991, prod. Paul Kolderie and Sean Slade) ♪♪♪♪, are both raucous affairs featuring numerous anthems to booze and boredom. *March 16-20, 1992* (Rockville, 1992, prod. Peter Buck) ♪♪♪♪ is a fine acoustic effort featuring Buck's minimal production and spotlighting dour white-gospel tunes and equally grim originals.

worth searching for: *The Long Cut + Five Live* (Sire/Reprise, 1993, prod. Brian Paulson and Tim Powell) ♪♪♪, the single from *Anodyne* plus a handful of rare live cuts featuring the full five-piece band.

▶▶ The Bottle Rockets, Blue Mountain, Whiskeytown, Old 97's, Waco Brothers

◀◀ Gram Parsons, Neil Young, Black Flag, Merle Haggard, the Clash

see also: *Son Volt, Wilco, Golden Smog*

Daniel Durchholz

The Undertones

Formed 1975 in Derry, Northern Ireland. Disbanded 1983

Feargal Sharkey, vocals; John O'Neill, guitar; Damian "Dee" O'Neill, guitar; Mike Bradley, bass; Billy Doherty, drums

It took the U.K. press a couple of years to discover the Irish music scene; when it did, The Undertones were one of the more distinctive acts. With a style that was partially influenced by rock's past, its sound was punky pop, with Sharkey's quavering vocals sounding as if they were about to give out. The group broke up in 1982, spawning Sharkey's solo career and the John O'Neill-led That Petrol Emotion.

what to buy: *The Undertones* (Sire/Rykodisc, 1979, prod. The Undertones and Roger Bechirian) ♪♪♪♪½ is filled with perfect pop gems such as "Jimmy Jimmy," "Teenage Kicks," "Here Comes The Summer" and "Get Over You."

what to buy next: *The Very Best of the Undertones* (Rykodisc, 1994, prod. Various) ♪♪♪♪, a solid overview of the group's too-brief career.

the rest: *Hypnotized* (Sire/Rykodisc, 1980) ♪♪♪½ *Positive Touch* (Harvest/Rykodisc, 1981) ♪♪♪ *The Sin Of Pride* (Ardeck U.K., 1983) ♪♪♪

worth searching for: *The Peel Sessions Album* (Strange Fruit, 1989) ♪♪♪♪, a nice shot of live Undertones recorded at the BBC.

solo outings:

Feargal Sharkey A Good Heart Is Hard To Find (Virgin, 1985) ♪♪♪♪ *Wish* (Virgin, 1988) ♪♪♪

▶▶ Supergrass, Oasis, The La's

◀◀ Them, The Beatles, The Kinks, The Stooges, Ramones

see also: *That Petrol Emotion*

Anna Glen

Urge Overkill

Formed 1986 in Evanston, Ill.

Nash Kato (born Nathan Katruud), guitar, vocals; Eddie "King" Roeser, guitar, bass, vocals; Pat Byrne, drums (1987); Blackie Onassis (born John Rowan, drums, vocals (1990-present)

The members of Urge Overkill decided they were rock stars from the start, and from their indie beginnings on they have camped it up with glam outfits, martinis chillin', convertibles, supermodels and the like. The group's sound began as rough-hewn punky rock but has grown into a smoother blend—equal parts power pop and classic rock, with all the posturing of the glitter era. Kato, the band's principal singer and songwriter, has a husky, appealing voice and has crafted some monster hooks. After a string of beloved independent releases and relentless touring, the band went big-time with with Geffen Records in 1993, scoring a modern rock radio hit with "Sister Havana." Urge enjoyed yet another another boost when director Quentin Tarantino used its version of Neil Diamond's "Girl, You'll Be a Woman Soon" on the hit soundtrack for movie, "Pulp Fiction."

what to buy: *Saturation* (Geffen, 1993, prod. the Butcher Brothers) is filled with melodic hooks and guitar crunch. A thoroughly enjoyable throwback to the days of shameless rock-star swagger.

what to avoid: *Exit the Dragon* (Geffen, 1995, prod. the Butcher Brothers) is, despite some decent tunes, a bummer: too much angst, too much Roeser, not enough energy.

the rest: *Strange, I* (Ruthless, 1986) *Jesus Urge Superstar* (Touch & Go, 1989) *Americruiser* (Touch & Go, 1990) *Supersonic Storybook* (Touch & Go, 1991)

worth searching for: *Stull* (Touch & Go EP, 1992, prod. Urge Overkill & Kramer) includes the group's breathy, campy take on Diamond's "Girl, You'll Be a Woman Soon," among other notable tracks.

▶▶ Supergrass, Superdrag

◀◀ Rolling Stones, Neil Diamond, David Bowie, Parliament-Funkadelic, Cheap Trick, Sweet, the Replacements

Simon Glickman

Uriah Heep

Formed 1970 in London, England

David Byron, vocals (1970-76, died Feb. 28, 1985); Mick Box, guitar; Ken Hensley, keyboards (1970-80); Paul Newton, bass (1970-71); Alex Napier, drums (1970-71); Keith Baker, drums (1971); Lee Kerslake, drums (1971-78, 1981-present); Mark Clarke, bass (1971-72); Gary Thain, bass (1972-76, died March 19, 1976); John Wetton, bass, vocals (1975-76); John Lawton, vocals (1976-78); Trevor Bolder, bass, vocals (1976-81, 1985-present); John Sloman, vocals, (1978-); Chris Slade, drums (1978-81); Greg Dechert, keyboards (1980-81); Bob Daisley, bass (1981-83); Pete Goalby, vocals (1981-88); Bernie Shaw, vocals (1988-present); John Sinclair, keyboards (1981-88); Phil Lanzon, keyboards (1988-present)

The heavy metal community cuts its bands a pretty wide berth; that's one way to explain the 70s success of Uriah Heep. Some will tell you this was the worst band in the history of rock 'n' roll, which is overstating the case a bit. But the Heep—named after a Charles Dickens character—displayed particularly lumbering quality, dynamic but seldom supple (evidence the suite-like sonic circus of "The Magician's Birthday"). And the late singer Byron's voice could be grating over extended listenings. That said, the group churned out a fair amount of workmanlike hard rock, especially during its 1970-74 heyday. Call it a poor man's Deep Purple. The group—now led by guitarist Box and drummer Kerslake—still has pockets of fans around the world, but it's been quite awhile since it released anything of more than middling quality.

what to buy: *The Best of Uriah Heep,* (Mercury, 1975, prod. Gerry Bron) though a bit skimpy—it lacks the big radio hit "Stealin' "—is still the best first, cautious step into the Heep realm.

what to buy next: The Heep peaked with the one-two punch of *Demons and Wizards* (Mercury, 1972/1989, prod. Gerry Bron) and *The Magician's Birthday,* (Mercury, 1972/1989, prod. Gerry Bron) albums that straddle the line between hard and art rock—which can be enjoyable or painful, depending on your taste.

what to avoid: *Still 'Eavy, Still Proud: Two Decades of Uriah Heep,* (Griffin, 1990/1994) WOOF! the latest Heep lineup is responsible for this misleadingly titled rip-off, on which the old hits are reprised in concert versions.

the rest: *Uriah Heep* (Mercury, 1970/1989) *Salisbury* (Mercury, 1971/1989) *Look at Yourself* (Mercury, 1971/1989) *Live* (Mercury, 1973/1989) *Sweet Freedom* (Mercury, 1973/Roadrunner, 1990) *Wonderworld* (Mercury, 1974/Roadrunner, 1990) *Fallen Angel* (Warner Bros., 1978/Castle, 1989) *Abominog* (Peak, 1982/1992) *Live in Moscow* (Griffin, 1988/1994) *Raging Silence* (Griffin, 1989/1994) *Different World* (Griffin, 1991/1994)

worth searching for: If you like the Heep, go big; the British box set *A Time of Revelation* (Essential, 1996, prod. Various) takes a luxurious (?) four-CD stroll through the band's career. And in a true Spinal Tap move, early copies misspelled the group name Uriah Heap on the spine.

▶▶ Queen, Scorpions, Dokken, Winger

◀◀ Deep Purple, the Yardbirds, Led Zeppelin, Emerson, Lake and Palmer

Gary Graff

Utopia

See: Todd Rundgren

U2

Formed 1978 in Dublin, Ireland

Bono Vox (b. Paul Hewson), vocals, guitar; The Edge (b. David Evans), guitar, keyboards, vocals; Adam Clayton, bass; Larry Mullen Jr., drums

Let the story of U2 be a lesson to you: if you're gonna dream, dream big. How else to account for the accomplishments of four lads from Dublin's Mount Temple High School, who grew up to be the biggest band in the world and then used their power to (in Bono's words) "f*** with the mainstream?" Their early work drew on the energy of punk, but exchanged the genre's no-future nihilism for an interest in progressive politics and Charismatic Christianity. After three albums of thundering arena rock (made, interestingly, before they played arenas), U2 began a long and fruitful collaboration with producers Brian Eno and Daniel Lanois, who tempered their bombast with washes of warm, ambient sound, and later, clanging metallic racket. Their most recent albums are among their most successful, but are also their most challenging sonically, which speaks to U2's continuing ability to reinvent themselves and to shape rather than merely react to current musical trends. Clearly, whichever way music may turn in the future, U2 will have some say in calling the tune.

what to buy: A dark turn for a band known for its open-heartedness, *Achtung Baby* (Island, 1991, prod. Daniel Lanois and Brian Eno) is the band's most complex and sophisticated work. Taking irony, excess, and media overload as its guiding principals, the album is still shot through with genuine emotion, most notably on songs such as "One" and "Love is Blindness." *The Joshua Tree*(Island, 1987, Daniel Lanois and Brian Eno), which marked the band's critical and commercial apotheosis, is a heady mix of chiming anthems examining the realms of self-analysis ("With or Without You," "I Still Haven't Found What I'm Looking For"), politics ("Bullet the Blue Sky") and drug addiction ("Running to Stand Still"). *War* (Island, 1983, prod. Steve Lillywhite) is the culmination of the band's early period, finding in Ireland's troubles the perfect subject for their message of peace, compassion and outrage as heard in "New Year's Day," "Sunday Bloody Sunday," and "40."

what to buy next: *The Unforgettable Fire* (Island, 1984, prod. Brian Eno and Daniel Lanois), is a moody gem whose rich, atmospheric aura is rent by the Martin Luther King tribute "Pride" and the equally passionate "Bad." *Rattle and Hum* (Island, 1987, prod. Jimmy Iovine), the soundtrack to the band's unintentionally self-deflating documentary, features the furious "Desire" plus nods to Billie Holiday, John Lennon and Bob Dylan, and "When Love Comes to Town," with a brilliant cameo by B.B. King. *Zooropa* (Island, 1993, prod. Flood, Brian Eno and the Edge) is U2's most diffuse and chaotic effort, yet it keeps the band on rock's cutting edge with the Edge's techno-rap "Numb" and a strikingly appropriate guest vocal by Johnny Cash. *Boy* (Island, 1980, prod. Steve Lillywhite), their auspicious debut, introduced the band's soaring sonic architecture and Bono's (then) guileless lyrics on "I Will Follow" and "Into the Heart."

the rest: *October* (Island, 1981) *Under a Blood Red Sky* (Island, 1983) *Wide Awake in America (EP)* (Island, 1985)

worth searching for: *Melon* (Island, 1995, prod. Various) and *Kiwi* (Island, 1995, prod. Various) were remix collections released only to the band's fan club, notable for how thoroughly the songs are recast while remaining remarkably true to the originals.

solo outings:

The Edge (with Michael Brook) Captive (Virgin, 1987) (with Jah Wobble and Holger Czukay): *Snake Charmer* (Island EP, 1983)

The Alarm, The Cult, Simple Minds, Our Lady Peace, Rhythm Corps

David Bowie, Brian Eno, Van Morrison, Bob Dylan, John Lennon, Massive Attack

see also: *Passengers*

Daniel Durchholz

Steve Vai

Born June 6, 1960, in Carle Place, N.Y.

One of the most talented musicians to survive the fret-shredding guitar explosion of the 80s, Vai is a virtuoso instrumentalist whose ability to meld artistic sensitivity with heavy metal chops has placed him among the most sought-after studio musicians in the business, as well as a popular solo artist. After picking up the guitar at age 14, Vai attended Berklee College of Music in Boston, augmenting his classwork by transcribing arrangements for Frank Zappa. That led to a job with Zappa's touring band, with gave Vai a job with his touring band and appearances on the Zappa albums *Ship Too Late to Save a Drowning Witch*, *The Man from Utopia* and *Thingfish* Vai's own career began with 1984's *Flex-Able*, which sold more than 250,000 copies without any promotion. Along with his solo albums, Vai has worked with the bands Alcatrazz and Whitesnake, as well as with former Van Halen singer David Lee Roth, John Lydon's Public Image Ltd., Ozzy Osbourne and Alice Cooper. Of late, however, Vai has concentrated on his own music, augmenting his albums with a highly regarded series of instructional books and videotapes.

what to buy: Fans of melodic, well-crafted solo guitar will find *Passion & Warfare* (Relativity, 1990, prod. Steve Vai) ♫♫♫♫ an essential part of their collections. The expressive, almost symphonic quality of tracks such as "Liberty," "The Riddle," and "Blue Powder" reflect the reverence and spirituality with which Vai approaches his playing. There are also plenty of searing examples of Vai's rock chops, including "The Animal," "The Audience is Listening" and "Greasy Kid's Stuff."

what to buy next: Though inconsistent, *Flex-Able* (Urantia, 1984, prod. Steve Vai) ♫♫♫♫ contains the foundation that Vai has built his reputation upon.

what to avoid: Whitesnake's *Slip of the Tongue* (Geffen, 1989, prod. Mike Clink and Keith Olsen) ♫ is a tired rehashing of the band's already derivative sound, with Vai simply stepping in to copy the playing of Adrian Vandenberg, who departed the band in mid-recording.

the rest: *Sex & Religion* (Relativity, 1993) ♫♫♫ *Alien Love Secrets* (Relativity, 1995) ♫♫♫♫

worth searching for: *Flex-Able Leftovers* (Relativity, 1984, prod. Steve Vai) ♫♫♫♫ contains the songs Vai recorded for *Flex-Able* but elected not to include on that release, despite the fact that they are more ambitious and enjoyable than most solo guitar albums released during the 80s.

▶▶ Dweezil Zappa, Tony MacAlpine, David Chastain, Joe Satriani, Eric Johnson

◀◀ Frank Zappa, Jeff Beck, Ritchie Blackmore, Tony Iommi

see also: *Whitesnake, Frank Zappa, David Lee Roth (Van Halen)*

Brandon Trenz

Ritchie Valens

Born Richard Steve Valenzuela, May 13, 1941, in Los Angeles, Calif. Died Feb. 3, 1959, in Mason City, Iowa.

Despite his lionized reputation after his death in the same plane crash that killed Buddy Holly, Valens was a minor figure in rock 'n' roll. He had a couple of singles under his belt and his first hit on the charts when that plane went down in a snowy Iowa cornfield. But don't try to tell that to any number of Mexican-American rock musicians in East Los Angeles or San Bernardino, where Los Lobos is not alone in keeping alive the name and spirit of the first Chicano rock star. Valens was an unschooled, intuitive 18-year-old musician when he went into Hollywood's historic Gold Star Studios to hold his first recording session with a band of seasoned professional sidemen. A year later, he was dead, leaving behind frustrating traces of promise, a couple of certified classics ("La Bamba," "Come On, Let's Go," "Donna") and a legend that only grew in the years since his death. The 16-song set, *The Best of Ritchie Valens,* (Del-Fi, 1988, prod. B. Keane) ♫♫♫♫ covers all the bases—slightly better than *The Ritchie Valens Story.* (Del-Fi, 1993) ♫♫♫ For a real immersion, there's a three-LP boxed set, *The History of Ritchie Valens,* (Del-Fi/Rhino, 1981) ♫♫♫ which contains all three albums that Valens recorded in his lifetime: *Ritchie Valens, Ritchie* and *In Concert at Pacoima Jr. High*

Joel Selvin

Dino Valente

See: Quicksilver Messenger Service

Franki Valli

See: Four Seasons

Van Halen

Formed 1974 in Pasadena, Calif.

Edward Van Halen, guitar, keyboards, vocals; Alex Van Halen, drums; Michael Anthony, bass, vocals; David Lee Roth, vocals (1974-84, 1996); Sammy Hagar, vocals, (1984-96)

With the possible exception of Aerosmith, Van Halen was the most important American hard rock band to emerge during the 70s. Edward Van Halen's blitzkrieg guitar style and string-tapping technique launched a thousand imitators, while Roth added a sense of comedy to a genre that generally took itself too seriously. But Roth left the band in 1985 to try to be a movie star (and wound up with a fading solo career) and was replaced by Hagar, a competent hard rock belter who'd honed his pipes with another guitar wizard, Ronnie Montrose. But while the Hagar-era Van Halen has been immensely popular, its meat-and-potatoes albums aren't as interesting the band's earlier output. Hagar left the band in 1996 after a spat over the rest of the group's decision to record some new tracks with Roth to include in a planned greatest hits album.

what to buy: *Van Halen* (Warner Bros, 1978, prod. Ted Templeman) &&&&& is a headbanger's paradise, brimming with muscular romps such as "Runnin' With the Devil," the Kinks' "You Really Got Me," "Jamie's Crying" and Eddie's brilliant guitar-gasm, "Eruption." *1984* (Warner Bros., 1984, prod. Ted Templeman) &&&&v found the band experimenting with synthesizers on the No. 1 hit "Jump" but still cranking out blazing guitar anthems like "Hot For Teacher" and "Panama."

what to buy next: *Women and Children First* (Warner Bros., 1980, prod. Ted Templeman) &&&& showed Roth at his most entertaining on "Everybody Wants Some" and "And the Cradle Will Rock." *OU812* (Warner Bros, 1988, prod. Van Halen and Don Landee), the best of the Hagar era albums, contains the stunning country-metal fusion "Finish What You Started."

what to avoid: *Van Halen Live: Right Here, Right Now,* (Warner Bros., 1993, prod. Van Halen and Andy Johns) && an all-too-typical live album complete with self-indulgent drum and bass solos.

the rest: *Van Halen II* (Warner Bros., 1979) &&&v *Fair Warning* (Warner Bros., 1981) &&&v *Diver Down* (Warner Bros., 1982) &&&, "5150" (Warner Bros., 1986) &&& *For Unlawful Carnal Knowledge* (Warner Bros., 1991 &&& *Balance* (Warner Bros. 1995) &&&v

worth searching for: The import CD-5 of "Jump" (Warner Bros., 1993) &&& from the live album, which features selections not included on the live album and works as an abbreviated version of the Van Halen live experience.

solo outings:

David Lee Roth Crazy From the Heat (Warner Bros. EP, 1985) &&&v *Eat 'Em and Smile* (Warner Bros., 1986) &&& *Skyscraper* (Warner Bros., 1987) &&v *A Little Ain't Enough* (Warner Bros., 1991) &&v *Your Filthy Little Mouth* (Reprise, 1994) &&v

▶▶ Randy Rhoads, Steve Vai, Joe Satriani, Skid Row, Bulletboys

◀◀ Led Zeppelin, Jimi Hendrix, Cream, Louis Prima

see also: *Sammy Hagar*

Thor Christensen

Johnny Van Zant

See: Lynyrd Skynyrd

Luther Vandross

Born 1951 in New York, N.Y.

Now known as an R&B balladeer who's found some success on the pop charts, Vandross started out as a session singer during the 70s, singing Army spots and backing up Carly Simon, Barbra Streisand and David Bowie—even helping to write (with Bowie and John Lennon) the art-rocker's 1975 hit "Fame." After singing on hits by R&B groups such as Chic and Change, Vandross scored his own record deal—releasing an album that surrounded his silky smooth tenor with up-to-date R&B sounds and evocative ballads. Vandross and his writing/production partners—Nat Adderly Jr. and former Miles Davis bassist Marcus Miller—crafted a signature sound that favored mid-to-slow tempo numbers with plenty of keyboard textures and room for his impressive vocal chops. Although he remained a solid R&B star through the 80s, it took the pop-styled hit "Here and Now" to court some crossover attention, though he's had middling success in that arena. But like fellow R&B/pop powerhouse Anita Baker, Vandross' sonic formula has narrowed to straightjacket in recent years, resulting in albums that often sound identical.

what to buy: As a distillation of all the qualities that have made Vandross a star, no single album does it better than *The Night I Fell In Love,* (Epic, 1985, prod. Luther Vandross and Marcus Miller) &&&&v which combines textured, atmospheric soul cuts such as the title track with an evocative take on Stevie Wonder's "Creepin'" and the boppy R&B hit "'Til My Baby Comes Home." For an overview, go to *The Best of Luther Vandross: The Best of Love,* (Epic, 1989, prod. Luther Vandross, Marcus Miller and Jacques Fred Petrus) &&&&v a double-disc set that's the best way to sample the early party hit "Bad Boys" and the majestic "Stop To Love."

what to buy next: Although it sounds a little dated 15 years later, Vandross' debut album *Never Too Much* (Epic, 1981, prod. Luther Vandross) &&&& bears the early signs of his trademark material—from the soaring title track to the legendary R&B lament "A House is Not a Home."

what to avoid: Much of Vandross' later records have been stifled by the very formula that made his early efforts so engaging. Nowhere is this syndrome more apparent than on *Songs,* (Sony, 1994, prod. Walter Afanasieff) **WOOF!** Vandross' collec-

What Album Changed Your Life?

"Sarah McLachlan's Fumbling Towards Ecstasy. I think her lyrics are really honest, really down to earth. I think her band is great and the production is really cool. That's a record I've been able to listen to over and over--we even took some ideas from it when we did our album."

Charlie Lowell (Jars of Clay)

tion of cover tunes that slaps his distinctive vocalese on songs such as Lionel Richie's "Hello," Heatwave's "Always and Forever" and a duet with Mariah Carey on "Endless Love."

the rest: *Forever for Always For Love* (Epic, 1982) *Busy Body* (Epic, 1983) *Give Me the Reason* (Epic, 1986) *Any Love* (Epic, 1988) *Power of Love* (Epic, 1991) *Never Let Me Go* (Epic, 1993)

worth searching for: Bowie's *Young Americans*, (RCA/Rykodisc, 1975, prod. Tony Viscontі) on which Vandross, sings, co-writes and arranges background vocals.

▶▶ Johnny Gill, Freddie Jackson, Alexander O'Neal

◀◀ Sam Cooke, Lionel Richie, Marvin Gaye

Eric Deggans

Vanilla Fudge

Formed 1967, as the Pigeons, in New York, N.Y. Disbanded 1970.

Vince Martell, vocals. guitar; Mark Stein, keyboards; Tim Bogert, bass; Carmine Appice, drums

Along with Iron Butterfly, Vanilla Fudge helped lay the foundation for heavy metal. Stressing production over songwriting, the group layered guitars, organ and thundering drums into a thick cloud of sonic excess. Vanilla Fudge began its recording career as a cover band, performing slow, drowsy versions of hits in an attempt to mimic the time-distorting effect of drugs. The formula eventually paid off with the Top 10 cover "You Keep Me Hangin' On," which was performed at about half the speed of the Supremes' hit. Nothing else by the group made much of a dent in the charts, and by 1969 the torch had been passed to Deep Purple and Led Zeppelin. *Psychedelic Sundae: The Best of Vanilla Fudge* (Rhino, 1993, prod. Shadow Morton, Vanilla Fudge and Adrian Barber) is the premier collection of the group's proto-heavy metal music. The album emphasizes covers ("You Keep Me Hangin' On," "The Look of Love," "Ticket To Ride" and "Season of the Witch"), but then half the fun is hearing these twisted variations on familiar themes. The compilation also contains an album and non-album singles discography as well as track annotations.

the rest: *Vanilla Fudge* (Atco/Rhino, 1967) *The Best of Vanilla Fudge Live* (Rhino, 1991)

Christopher Scapelliti

The Vapors

Formed 1978 in England. Disbanded 1981.

David Fenton, vocals, guitar; Howard Smith, drums; Edward Bazalgette, guitar; Steve Smith, bass, vocals

The Vapors helped usher in a new pop era with its hit, the essential "Turning Japanese"—a tightly wound, disturbing ode to masturbation. Surprisingly, the exuding sense of paranoia and isolation carries over throughout their out-of-print debut *New Clear Days* (United Artists, 1980, prod. Vic Coppersmith-Heaven), which marries brittle pop smarts with an aura of madness. Somehow connecting themes of war, adolescent pathos and Japan, it's strangely disquieting and bears little resemblance to the lightweight New Wave frenzy of the period. *The Vapors Anthology* (One Way, 1995, prod. Vic Coppersmith-Heaven) is something of a misnomer as it actually contains the entire debut plus a few extra songs tacked on at the end and cheap, redundant packaging. It does, however, keep "Turning Japanese" available.

Allan Orski

The Vaselines /Eugenius

Formed 1987 in Glasgow, Scotland

Eugene Kelly, vocals, guitar; Francis McKee, vocals, guitar; James Seenan, bass; Charles Kelly, drums

It's doubtful that anyone expected the brilliantly catchy/supremely silly Vaselines to become one of alternative rock's most influential bands. If a young Kurt Cobain had never discovered Kelly and McKee's sunny style of primitive-but-effective hooks and seemingly nonsensical lyrics, he might have never transformed his little sub-Melvins band Nirvana into the pop wunderkind that changed the world. Likewise, if Nirvana hadn't covered two Vaselines songs, Sub Pop wouldn't have released *The Way of the Vaselines: A Complete History.* (Sub Pop, 1992, prod. Various) ♪♪♪ At its best, the Vaselines utilized a variety of styles to create an emptyheaded pop excitement ("Jesus Doesn't Want Me For a Sunbeam," "Rory Rides Me Raw"); at its worst, the group made typical garage noise ("Sex Sux (Amen)"). Luckily, examples of the former outnumber the latter, as the Sub Pop collection attests.

Kelly went on to form Eugenius, a band whose greatest publicity came from a legal dispute with Marvel Comics over its original name, Captain America. Its two albums—*Oomalama* (Atlantic, 1992, prod. Jamie Watson and Eugenius) ♪♪♪ and *Mary, Queen of Scots* (Atlantic, 1994, Craig Leon) ♪♪♪½—dealt in the same power-pop vein as the Vaselines, but with less of its predecessor's shambling, unsteady charm.

Todd Wicks

Jimmie Vaughan

Born. March 20, 1951 in Dallas, Texas

The older sibling of the more famous Stevie Ray Vaughan, Jimmie made his reputation with the Fabulous Thunderbirds, incorporating his encyclopedic knowledge of blues licks into a setting contemporary enough to afford the band considerable popular success. Vaughan left the band in 1990, and the Thunderbirds never really were the same again. He and Stevie Ray got together for *Family Style* (Epic/Associated, 1990, prod. Nile Rodgers), ♪♪♪♪ a long-anticipated collaboration that was tinged with sadness due to Stevie Ray's death in a helicopter crash shortly before the album's release. "Tick-Tock," a call for peace and understanding cowritten by Jimmie, is *Family Style*'s enduring anthem. On his own, Vaughan released *Strange Pleasure,* (Epic, 1994, prod. Nile Rodgers) ♪♪♪½ an impressive solo bow that featured hard-charging raveups ("Boom-Bapa-Boom"), strutting instrumentals ("Tilt A Whirl") and smoky blues ("Love the World"). But the album's emotional centerpiece is "Six Strings Down," a harrowing acoustic number that envisions Stevie Ray as the newest member of an all-star blues band in heaven.

Daniel Durchholz

Stevie Ray Vaughan

Born October 3, 1954, in Dallas, Texas. Died August 26, 1990, in East Troy, Wisc.

Vaughan burst onto the national scene in 1983 with *Texas Flood,* a scorching, overdriven blues tornado that blew down the doors of popular music and proclaimed loud and clear that blues could actually be a potent force in the marketplace. Playing with deep blues feeling and a roof-shaking rock energy and virtuosity—and volume—Vaughan became a certified guitar hero and shone a light on many of his own heroes, notably Buddy Guy and Albert King. His rise also paved the way for the return of blues-based rockers such as the Allman Brothers Band. One thing that separated Vaughan from other earnest young bluesmen was that he also worshipped at the house of Jimi, and while his attempts at slavish Hendrix imitation were destined to fall flat, his understanding of Hendrix' more subtle, chordal elements informed all of his playing, allowing him to write gorgeous instrumentals like "Lenny" and "Riviera Paradise." Vaughan's career shot like a skyrocket, before hitting some seriously rocky roads as he wrestled with drug and alcohol abuse. In 1989, a new, clean SRV came out swinging for the fences, and his last two albums were by far his most focused, hinting that he was on the verge of reaching a whole new level of greatness when he died in a 1990 helicopter crash.

what to buy: Though it is at times downright jittery, Vaughan's debut, *Texas Flood* (Epic, 1983, prod. Stevie Ray Vaughan, Richard Mullen and Double Trouble) ♪♪♪½ remains a gritty summation of his strengths: hard-rocking shuffles ("Pride and Joy," "Love Struck Baby"), slow, nasty blues ("Texas Flood," "Dirty Pool"), overdriven guitar workouts ("Rude Mood," "Testify") and shimmeringly gorgeous instrumental masterpieces ("Lenny"). His last solo album, *In Step* (Epic, 1989, prod. Jim Gaines, Stevie Ray Vaughan and Double Trouble) ♪♪♪♪½ is just as passionate while also reflecting a new-found lyrical maturity as well as a musical and vocal confidence highlighted by "Riviera Paradise," probably Vaughan's most serene recording. *Family Style* (Epic, 1990, prod. Nile Rogers) ♪♪♪♪½ is as much brother Jimmie Vaughan's album as Stevie's (it's billed to both of them)—which doesn't make it any less great. Quite the contrary, the album contains some of the Vaughans' finest songs, more of *In Step*'s maturity and confidence and, of course, lots of serious guitar slinging. The posthumous *The Sky is Crying* (Epic, 1991, prod. Various) ♪♪♪♪ sketches out the contours of Vaughan's talents and influences, including Hubert Sumlin, Albert King, jazzman Kenny Burrell and, of course, Hendrix. Vaughan's breathtaking, instrumental "Little Wing" is here, as is his first recorded slide ("Boot Hill") and acoustic ("Life By the Drop") playing.

what to buy next: *Soul to Soul* (Epic, 1985, prod. Stevie Ray Vaughan, Double Trouble and Richard Mullen) is a fine, relatively relaxed outing. Once you're hooked you'll want to own *In the Beginning,* (Epic, 1992, prod. Wayne Bell) a rough, ragged, thoroughly intense 1980 live performance. The packaging even includes a rare photo of a bareheaded SRV!

what to avoid: *Live Alive* (Epic, 1986, prod. Stevie Ray Vaughan and Double Trouble) is, at times, downright painful to listen to, reflecting as it does a great artist's deterioration. Vaughan was a mess, strung out on drugs and alcohol, necessitating more overdubs than is proper for a live album, particularly for this fine a performer. Only SRV's subsequent resurgence prevents this from being a tragic album.

the rest: *Couldn't Stand the Weather* (Epic, 1984) *Greatest Hits* (Epic, 1995)

worth searching for: *Interchords* (Epic, 1992) a promotional CD released with *The Sky is Crying,* featuring interviews with Jimmie Vaughan and the members of double trouble, as well as snippets of songs and a few quotes from older SRV interviews.

▶▶ Kenny Wayne Shephard, Big Head Todd and the Monsters, Blues Traveler

◀◀ Albert King, Otis Rush, Buddy Guy, Eric Clapton, Jimi Hendrix, Lonnie Mack, Cream, Kenny Burrell

Alan Paul

Ben Vaughn

Born April 6, 1955 in Camden, N.J.

Part musicologist, part goofball and all heart, Vaughn is a rock 'n' roll purist who worships Sonny Bono and prefers AM radio to Surround Sound, the Goodwill to Tower Records and Duane Eddy to Eddie Vedder. Ever since forming the short-lived Ben Vaughn Combo in 1984, the New Jersey singer-songwriter-producer has merged odes to facial hair ("Growin' a Beard"), vintage cars ("El Rambler Dorado"), convenience stores ("Lookin' for a 7-11") and garage bands ("Big Drum Sound," "Rhythm Guitar") with hooks liberally lifted from rockabilly, surf music, British Invasion pop and Muscle Shoals R&B. And while Vaughn's quirky sense of humor makes him easy to shrug off as a clever novelty act, there's a genuine soul bubbling beneath the smirk: his affection for rock's roots shine through, whether he's recording basement tapes of vintage 60s instrumentals or producing the late Arthur Alexander's "Lonely Just Like Me." His penchant for pop culture metaphors can be as obscure as Dennis Miller's ("I'm Sorry But So Is Brenda Lee"), but there hasn't been any pop song in the last 10 years that has communicated the joyful buzz of puppy love like "Jerry Lewis In France" ("I feel like Jerry Lewis in France/when you hold me in your arms").

what to buy: The presence Marshall Crenshaw, Alex Chilton, Foster & Lloyd, John Hiatt, Peter Holsapple and Gordon Gano on *Dressed In Black* (Enigma, 1990, prod. Ben Vaughn) lends a boys-night-out exuberance to the Memphis undertones of "The Man Who Has Everything," the twangy lament of "Doormat," the unrequited crush of "Cashier Girl" and the greasy punch of "Words Can't Say What I Want to Say." *Mood Swings (90-'85 & More)* (Restless, 1992, prod. Ben Vaughn) is a handy compilation drawn from his four Restless/Enigma releases and features such essentials as "Jerry Lewis in France," "I'm Sorry But So Is Brenda Lee," "Daddy's Gone For Good" and both sides of his rare first single, "My First Band"/"Vibrato in the Grotto."

what to buy next: To appreciate the depths of Vaughn's soul (and his record collection), *Mono U.S.A.* (Bar/None, 1993, prod. Ben Vaughn) collects rollicking home-recorded 8-track covers of the Ventures' "Exploration in Fear," Tom T. Hall's "That's How I Got to Memphis," Willie Nelson's "Suffer in Silence," Link Wray's "Cross Ties," Lobo's "Big Red Kite" and 13 other obscurities that even the artists themselves probably don't remember recording.

what to avoid: *Kings of Saturday Night* (Sector 2, 1995, prod. Ben Vaughn and Kim Fowley) is a raucous, "Duets"-like collaboration between Vaughn and rock svengali Fowley in which the latter simply rants over backing tracks that Vaughn mailed to him. We assume Sinatra wasn't available.

the rest: *The Many Moods of Ben Vaughn* (Restless, 1986) *Ben Vaughn Blows Your Mind* (Restless, 1988) *Instrumental Stylings* (Bar/None, 1995)

worth searching for: *Bonograph: Sonny Gets His Share* (Bogus, 1991, prod. Carl M. Grefenstette), a tribute album to Sonny Bono, includes Vaughn's one-man version of "Koko Joe" and his liner notes that ask, "He wrote 'I Got You Babe' and still collects money from it. What've you done lately?"

▶▶ Pete Droge, Jack Logan, Jonny Polonsky, Skeletons, Los Straitjackets

Link Wray, Sonny Bono, Chuck Berry, the Kingsmen, Willie DeVille

David Okamoto

Suzanne Vega

Born July 11, 1959 in Santa Monica, Calif.

Vega grew up in New York, attending the prestigious High School of the Performing Arts. She continued at Barnard, where she began playing her own brand of folk songs at small clubs in Greenwich Village. Her light, whispery voice blended with haunting melodies and vivid imagery, building an underground following and, eventually, a larger audience. In 1984 she signed to A&M Records, and since then her career has evolved dramatically. Like Tom Waits, Vega began with sparse coffee-house folk and has firmly moved forward into new territory. Her 1985 debut revealed insightful lyrics, acoustic guitar playing reminiscent of Joni Mitchell and the solitary feel of her folk roots. Three albums later, her musical influences have provided her with the skill of successful risk-taking, with expanded instrumentation, more intricate melodies and even a collaboration with the dance group DNA. While this growth may not be fattening anybody's pockets, her influence as a creative force is incalculable. Her 1987 hit "Luka" helped female performers gain the recognition they long deserved, paving the way for artists such as Tracy Chapman, 10,000 Maniacs and Sarah McLachlan.

what to buy: Her debut, *Suzanne Vega* (A&M, 1985, prod. Steve Addabbo and Lenny Kaye) is still her most consistently moving work. This folky album opens with the lyricly wonderful "Cracking," a depiction of someone who is often on the edge of breaking down. The sparse "Straight Lines," the poppy "Marlene on the Wall" and the dark fable "Queen and the Soldier" make this album is a complete gem.

what to buy next: *Nine Objects of Desire* (A&M, 1996, prod. N/A) continues the sonic experiments Vega began with her 1992 album *99.9 °*, using driving, urban-style drum sounds, stong electric guitars and keyboards atop the poetic images that are her trademark. More than ever before, she uses eclectic layerings of backing vocals, experimental beats and exotic melodies as a vehicle to emphasise and compliment the incredible images that her songs evoke. *Days of Open Hand* (A&M, 1990, prod. Anton Sanko and Suzanne Vega) is another of her most ambitious albums. Here Vega successfully makes the jump from accomplished folkster to extraordinary musical artist, flaunting a string arrangement from Philip Glass, heavy use of a hammond organ and synthesizers for ambient effect and the eclectic rhythms of drums from around the world. *Solitude Standing* (A&M, 1987, prod. Steve Addabbo and Lenny Kaye) contains her two biggest hits, "Luka" and "Tom's Diner." The latter actually gained its notoriety three years later, when the DNA took Vega's vocal and added a strong techno beat and a few sound loops.

the rest: *99.9 °* (A&M, 1992, prod. Mitchell Froom and Suzanne Vega)

worth searching for: One of Vega's greatest attributes is her stage presence, which is never really displayed in her studio work. On the Australian import *Live in London* (A&M, 1986) we get to hear her sense of humor and excellent story-telling talents, as well as wonderful versions of "Left of Center," "Neighborhood Girls" and other songs.

Shawn Colvin, Tori Amos, 10,000 Maniacs, Tracy Chapman, Sarah McLachlan

Tom Waits, Ricky Lee Jones, Joni Mitchell, DNA

Joshua Zarov

Velvet Crush

Formed late 1980s in Providence, R.I.

Paul Chastain, bass and vocals; Jeffrey Borchardt, guitar; Ric Menck, drums

Among all the retro bands of the mid-90s, here's a group that's every bit as fresh as the original product. Velvet Crush fashions power-pop country-rock that combines the Anglo-pop stylings of Big Star with blazing Rickenbacker hooks redolent of the Byrds, dousing it liberally in the Southern mysticism of R.E.M. The trio's debut, *In the Presence Of,* (Ringers Lactate, 1991, prod. Matthew Sweet and Velvet Crush) showed a loose, free-form structure in which the group gamely practiced its talent for writing hook-filled tunes. Following a three-year absence, the band returned with *Teenage Symphonies to God,* (550 Music/Epic, 1994, prod. Mitch Easter and Velvet Crush) a stellar album featuring a dozen indelible pop masterpieces. Whether performing crunchy rockers ("Hold Me Up," "My Blank Pages," "Atmosphere"), wistful Byrds-like psychedelia ("Time Wraps Around You," "Weird Summer") or lilting country (a moving cover of Gene Clark's "Why Not Your Baby"), Velvet Crush brings new life to its musical traditions. This is a compelling and important work that deserves attention.

Christopher Scapelliti

Velvet Underground

Formed 1965 in New York, N.Y. Disbanded 1972.

Lou Reed (born Louis Firbank), vocals, guitar (1965-70); John Cale, viola, bass, keyboards (1965-68); Nico (born Christa Paffgen), vocals, (1966-67, died July 18, 1988); Sterling Morrison, bass, guitar (1965-71); Maureen "Moe" Tucker, drums, vocals (1965-70); Doug Yule, bass and vocals (1968-72); Billy Yule, drums (1970-72); Walter Powers, vocals (1970-72); Willie Alexander, guitar (1971-72)

No 1960s band had a greater influence on post-punk rock than the Velvet Underground. The group's musical innovations are as numerous as its record sales are minuscule, but perhaps most influential was its attitude: a single-minded, uncompromising and ultimately self-destructive vision that put the band at odds with everyone from recording engineers to record executives. Even its sole benefactor, Andy Warhol, got the boot after guiding the formation of the Velvets' notorious multimedia concerts, dubbed the Exploding Plastic Inevitable, and designing the famed banana cover for its first album, the 1967 *The Velvet Underground and Nico* At a time when even major bands such as the Beatles and Rolling Stones were genuflecting toward flower-power psychedelia and the ideal of a youth community, the Velvets sang about junkies and transvestites with dispassionate, almost clinical, insight, and spiked Reed's sublime three-chord melodies with feedback, drones and white noise. More than 20 years after the Velvets' dissolution (discounting a brief reunion tour of Europe in 1993), countless indie-rock bands have built and continue to build entire careers around a single aspect of their wide-screen sound.

what to buy: The band's four studio albums are essential to any complete rock library, beginning with *The Velvet Underground and Nico* (MGM/Verve, 1967, prod. Andy Warhol) 𝅘𝅥𝅘𝅥𝅘𝅥𝅘𝅥𝅘𝅥, virtually a blueprint of post-punk styles from pitiless noise-rock to poignant ballads such as the stunning "Pale Blue Eyes," sung with icy efficiency by the Germanic chanteuse Nico, whose inclusion was the sole concession to Warhol's managerial whims. With Nico and Warhol both out of the way, *White Light/White Heat* (MGM/Verve, 1968, prod. Tom Wilson) 𝅘𝅥𝅘𝅥𝅘𝅥𝅘𝅥𝅘𝅥 is an unsurpassed guitar exorcism, highlighted by the 17-minute landmark "Sister Ray." With the abrasive Cale gone, Reed was left free to explore his more melodic, subdued side on the gorgeous *The Velvet Underground* (MGM, 1968 prod. the Velvet Underground) 𝅘𝅥𝅘𝅥𝅘𝅥𝅘𝅥𝅘𝅥 *Loaded* (Atlantic, 1970, prod. Geoffrey Haslam, Shel Kagan and the Velvet Underground) 𝅘𝅥𝅘𝅥𝅘𝅥𝅘𝅥½ is the band's most determinedly pop-oriented effort, featuring the Reed masterpieces "Rock and Roll" and "Sweet Jane."

what to buy next: The five-CD box *Peel Slowly and See* (Polydor, 1995, prod. Various) 𝅘𝅥𝅘𝅥𝅘𝅥𝅘𝅥½ contains the four studio albums in their entirety, plus crucial unreleased material, live tracks and an hour's worth of 1965 rehearsals involving Reed, Cale and Morrison. *1969 Live* (Mercury, 1974) 𝅘𝅥𝅘𝅥𝅘𝅥𝅘𝅥½ captures the band at its best in lower-key, post-Cale mode.

what to avoid: The European-only release *Squeeze* (Polydor, 1972) WOOF! is essentially a Doug Yule solo album even though it was released under the Velvet Underground moniker.

the rest: *Live at Max's Kansas City* (Atlantic, 1972) 𝅘𝅥𝅘𝅥 *V.U.* (Verve, 1985) 𝅘𝅥𝅘𝅥𝅘𝅥𝅘𝅥 *Another View* (Verve, 1986) 𝅘𝅥𝅘𝅥𝅘𝅥 *The Best of the Velvet Underground: Words and Music of Lou Reed* (Verve, 1989) 𝅘𝅥𝅘𝅥½ *Live MCMXCIII* (Sire, 1993) 𝅘𝅥𝅘𝅥𝅘𝅥

solo outings:

Nico *Chelsea Girl* (Verve, 1967) 𝅘𝅥𝅘𝅥𝅘𝅥 *The Marble Index* (Elektra, 1969) 𝅘𝅥𝅘𝅥𝅘𝅥𝅘𝅥 *Desertshore* (Reprise, 1971) 𝅘𝅥𝅘𝅥𝅘𝅥½ *The End ...* (Island, 1974) 𝅘𝅥𝅘𝅥𝅘𝅥½ *Drama of Exile* (Aura, 1981) 𝅘𝅥𝅘𝅥 *Do or Die! Nico — in Europe — 1982 Diary* (ROIR, 1982) 𝅘𝅥𝅘𝅥𝅘𝅥½ *Camera Obscura* (Beggars Banquet/PVC, 1985) 𝅘𝅥𝅘𝅥𝅘𝅥 *The Blue Angel* (Aura, 1985) 𝅘𝅥𝅘𝅥𝅘𝅥½ *Behind the Iron Curtain* (Dojo, 1986) 𝅘𝅥𝅘𝅥𝅘𝅥 *Live in Tokyo* (Dojo, 1986) 𝅘𝅥𝅘𝅥𝅘𝅥 *Live Heroes* (Performance, 1986) 𝅘𝅥𝅘𝅥𝅘𝅥 *The Peel Sessions* (Strange Fruit EP, 1988) 𝅘𝅥𝅘𝅥½ *Hanging Gardens* (Restless, 1990) 𝅘𝅥𝅘𝅥𝅘𝅥

Maureen Tucker *Playin' Possum* (Trash, 1981) 𝅘𝅥𝅘𝅥𝅘𝅥 *MoeJadKateBarry* (50 Skidillion Watts EP, 1987) 𝅘𝅥𝅘𝅥𝅘𝅥 *Life in Exile After Abdication* (50 Skidillion Watts, 1989) 𝅘𝅥𝅘𝅥𝅘𝅥½ *I Spent a Week There the Other Night* (Sky, 1994) 𝅘𝅥𝅘𝅥𝅘𝅥𝅘𝅥 *Dogs Under Stress* (Sky, 1994) 𝅘𝅥𝅘𝅥𝅘𝅥½

▶▶ David Bowie, Mott the Hoople, Brian Eno, Roxy Music, Patti Smith, R.E.M., Sonic Youth, the Feelies, Luna, the entire punk-rock class of 1976, countless others...

◀◀ John Cage, La Monte Young, 50s doo-wop, "Louie Louie"

see also: *Lou Reed, John Cale*

Greg Kot

Tom Verlaine

See: Television

The Verlaines

Formed 1979 in Dunedin, New Zealand. Disbanded 1994.

Graeme Downes, Vocals, guitar, keyboards, oboe, piano; Jane Dodd,

bass (1979-88); Greg Kerr, drums (1981-82); Alan Haig, drums (1982-84); Robbie Yeats, drums (1984-89); Mike Stoodley, bass (1991-93); Greg Cairns, drums (1991-92); Darren Stedman, drums, (1993); Paul Winders, guitar, vocals (1993)

An ambitious band, The Verlaines set its sights above the usual pop-punk standards, creating a sound both romantic and furious. Like the symbolist poet the group is named after and inspired by, the aching voiced, classically trained frontman Downes spun sweeping tales of imploding relationships, drunks and melancholy outcasts with engaging melodicism. Largely ignored in the U.S., the band's output was remarkably consistent, and Downes songwriting skills always hovered around the flawless level. Rather than endure more commercial failure, Downes pulled the plug on the band after 1993's *Way Out Where*

what to buy: *Juvenilia* (Flying Nun, 1993, prod. Various) ♪♪♪♪ is a potent collection of the band's first EPs and a few extras. With the hammering immediacy of punk coupled with Downes' already poetic lyrics, it's a solid introduction to the band's early years. Keeping an eye on the mainstream, *Ready to Fly* (Slash, 1991, prod. The Verlaines and Victor Brbic) ♪♪♪♪ bears an acoustic-tinged grandeur that allows the scope of Downes' tales to reach an unencumbered vastness.

what to buy next: The group's final release, *Way Out Where* (Slash, 1993, prod. Joe Chiccarelli), ♪♪♪½ finds the band existing in name only, with Downes the only original member left. The darker and tougher edge of his doomed love songs here are truly the stuff to empty the Remy bottle with.

what to avoid: Lumbering under pretentious airs, *Hallelujah All the Way Home* (Homestead, 1989, prod. not listed) ♪♪½ lets most of the album's tunefulness simply get bogged down under its own artiness. For the dedicated fans only.

worth searching for: The out-of-print *Bird Dog* (Homestead, 1987) is arguably the band's creative peak. ♪♪♪♪

▶▶ Guided By Voices, Chris Knox, The Waterboys

◀◀ The Chills

Allan Orski

Veruca Salt

Formed 1992 in Chicago, Ill.

Louise Post, guitars, vocals; Stephen L. Lacharvicz, bass; Nina Gordon, guitars, vocals; Jim Shapiro, drums, vocals

Naming itself after the character in "Willy Wonka and the Chocolate Factory," Veruca Salt stormed onto the modern rock scene with its aptly titled sweetie pie hit "Seether" from its debut *American Thighs* (Minty Fresh/Geffen, 1994, prod. Brad Wood) ♪♪♪ If nothing else, you have to give credit to any band that can write a sexy ode to a comic book hero ("Spiderman '79"). But Veruca Salt succeeds in borrowing from fellow Chicago rockers Cheap Trick the ability to meld hard rock with bubblegum pop. Its follow-up, a four-song EP *Blow It Out Your Ass ... It's Veruca Salt,* (Geffen, 1996, prod. Steve Albini) ♪♪♪ hits even a little harder, which is a promising sign.

Christina Fuoco

The Verve

Formed 1991 in England. Disbanded 1995.

Richard Ashcroft, vocals; Nick McCabe, guitars; Peter Salisbury, drums; Simon Jones, bass

The Verve (or simple Verve) managed to evoke a number of influences without actually sounding like any of them—including Jimi Hendrix (especially his psychedelic outings), the Allman Brothers Band, Pink Floyd and Brian Eno. Most importantly, the group used these artists as inspiration and not as essential components in their music. The Verve's sound is defined with vast swirls of atmospheric guitars and reverb-drenched vocals atop subtle bass and drums. To say that this music is dreamy and psychedelic is an understatement; it is hypnotic and haunting and, at times, becomes nearly hallucinatory. Techno artists such as the Aphex Twin and Moby have achieved sonic psychotropy on a par with this, but what raises the Verve above such trance artists is its dedication to melody and song structure, and its use of traditional rock instruments. Unfortunately, the band (particularly singer Ashcroft) became as well-known for its indulgences and mercurial behavior as for its music, which led to a split in 1995.

what to buy: The Verve's debut album, *A Storm in Heaven,* (Vernon Yard, 1993, prod. John Leckie) ♪♪♪♪ is an enveloping ride that is most effective if listened to in a single sitting. While songs such as "Blue," "Butterfly" and "Slide Away" stand well enough on their own, the album as a whole works as a kind of psychedelic tone poem.

what to buy next: *A Northern Soul* (Vernon Yard, 1995, prod. Owen Morris and the Verve) ♪♪♪♪ will not disappoint fans of *A Storm in Heaven,* with sure signs of progress that makes the band's break-up all the more distressing.

the rest: *No Come Down* (Vernon Yard, 1994) ♪♪♪

worth searching for: The imported *The Verve EP* (Vernon Yard, 1992, prod. not listed) ♪♪♪ is relatively easy to find and worth the extra cash.

▶▶ Aphex Twin, Moby, Beck

◀◀ Jimi Hendrix, Pink Floyd, Brian Eno, Allman Brothers Band

Dave Galens

The Verve Pipe

Formed 1991 in East Lansing, Mich.

Brian Vander Ark, vocals, guitar; Brian Stout, guitar, vocals (1992-93); A.J. Dunning, guitars (1993-present); Doug Corella, percussion, keyboards (1995-present); Donny Brown, drums, vocals

A merging of two popular western Michigan bands—Johnny With An Eye and Water 4 The Pool—the melodic power-pop band The Verve Pipe attracted a grass roots following (via tours and independent releases) well before the release of its major label debut, *Villains*. (RCA, 1996, prod. Jerry Harrison) ♪♪♪♪ Frontman Vander Ark passionately delivers his shockingly vivid tales of cynical and bittersweet tales of love, while edgy, subtle keyboards textures and hypnotic bass and drums swirl around his effortlessly lush vocals. A mature effort that was one of the year's finest debuts.

the rest: *I've Suffered A Head Injury* (LMNOPop!, 1992) ♪♪♪ *Pop Smear* (LMNOPop!, 1993) ♪♪♪

Christina Fuoco

The Vibrators

Formed 1976 in London, England

Knox, vocals; Eddie, guitar; Pat Collier, bass (1977-78, 1982-85); John Ellis, guitar (1977-86); Gary Tibbs, bass (1978-80); Noel Thompson, bass (1985-86); Nigel Bennett, guitar (1990)

Opportunistic (and older) punkers, the Vibrators made one ripping album at the crest of the punk explosion. Unlike others, the band didn't split up when it fell out of favor, instead releasing a number of now-deleted albums featuring streamlined chargers that lost a little of their speed and fury along the way. The startling debut, *Pure Mania* (Columbia/Legacy, 1977/1991) ♪♪♪ features rudimentary but catchy songs, along with rude riffs that lend it a punchy that bears the test of time well. *The Power of Money: The Best of The Vibrators* (Continum Records, 1991) ♪♪♪ collects highlights from the debut as well as material from the later, otherwise out-of-print, work.

Allan Orski

Gene Vincent

Born Eugene Vincent Craddock, Feb. 11, 1935, in Norfolk, Va. Died Oct. 12, 1971, in Los Angeles, Calif.

Vincent, whose sad, lonely life ended in an early death, is mostly forgotten these days; even his gravesite is so neglected that the inscription on his marker is virtually unreadable. But how good were the early rock 'n' roll sides he cut for Capitol Records during the late 50s? Ask any collector who routinely pay hundreds of dollars for clean copies of his old albums. Although the success of his 1956 Top 10 hit, "Be-Bop-A-Lula," would never be repeated, he left behind a remarkably fine and consistent set of recordings, including some of the most openly erotic rock of its day. "Woman Love," the B-side to "Be-Bop-A-Lulu," was banned from radio because of Vincent's "suggestive" vocal. Country star Buck Owens started out as an original member of his backup band, the Bluecats, while Bluecats guitarist Cliff Gallup remains one of the most uncredited originators of the music, even though guitar maestro Jeff Beck cut an entire album of Vincent oldies in 1993, faithfully reproducing Gallup's original work on every track for one of the most sober and reverential tribute albums ever. Like his frequent sidekick Eddie Cochran—who was killed in the car crash that left Vincent's already crippled leg mangled for the rest of his life—Vincent occupied only a small corner of the world of rock 'n' roll in his time. But, man, did he hold that little corner down. His installment of *The Capitol Collectors Series* (Capitol, 1990, prod. Various) ♪♪♪♪♪ is one of the great reissues of 50s music, with 21 prime cuts from Vincent's 1956-59 Capitol sessions. Until Capitol starts putting out his original albums, this is the sole souvenir of the brief, bittersweet career of one of rock's forgotten greats.

Joel Selvin

Holly Vincent /Holly and The Italians/Oblivious

Born Holly Beth Vincent in the late '50s in Chicago, Ill.

The Italians: Holly Vincent, guitar, vocals; Steve Dalton, drums; numerous bass players

Author of one true rock 'n' roll classic, the 1980 single "Tell That Girl to Shut Up," Vincent formed the Italians in Los Angeles, then moved to England to sign a recording contract and earn her few minutes of fame. Though "Tell That Girl to Shut Up" is a terrific punk-rock kiss-off song, the band had severe personnel problems, couldn't find a compatible producer and Vincent's career more or less dwindled into obscurity. She resurfaced occasionally, with her early-90s band Oblivious and on a duet album with Concrete Blonde's ex-singer Johnette Napolitano. Vincent's first two albums—*The Right to Be Italian* (Virgin-Epic, 1981, prod. George "Shadow"

Morton and Richard Gottehrer) and *Holly and the Italians* (Virgin-Epic, 1982) (the latter's a solo album despite the title)—are out of print, so the curious have only Shake It Up! American Power Pop II *(Rhino, 1993, comp. Gary Stewart) for a taste, via "Tell That Girl to Shut Up." Oblivious she released* America, *(Daemon, 1993) while the Napolitano album is called* Vowel Movement. *(Mammoth, 1995)*

Steve Knopper

Violent Femmes

Formed 1981 in Milwaukee, Wisc.

Gordon Gano, guitar, vocals; Brian Ritchie, bass, guitar; Victor DeLorenzo, drums (1981-92); Guy Hoffman, drums (1992-present)

Other acts flirted with the idea, but the Violent Femmes perfected acoustic punk rock. Preacher's kid Gano doctored up country/gospel styles with his whacked-out poetry, while Ritchie thumped out funky jazz rhythms on a mariachi-styled bass and DeLorenzo scratched propulsive beats on a single snare drum. The trio experimented with different sounds on later albums, with varying degrees of success. But its most lasting style remains the twisted folk-punk it invented in the early 80s while busking on the sidewalks of Milwaukee's East Side.

what to buy: A true word-of-mouth sensation, *Violent Femmes* (Slash, 1983, prod. Mark Van Hecke) sold a million copies over 10 years without ever scratching the Billboard charts. Gano's nasal whine of a voice is an acquired taste, but psycho-nerd anthems such as "Add It Up," "Blister in the Sun" and "Kiss Off" have universal appeal.

what to buy next: *The Blind Leading the Naked* (Slash, 1986, prod. Jerry Harrison) adds hard-core punk and R&B to the mix with grand results. Don't judge *Why Do Birds Sing?* (Slash/Reprise, 1991, prod. Michael Beinhorn and the Violent Femmes) by the tepid remake of Culture Club's "Do You Really Want To Hurt Me:" the rest of the album, especially the PG-13 "Girl Trouble" and "American Music," is the Femmes in full glory.

what to avoid: Aside from the album-opening "Don't Start Me on the Liquor," there's little to be intoxicated by on *New Times* (Elektra, 1994, prod. Brian Ritchie and Gordon Gano)

the rest: *Hallowed Ground* (Slash, 1984) *3* (Slash, 1989) *Add It Up: 1981-1993* (Slash, 1993)

worth searching for: *Debacle: The First Decade* (Liberation/Slash, 1990) is an import collection that's a bit more straightforward than the domestic *Add It Up*

solo outings:

Gordon Gano (in Mercy Seat): *Mercy Seat* (Slash, 1987)

Brian Ritchie: *The Blend* (SST, 1987) *I See A Noise* (Chameleon/Dali 1990)

Victor DeLorenzo: *Peter Corey Sent Me* (Dali, 1990)

Frank Black, Jonny Polonsky, Liz Phair, Hammell on Trial

What Album Changed Your Life?

"Maybe the Clash's London Calling, just the impact of the first time I heard that record--I thought I wanted to join a band. I was probably 11 or 12 when it came out, but it really affected me when I was 13 or 15. I was going to see my first shows, and they had something I could listen to that I wanted to join. I saw the four guys onstage and said 'I want to be one of those guys.' The album was a soundtrack to that feeling."

Jakob Dylan (The Wallflowers)

Jonathan Richman, the Velvet Underground, the Carter Family

Thor Christensen

Visage

See: Magazine

Voice of the Beehive

Formed 1987 in London, England

Tracey Bryn (Belland), vocals, guitar; Melissa Brooke Belland, vocals; Martin Brett, bass, piano (1987-91); Mike Jones, guitar, vocals, keyboards, programming (1987-91); D.M. (Woody) Woodgate, drums, percussion, programming (1987-91)

Sisters and expatriate Californians Bryn and Belland front this group, which was conceived as a delightful amalgamation of West Coast and U.K. pop approaches. The original Voice of the Beehive incorporated elements of 60s girl group sugar, post-punk spice and a recognition that the world ain't always everything nice. The approach is best realized on *Let It Bee,* (London, 1988, prod. Pete Collins, Hugh Jones and Marvin Etzioni) an uneven but winning foray into the realm of hooks and heartache, with spunk and sass to spare. *Honey Lingers* (London, 1991, prod. Various) falls prey to too many cooks (seven different production credits?!) and a general slip into the realm of overly slick contemporary gloss. The band splintered after *Honey Lingers,* leaving the sisters to carry on for *Sex & Misery* ,(Discovery, 1995, prod. Peter John Vettese) on which Voice of the Beehive's original vim and vigor finally succumb to the temptation to sound more like a Madonna clone that will get airplay. The lyrics are heartfelt and personal; the music, sadly, is forgettable.

Carl Cafarelli

Chris von Sneidern

Born Dec. 6, 1965 in Syracuse, N.Y.

Although virtually unknown outside the insular world of pure pop fandom, von Sneidern (or CVS, as he's known) is a bona fide star among the pop cognoscenti, and he achieved this status in a staggeringly short period of time. After leaving his native central New York during the mid-80s, CVS served his apprenticeship with San Francisco-area bands the Sneetches and Flying Color before becoming friends with power pop legend Paul Collins. At Collins' urging, CVS began fronting his own Pop Gem Factory and releasing solo albums of unerring brilliance. *Sight & Sound* (Heyday, 1993, prod. Chris von Sneidern) sounds like some beyond-this-mortal-coil collaboration between Badfinger's Pete Ham and Big Star's Chris Bell. *Big White Lies* (Heyday, 1994, prod. Chris von Sneidern) continues in much the same irresistible vein, while *Go!* (Mod Lang, 1996, prod. Chris von Sneidern) offers further proof that CVS is one of the most accomplished and vital performers working in the pop idiom today. Furthermore, his work demonstrates that it's possible to be overtly influenced by the classic pop of the past and still create new work that is not a simple rehash. Pop Gem Factory, indeed.

Carl Cafarelli

Vulgar Boatmen

See: The Silos

John Waite /The Babys/Bad English

The Babys (1976-1981): John Waite (born July 4, 1955 in Lancashire, England), bass, vocals; Wally Stocker, guitar, vocals; Mike Corby, keyboards, vocals (1976-77); Tony Brock, drums, vocals; Jonathan Cain, keyboards, guitar, vocals (1978-81); Ricky Phillips, bass (1978-81) Bad English (1988-91): Waite; Cain; Phillips; Neal Schon, guitar; Deen Castronovo, drums

The focal point for all three of these entities is Waite, a reedy singer and self-styled bad boy who brings abundant attitude—a palpable vocal sneer—to even the prettiest songs. The Babys are the best of this lot; it's no accident that 14 of the 20 songs on *The Essential John Waite* (Chrysalis, 1992, prod. Various) are Babys selections, including modest hits such as "Isn't it Time," "Back on My Feet Again" and "Head First," as well as his own No. 1 smash from 1984, "Missing You." The short-lived Bad English, a meeting of the Babys and Journey, had neither the charm nor pop touch of the Babys; its albums—*Bad English* (Epic, 1989, prod. Richie Zito) and *Backlash* (Epic, 1991) —are bangy arena rock well after the genre became obsolete. Waite's solo offerings have been whittled down to his recent *Temple Bar,* (Imago, 1995, prod. Mike Shipley) a well-sung effort that wants for a good song or two—or 10.

see also: *Journey*

Gary Graff

The Waitresses

Formed late 1979 in Akron, Ohio

Patty Donahue, vocals; Mars Williams, reeds; Chris Butler, guitar; Dan Klayman, organ; David Hofstra, bass; Tracy Wormworth, bass; Billy Ficca, drums

Boasting an armful of smart-aleck one-liners and a funkified pop beat, The Waitresses became a surprise, albeit short-lived, sensation with the teasing "I Know What Boys Like" in 1982. Although Butler wrote the material, it was the pragmatic voice of Donahue that stamped the smirking but no-foolin' demeanor that identified The Waitresses on the group. *The Best of The Waitresses* (Polydor, 1980, comp. Bill Levenson and Chris Butler) is all that's left and contains everything essential, including the anti-yuletide "Christmas Wrapping" and the theme song to the 80s TV show "Square Pegs."

Allan Orski

Tom Waits

Born Dec. 7, 1949 in Pomona, Calif.

With a voice that sounds like it was soaked in a vat of bourbon, left hanging in the smokehouse for a few months and then taken outside and run over with car a few times, Waits is something of an acquired taste. Yet it's his songs that are the real selling point, and Waits' detailed accounts of losers with hearts of gold have won over the likes of Bruce Springsteen, Rod Stewart, Bette Midler, The Eagles, Screamin' Jay Hawkins, the Ramones, Johnny Cash, Bob Seger and Dion, all of whom have recorded his material. Starting out as the embodiment of dissipated hipster slackness, Waits reached a creative dead-end with that persona and proceeded to reinvent himself as a ravaged-voiced Howlin' Wolf acolyte backed by a combination of avant-rock and traffic noise. Not only did the change reinvigorate his music, it expanded his horizons; Waits has since performed in a stage production he wrote with his wife, Kathleen Brennan, and a filmed cabaret-style concert. He has also acted in a number of films, including "Short Cuts," "Ironweed," "Bram Stoker's Dracula," "Mystery Train" and "Rumblefish." Considering the risks he takes in all facets of his career, it's to Waits' credit that nearly every move he makes is worth paying attention to.

what to buy: The first two installments of a loose trilogy that also includes *Franks Wild Years, Swordfishtrombones* (Island, 1983, prod. Tom Waits) and *Raindogs* (Island, 1985, prod. Tom Waits) finds Waits writing the strongest material of his career. The sound is unsettling, to say the least, yet even through the odd instrumental textures, sprung rhythms and barked vocals, Waits' songs (including the Stewart hit "Downtown Train") come through loud and clear. *Bone Machine* (Island, 1992, prod. Tom Waits) ups the clatter quotient even further, and the material is Waits' most harrowing ever—including "Earth Died Screaming," "Dirt in the Ground" and "Jesus Gonna Be Here." On his debut album, *Tom Waits,* (Asylum, 1973, prod. Jerry Yester) the singer may be sentimental in the way people are after a few too many cocktails, and his voice slightly ravaged (though not so much as it would get on later albums), yet songs such as "Ol' 55," "Midnight Lullabye" and "Martha" are so good they transcend his shortcomings.

what to buy next: Many find Waits' monologue-laden live album *Nighthawks at the Diner* (Asylum, 1975, prod. Bones Howe) hopelessly schticky, but it's the album on which his early beatnik persona came into full flower, for good or ill. Waits tells hilarious tall tales and one-liners, cranks out some sidewalk sociology in verse form and even performs a few songs—notably a memorable version of Red Sovine's trucker epic "Big Joe and Phantom 309." *Small Change* (Asylum, 1976, prod. Bones Howe) kicks off with the syrupy yet effective "Tom Traubert's Blues," but things pick up fast with "Step Right Up," which finds Waits improvising a huckster's jive at a mile a minute. *Anthology of Tom Waits* (Asylum, 1985, prod. Jerry Yester and Bones Howe) offers a serviceable selection of Waits' years on Asylum, but there are too many omissions to make it essential.

what to avoid: *The Early Years* (Bizarre/Straight, 1991, prod. Bob Duffey) includes four songs that Waits re-recorded for *Closing Time,* but it's ultimately for curiosity seekers and diehard fans only—as is *The Early Years Volume 2* (Bizarre/Straight, 1992, prod. Bob Duffey)

the rest: *The Heart of Saturday Night* (Asylum, 1974) *Foreign Affairs* (Asylum, 1977) *Blue Valentine* (Asylum, 1978) *Heart Attack and Vine* (Asylum, 1980) *Franks Wild Years* (Island, 1987, prod. Tom Waits) *Big Time* (Island, 1988) *Night on Earth* soundtrack (Island, 1992) *The Black Rider* (Island, 1993)

worth searching for The soundtrack from Francis Ford Coppola's *One from the Heart'* (Columbia, 1982, prod. Bones Howe) pairs Waits' gutter growl against the honeyed crooning of country-music chanteuse Crystal Gayle—a terrible idea on paper, perhaps, but magic on disc.

▶▶ Rickie Lee Jones, Beck, Soul Coughing

◀◀ Chet Baker, Charles Bukowski, Captain Beefheart, Howling' Wolf

Daniel Durchholz

Junior Walker & the All-Stars

Formed 1964 in Detroit, Mich.

The original line-up consisted of Junior Walker (born Autry DeWalt; died Nov. 23, 1995 Battle Creek, MI) tenor sax and vocals; Vic Thomas, keyboards; Willie Woods, guitar; James Graves, drums

Mixing southern fatback funk with gritty vocals and hard-blowing tenor sax straight from the roadhouse, Arkansas-born Junior Walker became an unlikely mid-60's star at Motown. His wasn't the assembly-line "Sound Of Young America" that Berry Gordy had envisioned; in the beginning, Junior & The All Stars' groove was rawer and raunchier than anything else on the label (its single, "Shoot Your Shot," was banned from the airwaves during the Detroit Riots in the summer of '67). The group had immediate success with a series of classic singles - "Shotgun" and "Road Runner" among them - which established Walker, along with King Curtis and New Orleans' Lee Allen, as one of the legends of rock 'n' roll sax. Though he never again reached the frenetic heights of those early singles, Walker enjoyed a successful career with Motown well into the 70's, recording more mainstream fare such as "What Does It Take" and "These Eyes." He continued to play and tour until his death in 1995.

what to buy: One of the most influential R&B albums of the 60s is *Shotgun*. (Motown, 1965, prod. Berry Gordy and Lawrence Horn) ♪♪♪♪ The first side alone includes "Road Runner," "Shotgun," "Shake And Fingerpop," "Shoot Your Shot" and the much-covered, moody instrumental "Cleo's Mood." Aside from James Brown's band, this was the tightest, most raucous funk around in the mid-60's. For a complete career overview, *Nothing But Soul: The Singles (1962-1983)* (Motown, 1994, prod. Various) ♪♪♪♪ contains all the essential early singles as well as more polished later hits such as "What Does It Take," "Do You See My Love," "These Eyes" and "Way Back Home."

what to buy next: For a taste of Junior's late 60s live shows, check out *Junior Walker & The All-Stars—Live!* (Motown, 1969) ♪♪♪

what to avoid: The numerous and needlessly duplicated "best-of" sets Motown has churned out over the years; there are currently six Junior Walker "greatest hits" collections on CD. Stick with *Nothing But Soul*.

the rest: *Road Runner* (Motown, 1966) ♪♪♪ *Gotta Hold On To This Feeling* (Motown, 1967) ♪♪♪ *Home Cookin'* (Motown, 1968) ♪♪♪

worth searching for: An original vinyl pressing of the *Shotgun* album—a strong argument for the sonic superiority of the LP vs. the CD.

▶▶ Maceo Parker, Morphine, Prince, David Sanborn

◀◀ Illinois Jacquet, Louis Jordan, Coleman Hawkins, Ray Charles

Doug Pippin

The Walker Brothers

Formed 1964 in London, England. Disbanded 1968. Reunited 1975.

Not a duo, not a Walker in sight and definitely not British, the Walker Brothers - Americans John Maus, Scott Engel and Gary Leeds—found sudden fame in the midst of British pop mania of the mid-60s. Lush production and rich vocals made for a romantic swoon, and "The Sun Ain't Gonna Shine (Anymore)" and "Make It Easy on Yourself" are two certified and worthy hits from the era. Although success was short-lived, Scott Walker (Scott Engel) had a fairly successful solo career in England through the 70s. *Anthology: The Walker Brothers* (One Way, 1995) ♪♪♪♪ is a good overview of the hits period.

Patrick McCarty

Wall of Voodoo

Formed 1978 in Los Angeles, Calif. Disbanded 1989.

Stan Ridgway, vocals, keyboards, harmonica (1978-83); Marc Moreland, guitar; Bruce Moreland, bass, keyboards; Joe Nanini, percussion; Chas Gray, keyboards; Andy Prieboy, vocals (1983-90)

For a time at the dawn of the 80s, Wall of Voodoo straddled the line between avant-garde/industrial music and New Wave, eschewing the latter's good-timey attitude and the former's rejection of musicality. The result was a weird but compelling stew of spaghetti-western twang, ominous synthesizers, exotic percussion and dystopian visions. Holding it all together was Ridgway's side-of-the-mouth delivery, laced with irony but still a tad vulnerable. At its best, the band made anthems of alienation sweetened by wise-guy absurdity and off-kilter hooks. Wall of Voodoo enjoyed a moment of fame with the 1982 hit, "Mexican Radio," which appeared on their sophomore album *Call of the West* But the group lost its focus after Ridgway left for a solo career (and eventually a new group, Drywall) and was replaced by the far less interesting Prieboy.

what to buy: *Dark Continent* (I.R.S., 1981, prod. Jim Hill, Paul McKenna and Wall of Voodoo) 🦴🦴🦴🦴 remains the finest distillation of WOV's strange brew.

what to buy next: *The Ridgway Compilation: Songs That Made This Country Great* (I.R.S., 1992, prod. Various) 🦴🦴🦴🦴 gleans the best of his days with WOV as well as his equally interesting solo material.

what to avoid: By the arrival of *Seven Days in Sammystown,* (I.R.S., 1985, prod. Ian Brodie) 🦴🦴 the band was a mere shadow of its former self.

the rest: *Call of the West* (I.R.S., 1982) 🦴🦴🦴 *Happy Planet* (I.R.S., 1987) 🦴🦴 *Ugly Americans in Australia* (I.R.S., 1988) 🦴🦴 *Index Masters* (I.R.S., 1980/Restless, 1991) 🦴🦴🦴🦴

worth searching for: *Wall of Voodoo* (I.R.S. EP, 1980, prod. Wall of Voodoo) 🦴🦴🦴🦴 contains three strong originals and a smoldering electronic rendition of Johnny Cash's "Ring of Fire." *Granma's House* (I.R.S., 1984, prod. Various) 🦴🦴🦴🦴 is a British best-of that recaps the Ridgway years.

solo outings:

Stan Ridgway The Big Heat (I.R.S., 1986/1993) 🦴🦴🦴

▶▶ Soul Coughing, Moby, Medicine

◀◀ Johnny Cash, Ennio Morricone, Martin Denny, Les Baxter, Phillip Glass, Residents, Devo, Kraftwerk

Simon Glickman

The Wallflowers

Formed 1990 in Los Angeles, Calif.

Jakob Dylan, vocals, guitar; Rami Jaffee, piano, organ; Barrie Maguire, bass (1990-93); Peter Yanowitz, drums (1990-93); Tobi Miller, guitar (1990-95); Michael Ward, guitar (1995-present); Greg Richling, bass (1993-present); Mario Calire, drums (1995-present)

The Wallflowers are the answer to those who like the idea of roots rock but are repelled by the derivative poundings of its lesser practitioners. An exciting rock 'n' roll band—regardless of Dylan's lineage (yes, that's his father)—the Wallflowers rock with an organic authenticity and dense dramatic overtones. Much of the credit does belong to Dylan, whose lyrical insights and gruff delivery possess a striking maturity, and to Jaffee's understated elegance on the Hammond. The debut, *Wallflowers* (Virgin, 1992, prod. Various) 🦴🦴🦴 is a sprawling and indulgent snapshot recorded live in the studio. With many of the songs clocking in at epic length, the nearly 70-minute total becomes a test of one's attention span, though the more concise and sturdy songs such as "Ashes to Ashes" and the grotesque imagery of "Sugarfoot," plus the spare beauty of "Asleep at the Wheel" make the case for further inspection. A lengthy disappearance from the public eye (due to label and lineup changes) proved fruitful, as the band displays impressive growth on *Bringing Down the Horse* (Interscope, 1996, prod. T-Bone Burnett) 🦴🦴🦴🦴 From the opening bars on the sultry groove of "One Headlight" on, it's a fully realized return with a tighter, cleaner sound.

Allan Orski

Joe Walsh /The James Gang/Barnstorm

Born Nov. 20, 1947, Wichita, Kansas

Part guitar ace and part court jester, Walsh is one of the most unique personalities rock 'n' roll has produced—sometimes to a fault. He's scored hits on his own and with every band he's been in, from the James Gang to the Eagles. And his wobbly slide guitar signature has been hooked for sessions by Steve Winwood, B.B. King, Ringo Starr, Bob Seger, Richard Marx and Wilson Philips. Walsh is capable of writing some terrific songs ("Rocky Mountain Way," "Walk Away," "Help Me Through the Night," "Turn to Stone") but too often he lets his comic persona get the best of him, often to the detriment of the music.

what to buy: Walsh did right by *Look What I Did: The Joe Walsh Anthology* (MCA, 1995, prod. Various) 🦴🦴🦴🦴🦴. While his individual albums run the gamut from inconsistent to wretched, this 34-song set snares the best from James Gang, Barnstorm and his solo albums, showing both the fluid rocker and the rock 'n' roll funny man. The only glaring deletion is his taught rocker "In the City," which he recorded for *The Warriors* soundtrack and for the Eagles' *The Long Run* album.

what to buy next: Not much, really. *The Smoker You Drink, The Player You Get* (ABC/Dunhill, 1973, prod. Walsh and Bill Szymczyk) 🦴🦴🦴 is Barnstorm's defining moment, housing hot tracks such as "Rocky Mountain Way" and "Meadows." Humor dominates on *But Seriously Folks* (Asylum, 1978, prod. Szymczyk) 🦴🦴🦴—presumably because Walsh's more serious music was being made with the Eagles—but at least the jokes, particularly "Life's Been Good," are funny.

What Album Changed Your Life?

"(David Bowie's) Ziggy Stardust changed my life when I first heard that. That era--I was growing up, learning to play guitar, and it had all the elements of everything I wanted to hear in a band or an art or whatever. It didn't seem realistic; that's how good it was."

Phil Collen (Def Leppard)

what to avoid: Despite the popular title track, *Ordinary Average Guy* (Pyramid/Epic 1991) WOOF! is a bottom feeder on which Walsh seems to have run out of ideas on all fronts.

the rest: With the James Gang: *Yer Album* (Bluesay, 1968) ♪♪♪, *Rides Again* (ABC/Dunhill) ♪♪♪, *Thirds* ABC/Dunhill, 1970) ♪♪♪, *Live at Carnegie Hall* (ABC/Dunhill, 1971) ♪♪. With Barnstorm: *Barnstorm* (ABC/Dunhill, 1972) ♪♪. Solo: *So What* (ABC/Dunhill, 1975) ♪♪♪, *You Can't Argue With a Sick Mind* (ABC, 1976) ♪♪♪, *There Goes the Neighborhood* (Asylum, 1981) ♪♪, *You Bought It…You Name It* (Warner Bros., 1983) ♪♪, *The Confessor* (Warner Bros., 1985) ♪♪♪, *Got Any Gum* (Warner Bros., 1987) ♪♪, Songs For a Dying Planet *Pyramid/Epic, 1992)* ♪, Robocop: The Series Soundtrack *(Pyramid, 1995)* ♪♪. *With Albert Collins and Etta James:* Jump the Blues *(Verve, 1989)* ♪♪♪

▶▶ Georgia Satellites, Lynyrd Skynyrd, .38 Special, Brother Cane

◀◀ Chuck Berry, B.B. King, Albert Collins, T-Bone Walker, Pete Townshend, Keith Richards, Chet Atkins

see also: *The Eagles*

Gary Graff

Steve Walsh

See: Kansas

Wang Chung

Formed as Huang Chung, 1982 in London, England

Jack Hues, vocals, keyboards, guitar; Nick Feldman, bass, keyboards, vocals; Darren Costin (1982-84), drums, percussion, keyboards

The catchy "Dance Hall Days" made a big splash in 1984, with its awkward simplicity, deceptively sinister lyrics and sanitized synthesizer hooks. Along with its airs of pomposity, it neatly captures the era, as does the group's debut album *Points on a Curve* (Geffen, 1983, prod. Chris Hughes and Ross Cullum) ♪♪♪ The soundtrack for *To Live and Die in L.A.* (Geffen, 1984, prod. Wang Chung) ♪♪♪ finds the band playing above its own mediocre level. Besides the fine title track, Wang Chung's best song, the album blends atmospheric electronics into a chilly picture of L.A.'s underside. It's a tense and convincing album that successfully avoids most of Hues' arty ambitions.

the rest: *Mosaic* (Geffen, 1986) ♪♪ *The Warmer Side of Cool* (Geffen, 1989) ♪♪

Allan Orski

War

Formed 1969 in Long Beach, Calif.

Lonnie Jordan, vocals, keyboards, bass; Howard Scott, vocals, guitar; Charles Miller, woodwinds (1969-79); B.B. Dickerson, vocals, bass (1969-78); Harold Brown, drums, percussion (1969-83, 1993-present); Papa Dee Allen, vocals, keyboards (1969-88, died Aug. 30, 1988 in Vallejo, Calif.); Lee Oskar, harmonica (1969-92); Pete Rosen, bass (1969, died that year); Luther Rabb, bass (1978-84); Ricky Green, bass (1984-89); Pat Rizzo, reeds (1979-86); Ron Hammon, percussion (1979-present); Alice Tweed Smyth, vocals (1978-82); Tetsuya "Tex" Nakamura, harmonica (1993-present); Rae Valentine (born Harold Rae Brown, Jr.), programming (1993-present); Kerry Campbell, saxophone (1993-present); Sal Rodriguez, drums, vocals (1993-present); Charles Green, reeds (1993-present).

Some of the best groove music ever laid down was done by War during the 70s. With its Latin percussion and Angelino concerns, War was the Southwest's flagship entry into the funk fray. And it represented it well with memorable jams such as "Low Rider," "Cisco Kid," "The World Is a Ghetto" and more. War initially formed as a backup group for pro-footballer Deacon Jones and got the attention of U.K. rocker Eric Burdon, who was also looking for a backup group. Adding the Danish-born Oskar, whose harmonica brought a trademark sound the band, Burdon and War had a smash hit with "Spill the Wine." After two years and two albums, during which the group jammed with Jimi Hendrix the night before he died, the band bid Burdon adieu and went on to even greater accomplishments on its own. Despite numerous personnel changes and flagging sales—particularly during the 80s—War kept touring until the hip-hop community began embracing its old records. The group then set up an innovative lend-lease kind of arrangement, ensuring that a) it was compensated for the use of its music, and b) that it would be able to cash in on the newfound exposure.

what to buy: *All Day Music* (United Artists, 1971/Avenue, 1994) is an awesome coming of age album, with "Slippin' into Darkness" leading the way. *Anthology 1970-1994* (Avenue, 1994, prod. Various) touches all the essential moments and includes a version of "Don't Let No One Get You Down" with the Hispanic MC's.

what to buy next: *The World is a Ghetto* (United Artists, 1972/Avenue, 1992) has "The Cisco Kid" and the pointed, poignant title track as cornerstones for another superlative album. *Rap Declares War* (Avenue, 1992, prod. Various) is a fascinating look —through the vantage point of one group's music—at how hip-hop cleverly appropriates and blends older sounds into its mix.

what to avoid: *The Best of War...and More,* (Priority, 1987/Avenue, 1991) a skimpy, poorly chosen (no "The World is a Ghetto?") that deserves instant deletion from the catalog.

the rest: with Eric Burdon—*Eric Burdon Declares "War"* (MCA, 1970/Avenue, 1992) *The Black-Man's Burdon* (MCA, 1970/Avenue, 1992) *Love is All Around (Early Recordings)* (ABC, 1976/Avenue, 1992) *Best of Eric Burdon and War* (Avenue, 1995) as War—*War*(United Artists, 1971/Avenue, 1992) *Deliver the Word* (United Artists, 1973/Avenue, 1992) *War Live* (United Artists, 1974/Avenue, 1992) *Why Can't We Be Friends?* (United Artists, 1975/Avenue, 1992) *Greatest Hits* (United Artists, 1976/Avenue (gold disc), 1995) *Platinum Jazz* (Blue Note, 1977/Avenue Jazz, 1993) *Galaxy* (MCA, 1977/Avenue, 1993) *Outlaw* (RCA, 1982/Avenue, 1995) *Peace Sign* (Avenue, 1994)

worth searching for: The late 70s couplet *The Music Band* (MCA, 1979) and *The Music Band 2* (MCA, 1979) gave War a bit of a revival in the midst of its commercial doldrums.

▶▶ Groove Collective, Los Lobos

◀◀ Sly & the Family Stone

Lawrence Gabriel and Gary Graff

Jennifer Warnes

Born March 3, 1947 in Seattle, Wash.

A former background singer, "Smothers Brothers Comedy Hour" regular and soundtrack diva, Warnes has lived to tell the tale. Her singing style through the years has remained appealingly understated, yet it has left her at the mercy of her material—which hasn't always been as strong as it could be. Her early 70s Warner Bros. albums, *See Me* and *Jennifer*, are out of print, as are the Arista albums she recorded late in the decade, *Jennifer Warnes* and *Shot Through the Heart* Material from the latter two is gathered on *Best of Jennifer Warnes* (Arista, 1982, prod. Various), which is negligible except for the presence of the hits "Right Time of the Night" and "I Know a Heartache When I See One." Warnes gained fame recording soundtrack duets for "An Officer and a Gentleman" ("Up Where We Belong" with Joe Cocker) and "Dirty Dancing (I've Had The Time of My Life)" with Bill Medley), and her return to solo work produced *Famous Blue Raincoat: The Songs of Leonard Cohen* (Cypress, 1986, prod. C. Roscoe Beck and Jennifer Warnes), a stunning collection that makes Cohen's songs accessible without prettifying them too much. *The Hunter* (Private, 1992, prod. Jennifer Warnes, C. Roscoe Beck and Elliot Scheiner) features a number of assured originals as well as an eclectic mix of covers by the likes of Todd Rundgren, Donald Fagan, Leonard Cohen, and Mike Scott.

Daniel Durchholz

Was (Not Was)

Formed 1980, Detroit, Mich. Disbanded 1993.

Don Was (Fagenson), bass, etc.; David Was (Weiss), reeds, etc.; Sweet Pea Atkinson, vocals; Sir Harry Bowens, vocals; Donald Ray Mitchell, vocal; plus assorted side musicians

Utterly unclassifiable, Was (Not Was) is a combination studio project and rock/r&b collective whose offbeat lyricism—mostly from Weiss—nods to beat culture, Frank Zappa and Captain Beefheart. The Was brothers' anything goes sensibility brought together a wildly eclectic group of guests for its albums, including Ozzy Osbourne, Frank Sinatra Jr., Iggy Pop, Mel Torme, Leonard Cohen, Mitch Ryder, Marshall Crenshaw and members of the Knack, the MC5, Parliament-Funkadelic and Wild Cherry. A Top 10 hit with "Walk the Dinosaur" in 1989 took the group on the road, but Fagenson's Grammy winning production work—his credits include the Rolling Stones, Bonnie Raitt, Bob Dylan, the B-52's, Willie Nelson, Ringo Starr and the Highwaymen—

put the group on ice, and by the early 90s Was (Not Was) was on an extended hiatus.

what to buy: *What Up, Dog?* (Chrysalis, 1988) ♪♪♪♪ is Was (Not Was)'s shining moment. The guest list was interesting—Sinatra, Jr., and a co-writing credit to Elvis Costello—but this is the album where a true band identity surfaced thanks to the singers and to an ace group of Detroit players. The songwriting is solid, particularly on "Spy in the House of Love" and "Boy's Gone Crazy," and Weiss' psycho tone-poem "Dad, I'm in Jail" is tremendous comedy.

what to buy next: Either of *Dog's* predecessors—*Was (Not Was)* (Ze/Island, 1981) ♪♪♪ and *Born to Laugh at Tornadoes* (Ze/Geffen, 1983) ♪♪♪♪—are worthwhile. The latter is guest-drenched; check out Osbourne rapping on "Shake Your Head." The first album is a bit funkier and more subversive, with dance club hits such as "Out Come the Freaks" and "Tell Me That I'm Dreaming."

what to avoid: *Are You Okay?* (Chrysalis, 1990) ♪♪♪ isn't awful, but it's more convoluted than the group's other offerings and is therefore the last one to acquire.

worth searching for: *Hello, Dad...I'm in Jail* (Fontana, 1992) ♪♪♪♪ is a British best-of that captures the essential tracks and includes the updated "Shake Your Head" featuring Osbourne and actress Kim Basinger.

▶▶ None; Was (Not Was) is an unusually unique venture whose influence was more in spirit—any modern rock band with a touch of funk—than directly in music.

◀◀ 60s classic rock, Motown and Stax, 70s funk, Duke Ellington, Charlie Parker, John Coltrane, various world musics

Gary Graff

The Waterboys

Formed 1981 in London, England. Disbanded in 1993.

Mike Scott, vocals, guitar, piano, Hammond organ; Steve Wickham, fiddle, hammond organ, vocals; Anthony Thistlethwaite, saxaphone, mandolin, organ, harmonica; Colin Blakey, whistle, flute, Hammond organ, piano; Noel Bridgeman, drums, percussion; Jay Dee Daugherty, drums; Sharon Shannon, accordian, fiddle; Trevor Hutchinson, bass, bouzouki; Karl Wallinger, bass, keyboards; Roddy Lorimer, trumpet

The history of The Waterboys is the story of Mike Scott's ever evolving musical and spiritual quest. "I've always followed my heart or where my latest musical fascination is, which is rarely where popular trends have been going," says Scott. The band was characterized by a continually changing cast of characters supporting Scott, with one anchor being the musical versatility of Anthony Thistlethwaite. The Waterboys originated the "Big Music," an epic, sprawling, feverish sound of layered acoustic guitars, ecstatic horns, and charging, obscure, expansive poetics reminiscent of the mythmaking of Yeats and Blake. At its best, the music was transcendent, leading the listener into a new, exotic land brimming with imagery and feeling, and owed a debt to the earlier work of fellow shamans Patti Smith, Van Morrison, and Bruce Springsteen, as well as The Beatles. Scott then changed tactics for the band's fourth album, the astounding "Fisherman's Blues," bringing his Celtic passions to the forefront and toning down the Big Music. That particular "raggle taggle" version of the band broke up after two albums, The Waterboys became Scott and a slew of session players, and music returned to harder guitar riffs, with disappointing results. A recent solo outing by Scott is much closer to the spiritual essence he sought with "Fisherman's Blues," and on the tour supporting that album, Scott promised that next time around, he'd return with a band. So perhaps a new generation of The Waterboys is just around the corner.

what to buy: Different eras of The Waterboys produced distinctly different music. Early Waterboys is best sampled on *A Pagan Place* (Chrysalis, 1984, prod. Mike Scott) ♪♪♪♪ featuring the strumming acoustic majesty of the title cut. *This is the Sea* (Chrysalis, 1985, prod. Mike Scott and Mick Glossop) ♪♪♪♪♪ is a fully realized epic that showcased the Scott-Wallinger partnership and included the shimmering "This is the Sea," "The Whole of the Moon," "Spirit," and "Old England." Late Waterboys is captured in all its glory on *Fisherman's Blues* (Chrysalis, 1988, prod. John Dunford and Mike Scott) ♪♪♪♪♪ with its embrace of the Celtic tradition. Commencing with the luminous title cut, the album includes a stirring cover of Van Morrison's "Sweet Thing," and the last recorded song written by Scott and Wallinger (with Hutchinson), "World Party." A masterpiece from start to finish.

what to buy next: *Best of the Waterboys* (Chrysalis, 1991, prod. Mike Scott) ♪♪♪♪ is a good retrospective of the band, with the addition of "Killing My Heart" an early electric version of "When Ye Go Away" and live "Old England." *The Secret Life of the Waterboys* (Chrysalis, 1994, prod. Mike Scott) ♪♪♪♪ is a collection of unreleased Waterboys studio recordings, radio sessions, live tracks, and "lost" b-sides recorded between 1981 and 1985.

what to avoid: *Dream Harder* (Geffen, 1993, prod. Mike Scott and Bill Price) is a lackluster attempt to do The Waterboys without The Waterboys and is hopefully Scott's last attempt to become a guitar god.

the rest: *The Waterboys* (Ensign, 1983, prod. Mike Scott) *Room to Roam* (Ensign, 1990)

worth searching for: A variety of CD singles and 12-inch releases exist, most prominently from the *Fisherman's Blues* era on foreward. They include: *And a Bang on the Ear/Raggle Taggle Gipsy* (1989); *The Whole of the Moon/Golden Age Medley* (1991); *Fisherman's Blues/Medicine Bow* (Radio 1 Session/Lost Highway, 1991); *Bring 'em all in* (with three previously unreleased songs), all on Chrysalis; *The Return of Pan/Karma/Mister Powers* (Geffen, 1993).

solo outings:

Mike Scott: Bring 'em all in (Chrysalis, 1995)

Anthony Thistlewaite: Aesop Wrote a Fable (Rolling Acres, 1993)

Sharon Shannon: Sharon Shannon (Solid, 1991) *Out the Gap* (Solid, 1994)

▶▶ U2, Sinead O'Connor, World Party

◀◀ Bob Dylan, Patti Smith, The Beatles, Bruce Springsteen, Van Morrison, The Chieftains

see also: *World Party*

Martin Conners

Muddy Waters

Born McKinley Morganfield, April 4, 1915 in Rolling Fork, Miss. Died April 30, 1983 in Chicago, Ill.

"The blues had a baby," Waters sang in 1977, "and they named it rock and roll." It was *his* baby. Inspired by Robert Johnson, Son House and the other talented local bluesmen, the young McKinley Morganfield picked up an acoustic guitar and immediately established himself as a peer. Even as a young man, his voice was deep and charismatic; his untrained guitar tones on "Honey Bee" and "Rollin' Stone"—the latter inspired both the band and the Bob Dylan hit—sounded so new and out of the ordinary that they inspired such torch-carriers as Charlie Parker, Chuck Berry, Elvis Presley and Keith Richards. At a time when pop music was still defined by George and Ira Gershwin, such "black music" was considered dirty and uncouth, and Waters' gravely voice and forthright lyrics did little to combat this perception.

He didn't earn his legend until the 1950s, when he moved to Chicago and picked up an electric guitar. Recording for Chicago's Chess Records, the label at the right place at the right time, Waters developed a sharp, piercing blues sound that influenced generations of blues and rock players and launched the careers of harpist James Cotton and pianist Otis Spann, who both played in Waters' band. He reeled off countless classics - "Hoochie Coochie Man," "You Shook Me," "Got My Mojo Workin'," "Mannish Boy" - many written by Chess session bassist Willie Dixon. His career sagged slightly, and ironically, after Elvis Presley merged Waters' electric blues with Kentucky bluegrass music, but it picked up again when the Stones began dropping his name in America.

Waters performed with his proteges several times, including once at Chicago's still-thriving Checkerboard Lounge, and was a prominent figure in the 60s blues revival. In the 70s, he hooked up with guitar hero Johnny Winter and, playing his distinctive electric tones off Winter's spastic solos, found renewed creative power. He died in 1983 as perhaps the world's best-known and most influential bluesman. Others still base their entire career on the fact that they once played with him. And many thriving blues clubs, including Antone's in Austin, Texas, market themselves with huge pictures and T-shirts of Muddy Waters.

what to buy: It's tough to navigate Waters' 20-plus albums, many of which were released simply to promote a single or two, so the best starting point is the comprehensive career retrospective *The Chess Box*, (Chess/MCA, 1989, prod. Various) which has simply everything, plus critic Robert Palmer's must-read liner notes dissecting Waters' unique musical style. Another worthwhile collection is *The Best of Muddy Waters*, (Chess, 1958; Chess/MCA, 1987, prod. Various) which contains "I Can't Be Satisfied" and other studio tracks from 1948 to 1954.

what to buy next: To build a good Waters collection, it's advisable to sample a key album from every phase of his career. *Down on Stovall's Plantation* (Testament, 1966, prod. Alan Lomax) is a collection of folklorist Lomax' acoustic 1941 field recordings; the scholar was trying to find Robert Johnson in the Delta, but failed and was referred to the similar-sounding Waters instead. The 50s sides are best collected on *Trouble No More (Singles, 1955-1959)* (Chess/MCA, 1989, prod. Various) Waters' 60s material is less spontaneous, though *The*

Real Folk Blues (Chess, 1966/MCA, 1987, prod. Marshall Chess) ♪♪♪♪♪ contains "40 Days & 40 Nights" and "Mannish Boy," which influenced the Stones, Led Zeppelin, Bo Diddley and every living bluesman. The better-known version of *Mannish Boy*, at least the one rock radio stations still play from time to time, is off *Muddy Mississippi Waters Live*, (Blue Sky, 1979, prod. Johnny Winter) ♪♪♪♪ a fiery collection with Winter's electric guitar smashing dangerously into Waters' confident, perfectly timed chiming notes and friendly vocal growl.

what to avoid: Even Waters put out some lemons, most notably *The Muddy Waters Woodstock Album* (Chess, 1975, prod. Henry Glover) ♪, which gives the legendary upstate New York town a bad name.

the rest: *At Newport* (Chess, 1960; Chess/MCA, 1986) ♪♪♪♪ *Sings Big Bill Broonzy* (Chess, 1960) ♪♪♪ *Folk Singer* (Chess, 1964) ♪♪♪ Muddy, Brass and the Blues *(Chess, 1966; Chess/MCA, 1989)* ♪♪ Mud In Your Ear *(Chess, 1967; Chess/MCA 1989)* ♪♪ More Real Folk Blues *(Chess, 1967; Chess/MCA, 1988)* ♪♪♪♪ Fathers and Sons *(Chess, 1969)* ♪♪♪ They Call Me Muddy Waters *(Chess, 1971; Chess/MCA, 1990)* ♪♪ The London Muddy Waters Sessions *(Chess, 1972; Chess/MCA, 1989)* ♪♪♪ Can't Get No Grindin' *(Chess, 1973; Chess/MCA, 1990)* ♪♪ Hard Again *(Blue Sky, 1977)* I'm Ready *(Blue Sky, 1978)* ♪♪♪ Sweet Home Chicago *(Quicksilver/Intermedia, 1982)* ♪ Muddy & the Wolf *(Chess, 1982; Chess/MCA, 1986)* ♪♪ Rolling Stone *(Chess, 1982; Chess/MCA, 1984)* ♪♪♪ Rare and Unissued *(Chess, 1982; Chess/MCA, 1991)* ♪♪♪

worth searching for: The two-on-one CD combination of *Folk Singer* and *Sings Bill Broonzy*, (Chess/MCA, 1987) ♪♪♪♪ two of Waters' finest albums from the early 60s.

▶▶ Buddy Guy, Jimi Hendrix, Bob Dylan, the Rolling Stones, Led Zeppelin, PJ Harvey, Johnny Winter, Elvin Bishop, Paul Butterfield Blues Band, Allman Brothers Band, Eric Clapton

◀◀ Robert Johnson, Son House, Charley Patton

Steve Knopper

Roger Waters

See: Pink Floyd

Jack Waterson

See: Green on Red

Ben Watt

See: Everything but the Girl

Mike Watt

See: fIREHOSE

Weather Report

Formed 1970 in New York, N.Y. Disbanded 1985.

Josef Zawinul, keyboards; Wayne Shorter, saxophones; Miroslav Vitous, bass (1970-73); Alphonse Mouzon, drums (1970), Airto Moreira, percussion (1970); Eric Gravatt, drums (1971-1972); Dom Um Romao, percussion (1971-73); Ishmael Wilburn, drums (1972); Andrew N. White III, bass, French horn (1973); Herschel Dwellingham, drums (1973); Muruga, percussion (1973); Alphonso Johnson, bass (1973-75); Alyrio Lima, drums (1974); Ndugu (Leon) Chancler, percussion (1974); Chester Thompson, drums (1975); Jaco Pastorius, bass (1976-79); Alex Acuna, percussion (1976); Manola Badrena, percussion (1976); Peter Erskine, drums (1978-81); Victor Bailey, bass (1982-85); Jose Rossy, percussion (1982-85); Omar Hakim, drums (1982-85)

Led by Zawinul and Shorter—both part of Miles Davis's landmark jazz-rock experiments during the late '60s, Weather Report was a visionary band that managed to infuse its high-voltage jazz with rock 'n' roll excitement and world-music exoticism. Unlike many fusion experiments that fizzled, Weather Report's sound was compelling and seemed to sweep the listener along, prompting Zawinul to dub it "parade music." The unique sound and accessibility quickly earned a following beyond normal jazz aficionados. Zawinul, classically trained on the piano in his native Austria, created a vibrant, full-bodied sound using layers of cutting-edge synthesizers while the rhythm section built deep, complex foundations. Shorter, with his bebop jazz background, soared above and through the mix with sharp, angular saxophone lines. When Pastorius added his compositional skill and darting jazz-funk flourishes on fretless bass, Weather Report experienced its greatest commercial success, earning a gold record with 1977's *Heavy Weather* and the hit, "Birdland." Zawinul and Shorter announced in the spring of 1996 that they planned to reform Weather Report later in the year.

what to buy: *Heavy Weather* (Columbia, 1977, prod. Josef Zawinul, Jaco Pastorius and Wayne Shorter) ♪♪♪♪♪ is a compelling blend of ebullience ("Birdland," "Teen Town") and beauty ("A Remark You Made," "Harlequin"). The energy level nears meltdown status on *Mysterious Traveler*, (Columbia, 1974, prod.

Josef Zawinul) [3½ bones] with its adventurous title track and the mesmerizing "Nubian Sundance."

what to buy next: *Black Market* (Columbia, 1976, prod. Josef Zawinul and Jaco Pastorius) [4 bones] bristles with Latin and African rhythms and exotic melodies. The triumvirate of Zawinul-Shorter-Pastorius hits its compositional peak on *Mr. Gone,* (Columbia, 1978, prod. Josef Zawinul, Jaco Pastorius) [4 bones] creating high drama with instrumental music.

what to avoid: It took a few albums for Weather Report to find its form amid all those influences, so the first two discs, *Weather Report* (Columbia, 1971, prod. Josef Zawinul and Wayne Shorter) [1½ bones] and *I Sing the Body Electric* (Columbia, 1972, prod. Josef Zawinul and Wayne Shorter) [2 bones] offer too few glimpses into the magic ahead.

the rest: *Sweetnighter* (Columbia, 1973) [2½ bones] *Tale Spinnin'* (Columbia, 1975) [2 bones] *8:30* (Columbia, 1979) [2 bones] *Night Passages* (Columbia, 1980) [3 bones] *Procession* (Columbia, 1983) [2 bones] *Domino Theory* (Columbia, 1984) [3½ bones] *Sportin' Life* (Columbia, 1985) [3 bones] *This Is This* (Columbia, 1986) [4 bones]

worth searching for: Though Weather Report's best albums are unified pieces, a couple best-of collections allow for sampling of different periods in the group's evolution. Both Japan's *Star Box* (Sony, 1993, prod. Various) [3 bones] and Britain's *Weather Report: The Collection* (Castle, 1990, prod. Various) [3 bones] offer key tracks and good introductions to the group.

▶▶ Full Circle, Herbie Hancock, Chick Corea, Steps Ahead

◀◀ Miles Davis, Charlie Parker, Dizzy Gillespie, John Coltrane

see also: *Miles Davis*

David Yonke

Jimmy Webb

Born Aug. 15, 1946 in Elk City, Okla.

By his early 20s, Webb had already seen his songs covered by many of the top artists of the day, scoring a slew of Top 10 singles and a couple of Grammys in the process. Best known for the string of city-named hits he wrote for Glen Campbell—"By the Time I Get to Phoenix," "Wichita Lineman," "Galveston"—and for the melodramatic opus "MacArthur Park" sung by actor Richard Harris (and later by disco diva Donna Summer), Webb's songs have been recorded by a gamut that includes Frank Sinatra, Barbra Streisand and Isaac Hayes; modern rock groups such as R.E.M., Urge Overkill and Ghost of An American Airman have taken on "Wichita Lineman." Webb's career as a solo artist seems almost a completely separate entity from his career as a songwriter; of his biggest hits, the only one that appears on his own records is "Galveston" (and that in a dramatically rearranged form). He's released eight solo albums, though none of them met with any measure of commercial success. The most notable aspect of Webb's recorded output is his tendency to swing wildly between the ridiculous and the sublime, which is no surprise coming from the guy who wrote "MacArthur Park." As a songwriter, Webb has never been afraid to go way out on a limb both musically and lyrically; sometimes that means he falls flat, but when he nails it, there's probably no one alive today who can compare. That uneven essence pervades all of his solo records, though some ultimately hold up better than others.

What Album Changed Your Life?

"Patti Smith's Horses. Growing up in the South at the time that came out, I was indoctrinated with the Allman Brothers and Lynyrd Skynyrd. This was a whole new way of looking at pop music."

Peter Buck (R.E.M.)

what to buy: His best album is *Words And Music,* (Reprise, 1970, prod. Jimmy Webb) [4 bones] which includes "P.F. Sloan," a hidden gem of a tribute to one of Webb's favorite fellow tunesmiths, plus the three-part suite "Music For an Unmade Movie."

what to buy next: *Land's End,* (Asylum, 1974, prod. Jimmy Webb) [3½ bones]

And So: On (Reprise, 1971, prod. Jimmy Webb) [3 bones] and *El Mirage* (Atlantic, 1977, prod. George Martin) [3 bones] suffer for their inconsistencies, but each has its share of compelling tunes.

what to avoid: *Angel Heart* (Columbia, 1982, prod. Matthew McCauley and Fred Mollin) [1½ bones] seems to catch Webb's creative faculties at a particularly low ebb; it's no wonder he didn't release another album for 11 years after this one.

the rest: *Jim Webb Sings Jim Webb* (Epic, 1968) [2 bones] *Letters* (Reprise, 1972) [2½ bones] *Suspending Disbelief* (Elektra, 1993) [3 bones]

worth searching for: *Archive: 1970 to 1977* (WEA International, 1993, prod. Various) is an excellent European import that gathers most of the best cuts from Webb's 70s albums. Also worthy of mention is *Glen Campbell: The Songs of Jimmy Webb* (Capitol, 1974, prod. Jimmy Webb) the vocals are all Campbell's, but both artists are pictured on the cover, and it's the best album Campbell has ever recorded.

Glen Campbell, Art Garfunkel, Linda Ronstadt, the Fifth Dimension, Johnny Rivers, Amy Grant, Scud Mountain Boys, Zumpano

Elvis Presley, the Beatles, Brian Wilson, Joni Mitchell, George Gershwin

Peter Blackstock

Ween

Formed 1985 in New Hope, Pa.

Dean Ween (born Mickey Melchiondo), vocals, instruments; Gene Ween (born Aaron Freeman) Ween, vocals, instruments

This terminally wacky duo has the musical chops and wiseass sensibility that could have made them millions had they gone the Weird Al Yankovic route. But the brothers Ween are far more subversive than that. Rather than simply parody individual songs, they turn whole genres inside-out and upside-down, exterminating the boundaries of good taste with extreme prejudice and a 4-track tape deck. Their humor is sophomoric in the extreme, but then, they may have been sophomores when they formed the group. To give you an example, the surname Ween, they say, is a combination of the words wuss and penis. Still, if the mood catches you, these guys can be absolutely hilarious. And whether or not you like what they do, Ween can, at the very least, be a test case for a debate about what cheap recording equipment has wrought: is it the democratization of the music industry, or the end of music altogether?

what to buy: A hilarious goof from beginning to end, *God Ween Satan—The Oneness* (Twin/Tone, 1990, prod. Andrew Weiss) has something to offend nearly everyone. But ease off the PC meter and notice how deftly this duo deconstructs genres as various as gospel (in a hilarious hymn to their god, Boognish), mariachi, heavy metal and funk (a leering cover of Prince's "Shockadelica." A work of near-genius not despite its excess, but because of it.

what to buy next: The duo's technique was considerably refined by the time it recorded *Chocolate and Cheese,* (Elektra, 1992, prod. Andrew Weiss) and it takes on Philly soul ("Freedom of '76"), boneheaded 70s rock ("Take Me Away") and Pink Floyd-style instrumental excursions ("A Tear for Eddie"). "Spinal Meningitis (Got Me Down)" is more creepy than funny, though, and the happy carnival music in "The HIV Song" is either incredibly stupid or their bravest move yet. *The Pod* (Shimmy-Disc, 1991, prod. Andrew Weiss) —recorded at the Weens' apartment (hence the title)—is full of bad vibes, distorted vocals and near-stationary grooves. Still, "Strap on That Jammypac" is a merciless take on the blues, "Demon Sweat" a slab o' neo-Princian bedroom funk and "Pork Roll Egg and Cheese" offers a bit of twisted psychedelia.

what to avoid: The fact that Ween actually went out and hired a bunch of notable Nashville pros to record the country album, *12 Golden Country Greats* (Elektra, 1996, prod. Ben Vaughan) is actually funnier than anything that resulted from the sessions. It's a good joke, but one joke does not an album make.

the rest: *Pure Guava* (Elektra, 1992, prod. Ween)

worth searching for: Good luck finding it, but 500 copies of Ween's debut album, *Live Brain Wedgie!* (Bird o' Pray, 1987, prod. Ween) exist out there somewhere. Actually, only half is live, recorded in Trenton, N.J. The rest is early 4-track recordings, including "I Got a Weasel."

Beck

Prince, Captain Beefheart, Ozzy Osbourne, Alvin and the Chipmunks

Daniel Durchholz

Weezer /The Rentals

Formed 1992 in Los Angeles, Calif.

Rivers Cuomo, vocals, guitar; Brian Bell, guitar, vocals; Matt Sharp, bass, vocals; Patrick Wilson, drums

Weezer surprised the grunge- and punk-saturated modern rock world with its multi-platinum debut *Weezer,* (DGC, 1994, prod. Ric Ocasek) which owed more to Brian Wilson than to the Sex Pistols. Beefing up vulnerable power-pop tunes with massive guitars and drums, Weezer produced geeky anthems that made the world want to sing. Guided by the vision of wispy frontman Cuomo, the group enjoyed a string of hits—thanks in part to inventive videos by Spike Jonze—that included "Undone (The Sweater Song)," "Buddy Holly" and "Say It Ain't So." Cuomo's tunes at times address emotionally painful subject matter, but the band's energetic, melodic and brightly colored rock makes even the darkest songs uplifting. While Weezer took a hiatus before its second album, bassist Sharp moonlighted in the parodic new wave band The Rentals, whose *Return of the Rentals* (Maverick, 1995, prod. Matt Sharp and Tom Grimley) is good, retro fun.

Simon Glickman

Bob Weir

See: Grateful Dead

The Weirdos

Formed 1976 in Los Angeles, Calif.

John Denney, vocals; Dix Denney, guitar; Clif Roman, guitar, bass; Dave Trout, bass (1977-78); Bruce Moreland; bass (1978), Billy Ford Persons, bass (1979); Greg Williams; bass (1980), Flea (born Michael Balzary), bass (1989); Nickey Beat, drums (1977-1978, 1989); Danny Benair, drums (1979); Art Fox, drums (1980); Cliff Martinez, drums (1981), synthesizer (1989); Jerry Angel, drums (1989)

Simply put, the Weirdos were the most explosive punk rock band in America during the pre-hardcore late 70s. Let anyone who doubts it simply hear both sides of the group's classic 1977 single on Dangerhouse records, "We Got the Neutron Bomb"/"Solitary Confinement," and feel the burning hugeness of its attack. Along with the never-released Screamers, the Weirdos were also the top dogs and biggest draws on the pioneering L.A. punk scene of the time, its bizarre and zany clothing even landing the group national exposure in U.S. newsmagazines; singer John Denney was even known to dress in space-age astronaut gear to frequent record label A&R offices with demo tapes and promotional material. And his characteristic, arms-swinging, head-down, chicken-strut has often been thought of as the precursor to the silly "skank" dance favored by later 80s mosh-pit slam-dancers. More importantly, the true stars of that burgeoning time and scene left behind just enough music to document their raw, tumultuous power, incredible cool and amusing but keen and penetrating intelligence. Perhaps the aforementioned single is now as rare and as pricey as a Lou Gehrig autograph, as are its other 7" single and two 12" EPs. But the curious are well served by the knockout retrospective *Weird World, Time Capsule Vol. One, 1977-1981* (Frontier Records, 1991, prod. Various) In addition to the "Neutron Bomb" double-sided detonation and the highlights of their other releases, more than half of this 14-track collection is comprised of unreleased demos, providing a slice of history for even the oldest fan. Anyone wishing to hear pure punk power should check out the Dix Denney/Cliff Roman guitar assault on such previously undocumented juggernauts as "Message From the Underworld" and "Teenage." The unadulterated spirit of John Denney's wild voice throughout is another comet of sorts. Though for some reason *Volume Two* has never appeared as promised, those blown away by this retro are further advised to seek out a new compilation entitled *Live From the Masque: Forming* (Year One, 1996, prod. not listed), which features six live tracks from the Weirdos (as well as the Bags, the Germs and the Skulls) and too captures the original, vintage '77-'78 Weirdos at its most furious, wild glory. However, novices should approach the band's lone comeback album, *Condor* (Frontier Records, 1990, prod. by Dix Denney, John Denney and Clif Roman) with caution; though certainly no dud, the LP fails to completely rekindle the band's prior greatness. As an extra piece, however, the still fast and frenzied "Cyclops Helicopter" and "Shining Silver Light" can please.

Jack Rabid

Bob Welch

Born July 31, 1946 in Los Angeles, Calif.

Welch was a member of Fleetwood Mac for a few years (1971-74) but departed before the band went multi-platinum, making him only slightly better off than Pete Best. He first formed the short-lived group Paris, then launched a solo career that started strong with his hit remake of the Fleetwood Mac song "Sentimental Lady," which he followed with the peppy "Ebony Eyes." The hits dried up soon after, and Welch drifted into obscurity while his former bandmates went through the roof with almost unparalleled success. *Best of Bob Welch* (Rhino, 1991, prod. Various) collects his charting numbers, plus material from Paris. Taken together, Welch's talents as a guitarist and songwriter are evident; He's just never parlayed it to his benefit.

the rest: *Three Hearts* (Capitol/EMI, 1978/1996) *Greatest Hits* (Curb, 1994)

see also: *Fleetwood Mac*

Allan Orski

Paul Weller

See: The Jam

Mary Wells

Born May 13, 1943, in Detroit, Mich. Died July 26, 1992, in Los Angeles, Calif.

Motown's first bona fide star, Wells is remembered, perhaps unfairly, for her 1964 smash "My Guy." The song, one of many collaborations with Smokey Robinson, became her biggest seller and overshadowed everything else. She didn't have much luck after her bitter split with Motown, but she continued to record and perform until her death from throat cancer.

what to buy: *Looking Back* (Motown, 1993, prod. Various) is a two-disc set that offers the best representation of the singer's most famous period; all her hits came from the Motown years. "The One Who Really Loves You," "You Beat Me to the Punch" and "My Guy" are all here, in addition to interviews with friends and associates.

what to buy next: *Never, Never Leave Me/The 20th Century Sides* (Ichiban, 1996, prod. Various) reveals that Wells had more to say after "My Guy." Compiling material from sessions immediately after her Motown split, this has no big hits but plenty of decent lightweight soul. Wells' chirpy innocence had begun to subside a bit by this point, leading to more versatile interpretations.

what to avoid: The too-puny *Greatest Hits* (Motown, 1964)

the rest: *Motown Legends: You Beat Me to the Punch—My Guy* (ESX, 1994) *My Guy* (Motown, 1964/1989) *Ain't it the Truth* (Varese Vintage, 1994) *Dear Lover: The Atco Sessions* (Ichiban, 1995)

▶▶ The Supremes, Diana Ross, Martha and the Vandellas

◀◀ Smokey Robinson

Allan Orski

Wendy and Lisa

Formed 1986, Los Angeles, Calif.

Wendy Melvoin, guitar, bass, vocals; Lisa Coleman, keyboards, backing vocals

One of the first and most interesting spin offs from Prince's backup band The Revolution, Melvoin and Coleman started the act shortly after their royal employer gave them a pink slip in 1986. Friends since childhood, the two hooked up musically in the Revolution when Melvoin replaced guitarist Dez Deckerson in 1984 (Coleman had been backing Prince since 1979). Playing almost all the instruments on their self-named debut, the two presented a slick neo-psychedelic sound with just enough R&B to hint at their musical roots. Though their four albums progressed toward a rockier, band approach - with notables such as Michael Penn and k.d. lang helping out on 1990's *Eroica* their work went largely unnoticed commercially, despite presaging a nod toward funky psychedelia that artists continue to mint today. The debut, *Wendy and Lisa* (Columbia, 1987, prod. Bobby Z., Wendy Melvoin and Lisa Coleman) remains the pair's finest work, featuring an atmospheric blend of psychedelic rock and soul that goes down like a gentle dream. Songs such as "Chance to Grow" and "Blues Away" ride a sophisticated groove with spot-on playing. Then things get funky with the wah-wah guitar-spiced "Light."

the rest: *Fruit at the Bottom* (Columbia, 1989) "Re-Mix-in-a-Carnation (Virgin, 1991) *Eroica* (Virgin, 1990)

Eric Deggans

Leslie West

See: Mountain

Wham!

See: George Michael

Whipping Boy

Formed 1989 in Dublin, Ireland

Ferghal McKee, vocals; Paul Page guitar; Myles McDonnell bass; Colm Hassett drums

Though they're at present virtually unknown here, this Irish quartet's second album, *Heartworm* (Columbia, 1996, prod. Wayne Livesey) indicates it's one of the most important new bands to emerge from the U.K. The group was introduced to the English public when the album's second single, "We Don't Need Nobody Else," caught fire behind some nervy, controversial lyrics on the subject of domestic violence. The single hit the charts, and its success helped propel *Heartworm* into several "year's best" lists in the U.K. press. Those fans who were thus enticed to pick up the LP found that song—as well as succeeding hits ("Twinkle" and "When We Were Young") were cogs in a dramatic, gripping, varied album—the sort that unfolds for an hour, one that must be taken in as a flowing whole. Beyond the intelligence and the memorable songwriting, one encounters elusive undercurrents that have always defined the finest U.K. post-punk, such as "154" Wire, Joy Division, early Echo & the Bunnymen, The Sound, early Stone Roses and Pale Saints. These undertones are everywhere, sonic moods so enticing and oddly foreboding that they make *Heartworm* a truly special LP. It's a promising beginning for Whipping Boy in the U.S.; the group has little of equal substance to show for its first seven years, which should steer new converts away from the expensive imports of its U.K. and European recordings.

Jack Rabid

Ian Whitcomb

Born July 19, 1941 in Surrey, England

Proving that with the right accent (British) and the right hairstyle (over the ears) at the right time (summer of '65) *anything* was possible on the U.S. charts, Whitcomb—while still ostensibly studying political science at Trinity College in Dublin—had a Top 10 hit with an innocuous little song ("You Turn Me On") full of barrelhouse piano and heavy breathing. He was duly summoned to Hollywood to appear on all the pop shows of the day and to tour with all the other pop stars of the moment. He never again visited the Top 40, but Whitcomb remained in Southern California, carving out a career for himself as a record producer, television producer, radio host (currently on NPR) and all-around musicologist. His 1983 book "Rock Odyssey" remains a definitive study of popular music in the 60s, and his best-selling "After The Ball" covers every aspect of pop from rock to his beloved ragtime. He has continued making records of his own since '65, if of a decidedly non-rock nature, and continues to sell his wares through a post office box high in the Hollywood hills. *This Sporting Life* (Rev-Ola, 1994, prod. Various) contains "You Turn Me On," as well as the many failed but delightful attempts at a follow-up.

Gary Pig Gold

James White

See: James Chance

Maurice White

See: Earth, Wind & Fire

White Zombie

Formed 1985 in New York, N.Y.

Rob Zombie (born Robert Straker), vocals; John Ricci, guitar (1985-89); Sean Yseult, bass; Ivan dePrume, drums (1985-93); Jay "J." Yuenger, guitar (1989-present); Phil "Philo" Buerstatte, drums (1993-95); John Tempesta, drums (1995-present)

It's no wonder MTV's Beavis and Butt-head championed this band; it's the realization of every headbanger's wet dream, a blazing, over-the-top band that can't seem to create enough spectacle in its live shows and that hasn't met an album title too long to like. White Zombie first made its mark in the New York rock/industrial underground, putting some groove and swing behind its crunchy guitar licks and sledgehammer drums. *Make Them Die Slowly* (Caroline, 1989, prod. Bill Laswell) was a good meeting of warped minds with clever sonic mastermind Laswell, but the album wanted for some better songs. Those came on *La Sexorcisto: Devil Music Vol. 1*, (Geffen, 1992, prod. Andy Wallace) a tough, roiling soundscape best realized on the Grammy winning "Thunder Kiss '65" and "Black Sunshine," which features a guest vocal by Iggy Pop. *Astro-Creep 2000: Songs of Love, Destruction and Other Synthetic Delusions of the Electric Head* (Geffen, 1995, prod. Terry Date and White Zombie) loads up with samples, tape loops and a variety of sound effects, never obscuring the group's playing but dressing it up in darker, more visceral moods. *Supersext* (Geffen, 1996, prod. Various) is an album of remixes.

Gary Graff

Whitesnake

Formed 1978 in Yorkshire, England

David Coverdale, vocals; Micky Moody, guitar (1978-83); Bernie Marsden, guitar (1978-82); Brian Johnston, keyboards (1978); Neil Murray, bass (1978-82, 1983-87); David Dowle, drums (1978-79); Jon Lord, keyboards, (1978-84); Ian Paice, drums (1979-82); Mel Galley, guitar (1982-84); Colin Hodgkinson, bass (1982-83); Cozy Powell, drums (1982-85); John Sykes, guitar (1983-87); Richard Bailey, keyboards (1984-85); Don Airey, keyboards (1985-); Aynsley Dunbar, drums (1985-87); Adrian Vandenberg, guitar (1987-present); Vivian Campbell, guitar (1987-88); Rudy Sarzo, bass (1987-present); Tommy Aldridge, drums (1987-90); Steve Vai, guitar (1988-90); Denny Carmassi, drums (1994-present); Warren De Martini, guitar (1994-present)

Whitesnake was actually the name of Coverdale's first solo album after leaving Deep Purple in 1976; two years later, he figured it would also make a good name for a band. Whitesnake went through a few phases of development, taking a bluesy hard rock approach at first, then coming closer to the Purple sound after the addition of Paice and Lord from that band. Whitesnake finally hit pay dirt in 1987 with the multi-platinum *Whitesnake* album—whose sales were driven by catchy pop-metal songs from the Coverdale/Sykes team and by videos that featured Coverdale's attractive then-fiancé, Tawny Kitaen. The ride didn't last long, though; one more album and the band

What Album Changed Your Life?

"I definitely love the first New York Dolls album. I loved it. That was one of the albums I'd always listen to a lot. I really got off on it, y'know?"

Steve Jones (Sex Pistols, Neurotic Outsiders)

was on hiatus while Coverdale—long lambasted as a Robert Plant wannabe—recorded an album and toured with former Led Zeppelin guitarmeister Jimmy Page. Another version of the band toured Europe after that venture, however, so we may still have Whitesnake to kick around.

what to buy: Three years before *Whitesnake,* the group's *Slide it In* (Geffen, 1984, prod. Martin Birch) ♪♪♪♪ was a harbinger of things to come, but without the slick pop sheen that rendered the group's later albums a bit anonymous. *Greatest Hits* (Geffen, 1994, prod. Various) ♪♪♪ is a good overview of the Whitesnake radio experience.

what to buy next: *Whitesnake* (Geffen, 1987, prod. Mike Stone and Keith Olsen) ♪♪♪ is tuneful enough, and a definitive piece from one of those odd periods when mainstream tastes turned towards hard rock.

what to avoid: The ballyhooed addition of super-guitarist Vai for *Slip of the Tongue* (Geffen, 1989, prod. Mike Clink and Keith Olsen) ♪♪ was a mixed blessing, as his freewheeling style wasn't a crisp fit with Whitesnake's more regimented direction.

the rest: *Snakebite* (Geffen, 1978) ♪♪♪ *Saints and Sinners* (Geffen, 1982) ♪♪♪

worth searching for: *Live...In the Heart of the City* (Mirage, 1980) ♪♪♪ is a good document of the early, more rough 'n' tumble Whitesnake.

▶▶ Extreme, Queensryche, Spinal Tap

◀◀ Deep Purple, Led Zeppelin

see also: *Deep Purple, Jimmy Page*

Gary Graff

Whitford-St. Holmes

See: Aerosmith

Chris Whitley

Born August 31, 1960, Houston, Texas

Whitley's modest number of albums belies the long road his career has taken. Constantly uprooted and moved throughout the South as a child, he began playing guitar and eventually discovered the National Steel guitar and dobro. Whitley served a long stint busking in New York, then moved to Belgium and experimented with blues and funk. Upon returning to America, he met producer Daniel Lanois (U2, Peter Gabriel), scored a record deal and recorded his heralded debut *Living with the Law* (Columbia, 1991, prod. Daniel Lanois) ♪♪♪♪, a stark but gorgeous album that explored a rusty, burned-out Americana. After rave reviews for this rootsy affair—fans should also check out the partially live CD-5 for "Poison Girl" (Columbia EP, 1992) ♪♪♪♪—he turned his reputation on its head by fronting a loud, droning rock trio for his heavier sophomore effort, *Din of Ecstasy.* (Columbia, 1995, prod. Malcom Burn) ♪♪♪♪ Although the buzz around Whitley had died down, the album was also well-received.

Todd Wicks

The Who

Formed 1964, London, England

Peter Townshend, guitar, vocals; Roger Daltrey, vocals; John Entwistle, bass, vocals; Keith Moon, drums (1964-1978) (d. September 7, 1978); Kenney Jones, drums (1979-82); Simon Phillips, drums (1989).

Originally a straightforward R&B band that played for England's short-lived mod subculture, the Who gradually developed a creative and forceful style that led the British Invasion's second wave and gave them lasting fame. Chief songwriter Townshend, an angry young Brit with a big nose and an inferiority complex, spontaneously began smashing his electric guitar at London's Marquee Club; Moon, who joined the band after vaulting on stage and announcing he could best the Who's original drummer, Doug Sandom, followed Townshend's cue and regularly destroyed his drum kits. Daltrey and Entwistle, the band's talented role players, watched the smoke and violence with bemusement.

Eventually Townshend went from writing powerful little pop songs—always with Moon's barely controlled percussion explosions in the background—to more lofty artistic ventures. He wrote *Tommy,* a rock opera, then followed it with the failed spiritual project *Lifehouse,* whose remnants eventually became the classic album *Who's Next.* As the Who's live show grew legendary and lured stadium crowds, Townshend's maturity overcame him; he tried to sing about growing up, spirituality and his personal drug and drinking problems. Some of this inspiration produced great rock 'n' roll, but after Moon died of a drug overdose in 1978, his vibrancy dwindled away.

After several uninspired tours with ex-Faces drummer Kenney Jones, the Who broke up in 1982, then did a bloated reunion tour full of professional backup musicians in 1989. Townshend still puts out solo albums and has turned his attention to the theater; he recreated *Tommy* as a Broadway musical in 1994. And in 1996 The Who were set to reunite for a special performance of its other rock opera, *Quadrophenia*, in England.

what to buy: *Meaty Beaty Big and Bouncy* (MCA, 1971, prod. Various) collects "My Generation," "Substitute," "Magic Bus," "I Can't Explain" and all the Who's exhilarating 60s singles. *Who's Next*, (MCA, 1971, prod. Glyn Johns and The Who; expanded 1995) with "Baba O'Riley" and "Won't Get Fooled Again," gave the band rock-radio staying power. The rock opera *Tommy* (MCA, 1969, prod. Kit Lambert) is valuable more for the concept than the music, though Moon's brilliant, propulsive drumming overcomes weak production. Townshend's confessional *The Who by Numbers*, (MCA, 1975, prod. Glyn Johns) the still fresh *The Who Sell Out* (MCA, 1967, prod. Kit Lambert) and *Live at Leeds* (MCA, 1970, prod. The Who; expanded 1995, prod. Jon Astley) are also essential.

what to buy next: The soundtrack from the film *The Kids Are Alright* (MCA, 1979, prod. Entwistle) is a charming, funny collection of outtakes and concert weirdness, including highlights from the band's Woodstock performance. *Who Are You*, (MCA, 1978, prod. Glyn Johns and Jon Astley) recorded just before Moon's death, is the original band's last gasp. Completists will enjoy the thorough *Thirty Years of Maximum R&B* (MCA, 1994, prod. Jon Astley, Chris Charlesworth and Bill Curbishley) box set, which includes everything you need plus hilarious live Townshend diatribes.

what to avoid: Anything with Kenney Jones' name, including *Face Dances* (MCA, 1981, prod. Bill Szymczyk) and *It's Hard* (Warner Bros., 1982, prod. Glyn Johns).

the rest: *The Who Sings My Generation* (Decca, 1965) *Happy Jack* (Decca, 1966) *Magic Bus—the Who on Tour* (Decca, 1968), *Quadrophenia* (MCA, 1973) *Odds and Sods* (MCA, 1974) *Who's Greatest Hits* (MCA, 1983) *Who's Last* (MCA, 1984) *Who's Missing* (MCA, 1985) *Two's Missing* (MCA, 1987) *Who's Better, Who's Best* (MCA, 1988) *Join Together* (MCA, 1990).

worth searching for: The reissues of *Tommy, Live at Leeds, Sell Out* and others, which came out in the mid-90s with perfect production and well-chosen bonus tracks.

solo outings:

John Entwistle *Smash Your Head Against the Wall* (Decca, 1971) *Whistle Rymes* (Decca, 1972) *Rigor Mortis Sets In* (Track, 1973) *Mad Dog* (Track, 1975) *Too Late the Hero* (Atco, 1981)

Keith Moon *Two Sides of the Moon* (MCA, 1975),

Roger Daltrey *Daltrey* (MCA, 1973) *Ride a Rock Horse* (MCA, 1977) *One of the Boys* (MCA, 1977) *McVicar* soundtrack (Polydor, 1980) *Under a Raging Moon* (Atlantic, 1985) *Can't Wait to See the Movie* (Atlantic, 1987) *The Best of Rockers and Ballads* (Polydor, 1991) *Rocks in the Head* (Atlantic, 1992) *A Celebration: The Music of Pete Townshend and the Who* (Continuum)

Iggy and the Stooges, The Sex Pistols, the Jam, Too Much Joy, Nirvana

James Brown, Mose Allison, Sonny Boy Williamson, Rolling Stones, Kinks, Beatles, Ventures, Gene Krupa

see also: *Pete Townshend*

Steve Knopper

Jane Wiedlin

See: The Gogos

Wilco

Formed 1994 in Chicago, Ill.

Jeff Tweedy, vocals, guitar; Ken Coomer, drums; John Stirratt, bass, vocals, guitar, piano, organ; Max Johnston, guitar, vocals, fiddle, mandolin, banjo; Jay Bennett, guitar.

After guitarist and cofounder Jay Farrar left Uncle Tupelo in 1994, the rest of the band soldiered on under a new moniker and Jeff Tweedy's leadership. *A.M.* (Reprise, 1995, prod. Brian Paulson and Wilco) contains a preponderance of breakup tunes (directed at Farrar, perhaps?), including "I Must Be High" and "Box Full of Letters." Bottle Rockets guitarist Brian Henneman provides some fine lead work (ex-Titanic Love Affair guitarist Bennett joined the group after the album was cut), and most of the songs chug along in a pleasant mid-tempo fashion. But Tweedy's voice is plainly shot on several tracks, and it sounds as if the album were recorded before the band had fully rallied around Tweedy. Better luck next time.

see also: *Uncle Tupelo, Golden Smog, Wilco*

Daniel Durchholz

Wild Kingdom

See: The Dictators

Webb Wilder

Born May 19, 1954, in Hattiesburg, Miss.

A tall, balding, bespectacled white guy in a state trooper's hat might seem a man least likely to be a wild rock 'n' roller, but Wilder has turned his odd looks into an effective schtick. Playing deadpan with his deep baritone voice, Wilder has created a body of work he sometimes calls "hillbilly gothic"—a weird mixture of country, blues and psychedelic-era rock. His band has evolved from Webb Wilder and the Beatnecks to simply Webb Wilder, and most recently Webb Wilder and the NashVegans. But the elements have remained largely the same: power chords, wild twangy guitar and a large dose of novelty. He's also come up with one of the best credos in the business: "Work hard, rock hard, eat hard, sleep hard, grow big, wear glasses if you need 'em."

what to buy: *It Came From Nashville,* (Watermelon, 1986/1993, prod. R.S. Field) Wilder's first album, combines instrumentals and songs filled with deadpan Southern humor. The best is "Poolside" (co-written by Kevin Welch), in which Wilder lists his summertime rules: "no running, no pushing, no profanity and no dogs." The updated version of the album includes four extra tracks.

what to buy next: *Town & Country* (Watermelon, 1995, prod. R.S. Field, Mike Janas, Webb Wilder and the NashVegans) was originally conceived as a driving tape in which one band performs all the songs. The result is a wild cover album that ranges from the Flamin' Groovies ("Slow Death") to Rodney Crowell ("I Ain't Living Long Like This").

what to avoid: The vinyl version of *It Came From Nashville* (Racket, 1986, prod. R.S. Field), which is improved with the CD version's extra tracks.

the rest: *Hybrid Vigor* (Demon, 1984) *Doo Dad* (Praxis/Zoo, 1991) *Acres of Suede* (Watermelon, 1996)

Omar and the Howlers, the Leroi Brothers

The Rolling Stones, ZZ Top, Howlin' Wolf

Brian Mansfield

Dar Williams

Born Dorothy Snowdon Williams, April 19, 1967 in Mount Kisco, N.Y.

Williams is the quintessential female folk singer of the 90s, capturing society's awkward social transitions as well as the timeless "big questions" with graceful melodies and intelligent, often wry, lyrics. The daughter of a Yale-educated medical writer and a Vasser grad who raises funds for Planned Parenthood, Williams enjoyed a cozy childhood in an upscale Manhattan suburb. A sensitive soul with a crystalline alto voice and a keen eye for the comical, she wrote her first song at age 11 but shied away from performing until, at age 23, she managed to overcome a serious case of stage fright and hit the Boston coffeehouses. Gender roles, relationships and stereotypes—from the innocence of childhood androgyny to a sexist boyfriend with roving eyes—are prime targets for Williams' lyrical twists. But she just as easily spins metaphorical tales about the deeper, more subtle tensions and pleasures of life, with either a delicate tug at the heartstrings or a humorous elbow in the ribs. Arrangements are generally kept simple, focusing on Williams' silky voice underpinned by her acoustic guitar, although some tunes feature a full band and, on one, you'll even hear a digeridoo. Her second release, *Mortal City,* (Razor & Tie, 1996, prod. Steven Miller) is her bits, offering a brilliant balance of depth and levity, delicacy and strength. On the boisterous "As Cool As I Am," the narrator dumps her lecherous boyfriend and regains her pride. "This Was Pompeii" likens one of history's most deadly, unforeseen disasters with the ashes of a failed relationship. Williams' debut, *The Honesty Room,* (Burning Field Music, 1994/Razor & Tie, 1995, prod. Dar Williams, Adam Rothberg, David Seitz and Brooks Williams) has charm and wit but is much more straightforward and less ambitious than *Mortal City.*

David Yonke

Freedom Williams

See: C&C Music Factory

Hank Williams Sr.

Born Hiriam King Williams, Sept. 17, 1923 in Mount Olive, Alabama. Died Jan. 1, 1953.

Though Williams died before he turned 30 and recorded for

barely six years, he created a mythology as large as those of Elvis Presley or the Beatles in rock. Every songwriter covets his ability to pierce the soul with minimally drawn lines. Every performer craves the kind of charisma that would get them a half-dozen encores at the Grand Ole Opry. And every singer with self-destructive tendencies uses Williams as the measuring glass against which he compares his ability to drink himself to death. The Alabama-born son of a railroad engineer, Williams became a star of the Grand Ole Opry between 1949 and 1952 after stints with radio shows in Shreveport, La., and Montgomery, Ala. He has been inducted into both the Country Music and Rock and Roll Halls of Fame. He also recorded as Luke the Drifter.

what to buy: *40 Greatest Hits.* (Polydor, 1978, prod. Fred Rose) Like the Beatles, every single—and then some—in Williams' catalog has become a standard in its genre, making this 1978 collection the best place to start delving into Williams material, both musically and contextually.

what to buy next: It's up for grabs, depending on what you want, because most of Williams compilations will include some cuts from *40 Greatest Hits. The Original Singles Collection ... Plus* (Polydor, 1990, compilation prod. Colin Escott) expands the Williams ouevre to three discs but, deceptively, doesn't include many of Williams' singles with his wife Audrey. *Health & Happiness Shows* (Mercury, 1993, no producer listed) contains eight radio performances from 1949.

what to avoid: *24 Greatest Hits* (PolyGram, 1976) and *24 Greatest Hits Vol. 2*, (Polydor, 1977) two collections of posthumously overdubbed recordings. The original versions of all these songs are available elsewhere, rendering these collections superfluous. Mercury targeted the alternative-rock crowd with *Alone and Forsaken* (Mercury, 1995), which features Williams most angst-ridden tunes. Matt Johnson, who had recorded a Williams tribute album, *Hanky Panky*, (Epic, 1995, prod. Matt Johnson and Bruce Lampcov) with his group The The, opened *Alone and Forsaken* with a monologue that insulted the many country fans who didn't need to have Williams' greatness explained to them.

the rest: *Greatest Hits* (Polydor, 1963) *Beyond the Sunset* (Polydor, 1963) *Very Best Of* (Polydor, 1963) *Wait for the Light to Shine* (Polydor, 1963) *I Saw the Light* (Polydor, 1968) *Hank Williams Live at the Grand Ole Opry* (MGM, 1976) *Rare Takes and Radio Cuts* (Polydor, 1984) *On the Air* (Polydor, 1985) *I Ain't Got Nothin' but Time, December 1946-August 1947* (Polydor, 1985) *Lovesick Blues, August 1947-December 1948* (Polydor, 1985) *Lost Highway, December 1948-March 1949* (Polydor, 1986) *I'm So Lonesome I Could Cry, March 1949-August 1949* (Polydor, 1986) *Long Gone Lonesome Blues, August 1949-December 1950* (Polydor, 1987) *Hey, Good Lookin', December 1950-July 1951* (Polydor, 1987) *Let's Turn Back the Years, July 1951-June 1952* (Polydor, 1987) *I Won't Be Home No More, June 1952-September 1952* (Polydor, 1987) *Rare Demos: First to Last* (Country Music Foundation, 1990) *I Saw the Light* (PolyGram Special Markets, 1994) *The Hits Volume Two* (Mercury, 1995) *Low Down Blues* (Mercury, 1996, compilation prod. Kira Florita and Colin Escott)

worth searching for: *The Collectors' Edition* (Mercury, 1987) This eight-disc, limited-edition set—available only through Tower Records—collected the individual volumes that contained almost every recording Williams made for MGM in chronological order. *The Legend of Hank Williams*, (Mercury, 1996 prod. Joseph Wilson) an abridgement of Colin Escott's Willliams biography read by Sammy Kershaw. Includes music.

Hank Williams Jr., Jimmie Dale Gilmore, every male country singer since

The Carter Family, Roy Acuff

Brian Mansfield

Hank Williams Jr.

Born Randall Hank Williams, May 26, 1949, Shreveport, La.

Hank Williams Jr. has lived long enough to play out the complexities of the Williams bloodline on record in a way his father never got to. Not quite four years old when his father died, Hank Jr. had his first chart hit at age 14 with a rendition of daddy's "Long Gone Lonesome Blues." That record set the tone for his career: Williams had to emerge from one of the longest shadows in musical history, and it nearly killed him to do it. Nearly every one of Hank Jr.'s albums contains either a song written by Hank Sr. or one about his relationship to the father he barely knew—including the macabre posthumous duet on "There's a Tear in My Beer" that Hank Jr. fashioned in 1989. For a long time, it seemed that Hank Jr. would fall victim to the same substance abuse problems that killed his father, and many fans expected him to do just that to keep the legacy going. Eventually, Williams distinguished himself as a redneck Southern rocker, though he had recorded for more than a decade before he reached that point. He's actually a better singer than his dad, but his material varies wildly. His ability to draw rock and country crowds together—not to mention football fans thanks to his theme song for ABC's "Monday Night Football"—made him one of country's biggest stars during the late '80s, when he won the Country Music Association's Entertainer of the Year award twice.

what to buy: *Hank Williams, Jr. & Friends* (MGM, 1975, prod. Dick Glasser) was the first of his Southern rock albums, and with it he began to tie the outlaw country of Willie Nelson and Waylon Jennings to the Southern rock of Lynyrd Skynyrd and Charlie Daniels. Daniels, the Marshall Tucker Band's Toy Caldwell and Chuck Leavell of the Allman Brothers Band appear on this album, which contains the hits "Stoned at the Jukebox" and "Living Proof."

what to buy next: *Family Tradition* (Elektra/Curb, 1979, prod. Ray Ruff, Jimmy Bowen and Phil Gernhard) continued in the Southern rock/outlaw vein, expecially with title track hit. *Hank Williams Jr.'s Greatest Hits,* (Warner Bros./Curb, 1982, prod. Jimmy Bowen) collects Williams hits from 1979-82—among them "Whiskey Bent and Hell Bound" and "A Country Boy Can Survive"—and is probably the best single-disc Williams anthology.

what to avoid: *Eleven Roses* (Polydor, 1972, prod. Jim Vienneau) is one of Williams' weakest efforts from his early period, with none of the attitude that would show itself later. That attitude, though, only carries Williams so far and makes him wildly uneven. *Lone Wolf* (Warner Bros./Curb, 1990, prod. Barry Beckett, Hank Williams Jr., Jim Ed Norman) is dull, by-the-numbers Southern rock, while *America (The Way I See It)* (Warner Bros./Curb, 1990, prod. Jimmy Bowen, Barry Beckett, Hank Williams Jr., Jim Ed Norman) is a collection of Williams politically (feeble) minded material that rides the fence between blindly patriotic and offensive.

the rest: Hank Williams Jr. Has recorded more than 50 albums, and when you factor in repackagings and collections, he appears on more than 100. The most important of those albums include: *Your Cheatin' Heart* (MGM, 1965) *14 Greatest Hits* (Polydor, 1976) *One Night Stands* (Warner/Curb, 1977) *The New South* (Warner Bros., 1978) *Whiskey Bent and Hell Bound* (Elektra, 1979) *Habits Old and New* (Elektra, 1980) *Rowdy* (Warner Bros./Curb, 1981) *The Pressure Is On* (Warner Bros., 1991) *High Notes* (Warner Bros./Curb, 1982) *Man of Steel* Warner Bros./Curb, 1983) *Strong Stuff* (Warner Bros./Curb, 1983) *Major Moves* (Warner Bros./Curb, 1985) *Five-o* (Warner Bros./Curb, 1985) *Greatest Hits, Vol. 2* (Warner Bros./Curb, 1985) *The Early Years 1976-1978* (Warner Bros./Curb, 1986) *Montana Cafe* (Warner Bros./Curb, 1986) *Born to Boogie* (Warner Bros./Curb, 1987) *Hank "Live"* (Warner Bros., 1987) *Hank Williams Jr.'s Greatest Hits* (Polydor, 1987) *Standing in the Shadows* (Polydor, 1988) *Wild Streak* (Warner Bros., 1988) *Greatest Hits III* (Warner Bros./Curb, 1989) *Pure Hank* (Warner Bros., 1991) *The Best of Hank Williams Jr., Vol. 1-Roots & Branches* (Mercury, 1992) *Living Proof: The MGM Recordings, 1963-1975* (Mercury, 1992) *The Bocephus Box: The Hank Williams Jr. Collection, 1979-1992* (Curb/Capricorn, 1992) *Maverick* (Capricorn, 1992) *Hank Williams/Hank Williams Jr.* (K-Tel, 1992) *The Best of Hank and Hank* (Curb/CEMA, 1992) *Out of Left Field* (Capricorn, 1993) *Hog Wild* (Curb, 1995) *Aka Wham Bam, Sam* (Curb, 1996)

worth searching for: *Live at Cobo Hall, Detroit,* (Polydor, 1969, prod. Jim Vienneau) an impressive live album from his pre-Southern rock days.

Steve Earle, Travis Tritt, the Kentucky HeadHunters

Hank Williams Sr., Charlie Daniels, Lynyrd Skynyrd, the Marshall Tucker Band

Brian Mansfield

Lucinda Williams

Born January 26, 1953, in Lake Charles, La.

Something of a roots-music purist when she made her first recordings during the late 70s, Williams took a long hiatus before emerging nearly a decade later as an accomplished singer-songwriter. Since then, she has demonstrated tremendous breadth and sensitivity on a handful of releases. Though others, notably Mary Chapin Carpenter and Patty Loveless, have scored hits with her songs, commercial success has for the most part eluded Williams as a recording artist, except within the narrow "Americana" format. Too country for rock and too eclectic for country, she has nonetheless blithely forged ahead, showing equal facility with others' work and with her own heartfelt, well-crafted compositions. She signed a deal with Rick Rubin's American Recordings in 1994; the label kept fans waiting well into 1996 for a release.

what to buy: *Lucinda Williams* (Rough Trade, 1988, prod. Gurf Morlix) shows Williams's impressive range, from smoldering blues to folky pop.

what to buy next: *Sweet Old World* (Chameleon, 1992, prod. Lucinda Williams) is an exceptional collection of songs performed with soul and sensitivity. It features a powerful version of Nick Drake's "Which Will."

what to avoid: *Ramblin'* (Smithsonian/Folkways, 1978, prod. Tom Royals) was recorded before the singer-songwriter had really forged her own artistic identity.

the rest: *Happy Woman Blues* (Smithsonian/Folkways, 1980) *Passionate Kisses* (Rough Trade EP, 1989)

worth searching for: "Main Road," her contribution to the Victoria Williams (no relation) tribute/benefit album *Sweet Relief,* (Chaos, 1993, prod. Gurf Morlix) is one of the standout cuts on that impressive anthology.

▶▶ Michelle Shocked, Nanci Griffith, Matraca Berg, Gillian Welch

◀◀ Hank Williams, Leadbelly, Loretta Lynn, Patsy Cline, Joan Baez, Joni Mitchell

Simon Glickman

Victoria Williams

Born 1959 in Forbing, La.

With her unusual, high-pitched voice and obviously quirky sensibility, Williams might seem at first like another indie-pop novelty. A few spins of her records, however, indicate a major artist. A superb songwriter and distinctive vocalist, Williams achieved a great deal of press coverage in 1993 and 1994 when she battled multiple sclerosis. Though her struggle against the disease has been an inspiring one—some major rock artists contributed versions of her songs to the tribute/benefit album *Sweet Relief* in 1993—her work has been somewhat overshadowed by the story. She grew up in Louisiana and attended college there. After trekking around the country, playing her songs for hikers, punks and anyone else who'd listen, Williams made her way to Los Angeles, where she waited tables and performed when she could. At last she signed with Geffen, but her debut album sold poorly, as did her subsequent, critically acclaimed effort with Rough Trade. It wasn't until the release of *Sweet Relief*—featuring contributions from Lou Reed, Pearl Jam, Soul Asylum and many others—that she became better known in the pop world. Her subsequent albums have enjoyed greater attention, though she has remained a bit too unique for the mainstream. Even so, her version of the standard "What a Wonderful World" graced a commercial for Microsoft computer software. She is the subject of the song "Miss Williams' Guitar," by the Jayhawks, of which her husband Marc Olson was a member.

A progressive, homespun Christian, Williams spins compassionate tales of friends, family and nature that evince both childlike wonder and old-soul wisdom. Musically, she draws from an extraordinary pool of influences—gospel, country, folk, acid rock, pop—to create works that never seem derivative. Her live performances reach levels of intimacy and spontaneity that are rare in contemporary music.

Loose (Mammoth, 1994, prod. Paul Fox) is Williams's most engaging collection—which is saying something. While it is governed, like the earlier albums, by her luminous world view, her experiences with illness and loss give everything greater heft.

the rest: *Happy Come Home* (Geffen, 1987) *Swing the Statue!* (Rough Trade, 1990) *This Moment: Live in Toronto* (Mammoth, 1995)

Simon Glickman

Marty Willson

See: The Church

Brian Wilson

Born June 20, 1942, in Inglewood, Calif.

Though he earned superstar status as the musical director, composer and songwriter for the Beach Boys, Wilson has enjoyed far less recognition for his solo work. This is understandable, since his recordings as a solo artist began some 20 years after his best work with the band. Indeed, his solo releases have been more significant as milestones of his recovery from years of drug-aided emotional trauma than as artistic benchmarks. Even so, the film and album *I Just Wasn't Made for These Times* demonstrate Wilson's profound importance as a pop innovator; the genres known as chamber pop and power pop are unthinkable without him.

Born and raised in Southern California, Wilson turned to music as a refuge from a troubled home life. His growing ambitions took the Beach Boys from pop ditties about cars, girls and surfing to masterworks as *Pet Sounds* and "Good Vibrations" before a combination of career pressures, familial abuse and drugs led to a psychological collapse that nearly destroyed him. After years of struggle—and the controversial assistance of therapist Dr. Eugene Landy—Wilson emerged in the 80s as a still-damaged but reasonably functioning person, and at last made a solo album in the latter part of the decade. Wilson has continued to wrangle with his family—cousin Mike Love successfully sued for co-writing credits and royalities for many Beach Boys hits—but by the mid-90s Wilson was hailed as a genius by both critics and legions of young bands.

what to buy: *I Just Wasn't Made for These Times* (MCA, 1995, prod. Don Was) features illuminating solo renditions of some of Wilson's greatest Beach Boys songs. It's no surprise that even stripped of their brilliant arrangements and dazzling harmonies, the songs hold up quite nicely.

the rest: *Brian Wilson* (Reprise, 1988) (with Van Dyke Parks): *Orange Crate Art* (Warner Bros., 1995)

worth searching for: Bootleg copies of *Sweet Insanity,* the wonderful, Don Was-produced follow-up to *Brian Wilson* that Warner Bros. unbelievably opted not to release.

The Beatles, Move, Hollies, Badfinger, Cheap Trick, Pixies/Frank Black, John Wesley Harding, Sonic Youth, Matthew Sweet, Posies, Aimee Mann, Jellyfish, Weezer, Eric Matthews, Cockeyed Ghost, the Negro Problem, Wondermints

George Gershwin, the Four Freshmen, Phil Spector, the Beatles

see also: *The Beach Boys, Van Dyke Parks*

Simon Glickman

Carnie and Wendy Wilson

See: Wilson Phillips

Chris Wilson

See: The Flamin' Groovies

Jackie Wilson

Born June 9, 1934 in Detroit, Mich. Died Jan. 21, 1984 in Mount Holly, N.J.

Reputedly the most exciting, acrobatic live performer of his time, Wilson could sizzle when he sang. His darting, arching shrieks sound like exposed nerves. His greatest recording, "(Your Love Keeps Lifting Me) Higher and Higher," could well be the best single ever made. But Wilson's body of work is riddled with work far less sublime; under the dubious influence of a manipulative manager and insensitive record label, this great vocal talent was wasted on projects as odious as an entire album of Al Jolson songs. His longings for conventional show business respectability may have mirrored the mores of his generation of black entertainers, but it meant that Wilson would leave behind a recorded legacy more frustrating for what might have been than what he actually accomplished.

A onetime professional boxer, he apprenticed as lead tenor with Billy Ward and the Dominoes, replacing the estimable Clyde McPhatter in the lineup. His earliest pop records, which were also the first hits for Motown's Berry Gordy Jr., throbbed with his incessant pleading vocals. But after parting ways with Gordy, he fell under the unenlightened artist and repertoire direction of Brunswick Records, the same people that gave you Buddy Holly with strings. His singles had stopped making the charts at all when "Higher and Higher"—a record Wilson cut with moonlighting Motown sidemen behind him—blasted off in 1965, setting the stage for what could have been one of the more extraordinary comebacks in soul history.

His decision the following year to leave his longtime, mob-affiliated manager, who also happened to own Brunswick Records, may have sabotaged that possibility. The murder of his 16 year-old son, Jackie Wilson Jr., in 1969 turned Wilson into a further tragic figure. But the story gets downright Dickensian after his on stage collapse from an apparent heart attack in 1975 at the Latin Casino in Cherry Hill. N.J. Shipped out of the emergency room in a coma, possibly the product of improper medical care, Wilson lay speechless and motionless in a hospital bed while a long forgotten ex-wife and attorneys began fighting over his inert body. When it became apparent there was no money anyway, Wilson wound up a ward of the state, alone, abandoned, comatose for eight years before he finally died.

what to buy: The high points of fifteen years of recording can all be found on *The Jackie Wilson Story* (Epic, 1983, prod. Various) a 24-song collection that qualifies as one of the backbones of modern soul music.

what to buy next: The three-disc boxed set, *Mr. Excitement* (Rhino, 1992, prod. Various) covers the Jackie Wilson legacy in considerable detail that mixes his key singles with album tracks, including collaborations with Count Basie and the Chi-Lites.

what to avoid: *Merry Christmas From Jackie Wilson* (Brunswick 1963/Rhino, 1991, prod. Nat Tarnapol) is not only a lame Wilson album, recorded at the nadir of his career, but not a very good Christmas album either.

the rest: *Live at the Copa* (Brunswick, 1962/1995) *The Very Best of Jackie Wilson* (Rhino, 1994) *Higher and Higher* (Rhino, 1995)

worth searching for: An X-rated version of the duet with LaVern Baker, "Think Twice," has been only infrequently bootlegged.

Elvis Presley, Marv Johnson, Michael Jackson

Clyde McPhatter, Little Willie John, Roy Hamilton

Joel Selvin

Kim Wilson

See: The Fabulous Thunderbirds

Wilson Phillips

Formed 1989 in Los Angeles, Calif. Disbanded 1993.

Chynna Phillips, vocals; Carnie Wilson, vocals; Wendy Wilson, vocals

They came from a 24-karat gene pool that had already spawned "God Only Knows" and "California Dreaming;" the trio's parents included Beach Boy Brian Wilson and the Mamas and Papas' John and Michelle Phillips. The debut, *Wilson Phillips* (SBK, 1990, prod. Glenn Ballard) is a collection of tautly constructed pop tunes, mesmerizing vocal harmonies and flawless production. It isn't the second coming of anything profound, but a recording that sounds this good and effortless deserves praise.

the rest: *Shadows and Light* (SBK, 1992)

solo outings:

Chynna Phillips: Naked and Sacred (EMI, 1995,)

Carnie and Wendy Wilson: Hey Santa! (SBK, 1993)

Patrick McCarty

Winger

Formed 1986 in New York, N.Y.

Kip Winger, vocals, bass; Reb Beach, guitar; Paul Taylor, guitar (1986-89); Rod Morgenstein, drums; John Roth, guitar (1990-93)

Sportin' a studmuffin's hunk appeal and a pop metal safety valve, Winger emerged from Alice Cooper's band all set to charge the MTV airwaves with his new group. Like most hair bands of the same vintage, Winger found its niche in power ballads; Kip Winger could pen reasonably engaging melodies, but there was no disguising the generic rockers. The metal backlash overtook the band as the decade drew to a close. *Winger* (Atlantic, 1989, prod. Beau Hill) is the group's most successful album and contains Kip Winger's best ballad, "Headin' For a Heartbreak." There is no excuse for attempting Hendrix's "Purple Haze," however. *In the Heart of the Young* (Atlantic, 1990, prod. Beau Hill) follows the same course with a heavier dose of ballads. Why mess with a sure thing, after all? *Pull* (Atlantic, 1993, prod. Mike Shipley) actually has New Age harpist Andreas Vollenweider on board. Everyone out of the pool.

Allan Orski

What Album Changed Your Life?

"I don't think there is such an animal."

Meat Loaf

Wings

See: Paul McCartney

Edgar Winter

Born Dec. 28, 1946, in Beaumont, Texas

Winter may have composed "Frankenstein," that monster of hard rock redundancy, but fans should rejoice that he first formed White Trash. The band was meaner looking than a half-dozen Jerry Lee Lewises and twice as rocking. Winter, who is guitar great Johnny Winter's younger brother, is a multi-instrumentalist; his sax and keyboard work is complex, and his technique sways between subtle and ferocious. His vocals could peel a banana or soothe a fevered baby. His take of "Tobacco Road" from his debut album *Entrance* (Epic, 1970) is nearly unhinged and completely unforgettable. But for all of his talents, Winter's recordings since the 70s have been sporadic in both volume and quality.

what to buy: *Edgar Winter's White Trash* (Epic, 1971/1989, prod. Rick Derringer) covers hard rock, soul, funk and blues—often at a blistering pace. The impassioned "Save the Planet" and melodic "Where Would I Be" accompany a salvo of rocking R&B in "I've Got News for You" and "Give It Everything You Got."

what to buy next: *The Edgar Winter Collection* (Rhino, 1989, prod. Various) samples from Winter's 70s catalog and highlights his most familiar work. "Frankenstein" is part of Winter's hard rocking *They Only Come Out at Night,* (Epic, 1972, prod. Rick Derringer) which also spawned the play-it-'till-it-melts "Free Ride."

what to avoid: *The Real Deal.* (Intersound, 1996) Flawless playing can't overcome this sterile recording, which is as clinical as a jingle house.

the rest: *Entrance* (Epic, 1970/1992) *Roadwork* (Epic, 1972/1989) *Shock Treatment* (Epic, 1974/Lebacy, 1990) *Together:Live* (with Johnny Winter) (Blue Sky, 1970/Epic, 1992) *I'm Not a Kid Anymore* (Thunderbolt, 1994)

worth searching for: On Johnny Winter's *Hey, Where's Your Brother?,* (Point Blank, 1992) Edgar provides keyboard, sax and vocal support on his big brother's strongest gig in the 90s.

▶▶ Stevie Wonder. Rare Earth

◀◀ Johnny Winter, Blood, Sweat & Tears, the Blues Project, Sly & the Family Stone, Them

Patrick McCarty

Johnny Winter

Born Feb. 23, 1944, in Leland, Miss.

Albino blues guitarist Johnny Winter was already a journeyman by 1968, when fame beckoned from the rock 'n' roll crowd via a feature in Rolling Stone magazine. Raised in Texas, Winter helped familiarize white rock audiences with traditional blues by incorporating rock into his music. Winter's first few rock recordings made him a top draw, and he played at the legendary Woodstock festival and other high-profile gigs. While Winter semi-retired in 1972 to recover from heroin addiction, his brother Edgar formed White Trash with the rest of Johnny's band; they had a bright but brief rock career that actually eclipsed Johnny's fame, and Johnny didn't repeat his early success until he started working with Muddy Waters in 1977 as a sideman and producer. Two Winter-produced Waters albums won Grammy Awards, and Winter stayed with the elder bluesman until his death in 1983. Winter has continued to ply his blues- rock by touring and recording for various labels with varying degrees of success. Not a prolific writer, Winter's skill lies most in putting his stamp on other people's tunes. In 1986, he became the first white artist inducted into the Blues Foundation's Hall of Fame.

what to buy: *Johnny Winter And...Live* (Columbia, 1971, prod. Johnny Winter and Rick Derringer) busted him out as big as he would get. With the help of backup guitar ace Derringer, Winter rips through "Jumping Jack Flash" and rocks out the blues on "Good Morning Little Schoolgirl." *Guitar Slinger* (Alligator, 1983, prod. Various) avoids the rock pyrotechnics as a group of veteran blues sidemen give full support to the rootsier side of Winter. Check out his slide guitar work on "It's My Life, Baby" and "Iodine in My Coffee."

what to buy next: After laying off to kick heroin, Winter sent a message with *Still Alive and Well* (Columbia, 1973, prod. Rick Derringer) He rocks hard, and even though "Too Much Seconal" and "Cheap Tequila" warn against substance abuse, it doesn't preach. *Serious Business* (Alligator, 1985, prod. Various) is solid Texas roadhouse music. "Master Mechanic" proves Winter is a master guitarist.

what to avoid: *Captured Live* (Blue Sky, 1976, prod. Johnny Winter) finds Winter still trying to climb the rock mountain before turning back to the blues. It's journeyman work, but unexciting.

the rest: *Johnny Winter* (Columbia, 1969) *Second Winter* (Columbia, 1970) *Johnny Winter And* (Columbia, 1971) *Nothin' But the Blues* (Blue Sky, 1977) *Third Degree* (Alligator, 1986) *The Winter of '88* (MCA, 1988) *Let Me In* (Charisma, 1991) *Scorchin' Blues* (Legacy, 1992) *Hey, Where's Your Brother* Point Blank, 1992) *A Rock 'n' Roll Collection* (Columbia Legacy, 1994)

worth searching for: The bootleg *Texas International Pop Festival* (Oh Boy) captures a seminal Winter performance on home turf, highlighted by a burning, nearly 13-minute take of "Mean Mistreater."

▶▶ Stevie Ray Vaughan, Jimmie Vaughan, Eric Johnson, Edgar Winter

◀◀ T-Bone Walker, Albert Collins, Chuck Berry, Muddy Waters, Keith Richards

see also: *Muddy Water, Edgar Winter, Rick Derringer*

Lawrence Gabriel

Steve Winwood

Born May 12, 1948, in Birmingham, England

Before there was a Little Stevie Wonder, there was a Little Stevie Winwood, belting out "Gimme Some Lovin' " and "I'm a Man" with the Spencer Davis Group when he was still a teenager. Schooled in jazz and R&B, Winwood clearly had ambitions, and he pursued them with zest, leaving Davis for the adventurous Traffic, during which he also collaborated with Cream's Eric Clapton and Ginger Baker in Blind Faith. Following Traffic's demise, Winwood worked with Japanese composer Stomu Yamashta before launching a solo career that would go from halting to enormously successful—first hitting with his *Arc of a Diver* album in 1980 and then in an even bigger way six years later with *Back in the High Life.* Over the years, Winwood perfected a seamless blend of his jazz and R&B roots with pop, rock, folk and world music; at its best, Winwood's music is transendent, at it's worst it seems stiff and formulaic. In 1994 he re-formed Traffic with singer-drummer Jim Capaldi, but it's doubtful that reunion will completely scotch Winwood's solo work.

what to buy: The box set *The Finer Things* (Island/Chronicles, 1995, prod. Various) ♪♪♪♪♪ is so comprehensive it's absolutely essential, tracing Winwood's career from Spencer Davis to his latest solo ventures. It may be the one piece you need own, but *Arc of a Diver* (Island, 1980, prod. Steve Winwood) ♪♪♪♪½—an evocative, one-man-band project—should be heard in its entirety, too.

what to buy next: *Back in the High Life* (Island, 1986, prod. Russ Titleman and Steve Winwood) ♪♪♪♪ provided Winwood's commercial breakthrough with a string of hits such as "Higher Love," "The Finer Things" and the title track, and even the non-hits—"Wake Me Up on Judgment Day," "Split Decision"—rank high in his songbook.

what to avoid: *Refugees of the Heart* (Virgin, 1990, prod. Steve Winwood) ♪♪ showed that the hit formula Winwood discovered in the mid-80s was pretty well tapped out.

the rest: *Steve Winwood* (Island, 1977) ♪♪♪½ *Talking Back to the Night* (Island, 1983) ♪♪½ *ChroniclesMDBO* (Island, 1987) ♪♪♪ *Roll With It* (Virgin, 1988) ♪♪♪

worth searching for: *Go,* (Island, 1976) ♪♪♪ Winwood's first collaboration with Yamshta, an intriguing exploration of World Music and pre-techno ambience.

▶▶ Michael Penn, Michael Bolton, Bryan Adams, Tina Turner

◀◀ Ray Charles, the Beatles, Stax, Derek & the Dominos, Fairport Convention

see also: *Traffic, the Spencer Davis Group, Blind Faith*

Gary Graff

Wipers

Formed 1977 in Portland, Ore.

Greg Sage, guitar, bass and vocals; Dave Koupal bass (1977-81); Greg Davidson, bass (1981-89); Sam Henry, drums (1977-81); Brad Naish, drums 1981-86); Steve Plouf, drums (1986-present)

What man or band has released ten extraordinary studio albums over 18 years and has even been covered on record by Nirvana (twice!), Hole, Sonic Youth's Thurston Moore and Dinosaur Jr.'s J. Mascis (some as part of a tribute LP, *Fourteen Songs For Greg Sage & The Wipers*), yet most have (likely) never heard of him? The answer is Greg Sage, whose 10 albums—eight with Wipers and two under his own name—form a body of consistently mind-blowing work unmatched over such a long period of time in this country. So why is Sage such a no-name, despite being misleadingly tagged as a "Godfather of Northwest Grunge?" Simply put, the lanky, incredibly talented guitarist is one of the last of the fiercely independent punk-era nonconformists still running afoul of the bogus, ludicrous star-making machine that is alterna-rock. He hates it and shuns it; the man won't even sit for publicity photos. But if his music must speak for itself, it speaks in deafening tones. From Sage's earlier, punk-influenced albums to his more moody, methodical works of the late 80s and early 90s, Sage is a veritable guitar magician, producing his own rough-and-ready LPs in studios he builds. Finally, name another artist 18 years into his career whose later work is every bit as aggressive, vital and genuinely stunning as his younger days? In fact, *The Herd* is 1996's finest rock LP by anyone, a rare and unappreciated knockout right under our noses. Will anyone outside of Continental Europe, where he is a loved legend who packs halls and theaters (not surprisingly, it's the only continent Sage will still tour), notice?

what to buy: Hands down, *Youth of America* (Restless, 1981, prod. Greg Sage) ♪♪♪♪♪ is a monster; the 11-minute title track ranks up with the finest, most awe-inspiring pieces of music ever released in America. *The Herd* (Tim Kerr, 1996, prod. by Greg Sage) ♪♪♪♪½ which smolders from start to finish; don't miss "Psychic Vampire" and "Wind the Clock Slowly." For the more reflective side of Sage's piston-pumping rock, *Follow Blind* (Restless, 1987, prod. Greg Sage) ♪♪♪♪ is highlighted by

Sage's doomsday chords on the title track and surprising neo-Joy Division bass tones.

what to buy next: Sub Pop smartly reissued the rockin' debut, *Is This Real?* (Park Ave., 1979, prod. Greg Sage) which produced both songs Kurt Cobain and Co. covered on record, "Return of the Rat" and "D7," plus the pop gem, "Mystery." *Silver Sail* (Tim Kerr, 1993, prod. Greg Sage) is more of the reflective bent, mixing in surf and spaghetti western. *The Best of The Wipers and Greg Sage* (Restless, 1990) provides a solid overview for newcomers mixed with a few rare singles tracks for old fans.

what to avoid: *Wipers Live* (Enigma, 1985, prod. Greg Sage) is the least essential, though even this is of interest since it includes three songs never recorded in the studio.

the rest: *Land of the Lost* (Restless, 1986) *The Circle* (Restless, 1988)

worth searching for: The hard-to-find third album, *Over The Edge,* (Braineater, 1983, prod. by Greg Sage) whose first three songs are also consummate Wipers' blowout guitar hooks.

solo outings:

Greg Sage: Straight Ahead (Enigma, 1985) *Sacrifice (For Love)* (Restless Records, 1991)

Nirvana , Hole, Sonic Youth, Dinosaur Jr, Mudhoney, The Melvins, Screaming Trees, Pearl Jam

Jimi Hendrix, Dick Dale, The Ventures, The Yardbirds, The Wailers, The Kingsmen, The Raiders

Jack Rabid

Wire

Formed 1976 in London, England. Disbanded 1980. Reformed 1986.

Colin Newman, vocals; Bruce Gilbert, guitar; Graham Lewis, bass, vocals; Robert Gotobed (born Mark Field), drums

In contrast to the working-class snarl of most British punk circa 1977 —all you needed to form a band was bad teeth, a couple of strategically inserted safety pins and three chords — Wire offered a more distanced, coolly cerebral but no less enthralling approach. Befitting the members' art-school backgrounds, the group recorded songs with titles such as "French Film (Blurred)" and "Reuters," the latter about a news agency reporter whose last dispatch closes the song: "This is your correspondent, running out of tape, gunfire's increasing, looting, burning, rape." The minimalist music was as terse as most punk bands', particularly on the debut album, *Pink Flag.* But the group's debt to the avant-garde quickly became evident with the more experimental textures on the increasingly expansive follow-ups, such as the superb *Chairs Missing* and the less involving *154.* After releasing these three poor-selling but highly influential discs, the group broke up, only to reconvene in 1986 as an angular synth-pop band. Refusing to indulge fans with its punk-era "hits" while on tour, Wire even went so far as to hire an opening band, the Ex-Lion Tamers (named after a song on *Pink Flag*), to play them. Drummer Gotobed, frustrated by the machine-dominated approach, quit in 1991, and the group dropped the last letter of its name to record what appears to be its final album, *The First Letter.*

what to buy: *Pink Flag* (Restless Retro, 1977, prod. Mike Thorne) is one of the essential documents of British punk, though it's not really a punk record. Whereas bands such as the Sex Pistols and Clash viewed punk as a means of reclaiming rock 'n' roll's essence, Wire were arty minimalists lumped in with punk by default because of its fondness for fat-free arrangements, terse melodies and fast, stuttering rhythms. The 21 tracks span all of 35 minutes, and not one is wasted. The follow-up, *Chairs Missing,* (Restless Retro, 1978, prod. Mike Thorne) lengthens the songs and broadens the sonic palette to include keyboards, synthesizers and even flutes without dulling the impact. "I am the fly in the ointment," the group accurately declares.

what to buy next: *On Returning (1977-79)* (Restless Retro, 1989, prod. Mike Thorne) collects most of the best of the first three discs (with the crucial exception of "Map Ref. 41 41N 93W" from *154*) and assorted singles from the band's most critical phase. *Wire 1985-1990: The A List* (Mute, 1993, prod. Various) is an insidiously catchy collection of singles and album tracks from the synth-pop years.

what to avoid: One would think that a document of the band's final live performance from its punk era would be riveting, but instead it's a sham. *Document and Eyewitness* (Mute, 1991) the bulk of which is from a 1980 concert, is a stunningly dreary avant-garde experiment.

the rest: *154* (Restless Retro, 1979) *Snakedrill* (Mute-Enigma EP, 1987) *The Ideal Copy* (Mute-Enigma, 1987) *Ahead* (Mute-Enigma EP, 1987) *The Peel Sessions* (Strange Fruit EP, 1987) *A Bell is a Cup Until It is Struck* (Mute-Enigma, 1988) *Kidney Bongos* (Mute-Restless EP, 1988) *Silk Skin Paws* (Mute-Restless EP, 1989) *It's Be-*

ginning To and Back Again (Mute-Enigma, 1989) *The Peel Sessions Album* (Strange Fruit-Dutch East India, 1991) *Manscape* (Mute-Enigma, 1990) *The Drill* (Mute-Elektra, 1991) As Wir—*The First Letter* (Mute-Elektra, 1991)

worth seeking out: Though at 18 tracks it contains 13 fewer cuts than the *On Returning* CD compilation, the vinyl-only *And Here It Is ... Again ... Wire* (Sneaky Pete Records, 1984) is a more judiciously chosen overview of the band's crucial early years, including some key songs left off the later collection.

REM, Sonic Youth, Husker Du, the Cure, Big Black, the Minutemen, Elastica

Greg Kot

Wire Train

Formed 1982 in San Francisco, Calif.

Kevin Hunter, vocals, guitar; Anders Runblad, bass; Kurt Herr, guitar (1982-85); Frederico Gil-Sola, drums (1982-84); Brian McLeod, drums (1985-92); Jeffrey Trott, guitar (1986-92)

Wire Train's pre-industry guitar jangle was noticeably out of sync with the emotionally repressed New Wave scene of the early 80s. Despite the group's capability to produce hit singles whose sincerity against the backdrop of the Reagan years was admirable, it remained more of a local phenomenon than a national act. With whirling guitars and heartfelt messages of societal ills, Wire Train came along at least five years too early. Despite a strong return in '92 with *No Soul No Strain,* (MCA, 1992, prod. Bill Bottrell) the band remained stuck between the cracks of new wave and alternative rock. *Last Perfect Thing: A Retrospective* (Columbia/Legacy, 1996, prod. Various) sets the Wire Train record straight, starting off with the ringing "Chamber of Hellos"—surely one of the best forgotten pop songs of 1984. *In a Chamber/Between Two Worlds* (Oglio Records, 1995, prod. David Kahne and Peter Maunu) contains both of the band's first two releases in their entireties, which gives pop miners a good bang for their buck. The latter's leaner edge contains some singles as fine as "Chamber," notably "Last Perfect Thing" and "Skills of Summer," as well as a warm version of Dylan's "With God on Our Side."

Allan Orski

Wizzard

See: The Move

Jah Wobble's Invaders of the Heart

See: Public Image Ltd. (PiL)

Peter Wolf

Born Peter Blankfield, March 6, 1946, in Bronx, N.Y.

The J. Geils Band's white-boy R&B ran toward the music's roots, but singer Wolf, a supporter of Boston's R&B scene since his days as a WBCN deejay, looked toward more modern sounds after leaving the group in 1983. He had some initial success with his solo outings—more, certainly, than the Wolf-less J. Geils Band—and placed three singles ("Lights Out," "I Need You Tonight" and "Come As You Are") in the Top 40. Subsequent releases have not been received as well, however, and have become more infrequent.

what to buy: Wolf had been writing songs with R&B singer Don Covay ("Lights Out") and Michael Jonzun of Boston hip-hoppers the Jonzun Crew when he was squeezed out of J. Geils. Those songs emerged on *Lights Out,* (EMI America, 1984, prod. Michael Jonzun and Peter Wolf) whose playful approach to the music proved an excellent foil for Wolf's white-funk jive.

what to buy next: On *Come As You Are,* (EMI America, 1987, prod. Peter Wolf, and Eric "E.T." Thorngren) Wolf continued to work with hot hip-hop producers—this time with Thorngren, who had come to fame remixing Grandmaster Flash's records. Wolf and Thorngren turn up the guitars while retaining the grooves, but beyond the title track and a couple other cuts, they can't maintain the party atmosphere in which Wolf has cut his best records.

what to avoid: Written and co-produced with two Nashville songwriters, *Up to No Good* (MCA, 1990, prod. Peter Wolf, Robert White Johnson and Taylor Rhodes) doesn't have the spark of his work with R&B musicians.

the rest: *Long Line* (Reprise, 1996)

worth searching for: The 12" dance mixes of "Lights Out" (EMI America, 1984, remixed by Francois Kevorkian) and "Come As You Are" (EMI America, 1987, remixed by Chris Lord Alge) are among the best rock remixes of the mid-80s.

Robert Palmer, Mick Jagger

The J. Geils Band, Bobby Womack, the Rolling Stones, Blondie, doo-wop

Brian Mansfield

Bobby Womack

Born March 4, 1944, in Cleveland, Ohio

Helping to fill the bill after Sam Cooke's death in 1964, Womack—who was Cooke's guitar player—embarked on a solo career. He wrote or co-wrote some key rock 'n' roll songs, played guitar on a lot of crucial sessions and had rumblings of R&B success, with a gritty soul voice and an advanced sense of soul writing and arrangement. When he and his brothers were signed to Cooke's label as the Womack Brothers, he changed their name to the Valentinos, and they tasted their first success with "Looking for a Love" and "It's All Over Now," which later became key hits for the J. Geils Band and the Rolling Stones, respectively. Lapses in his career were said to be caused by drug abuse; pronounced comebacks accompanied several clean-ups. After he helped out on more than a couple of Stones albums, the band repaid him when Ron Wood issued Womack's 1994 comeback on his own label and enlisted superstar rock friends to help out. Womack sees himself as a soul survivor in a field decimated over the decades. He's certainly been able to maintain a major-label career as his peers struggled, although the big fame has so far eluded him.

what to buy: The number of Womack titles currently in print is conspicuously spotty, with early 70s recordings much more readily available than mid- to late-80s successes. There's never been a loss in Womack compilations, though. *Only Survivor: The MCA Years* (MCA, 1996, prod. Various) stands out because it collects such otherwise unavailable songs as "I Wish He Didn't Trust Me So Much" and the stirring "I'll Still Be Looking Up to You (No Matter How High I Get)."

what to buy next: *The Poet,* (Beverly Glen Music, 1981/Razor & Tie, 1993, prod. Bobby Womack) the first of two strong *Poet* albums that mounted a comeback of sizzling R&B tracks such as "If You Think You're Lonely Now." *Midnight Mover: The Bobby Womack Collection* (EMI, 1993, prod. Various) covers so much ground—the first nine years of his solo recording career, over 11 albums for Minit/Liberty/United Artists from 1967-1975.

what to avoid: Although it boasts grittier production and a wonderful remake of the Temptations' "I Wish It Would Rain," Womack's last album for United Artists, *Safety Zone,* (United Artists, 1972/The Right Stuff-Capitol, 1994, prod. David Rubinson) ended with a dismal eight-minute disco stab, "I Feel a Groove Coming On."

the rest: *Communication* (United Artists, 1971/The Right Stuff-Capitol, 1994) *Understanding* (United Artists, 1972/The Right Stuff-Capitol, 1994) *Facts of Life* (United Artists, 1973/The Right Stuff-Capitol, 1994) *Looking for a Love Again* (United Artists, 1974/ The Right Stuff-Capitol, 1994) *The Poet II* (Beverly Glen Music, 1984) *Lookin' for a Love: The Best of Bobby Womack, 1968-1975* (Razor & Tie, 1993) *Resurrection* (Slide/Continuum, 1994)

worth searching for: *Someday We'll All Be Free* (Beverly Glen Music, 1985, prod. Bobby Womack and Patrick Moten) may be the best of the many out-of-print Womack titles. This could have been *Poet III* since it was his next in that series on that small label, boasting such workouts as "I Wish I Had Someone to Go Home To" and the Donny Hathaway-penned title song.

Womack & Womack, Tony Rice Project, Babyface

Sam Cooke, Wilson Pickett, Friendly Womack

Roger Catlin

Womack & Womack

Formed c. 1983.

Cecil Womack (born 1947), guitars, vocals; Linda Womack (born 1952), keyboards, vocals

The husband-and-wife duo of Womack & Womack bring a deep family tradition to their soulful music. Cecil started performing as a teenager with the Womack Brothers gospel group, which evolved into the influential R&B band the Valentinos and, in turn, launched brother Bobby Womack's solo career. And Linda is the daughter of Sam Cooke. Before partnering as performers, they wrote songs individually for artists such as Aretha Franklin and Teddy Pendergrass. In 1983, they produced their first album as a duo, called *Love Wars.* Interestingly, for a couple who appear to be the picture of domestic bliss on their album covers, Womack & Womack's lyrics often explore the tenuous realms of infidelity, betrayal and lost love. Though displaying a skilled sense of contemporary songwriting, the feeling and flavor of soul music's roots are crucial elements in all their work. This is mature, seasoned stuff—which probably explains their lack of airplay, and resultant journeys from one record label to another. *Love Wars* (Elektra, 1983, prod. Stewart Levine) remains their best, with a solid studio band adding muscle to classic soul grooves and well-crafted tunes. On *Conscience,* (Island, 1988, prod. Chris Blackwell and the Gypsy Wave Power Co.) a multi-layered Southern soul guitar mix gives a mellower feel to some of Womack & Womack's best material - including "Good Man Monologue," later covered by Bonnie Raitt and Delbert McClinton.

the rest: *Radio M.U.S.I.C. Man* (Elektra, 1985) *Family Spirit* (RCA, 1991) *Transformation to the House of Zekkariyas* (Warner Bros., 1993)

Doug Pippin

Stevie Wonder

Born Steveland Morris, May 13, 1950, in Saginaw, Mich.

Out of all the stars that came out of the Motown stable, Wonder's has shined the brightest and the longest. Already a star as Little Stevie Wonder in 1971, the maturing musician fought Motown president Berry Gordy for artistic control of his music—and won. Wonder went on to become the 800-pound gorilla of pop during the 70s, with a distinctive sound that borrowed freely from funk, rock, classical, jazz, country and even reggae. His immense genius absorbed it all into a precisely layered and melodic music that had no peer. From "Fingertips Part 2," his first hit at the age of 13, to "I Just Called to Say I Love You" and beyond, Wonder's oeuvre encompasses a treasure trove of ageless songs—"My Cherie Amour," "You Are the Sunshine of My Life," "Superstition," "Golden Lady." Paul Simon put it all in perspective when accepting a Grammy for 1975's *Still Crazy After All These Years* by thanking Wonder for not putting out a record that year. Wonder was instrumental in the campaign to get Martin Luther King Jr.'s birthday declared a national holiday and has been active in exposing African and Caribbean musicians to American audiences. Though not in the spotlight as much as before, Wonder is still a top pop star with the ability to put his finger on the pulse of the people and compose a tune that goes right to the heart of the matter.

what to buy: Wonder seemed an absolute pop music genius during the 70s, and *Innervisions* (Motown, 1973, prod. Stevie Wonder) is the pinnacle of that sensibility. Nearly every song—"Too High," "Golden Lady," "Don't You Worry 'Bout a Thing," "All in Love Is Fair"—is a classic. But it was the gritty "Living for the City" that really set folks on their ears. *Talking Book* (Motown, 1972, prod. Stevie Wonder) was almost as good; "Superstition" and "You Are the Sunshine of My Life" gave an inkling of what was to come.

what to buy next: A lot of folks thought Wonder had gone off the deep end when the double album *Songs in the Key of Life* (Motown, 1976, prod. Stevie Wonder) came out with its blend of funk and jazz influences, but it yielded hits such as "Sir Duke" and "Isn't She Lovely" to turn minds around. *Where I'm Coming From* (Motown, 1972, prod. Stevie Wonder) is the first album that Wonder had complete creative control over and the only one of his adult years that he gave significant songwriting space to someone else—then-wife Syreeta Wright. The album gave us "If You Really Love Me" and "Never Dreamed You'd Leave Me in Summer."

what to avoid: *Journey Through the Secret Life of Plants* (Motown, 1979, prod. Stevie Wonder) has well-crafted instrumentals that lean toward the New Age vibe but was outside the pop mainstream. It's a testament to Wonder's clout that Motown head Berry Gordy even allowed this to be released.

the rest: *The Jazz Soul of Little Stevie Wonder* (Motown, 1963) *With a Song in My Heart* (Motown, 1966) *Down to Earth* (Motown, 1967) *I Was Made to Love Her* (Motown, 1967) *Someday at Christmas* (Motown, 1967); *For Once in My Life* (Motown, 1968) *Greatest Hits, Volume 1* (Motown, 1968) *My Cherie Amour* (Motown, 1969) *Signed, Sealed and Delivered* (Motown, 1970) *Greatest Hits, Vol. 2* (Motown, 1972) *Music of My Mind* (Motown, 1972) *Fulfillingness First Finale* (Motown, 1974) *Hotter Than July* (Motown, 1980) *Original Musiquarium* (Motown, 1982) *The Woman in Red* soundtrack (Motown, 1984) *In Square Circle* (Motown, 1985) *Jungle Fever* (Motown, 1991) *Motown Legends: I Was Made to Love Her—Uptight* (ESX Entertainment, 1994) *Conversation Peace* (Motown, 1995) *Natural Wonder* (Motown, 1995)

worth searching for: The import *Essential Stevie Wonder* is the only comprehensive collection of Wonder's 1963-71 work, a period covered no single domestic release covers completely.

▶▶ Lionel Ritchie, Lenny Kravitz, Luther Vandross, Howard Jones, Michael Jackson

◀◀ Ray Charles, Duke Ellington, Smokey Robinson, Marvin Gaye, Frankie Lymon, Miles Davis

Lawrence Gabriel

The Wonder Stuff

Formed 1987 in Birmingham, England. Disbanded 1994.

Miles Hunt, vocals, guitar, harmonica; Malc Treece, guitar, vocals; Martin Gilks, drums; Rob Jones, bass (1987-89); Paul Clifford, bass

(1990-94); Martin Bell, fiddle, accordion, mandolin, guitar, sitar, keyboards (1989-94)

With a sharp wit and cynicism, the Wonder Stuff emerged with *The Eight Legged Groove Machine* (Polydor, 1988 prod. Pat Collier) 𝅘𝅥𝅘𝅥𝅘𝅥𝅘𝅥 while the British press focused on the arrogant self-confidence of frontman Hunt, the Wonder Stuff made its case with strong melodies, killer pop hooks, a bit of a mean spirit and a sharp sense of humor. This continued with on *Hup*, (Polydor, 1989, prod. Pat Collier) 𝅘𝅥𝅘𝅥𝅘𝅥𝅘𝅥 which moved a bit towards the psychedelic, though the foundation remained rooted in power pop filled with rich harmonies and spiky arrangements. *Never Loved Elvis* (Polydor, 1991 prod. Mick Glossop) 𝅘𝅥𝅘𝅥𝅘𝅥𝅘𝅥 delivers more wonderful pop smarts and the single "Welcome To The Cheap Seats," which achieved modest airings on MTV, thanks partially to Kirsty MacColl's guest spot in the video. Long touring around the world and European festivals showcased the band's raw energy on stage but never delivered as big an audience in America as it did in its homeland. *Construction For The Modern Idiot* (Polydor, 1993, prod. Pat Collier)𝅘𝅥𝅘𝅥𝅘𝅥𝅘𝅥 was a bit off the mark from previous releases, while the retrospective *If The Beatles Had Read Hunter...The Singles* (Polydor, 1994 prod. Pat Collier and Mick Glossop) 𝅘𝅥𝅘𝅥𝅘𝅥𝅘𝅥 delivered the U.K. singles in one package and is the next stop after *Groove Machine*

John Nieman

Ron Wood

Born June 1, 1947 in Hillingdon, England

A consummate support player, Wood has made a career out of playing second-fiddle to bigger stars with bigger egos. He was the original bass player in the Jeff Beck Group, largely because Beck didn't want another guitarist in the band and Wood was no match for Beck's six-string virtuosity. He did switch to guitar when he joined the Small Faces in 1968 with another disgruntled Beck group member, singer Rod Stewart. They guided their new group, renamed the Faces, to fame and fortune from 1969-75, perfecting a scuzzy, boozy, ballroom-style rock 'n' roll. The rooster-haired Wood happily served as the ostentatious Stewart's foil, quietly becoming a formidable rhythm and slide player. But Stewart's solo work proved more popular than the band's, particularly in America, turning the Faces' smiles to frowns. Wood released his own solo album, *I've Got My Own Album to Do*, in 1974. But his output has been sporadic since then, largely because he left the Faces to become Mick Jagger and Keith Richards' junior partner in the Rolling Stones in time for their North American tour in 1975. Wood ended a 12-year gap between solo albums with the release of *Slide on This* in 1992. Unfortunately, collector's will have some trouble finding Wood's solo stuff, since most of it is out of print. Warner Bros. has reissued his first two albums, and copies of *Slide on This* and the live album culled from the subsequent solo tour is still floating around.

what to buy: *Slide on This* (Continuum, 1992) 𝅘𝅥𝅘𝅥𝅘𝅥 is the most accomplished of Wood's six solo efforts. It's louder, brasher, bluesier and more confident than anything he's ever done, largely because he enlisted the soulful Bernard Fowler, who ably assisted the Stones on their *Steel Wheels* and *Voodoo Lounge* albums and tours, as a songwriting partner and singer.

what to buy next: *I've Got My Own Album to Do* (Warner Bros., 1974) 𝅘𝅥𝅘𝅥𝅘𝅥 features guest appearances by Jagger and Richards.

what to avoid: *1234* (Columbia, 1981) 𝅘𝅥 is a real dog of an album, seemingly thrown together and without any discernible focus.

the rest: *Now Look* (Warner Bros., 1975) 𝅘𝅥𝅘𝅥 "Mahoney's Last Stand" soundtrack (with Ronnie Lane) (Atco, 1976) 𝅘𝅥𝅘𝅥 *Gimme Some Neck* (Columbia, 1979) 𝅘𝅥𝅘𝅥𝅘𝅥 *Slide on This Live: Plugged and Standing* (Continuum, 1993) 𝅘𝅥𝅘𝅥

worth searching for: Hardcore Wood fans should track down *Live at the Ritz* (Victory Music, 1987) 𝅘𝅥𝅘𝅥 a now out-of-print concert album taken from Wood's 1986 club tour with his idol, Bo Diddley. It includes Diddley classics such as "Who Do You Love" and Wood's own howling version of "Honky Tonk Women."

▶▶ The Black Crowes, Oasis

◀◀ Bo Diddley, Howlin' Wolf, Muddy Waters, Keith Richards

see also: *The Rolling Stones, the Faces*

Doug Pullen

Roy Wood

See: The Move

World Party

Formed 1986 in London, England

Karl Wallinger, vocals, keyboards, guitars, bass; Chris Sharrock, drums (1992-93); Dave Catlin-Birch, guitars (1992-93)

Derivative and hippyesque, yet well-crafted and often soulful, the music of World Party ranks about as high as pop can get without actually seeming to have lasting value. It's doubtful that anyone will ever have a hit cover version of any of Wallinger's songs, yet there's much to enjoy on each of his group's four official releases. He has been knocked for his lyrics, which often fancifully chide mankind for wreaking environmental havoc and being generally inconsiderate to each other, and yet he has stuck to his guns, keeping his focus throughout his career. For the most part, World Party is a Wallinger solo project on whose albums he has always had numerous guests (including a very young Sinead O'Connor on backing vocals for one cut on the group's 1986 debut). After a stint as keyboardist for Scotch/Irish rockers The Waterboys around the time of their gloriously over-the-top *This Is The Sea* album in 1985, Wallinger concocted *Private Revolution* as World Party's debut in 1986, pulling stylistic elements from Bob Dylan, Van Morrison, the Beatles and the Stones. He leaned a little more toward Morrison and the Beatles on 1990's *Goodbye Jumbo*, before getting slightly interested in the sassy funk of Prince, first on 1991's "Thank You World" EP, and then more so on 1993's riskier but less accomplished *Bang!*

what to buy: The first half of *Private Revolution* (Ensign/Chrysalis, 1986, prod. Karl Wallinger) ♪♪♪♪ remains Wallinger's greatest achievement to date. Haunting, soulful and brimming with convincingly righteous indignation, those first six tunes run the gamut from sassy dance-pop (the title track) to moody R&B-rock (the wonderful "Ship of Fools") to the beautiful but almost creepy "All Come True." The rest of the album slips a bit—the cover of Dylan's "All I Really Want to Do" only proves once again that Dylan wrote most of his stuff with his own style in mind, and that most others can't hack it—but not enough to tarnish the work as a whole.

what to buy next: Although it lacks the level of atmospheric cohesion that made the first half of *Private Revolution* so compelling, *Goodbye Jumbo* (Ensign/Chrysalis, 1990, prod. Karl Wallinger) ♪♪♪♪ includes several standout songs and a great deal of heart. The Stones-y R&B-pop of "Way Down Now" and the Van Morrison-like balladry of "Sweet Soul Dream" are highlights, but perhaps most impressive is the surprisingly soulful "Ain't Gonna Come Till I'm Ready."

what to avoid: With Sharrock and Catlin-Birch on board, *Bang!* (Ensign/Chrysalis/ERG, 1993, prod. Karl Wallinger and Steve Lillywhite) ♪♪♪ is Wallinger's attempt at developing a more band-based sound. Somehow, though, the album drags, as too many songs go on too long. Still, "Give It All Away" is the group's wildest funk-dance workout and "Is It Like Today" makes for good, melancholy pop.

the rest: *Thank You World* (Chrysalis EP, 1991, prod. Karl Wallinger) ♪♪♪

worth searching for: The promo-only *History of the World* (Ensign/Chrysalis/ERG, 1993, prod. Karl Wallinger, Steve Lillywhite) ♪♪♪♪ serves as a well-balanced greatest hits of sorts, though the moody flow of the individual albums is lost somewhat.

▶▶ Lenny Kravitz, Ben Folds Five

◀◀ The Beatles, Bob Dylan, Van Morrison, Prince, the Rolling Stones, the Beach Boys

Bob Remstein

What Album Changed Your Life?

"I think Joni Mitchell's Miles of Aisles was probably the turning point where I realized that being a singer was one thing and being a sonwriter was another, and that songwriting was very, very important."

k.d. lang

Link Wray

Born Lincoln Wray, May 2, 1935 in Dunn, N.C.

Wray made history by punching holes in his amp speaker and playing his version of the stroll, a popular early rock dance, during the 50s. The result was "Rumble," one of the most menacing, raunchy instrumentals ever cut. It was his greatest moment, though he would continue making music well into his 60s. Wray's distorted, twangy, tremolo-laden guitar tone—a demonic version of Duane Eddy's—would embolden countless guitar players in ensuing years; as a result, Wray has been credited as a founding father of both heavy metal and punk rock.

Wray and his brothers Vernon and Doug first formed a band with bassist Short Horton during the 50s, playing country and rockabilly for dances and entertaining thoughts of becoming studio session players. After Korean War service and the loss of a lung to tuberculosis, Wray returned to music and embarked on a recording career that sent him from one label to the next through the 60s. A gruff but compelling singer, Wray actually assayed a variety of styles, including bluegrass and blue-eyed soul. Despite a well-publicized comeback attempt during the early 70s, he has remained an underground artist ever since.

what to buy: *Mr. Guitar* (Norton, 1995, prod. Various) is an exhaustive two-disc collection of Wray's killer early instrumentals; there's enough guitar raunch here for any lost weekend.

what to buy next: *Rumble: The Best of Link Wray* (Rhino, 1993, prod. Various) is a fine one-disc compilation for those on a limited budget.

what to avoid: *Bullshot*, (Visa, 1979, prod. Richard Gottehrer) the title of which may have been misspelled.

the rest: *Link Wray & the Wraymen* (Edsel, 1960) *Jack the Ripper* (Swan, 1963) *Link Wray* (Polydor, 1971) *Be What You Want To* (Polydor, 1973) *Beans and Fatback* (Virgin, 1973) *The Link Wray Rumble* (Polydor, 1974) *Interstate 10* (Caroline, 1975) *Stuck in Gear* (Virgin, 1976) *Robert Gordon and Link Wray* (Private Stock, 1977) *Fresh Fish Special* (Private Stock, 1978) *Good Rockin' Tonight* (Visa, 1985) *Original Rumble* (Ace, 1989) *Walkin' with Link* (Epic, 1992) *Indian Child* (Sony (Denmark), 1993)

worth searching for: *Guitar Preacher: The Polydor Years* (Polydor, 1995, prod. Bill Levenson) is an impressive two-disc anthology of Wray's rootsier, more song-oriented side. It still features a lot of hair-raising guitar work.

Pete Townsend, Jeff Beck, Tom Waits, Southern Culture on the Skids

James Burton, Duane Eddy, Dick Dale, Howlin' Wolf

Simon Glickman

Gary Wright /Spooky Tooth

Formed 1967 in London, England. Disbanded 1975.

Gary Wright (born April 26, 1943 in Creskill, N.J.) keyboards, vocals (1967-70, 1972-75); Mike Harrison, vocals, keyboards (1967-75); Luther Grosvenor, guitar (1967-72); Greg Ridley, bass (1967-69); Mike Kellie, drums (1967-72); Andy Leigh, bass; Henry McCullough, guitar (1970-72); Chris Stainton, keyboards (1970-72); Alan Spenner, bass (1970-72); Mick Jones (1972-75); Chris Stewart, bass (1972-75); Bryson Graham, drums; Mike Patto, keyboards, vocals (1975, died March 4, 1979); Val Burke, bass, vocals (1975)

New Jersey native Wright was a child actor and performed on Broadway in the musical "Fanny" before attending college in Berlin and eventually working his way to England. As a founding member of Spooky Tooth, he brought an experimental edge to his keyboard technique; to further his vision, he hired French electronic music pioneer Pierre Henry to participate on Spooky Tooth's 1970 album *Celebration*, marking a huge but successful departure both artistically and commercially. Spooky Tooth suffered from frequent lineup changes and a lack of commitment to recording, which resulted in lots of weak albums. Wright enjoyed the most notable solo career, but guitarist Jones had the most success, forming the group Foreigner and producing albums for Billy Joel and Van Halen. Grosvenor joined Stealers Wheel and, later Mott the Hoople.

what to buy: *Spooky Two* (A&M, 1969, prod. Jimmy Miller) is the band's best and most focused album.

what to buy next: When Spooky Tooth truly called it quits in 1975, Wright followed with his platinum-selling solo effort *The Dream Weaver*, (Warner Bros., 1975) which garnered two Top 10 hits, the title track and "Love Is Alive."

what to avoid: *The Mirror* (Island/Griffin, 1974) showed the reconstituted Spooky Tooth had little to say and nowhere to go. On *First Signs of Life*, (Worldly Music, 1995, prod. Gary Wright) WOOF! Wright spoils the Brazilian-flavored percussive edge with his penchant for naval-gazing and keyboard-noodling.

Deep Purple, Uriah Heep, the Waterboys, Talk Talk

Spencer Davis Group, Terry Reid

see also: *Foreigner, Mott the Hoople, Gerry Rafferty/Stealers Wheel*

Patrick McCarty

Richard Wright

See: Pink Floyd

Robert Wyatt

Born 1945 in Bristol, England

Almost wholly undiscovered by Americans throughout his 30-year career, Wyatt is among the most durable of Britain's musical artists, having transited his years as the drummer for the progressive art-rock group Soft Machine to build a solo career of lush, meditative music punctuated by the occasional odd British hit. His music is almost always pleasantly eccentric, graced by Wyatt's distinctive, frail tenor, a lovely voice that has a child's boldfaced, unassuming honesty. Wyatt's solo career suffered an immediate setback when, shortly after the release of his debut, 1970's *The End of an Ear*, a fall from a window left him permanently paralyzed from the waist down. Wyatt devoted his talents to keyboards and returned in 1974 with back-to-back oddities, the star-studded *Rock Bottom* and *Ruth is Stranger than Richard* (1975). For all the frequently primal eccentricities of his music, Wyatt has scored several mainstream U.K. hits over the years, first with a straight version of the Monkees' "I'm a Believer" in 1974, and again during the early 80s with "Shipbuilding," a song about the Falklands war written for him by producer Clive Langer and Elvis Costello. His music became more stridently political during Margaret Thatcher's reign as Britain's prime minister, but he kept clear of vicious sniping, focusing instead on the human costs of politics and war. Wyatt continues to write, paint and make music when he wants to, seemingly oblivious to the expectations of the music industry. He remains today as he was in the Soft Machine, an uncommonly devoted artist marching to a different drummer.

what to buy: *Rock Bottom/Ruth is Stranger than Richard* (Virgin, 1981, prod. Nick Mason and Robert Wyatt) ♪♪♪♪ is a highly prized repackaging of Wyatt's second and third solo albums. *Rock Bottom* is a lovely and at times haunting record dealing (as the title suggests) with Wyatt's recovery from his paralyzing fall. *Ruth/Richard* is, by comparison, a lively and much brighter record on which Wyatt further experiments with jazz and pop; the jaunty opener, "Soup Song," is a particularly fun and memorable track. *Nothing Can Stop Us Now/Old Rotten Hat* (Gramavision Records, 1994, prod. ??) ♪♪♪♪ is another double-reissue of albums from 1981 and 1985, respectively. Wyatt's political voice emerges to present some of his most rewarding songs, including "Stalin Wasn't Stallin'," the Billie Holiday standard "Strange Fruit" and his expressive rendition of "Shipbuilding."

what to buy next: If either of the above CDs motivates you, then dig deep into your pockets for *Going Back a Bit: A Little History of Robert Wyatt* (Virgin, 1994, prod. Various) ♪♪♪♪♪ Although a somewhat pricey offering (a double CD and an import), it more than compensates with 29 tracks that span Wyatt's career from Soft Machine and Matching Mole to his solo years, including collaborations with Brian Eno and others. It's an excellent overview of a wide and varied career, providing a sense of chronology and strong recognition of Wyatt's unique talents.

what to avoid: Despite its value to hard-core Wyatt fans, neophytes will probably be put off by *Flotsam Jetsam* (Rough Trade, 1994, prod. Various) ♪♪♪♪, a terrific collection of out-takes and oddities from 1968-90. The CD does a fine job filling in the cracks in Wyatt's career, serving up snippets of his work with avant-garde artists Dagmar Krause and Lol Coxhill as well as with Jimi Hendrix (with whom Soft Machine toured America in 1968); unfortunately, Wyatt takes a back seat to the many stellar talents in evidence throughout the album.

the rest: *Rock Bottom* (Blue Plate, 1974) ♪♪♪ *The Animals Film Soundtrack* (Rough Trade, 1982) ♪♪♪ *The Peel Sessions* EP (Dutch East India, 1987) ♪♪♪♪ *Dondestan* (Gramavision Records, 1991) ♪♪♪♪ *A Short Break* (UK Voiceprint, 1992) ♪♪♪ *Flotsam Jetsam* (Rough Trade, 1994) ♪♪♪♪ *Mid-Eighties* (Gramavision Records, 1994) ♪♪♪♪

worth searching for: *The End of an Ear* (Sony Belgium, 1970, prod. Robert Wyatt) ♪♪♪ is Wyatt's wonderful solo debut. Featuring a loose improvisational jazz style and plenty of odd scat singing, it's a tempting listen that gives a strong indication of where Wyatt would be going in the future.

▶▶ Fred Frith, Ivor Cutler, Henry Cow, Kevin Ayers, Steve Hillage, John Cale, Brian Eno, Phil Manzanera, Elvis Costello, The Residents, Ozric Tentacles

◀◀ David Allen, Pink Floyd, Soft Machine, Matching Mole, Gong, Caravan

see also: *Soft Machine*

Christopher Scapelliti

Steve Wynn

See: The Dream Syndicate

X /John Doe/Exene Cervenka/Knitters

Formed 1977 in Los Angeles, Calif.

John Doe (born XX), vocals and bass; Exene Cervenka, vocals; Billy Zoom, guitar (1977-85); D.J. Bonebrake, drums; Tony Gilkyson, guitar (1985-present); Dave Alvin, guitar (1987)

Not since the Who has any rock 'n' roll band crashed its individual parts together with such force. When word of British punk rock leaked to America's coasts, Los Angeles suburban teens were among the first to embrace it. X, led by the husband-wife team of regular guy Doe and tortured, screechy poet Cervenka, became the shining star of West Coast punk. It helped that guitarist Zoom could play rockabilly riffs straight from old Link Wray records, but juiced up so fast they were exhilaratingly incomprehensible. Bonebrake's metronomic drumming was worthy of his forebearer, Elvis Presley drummer D.J. Fontana. And the whole group had, with influence from the Blasters' Dave Alvin and early patron Ray Manzarek of The Doors, a keen sense of American music history to make everything more interesting. For awhile, Doe and Cervenka while, sang Johnny Cash-June Carter ballads at L.A. coffeehouses—appropriate, since X sometimes sounds like a sped-up, angst-ridden version of "Jackson."

Eventually, Zoom left the band, replaced by the talented but more professional Gilkyson, and after a few of rock's most propulsive albums, the band eased slowly into older age. Its social conscience, always bubbling under the surface, grew into sometimes preachy ballads. Cervenka and Doe divorced during the late 80s, and their relationship regularly drove the members apart, then brought them back together. The group reunited for good in 1994 and still has interesting things to say, even if, regrettably, there will never be another "The Phone's Off the Hook, But You're Not."

what to buy: The first four albums are up there with the peak runs of Bob Dylan, the Rolling Stones and the Beatles in terms of career consistency. *Los Angeles,* (Slash, 1980, prod. Ray Manzarek) with its barely decipherable stories of underground L.A. life and contempt for boring people, has the title track, "Sex and Dying in High Society" and "Johnny Hit and Run Paulene." *Wild Gift* (Slash, 1981, prod. Ray Manzarek) is a fine continuation, with even more great songs—including the L.A. punk anthem "We're Desperate," "Adult Books" and "Back 2 the Base." In *Under the Big Black Sun,* (Elektra, 1982, prod. Ray Manzarek) you can actually start hearing the lyrics. *More Fun in the New World* (Elektra/Asylum, 19843, prod. Ray Manzarek) is X's most effective blending of standing-up-for-the-oppressed ideals and rock 'n' roll—"The New World" name-drops Detroit and Gary, Ind., in the most blunt possible way.

what to buy next: *See How We Are* (Elektra/Asylum, 1987, prod. Alvin Clark) reunites an older X, musing poignantly about the plight of the poor. Dave Alvin's classic "Fourth of July" appears for the first time on record. *Ain't Love Grand* (Elektra/Asylum, 1985, prod. Michael Wagener) is pristinely polished, which is jarring for an X album, but its wonderful love song "Burning House of Love" almost makes up for it. The Knitters, the band's short-lived country alter ego, seemed weird at the time, but *Poor Little Critter on the Road* (Slash, 1985, prod. the Knitters) holds up surprisingly well today.

what to avoid: *Hey Zeus!* (Big Life/Mercury, 1993, prod. Tony Berg) is another reunion album, which means trouble and weak, blandly political songs about war and other controversial subjects. *Live at the Whisky A Go-Go on the Fabulous Sunset Strip* (Elektra/Asylum, 1988, prod. Alvin Clark) goes downhill right after Doe drawls his funny introduction; it was the wrong concert to record.

the rest: *Unclogged* (Infidelity Records, 1995, prod. X)

worth searching for: Both *Dangerous* compilations (Frontier, 1991 and 1992, prod. Various) contain just one X classic each, but in the context of Los Angeles' vibrant late 70s/early 80s punk scene. It also has tracks from Randoms, Weirdos, Avengers, Bags, Alley Cats, Black Randy and Eyes.

solo outings:

Exene Cervenka *Twin Sisters* (Freeway, 1985) *Old Wives' Tales* (Rhino, 1989) *Running Scared* (Rhino, 1990) *Surface to Air Serpents* (213CD, 1995)

John Doe *Meet John Doe* (DGC, 1990) *Kissingsohard* (Rhino/Forward, 1995,)

Hole, Uncle Tupelo, Mekons, Sonic Youth, Minute Men, Social Distortion, Pixies

Johnny Cash and June Carter, the Sex Pistols, Ramones, the Clash, the Who, the Blasters, Elvis Presley, the Patti Smith Group

Steve Knopper

X-Ray Spex

Formed 1977 in London, England. Disbanded 1980.

Poly Styrene (born Marion Elliot), vocals; Jak Airport, guitar; Steve Rudan, sax; Paul Dean, bass; B.P. Hurding, drums; Laura Logic, sax (1977)

Though only a band for three years, X-Ray Spex made a lasting impact on the punk scene. Styrene's wild, banshee-style singing was punctuated by saxophones and fast pop melodies. "Oh Bondage Up Yours" announced the group's punk attitude with a bang, but it was "Identity" from *Germ Free Adolescents* (EMI, 1978, prod. Falcon Stuart) that transcended raw aggression and sent it into hyperspace.

Anna Glen

XTC /The Dukes of Stratosphear

Formed 1977 in Swindon, Wiltshire, England

XTC—Andy Partridge, guitar, vocals; Colin Ivor Moulding, guitar, bass, vocals; Barry Andrews, keyboards (1977-79); Dave Gregory, guitar, keyboards, vocals (1979-present); Terry Chambers, drums (1977-1983). The Dukes of Stratosphear—Sir John Johns (Andy Partridge), guitar, vocals; The Red Curtain (Colin Moulding), bass, vocals; Lord Cornelius Plum (Dave Gregory), guitar, keyboards and vocals; E.I.E.I. Owen (Ian Gregory), drums

It's hard to put a finger on XTC. It is either one of the most creative rock bands to come along or simply a capable re-inventor of rock's more original creators. Like John Lennon and Paul McCartney (who are obvious influences here), Partridge and Moulding write in distinctively different but complementary styles. Partridge is usually quirky and more rock-influenced, while Moulding is the quieter, more folk-touched of the pair. During its lengthy career, XTC has pursued a broad range of styles, including new wave (1977-79), pop-rock (1979-81), neofolk (1982-83) and a synthesis of Beatles and Beach Boys influences (1984-present). Despite such obvious derivation, the group has produced hook-laden and highly durable music at each stage of its development. Since Chamber's departure in 1983, XTC has performed as a trio, with drumming support from such notable sidemen as the Tubes' Prairie Prince and former Glitter Band member Pete Phipps. The Dukes of Stratosphere is a pseudonymous project undertaken by XTC and producer John Leckie in 1985. With meticulous detail and a good deal of humor, the group creates mock psychedelic music in the same self-conscious way the Rutles ransacked the Beatles' legacy. What could have been a one-joke farce turns out to be an enjoyable and highly listenable romp. Interestingly, for all of its tongue-in-cheek nature, the Dukes' first release (a six-song EP) actually outsold XTC's previously released album, *The Big Express*

what to buy: *Skylarking* (Geffen, 1986, prod. Todd Rundgren) is a masterful collection of songs seamlessly woven in one continuous thread, a la *Sgt. Pepper's Lonely Hearts Club Band* Rundgren's production is well attuned to the group's own influences and offbeat sensibilities. More to the point, the songs-a mixture of pop-rock, neofolk and lush orchestrations-are simply superb, particularly "Earn Enough for Us," "Big Day" and the surprising hit single "Dear God." Of XTC's early catalog, *Drums & Wires* (Geffen, 1979, prod. Steve Lillywhite) is among the best. Partridge tones down his idiosyncratic tendencies ever so slightly to turn in terrific and lively pop on "Life Begins at the Hop," "When You're Near Me I Have Difficulty" and "Roads Girdle the Globe". Moulding's stellar offerings include "Ten Feet Tall" and the British hit "Making Plans for Nigel."

what to buy next: *The Compact XTC—The Singles 1978-85* (Virgin, 1985, prod. Various) is a handy repackaging of 18 A-sides from the group's output of singles, including the hyperkinetic rave-up "Science Friction," "Statue of Liberty" and Partridge's beautifully bucolic "Senses Working Overtime." It's a great way to investigate the group's earlier work without making a huge investment. For a fun time, check out *Chips from the Chocolate Fireball,* (Geffen, 1988, prod. John Leckie) a one-disc compilation of the two Dukes of Stratosphear releases—the EP *25 O'Clock* and the album *Psonic Psunpot,* both of which were also released as individual CDs. For all of the group's intended satire, many of the songs ("Vanishing Girl," "Have You Seen Jackie" and "Brainiac's Daughter") are brilliantly rendered and stand up quite nicely on their own.

what to avoid: Released in the same year as the group's wonderfully frenetic debut LP, *Go 2* (Geffen, 1978, prod. John Leckie) sounds forced and uneven. Aside from the infectious single "Are You Receiving Me?", the songs are merely curious reminders of punk's quirkier side.

the rest: *White Music* (Geffen, 1978) *Black Sea* (Geffen, 1980) *English Settlement* (Geffen, 1982) *Waxworks: Some Singles 1977-1982* (Geffen, 1982) *Mummer* (Geffen, 1984) *The Big Express* (Geffen, 1984) *Oranges & Lemons* (Geffen, 1989) *Rag & Bone Buffet (B-Side & Rarities)* (Geffen, 1990) *Nonsuch* (Geffen, 1992) The Dukes of Stratosphear: *25 O'Clock* (Virgin, 1985) *Psonic Psunspot* (Geffen, 1987)

worth searching for: *Skylarking Demos and Others* (Extatic, 1995, prod. Various) reconstructs nearly the entire "Skylarking" album in demo form, adding on, for good measure, a number of studio outtakes from various projects, including the Dukes of Stratosphear. Good performances and high-quality recording make this a particularly interesting look behind one of XTC's best albums.

solo outings:

Andy Partridge Mr. Partridge: Take Away/The Lure of Salvage (Virgin, 1980) (with Harold Budd) *Through the Hill* (Gyroscope/Caroline, 1994)

The B-52s, The Buzzcocks, Wire, Husker Du, The La's, The Pursuit of Happiness, Blur

The Beach Boys, the Beatles, Bob Dylan, Pink Floyd, Todd Rundgren

Christopher Scapelliti

Xymox

Formed 1983 in Nijmegan, Holland

Ronny Moorings, vocals, guitars; Anke Wolbert, bass, vocals; Pieter Nooten, synthesizers

Xymox, founded as Clan Of Xymox, was a mid-80s signing to the 4AD label; if not for that, we may have never heard of the band. After all, being from the Netherlands isn't exactly conducive to making it in the music business. Unique for the spacious synthesizer sounds with an overtly baroque lean, the band differentiated itself from the pack of other arty industrial bands by introducing lush string arrangements and relying heavily on a acoustic steel guitar to customize its sound. While critically accused of overt pretentiousness and lack of talent, the band creates amazing atmospheres with minimal machinery and imbibes all of its work with an amazing emotional pull. No explanation has surfaced to explain the dropping of "Clan Of..." from the band's third album, which marked its departure from 4AD and its first U.S. release. Most of the its material can be found domestically at this point. *Clan Of Xymox* (4AD, 1985, prod. Xymox and Ivo Watts Russell) is the band's first full-length effort, solid from start to finish, with everything art-dance music lovers look for—angst-ridden lyrics, stunning synth washes and brooding guitar sounds. "Stranger" and "A Day" are dance floor classics.

the rest: *Medusa* (4AD, 1986) *Twist Of Shadows* (Wing/PolyGram, 1989) *Phoenix* (Wing/PolyGram, 1991)

Tim Davis

Weird Al Yankovic

Born Alfred Matthew Yankovic, Oct. 23, 1959 in Lynwood, Calif.

A rocker or a mocker? The latter, thank you—and a damn good one at that. Figuring that he wouldn't be the next Elton John on his instrument of choice—accordion—Yankovic chose the parody path and for the past 17 years has been twisting the biggest hits of the day into clever and wickedly twisted ditties. It started with "My Bologna," his re-write of the Knack's "My Sharona," that received airplay from syndicated radio host Dr. Demento. By the time Demento aired "Another One Rides the Bus" (Queen's "Another One Bites the Dust"), Yankovic has his own recording deal. Over the years he's taken on Michael Jackson, Madonna, Nirvana—you're not a pop phenomenon until Weird Al has messed with one of your songs. And his assorted polka medleys of rock 'n' roll classics are even better than the individual parodies. Yankovic only missteps with his originals, which are occasionally funny but never quite hit the zeniths of his whacko covers.

what to buy: *In 3-D* (Scotti Bros., 1984/1991, prod. Rick Derringer) made Yankovic a phenomenon himself as he grabbed Jackson's coattails with "Eat It" ("Beat It") and also scored with "I Lost on Jeopardy" (Greg Kihn's "Jeopardy"). *The Food Album* (RCA, 1993, prod. Al Yankovic and Rick Derringer) and *The TV Album* (Scotti Bros., 1995, prod. Al Yankovic and Rick Derringer) are hysterical thematic albums that are considerably better than Yankovic's skimpy greatest hits collection.

what to buy next: If you're willing to splurge for more than one Yankovic collection, why not live large with the box set *Permanent Record.* (Scotti Bros., 1994, prod. Al Yankovic and Rick Derringer) Is four discs a bit much? Yeah, but too much Weird Al is better than too little.

what to avoid: He decided to push the originals a bit too hard on *Even Worse,* (Scotti Bros., 1988/1991, prod. Rick Derringer) and it's tough to compete with a good parody like "Fat" (Jackson's "Bad").

the rest: *Weird Al Yankovic* (Rock 'n' Roll/Scotti Bros., 1983/1991) *Dare to Be Stupid* (Scotti Bros., 1985/1991) *Polka Party!* (Scotti Bros., 1986/1991) *UHF/Original Motion Picture Soundtrack and Other Stuff* (Scotti Bros., 1989) *Greatest Hits* (Scotti Bros., 1991) *Off the Deep End* (Scotti Bros., 1992) *Alapalooza* (Scotti Bros., 1993) *Bad Hair Day* (Scotti Bros., 1996)

worth searching for: Weird Al speaks—yes, speaks—as a narrator for a high-minded children's recording of Prokofiev's—yes, Prokofiev's—*Peter & the Wolf.* (CBS Masterworks, 1992) ♪♪♪♪ There's not an accordion within earshot.

⏩ The Presidents of the United States of America

⏪ Alan Sherman, Barnes and Barnes, Frankie Yankovic (no relation)

Gary Graff

The Yardbirds

Formed 1963 in London, England. Disbanded 1968.

Keith Relf, harmonica, vocals (died May 14, 1976); Paul Samwell-Smith, bass; Chris Dreja, guitar, bass, vocals; Jim McCarty, drums; Anthony "Top" Topham, guitar (1963); Eric Clapton, guitar (1963-64); Jeff Beck, guitar (1964-67); Jimmy Page, guitar (1966-68)

If only for featuring Clapton, Beck and Page as successive lead guitarists, the Yardbirds earned a place in rock history. But—primarily due to that Guitar God threesome—the band also brought an inventiveness to British Invasion blues-rock that would only be surpassed by the Rolling Stones and Cream. Clapton left the band early, complaining of commercialism, though not before contributing to its first hit, "For Your Love." Beck took over, and the Yardbirds sound took off with a series of classic singles built around his groundbreaking guitar leads, feedback textures and experiments with Eastern scales—"Shapes Of Things" and "Over Under Sideways Down" among them. For a short time, Beck and Page shared lead guitar duties, creating the band's last great single, "Happenings Ten Years Time Ago." Page took over for one final album before departing for Led Zeppelin (originally billed as the New Yardbirds). Relf went on to form Renaissance, and Samwell-Smith became a producer—though he, McCarty and Dreja formed a new band, Box of Frogs, during the mid-80s. Over time, however, the Yardbirds' music continues to influence countless guitar-slingers.

what to buy: Two collections provide a good introduction to the Yardbirds' music. *Greatest Hits, Vol. 1: 1964-1966* (Rhino, 1986) ♪♪♪♪♪ contains essential tracks—"For Your Love", "Heart Full Of Soul," "I'm A Man," "Shapes Of Things"—through the band's mid-career. *Vol. 2: Blues, Backtracks & Shapes Of Things* (Sony, 1991) ♪♪♪♪ is a two-CD set that fills in many of the remaining gaps, with a number of live and rare cuts as a bonus. (Because of a long-unsettled court case, most of the Yardbirds' original master tapes are unavailable. Nearly all the cuts existing on the band's CDS are taken from safety tapes and other sources, so don't expect excellent fidelity.)

what to buy next: To hear the gritty, pre-hits Yardbirds live, with Clapton on guitar, check out *Five Live Yardbirds* (Epic U.K., 1964/Rhino, 1988, prod. Giorgio Gomelsky) ♪♪♪ The Beck-Page incarnation of the group turns in an awesome instrumental, "Stroll On," on the soundtrack to "Blow-Up" (Rhino, 1966) ♪♪♪♪

what to avoid: A number of not-so-great greatest hits collections. Stick with the recommendations.

the rest: *Vol. 1: Smokestack Lightning* (Sony, 1991) ♪♪♪♪ *Yardbirds Little Games Sessions & More* (EMI, 1992) ♪♪♪

worth searching for: Perhaps the finest Yardbirds album is only available as an import, but it's worth the hunt. *Roger The Engineer* (Edsel U.K., 1966, prod. Paul Samwell-Smith and Simon Napier Bell) ♪♪♪♪♪ finds Beck and Page together at the helm and the band taking its most successful experimental forays. It is also the only Yardbirds album made from the original masters, and the sound is superb. Less stunning, but of some historical value, is the Yardbirds' collaboration with hero Sonny Boy Williamson on the import-only *With Sonny Boy Williamson* (Edsel U.K., 1966) ♪♪♪

⏩ Jeff Beck Group, Led Zeppelin, the Allman Brothers Band, the Grateful Dead

⏪ Sonny Boy Williamson, Jimmy Reed, Alexis Korner

see also: *Led Zeppelin, Jeff Beck, Eric Clapton, Jimmy Page, Cream, Renaissance*

Doug Pippin

Yaz

See: Alison Moyet

Yes

Formed 1968 in London, England. Disbanded 1980. Reformed 1983.

Jon Anderson, vocals (1968-80, 1983-89, 1991-present); Chris Squire, bass, vocals; Peter Banks, guitar (1968-69); Tony Kaye, keyboards (1968-71, 1983-present); Bill Bruford, drums (1968-72, 1991); Steve Howe, guitar, vocals (1969-81, 1991-present); Rick Wakeman, keyboards (1971-74, 1976-80, 1991); Alan White, drums (1972-present); Patrick Moraz, keyboards (1974-76); Trevor Horn, vocals (1980); Geoff Downes, keyboards (1980); Trevor Rabin, guitar (1983-94)

A shining example of both the zeniths and nadirs of progressive rock, Yes has plied its symphonic, fussy craft since the late 60s with a rotating crew of players. Initially influenced by the Beatles and Simon and Garfunkel, singer Anderson, bassist Squire and others began work on a rock-jazz-folk-classical hybrid during the peak of psychedelia; indeed, the group's first major gig was an opening spot for acid-rock trio Cream's farewell concert. By the time Yes emerged as an arena-filling act, the 70s had begun and pomp-rock was in full flower. The arrival of keyboardist Wakeman, whose incessant noodling on the synthesizer was unshackled by taste, pushed the band to previously unimagined peaks of pretension. With its lengthy, mind-expanding excursions, instrumental pyrotechnics and trippy Roger Dean album covers, the band became poster children of progressive rock alongside Pink Floyd, Emerson, Lake and Palmer, Genesis, Jethro Tull and other kindred spirits. That said, Yes also made some transcendently lovely music. Lineup changes have affected the sound over the years—the New Wave touches provided by Buggles Horn and Downes, Rabin's slick album-rockcraft—and for awhile some members (Anderson, Bruford, Wakeman and Howe) struck out on their own rather than be part of all that. But Yes remains, though its most recent output makes one wonder if that's such a good thing.

what to buy: *The Yes Album* (Atlantic, 1971, prod. Eddie Offord) is crammed with inventive, dynamic rock that borrows from jazz, English folk and myriad other forms. It's notable especially for the long-form rockers "Starship Trooper" and "Yours Is No Disgrace."

what to buy next: Despite the ominous import of their excesses, *Fragile* (Atlantic, 1971, prod. Eddie Offord) and *Close to the Edge* (Atlantic, 1972, prod. Eddie Offord) show Yes at a creative and commercial peak, and both include some of their most majestically beautiful work. The earlier *Time and a Word* (Atlantic, 1970, prod. Tony Colton) shows the band in an ambitious but not overweening stage of its development.

what to avoid: Start by dodging the high school reunion-style *Union*, (Arista, 1991, prod. Jonathan Elias) WOOF! which suggests that the quality of a modern Yes recording may be inversely proportional to the number of players (eight) on it. And stay far, far away from *Symphonic Music of Yes* (RCA, 1993, prod. Alan Parsons) WOOF! which features the London Philharmonic and English Chamber Orchestras and is an object lesson in why progressive rock died of its own bloat.

the rest: *Yes* (Atlantic, 1969) *Yessongs* (Atlantic, 1973) *Tales from Topographic Oceans* (Atlantic, 1973, prod. Eddie Offord) *Relayer* (Atlantic, 1974) *Yesterdays* (Atlantic, 1975) *Going for the One*, (Atlantic, 1977) *Tormato* (Atlantic, 1978) *Drama* (Atlantic, 1980) *Yesshows* (Atlantic, 1980) *Classic Yes* (Atlantic, 1982) *90125* (Atco, 1983) *Big Generator* (Atco, 1987) *Yesyears* (Atco, 1991) *Yesstory* (Atco, 1992) *Highlights: The Very Best of Yes* (Atlantic, 1993) *Talk* (Victory, 1994, prod. Trevor Rabin) WOOF! *Keys to Ascension* (CMC, 1996)

worth searching for: *Affirmative: The Yes Solo Family Album*, (Connoisseur, 1993, prod. Various) an import that some of the best material from the individual Yes members' myriad solo albums.

solo outings:

Anderson, Wakeman, Bruford and Howe: *Anderson, Wakeman, Bruford and Howe* (Arista, 1989) *An Evening of Yes Music Plus* (Herald, 1994)

Jon Anderson: *Olias of Sunhillow* (Atlantic, 1976) *Song of Seven* (Atlantic, 1980) *Animation* (Mercury, 1982) *In the City of Angels* (Columbia, 1988) *Change We Must* (Angel/EMI, 1994) *Deseo* (Windham Hill, 1994) *Angels Embrace* (Higher Octave, 1995) *Toltee* (High Street, 1996)

Jon (Anderson) and Vangelis: *Short Stories* (Mercury, 1980) *The Friends of Mr. Cairo* (Mercury, 1982) *Private Collection* (Mercury, 1983) *The Best of Jon and Vangelis* (Mercury, 1984)

Steve Howe: *Beginnings* (Atlantic, 1975/1994) *The Steve Howe Album* (Atlantic, 1979/1994) *Turbulence* (Relativity, 1994) *Not Necessarily Acoustic* (Herald, 1994)

Trevor Rabin: *Can't Look Away* (Elektra, 1989)

Chris Squire: *Fish Out of Water* (Atlantic, 1975)

Rick Wakeman: *Six Wives of Henry VIII* (A&M, 1973) *Journey to the Center of the Earth* (A&M, 1974) *Myths and the Legends of King Arthur and the Knights of the Round Table* (A&M, 1975) *1984* (Griffin, 1981/1994) *Cost of Living* (Griffin, 1994) *Greatest Hits* (Herald/Caroline, 1994) *Wakeman with Wakeman: The Official Bootleg* (Griffin, 1994) *Almost Live in Europe* (Griffin, 1995) *Live at Hammersmith* (Griffin, 1995) *The Classical Connection* (Griffin, 1995) *The Classical Conection II* (Griffin, 1995) *Romance of the Victorian Age* (Griffin, 1995) *Country Airs* (Griffin, 1995) *Night Airs* (Griffin, 1995) *In Concert* (KBFH, 1996)

Rush, Starcastle, Dream Theater, Queensryche

The Beatles, the Byrds, Simon and Garfunkel, Move, the Moody Blues, Genesis, post-bop jazz

see also: *Asia, King Crimson, Moody Blues, Rick Wakeman*

Simon Glickman and Gary Graff

Yo La Tengo

Formed 1985 in Hoboken, N.J.

Ira Kaplan, guitar, vocals; Georgia Hubley, drums, vocals; James McNew, bass (1991-present); Dave Rick, bass (1985); Mike Lewis, bass (1986); Stephan Wichnewski, bass (1986-89); Wilbo Wright, bass (1990); Gene Holder, bass (1990-1991)

Kaplan and Hubley spent their early dates playing songs together in a New Jersey apartment and ended up with a marriage and a band. Named for the way a Spanish baseball player says "I've got it", Yo La Tengo is a perennial indie band, a favorite among serious music fans and college radio types. Like a new version of the Velvet Underground (Yo La Tengo members actually portrayed the VU in the film "I Shot Andy Warhol") the band vacillates between gentle folk pop and noise, often ending up with a hybrid of understated vocals, layered guitar drone experiments and the occasional noise squall.

what to buy: Smooth transitions between a hushed ballad like "Don't Say A Word (Hot Chicken #2)" and the noisy "(Straight Down To The) Bitter End" on *Electr-O-Pura* (Matador, 1995, prod. Roger Moutenot) show Yo La Tengo at peak form.

what to buy next: Kaplan was a former music critic, and it shows on his selections of songs for *Fakebook*, (Bar None, 1990, prod. Gene Holder) a collection of mostly cover tunes filled with obscurities by the Flamin' Groovies, NRBQ and Daniel Johnston. It's not especially representative of the band, but it is a lot of fun.

what to avoid: *May I Sing With Me* (Alias, 1992, prod. Gene Holder) is weighed down with too many lengthy guitar solos.

the rest: *Ride The Tiger* (Matador, 1986) *President Yo La Tengo/New Wave Hot Dogs* (Matador, 1989) *Painful* (Matador, 1993)

worth searching for: *Camp Yo La Tengo* (Matador EP, 1995, prod. Roger Moutenot) is a four-song set that includes interesting remakes of two songs from *Electr-o-Pura.*

The Velvet Underground, Sonic Youth

Jill Hamilton

Dwight Yoakam

Born Oct. 23, 1956 in Pikesville, Ky.

When Yoakam released his debut album in 1986, the Nashville establishment branded him a punk: True, he did cut his teeth doing gigs with noisy L.A. roots-rockers like the Blasters, and he was openly hostile in interviews toward mainstream country music. But that hardly qualified him as a punk. His music has always been pure country, in the mode of Buck Owens and Merle Haggard. Working closely with guitarist-producer Pete Anderson, the singer has turned out some of the best neo-traditional country albums of the past decade.

what to buy: *Gone* (Reprise, 1996, prod. Pete Anderson) is Yoakam's most fully realized collection—an ambitious mix of hard-core country, psychedelic guitars, string sections and mariachi horns. The more traditional *If There Was A Way* (Reprise, 1990, prod. Pete Anderson) boasts such gems as "You're The One" and "Nothing's Changed Here," while *Buenos Noches From A Lonely Room* (Reprise, 1988, prod. Pete Anderson) is Yoakam's melancholy masterwork featuring loving remakes of Owens' "Streets of Bakersfield" and Johnny Cash's "Home of the Blues."

what to buy next: *Hillbilly Deluxe,* (Reprise, 1987, prod. Pete Anderson) Yoakam's second album, spawned a flurry of hits, including "Always Late With Your Kisses," "Little Ways" and Elvis Presley's "Little Sister." *Lookin' For a Hit* (Reprise, 1989, prod. Pete Anderson) is a fine primer, with a bonus remake of the Flying Burrito Brothers' "Sin City" as a duet with k.d. lang.

what to avoid: None of the songs on *Dwight Live* (Reprise, 1995, prod. Pete Anderson) come close to matching the versions on his studio albums.

the rest: *Guitars, Cadillacs, Etc., Etc.* (Reprise, 1986) *This Time* (Reprise, 1993)

worth searching for: The *White Sands* soundtrack, (Morgan Creek, 1992) which features music composed by Yoakam.

Travis Tritt, the Mavericks, Uncle Tupelo

Buck Owens, Hank Williams, Hank Snow

Thor Christensen

What Album Changed Your Life?

"The one record that really got me in gear was this Terry Reid record. It had this white cover; I don't even think it had a title, but it's got that song Speak Now or Forever Hold Your Peace' that Cheap Trick covered on its first record. He's one of my favorite male rock vocalists, outside of Nat King Cole."

Tommy Stinson, Replacements, Perfect

Young Fresh Fellows /Scott McCaughey/The Minus Five

Formed 1983 in Seattle, Wash.

Scott McCaughey, guitar, vocals; Jim Sangster, bass; Tad Hutchison, drums; Chuck Carroll, guitar (1983-88); Kurt Bloch, guitar (1989-present)

When the Young Fresh Fellows released *The Fabulous Sounds of the Pacific Northwest* in 1984, the Seattle scene was but a glimmer in the eyes of future Sub Pop moguls Bruce Pavitt and Jonathan Poneman. By the time Sub Pop, Nirvana, Soundgarden and the like entered the picture during the late 80s, the Fellows had already put out a couple of records on a homegrown indie label (PopLlama) and were touring the country, helping to lay a foundation for the flurry of Seattle activity that followed. The Fellows were often as loud and raucous as any band in town, but instead of relying on punk and metal, the music drew inspiration from 60s pop and garage-rock sounds both classic (the Kinks) and obscure (the Flamin' Groovies). Furthermore, the group's attitude has always forsaken angst-ridden doom 'n' gloom in favor of happy-go-lucky hijinks a la the Replacements (it's fitting, then, that the Fellows played at Mats frontman Paul Westerberg's wedding reception). Though YFF is still a going concern, the group's recorded output has slowed in recent years as its members have become more involved with other projects—Bloch with punk-pop band the Fastbacks, Sangster with country-rockers the Picketts and McCaughey as a sideman with R.E.M.

what to buy: *This One's for the Ladies* (Frontier, 1989, prod. Conrad Uno) ♪♪♪♪½ captures the group at its best and makes a solid argument that it deserves to be considered among the best rock 'n' roll bands of its day. McCaughey originals such as "Carrothead" and "Miss Lonelyhearts" are would-be pop classics that fit right alongside a perfect cover of the Kinks' "Picture Book." *The Men Who Loved Music* (Frontier, 1987, prod. Conrad Uno) ♪♪♪♪ is a close second and a bit more whimsical, offering up the hilarious "Hank, Karen and Elvis" plus the classic anthem "My Friend Ringo" (the latter written by Charlie Chesterman of Scruffy The Cat). *Electric Bird Digest* (Frontier, 1991, prod. Butch Vig) ♪♪♪♪ may be the strongest of the bunch strictly in terms of songwriting.

what to buy next: The band's first two albums—*The Fabulous Sounds of the Pacific Northwest* (PopLlama, 1984, prod. Conrad Uno) ♪♪♪ and *Topsy Turvy* (PopLlama, 1985, prod. Conrad Uno) ♪♪♪—find its songwriting abilities not quite fully developed, but both albums contain a sense of youthful innocence that make them wholeheartedly enjoyable outings.

what to avoid: *Totally Lost*, (Frontier, 1988, prod. Conrad Uno) ♪♪½ recorded just before founding member Carroll decided to leave the band, is the most uneven of the band's efforts, though it still contains a handful of worthwhile songs.

the rest: *It's Low Beat Time* (Frontier, 1992) ♪♪♪ *Refreshments* (Frontier EP, 1986) ♪♪♪

worth searching for: *Somos Los Mejores*, (Munster, 1991, prod. Various) ♪♪♪♪ a vinyl-only Spanish import that collects many highlights from the Fellows' catalog.

solo outings:

Scott McCaughey: My Chartreuse Opinion (East Side Digital, 1989) ♪♪♪

The Minus Five (McCaughey plus R.E.M.'s Peter Buck and the Posies' Ken Stringfellow): *Old Liquidator* (East Side Digital, 1994) ♪♪♪½

▶▶ Presidents of the United States of America, the Posies, Scruffy the Cat, Stumpy Joe

◀◀ The Kinks, the Flamin' Groovies, the Sonics, the Beatles, the Replacements

Peter Blackstock

James Young

See: Styx

Jesse Colin Young /The Youngbloods

Formed 1965 in Boston, Mass. Disbanded 1972.

Jesse Colin Young (born Perry Miller, Nov. 11, 1944 in New York, N.Y.), vocals, bass, guitar; Jerry Corbitt, guitar (1965-69), vocals; Joe Bauer, drums; Banana (born Lowell Levinger) guitar, keyboards; Michael Kane, bass (1971-72)

Before forming the Youngbloods, Young recorded two folk albums, *The Soul of a City Boy* (Capitol, 1964/One Way, 1995, prod. Bobby Scott) and *Youngblood* (Mercury, 1964, prod. Bobby Scott). The former album was rough, but his vibrant energy is still appealing. The group's 1967 debut, Youngbloods, included the hit "Grizzly Bear" and the Dino Valente-penned hit "Get Together," which became the Youngblood's anthem with its open-sounding instrumentation and comfortable, laid-back style set the tone for many of Young's future compositions with the band and on his own.

what to buy: As a trio, the Youngbloods' *Elephant Mountain* (RCA/Mobile Fidelity, 1969) is by far the group's best effort. With fine instrumental rapport and trippy little accents, it's a clever melding of introspective, rocking and romantic elements. After this, the group became something of a one-trick pony.

what to buy next: *The Best of Jesse Colin Young: The Solo Years* (Rhino, 1991, prod. Various) showcases Young at his best, without a bevy of indulgences. His best solo recording remains *Song for Juli* (Warner Bros., 1973/Ridgetop, 1993, prod. Jesse Colin Young). A warm smile of a song, "Morning Sun," opens the disc, while his rock- and jazz-inflected "Ridgetop," with its multiple instrumental layers and tempos, is a terrific song.

what to avoid: Young's *Swept Away* (Ridgetop, 1994) **WOOF!**, which is overblown, gushing and relentlessly soft-headed.

the rest: The Youngbloods—*Best of* (RCA, 1988); Jesse Colin Young—*Together* (Raccoon, 1972/Edsel, 1996) *Light Shine* (Warner Bros., 1974/Ridgetop, 1994) *Songbird* (Warner Bros., 1975/Ridgetop, 1994) *On the Road* (Warner Bros., 1976/Ridgetop, 1995) *Love on the Wing* (Warner Bros., 1977/Edsel, 1996) *Makin' it Real* (Ridgetop, 1993) *Crazy Boy* (Ridgetop, 1995) *The Highway is for Heroes* (Edsel, 1996)

worth searching for: The group's 1967 debut, *Youngbloods*, included the hit "Grizzly Bear" and the Dino Valente-penned hit "Get Together," which became the Youngblood's anthem with its open-sounding instrumentation and comfortable, laid-back style set the tone for many of Young's future compositions with the band and on his own.

▶▶ Boz Scaggs, Kenny Rankin

◀◀ Beatles, Tom Rush, Kingston Trio

Patrick McCarty

Neil Young

Born November 12, 1945 in Toronto, Ontario, Canada

Few musicians have been as influential in as broad a manner as Young, whose three-decade career has been remarkably varied. He's both the godfather of grunge and the uncle of Unplugged. As a member of Buffalo Springfield, he helped create the folk-rock genre. With Crazy Horse, he introduced the ragged, powerful, three-chord-and-a-cloud-of-dust approach that mutated into grunge. His 1972 album *Harvest* cross-pollinated country and rock. And his hits "Old Man" and "Heart Of Gold" are essential sensitive-guy-on-the-beach acoustic fare. Though some of Young's incursions into alien fields such as rockabilly and straight country have been less than successful—and who knows what the Mynah Birds, his early 60s band with Rick James, sounded like—each foray has re-energized him, allowing him to return to his classic styles with renewed vigor. After a prolonged fallow period during the 80s, Young returned with a vengeance with 1989's *Freedom* and has been more or less going strong ever since.

what to buy: *Decade* (Reprise, 1977, prod. Neil Young and David Briggs) was a boxed set before its time, a three-album, two-CD summation of Young's career from 1966-75 that gives an excellent overview and should help guide you through the rest of the early catalog. *After the Gold Rush* (Reprise, 1970, prod. Neil Young and David Briggs) is a great mix of Young's two selves, with rockers such as "Southern Man" alongside ballads like "Tell Me Why," not to mention the glorious title track. *Everybody Knows This is Nowhere* (Reprise, 1969, prod. Neil Young and David Briggs) is Young's quintessential Crazy Horse album, featuring the extended guitar workouts of "Down by the River," "Cinnamon Girl" and "Cowgirl in the Sand." *Tonight's the Night* (Reprise, 1975, prod.

Neil Young and David Briggs), with its harrowing images of violence and drug addiction after losing two close friends—including original Crazy Horse guitarist Danny Whitten—is one of rock's scariest albums ever.

what to buy next: *Harvest* (Reprise, 1972, prod. Eliot Mazer and Neil Young) is Young's most popular album for good reason, though it's docked one bone for the presence of two horribly overwrought orchestral numbers. The rest is pure gold. *Rust Never Sleeps* (Reprise, 1979, Neil Young, David Briggs and Tim Mulligan) and *Weld* (Reprise, 1991, prod. Neil Young and David Briggs) are two great live albums—the former a collection of awesome new songs, the latter serving notice of Young's turn-of-the-decade return to form. *Tonight's the Night Harvest Moon* (Reprise, 1992, prod. Neil Young and Ben Keith) — a sequel of sorts to *Harvest*—marks a delightful return to acoustic music.

what to avoid: Young has made many missteps along the way, but his biggest failures were wild stabs at different genres—including electronic music on *Trans* (Geffen, 1982, prod. Neil Young, David Briggs and Tim Mulligan) and rockabilly on *Everybody's Rockin'* (Geffen, 1983) *Mirror Ball,* (Reprise, 1995, prod. Neil Young and David Briggs) his collaboration with Pearl Jam, was a leaden bore, with undeveloped songs to boot.

the rest: *Neil Young* (Reprise, 1969) *Journey Through the Past* (Reprise, 1972) *Time Fades Away* (Reprise, 1973) *On the Beach* (Reprise, 1974) *Zuma* (Reprise, 1975) *American Stars 'n Bars* (Reprise, 1977) *Comes a Time* (Reprise, 1978) *Live Rust* (Reprise, 1979) *Hawks & Doves* (Reprise, 1980) *Old Ways* (Geffen, 1985) *Landing on Water* (Geffen, 1986) *Life* (Geffen, 1987) *This Notes for You* (Reprise, 1987) *Freedom* (Reprise, 1989) *Ragged Glory* (Reprise, 1990) *Arc* (Reprise, 1991) *Lucky Thirteen* (Geffen, 1993) *Unplugged* (Reprise, 1993) *Sleeps with Angels* (Reprise, 1994) *Broken Arrow* (Reprise, 1996)

worth searching for: Besides Young contributions to some recent Randy Bachman records (we just had to throw that in), there are myriad bootlegs of Young concerts and unreleased material. One of the great ones is *Chrome Dreams,* an acetate copy of an album Young worked on during 1975-76. The album never came out, but the songs—including "Pocahontas," "Too Far Gone," "Sedan Delivery" and "Powderfinger"—made their way onto other albums.

▶▶ Dinosaur Jr., Joe Henry, Uncle Tupelo, Sonic Youth, Pearl Jam, America, the Replacements

◀◀ Bob Dylan, Jimi Hendrix, Gram Parsons

see also: *Crosby, Stills, Nash and Young; Crazy Horse*

Alan Paul

Paul Young

Born Jan. 17, 1956 in Luton, England

The son of an auto plant worker who logged some time in the factory himself,Young merged a simultaneous affection for New Wave rock and 60s soul into a singular solo voice during the 80s. Gaining early notice as lead vocalist for the British soul/horn band the Q-Tips, Young was signed to a solo deal by CBS Records in 1981 and immediately presented an expert blend of the New Wave and dance sounds of the day with old-time soul vocal gymnastics. His next efforts further refined that signature sound, blunting the force of his soul sources with increasing amounts of pop flavor. Though a passable songwriter himself, most of Young's big hits were covers of other artists' material, from Marvin Gaye to Hall & Oates. Unfortunately, the proportion of slickness to soul in his records kept tilting toward pop blandness until U.S. listeners—who had never fully embraced him, anyway—stopped caring.

what to buy: Young's debut, *No Parlez* (Columbia, 1983, prod. Laurie Latham) is both his most eclectic and impressive recorded effort, bridging the gap between arty New Wave and funky soul sounds in a vibrant new way. From the dreamy cover of Marvin Gaye's obscure ballad "Wherever I Lay My Hat" to the drum machine and sequencer-fed dance excursion "Sex" and atmospheric lead-off single "Come Back and Stay," this record offers an inspired mix of styles unified by Young's own impassioned blue-eyed soul vocal licks.

what to buy next: His second album, *The Secret of Association*, (Columbia, 1985, prod. Laurie Latham) is the only other Young record that doesn't completely sacrifice passion for precision, as the singer allows a little funky heat to build on cuts like the fretless bass-fueled dance workouts "I'm Gonna Tear Your Playhouse Down," "Bite the Hand That Feeds" and "Hot Fun." But the only hit here, a pop-ified cover of Darryl Hall's "Everytime You Go Away," hints of the mistakes to come.

what to avoid: The rest of Young's catalog, basically. The singer seemed to turn his back on the very soul influences that made him a success in the first place—with *Between Two Fires* (Columbia, 1986, prod. Hugh Padgham, Paul Young and Ian Krewley) WOOF! drowning in its own pop slickness (and a preponderance of Young-penned tunes) and *Other Voices* (Columbia, 1990, prod. Various) WOOF! rocking out on a collection of forgettable songs.

the rest: *From Time to Time/The Singles Collection* (Columbia, 1991) ♪♪♪½

worth searching for: A rare recording of a pre-stardom Young performing with the Q-Tips in concert, *Live At Last* (Stoic Records/Rewind Records, 1984) ♪♪♪ is available as an import and offers early versions of the singer's take on Smokey Robinson's "Tracks of My Tears" and his own strongest original tune, "Broken Man."

▶▶ George Michael, Maxwell, Tony Rich

◀◀ Rod Stewart, Paul Rodgers, Robert Palmer, Smokey Robinson, Marvin Gaye, Darryl Hall

Eric Deggans

Rusty Young

See: Poco

Young Marble Giants

Formed late 1970s in Cardiff, Wales. Disbanded 1981.

Alison Statton, vocals; Philip Moxham, bass; Stuart Moxham, guitar, organ

Taking its cue from some idealized notion of a beatnik coffee house, Young Marble Giants confabulate in a hushed, candle-lit mood of studied bohemian minimalism. Statton's gentle, low-key vocals mesh neatly with the Moxham brothers' jazz stylings in a manner that anticipates Everything But the Girl. *Colossal Youth* (Crepuscule, 1980, prod. Young Marble Giants and Dave Anderson) ♪♪♪ is the off-beat result, a slip of an album whose lo-fi ambience makes scarcely a ripple in your double latte. Apparently the members couldn't keep their blood pressure low enough to pursue another album. Under the guise of Gist, Stuart Moxham released "Embrace the Herd" (out of print) with assistance from brother Phil, Statton and others. Statton went on to form the neo-avante-garde jazz group Weekend and later teamed up with Ian Devine as one half of Devine & Statton.

see also: *Weekend, Devine & Statton*

Christopher Scapelliti

The Young Rascals /The Rascals

Formed 1965 in New York, N.Y. Disbanded 1972.

Felix Cavaliere, vocals, keyboards; Dino Danelli, drums; Eddie Brigati, vocals (1965-71); Gene Cornish, guitar (1695-71); Buzzy Feinten, guitar (1970-71); Robert Popwell, bass (1971-72); Ann Sutton, vocals (1971-72)

With three-part vocal harmonies, rooted in R&B and floating atop an ocean of sound from Cavaliere's Hammond B-3 organ, the Young Rascals were one of the original "blue-eyed soul" bands, bringing the energy and excitement of R&B to the masses by covering Wilson Pickett, Sir Mack Rice and other soul stirrers. Wearing Little Lord Fauntleroy outfits at nightclub gigs across Long Island, Manhattan and New Jersey, the Young Rascals offered an American alternative to the British invaders. The band's uptempo cover of the Olympics' "Good Lovin'," its first No. 1 single, erupts with such rhythmic fury that it endures as one of the greatest dance-rock numbers ever recorded. The band tried a softer touch with the syrupy "Groovin'," another chart-topper that, unfortunately, marked a shift away from raw R&B to polished pop. In 1967, the Rascals dropped the "Young" from its name and the knickers from their stage show, seeking a maturity and awareness appropriate to the times. It was a good fit for a while, as heard in "See," "Ray of Hope" and "People Got To Be Free," the group's last No. 1 hit. The Rascals experimented with lengthy jazz episodes—working with guests such as Dave Sanborn, Ron Carter, Hubert Laws and Alice Coltrane—before fading in the charts and dissolving in 1972. There have been periodic, short-term reunions since.

what to buy: *Time Piece: The Rascals' Greatest Hits* (Atlantic, 1968, prod. the Rascals) ♪♪♪♪♪ crystallizes the band's most exuberant years into one tidy package of essentials ("Good Lovin'," "Mustang Sally," "I Ain't Gonna Eat Out My Heart Anymore," "You Better Run" and "Groovin'"). The two-disc, 44-song set *The Rascals Anthology 1965-1972* (Rhino, 1992, prod. Various) ♪♪♪♪½ is also a superb overview from Young Rascals to the old, the good, the not-so-good, and the awful ("Real Thing," "Brother Tree").

what to buy next: Even though the group only wrote one of the tunes, its debut album *The Young Rascals* (Atlantic, 1966/Warner Special Products, 1988, prod. the Young Rascals, Tom Dowd and Arif Mardin) ♪♪♪♪ can't be beat for sheer energy and exuberance.

what to avoid: After Brigati and Cornish left, the Rascals lost its

R&B heart and replaced it with an artificial jazz pump. Pull the plug on the lifeless *Peaceful World* (Atlantic, 1971, prod. Felix Cavaliere) **WOOF!** and *The Island of Real.* (Atlantic, 1972, prod. Felix Cavaliere) **WOOF!**

the rest: *Groovin'* (Atlantic, 1967) *Collections* (Atlantic, 1966/Warner Special Products, 1988) *Once Upon a Dream* (Atlantic, 1968/Rhino, 1993) *Freedom Suite* (Atlantic, 1969/Rhino, 1993) *See* (Atlantic, 1969) *Search and Nearness* (Atlantic, 1971) *The Ultimate Rascals* (Warner Special Products, 1986) *Groovin'* (Warner Special Products, 1988) *The Very Best of the Rascals* (Rhino, 1993) *Good Lovin'* (Rhino, 1993)

solo outings:

Felix Cavaliere: *Felix Cavaliere* (Bearsville, 1974) *Destiny* (Bearsville, 1975) *Treasure* (Epic, 1976) *Castles in the Air* (Epic, 1980) *Dreams in Motion* (Karambolage, 1994)

Eddie Brigati: *Brigati* (Elektra, 1976)

▶▶ Hall and Oates, Huey Lewis & the News, Robert Palmer, Gin Blossoms

◀◀ Ray Charles, Booker T. Jones, Stax-Volt, Motown

David Yonke

The Youngbloods

See: Jesse Colin Young

Z

Formed 1994, Los Angeles, Calif.

Ahmet Zappa, vocals; Dweezil Zappa, guitar, vocals; Mike Keneally, guitar, vocals; Bryan Beller, bass; Scott Thunes, bass; Joe Travers, drums

Being the children of Frank Zappa is likely an experience like no other, as the first names of Zappas Ahmet and Dweezil will attest. Yet there's nothing like the career boost offered by growing up around a genius who happens to have his own record company, as evidenced by the existence of Dweezil's solo albums and the pair of albums by Z. *Shampoohorn* (Barking Pumpkin, 1994, prod. Dweezil Zappa) contains plenty of crunch and funky metal shenanigans, with in-joke lyrics of the sort the old man used to do—and flash guitar courtesy of Dweezil, who's a chip off the old block, or at least a chip off the old block's sidemen, like Steve Vai. There's a few yuks to be had, but there's not a lot else to recommend the album. *Music for Pets* (Zappa, 1995, prod. Dweezil Zappa) carries on in pretty much the same vein.

Daniel Durchholz

Robin Zander

See: Cheap Trick

Frank Zappa

Born Frank Vincent Zappa, Dec. 21, 1940 in Baltimore, Maryland. Died Dec. 4, 1993 in Los Angeles, Calif.

Singer, songwriter, conceptualist, composer, theoretician, would-be politician, guitar god, satirist, record-company scofflaw, ruthless bandleader and all-around iconoclast. There were many Frank Zappas, but still not enough of him to go around. His groundbreaking works from the mid-to-late 60s with the Mothers of Invention blew open the doors for rock experimentalism, and, while others succeeded in work of a similar vein, no one ever bettered him, save perhaps his old running buddy Captain Beefheart. Zappa's muse took him far afield from rock's limiting instrumentation and 4/4 beat; before there was such a thing as fusion, his work approached electrified jazz, and as early as *Freak Out!* he was flirting with orchestral compositions. His talent in that genre would come into full flower on *London Symphony Orchestra* and *The Yellow Shark.* Yet, however complex his music got, Zappa never lost touch with some of rock 'n' roll's cornerstones, such as doo-wop music and "Louie Louie," which he would occasionally sprinkle into his music, if only as a humorous aside. An intimidating and demanding bandleader, Zappa brought the best out of his musicians, and today, time spent in a Zappa band is an accolade worn like a badge of honor. His list of sidemen includes Lowell George, Aynsley Dunbar, Steve Vai, Adrian Belew, Terry Bozzio and Vinnie Colaiuta. Zappa's controversial material and sometimes scatological humor made him too hot to handle for most mainstream record companies, so he formed his own label during the late 70s and continued to release his music through it for the remainder of his life. Undeniably one of rock's most influential guitarists, in the 80s, Zappa put down the instrument for good in favor of the synclavier, a computerized keyboard on which he could realize his compositions all by himself; *Jazz From Hell* is the most impressive display of his prowess on the instrument. A passionate advocate of free speech, Zappa took part in the infamous congressional hearings in 1985, which led to the stickering of rock albums with parental warnings. Zappa's testimony exposed the congressmen and their social climbing wives as the fools they were (and are). The hearings are excerpted to hilarious effect on a cut from *Frank Zappa Meets the Mothers of Prevention.* As beloved in Europe as he was scorned in America, Zappa was named Czechoslovakia's cultural liaison to the West by President Vaclav Havel in 1990. A relentless workaholic who smoked cigarettes and drank coffee incessantly, Zappa died of prostate cancer at age 52. There will never be another like him. (Note: Between the past decade, Rykodisc re-issued all of Zappa's catalog. The original label and release information is noted below.)

what to buy: Less than a year after the Summer of Love, Zappa stepped forward to report he had met the enemy and it is us. *We're Only in It for the Money* (Verve, 1968, prod. Frank Zappa) is a savage attack on all things smelling of patchouli; the cover satirizes *Sgt. Pepper,* but the music—spoken sections, white noise and sound-bite montages—scores a direct hit on the America that so desperately wanted to be hip. A year before Miles Davis' *Bitches Brew,* Zappa's *Hot Rats* (Bizarre/Reprise, 1969, prod. Frank Zappa) presaged jazz-rock fusion with some of Zappa's best instrumental tracks, including "Peaches En Regalia." Captain Beefheart contributes vocals on "Willie the Pimp." Not necessarily one of his best albums, *Apostrophe* (DiscReet, 1974, prod. Frank Zappa) is certainly among his best-known, thanks in large part to the FM rock staples "Cosmik Debris" and the suite comprising "Don't Eat the Yellow Snow" and "St. Alphonso's Pancake Breakfast." *Apostrophe* was Zappa's sole gold record, and the only one to crease the Top 10. Of Zappa's orchestral recordings, *The Yellow Shark* (Barking Pumpkin, 1993, prod. Frank Zappa) is the most entertaining; performed by the 26-member Ensemble Modern, the album was released just a month before Zappa's untimely death. It includes "Uncle Meat," "Welcome to the United States" and a breathtaking version of "G-Spot Tornado." The long, experimental pieces and obscure personal references make *Uncle Meat* (Bizarre/Reprise, 1968, prod. Frank Zappa) Zappa's most demanding opus outside of his strictly classical work. It includes "Dog Breath Variations" and "King Kong." Novices, on the other hand, may want to begin with *Strictly Commercial: The Best of Frank Zappa,* (Rykodisc, 1995, prod. Frank Zappa) a collection of his humor-oriented vocal material. Zappa's expansive material resists abridgment, though, and true Frank-ophiles will likely want the uncut stuff.

what to buy next: The most audacious debut album in rock history, *Freak Out!* (Verve, 1966, prod. Tom Wilson) was originally released as a double album, one of them containing deft parodies of the teen exploitation music of the day and the other a wildly anarchic experimental piece featuring tape collage experiments and moments of sheer brilliance. *Burnt Weeny Sandwich* (Bizarre/Reprise, 1969) and *Weasels Ripped My Flesh* (Bizarre/Reprise, 1970, prod. Frank Zappa) are two volumes of a projected career retrospective that never materialized, but they're Zappa's most consistently great albums. *Weeny* contains "WPLJ" and "The Little House I Used to Live In," while *Weasels* has "Eric Dolphy Memorial Barbecue" and "My Guitar Wants to Kill Your Mama." An extraordinary display of Zappa's instrumental prowess can be found on *Shut Up 'N Play Yer Guitar,* (Barking Pumpkin, 1981, prod. Frank Zappa) *Shut Up 'N Play Yer Guitar Some More* (Barking Pumpkin, 1981, prod. Frank Zappa) and *Return of Son of Shut Up 'N Play Yer Guitar,* (Barking Pumpkin, 1981, prod. Frank Zappa) a collection of solos that's now available on Rykodisc as a two-CD set. You can argue with the methodology of Zappa's *You Can't Do That On Stage Anymore,* a six-volume retrospective (available separately) of his live work; performances from different concerts (different years, even) were spliced together, resulting in a performance that never was, but you can't argue with the consistently high quality of the set. *Vol. 1* (Barking Pumpkin, 1988, prod. Frank Zappa) is representative of the series.

what to avoid: The compilations *Mothermania* (Verve, 1969) and *The Worst of the Mothers,* (Verve, 1969) WOOF! which unsuccessfully attempt to excerpt Zappas long-form experiments, are justifiably out of print. *The Man From Utopia* (Barking Pumpkin, 1983, prod. Frank Zappa) has some interesting instrumental work, but mainly features Zappa in an annoying sing-song vocal mode. Zappa's long-winded Broadway parody, *Thing-Fish* (Barking Pumpkin, 1983, prod. Frank Zappa) never really takes off. On *Francesco Zappa,* (Barking Pumpkin, 1984, prod. Frank Zappa) WOOF! the 20th century Zappa performs the music of the 18th century Zappa on the synclavier keyboard. Beware: This recording may induce fond memories of *Switched-On Bach.*

the rest: *Absolutely Free* (Verve, 1967, prod. Tom Wilson) *Lumpy Gravy* (Bizarre/Reprise, 1967, prod. Frank Zappa) *Cruising With Reuben & the Jets* (Verve, 1968, prod. Frank Zappa) *Chungas Revenge* (Bizarre/Reprise, 1970, prod. Frank Zappa) *The Mothers: Fillmore East, June 1971* (Bizarre/Reprise, 1971) *Just Another Band From L.A.* (Bizarre/Reprise, 1972, prod. Frank Zappa) *Waka/Jawaka* (Bizarre/Reprise 1972, prod. Frank Zappa)

The Grand Wazoo (Bizarre/Reprise 1972, prod. Frank Zappa)

What Album Changed Your Life?

"It was the Townes Van Zandt album, Our Mother the Mountain. It was maybe the first place that sounded like a real blend of country and folk. It had several songs on it that I learned and made part of my repertoire for the next 15 years."

Jimmie Dale Gilmore

Over-Nite Sensation (DiscReet, 1973) *Roxy & Elsewhere* (DiscReet, 1974, prod. Frank Zappa) *One Size Fits All* (DiscReet, 1975, prod. Frank Zappa) *Bongo Fury* (with Captain Beefheart) (DiscReet, 1975, prod. Frank Zappa) *Zoot Allures* (DiscReet, 1976, prod. Frank Zappa) *Zappa in New York* (Barking Pumpkin, 1978, prod. Frank Zappa) *Studio Tan* (DiscReet, 1978, prod. Frank Zappa) *Sleep Dirt* (DiscReet, 1979, prod. Frank Zappa) *Sheik Yerbouti* (Zappa, 1979, prod. Frank Zappa) *Orchestral Favorites* (DiscReet, 1979, prod. Frank Zappa) *Joes Garage* (Zappa, 1979, prod. Frank Zappa) and *Joes Garage Acts II & III* (Zappa, 1979, prod. Frank Zappa) (now avail on Ryko as a 2CD set) Tinseltown Rebellion (Barking Pumpkin, 1981, prod. Frank Zappa) *You Are What You Is* (Barking Pumpkin, 1981, prod. Frank Zappa) *Ship Arriving Too Late to Save a Drowning Witch* (Barking Pumpkin, 1982, prod. Frank Zappa) *Baby Snakes* (Barking Pumpkin, 1983, prod. Frank Zappa) *London Symphony* Orchestra (Barking Pumpkin, 1983, prod. Frank Zappa) (now available as expanded 2CD set on Rykodisc) *The Perfect Stranger: Boulez Conducts Zappa* (Angel/EMI, 1984, prod. Frank Zappa) *Them or Us* (Barking Pumpkin, 1984, prod. Frank Zappa) *Does Humor Belong in Music?* (EMI Euorpe, 1984, prod. Frank Zappa) *Frank Zappa Meets the Mothers of Prevention* (Barking Pumpkin, 1985, prod. Frank Zappa) *Jazz From Hell* (Barking Pumpkin, 1986, prod. Frank Zappa) *Guitar* (Barking Pumpkin, 1988, prod. Frank Zappa) *You Cant Do That On Stage Anymore Vol. 2: The Helsinki Concert* Barking Pumpkin, 1988, prod. Frank Zappa) *Broadway the Hard Way* (Barking Pumpkin, 1989, prod. Frank Zappa) *You Cant Do That On Stage Anymore Vol. 3* (Barking Pumpkin, 1989, prod. Frank Zappa) *Make a Jazz Noise Here* (Barking Pumpkin, 1991, prod. Frank Zappa) *You Cant Do That On Stage Anymore Vol. 4* (Barking Pumpkin, 1991, prod. Frank Zappa) *The Best Band You Never Heard in Your Life* (Barking Pumpkin, 1991, prod. Frank Zappa) *Playground Psychotics* (Barking Pumpkin, 1992, prod. Frank Zappa) *You Cant Do That On Stage Anymore Vol. 5* (Barking Pumpkin, 1992, prod. Frank Zappa) *You Cant Do That On Stage Anymore Vol. 6* (Barking Pumpkin, 1992, prod. Frank Zappa) *Ahead of Their Time* (Rykodisc, 1993, prod. Frank Zappa) *Civilization Phaze III* (Barking Pumpkin, 1994, prod. Frank Zappa) *The Lost Episodes* (Rykodisc, 1996, prod. Frank Zappa)

worth searching for: *200 Motels* (United Artists, 1971, prod. Frank Zappa) is the only album Rykodisc has not been able to secure the rights to for reissue, and while not an essential purchase, it deserves a place in the canon. In an attempt to outflank bootleggers, Zappa pulled a number of illegal recordings off the market and released them himself, resulting in a series his most devoted fans will want to own. They include *Piquantique,* (Foo-Eee, 1991) *Saarbrucken,* (Foo-Eee, 1991) *Tis the Season to be Jelly,* (Foo-Eee, 1991), *Unmitigated Audacity,* (Foo-Eee, 1991) *Any Way the Wind Blows,* (Foo-Eee, 1991) *Freaks & Motherfu*#@%!,* (Foo-Eee, 1991) *The Ark* (Foo-Eee, 1991) and *As An Am.* (Foo-Eee, 1991) They vary in sound and musical quality, but are each of sufficient historical interest to rate A second batch is available in the box set *Beat the Boots #2.* (Foo-Eee, 1992)

Captain Beefheart, Matt Groening, Eugene Chadbourne, Uz Jsme Doma, the Persuasions, Wild Man Fischer, Pulnoc

Edgard Varese, Spike Jones, Eric Dolphy, Karlheinz Stockhausen, Johnny Guitar Watson, Thomas Paine

Daniel Durchholz

Peter Zaremba

See: The Fleshtones

Martin Zellar /Gear Daddies

Born June 14, 1963 in Austin, Minn.

Since they hailed from Minnesota, the Gear Daddies were often lumped in with the Replacements, Husker Du and Soul Asylum. That left leader Martin Zellar compared to such alt-rock pillars as Paul Westerberg, Bob Mould and Dave Pirner, even though his tastes were more country and his viewpoint was more compassionate. The raspy-voiced Zellar's twangy ruminations on the battered egos and shattered dreams of blue-collar middle America include compelling portraits of blissfully naive housewives, abandoned mothers, self-pitying alcoholics and bored teenagers that never deteriorate into caricatures. Since the 1992 breakup of the Gear Daddies, Zellar has launched a promising solo career that reflects a more-focused sound and a more authoritative point of view. And while he's abandoned old habits (he quit drinking in 1990) and a healthy portion of his older material (don't ever expect to hear "Zamboni" again), Gear Daddies fans will still recognize his staunch roots-rock allegiance and unrivaled ability to mine that fertile gray area that lies between desperation and hope.

what to buy: Zellar's solo debut, *Born Under,* (Rykodisc, 1995, prod. Martin Zellar and Steve McKinstry) broadens his bar-band roots with cellos, organs, accordions and mandolins. "Problem Solved," "Something's Gotta Happen" and "Cross My Heart" aren't about lonesome losers so much as ego-bruised, guilt-wracked underdogs trying to muster the inner strength for one last stand. The guitars and lyrics of *Martin Zellar and the Hardways* (Rykodisc, 1996, prod. Tom Herbers) boast a sharper bite, thanks mostly to the seasoned clout of the Hardways, who drive the sardonic commentary of "Big Sandals," the harrowing hate-crime tale of "Guilty Just the Same" and a rowdy bonus-track leftover from the Gear Daddies days called "Frog Fightin' Drunk."

what to buy next: Of the Gear Daddies' output, it's a tossup between the twangy *Let's Go Scare Al* (Polygram, 1988, prod. Jim Walsh), which includes "She's Happy" and "Boys Will Be Boys," and *Billy's Live Bait,* (Polygram, 1990, prod. Tom Herbers and Gear Daddies) which rocks much harder and offers the hockey-rink anthem "Zamboni" as an unlisted bonus track.

the rest: *Can't Have Nothin' Nice* (Crackpot, 1992)

worth searching for: The promotional "Lie to Me" CD single (Rykodisc, 1995, prod. Martin Zellar and Steve McKinstry) adds Zellar's straight-faced cover of Neil Diamond's "If You Know What I Mean" and spirited take on the Cars' "My Best Friend's Girl" as B-sides

The Band, Buck Owens, Bruce Springsteen

David Okamoto

Warren Zevon

Born Jan. 24, 1947 in Chicago, Ill.

You couldn't blame Zevon if he regards the term singer/songwriter as an epithet. Unlike his terminally mellow El Lay brethren Jackson Browne (who produced Zevon's early albums), the Eagles, J.D. Souther, et al, Zevon's tales of life on the left coast are fraught with excess, violence and nearly every sort of mayhem imaginable. But his songs are literate and literary (novelists Thomas McGuane and Carl Hiaasen have been cowriters), and Zevon seems more influenced by other media, such as the films of Sam Peckinpah or the novels of F. Scott Fitzgerald and Raymond Chandler, than he is by other musicians. And while there's plenty of macho posturing on his albums, he has his tender side, too. Besides, his bluster is almost always accompanied by a gallows humor that is second to none in rock and roll.

what to buy: *Warren Zevon* (Asylum, 1976, prod. Jackson Browne) is one of the great albums of the '70s, a virtual concept album about a culture, and its individual inhabitants, spinning out of control. Some of the songs were first popularized by Linda Ronstadt ("Hasten Down the Wind," "Poor Poor Pitiful Me" and "Mohammed's Radio"), but Zevon's versions are grittier and more desperate. Zevon's dark streak runs rampant on *Excitable Boy,* (Asylum, 1978, prod. Jackson Browne and Waddy Wachtel) notably on the title track about an eternally coddled sociopath. The album is uneven, but it contains some of his best-known songs, including the hit "Werewolves of London," "Roland the Headless Thompson Gunner" and "Lawyers, Guns And Money." *I'll Sleep When I'm Dead: The Warren Zevon Anthology* (Rhino, 1996, prod. Various) is a career-spanning retrospective that hits all the high points of Zevon's career and includes some tracks from the highly sought-after live album *Stand in the Fire* (see Worth Searching For).

what to buy next: *Sentimental Hygiene* (Virgin, 1987, prod. Warren Zevon, Andrew Slater and Niko Bolas) finds Zevon back in fighting form after a long struggle with alcoholism. "Detox Mansion" "Trouble Waiting to Happen" and "Bad Karma" offer an unsentimental and often hilarious account of his ordeal. "The Factory" veers into Springsteen territory, while "Boom Boom Mancini" offers a more concise sketch of boxing's attraction/repellence than Joyce Carol Oates or Norman Mailer could ever dream of. *Bad Luck Streak in Dancing School* (Asylum, 1980, prod. Warren Zevon and Greg Ladanyi) finds him reworking themes of mercenary violence ("Jungle Work)" and personal demons ("Bad Luck Streak in Dancing School"), but Zevon's wit buoys the album, particularly on "Play It All Night Long," a devastating caricature of the popular notion of going "back to the country."

what to avoid: Zevon's first, *Wanted—Dead or Alive,*(Imperial, 1969/One Way, 1996, prod. Kim Fowley) **WOOF!** an album so bad that, after it flopped, Zevon turned to writing jingles for the likes of Chevrolet and Gallo wine.

the rest: *A Quiet Normal Life: The Best of Warren Zevon* (Asylum, 1986) *Transverse City* (Virgin, 1989) *Mr. Bad Example* (Giant, 1991) *Learning to Flinch* (Giant, 1993) *Mutineer* (Giant, 1995)

worth searching for: *Stand in the Fire* (Asylum, 1980, prod. Warren Zevon and Greg Ladanyi) and *The Envoy,* (Asylum, 1982, prod. Waddy Wachtel, Greg Ladanyi, and Warren Zevon) two albums from Zevon's early period that are inexplicably unavailable on CD. *Stand* is one of the great live albums, on which Zevon and his band of unknowns can barely contain their excitement. Never one to settle for the usual rock and roll subjects, Zevon wrote the title track of *The Envoy* as a tribute to shuttle diplomat Philip Habib.

Linda Ronstadt, Don Henley, R.E.M., Counting Crows, Camper Van Beethoven

Bob Dylan, Jackson Browne, Leonard Cohen

see also: *Hindu Love Gods*

Daniel Durchholz

The Zombies

Formed 1963 in Hertfordshire, England. Disbanded 1967.

Rod Argent, keyboards, vocals; Colin Blunstone, vocals; Paul Atkinson, guitar; Hugh Grundy, drums; Paul Arnold, bass (1963-64); Chris White, bass (1964-67)

The Zombies stood out from the horde of pop-rock bands grouped under the British Invasion umbrella by virtue of its jazzy, syncopated arrangements, minor-key melodies and burnished harmonies. Though the music was more challenging than that made by most of their peers, the band nonetheless scored two huge hits right out of the box, "She's Not There" and "Tell Her No." It struggled for several years during the tumultuous mid-60s and didn't enjoy its next hit, "Time of the Season," until after it disbanded. Argent went on to front a band that bore his name; Blunstone had a spotty solo career and Grundy and Arnold eventually made their way out of the music biz.

Thanks to gorgeous songcraft, sexy and unusual harmonies, and Argent's skillful keyboard work, the Zombies' finest creations are in the same league with the Beatles, Beach Boys and Kinks, and the group's influence is readily apparent in contemporary power pop. In 1994 the group was even the subject of the form's ultimate honorific, a tribute album—*The World of the Zombies* (Popllama).

what to buy: A couple of anthologies capture the peaks of a group that for the most part lived and died by singles. *Time of the Zombies* (Epic, 1973, prod. Various) is an excellent place to start, though some Zombiephiles consider *Greatest Hits* (Digital Compact Classics, 1990, prod. Kenny Jones) to be superior.

what to buy next: *Odyssey and Oracle* (Date, 1968/Rhino, 1987, prod. the Zombies) is the one Zombies release that was actually structured as an album and not a collection of singles, and it contains some of the band's trippiest, most sparkling pop.

the rest: *Begins Here* (Decca, 1965) *Live on the BBC: 1965-67* (Rhino, 1985) *Greatest Hits/Greatest Recordings* (Transluxe, 1995)

worth searching for: The import *Singles A's and B's,* (See For Miles, 1992) with B-sides that offer further proof the Zombies had more to offer than its singles.

The Doors, the Left Banke, the Hollies, the Move, Elvis Costello, the Balancing Act, Young Fresh Fellows, Jellyfish, the Posies, Zumpano, Wondermints, Spanish Kitchen

George and Ira Gershwin, Cole Porter, Phil Spector, the Beatles, the Beach Boys

see also: *Argent*

Simon Glickman

ZZ Top

Formed 1969 in Houston, Texas

Billy Gibbons Jr., guitar, vocals; Frank Beard, drums; Dusty Hill, bass, vocals

Few bands have enjoyed the longevity and steady personnel of Texas blues-rock-pop band ZZ Top. And working together has paid off, as the trio has improved over the years rather than fading away. Its psychedelic blues-rock led it to national stardom with 1973's *Tres Hombres* and it stayed on the charts until 1976 when, due to label problems, the group stopped playing and even jamming together. After changing labels, it tossed off a killer blues rock album, *Deguello,* then recreated themselves; Gibbons' trademark licks were still in there, but the sound embraced synthesizers while the band adapted to the MTV generation with its huge beards and humorous videos filled with leggy models. The resultant *Eliminator* in 1983 pumped the trio to superstar status with the hits "Legs," "Sharp Dressed Man" and "Gimme All Your Lovin.' " ZZ Top rode that formula until it sputtered out during the early 90s, at which point it began reverting back to its blues-rock roots.

what to buy: Coming off a two-year layoff, the guys laid it on the line for *Deguello,* (Warner Bros., 1979, prod. Bill Ham) showcasing deep blues like "Dust My Broom" and funky fun on "Cheap Sunglasses"—kink, kitsch and some searing guitar riffs. They just kept rolling, and *Eliminator* (Warner Bros., 1983, prod. Bill Ham) let anybody who hadn't heard of them yet in on the secret.

what to buy next: *Tres Hombres* (London, 1973/Warner Bros., 1987 prod. Bill Ham) catches the band as it was coming into the spotlight, when its idea of a jam was "Beer Drinkers and Hell Raisers." If you just want to skim the hits, *ZZ Top's Greatest Hits* (Warner Bros., 1992, prod. Bill Ham) covers all the bases and adds a cover of Elvis Presley's "Viva Las Vegas."

what to avoid: The only questionable product is *Six Pack,* (Warner Bros., 1987, prod. Bill Ham) a CD compilation of the first six albums remixed with drum samples that lost some of the earthiness of their sound.

the rest: *ZZ Top* (London, 1970/Warner Bros., 1987) *Rio Grande Mud* (London, 1972/Warner Bros., 1987) *Fandango!* (London, 1975/Warner Bros., 1987) *Tejas* (London, 1976/Warner Bros., 1987) *The Best of ZZ Top* (London, 1977/Warner Bros., 1987) *El Loco* (Warner Bros., 1981) *Afterburner* (Warner Bros., 1985) *Recycler* (Warner Bros., 1990) *Antenna* (RCA, 1994) *One Foot in the Blues* (Warner Bros., 1994) *Rhythmeen* (RCA, 1996)

worth searching for: *A Taste of the ZZ Top Six Pack,* (Warner Bros., 1987, prod. Bill Ham) a lively 13-song promotional sampler from the first six albums.

Stevie Ray Vaughan, Big Head Todd and the Monsters

Johnny Winter, Lightning Hopkins, T-Bone Walker, Cream

Lawrence Gabriel

If you can't get enough rock, we've listed popular books and magazines you can check out for further information. We've also listed a whole bunch of, mostly official, band websites for specific artist information, as well as select general rock music websites that the Hound especially likes.

Books

All Music Guide to Rock
Michael Erlewine, Vladimir Bogdanov, and Chris Woodstra, 1995, Miller Freeman Books, $24.95

The Billboard Book of Number One Albums
Craig Rosen, 1996, Billboard Books, $21.95

From Velvets to Voidoids: A Pre-Punk History for a Post-Punk World
Clinton Heylin, 1993, Penguin

Hollywood Rock
Marshall Crenshaw, 1994, Harper Perennial, $15.00

The Penguin Encyclopedia of Popular Music
1990, Penguin Books, $20.00

The Rock and Roll Almanac
Mark Bego, 1996, Macmillan, $12.95

Rolling Stone Album Guide
Patricia Romanowski, Holly George-Warren, 1995, Straight Arrow Press/Random House, $20.00

Spin Alternative Record Guide
Eric Weisbard with Craig Marks,1995, Vintage Books $20.00

Trouser Press Record Guide
Ira A. Robbins, 1994, Collier Books/Macmillan, $20.00

Unsung Heroes of Rock 'n' Roll
Nick Tosches, 1984, Charles Scribner's Sons

Magazines

Alternative Press
6516 Detroit Ave., Ste. 5
Cleveland, OH 44102
$19.95/12 issues. Provides coverage of progressive music with attention given to regional bands as well as national acts. Contains interviews and features written for a young adult audience.

Billboard Magazine
One Astor Plaza
1515 Broadway
New York, NY 10036
$265/annual rate. Published weekly, except for the last week in December. Covers music, video and home entertainment news.

CMJ New Music Report
245 Great Neck Rd.
Great Neck, NY 11021
Weekly trade mag covers a variety of musical styles, including hip-hop, metal and worldbeat.

Creem
John T. Edwards Publishing, Ltd.
28 W. 25th St.
New York, NY 10010
$3.50 per issue/9 issues yearly. Covers personalities in all types music, including rock, pop, jazz, rap, and alternative.

Q
PO Box 500
Leicester LE99 0AA, England
English monthly covers features and includes reviews.

Rolling Stone
1290 Avenue of the Americas, 2nd. Fl.
New York, NY 10104
$25.95/24 issues. Reports on various aspects of popular culture including film, politics, and especially music. Covers music of all genres with a focus on rock.

Spin
6 West 18th St., 8th Fl.
New York, NY 10011
$18.00/12 issues. Covers fashion, politics, popular culture, and music with an alternative perspective. Focuses on progressive music geared to young adults.

Web Pages

General Rock Music Sites

http://imusic.com/
http://www.iuma.com/
http://www.stl-music.com/gen.html
http://rocktropolis.com/
http://mtv.com/
http://www.musiccentral.msn.com/
http://www.addict.com/ATN/
http://american.recordings.com/wwwofmusic/ubl/ubl.shtml
http://bmi.com/
http://www.billboard-online.com
http://www.icemagazine.com/ice/docs/home.html
http://www3.pgh.net/~rockreporter/
http://www.nj.com/arts/music/sos/
http://www.rockhall.com/
http://xp.nyu.edu/~jonathan/rocksong.html
http://www.angelfire.com/free/MusicMania.html
http://sjcpl.lib.in.us/homepage/Reference/Rockweb/MUSIC.HTML
http://www.ans.se/musiccorner/
http://www.rockweb.com/features/house-of-boo/
http://homepage.cistron.nl/~edmar/
http://www.pncl.co.uk/subs/julianw/list.html

ABBA

http://spider.media.philips.com/polydor/artists/abba.html
http://phymat.bham.ac.uk/ABBA/

Paula Abdul

http://www.southwind.net/~ksims/abdul/Abdul.html

AC/DC

http://www.elektra.com/artists/acdc/acdc.html
http://www.ping.be/~ping2623/acdcpage.html
http://www.sdstate.edu/~cc92/http/acdc.html

Ace of Base

http://www.aristarec.com/aob/home.html
http://www.dacc.cc.il.us/~mulberry/music/aceofbase/aceofbase.html

William Ackerman

http://www.windham.com/ourmusic/artist_pages/ackerman.empty.byartist.html

Bryan Adams

http://www.glue.umd.edu/~xiaoqin/music/adams.html

Aerosmith

http://www.sony.com/Music/ArtistInfo/Aerosmith.html
http://coos.dartmouth.edu/~joeh/
http://pandora.st.hmc.edu/Aerosmith/
http://pages.prodigy.com/aerosmith/aerocove.htm
http://www.hooked.net/users/noelh/aero.HTML

Afghan Whigs

http://www.elektra.com/artists/afghanwhigs/afghan.html

a-ha

http://www.wwiv.com/a-ha/
http://chu-domo.mit.edu/a-ha/a-ha.html

The Alarm/Mike Peters

http://www.demon.co.uk/alarmpo/

Algebra Suicide

http://users.aol.com/barnabas01/algebra.htm

Alice Donut

http://www.users.interport.net/~mjung/Albums.html

Alice in Chains

http://www.music.sony.com/Music/ArtistInfo/AliceInChains/
http://www.proaxis.com/~mcoleman/aliceinchains/

Alien Sex Fiend

http://www.zynet.co.uk/steelwolf/ignore/

All

http://www.lava.net:80/~sanner/

All About Eve

http://www.concentric.net/~Mikusko/eves/index.shtml

The Allman Brothers

http://www.music.sony.com/Music/ArtistInfo/AllmanBrothersBand.html
http://www.netspace.org/allmans/

Marc Almond

http://www.iti.gov.sg/almond/
http://www.why.net/home/torero/marcpage.html

Herb Alpert

http://www.geffen.com/almo/herbalpert/

Alphaville

http://www.netcns.com/~dan/av/

Amazing Rhythm Aces

http://members.aol.com/fhah/index.html

America

http://www.pacificrim.net/~wahlgren/

American Music Club/Mark Eitzel

http://www.wam.umd.edu/~ljason/amc/

Tori Amos

http://www.atlantic-records.com/Tori_Amos/
http://hubcap.clemson.edu/~watts/tori.html
http://cctr.umkc.edu/user/cgladish/tori.html
http://gto.ncsa.uiuc.edu./khawkins/tori.html

Jon Anderson

http://www.windham.com/ourmusic/artist_pages/anderson.empty.byartist.html

Laurie Anderson

http://www.c3.lanl.gov:8080/cgi/jimmyd/quoter?home
http://www.voyagerco.com/LA/VgerLa.html

Angel

http://www.wintermute.co.uk/users/babylon/apage.htm

Adam Ant

http://www.uhs.uga.edu/Adam_Ant/Adam.html
http://www.interlog.com/~nmkelly/A-Ant/Adam.html

Anthrax

http://www.elektra.com/artists/anthrax/anthrax.html
http://www.fanbase.com/anthrax/
http://www.ollusa.edu/academic/sbpa/cishome/students/cardenas/anthpage.htm

Aphex Twin
http://hyperreal.com/music/artists/aphex_twin/

Arc Angels
http://www.cityscape.co.uk/users/du27/index.html

Archers of Loaf
http://www.wku.edu/~jonesrw/archers/go_loaf.html

Joan Armatrading
http://www.rahul.net/hrmusic/artists/jaart.html

Army of Lovers
http://www.enqueue.com/aol/

Art of Noise
http://weber.u.washington.edu/~wbwolf/AON.html

Asia
http://www.globalnet.co.uk/~asia/
http://www.clo.com/~dave/

Chet Atkins
http://www.chetatkins.com/

Atlanta Rhythm Section
http://apts178.residence.gatech.edu/052/arshome.html

Auteurs
http://www.niweb.com/music/auteurs/

Aztec Camera
http://homepage.interaccess.com/~hawkfan/aztec.htm

The B-52's
http://www.dur.ac.uk/~d43e4d/b-52s.html
http://www.york.ac.uk/~dwe101/b52s/
http://www.ozemail.com.au/~peterv/b52s/index.html

Babes in Toyland
http://www.RepriseRec.com/BabesInToyland
http://www.nvg.unit.no/~hersir/babes.html

Bad Brains
http://www.networkamerica.com/~whatsup/brains/index.html

Bad Religion
http://www.atlantic-records.com/bad_religion/
http://r2d2.ucsd.edu/br/
http://www.htu.se/~ti95co/bad_religion/

Joan Baez
http://baez.woz.org/

Bailter Space
http://www.matador.recs.com/bios/bio_bailter.html

Marcia Ball
http://members.gnn.com/JDarby/marcia.htm

The Band
http://www.theband.com/mirror/

The Bangles
http://sipi.usc.edu/~clare/Bangles.html

Barenaked Ladies
http://www.RepriseRec.com/Reprise_HTML_Pages/BNLFolder/Barenaked-Ladies
http://www.cs.fredonia.edu/~ludw1080/WWW/Barenaked/BareNaked.html

Basia
http://www.sony.dreammedia.com/Epic/artistdetail.qry?artistid=12
http://www.eden.com/%7Ecombee/basia/

The Beach Boys
http://overlord.dmv.com/~atroxi/bb.html

The Beastie Boys
http://www.nando.net/BeastieBoys/
http://www.hooked.net/users/clayton/links.html

Beat Farmers
http://orpheus.ucsd.edu/sdam/artists/bf/

The Beatles
http://pages.prodigy.com/mervis/beatle.htm
http://www.primenet.com/~dhaber/beatles.html
http://www.calweb.com/~gerrito1/beatles/
http://falcon.jmu.edu/~karschsp/beatles/index.html
http://www.neca.com/~mikem/beat.html

Beck
http://www.geffen.com/beck/
http://www.rain.org/~truck/beck/
http://www.netrail.net/~smack/beck/

Jeff Beck
http://www.music.sony.com/Music/ArtistInfo/JeffBeck.html

The Bee Gees
http://www.columbia.edu/~brennan/beegees.html
http://home.cc.umanitoba.ca/~umwalter/

Bel Canto
http://math-www.uio.no/bel-canto/

Adrian Belew
http://wl.iglou.com/hermit/adrian/

Belly
http://www.RepriseRec.com/Belly
http://www.evo.org/html/group/belly.html
http://www.stack.urc.tue.nl/~conrad/belly/
http://shoga.wwa.com/~foss/belly/
http://www.escape.ca/~skinner/belly/belly_.html

Ben Folds Five
http://oeonline.com/~maynard/bff/

Pat Benatar
http://www2.southwind.net/~jcross/benatar/
http://www.netgate.net/~bmeier/benatar.html

Heidi Berry
http://www.evo.org/html/group/berryheidi.html

Better than Ezra
http://www.elektra.com/artists/better/better.html
http://www.ezra.org/

Bettie Serveet
http//www.atlantic-records.com/Bettie_Serveet/
http://www.evo.org/html/group/bettieserveert.html
http://www.xs4all.nl/~gdvlugt/bettie/hoofd.html

Big Audio Dynamite
http://www.radioactive.net/BANDS/BAD/index.shtml

Big Bamboo
http://www.realitycom.com/bamboo/

Big Country
http://www.cs.clemson.edu/~junderw/music/bc/

Big Head Todd & the Monsters
http://www.phoenix.net/USERS/cbyrne/bhtmhome.html

Big Star
http://comp.uark.edu/~cbray/bigstar/index.html

Bikini Kill
http://www.columbia.edu/~rli3/music_html/bikini_kill/bikini.html

Birthday Party
http://www.evo.org/html/group/birthdayparty.html

Stephen Bishop
http://www.genoagrp.com/genoagrp/stephen_bishop/

Bjork
http://www.elektra.com/artists/bjork/bjork.html
http://www.bjork.co.uk/bjork/

Black Crowes
http://www.rockweb.com/rwi/listeners/black-crowes/
http://www.tallest.com/

Black Flag
http://pages.nyu.edu/~vqd6140/flag.html

Black Sabbath
http://www.apogee1.com/sabbath/sabbath.htm

Frank Black
http://www.evo.org/html/group/blackfrank.html
http://beaker.nmsu.edu/spaceman/fb/

Ritchie Blackmore
http://www.webstars.com/webstars/ritchie/

Blake Babies
http://wwwvms.utexas.edu/~slowdog/index.html

Blind Melon
http://www.fanbase.com/blindmelon/melon.htm
http://www.students.uiuc.edu/~strougal/melon.html
http://www.oberlin.edu/~mbadanes/melonhome.html

Blondie/Debbie Harry
http://anansi.panix.com/userdirs/jessamin/
http://www3.primenet.com/~lab/DHDeborahHarry.html

Michael Bloomfield
http://www.bluespower.com/arbn.htm

Blue Oyster Cult
http://www.sony.com/Music/ArtistInfo/BOC/

Blue Rodeo
http://pathfinder.com/wmgca/bluerodeo/index.html
http://www.bluerodeo.com/

The Blues Brothers
http://www.nta.no/brukere/kol/bb/

Blues Traveler
http://www.bluestraveler.com/
http://www.sgi.net/bluestraveler/

Blur
http://www.parlophone.co.uk/blur/

Bo Deans
http://www.repriserec.com/Reprise_HTML_Pages/BoDeansFolder/BoDeans

Tommy Bolin
http://www.primenet.com/~trix/bolin.htm

Michael Bolton
http://www.music.sony.com/Music/ArtistInfo/MichaelBolton/index.html
http://www.cs.neu.edu/home/shiney/bolton/bolton.html

Bon Jovi
http://www.polygram.com/bonjovi/
http://www2.s-gimb.lj.edus.si/peter/bj/bj.html

Boo Radleys
http://www.geocities.com/Broadway/3308/boorad.htm

Betty Boo
http://www.ling.uu.se/~bengt/boo.html

Boston
http://www.nd.edu/~grand/rachel/boston.html

Bottle Rockets
http://www.tagrec.com/Bottle.html

David Bowie
http://liber.stanford.edu/~torrie/Bowie/BowieFile.html

Brad
http://www.music.sony.com/Music/ArtistInfo/Loosegroove/brad.htm

Billy Bragg
http://noel.pd.org/~usul/billy-bragg.html

The Breeders
http://www.elektra.com/artists/breeders/breeders.html
http://www.vuse.vanderbilt.edu/~burketrd/breeders.htm
http://www.evo.org/html/group/breeders.html

Jackson Browne
http://www.elektra.com/artists/browne/browne.html
http://www.west.net/~jrpprod/jackson_browne.html

Jeff Buckley
http://www.sony.com/Music/ArtistInfo/JeffBuckley.html
http://www.goodnet.com/~gkelemen/jeffhome.html

Buffalo Tom
http://www.cjnetworks.com/buffalo_tom/

Jimmy Buffett
http://www.homecom.com:80/buffett/
http://www.hepcat.com/buffett/bank.html

The Buggles
http://tiger.coe.missouri.edu/~patrick/buggles/

Bush
http://www.bushonline.com/
http://angelfire.com/free/bush.html
http://ece.wpi.edu/~derekh/bush/

Kate Bush
http://www.acy.digex.net/~dobenson/the_muse.html
http://www.aitec.edu.au/ExplV/

The Butthole Surfers
http://www.ifi.uio.no/~haavardh/butthole.html
http://www.ods.de/butthole/surfers.html

The Buzzcocks
http://www.cityscape.co.uk/users/ac46/

The Byrds
http://www.uark.edu/~kadler/rm-cguinn/
http://www.q-net.net/~rrussell/Byrds/

David Byrne
http://www.bart.nl/~francey/th_db.html

C & C Music Factory
http://www.golden.net/~rarcher/do-main/index.htm

Cabaret Voltaire
http://www.bath.ac.uk/~mapnjd/Music/cabaretVoltaire.html

Camel
http://ng.netgate.net/~jsp/camel/camelpage.html

Candlebox
http://www.candlebox.com/
http://vulture.creighton.edu/~pfinn/cbox.html

Captain & Tennille
http://www.vcnet.com/moonlight/

Captain Beefheart
http://www.rit.edu/~jcs1589/hpr/

Carcass
http://rhf.bradley.edu/~muslhead/carcass.html

Mariah Carey
http://www.southwind.net/~ksims/VOL.html
http://www.serve.com/mriahfan/tralala/tralala.html
http://www.oecn.ohio.gov/~sr-baker/mcarey.html

Mary Chapin Carpenter
http://www.music.sony.com/Music/ArtistInfo/MaryChapinCarpenter.html
http://members.aol.com/djcoplien/mcc/index.html
http://www.dopig.uab.edu/people/ctichenor/chapin.html

The Carpenters
http://home.earthlink.net/~eeyore/

The Cars
http://www.cs.hmc.edu/~me/cars/cars.html

Carter the Unstoppable Sex Machine
http://pinky.math.uiuc.edu/carter_usm/

Peter Case
http://www.buzznet.com/petercase/

Johnny Cash
http://www.catt.ncsu.edu/www_projects/Cash/cash.html
http://american.recordings.com/American_Artists/Johnny_Cash/cash_home.html

Nick Cave/Bad Seeds
http://www.maths.monash.edu.au/people/brett/nick/nick.html
http://members.aol.com/cycho/cave/index.html

Eugene Chadbourne
http://www.math.duke.edu/~priley/chadbourne.html

Harry Chapin
http://www.fn.net/~jmayans/chapin/index.html

Tracey Chapman
http://www.elektra.com/artists/chapman/chapman.html
http://www.rrze.uni-erlangen.de/~sz1526/tracy.html

The Charlatans UK
http://www.ifi.uio.no/~eirikg/Charlatans.html

Charm Farm
http://www.rust.net/~charm/index.html

Cheap Trick
http://users.aol.com/melkel/

Neneh Cherry
http://remus.rutgers.edu/~ghuliani/neneh.html

Chicago
http://www.chirecords.com/
http://www.cyberspace.com/adrock/

China Crisis
http://www.tgraph.com/china.htm

The Choir
http://www.cen.uiuc.edu/~mr-gates/choir.html

The Church
http://www.cen.uiuc.edu/~mr-gates/choir.html

Eric Clapton
http://http.bsd.uchicago.edu/~d-hillman/welcome.html
http://mars.superlink.net/user/wnuck/clapton.html

The Clash
http://www.primenet.com/~jen-dave/clash/clash.htm
http://www.well.com/user/jeffdove/clash.html

George Clinton/Funkadelic/Parliament
http://ourworld.compuserve.com/homepages/PJebsen/homepage.htm
http://www.duke.edu/~eja/pfunk.html

Bruce Cockburn
http://users.aol.com/fxbrusca/bruce.htm
http://www.fish.com/music/bruce_cockburn/

Joe Cocker
http://www.music.sony.com/Music/ArtistInfo/JoeCocker.html

Cocteau Twins
http://205.147.5.69/
http://www.evo.org/html/group/cocteautwins.html

Leonard Cohen
http://www.music.sony.com/Music/ArtistInfo/LeonardCohen.html
http://ccat.sas.upenn.edu/cpage/Leonard_Cohen/

Jude Cole
http://www.castle.net/~becker/music/judecole/judecole.htm

Paula Cole
http://cpcug.org/user/titusb/pcole/

Collective Soul
http://www.atlantic-records.com/Collective_Soul/
http://edge.edge.net/~wgrisard/soul/realsoul.html

Phil Collins
http://www.brad.ac.uk/~agcatchp/pc/collins.html

Shawn Colvin
http://www.music.sony.com/Music/ArtistInfo/ShawnColvin.html

Combustible Edison
http://www.subpop.com/bands/combustible/comed/

Come
http://www.matador.recs.com/bios/bio_come.html

Commander Cody
http://www.awpi.com/Commander-Cody/

Concrete Blonde
http://web.cs.ualberta.ca/~mah/CB/

Continental Drifters
http://www.bangos.com/BLUROSO/artists/ContiDri/codr.htm

Alice Cooper
http://www.sbbs.se/hp/lare/cooperfile.html
http://www.sn.no/~embla/acpage.html
http://www.dur.ac.uk/~d3hu71/music/cooper.alice/

Cop Shoot Cop
http://www.columbia.edu/~egn2/csc.html
http://www.lap.umd.edu/harper/csc/csc.html

Julian Cope
http://www.fsa.ulaval.ca/personnel/gaumondp/cope/index.html

Corrosion of Conformity
http://www.prairienet.org/~kiadm/coc.html

Elvis Costello
http://www.wbr.com/elvis/
http://east.isx.com/~schnitzi/elvis.html

Counting Crows
http://www.monmouth.com/~jkochel/crows.html
http://www.primenet.com/~ztv/crows.html

Cowboy Junkies
http://www.geffen.com/cowboyjunkies/
http://www.compulink.co.uk/~sparks/cj_home.htm

Cracker/Camper Van Beethoven
http://sal.cs.uiuc.edu/~tdsmith/cracker.html
http://www.upx.net/~basehead/cvb.html

The Cranberries
http://www.nada.kth.se/~d90-fgi/Cranberries/index.html
http://www.bright.net/~shwendel/
http://pages.prodigy.com/crannews/welcome.htm

Cranes
http://busop.cit.wayne.edu/www/cranes/home.htm

Crash Test Dummies
http://www.qbc.clic.net/~krystall/ctd/

Cream
http://www.fas.harvard.edu/~daraujo/cream.html

Creedence Clearwater Revival
http://www.jyu.fi/~petkasi/ccr.htm

Marshall Crenshaw
http://www.primenet.com/~jeffcdo/crenshaw.htm

Crosby, Stills & Nash
http://www.alpha.nl/CSN/

Sheryl Crow
http://www.wintermute.co.uk/~cicely/sheryl/

Crowded House
http://www.bath.ac.uk/%7Ema4adas/ch/
http://www.etext.org/Mailing.Lists/house/

The Cult
http://www.coastnet.com/~jtaylor/cult.html

Culture Club/Boy George
http://www-personal.umich.edu/~geena/boygeorge.html

The Cure
http://www.the-cure.com/
http://ezinfo.ucs.indiana.edu/~ncosgray/home.html
http://www.elektra.com/artists/cure/cure.html
http://www-acc.scu.edu/~btrott/cure/other/other.html

Curve
http://www.stack.urc.tue.nl/~conrad/curve/

Cutting Crew
http://www.io.org/~twg/cc/cuttcrew.html

Cypress Hill
http://www.music.sony.com/Music/ArtistInfo/CypressHill/index.html
http://reality.sgi.com/sprout/vibrations/cypress/index.shtml

The Damned
http://www.thebeach.com/damned/

Danzig
http://american.recordings.com/American_Artists/Danzig/index.shtml

Terence Trent D'Arby
http://www.sony.com/Music/ArtistInfo/TTD/

Miles Davis
http://charlotte.acns.nwu.edu/larryt/miles/milestones.html
http://www.wam.umd.edu/~losinp/music/ahead.html

Spencer Davis Group
http://fas-www.harvard.edu/~stribble/sdg.html

Deacon Blue
http://ourworld.compuserve.com/homepages/Deacon_Blue/

Dead Can Dance
http://www.evo.org/html/group/deadcandance.html
http://www.nets.com/dcd/

Dead Kennedys
http://tahoma.cwu.edu:2000/~gossardr/dk_html/dk.html

Dead Milkmen
http://ucunix.san.uc.edu/~hobbscf/milkmen/Milkmen.html
http://www.phlab.missouri.edu/~c510292/dead.milkmen/
http://twintone.com/restless/milkmen.html

Death
http://www.geom.umn.edu/~bmeloon/music/bandinfo/death.html

Chris DeBurgh
http://www.crl.com/~jderouen/cdeb/

Deep Purple
http://www.deep-purple.com/

Def Leppard
http://www.xs4all.nl/~eldritch/leppard.html
http://www.realtime.net/~denece/

Ani DeFranco
http://www.cc.columbia.edu/~marg/ani/
http://www.columbia.edu/~dg137/ani.html

Defunkt
http://www.fred.net/jbowie/defunkt.html

Del Amitri
http://del-amitri.linex.com/

Cathy Dennis
http://www.en.com/users/rodneye/cathyd.html

Depeche Mode
http://www.commline.com/
http://www.thedaily.washington.edu/staff/martin/mode.net/

Devo
http://www.nvg.unit.no/~optimus/devo/

Diamond Head
http://www.iuma.com/SOB/html/Diamond_Head/Diamond_Head.html

Neil Diamond
http://www.music.sony.com/Music/ArtistInfo/NeilDiamond.html
http://www.diamondville.com/
http://users.aol.com/klerxt/diamondhome.html

Bo Diddley
http://www.codeblue-records.com/diddley.html

Dinosaur Jr.
http://www.RedBrick.dcu.ie/~wibble/dinosaur.jr/index.html

Celine Dion
http://www.music.sony.com/Music/ArtistInfo/CelineDion.html
http://www.netrover.com/~eyevet/celine.html
http://wwwbacc.ift.ulaval.ca/~beauregs/celine/celine_a.html

Dire Straits/Mark Knopfler
http://www-iwi.unisg.ch/~tgygax/ds/index.html
http://www.physics.sunysb.edu/~gene/DS/DS.html
http://www.mark-knopfler.com/

Dokken
http://www.sony.com/Music/ArtistInfo/Dokken/

Thomas Dolby
http://www.kspace.com/KM/spot.sys/Dolby/pages/bio.html
http://flatearth.tdolby.com/

Anna Domino
http://www.walrus.com/~lode/domino/

Donovan
http://www.dur.ac.uk/~d416bb/don/index.html

The Doors
http://www.elektra.com/artists/doors/doors.html
http://www.nwmissouri.edu/~0211170/doors.html
http://www.serv.net/~briansn/doors.html

Dramarama
http://remus.rutgers.edu/~jcf/Drama/drama.html

Dread Zeppelin
http://www.primenet.com/~doeppel/dread/dread.html
http://www.dreadzeppelin.com/

Dream Syndicate
http://www.geofysik.aau.dk/~thomas/wynn/ds.htm

Dream Theater
http://www.elektra.com/artists/dream/dream.html
http://www.cs.brandeis.edu/~mikeb/dt.html

Drivin' N' Cryin'
http://www.geffen.com/dnc/
http://www.auburn.edu:80/~youngdr/dnc/dnc.html

Pete Droge
http://american.recordings.com/American_Artists/Pete_Droge/droge_home.html

Duran Duran
http://hal.cs.uiuc.edu/~smarch/Duranduran.html
http://www.chapman.edu/students/mathur/duran.html

Bob Dylan
http://www.ideasign.com/~nh/
http://bob.nbr.no/
http://www.execpc.com/~billp61/boblink.html

Eagles
http://www.worldonline.nl/~annetted/eagles.html

Ronnie Earl
http://www.wcnet.org/~kjenkins/DIR_ronnieearl/pg_RonnieEarl.html

Steve Earle
http://www.mcs.net/~lisa/EARLE/steve.htm

Sheena Easton
http://remus.rutgers.edu/~ghuliani/sheenapage.html
http://www.kaiwan.com/~namboun/sheena.html
http://www.planet.eon.net/~jim/sheena.html

Echo & the Bunnymen
http://www.netaxs.com/~jgreshes/echo.html

Echobelly
http://www.music.sony.com/Music/ArtistInfo/Echobelly.html
http://www.echobelly.com/
http://www.grfn.org/~mod/echobelly/

Jonathan Edwards
http://www.bicoastal.com/jedwards/

Einsturzende Neübauten
http://www.uib.no/People/henrik/neubauten/

Elastica
http://www.geffen.com/elastica/
http://www.actwin.com/lineup/

Electric Light Orchestra
http://rampages.onramp.net/~myersrj/elo.html

Joe Ely
http://www.ely.com/

Emerson, Lake & Palmer
http://bliss.berkeley.edu/elp/

EMF
http://www.rise.co.uk/emf/

The English Beat
http://www.best.com/~sirlou/uk-beat.html

Enigma
http://www.stud.his.no/~joarg/Enigma.html

Brian Eno
http://www.hyperreal.com/music/artists/brian_eno/

Enya
http://www.bath.ac.uk/~ccsdra/enya/homepage.html

Erasure
http://www.elektra.com/artists/erasure/erasure.html
http://www.europa.com/~carl/erasure_home/

Eric's Trip
http://www.subpop.com/bands/ericstrip/et.html

Roky Erickson
http://www.hyperweb.com/roky/roky.html

Gloria Estefan
http://www.music.sony.com/Music/ArtistInfo/GloriaEstefan.html
http://www.almetco.com/estefan/gloria-1.html

Melissa Etheridge
http://www.polygram.com/metheridge/
http://fanasylum.com/melissa/
http://www.wchat.on.ca/queen/me.htm

Eurythmics
http://imv.aau.dk/~vibber/Eurythmics/Index.html

Everclear
http://www.geocities.com/Paris/2068/
http://www.columbia.edu/~akn7/everclear.html

Everything But the Girl
http://www.ebtg.com

Extreme
http://www.eecs.nwu.edu/~dble-play/extreme.html
http://mars.superlink.net/user/jkramer/extreme.html

The Fabulous Thunderbirds
http://www.quadralay.com/www/Austin/AustinMusic/TBirds/TBirds.html

Fairport Convention
http://www.NovPapyrus.com/fairport/

Faith No More
http://www.RepriseRec.com/FaithNoMore
http://cv.org/index.html

Marianne Faithfull
http://www.planete.net/~smironne/

Mylene Farmer
http://www.geocities.com/Hollywood/2743/mylene.html
http://www.bart.nl/~rdelfgou/farmer.html

Fastbacks
http://nis-www.lanl.gov/~rebecca/fastbacks.html

Melissa Ferrick
http://www.best.com/~kluce/mf.htm

Bryan Ferry
http://www.scp.caltech.edu/~bryan/roxy/

The Figgs
http://www.ithaca.edu/shp/shp97/amontg01/

Firehouse
http://www.ntplx.net/~drieston/firehse.html

The Fixx
http://www.cc.gatech.edu/aimosaic/students/Psych-students/Byrne/Fixx/

The Flamin' Groovies
http://www.webcom.com/~smholt/groovies/

The Flaming Lips
http://www.wbr.com/flaminglips/
http://blake.oit.unc.edu/~beastie/flips/

Fleetwood Mac
http://www.primenet.com/~jkenney/fm/fm.htm

Fleshtones
http://idun.unl.ac.uk/~hfa9colemas/fhof.htm

Flipper
http://american.recordings.com/American_Artists/Flipper/flipper_home.html

A Flock of Seagulls
http://snhungar.kings.edu/AFOS.html

Flop
http://www.music.sony.com/Music/ArtistInfo/Flop.html

Foetus
http://www.music.sony.com/Music/ArtistInfo/Foetus.html
http://members.gnn.com/foetusuber/foetus.html

Dan Fogelberg
http://www.lookup.com/Homepages/77340//fogelberg.html

Foghat
http://www.olywa.net/ralph/foghat.htm

Foo Fighters
http://www.foofighters.com/foo/
http://www.clever.net/foo/
http://www.shu.edu/~bochicvi/foo/foo.html

Steve Forbert
http://dip1.ee.uct.ac.za/music/steve_forbert.html

Julia Fordham
http://www.comp.vuw.ac.nz/~ectophil/jules/

Peter Frampton
http://www.frampton.com/

Frankie Goes to Hollywood
http://www.cs.rulimburg.nl/~antal/fgth/fgth-home.html

Free
http://ernie.bgsu.edu/~adavoli/jb/free/free.html

Frente!
http://www.mammoth.com/mammoth/frente.html

Robert Fripp
http://www.cs.man.ac.uk/aig/staff/toby/et/

Front 242
http://www.waste.org/~terje/front242/

Fugazi
http://www.prism.gatech.edu/~gt1976a/fugazi.html

The Future Sound of London
http://raft.vmg.co.uk/fsol/

G. Love & Special Sauce
http://www.music.sony.com/Music/ArtistInfo/GLoveAndSpecialSauce.html

Peter Gabriel
http://geffen.com/gabriel.html
http://www.cs.clemson.edu/~junderw/pg.html

Galactic Cowboys
http://www.cedarville.edu/student/s1133627/gcowboys.htm
http://ewi.ewi.org/~rroberts/gc/

Diamanda Galas
http://www.sundial.net/~endless/Diamanda.html

Galaxie 500
http://www.intr.net/mlangley/galaxie500/

Rory Gallagher
http://www.hut.fi/~khagelbe/rory.html

Jerry Garcia
http://www.rockweb.com/rwi/jerrytribute/

Danny Gatton
http://www.wam.umd.edu/~sgorospe/Gatton/gatton.html

Marvin Gaye
http://weber.u.washington.edu/~randman/marvin.html

Gene
http://www2.e.kth.se/~e93_jge/Public/gene_unof_home.html

Genesis
http://www.uio.no/~tholter/genesis.html
http://www.brad.ac.uk/~agcatchp/gen_home.html

Gentle Giant
http://www.cs.umass.edu/~barrett/gentlegiant.html

Georgia Satellites
http://fly.hiwaay.net/~dderrick/satellites.html

Lisa Germano
http://www.yankee-siam.com/lisa/lisa.html
http://www.evo.org/html/group/germanolisa.html

Jimmie Dale Gilmore
http://monsterbit.com/jdg/

Gin Blossoms
http://www.prairienet.org/~eharty/gin_blossoms.html

The Go Betweens
http://ourworld.compuserve.com/homepages/Skeleto/

The Go-Go's
http://www.geocities.com/SunsetStrip/3981/

Godflesh
http://www.music.sony.com/Music/ArtistInfo/Godflesh.html
http://rachel.albany.edu/~teo011/godflesh.html

The Golden Palominos
http://ux1.cso.uiuc.edu/~apasulka/gopals/

Gong
http://prog.ari.net/prog/Bands/Gongwyatt/gonghome.html

Goo Goo Dolls
http://www.wbr.com/googoodolls/
http://www.rpi.edu/~velks/GOOGOODOLLS.html

Steve Goodman
http://tigger.cc.uic.edu/~tobyg/sg/good.html

John Gorka
http://www.windham.com/ourmusic/artist_pages/gorka.empty.byartist.html

Grant Lee Buffalo
http://www.fas.harvard.edu/~visel/glb/
http://www.uq.edu.au/~zzsmiffs/GLB/grant.html

Grateful Dead
http://grateful.dead.net/
http://www.u.arizona.edu/~timothys/gd101.html
http://www.cs.cmu.edu/~mleone/dead.html

Great White
http://www.usa.net/~shortdog/great_white/great.html
http://web.syr.edu/~reharnoi/gw.html

Green Day
http://www.RepriseRec.com/Reprise_HTML_Pages/GD_folder/GreenDay
http://www.teleport.com/~ozzzy/

Nanci Griffith
http://www.elektra.com/artists/griffith/griffith.html
http://www.rahul.net/frankf/nanci.html
http://www.sover.net/~rschrull/ngriffith/gchpage.html

Guns N' Roses
http://www.teleport.com/~boerio/gnr-home.html

Arlo Guthrie
http://www.clark.net/pub/downin/cgi-bin/arlonet.html

GWAR
http://www.neckar-alb.de/gwar/Gwar.html
http://www.iuma.com/gwar/

Nina Hagen
http://www.primenet.com/~spork/nina/

Half Japanese
http://www.onr.com/user/java/halfjap.html

Hall & Oates
http://www.pair.com/iwc/hall_oates/
http://www.access.digex.net/~joe/h_and_o.html

Kristen Hall
http://www.windham.com/ourmusic/artist_pages/hall.empty.byartist.html

Peter Hammill
http://anjovis.tky.hut.fi/~ola/music/hammill/

Hanoi Rocks
http://pilleri.spt.fi/~jukka/index.html

John Wesley Harding
http://lemur.magnet.com/~alaken/wes/

Roy Harper
http://www.bilpin.co.uk/stormcock
http://www.helsinki.fi/~akoskine/royharper.html

Emmylou Harris
http://www.elektra.com/artists/harris/harris.html
http://www.nashville.net/~kate/

Mickey Hart
http://grateful.dead.net/band_members/mickey/mh.html

P.J. Harvey
http://www.louisville.edu/~jadouro1/pjh/
http://hamp.hampshire.edu/~temS95/pollyj.htm

Juliana Hatfield
http://www.public.asu.edu/~masonfox/juliana/juliana.html

Sophie B. Hawkins
http://weber.u.washington.edu/~meisner/sophie.html
http://www.wam.umd.edu/~xiaoqin/music/sophie.html

Hawkwind
http://ourworld.compuserve.com/homepages/hawkwind/

Heart
http://www.imt.net/~scooter/Heart.html
http://users.aol.com/mongernet/heart/corner.html

Heaven 17
http://www.path.unimelb.edu.au/~new_wave/17.html

Michael Hedges
http://www.windham.com/ourmusic/artist_pages/hedges.empty.byartist.html

Helium
http://www.matador.recs.com/bios/bio_helium.html
http://www.princeton.com/sbatten/helium/index.html

Hellecasters
http://ro.com/~craigs/camphlle.html

Helmet
http://r2d2.ucsd.edu/helmet/index.html

Jimi Hendrix
http://www.wavenet.com/~jhendrix/
http://www.parks.tas.gov.au/jimi/jimi.html
http://www.prism.gatech.edu/~gt1787a/jimi/index.html
http://www.primenet.com/~mikef1/jimi/jimi.html
http://www.inslab.uky.edu/MailingLists/hey-joe.html

Don Henley
http://members.aol.com/ivyrain/don.htm

John Hiatt
http://www.grooves.com/Discs/10/Html/hiatt.html

Dan Hicks
http://www.ns.net/~chaler/hicks.html

Peter Himmelman
http://www.princeton.edu/~shiny/ph/

His Name Is Alive
http://www.evo.org/html/group/hisnameisalive.html

Robyn Hitchcock
http://www.teleport.com/~capuchin/fegmaniax/

Hole
http://www.albany.net/~rsmith/hole.html
http://www.geffen.com/hole/
http://www.umd.umich.edu/~haibachi/Hole/hole.html

The Hollies
http://www.cae.wisc.edu/~gansler/hollies/hollies.htm

Buddy Holly
http://www.cmgww.com/music/holly/holly.html

The Hoodoo Gurus
http://www.i2020.net/~grendel/gurus.htm

The Hooters
http://www.pitt.edu:81/~shsst12/Hooters1.html

Hootie & the Blowfish
http://www.hootie.com/
http://www.atlantic-records.com/Hootie_&_The_Blowfish/
http://www.thecore.com/~webuser/hootie_html/Hootie.html
http://www.indy.net/~bstegner/hootie/h&btitle.html

Bruce Hornsby & the Range
http://www.tc.umn.edu/nlhome/m097/danio100/bruce/
http://members.aol.com/brhornsby/index.html

Hot Tuna
http://www1.mhv.net/~federici/jorma2.htm

House of Pain
http://www3.tcd.ie/~oreilltj/house.html

Penelope Houston
http://www.iuma.com/IUMA/band_html/Houston,_Penelope.html

Whitney Houston
http://www.aristarec.com/whitney/home.html
http://ourworld.compuserve.com/homepages/Exhale_Tonight/

Human League
http://www.elektra.com/artists/humanleague/human.html
http://www.cityscape.co.uk/users/bt18/human.html

Hunters & Collectors
http://www.mpce.mq.edu.au/~brendan/music/hunnas.html

Janis Ian
http://www.nauticom.net/www/hyperguy/janis.html

Icehouse
http://cc-server9.massey.ac.nz/~bfoster/icehouse/

Incredible String Band
http://dspace.dial.pipex.com/town/square/ac455/index.htm

Indigo Girls
http://www.music.sony.com/Music/ArtistInfo/IndigoGirls.html
http://pages.prodigy.com/Indizone/index.htm

http://www.hidwater.com/lifeblood/ig.html

Information Society
http://acm-www.creighton.edu:80/~duke/insoc/
http://www.c2.net/~ricochet/insoc/

Inspiral Carpets
http://fbox.vt.edu:10021/D/ddouros/ic/moo.html

INXS
http://www.columbia.edu/~sbs34/inxs.html
http://www.public.iastate.edu/~mystify/inxs.html

Iron Maiden
http://www.ironmaiden.co.uk/maiden
http://www.cs.tufts.edu/~stratton/maiden/maiden.html

Chris Isaak
http://www.repriserec.com/ChrisIsaak/
http://fly.hiwaay.net/~mdlatham/isaak.html

The Isley Brothers
http://www.his.com/~vincentl/isleys.htm

Janet Jackson
http://www.mit.edu:8001/people/agoyo1/janet.html
http://fanasylum.com/janet/

Joe Jackson
http://www.cryst.bbk.ac.uk/~ubcg5ab/JJ/joe.html

Michael Jackson
http://www.sony.com/Music/MichaelJackson.html
http://www.qns.com/~scottb/homepage.htm
http://www.ozemail.com.au/~gwoody/
http://fred.net/mjj/

Rick James
http://www.weblive.com/stars/rickjames/

Jane's Addiction
http://uhavax.hartford.edu/~mschulman/shock.html

Jason & the Scorchers
http://edge.edge.net/~hpeek/scorch.html

Jawbox
http://www.his.com/~desoto/jawbox.html

The Jayhawks
http://american.recordings.com/American_Artists/Jayhawks/jayhawks_home.html

Jefferson Airplane/Jefferson Starship
http://grove.ufl.edu/~number6/Jefferson.Airplane/airplane.html
http://www.jstarship.com/

Jellyfish
http://comp.uark.edu/~cbray/jelly/

The Jesus Lizard
http://theochem.uwaterloo.ca/~crowell/jl/

The Jesus & Mary Chain
http://american.recordings.com/American_Artists/Jesus_And_Mary_Chain/jamc_home.html
http://www.chilepac.net/~covicius/JesusAndMaryChain/

Jethro Tull
http://www.illumin.co.uk/chrysalis/tuldex.html
http://www4.ncsu.edu/~rmoneill/tull/tull.html
http://remus.rutgers.edu/JethroTull/

Joan Jett
http://www.wbr.com/joanjett/
http://www.paston.co.uk/blackheart/joanjett/

Jewel
http://www.atlantic-records.com/Jewel/
http://www.nebula.net/~lazlo/jewel/
http://www.umd.umich.edu/~fyd/Jewel/Jewel.html

Billy Joel
http://www.zanzibar.com/
http://www.rpi.edu/~goodsd/BJ/billy.html
http://members.aol.com/bjwebpage/index.html

Elton John
http://itchy.faa.uiuc.edu/elton.html
http://www.rpi.edu/~bodohd/elton.html

Eric Johnson
http://www.inetport.com/~jdekan/eric/

Freedy Johnston
http://www.elektra.com/artists/freedy/freedy.html

Howard Jones
http://www.amug.org/~hojoinfo/index.html

Tom Jones
http://www.kspace.com/jones/

Janis Joplin
http://www.dur.ac.uk/~d416bb/serge/main.htm
http://www.dartmouth.edu/~modred/janis.html

Journey
http://webcom.net/~sdlake/journey.html

Joy Division
http://www.wbr.com/JoyDivision
http://slashmc.rice.edu/ceremony/ceremony.html

Judas Priest
http://www.edu.isy.liu.se/~c93patwe/priest/

The Judybats
http://copper.ucs.indiana.edu/~mrstone/judybats.html

Brenda Kahn
http://mindlink.bc.ca/a404/brenda.htm

Kansas
http://www.traveller.com/~rew/kansas.html

K.C. & the Sunshine Band
http://www.geocities.com/Hollywood/4471/kc.htm

Tommy Keene
http://www.matador.recs.com/bios/bio_tommy.html

Nik Kershaw
http://www.ida.com.au/~drew/kershaw/

Killing Joke
http://onyx.dartmouth.edu/~dupras/kj/kj.html

King Crimson
http://www.cs.man.ac.uk/aig/staff/toby/et/
http://www.rockslide.com/crimson/

King Diamond
http://www.atcon.com/staff/petef/king.diamond/

King Missle
http://www.con.wesleyan.edu/~cooper/missile/kingmissile.html

King's X
http://www.willamette.edu/~gsweeten/kingsx/
http://mars.superlink.net/user/jkramer/kingsx.html

B.B. King
http://bbking.mca.com/
http://www.worldblues.com/

The Kinks
http://www.inetbiz.com/blackmon/

Kiss
http://asylum.cid.com/aure/kiss/
http://www.buffnet.net/~toefer/
http://www.westnet.com/~gizmad/kiss.html
http://www.nextlevel.com/firehouse/
http://www.wku.edu/www/kiss.html

KIX
http://www.microserve.net/~chuck/kix/kix.html

KLF
http://www.york.ac.uk/~ph100/HTML.Mike/KLF.html
http://www.edu.isy.liu.se/~d91johol/KLF/

KMFDM
http://www.xnet.com/~kmfdm/
http://www.phlab.missouri.edu/~c510292/kmfdm/

Kraftwerk
http://www.cs.umu.se/tsdf/KRAFTWERK/

Lenny Kravitz
http://www.vmg.co.uk/lennykravitz/
http://ourworld.compuserve.com/homepages/kilmernock/circus.htm

Kyuss
http://www.elektra.com/artists/kyuss/kyuss.html

Laibach
http://stud1.tuwien.ac.at/~e9002080/level1/Industrial/laibach.html

k.d. lang
http://www.infohouse.com/obvious-gossip/
http://www.wbr.com/kdlang/

Last Poets
http://www.trilliumproductions.com/tlphp.htm

Bill Laswell
http://www.hyperreal.com:80/music/labels/axiom/

Cyndi Lauper
http://www.htw-dresden.de/~sfw2010/cyndi/welcome.htm
http://www.shebute.com/Vlab/cl/

Led Zeppelin
http://www.pathcom.com/~rapallof/emagic.html
http://www.dnaco.net/~buckeye/lz.html
http://cadman.cit.buffalo.edu/~bhaga-z/
http://www.tdx.org/~fagan/zep/
http://acs5.bu.edu:8001/~buddha/ledzep.html

The Left Banke
http://members.aol.com/bocad/leftbank.htm

The Lemonheads
http://www.students.uiuc.edu/~cfwillis/lemonheads.html

John Lennon
http://www.missouri.edu/~c588349/john-page.html
http://www.ecnet.com/home/akira/

Julian Lennon
http://www.feline.org/feline/valotte.html

Annie Lennox
http://www.aristarec.com/annie/home.html

Level 42
http://kumo.swcp.com/synth/level42/
http://www.worldmachine.com/level42/

Huey Lewis & the News
http://www.prism.gatech.edu/~jw157/hl/

Jerry Lee Lewis
http://www.elektra.com/artists/jerrylee/jerry.html
http://members.tripod.com/~Jerry9/Fire.htm

Gordon Lightfoot
http://www.mmlc.nwu.edu/~mfifer/lightfoot/index.html

The Lightning Seeds
http://techst02.technion.ac.il/~c1021351/Seeds/seeds.html

Little Feat
http://www.ultranet.com/~amygoode/FEATS.HTML

Live
http://live.cerf.net/
http://www.dru.nl/live.html

Living Colour
http://www.willamette.edu/~cwick/living_colour.html
http://www.megaton.com/host/LivingColour/

Nils Lofgren
http://www.rockhouse.com/nils/

Lords of Acid
http://american.recordings.com/American_Artists/Lords_Of_Acid/lords_home.html
http://www.ee.fit.edu/users/ccurtis/lords/

Los Lobos
http://www.wbr.com/loslobos/

Love and Rockets
http://american.recordings.com/American_Artists/Love_And_Rockets/loverox_home.html
http://www.vistech.net/users/jameson/lr/

Lyle Lovett
http://pathfinder.com/curb/Artists/ll.html
http://www.geocities.com/SoHo/1192/lyle.html

L7
http://www.directnet.com/Crash/Music/L7/

Lulu
http://www.oberlin.edu/~gjohnson/lulu/lulu1.html

Lydia Lunch
http://www.musicwest.com/MW/Artists/L/LydiaLunch/index.html
http://www.evo.org/html/group/lunchlydia.html

Lush
http://mugwump.ucsd.edu/bkeeley/play-stuff/lush/lush.html
http://www.evo.org/html/group/lush.html

Lynyrd Skynyrd
http://www.ici.net/cust_pages/tsoares/skynyrd.html

Madness
http://www.uea.ac.uk/~u9530037/madness/
http://huizen.dds.nl/~dag/madness/

Madonna
http://www.wbr.com/madonna
http://www.buffnet.net/~steve772/maddy.html
http://www.geocities.com/Hollywood/2837/
http://www.mit.edu:8001/people/jwb/Madonna.html
http://www.cbvcp.com/c2/madonna.html

Magnapop
http://www.comland.com/~darrend/magnapop.htm

Yngwie Malmsteen
http://www.lewisentertainment.com/yngwie/ym_home.htm
http://pd.net/yngwie/

Aimee Mann
http://www.geffen.com/aimeemann/

Manic Street Preachers
http://www.cs.nott.ac.uk/~jwl/Manics/
http://www.niweb.com/tony/manics/

Marilyn Manson
http://www.pangea.ca/~sinful/MarilynManson/index.html

Marillion/Fish
http://www.mv.com:80/users/hogarth/Marillion/
http://www.let.ruu.nl/~jeroen/web/
http://www.livjm.ac.uk/fish/

Bob Marley
http://student-www.uchicago.edu/users/djrivera/marley.html

Dave Mason
http://members.aol.com/ditum/index.htm
http://members.aol.com/smacdoug/index.htm

Material Issue
http://freakcity.slu.edu/

Johnny Mathis
http://www.sony.com/Music/ArtistInfo/JohnnyMathis/

Dave Matthews Band
http://liberty.uc.wlu.edu/~ajacob/dmb/

Mazzy Star
http://www.unc.edu/~hondo/mazzy.html

MC5
http://ourworld.compuserve.com/homepages/rauk/mc-5.htm

MC 900 Ft. Jesus
http://american.recordings.com/American_Artists/MC_900FT_Jesus/mc_home.html

Paul McCartney
http://www.halcyon.com/marieg/paul.html

Maria McKee
http://www.geffen.com/maria/
http://www.hgs.se/~nf95166/index.htm
http://www.zipnet.net/users/bourbeau/diva.html

Sarah McLachlan
http://www.nettwerk.com/artists/SarMc.html
http://shakti.trincoll.edu/~kthompso/sarah/visual.html
http://members.aol.com/froggyjen/sarah/sarah1.htm
http://www.webcom.com/~donh/sarah/

James McMurty
http://www.imperium.net/~echidna/

Meat Loaf
http://www.voicenet.com/~hlavacek/index.html

Meat Puppets
http://www.polygram.com/polygram/island/artists/meat_puppets/

Mega City Four
http://www.cityscape.co.uk/users/fm93/badmoon/megacityfour/mega.html

Megadeth
http://caprec.digilink.net/Megadeth/megadeth.html
http://www.cs.vu.nl/~rfennema/megadeth/

The Mekons
http://www.gold.net/ellipsis/mekons/

John Cougar Mellencamp
http://spruce.evansville.edu/~tb8/mellencamp.html

Melvins
http://www.community.net/~buster/melvins.html

Men without Hats
http://www.mit.edu:8001/people/tobye/mwh/mwh.html

Natalie Merchant
http://www.elektra.com/artists/merchant/merchant.html
http://www.primenet.com./~infomas/natalie.html

Metal Church
http://www.rt66.com/sloppy/metal_church/index.html

Metallica
http://www.elektra.com/artists/metallica/metallica.html
http://www.galstar.com/~cfh/metal.html
http://spock.pluggnet.se/~metalman/index.html

George Michael
http://www.iwo.com/gmichael/
http://www.ozemail.com.au/~alhatu/gm.htm

Bette Midler
http://www.interactive8.com/bette/
http://www.cdc.net/~bparcrtv/bette.html

Midnight Oil
http://www.stevens-tech.edu/~dbelson/oilbase/

Mike & the Mechanics
http://www.brad.ac.uk/~agcatchp/mr/rutherford.html

Milla
http://www.emirec.com/milla/

Steve Miller Band
http://www.stevemillerband.com/
http://sac.uky.edu/~mcabboo/index.html

Ministry/Revolting Cocks
http://www.wbr.com/Ministry
http://pulsar.cs.wku.edu/~gizzard/ministry.html
http://pubweb.acns.nwu.edu/%7epenielse/revco.htm

Miranda Sex Garden
http://bock.physics.sunysb.edu/~jng/msg/

The Misfits
http://watt.seas.virginia.edu/~msk4m/

Mr. Big
http://www.electriciti.com/mrbig/index.html

Joni Mitchell
http://www.well.com/user/wallyb/jonihome.html

Moby
http://www.elektra.com/artists/moby/moby.html
http://mindvox.phantom.com/~hymn/moby.html

Moby Grape
http://www.geocities.com/Sunset-Strip/1256/

Modern English
http://www.evo.org/html/group/modernenglish.html

The Monkees
http://www.primenet.com/~flex/monkees.html
http://www.csam.montclair.edu/~colli/monkees.html

Moody Blues
http://is.usmo.com/~sojourn/
http://kbt.com:80/moodies/

Gary Moore
http://www.bourgoin.holowww.com/GM/

Morbid Angel
http://www.globaldialog.com/~leda/ma/index.html

Alanis Morissette
http://www.RepriseRec.com/Alanis
http://www.geekweb.com/~prsitko/
http://www.PERnet.net/~rbarrow1/alanis.htm
http://www.sgi.net/alanis/

Morphine
http://www.ai.mit.edu/~stevec/morphine/morphine.html

Van Morrison
http://www.harbour.sfu.ca/~hayward/van/van.html

Morrissey
http://www.RepriseRec.com/Morrissey
http://www.public.iastate.edu/~moz/

Steve Morse
http://www.windham.com/ourmusic/artist_pages/steve_morse.empty.byartist.html

Motley Crüe
http://www.elektra.com/artists/motley/motley.html
http://www.io.org/~motley1/m.crue/cruepage.html

Motorhead
http://fermi.clas.virginia.edu/~sha3u/motorhead/motorhead.html

Mountain
http://www.lewisentertainment.com/mountain/mtnhome.htm

The Move
http://www.ici.net/cust_pages/bad/move.html

Mudhoney
http://www.RepriseRec.com/Mudhoney

The Muffs
http://www.RepriseRec.com/The-Muffs

Elliott Murphy
http://www.bangos.com/bluroso/artists/murphy/elliott.htm

Peter Murphy
http://www.atlantic-records.com/Peter_Murphy/
http://www.itis.com/murphy/

My Bloody Valentine
http://www.triplo.com/mbv/index.html

My Life with the Thrill Kill Kult
http://pulsar.cs.wku.edu/~draven/tk.html

Naked Raygun
http://www.tezcat.com/~gdd/raygun.html

Nelson
http://www.geffen.com/nelson/

The Neville Brothers
http://www.comm.net/nevilles/
http://www.his.com/~georgeg/neville.html

New Kids on the Block
http://www.colby.edu/personal/jhbrown/nkotb.html
http://www.nkotb.com/

New Model Army
http://www.interlog.com/~cb/

New Order
http://slashmc.rice.edu/ceremony/ceremony.html

Randy Newman
http://weber.u.washington.edu/~jcoan/RN/index.html

Olivia Newton-John
http://www-leland.stanford.edu/~clem/

Stevie Nicks
http://web2.airmail.net/jkinney/

Nico
http://www.geocities.com/Paris/1781/index.html

Night Ranger
http://www.concentric.net/~eclcons/kdavis/Nightranger/

Harry Nilsson
http://www.magicnet.net/~rasmith/nilsson.html

Nine Inch Nails
http://nothing.nin.net/
http://uslink.net/~cpunut/nin.html
http://WWW.PRAIRIENET.ORG/~konkers/ninfaq.html

Nirvana
http://seds.lpl.arizona.edu/~smiley/nirvana/home.html

http://www.walrus.com/~dreamlog/nirvana/
http://www.westol.com/~cheese18/nirvana.html
http://www2.cybernex.net/~seiji/nirvana.html

Ted Nugent
http://thunder.indstate.edu/h5/jn-gonzo/.nuge.html
http://www.outdoors.net/tednugent/index.html

Gary Numan
http://www.numan.co.uk/
http://www.nuzone.org.uk/

Laura Nyro
http://www-unix.oit.umass.edu/~glens/nyro.html

Oasis
http://www.oasisinet.com/
http://www.uea.ac.uk/~u9530053/oasisteria.htm

Phil Ochs
http://www.cs.pdx.edu/~trent/ochs/

Sinead O' Connor
http://www.engr.ukans.edu/~jrussell/music/sinead/sinead.html

Offspring
http://members.tripod.com/~Jetter/TheOffspring

Oingo Boingo
http://www.oingoboingo.com/

Yoko Ono
http://yoko.com/

Orb
http://www.hyperreal.com:80/music/artists/orb/www/

Roy Orbison
http://stm1.chem.psu.edu/~krk/orbison/RoyOrbison.html

Orbital
http://www.york.ac.uk/~wjb101/orbital/

Orchestral Manoeuvres in the Dark
http://www.accessone.com/~fester/index.htm

Joan Osborne
http://www.rockweb.com/bands/joan-osborne/
http://members.aol.com/drldeboer2/htm/jo.htm

Ozzy Osbourne
http://www.music.sony.com/Music/ArtistInfo/OzzyOsbourne.html
http://ourworld.compuserve.com/homepages/MITCH_VANBEEKUM/

The Oysterband
http://www.sussex.ac.uk/Users/kcci1/Oysterband/

Pale Saints
http://www.evo.org/html/group/palesaints.html

Pantera
http://www.elektra.com/artists/pantera/pantera.html
http://www.umd.umich.edu/~alfieii/pantera/pantera.html
http://gwis2.circ.gwu.edu/~pantera/music/Pantera/

Graham Parker
http://reality.sgi.com/employees/howells/gparker.html

Alan Parsons Project
http://www.roadkill.com/APP/

Gram Parsons
http://www.primenet.com/~klugl/gramhome.html

Pavement
http://www.matador.recs.com/bios/bio_pavement.html
http://www.pitt.edu/~rabst59/pave/pave.html

Pearl Jam
http://dst.net/pj/
http://users.aol.com/pearljam92/rockin/pj/pj.htm
http://www.hamline.edu/personal/matjohns/pearljam/index.html
http://www.geocities.com/Hollywood/1889/
http://Shinbone.Psych.Brown.Edu/pj/zine/release.html

Pell Mell
http://www.geffen.com/pellmell/

Michael Penn
http://www.proex.com/t-bone/m_penn/m_penn.htm

Pere Ubu
http://www.dnai.com/~obo/ubu/index.html

Pet Shop Boys
http://www.dsv.su.se/~matsbjo/psb/psbhome.html
http://home.interlynx.net/~rwerner/psb/

Tom Petty & the Heartbreakers
http://www.sbbs.se/com/home/est/petty/indiana.html

Liz Phair
http://www.matador.recs.com/bios/bio_liz.html
http://www.armory.com/~fisheye/lpml.html

Sam Phillips
http://www.niweb.com/tony/sam/

Phish
http://www.elektra.com/artists/phish/phish.html
http://www.sccs.swarthmore.edu/~josh/Phish.html

Pink Floyd
http://www.music.sony.com/Music/ArtistInfo/PinkFloyd.html
http://humper.student.princeton.edu:80/floyd/
http://www.mtnlake.com/~robp/floyd1.html
http://www.smartlink.net/~migre.v/floyd/
http://www.vnet.net/users/pinkflyd/pf/

Pixies
http://www.eis.enac.dgac.fr:8001/~biel/pixies/

Pizzacato 5
http://www.matador.recs.com/bios/bio_p5.html
http://www2.hawaii.edu/~evaldez/pizzicato5/pizzicato5.htm

Plasmatics
http://www.io.com/~triske/plasma.html

Plastikman
http://www.rpi.edu/~desais2/plastikman.html

PM Dawn
http://www.eelab.newpaltz.edu/~harple31/pm.dawn/index.html

The Pogues
http://140.249.8.212/pogues/
http://www2.linknet.net/deadair/pogues/

Poi Dog Pondering
http://www.poiHQ.com/poi/

Poison
http://www.io.org/~lindaw/Poison.html

The Police
http://mail.bcpl.lib.md.us/~mmugmon/message.html
http://violet.berkeley.edu:8080/

Porno for Pyros
http://www.wbr.com/pornoforpyros/

Portishead
http://gladstone.uoregon.edu/~jbunik/portishead.html

The Posies
http://www.slumberland.com/dear23.html

Poster Children
http://www.prairienet.org/posterkids/

Prefab Sprout
http://www.xs4all.nl/~elfasih/muziek/prefabs.html

The Presidents of the United States of America
http://www.sony.com/Music/ArtistInfo/Presidents/

Elvis Presley
http://members.aol.com/elvisnet/index.html
http://sunsite.unc.edu/elvis/elvishom.html

The Pretenders
http://www.wbr.com/pretenders

Primal Scream
http://www.music.sony.com/Music/ArtistInfo/PrimalScream.html

Primus
http://www.primussucks.com/
http://www.serve.com/Philm/suck.htm

Prince
http://www.nuvo.net/hammer/prince.html
http://www710.univ-lyon1.fr/%7Eburzlaff/uptown.html
http://members.aol.com/trupfan/alphabet.htm

Public Enemy
http://spider.media.philips.com/defjam/artists/pe/enemy.html

Public Image Ltd.
http://www2.ucsc.edu/people/liston/pil/

Pulp
http://www.rise.co.uk/pulp/

The Pursuit of Happiness
http://www2.excite.sfu.ca/jot/tpoh/

Pylon
http://www.mindspring.com/~dfish/pylon/index.html

Queen
http://www.hollywoodrec.com/HollywoodRecords/Musicians/Queen/queen_homepg.html
http://queen-fip.com/
http://iinet.net.au/~orchard/
http://members.gnn.com/RVQueenFC/rvmain.htm

Queensrÿche
http://www.emirec.com/qryche/
http://www.mcs.net/~ryche/

Quicksilver Messenger Service
http://www.epix.net/~brett/qms/qms1.html

Radiohead
http://www.abacom.com/~jfdufour/

Rage Against the Machine
http://www.music.sony.com/Music/ArtistInfo/RageAgainstTheMachine.html
http://www.geocities.com/SunsetStrip/3440/index.html

Railway Children
http://www.cityscape.co.uk/users/ej77/TRC.html

The Ramones
http://www.radioactive.net/BANDS/RAMONES/index.shtml
http://www.albany.edu/~orrin/ramones.html

Chris Rea
http://www.elektra.com/artists/rea/rea.html

Red Hot Chili Peppers
http://www.wbr.com/chilipeppers
http://www.treknet.is/saemund/redhot.htm
http://members.gnn.com/BSnow/venus.htm

Red House Painters
http://www.dhp.com/~ash/rhp/

Otis Redding
http://ernie.bgsu.edu/~adavoli/otis.html

The Reducers
http://members.aol.com/Reducers/index.html

Lou Reed
http://www.poiHQ.com/loureed/

Terry Reid
http://pilot.msu.edu/user/hernan49/links/terry/tr_index.htm

R.E.M.
http://www.stipey.com/
http://www.inmind.com/people/teague/rem.html
http://www.panix.com/~spyro/rem/remhome.html
http://www.svs.com/rem/

The Rembrandts
http://www.elektra.com/artists/rembrandts/rembrandts.html
http://home.navisoft.com/rembrandts/page1.html

Renaissance
http://www.peabody.jhu.edu/~gaines/renaissa.htm

REO Speedwagon
http://icradio.su.ic.ac.uk/music/bands/reo/
http://members.aol.com/REOphile/index.html

The Replacements/Paul Westerberg
http://www.novia.net/~matt/sky/skyway.html
http://users.aol.com/paulspage/main.htm

The Residents
http://www.csd.uwo.ca/Residents/

Paul Revere & the Raiders
http://www.cris.com/~msmoo/revere/prr.html

Cliff Richard
http://www.starnet.com.au/~shep-pard/2cliff.html

Keith Richards
http://www.ts.umu.se/~krl/keef.html

Jonathan Richman/Modern Lovers
http://harp.rounder.com/rounder/artists/richmanjonathan/richman.html

Ride
http://weber.u.washington.edu/~fearless/ride.html
http://ucsub.colorado.edu/~grier/ride.html

Tom Robinson Band
http://www.demon.co.uk/control/tr.html

Rocket from the Crypt
http://www.resource.com/rocket/

The Rolling Stones
http://www.stonesworld.com/
http://camel.conncoll.edu/ccother/sf.folder/exile/exile.html
http://homepage.seas.upenn.edu/~demarco/stones/breakfast.html
http://www.stones.com/
http://www1.primenet.com/~jaaiii/

Linda Ronstadt
http://www.elektra.com/artists/ron-stadt/ronstadt.html
http://ourworld.compuserve.com/homepages/eric_herni/

Diana Ross
http://dianaross.com/

Roxette
http://www.icon.co.za/~tider/

Roxy Music
http://www.scp.caltech.edu/~bryan/roxy/

The Runaways
http://www.ite.his.se/ite/~c95chrha/secrets.html

Todd Rundgren
http://www.roadkill.com/todd/trconn

Rush
http://syrinx.umd.edu/rush.html
http://www.pb.net/usrwww/w_beaker/rush.html

Leon Russell
http://users.aol.com/leonrussel/leonaol.htm

The Rutles
http://www.primenet.com/~dhaber/rutles.html

Sade
http://www.music.sony.com/Music/ArtistInfo/Sade.html
http://www.diku.dk/~terra/sade/

Saga
http://www.bonaire.com/saga014.html

The Samples
http://gladstone.uoregon.edu/~jtor-bert/samples/samples.html

Santana
http://www.santana.com/

Joe Satriani
http://www.satriani.com/

School of Fish
http://www-scf.usc.edu/~mmaramot/sof_home-page.html

Klaus Schulze
http://www.eecs.uic.edu/~jstam-ato/ks/klaus_schulze.html

Scorpions
http://www.csc.tntech.edu/~ggmor-ton/scorpion.html

Screaming Trees
http://www.sony.dreammedia.com/Epic/artistdetail.qry?artistid=150

Seal
http://www.wbr.com/seal/
http://pantheon.cis.yale.edu/~ariedels/seal.html

Seam
http://www.citynet.net/personal/mick/index.htm

Sebadoh
http://www.cafeliberty.com/se-badoh/

Seefeel
http://hyperreal.com/music/artists/seefeel/seefeel.html

The Seekers
http://www.dur.ac.uk/~d3fube/Seekers.html

Bob Seger
http://walden.mo.net/~rhall/seger.html
http://www4.ncsu.edu/~kreimer/WWW/seger.html

Sepultura
http://www.lut.fi/~moro/sepu.html

Sex Pistols
http://www.sexpistols.com/
http://www.atlas.co.uk/tibco/

Shamen
http://w3.adb.gu.se/~s94dalle/shamen.html

Shampoo
http://www.io.org/~peterw/Sham-poo/Shampoo.html

Sheila E.
http://www.viainc.com/sheilaE/

Shonen Knife
http://www.netropolis.net/shonen/knife/shrine.htm

Shudder to Think
http://www.pitt.edu/~jlrst55/shud

Jane Siberry
http://www.RepriseRec.com/JaneSi-berry
http://malletp.psyc.queensu.ca/siberry/

Simon & Garfunkel
http://www.dur.ac.uk/~d213ga/

Carly Simon
http://www.aristarec.com/carly/home.html
http://www.ziva.com/carly/

Paul Simon
http://www.best.com/~rlai/Paul-Simon.html

Simple Minds
http://matahari.cv.com/people/Simon.Cornwell/simple_minds/

Simply Red
http://www.elektra.com/artists/red/red.html
http://www.simplyred.co.uk/

Frank Sinatra
http://www.io.org/~buff/sinatra.html
http://www.sinatra.com/club/

Siouxsie & the Banshees
http://www.vamp.org/Siouxsie/

Sisters of Mercy
http://www.cm.cf.ac.uk/Sisters.Of.Mercy/

Skid Row
http://www.atlantic-records.com/Skid_Row/
http://fanasylum.com/skidrow/

Skinny Puppy
http://www.cling.gu.se/~cl3polof/central/

Slade
http://www.tdh.no/~stromo/slade.html

Slayer
http://american.recordings.com/American_Artists/Slayer/slayer_home.html

Sloan
http://www.iaw.on.ca/seant/sloan/sloan.html

Slowdive
http://www.musicbase.co.uk/music/creation/slowdive/

Sly & the Family Stone/GrahamCentral Station
http://www.columbia.edu/~jhd10/funkpub/family.html

Smashing Pumpkins
http://www.cae.wisc.edu/~agnew/sp.html
http://www.muohio.edu/~carmance/sp.html
http://cs.gfc.edu/~snickeso/sp/index.html
http://home.sol.no/floy/music.htm

Patti Smith
http://www.access.digex.net/~fi/patti.htm

Chris Smither
http://www.intermarket.net/~stessa/smither/

The Smiths
http://www.public.iastate.edu/~moz/

Jill Sobule
http://www.atlantic-records.com/Jill_Sobule/

Social Distortion
http://www2.globaldialog.com/sxdx/sxdx.html

Soft Cell
http://www.iti.gov.sg/almond/

Son Volt
http://chattanooga.net/~mlumley/son_volt/son_volt.htm

Sonic Youth
http://www.geffen.com/sonic-youth/
http://mmm.mbhs.edu/~wdeng/sy.html

Soul Asylum
http://www.music.sony.com/Music/ArtistInfo/SoulAsylum.html
http://www.achilles.net/~tedd/sapage.html

Soundgarden
http://www.sgi.net/soundgarden/
http://www.rocktropolis.com/Soundgarden/index.html

John David Souther
http://ourworld.compuserve.com/homepages/eric_herni/souther.htm

Southside Johnny & the Asbury Jukes
http://pease1.sr.unh.edu/1/southside/

Spacemen 3
http://www.pacificnet.net/~xibalba/sp3/spacemen3.html

Sparks
http://www.skynet.co.uk/doremi/sparks/

The Specials
http://www-scf.usc.edu/~keep/

Spin Doctors
http://www.sony.dreammedia.com/Epic/artistdetail.qry?artistid=162
http://www.levity.com/spindoctors/index.html

Spinal Tap
http://www.spinaltap.com/
http://www.voyagerco.com/spinaltap/

Spirit
http://kspace.com/spirit

Spiritualized
http://www.spiritualized.com/

Split Enz
http://www.aswas.com/splitenz/

Sponge
http://www.sony.com/Music/ArtistInfo/Sponge/

Rick Springfield
http://www1.aksi.net/~luvs2luv/rick.htm

Bruce Springsteen
http://www.music.sony.com/Music/ArtistInfo/BruceSpringsteen.html
http://www.helsinki.fi/~tsmalmbe/bruce_springsteen/bruce.htm
http://www.iac.es/galeria/msteineg/bruce.html
http://www.everyday.se/people/pac/oscar/bruce/
http://www.mcs.net/~kvk/luckytown.html

Squeeze
http://songwriting.com/squeeze

Ringo Starr
http://web2.airmail.net/gshultz/

Status Quo
http://www.sn.no/~qwerty/quo.html

Steely Dan
http://pathfinder.com/steelydan
http://www.seanet.com/Users/stalfnzo/steeldan.html
http://pages.prodigy.com/steelydan/

Stereolab
http://www.maths.monash.edu.au/people/rjh/stereolab/

Cat Stevens
http://www.dashing.com/dash/cat/index.html
http://www.oberlin.edu/~amarcus/cat/cat.html

Al Stewart
http://www.fish.com/music/al_stewart/

John Stewart
http://www.sfo.com/~wondrdog/jstewart/

Rod Stewart
http://www.wbr.com/rodstewart/

Stiff Little Fingers
http://www.dcez.com/~ssexton/slf/

Sting
http://www.Rocktropolis.com/Sting/index.html
http://www.ot.com/sting/

http://www.rrz.uni-koeln.de/wiso-fak/wisostatsem/autoren/sting/index.html

Stone Roses
http://geffen.com/sroses.html
http://www.cm.cf.ac.uk/User/J.R.Candy/roses.html

Stone Temple Pilots
http://gpu.srv.ualberta.ca/~vchan/stp.html
http://www.mlode.com/~guzzetta/stp/stp.html

Strangelove
http://www.geocities.com/SunsetStrip/1119/strange.htm

The Stranglers
http://users.colloquium.co.uk/~g_smith/strangle.htm

Syd Straw
http://ourworld.compuserve.com/homepages/gregoryp/syds.htm

The Stray Cats
http://human1.comp.kyutech.ac.jp/~tsubu/cats/

Styx
http://www.tiac.net/users/kat/Styx/index.html

The Subdudes
http://www.the-subdudes.com/

Suede
http://members.aol.com/SuedeNet/index.htm

Suicidal Tendencies
http://www.music.sony.com/Music/ArtistInfo/SuicidalTendencies.html

Donna Summer
http://innovationstation.psych.yorku.ca/Zone/

The Sundays
http://165.154.1.3/~jacke/sundays.html

Superchunk
http://www-personal.umich.edu/~mransfrd/superchunk/

Supergrass
http://www.cee.hw.ac.uk/~ceebsm/Supergrass/

Supersuckers
http://www.isl.net/~runyon/suckers.html

Supertramp
http://huizen.dds.nl/~suptramp/

Swans
http://www.netreach.net/~bishop/swans/swans.html

Sweet
http://www.u-net.com/~thesweet/

Matthew Sweet
http://www.afn.org/~afn04314/msweet.htm
http://www.cen.uiuc.edu/~e-dahl/newmenu.htm

David Sylvain
http://dut002.tudelft.nl/~keesjan/music/sylvian/index.html

Talk Talk
http://www.mpce.mq.edu.au/~brendan/music/talktalk.html

Talking Heads
http://www.bart.nl/~francey/th.html
http://penguin.cc.ukans.edu/Heads/Talking_Heads.html

Tangerine Dream
http://www.oslonett.no/~mmoen/tadream/

James Taylor
http://www.music.sony.com/Music/ArtistInfo/JamesTaylor.html
http://www.shore.net/~jrisberg/JT.html

Tears for Fears
http://www.sony.com/Music/ArtistInfo/TearsForFears/
http://users.aimnet.com/~markg/tears4fears/
http://www.luminet.net/~tsonsall/

Teenage Fanclub
http://www.geffen.com/teenage/

10cc
http://www.pacifier.com/~mikes/10cc/10cc.html

10,000 Maniacs
http://www.elektra.com/artists/maniacs/maniacs.html
http://www.maniacs.com/home/
http://ally.ios.com/~jec/

Ten Years After
http://www.bekkoame.or.jp/~tadatk/music/tenyrsaftr.html

Tesla
http://taurus.cira.colostate.edu/tesla/tesla.html

Texas
http://huizen.dds.nl/~miura/texas/texas.htm

that dog
http://www.geffen.com/thatdog/

The The
http://www.music.sony.com/Music/ArtistInfo/TheThe.html
http://www.io.com/~fabiol/the_the.html

Therapy?
http://www.compapp.dcu.ie/~c2dclark/therapy/home.html

They Might Be Giants
http://www.elektra.com/artists/tmbg/tmbg.html
http://www.tmbg.org/

Thin Lizzy
http://www.uncg.edu/~edpoole/

Thinking Fellers Union Local #282
http://www.matador.recs.com/bios/bio_tful.html

.38 Special
http://www.38special.com/

This Mortal Coil
http://userwww.sfsu.edu/~hhngo/tmc/This.Mortal.Coil.html

The Thompson Twins/Babble
http://www.interlog.com/~ditko37/ttwins.html
http://www.austech.com.au/entertain/babble/babble.html

Richard Thompson
http://www.mel.dit.csiro.au/~sfy/RT/

Throbbing Gristle
http://www.ing.umu.se/~da95jhn/tg.html

Throwing Muses
http://www.evo.org/html/group/throwingmuses.html

The Time
http://morra.et.tudelft.nl/npn/music/the_time/

Tindersticks
http://huizen.dds.nl/~totos/tinder.htm

Toad the Wet Sprocket
http://www.music.sony.com/Music/ArtistInfo/Toad/index.html
http://www.prairienet.org/arts/listen/toad.html

Too Much Joy
http://www.cybercom.net/~jesse/tmj/

Toto
http://www.euronet.nl/users/sazias/

Tower of Power
http://www.rock.n.roll.com/TOP/

Traffic
http://www.fas.harvard.edu/~stribble/sw/traffic.html

Tragically Hip
http://www.thehip.com/thehip.htm
http://www.tuns.ca/~hillba/hip.html

Transvision Vamp
http://web.syr.edu/~smsinger/trans.htm

Tina Turner
http://riverland1.riv.nl/emi/pop/tinaturner/t1.htm

Twisted Sister
http://exo.com/~bobn/sister.html

Type O Negative
http://lx1.benp.wau.nl/people/jgkoops/typeo.html

U2
http://www.panix.com/~henryw/zootv/index.html
http://www.il.ft.hse.nl/~jinx/u2/
http://www.students.uiuc.edu/~mahieu/zootv.htm
http://boris.qub.ac.uk/tony/u2/
http://www.panix.com/~henryw/new/u2/

UFO
http://www.csv.warwick.ac.uk/~masai/ufo/
http://www.leonardo.net/wagamama/ufopage/index.html

U.K. Subs
http://www.nol.net/~dfx/uksubs.html

James Blood Ulmer
http://www.music.sony.com/Music/ArtistInfo/JamesBloodUlmer.html

Ultra Vivid Scene
http://www.evo.org/html/group/ultravividscene.html

Ultravox
http://www.geocities.com/SiliconValley/9463/fixion.html

Uncle Tupelo
http://www4.ncsu.edu/eos/users/s/sdhouse/Mosaic/uncle-tupelo.html
http://www.webcom.com/~gumbo/uncle-tupelo.html

Unrest
http://faraday.clas.virginia.edu/~alb7j/
http://www.evo.org/html/group/unrest.html

Urge Overkill
http://www.geffen.com/uo/
http://www.fanbase.com/urgeoverkill/
http://www.tezcat.com/~andy/urge/

Uriah Heep
http://home.pacific.net.sg/~hani/heep1.htm

Steve Vai
http://www.vai.com/
http://www.kumar.net/ace/sv/
http://www.cs.trinity.edu/~kclark/vaitop.html
http://www.hit.no/~u952640/vaieng.html

Van Der Graaf Generator
http://www.compusmart.ab.ca/tbennett/hammill.htm

Luther Vandross
http://www.music.sony.com/Music/ArtistInfo/LutherVandross.html

Ben Vaughn
http://www.webxfm.com/vaughn.html

Jimmie Vaughan
http://www.music.sony.com/Music/ArtistInfo/JimmieVaughan.html

Stevie Ray Vaughan
http://members.aol.com/SRVMemFund/MVaughan.htm
http://www.pla-net.net/~dreppa/
http://carmen.murdoch.edu.au/~adriang/
http://www.clark.net/pub/tzamer/
http://http.tamu.edu:8000/~tma2280/srv/index.html

Suzanne Vega
http://www.vega.net/

Velvet Crush
http://www.music.sony.com/Music/ArtistInfo/VelvetCrush.html

Verlaines
http://www.flyingnun.co.nz/verlaines.html

Veruca Salt
http://www.cyberia.com/pages/david/veruca/
http://www.gordian.com/users/daniel/veruca/
http://www.geffen.com/veruca.html/

The Verve
http://cygnus.campbellsvil.edu/~wisen/annie/verve/verve.html
http://www.odc.net/~ssharma/verve/
http://www.vmg.co.uk/hut/theverve/

Violent Femmes
http://www.gl.umbc.edu/~mmerry2/femmes.html

Tom Waits
http://www.nwu.edu/waits/

Wall of Voodoo
http://student.uq.edu.au/~s323140/Prieboy.html
http://www.primenet.com/~drywall/

Joe Walsh
http://www.joewalsh.avnet.co.uk/eagles/

Waltons
http://www.io.org/~waltons/
http://pathfinder.com/@@Bye85QUAWenjgVPg/wmg-ca/waltons/index.html

Jennifer Warnes
http://www.megabaud.fi/~ja/cohen/cover1.html

Warrant
http://www.li.net/~bladez/warrant/warrant.html

The Waterboys
http://www.cs.uml.edu/~nmoreau/water.scott/water.shtml
http://www.morningstar.com/bilbo/waterboys.html
http://www.emirec.com/mikescott/

Crystal Waters
http://ubmail.ubalt.edu/~rmills/cwaters.html

The Wedding Present
http://www.ncinter.net/~jamiem/weddoes/
http://huizen.dds.nl/~chester/wpindex.htm
http://www.westnet.com/weddoes/

Ween
http://www.sarcasm.com/Ween/
http://pathfinder.com/@@Bye85QUAWenjgVPg/elektra/artists/ween/ween.html
http://www.ods.de/butthole/ween.html

Weezer
http://www.thursby.com/~nelson/lee/weezer.html
http://www.contrib.andrew.cmu.edu/~km6b/weezer.html
http://users.icanect.net/~jarac//weezer/weezer.htm
http://alpha.wcoil.com/~foolio/

Ian Whitcomb
http://www.colorado.net/picklehead/ian.html

White Zombie
http://www.geffen.com/planetzombie/
http://www.gac.edu/~dkuster/zombie/index.html
http://fanasylum.com/zombie/
http://www2.acs.oakland.edu/~kmhanser/zombie/old.index.html

Whitesnake
http://www.st.rim.or.jp/~kino1989/Coverdale/

Chris Whitley
http://www.music.sony.com/Music/ArtistInfo/ChrisWhitley_Biography.html
http://www.bhm.tis.net/~lowga/

The Who
http://www.riverdale.k12.or.us/students/jackr/who.html
http://www.siggroup.com/thewho.html
http://206.72.136.6:80/thewho/albums/
http://www.xmission.com/~legalize/who-gallery.html

Widespread Panic
http://iweb.www.com/wsp/index.html
http://www.netspace.org/Widespread/
http://www.wwisp.com/~cryptcl/wsphome.htm

Kim Wilde
http://www.bart.nl/~bieleman/KimWilde.html

Webb Wilder
http://www.nd.edu/~kdrew/WW.html
http://atlantis.austin.apple.com/people.pages/cgibbons/Wilder/Last.of.the.Full.Grown.Men.html
http://www.warez.com/dizzyj/wwwwwww.html

Dar Williams
http://www.wolfenet.com/~optica/honesty.html
http://www.panix.com/~tneff/dar/

Hank Williams
http://www.cmgww.com/music/hank/hank.html

Hank Williams Jr.
http://ucunix.san.uc.edu/~roundsda/hankhome.html

Linda Williams
http://www.tc.umn.edu/nlhome/m161/schn0170/lw/index.html

Victoria Williams
http://www.atlantic-records.com/Victoria_Williams/
http://www.daenet.com/vw/

Wilson Philips
http://www.cdc.net/~bpar/wilson-phillips.html
http://www.mit.edu:8001/people/jwb/wp.html

Brian Wilson
http://gladstone.uoregon.edu/~mwheeler/beach_boys.html
http://www.mca.com/mca_records/library/bios/bio.wilson.html

Jackie Wilson
http://www.rockhall.com/induct/wilsjack.html

Winger
http://users.aol.com/plsdee/private/winger.htm
http://www.cityscape.co.uk/users/et92/rock/winger.htm

Steve Winwood
http://www.fas.harvard.edu/~stribble/sw/index.html

The Wipers
http://www.pitt.edu/~mxjst3/pages/wipers.html

Wonder Stuff
http://cernan.ecn.purdue.edu/~malasky/

Roy Wood
http://www.ici.net/cust_pages/bad/woody.html

Gary Wright
http://www.primenet.com/~dreamw/

Robert Wyatt
http://prog.ari.net/prog/Bands/Gongwyatt/wyatt.home.html
http://ecmrecords.com/ecm/artists/814.html

X
http://www.cyberg8t.com/gene/

X-Ray Spex
http://www.terrapin.co.uk/xrayspex/

XTC
http://www.users.dircon.co.uk/~nonsuch/bungalow.htm
http://www.charm.net/~duke/xtc/beatown.html
http://reality.sgi.com/employees/relph/chalkhills/

Xymox
http://www.evo.org/html/group/clanofxymox.html
http://mcmuse.mc.maricopa.edu/~xymox/xymox.html

The Yardbirds
http://mars.superlink.net/user/wnuck/Hist/yardbirds.html

Yellow
http://www.yello.space.net/yello/
http://www.geocities.com/SunsetStrip/3040/

http://www.primenet.com/~spork/yello/index.html

Yellow Magic Orchestra
http://www.tezcat.com/~klee/ymo.html

Yes
http://www.wilmington.net/yes/
http://www.yesmag.com/yesmag/
http://www.worldaccess.nl/~yescomm/
http://www.adept.net/bizlinks/howefans/turb/trblnce.htm

Yo La Tengo
http://www.muohio.edu/~plattgj/ylt/
http://www.matador.recs.com/bands/ylt/index.html
http://www.mordor.com/neslon/music/faves/index.html#ylt
http://www.atlantic-records.com/Yo_La_Tengo/

Dwight Yoakman
http://www.iac.net/~sharonv/dwight.html
http://www2.netdoor.com/~keifer/dy.html
http://www.southside.org/~thorpedo/etoilenoir/

Young Fresh Fellows
http://www.accessone.com/~jmiller/yff/

Young Gods
http://www.fys.uio.no/~bor/diskog/gods.html

Neil Young
http://HyperRust.org/
http://ourworld.compuserve.com/homepages/nyas/
http://www.guitarworld.com/perm.archives/history/hs.neil.html
http://www.iuma.com/Warner/html/Young,_Neil.html

Frank Zappa
http://www.zappa.com/
http://www.fwi.uva.nl/~heederik/zappa/
http://www.caos.kun.nl/zappa/
http://www.cpeq.com/~evilbob/zappa.html
http://www.rockhall.com/induct/zappfran.html

Martin Zeller
http://www.stolaf.edu/people/anderswa/martin/main.html

Warren Zevon
http://sushi.st.usm.edu/~hamorris/zevon.html

John Zorn
http://mars.superlink.net/marko/jz.html
http://www.nwu.edu/WNUR/jazz/artists/zorn.john/discog.html

ZZ Top
http://www.cen.uiuc.edu/~pzurich/zztop.html

They're the K-Tel collections of the 90s — lots of stars, lots of hits, a seemingly random rate of production. They're tribute albums, and the music industry loves 'em. But since the late 80s, when the first tribute came out, they've ballooned into a significant trend that often results more in product than in actual artistic events. In other words, there's far more wheat than chaff, so hopefully this section will help guide you towards the best picks.

Arthur Alexander

what: *Adios, Amigo* (Razor & Tie, 1994)

why: A fine songwriter ("Anna (Go to Him)," "Burning Love") who was never rightly celebrated while he was alive.

who: Roger McGuinn, Elvis Costello, Graham Parker, Nick Lowe

who?!: Corey Glover of Living Colour

Bauhaus

what: *The Passion of Covers* (Cleopatra, 1996)

why: Everyone needs a good mope now and again.

who: The Shroud, Ikon, Wreckage

who?!: Fahrenheit 451 with Eva O

Jeff Beck

what: *Jeffology* (Shrapnel, 1996)

why: A bunch of contemporary hard rock guitarists take a shot at solos they only wish they could play.

who: Def Leppard's Phil Collen and Vivian Campbell, Toto's Steve Lukather, Dokken's George Lynch

who?!: Motley Crue's Mick Mars on "Happenings Ten Years Ago."

The Bee Gees

what: *Melody Fair* (Eggbert, 1994)

why: Enough strong tunes to make you forget the white polyester suits.

who: Young Fresh Fellows, Phil Seymour, Material Issue, the Fastbacks

who?!: The Insect Surfers

Black Sabbath

what: *Relativity in Black* (Columbia, 1994)

why: It was the most influential hard rock band this side of Led Zeppelin.

who: Megadeth, White Zombie, Ozzy Osbourne, Faith No More

who?!: Ugly Kid Joe

Otis Blackwell

what: *Brace Yourself* (Shanachie, 1994)

why: Another great but underappreciated songwriter.

who: Frank Black and the Stax Pistols, Deborah Harry, Dave Edmunds, Chrissie Hynde

who?!: Paul Rodgers

The Byrds

what: *Time Between* (Comm., 1993)

why: It gave all the participants a good excuse to buy Rickenbacker guitars.

who: Dinosaur Jr., Richard Thompson, Thin White Rope, Giant Sand

who:?! buck-hitchcock thing

The Carpenters

what: *If I Were a Carpenter* (A&M, 1994)

why: It had to be a joke; these cool groups don't *really* like the Carpenters, do they?

who: Matthew Sweet, Cracker, Redd Kross, Cranberries

who?!: Shonen Knife doing "Top of the World."

Vic Chesnutt

what: *Sweet Relief II: Gravity of the Situation* (Columbia, 1996)

why: Another benefit for the musician's health care fund.

who: R.E.M., Soul Asylum, Live, Smashing Pmpkins, Indigo Girls

who?!: Joe Henry and Madonna (she's his sister-in-law).

Leonard Cohen

what: *I'm Your Fan* (Atlantic, 1991)

why: Cohen's material lends itself to strong, distinctive interpretations.

who: R.E.M., the Pixies, Lloyd Cole, Nick Cave

what?!: Dead Famous People doing "True Love Leaves No Traces."

Leonard Cohen

what: *Tower of Song* (A&M, 1995)

why: Ditto, though this big-name oriented tribute is a touch less interesting and daring than its predecessor.

who: Sting, Tori Amos, Billy Joel, Don Henley

what?!: A U2-less Bono doing "Hallelujah."

Alice Cooper

what: *Welcome to Our Nightmare* (TRI, 1993)

why: Secret fantasies about playing with boa constrictors and hacking up baby dolls.

who: Dramarama, the Hangmen, Cold Ethyl, Shadow project

who?!: Cold Ethyl

The Damned

what: *Another Damned Seattle Compilation* (Dashboard/Hula Girl, 1991)

why: They had more songs to choose from than the Sex Pistols.

who: Mudhoney, the Posies, Flop, Hammerbox

who?!: Coffin Break doing "Love Song"

Deep Purple

what: *Smoke on the Water* (Shrapnel, 1994)

why: License to throw a Ritchie Blackmore-style temper tantrum.

who: Yngwie Malmsteen, Winger, Dokken

who?!: Ritchie Kotzen

John Denver

what: *Minneapolis Does Denver* (October, 1995)

why: Extreme hockey withdrawal after the North Stars left for Dallas.

who: Fat Tuesday, John Casey, Tina & the B-Side Movement

who?!: Juggernaut doing "Fly Away"

The Eagles

what: *Common Thread* (Giant, 1993)

why: Modern country stars pay well-deserved propers to the Eagles.

who: Travis Tritt, Little Texas, Diamond Rio, Brooks & Dunn

who?!: Tanya Tucker

Roky Erikson

what: *Where the Pyramid Meets the Eye* (Sire, 1990)

why: A well-intentioned and successful effort to give Erikson a bit of mainstream spotlight.

who: R.E.M., John Wesley Harding, Bongwater,

who:?! ZZ Top

John Fogerty

what: *Wrote a Song For Everyone* (Rubber Rabbit/Pravda, 1995)

why: Maybe they thought these weak performances would jar him out of his writer's block.

who: Steve Wynn, Peter Zaremba, the Cole Porters

who?!: Al Perry & the Cattle doing "Fortunate Son."

Ace Frehley

what: *Spacewalk* (Shrapnel, 1996) WOOF!

why: Didn't it bother anybody that they had to use a bunch of songs that Gene Simmons and Paul Stanley wrote?

who: Gilby Clarke, Scott Ian, Tracii Guns, members of Skid Row and Pantera

who ?! Ace Frehley — on his own tribute album?

Genesis

what: *The River of Constant Change* (Mellow/Phantom, 1995)

why: Maybe *this* is the real reason Phil Collins left the band.

who: Galahad, Evolution, Algebra

who?!: Notturno Concertante

The Germs

what: *A Small Circle of Friends* (Grass, 1996)

why: 'Coz all those Nirvana and Foo Fighters fans are wondering about this other band Pat Smear was in.

who: The Posies, Matthew Sweet, Flea, L7, Mike Watt and J Mascis

who?!: The Puzzle Panthers (with Sonic Youth's Thurston Moore and the Beastie Boys' Mike D.)

Berry Gordy

what: *Memories, Music, Magic of Motown* (Motown, 1995)

why: A back-up product in case the audio version of his autobiography didn't sell.

who: Smokey Robinson, Stevie Wonder, Four Tops, Temptations, Diana Ross

who?!: Shanice

The Grateful Dead

what: *Deadicated* (Arista, 1991)

why: 'Coz, like Alice Cooper, they love the Dead.

who: Bruce Hornsby, Warren Zevon, Suzanne Vega, Lyle Lovett

who?!: Jane's Addiction doing "Ripple"and a group called the Harshed Mellows, which features members of the Georgia Satellites and Tom Petty's Heartbreakers.

Merle Haggard

what: *Tulare Dust: A Songwriters' Tribute to Merle Haggard* (Hightone, 1994)

why: Someone actually had the rare idea of doing a tribute that actually illuminated the subject's work.

who: Dwight Yoakam, Peter Case, Joe Ely, Lucinda Williams, Dave Alvin
who?!: Barrence Whitfield

Jimi Hendrix
what: *If 6 Was 9* (Comm., 1991)
why: There is no limitation on ways to cash in on the Hendrix legacy.
who: XTC, Monks of Doom, Giant Sand
who?!: Bevis Frond

Jimi Hendrix
what: Stone Free (Warner Bros., 1993)
why: There's *still* no limitation on ways to cash in on the Hendrix legacy.
who: Eric Clapton, Jeff Beck and Seal, PM Dawn
who?!: Body Count doing....

John Hiatt
what: *Love Gets Strange* (Rhino, 1993)
why: Lots of artists have recorded Hiatt's songs more successfully than he has.
who: Dave Edmunds, Marshall Crenshaw, Bonnie Raitt, Emmylou Harris
who?!: Johnny Adams

The Hollies
what: *Hollies in Reverse* (Eggbert, 1995)
why: Nobody could get too excited about a Merseybeats tribute.
who: The Posies, Tommy Keene, Bill Lloyd, Material Issue, Continental Drifters
who?!: Carla Olson

Buddy Holly
what: *Not Fade Away (Remembering Buddy Holly)* (MCA, 1995)
why: They just wanted to prove how good Holly really was.
who: Los Lobos, Waylon Jennings and Mark Knopfler, Todd Snider, The Band
who?!: Buddy Holly and the Hollies

Husker Du
what: *Twin Cities Replay: Zen Arcade* (Syn, 1993)
why: *Zen Arcade* was such a great album that these Minneapolis bands were moved to re-create it.
who: Hammerhead, Zuzu's Petals, God's Favorite Band
who?!: Janitor Joe

Joy Division
what: *End* (Virgin, 1995)
why: Everyone needs another good mope now and again.
who: Moby, Girls Against Boys, Versus
who ?!: Starchildren (aka Smashing Pumpkins)

Carole King
what: Tapestry Revisited (Atlantic, 1995) WOOF!
why: Good question.
who: Rod Stewart, Celine Dion, Aretha Franklin, Amy Grant
who?!: The Bee Gees

The Kinks
what: Shangri-La (Imaginary, 1991)
why: Look, ma; I can play the three chords to "You Really Got Me," too.
who: Fleshtones, Chesterfield Kings, the Mock Turtles
who?!: Village Green Preservation Society

Kiss
what: *Kiss My Ass* (Mercury, 1994)
why: Revlon had a good idea for boosting its stock.
who: Lenny Kravitz, Gin Blossoms, Anthrax, Extreme
who?!: Garth Brooks (with Kiss) doing "Hard Luck Woman."

Led Zeppelin
what: *Stairways to Heaven* (Atlantic, 1995) WOOF!
why: Why *wouldn't* everyone want to hear an album of "Stairway to Heaven" covers?
who: Nobody
who?!: Rock Lobsters, everybody else

Led Zeppelin
what: *Enconium* (Atlantic, 1995)
why: Just in case folks *didn't* want an album of "Stairway to Heaven" covers.
who: Stone Temple Pilots, Hootie & the Blowfish, Robert Plant and Tori Amos
who?!: Duran Duran doing "Thank You."

John Lennon
what: *Working Class Hero* (Hollywood, 1995)
why: They all owe Lennon something — except perhaps the decency to stay away from his songs.
who: Cheap Trick, Sponge, Collective Soul, Blues Traveler, Mary Chapin Carpenter
who ?!: George Clinton doing "Mind Games."

Lynyrd Skynyd
what: *Skynyrd Frynds* (MCA, 1994)
why: Next to the Eagles, Skynyrd was modern country's greatest touchstone.
who: Travis Tritt, Hank Williams Jr., the Mavericks
who?!: Wynonna Judd doing "Free Bird."

Bob Marley
what: One Love (Verve, 1996)
why: Someone thought Marley's transcendent reggae lent itself to acid jazz treatments.
who: Tony Remy, Juliet Roberts, Omar
who?!: Cleveland Watkiss featuring Project 23

Curtis Mayfield
what: *People Get Ready* (Shanachie, 1993)
why: His songs deserve to be covered as many times as possible.
who: Don Covay, Delbert McClinton, Jerry Butler, David and Jonathan Sanborn, Huey Lewis & the News, Bunny Wailer
who?!: Michael Hill and Vernon Reid

Curtis Mayfield

what: *Tribute to Curtis Mayfield* (Warner Bros., 1994) 3.5 bones

why: Well, almost as many times as possible.

who: Eric Clapton, Bruce Springsteen, Lenny Kravitz, Whitney Kravitz

who?!: Public Enemy

Minutemen

what: *Our Band Could Be Your Life* (LIT, 1997) not available for rating.

why: Unsung hero of modern rock is overdue for a salute.

who: Hazel, Meat Puppets, Jawbox, Seam

who?!: Overpass

The Monkees

what: *Here No Evil* (Long Play, 1992) 3.5 bones

why: Mike Nesmith let 'em all wear his hat for a day if they contributed a track.

who: Peter Holsapple, Magnapop, Mitch Easter, the Vulgar Boatmen

who?!: Boise and Moss with A Side of Hamm

Van Morrison

what: *No Prima Donna* (Polydor, 1994) WOOF!

why: Van must not have been having a beautiful vision when he helped helm this turkey.

who: Sinead O'Connor, Elvis Costello, Marianne Faithfull

who?! Actor Liam Neeson doing "Coney Island."

Willie Nelson

what: *Twisted Willie*(Justice, 1996) 4 bones

why: If Johnny Cash can be rumored for Lollapalooza, why can't fellow Highwayman Nelson get the modern rock treatment?

who: Johnny Cash, the Reverend Horton Heat, X, Waylon Jennings

who?!: Jello Biafra with Life After Life.

Gram Parsons

what: *Commemorativo* (Rhino, 1993) 4 bones

why: Just another reminder of what a great influence he was on two more generations of rockers.

who: Uncle Tupelo, Bob Mould, Steve Wynn, Something Happens

who?!: The Mekons

Tom Petty

what: *You Got Lucky* (Scotti Bros., 1994) 1 bone

why: They wanted to find out just how hard it really is to do Petty's songs well.

who: Throneberry, Loud Lucy, Fig Dish

who?!: Everclear (unknown when the album came out).

Pink Floyd

what: *Saucerful of Pink* (Cleopatra, 1995) 3 bones

why: The industrial crowd figured Roger Waters might need some $$$ after his legal battles with his former bandmates...

who: Psychic TV, Ron Geesim, Alien Sex Fiend, Hawkwind's Nik Turner

why:?! Leather Strip doing "Learning to Fly."

Pink Floyd

what: *The Moon Revisited* (Magna Carta, 1995) 2 bones

why:...So did this batch of unknowns.

who: Cairo, Shadow Gallery, Magellan, Enchant

who?!: World Trade

Doc Pomus

what: *Till the Night is Gone* (Rhino, 1995) 4 bones

why: Pomus' songs are great, that's all.

who: Lou Reed, Bob Dylan, The Band, Brian Wilson

who?!: Shawn Colvin doing "Viva Las Vegas."

Cole Porter

what: *Red, Hot and Blue* (Chrysalis, 1990) 4 bones

why: A good cause (AIDS research and relief) and a great batch of tunes for these rockers to get their hands on.

who: U2, Sinead O'Connor, David Byrne, Neville Brothers

who?!: Debbie Harry and Iggy Pop doing "Well Did You Evah."

Elvis Presley

what: *It's Now or Never* (Polydor, 1994) 2 bones

why: It was inevitable, but never would have been preferable.

who: Bryan Adams, U2, Chris Isaak, Melissa Etheridge, Michael Bolton

who?! **Michael Hutchence with NRBQ.**

The Ramones

what: *Gabba Gabba Hey* (TRI, 1991) 3 bones

why: You can't *not* love the Ramones; it's the 27th amendment, isn't it?

who: Bad Religion, Flesheaters, L7, Mojo Nixon

who?!: The Creamers

Sisters of Mercy

what: *First, Last and Forever* (Cleopatra, 1993) 3.5 bones

why: The Joy Division tribute was already taken.

who: Halo, Wreckage, The Shroud

who?!: Prophetess

Bruce Springsteen

what: *Cover Me* (Rhino, 1989) 4 bones

why: Someone needed to get all these Boss songs, recorded by others, on one disc.

who: Greg Kihn, Patti Smith Group, Dave Edmunds, Southside Johnny & the Asbury Jukes

who?!: The Hollies doing "4th of July, Asbury Park (Sandy)."

Richard Thompson

what: *Beat the Retreat* (Capitol, 1994) 4.5 bones

why: Nobody can play guitar like him, but they all keep trying.

who: Bob Mould, R.E.M., Bonnie Raitt, X

who ?! Dinosaur Jr.

Stevie Ray Vaughan

what: *A Tribute to Stevie Ray Vaughan* (Epic, 1996)

why: A chance to celebrate the late guitar whiz' life with dignity and hot licks.

who: Eric Clapton, Bonnie Raitt, Buddy Guy, Dr. Vaughan, Jimmie Vaughan, B.B. King

who?!: Believe it or not, they all fit.

Tom Waits

what: *Step Right Up* (Manifesto, 1995)

why: Why should Rod Stewart and Bob Seger get to have all the fun?

who: 10,000 Maniacs, Tim Buckley, Alex Chilton

who?!: Violent Femmes doing "Step Right Up."

Victoria Williams

what: *Sweet Relief* (Chaos/Columbia, 1993)

why: The original; even better than the Vic Chesnutt sequel.

who: Pearl Jam, Soul Asylum, Jayhawks, Matthew Sweet

who?!: Victoria Williams

Wire

what: *Whore* (WMO, 1996)

why: The group deserves more credit for its impact on the modern rock scene.

who: Lush, My Bloody Valentine, Godflesh, Mike Watt

who?!: Fudge Tunnel

XTC

what: *Testimonial Dinner* (Thirsty Ear, 1995)

why: Great songs that should have been hits on their own.

who: Sarah McLachlan, Freedy Johnston, the Verve Pipe, Joe Jackson

who?!: Ruben Blades

Neil Young

what: *The Bridge* (Caroline, 1989)

why: One of the original tribute albums, and we can't think of a more appropriate subject.

who: The Pixies, Soul Asylum, Dinosaur Jr., Nick Cave

who?!: Henry Kaiser's medley of "The Needle and the Damage Done/Tonight's the Night."

Neil Young

what: *Borrowed Tunes* (Sony Canada, 1994)

why: An inspired concept; one disc of acoustic material, another of electric.

who: Jeff Healey Band, Cowboy Junkies, Blue Rodeo, the Waltons

who ?!: Our Lady Peace doing "Needle and the Damage Done."

The Zombies

what: *The World of the Zombies* (popLlama, 1994)

why: Who knew what a following the Zombies had in the Pacific Northwest and Canada?

who: The Posies, Zumpano, Young Fresh Fellows, Flop

who?!: Steam King doing "She's Not There."

The following is a list of selected record labels and their locations or e-mail addresses.

A Gentle Wind
PO Box 3103
Albany, NY 12203

A&M Records
1416 N. LaBrea
Hollywood, CA 90028

Ace Records, Ltd.
48 - 50 Steele Road
London, NW10 7AS
England

Acorn Music
5332 Colleve Avenue Suite 101
Oakland, CA 94618-2805

Acoustic Disc Box 4143
San Rafael, CA 94913

Acoustic Music Records
Postfach 1945
D-49009 Osnabruck, Germany

Acoustic Music Records
1610 Crestview
Seal Beach, CA 90740

Acoustics Records
PO Box 350
Reading RG6 7DQ
Berkshire, United Kingdom
email:100711.1732@compuserve.com

Adelphi/Genes CD Company
PO Box 7688
Silver Spring, MD 20907

Adobe Records
PO Box W
Shallowater, TX 79363

Africassette
PO Box 24941
Detroit, MI 48224
email:
rsteiger@africassette.com

Agua Azul Records
PO Box 161556
Austin, TX 78716

Airborne Records
10 Music Circle South
Nashville, TN 37203

Alacazam! Records
Box 429
Waterbury, VT 05676-0429

Albertine Records
PO Box 154
Vauxhall, NJ 07088

Alcazar Records
Box 429
Waterbury, VT 05676-0429

Alias Records
10153 1/2 Riverside Drive, #115
Toluca Lake, CA 91602

Alligator Records
PO Box 60234
Chicago, IL 60660

Almasud Records
c/o Joao Mauricio Marques
Rua do Bom Sucesso
Beco do Ribeiro, 7
9000 Funchal
Madeiram, Portugal
email: almasud@madinfo.pt

Alternative Tentacles
PO Box 419092
San Francisco, CA 94141-9092

Amalthea Records
Box 286
20122 Malmö, Sweden

Amazing Records
PO Box 2164
Austin, TX 78768

American Gramaphone Records
9130 Mormon Bridge Road
Omaha, NE 68152

American Melody
PO Box 270
Guilford, CT 06437

American Recordings
3500 W. Olive Avenue, Suite 1550
Burbank, CA 91505

AMMP
Alam Madina Music Productions
74 Broadmoor Avenue
San Anselmo, CA 94960

Amigo Musik Finland Ab
Cygnaeuksenkatu 12
FIN-00100 Helsinki, Finland

Amoeba Records
5337 LaCresta Court
Los Angeles, CA 90038

Angel Records
810 Seventh Avenue
New York, NY 10019

Antone's
500 San Marcos Street, Suite 200
Austin, TX 78702

Appleseed Recordings
PO Box 2593
West Chester, PA 19380
email: folkradicl@aol.com

ARC Music Productions International
PO Box 111, East Grinstead
West Sussex RH19 4FZ
England

ARC Music US
PO Box 2453
Clearwater, FL 34617-2453

Arhoolie Records
10341 San Pablo Avenue
El Cerrito, CA 94530

Arista Records
6 West 57th Street
New York, NY 10019

Asylum Records
1906 Acklen Avenue

Nashville, TN 37212

Atlantic Recording Corporation
75 Rockefeller Plaza
New York, NY 10019

Atlantica Music
1819 Granville Street, 4th Floor
Halifax, NS B3J 3R1
Canada

Atomic Theory Records
106 West 49th Street
Minneapolis, MN 55409

Attic Records
102 Atlantic Avenue
Toronto, ON M6K 1X9
Canada

Augusta Heritage Center
Davis & Elkins College
Elkins, WV 26241

Aural Tradition Records
3271 Main Street
Vancouver, BC V5V 3M6
Canada

Australian Music International
253 West 18th Street, Ground Suite
New York, NY 10011

Avenue Records
145 West 57th Street, 14th Fl.
New York, NY 10019

Awareness Records
6 Vernon Avenue
London SW20 8BW
England

Axiom Records
400 Lafayette Street, 5th Floor
New York, NY 10003

Azra International
Box 459
Maywood, CA 90270

Azure Records
PO Box 38
Washington, VA 22747

B&R Heritage Enterprises
PO Box 3
Iona, NS B0A 1L0, Canada

Backshift Music
103 Oldham Road
Ripponden, Sowerby Bridge
West Yorkshire HX64EB
England

Bar/None
PO Box 1704
Hoboken, NJ 07030

Barraka el Farnatshi
Postbox 140
4020 Basel, Switzerland

Batish Records
1310 Mission Street
Santa Cruz, CA 95060
email: batish@cruzio.com

BCN Records
PO Box 3129
Peabody, MA 01961

Beacon Records
8033 Sunset Blvd., Suite 392
Los Angeles, CA 90046

Bear Family Records
PO Box 115
42864 Vollersode, Germany

Beautiful Jo Records
86 Marlborough Road
Oxford OX1 4LS
England

Betrayal Records
J.A.F. Box 7131
New York, NY 10116

Bewilderness Records
PO Box 27283
Raleigh, NC 27611

BGO Records
PO Box 22
Bury St. Edmunds
Suffolk IP28 6XQ
England

Bizarre/Straight Records
740 North La Brea Avenue
Hollywood, CA 90038

Black Sun
PO Box 30122
Tucson, AZ 85751
email: 72120.3673@compuserve.com

Black Top Records
email: info@rounder.com

Blackthorne Records, Ltd.
35 Stanley Avenue
Beckenham, Kent BR3 2PU
England

Blind Pig Records
PO Box 2344
San Francisco, CA 94126

Blix Street Records
PO Box 1129
Burbank, CA 91507
email: BlixStreet@aol.com

Blue Planet Records
PO Box 2074
Boulder, CO 80306
email: planet@bluegrass.com

Blue Plate Music
33 Music Square West, #102-A
Nashville, TN 37203

Bluestein Family Tapes & Records
4414 E Alamos/ Fresno, CA 93726

Blue Thumb Records
555 West 57th Street, 10th Floor
New York, NY 10019

Boucherie Productions
15bis, rue de Plateau
75019 Paris, France

Boyjay Records
496A Hudson Street
New York, NY 10014

Brambus Alexanderstraße 14
Postfach 216
CH-7001 Chur, Switzerland

Brentwood Bluegrass
One Maryland Farms, Suite 200
Brentwood, TN 37027

Bridge Records
JAF Box 1864
New York, NY 10116

Buda Musique
188, bd Voltaire
75011 Paris, France

Buddah Records
1540 Broadway, 27th Floor
New York, NY 10036

Bullseye Blues
email: info@rounder.com

Burnside Records
3158 E. Burnside
Portland, OR 97214
email: burnside@teleport.com

John C. Campbell Folk School
Rt 1, Box 14A
Brasstown, NC 28902

Canyon Records
4143 North 16th Street, Suite #6
Phoenix, AZ 85016

Capitol Nashville
3322 West End Avenue
Nashville, TN 37203

Capitol Records
1750 North Vine Street
Hollywood, CA 90028-5274

Caroline Records
114 W. 26th Street
New York, NY 10001

Carpe Diem Records
email:
carpediem@dmusic.com

Castle USA
352 Park Avenue S. 10th Floor
New York, NY 10010

Castle Communications
29 Barwell Business Park
Leatherhead Road
Chessington, Surrey KT9 2NY
England

Celestial Harmonies
PO Box 30122
Tucson, AZ 85751
email: 72120.3673@compuserve.com

Celtic Heartbeat Atlantic Recording Corporation
75 Rockefeller Plaza
New York, NY 10019

Celtic Music CM Distribution
4 High Street
Starbeck, Harrogate
North Yorkshire HG1 7HY
England

Chameleon Music Group
36 24th Avenue
Venice, CA 90291

Charisma Records America
1790 Broadway, 20th Floor
New York, NY 10019

Charly Records
156-166 Ilderton Road
London SE15 1NT
England

Le Chasse-Mareé
Abri du Matin
29100 Douarnenez, France

Chiswick Records
48 - 50 Steele Road
London NW10 7AS England
Chrysalis Records
645 Madison Avenue
New York, NY 10022-1010

City of Tribes
3025 17th Street
San Francisco, CA 94110-1334

City Spark
921 W. 44th Street
Kansas City, MO 64111-3511

Claddagh Records@16b:
Dame House
Dame Street
Dublin 2, Ireland
email: info@rounder.com

Cleopatra Records
8726 S. Sepulveda, Suite D-82
Los Angeles, CA 90046

Clever Sheep Records
PO Box 331
Ardmore, PA 19003

CMH Records@16b:
PO Box 39439
Los Angeles, CA 90039-0439

CMP
140 West 22nd Street, Suite 7B
New York, NY 10011

Coconut Grove Recording Company
2980 McFarlane Road, Suite 211
Coconut Grove, FL 33133

Cold Cuts
PO Box 2974
Denver, CO 80201-2974

Columbia Records
PO Box 4450
New York, NY 10101-4450

Common Ground
The Redesdale Centre
Elsdon, Northumberland, U.K.

Compass Records
117 30th Avenue South
Nashville, TN 37212-2507
email: smlwrld@aol.com

Compass Rose Music
PO Box 1501
Bennington, VT 05201
email: mangsen@sover.net

Cooking Vinyl America
PO Box 311
Port Washington, NY 11050

Cooking Vinyl Records
PO Box 1741
London W9 3LA
England

Coop Breizh Kerangwenn
29540 Spezet
Brittany, France

Copper Creek
PO Box 3161
Roanoke, VA 24015

Corason
email: info@rounder.com

Cornbelt Records
Box 3452
Madison, WI 53704

Country Heritage Productions
RR1, Box 320
Madill, OK 73446

Country Music Foundation Records
4 Music Square
East Nashville, TN 37203

County Records
Box 191
Floyd, VA 24091

Crammed Discs
43 rue Général Patton
1050 Brussels, Belgium

Crapstone Records
The Firs, Crapstone
Yelverton, Devon PL20 7PJ
U.K.

Cross Border Media
10 Deer Park
Ashbourne
Co. Meath, Ireland

Culburnie Records
PO Box 219
Nevada City, CA 95959
email: Culburni@oro.net

Culburnie Records
PO Box 13350
Jedburgh TD8 6YA
Scotland
email: 100046.1746@compuserve.com

Cuneiform Records
PO Box 8427
Silver Spring, MD 20907

Cypress Records
1523 Crossroads of the World
Los Angeles, CA 90028

Daemon Records
PO Box 1207
Decatur, GA 30031

Dambuster Records
24 Mercer Row
Louth, Lincolnshire LN11 9JJ
England

Dancing Cat Records
PO Box 639
Santa Cruz, CA 95061

Dancing Dog Music
PO Box 4427
Austin, TX 78765-4427
email: mesa@eden.com

Dara
c/o Dolphin Traders
56 Moore Street
Dublin 1, Ireland

Dara Records U.S.A.
235 E. 84th Street, Suite 32
New York, NY 10028

Daring Records
PO Box 793
Marblehead, MA 01945
email: info@rounder.com

Dargason Music
PO Box 189
Burbank, CA 91503

D&D Records
PO Box 847
Montrose, CA 91020

Dejadisc
537 Lindsey Street
San Marcos, TX 78666

Delmark Records
4121 N. Rockwell Street
Chicago, IL 60618-2822

Deluge Records
PO Box 2877
Waterville, ME 04903
email: info@deluge-records.com

Demon Records
Canal House
Set Star Estate
Transport Avenue
Brentford, Middx. TW8 0QP
England

Denon Canada Inc.
17 Denison Street
Markham, ON L3R 1B5
Canada

Digelius Music
Laivurinrinne 2
00120 Helsinki, Finland
email: pap@dighoe.pp.fi

Dirty Linen
PO Box 66600
Baltimore, MD 21239-6600

Discovery Records
2034 Broadway
Santa Monica, CA 90404
email: info@discoveryrec.com

Disques Dreyfus
26, av. Kleber
75116 Paris, France

Walt Disney Records
500 South Buena Vista Street
Burbank, CA 91521

Discos Camiantes
PO 411082
San Francisco, CA 94141

Distant Sound Records
PO Box 971534
Yipsilanti, MI 48197

Don't Records
PO Box 11513
Milwaukee, WI 53211
email: dont@execpc.com

Dorian Recordings
8 Brunswick Road
Troy, NY 12180-3795

Dos Records
500 San Marcos Street, Suite 200
Austin, TX 78702

Dragon Records
5 Church Street
Aylesbury, Buckinghamshire
U.K.

Duckworth Distribution Ltd.
198 Duckworth Street
St. John's, NF, A1C 1G5
Canada
email: rbuck@nfld.com

Dunkeld Records
Cathedral Street
Dunkeld, Perthshire PH8 0AW
Scotland

Dutch East India Trading/Strange Fruit Records
PO Box 800
Rockville Center, NY 11571-0800

Dynamic Recording Studio
c/o Dave Kaspersin
2844-46 Dewey Avenue
Rochester, NY 14616
email: drk@dynrec.com

EarthBeat!
PO Box 1460
Redway, CA 95560-1460

Earthworks/Caroline Records
114 W. 26th Street
New York, NY 10001

Earwig Music Co.
1818 West Pratt Blvd.
Chicago, IL 60626

Eastern Front Records
7 Curve Street
Medfield, MA 02052
email: EastFront1@aol.com

East Side Digital
530 N. 3rd Street
Minneapolis, MN 55401

ECM Records Worldwide Plaza
825 Eighth Avenue
New York, NY 10019

Eino Ab
Papinkuja 2 B 32
00530 Helsinki, Finland

Elektra/Nonesuch Records
75 Rockefeller Plaza
New York, NY 10019

Ellipsis Arts
20 Lumber Road
Roslyn, NY 11576

Energy Records
545 8th Ave. 17th Fl.
New York, NY 10018

Enigma/Retro
PO Box 3628
Culver City, CA 90232-3628

Epic
1801 Century Park West
Los Angeles, CA 90067

Erde Records
Postfach 20 02 44
5060 Bergisch Gladbach 2
Germany

Escalibur
29540 Spezet
Brittany, France

Essential Records
4200 Wisconsin Ave. ,NW,
Suite 106 - Box 800
Washington, DC 20016

Ethnic/Auvidis Records
Harmonia Mundi USA
2037 Granville Avenue
Los Angeles, CA 90025-6103

Exile Records
Koethener Str. 38
1000 Berlin 61
Germany

Familiar Records
7B Farnaby Road
Bromley, Kent BR1 4BL
England

Fantasy Records
Tenth and Parker
Berkeley, CA 94710

Fat Cat Records
1 Holly Terrace
York YO1 4DS
England

Fat Wreck Chords
PO Box 460144
San Francisco, CA 94146

Fellside Recordings
15 Banklands
Workington, Cumbria CA14 3EW
U.K.

Festival Records
21 Halifax Road
Ripponden
Halifax, West Yorkshire HX6 4AH
England

Feuer und Eis Musikverlag
Fuldastr. 40m
4130 Moers 1, Germany

Fflach Llys-y-Coed
Heol Dinbych-y-Pysgod
Aberteifi, Dyfed
Wales SA43 3AH
U.K.

Fifth Column
PO Box 787
Washington, DC 20044

Fire Ant Music
2009 Ashland Avenue
Charlotte, NC 28205
email: Fireants@aol.com

Firebird Arts & Music
PO Box 30268
Portland, OR 97294-3268

First Nations Music
Wawatay Recordings
3025 Kennedy Road, Unit 3A
Scarborough, ON M1V 1S3
Canada
email: oka@inforamp.net

First Warning Records
594 Broadway, Suite 1104
New York, NY 10012

Fish Tail Records
PO Box 2561
Iowa City, IA 52244

Flat Five
PO Box 8127
Roanoke, VA 24014

Flannel Jammies
3160 Thorp Street
Madison, WI 53714

Fledg'ling Records
PO Box 547
London SE26 4BD
England

Flyin' Cloud Records
c/o Flyin' Cloud, Inc.
168 Glenridge Drive
Eden, NC 27288
email: mediaman@vnet.net

Flying Fish Records
email: info@rounder.com

The Folk Corporation
9 Victoria Road
Maldon, Essex CM9 5HE
England

Folk Era Productions
705 S. Washington Street/
Naperville, IL 60540
email: FolkEra@aol.com

Folk-Legacy Records
Box 1148
Sharon, CT 06069

Folksound/Roots Records
250 Earlsdon Avenue North
Coventry CV5 6GX
England

Fortuna Records
PO Box 32016
Tucson, AZ 85751

Four Dots
Box 233
Denton, TX 76201

Fresh Fruit Records
369 Montezuma, #209
Santa Fe, NM 87501
Front Hall Records
PO Box 307
Voorheesville, NY 12186

Fundamental Records
Box 2309
Covington, GA 30209

Fuse Records
32 Nethergreen Road
Sheffield S11 7EJ
England

Gadfly Records
Box 5231
Burlington, VT 05402
email: gadfly1@aol.com

Gael-Linn Records
26 Merrion Square
Dublin 2, Ireland

Gajo Records
PO Box 140777
Dallas, TX 75214

Gazell Records
PO Box 527
Mansfield Center, CT 06250

Geffen Records
9130 Sunset Blvd.
Los Angeles, CA 90069

Genes CD Co.
PO Box 7778
Silver Spring, MD 20907

Giant Records
8900 Wilshire Blvd.
Beverly Hills, CA 90211-1906

Gifthorse Records
PO Box 1129
Burbank, CA 91507
email: BlixStreet@aol.com

Giga Folkmusik HB
Borsheden
S-780 40 Mockfjard, Sweden

Glitterhouse Records
Grüner Weg 25
37688 Beverungen, Germany

Global Music Centre
Mikkolantie 17
FIN-00640, Helsinki, Finland

Global Pacific Records
PO Box 2001
Sonoma, CA 95476

Global Village Music Box
2051 Cathedral Station
New York, NY 10025

Globe Records
PO Box 5523
Mill Valley, CA 94942

GlobeStyle Records
48-50 Steele Road
London NW10 7AS
England

Go-Kart Records
PO Box 20
Prince St. Station New York, NY 10012

Gourd Music
PO Box 585
Felton, CA 95018

Grand Royal
PO Box 26689 - Dpt. CRC
Los Angeles, CA 90026

Grateful Dead Records
PO Box X
Novato, CA 94948

Great American Music Hall
859 O'Farrell Street
San Francisco, CA 94109

Great Divide Records
178 West Houston Street, Suite 9
New York, NY 10014

Great Northern Arts, Ltd.
114 Lexington Avenue
New York, NY 10016

Great Southern Records
PO Box 13977
New Orleans, LA 70815

Greener Pastures Records
70 Route 202 North
Peterborough, NH 03458

Greenhays Records
PO Box 361
Port Washington, NY 11050
email: info@rounder.com

Green Linnet Records
43 Beaver Brook Road
Danbury, CT 06810
email: grnlinnet@aol.com

Greentrax Records
Cockenzie Business Centre
Cockenzie, East Lothian EH32 0HL3
Scotland :

Ground Swell Records
PO Box 245, Central Station
Halifax, NS B3J 2N7
Canada

GTD Heritage Recordings
Ballybane Industrial Estate
Galway, Ireland

Guardian Records
810 Seventh Avenue
New York, NY 10019

Gwerz Pladenn
Coop Breizh
29540 Spezet
Brittany, France

Gypsy Moth Records
Box 1285
New Haven, CT 06505

Gyroscope Records
Caroline Records
114 W. 26th Street
New York, NY 10001

Halshaw Music
37 Catherine Street
Macclesfield, Cheshire SK11 6ET
England

Hands on Music
PO Box 48
Cirencester, Gloucestershire
GL7 7HW
England

Hannibal-Rykodisc
Shetland Park
27 Congress Street
Salem, MA 01970

Happas Records
129A Hamilton Place
Aberdeen AB2 4BD Scotland

Harbourtown Records
PO Box 25
Ulverston, Cumbria LA12 7UN
England

Harmac, Ltd.
67 Amiens Street
Dublin 1, Ireland

Harmonia Mundi USA
2037 Granville Avenue
Los Angeles, CA 90025-6103

Hear Music
560 Harrison Street, Suite 501
Boston, MA 02118

Heartbeat
info@rounder.com

Hearts of Space
PO Box 31321
San Francisco, CA 94131

Henry Street
email: info@rounder.com

Heyday Records
2325 3rd Street #339
San Francisco, CA 94107

Hi, Folks! Records
Res. Sagittario
133 Milan 2 - Via F.lli Cervi
20090 Segrate (MI) Italy

Higher Octave Music
23715 West Malibu Road, Suite 358
Malibu, CA 90265

High Street Records
See Windham Hill Records

Hightone Records
220 4th Street, #101
Oakland, CA 94607

High Water Recording Company
c/o Music Department
Memphis State University
Memphis, TN 38152

High Windy Audio
PO Box 553
Fairview, NC 28730

Hobo Star Music
PO Box 387
Jersey City, NJ 07303-0387

Hobson's Choice Music
176 Ribblesdale Road
Streatham, London SW16 6QY

Hokey Pokey Records
PO Box 547
London SE26 4BD
England

Hollywood Records
Animation Bldg 3E8
500 S. Buena Vista
Burbank, CA 91521

Homeboy Cassettes
134 Lewis Street
New Brunswick, NJ 08901

Homecoming Records
PO Box 2050
Malibu, CA 90265-7050

Homespun Tapes
Box 694
Woodstock, NY 12498

Hopeless Records
15910 Ventura Blvd. 11th Fl.

Encino, CA 91436-2804

Hopewell Records
Box 297
Hadley, MA 01035

HTD Records
70 Bridgen Road
Bexley, Kent DA5 1JG
England

Hudson River Company
PO Box 609/ Averill Park, NY 12018

Humming Bird Records
1921 Walnut #1
Berkeley, CA 94704

Hypertension Music
St. Benedictstraße 5
20149 Hamburg, Germany

Hypertension Music
PO Box 2259
London E17 4RD, England

Hypnotic Records
96 Spadina Avenue, 9th Floor
Toronto, ON M5V 2J6
Canada

Ichiban Records
PO Box 721677
Atlanta, GA 31139-1677

Imaginary Records
28 Hopwood Avenue
Heywood, Lancashire OL10 2AX
England

Inedit
Harmonia Mundi USA
2037 Granville Avenue
Los Angeles, CA 90025-6103

Intuition Music
636 Broadway #1218
New York, NY 10012

Invisible Records
PO Box 16008
Chicago, IL 60616-6008

Iona Records
27-29 Carnoustie Place
Scotland Street, Glasgow G5 8PH
Scotland

Indian House
PO Box 472
Taos, New Mexico 87571

Interra
180 Varick Street
New York, NY 10014

Interworld Music Associates
RR 3, Box 395-A
Brattleboro, VT 05301-8537

I.R.S. Records
3520 Hayden Avenue
Culver City, CA 90232

Island Records
825 Eighth Ave
New York, NY 10019

Island Records
400 Lafayette Street
New York, NY 10003

Joplin & Sweeney Music
334-B North Santa Cruz Avenue
Los Gatos, CA 05030

June Appal
Box 743
Whitesburg, KY 41858

Just A Memory
5455 Pare, #101
Montreal, PQ H4P IP7
Canada

Justice Records
PO Box 980369
Houston, TX 77098-0369

Justin Time Records
5455, rue Paré, Suite 101
Montréal, Quebec H4P 1P7
Canada

Kansanmusiikki-Instituutti
SF-69600 Kaustinen, Finland

Kells Records
64 New Hyde Park Road
Garden City, NY 11530

Keltia Musique
1 Place Au Beurre
29000 Quimper, France

Kennebunk River Productions
Box 860
Kennebunk, ME 04043

Kereshmeh Records
12021 Wilshire Blvd. #420
Los Angeles, CA 90025
email: sdy@kereshmeh.com

Kicking Mule Records
PO Box 158
Alderpoint, CA 95411

Kill Rock Stars
120 NE State St. #418
Olympia, WA 98501

Klub Records
9 Watt Road
Hillington Ind. Est.
Hillington, Glasgow G52 4RY
Scotland

Knitting Factory
74 Leonard Street
New York, NY 10013

KRL
9 Watt Road
Hillington Ind. Est.
Hillington, Glasgow G52 4RY
Scotland

Koch
International 2 Tri Harbor Court
Port Washington, NY 11050-4617

Ladyslipper
PO Box 3124
Durham, NC 27715

Laika Records
Arroder Weg 96
D-33619 Bielefeld, Germany

Lake
15 Banklands
Workington, Cumbria CA14 3EW
U.K.

La Louisianne Records
PO Box 52131
Lafayette, LA 70505-2131

Lanor Records
PO Box 233
Church Point, LA 70525

Lapwing Records
8 Queen's Gardens
Edinburgh EH4 2DA
Scotland

Larrikin
PO Box 162
Paddington NSW 2021
Australia

Legacy International
Box 6999
Beverly Hills, CA 90212

Hal Leonard Publishing Corp.
PO Box 13819
Milwaukee, WI 53213

Lightyear Entertainment
350 Fifth Avenue, Suite 5101
New York, NY 10118

Line
PO Box 605220
D-2000 Hamburg 60
Germany

Linn Records
Floors Road
Waterfoot, Eaglesham
Glasgow G76 0EP
Scotland

Lismor Recordings
27-29 Carnoustie Place
Scotland Street
Glasgow G5 8PH
Scotland

Little Dog Records
223 W. Alameda, Suite 101
Burbank, CA 91502

Living Music
PO Box 72
Norfolk Road
Litchfield, CT 06759
email: pwclmr@aol.com

Lochshore/Klub Records
9 Watt Road
Hillington Ind. Est.
Hillington, Glasgow G52 4RY
Scotland

London Records
825 Eighth Avenue
New York, NY 10019

Loose Cannon
825 Eighth Avenue
New York, NY 10019

Luaka Bop
Box 652, Cooper Station
New York, NY 10276

Lyrichord Discs
141 Perry Street
New York, NY 10014

Maggie's Music
PO Box 4144

Annapolis, MD 21403

Magna Carta
208 E. 51st Street, Suite 1820
New York, NY 10022

Making Waves-Spindrift
24 Mercer Row
Louth, Lincolnshire LN11 9JJ
England

Makoché
PO Box 2756
Bismarck, ND 58502

Malaco Records
3023 W. Northside Drive
Jackson, MS 39213

Dave Mallinson Publications
3 East View
Moorside
Cleckheaton, West Yorkshire
BD19 6LD
England

Mammoth Records
75 Rockefeller Plaza
New York, NY 10019

Mango (Island) Records
825 Eighth Avenue
New York, NY 10019

Marigold Records
PO Box 54552
Avenue Fairlawn R.P.O.
1771 Avenue Road
Toronto, ON M5M 4N5
Canada

Marimac Recordings
PO Box 447
Crown Point, IN 46307

Marlboro Records
PO Box 808
Unionville, PA 19375

Jim Martin Productions
PO Box 152
Saint Albans, WV 25177

Mass Publishing
PO Box 377
851 06 Sundsvall, Sweden
email: mass@mkv.mh.se

Matador Records
676 Broadway
New York, NY 10012

Matchbox
Chipping Manor
Wooten-under-edge
Glos. GL12 7AD
England

MA Records
70 Universal City Plaza
Universal City, CA

MCA Nashville
60 Music Square E
Nashville, TN 37203-4325

Mercator/Caroline Records
114 W. 26th Street
New York, NY 10001

Mercury Records
825 Eighth Avenue
New York, NY 10019

Mesa/Bluemoon Recordings
209 E. Alameda Avenue, Suite 101
Burbank, CA 91502

Metal Blade Records
2345 Erringer Rd. Suite 108
Simi Valley, CA 93065-2200

Midnight International Records
Box 390
Old Chelsea Station
New York, NY 10011

Mighty Boy Ltd.
59 Abercrombie Street
Chippendale, Sydney, NSW 2008
Australia

Milan Entertainment
1540 Broadway, 29th Floor, Suite D
New York, NY 10036

Mille-Pattes
503, rue Archambault
Joliette, PQ J6E 2W6
Canada

Mipu Music
Lönnrotinkatu 15 C 24
00120 Helsinki, Finland

Miramar Recordings
200 Second Avenue West
Seattle, WA 98119

MNW Records
Box 535
S-183 25 Täby, Sweden

Mo' Wax
PO Box 9331
London N1 0TQ
England

Mobile Fidelity Sound Lab
1260 Holm Road
Petaluma, CA 94952-1181

Monkey Hill
804 Spain Street
New Orleans, LA 70117
email: monkeyhill@aol.com

Monster Music
274 Wattis Way
South San Francisco, CA 94080-6761

Mooncrest Records Ltd.
Twyman House
31-39 Camden Road
London NW1 9LE
England

Moose Records
2146 Gerrard Street East
Toronto, ON M4E 2C2
Canada

Mountain Railroad
3355 W. El Segundo Blvd.
Hawthorne, CA 90250

Mouthpiece Records
106 West 49th Street
Minneapolis, MN 55409

Mrs Ackroyd Records
PO Box 95, South District Office
Manchester M20 4LB
England

Mrs Casey Records
PO Box 296
Aylesbury, Bucks HP19 3TL
England

MTI Music
369 Montezuma, #313
Santa Fe, NM 87501

Mudball Records
PO Box 1054
Salem, OH 44460

Mulligan Records
19 Stephen's Lane
Upper Mount Street
Dublin 2, Ireland

Multicultural Media
RR3 Box 6655
Granger Road
Barre, VT 05641
email: mcm@multiculturalmedia.com

Munich Records America
Stuart-Meyers Group
PO Box 2242
Austin, TX 78768

MUSA
522 McAdam Avenue
Winnipeg, MB
Canada R2V 0A9

Music of the World
PO Box 3620
Chapel Hill, NC 27515-3620

Music for Little People
PO Box 1460
1144 Redway Drive
Redway, CA 95560

Musical Heritage Society
1710 Highway 35
Ocean, NJ 07712

Musikfolk
PO Box 339
West Byfleet, Surrey KT14 7YP
England

Music Masters
1710 Highway 35
Ocean, NJ 07712

Music & Words
MW Records PO Box 1160
3430 BD Nieuwegein, The Netherlands
email:
muwohans@knoware.nl

Mutant Rengade Records
PO Box 3445
Dayton, OH 45401

Mute Records
136 West 18th Street
New York, NY 10011

Narada
4650 N. Port Washington Road
Milwaukee, WI 53212-1063

Nature Recordings
PO Box 2749
Friday Harbor, WA 98250

Network Medien
GmbH Merianplatz 10
D-60316 Frankfurt am Main
Germany

New Albion Records
584 Castro #515
San Francisco, CA 94114

New Alliance Records
PO Box 1389
Lawndale, CA 90260

New Weave Records
PO Box 17553
Portland, OR 97217

New World Records
701 Seventh Avenue
New York, NY 10036

Nico Polo
"Braylands," St. Peters Road
Northney, Hampshire PO11
oRT
England

Night River Records
103 North Highway 101 #1013
Encinitas, CA 92024

Nimbus Records
PO Box 7427
Charlottesville, VA 22906-7427

Nomad
Music of the World
PO Box 3620
Chapel Hill, NC 27515-3620

No Masters Voice Cooperative Ltd.
78 Moorgate Road
Rotherham S60 2AY
England

Nor-CD
Hammerstads gate 48
0363 Oslo, Norway

Northeastern Records
PO Box 3589
Saxonville, MA 01701-06051

North Star Records
22 London Street
Providence, RI 02818-3628

Noumenon Records
PO Box 287
Mt. Sunapee, NH 03722

Ocora
Harmonia Mundi
2037 Granville Avenue
Los Angeles, CA 90025-6103

Oh Boy Records
33 Music Square West, #102-A
Nashville, TN 37203

OKra Records
1992-B N. High Street
Columbus, OH 43201

Olarin Musiikki Oy
Pl 20
02211 Espoo, Finland

Old Bridge Music
PO Box 7
Ilkley, W. Yorks. LS29 9RY
England
email: 100646.1316@compuserve.com

Old Dog Records
Hill Farm
Gilmorton Lane
Misterton, Nr. Lutterworth
Leicestershire LE17 4LD
England

Olivia
4400 Market Street
Oakland, CA 94608

Oenoke Records@16b:
65 High Ridge Road Suite 439
Stamford, CT 06905

Omnium Recordings@16b:
PO Box 7367
Minneapolis, MN 55407

1-800-PRIME CD
111 East 14th Street, Suite 300
New York, NY 10003

On the Spot/Private Music
8750 Wilshire Blvd.
Los Angeles, CA 90211

101 Records
PO Box 101
Heswall, Wirral
Merseyside L60 5TE
U.K.

Original Music
Box 190
Tivoli, NY 12583
email: orimu@aol.com

Orleans Records
828 Royal Street
New Orleans, LA 70116

Osmosys Records
Unit 5, Cirrus
Glebe Road
Huntingdon PE18 7DX
England

Outer Green Records
PO Box 416
South Paris, ME 04281-0416

Out There Records
PO Box 543
Norman, OK 73070

Pacific Arts Corporation
11858 La Grange Avenue
Los Angeles, CA 90025

Paget Press
115 Highland Drive
Seattle, WA 98109
email: bananafish@paget.com

PAN Records
PO Box 155
2300 AD Leiden, Netherlands

Paradox Records
PO Box 4124
27 Mountain Blvd., Suite 8
Warren, NJ 07060-0124

Parachute/Mercury/PolyGram
11150 Santa Monica Blvd,
Suite 1000
Los Angeles, CA 90025

Park Records
20 Raleigh Park Road
North Hinksey, Oxford OX2
9AZ
England

Passenger/Caroline Records
114 W. 26th Street/ New York,
NY 10001

Pax Records
78 Park Place
East Hampton, NY 11937

Peerless Music
260 Adelaide Street E., Box
#163
Toronto, ON M5A 1N1
Canada

The Pennywhistler's Press
PO Box 2473
New York, NY 10108

Philo
email: info@rounder.com

Phonogram, Ltd.
Chancellors House
Chancellors Road
Hammersmith, London W6
England

Pigeon Inlet Productions
PO Box 1202, Station C
St. John's, NF A1C 5M9
Canada

Pinecastle Records
5108 S. Orange Avenue
Orlando, FL 32809
email: pinecast@innet.com

Pläne, GmbH
Postfach 10 31 51
4600 Dortmund 1
Germany

Planet Bluegrass
1539 Pearl Street, Suite 200
Boulder, CO 80302
email: planet@bluegrass.com

Pleemhead
PO Box 1342
Claremont, CA 91711

Plump Records
30 W. 21st Street, 7th Floor
New York, NY 10010-6905
email: plumprec@aol.com

Point Records
Polygram Records
825 8th Avenue
New York, NY 10019

Pointblank/Charisma@16b:
1790 Broadway, 20th Floor
New York, NY 10019

Pointblank Records
Virgin Records
338 N. Foothill Road
Beverly Hills, CA 90210

Poke Records
54 Cambridge Road
St. Albans, Herts. AL1 5LD
England

Polaris Records
2350 Laurel Canyon Blvd.

Los Angeles, CA 90046-1505

PolyGram Records
825 8th Avenue
New York, NY 10019

Popron
Jeremi sova 947
155 00 Praha - Stodulky,
Czech Republic

Power Records
Oy Launeenkatu 82
15610 Lahti, Finland

PRA Records
1543 Seventh Street, 3rd Floor
Santa Monica, CA 90401

Prairie Smoke Records@16b:
250 W. 99th Street
New York, NY 10025

Private Music
8750 Wilshire Blvd.
Los Angeles, CA 90211

Profile Records
740 Broadway
New York, NY 10003

Propinquity Records
PO Box 9036
Denver, CO 80209

Pure Records
17 Darton Road
Cawthorne, Barnsley S75 4HR
England

Putumayo World Music
627 Broadway
New York, NY 10012

Pyramid Records (Canada)
512 Roxton Road
Toronto, ON M6G 3R4
Canada

Pyramid Records (U.S.)
1107 Biscayne Blvd. Suite 200
Miami, FL 33161

Qbadisc
PO Box 1256, Old Chelsea Station
New York, NY 10011

Quarterstick Records
PO Box 25342
Chicago, IL 60625

Rabbit Ears
One Turkey Hill Road S.
Westport, CT 06880
email: email@rabbitears.com

Razor & Tie Music
214 Sullivan Street, Suite 5A
New York, NY 10012

RDR Promotions
Box 2294 Stn. "B"
Scarborough, Ontario M1N 2E9
Canada

Reach'n Records
The Bassment Store
80 Oxford Street
Darlinghurst, NSW 2010
Australia
email: Reach@mello.com.au

RealWorld/Caroline Records
114 W. 26th Street
New York, NY 10001

Rebel Records
PO Box 3057
Roanoke, VA 24015

Reckless Records
1401 Haight Street
San Francisco, CA 94117

Red House Records
PO Box 4044
St. Paul, MN 55104

Red Pajamas
33 Music Square West, Suite 102A
Nashville, TN 37203

Relativity Records
3420 Ocean Park Blvd Suite 3050
Santa Monica, CA 90405-3305

Release

PO Box 251

Millersville, PA 17551

Relix Records
PO Box 92
Brooklyn, NY 11229

Reprise
3300 Warner Blvd.
Burbank, CA 91505-4694

Resounding Records
Box 205, Loretto Station
3001 So. Federal Boulevard
Denver, CO 80236

Resource Records
Box 535
S-183 25 Täby, Sweden

Restless Records
1616 Vista Del Mar
Hollywood, CA 90028-6420

Rhiannon Records
20 Montague Road
London E8 2HW
England
email: 100517.2142@compuserve.com

Rhino Records
10635 Santa Monica Blvd.
Los Angeles, CA 90025

Rhythm Safari
5252 Van Nuys Blvd.
Van Nuys, CA 91401-5617

Righteous Babe Records
PO Box 95, Ellicott Station
Buffalo, NY 14205-0095

Rio Records
11858 La Grange Avenue
Los Angeles, CA 90025

Rising Son Records
PO Box 657
Housatonic, MA 01236-0657
email: rsrhq@aol.com

Riverboat Records
Basement, 110 Netherwood Road
London N14 0BQ
England

The Road Goes On Forever
PO Box 12
Barnet, Herts. EN4 8PT
England

Roadrunner Records
536 Broadway
New York, NY 10012

Robi Droli
16, Strada Roncaglia
15040 S. Germano, Italy

Rockadillo Records
Keskustori 7 A 11
SF 33100 Tampere, Finland

Rogue Record
PO Box 337
London N4 1TW
England
email: froots@cityscape.co.uk

ROIR
611 Broadway, Suite 411
New York, NY 10012

ROM Records
PO Box 491212
Los Angeles, CA 90049

Rooster Blues Records
232 Sunflower Avenue
Clarksdale, MS 38614
email: info@rounder.com

Rotten Records
PO Box 2157
Montclair, CA 91763-0657

Rounder Records
1 Camp Street
Cambridge, MA 02140
email: info@rounder.com

Round Records
PO Box 3243
Norwood, SA 5067
Australia

Round Tower Music
16 Upper Grand Canal Street
Dublin 4, Ireland

Rykodisc
Shetland Park
27 Congress Street
Salem, MA 01970

Rykodisc
PO Box 2401
London W2 5SF
England

Safehouse Records
PO Box 5349
West Lebanon, NH 03784-5349

(Saga) Technosaga sa
Dolores Armengot, 13
28025 Madrid, Spain

Sage Arts
Littlefield Farm
14311 Stehr Road
Arlington, WA 98223

Sain Records
Llandwrog, Caernarfon
Gwynedd, Wales LL54 5TG
U.K.

St. Christopher Records
7615 West Touhy
Chicago, IL 60648

Sampler Records
PO Box 19270
Rochester, NY 14619

Sandstock Music
PO Box 57
Charlestown NSW 2290
Australia

Sandy Flat Music
PO Box 51056
Denton, TX 76206

Saydisc Records
Chipping Manor
The Chipping
Wotton-Under-Edge, Glos.
GL12 7AD
England

Scenesc of Records
PO Box 88
Northampton, MA 01061
email: chip.reynolds@the-spa.com

Schoolkids Records
523 E. Liberty
Ann Arbor, MI 48104

Scotti Brothers Records
2114 Pico Blvd.
Santa Monica, CA 90405

Scratch Records
PO Box 5381
Whitehorse, Yukon Territory, Y1A 4Z2
Canada

See For Miles
PO Box 328
Maidenhead, Berkshire SL6 2NE
England

Several
c/Tucán, 2
28025 Madrid, Spain

Shamrock Records
Altwaidhofen 37
A-3830 Waidhofen
Thaya, Austria

Shanachie Records
37 East Clinton Street
Newton, NJ 07860
email:
shanachie@haven.ios.com

Shed Records
PO Box 252
Iowa City, IA 52244-0252

Sheffield Lab
PO Box 5332
Santa Barbara, CA 93150

Sierra Records
PO Box 5853
Pasadena, CA 91107

Signature Sounds
PO Box 106
Whately, MA 01093
email: ssrc2@aol.com

Silence Records
S-670 41 Koppom, Sweden

Silent Planet Records
PO Box 150922
Nashville, TN 37205
email: dk@slntplanet.com

Silex Records
39 avenue Paul Vaillant Couturier
94250 Gentilly, France

Silex Records
Harmonia Mundi USA
2037 Granville Avenue
Los Angeles, CA 90025-6103

Silvertone Records
137-139 W. 25th Street
New York, NY 10001

Silver Wave Records
PO Box 7943
Boulder, CO 80306

Singsong, Inc.
PO Box 6371
St. John's, Newfoundland A1C 6J9
Canada

Sire/Warner Brothers Records
75 Rockefeller Plaza
New York, NY 10019

Sjelvar Records
HB
Närlunda Gårdsväg 20
S-178 34 Ekerö, Sweden

Skellig Records
Haupstr. 9
7111 Parndorf, Austria

Sky Records
PO Box 724677
Atlanta, GA 31139-1677

Slap-A-Ham Records
PO Box 420843
San Francisco, CA 94142-0843

Slash/Warner Brothers Records
PO Box 48888
Los Angeles, CA 90048

Slask
Box 27
S-430 84 Styrsö, Sweden

Small World Music
117 30th Avenue South
Nashville, TN 37212-2507
email: smlwrld@aol.com

Smithsonian Folkways
414 Hungerford Drive Suite 444
Rockville, MD 20850
email: Folkways@aol.com

Snow Goose Records
Woodburn Road, RR #1
Hannon, Ontario L0R 1P0
Canada

Snowplow Records
309 11th Street, C1
Union City, NJ 07087

Snowy River Records
Box 4655, Station E
Ottawa, Ontario K1S 5H8
Canada

Some Bizarre
166 New Cavendish Street
London W1, England

Sona Gaia
4650 N. Port Washington Road
Milwaukee, WI 53212

Sonet Records
78 Stanley Gardens
London W3 7SN
England

Songhai Empire Records
Rockefeller Center Station, PO Box 4236
New York, NY 10185-0036

Sonic Bubblegum
PO Box 35504
Brighton, MA 02135

Sonic Edge Records
14755 Ventura Blvd., Suite 1776
Sherman Oaks, CA 91403

Sonifolk
Calle Fernando el Católico, 58
Sotano Interior "A"
28015 Madrid, Spain

Soul-eyed Bear Records
PO Box 1327, Canal Street Station
New York, NY 10013-0867

Soundbox Records
345 Riverside Drive, 6A
New York, NY 10025

Soundings of the Planet
PO Box 43512
Tucson, AZ 85733

Sound Wave Records
3115 Ocean Front Walk
Marina Del Rey, CA 90202

The Sparrow Corporation
PO Box 5010
Brentwood, TN 37024-5010

Special Delivery Records
50 Stroud Green Road
London N4 3EF
England

Spindletop Records
11115 Magnolia Blvd.
N. Hollywood, CA 91601

Spiv Records
PO Box 35
South East P.D.O.
Manchester, M18 8JY
England

Spring Records
50 Shore Road
Rostrevor, Co. Down
Ireland

Squeezer
5 Mill Street
Aston-On-Clun
Craven Arms, Shropshire SY7 8EN
England

SST
PO Box 1
Lawndale, CA 90260

Steam Pie Records
17 The Grove, Pontllanfraith
Blackwood, Gwent NP2 2Q
Wales

Stern's
598 Broadway
New York, NY 10012

Stern's
74/75 Warren Street
London W1P 5PA
England

Stony Plain Records
PO Box 861
Edmonton, AL T5J 2L8
Canada

Strictly Country Records
PO Box 91
Coventry, CT 06238

Strictly Country Records
Postbus 32
9540 AA Vlagtwedde, Netherlands

Subharmonic
180 Varick Street
New York, NY 10014

Sub Pop
1932 First Avenue, Suite 1103
Seattle, WA 98101

Sugar Hill Records
PO Box 55300
Durham, NC 27717-5300

Sundazed Music
PO Box 85
Coxsackie, NY 12051

Sümertone Records
PO Box 22184
San Francisco, CA 94122

Sundown Records
PO Box 241
Newbury Park, CA 91320

Survival Records
PO Box 888
Maidenhead, Berks. SL6 2YQ
England

Swallow Records
Drawer 10
Ville Platte, LA 70586

Swamptone
PO Box 441388
Somerville, MA 02144

Sygnet
Swan Arcade
78 Moorgate Road
Rotherham S60 2AY
England

Tangible Music
PO Box 340
Merrick, NY 11566-0340
email: info@tangible-music.com

Tara Records
8 Annes Lane
Dublin 2, Ireland

Taxim Records
Am Dobben 3
D-27330 Asendorf, Germany

Temple Records
Shillinghill,
Temple, Midlothian EH23 4SH
Scotland

Terrapin Trucking
15 Park Road
Crouch End, London N8 8TE
England

Texas Hotel
Box 72449
Davis, CA 95617

Third Gear Records
PO Box 251481
West Bloomfield, MI 48325

Tim Kerr Records
PO Box 42423
Portland, OR 97242

Tipitina's Records
501 Napoleon Avenue
New Orleans, LA 70115-1546

Tone-Cool Records
129 Parker Street
Newton, MA 02159

Topic Records Ltd.
50 Stroud Green Road
London N4 3EF
England

Touch
13 Osward Road
London SW17 7SS
England

Touch and Go Records
PO Box 25520
Chicago, IL 60625

Tradition
Shetland Park
27 Congress Street
Salem, MA 01970

Traditional Crossroads
PO Box 20320, Greeley
Square Station
New York, NY 10001-9992
email: tradcross@aol.com

Trailer Records
email: trailer@avalon.net

Trampoline Records
PO Box 20811
Ferndale, MI 48220-0811

Tranquilla Music
106 Chelsea Street, NW
Calgary, Alberta T2K 1N9
Canada

Transatlantic Records
52 Red Lion Street
London WC1
England

Triloka Records/Worldly Music
306 Catron
Santa Fe, NM 87501

TriStar/Sony Music
550 Madison Avenue
New York, NY 10022-3211

True North Records
151 John Street, Suite 301
Toronto, Ontario M5V 2T2
Canada

Turn of the Century Records
PO Box 65
New Britain, CT 06050-0065

Turquoise Records
PO Box 947
Highway 931
Whitesburg, KY 41858

TVT Records
23 E. 4th St.
New York, NY 10003

Twah!
Schutzenstr. 31
23558 Lübeck, Germany

Twin/Tone Records
2541 Nicollet Avenue South
Minneapolis, MN 55404

Universe Records
PO Box 73
Kenmore, NY 14217

Utility Records
325 E. 21st Street #5
New York, NY 10010

Vanguard Records
Welk Record Group
1299 Ocean Avenue
Santa Monica, CA 90401,
email: vanguardrec@aol.com

Varrick Records
email: info@rounder.com

Vertebrae Records
2301 Whispering Drive
Indianapolis, IN 46239

Vertigo/Phonogram Ltd.
Chancellors House
Chancellors Road
Hammersmith, London W6
England

Village Pulse
2318 Second Avenue
Seattle, WA 98121
email: adama@oz.net

Virgin Records
9247 Alden Drive
Beverly Hills, CA 90210

Virgin Records
30 West 21st Street, 11th Floor
New York, NY 10010

Volcano Records
PO Box 368
Boston, MA 02134

Voyager Recordings & Publications
424 - 35th Avenue
Seattle, WA 98122

Waldoxy Records
PO Box 16926
Jackson, MS 39236-6926

Warner/Reprise
3300 Warner Blvd.

Burbank, CA 91505-4694

Warner Music Canada
1810 Birchmount Road
Scarborough, Ontario M1P 2H1
Canada

Waterbug
PO Box 6605
Evanston, IL 60204

Waterlily Acoustics
PO Box 91448
Santa Barbara, CA 93190
Watermelon Records
PO Box 402088
Austin, TX 78704

Wayside Music
PO Box 6517
Wheaton, MD 20906

Wax Trax!
1653 N. Damen
Chicago, IL 60647

Weasel Disc Records
1459 18th Street No. 140
San Francisco, CA 94107

Wedgie Records
30586 Paddington Court
Salisbury, MD 21804
email: tporter@shore.intercom.net

Wergo Records
GmbH Weihergarten 5, Postfach 3640
D-6500 Mainz 1, Germany

Westpark Music
PO Box 260-227
Rathenauplatz 4
D-500 Köln, Germany

Westworld
PO Box 43787
Tempe, AZ 85737

What Are Records? (W.A.R.?)
2401 Broadway
Boulder, CO 80304

Whirlie Records
Greenside House
25 Greenside Place
Edinburgh EH1 3AA
Scotland

Windham Hill Records
8750 Wilshire Blvd.
Beverly Hills, CA 90211

WindSong International
Electron House
Cray Avenue, St. Mary Cray
Orpington, Kent BR5 3RJ
England

Windy Records
216 West 89th Street, Box 39
New York, NY 10024

W.I.N. Records
PO Box 26811
Los Angeles, CA 90026-0811
email: winrecords@aol.com

Winter Harvest
PO Box 60884
Nashville, TN 37206

Wisdom Tree Records
PO Box 410
Bradford, NH 03221

Wizmak Production
PO Box 477
Wingdale, NY 12594

Woodnight Records
PO Box 6285
St. Johns, Newfoundland A1C 6J9
Canada

Woodworm Records
PO Box 37
Banbury, Oxon OX16 8YN
England

Woodpecker Records
PO Box 815
York, ME 03909
email: info@woodpecker.com

World Circuit Ltd.
35A Station Crescent
London N15 5B6
England

World Disc Music
PO Box 2749
Friday Harbor, WA 98250

The World Music Institute
109 W. 27 Street
New York, NY 10001

WPS Records
44 Avon Street
Coventry, CV2 3GL
England

Wundertüte Musik
Am Hirtenberg 14
37136 Bösinghausen, Germany

Xenophile
43 Beaver Brook Road
Danbury, CT 06810
email: grnlinnet@aol.com

Xource Records
Box 535
S-183 25 Täby, Sweden

Y&T Music
5753 S.W. 40 Street
Miami, FL 33155

Yazoo Records
Shanachie Records
37 East Clinton Street
Newton, NJ 07860
email:
shanachie@haven.ios.com

Zane Records
162 Castle Hill Reading Berks
RG1 7RP
England

Zanman Records
525 Welty Avenue
Rockford, IL 61107

Zassafras Records
PO Box 1000
Gravette, AR 72736

Zero Hour Records
14 West 23rd Street, 4th Floor
New York, NY 10010

Zimbob, Inc.
PO Box 2421
Champaign, IL 61825

Zoo Entertainment
8750 Wilshire Blvd.
Beverly Hills, CA 90211

The Influences Index corresponds to the Fast Forward and Rewind symbols included in some entries. This index acts as a unified record of the musical roots that influenced each band or artist (denoted by the Rewind symbol ⏪) and notes acts who are similar in nature to or were influenced by the artist(s) named (denoted by a Fast Forward symbol ⏩). Artists listed under the main entry are not limited to the rock genre only, and any of a number of musical genres may be listed as well.

ABBA

⏩ Ace of Base
⏪ Archies
⏩ Bjorn Again
⏪ Blue Swede
⏩ Erasure
⏪ Fifth Dimension
⏪ 1910 Fruitgum Co
⏩ Real McCoy

ABC

⏪ David Bowie
⏩ Love Jones
⏩ George Michael
⏪ Motown
⏩ Pulp
⏪ Roxy Music

Paula Abdul

⏩ Mariah Carey
⏩ Gillette
⏪ Janet Jackson
⏪ Madonna
⏪ Donna Summer

AC/DC

⏩ Rhino Bucket
⏪ Cream
⏩ Cult
⏩ Guns N' Roses
⏩ Joan Jett
⏪ Led Zeppelin
⏩ Soundgarden
⏪ Who
⏪ Yardbirds

Bryan Adams

⏪ Beatles
⏩ Bon Jovi
⏪ Joe Cocker
⏪ John Mellencamp
⏪ Fleetwood Mac
⏪ Guess Who
⏩ Michael McDermott
⏩ Steve Perry
⏩ Skid Row
⏪ Bruce Springsteen

Aerosmith

⏩ Die Kreuzen
⏩ Guns N' Roses
⏪ Led Zeppelin
⏩ Ratt
⏪ Rolling Stones
⏩ Tesla
⏪ Yardbirds

Afghan Whigs

⏪ Beatles
⏩ D Generation
⏪ Hüsker Dü
⏩ Howlin' Maggie
⏪ Motown
⏩ Jonny Polonsky
⏪ Replacements
⏩ Super 8

Agent Orange

⏩ Adolescents
⏩ Christian Death
⏪ Fear
⏪ Jefferson Airplane
⏪ Minor Threat
⏪ Sex Pistols
⏩ Game Theory
⏪ Ventures

a-ha

⏩ Ace of Base
⏪ David Bowie
⏪ Duran Duran
⏪ Roxy Music
⏪ Simple Minds

Air Supply

⏪ Captain and Tennille
⏩ Mariah Carey
⏩ Christopher Cross

Alarm

⏪ Clash
⏩ Hothouse Flowers
⏩ Midnight Oil
⏪ Sex Pistols
⏪ U2

Arthur Alexander

⏪ Eddy Arnold
⏩ Beatles
⏪ Clovers
⏩ Ry Cooder
⏩ Elvis Costello
⏩ Marshall Crenshaw
⏪ Drifters
⏩ Bee Gees
⏩ Humble Pie
⏪ Elmore James
⏪ B.B. King
⏪ Junior Parker
⏩ Otis Redding

◀◀ Jimmy Reed
▶▶ Rolling Stones
▶▶ Rod Stewart
▶▶ Ike & Tina Turner
◀◀ Billy Ward and the Dominos
◀◀ Hank Williams

Alice in Chains
◀◀ Black Sabbath
▶▶ Bush
▶▶ Hootie and the Blowfish
▶▶ Korn
◀◀ Led Zeppelin
◀◀ Metallica
◀◀ Nirvana
◀◀ Pearl Jam
▶▶ Stone Temple Pilots

Allman Brothers Band
▶▶ Black Crowes
▶▶ Black Oak Arkansas
◀◀ Cream
◀◀ Miles Davis
▶▶ Eagles
◀◀ Albert King
▶▶ Little Feat
▶▶ Lynyrd Skynyrd
▶▶ .38 Special
◀◀ Bob Willis and the Texas Playboys

Herb Alpert
▶▶ Baja Marimba Band
▶▶ Chicago
▶▶ Dirty Dozen Brass Band
▶▶ Chuck Mangione
▶▶ Hugh Masekela
▶▶ Sergio Mendes
◀◀ Louis Prima
◀◀ Tito Puente

Dave Alvin
▶▶ Big Sandy & His Fly Right Boys
◀◀ Sonny Burgess
▶▶ Reverend Horton Heat
▶▶ Jason & the Scorchers
◀◀ Big Joe Turner
◀◀ Hank Williams

Ambitious Lovers
◀◀ Derek Bailey
◀◀ James Brown
▶▶ David Byrne
◀◀ Caetano Veloso
▶▶ Cameo
◀◀ Gilberto Gil

America
◀◀ Jackson Browne
▶▶ Clark & Hillman
◀◀ Crosby, Stills, Nash and Young
◀◀ Eagles
▶▶ Firefall
▶▶ McGuinn
◀◀ Poco
◀◀ the Kingston Trio
◀◀ James Taylor

American Music Club
◀◀ Big Starr
◀◀ Tim Buckley
◀◀ Nick Drake
▶▶ Idaho
◀◀ Love
▶▶ Red House Painters
▶▶ Swell

Eric Anderson
▶▶ Jackson Browne
◀◀ Bob Dylan
◀◀ Woody Guthrie
▶▶ James McMurtry
▶▶ John Mellencamp
▶▶ Tom Petty
▶▶ Bruce Springsteen
▶▶ James Taylor
◀◀ Hank Williams

Laurie Anderson
▶▶ Adrian Belew
◀◀ William S. Burroughs
◀◀ Brian Eno
◀◀ experimental theater
▶▶ Mae Moore
◀◀ Talking Heads

Animals
▶▶ Blue Oyster Cult
◀◀ John Lee Hooker
◀◀ Alex Korner
▶▶ John Mellencamp
▶▶ Bruce Springsteen

Paul Anka
◀◀ Nat King Cole
▶▶ Neil Diamond
▶▶ Julio Iglesias
▶▶ Barry Manilow
◀◀ Frank Sinatra

Adam Ant
▶▶ Bogmen
▶▶ Elastica
◀◀ Kiss
◀◀ New York Dolls
▶▶ Sigue Sigue Sputnik

Antenna
◀◀ Buffalo Tom
◀◀ Feelies
◀◀ R.E.M.
◀◀ Keith Richards
◀◀ Velvet Underground

Anthrax
◀◀ Black Sabbath
◀◀ Alice Cooper
◀◀ Fishbone
▶▶ Gravity Kills
▶▶ GWAR
◀◀ KISS
▶▶ Megadeth
◀◀ Metallica
◀◀ Motorhead
◀◀ Ted Nugent
◀◀ P-Funk
▶▶ Pantera
◀◀ Public Enemy
◀◀ Ramones
▶▶ Red Hot Chili Peppers
◀◀ Sex Pistols
▶▶ Slayer
▶▶ Type O Negative

Joan Armatrading
▶▶ Tracy Chapman
▶▶ Dionne Farris
◀◀ Joni Mitchell
◀◀ Odetta

Louis Armstrong
▶▶ Bix Beiderbecke
▶▶ Blood, Sweat & Tears
◀◀ Buddy Bolden
▶▶ Chicago
▶▶ Dizzy Gillespie
◀◀ Kid Rena
▶▶ Wynton Marsalis
◀◀ Joe "King" Oliver
▶▶ Buster Poindexter
▶▶ Victoria Williams

Arrested Development
▶▶ Basehead
◀◀ De La Soul
▶▶ Digable Planets
◀◀ Dream Warriors
▶▶ Fugees
◀◀ Gangstarr
◀◀ Jungle Brothers
◀◀ Public Enemy
◀◀ Sly & the Family Stone
▶▶ Spearhead

Art of Noise
◀◀ John Cage
▶▶ 808 State
◀◀ environmental noise recordings
▶▶ Future Sound of London
▶▶ Global Communication
◀◀ Kraftwerk
◀◀ Mike Oldfield
▶▶ Orb
▶▶ William Orbit
▶▶ Severed Heads
▶▶ Shinjuku Thief
◀◀ Tangerine Dream
▶▶ Yello

Asia
▶▶ Dream Theater
◀◀ Emerson Lake and Palmer
◀◀ Kansas
◀◀ King Crimson
▶▶ Marillion
▶▶ Saga

- Styx
- Yes
- Zebra

Asleep at the Wheel

- Count Basie
- Merle Haggard
- Phil Harris
- Alison Krauss
- Lyle Lovett and His Large Band
- Mark O'Conner
- Marty Stuart
- Bob Wills

Association

- Bread
- Byrds
- Carpenters
- Kingston Trio
- Mamas & The Papas
- Peter, Paul & Mary
- Simon & Garfunkel
- Up with People
- Weavers

Aswad

- Big Mountain
- Freddie McGregor
- Patra
- Toots and the Maytals

Average White Band

- Brian Auger
- James Brown
- K.C. & the Sunshine Band
- Ben E. King
- Little Steven & the Disciples of Soul
- Prince
- Tower of Power

Aztec Camera

- Byrds
- Elvis Costello
- Dire Straits
- Nick Heyward
- The Housemartins
- The Style Council
- 10,000 Maniacs

Babes in Toyland

- Hole
- Pixies
- Pretenders
- 7 Year Bitch
- Sonic Youth
- Stooges
- Veruca Salt

Bachman-Turner Overdrive

- Box Tops
- Free
- Smithereens
- Soundgarden
- Stone Temple Pilots
- Who

Bad Brains

- Babe the Blue Ox
- Bad Religion
- Beastie Boys
- Clash
- Consolidated
- Cornershop
- Damned
- Goldfinger
- Living Colour
- Mahavishnu Orchestra
- Bob Marley
- Parliament/Funkadelic
- Ramones
- Return to Forever
- Sex Pistols
- Sting

Bad Company

- Black Crowes
- Bon Jovi
- Def Leppard
- Fleetwood Mac
- Free
- Alexis Korner
- Led Zeppelin
- Yardbirds

Bad Religion

- Bad Brains
- Buzzcocks
- Clash
- Crass
- NOFX
- Offspring
- Pennywise

Badfinger

- Beatles
- Del Amitri
- Herman's Hermits
- Manfred Mann
- Oasis
- Suede
- Teenage Fanclub

Joan Baez

- Mary Chapin Carpenter
- Tracy Chapman
- Bob Dylan
- Woody Guthrie
- Indigo Girls
- Odetta
- Dar Williams

Bailter Space

- Band of Susans
- Come
- Nirvana
- Sonic Youth
- Stooges
- Television
- Velvet Underground

Hank Ballard

- Gene Autry
- James Brown
- Five Royales
- John Fogerty
- Jimmy Rushing
- Swamp Dogg

Bananarama

- Chiffons
- Go-Go's
- Mamas and the Papas
- Milli Vanilli
- Wilson Phillips
- Shangri-La's

Band

- Chuck Berry
- Bobby "Blue" Bland
- Booker T and the MGs
- Eric Clapton
- Marvin Gaye
- Clarence "Frogman" Henry
- Impressions
- Long Ryders
- McGuinness-Flint
- Miracles
- Graham Parker
- Rumour
- Son Volt
- subdudes
- Uncle Tupelo
- Wilco

Band of Susans

- aMiniature
- Rhys Chatham
- Joy Division
- Live Skull
- Psychedelic Furs
- Rolling Stones
- Wire

Bangles

- Beatles
- Big Star
- Gin Blossoms
- Go-Go's
- Hole
- L7
- Mamas and the Papas
- Veruca Salt

Barenaked Ladies

- B-52s
- Beach Boys
- Beatles
- Bruce Cockburn

Dave Bartholomew

- Louis Armstrong
- Dirty Dozen Brass Band
- Louis Jordan
- Paul McCartney
- Fats Pinchon
- Allen Toussaint

Basia

- ◀◀ Gloria Estefan
- ◀◀ Astrud Gilberto
- ◀◀ Sade
- ▶▶ Lisa Stansfield
- ▶▶ Swing Out Sister

Bauhaus

- ▶▶ Alien Sex Fiend
- ◀◀ David Bowie
- ◀◀ John Cale
- ▶▶ Christian Death
- ▶▶ Sisters of Mercy
- ◀◀ Pere Ubu

Be Bop Deluxe

- ◀◀ Jeff Beck
- ◀◀ David Bowie
- ▶▶ Fixx
- ▶▶ A Flock of Seagulls
- ◀◀ Jimi Hendrix
- ◀◀ Roxy Music
- ▶▶ Joe Satriani

Beach Boys

- ▶▶ Beatles
- ◀◀ Chuck Berry
- ▶▶ Byrds
- ▶▶ Eagles
- ◀◀ Everly Brothers
- ◀◀ Four Freshmen
- ▶▶ Jan and Dean
- ◀◀ Lettermen
- ▶▶ Porno For Pyros
- ◀◀ Phil Spector

Beastie Boys

- ▶▶ Consolidated
- ▶▶ Disposable Heroes of Hiphoprisy
- ▶▶ G. Love and Special Sauce
- ◀◀ Led Zeppelin
- ◀◀ Public Enemy
- ◀◀ Run-D.M.C.

Beat Farmers

- ▶▶ Backsliders
- ◀◀ Flying Burrito Brothers
- ▶▶ Go to Blazes
- ▶▶ Old 97s
- ◀◀ Rolling Stones
- ▶▶ Uncle Tupelo
- ◀◀ Neil Young

Beat Happening

- ▶▶ Beck
- ◀◀ Doors
- ▶▶ Nirvana
- ▶▶ Spinanes
- ◀◀ Stooges

Beat

- ◀◀ Beatles
- ◀◀ Byrds
- ◀◀ Hollie
- ▶▶ Material Issue
- ▶▶ Plimsouls
- ▶▶ Romantics
- ▶▶ Rubinoos
- ◀◀ Shoes
- ◀◀ Dwight Twilley

Beatles

- ◀◀ Arthur Alexander
- ▶▶ Badfinger
- ◀◀ Chuck Berry
- ▶▶ Big Star
- ◀◀ Coasters
- ▶▶ Crowded House
- ▶▶ dBs
- ◀◀ Lonnie Donegan
- ◀◀ Everly Brothers
- ◀◀ Buddy Holly
- ▶▶ Jam
- ◀◀ Little Richard
- ▶▶ Oasis
- ◀◀ Roy Orbison
- ◀◀ Carl Perkins
- ◀◀ Elvis Presley
- ▶▶ Squeeze
- ▶▶ Utopia
- ▶▶ XTC

Beau Brummels

- ◀◀ Beatles
- ▶▶ Del Amitri
- ◀◀ Searchers
- ▶▶ Toad the Wet Sprocket

Jeff Beck

- ◀◀ James Burton
- ◀◀ Cliff Gallup
- ◀◀ Buddy Guy
- ◀◀ Les Paul
- ▶▶ Vernon Reid
- ▶▶ Joe Satriani
- ▶▶ Eddie Van Halen
- ▶▶ Stevie Ray Vaughan

Bee Gees

- ▶▶ Air Supply
- ◀◀ Beach Boys
- ◀◀ Beatles
- ▶▶ Bread
- ▶▶ Yvonne Elliman
- ◀◀ Four Freshmen
- ▶▶ Andy Gibb
- ◀◀ Kingston Trio
- ▶▶ Mr. Mister

Adrian Belew

- ◀◀ Beatles
- ▶▶ Beck
- ▶▶ John Frusciante
- ◀◀ King Crimson
- ◀◀ Frank Zappa

Pat Benatar

- ▶▶ Melissa Etheridge
- ▶▶ 4 Non Blondes
- ◀◀ Janis Joplin
- ▶▶ Scandal
- ◀◀ Grace Slick
- ◀◀ Patti Smith

Brook Benton

- ▶▶ Ray Charles
- ◀◀ Nat King Cole
- ▶▶ Etta James
- ▶▶ Clyde McPhatter
- ◀◀ Arthur Prysock
- ◀◀ Frank Sinatra
- ▶▶ Joe South

Chuck Berry

- ▶▶ Beach Boys
- ▶▶ Beatles
- ▶▶ Bob Dylan
- ◀◀ Louis Jordan
- ▶▶ Rolling Stones
- ◀◀ T-Bone Walker
- ◀◀ Muddy Waters
- ◀◀ Hank Williams

B-52's

- ◀◀ Dick Dale
- ▶▶ Deee-Lite
- ▶▶ Cibo Matto
- ◀◀ Ricky Ricardo
- ◀◀ Shangri-La's
- ▶▶ Technotronic
- ◀◀ Yoko Ono

Big Audio Dynamite

- ◀◀ Chicago house music
- ◀◀ Clash
- ◀◀ Detroit techno
- ▶▶ EMF
- ▶▶ Jesus Jones
- ▶▶ Soup Dragons
- ◀◀ Who

Big Chief

- ◀◀ James Brown
- ◀◀ MC5
- ◀◀ Parliament-Funkadelic
- ◀◀ Stooges

Big Head Todd and the Monsters

- ◀◀ Blues Traveler
- ◀◀ Albert Collins
- ◀◀ Buddy Guy
- ▶▶ Dave Matthews Band
- ▶▶ Rusted Root
- ◀◀ Sly and the Family Stone
- ◀◀ Stevie Ray Vaughan
- ▶▶ Widespread Panic

Big Star

- ◀◀ Badfinger
- ◀◀ Beach Boys
- ◀◀ Beatles
- ◀◀ Booker T. and the MGs
- ◀◀ Byrds
- ▶▶ Elvis Costello
- ▶▶ Marshall Crenshaw

- ⏩ dB's
- ⏩ Game Theory
- ⏪ Hollies
- ⏩ Jellyfish
- ⏩ Tommy Keene
- ⏪ Kinks
- ⏩ Letters to Cleo
- ⏩ Loud Family
- ⏩ Aimee Mann
- ⏪ Moby Grape
- ⏪ Move
- ⏩ Posies
- ⏩ R.E.M.
- ⏩ Raspberries
- ⏪ Otis Redding
- ⏩ Replacements
- ⏪ Rolling Stones
- ⏩ Matthew Sweet
- ⏩ Teenage Fanclub

Birthday Party

- ⏪ Doors
- ⏩ Sex Pistols
- ⏪ Stooges

Elvin Bishop

- ⏩ Canned Heat
- ⏪ Albert Collins
- ⏪ Lightinin' Hopkins
- ⏪ Elmore James
- ⏪ Albert King
- ⏪ B.B. King
- ⏪ Freddie King
- ⏩ Jimmie Vaughan
- ⏩ Stevie Ray Vaughan

Bjork

- ⏪ Cocteau Twins
- ⏪ Dead Can Dance
- ⏩ Dee-Lite
- ⏪ Joy Division
- ⏩ Pizzicato 5
- ⏩ Shelleyan Orphan
- ⏪ Siouxsie and the Banshees

Frank Black

- ⏪ Beatles
- ⏩ Belly
- ⏪ David Bowie
- ⏪ Dick Dale & His Del-Tones
- ⏩ Dinosaur Jr.
- ⏩ Feelies
- ⏩ Flaming Lips
- ⏩ Hüsker Dü
- ⏩ Lemonheads
- ⏩ Nirvana
- ⏩ Pixies
- ⏩ Jonny Polonsky
- ⏪ Iggy Pop
- ⏪ Ramones
- ⏪ Jonathan Richman
- ⏩ Sonic Youth
- ⏩ Sugarcubes
- ⏩ Throwing Muses
- ⏪ Velvet Underground
- ⏪ Ventures
- ⏩ Weezer
- ⏪ Brian Wilson

Black Crowes

- ⏪ Aerosmith
- ⏪ Allman Brothers Band
- ⏩ Blues Traveler
- ⏪ Faces
- ⏪ Humble Pie
- ⏪ Led Zeppelin
- ⏪ Little Feat
- ⏩ Primal Scream
- ⏩ Quireboys
- ⏪ Rolling Stones
- ⏪ Rod Stewart
- ⏪ War
- ⏩ Widespread Panic

Black Flag

- ⏩ Circle Jerks
- ⏩ Green Day
- ⏩ Wayne Kramer
- ⏪ MC5
- ⏩ NOFX
- ⏩ Offspring
- ⏩ Pennywise
- ⏪ Ramones
- ⏪ Sex Pistol
- ⏪ Stooges

Black 47

- ⏪ Booker T. and the Mgs
- ⏪ Enemy Orchard
- ⏩ Goats Don't Shave
- ⏪ Pogues
- ⏪ Bruce Springsteen
- ⏪ Them

Black Sabbath

- ⏩ Anthrax
- ⏪ Bela Lugosi
- ⏪ Cream
- ⏩ Megadeth
- ⏩ Metallica
- ⏪ Muddy Waters
- ⏩ Nirvana
- ⏩ Soundgarden

Black Uhuru

- ⏪ Burning Spear
- ⏩ Fugees
- ⏩ UB40
- ⏪ Wailers

Ruben Blades

- ⏪ Celia Cruz
- ⏪ Fania All Stars
- ⏩ Victor Manuel
- ⏩ Robbie Robertson
- ⏩ Jon Secada

Blake Babies

- ⏪ Buffalo Tom
- ⏪ Feelies
- ⏩ Lemonheads
- ⏪ R.E.M.
- ⏪ Keith Richards
- ⏩ Jill Sobule
- ⏪ Velvet Underground

Blondie

- ⏩ Bangles
- ⏩ Echobelly
- ⏩ Elastica
- ⏩ Letters to Cleo
- ⏩ Sleeper

Blood, Sweat and Tears

- ⏪ Beatles
- ⏪ Blues Project
- ⏩ Michael Bolton
- ⏩ Brecker Brothers
- ⏩ Chicago
- ⏪ Count Basie
- ⏪ Electric Flag
- ⏪ Duke Ellington
- ⏪ Ike Turner's Kings of Rhythm
- ⏩ Stevie Wonder

Luka Bloom

- ⏪ Joan Armatrading
- ⏪ Boomtown Rats
- ⏩ Tracey Chapman
- ⏪ Cowboy Junkies
- ⏩ Hothouse Flowers
- ⏪ Joni Mitchell
- ⏩ Sinead O'Connor
- ⏪ Michelle Shocked
- ⏪ Susan Vega

Michael Bloomfield

- ⏩ Peter Green
- ⏪ Robert Johnson
- ⏪ Muddy Waters
- ⏩ Shuggie Otis

Blue Aeroplanes

- ⏩ Nick Cave and the Bad Seeds
- ⏪ Leonard Cohen
- ⏪ Fairport Convention
- ⏪ Velvet Underground
- ⏪ Paul Winter Consort

Blue Öyster Cult

- ⏩ Def Leppard
- ⏩ Judas Priest
- ⏪ Led Zeppelin
- ⏩ Metallica
- ⏩ Minutemen/fIREHOSE
- ⏪ Steppenwolf

Blues Brothers

- ⏪ Blues Project
- ⏩ Blues Traveler
- ⏪ James Brown
- ⏪ Ray Charles
- ⏪ Stax
- ⏩ Treat Her Right
- ⏪ Sonny Boy Williamson

Blues Project
- ◀◀ Chuck Berry
- ▶▶ Blood, Sweat & Tears
- ◀◀ Willie Dixon
- ◀◀ Bob Dylan
- ◀◀ Rolling Stones
- ▶▶ Seatrain
- ◀◀ Muddy Waters

Blues Traveler
- ◀◀ Allman Brothers Band
- ◀◀ Blues Brothers
- ◀◀ Grateful Dead
- ▶▶ Joan Osborne
- ◀◀ David Peel
- ▶▶ Screaming Cheetah Wheelies
- ▶▶ Spin Doctors
- ▶▶ Why Store

Blur
- ◀◀ Buzzcocks
- ▶▶ Elastica
- ◀◀ Jam
- ◀◀ Kinks
- ▶▶ Shed Seven
- ▶▶ These Animal Men
- ◀◀ Who
- ◀◀ XTC

Bodeans
- ◀◀ Band
- ▶▶ Big Head Todd & The Monsters
- ◀◀ Buffalo Springfield
- ◀◀ Byrds
- ◀◀ Everly Brothers
- ▶▶ Jayhawks
- ▶▶ Freddy Jones Band
- ▶▶ Son Volt and the Bottle Rockets
- ▶▶ Uncle Tupelo
- ▶▶ Wilco

Tommy Bolin
- ◀◀ Jeff Beck
- ◀◀ David Bowie
- ◀◀ Eric Clapton
- ◀◀ Jimmy Hendrix
- ▶▶ Motley Crue
- ◀◀ Elvis Presley
- ▶▶ Randy Rhodes
- ▶▶ Eddie Van Halen
- ▶▶ Stevie Ray Vaughan

Michael Bolton
- ▶▶ Mariah Carey
- ▶▶ Celine Dion
- ◀◀ Al Jolson
- ◀◀ Patti LaBelle
- ◀◀ Otis Redding
- ◀◀ Percy Sledge

Bon Jovi
- ◀◀ Aerosmith
- ◀◀ Asbury Jukes
- ◀◀ Cheap Trick
- ◀◀ Alice Cooper
- ◀◀ Kiss
- ▶▶ Poison
- ▶▶ Ratt
- ◀◀ Bruce Springsteen
- ▶▶ Warrant
- ▶▶ Winger

Bongos
- ◀◀ Beatles
- ◀◀ Marc Bolan
- ◀◀ Donovan
- ▶▶ Michael Penn
- ◀◀ Velvet Underground

Karla Bonoff
- ▶▶ Kathy Mattea
- ◀◀ Laura Nyro
- ◀◀ Stone Poneys
- ◀◀ Wendy Waldman
- ▶▶ Wynonna
- ▶▶ Trisha Yearwood

Bonzo Dog Band
- ◀◀ Beatles
- ◀◀ Spike Jones
- ▶▶ Monty Python
- ▶▶ Rutles
- ▶▶ Weird Al Yankovic

James Booker
- ▶▶ Allen Toussaint
- ▶▶ Henry Butler
- ◀◀ Frederic Chopin
- ▶▶ Dr. John
- ◀◀ Louis Moreau Gottschalk
- ◀◀ Meade Lux Lewis
- ▶▶ Little Richard
- ◀◀ Jelly Roll Morton
- ◀◀ Professor Longhair
- ◀◀ Huey "Piano" Smith
- ◀◀ Tuts Washington
- ▶▶ George Winston

Booker T. And the MG's
- ◀◀ Cannonball Adderley
- ▶▶ Elvis Costello and the Attractions
- ▶▶ Creedence Clearwater Revival
- ◀◀ Mar-Keys

Boston
- ◀◀ Beatles
- ▶▶ Foreigner
- ◀◀ Led Zeppelin
- ▶▶ Night Ranger
- ▶▶ Survivor
- ◀◀ Yes

Jean-Paul Bourelly
- ◀◀ Miles Davis
- ◀◀ Jimi Hendrix
- ◀◀ John McLaughlin
- ▶▶ Milo Z
- ◀◀ Wes Montgomery
- ◀◀ Jimmy Page
- ◀◀ Sly & the Family Stone
- ◀◀ Muddy Waters
- ◀◀ Frank Zappa

Bow Wow Wow
- ◀◀ Adam and the Ants
- ▶▶ Belly
- ◀◀ Bo Diddley
- ▶▶ Oingo Boingo
- ◀◀ Sex Pistols
- ▶▶ Siouxsie and the Banshees

David Bowie
- ▶▶ Duran Duran
- ◀◀ Easybeats
- ◀◀ Kinks
- ▶▶ Nirvana
- ◀◀ Pink Floyd
- ▶▶ Smashing Pumpkins
- ▶▶ Smiths
- ▶▶ Suede
- ◀◀ Who
- ◀◀ Yardbirds

Billy Bragg
- ◀◀ Clash
- ◀◀ Elvis Costello
- ◀◀ Woody Guthrie
- ▶▶ Hammell On Trial
- ▶▶ John Wesley Harding

Laura Branigan
- ◀◀ Irene Cara
- ◀◀ Hall and Oates
- ▶▶ Alanis Morrisette
- ▶▶ Joan Osborne
- ◀◀ Donna Summer
- ◀◀ Tina Turner

Brave Combo
- ▶▶ New Orleans Klezmer All Stars
- ◀◀ You name it

Bread
- ▶▶ Air Supply
- ▶▶ America
- ◀◀ Association
- ◀◀ Chet Atkins
- ◀◀ Beatles
- ▶▶ Chris von Sneidern
- ▶▶ Matthew Sweet

Breeders
- ◀◀ Beach Boys
- ▶▶ Belly
- ▶▶ Juliana Hatfield
- ◀◀ Hüsker Dü
- ◀◀ Jesus and Mary Chain
- ◀◀ Raincoats
- ◀◀ Ramones
- ◀◀ Replacements
- ◀◀ Throwing Muses
- ◀◀ Who

David Bromberg
- ◀◀ Beatles
- ◀◀ Rev. Gary Davis
- ◀◀ Bob Dylan
- ▶▶ David Grisman

- ◀◀ Jerry Jeff Walker
- ▶▶ Chris Whitley

Bronski Beat

- ▶▶ Cathy Dennis
- ◀◀ Thelma Houston
- ◀◀ Giorgio Moroder
- ◀◀ Alison Moyet
- ▶▶ Cece Peniston
- ◀◀ Q-Feel
- ◀◀ Donna Summer

Arthur Brown

- ▶▶ David Bowie
- ▶▶ Alice Cooper
- ◀◀ London's West End theaters
- ▶▶ Sensational Alex Harvey Band

James Brown

- ▶▶ Afrika Bambaataa
- ◀◀ Hank Ballard & the Midnighters
- ◀◀ Roy Brown
- ◀◀ Ray Charles
- ▶▶ Chic
- ▶▶ George Clinton
- ▶▶ Bootsy Collins
- ◀◀ Bo Diddley
- ◀◀ Dominos
- ▶▶ Eric B. and Rakim
- ◀◀ Five Royales
- ▶▶ Hammer
- ◀◀ Wynonie Harris
- ▶▶ Isaac Hayes
- ▶▶ Jimi Hendrix
- ▶▶ Michael Jackson
- ▶▶ Mick Jagger
- ◀◀ Louis Jordan
- ▶▶ Parliament-Funkadelic
- ▶▶ Prince
- ▶▶ Otis Redding
- ▶▶ Sly and the Family Stone
- ▶▶ Rod Stewart
- ▶▶ Peter Wolf (J. Geils Band)

Jackson Browne

- ◀◀ Eric Andersen
- ▶▶ Garth Brooks
- ◀◀ Leonard Cohen
- ▶▶ Natalie Merchant
- ▶▶ Alanis Morissette
- ◀◀ Phil Ochs
- ▶▶ David Wilcox

Jack Bruce

- ▶▶ Jack Casady
- ▶▶ Stanley Clarke
- ◀◀ Willie Dixon
- ◀◀ Dizzy Gillespie
- ▶▶ Geddy Lee
- ◀◀ John Mayall
- ▶▶ Ozzy Osbourne
- ◀◀ Charlie Parker
- ▶▶ Jaco Pastorius
- ▶▶ Robert Plant
- ▶▶ Rob Wasserman

Lindsey Buckingham

- ◀◀ Clash
- ▶▶ Marshall Crenshaw
- ◀◀ Kingston Trio
- ◀◀ Sex Pistols
- ▶▶ John Stewart
- ▶▶ Matthew Sweet
- ◀◀ Brian Wilson

Tim Buckley

- ▶▶ Bono
- ▶▶ Jeff Buckley
- ◀◀ John Coltrane
- ◀◀ Miles Davis
- ◀◀ Bob Dylan
- ◀◀ Leadbelly
- ▶▶ Patti Smith
- ▶▶ This Mortal Coil

Buffalo Springfield

- ◀◀ Beatles
- ◀◀ Byrds
- ▶▶ Crosby, Stills and Nash
- ▶▶ Eagles
- ◀◀ Everly Brothers
- ▶▶ Flying Burrito Brothers
- ▶▶ Loggins and Messina
- ▶▶ Poco
- ▶▶ Linda Ronstadt
- ▶▶ Uncle Tupelo
- ▶▶ Warren Zevon

Buffalo Tom

- ▶▶ Grant Lee Buffalo
- ◀◀ Dinosaur Jr.
- ◀◀ Hüsker Dü
- ◀◀ Mission of Burma

Jimmy Buffett

- ▶▶ Blues Traveler
- ◀◀ Gamble Rogers
- ▶▶ Iguanas
- ◀◀ Benny Spellman
- ▶▶ subdudes
- ◀◀ Irma Thomas
- ◀◀ Jerry Jeff Walker

Solomon Burke

- ◀◀ Robert Blair and the Fantastic Violinaires
- ◀◀ Rev. Julius Cheeks
- ▶▶ Otis Redding
- ▶▶ Bruce Springsteen
- ▶▶ Joe Tex

T-Bone Burnett

- ◀◀ Elvis Costello
- ▶▶ Counting Crows
- ◀◀ Bob Dylan
- ▶▶ Los Lobos
- ▶▶ Sam Phillips

Kate Bush

- ▶▶ Tori Amos
- ◀◀ Celtic folk music
- ◀◀ Sandy Denny
- ◀◀ Fairport Convention
- ◀◀ Peter Gabriel
- ◀◀ Genesis
- ◀◀ Moody Blues
- ▶▶ Sinead O'Connor
- ▶▶ Dolores O'Riordian (the Cranberries)
- ◀◀ Pink Floyd
- ▶▶ Siouxsie Sioux (Siouxsie and the Banshees)

Jon Butcher Axis

- ◀◀ Jeff Beck
- ◀◀ Jimi Hendrix Experience
- ▶▶ Living Colour
- ◀◀ Pat Metheny
- ◀◀ Mahogany Rush
- ◀◀ Robin Trower

Paul Butterfield Blues Band

- ▶▶ Aerosmith
- ▶▶ Bad Company
- ▶▶ Black Crowes
- ▶▶ Blood, Sweat and Tears
- ◀◀ Buddy Guy
- ▶▶ Chicago
- ▶▶ Electric Flag
- ▶▶ Fabulous Thunderbirds
- ◀◀ Little Walter
- ◀◀ Muddy Waters
- ◀◀ Junior Wells
- ◀◀ Sonny Boy Williamson

Butthole Surfers

- ▶▶ Alice Donut
- ▶▶ Cherubs
- ◀◀ Fall
- ◀◀ Flipper
- ◀◀ Hawkwind
- ▶▶ Reverend Horton Heat
- ▶▶ Killdozer
- ▶▶ NoMeansNo
- ◀◀ 10cc
- ▶▶ Ween

Buzzcocks

- ▶▶ Hüsker Dü
- ▶▶ Magazine
- ◀◀ Ramones
- ◀◀ Sex Pistols
- ◀◀ Stooges
- ◀◀ Television

Byrds

- ▶▶ Beatles
- ◀◀ Beatles
- ▶▶ Blue Oyster Cult
- ▶▶ Buffalo Springfield
- ◀◀ John Coltrane
- ▶▶ Elvis Costello & the Attractions
- ▶▶ Crosby, Stills & Nash
- ▶▶ Desert Rose Band
- ▶▶ Bob Dylan
- ◀◀ Bob Dylan

- ⏩ Eagles
- ⏩ Flying Burrito Brothers
- ⏩ Gin Blossoms
- ⏪ Merle Haggard
- ⏩ Jayhawks
- ⏪ New Christy Minstrels
- ⏩ Tom Petty & the Heartbreakers
- ⏩ Poco
- ⏩ R.E.M.
- ⏩ Searchers
- ⏪ Ravi Shankar
- ⏩ Son Volt
- ⏩ Soul Asylum
- ⏩ Uncle Tupelo
- ⏩ Wilco

David Byrne

- ⏪ Terry Allen
- ⏪ Desi Arnaz
- ⏩ Beck
- ⏩ Hayden
- ⏩ Primitive Radio Gods
- ⏪ Robert Wilson

J.J. Cale

- ⏪ Chet Atkins
- ⏩ John Campbell
- ⏩ Eric Clapton
- ⏩ Dire Straits
- ⏪ Grand Ole Opry
- ⏩ Uncle Tupelo
- ⏩ Wilco

John Cale

- ⏪ Beach Boys
- ⏪ Beatles
- ⏪ John Cage
- ⏩ Nick Drake
- ⏩ Brian Eno
- ⏩ Robert Fripp
- ⏩ King Crimson
- ⏩ Pink Floyd
- ⏩ Roxy Music
- ⏩ Patti Smith
- ⏩ Television
- ⏪ Velvet Underground
- ⏩ Tom Verlaine
- ⏩ Tom Waits
- ⏩ Robert Wyatt
- ⏪ LaMonte Young

Call

- ⏩ Alarm
- ⏪ Clash
- ⏪ Joy Division
- ⏩ nine inch nails

Camel

- ⏩ Cocteau Twins
- ⏩ Dead Can Dance
- ⏩ Enya
- ⏪ Genesis (with Peter Gabriel)
- ⏪ King Crimson
- ⏪ Pink Floyd (with Syd Barrett)
- ⏪ Procol Harum

Camper Van Beethoven

- ⏩ Dead Milkmen
- ⏪ Grateful Dead
- ⏪ Indian raja music
- ⏪ Jan & Dean
- ⏪ Bob Marley
- ⏩ Mighty Mighty Bosstones
- ⏪ Tom Petty
- ⏩ Presidents of the United States of America
- ⏪ R.E.M.
- ⏪ Specials
- ⏩ Sublime

Canned Heat

- ⏩ Blues Traveler
- ⏩ Fabulous Thunderbirds
- ⏩ Grateful Dead
- ⏪ John Lee Hooker
- ⏪ Howlin' Wolf
- ⏪ Sonny Boy Williamson

Captain Beefheart & His Magic Band

- ⏩ Nick Cave
- ⏩ Eugene Chadbourne
- ⏪ Ornette Coleman
- ⏪ Bo Diddley
- ⏪ Eric Dolphy
- ⏩ PJ Harvey
- ⏪ Howlin' Wolf
- ⏩ Residents
- ⏩ Sonic Youth
- ⏪ Karlheinz Stockhausen
- ⏪ Sun Ra
- ⏩ Tom Waits

Mariah Carey

- ⏩ Toni Braxton
- ⏪ Irene Cara
- ⏩ Celine Dion
- ⏪ Whitney Houston
- ⏪ Minnie Ripperton

Mary Chapin Carpenter

- ⏪ Beatles
- ⏩ Suzy Bogguss
- ⏪ Carlene Carter
- ⏪ Rosanne Cash
- ⏩ Shawn Colvin
- ⏪ Bob Dylan
- ⏩ Patty Loveless
- ⏪ Joni Mitchell
- ⏩ Dar Williams
- ⏩ Trisha Yearwood

Carpenters

- ⏩ Air Supply
- ⏪ Association
- ⏪ Burt Bacharach
- ⏪ Beatles
- ⏩ Sheryl Crow
- ⏪ Mantovani

Paul Carrack

- ⏩ Michael Bolton
- ⏪ Ray Charles
- ⏩ Little River Band
- ⏪ Otis Redding
- ⏪ Jackie Wilson

Joe "King" Carrasco

- ⏪ Flaco Jimenez
- ⏩ Flaco Jimenez
- ⏪ ? and the Mysterians
- ⏩ Doug Sahm
- ⏪ Sam the Sham & the Pharoahs
- ⏪ Sir Douglas Quintet
- ⏩ Texas Tornados

Jim Carroll

- ⏩ Alice in Chains
- ⏪ Leonard Cohen
- ⏪ Jim Morrison
- ⏪ Graham Parker
- ⏩ Pearl Jam
- ⏪ Lou Reed
- ⏪ Sex Pistols
- ⏩ Soundgarden
- ⏪ Bruce Springsteen

Cars

- ⏩ Afghan Whigs
- ⏩ Bad Religion
- ⏪ Blondie
- ⏩ Lloyd Cole
- ⏪ Kraftwerk
- ⏪ Modern Lovers
- ⏩ Matthew Sweet
- ⏪ Talking Heads
- ⏪ Velvet Underground
- ⏩ Weezer

Clarence Carter

- ⏩ Aerosmith
- ⏪ Solomon Burke
- ⏩ Rick James
- ⏩ R. Kelly
- ⏪ Lightnin' Hopkins
- ⏪ Otis Redding
- ⏩ Keith Sweat

Peter Case

- ⏪ Blind Lemon Jefferson
- ⏩ Alejandro Escovedo
- ⏪ Woody Guthrie
- ⏩ Replacements

Johnny Cash

- ⏩ Carlene Carter
- ⏪ Carter Family
- ⏩ Rosanne Cash
- ⏩ Bob Dylan
- ⏩ Waylon Jennings
- ⏩ Kris Kristofferson
- ⏪ Louvin Brothers
- ⏩ Nick Lowe
- ⏪ Jimmie Rodgers
- ⏩ Bruce Springsteen

- ▶▶ Marty Stuart
- ▶▶ Hank Williams Jr.

Rosanne Cash
- ▶▶ Mary Chapin Carpenter
- ▶▶ Shawn Colvin

Nick Cave and the Bad Seeds
- ▶▶ Tori Amos
- ◀◀ Clash
- ◀◀ Leonard Cohen
- ◀◀ Doors
- ◀◀ Nick Drake

Chad & Jeremy
- ▶▶ Boyce & Hart
- ◀◀ Everly Brothers
- ◀◀ Flanders & Swann
- ◀◀ Peter,Paul & Mary
- ▶▶ Proclaimers
- ▶▶ Wham!

Chambers Brothers
- ◀◀ Animals
- ◀◀ James Brown
- ▶▶ George Clinton
- ◀◀ Wilson Pickett
- ◀◀ Otis Redding
- ▶▶ Run DMC
- ▶▶ Sly and the Family Stone
- ▶▶ War

Chameleons
- ▶▶ Afghan Whigs
- ▶▶ Bush
- ◀◀ Peter Gabriel/Genesis
- ▶▶ Green Day
- ▶▶ James
- ◀◀ Joy Division
- ◀◀ King Crimson
- ▶▶ Smiths

James Chance
- ◀◀ Albert Ayler
- ◀◀ James Brown
- ▶▶ Bush Tetras
- ▶▶ Defunkt
- ▶▶ Living Colour
- ▶▶ Minutemen
- ▶▶ Raybeats
- ▶▶ Tar Babies
- ◀◀ Teenage Jesus & the Jerks

Harry Chapin
- ▶▶ Mary Chapin Carpenter
- ▶▶ Sheryl Crow
- ▶▶ James McMurtry
- ▶▶ John Mellencamp
- ◀◀ Phil Ochs
- ◀◀ Pete Seeger

Tracy Chapman
- ◀◀ Joan Armatrading
- ◀◀ Joan Baez
- ▶▶ Ani DiFranco
- ▶▶ Dionne Farris
- ▶▶ Patty Griffin
- ▶▶ Jewel
- ◀◀ Joni Mitchell
- ▶▶ Poe

Charlatans UK
- ▶▶ Bluetones
- ◀◀ Deep Purple
- ▶▶ Milltown Brothers
- ▶▶ Northern Uproar
- ◀◀ Rolling Stones
- ◀◀ Who
- ◀◀ Stevie Wonder

Ray Charles
- ◀◀ Count Basie
- ◀◀ Charles Brown
- ▶▶ Joe Cocker
- ◀◀ Nat "King" Cole
- ◀◀ Grand Ole Opry
- ◀◀ Claude Jeter
- ▶▶ Billy Joel
- ◀◀ Louis Jordan
- ▶▶ Van Morrison

Cheap Trick
- ◀◀ Beatles
- ▶▶ Johnny Bravo
- ▶▶ Enuff Z'Nuff
- ▶▶ Material Issue
- ◀◀ Move
- ◀◀ Who

Vic Chesnutt
- ◀◀ Leonard Cohen
- ◀◀ Bob Dylan
- ▶▶ Joe Henry
- ▶▶ Gillian Welch
- ▶▶ Victoria Williams

Chic
- ▶▶ Philip Bailey
- ▶▶ Blondie
- ▶▶ David Bowie
- ◀◀ James Brown
- ▶▶ Duran Duran
- ▶▶ Bryan Ferry
- ▶▶ Peter Gabriel
- ▶▶ Mick Jagger
- ▶▶ Al Jarreau
- ▶▶ Madonna
- ▶▶ Robert Palmer
- ◀◀ Parliament/Funkadelic
- ▶▶ Queen
- ▶▶ Diana Ross
- ▶▶ Sister Sledge
- ▶▶ Sugarhill Gang
- ◀◀ Sylvester

Chicago
- ◀◀ Herb Alpert & the Tijuana Brass
- ▶▶ American Breed
- ◀◀ Blood, Sweat & Tears
- ◀◀ Electric Flag
- ◀◀ Maynard Ferguson
- ▶▶ Grass Roots
- ▶▶ UB40
- ▶▶ Uptown Horns

Chills
- ◀◀ Cocteau Twins
- ▶▶ Cranberries
- ◀◀ Easybeats
- ▶▶ Posies
- ◀◀ Split Enz
- ▶▶ Sundays

Alex Chilton
- ◀◀ Beatles
- ▶▶ dB's
- ▶▶ Posies
- ▶▶ R.E.M.
- ◀◀ Otis Redding
- ▶▶ Replacements

Chipmunks
- ▶▶ Geddy Lee (Rush)
- ◀◀ "The Wizard of Oz" and all of your favorite singers

Church
- ◀◀ Beatles
- ◀◀ David Bowie
- ◀◀ Byrds
- ◀◀ Cocteau Twins
- ◀◀ Leonard Cohen
- ◀◀ Fall
- ▶▶ Galaxie 500
- ▶▶ Luna
- ▶▶ Lush
- ▶▶ Ride
- ▶▶ Slowdive
- ▶▶ Stone Roses

Circle Jerks
- ▶▶ Agent Orange
- ▶▶ Bad Religion
- ◀◀ Cramps
- ▶▶ Dead Kennedys
- ◀◀ Dictators
- ▶▶ Hüsker Dü
- ◀◀ Jefferson Airplane
- ◀◀ Kinks
- ◀◀ Rolling Stones
- ◀◀ Sex Pistols
- ◀◀ XTC

Eric Clapton
- ▶▶ Allman Brothers Band
- ◀◀ The Band
- ◀◀ Jimi Hendrix
- ◀◀ J.J. Cale
- ◀◀ Albert King
- ◀◀ Freddie King
- ▶▶ Stevie Ray Vaughan
- ◀◀ Muddy Waters

Petula Clark
- ▶▶ Carpenters
- ▶▶ Olivia-Newton John
- ◀◀ Lulu

⏩ Anne Murray
⏩ Linda Ronstadt

Clash
⏪ David Bowie
⏪ Eddie Cochran
⏪ Bo Diddley
⏩ Green Day
⏪ Junior Marvin
⏩ Nada Surf
⏩ Pogues
⏪ Ramones
⏩ Rancid
⏪ Sex Pistols
⏪ Who

Johnny Clegg & Savuka
⏪ Aswad
⏪ Ladysmith Black Mambazo
⏪ Mahlathini & the Cinderella Queens
⏩ Dave Matthews Band
⏪ Men At Work
⏪ Police
⏩ Rusted Root
⏩ Paul Simon (circa "Graceland")

Jimmy Cliff
⏩ Big Mountain
⏪ Desmond Dekker
⏩ English Beat
⏩ Maxi Priest
⏩ Third World
⏪ Toots and the Maytals
⏩ UB40

Patsy Cline
⏩ Mary Chapin Carpenter
⏩ Cowboy Junkies
⏩ k.d. lang
⏩ Loretta Lynn
⏩ Dolly Parton
⏪ Cole Porter
⏩ Linda Ronstadt
⏪ Hank Williams
⏩ Lucinda Williams
⏪ Bob Wills

George Clinton
⏪ James Brown
⏩ Digital Underground
⏩ Dr. Dre
⏩ Eric B & Rakim
⏩ Groove Collective
⏪ Screamin' Jay Hawkins
⏩ Prince
⏩ Red Hot Chili Peppers
⏪ Sun Ra
⏪ Ike Turner

Eddie Cochran
⏩ Paul McCartney
⏩ Ricky Nelson
⏪ Elvis Presley
⏩ Brian Setzer

Bruce Cockburn
⏩ Billy Bragg
⏪ Bob Dylan
⏩ Mark Heard
⏪ Gordon Lightfoot
⏩ Tragically Hip
⏪ Weavers

Joe Cocker
⏩ Bryan Adams
⏪ Beatles
⏪ James Brown
⏪ Ray Charles
⏩ Roger Daltrey (the Who)
⏪ B.B. King
⏩ Robert Palmer
⏪ Big Joe Turner
⏩ Kim Wilson (Fabulous Thunderbirds)

Cocteau Twins
⏩ Tori Amos
⏪ Kate Bush
⏩ Cranes
⏩ Curve
⏩ Dead Can Dance
⏪ Joy Division
⏪ Simple Minds
⏪ Siouxsie and the Banshees
⏩ This Mortal Coil

Leonard Cohen
⏪ Jacques Brel
⏩ Nick Cave
⏪ Bob Dylan
⏪ Leadbelly
⏩ Morrissey
⏩ Sisters of Mercy
⏪ Hank Williams

Lloyd Cole
⏪ Beatles
⏪ Big Star
⏪ Leonard Cohen
⏪ Elvis Costello
⏪ Nick Drake
⏩ Pete Droge
⏪ Bob Dylan
⏪ Al Green
⏪ Lou Reed
⏩ Toad the Wet Sprocket
⏪ Jimmy Webb
⏪ Hank Williams
⏪ Neil Young

Bootsy Collins
⏪ James Brown
⏪ George Clinton
⏩ Flea (Red Hot Chili Peppers)
⏪ Larry Graham
⏩ Rick James
⏩ T.M. Stevens

Judy Collins
⏩ Cowboy Junkies
⏪ Bob Dylan
⏪ Woody Guthrie
⏩ Emmylou Harris
⏩ Linda Ronstadt
⏪ Pete Seeger

Phil Collins
⏪ Earth Wind and Fire
⏪ Peter Gabriel
⏩ Howard Jones
⏩ Mike + the Mechanics
⏪ Motown
⏩ Seal

Shawn Colvin
⏩ Jewel
⏩ Amanda Marshall
⏩ Natalie Merchant
⏪ Joni Mitchell
⏪ Suzanne Vega
⏪ Tom Waits

Come
⏪ Live Skull
⏪ Rolling Stones
⏪ Swans
⏪ Velvet Underground
⏩ Steve Wynn
⏪ Neil Young

Commander Cody and His Lost Planet Airmen
⏩ Asleep At the Wheel
⏪ Dave Dudley
⏩ Nick Lowe
⏪ Moon Mullican
⏪ Bob Wills

Commodores
⏩ Steve Arrington
⏩ Frankie Beverly & Maze
⏪ Blood, Sweat & Tears
⏪ James Brown
⏩ Prince
⏪ Sly & the Family Stone
⏪ Temptations

Concrete Blonde
⏪ James Brown
⏪ Leonard Cohen
⏩ 4 Non Blondes
⏩ Alanis Morissette
⏪ Pretenders
⏪ Patti Smith

Connells
⏪ dBs
⏩ Gin Blossoms
⏩ Jayhawks
⏩ Freddy Jones Band
⏪ R.E.M.
⏩ Son Volt
⏩ Wilco
⏪ Wire Train

Continental Drifters
◀◀ Band
◀◀ Byrds
▶▶ Jayhawks
◀◀ Nitty Gritty Dirt Band
◀◀ Gram Parsons
▶▶ Son Volt
▶▶ subdudes
▶▶ Wilco

Ry Cooder
▶▶ Jim Dickinson
◀◀ Sleepy John Estes
◀◀ Golden Gate Quartet
▶▶ John Hiatt
◀◀ Blind Willie Johnson
▶▶ Daniel Lanois
◀◀ Little Walter
▶▶ Los Lobos
◀◀ Gabby Pahinui
▶▶ Robbie Robertson
◀◀ Joseph Spence

Sam Cooke
◀◀ Charles Brown
▶▶ Marvin Gaye
◀◀ R.H. Harris
▶▶ Steve Perry
▶▶ Otis Redding
▶▶ Rod Stewart
◀◀ Kylo Turner

Alice Cooper
◀◀ Crazy World of Arthur Brown
▶▶ Guns N' Roses
▶▶ Gwar
◀◀ Boris Karloff
▶▶ Kiss
◀◀ Little Richard
◀◀ Bela Lugosi
◀◀ MC5
▶▶ Motley Crüe
▶▶ Ozzy Osbourne
◀◀ Stooges

Julian Cope
◀◀ Syd Barrett
◀◀ Doors
▶▶ Icicle Works
▶▶ Inspiral Carpets
◀◀ Jam
◀◀ Kinks
▶▶ Outfield
▶▶ Psychedelic Furs

Stewart Copeland
▶▶ Jars of Clay
▶▶ Manu Katche
◀◀ Edgar Varese
◀◀ Frank Zappa

Corrosion of Conformity
▶▶ Alice in Chains
◀◀ Black Flag
◀◀ Black Sabbath
◀◀ MC5
▶▶ Pantera
◀◀ Samhain
◀◀ Lynyrd Skynyrd
▶▶ Soundgarden
◀◀ ZZ Top

Elvis Costello
◀◀ Band
◀◀ Beatles
◀◀ Booker T. & the MGs
◀◀ Byrds
◀◀ Johnny Cash
◀◀ Bob Dylan
◀◀ George Jones
◀◀ Motown
◀◀ Randy Newman
◀◀ Gram Parsons
◀◀ Rolling Stones
◀◀ Brinsley Schwarz
◀◀ Bruce Springsteen
◀◀ Stax
◀◀ Van Morrison
◀◀ Hank Williams

Country Joe and the Fish
▶▶ B-52's
◀◀ Big Brother and the Holding Company
▶▶ Boomtown Rats
◀◀ Reverend Gary Davis
◀◀ Woody Guthrie
▶▶ Tom Robinson Band

Cowboy Junkies
◀◀ Patsy Cline
▶▶ Dead Can Dance
▶▶ Lisa Germano
◀◀ Velvet Underground
◀◀ Hank Williams

Cramps
◀◀ Hasil Adkins
◀◀ Ed Gein
▶▶ Reverend Horton Heat
▶▶ Jason and the Scorchers
◀◀ Ed Wood

Cranes
◀◀ Cocteau Twins
◀◀ Foetus
◀◀ Joy Division
◀◀ Lydia Lunch
▶▶ Mazzy Star

Robert Cray
◀◀ Eric Clapton
◀◀ Albert Collins
◀◀ Howlin' Wolf
◀◀ B.B. King
◀◀ Magic Sam
▶▶ Kenny Wayne Shepherd
◀◀ Hubert Sumlin
▶▶ Joe Louis Walker
◀◀ Johnny "Guitar" Watson
◀◀ O.V. Wright

Crazy Horse
▶▶ Black Crowes
◀◀ Buffalo Springfield
▶▶ Jayhawks
◀◀ Rolling Stones
◀◀ Yardbirds

Cream
◀◀ Willie Dixon
▶▶ Jimi Hendrix Experience
◀◀ Robert Johnson
◀◀ Alexis Korner
▶▶ Mountain
◀◀ Charlie Parker
▶▶ Van Halen
◀◀ Muddy Waters
▶▶ ZZ Top

Creedence Clearwater Revival
◀◀ Booker T. and the MGs
▶▶ Hollies
◀◀ Little Richard
◀◀ Elvis Presley
▶▶ Bob Seger
▶▶ Bruce Springsteen

Marshall Crenshaw
◀◀ Arthur Alexander
◀◀ Beatles
▶▶ BoDeans
◀◀ Everly Brothers
◀◀ Buddy Holly
▶▶ Hootie & the Blowfish
◀◀ Motown
▶▶ Matthew Sweet
▶▶ Toad the Wet Sprocket

Jim Croce
▶▶ Jackson Browne
▶▶ Dan Fogelberg
◀◀ Gordon Lightfoot
▶▶ Lyle Lovett
▶▶ Don McLean
◀◀ Joni Mitchell
◀◀ Paul Simon
▶▶ Cat Stevens
◀◀ James Taylor
▶▶ Jesse Winchester

Crosby, Stills and Nash
▶▶ America
◀◀ Beatles
◀◀ Bob Dylan
▶▶ Eagles
◀◀ Everly Brothers
▶▶ Michael Hedges
◀◀ Fred Neil
▶▶ Poco

Crowded House
◀◀ Beatles
◀◀ Byrds
◀◀ Everly Brothers
▶▶ Oasis
◀◀ Procol Harum
▶▶ Rembrants
◀◀ Split Enz

Julee Cruise
- Tori Amos
- Cocteau Twins

Cult
- AC/DC
- Alice in Chains
- Bush
- Candlebox
- Doors
- Guns N' Roses
- Killing Joke
- Led Zeppelin
- Sex Pistols

Culture Club
- Bow Wow Wow
- David Bowie
- Madonna
- Pulp
- Queen
- Right Said Fred
- Rupaul
- Village People

Cure
- Essence
- Genesis
- Jesus & Mary Chain
- Joy Division
- Sex Pistols
- Siouxsie And The Banshees

Cypress Hill
- Funkdoobiest
- House of Pain
- Kid Frost
- Mellow Man Ace
- N.W.A.

Dick Dale
- Chet Atkins
- Beach Boys
- Chuck Berry
- Chantays
- Duane Eddy
- Jimi Hendrix
- Link Wray
- Man ... Or Astroman?
- Metallica
- Merle Travis
- Van Halen
- Ventures

Damn Yankees
- Bon Jovi
- Foreigner
- Hootie and the Blowfish
- Journey
- Kiss
- Motley Crüe
- Ted Nugent
- Poison
- REO Speedwagon
- Styx
- Warrant

Damned
- Germs
- NOFX
- Offspring
- Ramones
- Sensational Alex Harvey Band
- Stooges

Charlie Daniels Band
- Alabama
- Allman Brothers Band
- Brooks & Dunn
- Merle Haggard
- Waylon Jennings
- Little Texas
- Oak Ridge Boys
- Lynyrd Skynyrd
- Marshall Tucker Band
- Hank Williams Jr.

Danzig
- AC/DC
- Black Sabbath
- Led Zeppelin
- Metallica
- Slayer

Terence Trent D'Arby
- Marvin Gaye
- Lenny Kravitz
- Living Colour
- Prince
- Rolling Stones
- Seal
- Stevie Wonder

Bobby Darin
- Harry Connick, Jr.
- Bing Crosby
- Burton Cummings
- Ella Fitzgerald
- Billy Joel
- Brian Setzer
- Frank Sinatra

Miles Davis
- James Brown
- Cannonball Adderley Quintet
- Ornette Coleman
- Grassy Knoll
- Herbie Hancock
- Jon Hassell
- Ice Burn
- Bill Laswell/Material
- Mahavishnu Orchestra
- Charlie Parker
- Vernon Reid/Living Colour
- Sly & the Family Stone
- Karlheinz Stockhausen
- Weather Report
- Freddie Webster

Taylor Dayne
- Mariah Carey
- Celine Dion
- Janet Jackson
- Madonna
- Donna Summer

dB's
- Beatles
- Big Star/Alex Chilton
- Continental Drifters
- Elvis Costello
- Grass Roots
- Individuals
- Nazz
- R.E.M.
- Schramms
- Wygals

De La Soul
- Jungle Brothers
- KRS-One
- Ritz Brothers
- Stetsasonic
- A Tribe Called Quest

Deacon Blue
- Jackson Browne
- Go-Betweens
- Goodbye Mr. Mackenzie
- Oasis
- Prefab Sprout
- Simple Minds

Dead Can Dance
- Johan Sebastian Bach
- Bauhaus
- chamber orchestras
- Cindytalk
- Cocteau Twins
- Deep Forest
- Enigma
- Enya
- Gregorian chants
- Le Mystere De Voix Bulgare
- medieval minstrels
- Sisters Of Mercy
- SPK
- This Mortal Coil

Dead Kennedys
- Avengers
- Bikini Kill
- Black Flag
- Dickies
- Disposable Heroes of Hiphoprisy
- Germs
- Ice-T
- MC5
- Iggy Pop
- Rage Against the Machine
- Sex Pistols
- X

Dead Milkmen
- Beastie Boys
- Dead Kennedys
- King Missile

- ◀◀ Minutemen
- ▶▶ Presidents of the United States of America
- ◀◀ Run-D.M.C.
- ◀◀ They Might Be Giants
- ▶▶ Too Much Joy

Deep Purple

- ◀◀ Animals
- ▶▶ Dio
- ▶▶ Dokken
- ▶▶ Guns 'N Roses
- ▶▶ Iron Maiden
- ◀◀ Johnny Kidd & the Pirates
- ◀◀ Mahler
- ▶▶ Metallica
- ▶▶ Rainbow
- ◀◀ Screaming Lord Sutch & the Savages
- ▶▶ UFO
- ▶▶ Whitesnake
- ◀◀ Yardbirds

Def Leppard

- ◀◀ AC/DC
- ◀◀ Beatles
- ▶▶ Bon Jovi
- ◀◀ Boston
- ▶▶ Candlebox
- ◀◀ Kiss
- ▶▶ Poison
- ▶▶ Ratt
- ◀◀ Slade
- ◀◀ Sweet
- ▶▶ Shania Twain

Del Fuegos

- ▶▶ Afghan Whigs
- ◀◀ Chuck Berry
- ◀◀ Bo Diddley
- ▶▶ Jayhawks
- ◀◀ Tom Petty and the Heartbreakers
- ◀◀ Stax

Depeche Mode

- ◀◀ Cabaret Voltaire
- ▶▶ Erasure
- ◀◀ Kraftwerk
- ▶▶ Orb
- ▶▶ Orbital
- ▶▶ Recoil
- ◀◀ Silicon Teens
- ▶▶ Soft Cell
- ◀◀ Throbbing Gristle
- ▶▶ Yaz

Rick Derringer

- ▶▶ Bryan Adams
- ◀◀ Chuck Berry
- ◀◀ Kingsmen (Johnny Winter)
- ▶▶ Cyndi Lauper
- ◀◀ Jerry Lee Lewis
- ◀◀ Carl Perkins
- ▶▶ Slash (Guns 'N Roses)
- ▶▶ Billy Squier
- ◀◀ Edgar Winter

Devo

- ▶▶ Tony Basil
- ◀◀ Can
- ◀◀ Brian Eno
- ▶▶ Foo Fighters
- ◀◀ Robert Fripp
- ◀◀ Kratfwerk
- ▶▶ Nirvana
- ▶▶ Residents
- ◀◀ Rolling Stones
- ▶▶ They Might Be Giants

Neil Diamond

- ▶▶ Michael Bolton
- ◀◀ Bob Dylan
- ◀◀ George and Ira Gershwin
- ▶▶ Barry Manilow
- ▶▶ Mary's Danish
- ◀◀ Elvis Presley
- ◀◀ Barbra Streisand
- ◀◀ Hank Williams

Dictators

- ◀◀ Blue Oyster Cult
- ▶▶ Circle Jerks
- ◀◀ Flamin' Groovies
- ◀◀ Kinks
- ▶▶ Motley Crüe
- ◀◀ Mott the Hoople
- ▶▶ Ramones
- ◀◀ Seeds
- ◀◀ Stooges
- ▶▶ Surf Punks
- ▶▶ Twisted Sister
- ◀◀ Who

Bo Diddley

- ▶▶ Bow Wow Wow
- ▶▶ Eric Burdon
- ▶▶ Jimi Hendrix
- ▶▶ Buddy Holly
- ◀◀ John Lee Hooker
- ◀◀ Louis Jordan
- ◀◀ Muddy Waters
- ▶▶ Elvis Presley
- ▶▶ Rolling Stones
- ▶▶ U2

Ani DiFranco

- ◀◀ Tracy Chapman
- ◀◀ Fugazi
- ◀◀ Rickie Lee Jones
- ◀◀ Joni Mitchell
- ▶▶ Alanis Morissette
- ▶▶ Dar Williams

Dinosaur Jr.

- ▶▶ Afghan Whigs
- ◀◀ Black Flag
- ▶▶ Buffalo Tom
- ◀◀ Cure
- ▶▶ My Bloody Valentine
- ◀◀ R.E.M.
- ▶▶ Sebadoh/Folk Implosion
- ◀◀ Velvet Underground
- ◀◀ Neil Young

Dio

- ◀◀ Arthur Brown
- ▶▶ Chris Cornell (Soundgarden)
- ◀◀ King Crimson
- ◀◀ Deep Purple
- ▶▶ James Hetfield (Metallica)
- ◀◀ Led Zeppelin
- ▶▶ Dave Meniketti (Y&T)
- ◀◀ Rainbow
- ▶▶ Geoff Tate (Queensryche)
- ▶▶ Eddie Vedder (Pearl Jam)

Dion

- ◀◀ Cadillacs
- ◀◀ Del-Vikings
- ▶▶ Billy Joel
- ◀◀ Orioles
- ▶▶ Lou Reed
- ▶▶ Paul Simon

Celine Dion

- ◀◀ Mariah Carey
- ▶▶ Donna Lewis
- ◀◀ Carly Simon
- ◀◀ Barbra Streisand

Dire Straits

- ◀◀ Chet Atkins
- ▶▶ Aztec Camera
- ▶▶ Mary Chapin Carpenter
- ◀◀ Ry Cooder
- ◀◀ Bob Dylan
- ▶▶ John Hiatt
- ▶▶ Mavericks
- ◀◀ Van Morrison

Dirty Dozen Brass Band

- ◀◀ Olympia Brass Band
- ▶▶ Rebirth Brass Band

Divinyls

- ◀◀ AC/DC
- ◀◀ Pat Benatar
- ▶▶ Hole
- ▶▶ Magnapop
- ◀◀ Rolling Stones

Dixie Dregs

- ▶▶ Col. Bruce Hampton & the Aquarium Rescue Unit
- ◀◀ Flock
- ▶▶ Michael Hedges
- ◀◀ Mahavishnu Orchestra
- ◀◀ Weather Report
- ◀◀ Frank Zappa

Don Dixon

- ▶▶ Hootie & the Blowfish
- ▶▶ Marti Jones
- ◀◀ Nick Lowe
- ◀◀ Searchers
- ◀◀ Percy Sledge

DNA
- ◀◀ Derek Bailey
- ▶▶ Bill Frisell
- ▶▶ Lounge Lizards
- ▶▶ Marc Ribot
- ◀◀ Television
- ◀◀ Pere Ubu
- ▶▶ John Zorn

Dr. John
- ▶▶ Marcia Ball
- ◀◀ James Booker
- ◀◀ Joe Liggins
- ▶▶ Neville Brothers
- ◀◀ Professor Longhair
- ▶▶ Radiators
- ◀◀ Huey (Piano) Smith
- ◀◀ Tuts Washington

Dokken
- ◀◀ AC/DC
- ◀◀ Black Sabbath
- ◀◀ Judas Priest
- ◀◀ Ozzy Osbourne
- ◀◀ Van Halen

Thomas Dolby
- ▶▶ Beck
- ◀◀ George Clinton
- ▶▶ Trent Reznor
- ▶▶ Self
- ◀◀ Gary Wright
- ◀◀ Frank Zappa

Fats Domino
- ▶▶ Bruce Hornsby
- ▶▶ Billy Joel
- ◀◀ Louis Jordan
- ▶▶ Neville Brothers
- ◀◀ Professor Longhair
- ▶▶ Paul Simon
- ▶▶ Allen Toussaint
- ◀◀ Big Joe Turner
- ▶▶ Van Morrison

Donovan
- ◀◀ Beatles
- ▶▶ David Crosby
- ◀◀ Bob Dylan
- ▶▶ Housemartins
- ▶▶ XTC/Dukes of Stratosphear

Doobie Brothers
- ◀◀ Allman Brothers Band
- ▶▶ Black Crowes
- ▶▶ Georgia Satellites
- ◀◀ Moby Grape
- ◀◀ Hot Tuna
- ▶▶ Screaming Cheetah Wheelies

Doors
- ◀◀ Bertolt Brecht
- ▶▶ Cult
- ◀◀ Willie Dixon
- ◀◀ Howlin' Wolf
- ▶▶ INXS
- ▶▶ Jane's Addiction
- ▶▶ Lords of the New Church
- ▶▶ Marilyn Manson
- ◀◀ Jimmy Reed
- ▶▶ Patti Smith

Lee Dorsey
- ◀◀ Ray Charles
- ▶▶ Devo
- ▶▶ Robert Palmer
- ▶▶ Pointer Sisters
- ◀◀ Professor Longhair

Nick Drake
- ◀◀ Beatles
- ▶▶ Jeff Buckley
- ◀◀ Tim Buckley
- ▶▶ Cure
- ◀◀ Bob Dylan
- ▶▶ Mark Eitzel
- ◀◀ Tim Hardin
- ▶▶ J Mascis
- ◀◀ Joni Mitchell
- ▶▶ R.E.M.
- ◀◀ John Renbourn
- ▶▶ Smiths
- ▶▶ Paul Weller

Dramarama
- ◀◀ Blondie
- ◀◀ dB's
- ▶▶ Gin Blossoms
- ◀◀ Mott the Hoople
- ◀◀ New York Dolls
- ◀◀ Rolling Stones
- ▶▶ Tragically Hip
- ▶▶ Velvet Crush
- ◀◀ Neil Young

Dread Zeppelin
- ▶▶ Are you kidding? Nobody sounds like these guys
- ◀◀ Led Zeppelin
- ◀◀ Bob Marley
- ◀◀ Spinal Tap
- ◀◀ Vegas-era Elvis Presley
- ◀◀ Weird Al Yankovic

Dream Syndicate
- ▶▶ American Music Club
- ▶▶ Continental Drifters
- ◀◀ Brian Eno
- ▶▶ R.E.M.
- ▶▶ Red House Painters
- ◀◀ Rolling Stones
- ◀◀ Velvet Underground
- ◀◀ Neil Young

Drifters
- ▶▶ Boyz II Men
- ▶▶ Four Tops
- ◀◀ Ink Spots
- ◀◀ Orioles
- ▶▶ Parliaments
- ◀◀ Ravens
- ▶▶ Temptations

Drivin' N' Cryin'
- ▶▶ Black Crowes
- ◀◀ John Denver
- ◀◀ Bob Dylan
- ▶▶ Indigo Girls
- ◀◀ Ramones
- ◀◀ Hank Williams

Duran Duran
- ▶▶ Blur
- ◀◀ David Bowie
- ◀◀ Chic
- ▶▶ Hole
- ▶▶ Live
- ◀◀ Roxy Music
- ◀◀ Sex Pistols
- ▶▶ Stone Temple Pilots

Bob Dylan
- ▶▶ Joan Baez
- ◀◀ Joan Baez
- ▶▶ Garth Brooks
- ▶▶ Byrds
- ◀◀ Woody Guthrie
- ▶▶ Joe Henry
- ◀◀ Leadbelly
- ◀◀ Little Richard
- ▶▶ John Mellencamp
- ▶▶ Joan Osborne
- ▶▶ Tom Petty & the Heartbreakers
- ◀◀ Elvis Presley
- ▶▶ Bob Seger
- ▶▶ Sonny & Cher
- ▶▶ Bruce Springsteen
- ◀◀ Weavers
- ◀◀ Hank Williams

Eagles
- ◀◀ Beatles
- ▶▶ Garth Brooks
- ◀◀ Byrds
- ◀◀ Everly Brothers
- ▶▶ Vince Gill
- ▶▶ Gin Blossoms
- ▶▶ Jayhawks
- ▶▶ Mavericks
- ◀◀ Gram Parsons
- ▶▶ Travis Tritt
- ▶▶ Uncle Tupelo
- ◀◀ Hank Williams

Steve Earle
- ◀◀ Bob Dylan
- ◀◀ Waylon Jennings
- ▶▶ Todd Snider
- ◀◀ Bruce Springsteen
- ▶▶ Travis Tritt
- ◀◀ Townes Van Zandt
- ▶▶ Dale Watson

Earth Wind & Fire
- ▶▶ Brand New Heavies
- ▶▶ Brothers Johnson
- ◀◀ James Brown

- ▶▶ Incognito
- ◀◀ Ohio Players
- ▶▶ Kim Pensyl
- ◀◀ Sly & the Family Stone

Echo & the Bunnymen

- ◀◀ Beatles
- ◀◀ Doors
- ▶▶ Happy Mondays
- ▶▶ Oasis
- ▶▶ Stone Roses
- ▶▶ Suede

Eddie & the Hot Rods

- ▶▶ Buzzcocks
- ◀◀ Dr. Feelgood
- ▶▶ Graham Parker and the Rumour
- ▶▶ Rockpile
- ◀◀ Rolling Stones
- ◀◀ Bob Seger
- ◀◀ Who

Eddie Floyd

- ▶▶ Eric Clapton
- ▶▶ Commodores
- ◀◀ Sam Cooke
- ▶▶ Rick James
- ◀◀ Lou Rawls
- ◀◀ Otis Redding
- ▶▶ Bruce Springsteen
- ▶▶ Toots and the Maytals

Duane Eddy

- ◀◀ Chet Atkins
- ◀◀ Jerry Byrd
- ▶▶ John Entwistle
- ▶▶ John Fogerty
- ▶▶ George Harrison
- ◀◀ Les Paul
- ▶▶ George Thorogood

Dave Edmunds

- ◀◀ Chet Atkins
- ◀◀ Chuck Berry
- ▶▶ Blasters
- ▶▶ Bottle Rockets
- ◀◀ Everly Brothers
- ◀◀ Les Paul and Mary Ford
- ◀◀ Jerry Lee Lewis
- ◀◀ Smiley Lewis
- ◀◀ Ricky Nelson
- ◀◀ Elvis Presley
- ▶▶ Stray Cats
- ◀◀ Gene Vincent

Electric Light Orchestra

- ◀◀ Beatles
- ▶▶ Enya
- ▶▶ Eurythmics
- ◀◀ Move
- ◀◀ Roy Orbison
- ▶▶ Traveling Wilburys

Eleventh Dream Day

- ▶▶ Grunge
- ◀◀ Television
- ◀◀ Neil Young

Joe Ely

- ▶▶ Alejandro Escovedo
- ◀◀ Buddy Holly
- ▶▶ Sun Volt
- ▶▶ Uncle Tupelo
- ◀◀ Hank Williams

Emerson, Lake & Palmer

- ▶▶ Asia
- ▶▶ David Bowie
- ▶▶ Depeche Mode
- ▶▶ Kansas
- ◀◀ King Crimson
- ◀◀ Jerry Lee Lewis
- ▶▶ Mission UK
- ◀◀ Nice
- ◀◀ Charlie Parker
- ◀◀ Prokofiev
- ▶▶ U2
- ▶▶ Yes

English Beat

- ◀◀ Prince Buster
- ◀◀ Desmond Dekker
- ▶▶ Barenaked Ladies
- ▶▶ Dave Matthews Band
- ▶▶ Rancid
- ◀◀ Smokey Robinson
- ◀◀ Sly and the Family Stone

Brian Eno

- ▶▶ David Arkenstone
- ▶▶ Michael Brook
- ◀◀ John Cage
- ◀◀ King Crimson
- ◀◀ Soft Machine
- ▶▶ Talking Heads
- ▶▶ U2

John Entwistle

- ◀◀ Bob Bogle
- ▶▶ Jack Bruce
- ◀◀ Duane Eddy
- ▶▶ Bruce Foxton
- ◀◀ Boris Karloff
- ▶▶ Geddy Lee

Enuff Z'nuff

- ◀◀ Badfinger
- ◀◀ Beatles
- ◀◀ Cheap Trick
- ▶▶ Jellyfish
- ◀◀ Mott the Hoople
- ◀◀ Off Broadway

Erasure

- ◀◀ Abba
- ◀◀ Depeche Mode
- ▶▶ Electronic
- ▶▶ New Order
- ▶▶ Simply Red
- ◀◀ Yaz/Yazoo

Roky Erickson

- ◀◀ Black Sabbath
- ▶▶ Daniel Johnston
- ▶▶ Katy McCarty
- ◀◀ 13th Floor Elevators
- ▶▶ R.E.M.

Alejandro Escovedo

- ◀◀ Blasters
- ▶▶ Bottle Rockets
- ◀◀ Jimmie Dale Gilmore
- ◀◀ Buddy Holly
- ▶▶ Jason and the Scorchers
- ◀◀ Iggy Pop
- ▶▶ Uncle Tupelo
- ◀◀ Richie Valens
- ▶▶ Wilco
- ◀◀ X

Gloria Estefan

- ◀◀ Herb Alpert & the Tijuana Brass
- ◀◀ Aretha Franklin
- ▶▶ Debbie Gibson
- ◀◀ Carmen Miranda
- ◀◀ Tito Puente
- ◀◀ Donna Summer

Melissa Etheridge

- ▶▶ Sheryl Crow
- ◀◀ Janis Joplin
- ▶▶ Sass Jordan
- ◀◀ John Mellencamp
- ▶▶ Alanna Myles
- ▶▶ Joan Osborne
- ◀◀ Suzi Quatro
- ◀◀ Bruce Springsteen

Eurythmics

- ◀◀ Can
- ◀◀ Aretha Franklin
- ▶▶ Garbage
- ◀◀ Kraftwerk
- ◀◀ Lene Lovich
- ▶▶ Roxette

Everly Brothers

- ▶▶ Beatles
- ◀◀ Louvin Brothers
- ▶▶ Simon and Garfunkel
- ◀◀ Stanley Brothers

Everything But the Girl

- ▶▶ Eddi Reader
- ◀◀ Stan Getz
- ◀◀ Astrud Gilberto
- ◀◀ Massive Attack
- ▶▶ Tanita Tikaram

Extreme

- ◀◀ Beatles
- ▶▶ Deftones
- ▶▶ Dream Theater
- ◀◀ ELO
- ▶▶ Jars of Clay
- ◀◀ Queen
- ◀◀ Red Hot Chili Peppers
- ▶▶ Spacehog

- Van Halen

Fabulous Thunderbirds

- Bo Diddley
- Freddie King
- Red Devils
- Slim Harpo
- Stevie Ray Vaughan and Double Trouble
- Muddy Waters

Faces

- Black Crowes
- Sam Cooke
- Lonnie Donnegan
- Jerry Lee Lewis
- London Quireboys
- Elvis Presley
- Otis Redding
- Muddy Waters

John Fahey

- William Ackerman
- Julian Bream
- Robert Johnson
- Jorma Kaukonen
- Leo Kottke
- Leadbelly
- Lightin' Hopkins
- Richard Thompson

Fairport Convention

- Andy and The Marksman
- Bradford F.C. and The Pyramid
- Byrds
- Captain Rugeley's Blues
- Chieftains
- Dire Straits
- Doctor K's Blues Band and Ethnic Shuffle Orchestra
- Donovan
- Nick Drake
- Bob Dylan
- King Crimson
- Led Zeppelin
- Joni Mitchell
- Pentangle
- Pioneers
- Soft Machine
- Steeleye Span
- Jethro Tull
- Whippersnapper

Faith No More

- Black Flag
- John Zorn/Naked City
- Black Sabbath
- William S. Burroughs
- Roky Erikson
- Parliament
- Primus
- Public Enemy
- Therapy?
- Tool
- Tom Waits
- White Zombie
- Frank Zappa

Marianne Faithfull

- Joan Baez
- Bjork
- Everly Brothers
- Buddy Holly
- Rickie Lee Jones
- Charlie Parker

Fall

- Can
- Faust
- Joy Division
- Kinks
- Pavement
- Public Image Ltd
- Sex Pistols
- Sonic Youth
- Sugarcubes
- Swans
- Trumans Water
- Velvet Underground
- Gene Vincent

Feelies

- Beatles
- Brian Eno
- Luna
- Monkees
- R.E.M.
- Rolling Stones
- Patti Smith Group
- Velvet Underground
- Wake OoLoo
- Wild Carnation
- Wire
- Yo La Tengo
- Neil Young

Bryan Ferry

- a-ha
- ABC
- Tony Bennett
- David Bowie
- Edwyn Collins
- Duran Duran
- Frank Sinatra

54.40

- Hunters & Collectors
- R.E.M.
- Tragically Hip

Firefall

- Brooks & Dunn
- Byrds
- Flying Burrito Brothers
- Poco
- Shenandoah

fIREHOSE

- Blue Oyster Cult
- Clash
- Ornette Coleman
- Dils
- Bob Dylan
- Effigies
- Richard Hell & the Voidoids
- Jane's Addiction
- Tar Babies
- Universal Congress of..
- UYA
- Victim's Family
- Wire

Fishbone

- James Brown
- Living Colour
- Curtis Mayfield
- Rush
- Sly Stone
- Weapon of Choice

Fixx

- David Bowie
- Erasure
- Howard Jones
- Gary Numan
- Ultravox

Flamin' Groovies

- Beach Boys
- Beatles
- Byrds
- Eddie Cochran
- Hoodoo Gurus
- Tommy Keene
- Long Ryders
- Lovin' Spoonful
- Plimsouls
- R.E.M.
- Rolling Stones
- Sneetches
- Phil Spector

Flaming Lips

- Syd Barrett
- Echo and the Bunnymen
- Hawkwind
- Pavement
- Plastic Ono Band
- Presidents of the United States of America

Fleetwood Mac

- Tori Amos
- Beach Boys
- Elmore James
- Etta James
- John Mayall
- Matthew Sweet

Fleshtones

- Dick Dale
- Dead Milkmen
- Dictators
- Green Day
- Mighty Mighty Bosstones
- Monks

◀◀ Zombies

Fluid

▶▶ Baldo Rex
◀◀ David Bowie
▶▶ L7
◀◀ MC5
▶▶ Nirvana
◀◀ Iggy Pop
◀◀ Sex Pistols
◀◀ Troggs

Flying Burrito Brothers

◀◀ Byrds
▶▶ Desert Rose Band
▶▶ Eagles
▶▶ Jayhawks
◀◀ Memphis/Muscle Shoals soul
▶▶ Gram Parsons
▶▶ Son Volt
▶▶ Uncle Tupelo
▶▶ Wilco
◀◀ Hank Williams

Dan Fogelberg

◀◀ Jackson Browne
◀◀ Cascades
◀◀ Bruce Cockburn
▶▶ Dan Hill
▶▶ James McMurtry
◀◀ James Taylor
▶▶ David Wilcox

John Fogerty

◀◀ Creedence Clearwater
▶▶ Dave Edmunds
◀◀ Dave Edmunds
▶▶ Southern Culture On the Skids

Foghat

▶▶ Badlands
◀◀ Chuck Berry
▶▶ Black Crowes
▶▶ Brother Cane
◀◀ Savoy Brown
◀◀ Willie Dixon
◀◀ Fleetwood Mac
▶▶ Georgia Satellites
◀◀ John Lee Hooker
◀◀ Howlin' Wolf
▶▶ Lenny Kravitz
◀◀ John Mayall's Bluesbreakers
▶▶ Pearl Jam
◀◀ Rolling Stones

For Against

◀◀ Comsat Angels
▶▶ Half String
◀◀ Joy Division
◀◀ Lowlife
▶▶ Scenic
▶▶ Springhouse

Steve Forbert

◀◀ Chuck Berry
◀◀ Bob Dylan
▶▶ Joe Henry
▶▶ Will T. Massey
▶▶ Michael McDermott
◀◀ Jimmie Rodgers

Lita Ford

◀◀ Black Sabbath
◀◀ Jimi Hendrix
▶▶ Hole
▶▶ L7
◀◀ Motorhead
◀◀ Suzi Quatro
▶▶ 7 Year Bitch
◀◀ Slade

Foreigner

▶▶ Cutting Crew
◀◀ Jefferson Airplane
◀◀ Elton John
▶▶ Loverboy
◀◀ Mountain
◀◀ Shadows
◀◀ Spooky Tooth
▶▶ Survivor

Four Seasons

▶▶ Beach Boys
▶▶ Beatles
◀◀ Drifters
▶▶ Billy Joel
◀◀ Penguins
◀◀ Platters

Four Tops

▶▶ Boyz II Men
◀◀ Drifters
◀◀ Moonglows
◀◀ Orioles
▶▶ Darius Rucker (Hootie and the Blowfish)
▶▶ Temptations

Peter Frampton

▶▶ Bryan Adams
◀◀ Beatles
▶▶ Tom Cochrane
◀◀ Searchers
◀◀ Shadows

Frankie Goes to Hollywood

◀◀ Burt Bacharach
◀◀ Duran Duran
▶▶ Pet Shop Boys
▶▶ Seal
◀◀ Sex Pistols
▶▶ Sigue Sigue Sputnik
◀◀ Village People

Aretha Franklin

▶▶ Anita Baker
◀◀ Ruth Brown
◀◀ Sam Cooke
◀◀ Rev. C.L. Franklin
▶▶ Whitney Houston
▶▶ Chaka Khan
◀◀ Celia Ward

Free

▶▶ Backstreet Crawler
▶▶ Bad Company
▶▶ Foreigner
◀◀ John Lee Hooker
▶▶ Kiss
◀◀ John Mayall's Bluesbreakers
◀◀ Rolling Stones
◀◀ Sonny Boy Williamson
◀◀ Yardbirds

Robert Fripp

◀◀ Beatles
◀◀ Phillip Glass
◀◀ Jimi Hendrix
▶▶ His Name Is Alive
▶▶ Iceburn
▶▶ Living Colour
◀◀ John McLaughlin
▶▶ Orb

Fugazi

◀◀ Dead Kennedys
◀◀ Descendents
▶▶ Guns N' Roses
◀◀ Minutemen
◀◀ Motorhead
▶▶ Nada Surf
▶▶ Nirvana
▶▶ Offspring
▶▶ Pearl Jam
◀◀ Queen
◀◀ Sex Pistols
▶▶ Soundgarden

Future Sound of London

◀◀ Brian Eno
◀◀ Master Musicians of Jajouka
▶▶ Small Fish With Spine
◀◀ Tangerine Dream

Peter Gabriel

◀◀ David Bowie
▶▶ Paula Cole
◀◀ Sam Cooke
◀◀ King Crimson
◀◀ Brian Eno
▶▶ Daniel Lanois
▶▶ George Michael
▶▶ Youssou N'Dour
◀◀ Otis Redding

Rory Gallagher

◀◀ Bo Didley
◀◀ Albert King
◀◀ Freddie King
▶▶ Gary Moore
◀◀ Muddy Waters
▶▶ George Thorogood & The Destroyers

Game Theory

◀◀ Big Star
◀◀ dB's
▶▶ Posies

◀◀ Roxy Music
▶▶ Ultra Vivid Scene

Gang of Four
◀◀ James Brown
▶▶ Disposable Heroes of Hiphoprisy
◀◀ Funkadelic
◀◀ Jimi Hendrix
◀◀ Marxism-Leninism
◀◀ Mekons
▶▶ Ministry
▶▶ Nine Inch Nails
▶▶ Rage Against the Machine
▶▶ Red Hot Chili Peppers
◀◀ Sex Pistols
◀◀ Pere Ubu

Gang Starr
◀◀ Roy Ayers
▶▶ Bahamadia
▶▶ Buckshot LeFonque
◀◀ Donald Byrd
◀◀ Miles Davis
▶▶ Digable Planets
▶▶ Dream Warriors
◀◀ Eric B and Rakim
▶▶ Jeru the Damaja
▶▶ Ronny Jordan
◀◀ Jungle Brothers
◀◀ Poor Righteous Teachers
▶▶ Roots
◀◀ Lonnie Liston Smith
▶▶ A Tribe Called Quest
▶▶ Us3

Art Garfunkel
▶▶ Babyface
◀◀ Beach Boys
▶▶ Stephen Bishop
▶▶ Jackson Browne
◀◀ Sam Cooke
◀◀ Judy Garland
▶▶ Bobby Kimball

Danny Gatton
◀◀ Chet Atkins
▶▶ Junior Brown
◀◀ Dave Brubeck
◀◀ Roy Buchanan
◀◀ Charlie Christian
◀◀ Roy Clark
◀◀ Duane Eddy
▶▶ Vince Gill
◀◀ Albert Lee
◀◀ Les Paul
◀◀ Carl Perkins
▶▶ Brian Setzer
◀◀ Thelonius Monk
◀◀ Gene Vincent

Marvin Gaye
▶▶ Frankie Beverly
◀◀ Capris
◀◀ Ray Charles
◀◀ Nat King Cole
▶▶ Terence Trent D'Arby
▶▶ El DeBarge
◀◀ Billie Holiday
▶▶ Rick James
◀◀ Little Willie John
◀◀ Clyde McPhatter
◀◀ Orioles
◀◀ Frank Sinatra
▶▶ Al B. Sure!
▶▶ Keith Sweat
◀◀ Rudy West
▶▶ Barry White
▶▶ Stevie Wonder

J. Geils Band
▶▶ Aerosmith
◀◀ James Brown
◀◀ Bill Haley & the Comets
◀◀ John Lee Hooker
▶▶ Iron City Houserockers
◀◀ John Mayall
◀◀ Motown
◀◀ Rolling Stones
▶▶ Bruce Springsteen and the E Street Band
▶▶ Michael Stanley Band
◀◀ Stax
▶▶ Blues Traveler
◀◀ Jackie Wilson
◀◀ Yardbirds

Genesis
◀◀ Beatles
▶▶ Kansas
◀◀ King Crimson
◀◀ Jonathan King
▶▶ Marillion
◀◀ Procol Harum
▶▶ Saga
▶▶ Styx

Lisa Germano
◀◀ Indigo Girls
▶▶ Michelle Malone
◀◀ Aimee Mann
▶▶ Mae Moore
◀◀ Patti Smith

Jimmy Dale Gilmore
▶▶ Iris DeMent
◀◀ Buddy Holly
▶▶ Jim Lauderdale
◀◀ Willie Nelson
◀◀ Roy Orbison
◀◀ Jimmie Rodgers
▶▶ Gillian Welch
▶▶ Kevin Welch
◀◀ Hank Williams

Girls Against Boys
◀◀ Fugazi
◀◀ Ministry
◀◀ Einstrüzende Neubauten
◀◀ Skinny Puppy
◀◀ Soulside

Gary Glitter
◀◀ David Bowie
▶▶ Def Leppard
▶▶ Joan Jett
▶▶ Kiss
▶▶ Oasis
◀◀ T. Rex

Go-Betweens
◀◀ Cure
▶▶ Deacon Blue
◀◀ Bob Dylan
◀◀ Echo and the Bunnymen
▶▶ Downy Mildew
▶▶ Poi Dog Pondering

Go-Go's
▶▶ Bangles
▶▶ Bikini Kill
◀◀ Chordettes
◀◀ Germs
◀◀ Shangri-La's
▶▶ Tiger Trap

Go West
◀◀ Earth Wind and Fire
◀◀ Gary Numan
◀◀ Smokey Robinson

Golden Palominos
▶▶ Jeff Buckley
◀◀ Cocteau Twins
◀◀ DNA
◀◀ Bill Laswell
◀◀ Steely Dan
▶▶ Matthew Sweet
◀◀ David Sylvian
▶▶ Hector Zazou

Goo Goo Dolls
◀◀ Cheap Trick
▶▶ Goldfinger
◀◀ Replacements
▶▶ Triplefast Action

Steve Goodman
◀◀ Big Bill Broonzy
◀◀ Jethro Burns
◀◀ Bob Dylan
▶▶ Steve Forbert
◀◀ Bob Gibson
◀◀ Woody Guthrie
▶▶ James McMurtry
▶▶ Michael Penn
◀◀ Josh White
◀◀ Hank Williams
◀◀ Bob Wills

John Gorka
▶▶ Peter Keane
▶▶ Bill Morrissey
◀◀ Stan Rogers

Grand Funk Railroad
▶▶ Bon Jovi
▶▶ Boston

◀◀ Cream
▶▶ Foreigner
◀◀ Hendrix
▶▶ Kiss
◀◀ Motown
▶▶ Soul Asylum

Grateful Dead
▶▶ Allman Brothers
▶▶ Blues Traveler
◀◀ Cannon's Jug Stompers
◀◀ Bob Dylan
◀◀ Le Hot Club de France
▶▶ Los Lobos
▶▶ Phish
◀◀ Jimmy Reed
◀◀ Rolling Stones
▶▶ Spin Doctors

Al Green
▶▶ Otis Clay
◀◀ Sam Cooke
▶▶ Terence Trent D'Arby
◀◀ Clyde McPhatter
▶▶ Prince
◀◀ Otis Redding
▶▶ Luther Vandross

Green Day
◀◀ Buzzcocks
◀◀ Cheap Trick
◀◀ Clash
◀◀ Dickies
◀◀ Only Ones
◀◀ Ramones
◀◀ Redd Kross
◀◀ Undertones

Green on Red
▶▶ Blue Mountain
◀◀ Faces
▶▶ Son Volt
▶▶ Uncle Tupelo
◀◀ Violent Femmes
◀◀ Neil Young

Clive Gregson & Christine Collister
◀◀ Sandy Denny
◀◀ Nick Drake
▶▶ John Wesley Harding
▶▶ Matt Keating
▶▶ Eleanor McEvoy
◀◀ Richard & Linda Thompson
◀◀ Hank Williams

Nanci Griffith
◀◀ Judy Collins
▶▶ Iris DeMent
◀◀ Carolyn Hester
◀◀ Tom Paxton
◀◀ Bill Staines
◀◀ Weavers
▶▶ Gillian Welch
▶▶ Lucinda Williams

Joe Grushecky
▶▶ Hootie & the Blowfish
◀◀ Rockets
◀◀ Mitch Ryder & the Detroit Wheels
◀◀ Bruce Springsteen
◀◀ Stax-Volt

Guess Who
◀◀ Beatles
▶▶ Blues Traveler
▶▶ Del Amitri
◀◀ Gerry and the Pacemakers
◀◀ Buddy Holly
▶▶ Pearl Jam
▶▶ Queen
◀◀ Big Joe Turner

Guided by Voices
◀◀ Damned
◀◀ Genesis
◀◀ Jam
◀◀ Pink Floyd
▶▶ Presidents of the United States of America
◀◀ Sex Pistols
◀◀ Who

Guns N' Roses
◀◀ AC/DC
◀◀ Aerosmith
◀◀ David Bowie
◀◀ Brian Eno
◀◀ Nazareth
◀◀ Rolling Stones
◀◀ Frank Zappa

Arlo Guthrie
▶▶ Jackson Browne
◀◀ Bob Dylan
▶▶ Eagles
◀◀ Woody Guthrie
◀◀ Leadbelly
▶▶ John Mellencamp
▶▶ Tom Petty
◀◀ Pete Seeger

Gwar
▶▶ "Beavis and Butt-head"
◀◀ Alice Cooper
◀◀ Dead Kennedys
◀◀ Kiss
▶▶ Marilyn Manson
◀◀ Motorhead
▶▶ My Life With the Thrill Kill Kult
▶▶ nine inch nails
◀◀ Tubes

Sammy Hagar
◀◀ Foghat
▶▶ Journey
◀◀ Kiss
▶▶ Loverboy
◀◀ Montrose
▶▶ Van Halen

Bill Haley
▶▶ Pat Boone
◀◀ Louis Jordan
◀◀ Carl Perkins
▶▶ Ramones
▶▶ Bruce Springsteen
◀◀ Big Joe Turner
◀◀ Bob Wills

Darryl Hall & John Oates
▶▶ Boyz II Men
▶▶ Charles & Eddie
◀◀ Gamble & Huff
◀◀ O'Jays
◀◀ Sam and Dave

Col. Bruce Hampton
▶▶ Blues Traveler
◀◀ Captain Beefheart
▶▶ Dave Matthews Band
◀◀ Root Boy Slim
▶▶ Screaming Cheetah Wheelies
◀◀ Frank Zappa

Happy Mondays
◀◀ Beatles
◀◀ Bee Gees
◀◀ Donovan
▶▶ Farm
◀◀ Curtis Mayfield
▶▶ Northern Uproar
▶▶ Northside

John Wesley Harding
◀◀ Elvis Costello
◀◀ Bob Dylan
◀◀ Phil Ochs

Emmylou Harris
◀◀ Carter Family
▶▶ Cowboy Junkies
◀◀ Hazel and Alice
▶▶ Alison Krauss
◀◀ Louvin Brothers
▶▶ Mavericks
◀◀ Buck Owens
◀◀ Gram Parsons
◀◀ Tom Rush

George Harrison
◀◀ Chet Atkins
◀◀ Beatles
▶▶ Crowded House
▶▶ Jeff Lynne
▶▶ Grant McLennan
◀◀ Carl Perkins
◀◀ Ravi Shankar
▶▶ Paul Simon

Juliana Hatfield
▶▶ Magnapop
▶▶ Alanis Morissette
◀◀ R.E.M.
◀◀ Replacements
◀◀ Patti Smith

◀◀ 'til Tuesday
◀◀ X

Richie Havens
◀◀ Beatles
▶▶ Tracy Chapman
◀◀ Sam Cooke
◀◀ Bob Dylan
▶▶ Ben Harper
▶▶ Hootie and the Blowfish
◀◀ Robert Johnson
◀◀ Leadbelly
◀◀ Muddy Waters

Isaac Hayes
◀◀ Burt Bacharach
◀◀ Brook Benton
◀◀ Nat King Cole
▶▶ Cypress Hill
▶▶ Terence Trent D'Arby
▶▶ Gamble and Huff
▶▶ Marvin Gaye
▶▶ Al Green
▶▶ Lenny Kravitz
◀◀ Henry Mancini
◀◀ Motown
▶▶ Teddy Pendergrass
◀◀ Wilson Pickett
▶▶ DJ Quik
◀◀ Percy Sledge
◀◀ Rufus Thomas
▶▶ Barry White

Jeff Healey Band
◀◀ Jeff Beck
◀◀ Eric Clapton
◀◀ Willie Dixon
◀◀ John Lee Hooker
◀◀ Stevie Ray Vaughan

Heart
▶▶ 4 Non Blondes
◀◀ Janis Joplin
◀◀ Led Zeppelin
◀◀ Joni Mitchell
▶▶ Alannah Myles
▶▶ Veruca Salt

Michael Hedges
◀◀ Martin Carthy
▶▶ Craig Chaquico
▶▶ Ben Harper
◀◀ Leo Kottke
◀◀ John Martyn
◀◀ Edgar Varese
▶▶ Chris Whitley

Richard Hell & the Voidoids
◀◀ Charles Baudelaire
◀◀ Captain Beefheart
▶▶ Contortions
▶▶ DNA/Arto Lindsay
▶▶ Matthew Sweet
▶▶ Minutemen
◀◀ Arthur Rimbaud
▶▶ Sex Pistols
▶▶ Sonic Youth
◀◀ Stooges
◀◀ Velvet Underground/Lou Reed

Jimi Hendrix
◀◀ Beatles
◀◀ Chuck Berry
▶▶ Eric Clapton
▶▶ Miles Davis
◀◀ Bob Dylan
◀◀ Buddy Guy
◀◀ Howlin' Wolf
▶▶ Ernie Isley
◀◀ Robert Johnson
◀◀ Freddie King
▶▶ Lenny Kravitz
▶▶ Prince
▶▶ Carlos Santana
▶▶ Sly Stone
▶▶ Robin Trower
▶▶ Van Halen
▶▶ Stevie Ray Vaughn
◀◀ Yardbirds

Nona Hendryx
▶▶ Tasmin Archer
▶▶ Neneh Cherry
◀◀ Eurythmics
▶▶ Lisa Lisa & Cult Jam
◀◀ Mavis Staples

Don Henley
▶▶ Bryan Adams
◀◀ Byrds
◀◀ Leonard Cohen
▶▶ Sheryl Crow
◀◀ Bob Dylan
▶▶ Mojo Nixon
◀◀ Gram Parsons
▶▶ Tom Petty
◀◀ Henry David Thoreau

John Hiatt
◀◀ Ry Cooder
◀◀ Elvis Costello
◀◀ Bob Dylan
▶▶ Joe Henry
◀◀ Bob Seger
▶▶ Bob Seger
◀◀ Stax/Volt soul
▶▶ Syd Straw

Dan Hicks
◀◀ Andrews Sisters
◀◀ Charlatans
▶▶ Thomas Dolby
◀◀ Le Hot Club de France
▶▶ Pointer Sisters

Peter Himmelman
◀◀ Elvis Costello
◀◀ Bob Dylan

His Name is Alive
◀◀ Big Star
◀◀ Cocteau Twins
◀◀ Brian Eno
◀◀ Phillip Glass
◀◀ Guided By Voices
◀◀ King Crimson
◀◀ King Tubby
◀◀ Led Zeppelin
◀◀ Colin Newman
◀◀ Karlheinz Stockhausen
◀◀ This Mortal Coil
◀◀ Brian Wilson

Robyn Hitchcock (And the Egyptians)
◀◀ Syd Barrett
▶▶ Blur
▶▶ Crowded House
▶▶ Pete Droge
◀◀ Bob Dylan
▶▶ Everclear
◀◀ John Lennon

Hollies
▶▶ Barenaked Ladies
▶▶ Crosby, Stills and Nash
◀◀ Everly Brothers
◀◀ Buddy Holly
▶▶ Material Issue
▶▶ Posies

Buddy Holly
◀◀ Hank Ballard
▶▶ Beatles
▶▶ Waylon Jennings
◀◀ Elvis Presley
▶▶ Rolling Stones
▶▶ Bobby Vee
◀◀ Hank Williams

Hoodoo Gurus
◀◀ Cramps
▶▶ Jellyfish
◀◀ Kinks
◀◀ Skyhooks
▶▶ Smithereens
◀◀ Turtles

John Lee Hooker
▶▶ James Brown
▶▶ Savoy Brown
▶▶ Canned Heat
▶▶ George Clinton
▶▶ Robert Cray
◀◀ Robert Johnson
▶▶ John Mayall
◀◀ Charley Patton
▶▶ Bonnie Raitt
▶▶ George Thorogood

Hooters
◀◀ Band
▶▶ Hot House Flowers
▶▶ Levellers
◀◀ Bruce Springsteen

Bruce Hornsby
- Bob Dylan
- Ben Folds Five
- Grateful Dead
- Keith Jarrett
- Bonnie Raitt
- Steely Dan

Hot Tuna
- Jeff Buckley
- Rev. Gary Davis
- Jeff Healey
- Mississippi John Hurt
- Keb' Mo'
- Scott LeFaro
- Chris Whitley

Hothouse Flowers
- 54.40
- U2
- Waterboys

House of Love
- Beatles
- Chapterhouse
- Church
- Echo & the Bunnymen
- Ride
- Smiths
- Stone Roses
- Velvet Underground

Housemartins
- Blur
- Clash
- English Beat
- Green Day
- Kinks
- Oasis
- Specials
- Supergrass

Whitney Houston
- Brandy
- Toni Braxton
- Mariah Carey
- Aretha Franklin
- Cissy Houston
- Chaka Khan
- Diana Ross
- Dionne Warwick

Howlin' Wolf
- Jeff Beck
- Eric Clapton
- Cream
- Willie Dixon
- Doors
- Robert Johnson
- Led Zeppelin
- John Mayall
- Charley Patton
- Sonny Boy Williamson
- Yardbirds

Humble Pie
- Beatles
- Black Crowes
- Cry of Love
- Willie Dixon
- Foghat
- John Lee Hooker
- Ted Nugent
- REO Speedwagon
- Spooky Tooth

Ian Hunter
- David Bowie
- Elvis Costello
- Def Leppard
- Bob Dylan
- Great White
- Little Richard
- Graham Parker
- Smashing Pumpkins

Hunters & Collectors
- Bad Manners
- Nick Cave
- Gang of Four
- Hoodoo Gurus
- Kinks
- Lords of the New Church
- Midnight Oil

Hüsker Dü
- Black Flag
- Nirvana
- Pixies
- Soul Asylum

Janis Ian
- Joan Baez
- Tracy Chapman
- Shawn Colvin
- Rev. Gary Davis
- Ronnie Gilbert
- Suzanne Vega

Icehouse
- David Bowie
- Cars
- Cutting Crew
- Alan Parsons Project
- Roxy Music
- Talk Talk
- Tears For Fears
- Ultravox

Billy Idol
- Beatles
- Buzzcocks
- Clash
- Green Day
- Offspring
- Sex Pistols
- Sigue Sigue Sputnik
- Siouxsie and the Banshees
- Sisters of Mercy

Indigo Girls
- Disappear Fear
- Bob Dylan
- R.E.M.
- Simon and Garfunkel
- Story

Inspiral Carpets
- Doors
- Fall
- Joy Division
- Oasis
- Supergrass

INXS
- Charm Farm
- Jesus Jones
- Rolling Stones
- Roxy Music

Iron Butterfly
- Animals
- Black Sabbath
- Blue Cheer
- Alice Cooper
- Judas Priest
- Kiss
- Troggs
- Yardbirds

Iron Maiden
- Black Sabbath
- Deep Purple
- Led Zeppelin
- Megadeth
- Metallica
- Slayer

Chris Isaak
- Eddie Cochran
- Marshall Crenshaw
- Neil Diamond
- Roy Orbison
- Elvis Presley
- Dwight Yoakam

Isley Brothers
- Boyz II Men
- James Brown
- Sam Cooke
- Drifters
- Funkadelic
- Jimi Hendrix
- Bone Maxwell
- Sly & the Family Stone

Jackson 5
- Boys II Men
- James Brown
- Jodeci
- Frankie Lymon
- New Edition
- Smokey Robinson
- Temptations
- Jackie Wilson

Janet Jackson
- Paula Abdul

- ◀◀ Michael Jackson
- ◀◀ Madonna
- ◀◀ Prince
- ◀◀ Diana Ross
- ▶▶ Jody Watley
- ▶▶ Karyn White

Joe Jackson

- ◀◀ Bob Dylan
- ▶▶ Ben Folds Five
- ◀◀ Louis Jordan
- ◀◀ Cole Porter

Michael Jackson

- ◀◀ James Brown
- ◀◀ Gene Kelly
- ◀◀ Diana Ross
- ◀◀ Jackie Wilson

Jam

- ◀◀ Beatles
- ◀◀ Booker T & the MGs
- ▶▶ Billy Bragg
- ▶▶ Clash
- ▶▶ Elvis Costello
- ◀◀ Free
- ◀◀ Kinks
- ◀◀ Curtis Mayfield
- ◀◀ Motown
- ▶▶ Oasis
- ◀◀ Small Faces
- ▶▶ Sugar
- ◀◀ Traffic
- ◀◀ Who
- ◀◀ Steve Winwood

James

- ▶▶ Altan
- ◀◀ Nick Cave
- ▶▶ Levellers
- ◀◀ Patti Smith
- ◀◀ Neil Young

Elmore James

- ▶▶ Allman Brothers
- ▶▶ Jimi Hendrix
- ◀◀ Robert Johnson
- ▶▶ B.B. King
- ◀◀ Robert Nighthawk
- ▶▶ Rolling Stones
- ▶▶ George Thorogood
- ▶▶ Stevie Ray Vaughan
- ◀◀ Muddy Waters
- ◀◀ Sonny Boy Williamson
- ▶▶ Johnny Winter

Etta James

- ◀◀ Hank Ballard
- ◀◀ Billie Holiday
- ▶▶ Janis Joplin
- ▶▶ Tina Turner

Rick James

- ◀◀ James Brown
- ▶▶ Jodeci
- ◀◀ Parliament-Funkadelic
- ▶▶ Prince
- ◀◀ Sly & the Family Stone
- ▶▶ 2 Live Crew

Tommy James & the Shondells

- ◀◀ Beatles
- ▶▶ Five Americans
- ▶▶ Grass Roots
- ◀◀ Jefferson Airplane
- ▶▶ Monkees
- ◀◀ Motown
- ▶▶ 1910 Fruitgum Company
- ◀◀ Elvis Presley
- ▶▶ Paul Revere & the Raiders
- ▶▶ Tommy Roe
- ▶▶ Strawberry Alarm Clock
- ▶▶ Troggs
- ▶▶ XTC/the Dukes of Stratosphear

Jan & Dean

- ◀◀ Dion & the Belmonts
- ▶▶ Flo & Eddie
- ◀◀ Four Freshmen
- ▶▶ Hall & Oates
- ◀◀ Laurel & Hardy
- ◀◀ Lettermen
- ◀◀ Frankie Valli & the Four Seasons

Japan

- ◀◀ Bebop Deluxe
- ◀◀ David Bowie
- ◀◀ Can
- ▶▶ Depeche Mode
- ◀◀ Brian Eno
- ▶▶ Bill Nelson
- ◀◀ Lou Reed and the Velvet Underground
- ◀◀ Roxy Music
- ▶▶ Midge Ure and Ultravox

Jason and the Scorchers

- ▶▶ Bottle Rockets
- ◀◀ Johnny Cash
- ▶▶ Golden Smog
- ◀◀ Mekons
- ◀◀ Gram Parsons
- ◀◀ Ramones
- ▶▶ Social Distortion
- ▶▶ Uncle Tupelo
- ◀◀ Hank Williams Sr.

Jayhawks

- ▶▶ Golden Smog
- ▶▶ Joe Henry
- ◀◀ Gram Parsons
- ▶▶ Son Volt
- ▶▶ Wilco
- ▶▶ Victoria Williams
- ◀◀ Neil Young

Jefferson Airplane

- ◀◀ Eric Dolphy
- ◀◀ Bob Dylan
- ▶▶ Jefferson Starship (ugh)
- ◀◀ Otis Redding
- ◀◀ Weavers

Jefferson Starship

- ◀◀ Jefferson Airplane
- ▶▶ Jefferson Starship: The Next Generation

Jesus and Mary Chain

- ◀◀ Beach Boys
- ◀◀ Jimi Hendrix
- ▶▶ My Bloody Valentine
- ▶▶ Ride
- ◀◀ Phil Spector
- ▶▶ Teenage Fanclub
- ◀◀ Velvet Underground

Jesus Lizard

- ◀◀ Birthday Party
- ◀◀ Led Zeppelin
- ◀◀ Yow-Sims band Scratchsims Acid

Jethro Tull

- ◀◀ Bach
- ◀◀ Beatles
- ▶▶ Bloodwyn Pig
- ◀◀ Fairport Convention
- ▶▶ Heart
- ◀◀ Rahsaan Roland Kirk
- ◀◀ Move
- ▶▶ Spinal Tap
- ◀◀ Sonny Boy Williamson

Joan Jett

- ▶▶ Babes in Toyland
- ▶▶ Bikini Kill
- ◀◀ David Bowie
- ◀◀ Gary Glitter
- ▶▶ L7
- ◀◀ Rolling Stones
- ◀◀ 60s bubblegum

Billy Joel

- ◀◀ Beatles
- ▶▶ Garth Brooks
- ◀◀ Ray Charles
- ◀◀ Dion & the Belmonts
- ◀◀ Bob Dylan
- ◀◀ Four Seasons
- ◀◀ George & Ira Gershwin
- ▶▶ Amy Grant
- ◀◀ Elton John
- ▶▶ Barry Manilow
- ▶▶ Richard Marx
- ◀◀ Rolling Stones

David Johansen

- ◀◀ Four Tops
- ▶▶ modern lounge movement
- ◀◀ Louis Prima
- ◀◀ Rolling Stones

Elton John

- ◀◀ Beatles
- ▶▶ Phil Collins
- ◀◀ Lee Dorsey

- Duke Ellington
- Ben Folds Five
- Guns N' Roses
- Jellyfish
- George Michael
- Motown
- Rolling Stones
- Leon Russell
- Stax
- Suddenly Tammy!
- Fats Waller

Eric Johnson

- Chet Atkins
- Beatles
- Jeff Beck
- Eric Clapton
- Cream
- Dixie Dregs
- Nokie Edwards
- Eric Gale
- Danny Gatton
- Billy Gibbons (ZZ Top)
- Jimi Hendrix
- Elmore James
- Freddie King
- Shawn Lane
- Ian Moore
- Vinnie Moore
- Steve Morse
- Rolling Stones
- Joe Satriani
- Merle Travis
- Steve Vai
- Stevie Ray Vaughn
- Johnny Winter
- Yardbirds

Johnnie Johnson

- Count Basie
- Earl "Fatha" Hines
- Elton John
- Ian McLagan (Faces)
- Bud Powell
- Ian Stewart (Rolling Stones)

Daniel Johnston

- Beach Boys
- Beatles
- Dead Milkmen
- Bob Dylan
- Roky Erickson and 13th Floor Elevators
- Jerry Lee Lewis
- Kathy McCarty
- Nirvana
- Pearl Jam
- Sonic Youth
- Yo La Tengo
- Neil Young

Grace Jones

- Joan Armatrading
- Wally Badarou
- Black Box
- David Bowie
- Fine Young Cannibals
- Gloria Gaynor
- Normal
- Robert Palmer
- Pretenders
- Andrea True

Howard Jones

- Depeche Mode
- Donnie Iris
- Joy Division
- Kraftwerk

Marti Jones

- Petula Clark
- Judy Collins
- Jackie DeShannon
- John Doe
- Bonnie Raitt
- Dusty Springfield

Rickie Lee Jones

- Sheryl Crow
- k.d. lang
- Joni Mitchell
- Laura Nyro
- Suzanne Vega
- Tom Waits

Tom Jones

- Michael Bolton
- Buster Poindexter
- Elvis Presley
- Wham!

Janis Joplin

- Mariah Carey
- John Coltrane
- Melissa Etheridge
- Lightnin' Hopkins
- Memphis Minnie

Journey

- Bad English
- Michael Bolton
- Boston
- Queen
- Santana
- Survivor
- Whitesnake

Joy Division

- American Music Club/Mark Eitzel
- Bauhaus
- David Bowie
- Cure
- Kraftwerk
- Moby
- New Order
- nine inch nails
- Nirvana
- Red Lorry Yellow Lorry
- Sex Pistols
- Sisters of Mercy/The Mission U.K.
- Teardrop Explodes/Julian Cope
- Velvet Underground

Judas Priest

- Accept
- Anthrax
- Black Sabbath
- Cream
- Iron Maiden
- Led Zeppelin
- Metallica
- Pantera
- Scorpions
- Slayer
- Tool
- Venom
- White Zombie
- Who

Brenda Kahn

- Clash
- Elvis Costello
- Roger Manning
- Phil Ochs
- Pretenders
- Lou Reed
- Michelle Shocked
- Bessie Smith
- Dave Van Ronk
- X-Ray Spex

Kansas

- Dave Brubeck
- Humble Pie
- Elmore James
- B.B. King
- King Crimson
- Ramsey Lewis
- Livgren-Hope Christian rock band AD
- Moody Blues
- Procol Harum
- Shooting Star

Katrina and the Waves

- Ace of Base
- Bangles
- Soft Boys
- Dusty Springfield

KC and the Sunshine Band

- Anita Ward
- Chic
- George Clinton/Parliament-Funkadelic
- Fine Young Cannibals
- Gwen Guthrie
- Gwen McCrae
- Miami Sound Machine
- Tito Puente
- Sylvester
- Betty Wright

Tommy Keene
- Beatles
- Big Star
- Byrds
- Gin Blossoms
- Let's Active
- Shoes
- Superchunk
- Matthew Sweet
- Teenage Fanclub
- Velvet Crush
- Who
- Young Fresh Fellows

Paul Kelly
- Raymond Carver
- Elvis Costello
- Bob Dylan
- John Mellencamp
- Graham Parker

Nik Kershaw
- Chesney Hawkes
- Elton John
- Gary Numan

Kid Creole and the Coconuts
- Cab Calloway
- Gloria Estefan
- Machito and His Afro-Cubans
- Buster Poindexter

Killing Joke
- Can
- Filter
- Joy Division
- Kraftwerk
- Ministry
- nine inch nails

Albert King
- Eric Clapton
- Billy Gibbons
- Buddy Guy
- Jimi Hendrix
- B.B. King
- Jimmy Reed
- Otis Rush
- Stevie Ray Vaughan
- T-Bone Walker

B.B. King
- Blind Lemon Jefferson
- Clarence "Gatemouth" Brown
- Eric Clapton
- David Gilmour
- Buddy Guy
- Lonnie Johnson
- Albert King
- Django Reinhardt
- Otis Rush
- Kenny Wayne Shepherd
- Stevie Ray Vaughan
- T-Bone Walker

Carole King
- Tori Amos
- Doc Pomus
- Bonnie Hayes
- Mort Shuman
- Carly Simon

Freddie King
- Eric Clapton
- Jimi Hendrix
- Robert Jr. Lockwood
- Otis Rush
- Eddie Taylor
- Stevie Ray Vaughan

King Crimson
- Bad Company
- Beatles
- Emerson Lake & Palmer
- Foreigner
- Helmet
- Jimi Hendrix
- His Name Is Alive
- Iceburn
- Living Colour
- John McLaughlin
- No Man
- Porcupine
- U.K.

King Curtis
- Earl Bostic
- Clarence Clemons
- Arnett Cobb
- Illinois Jacquet
- Leroi Moore (Dave Matthews Band)

King Missile
- Maggie Estep/I Love Everybody
- Allan Ginsburg
- Bob Holman

King Sunny Ade
- Johnny Clegg
- Peter Gabriel
- IK Dairo
- Kotoja
- Segun Adewale
- Tunde Nightingale

King's X
- Beatles
- Eye and I
- Follow For Now
- Living Colour
- Petra

Kingston Trio
- Brothers Four
- Bob Dylan
- Gateway Singers
- Journeymen
- Limelighters
- Roger McGuinn
- Chad Mitchell Trio
- New Christy Minstrels
- Peter Paul and Mary
- Pete Seeger
- Serendipity Singers
- Simon and Garfunkel
- Weavers

Kinks
- Beatles
- Big Bill Broonzy
- Blur
- Charles Dickens
- Jam
- Little Richard
- Pulp
- Who

Kiss
- Beatles
- Alice Cooper
- Crazy World of Arthur Brown
- Def Leppard
- Misfits
- Motley Crue
- Motorhead
- Poison
- Quiet Riot
- Ratt
- Lou Reed

Klaatu
- Beatles
- Jellyfish
- Utopia

KMFDM
- Einstürzende Neubanten
- KLF
- Ministry
- My Life With the Thrill Kill Kult
- nine inch nails
- Pig
- Skinny Puppy

Knack
- Beatles
- Herman's Hermits
- Jellyfish
- Kinks
- Plimsouls
- Posies
- Romantics
- Turtles
- 20-20

Kool and the Gang
- Con Funk Shun
- Miles Davis
- Dazz Band
- Digable Planets
- Marvin Gaye
- Isley Brothers
- Rashaan Roland Kirk
- Living Colour
- Mandrill
- Manu Dibango

◀◀ Horace Silver
▶▶ Slave
◀◀ Sly and the Family Stone
▶▶ Time

Leo Kottke
◀◀ Chet Atkins
◀◀ Roy Clark
▶▶ Ry Cooder
◀◀ Rev. Gary Davis
▶▶ Jorma Kaukonen
◀◀ Carl Perkins
▶▶ Chris Whitley
▶▶ Edward Wright

Kraftwerk
▶▶ David Bowie
◀◀ John Cage
▶▶ Brian Eno
◀◀ Phillip Glass
▶▶ Orb
▶▶ Orbital
▶▶ Tangerine Dream

Lenny Kravitz
◀◀ Jimi Hendrix
◀◀ Led Zeppelin
◀◀ Living Colour
▶▶ Self

k.d. lang
▶▶ Mary Chapin Carpenter
◀◀ Patsy Cline
▶▶ Melissa Etheridge
◀◀ Julie London
◀◀ Minnie Pearl
▶▶ Trisha Yearwood

Last Exit
◀◀ Albert Ayler
◀◀ John Coltrane
▶▶ William Hooker
◀◀ Blind Willie Johnson
▶▶ Thurston Moore and Lee Ranaldo of Sonic Youth
▶▶ Naked City

Bill Laswell/Material
▶▶ Arthur Baker
◀◀ John Coltrane
▶▶ Mitchell Froom
▶▶ Golden Palominos
◀◀ Jimi Hendrix
▶▶ Nona Hendryx
◀◀ Mad Professor
▶▶ Ben Neill
▶▶ Orb
◀◀ Parliament-Funkadelic/George Clinton
◀◀ Sonny Sharrock
▶▶ DJ Spooky

Cyndi Lauper
▶▶ Bjork
◀◀ Marlene Dietrich
◀◀ Shelley Fabares
◀◀ Bette Midler

Led Zeppelin
▶▶ AC/DC
▶▶ Aerosmith
▶▶ Bad Company
◀◀ Beatles
◀◀ Chuck Berry
▶▶ Black Sabbath
▶▶ Bonham
▶▶ Alice Cooper
▶▶ Cult
◀◀ Willie Dixon
◀◀ Fairport Convention
▶▶ Great White
▶▶ Guns N'Roses
◀◀ Buddy Guy
◀◀ Howlin' Wolf
◀◀ Robert Johnson
◀◀ B.B. King
▶▶ Kingdom Come
◀◀ Little Richard
▶▶ Mötley Crüe
▶▶ Joni Mitchell
◀◀ Elvis Presley
◀◀ Otis Redding
◀◀ Rolling Stones
▶▶ Rush
▶▶ Soundgarden
▶▶ Van Halen
▶▶ Whitesnake
◀◀ Sonny Boy Williamson

Lemonheads
▶▶ Cracker
▶▶ Everclear
▶▶ Gin Blossoms
◀◀ Ramones
◀◀ Replacements
◀◀ Sex Pistols
◀◀ Neil Young

John Lennon
◀◀ Chuck Berry
◀◀ Lonnie Donnegan
◀◀ Buddy Holly
▶▶ Billy Joel
▶▶ Elton John
◀◀ James Joyce
▶▶ Lenny Kravitz
▶▶ Julian Lennon
▶▶ Oasis
◀◀ Gene Vincent

Level 42
▶▶ Brand New Heavies
◀◀ Stanley Clarke
◀◀ Chick Corea
◀◀ Herbie Hancock's Headhunters
◀◀ Return to Forever

Jerry Lee Lewis
▶▶ Jason and the Scorchers
▶▶ Billy Joel
▶▶ Elton John
▶▶ Kentucky HeadHunters
▶▶ Iggy Pop
◀◀ Elvis Presley
◀◀ Charlie Rich
▶▶ Bruce Springsteen

Huey Lewis and the News
▶▶ Blues Traveler
◀◀ Clover
◀◀ Elvis Costello
◀◀ doo-wop
▶▶ Bruce Hornsby
▶▶ Nick Lowe
◀◀ Motown
◀◀ Brinsley Schwartz

Gordon Lightfoot
▶▶ Harry Chapin
▶▶ Tracey Chapman
▶▶ Nancy Griffith
◀◀ Woody Guthrie
▶▶ Janis Ian
▶▶ James Taylor

David Lindley
▶▶ Black Crowes
▶▶ Bottle Rockets
◀◀ James Burton
◀◀ Clifton Chenier
◀◀ Ry Cooder
◀◀ King Curtis
◀◀ Duane Eddy
◀◀ Fendermen
▶▶ Hooters
◀◀ Gabby Pahinui
◀◀ Pioneers
◀◀ Sam the Sham and the Pharoahs
◀◀ Huey "Piano" Smith
◀◀ Ventures
▶▶ Chris Whitley
◀◀ Yellow Magic Orchestra

Little Feat
◀◀ Beatles
▶▶ Black Crowes
▶▶ Blind Melon
◀◀ Byrds
◀◀ Canned Heat
▶▶ Elvis Costello
◀◀ Lee Dorsey
▶▶ Emmylou Harris
◀◀ John Lee Hooker
◀◀ Howlin' Wolf
▶▶ Daniel Lanois
◀◀ Meters
▶▶ Linda Ronstadt
◀◀ Muddy Waters
◀◀ Hank Williams

Little Richard
◀◀ Roy Brown
◀◀ Cab Calloway
▶▶ John Fogerty
▶▶ Michael Jackson
▶▶ Paul McCartney
▶▶ Prince

⏩ Otis Redding

Little Steven

⏩ Bon Jovi
⏪ Cream
⏪ doo wop
⏪ Motown
⏪ Rolling Stones
⏩ Southside Johnny
⏪ Stax
⏪ Hank Williams
⏪ Yardbirds

Live Skull

⏩ Band of Susans
⏩ Come
⏪ Joy Division
⏪ Killing Joke
⏪ Psychedelic Furs
⏩ Rein Sanction
⏪ Sonic Youth
⏪ Swans

Living Colour

⏪ Bad Brains
⏪ Fishbone
⏩ Fugees
⏪ Jimi Hendrix
⏩ I Mother Earth
⏩ Me'Shell NdegeOcello
⏪ Parliament/Funkadelic

L.L. Cool J

⏪ Kurtis Blow
⏩ Big Daddy Kane
⏩ Notorious B.I.G
⏪ Run D.M.C
⏪ Whodini

Nils Lofgren

⏪ Chuck Berry
⏩ Eric Johnson
⏪ Rolling Stones
⏩ Bruce Springsteen
⏩ Stevie Ray Vaughan
⏩ Paul Westerberg
⏪ Neil Young

Loggins and Messina

⏪ Bread
⏩ Buckingham Nicks
⏩ Captain and Tennille
⏩ Fleetwood Mac
⏪ Poco
⏪ Simon and Garfunkel

Lone Justice

⏪ Byrds
⏩ Cowboy Junkies
⏩ Sheryl Crow
⏪ Flying Burrito Brothers
⏪ Aretha Franklin
⏩ Jayhawks
⏪ Janis Joplin
⏪ Tom Petty and the Heartbreakers
⏩ Uncle Tupelo

Los Lobos

⏩ Blazers
⏪ Sir Douglas Quintet
⏪ Ritchie Valens

Lounge Lizards

⏩ Ambitious Lovers
⏪ Dollar Brand
⏩ Golden Palominos
⏩ Jazz Passengers
⏩ Medeski Martin & Wood
⏪ Charles Mingus
⏪ Thelonious Monk
⏪ Peter Apfelbaum's Heiroglyphics Ensemble
⏩ Spanish Fly
⏩ Squirrel Nut Zippers

Love and Rockets

⏪ Bauhaus
⏩ Christian Death
⏪ Jazz Butcher
⏩ Ministry
⏪ New Order
⏩ Sisters of Mercy
⏪ Smiths
⏪ Tones on Tail

Loverboy

⏪ Boston
⏪ Foreigner
⏩ Poison
⏩ Skid Row
⏪ Styx
⏩ Warrant

Lyle Lovett

⏩ Beck
⏪ Ray Charles
⏪ Guy Clark
⏩ Hayden
⏪ Randy Newman
⏪ Townes Van Zandt

Lovin' Spoonful

⏩ Crosby, Stills and Nash
⏪ Rev. Gary Davis
⏩ Eagles
⏪ Mississippi John Hurt
⏪ Fred Neil
⏩ Poco
⏪ Weavers

Nick Lowe

⏪ Chuck Berry
⏪ Johnny Cash
⏩ Elvis Costello
⏩ Don Dixon
⏩ Francis Dunnery
⏪ Everly Brothers
⏩ John Hiatt
⏪ Carl Perkins

L7

⏪ Babes in Toyland
⏩ Bikini Kill
⏪ Black Sabbath
⏩ Bratmobile
⏩ Hole
⏪ Holly and the Italians
⏩ Alanis Morrissette
⏪ Motorhead
⏪ Nirvana
⏩ Pearl Jam
⏪ Iggy Pop
⏪ Sex Pistols
⏪ X

Lush

⏪ Beach Boys
⏪ Cocteau Twins
⏩ Cranes
⏩ Medicine
⏪ My Bloody Valentine
⏩ Slowdive
⏪ Phil Spector

Lynyrd Skynyrd

⏪ Allman Brothers Band
⏩ Black Crowes
⏪ Cream
⏩ Molly Hatchet
⏪ Led Zeppelin
⏩ Metallica
⏪ Rolling Stones
⏩ .38 Special
⏪ Yardbirds
⏩ Zakk Wylde

Lyres

⏩ Del Fuegos
⏪ Kinks
⏪ ? and the Mysterians
⏪ Shadows of Knight
⏪ Standells

Kirsty MacColl

⏪ Billy Bragg
⏩ Billy Bragg
⏪ Patsy Cline
⏪ Elvis Costello
⏪ Pretenders
⏪ Rockpile
⏪ Smiths
⏩ Tracey Ullman

Ashley MacIsaac

⏪ Chieftains

Madonna

⏪ Crystals
⏩ Terence Trent D'Arby
⏩ Celine Dion
⏩ En Vogue
⏪ Aretha Franklin
⏪ Billie Holiday
⏩ Whitney Houston
⏪ Michael Jackson
⏪ Cyndi Lauper
⏩ Alanis Morrissette

- ⏪ Elvis Presley
- ⏪ Donna Summer
- ⏩ TLC
- ⏪ Tina Turner

Magazine
- ⏪ Buzzcocks
- ⏪ Captain Beefheart
- ⏪ Fyodor Dostoevsky
- ⏪ Franz Kafka
- ⏩ Negro Problem
- ⏩ Radiohead
- ⏪ Sex Pistols
- ⏪ Sly and the Family Stone

Taj Mahal
- ⏪ Sleepy John Estes
- ⏪ Mississippi John Hurt
- ⏩ Keb' Mo
- ⏩ Vinx

Yngwie Malmsteen
- ⏩ Darrell Abbott (Pantera)
- ⏪ Bach
- ⏩ Jennifer Batten
- ⏪ Beethoven
- ⏪ Ritchie Blackmore
- ⏪ Jimi Hendrix
- ⏪ Steve Hillage
- ⏪ Paganini
- ⏩ Slash
- ⏪ Vivaldi
- ⏩ Zakk Wylde

Mamas and the Papas
- ⏪ Beatles
- ⏪ Everly Brothers
- ⏩ Manhattan Transfer
- ⏪ Rick Nelson
- ⏩ Wilson Phillips
- ⏪ Weavers

Aimee Mann
- ⏪ Beatles
- ⏪ Byrds
- ⏪ Elvis Costello
- ⏩ Crowded House
- ⏩ Juliana Hatfield
- ⏩ Michael Penn
- ⏩ Sam Phillips
- ⏪ Pretenders
- ⏩ Jules Shear
- ⏪ Squeeze

Manfred Mann
- ⏩ Asia
- ⏪ Beatles
- ⏪ Lonnie Donegan
- ⏪ Bob Dylan
- ⏩ Emerson, Lake & Palmer
- ⏪ Bruce Springsteen

Phil Manzanera
- ⏩ Adrian Belew
- ⏪ Charlie Christian
- ⏪ Charles Mingus
- ⏩ Andy Taylor (Duran Duran)
- ⏪ Edgar Varese

Teena Marie
- ⏩ Mariah Carey
- ⏪ Aretha Franklin
- ⏪ Rick James
- ⏩ Madonna
- ⏪ Prince
- ⏩ Lisa Stansfield
- ⏩ Wendy & Lisa

Marillion
- ⏩ Dramarama
- ⏩ Dream Theatre
- ⏪ Emerson, Lake & Palmer
- ⏪ Genesis
- ⏪ King Crimson
- ⏪ Moody Blues
- ⏩ Queensryche
- ⏪ Yes

Bob Marley and the Wailers
- ⏪ Desmond Dekker
- ⏩ English Beat
- ⏩ Lucky Dube
- ⏩ Ziggy Marley and the Melody Makers
- ⏪ Skatalites
- ⏩ UB40

Ziggy Marley & the Melody Makers
- ⏩ Big Mountain
- ⏪ Earth ,Wind and Fire
- ⏩ Fugees
- ⏪ Jacksons
- ⏪ Bob Marley
- ⏪ New Edition
- ⏩ Spearhead
- ⏪ Wailers

Martha and the Vandellas
- ⏩ Pointer Sisters
- ⏪ Della Reese
- ⏩ Salt-N-Pepa
- ⏩ Supremes
- ⏩ TLC

John Martyn
- ⏪ Harold Arlen
- ⏪ Louis Armstrong
- ⏩ Eric Clapton
- ⏩ Phil Collins
- ⏪ Tim Hardin
- ⏪ Billie Holiday
- ⏩ Robert Palmer
- ⏩ Richard Thompson

Dave Mason
- ⏪ Beatles
- ⏪ Eric Clapton
- ⏩ Joe Cocker
- ⏩ Delaney & Bonnie
- ⏪ Jimi Hendrix
- ⏪ Stephen Stills

Material Issue
- ⏪ Big Star
- ⏪ Hollies
- ⏪ Sweet

Iain Matthews
- ⏩ America
- ⏩ England Dan & John Ford Coley
- ⏪ Peter & Gordon
- ⏩ Seals & Crofts
- ⏪ Simon & Garfunkel
- ⏪ Jimmy Webb

John Mayall
- ⏩ Blues Traveler
- ⏩ Savoy Brown
- ⏩ Fabulous Thunderbirds
- ⏩ Foghat
- ⏪ Howlin' Wolf
- ⏪ Little Walter
- ⏪ Muddy Waters
- ⏩ Rolling Stones

Curtis Mayfield
- ⏩ D'Angelo
- ⏪ Drifters
- ⏩ Maxwell
- ⏩ Tony Rich
- ⏩ Seal
- ⏪ Soul Stirrers

Paul McCartney
- ⏩ Blur
- ⏪ Sammy Cahn
- ⏪ Eddie Cochran
- ⏪ Fats Domino
- ⏪ George and Ira Gershwin
- ⏪ Buddy Holly
- ⏩ Jellyfish
- ⏪ Jim Mac Jazz Band
- ⏩ Oasis
- ⏪ Elvis Presley

Kathy McCarty
- ⏩ Dead Milkmen
- ⏪ Robyn Hitchcock
- ⏪ Daniel Johnston
- ⏪ Minutemen
- ⏪ Raincoats
- ⏪ Sonic Youth
- ⏪ Talking Heads
- ⏩ Yo La Tengo

MC5
- ⏪ Amboy Dukes
- ⏩ Bad Brains
- ⏪ Chuck Berry
- ⏩ Black Flag
- ⏪ John Coltrane
- ⏩ Alice Cooper
- ⏩ Guns N' Roses
- ⏩ Kiss

- ▶▶ Metallica
- ▶▶ Modern Lovers
- ▶▶ Motörhead
- ◀◀ New York Dolls
- ▶▶ Presidents of the United States of America
- ◀◀ Rolling Stones
- ▶▶ Rollins Band
- ◀◀ Mitch Ryder & the Detroit Wheels
- ◀◀ Bob Seger
- ▶▶ Sex Pistols
- ▶▶ Slayer
- ◀◀ Stooges
- ◀◀ Velvet Underground

Kate and Ann McGarrigle

- ◀◀ Carter Family
- ▶▶ Iris DeMent
- ▶▶ Nanci Griffith
- ◀◀ Joni Mitchell
- ◀◀ Maria Muldaur
- ▶▶ Roches

Don McLean

- ▶▶ Garth Brooks
- ◀◀ Bob Dylan
- ◀◀ Tim Hardin
- ▶▶ Jewel
- ▶▶ James McMurtry
- ◀◀ Phil Ochs
- ◀◀ Pete Seeger
- ◀◀ Roger Whittaker

James McMurtry

- ◀◀ Lou Reed
- ◀◀ Bruce Springsteen

Meat Loaf

- ▶▶ Bon Jovi
- ◀◀ Phil Spector
- ◀◀ Bruce Springsteen
- ◀◀ Richard Wagner

Meat Puppets

- ◀◀ Black Flag
- ◀◀ Blue Oyster Cult
- ◀◀ Buck Owens
- ◀◀ Byrds
- ◀◀ Captain Beefheart
- ▶▶ Nirvana
- ▶▶ Overwhelming Colorfast
- ◀◀ ZZ Top

Mega City Four

- ◀◀ Buzzcocks
- ▶▶ Doughboys
- ◀◀ Hüsker Dü
- ▶▶ Leatherface
- ▶▶ Les Thugs
- ◀◀ Replacements

Megadeth

- ◀◀ Black Sabbath
- ▶▶ Corrosion of Conformity
- ◀◀ Dead Boys
- ▶▶ Entombed
- ◀◀ Iron Maiden
- ▶▶ Pantera
- ◀◀ Sex Pistols
- ▶▶ White Zombie

Mekons

- ◀◀ Band
- ◀◀ Johnny Cash
- ▶▶ Ex
- ▶▶ Handsome Family
- ▶▶ Palace Brothers
- ▶▶ Pogues
- ◀◀ Sex Pistols
- ◀◀ Ernest Tubb
- ◀◀ Hank Williams

Melanie

- ◀◀ Joan Baez
- ▶▶ Jewel
- ▶▶ Alanis Morissette
- ▶▶ Olivia Newton-John
- ◀◀ Odetta
- ◀◀ Ronettes
- ◀◀ Dusty Springfield

John Mellencamp

- ◀◀ James Brown
- ◀◀ Humble Pie
- ▶▶ Michael McDermott
- ▶▶ James McMurtry
- ◀◀ Rolling Stones
- ◀◀ Mitch Ryder and the Detroit Wheels
- ▶▶ Uncle Tupelo
- ◀◀ Van Morrison

Metallica

- ◀◀ Black Sabbath
- ▶▶ Danzig
- ◀◀ Iron Maiden
- ◀◀ Killing Joke
- ▶▶ Megadeth
- ◀◀ Misfits
- ◀◀ Queen
- ◀◀ Sex Pistols
- ▶▶ Slayer

Meters

- ▶▶ Beastie Boys
- ◀◀ Booker T. and the MGs
- ◀◀ James Brown
- ▶▶ De La Soul
- ▶▶ Neville Brothers
- ▶▶ Parliament-Funkadelic
- ▶▶ Prince
- ▶▶ Red Hot Chili Peppers
- ◀◀ Allen Toussaint

George Michael

- ▶▶ Babyface
- ◀◀ Aretha Franklin
- ◀◀ Elton John
- ▶▶ Seal
- ▶▶ Take That
- ◀◀ Stevie Wonder

Midnight Oil

- ◀◀ Clash
- ◀◀ Easybeats
- ▶▶ Inxs
- ▶▶ Love and Rockets
- ▶▶ silverchair
- ◀◀ Split Enz

Steve Miller

- ◀◀ Beatles
- ▶▶ Big Head Todd and the Monsters
- ▶▶ Blues Traveler
- ◀◀ Cream
- ▶▶ Omar and the Howlers
- ◀◀ Jimmy Reed
- ▶▶ Spin Doctors

Ministry

- ◀◀ Cabaret Voltaire
- ▶▶ Filter
- ▶▶ Gravity Kills
- ▶▶ KMFDM
- ◀◀ Einsturzende Neubauten
- ▶▶ nine inch nails
- ◀◀ Sex Pistols
- ◀◀ Throbbing Gristle

Misfits

- ◀◀ Damned
- ▶▶ Danzig
- ▶▶ Guns 'n' Roses
- ◀◀ Kiss
- ◀◀ Ramones
- ▶▶ Samhain
- ▶▶ Sepultura
- ▶▶ Slayer

Joni Mitchell

- ▶▶ Tori Amos
- ▶▶ Tracey Bonham
- ◀◀ John Coltrane
- ▶▶ Shawn Colvin
- ◀◀ Crosby, Stills & Nash
- ◀◀ Dizzy Gillespie
- ▶▶ Jewel
- ▶▶ Milla Jovovich
- ▶▶ Sarah MacLachlan
- ◀◀ Charles Mingus
- ▶▶ Alanis Morissette
- ◀◀ Motown
- ▶▶ Prince
- ▶▶ Seal
- ◀◀ James Taylor

Moby

- ▶▶ Aphex Twin
- ◀◀ Arvo Part
- ◀◀ Bad Brains
- ◀◀ Brian Eno
- ▶▶ Goldie
- ◀◀ Orb
- ◀◀ Saint Etienne
- ◀◀ Donna Summer

◀◀ Tangerine Dream
▶▶ Tricky

Moby Grape

◀◀ Beatles
◀◀ Buffalo Springfield
◀◀ Byrds
▶▶ Gin Blossoms
▶▶ Golden Smog
◀◀ Jefferson Airplane
▶▶ Wilco

Eddie Money

▶▶ Bryan Adams
◀◀ Chuck Berry
▶▶ Michael Bolton
◀◀ Eric Burdon (Animals)
▶▶ Peter Cetera
◀◀ Sam Cooke
▶▶ John Mellencamp
◀◀ Motown
◀◀ Elvis Presley
▶▶ Jon Secada
◀◀ Stax
◀◀ Rod Stewart

Monkees

▶▶ Archies
▶▶ Barclay James Harvest
◀◀ Beatles
◀◀ Beatles
▶▶ Big Star
▶▶ Electric Light Orchestra
▶▶ Fairport Convention
▶▶ Genesis
▶▶ Go-Go's
◀◀ Herman's Hermits
◀◀ Hollies
◀◀ Buddy Holly
▶▶ Josie & the Pussycats
◀◀ Motown
▶▶ Partridge Family
◀◀ Elvis Presley
▶▶ Sex Pistols
▶▶ Yes

Gary Moore

◀◀ Albert Collins
◀◀ Fleetwood Mac
▶▶ Colin James
◀◀ Elmore James
◀◀ B.B. King
◀◀ John Mayall's Bluesbreakers
▶▶ Metallica
▶▶ Randy Rhoads
▶▶ Kenny Wayne Shepherd
◀◀ Hubert Sumlin
▶▶ Stevie Ray Vaughan

Van Morrison

◀◀ Mose Allison
▶▶ Joan Armatrading
▶▶ Band
◀◀ James Brown
◀◀ Solomon Burke
◀◀ Ray Charles
◀◀ Sam Cooke
▶▶ Elvis Costello
▶▶ Counting Crows
▶▶ Dexy's Midnight Runners
◀◀ Bo Diddley
◀◀ Bob Dylan
◀◀ Slim Harpo
◀◀ John Lee Hooker
◀◀ Johnny and the Pirates
▶▶ Rickie Lee Jones
▶▶ Mark Knopfler
◀◀ Alexis Korner
◀◀ Leadbelly
◀◀ Curtis Mayfield and the Impressions
▶▶ John Mellencamp
◀◀ Muddy Waters
▶▶ Sinead O'Connor
▶▶ Graham Parker & the Rumour
▶▶ Bob Seger
▶▶ Bruce Springsteen
▶▶ Rod Stewart
◀◀ Sonny Terry and Brownie McGhee
▶▶ U2
◀◀ Sonny Boy Williamson
◀◀ Jackie Wilson

Morrissey

◀◀ David Bowie
▶▶ James
▶▶ Judybats
◀◀ Kinks
▶▶ La's
◀◀ New York Dolls
◀◀ Lou Reed
▶▶ Sundays
◀◀ Velvet Underground

Motörhead

▶▶ Anthrax
▶▶ Bad Religion
◀◀ Black Sabbath
▶▶ Body Count
◀◀ Alice Cooper
◀◀ Count Five
▶▶ Guns N' Roses
◀◀ MC5
▶▶ Megadeth
▶▶ Metallica
▶▶ Ministry
◀◀ Ted Nugent
◀◀ Iggy Pop
◀◀ Ramones
▶▶ Slayer
▶▶ Soundgarden
◀◀ Who
◀◀ Yardbirds

Mötley Crüe

◀◀ Black Sabbath
◀◀ Boston
◀◀ Cheap Trick
◀◀ Alice Cooper
◀◀ Foreigner
▶▶ Guns N' Roses
◀◀ Kansas
◀◀ Kiss
▶▶ Ratt
▶▶ Ugly Kid Joe
▶▶ Warrant

Mott the Hoople

▶▶ Clash
◀◀ Bob Dylan
▶▶ Generation X
◀◀ Little Richard
◀◀ Rolling Stones
▶▶ Sex Pistols
◀◀ Sir Douglas Quintet

Bob Mould

▶▶ Boo Radleys
▶▶ Breeders
◀◀ Hüsker Dü
▶▶ Magnapop
▶▶ Medicine
◀◀ Minutemen
▶▶ Nirvana
▶▶ Offspring
▶▶ Pixies
◀◀ Ramones
◀◀ Sex Pistols
◀◀ Television
◀◀ Richard Thompson

Mountain

▶▶ AC/DC
▶▶ Black Sabbath
◀◀ Cream
◀◀ Jimi Hendrix Experience
▶▶ Nazareth
▶▶ Uriah Heep

Move

◀◀ Bach
◀◀ Beach Boys
◀◀ Beatles
▶▶ David Bowie
▶▶ Cheap Trick
▶▶ Elvis Costello
◀◀ Donovan
▶▶ ELO
▶▶ Jellyfish
◀◀ Kinks
◀◀ Motown
▶▶ Posies
▶▶ Queen
◀◀ Stax
▶▶ T. Rex
▶▶ Teenage Fan Club

Alison Moyet

▶▶ Blue Nile
◀◀ Depeche Mode
▶▶ Erasure
▶▶ Eurythmics
◀◀ Joy Division

- Kraftwerk
- Annie Lennox

Mudhoney

- Billy Childish
- Green River
- Nirvana
- Ramones
- Jon Spencer Blues Explosion
- Stooges
- Tad

Muffs

- Bad Religion
- Green Day
- Hole
- Joan Jett
- L7
- NOFX
- Offspring
- Ramones

Maria Muldaur

- Mary-Chapin Carpenter
- Sheryl Crow
- Alison Krauss
- Linda Ronstadt
- Weavers

Peter Murphy

- David Bowie
- John Cale
- Edwyn Collins
- Bryan Ferry
- Japan
- David Sylvian

My Bloody Valentine

- Beatles
- Chapterhouse
- Cocteau Twins
- Curve
- Brian Eno
- Philip Glass
- Lush
- Ride
- Seefeel
- Slowdive
- Sonic Youth

My Life with the Thrill Kill Kult

- Big Stick
- Death in June
- Electric Hellfire Club
- KMFDM
- Legendary Pink Dots
- Lords of Acid
- Meat Beat Manifesto
- Ministry
- Pigface
- Luc Van Acker

Nazareth

- Deep Purple
- Krokus
- Led Zeppelin
- Mötley Crüe
- Mountain
- Sensational Alex Harvey Band

Rick Nelson

- Eagles
- Fleetwood Mac
- Dale Hawkins
- Nelson
- Carl Perkins
- Elvis Presley

Neville Brothers

- Angelo and Boyz II Men
- Ray Charles
- Black Crowes
- Lee Dorsey
- Gospel
- Elton John
- Daniel Lanois
- Meters
- Professor Longhair

New Edition

- Cameo
- Four Tops
- H-Town
- Jackson 5
- Janet Jackson
- New Kids on the Block
- Solo
- Time

New Kids on the Block

- Bay City Rollers
- Jackson Five
- Marky Mark
- Milli Vanilli
- New Edition

New Order

- Charlatans U.K.
- Cure
- Brian Eno
- Joy Division
- Kraftwerk
- Love
- Pet Shop Boys
- Stone Roses
- Sylvester
- Underworld
- Velvet Underground

New Riders of the Purple Sage

- Byrds with Gram Parsons
- Eagles
- Flying Burrito Brothers
- Gene Clark
- Ozark Mountain Daredevils
- Seatrain
- Marshall Tucker Band

New York Dolls

- David Bowie
- D Generation
- Guns N' Roses
- Rolling Stones
- Sex Pistols
- Stooges

Randy Newman

- Fats Domino
- Stephen Foster
- George and Ira Gershwin
- Lyle Lovett
- Lionel and Alfred Newman
- Timbuk 3

Olivia Newton-John

- Cilla Black
- Sandra Dee
- Debbie Gibson
- Lulu
- Kylie Minogue
- Tiffany

Stevie Nicks

- Tori Amos
- Toni Childs
- Janis Ian
- Melanie

Harry Nilsson

- Burt Bacharach
- Beach Boys
- Beatles
- Marshall Crenshaw
- Gershwin
- Gin Blossoms
- Jellyfish
- Little Richard
- Aimee Mann
- Randy Newman
- Van Dyke Parks
- Cole Porter
- Posies
- Semisonic
- Jennifer Trynin
- Hank Williams

Nine Inch Nails

- Black Sabbath
- Butthole Surfers
- Can
- Filter
- KMFDM
- Kraftwerk
- Ministry
- Motörhead
- Rage Against the Machine
- White Zombie

Nirvana

- David Bowie
- Bush
- Cheap Trick
- Everclear
- Flipper
- Hüsker Dü
- Leadbelly
- Melvins

- Pearl Jam
- Presidents of the United States of America
- Raincoats
- Replacements
- Sonic Youth
- Stone Temple Pilots
- Vaselines
- Who

Nitty Gritty Dirt Band

- Byrds
- Carter Family
- Rosanne Cash
- Rodney Crowell
- Foster & Lloyd
- Buddy Holly
- Jim Kweskin Jug Band
- Michelle Shocked
- Travis Tritt
- Uncle Tupelo
- Weavers
- Hank Williams Jr.

Mojo Nixon

- James Brown
- Foghorn Leghorn
- Howlin' Wolf
- Jerry Lee Lewis
- Reverend Billy C. Wirtz

NRBQ

- Beatles
- Chuck Berry
- Blue Rodeo
- Johnny Cash
- Charlie Christian
- Eddie Cochran
- Duane Eddy
- Everly Brothers
- Golden Smog
- Jayhawks
- Jerry Lee Lewis
- Little Richard
- Thelonius Monk
- Carl Perkins
- Elvis Presley
- Rolling Stones
- Spike Jones
- Steely Dan
- Cecil Taylor
- Uncle Tupelo
- Hank Williams Sr.

Ted Nugent

- Aerosmith
- Chuck Berry
- Cry of Love
- Duane Eddy
- Jimi Hendrix
- Jackyl

Gary Numan

- David Bowie
- Deee-Lite
- Brian Eno
- Kraftwerk
- Orb
- Orbital
- Underworld

Laura Nyro

- Joan Baez
- Blood, Sweat & Tears
- Leonard Cohen
- Judy Collins
- Des'ree
- Bob Dylan
- 5th Dimension
- Aretha Franklin
- Rickie Lee Jones
- Chaka Kahn
- Carole King
- Carole King
- Labelle
- Joni Mitchell
- Alanis Morissette
- Randy Newman
- Todd Rundgren
- Carly Simon
- Barbra Streisand

O'Jays

- Boyz II Men
- Sam Cooke
- Drifters
- Isley Jasper Isley
- Levert
- Mascots
- New Edition
- Keith Sweat
- Jackie Wilson

Maura O'Connell

- Mary Black
- Mary Coughlan
- Little Feat
- Delores O'Riordan (the Cranberries)
- Bonnie Raitt

Sinead O'Connor

- Clannad
- Cranberries
- Enya
- In Tua Nua

Ohio Players

- Bar Kays
- Cameo
- Guy
- Isley Brothers
- Prince
- Sly & the Family Stone
- Time

Oingo Boingo

- Devo
- Madness
- Mighty Mighty Bosstones
- No Doubt
- Presidents of the United States of America
- XTC
- Frank Zappa

Yoko Ono

- Albert Ayler
- B-52s
- Cathy Berberian
- John Cage
- Death of Samantha
- Diamanda Galas
- Nina Hagen
- Lene Lovich
- Cibo Matto
- Patty Waters
- Shonen Knife
- LaMonte Young

Orb

- Chemical Brothers
- Brian Eno
- Fripp
- Future Sound of London
- Justified Ancients of Mumu
- KLF
- Kraftwerk
- Mad Proffesor
- Orbital
- Pink Floyd
- Skylab
- Vapoursapce

Roy Orbison

- Chris Isaak
- Mavericks
- Elvis Presley
- Bruce Springsteen
- Hank Williams

Orbital

- Archies
- Kate Bush
- Crass
- Dead Kennedys
- Drum Club
- Kraftwerk
- Pressure of Speech
- Tangerine Dream

Orchestral Manoeuvres in the Dark

- ABC
- Arcadia
- David Bowie
- Buggles
- Duran Duran
- A Flock of Seagulls
- Human League
- Gary Numan
- Roxy Music
- Soft Cell
- Spandau Ballet
- Talk Talk

- Ultravox

Ozzy Osbourne
- Black Sabbath
- Alice Cooper
- Danzig
- Tubes
- W.A.S.P.
- White Zombie

Outfield
- Alarm
- Boston
- Bush
- Hootie and the Blowfish
- Rembrandts
- Scorpions
- Styx
- U2

Outlaws
- Allman Brothers Band
- BlackHawk
- Eagles
- Georgia Satellites
- Henry Paul Band
- Poco
- Screaming Trees

Oyster Band
- Clash
- Fairport Convention
- Pentangle
- Pogues
- Spirit of the West

Jimmy Page
- Eric Clapton
- Willie Dixon
- Jimi Hendrix
- Howlin' Wolf
- Albert King
- Alex Lifeson
- Brian May
- Slash
- Eddie Van Halen
- Muddy Waters

Robert Palmer
- Tony Bennett
- James Brown
- Billie Holiday
- Ronald Isley
- Mr. Mister
- Wilson Pickett
- Nina Simone
- Mel Torme
- Toto

Pandoras
- Babes in Toyland
- Chocolate Watch Band
- 4 Non-Blondes
- Hole
- Kinks
- Lunachicks
- Pretty Things
- Rolling Stones
- Sonics
- Standells
- Them

Pantera
- Black Sabbath
- Clutch
- Metallica
- Prong
- Suicidal Tendencies

Graham Parker
- Frank Black
- Billy Bragg
- Brinsley Schwarz
- Sam Cooke
- Elvis Costello
- Dion
- Bob Dylan
- Dave Edmunds
- John Wesley Harding
- John Hiatt
- Joe Jackson
- Jam
- Nick Lowe
- Motown
- Tom Petty
- Pretenders
- Rockpile
- Bruce Springsteen
- Van Morrison

Maceo Parker
- Brecker Brothers
- Ray Charles
- Clarence Clemons
- John Coltrane
- Charlie Parker
- Tower of Power

Van Dyke Parks
- Richard Davies
- Stephen Foster
- High Llamas
- Leadbelly
- Eric Matthews
- Medicine
- Negro Problem
- Phil Spector
- Tin Pan Alley
- Trinidadian music
- Victoria Williams
- Witch Hazel

Alan Parsons
- M
- Manfred Mann's Earth Band
- Pink Floyd
- Queen
- Donna Summer
- Tangerine Dream
- Wings

Gram Parsons
- Bottle Rockets
- Byrds
- Eagles
- Merle Haggard
- Emmylou Harris
- Jayhawks
- Elvis Presley
- Son Volt
- Uncle Tupelo
- Wilco
- Hank Williams

Pavement
- Fall
- Free Kitten
- Guided By Voices
- Hüsker Dü
- Iggy Pop
- Silver Jews
- Sonic Youth
- Velvet Underground

Pearl Jam
- Allman Brothers Band
- Beatles
- Black Sabbath
- Bush
- Led Zeppelin
- silverchair
- Stone Temple Pilots

Ann Peebles
- Toni Braxton
- Otis Clay
- Sam Cooke
- Aretha Franklin
- Mahalia Jackson
- Annie Lennox

Pentangle
- British folk
- Clannad
- Corrs
- Miles Davis
- Nick Drake
- Duke Ellington
- John Martyn
- Charlie Parker

Pere Ubu
- Big Black
- Can
- Captain Beefheart
- Henry Cow
- Hüsker Dü
- Pixies
- R.E.M.
- Red Crayola
- Stooges

Carl Perkins
- Beatles
- John Fogerty
- Ricky Nelson

◀◀ Elvis Presley
▶▶ Stray Cats
◀◀ Ernest Tubb
◀◀ Muddy Waters

Pet Shop Boys
▶▶ Electronic
◀◀ Human League
◀◀ Kraftwerk
◀◀ New Order
◀◀ Smiths

Tom Petty and the Heartbreakers
◀◀ Chuck Berry
◀◀ Byrds
◀◀ Del Shannon
◀◀ Bob Dylan
▶▶ Georgia Satellites
◀◀ Kingsmen
◀◀ Outsiders
▶▶ Pearl Jam
▶▶ Plimsouls
▶▶ Phil Seymour
▶▶ Wallflowers

Liz Phair
▶▶ Tracy Bonham
▶▶ Ben Lee
▶▶ Alanis Morissette
◀◀ Rolling Stones
◀◀ Smashing Pumpkins
◀◀ Patti Smith
▶▶ Jennifer Trynin
◀◀ Urge Overkill
◀◀ Suzanne Vega

Sam Phillips
◀◀ Beatles
◀◀ T Bone Burnett
◀◀ Elvis Costello
▶▶ Crowded House
◀◀ Bob Dylan
◀◀ Fleetwood Mac
▶▶ Juliana Hatfield
◀◀ John Hiatt
▶▶ Aimee Mann
▶▶ Stevie Nicks
▶▶ Joan Osborne

◀◀ Pretenders
◀◀ Squeeze
▶▶ Suzanne Vega

Phish
▶▶ Blues Traveler
◀◀ Grateful Dead
▶▶ Spin Doctors
◀◀ Sun Ra
◀◀ Frank Zappa

Wilson Pickett
◀◀ Hank Ballard & The Midnighters
▶▶ Commitments
▶▶ Teddy Pendergrass
◀◀ Soul Stirrers
◀◀ Swan Silvertones
▶▶ Bobby Womack

Pink Floyd
◀◀ Beach Boys
◀◀ Beatles
◀◀ Early British blues and jazz
▶▶ Focus
▶▶ Genesis
▶▶ Kansas
▶▶ Orb
▶▶ Orbital
▶▶ Roxy Music

Gene Pitney
▶▶ Chris Isaak
◀◀ George Jones
◀◀ Johnny Ray
▶▶ Soft Cell

Pixies
▶▶ Belly
◀◀ Dick Dale & His Del-Tones
▶▶ Dinosaur Jr.
▶▶ Feelies
▶▶ Flaming Lips
▶▶ Hüsker Dü
▶▶ Lemonheads
▶▶ My Bloody Valentine
▶▶ Nirvana
◀◀ Iggy Pop
◀◀ Ramones
▶▶ Sonic Youth

▶▶ Sugarcubes
▶▶ Throwing Muses
◀◀ Velvet Underground
◀◀ Ventures
▶▶ Weezer

Pizzicato Five
▶▶ Dee-Lite
◀◀ disco
◀◀ Esquivel
▶▶ Esquivel
◀◀ James Bond movie themes
▶▶ St. Etienne
◀◀ Sly & the Family Stone

Robert Plant
▶▶ David Coverdale
◀◀ Donovan
◀◀ Tim Hardin
◀◀ Howlin' Wolf
◀◀ Little Richard
▶▶ Bret Michaels
◀◀ Muddy Waters
▶▶ Vince Neil
◀◀ Keith Relf
▶▶ Axl Rose

Platters
◀◀ Bobby Bland
▶▶ Boyz II Men
◀◀ Ink Spots
▶▶ Huey Lewis & the News
▶▶ New Edition

Poco
◀◀ Buffalo Springfield
◀◀ Byrds
◀◀ Everly Brothers
◀◀ Flatt & Scruggs
◀◀ Flying Burrito Brothers
▶▶ Foster & Lloyd
▶▶ Alison Krauss & Union Station
▶▶ New Grass Revival
▶▶ Son Volt
▶▶ Uncle Tupelo
▶▶ Wilco

Pogues
◀◀ Chieftains

◀◀ Clancy Brothers
◀◀ Clash
▶▶ Cranberries
▶▶ Drovers
▶▶ Levellers
◀◀ Sex Pistols

Poison
◀◀ AC/DC
▶▶ Cry of Love
◀◀ Journey
◀◀ Kansas
◀◀ Kiss
▶▶ Ratt
▶▶ Warrant
▶▶ Winger

Police
◀◀ Beatles
◀◀ Miles Davis
▶▶ Goldfinger
◀◀ Bob Marley
▶▶ Men at Work
▶▶ Rancid
▶▶ Samples
◀◀ Wayne Shorter
▶▶ Wang Chung

Iggy Pop
◀◀ Animals
▶▶ Black Flag
▶▶ Damned
▶▶ Danzig
◀◀ Doors
▶▶ Metallica
▶▶ Misfits
◀◀ Motown
▶▶ Ramones
◀◀ Rolling Stones
◀◀ Mitch Ryder & the Detroit Wheels
▶▶ Sex Pistols

Prefab Sprout
◀◀ Aztec Camera
▶▶ Lloyd Cole
▶▶ Deacon Blue
▶▶ Everything But the Girl
▶▶ Gavin Friday
◀◀ Antonio Carlos Jobim

◀◀ Frank Sinatra
◀◀ Steely Dan

Elvis Presley
◀◀ Eddy Arnold
▶▶ Band
▶▶ Beach Boys
▶▶ Beatles
◀◀ Chuck Berry
▶▶ Blasters
◀◀ Roy Brown
◀◀ Carter Family
▶▶ Johnny Cash
▶▶ Elvis Costello
◀◀ Arthur (Big Boy) Crudup
▶▶ Bob Dylan
◀◀ Lowell Fulson
▶▶ Elvis Hitler
▶▶ Buddy Holly
◀◀ Ink Spots
▶▶ Billy Joel
◀◀ Little Richard
▶▶ Living Colour
▶▶ Janis Martin
◀◀ Bill Monroe
▶▶ Mojo Nixon
▶▶ Roy Orbison
▶▶ Carl Perkins
▶▶ Public Enemy
◀◀ Jimmie Rodgers
◀◀ Frank Sinatra
◀◀ Hank Snow
▶▶ Bruce Springsteen
▶▶ Stray Cats
◀◀ Big Mama Thornton
▶▶ U2
◀◀ Hank Williams Sr.
▶▶ Dwight Yoakam
▶▶ we should have just listed everyone...

Pretenders
◀◀ Beatles
◀◀ Byrds
◀◀ Elvis Costello
▶▶ Divinyls
▶▶ Elastica
◀◀ Jimi Hendrix
◀◀ Kinks
▶▶ Nick Lowe
◀◀ Nick Lowe
▶▶ Alanis Morrisette
◀◀ Suzi Quatro
▶▶ Rockpile
▶▶ Scandal/Patti Smyth
◀◀ Patti Smith
◀◀ Who

Primus
◀◀ Dead Milkmen
◀◀ Metallica
▶▶ Presidents of the United States of America
▶▶ Rage Against the Machine
◀◀ Red Hot Chili Peppers
◀◀ Residents
◀◀ Rush
◀◀ Talking Heads
◀◀ Tom Waits

Prince
◀◀ Beatles
◀◀ James Brown
▶▶ dance/funk artists of the 1980s
◀◀ Jimi Hendrix
◀◀ Rolling Stones
◀◀ Carlos Santana
◀◀ Sly and the Family Stone
▶▶ Time
▶▶ Vanity 6

John Prine
◀◀ Chuck Berry
◀◀ Carter Family
▶▶ Cowboy Junkies
◀◀ Bob Dylan
▶▶ Nanci Griffith
▶▶ Iris Dement
◀◀ Jerry Lee Lewis
◀◀ Hank Williams

Proclaimers
◀◀ Buzzcocks
◀◀ Everly Brothers
▶▶ Green Day
◀◀ Buddy Holly
▶▶ Jackopierce
▶▶ Lowen and Navarro
◀◀ Plimsouls
◀◀ Tom Robinson Band
◀◀ Romantics

Procol Harum
◀◀ J.S. Bach
▶▶ Electric Light Orchestra
▶▶ Genesis
▶▶ Kansas
◀◀ Shangri-Las

Professor Longhair
◀◀ Albert Ammons
▶▶ James Booker
▶▶ Fats Domino
▶▶ Dr. John
▶▶ Bruce Hornsby
◀◀ Pete Johnson
▶▶ Jerry Lee Lewis
◀◀ Meade Lux Lewis
▶▶ Little Richard
◀◀ Big Maceo
▶▶ Art Neville (and the Neville Brothers)
▶▶ Elvis Presley
▶▶ Huey "Piano" Smith
▶▶ Allen Toussaint
▶▶ Jason D. Williams
◀◀ Jimmy Yancey

Prong
◀◀ Black Flag
▶▶ Body Count
◀◀ Living Colour
◀◀ Megadeth
◀◀ Metallica
▶▶ nine inch nails
▶▶ Pantera
▶▶ White Zombie

Psychedelic Furs
◀◀ Beatles
◀◀ Joy Division
▶▶ Live Skull
▶▶ Sisters of Mercy
◀◀ Velvet Underground

Public Enemy
◀◀ Anthrax
▶▶ Boo-Yaa T.R.I.B.E.
◀◀ Boogie Down Productions
◀◀ James Brown
▶▶ Geto Boys
◀◀ Kurtis Blow
◀◀ Last Poets
▶▶ Rage Against the Machine
◀◀ Gil Scott-Heron
▶▶ Tricky

Public Image Ltd. (PiL)
▶▶ Glenn Branca
◀◀ psychedelic rock
◀◀ Sex Pistols
▶▶ U2
◀◀ Yoko Ono

Pure Prairie League
▶▶ Clint Black
▶▶ Garth Brooks
◀◀ Byrds
◀◀ Creedence Clearwater Revival
◀◀ Flying Burrito Brothers
▶▶ Vince Gill
▶▶ Little Feat

Pursuit of Happiness
▶▶ Breeders
▶▶ Pixies
◀◀ Todd Rundgren
◀◀ Television
▶▶ Veruca Salt

Queen
◀◀ David Bowie
◀◀ Maria Callas
▶▶ Def Leppard
▶▶ Guns N' Roses
◀◀ Led Zeppelin
▶▶ Annie Lennox
▶▶ George Michael
◀◀ Liza Minnelli
◀◀ Mott the Hoople
▶▶ Oasis
▶▶ "Wayne's World"

Queensryche
▶▶ Alice in Chains

⏪ Kansas
⏩ Pearl Jam
⏪ Pink Floyd
⏪ Styx

Quicksilver Messenger Service
⏩ Blues Traveler
⏪ Charlatans
⏩ Copperhead
⏩ Man
⏪ Righteous Brothers
⏪ Buffy St. Marie

Quiet Riot
⏩ Dokken
⏪ Kiss
⏩ Ratt
⏪ Slade
⏪ Van Halen
⏩ Winger

Rage Against the Machine
⏪ Beastie Boys
⏪ Black Sabbath
⏪ Body Count
⏪ Clash
⏩ Deftones
⏪ Fugazi
⏪ Ice Cube
⏩ Korn
⏪ Led Zeppelin
⏪ MC5
⏪ Minor Threat
⏪ Public Enemy
⏪ Red Hot Chili Peppers
⏩ Salmon
⏪ Sex Pistols
⏪ Youth of Today

Rainbow
⏩ Accept
⏩ Alcatrazz
⏪ Jeff Beck Group
⏪ Ludwig van Beethoven
⏪ Deep Purple
⏩ Dokken
⏩ Metallica
⏪ Richard Wagner

⏪ Yardbirds

Bonnie Raitt
⏪ Joan Baez
⏩ Pat Benatar
⏩ Sheryl Crow
⏩ Melissa Etheridge
⏩ Melissa Ferrick
⏪ John Lee Hooker
⏪ Howlin' Wolf
⏪ Mississippi Fred McDowell
⏪ Muddy Waters
⏪ Odetta
⏩ Joan Osborne
⏪ Sippie Wallace

Ramones
⏪ Beach Boys
⏩ Green Day
⏩ Pansy Division
⏩ Shonen Knife
⏪ Phil Spector
⏪ Trashmen

Rare Earth
⏩ Commodores
⏩ Funkadelic
⏪ Pink Floyd
⏪ Procol Harum
⏪ Sly & the Family Stone
⏪ Temptations
⏩ Was (Not Was)

Ratt
⏪ Aerosmith
⏪ Alice Cooper
⏪ Journey
⏪ Kiss
⏩ Meat Loaf (part II)
⏪ Rolling Stones
⏩ Skid Row
⏪ Styx
⏩ Ugly Kid Joe

Johnnie Ray
⏩ Dexy's Midnight Runners
⏪ Billie Holiday
⏪ Ivory Joe Hunter
⏩ Tom Jones

⏪ Frankie Laine
⏩ Anthony Newley

Chris Rea
⏩ Del Amitri
⏪ Neil Diamond
⏪ Dire Straits
⏪ Robert Palmer
⏪ Gerry Rafferty
⏩ Curtis Stigers

Red Hot Chili Peppers
⏩ Anthrax
⏩ Body Count
⏩ Fishbone
⏪ Flipper
⏪ Jimi Hendrix
⏪ Minutemen
⏩ Onyx
⏪ Parliament-Funkadelic
⏩ Pearl Jam
⏩ Primus
⏩ Rage Against the Machine
⏪ Sex Pistols
⏪ Stevie Wonder

Red House Painters
⏩ Jeff Buckley
⏪ Tim Buckley
⏪ Leonard Cohen
⏪ Nick Drake
⏩ Mark Eitzel
⏩ Spain
⏪ Velvet Underground

Redd Kross
⏪ Beach Boys
⏪ Beatles
⏪ Carpenters
⏪ Cheap Trick
⏩ Green Day
⏩ Jellyfish
⏪ KISS
⏩ Lemonheads
⏪ Ramones
⏪ Raspberries
⏪ Phil Spector
⏩ Stone Temple Pilots
⏩ Teenage Fanclub

Otis Redding
⏪ Solomon Burke
⏪ Sam Cooke
⏩ Al Green
⏩ Mick Jagger
⏩ Janis Joplin
⏪ Little Richard

Lou Reed
⏩ Nick Cave
⏪ Don Cherry
⏩ Kurt Cobain
⏪ Ornette Coleman
⏪ Bob Dylan
⏩ Ian Hunter
⏪ Doc Pomus
⏩ R.E.M.
⏩ Patti Smith
⏪ Andy Warhol

R.E.M.
⏩ Drivin' N' Cryin'
⏩ For Squirrels
⏩ Gin Blossoms
⏩ Hootie and the Blowfish
⏪ New York Dolls
⏪ Patti Smith
⏪ Soft Boys
⏪ Television
⏩ Toad the Wet Sprocket
⏪ Pere Ubu
⏪ Velvet Underground
⏪ Wire

REO Speedwagon
⏪ Allman Brothers Band
⏪ Beatles
⏪ Chuck Berry
⏩ Boston
⏪ Creedence Clearwater Revival
⏩ Journey
⏩ Kenny Loggins
⏩ Eddie Money
⏩ Mr. Mister
⏩ Starcastle

Replacements
⏪ Big Star
⏪ Black Flag

- ⏩ Cracker
- ⏪ Faces
- ⏩ Goo Goo Dolls
- ⏪ Kinks
- ⏩ Nirvana
- ⏪ Ramones
- ⏪ Sex Pistols
- ⏩ Soul Asylum
- ⏩ Wilco

Residents
- ⏪ Beatles
- ⏪ Captain Beefheart
- ⏩ Half Japanese
- ⏩ Primus
- ⏪ Edgar Varese

Paul Revere & the Raiders
- ⏩ Pat Benatar
- ⏪ Spike Jones
- ⏪ Jerry Lee Lewis
- ⏩ John Mellencamp
- ⏩ Monkees
- ⏪ Little Richard
- ⏩ Bruce Springsteen

Marc Ribot
- ⏪ Derek Bailey
- ⏩ Danny Blume (Liminal)
- ⏪ Captain Beefheart
- ⏪ Frantz Casseus
- ⏪ Eugene Chadbourne
- ⏪ Bill Frisell
- ⏪ Fred Frith
- ⏪ Jimi Hendrix
- ⏪ Arto Lindsay
- ⏩ Brad Schoeppach (Babkas, Paradox Trio)
- ⏩ David Tronzo
- ⏪ John Zorn

Jonathan Richman
- ⏩ Beck
- ⏪ Chuck Berry
- ⏩ Ben Lee
- ⏩ Poi Dog Pondering
- ⏪ Velvet Underground
- ⏪ Ventures

Ride
- ⏩ Chapterhouse
- ⏪ Echo & the Bunnymen
- ⏪ House of Love
- ⏪ Jesus & Mary Chain
- ⏪ My Bloody Valentine
- ⏩ Revolver
- ⏩ Rosemary's

Righteous Brothers
- ⏪ Ray Charles
- ⏪ Don and Dewey
- ⏩ Hall and Oates
- ⏩ Walker Brothers

Johnny Rivers
- ⏪ Mose Allison
- ⏪ Chuck Berry
- ⏪ Jimmy Clanton
- ⏩ Doobie Brothers
- ⏪ Dick Holler
- ⏪ Jerry Lee Lewis
- ⏪ Trini Lopez
- ⏩ John Mellencamp
- ⏩ Tom Petty & the Heartbreakers
- ⏪ Elvis Presley
- ⏪ Jimmy Reed
- ⏩ Bob Seger

Smokey Robinson and the Miracles
- ⏩ Babyface
- ⏪ Sam Cooke
- ⏩ Terence Trent D'Arby
- ⏩ Michael Jackson
- ⏩ Paul McCartney
- ⏪ Clyde McPhatter
- ⏪ Jackie Wilson

Tom Robinson Band
- ⏩ Elvis Costello
- ⏩ Pansy Division
- ⏪ Bob Dylan
- ⏩ John Wesley Harding
- ⏪ Kinks
- ⏩ Me'Shell Ndegeocello
- ⏪ Todd Rundgren
- ⏪ Who

Roches
- ⏪ Madrigal singing
- ⏪ Kate and Anna McGarrigle
- ⏩ Murmurs
- ⏪ Simon and Garfunkel
- ⏩ Story

Rocket from the Crypt
- ⏩ Back Off Cupids
- ⏪ Beatles
- ⏪ Black Flag
- ⏩ Lucy's Fur Coat
- ⏪ Graham Parker
- ⏪ Ramones

Rolling Stones
- ⏩ Aerosmith
- ⏪ Beatles
- ⏪ Chuck Berry
- ⏩ Black Crowes
- ⏪ Sam Cooke
- ⏪ Willie Dixon
- ⏩ Guns N' Roses
- ⏪ Buddy Holly
- ⏩ New York Dolls
- ⏪ Muddy Waters

Henry Rollins
- ⏪ Bad Brains
- ⏪ Black Sabbath
- ⏪ Charles Bukowski
- ⏪ Led Zeppelin
- ⏩ Pearl Jam
- ⏩ Soundgarden

Romantics
- ⏪ Beatles
- ⏪ Buzzcocks
- ⏪ Easybeats
- ⏩ Green Day
- ⏪ Kingsmen
- ⏪ Monkees
- ⏩ Offspring
- ⏩ Plimsouls
- ⏩ Proclaimers
- ⏪ Rockpile
- ⏩ Shoes
- ⏪ Them

Linda Ronstadt
- ⏪ Lola Beltran
- ⏩ Rosanne Cash
- ⏪ Patsy Cline
- ⏩ Celine Dion
- ⏪ Elvis Presley
- ⏩ Trisha Yearwood

Diana Ross
- ⏩ Brandy
- ⏩ Cher
- ⏪ Ella Fitzgerald
- ⏪ Billie Holiday
- ⏪ Smokey Robinson
- ⏩ Donna Summer
- ⏩ Dionne Warwick

Roxette
- ⏩ Ace of Base
- ⏪ Beatles
- ⏪ Eurythmics

Roxy Music
- ⏩ ABC
- ⏩ Adam and the Ants
- ⏪ Humphrey Bogart
- ⏪ Brecht-Weill
- ⏩ Cars
- ⏩ Combustible Edison
- ⏩ Duran Duran
- ⏪ Billie Holiday
- ⏪ King Crimson
- ⏩ New York Dolls
- ⏪ Velvet Underground

Royal Crescent Mob
- ⏪ James Brown
- ⏪ Dead Kennedys
- ⏩ Infectious Grooves
- ⏩ Mind Funk
- ⏪ Ohio Players
- ⏪ Stooges

Rufus
- ⏩ Mary J. Blige
- ⏪ Betty Carter
- ⏩ Faith Evans
- ⏪ Aretha Franklin
- ⏪ Gladys Knight
- ⏩ Monica

Run-D.M.C.

⏪ Aerosmith
⏪ Afrika Bambaataa
⏩ Beastie Boys
⏪ James Brown
⏪ Grandmaster Flash
⏪ Kool DJ Herc
⏩ N.W.A.
⏪ Parliament-Funkadelic
⏩ Public Enemy
⏪ Queen
⏩ Rage Against the Machine

Runaways

⏩ Bangles
⏩ Go-Gos
⏩ L7
⏪ Suzi Quatro
⏪ Slade
⏪ T. Rex

Todd Rundgren

⏪ Beach Boys
⏪ Beatles
⏪ Doo-Wop
⏩ Electric Light Orchestra
⏩ Hall & Oates
⏪ Jimi Hendrix
⏩ Madonna
⏩ Meat Loaf
⏪ Motown
⏪ Move
⏩ Prince
⏩ Queen
⏩ Tubes
⏪ Stevie Wonder
⏩ XTC

Rush

⏪ Guess Who
⏪ King Crimson
⏪ Led Zeppelin
⏪ Move
⏩ Primus
⏪ Buddy Rich
⏩ Triumph
⏪ Yes
⏩ Zebra

Leon Russell

⏪ Clarence "Gatemouth" Brown
⏪ J.J. Cale
⏪ Bob Dylan
⏩ Richie Havens
⏩ Bruce Hornsby

Mitch Ryder

⏪ Gary U.S. Bonds
⏩ Iron City Houserockers
⏪ Little Richard
⏩ John Mellencamp
⏩ Rockets
⏩ Bruce Springsteen
⏪ Big Joe Turner
⏪ Jackie Wilson

Sade

⏩ Des'ree
⏪ Marvin Gaye
⏪ Billie Holiday
⏩ Me'Shell Ndeg'eocello
⏪ Nina Simone

St. Etienne

⏪ ABBA
⏪ Adam Ant
⏪ Bee Gees
⏩ Boo Radleys
⏩ Charlatans
⏪ Fall
⏪ Jam
⏪ Monkeys
⏩ Shara Nelson
⏪ Neil Young

Saints

⏩ Celibate Rifles
⏪ Eddie Cochran
⏪ Easybeats
⏩ Leaving Trains
⏪ Pretty Things
⏩ White Flag

Ryuichi Sakamoto

⏪ African and Arabian folk music
⏪ David Byrne
⏩ Deee-Lite
⏪ Brian Eno
⏪ Erik Satie
⏪ Japanese
⏪ Material
⏪ Maurice Ravel
⏪ Bill Nelson
⏩ Pizzicato 5
⏪ Prince
⏪ Sergio Mendes
⏩ Soul Coughing

Sam and Dave

⏩ Blues Brothers
⏪ Sam Cooke
⏩ Elvis Costello
⏩ Fabulous Thunderbirds
⏩ Righteous Brothers
⏪ Sims Twins
⏩ Bruce Springsteen
⏪ Jackie Wilson

Samples

⏪ Grateful Dead
⏪ Bob Marley
⏪ Police
⏩ Ugly Americans
⏩ Why Store

Santana

⏩ Azteca
⏪ John Coltrane
⏪ Miles Davis
⏪ Peter Green
⏩ Journey
⏩ Malo
⏪ Olatunji
⏪ Tito Puente
⏪ Willie Bobo

Joe Satriani

⏪ Jeff Beck
⏪ Jimi Hendrix
⏩ Megadeth
⏩ Metallica
⏪ Pat Metheny
⏪ Jimmy Page
⏩ Pantera
⏩ Steve Vai
⏪ Johnny Winter

Savoy Brown

⏩ Allman Brothers Band
⏩ Fabulous Thunderbirds
⏩ Foghat
⏪ John Lee Hooker
⏪ John Mayall's Bluesbreakers
⏩ Nighthawks
⏩ George Thorogood and the Destroyers
⏪ Yardbirds
⏩ ZZ Top

Boz Scaggs

⏩ Michael Bolton
⏩ Phil Collins
⏩ Huey Lewis & the News
⏪ Lightnin' Hopkins
⏪ Steve Miller Band
⏪ Motown
⏪ Dan Penn
⏪ Lou Rawls
⏩ Tony Rich

Scorpions

⏪ Beatles
⏩ Def Leppard
⏩ Dokken
⏪ Kinks
⏩ Metallica
⏪ Rolling Stones
⏩ Spinal Tap
⏩ Warrant
⏪ Who

Screaming Trees

⏪ Leonard Cohen
⏩ Darkside
⏪ Lee Hazelwood
⏪ Love
⏩ Luna
⏪ Spirit

Scritti Politti

⏩ Ace of Base
⏪ Beatles
⏪ Fall
⏪ Gang of Four
⏪ Al Green
⏪ Kraftwerk

⏩ Madonna
⏪ Motown
⏩ Pet Shop Boys

Sebadoh
⏪ Dinosaur Jr.
⏪ Flipper
⏪ Husker Du
⏪ Minutemen
⏩ Nirvana
⏩ Liz Phair
⏪ Replacements
⏪ Sex Pistols
⏩ Smashing Pumpkins
⏪ Stooges
⏩ Superchunk
⏪ Velvet Underground
⏪ Neil Young

Seeds
⏩ Dukes of the Stratosphere
⏪ Electric Prunes
⏩ Green River
⏩ Replacements
⏪ Rolling Stones
⏪ Shadows of Knight
⏩ Soul Asylum
⏪ Standells
⏪ Yardbirds

Bob Seger
⏪ Chuck Berry
⏩ Garth Brooks
⏪ Rodney Crowell
⏪ Bob Dylan
⏩ Eagles (Glenn Frey)
⏪ John Fogerty
⏩ John Mellencamp
⏪ Wilson Pickett
⏩ Bruce Springsteen
⏩ Michael Stanley
⏪ Van Morrison
⏪ Hank Williams

Sex Pistols
⏩ Black Flag
⏩ Green Day
⏩ Minutemen
⏪ Monkees
⏩ Nirvana
⏪ Ramones
⏪ Who

Sham 69
⏩ Angelic Upstarts
⏪ Chelsea
⏩ Cockney Rejects
⏩ Minor Threat
⏪ Sex Pistols
⏪ Yardbirds

Del Shannon
⏪ Bobby Freeman
⏪ Bill Haley
⏪ Buddy Holly
⏪ Roy Orbison
⏩ Tom Petty
⏩ Bonnie Raitt
⏩ Bruce Springsteen
⏩ Dwight Twilley

Sandie Shaw
⏪ Cilla Black
⏩ Petula Clark
⏩ Marianne Faithfull
⏩ Mary Hopkin
⏩ Nico
⏩ Smiths
⏪ Dusty Springfield
⏪ Dionne Warwick

Jules Shear
⏪ Beatles
⏩ Frank Black
⏪ Byrds
⏩ Goo Goo Dolls
⏪ Roy Orbison
⏩ Jonny Polonsky

Sheila E
⏪ Azteca
⏩ Dionne Farris
⏩ Me'Shell NdegeOcello
⏪ Prince
⏪ Tito Puente
⏪ Santana
⏩ Crystal Taliefero

Michelle Shocked
⏪ Guy Clark
⏩ Ani DiFranco
⏪ Woody Guthrie
⏩ Liz Phair
⏪ Jean Ritchie

Shoes
⏪ Badfinger
⏪ Beatles
⏩ Figgs
⏪ Grin
⏩ Material Issue
⏪ Raspberries
⏩ Urge Overkill

Shonen Knife
⏪ Beach Boys
⏪ Beatles
⏩ Boredoms
⏪ Buzzcocks
⏪ Byrds
⏩ Nirvana
⏪ Ramones
⏩ Redd Kross
⏪ XTC

Jane Siberry
⏪ Laurie Anderson
⏪ Kate Bush
⏩ Innocence Mission
⏩ Sarah McLachlan
⏪ Joni Mitchell
⏩ Story

Dick Siegel
⏩ John Doe (X)
⏪ Dr. John
⏪ Bob Dylan
⏩ Mark Eitzel
⏩ Townes Van Zandt

Silos
⏩ Beat Happening
⏪ Buffalo Springfield
⏪ Johnny Cash
⏪ Buddy Holly
⏪ Waylon Jennings
⏩ Son Volt
⏩ Uncle Tupelo
⏩ Wilco

Simon and Garfunkel
⏪ Beach Boys
⏩ Jackson Browne
⏩ Mary Chapin Carpenter
⏩ Jim Croce
⏩ Sheryl Crow
⏪ Bob Dylan
⏪ Everly Brothers
⏩ George Harrison
⏩ Joe Henry
⏪ Kingston Trio
⏪ Peter, Paul and Mary
⏪ Pete Seeger
⏩ James Taylor
⏪ Weavers

Carly Simon
⏪ Judy Collins
⏩ Yvonne Elliman
⏪ Carole King
⏩ Melissa Manchester
⏪ Joni Mitchell
⏩ Olivia Newton-John
⏪ Laura Nyro
⏩ Helen Reddy
⏪ Cat Stevens
⏪ James Taylor
⏪ William Butler Yeats

Paul Simon
⏪ Beach Boys
⏩ Jackson Browne
⏩ Mary Chapin Carpenter
⏩ Jim Croce
⏩ Sheryl Crow
⏪ Bob Dylan
⏪ Everly Brothers
⏩ George Harrison
⏩ Joe Henry
⏪ Kingston Trio
⏪ Peter , Paul and Mary
⏪ Pete Seeger
⏩ James Taylor
⏪ Weavers

Simple Minds
⏩ Call

◀◀ Peter Gabriel
◀◀ Genesis
▶▶ Jars Of Clay
◀◀ King Crimson
◀◀ Roxy Music
▶▶ Tears For Fears
▶▶ U2
▶▶ Zerra One

Simply Red
▶▶ Rick Astley
▶▶ Committments
◀◀ Dells
◀◀ Harold Melvin and the Blue Notes
◀◀ Bobby Purify
◀◀ Smokey Robinson
▶▶ Lisa Stansfield

Siouxsie and the Banshees
▶▶ Cure
▶▶ Hole
▶▶ Alanis Morissette
◀◀ New York Dolls
◀◀ Ramones
◀◀ Sex Pistols

Sir Douglas Quintet
◀◀ Bobby (Blue) Bland
▶▶ Joe (King) Carrasco and the Crowns
▶▶ Elvis Costello and the Attractions
▶▶ Creedence Clearwater Revival
◀◀ Freddie Fender
◀◀ Howlin
◀◀ Santiago Jimenez Sr.
◀◀ Little Sunny and the Skyliners
▶▶ Mouse and the Traps
◀◀ Junior Parker
▶▶ ? and the Mysterians
◀◀ Jimmy Reed
▶▶ Sam the Sham and the Pharoahs
▶▶ Uncle Tupelo
◀◀ T-Bone Walker
◀◀ Hank Williams
◀◀ Wolf

Skid Row
◀◀ Bon Jovi
▶▶ Bush
◀◀ Guns N' Roses
◀◀ Jimi Hendrix
▶▶ Alanis Morrissette
◀◀ Mötley Crüe
◀◀ Poison
◀◀ Ramones
◀◀ Sex Pistols
▶▶ Ugly Kid Joe
◀◀ Warrant

Skinny Puppy
◀◀ Cabaret Voltaire
◀◀ Chrome
▶▶ Marilyn Manson
▶▶ Ministry
▶▶ nine inch nails
◀◀ Throbbing Gristle

Slayer
◀◀ Black Sabbath
▶▶ Cannibal Corpse
◀◀ Deep Purple
▶▶ Entombed
◀◀ Minutemen
▶▶ Sepultura

Slowdive
◀◀ Byrds
◀◀ Cocteau Twins
◀◀ Brian Eno
▶▶ Garbage
◀◀ Lee Hazlewood
▶▶ Medicine
◀◀ My Bloody Valentine
▶▶ St. Etienne

Sly and the Family Stone
◀◀ Lenny Bruce
▶▶ Miles Davis
▶▶ Funkadelic
▶▶ Prince
▶▶ Red Hot Chili Peppers
◀◀ Otis Redding
◀◀ Swan Silvertones
▶▶ Temptations
▶▶ Stevie Wonder

Smashing Pumpkins
◀◀ Black Sabbath
◀◀ Boston
▶▶ Bush
◀◀ Cheap Trick
▶▶ Dig
◀◀ Kiss
▶▶ Alanis Morissette
◀◀ Nirvana
◀◀ Pixies
▶▶ silverchair
◀◀ Soundgarden
▶▶ Sponge
▶▶ Stone Temple Pilots
▶▶ Tripping Daisy
◀◀ Velvet Underground

Patti Smith
▶▶ Bjork
▶▶ John Cale
◀◀ Leonard Cohen
◀◀ Doors
◀◀ Bob Dylan
▶▶ P.J. Harvey
◀◀ Jimi Hendrix
▶▶ Hole
◀◀ Iggy & the Stooges
▶▶ Marianne Faithfull
◀◀ Joni Mitchell
▶▶ Alanis Morissette
◀◀ Nico
▶▶ Nirvana
▶▶ Yoko Ono
▶▶ Liz Phair
◀◀ Plastic Ono Band
▶▶ Iggy Pop
▶▶ Pretenders
▶▶ R.E.M.
▶▶ Lou Reed
◀◀ Rolling Stones
▶▶ Bruce Springsteen
▶▶ Sugarcubes
▶▶ Television
▶▶ Television
◀◀ Velvet Underground

Smithereens
◀◀ Beach Boys
◀◀ Beatles
▶▶ Better Than Ezra
◀◀ Black Sabbath
◀◀ Hollies
◀◀ Kinks
▶▶ Muzzle
▶▶ Weezer

Smiths
◀◀ David Bowie
▶▶ Jeff Buckley
◀◀ Jam
▶▶ James
◀◀ New York Dolls
◀◀ Nico
▶▶ Oasis
▶▶ Ride
◀◀ Roxy Music
▶▶ Stone Roses
▶▶ Sundays

Patty Smyth
◀◀ Pat Benatar
▶▶ Sheryl Crow
▶▶ Garbage
▶▶ Magnapop
▶▶ Alanis Morrissette
▶▶ Joan Osborne
◀◀ Bonnie Raitt

Phoebe Snow
▶▶ Tracy Chapman
◀◀ Sandy Denny
◀◀ Joni Mitchell
◀◀ Laura Nyro
▶▶ Suzanne Vega
▶▶ Dar Williams

Social Distortion
▶▶ Jason and the Scorchers
▶▶ Son Volt
▶▶ Uncle Tupelo
▶▶ Wilco

Soft Boys
◀◀ Syd Barrett
◀◀ Bob Dylan
▶▶ Robyn Hitchock & the Egyptians
▶▶ Katrina & the Waves

◀◀ John Lennon
▶▶ R.E.M.

Soft Machine
◀◀ Ornette Coleman
◀◀ Miles Davis
▶▶ Kansas
◀◀ Pink Floyd
▶▶ Steely Dan
▶▶ Sting

Sonic Youth
◀◀ Glenn Branca
◀◀ Rhys Chatham
◀◀ John Coltrane
◀◀ DNA
◀◀ Einsturzende Neubauten
◀◀ Richard Hell & the Voidoids
▶▶ Hole
▶▶ Live Skull
▶▶ Nirvana
◀◀ Sonny Sharrock
▶▶ Sloan
◀◀ Sun Ra
◀◀ Television
◀◀ Velvet Underground
▶▶ Neil Young

Sonny and Cher
▶▶ ABBA
▶▶ Captain and Tennille
▶▶ Madonna
◀◀ Louis Prima and Keely Smith
◀◀ Phil Spector

Sons of Champlin
◀◀ Bobby Bland
▶▶ Chicago
◀◀ Lou Rawls
◀◀ Johnny Smith
▶▶ Tower of Power
▶▶ Lee Ritenour (Champlin's vocal on the Stevie Wonder song

Soul Asylum
▶▶ Afghan Whigs
▶▶ Dharma Bums
▶▶ Gin Blossoms
◀◀ Hüsker Dü
◀◀ Buck Owens
◀◀ Replacements
◀◀ Rolling Stones

Soundgarden
▶▶ Alice in Chains
◀◀ Black Sabbath
▶▶ Bush
◀◀ Killing Joke
◀◀ Led Zeppelin
◀◀ Melvins
▶▶ Mudhoney
▶▶ Pearl Jam
▶▶ Screaming Trees
▶▶ silverfish

Soup Dragons
▶▶ Charlatans U.K.
▶▶ Happy Mondays
▶▶ Jesus Jones
◀◀ Pretty Things
◀◀ Procol Harum
◀◀ Rolling Stones
▶▶ Stone Roses
◀◀ Thompson Twins

Southside Johnny & the Asbury Jukes
◀◀ Gary U.S. Bonds
◀◀ James Brown
◀◀ Coasters
◀◀ Drifters
▶▶ Iron City Houserockers
▶▶ Little Steven & the Disciples of Soul
▶▶ Jack Mack & the Heart Attack
◀◀ Wilson Pickett
◀◀ Bruce Springsteen

Spanic Boys
◀◀ Chet Atkins
▶▶ Blazers
◀◀ Everly Brothers
▶▶ Rosie Flores
▶▶ Wayne Hancock
◀◀ Jimi Hendrix
◀◀ Buddy Holly
◀◀ Los Lobos
◀◀ Elvis Presley
▶▶ Big Sandy and the Fly-Rite Boys
◀◀ Richie Valens
◀◀ X

Sparks
▶▶ B-52's
◀◀ Captain Beefheart
◀◀ Commander Cody
◀◀ Todd Rundgren
▶▶ Talking Heads
◀◀ Frank Zappa

Phil Spector
▶▶ Beach Boys
▶▶ Beatles
◀◀ Gary U.S. Bonds
◀◀ Drifters
▶▶ Steve Lillywhite
◀◀ Frankie Lymon and the Teenagers
▶▶ Ramones
▶▶ U2

Jon Spencer Blues Explosion
▶▶ Beck
▶▶ Big Ass Truck
◀◀ Gibson Brothers
◀◀ James Brown
◀◀ Johnny Burnette
◀◀ Cramps
◀◀ Hound Dog Taylor
◀◀ Jerry Lee Lewis
◀◀ Elvis Presley
◀◀ Stax/Volt
◀◀ Stooges

Spin Doctors
◀◀ Blues Traveler
◀◀ Grateful Dead
◀◀ Steve Miller Band
◀◀ Parliament-Funkadelic
▶▶ Screaming Cheetah Wheelies
▶▶ Ugly Americans
▶▶ Why Store

Spinners
▶▶ Dazz Band
◀◀ Drifters
◀◀ Major Lance
▶▶ Maze
◀◀ O'Jays
◀◀ Smokey Robinson and the Miracles
◀◀ Temptations
▶▶ Trammps

Spirit
▶▶ Firefall
▶▶ Jo Jo Gunne
▶▶ Heart
◀◀ Jimi Hendrix
◀◀ Gerry Mulligan
◀◀ Rising Sons
◀◀ Thelonious Monk
◀◀ Weavers

Split Enz
◀◀ Beatles
▶▶ Boom Crash Opera
◀◀ David Bowie
▶▶ Crowded House
▶▶ Phil Keaggy
◀◀ Roxy Music
▶▶ Schnell Fenster
▶▶ That Petrol Emotion

Spongetones
▶▶ Dave Clark Five
▶▶ Marshall Crenshaw
▶▶ Hollies
▶▶ Jellyfish
▶▶ Knickerbockers
▶▶ Searchers

Dusty Springfield
▶▶ Blondie
▶▶ Elvis Costello
◀◀ Sandy Denny
▶▶ Echobelly
◀◀ Fontella Bass
◀◀ Aretha Franklin
◀◀ Leslie Gore
▶▶ Chrissie Hynde
◀◀ Lulu
▶▶ Pet Shop Boys
◀◀ Diana Ross

Bruce Springsteen
▶▶ Bryan Adams

- Chuck Berry
- John Cafferty
- Creedence Clearwater Revival
- Bob Dylan
- Melissa Etheridge
- Will T. Massey
- John Mellencamp
- Roy Orbison
- Van Morrison

Squeeze
- Crowded House
- Del Amitri
- Gin Blossoms
- Odds

Billy Squier
- Bon Jovi
- Def Leppard
- Dokken
- Kiss
- Led Zeppelin
- Queen
- Quiet Riot
- Rick Springfield
- Winger

Staple Singers
- Arrested Development
- Ray Charles
- Sam Cooke
- Aretha Franklin
- Howlin' Wolf
- Impressions
- Mahalia Jackson
- Madonna
- Me'Shell Ndegeocello
- Charley Patton
- Prince
- Salt-n-Pepa
- Spearhead
- Talking Heads

Ringo Starr
- Phil Collins
- Micky Dolenz
- Anthony Newley
- Roy Rogers

Stealers Wheel
- Beatles
- Everly Brothers
- Hollies
- Proclaimers

Steely Dan
- China Crisis
- Deacon Blue
- Duke Ellington
- Rickie Lee Jones
- B.B. King
- Charlie Parker
- Stax-Volt

Steppenwolf
- Animals
- Chuck Berry
- Blue Oyster Cult
- Boston
- Bob Dylan
- Kiss
- Led Zeppelin
- Pete Seeger
- Sonny Boy Williamson
- Yardbirds

Stereolab
- Brazil-pop
- Cardigans
- Cornershop
- Martin Denny
- Neu!
- Throbbing Gristle
- Tortoise
- Trans Am
- Ui
- Velvet Underground
- Brian Wilson

Cat Stevens
- Jackson Browne
- Bob Dylan
- Joe Henry
- Paul Simon
- James Taylor
- 10,000 Maniacs

Al Stewart
- Donovan
- Bob Dylan
- Nick Gilder
- Rupert Holmes
- King Crimson
- Alan Parson Project
- Sting

John Stewart
- Beat Farmers
- Lindsey Buckingham
- Cumberland Three
- Dave Guard
- Kingston Trio

Rod Stewart
- Dan Baird
- Bash and Pop
- Black Crowes
- Sam Cooke
- Otis Redding

Sting
- Beatles
- Gil Evans
- Gilberto Gil
- Peter Himmelman
- Bob Marley
- Dave Matthews Band
- Samples

Stranglers
- Doors
- Green Day
- Richard Hell and the Voidoids
- Kinks
- Daniel Lanois
- L7
- Rolling Stones
- Sonic Youth

Strawbs
- Beatles
- Bob Dylan
- Fairport Convention
- Hollies
- Alan Parsons Project
- Jethro Tull

- Weavers

Stray Cats
- Bottle Rockets
- Eddie Cochran
- Elvis Presley
- Royal Crown Revue
- Uncle Tupelo
- Gene Vincent

Style Council
- Big Audio Dynamite
- Chiefs of Relief
- Communards
- Everything But the Girl
- Marvin Gaye
- Dexter Gordon
- Guru
- Curtis Mayfield
- Modern Jazz Quartet
- Steely Dan
- US3

Styx
- Asia
- Beatles
- Chicago
- Cure
- Depeche Mode
- A Flock of Seagulls
- Smashing Pumpkins
- Starcastle
- Yes

Subdudes
- Band
- Eric Clapton
- Continental Drifters
- Earl King
- Neville Brothers
- Bonnie Raitt
- Wild Tchoupitoulas

Suicidal Tendencies
- Anthrax
- Back Flag
- Corrosion of Conformity
- D.R.I.
- Faith No More

Donna Summer

- Paula Abdul
- Irene Cara
- Taylor Dayne
- Aretha Franklin
- Gloria Gaynor
- Mahalia Jackson
- Grace Jones
- Kraftwerk
- Madonna
- Nico

Andy Summers

- Syd Barrett
- Adrian Belew
- Steve Farris (Mr. Mister)
- David Gilmour
- Allan Holdsworth
- Steve Howe
- Samples

Sun Ra

- Art Ensemble of Chicago
- George Clinton/Parliament/Funkadelic
- Duke Ellington
- Fletcher Henderson
- Phish
- Michael Ray and the Cosmic Krewe

Superchunk

- Buzzcocks
- Helium
- Hüsker Dü
- Polvo
- Ramones
- Sex Pistols
- Tsunami

Supertramp

- Beatles
- Willie Dixon
- Jellyfish
- Judybats
- Dusty Springfield

Supremes

- Bananarama
- Chiffons
- Go-Go's
- J. Geils Band
- Shangri-las

Matthew Sweet

- Beatles
- dB's
- Raspberries
- Teenage Fanclub
- Television
- Velvet Crush
- Neil Young

David Sylvian

- Aphex Twin
- David Bowie
- Can
- Holger Czukay
- Depeche Mode
- Brian Eno
- Bryan Ferry/Roxy Music
- Gong
- King Crimson
- Moby
- Bill Nelson/Bebop Deluxe

T. Rex

- David Bowie
- Gary Glitter
- Love and Rockets
- Replacements
- Soup Dragons

Talking Heads

- Big Audio Dynamite
- Blancmange
- John Cage
- Love and Rockets
- Modern Lovers
- Mothers of Invention
- Parliament-Funkadelic
- R.E.M.
- Ramones
- Rusted Root

Tangerine Dream

- Dancing Fantasy
- Devo
- Brian Eno
- Klaus Schulze
- Kraftwerk
- New Order
- Software

James Taylor

- Beatles
- Garth Brooks
- Jackson Browne
- Bob Dylan
- Carole King
- Simon & Garfunkel

Tears for Fears

- Oleta Adams
- Bauhaus
- Beatles
- Kraftwerk

Television

- Allman Brothers Band
- Beach Boys
- Big Star
- Blondie
- David Bowie
- Breeders
- Cars
- John Coltrane
- Miles Davis
- dBs
- Durutti Column
- Bob Dylan
- Eleventh Dream Day
- Roky Erikson
- Feelies
- Game Theory
- Heartbreakers
- Robyn Hitchcock/Soft Boys
- Led Zeppelin
- Material Issue
- My Bloody Valentine
- Charlie Parker
- Pixies
- Posies
- R.E.M.
- Sonic Youth
- Matthew Sweet
- Urge Overkill
- Velvet Underground
- XTC
- Neil Young

Temptations

- Commodores
- Drifters
- Falcons
- Jackson 5
- Maze
- Ohio Players
- Soul Stirrers

10cc

- Badfinger
- Bare Naked Ladies
- Beach Boys
- Beatles
- Hollies
- They Might be Giants

10,000 Maniacs

- Fairport Convention
- John and Mary
- Bob Marley
- Nields
- R.E.M.
- Patti Smith

Ten Years After

- Molly Hatchet
- Jimi Hendrix
- John Lee Hooker
- John Mayall's Bluesbreakers
- George Thorogood and the Destroyers
- Stevie Ray Vaughan

Tesla

- AC/DC
- Aerosmith
- Def Leppard
- Guns N' Roses
- Led Zeppelin
- Poison
- Queen
- Rolling Stones
- Rush

The The

- ◀◀ Julian Cope
- ◀◀ Doors
- ▶▶ Echo and the Bunnymen
- ◀◀ Pink Floyd
- ▶▶ Smiths
- ◀◀ Teardrop Explodes
- ◀◀ Hank Williams
- ▶▶ XTC

Therapy?

- ◀◀ Alice In Chains
- ▶▶ Biohazard
- ◀◀ Black Sabbath
- ▶▶ Bush
- ◀◀ Faith No More
- ▶▶ Gravity Kills
- ◀◀ Metallica
- ◀◀ Nirvana
- ◀◀ Slayer
- ◀◀ Soundgarden
- ▶▶ Stone Temple Pilots
- ▶▶ Type O Negative
- ▶▶ White Zombie

They Might Be Giants

- ◀◀ Burt Bacharach
- ▶▶ Barenaked Ladies
- ◀◀ Beach Boys
- ◀◀ Beatles
- ◀◀ dBs
- ▶▶ Ben Folds Five
- ▶▶ Negro Problem
- ◀◀ Monty Python
- ◀◀ Spinal Tap
- ◀◀ Tin Pan Alley
- ◀◀ Frank Zappa

Thin Lizzy

- ▶▶ Bon Jovi
- ▶▶ Metallica
- ▶▶ Graham Parker
- ◀◀ Bob Seger
- ◀◀ Van Morrison

.38 Special

- ◀◀ Allman Brothers Band
- ◀◀ Beatles
- ▶▶ Garth Brooks
- ◀◀ Lynyrd Skynyrd
- ◀◀ Molly Hatchett
- ▶▶ Mavericks
- ▶▶ Travis Tritt

This Mortal Coil

- ◀◀ Bauhaus
- ◀◀ Breathless
- ▶▶ Cocteau Twins
- ▶▶ Colourbox
- ▶▶ Dead Can Dance
- ◀◀ Legendary Pink Dots
- ◀◀ Modern English
- ▶▶ Pixies
- ▶▶ Wolfgang Press

Richard Thompson

- ▶▶ Jeff Buckley
- ▶▶ Elvis Costello
- ▶▶ Dire Straits
- ◀◀ Nick Drake
- ◀◀ Bob Dylan
- ◀◀ Fairport Convention
- ◀◀ Jimi Hendrix
- ◀◀ Wes Montgomery
- ◀◀ Django Reinhardt
- ◀◀ Van Morrison
- ▶▶ Womack & Womack

Thompson Twins

- ◀◀ David Bowie
- ▶▶ Neneh Cherry
- ▶▶ Depeche Mode
- ▶▶ Thomas Dolby
- ▶▶ Howard Jones
- ◀◀ Roxy Music
- ◀◀ Talking Heads

George Thorogood and the Destroyers

- ◀◀ Chuck Berry
- ▶▶ Black Crowes
- ◀◀ Bo Diddley
- ◀◀ Duane Eddy
- ▶▶ Fabulous Thunderbirds
- ◀◀ John Lee Hooker
- ▶▶ Nighthawks

Three Dog Night

- ▶▶ America
- ◀◀ Beatles
- ▶▶ Bo Donaldson & the Heywoods
- ◀◀ Four Tops
- ◀◀ Laura Nyro
- ▶▶ Paper Lace
- ◀◀ Otis Redding

Throwing Muses

- ◀◀ Beatles
- ▶▶ Belly
- ▶▶ Breeders
- ▶▶ Buffalo Tom
- ▶▶ PJ Harvey
- ◀◀ Led Zeppelin
- ◀◀ Joni Mitchell
- ◀◀ Modern Lovers
- ▶▶ Pixies
- ▶▶ Sebadoh
- ◀◀ Sex Pistols
- ◀◀ Siouxsie and the Banshees
- ◀◀ Sonic Youth
- ▶▶ Superchunk
- ◀◀ Velvet Underground
- ▶▶ Veruca Salt
- ▶▶ Voice of the Beehive
- ◀◀ X-Ray Spex

'Til Tuesday

- ◀◀ Beatles
- ◀◀ Byrds
- ◀◀ Elvis Costello
- ▶▶ Crowded House
- ▶▶ Juliana Hatfield
- ▶▶ Sam Phillips
- ◀◀ Pretenders
- ▶▶ Jules Shear
- ◀◀ Squeeze

Timbuk 3

- ◀◀ Leonard Cohen
- ▶▶ Penelope Houston
- ▶▶ Luscious Jackson
- ◀◀ Jim Kweskin Jug Band
- ▶▶ Lisa Loeb
- ▶▶ Mary Lou Lord
- ◀◀ Talking Heads
- ◀◀ Muddy Waters

Time

- ▶▶ Chuckii Booker
- ◀◀ James Brown
- ◀◀ Ohio Players
- ◀◀ Parliament/Funkedelic
- ◀◀ Prince
- ▶▶ Tony Toni Tone
- ▶▶ Wooten Brothers

Toad the Wet Sprocket

- ◀◀ Beatles
- ▶▶ Better Than Ezra
- ◀◀ Crosby, Stills and Nash
- ▶▶ Gin Blossoms
- ◀◀ Nanci Griffith
- ▶▶ Hootie and the Blowfish
- ◀◀ R.E.M.
- ▶▶ Verve Pipe

Too Much Joy

- ◀◀ Clash
- ▶▶ Cracker
- ◀◀ Dead Milkmen
- ◀◀ Tom Petty
- ▶▶ Presidents of the United States of America
- ◀◀ Records
- ▶▶ Weezer
- ◀◀ Who

Toto

- ◀◀ Beatles
- ◀◀ Jimi Hendrix
- ▶▶ Mr. Mister
- ◀◀ Shadows
- ▶▶ Tubes

Allen Toussaint

- ▶▶ Boz Scaggs
- ◀◀ Fats Domino
- ▶▶ Neville Brothers
- ◀◀ Professor Longhair

Tower of Power

- ◀◀ James Brown
- ▶▶ Cameo
- ▶▶ Incognito
- ◀◀ Stan Kenton

- ◀◀ Otis Redding
- ◀◀ Sam & Dave
- ◀◀ Sly & the Family Stone
- ▶▶ Uptown Horns
- ▶▶ Weapon of Choice

Pete Townshend

- ▶▶ Kurt Cobain
- ◀◀ Meher Baba
- ◀◀ Rolling Stones
- ◀◀ Stephen Sondheim
- ▶▶ U2
- ▶▶ Eddie Vedder
- ▶▶ Paul Weller
- ◀◀ Sonny Boy Williamson

Traffic

- ◀◀ Beatles
- ◀◀ Ray Charles
- ◀◀ Fairport Convention
- ▶▶ Fleetwood Mac
- ▶▶ Grateful Dead
- ◀◀ Procol Harum
- ◀◀ Spencer Davis Group
- ▶▶ Steely Dan
- ▶▶ Toad the Wet Sprocket
- ▶▶ Tragically Hip
- ◀◀ Zombies

Tragically Hip

- ◀◀ Band
- ◀◀ Gordon Lightfoot
- ▶▶ Live
- ◀◀ Joni Mitchell
- ▶▶ Our Lady Peace
- ◀◀ Rolling Stones
- ◀◀ Yardbirds
- ◀◀ Neil Young

Robin Trower

- ◀◀ Jimi Hendrix
- ▶▶ Eric Johnson
- ◀◀ Robert Johnson
- ◀◀ Jimmy Page
- ▶▶ Vernon Reid
- ▶▶ Joe Satriani
- ▶▶ Steve Vai

Tubes

- ◀◀ Kiss
- ▶▶ Meat Loaf
- ◀◀ New York Dolls
- ▶▶ Pet Shop Boys
- ◀◀ Frank Zappa

Marshall Tucker Band

- ◀◀ Allman Brothers Band
- ◀◀ Atlanta Rhythm Section
- ▶▶ Black Crowes
- ◀◀ Johnny Cash
- ◀◀ Grateful Dead
- ◀◀ Waylon Jennings
- ▶▶ Sea Level

Big Joe Turner

- ▶▶ Chuck Berry
- ▶▶ James Brown
- ▶▶ Mick Jagger
- ▶▶ Little Richard
- ▶▶ Otis Redding
- ◀◀ Jimmy Rushing
- ▶▶ Sam and Dave
- ▶▶ Bruce Springsteen

Ike and Tina Turner

- ▶▶ Nona Hendryx
- ▶▶ Chaka Khan
- ◀◀ Bessie Smith
- ▶▶ Donna Summer
- ◀◀ Big Mama Thornton

Turtles

- ▶▶ Barnes & Barnes
- ▶▶ Cheap Trick
- ▶▶ Evaporators
- ◀◀ Four Preps
- ◀◀ Mothers of Invention
- ◀◀ Stan Freberg

20/20

- ◀◀ Beatles
- ▶▶ Tommy Keene
- ▶▶ Martin Luther Lennon
- ◀◀ Raspberries
- ▶▶ Adam Schmitt
- ▶▶ Matthew Sweet
- ◀◀ Dwight Twilley Band

UB40

- ▶▶ Big Mountain
- ▶▶ Chrissie Hynde
- ◀◀ Gregory Isaacs
- ◀◀ Bob Marley
- ▶▶ Rancid
- ◀◀ Bim Sherman

James Blood Ulmer

- ▶▶ Jon Butcher
- ◀◀ Ornette Coleman
- ▶▶ Helmet
- ◀◀ Jimi Hendrix
- ▶▶ Jon Spencer Blues Explosion

Uncle Tupelo

- ◀◀ Black Flag
- ▶▶ Blue Mountain
- ▶▶ Bottle Rockets
- ◀◀ Clash
- ◀◀ Merle Haggard
- ▶▶ Old 97's
- ◀◀ Gram Parsons
- ▶▶ Waco Brothers
- ▶▶ Whiskeytown
- ◀◀ Neil Young

Undertones

- ◀◀ Beatles
- ◀◀ Kinks
- ▶▶ La's
- ▶▶ Oasis
- ◀◀ Ramones
- ◀◀ Stooges
- ▶▶ Supergrass
- ◀◀ Them

Urge Overkill

- ◀◀ David Bowie
- ◀◀ Cheap Trick
- ◀◀ Neil Diamond
- ◀◀ Parliament-Funkadelic
- ◀◀ Replacements
- ◀◀ Rolling Stones
- ▶▶ Superdrag
- ▶▶ Supergrass
- ◀◀ Sweet

Uriah Heep

- ◀◀ Deep Purple
- ▶▶ Dokken
- ◀◀ Emerson
- ◀◀ Lake and Palmer
- ◀◀ Led Zeppelin
- ▶▶ Queen
- ▶▶ Scorpions
- ▶▶ Winger
- ◀◀ Yardbirds

U2

- ▶▶ Alarm
- ◀◀ David Bowie
- ▶▶ Cult
- ◀◀ Bob Dylan
- ◀◀ Brian Eno
- ◀◀ John Lennon
- ◀◀ Massive Attack
- ▶▶ Our Lady Peace
- ▶▶ Rhythm Corps
- ▶▶ Simple Minds
- ◀◀ Van Morrison

Steve Vai

- ◀◀ Jeff Beck
- ◀◀ Ritchie Blackmore
- ▶▶ David Chastain
- ◀◀ Tony Iommi
- ▶▶ Eric Johnson
- ▶▶ Tony MacAlpine
- ▶▶ Joe Satriani
- ▶▶ Dweezil Zappa
- ◀◀ Frank Zappa

Van Halen

- ▶▶ Bulletboys
- ◀◀ Cream
- ◀◀ Jimi Hendrix
- ◀◀ Led Zeppelin
- ◀◀ Louis Prima
- ▶▶ Randy Rhoads
- ▶▶ Joe Satriani
- ▶▶ Skid Row
- ▶▶ Steve Vai

Luther Vandross

- ◀◀ Sam Cooke
- ◀◀ Marvin Gaye

- Johnny Gill
- Freddie Jackson
- Alexander O'Neal
- Lionel Richie

Stevie Ray Vaughan

- Big Head Todd and the Monsters
- Blues Traveler
- Kenny Burrell
- Eric Clapton
- Cream
- Buddy Guy
- Jimi Hendrix
- Albert King
- Lonnie Mack
- Otis Rush
- Kenny Wayne Shephard

Ben Vaughn

- Chuck Berry
- Sonny Bono
- Willie DeVille
- Pete Droge
- Kingsmen
- Link Wray
- Jack Logan
- Los Straitjackets
- Jonny Polonsky
- Skeletons

Suzanne Vega

- Tori Amos
- Tracy Chapman
- Shawn Colvin
- DNA
- Ricky Lee Jones
- Joni Mitchell
- 10,000 Maniacs
- Tom Waits

Velvet Underground

- David Bowie
- John Cage
- Brian Eno
- Feelies
- 50s doo-wop
- La Monte Young
- "Louie Louie"
- Luna
- Mott the Hoople
- R.E.M.
- Roxy Music
- Patti Smith
- Sonic Youth
- entire punk-rock class of 1976

Verlaines

- Chills
- Guided By Voices
- Chris Knox
- Waterboys

Verve

- Allman Brothers Band
- Aphex Twin
- Beck
- Brian Eno
- Jimi Hendrix
- Moby
- Pink Floyd

Violent Femmes

- Frank Black
- Carter Family
- Hammell on Trial
- Liz Phair
- Jonny Polonsky
- Jonathan Richman
- Velvet Underground

Tom Waits

- Chet Baker
- Beck
- Charles Bukowski
- Captain Beefheart
- Howling' Wolf
- Rickie Lee Jones
- Soul Coughing

Junior Walker & the All-Stars

- Ray Charles
- Coleman Hawkins
- Illinois Jacquet
- Louis Jordan
- Morphine
- Maceo Parker
- Prince
- David Sanborn

Wall of Voodoo

- Johnny Cash
- Martin Denny
- Devo
- Phillip Glass
- Kraftwerk
- Les Baxter
- Medicine
- Moby
- Ennio Morricone
- Residents
- Soul Coughing

Joe Walsh

- Chet Atkins
- Chuck Berry
- Brother Cane
- Albert Collins
- Georgia Satellites
- B.B. King
- Lynyrd Skynyrd
- Keith Richards
- .38 Special
- Pete Townshend
- T-Bone Walker

War

- Groove Collective
- Los Lobos
- Sly & the Family Stone

Was (Not Was)

- John Coltrane
- Duke Ellington
- Motown and Stax
- Charlie Parker
- 70s funk
- 60s classic rock
- various world musics

Waterboys

- Beatles
- Chieftains
- Bob Dylan
- Sinead O'Connor
- Patti Smith
- Bruce Springsteen
- U2
- Van Morrison
- World Party

Muddy Waters

- Allman Brothers Band
- Elvin Bishop
- Buddy Guy
- Paul Butterfield Blues Band
- Eric Clapton
- Bob Dylan
- PJ Harvey
- Jimi Hendrix
- Robert Johnson
- Led Zeppelin
- Charley Patton
- Rolling Stones
- Son House
- Johnny Winter

Weather Report

- John Coltrane
- Chick Corea
- Miles Davis
- Full Circle
- Dizzy Gillespie
- Herbie Hancock
- Charlie Parker
- Steps Ahead

Jimmy Webb

- Beatles
- Glen Campbell
- Fifth Dimension
- Art Garfunkel
- George Gershwin
- Amy Grant
- Joni Mitchell
- Elvis Presley
- Johnny Rivers
- Linda Ronstadt
- Scud Mountain Boys
- Brian Wilson
- Zumpano

Ween

- Alvin and the Chipmunks
- Beck
- Captain Beefheart
- Ozzy Osbourne
- Prince

Mary Wells

- Martha and the Vandellas
- Diana Ross
- Smokey Robinson
- Supremes

Whitesnake

- Deep Purple
- Extreme
- Led Zeppelin
- Queensryche
- Spinal Tap

Who

- Mose Allison
- Beatles
- James Brown
- Iggy and the Stooges
- Jam
- Kinks
- Gene Krupa
- Nirvana
- Rolling Stones
- Sex Pistols
- Too Much Joy
- Ventures
- Sonny Boy Williamson

Webb Wilder

- Howlin' Wolf
- Leroi Brothers
- Omar and the Howlers
- Rolling Stones
- ZZ Top

Hank Williams Sr.

- Roy Acuff
- Carter Family
- Jimmie Dale Gilmore
- Hank Williams Jr.
- every male country singer since

Hank Williams Jr.

- Charlie Daniels
- Steve Earle
- Kentucky HeadHunters
- Lynyrd Skynyrd
- Travis Tritt
- Marshall Tucker Band
- Hank Williams Sr.

Lucinda Williams

- Joan Baez
- Matraca Berg
- Patsy Cline
- Nanci Griffith
- Leadbelly
- Loretta Lynn
- Joni Mitchell
- Michelle Shocked
- Gillian Welch
- Hank Williams

Brian Wilson

- Badfinger
- Beatles
- Beatles
- Cheap Trick
- Cockeyed Ghost
- Four Freshmen
- George Gershwin
- Hollies
- Jellyfish
- Aimee Mann
- Eric Matthews
- Move
- Negro Problem
- Pixies/Frank Black
- Posies
- Sonic Youth
- Phil Spector
- Matthew Sweet
- Weezer
- John Wesley Harding
- Wondermints

Jackie Wilson

- Roy Hamilton
- Michael Jackson
- Little Willie John
- Marv Johnson
- Clyde McPhatter
- Elvis Presley

Edgar Winter

- Blood, Sweat & Tears
- Blues Project
- Rare Earth
- Sly & the Family Stone
- Them
- Johnny Winter
- Stevie Wonder

Johnny Winter

- Chuck Berry
- Albert Collins
- Eric Johnson
- Keith Richards
- Jimmie Vaughan
- Stevie Ray Vaughan
- T-Bone Walker
- Muddy Waters
- Edgar Winter

Steve Winwood

- Bryan Adams
- Beatles
- Michael Bolton
- Ray Charles
- Derek & the Dominos
- Fairport Convention
- Michael Penn
- Stax
- Tina Turner

Wipers

- Dick Dale
- Dinosaur Jr.
- Jimi Hendrix
- Hole
- Kingsmen
- Melvins
- Mudhoney
- Nirvana
- Pearl Jam
- Raiders
- Screaming Trees
- Sonic Youth
- Ventures
- Wailers
- Yardbirds

Wire

- Big Black
- Cure
- Elastica
- Hüsker Dü
- Minutemen
- R.E.M.
- Sonic Youth

Peter Wolf

- Blondie
- doo-wop
- J. Geils Band
- Mick Jagger
- Robert Palmer
- Rolling Stones
- Bobby Womack

Bobby Womack

- Babyface
- Sam Cooke
- Wilson Pickett
- Tony Rice Project
- Womack & Womack
- Friendly Womack

Stevie Wonder

- Ray Charles
- Miles Davis
- Duke Ellington
- Marvin Gaye
- Michael Jackson
- Howard Jones
- Lenny Kravitz
- Frankie Lymon
- Lionel Ritchie
- Smokey Robinson
- Luther Vandross

Ron Wood

- Black Crowes
- Bo Diddley
- Howlin' Wolf
- Oasis
- Keith Richards
- Muddy Waters

World Party

- Beach Boys
- Beatles
- Bob Dylan
- Ben Folds Five
- Lenny Kravitz
- Prince

◀◀ Rolling Stones
◀◀ Van Morrison

Link
▶▶ Jeff Beck
◀◀ James Burton
◀◀ Dick Dale
◀◀ Duane Eddy
◀◀ Howlin' Wolf
▶▶ Southern Culture on the Skids
▶▶ Pete Townsend
▶▶ Tom Waits

Gary Wright
◀◀ Spencer Davis Group
▶▶ Deep Purple
◀◀ Terry Reid
▶▶ Talk Talk
▶▶ Uriah Heep
▶▶ Waterboys

Robert Wyatt
◀◀ David Allen
▶▶ Kevin Ayers
▶▶ John Cale
◀◀ Caravan
▶▶ Elvis Costello
▶▶ Henry Cow
▶▶ Ivor Cutler
▶▶ Brian Eno
▶▶ Fred Frith
◀◀ Gong
▶▶ Steve Hillage
▶▶ Phil Manzanera
◀◀ Matching Mole
▶▶ Ozric Tentacles
◀◀ Pink Floyd
▶▶ Residents
◀◀ Soft Machine

X
◀◀ Blasters
◀◀ Johnny Cash and June Carter
◀◀ Clash
▶▶ Hole
▶▶ Mekons
▶▶ Minute Men
▶▶ Pixies
◀◀ Elvis Presley
◀◀ Ramones
◀◀ Sex Pistols
◀◀ Patti Smith Group
▶▶ Social Distortion
▶▶ Sonic Youth
▶▶ Uncle Tupelo
◀◀ Who

XTC
◀◀ Beach Boys
◀◀ Beatles
▶▶ Blur
▶▶ B-52s
▶▶ Buzzcocks
◀◀ Bob Dylan
▶▶ Hüsker Dü
▶▶ La's
◀◀ Pink Floyd
▶▶ Pursuit of Happiness
◀◀ Todd Rundgren
▶▶ Wire

Weird Al Yankovic
◀◀ Barnes and Barnes
▶▶ Presidents of the United States of America
◀◀ Alan Sherman
◀◀ Frankie Yankovic (no relation)

Yardbirds
◀◀ Alexis Korner
▶▶ Allman Brothers Band
▶▶ Jeff Beck Group
▶▶ Grateful Dead
▶▶ Led Zeppelin
◀◀ Jimmy Reed
◀◀ Sonny Boy Williamson

Yes
◀◀ Beatles
◀◀ Byrds
▶▶ Dream Theater
◀◀ Genesis
◀◀ Moody Blues
◀◀ Move
◀◀ post-bop jazz
▶▶ Queensryche
▶▶ Rush
◀◀ Simon and Garfunkel
▶▶ Starcastle

Yo La Tengo
◀◀ Sonic Youth
◀◀ Velvet Underground

Dwight Yoakam
◀◀ Hank Snow
▶▶ Mavericks
◀◀ Buck Owens
▶▶ Travis Tritt
▶▶ Uncle Tupelo
◀◀ Hank Williams

Young Fresh Fellows
◀◀ Beatles
◀◀ Flamin' Groovies
◀◀ Kinks
▶▶ Posies
▶▶ Presidents of the United States of America
◀◀ Replacements
▶▶ Scruffy the Cat
◀◀ Sonics
▶▶ Stumpy Joe

Jesse Colin Young
◀◀ Beatles
▶▶ Boz Scaggs
◀◀ Kingston Trio
▶▶ Kenny Rankin
◀◀ Tom Rush

Neil Young
▶▶ America
▶▶ Dinosaur Jr.
◀◀ Bob Dylan
◀◀ Jimi Hendrix
▶▶ Joe Henry
◀◀ Gram Parsons
▶▶ Pearl Jam
▶▶ Replacements
▶▶ Sonic Youth
▶▶ Uncle Tupelo

Paul Young
◀◀ Marvin Gaye
◀◀ Darryl Hall
▶▶ Maxwell
▶▶ George Michael
◀◀ Robert Palmer
▶▶ Tony Rich
◀◀ Smokey Robinson
◀◀ Paul Rodgers
◀◀ Rod Stewart

Young Rascals
◀◀ Booker T. Jones
◀◀ Ray Charles
▶▶ Gin Blossoms
▶▶ Hall and Oates
▶▶ Huey Lewis & the News
◀◀ Motown
▶▶ Robert Palmer
◀◀ Stax-Volt

Frank Zappa
▶▶ Captain Beefheart
▶▶ Eugene Chadbourne
◀◀ Eric Dolphy
▶▶ Uz Jsme Doma
▶▶ Matt Groening
◀◀ Spike Jones
◀◀ Thomas Paine
▶▶ Persuasions
▶▶ Pulnoc
◀◀ Karlheinz Stockhausen
◀◀ Edgard Varese
◀◀ Johnny Guitar Watson
▶▶ Wild Man Fischer

Martin Zellar
◀◀ Band
◀◀ Buck Owens
◀◀ Bruce Springsteen

Warren Zevon
◀◀ Jackson Browne
▶▶ Camper Van Beethoven
◀◀ Leonard Cohen
▶▶ Counting Crows
◀◀ Bob Dylan
▶▶ Don Henley
▶▶ R.E.M.
▶▶ Linda Ronstadt

Zombies
▶▶ Balancing Act
◀◀ Beach Boys

- ◀◀ Beatles
- ▶▶ Elvis Costello
- ▶▶ Doors
- ◀◀ George and Ira Gershwin
- ▶▶ Hollies
- ▶▶ Jellyfish
- ▶▶ Left Banke
- ▶▶ Move
- ◀◀ Cole Porter
- ▶▶ Posies
- ▶▶ Spanish Kitchen
- ◀◀ Phil Spector
- ▶▶ Wondermints
- ▶▶ Young Fresh Fellows
- ▶▶ Zumpano

ZZ Top

- ▶▶ Big Head Todd and the Monsters
- ◀◀ Cream
- ◀◀ Lightning Hopkins
- ▶▶ Stevie Ray Vaughan
- ◀◀ T-Bone Walker
- ◀◀ Johnny Winter

The Producer Index lists individual producers of the various recommended albums listed in artist entries, where a producer is noted. The albums under each producer are listed alphabetically, with the name of the entry it can be found in following in italics. This is not a comprehensive list of all rock album producers, just those albums where producers are noted in this book. If an album is produced by more than one individual, the album name will be listed separately under each of the individuals or groups who produced it.

Vinnie Paul Abbott
The Great Southern Trendkill *Pantera*
Vulgar Display of Power *Pantera*

ABC
Beauty Stab *ABC*
The Lexicon of Love *ABC*

Mark Abel
Drums Along the Hudson *The Bongos*

Rod Abernathy
The Accelerators *The Accelerators*

Alton Abraham
The Magic City *Sun Ra*

Daniel Abraham
Big Thing *Duran Duran*

Alan Abrahams
Dance *Pure Prairie League*

Mark Abramson
East-West *The Paul Butterfield Blues Band*
In My Life *Judy Collins*
Whales & Nightingales *Judy Collins*
Wildflowers *Judy Collins*

AC/DC
Flick of the Switch *AC/DC*

William Ackerman
Breakfast in the Field *Michael Hedges*

Ed Ackerson
He's After Me *The Hang Ups*

Bryan Adams
Bryan Adams *Bryan Adams*
Cuts Like a Knife *Bryan Adams*
18 til I Die *Bryan Adams*
Into the Fire *Bryan Adams*
Live! Live! Live! *Bryan Adams*
Reckless *Bryan Adams*
Waking Up the Neighbours *Bryan Adams*
You Want It, You Got It *Bryan Adams*

Dave Adams
Darker Days *The Connells*

Joe Adams
Modern Sounds in Country and Western Music *Ray Charles*
Modern Sounds in Country and Western Music, Vol. 2 *Ray Charles*

Terry Adams
Johnnie B. Bad *Johnnie Johnson*
Message for the Mess Age *NRBQ*

Steve Addabbo
Ghosts Upon the Road *Eric Anderson*
Solitude Standing *Suzanne Vega*
Steady On *Shawn Colvin*
Suzanne Vega *Suzanne Vega*

King Sunny Ade
Ajoo *King Sunny Ade*
Live At the Hollywood Palace *King Sunny Ade*

Lou Adler
A Natural Woman: The Ode Collection 1968-1976 *Carole King*
Changes/Rewind *Johnny Rivers*
Here We A Go Go Again *Johnny Rivers*
Johnny Rivers at the Whiskey A Go Go *Johnny Rivers*
Johnny Rivers in Action *Johnny Rivers*
Meanwhile Back at the Whiskey *Johnny Rivers*
Tapestry *Carole King*
The Johnny Rivers Anthology: 1964-1977 *Johnny Rivers*

Aerosmith
Rocks *Aerosmith*

Walter Afanasieff
Celine Dion *Celine Dion*
Face the Music *New Kids on the Block*
Mariah Carey *Mariah Carey*
Merry Christmas *Mariah Carey*
MTV Unplugged *Mariah Carey*
Songs *Luther Vandross*

Afghan Whigs
Big Top Halloween *The Afghan Whigs*
The Uptown Avondale *The Afghan Whigs*

Peter Afterman
Honeymoon in Vegas *Elvis Presley*

a-ha
Scoundrel Days *a-ha*

Brian Ahern
Cimarron *Emmylou Harris*
Johnny 99 *Johnny Cash*

Roses in the Snow *Emmylou
Harris*

Chuck Ainlay
Fervor *Jason and the
Scorchers*

Dino Airali
Phoebe Snow *Phoebe Snow*

Matt Aitken
Hold Me In Your Arms *Rick
Astley*

Will Akerman
Jack's Crows *John Gorka*

John Alagia
Remember Two Things *Dave
Matthews Band*

Steve Alaimo
KC & The Sunshine Band...And
More *KC and the
Sunshine Band*

Howie Albert
High on the Hog *Black Oak
Arkansas*
Something Magic *Procol
Harum*

Ron Albert
High on the Hog *Black Oak
Arkansas*
Something Magic *Procol
Harum*

Steve Albini
After Murder Park *The Auteurs*
Down *The Jesus Lizard*
In Utero *Nirvana*
Laboratory of Sound *The
Fleshtones*
Liar *The Jesus Lizard*
Pure *The Jesus Lizard*
Salt *Veruca Salt*
Surfer Rosa *The Pixies*
Under the Bushes Under the
Stars *Guided by Voices*

John Alcock
Jailbreak *Thin Lizzy*
Tales From The Ox: The Best
Of John Entwistle *John
Entwistle*
Whistle Rymes *John Entwistle*

Chris Lord Alge
Come As You Are *Peter Wolf*

Alice In Chains
Jar of Flies *Alice in Chains*

Cameron Allan
Icehouse *Icehouse*

David M. Allen
Earth *Matthew Sweet*
Strange Times *The
Chameleons*

John Allen
Association 1995: A Little Bit
More *The Association*

Allman Brothers Band
Brothers and Sisters *Allman
Brothers Band*

Tom Allom
On Through the Night *Def
Leppard*
Priest ... Live! *Judas Priest*
Screaming for Vengeance
Judas Priest

Herb Alpert
Classics, Vol. 1 *Herb Alpert*
Rise *Herb Alpert*

Alpha Band
The Statue Makers of
Hollywood *The Alpha
Band*

Billy Altman
Joe "King" Carrasco and the
Crowns *Joe "King"
Carrasco*

Dave Alvin
Blue Blvd. *Dave Alvin*
Interstate City *Dave Alvin*
Museum of Heart *Dave Alvin*
Tennessee Border *Sonny
Burgess*

Eric Ambel
Loud & Lonesome *The Del
Lords*
The Brooklyn Side *The Bottle
Rockets*

Ambrosia
One Eighty *Ambrosia*

AMC
San Francisco *American Music
Club*

Michael Amicone
Listen, Listen: The Best of
Emitt Rhodes *The Merry-
Go-Round*

David Anderle
Golden Shower of Hits *Circle
Jerks*
Who Knows Where the Time
Goes *Judy Collins*

Dale Anderson
Ani DiFranco *Ani DiFranco*

Dave Anderson
Blind *The Sundays*
Colossal Youth *Young Marble
Giants*

Eric Anderson
Ghosts Upon the Road *Eric
Anderson*

Ian Anderson
Aqualung *Jethro Tull*
Benefit *Jethro Tull*
Stand Up *Jethro Tull*
Thick as a Brick *Jethro Tull*

Laurie Anderson
Bright Red *Laurie Anderson*
Home of the Brave *Laurie
Anderson*
Strange Angels *Laurie
Anderson*
United States Live *Laurie
Anderson*

Pete Anderson
Buenos Noches From A Lonely
Room *Dwight Yoakam*
Captain Swing *Michelle
Shocked*
Dwight Live *Dwight Yoakam*
Gone *Dwight Yoakam*
Hillbilly Deluxe *Dwight
Yoakam*
If There Was A Way *Dwight
Yoakam*
Short Sharp Shocked *Michelle
Shocked*
The American in Me *Steve
Forbert*

Benny Andersson
Arrival *ABBA*
Gold *ABBA*
More ABBA Gold *ABBA*
Ring Ring *ABBA*
Thank You for the Music *ABBA*

Barry Andrews
Dancing Years *Gang of Four*
Oil & Gold *Gang of Four*

Punch Andrews
Against the Wind *Bob Seger*
Live Bullet *Bob Seger*
Night Moves *Bob Seger*
Stranger in Town *Bob Seger*

Johnny Angel
The Dogmatics: 1981-86
Dogmatics

Animal Logic
Animal Logic II *Stewart
Copeland*

John Anthony
For Your Pleasure *Roxy Music*

Anthrax
Among the Living *Anthrax*
Attack of the Killer B's (EP)
Anthrax
Spreading the Disease
Anthrax
State of Euphoria *Anthrax*

Mike Appel
Born to Run *Bruce
Springsteen*
Greetings from Asbury Park,
N.J. *Bruce Springsteen*
The Early Years *Bruce
Springsteen*
The Wild, the Innocent and
the E Street Shuffle *Bruce
Springsteen*

Rod Argent
Late Night Grande Hotel *Nanci
Griffith*

Art of Noise
(The Art of Noise!) *The Art of
Noise*
In Visible Silence *The Art of
Noise*

Robert Ash
The B-52's *The B-52's*

Ash
1977 *Ash*

Peter Asher
Hasten Down the Wind *Linda
Ronstadt*
Heart Like a Wheel *Linda
Ronstadt*
In My Tribe *10,000 Maniacs*

Bill Bottrell
Aliens Ate My Buick *Thomas Dolby*
No Soul No Strain *Wire Train*
Tuesday Night Music Club *Sheryl Crow*

David Bottrill
The First Day *Robert Fripp*
The Woman's Boat *Toni Childs*

Jean-Paul Bourelly
Jungle Cowboy *Jean-Paul Bourelly*
Trippin' *Jean-Paul Bourelly*
Saints & Sinners *Jean-Paul Bourelly*

Dennis Bovell
Cut *The Slits*

Jimmy Bowen
America (The Way I See It) *Hank Williams Jr.*
Family Tradition *Hank Williams Jr.*
Hank Williams Jr.'s Greatest Hits *Hank Williams Jr.*
Last Mango in Paris *Jimmy Buffett*

David Bowie
Aladdin Sane *David Bowie*
All the Young Dudes *Mott the Hoople*
Heroes *David Bowie*
Never Let Me Down *David Bowie*
Raw Power *Iggy Pop*
Scary Monsters *David Bowie*
Station To Station *David Bowie*
The Idiot *Iggy Pop*
The Rise and Fall of Ziggy Stardust and the Spiders from Mars *David Bowie*
Ziggy Stardust... *David Bowie*

Chris Boyd
North on South St. *Herb Alpert*

Joe Boyd
Dancer with Bruised Knees *Kate and Ann McGarrigle*
House Full *Fairport Convention*
Junco Partner *James Booker*
Kate & Anna McGarrigle *Kate and Ann McGarrigle*
Liege and Leaf *Fairport Convention*
Maria Muldaur *Maria Muldaur*
Richard Thompson Live! (More or Less) *Richard Thompson*
Shoot Out the Lights *Richard Thompson*
The Wishing Chair *10,000 Maniacs*
Time of No Reply *Nick Drake*
Unhalfbricking *Fairport Convention*
Waitress In a Donut Shop *Maria Muldaur*
What We Did on Our Holidays *Fairport Convention*
Workers Playtime *Billy Bragg*

Jim Boyer
Kohuept (In Concert) *Billy Joel*

John Boylan
Boston *Boston*
Full Moon *Charlie Daniels Band*
Great Buildings *The Rembrandts*
Kermit Unplugged *Ozzy Osbourne*
Million Mile Reflections *Charlie Daniels Band*
Quarterflash *Quarterflash*
Two Lane Highway *Pure Prairie League*

Owen Bradley
Hungry for Love: Her First Recordings, Vol. 2 *Patsy Cline*
Rockin' Side: Her First Recordings, Vol. 3 *Patsy Cline*
The Great Buddy Holly *Buddy Holly*
The Patsy Cline Story *Patsy Cline*
Walkin' Dreams: Her First Recordings, Vol. 1 *Patsy Cline*

Delaney Bramlett
Eric Clapton *Eric Clapton*

John Brand
High Land, Hard Rain *Aztec Camera*

Brand X
Xtrax *Phil Collins*

Brave Combo
It's Christmas, Man! *Brave Combo*
Musical Varieties *Brave Combo*
No, No, No, Cha Cha Cha *Brave Combo*
Polkas for a Gloomy World *Brave Combo*

Stephen Bray
True Blue *Madonna*

Victor Brbic
Ready to Fly *The Verlaines*

Bread
Retrospective *Bread*

David Brewis
Swoon *Prefab Sprout*

David Briggs
After the Gold Rush *Neil Young*
Decade *Neil Young*
Everybody Knows This is Nowhere *Neil Young*
Mirror Ball *Neil Young*
Nils Lofgren *Nils Lofgren*
Rust Never Sleeps *Neil Young*
The Twelve Dreams of Dr. Sardonicus *Spirit*
Tonight's the Night *Neil Young*
Trans *Neil Young*
Weld *Neil Young*

Jon Brion
I'm with Stupid *Aimee Mann*
Whatever *Aimee Mann*

Neil Brockbank
The Impossible Bird *Nick Lowe*

Ian Brodie
Seven Days in Sammystown *Wall of Voodoo*

Bruce Brody
Life is Sweet *Lone Justice*

Bruce Bromberg
Bad Influence *Robert Cray*
Blue Blvd. *Dave Alvin*
Jimmy Dale Gilmore *Jimmy Dale Gilmore*
Museum of Heart *Dave Alvin*
Strong Persuader *Robert Cray*

David Bromberg
How Late'll Ya Play Til? *David Bromberg*
Out of The Blues: The Best of David Bromberg *David Bromberg*

Gerry Bron
Demons and Wizards *Uriah Heep*
The Best of Uriah Heep *Uriah Heep*
The Magician's Birthday *Uriah Heep*

Michael Brook
When I Was a Boy *Jane Siberry*

Ernie Brooks
Party Girl, Broken Poets *Elliot Murphy*

Harvey Brooks
Quicksilver Messenger Service *Quicksilver Messenger Service*

Isley Brothers
3 + 3 *Isley Brothers*
In the Beginning . . . *Isley Brothers*
The Heat Is On *Isley Brothers*

Ian Broudie
Smart *Sleeper*

Michael Brovsky
Must Notta Gotta Lotta *Joe Ely*

Ric Browde
Look What the Cat Dragged In *Poison*

Earle Brown
Copperhead Road *Steve Earle*

James Brown
Live at the Apollo *James Brown*
Messing with the Blues *James Brown*
Slaughter's Big Rip-Off *James Brown*
Soul Pride: The Instrumentals 1960-1969 *James Brown*

Steve Brown
Pogue Mahone *The Pogues*

Terry Brown
2112 *Rush*
All the World's a Stage *Rush*

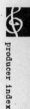

Time For Mercy *Jann Arden*

Neneh Cherry
Homebrew *Neneh Cherry*

Rick Chertoff
Nervous Night *The Hooters*
Never Enough *Patty Smyth*
Relish *Joan Osborne*
Tongues and Tails *Sophie B. Hawkins*
Zig Zag *The Hooters*

Vic Chesnutt
Drunk *Vic Chesnutt*

Leonard Chess
After School Session *Chuck Berry*
Chuck Berry is on Top *Chuck Berry*
Chuck Berry On Stage *Chuck Berry*
Missing Berries: Rarities, Vol. 3 *Chuck Berry*
More Rock 'n' Roll Rarities *Chuck Berry*
One Dozen Berrys *Chuck Berry*
Rock 'n' Roll Rarities *Chuck Berry*
St. Louis to Liverpool *Chuck Berry*
The Chess Box *Chuck Berry*
The Great Twenty-Eight *Chuck Berry*
Whose Muddy Shoes *Elmore James*

Marshall Chess
Fleetwood Mac in Chicago 1969 *Fleetwood Mac*
The Real Folk Blues *Muddy Waters*

Phil Chess
After School Session *Chuck Berry*
Chuck Berry On Stage *Chuck Berry*
Missing Berries: Rarities, Vol. 3 *Chuck Berry*
More Rock 'n' Roll Rarities *Chuck Berry*
One Dozen Berrys *Chuck Berry*
Rock 'n' Roll Rarities *Chuck Berry*
St. Louis to Liverpool *Chuck Berry*
The Chess Box *Chuck Berry*
The Great Twenty-Eight *Chuck Berry*
Whose Muddy Shoes *Elmore James*

Joe Chiccarelli
Postcards from the Arctic *Springhouse*
San Francisco *American Music Club*

Toni Childs
House of Hope *Toni Childs*
The Woman's Boat *Toni Childs*

Alex Chilton
Bad Music for Bad People *The Cramps*
High Priest/Black List *Alex Chilton*
Songs the Lord Taught Us *The Cramps*

Nicky Chinn
Your Mama Won't Like Me *Suzi Quatro*

Ciccone Youth
The Whitey Album *Madonna*

Circle Jerks
Golden Shower of Hits *Circle Jerks*
VI *Circle Jerks*
Wönderful *Circle Jerks*

Eric Clapton
From the Cradle *Eric Clapton*

Alvin Clark
Live at the Whisky A Go-Go on the Fabulous Sunset Strip *X*
See How We Are *X*

Bernie Clark
High Land, Hard Rain *Aztec Camera*

Dave Clark
The History of the Dave Clark Five *Dave Clark Five*

Tony Clarke
Days of Future Passed *The Monkees*
Every Good Boy Deserves Favour *The Monkees*
On the Threshold of a Dream *The Monkees*
Seventh Sojourn *The Monkees*

The Clash
Sandanista Now! *The Clash*
The Clash *The Clash*

Al Clay
Teenager of the Year *Frank Black*

Lester Claypool
Join the Army *Suicidal Tendencies*

Josh Clayton-Felt
Inarticulate Nature Boy *School of Fish*

Bob Clearmountain
Catholic Boy *Jim Carroll*
Cuts Like a Knife *Bryan Adams*
Escape Artist *Garland Jeffreys*
Into the Fire *Bryan Adams*
Of Skins and Heart *The Church*
Reckless *Bryan Adams*
You Want It, You Got It *Bryan Adams*

Jack Clement
Hittin' that Jug! The Best of Sonny Burgess *Sonny Burgess*
The Sun Years *Johnny Cash*
Water From the Wells of Home *Johnny Cash*
We Wanna Boogie *Sonny Burgess*

Keith Cleversly
Transmissions from the Satellite Heart *Flaming Lips*

Jimmy Cliff
I Am the Living *Jimmy Cliff*
In Concert - The Best of Jimmy Cliff *Jimmy Cliff*

Doug Clifford
Daydreaming at Midnight *Sir Douglas Quintet*

Mike Clink
Appetite For Destruction *Guns N' Roses*
Rust in Peace *Megadeth*
Slip of the Tongue *Whitesnake*
Use Your Illusion II *Guns N' Roses*

George Clinton
Freaky Styley *Red Hot Chili Peppers*
Funkadelic's Greatest Hits *George Clinton*
Maggot Brain *George Clinton*
Mothership Connection *George Clinton*
New Spark (For an Old Flame) *Johnny Powers*
One Nation Under a Groove *George Clinton*
Stretching Out in Bootsy's Rubber Band *Bootsy Collins*
The Electric Spanking of War Babies *George Clinton*
Ultra Wave *Bootsy Collins*

Jeremy Clyde
Of Cabbages And Kings *Chad & Jeremy*

Gary Cobain
Accelerator *Future Sound of London*
Humanoid *Future Sound of London*
ISDN *Future Sound of London*
Tales of Ephidrena *Future Sound of London*

Ed Cobb
Best of the Standells *The Standells*
Dirty Water *The Standells*
No Way Out *The Chocolate Watch Band*
One Step Beyond *The Chocolate Watch Band*
The Hot Ones *The Standells*
The Inner Mystique *The Chocolate Watch Band*
Try It *The Standells*
Why Pick on Me *The Standells*

William E. Cobham Jr.
Spectrum *Tommy Bolin*

The Cocteau Twins
Garlands *Cocteau Twins*

Rod Coe
(I'm) Stranded *The Saints*

Tommy Cogbill
Rainbow Road: Arthur Alexander: The Warner Brothers Recordings *Arthur Alexander*
The Ultimate Box Tops *Alex Chilton*

Give the People What They Want *The O'Jays*
Love Train: The Best of The O'Jays *The O'Jays*

David Gamson
Cupid & Psyche '85 *Scritti Politti*
Peace Beyond Passion *Me'Shell Ndegeocello*
Plantation Lullabies *Me'Shell Ndegeocello*
Provision *Scritti Politti*

Gang of Four
Solid Gold *Gang of Four*

Gordon Gano
New Times *Violent Femmes*

Don Gant
Living and Dying in 3/4 Time *Jimmy Buffett*

Val Garay
Live at the China Club *Dramarama*

Art Garfunkel
Angel Clare *Art Garfunkel*
The Concert in Central Park *Simon and Garfunkel*

Nick Garside
James *James*
Life *Inspiral Carpets*

G.G. Garth
Hungry for Stink *L7*
Rage Against the Machine *Rage Against the Machine*

Green Gartside
Cupid & Psyche '85 *Scritti Politti*
Provision *Scritti Politti*

Albert Garzon
Goldfish Don't Talk Back *Brenda Kahn*
Hope Chest *10,000 Maniacs*

David Gates
Goodbye Girl *Bread*
Guitar Man *Bread*
Lost Without Your Love *Bread*
Love is Always Seventeen *Bread*
On the Waters *Bread*

Humberto Gatica
Celine Dion *Celine Dion*

Danny Gatton
88 Elmira St. *Danny Gatton*
Cruisin' Deuces *Danny Gatton*
Unfinished Business *Danny Gatton*

Bob Gaudio
Little Shop of Horrors *The Four Tops*

David Gavurin
Blind *The Sundays*

Marvin Gaye
Let's Get it On *Marvin Gaye*
Midnight Love *Marvin Gaye*
What's Going On *Marvin Gaye*

Gear Daddies
Billy's Live Bait *Martin Zellar*

Don Gehman
Scarecrow *John Mellencamp*
the subdudes *The Subdudes*
The Lonesome Jubilee *John Mellencamp*
Uh-huh *John Mellencamp*

Greg Geller
Bronx Blues: The Columbia Recordings *Dion*

General Public
. . All the Rage *English Beat*

Genesis
..And Then There Were Three... *Genesis*
A Trick of the Tail *Genesis*
Abacab *Genesis*
Seconds Out *Genesis*
Selling England by the Pound *Genesis*
The Lamb Lies Down on Broadway *Genesis*

Lowell George
Dixie Chicken *Little Feat*
Shakedown Street *Grateful Dead*
Waiting for Columbus *Little Feat*

The Georgia Satellites
In the Land of Salvation and Sin *Georgia Satellites*

Neil Geraldo
Based on a True Story *The Del Lords*
True Love *Pat Benatar*

Lisa Germano
Geek The Girl *Lisa Germano*
Happiness *Lisa Germano*
On the Way Down From the Moon Palace *Lisa Germano*

Phil Gernhard
Family Tradition *Hank Williams Jr.*

Birger Gesthuisen
World Out of Time Vol. 2: Henry Kaiser and David Lindley in Madagascar *David Lindley*
World Out of Time: Henry Kaiser and David Lindley in Madagascar *David Lindley*

David Getz
Cheaper Thrills *Janis Joplin*

Chris Gilbey
Of Skins and Heart *The Church*

Andy Gill
Entertainment! *Gang of Four*
Mall *Gang of Four*

Verna Gillis
Live from Soundscape *Bill Laswell/Material*

Voyle Gilmore
At Large *Kingston Trio*
Live at the Hungry I *Kingston Trio*
String Along *Kingston Trio*
The Capitol Years *Kingston Trio*
The Kingston Trio *Kingston Trio*

David Gilmour
The Division Bell *Pink Floyd*
The Wall *Pink Floyd*

Gin Blossoms
Congratulations I'm Sorry *Gin Blossoms*
New Miserable Experience *Gin Blossoms*
Up and Crumbling *Gin Blossoms*

Greg Ginn
In My Head *Black Flag*
MinuteFlag *fIREHOSE*
Who's Got the 10 1/2? *Black Flag*

Lou Giordano
Copper Blue *Bob Mould*
Eventually *The Replacements*
Ring *The Connells*
The Way to Salvation *King Missile*

Nick Giordano
Beaster *Bob Mould*
Besides *Bob Mould*

Gabrielle Glaser
Natural Ingredient *Luscious Jackson*

Dick Glasser
Hank Williams, Jr. & Friends *Hank Williams Jr.*

Pete Glenister
Hoodoo *Alison Moyet*

Jim Glennie
James *James*

The Glimmer Twins
Flashpoint *Rolling Stones*
Love You Live *Rolling Stones*
Some Girls *Rolling Stones*
Still Life *Rolling Stones*
Stripped *Rolling Stones*

Jeff Glixman
Leftoverture *Kansas*
Odyssey *Yngwie Malmsteen*
Part 2 *Electric Light Orchestra*
Seventh Star *Black Sabbath*

Mick Glossop
Crashes *The Records*
Friends *The Bolshoi*
This is the Sea *The Waterboys*

Henry Glover
Fever: The Best Of Little Willie John *Little Willie John*
Mister Little Willie John *Little Willie John*
Sure Things *Little Willie John*
The Muddy Waters Woodstock Album *Muddy Waters*

Roger Glover
Down to Earth *Rainbow*
Razamanaz *Nazareth*

Bryce Goggin
Don't Ask Don't Tell *Come*

Hard to Earn *Gang Starr*
Jazzmatazz Vol. II: The New Reality *Gang Starr*
No More Mr. Nice Guy *Gang Starr*

Robin Guthrie
Gala *Lush*
Spooky *Lush*

Hüsker Dü
Land Speed Record *Hüsker Dü*
New Day Rising *Hüsker Dü*

Sammy Hagar
Welcome to the Neighborhood *Meat Loaf*

Frans Hagenaars
Lamprey *Bettie Serveert*
Palomine *Bettie Serveert*

Stephen Hague
Cloudland *Pere Ubu*
Fenętiks *Jules Shear*
Got No Breeding *Jules Shear*
Please *Pet Shop Boys*
Read My Lips *Bronski Beat*
The House of Love (Butterfly) *The House of Love*
The Innocents *Erasure*

Lew Hahn
From Luxury to Heartache *Culture Club*

Diane Haig
Motown Legends: War-Twenty Five Miles *Edwin Starr*

Luke Haines
New Wave *The Auteurs*
Now I'm A Cowboy *The Auteurs*

Roy Halee
Angel Clare *Art Garfunkel*
Blood, Sweat & Tears 3 *Blood, Sweat and Tears*
New York Tendaberry *Laura Nyro*
Nurds *The Roches*
Paul Simon *Paul Simon*
Picture Perfect Morning *Edie Brickell & New Bohemians*
The Concert in Central Park *Simon and Garfunkel*
To the Heart *Marc Almond Band*

Darryl Hall
Private Eyes *Darryl Hall & John Oates*
Voices *Darryl Hall & John Oates*

Doug Hall
The Number of the Beast *Iron Maiden*

Ellis Hall
Power *Tower of Power*

Norman Hall
Supertramp Live '88 *Supertramp*

Rick Hall
Sixty Minutes with Clarence Carter *Clarence Carter*
Snatching it Back: The Best of Clarence Carter *Clarence Carter*

Stuart Hallerman
Pussy Whipped *Bikini Kill*

Mark Hallman
Skeleton Keys *Iain Matthews*
The Dark Ride *Iain Matthews*
Walking a Changing Line: The Songs of Jules Shear *Jules Shear*
Walking A Changing Line *Iain Matthews*

Neil Halstead
Just For A Day *Slowdive*

Bill Halverson
Hangin' On by a Thread *The Texas Tornados*
How's Tricks *Jack Bruce*
So Far *Crosby, Stills and Nash*
Stephen Stills *Crosby, Stills and Nash*
Texas Tornados *The Texas Tornados*
Zone of Our Own *The Texas Tornados*

Bill Ham
A Taste of the ZZ Top Six Pack *ZZ Top*
Deguello *ZZ Top*
Eliminator *ZZ Top*
Six Pack *ZZ Top*
Tres Hombres *ZZ Top*
ZZ Top's Greatest Hits *ZZ Top*

Ken Hamann
Dub Housing *Pere Ubu*
Terminal Tower: An Archival Collection *Pere Ubu*
The Modern Dance *Pere Ubu*

Paul Hamann
Cloudland *Pere Ubu*
One Man Drives While the Other Man Screams *Pere Ubu*
Terminal Tower: An Archival Collection *Pere Ubu*
The Tenement Year *Pere Ubu*

Tom Hamilton
Create Your Friends *Lemonheads*
Lick *Lemonheads*

Jan Hammer
Jeff Beck with the Jan Hammer Group Live *Jeff Beck*

John Hammond
The Freewheelin' Bob Dylan *Bob Dylan*

Lee Hammond
Dream Letter: Live In London, 1968 *Tim Buckley*

John Hampton
Congratulations I'm Sorry *Gin Blossoms*
New Miserable Experience *Gin Blossoms*
Songs from the Film *Tommy Keene*

Michael Hampton
Rites of Spring *Fugazi*

Robin Hancock
Cyberpunk *Billy Idol*

Martin Hannett
Closer *Joy Division*
Hallelujah *Happy Mondays*
Power, Corruption and Lies *New Order*
Still *Joy Division*
Substance *Joy Division*
The Correct Use of Soap *Magazine*
Unknown Pleasures *Joy Division*

Barry Hansen
The Essential John Fahey *John Fahey*

John Hanti
Live in New York *James Chance*

Paul Hardiman
Rattlesnakes *Lloyd Cole*

Daize Harding
Whenever You Need Somebody *Rick Astley*

John Wesley Harding
God Made Me Do It: The Christmas EP *John Wesley Harding*

Joe Hardy
Here Come the Snakes *Green on Red*
In the Land of Salvation and Sin *Georgia Satellites*
Songs from the Film *Tommy Keene*
The Hard Way *Steve Earle*

Mark Harman
Rose of Cimarron *Poco*

Ben Harper
Fight For Your Mind *Ben Harper*
Welcome to the Cruel World *Ben Harper*

Tim Harper
Weird Food And Devastation *The Connells*

Andre Harrell
Uptown MTV Unplugged *Jodeci*

Emmylou Harris
Angel Band *Emmylou Harris*
The Ballad of Sally Rose *Emmylou Harris*

James Harris III
Control *Janet Jackson*
Heart Break *New Edition*
Rhythm Nation 1814 *Janet Jackson*

Jody Harris
Escape *Robert Quine*

Tony Harris
You, the Night . . . & the Music *Gallon Drunk*

George Harrison
Encouraging Words *Billy Preston*

Matt Hyde
Good God's Urge *Porno for Pyros*
Porno For Pyros *Porno for Pyros*

Chrissie Hynde
Packed! *The Pretenders*

Janis Ian
Breaking Silence *Janis Ian*

Bruce Iglauer
Showdown! *Robert Cray*

Aki Ikuta
Playing the Orchestra *Ryuichi Sakamoto*

Indigo Girls
1200 Curfews *Indigo Girls*

Infinity Inc.
The Magic City *Sun Ra*
The Night of the Purple Moon *Sun Ra*

Bill Inglot
Anthology *Four Seasons*
Dream Letter: Live In London, 1968 *Tim Buckley*
It's About Time *The Pandoras*
Missing Links *The Monkees*
Nuggets: Classics from the Psychedelic 60s *Count Five*
Peek-a-Boo *NRBQ*
Retrospective *Bread*
The Best of the Bobby Fuller Four *The Bobby Fuller Four*
The Isley Brothers Story, Vol. 1: Rockin' Soul *Isley Brothers*
The Johnny Rivers Anthology: 1964-1977 *Johnny Rivers*

Neil Innes
The Rutles *The Rutles*

At'c Inoue
Keepin' Dah Funk Alive 4 1995 *Bootsy Collins*

Inspiral Carpets
Life *Inspiral Carpets*

INXS
Full Moon, Dirty Hearts *INXS*

Tony Iommu
Headless Cross *Black Sabbath*

Jimmy Iovine
Bella Donna *Stevie Nicks*
Damn the Torpedoes *Tom Petty and the Heartbreakers*
Dead Ringer *Meat Loaf*
Hard Promises *Tom Petty and the Heartbreakers*
Lone Justice *Lone Justice*
Making Movies *Dire Straits*
Matters of the Heart *Tracy Chapman*
Raindancing *Alison Moyet*
See the Light *Jeff Healey Band*
The Distance *Bob Seger*

Iron Maiden
The Number of the Beast *Iron Maiden*

Robert Irving III
Time After Time *Miles Davis*

Bob Irwin
A Rave Up with . . . The Knickerbockers *The Knickerbockers*
Don't Say That I Ain't Your Man! *Michael Bloomfield*
Jerk and Twine Time *The Knickerbockers*
Lies *The Knickerbockers*
Surfin' Bird *Surf Music*
Tighten Up Your Wig: The Best of John Kay & Sparrow *Steppenwolf*
Twist and Shout *Isley Brothers*

Jonathon Isley
Please Panic *The Silos*

David J
Crocodile Tears and the Velvet Cosh *Love and Rockets*
On Glass *Love and Rockets*

J. Geils Band
Blow Your Face Out *J. Geils Band*
Monkey Island *J. Geils Band*

Al Jackson
Born Under a Bad Sign *Albert King*
Live Wire/Blues Power *Albert King*
Wednesday Night in San Francisco *Albert King*

Janet Jackson
Control *Janet Jackson*
Rhythm Nation 1814 *Janet Jackson*

Joe Jackson
Blaze of Glory *Joe Jackson*
Jumpin' Jive *Joe Jackson*
Night and Day *Joe Jackson*
Night Music *Joe Jackson*
Stranger Than Fiction *Joe Jackson*

Al Jackson Jr.
Good to Me *Otis Redding*

Michael James Jackson
Creatures of the Night *Kiss*

Michael Jackson
Off The Wall *Michael Jackson*

Jacksons
Destiny *Jackson 5*
Triumph *Jackson 5*

Erik Jacobsen
Anthology *Lovin' Spoonful*
Best of the Lovin' Spoonful Volume 2 *Lovin' Spoonful*
Best of the Lovin' Spoonful *Lovin' Spoonful*
Daydream *Lovin' Spoonful*
Do You Believe In Magic *Lovin' Spoonful*
Forever Blue *Chris Isaak*
Hums of the Lovin' Spoonful *Lovin' Spoonful*
San Francisco Days *Chris Isaak*
Silvertone *Chris Isaak*

Daniel Jacoubovitch
Rockin' Eighty-Eights *Johnnie Johnson*

Mick Jagger
She's the Boss *Mick Jagger*
Wandering Spirit *Mick Jagger*

Jam Master Jay
Back From Hell *Run-D.M.C.*

The Jam
Sound Affects *The Jam*
The Gift *The Jam*

Bob James
Nightwatch *Loggins and Messina*

Ethan James
Double Nickels on the Dime *fIREHOSE*
if 'n' *fIREHOSE*

Michael James
Son of Sam I Am *Too Much Joy*

Rick James
Bustin' Out of L7 *Rick James*
Come Get It *Rick James*
Street Songs *Rick James*
The Flag *Rick James*
Throwin' Down *Rick James*

James
Seven *James*

Nick Jameson
Fool For the City *Foghat*
Zig-Zag Walk *Foghat*

Mike Janas
Town & Country *Webb Wilder*

Jane's Addiction
Jane's Addiction *Jane's Addiction*

McCloud Janney
Nineties vs. Eighties *Girls Against Boys*

John Jansen
Adventure *Television*
Beat Hotel *The Bongos*
New Sensations *Lou Reed*
Numbers With Wings *The Bongos*

Japan
Tin Drum *Japan*

Rick Jarrard
Harry *Harry Nilsson*

Felton Jarvis
As Recorded at Madison Square Garden *Elvis Presley*
Elvis Country *Elvis Presley*
From Elvis in Memphis *Elvis Presley*
Recorded Live on Stage in Memphis *Elvis Presley*

S. Jarvis
Sleazy Roadside Stories *Commander Cody and His Lost Planet Airmen*

Scott Jarvis
Some Old Bullshit *Beastie Boys*

The Ghost of Tom Joad *Bruce Springsteen*

Jon Plum
Candlebox *Candlebox*
Lucy *Candlebox*

J.P. Plunier
Fight For Your Mind *Ben Harper*
Welcome to the Cruel World *Ben Harper*

PM Dawn
Jesus Wept *PM Dawn*
Of the Heart, of the Soul and the Cross: The Utopian Experience *PM Dawn*
The Bliss Album...? *PM Dawn*

Poco
Rose of Cimarron *Poco*

Richard Podolor
Harmony *Three Dog Night*
Look Out *20/20*

Poi Dog Pondering
Wishing like a Mountain and Thinking like the Sea *Poi Dog Pondering*

The Police
Ghost in the Machine *The Police*
Regatta de Blanc *The Police*
Synchronicity *The Police*
Zenyatta Mondatta *The Police*

Dug Pomeroy
Some Old Bullshit *Beastie Boys*

Doc Pomus
Blues Train *Big Joe Turner*

Vini Poncia
Scandal *Patty Smyth*

Lee Popa
UAIOE *KMFDM*

Steve Popovich
Heaven and Hull *Mick Ronson*

Page Porrazzo
Rock Animals *Shonen Knife*

Bob Porter
Blues Train *Big Joe Turner*
1959-1965 All-Time Greatest Hits and More *The Drifters*

David Porter
Soul Men *Sam and Dave*

John Porter
Hatful of Hollow *The Smiths*
School of Fish *School of Fish*
Talking With the Taxman About Poetry *Billy Bragg*
The Queen Is Dead *The Smiths*
The Smiths *The Smiths*
Wrapped in Sky *Drivin' N' Cryin'*

Robie Porter
Greatest Hits *Air Supply*
Lost in Love *Air Supply*

Portishead
Dummy *Portishead*

Robert Poss
Here Comes Success *Band of Susans*
Hope Against Hope *Band of Susans*
The Powerful Veil *Band of Susans*
The Word and the Flesh *Band of Susans*
Wired for Sound *Band of Susans*

Chris Potter
Magic Bullets *Mega City Four*
Soulscraper *Mega City Four*

Andrew Powell
Lionheart *Kate Bush*

Cozy Powell
Headless Cross *Black Sabbath*

Tim Powell
The Long Cut + Five Live *Uncle Tupelo*

Timothy Powell
Back on the Bus Y'all *Indigo Girls*
The House of Love Live *The House of Love*

Bob Power
Plantation Lullabies *Me'Shell Ndegeocello*

Steve Power
Strip-Mine *James*

Johnny Powers
New Spark (For an Old Flame) *Johnny Powers*

Bud Prager
Classic Hits Live *Foreigner*

David Prater
Feeding off the Mojo *Damn Yankees*

Prefab Sprout
Swoon *Prefab Sprout*

Elvis Presley
Frankie and Johnny/Paradise, Hawaiian Style *Elvis Presley*
Fun in Acapulco *Elvis Presley*
Girl Happy/Harum Scarum *Elvis Presley*
His Hand In Mine *Elvis Presley*
Loving You *Elvis Presley*

Steve Presti
Skank for Brains *The Suicide Machines*

Billy Preston
Encouraging Words *Billy Preston*
The Best of Billy Preston *Billy Preston*

Richard Preston
Liberty Belle and the Black Diamond Express *The Go-Betweens*

Bill Price
Darklands *The Jesus and Mary Chain*
Dream Harder *The Waterboys*
The Clash *The Clash*

Primus
Pork Soda *Primus*
Sailing the Seas of Cheese *Primus*
Tales from the Punch Bowl *Primus*

Prince
Around the World In a Day *Prince*
Chaos & Disorder *Prince*
Come *Prince*
Controversy *Prince*
Diamonds and Pearls *Prince*
Dirty Mind *Prince*
For You *Prince*
'Girl 6' Motion Picture Soundtrack *Prince*
Ice Cream Castle *The Time*
Love Symbol Album *Prince*
Lovesexy *Prince*
Music from 'Graffiti Bridge' *Prince*
1999 *Prince*
Parade (Music from the Motion Picture 'Under the Cherry Moon') *Prince*
Purple Rain *Prince*
Sign O' the Times *Prince*
The Gold Experience *Prince*
The Hits 1 *Prince*
The Hits 2 *Prince*
The Hits/The B-Sides *Prince*
The White Album *Prince*

John Prine
John Prine Live *John Prine*

Procol Harum
Something Magic *Procol Harum*

Spencer Proffer
Metal Health *Quiet Riot*
Pictures from the Front *Jon Butcher Axis*

Prong
Beg to Differ *Prong*

Psychedelic Furs
World Outside *The Psychedelic Furs*

Jack Joseph Puig
Amorica *The Black Crowes*
Bellybutton *Jellyfish*
Grits 'n' Gravy *The Black Crowes*
Spilt Milk *Jellyfish*
Three Snakes and One Charm *The Black Crowes*

John Punter
Gentlemen Take Polaroids *Japan*

John Purdell
No More Tears *Ozzy Osbourne*

Jimmy Pursey
Hersham Boys *Sham 69*
Tell Us the Truth *Sham 69*
The Game *Sham 69*
Volunteer *Sham 69*

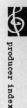

Ricochet *Tangerine Dream*
Rubycon *Tangerine Dream*
Shy People *Tangerine Dream*
Tangents: 1973-1983 *Tangerine Dream*
Zeit *Tangerine Dream*

Mark Tanner
After the Rain *Nelson*
Because They Can *Nelson*

Tar
Clincher *Tar*

Dave Tarling
In My Head *Black Flag*

Nat Tarnapol
Merry Christmas From Jackie Wilson *Jackie Wilson*

Alan Tarney
Hunting High and Low *a-ha*
Scoundrel Days *a-ha*
Take On Me *a-ha*

Nick Tauber
Thin Lizzy *Thin Lizzy*

Dallas Taylor
Manassas *Crosby, Stills and Nash*

Ian Taylor
Blues Alive *Gary Moore*
Blues For Greeny *Gary Moore*

Sam Taylor
Gretchen Goes to Nebraska *King's X*
Out of the Silent Planet *King's X*

Skip Taylor
Future Blues *Canned Heat*
Hooker 'N' Heat *John Lee Hooker*

Tears for Fears
The Seeds of Love *Tears for Fears*

Montie Temple
Good Lucky Killer *Royal Crescent Mob*
Omerta *Royal Crescent Mob*
13 Destruction *Royal Crescent Mob*

Temple of the Dog
Temple of the Dog *Pearl Jam*

Ted Templeman
St. Dominic's Preview *Van Morrison*
Best of the Doobies *The Doobie Brothers*
Listen to the Music *The Doobie Brothers*
1984 *Van Halen*
Sailin' Shoes *Little Feat*
Takin' It To the Streets *The Doobie Brothers*
The Best of the Doobies Volume II *The Doobie Brothers*
The Spotlight Kid/Clear Spot *Captain Beefheart & His Magic Band*
Toulouse Street *The Doobie Brothers*
Van Halen *Van Halen*
Women and Children First *Van Halen*

10cc
Greatest Hits, 1972-78 *10cc*
How Dare You *10cc*
The Original Soundtrack *10cc*
Two Classic Albums by 10cc *10cc*

10,000 Maniacs
Hope Chest *10,000 Maniacs*

Ten Years After
Cricklewood Green *Ten Years After*

Brian Tench
Junk Culture *Orchestral Manoeuvres in the Dark*

Joe Terry
No Trespassing *The Roches*

The Texas Tornados
Hangin' On by a Thread *The Texas Tornados*
Zone of Our Own *The Texas Tornados*

Ed E. Thacker
Great Buildings *The Rembrandts*

that dog
that dog *that dog*
Totally Crushed Out *that dog*

Therapy?
Caucasian Psychosis *Therapy?*
Hats Off to the Insane *Therapy?*

They Might Be Giants
Apollo 18 *They Might Be Giants*

Bob Thiele
Rockabilly Boogie *Johnny Burnette*
What A Wonderful World *Louis Armstrong*

Thin Lizzy
Live and Dangerous *Thin Lizzy*

David Thoener
After the Rain *Nelson*

Chris Thomas
All the Best Cowboys Have Chinese Eyes *Pete Townshend*
Empty Glass *Pete Townshend*
For Your Pleasure *Roxy Music*
Grand Hotel *Procol Harum*
Hormonally Yours *Bananarama*
Kick *INXS*
Learning to Crawl *The Pretenders*
Never Mind The Bollocks Here's The Sex Pistols *The Sex Pistols*
Paris 1919 *John Cale*
Power in the Darkness *Tom Robinson Band*
Siren *Roxy Music*
Stranded *Roxy Music*
The Pretenders *The Pretenders*

Ken Thomas
Drums Along the Hudson *The Bongos*
Playing with a Different Sex *The Au Pairs*

Marvell Thomas
Hot Buttered Soul *Isaac Hayes*

Terry Thomas
Bust a Nut *Tesla*

D. Clinton Thompson
Jonathan Goes Country *Jonathan Richman*

Marc Anthony Thompson
Shrek *Marc Ribot*

Mayo Thompson
Brave Words *The Chills*

Richard Thompson
I Want to See the Bright Lights Tonight *Richard Thompson*

Steve Thompson
Electriclarryland *Butthole Surfers*
Four *Blues Traveler*
The Great Radio Controversy *Tesla*

Alan Thorn
Gossip *Paul Kelly*

Tracey Thorn
Acoustic *Everything But the Girl*
Amplified Heart *Everything But the Girl*
Language of Life *Everything But the Girl*

Alan Thorne
Comedy *Paul Kelly*
Stoneage Romeos *The Hoodoo Gurus*

Mike Thorne
Chairs Missing *Wire*
On Returning (1977-79) *Wire*
Pink Flag *Wire*

Eric "E.T." Thorngren
A Night to Remember *Cyndi Lauper*
Come As You Are *Peter Wolf*

Throwing Muses
Limbo *Throwing Muses*

Colin Thurston
Duran Duran *Duran Duran*
Rio *Duran Duran*
White Feathers *Kajagoogoo*

David Tickle
Divinyls *Divinyls*
True Colors *Split Enz*
Union *Toni Childs*
Waiata *Split Enz*
Wonderful *Adam Ant*

Timbuk 3
Edge of Allegiance *Timbuk 3*
Espace Ornano *Timbuk 3*
Looks Like Dark to Me *Timbuk 3*

The Category Index represents an array of categories put together to suggest just some of the many groupings under which rock music and rock band names could be classified. Category names are followed by artist/band entries in alphabetical order. The Hound welcomes your additions to the existing categories in this index and also invites you to send in your own funny, sarcastic, prolific, poignant, or exciting ideas for brand new categories.

Acronyms Only
AC/DC
DMZ
DNA
DOA
EMF
G.B.H.
The GTO's
INXS
U2
UB40
UFO
XTC
X
Z

All-Girl Groups—Contemporary
The Angels
Babes in Toyland
Bananarama
The Bangles
The Go-Go's
Indigo Girls
L7
Lunachicks
Slits

All-Girl Groups—Historical
Martha & The Vandellas
Shirelles
The Supremes

All the Rage
Angry Samoans
Rage Against the Machine
Rage to Live
Violent Femmes

Am I Blue
Babe the Blue Ox
Blue Aeroplanes
Blue Angel
Blue Cheer
Blue Nile
Blue Oyster Cult
Blues Project
Blue Rodeo
Blue Ruin
Bluebells
The Blues Brothers
Blues Magoos
Blues Traveler
Paul Butterfield Blues Band
Deacon Blue
Moody Blues
Screaming Blue Messiahs
Jon Spencer Blues Explosion
Swinging Blue Jeans

Amazin' Adjectives
Amazing Rhythm Aces
Average White Band
Angry Samoans
Ambitious Lovers
Bad Brains
The Beautiful South
Cheap Trick
Combustible Edison
Inspiral Carpets
L.A. Guns
Lightning Seeds
Luscious Jackson
Thunderclap Newman
Pale Saints
Simple Minds
Swinging Blue Jeans
Violent Femmes

American Folk Rock
Alpha Band
America
American Flyer
Tori Amos
Joan Baez
Luka Bloom
The Byrds
The Beau Brummels
Buffalo Springfield
Tracey Chapman
Shawn Colvin
Crosby, Stills and Nash
Bob Dylan
Richard & Mimi Farina
Dan Fogelberg
Steve Forbert
Janis Ian
Indigo Girls
Love
The Lovin' Spoonful
James McMurtry
John Mellencamp
Joni Mitchell
Phil Ochs
Peter, Paul & Mary
Simon & Garfunkel
Cat Stevens
Neil Young

American Neo-Punk
All
Angry Samoans
Babes in Toyland
Big Drill Car
Fugazi
Green Day
Hole
L7
Offspring
Prong
Rancid
Roches
Rocket from the Crypt
Superchunk

American Punk
Adolescents
Agnostic Front
Agent Orange
Bad Religion
Black Flag
Blondie
Butthole Surfers

The Who
Yardbirds
The Zombies

British Invasion—Second Wave
Cream
Jeff Beck
Fleetwood Mac
The Jimi Hendrix Experience
Led Zeppelin
Pink Floyd
Rod Stewart
Traffic

British Punk
Adverts
Alien Sex Fiend
Alternative TV
The Anti-Nowhere League
The Buzzcocks
The Clash
Elvis Costello
The Damned
G.B.H.
Generation X
The Jam
Public Image Ltd. (PiL)
The Sex Pistols
The Undertones
The Vibrators
X-Ray Spex

BritPop Spotlighters
Blur
The Boo-Radleys
Blur
Depeche Mode
Erasure
Gene
Happy Mondays
House Martins
Lush
Oasis
Pulp
Radiohead
Ride
Shakespear's Sister
Smiths
Suede
Supergrass
The Verve

California Psychedelia
Davie Allan
Beach Boys
Big Brother & The Holding Company
Captain Beefheart
Country Joe and the Fish
Creedence Clearwater Revival
Crosby, Stills and Nash (& Young)
Doors
Roky Erickson/13th Floor Elevators
Grateful Dead
Hot Tuna
Iron Butterfly
Janis Joplin
Jefferson Airplane
Moby Grape
Phish
Quicksilver Messenger Service
Santana
Sly & The Family Stone
Vanilla Fudge
Frank Zappa
Canada
Bryan Adams
Jan Arden
Bachman-Turner Overdrive
The Band
Barenaked Ladies
Blue Rodeo
Crash Test Dummies
Bruce Cochburn
54-40
Foster & Lloyd
Guess Who
k.d. lang
Loverboy
McGarrigles
Ashley McIssac
Sarah McLachlan
Joni Mitchell
Alanis Morissette
Rush
Jane Siberry
Skinny Puppy
Sloan
Tragically Hip
Neil Young

Car Crazy
Accelerators
Asleep at the Wheel
Big Drill Car
The Cars
Crash Test Dummies
Drivin' N Cryin'
Dumptruck
Eddie & the Hot Rods
The Fabulous Thunderbirds
Mike and the Mechanics
Motorheads
Motors
Red Lorry Yellow Lorry
REO Speedwagon
Traffic

Cave Rock
Barbarians
Fine Young Cannibals
Gwar
The Missing Links
The Savages

Celtic-Influenced
A House
The Alarm
Black 47
Luka Bloom
Blue Nile
Kate Bush
Johnny Clegg
Crash Test Dummies
Cranberries
Deacon Blue
Dead Can Dance
Del Amitri
Devlins
An Emotional Fish
Enya
Fairport Convention
Bob Geldof
Hothouse Flowers
Kirsty Macoll
Ashley McIsaac
Loreena McKennitt
McGarrigles
Mekons
Sinead O'Connor
Maura O'Connell
The Oyster Band
Pentagle/Bert Jansch
Pogues
Proclaimers
Rod Stewart
Richard Thompson
U2
The Waterboys
World Party

Chicago
Chuck Berry
Michael Bloomfield
Blues Brothers
The Buckinghams
Jerry Butler
Paul Butterfield Blues Band
Gene Chandler
Cheap Trick
Chicago
Sam Cooke
The Dells
Bo Diddley
Earth, Wind & Fire
Buddy Guy
Howlin' Wolf
Major Lance
Curtis Mayfield and the Impressions
Ministry
New Colony Six
Liz Phair
Jimmy Reed
Shadows of Knight
Smashing Pumpkins
Styx

Cities & States
Boston
Buffalo Tom
Chicago
The Future Sound of London
Georgia Satellites
Grant Lee Buffalo
Hanoi Rocks
Kansas
L.A. Guns
London Suede
New York Dolls
Ohio Express
The Ohio Players
Mitch Rider and the Detroit Wheels

Country Cross-Over
The Beau Brothers
Steve Earle
Joe Ely
Everyly Brothers
The Flying Burrito Brothers
Jimmy Dale Gilmore
Arlo Guthrie
k.d. Lang
Lyle Lovitt
Poco
Gram Parsons
Ween
Hank Williams Sr.
Hank Williams Jr.
ZZ Top

Dancin' Shoes
ABBA
Paula Abdul
Ace of Base
a-ha
Animotion
Aphex Twin
A.R. Kane

Army of Lovers
Arrested Development
Art of Noise
B-52s
Bananarama
Bee Gees
Chubby Checker
Neneh Cherry
Chic
Culture Club
Deee-Lite
Enigma
Erasure
Everything But the Girls
Frankie Goes to Hollywood
Future Sound a Lodon
Janet Jackson
Michael Jackson
K.C. and the Sunshine Band
Lords of Acid
The Orb
Orbital
Plastikman
Primal Scream
Prince
Diana Ross
Donna Summer

Dead Heads?
Dead Boys
Dead Can Dance
Dead Kennedys
Dead milkmen
Death
The Grateful Dead
Grim Reaper
Napalm Death
Stormtrooper of Death
Suicidal Tendancies
Suicide
Suicide Machines
The Undead

Detroit
Lavern Baker
Brownsville Station
Charm Farm
The Civilians
George Clinton
Alice Cooper
Marshall Crenshaw
The Four Tops
Aretha Franklin
Iggy and the Stooges
Marvin Gaye
Grand Funk Railroad
The Knack
Madonna
Martha and the Vandellas
MC5
The Miracles
Ted Nugent
Rare Earth
The Romantics
Mitch Ryder and the Detroit Wheels
? & the Mysterians
Jack Scott
Bob Seger and the Silver Bullet Band
Patti Smith
The Spinners
Sponge
The Supremes
The Temptations
Verve Pipe
Junior Walker and the All Stars
Was (Not Was)
Jackie Wilson
Stevie Wonder

Dixieland Jams
The Allman Brothers Band
The Amazing Rhythm Aces
The Atlantic Rhythm Section
The Black Crowes
The Dixie Dregs
Charlie Daniels Band
The Georgia Satellites
Lynyrd Skynyrd
The Outlaws
Phish
Marshall Tucker Band
The Dave Matthews Band
Molly Hatchett
.38 Special
Widespread Panic

Double Vision
ABBA
G.G. Allin
Bee Gees
Duran Duran
The Go-Go's
Goo Goo Dolls
Kajagoogoo
B.B. King
L.L. Cool J
Liquid Liquid
Oingo Boingo
Talk Talk
The The
Twenty Twenty
Was (Not Was)
Yo-Yo
ZZ Top

Dubbed "Loudest" Band
Einstürzende Nubaeuten
Fugazi
Led Zeppelin
Pantera
Rage Against the Machine
The Ramones
Sonic Youth
Spinal Tap

Everything Old is New Again
Edie Brickell & New Bohemians
Club Nouveau
Modern English
Modern Lovers
New Colony Six
New Edition
New Kids on the Block
New Model Army
New Order
New Raiders of the Purple Sage
New York Dolls
Lords of the New Church

Experimental
Amazing Blondel
Laurie Anderson
Ginger Baker
Beck
David Bowie
Brian Eno
Einstürzende Nubaeuten
Dead Can Dance
Robert Fripp
Peter Gabriel
King Missle
Kraftwerk
Tangerine Dream
They Might Be Giants
Yoko Ono
The Velvet Underground
Frank Zappa

Garage
Chocolate Watch Band
Count Five
Electric Prunes
Fuzztones
The Lemon Drops
The Kingsmen
MC5
Music Machine
Mystic Tide
New Colony Six
The New York Dolls
Pandoras
The Pumains
? & the Mysterians
Rising Storm
The Seeds
Shadows of Knight
Sonics
The Standells
The Stooges
Thee Fourgiven
Them
13th Floor Elevators
The Troggs

Georgia on My Mind
Allman Brothers Band
Arrested Development
Atlanta Rhythm Section
B-52s
Black Crowes
Ray Charles
Georgia Satellites
Indigo Girls
Little Richard
Otis Redding
R.E.M.
Joe South

Glam Rock
Cinderella
Def Leppard
Extreme
Firehouse
Gary Glitter
Great White
Jon Bon Jovi
Kiss
Mötley Crüe
New York Dolls
Poison
Suzi Quatro
Skid Row
Slade
Slaughter
Sweet
T-Rex
Tesla
Twisted Sister
Warrant
White Lion
Whitesnake
Winger

Gothic Rock
All About Eve
Bauhaus
The Church
The Cure
Joy Division

The Grassroots
Guns N' Roses
Ice-T
Jane's Addiction
L.A. Guns
Los Lobos
Megadeath
Mötley Crüe
N.W.A.
Righteous Brothers
Linda Ronstadt
Social Distortion
Steely Dan
Turtles
Warrant
X

Late Great Guitarists
Roy Buchanan
Rory Gallagher
Jerry Garcia
Danny Gatton
Jimi Hendrix
Mick Ronson
Stevie Ray Vaughan

Literate and Lovin' It
All About Eve
Better Than Ezra
Blake Babies
Cocteau Twins
Dharma Bums
Grapes of Wrath
Hothouse Flowers
Last Poets
Pere Ubu
Sam I Am
Shakespear's Sister
Soft Machine
Steely Dan
Trip Shakespeare
Uriah Heep
The Velvet Underground

Little Big Man
Big Brother & the Holding Company
Mr. Big
Zoot Money's Big Roll
Lee Rocker's Big Blue
Big Joe Turner
Big F
Big Audio Dynamite
Big Black
Big Bopper
Big Boys
Big Chief
Big Country
Big Dish
Big Drill Car
Big Head Todd & the Monsters
Big Star
Little Willie John
Little Anthony & the Imperials
Little Eva
Little Feat
Little Richard
Little River Band
Little Steven & the Disciples of Soul
Little Village
Little Esther Phillips
Stiff Little Fingers

Lo-Fi
Beat Happening
Beck
Pussy Galore
Grifters
Guided by Voices
Daniel Johnston
Pavement
Palace Bros.
Portastatic
Liz Phair
Royal Trux
Sebadoh
Silver Jews
Smog
Skip Spence (Moby Grape)
Superchunk
Velvet Underground

Math
A Certain Ratio
Algebra Suicide
Circle Jerks
Curve
Arc Angels
Pentangle
360's

Memphis
Big Star
Bobby Bland
Booker T. & the MG's
Sonny Burgess
Johnny Cash
Al Green
Jerry Lee Lewis
B.B. King
Roy Orbison
Carl Perkins
Elvis Presley

Military Maneuvers
Agent Orange
Captain & Tenille
Captain Beefheart
Colonel Abrams
Comander Cody & His Lost Planet Airmen
Cutting Crew
Ray Columbus and The Invaders
Col. Bruce Hampton & The Aquarium Rescue Unit
Major Lance
Music Explosion
New Model Army
Paul Revere and The Raiders
Royal Cresent Mob
Slayer

Minneapolis
Babes in Toyland
Bob Dylan
Hüsker Dü
Jayhawks
Prince
The Replacements
Soul Asylum
The Time
Vanity Six

Most Bizarre Names
Alien Sex Fiend
An Emotional Fish
Big Head Todd & the Monsters
Celibate Rifles
The Chocolate Watch Band
The Dickies
Echo and the Bunnymen
Frightwig
Kinky Friedman & The Texas Jewboys
My Life With the Thrill Kill Kult
Ned's Atomic Dustbin
Orchestral Manoeuvres in the Dark
The Pursuit of Hapiness
Psychedelic Furs
Temple of the Dog
Therapy?
Toad the Wet Sprocket
Urge Overkill
Was (Not Was)

Most Depressing Bands
Bauhaus
Joy Division
Ministry
Morrissey
My Bloody Valentine
Nine Inch Nails
Nirvana
Pearl Jam
Portishead
R.E.M.

Most Pretentious Names
Carter the Unstoppable Sex Machine
Electric Light Orchestra (ELO)
An Emotional Fish
Hindu Love Gods
His Name Is Alive
Orchestral Maneuvers in the Dark (OMD)

Mouth Watering Good
Chocolate Watch Band
The Cranberries
Cream
The Electric Prunes
Green Jelly
Jellybean
The Raspberries
Red Hot Chili Peppers
Smashing Pumpkins
Vanilla Fudge

Music By Numbers
The B-52's
Black 47
5th Dimension
54-40
The "5" Royales
Front 242
Galaxie 500
Heaven 17
The Jackson 5
L7
Level 42
Local #282
M.C. 900 Ft Jesus
MC5
100 Proof (Aged in Soul)
Pizzacato 5
Sham 69
Spacemen 3
10cc
10,000 Maniacs
The 360's
.38 Special
Timbuk 3
U2
UB40

MusicHound Diner
Busboys
Sam Cooke
Cracker
Green Jelly

Humble Pie
Ice T.
Kitchens of Distinction
G. Love and Special Sauce
Meatloaf
The Platters
Salt N' Peppa
Waitresses

Named After Movies/ TV Shows or Characters
All About Eve
Bambi Slam
The Boo Radleys
Cinderella
Dash Rip Rock
Duran Duran
Faster Pussycat
Fine Young Cannibals
Jody Foster's Army
Mudhoney
My Bloody Valentine
Pussy Galore
The Stooges
Veruca Salt
Zu-zu's Petals

The "New" Dylans
Eric Anderson
Tim Buckley
Tracey Chapman
Elvis Costello
Steely Dan
Jakob Dylan
Steve Forbert/artist
Bob Geldof
Elliot Murphy
Prince
John Prine
Patti Smith
Bruce Springsteen
Eddie Vedder (Pearl Jam)

The New Orleans Sound
Dave Bartholomew
Fats Domino
Lee Dorsey
Down
Dr. John
The Meters
The Neville Brothers
Allen Toussaint

New Wave
ABC
Marc Almond
Adam Ant
Blondie
Buggles
The Cars
Culture Club
Devo
Dexys Midnight Runners
Duran Duran
Thomas Dolby
The Fixx
A Flock of Seagulls
Haircut 100
Joy Division
Kajagoogoo
Lene Lovich
Magazine
Men Without Hats
Men at Work
New Order
Police
The Slits
Split Enz
Talking Heads
Thompson Twins
XTC

Offspring
Bonham
Jeff Buckley
Julain Lennon
Nancy Boy
Nelson
Wallflowers
Hank Williams, Jr.
Wilson Phillips

Ohio
Bootsy Collins
The Dead Boys
Devo
The James Gang
Tommy James & the Shondells
Isley Brothers
Nine Inch Nails
Ohio Express
Ohio Players
O'Jays
The Outsiders
Pere Ubu
The Pretenders
The Raspberries

One of the Grrrls
Babes in Toyland
Ani DiFranco
Hole
Joan Jett
L7
The Runaways
Slits

Onomatopoeia
Bif Band Pow!
Bl'ast
Blurt
Bow Wow Wow
Gong

Oxymorons
Golden Smog
Happy Mondays
Iron Butterfly
Joy Division
Led Zeppelin
Quiet Riot
Yeah Yeah Noh

Politically Astute
Jackson Browne
The Clash
Bruce Cockburn
Creedence Clearwater Revival
Bob Dylan
Marvin Gaye
Grandmaster Flash
Don Henley
Garland Jeffreys
John Lennon
Little Steven
MC5
John Mellencamp
Yoko Ono
Public Enemy
Tom Robinson
Gil Scott-Heron
The Sex Pistols
Bruce Springsteen
Sting
Neil Young

Punk Grandparents
The Animals
MC5
Patti Smith
The Stooges
The Velvet Underground

Rhythm Nations
America
Asia
Afrika Bambaataa
Gary "U.S." Bonds
China Crisis
Europe
Japan
Mission UK
Mission of Burma
U.K. Decay
U.K. Subs

Rockabilly
Hasil Adkins
The Blasters
Johnny Burnette
Eddie Cochran
Bill Haley
Dale Hawkins
Buddy Holly
Wanda Jackson
Jerry Lee Lewis
Ricky Nelson
Roy Orbison
Carl Perkins
Elvis Presley
Reverand Horton Heat
Stray Cats/Brian Setzer
Gene Vincent

Rockin' & Rollin'
Bl'ast
Des'ree
Drivin' N Cryin'
E'bn O'zn
Enuff Z'nuff
Guns N' Roses
Screamin' Jay Hawkins
Howlin' Wolf
The Lovin' Spoonful
The Rockin' Ramrods

Roots Rock
The Band
The Blasters
Blue Rodeo
The Bodeans
Gary U.S. Bonds
T. Bone Burnette
John Cafferty & the Beaver Brown Band
Peter Case/Plimsouls
Eddie Cochran
The Connells
Cowboy Junkies
Cracker/Camper Van Beethoven
Marshall Crenshaw
Sheryl Crow
The Dbs/Chris Stamey/Peter Holsapple
Willy DeVille
Bo Diddley
Dire Straits
Drivin' N Cryin'
Pete Droogе
Bob Dylan
Steve Earle
Everly Brothers
Fabulous Thunderbirds

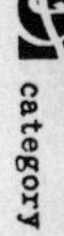

John Fogerty/Creedence Clearwater Revival
Steve Forbert
Foster & Lloyd/Bill Lloyd
Danny Gatton
Gin Blossoms
Grass Roots
Joe Grushecky and the Iron City Rockers
John Wesley Harding
John Hiatt
Hooters
Chris Isaak
Jason & the Scorchers
Jayhawks
Freedy Johnston
Marti Jones
Nils Lofgren
Lyle Lovett
Lovin' Spoonful
Dave Matthews
Maria McKee/Lone Justice
James McMurtry
John Mellencamp
Randy Newman
Willie Nile
Graham Parker
Michael Penn
Tom Petty & The Heartbreakers
John Prine
Bob Seger
Del Shannon
Michelle Shocked
Social Distortion
Southside Johnny & the Asbury Jukes
Spanic Boys
Bruce Springsteen
Syd Straw
Timbuk 3
Traveling Wilburys
Uncle Tupelo/Son Volt/Wilco
Lucinda Williams

Round Midnight
Hank Ballard & the Midnighters
Dexys Midnight Runners
Midnight Oil

Scandinavian Death Metal
Emperor
Mayhem
Mercyful Fate

Seattle Sound
Alice in Chains
Candlebox
Judy Collins
Foo Fighters
Heart
Jimi Hendrix
Mudhoney
Nirvana
Pearl Jam
Screaming Trees
Sebadoh
Soundgarden

See Ya at CBGBs
Blondie
Heartbreakers
Richard Hell
Mink Deville
Ramones
Patti Smith
Talking Heads
Television

Sex & Drugs & Rock 'n' Roll
Alien Sex Fiend
Barenaked Ladies
Buzzcocks
Carter the Unstoppable Sex Machine
Cheap Trick
Come
Gary Lewis and the Playboys
Green Day
Helium
Hole
Hooters
Human Sexual Response
Lords of Acid
Loverboy
Lovin' Spoonful
Miranda Sex Garden
Prong
Scratch Acid
Sex Pistols
Sham 69
Slits
Steely Dan
10cc
Tool

Shoe Gazers
Blur
Charletons U.K.
Happy Mondays
Inspiral Carpets
My Bloody Valentine
Portishead
Stone Roses
Suede

Sonic Boom
Amps
Helmet
Jesus and Mary Chain
Kyuss
Live Skull
Lush
My Bloody Valentine
Pixies
Ride
Smashing Pumpkins
Sonic Youth
Swervedriver
Tsunami

Southern Alternative Rock
The B-52's
Edie Brickell & New Bohemians
Collective Soul
The Connells
The dB's
Don Dixon
Gin Blossoms
The Golden Palominos
Grapes of Wrath
Hootie and the Blowfish
Bruce Hornsby & the Range
Indigo Girls
Jason & the Scorchers
Marti Jones
Let's Active
Sidewinders
Darden Smith
Syd Straw
Uncle Tupelo/Son Volt/Wilco
Victoria Williams

Spirit of the West
Blood on the Saddle
Cowboy Junkies
Galactic Cowboys
Go West
Lazy Cowgirls
Pure Prairie League

Stax-Volt/Motown
The Bar-Kays
Archie Bell & The Drells
William Bell
Booker T. & The Mgs
James Brown
Shirley Brown
Solomon Burke
Ray Charles
The Contours
Sam Cooke
The Crests
The Elgins
The Fantastic Four
The Four Tops
Aretha Franklin
Marvin Gaye
Al Green
Isaac Hayes
The Isley Brothers
The Jackson 5
Rick James
Albert King
Ben E. King
Curtis Mayfield & The Impressions
Martha & the Vandellas
The Miracles
The Originals
Wilson Pickett
Rare Earth
Otis Redding
Sam & Dave
Staple Sisters
Edwin Starr
The Supremes
Johnnie Taylor
The Temptations
Carla Thomas
Jackie Wilson
Stevie Wonder

Surf Groups
The Astronauts
Beach Boys
The Bel-Airs
Challengers
Chantays
Dick Dale & The Deltones
Jan and Dean
Original Surfaris
The Pyramids
The Revers
The Rip-Chords
The Sentinals
The Tornados
The Trashmen
Gary Usher
The Ventures

Teen Heartthrobs
Paul Anka
Rick Astley
The Beatles
Johnny Burnett
Bobby Darin
Dion & the Belmonts
Ral Donner
Donovan
Fabian

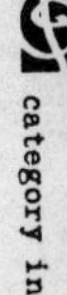

The enclosed CD sampler from The RCA Records Label® includes these up and coming artists:

Babe the Blue Ox

Born of a shared musical outlook and college friendship between Rose Thompson, Tim Thomas, and Hanna Fox, Babe the Blue Ox doesn't conform to strict genre classification. Drawing from a myriad of influences that range from P-Funk to Pere Ubu to Dwight Yoakum, their sound covers the spectrum from art-rock to blues to punk, often in one song. Critics and fans have embraced their on odd syncopations, off-beats, eclectic influences, and high energy. Their major-label debut, *People*, follows three successful indie releases.

Robert Bradley's Blackwater Surprise

The mean streets of Detroit are famous for the music they spawned—from Motown to Iggy Pop—and now Robert Bradley's Blackwater Surprise proudly carries on the Detroit tradition. Forty-six-year-old lead singer Bradley made his living as a street singer in the Motor City for 23 years before he hooked up with ex-Second Self members Michael Nehra, Andrew Nehra, and Jeff Fowlkes to form the core of Blackwater Surprise. Joined by Jimmy Bones on keyboards, the band recently recorded its 11-song debut album that features Bradley's "gutbucket" voice and musical influences that range from classic Motown to Stax, gospel, blues, funk, and rock and roll.

Zoe

Although young, versatile 27 year old singer/songwriter Zoe Pollock has actually had over a decade in the business already, touring at 16 as a frontwoman for a soul band. Combining such eclectic influences as jazz, Celtic folk, and traditional rock, the London-born artist had big success in the British carts with dance-oriented singles but quickly tired of limiting herself to the genre. After spending the next few years traveling to places such as India and Ireland, the traditional musics she heard there are evidenced in many of the songs on her RCA debut, *Hammer*.

REPUBLICA

Led by vocalist Saffron and keyboardists Tim Dorney and Andy Todd, Republica is leading the rebellion against the angst-ridden pop that has dominated the British music scene in recent years. Describing their music as "techno-pop punk rock," Saffron says that the band relies heavily on clever lyrics, identifiable melodies, and relentless, driving upbeat music. Lead guitarist Johnny Male and drummer Dave Barborossa round out a lineup that has already created a stir in England with its live shows and is now climbing the charts in the States with its self-titled first album and blistering debut single "Ready to Go."

Skold

Originally from Sweden, the Los Angeles based artist's eponymous debut album boasts an innovative sound, fusing the high production value found in dance music with the spirit and creativity of rock. Skold worked with a variety of notable producers in creating this unique sound, including producers of such acts as Killing Joke, Ministry, nine inch nails, and Danzig. His music touted as "technologically enhanced grittiness," Skold says, "We were constantly finding new ways of recreating old ideas and deliberately ruining perfectly nice sounds. In the end, it only comes down to the song and what the production does for it."

Delinquent Habits

This Latin influenced band adds hip-hop appeal to many of their songs to create their funky, new sound. Combining techniques of sampling island records, jungle sounds, ethnic music and dj'ing techniques like scratching, this band puts a new spin on every track of it's self-titled album.

musicHound **notes**

musicHound **notes**

musicHound **notes**

musicHound **notes**

musicHound **notes**

musicHound **notes**

musicHound **notes**